ENCYCLOPAEDIA
OF
MODERN MANAGEMENT TECHNIQUES

ENCYCLOPAEDIA OF MODERN MANAGEMENT TECHNIQUES

Volume 1

Edited by

A. K. Chaudhary

ANMOL PUBLICATIONS PVT. LTD.

NEW DELHI-110 002 (INDIA)

ANMOL PUBLICATIONS PVT. LTD.
4374/4B, Ansari Road, Daryaganj
New Delhi-110 002

Encyclopaedia of Modern Management Techniques

First Edition 1999
ISBN 81-261-0321-3 (Set)

PRINTED IN INDIA

Published by J. L. Kumar for Anmol Publications Pvt. Ltd., New Delhi-110 002 and Printed at Mehra Offset Press, Delhi.

Contents

Preface

There were two aspects to development technical and human. Organizations had usually been more sensitive to possibilities offered to them by the achievements of modern technology than to the refinements of human behaviour as revealed by the sciences of Sociology and Psychology. On the other hand, lessons drawn from experience showed that technical innovations driving from the engineering sciences encountered considerable resistance unless supported by corresponding changes in human attitudes and behaviour. In an era of rapid change, the improvement of management in its human aspect had become a critical issue. It was important to make full use of the findings of social sciences which endeavoured to be instrumental in giving guidance in behaviour of individuals and groups in varying circumstances. Organisations should, therefore, be conceived as complex, socio-technical systems whose management required both technical skills and insight into the motives of human behaviour.

It is widely agreed that manipulation and lack of integrity produce strong negative side-effects and reduce organizational effectiveness. With this important value commitment the organization may shift their styles and climate from one of direction, control an d surveillance to one of providing help, support and instruction. Mutuality and collaboration between the leaders and the led, self control and mutual support are essential for creating air organic organization.

The most important factor for the success of any organization is its leadership political and administrative. Leadership is an important means of converting or processing programme inputs into output such as goods and services. That is why, it has been rightly said that "Put a good man in a bad set up, he will push through. Put a bad man in a good set up he will make the mesh of the whole situation." No technique can help those administrators who have faith in their work and its best performance. Even poorly devised machinery may be made to work if it is manned with trained, intelligent imaginative and devoted staffs. On the other hand, the best planned organization may produce unsatisfactory results, if it is operated by mediocre or disgrantled people. So, we must find out such administrators who possess the following qualifications : competence, missionary-zeal, the capacity to motivate other people, the capacity to communicate with others, the ability to get along with colleagues and the people, cultural adaptability, the capacity to organize and manage, the capacity to inspire confidence in others, patience and dignity. Besides, they must have faith in the ideal of their work, be willing to accept hardships and prepare to work in a spirit of service. Their ambition and enthusiasms should not be dampened by local conditions which may not provide them with the necessary facilities. Unfortunately, the sense of dedication has been the crassest casualty of the prevailing atmosphere of cynicism bred by increasing propensity towards expediency.

An attitude of dedication to the goals of an organization should be an indispensable trait of the top leaders. This is their primary source of self-confidence to operate and function effectively and effectively to build self-confidence in themselves and in turn in the public. It is not just performing development linked administrative duties; it is taking action and encouraging people to take action required to bring about structural change and growth in the economy. This needs to be supplemented by his belief in the organizational goals. In such a situation, Management Techniques can generate and help in promoting efficiency.

Editor

1

Resource Management and Techniques

The resource management process begins with the appraisal of resources required by an organization to create and consummate exchange relationships. It involves synthesis of all resources and activities required to attain objectives, and it recognizes the different kinds of skills required to perform the various activities. To frameworks are helpful to managers in improving the effectiveness and efficiency of the resource management process. One classified resources according to what is needed to provide utility to the producer, user and society at large. The other considers the *uses* of resources required to implement strategies for the delivery and receipt of satisfactions of all involved in the exchange system. The process *ends* with the delivery of added value and satisfaction. We continue to use the exchange system as the vehicle for discussing and analyzing the process of resource management. We adopt this perspective because acquisition of resources necessitates exchange. Additionally, almost everything the organization does is ultimately focused on the exchanges system. For example, even the courtship of stockholders and the public in general through owner relations and public relations departments is at least indirectly concerned with some facet of the exchange system.

The exchange cycle is a pattern of recurring events or activities that take place as good move through the exchange system, and this chapter discusses its first two stages. These are concerned with resource appraisal and the synthesis of the input, throughout and output segments of that cycle. The resource management process begins with the decision to add value to a mix of resources by modifying them to satisfy demand for an organization's product/service. This decision concerns the demand side of marketing and leads first to marketing decisions related to the exchange system. Marketing is a human process of identifying, creating and consummating desired exchange relationships. The nature and performance of marketing activities is a marketing-specific adaptation of those activities previously attributed to management in general. The first of those activities is deployment of marketing resources to attain the organization's marketing objectives. This involves the adaptation of the external marketing environment in order to create and consummate exchange relationships. The second is the deployment of marketing resources to adapt the organization to the environment to facilitate creation and consummation of exchange relationships. The third is to relate the marketing resources and environment to the stimulation of innovation in creating, consummating and rewarding exchange relationships.

With marketing as the lead activity in creating and consummating exchange relationships, the function of marketing resource management is to acquire and manage resources to assure that the marketing efforts of those involved in all phases of the exchange system are supported effectively and efficiently. The multidimensional features of the exchange system necessitate a multidimensional orientation. A constituency or customer orientation is needed to develop exchanges, a general management orientation to facilitate them and a financial orientation to control and reward them.

The definition of marketing as creating and consummating desired relationships establishes that marketing has both a demand side is involved in the creation of exchanges of goods and services through the discovery of opportunities for exchange. The supply side is involved in the creation of exchange systems capable of satisfying these additional demands.

The discovery of opportunities for exchange and the response to them may take the form of (1) creating demand for new products, as was done with the personal computer; (2) creating new uses for existing products, a process still occurring for nylon after nearly 50 years; (3) capturing a special market niche for re-manufacturing heat transfer equipment in the aerospace industry, as Lori of Tulsa did; or (4) head-to-head competition to gain market share, as was the case when Sears introduced the Discover credit card.

Creating and consummating exchange implies that value has been added to goods and services. In most cases there is no question that value has been added in the exchange process. However, some marketing critics question whether such costs as advertising, expensive packaging, or a "frill" added to a product adds value. A few years ago, small rocks were polished and very successfully sold as Pet Rocks to be fondled. We prefer merely to acknowledge the controversy over value added and summarily dismiss it. Value is in the eye of the buyer, and a lot of people who bought Pet Rocks apparently found value in them. When people exchange dollars for products, they must see more value in the products than they do in the dollars they give up.

Fundamentally, value is added by a useful change in form, time, place or possession utility. Form utility: the form of raw stone is changed to a lovely sculpture. Time utility: today's news is delivered today. Place utility: we don't have to drive to Detroit to buy a car. Possession utility: the satisfaction derived from owning a new refrigerator. We now turn to that portion of the resource management process that involves synthesis of effort. In that discussion, we will elaborate and expand upon some of the points raised above.

The process involves synthesis

This discussion of synthesis of effort centers on the input, throughput and output activities of the exchange system. These activities are affected by and cause environmental conditions actively involved in the creation and use of resources. The outer rim of the large circle shows the input segments of raw materials and production and the throughput of the marketing channel. These lead to the output to users through the maze of competition.

The primary guiding principles of synthesis is the principle of coordination. This principle says any activity or action that could have an impact on another department in an organization or an outside shared interest group should first be discussed or reviewed with that entity. Coordination, as such, is not resource planning, but the result of it. Nonetheless coordination activities can be source of ideas for resource planning. Planning involves the writing of the script for the future of an organization, while coordination is the directing of the script and thus the monitoring of the actors that act out the resource management plan. The purpose of coordination is to harmonize, balance and synchronize the flow of input, throughput and output.

Like so many other managerial concepts and activities, coordination and its associated activities are managerial resources. The recipe for that concept and its use calls for large amounts of common sense seasoned liberally with such managerial attributes as leadership, experience, the power of persuasion and even the frequent use of managerial power. The coordination process falls into place, or is put in place, and the members of a coordinating group and its objectives emerge when one question is answered: what departments and organizations are affected by a decision? That makes coordination sound easy, and the faster it is said, the easier it sounds. Human failings are the only things that make coordination difficult. The easiest of those failings to deal with is caused by oversights such as the failure to include suppliers or intermediaries in strategic planning and decision systems.

The input of materials, parts and supplies to the exchange system is the result of interactions of purchasing units in the organization and supplying organizations. The strategies of these suppliers concerning certain elements of the environment determine the input strategies of the purchasing department(s).

The organization and its resource environment

One set of critical decisions pertains to how the organization is to acquire the resources to provide the necessary input of materials. Answers to such questions as these will help define resource acquisition strategies: what sources of supply will be used; how many, and what kinds of vendors; what relationships are to be established with vendors? In recent years, many companies who formerly used many vendors and carriers have reduced the number to a few in order to better coordinate and control quality of materials and service and to arrange for long-term relationships.

Another critical decision centers on the degree of vertical integration which is desirable. For example, should the organization make or buy certain materials or parts? Should it own or lease transportation equipment, or depend on for-hire carriers? The same question arises about distribution centers. Answers to these questions determine the degree of vertical integration, which in turn influences the coordination strategies employed.

The organization and its market and competitive environment.

A second set of decisions will be made if the objectives relate to a market. For example, the market may demand high quality and reliability and be willing to pay a high cost. If the product is clothing, both the choice of cotton, wool or synthetic fibers and the quality of the fibers chosen will be important. Accordingly, the purchase of raw materials has to be coordinated with those who design quality into a product, and with the marketing people who identify the target markets for various levels of quality. Competitive factors enter the decision also. For competitive reasons, an organization may think it is necessary to have a product line with several price and quality levels. These needs should be coordinated among production, marketing, design and material management departments.

The organization and its ecological environment

A third set of decisions relates to protection of the ecological environment. Examples include the disposal of wastes from the production process and the choice of packaging materials and their biodegradability. Because of the environmental effects of disposal of waste generated in the production process, it is important to coordinate materials acquisition with those in the organization who are responsible for environmental production. If the organization is concerned about disposal problems, similar coordination is necessary in selecting the types of material used in the product itself. For example, the problem of disposing of disposable diapers is an important concern, to the point that diaper washing services are experiencing a boom.

The marketing support system.

The marketing support system is an intangible resource which will foster coordination with other organizations; the essence of the marketing support system concept is that organizations and their activities in the exchange system are interdependent and that their individual and collective function is to support the marketing effort of one another. This support function begins on the input side by meshing the objectives and activities of vendors and purchasers. It continues within an organization, as well as among the organization and intermediaries.

Michiel R. Leenders and David L. Blenkhorn have the most complete discussion of marketing support system type buyer-seller relationships that we have seen. What we call the marketing support system, they call *reverse marketing* because the concept implies that the same marketing concepts applied to customers should be applied to suppliers. Their book documents successful and failed reverse-marketing efforts, and the checklists and illustrations provide excellent bases for the coordination of input of materials.

The Massachusetts Institute of Technology Commission on Industrial Productivity called attention to six key similarities among the "best practice" firms it studied, two of which were the importance of extending the arms of the firm forward to the customer and backward to suppliers. The Commission reported that all of the successful firms it observed are attempting to establish closer ties with their customers. These ties proved to be valuable in several ways. They enable the companies to pick up signals from the market, respond more easily to different market segments and shifts in the market and redeploy resources to new uses more rapidly.

The Commission also fund that all of the "best-practice" firms observed had developed close, tightly coordinated relations with suppliers. This coordination was achieved both through the use of coercive power and new forms of cooperation and negotiation. The benefits flowed in both directions. For example, one company reduced its inventory radically, partially through just-in-time delivery, even though sales doubled. In exchange, the company reduced the number of its suppliers 50 percent, "foregoing the assurance of low prices that competition had once produced..."

Some retailers, especially grocery stores, have followed the practice of allowing vendors to arrange shelf and other displays of merchandise the store had bought. An experiment begun in the summer of 1989 added new dimensions to this practice and raised it to a higher level of vendor-purchaser cooperation. Wal-Mart Stores, Inc. and some of its suppliers began testing an experimental "vendor store" in a newly opened Wal-Mart. The vendors were allocated more space than usual and allowed to select, display and generally merchandise their own products in an in-store boutique-type setting commonly used in department stores. This illustrates how purchasers and vendors attempt to lean from each other, and how each supports the marketing effort of the other.

The input of production to the exchange system is also the result of the interaction of the design, marketing, materials management and other departments. Unfortunately, much of the interaction takes place haphazardly, almost as if the word "coordination" were not in the managerial vocabulary. One facet of the problems caused by lack of coordination was described by Jerry Myers, general manager of the automotive sector of TRW. *Forbes* quoted him: "A few years ago the American auto makers would throw a component design over the transom and say, 'Build it!' Increasingly, the parts suppliers are becoming part of the design process itself." At the other end of the spectrum, customers are being brought into the production process to help coordinate effort and assure quality. One steel company keeps a representative at a Honda plant in Maryland to help in the coordination and problem-solving processes.

It is paradoxical that co-ordination arrangements seem to be easier to set up externally with suppliers and customers than internally among departments. Three cultural forces seem to hamper internal coordination. One is that the production process is often perceived as a series of discrete steps each separated in time and according to which manager controls it. The first step is to design the product, and even within the design department, coordination may be hampered by a requirement that the design be approved by several layers of management, each of which may make changes. After that step is complete, the next department in the process goes through the same routine. A second cultural force that hampers internal coordination is the organization structure that physically, operationally and emotionally separates the activities from one another without providing for lowering departmental barriers. The third coordination killer is turf protection. Too many department managers believe they are kings, and that personnel from other departments are invading warriors that must be fought off.

The study of the MIT Commission on Industrial Productivity found that flatter and less-compartmentalized organizations permit greater cross-functional integration. The Commission said that Ford was the first American automobile company to use cross-functional teams for the development and introduction of a new model. Illustrative of this philosophy was the team for the creation of the Taurus, which included people from planning, design, engineering, manufacturing and marketing. The specialists worked simultaneously with each other rather than serially, and more or less independently.

The Commission also stated that many companies have difficulty in achieving cross-functional integration. It added that, "Successful implementation typically requires a change in company culture that encourages and supports participation, teamwork and decision making at lower levels of the organization." The MIT Commission implicitly recognized that company culture was a resistance, and that a new management philosophy was needed to transform this resistance into a resource.

Materials management

The decisions about materials concern purchasing, logistics and inventory management activities. Emphasis is on three things: coordinating decisions about the specifications of the materials, parts and supplies; coordinating decisions about managing the processes concerned with acquisition and holding the materials until they are ready for use; and coordinating decisions about holding and physically distributing finished products. Even though many of the actual decisions in materials management are operational, they should be made within a framework of strategic decisions previously coordinated with other departments. For example, the economic order quantity decision should be partially influenced by a strategic marketing decision based on the extent to which the market would stand for back orders because of depleted safety stock.

The importance of coordination of the elements of materials management with the production process is illustrated with two examples. In one company a raw material was received in paper bags. The Vice President—Traffic worked cooperatively with production, suppliers and carriers and arranged for the material to be shipped in bulk and stored in a tank in the plant. The result was lower cost of the material, lower handling costs at the plant and elimination of the cost of holding and disposing of waste paper.

In another case the coordination of packaging with production resulted in a paper napkin manufacturer reducing its packaging, handling and transportation costs significantly. The napkins were compressed to allow about one-third more napkins in each box. Fewer boxes were required; labor costs for movement from the production line and loading for storage and shipment were reduced; transport costs were reduced because of heavier loads that met minimum shipping weights; and warehousing costs were reduced because more napkins could be stored per cubic foot.

Marketing

The coordination between marketing and production as an input to the exchange system covers a long list of joint concerns. One such concern is product design. The design, size, shape, color and packaging of the product are all marketing-related matters that need to be coordinated with production. If left alone in its decision making, production departments would make completely rational production decisions based on cost that could well be marketing disasters.

Take waste baskets for example. With no concern for marketing considerations, production departments would probably have rectangular or square basket to minimize material waste, and one size and color to minimize production costs. Imagine the trouble marketing would have trying to market that product for use in executive offices; by clerical desks; on shop floors; and in bedrooms, bathrooms, family rooms and kitchens. By the same token, if marketing considerations were ignored, the rational production decision for packaging products to appear on retailers' shelves would be strictly utilitarian. The boxes for perfume would be much like those containing spark plugs destined for an auto parts store's inventory. Another major concern is pricing. In this regard, marketing input into the production decision will influence durability of the product and thus its price. Also various degrees of quality will allow a series of prices. And, as pointed out before, marketing has a very strong interest in the timing and length of production runs because of their impact on safety stock of inventory to keep stock-outs at an economic minimum. This leads to the need for coordination with the finance department.

Finance and production

Each of the above illustrations of coordination with materials management and marketing has financial implications. Since inventory is such a significant part of the working capital of a company, the finance department has an acute interest in policies for the management of both raw material and finished goods inventory. In addition, not only the acquisition of production resources but also the method of financing this acquisition are important factors to be coordinated.

Production-finance coordination should be established at both ends of the production process and in the middle. Finance people should be a part of the raw material inventory decision at the start of the production process for two reasons. The department has to provide working capital to buy materials and fixed facilities for storing them. Finance has to arrange the flow of funds for machinery, buildings and labor, as well as other operating costs. Furthermore, the most economical method of acquiring production resources often depends on careful financial analyses. For example, finance people can help determine the economics of buying resources or leasing them. And, if a decision to lease is made, the terms and conditions of the lease may require financial input. Altogether, strategies for the input to the exchange system are a complex mix of strategic, managerial and operational decisions. They require a complex system to coordinate the efforts of many different departments of the organization. Many organizations manage to get by without all of this coordination. Unfortunately, because of uncoordinated efforts, many also have lost both domestic and international markets.

Coordination of throughput

The throughput of the exchange picks up where the input leaves off, with the coordination of internal activities related to the production of goods and services, and it deals with all of those activities in the marketing channel that position goods and services for use. There is a remarkable lack of coordination of strategies among suppliers, manufacturers, wholesalers, carriers and retailers. The typical manufacturer recognizes the need for all of the activities required to position goods for the user, but few recognize either the role of intermediaries as off-balance sheet resources of one another and how to capitalize on these resources.

Saturn is one company that does recognize suppliers as off-balance sheet resources. Quality is especially important to Saturn because it produces the new automobiles of General Motors designed to be GM's answer to Japanese cars. Saturn has done two things to build its reputation for quality. One is the previously very rare example of replacing rather than repairing 1,836 cars with various problems. The other is the increasingly popular step of asking vendors to do more engineering and design of parts.

There seems to be a trend by large companies to create new intermediaries as off-balance sheet resources to perform a wide range of services. Work is farmed out to other firms because it can be done better, cheaper or faster (or all three!) than by the company concerned. For example: National Steel Corporation spun off its mail room to a company that also does its major copying work; J.P. Morgan & Co. and Bank America Corporation, among others, are turning over certain "back room" activities to another company; and major refiners such as Mobil and Chevron are farming out the work required to maintain and overhaul their refineries.

The earlier discussion emphasized that the function of each channel member is to support the marketing effort of all the others, and thus create a marketing support system. Two things are required to accomplish this. First, each channel member needs to recognize that its self-interest is in marketing with others, and not just distributing to or acquiring goods from them. Second, this requires the development of inter-organizational resource use strategies.

Coordination of output

The final part of the organization's role in the exchange system is played in the competitive marketplace where each organization's exchange system interacts with those of its competitors.

Raw materials

The output segment of the exchange system, for undifferentiated raw materials is a special case, because no one producer can command a higher price or influence sales by advertising or anything else. However, there are exceptions where a particular relationship yields a higher utility to the buyer or seller, thereby justifying a special price. For example, a given coal producer may negotiate special prices, quantities and terms of delivery with a large coal user. A wheat farmer may do business with a certain grain buyer, or an oil producer may sell to a given buyer.

Marketing, media and finance

By the time the output segment of the exchange system has been reached, almost all of the necessary and desirable coordination of activities should have been accomplished. That includes most of the elements of competitive strategy aimed at target markets. For example, product design will have been coordinated, as will various elements of customer service, including where the user can buy the product and get service for it, as well as inventory, price and other policies. About the only addition at this stage is the promotional program. That program may involve advertising, or special terms of sale such as quantity discounts and financing terms. Or, it may involve the use of coupons or special arrangements with a retailer for shelf space.

The coordination for this competitive program is generally handled as a part of the marketing activity. It involves coordinating dates of advertising with media people and inventory and logistics managers to be sure the product is available. If special financial considerations are involved, they will have to be coordinated with the finance department. For example, special factory rebates and interest rates are often an important part of competitive strategy employed by automobile companies.

Coordination of quality

Coordination is the single largest determinant of the quality of goods and services.

Most of the opportunities to provide—or fail to provide—quality appear in the coordination processes associated directly with the input, throughput and output segments of the system. Quality is a highly subjective concept. According to the dictionary, quality refers to the degree of excellence a thing possesses. Excellence in turn in defined as something in which a person or thing excels. But excels compares with what? The term may be applied to a 12-year-old who is the best baseball player in his age group, or to a major league player. Irrespective of the dictionary definition, quality is the degree to which the expectations of the user are satisfied. This is clearly a marketing-based definition. Because we define quality as the degree to which the expectations of the user are satisfied, and because we believe that the key to meeting user expectations is management of the input and throughput segments, we adopt a "process-customer" framework for the management of quality.

Elements of process-customer satisfaction

The essence of the concept is that each process is not only a customer, but that it has a customer. This means that each process in the long chain of processes that extends from the design of the product through to the user has to be satisfied by the preceding process, as do all relevant subsequent processes. These processes have to be performed anyway, so they are best performed to the satisfaction of subsequent recipients of the product. Normally no new steps are required to build satisfaction (quality) into the process. All that is required is that employees care enough to do quality work the first time and make better use of the skills required for the process.

The first step is to define in the planning process what level of quality in the product or service is desired in order to provide satisfaction to the ultimate user. This involves defining the quality the user wants in the package of the Four Ps of marketing: product, place, promotion and price.

The second step in installing a process-customer satisfaction approach to quality assurance is a test of the quality of managerial leadership. It tests the ability of managers to plan, organize and implement the program and to overcome the resistance to change by both managers and other employees. The challenge is to provide supervision and control of quality over each of perhaps thousands of separate processes.

The third step is to define the desired level of quality required in materials, parts and supplies. Despite the multi-dimensional aspects of quality, these steps are relatively easy. Standards can be set to meet customer needs for the proper mix of durability, reliability, purity, performance, workmanship or other requirements for pleasing the customer. Decisions about quality related to the Four Ps of marketing are important at the planning stage. Some adjustments can occur in the production process to change quality for different markets. However, if the desired levels of quality are not designed into the process at the outset, fine tuning of production is difficult. Many people, including us, have written and spoken in glowing terms about the Japanese approach to quality assurance. Also, many people, excluding us, have, directly or by implication, suggested that American manufacturers adopt the Japanese approach. Our position is that just because a method works for the Japanese doesn't mean it will work for Americans.

The wrong question to ask is, "How can we transfer the Japanese experience to the U.S.?" The Japanese approach is mostly irrelevant except in one respect. The only issue American producers should be concerned with is improving their effectiveness, efficiency and quality in order to improve their competitiveness. Therefore, the proper question to ask about quality is, "How can we improve our quality as one way to help make us more competitive?" In searching for the answers, the Japanese experience becomes relevant, as do the experiences of all other foreign and domestic manufacturers. American producers should explore these various approaches to quality, adapt them to their situations, and adopt them where appropriate. The only Japanese approach we should copy is the one they are said to use: copy or adapt goods and processes used elsewhere when they will improve the effectiveness, efficiency, quality and profitability of your output.

Synthesis of strategic elements

Synthesis of putting together parts so as to form a whole. This is what managers do in the acquisition, creation and use of resources. They synthesize the elements of supply and demand and the organizational effort, activities and strategies necessary to manage supply and demand. Because strategic planning is the first step in management, the broad elements of planning are used as building blocks in the synthesis required in resource creation and use.

Building blocks of synthesis

Several types of synthesis involved in resource creation and use for resource management. The strategic elements of the function, mission, objectives and strategies concerned with that synthesis. The synthesis of the several strategic elements of demand and supply, effort, activities and strategies is a multi-stage process. The elements of each stage are synthesized, and then the several stages are synthesized. For example, the first building block is the function. It consists of demand and supply which are synthesized through the process to attain results. This is shown by the arrows depicting a horizontal flow of the action from the strategic element to the process to the expected results.

The process of synthesis continues with other building blocks: objectives to synthesize activities and the synthesis of strategies. Together, these are the elements involved in the formulation of strategy. The obvious next series of steps shown would be those related to the implementation of strategy.

The function of synthesis is to attempt to reconcile the wants of the market (demand) with supplying goods and services to satisfy those wants. The process involved the acquisition of resources that are necessary to bring the demand and supply into balance, thereby managing change.

Generally, this is done when the organization discovers an opportunity or problem and sets out to develop the capability to exploit the opportunity or solve the problem. It is likely that most products fall in this category. Examples range from the development of gunpowder to the search for a cure for the cold. Several modern examples drawn from the preoccupation of the market with health include the development of exercise equipment and clothing, cholesterol-free bread, smoke-free hotel rooms, and human organ transplants.

Sometimes the state of the art (supply) is the leader, and the organization sets out to create a market for a product or service it has developed. Technology-related examples include the development of the many products based on nylon, the copying machines, the familiar yellow "Post it" papers, and the all-waiting services of the telephone companies.

Then there are those situations where both the state of the art and the state of the wants (demand) are influenced by some outside force such as government edict. Examples from the automotive field include standards for control of pollution emissions, fuel consumption and safety. These edicts forced companies to develop and users to buy catalytic converters, fuel-efficient automobiles, and automatic seat belts.

The mission of synthesis is to attempt to coordinate the effort and skills of all of those involved in the use of resources to help attain the desired ends of the organization.

The objectives of synthesis are derived from the mission and relate to the synthesis of activities involving the use of resources. Those activities discussed centered on those created as a means tot he desired ends associated with the exchange system. The strategies of synthesis are those designed to bring about the coordination of the various segments of the exchange system that should result in attaining the objectives of all shared interest groups.

General conceptual and operating results. The objectives of synthesis is to create a whole by potting together several parts. The overall result of this multi-stage process is a basis for resource management. Conceptually, a resources base has been established for strategic planning and management which makes operational and meshing of strategies for resource acquisition and use. Second, the synthesis of effort focuses on resources as the forces that drive the functional activities of the organization and establishes a basis for meshing the strategies of all shared interest groups.

Third, the synthesis of functional activities integrates all off-balance sheet resources, processes and the external environment into a coherent management program. This results in a change in interorganizational relationships in which cooperation among exchange system members replaces power as the basis for getting things done. Power becomes an action tool only where cooperation fails. Fourth, because of the synthesis of strategies, the organization becomes a managerial resource system in an exchange system of shared interest groups, all of which are working toward a common marketing goal. Therefore, these shared interest groups become a marketing support system that supports the marketing effort of each member of the exchange system, thus improving the efficiency and effectiveness of that system. The discussions in this chapter have centered on resource management to improve the effectiveness and efficiency of individual organizations—a micro-management perspective. But we believe that the importance of the resources perspective far transcends its impact on an organization. We believe that the macroeconomic effects of the concept are significantly more important because of their impact on improving the competitive posture of our nation as a whole, thus leading to the creation of a higher quality of life.

Strategic planning is the process of deciding on objectives of the organization, on changes in these objectives, on the resources used to attain these objectives, and on the policies that are to govern the acquisition, use, and disposition of these resources." His definition of strategy corresponds to Andrews', in that he uses the term strategic planning to identify a process that is concerned with "the formulation of long range, strategic plans are policies that determine or change the character or direction of the organization." George A. Steiner's conceptual model of the structure and process of strategic planning has three major sections: (1) premises, (2) formulation of plans and (3) implementation and review of plans, Premises are statements that serve as the bases for developing a plan, and relate to the total environment of the organization. They are generally derived from the basic beliefs of manages and from an audit of the situation the organization finds itself in or wants to be in. Steiner identifies four broad sources of planning premises:

1. The expectations of major outside interests such as society as a whole, stockholders, customers and suppliers;
2. The expectations of the inside interests of all employees;
3. The data base concerned with the past, present and future; and
4. Evaluations of company strengths and weaknesses, and of the opportunities and threats lurking in the environment.

The fourth source of premises, the evaluation of strengths, weaknesses, opportunities and threats (SWOT) is a central element in strategic planning systems. A firm's resources and the way they are used are its strengths. Whether the strength is tangible—as from a modern production facility—or intangible—as from a strong corporate culture that produces teamwork—the strength is a resource. A firm's weaknesses are the result of resistances that must be overcome. An out-of-date and unreliable computer is a tangible weakness, and a demoralized labor force is an intangible weakness, but the central strategic imperative is to overcome the resistances and eliminate the weaknesses, with the capability developed in the process of overcoming that weakness becoming another resources. The best-developed and executed strategic plans provide strategic direction for transforming weaknesses into strengths by converting resistances to resources. For example, poor customer, employee or public relations are clearly resistances that can be converted to resources by a change in management policies and application of effort.

Marketing opportunities evolve from changes in the social, technological, competitive, legal/political, ethical, economic or physical environment; therefore, they evolve largely from the external environment. Such changes often come as threats, but resourceful marketers can often turn threats into opportunities. For example, grocery store managers see changes in the public's eating habits as opportunities to develop in-store delicatessens and restaurants, expand frozen food departments and market an increased assortment of fast and easy-to-prepare, high-quality food items. Conversely, some threats may represent such a strong resistance that withdrawal or avoidance of a particular market is the best strategy. Four types of threats should be viewed as resistances because they:

1. *impede a strategy's implementation*. Babcock and Wilcox is developing a new type of nuclear reactor to generate electricity; if anti-nuclear power legislation is passed, then the company will not be able to implement its new product strategy.
2. *increase a strategy's risks*. A firm may be planning to double its production capacity for dishwashers as a step toward increasing market share. It recognizes that most dishwashers are purchased with new homes, but as the economic forecast for new home construction becomes more volatile each month due to troubles in the economy, the risk of doubling capacity and seeking higher market share is increased.
3. *increase the resources needed to implement a strategy*. A firm developing a new drug may learn that the government requires two additional years of premarket testing before the drug can be commercially produced and marketed.
4. *reduce financial performance expectations*. A microchip manufacturer could be threatened by the announcement that large Taiwanese and South Korean firms plan to enter the market and concentrate their selling efforts in U.S. and European markets.

A firm's opportunities and threats are resource or resistance based. An opportunity could be externally based, as in a rapidly growing market—or internally based, if created by the early retirement of managers who have been blocking progress. In either case, such an opportunity is a source of support or aid (a resource). A threat could be external, as from pending legislation that would significantly increase costs, or it could be internal, from a group of disgruntled employees seeking to undermine morale. Clearly, in both cases a resistance is present. The best strategic plans will capitalize on opportunities since they are a source of aid, and transform threats into opportunities or resistances into resources.

Perhaps one of the most difficult challenges for senior management is to have the insight and wisdom to view threats as opportunities, or to be able to take a resistance and make it a resource. In this regard, it is important to acknowledge that almost every market opportunity an organization encounters originates in the firm's external environment.

Premises underlying resource management

Remember, resource management is a concept that positions an organization as a managerial resource system driven by the relevant tangible and intangible resources of both the internal and external environments, and resources are those tangible and intangible assets of all types that an organization depends upon for aid and support, and that serve as a means of attaining its objectives.

A series of premises about resource management is deriven from Zimmermann's concepts developed to apply to the broad spectrum of natural, human and cultural resources. Here we are sing these concepts as the basis for making resource management central to the management of organizations. Zimmermann wrote of natural, human and cultural resources and resistances that stand in the way of exploiting the three types of resources. His focus was on the interactions of these three types of resources and their accompanying resistances that result in resources becoming sources of aid and support to mankind and as means to satisfying wants and needs.

Premise 1

An organization's resources are packages of tangibles and intangibles, with people and ideas at their center.

Zimmermann on resources. Zimmermann cited several dictionary definitions of resources to show that they result from an interaction between man and nature (his environment). That interaction exists when man is searching for a means to attain given ends such as the satisfaction of individual wants and the attainment of social objectives. Resources also result from the man-environment interaction because man has the capacity to take advantage of opportunities or to extricate himself from difficulties.

For centuries, resources were absorbed into the market process by being reduced to the working tools of the entrepreneur-capitalist as "land, labor and capital." Or, resources were recognized because of their effects on costs, price, supply and demand. Release from these confining perspectives opens an almost infinite number of options for resource utilization. Resources should be acknowledged as means to the ends for all elements of society; perceived more accurately in their natural, human and cultural senses; and recognized for the technological, economic and social roles they perform. The narrow view of resources has led to several misconceptions about them. Probably the most important misconception Zimmermann saw was the tendency to identify resources with tangible things to the exclusion of intangible such as knowledge, freedom and wise policies. This has led to a preoccupation with natural resources to the general exclusion of cultural and human resources. It also led to thinking of resources as single assets instead of as an interacting system creating resources.

For example, to think of coal as a single asset is misleading. Until a broad spectrum of circumstances coalesce, coal is a nothing: "neutral stuff" at its best, a resistance at its worst. A complex set of forces is required before coal becomes a resource: among them are need; local; technological resources to mine and use it; the economics of cost, price and use; and institutions to produce, market and use it.

In turn, Zimmermann said that this preoccupation with specific physical assets created the false perception that resources are static, instead of being as dynamic as the changes in knowledge, the environment and economics. Technological breakthroughs that enable an oil operator to lift more barrels of oil at the same or at a lesser cost, a refiner to extract more usable products per barrel, a chemist or manufacturer to provide more miles per gallon from gasoline, an engineer to improve engine performance or a designer to reduce weight all effectively increase the amount of oil available.

An organization's resources. Our first premise about resource management is that a firm's resources are packages of tangibles and intangibles, with people and ideas at their center, used to attain the ends of an organization by overcoming natural, human and cultural resistances to attaining those ends. Thus, an organization is an institutional resource system operating within an environmental resource system, both of which are governed by a managerial resource system. The resources of all of those systems include all of the tangible and intangible things that the organization depends on for aid and support and that serve as means to attain its objectives.

Related to this first premise, we identify four groups of an organization's resources not listed on the asset side of the balance sheet. Among these off-balance sheet resources we count the *people* with a role in the operation of the organization including its employees, owners and consultants, as well as the skills of those people. Also included is the superb teamwork that results from another resource, the *esprit de corps* of the organization and its collective competencies. These off-balance sheet resources include the *concepts* related to the management of the firm; among these are management science, the concepts of auditing and human relations, and the marketing concept itself.

A third group of resources consists of various kinds of *institutions* that serve, and are served by, a firm, including suppliers, distributors, financiers, advertising agencies and the like. *Markets,* both actual and potential, make up the fourth group of resources. The markets also perform another role, for they are among a group we call *arbiters of society* that individually and collectively pass judgment on the firm, its offering and its actions. And of course people are included; those people who create and apply the concepts, who perform the work of the institutions, and who make up the markets, including dissatisfied customers who, through their complaints, cause the firm to improve the quality of the product and or service. These resources also include dissatisfied shareholders who stimulate improvement of the effectiveness, efficiency and profitability of the organization. And, of course, the sol-called corporate raiders often serve as resources for shareholders, even though management may view them as resistances.

In addition to these four groups of off-balance sheet resources, there are those that appear on the balance sheet as assets, liabilities and the elements of net worth. Clearly, cash, accounts receivable, inventory and other assets are resources. Even accounts and notes payable as well as common stock and bonds are resources or the representations of resources. They, along with the net worth or stockholders equity may be used as means to the organization's ends. To summarize: the resources of an organization are its people, concepts, institutions markets and assets, whether tangible or intangible. All are parts of the environment in which the firm operates, and, except for human resources, all of the off-balance sheet resources are cultural resources, including the skills of the people.

Premise 2

The effective management of the environmental resource system calls for the management of two sets of resource packages, physical and cultural, to serve as a means to the organization's ends.

Zimmermann on fund and flow Resources. Our first premise identified certain off-balance sheet resources as cultural resources to managerial activities, and apply them to physical and cultural resources that are available and thus useful. Zimmermann found the commonly held distinction of renewable and non-renewable to be useful as a basis for appraising physical and cultural resources. He characterized renewable ones as flow resources and non-renewable ones as fund resources, although he recognizes some problems with this characterization. For example, soil fertility is typically a renewable or flow resource, but through continuous cultivation of plants that deplete certain elements in the soil, it may become a fund resource subject to depletion. Also, while cola and iron are both non-renewable fund resources, iron converted to steel may be remelted and reused. Finally, salmon are one of the most unusual, determined and location-specific renewable resources in existence. In returning from the sea to the streams where they were hatched, to renew themselves through the next generation, salmon must overcome powerful man-made and natural resistances to their progress.

We have also pointed out that Zimmermann emphasized the role of culture, especially man's wisdom, in resource availability. For example, "Man's own wisdom is his premier resource—the key resource that unlocks the universe." Again: "The problems of resource adequacy for the ages to come will involve human wisdom more than it will involved limits set by nature." Because wisdom implies superior judgment and understanding based on broad knowledge, it rests also on the availability of good information. Our second premise is that the effective management of the environmental resource system calls for the management of two sets of resource packages to serve as means to the organization's ends. There are two sets of ends to be attained and two sets of managerial cultural resources. This subject is discussed here in a conceptual context.

One set of resources consists of physical resources; the other is made up of cultural resources. In Chapter 8 we refer to them as operand and operant resources, respectively. These two types of resources are interdependent. The *basis* for differentiation is that one is a physical or tangible thing to be operated or used, while the other is mostly a cultural or intangible skill that is applied to the operation or use of the physical resource—thus the operand-operant relationship. The *reason* for the differentiation is that by separating the two elements, more relevant analyses and generalizations can be made so that each can be managed more effectively.

For example, unless physical and cultural resources are separated for analysis, it is difficult to generalize about cause and effect of variations in the quality of output. If an operator and machine are not producing as expected, to find out why, they and the materials used have to be analyzed separately. Does the fault lie with the operator's skill, or is the machine inadequate or are the wrong materials used? With the disaggregation, analyses of and generalizations about each type of resource *and the resistances to its use* may be made that are applicable for the operator but not for the machine or materials. Specifically, and relatively simply, differences in performance may be explained by some combination of differences in the quality of the physical resources, differences in the quality of cultural resources, and differences in the nature of resistances of resource use.

Why does one set of machines turn out higher-quality products at lower cost than another set? Quality may be explained by several factors, including better-quality raw materials or better-quality machines. Better quality of labor operating the machine may also be a factor. Lower cost may also be explained by several factors, including better quality of labor, better plant layout and design, more effective management of inventories, more effective management of labor, or better control systems in general.

General similar-quality physical resources, the quality of cultural resources and their use, and the nature of resistances to resource use, explain differences in the quality of performance. Even in comparing two organizations, the one with inferior-quality physical and cultural resources may perform more effectively and efficiently than the other. Therefore, the quality of at least three types of resources must be appraised: physical (the operand), cultural (the operant) and cultural resource applications (the operation).

Before proceeding, we apply the notion of differentiation between physical and cultural resources in a series of familiar settings:

1. *American Japanese automobile competition.* To avoid the influence of import quotas, exchange rates and similar complicating factors, we place the Japanese factory in the United States. Both the Japanese-managed plant and the American-managed one use the same sorts of buildings, machines, tools and other physical resources. Both draw from the same general labor pool and have access to the same cultural concepts of market research and production, materials, financial, marketing and information management, Yet according to the conventional wisdom, the Japanese produce a better car at lower cost than the Americans. Of course, the explanation lies in the management of the *use* of the cultural resources.

2. *A portion of a large organization acquired by its managers and employees in a buyout.* After the buyout, the physical resources may remain the same, but the cultural resources and the resistance to effective resource use may both be diminished. The new company may not have access to the range of expertise formerly available to it as a division of a large company. However, the cultural resistances may also be reduced as the attitude of workers change, and as the number of layers of management and other bureaucratic impediments are reduced, Improved efficiency and effectiveness may be the result of improved ability to use cultural resources as operants through the removal of some cultural resistances.

3. *A government activity compared with private operations.* When the private sector can perform more effectively and efficiently than the public sector, the explanation may have nothing to do with either physical or cultural resources. The government operated utility, whether garbage service or security service, may have exactly the same quality and quantity of resources as private operators. The explanation for the difference may lie in resistances that the private sector does not encounter, which may range from political appointment of managerial hacks to the public demand for unprofitable services. It may include overstaffing because of the lack of competitive discipline or cross-subsidy of other services. This is a case of cultural resistances to the effective and efficient use of both physical and cultural resources.

4. *A firm with fewer and inferior physical and cultural resources performing more effectively than a better-endowed organization.* In many cases, the small firm has access to fewer and inferior physical and cultural resources. This may cause greater resistances to the use of both kinds of resources. When these firms perform more effectively than their better-endowed counterparts, it may be for any of several reasons, starting with luck. They may be able to move more rapidly to change direction; they may be able to operate in smaller market niches; they may be more motivated. In short, while they have fewer and perhaps inferior physical and cultural resources of the "typical" type,

they may have more cultural resources of a very special type. We have already alluded to the ends to be attained by the two sets of resource packages. Actually, the two resource packages are joint means to only one set of ends, those of the organization as a whole. Even so, each package is a means to an intermediate end of its own. The end to be attained by the physical resources is to have the facilities in place used throughout the acquisition process. Similarly, while the cultural resources must also be available or acquired, their end is the use and control of the physical resources to attain the ends of the organization. Thus, one end is to acquire resources effectively and efficiently while the other is to use them effectively and efficiently.

There are two reasons for this somewhat forced disaggregation of ends, one of which is to emphasize the differences in the nature of the two sets of resource packages. The other is to underscore the fact that the cultural resources make the difference in performance of two organizations. Another perspective of this: a skilled carpenter can often do a better job with second-rate materials and tools than an unskilled person can with first-class materials and tools.

The two sets of managerial cultural resources need to be discussed briefly here in the present context. The first set includes all of the relevant managerial concepts including theories of human, consumer, organization and interorganization behaviour; concepts of marketing, managerial accounting and money management; tools of statistical, market and economic analysis; and many, many others. The second set includes the managerial skills required to use those theories, concepts and tools in dealing with strategic, managerial and operational matters concerning the organization.

Premise 3

Managerial and cultural forces affect resource availability.

Resources are dynamic functional concepts that evolve out of the interaction of nature, man and culture. This implies that *resources are not, they become*. It also implies that they are not static, but expand and contract in response to human wants and human culture that can convert "neutral stuff" and resistances into want-satisfying resources. The oil sands, the arid regions and the wild rubber trees were all in place millenia before humans leaned how to use them. People did not know of the oil sands; so they could not be resources until mankind and culture discovered them and combined forces to find a way to use them economically. The arid regions, if anything, were a resistance until that same combination brought water from underground and distant sources to covert some of these areas to great agricultural resources. The wild rubber trees neither particularly helped nor hurt mankind until those cultural forces converted these trees to resources. Then, culture played a dirty trick. The development of synthetic rubber reconverted a good portion of the vastly improved and now-cultivated rubber trees back into neutral stuff.

So, resources are not—not until mankind finds an economic or social use for them. Then, they "become." In many respects, the study of resources is the study of overcoming resistances to their use. Also, resources may ultimately revert to being a "not" and perhaps even a resistance, as, for example, the toxic wastes requiring disposal after their resource elements are extracted.

As for the future, both outer space and undersea exploration hold promise of many mineral resources. For now, they are either "neutral stuff" or "potential resources" because of technological, economic and cultural resistances to their development. Also, cultural resistances deter the mining of metal modules from the sea bed because nations are unable to agree on fundamental matters of ownership and benefit from the mining. Our third premise implies that the resources of an organization are dynamic rather than static. We have just seen how they may expand or contract in response to cultural or other stimuli. Those stimuli may also improve or impair the quality or resources by making them more or less able to perform the role expected of them.

It is probably fair to say that, with the possible exception of people, an organization's greatest resources are the off-balance sheet resources in its external environment. It can even be argued that people exist in the external environment because the organization does not own them; they must be attracted to the organization. The external environment is actually the source from which internal resources originate: money, supplies, materials, concepts, etc. Similarly, the environment probably shelters the greatest resistances to attaining an organization's objectives: competitors, laws, customers, middlemen and so forth. With the exception of people, a large portion of the resources of an organization's internal environment is identified and valued on the balance sheet. Financial statements, and their uses, emphasize the differences between assets and resources, liabilities and resistances, and static and dynamic characteristics of resources, resistances and the environment.

Several things about the balance sheet the other financial statements give the false impression that resources are static and that they exist in a static environment. The practice of valuing certain assets as the lower of cost or market at a particular moment reinforces that notion, as does such terminology as fixed assets and long-term liabilities. Furthermore, balance sheets record value for assets of many companies, such as some steel mills, when they are actually liabilities because they operate at a loss and drain the resources of the companies until they are closed. Also, the balance sheets of many financial institutions in the 1980s not only gave the false impression that certain of their assets were static, but also called things assets that were not, In mid-1987 several major banks rectified this situation in part by writing off a portion of their uncollectable loans to Third World countries. Similarly, regularly agencies temporarily adopted new procedures to deal with bad loans in order to prevent widespread failure of banks and savings and loan companies.

Accountants, in effect, stop time and report on the way things were, which implies a preoccupation with the deal hand of the past. Accounting rules required steel mills that were losing money, and were in effect a liability, to be shown as assets on the balance sheet. When they were written off, some of the value on the balance sheet had to be shown as a loss, even though the corporation realized a net gain when the losses stopped. The same can be seen in the write-off of problem loans. The stock market saw the accounting loss as a corporate gain because share prices rose. For example, after Citicorp reduced its reported income in order to raise its loan loss reserve in 1987 $3 billion, the price of the stock rose about 24 percent.

Accountants, as creators, users and interpreters of financial statements, and financial analysts, as users and interpreters, understand and notice the effect of a dynamic environment on resources. They watch—and eventually record the event—as assets turn into liabilities for one group and greater assets for another; as debt as a liability becomes an asset; and as inventory as an asset becomes a liability. Let's explore these observations further.

Dynamic market conditions may place such a high value on the fixed assets of a company that one of two things may happen. First, financial analysts and investors see an opportunity for a takeover attempt because of the low book value of these assets. Thus, the higher price offered for stock may enhance the value of the resources for owners. Or the undervalued fixed assets may become a "liability" to managers who want to resist the takeover. Second, the managers may see an opportunity to sell the fixed assets and use the proceeds to create current assets such as cash or inventory. The wave of mergers, corporate raids and restructuring, leveraged buyouts by managers, and the payment of "greenmail" (paying potential raiders who own large blocks of stock to go away) illustrate both of these points. They also illustrate that price per share and book value per share are often far apart and often fluctuate.

On the other hand, a change in demand or technology may convert some current assets consisting of newly obsolete inventory into a "liability." Or, defaulted accounts and notes receivable convert both current and long term assets into "liabilities" (handicaps). On the other hand, relatively low accounts and notes payable on the liability side may become major assets, or resources, because they may be increased substantially to enable the company to acquire other resources. Writing down obsolete inventories and reducing book value to reflect current market conditions have led many companies tot he bankruptcy courts.

Several points emerge from this discussion. First, the dynamic character of the environment is an important force in contributing to the dynamic nature of resources, and the reverse is true also. Second, things are not always just assets and liabilities as the balance sheet says they are. Even though an item is labeled a liability, it may be a powerful resource, and the reverse is true for an asset. The dynamic nature of the environment will be influential in making the determination.

We are not suggesting that accountants change accounting terminology or techniques; we are advocating that managers develop a broader resources perspective of assets and liabilities, one that would enable them to view liabilities as potential resources, and assets as potential resistances, without upsetting the American Institute of Certified Public Accountants, the SEC or the IRS. Long ago, financial analysts adopted this perspective, and began plugging into their analyses, especially those related to mergers and acquisitions, the "value" of such off-balance sheet resources as brand names, quality of distribution systems and managerial competence.

Third, the dynamic nature of the environment underscores the importance to managers of creating an environmental signal corps in their firms. Fourth, the failure of many managers to anticipate or respond to environmental changes is at the root of the problems of the industries discussed earlier. The successes of many companies can be explained by the fact that many managers did anticipate, respond to, and even created environmental change—especially in high-technology industries.

Premise 4

The state of the wants and the state of the arts drive resource management.

Two sets of interdependent criteria influence the appraisal of resources: the state of the wants (demand) and the state of the arts (supply). The former reflects many things, and ranges from the expression of basic human needs for food, clothing and shelter, tot he enlargement of those basic needs by individual wants that eventually result in the production of modern goods and services. The state of the wants extends to include larger social objectives related to such things as health, eduction and welfare, culmination in higher aspirations represented by such terms as life, liberty and the pursuit of happiness; and improved quality of life; ad peace, security and opportunity. The state of the arts represents the attainment level of human capacity to deal with both technology and social organization. In brief, it represents how well an organization can meet the wants of the market.

The elements of these criteria of resource appraisal are not fixed; both the state of the wants and state of the arts are in a constant state of change. In fact, a change in one is often induced by a change in the other, and resources are in a constant flux, reflecting changing capacities of mankind and changing definitions of needs. The appraisal of resources in the context of the state of the wants and the state of the arts is the central feature of the functional theory of resources. The appraisal is of the natural, human and cultural resources as means to ends, and of the resistances that must be overcome before the desired ends can be attained. Since resources available to us evolve out of the working combination of their natural, human and cultural aspects, the study of resources falls into separate fields that require the services of specialized groups.

1. The basic scientists are the fact-finders of society. They reveal the secrets of nature and answer such questions as: What is it? Where is it? How is it, and why? How

does it behave, and why? Their work is objective and detached from the human viewpoint. They deal with "neutral stuff" that may or may not be useful to mankind.

2. The applied scientists are the technicians of society. Their function is to apply their knowledge to the findings of the pure scientists in order to determine what is technically feasible, and to answer the question, what can we do with it? They separate the feasible from the unfeasible or the not yet feasible.
3. Entrepreneurs and managers are the economic risk-takers of society. They determine and test the economic feasibility by asking whether those things found to be technically feasible are potentially profitable. Their question is, how should it be used to yield the highest return to private enterprise? They seek to differentiate the profitable from the unprofitable, or the more profitable from the less profitable. We must also include here the entrepreneurs and managers of such non-profit organizations as social, political and religious institutions that have different tests of technical feasibility and profitability.
4. Economists and other social scientists are the evaluators of society. Their function is to help shape the grand strategy of resource use to encourage the highest and wisest application of scarce resources to alternate ends. In doing so, they try to distinguish between good and bad, and between that which promotes the common good and that which harms. Their questions center on how the resources should be used to yield the highest return to society and/or the organization.

Probably the second application of the systems approach (after *Genesis)* was in the field of resource use as practiced by primitive man. Modern society raised that approach to a high art because no one person or group can fully understand and appraise resources. As the simplified exposition shows, the appraisal of resources proceeds:

- from the knowledge of the facts of nature and culture,
- to the determination of technical feasibility,
- to the determination of profitability,
- to the formulation of social-economic based public strategy.

And, of course, the appraisal process and criteria are related tot he state of the wants and the state of the arts.

Resource management requires synthesis. Our fourth premise has several facets. First, the state of the wants (demand), the state of the arts (supply) and the management of resources related to them are the forces that drive the creation and management of economic, technological and social (and anti-social!) organizations. Second, resource management involves synthesizing natural, human and cultural resources and overcoming resistances to the exploitation of each of those categories of resources.

This means that resource management requires the ability to synthesize and manager resources related tot he input, throughput, output and support efforts of the organization that are designed to attain its objectives.

Third, marketing resources are deeply involved with the state of the wants in identifying, creating and satisfying demand. Also, they are more than casually involved in tailoring certain elements of the state of the arts so that supply and demand are meshed. Accordingly, marketing resources occupy a pivotal position as the means to the ends of both the market and the organization. When those resources deliver satisfactions to the market to attain users' objectives, they are the major force in helping to attain the objectives of the organization. Because of the pivotal position of marketing, a marketing resource management concept will enlarge and strengthen the foundation for a resource based strategy of the organization.

Premise 5

Resource management is management of functions.

Because they reflect human appraisal that something can be relied on for aid and support, it is emphasized that resources are abstractions. The word resource does not refer to a thing or substance, but to a function that the thing or substance performs or to an operation in which it may take part in order to attain desired ends.

The management of functions. Out fifth premise is that the primary mission of resource management is the management of functions and resource packages (or systems) to attain given ends. The management of activities, tasks or "men, money and machines" are at best secondary to the primary mission.

This implies an hierarchical structure that underlies getting things done. We refer to that structure as *the functional continuum of management.* It starts with determining the function of the business or undertaking, and moves through the strategic, managerial and operational roles of management. In so doing, it differentiates among functions, activities and tasks. This differentiation also draws distinctions between the among what a company produces, markets and sells. The management of functions and resource packages avoids the all-too-common practice of starting the formulation of strategy at the wrong level in the process of strategic management.

A simple example will provide a basis for differentiation. The *function* of a police department is to help preserve the peace of the community and protect the public. In so doing, it engages in several *activities* such as sponsoring anti-crime educational programs and patrolling the streets. Among other things, in engaging in their patrol activities, police officers perform such diverse *tasks* as ticketing speeders, checking to see if store doors are locked and "helping little old ladies across the street."

Four industries are outlined to further differentiate among the concepts. Two of the industries, fast foods and cosmetics, appear to have decided the true nature of their businesses, and have sorted out the distinctions between what their businesses are and what they produce and market. They have also recognized the difference between what they market and what they sell. Managers of firms in these two industries can base the formulation of their financial, marketing, production and other strategies on the functions they perform rather than on heir operational processes. As a result, their function, what they produce, what they market and what they sell are all defined in terms of what they do.

The extensive deregulation of motor carriers began in the late 1970s with dramatic changes in policies of the Interstate Commerce Commission. Those changes allowed greater freedom in rate-making, and permitted new companies to enter the relatively closed competitive environment. Even more drastic changes followed congressional action in 1980. These changes coupled with a depressed economy resulted in bankruptcy for many carriers, while some of the survivors began to sort out the differences between operations-based strategy and strategically based operations. Most motor carrier managements appear to have based their strategies on the operational processes involved in moving goods from here to over there, almost as if goods are moved just for the sake of moving them. In the ordinary course of events, there is only one reason goods are moved: to meet the requirements of the marketing programs of customers and customers' customers. Therefore, carriers are not in the transportation business; they are in the marketing support business and engage in several transportation-related activities to support the marketing efforts of their customers and their customers' customers. While the carriers may sell transportation services, they market that marketing support that provides time and place utility and logistics management.

In his classic article of three decades ago. Theodore Levitt addressed the subject of "Marketing Myopia." He urged managers to define their organizations broadly in order to take advantage of opportunities, using the railroads as examples of companies with marketing myopia because they defined themselves too narrowly. Levitt sad the railroads had foreclosed many opportunities by not identifying their business as the transportation business instead of the railroad business.

Professor Levitt suggested that the railroads should have defined their business in terms of their activities (transportation). Instead, we believe that all organizations, including freight carriers, whether for-hire or private, should define their businesses even more broadly in terms of their function. As was pointed out above, carriers are in the business of supporting the marketing effort of their customers and their customers' customers. Their function is *marketing support.* Transportation is only one of the activities carriers engage in to provide that support, and transportation resources are only one set of resources available to fulfill the function of marketing support. Other activities include using conceptual resources to provide expert advice on distribution, using information resources to inform shippers about location of their shipments and time of arrival, and using other managerial resources to assure quality performance and customer service. *Marketing myopia* was only part of the problem plaguing the railroads; it was only a symptom. *Resource myopia* was the problem, or *functional myopia.* The actual and normative perceptions of most bank managements, are roughly parallel to those ascribed to motor carrier managements, where today the money storage or rental role perceptions still used by many bank managers are a proven route to competitive failure against managers practicing a financial services approach. As with the motor carriers and several other industries, the bank management disaster caused by unwise real estate and oil loans, among other things, was largely self-induced and stemmed from similar causes: failure to read persistent environmental signals; a myopic view of what business they were in; and, as a result, no functionally based strategies underlying their operating strategies.

We also show what we see as the proper normative perceptions of these concepts for bankers and motor carriers. If these perceptions are used, the managerial perception of the *function* of the company or *definition* of what business the company is in becomes the foundation of all that follows. That function and business definition are the joint springboard for the strategic and managerial concepts, upon which, in turn, operations are based.

The result of the normative approach is that strategic matters become dominant, and operations processes reflect those strategic considerations. Thus, the process of "what the people do" is driven by strategic objectives related to resource use, finance, production and marketing. There is a vast difference in the results of this approach which expands their opportunities and thus resources, census one where "what the people actually do" is determined only by operational needs, with true strategic objectives absent. There is now evidence that both motor carriers and banks, especially banks, are using the normative approach in increasing numbers.

Premise 6

Resource management is management of environments.

Environment management. Our sixth premise, derived from Zimmermann's concepts discussed above, is that managerial responsibilities center on the three basic activities in *managing the environment:* (1) those related to the product itself as well as the processes required to get it to users, (2) those related to customer service, and (3) those related to managerial innovation. These activities involve the application of culture tot he environment, the adaptation of the organization tot he environment and the adaptation of the environment to the needs of the organization. This premise is based on our belief that the function of management as it fulfills its role is to acquire and manage resources in order to find and exploit opportunities, find and solve problems, and manage change.

Both the function of management and the basic activities for which managers are responsible have several implications for resource systems, resources of organizations and environmental management. Rather than dealing with only one system, managers deal with several resource systems with different functions, the first of which is the managerial resource system, a multilevel, multifaceted system managing the environmental resource system. These two systems include such diverse resources as vendors, the production system, the marketing channel system and many others, and management needs strategies for the management of the functions of each of the systems as the basis for management of activities and tasks—or a functional approach to management. There are a number of interrelated considerations involved in environmental management. First, drawing a distinction between the external and internal environments is an artifact of classification that may do more harm than good if applied carelessly, because that split detracts from the unity of resources and the wholeness of the system. For example, today, Firm A may use Firm B, an independent wholesaler who is by definition a part of the external environment. Tomorrow, A may acquire B, which would then become a part of its internal environment. The function of B will not change; it still will need to support the marketing efforts of A and A's customers.

Second, the off-balance sheet resources of an organization deserve at least as careful managerial attention as the balance sheet resources. These off-balance sheet resources may be intangibles, such as an inventory management concept or the marketing concept, or they may be such institutions as the wholesaler in the example above, or even the market for the output of the organization. Thus, the effective integration of managerial effort requires that the two types of resources be meshed.

A third and related consideration has to do with the difference between coping with the environment and managing it. Essentially, this is the difference between the acceptance of a static situation and an active approach, to attempt to manage the organization's destiny. All of the elements of the environment should be considered potentially variable and therefore subject to being controlled, including laws that may be changed, suppliers whose policies my be meshed, or finding ways of bypassing environmental situations that cannot be controlled.

Premise 7

Comparative advantage may lead to competitive disadvantage

Once more, we use Zimmermann's general resources perspectives as a backdrop. His belief that "Man's own wisdom is his premier resource—the key resource that unlocks the universe" was the central thought underlying those general perspectives. Premise 7 is a synthesizing premise. It is derived from and integrates the conceptual and operational features of the other six premises. In addition, it is a premise that provides the basis for selecting the way in which the principle of absolute and comparative advantage is used. A valuable, widely used, and very dangerous tool for resource allocation, misguided managerial use of this principle may so seriously impair the development of an organization's technological expertise and core competency as to jeopardize its future.

Resources, comparative advantage and competitiveness. Our seventh premise is that setting priorities for resource allocation on the basis of either absolute or comparative advantage may be counterproductive or even destructive, where absolute and comparative advantage are often used to determine whether certain resources will be allocated to produce parts of a product in-house or whether managers will turn to external suppliers. Absolute and comparative advantage are useful aids in make-or-buy decisions. A firm has an absolute advantage if it can make Product A five percent cheaper than an external supplier. It has an absolute advantage in making Product B if its costs are 35 percent lower than those of the other firm, but it also has a comparative advantage in making Product B because its manufacturing costs are comparatively lower for B than for A. The potential supplier has an absolute disadvantage in making both products, but its comparative disadvantage is less for Product A.

This situation suggests two alternatives for the low-cost producer: either make both products, or make Product B in which it has a comparative advantage and buy Product A. It also suggests similar alternatives for the high-cost producer: either buy both products or buy Product B where the comparative disadvantage is greatest and make Product A. However, for both rims, the application of absolute and comparative advantage may be either an extremely wise use of resources, or destructive for one or both.

To illustrate this point, we first look at the application of the principle of advantage to trade between nations, and then apply it to trade between organizations. A few phrases illustrate the point: you specialize in bananas; we specialize in steel; we trade. You produce oil; we buy and refine it; we sell you cars and gasoline. You mine iron ore; we refine it and sell you washing machines. Each nation should do only what it does best. One nation should specialize and become "hewers of wood and drawers of water" and sell to another that is more efficient at producing energy, steel and manufactured goods. This was the basis for colonial policy, including that of Great Britain for the American colonies. Often the result is that the hewers of wood and drawers of water fasten poverty on themselves and enrich their trading partners by shipping raw materials to the industrial nations where greater value is added. The escape this poverty potential, the American colonies rebelled, and the oil-producing countries of the Middle east designed the OPEC cartel. Now let's return to our original illustrations of Products A and B and give them some specific names to illustrate both the good and bad aspects of applying the concept of advantage, Let Product A be wheel capable of being produced five percent cheaper than a potential supplier's and Product B, wheel covers 35 percent cheaper. If our firm has limited resources, it makes sense to buy the wheels and make the wheel covers. This results in a switch from sing balance sheet and internal resources to using suppliers in the external environment as off-balance sheet resources. In this situation everyone is probably better off.

But what if Product A consists of the internal technology of a computer and Product B is the external shell? Again, that depends on our organization's business definition. If it defines itself primarily as a computer parts assembled instead of a developer and manufacturer of computers, the strategy is still appropriate. However, there is a risk that the vendor may decide to get into the assembly business also, despite its comparative disadvantage.

Now we change the assumption for a different illustration. Assume that we aspire to be a computer developer and manufacturer and that Product A is a high-technology product that costs us 15 percent more to produce that to buy from others. The decision here is no so clear-cut. If we buy that part, we lose whatever competitive edge we originally had, as continued product improvement makes our skills obsolete.

Core competencies are at the heart of decisions of this type. These points and their implications are carefully considered and effectively illustrated in *Harvard Business Review* article by C.K. Prahalad and Gary Hamel. The authors make a strong case for their thesis that in the 1990s executives will be judged on their ability to deal with what they all "core competencies" that make growth possible. To deal effectively with the core competencies, those executives will have to "rethink the concept of the corporation itself." They add that, "Both the theory and practice of Western management have created a drag on our forward motion. It is the principles of management have created a drag on our forward motion. It is the principles of management that are in need of reform." They point to the treasured concept of Strategic Business Units (SBUs) as an element most in need of reform because of the parochial attitudes developed toward ownership of resources and competencies and the difficulty of coordination effort across SBU boundaries.

The authors of the article draw an analogy between a diversified corporation and a tree. The root system of the tree is the equivalent of the core competencies; the trunk and large limbs are the core products; and the leaves, flowers and fruit are end products.

Core competencies are streams of technology and expertise that spawn a wide range of products presently produced, as well as those not yet visualized. For example, the core competency Honda developed in engine and powertrain manufacturing led to its advantage in several businesses: automobiles, generators, lawn mowers and motorcycles. Core competencies are seen as the collective learning of the organization that enables coordination of diverse skills of different people in different parts the organization.

This means that core competencies are resources of the organization and do no "belong" to any one department, product group or SBU. In turn, all those concerned are required to transcend traditional organizational boundaries in their thinking, efforts and loyalty. Because people at all levels and functions or activities of all kinds are involved, effective organization-wide communication is necessary to assure coordination of effort and enhancing of core competencies. Core products are those that flow from the core competencies, and are the major components of end products and the major contributors to their value. For example the ability of Casio to make things in miniature plus its competence in display systems converged to enable it to be in such businesses as calculators, monitors, and miniature television sets. Core competence and comparative advantage do not make good bedfellows for the long run. For example, "Outsourcing can provide a short-cut to a more competitive product, but it typically contributes little to building the people-embodied skills that are needed to sustain product leadership." Pralahad and Hamel pointed out that Chrysler has tended to view engines and power trains as just one more component, and as a result Chrysler is becoming increasingly dependent on Mitsubishi and Hyundai. This situation illustrates our point about the dangers of seeking external suppliers based on absolute or comparative advantage (or disadvantage). It also illustrates the point made by the authors of the cited article when they wrote, "...to many companies have unwittingly surrendered core competencies when they cut internal investment in what they mistakenly thought were just `cost centers' in favor of outside suppliers."

Implications of comparative advantage and competitive disadvantage

Five major points emerge from the discussion of this premise.

1. The other six premises underlying resource management are in some ways free-standing but also are interrelated. The discussion of absolute and comparative advantage and core competencies re-emphasizes the points made in Premises 1,2, and 3 that resources are more than balance sheet items, that physical and cultural resources are different, and that managerial and cultural forces affect resource availability.

Also, the discussion of core competencies and products re-emphasizes Premises 4,5, and 6 that resource management is driven by the state of the arts (and wants), that it involves the management of functions such as core competencies, and that it is concerned with the management of internal and external environments to create a structure for developing and nurturing core competencies.

2. This seventh premise shows the actual and potential managerial abuse of some very valuable concepts, such as the management of cost and profit centers, the principle of absolute and comparative advantage, and strategic business units. The abuse has taken the form of creating a series of departments, product groups or SBUs that are parochial in nature, discrete and independent in structure, and act as if they do not work for the same firm.

3. Both practicing managers and management theorists need to rethink the structure of the organization and the theory underlying it to make them more consistent with the real world of competitiveness. They need to develop theories and

structures that place a high value on the coordination of effort and integration of activities.

4. This premise also shows that both managers and academics need to stop insisting that some functional activity be the driving force of an organization. The core competencies are major resources of the organization, and for the concept of core competencies and products to have any significant role in maintaining competitiveness, the resources underlying their development and nurturing must be the forces that drive the organization.

5. The core competencies are jeopardized by the three strategic oversights of management related to managerial processes, off-balance sheet resources, and the external environment; and the failure of managers to deal effectively with core competencies is a major cause of the strategic oversights. For example, the managerial processes in coordination of effort are stifled by the parochial views fostered by management of an organization structure that overvalues the independence and relative autonomy of departments, product groups, and SBUs.

While we have made much of the value of dealing with off-balance sheet resources—particularly those in the external environment—too much of a good thing can be destructive.

Preparing for resource management

We prefer to think that we are not practicing managerial heresy, but are moving into the realm of managerial heterodoxy. One way to prepare for resource management is to have resources replace such functional activities as finance, marketing and production as the conceptual driving force of organizations. Another way is to recognize that balance sheet terminology is unsuitable and misleading as a basis for resource management because some assets may actually be liabilities, and *vice versa*. A third way is to recognize that some off-balance sheet resources, such as a marketing channel network or reliable vendors, may be more valuable to the organization than certain balance sheet assets, such as a money-losing branch plant. A fourth option is to recognize that the strategic management of the processes required to transform an idea into a user-satisfying good or service is at least as important as the strategic management of the product. A manager that recognizes all four of these viewpoints will be well along the path to preparing for the management of resources.

With the business environment changing as rapidly as it is, few strategies will remain optimum for very long. Therefore (1) continuous adjustment is required to keep something from *becoming broke*; (2) continuous fixing is necessary to repair the inevitable imperfections of the adjustment process; and, consistent with the GE idea, we should be working at making it *steadily better* anyway.

The Japanese attitude seems to be. "It is always broke; so fix it continuously." This is reflected in their concept of *kaizen*, the gradual improvement toward a goal.

The concept is implemented by employees at all levels who are responsible for seeking improvements in both the product and the process as a way of reducing cost and improving quality and productivity. Accordingly, we echo GE's charge to accept change before change is necessary. But the reactive acceptance of change is not enough. Managers should be proactive in seeking it out and inducing it. And, a resource-based management style will be a stimulant to proactive change.

Managing resources should be no more difficult than managing functional activities. The difficulty is in departing from orthodox ways of thinking and doing things "as usual," where the comfort index is high even though the effectiveness and efficiency index usually is lower than it should be. To help prepare for the management of resources based on the resource management concept, we first examine some desirable managerial perspectives of resources and functional activities. Subsequently, we look at the need for analysis and synthesis of some of the factors involved in the processes of resource creation and use.

Management of resources Vs. management of functional activities

The *elements* of the framework of resource management were discussed, and the *process* of resource management was introduced. Both the framework and the process and considered in more detail in this and the following chapter.

The management of resources and the management of functional activities cannot reasonably be separated; the question is one of focus. Managers must focus on using resources effectively to attain an objective, and on the efficiency with which those resources are used to perform the functional activity to attain that objective. This is the essence of resource management; both resources and functional activities get attention. Alternatively, managers may focus on the effectiveness and efficiency with which a function activity is performed to attain an objective—the essence of activity management. The primary focus is on the activity, but the effective use of resources is given secondary attention.

We have previously referred to companies, especially those involved in the marketing channel, that are generally activity-oriented. Also, we have discussed companies that were marketing-activity-, sales-activity-, or production-activity-oriented. All of these companies were myopic. We will now provide some specific examples of how the myopic activity approach results in the undermanagement and relatively ineffective use of resources, with suboptimal financial performance.

A look at what happened between two members of a marketing channel illustrates the difference. One member was an activity-driven large shipper in the North; the other was a resource-driven small warehouseman in the South. The typical shipment to the warehouseman consisted of several hundred cartons of the same product. They were to be delivered on specified dates to about 20 consignees, some of whom received a dozen cartons and some several dozen. Each carton was individually addressed. Both the shipper and the consignees were happy with what they thought was the efficiency of the activity. To small warehouseman met the time requirements. Sorting all those cartons took an extraordinary amount of time and warehouse sorting space which the shipper paid for, and on which the warehouseman made a profit. While the total number of cartons usually tallied, sometimes the shipper addressed too many to some consignees and too few to others. The warehouseman eventually persuaded the shipper to conserve resources by not addressing each carton, and by telling the warehouseman who got how many packages. The warehouseman eliminated the sorting, conserved resources, and was able to offer a rate reduction of about 20 percent.

In addition to saving on warehouse charges, the shipper save by not having to stencil several hundred packages. It had been very difficult to get the shipper to change, but he was very pleased when he did. Consignees were happier too because they always got the right number of cartons. The former approach emphasized the activity, and measured its effectiveness by on-time delivery. The new approach emphasized resource management and measured its effectiveness by the reduced resources required to perform the activity as well as before, and to do it less expensively.

Another potential customer of the warehouseman had exactly the same process but with a different product. When the warehouseman proposed the same approach, that shipper had a problem accepting it because his system worked well. ("It ain't broke.") He delayed doing anything until he could check with the first customer to see how things worked out. The point, of course, was that the warehouseman was resource-driven, while the shipping customers were activity-driven. Also, the customers were using a process required when they used common motor carriers who needed addresses on each carton. When the activity changed from motor carrier to warehouseman, they retained the old process. It was "broke," but they didn't know it!

A third and more dramatic illustration involved the same warehouseman and a shipper in a nearby town who wanted his goods warehoused and ultimately shipped. The shipper asked for a bid that called for the warehouseman to pick up the goods each afternoon—because that was the way the shipper had always performed that activity. The warehouseman proposed a resource-oriented variation that the shipper could live with. The warehouseman had a truck on an assigned daytime route that was idle all night. He proposed to spot a trailer at the factory to be loaded by the shipper. The warehouseman would leave an empty and take away the full trailer about 2:00 a.m. each morning. By getting more use out of the tractor-trailer combination, he was able to offer a substantially lower charge than if it had been done the "normal" way. The shipper's resources were also used more effectively because the shipment could be prepared at slack times during the day instead of having to be ready for a scheduled pick-up.

In a *Harvard Business Review* article, James Brian Quinn and his coauthors examined the way some technology-based companies are shifting their strategic focus on resources and activities. Those companies—among them Apple, Honda and Merck—are moving to less-integrated organizations, building their strategies around highly developed service skills rather than around products. Such companies identify the core activities for which they have or an develop unusually capabilities *(core competencies)*. Other activities are then farmed out to other companies with superior resources. For example, General Motors arranged for PPG Industries to manage and operate the paint departments in its assembly plants. Master Card and Visa have arranged for American Express to process much of the work related to customer charges and transactions. Apple began by manufacturing as little as possible and concentrating on design and control of its products concepts, appearance and key software.

This shift from using internal resources to using external off-balance sheet resources to perform activities in which an organization has either an absolute or comparative disadvantage has several implications. First, it frees resources for use in the activities retained. Second, it gives the company greater flexibility in adding or dropping products. Third, because of lower costs and perhaps better quality from external sources it improves a company's competitive and profit position as long as no core competencies are sacrificed.

In the best of all worlds, resources and activities would be given equal emphasis, as we sometimes suggest. However, managers do not live in the best of worlds. Two "Equals" are seldom truly equal: one is almost always "more equal" than the other and is dominant. Accordingly, we position resource manage-ment as the dominant force over functional activity management. We do so because if functional activity management is dominant, resource management may be short-changed. However, if resource management is dominant, activity management is given proper consideration.

Focus on human resources. Employee involvement (EI) is one narrow and specialized example of giving primary attention to the management of resources rather than to the management of functional activities. EI is also known by several other names, including worker participation, quality circles and jointness (in the automobile industry). In EI, management focuses on the management of human resources rather than on the activities. This approach to resource management is not new to many companies in both manufacturing and other operations.

While many variations on the basic theme exist, one version of EI creates teams of five to 15 people. The workers may rotate jobs and produce an entire product or service with relatively little managerial supervision. The teams may even take over a wide range of managerial duties including some aspects of customer service, work/ vacation scheduling, and ordering materials. In some cases, unions seek roles in decisions affecting production scheduling, capital expenditures and the introduction of new technology.

Integrating resource and functional activity management

The CSX Corporation is the result of several mergers and acquisitions in the early 1980s. The major merger was between two regional railroads that roughly blanket the area east of Chicago and Mobile, excluding the area north of Philadelphia. In its 1985 reorganization, CSX rejected the typical activity-based structures of railroads that, "tend toward a mentality of run the trains first, serve the customer second, and then make a profit if you can." Instead, it looked to the functions of its several groups of resources to design what it calls a "component structure" and "a market-driven organization." By so doing, CSX positioned itself as being in the business of supporting the marketing effort of its customers.

What CSX calls a component structure, we call a resource-based structure. What it calls a market-driven organization, we call a resource-driven marketing support organization. The differences in terminology are unimportant.

A resource-based organization structure. This discussion of the CSX organization structure concerns only the transportation group and how it focuses on resource management rather than functional activity management. Seven groups were created, four of which are concerned with transportation. The other three are concerned with technology (information systems and communication), properties (real estate and hotel interests) and energy (mineral, transmission and exploration). CSX later disposed of the resorts, pipelines, and oil and gas operations because they diverted management attention from the core businesses. One of the four transportation groups, American Commercial Lines (ACL) is a barge line and was held out of the other three transportation groups in accordance with an Interstate Commerce Commission decision.

Each of the three transportation groups is headed by a President-CEO who is held responsible for fulfilling carefully identified functions. The activities of the groups are "coordinated, integrated, and monitored" by the Transportation Operator Groups (TOG). The Presidents-CEOs of the three groups are members of TOG. The other members are the highest officers of CSX: The Chairman-CEO, Vice Chairman, President and Senior Vice President-Corporate Development. *CSX Distribution Services* defines and implements the marketing support effort of the company. All of the marketing resources and activities are centered in this group. It is responsible for all activities that involve transportation customers. This group is the customer of CSX Transport and depends on it as an off-balance sheet resource in fulfilling its function. *CSX Transport* supports the marketing effort of its customer, CSX Distribution Services. It is responsible for delivering transportation services to customers of the carrier and supervises all resources and activities related to delivering those services. To meet its responsibilities, it depends on CSX Equipment as its vendor—an off-balance sheet resource of CSX Transport. *CSX Equipment* has the function of supporting the operation effort of one of its customers. CSX Transport. It owns all of the equipment-related resources and is responsible for acquiring, maintaining and supplying them to CSX Transport as one of the latter's off-balance sheet resources. The creation of these three groups separated resources according to their respective interrelated functions, or as Chairman Watkins put it, by component. The separation of marketing effort, transportation activities and equipment ownership enables each group to concentrate on the effective acquisition and use of its own resources in fulfilling its function. The TOG monitors coordination and integration of effort to resolve differences.

Watkins said the structure helps CSX avoid the classic big organization problems. It also gives, "an opportunity to leverage special competitive advantages while producing a market-driven organization; integrated customer service; and dramatically improved accountability for costs, revenue, profits and asset utilization." In this sense, when CSX reorganized itself, it created a new resource in the form of an organization structure on which the several parts could draw for support of their own efforts. The CSX Corporation had essentially the same resources before and after the reorganization: customers, concepts, people, equipment and facilities. Before the reorganization, all resources were focused on the activities related primarily to running the trains and selling transportation to move goods from here to over there.

The reorganization was based on two new perspectives. First, CSX was not in the transportation business. It was to be in the marketing support business, or an Watkins put it, it was to become a market-driven organization. Second, the focus shifted from activities to the resources required to perform them. This focus shifted attention to customers as basic resources; marketing and operation concepts as guides to managing customers; and people, equipment and facilities as ways to implement the concepts. The effect of the new perspectives and the reorganization was that CSX became a marketing-resource-driven organization that perceives itself as a marketing support system. Even its transportation production resources and its equipment resources are considered to be marketing resources.

A resource-driven marketing support organization. CSX published a special report on its marketing program, quoted in the discussion below, based on an interview with Aden Adams, Vice President-Marketing for CSX Distribution Services. That report shows how the company applied a series of conceptual resources with a hierarchical structure that flows from the resource management concept down to the marketing support concept, the marketing concept and the target marketing concept. Adams established the *resource management* orientation when he said: "But what we are really trying to do with marketing is improve our profit margin and concentrate on the most profitable use of our assets and people." Taken out of context, that statement could be interpreted as implying that profit is everything and the customer be damned. However, in the context of the *marketing support* orientation of CSX, the real meaning of the statement emerges. Adams said they have so many customers with differing needs that they have many different approaches to the common goal of finding the competitive advantage that makes the customer want to use CSX. He stressed the CSX approach of interacting with its environment and developing ways to adapt to circumstances it faces. Previous comments about the organization structure also show the marketing support orientation.

This interactive process leads to the application of Adams' view of the *marketing concept*: "reaching out to find customers and then designing ways for an organization to satisfy them." CSX uses an elaborate system of market segmentation as the first step in applying the *target market* concept. It identified 149 market segments and assigned them to a classification reflecting a market's attractiveness to the company. The classifications are the well-known grow, hold, harvest and exist. Three criteria are used to decide whether to pursue a given segment: whether CSX can serve it effectively and economically; whether the market is growing, stable or shrinking; and whether competitors can serve the segment better.

The Four Ps of marketing—product, place, price and promotion—are used in the second step of the target market concept. The *product* is now considered to be distribution services, a total package of services, "not just moving freight from point A to point B." The package that is being marketed includes billing, claims, information, expert advice on logistics and special equipment. The package of services may extend beyond rail service to combine long-haul rail movements with bulk storage and local truck delivery. The nearly 100 bulk and non-bulk facilities are resources that were created to further improve marketing activities. They include not only bulk and general merchandise warehouses, but specialized auto, steel distribution and lumber centers.

The CSX version of the *place* element is a variation on what marketing people usually think of place—channels of distribution. To CSX, place means how and where it is most profitable to operate. *Price* is determined by the interaction of competition and customer requirements. It starts with cost as a floor, and ends with market conditions. "We can't charge every customer the same price for every service because every customer has different needs." *Promotion* includes the selling process in all its forms—personal sales, telemarketing and advertising. Adams stressed that the other elements will not work without effective promotion.

In addition to the external marketing program, internal marketing is a part of the coordination process. Initially, internal marketing was overlooked. Adams said they were so busy with external marketing that they hadn't spent much time explaining what they do and why. He said, "some people may think we are trying to force other departments to spend a lot of money satisfying customers with costly, special service."

All of the activities CSX performed before the reorganization are still performed. However, the focus has shifted from running the trains to selling transportation service to keep them running. The focus is now on the effective acquisition, integration and use of resources—human, physical, conceptual and organi-zational--required to support the marketing effort of its customers. In short, it focuses on being a resource-driven marketing support system.

Resource creation and use

The environment is the provider, processor and user of various mixes of the materials and conditions found in nature; people with wants, needs and abilities; and such cultural resources as capital (including money, machines and facilities), vendors, facilitation institutions, knowledge, skills and wisdom. Ultimately, that environment is the fountainhead of all resources, and a two-phase framework will simplify the necessary environmental analysis. The first phase involves a framework for synthesis of the work in the resource creation process by: the basic scientists who discover things; the applied scientists and technologists who develop techniques for their use; the business people who make them economically profitable; and the social scientists who examine things from the perspective of society. Resource creation is truly where the sciences meet. The second phase involves a framework for the deployment and use of production and marketing resources through the input-throughput-and-output steps of the managerial process. This phase is where the functional activities meet. These two frameworks will help managers sort out: (1) the synthesis of the resource creation process' elements and (2) the integration of the steps in resource use in production-and marketing-related activities.

Resource creation: where the sciences meet

In today's complex world it is difficult to name even one resource that is available to managers just for the taking. The oceans as transport facilities come the closest we can think of, but even before they can be used, ships have to enter them from the port and harbor resources created for that purpose. For all practical purposes, all resources of the modern organization have to be created. In fact, throughout recorded history most resources have always been created. Oceans themselves were neutral matter except for food and resistances until vessels were created that could navigate them. It is true that resources are created when materials and conditions in nature are the basis for products to satisfy the wants and needs of people. This is also true for such diverse products as environmentally safe pesticides, a device to replace a person's limb lost in an accident, an improved hair shampoo or a replacement for existing metals.

Resource creation calls for the synthesis of effort of scientists, technicians, managers social scientists and many arbiters who pass judgment on the results. Synthesis of effort for resource creation may start in the mind of a researcher who has no particular end in mind for it. Or it may start with the recognition of some need such as the need for a new vaccine. Or, it may start serendipitously. A biologist told one of the authors that one of his jobs as a graduate assistant was to keep mold from forming on bacteria cultures because it kills the bacteria and ruined the research. His counterparts in universities all over the world were doing the same thing—until

Fleming discovered that the mold was the basis for what was to become penicillin. The responsibility for resource creation belongs to management—not to scientists, engineers or social scientists. Unless management provides motivation and creates a working environment in which creativity and research can flourish, new resource creation will be limited, Inventors working alone are a different story; they provide their own motivation and environment.

Synthesis of effort in the creation and use of resources, and the role of people and their knowledge in that synthesis are constantly recurring themes in all of Zimmermann's work. We pointed out above that several diverse groups are involved in creating resources, including scientists, technicians, managers and social scientists. Others involved include lawmakers who pass enabling legislation or provide subsidies, lobbyists who try to influence the lawmakers one way or another and activist groups who take their case to the people. Zimmermann summarized the importance of synthesis in the last paragraph of his book:

If the preceding discussion has led to any vital conclusion, it is the altogetherness of things. In this inextricable mesh of forces and conditions, man appears as the responsible agent. The problems of resource adequacy for the ages to come will involve human wisdom more than it will involve limits set by nature.

Nature of the synthesis. The synthesis of effort in creating resources is typically done sequentially. The first set of things pertains to resource appraisal and is shown in the first column, which lists the types of services required for appraisal, the sequence of the appraisal process, and the function and activities undertaken by the appraisers. A new theory of human behavior and a pest-resistant type of plant. However, with a few word changes, it also applies to the creation of other types of resources such as a concept of managerial accounting or a process for improving the quality of goods.

An example shows that common sense is the basic tool used in the synthesis of effort in resource creation. If it is desirable to know more about the role of bacteria in breaking down compounds, naturally the services of scientists in bacteriology and related fields and needed. These scientists proceed from their knowledge of the facts of nature, and their function is to determine what is available. Their activities center on discovery and telling the secrets of bacteria.

The someone begins to think of applications. Perhaps it is the research scientist or an applied scientist or technician—or both—who picks up on some facet of that knowledge that shows the effect of certain bacteria on oil-bearing sands. The effort of the applied scientist is then devoted to determining the technical feasibility of using bacteria to release oil from its hiding place, and in doing so is helping to refine and define the concept of the original research scientist.

Other scientists-technicians may pick up on a facet of the new knowledge that shows that another strain of bacteria "eats" other compounds and determines the technical feasibility of using bacteria to clean up oil spills. The next phase is to test the process to determine its economic feasibility. This requires the services of managers to help set up experiments and determine the return on investment and develop the product for the market. As this is being written, arrangements are being made by the developers to test, in an old oil field, the use of bacteria in releasing oil from its sands. If it proves to be economically feasible, the next step is for social scientists to determine several aspects of social and economic strategy to determine how the process should be used and its benefit to society.

At any time between discovery and exploitation the arbiters may begin to evaluate the implications of the process for the economy and society. At some point, governments, conservationists and others will get into the act. Depending on what their conclusions are, one group may try to inhibit the process while another may try to encourage it. The net effect, if we are lucky, will be to balance the usefulness and profitability of the new product or process with possible harmful side effects.

The discussion of the synthesis of effort has made the process look deceptively easy in three respects. First, while we think the situation justifies our action, we disposed of the problem of creating the necessary environment by saying, in effect, "Go to the library and look it up." Second, the point was made that common sense is the major tool required to synthesize effort. As if there were no spill-over among them. Again, common sense comes into play to force recognition that the groups and actions that appear to be isolated from one another cannot be isolated.

Steps in the synthesis of effort. The following is a summary of the six steps involved in a systematic approach to the synthesis of effort in the creation of resources.

1. Design an organizational environment conducive tot he creation of new resources. Among other things, this reflects a willingness and commitment of management to adapt to and manage change. Two problems can be encountered in the implementation of this step. One is the resistance to change that is characteristic of many organizations and is often embedded in the culture of an industry, an organization, and/or of individuals. The other centers on the leadership required to manage the incredibly co-mplex task of identifying and bringing together the elements of the desired environment. Even the after-the-fact case histories of companies whose leaders have created such environments—some of which were cited above—make the process look deceptively easy.

2. In that environment, prove the scientists with the tools, direction, freedom of investigation, rewards and controls to answer the questions relevant to the organization's interests about what is available. Despite the neat boxes, communication systems among the scientists, engineers, marketing and production people are not just desirable, but essential to provide some direction for the scientists and to furnish a basis for integrated effort.

3. In that environment, provide the engineers and other technicians with tools appropriate to their work, give them more specific direction than is provided the scientists and establish rewards and controls to answer questions related to feasibility, reliability and safety. Communication between the technicians and other managers is even more important to the synthesis of effort at this stage than in step 2. Alternative designs can help or hinder both the production and marketing processes.

4. The next relevant question has to do with economic feasibility, raises even more questions and requires the synthesis of completely different kinds of effort. The finance people are brought in to determine whether the new resource or product can be financed. Before they can make their determination, questions about the volume-cost-price relationships have to be answered by production, marketing and management science people. And those answers are not firm because they are only estimates based on estimates. The estimated amount to be produced will influence the estimates of unit costs, which will influence estimates of possible prices, which go full circle and influence the amount to be marketed and thus produced. In this step, managers and analysts have to anticipate some of the questions that are raised in the fifth and sixth steps. Even though these questions take place outside the organization, the firm's effort has to be synthesized with what outside organizations might do.

5. The fifth step will take place whatever the organization may think about it. The relevant question here is to determine how the resource should be used from the point of view of society.

6. The sixth step is related to the fifth. The questions here relate to whether the new resource or product should be introduced, and if so, under what conditions and with what types of controls, subsidies or limitations. The types of products on which society wants controls include new drugs, cars that are perceived to be unsafe, nuclear power plants, coal-fired power plants, artificial hormones to increase milk production and many others.

This discussion has centered on the nature of the effort to be synthesized in resource creation and the steps in the synthesis of that effort. It has been concerned with the environment as the provider of resources. Now we turn to examine the nature and elements of the environment as a processor and user of resources.

It will become evident that resource creation is an integral part of resource use. This is a discussion of only one very broad segment of resource use: input, throughput and output management (ITO management). Several other major subsets of resource use not specifically covered are the management of resource systems; information; and financial, human and physical resources such as buildings, machinery and equipment. However, discussion of management either embraces most of those subjects or alludes to them.

Some Characteristics of the exchange system. Goods and services are produced to be exchanged for money or something else of value. Therefore, except for purely housekeeping activities, the exchange system is critical to almost everything the organization does. The exchange process of a given organization starts with the acquisition of raw materials, parts and supplies and ends with a finished product being completely consumed, or that part not used up being sent to the junk yard or disposal site.

The input-throughput-output systems of the organization are different from those of the exchange system. Generally, for the organization, materials and labor are considered to be the inputs; production processes the throughput; and finished goods and services the output. However, as explained below, when the organization is considered to be a part of the exchange system, a different perspective of these segments is required. *Input* to the exchange system is the acquisition of materials and the production of goods and services. *Throughput* consists of the activities that take these goods and services from the end of the organization's production line, add value to them, and position them for acquisition by the user. The *output* segment of the system consists of the organization's competitors and the buyers of goods and services, where the exchange cycle ends when the goods are used and waste products suitably discarded.

Considering input, throughput and output from the perspective of the exchange system, rather than from that of the organization, makes it easier to develop integrated strategies for the system. These strategies will acknowledge the exchange system and its members as resources of the organization. They also will acknowledge the support role that each member of the system performs for other members, and that each are both customers and have customers in the system. Several other things about the exchange system should be noted.

Decisions affect most members of the system. Regardless of where their positions are in the input-throughput-output segments of the system, almost all of those involved in the system are affected by many, most or all of the actions or decisions of almost any other member of the system. For example, note the effect on inventory, transportation and other policies of those doing business with an organization that has adopted the JIT concept of inventory management.

Vendors have to adjust their own marketing, inventory and logistics activities. Customer service provided by vendors takes on a new meaning. No longer can they promise the customer that just 90 percent of the deliveries will be made on time. The new figure is 100 percent or the customer has to shut down the plant/ This means a new policy for deciding on safety stocks of inventory, possibly a new location for inventory or even of the factory, and new financial requirements to implement the inventory policy.

Furthermore, arrangements with warehousemen and transportation companies will be required to assure timely delivery to the customer. These arrangements may extend to the vendor setting up its own private warehouse and private carrier. In addition, the vendor may need new arrangements with financial agencies. All of these changes from the vendor's side may or may not mean increased costs to the vendor. The organization installing the JIT system has done so to lower costs. Accordingly, the buyers of finished goods and business owners are affected by the impact of lower costs on price and profit.

Not just one exchange system. An organization with several products or services and several users may have multiple exchange systems because of the variety of input-throughput-output resources. For example, a food processor may have multiple output segments and thus multiple throughput segments of the system. That processor may have its own national brand to be sold to householders through wholesalers and retailers. It may also put a grocer's private label on some of the output and sell directly, or package the product in large containers for distribution to institutions and restaurants.

A vendor of raw materials, machinery or supplies that are inputs to one system will have its own vendors and production activities as its input segment of its exchange system. Also, it will have its own throughput and output segments. The raw material vendor has some interesting differences from other vendors. Its input of raw materials is a combination of the rights to mine, grow or cut products and the finished products of other producers. Those products are mining, agricultural and timber-cutting equipment. Their production input is not much different from that of other producers. Its output role in the system differs in that coal, ore, oil, wheat and lumber are mostly sold on the basis of some grading system that identifies product quality. This means that the product of a givèn grade from one producer is not substantially different from that of another producer. Even though past and future references are to *the* exchange system and an organization's exchange system, there are many systems, and each member of one organization's system has his or her own system.

Even though some terminology of manufacturing is used, services have their exchange system. This has been reflected in the fairly consistent use of the words goods and services. One reason is that much of the work of the exchange system is done by such service organizations as wholesalers and transportation companies. Also, accounting, legal, advertising, banking and other service organizations have their own exchange systems. For example, the raw material input of the accountant's exchange system is numbers. The production input results in the creation of balance sheets, productivity analyses and audit reports. The throughput involves timely delivery of quality work. The output segment has to do with the use made of reports by clients.

The marketing channel is a part of the exchange system. The flow of goods through the manufacturing-wholesaling-retailing-consumer elements of the channel is usually depicted as a linear system. While that approach accomplishes its purpose, it does not consider the interaction of resources that takes place in the exchange system. That system is more accurately portrayed as a system of interdependent subsystems that interact with each other throughout the exchange process.

Information resource management

The development and implementation of information applications is an organizational change process. Organizational procedures and processes change as a result of or in connection with new information systems. Jobs and tasks are altered. The development and implementation of applications therefore should be managed in order to achieve desired results without undesirable organizational and behavioral consequences. The basic approach to application development management is the system development life cycle, but other strategies are in use. The development approach to a specific application and the application development environment.

Organizations usually follow quality assurance procedures for manufacturing operations, but frequently do not apply the same principles to information systems. Control and quality assurance producers can be applied within the organization to assure information system quality. Analysis of value of information systems and post-audit evaluation of application are methods for applying cost and benefit criteria to information system applications. There are also methods to evaluate existing and proposed hardware and software. The purpose of this chapter is to describe the process of system design and implementation. It focuses on action-oriented techniques for carrying out the process of design and managing it. The underlying theme of the chapter is that different strategies are available for the design and implementation of information systems, and the selection of the appropriate strategy depends on the situation. In the first section, a contingency approach to choosing the appropriate development strategy is described. In the following sections two major system development strategies are discussed.

Information requirements determination may employ a variety of techniques, the appropriate technique being dependent on the situation. Development should encompass a process to accommodate requirements changes and provide assurance that the application as developed is an accurate and complete reflection of user requirements. A fundamental purpose for application development methods is therefore *requirements development assurance.* However, application development approaches or strategies differ in their power to achieve requirements assurance. A contingency approach to choosing the appropriate strategy is described below. Once a strategy is selected, methods appropriate to it can be selected. Subsequent sections of this chapter describe the prototyping and life cycle development methods and relate them to the contingency approach to requirements development assurance.

The underlying basis for the selection of a requirements determination strategy was uncertainty as to the ability of users and developers to know and elicit requirements. In the selection of an appropriate development strategy to assure correct and complete application development, there is uncertainty of requirements prior to and during development. During application development, four contingencies affect the degree of uncertainty with respect to achievement of an application to deliver "real" information requirements.

1. *Project size*: The project size contingency has two characteristics: duration and total cost. These characteristics are usually, but not necessarily, collinear; that is, a high-cost project usually requires an extended time period. Large project size increases the difficulty of assuring that requirements are met because of the number of persons involved in establishing and modifying requirements, the volume and complexity of communications, and changes over time in both user and developer personnel.
2. *Degree of structuredness*: One dimension of the Gorry and Scoot Morton framework for information systems is the relative structuredness of the decisions to be supported by an information system. Uncertainty about the structure of the decision process or other process to be supported is thus an important factor in uncertainty about initial requirements and about alteration of those requirements during development.
3. *User task comprehension*: Distinct from degree of structuredness is the comprehension that the user or users have of the task to be performed by the information system. User task comprehension affects requirements determination and development uncertainty in much the same way as the degree of structuredness. If users have a low degree of understanding, or do not agree on the task for which a system is intended, the level of uncertainty for accuracy and completeness both in initial requirements and requirements modification is high.
4. *Developer-task proficiency*: Developer-task proficiency is a measure of the specific training and experience brought to the project by the development staff: project management, liaison staff, systems analysts, systems designers, programmers, and so on. It is not a measure of ability or potential but rather of directly applicable experience. This contingency indicates the degree of certainty with which the developer will be able to understand requirements accurately and completely and develop an application to achieve them.

A common organizational response to requirements development uncertainty is to add control by adopting a single requirements development assurance method. Rather than forcing all projects to use a single requirements development assurance strategy, an alternative approach, which recognizes the differences in project-related factors, is as follows:

1. Measure contingencies and determine the level of development uncertainty.
2. Select a development assurance suitable for the observed level of uncertainty.

Four basic development assurance strategies, and the contingencies under which they are appropriate, are described below:

1. *Acceptance assurance strategy:* This strategy is to accept user statements of requirements as complete, correct, and firm and to develop as defined. There are no procedures to gain assurance that initial requirements are correct or complete or that requirements do not change during development. Examples of appropriate use of the "accept" strategy are file conversions, reports from existing files or databases, and some simple, single-user decision models. The contingencies these examples have in common are small size, high degree of structure, users who understand what the systems are to do, and developers who are experienced in this kind of task. When appropriate, the acceptance assurance strategy will lead to greater responsiveness to users who have well defined needs, elimination of frustrating assurance procedures for such users, and an increase in development efficiency.

2. *Linear assurance process*: If application requirements can be determined through a straightforward process with little or no subsequent modification, a suitable assurance strategy is to proceed from requirements specification to final development. As each step is completed, there are assurance procedures to verify conformance with requirements. There are "sign offs" to this effect. This is a linear assurance process and is used in most formal life cycle methodologies. The linear assurance process is an effective strategy under a combination of contingencies that lead to a very low level of requirements changes after the initial sign-off on specifications. Application requirements for systems that are highly structured and for which user task comprehension and developer task proficiency are high may be effectively developed by this process. If the system is also small and involves only one or a few users, the linear assurance strategy may be effectively equivalent to an acceptance assurance strategy. On the other hand, requirements achievement for even a relatively small system might not be assured by this process if the decisions to be supported are relatively unstructured, the user does not comprehend the task, or the developers have not previously produced such a system.

3 *Iterative assurance process*: Where requirements uncertainty during development is moderately high, the linear assurance strategy may not assure that application development meets real information requirements. For such applications, the linear assurance process of traditional life cycle methodologies can be modified to include iteration. Whenever requirements are found to be wrong or inadequate during development, the specifications are revised by a return to the requirements determination process with users. The sequence of activities in the life cycle can therefore be repeated as often as necessary in order to obtain the requirements and develop a system to achieve them. This approach assumes that a correct and complete specification of requirements can be obtained if sufficient iterations are

used. Examples where the iterative assurance process is applicable are large multiple-user systems and application areas that are new to the user or developer organization.

4 *Experimental assurance process*: A high level of requirements and achievement uncertainty during development may indicate the need for an experimental assurance process in which requirements development assurance is obtained through actual user experience with the system being developed. This experience is achieved by prototyping or simulation of the application. The prototype design method reduces uncertainty by producing successive approximations. Users and developers can readily identify the shortcomings of a prototype even when they were unable to specify application requirements in advance. Examples of applications with high uncertainty include decision support systems for upper management, interactive forecasting models, and unstructured systems to be implemented for multiple users. Conscious selection of the experimental assurance strategy may be the only effective approach to assurance that requirements are met when the level of uncertainty is very high.

A contingency model for selection of a development assurance strategy selection is depicted. Application of the contingency model require measurement of the level of each contingency, estimation of the overall level of uncertainty determined by the contingencies, and selection of an appropriate strategy.

Note that, putting aside the acceptance assurance strategy, there are two general approaches to proactive application development requirements assurance: application development life cycle and an experimental, prototyping approach. Prototyping is described below; the traditional system development life cycle method is described in subsequent sections of this chapter.

The strategy of experimental assurance in development of information system applications may be achieved by an evolutionary design method commonly called *prototyping*. Prototyping is used when requirements are difficult to specify in advance or when requirements may change significantly during development. The prototyping methodology is based on the simple proposition that people can express what they like or do not like about an existing application system more easily than they can express what they think they would like in an imagined, future system. A prototyping methodology is initiated by a user who conceives of a problem or an opportunity to be solved by an information system. The user seeks assistance from a professional system designer who is competent in the prototyping methodology.

Prototyping an application system is basically a four-step process, as described below and depicted in. There are two significant roles: the user and the system designer.

Step 1: Identify the user's basic information requirements: In this stage, the user articulates his or her basic needs in terms of output from the system. The designer's responsibility is to establish realistic user expectations and to estimate the cost of developing an operational prototype. The data elements required are defined and their availability determined. The basic models to be computerized are kept as simple as possible.

Step 2: Develop the initial prototype system: The objective of this step is to build a functional interactive application system that meets the user's basic stated information requirements. The system designer has the responsibility for building the system using very high level development languages or other application development tools. Emphasis is placed on speed of building rather than efficiency of operation. The initial prototype responds only to the user's basic requirements; it is understood to be incomplete. The early prototype is delivered to the user.

Step 3: Use of the prototype systems to refine the user's requirements: This step allows the user to gain hands-on experience with the system in order to understand his or her information needs and what the system does and does not do to meet those needs. It is expected that the user will find problems with the first version. The user rather than the designer decides when changes are necessary and thus controls the overall development time.

Step 4: Revise and enhance the prototype system: The designer makes requested changes using the same principles as stated in step 2. Only the changes the user requests are made. Speed in modifying the system and returning it to the user is emphasized.

All illustrated in step 3 and 4 are iterative. The number of iterations may vary considerably. There may be one of two reasons that iterative modification is ceased. First, the user determines that the prototype is not useful and the working prototype is discarded. Second, the user is satisfied with the system and it becomes an "operational prototype." It may be modified at a later stage, but at this point it is considered usable any may be distributed to other users. Alternatively, it may "seed" the idea of a new major application and be used to provide initial specifications for the application development effort.

The prototyping methodology, as outlined above, has several significant advantages in development of applications having high uncertainty as to requirements:

- Ability to "try out" ideas without incurring large costs
- Lower overall development costs when requirements change frequently
- The ability to get a functioning system into the hands of the user quickly
- Effective division of labor between the user professional and the MIS professional
- Reduced application development time to achieve a functioning system
- Effective utilization of scarce resources

A major difficulty with prototyping is management of the development process because of frequent changes. Also, there may be a tendency to accept a prototype as the final product when it should only be the basis for a fully-specified design. For example, a prototype may no handle all exceptions or be complete as to controls. It "works," but it is not complete.

Variations on the prototyping model

The model described above assumes only two participants: a user who is a functional expert and a system designer who is expert at the development of prototypes. The prototyping methodology may be modified to accommodate a greater number of participants. Multiple users may be involved in prototype development when the application is useful across a broad area with many different user, or when it is so complex as to require input from several specialists. Both situations require added time for communications and negotiation among users. They do not significantly affect the designer's time required to build the prototype. If an application requires complex technical or analytical skills, it may be necessary to have more than one designer, and this may add time to the prototype-building process.

As users become more familiar with very high level development languages and gain experience with the use of prototypes, it will become more common for the user to also function as the system designer. In such cases, it is important that the user have access to computing resources. One approach is a service organization such as an information center.

Life cycle approach to application system development

Although there are a growing number of applications that should be developed using an experimental process strategy such as prototyping, a significant amount of new development work continues to involve major operational applications of broad scope. The application systems are large and highly structured. User task comprehension and developer task proficiency are usually high. These factors suggest a linear or iterative assurance strategy. The most common method for this large class of problems is a *system development life cycle model* in which each stage of development is well defined and has straightforward requirements for deliverables, feedback, and sign-off. The system development life cycle is described in detail since it continues to be an appropriate methodology for a significant part of new development work.

The basic idea of the system development life cycle is that there is a well-defined process by which an application is conceived, developed, and implemented. The life cycle gives structure to a creative process. In order to mange and control the development effort, it is necessary to know what should have been done, what has been done, and what has yet to be accomplished. The phases in the system development life cycle provide a basis for management and control because they define segments of the flow of work which can be identified for managerial purposes and specify the documents or other deliverables to be produced in each phase.

The phases in the life cycle for information system development are described differently by different writers, but the differences are primarily in amount of detail and manner of categorization. There is general agreement on the flow of development steps and the necessity for control procedures at each stage.

The information system development cycle for an application consists of three major stages:

Definition

Development

Installation and operation

The first stage is the process which defines the information requirements for a feasible cost-effective system. The requirements are then translated into a physical system of forms, procedures, programs, etc., by system design, computer programming, and procedure development. The resulting system is tested and pout into operation. Not system is perfect, so there is always a need for maintenance changes. To complete the cycle, there should be a post audit of the system to evaluate how well it performs and how well it meets cost and performance specifications. The three stages of definition, development.

At completion of each phase, formal approval sign-offs are required from the users as well as from the manager of project development. Each phase also results in formal documentation. The information system development cycle can follow an iterative assurance strategy. For example, the review after the physical design phase may result in cancellation or continuation, but it may also result in going back to prepare a new conceptual design.

It is instructive to note that upon completion of coding of programs and beginning of program testing, the application is probably only about 60 percent complete. For example systems involving much testing, completion of coding may mark about the halfway point. Many errors in estimation of project completion dates can be attributed to failure to allocate adequate time to program testing and conversion.

The life cycle definition stage

Ideally, a major system development project is conceived as a component of the information systems planning process, but a proposal may come from other sources such as users and data processing personnel. After a project is proposed, the next step in the definition stage is feasibility assessment, which is discussed briefly here. Once a proposed alternative is approved, the next phase is information requirements analysis. Following requirements analysis, a conceptual design phase produces a high-level design emphasizing the application as seen by its users.

Upon completion of the definition stage most of the key decisions that affect the user have been made. The definition stage is therefore critical in making sure the application will meet user needs. Although perhaps only 25 percent of total efforts has been expended, the important decisions that shape the remainder of the effort are in place. The definition stage must therefore not be neglected if applications are to satisfy the users. In a study by McKeen, it was found that projects which spend more time in the definition phase were more successful regardless of the outcome measure used. Both user satisfaction and ability to develop the application within budget were enhanced.

Proposal definition

The proposal definition phase is not necessary if the application was defined as part of information system planning. Otherwise, a simple procedure may be used for proposal of an application. Proposals may be for entirely new applications or for enhancements to existing applications. The proposal should not be complex but in a short one-or two-page document should provide sufficient justification to support a decision to proceed with a feasibility analysis. Examples of items that may be included are the following:

- identification of those proposing the project and others who have an interest in the application;
- The organizational need for or benefit from the application (the business reason);
- Organizational support (budget, sponsor, management support, etc);
- Schedule considerations (date needed, availability of user personnel, etc.).

Following user management approval, the proposal is reviewed by the management authority responsible for allocating information system development resources (user management, a steering committee, or the information systems executive).

Feasibility assessment

When a new application is proposed, it normally goes through a feasibility study before it is approved for development. If the application is part of the predefined MIS master plan, it still should go through the feasibility assessment phase in order to evaluate alternative approaches to its development, even through the general idea has been approved with the rest of the plan. If a proposal is submitted outside of the plan, the feasibility study includes whether it is consistent with the existing plan and whether it should override the priorities of other applications already planned.

Five types of feasibility are addressed in the study. They result in recognition of both the benefits and risks inherent in the development and implementation of the proposed application system:

1. *Technical feasibility*: Can the proposed application be implemented with existing technology? Analysis of project risk relative to technical feasibility includes not only whether the technology is available on the market but also its "state of the art" both in absolute terms and relative to the company's current technical sophistication.
2. *Economic feasibility*: Will the system provide benefits greater than the costs? The feasibility study presents intangible as well as tangible benefits in a formal way. A relatively detailed analysis of the costs of both development and operations of the various alternatives is also presented.
3. *Motivational feasibility: The* probability that the organization is sufficiently motivate to support the development and implementation of the application with necessary user participation, resources, training time, etc. This motivation is usually demonstrated by an owner or champion for the application who has sufficient organizational power to provide the resources and motivate others to assist and cooperate.
4. *Schedule feasibility*: The probability that the organization can complete the development process in the time allowed for development. Adding development resources does not always reduce the development time; in fact, adding staff who cannot be used effectively may impede development because of time spent in communication.
5. *Operational feasibility*: Will it work when installed? This analysis may involve a subjective assessment of the political and managerial environment in which the system will be implemented. In general, the greater the requirements for change in the user environment in which the system will be installed, the greater the risk of implementation failure.

The feasibility study may be staffed in different ways. Some alternatives are:

1. Evaluation group with representatives from users, information systems, and other groups affected by the system. The head of the study group may be user or from information systems.
2. Evaluation person or group from information systems.
3. Evaluation person or group from users.

Each of the alternatives has advantages and disadvantages, and the selection of the staff for evaluation may depend on the type of the project and the organizational culture with respect to responsibility. For example, an evaluation group with many representatives has advantages when the application will have significant impact on several groups or on the fundamental operations of the organization. The evaluation by information systems may be appropriate for highly centralized organizations in which the evaluation is primarily technical. The feasibility evaluation by users is consistent with user responsibility for information system resources. It establishes user commitment to the new system, and requires that user management be "sold" by the user evaluators.

The feasibility report covers items such as the following:

- General description of the application
- Expected development schedule
- Schedule of resources and budget required for development
- Schedule of expected cost and benefits from operations
- Summary of evaluation with respect to technical, motivational, schedule, and operational feasibility

If the feasibility study includes several alternatives, the report should present the budget, expected benefits, schedule of resources required, etc., for each (including the alternative of "do nothing"). The choice of alternative is based on the relative feasibility of each of the alternatives. For instance, the following alternatives were considered for an accounts receivable system for one division of a large multidivisional company (after rejecting "do nothing"):

1. Dedicated minicomputer system with modification of a purchased software package
2. A minicomputer system for data entry with processing on the central computer using a generalized transaction processing package.
3. Online data entry to the central computer using an accounts receivable system developed by another division and modified as required.

The feasibility report is reviewed by the management of information systems and by the requesting department. If not part of the master plan, it may also be reviewed by the information systems steering committee. Once the feasibility study has been accepted and an alternative is approved, information requirements analysis can begin.

Information requirements analysis

A contingency approach to selecting one or more methods for determining information requirements was outlined. In order to effectively obtain a complete and correct set of requirements, it is necessary to use a method or methods that take into account the extent to which requirements are already known versus their needing to be searched out or discovered.

The result of the information requirements analysis or requirements determination phase of the application development life cycle is a report detailing the requirements for the application. The requirements consist of items such as the following:

- Reports (including the data items on the reports)
- Queries (both regular and ad hoc)
- Conceptual schema for database (From data modeling or other analysis)
- Functional requirements (including operational characteristics)
- User interface requirements

Conceptual design

In the proposal definition, some user needs were specified; in the feasibility assessment phase, additional requirements were identified and some fairly general design alternative were evaluated. The information requirements analysis phase elicited and documented a more detailed set of requirements. The conceptual design phase establishes a more complete user-oriented design for the application.

It is useful to divide application design into a conceptual design phase and a physical design phase. These two phases can also be characterized as external design and internal design or general design and detailed design. The conceptual design emphasizes the application as seen by those who will operate or use the outputs of the system; the physical design translates those requirements into specifications for implementing the system. The conceptual design establishes the inputs and outputs, functions to be performed by the application, and audits and controls. In general terms, conceptual design treats the actual processing functions as "black boxes" physical design specifies the actual processing given in conceptual design. Conceptual versus physical designs in application development are loosely analogous conceptual versus physical modeling in database development.

Typical contents of a conceptual design report are the following:

- User-oriented application description. Documents the flow of the application activities through the organizational units providing inputs and using outputs.
- Distinguishes manual operations from automated operations performed by the application system.
- Inputs for the application with general description of each (visual display screens, source documents, forms, queries, etc.)
- Outputs produced by the application with general description of each (visual display screens, query responses, printed outputs, reports, etc.)
- Functions to be performed by the application system.
- General flow of processing with relationships of major programs, files, inputs, and outputs.
- Outlines of operating manuals, user manuals, and training materials needed for the application.

- Audit and control processes and procedures for ensuring appropriate quality in the use and operation of the application.

The life cycle development stage

The development stage of the system development life cycle consists of four classes of activity which may occur somewhat concurrently: physical system design, physical database design, program development, and procedure development.

Physical system design

The physical system design phase, also called internal or detailed design, consists of activities to prepare the detailed technical design of the application system. The physical system design is based on the information requirements and the conceptual design. In turn, it provides the basis for physical database design, program development, and procedure development. Testing is sometimes defined ad a separate phase, but testing is really part of each phase. Some life cycles include physical database design in the physical system design phase; however, since the trend is toward more independence between programs and data and specialized skills are often required for physical database design, it is considered a separate design phase in this explanation. The results of the physical system design phase are specifications and designs for the following;

- System design showing flow of work, programs, and user functions
- Control design showing controls to be implemented at various points in the flow of processing
- Hardware specifications for the applications if new hardware is required
- Data communications requirements and specifications
- The overall structure of programs required by the application with procedural specifications on functions to be performed by each
- Security and backup provisions
- An application test quality assurance plan for the remainder of the development.

The physical system design work is performed by systems analysts and other technical personnel. Users may participate in this phase, but much of the work requires data processing expertise instead of user function expertise.

The work of the physical system design phase is to take the fairly high level, user-oriented requirements of the conceptual design phase and produce a specific technical design. This process is generally one of defining the "black boxes" that will produce the required outputs based on the inputs defined in conceptual design. There are a number of different methods an analyst may employ.

By supporting the systematic process of expanding the level of detail and documenting the results, the methods aid in reducing the complexity and cost of developing application systems and in improving the reliability and modifiability of the designs.

Generally, physical system design techniques achieve simplicity by subdividing the application system into small, relatively self-contained modules. System modules can be programs or procedures which are subsections of programs.

System complexity is reduced because each module can be developed, coded, and tested relatively independently of the others. Reliability and modifiability are enhanced because a change can be made to a system module with minimal, well-understood effects on the rest of the system. The techniques are thus based on well-understood principles of systems theory.

Some of the available techniques are summarized below:

Techniques	Description
Top-down design	A processing unit is defined by a general statement of its purpose then broken down into smaller and smaller refinements. The design is depicted as a hierarchy chart with general control modules at the top and detailed modules at the bottom. The resulting program is also structured.
Structured design	Each, module of a program is defined by the specific function it performs. Emphasis is on decoupling or minimizing the integration between modules; each module is highly cohesive, meaning all the statements within it are functionally related. Structure charts, similar to hierarchy charts, show module definition. The transformation of data is represented by data flow diagrams.
SADT	Systems Analysis and Design Technique is a proprietary system utilizing a graphical modeling language to describe, in a top-down fashion, the functions of the system and the data utilized.
HIPO	Hierarchy-Input-Process-Output is a documentation technique which can also be used to communicate system specifications to project participants throughout the design process. The three types of charts, each depicting a finer level of detail.
Warnier-Orr	The methodology was originally developed in France by Warnier; it has been adapted and expanded by Orr. The methodology assists in defining the hierarchical structure of systems. It can be used in defining the logical structure of the processing system, data structures, and control structures and flow of control in programs.

The objectives of these examples of techniques for detailed design are similar, but each has unique features for defining and communicating system specifications. They can be used in communicating the design specifications to users, although they are not necessarily easy to understand for a person untrained in the technique. Another advantage of these physical design approaches is that they support the use of *structured programming*, to be described later in this chapter. One problem with all of the techniques is that they require a large investment in training analysts and converting to the new procedures. Each requires a rather complete commitment and changeover; it is not easy to "borrow" elements from each and combine them.

Since the early 1960s there has been ongoing experimental work in techniques for automating the system design process. The intent of these efforts has been to provide a means for specifying the information requirements of a system and automatically generating program code and database specifications. The problem is to develop a requirements language which is rich enough to provide the necessary information yet easy to understand. Another problem is developing adequate tools to generate code and organize data structures automatically.

The most comprehensive research project to date has been ISDOC at the University of Michigan. The ISDOS approach begins with a problem definer who defines the information needed, specifies timing and volume requirements, and provides algorithms and logic to produce output. The requirements are written in a Problem Statement Language. The software system analyzes the problem statements and in a limited sense performs system design, complies programs, organizes files, and directs execution of the resulting application system. In other words, information requirements statements. The ISDOS system thus performs tasks associated with physical system design, physical database design, program development, some procedure development, conversion, and operation phases of the system development life cycle. The system is in limited experimental use.

Physical database design

The approach to physical database design for an application depends on the existing database and the approach followed for database requirements determination. There are three major approaches to meeting the data requirements for a an application.

1. *Create a new physical life or database:* This is appropriate if no database is used or a database is dedicated to the application; in either case the application "owns" the data and objectives of a database are violated. New data may be required and the files or database must be designed and created from data collected specifically for the application.

2. *Using and modifying an existing database*: This method is appropriate if an evolutionary strategy for database development is followed. It may require special functions to be evoked by the database administrator for restructuring the existing database as well as adding necessary data.

3. *Access an existing database by means of a user schema*: This approach is possible if a

complete conceptual model of the enterprise, anticipating new application needs, was used as the basis for physical database design. New data may need to be added to the database, but the connection between the logical description of the data needed by the application and the physical database is easily made through the database management software.

The third alternative assumes that a complete data model of the enterprise will anticipate further application requirements. The second alternative is more likely even if a data modeling approach to database definition was followed. Fortunately, one of the advantages of database management systems is that the database can be restructured to accommodate evolutionary application requirements.

Program development

A primary output of the physical design process is a set of specifications that define programming tasks. The goal of the program development phase is to code and test programs required for the application. Testing of each module is performed on test data representing a fairly complete set of variations in input data in the user environment.

Problems encountered during the programming phase are typically a result of lack of complete specifications provided during conceptual or physical design. This often results in extensive reprogramming efforts when specifications are changed. The techniques for formalizing the conceptual and physical design process are aimed at alleviating this problem. Another problem in this phase is inadequate program testing prior to system test and conversion. A number of program development techniques reduce program complexity and aid in achieving program correctness. Important examples are modularity, structured programming, application generators, and tailoring of application packages.

The concept of *modularity* has already been discussed. The practice of subdividing a program into small, relatively well defined modules is generally accepted. Modularity aids in reducing program complexity and in enhancing reliability and modifiability. In most programming languages, modules can be programmed as subprograms with well-defined procedures for passing data values between them. Each module can be coded and tested by itself before begin integrated and tested with other modules.

In *structured programming*, a small set of basic coding structures is used for all program code, which generally results in programs that are straightforward in flow of logic. Structured programming is related to modularity in that use of the coding structures ensures well-defined modules. Structured programming is often termed "GOTO-less" programming because GOTO statements are discouraged or prohibited. The reason is that use of GOTOs can introduce unnecessary complexity. However, structures results in code which does not require GOTOs.

Testing represents a critical factor in application development. It can take up from 15 to 50 percent of the total development effort depending on the size and complexity of the application. Formal approaches to system testing involve a discipline which begins early in the program development phase. There are three distinct phases of program testing:

1. *Module testing*: Each individual program module is tested using dummy routines for calls to other modules.
2. *Integration testing*: Group of program modules are tested together to determine if they interface properly. This may be done incrementally as they are developed until the entire program system is tested.
3. *System testing*: This involves testing of the complete set of application programs.

There is debate over what constitutes a correct or adequately tested program. Some errors will be revealed only after the system is in production; however, a system that is put into production with too many errors can be disastrous in terms of corrective activity required and organizational acceptance of the application. Criteria for program correctness vary widely and tend to be related to the method of generating test data.

It is useful to distinguish between reliability and correctness for programs. A *correct* program meets specification; a *reliable* program operates in an acceptable manner under both intended and unintended input data and operating conditions. In other words, a reliable program will perform satisfactorily under a wide range of correct and incorrect inputs; a correct program need only perform satisfactorily as long as the inputs are as specified.

An alternative approach to application development with high potential payoff in productivity is to purchase generalized software packages and modify them to meet the unique needs of the organization. Many applications, such as payroll, have similarities across organizations and across industries, suggesting the possibility of using generalized software instead of writing unique application software. There are tow alternative approaches to the use of generalized application software packages:

1. *Have organization adapt to the package*: The application software producers are fixed and the operating procedures of the organization are modified to conform to the software. This alternative may be desirable for an organization with applications where there are no significant unique organizational requirements or internal training is less expensive than modifying the software. Another situation is when cost limits or the urgency for the system to be implemented offsets the benefits of unique requirements that can be obtained only through delay and extra cost associated with unique application development. Small business, for example, can frequently afford the cost of conforming to a package but not the cost of unique development.

2. *Adapt package to organizational needs*: Recent trends, accepted by software vendors and purchasers, have been to provide general packages that can be easily modified because of modular design to fit unique organization requirements. The increasing cost of software development relative to packages makes it cost-justifiable to purchase a package and spend the same amount as the acquisition cost to modify it. Some vendors "tailor" packages themselves; others provide the source code for their clients to modify. The tailoring alternative is suited for situations in which the essential features are found in a package, but the purchasing organization desires unique features.

When the choice is made to purchase a software package rather than to develop in-house, it is still important to have complete, accurate system design specifications. The specifications provide the guidelines for evaluating different software packages and choosing the one that most closely meets the specifications. They also dictate how the chosen package should be modified, providing a basis for estimating the cost of modifications and assuring that it is done adequately.

Procedure development

Procedure development can take place concurrently with program development. Procedures should be written for all personnel who have contact with the system. This includes the following:

1. *Primary users*: This includes instructions for how to interpret a report, how to select different options for a report, etc. If the user can execute the system directly, as in online queries, it includes detailed instructions for accessing the system and formulating different types of queries.
2. *Secondary users*: This includes detailed instructions on how to enter each kind of input. It is more oriented to "how to" and less to "what" for different inputs.
3. *Computer operating personnel*: There are generally maintenance procedures to be performed by computer operators and/or control personnel. Procedures include instructions for quality assurance, backing up system files, maintaining program documentation, etc.
4. *Training procedures*: In some cases, a separate training manual or set of training screens is developed for the implementation stage and subsequent training.

One of two groups may be responsible for writing procedures: analysts or users. The advantages of analyst-written procedures are technical accuracy, project control over completion, and conformance to the overall documentation; disadvantages are the tendency of analysts to write in technical jargon or technical abbreviations and to assume users have knowledge of the technical environment. The advantages of user-written procedures are an appropriate level of technical description and instructions that are understandable; disadvantages are the difficulty of assuring clear, complete instruction. A mixed strategy is one in which analysts and users work together to produce a technically correct, understandable manual. An effective procedures manual, one that communicates well and can be referenced easily, must be well designed. Several alternative layouts are shown. Conditions under which are most appropriate are the following.

Format	*Conditions for use*
Conventional	Sequenced set of instructions for one job title or unit. Possible use for policy statements
Playscript	Sequenced set of instructions involving several job titles or units.
Caption	Unsequenced procedures or policies
Matrix	Two conditions determine a procedure or an action.
Decision	Several conditions and one or more procedures or actions.
Live specimen	Supplement for all of above.
Flowchart	Supplement to playscript, matrix, or decision table.

It is important that procedures be kept current to coincide with changes to the information system. A document numbering system that ties procedures to particular programs, modules, or data files is useful for this purpose.

The third stage of the information system development life cycle begins with conversion to the new application system. The rest of the system development life cycle refers to the life of the system in use. After the system is in production, changes and enhancements are made during the operation and maintenance phase of the system. Periodically, a post audit of the system is conducted; based on this activity, the system may be modified, enhanced, or replaced.

Conversion

Conversion to the new application system begins after all programs and procedures have been prepared and individually tested. Three major activities prepare for actual conversion: acceptance testing, file building, and user training.

Acceptance testing is testing of the completed application and comparing it to specifications. It verifies to the user that the system meets performance criteria and operation requirements. The testing includes user inputs, operating and control procedures, and outputs. Differences between what users expected and what the system delivers are identified and resolved. The acceptance test was developed as part of the planning for the system.

File building refers to the collection and conversion to machine-readable form of all new data required by the application. File building can be a long and tedious process, and careful planning is important. *Ad hoc* file conversion programs may be employed if the required data is already in computer-readable form. If not, the data must be gathered, coded, and entered into the database. Sufficient time and human resources should be provided to "clean up" the data, that is, remove inaccuracies and inconsistencies and make the data complete. *User training* may be relatively straightforward or a critical effort, depending on the degree to which the new application system affects existing jobs. If techniques such as job design are used, training will involve substantial reorientation of the users to their jobs. Proper user training is an important factor in overcoming user resistance to new systems. In a later section of this chapter, training as a subset of the implementation or change process will be discussed.

Conversion from the old system to the new takes place after acceptance testing, file building, and user training are complete. Conversion can be accomplished in several ways. The most careful method is to run the old and new systems in parallel; the new system is run under actual conditions and the results are compared with the old system for reliability and accuracy. After the new system has shown consistent results for a reasonable period of time it becomes operational and the old system is dropped. The drawback to this method is that it is expensive; both machines and employees work double time. Machine time can be costly if new hardware is replacing old and both must be maintained. More important, employees are required to perform essentially two full-time jobs, one of them being new and unfamiliar. Moreover, if the system has not been sufficiently tested and errors are detected during conversion, costly delays and employee frustration can cause serious problems.

If parallel processing of the old and new systems is not feasible, the new system should be tested under simulated conditions of full volume before cutting over from the old. Complete cutover is often referred to as "burning the bridges" because it is usually impossible to return operations to the old system once cutover takes place. Problems with the new system are corrected by "brute force" since no alternative is available. This is frequently a risky strategy, especially for systems such as payroll where very little delay can be tolerated. If possible, conversion should take place gradually, one portion of the system at a time.

Conversion turns to disaster

A shoe manufacturer and importer, a division of a large company, waned a computer. The company hired a consultant to recommend computer hardware, prepare programs, and convert company records. The invoicing and inventory systems were to be the first applications, followed by accounts receivable and accounts payable.

The first computerized invoices resulted in customer complaints. The inventory reports could not be compared with the parent company reports. The consultant was terminated, and he filed a lawsuit for fees due.

Some errors in development were highlighted in pretrial discovery:

1 The company had no experience with computers but still decided to implement all major applications at one time.

2 The manual system of inventory control had been developed by employees without formal training, resulting in somewhat unique features. The consultant never fully understood the existing system.

3 Live data items were used in the testing. This produced huge test outputs which could not be checked adequately.

4 The parent company system and the company's new system were not compatible, so the parent company inventory files were not copied. Instead, temporary input clerks were brought in to prepare data, but no programs were available to validate this input. The input data quality was poor.

5 No audit trails were included to identify corrections. No one knew what has changed or who made the changes.

6 No company personnel were assigned to the project. Lower-level employees were afraid to contradict the consultant; high-level employees refused to participate at all.

Operation and maintenance

When the system appears to be operating without difficulty it is turned over to the information processing production function. This often requires not only approval by the user stating that they system meets predefined acceptance criteria, but also approval of the system operations and maintenance groups stating that it meets standards for documentation and maintainability.

Any subsequent changes in the application are handled as maintenance. Maintenance of an application can be classified as repairs or enhancements. Repairs are required when incomplete or incorrect coding renders the application defective. Enhancements are additions or improvements. Repairs dominate the maintenance activity for the first few months of operation. Later, most of the maintenance is enhancement. Sometimes maintenance is performed by the system developers, but often it is the responsibility of a separate maintenance group.

Post audit

A desirable part of the system development life cycle is a review of the application after it has been in operation for a period, such as a year. An audit team with representatives from users, development, maintenance, operations, and perhaps internal audit review the operation, use, cost, and benefits of the application. Recommendations from a post application and suggestions for improving the development process on subsequent applications.

Project management

When an information system project is approved, its consequences are not certain; there are risks associated with it. The anticipated benefits may not be achieved, costs may be higher than planned, time for implementation may be greater than estimated, or performance of the hardware and software may be lower than anticipated. There are three factors, recognizable prior to implementation, that affect the inherent risk in a project: size, the degree of structure of tasks to be automated, and the level of technology of the project relative to the organization. Note that the first two are similar to the factors contributing to uncertainty of information requirements. The level of company-relatively technology introducers risk in system implementation but is relatively independent of requirements definition. Using combinations of high and low for these three factors, there are eight possible risk estimates for projects.

Relatively level of technology used	*Structure*	*Size*	*Risk*		
Low	High	Large	Low		
		Small	Very low		
	Low	Large	Low		
		Small	Very low		
High	High	Large	Medium		
		Small	Medium-		low
	Low	Large	Very	high	
		small	High		

In other words, a large project using high technology for an application having low structure for the tasks to be automated has a very high risk. A small project using a low relative technology and high structure for tasks has a very low risk. The contingency approach to project management is to organize and manage a project according to the level of risk in the project. Four types of tools and techniques are applied to obtain appropriate project management.

1. External integration tools and techniques to link the project with users. Examples are user project managers, users on project team, and user steering committee.
2. Internal integration tools and techniques to keep the project team working as a unit. Examples are project review meetings, minutes, and team participation in decisions.
3. Formal planning tools and techniques to structure and sequence tasks. Examples are critical path scheduling, milestones, and project approval processes.
4. Formal control tools and techniques to evaluate progress. An example is a series of formal status reports with variance analysis.

In general, the lower the structure of the tasks to be automated, the greater the need for high levels of external integration with user involvement. High level of technology relative to the organization generally is aided by high internal project integration and fairly low formal planning and control. High formal planning and control tend to be most useful for large projects with low technology.

Management may choose a portfolio of projects to balance the overall development risk. Typically, a high-risk project will also have the greatest expected benefits if implemented successfully. For instance, a balanced portfolio might include one or two high-risk, high-benefit applications as well as several low-risk applications with more modest expected benefits. A mixture of projects with different risks and different project organization and management will allow an organization to achieve acceptable results while taking some risks to implement large projects, unstructured projects, and using relatively high technology.

2
Planning

Management by Objectives (MBO) is at once a method of performance appraisal and a technique of organisational planning and control. It is a top down control technique whereby corporate objectives are segmented into departmental targets and then into objectives for individual employees. Superiors and subordinates meet and jointly agree subordinates' job specifications and goals, preferably in quantitative terms. MBO supposedly motivates employees through involving them in the determination of objectives, and should help them develop their individual careers. Subordinates who exceed their targets will experience a sense of satisfaction in their achievements. Causes of success can be isolated, analysed, and applied elsewhere. The concept is not new: in Britain it has been formally applied in military administration since 1914—and informally since long before then. MBO imposes disciplined and logical approaches to decision taking. It forces managers to consider carefully the nature of their objectives, the factors affecting attainment of objectives, possible barriers, and all the alternatives available. Three management theorists in particular have recommended the use of MBO in business situations. Peter Drucker's contribution is perhaps the best known.

According to Drucker, there are in business 'natural' forces militating against the emergence of common objectives. These 'factors of misdirection', Drucker argued, are managerial specialisation, hierarchical management structures and differences in the work and perceptions of individual managers. Thus, management should consciously seek to direct the activities of all the organisation's employees towards the attainment of one common goal and MBO would result in the integration of corporate and personal objectives. Managers would be able, he suggested, to control and improve their own performances since, in Drucker's words, 'self control means stronger motivation..higher performance and broader vision'. John Humble saw MBO as a means for linking companies desires for profits with managers' desires to contribute to decision-making and to develop their careers. He recommended a hierarchical system of objectives, initiated by the organisation's chief executive and starting from its corporate plan. Schemes should include targets for divisions, sections, departments and individuals. Action plans were needed, the preparation of which required systematic analysis of tasks and agreement on appropriate performance standards. Thus, managers should consult with subordinates to agree priorities and to establish the resources and authority needed to achieve objectives. This participative aspect of MBO caused Douglas McGregor's to advocate consultative MBO systems. In McGregor's view, an ideal MBO system would enable individuals to identify and pursue personal objectives in harmony with the needs of the enterprise. Through participation, managers appreciate the organisation's wider objectives and understand their personal contributions towards achieving them.

Once targets have been agreed, progress towards their attainment must be systematically monitored. This will be possible only if the targets set are clear and precise. Senior management is compelled, therefore, to elucidate its objectives, publicise them and pinpoint the criteria used in their formulation. Targets should be reasonably attainable, since unrealistic targets will never be met and, in consequence, the entire programme will fail. Objectives can be specified at three levels: routine, developmental and for innovative effort. A sales manager, for example, might have a routine target of maintaining existing custom, a developmental target involving a launch of a new product and innovative targets concerned with location of new market opportunities, establishment of a new distribution system and the identification of demands for new goods. Objectives must be clearly defined: ambiguous phrases such as 'seeking' to increase profits' or 'reducing costs' are inadequate. Targets must be specific and, if possible, expressed in numerical terms. What constitutes 'adequate' as opposed to 'excellent' performance should be explicitly stated. Impossibly high targets must be amended.

Subordinates require resources, authority and facilities in order to attain their targets. Resource requirements can be listed in, MBO action plans drafted jointly by superior and subordinate which set out all the facilities, information and patterns of behaviour necessary for successful implementation of accepted objectives. The aim is to integrate the corporate goals of the firm with the personal aspirations of the individual manager, hopefully isolating those areas of his or her work that will enable individual effort to contribute most towards the attainment of broader company-wide objectives. At the end of each review period superior and subordinate meet to ascertain how far the action plan has been implemented and to discuss difficulties encountered. Both superior and subordinate suggest ways of improving performance and a further action plan for the next period is prepared. A convenient way to begin a action plan is with the superior making the statement, 'Your targets will be considered to have been met if...', and then filling in the rest of the sentence according to the requirements of the situation. The advantages of management by objectives are summarised below:

- it forces all employees to think carefully about their roles and objectives, about why tasks are necessary and how best to get things done.
- targets are clarified and mechanisms are created for monitoring performance
- crucial elements are identified in each job. This information is useful for determining training and recruitment needs.

- personal achievements of subordinates are recognised and rewarded
- superiors and subordinates are obliged to communicate. In consequence, superiors can quickly identify which subordinates, are ready for promotion and the help they will need in preparing themselves for this
- performance is appraised against quantified targets, not subjective criteria
- there is forced coordination of activities, between departments, between junior and senior management, and between short and long term goals.

MBO systems require effective management information systems in order to assess the effects of subordinates activities and the system should be sufficiently flexible to enable rapid revision of individual targets as environmental circumstances change. There are, of course, problems associated with MBO, including.

- the danger of meaningless attempts to quantify activities that are innately unquantifiable. How, for example, could the objectives of a manager whose role is purely advisory be expressed in numerical terms?
- possible encouragement of myopic emphasis on immediate quantifiable goals to the detriment of nebulous but nonetheless important longer-term objectives
- difficulties created through subordinates not being given the information, resources or authority necessary for completion of tasks allocated to them
- the enormous amount of time consumed by regular consulations between higher and lower executives. A dictatorial system whereby superiors simply impose targets on subordinates, without consultation, might be more efficient. Moreover, firms operating in highly uncertain, rapidly changing market environments may need to alter their objectives so frequently the MBO procedures become impractical
- tendencies of senior managers to pay more attention to subordinates' personal qualities than to the work done by them
- possible concentration of effort on the achievement of individual rather than departmental targets.

MBO at the departmental level

If you have to implement a management by objectives programme you will need to draft a precise and comprehensive statement of your departmental aims. Do this yourself, but send copies to all your subordinates and to your immediate superior together with covering memorandum asking for comment. Emphasise in the momorandum that your statement represents only your own personal and provisional view, and that it *will* be amended following discussions. Split the statement into two sections—one for the 'central aim' of the department, the other for 'specific objectives'. The central aim is a statement of the reason for your department's existence. It should relate directly to wider organisational aims dictated by higher levels of authority. Without a clearly specified central aim it is impossible to determine particular tasks that need to be done and the resources and authority necessary for their completion. If you cannot specify what you want your department to achieve, you will not be able to define meaningful targets for subordinates.

Hold a briefing session to inform your colleagues of the existence of the exercise. Then have a departmental meeting at which each subordinate can present his or her own interpretation of the central aim. Identify differences in various peoples' perceptions of this (write out the contrasting interpretations on a wall chart or flip pad if you have one) and have your subordinates openly state their views. A representative from senior management should be present in order to arbitrate whenever serious disagreements emerge. It is appropriate for a senior management representative to be present since he or she can relate the various interpretations of the department's role presented at the meeting to fundamental organisational goals. At the end of the meeting you should have an agreed position about what the department exists to do. It is very difficult to run a department whose members cannot concur on its basic purpose. If agreement cannot be reached, senior management will have to impose a settlement.

After the meeting, write out a list of all the tasks that will have to be done to achieve the central aim and alongside each item write a prediction of the consequences for the central aim if that task is not completed satisfactorily. Ensure that each task relates directly to the central aim. Now allocate these tasks to subordinates according to your opinion of their ability to undertake them. List the skills and experience needed to perform tasks, noting the personal strengths and weaknesses of the individuals to whom particular tasks have been allocated. Discuss the allocations with each subordinate, in private, on a one-to-one basis. Negotiate acceptance of specific achievement targets, noting subordinates' reservations and objections. You need to ensure that someone has a target relating to *every single objective*. Record this action plan formally in a typewritten document and file it for further reference.

Management audits.

Policies and procedures are effective in achieving organisational aims only if they relate to targets and to be relevant they must be up to date. Management auditing is the term used to describe the systematic analysis of the efficiency of policies adopted and procedures applied in attaining goals. Audits should be comprehensive (looking at all aspects of the firm's operations and not just some of them) and regular. As well as undertaking audits at predetermined intervals (say once every two or three years for a thorough investigation), audits are needed whenever external situations or internal circumstances significantly change. Business environments are dynamic in nature—they evolve, alter unexpectedly, generate new opportunities and make irrelevant some existing activities. The purpose of a major audit is to reorganise resources— material, financial and human—and redirect effort towards the more efficient attainment of currently pressing organisational goals. Minor audits, taking one department at a time, might be completed between major analysis. Large firms sometimes hire outside consultants to conduct management audits, on the grounds that outsiders will be more objective in their approach.

Auditing, planning, MBO and performance appraisal are all parts of the same package of management activity. Planning and the specification of departmental and individual targets have meaning only if current administrative procedures are adequate for implementing the targets set. Two types of audit are needed: internal and external. External audits examine the general environments, legal (the effects of changes in employment law for example), economic, market opportunities, behaviour of competitors etc. that surround the organisation. Internal audits investigate operational systems inside the enterprise and are the type of audit with which executive managers are usually concerned. Often, checklists are issued to department heads in order to gather information on the relevance of sectional activities, on the flow of work through sections and on relationships between resource inputs and departmental productivity. Standard work study techniques are frequently used to analyse efficiency during audits. A typical audit will examine such things as:

Management style and communications; whether organisation charts and job specifications are up to date; whether organisational and departmental objectives are understood by all department members; possible duplication of activities; operational efficiency with sections; plant and/or office layout;

Monitoring activity

Setting targets is not of itself sufficient to ensure that an organisation will function efficiently. Organisations need to be *controlled,* i.e monitored to ensure that targets are met. You need to establish what information needs to be collected for control purposes, by whom it should be gathered and when. Note how much time and money might be spent on compiling control data. It is essential therefore that the information collected have a definite and valuable use. In general, the less expensive the control process the better, so that automatic control systems requiring only minimal human intervention are normally preferred. Control has three aspects: information input, data evaluation and feedback to the controlling authority. Rapid feedback is essential. Otherwise problems could develop faster than the controller's ability to correct them. Obviously, corrective action should always be taken when targets are not achieved. What is the point of installing a control mechanism only to ignore the deficiencies it reveals?

Ultimate responsibility for control necessarily lies with top management, which will delegate appropriate control duties. The first stage in the control process is to use information gathered from a management audit to describe all current activities. This constitutes the *input* of the system, which is then compared with existing targets and, if necessary, corrective action is taken or targets amended to more realistic levels. Problems inevitably occur, among them the possibilities that:

- current activities might not be reported accurately, comprehensively, or in sufficient detail
- inappropriate criteria might have been used in setting initial performance objectives, resulting in unattainable targets which render the entire system inoperable.
- historical records of relevant activities may be inadequate
- information retrieval systems could be faulty.

Control methods

Control process link inputs to outputs and provide feedback. They measure current activities, compare them with activities specified in plans and correct deviations from predetermined norms. Managers are likely to encounter three methods of practical control: budgeting, compilation and analysis of control ratios and the analysis of 'standard' costs. Budgeting and standard costing are dealt with in chapter seven of volume two, and various key ratios are discussed under the subject headings to which they relate. There are, however a number of general comments on ratio analysis that are worth making at this point.

Ratio analysis

Preparation and monitoring of operational ratios permits the comparison of relative performance figures (rather than absolute amounts) over time. Each department must choose the ratios most relevant to its needs. A credit control department for instance will be interested in the ratio of bad debts to sales, while production managers will want to measure (among others) ratios of costs to outputs and average inventory to purchases. Personnel specialists will compute labour turnover indices (e.g. the number of employees with more than one year's service divided by the total number of people employed one year ago) and figures for revenue per person employed. Other important ratios are value added per employee, wage cost per unit of production, actual performance divided by target performance (for various variables) and value added per unit of plant or machinery.

'Normal' values for key ratios may be predetermined and acceptable deviations specified. Management by exception procedures can then be applied. Ratio analysis has much to offer as a technique of management control, since ratios can be used to show interrelationships between functional activities and large volumes of data that can be summarised into a few easily understood figures. Note however that a ratio consists of both a numerator *and* a denominator—an increas in one has an effect equivalent to a decrease in the other. Thus, a ratio that is reasonably constant over time might conceal large but counterbalancing disturbances in the variables that make up the ratio an these movements might be important and deserve close investigation.

A ratio should be relevant to the purpose for which it is intended and should be computed consistently. Where data definitions vary, ratios calculated using different criteria should not be compared. Different firms measure variables in contrasting ways. Accordingly, cross firm or industry ratio comparisons ought not to be attempted unless comparable measurement techniques are guaran-teed. Some firms value stock at cost, others at replacement value; some firms use straightline methods for depreciating fixed asset values, others use the method of diminishing balance. Ratios should not be interpreted in isolation, but compared with norms or targets and their constituent elements periodically examined in depth.

Feedforward and feedback

A good control system will be flexible and thus capable of easy adjustment as circumstances change. Environments, corporate objectives and organisa-tional climates alter over time-market conditions change, competing firms enter and leave industries. Equally, a control system should be clear and easily understood by those who use it: complicated formulae, statistics, graphs etc. can obscure simple issues.

Flexible, understandable systems will generate feedback informing controllers of the consequences of their decisions. Feedback, however, is retrospective—when the information arrives it may be too late to remedy malfunctions. It is better, therefore, that control processes contain predictive elements so that future problems can be forecast in advance and measures taken now to overcome them. Accordingly, control theorists increasingly focus their attention on feedforward, as opposed to feedback, systems. These are 'future orientiated', meaning that current activities are altered today according to forecasts of future events. In other words, likely eventualities are predicted and policies introduced now to overcome the difficulties they might cause. Thus, for example, management might predict today that future sales will fall because of increased marketing activity by a major competitor. Consequently, the firm alters its marketing policies, increases its advertising and public relations expenditure and generally intensifies its selling efforts to counteract the forecast decline in sales. Whereas feedback systems concentrate on initiating remedial actions at the output stage, feedforward schemes centre on decision-making in the input period. If inputs differ from activities necessary to overcome predicted difficulties, they are altered in appropriate ways. The success of a feedforward system depends ultimately on the accuracy of forecasts and business forecasts in particular are notoriously unreliable. There are so many variables involved: alterations in public taste, government policy, behaviour of competitors etc. and all are liable to change at any time.

Monitoring techniques

You can adopt various approaches to the monitoring function. The essential choice is between continuous involvement or the adoption of an arm's length 'management by exception' (MBE) approach. The latter was first advocated by F.W. Taylor in his book, *The Principles of Scientific Management*, published in 1911. Subordinates, Taylor argued, should submit to their superiors only brief, condensed reports on normal operations, but extensive reports on deviations from past average performance or targets set by higher management. Once established, standards should be monitored through picking out significant deviations from predetermined norms. Exceptionally good or bad results would be analysed in depth, but reasonable deviations from standard performance would not be questioned. Thus, routine matters would be dealt with at lower levels, leaving higher—level managers free to devote their time to unusual problems and policy issues.

Management by exception has been popular because of the enormous volume of information continuously generated within firms and the physical impossibility of continuously monitoring actual activities. Thus data could be collected continuously but analysed periodically(weekly, monthly, quarterly, annually). By specifying tolerable deviations from target performance and intervening only if the limits of tolerable deviation were exceeded, management could avoid becoming immersed in trivial issues and instead reserve its time and efforts for more demanding problems.

There are, however, several difficulties associated with MBE. First, there are time lags between the moment a problem arises, the moment it is noticed and the time remedial action is implemented. Manufacturing cost data, for example, may be collated and analysed once a month if a particular production line develops a fault and begins to generate unacceptably high expenses at the start of the month, the situation will not be recognised until the moth's end. Then there is a further delay before a report goes to higher management, followed by another lag until corrective action is taken and during these delays high extra costs are being incurred. The second major problem is that since 'acceptable' deviations from target performance are tolerated without investigation, it is possible for a particular activity to be perpetually above or below standard by a relatively small amount without the fact ever being reported. Hence minor defects continue and overall performance is constantly lower than could be the case. Equally, the cause of consistently superior performance just below the upper reporting boundary will not be examined; there is no mechanism for isolating the factors contributing to high achievement and applying these factors elsewhere.

Continuous monitoring, on the other hand, is today much easier than it was because of the availability of increasingly powerful desktop computer systems. Information on costs, outputs, revenues and other relevant variables can be immediately analysed at the moment of collection and existing summaries can be updated at once. Trends in costs and outputs can be picked up, hour by hour, as they occur. Managers in control of a computerised system can requisition information at will and order its presentation in any one of a variety of alternative forms. Problems are highlighted instantly—they will be observed on the appropriate manager's visual display unit whenever he or she types into the system a command to update information on current activities. Production lines which begin to produce defectives; labour and materials costs which start to get out of hand; increasing overheads; falling sales etc. can be identified as they happen so that remedial action can be applied at once. Functions such as stock taking, collation of production figures or the preparation of management accounts can be undertaken on a continuous basis. Stock can be coded and computer controlled, using mark sensitivity devices, raw materials can be recorded as they are used and each item of production can be automatically recorded and categorised as it leaves a department. Original accounting documents such as invoices, credit notes, sales vouchers and cheques received and paid may simultaneously be recorded and integrated into the input data for the programme which prepares the firm's final accounts. Interim statements of these accounts will be available instantly.

In a non-computerised system, monitoring may be undertaken in several ways. You must accept that the time and cost of collecting useful information requires you to be highly selective in the data you collate. First, decide *which* targets you most want to monitor and assess the cost of control (collecting figures, meetings, discussions with subordinates etc.). Ask your self what would happen if you did not bother monitoring specific activities? What questions will the information collected answer and are those questions really worthwhile? Then you must decide how to gather the information — whether to do it yourself or delegate the task to a subordinate. In the latter case you must issue clear and precise instructions about how, when and where the data are to be collected and you need to ensure that the person to whom you entrust the responsibility is reliable and competent at these tasks.

Management information systems

An efficient management information system (MIS) will enable management to plan, coordinate, organise and control its activities. Information systems collect, store and retrieve data. In the past, the volume of data handled within a system has been constrained by limitations on available clerical labour and the inability of many people to comprehend and assimilate large quantities of information. Hence, various summary statistics were developed to ease the burdens of data collection and interpretation. Standard costing is a good example of attempted budgetary control through the preparation of a small number of concise variances to summarise expenditures and compare them with predetermined norms. Likewise, many financial accounting procedures have been designed to enable easy checking of the accuracy of bookkeeping entries and to facilitate periodic extraction of summary data on sales, creditors, discounts received and given and so on. Aggregate figures only were available, however, because of the difficulties and expenses of cross-tabulation. Comprehensive detailed analyses with respect to various categories and sub headings were not generally possible.

Computerisation has cut the costs of data collection and has made easy the reduction of large amounts of data into summary numbers. Cross-tabulation has become effortless and the precise form in which data are presented can be chosen at will. A great benefit of computerised data processing is the integration at source of each piece of information into the management control system of the entire organisation. Data are recorded once but then used for many different purposes in different departments. Thus, information on production costs will be diffused simultaneously to the accounts department, production planning and control, costing department, the purchasing manager, stores and stock controllers and any other interested party. The data will be presented to each of these recipients in a form which is precisely relevant to their particular needs. It is not necessary for several departments to collect and prepare what is essentially the same information. This has implications for the structure of departmentalisation within the firm, since many functions which previously were independent may, with the assistance of an integrated data presentation network, be combined.

The installation of an MIS might, at first sight, appear to be a relatively straightforward task. There are only a few factors to consider—when, how and to whom information should be transmitted and how best to summarise data in a form that enables fast and accurate evaluation prior to taking decisions. In practice, however, difficulties emerge, including the following.

- relevant information might not reach the right people. Managers commonly assume that colleagues and subordinates have been informed of particular facts when, actually, they have not. Transmission of evry piece of information that might be relevant to an individual is not feasible; otherwise the firm would devote all its time, energy and resources to transmitting message, most of which were of little practical use. Thus, choices have to be made, and dangers exist that the wrong people will receive information;
- breaks in the chain of command. Information should flow vertically through the enterprise from its top to its bottom via channels illustrated in its organisation chart. Often, information bottlenecks occur at supervisory and middle management levels since supervisors and middle managers not only receive information from above(and have to decide whether to act on it) but also collect feedback from lower levels. If a supervisor fails to act on relevant information received, the chain of command is broken-policies are not implemented; feedback on the success or failure of policies is not transmitted to higher authority
- horizontal flows of information among colleagues of equal rank may be interrupted if certain individuals deliberately conceal information or, through incompetence, do not pass it on.

The effectiveness of an MIS should be evaluated against its ability to assist in taking decisions: operations decisions, long and short term planning, budgeting, investment decisions, and so on. Information generated is often used to compare things (costs, alternative possibilities, environmental circumstances, etc.) in new and meaningful ways. There is little point in creating extra information the substance of which is already known. Strategic information needed for long range planning must often be obtained from external sources, and involve market and marketing researche, as well as the analysis of microeconomic indicators, investigations of outside sources of supply of labour, raw materials, finance etc. Such information may be extremely inaccurate and should be treated with caution. Internally generated information used for tactical decision-making and operational control should, in principle, not contain serious errors. Records of output, expenditures, wage payments, labour turnover and so on result from written reports, direct observation, face to face or telephone messages or from completion of check lists or questionnaires, but even these data might be flawed. Miscounting of items is common, delays occur in registering information contained in documents (invoices for example), while questionnaires and check lists, however well designed, may be quickly and haphazardly completed on the shop floor.

Databases

A database (DB) is a pool of information. A DB program (of which there are several varieties) will sort that information into predetermined categories, select and display items according to one or more criteria, perform mathematical functions on data and present information in some chosen form (lists, bar charts or pie diagrams, report formats, financial accounts etc.). Modern programs, even the least expensive (they begin at around 20pounds) can hold so many entries (the simplest can store at least 75,000 items) that capacity is not a limiting factor. Rather, the functions to be performed determine the requirements of an appropriate DB system for a particular firm.

Information on (say) all a firm's customers can be put into a customer *file*. Similar files can be created around other aspects of the business. The DB itself is the aggregate of these files. *A record* is a self contained set of information within a file. Suppose for example you had a file of names and addresses of customers, then each name and address would be a separate record. The records themselves are made up of *fields*. Thus, in a name and address, the name is one field and the postcode another. You must define your fields carefully because they are used to identify particular records. If for instance you have a separate field for the town in each address then later on you will be able to extract all address within any specified town.

The most expensive database have a relational facility whereby one file is related to another. For example, you could relate customer's names and address to how much each customer purchased from you during the previous year, or a file for sales people's orders could be related to a file for the expenses they claim. A search of a database is undertaken across one or more fields, such as, 'All customers in London with names beginning with the letter A and who spent more than—100 with this company last year'. The cheaper the program, the fewer fields can be examined at any one time. More expensive systems (though none cost more than a couple of hundred pounds) offer, in effect, self- contained MIS record keeping facilities.

Information within a DB can be organised 'dimensionally' as well as 'hierarchically'. To conceptualise this data, think of a hierarchical information system as a tree, with a main trunk, branches, twigs and leaves. There is only one route to each leaf, via the trunk, branch and twig system. In a relational system however, you can go not only to a single leaf, but to any number of them simultaneously. Thus, for example, a garage stock control system would, using a hierarchical system, identify stock *first* by assembly type (bodywork, electrics etc.), *then* by sub-assembly (doors, lighting, ignition and soon), *then* by make of car and *finally* by specific part. With a relational stock control system on the other hand you do not need to go through this tedious information gathering procedure. The order in which you identify the features of an item can be reversed or mixed up and still lead to the correct component. In this particular example, the problem is how to reorder, automatically, for many parts for many models from many suppliers. Here, you would simply create three files: a stock item file; a suppliers' file with supplier's names, address, prices, terms etc.; a purchase order file containing past details and who can supply them. Each time a part is recorded as having been withdrawn from stock, the stock item file will be automatically updated and if the withdrawal causes stocks of that item to fall below a present limit then, via relational linkages to the other fields, a supplier will be identified and a purchase order with the supplier's name and address automatically printed out.

Spreadsheets

Increasingly, database information is inputted from 'spreadsheets'. A spreadsheet is simply a grid containing data and formulate which process the data. It performs functions that could not be achieved using manual methods, even with calculators. The common analogy is to compare spreadsheets with accounting ledgers, except that the spreadsheet does all the adding and subtracting, juxtaposition of entries etc. instantly and automatically. Spreadsheets can be used, moreover, for nearly all other management information applications. The concept predates computers; accountants long ago devised standardised specially lined paper to assist inexperienced clerks prepare accounting statements, but the hard arithmetic then had to be done by hand. Following the arrival of personal computers it soon became possible to purchase electronic spreadsheets which not only organised data in predetermined ways, but which also did the arithmetic. The calculating speed and power of a computer was combined with spreadsheet layouts.

A computer based sepreadsheet comprises a matrix of cells (entries) located by horizontal and vertical grid references. Data can be moved around and arithmetically manipulated. Subtotals can be extracted at will. A particularly useful attribute of the modern electronic spreadsheet is its ability to complete projections at the touch of a button, i.e. you can change your assumptions about various factors and observe the effects. For example, if your spreadsheet has been programmed to calculate the manufacturing cost of an item you can ask the question, 'What if labour costs increase by five per cent and the cost of raw material falls by two per cent ?', and receive an answer at once since the computer will automatically and instantly recalculate all relevant figures. Output from spreadsheets can often be used as inputs to files in other programmes and information may be presented graphically, as well as in lists and tables and pre-formatted reports. Spreadsheets are today widely used in industry and commerce for accounting, statistical analyses, financial modelling, cash flow forecasting and business planning generally.

Organisation analysis and planning

The analysis and planing of organisations is seen increasingly as being part of the personnel function. Analysis is important not only to provide the foundation for planning the most appropriate type of organisation to meet objectives and circumstances, but also so that the management development needs of teams of managers may be identified.

Organisation structures are about people, their relationships as individuals and as members of working groups; the relationships between groups; the way in which people communicate; the methods by which authority and responsibility are exercised by them; and their roles as managers, supervisors and employees. There can be little doubt, therefore, that those who work in the personnel field should be in a position to contribute significantly to organisation analysis and planning. Before looking further at the problems involved, it will be useful to review briefly the *three main theories of organisation which have developed through the twentieth century*. The first was the classical theory which embodied a set of principles throught to be applicable to all organisations. *The second was the human relations theory,* which focused on raising performance in the enterprise by improving human relaions. *The third, which has current credence, is the systems theory,* in which organisations are viewed as analogous to physical organisms in that they take something from the environment, convert it and in turn contribute back to the environment.

The classical theory

The classical theory prescribed the following principles for the design of organisation structures.

1. *Work should be grouped (departmentation) into the smallest number of different functions* required for the objectives of the concern to be effectively and efficiently achieved.

2. *Each employee should have one boss only.*

3. *Responsibility* for specific tasks should be exacted from one individual rather than several. Within a company or other form of enterprise responsibility may be regarded as the acceptance by a subordinate of instructions from a superior and his obligation to undertake the duties involved. *Responsibility cannot be delegated.* It

is owed by a subordinate to his superior, and he does not escape from it by assigning the duties involved to one or more of his own subordinates. The cabinet minister, divisional manager and brigadier cannot avoid total responsibility for the effectiveness, respectively, of ministry, division and brigade. It is therefore imperative that responsibility should be exacted from one man for the sales performance of a company, another for manufacturing, another for purchasing, and so on. Although each of these men is responsible for effective performance within various spheres of their own functions. For example, the Company Sales Manager would hold the Northeastern District Sales Manager responsible for sales performance within that district. In this instance although the Company Sales Manager holds his subordinate North-eastern District Sales Manager responsible for sales in that area he does not evade overall responsibility himself. Just as the Managing Director by exacting responsibility from the Campany Sales Manager for overall sales performance does not, by so doing, evade responsibility for the success or otherwise of the enterprise as a whole.

4. *Authority should be delegated.* The position of managers is made real by the delegation of authority to them. In any organisation structure where relationships exist between superior and subordinate the delegation of authority at each level in the hierarchy is essential. The objectives of a concern organised on a departmental basis could not be effectively and efficiently attained without the delegation of authority.

The concept of authority delegation requires that every position within the organisation structure is clearly defined and authority relationships specified. It is important for all sunordinated to be aware of the extent of their own authority, and the degree to which matters must be reffered to a superior because they are outside the subordinate's authority.

5. *Lines of command should be as short as possible, given the size of* the concern and the degree to which authority is centralised or decentralised, so that instructions and policy directives are not misunderstood.

6. Optimum spans of control should exist for all employees responsible for managing and supervising work groups. The determination of an optimum span of control is difficult, and to some extent, of course, it depends on the type of work being undertaken by the group. It is probably easier for a foreman supervising a semi-skilled work force engaged on batch production to control more subordinates than the leader of a team of men engaged in fundamental scientific research. This is because the batch production foreman is supervising employees engaged on clearly established work which is largely repetitive. In the case of the research team, each subordinate may be less sure of the goals of his work group; and policies, procedures and authority may be less clearly defined. In such circumstances much more of the supervisor's time, inevitably, will be taken up in guidance and clarification.

The extent to which authority can be delegated is one of the crucial factors in determining the size of the span. The more a superior is able to delegate authority to his subordinates to undertake their task effectively and efficiently, the less of his time will be required in directly supervising, and consequently the greater his span of control can be.

The degree to which on-the-job training is necessary has an impact on the number of subordinates that one man can control. The on-the-job training in specific company techniques required for cost clerks (even if they have done similar work in another company before) is usually significantly greater than that required in training semi-skilled production workers. It is likely, therefore, that the span of control will be smaller in the case of the office supervisor controlling cost clerks than the production foreman controlling the production workers.

7. Authority is derived from the position held in the formal organisation.

It has become clear from research and experience that such factors as tasks, technology and people affect the ways in which attempts are made to implement these 'classical principles'. For example, in some concerns employees have more than one boss: in particular in some research and development activities where employees may be working on a number of different projects they report to several different managers. Spans of control are found, in practice, to vary in size considerably; nevertheless they are managed successfully. Responsibility is sometimes delegated or relinquished when specialists within a team have expertise which the formal boss does not enjoy; it remains possible however to require such specialists to be accountable for their actions. Increasingly, particularly in organisations of professional workers, authority is seen to be dervied from personal abilities rather than from formal positions in the hierarchy.

The human relations theory

The development of this theory stemmed in the main from the Hawthorne experiments. *Like the classical theory it was prescriptive*, but rather than setting out a series of principles of formal organisation it *postulated that performance of individuals in enterprises could be improved by concentration on good human relations.* In particular the following were recommended:

1. Managers should be consultative rather than authoritarian.
2. Employees should, whenever possible, have some influence on management decision-making.
3. Good human relations and leadership training are required to achieve improvements in organisational performance.
4. Every effort should be made to create satisfying work groups.
5. Social and psychological rewards for employees are as important as economic rewards.

Many attempts are made to improve performance by the application of such concepts. However, as in the case of the classical theory principles, one has to beware of regarding them as of universal applicability. For instance, in high risk conditions, such as civil airline flying, work has to be closely monitored, a high degree of task specialisation is unavoidable and management style tends to be authoritarian rather than consulative. In other words the nature of the task and the technology, in this simple illustration, influence the formal organisation structure and limit the extent to which human relations prescriptions for organisational improvement are likely to be helpful.

The systems theory

The notion of systems is in common use in biology. Organisms (e.g. animals), import air, food, water and information from their envronments; they convert these for mental and physical functioning, and export activities and waste products back into their environments. In the process the organisms change in various ways. Similarly organisations import resources such as raw materials, components, employees, energy, ideas and services, convert them and export finished products and services back to the environment. An environment such as a nation consists of many systems—for example, companies, hospitals, schools, local authorities, club and charities—all of which to some extent are dependent on other system: the outputs of some systems are the inputs of others. Each system (i.e each organisation) has to produce outputs that other systems require. If a system's output is no longer needed then it will die, or change in some way to provide new or modified outputs that are now required.

Organisations which are capable of changing to meet new or altered circumstances in their environment are known as open systems. In contrast, organisations which are insufficiently sensitive to changes taking place in their environment and do not modify or radically alter their input, conversion and output processes to meet new or altered needs are known as closed systems. All organisations consist of many sub-systems which are interdependent; the output of one is the input another. A change in any one subsystem therefore leads to the need for changes in other when the need for such further changes is not sufficiently appreciated by the employees involved then difficulties such as absenteeism, lack of cooperation or indeed sabotage may occur. This is not uncommon when new procedures, such as employee appraisals or budgetary control, are introduced into organisations. A good deal of work has been done in recent years to aid our understanding of organisations, and much of it has been based, in one way or another, on treating organisations as systems. One framework for analysing organisations and some examples of research work undertaken follow.

An analytical framework for organisations based on systems thinking.

Drake and Smith in their book *Behavioural Science in Industry* provide a useful framework for the analysis of organisations. They show that an organisation may be viewed in term of four interdependent elements:

1. Task: for example, specific goals in relations to its environment.
2. *Technology*: for example, equipment and processes.
3. *Structure*: for example, size and formal relationships.
4. *People*: for example, skills, knowledge, personalities and motivation of employees.

The elements are interdependent because changes in any one of them will lead to changs in the others. The characteristics of each elements help to determine the characteristics of the others. For example, the tasks of an organisation helps to determine the types of production processes to be used. The technology calls for specific skills and knowledge and thus work groups and the relationships of personnel are influenced. The size and geographical locations of units of a business may have an important influences on its informal organisation structure.

The four elements interact to influence the character of the three major processes of an organisation. These are control, integration and boundary regulation The processes may be defined briefly as follows:

Control: The methods by which the organisation ensures that individuals perform their work activities so that tasks are completed satisfactorily.

Integration: The ways in which the relationship components of roles are defined and regulated.

Boundary regulation: The extent to which the internal behaviour of the organisations needs to be 'open' to its environment so that changes in its task, structure and technology occur and guarantee its survival.

Socio-technical systems

Researchers at the Tavistock Institute of Human Relations first used the term 'socio-technical system' when they undertook some research work in the coal mining industry. They showed that only by considering both the social and the technical sub-systems of an organisation when changes are introduced may potential problems be mitigated. The requirements of both sub-systems have to be considered carefully; that is, the people (the social system) have to be related to the task (the technical system). Often organisations mistakenly consider only the requirements of the technical system and treat the social system as an adjunct to it. In the Durham coal field small group organisation existed before mechanisation. Known as single place working, miners were all-round workers performing, in small groups which were self-selected, the full cycle of extracting coal. They used hand tools, were paid as a group and worked without close supervision. Subsequently, the conventional longwall method of coalmining was introduced: the cycle of preparing an area for coal extraction, cutting and removing coal with the aid of conveyors and moving machinery, and clearing new roadways was undertaken over three shifts. Each shift undertook a specialised task which followed sequentially from the one undertaken by the previous shift. Each worker was aid an individual incentive which was quite independent of those paid to othrs on his own shift or those on other shifts. The social consequence of this method of working was the evolution of separate task groups with different customs, less effective work-team relationships and closer and more coercive supervision than previously. Conflict between work groups, workers and workers, and workers and managment increased.

An experimental 'composite longwall' system was then tried. Self-selected groups of miners allocated themselves to tasks and shifts over a twenty-four hour preparation and production cycle. A group incentive payment based on the aggregate level of output was introduced. Task versatility rather than task specification was encouraged. Thus responsibility was placed in the entire group for all aspects of the work. Work-groups relations improved, interchange between tasks occurred, each shift started where the previous shift finished, whatever stage in the preparation and production cycle had been reached. The miners enjoyed a higher level of autonomy and more varied tasks than with the conventional longwall systm. Voluntary absence, sickness and accident rates were lower and productivity was higher with the composite than with the conventional longwall system.

Clearly in this example the composite longwall organisation reflected a concern on the part of the planners with both the technical, and social sub-systems. On the other hand, the conventional longwall organisation reflected a concern only with the technical aspects of preparation and production, with people viewed as appendages to the operation.

Formal and informal organisation and the effects of technologies

The notion that it is possible to view 'organisation' in two ways has developed over the last few decades. On the one hand there is the formal organisation structure which comprises the set of relationships, disposition of authority, the spans of control and command hierarchy defined and laid down by management. The informal organisation, on the other hand, comprises the actual relationships which exist between groups and individuals, which may or may not correspond with the formally established structure.

Until the last fifteen to twenty years the industrial sociologists concentrated their attention on informal organisation. Joan Woodward, a sociologist, suggested in her book *Industrial Organisation* that this was acceptable to the managers of the time and to the formal organisation theorists because it was believed that although formal organisation structures might have been very carefully planned, the behaviour of human beings involved might have prevented them from working successfully. In such circumstances the social scientists, following their investigations into informal organisation, could indicate the apparent reasons for failure.

However, E.F. L. Brech (whose book *Organisation: the Framework of Management* is devoted to the problems of establishing sound formal organisation structures and follows the classical principles of organisation) has argued that the problem was wrongly focused in the minds of many sociologists because they studied companies which had no known organisation structure and certainly no defined managerial and supervisory roles. In other words the informal channels were the only ones which could be used. Brech argues that provided a sound organisation structure is designed the formal and inflrmal channels should work in harmony. It is interesting to note that Woodward indicated that in her empirical research into organisation in 100 firms in South Essex in the 1950s it was not possible to distinguish informal and formal organisation in any meaningful way. Her work was among the first by industrial sociologists in Britain which did not concentrate simply on the question of informal organisation, and it was particularly important because it demonstrated clearly that technology affects organisation and organisation affects behaviour. It showed that for each of the main types of production (one off or unit large-batch, mass-production, and process or continous flow) there tends to be a different organisation pattern. The number of levels of management, the ratio of managers and supervisors to total employees, the ratio of staff to manual workers, and the spans of control of manager and supervisors were similar within each method of production investigated but differed from system to system. Hence the close relationship between the organisation structure and the technology of the industry. Industrial relations in unit and process production were better than those in large batch and mass production. It was felt that one reason for this might be the smaller spans of control of first line supervisors in unit and process work and hence smaller working groups. The essential point is that behaviour was shown to be affected by organisation structure and structure affected in its turn by technology.

Some sociologists have argued that the findings of Woodward and her research associates offer a serious challenge to the organisation principles developed by the formal theorists. They claim that the formal or classical organisation theorists have generalised about the means of coordinating tasks without reference to the particular tasks involved. Thus a piece of research work which demonstrates the significance of technological factors in affecting the shape of organisation must, *ipso facto,* indicate that the formal classical organisation principles hitherto developed are iradequate.

Technical and Social systems and an organisations's environment

Burns and Stalker in *The Management of Innovation* argue that it is possible to identify two contrasting forms of organisation, a mechanistic structure appropriate to stable conditions and an organic one suitable for changing circumstances and new problems and courses of action. Their theory is based on research in companies mainly engaged in the development of electronic devices and shows that there are appropriate structures, organic and mechanistic, to match the environmental influence of scientific discoveries and techniques and markets.

A mechanistic organisation is characterised by a high degree of task specialisation: precise definitions of jobs and technical methods; a hierarchic structure of control, authority and communications a tendency for the major interactions to be between supervisors and subordinates (i.e. vertical relationships); a tendency for operations to be governed by direct instructions from superiors; and an emphasis on the importance of loyalty and obedience to superiors. On the other hand an organic structure is characterised by a low degree of task specialisation; the continual redefinition of jobs and methods; a network structure of control, authority and communications; lateral communications; commitment to tasks and the technical ethos being more highly valued than loyalty and obedience; and the spread of commitment to the organisation as a whole rather than to specific tasks or departments.

Burns and Stalker show that as well as considering an organisation's system of work activities, including the predominant technology and the social system, attention must be paid to the relationship of the organisation with its environment. In a highly dynamic environment it appears that organic structures are appropriate whereas when the environmental or external circumstances are relatively stable then mechanistic structures are preferable.

Examples of two contrasting formal organisation structures

In some large concerns working in stable environmental conditions it is likely that the formal organisation structures will be mechanistic and be based to some degree on the formal classical organisational principles described earlier. Furthermore, the structures are likely to embody the concepts of line, staff and functional relationships.

Line management is a direct superior—subordinate authority relationship. A staff relationship, on the other hand, is advisory and hence the managing director may have a personnel manager to advise him on industrial relations matters. At the same time the personnel manager will be in a line management authority relatonship with his own subordinates. Some divisions or departments are primarily line in character, whereas others are primarily staff in terms of their relationship with the corporate body. Indeed in some companies the organisation charts are drawn in such a way that each type of funtion becomes immediately apparent. The thick line joins those functions (development, manufacturing and sales) which are directly related to the objetives of the enterprise, that is the products must be developed, manufactured and sold to ensure that the company stays in business. The finance, personnel and public relations functions, however, may be regarded as being primarily staff in character. Too much should not be made of these broad classifications which relate individual divisions and departments to the corporate whole, as many managerial position have both line and staff relationships with others.

It is important for individuals within such an organisation structure to know when they are acting in a line and when in a staff capacity. When they are acting in a staff capacity they can only advise and attempt to persuade others of their ideas and views.

In many large companies counterpart functions exist at two or more levels. Just as the managing director of a large company may have a company peronnel manager to advise him on industrial relations and personnel matters for the company as a whole, so, if the company has several products each developed, manufactured and sold in separate divisions, each divisional manager might have his own personnel manager to advise him on industrial relation and personnel matters within the devision. The thick line denotes line relationships and the thin line staff relationships. Policies and procedures are established in the departments under the direct control of the company manaager and implemented in the counterpart functions in the divisions.

In order that overall company objectives may be met, the central personnel department would have a number of responsibilities to fulfil which might include the development of policies and procedures for recruitment, wages and salaries administration, organisation and personnel planning and training. Through the procedures, the central personnel department ensures that divisional personnel departments undertake their duties in accordance with company policy. The control which is exercised from the centre in this way is known as functional contol. The prime control comes through the diect lone of command from superior to subordinate. The divisional manager is in complete charge of his division subordinate. The divisional manager is in complete charge of his division and may overrule the advice of his specialist personnel lmanager even though such advice is in accordance with instructions from the central personnel department. If the divisional personnel manager is overuled by te divisional manager then the company personnel manager will get to know sooner or later, when this happens he could, if he felt that the company would suffer unduly from the divisional manager's decision to overrule functional instructions, take the matter up with the managing director for a decision. Whilst a manager acting in a staff capacity may be functionally responsible to his counterpart staff level above him, his prime responsibility is to his own immediate line superior.

In contrast, in concerns working in rapidly changing environments and where the employees are highly qualified, it is possible that the formal organisation structures, if they exist at all, will be based on the concept of project teams. This type of structure, often known as a matrix organisation, differs in a number of fundamental ways from the line, staff and functional organisation based on the classical principles. For instance, it is possible for employees to have more than one boss in that they may find themselves working in two or more different project teams and they may have a 'specialism' boss as well as a 'project' boss. Responsibility for the successful completion of tasks might be shared rather than extacted from one individual; and authority is more likely to be a function of expertise in relation to the requirements of the task rather than derived from formal status. Matrix organisations may be found, for example, in research and development companies, or departments of companies, management consultancy firms, institutes providing management education and in the provision of computer services. Perhaps the best known martix organisation structure existed at NASA, the American space operation. There are a number of managers of specialist activities such as personnel, accounting, marketing and operational research. These managers are responsible for developing and maintaining professional standards of consultancy in the specialism concerned. In a sense they are 'people' managers. The project managers, on the other hand, are responsible for preparing proposals and managing cosultancy projects within the sector of the economy for which they are responsible. They call on specialists from the appropriate 'poeple' managers' departments to join multi-disciplinary project teams as required.

Manpower planning and recruitment

Manpower planning is concerned with forecasting future requirements of all types and levels of employee and with attempting to match these with forecasts of the likely availability of such employees. Simply put it is about labour supply and demand. Emphasis is sometimes placed on another aspect of manpower planning emanating from economic difficulties with which Britain has been faced during the past thirty years. This is the problem of manpower utilisation. There are many possible reasons for Britain's economic difficulties, a discussion of which is outside the scope of this book, but there is little doubt that one of the contributing factors is the wasteful use of manpower. This is particularly apparent from comparisons with other advanced industrial nations. Full employment, which has been an objective largely achieved, of all governments since the Second World War disguises a serious situation of underemployment which is occurring in many profitable industries as well as in those which have ceased to operate on a fully economic basis. This misuse of labour is generally considered to be due both to inadequate management and to labour restrictive practices. Traditional methods of tackling jobs and deploying labour, too rigid demarcations between people doing similar jobs, overmanning and inadequate maintenance planning are all examples of causes of labour under-employment. Manpower planning has inevitably come to be concerned with these matters.

Manpower planning is a very difficult job. It is particularly so in business enterprises which are often subject to forces outside their control, such as political and economic changes. In addition, the objectives of the enterprises themselves may legitimately alter. Forecasts of manpower requirements and availability therefore need to be regularly adjusted. Manpower plans cannot be like engineering blueprints for they must be ever changing to meet new circumstances.

Analysis of current manpower utilisation

The first step in manpower planning is to prepare a complete analysis of present manpower. Statistics on the total number of employees must be prepared in a variety of ways, each providing valuable basic information for planning purposes. Examples of the various classifications which may be used are:

Managers, supervisors and operatives by department, function, process or product (or other appropriate subpopulation).

Direct and indirect labour.

Jobs and skills, following job analysis.

Payroll, e.g. hourly, weekly, monthly, managerial.

Age, sex and length of service.

Qualifications.

As well as the provision of these basic statistics on the present total manpower deployment, there is considerable value in unearthing a range of other facts about labour utilisation. Examples of these include:

(a) How much overtime is worked by department, function, product, process, etc.? How many man hours does this represent? Is overtime worked in specific departments on a consistent basis, how many extra men would have to be recruited to eliminate it, and how much money in overtime premiums would be saved?

(b) To what extent is indirect labour engaged, for example, on maintenance work fully utilised? Over a period of one year, say, how many hours are actually worked out of the total work time available?

(c) What proportion of labour is engaged in anticipation of future business or to meet the demands of peak production periods only?

(d) If manpower budgets have been previously prepared, to what extent do actual manpower figures exceed or fall short of these budgets? To what extent, if it can be measured, do such overages and shortfalls adversely affect or improve performance?

(e) What is the current relationship between increases in output and increases in remuneration? Do piece work and bonus schemes have any measurable impact on output?

Further useful information relating to current manpower utilisation may include the number of employees undergoing training, the difficulty or ease in recruiting specific grades of employee, average monthly engagements and resignations by sub-populations, and analysis of absenteeism.

Forecasts of requirements and availability

Projections of requirements serve little purpose if unrelated to studies of how existing manpower is utilised. Irrespective of technological innovation and change, it is important for forecasts of manpower requirements to be closely related to studies aimed at reducing underemployment. For the moment we will concentrate on the problem of forecasting requirements whilst taking utilisation as fixed.

Consideration of the problems associated with forecasting manpower requirements and availability may be divided into two—forecasting labour requirements and forecasting managerial and supervisory requirements specifically. In order to establish realistic manpower objectives for one year ahead, two years ahead and say five years ahead account must be taken of the effects of automation, expansion plans, centralisation or decentralisation of authority, functions becoming obsolete and the projected rate of manpower wastage. Access to marketing forecasts and information relating to consumer expenditure patterns is also essential. This particular aspect of planning needs to be periodically revised in the light of changes in policy which may or may not be due to forces outside the control of the organisation.

Forecasting the availability and supply of labour calls for continuous studies on a national and local basis to ascertain, for example, population, education, transport, social service and migratory trends. Detailed statistics on the present and predicted availability of various categories of employees within the locality, e.g. female workers, skilled men, school leavers of varying ages and qualifications, should be collected and analysed.

These are the initial steps which need to be taken in ascertaining the supply and demand of labour. They are difficult steps to take but do provide worthwhile information to help management take more sensible decisions. Some aspects of forecasting are comparatively easy. Given a detailed analysis of the current manpower situation, wastage due to retirements, deaths, accidents and resignations can be calculated reasonably accurately on the basis of current trends and on analysis of the age structure. With the help of a computer information on the degree of correlation between wastage and such matters as employee travelling distances, changes in rates of remuneration, fringe benefits, training opportunities, overtime working and the degree of job specialisation may be assessed.

There are special problems associated with forecasting the availability and requirements of manpower for supervisory and managerial positions. This may be regarded as part of the overall problem of what is commonly known as 'management development'. From employee assessment reports and organisation charts, information on the manpower considered promotable to managerial and supervisory positions and the positions which will need at some time to be filled is available.

The first step in forecasting succession requirements is often the use of charts to pinpoint those jobs, given current organisation structures, which will fall vacant over the next few years because the incumbents will be retiring. In addition, the chain reactions of anticipated promotions has to be taken into account and forecasts of positions which will require filling at subordinates levels in the hierarchy will have to be made. It is useful for estimates of supervisory and managerial requirements arising from premature deaths, sickness and resignations to be built into the longer term forecasts. This involves projecting past trends into the future. Future requirements due to proposed organisation changes must also be taken into account. Centralisation or decentralisation, the effect of functions becoming obsolete, and expansion plans are among the factors which influence organisation structures.

One of the simplest and most effective ways of comparing the requirements with the availability situation is the use of replacement organisation charts depicting the current organisation and showing present incumbents of positions, their ages and grades, and the names, ages and grades of potential replacements. These may be obtained from analysis of employee assessment reports, appraisal interviews and discussions with appropriate line managers. Those considered to be qualified and ready for immediate promotion are depicted, and in addition the names of those employees who, with further training, experience and development, should be ready for promotion in say two years and possibly five years time. Given the current organisation structure, such replacement charts will show up those positions for which there is a weak replacement situation. It is then possible to pursue appropriate training, recruitment and deployment policies to ensure that the placement weaknesses are remedied.

In addition, it is useful for organisation charts to be prepared showing anticipated organisation changes over, say, the next five years. Once again the weak replacement areas will be readily identified and remedial action may be taken. Naturally the replacement situation for supervisory and managerial positions must be reviewed regularly in the light of reassessments of employees' potential, resignations and changes in organisation.

Improving labour utilisation

The other important function of manpower planning is to assess the degree to which current manpower in an organisation is fully utilised or under-employed. Clearly there are substantial economies to be realised through manning reductions, and experience and economic studies have shown the advantages of carefully devised labour/capital ratios. The problem of increasing productivity is unquestionably one to which the manpower planner should address himself.

Although economists generally believe that one of the keys to raising productivity is a higher rate of capital investment, it is also considered that a significant contribution comes from a rise in the level of individual work performance. Higher levels of performance seem to come primarily through changes in working methods and improvements in the way that work is organised. This would appear to be a much more realistic and practical way to increase productivity (raising the level of output per head) than exhortations to harder work.

Where plant productivity bargains have been made between management and trade unions the types of changes in methods and organisation of work which have been established have included:

1. Reductions in the number of craftsmen mates on maintenance work.

2. Substantial reductions in overtime working which had hitherto been unquestioningly accepted as necessary and had developed into an institution, resulting in considerable underemployment during normal working hours.
3. Reductions in manning scales.
4. Increases in work interchangeability by the relaxation of demarcation lines.
5. Transfers of simple maintenance jobs from craftsmen to production operatives.
6. Greater departmental redeployment of labour, and retraining.

Before management can bargain with trade unions for such productivity improvements, it has to undertake comprehensive studies to discover precisely where, for example, underemployment and overmanning may be reduced. This is an area in which the manpower planners have a clear role to play. It is for them to assess, in consultation with other appropriate experts such as work study engineers, the degree to which overtime working has become unnecessary but institutionalised, to identify labour restrictive practices, to ascertain where manning scales might be reduced and to work out the positive advantages of greater redeployment of labour within the organisation. Job analysis records provide useful basic material for this task. The facts can then be given to management for use in productivity bargains with the trade unions, or for implementation immediately if the employees are not represented by unions or if joint consultative machinery does not exist.

Clearly, whether trade unions are involved or not, when management has evidence from manpower planners that a better utilisation of labour is feasible, it may be necessary for it to offer higher rewards if it wishes to see the changes accepted and implemented. Much under-employment, particularly of the sort leading to institutionalised overtime working, may very well be due to low basic wages. There is evidence to suggest that substantial increases in basic pay, coupled with far-reaching changes in working methods and practices, give rise to significant improvements in productivity. (However, productivity bargaining conflicts with concepts of equitable payment. In February 1960 Esso offered its 2, 400 wage earners at the Fawley refinery a 40 per cent wage increase spread over two years in return for changes in working practices. These included an overtime cut form 18 per cent to 2 per cent, a reduction in the working week from 42 hours to 40 hours, the redeployment of craftsmen, the upgrading of craftsmen's mates and the relaxation of job demarcation lines. In negotiation the majority of the proposals were agreed to by the trade unions concerned. The results make interesting reading. Productivity of maintenance workers increased by 50 per cent, the average working week on maintenance dropped from 50 to 42½ hours, process workers' productivity increased by 45 per cent to 10½ per cent and at the end of 1962, compared with 1959, 12 pound million more plant was being operated and maintained by a labour force reduced from 2,461 to 2,266 employees. In return the employees enjoyed an increase in average hourly earnings of about 35 per cent compared with a 20 per cent rise for the oil industry as a whole.

Manpower planning and the computer

Manpower planning can only be based on a comprehensive range of data, as is suggested above. The computerisation of payrolls has provided a realistic basis on which to work; realistic in terms of accommodating a large amount of cost. Without computers to process information at speed, manpower planning on any significant scale would be a non-starter. The alternative of manual clerical effort is a burden beyond justification for all except very small organisations. Although the purchase of a computer is outside the scope of many small to medium-sized organisations, there is a good case for them to buy time on some other organisation's computer so that manpower data may be processed.

Personnel information, suitably coded, ranging through job title, age, qualification, employee assessment, grade, length of service, remuneration, reason for resignation, etc., may be stored on a computer tape. Rapid analyses can be undertaken such as manpower audits, labour turnover by function, process or other subpopulation, age/qualification distributions by subpopulation for career planning the number of employees ahead or behind the average salary/age for the grade. As data is built up over a period of time and analysed regularly, predictions about the future become easier and safer to make. Forecasts of the number of employees to be recruited, promoted, trained or redeployed in given year in specific functions or departments become feasible.

Progress reporting

Few people would maintain that planning is going to provide foolproof forecasts of manpower supply and demand or of optimum utilisation of labour. There can be no hope of 100 per cent success in the foreseeable future. Plans, however well founded on detailed data and analysis, will fail in part and sometimes wholly through unforeseen changes in external circumstances. Nevertheless, this should not be an excuse for throwing manpower planning out of the window. It is better to have charted the way and obtained the broad picture upon which predictions may be made, and to be therefore in a position to understand exactly where and why things have gone wrong, than to be the unknowing victim of forces which are completely outside ones control.

It is also helpful for regular reports to be prepared, comparing actual performance and results achieved with the manpower plan originally established. On the basis of such reports, revised plans or parts of plans may be prepared and improvements in planning techniques accordingly achieved. Above all, those concerned should beware of producing plans which are too ambitious. Plans should be tailor-made to realistic objectives. It is better for a plan incorporating fairly generous statistical confidence limits (i.e. a range of statistical predictions within which the actual achievement is likely to occur) to be established, rather than one which attempts to be too precise and which therefore may prove totally inadequate as a basis for management decisions.

Recruitment

To an increasing extent, it is true to say that any organisation is only as effective as its work force. It must follow from this that an efficient process of staff selection is of considerable value in building up a competent work force. However, selection can only take place if there are sufficient applicants for each vacancy to make such selection a reality. Thus it can be seen that a successful recruitment policy is the essential precursor to both an efficient selection procedure and an effective work force. Many organisations appear unaware of this, and do nothing towards the formalisation of a positive recruitment policy. They work on a purely *ad hoc* basis, changing their methods of recruitment or keeping them static without reference to any previous experience of success or failure of particular methods. In periods of full employment, with a tight labour market it is more than ever necessary to have such a policy.

Basic essentials of recruitment policy

In order to have consistency throughout an organisation, it is necessary to lay down certain principles as guide lines for both management and staff. The first basic principle is the organisation's attitude towards filling vacancies, whether from within or from outside. If the organisation is strongly unionised, it is probable that a policy of promotion from within whenever possible has been agreed with the unions. Following on this, it is necessary to agree on the method of selection for promotion, be it seniority, experience or merit, or a combination of two or more of these criteria.

There are several advantages to a policy of promotion from within.

These include:

(a) the maintenance of high employee morale, as employees know they have the opportunity to advance upwards through the organisation;

(b) reduced labour turnover, as employees do not find it necessary to leave in order to progress in their careers;

(c) the selection procedure is simplified, as the personnel department will have records of the skills and abilities of each employee, and management will have had previous experience of their behaviour and attitudes;

(d) both the number of new entrants to the organisation and the number of different levels of entry are reduced.

There are also certain disadvantages to such a policy, including:

(a) the necessity for a more intensive planned training programme for the development of existing employees, which can be expensive for a small or medium-sized company;

(b) the danger of taking in at entry level workers who have the ability to rise within the organisation, and then being unable to promote them fast enough to prevent their frustration, and thus losing them;

(c) perhaps most important of all, the dangers of 'in-breeding', when all senior posts are filled from within by employees who have been trained over the years by their superiors in their own ways of working; this tends to perpetuate old-fashioned ideas, and prevent new methods being introduced. The organisation can develop a very rigid outlook, highly resistant to change and unable to adapt to new conditions, if it adheres strictly to such a policy.

It would appear, therefore, that the best policy of promotion would be one which promoted from within when the necessary talent and experience was available, but which also specified that a certain proportion of supervisory and managerial posts must be filled from outside, in order to bring new ideas and vigour into the organisation at regular intervals, or when the position concerned could not be filled from the available talent within the enterprise.

Sources of recruitment

If the vacancy cannot be filled by the transfer or promotion of an existing employee, or if there is a general expansion of the labour force within the organisation, or if the vacancy is at one of the general entry levels, it is necessary for the personnel department to us an outside source to provide the appropriate worker.

One source which perhaps may not strictly be defined as 'outside' is the nomination of new workers by existing employees, usually their friends or relatives; such nominations can be of great use to the personnel department, as it is unlikely that a good worker will, recommend an unreliable on whose performance would reflect on his own abilities. Some organisations actively encourage such nominations, awarding bonuses to those employees whose nominations are accepted and remain with the company for a specified minimum period.

Depending on the state of the labour market, the personnel department may have a considerable number of casual applications for employment from people who just walk in, or write in, to enquire whether there are any vacancies. These unsolicited applications are often sufficient to fill unskilled vacancies at the lowest entry level, particularly if the organisation has a good reputation locally and is known to have a policy of training and promotion from within. This factor of the prestige and 'public image' of the organisation is of tremendous importance for the recruitment of the best available workers. There are organisations whose reputation is so high that they never have to advertise or use any other form of recruitment, except for specialist staff, as they always have a waiting list of people anxious to work for them.

Employment offices and job centres of the Employment Services Agency are the most important source of unskilled and semi-skilled labour in this country. Practically all unemployed labour is registered with them, and they are able to pass information regarding labour requirements to their other offices throughout the country, thus encouraging labour mobility from high unemployment areas to areas where there is a shortage of labour. They work closely with the Training Services Agency which is responsible for the retraining of labour and for the payment of special allowances to workers undergoing retraining. There is a tendency, however, for only the unskilled and semi-skilled to use the employment offices; few technical, supervisory or administrative posts are filled from this sources although the Manpower Services Commission provides special services—and the numbers using this are rising. The advantages of using local employment offices as a source of labour supply include their nation wide coverage, their knowledge of local requirements and availability of labour, and the fact that no charge is made to employer or employee for their services, except in the case of the Professional and Executive Recruitment Service, where the employer pays a fee.

The chief source of recruitment of school leavers and young people under the age of eighteen is the Careers Service run by the local education authorities. Personnel managers generally have very close links with the local careers officer, discussing future requirements and organising visits to their companies by school leavers, to interest them in the range of opportunities available.

A similar type of activity is often used in liaison with the local schools, as schools recruitment is a valuable source of new labour. Each year, usually in the spring, personnel manager or a senior member of management visits the schools to give a talk on the opportunities available in his firm, and to answer questions and distribute literature. This is often followed up by a visit to the company by any interested pupils. This method is useful for the selection of the best available candidates for apprenticeships, and for girls to be trained as typists, telephonists or clerks.

Graduate and specialist staff

Because of the difficulties of recruiting adequate numbers of scientific and technical staff many organisationas now place great emphasis on college and university recruitment campaigns. These are arranged in liaison with the appointments officer of a college, who will announce the proposed visit of representatives of a certain organisation and arrange a schedule of interviews with any students interested in learning more about the opportunities available in that organisation. Very often a team of representatives from the company, usually the personnel manager and one or two senior managers, will visit a college or university, and will even short-list there any potential candidates for vacancies in their company and arrange for further interviews for them at headquarters. In this way the cream of graduates are acquired by enterprising organisations even before graduation; this method is considered so valuable that the larger organisations even have one member of the personnel staff whose entire responsibility is graduate recruitment. Organisations which are too small for this system often produce bulletins, brochures and other informational material which is supplied to the appointments officer for distribution to any interested students.

Private employment agencies have expanded enormously over the past twenty years and are now the main source of supply of office workers such as typists, secretaries, clerks and telephonists. They profess to do a certain amount of initial screening of candidates before sending them to the organisation for interview, but such screening varies very much in its effectiveness. They normally charge the employer for their services, their charges ranging from one week's to one month's salary.

A further expansion in this field had been the establishment of agencies for the provision of more senior personnel, ranging from technical specialists to managing directors. These agencies are often linked to a management consultant firm, and have contacts throughout the country. Again they provide an initial selection service, and send only a short list of suitable candidates to the organisation concerned. Sometimes they carry out the entire recruitment and selection process when a very senior employee is required, particularly for a small firm without a sophisticated personnel department. The reputable agencies use the most up-to date selection techniques, and can save a tremendous amount of work for the personnel department requiring senior staff. Their only serious disadvantage would appear to be the cost—they usually charge at least one-eighth of the annual salary of the person appointed.

A special kind of agency which is sometimes used for recruitment of senior staff carries out a procedure known as 'executive search' or 'head hunting'. Having identified the requirements of the job to be filled, the agency does not advertise the vacancy, but instead approaches those individuals whom it considers to be suitable and who might be interested in the post. Such people come to the attention of these agencies mainly through personal contacts in employing organisations. In this way it taps a market of people who are not actively looking for a change of job, but whose talents are perhaps scarce and just those required in the vacant position. Specialist agencies also exist, often associated with professional associations, which maintain lists of people who are interested in changing jobs and which circulate to interested members of their association details of vanancies, which have been notified to them. Such agencies are useful when attempting to recruit accountants, designers, personnel officers and other specialists.

A similar specialist source is the union—there are certain trades where it is impossible to recruit new staff except through the appropriate trade union. The printing trade is an example of this system, where the union must first be approached regarding any vacancy and only if it is unable to supply a worker may the company use any other source of suitable labour.

Recruitment by advertisement

Advertising is a very common method of recruitment which has expanded greatly over recent year. So much expertise is now required in the design, layout, placement and wording of staff advertise—ments that some organisations have put them in the hands of their advertising departments or agencies. A great deal of money can be wasted by the bad design of advertisements or by placing them in unsuitable media. As a general rule, local evening papers are the best media for advertising lower level office vacancies and certain semi-skilled and skilled jobs, while the 'serious dailies and Sunday papers are used for more senior posts or those requiring academic qualifications. Again, certain weekly publications and specialist journals are used for advertising technical or specialist posts.

The use of box numbers with anonymous advertisements for vacancies should be avoided whenever possible. The chief disadvantage of this method is a reduction is the number of applications' most applicants; want to know for whom and where they would be working, and many may be put off in case they find they have applied for a post in their own company. Reasons for the use of box numbers include (a) that the company does not wish its present employees to know either what vacancies exist, or what rates of pay it is offering, and (b) that the company does not want to publicise a high rate of turnover of a particular grade of staff, (e.g. salesmen). Conversely an organisation with a prestige name or a reputation as good employer will gain much from the use of its name in its advertisements for staff.

Many other sources of recruitment are used on a small scale, such as advertisements on commercial television and radio, notices outside factories and stores listing vacancies, and even the travelling recruiter who goes as far as field as Canada and the United States of America to persuade British graduates to return to posts at home.

Publicity material has become much more sophisticated over the past few years, with glossy brochures describing career prospects and employment opportunities often incorporated with a short history of the company; these booklets are generally aimed at students and circulated to schools careers teachers and college appointments officers. With the implementation of the Sex Discrimination Act 1975, and the Race Relations Act 1976, it is essential that recruitment advertising material could not be interpreted as discriminating against anyone on grounds of sex, colour, race or nationality.

The use of job analysis in recruitment

It is desirable, when planning a recruitment campaign or designing an advertisement, to have a clear and detailed picture of the vacancy or vacancies to be filled. Job analysis can be of great assistance at this stage by providing a clear and detailed description both of the job itself and a specification of the attributes required of the job holder. The advertisement should be so worded that it does not mislead prospective applicants about the content and prospects of the job in question, yet it should be able to attract a sufficient number of suitable applications.

A particular problem exists when recruiting management trainees such as eighteen-year-old grammar school leavers or university graduates, where a specific job is not in immediate view but where the area in which the trainee can develop may depend on his own aptitudes or the direction in which the organisation expands. In this instance, only a very general description of the prospects and potential within the organisation should be used in the recruitment campaign and advertisements.

Cost analysis

There are then numerous avenues which can be explored in order to obtain as large a number of applicants as possible for each vacancy, but it is necessary continually to evaluate the results of every recruitment campaign in order to identify those sources and methods which are the most efficient and the most economical. Records of results must be maintained in order to ensure value for money expended.

It is not sufficient to keep a check on the number of applicants resulting from a particular advertisement or promotional visit. It is also essential to record the number of suitable applicants worthy of short-listing and the number of applicants actually appointed. One advertisement may bring in fifty applications, none of which are suitable, while another may only bring in ten, all of which are worth following up.

Long-terms planning

As with all other aspects of the manpower plan within an organisation, long-term forecasting of staffing requirements is essential for the effective use of recruitment techniques. It is useless to expect to find a particular well qualified or highly experienced worker within the space of a few days, and it is necessary for management to understand that they must put in their staffing requisitions well in advance of requirements. It has been estimated that it can take up to ten weeks to fill even a junior supervisory post, and more senior posts many take considerably longer.

The labour market situation has also to be taken into account when attempting to attract new recruits. Are the wage or salary scales offered sufficiently attractive to persuade workers to move to a new job? Are other benefits to be included, such as costs of removal, assistance with mortgages or temporary housing to encourage people to move from one part of the country to another? Is your organisation willing to take on untrained or unqualified personnel, and train or retrain them at the organisation's expense? Such policy decisions are of growing importance as the demand for skilled and technically trained personnel continues to increase and as the state places more and more emphasis on training within industry.

Nature of planning

The essential nature of planning can be highlighted by four major principles:

1. Contribution to purpose and objectives
2. Primacy of planning

3. Pervasiveness of planning, and
4. Efficiency of plans.

The purpose of every plan and all derivative plans is to facilitate the accomplishment of enterprise purpose and objectives. This principle derives from the nature of organized enterprise, which exists for the accomplishment of group purpose through deliberate cooperation. As shown in since managerial operations in organising, staffing, leading, and controlling are designed to support the accomplishment of enterprise objectives, planning logically precedes the execution of all other managerial functions.

Although all the functions intermesh in practice as a system of actions, planning is unique in that it establishes the objectives necessary for all group effort. Besides, plans must be made to accomplish these objectives before the manager knows what kind of organization relationships and personal qualifications are needed by those who fill positions, along which course subordinates are to be directed and led, and what kind of control is to be applied. And, of course, all the other managerial functions must be planned if they are to be effective.

Planning and control are especially inseparable-the Siamese twins of management. Unplanned action cannot be controlled, for control involves keeping activities on course by correcting deviations from plans. Any attempt to control without plans would be meaningless, since there is no way for people to tell whether they are going where they want to go-the task of control-unless they first know where they want to go-the task of planning. Plans thus furnish the standards of control.

Pervasiveness of Planning Planning is a function of all managers, although the character and breadth of planning will vary with their authority and with the nature of policies and plans outlined by their superiors. It is virtually impossible to so circumscribe their area of choice that they can exercise no discretion. Unless they have some planning responsibility, it is doubtful that they are truly managers.

Recognition of the pervasiveness of planning goes far in clarifying the attempt on the part of some students of management to distinguish between policy making (the setting of guides for thinking in decision making) and administration, or between the "manager" and the "administrator" or "supervisor." One manager, because of his or her authority delegation or position in the organization, may do more planning or more important planning than another, or the enterprise than that of another. However, all managers-from presidents to supervisors-plan. The supervisor of a road gang or a factory crew plans in a limited area under fairly strict guidelines and procedures. Interestingly, in studies of work satisfactions, a principal factor found to account for the success of supervisors at the lowest organization level has been their ability to plan.

Efficiency of Plans The efficiency of a plan is measured by the amount it contributes to purpose and objectives as offset by the costs and other unsought consequences required to formulate and operate it. A plan can contribute to the attainment of objectives, but at too high or unnecessarily high costs. This concept of efficiency implies the normal ration of input to output, but goes beyond the usual understanding of inputs and outputs in terms of dollars, labor-hours, or units of production to include such values as individual and group satisfactions.

Many managers have followed plans, such as in the acquisition of certain aircraft by airlines, where costs were greater than the revenues obtainable. There have actually been some aircraft with which an airline found it could not make money. Companies have inefficiently attempted to attain objectives in the face of the unsought consequence of market unacceptability, as happened when a motor car manufacturer tried to capture a market by emphasizing engineering without competitive advances in style. Plans may also become inefficient in the attainment of objectives by jeopardizing group satisfactions. The new president of a company that was losing money attempted quickly to reorganize and cut expenses by wholesale and unplanned layoffs of key personnel. The result in fear, resentment, and loss of morale led to so much lower productivity as to defeat his laudable objective of eliminating losses and making profits. And some attempts to install management appraisal and development programs have failed because of group resentment of the methods used, regardless of the basic soundness of the programs.

Types of plans

The failure of some managers to recognize the variety of plans has often caused difficulty in making planning effective. It is easy to see that a major program, such as to build and equip a new factory, is a plan. But what is sometimes overlooked is that a number of other courses of future action are also plans. Keeping in mind that a plan encompasses any course of future action, we can see that plans are varied. They are classified here as purposes or missions, objectives, strategies, policies, procedures, rules, programs, and budgets. The nature of these may be expressed as a hierarchy, as shown.

Purposes of Missions If it is to be meaningful, every kind of organized group operation has, or at least should have, a purpose or mission. In every social system, enterprises have a basic function or task which is assigned to them by society. The purpose of businesses generally is the production and distribution of economic goods and services. The purpose of a state highway department is the design, building, and operation of a system of state highways. The purpose of the courts is the interpretation of laws and their application. The purpose of a university is teaching and research.

Although this book does not do so, sometimes distinctions are drawn between purposes and missions. While a business, for example, may have a social purpose of producing and distributing economic goods and services, it may accomplish this by fulfilling a mission of producing certain lines of products. The mission of an oil company like Exxon is to search for oil and to produce, refine, and market petroleum and a wide variety of petroleum products, from diesel fuel to chemicals. The mission of the Du Pont Company has been expressed as "better things through chemistry," and Kimberly-Clark (noted for its Kleenex trademark) regards its business mission as the production and sale of paper and paper products.

It is true that in some businesses and other enterprises the specific purpose or mission often becomes fuzzy. In some of the larger conglomerates, such as Litton Industries, a product line mission does not appear to exist. However, many of the conglomerates have regarded their mission as "synergy," which is accomplished through the combination of a variety of strengths and weaknesses. Some businesses never make clear to themselves or their organizations what their purpose or mission is, and many nonbusiness enterprises have likewise not always made this clear. It would, for example, be difficult to get a very clear notion of the mission of the Department of State, the Department of the Interior, or the Interstate Commerce Commission, to mention a few. Even some nonprofit foundations seem to the observer to have an obscure mission. One cannot help but wonder, for example, what the mission of the very large Ford Foundation is.

It can hardly be doubted that a clear definition of purpose or mission is necessary in order to formulate meaningful objectives. While every business should know the answer to the question, What is our business and what should it be? Many business executives have difficulty finding the answer.

The correct approach requires, first, that a business define who its customers are and what their attitudes and expectations are. This is a simple approach, but it often poses difficulties, as the railroads apparently found when they realized that they had too long looked upon themselves as being in the railroad business rather than the transportation business. However, every kind of enterprise in a society should know who its customers are and what they expect. Nonbusiness enterprises, in a very real sense, also have customers. Is not the public the "customer" of government agencies, and are not the parishioners the "customers" of a church?

It is sometimes thought that the mission of a business, as well as its objective, is to make a profit. It is true that every kind of enterprise must have, as was pointed out in the first chapter, a "surplus"-in business, "profit"-goal or objective if it is to survive and do the task society has entrusted to it. But this basic objective is accomplished by undertaking activities, going in clear directions, achieving goals, and accomplishing a mission.

Objectives objectives, or goals, are the ends toward which activity is aimed. They represent not only the end point of planning, but the end toward which organizing, staffing, leading, and controlling are aimed. While enterprise objectives constitute the basic plan of the firm, a department may also have objectives, but the two sets of goals may be entirely different. For example, the objective of a business might be to make a certain profit by producing a given line of home entertainment equipment, while the goal of manufacturing department might be to produce the required number of television sets of a given design and quality at a given cost. These objectives are consistent, but they differ in that the manufacturing department alone cannot ensure accomplishing the company's objective.

The nature of objectives and their relationship to planning are discussed in the following chapter. It is enough to emphasize here that objectives, or goals, are plans and that they involve the same planning process as any other type of planning. Even though they are also end points of planning. A sales goal, for example, cannot be guessed at or wished for; it must be determined in the light of purpose and circumstances. Likewise, a plan to accomplish a certain sales goal will have within it, or as derivatives of it, project or departmental goals.

Strategies For years the military used "strategies," or "grand plans" to mean plans made in the light of what it believed an adversary might or might not do. While the term "strategies" still usually has a competitive implication, it has been increasingly, used to reflect broad overall concepts of an enterprise operation. Strategies, therefore, most often denote a general program, of action and an implied deployment of emphasis and resources to attain comprehensive objectives. Anthony defines them as resulting from "the process of deciding on objectives of the organization. On changes in these objectives, on the resources used to attain these objectives, and on the policies that are to govern the acquisition, use, and disposition of these resources. And Chandler defines a strategy as "the determination of the basic long-term goals and objectives of an enterprise, and the adoption of courses of action and the allocation of resources necessary to carry out these goals.

Thus, a company may have an objective of profitable growth at a certain percentage per year. Supportive of this might be a determination that the company will be of a certain kind, such as a transportation company rather than a railroad company, or a container company rather than a paper box manufacturer. A strategy might include such major policies as to market directly to customers rather than through distributors, or to concentrate on proprietary products, or to have a full line, such as General Motors decided to save years ago for its automobile business.

The purpose of strategies, then, is to determine and communicate, through a system of major objectives and policies, a picture of what kind of enterprise is envisioned. Strategies show a unified direction and imply a deployment of emphasis and resources. They do not attempt to outline exactly how the enterprise is to accomplish its objectives, since this is the task of countless major and minor supporting programs. But they are a useful framework for guiding enterprise thinking and action. This usefulness in practice and importance in guiding planning do, however, justify their separation as a type of plan for purposes of analysis.

As a matter of fact, most strategies, particularly in business, do fit the traditional military concept by including competitive considerations. In the 1950s and later, the German Volkswagen Company, for example, selected the strategy of offering on the highly competitive American market a low-priced small car getting high mileage per gallon of fuel, easy to drive in congested areas and easy to park, in order to meet a demand by consumers who were not being served in these respects by native manufacturers. In this strategy were all the elements of the traditional military concept: (1) competitors, (2) a market not large enough to satisfy all competitive manufacturers, and (3) a gap that offered an adversary an opportunity. But even this kind of strategy is not entirely an independently separate type of plan because it is actually a combination of objectives (to secure a given market share), a major policy (produce and market a small, low-priced car), and various programs (for example, exporting and marketing).

Policies Policies, also, are plans in that they are general statements or understandings which guide or channel thinking and action in decision making. One can hardly refer to all policies as "statements," since they are often merely implied from the actions of managers. The president of a company, for example, may strictly follow-perhaps for convenience rather than as policy-the practice of promoting from within; the practice may then be interpreted as policy and rigorously followed by subordinates. In fact, one of the problems of all managers is to make sure that subordinates do not interpret as policy minor decisions which they make without intending these decisions to serve as precedents.

Policies limit an area within which a decision is to be made and assure that the decision will be consistent with the contributive to objectives. Policies tend to predecide issues, avoid repeated analysis, and give a unified structure to other types of plans, thus permitting managers to delegate authority while maintaining control. For example, the Western Pacific Railroad has had the policy of acquiring industrial land to replace all acreage sold along its right of way. This permit the manager of the land department to develop acquisition plans without continual reference to top management, which is nevertheless furnished with a standard for control.

Policies ordinarily exist on all levels of the organization and range from major company policies through major departmental policies to minor or derivative policies applicable to the smallest segment of the organization. They may also be related to functions-such as sales and finance-or merely to a project-such as that of designing a new product with materials to meet a specified competition.

The varieties of policies are legion. Examples are departmental policies to hire only university-trained engineers or to encourage employee suggestions for improved cooperation, and company policies to promote from within, to confirm strictly to a high standard of business ethics, to compete on a price basis, to insist on fixed rather than cost-plus pricing.

Being guides to thinking in decision making, it follows that policies must allow for some discretion. Otherwise, they would be rules. Too often policies are established as a kind of Ten Commandments which leave no room for discretion. Although the discretion area, in some instances, is quite broad, it can be exceedingly narrow. For example, a policy to buy from the lowest of three qualified bidders leaves for discretion only the question of which bidders are qualified; a requirement to buy from a certain company, regardless of price or service, is a rule.

Because policies are so often misunderstood, the authors have selected examples from a company's policy manual. It will be noted in each case that there is an area for a person in a decision-making capacity to use discretion. The following are interesting examples:

1. Gifts from Suppliers Except for token gifts of purely nominal or advertising value. No employee shall accept any gift or gratuity from any supplier at any time. (What is "token" or "nominal"?)
2. Entertainment No officer or employee shall accept favors or entertainment from an outside organization or agency which are substantial enough to cause undue influence in his or her selection of goods or services for the company. (What is "substantial" or "undue"?)
3. Outside Employment It is improper for any employee to work for any company customers, or for any competitors, or for vendors or suppliers of goods or services to the company; outside employment is further prohibited if it: (a) results in a division of loyalty to the company or a conflict of interests, or (b) interferes with or adversely affects the employee's work or opportunity for advancement in the company. (What is meant by a "division of loyalty," "conflict of interest," or "adversely"?)
4. Pricing Territorial division managers may establish such prices for the products under their control as they deem in a division's interest so long as (a) these prices result in gross profit margins for any line of products which are consistent with an approved profit plan, (b) price reductions will not result in detrimental effects on prices of similar products of another company division in another state or country, and (c) prices meet the legal requirements of the state or country in which the prices are effective. (What are "consistent," "detrimental," or "legal requirements"?)

The area of discretion in most of these policies is fairly general. However, in the pricing policy shown, the discretion area is fairly specifically defined. Likewise, in the outside employment policy, that portion dealing with employment with any vendors or suppliers leaves no discretion and is, consequently, a rule.

Policy should be regarded as a means of encouraging discretion and initiative, but within limits. As shown in the amount of freedom possible will naturally depend upon the policy, which in turn reflects position and authority in the organization. The president of a company with a policy of aggressive price competition has a broad area of discretion and initiative in which to interpret and apply this policy. The district sales manager abides by the same basic policy, but the interpretations made by the president, the vice president for sales, and the regional sales manager become derivative policies which narrow the district sales manager's scope to the point where, for example, he or she may be permitted only to approve a special sale price to meet competition and not exceeding a 10 percent reduction.

Making policies consistent and integrated enough to facilitate the realization of enterprise objectives is difficult for many reasons. First, policies are too seldom written and their exact interpretations too little known. Second, the very delegation of authority that policies are intended to implement leads, through its decentralizing influence, to widespread participation in policy-making and interpretation, with almost certain variations among individuals. Third, it is not always easy to control policy because actual policy may be difficult to ascertain and intended policy may not always be clear.

Procedures Procedures are plans in that they establish a customary method of handling future activities. (They are truly guides to action) rather than to thinking; and they detail the exact manner in which a certain activity must be accomplished. Their essence is chronological sequence of required actions.

Their pervasiveness in the organization is readily apparent. The board of directors follows many procedures quite different from those of the supervisors; the expense account of the vice president may go through quite different approval procedures from that of the salesperson; the procedures for carrying out vacation and sick leave provisions may vary considerably at various levels of organization. But the important factois that procedures exist throughout an organization, even though, as one might expect, they become more exacting and numerous in the lower levels, largely because of the necessity for more careful control, the economic advantages through specialization of spelling out actions in detail, the reduced need for discretion, and the fact that routine jobs lend themselves to obtaining greater efficiency through prescription of what is thought to be the one best way.

As in other types of plans, procedures have a hierarchy of importance. Thus, in a typical corporation, one may find a manual of "Corporation Standard Practice" outlining procedures for the corporation as a whole, a manual of "Division Standard Practice," and special sets of procedures for a department, a branch, a section, or a unit.

Procedures often cut across department lines. For example, in a manufacturing company, the procedure for handling orders will almost certainly encompass the sales department (for the original order), the finance department (for acknowledgment of receipts of funds and for customer credit determination), the accounting department (for recording the transaction), the production department (for order to produce or authority to release from stock), and the traffic department (for determination of the shipping means and route)

The relationship between procedures and policies may best be indicated by a few examples. Company policy may grant employees vacations; procedures established to implement this policy will schedule vacations to avoid disruption of work, set methods and rates of vacation pay, maintain records to assure each employee a vacation, and provide means of applying for the vacation. A company may have a policy of shipping orders quickly; particularly in a large company, careful procedures will be necessary to ensure that orders are handled in a specific way. Company policy may require clearance by the public relations department of public utterances of its employees; to implement this policy, procedures may be established to obtain clearance with a minimum of inconvenience and delay.

Rules are plans in that they are required actions which, like other plans, are chosen from among alternatives. They are usually the simplest type of plan. Rules are frequently confused with policies or procedures. A rule requires that a specific and definite action be taken or not taken with respect to a situation. It is thus related to a procedure in that it guides action but specifies no time sequence. As a matter of fact, a procedure could be looked upon as a sequence of rules. A rule, however, may or may not be part of a procedure. For example, "no smoking" is a rule quite unrelated to any procedure; but a procedure governing the handling of orders may incorporate the rule that all orders must be confirmed the day they are received. This rule allows no deviation from a stated course of action and in no way interferes with the procedure for handling orders. It is comparable to a rule that all fractions over half an ounce are to be counted a full ounce or that inspectors in the receiving department must count or weigh all materials and compare these against the purchase order. The essence of a rule is that it reflects a managerial decision that certain actions be taken-or not be taken.

Rules should be carefully distinguished from policies. The purpose of policies is to guide thinking in decision making by marking off areas of discretion. Although rules also serve as guides, they allow no discretion in their application. Many companies and other organization think they have policies when they really spell out rules. The result is confusion as to when a person may use his or her judgment, if at all. This can be dangerous. Rules and procedures, by their very nature, are designed to restrict thinking and should of course be used only when we do not want people in an organization to use their discretion.

Programs are a complex of goals, policies, procedures, rules, task assignments, steps to be taken, resources to be employed, and other elements necessary to carry out a given course of action; they are ordinarily supported by necessary capital and operating budgets. Programs may be as major as that of the Du Pont Company to acquire Conoco, and $8 billion oil and coal company, or the 5-year program embarked upon by the Ford Motor Company several years ago to improve the status and quality of its thousands of supervisors. Or they may be as minor as a program formulated by a single supervisor in a parts manufacturing department of a farm machinery company to improve the morale of workers.

A primary program may call for many derivative programs. For example, an airline program to invest in new jets, costing hundreds of millions of dollars for the aircraft and the necessary spare parts, requires many derivative programs if the investment is to be properly used. A program for providing the maintenance and operating bases with spare components and parts must be developed in detail. Special maintenance facilities must be prepared, and maintenance personnel trained. Pilots and flight engineers must also be trained, and, if the new jets mean a net addition to flying hours, flight personnel trained to handle the new airplanes and their schedules, as service is expanded to new cities in the airline's system. Advertising programs must give adequate publicity to the new service. Plans to finance the aircraft and provide for insurance coverage must be developed.

These and other programs must be devised and effected before any new aircraft are received and placed in service. Furthermore, all these programs necessitate coordination and timing, since the failure of any part of this network of derivative plans means delay for the major program with consequent unnecessary costs and loss of revenues. Some of the programs, particularly those involving hiring and training of personnel, can be accomplished too soon as well as too late, since needles expense results from employees being available and trained before their services are required.

Thus one seldom finds that a program of any importance in enterprise planning stands by itself. It is usually a part of a complex system of programs, depending upon some and affecting others. This interdependence of plans makes planning very difficult. The results of poor or inadequate planning are seldom isolated, for planning is only as strong as its weakest link. Even a seemingly unimportant procedure or rule, if badly conceived, may wreck an important program. Coordinated planning requires extraordinarily exacting managerial skill. It truly requires the most rigorous application of systems thinking and action.

Budgets A budget as a plan is a statement of expected results expressed in numerical terms. It may be referred to as a "numberized" program. As a matter of fact, the financial operating budget is often called a "profit plan". It may be expressed either in financial terms or in terms of labor-hours, units of product, machine-hours, or any other numerically measurable term. It may deal with operations, as the expense budget does; it may reflect capital outlays, as the capital expenditures budget does: or it may show flow of cash, as the cash budget does.

Since budgets are also control devices, the principal discussion of them is reserved for the chapters on control. However, making a budget is clearly planning. It is the fundamental planning instrument in many companies. A budget forces a company to make in advance-whether for a week or 5 years-a numerical compilation of expected cash flow, expenses and revenues, capital outlays, or labor or machine-hour utilization. The budget is necessary for control, but it cannot serve as a sensible standard of control unless it reflects plans.

Budgetary planning does vary considerably in its accuracy, extent of detail, and ways of developing budgets. Some budgets are made to vary with possible levels of output of an enterprise; these are called "variable" or "flexible" budgets. Another approach that has been widely (but not always successfully) used by government agencies has been referred to as "program budgets." The idea behind this type of budgeting is that each agency and department of it will identify program goals sought, then develop detailed planning programs needed to meet these goals, and finally "numberize" or "dollarize" the needed programs. It is easy to see that this kind of budget, where it is done well, goes far in forcing a fairly detailed and complete degree of planning. Still another type of budgeting, which really combines variable and program budgeting, has been given the attractive name "zero-base budgeting." In this approach, the objectives sought and the work found necessary for their accomplishment are put up in "work packages" as though the budget planner were starting from the beginning, or "base zero." The impetus to make planning more complete may be readily seen from this approach.

As a matter of fact, the principal advantage of budgeting is that it makes people plan; and because it is usually in the form of numbers, it forces a degree of definiteness in planning.

Steps In planning

Although the steps in planning are presented here in connection with major programs such as the acquisition of a plant or a fleet of jets or the development of a new product, essentially the same steps would be followed in any thorough planning. As minor plans are usually simpler, certain of the steps are more easily accomplished, but the following practical steps are of general application. These steps are diagramed. Obviously, the discriminating manager would not use $100 worth of time used to make a planning decision involving millions of dollars.

1. *Being aware of opportunities* Although preceding what is usually considered to be actual planning, the awareness of an opportunity is the real starting point for planning. It includes a preliminary look at possible future opportunities and the ability to see them clearly and completely, a knowledge of where we stand in the light of our strengths and weaknesses, and understanding of why we wish to solve uncertainties, and a vision of what we expect to gain. Setting realistic objectives depends on this awareness. Planning requires realistic diagnosis of the opportunity situation.

2. *Establishing objectives* The second step in planning is to establish objectives for the entire enterprise and then for each subordinate unit. Objectives specifying the results expected indicate the end points of what is to be done, where the primary emphasis is to be placed, and what is to be accomplished by the network of strategies, policies, procedures, rules, budgets, and programs.

Enterprise objectives should give direction to the nature of all major plans which, by reflecting these objectives, define the objectives of major departments. Major department objectives, in turn, control the objectives of subordinate departments, and so on down the line. The objectives of lesser departments will be better framed, however, if subdivision managers understand the overall enterprise objectives and the implied derivative goals, and if they are given an opportunity to contribute their ideas to them and to the setting of their own goals.

3. *Premising* A third logical step in planning is to establish, obtain agreement to utilize, and disseminate critical planning premises. These are forecast data of a factual nature, applicable basic policies, and existing company plans. Premises, then, are planning assumptions-in other words, the expected environment of plans in operation. As was discussed in, the external environment of an enterprise can be quite complex. Even the internal environment of an organization must be carefully considered when plans are drawn up. The premising step leads to one of the major principles of planning: The more individuals charged with planning understand and agree to utilize consistent planning premises, the more coordinated enterprise planning will be.

Forecasting is important in premising: What kinds of markets will there be? What quantity of sales? What prices? What products? What technical developments? What costs? What wage rates? What tax rates and policies? What new plants? What policies with respect to dividends? How will expansion be financed? What political or social environment?

Some premises forecast policies not yet made. For example, if a company has no pension plan and no policy with respect to one, planning sometimes must premise whether such a policy will be set and, if so, what it will contain. Other premises naturally grow out of existing policies or other plans. For example, if a company has a policy of paying out no more than 3 percent of its profits, before taxes, for contributions, and if there is no reason to believe that this policy will be changed, the policy becomes a planning premise. Or, if a company has made large investments in special purpose fixed plant and machinery, this becomes an important planning premise.

A difficulty of establishing complete premises and keeping them up to date is that every major plan, and many minor ones, become a premise for the future. The plan to establish a factory in Kansas City, for example, becomes a premise for plans in which plant location is important. Similarly, it would make little sense for a Denver local bus line to premise future plans on Florida markets. And when an airline equips its long-haul routes with one type of aircraft for which it builds maintenance and overhaul facilities, these becomes critical premises for other plans.

As one moves down the organization hierarchy, the composition of planning premises changes somewhat. The basic process will be the same, but old and new major plans will materially affect the future against which managers of lesser units must plan. A superior's plans affecting a subordinate manager's area of authority become premises for the latter's planning. Because the future environment of plans is so complex, it would not be profitable or realistic to make assumptions about every detail of the future environment of a plan. Therefore, premises are, as a practical matter, limited to those which are critical, or strategic, to a plan, that is, those which most influence its operation.

It would be surprising if all members of a company's management at all levels agreed independently about the company future. One manager might expect world peace to last 10 years; another, world war for the same period. One manager might expect prices to go up 10 percent in 5 years; another, 50 percent; and another might expect prices to drop.

Lack of planning coordination, through use by managers of different sets of premises, can be extremely costly. The use of consistent premises should, therefore, be agreed upon. A single standard for the future is necessary for good planning, even though this standard includes several sets of premises, with the instruction that different sets of plans be developed on each. Some companies, for example, customarily develop plans in prospect of both peace and war, so that, regardless of what occurs, the company will be ready. Obviously, however, a plan actually put into operation for any future period can use only one set of premises if coordination of its elements is to be achieved. Since agreement to utilize a given set of premises is important to coordinated planning, it becomes a major responsibility of managers, starting with those at the top, to make sure that subordinate managers understand the premises upon which they are expected to plan. It is not unusual for chief executives in well-managed companies to force top managers with differing views, through group deliberation, to arrive at a set of major premises that all can accept. But whether they are acceptable to all or not, no chief executive can afford to chance a situation where lieutenants are planning their portions of the company's future on substantially different premises.

4. *Determining alternative courses* The fourth step in planning is to search for and examine alternative courses of action, especially those not immediately apparent. There is seldom a plan for which reasonable alternatives do not exist, and quite an alternative that is not obvious proves to be the best.

The more common problem is not finding alternatives, but reducing the number of alternatives so that the most promising may be analyzed. Even with mathematical techniques and the computer, there is a limit to the number of alternatives that may be examined. It is therefore usually necessary for the planner to reduce by preliminary examinations the number of alternatives to those promising the most fruitful possibilities or by mathematically eliminating, through the process of approximation, the least promising ones.

5. *Evaluating Alternative* Courses Having sought out alternative courses and examined their strong and weak points, the fifth step is to evaluate them by weighing the various factors in the light of premises and goals. One course may appear to be the most profitable but require a large cash outlay and a slow payback; another may be less profitable but involve less risk; still another may better suit the company's long-range objectives.

If the only objective were to maximize profits in a certain business immediately, if the future were not uncertain, if cash position and capital availability were not worrisome, and if most factors could be reduced to definite data, this evaluation should be relatively easy. But typical planning is replete with uncertainties, problems of capital shortages, and intangible factors, and so evaluation is usually very difficult, even with relatively simple problems. A company may wish to enter a new product line primarily for purposes of prestige; the forecast of expected results may show a clear financial loss, but the question is still open as to whether the loss is worth the gain in prestige.

Because the number of alternative courses in most situations is legion and the numerous variables and limitations may be complex, evaluation can also be exceedingly difficult. Because of these complexities, the newer methodologies and applications of operations research and analysis, discussed, are helpful. Indeed, it is at this step in the planning process that operations research and mathematical and computing techniques have their primary application to the field of management.

6. *Selecting a Course* The sixth step, selecting the course of action, is the point at which a plan is adopted-the real point of decision making. Occasionally an analysis and evaluation of alternative courses will disclose that two or more are advisable, and the manager may decide to follow several courses rather than a single course.

7. *Formulating Derivative Plans* At the point where a decision is made, planning is seldom complete, and another step is indicated. There are almost invariably derivative plans required to support the basic plan. In the case where an airline decided to acquire a fleet of new planes, this decision was the signal for the development of a host of derivative plans dealing with the hiring and training of various types of personnel, the acquisition and positioning of spare parts, the development of maintenance facilities, scheduling and advertising, financing and insurance.

8. *Numberizing Plans by Budgeting* After decisions are made and plans are set, the final step to give them meaning, as indicated in the discussion above on types of plans, is to numberize them by converting them to budgets. The overall budgets of an enterprise represent the sum total of income and expenses, with resultant profit or surplus, and budgets or major balance sheet items such as cash and capital expenditures. Each department or program of a business or other enterprise can have its own budgets, usually of expenses and capital expenditures, which tie into the overall budget.

If done well, budgets become a means of adding together the various plans and also important standards against which planning progress can be measured. As such, budgets will be discussed below in connection with managerial control.

As one moves down the organization hierarchy, the composition of planning premises changes somewhat. The basic process will be the same, but old and new major plans will materially affect the future against which managers of lesser units must plan. A superior's plans affecting a subordinate manager's area of authority become premises for the latter's planning.

Because the future environment of plans is so complex, it would not be profitable or realistic to make assumptions about every detail of the future environment of a plan. Therefore, premises are, as a practical matter, limited to those which are critical, or strategic, to a plan, that is, those which most influence its operation.

It would be surprising if all members of a company's management at all levels agreed independently about the company future. One manager might expect world peace to last 10 years; another, world war for the same period. One manager might expect prices to go up 10 percent in 5 years; another, 50 percent; and another might expect prices to drop.

Lack of planning coordination, through use by managers of different sets of premises, can be extremely costly. The use of consistent premises should, therefore, be agreed upon. A single standard for the future is necessary for good planning, even though this standard includes several sets of premises, with the instruction that different sets of plans be developed on each.

Some companies, for example, customarily develop plans in prospect of both peace and war, so that, regardless of what occurs, the company will be ready. Obviously, however, a plan actually put into operation for any future period can use only one set of premises if coordination of its elements is to be achieved.

Since agreement to utilize a given set of premises is important to coordinated planning, it becomes a major responsibility of managers, starting with those at the top, to make sure that subordinate managers understand the premises upon which they are expected to plan. It is not unusual for chief executives in well-managed companies to force top managers with differing views, through group deliberation, to arrive at a set of major premises that all can accept.

But whether they are acceptable to all or not, no chief executive can afford to chance a situation where lieutenants are planning their portions of the company's future on substantially different premises. The more common problem is not finding alternatives, but reducing the number of alternatives so that the most promising may be analyzed. Even with mathematical techniques and the computer, there is a limit to the number of alternatives that may be examined. It is therefore usually necessary for the planner to reduce by preliminary examinations the number of alternatives to those promising the most fruitful possibilities or by mathematically eliminating, through the process of approximation, the least promising ones.

3

Decision Making

Consider the following statements:

1. If accounting information is not considered relevant by a decision-maker to a decision under consideration, a change in the accounting information will not affect his decision.
2. The conception of accounting information held by a decision-maker-his opinion on how well the accountant and accounting system measures significant attributes and characteristics of factors affecting and affected by a decision-will affect the weight given to accounting information in the decision process when other information is available.
3. The availability of other information will be an important determinant of the weight assigned by a decision-maker to accounting information in the decision process.

Each of these statements has many characteristics of a truism. Many more like them, each concerned with the relationship between accounting systems, accounting information, decision-makers, and decision-making could be easily constructed. Though behavioral relationships on which such statements rest are potentially important to the development of accounting theory and the design of information-decision systems, the study of those relationship is in the earliest stages.

Relatively little is known about the way in which information is used in decision-making, and without such knowledge it is difficult to predict the diverse effects which different accounting systems or information will have on decisions. A model developed below explicitly identifies and relates some factors which may determine when decisions are affected by accounting systems and information. The hypotheses on which this model is based are intended to stimulate and direct part of the study of accounting and decision-making. While the model is not tested here, some implications of the hypothesized relationships for both accounting theory and accounting systems are discussed.

Rationales for research on decision-making and behavior by accountants

The problems that demand new research in behavioral aspects accounting are familiar to almost all who have studied economics and accounting. The relationship between available information and decision is basic to economic theories of decision-making. Knowledge about costs, prices, and competitors is assumed in almost all traditional theory, and much effort has been directed toward developing models of decision-making for use when information about one or more of these factors is unknown. As these models have been explored and modified, and as new procedures for analysis of alternative courses of action have been developed, new attention has been given to the role of data as determinants of decisions.

Accounting systems of firms are important sources of information for business decision-making. The information which systems provide for decision-making can be grouped in three classes: financial statements,quantitative reports on selected aspects of operations, and special analyses. Information from each class can be grouped with information from another or with information from sources outside the accounting system in the set of information used by a decision-maker.

Almost al;l accounting information is affected by the body of rules and procedures called generally accepted accounting principles. Efforts to develop and improve generally accepted accounting principles have been underway since the 1930's, and since 1960 these efforts have found vigorous support from the accounting profession. Thus far, these efforts have not been notably successful, for there are few, if any, base, on which all accountants can agree to select among alternative general principles.

It is possible that much of the effort directed toward resolution of controversy about generally accepted accounting principles has been premature or misdirected. Accounting is a service activity carried out to provide information for decisions within and about business firms. Analyses of alternative sets of generally accepted accounting principles have often been based on the assumption that the relationship between an accounting report or information contained therein and each decision is direct. But this assumption has not been tested, and alternative hypotheses abound. When these have been tested and efforts to develop generally accepted accounting principles can be based upon knowledge of the manner in which accounting affects decisions about business activity, new and important criteria for selecting among alternative methods and alternative systems will be available.

Defining accounting systems and information

One complication in the task of relating accounting information to decision-making is the fact that "accounting systems" are diverse and "accounting information" describes many different sets of data and information. For purposes of this paper, an "accounting system" will refer to the methods by which financial data about a firm or its activity are collected, processed, stored and/or distributed to members of the firm or other interested parties. It is possible to consider that any data or information which are obtained from or created in the accounting system of a firm are accounting information, whether contained in a financial statement, a special report, or verbal statement. However, for our immediate purposes, that interpretation is too broad to be useful. Hereafter, "accounting information" will refer to written information of the type that might be contained in a complete or partial financial report-balance sheet, income statement, or funds flow statement-though in many cases this limitation is not critical to the discussion.

The relevance of accounting information for decision-making

By definition, decisions affect future events, for future actions are determined as a decision is made. In the case of management decisions, decisions may affect only a single event or they may affect all events subsequent to the decision. But no event which has been completed can be altered by a decision. Furthermore, accounting information, in the sense that we are using that term here, focuses on past events. Accounting cannot change events or their effects unless it is through the decision process where future events and their effects are determined. Decision-making and accounting information focus on different time periods except to the extent that the decision process employs accounting information. An important question then is, when is accounting information relevant for decision-making?

In a recent paper, Ijiri, Jaedicke, and Knight have provided a framework which is extremely useful as a basis for discussing the relationship of accounting information and decision processes. They represent a decision process as a function that relates a set of decision inputs to a unique set of decisions. Symbolically,

Here z_2, z_2,...., z_n are set of decisions based upon inputs, x_1, x_2,....,x_n, according to a decision rule, h. Each set Z and X, must contain at least one element, but there is no requirement that the number of inputs be equal to the number of decisions.

Selection of a particular decision rule by a decision-maker is affected by many factors, among them his analytical capabilities and objectives. The rule associates inputs with decisions and selection of a decision rule establishes the degree to which objectives will be met by the expected effects of a particular set of decisions. The decisions-maker explores the relationships between decisions and objectives prior to the selection of a rule by analysis and through evaluation of the effects of past events similar to those contemplated in the future.

If accounting information affects decisions, it does so through a decision rule which relates decisions to inputs, which include accounting information. The decision-maker uses or selects a decision rule which relates inputs to decisions in a manner consistent with his experience, perceptions, and his objectives. Suppose we let x_1 represent consistent accounting information, one element of a set of all decision inputs available at the time a set of decisions is to be made. The decision rule weights each decision input. which determines each decision in the set Z, and the weight assigned to x_1 will determine what effect, if any, accounting information has on decisions affecting future events. All other decision inputs, x_2 through x_m are also weighted by the decision rule, and each affects the resulting set of decisions. These inputs may provide nonfinancial information essential to decisions, and in some cases their weights will overwhelm any possible effects of accounting information.

In selecting a decision rule, the decision-maker must consider all inputs available and their relevance to the set of decisions to be made. It is the decisions-maker who decides whether any input is relevant or not. The perceived relevance of the decision inputs to the decisions at hand determine whether the decision rule selected will apply a weight different from zero to accounting information. If a weight different from zero is applied, accounting information may affect decisions, if not, decisions will not be affected by accounting information. Therefore, we hypothesize: if accounting information is perceived as irrelevant for the set of decisions to be made, accounting information will not affect decisions; if accounting information is perceived as relevant to the set of decisions to be made, it may affect decisions.

The role of the decision-maker's conception of accounting

Accounting is a systematic process of providing information about wealth and the effects of economic events. The methods, rules, and procedures that comprise accounting are here assumed to be familiar to the reader. However, there are reasons to believe that accounting is different things to different participants in economic events, and if so, the conceptions of accounting held by individuals or organizations may influence the impact of accounting information on behavior.

Away from reality, accounting can be regards as a perfect measure. A perfect measure can be defined as a measure where there is a zero probability that the true measurement of an attribute differs from the reported measurement. We can assume that identifiable objects and legal rights have value and that these values are enhanced or destroyed as economic events occur, and we can assume that these values and effects are measurable. To many persons, accounting practice, carried out by trained observers applying consistent and objective methods of measurement and attested to by independent agents, holds the image of a perfect measure applied buy professionals. There is an aura of authenticity that surrounds accounting data, and to the untrained user of information, accounting may appear to be a perfect source. We must recognize, however, that few, if any, of the persons who have processed or reviewed the data and the procedures that have converted it to information would consider it perfect.

More realistically, accounting can be considered as a process by which the value or effects of events is reported as a accurately as possible but without pretense of being a perfect measure. Here, this conception of accounting will be referred to as an "imperfect measure". Such a measure is defined when the probability that the true value differs from the reported value is greater than zero. This conception is probably closest to that held by most practicing accountants. Errors and inaccuracy in the process of measuring, counting, and reporting are inevitable, and most persons who are familiar with accounting measures and procedures are familiar with these problems. This notion may cause accounting to have a different impact on behavior than the "perfect measure" notion. It allows for a "margin of disbelief" that may in some cases affect the kind of action taken as accounting information is used in decision processes.

A third conception of accounting is fundamentally different from the "perfect measure" or "imperfect measure" notions advanced above. Accounting information may be a goal for actors in economic events. When a businessman seeks profit, he does so for many reasons. For some purposes, the profit reported by accounting is far more important to the businessman or manager than the "true" or "perfectly measured" profit. Modern business organization has given this conception of accounting wide significance, and the implications of this notion for accounting warrant close examination.

Accounting becomes a goal when rewards or satisfactions accrue to a decision-maker as a result of accounting informations, and the relationship of the true measure to the reported measure is unimportant. For example, if a manager hopes to advance and feels he will be promoted if he can effect cost reductions, and if accounting information will provide the basis for determining whether costs have been reduced, then it is the accounting information which shows reduced costs that becomes the goal. Likewise, where management is rewarded by stockholders with salary and prerequisites on the basis of reported earnings or growth, the reports which result in these rewards may become more important-the goal of management decision-makers-than the long-run earnings or healthy growth which the stockholders really intend to reward.

While not exclusive, this brief recognition of diverse conceptions of accounting seems essential to understanding the effects of accounting information on behavior and decision-making. Below it will be assumed that any individual in a decision situation conceives accounting information either as a goal or at a point on a continuum on which accounting varies from a perfect measure to an imperfect one. This assumption is necessary to state a second set of hypotheses relating accounting information and decisions: the conception of accounting held by a decisions-maker will affect his selection of a decision rule to be used in reaching a set of decisions. This hypothesis can be further specified by stating it in two parts:

1. If accounting information is both a decision input and an objective sought by a decision-maker, accounting information will affect decisions.

2. The more a decisions-maker conceives accounting as being a perfect source of information, the more likely the decision-maker will select decision rules that weight accounting heavily, and the more likely accounting information will affect decisions.

Classifying decisions-makers

Because accounting information can be conceived as a goal, and because accounting information is determined in part by an accounting system, a classification of decisions-makers provides insight into a final effect which accounting information may have on the set of decisions selected by the decisions-makers. Three classes are suggested; first, decisions-makers within the firm who make decisions both about operations and about the accounting system used to prepare reports; second, decision-makers within the firm who can make operating decisions but who cannot affect the methods used to prepare reports; and third, those outside of the firm who make decisions about the firm which may affect its environment and operations but who have no direct control over the operation of the firm or any activities in which it is engaged. The reasons for separating the first two classes of decision-makers, both of which are internal to the firm, will later become more obvious.

The first class of decision-makers is comprised of top management. Financial reports are the reports of this group and they are responsible for their preparation and presentation. If a choice must be made between accounting methods, this group is responsible for making that decision. This means that the set of possible decisions available to this class of decision-makers includes modification of the accounting system.

The second class of decision-makers is distinguished from the first only in one important way. Their position in the organization precludes their determining the information included in accounting reports by modifying the accounting system. However, they make decisions about the activities of the firm and we can assume that accounting information enters into their decisions processes. They can, of course, influence the content of accounting information by their decisions about activities. In which case accounting information may be affecting decisions.

The distinction between top management, who may affect accounting information, and internal decision-makers who cannot, is most critical where accounting information is conceived as a goal. The decision function for such managers may contain important options between operating decisions and decisions to change the methods by which accounting information is prepared. In any event, decisions are affected, but predicting directions of the effects is much more complicated than it is for decision-makers who do not have authority to modify accounting methods or procedures. Requirements for independent audits and certification of consistency in methods between accounting periods reduces the significance of the two levels of management, though few would argue that this requirement is such that the effects of top management's discretion in accounting can be ignored.

The third class of decision-makers consists of several sets of interested outsiders. Investors, legally the owners of the firm but in fact usually somewhat removed from it, are ostensibly the group for which accounting information in published form is prepared. Creditors, in some cases merely another class of investors, usually seek the same information. A third major set of outsiders consists of government agencies who seek bases for taxation, regulation, and economic analysis. Each of these sets of outsiders makes decisions that may affect the firm and its operations, and to the extent that accounting information is utilized as part of their decision processes, it will affect these decisions. However, the goals of the decisions-makers external to the firm presumably may differ from the objectives of the firm or objectives which concern decision-makers within the firm. This possibility makes analysis of effects of accounting information on decisions of this class of decision-makers very difficult.

Nevertheless, the classification of decision-makers yields an important hypothesis: if a decision-maker can affect the accounting system as well as the activities of the firm, and if he conceives accounting information as a goal, accounting information will affect decisions about either or both the accounting system and operations.

Non-accounting information

The final hypothesis to be introduced in this model concerns the role played by information which is not a product of the accounting system in determining the impact of accounting information on decisions. Above, accounting information was defined as information of the type that might be contained in a conventional financial report. In many respects, the effects of non-accounting information on decisions can be analyzed in the same framework as accounting information. However, the importance of non-accounting information here is that it may determine the effects of accounting information on decisions.

If non-accounting information becomes a goal or is perceived as having special relevance for decisions undergoing evaluation, the impact of accounting information will be reduced. If non-accounting information is not relevant to decisions, the effects of relevant accounting information will be enhanced. Therefore, we hypothesize: the impact of accounting information on decisions is affected by the perceived relevance of other information also available to the decision-maker.

A model for analyzing the effects of accounting information on decisions

The hypotheses developed above are all summarized and their interrelationships are made clear. Rather than restate all hypotheses or describe the model in detail, a summary of hypotheses which lead to the principal outcomes predicted by the model will be used to reveal the interrelationships within it.

1. Accounting information will either affect decisions or affect decisions about the accounting system if:

   (a) accounting information is relevant to decisions; and

(b) the decisions-maker conceives accounting as a goal;

(c) the decisions-maker is a member of the firm who can control the selection and operation of the accounting system.

II. Accounting information will affect decisions if:

(a) accounting information is relevant to decisions;

(b) the decision-maker conceives accounting as a goal; and

(c) the decision-maker is a member of the firm who cannot control the selection and operation of the accounting system;

(c2) the decisions-maker is external to the firm;or

(b2) the decision-maker conceives accounting as a perfect measure;

(c) non-accounting information is not relevant to the decision.

III. Accounting information may affect decisions if;

(a) accounting information is relevant to decisions;

(b1) the decision-maker conceives accounting as a perfect measure; and

(c) non-accounting information is relevant to the decision;

(b2) the decision-maker conceives accounting as an imperfect measure; but

(c) non-accounting information is not relevant to the decision.

IV. Accounting information will not affect decisions if:

(a1) accounting information is not relevant to decisions; or

(a2) accounting information is relevant to the decisions; but

(b) the decision-maker conceives accounting information as an imperfect measure; and

(c) non-accounting information is relevant to the decision.

Some further exploration of the model

The flow chart format used in figure 1 is extremely demanding and, possibly, too restrictive. This format demands that we state precisely what will happen at each branch of the model. Yet there appear to be some situations in which it would be more satisfactory to think in terms of effects along a continuum.

Examine, for example, the lower right-hand portion of figure 1, where the model predicts the impact of other information when accounting has been perceived as relevant and when the decision-maker perceives accounting information as being either perfect or imperfect. The model predicts that accounting information perceived as perfect may have some effect on decisions. However, when the decision-maker perceives accounting information as being something less than perfect, the impact of other information becomes less certain. The degree of conceived imperfection and the amount and quality of other information are important variables in such cases. Likewise, even in cases where accounting information is perfect, and other information is relevant, the decision might be affected, but not altered, by accounting information. Similar questions can be raised at other points and simply reinforce conclusions about the need for testing the hypotheses on which this model is based.

While these uncertain conclusion beg for clarification and discriminating research, they are perhaps the least interesting. In cases where decisions may be little affected by accounting information, the choice of a particular accounting system, or particular accounting methods used in that system, may be of little importance. It is at the other extreme, where the model predicts that accounting information will affect decisions that the choice of accounting systems and methods becomes critical.

Interaction within the model

Further complications in interpreting or using the model stem from possible interaction between the method of accounting used and/or the accounting system developed and the perceived relevance of accounting for decision-making purposes. If the decision-maker feels that a particular method or system of accounting is inappropriate as a basis foe measurements relating to a particular problem, he will be led to a position where the effective accounting information will be reduced. Unless we know something about the particular class of decision-makers and their perceptions of accounting methods, it is difficult to predict whether any examination of the conception of accounting held by the decision-maker will be of importance. Likewise, if the method chosen, or the process of selecting a method, affects the conception of accounting held by the decision-makers, then this will affect the relationship between a particular method and decisions.

The proposal made here to recognize relevance as a primary determinant of the effect of accounting on decision-making is not new. The degree of relevance has frequently been suggested as a basis for choosing between alternative accounting methods and forms of accounting information. This has been particularly true in the literature relating to accounting within the firm, where it is frequently asserted that those methods that result in revelation of cost-volume-profit relationships are most appropriate. Likewise, in the recent Statement of Basic Accounting Theory, formulated by a committee of the American Accounting Association, relevance is proposed as a primary standard for selecting among alternative forms of accounting information.

However, the meaning of relevance appropriate for its use as a criterion in the development of accounting methodology and theory is not clear. While users are frequently the point of reference in analyses employing "relevance", the determination of "relevant information" is left to the accountant, who uses some standard, generally accepted model for decision-making as the criterion in determining what should be reported. In the formulation which has been presented above, relevance is determined by the user of the information, and the effect of this choice creates several problems which require careful consideration before this criterion is employed.

If the user determines relevance, we should expect that, in some cases, what the user feels is relevant would not be relevant in those standard, accepted models with which we are familiar, such as those drawn from economics. Suppose the accountant knows the objectives of the firm and those objectives correspond to those in an accepted model of decision-making, but the decision-maker feels the relevant information is different from that called for by the model. The accountant may be placed in a position of second guessing the user, in order to provide the data that will allow him to make a correct decision, because the user's idea of what information is relevant is wrong from the standpoint of the decision models. This is a position in which I believe most accountants would feel somewhat uncomfortable.

We must also be concerned with the possibility that the conception of accounting held by the decision-maker affects the perception of relevance to a significant degree. The more a decision-maker conceives of accounting as being perfect, the more relevant accounting information is likely to be for decision-making purposes, and the more importance can be attached to the part that accounting systems and methods will play in the decision-making process. In so far as this writer is aware, this relationship has seldom been considered, and never carefully explored.

If the hypotheses developed in this paper are valid, then it is clear that relevance alone cannot serve as a primary standard for the development of accounting theory and methods. If accounting is to serve users of accounting information then something besides whether or not the data is relevant must be known. These hypotheses would lead us to believe that critical variables are the conception of accounting held by a decision-maker and the perceived relevance of other kinds of information to the problems under examination at the time the user chooses to employ or not to employ accounting information.

Some examples of the use of relevance and the conception of accounting as bases for accounting systems development

Suppose that research fails to lead to rejection of the hypotheses presented above, and consider a case in which we are concerned with designing an appropriate accounting system to facilitate effective decision-making. Imagine that the organization in question is a business firm. Among the products of an accounting system are financial statements issued at regular intervals. These intervals may vary in length from very short periods to relatively longer periods; that is, financial statements may be prepared for internal use as frequently as daily or weekly, or they may be issued less often, perhaps annually, to employees of the firm. It is possible to hypothesize that the more frequently financial reports are issued and attention is drawn to the financial condition of the firm, the more relevant accounting information will appear to people within the firm who are making decisions about prices, promotion policies, and production quantities. Yet, for many decisions of this type, we might argue that other information would be more important and relevant . Therefore, we might be led to situation in which we wish to reduce the perceived relevance of accounting information by reducing the frequency of reports, so that decision-makers within the firm would rely more heavily on other information which would allow their decisions to be more appropriate for the conditions under which the firm was operating.

Consider pricing decisions. In general, economists and other analysts would agree that the financial condition of the firm is not necessarily an appropriate basis for choosing a price strategy and selecting terms of sale. However, if financial statements are issued very frequently, thus enhancing their perceived relevance, and the conception of accounting held by decisions-makers is such that we might expect accounting information to have some effect, then favorable or adverse profit information and/or other financial information might affect decisions with respect to price. It is possible, then, that by developing an accounting system in which the frequency of reporting reduce the perceived relevance of accounting information we could improve pricing decisions in the firm.

In other cases, we might come to an opposite conclusion. In decision making related to the acquisition and management of working capital, the availability of frequent information on the status of assets and liabilities of the firm may be very important, and we might chose to issue reports to persons concerned with these matters very frequently in hopes of increasing the efficiency of such decisions.

The point of these examples is that changes in the accounting system may affect perceived relevance of accounting information and may determine the effect of accounting information on decisions, and furthermore, that the interactions between relevance and conceptions of accounting which we have considered above may be important also. In designing an accounting system, relying on cliches like ".... the more information, the better...." may lead to surprising results.

Consider another example, in which we are concerned with a choice between alternative accounting methods for reporting on a particular class of assets or liabilities. For sake of illustration, let us consider a choice between two alternative inventory valuation methods-LIFO and FIFO. Assuming that the reader is familiar with the characteristics of these methods, we can quickly conclude that in cases where prices are changing frequently that LIFO will reveal through the income statement the effects of these changes on the profitability of the firm more rapidly than FIFO. To the extent that this is important for the types of decisions being made, this model might provide us with the basis for preferring one method of accounting for inventories over another.

Let us assume that the prices of raw materials for the production process or the price of goods to be resold is rising. From the standpoint of decision-makers within the firm, this is important information, and information which we would expect to be important for decision-making purposes within the firm. To the extent that the decision-maker felt accounting information was relevant to his decisions, a conception of accounting as perfect information would make the choice of LIFO more important than if the decision-maker's conception of accounting information was that it was an imperfect measures. If accounting information is not perceived as relevant, or if the decision-maker feels accounting measures are imperfect and other information is also relevant for decision-making , the choice of inventory valuation methods is unlikely to affect decisions.

Here also we can consider the possible usefulness of this model for evaluating the selection of a method for reporting to external users. Assume that external users feel accounting information is relevant for their decisions. The more perfect their conception of accounting, the more likely that the choice between methods of accounting will affect their decisions. If the current performance of the firm is important to external users because they wish to use it as a basis for decisions, then LIFO may be more appropriate than FIFO for inventory valuation purposes.

In either of these last two cases. If accounting information were perceived as being irrelevant and/or if accounting information were conceived as being so imperfect a measure that it is not weighted heavily by the decision rule, then a decision on an inventory valuation method might not be very important. Such would be the case in any choice between accounting systems or methods. The implication of this is, I believe, quite clear: until we know more about the conditions that affect perceived relevance of accounting information for decision-making and until we know more about the conceptions of accounting held by users we do not have adequate bases on which to reduce diversity in accounting or to increase it selectively.

Implications for further research

It is clear that a great deal more research about behavioral relationships between accounting and decision-making is required. The hypotheses which comprise the model presented here demand that we learn more about the factors that influence a decision-maker's perception of the relevance of accounting information. We need to know more about the conceptions of accounting held by individuals, both within business enterprises and external to them and it would be useful also to know more about the magnitudes of difference required before perceptions of relevance and conceptions would be affected.

One way of finding data about these variables would be to g into the field and do field research about the perceived relevance of accounting for various decision problems. Some attempts have been made in this direction, and while the results are still inconclusive, they provide a basis for the design of further studies. It is also necessary that something be learned about the conceptions of accounting held by users. Is it true that the majority of users feel accounting is a valid and good source of information? Or do most experienced users of accounting information conceive of accounting as being imperfect in the sense that the term is used here, and hence, the types of decisions made about accounting systems and accounting methods are relatively unimportant?

Another approach to this type of problem is the experimental approach, where in a laboratory or a simulated environment, we place people in alternative conditions in hopes of comparing their behavior under the conditions we have created. This, in my opinion, provides a most promising avenue for testing some of the hypotheses we have created in this study.

Consider, for example, an experiment to determine if the relevance of accounting information is a determinant of the effect of that information on decision-making. We could, for example, take a sample group and partition it to obtain a control section and an experimental section. The experimental section could be instructed as to the types of situations in which, given generally accepted models of decision-making, accounting information is relevant. Having provided this background, this group could then take part in a simulated exercise-a business game-in which accounting information and other information are controlled. The decisions of the groups could be compared, and if there were differences, there might be reasons to believe that when accounting information is perceived as being relevant,. it will have an effect and that relevance, then, is something that can be affected through educational experiences.

In like manner, it should be possible to explore in the laboratory the effect of conception of accounting. After determining through tests or interviews the conceptions of accounting held by subjects, we could partition the group in such a way that those having another conception of accounting serve as an experimental group.

Experiments of the type proposed above would have to be replicated many times before we could employ the findings with confidence. Nevertheless, the "obvious" character of the hypotheses developed here gives hope that they may provide keys to new criteria for use in the design of accounting systems and reports.

Make or Buy Decision

The relationship between a library or information unit and a supplier can cover a whole range of associations from a single order that goes disastrously wrong to a long and mutually rewarding association in which the library is provided with material reliably and on time, and the supplier receives a just financial payback. It is the librarian's role to ensure that the organization being served achieves the best possible outcome from the association, although the problem is, of course, that the 'best' is defined by a cumulation of requirements that each supplier must meet in order to have a satisfied client. An unsatisfied client not only produces irritations and eventually a loss of business, but the poor reputation of the supplier may spread of other potential clients.

Some of the criticism may be unjustified, resulting from unreasonable expectations by the library. It is therefore in the interests of the supplier as much as the supplied that the two parties agree on the materials to be supplied, services on offer, and conditions of delivery. While contract law has developed to define many of these relationships, it often manages to achieve the dual sins of being both too detailed and too crude in its methods. For instance, in an obscure on-line service you use twice a year there may be three pages of microscopic detail in a contract, whereas the definitions of service provision between you and your main supplier of books and journals may be very brief and lacking in detail. Can you find your contract now? If you can find it, you keep it with you at all times. But is it still relevant?

Cost differentials are often limited in book and journal supply, and the service elements of the relationship governed by unwritten and changing circumstances. The apparent efficiency of the library can be greatly influenced by the ability of the supplier to produce the items required on time. This chapter considers some of the most important elements in the selection of suppliers, the relevance of the continuing relationship, and the mutual support that produces good quality results. We look at what it is worth in terms of saving the time of the library, saving money, and delivering faster than the next supplier. The problem for the supplier is, of course, that they can provide any level of service that the client requires, but at a cost either in terms of money or as a depletion of facilities. In many ways it is the client's responsibility to make clear exactly what is required in a structured way so that the potential supplier can produce a package that states costs and service, and which can be measured and monitored effectively.

The process of selection implies some form of competition, either directly in terms of a tendering process, or in terms of measuring the comparative performance of different sources. The client therefore needs to be able to determine the value and types of service, how this is to be measured and over what period, and the way in which samples, analyses and the results of analyses are to be determined. Added to this will be the opinions of other users of the supplier, and the ways in which they match or do not match needs.

Our 'supplier' may be one of any number of sources for the materials and services we require. Of course, there is a continued debate in the mind of anyone charged with purchasing—go to source or use an agent. In the end the decision is usually taken out of our control, for which many of us are grateful. Certain sources of supply decide that they trade only directly with the final receiver of the material, a not uncommon attitude among those who produce market analyses, while others insist that an appointed agent must be the access route within a particular geographical area.

Between these two extremes the purchaser can, however, exercise considerable judgement on the sources for information and the techniques and methods those suppliers use.

The initial reaction of those who see library systems for the first time is often 'Why use an agent? It's quicker to go direct." It is only after some thought that the overheads involved in a total 'source from originator' policy appear to be less attractive. We perhaps dismiss this naive approach too easily, since it often emanates from senior members of the organization who may go away unconvinced by a dismissive librarian. Time spent discussing the priorities for employee time not only answers specific queries, but transmits to the receiver that the librarian understands the need to manage their operations effectively.

Single or multiple suppliers?

The decision on the number of suppliers to use, one or many, is often taken from the library, since there are inevitably suppliers who will not deal with an agent and insist that orders come from source. For the majority of orders which pass through the system, however, the client, i.e. the library, does have the choice as to whether only one main supplier is employed, or two or more. The ability to match two suppliers against each other is at first attractive, but will the comparison be fair, since it can be difficult to directly measure success unless they all receive an even distribution of orders in terms of quantity and difficulty? The multiple supplier situation can be difficult to evaluate, but the monopoly supplier is even more of a problem as no comparison can be made except by inference from colleagues whose data will be difficult to interpret. The rationale for the monopoly situation is the greater influence that the client has, but that in turn leaves the library dependent on one source. Any efforts to improve the service of such a supplier are fraught with difficulties, since a basis for comparison does not exist.

The suppliers we deal with here fall into three broad areas:

- suppliers of single order items such as books, reports and similar documents, equipment, etc.
- suppliers of repeat business such as journals and standing orders
- suppliers of services.

Criteria for choosing suppliers

In many ways, the library being served by a trader is not in a simple client-seller relationship. The library serves a company or other organization which is supported by its orders and accounts department. While these are themselves designed to provide a service to other parts of the organization, their relationship with the rest is deeply affected by the reliance which is placed on accounts to ensure that the flow of resources in and out of the organization is regulated to provide for the continuation and development of the company. What others may see as a simple clerical procedure masks the complexities of company law and cash flow. Anything another section can do to minimize perturbations in the systems that govern the financial dealings of the organization will earn appreciation from these custodians of the purse, and be repaid many times. First, of course, one needs to gain the confidence of the accountants, establishing a relationship in which mutual skills are respected and built up to provide for the smooth running of company systems and the reduction of individual work problems.

On normal order and payment routines, techniques and systems need to be established with primary suppliers that match the requirements of the company's accountants. Every slide in the system produced by a non-standard accountancy procedure results in a disproportional amount of effort for all. Suppliers need to understand the company's accountancy needs in detail, and the consequences to the organization of not meeting them. Such three-way co-operation enables company employees to focus on those areas where compliance with the organization's needs are not so easily established. There will be suppliers with whom it is difficult to build up such a relationship, including the large on-line hosts, government publishers, and organizations which demand direct orders and will not go through agents. With these sources, which often operate within their own intricate and usually mystifying methods, the 'mutual aid method' built up with the internal accounting section when dealing with regular suppliers will smooth the handling of these difficult to administer accounts.

Other aspects of the payments systems that are of concern include the amount of time from invoicing to payment expected by the supplier, any penalties for late payment, and any incentives for early payment. While many companies operate on the basis of paying only at the last moment, in the supply areas in which we exist the cash flow of the supplier may materially affect delivery performance.

Foreign currency transactions are a major problem for companies unused to operating in the international arena, and providing invoices in the local currency for materials from many sources is one of the most 'value added' services a supplier can render. Converting currencies, obtaining orders, and clearing cash through foreign banks not only save time and effort, but reduce risks for the purchaser. The costs of such activities must, however, be borne by someone, and the purchase price may be heavily loaded to recover the time that has been expended. From time to time correspondence appears in the library press which indicates differences in prices for the same item by as much as 100% for the end purchaser. On sets of expensive specialist encyclopaedia and continuing series this difference can amount to a significant sum.

Understanding the basis on which suppliers charge for foreign material can therefore save thousands over the course of a year. Suppliers with established links in the countries in which the material you are seeking is published stand the best chance of obtaining such material at a good price, and also in reasonable time. How and whether they pass on the financial benefits or costs is a matter of negotiation between them and you. You should at least know on what basis currency conversion rates are calculated, and how any supplement for foreign material is introduced. Without this you cannot even begin to assess the costs and benefits of the service you are seeking.

Bibliographically speaking

The timely and accurate provision of material relies to a large extent on the accuracy and completeness of the information generated by the originator of an order and the ability of the supplier to reinforce and supplement this information. Many suppliers see the provision of an accurate and complete bibliographic service as a major feature in their strategy. Evaluating the strength and utility of such services is one of the most difficult aspects of customer/supplier relationships. In many cases the customer may be supporting a service which is not really required. Often the information given on a customer's original order is sufficient and accurate enough to enable the item to be supplied immediately. On others the very nature of the material and lack of information may defeat the intermediate supplier just as much as the originator.

On the other hand, the supplier that can rapidly locate and supply an obscure, urgently required item scores well. Only experience can provide a guide to the benefits using any one supplier can bring to such a situation, although information on the skills and sources available to them will give a strong clue. There is, however, little benefit from receiving a service you do not need, and if you have confidence in your own bibliographic resources you should find a supplier who will offer alternative plus points. A mutual understanding of the bibliographic tools regularly employed by both parties and a common set of codes to denote sources checked will at least prevent needless duplication of effort and eliminate time wasted in repeated checking.

A supplier must decide to what extent the client is driven by price, and to what extent by the level of service on offer. The problem is, of course, that the needs of each client are different, and the needs of those individual clients vary depending on their end users. This is an almost impossible problem for the supplier to solve without adequate information from the client, since without this information the supplier is being asked to make a value judgement about an unknown end use. Tactics employed include librarians trusting that supplier goodwill be generated by placing regular orders and suppliers making a feature of rapid service at a premium price, e.g. same day delivery of new HMSO materials. An alternative to either of these tactics is to establish an understanding between the normal supplier and the client on a *modus operandi* for urgent orders. Many delays can be minimized if a basic set of rules is negotiated between both parties on the procedures each will follow if an item is designated urgent. If the proportion of urgent to non-urgent orders is also broadly agreed as a percentage of overall trading, rapid delivery may be achieved when needed at a negligible premium price. The occasion when your Managing Director calls for an obscure document required yesterday is not the time to start talks with your suppliers.

In addition to determining price and delivery such negotiations may cover:

- who is the client's organizations can declare an item urgent
- the level of information supplied about the item.
- any special protocols for delivery. For example, should all urgent orders be faxed through to the supplier to avoid any misunderstandings a telephone call might introduce?

Even with the urgent action specialist suppliers, clearance of credit and an understanding of their trading techniques can be as effective as any other element in ensuring prompt service. While the aim of all suppliers is to deliver items required at an appropriate time, the efficient notification of possible delays has great value. Not only does it reduce the frustration of the client, but it enables them to plan for the delay. Reports on the factors involved in a delay need to be in a form which is easily assimilated into the client's own record system, and in a form that can be transmitted on to their users with the minimum of effort. The client and the supplier need to establish the events and timescales that lead to the production of reports, and the regularity with which they are produced should an item have a long delay. There should be arrangements made to cover situations where prices are above those predicted by the library.

Stock exchange

Most of the time the fact that a supplier holds stock may not be relevant, since the normal distribution system will enable the supplier to order directly from source and to deliver in what the client perceives is a satisfactory timescale. The stockholder has additional overheads in terms of the stock itself and the storage needed to hold it in readiness for orders. By definition, they will have material on the shelves that is going to be in demand and is therefore in the category of 'less difficult to obtain' material. The non-stockholder can concentrate staff on ordering material rather than supporting that which is in stock, and as a result may have a quicker turnaround on the majority of orders not recovered from stock and at a lower cost. The selection of a specialist stockholder thus becomes one of the more finely balanced decision making activities, since their value lies in their ability to 'second-guess' your needs—which they are unlikely to know unless you have been a customer over a considerable period. A sample from some recent orders to your existing supplier can provide an indication of the potential a supplier has in your field for immediate delivery. However, remember that urgently required material may not be mainstream in your subject area, but may be specialist material such as government documents or standards.

An efficient selective dissemination of information (SDI) service on new publications within the library's interest domain provides the supplier's client with an economical method of checking that the library is keeping up with new material. If this information is supplied in a form that matches the library's administrative systems, perhaps as paper slips or a machine readable file, the service can become an integral element in the library's information provision activities.

A good supplier should be able to provide assistance during stock building and editing by the production of lists of suitable material both in stock and not in stock but in print. An inspection service provides this type of support on a continuing basis, although care is needed in establishing the exact conditions under which the service is provided.

The benefits of a book servicing facility will be dependent on the amount of material acquired in a year. For some the amount of inhouse time saved by a supplier placing stationary and stamps in new material will be insignificant, while for others the savings enable other tasks to be accomplished in-house that could otherwise not be carried out. Similarly, differences in the charges made for these activities may be a significant element in selecting a supplier. Delivery costs, packaging, etc., all add to costs. In the end it is the price at the bottom of the invoice that we need to concentrate on.

Delivery is a matter not only of efficient service to your clients, but has a direct effect on the allocation of staff resources. A delivery cycle which is unreliable, sporadic and infrequent leaves the purchaser with the inability to plan work loads and causes delays right up to the final payment of invoices. Even if we cannot control individual one-off suppliers, we should be able to obtain a reasonable delivery arrangement from regular ones.

Contract renewal

Few events fill the manager with more dread than going out to contract for the supply of periodicals and standing orders through an agent. Among the most prominent of the more hated experiences is managing the process which stems from using a new agent, i.e. the transition period from the old supplier. While some organizations leave the style and timing for going through the tendering process to the information officer or librarian, in other this event appears to be just the opportunity for the company purchasing officers to show off their skills. If the organization's style is to utilize the talents of purchase/order departments fully in the process, then the secret is, of course, to involve them on your terms. Indeed, such sections have skills that are important and useful, they just perhaps need some moderating.

Seize the initiative by approaching the relevant person early on in the process, and making it clear you value and respect their professional help. A clear understanding of aspects of a tender not directly concerned with price is important. By making a list of these points and placing an estimate of value on them you will be able to more easily isolate the differences between one quotation and another. Having established a document based not only on price but on system responses, such as dealing with missing issues, invoices, credit arrangements, etc., suppliers can be asked to present their offerings. An established track record with similar clients is an important element. Some quantification of the cost of switching from the existing source should be made, and of the help a prospective supplier could give in effecting the transfer. This is a good point at which to discuss the results of any possible change of supplier with the current agent. While the tendering process is being conducted, the existing supplier is much more likely to agree the possible ending of a relationship on amicable terms.

When tenders are examined they can be evaluated against your criteria and the successful agent established. One of the options in this process will of course be a fully estimated and costed alternative to conducting the purchase of periodicals and standing orders directly from source. Once the decision on a supplier has been made, 'those who failed to get the contract should be informed of the reasons for their failure, provided company policy permits this. Such feedback gives those unsuccessful suppliers an opportunity to improve their techniques and increase the chances of success next time. One of the advantages of having an established cycle of going out to tender and communicating this to suppliers is that those who lose out on the current evaluation know the framework in which another opportunity will arise.

Measuring the differences

Determining the 'best' supplier for a service depends on the ability to measure the performance of the organization itself against a set of criteria. The assessment of the supplier's performance against those criteria which are the most sensitive produces a set of performance indicators. Performance indicators have been widely advocated by those who control library budgets in all sectors, so developing them for libraries to use in comparing their performance to other libraries gives a new insight into their relevance, as well as helping to define a set of measurable objectives for suppliers to fulfill.

Our supplier performance indicators can be developed from the criteria already discussed. They will enable the library both to compare the supplier against targets assigned to individual companies, and to compare one company with another.

Even with a small throughput of new material the ability to answer the question 'How well does my supplier do?' except in the most general terms, requires the processing power that a computer can give. This sounds relatively easy: but a package-there are enough acquisition and order modules available for even small operations to implement. Unfortunately, most of these see the type of management information we need as secondary to the task of processing transactions, such as posting an order or invoice to the system. The position is beginning to change, but the requirement for complex analysis of time is still a challenge that many systems are unable to meet. Even if such analysis is possible, be careful that differences in suppliers are not masking differences in environments and demands. The amount of effort required for such a sophisticated approach needs to be matched by benefits which may not be in the delivery of all materials x days early, but in the arrival of just one important item on time as a result of knowing who best to choose for the order.

Automating your suppliers

It is, of course, one of the tenets of modern library automation that automating the links between supplier and library will lead to improved cost efficiency and service effectiveness. This is simpler to say than to achieve given that there are currently few operational standards to which suppliers can provide a common interface. Some are in the process of development, but until these have reached full international standards status, linking your automated system to that of your supplier is a matter of negotiation. Where you use several suppliers, each of which has a number of other clients, a standard method of communication may seem impossible. A simple file transfer format such as a series of fields in sequential order in ASCII file format may, however, produce an interim measure that provides a pay off in terms of staff time saved at both the library and the supplier, and which more than recoups the effort expended in developing such a system. Not only does such downloading of files in the form of discs or through electronic mail speed up clerical processes, but it leads to greater accuracy by eliminating keyboarding and rechecking data.

Remote hosts

The term remote database was coined to define the geographic relationship between the information store and the end user. It is often also an accurate description of the type of relationship enjoyed by the user. Such hosts have very carefully defined terms and conditions of service, originally developed with little thought to the user, which can be imposed quite easily by threat of removing the service instantly using the database password administration system. 'Invalid password' or 'access denied' can be the first indication one has that the organization's accounts system has failed to make a payment on time.

Some of these database hosts were originally targeted on individuals rather than companies, or were set up for the US market where the use of credit cards for business accounts is much more widespread. The payment method is therefore geared to this, and other methods of handling accounts are treated as secondary. Attempting to persuade your organization to have a charge account or credit card for such payments is probably a challenge which you see as having limited prospects of success, but it is worth thoroughly enumerating the benefits of such a tactic as the advantages to your organization could easily outweigh any company general policy about payments made this way. There is little you can do to establish an easy relationship with these remote on-line suppliers, but some planning may help.

Individual problems can be more easily dealt with if a local agent or office is in place. Failing this, try to establish the name and location of a person who will deal with any problems you have at the host. A fax number will yield great benefits in establishing rapid communications, as will the electronic mailbox of the link person if the on-line host includes e-mail in its facilities. Changing a supplier's administrative and accounting procedures which are wasteful and inconvenient for the end user by taking up the matter as an individual client is perhaps the method least likely to work. Rather more profitable is to join a user group: both groups designed around particular hosts and more general on-line user groups enable pressure to be applied and problems to be dealt with in a concerted and organized way. Suppliers are then much more likely to act.

Purchasing automated systems

Until a comparatively few years ago the largest contract and purchase that a library needed to be involved in was the periodic review of journal subscriptions. Now, the purchase of automated systems and their attendant maintenance equal and surpass this. The problem is, of course, that while journals are an area every librarian has confidence in, the supply of automated systems produces less confidence and may be heavily biased by company policy on information technology. In addition to the involvement of orders and accounts staff, computing staff may also become involved.

Not that the basic principles of purchase change, but new factors are introduced. A specification of requirements is still needed, and tenders invited and measured on the basis of costs and services, in this case facilities and performance. Questions of deliverables and support are, however, even more important than in normal purchase arrangements. There is also the need to define the requirements for systems now and also over the next five to ten years. There is not usually the luxury of being able to carry out an annual review in this area, and cut or increase facilities to match the budget. Money will still have to be found to support the system in five years' time no matter what level the disposable budget. It is at this point that we need to discuss the full cost of system support over the period of its planned use—its life-cycle cost, including input from your own personnel. While suppliers are often cautious about projecting forward such figures, they become less sensitive to the matter if they understand that every potential supplier has to produce some justified data.

Two of the main reasons that computer system installation plans go wrong are over-specification and 'vapourware'. These exemplify a simple but often repeated problem of not building a relationship with potential suppliers. Both result from the failure to achieve an understanding of the balance between facilities, investment and growth. By over-specifying a system in a tender document, the library may eliminate perfectly suitable and often superior systems from competing. At first sight it may seem a good tactic to specify every possible facility you may wish to use eventually, and require it to be immediately available. In this way, each potentially useful element in the system can be seen to work before purchase. Without such an approach you could be buying 'vapourware', i.e. a part of the system which, although planned, does not exist as a product.

Both approaches lead to failure. The first assumes that your unit will take up all the elements in the system almost immediately, probably something which it is organi-zationally unable to do. In the period between contract signing and uptake of service, some products may have moved on in specification and so no longer match your needs. One of the rival systems originally rejected may now appear to be more suitable. On the other hand, buying on a company's promises of future products can lead to disappointment if the plans are not fulfilled on schedule.

The careful potential system purchaser discusses the department's mid-term plans and resources, levels to build a picture of implementation for the system. In this way, both parties can establish event points along a pathway to full system adoption and mark those points in such a way that each understands the other's role and obligations. Such a policy will also enable each party to assess the needs for hardware growth and upgrade during the life of the system.

Computer systems require a high level of support, both hardware and software, over their life time. The potential purchaser needs to know just how that support is to be offered, and the terms under which it is offered. Some protection needs to be given to the client if the company should fail, such as access to the computer code used and the availability of alternative maintenance sources.

Using information brokers

The information broker's role in an organization's information unit can be ambivalent. On the one hand they may be seen as an aid, while on the other they may appear to be potential alternative sources of information for the parent organization.

The broker has a definite role within an established information unit, able to provide a service within three broad areas: the provision of specialist skills which it is not economic for the unit to support, access to sources that the company may not have directly, and the delivery of information under time constraints that the information unit may be unable to meet because of a sudden temporary upturn in demand.

The cost to an information unit of supporting certain skills with training and practice can be high if the source concerned is little used. Taking all these staff and support costs into consideration, a broker's 'value added' fee may be economical. Brokers acting as third parties can trace information where a direct approach may be rejected.

Although brokers will of course act on a one-off call basis to a standard set of conditions and a fee, building up a relationship with a broker will enable you to assess their talents and be better able to decide when they should be called in. You need to know how each broker handles an enquiry. Do they specialize in certain areas—most do—and what action is taken if an enquiry does not match their skills profile? Some will direct clients to other sources; if so, who do they recommend and why? Do they have reciprocal arrangements with these other sources?

Alternatively, do they sub-contract work to others under their own trading name? If so, to whom, and is the client told when this is done and to whom the work is sent? If the broker uses people who do not work exclusively for them, then who else do they work for, and to whom are they connected? While brokers will not knowingly break a confidence, a chain of people that extends to the interests of a rival company is to be avoided. A chain of subcontractors will also add to cost overheads and make dealing with any subsequent matters that may arise out of the initial enquiry difficult.

Who needs a consultant?

The role of consultants is often maligned by those who have experienced the arrival, and subsequent departure, of a person who seems full of instant answers but has no responsibility for any outcomes of recommendations. Such experiences are usually the fault of the organizations bringing in the consultant rather than the consultants themselves.

A consultant may be brought in for particular skills, to bring a new approach to a problem, perhaps by looking at a reorganization; or may be asked to give a second opinion on a situation or suggestion. To develop good relations with a consultant one needs to understand the nature of the consultancy, be able to communicate this effectively, and be able to structure the outcome so that any recommendations can be effectively examined by the organization's management, commented on, and appropriate action taken.

The whole process is more likely to develop smoothly if it is the information manager rather than anyone else in the organization who decides that a consultant should be employed within the unit. If this is followed up with a short-list of possible individuals who could fulfil the role, then the initiative, once established, can be built on.

A document setting out the contractual terms of the consultancy and a definition of the area to be covered will enable the short-list of possible consultants to respond with a quotation on the size and cost of the work. When the consultant has been selected they will need more detailed background on the existing situation, the organization, and the roles and relationships between people within it. The success of a consultancy stems to a large extent from building mutual confidence between the consultant and those within the organization with whom they come into contact.

The consultant will understand this, and work towards it as a major goal in achieving the stated aims of the mission. It is those who have never experienced such a situation, or those who have been involved in a poor consultancy, who need support, and it is the section leader who can best provide this through a knowledge of the motivations of those who will be most affected by any outcome. The consultant is only too aware of being both a temporary employee and someone who may change the local environment drastically, both at the same time.

Make or buy decisions?

Retailers and wholesalers normally buy the merchandise they sell rather than manufacturing it themselves. The appliers not only to small distributors, but also to the large chain stores which often not only select merchandise from what is available, but also draw up specifications themselves. While doing this they are talking to suppliers and finding firms which can supply goods to their specifications.

There are exceptions. Some retailers use backward integration into products or packaging to improve their competitive position, and some manufacturers aim to strengthen their competitive position by forward integration into distribution. Breweries, which are beer manufacturers, often own most of their retail outlets, and many filling stations are common in the superstores, an exception to the normal policy which is for shops to buy rather than make.

Manufacturers on the other hand normally make the products they sell, although a few products may be bought in to complete a range. They manufacture them from pats and material which are either produced internally or brought out, so that make-or-buy decisions have to be made at each stage in formulating manufacturing strategy. Outside processing may be used in addition to or instead of internal processing. Subcontracting also requires make-or-buy decisions.

Tactical and strategic

Every time an organization a purchase order or an internal make order, somebody must have decided whether the item is to be bought or made. Deciding whether to make or buy is, in principle, a top management decision. Yet, in practice, decisions of this kind seem to be taken routinely without reference to higher authority or to any written policy guide.

The fact is that every organization has a definite policy about what it makes and what it buys,. Make-or-buy decisions taken at departmental level ate those which simply apply the existing policy. It is only when there are reasons to change the policy that the decision needs to be made at higher levels where strategy is decided.

The existing policy is expressed by the facilities actually available for making goods. Decisions to make internally goods that can be made economically on those facilities, and to buy those that cannot, are routine applications of the existing policy. However, routine does not quite complex, since company custom, prejudice, costing conventions and other partly arbitrary considerations are involved.

Changes in policy, such as extensions to plant facilities, or divesting existing manufacturing facilities, are also complex decisions.

Routine Make-or-buy decisions

Large organizations sometimes set up a make-or-buy committee, with representatives from design, production, buying and costing departments. Deciding which parts can be made economically on available plants of course simpler than deciding whether or not to invest in new plant, and the decisions have a shorter time-span -they can often be reversed the next time the item is required. The economics of particular cases can be complicated, especially when capacity is fully employed and the question is which parts to subcontract. As new suppliers appear or new processes are introduced, the make-or-buy cost balance may alter.

There are two main reasons why a factory buys out parts which it is equipped to make in : the first is that it can often buy cheaper than it is make, and the seconds that it may not be able to make all it needs of the sort of part for which its plant is suitable because it has not got enough plant. This capacity shortage may result from a rush of orders, or form an expansion in sales which is outrunning the expansion in manufacturing facilities, or it may result from a deliberate policy of gearing capacity to *average* output and subcontracting exceptionally high output in order to run the factory at a stable base load.

How can a factory buy parts cheaper than it can make them, if it is equipped with suitable plant, when the buy price must include the seller's selling expenses, distribution expenses and profit? The short answer is through specialization. This enables the specialist supplier to get long runs and use special tackle. Any machine shop can turn black steel bar into bright bar, but it is less expensive to buy bright bar in the first place if that is what wanted. Any machine shop can make a while metal bearing but costs will be reduced substantially if one of the wide range of commercially available standard designs can be adopted. Many parts can be made in any machine shop in short runs on general purpose plant. But making them in long runs in special purpose equipment enables the specialist suppliers to take his profit and deliver the product to the buyer's door., often through distributors who also have costs to cover and profits to take, at a selling price that many actually be lower than the buyer's bare direct cost for making in.

But specialization extends beyond tooling up for long runs. The motor car industry buys in quantities which give long runs on single order, and has never been slow to equip itself with special plant, yet it supports a host of specialist suppliers employing between them four times as many people as the motor car firms themselves. Some of these suppliers are large firms but may are tiny concerns in the backstreets of Birmingham and the Black Country. How can a gasket supplier employing a hundred or so people sell successfully to a motor car manufacturer whose qualified design staff alone heavily outnumbers the whole payroll of the gasket manufacturer? Why does the motor manufacturer not buy out the gasket firm?

The fact is that specialization does not stop at the plant, the process and the product, it extends to research and management too. In buying out components such as gaskets and lamps and brakes vehicle manufacturers are buying research and development as well as components. This enables them to benefit from a suppliers specialist design talent and trade knowledge based on experience in the service of the whole industry.

In general therefore most factories concentrate their research facilities, talents, and development on the main product, and buy from, rather than compete with, suppliers who have specialized in the accessories and subsidiary parts they require. But there are plenty of exceptions to this rule. Make-or-buy decisions are based on facts which may alter, when buyers and others concerned should request a reappraisal in the light of changes and developments both in their own plant and outside.

Make-or-buy questions involving capital investment

Serious problems in *quality, delivery or price* or in guaranteeing *continuity* of supplies, sometimes justify the purchasing manager in making a recommendation that consideration should be given to investing new manufacturing facilities in order to switch items from purchase to production. Such a recommendation will usually be made with reluctance, because it could be constructed as an easy way out of a purchasing problem, because it does involve some loss of flexibility, and because of course it builds up someone else's empire, at the expense of one's own.

Ensuring that very tight quality specifications are met by making the parts within the organization is a traditional approach to quality problems. For instance, spool Axminster carpets with floral patterns may use 60 or 70 different hues. Getting these colours right requires great and repeatable accuracy in the dyeing of the yarn. It is quite easy for two shades of green to diverge slightly from the standards and become indistinguishable. Consequently many firms which weave spool Axminster operate their own dyehouses despite the facts that seeing is a specialist trade and a very different one from weaving and that there are many textile dyeing and finishing firms producing high quality work. Supplier development to meet difficult quality standards is an alternative approach.

Delivery problems have prompter firms to take over their suppliers in seller's market conditions, in order to ensure supplies of sufficient quantities at the time required.

Price problems can sometimes be solved by threatening to make the part in internally instead of purchasing it. The threat is often implied. The buyer insists on cost breakdowns from the supplier. He cost estimator, who usually sits in on the negotiation, adopts the position that these are the costs which apply in *your* (the supplier's) industry. Nobody has to spell out that these are the costs which *we* (the purchaser) estimate we should incur if we decide to make it ourselves. There has to be a serious possibility that the purchaser will embark on manufacture if necessary, for this tactic to be effective.

Continuity of supplies can be a problem in bilateral oligopoly markets. The motor car industry is rich in examples of situations where two or three firms supply some speciality item to the whole trade. If one or other of the vehicle manufacturers decides to increase its security by taking over one of the supplier firms, the result is a sharp decrease in the security of the other vehicle of manufacturers. Many years ago there were to or three specialist suppliers of steel pressings who made car bodies for the whole British motor car industry. A long strike at the firm which supplied car bodies to Jowett Cars forced this estimable little manufacturer to close down. Ford Motor pondered this situation, and decided to take over their main body supplier-not, as the chairman explicitly stated in his annual report, because of any dissatisfaction with their quality, delivery or price:

> For many years Briggs supplied with almost all body requirements. A car body today costs about 40% of the total cost of a car.....We are generally indebted to Briggs Motor Bodies Ltd for their unfailing cooperation in meeting so successfully all demands we have made on them, sometimes under conditions of considerable difficulty. Nevertheless our great dependence on their supplies has been of increasing concern to us.

Before making a recommendation to solve problems in quality, deliver, price continuity by embarking on substantial capital expenditure so that the items can be manufactured it, would be prudent to ask some searching questions, for instance: What have we done already to solve the problem? What else could we try apart from making in? Is it, really a permanent difficulty or might it clear itself up in, say a year? What it involve? Could we absorb all the output ourselves? If we could make it pay only by selling part of the output, is this the sort of business we want to go into? Should we aim at making the shore of our requirements, or at making part and buying part? Would this harm or help our relations with suppliers?

Suppliers within the group

Top management must decide what plant will be provided and hence what goods can be made, and what plant will not be provided and hence what things must be bought out. This is because there is no general rule, policy depends largely on what skills and talents the management has and where its interest lie, as well as on what funds are available and on the strict economics of the situation.

Policy may also be affected by the nature of the industry. In old and declining industries there may sometimes be a tendency for successful firms to acquire their suppliers in order to eke out a slim profit margin by vertical integration. In expanding industries horizontal integration, broadening the end-product, may provide a better return on investment. But the difference between firms in a single industry is far greater than the difference between industries. In every industry there are firms that have diversified. There are also firms that have not been saved from failure by specialization, and firms that have diversified and still failed. There is one firm making nothing but a parents for parrots, a specialization so extreme as to strike awe in the beholder; at other extreme great like Imperial Chemical Industries produce paint, plastics, Wallpaper, dyestuffs, metals: a score or more of socialist product groups.

Diversification on this scale brings purchasing problems of its own. When one division buys the product of another division in the group, the operation is intermediate between making in and buying out. In the short term the price paid may not matter much, since it is like transferring money from one of your suits to another; the more stays in the group. But in the long term interdivisional pricing does matter and does affect group profitability; because of its effect on relative profitability of divisions it affects the allocation of resources between divisions. Price bargaining between the divisions of a great corporation is consequently often as keen as price bargaining between the company and its outside suppliers. In theory at least the buying division is often free to place its orders with an outside source if the supplier within the group cannot match market price. But in practice this freedom is far from absolute.

Research into the policies of 193 companies in the United Kingdom revealed that large firms, and firms with a decentralized management style, gave considerably more freedom to buyers in this respect than others did.

Transfer Prices

Large concerns have to find some way to set transfer prices —the prices at which goods manufacturing one division are transferred as supplies to another division. In highly centralized firms these prices are set centrally in three-quarters of cases. This is said to be because only central staff have enough information to set prices properly. In multinational companies rates and different tax laws, and may be set with the main object of reducing the total tax liability of the company.

Prices *negotiated* between selling division and buying division are not always a happy solution. If the seller is compelled to sell internally his negotiating position is poor. Personalities and positions in corporate hierarchies complicate matters. A great deal of time can be taken up by these internal negotiations. Yet some negotiation is necessary, and purchasing managers may try to negotiate a discount off market price where this is the basis chosen for transfer pricing on the groups that market price includes selling overheads such as advertising and salesmen which an internal supplier does not need to incur.

Market, price, and full cost of production, emerge as the two most widely used methods of setting transfer prices. Market price is preferred when firms are interested in divisional profitability, and production cost when they are more interested in the profitability of the product. Setting up product divisions as profit centres is the standard method of running large manufacturing businesses. The authority and the accountability of the division chief cannot be quite as untrammeled as that of the managing director of an independent business. If it were, the whole firm would degenerate into a collection of separate units gaining nothing by association. But within defined limits, and subject to central or corporate management's reservation of certain matters such as source of finance and major capital expenditure, division chiefs have a gooc leal of autonomy so long as they earn acceptable returns on the assets they employ. 'his is why it matters to them how prices are fixed for goods or services supplied by one goods of the company to another division. If Division A supplies goods to Division B at an excessively high price, then Division A is profitable and its return on assets is high. It gets all the finance it wants.

In principle the fairest approach is to charge opportunity costs, that is, what the seller division could charge on outside customer, or what the buyer division would have to pay an outside supplier-market price, in fact; but this is not easy to establish unless the item is a standard price-list part. With made-to-order castings, forging fabrications, the price may be determined by selling some of the output, and buying some of the input, extremely.

The *stated* policy may then be to buy from the best source, inside or outside the company. Buying departments get dispirited when they find what seems a better source outside the company only to see their decision to switch to an outside supplier overruled. but the *real* policy may in fact be to sell the output of the supplier division at opportunity cost. This is equal to outside supplier price when the internal supplier division is fully employed but it would change downwards if the division had unused capacity.

Cyert and March describe the real-world firm as a collation of participants in which conflict is only partly resolved. When divisional results depend partly on how well a division has coped with external circumstances and partly on the transfer payments they have managed to arrange with other divisions, prices result in practice from a permanent bargaining process, rather than from the solution of a theoretical problem in resource allocation, performance desegregation or most distribution and divisions whose results are poor will bargain hard for better results. In general we should rules that (1) have some crude face validity and (2) have shown some historical viability. We should find that they are the focus of conflict between sub-units in the same way as other allocative devices.

Subcontracting and outside processing

In the construction industries, the normal practice is for a single main contract to be signed with one firm, often after a competitive tendering procedure. The main contractor then places subcontracts with a number of specialist firms to carry out parts of the work. Subcontractors may be nominated by the customer (or client, or purchaser, as the organization placing the contract is customers called), or decided on by the main contractor, possibly subject to the approval of the customer. Many terms of the main contract may be passed on to subcontractors by incorporating them in the contracts made with them by the main contractor, and additional special terms may also be inserted in subcontracts.

In other industries, the term subcontracting is used for outside processing. This means arranging for work to be done or parts to be made by outside suppliers which could in principle be done internally on the organization's own facilities. It may be work normally undertaken by the buyer which has, when order books are full, to be framed out if delivery dates are to be met. Or it may be work which could in principle be undertaken by the purchaser, but which as a matter or policy is given to outside contractors. Security, and running the canteen, are two common examples.

Subcontracting of this kind involves the purchase department because it is kind of purchasing goods are supplied or work done in accordance with a contract and payment has to be made. Nearly always it is a combined operation in which other departments are also involved. Production planning and control will naturally be involved if what is purchased is capacity rather than components as such, a short-term extension of the manufacturing facilities. Much of the detailed planning and progressing may be undertaken by production control as an extension of their normal work. Quality control will also be involved since the subcontracted work may be inspected just as if the work had been done in house.

4

Motivation

The classical approach about motivation labelled Theory X by McGregor. takes a rather unkind view of people's nature. Among its assumptions are:

1. Men and women are motivated primarily by economic considerations and will do whatever obtains the greatest economic gain.
2. The organization, as controller of economic incentives, must deal with its passive employees through manipulation, direction, threat, and coercion to motivate them toward achievement of organizational goals.
3. People's emotions are essentially irrational and must be prevented from interfering with their rational for economic rewards.
4. Organizations must be designed in such a way that people's irrational emotions are under maximum control.

Within these four assumptions lie four more implications which McGregor makes explicit:

5. Men and women are inherently lazy, dislike and try to avoid work, and must be motivated by external forces.
6. People's natures are antithetical to organizational goals, hence they must be carefully monitored and controlled to insure that they contribute to organizational goal achievement.
7. Being essentially irrational, people are basically incapable of self-direction or self-control.
8. *However,* there are two kinds of people: those fitting the preceding descriptions, and those who are self-motivated, self-controlled, and dominated by reason rather than emotion. The fortunate few falling into the second group must assume managerial responsibilities over the irrational masses.

While Theory X organizations still exist in our society, for the most part, happily, the "organization mind" has moved beyond these Neanderthal assumptions.

The human relations approach, with its focus on people's social nature, has another set of assumptions concerning human motivation. From the evidence collected by the Hawthorne studies, Mayo developed a description of people's nature quite different from the description inherent in Theory X:

1. People are motivated primarily by social needs and obtain their basic identities through their relations with others.
2. As a result of the industrial revolution and the rationalization of work, the work itself has become rather meaningless; thus satisfaction comes to workers only through their relationships on the job.
3. Men and women are more responsive to the social pressures exerted by their peers than they are to influences coming from those in managerial positions.
4. The extent to which workers are responsive to management is a function of the extent to which management can meet the workers' social needs.

These assumptions consider people not in terms of task behaviours—the approach taken by Theory X—but in terms of relationships with their peers. The primary function of the organization, then, is to provide relationships as satisfying as possible, for only if satisfactory relationships exist will the workers' productivity be maximized.

The most recent approach to organizational theory, the systems approach, has developed in coincidence with the formulation of Theory Y, presented by McGregor as a more realistic view of people's nature. Combining elements of the classical and human relations approaches, Theory Y holds that:

1. Work is as natural to people as play or rest, not something that people by nature dislike and avoid.
2. People are essentially self-motivated and self-controlled; externally imposed incentives and controls may be unnecessary or (if they threaten the worker) counterproductive.
3. There is no inherent conflict between human motives and organizational goals. If given the chance, and if properly rewarded, people voluntarily will integrate organizational goals with personal goals and become committed to organizational success.
4. People are both complex and highly variable. They possess many motives which interact in complex patterns and change in importance from time to time and situation to situation.
5. People are capable of learning new motives through their organizational experiences, making their ultimate motivational patterns a product of the interaction between their initial needs and their job experiences.

6. Satisfaction and productivity spring from several sources, including the nature of the task to be performed, the abilities and experiences of the workers themselves, and the nature of the other organizational members.
7. The ability and desire to exercise creativity and imagination rest not only at the organization's higher levels but within workers at every level of the hierarchy.
8. Every worker has potential untapped by organizational life.

This third set of assumptions emphasizes people's complex motivational natures and their responsiveness to situational influences. Our purpose in this chapter is to analyze human motivation in some depth, to determine the general system of motivation underlying human behaviour and to assess one particularly potent motivational force, the presence of other people. We shall consider in turn some "drive-reduction" theories of motivation, some "reinforcement" theories, and "social facilitation," or the effects produced by the presence of others.

Motivation theories

Before examining specific theories of motivation, we must understand the distinctions between some related concepts. The first are *motive* and *incentive.* As used here, a motive (or drive) is considered the internal force or need which produces external behaviour. A worker who consistently "talks back" to one's supervisor, for example, may be manifesting one's "security" motive by reassuring oneself through self-assertion. An incentive, on the other hand, is external to the individual and is perceived to be useful in fulfilling some motive. Money is a common incentive, seen by workers as useful in achieving status and security. Drive-reduction theories are concerned primarily with the motives generating human behaviour; reinforcement theories concentrate more upon the external incentives to which people respond.

A second distinction must be made between types of motives or drives. While there are a variety of ways to classify motives, one widely used method is to divide them into *primary* or physiological needs and *secondary* or social and psychological needs. Primary drives include the needs for water, food, air, sex, sleep, and proper temperature. While these drives are universal, they vary in intensity from person to person and, within an individual, from time to time. And they are conditioned by experience; someone who typically sleeps eight hours nightly develops a need for that much sleep, while someone used to sleeping only six hours needs only that amount.

Secondary needs are more difficult to specify and will occupy most of our attention in this section. These needs are typically learned through social interaction, vary widely across individuals and situations, operate in interacting sets rather than individually, involve nebulous feelings rather than tangible physical sensations, and are hidden from conscious recognition. These motives also affect behaviour profoundly and thus are the primary concern of management when considering the best methods by which to maximize worker productivity and satisfaction. To illuminate the roles of primary and, particularly, secondary motives or drives, we turn now to specific drive-reduction theories of human motivation.

The Maslow system

Perhaps the most widely cited drive-reduction system is that suggested by Abraham Maslow. In his view, people have five basic needs: physiological needs, safety and security needs, social needs, esteem needs, and self-actualization or self-fulfillment needs. Moreover, these needs are arranged in a hierarchy of pre-potency; only when the needs at one level are satisfied can the needs at the next level be activated.

At the bottom of the hierarchy are physiological needs, or the motives we labelled primary needs. As their position in the hierarchy suggests, these needs are the individual's first concern. Only when one's drives for food, water, air, and so on are relatively satisfied will one's safety and security needs become activated. On this second level, the person's concern for safety and security demand that his or her physical well-being not be threatened and that the future be relatively predictable. Workers thus demand a measure of safety in their working conditions to protect their health, and they expect provisions to be made for their physiological needs should they become unable to provide for themselves. When safety and security have been attained, social needs are activated. On this level the individual seeks inclusion by others, affection from them, and interaction with them. As human relations theorists have demonstrated, resolution of this drive is an important determinant of organizational behaviour. Level four, esteem needs, can be subdivided into the drives to receive esteem from others and the need to hold one's self in esteem. These clearly are related; thinking well of one's self generally is predicated upon receiving favourable responses from others. Finally, when self-esteem and esteem from others are adequate, the highest level of needs, self-actualization, becomes activated. This is a drive to become all that one is capable of becoming—to fulfil one's potential. Since people usually are busy striving to fulfil levels three and four, we rarely see this fifth level manifested. Nevertheless, such behaviours as choosing an occupation to serve others more than self and completing a task simply to obtain the satisfaction such completion provides are manifestations of this level of motivation.

An examination of everyday behaviour suggests the validity of Maslow's system. In a burning theatre, for example, the people present are little interested in the satisfaction inherent in leaving a theatre, maintaining good relations with other panic-stricken patrons, or even having adequate life insurance coverage. They are interested only in self-preservation, and all higher needs are irrelevent. Empirical research has validated our common-sense conclusions. Porter studying managers at a variety of organizational levels in fourteen countries, found that in the United States and Britain (but not, surprisingly, in the other countries) the hierarchical satisfaction of needs seems to occur as Maslow hypothesizes. Beer found that when female clerks were forced to arrange needs in a hierarchy they tended to arrange them in accordance with Maslow's predictions. Evidence exists, then, suggesting that Maslow is correct both in his listing of drives and the hierarchy in which he arranges them.

The Herzberg system

A second frequently mentioned motivational system was proposed by Herzberg and his associate who based their theories upon data obtained from interviews of 200 engineers and accountants in the Pittsburgh area. The employees were asked to recall a time when they felt particularly good or particularly bad about their jobs and to describe the conditions which led to those feelings. Content analysis of the interviews demonstrated that certain job characteristics led to job satisfaction while other characteristics led to dissatisfaction. Job achievement usually produced satisfaction, for example, but lack of achievement did not seem to create dissatisfaction. Conversely, poor working conditions led to dissatisfaction but good conditions did not guarantee satisfaction. Satisfaction and dissatisfaction thus appear not to be simple opposites, and this in turn necessitates a two-factor theory of motivation.

From his interviews, Herzberg concluded that some job conditions are related only to dissatisfaction; they do not serve to motivate workers but cause discontent when absent. These conditions he called *maintenance factors*, for they serve to maintain satisfaction among workers. An alternative term, hygiene factors, reflects their parallel to the "preventive" aspects of medicine; they do not guarantee health or satisfaction. But they guard against the emergence of certain dissatisfaction.

Another set of job conditions serves to build satisfaction when present but not to produce discontent when absent. These Herzberg called *motivators* or satisfiers. Included among these factors are achievement, recognition, advancement, potential for personal growth, responsibility, and the nature of the work, itself. They are termed motivators because they are actively sought after by workers and thus exert considerable control over workers' behaviours.

Herzberg's system seems to parallel the distinction we made between motives and incentives. Motivators, as Herzberg describes them, are internal needs producing outward behaviours. Maintenance factors, which include salary, company policy and administration, relations with colleagues, job security, and working conditions, seem to be more related to the environment and thus act as incentives. Although motives and incentives are not exact equivalents with maintenance and motivator factors, this comparison seems to clarify the distinction Herzberg makes.

Two additional concepts which parallel Herzberg's system are those of *intrinsic* and *extrinsic* motivators. Intrinsic motivators are those aspects of the job which by their very nature provide the individual with rewards. The satisfaction of completing a task, for example, is a reward obtained intrinsically from the nature of the task itself. Similarly, the golfer who shoots a hole-in-one obtains significant reward from having done the act. Extrinsic rewards, on the other hand, are not directly related to the task, coming after the job has been completed and occurring apart from the task itself. If our lucky golfer had bet on the shot, he would have had the additional, extrinsic satisfaction of pocketing the cash. As our discussion suggests, motivators seem analogous to intrinsic motivators while maintenance factors parallel extrinsic motivators.

While the figure illustrates the similarities between the systems, there also are important differences. Maslow argues that any need can motivate if it is unsatisfied; Herzberg believes that only the higher-order factors serve as motivators. Maslow suggests that lower levels must be satisfied before concern shifts to higher level needs, while Herzberg indicates that unsatisfied needs can exist and be influential in both the motivational and maintenance areas simultaneously. Despite their differences, the Maslow and Herzberg systems have much in common; drawing comparisons between the two serves to clarify both.

Considerable empirical evidence exists to support the Herzberg system. Herzberg himself provides a summary of research through 1966 in which he cites a number of studies supporting the two-factor theory. Of the studies in his review, however, only those using Herzberg's interview methodology clearly support his theory; those using other procedures provide less definite substantiation. Other studies, such as those by Dunnette, Campbell, and Hakel, Hulin and Smith, Hinrichs and Mischkin and Evans have indicated that Herzberg's theory is "method bound" provable only when Herzberg's method is used. While Herzberg lists interpersonal relations as a maintenance factor, research by Allen and Centers and Bugental suggests that for women peer relationships often serve as motivational forces. Despite the imposing amount of evidence supporting Herzberg's theory, then, certain modifications seem in order.

Two further shortcomings in the Herzberg system need specification. First, neither this system nor the one offered by Maslow establishes any connection between the individual's drive-reduction and achievement of organizational goals. While this relationship generally is acknowledged, the Maslow and Herzberg systems imply that drive-reduction and organizational goal achievement operate independently. Second, neither theory can readily deal with the problem of individual differences in motivation. Indeed, Maslow admits that his model may not hold for persons with particular experiences—which makes his model rather unreliable in prediction since any case not adhering strictly to his principles may be dismissed as one of those unusual cases. The same problem is present in the Herzberg formulation. Nevertheless, both Herzberg and Maslow contribute to our understanding of human motivation.

The Vroom system

As early as 1955, Brayfield and Crockett postulated a connection between satisfaction, motivation, and organizational success:

> It makes sense to us to assume that individuals are motivated to achieve certain environmental goals and that the achievement of these goals results in satisfaction. Productivity is seldom a goal in itself but is more commonly a means to goal attainment. Therefore we might expect high satisfaction and high productivity to occur together when productivity is perceived as a path to certain important goals and when these goals are achieved.

Support was given to this notion by Georgopoulas, Mahoney, and Jones, who found motivation and productivity to be functions of the goals for which the individual is striving and the utility of work-related behaviour in achieving those goals.

This principie was expanded and developed by Vroom into a system of motivation. He defined motivation as a "process governing choices, made by persons or lower organisms, among alternative forms of voluntary activity". The basic elements of Vroom's system are presented, which illustrates a situation where an individual is faced with a set of alternative first-level outcomes from which to choose—with these outcomes in turn associated with potential second-level outcomes.

According to Vroom, motivation to perform a particular action at a particular time is a function of the anticipated values of all possible outcomes of the action, multiplied by the strength of the person's expectation that his or her action will achieve the desired outcome. These factors Vroom terms valence and expectancy. Valence denotes the anticipated value of an outcome and is considered to be the strength of a person's preference for one outcome over the others. Expectancy is the extent to which the individual believes that a particular act will be followed by a particular outcome: the stronger the belief, the greater the expectancy. A third factor closely related to expectancy is the concept of *instrumentality*. While expectancy considers the relationship between first-level outcomes, instrumentality notes the relationship between action and first-level and desired second-level outcomes. In other words, if achievement of a first-level outcome were useful in attaining a more long-range outcome, an individual might consider working harder to impress a foreman expecting that this would lead to promotion and higher status.

Assume, for example, that our ultimate goal in life is to make as much money as possible. In our present job a number of first-level outcomes are available: being fired, being demoted, being promoted, being given a testimonial dinner, and being given a raise. Only two of these first-level outcomes could result in more money—the promotion and the raise-and only the raise is certain to have that effect. Raises thus are highly instrumental in achieving our second-level goal. And we greatly prefer a raise over the other first-level outcomes available: firing will cut off all income, demotion will reduce income, promotion gives status but little salary increase, and ham steaks and testimonial speeches make us nauseous. Thus valency also is high. We come, then, to the specific behaviours in which we can engage. We could punch a foreman, but that rarely produces raises. We could work harder, but such efforts often are overlooked. We could marry the company president's daughter, and since our experience suggests that everyone marrying the company president's daughter gets a raise, our expectation of goal achievement though that behaviour would be extremely high. Given all these interrelationships between second-level outcomes, first-level outcomes, and specific behaviours, we can be reasonably certain what our future behaviour will be.

Because of its comparative recency, Vroom's system is only beginning to receive empirical support. Vroom himself conducted a study in which he attempted to predict graduating college students' organizational choices on the basis of their instrumentality-goal index scores, which reflect the extent to which the students perceived membership in particular organizations as instrumental in achieving their desired goals. The obtained evidence generally supported his theory. Similarly, Galbraith and Cummings successfully used the model to predict worker productivity, Hill used an adaptation of the Vroom system to accurately predict workers' job-selection behaviours, and Lawler and Porter confirmed Vroom's predictions concerning the ways in which goals influence effort. A variety of questions about Vroom's system remain unanswered; nevertheless, evidence is accumulating in support of his theory.

Like the Maslow and Herzberg systems, Vroom's model is not without shortcomings. He is unable to account for individual differences in personality, nor is he able to represent the common situation in which someone strives for a complex network of many interrelated outcomes rather than just one. Moreover, we do not know which goals have positive valence in work situations or how much difference is needed in motivation before one outcome will be preferred and striven for over another. Despite such shortcomings the Vroom model does take into account individual differences in motivation, and, since achievement of organizational goals often is a first-level outcome useful in achieving personal second-level outcomes, the theory allows a relationship between individual and organizational goals. In these respects, the Vroom system seems a better theory of human motivation in organizations than the systems offered by Maslow and Herzberg.

Other drive-reduction theories

While the systems developed by Maslow, Herzberg, and Vroom seem the most sophisticated systems presently available, other theorists have offered formulations which lend additional insight into the needs which motivate people. One of the earliest and most comprehensive inventories of human drives was presented by Murray, who listed 28 social needs:

1. Acquisition—to gain possessions and property

2. Conservance—to collect, preserve, repair, and protect things
3. Order—to arrange and organize things; to be clean
4. Retention—to hoard or keep things; to be frugal
5. Construction—to build
6. Superiority—to hold power over people and things, to receive recognition
7. Achievement—to accomplish, to overcome
8. Recognition—to receive praise, respect, prestige
9. Exhibition—to receive attention, to amuse, excite, or shock
10. Inviolacy—to maintain privacy, self-respect, reputation, psychological "distance"
11. Inferiority avoidance—to avoid failure, ridicule, or shame
12. Defendance—to justify actions, offer explanations, or defend self
13. Counteraction—to retaliate, defend self through attack, or accomplish particularly difficult goals
14. Dominance—to influence or control others, to persuade, to lead, to organize others, to restrain others
15. Deference—to admire, follow, cooperate, or serve
16. Similance—to empathize, imitate, or emulate
17. Autonomy—to resist influence, maintain independence
18. Contrarience—to be unique, unconventional, different
19. Aggression—to assault, injure, punish, ridicule
20. Abasement—to surrender, comply, self-deprecate, grovel
21. Blamaviodance—to avoid blame or punishment through proper behaviour
22. Affiliation—to form associations, to join, to belong
23. Rejection—to snub, exclude, ignore, or discriminate
24. Nurturance—to nourish, aid, protect, or "mother"
25. Succorance—to seek aid, protection, sympathy
26. Play—to relax, amuse self, laugh, joke, release tension
27. Cognizance—to learn, explore, satisfy curiosity
28. Exposition—to demonstrate, instruct, explain, teach

The arousal of any one of these needs, Murray concluded, produces behaviour designed to achieve need reduction.

Considerably simpler is the need system offered by Argyle, who suggests seven "roots of social behaviour":

1. Nonsocial drives producing social behaviour—basic biological drives such as hunger and thirst plus other acquired drives such as the need for achievement and the need to obtain information about one's environment.
2. Dependency—the need for "close and submissive" relations with others
3. Affiliation—the need for inclusion, belongingness, and moderate levels of intimacy
4. Dominance—the need to control the behaviours of others and to achieve status and recognition
5. Sex—the need for intimacy and affection
6. Aggression—the need to harm others physically, verbally, or in other ways.
7. Self-esteem and self-consistency—the need for approval from others, for a good self-concept, and for a clear, distinct, and consistent self-image.

Like Murray, Argyle suggests that human behaviour takes its roots in these drives as people actively seek to reduce them whenever they are aroused.

Simpler still is McClelland's three-part view of motivation. He holds that individuals seek achievement, affiliation, and power. By having people interpret ambiguous pictures and content analyzing those interpretations, McClelland discovered consistent behavioural patterns related to these three needs. Those high in achievement drives seem to prefer situations in which they take personal responsibility for finding solutions to problems, to set moderate achievement goals, to be willing to take risks, and to desire feedback concerning their performance. An individual having a high motivation for affiliation seeks the company of others, tries hard to be liked, actively promotes harmonious interpersonal relationships in groups, and offers help and support to others. Finally, a high power motivation is manifested by active attempts to win arguments, to persuade others, and to lead others toward goal achievement.

Taken alone, the systems of Murray, Argyle, and McClelland seem relatively sterile, providing only lists of drives which at any given time may or may not motivate an individual. Yet these systems do add something to the model suggested by Vroom. In that model, Vroom makes little statement concerning the nature of second-level outcomes. It seems likely, however, that those outcomes might well consist of some or all of the drives listed by Murray, Argyle, or McClelland. If, for example, we have a strong drive for power, reduction of that drive might be our preferred second-level outcome. We then would strive for a first-level outcome we perceive useful in achieving power, performing behaviours we perceive likely to achieve that outcome.

It may be that the most complete understanding of motivation can be achieved through some combination of Vroom's model, Murray, Argyle, and McClelland's need lists, and Maslow and/or Herzberg's suggestions concerning the order in which those needs occur and the functions they play. A system considering needs as second-level outcomes, arranging those needs into a hierarchy of prepotency, classifying them according to maintenance or motivation functions, specifying the instrumentality of certain first-level outcomes in achieving the second-level needs, measuring the valence of the first-level outcomes, and assessing the expectancy that a certain action will achieve the preferred first-level outcome, ultimately may provide a definite theory of human motivation.

Reinforcement theories of motivation

In drive-reduction theories the central assumption is that people have internal tensions or needs which, when aroused, produce behaviour. Motivation is thus seen as moving through an "inside need-outward behaviour" pattern. An alternate view of motivation, however, views the process as occurring in the opposite order, with outside behaviours leading to internal feelings. Essentially these *reinforcement* theories see motivation as a three-step process: we behave, observe the effects our behaviour produces, and then either repeat the behaviour or discontinue it.

Reinforcement theory finds its roots in the thought of Epicurus and Aristippus, Greek philosophers living several hundred years before Christ. In their view, human motivation revolves around a single principle: that man seeks pleasure and avoids pain. This philosophy, called hedonism, later was adopted by the Western philosopher Jremy Bentham, who wrote that human behaviour is "under the governance of two sovereign masters, pain and pleasure." Born thirty years after Bentham's death was Sigmund Freud, whose concept of the *primary process* embodied the search for pleasure and avoidance of pain. In his view, behaviour is a by-product of the conflict between the Id's desire for pleasure and the multitude of obstacles placed by society in the path of the pleasure-seeker, Thorndike, on the other hand, saw the pleasure-pain principle as the key to human learning, discovering that organisms learn behaviours which produce pleasure or escape from pain and discontinue behaviours which cause pain. His conclusion that "pleasure stamps in pain stamps out" has come to be known as the Law of Effect.

The most recent and most comprehensive formulation of the hedonistic view of motivation is the one by B.F. Skinner. Skinner developed the concept of *operant conditioning*, which, simply stated, dictates that behaviours receiving pleasurable responses will be repeated while behaviours producing pain will be stopped. Perhaps this principle can be clarified through an example: A pigeon is placed in a small cage. It struts around, exploring its environment, and in a random movement brushes its head against a small bell attached to one wall. Suddenly a grain of birdseed appears in a tray below. Since the bird has not eaten for some time, it happily gobbles the bit of seed. It resumes its random, exploratory movements and again brushes close to the bell. Again food appears, and again the bird receives a modicum of pleasure. Soon, after this process has been repeated a few times, a behavioural pattern will emerge. The pigeon pecks the bell more quickly, with decreasing amounts of random behaviour occurring between the reception of food and the next peck of the bell. Ultimately the pigeon performs only two behaviours: pecking the bell and hogging the seeds. The experimenter may then withhold the grain; the pigeon will continue to peck the bell with great vigour, still expecting the reward to be delivered. If, however, that reward is withheld long enough, the bell-pecking behaviour eventually will disappear. The pigeon is therefore at the mercy of its environment, which may withhold or give rewards, choose the behaviours to be reinforced, and thus control the bird's behaviour.

While the principle of reinforcement seems to hold true in virtually every situation, several aspects of the reinforcement employed are influential in determining the more specific effects of conditioning upon behaviour. First, *amount* of reinforcement affects the results: the more reinforcement the subject is given, the faster the subject learns the reinforced behaviour. Second, *delay* of reinforcement is important: reinforcement given immediately after the desired response is performed has more impact upon learning than does reinforcement given after some delay. Indeed, the principle seems to be that the closer the reinforcement follows the desired behaviour, the more quickly that behaviour becomes conditioned. Third, *schedule* of reinforcement has an impact: does reinforcement follow every performance of the behaviour? every other performance? every tenth, sixteenth, or fiftieth? Research findings indicate that the schedule of reinforcement influences two things: speed of learning and resistance to extinction. Speed of learning is fastest when reinforcement is given on a 100-per cent schedule. Extinction occurs fastest when reinforcement stops altogether. Partial reinforcement produces slower learning, but the response persists even when reinforcement no longer occurs. The most powerful reinforcement schedule is the "variable ratio" procedure, in which reinforcement occurs randomly after performance of the desired behaviour. In this situation learning occurs relatively slowly, but when reinforcement stops the behaviour persists over literally hundreds of further trials. Apparently the subject, accustomed to receiving reinforcement only occasionally and unpredictably keeps trying in the hope that reinforcement will again resume.

To understand more thoroughly this principle of reinforcement scheduling, consider that prototype of reinforcer for human "pigeons," the slot machine. The response desired by the slot machine's owner is for us to insert money and pull the handle. The initial performance of the response is learned through observation: we see other dummies pulling handles and receiving reinforcement, so we decide to try it too. At this point the issue becomes the extent to which our behaviour persists. If we were reinforced every time we pulled the handle, so that we won money the first ten times we played, we probably would be rather enthusiastic about slot machines. Should the reinforcement then stop completely, our enthusiasm would rather quickly disappear and we would "quit while we're ahead," discontinuing the response. Suppose, however, we were rewarded every fifth time we played. We would become enthusiastic more slowly, but we would continue playing longer after the reinforcement stopped altogether because we had not come to expect success with every try. But slot machines do not reinforce on 100-per cent or a fixed-rations schedule. Slot machine manufacturers, in their infinite wisdom, apparently realize that the most potent schedule of reinforcement is no schedule at all—that is, random reinforcement of behaviour. Occasionally we will be reinforced on consecutive trials; more often we will go several trials without success. Whatever the sequence, we discover that re-inforcement is unpredictable and that, even though we fail—this time, success surely will come with the next pull. In this situation, then hope indeed springs eternal—at least until our funds are exhausted and our credit runs out. Under extreme pressure the author will admit that fishing operates on the same principle and consumes as much money—just before he makes his next cast.

But what have pigeons and slot machines to do with organizational communication? Actually, communication behaviours can both condition and be conditioned. This first was illustrated by Verplanck, whose confederates conducted 24 conversations lasting 30 minutes each. During the first 10 minutes of a conversation, the confederate counted the number of times the subject used statements of opinion ("I think" or "It seems to me"). During the second 10 minutes the confederate began to apply reinforcement, agreeing with every opinion statement the subject made. Finally, during the last 10 minutes the confederate tried to extinguish opinion statements by either disagreeing with every such statement or failing to respond at all. The results fit Skinner's predictions almost perfectly, opinion statements increased significantly during the reinforcement period and decreased to almost zero when punishment was applied.

A remarkable number of studies have demonstrated the same principle. Matarazzo et al. were able to control the length of time the subjects spoke simply by providing slight affirmative head nods. Other researchers have conditioned plural nouns, first person pronouns, certain types of verbs, and a variety of non-verbal movements through the use of such reinforcers as "mmm-hmm," "good," smiles, nods, and forward leans, and such extinguishers as "huh-uh" and head shakes. In each of these studies verbal and nonverbal responses were used to condition the subject's communication behaviours.

We suggested earlier that reinforcement theories are an alternative to drive-reduction theories. Perhaps "supplement" would have been a more accurate description. Reinforcement theories have something to offer drive-reduction theories, which in turn can contribute to the development of an improved reinforcement theory. One criticism often levelled at reinforcement theory concerns Skinner's use of explanation. When a pigeon is trained to peck a bell, Skinner suggests that the bell-pecking behaviour can be explained in terms of the reinforcement ratio and timing: if we chart the two, we have explained bell-pecking behaviours. In fact, argues Gergen, such an explanation is analogous to claiming that when one has located certain mushrooms which cause death when eaten, one has explained deaths which occur from ingesting certain mushrooms. In fact, the true explanation lies in the physiological processes triggered by the mushroom. But Skinnerian explanations leave no room for internal processes. It is here that drive-reduction theories become useful; reinforcers are reinforcing because they resolve some internal motive. The pigeon's need for food makes bird seed reinforcing to it; Verplanck's subjects' desires for self-esteem caused them to respond to positive communications. Drive-reduction theories thus can make a valuable contribution to reinforcement systems.

Reinforcement theorists similarly have something to offer drive-reduction systems. Often the question is asked, Where do drives come from? In the instance of the drive for dominance, two explanations might be offered. First, an adherent to the Darwinian theory of evolution might argue that, since natural selection allows only the fittest and most dominant of the species to survive, the trait dominance has been passed to us through heredity. A more likely explanation, however, is that dominance is learned through reinforcement of behaviours. Perhaps, as children, we discovered that it is pleasurable to exert control over others or to be regarded as a leader. Thus the need for dominance grew within us through repeated performances and reinforcements of dominant behaviours.

Thus reinforcement theory provides a practical application for drive-reduction theories. If, in the organization, we have certain behaviours which we want workers to perform, we can "stamp in" those behaviours by reinforcing them. If we have certain behaviours which we want workers to avoid, we can extinguish them through punishment. Interestingly, rewards and punishments are effectively administered through communication.

General aspects of performance

Research suggests that group and individual performances differ in three general areas: judgment, problem solving, and learning. Studies in the first area, judgment, have focused upon two issues: whether the quality of group judgment exceeds the average quality of judgments made by individual members and whether the quality of group judgment exceeds the judgment quality of the best group member. Gordon found groups to exceed individuals in making aesthetic judgments and estimating weights, Jenness found groups superior in estimating the number of beans in a bottle, and Gurnee found group judgments superior on a written true-false test. This judgmental superiority of groups seems to spring from the greater number of estimates contributing to the judgment, the range of knowledge possessed by the membership, and the greater confidence inspired by group interaction. It also seems consistent with the social facilitation principle. However, some qualification of the group superiority principle is necessary: the kind of task seems an important determinant of whether group judgment is superior to that of individuals. Marston found group judgments of what occurred during a staged classroom incident to be less accurate than individual judgments. Nevertheless, group judgments generally seem superior to those exhibited by average group members.

The answer to the second issue—whether groups are better than the best individuals—seems to be no. While under some circumstances group performance might exceed that of any individual in the group. Jenness and Gurnee both found that the judgments of capable individuals usually equalled or exceeded those of the entire group.

A second area of performance is problem solving. In investigations of problem solving, comparisons are made either between performances by individuals working alone and performances by the same individuals working in groups, or between performances of single individuals and performances of other individuals in groups. These investigations have shown with remarkable consistency that groups produce more and better solutions to problems that do individuals, although the time taken to arrive at such solutions has not been shown to be shorter for either groups or individuals. A variety of explanations have been offered for these findings. Marquart suggested that the summation of individual contributions added up to a superior conclusion, Barnlund offered that critical thinking in groups led to the rejection of erroneous suggestions and that the group setting generated greater interest in the task; Watson pointed to the influence of the ablest group member in improving the other members' performances; Thorndike attributed the result to the influence of the most confident member; and several researchers suggested that group superiority stems from the greater amounts of information available to the group members. To these explanations we might add the principles underlying social facilitation; the evaluation implicit in the presence of other group members may have enhanced the problem-solving behaviours of individual subjects.

Group and individual learning comprises a third area of performance differences. Again, consistent results have emerged. When group members work together on a task, learning among the members occurs more quickly in the group situation than when the members work individually. The type of task may determine differences in learning, however: Yuker notes that group superiority occurs when the members can work without getting in each other's way, when the material to be learned can be augmented by the addition of individual contributions, and when parts of the material to be learned are interdependent. Generally, though, these results are consistent with the social facilitation theory. When all members are engaged in a learning task and implicitly judging one another according to how quickly each member learns, improvement should occur more quickly than in non-social situations.

On the whole, then, group performance seems to exceed individual performances in judgment, problem solving, and learning. These effects are modified somewhat by the type of task involved and the motivations of individual group members, but in general experimental results conform to predictions implicit in social facilitation theory.

Brainstorming

A technique becoming increasingly popular in organizational settings is that of *brainstorming,* used to generate new and radical solutions to problems. Basically, this technique involves three rules: ideas are to be expressed without regard to quality, no expression of evaluation may be made by any group member concerning any suggestion, and elaboration upon preceding ideas is encouraged. While the amount of research is limited, findings generally suggest that this technique is an effective producer of innovative ideas. Meadow, Parnes, and Reese instructed subjects working both in groups and alone to suggest as many uses as possible for a broom and a coathanger, and they found groups to generate about twice as many good ideas as did individuals when those groups were given brainstorming instructions. Cohen, Whitmyre, and Funk produced similar results with individuals working in pairs. However, studies by Taylor, Berry, and Block and Dunnette, Campbell, and Jaastad found no differences between the ideas generated by brainstorming groups and by individuals working alone under brainstorming instructions. Unlike the Meadow *et al.* and Cohen *et al.* studies, the latter two imposed a time limit upon the subjects. As Shaw suggests, groups can generate ideas indefinitely while individuals run dry after a timc; thus the results obtained by Taylor *et al.* and Dunnette *et al.* may reflect the time limitations rather than actual behavioural patterns.

Behavioural sciences for management

Management is concerned with the optimum utilization of various resources for the attainment of organizational goals and objectives. The proper management of human resources plays an important role for attaining such objectives. Here it is imperative for managers to have an insight into the nature and the complex behaviour pattern of individuals working in an organization. It is very difficult to analyse human behaviour. He may behave today as per our expectations but tomorrow his behaviour may be different. Lavitt, has made certain fundamental assumption about human behaviour. He has classifies behaviour behaviour as:

(i) Caused behaviour

(ii) Motivated behaviour

(iii) Goal oriented behaviour

These assumptions rule out randomness and prove that human behaviour is always due to some reason or that behaviour is a dependent factor. Thus the social scientists have developed methods to analyse human behaviour. The science which analyses the cause and effect of human activity in behavioural science. Behavioural science analyses why people behave as they do, thus help one to understand the reason and characteristics of past behaviour and tries to make an individual or a group to behave in a desired manner. Behavioural science makes one understand, predict, change and control behaviour of individual or groups. This subject brings together, from variety of disciplines, those concepts, theories and researches that may be useful to people in making decisions about the behaviour of individual and group. Behavioural science integrates concepts and theories from psychology, sociology, anthropology, social psychology, economics and political science that can be useful in better understanding, predicting the factors having an impact on the behaviour of the individuals or group.

Basic areas of behavioural science

The basic areas of behavioural science comprises of some of long-familiar academic disciplines. Certain of them, however, may be placed closer to the core of the entire field than others. Anthropology, Psychology, and Sociology are generally regarded as being in the center while Economics, Political Science and Jurisprudence are more at the periphery. While classification systems vary, a recent attempt to organize behavioural science literature, encourages just such an orbital organization of disciplines around psychology as the core.

Anthropology

Anthropology is the study of man and his works. While this definition is certainly broad, the anthropologist have traditionally emphasized study of primitive (or, better, preliterate) societies in order to learn about man and his activities from early times to the present. The problems faced by the subgrouping. Archeology analyses the remains of past civilisations. Physical Anthropology studies the biological features of man and traces evolutionary patterns.

Social Anthropology focuses on the forms of culture or technology and the impact they have on individuals and groups. Linguistics in the study of speech and relationships among languages. With the interesting culture and civilizations, or the concern with change in society, anthropologists may be called on to transfer information from basic studies to more applied areas. Much of this fundamental concern with man affects all phases of human activity at home and abroad. Strong cultural bases exist for war, peace, and mundane consumer behaviour. Even designers of rapid transit systems must take into account anthropometric data as they decide on the measurements of seats and aisles.

Psychology

The term psychology comes from the Greek word psyche, the soul or spirit. This is a misleading description of the discipline today even though it fits the image generally held by people when they define the field as 'study of the mind'. The mind is obviously not amenable to study through the scientific approach; psychologists study behaviour. The term behaviour includes not only surface acts, which can be noted and measured, but extends also to those activities that constitute the 'phenomenal' (experiential) aspects of the situation. Psychologists are concerned with concepts such as learning, sensation and perception, motivation, personality, attitudes, thinking, and problem solving all within the framework of behaviour. The areas of interest within psychology are so numerous that it is difficult to comprehend this array. In its development the field emerged electically from various 'schools' or theoretical approaches. The differences, heatedly argued in the past, are no longer crucial though the flavour of psychology today shows some influences of the differentiations. John B. Watson's emphasis on behaviour, and only behaviour, remains as the core of psychology though the field has moved far from this extreme position. Psychoanalytic theory remains Freud's extensive contribution to the field. Still further kinds of dynamic theories are Gestalt psychology with its integrative organizational approach, and the newer views of man as a 'self-actualizer' or as 'standing out in the world' and experiencing it, according to the existential or phenomenological approach.

While the focus of psychological research is on the basic core areas of learning and motivation, the immediate applications to the areas of business, government, and education are being made continuously. The fundamentals of human behaviour are of practical interest in selection and training, communication in school and industry, and in most management and marketing situations. The applied psychologist may be testing applicants in the personnel department, but he probably will be even more interested in a topic like 'motivation in the work group' to which he would apply concepts gained from basic research in physiological, social, and industrial psychology. In the same way, today's psychologist would be interested in the areas of individual and group decision making, patterns of influence and change in organizations, group processes vocational choice and satisfaction, programmed instruction, attitudes and values in consumer and mass media situations, or in conditions of human performance.

Sociology

Sociology is the study of the behaviour of people in groups 'Sociology is the scientific study of patterned, shared human behaviour... the ways in which people act toward one another'. From Comet to Durkheim, Cooley, Max Waber, and present-day sociologists, the emphasis has been on social groups, social behaviour, society, customs, institutions, status, social class, social mobility, and prestige. Specific areas of study that constitute special subfields, can be listed as follows, Urban and rural sociology, the sociology of race and ethnic relations, demography, communications, research on public opinion and attitude studies, collective behaviour, the study of occupations, the sociology of medicine and social psychiatry, and social disorganization and deviant behaviour are among the subfields in which considerable research and study are being undertaken. Substantial attention is also given to such subdisciplines as political sociology, the sociology of religion, educational sociology, the sociology of art, the sociology of knowledge, and sociology of science and invention.

For the citizen at large, as well as, for the professional worker in many fields, the sociologist can provide a basis for action in everyday situations. Problems of segregation, law enforcement, labour-management unrest, mobility of labour, juvenile delinquency, urban or rural dynamics, and interaction in an industrial work group represent only a few areas of application of the research techniques and conceptualizations available in this discipline.

Economics

The definitions of economics illustrated the current diversity of opinion as to what economics really is. The following broad definition by Von Mises may be contrasted with a more specific one given later. Economics, as a branch of the more general theory of human action deals with all human action, i.e., with man's purposive aiming at the attainment of ends chosen, whatever these ends may be. 'A more specifically delineated definition has', economics as 'the study of how the goods and services we want get produce, and how they are distributed among us'. This we call economic analysis. Equally economics is the study of how we can make the system of production and distribution work better. This we call economic policy.

The behavioural science features of economics cut across all the traditional categories used to subdivide the field, though the behavioural bases may be more evident in the areas of consumer economics or decision-making theory or finance. The approach toward economic behaviour, to qualify as a behavioural science, is described by Katona as the study of the actions of people who play a role in economic trends. In economic psychology one must not only 'analyze the results of human behaviour (but) also... study the decision makers and the process of decision making, because motives, attitudes, and opinions influence actions and thereby what happens in and to the economy'. Strict views of economics as the study of the 'economic man' whose behaviour is postulated as rational in striving for maximum utility under 'perfect competition' is not, except in a complementary fashion, a part of the behavioural approach. Nor is a limitation to the behaviour of commodities rather than of people included in this framework. Concern with actual decision making processes and their results in the entire input-output system marks the behavioural approach in economics.

Political science

Political science studies the behaviour of individuals and groups within a political setting. The approaches may vary from studies of the structure of a government unit to the description and analysis of actual behaviour of members of that political organization. The latter aspect is more behavioural than the former. Indeed, a classification system or a structuring of a situation can hardly qualify as behavioural. The earlier emphasis on political philosophy is less and less, a significant part of today's scene, especially in the United States. Lasswell, illustrates the differences between the 'science of politics which calls for the systematic statement of theory and the use of empirical methods of gathering and processing data and the philosophy of politics which justifies preferences'.

The behaviourally oriented political scientist will eschew philosophy and will search for the empirical bases of behaviour in politics and political parties, public opinion, pressure groups, public administration, voting, legislative activity, judicial decision making, organization and institutions, culture and government, comparative systems, and international relations. The full scope of the field may be appreciated in a work like 'Political Behaviour: A reading in Theory and Research', edited by Eulau, Eldersveld, and Janowitz. Theory in the behavioural approach is not ignored but emphasized. It is, furthermore, theory in the true sense and not a verbal substituted for the work 'speculation'.

Application of behavioural science

The knowledge of behavioural science had become of much importance for all the professional areas like, education, psychiatry, marketing, management, administration etc. If managers are able to understand, predict and direct changes and control the behaviour of their subordinates they are considered effective. Hence its concepts are now used in the following areas:

Education

The professional interests and activities in pedagogy are based on the basic findings of many of the fields of behavioural science, notably, psychology and sociology, Principles of learning and retention, growth and development, along with numerous other bits of information must be part of the reservoir of knowledge of the teacher in and the administrator of the educational endeavor. In addition, further understanding of social dynamics of the group and the community are proving to be an important requirement for anyone in today's educational structure.

Psychiatry

The diagnosis and treatment of nervous and mental disorders is the province of psychiatry. The psychiatrist is a medical doctor who has spent some time in learning the fundamental bases of human behaviour in order that he may be able to treat the afflictions of his patients. He must gather and apply as much behavioural science knowledge as he can but, since he is clinical practitioner, his direct involvement in basic behavioural research activities is minimal. This is more often the province of the psychologist, the analysis of and therapy for problems of a psychological nature. A psychoanalyst (to help clear up another common point of confusion) is a psychiatrist who follows, more or less, the methods of treatment originally formulated by Sigmund Freud.

Marketing

The applications of behavioural science principles and results can be very useful in specific areas of business activity, among them, is one of marketing activity. In the dynamic mechanisms of flow of goods and services from producer to consumer, the awareness of the nature of individual and social processes had immediate or long-range contribution to the success or failure of the enterprise in promoting its products. Consumer choice behaviour often is a critical condition; the nature of influence and the channels involved represent leading topics for behavioural research in this area. Innovation and the diffusion of new products, creativity and the learning of responses are not less important social and individual phenomena that contribute to the total marketing process.

Management

The accomplishment of organizational tasks through coordination of the activities of others is the job of the manager. Since this role depends so heavily on the action of other people, it might be guesses readily that behavioural concepts and findings are crucial for the completion of managerial tasks. Motivation, learning, perception, Inter-personal relation and other basic facets of individual behaviour from the foundations for effective performance in business organizations. The additional variables involved in such group and aggregate activity make it advisable for the would-be manager to acquaint himself with concepts of social behaviour as well. Becoming even more crucial these days is the awareness of the broader environmental factors and dynamics that arise beyond the immediate organization and yet affect it in its functioning in the community and society.

Administration

The field of administration is considered by some to be synonymous with management. Where a distinction between the two is made, administration is considered by most writers to be the activity of policy making or planning while management is the execution of such policy. Since the two functions are virtually inseparable, it would seem to be valid to consider management and administration as one and the same.

Administration has been use, however, to describe the functioning of coordinators or managers in the public sector or those executives in organizations such as hospitals or schools. Public administration has been an active professional area, and medical administration has been growing rapidly. Educational administration has developed almost exclusively under the aegis of schools of education and their pedagogical orientation.

Recent trends indicate growing recognition of the common base of specific areas of administrative activity. This reinforces some earlier positions reflecting the commonality of fundamental concepts underlying the variations found in specific locales. A pioneering effort by Litchfield sketched the basic creed as being that 'administration and the administrative process occur in substantially the same generalized form in industrial, commercial, civil, educational, military, and hospital organization'. Support for the whole area of administration as a significant entity is developing reorganization of professional curricular or colleges as well.

People

People make up the internal social system of the organization. They consist of individuals and groups, and large groups as well as small ones. There are unofficial, informal groups and more official, formal ones. Groups are dynamic. They form, change, and disband. The human organization today is not the same as it was yesterday, or the day before. People are the living, thinking, feeling beings who created the organization. It exists to achieve their objectives. Organizations exist to serve people. People do not exist to serve organizations.

Structure

Structure defines the official relationships of people in organizations. Different jobs are required to be accomplished through an organization's activities. The activities are performed by different people at different level. There are managers and employees, accountants and assemblers. These people have to be related in some structural way so that their work can be effective. The main structure related to power and to duties. For example, one person has authority to make decisions that affect the work of other people. This relation of power and responsibility is structure. The relationship has a definite influence on the behaviour of the person who does the work.

Technology

Technology provides the physical and economic resources with which people work. They cannot accomplish much with their bare hands, so they build, buildings, design machines, create work processes, and assemble resources. The technology that results has a significant influence on working relationships. An assembly line is not the same as a research laboratory, and a steel mill does not have the same working conditions as a hospital. The great benefit of technology is that it allows people to do more and better work, but it also restricts people in various ways. It has costs as well as benefits. The technology by its operational results influence the behaviour in organization.

Environment

All organizations operate within an external environment. A single organization does not exist alone. It is part of a larger system that contains thousands of other elements. All these mutually influence each other in complex system that becomes the life-style of the people. Individual organizations, such as a factory or a school, cannot escape being influenced by this external environment. It influences the attitudes of people, affects working conditions, and provides competition for resources and power. It must be considered in the study of human behaviour in organization.

organizational behaviour

Origin

Human relationships have existed since the beginning of time, the skill of trying to deal with them in the complex organizations is relatively new. In ancient days people worked alone or they worked in such small grounds that their work relationships were simple and easier to be handled. It has been popular to assume that under these conditions people worked in a Utopia of happiness and fulfillment, but this assumption is largely a nostalgic reinterpretation of history. Actual conditions were brutal and backbreaking. People worked from dawn to dusk under intolerable conditions, of filth, danger, and scarcity of resources. They had to work in those conditions as they had to survive, so they had little time to think for job satisfactions.

Even after the industrial revolution. The condition of people did not improve, but at least the seed was planted for potential improvement. Industry created a surplus of goods and knowledge that eventually gave workers increased wages, shorter hours, and more work satisfaction. In this new industrial environment. Robert Owen, a young Welsh factory owner, about in the year 1800, was one of the first to emphasize human needs of employees. He refused temperance and improved their working conditions. This could hardly be called modern organizational behaviour, but it was a beginning. He was called 'the real father' of personnel administration by an early writer.

Early development

In the early 1900s F. W. Taylor generated interest in people at work. He is often called 'the father of scientific management', and the changes he brought to management paved the way for later development of organizational behaviour. His work eventually led to improved recognition and productivity for industrial workers. He pointed out that just as there was a best machine for a job, so were there best ways to do the jobs. To be sure, the goal was still technical efficiency, but at least management was awakened to the importance of one of its neglected resources, the human being.

Taylor's major work was published in 1911. During that decade interest in human conditions at work was accelerated by First World War. The National Personnel Association was formed, and later, in 1923, it became the American Management

Association, carrying the subtitle 'Devoted Exclusively to the Consideration of the Human Factor is Commerce and Industry'. During this period Whiting Williams was studying workers while working with them, and in 1920 he published a significant interpretation of his experience, What's on the Worker's Mind.

human relation phase

Elton Mayo and F. J. Roethlisberger at Harvard University gave academic stature to the study of human behaviour at work. They applied keen insight, straight thinking, and sociological backgrounds to industrial experiments at the Western Electric Company, Hawthrone Plant. The result was the concept that an organization is a social system and the worker is indeed the most important element in it. Their experiments showed that the worker is not a simple tool but a complex personality interacting in a group situation that often is difficult to understand.

To Taylor and his contemporaries, human problems stood in the way of production and so should be removed. To Mayo, human problems become a broad new field of study and an opportunity for progress. He is recognized as the father of what was then called human relations and later became known as organizational behaviour. Taylor increased production by rationalizing it. Mayo and his followers sought to increase production by humanizing it.

The Mayo-Roethlisberger research has been strongly criticized as being inadequately controlled and interpreted, but its basic ideas, such as a social system within the work environment, have stood the test of time. The important point is that it was substantial research about human behaviour at work, and its influence was widespread.

Expanding popularity

The support of business and academic leaders led to a surge of interest in human relations and in modern days the subject became very popular. Some of the reasons for its popularity were as follows:

1. There was a cultural lag in understanding the human side of organizations so that heavy emphasis was needed to catch up with progress in engineering, production, sales and finance. Management saw this inbalance and wanted to improve the situation.

2. A large amount of research followed the work of Mayo and Roethlisberger, giving managers new knowledge for building more effective organizations.

3. Social forces brought increasing pressures for an improved human climate in organizations. Labour unions gained strength and pressed for a better working environment. Minority groups insisted upon a better climate for their members. Workers also were better educated and expected an improved, more human quality of leadership in organizations. Generally there was a change in social

attitudes that required more social responsibility from organizations in dealing with all types of people, including their employees.

4. The work environment itself became more complex, requiring more attention from management to make it operate effectively. Increasing organization size added to the complexity of work. Although it is relatively easy to get ten employees to work together, it is more difficult to have a hundred do so, and very complicated to have a thousand employees working together. Increased specialization also contributed to the complexity of work. As organization size increased and technology advanced, more intense specialization developed, and employees became, less able to understand the whole product or service that they helped produce.

The increasing emphasis on people at work was a result of trends that has been developing over a long period of time. It helped to bring human values back into balance with other values at work. The unfortunate part of the situation, however, was that human relations grew so fast that much faddism and shallowness developed. Some practitioners began to emphasize the big smile, 'being nice to people', and 'keep them happy', while at the same time subtly trying to manipulate employees. One humorist observed, "we have moved from the 'invisible hand' of Adam Smith's economics to the 'lad hand' of human relations". These practices led to well-deserved criticisms.

The term "human relations" gradually lost favour, although it continues to be used—especially at the operating level—because of its appropriateness. An example is the statement. "The supervisor is effective-based, the new term that arose to describe it was "organizational behaviour".

Theory X and theory Y

A powerful influence for maturity in organizational behaviour was Douglas McGregor's Theory X and Theory Y. These two theories clearly distinguished traditional autocratic assumption about people (Theory X) from more behaviourally based assumptions about people (Theory Y). The usefulness of the McGregor theories is his convincing argument that most management actions flow directly from whatever theory of human behaviour managers hold. Philosophy controls practice. Management's personnel practices, decision making, operating practices, and even organizational design flow from assumptions about human behaviour. McGregor pointed out that Theory X was the set of assumptions held by most managers at that time. Even though they did not explicitly state their assumptions, they implicitly held them, because the kinds of actions they took came from Theory X.

Theory X implies an autocratic approach to managing. As shown below, it assumes that most people dislike work and will try to avoid it, if possible. They engage in various work restrictions because they are lazy and indolent. They are self-centered, indifferent to organizational needs, and resistant to change. The common rewards given by organizations are not enough to overcome their dislike for work, so the only way that management can secure high employee performance is to coerce, control, and threaten them. Theory Y implies a humanistic and supportive approach to managing people. It assumes that people are not lazy and indolent. Any appearance they have of being that way is the result of their experiences with organization; but if management will provide the proper environment to release their potential, work will become as natural to them as play or rest. They will exercise self-direction and self-control in the service of objectives to which they are committed. Management's role is to provide an environment in which the potential of people can be released at work.

McGregor's argument was that management had been ignoring the facts about people. It had been following an outmoded set of assumptions about people because it adhered to Theory X when the facts are that most people are closer to the Theory Y set of assumptions. There are important differences among people, so a few may come closer to Theory X, but nearly all employees have some Theory Y potential for growth. Managers had failed to recognize this potential; consequently, their policies and practices failed to develop it. The result was that many people regarded work as a curse on humankind instead of an opportunity for growth and fulfillment. Management needed to change to a whole new theory of working with people: Theory Y.

Fundamental concepts

Every field of social science (or even physical science) has a philosophical foundation of basic concepts that guide its development. In accounting, for example, a fundamental concept if the "for every debit there will be a credit". The entire system of double-entry accounting was built on this philosophy when it replaced single-entry book-keeping many years ago.. In physics, a basic philosophy is that elements of nature are uniform. The law of gravity is supposed to operate uniformly in Tokyo and London, and an atom of hydrogen is supposed to be identical in Moscow and Washington, but the same cannot be said for people.

Organizational behaviour deals with a set of fundamental concepts revolving around the nature of people and organizations. A summary of these ideas are being mentioned hereafter.

The nature of people

— Individual differences

— A whole person

— Caused behaviour (motivation)

— Value of the person (human dignity).

The nature of organizations

— Social systems

— Mutual interest

Result—Holistic organizational behaviour

The nature of people

In behavioural science there are four are four basic assumptions: regarding nature of people; individual differences, a whole person, caused behaviour (motivation), and value of the person (human dignity).

1. *Individual difference*: People have much in common (they become excited or they are grieved by the loss of a loved one), but each person in the would is also individually different. On the hills of Greenland lie billions of tiny snowflakes; yet we are reasonably sure that each is different. On the planet Earth are billions of complex people who are likewise all different (and we expect that all who follow will be different): Each one is different from all others, probably in millions of ways, just as each of their fingerprints is different, as far as we know. And these differences are usually substantial rather than meaningless. Think, for example, of a person's billion brain cells and the billions of possible combinations of connections and bits of experience that could be stored therein. All people are different. This is a fact supported by science.

The idea of individual differences comes originally from psychology. From the day of birth, each person is unique, and individual experiences after birth make people even more different. Individual differences mean that management can get the greatest motivation among employees by treating them differently. If it were not for individual differences, some standard, across-the-board way of dealing with employees could be adopted, and minimum judgment that justice and rightness with employees shall be individual, not statistical.

Because of individual differences, organizational behaviour philosophy, like democratic political philosophy, begins with the individual. Only a person can take responsibility and make decisions; a group by definition cannot do so. A group is powerless until individuals act therein.

2. *A Whole person*: Although some organizations may wish they could employ only a person's skill or brain, all that they can employ is a whole person, rather than certain separate characteristics, Different Human traits may be separately studies, but in the final analysis they are all part of one system making up a whole person. Skill does not exist apart from background or knowledge. Home life is not totally separable from work life, and emotional conditions are not separate from physical conditions. People function as total human beings.

For example, a supervisor wanted Mrs. Vimala to work overtime on Wednesday night on a rush report. Mrs. Vimala had the necessary knowledge and skill for the job. She also wanted the overtime pay. However, from her point of view a social obligation made it impossible for her to work that night. The date was her tenth wedding anniversary, and an anniversary party was scheduled with a few friends at her house. This anniversary was important to her, so her supervisor had to consider her needs as a whole person, not just a worker.

When management practices organizational behaviour, it is trying to develop a better employee, but also it wants to develop a better person in terms of growth and fulfillment. Research suggests that jobs do shape people somewhat as they perform them, so management needs to be concerned about its effect on the whole person. Employees belong to many organizations other than their employer, and they play many roles outside the firm. If the whole person can be improved, then benefits will extend beyond the firm into the larger society in which each employee lives.

3. *Caused behaviour*: From psychology we learn that normal behaviour has certain causes. These may related to a person's needs and the consequences that result from acts. In the case of needs, people are motivated not by what we think they ought to have but by what they themselves want. To an outside observer a person's needs may be illusory or unrealistic, but they are still controlling. This fact leaves management with two basic ways to motivate people. It can show them how certain actions will increase their need fulfillment, or it can threaten decreased need fulfillment unless they follow a required course of action. Clearly a path toward increased need fulfillment is the better approach.

4. *Value of the person (human dignity)*: This concept is of a different order from the other three because it is more an ethical philosophy than a scientific conclusion. It confirms that people are to be treated differently from other factors of production because they are of a higher order, they want to be treated with respect and dignity—and should be treated this way. Every job, however simple, entitles the people who do it to proper respect and recognition of their unique aspirations and abilities. The concept of human dignity rejects the old idea of using employees as economic tools.

Ethical philosophy is reflected in the conscience of humankind confirmed by the experience of people in all ages. It recognizes each individual. Since organizational behaviour always involves people, ethical philosophy is involved in one way or another in each action. Human decisions cannot, and should not, be made apart from values.

Conceptual models for human behaviour

Since Behavioural Science is concerned with understanding and prediction human behaviour, philosophers, theologians, politicians, scientists, managers, and the person on the street have been and still are preoccupied with the idea of developing techniques to final what is the real nature of human being? Are people good or bad, rational or irrational, free or biased? A number of studies have been made in this area. However, the true nature of human behaviour is largely most unfounded and still open for discussion and research.

Scholar or lay person, everyone has had abundant experience in living and dealing with, reading about, and observing fellow human beings. A normal outgrowth of this lifetime of experience is that everyone has a definite opinion about human behaviour. Unfortunately, when common-sense approaches to human behaviour are put to the test of science, they are often proved wrong. Yet, it is through the applications of science that human behaviour can best be understood.

The behavioural scientist analyses human behaviour on the basis of scientific methodology. The major goal of behavioural science is to understand behaviour. On the other hand, philosophers, theologians, and managers are interested primarily in evaluating behaviour. The emphasis, on understanding versus evaluation is the major difference between the behavioural sciences and the other approaches used in analysing human behaviour. The objective of any science is to discover truth and develop understanding. Scientists always attempt to divorce their own value judgments from this quest. The following models take an understanding, not an evaluating approach to the overall nature of human behaviour. These models serve as important background information for developing a specific model for organizational behaviour.

Freudian psychoanalytic model

The Freudian approach relies on a psychoanalytic or conflict model of humans. At least in Western culture, the conception of people being in constant inner conflict is one of the oldest explanations. The conflict model portrayed primitive humans constant inner struggle between good and evil. Good (angels) and evil (devils) were believed to be competing for the domination of the body and soul. Common sayings, such as "He is possessed by the devil" or "She is a little angel", reflect this view. Under this model, individuals are merely innocent bystanders and the situation completely overwhelms them. This primitive view of conflict still exists in many parts of the world, even within subcultures of highly developed countries. Obviously, the primitive good-evil conflict model cannot be substantiated by scientific methodology. It is based on magic and the supernatural, which are outside the realm of science.

A more meaningful, comprehensive, and systematically based conflict model stems from the theories of Sigmund Freud. These theories can be summarized into that can be called the psychoanalytic model. Although Freud is most closely associated with the model, others, such as Carl Jung, Alfred Adler, Karen Horney, and Eric From, who all broke away from Freud, made additional contributions and extended the model.

Clinical techniques were used primarily to develop the psychoanalytic model. Through the clinical techniques of free association and psychotherapy, Freud noted that his patients' behaviour could not always be consciously explained. This clinical finding led him to conclude that the major motivating force in humans is unconscious in nature. The personality structure can be explained within the unconscious framework. Freud believed, by three interrelated, but often conflicting, psychoanalytic concepts: the id, the ego, and the superego.

(i) *The Id*: the id is the core of the unconscious. It is the unleashed, raw, primitive, instinctual drive of the freudion model. The id constantly struggling for gratification and pleasure is manifested mainly through the libido (sexual urges) or aggression. The libido strives for sexual relations and pleasure, but also for warmth, food, and comfort. Aggressive impulses of the id are destructive and include the urges to fight, dominate, and generally destroy. In a conflict sense, the id incorporates life instincts that compete with its death instincts. As individuals develop and mature, they learn no control the id. But even then it remains a driving force throughout life and an important source of thinking and behaving.

(ii) *The Ego*: Whereas the id represents the unconscious, the ego is the conscious. It is the logical part of the Freudian model and is associated with the reality principle. The ego keeps the id in check through the realities of the external environment. The ego is constituted so that it can interpret reality for the id through intellect and reason. Instrumental behaviour, such as dating or looking for food, is developed by the ego to satisfy the needs of the id. However, many conflict situations arise between the id and the ego because the id demands immediate pleasure while the ego dictates denial or postponement to a more appropriate time and place. In order to resolve the conflicts, the ego gets support from the superego.

(iii) *The Superego*: The superego is the third element of the Freudian model. It can best be depicted as the conscience. The superego provides the norms that enable the ego the determine what is right or wrong. The superego conscience should not be confused with the conscious aspects of the ego. In fact according to Freud, the superego is mostly unconscious.

The person is not aware of the workings of the superego. The conscience is developed by absorption of the cultural values and morals of a society. Accordingly, the parents have the most influence on the development of the superego. After resolving the Oedipus of Electra complex (love of parent), the child will unconsciously identify with the parents' values and morals.

The superego aids the person by assisting the ego to combat the impulses of the id. However, in some situations the superego can also be in conflict with the ego. An example is the situation where the reality-seeking ego violates the conscience. The conflict between ego and conscience provokes the wrath and vengeance of the largely unconscious superego. The inevitable struggle between the id, ego, and superego makes this to be called as a conflict model of behaviour.

The freudian model in perspective

Freud's model is characterized by the conflicting personality constructs (id, ego, and superego) and unconscious motivation. Psychological adjustment occurs only when the ego properly develops to resolve the conflicts stemming from the id and superego. The ego concept implies that humans are rational, but the id, the superego, and unconscious motivation give the impression that humans are very irrational. In the Freudian model, behaviour is based on emotion. If the ego cannot control the id, the person is an aggressive, pleasure-seeking menace to society. If the id is too severely checked by the ego, the person is equally maladjusted. Moreover, if the superego is very strong, the result may be acute anxiety and guilt.

Freud has had a great impact in many areas of twentieth-century thought. He had a great influence on treatment techniques for the mentally ill, and he did make some contribution to the understanding of human behaviour. His ideas have proved to be very far-reaching and long-lasting. Yet, today he is criticized as much as he is praised. Most of the criticism centres on the overemphasis given to sexual motivation.

From a behavioural science viewpoint, however, the most valid criticism of the Freudian model is that it is not based on empirically verifiable facts. The psychoanalytic elements are largely hypothetical constructs and not measurable, observable items for scientific analysis and verification. The id, ego, and superego are primarily a "black box" explanation of humans. This is why most modern behavioural scientists reject the psychoanalytic model as the total explanation of human personality and behaviour. Nevertheless, important insights into personality structure and the ideas of unconscious motivation are significant contributions and they serve as important tool for understanding specific behaviours of human being.

Existentialistic model

Existentialism, broadly defined as the search for meaning, is based on the analysis of existence and being. The existentialistic model is not a behavioural science model. Its roots lie more in the realm of philosophy and literature and are not scientifically based. Existentialism is European in origin and can be traced to the writings of the philosophers Kierkegaard, Nietzsche, and Schopenhauer. Among the philosophers with an existentialist orientation are Martin Heidegger, Martin Buber, and Jean-Paul Sartre. The best-known American spokesman had been Rollo May. May and Sartre, in particular, have been critical of the usual scientific approaches that are employed to gain an understanding of humans. They are afraid that a scientific behavioural analysis may destroy or lose sight of the person's true nature or "being".

Existentialists see a breakdown of traditional norms and the ties that individuals have traditionally with society. For example, Rollo May views people as suffering from unconstructive anxiety. He defines "unconstructive" or "neurotic" anxiety as the "Shrinking of consciousness, the blocking off of awareness; and when it is prolonged it leads to a felling of depersonalization and apathy" which is "the state, to a greater or lesser degree, of those who have lost, or never achieved, the experience of their own identity in the world." This feeling of "depersonalization and apathy" is what Durkheim referred to a asnomie.

In modern times the individual is faced with a very large, urbanised environment. The existentialist believe that the depersonalizing effects of this environment force individuals to determine their own destiny. People shape their own identity and make their "existence" meaningful and worthwhile to themselves. This process is accomplished through the individual's experience of being. Coleman views this being as "a matter of commitment to increased self-awareness and self-direction, to true communication with others, to concern with values and evaluation and to acceptance of the responsibility for making choices and directing his own destiny."

The emphasis attached to self-awareness and action in the existential scheme is different from that in the psychoanalytic model. Existentially, people seek self-awareness, direction, and control. What they make of this existence is entirely up to them. The existentialist approach maintains that people have free will to chart their existence and being.

The impact of the existential model

The existentialist approach becomes very relevant in a society suffering from environmental and moral decay. In world that is overpopulated, undernourished, polluted, ravaged by war and crime, with racial injustice and poverty rampant amidst affluence and material excess, it is extremely difficult for an individual to carve out a meaningful existence. The problem is compounded if the old, tradition-bound values of the past linger on as nommas for the present although they are irrelevant and incapable of practical application under current conditions or in the foreseeable future.

Certainly some aspects of the modern Indian scene seem directly relevant to an existentialist approach. Similarly, on a micro level, human behaviour in organizations seems appropriated for existentialist existence may be a severe challenge for an individual faced with the characteristics of the modern formal organization. Although not scientifically based and not conceptually integrated into this book, existentialism provides some very useful insights. It can be effectively used to set a tone and to supplement more scientifically based discussions of human behaviour.

Cognitive model

The psychoanalytic and existentialistic models are on the fringe of the study of human behaviour. Two more scientifically based models can also be used to explain human behaviour. Although other names are sometimes applied and there are many other distinct models contained within each, these two important models of human behaviour are the cognitive and the behaviouristic.

The cognitive model of human behaviour has many sources of input. The gestalt and phenomenological schools of thought in psychology provide a historical base for the cognitive approach. In general, the cognitive model came about as a reaction to the other models of human behaviour. In particular, pioneering Psychologists such as Edward Tolman became disenchanted with the psychoanalytic models. They felt that the Freudian conception placed too much emphasis on negative, irrational, and sexually motivated behaviour and that the behaviouristic model was too deterministic and mechanistic. The alternative that was proposed gave humans much more 'credit' than the other models. The cognitive model emphasizes the positive and free-will aspects of human being and utilizes concepts such as expectancy, demand, and incentive.

The work of Tolman, in particular, can best demonstrate the cognitive approach. He felt that behaviour is always purposive, it is directed toward a goal. In his laboratory experiments, he found that animals learned to expect that certain events will follow one another. For example, rates learned to behave as if they expected food when a certain cue appeared. Thus, to Tolman learning consisted of the expectancy that particular event will lead to a particular consequence. This expectancy concept, of course, implies mentalistic phenomena. In other words, the cognitive explanation implies that the organism is thinking about or is conscious or aware of the goal. Behaviour is base on these cognitions.

Contemporary psychologists, such as Robert Bolles, carefully point out that a cognitive concept such as expectancy "does not reflect a guess about what is going on in the animal's mind: it is a term that describes the animal's behaviour." For example, even though Tolman use concepts such as expectancy, he considered himself a behaviouristic models are not as opposite as they appear on the surface and sometimes are made out to be. Yet despite some conceptual similarities, there has been a controversy through the years in the behavioural sciences on the relative contributions of the cognitive versus the behaviouristic model. Although the sequence is revised (only recently have behaviouristic models been proposed in organizational behaviour because of the dissatisfaction with the cognitive approach) the controversy has carried over into the field of organizational behaviour. Before discussing the input that the cognitive model can make to organizational behaviour, it is necessary to understand fully the behaviouristic model.

Behaviouristic model

Its roots can be traced to the work of Pavlov and Watson. These pioneering behaviourists stressed the importance of dealing with observable behaviours instead of the elusive mind that had preoccupied the earlier structuralists and functionalists. They used classical conditioning experiments to formulate the stimulus-response (S.R) explanation of human behaviour. Both Pavlov and Watson felt that behaviour could be best understood in terms of S-R. A stimulus elicits a response. They concentrated mainly on the impact of the stimulus and felt that learning occurred when the S-R connection was made.

Modern behaviourism marks its beginning with the work of B.F. Skinner. Skinner is generally recognized as the most influential living psychologist. He felt that the early behaviourists helped to explain respondent behaviours but not the more complex operant behaviours. In other words, the S-R approach helped to explain physical reflexes [e.g., when stuck by a pin (S), the person will flinch (R); or when tapped below the kneecap (S), the person will extend the lower leg (R)] and certain emotional reactions [e.g., a loud noise (S) will lead the person to cry out (R). On the other hand, Skinner found through his operant conditioning experiments that the consequences of a response could better explain most behaviours than could eliciting stimuli. He emphasized the importance of the R-S relationship. The organism has to operate on the environment in order to receive the desirable consequence. The preceding stimulus does not cause the behaviour. For Skiner, behaviour is a function of its consequences.

However, it is important to understand that the behaviouristic model is environmentally based. It implies that cognitive processes such as thinking, expectancies, and perception do not play a role in behaviour. However, as in the case of the cognitive having behaviouristic concepts, some psychologists feel that there is room for cognitive variables in the behaviouristic model. Nevertheless, as the cognitive model had been accused of being mentalistic, the behaviouristic model has been accused of being deterministic. Cognitive theists argue that the S-R model, and to a lesser degree the R-S model, are much too mechanistic an explanation of human behaviour. A strict S-R interpretation of behaviour seems justifiably open to the criticism of being too mechanistic, but because of the scientific approach that has been meticulously employed by behaviourists, the operant model in particular has made a tremendous contribution to the study of human behaviour.

An eclectic model for organizational behaviour

Organizational behaviour has the advantage of being a relatively young and growing field of study. It can legitimately borrow, in an eclectic manner, the best from the various established models of human behaviour. At one point in its early development, the field of organizational behaviour have taken a humanistic, cognitive approach. For example, Douglas McGregor and Rensis Likert depended mainly on a cognitive approach in their writings on organizational behaviour. In the last couple of years, the behaviouristic model had begun to be utilized in the theorizing and research on organizational behaviour. In many ways, what the field of organizational behaviour has been going through in recent years is a replay of the behaviouristic-versus-cognitive controversy that has been and, in many respects, still is going on in psychology. Now, in organizational behaviour, the time seems to have come to recognize the contributions of both models and to begin to synthesize and integrate both approaches into a meaningful model of organizational behaviour.

The goals of the organizational behaviour model

As stated earlier, the goal of the models presented so far is to better understand, not evaluate, the complex phenomena called human behaviour. Understanding human behaviour in organizations is also a vital goal for a model of organizational behaviour. In addition, however, because organizational behaviour is more of an applied field than is psychology, other desirable goals besides understanding are prediction and control. The study of organizational behaviour serves as the basis for modern human resource management. Predicting and controlling human resources are critical to the goals of moderns management. Thus, the goals of a model of organizational behaviour are to understand, predict, and control human behaviour in organisations.

The cognitive approach seems essential to the understanding of organizational behaviour. The behaviouristic approach can also lead to understanding, but perhaps even more important is the contribution it can make to prediction and control. On the basis of Edward Thorndike's classic law of effect, the behaviouristic model would say that organizational behaviour followed by a positive or reinforcing consequence will be strengthened and increased in subsequent frequency, and organizational behaviour followed by an unpleasant or punishing consequence will be weakened and decrease in subsequent frequency. In any event, if the threefold goals of understanding, prediction, and control are to be met by a model of organizational behaviour, both the cognitive and the internal causal factors which are cognitively oriented and the external environmental factors which are behaviouristically oriented are important to the understanding, prediction, and control of organizational behaviour.

The S-O-B-C model

An S-O-B-C model can be formulated to incorporate both cognitive and behaviouristic approaches. The S-O-S portion is largely an extension of the widely recognized S-O-R model of psychology. The addition of the consequence (C) is given recognition by the industrial psychologist Norman Mailer in his S-O-B-A model. The S-O-R model incorporated both cognitive and behaviouristic thinking. The human organism (O) plays an active mediating or interventing role between stimulus and response. The O is inserted into the classic behaviouristic S-R model, thus producing the S-O-R version. This O is viewed as a mediating, maintenance, and adjustment function between stimulus (S) and response (R). Floyd Ruch states that the O is "constantly active, scanning its own actions, seeking certain conditions and avoiding other".

As a maintenance function, the organs of the O are responsible for its health and growth. The three primary categories of maintenance organs are the receptors, connectors and effectors. Behaviour is mediated by neutral activity. The nervous system serves as connectors for the receptors of stimuli (sense organize) and the effectors of behaviour (muscles and glands). Significant breakthroughs have already occurred, and many scholar students of behaviour feel that the key area for future understanding of behaviour lies in this mediation monitors people's activities in the environment so that they can overcome obstacles and thus satisfy their needs.

The variables in the model

An underlying theme throughout the various models of human behaviour is the relative importance of heredity versus environment. Although different terns are sometimes used and there are differing degrees of emphasis, the psychoanalytic, existentialistic, cognitive, and behaviouristic models have all entered the controversy. Almost all psychologists agree that both heredity and environment play a role in behaviour, but a disagreement revolves around the comparative importance of each. In reality, the argument is self-defeating. It is impossible to separate heredity completely from environment for scientific analysis.

Human behaviour is more a function of the psychological process than of the physiological ones. Form the moment of birth, learning, perception, and motivation are an integral part of the person. Naturally, these processes do not operate as isolated, separate entities any more than do the physiological mechanisms of the body. The human being functions as a whole, not as series of parts. The psychological processes, taken as a whole, are included in the concept of personality. The latter concept plays a very major role in understanding behaviour.

The recognition of the psychological process and personality as essential parts of the human being marks a major departure from a strict hereditary or physiological interpretation. For the purpose of developing a model of organizational behaviour, the person is considered to be made up of the both the physiological and psychological processes. Both are important variables of human behaviour, although the psychological variables are considered here to have relative much more influence on organizational behaviour.

The environment variable: The environment is the other variable mentioned in the Lewin's equation for behaviour. In the most basic and narrow sense, the environment consists of a stimulus. Common stimuli include lights, sounds, odors, pinpricks, and persons. In a strict S-R behaviouristic interpretation, such stimulu (S) play the crucial role in eliciting behaviour. Stimuli guides humans into action, interrupt what they are doing, and direct their choices. In this classical behaviouristic view, the immediate stimulus in the primary causal factor in behaviour. In the more modern operant view, the stimulus serves as the antecedent cue which emits (not causes) the behaviour. However, it must also be remembered that the contingent consequence is also a stimulus (R-S), and in the operant approach behaviour is a function of its consequences.

The immediate stimulus is a basic element in the S-O-B-C model, but it is not equated with the total environment. The more comprehensive environment is represented in the S-O-B-C model in the S and the C. The S includes the immediate stimulus but also the broader physical, sociocultural, and technological environment. The C in the model is also an environmental variable. As in the operant behaviouristic model, the person must operate on the environment in order to obtain certain consequence. This is the contingent-consequence emphasis from modern behaviourism, but the C also includes broader-based dynamics (e.g., conflict) and applications (e.g., appraisal) as part of the environmental consequences of organizational behaviour.

The behaviour variable: Perhaps the best way to describe the behaviour variable is to state what it is and what it is not. Behaviour is anything that the human does: it is not something that is done to the person. The nature of behaviour can be clarified by analyzing two sets of examples of behaviour. In the first set are five possible behaviours of an assembly-line worker in a widget factory:

1. The worker started the machine.
2. The worker produced many widegets.
3. The worker did not produce many widgets.
4. The worker came to work late.
5. The worker came to work on time.

In these five instances the worker did something. Thus, according to the simple definition, the examples are forms of behaviour. However, before jumping to this conclusion, a refinement is necessary. Each of the five examples implies and outcome to the worker's behaviour rather than the actual overt (outward) or covert (inward) behaviour. In understanding the behavioural variable, it is extremely important to separate the actual behavioural events form the outcomes of these events. The same five examples can be translated into more precise behavioural events in the following manner:

1. The worker pushed the button.
2. The worker moved his or her arms and hands very fast.
3. The worker moved his or her arms and hands very slowly.
4. The worker walked very slowly from the parking lot.
5. The worker walked very fast from the parking lot.

This second set of examples describes the specific, overt behaviour, not outcomes of the behaviour.

Specific behavioural events and the patterns of these specific behaviours are what are included in the S-O-B-C model. There may be many reasons for the outcomes of behaviour. In the first set of examples, there are a number of possible reasons why the machine started, why productivity was high or low and why the worker did or did get to work on time?

Because of these many possibilities, plus the chance factor, it is extremely difficult to make an analysis of the outcomes of behaviour. On the other hand, specific, observable behavioural events and their patterns provide useful data in order to analyze the S-O interaction which precedes the behaviour and the consequences that follow the behaviour. Such an analysis of the S-O antecedent and the consequences is crucial to the understanding, prediction, and control of the behaviour.

The interactive connections and feedback loops: First the interactive connection between S and O. This interactive process must occur between the situation and the person before behaviour results. Merely placing the S and O together is not enough. The interaction usually takes the form of the O's cognitive interpretation of the immediate S. This type of interaction can be thought of as the process of perception. However, this is only one simple form of interaction. In the S-O-B-C model the perceptual process is part of the O, along with the other psychological processes of learning and motivation. When the influence of the physiological being and personality and the greatly expanded conception of S are added, the complexity of the interaction between the S and O becomes clear. Yet, in abstract, simplistic terms, the S-O can be thought of as the antecedent of behaviour in the S-R interaction should not be thought of as causing the behaviour in the S-R sense. Instead, S-O should be thought of as preceding the behaviour, with the S serving as an emitting cue for the behaviour, the O as the mediating physiological and cognitive processes, and the—as the complex interactive effect between the S and O that leads to (not causes) the behaviour.

The second important connection in the S-O-B-C model is the B-C relationship. This is an outgrowth of the R-S relationship of the operant model in behaviouristic psychology. One key to the connection between behaviour and its consequence is the contingency concept. A contingent relationship, is an "if-then" relationship. As used here, this simply means that the person's behaviour is affected by its contingent consequences. If the person behaves in a certain way, then a particular consequence will follow. Such contingent consequences can be used to predict and control behaviour.

The feedback loops from the consequence to the person and the situation are also important to the model. These feedback loops, shown as the dashed lines show that the consequences affect the person's cognitions and the situational cues. In the simplest sense, these feedback loops can be thought of as learning. Based on the consequences of behaviour, the person's (O) perceptions and motives will be affected and situational cues (S) will become associated with or even change on the basis of certain consequences. However, just as the interaction between S and O involves more than perception, the feedback loops from C to O and S involve more than learning. Furthermore, just as perception is placed in the O portion of the model, so is learning. The S-O-B-C model is much more comprehensive than and not as rigorous as the behaviouristic and cognitive models upon which it is based.

A conceptual framework for the study of organizational behaviour

The S-O-B-C model can serve as the conceptual framework for the study of organizational behaviour. The model attempts to synthesize the cognitive and behaviouristic explanations of human behaviour. In a very simplified summary, the S-O represents the causal, mainly cognitive factors in behaviour, and the B-C represents the modern behaviouristic emphasis on the role that consequences play in behaviour. The addition of the S in the antecedent to the behaviour and the feedback loops from the C to the O and the S represent the attempt to integrate both cognitive and behaviouristic variables. The S-O portion of the model primarily contributes to the goal of understanding organizational behaviour, and the B-C primarily contributes to the goals of prediction and control of organizational behaviour.

Obviously, the S-O-B-C model briefly summarized above is only a "barebones" sketch of the complexities of human behaviour. The purpose of the model, as with any model, is to identify the important variables and show how they relate to one another. particularly with the field of organizational behaviour, which is still developing and searching for a theoretical base, such a model is extremely important for structuring study and further development.

The formal organization

The formal organization, of course, is the most important situational environment for the study of organizational behaviour. Viewing the organization as a system, there are three subsystems that are especially important to the study of organizational behaviour. The first, the structure, serves as the skeleton for the formal organizational system. Structure allows the other subsystems, management processes and technology to operate. The bureaucratic model best represents the classical organization structure. Extensions and modifications of the bureaucratic model, such as centralization-decentralization, horizontal-vertical, departmentation, and line-staff, also have an important role in classical organization structures.

Interacting and interdependent with the organization structure are the management processes. e.g. organizing, commanding, coordinating, and controlling, on the other hand the dynamic process are more pertinent and meaningful, which includes decision making, communication, and control. Although presented as part of the external environment, technology is also a vital subsystem of the formal organizational system. Used in this organizational context, "technology" means the internal technological environment that is used to attain the objectives of an organization. It includes productive operations, technologies such as mechanization and cybernation and, of course, computers. The technological subsystem affects and is affected by the organization structure and management processes.

Organizational participants

Organizational participants or employees are plugged into the O portion of the model. Analogous to the formal organization, these participants can be conceptualized as a system, consisting of three primary subsystems: physiological structure, psychological process, and personality. For discussion purposes, these subsystems can be made analogous to the three subsystems of the formal organization. For instance, the physiological structure related to and serves the human as the structure related to and serves the formal organization. The physiological structure consists of basic units of heredity and includes the nervous system, sense organs, muscles, and glands.

Analogous to the management processes of the formal organization are the participant's psychological process of perception, learning, and motivation. These processes are at the very heart of the study of organizational behaviour. They are probably more viral than any other single part of the overall framework to the understanding of organizational behaviour. However, just as separating the processes from there formal organization is largely artificial, so is abstracting the psychological processes from the total human being. Organizational participants behave as a whole, not as a collection of separate parts or processes. When the individual is viewed as this whole, the study of behaviour becomes involved with personality. Personality is to the organizational participant as technology is to the formal organization. Both personality and technology pervade their respective entities and are vitally responsible for the outputs. The study of the development and structure of personality is therefore very important to the understanding of organizational behaviour.

Just as the systems concept was shown to be relevant to the formal organization, the same concept seems applicable in relating the parts of the human being. The biological-physiological structure, psychological processes, and personality are related to one another and, analogously, to the formal organization subsystems in the manner. The primary base for the organizational participant (formal organization) is the personality (technology). Interaction with and supporting the personality (technology) are the physiological structure (organization structure) and the psychological processes (management processes). It must be realized that the triangular model represents only a very highly simplified abstraction, but it does serve as a starting point for the elementary understanding of the very complex organizational and human variables that make an input into understanding organizational behaviour.

Organizational consequences

The study of the formal organization and the organizational participant lead to the better understanding of organizational behaviour. The study of the organizational consequences, on the other hand, can help better predict and control organizational behaviour. Again the reader should be reminded that this is a highly simplified generalization. Cognitive theorists are beginning to provide ways to predict and control behaviour, and behaviouristically oriented theorists are certainly contributing on the better understanding of behaviour. Nevertheless, the emphasis in the S-O is for understanding and in the B-C is for prediction and control.

Certain dynamics and human resource management applications are especially relevant environmental consequences. The dynamics of groups, informal organization, conflict, change, job satisfaction, leadership, and power are particularly important consequences in the study of organizational behaviour. The application of managerial techniques in the areas of selection, job design, appraisal, applied behavioural analysis, and organization development can be fed back and change the formal organizational situation and, through learning, the organizational participant. In other words, these managerial applications can lead to the goals of prediction and control of organizational behaviour.

Behavioural sciences for management

The assessment of the relevance of the behavioural sciences to management confronts us with an immediate paradox. Organisations are composed of people producing things for other people; hence, any science of people would appear to be totally relevant to what happens in organisations. Yet the behavioural sciences are relatively little utilised by managers if one considers that full potential of their applicability. If the behavioural sciences are so relevant to managerial problems, why are they not more fully utilised? The answer is complex and multifaceted.

First of all, every manager by virtue of his own experience as a person, believes himself to be something of an expert and authority on people. He would be the first to acknowledge that the managerial job involves all kinds of people problems, but he might also argue that he known from his own experience how to deal with most of those problems. For the manager to accept the input of the behavioural scientist requires some admission that he is not as expert in handling people problems as he might like to believe.

Second, the behavioural sciences have accumulated a body of knowledge but have done a poor job of communicating this knowledge. They have played the science game, which involves the erroneous assumption that once some findings are published in a technical journal, it is someone else's responsibility to figure out how to use the knowledge. Until recently, behavioural scientists have not been willing to take their knowledge and know-how out into the organisational world, translate what they know into language that the manager can understand, and help the manager to utilise the knowledge in solving managerial problems. Third, behavioural scientists have tended to study problems that they thought were important, rather than those that managers who had to deal with people problems thought were important. To a considerable extent this approach was a necessary and legitimate one in developing the field. behavioural scientists had to work within the context of theories and methods they could handle. Managerial problems often were too difficult and complex to encompass, and so were not studied. Managers rightly complained that much of the knowledge accumulated was trivial and irrelevant, or at least, they could not see the relevance, the behavioural scientist was too busy with his next piece of research to show the manager where the relevance lay.

Fourth, in those cases in which behavioural scientists have been called in to help with organisational and managerial problems, it has been very difficult to evaluate the results of their efforts. Just as it has been difficult to a control group, so it has been difficult to determine whether the efforts of psychologists to improve the quality of managerial decisions were actually paying off. The person being helped might feel the help was well worth it, solid evidence. In fact, he could make the valid argument that if a manager had committed himself to using some new approach, he was usually psychologically biased toward seeing good results, since it was his own decision edge against hard criteria, but as yet we have not solved the problem of how to carry out good evaluation research in a setting in which it is not possible to control all the other factors affecting the situation.

In what areas are the behavioural sciences relevant to management? The answer is—in all areas—but this answer is not very helpful without some categorisation of what these areas are. We can conceive of the manager's job as being concerned with the processing of three kinds of basic resources 1. Money or financial resources; 2. People or human resources 3. Information of various kinds. The managerial job is to utilise information, money and people in the service of some task or goal. Most of the decisions that the manager makes involve putting together the right mix of human, financial, and information resources to transform some kinds of raw material into useful products and/or services. The behavioural sciences have a potential relevance to the utilisation of all three of these resource areas, although traditionally they have been linked only with the utilisation of human resources.

It was with the Hawthorne studies of the 1920, when industrial sociologists first began a serious inquiry into the nature of work and worker relations, that the individualistic, economic man assumptions began to be seriously challenged. The sociologists moved into the plant and used observational techniques to gather their data. They discovered among other things that workers tended to from close ties to other workers and these group relations influenced the work in important waves. For example, the production workers in the Hawthorne plant of the Western Electric Co. formed their informal groupings first around the geographical layout of the room. Once the group had been formed developed various home same of which were in direct violation of company procedures. Different classes of workers were forbidden to trade jobs because industrial engineering had designed the jobs to match the skills of the particular worker's yet the men routinely traded jobs to reduce their monotony and were clearly able to do one another's work. The company paid on the basis of a regular output of units from the group and the records showed a "straight-line output" of so units per day, the observer noted that the workers would overproduce on one day and store part of their output and add it to their work on another day when for one or another reason they underproduced. The supervisor of the group was required to report irregularities and enforce company policy; the workers had a norm that any supervisor who was "officious" was not part of the gang and found ways to make his life so unpleasant that the officious ones left until someone who would let the workers do it their own way ended up with the group.

Worker output was assumed by the company to reflect individual ability and the pay structure: the observer noted that the group had a norm of "a fair day's work for a fair day's pay" and that individual worker output related more closely to group membership than individual ability. That is, there were two sub-groups in the total group one of which saw itself as highest status than the other: All of its members produced at or near the norm. The other sub-group in reaction to their lower status deliberately underproduced in order to get back at the others. Those workers who were markedly overproductive or underproductive relative to the norm, turned out to be social isolates to belong to neither group.

The company had an inspector in each group to control quality. If the inspector challenged any of the group's sabotage norms or threatened to report its activities, the group found ways to sabotage the equipment in such a way that it would pass inspection but break down later, thus forcing the inspector to cooperate. All this was going on in a group that was performing quite adequately by management standards. Productivity was reasonably good, there was excellent morale partly because the group felt it was allowed to do things its own way and quality reached acceptable standards. But clearly, any resemblance between the economic man model of the early industrial psychologist and these workers was purely coincidental.

Subsequent studies of worker behavior in industrial repeatedly confirmed the finding of the Hawthorne studies and let to a different set of assumptions about "human nature" and lunched the human relations approach to managing people. Both psychologists and sociologists began to attack the dehumanizing aspects of bureaucratic forms of organization and the scientific management approach. There was a flurry of programs to teach foremen how to understand their people better how to accept groups among workers and to facilitate informal organization rather than trying to break up as the assembly line had done in many instances how to involve workers in decision making on those aspects of their job that were under their control how to be their subordinate's friend and champion rather than merely his boss.

With the aid the behavioural scientific the pendulum swung completely from a very depersonalized view of man to an overpersonalized one industrial psychologists developed concepts that focused on concern for people rather than the job production and it was assumed that it such concern strengthened people's morale, it surely would pay off in greater productivity. Some companies set up counseling programs that would allow workers to air frustrations to a supportive neutral person in an effort to humanize the industrial environment even more.

This "human relations movement," which held sway in the 1930s and 1940s has left a strong residue of important concepts research findings and values about the role of the individual in the large organizations. Much of its philosophy and value system was embodied in the writings of Likert, Mcgregor, Argyris, and others, who saw the need for a theory that put some faith in human capacities and potentials. Mcgregor put it most clearly in his Classic The Human Side of Enterprise, published in book from in 1960 although the given manager could build his approach on one of two basic sets of assumptions: theory X, an Essentially cynical negative view of man, and theory Y, an essentially idealistic positive view of man.

According to theory X, man is lazy, self-seeking can only be motivated by economic incentives and must be controlled by management because he would not voluntarily work toward organizational goals. According to the theory Y, man is capable of self direction and self-control will integrate his efforts with those of the organizations if his inner needs for a sense of meaning and worth in his job are met, and if his basic needs for physical and economic security are satisfied. McGregor's key argument was that if a manager held a theory X set of assumptions he would tend to develop a managerial style not unlike that of the scientific management school, involving a tightly structured job situation and controls and that it if he managed subordinates in this manner they would learn to behave according to the theory X assumptions. That is they would feel that the manager had a cynical view of them and would therefore respond with an anti-management attitude. For many workers such an attitude would be supported by their union and by their previous history or the attitudes of their parents who might have been involved for several generations in labour-management disputes. In other words Mcgregor acknowledged that much of worker behavior fitted theory X assumptions, but that such behavior was learned behavior not inherent "human nature." If one looked at the accumulated research findings of the behavioural scientists, one would find that human nature is much more consistent with theory Y, and one could find evidence of this point in studies attempted to involve workers more and found very positive responses to such attempts.

One of the real weaknesses of the human relations approach was its tendency to forget the task that people were working on and the organization structure and technology that related to this task, Sociologists like George Homans, William Whyte, and Conrad Arensberg in this country, and Eric Trist and Kenneth Rice England began series of studies that led to the concept of "socio-technical systems." A concept that tries to acknowledge explicitly that the nature performing that task are integrally related. In other words, human relations occur within an environment that is itself determined by technology culture, organization structure and specific work settings. Even in the Hawthorne studies it was evident that the groups that emerged reflected the layout of the room and the nature of the jobs. Eric Trist's work on the conversion from short-wall to longwall coal mining methods facilitated by the invention of long-wall mining machinery is a landmark comparable to the Hawthorne studies.

Trist showed that the technology of short wall mining required a vertically integrated effect among the men who cut, loaded, and carried the coal away in tubs.

These groups developed very close relations which carried over into their life of the job and met important needs, such as reducing the anxiety of working underground. The long-wall method involved a larger group of men under a supervisor working on a machine that did most of the cutting. The men were spread out, which made social contact difficult and thus undermined the close relations that the short-wall method had fostered. It was then discovered that the men did not like the description of those close relationships and that the greater tension of working in the mine could not be worked through as well in the larger groups as it had been in the smaller ones. The work lost much of its meaning and the miners became less committed, which showed up in lower productivity, greater carelessness, and less maintenance of the equipment. Thus, the new technology did not in fact produce more coal because of the description of the social structure of the workers. Only when this factor had been recognized and a new kind of training program set up to deal with the social factors could the technology began confirmed these kinds of findings in a variety of settings and emphasized the need to think both about task (technology) and human factors. Consideration of either one alone failed to solve the productivity problem, and also failed to solve the morale problem.

Just as economic man as a model of the individual person in the organization proved to be an oversimplification, so social man also proved to be an oversimplification. Increasingly the emphasis of the behavioral scientist shifted to the nature of the work itself, and the degree to which there was potential in the work for the fulfillment of man's basic need to use his skills, abilities, and talents. Man's also needs for contact with other workers was only part of the story; man also needed work that was inherently meaningful and contributory.

Many of the studies that had argued for participation on the part of workers could be interpreted to mean that participation did not so much fulfill the worker's social need as it fulfilled his needs to be meaningful involved in his work's. Workers in highly automated industries could still be meaningfully involved if they had a high degree of responsibility, such as the operator in an automated oil refinery; but if the worker was on an assembly line attaching one small part to a complex product all day long he would gradually lose his sense of involvement and began to feel that if work was that meaningfulness, he might at least seek more economic rewards and get meaning in off-the-job leisure time activities.

The human relations movement now shifted to a concern for job enrichment job enlargement and more worker involvement in planning the work. Human relations still a popular activity but the content of the programs has shifted away from training managers simply what the task and human requirements are in the socio-technical systems of their organization and how to change not only their management style but also the organization structure, the reward system and the culture of the organization toward more effective total utilization of human resources. This more broad approach has led to what is currently called organization development.

Group and Intergroup Problems. A technology has became more complex, organizations have found themselves having to divide the labour among more and more different specialists. In a simple technology, the hierarchy of authority could adequately handle the integration problem i.e., the manager one or two levels up could collect information from production, engineering, and marketing and make reasonably good product and/or marketing decisions. However, as technology became more complex the manager could not comprehend all the issues and could not process all the information needed to make a decision. To some extent the resulting greater information processing need has been dealt with by more effective computer-supported information and control systems. But the problem of how to make a good decision involving technical specialties which the manager could not himself totally comprehend could not be solved by this means. Increasingly; therefore, organizations have had to rely on decision mechanisms that involved brining together the representatives of several specialities and conducting group meetings to acquire all the information and coverall the issues. The manager of the group might then choose one of a number of decision-making style-just listening and then deciding making tentative decisions for the group to react to; giving alternatives among which the group might choose or giving the group complete decision-making power-but in one way or another he had to use a group in support of the decision process.

For the manager who was brought up in the traditional management approach the use of meetings and groups was often award and uncomfortable. If the group did not work well, the manager often blamed the group decision method failing to recognize that it was his approach to the group that might have caused the problem. The behavioural scientists, particularly those who were expect in group dynamics, found themselves developing methods that would aid managers to learn how to be effective members and leaders of groups, and how to make group decision process more effective. The great popularity of T-group throughout the 1950s and 1960s resulted in part from the need of managers in organization to learn more about groups and how to work in them. Whereas earlier studies of groups among workers treated them as part of the informal system to be tolerated because it met interpersonal needs of workers, the emphasis now shifted to groups as formal organizational mechanisms for solving problems and making decisions. The group a management tool rather than a worker phenomenon, and behavioral scientists more of their attention on the role of management groups in increasing organization effectiveness. This trend has continued unabated and will continue as organizations become more and more complex.

With the recognition of groups as essential elements of organization structure has come the additional recognition that groups within organizations could either work in support of one another or actually get in one another's way, it has always been recognized that problems arise in the flow of work from engineering to production to sales and back to engineering via new marketing information. Each functional grouping tends to develop a particular approach to problems based on the background of the people in it and the kind of environment in which they work. If the reward system of the total organization is such that each function does its best as it sees it there are strong pressures set up for grouping in the organization to complete with one another. If they compete there are then strong tendencies set up to hide information to try to blame errors on other groups (throw the dead cat in the neighbour's yard), and to fail to perceive how a decision that is good within a given function might that can't be built, production subverts quality requirements or elegant products order to get out large numbers within the schedule and at the cost production blames sales for making unrealistic commitments to customers on delivery times or special alternation and so on.

As the competition among functional groups has become recognized management has invented compensatory devices such as integrating departments like production engineering, or product terms, which embrace representatives from all the functions under a product manager. At a higher level of integration, organizations have invented project management or divisionalisation to integrate whatever specialities are needed, even if that meant breaking up the functional departments. In each of these cases new groups are created that must learn to work together effectively, often requiring the aid of behavioral scientists in training the members of the group as a whole.

Where such new grouping are not possible or where new levels of competition arise that the total organization considers destructive behavioural scientists have adapted conflict resolution methods to the study and amelioration of inter-group conflicts. Special kinds of workshops meeting or training activities have been developed to help groups that have problems with one another or explore those problems historically to set new and integrative goals and to develop methods for achieving more collaboration in achieving the goals. Such methods have also been applied in reducing headquarters/field problems, in facilitating mergers and in introducing new management terms into organizations.

Organization structure and design problems. the traditional role of the behavioral scientists working in organizations was to work on individual or group problems that were identified by higher levels of management. Often the behavioral scientist helped to identify such problems by working with these higher levels but only rarely did he get involved in top level corporate issues and problems of organizational strategy and tactics. The main reason, suspect is that he had relatively little to contribute to this area up until the last ten or twenty years when his theories and research methods developed to the point where they could encompass organizations as total systems and began to help the top manager to think through total organizational problems. If the organization had problems about how to set goals how to structure itself or how to adapt to changing environmental conditions, it typically turned to planners or management consultants who might or might not have been exposed to any psychology sociology, or anthropology. As the business schools introduced more of the behavioral sciences more research was done on organizational problems, and more links were developed with top management.

Much of the theorizing about organization structure and design has come from the studies of socio-technical systems already referred to. A number of empirical studies were done of effective and ineffective companies in different kinds of industries, and it was found that effective structure varied as a function of the type of task and type of environment in which the company existed. Highly stable and predictable tasks in fairly stable environment were most effectively dealt with by companies that had tightly structured formal hierarchies-i.e., that were coordinated from power centers at the very top of the organization; complex tasks in fairly turbulent or less predictable environments were most effectively handled by companies that had fairly decentralized structures with a high degree of diffusion of decision-making power and a greater use of lateral coordinating structures such as project teams or integrated divisions rather than functionally organized departments. The significance of these studies has been that an area that had traditionally been considered to be far too complicated to be studied empirically and had been relegated to men of wisdom and experience, has increasingly come to be clarified by theories and researchers.

The essence of most of the theories is that one must view the organization as total system in interaction with its environment, and must apply criteria of effectiveness that apply to systems as whole i.e., the ability to survive and grow in the face of environmental change through better sensing of what change occurs better ingestion and digestion of relevant information, better ability to make internal changes to adapt to new information, and better ability to obtain valid feedback on changes made. Profits return on investment turnover etc., are all still critical measures of performance, but they are increasingly to be viewed only as symptoms of organizational health that must be supplemented by other basic criteria. Behavioral scientists have not only developed theoretical and research tools for studying organizational structure and design but have also developed methods for improving organizational performance by helping organizations intervene effectively in their human and informational processes. This area has come to be known as organization development and will be discussed next.

Problems of Organization Improvement Through Organization Development. The field of organization development (O.D) is recent and as yet not well defined it is distinguished by the fact that is heavily based on behavioral science concepts and methods heavily committed to viewing the organization as total system and heavily committed to improving the long range effectiveness of organizations through constructive interventions in organizational processes and structures. There are some variations in the approaches of different O.D. practitioners; hence a particular methodology that is associated with the field cannot as yet be defined. But scme of the different methods that have been developed and that are used in varying combinations depending on the kind of organizational problems that are being worked on and the style of the consultant can be outlined. Incidentally most organization development work is being carried out by consultants who function from inside the organization (they may be members of a corporate staff group or a separate O.D. department) and/or who are brought in from outside the organization directly by line management or by the internal consultant. Usually the inside and outside man will from a team to carry out the project.

The essential elements underlying any organization development effort are that it be long-range in its orientation that it involve efforts to improve the overall effectiveness of the total organization, that it concern itself with the total system not only part of it, even through a given activity may occur in only one part of the organization, and that the diagnostic and intervention steps be shared by both the line managers and the consultants. In other words, one cannot come in as an outsider and do organization development work, but one can help line managers improve their organization by working closely with them in helping them to diagnose their problems and helping them to invent appropriate interventions or changes.

Most of the actual activities of organization development projects derive from what Kurt Lewin called "action research." The basic idea is that one cannot study a system like an organization without a changing it by the very act of studying it, but that this should not be seen as a disadvantage so much as an opportunity. In other words, one can learn the most about an organization in the process of trying to change it. Interventions to produce change and diagnosis of what changes are needed are thus completely inter-twined with each other even though most O.D practitioners talk as if diagnosis preceded intervention. With this background comment we can look at some of the specific techniques used:

1. *Survey feedback methods*—Some portion of the organization is interviewed and/or given questionnaires dealing with various aspects of organizational process morale, the reward system, management style, etc., and the data are fed back to one level at a time in a series of meetings that involve (a) an analysis of the results and (b) planning of remedial measures by every level of the organization. It is this last step that differentiates the use of these methods in O.D. program from the more traditional attitude surveys carried on in industry.
2. *Team building and team training methods*—most of these methods are coordinated with individual management development activities and are distinguished by the fact that the group being trained is selected on the basis that they will have to work together in the organization. Thus, it one highly relevant to give team training to the members and leader of that teams as an aid to making it effective. One version of such methods that has achieved considered prominence is the use of the "managerial grid" in team training programs.

3. *Job enrichment and job enlargement*—a number of O.D. practitioners are putting their primary focus on training programs that facilitate redesigning the work itself toward jobs that are more interesting and involving to the people in the organization. Where such work would traditionally have been done by industrial engineers aiming at work simplification these programs put more emphasis on involving the organization as a whole in redesigning its own work.
4. *Sensitivity training*—the use of T-groups encounter groups and sensitivity groups antedates organization development by ten to fifteen years. The real growth of such groups was supported by their key role in individual management development programs although the use of the method in a number of companies in combination with team training produced major impacts on the organization as whole. Such groups are often used as part of an overall effort and are combined with other techniques mentioned above but they are by themselves rarely sufficient to produce major organizational change. They have their biggest impact in unfreezing some of the attitudes of managers and making them more amenable to other kinds of interventions.
5. *Process consultation*—this concept cuts across many of the others in that it is more of an approach to how to work with the organization in what ever specific methods one uses. The basic idea is that the consultant should not really function as an expert on what the organization is trying to do but should help the organization to improve whatever human and informational processes it is using in accomplishing its goals. If the goals or decision processes are themselves not focusing on how they are working together. The consultant's expertness lies in his ability to help the organization to help itself.

There are many other specific kinds of techniques that have acquired labels and become part of the kit-bag of the organization development consultant but most of them are closely related to one of the five categories just outlined. It should be said in concluding this section that although the behavioral scientist functioning as an inside or outside consultant plays a key role in facilitating organization development, it must be the line managers who take the initiative and manage the project if real organization improvement is to result.

Utilization of Financial Resources

Budgeting Most managers are involved as part of their job in developing budgets and administering those budgets a system of financial controls. The budgets are typically built on the basis of information that is supplied by subordinates and checked by the manager. Once the budget is made the manager is typically involved in selling that budget to a higher level in the organization. Both the building and selling of the budget involves multiple integration among many people, creating multiple opportunities for psychological distortions misinformation overselling and inter-group competition for scarce resources.

The behavioural scientist is not really needed to convince one manager that these things occur: if he has any experience in organizations he has switnessed them with dismay. Where the behavioral scientist often can contribute, however is in helping the manager to understand why people behave in these situations the way they so and how the manager might set up a situation that would reduce distortion, misinformation and destructive competition. For example most managers are well aware that if they do not spend all the money that they asked for in their budget their boss will assume that they padded the budget and will cut the next year's budget by a certain amount. they will tell their own subordinates to find ways of using up the resources or concealing them by investing them in "Kitties" to be used later. Yet they will expect those same subordinates to give them accurate information when the subordinates are submitting their own budgets.

The behavioural scientist can bring to bear the knowledge that people will adapt very efficiently to how the organization's reward system or normal work, and that if the subordinate's behavior is to be made more "rational" the boss's own behavior will have to set a climate in which such rational behavior is rewarded. Sometimes this means that the normal or climate emanating from the every top of the organization have to be reexamined and rebuilt. We have seen organizations spend literally months developing presentations to accompany budgets and business plans, where the sole purpose was to get top management to agree while top management tried to figure out as best they could how the different groups competing for resources were trying to fool them. Yet those top managers did not see any connection between their own management style and the behavior of their subordinates.

Financial controls When we examine the area financial controls a similar picture emerges. the organization designs an information system that will provide accurate figures on costs on schedules, on inventory and the like and then typically assumes that it can accurately measure the progress of different departments against these figures. Let us look at how the process often works. In most organizations the control functions are given to a special staff unit like the accounting department which collects and centralizes information across a number of operating departments. A higher level of management typically scans the information and raise questions about those departments that show irregularities. The questions come back down the chain of command until the responsible worker or manager is confronted by this boss with a question concerning the irregularity.

Such a system has several psychological consequences that have been observed by behavioral scientists, but are less visible to the managers (1) Workers and lower level managers become highly dependent on the system and cease to monitor their own areas as closely as they should; they develop the attitude that if they are not doing their job the control system will let them know soon enough, hence why worry about it; (2) Workers and lower-level managers become resentful that they are called on the carpet by their boss for things that they may already have known about and fixed or that they feel they should have been told about in order to fix without involving higher levels of management; (3) Workers and lower level managers treat the accountants and representatives of other control functions as an enemy to be beaten rather than as an ally in getting a job done better; often they hide information or falsify it to make their operation look better than it is in order to avoid being penalized. these responses are normal given the system as it is set up. the scientist can help the higher-level manager analyze the system its impact on people and how to change it if the impact is undesirable.

Budgeting and control processes involve financial operations within the firm. Another aspect of financial management has to do with investments cash flow and the like wherein a person or small group has to make sound decisions given the company's particular needs and situation. A number of studies have been undertaken in recent years attempting to understand how individuals make investment decisions and how such decisions can be improved. Such studies have typically combined the talents of the econometrician the information systems expert and the behaviorally oriented psychologist. Sophisticated techniques involving simulation of the decision-making process have been undertaken with as yet limited but promising results. Within the next decade we should see the development of decision support systems that will help the individual decision-maker analyze his own problem-solving process will reveal his biases and help him to correct errors and generally improve decision quality.

Although the role of the behavioral scientists in helping the manager deal with his financial management is not as yet well accepted, there is an increasing need for managers to recognize the interaction between people or investment plan, as long as people are involved in carrying it out and in contributing the raw data with which the system operators there will be a need to examine how people feel about and use the system in order to examine its utility to the organization. The behavioral scientist will play a key role in helping the manager to make such as assessment.

Utilization Information

The manager makes his basic decisions on the basis of information that he acquires directly from his own experience is given by subordinates peers, and supervisors, and digs out of financial, marketing and other analyses made available to him. The quality of his decisions cannot be better than the quality of his information; hence real attention must be given to the process by which the manager acquires evaluates, and digests information. Behavioural scientists have played two roles in this process: (1) the have aided in the acquisition of information; and (2) they have the process of information digestion, interpretation and utilization in the decision making process.

Information acquisition One of the major research tools of psychologists has been use of interviews and questionnaires to obtain information on beliefs attitudes values to the marketing man; hence the field of market research has developed around advances in survey design statistics, and more subtle methods of obtaining information about consumer behavior such as motivation research. Most market research departments in organization and most advertising agencies employ behavioral scientists to obtain information about customers and to utilize this information in designing advertising and marketing strategies.

Behavioural scientists are also used to gather data about the morale of employees and in connection with organization development efforts their attitudes towards various organizational and managerial issues. Usually such information is gathered by an outside consulting agency, but many large corporations maintain a full-time in house staff to do continuous attitude and morale survey of their employees.

Information Processing and Decision-making The way in which the manager acquires processes and utilizes information in making decisions has only come under scrutiny by behavioral scientists in the last decade or so but it is one of the most promising and fruitful areas for future study and application. Several approaches have been used. Psychologists interested in learning thinking and problem-solving have attempted to apply some of their theories and research methods to understanding and simulating how managers make their decisions. Herbert Simon's work stands out as managerial decision-making is characterized by "satisficing" rather than maximizing. In other words the manager typically operates with imperfect and incomplete information under time pressure and tends therefore to seek a solution that will suffice which will get the job done rather than a solution that will be the best possible one under the circumstances. Simulation of managerial decision-making has so far limited itself to manageable areas like investment decisions but in these areas considerable understanding has been acquired of how the manager obtains and digests information what kinds of assumptions or premises he holds and how these entire into his decisions.

Another approach has been take problems-solving models that either an individual person or group can use and build a training program around them to improve individual and group decision-making. The Kenpner Tregoe program is perhaps the best known of these although sensitivity training programs also typically devote some percentage of their time to improving decision processes. Process consultation is heavily involved in observing how groups process information and make decisions and in helping managers to improve this process by learning to observe their own processes, and to improve them. The use of business games and complex business simulations can be put into this same category. Usually behavioral scientists are involved in the initial design and construction of the game in the way in which it is used as an educational aid, and in helping individuals or groups learn from their experience in playing the game.

A third approach which is perhaps the most existing one is for the behavioral scientist to collaborate with information system design experts in building better information and decision support systems.. This whole area has been revolutionized by the computer and its true potential is only now beginning to be understood. For example in its early history the glib assumption was made that the more information the manager had about everything and the quicker he could get it the better off he would being at interesting but irrelevant information are only now beginning to be recognized. For example a computerized information system can give a division manager detailed performance information on each of his operating department of which there may be great many three or four levels below him e.g., a president of a super-market chain getting information on each of several hundred stores. From the point of view of the system designer such access to information may be a virtue of the system. From the point of view of the analyst of managerial decision-making such access may be a disaster in that it would seduce the president into preoccupations that should be the responsibility of subordinates.

More sophisticated information system designers working with behavioural scientists are beginning to ask questions about what kind of information and what quantity of information the manager should have to optimize his decision processes. May be each level should get detailed information only about the level below it with everything below that aggregated to prevent managers from getting lost in irrelevant detail and from getting involved in levels too far below them. The kinds of control system problems that were outline in the preceding section often derive from an information system that makes detailed information about lower levels available at too high a level.

The behavioural science view has also entered information design thinking in terms of the integration between the from in which the information is displayed and the kind of decision-making grouping that is needed. For example if the task requires intensive effort from an individual manager using multiple information sources, he may be able to work successfully with well-designed computer printouts written summaries and other materials that he can read at his leisure. If the task required team effort in interpreting complex information and in reaching a decision it may be more appropriate to design visual displays that can be viewed simultaneously by a number of managers. In one study of the installation of such a system it was found that the visual display terminal encouraged a group of managers to get together and begin to work as team in a situation in which it was initially unlikely that they would have gotten together, even though the task they were working on required it.

What is behavioral science? The definition can be given verbally but then must be repeated through applications to everyday events to make it more meaningful. Behavioral science is the systematic study of behavior-what "is" rather than what ought to be. It is, therefore empirical and not speculative instead of relying on what individual notions of behavior might be the behavioral scientist gathers data to find out what is so or not. This "hard-nosed" empiricism is often missed by many who believe that one can stop after reading about McGregeo Maslow Herzberg or others.

As a result of limiting themselves to a few more popular points readers misjudge the main thrust of the discipline and call it qualitative normative value oriented or even one focusing solely on participative approaches to group functioning. That it is not Behavioral science entails rigorous research design unbased data collection organization of results and analytical attempts at ordering the data in order to add to the cumulative reservoir of knowledge that makes for human progress. Even the "humanistic" among the behavioral scientists did not reach the results they did" off the tops of their heads.

The additional common feeling that behavioural science is not in the same league as the "hard" sciences is related to the stereotypes stemming from the symbols associated with physical science laboratories Lab coats and test tubes do not a scientist make nor does one have to process such apparatus to be a scientist. It may be and often is much more difficult together good data in the complex area of human behavior than in other settings. Behavioral scientists often wish they had the opportunity to regulate and very circumstances as readily as physical and chemical conditions. Behavioral researches just have to try harder.

Behavioral science is just that a science because it shares certain characteristics with other science. Using the scientific method involves.

!. being systematic

2. in gathering data

3. that can be ordered

4. for *analysis*

5. and *communicated*

6. to add to the cumulative fund of knowledge

It relies on basic premises and then develops hypotheses or educated guesses that must be checked to determine whether the results call for an acceptance or rejection of the statement of relationships in the data. A more general theory can develop and give rise to further hypotheses to be tested. The word "theory" may cause many managers to "turn out" since it has long carried the connotation of impracticality. Yet each of us is constantly a theorist to one extent or another (the manager often without realizing it) in that we do construct shorthand explanations for relationships among events and no this basis try to predict results. Things would not make much sense otherwise. As Kurt Lewin was once said to have remarked "there is nothing as practical as a good theory." Behavioural science may not have enough good theory yet but the work proceeds.

Now to the specifics, of which there are many too many. Just as Schein could use the argument that there is very little space in which to cram in all that case here.

Trade offs can be attempted however. A good place to make room would be to reduce the discussion of theory X and theory Y. If there is one thing that managers these days have heard about behavioural science it's X and Y. Start instead with the a, b, and c and go all the way to z. The same tendency incidentally exists in academic publications and in college classrooms. An instructor-researcher teaching or writing on "behavioral science" has a tendency to focus on his narrow area of interest and send the student away with the feeling that this little bit was all there was to behavioral science.

The elements of individual behaviour are often glossed over. Students and managers discuss organization with out a clear knowledge of the fundamentals of human behavior. People who should know better make statements like "managers must motivate" which miss the entire point about how internal a factor motivation is. "Communicate" stimulates much discussion in management without a clear knowledge of what communication really is. Not one in ten in the target group is likely to know the first thing about semantics or other basic bits of knowledge.

Although the in-house group applications of behavioural science have been covered quite well by Schein, what is bothering more and more managers these days is the challenge from forces external tot he corporation. The social issues in the larger environment often tax and perplex the executive more than the usual and familiar problems he is used to facing within the organization. This is unknown territory and there has been little management training or development along these lines. It may be that corporations have failed to respond to respond to the challenges of a changing environment because they have not yet recognized public values as part of their own: they still see society as composed of independent sub-systems rather than as a larger, unified system. The interrelatedness of all activity of the corporation and its environment necessitates an awareness of the dynamics of social forces on the part of the executive.

Discussion of social patterns presuppose, however, the prior understanding of the interrelatedness of individual and group behavior. Culture, for instance, is a concept based on aggregates, but the transmission of culture through interpersonal channels or as the result of geographic mobility can be grasped well only if one understands individual development and the differences that can result from it. The broad and basic pattern of social life that we call culture, with all its attitudes and material possessions, is not passed on unchanged. The mediation by intermediate transmitters in the environment or by the family is critical. Can one really understand the Protestant Ethic, Black attitudes, reactions to welfare programs, women's lib, or any other contemporary social factor without some pre-awareness of the dynamics of culture and its transmission (a knowledge established on the basis of empirical data and not on biases, fictions, or stereotypes)? Social structure and process are easily seen in ongoing events. Someone with middle-class values who puts a high premium on education and achievement, for instance, may find it difficult to comprehend actions that arise from other values. To make it even more complex recently, sons and daughters of the establishment or newer managers in the corporation have been questioning the goals and values of the system into which they were born or moved into. Mobility, both geographic and generational, puts further stresses on familiar ties (ask today's manager about transfers within the company). Broader questions of population movements and the changing composition of the populace concern the average thinking citizens, but these matters interest the organizational planner, personnel administrator, and the marketer even more. What are people like in terms of age, sex, education, or occupation are only the beginning questions.

The processes of social change are even more pertinent for the administrator. The manager has often been called a change agent and this function of organizational behavior has been termed the most important aspect of management. The internal requirements for change may rest approximately on individual and small-group dynamics, but they are reflections of broader patterns of social change. Discordant consequences of change in society manifest themselves in conflict and disintegration in individuals and groups. Whether it takes place as industrial strife in various kinds of industries or in other moves toward power, a manager feels the impact keenly.

Behavioural science contributions to an understanding of politics and law range from establishing a basic framework of concepts to recognizing applications in specific situations. Managers do not need to be told, perhaps about the impact of law and politics in the functioning of their organizations. What does not telling is something like the relationship between personality and politics, attitudes or other characteristics or political agents, variables in participation, voter preference patterns, and other specific aspects of politics. In the law, an understanding of the behavioral basis of the legal process should be gained before (or instead of) substantive rules of law are memorized. What is the purpose of law? What are concepts of control and how it is achieved? What is basic to the functioning of an ordered society? Does punishment deter? Can law induce social change or is it the other way around? How do agents of public government and private government (corporation, colleges, etc.) relate to one another? What are the consequences of attempting to balance concerns for the consumer and the development of the economy?

We can come full circle now to the prior discussion of organizational behavior and add an interface with the environment that is part of the everyday functioning of virtually every corporation-the market. What makes the consumer tick and how does the message get across to him? The fundamental influence process in marketing and advertising involves all aspects, from mass communication at one end of the spectrum to a one-to-one personal relationship at the other. It can be the knowledge that is most crucial to the continuing existence of the organization and the manager's job.

All the above may really be leading up to the fundamental questions faced in viewing the role of the person in an organization and in society. Addressing oneself to the problem of quality of life on an individual basis or in the broader environment is often cast, for business, in terms of social responsibility. The critical questions lie, however, in determining the behavioral elements of identity, equality, privacy, security, and other primary or secondary needs. All this part of the job of the behavioral scientist and may even be his most important task in the long run.

The extensive and impressive itemization of behavioral science contributions to management theory and practice by Edgar Schein adds to the enigma of managerial neglect and underutilization of such contributions. Certainly, the four reasons cited for this lack of utilization are valid, but two others might be added. In the first place, there is a considerable lack of unanimity among behavioral theorists about normative prescriptions for management. Harold Koontz pointed out long ago that there exists a "management theory jungle" with multiple and often conflicting proposals from practicing managers, functionalists, behaviourist, mathematicians, and decision theorists. Among behavioral scientists there are the psychologists, who have a more individualistic approach and often set forth normative prescriptions, and the sociologists, who attempt to explain how organizations and groups form and adapt, frequently without making specific recommendations. Within these two broad groups, different emphases are advocated-some say that the important factor is the design of the job whereas others say that power and politics should constitute the focal point of analysis and action. Thus, a fifth possible reason for the limited use of behavioural science contribution among practicing managers about which behaviourist to believe.

One final suggestion can be made concerning the puzzle of nonuse. Had been asked to prepare the original statement, contributions of behavioral science for managers, we would have substantially duplicated Edgar Schein's material, but my orientation would have been slightly different. Our perspective would have advocated the position, attitude, and problems of the manager. Utilizing the contributions of early management theorists, the statement that a manager must (1) plan, (2) organize, (3) direct, and (4) control the work of others provides some insight into the nature and demands of his task. Thus, the question could be asked of the behaviourists, "How can you help me perform these tasks?" In general, as Schein's statement shows, the behaviorists have been most helpful in the "people-oriented" functions of organizing and directing. In organizing, we are concerned with establishing conditions necessary for effective accomplishment of goals. This would encompass designing jobs, obtaining personnel, differentiating structure, and developing effective interpersonal and intergroup relations. As Schein points out, the early behaviorists were industrial phycologists who provided direct assistance in selecting personnel to fit predetermined jobs. This approach has since been enlarged to include study and recommendations in such areas as job enrichment, socio-technical systems, and organization development. In similar fashion, the behaviorists have made substantial contributions with respect to the directing function. Direction can be defined broadly as the process of initiating action, and is sometimes termed "motivation." It is readily apparent that this is a subject of vital concern to behaviorists and perhaps does not receive the space in Schein's statement that it deserves. McGregor's theory was appropriately emphasized, but it, in turn, rests partially on the underpinning of Maslow's hierarchy of needs, showing a sequential development of human needs that the manager can utilize in motivating employees. To motivation can be added expectancy theory. The actual effect of a manager's attempt to motivate another person comes from that person's assessment of (1) the anticipated value of the perceived outcome of the behavior wanted by the manager, and (2) the strength of the expectancy that the act will actually result in a realization of the outcome. The Maslow hierarchy may well explain that a particular person is currently interested in monetary rewards. But if that person does not believe that the higher output desired by the manager will actually bring about an appropriate increase in his compensation, it is not likely that he will be motivated. Thus, the behaviorist has aided the manager in assessing current employee needs, analyzing incentive schemes to ascertain how they fit these needs, and developing educational and action programs that will demonstrate to the employee that the reward is effectively connected to the behavior desired.

Although Schein did devote a portion of his paper to information and financial control, most of it was concerned with detailing the contribution in the human resources area. Thus, most of the works has been in relation to the organizing and directing functions of management. The behaviorists have not been of equal help in the planning and control functions. To many managers who are concerned with immediate results, the effective execution of the planning and controlling functions will make a far greater contribution to success than those dealing with establishing and maintaining the human organization that carries out the necessary work. What is the necessary work? What should be the goal of the organization? Should a company manufacture this product and compete in that market? What technology should be used, and what should be developed in the future? And after undertaking operations, is the system under control? Is enough of the right information coming through soon enough to avoid disaster if not mediocrity?

Managers are all too willing to discuss the human elements of organization and deliver speeches about human values to civic groups, but many feel that the essentials to success lie else where. In a survey of over 1,000 business managers. George England attempted to determine the goals that they deemed important as well as those regarded as essential to the success of an enterprise. With respect to the goals of efficiency, productivity, profit, growth, and stability, from 60 to 80 per cent felt that these were both important and essential. With respect to the goal of employee. With respect to the goal of employee welfare, 65 per cent felt it to be important, but only 20 per cent deemed it essential. There seems to be a kind of credibility gap between behaviorists and practicing managers. Despite the research that "proves" a cause-and-effect relationship between behaviorally recommended practices and managerially valued results such as productivity, managers tend to give only lip service to the findings of behavioral scientists. The cynical observer would conclude that behavioral practices that are pushed by labor unions or demanded by government laws or edicts will constitute the majority of behavioral contributions actually placed into practice.

This writer joins Edgar Schein in contending that the body of knowledge in the behavioral sciences has not been well marketed. Certainly the organization and direction of all types of institutions could be improved by a greater utilization of the behavioral sciences. There is a considerable overlap between the interests of the manager in productivity and efficiency, and the interests of individuals and groups in satisfaction and self-actualization. However, this writer is not among those who believe that there is a complete overlap, that what is best for the organization is best for the individual, or that a maximum concern for output can always be aligned with a maximum concern for people. But the overlap is far greater than many practicing managers believe. And it is up to the behaviourists to prove its existence through research, and to convince the manager of this fact through an appropriate marketing job. In the areas outside the overlap, if certain behavioural recommendations are to be implemented, it will require the external forces of unions and government, or perhaps the internal force of conscience and personal codes of ethics. And similarly, in other areas outside the overlap, if certain managerial demands are to be implemented, disciplinary action or the politics of compromise or purchase will be required.

In dealing with the human resources area, Schein emphasized developing an effective organization. Although Schein's itemization of behavioral contribution was comprehensive, it is important to recognize a philosophical difference between certain organization phychologists and organization sociologists. The organization psychologists are perhaps better known to managers because of their consulting activities and their publication of articles in periodicals oriented toward business management. Management should therefore structure the firm in a more participatory, trusting, and open manager. Specific suggestions would include abandoning time clocks, self-evaluation in merit rating, joint determination of job goals, and substituting consultative relationships for surveillance relationships between line and staff. Argyris, in his well-known maturation theory, recommended that organizations be restructured to reduce the clash of interests between mature personalities and traditionally managed institutions. Specific recommendations included design of jobs that permit closure and self-actualization and increased subordinate participation in management decisions. Likert approached the problem by delineating alternative leadership styles ranging through coercive autocracy, benevolent autocracy, and consultative management, to the participative group. The last style, be suggested, was most effective because it ensured the greatest degree of subordinate involvement. Similarly, in Blake and Mouton's Management Grid, the single style most recommended is the 9,9 type wherein the manager exhibits a maximum concern for output simultaneously with a maximum concern for people. The Herzberg motivator-hygiene theory contends that job content variables tend to elicit greater motivation than environmental factors. Specific recommendations to the manager would include redesign of jobs to permit closure and self-determination of methods, pace, and quality. It should be readily apparent that these recommendations are entirely compatible with McGregor's theory Y, Argyris's maturation concepts, Likert's participative group and supportive style, and the 9,9 position of Blake and Mouton. Visualize the type of organization that would be created-one that is open, honest, trusting, participative, problem-solving, supportive, self-controlling, and collegial.

The efforts in the field of organization development as described by Schein are in line with the above theories. The survey feedback method provides data concerning morale and management style with the implication that the manager alter his approach in the direction of the values of McGregor, Argyris, and the others. Team building, team training, job enlargement, job enrichment, and sensitivity training are similarly oriented toward recognition and development of theory Y personnel and relationships. Thus, the theories and implementations of this well-known group of organization psychologists are heavily normative in the direction of a more participative type of management. There seems to be only limited recognition of different types of personnel available and state of technology utilized.

On the other hand, a second group of behaviorists, who might be termed "organization sociologists," appear to be less normative and more tolerant of varying management approaches. Outstanding within this group would be James D. Thompson. Charles Perrow, and Joan Woodward, Central to the approach of this group is an analysis of varying types of technology that are utilized to accomplish organization objectives. In considering the variety of activities and the degree of uncertainty regarding cause-and-effect relations in the performance of such activities. Perrow establishes two extreme types of technology-routine and nonroutine and two hybrid, intermediate types-craft and engineering. The manager's task, according to Thompson, is the "Co-alignment of technology and task environment with a viable domain, and of organization design and structure appropriate to that domain. Thus, the implication is that routine technology will demand more centralized and autocratic management approaches, whereas the nonroutine will call for the type of organizational action envisioned by the McGregor, Likert, Argyris group. The normative prescription of this group of behaviourists is to co-align the technology, structure, and decision strategies. Certainly, if one attempted to manage a research and development unit in an autocratic fashion, there would be little co-alignment. And in this the organization psychologists would agree. But if one attempted to manage an automobile assembly line in a participative fashion, there would also be little co-alignment. But here the organization psychologists perhaps would not agree. Although many behaviorists have criticized early classical management theorists for proposing the determination and enforcement of the "one best way" of operating perhaps some of them are similarly vulnerable for proposing the one best management style or the one best type of interpersonal or inter-group relationship. In Woodward's famous study of business firms in England, she could make sense of her findings only when she correlated managerial practices with the various types of technology utilized.

As the final point in this critique, this writer is in full agreement that the significant future contributions of the behavioral sciences should lie in the information and control areas of management. As suggested above, many managers view these aspects of their jobs as more connected to immediate success. But even in this regard, the behavioral contribution might be regarded as peripheral and only supplementary by the manager. For example, Schein suggests that the behaviorist approach can be used in establishing better information and decision support systems. He points out specifically that behavioural data should be collected to supplement the usual economic and technical data, and that too much technical and economic data might make higher levels of management become too centralized and autocratic toward lower levels. Although this behavioral attitude should assist in the creation of a more comprehensive and balanced system, the same credibility gap between manager and behaviorists still is likely to persist. The behavioural model implied in this case is a decentralized, participatory one.

Similarly, in the control area, the behaviorists point out the numerous negative consequences of particular control systems that are unbalanced, excessively tight, and enforced through overt or covert threats. Again, this is a valued and legitimate contribution, but its role is supplementary to the task of establishing the content and level of control standards to be administered by the manager. When we get to the actual process of how managers utilize information in making decisions of all types, whether behaviourally, classically, or otherwise oriented, this writer fully agrees that this "is one of the most promising and fruitful areas for future study and application."

Communication and Motivation

The abundance of motivational theories from which managers can choose testifies to the fact that employee motivation remains one of the most fascinating but perplexing areas of managerial concern. Few employees work to their full ability; in fact, studies show that in some cases workers can perform at only 20 to 30 per cent of their ability without being fired and that average employees work at only two-thirds of their capacities. A machine that produced so poorly would be repaired or replaced. What can managers of human resources do to overcome this waste and inefficiency?

Frankly, the values of all the different motivational theories can be seriously questioned. To quote Odiorne, "Has all of the talk and work on teaching motivational theory been overdone? I'd like to suggest that it has." Leidecker and Hall review the major motivational theories and state that when these theories are applied in the "real world," the results are often negative or, at best, neutral.

Miller made a comprehensive effort to determine if different motivational theories had an impact in the organization. Miller analyzed three different organizations that applied three different between motivational concepts and concluded that there was little difference between the companies. He further concluded that the main problem was that the theories were misapplied for two possible reasons (1) the degree of expertise required to implement the theories is beyond most professional managers, and (2) the theories are not applicable to all individuals in all situations. Miller contends that many proponents of motivational theories encourage managers to fit round theories into square holes.

Because motivational theory is so difficult to implement, more and more companies are seeing that the link between motivation and performance improvement is communication. Such companies as Oneida Silversmiths, National Can Corporation, New York Life Insurance, and Kohler have initiated programs that stress communication as the critical element in employee motivation.

Why do these companies stress communication when considering employee motivation? Effective communication is what managers use to improve an employee's sense of self-worth by showing recognition, reinforcing a job well done, and providing a general sense of support. Communication is the tool that is available to every manager. Not every manager can give an employee a raise or use a promotion as an incentive; however, every manager can use effective motivational communication. This chapter shows specifically how communication is the central ingredient in the motivational process and presents techniques that every manager can use to improve performance in the workplace.

The basic elements in employee motivation

Although motivational theories can become rather complex and their applicability can be questioned, fortunately the volumes of research have led to some simplified conclusions that are easy to understand and apply. The following performance model presents these results in a simplified manner and follows the advice of Terpstra- "borrow from the best.' The model integrates the popular models presented by Vroom, B.F. Skinner, Locke, Herzberg, and Maslow. Rather than introduce another motivational model, we propose to provide a framework for strategic communication that managers can implement for improved motivation.

Rewards-efforts

Thorndike's law of effect, one of the only unequivocably established laws of human behaviour, simply states that a behaviour that results in a pleasurable outcomes tends to be repeated, whereas a behaviour that results in a non-pleasurable outcome tends not to be repeated. The value of the reward and the probability of obtaining the reward determine the amount of effort that an employee will exert on the job. The greater the reward for workers, the greater their effort. In addition, workers often do not know what the probability is of obtaining the desired reward when they perform in a certain manner. Increased probability of success leads to increased effort. We may analyze rewards in many ways, but one of the more universally accepted approaches is in terms of needs; people have needs, and when these needs are satisfied as the result of some behaviour, a pleasurable or satisfying feeling—a reward-results.

Langer distinguishes three classes of needs: physical, social, and egotistical. The physical needs are for food and water, for air, temperature control, sleep, elimination, and the like. Social needs are those that are satisfied only in relationship with other people. The affiliation drive—the need to associate with others—is an example of this. We have all seen a tremendous need to conform expressed by an individual at one time or another. This is an example of affiliation or social need.

Egotistical needs differ from social needs in their orientation. Even though the social needs are instrumental in gratifying egotistical needs, these needs are directed toward the maintenance or enhancement of one's ego or one's self. Fulfilling these needs makes people feel good about themselves. Among the goals of egotistical needs are to achieve, to be important, dominant, autonomous, to be "somebody." Recognition, prestige, esteem, fame, status, and reputation are among the common means for gratifying egotistical needs. For instance, people often feel like they are "somebody" when they have accomplished something for the first time, even if nobody else knows about it.

How does all this relate to the manager who is trying to motivate employees to improve work performance? It suggests that a manager or supervisor can help an employee meet many of his needs. For example, the affiliation need can be met by communicating to employees that they "belong" to the work group. It means involving new employees in group projects where others listen to their views as soon as the new employees join the company. It means letting employees participate in decisions rather than just telling them what their job duties are. It also means taking the time to visit with them about things important to them—family, hobbies current events—in addition to job-related activities. Verbal interaction is extremely important in the affiliation motive and goes a long way toward motivating an individual to meet group goals.

The manager who blocks an employee's need to belong is one who develops intense competition between employees, does not keep employees equally informed on important matters, or may even isolate certain employees for privileged information. This manager also eliminates opportunities for group decision-making and attempts to keep employees isolated on important matters. This type of manager assumes the central role of total responsibility and credit and blocks any efforts to the group or gain a sense of achievement. On the other hand, the operation of the effective manager communicates in a manner that assists employees to meet their need to belong.

A manager can help employees satisfy their egotistical needs by communicating their importance to the company and recognizing them as individuals. Two out of three companies have formal recognition programs, and most personnel managers believe that recognition programs help keep and motivate employees. But it is often difficult to make formal programs effective at the individual level. Thus, the free trip to Hawaii gives a lot of recognition to one employee, but what about all the others? This is why each manager is so important at the individual level. At that level he can give individual recognition by simply asking employees for their ideas and listening to them. Such recognition makes an individual feel worthwhile and important to the company. For this reason, the concepts of participation and quality circles have become such popular concepts with American management. Let us take a quick look at quality circles.

This concept, a take-off on Japanese management practice, involves small groups of people who regularly do similar work. The groups meet to identify and analyze causes of problems and recommend their solutions to management. But for the quality circles to really work, effective managers must coordinate them. Larry Nelson, a consultant specializing in quality circles, maintains that the following participant conduct is important for a circle to be effective:

- Listen to, and show respect for the views of other members.
- Critique ideas, not persons.
- Treat everyone as equal.
- Ensure that credit is given to those to whom it is due.

As these suggest, each person is recognized as important to the process.

In the business section of a Tokyo newspaper, Tateo Tsunemi, a Japanese expert on American business, recently indicated many American business managers on the grounds of their dictatorial approach toward workers. These managers do not understand the mentality of the workers and they do not necessarily have confidence in the workers in the way that their Japanese counterparts do. Obviously, managers must show that they trust their employees to communicate a sense of recognition and importance.

Some managers believe that they show adequate recognition to employees by saying "good morning" or by telling them occasionally that they have done a good job. Of course, this is important, but a manager shows a more meaningful level of recognition by asking the employees questions, by listening to the employees, and by refraining from criticism when small errors are made.

The real impact communication can have as a tool for recognizing employees was verified by a quality control manager in a food processing plant. This manager has 32 people either directly or indirectly reporting to her. She listed each person's name in a small book. She then made a special point of talking to each person individually about something other than immediate work at hand at least once a week. The manager knew that with 32 people it would be easy to omit certain employees, so she put a checkmark after the person's name after the conversation. This meant that she took special care to recognize each person individually at least once a week even though it was a large department. The prevailing atmosphere within the department was one of trust and cooperation, and the manager was recognized by the plant manager for the fine performance in the department.

Clearly, through effective communication a manager can help an employee meet social and egotistical needs. But let us look at a common notion that has not been explored: money's role as motivator.

Money as a form of reward

We could develop a lengthy debate about the relative importance of money as a motivator. While one research study could be cited about salary's effects on turnover, other research would indicate that many employees will actually stay on a particular job when they could change for increased salaries. The critical fact is that the monetary compensation must be related to immediate performance, and this is where most compensation programs have failed. While merit programs are designed to overcome this problem, unfortunately, most merit pay systems have failed. Significantly, employees are unable to perceive a direct relationship between pay and performance.

Besides, the average manager is really helpless to use money as a reward. Assume that a company uses a merit system contingent upon an annual performance review. Employees find it extremely difficult to relate a specific performance that took place 11 months prior to a merit increase of may be 5 per cent. Of course, not only is a manager severely limited in the amount of merit pay that may be granted, but the merit pay will have little impact on take-home pay or earning power in times of high inflation. In face, many managers may feel compelled to administer merit increases near the allowable maximum to even mediocre performers just to allow employees to keep pace with the high rate of inflation.

Because of the nature of merit systems in an era of inflation, money is really a negative rather than a positive motivational device. Employees may operate more from a fear of not receiving a customary increase rather than for extra incentive. Fear may develop because the salary is important just to meet the physical needs of having food, shelter, and clothing. This is not to say that money is not important when considering motivation; rather, it is to say that monetary rewards are not viable alternatives for the average manager considering ways to motivate employees to exert greater effort on the job.

A manager will succeed more by using effective communication to emphasize the social and egotistical needs. Also, when managers emphasize the probability of obtaining a reward, they meet with greater success in their efforts to improve employee performance.

Probability of obtaining a reward

Regardless of the value of the reward to an employee, she must know the probability of obtaining that reward. One way for a manager to do this is to establish procedural models that tell employees that if they perform as expected, rewards will follow. For instance, if Mary, an accountant, prepares a report, she should present it to the executive group. This will help her to fulfil her need for recognition and show her that her work is important. Also, it lets employees know that if they make a suggestion, they will be listened to. Such practice recognize a person as an individual.

Another way of letting an employee know what the probability is of obtaining a reward is to tell him. For instance, "Mark, in the past we have had difficulty getting the test on the magnesium components done on time. I know this is a long, tedious job, so is you get it all completed by Tuesday, you can make the report to the plant manager's staff." Another example would be, "Rex, when you master the use of this computer program, I will see if we can send you to a special training program on the new system." On a different level, a manager might tell a new engineer that two of the last four engineers who worked in this area were given special corporate research projects where they received high exposure.

Of course, a manager may not know the probability of an employee obtaining a particular reward when the employee performs in a satisfactory manner. For instance, a young salesperson may want a more responsible sales director position. Unfortunately, the manager may not know if or when such a position might become available. Candor is important in these situations, and the manager should avoid the temptations of false promises or deception.

Understanding Employee's Goals

But how can a manager learn to understand the individual needs and suitable rewards for an employee? Even a psychologist can spend months with clients without fully understanding them. One occasionally hears another say that she has been married years and still cannot figure out her husband. The interesting and fascinating aspect of people is their unpredictability.

An excellent way for managers to understand their employees better is to spend time visiting with them. As people spend more time with each other, they feel more comfortable with one another and are consequently more inclined to relate private feelings and needs. Such cannot be accomplished in an annual performance review where a manager says little that is more specific than, "What are you looking for in your job?" With time and effort, managers can develop a sense of openness and trust in communication. Managers developing an open communication climate need to listen to employees without being quick to criticize. One need not try to play the role of a psychologist. As employees become more open, they will relate the importance of group or individual recognition, the type of achievements they feel best about, and the type of work they most enjoy. Employees will also feel freer to state their complaints to a listening manager—an invaluable way in which to understand employees better. In such cases, employees will often complain about needs the present situation does not satisfy.

Job Knowledge

Effort alone, no matter how great, cannot guarantee high level of performance. Besides effort, one needs job knowledge, which results from two separate factors: (1) abilities and skills; and (2) clear instructions and expectations. With thee extra elements added, our performance model now looks like Figure.

Abilities and Skills

Managers often assign employees to a job because they have assumed that the employees know how to perform it. Ironically, when their performance is rated sub-standard, these employees may be accused of being poorly motivated or sloppy when in fact they lacked the requisite ability or skill. This situation arises frequently when a manager assumes that an employee has the appropriate skill and the employee is afraid to admit that he cannot do the job.

Consider an employee, Bill, who joined the office staff of an insurance company shortly after graduating from a business school. While in school Bill had some experience, three day's training, on a word processing system. During the interview, Bill's boss asked him if he knew how to operate a word processor; he quickly replied that he did. Now that he is on the job, he has been asked to complete a report using a new word processing system in the office. Unfortunately, the new system is entirely different from the one bill trained on. After all, he has just started the job and is afraid of looking slow or unskilled. When the manager asks Bill if he thinks he will have any trouble, Bill acts enthusiastically about the project. Clearly, this could be the beginning of many problems.

How can a manager prevent such a problem? Taking the safe route and always assuming that subordinates cannot do a job may only insult the subordinates by casting doubt on their skills. At the same time, it is dangerous to assume that people can do something they cannot. The answer is open, trusting communication. A manager must establish a climate in which a subordinate can admit deficiencies without fear of criticism. The climate established should be "What can we do to improve? "rather than a climate that continually challenges people to prove their self-worth.

Managers establish this climate by resisting the urge to criticize every time subordinates err. Continuous criticism will force a person to hide inabilities. Also, employees should have the opportunity to ask questions even when it appears that they should already know the answers. One can quickly inhibit questions by acting as if they are so simple that everyone should know the answers.

The tactful use of open-ended questions is also important when determining if a person has the appropriate skills to do a job. Rather than saying, "Bill, can you type up the report on the word processor? it is better to say, "I know you haven't been here long. How confident are you on this work processor?" Another approach might be, "Bill, how do we set up this process; it's been a while since I've looked at it." Doing so gives the manager an opportunity to work together to determine Bill's level of knowledge without directly challenging him.

Clearly, a manager must determine the abilities and skills of employees without threatening the employees. A manager must be able to listen carefully and ask open-ended, non-threatening questions. If a person has successfully completed the job before, then it is possible to confidently assume that it can be done again. However, if this is not the case, effective communication helps to ensure that the employee possesses the necessary skills.

Clear instructions and expectations

Of course, hard work and excellent skills are of no avail when a person is doing the wrong thing. Not only must employees receive clear instructions, they must clearly know what is expected of them. Feedback is the key here, and questioning is the most important skill a manager possesses to obtain feedback.

It is not enough simply to ask if the instructions are clear. "Are you clear on what you are supposed to do how? is a closed question to which most people will respond "yes," probably thinking that if they are not completely clear, they will probably be able to figure it out once they start the job. They may fear that admitting that they are not clear on the instructions indicates they did not understand the assignment or were not listening. Another tactic, constantly asking an employee to repeat the instructions, may be interpreted as a challenge or even as an insult to the employee's intelligence. A manager must strategically vary communications to obtain feedback on instructions given.

One way to achieve this is by taking the responsibility for instructions rather than putting the responsibility on the receiver of the instructions. For instance, after giving instructions, a manager might say, "This is a complicated assignment, and I'm not sure I've given you all the information I need to. Would you please summarize it for me just to make sure that I've covered everything." This tactful practice is less challenging to the receiver than is that of asking closed questions and puts the responsibility on the sender of the message. Another strategy might be to say, "Sometimes I forgot important parts when giving instructions; tell me exactly what you're going to do now just to make sure that I haven't skipped anything." Once again the sender takes responsibility for the message's accuracy. This strategy not only assures greater clarity of the message, but it serves to help meet the ego needs of the subordinate. It shows that the subordinate is important and that his or her thoughts are important to the completion of the task. Managers establish a cooperative climate rather than a "tattletale' climate in which the subordinate is always responsible for any errors that may result.

To determine if instructions are clear, a manager should check for the three C's. Is the instruction complete, concise, and concrete? For example, the instruction. "Take care of the shipment of new shirts when you get a chance," does not meet the C's. It may seem adequate because a manager may assume that the subordinate is thinking along the same lines. The instruction could be clearer: "Count the shipment of new shirts to make sure they're the same as the billing order. If they match the billing, place them on the appropriate shelves. If there are any discrepancies, let me know. This work needs to be done before noon when we begin to have heavier customer traffic." While this second instruction takes more time and effort than the first, it meets the C's . If this instruction were not complete, the shirts might not be placed on a shelves until the end of the day, at which time the manager might think that the employee was not motivated.

Of course, many jobs are more ambiguous, and the employees have a great deal of freedom to determine what they should be working on and when they should do it. Even though managers and employees do not have constant contact in these jobs, feedback is still important. According to Scanlon, the value of feedback varies according to the time interval between results, the extent to which the feedback deals with the total situation, and the extent to which it dwells on matters under the worker's control. This is the essence of establishing expectations through feedback.

An effective manager must periodically establish expectancies at a time interval appropriate to the nature of job. Simply stating from time to time "You're doing a fine job" does not meet the elements of the C's, and formal yearly performance review is too great a period of time between feedback. A periodic conversation dealing with specific expectations of the job helps to guarantee continued performance. In fact, the element that makes sports so exciting is that a definite scoring system provides feedback. The players know exactly where they stand relative to the goals and know what they have to do to win the game. Most jobs do not have a precise scoring system, but an insightful manager can provide accurate and timely feedback.

This feedback needs to be provided at both a micro and a macro level. As suggested by Scanlon's comment, feedback must deal with the total situation as well as with the elements within the situation. It is valuable feedback for an accountant to know that his or her audits are taking longer than they should; however, an in-depth discussion may reveal what particular type accounts or systems are causing the problem. Then, too, the person needs to know precisely the areas in which he is doing excellent work as well. The final important element of expectations and feedback is that they should deal with those elements of the job over which the person has control. It would be extremely demotivating to tell sales clerks that sales are declining and that they should be selling more when the problem really lies in the fact that fewer customers are entering the store. Employees cannot be expected to control every element of their job, so feedback should relate only to those elements under their control. If elements outside an employee's control have profound impacts on her performance, demotivation may result unless her manager analyzes the next element of the performance model.

Cooperation and materials

Satisfactory job performance is not merely a product of effort and job knowledge. We also need cooperation from others along with the necessary tools. Imagine an accountant who works hard, is highly skilled, knows what is expected, but cannot get the necessary figures to complete his job. The cooperation of others with him is essential. While individual employees are responsible in part for developing a cooperative work environment, the manager often plays the critical role.

A manager can develop cooperation in several different ways. First because managers generally have higher visibility and credibility in the organization than do their subordinates, managers can represent their subordinates in an effort to sell their projects and gain support. Second, a manager can call a group of employees together and analyze ways that the group can develop a cooperative effort. She may use integrative problem-solving strategies discussed in the chapter on conflict management as well as the group meeting formats presented in the chapter on meetings. Regardless of the approach used, skilful communication is required.

Let us look at an example of developing cooperation. A company was about to introduce a new product and required that at least one member of the marketing staff attend product introduction meetings held throughout the country. The product marketing manager for the company stated that at least one member of the corporate staff must attend one introductory meeting even though it would be inconvenient. The corporate staff already spent a great deal of time travelling, and summer vacations were approaching; consequently, cooperative spirits were not high.

The manager developed cooperation by having a meeting to discuss the schedule rather than "drawing straws" as suggested by one of the staff. During this meeting, each person listed the best time for his or her to travel. All the participants compared dates and arranged cooperative agreements on travel times. The manager listened to possibilities, asked for cooperation, and thus motivated the employees to work together.

A manager who successfully develops a cooperative work group not only reduces barriers to performance but also enables employees to meet their social needs. When employees see that they can help one another meet their social needs, a higher level of communication will exist among them. This communication, in turn, will foster a feeling of interdependence among group members, because they will see themselves as sharing certain goals that no single individual could achieve alone.

Employees must also have the tools needed to complete the job if they are to remain motivated and maintain a high level of performance. Sometimes it seems that subordinates are always "griping" about inadequate materials or old, worn-out equipment. These complaints put the manager in a awkward position because budget restraints often do not allow for the equipment and materials that subordinates would like to have. So what can a manager do? Communication is once again important. First, it is important to listen thoroughly to the concerns of the employees without making premature decisions. Once the situation is fully understood, it is important that a manager explain why the new equipment can or cannot be purchased.

Managers often tend to blame the inability to purchase on the budget or top management. While this is an easy out for the manager, it does little for the frustrated employee who must work without that equipment. Giving a complete explanation of future possibilities for the equipment, discussing other alternatives that may be taken, and describing why other equipment may have a priority will prevent an employee from becoming demotivated due to equipment inadequacies. This also indicates to the employee that management is aware of the problem; even though no action is taken, at least management is listening.

The role that communication plays in obtaining necessary tools and equipment is demonstrated by a situation in which a secretary kept asking for a simple word processing system. Jerry was presently using an electronic typewriter, so it would not be too expensive to move up to a word processor. The move would increase productivity and probably reduce the number of complaints receive about the slow level of productivity. Unfortunately, top management would not approve the word processor. Subsequently, Jerry was asked to write a rationale for the equipment so that the manager could again present the request to top management. Furthermore, Jerry was asked to accompany the manager when making the request. Once again the request was denied, but Jerry received a complete explanation firsthand and had an opportunity to ask questions. In addition, Jerry held a meeting with all those who produced the work Jerry typed to make clear what could be expected with the present equipment.

Instrumentality

Instrumentality is the degree of assurance that an employee feels that performance will lead to rewards. The discussion has already emphasized the importance of rewards as well is expectations; however, the relationship among expectations, performance, and rewards is so important that it reserves special attention. Also, this relationship is directly controlled by the managerial communication process and is affected by past experiences, by organizational policies and by the relationship between the manager and subordinate. It is this last component—the manager-subordinate relationship—that an individual manager can use best to improve the motivational process.

The first aspect of this relationship to consider is that both the manager and subordinate have expectations that they communicate to one another. Similarly, in George Bernard Shaw's classic play, Pygmalion, Professor Henry Higgins had high expectations for Eliza Doolittle and turned the guttersnipe into an elegant lady. The professor communicated his high expectations to the lady, and these led to positive results.

In one study, supervisors received what they thought were test results on employees whom they were to begin supervising. The survey found that those employees whose supervisors had high expectations as a result of their "higher" test scores actually performed better than those employees whose supervisors had lower expectations. A number of studies have also demonstrated that a teacher's expectations of his students appears to influence directly the student's performance. Similarly, the expectations of coaches and fellow players appear to influence directly an athlete's performance.

Just as the manager communicates expectations to her subordinate, subordinates expect a certain reward based on their level of performance. This reward expectation is based on communication from the managers and past experience. After an employee has performed and received a reward, the level of expected reward is adjusted accordingly. In other words, the reward an individual receives acts as a feedback loop and affects the amount of reward expected for future effort. The feedback loop can be put in the model so it now looks like this. It is easy to see that the reward a person receives affects the expected rewards for future behaviour, which in turn affect the future effort.

An employee can enter a situation highly motivated, but soon become disillusioned and demotivated when he received reward is not consistent with the expected reward. Because of the relationship between expected and received rewards, it is critical that an employee not receive false promises or foster unrealistically high expectations. At the same time, it is important to relate rewards directly to performance so that a person knows why he is receiving the rewards. Managers create accurate expectations and reduce uncertainty through frequent communication and follow-up. These factors help employees to understand what tasks they must perform and the level of performance required for reward. Remember, uncertainly is demotivating.

The direct and immediate feedback also makes it clear to employees that they experience the results of their performance—either negatively or positively. When employees do not know why they are penalized, they may become confused, disillusioned, and demotivated; the same is true for a reward. Consider a small boy who gets in a fight with the neighbour's child. The boy's mother punishes him by saying that he will receive a spanking from his father when the father comes home from work. Six hours later the father comes home and spanks the small boy. Unfortunately, by then the boy has forgotten why he is being paddled, or, even worse, the boy has just cleaned up his room. The poor boy may think he is getting paddled for clearing his room.

This is extreme example, of course. But the point is that employees must be told why they are receiving a reward or a penalty as soon as possible after the appropriate or inappropriate behaviour.

Managerial communication is important here in several ways. First, employees must clearly understand policies and procedures. In one situation an employee voluntarily began to work with a junior achievement group. He stated that he was representing his company in this activity. Unfortunately, he was reprimanded for announcing this connection because he was told, he could not officially represent the company without the public relations director's prior approval. The fact that the company policies were not communicated to him resulted in a penalty for exerting extra effort.

Another common example of instrumentality involves the relationship between promotions and performance. In many organizations, seniority almost automatically leads to an upgrade in title. For instance, nurses may move up in classification, teachers may become tenured, and engineers may move from a junior-to a senior-level classification. But in many instances, the employees did not know exactly what is expected of them other than longevity; consequently, when a person does not receive an upgrade for some unknown reason, frustration and bitterness may result. Clear communication between managers and subordinate ensures clear expectations and an understanding of either the rewards or penalties received. The reward-penalty structure should operate as feedback, not as a surprise! The model we have been examining shows that employee motivation is not a simple matter. A manager cannot read about a motivational theory in the hope that this will be the key to the problem. The real key is effective, strategic communication. Theory has minimal value unless a manager is an effective communicator. All the different elements of the model must be analyzed to help establish a motivational climate which can be established through strategic communication. While this model helps to explain how effective communication can facilitate the motivational process, it is clearly helpful to be able to diagnose a situation where performance does not meet expectations. The following discussion presents a concrete way in which the model can be used to diagnose a situation.

Diagnosing performance problems

A formalized approach helps when a manager faces a performs problem. The following diagnostic scheme, adapted from Mager and Pipe, should help to pinpoint the exact nature of the problem. The most efficient strategy for understanding the nature of a problem is to ask the people involved the six critical questions presented here. As you review these questions, remember the importance of open-ended questions. Closed questions, those that can be answered with a "yes" or "no", do not provide the required in-depth information. Also avoid leading questions whose answer may support a previous bias or inclination while completely hiding the real problem.

In some situations, questions can also be a threat. Questions should be put in such a context to make it clear that the manager is seeking to improve performance so that organizational and personal goals can be met. Unfortunately, questions too often sound like an attempt to indict an individual, so it is important for managers to remain positive and sensitive to the perceptions of employees.

The following six questions are presented in a sequential, additive fashion. This means that if the managers ask themselves the questions as well as ask their employees in the sequence presented here, the answers should combine to develop an understanding. The answer to one question should add to the meaning and significance of the next one, and so on.

QUESTION 1: Does the performance really make any difference?

A subordinate's performance may be personally irritating to a manager without really affecting the organizational goals. For instance, an employee may come to work dressed in a manner considered inappropriate by a manager, but this dress may not affect overall performance. Another person may have a messy desk while the manager takes pride in a neat, well-organized office. Such mannerisms can irritate without affecting overall performance.

One way to determine if an element of performance really is critical is to ask a fellow manager who may be more objective. If asked about a particular behaviour in an open, nonleading manner, the other manager may reveal that the behaviour is nothing more than a personal irritant to the first manager. Then , too, it may become apparent that the performance really does need rectifying. When this is the case, the second question is appropriate.

QUESTION 2: Precisely what is the desired behaviour?

As we saw earlier under criteria a feedback, concrete criteria need to be established. What precise quality and quantity are expected? Such terms as soon, good, many, nice, fast, and acceptable mean little in discussion of performance. A person explains little by saying, "You aren't getting the reports done fast enough, and they aren't accurate." Compare the last communication with the following: "The last two reports were submitted one day after the expected completion date. Also, they both had incorrect accumulated discount figures." The second explanation provides a clear understanding of the problem. However, it still does not indicate what the manager expects. Is half-a-day late acceptable? How may errors are acceptable? Be precise on the quality and quantity of the desired behaviour.

Managers sometimes feel that performance is not up to par, but they are not really sure why. A deeper analysis may indicate that the manager does not really know what he wants in this situation. It can be difficult to determine exactly what one expects, but it is necessary to analyze performance problems accurately.

QUESTION 3: Does the employees now what is expected ? How can a manger be sure?
As simple as it seems, lack of employee understanding is the problem that causes many performance breakdowns. Do not assume. Ask employees what they believe is expected of them. Do not settle for general terms. Large discrepancies between a manager's and a subordinate's perceptions may be revealed in a short exchange of expectations.

The importance of clear goals cannot be overemphasized. It does not take extensive research to substantiate the fact that goals are easier to meet when they are well defined and observable than when they are not. Employees cannot be expected to perform when they have knowledge of the goals or the reasoning behind them. Unclear goals can cause problems. For example, a fields sales force was given an urgent message. Headquarters wrote letter to all the field people saying that product A was tremendously overstocked and that the finance charges on the inventory were creating a burden. Management urged sales personnel to push this item. As a result, the sales staff took orders for all the items in three weeks. Unfortunately, they granted liberal discounts and ignored the other products, all factors that placed an even greater burden on the company. Management failed in relating goals to the salespeople clearly and completely.

If any first three questions results in a negative answer, further questions are not necessary. For instance, if the manager is not sure what is expected or cannot be sure the employees know, she must establish clear expectations. This would require an analysis of the job and a meeting between the manager and employee to compare job expectations. Skilfully managed communication that results in an open and trusting environment is required for job expectations to be compared successfully.

Once everyone involved is clear on the expectations, performance should probably improve. If after a period of time performance does not improve, it would be necessary to add the next question in the sequence to the performance analysis.

QUESTION 4: Has the desired behaviour even been performed before?
It is easy to assume that employees could perform a certain job if they wanted to, but a manager cannot be sure that employees have the appropriate ability and skill unless they have done it before. Employees who have not fully met the goal before they

require training. However if the job has been done before, but performance is now slipping, incentives or rewards are the problem.

How can a manager determine whether it is lack of skills or lack of incentive at the root of a performance problem? It may be necessary to ask previous supervisors or to investigate previous performance information.

QUESTION 5: ***Is adequate cooperation being received, and are the necessary tools and equipment present?***

We discussed the question of adequate cooperation and equipment earlier when presenting the model, but it is easy to overlook this concern. When analyzing a performance problem, manager tend to miss the obvious and make the entire situation much more complicated than necessary.

Listening may be particularly critical when attempting to determine if lack of cooperation or an equipment shortage is a problem. Employees will often blame poor performance on a lack of cooperation or equipment because they are easy excuses. Interactive listening to both the subordinates and other key employees helps a manager to determine if employees are making excuses or if these are the real cause of the performance problem.

If the first five questions do not resolve the problem, a manager needs to move on to the next question. After asking each of these questions in a sequential manner, a manager can be sure that the motivational model has been applied in a systematic manner in the attempt to understand a performance problem.

QUESTION 6: ***Are the employees being rewarded for satisfactory performance?***

The question of adequate reward for satisfactory performance actually involves three different questions: (1) Are rewards being received for performance? (2) Can employees see the relationship between performance and rewards? and (3) Is there a possibility that penalties are received for performance?

We discussed the first and second questions when presenting the model; we focus here on the third: Are employees receiving a penalty or rewards? Each week the production supervisors were required to fill out the timesheets for all their employees, but their carelessness resulted in many payroll errors. In fact, the supervisors were making so many errors that payroll had to add a clerk just to correct the errors. The production manager wrote a memo to all the supervisors about the importance of the timesheets, but this did little good. When the payroll manager again confronted the production manager about the problem, the production manager said that the supervisors simply disliked paperwork and there probably wasn't any way to motivate them to do it. A quick analysis revealed that there was no reason for the supervisors to complete the timesheets accurately. In fact, they would be penalized for doing so. They submitted timesheets on Friday afternoons, a busy production time for the supervisors. If the supervisors went through the timesheets quickly, they saved time and the payroll department would correct the errors anyway. In other words, they were penalized for performing in the manner requested of them. Once the supervisors learned payroll would no longer correct the errors, they turned in the timesheets error free. What supervisor wants to meet an employee who does not receive pay for the total number of hours worked?

From this example, it is clearly possible that a person will benefit from not performing in the desired manner. Managers must remain alert to the existing possibilities.

The six questions we have just examined should help managers to use the model when diagnosing a performance problem. If managers ask each of these questions, they can be assure that they have taken a systematic approach to understanding the total situation.

So far this discussion has been from the perspective of a manager trying to increase the motivational level and productivity of subordinates. However, a manager also needs to be concerned with motivating employees in the organization other than those who have a direct reporting relationship to the manager. An alternative may be to say that a manager is concerned with influencing others to act in a particular way. To influence others, the manager must understand the power base and communicate accordingly.

Power and Influence

Power can be defined as the capacity to apply "any force that results in behaviour that would not have occurred if the force had not been present." This force can originate from the individual, the organization, or the specific situation. Not all managers are able to use their power or force to influence. In fact, some managers shy away from the *concept* of power because it seems to be "undemocratic". Of course, some basis of power is usually implemented, but often it is done incorrectly since some managers do not even know they are using it.

The first step in using power correctly to influence others is to recognize the different types of power that a manager may possess. The same manager may have access to several types of power resources or may depend on a single resource to accomplish many power relationships. French and Raven suggest the five sources detailed in the paragraphs that follow. This discussion can serve as a comprehensive reference.

Reward power

Reward power grows out of the ability to give income, praise, recognition, promotion, or other valuable tangibles and intangibles. People in an organization generally know who has the power to sign vouchers or give raises; they know whose compliments are a sign of high status. We analyzed this kind of power extensively while discussing the performance model.

Coercive power

Coercive power is the opposite of reward power in that coercive power is based on fear. A manager who can give out a reward in a given situation can also use coercion—if only by withholding rewards. People may work hard to avoid embarrassment or scorn.

The power to reward and coerce are tangible resources when a manager is directly responsible for an employee. But what happens when a manager has no direct control? Obviously one cannot give a raise to, or fire, or suspend a fellow manager. In this situation, conformity and identification are strong motives and operate together. One person identifies with another when he feels that the other person has some quality that is desirable, appealing, or worth imitation. This identification will influence a person to act like another and meet his requests. In turn, this identification often leads to conformity.

The need to identify and conform can lead to peer pressure, which is a powerful management tool. The makers of T.V. commercials use celebrities in the hope that a customer will identify with them. Many commercials imply, "Wouldn't you like to be like this hero; everyone else is. Surely you don't want to be different." Likewise, a peer may be influenced by saying, "Ruth, all the other managers are sending a representative to the safety meeting. Even the V.P. of finance is going to have a representative present. Whom will you be sending?

Peer pressure is a subtle source of reward and coercive power that should not be overlooked. Consider, for example, a manager of accounting who was having a difficult time convincing the production department heads to send their supervisors to a quarterly meeting in which the topic was the paperwork required by the accounting department. She decided to use the power of identification and conformity. She first went to one of the most senior and respected department heads and asked what the best time would be for a meeting. She then asked this manager to ask a fellow manager if he would agree that this was the best time. Both managers agreed on the time and also agreed to send the notice about the next meeting to their fellow managers. She had perfect attendance at the next meeting! To do this, then, the accounting manager began where she had the greatest influence and then used conformity and peer pressure to acquire the desired results. Remember that the power to reward and the power to coerce are really the flip sides of this same coin, so they can be used in similar manners.

Legitimate Power

Legitimate power is the power usually associated with one's position or role in the company. It is the power of the title, rather than of the individual, and it can be transferred from one individual to another. Clearly, this power and the powers just detailed begin to overlap because legitimate power is usually associated with some power to reward and coerce. However, close examination often reveals that some positions with prestigious titles may have little legitimate power. For instance, a chairman of one corporatewide social responsibility committee has so little power that members do not even bother to attend meetings. Also, many organizations have a manager of production planning, but the position is given little power to go with the title. On the other hand, a manager of engineering has the power to change work schedules or project priorities due merely to the power given the position.

Export power

Export power arises from the knowledge, skill, or experience of the leader, the leader's ability to relate that expertise to a given work situation, and the extent to which the leader is perceived as having expertise. Expert power is difficult to assess, but important nonetheless. While a certain degree of reward, coercion, and legitimate power is inherent in the organizational structure, expert power depends entirely upon the person granting the power.

Expert power can be granted or taken away with the same degree of ease. For instance, the manager of a research and development group might have a lot of technical expert power with fellow managers. However, if she makes a significant error, all her power may suddenly vanish. At the same time, a manager may have a lot of expert power when dealing with one individual, but very little power with another. Expert power strictly depends upon the perceptions of people in the organization.

Managers probably use expert power more than they realize. Since others assume that an accounting manager knows more about accounting than anyone else, others will attend to any suggestions he makes along those lines. The same is true with most positions in an organization.

Trouble can develop, however, when one person assumes that he has power in a way or area that others do not perceive. For instance, what if an engineer makes a suggestion and believes that others will be influenced by expert power only to find that they are not. The engineer may attempt to "force" the issue of her expertise, but the others may then feel that the engineer is being arrogant.

A self-appraisal can help one be effective with expert power in relationships with others. Remember that expert power is based on others' perceptions; what one may see as expert, another may not. When a manager has completed a realistic self-appraisal, she should be able to use it to influence others without the fear of appearing arrogant.

Referent power

The last category of power, referent power, may be the most difficult to identify. Referent power is related to the attractiveness or appeal one person has to others. An intangible part of a leader's personal makeup, it makes him special to others. It may be charisma, or personal magnetism, or some other undefinable quality. Historians say that President Kennedy had a high degree of referent power. In this context, person's attractiveness is determined by the way in which the person conveys a trusting and positive image, nebulous terms to put into operation. They only way a person can gauge referent power is through careful observation of others. a manager needs to ask, "How do others react to me? to assess the degree of referent power possessed.

The key to using any of these types of power is for one to identify the power he has and know when to use it, yet many managers fail. Either they do not recognize the fact that they have the power, or they attempt to use it when they do not really have it.

To become more effective in the use of power, a person should analyze how and why she presently attempts to influence others. This will help to identify the type of power being used. One should identify the type of power used and assess the efficiency of its application and the possibility of using other types. By being socially aware and by continually analyzing, one can be assured that the influence and communication flow from the correct power base.

Motivating and controlling the sales office team

The sales office manager's job is to get things done through people and too make his department a good place in which to work. Here are a number of good ideas aimed at helping the sales office manager to build the alert, effective and responsible staff he needs to be able to do his job better.

Put the emphasis on skill, not rule

Judge your own actions and those of others by their effects. That is to say, effects in terms of both increasing the competitive strength of your department and the satisfaction of the human needs of the people who work in it. Go easy on rules in running your department, for doing it by the book is often not the most effective way. If an unorthodox solution works well and pleases the people who use it, don't discount it because it doesn't appear in the manual of rules and procedures.

Set a high standard within your department

Most people enjoy working in the best team. They like to feel that their leader is firm but fair. Provided the standards are reasonable and attainable, and provided their leader shows them how, most people in the team will stretch out to attain the attainable. To achieve this the supervisor must, of course, set the most excellent example. If he is irregular in his work habits, bad at expressing himself, careless about facts, bored in attitude, and generally lethargic—then it is certain that his staff will be likewise. High performance standards are a key factor in motivating people.

Know your subordinates individually

Continuous study of individuals is a must for getting things done through people.

Motives and attitudes are important tools for the executive, and they can be determined only through study. Since security is one of the main job satisfactions of most people, giving recognition to the contribution of others and to their roles is a useful starting point in getting the best out of people. Individuals to vary widely in their personal characteristics. Well-timed praise may spur one person to new heights of achievement, whereas it may only inflate another. A better key to the latter's of achievement, whereas it may be constructive criticism. A third individual may wilt under any kind of criticism and some other approach is needed. The skilled executive constantly hunts for the right method for each of his people. For this reason, the tactful drawing out of subordinates can often supply valuable information for understanding them. Do remember that people often act on the basis of non-logical emotion, even though they try to appear completely logical.

Try to listen thoughtfully and objectively

The sales office manager who knows his people—their habits, worries, ambitions and pet prides—comes to appreciate why they behave as they do and what motives stir them. The best and fastest way to know them is to get them to talk freely, without fear of ridicule or disapproval. The manager should try to understand how others feel on a subject, whether or not he feels the same way. He should never dominate a discussion or a meeting by doing all the talking himself. If he starts to say something at the same time as the person he is talking to, he should give way and allow the other person to speak first. One objection to the idea of being a good listener is that it takes time to draw people out. The answer is that it takes time to plan too. Both are essential to a manager's job, and the time invested will pay big dividends.

Be considerate

Few things contribute more to building a fine well-motivated team than a considerate team leader. Try to be calm and courteous towards your people and consider the effects on them of any decisions you make. Take into account the problems they have of their own, both business and domestic and try to build up their pride in their work and their self-respect. Start by treating personal characteristics as assets and by being careful not to trample on them.

Be consistent

If you fly off the handle you are likely to frighten your people into their shells. If you vacillate wildly in reaction, mood and manner you will probably bewilder them. Neither sort of behaviour can win you the confidence and co-operation of your people—and you must have this to get things done.

Give your people objectives and a sense of direction

Your people should know where they are now, where they are going, by what route they are going, what time they should arrive and the type of obstacles likely to be encountered on the way. They need this information to plan their time intelligently and too work effectively. Always make clear the relationship between the day-to-day work of sales office employees and the larger sales division and corporate objectives. For example, don't ask to analyse the variable costs of their operation unless at the same time you make it clear that the project is part of a long-range plan to provide leeway for salary increases, and that the knowledge they provide will help strengthen the operating efficiency of the company.

Give directions in terms of suggestions or requests

If your people have initiative and ability, you will vastly better results in this way than by issuing orders or commands. Issue the latter only as a last resort. If you have to give orders all the time, maybe you should look for some different assistants, or perhaps examine closely the way you have been handling your own job. Always be sure to tell why you want certain jobs done. Informal oral explanations are often much better than formal written ones, so let the individual circumstances be your guide here.

Delegate responsibility for details to people

This is another obvious point that is frequently overlooked. Delegating responsibility is basic to competent administration and you are not doing your real job as an executive if you fail to delegate. If, as a sales office manager, you insist on keeping your hand in details, you discourage your people by competing with them. Moreover, by doing everything yourself you prevent your people learning to make their own decisions. Sooner or later the more capable people will leave, and the others will sit back quite happy and let you do all the work. Ultimately you will have little or no time for the important thinking and planning which are so important in your job. Think of your people as working with you—not for you.

Show your staff that you have faith in them

People tend to perform according to what is expected to them. If they know that you have confidence in them to do a first-rate job, that is what they will usually try to give you.

Keep your people well informed

Bring them up to date constantly regarding new developments and let them know well in advance whenever changes are in the offing. As members of a team they are entitled to know what is going on. If they do, their thinking will be more closely geared to reality and their attitudes are bound to be more flexible. Give them enough information about conditions and events within the company and the industry to enable them to see themselves and their work in true perspective.

Let your people in on your plans at an early stage

It is, of course, true that some plans cannot be discussed far in advance. They should, though, be discussed with subordinates before they appear in final form. It will give you people that all-important chance to participate. Furthermore, because they will have taken part in shaping the plan, it will be as much theirs as yours, and their sense of commitment will be much greater. Hence they will tend to carry out the plan with real vigour and enthusiasm.

Ask your people for their counsel and help

Bring them actively into the picture. It will help give them a feeling of belonging and will build their self-confidence. It will often make them anxious to work harder than ever. What is even more important is that they may well have excellent and usable ideas which may never be utilised unless you ask for them.

Give a courteous hearing to ideas

Many ideas may sound shallow and badly thought through to you, but it is most important not to react in an impatient or scornful manner. There is no surer way to discourage original thinking than to dispel or ridicule a suggestion or idea expressed by a subordinate. His next idea may be the very one you want, so make it easy for that important idea to come to you.

Give your people a chance to take part in decisions

When your people feel they have had a say in decisions, they are more likely to go along with them in a co-operative way. If they agree with the decision, they will look upon it as their own and back it to the hilt. If they don't agree, they may still back it more strongly than otherwise because of the fact that their point of view was taken into full and fair consideration.

Tell the originator of an idea what action was taken and why

If you do, he'll study other problems and suggest how to solve them. If his idea is accepted he will be encouraged by seeing the results of his suggestion taking effect. If his idea is not adopted. He will accept that fact more readily and with fuller understanding if you show him that the reasons for rejection are clear and sound. In addition, knowing why his idea was impractical will help the suggester analyse the next problem more clearly.

Try to let people carry out their own ideas

It sometimes happens that equally good suggestions on a particular problem come from two individuals at the same time, one person directly responsible in the situation and the other essentially detached from it. In such cases it is usually desirable to choose the recommendation of the person who will have the responsibility of carrying it out. It is good management practice therefore, to keep your people constantly aware of your willingness to let them work out their own solutions to problems in their particular operating areas.

Most people need to think that their job is important. Many not only have to feel that they have an important job, but are essential in it before they start to operate really well.

The days of "treat 'em rough and tell 'em nothing" have passed. A system providing for periodic ratings for employees is the first step. However, the full value of such a system is only realised when ratings are discussed with each person individually so that each can bolster weak points, clear up misunderstandings and recognise his particular talents.

This may, perhaps seem obvious, but managers in thousands of organisations forget to do it every day. Reprimands in the presence of others cause humiliation and resentment instead of a desire to do better next time. Criticising a subordinate when people from his department are present undermines his morale, his authority, and his enthusiasm to do his best for his manager and his company.

First of all—get the facts. Review them with those concerned and reach agreement on them. Then be ready to suggest a constructive course of action for the future. When you criticise, do concentrate on the method and on results rather than on personalities. If you can precede the criticism by a bit of honest praise, then so much the better. Note, however, that some executives tend to do this so regularly, so insincerely and so unimaginatively that the compliments lose their value.

Most people thrive on appreciation. Praise before others often has a multiple impact. It tends to raise morals, increase prestige and strengthen self-confidence important factors in the development of your people. But do be sure that those you praise are really the ones who deserve it, and that you don't encourage "credit grabbing."

Taking credit yourself which really belongs to one of your people tends to destroy his initiative and willingness to take responsibility. Giving him fair recognition for what he does has a double benefit. He gets appreciation for doing a good job, and you get the help and support of loyal and well-motivated staff. If you take all the bows when someone else has played the leading role, you can expect to rapidly lose the respect of your people.

In small doses, griping can act as a safety valve for your people. If they worked under a perfect administrator they would probably still complain, just because he was perfect. Vicious personal sniping though, is another matter, and here you should take every possible action to have the cause discovered and rooted out. Remember too, that without some dissatisfaction there would be little incentive to do or get something better.

Every person in the sales office should have a detailed job description, and each item of the job description should be linked to specific standards of performance as in the following example.

To liaise with production and sales departments regarding stock availability. To handle all incoming calls from customers and route to the correct department.

Standards of performance in relation to the above are attained when:

1 The company becomes renowned for its excellent customer relations and customer services.

2 The percentage of complaints that cannot be handled at the customer relations officer's desk is not more than (state %).

3 The sales force look upon the function of customer relations as a vital part of their "backing."

Obviously, the more specific you can be in setting sales office standards of performance the better. Once these standards have been worked out, discussed and accepted by individuals, then their performance in relation to the standards must be continually observed and discussed with them, applying many of the principles of good management and good leadership already discussed.

Does he recognise ability in others?

Every manager should be constantly appraising the performance of his people. After all, it is his prime function to produce results through others, and the quality of the results is almost completely dependent on the quality of the people who do the work. Many managers in small offices tend to have personal likes and dislikes concerning each of their employees, but as the team increases in size it is most important to develop good assessment procedures based upon the most realistic standards.

A sound merit rating programme must be based on the following factors:

1 It must be as simple as possible and based on principles which are seen to be fair and fully understood by all. There should be a minimum of red tape.

2 It must, where possible, give both qualitative and quantitative measures. This means the procedure must show in quantitative terms where the individual stands in relation to others in his unit, for example:

   1 Number of customer complaints handled.

   2 Number of promotional telephone calls made.

   3 Number of sales office errors.

   4 Number of days worked—and so on.

and it should also give an indication of why he has that particular ranking, what are his strong points and what are his weaknesses.

3 It must be flexible so that special or temporary factors which may be affecting the person's performance will be investigated thoroughly, and so that the permanence of their nature can also be evaluated.

4 It must be thorough because a hurried, superficial rating is worthless. The very nature of the rating procedure itself must require the supervisor to explore fully every aspect of the employee's job performance. This means that any rating procedure which is susceptible to misuse—for example, the hurried checking off of categories—must be avoided.

5 It must provide definite control over personal biases prejudices. Everyone has personal feelings which may influence his appraisal, yet few merit rating procedures contain any kind of built-in control to prevent baises and prejudices from creeping into a supervisor's evaluation. Mere warnings about such happenings during training sessions are not nearly enough. On-the-spot control is essential.

6 It should provide for two or more independent evaluations of each person although this is sometimes difficult to arrange. In any event, the merit rating of every individual should be discussed at some length with the rater's manager before the rating is finalised. In this way the manager can satisfy himself that the rating is being made in an objective and unbiased manner, and can take an interest in all the things the supervisor is (hopefully) doing to train and develop the person being assessed.

With regard to the important rating discussion, the following suggestions may prove most helpful:

1 Arrange to talk to the employee when interruptions will be at a minimum. Neither of you should feel rushed.

2 Be sincere so that the employee will have confidence in you and feel that you are really interested in his welfare. Your attitude can make or break the success of the whole rating programme.

3 Make a definite appointment well ahead of time, so that the employee realises the importance of the occasion.

4 Conduct the conselling interview where you will not be overheard—in a private office if possible.

5 Explain thoroughly the rating programme and what can be attained for his own good and for the good of the company.

6 Talk frankly about each factor. With the exception of the back page, let the employee see the rating form and where you have placed your checkmarks.

7 Mention good points as much as you do the poor ones. Let him know why he has a good rating or a poor one.

8 Be open-minded. If you feel that a rating is wrong, admit it and then change it.

9 Record what you told the employee and what his reactions were at the close of the discussion.

A typical merit rating system for a sales office manager is as follows:

How do you rate the manager with respect to the quality of work he turns out, and the neatness and accuracy evident in the job he does?

a Careless. Tends to repeat the same type of errors.

b Work is sometimes poor because of errors or untidiness.

c Usually turns out acceptable work. Not many errors.

d Checks and observes his work. Quality of the finished product can be relied upon.

e Work of the highest quality. Errors, if any, extremely rare.

How would you rate this person with respect to the speed with which he works? Is he a fast worker who turns out a large amount of work, or does it take him an unusually long time to complete a job?

a Exceptionally fast worker. Turns out large volume of work.

b Gets his work done promptly.

c Works at moderate speed. Good output on repetitive work.

d Tends to let work pile up. Has difficulty in keeping pace.

e Volume of work done is unsatisfactory. Slow.

a Brilliant and keen mind coupled to an eagerness to learn.

b Quick to grasp new ideas and methods.

c Learns in a satisfactory manner.

d Learns new methods and procedures by excessive repetition.

e Slow in learning even simple procedures. Needs constant guidance.

a Does not accept responsibility.

b Assumes responsibility without necessary qualifications.

c Assumes responsibility only on matters within his own sphere.

d Takes full share of responsibility in keeping with good judgement.

e Takes more than his share of responsibility.

a Extremely careless. Makes many mistakes.

b Work of uneven quality ranging from good to poor.

c Does what is expected of him. Sometimes requires follow-up.

d Very industrious. Requires little follow-up.

e Extremely reliable. Consistently does an excellent job.

a Is enthusiastic and sold on the organisation. Any criticism he makes is constructive and in keeping with good judgement.

b Happy in the job. Is satisfied with the organisation.

c Seems to be fairly happy with the job and with the company.

d Shows little interest in either the job or the company.

e Is disgruntled and depressed. Not in accord with many policies.

a Outstanding ability to work with people at all levels.

b Co-operates willingly and generally wins co-operation from others.

c Co-operates with others sometimes, but only when really necessary.

d Has difficulty in working with others.

e A very poor attitude in dealing with others.

a Lacks self-confidence, extremely reluctant to commit himself.

b Slow or reluctant to make decisions or makes decisions on matters for which he is not qualified.

c Makes necessary decisions only on matters within his own sphere.

d Makes decision based upon sound reasoning.

e Makes timely decisions based upon sound reasoning. Creates confidence in his ability.

a Needs constant guidance. Cannot see the wood for the trees.

b Often confused as to the relevant importance of factors.

c Good at analysing data and for most part gives proper emphasis to each factor.

d Alert. Correctly weighs important factors.

e Keenly analytical. Has a special ability in this area.

a Vivid imagination. Visualises future possibilities and methods.

b Active imagination. Keeps one step ahead of current problems.

c Quite satisfactory. Visualises his situation and what of others.

d Only sees the immediate situation. Does not think ahead.

e Entirely lacking in imagination.

a Confused with detail. Tries to do it all himself.

b Often fails to properly apportion work and authority. Frequently lacks time for important matters.

c Most often gets things done, though is often late in attainment of deadlines.

d Gets things done and usually within the required time limits.

e Superb ability in getting projects completed on time.

a Outstanding ability to evaluate and develop subordinates. Builds men.

b Good appraiser and developer of men.

c Recognises strong and weak qualities in his people and usually develops them well.

d Usually overlooks both strong and weak traits in his people.

Seldom makes any attempt to develop them.

e Fails completely to either appraise or develop his people.

a Apt to claim the credit for all good work done in his department. Seldom commends an employee for good work.

b Overlooks giving credit to others except when it is brought to his attention.

c Is usually fair in recognising the good work of others.

d Gives credit where it is due.

e Gives timely recognition to each individual's work, both to outsiders and to the employee.

How would you rate this individual with respect to his potential for future growth in the company? Does he seem to have attained the limit of his development? Or does he show evidence of a capacity for growth well beyond his present job level?

a Very good potential for advancement. Tends to raise the level of the job he now holds. Always alert to opportunities for self-improvement.

b Fairly good possibilities for promotion. He is eager to learn and accept greater responsibility.

c Becoming more valuable in his present job with experience but unlikely he will develop much beyond his present level.

d Very limited capacity for growth.

e He is slipping backwards and is quite a serious problem in his present assignment.

Maintaining sales office discipline

Here are some final pointers on merit rating in the sales office:

1 Top management must approve the rating system and be really interested in making it a success.

2 Managers, supervisors and employees must be thoroughly sold on the purpose of merit rating, and they must realise that management is sincere in its intention to use it only in the interests of developing staff towards greater job satisfaction through improved and altogether more professional performance.

3 Rating forms should be carefully designed and kept flexible. Frequent change is not a bad thing provided that each change brings a definite improvement.

4 The plan should be only part of a complete employee and supervisor training and development programme.

5 Ratings should be considered only indicative, never final.

6 Thorough training is necessary for all those who will carry out ratings and the resultant conversations with subordinates.

7 All ratings should be discussed with employees by the raters.

8 Provision should be made for appeal from ratings.

9 Ratings should be reviewed at regular intervals. Programmes must be kept to some kind of regular schedule.

10 The forms and the whole plan should be kept fluid and liable to constant improvement.

11 Ratings should be validated by comparison with the performance of others on the job rated.

12 Interviews with employees should always be strictly in private. Ratings should never be discussed with those not connected with the administration of the programme.

13 All raters should be familiar with every factor and definition of the factors in the rating form.

14 An inaccurate or badly conducted rating is far worse than no rating at all.

One of the great drawbacks to good supervision is the difficulty most managers seem to have in reprimanding an employee when the occasion demands, and no company should neglect the important task of training their managers to interview for correction. Discipline is an important force for getting things done, and where discipline is lacking, morale is usually low and the standard of work produced is low. Good discipline does not necessarily mean a tough, rough manager—but it does mean complete adherence to a number of entirely reasonable "standards of behaviour and performance."

Managers must be alert to remove any factor which encourages subordinates to violate regulations or to deviate from the standards which have been accepted as reasonable and fair by everyone.

Under normal conditions, reprimanding should take the form of private counselling, as previously described, remembering that the prime objective is that of securing better performance from the employee without creating resentment or dissatisfaction in the process. Therefore we must draw a careful distinction between the reprimand and the rollocking.

Reprimand	*Rollocking*
Given when calm.	Given when angry.
When sure it is deserved.	Without checking facts.
With worker and boss alone.	In front of others.
Straightforward, no swearing.	Uses strong language.
Uses encouragement to do better.	Makes man angry or discouraged.
Leaves man anxious to improve.	Leaves him beaten or resentful.

Planning the interview for correction purposes is as important as planning for any other type of interview. The manager who follows a well-thought-out plan will never regret things he may have said unplanned in the heat of the moment - or for things left undone until they were too late to be effective. The following outline should be used in preparing for this type of interview:

Before the interview

1 Get all the facts.

2 Evaluate the facts.

3 Organise the facts into a plan of action.

4 Arrange for the interview.

During the interview

1 Give the reasons for the reprimand.

2 Give the employee an opportunity to explain his views.

3 Keep cool under all circumstances.

4 Focus the attention on the situation, rather than the person at fault.

5 Don't make threats, use sarcasm or display authority.

6 Talk straight.

7 Be constructive at all time - point out ways to improve.

8 Encourage the employee and express confidence in his desire and ability to improve.

After the interview

1 Follow up and give praise for improvement.

2 Indicate by casual contacts that the friendly relationship has not been impaired.

Here is a reprimand checklist to help pinpoint the causes of the problems which make reprimanding necessary:

1 Did not know what was expected.

a Full details of the job never properly explained.

b Details were explained, but forgotten.

c Sufficient explanation of policies and standards not given.

d Policies and standards were explained, but forgotten.

2 Did not know how to do what was expected.

a Had improper or inadequate instruction.

b Had insufficient practise.

c Too complicated to remember.

d Did not pay attention to instructions.

3 Could not do what was expected.

a Too much skill and training required.

b Lacks background of education.

c Lacks background of experience.

d Illness.

e Fatigue.

f Nervousness.

g Worry.

h Insufficient intelligence.

i Did not have time.

j Was not permitted to perform duties required.

4 Would not do what was expected.

a Duties were too unpleasant.

b Angry with supervisor/manager.

c Just didn't feel like it.

d Against it because of personal principles.

e Not in line with company policies.

f Wants to be transferred.

g Wants to be discharged.

h Was not part of the job as he understood it.

i No one else follows the rule.

j Wanted to have some fun.

k Job was too monotonous.

l Preferred to do another job first.

m Didn't see any sense in it.

n Preferred to do things the old way.

5

Office Management

Organisation can be defined as 'the structure of relationships and responsibilities, authorities and duties by means of which the work to be done and the personnel and means to do it are brought together and coordinated.' It is, then, a structure or basic framework within which an enterprise is enabled to work, its purpose being to create an arrangement of responsibilities, authorities and duties through which this work can be efficiently carried out. Effective organisation relies heavily on effective direction and careful delegation, both of which were examined under the heading of 'Command'. It would be useful at this point, then, to give definitions to the terms 'responsibility', 'authority' and 'duty', as they are so important to the understanding of organisation and delegation:

Responsibility is the obligation to ensure that authority is property used and duties properly performed. It normally carries the right to delegate authority and duties, but cannot itself be delegated, flowing from the bottom to the top of the organisational structure. However, at each level of delegation the delegate is responsible to the delegate for the proper performance of the work delegated: 'accountability' is, perhaps, a better term here than 'responsibility.' As has been pointed out already, responsibility or accountability must always be accompanied by the requisite authority to direct the activities of subordinates in the pursuit of the work delegated. Authority is the right to require subordinates to perform duties allocated to them. It is essential that the subordinates staff concerned know that is authority exists and its extent. Duty is the obligation to carry out the instructions of those in authority. Orders are not, of course, necessarily given specifically; the work to be done may be inherent in the procedures and systems being carried out, and the worker must act on implicit as well as explicit instructions.

In very many undertaking the organisation has grown rather than been planned, and this is understandable where a firm or a department-has expanded from small beginnings. However, this does not produce the most efficient organisation structure, and to plan for efficiency it is necessary to apply certain clearly recognised rules. These are:

1. Determine the activities necessary to attain the desired objectives.
2. Divide these activities into logical work areas.

3. Appoint a leader to each work area.
4. Determine the number of staff required for each work area and appoint these to operate under the appropriate leaders.
5. Determine the necessary equipment for each section and make the necessary provision.
6. Ensure proper coordination between all sections of the organisation by the provision of adequate procedures and communication systems.
7. Clearly define and set the extent and limits of responsibility, authority and duty is respect of all members of the organisation.
8. Ensure that senior members of staff have the authority to delegate, and also that they make provision for understudies where appropriate.

It will be seen that, ideally, organisation should be planned from the bottom, or at least from the bottom level of supervision. However, in reality this is very rarely practicable because by the time the necessity for a formal structure is recognised, usually through the growth of the concern, some form of organisation pattern has already been established. Nevertheless, when organisation does become necessary the rules set out above should be taken into account.

It is usual to classify forms of organisation into specific types so far as theory is concerned, but it must be realised that in actual practice it is rare to find any particular pattern in its pure theoretical form. The first and easiest type is line organisation—also called military, scalar or vertical organisation.

Line organisation

Here the concern is divided into departments, each department having a controlling head. Accountability for the activities of the department is vested in the head of the department by top management, from who he also derives his authority to control the department. Authority then flows downwards through the supervisory strata to the lowest level of supervision. In this way there is direct management control from the very top of the organisation, departmentally, to the bottom. This form of organisation has the following advantages and disadvantages:

Advantages

1. It is simple and readily understood.
2. It promotes rapid decisions because of the direct nature of the chain of command.
3. For the same reason it simplifies coordination between personnel in the same department.
4. Effective delegation is facilitated, and because of the direct line of control inspection of the work of delegates is relatively easy to arrange and maintain.

5. All members of the department can be made aware of, and readily understand, their position and status in the departmental hierarchy.
6. Staff discipline is easier to maintain than in other forms of organisation.
7. The extent of responsibility, authority and duties can be clearly defined and recognised by those concerned.

Disadvantages

1. It is potentially rigid and inflexible because each department is virtually self-contained and there are limited opportunities to gain experience of other departments.
2. Its effectiveness is very much dependent on the capacity of the head of departmental.
3. For the same reason, expansion of the department may prove difficult.
4. Cooperation and coordination between different departments may prove difficult, and is very much dependent on the attitude of the departmental head.

Functional organisation

A second form of organisation is functional organisation, also called horizontal or lateral organisation and occasionally staff organisation. In this pattern the various functions of the undertaking are determined and an expert in each is appointed, who will be responsible for his special function irrespective of in what department any aspect of it is carried out. Thus he will be in direct contact with supervisors and staff in operating departments and authorised to give them direct instructions in regard to his special function without reference to their line supervisors.

If, for instance an accountant is appointed as the functional chief in regard to finance, he will have the right to direct sales staff to refrain from taking orders from customers without reference to the sales manager. Equally, he will have the authority to instruct a purchasing clerk to avoid buying from a specific supplier without reference to the chief buyer. In both cases there is an element if finance and so they come within the accountant's functional orbit. However, both cases also come within other functional areas, the first being sales and the second purchasing. It will be immediately obvious that operating staff in such circumstances are subject to directions from several sources, some of which may be conflicting, and the while departmental supervisors and managers still have responsibility for discipline their authority is diluted so far as other areas of their accountability are concerned.

It is argued that in functional organisation line supervisors do not have to be so capable as in the purely line form as the functional aspects of their departments' activities are taken over by experts separate from their departments. Be that as it may, this type of organisation can be very confusing to the workers as they can become unsure as whose instructions they should give priority. This problem can be ameliorated to some extent by putting clearly defined limits on the authority of the functional specialists, and making sure these limits are known and understood by all concerned.

Because of the difficulties inherent in this form of organisation it is not commonly found in practice: nevertheless its advantages should be stated.

Advantages

1. The knowledge and experience of functional experts are utilised in the direct control of the operations of the concern.
2. The specialists are able to concentrate more fully on their functions since they are not concerned specifically with running the operational departments and so their time is not dissipated by disciplinary and other problems associated with line management.
3. The organisation is able to grow without radical alternation to its organisation structure.

Disadvantages

1. No clear lines of authority are apparent, making control and coordination difficult. The result of this is that:
2. Responsibility for failure may be difficult to establish and so remedies may no be easy to apply.
3. It can be uneconomic because of the large number of high-salaried experts engaged.
4. It can be confusing to the workers, as explained above.

Line and staff organisation

A third basic type of organisation is line and staff, which attempts to combine the benefits of the previous two. In this form of organisation there are, again, functional experts appointed but in this instance they have no executive powers and act in an advisory capacity only. The result of this is that the line managers and supervisors maintain direct control and authority over the members of their departments but also have available to them expert knowledge to assist their departments in the effective operation of their functional areas. As obvious example is that of a personnel manager (staff) advising an accountant (line) in the recruitment of new members of staff. Line and staff organisation is the type most commonly found and can be said to be the most generally efficacious. It has, of course, advantages and disadvantages, which are:

Advantages

1. Direct lines of responsibility and authority are maintained.

2. Control of departments remains with the departmental heads.
3. The advantage of having specialist knowledge and experience available to line managers and supervisors promotes departmental efficiency.
4. Departmental and interdepartmental coordination and cooperation are facilitated because the 'specialists' interests spread throughout the undertaking.

Disadvantages

1. Line officers are not bound to follow the advice of the staff officers, and sometimes do not. This can lead to inefficiencies and a waste of the expensive skills of the expert functional specialists.
2. Staff officers can sometimes try to usurp the authority of line officers, which can lead to bad feeling. It can also result in some diminution of the authority of the line managers and supervisors over their staff.
3. This form of organisation can be confusing for the workers, especially where there is a sharp difference of opinion between the line and the staff officers.

Whilst staff officers can operate in any of the traditional management functions, such as finance, marketing and so on, most are to be found in what might be called the newer professional areas such as organisation and method, personnel management and industrial relations, and operational research. All of these specialisms require a high degree of training and a thorough experience for them to be effectively practised. It is, therefore, unlikely that line managers and supervisors, thoroughly engaged as they are in the day-to-day operations of their organisation, would have the opportunity to acquire the necessary expertise to function as staff officers.

Equally, because of the concentration required to achieve thorough training and experience in their own particular fields, which tends to preclude their gaining experience of day-to-day operations in line departments, staff officers may not be adequately equipped to carry line responsibility and authority. Hence, the line and staff pattern is seen to be an ideal organisation form.

Committee organisation

A fourth type of organisation, which has become increasingly evident in recent years, is committee organisation. Whilst formerly largely confined to non-profit-making undertaking and institutions, and also to bodies subject to public accountability such as local government, it is now in some measure to be found in industrial and commercial enterprises. A board of directors is, of course, a committee, but lower down the management chain committees deliberate on matters that used to be the province of one executive. This has come about chiefly for two reasons: first because modern business is much more worker participation in management decisions, particularly in matters directly concerning the labour force.

Committee organisation occurs where management decisions are formulated by a group instead of being made by an individual. Members may be *appointed* or may be *elected,* according to the regulations of the body concerned. It is, of course, quite impossible for an organisation to be managed entirely by committee and of necessity some other form of organisation such as pure line or line and staff is required where individuals at various supervisory levels put into effect decisions taken in committee. It must also be said that some committees can become merely the reinforcing mouthpiece of a strong committee member: this is not uncommon in boards of directors, where a forceful managing director or chairman may constantly subdue his fellow directors to his point of view.

The advantages and disadvantages of committee organisation may be put as follows:

Advantages

1. More than one point of view on any problem can be considered.
2. the advice of experts on particular matters can be made available.
3. Full discussion and consideration can be given to any problem before the organisation is committed to particular solution.
4. Because committee members normally come from different activity areas it is likely that the implementation of decisions will be well coordinated and that cooperation between different sections of the organisation will be better assured.

Disadvantages

1. Because of the number of people involved and the sometime lengthy discussions that take place, committees are often slow in reaching decisions.
2. Because of the collective nature of committees no individual responsibility can be fixed for decisions reached, and so no individual accountability for failure can be apportioned.
3. Decisions are likely to be the result of compromise and are therefore likely to lead to less positive action than would be the case where an individual made the decisions.
4. Differences of opinion between members of the committee may result in decisions being postponed to another meeting, with the result that day-to-day operations may suffer.
5. It is often not possible to obtain rapid decisions from individual members of a committee where urgent action may be required, on the grounds that no authority is vested in individuals.

It has been said that a camel is a horse designed by a committee and this statement gives a very good idea of the way some people view the way committee organisation works.

Centralisation and decentralisation

An examination of organisation patterns would not be complete without a look at the questions of centralisation and decentralisation. Centralisation can be defined as the grouping of specialised functions or office services into one servicing unit and under unified control. Thus we have centralised accounting and centralised purchasing as examples of centralised functions, and centralised typing and centralised filing as examples of centralised office services.

The increasing size and complexity of modern undertakings and the widespread use of computers have encouraged the extensive adoption of centralisation for the following reasons:

1. Really competent managers are hard to find and centralisation makes the best use of their talents.
2. Standardisation of systems and methods can be achieved, which facilitates the setting of performance standards, leading to effective supervision and control.
3. There is an increase, in specialisation and hence the development of greater competence.
4. The problem of servicing peak load is eased because periods of pressure will not coincide in different sections of the undertaking.
5. It is administratively convenient to have control of a function or service in one place.
6. Machines and equipment are most fully, and therefore economically, used.
7. Staff training is simplified because personnel are employed where their particular function or service is concentrated.

Against these very real advantages of centralisation must be set equally real disadvantages, which may be enumerated as follows:

1. It results in a rigid-structure with little flexibility which is slow to accommodate change when necessary.
2. In the larger undertaking there usually develops a long chain of command with many intermediate levels of management and supervision which, in turn, results in communication difficulties and slow response to management decisions.
3. Often decisions are taken a long way from the operation centre they effect, and such decision may not take into account special conditions.
4. Staff may not easily be able to identify with the distant central management control of their function and morale may suffer in consequence.

5. Local managers and supervisors may have little discretion to act on their own initiative, which may dampen the enthusiasm of the talented. This in turn may lead to the loss to the organisation of able people.
6. Of necessity the organisation will be in some measure bureaucratic with the inevitable increase in administrative paperwork and records.
7. There is a real danger that staff will form a restricted view of the organisation, bounded by their own particular function. This leads to a narrowing of their experience, an inflexible attitude to any spread of duties and difficulty in transferring them to other types or areas of work should the occasion arise. It may also, of course, result in a reduction in their prospects of promotion.

Decentralisation is, of course, the opposite to centralisation. Here each division or department is in control of the running of all the functions which impinge upon it and of all the office services required to enable it to operate. Undertakings where there are many branches, for example, in total decentralisation—or departmentalisation as it is sometimes called—each branch would be entirely responsible for its buying, selling, credit control, office services and other aspects of its operation. When decentralisation takes place where the whole organisation is on one location, each department or division will also have total control, operating its own buying, staff recruitment secretarial and filing services and so on.

In such cases the advantages and disadvantages accruing may be said to be the reverse of those given for centralisation, and there is, therefore, no need to enumerate them again. Certainly more able departmental management and supervision are required, and all staff members are exposed to a wider range of experience. However, it must also be said that departments can become very departmental-minded and show some inflexibility in the relationships with other sections of the organisation. Where decentralisation is absolute, which is not a common phenomenon by any means, the organisational structure is very likely to be decidedly of the line form.

Perhaps the most difficult aspect of decentralisation is that of final control—that is, control by top management. Lack of common standards, piecemeal buying, different office systems and the like make control difficult. One solution is to have certain functions—such as purchasing, staff training, accounting and others—centralised, leaving the more localised functions such as selling, departmental recruitment and secretarial assistance in the hands of each separate section. Another is to ensure cohesion and coordination of the whole undertaking's activities by means of functional and servicing committees, very efficient communication systems and positive inspection and checking procedures as discussed under delegation.

In actual practice, in order to try to obtain the best of both worlds, most organisations operate on a mixture of both centralisation and decentralisation according to their individual problems and requirements. It must be said, however, that the increasing use of the computer has tended to require the centralisation of many operations, particularly those of accounting buying and similar functions where there is a significant measure of standardisation.

Organisation charts

The organisational pattern of an undertaking can most clearly be illustrated by means of a chart, and examples of organisation charts have been. These are presented in what is known as the horizontal pattern. This pattern is easy to read and understand. Line authority and responsibility are simple to recognize, connections being made by solid lines. Where it is required to show functional relationships, such as in line and staff organisation, then these can be indicated by broken or dotted lines. Generally speaking, though this is by no means universal, posts of equal authority and accountability are drawn at the same levels: alterations from this practice usually occur through lack of space on the paper rather than by deliberate intent.

The benefits accruing from organisation charts are that they present the organisation pattern in a simplistic form, and few members of the organisation will not be able to understand from such a presentation where they stand in the organisation scheme. In addition, when such charts are constructed they require the designer to examine the organisation very carefully before committing anything to paper, and such analysis will often draw attention to anomalies in the organisation plan and to overlapping duties and responsibilities. However, to be effective, a chart must not be too complicated: only by being kept reasonably simple, and in consequence, bearing only the minimum of lines and titles, will it be most effective. Besides the horizontal type, there are various other forms of organisation chart, including those drawn in a circular fashion and those having concentric circles. Most are confusion except to the specialist and need not concern us here. However, one other form is worth looking at, and this is the vertical organisation chart. It is most useful where it is necessary to show a very large number of departments and subdivisions, but is less easy to read than the horizontal form. An example of this type of chart is given.

Relationships

All forms of organisation give rise to relationships between members, and these can be categorised into four types as follows:

1. *Direct:* also known as the line or executive relationship, this occurs between controllers and the controlled. It is the relationship existing down the chain of command, as exemplified in line organisation. Thus the chief accountant has a direct relationship with his assistant accountant and the office administrator with his typing supervisor.
2. *Indirect:* Also known as the functional relationship, this occurs where a specialist is responsible for seeing that a function meets a suitable standard throughout an

organisation, though his powers are advisory only and not executive. Thus the personnel officer has an indirect relationship with all operational departments: he may advice on and assist in the recruitment to staff, of example, but he has no authority to make appointments.

3. *Staff:* This is a particularly difficult relationship for the person concerned, and exists between and executive and his personal assistant. The personal assistant has no delegated authority to make decisions of his own or on behalf of his chief. The problem with this relationship is that other members of the organisation consider that the personal assistant has authority and powers as though he were his chief's deputy, which he is not: in practice this often is the cause of much misunderstanding. being the assistant to the sales manager is not the same as being the assistant sales manager: the latter implies some delegated authority.

4. *Lateral:* Between departments there must be relationships existing between staff at the same levels. This is absolutely necessary for there to be effective cooperation and coordination between them. These are lateral relationships, also known as horizontal relationships, and they exist for the purposes of collaboration: there is no direct authority flowing and activities are agreed by consent. Thus there is a lateral relationship between the accountant and the sales manager, perhaps on matters of credit control; or between the sales clerk and the despatch clerk to satisfy a customer's special delivery requirement.

Normally a person in an organisation will be subject to more than one type of relationship and sometimes it is not easy to separate the activities of one from the powers and requirements of the other. For instance, in a small firm the personal assistant to the managing director, which is a staff relationship, may also act as office manager, which post has line authority. It is often difficult for other members of the organisation to appreciate that, whereas the office manager has responsibility and authority to make decisions within the scope of office administration, he or she is not empowered to so act on behalf of the managing director.

Let us, now, know what is division of activities and allocation of duties, authority and responsibility. Division of activities mean establishing different departments or sections. Allocation of duties mean assigning duties to the departments or sections so established. Authority means right to make decisions and to take action. 'Responsibilities' refer to the area of work for which one is answerable.

For example is we have to organise an office first of all we will find what work is to be done. Then we will decide how this work should be divided among different sections, for example the work of typing will be given to type section and the work of keeping accounts will go to accounts section. The next step will be to assign duties to employees, for example the duty of writing up the cash book will be given to the cashier and the duty of maintaining ledger will be assigned to an accounts clerk. For performance of duties the officials will be granted authority, for example the accountant will be given authority to manage the affairs of the accounts department. The last step will be to fix responsibilities of employees so that they know the area for which they will be accountable, for example the accountant will be held responsible if the balance sheet is not ready in time or the work of accounts section is not properly carried out.

Office organisation is a dynamic process. Like all organising, office organising is a changing and dynamic process. It is not a static phenomenon. Changes in the organisation of an office take place for many reasons like a change in the objective of an enterprise, change in personnel ad changes in environments which take place outside the office or the enterprise. Changes in political set up or scientific inventions are the examples of changing environments. Organising is an active or living entity, it is not a passive or rigid concept. An efficient office manager has to change his organisation from time to time in order to meet the current requirements. A type of organisation found most suitable at one time may not remain so later. For example the organisation pattern may have to be changed if a very capable office manager has left the job or the organisation changes its objectives. For example if a selling house starts the work of manufacture also the organisation will need a change.

Principles of office organisation

For proper management of any business house it is very necessary that the office should be organised in a perfect manner. Some basic principles have to be observed when organising an office. These principles are:

1. *Defining objectives*: While organising one should be clear about his objectives and know precisely what is to be done or what is to be achieved by each department or function.

2. *Division of work*: Once we are clear about our objectives the next step will be to divide the work in such a way that the objective is need of specialisation which requires division of work. In short the work to be done should be so divided that the objective is achieved in an efficient manner.

3. *Parity of authority and responsibility*: If somebody is giving the responsibility to do a job he should be given enough authority so that he may be able to discharge his responsibility. For instance if a subordinate is made responsible to construct a house, but not given an authority to spend more than Rs. 100/- without the sanction of the boss, the subordinate will not be able to discharge his responsibility. His responsibility does not commensurate with authority.

4. *Unity of command*: Every subordinate should be immediately responsible to one and not several supervisors. If there are too many bosses to guide and supervise the subordinate he will get confused and will not be able to do anything.

5. *Span of control*: Only as many subordinates should be placed under one supervisor as many he can effectively supervise. No definite number can be fixed for this

purpose. It will depend on the nature of work to be done by the subordinate, capability of the supervisor and other circumstances.

6. *Number of levels of management*: The number of levels of management should be reduced to minimum. There should not be a long chain of supervisors between the worker and the top management. Too many levels of management make both upward and downwards communication difficult. It means that the directions of management will reach the subordinates late and not so correctly. In the same manner whatsoever may a subordinate wants to convey to the top management will be communicated after quite a long time and the communication may perhaps not be so accurate because of many intermediaries.
7. *Balance between centralisation and decentralisation*: Absolute centralisation or decentralisation are the two extremes. To achieve the best results it is necessary to have judicious admixture of both central and local supervision. The proportion of each will depend on the nature of work, the historical evolution and the type of institution concerned.
8. *Even distribution of work*: It should be seen that different subordinates are assigned equal work. No one should be over or under worked.
9. *Laying down task and functions*: The responsibilities and duties assigned to every should be clearly defined so that every body knows what work he is to do and no work remains unassigned.
10. *Flexibility*: The organisation structure should be flexible. It should be capable of being adopted to changing circumstances.
11. *Continuity*: The structure of the organisation should be such that it able to maintain a continuous supply of required personnel and equipment. Continued existence of the enterprise should be ensured through readjustment of plans and procedures, when needed.
12. *Efficiency*: The goal of the organisation should be attained at minimum cost it is the real test of efficiency. The organisation should provide work satisfaction to the workers so that they become more efficient.
13. *Simplicity*: An enterprise should be organised in such a manner that every employees can follow the laid down procedures and methods without difficulty. Simplicity makes the organisation more effective.
14. *Facilitation of leadership*: The structure of the organisation should be so deviced that there is enough opportunity for the management to give effective lead to the enterprise.

Technique of organisation

Following steps are needed to organise or recognise an office:

1. The objective or the purpose of the office has to be studied.
2. Total volume of the work is assessed. Staff requirements for each job are estimated.
3. Decision has to be taken regarding method of grouping whether it is to be homogeneous like.
4. Decision is taken on the degree of specialisation to be used in the allocation of work.
5. Decision has to be taken about the size of work-groups, span of control i.e., how many subordinates are to be put under one supervisor.
6. Consider the results of inter-action of one worker with another, one group with another. The grouping of workers should be such that relations in between them are cordial. Clash of personalities should be avoided.
7. Allocation duties, responsibilities and authority. The final stage is the preparation of the organisational chart.

Types or systems of organisation

For smooth working of a large enterprise where a large number of people are employed, the activities to be performed have to be divided into groups of functions. It goes without saying that these activities ultimately have to be done by men that is the employees. The basic question in organisation is therefore, to organise men.

By organisation of men we mean the creation of well defined organisation structure that points out who does what work, who is responsible to whom and who has authority over whom? Formally stating, organisation structure is the set of formal planned relationship between groups of related functions and between the physical factors and personnel required for the performance of these functions. The main aim of setting up of an organisation structure is to facilitate managers in functioning effectively and smoothly.

There are four main kinds of organisation structure or organisation:

(i) Line organisation

(ii) Functional organisation, and

(iii) Line and staff organisation

(iv) Committee organisation

The line organisation

This is the oldest method which has been followed in its pure form in military till recently. Under this system authority flows from the top to bottom. Directions are issued by the higher authority and are conveyed to the persons responsible for executing them through the chain of command. The highest officer gives order to his immediate subordinate who to his next subordinate and so on.

The application of this system is in the manner that the business is divided into a number of departments or units which is headed by a departmental executive or head. The chief executive, who may be the general manager or managing director, issues orders to the departmental heads who in turn transmit them to their immediate subordinates and the subordinates transmit them to the workers.

In line organisation promotions and demotions of subordinate depend on the recommendations of his immediate superior. A subordinate will receive all this instructions from his immediate superior and will directly be responsible to him. No subordinate can approach any higher authority except through his immediate boss. Suppose there are eight accounts clerks who work under an accountant, under the line organisation all these eight clerks will work under the supervision of the accountant who will watch their progress, maintain control over them, write their confidential report etc. The clerks will be responsible to the accountant and forward all their difficulties to him.

Merits

1. *Simple* This is very simple and easily understood by employees.
2. *Discipline.* It ensures very good discipline. There is no confusion about orders, they come from a single person to whom the employee is accountable. Everybody in the organisation knows to whom he is responsible and who is responsible to him.
3. *Quick decisions.* This system facilitates quick decisions. The subordinate reports the matter to his immediate boss who gives on the spot decision.
4. *Flexibility.* Each executive or supervisor has sole responsibility of his own department or section with the result that he can adjust his department or section to changing situations.
5. *Unity of command.* As the subordinates receive orders from one boss only there is no dual subordination and hence no confusion.
6. *Definite Responsibility.* In line organisation responsibility of every person is definite, he can be held responsible for unsatisfactory results.
7. *Economy.* There are no staff functionaries everybody is involved in production work hence there are no unnecessary overheads in the shape of salaries of specialists. This leads to economy.
8. *Control:* Management can exercise effective control over the activities of workers.
9. *Stable:* This system is quite stable.

Demerits

1. *Top managers overworked:* Under this system top executives are generally overworked. They remain so much engrossed in the routine work that they hardly get time to pay attention to more important functions like planning and directing.

2. *Lack of specialisation*: Under his system every supervision is responsible for providing all kinds of guidance to the subordinate may it relate to repair of machine, quality of product or techniques of work. Of course, a supervisor can not be master of everything. Moreover, he has to do overall planning, execution, control of his department or unit also. He can not be expert in all these aspects of managerial task.

2. *Lack of communication:* There is usually no communication from lower ranks to higher executive with the result that top management is neither in a position to know the difficulties and problems of workers nor is able to take advantage of ideas of man directly concerned with work.

4. *Nepotism and favouritism:* The supervisor may judge people from his own personal angle rather than from the angle of the organisation. Efficient people may be left behind and in efficient flaterers may get promotion.

5. *Dictatorial:* Because a subordinate's promotion and demotion depends on his immediate superior the system places him absolutely at the mercy of his superior. The system requires absolute obedience on the part of subordinate towards his boss. All these factors make managers dictators and semi-Gods, not cooperative leaders.

6. *Unstability*: If a few top executives leave the enterprise it becomes difficult to fill the gap immediately. The result of this is that the enterprise gets crippled.

7. *Inflexible:* It is a rigid and inflexible form of organisation.

Though there are many demerits and drawbacks of line organisation yet it still plays a vital role in small organisations. It is serious mistake to underestimate its importance. It is the most suitable form of organisation when the business is small and work is of simple and routine nature. All other systems of staff organisation are simply off-shoots of line organisation.

Functional organisation

It was F.W. Taylor who gave the concept of functional organisation. A worker under functional organisation is not guided by one supervisor, as in the case of line organisation, but by many specialists who are incharge of separate functions. Each specialist or supervisor has control over a particular function no matter wheresoever that function is performed. For example, a finance manager will have the right and the power to command all the subordinates on all matters relating to finance. The result of all this is that each worker instead of being supervised by one supervisor receives his orders from a group of specialised supervisors.

Characteristics of functional organisation

Following are the main characteristics of functional organisation:

(a) Each work is divided into specified functions.

(b) There is a separate supervisor for each function, he has right to give orders regarding that function wheresoever that function is performed in the enterprise.

(c) If anybody in the enterprise has to take any decision relating to a particular function, it has to be in consultation with the functional specialist.

Merits

Functional organisation offers following advantages:

1. *Specialisation:* Under this type of organisation maximum use can be made of the services of the experts. There is separate supervisor for each function who is a specialist in the field and can tender correct advice. For example a personnel manager can tender best advice regarding recruitment, training etc. of people in the enterprise.
2. *Higher efficiency:* As different specialised functions are performed by experts in their own fields, it makes for higher degree of efficiency.
3. *Separation of mental and manual jobs:* This system separates manual and mental functions with the result that unskilled employees can be entrusted with manual work while more intelligent and qualified people can be spared for mental work.
4. *Lightens the burden of executives:* As in the case of line organisation, executives, and supervisors, under this system, are not overloaded with too many routine duties. They concentrate on one function alone, with the result that the quality and standard of supervision is much better.
5. *East in decision making:* As the specialist of a function can give his decision about a problem on the spot without referring it to decisions are uniform too.

Demerits

Following are the main drawbacks of Functional organisation:

(1) *Confusing:* This type of organisation structure can be confusing to the workers and muddling to the management. Every specialist may give his own orders bearing in mind his own function without taking into account the overall picture. It violates the principal of unity of command. As the subordinates get orders from different bosses it makes the operative task quite difficult.

(2) *Uneconomic:* If the system becomes too elaborate it proves quite expensive. If a large number of specialists are employed it adds to the salary bill.

(3) *Diluted Responsibility:* If the results are unsatisfactory responsibility for this cannot

be fixed on anyone. Every specialist can say that he had performed his function well, the others who are at fault.

(4) *Loose discipline:* It weakens the position and influence of line supervisor which complicates the problem of discipline at lower levels of the organisation.

(5) *Difficulty in coordination:* Since the specialists operate independent of each other it becomes difficult to co-ordinate their activities.

(6) *Does not train employees to fill top positions:* Under this system there are specialists for different unctions who get experience in one function only hence it does not train new managers to shoulder overall responsibilities of the enterprise.

Functional type of organisation has been criticized by both business experts and scholars. It is believed that in its pure form it is an unpracticable organisation system. Entire business is bound to collapse if advice of every expert is put into practice. This type of organisation creates a lot of problems if adopted at lower level. It can bring good result if practised only at higher levels.

Line and staff organisation

This system is a compromise between pure line system and pure functional system. This system implies the combined role of line and the staff (the persons who only advise about during the job) in attaining the objectives of the enterprise. To understand the structure of this system let us imagine, for the time being, that there is line system only. As the line officers are not expected to be experts in all the fields they are given advice about special matters by experts who are called staff. So we see that under line and staff system there are two types of employees, the line people i.e. those who are directly responsible for the performance of the work and staff people i.e. those who provide expert advice to line people and are not directly concerned with production.

Allen has brought out the distinction between line and staff in these words, "Line refers to those positions and elements of the organisation which have the responsibility and authority and are accountable for accomplishment of primary objectives. Staff elements are those which have responsibility and authority for providing advice and service to the line in attainment of objectives."

In modern business a manager has to face so varied and complex problems that he cannot possibly be master of them all by himself. He may not know much about subjects as budgetary controls, motivation, operational research, psychological tests etc. Specialised knowledge about various aspects of running the business is needed at all levels of management. This specialised knowledge can be provided best by highly trained and experienced internal consultants called staff functionaries. It should be borne in mind that the line and staff functions cannot be put under water-tight compartments. One function may be a line function in one organisation and staff function in another.

Merits

Following are the main advantages of line and staff system:

1. *Improvement in operational efficiency:* Staff personnel who are experts in their fields provide able guidance to managers which helps in increasing operational efficiency. Moreover, a line supervisor cannot be competent enough to provide guidance to his subordinates in every kind of matter, he can take the help of staff.
2. *Reduction in burden of line executives:* It enables line executives to concentrate on important tasks like managerial planning, control and decision making. The burden of finding solutions for problems concerned with technology, finance, personnel administration can be left to staff functionaries.
3. *Unity of command:* Under this system the experts provide special guidance without giving orders, it is the line manager who only has got the right to give orders, the result is that the enterprise takes advantage of functional organisation while maintaining the unity of command i.e. one subordinate receiving orders from one boss only.
4. *Training to line executives:* From the process of continuously receiving advice from experts line managers get education in specialised fields, gradually they develop their own knowledge and skill and prove capable managers of tomorrow.
5. *All the advantages of line organisation:* Because the basis of this system is line authority relationships, it offers all the advantages of line organisation.

Demerits

1. *Staff advice is not always practical:* When the staff advises managers they do not take an overall view of the situation, being specialists of their own field they consider their function as the only important thing and offer based advice.
2. *Conflict between line and the staff:* There is often a conflict between the line and the staff. Line people complain that staff gives impractical and irresponsible advice from their ivory towers of specialisation while staff complain that line people do not take full advantage of their special knowledge.

   Line managers complain that if something goes wrong, the staff blames them for the result while they will claim all the credit for anything that is good. The line people rightly complain that the staff has right to give advice but shoulders no responsibility. The staff say that their advice is not taken seriously because they have no right to implement their recommendations.
3. *Centralisation:* When the line managers are assured of continuous advise of staff they leave the task of thinking and planning to them and develop a habit of not taking initiative. Sometimes line officers start relying too much on staff advice even in respect of minor routine matters.

4. *Expensive.* Employment of specialists is quite expensive, experts generally demand higher remuneration. Staff, many a time unnecessarily increases paper work of the line.

Committee organisation

A group of persons entrusted with discharging the assigned functions collectively is called a committee. Committee type of organisation is rarely found to exist in its pure form. It is generally found to co-exist with line and staff type of organisation. The Board of Directors of a company is an example of Committee Organisation. This form of organisation is suitable for taking decisions on policy matters or laying down broad objective for the enterprise. The basic objective of committee is to get a more comprehensive view of a given problem than can be obtained by a single person. Committee Organisation is in existence in varying degree in different concerns.

Merits

1. The decision of committees are based on expertise and knowledge of large number of persons hence they are more balanced than individual decisions. It promotes new ideas.
2. Committee Organisation facilitates a coordination between the activities and views of different departments. It saves time taken in transmission of essential information. Participants can know the views of various participants through their speeches.
3. Participating members inculate the sense of participation and feel duty bound to implement the decision taken by them in committee meetings.
4. It provides an excellent medium of discussion, education and of communication between management and workers.
5. It facilitates dispersal of authority. Too much concentration of power at one point is eliminated.
6. Committee management system ensures continuity of administration because changes in the constitution of committees are few and gradual.

Demerits

1. No single person can be held responsible for the decisions of the committees.
2. The decisions have to wait for committee meetings and hence are not prompt.
3. Committee decisions are generally weak because they are the result of compromise.
4. Calling and arranging meetings is quite expensive.
5. Sometimes an aggressive minority group is able to force decisions on weak and indifferent majority.

The ideal organisation

There is no ideal type of organisation which can be called as optimum type. There are various types of organisations and there are many admixtures of different types. The best is that which suits the need of the enterprise the most, the one which will facilitate the flow of work and effectively fulfil the demands of the institution concerned. A type of organisation found best at one time may not be found so later. It is a dynamic concept.

Factors determining—What type of organisation

Following are the main factors which influence the type of organisational set-up in a business concern:

(1) *Size of business*: The most important factor is the size of the business. If the size of the business is small, line type of organisation is the best and the cheapest but if the business is big, an elaborate system like line and staff type combined with committee type of organisation will be found more suitable. If there are many independent departments in an enterprise the organisation can be on the basis of products also. For example Modi's may have separate organisations for cloth, tyres, paints etc.

(2) *Nature of business:* A temporary organisation, established for a short period, for example for completing a particular contract, will have a type of organisation which will not be elaborate while a well established and old enterprise will need elaborate and mixed type of organisational set up.

(3) *Continuity:* An enterprise having steady flow of work throughout the year and permanence of structure will have complex and elaborate system of organisation as compared to one where requirements are fluctuating from time to time or season to season.

(4) *Geographical Location:* Geographical location of different units of the enterprise will also influence the type of organisation. If different units are situated hundred of miles apart, there may be separate staff for each unit which cannot be on elaborate scale. If all the units are located in one city or locality the system of organisation can be more complex.

(5) *Type of workers and degree of mechanisation:* If in any enterprise the ratio of unskilled workers to administrative staff is high there will be the need of more and close supervision and hence the need for line organisation. In the case of skilled workers close supervision is not necessary; here staff type of organisation may suit better. The type of organisation will also vary according to the amount of machinery used in office and workshops.

(6) *Approach of management:* The approach of management, whether it believes in participative or autocratic management will also be reflected in the type of organisational structure adopted.

Authority and responsibility

Authority

It is not possible to achieve the desired object (running the office efficiently in our case) unless the managers have the authority to get things done from their subordinates. Authority is an essential element of management.

Our next question is, what is authority? Authority is the right to act or to exact action by others, within a prescribed area. As Koontz and O'Donell put it "authority is the power to command others to act or not to act in a manner deemed by the processor of the authority, to further enterprise or departmental purpose. According to Herbert Simon "authority is the power to make decisions which guide the actions of others." It in relationship between two individuals one 'superior' and the other 'subordinate'. The person who makes decisions is the 'Superior' and the person who accepts them and is guided by them is called the 'Subordinate'.

Sources or types of Authority. There are three sources of authority:

(a) Formal structure of organisation.

(b) Acceptance of authority by others, and

(c) Technical competence.

(a) *Formal structure of organisation:* The relative position of a person in the organisation structure normally determines the degree of authority from formal viewpoint. Managers at each level of organisation derive their authority from authorities of higher levels. Every organisation has a chain of command consisting of relationships of authority. For example an Accounts Officer derives his power from his higher authorities because of his position in the formal structure.

(b) Acceptance of authority by others: According to this concept authority is that power which the subordinates accept that their superior possesses.A supervisor may apparently have authority over his subordinates but the ultimate enforcement of that may be modified by real acceptance of that authority by the subordinates. It may not be possible to gain enthusiastic cooperation from subordinate despite the formal authority of the superior unless subordinates accept that the superior really has that authority.

(c) *Technical competence:* Sometimes a person may have authority because he is technically more competent and others seek his guidance and advice. A person may have little or no formal authority by reason of his position in the formal structure but may posses extensive authority due to his integrity, knowledge and skill. For example a person may be a mere mechanic in his organisation but even engineers may seek his advice. Here the mechanic has authority because his competence in his field.

Responsibility

Responsibility means the obligation of a subordinate to perform the duty assigned to him. When any person assumes authority to perform certain task he also becomes responsible for its performance. In the context of delegation of authority, responsibility is used in the sense of accountability or obligation.

Responsibility has two parts:

(1) The obligation to secure results and (2) The accountability to the person from whom the authority is received. For example when a superior assigns some task to a subordinate and grants him the required authority the subordinate is (a) under obligation to do the assigned task, and (b) be responsible for results.

Ordinarily in the normal functioning of an organisation responsibility is continuing one, every employee is responsible for something otherwise there will be no need for him. This means that every subordinate is under obligation to discharge his functions, as required by his superior continuously.

Accountability

Accountability is the obligation to carry out responsibility and exercise authority in terms of established standard. It is the obligation to account for, and report upon, the discharge of responsibility or use of authority. Accountability applies both to the obligation to perform work and to exercise authority. For example if a person has taken a loan he is responsible for its return as per the terms of loan, similarly a person who is delegated authority and responsibility has an obligation to fulfil his obligation in terms of established standard.

Accountability always *flows upward,* that is, a person who has been delegated authority is accountable to his superiors. A person can be held accountable only to the *extent* that he is delegated responsibility and authority. An important thing to note is that *accountability cannot be delegated.* The delegator remains accountable for the acts of person to whom authority has been delegated.

Accountability is unitary. A subordinate can be accountable only to one superior for delegated responsibility and authority. If a person reports to two bosses on the same responsibility confusion and friction inevitably result. For determining accountability the delegator has to *set standards of performance.* Accountability is meaningful only if the measure of performance can be spelled out in specific terms.

Delegation of authority

When the work of an executive increases to such an extent that he cannot hope to cope up with it the only remedy in such case is that he should divide his less important work among his subordinates. The process of dividing is referred to as 'delegation'. According to Terry "conferring authority from one executive or organisational unit to another in order to accomplish particular assignment".

Allen states "Delegation is the process the manager follows in his dividing up work entrusting part of it to his subordinates and establishing conditions that will enable him to hold them accountable for performances.

By this process the manager can get help from others. Delegation is the ability to get results through others, for example if the administrative officer of a company delegates work relating to granting of leave to clerks etc. to superintendent of administration, it will be delegation. Similarly if the general manager allows departmental heads to incur an expenditure up to Rs. 1000/- without his prior sanction it will be known as delegation.

Without delegation the chief executive will wear out. Doctors point out that ulcers (stomach boils), heart attacks and many other psychoso-matic ailments are caused by strain, tension and worries and persist because the affiliated manager is not able to distinguish between what is important on his job and what is not.

It is now widely acknowledged that delegation of authority is one of the surest and best methods of getting better results. Delegation can be one of management's best technique for satisfying subordinates and motivating them to better performance. Delegation enables the managers to divide their workload to others thus leaving them free to concentrate or more important problems of management. Allen remarks "once a man's job grow beyond his personal capacity his success lies in his ability to multiply himself through other people." Delegation also influences the nature of relationship between the manager and his subordinates, the subordinate does not merely remain an obedientiary, he also becomes responsible for results.

Elements or process of delegation

Delegation is the entrustment of responsibility and authority to another and the creation of accountability for performance. This process involves three basic actions.

(i) *Assigning of duties:* The superior assigns duties to his subordinates, the delegator tells his subordinates what they have to do, for example an overseer may be assigned the duty of constructing a house by the chief engineer.

(ii) *Granting of authority:* For the performance of the assigned work the delegator grants authority to his subordinate. For example the chief engineer may authorise an overseer to purchase all the material necessary for the construction of the house.

(iii) *Creation of an obligation:* The subordinate is under an obligation to complete his job. For example the concerned overseer will be accountable for the construction of the house.

Basic principles of delegation

Delegation can be successful only when certain basic principles are followed. These principles are:

1. *Authority should commensurate with responsibility:* The degree of authority granted to the subordinate should be in proportion to the duties assigned. It is not correct to say that authority should be equal to responsibility. A person can never be given exactly as much authority as the assigned work, some authority has to be withheld and cannot be delegated. For example a director of personnel delegates responsibility for wage and salary matters to the manager of wage and salary but he must withhold authority for overall planning, organisation, coordination, motivation and control relating to wage and salary. Authority can only be delegated commensurate with responsibility.
2. *Responsibility cannot be delegated:* When the delegator delegates authority to the subordinate responsibility for accomplishment still rests with him. The person making the delegation always remains accountable to his superiors for that which he has delegated. Since responsibility can not be delegated, the delegated, the delegator is accountable for the acts of subordinate. But such rigidity of principle can be modified by common sense in any particular instance.
3. *There should be no dual subordination:* For delegated authority and responsibility each person should be accountable only to one superior. If a subordinate reports to two superiors on the same responsibility, confusion and friction inevitably result. In case of dual responsibility the subordinate is never sure which superior will ask him to account for specific activity. Since demands of different superiors can be much different, he can never satisfy two different bosses even if he may handle the problems in any manner whatsoever. The subordinate may receive conflicting orders and may not be able to please any boss.

What can be delegated and what cannot be?

It is difficult for every manager to decide what part of his job can be entrusted to others and which things he must perform himself. If the manager performs all the duties which he can easily delegate, he will find himself buried in routine work. If, on the other hand, he delegates responsibility and authority which he should exercise himself it will jeopardise his leadership and bring disorganisation and conflicts. To avoid the two extremes the manager should analyse his job and determine:

(i) tasks which cannot be delegated (job of planning, controlling, policy making and co-ordination);

(ii) tasks which can be delegated to others (the job of administration of policies);

(iii) tasks which are of routine nature and must be delegated.

The work of routine nature, which does not relate to policy making or controlling should be delegated. A large part of executive work consists of activities which are subsidiary to his primary task, for example the work like that of granting sanction etc. within the frame work of laid down policies should be delegated.

There are certain tasks which can be delegated but with care. These relate to administration of policies. Where the policies have been decided before hand and they have to be implemented only such work can be delegated. It is essential that even such tasks should be delegated only if the anger has confidence in his subordinates and the subordinates have been properly developed to accept those responsibilities.

Certain tasks cannot be delegated. No manager can effectively delegate responsibility and authority for initiating and making final decisions for planning, organising, coordinating, motivating and controlling. The manager must reserve responsibility and authority for establishing and interpreting plans. The manager must himself decide what organisation structure he needs to accomplish his goal. The manager must himself exercise decisions regarding motivation i.e. about final selection, compensation and training of his subordinates. To know, assess and reconcile all the interests involved and to evaluate the work accomplished and to take corrective action, the manager should not delegate responsibility and authority for coordination and control.

How much authority should be delegated?

Just man's legs should be long enough to reach the ground, and no longer, enough responsibility and authority should be delegated to a position to enable the incumbent to accomplish whatever objectives are set for him. Only as much responsibility and authority should be delegated that will enable the subordinate to accomplish the desired objective. So how much should be delegated will depend on objectives to be achieved. It is essential that enough authority should be delegated for the individual to reach the performance standards that have been set for his work. For example if the salesman has been given responsibility of selling products of the company, he must be given power to approach customers in the name of company, promise timely delivery etc. If the manager who delegates thinks that more powers should be delegated to salesman like hiring automobiles, organising displays, selling on credit, he will have to decide about this policy considering all relevant factors like abilities of salesman, type of product, peculiarities of the market etc.

Difficulties in delegation

Many problems crop up when the delegators delegate powers to the subordinates. It is not a simple process. The difficulties arise due to the suspecting attitude of the delegator and fear of shouldering responsibility of the subordinate to whom the power is delegated. The main difficulties are:

On the part of the delegator or the boss

(i) *I can do it better approach:* Most of the executives have a notion that it is only they who can do the job in a perfect manner. They always think they could have done better and hesitate to delegate authority.

(ii) *Desire to dominate:* Some bosses have the habit of dominating and hence would like to do everything by themselves. They will not like their subordinates to enjoy any power.

(iii) *Lack of ability to direct:* For effective delegation the subordinates has to be told the objective he is to achieve and how he is to achieve. Sometimes the boss may like to delegate authority but may not be able to guide the subordinate about his role and communicate to him the essential features of his plan.

(iv) *Lack of confidence in subordinate*: If the boss has no confidence in the subordinate he will not like to delegate authority even if he may agree that delegation is necessary.

(v) *Conservative attitude of the boss or cautious temperament:* If the boss is conservative in attitude and is not willing to take any risk he will never think of delegating any power or authority.

(vi) *No-appreciation of problems of the department.* Some managers are not competent enough to asses problems arising out of non-delegation of authority. They do not realize when the time to delegate has come.

On the part of the subordinate

Many a times the boss is willing to delegate authority and wants to lighten his work but the subordinate is not willing to assume responsibility due to following reasons:

(i) *Lack of self-confidence:* If the subordinate lacks confidence and thinks that he will not be able to shoulder the responsibility, he will be unwilling to assume any authority. Some subordinates lean too much on their superiors. They are afraid of holding independent charge.

(ii) *Fear of criticism:* If the subordinate has been unduly criticised while taking decisions on account of minor mistakes in the past he will not like to do that thankless job again and will refrain from accepting powers.

(iii) *Absence of positive incentives:* Shouldering responsibilities is a burdensome job. A subordinate will hesitate in accepting additional work delegated to him if he does not get a positive reward.

(iv) *Non-availability of information or resources to perform the assigned duty:* If the subordinate does not possess sufficient information and resources to perform the assigned job he will hesitate to accept responsibility and authority.

How to secure better delegation?

Every manager will be interested in knowing methods by which delegation will work more effectively and smoothly. On the one hand the person who has delegated the authority should feel that the delegation has saved him from unnecessary work without any risk or anxiety and on the other hand the subordinate should feel happy about the responsibility he has undertaken. Delegation should also help the organisation being carried on smoothly.

Following steps will help in achieving better delegation of authority:

1. *Goals should be clearly established*: Every person to whom the task is delegated wants to know, "Why I am being asked to do the job?" Only when the subordinate clearly knows the objective of the work can be put his heart into it.
2. *Responsibility and authority should be clearly defined:* A manager can perform well when he knows what his job is and how much authority he possesses. A subordinate can understand what his superior expect from him only when his responsibility and authority is clearly defined.
3. *Subordinates should be motivated:* Motivation is the moving force in delegation. If the delegator wants that his subordinates should do what he wants to get done through them willingly and enthusiastically he should motivate them. He should provide them incentives.
4. *Maintain rapport with subordinate:* There are chances that the subordinate might not have understood his role, responsibility or authority and he may come to the boss for clarification again and again. This will defeat the very purpose of delegation. The other extreme can be that the superior does not allow access to the subordinate till he has completed his task, this is also not desirable. A middle course will be that the superior consciously plans for guidance and coaching of the subordinate and maintains communication with him.
5. *Provide training to subordinates:* The process of helping managers to develop ability in delegation is difficult. Subordinates should be trained to accept delegation. The performance of the subordinate should be watched and appraised and advice should be offered when necessary. Coaching on the job is a good method of training.

Centralisation versus decentralisation

When organising a decision has to be taken whether there should be centralisation or decentralisation. A brief discussion about both these concepts follows :

Centralisation

Centralisation means, reservation of authority at central points within the organisation. Centralisation denotes that a majority of decisions regarding the work being performed are not made by those doing the work but at a point higher in the organisation. This means that large portion of managerial work is done at the top executive level.

Advantages of centralisation

Following are the advantages of centralisation of authority:

1. *Encouragement to individual leadership:* Under centralisation the power to take decisions rests with one or a few persons. If some body is the owner of a business

and takes all decisions about it himself, he will develop into a fine manager and competent leader.

2. *Effective control:* Because the power to take decisions lies in the hands of few people at the top and not at lower levels, it is possible to maintain an effective control over the activities of the organisation. Decisions by few are controllable, they are likely to be less contradictory.

3. *Coordination and uniformity:* If the decisions are taken by few people they will be uniform and will be helpful in maintaining coordination between different departments. Decisions by few top level managers will be harmonious and will help in formation of uniform policies.

4. *Immediate decision in case of emergency:* If the authority is centralised, immediate, on the spot decision can be taken on urgent matters, which is not possible in the case of decentralisation. In decentralised set-up lower level executive refrains from taking decision in important matters which causes delays.

5. *Secrecy:* It is easy to maintain secrecy about decisions taken by a few top level executives. In decentralised set-up decisions are taken at lower levels and become known to so many people that it becomes difficult to maintain secrecy about them.

Decentralisation

Decentralisation means delegation of power to take business decisions at lower levels of management. The lower the rank of the executives who make decisions the greater is the degree of decentralisation. In decentralised units authority is exercised as near as possible to the point where problems originate.

According to Allen: *"Decentralisation is the systematic and consistent delegation of authority to the levels where the work is performed"*. Leomard D. White states "The process of decentralisation denotes transference of authority from the higher level to a lower level". Decentralisation has also been defined as "a situation in which ultimate authority to command and ultimate responsibility for results is localised as far down in the organisation as efficient management of the organisation permits". Decentralisation should not be confused with physical separation. Physical separation means locating plants or factories away from offices, for example the head office may be in New Delhi and plants or factories at Agra and Kanpur. If the authority to take decisions still vests in head office, it is dispersion and not decentralisation. Following are the advantages and disadvantages of decentralised organisation in general:

Advantages of decentralised organisation

1. *Relieves the top management:* In Decentralised set-up subordinates share the burden of decision-making with the result that the top executive gets more time to concentrate on important issues likes planning, coordinating and control.

2. *Training of managers:* Under decentralisation the junior executives incharge of various units get training indecision making which makes them capable of handling higher responsibilities later.

3. *Team spirit:* Decentralisation promotes team spirit among workers working in different units. A local managers can weld their men into a well-knit group.

4. *Development of new techniques:* Decentralisa-tion encourages diversification of activities and development of new products. If more people are involved in decision making they can think of new lines and products.

5. *Prompt action:* In a decentralised structure subordinate executives can make timely decisions without asking for the approval or direction of superiors. This increases flexibility and permits more prompt action.

6. *Better decisions:* In decentralisation decisions are taken by those who are closer to the point of operative performance and familiar with the requirements of local situation hence the decisions are better.

7. *Location of trouble spots:* Under decentralisation inefficient departments can easily be singled out by scrutiny of their individual results. Remedial measures can quickly be taken.

Disadvantages of decentralised organisation

1. *Duplication of work:* Decentralisation involves duplication or overlapping of work. Provision of certain common functions and equipment has to be made in each unit, this increases the cost of operations.

2. *Difficulty in co-ordination:* Decentralised set up also creates the problem of coordination which sometimes becomes difficult. It may hamper adoption of uniform policies.

3. *Shortage of competent managers:* It is difficult to find competent managers who can be entrusted with power of decision making in every decentralised unit.

4. *Discouragement to specialisation*: It is unsuitable for the development of specialised services, for example service like maintenance of accounts or recruitment and training of staff have to be performed at central level. It may prevent utilisation of cost-saving effect of specialisation.

5. *Does not permit full utilisation of specialised staff:* A decentralised structure does not permit full and optimum utilisation of highly qualified staff. For example the services of a research scientist or a financial adviser can be best utilised when there is centralisation.

Factors affecting decentralisation

No organisation can be fully centralised or fully decentralised. We will find a mixture of centralisation and decentralisation in, practically, all organisations; in some organisations there may be more decentralisation than in others, the difference will be of degree only. Now we consider the factors on which this degree of decentralisation varies. Following are the limitations which affect the degree of decentralisation:

1. *Importance of decision:* If the decisions are important and can involve heavy financial expenditure or risk, authority to take such decisions can not be decentralised. Similarly decisions having implication on long term policy matters can also not be delegated to lower levels.

2. *Desirability of having uniformity in policies:* If it is desired that there should be uniformity in decisions of different departments, the authority will have to be centralised.

3. *Size*: If the organisation is of large size the authority in such a case has to be decentralised. It becomes essential to delegate authority to lower level executive if there are many executives in the organisation or there is long chain of command.

4. *History of the organisation and outlook of management:* If the organisation has become big from a small sized organisation, there will be tendency for greater of centralisation. The owners who had been taking all the decisions themselves previously, will continue to do so even if the size of the organization might have increased manifold. If the management does not have faith in democratic set-up and want to reserve all authority in its own hands, the degree of decentralisation in such organisations will be low.

5. *Availability of capable managers:* In decentralisation there is need of capable managers who can take decisions and such managers are not available in large numbers in every organisations. Non availability of capable managers results in centralisation of authority.

6. *Availability of control devices:* Management would not hesitate to delegate authority (which leads to decentralisation), if effective control devices are available in organisation. Through control devices management can check and correct wrong decision soon. Decentralisation is practiced only when effective control can be exercised on subordinates.

7. *Changing environments:* If circumstances or technology undergoes quick changes at local level, decentralisation of authority becomes a necessity. Organisations not subject to change can manage to do with centralisation.

Centralisation and decentralisation of office services

A big organisation can have many departments like sales, purchase, accounts, personnel, marketing etc. There is a need to provide office services to these departments. Some of the clerical services can no doubt be provided in each department but there are many services which can be conveniently provided at a centralised place called *general office*. The common office services are:

(i) Handling of incoming and outgoing mail;

(ii) Typing and duplicating;

(iii) Communication;

(iv) Filing and indexing;

(v) Provision of stationery and supplies;

(iv) Control and use of forms;

(vii) Reception of visitors;

(viii) Employment and training of clerical staff.

These office services are needed by all the departments. Efficient provision of these services can lead to economy and make a considerable contribution towards the efficiency of the organisation. If there is any mismanagement of these services, perhaps, the best efforts of all the departments may prove ineffective.

Looking at the importance of office services, the management has to decide whether these common services should be performed in each department for itself or should be centralised at one place known as the central office.

Centralisation of office services: Means physical concentration of common office services at one place which is called "general office". The general office is put under the control and supervision of Office Manager. Under this arrangement all the office work of different departments like that of typing, receipt and dispatch of letters, filing, indexing is done in the general office. For example it will be centralisation of office services if the typing work of the whole organisation is done in a 'central typing pool.'

Decentralisation of office services: Implies that each department of the organisation will make its own arrangements for common office services. For example if every department handles its own filing and indexing, keeps its own typewriters and office equipment, it will be known as decentralisation of office services.

The current trend appears towards centralisation. Use of specialised machines, computers and the desire to reduce office heads are the major reasons for this trend.

Advantages of centralisation of office services

The advantages of centralisation of office services include:

1. *Equitable distribution of work load:* If office services are provided in each department, work in some departments may be more and a little in other departments Staff in some departments may sit idle while there may be delays due to overwork in other departments. In centralisation the work can be equitably distributed among the staff so that nobody sits idle and nobody is overworked. There can be optimum use of the office machinery and equipment also. Modern

office machines and appliances are expensive, these cannot be provided in each department separately. There is the problem of operating these machines. Services of operators of office machines can be fully utilised if there is centralisation of office service.

2. *Decrease in cost of performing office work:* Due to centralisation supervisory costs are lowered. Centralisation leads to reduction in investment on office machines, the cost on their maintenance is also lowered. Due to lesser need for machines and equipment and men the amount of floor area required is frequently reduced. If one typewriter and one typist is needed in each of the eight departments, in case of decentralisation perhaps the same work could be done by six typewriters and six typists in the case of central typing pool.
3. *Training of office employees is expedited.* New employees can be easily trained by putting them in centralised groups without affecting the operations of the group seriously. The old employees who by experience become specialists in their respective fields can impart training to the newcomers.
4. *Specialisation is possible.* Because the same employees have to do the same work again and again they become experts in that work, this leads to more efficiency and reduction in costs.
5. *Better Supervision is possible:* As the employees are put under the supervision of a person who is a specialist in that field, better supervision is possible. For example a production engineer cannot supervise the work of a typist as efficiently as an incharge of typing section can do.
6. *Duplication of work is avoided:* If office functions are performed in each department there will be the need for separate equipment and staff for each department. This can lead to duplications of work and equipment and may require extra investment.
7. *Leads to standardisation of work and equipment:* As all the employees doing the same work, work under the supervision of same executive, at the same place by same methods and by same type of equipment, there can be better conformity to the standards. This can lead to better maintenance of machines and equipment also.
8. *Even flow of work:* If the office work of different departments is done within respective departments there are chances that in some departments there may be more work in one season and little in another with the result that the staff in different departments may be overworked at one time and may remain idle at other time. In the case of centralised services the quantum of work at any time remains even because extra work relating to one department may be offset by lesser work of some other department.

Disadvantages of centralisation of office services

There are many who feel that better results are obtained by non-centralised or decentralised arrangement of office work. Too rigid central control may encourage frustration and inflexibility. Remote control has many evils too. Following are the main drawbacks or disadvantages of centralised system of office services:

1. *Secrecy cannot be maintained:* Much office work is confidential and should not go out of the concerned department. There is greater possibility of leakage of business secrets if the work is entrusted to central office.
2. *It may cause delays:* Performance of office functions at one place can lead to delays. The central office cannot appreciate the urgency of work relating to other departments.
3. *Departmental specialisation is not possible:* Under centralisation the work is performed by those not familiar with the detailed requirements of a particular department with the result that work of specialised nature cannot be performed efficiently at the central office. Even minor changes and corrections can not be made on the spot. For example a typist of the accounts department will be much more familiar with technicalities of the accounts department rather than a typist of the general pool.
4. *Lack of departmental loyalties:* When the work is done at departmental level the employees develop a sense of belonging and try to do the work of their department in a better way. There is a kind of inter-departmental competition to perform better but this spirit is missing if the work is performed at central level.
5. *Encouragement to redtapeism*: Under centralisation of office services the rules, procedures and systems get standardised and are strictly followed, the result of which is that clerks lay more emphasis on following the rules rather than doing the work. This encourages redtapeism resulting in low productivity. Under centralised system of office services the employees get so much entangled in redtapeism that they forget to care about special needs or technical requirement of different departments.

Advantages of decentralisation of office services

The main advantages of decentralisation:

1. *Recruitment can be according to the needs of the particular department:* The staff can be recruited according to the needs of the individual department, recruitment tests can be shaped accordingly.
2. *Saving in time and efficiency:* Persons working in different departments get will acquainted with the work of their departments and hence can do the work promptly and efficiently. For example reminders for recovery of debts can be sent more quickly by accounts department without much red tape than by central office. Depending on central office for all office services causes delays due to transitions and formalities. Decentralisation avoids these delays.

3. *Maintenance of secrets:* It is easier to preserve business secret if there is decentralisation because employees who are trustworthy and have departmental loyalty can keep the secrets better as compared to persons working in general office. In central office everything comes to the notice of a number of persons and hence nothing can remain secret.

4. *Promotion of departmental loyalties:* Persons working in one department develop loyalty to that department and try to prove their own department better than others. This promotes healthy spirit of competition resulting in increased efficiency.

5. *Better morale:* Decentralisation creates better morale of the departmental employees. A small number of workers employed in a department can know each other better and develop team spirit, a sense of participation and achievement. The supervisor can know his subordinates more intimately and can appreciate their problems better. All this leads to better human relations and motivate employees.

Disadvantages of decentralisation of office services

The advantages of centralisation are obviously the disadvantages of decentralisation. For quick reference these have been summarised below:

1. *Uneven distribution of work-load:* In decentralisation work load cannot be distributed equitably. Some departments may have little work while in other there may be a heavy rush of work which may cause delays.

2. *Under utilisation of machines and equipment:* If office services are performed in each department every department will need a separate set of machines and equipment which may not be used to full capacity. If eight calculators are required under decentralisation the same work may be done by two calculators in the case of centralisation.

3. *Increase in office costs due to duplication:* Duplication of work machines are equipment results in increased office costs.

4. *Lack of specialisation:* Under decentralisation employees working in different departments have to do all kind of work relating to their departments, this does not permit division of labour and specialisation. Under centralisation a set of employees do the same type of work relating to all departments again and again and become experts in that. It leads to efficiency and adherence to standards.

5. *Lack of coordination and integration:* As different departments work independently of each others they do not know what is happening in other departments so they can not develop a team spirit. For example if reminders for recovery of debt are issued by the central office, it may not knew the standing of a particular valued customer and may annoy him by issuing harsh reminders for early payment much

to the displeasure of sales department. All this results in poor coordination and affects over all efficiency of the organisation.

6. *Difficulty in supervision:* Under decentralis-ation of office services the departmental heads have to exercise control on employees doing office work in their departments and since they are not expert in office work they are unable to exercise effective control over the work of such employees.

7. *No solution for over or under work due to seasonal changes:* The office work in different department is not equal throughout the year, at some time it is less while at others it is more. With fixed number of office employees in each department it is not possible to maintain smooth flow of work, in some periods there may be a backlog of work and in some others the employees might have to remain idle.

Factors affecting centralisation or decentralisation of office services.

To what extent can office services be centralised or decentralised will depend on the following factors:

1. *Size of the Organisation:* Only a big organisation can think of decentralisation of office services. There is no use of decentralised office services in a small organisation having few departments.

2. *Cost:* Any organisation will think of decentralised office service only when benefits arising from it in monetary terms are more than the cost involved in providing separate office service in each department. Cost consideration is a limiting factor on the degree of decentralisation of office services.

3. *Nature of business:* If the nature of business is such that there is not much need of office services in different departments, the management will not think of decentralisation of office services. In an organisation engaged in production of goods only there will hardly be any need of office services in each department while in an insurance company there will be need for office service in each and every department.

4. *Dispersal of operations:* Decentralisation of office services becomes essential if different departments are geographically dispersed i.e. they are situated at distance from each other.

5. *Need for specialised personnel or equipment:* Centralisation of office services becomes essential if costly equipment or specially qualified people are needed to do the office work. For example it is not possible to provide a computer and a programmer in each and every department of the organisation.

6. *Convenience of control:* Under decentralised system of office services it becomes difficult to maintain effective control on office work being performed in different departments of the organisation. It is not proper to provide decentralised office service to each department if strict adherence to office systems and procedures is

thought essential. Contrary to this if office systems and procedure are well defined and have been found practical and foolproof it facilitates decentralisation of office services.

Whether centralisation or decentralisation of office services

Complete centralisation and complete decentralisation of office service are the two extremes but none of these extremes is ideal. Whether to have centralisation or decentralisation of office services, and to what extent, will depend on the nature and type of the business of the enterprise. The management has to consider the pros and cons of both the systems from its own angle.

To obtain the best results it is necessary to have a judicious mixture of both central and local administration. The proportion of each will vary from one organisation to another dependent on the nature of work, the historical evolution and the type of the institution concerned. Some services of specialised nature concerning a particular department alone should be provided in that department locally while some services required by all the departments, which can be effectively performed at a central place should be provided centrally.

Which office services to be centralised and which to be decentralised

It is a matter of discussion as to which office services should be centralised and which should be decentralised. It is difficult to provide a definite answer to this question. It will depend on nature and size of the organisation and the cost involved in decentralisation. Office services which are usually, centralised are:

(a) communication services,

(b) telephone, telex and local mail services,

(c) routine correspondence,

(d) stocking, purchasing and issuing stationery,

(e) reception and public relations,

(f) office personnel management,

(g) duplicating and printing,

(h) maintenance and repair of office machines and equipment, and

(i) safety of old records.

The offices services which are generally, decentralised, are:

(i) departmental correspondence,

(ii) custody and maintenance of current records of different departments,

(iii) special stationery required by a particular department,

(iv) attendance and leave record of employees working in a department

Office administration is part of general management and the same principles of management apply. If will be as well, therefore, to take a look at management as the whole and we will start with the definition. There are many definitions of management—almost as many as there are writers on the subject—but a brief one, which is to the point, is as follows: Management is the art or skill of directing human and material resources in the attainment of a specified goal or goals. This definition is apt for the management of any organization or enterprise, and in the sphere of business might be construed as being concerned with adherence to the policies laid down by the board of directors.

It will be noticed that this definition is concerned with the deployment of resources and not the actual manipulation of them: in other words, management is the art or skill of getting things done rather than actually doing them. From this it may be deduced that management is a skill in its own right and quite outside any other technical skills and knowledge a particular manager may have. Thus a manager may be a very successful salesman when he is using his experience and technical knowledge to persuade costumers to buy, but he is not acting as a salesman when he is directing the activities of his team of sales representative; there he is exercising his management skills to organise and coordinate their activities. It is generally accepted that all positions with any element of supervision have a management component, and that the proportion of this component compared with the technical aspect increases with the rank of the holder of the office.

The need to develop management as a separate study probably came about because of the increasing size of corporate undertakings. Up to the beginning of the nineteenth century the owner or owners of a business also managed it and personally directed the efforts of the work-force. Thus there were two divisions, capital and labour. However, the invention and development of new machines and products gave rise to the need for greater amounts of investment, sums the size of which were beyond the capacity of private owners. This led to the floating of numerous joint stock companies, a process encouraged by a series of Companies Acts starting in 1844 which afforded protection to shareholders by limiting their liability to the extent of their investment. This development also led to a three-division arrangement: capital, which was largely absentee; management, which provided little or no capital; and labour. It is important, at this point, to have a look at the terms administration and management. Some authorities try to draw a distinction between the two and others use the terms interchangeably: even the great Henri Fayol was not entirely consistent in this matter. If there is a distinction between the functions of an administrator and a manager, it is a very fine one and there are no definitions that separate them conclusively. In this work the words are used synonymously.

The elements of management

Although there have been many attempts to spell out the content of management, for the most part they merely subdivide the five elements

1. Planing
2. Organization
3. Direction
4. Coordination
5. Control

Planning

The board of directors of a concern sets down the policy of the enterprise and the objective or objectives which should be achieved. Such achievement can, however, be made only by planning the courses of action which need to be taken, and these in turn can be developed only on the basis of likely events and performance both internally and in the world at large. Hence, besides the making of policy, the planning element involves both short-term and long-term forecasting.

As it is impossible to see into the future, forecasting is based on past events and the estimating of likely trends arising out of these events. So far as the business itself is concerned, the past performance of the various functional departments can be ascertained and the results analysed and extrapolated into the future.

The external factors likely to affect planning and thus requiring to be taken into account in forecasting are chiefly the economic and the political situations. These are the most difficult areas in which to make prediction and, again, past history is the only guide. As planning can be done only on the basis of forecasts, and the these are, at best, carefully considered opinion drawn from past experience, albeit opinions of experts, it is necessary that all plans have an element of flexibility so that they can be modified in the light of changed circumstances. Naturally, the longer the term over which plans are drawn up, the longer the term of forecasting must be and so the less accurate it will be. Consequently, the longer the term of planning the more ready management must be to modify its plans and to change its approach and even, perhaps, its original objectives.

Organisation

This is the framework within which the enterprise brings together all the elements of production so that its objectives can be achieved as efficiently as possible. It is concerned with personnel, equipment, materials and premises so that they are made available to further the progress of the undertaking. Under this heading management must determine what work has to be done, how it is to be done and who is to do it. This aspect of management, particularly in regard to office administration, is dealt with more fully.

Direction

It is the natural circumstance of any human group enterprise that it operates under a leader, a fountain-head from which the group may take directions. This apples equally to any business enterprise as it does to any other human activity. It is also true that any organization is likely to be most efficient if the responsibility for direction is centered in one office. This is what is known as unity of command. Every limited company has a managing director who represents the board of directors in the running of the concern, and who is seen as the centre of responsibility and authority, and as the final arbiter in cases of dispute. Equally, each department has its own head who is, or should be, soley responsible for the efficient running of his function, accountable in the final analysis to the managing director and ultimately through him to the board of directors.

Where unity of command does not exist, as in cases where there are joint managing directors with equal authority, or in partnerships where two or more partners have equal powers confusion is apt to result to the detriment of the efficiency of the organisation. Command in connection with non-military activities is, perhaps, a strong term, and embraces not only the giving of direct instructions, but also operating by means of persuasion and consultation.

It is important to remember that however the policies of the organisation are achieved, the ultimate responsibility for success lies with the head of the concern. He must delegate some of his authority to the executives under him and they in turn will have to delegate some of their authority to their subordinates. Nevertheless, each level of delegated authority is accountable to the one above, from whence the authority was derived, and so this accountability flows right up the management hierarchy until it finally stops at the top, where final responsibility lies.

Delegation

No one person can possibly perform all the functions required to run an organisation so it is necessary to pass some of the work down to subordinates, who in their turn have to pass some down to their subordinates. A sole trader making concrete fence posts will initially do all his own buying, selling, accounting and making. As his business grows he will find that he cannot encompass all of these functions within the time available to him. At some point he will have to give up one or two of the functions and engage staff to carry them out. This process will carry on as the business becomes larger until each function will be the responsibility of a departmental head. Further growth will then cause each departmental head to delegate some of his work to responsible subordinates. The main purpose of delegation, therefore, is to prevent a manager or supervisor at any level from becoming overwhelmed by detail and so depriving him of the time necessary to pursue his primary function of managing or supervising.

Delegation also permits the bringing in of specialist knowledge in particular areas of the business—for instance, in production or design.

Delegation is the act of appointing someone to act on the delegator's behalf and with his authority, and the following factors must be borne in mind:

1. The limits of the delegate's authority and duties must be clearly defined and understood.
2. Besides having the requisite technical ability and experience, the delegate must also have such personal qualities as self-confidence, ability to solve common day-to-day problems without recourse to his principal, and the aptitude to work well with those now subject to his authority.
3. The delegate is responsible to the delegator, and the authority given must be commensurate with the responsibility. It is unless and absurd to give a delegate the responsibility of carrying out various duties without at the same time giving him the necessary amount of authority to accomplish these duties.
4. All those subject to the delegates' authority should be made aware of the appointment and of the extent of the delegate's powers.
5. The delegator himself, having made the appointment and having ascertained that the delegate is capable of carrying out his duties competently, should interfere as little as possible.
6. Despite the statement in 5 above, the delegator of course still has the responsibility for the delegated work and must ensure that it is effectively carried out. Some form of inspection is, therefore, a necessary corollary of delegation. At lower levels this may be, indeed, overt checking, but at higher levels less obvious checking must be used.

Span of control

Inherent in the question of delegation is the management concept of span of control, sometimes termed span of management. Simply, this means the number of persons a manager or supervisor can effectively control, and is based primarily on the fact that as the numbers supervised increase so the number of relationships and cross-relationships increase disproportionately. As a general rule, the span of responsibility is taken as about six subordinates and is normally applicable to the control of supervisory staff at all levels but not to the supervision of operating personnel where they are all doing very similar tasks. Additionally, by the very nature of things, the span of control narrows as it reaches the higher levels of management. It is, therefore, important to remember that there can be no specific number of subordinates quoted as the ideal or even the normal. The number involved, in fact, depends very largely on the following circumstances:

1. The abilities of the subordinates: if they are skillful and well trained they need less supervision and therefore more can be managed than if they need tight control.
2. The complexity of the work being done: simply jobs need little supervision, thus increasing the span of control; complex work requires closer supervision, so reducing the number able to be supervised.

3. The effectiveness of communications: if the supervisor is able to give clear and understandable advice and instructions then he will be able to handle more people than if he cannot make himself clear. Equally, worker's' ability to make themselves understood is an important factor, and one that is quite significant in out multiracial society.

4. The personality and ability of the supervisor himself: if he is understanding and patient and has some human insight then he will generate loyalty which will reduce the problems of supervision; if, on the other hand, he is abrasive he may find his workers reluctant to cooperate with him. Equally, if he is fully conversant with the work of his section or department and is technically competent then he will earn the respect of his staff and close supervision will be less necessary than if he is not. These facts have a great bearing on the span of control.

5. The consistency of operations: where systems and procedures remain constant and uniform over long periods it is easier to control a larger staff than if methods are subject to continual change.

6. Staff turnover: constantly changing staff leads to difficulties in effective supervision because of the need for new workers to be trained and to gain experience. The closer supervision required means that fewer can be managed.

Difficulties in delegation

The chief difficulties in delegation are those mentioned above under span of control, but there are other factors which impede or limit delegation or its effectiveness.

Often there is a measure of under-delegation, which means that individual managers or supervisors are caught up in an excessive amount of detail leaving them insufficient time to concentrate on their prime function of direction or command. Under-delegation is also the result of an individual manager not having the ability to delegate: he is responsible for the effective performance of the work of his team and feels he must be personally involved in all aspects of it. This is a personality trait very difficult to overcome: even where such a manager does delegate authority for some of his function he still interferes with the member of staff to whom he has delegated this part of his work, to the detriment of his own and his subordinate's performance and often to the detriment of relations between the two as well. Further, this over-inspection may be construed as mistrust of the delegate's ability which will reflect adversely on the control he can exercise over the staff under him.

Equally, it is possible to over-delegate. IN such a case the manager concerned may be left with little to do but to call for reports and pursue other forms of inspection. Over-delegation has two effects: there will probably be an increase in paperwork which is needed to ensure that the delegated work is being properly carried out, and members of staff may resent the over-delegation, seeing it as a way of 'passing the buck', of laziness on the part of their manager, or simply of his incompetence. In any case it does nothing to further good management/staff relations. Effective delegation is also difficult where the undertaking suffers from poor organisation. Good delegation requires that the powers delegated are precisely defined. Where organisation is such that managers' terms of reference are vague, where areas of authority are not clearly determined and known, where divisions of responsibility are not properly laid down, where there are inadequate channels of communication, and where policies are not precisely formulated, then managers are not able to define clearly what they expect of their delegates. Any of these deficiencies impede effective delegation and limit a manager's capability in this respect.

Coordination

This involves the synchronizing of effort of all the elements concerned in achieving an objective: in fact, it might be termed 'organisation in time' because proper timing is the essence of effective coordination. Co-ordination should start at the planning stage of any project and requires the full cooperation of all those participating in the pursuit of the given objectives. Above all, it requires good communication at all levels, both vertically and horizontally, and also the installation of control mechanisms vertically and horizontally, and also the installation of control mechanisms vertically and horizontally, and also the installation of control mechanisms to indicate where failure is likely to occur.

The need for effective coordination has become greater since the development of ever more complex organizations of all sorts, which have of necessity entailed the division of labour and the setting up of largely independent functional units. For example, the launching of a new product will create the need for an advertising campaign, supported by an appropriate sales drive, but the success of the launch will also depend upon the coordination of the manufacturing effort so that production coincides with marketing requirements.

Similarly, the provision of the necessary labour and materials which entails the availability of the requisite finance, must also be timed so that the new product, in the proper quantities, is ready in time for expected customer demand created by the advertising and selling effort. In a substantial modern organisation, each of these elements will probably be under the control of a separate functional head and effective coordination of all their efforts is vital for the success of the project. It is, of course, at the planning stage that the required coordination will be decided, but constant monitoring will be necessary to ensure that this is being maintained so that any default can be rectified without delay. Such monitoring is a function of the communication system.

Difficulties and problems of adherence to schedules, which are often basic to the coordination effort, can be discussed formally at meetings, or in an informal manner by face-to-face discussions by senior members of departments concerned. Otherwise any other appropriate method of communication can be used.

Control

Any enterprise can succeed in attaining its objectives only if its policies and plans are adhered to, and it stays on its selected course. In order to maintain this adherence it is necessary to institute controls. However, controls can be effective only if there are standards set against which performance can be measured so that deviation is brought to light. Such standards may be classed under the broad headings of quantity, quality and time, and checks should be instituted to ascertain that the set standards are achieved and maintained. Such checks involve the establishment of the necessary instruments to carry them out, and include work study, organisation and method, internal audit and internal check, inspection departments, sales targets and many other methods.

Organisation Structure

As the business grows, there comes a point when one man can no longer exercise personal control; departments are formed so that the task of management is shared. The manager, by now known as the general manager or managing director, is still in control, but his control is indirect. Responsibility for the work of departments has been delegated, together with the authority to make decisions and take action. An organization has been created. As the business grows still larger and more departments are created, the comes a point when there are too many managers directly responsible to the general manager. The number of direct subordinates is termed the 'span of control'; this must be such that the manager in charge has time to meet them and deal with their problems. If he is too busy, the business will suffer. What the span of control should be is dependent on the facts of the case. When growth causes the span to exceed what is efficient, an additional level of management is introduced.

Office services in relation to the organization

In any organization, 'the office' may mean different things to different people. To the salesman, it may mean the marketing manager and his supporting office staff; to a branch manager, it may mean head office; to the factory operative, it may mean the foreman's office. Often one hears that 'the office says we have to do it', as though the office had authority to give orders. In considering the office in relation to the organization, it is necessary to separate completely the concepts of management which decides and exercises authority, and the office which is a servant acting on behalf of management.

To those studying administration, or already responsible for the provision of office services, the office must be seen in wide terms; as anywhere where clerical work is done. The simple organization charts shown above, although they express the truth in broad terms, do not give the whole truth. They suggest that the administrative functions are in the hands of the office manager, whilst his colleagues are solely concerned with purchasing, production and marketing. In fact, all are involved in one way or another in the operation of clerical systems.. The office manager undoubtedly has the principal responsibility, but he cannot fulfil this without the help of other managers, supervisors and, indeed, operative staff.

The main office relies on other departments for most of the data it processes. The facts of what happens in the course of business can only be reliably recorded by those present when incidents occur. The purchasing officer provides copies of the orders he places; the storeman records the goods he receives; the factory operative records time spent and goods produced; the salesman writes out a customer's order; the van driver obtains the receipt for goods delivered and so on. The responsibility for the complete collection and accurate recording of these facts rests with the managers of the various departments where activity takes place.

Often, production, sales and other departments need immediate information which involves clerical work, if only to summarize the events of the day. In a factory, the supervisors may have to observe the rate of production from hour to hour. The marketing manager may need summaries of orders and despatches so as to assess the effects of these on available stocks. It is, therefore, not unusual for there to be small departmental offices in addition to the main office. Where an organization is highly computerized, these small offices may assume great importance: equipped with terminals, they can feed data directly into a central computer where stored information is held in a data-bank, available for all purposes. They can also extract information from the computer without calling on the services of the main office.

Whether clerical work is done manually or by computer, there must be co-ordination of systems and services. Each department cannot be left to devise its own methods and operate independently. The data used departmentally are the same data that are needed for the central accounting and recording processes. In the interests of efficiency, office work, wherever it is done, must be seen as part of one whole administrative process.

The provision of office services is a specialist function, having its own skills and its own body of knowledge. It cannot be expected that managers trained in disciplines such as engineering, chemistry or marketing shall also be expert in record-keeping, data processing or communications. In any organization there should be one authority the office or administrative manager, by whatever title he may be known responsible for the provision of central services, for the principal systems and for the machines and equipment wherever used.

If an effective office service is to be provided for management there must be full co-operation between the office manager and the managers of other functions. The records maintained should present a picture in words and figures of the activities of the business. It should be possible from the records to trace every transaction, every movement of goods, and every expense that has been incurred, and if these records are to be of proper value they must be kept in a form which truly reflects the business.

For example, records of revenue and expenditure should be so maintained that it is possible to show them in relation to the delegation of responsibility within the organization. The financial effect of any decision taken by an individual manager should be capable of being made known without undue special work. It is clearly not possible for the office manager to provide records which give a proper picture of the business unless he is taken fully into the confidence of the general manager and functional managers. He must be kept fully informed of plans as they are made, and alterations as they are put into effect. His task is then to ensure that the work of the offices is so directed that the facts will be available when they are wanted.

The office manager, by constant consultation with other managers, must be able to know what information is likely to be necessary so that adequate records only may be kept. Some offices, tend to keep records 'just in case they are wanted', or to perpetuate records which are no longer useful. This can only lead to excessive cost. There must be agreed routine statements which will be produced to meet the normal requirements of management, and there must be an understanding as to the type of special information which may from time to time be required and the degree of urgency with which it must be produced.

Centralization of office control

It has been argued above that, in the interests of efficiency, all office work Should be co-ordinated by one office manager, even though some parts of it may be done in departmental offices not under his control. In some organizations, the principal office manager is given full responsibility for all offices, including those attached to operative departments. He is required to organize, equip, staff and manage these offices, providing such services as the depart- mental or functional manager may reasonably demand. Taking the simplest example of organization given above, the situation may be illustrated thus, the dotted lines indicating responsibility for providing service. Again, it is emphasized that the office is not an end in itself but a service. If the service is best given by decentralization of offices then they should be decentralized, but this does not mean that those offices must be managed independently. A specialist office manager can control a group of small offices in just the same way as a sales manager can control groups of salesmen operating away from head office over a wide area.

Delegation

Authority resides with the board of directors and is delegated to the managing director and down to all those in the company until they all have the requisite amount of authority to carry out their allotted work.

Delegation is the process whereby an individual or group transfers to some other individual or group the duty of carrying out some particular action and, at the same time, taking some particular decision. It means, in effect, entrusting some part of the work of management to subordinates. Irresponsibility is not, however, surrendered, as no manager relieves himself of ultimate responsibility by delegating. The work is delegated and the superior holds the subordinate accountable to him. The subordinate is responsible for doing the job, it is the superior's responsibility to see the job is done.

When authority is delegated, all it means is that someone has been granted permission to do something; the superior must ensure that the subordinate has sufficient authority to do the job and that he has been told how the authority is to be used. Delegation can therefore be briefly stated to be a process whereby a manager:

(a) assigns duties to his subordinates;

(b) grants them authority to make commitments to the extent thought necessary to enable duties to be carried out;

(c) creates an obligation on the part of each subordinate for the satisfactory performance of the job.

Responsibilities should be clearly defined at all levels before work can delegated.

Reasons for delegation

(a) Lack of time or energy.

(b) Complexity of rules and new techniques means specialists are needed.

(c) Need for training for management succession.

It is noteworthy that a superior cannot delegate all his authority, otherwise he passes his position to his subordinate. When a superior delegates he is taking a calculated risk on the abilities of his subordinate. Supervision is needed but should not be too close as this tends to stifle initiative. Many managers fear to delegate because of the possible incompetence of subordinates.

Delegation is therefore an art and the following points should be noted:

(a) A manager should ensure that the subordinate accepts and understands what is involved.

(b) After giving an outline of the job, the control limits and the desired standards, a manager should leave his subordinate to do the job.

(c) Checking should be done periodically, and the superior should be willing to listen to the ideas of subordinates.

(d) Authority must be given to subordinates, as a manager cannot make all the decisions himself. He must trust subordinates to do their job, and delegate to them those matters which the subordinate is most competent to deal with, even though the manager can make better decisions than his subordinate.

It is worth noting that because of the use of modern equipment and the linking up with the telephone network, delegation of office functions to more dispersed units may occur. Management control can still be maintained by building in the system controls and safeguards using the speed and accuracy of the electronic equipment.

Factors affecting the degree of delegation

Cost of decision: The more costly the action to be decided upon, the more probable it is that the decision will be made higher up. For example, a decision to purchase a computer will be made higher up the scale of authority than a decision to buy a typewriter.

Need for uniformity of policy: The greater the need for uniformity, the greater the amount of centralization. For example, there often is a need to treat all customers alike. But too much uniformity means local knowledge is not used and initiative is stifled.

History of the firm: This could be an important factor as there is a tendency to retain decentralized authority, particularly at first, when a firm amalgamates and consolidates with other firms, whereas if a firm has grown up from a small group, there is a tendency to centralize. The philosophy of management is also important; for example, Henry Ford senior, the American motor car manufacturer, was very keen on centralization and, wherever possible, made every major decision himself.

Availability of capable managers: If there are few managers of quality there will be less decentralization of authority. The solution here lies in efficient training and decentralization is a good method of obtaining management experience.

Size of firm The larger the firm, the more complex the organization and the greater the difficulty in co-ordination. Decisions are more slowly reached and therefore more costly; decentralization can reduce this problem.

Controls available: If control techniques are good, management will be keener to delegate authority. If a subordinate can be controlled easily, a manager is more likely to delegate authority to him.

Span of control

A department is a specific area or branch over which a manager has authority for the performance of specified variables. Departmentation is necessary as a single person is unable to manage 'too many' subordinates, i.e., his span of control is too wide. This span of control or, preferably, span of management responsibility is simply the number of subordinates that an executive supervises. It is important to note that the phrase refers to executive or supervisory subordinates over whom an individual has authority, and not to subordinate operating personnel. There are of course other factors than the number of subordinates to consider, e.g. the abilities of supervisors and subordinates.

Spans of control vary widely from two to over twenty. The number varies with such factors as:

(a) the nature of the work, e.g. the more repetitive the work, the greater the number that can be controlled;

(b) the ability and training of subordinates and supervisors;

(c) the degree of delegation exercised;

(d) the effectiveness of communications and also physical proximity.

The problem then arises, that, if the span of control is restricted, information must then be carried through several levels of officials for decision and then back downwards in the form of instructions. This may cause undue delay and lead to the label of 'red tape' being given. Extremely tall or flat structures are the exceptions and usually growth is directed so that the dimensions are kept in reasonable balance. An important objective of organizational planning should be simplicity; this helps communications and can reduce overhead costs. A recent trend has been the tendency towards flatter structures where a manager is seen to co-ordinate the work of peers rather than directing the work of subordinates. In any large organization a large amount of basic facts, from which organizations make their decisions, start close to the bottom of the organizational hierarchy. If decision-making can be more automated it means that the lower levels of an organization can be removed and replaced by machines which will pass on the required information. This might possibly result in flatter structures. The less discretion there is for making decisions in a process, the more likely it is that the process will be automated, and this might lead to fewer people being involved in decision-making activities.

Office communication

The typewriter is the most commonly used and best known of office machines and as such requires no general description. The standard model is designed for use in typing correspondence and reports on quarto, foolscap or A4 size paper and is satisfactory for most general office work. This basic standard machine can be modified in a number of different ways in order to meet special requirements. Most machines are fitted with a single type, usually Roman, but a variety of other styles is available. There are also typewriters which permit several styles of type to be used. . The printball bearing the type required can be dropped into position in the machine. As a key is depressed the ball is turned until the required character is in position, when the printing action takes place.

Different sizes of type require different horizontal spacing. Ten letters to the inch (Pica) and twelve letters to the inch (Elite) are the most common. Most machines are restricted to one horizontal spacing but some printball machines can work at either ten or twelve letters to the inch. Printball units can also be provided for universal, technical, chemical and mathematical symbols.

The standard spacing of lines is six to the inch, variable by the operation of a lever to three lines to the inch and two lines to the inch (treble spacing). Machines are also available which provide for half-line spacing or for four lines to the inch. Double spacing is commonly used in typing drafts, when room must be left between the lines for any corrections which may be necessary. Where office forms are duplicated from typewritten masters, adequate space must be left for any entries which will subsequently be made by hand. Double spacing is the usual allowance for this purpose, but four lines to the inch is often sufficient.

The platen (roller) on a standard machine is usually between ten and eleven inches wide, a size well suited to take letter paper, envelopes, labels, and the majority of office forms. Where, however, large sheets of paper have to be used, as for legal documents, balance sheets, or involved statistical reports, a wider carriage is necessary. Carriages are obtainable in a variety of standard sizes, but for exceptional widths it may be necessary to modify the typewriter to carry the additional weight. On some typewriters, the carriage moves in relation to the type position; on others, a type-head moves along the length of the carriage.

Every office typewriter is fitted with some device to enable the typist to stop the carriage or type-head at predetermined positions, as an aid to setting out work accurately and quickly. In its simplest form, the tabulator consists of a rack at the back of the carriage on which small forked 'stops' can be fitted at any required point. When tabulating to insert figures in the columns of a form, for example, the typist has only to depress a key to cause the carriage or type/head to move and stop at the next column. Some machines are fitted with a more elaborate device, permitting the stops to be set from the keyboard simply by moving the carriage to the required position and depressing a key or lever. A further refinement is the provision of a series of tabulation keys which permit the carriage to be stopped at any one of a number of positions within a column. If, for example, the figure 10 has to be inserted, a key is depressed which will cause the carriage to stop two spaces from the right-hand side of the column. Other keys cause the carriage to stop at the correct position for typing 100s, 1000s and so on.

The typewriter imprint is normally made by type striking the paper through an ink-impregnated ribbon or coated plastic film. Ribbons may be of one or two colours, e.g. black and red, the colour being selected by means of a lever on the machine. Black and white ribbons are available, the white portion being used to conceal errors by over-typing, after which the correct characters are superimposed. Alternatively, some machines carry a separate white ribbon which can be brought into action when required.

There are also film ribbons which give high-quality impression by transferring a portion of the film to the paper. On some typewriters, there is a device which removes the film from the paper when an error has been made. Portable typewriters are machines, whether manual or electric, are of fighter construction than the standard typewriters. They are useful for casual office use and when travelling.

Manual and electric typewriters

In an electric typewriter, which should be regarded as the normal, both type and carriage movements are power actuated and only a slight depression of the keys is necessary. As compared with the manual machine, it offers the following advantages:

(a) Type impression is perfectly even.

(b) More carbon copies are obtainable.

(c) Typists can maintain a higher daily output.

There are typewriters which permit the use sizes of type. Instead of type being carried on bars, it is On a block or printball which is dropped into position on the machine. As a key is depressed the block is turned until the required character is in position, when the printing action takes place. Type blocks can easily be interchanged without removing the paper from the platen, thus permitting a variety of type styles to be used on one sheet of paper as required. These machines are of particular value in preparing company and management accounts and for laying out involved statistical reports, when the range of type styles can be used to distinguish one set of figures from another, and to give whatever emphasis may be required.

Electronic typewriters

The difference between clectro-mechanical typewriters and electronic type- writers is that an electrical machine has no moving parts only micro-electronic circuits. When a key is depressed a digital code is passed to the type-head instructing it what to do. There are a reducing number of electro-mechanical typewriters being produced; they use spherical printheads shaped like 'golf balls'. Most electronic machines have a round printwheel known as a 'daisy wheel'.

Many typists still prefer golf ball machines, but the trend of sales is fairly heavily towards electronic machines using daisy wheels. Ribbon costs though are lower on golf ball machines. Electronic typewriters have more features, which can increase typing productivity and presentation; they are also quieter and can offer scope for upgrading and for linking with microcomputers.

Usage

Consider whether the usage will be light or heavy; if it will be used many hours a day, continuously, then a heavy duty type will be needed.

Memory type

All have memories of some sort and the three main types are:

(a) *Correction-only machines*. They have small memories that hold (from about six to a few hundred characters) what has just been typed. Corrections can be made by single key-strokes which lift off errors and allow the correct letters to be replaced. These machines have other features but do not have memories that can store text for playing back and editing.

(b) *Phrase-store machines.* These allow phrases, paragraphs often used, short letters, etc to be automatically typed and merged with other text items. The memory could be over 1000 characters.

(c) *Editable machines.* They have much larger memories. Text can be stored and edited. Changes can be made character by character and simple machines have a single-line display of about 30 characters to enable a line to be verified or corrected. If a great amount of text editing needs to be done then a screen word processor is needed and not a memory typewriter.

Final choice

Most people will be satisfied with a machine that does corrections only as most typewriters are only used a few hours a day. If a memory is needed, a basic editable typewriter with a 5000 character store should be adequate. Do not pay more for advanced text editing or a larger memory unless there is a real need for these features.

Features of electronic typewriters

Most features are set out below and show why electronic machines are SO popular with typists and managers.

Automatic lift-off correction: Electronic typewriters have a correction memory, which remembers the characters that have just been typed. Correction occurs by pressing a key to backspace the print element and then automatically lifts off the characters that are incorrect. Some machines can only correct a few characters, some can correct on one line, others can correct characters spread over several lines

Line display: Many machines have an LED (light emitting diode) display which shows from 10 to 40 characters, allowing corrections to be made on the display before printing. Words in the memory can be recalled on the line display (scrolled) to allow checking or changing to be made. It is usually better to buy an editable machine with a line display.

Proportional spacing and pitches: The number of characters that can be typed in one inch is called the 'pitch'. Most electronics offer two pitches as standard; pitches can be 10, 12 or 15. Proportional spacing varies the number of characters in one inch in proportion to their individual size, producing a neat effect.

Editing features: Basic editing is corrections made character by character, so it can be slow if one wishes to delete a number of words. It is not easy to move words or sentences within a document as it has to be deleted first and then typed in again. More expensive machines allow deletion of blocks of text, or movement from one part to another. Some have a 'mailmerge' facility.

Carriage length: The carriage length tells you the maximum paper width that you can insert.

Bold print: This is found mainly on heavy duty machines and the effect is caused by the daisy wheel hitting the ribbon twice, the second strike being slightly to one side, giving a double image effect. On some machines the effect is very clear and neat.

Justification: The right-hand margin automatically.

Automatic underlining: As words are typed they are automatically underlined, there is no need to go back later and do this.

Centring: Headings etc. can be automatically centred at the touch of a key. This occurs mainly on heavier duty machines.

Decimal tabulation: Columns of decimal figures can be automatically lined up on a decimal point.

Half-space key: Movement is by half a space; thus for example correction of a spelling mistake by inserting a letter which had been omitted, can be done.

Automatic paper feed: This is the automatic feed of a sheet of paper into a preset position. The paper is then ready for typing.

Automatic repeat key: If a finger remains on a key, it continues to type.

Automatic carriage return: Every time the end of a line is reached the print wheel is automatically moved to the next line. Typing does not have to stop while this happens, as characters typed are held in the machine's buffer memory and then typed when the carriage is positioned on the next line.

Block indent: A block of text, or paragraph can be automatically indented, which can improve presentation.

Form memory: The layout of forms can be stored. By pressing a key, positions can be moved quickly, up, down and across, a very useful feature for preprinted forms.

Vertical line tabulation: When movement occurs from one tabulation position to another, a vertical line can be printed automatically.

Typewriters linked to microcomputers

Typewriters can be interfaced with a microcomputer so that they serve as a printer, or an input terminal. Most typewriter manufacturers provide for this, but it is important to have the correct interface type. Short memos and letters are usually simpler, quicker and cheaper to do on a typewriter. Using a typewriter as a printer for low volume of output is economical although rather slow. In addition ribbon costs will probably be higher, than if a dedicated (or purpose-built) printer is used.

The *Microwriter* has only six keys and is about 9 x 4 inches in size. The keys are positioned so that they line up with the fingers of one hand. On the top is a 14-character liquid crystal display and at each end are sockets for connection to a TV or monitor, printer, tape-recorder and power adaptor. To obtain letters or numbers two keys at a time have to be depressed together. To handle punctuation and other word processing commands there are four shifts, or settings. The 8 k bytes of memory holds about 5 pages of A4 size typescript. Speeds of about 50 words per minute are possible. A TV interface is needed to display up to 24 lines of text at any time and up to 60 characters on any one line. This is a useful, portable system which can be used by persons without too much effort once the 'rules' are learned. A number of printers can be attached to give good results.

Typewriter Ribbons

Most typewriters can use ribbons from various manufacturers. Prices can vary greatly. At present most golf ball typewriters use the same ribbon type, whilst most electronic typewriters have a very restricted use of type of ribbons. Most electronic typewriters use different ribbons to 'golf ball' machines. It is wise to examine prices of different dealers to get reasonable value. Fabric ribbons are more economical, but typing quality- is poorer. Carbon film ribbons giving good-quality print are used more often.

Continuous stationery

When long runs of routine forms, such as invoices, are being filled in by a typewriter, a considerable—proportion of the typist's time is occupied in interleaving carbon paper and inserting forms in the machine. These preparatory operations can be greatly reduced by the use of continuous stationery. An attachment is fitted to the typewriter carriage to take a quantity of forms printed on a long strip of paper which is usually folded in a zigzag formation. Successive forms are thus fed into the machine with no more effort than is needed to turn the platen. The backs of the original and all but the last of the copies can be coated with carbon, or a device fitted which enables sheets of carbon paper or ribbons to be used again and again, by drawing them down into the next set of forms after each typing operation is completed. Use can also be made of chemically impregnated paper which produces copies without requiring carbon paper or backing.

Word processing

Automatic typewriters of various kinds have been available for many decades. The term 'Word processing' has been introduced to describe automatic typing processes which make use of electronic and magnetic equipment similar to that employed in data processing. To review systems of word processing it is helpful to examine in turn three basic processes:

(a) the initial recording of the text;

(b) the recall of the text from the magnetic record; and

(c) the final typing of the document required for use.

Initial recording

Whatever is entered on the keyboard can be made into both a visible record and a magnetic record.

Visible records All word processing machines produce a typewritten record but some also have a separate display screen or a display panel built into the machine on which illuminated characters appear. Where a screen or panel is available the operator can delay the production of the typewritten record until a visual cheek has been made.

Magnetic records: There are three types of magnetic record: a magnetic card which can hold up to 12 000 characters but which often, for convenience, is used to hold the contents of one page, a magnetic tape cassette which can hold up to 125000 characters, and a diskette which can hold up to 250000 characters.

All word processing machines have an electronic store or memory, and for this reason they are sometimes called *memory* typewriters. The store has two purposes: to hold a program of operating instructions and to hold part or all of the text.

The program relates to the entry of the text and ensures that when the text is recalled from the magnetic record and typed automatically, the machine follows the original operator's instructions as to line length, paragraphing, column headings, tabulations, etc. The extent to which text is held in the store depends upon the system. Where there is a screen or panel, the store must be able to hold at least that part of the text being so displayed. Figure 5.4 illustrates a machine that operates with magnetic cards for external storage, and has an internal electronic store for 8000 characters. Some systems are able to hold large quantities of text in a central computer. In this kind of system, which uses what is called shared logic, the computer is served by several connected keyboards. Each keyboard may have typing capacity or the computer may be linked to a fast printer.

Recall

An important feature of word processing is the ease with which it is possible 1recall parts of the text from a magnetic record so as to make amendments, to add information or to retrieve information. For such purposes it is necessary to be able to transfer into the electronic store a particular page, paragraph, line, word or item of information. There are various ways of doing this of which the following are examples. With a magnetic card or a cassette every paragraph can be given a code number which appears on all drafts but which is omitted from the final document. The program automatically associates the number with the exact location in the magnetic record of the corresponding text. When it is required to make an alteration the operator places the appropriate card or cassette in the reader on the machine and:

(a) enters through the keyboard the reference number of the paragraph to be brought into the store;

(b) counts and enters the number of lines and the number of words along the relevant line to the point at which a change is to be made; and

(c) enters instructions to delete from, or add to, the text.

Working automatically under the operating instructions in the store, the System makes the changes and adjusts the spacing in the rest of the paragraph to allow for the change. When recalling and editing text with the aid of a display screen, the entry of the paragraph number brings the whole paragraph on to the screen, or as much of it for which there is capacity on the screen. The text can then be scrolled back and forth until the line to be altered is at the top of the screen. A dot of light is moved along the line until the point is reached where the change is to be made. As soon as the entry has been made a key is depressed and the revised and respaced paragraph appears immediately on the screen.

With a system using a diskette it is possible to locate a point in the text by merely entering into a part of the store a phrase from the text of sufficient length to identify it; if the phrase is used more than once it will locate each use in turn. One system which uses a diskette has a display panel in which the phrase is displayed for checking and, when that phrase is located in the text, it can also be scrolled back and forth in the panel to display the text on either side.

Producing results

Since the final document is produced automatically the printing speed is important. The conventional type basket is never used and the printball, working at a speed of 15 characters a second has largely been replaced by the daisy wheel printer (Fig. 5.5) which works at 52 characters a second. It has 80 flexible spokes each with a different character or sign on one face at the end of the spoke. It is rotated back and forth at high speed to bring each required letter into place whereupon the spoke head is struck with a hammer. Like the printball the daisy wheel is interchangeable with different styles of type.

An even faster device is the ink jet printer. This is a separate free standing printer and the process is to squirt a stream of magnetized ink particles on to the paper; magnetic deflection ensures that these particles hit the paper in the shape of the required characters. The speed of printing is 90 characters a second. In a large installation this item may be justified because it enables the typewriters to be used only for composing and editing and does not leave an operator idle whilst the machine automatically types the final work.

Applications

Wherever typists are engaged in work that involves extensive repetition, word processing is likely to offer advantages. Many kinds of typing incur a great deal of repetition. The preparation of technical reports, specifications, legal documents, manuals, minutes and a variety of long reports often causes extensive textual amendments. A draft is typed and returned to the author for checking and amendment; this may require the retyping of whole pages if not an entire report. The cycle may be repeated several times and involve many different people whose views have to be taken into account before the finished document is released. Moreover, every time a report is retyped there is the possibility of a new error being made. Much routine correspondence is highly repetitive particularly in matters such as a direct mail sales promotion, requests for quotations, and debt collection, where there is an attempt to 'personalize' what are in fact form letters. With word processing systems it is possible to merge form letters from one magnetic record with addresses and variable information either from another magnetic record or from a part of the memory where the information will have been entered in advance through the keyboard.

Word processing also has advantages to offer in the maintenance of, and data retrieval from, directories, lists, client and prospect files, inventories, staff records and a variety of other lengthy records that are subject to constant change and also where selection may involve the application of criteria.

Punched hole records

An earlier form of automatic typewriter is controlled by punched paper tape or edge punched cards. On these machines at the same time as a proof page is typed, a paper tape or card is punched. Tape and cards can be fed into the reader to control the type, spacing and carriage movements and the recording can include instructions to stop at required points so that names and addresses and non-standard text can be inserted through the keyboard in the ordinary way.

Summary of types of word processing equipment

(a) An electronic typewriter with a fairly large memory but without a screen or external disk drives.

(b) A word processor without a screen but with disk drives. This is similar to (a) above.

(c) Upgrading an electronic typewriter by attaching a screen.

(d) A microcomputer which uses word processing software (e.g. WordStar).

(e) A dedicated word processor. This is really a computer which has been built for word processing. Such a 'stand-alone' machine uses a single screen but is capable of linking in a cluster. These are more costly but more easy to operate (user-friendly).

The visible part of a system is called the 'hardware'. The 'software' is the program that determines what the system is capable of doing within the parameters of the hardware. Manufacturers of dedicated word processors (i.e. machines which are purpose built for word processing) offer their own software which is included in the system. Some confusion exists in the difference between word processors and micro-computers. Almost all computers can be used as a word processor. They can be programmed for different applications and one of these is word processing. Machines that are purpose built for word processing are known as 'dedicated systems'. At one period all dedicated word processors could only do word processing, so it was easy to distinguish between them and computer systems. Now they can run programs for other applications, financial planning for example, so it is not so easy to classify them.

There are still machines which are primarily intended for word processing; they have a keyboard specially designed so that you only need to press one key to perform a particular editing function, e.g. insert, delete, move. With other machines you probably have to press a command key and another to insert or move an item. The use of dedicated keys is one of the main differences between microcomputers and dedicated word processors. In both cases something which is typed on a keyboard appears on a screen, and this can be stored on a disk or printed on a separate printer connected by a cable.

Three types of word processors

Without a screen

These usually have a single line display. They look like a typewriter and are generally slower in operation as few of them can input text and print something else simultaneously. This facility (called concurrent printing) is generally standard on screen-based machines. Usually the printer is built into the same unit as the keyboard, just like a typewriter. They usually have some sort of external memory to store text, e.g. disks or tape. Few screenless word processors —can 'communicate' with other machines, although this facility is becoming more prevalent. The sending of text over a cable or telephone line to another word processing machine is an important development. A number of manufacturers have taken electronic typewriters and added disk storage to make a screenless word processor.

Word processor with screen

A screen simplifies text editing. They have free standing printers which can print while material is being inserted on the keyboard (i.e. concurrent printing), These machines have 'software' to drive them (i.e. a floppy disk incorporates the program that determines what the system can do). Changing disks can upgrade the program to incorporate new improvements. Screenless word processors usually have programs built into the machine's hardware, and cannot be changed. Such a system is expandable; two or three screens can be added and share a printer, or sometimes they can share central disk storage.

Shared logic word processors

Extra terminals can be added which share the main program, processor and central disk storage. Each terminal is incapable of performing any word processing function without connection to the share logic or central processing unit.

Computers and dedicated word processors

A number of years ago, if word processing was the main usage, a dedicated machine was easier to operate as compared with computers using a word processing package. Computers were favoured particularly as applications other than word processing were possible. Now computers have been modified to make word processing easier, and dedicated word processors have software to allow other operations to be run (e.g. payroll, stock control).

Choosing a word processor

This is not easy as there are very many variables involved (i.e. over 40 different performance capabilities) but the following information will be of assistance.

Automatic functions

These have been described

(a) automatic lift-off correction, centring of headings;

(b) automatic underlining, carriage return;

(c) automatic paper feed, repeat key;

(d) automatic decimal alignment of columns and numbers.

Memory functions

Word processors have memory capabilities far greater than electronic typewriters, which usually only store a few words.

Storage functions

Typed material can be permanently stored by using cards, tapes, diskettes or cassettes. This enables documents to be printed, stored, re-edited and then printed again. The saving on re-usable reports or contracts is great.

Communication functions

Stand-alone machines can be directly connected to each other to form a communication network, which can transmit messages and documents from machine to machine. This is easier if transfer is between identical machines. A word processor can also be connected to a mainframe computer, intelligent photocopier or typesetter, so data and documents can be transmitted at high speed. This can be costly as dissimilar machines may have different machine codes, which have to be connected to other codes before transmission.

The transmission of data over telephone lines (electronic mail) between word processor and computers is very convenient and is quicker and cheaper than telex. This method needs a device to connect a system to the telephone to transmit documents over telephone lines; such a device is called a modem.

Display functions

The ability to see words displayed (either one line or half a page) allows checking and correcting before printing. For a large display a more expensive machine will be needed. Some machines hold a full page and some display material from two different pages on one screen.

Additional functions

Words can be checked against a preprogrammed dictionary which highlights words that do not match. Some systems suggest alternate words to the words that have been used. Some word processors are programmable and perform other tasks involving processing of data. They can accept instructions in various programming languages, e.g. Basic, Cobol, and accept software to run packages on accounting and stock control.

Main Functions and Features of a Word Processor

Display features

(a) *Buffer memory*. Some of the memory is used to hold information that is being displayed, before it is stored.

(b) *Cursor*. An indicator showing the operator where the next character will be input or where editing is being performed.

(c) *Character size control*. The operator can enlarge or reduce character size to help to view or display more characters.

(d) *Code display*. Ability to display or not to display codes, e.g. change format, or start underlines.

(e) *Format display*. Screen should ideally show the document as closely as possible to the final appearance in print.

(f) *Screen size*. Standard size allows 24 lines of 80 characters. This can go up to full page display.

(g) *Scrolling*. Horizontal and vertical rolling of text. This should be very smooth and fast so as to move easily between pages.

(h) *Highlighting*. Material being manipulated can be highlighted.

(i) *Windows*. Separation of screen into different sections to enable comparisons and alterations to various parts of documents.

Basic functional features

(a) *Document index*. Documents should be logged or named for accessing or storage. Index should be available on disk, with easy access.

(b) *Format master*. Formats control the layout and text of a page, these include line spacing, margins, tabs, justification, type size and style.

(c) *Background*. This function is a job that can be performed while another is running.

For example, printing can be a background function, so while a document is being printed another one can be inserted.

(d) *Form input.* This enables a form which is often used to be set into memory so that movement from one area to another can be controlled by using only one key.

(e) *Keystroke memory.* The ability to set up and store a group of commands and recall them with one keystroke.

(f) *Machine dialogue.* Ways in which a machine allows an operator to select and perform tasks. Efficiency is assisted by

(1) Special keys (function keys), clearly labelled, which perform involved editing operations with few keystrokes. (3) A list of options (menus) shown on display which enable the operator to select from various functions. They are helpful for beginners but experienced operators try and bypass them.

Input of text features

(a) *Automatic carrier return.* With this the word processor automatically ends the line at a margin and words which extend over the margin are 'wrapped around' to the next line. The operator therefore does not have to make line-end decisions.

(b) *Automatic centring.* One keystroke will position cursor between margins and centre text at this point.

(c) *Emboldening.* Here the print strikes again at the same keystroke to darken the print. Some machines can darken print in one keystroke.

(d) *Columns.* Text can be inserted in columns which is very useful for statistical or accounting data.

(e) *Headers and footers.* Specific data can be inserted by most word processors above/ below the area of text on each page and are useful for heading and numbering pages of reports.

(f) *Hyphenation.* This can be automatic at line ends. Some machines mark the words and allow the operator to hyphenate.

(g) *Indenting.* One keystroke will move paragraph.

(h) *Margins.* They should be completely adjustable.

(i) *Pagination.* Some machines will, after text has been typed, automatically paginate and number pages. Others require the operator to make page ending decisions.

(j) *Phrase storage.* Common phrases can be recalled and inserted by pressing pre-defined keys (e.g. standard letter endings or paragraphs).

(k) *Underlining.* Once the beginning and end of the text to be underlined is noted the underlining is automatic.

Editing features

(a) *Copy.* Copying text from one part to another of a document or diskette.

(b) *Delete.* A block of type from one character to a whole page may be deleted and the other data is automatically closed up.

(c) *Editrace.* This shows where alterations or deletions have been made.

(d) *Global search or replace.* The ability to find all the number of times a string of characters occur in document (e.g. a word). This can then be altered or deleted automatically. Some machines are slow or are not very-cot operating this feature.

(e) *Index generator.* This is where specified words are automatically listed together with page and line numbers. This is available on more expensive models.

(f) *Input/edit.* Most machines allow editing at the same time as inputting the original document.

(g) *Insert.* The insertion of new text in the existing material. The machine should then automatically adjust the rest of the material in the paragraph.

(h) *Merge.* Variables in one document can be merged with text from another. The most common is personalizing one letter to a mailing list of names and addresses.

(i) *Move.* Text can be moved from one place to another within a document or from one document to another.

(j) *Random access.* The ability to move to specified points in a document bypassing intermediate text.

(k) *Go to or jump.* The ability to jump to a numbered line or page.

(l) *Find or search.* The ability to locate automatically and go to a selected string of characters.

(m) *Recovery.* The ability to retrieve text after it has been accidentally deleted.

(n) *Repagination reformat.* Where material is added or deleted in a document, the machine automatically alters the page make-up of the document.

(o) *Spelling.* Many machines have access to a dictionary of words so that misspelled words can be located and highlighted. Special or technical words can usually be added to the dictionary. Sometimes alternative words are offered.

Printing features

(a) *Graphics.* Display and printing to represent elements of graphs, e.g. a chart or table produced automatically.

b) *Diagnostic.* Lights show the end of essential features (e.g. end of ribbon, paper, printer failure).

(c) *Paper feeders.*

(1) Tractor feeders use continuous perforated forms, which can be torn into separate sheets. (2) Sheet feeders are more expensive than tractor feeders and handle separate sheets.

(d) *Paper width.* The carriage should be adjustable to allow different widths of paper,

(e) *Printing queuing.* The ability to enable a number of documents to fine up in order for printing. Where there is only one printer and several word Processors, this feature controls the order of printing from the various machines.

(f) *Simultaneous printout.* Here the printing can be running while another document is being prepared..

(g) *Spacing.* Should be adjustable between lines and also adjustable between characters to allow for different types of pitch and justified printout.

(h) *Speed.* Measurement of printing speed is usually in characters per second (cps) or words per minute (wpm). A rough guide is, up to 60 cps for print wheels and 80 cps for inkjet, and 50 pages a minute for laser printers.

(i) *Typestyles.* Better quality printers have a variety of typefaces and sizes which are easily interchangeable (e.g. elite, pica, italic).

Other features

(a) *Communications.* Ability to send and receive messages etc. from other computers and databases.

(b) *General computer capability.* Special software enables some word processors to function like standard computers and allow programming and other software applications including numerical data.

Ergonomic features

Machine design must be related to human needs, relating the physical characteristics of machines and their ease and pleasantness of use.

(a) Keyboards. Must be easy to use and read. Some are detachable and can be positioned to suit the operator.

(b) Screen

(1) Colour. Many word processors show bright green characters on a dark background, or white on a black background. Bronze characters on a dark background are becoming popular. Tinted glass can be placed over the screen to suit individual requirements. (2) Height and angle. These can be adjusted in some word processors.

(c) Dedicated command keys. These aid the operator.

(d) Desks. Should be at correct height with ease of use for disk drives and copyholders.

Word processing is the production of typewritten materials by using automated dictation transcription and typewriting machines. Input comes in the form of longhand, copy typewriting, or dictated material. Dictation can now be recorded magnetically and transferred to a central point by wire rather than be carried by hand. Material received is transcribed and stored in the memory of an automatic typewriter. While in the memory of the typewriter, material can be changed. When acceptable, it can be printed automatically at high speed.

Printers

The printer is the only predominantly mechanical part of a word processor system. It usually needs the most servicing and is a very expensive component of a word processor.

The features to note, other than price, are:

(a) *Speed.* Although the slowest printer is faster than a typist, long documents do take a long time. Faster printers may not produce good quality work.

(b) *Quality.* Ideally high-quality printing, as found on a standard typewriter, is required. The cheapest and slowest letter-quality printers use a 'golf ball' printing element (12-15 cps). Most letter-quality printers use a print wheel using a hammer to strike the rotating print element against the paper (30-60 cps). Plastic print wheels are faster and cheaper usually, but less durable and of lower quality than metal ones.

Types of printer

Matrix

These printers impact a group of small dots on to paper so that they merge to form characters. These are faster than letter-quality printers (85 cps). Quality is generally poor but they are in common use. Double-density matrix printers use a finer dot structure, producing better-quality characters.

Ink jet and laser

Both are systems that print ink on to a page without impacting against paper.

Electronic LCD/image

These are basically photocopying machines that 'copy' electronically stored information and are often called 'intelligent copiers'. They use a laser beam controlled by the word processor, placing images of characters on to the copying drum. They are new but have great potential, producing good quality at high speeds as well as copying normal material.

Printer feeders

Single feed, gravity or friction feeders are all right for single-letter word Processor applications, but are rather slow for use in volume applications. So feeders of multiple-sheets are needed:

(a) Tractor feeders have fan-fold paper with holes on the outside engaging on sprocket mechanisms to hold the paper while moving through the printer. Perforated tractor strips are tom off after printing. These are basically cheaper and quite reliable, but require special paper.

(b) Sheet feeders are bins which hold a hundred or more sheets or envelopes feeding them singly into the printer. They are dearer but more convenient than tractor feeders.

It is important to select manufacturers that are reputable and have good financial bases. They must have a good support system and training pro- grammes. Reliability of equipment and good support are essential and questions to local users are well worth while. Quick response time for servicing is vital. All of the above together with possible upgrades and length of warranty could form the basis of a check-list for machine support and repair.

Finally, there are some savings—the possible reduction in secretarial assistance, saving on time in revision or producing detailed contracts, electronic mail savings (eliminating telex and phone calls). Paper and printing time can be saved by working with a word processor screen.

Dictation

There is an art in dictation which every manager should cultivate; it consists, broadly, in being sure in advance what ideas are to be expressed and in being able to put those ideas into good English. Too many writers of business letters still rely on hackneyed phrases—the so-called 'business English'. It is only too easy to memorize and use such expressions as:

'Reference yours of the 15th inst.

'Yours of the 15th inst. to hand..

'Your esteemed instructions received

'We would advise you... and to finish by assuring the addressee of 'our best attention at all times'. The effect of these well-worn and often curiously ungrammatical sentences can scarcely convey to the recipient the writer's desire to give real thought and personal attention to his affairs. Constant practice and self-criticism are necessary in order to be able to dictate letters fluently which are pleasing to read and which reflect the true personality of the writer.

Dictating machines

Dictating machines provide a means whereby correspondence, reports, instructions, etc. can be recorded as speech and later transcribed by an audio-typist. Records may be inscribed, as where grooves are cut in a plastic belt or disk, or magnetic on tape, disk, or belt. Inscribed records are permanent and cannot be corrected during dictation. They can, however, be stored with little danger or deterioration or accidental erasure. Some inscribed records can be shaved to remove the grooved surface and then re-used, the number of times depending on the thickness of the material. Magnetic records can be erased and corrected during dictation. They can also be erased and re-used, possibly hundreds of times.

In addition to machines for desk use, there are portable models, some being small enough to be carried in the pocket.

There is advantage in standardizing the type of record used in an organization for both desk and portable machines. If, for example, all recording is done on standard magnetic-tape cassettes, it can be transcribed in any department.

Whatever the type of machine, facilities are provided whereby the dictator can start and stop the record instantly. By stopping the record when making even a brief pause in dictation, the whole surface can be used. The running times of records vary and may be classified as short duration (about 10 minutes), medium duration (10-20 minutes) and long duration (more than 20 minutes). If, in the course of recording, the dictator wishes to hear the record, this can be played back immediately. Magnetic records can be erased and corrected; inscribed records cannot be erased and corrections are usually indicated to the typist on a paper slip showing which parts are to be ignored and which substituted.

Whilst dictating machines can be operated after very little practice, executives are well advised to listen critically to their own recordings and take pains to— enunciate their words carefully. Carelessness in dictation leads to errors in transcription or, at the best, the wasting of time by the typist in listening to the record a second or third time in endeavouring to pick out an indistinct word or Phrase. Typists who transcribe from dictating machines should be encouraged to express their difficulties, and to offer criticism of the dictation.

Skills required in dictating

(a) Ensure correct controls are switched on for recording-and-all relevant papers are to hand clearly and distinctly.

(b) Give identity at start of dictation, speak

(c) Indicate number of copies required, size and type of paper, style (i.e. double spacing) and the size of envelope needed for special enclosures.

(d) Use index slip to note any alterations as well as on recording.

(e) Give spellings of unusual or specialized names and dictate references, name and addresses of addressee and post code.

(f) Dictate amounts of money with £ sign first and special punctuation instructions.

(g) The end of dictation should be indicated and any special distribution of copies.

Transcribing

The audio-typist hears the record through earphones, stopping and starting the machine by hand or pedal controls. The typist starts the record, listens, and types. Whilst some may require to stop the record before typing, experienced typists working from good records are able to listen and type simultaneously. Provision is made on the machine for the typist to be able to listen to any selected portion of the record without going back to the beginning.

With special attachments, dictating machines can be connected so as to record telephone messages and conversations. By using a suitable microphone, they can also be used to record speeches and the proceedings of meetings.

If adequately packed, records can be sent through the post without risk of damage. Salesmen can, for example, dictate their reports and orders on portable machines and send the records for transcription at head office. Reports may, in fact, be heard and never transcribed. If a report is to be preserved for a time the record itself can be filed. With the aid of portable machines, inventories of stock, etc. can be dictated whilst moving from place to place.

These are but a few examples of the many ways in which speed recording can be used to save time and paperwork.

Stenographic machines

These are machines which enable an operator to take dictation, recording it in type. Each line on the paper tape represents a syllable printed by the simultaneous depression of the appropriate combination of keys on the machine. The machine is easily portable and skilled operators can attain very high speeds. The operator does not usually transcribe from the tapes which he has prepared; they are passed to copy typists who can be quickly trained to read and type from them. Stenographic machines are particularly suited for the reporting of meetings, as the tape can be passed to typists from time to time during the course of the meeting, the typing proceeding almost simultaneously.

Comparison of shorthand with dictating machine

The shorthand systems in common use are of two main types:

(a) Those which can be written at high speeds, but only after extensive training and practice.

(b) Those, often based on the normal alphabet, which are more easily learned but cannot be written so quickly.

The ability to write at high speed is important in verbatim reporting, but the slower systems are often found to be adequate for general purposes. The practice of dictating business correspondence etc. to a shorthand writer is giving way to the use of dictating machines because they offer the following principal advantages:

(a) The typist need not be present during dictation.

(b) Dictation can be recorded item by item as matters arise.

(c) Dictation can be recorded away from the office.

(d) Recordings may be sent by post for transcription.

(e) Transcription by an audio-typist from a good recording can be than transcription from shorthand notes.

Because of (a) and (e), above, the output of an audio-typist may be as much as double that of a shorthand-typist.

Selecting dictating equipment

A good desk-top machine is available for under £200 and there is every evidence that greater efficiency is possible with dictating machines as compared with shorthand dictation.

The main features to consider in selecting a dictating machine are:

(a) The type of cassette tape used. Portable machines use a 'mini-cassette' giving 15 minutes recording time on each side of the tape. The arrival of a micro-cassette' allowing up to one hour's recording time on each side of the cassette has proved very popular.

The micro-cassette is very like ordinary cassettes, which are 'capstan driven', that is the tape is pulled through evenly. Mini-cassettes give a more inconsistent recording speed. One spool pulls the tape from the other spool so the quality of the sound can suffer. At present there is a bias towards the older system of mini-cassettes as there are a lot of these machines in use. This means that some manufacturers offer both mini and micro-cassettes.

(b) Whether to buy desk top or (hand-held) portable machines. Portable are cheaper and easy to transport. Desk top are clearer, but usually last longer and are more reliable. They also offer additional features, e.g. a hand-held microphone.

(c) Ease of use. European and American machines tend to be easier to use but are more expensive. Japanese machines have more features and are cheaper, but some makes a little more difficult to operate.

(d) Servicin ırrangements and price. Most business equipment dealers offer reliable servicing arrangements and most brands can be purchased below list price.

(e) Indexing. It is useful to mark the beginning and end of each letter to assist the typist. Indexing can be via a sound or visual index. The more expensive machines automatically index, often by flashing lights, but these may not be worth the extra cost.

(f) Other features include fast forward and reverse, pause, manual or automatic record level control, wait, automatic voice stop or start, automatic backspace (useful for transcribing).

Secretarial duties

It is not to be expected that private secretaries will understand as much about the business in hand as an executive, but they should have some understanding of the significance of the correspondence, reports, and instructions which pass through their hands. They should be able to fulfil some or all of the following duties:

(a) Receive visitors and, if necessary, turn them politely away.

(b) Receive and give messages verbally or by telephone, with understanding of their significance.

(c) Compose routine replies to letters and memoranda.

(d) Punctuate and correct grammar in transcribing dictation.

(e) Maintain a filing system.

(f) Keep an engagement diary, and see that engagements are fulfilled or other suitable action taken.

(g) Operate a reminder system to ensure that necessary work is done at the due time.

(h) Arrange business journeys, make reservations, obtain tickets, and prepare itineraries.

(i) Arrange meetings by making contact with a number of executives or their secretaries to find mutually convenient dates.

Personal assistants

In some businesses, senior-private secretaries are trained to act as personal assistants, relieving the executive of work which otherwise he could have to do personally. In this capacity, they should also be able to do the following:

(a) Gather and collate information from within the business and from outside.

(b) Draft reports, memoranda, etc. for the executive.

(c) Draft proposals for the executive to amend or approve.

(d) Act as secretary to management meetings, drafting agenda, minutes etc.

Centralized typing services

Where each executive has his own typist, there is inevitably wasted time because the flow of typing work is not steady. On some days, the typist may be hard-pressed; on others, she may have little or nothing to do, perhaps because the executive is away from his office. In any case, it is rare for an executive to generate enough work to keep one typist fully occupied, even if her work is supplemented by other secretarial duties. This problem may be overcome by providing a typing or secretarial service to a number of executives or departments from a central department or 'pool'. The advantage to be gained are as follows:

(a) The total number of typists is reduced, sometimes by as much as half.

(b) Expert supervision becomes possible.

(ç) Typists can be trained to do a wider variety of work.

(d) Difficulties arising from absence are reduced.

(e) Working conditions can be suited to the needs of typists.

(f) Work can be allocated according to individual ability and experience.

(g) A wider range of machines and equipment can be made available because they can be shared.

On the other hand, there are disadvantges, for example:

(a) continuity of understanding is lost, because the work of one executive is not always dealt with by the same typist.

(b) the executive does not have the assistance of a private secretary immediately available.

The success or otherwise of the system depends to some extent on the complexity of the work. It has been found that the typing pool is a very efficient way of dealing with routine correspondence. It does not, however, provide a Satisfactory substitute for the private secretarial service, which is generally retained for the higher executives. Although a centralized typing service may provide shorthand writers, dictating machines are more commonly used. The executive may dictate to a machine in his own office and send the record to be transcribed by the pool. Alternatively, the dictating machines may be installed centrally in the pool, being connected to the executives' offices by special circuits or through a private automatic telephone system. In the latter case, remote control permits the dictator to start and stop the machine and to play back his recording. The number of machines required is, of course, reduced. Two remote systems can be adopted:

(a) Tandem, in which each typist has two machines, so that one is available for recording whilst the other is being used for transcription.

(b) Bank or exchange, in which executives are connected to one of a number of dictating machines, from which the records are removed when full and passed to the typists for transcription.

In either case, connection with a machine may be automatic or controlled by a supervisor.

Computer-assisted typing pools

Where the nature and volume of work warrants it, the conventional typewriter can be replaced by a keyboard and visual-display screen connected with a computer. The typists firstly key in instructions as to margin, tabulation positions, etc., which are confirmed on the screen. The text is then typed in the ordinary way but without regard to line length which is automatically adjusted by the computer program. When a new paragraph is to be started or work is to be tabulated, it is sufficient to depress a control key. When a page is complete, the computer commences a new one without specific instructions.

What has been typed can be seen immediately on the screen. Corrections can easily be made by back-spacing to the required position and deleting or typing in. The computer automatically adjusts the position of the unaltered text to show the corrected version on the screen. When one task is complete, it is stored by the computer and the typist is immediately free to proceed with the next. Up to this stage there is nothing on paper.

An independent operator feeds paper (or continuous stationery) into a number of automatic typewriters which, under control of the computer, type accurately and at high speed. The computer checks the length of words and determines when to start a new line or a new page. If required, the first typing on paper can be treated as a draft for correction, whilst the computer file retains its recording. When the corrected draft is sent back to the pool, a typist recalls the recorded text to the screen and makes the required alterations. The final version is then produced on an automatic typewriter in the same way as was the draft.

If you are like most of us, you spend more time communicating than doing anything else. Probably you spend a large part of each day talking and listening. And when you are not talking or listening you are likely to be communicating in other ways—reading, writing, gesturing, drawing. Or perhaps you are just taking in information by being, or feeling, or smelling. All of these activities are forms of communication; and certainly you do them throughout most of your conscious moments.

Something we do so much must be important. Probably it is the most important of all our activities. It is easy to see that communication is the activity which has enabled us to develop the civilized society we know today. It is one activity which we human beings clearly do better than the other forms of life on earth; and largely it explains our dominant role. It is the activity which has enabled us to organize—to work in groups. And through organization we have been able to overcome barriers to our existence which individually we would not have been able to overcome. But there is no need to discuss further how communication contributed to the development of us human beings. Its role is obvious to us all. We need only to conclude that communication is extremely vital to our success and well-being in civilized society.

Just how much communicating a business organization needs depends on a number of factors. The nature of the business certainly is one. Some have much greater need to communicate than do others. The organization plan of the company also affects the volume of communication, for much of the information flow is provided by the structure.

Also, the people who make up the organization affect the volume of communication. As we shall point out later, every human being is different. Each has different communication needs and abilities. Thus, varying combinations of people will produce varying needs for communication.

Although the communication needs vary by company, people in organizations communicate more than most of us suspect. According to one generally accepted estimate, between 40 and 60 per cent of the work time spent in a typical manufacturing plant involves some phase of communication. Of course, these percentages are only averages. Some employees spend much more of their time communicating. In fact, the higher up the organization structure the employee is, the more communicating he or she is likely to do. Typically, top executives spend from 75 to 95 per cent of their time communicating. Unskilled labourers, on the other hand, need to communicate little to do their work.

Without question, communication is important to the business organization. Because it is important, it stands to reason that business wants its communication to be well done. But all, too rarely is business satisfied with what it gets. Unfortunately, to use the often quoted words of an authority in the field, "Of all the things business executives do, they are worst at communicating".

The role of communication in organized activities is perhaps best explained by illustration of a real situation. By design, our illustration is both detailed and scant. It is detailed because it is made up of illustrations of the minute and specific communication events which occur in business. It is scant because at best it covers only a sample of the almost infinite number of events.

For this review we could select any organization, as communication is vital to every conceivable type. Our choice is the Typical Company, manufacturer of a line of quality whatsits. The Typical Company is moderately large, with scores of departments and hundreds of workers doing a thousands and one tasks. It employs crews of salespeople who sell the manufactured whatsits to wholesalers all over the country. Like most companies in its field. Typical works to help move its products from wholesaler to retailer and from retailer to the final consumer. And it works to keep the consumer happy with the purchase. The Typical Company is indeed typical.

Our review begins with the workday of Dan D. Worker, a clerk in Typical's order department. Dan's communication activities begin each day the moment he awakens. But for our purposes we shall pick up Dan's activities as he rides to work in a car pool with three of his co-workers. Of course, Dan and the members of his car pool communicate as they travel. Obviously, communication has a social use, and riding to work is a form of social occasion for Dan and his friends.

Most of their talk is about trivial matters. They talk primarily to entertain and to while away the time. There is joke or two, some comments about politics, a few words about a coming football game, and some raves about the new woman at the company switchboard. Such talk, of course, is of little direct concern to Typical except perhaps as the talk affects the general happiness and welfare of the company's workers.

In time, the conversation drifts to subjects more pertinent to Typical and its operations. Someone mentions a rumour about a proposed change in promotion policy. Then Dan and the others being in their own collection of rumours, facts, and opinions on the subject. And in the process they form opinions and work up emotions concerning the Company and its policies. This communication activity has little to do with manufacturing whatsits, nor is it related to Dan's duties at Typical . But it has affected Dan's outlook, and he just might not put out very much work for Typical today or any other day. He might not trust Typical quite so much the next time the union contract problem comes up.

When the four reach the plant, the gate guard receives the message communicated by the green sticker on the windshield and waves the car through. They drive past the most convenient parking spaces, for they receive clearly the message on signs at these sites: "Reserved for the President." "Reserved for the Sales Manager," "Reserved for the Production Superintendent," and so on. As Dan enters his work area, he files past the time clock punches his card thereby communicates to the payroll department a record of his attendance.

As Dan enters his work area, he engages in more social communication. He exchanges "good mornings" with each of his colleagues, and he makes small talk with two of them as they wait for the Company whistle to communicate the message that it is time for work to commence. Although this small talk with associates has little to do with manufacturing whatsits, it helps to create a happy and friendly attitude among Dan and his co-workers. And such an attitude can be conducive to productivity.

When the 9 o'clock whistle, blows, Dan begins his work as order clerk. The morning mail, already delivered to his desk, produces first an order from one of Typical' salespeople in the field. Using the computer terminal at his work station, Dan enters the pertinent information: quantities, types, salesperson credited, sales district, purchaser identification, and such. As a part of the Company's data base, this information will become a part of a number of reports programmed to serve the information needs of Typical's employees. Shipping department workers will get the information they need to fill the order. Sales managers will receive summary reports of the activities of their salespeople. Production planners will receive the inventory and product demand information they need to work out production schedules. And the top executives will get the overall activity reports which give them the performance information they need in guiding Typical's course.

Among those in the shipping department who will receive the order information is Geraldine peevy, the department secretary. One of Ms. Peevy's duties is to send the shipping details to the customers in specially adapted acknowledgment letters. The Typically company uses a specially adapted letter rather than a routine from acknowledgment because the firm recognizes the goodwill-building effect of making every communication contact as favourable as possible. Obviously, individually composed letters are expensive; so Ms. Peevy cheats a little by selecting from a half dozen basic form letters stored in the memory of her word processor. Of course, the word processor will reproduce the letter and adapt it to the one customer.

Contents of the next envelope Dan opens are not so positive as the first. This one is a note from a Typical salesperson in the field who reports on a difficulty a customer is having with a whatsits. Using his computer terminal, Dan enters the pertinent facts into the Company's data base. There it will become a part of summary reports which may be useful to production control and product design. Then Dan forwards this message through interplant mail to the customer services department. Here Typical's individualized attention will be given to the problem, for Typical knows that it is good business to keep its customers satisfied. Probably someone in customer services will communicate with some of Typical technical personnel in an effort to find the cause of the difficulty. Then they will pass on their findings to the salesperson in the field, who will personally visit the customer to report the information.

Occasionally, such problems cannot be so easily solved. When a whatsit is defective, for example, customer services will make a fair and speedy adjustment. Or if the defect oceurs frequently enough, a full-scale investigation may result. Possibly one or more of the company's technical specialists will be assigned to the problem, and they will spend days or weeks or even longer periods searching for the answer to the problem. When they find the answer, they will communicate this information through some form of written report.

As Dan opens the third envelope, he recognizes the familiar off- colour brown of employee relations stationery. Inside he finds a printed memorandum with an instruction sheet attached. This memorandum, signed by the president, explains the new promotion plan Dan and his friends discussed on the way to work. The instructions tell Dan to post the memorandum on the department bulletin board. As Dan posts the memorandum, he reads the Company's explanation. There is much in it that he had not considered before, and some of the "facts" his friends used in their arguments are strongly refuted. Dan is now somewhat confused, but he begins to feel that the company may have a point or two.

On the way back to his desk, Dan passes the office of Mary Kapel. Last week, Mary was promoted to chief order clerk-a job Dan had wanted. Dan observes Mary sitting at her large double-pedestal desk. He sees Mary's name printed on the door, and he observes the carpeting on the floor. These objects clearly communicate to Dan a message of Mary's success. Mary is busily working and does not see Dan go by. "That stupid, puzzled look on her face shows she doesn't know what she's doing," Dan thinks "She sits at her desk so high and mighty". Mary certainly communicates a lot to Dan, and without saying a word.

Dan passes the water cooler where James Hooker and another worker are standing. Dan does not care much for Hooker. In fact, he has had a few run-ins with the man since Hooker joined Typical three weeks ago. Dan cannot explain exactly what went wrong. At the beginning Hooker appeared to be a pleasant enough chap. He and Dan had lunch together that first day. But soon after that time Hooker started to find fault with some of the work procedures in the department. He even pointed out some things that Dan could do "to improve operations." As Dan saw it, there was little a neophyte like Hooker could tell a man who had been on the job for almost 20 years.

As Dan passes the cooler he waves his hand slightly in a feeble gesture of recognition. Hooker responds halfheartedly with a nod of the head. these simple gestures clearly communicate how these men feel about each other Dan's thoughts now are even more hostile. He wonders how long it is going to take John Riley, his department head, to notice how much time Hooker spends at the water cooler, in the rest room, and at coffee. Yesterday Dan saw Hooker getting ready to go home for the day a full ten minutes before quitting time. As Dan sees it, Riley must like Hooker. The two talk together a lot, and Riley has accepted a number of Hooker's suggestions. But Riley always has had his favourites, Dan thinks.

Dan returns to his desk; but before he can resume his work, Riley walks up. "Have you given any more thought to that reporting procedure change we talked about yesterday?" Riley asks.

Riley is referring to a change he has had in mind for quite a few years. Last week he asked Hooker to do some research on the possibilities of the procedure. It was then that Hooker talked with Dan about the plan, and it was then that the two had another one of their run-ins.

Riley's words bring Dan's temper to a slow boil. "Riley certainly is sold on that asinine idea of Hooker's," he thinks to himself. "Sure, it will save time now, but it won't give us much information. Bur you can't fight city hall." Dan forces a smile which belies his inward feeling as he responds; "Yes, I have, Mr. Riley. It's a great idea. We should put it into effect right away."

Reviewing Dan's activities, we find that most of what he does involves communication in one way or another. Some of the forms of communication are easily recognized, such is speaking, listening, reading, and writing. But some are more subtle. Primarily these are the nonverbal types. One form is body motions. Another is the communication message made by how far or close people stand when communicating. Then there are the communications we make through facial expressions. As we noted above, even objects like desks and carpeting communicate, and so can people just by being seen. In fact, it is impossible for people knowingly in the presence of each other not to communicate.

Clearly, Dan communicated more that first meets the eye. From the moment he left home to the moment he looked at his watch, Dan was giving, receiving, or handling information. Nothing that he did directly involved making whatsits, which, of course, is the Typical Company's main reason for being. Yet there is no question of the importance of his activities to Typical's operations. Obviously, Dan's work assignment more directly involves communication that do many other assignments at Typical. But there are many other communication-oriented assignments in the company; and every Typical employee's workday is spotted in varying degrees with communication in one form or another. If we were to trace the workdays of each Typical employee and combine our findings, we would come up with an infinitely complex picture of the communication that goes on at Typical. We would see that communication truly plays a major role in Typical's operations.

Internaloperational communication

The importance of communication in business becomes even more apparent when we consider the communication activities of an organization from an overall point of view. As we can see from a review of Dan's half hour at Typical, these activities fall into three broad categories of communication; internal-operational, external-operational, and personal. Internal-operational communication consists of the structured communication within the organization directly related to achieving the organization's work goals. By "structured" we mean that such communication is built into the organization's plan of operation. By the "organization's work goals" we mean the organization's primary reasons for being—to sell insurance, to manufacture nuts and bolts, to construct buildings, and the like.

The Typical Company, to use a familiar example, has as its major work goals the making and selling of whatsits. In achieving these work goals, it has an established plan of operation, and communication plays a major role in this plan. More specifically, each of Typical's employees has an assignment in the plan. For the plan to work, some communicating must be done. In some of he assignments certain working information is needed. And so that all assignments may be performed as a harmonious and unified effort, certain coordinating information must be communicated. All this information flow is internal-operational communication.

Specifically, internal-operational communication is carried out through any number of structured activities. In the Typical Company, for example, much of the internal-operational information is entered into the Company computer to become a part of the company's data base. From the data base, programmed reports are developed to give each operations department the information it needs. For example, sales reports and inventory records combine to communicate reduction needs to the production planning department. Then the production planning department communicates this need to the various production departments through a strategically planned work schedule.

Within each production unit and between production units there is, of course, additional communicating that must go on. Superiors make decisions and transmit them to subordinates. Departments exchange information, and workers communicate working informations with each other. Memoranda are written, reports are prepared, conversations are held, all in the process of coordinating efforts and supplying the information needed to achieve the organization's goals. In every division of the company and in every activity, similar internal-operational communication occurs.

External-operational communication

External-operational communication is that part of an organization's structured communication which is concerned with achieving the organization's work goals and which is conducted with people and groups outside the organization. It is the organization's communication with its public—its suppliers, service companies, customers, and the general public.

Into this category fall all of the organization's efforts at direct selling—the sales representative's sales spiel, the descriptive brochures, the telephone callbacks, the follow-up service calls, and the like. Included also are all of an organization's advertising efforts. For what is advertising but a deliberate, structured communication with an organization's publics? Radio and television messages, newspaper and magazine space advertising, and point-of-pur-chase display material obviously play a role in the organization's plan to achieve its work objective. Also falling into this category is all an organization does to enhance its public relations. This includes its planned publicity, the civic-mindedness of its management, the courtesy of its employees, the condition of its physical plant. All these and many more communication efforts combine to make up the organization's external-operational communication.

The extreme importance of an organization's external communications hardly requires supporting comment. Certainly, it is obvious that any business organization is dependent on people and groups outside itself for its success. It is an elementary principle of business that, because a business organization's success is dependent on its ability to satisfy the needs of customers, it must communicate effectively with these customers. It is equally elementary that in today's complex business society, organizations are dependent on each other in the manufacturing and distribution of goods as well as the sale of services. And this interdependence necessarily brings about needs for communication. Just as with international communication, these outside communications are vital to an organization's operation.

Personnel communication

Not all the communication that goes on in an organization is operational, however. In fact, much of the communication in an organization is without purpose as far as the organization is concerned. Such communication may be classified as personal.

Personal communication is all that incidental exchange of information and feeling which human beings engage in whenever they come together. Human beings are social animals. They have a need to communicate, and they will communicate even when they have little or nothing to express.

Much of the time friends spend with each other is spent in communication, for it is simply the thing to do when people get together. Even total strangers are likely to communicate who they are placed in a position together, as for instance on a plane trip, in a waiting room, or at a ball game. Such personal communication also takes place in the work situation, and it is a part of the communication activity of any business organization. Although not a part of an organization's plan of operation, personal communication can have a significant effect on the success of this plan. This effect is a result of the influence personal communication can have on the attitudes, opinions, and beliefs of the members of the organization.

Attitudes of the organization members toward the organization, their fellow employees, and their assignment directly affect the members' willingness to do their assigned tasks. And the nature of conversation in a work situation affects attitudes. In a work situation where heated words and flaming tempers often are present, the participants are not likely to make their usual productive effort. Likewise, a rollicking, jovial work situation is likely to have an equally adverse effect on productivity. No doubt somewhere between these extremes the ideal productive attitudes lie.

Also affecting the organization members' work attitudes is the extent of personal communication permitted the members. Absolute denial of the communication privilege could lead to some degree of emotional upsets, for people hold dear their right to communicate. On the other hand, excessive personal communication could interfere directly with their work effort. Probably somewhere in the middle-ground area lies the optimum policy toward personal communication.

Personal communication also can help to form attitudes and beliefs, which are stronger and have more lasting effects on the mind than opinions. As was illustrated in the preceding account of Dan's workday at Typical, Dan and his car-pool friends spent some of their conversation time discussing a proposed new policy for Typical. And in talking, each helped to crystallize the opinions of the others. It is in this way that all members of an organization determine much of what they think about their organization, their co-workers, and their work situation in general. What they think can affect their relationships with organization. And what they think can have a direct influence on productivity.

Communication network of the organisation

Looking over all of an organization's communication, we see most complex mass of information flow. We see an organization literally feeding on a continuous supply of information. More specifically, we see dozens, hundreds, or even thousands of individual members engaging in untold numbers of communication events throughout each working day. The picture of this network of information flow is infinitely complex.

In simplified form, this infinitely complex information flow in a modern-day organization may be likened to the network of arteries and veins in the body. Just as the body has arteries, the organization has well-established channels of information flow. These are the formal and established channels of communication—the main line of the organization's operational communication. Included here are the reports, records, and other forms which supply working information to the various parts of the organization; the orders, instructions and messages which flow up and down the organization's authority structure; and the letters, sales presentations, advertising, and publicity which go to an organization's publics. These main channels do not just happen; they are carefully thought out, or at least they should be. In the modern office, these channels are formed by computer information systems. Information from work stations is put into the company's data base. And from the data base the information can be assembled at the work station needing it.

Our overview also shows us a secondary network of information flow corresponding to the veins of the body. This is the network made up of the thousands upon thousands of personal communications which take place in any organization. Such communications follow no set pattern but rather form an intricate and infinitely complex web of information flow linking all of the members of the organization in one way or another.

The complexity of the network cannot be overemphasized, especially in the larger organizations. Typically it is not a single network at all. Rather, it is a complex relation of smaller networks made up of groups of people. The relationships are made even more complex by the fact that the people in the organization may belong to more than one of these groups, and group memberships and the linking between groups are continually changing. Truly, the network structure in a large organization is so complex as to defy description.

Known as the "grapevine" in management literature, this informal communication system is far more effective than a first impression might indicate. Certainly it consists of much gossip and rumour, for this is the nature of human conversation. And it is as fickle and inaccurate as the human beings who are a part of it. Even so, the grapevine carries far more information than the formal communication system; and on many matters it is more effective in determining the course of an organization. Wise managers recognize the presence of the grapevine. Thy learn who the talk leaders are; and they communicate to them the information that will do the most good for the organization. That is, they keep in touch with the grapevine, and they turn in into a constructive tool.

From the preceding review it appears that much of the communication that goes on in organizations is written communication—letters, memoranda, reports, and such. Thus, it is vital that we address a question that sometimes is heard. It is the question of the role of written communication in the years ahead. The evidence suggests that we are moving rapidly into the age of automated communication—the age of the paperless office. This will be a time when there will be no letters, no reports, no files. Instead, each work station in an organization will be equipped with a computer terminal, or perhaps a microcomputer. As a result, internal-operational communications will be done primarily through computers. In the short run, a company's written external-operation communications will be done through the word-processing capabilities of the computer; and they will be in paper form. But in time, company-to-company computer link-ups will develop; and in more time there will be consumer-to-company link-ups. The result will be that computes-to-computer communication will replace conventional letters.

Although it is impossible to say with certainly what the future holds,it appears reasonable to say that computer technology will bring about revolutionary changes in communication. In fact, revolutionary changes are occurring now; and probably they will continue to occur at an accelerating rate. But we must keep in mind that these changes are primarily in the nature of the transmission- not in the messages communicated. There is no evidence which even remotely suggests that the needs for the messages communicated in letters, reports, and memoranda will decrease. And of even greater importance, there is absolutely no evidence to suggest that these messages can be handled in a way which does not require the basic writing skills. Clearly, business writing is here to stay. In fact, the increasing complexity of the technological world of the future is likely to require more—not less—of it.

The foregoing review merely skims the surface; yet, hopefully, it has given you an appreciation of the importance of communication to yourself and to organizations. It has shown you how extensive communication is, how it permeates every segment of the organization in a most intricate and complex way. And it has shown you that good communication is vital to the successful operation of an organization. These conclusions, combined with the convincing evidence that most organizational communication is not well done, should lead you to yet another conclusion: that communication is an area deserving increased study by those concerned with improving the operations of an organization.

In the following pages such a study is undertaken. Its approach is first to gain an understanding of what communication is—how it works and how it does not work. The material covered here borrows from many disciplines—from psychology, sociology, and linguistics. But primarily it borrows from the relatively new discipline of general semantics. Perhaps the term *general semantics* requires definition, for the generally used meanings of the two words in the term do not apply in this case. In a simplified sense, general semantics concerns the study of reality, of our perception of reality, and of how we relate to our perceptions in words, thoughts, and actions. Its emphasis is one recognizing the true nature of reality. Much of the source material for this review is highly sophisticated, but every effort has been made to simplify it. Perhaps some people will look upon it as being oversimplified.

After establishing a foundation of understanding, our study shifts to applications of this theoretical material to the real-life activities of an organization. For reasons of course design, much of the material concerns written communication. Specifically, we shall emphasize the areas of correspondence and report writing, for these are vital areas in today's business organization. We shall give some emphasis to other areas, especially oral communication. It should be apparent, however, that this coverage is far from complete. The almost infinite nature of the subject makes it so. Even so, the applications presented should show you the ways to handle the theoretical material in your day-to-day work in business.

Oral communication

Since managers spend as much as 50 per cent of their working day listening, they should be accomplished in this skill. Yet, too often we hear such comments as "Bob just doesn't" or "Barbara is hard to work with because she never takes the time to listen" or somebody wasn't listening." In fact, of the four primary communication skills needed for effective management—reading, writing, speaking, and listening-listening is used the most frequently and yet receives the least attention from educators.

A number of essential managerial skills involve listening. First, much of the data necessary for decision making comes through listening to employees, yet poor listeners miss important information. Second, listening makes a person more dependable: people who listen well follow directions better, make fewer errors, say foolish things less often, and generally become the kind of person others will ask for advice or direction. Third, good listeners are more respected and liked by those they work with. Managers who listen compliment those they listen to, in effect telling them they are worthy people. This trait can lead to harmonious labour relations since employees generally trust and support managers who "listen them out."

Fourth, better listening enables a manager to be better informed overall and more sophisticated. Sophistication comes not from talking but, rather, by learning about the world around one. Fifth, good listening spares a person many embarrassments. In many situations, people may miss a name because of poor listening, or they may need to have critical information repeated because of "daydreaming". Worse yet, a direct question may be unanswered because of inept listening. Such embarrassing situations can quickly label a manager as unconcerned or even apathetic.

Ultimately, the major reason for developing effective listening is to promote understanding between people. People who need to be heard not only for their own emotional well-being but to be understood create gaps by not listening. Mutual understanding is required in any work group.

Listening is not just hearing, and the effective manager differentiates between the two. Hearing is mechanical, an automatic sort of thing often difficult to avoid. A horn blaring, heavy construction equipment groaning, children shouting in a playground—all these sounds, plus others, may be heard even though they are not listened to actively. Hearing usually requires little special physical or mental effort.

By contrast, listening results from a concentrated effort; it requires both physical and mental effort. Listening requires a special effort because physical and psychological factors work against the process. In this chapter we review those physical and psychological barriers to listening and then analyze techniques to reduce these barriers.

Physical barriers to listening

One of the greatest physical barriers to listening arises from our own limitations. The trouble is that people speak approximately 25 per cent as fast as they think. Thus, while most Americans speak at a rate of about 125 words per minute, they are able to think at least four times that fast. As a result, instead of listening carefully, some people tend to think about other things and devote only a fraction of their capacity to taking in what is said. They become impatient with the slow rate of the spoken word and begin to concentrate on topics other than the words being spoken and daydream to remain stimulated. This problem may be referred to as the 25 to 75 problem: a person requires only 25 per cent of his mental time for listening while he spends the remaining 75 per cent on unrelated ideas. No wonder some find it hard to get their attention back to the main topic.

A second type of physical barrier arises from internal distractions that cannot be ignored. Our autonomic nervous system involuntarily pays attention to certain events such as a headache, sore feet, or an empty stomach. It is difficult to divide attention between these internal involuntary distractions and concentrated listening. A third physical barrier to listening is any overpowering noise that may compete with the main topic of interest. It is hard to listen to a subordinate who speaks softly in a noisy foundry or to a phone conversation mixed with static on the phone line. In these situations, separating the speaker's voice from all the surrounding noise can be exhausting. These physical barriers are not the only ones to effective listening. Psychological barriers can be equally burdensome.

Psychological barriers to listening

A major psychological barrier to listening is lack of motivation. Many find maintaining the continuous motivation required for listening a challenge. The need for motivation stands out when one recalls the speed of the thought process compared with that of speech. During the 75 per cent of time when the mind is not being stimulated with words, motivation for listening is a challenge. Managers who should be listening may be day-dreaming, making private plans, or even focusing on an emotional problem. During that 75 per cent void many things can take place that overpower the 25 per cent listening.

Researchers have long known that motivation or incentive is a prevalent problem in the listening process. Research completed almost 30 years ago demonstrated that people score better on listening achievement tests when they know in advance that they are going to be tested than when they think they are just supposed to listen. More recent research has also indicated that scores on listening tests rise as the incentive to listen increases. Since listening is hard work, we can expect greater effort when the goal is known, and listeners can observe a positive outcome of the effort. This is why the listening goal discussed later is so important.

Another psychological barrier may be termed "detouring." The listener may become distracted by mannerism, phrase, or concept and detour toward the distraction. This distraction then stimulates thought on another subtopic more interesting than the central point of the message; consequently, thoughts detour to the more interesting topics.

The "debate" represents a third type of barrier. A listener may suddenly find herself disagreeing with the speaker and begin to plan her rebuttal. As she plans the rebuttal, she blocks out the listener and misses his message. For instance, a manager listening to complaints from another department might prepare a rebuttal as the other person explains the incident. As a result, the manager creates a defensive climate and misses the most important information.

Time, an important factor in every manager's day, can also be a barrier to listening for busy managers. "I just don't have time to listen to this" is a common reaction for managers at one time or another. The saying, "time passes quickly when you're having fun," is really true; being involved in an interesting conversation can use more time than a person realizes. However, time is relative and seems to drag on and on when people have to listen to something in which they have no interest. When listening appears to take too much time, managers tend to stop listening.

Hasty conclusion is one way some terminate listening. This time pressure may lead to the tendency to judge, evaluate, approve, or disapprove a person's statement too hastily. To achieve real communication, resist me temptation to form hasty conclusions.

Perhaps the greatest psychological barrier is lack of willingness. A manager may not want to listen. Before listening is even required, he may have lost any desire to listen. A lack of willingness to listen is an attitude that supersedes all other barriers—both physical and psychological.

Since we have already discussed motivation as a barrier to listening, we must differentiate willingness from motivation. These concepts are closely related, but for the purposes of this discussion, assume that a lack of willingness develops before listening even begins. This is why it supersedes all other barriers. If a person consciously or unconsciously decides not to listen, listening skills are obviously of no advantage.

Why would a manager lack the willingness to listen? Several reasons explain this unfortunate condition. First, most people would rather talk than listen, and even when they ask a question, they often break into the first sentence of the response with another question or an argument. Second, the listener may quickly stereotype the speaker as one who talks a lot but has little to say; consequently, the listener believes that the person has little of value to say. Third, a listener may lack willingness because he may not want to receive negative information. For the speaker who bears "bad tidings," what incentive is there to listen? Defensive behaviour relates closely to this. Some managers consider the slightest attack on one of their opinions as an attack on them personally; consequently, they will rise, sometimes almost obsessively, to the defense. This defense often involves verbal attacks that preclude the possibility for listening.

This is only a summary of the many barriers to listening. Nevertheless, research indicates that we can improve listening skills. When managers strategically analyze the critical components of communication and apply the techniques suggested in the following section, their listening skills and effectiveness as managers will improve.

General techniques for improved listening skills

Let us first look at the different types of listening to be able to adapt techniques to the appropriate situation and three levels of listening intensity for both types.

For the purposes of this discussion, active listening occurs in situations in which a manager has little or no opportunity to interact verbally with the speaker. People in a large audience use active listening as do those listening to a recorded message or reviewing an audio-visual replay. People use interactive listening when they have the opportunity to interact verbally with the speaker by asking questions or summarizing. Interactive listening occurs with a manager involved in a conversation with one other individual or in a meeting with many people.

The level of intensity at the side reflects the relevance, the importance, or the significance of the information involved. Listening has basically three levels of intensity. Casual or marginal listening is used when the specific or technical information being discussed is not critical. Because no goal for specific information is established, a manager need not be as alert as in other situations. Casual listening occurs in social conversations or when listening to the radio.

The next level of intensity, factual listening, is necessary when specific information needs to be obtained. Probably the most common type of listening in business meetings and conferences, factual listening is the level that most people probably thinks of when they consider the topic of listening. At this level, the listener should ask questions and receive feedback to ensure effective communication.

A manager uses the empathetic level of listening when he wants to understand another person from that person's own internal frame of reference rather than from his own frame of reference. The empathetic listener tries to get inside the other's thoughts and feelings. The listener expresses empathy when he verbally and nonverbally communicates such messages as "I follow you," "I'm with you," or "I understand."

The empathetic level of listening is not easy to achieve because we naturally tend to advise, tell, agree, or disagree based on our own point of view. It is well worth the effort to become an empathetic listener, however. A speaker who sees that a manager is really trying to understand her meaning will trust the manager and be more willing to talk and explore problems. Empathetic listening can be such a powerful form of listening that, even when it is only partially attained, the mere attempt can be enough to open up communication.

When listening, the first thing a manager should do is determine the level of listening she needs to achieve. She can accomplish this by establishing a "listening goal," a specific statement of the purpose for listening. In the give-and-take of most communications, the need to adjust one's listening goal arises as the interchange develops. Conversations frequently start with talk about the weather or other topics unrelated to the purpose of the conversation. For example, what may have started out as a casual conversation with the general listening goal of getting suggestions for the next office social gathering may develop into a serious discussion on possible strategies for improving office performance. Knowing the listening goal permits one to adjust the strategy to the level of listening.

The act of writing out the listening goal is valuable: it forces the listener to analyze the purpose of the listening thoroughly. Also, when the goal is explicitly analyzed, it is easier to maintain the necessary motivation to reach the goal than when analysis is incomplete. As we saw earlier, motivation is often a major problem, so any technique that improves the motivational level is important.

Once she has established the level of listening, the manager must prepare herself physically and psychologically to listen. She should complete the following steps during the preparation state.

1. Pick the best possible place. While it is not always possible to change the place, the manager should not overlook better facilities when available.
2. Pick the best possible time. As with place, it is not always possible to change the time. However, the astute manager must be careful not to eliminate more favourable opportunities.
3. Think about personal biases that may be present.
4. Think about the physical and psychological barriers to listening.
5. Review the listening objectives.

A brief review of these five items shows why they are important in reducing the barriers to effective listening discussed earlier. First, selecting the best time and place helps one avoid the internal and external distractions. In addition, since time influences the psychological barriers of motivation, emotion, and willingness, the choice of time may significantly alter the outcome of the conversation.

However, is it polite to tell another that one cannot listen right at the moment? In a survey involving more than 200 different managers, the managers indicated that they would not be offended if someone asked them to wait for fear that important information might be missed. Of course, if time cannot be changed, it is important that the parties be aware of the barriers present and make a special effort to concentrate on the listening process.

A manager's biases may also have a drastic effect on the outcome of the communication. A manager unaware of personal bias may become selective and hear only what he wants to hear. The person may deal only with preconceived notions and even debate with the speaker on points of disagreement. For example, a manager who believes that women are unreliable may disregard any information indicating that a particular woman is reliable. The first step needed to control this psychological barrier of bias is awareness followed by recognition of the burden it places on the speaker-listener relationship.

Detouring, the psychological barrier that causes a listener to become distracted by a mannerism, phrase, or concept, is closely related to bias. A listener's negative bias toward a mannerism can totally distract from the content of the message. For instance, a speaker may place her hands over her mouth while speaking, or continually play with a cigarette, or look away from the listener. Such mannerisms can distract, and one needs to recognize them as just that—distractions. Mannerisms should not get in the way of messages.

Emotional words or phrases can also trigger listener bias. Such phrases as "typical accountant." "It really isn't my job," "we tried that before, and it didn't work," or "all engineers think alike" can lead to emotional responses. The danger in such phrases is that they cause a listener to hear different parts of a message. When a listener is caught by an emotional phrase, the internal emotional response may overpower the content of the message. Once again, the listener should be aware of the possible emotional responses and not let them distract from the message.

Again, it is important to review and be aware of the listening objective. Without the objective in mind, a manager may use casual listening when factual listening is required, or factual listening when empathetic listening would be more effective. The person who can state in one sentence the specific goal and the type of listening involved is well aware of the listening objective.

The manager who is physically and psychologically prepared to listen could use some specific techniques to improve listening. Let us look at some of them that are appropriate for active and interactive listening. The first techniques reviewed are the only possibilities available for active listening.

Techniques for active listening

One uses active listening in situations where interaction with the speaker is difficult or impossible. For example, a person who is sitting in a large audience or listening to a recording cannot interact. Since asking questions is generally not possible in these situations, a listener usually needs to have a clear and complete understanding of the message the first time around. An active listener should implement the following techniques.

Outline the message

A message usually has one or two main points with supporting information in the form of examples, specific figures, or descriptions. One good clue to the main points is the nonverbal techniques that the speaker uses when giving them; she might raise her voice, speak faster, repeat key words, or use gestures. Later discussion will detail nonverbal aspects that can be invaluable when identifying the main and supporting points. In the following example, note the emphasis on main and supporting points in a speech:

The electronic division was pleased with the successful introduction of four new products in the last year. All four of these products sold at a better rate than projected. We were especially pleased with the temperature sensor that sold 14 per cent above projections. This small sensor, which has many applications and is easy to install, should do as well or better next year.

Besides introducing four new products we expanded the Western Division's sales force by adding 16 high-quality salespeople. These salespeople were recruited from all over the United States, and we're confident of their ability to help us expand in the west. They all have a thorough understanding of the product and the changing nature of our industry.

No immediate changes are seen in the home implement division. It will be necessary to wait and see what happens with the entire housing industry. We're stable here since garage openers, intercom systems, and burglar protection devices are all holding their own. We developed a new burglar protection system that can be programmed by means of a digital device. This has been an interesting project to watch as it developed.

The main points in this example are the four new products, expansion of the Western Division's sales force, and a stable home implement market; the remainder of the message is supporting information. Separation of main and supporting points helps the listener to retain the critical information.

Summarise the message

Often, a speaker has some type of organization pattern that a listener may use to outline the message. For instance, a speaker may organize the message by pros and cons, advantages and disadvantages, likes and dislikes, similarities and differences, chronological events, or functional duties. Just as it is easier to remember the outline of a chapter rather than every word in it, it is easier to recall the outline of a spoken message rather than all the specifics.

Visualise the message

Another listening device is the summary, which can take the form of a mental picture of the main points. The summary need not contain elaborate sentences and details; in fact, simple words or sentence fragments may suffice. Summarization does not have to wait until the end of the message as it may be more efficient at major division points. The president's speech given earlier could be summarized in three phrases: (1) four new products in electronics, (2) 16 new salespeople in the western region, and (3) a stable home implement market.

The three techniques listed so far— differentiating between the main and supporting points, outlining, and summarizing—operate together for accurate listening. The effective use of a fourth technique assists in the development of the others.

Another tactic for active listening, to put the message into a picture, will help keep the listener's mind on the message. In fact, the beauty of this tactic is that it allows one to use some of that 75 per cent of the mental capacity not required to keep up with the message. Consequently, a person can commit more effort to listening, thus reducing the possibility of missing a major part of the message. Finally, the retention of the message improves because a picture can now be associated with it. In the annual meeting seen earlier, a manager might imagine the 16 new sales personnel in the western region as 16 little people running from different points of a U.S. wall map to California. Absurd as the device might be, these 16 little people running across a wall map will help the manager remember the main point of the message. Effective listeners are those who search a message for information that has special meaning for them. A topic is naturally more interesting and easier to concentrate on if it personally relates to the listener. In fact, those who relate the message to personal experiences ensure that the key elements of listening, willingness, and motivation are present.

The managers listening to the president in the previous example may also personalize the message by asking questions of themselves: "How will these four products affect my job?" "Will continued expansion of the electronic group affect me?" "Will those 16 new salespeople increase my work load for the western region?" "How will the stable market in the home implement group affect our division?" In answering these questions, the managers find how the message personally relates to them. Then, their incentive to listen to the message will increase as well.

All these techniques are strengthened when the listener takes notes. College students generally do not have to be convinced of the importance of notes, but they often lose this good habit once they have left the classroom. A listener can easily make short notations to help visualize and personalize a message. Not only do notes provide a written record of the communication, but they can provide valuable feedback that tells the listener just how well she is listening. If the notes are not well organized with main and supporting points, the listener probably has not mentally organized the message. If a quick review indicates that no notes have been taken for some time, the listener may find that his or her attention has been wandering.

Notes benefit a listener, too, because they keep her physically involved. We have seen that for naturally physically active humans, listening is a predominately mental activity. Since they are not physically active, many people get restless or impatient when listening for long periods of time. Rather than being satisfied by lighting a cigarette or playing with fingernails, this urge for physical activity might be channeled into note taking, which keeps a person involved with the business at hand.

Of course, note taking can be a problem for those people who overdo it. Not every word needs recording, and long sentences are not necessary. In fact, the possibility exists of concentrating on the notes to the extent that major components of the message are missed. Instead, jot down key words and phrases in outline form using abbreviations when possible.

Mnemonics may be used when jotting down abbreviated notes. One mnemonic device is the acronym, a combination of letters, each of which is the first letter of a group of words essential to the message. For instance, suppose that a person is presenting his main objection to taking additional training in computer programming.

The objection may stem from the cost, the individual's ability, and the time involved. The mnemonic CAT can be used to record these main ideas whenever the speaker refers to them. In this way, the listener records the main thoughts without becoming burdened by note taking. Later, the listener can rewrite the notes in more detail if an accurate record is needed. This rewriting has the added advantage of acting as a review of the major themes in the message.

A final thought on notes. The listener who takes notes indicates a sincere interest in both the message and the speaker. Notes require involvement, so the speaker will have a greater degree of confidence that listeners are paying attention to the message. The fact that it is important to demonstrate effective listening is discussed in more detail later.

Each of these techniques—identifying the main points, outlining. Summarizing, visualizing, personalizing, and note taking—is useful in either active or interactive listening. However, the techniques are especially critical in situations where the ability to ask questions and observe nonverbal message is limited. The ideal is to ask questions of the speaker for clarity without using them to replace the five techniques just discussed.

Questioning for improved interactive listening

In a variety of situations, the skillful use of questions adds immensely to a manager's ability to communicate. In fact, this book recommends several areas when questioning techniques are appropriate: listening, interviewing, conflict resolution, and coaching. Questions are important because they promote the two-way process of communication. Without the use of questions, feedback and mutual understanding are severely curbed.

Ask questions when the meaning of a message is either unclear or incomplete. When key words, phrases, or concepts are vague or when inconsistencies or contradictions appear, questions help to develop clarity. Listeners are not the only ones to benefit from questions, however; questions may also help a speaker to clarify his thoughts. In fact, a speaker might not be aware of an omission or distortion in a message until asked a question. When questioned, the speaker may be forced to reanalyze his own communication to the listener's benefit.

A manager must strategically determine the most appropriate questions for different situations to ensure mutual understanding. Three classifications of questions are appropriate to this discussion: open-closed; primary-secondary; neutral-directed.

The phrasing of an open-ended question gives the respondent an open choice of possible answers. At the other end of the spectrum is the closed question, which permits a narrow range of possible answers. An example illustrates this point. A frustrated employee has just described to his manager a major problem with a new project. In his agitation, the employee jumped from one point to another while describing the problem. Naturally, this disorderly description has made it difficult to listen, so the manager now needs to ask questions for both clarity and completeness of information. The following questions posed by the manager show the difference between open and closed questions.

What do you think are the major causes of the problem? (open)

Tell me more about it? (open)

Did you check the steam gauge? (closed)

Where do you think we should go from here? (open)

Would it be a good idea to wait until tomorrow? (closed). While open questions may generate additional information, they also allow possible digression. Closed questions are more direct and help one to focus on the problem. Nevertheless, the lack of openness may cause valuable information to be omitted since the answer is so narrow. Managers must use strategic analysis to determine the best choice of questioning style in each case.

Two other options open to managers are primary and secondary questions. A primary question is the first question that seeks clarification or more complete information on a topic. A manager may choose to follow up with a secondary question that probes to obtain still more specific information after the primary question has been answered. A secondary question is not merely an additional question; it seeks to get at a deeper level of information than the first or primary level. The following dialogue shows the strategic use of primary and secondary questioning.

Manager: Do you think you'll be able to have the analysis done by Wednesday? (primary)

Employee: That shouldn't be any problem if everything goes right for a change.

Manager: What would you be afraid of going wrong? (secondary)

Employee: The accounting information is hard to get sometimes.

Manager: What specific part is hard to get? (secondary)

Notice that each secondary question seeks further information on the preceding answer. Managers use the secondary question when they feel that they have not obtained sufficient information through the primary ones.

The third classification involves neutral versus directed questions. While a neutral question seeks information without attempting to lead the speaker to answer in a certain way, the directed question seeks to lead the speaker to a response the inquirer desires. A directed question, often referred to as a leading question, tries to pull the answer in a predetermined direction. Directed questions open with such phrases as "Doesn't it seem logical that...," or "Wouldn't you agree that ...," or

"Wouldn't you say..." Directed questions may be used to obtain confirmation or clarification on one specific point, whereas the neutral questions will obtain a more general response.

The use of an appropriate question adds clarity to communication because of the active two-way process that develops. Listening is clearly not a passive activity; rather, it requires the active involvement of the manager through the use of questions and other means.

Listening to nonverbal messages

People listen with their eyes as well as their ears. The renowned communication researcher Mehrabian found that only 7 per cent of a message's effect is carried by words; listeners receive the other 93 per cent through nonverbal means. After conducting extensive research, Bird-whistell suggested that spoken words account for no more than 30 to 55 per cent of all social interaction. Thus, any nonverbal sources of information available to listeners are worth reviewing. Nonverbal communication can be divided into facial expressions, postures, gestures, and spatial messages.

Facial expressions

Facial expression is probably the most universal form of human communication. A smile or frown is known around the world. The wide array of facial expressions used by such communication "experts" as Charlie Chaplin, Buster Keaton, and Jack Benny shows how diverse and dynamic this form of communication can be. Just as Charlie Chaplin developed different masks for the silent movies. Adults know the right expression for most communication circumstances. It is relatively easy to turn on and off such facial expressions as anger, disapproval, happiness, and fatigue. For this reason, the face is the most flexible source of nonverbal communication as well as the best at misrepresentation. A manager needs to be aware of the vast amount of information he can read from the face; however, he must be wary of the possibility that it can mask feelings or intent.

Usually, the eyes provide the first facial signal that a person notices. The expressions "shifty-eyed" or "evil-eyed" as descriptions of overall personality probably developed because of this powerful nonverbal cue. Eye contact is a carefully regulated human behaviour. People do not gaze too long without diverting their eyes because they have learned, probably nonverbally, that it is considered hostile, invest, or coercive to give an uninterrupted stare.

The amount of eye contact varies with the relationship between speakers. For example, a person will maintain more eye contact with a subject who is pleasing. People look more at others they like and seek to minimize eye contact with those they do not like. One's eye behaviour has also been linked to the level of anxiety present, a high rate of blinking indicating a high degree of anxiety. Furthermore, the pupils dilate in response to strong emotion of any sort, whether pleasurable or not."

An interesting eye-response test was run recently when a group of supervisors was shown pictures of men and women. Some of the faces on the pictures were retouched to make the pupils large, while other photos of the same persons had small pupils. Those looking at large-eyed pictures usually described the persons with such words as "warm," "loving," or "sincere." Those looking at the same faces, but with small pupils most often described them as "hard" "insincere," or "insensitive."

Managers can use these facts about eyes to improve their listening skills. Observations on eye contact and pupil size can help a manager to determine if an employee is possibly hostile, interested in a particular subject, nervous, or pleased. These cues let a manager listen beyond the spoken word. The facial muscles around the mouth, forehead, and cheeks are also important because they are so responsive. They make it possible to express pleasure, displeasure, contempt, or doubt. Thus, pulling down the corners of the mouth while furrowing the forehead can signal doubt. Anger may be displayed with an open square mouth or by lips pressed tightly together, accompanied by brows drawn together.

Most people are probably less accustomed to masking their posture than their facial expressions; thus, posture can serve as a reliable source of information for the manager. The way a person walks, stands, or sits can reveal a wealth of valuable information. Thus, a person can face one person, stand over another, or slump in front of or "give the shoulder" to another. It is possible to lean forward or recline backward, to lean to the right or the left, to sit erect, or to slouch. A person can open up in a sprawling, relaxed pose or be defensive with closed arms and legs locked in tight.

What does all this mean? No specific, irrevocable rules exist, but some general principles apply. First, a person is drawn toward something he or she likes. When a person leans toward a manager in conversation, it is often safe to assume that the person likes the manager. At the same time, since leaning forward may also indicate an aggressive attitude, the context should be considered.

Second, people position themselves in alignment with others. Frequently, the degree of mutual involvement corresponds to the degree that two people mutually align their heads, shoulders, and hips. People in conversation will often make subtle postural adjustments to one another to create their own preferred degree of alignment.

Third, crossed arms and legs generally characterize one who feels wary, distant, angry, or in some way uncomfortable. This posture may suggest that the body is closed off and protected. Of course, an isolated arm or leg cross alone is not enough evidence to judge closedness, because people have other reasons for crossing or uncrossing limbs such as a room's temperature or the need to rest a leg. It is the total posture of the body within a context that helps the manager to determine the openness or closedness of an individual. Thus, while one can read no concrete messages from posture, the observant and astute manager is better able to listen to the total message if he analyzes the posture of those involved in the communication.

Gestures

Gestures are another way a sender can complement the verbal communication and enable a receiver to understand the message better. When we see a person cupping her hands, pounding on her desk, waving her arms through the air, or pointing a finger while speaking on the phone, we are able to read the message she is sending. An interesting test of the importance of hands to speech requires a person to carry on a conversation while sitting on her hands. An exaggerated use of shoulder and head movement will result as a compensation for the loss of manual gestures.

You should remember that gestures frequently have different meanings in different cultures. The gestures discussed in this chapter are ones that the average American might easily recognize. At the same time, in another culture, the same gestures might have no meaning or one entirely different from that in the American culture. When involved in cross-cultural exchanges, managers are advised to learn some of the gestural vocabulary of the other cultural group.

Gestures can be used to emphasize or demonstrate a point, to regulate a conversation, to present a caring attitude, or to indicate a defensive or offensive orientation. In fact, many use gestures to emphasize key words in a message even as they use punctuation or underscoring in written statements. For example, "until the people upstairs The manager watching for these gestures finds it is easier to listen for the important points.

Some gestures look like what they demonstrate, such as the size or shape of an object. Such gestures are an attempt to draw a picture of an object, but others are more abstract. For instance, the upraised palms and shrugged shoulders gesture of "Who knows?" is abstract, but still easy to understand.

Speakers also use gestures to regulate the flow of the communication. When a person waves his hand upward or inward or cups his hand over the ear, it may be an indication to speak louder. A person can hold another speaker off by holding the other's arm or hand while making a point. Someone may also point to the listener, keep his hands out in space between himself and the listener, or poke a finger into the listener's shoulder. When people want to interrupt with their own point, they put their hand out as if to hold the person down. When people are not ready to answer, they may step back, screw their eyes closed, and scratch their heads in the hope of getting more time. An effective manager can determine the flow of the conversation by observing gestures and strategically adjusting the communication.

People also use gestures to show a caring attitude. Stroking or patting shoulders, arms, hands, heads, or cheeks, and slapping backs are examples of behaviors generally intended to convey good feeling and regard. These gestures relate so closely with caring that people in stress can often be seen giving such attention to themselves. The final type of gesture to be discussed indicates either a defensive or an offensive attitude. Movements such as hand rubbing hand clutching face rubbing lip pulling, or cuticle picking often reflect a perceived threat. Other defensive gestues that characterize protection include placing a hand to the throat, neck, head, or mouth. Offensive gestures may be clenched fists, a rapid forward movement of the arm, or a pushing motion. Of course, it is important to listen to the verbal message as well as the gestures of the speaker. However, just as some people speak in a monotone, it is possible that some will use no gestures to complement the verbal message. Thus, managers should observe all the different components of nonverbal communications.

Spatial messages

Edward Hall coined the word " proxemics" for the study of ways in which space, distance, and territory are components of human communication. Skill in reading proxemics can be valuable for managers listening to others in an organization. Through proxemics, one can determine how friendly, worried, or isolated another feels.

Hall identifies three types of space: feature fixed, semifixed feature, and informal. Feature-fixed space is the nonmoving and clearly defined space found in buildings and rooms. The permanent arrangement of buildings and, in turn, rooms considerably influences the communication environment. First, it reduce the degree to which people may vary their space to correspond to their attitude. For instance person may feel close to another and desire to move physically closer, however, if the chairs and tables are fixed, such a move would not be possible.

Semifixed space includes the movable objects such as tables and chairs and their arrangement. A flexible arrangement of furniture allows managers to observe how people arrange their environment and to listen for the messages being conveyed by the arrangement. For instance, when people are at ease with one another, they may move their chairs away from the table so it does not separate them. Research has found that people at right angles to each other produced six times as many conversations as face-to-face situations across a 36-inch span of table and twice as many as the side-by-side arrangement. Thus, two people seated at right angles to one another may be more predisposed to communication that others.

Informal space, perhaps most significant when considering managerial listening, encompasses the distances maintained in encounters with others. Informal space is divided into four distinct distances: intimate, personal, social, and public.

While these zones vary from one culture or group to another, this discussion will be in terms of the American culture. The first zone, intimate, involves fewer than 18 inches of space between two people. Those who feel close, safe, and secure with one another share this zone. A pat on the back or a hand on the shoulder occurs in this space in the business setting, the intimate zone is usually intentionally penetrated only for fleeting periods of time unless artificially enforced by close seating as in a conference setting or a theater.

The second zone is personal space, which ranges from arm's length to 3 to 4 feet from the body. While friends who feel ease with each other will share this space, strangers would probably feel some discomfort in this zone. The social zone extends from about 4 to 8 feet from the body and is the area in which most conduct ordinary business and social activity. In supervisor-subordinate relationships, anything closer than the social zone requires a special situation.

The public zone extends 8 to 10 feet from the body and is the area over which individuals exert little personal control. A person who moves to this zone may be signalling a lack of interest in the speaker or an unwillingness to become personal or social. Since distractions are a distinct possibility in this zone, listening is especially difficult for two people. It is better for two people to communicate in the social zone unless one of the participants is uneasy.

Para-language

The technical term for the vocal melody and the punctuation a person uses to change, emphasis, or reverse the meaning of words is paralinguistics or paralanguage. Paralanguage includes stress, pitch, rate, loudness, timber, inflection, rhyme, and enunciation—all the vocal nuances that accompany the verbal dimension of speech. Moreover, vocalizations that do not qualify as words, for example, laughing, crying, sighing, yawning, coughing, whispering, and the like, are also parts of paralanguage. Even silences, pauses, and hesitations can fall into this category.

Paralanguage can add richness, but also confusion when one listens to a message. A short sentence such as "I'll do it" may mean any on the following:

I' ll be really happy to do it.

I'll do it, but it's the last time.

You always make me do what you want.

All right you win.

Don't worry, I'll take care of it.

You're so dumb I'd better take care of it myself.

Which "meaning" is implied can usually be determined by the tone or inflection of the voice or by the stress placed on each separate word.

Robert J. McCloskey provided an interesting example of the relationship of paralanguage and listening. A former member of the State Department, he was known to have three distinct ways of saying, "I would not speculate. "Newsweek reported that "spoken without accent, it means the Department doesn't know for sure; emphasis on the 'I' means I wouldn't, but you may—and with some assurance, accent on 'speculate' indicates that the questioner's premise is probably wrong."

Effective managerial listening goes far beyond words then. Listening also involves the observation of facial expressions, posture, gestures, spatial arrangement, and paralanguage. One who does not attend to all these factors may miss important information. For instance, a manager may ask two subordinate if they have been able to work out a satisfactory system to share the services of a secretary. The subordinates say everything is fine, even as they both look at the floor, tense their muscles and lean away from each other. Manager listening beyond the words would see a clear need to pursue this matter further.

Demonstrating a listening climate

In addition to actually listening carefully, managers must also seem to be listening and establish a climate that demonstrates receptivity. Without this climate, the communication environment in an office can become like that in many homes:

Parent: Why don't you ever tell us what you are doing?

Child: I do, but you don't listen. You're always so busy.

Parent: We're never too busy to listen to you, but jut don't seem to want to tell us anything.

Are the parents too busy to listen, or do they just act too busy? The same is true with many managers. Is it possible that hey act too busy to listen? A manager may unintentionally establish a non-listening climate by subtle behaviour that says to the subordinate, "Why talk if nobody is listening?"

While a manager is responsible for a tremendous amount of information and spends as much as 50 per cent of her working day listening, she cannot listen if nobody is talking. Managers need to demonstrate a listening climate to motivate people to "open up." Consequently, managers should strive to eliminate listening habits that discourage communication. A listener demonstrating these behaviours is not exhibiting a positive communication climate; consequently, the speaker may not feel he is being listened to. This list can serve as a personal checklist for managers to see if they demonstrate any of the irritating behaviours.

This finding is especially revealing. Clearly, the listener needs to give undivided attention to the speaker who does not want to be rushed to complete the message. This fact relates to the "25-to 75" speaking-thinking differential discussed earlier. The listener's mind moves so much more rapidly than the spoken word that the listeners impatience may show as she attempts to complete the speaker's sentence. Even though the listener is paying attention, this impatience to complete the speaker's communication may develop a negative listening climate. The same is true when the listener works on something else while attempting to listen. The speaker may soon get the feeling that the message being delivered is not very important.

It is particularly important to demonstrate a positive climate when involved in empathetic listening. As discussed earlier in this chapter, an empathetic listener tries to understand the speaker's inner feelings. Most people have a very difficult time expressing their, so an en-couraging, supportive, receptive environment needs to be established. Feelings of relation, sadness or fear are more easily and willingly expressed when received in a congruent manner by a receiver whose behaviour demonstrates "I'm with you."

Unfortunately, incongrument listener behaviour is too often the norm. For instance, an employee enters a manager's office and says she has a major problem to discuss. Meanwhile, her manager is shuffling papers around of his desk while saying, 'Go ahead. I'll be listening while I get these forms finished up." What kind of an impression will the employee receive? The employee obviously thinks that her problem is important, but the manager acts as if his forms are as important, if not more so. As a result, he has established a negative listening climate with no demonstrated empathy. The manager should give full physical and psychological attention to the speaker by maintaining eye contact, leaning slightly toward the speaker, changing facial expression in relationship to the message, and taking notes. All are ways that demonstrate a positive listening climate.

ENCYCLOPAEDIA
OF
MODERN MANAGEMENT TECHNIQUES

ENCYCLOPAEDIA OF MODERN MANAGEMENT TECHNIQUES

Volume 2

Edited by

A. K. Chaudhary

ANMOL PUBLICATIONS PVT. LTD.

NEW DELHI-110 002 (INDIA)

ANMOL PUBLICATIONS PVT. LTD.
4374/4B, Ansari Road, Daryaganj
New Delhi-110 002

Encyclopaedia of Modern Management Techniques

First Edition 1999

ISBN 81-261-0321-3 (Set)

PRINTED IN INDIA

Published by J. L. Kumar for Anmol Publications Pvt. Ltd., New Delhi-110 002 and Printed at Mehra Offset Press, Delhi..

Contents

6

Organisational Development

The key assumptions about the nature of organizations are that they are social systems and that they are formed on the basis of mutual interest.

1. *Social systems*: Organizations are social systems; consequently, activities therein are governed by social laws as well as psychological laws. Just as people have psychological needs, they their group as well as by their individual drives. In fact, two types of social systems exist side by side in organizations. One is the formal (official) social systems, and the other is the informal social system.

The existence of a social system implies that the organizational environment is one of dynamic change, rather than a static set of relations as pictured on an organization chart. All parts of the system are interdependent and subject to influence by any other part. Everything is related to everything else.

The effects of the broader social system can be seen in the experience of a supervisor, Glenda Ortiz, Oritz disciplined an employee for a safety violation. The action was within the rules and considered routine by Oritz. However, the local union already was upset because of what it considered to be unfair discipline for safety violations in another branch of the company. It wanted to show sympathy for its fellow members in the other branch, and it also wanted to show management that it would not accept similar treatment in this branch. In addition, the Union President, Jimmie Swallen, was running for reelection, and the wanted to show members that he was protecting their interests.

The union encouraged the employee to file a grievance about Ortiz'a action, and the simple disciplinary matter became a complex labour relations problems that consumed the time of many people.

The idea of a social system provides a framework for analyzing organizational behaviour issues. It helps make organizational behaviour problems understandable and manageable.

2. *Mutual interest*: Mutual interest is represented by the statement "Organizations need people, and people also need organizations". Organizations have a human purpose. They are formed and maintained on the basis of some mutuality of interest among their participants. People see organizations as a means to help them reach their

goals, while at the same time organizations need people's help to reach organizational objectives. If mutuality is lacking, it makes no sense to try to assemble a group and develop cooperation, because there is no common base on which to build. Mutual interest provides a superordinate goal that unites the variety of needs that people bring to organizations.

We have seen that individuals work in group or in society. Some times the individual works in collaboration with others for accomplishing a work with the available resources. They work together with some understanding with each other and every one does some work with resources required for the accomplishment of work. The understanding and coming together is known an organization. Thus organization sets the relationship among people, work and resources. When-ever people join a common effort for some objective it takes the form of organization does not mean only group of individuals but the relation between the individuals working together for some common objective. Hence when goal-directed activities of individuals are coordinated rationally by assignment of duties and responsibilities, this rational coordination is called organization. Here it has been mentioned that it is the activities of individuals which is coordinated rationally and individuals function in a system, Katz and Khan mentioned that organization may be considered as a system of roles. In the system each individual has a specific role to play with each of the roles coordinated with more integrated Pattern. We may say that organization is a group of individuals rationally coordinated together on the basis of their activities to achieve a desired objective. The individuals coordinated together are assigned different roles but are integrated together. Organization thus implies structuring and integrating activities, that is people working or cooperating together in interdependent relationship. The notion of interrelatedness suggest a social system. Therefore we can say that organizations are: (1) Goal oriented, people with a purpose, (2) Psychosocial system, people interacting in group (3) technological system people using knowledge and techniques and (4) and integration of structured activities, people working together in patterned relationship.

Theories of organization

In the beginning the organization were simple based on some pattern and structures were also very simple but it has become increasingly complex hence a number of studies and theoretical propositions about organizations have been proposed from time to time. These theories can be grouped under three headings:

(1) Classical organization theories

(2) Neo classical theories and

(3) Modern theories

Classical theories

First man to give a systematic shape to formal organization was F.W. Taylor and later on Money and Reiley, E.F.L. Breach, Max Weber also contributed to the concept of the theory of organization. The classical writers start their reasoning by using examples of primitive organization. One of their favourite examples, for instance involves, a man who wants to move a stone that is too heavy for him. He arranges to secure the service of a second or the third man by offering a reward. When one pushes another pulls. This is the beginning of division of labour. When the first calls the signal of big heave, we have a primitive chain of command serving to integrate the different parts of the system. Form this simple example evolves the major part of the organization theory. The classical theories are, scientific Management theory, Webers Bureau-cratic theory, and Administrative theory.

Scientific Management theory: Taylors scientific management theory emphasised more on management concepts of research, standard, planning, control and cooperation. Taylor emphasized that there should be planning foreman and functional foreman which brought the beginning of division of labour. Taylor also same the phenomena of organizational chart, job descriptions, work standards leading to careful programming of each job and defining the responsibilities of managers. All these were the beginning of the threads of formal organization, and giving in future the concept of division of labour, delegation of authority etc. Taylor was more concerned with efficient functioning of the organization.

Structural theory: Another Classical writer is Heneri Fayol. He gave the 'Principles of Management. This body of theories has been sometimes known as departmentation or administrative management theory. These theories explain that the identification of tasks and their grouping together is the central point and essential for achieving the general purpose of the organization. These grouping of tasks or work may be done, on the basis of purpose, or process. Mooney tried to broaden this approach. He gave the 'principle of organization'. According to Mooney there are five principles of organization, perpendicular coordination, horizontal coordination, Leadership, delegation and authority. Each is considered to be the basic to all organizational activity and each is therefore a 'Universal principle of management'.

It may be mentioned that all of these principles relate to structure of relationship of activities in an organization. The ideas of these authors were developed around four major principles: (i) the coordinative principle which provided for a unity of action in the pursuit of common objective (2) the scalar principle, which emphasised hierarchical organizational form and authority (3) the functional principle, which organized tasks into departmental units and (4) the staff principle, which recognised the role of the management in the exercise of authority but provided a staff to gibe information and advices.

The ides were related to the development of pyramidal organizational structure with a clear delineation of authority, specialisation of tasks, coordination of activities and utilization of staff specialist. Applications of these concepts led to the establishment of a formal organization charts, position description and organizational manuals.

Bureaucratic theory

The third major contribution in the development of classical concept of organization was of Max Weber. Weber was a sociologist. He studied the administration of single organization and also the broad economic and social structure of society. His ideas concerning the bureaucratic organization were only a part of the total social theory. Weber conceived bureaucracy to be particular type of organization one that developed in a rational way to enable a society or economy to function effectively in a situation of rapid in crease in requirements. Bureaucracy is a style in which work is carried out under given rules. These activities are carried by people functioning in a hierarchy of authority systematically enforced and supported by documents. Thus the view of rational legal authority was basic to Webers concepts of bureaucracy. Rational legal authority is based on position within the organization and when it evolved into an organized administrative staff it takes the form of a bureaucratic structure. Weber suggests that the bureaucratic form of organization is the most efficient instrument of large scale administration that has ever been developed in the modern world.

The features of bureaucratic organization are: (1) division of labour based on functional specialisation (2) a well defined hierarchy of authority (3) a system of rule covering the rights and duties of positional incumbents (4) a system of procedure for dealing with work situation (5) impersonality of interpersonal relations and (6) promotion and selection for employment based on technical competence.

We have discussed the important classical of organization.

(1) The theories are based on unrealistic closed system assumption about organization. Organizations work in certain environment and are influenced by them which has been ignored in these theories.
(2) The classical theories were written by practitioners of management based upon their limited observation which could not be proved by empirical researches.
(3) March and Simon have described these theories as the 'machine model': Bennis suggests that the focus of the classical theory is on 'Organization without people'.

These theories were strongly influenced by the society of the time and the then existing ideologies. Inspite of these limitations the traditional theories represent an important part of organization theory. Many of them are still utilized in organizations. They serve as the foundation for more modern views of organization theory and management practice.

Neo classical theories

Many forces have affected the evolution of organization theory and management practice. New knowledge from the various field of social sciences and numerous empirical researches contributed a number of concepts which can be grouped under two categories (i) Behavioural science, which emphasized human aspect in organization and (ii) the management science which emphasized qualification. These two areas have influence on organizational theory.

Behavioural approach to organization theories

The behaviour scientists used open system approach to organization. They are concerned with the Psycho-social system the primary factor of the human component. The emphasis of behavioural approach is on human factor and the way people behave in organization. The behavioural approach is 'humanistic' approach.

There have been various attempts from behavioural scientists to give theories of organization. Important among them are; balance theory by Herbert Simon, Fusion Process theory by Wight Bakke, Role theory and Group theory by Rensis Likert. All these theories have emphasised the human aspect in organization.

In Balance theory simon explained that at all levels the participation of human being is essential. This theory also emphasized the need of balance between inducement and contribution for each participants. Bakke is of opinion that "The Organization to some degree remakes the individual and the individual to some degree remakes the organization". There is relationship of give and take between individual and organization. This theory prescribes some role for management and might for effective organizational structure. From the role concept given by W. Bakke another theory known as `Role theory' emerged. This theory sees organization as system of roles, and when these roles interact with one another, the organization could more realistically be pictured as a system of overlapping role sets.

According to this theory every individual in an organization has to perform a role and expects others to help him by supportive role. He thus will have certain expectations from others land self. These roles and interactions of roles taken together form the bases of organization.

Another important human approach theory is the 'group theory' given by Rensis likert. He explained organization as a group to group relationship with each individual serving as a linking pin. The Linking pin idea represents an actual model of organization structure. Every individual serves as a linking pin between units above and below his units in the organization. Thus every individual is a vital member of two groups. He is the leader of the lower group and a member of the upper unit. This theory provides organization an upward orientation. Likert suggested horizontal—Linkage for communication, motivation and cooperation. He suggested for staff groups also which will keep the groups coordinated with each other.

The more scientific behavioural theory of organization started from the research of Elton Mayo and his associated at Hawthorne plant of the Western Electric Company. The experiment provides an interesting picture of transition from scientific management to the early human relation movement in organization. Before behavioural approach, engineers and psychologist made investigations of the relationship of work environment to productivity, studies on fatigue, rest period and physical surroundings were prevalent. But Mayo's experiment and research studies proved that variables other than physical surroundings influence the output. It proved that psychological and sociological factors might have an important bearing not only on workers motivation but on output as well. Elton Mayo and F.J. Rothelisberger made experiments in relay assembly room, and bank wiring observation room. A series of studies were undertaken relating physical condition e.g. working condition, rest period, length of working day etc. It was found by Mayo that regardless of variations in Physical conditions production increased. The experiment proved that the increase in production was due to change in social relation, motivation and supervision of work. The experiment proved that social and psychological factors were more important in determining workers satisfaction and productivity. Further the second phase of Hawthorn experiment indicated that human and social factors in the total work situation were more important.

The third phase of Mayo's experiment in Band wiring room concerned with a small work group of 14 male workers. The informal group established production norms that were often in conflict with those set forth by management. The work group determined the output of each individual worker which the worker achieved. This indicated that production was more determined by social rather than aptitude and Physiological factor. It also proved that the informal social organization influence feelings roles and interactions between individuals in a more stronger way.

The early human relation approach was concerned for the people in organization. Scott calls it as Industrial Humanism. Mayo called for modification in Industrial system to give greater recognition to human values. The Human relation theories developed many concepts about organization such as:

1. The business organization is a social system as well as a technical-economic system. This social system defines individual roles and establishes norms that may be at variance with those of the formal organization.
2. The individual is not only motivated by economic incentives, but is motivated by diverse social and psychological factor. Behaviour is affected by feelings, sentiments, and attitudes.
3. The informal work group became a dominant unit of consideration. The group has an important role in determining the attitudes and performance of individual workers.
4. Leadership patterns based on the formal structure and authority of position in the organization under the traditional view should be modified substantially in order to consider Psychosocial factors. The human relationists emphasized 'democratic' rather than 'Authoritarian' leadership patterns.

5. The human relations school generally associated worker satisfaction with productivity and emphasized that increasing satisfaction would lead in increased effectiveness.
6. It is important to develop effective communication channels between the various levels in the hierarchy that allow the exchange of information. Thus 'participation' became an important approach of the human relations movement.
7. Management requires effective social skills as well as technical skills.
8. Participants can be motivated in the organization by fulfilling certain social psychological needs.

Neoclassical theory and organization design

According to neoclassical theory, the organization should be designed in such a way that meets the basic postulated of the theory as discussed above. The basic emphasis of neoclassical theory is on flat structure, decentralization, and provision of informal organization. It can be seen that this theory offers modifications over the classical organization structure. For example, it accepts the concept of span of control but emphasises on wide span of control to give a flat structure rather than narrow span of control resulting into tall structure as envisaged by the classical theory.

1. *Flat structure*: Neoclassical theory suggests flat structure as against tall structure. Neoclassicists feel that tall structure is against the human beings. It suffers from the following problems: communication problem increased differentiation between decision makers and implementers lack of motivation to people, and being expensive because too many level are added in the organization. As against this, flat structure with wide span of control is more suitable for motivating human beings in the organization; communication chain is shorter, and it is free from hierarchical control.

2. *Decentralisation*: Neoclassical theory suggests decentralisation in organization structure. Decentralisation is closely related to flat structure as wide span of control will result into horizontal increase of people. The decentralised structure offers various advantages and is in accordance with the various characteristics of human beings as identified by the neoclassicists.

3. *Informal organization*: A major departure of neoclassical theory from the classical theory is that the former recognises that in every formal organization, informal organization also exists. Formal organization structure represents as closely as possible the deliberate intention of its framers for the purpose of interactions. That are expected to take place among its members. The informal organization, on the other hand, is created because of the limitations the psychological needs. In can organization, the behaviour of members is determined with interaction of formal and informal organizations. Since a manager cannot control the informal control the

informal organization, he should make the best use of this in achieving the organization objectives.

Appraisal of neoclassical theory

Neoclassical theory has given a new dimension to the design and management of the organization. It has recognised such important factors which were almost ignored by classical theory like informal organization, informal leader, group norms, non-economic motivation, irrational behaviour and so on. All these factors are important in understanding the organizational behaviour. Thus neoclassical theory has tried to overcome many of the deficiencies of classical theory.

Neoclassical theory, however, is not free from shortcomings. It suffers from incompetency, a short-sighted perspective, and lack of integration among various facets of human behaviour studied by it. It has been criticised by many and criticisms range from 'human relations as a tool for cynical puppeteering of people's to 'human relations is no more than a trifling body of empirical descriptive information. 'In fact, neoclassical theory has been called bankrupt. The major problems in neoclassical theory are as follows:

1. Neoclassical theory lacks unified approach of organization theory.

   In fact, it is knot a new theory at all. What actually has been done in this theory is merely modification of classical concepts and models, Therefore, it a is merely concerned with organizational modification 'rather than organization transformation. Thus neoclassical theory suffers from the same problems as classical theory does.

2. Most of the assumptions of neoclassical theory on which it bases its recommendations for organizational design land operation are not true. The assumption that it is always possible to find out a solution that satisfies every body is not true. Thus if basic assumptions are not true, how can recommendations based on these be practical? In the organization, often there are sharp conflicts of interest among various groups in the organization that are structural and not merely psychological. This aspect has not been dealt adequately.

3. Various structures and formats of organizations given by neoclassicists are not applicable to all situations. It is true that while designing an organization, consideration should be give to the characteristics of people working in the organization but humanistic organization structure may have its own limitations. As will be seen later, a suitable organization structure is one which takes care of different variables which affect the organizational functioning and people may be one of the various factors.

Modern organization theory: Systems approach

Modern organization theory is a sophisticated and scientific way of explaining a complex organization. This theory is comparatively systematic and highly constructive. It is not an instantaneous or overnight development but it is a composite representation of various contribution from different disciplines for more than two decades. Modern organization theory can be understood in tow approaches, though both of them are interrelated. These are systems approach and contingency approach.

Modern organization theory, as a systems approach, is an integrative one which considers the organization in its totality. The study of a system must rely on a method of analysis involving the simultaneous variations of mutually dependent variables. This is what systems approach of organization theory offers. The concept and implications of systems approach to management has been presented. Here we are presenting the relevant aspects of systems approach for organizational design. These are subsystems in the organization and have their linking and structural arrangement.

Subsystems in organization

Every system has subsystems which are interrelated to constitute system as entity. Since the organization is a system, it contains various subsystems. Each subsystem is identified by certain objectives, processes, roles, structures, and norms of conduct. The various subsystems of the organization constitute the mutually dependent parts. These subsystems interact and through interactions create new patterns of behaviour that are separate from but related to the pattern specified by the original system. This is known as emerged behaviour. Since variables are interdependent, the true influence of altering one aspect of the system cannot be determined by varying it alone. Similarly when any of the subsystem fails to function properly, the impact on other subsystems is immediate and affects the total organization.

In an organization system, there are various ways of classifying subsystems. For example, each unit of the organization is a subsystem. There is another way of classifying subsystems which may be found in each functional unit. Accordingly there are various subsystems in the organization and have been classified in different ways. For example, Seiler has identified four components in an organization system: human inputs, technological inputs, organization inputs, and social structure and norms. Kast and Rosenzweig have identified five subsystems: goals and value subsystem, psychological subsystem, technical subsystem, structural subsystem, and managerial subsystem. Carzo and Yanouzas have identified three subsystems: technical subsystem, social subsystem, and power subsystem. The totality of these subsystems with their interconnections makes up the system of organization. However, within these subsystems, managerial subsystem should also be added so that managerial aspect is given due emphasis in designing the organization structure.

1. Technical subsystem

Technical subsystem is a vehicle for conduct of work in the organization. It refers to the knowledge required for the performance of tasks, including the techniques used in the transformation of inputs into outputs. The basic component of the technical subsystem is a group of tasks or activities that can be performed by an individual. In performing the tasks, the individual has to play a role involving decision making, communication, and other actions which relate him with other parts of the organization. Behaviour in the technical subsystem is governed by rules, procedures, policies and other prescriptions. The basic purpose of the behaviour regulation is to make sure that jobs are performed as planned and to stabilise behaviour so that organization members may develop reasonable expectations of others' work behaviour in the organization.

Technical subsystem, thus, constitutes the formal arrangement of the functions, relationships, and behaviour. However, behaviour in the organization is not explained fully by the technical subsystem alone, because there is a fundamental conflict between individual and the organization system resulting from the demand made by the system and the individual expectancies regarding the work he has to perform. Thus individual behaviour is modified by the existence of social subsystem. Unless this aspect is taken into account, behaviour cannot be predicted properly.

2. Social subsystem

Every organization has a social subsystem which is composed of individuals and groups in interaction. When people are set to perform their tasks, they develop some sort of informal relation ships. These relationships are not patterned on formal basis but are different. Because of these informal relationships, there may be modification of expectancies of behaviour. The informal organization expects certain norms of behaviour from its members and individuals have expectancies of psychological satisfaction they hope to derive from association with others on the job. Both these expectancies interact resulting into individuals modifying their behaviour according to group norms and the ground modifying what it expects from individuals because of the impact of their personality factors on group norms.

3. Power subsystem

Every organization has a power subsystem and people in the organization elaborate their behaviour through the power relationship. Power distribution in the organization is both formal an informal. That is why some people are more powerful in the organization and some people are powerless in spite of occupying the similar power centre. Power subsystem is important to transform a decision into action in the organization. Often there is hierarchy of power centres in the organization because people aspiring for power have varying degrees of success as they have varying degrees of control on the means by which the power can be acquired such as formal position, job importance, expertise, personal characteristics, and coalition of individuals in the organization.

4. Managerial subsystem

When organizational units are arranged and operated as a system, each subsystem is viewed as a distinct entity and its relationship or contribution to the next level in the hierarchical structure is programmed and measured, but always in consideration of total system. Since organizations are deliberate and purposive creations, their management should lead towards the realisation of their objectives. Management of a system involves tow processes: operation and review and control. Operation refers to conversion of inputs into outputs, commonly known as transformation or conversion process. In puts may be in the form of information, materials, and energy. These inputs are allocated according to plan. However, the distribution of these inputs is also affected by social subsystem and power subsystem, more by the latter one. Operation of a system requires some sort of review and control to make it sure that it is going as it has been planned. It there is any discrepancy, this is overcome so that results are as planned.

Since an organization has various subsystems, these should be linked properly so that the organization can work as an entity. The way an organization moves towards its equilibrium depends on the functional connectness of its various parts. Successful working of the whole system requires two conditions: (i) enough connecteness among various parts of the subsystems so that operation of one subsystem can activate another and contributions of all can contribute to the whole: (ii) enough separation of the subsystems can be achieved in the system as a whole. Various parts of the organization are interlinked by certain activities known as linking process. Basically there are three interlinking processes: communication, decision, and balance. Communication as linking process evokes the activation in various parts of organization. It also works as control and coordination mechanism linking the various decision centres in the organization so as to synchronise their functioning. Various parts of the organization interact among themselves through communication. The second linking process is decision which refers to selection of a in alternative based on some criteria. Thus the basic criteria of decision making provide uniformity in the working of various subsystems. The third process balance refers to an equilibrium mechanism whereby various parts of the organization are maintained in a harmonious structured relationship to each other. These three interlinking processes taken together will affect the functioning of individual subsystem as well as of the whole system.

Factors affecting organization structure

There are various factors which affect the working of an organization. Since the organization structure is part of working of the organization these factors affects the design of structure also. These factors may broadly be: classified as; environment, technology, people and size. The relative influence of these factors may vary from organization to organization because conditions for individual organizations differ. The managers have to take these factors into account while designing the structure. Below is given an analysis of how these factors affect organizational design.

An organization is an open system which works within a broader framework of its environment. The organization interacts continuously with its environment; it is affected by the environment and also affects the environment through organization's influence on environment is limited. In this interaction process, the environment affects the various organizational processes including organization structure. In fact an organization is affected by its environment in the same way as a subsystem of the organization is a subsystem of broader social system. Therefore, the organization must adapt itself according to the needs of the environment. For example, an organization can neither receive inputs from the environment nor can it give its outputs to the environment, if it fails to satisfy environmental requirements. Since organization structure is one of the major determinants of organization functioning, it must be able to satisfy the needs of the environment. For example, if the organization is working in a highly dynamic environment, it must provide adequate means to collect and interpret information from the environment. Naturally such a provision is made through organization structure.

There are two characteristics of environment which affect organizational design. There are environmental complexity and environmental variability. Environmental complexity refers to the heterogeneity of the environment. More diverse the relevant environmental activities and more in number, higher is the complexity. For a complex environment, the organization needs a design through which more information can be collected and processed to monitor the effort of environment. Such a design should be more sensitive to environment. Since there are limitations on human beings to collect and process the information, special unit for monitoring and processing such information is required.

Another feature of environment which is important for organizational design is environmental variability. Variability refers to the rate of change in environment. The degree of variability in environment affect the organizational design because the organization has to change itself in order to cope the requirements of changing environment. Higher is the variability in environment, higher is requirement of flexibility in organizational design. Flexibility in this case is required to (i) increase the organization's ability to preplan, (ii) increase its flexibility to adapt to its inability to preplan because of uncertainty in environment.

Various research studies have confirmed the role of environment in organizational design. Burns and stalker have studied 20 electronics firms in Great Britain and found a linkage between formal organization and its environment. Based on the findings of their research, they have differentiated two systems of management suitable for two types of environment. The mechanistic system is suitable for stable environment and organic system is suitable for dynamic environment. Mechanistic system is based on rigid prescriptions of behaviour patterns in the organization while organic system is based on flexible prescription.

The development of two systems in various organization operating under different environment is a proof of environmental impact on organizational design. The findings of Burns and Stalker have been confirmed by other researchers also. For example, Lawrence and Lorsch have found from their research in three different industrial environments—plastics, foods, and containers (having high, moderate, and low environmental diversity respectively)—that the environments of uncertainty and rapid rate of change place different requirements on the organizational design than do stable conditions. Effective organizational units operation in stable parts of environment are more highly structures while those in more dynamic parts of environment are less formal. Similarly Galbraith has found that the organization structure of the company changes over a period of time because of change in environment during the period. The implications of various research studies suggest that there is a positive relationship between environment and organization design. For stable environment, highly structured organization is required and for dynamics environment, less structured organization is required.

Technology is another factor which affects the design of organization structure. Though, broadly speaking, technology is one of the components of organizational environment, it may be studied separately because technology directly affects the task structure. As such technology is taken here in taken here in the context of task in the organization. Technology is a body of particular type of knowledge and related to direct problem solving inventions. It consists of equipments, machines, tools, set of activities methods or processes and layout, arrangements or patterns, etc. Technology is one of the most important physical variables affecting he work system. The structure of an organization and the division of its activities, the network of roles and role relationships have to relate intrinsically to the task to be performed. Technology limits the amount of discretion which people can be given in the organization.

The technology-organization relationship was brought to surface for the first time by the studies of woodward and her colleagues. They studied one hundred manufacturing firms in U. K. and structure of an organization. They classified the technology into three categories based on its complexity. These are (i) small batch and unit production (less technology complexity)., (ii) large batch and mass production (medium range complexity), and (iii) process or continuous production (highly complex technology). Technological complexity refers to the extent to which the production process is controllable and its results predictable. The study by woodward has given the following conclusions:

(i) The firms employing large batch and mass production technologies were characterised by mechanistic organization structures.

(ii) The process production and small batch and unit production technologies were characterised by organic structures.

Scott and others have found curvilinear relationships between technology and various dimensions of organization structure like number of levels and supervisory span of control. Thus various research studies relating to the relationship between technology and organization structure suggest that the type of technology will determine the type of organization structure.

The third factor which affects the organizational design is the type of people employed by the organization. Organization structure is the result of conscious action on the part of people who are engaged in the organization. As such, the form of organization structure is expected to reflect the thinking and the way of working of its people. The form of organization is a major source of satisfaction or dissatisfaction for the people in the organization. The requirements of different types of people differ considerably and these can be better met if suitable organization structure is designed. Moreover, the structure is the result of personality, values, and other effects of its framers. Thus to arrive at appropriate structure, the forces in people should be analysed. Such analysis may be made in two ways: forces in people in superior capacity and forces in people in subordinate capacity.

1. *Forces in superiors*: The design of an organization structure is greatly influenced by the personality factors of managers particularly at the higher levels. Higher level managers decide such crucial factors as the type of industry in which the organization should go, the basis on which it will face competition (such as price, quality, diversity of product line, service, etc.) structure of top management and organization structure. All such decisions have to be made in the context of relationship between the environment and managerial philosophy. Differences in managerial philosophy affect some of the basic variables of organization structure. Negandhi and stafen have found that two India textile mills have different philosophies differed on various structural considerations like delegation of authority, span of control, communication pattern, and employee morale. Thus the mill having log-term profit objective in terms of organization structure also. Similarly strategic decisions of top management also affect the choice of organization structure. For example, Chandler has found positive correlation between strategy and structure of an organization. Thus different types of organization structures can cope effectively with different types of strategies. Similarly the manager's feelings about the degree of autonomy and freedom required of their subordinates will have important impact on the form of organization structure. It the managers believe more in theory Y assumption, they will create structure which provide more autonomy, flexibility, and less control. On the other hand, if they believe in theory assumptions, they will create structure that puts more control, leaves less scope for autonomy and offers lesser flexibility. Further if the managers believe that their organization is to work as a change agent in the society, it is likely top be based on organic model. But if they believe that their organization has to react in the context of environmental factors, it is likely to be nearer to mechanistic structure.

2. *Forces in subordinates*: People working in the organization perform their work as subordinates and their need satisfaction perform their work as subordinates and their need satisfaction depends to a great extent by the type of organization structure. Since

people differ in many respects, a single organization structure cannot be suitable for all people. Thus different organization structures will be suitable for skilled and unskilled people, or professionals and non-professionals. This is so because both groups of people have different needs. Skilled and professional people are more involved in their job and are anxious for an opportunity to have high degree of autonomy on the job and opportunity to participate in decision making process relating to it. Thus professional people can better be managed by the organization structure which satisfied their needs for autonomy, less direct control, and participation in decision making. On the other hand, unskilled and non-professional people do not have such requirements. Therefore, organization structure should be different for two categories of people.

Size of an organization is another variable affecting the type of organization structure through the effect of size has not been conclusively proved. Theoretically specking, size of an organization influences its coordination, direction, control, and reporting system. Since all these are either the part of the organization structure or are affected by it, it can be said that size will affect the organization structure. When the size of the organization is small, interaction is confined to a relatively small group, communications is simpler and face-to-face, less information is required for decision making, and there is less need for formalisation of organizational relationships and processes.

Research findings on the impact of size on organization structure do not show similar results. Some studies confirm the relationship but some do not confirm this. Earnest Dale has found that larger organizations tend to decentralise as compared to smaller organizations. The finding of Pugh and his associates confirm the impact of size on structure. Large organizations tend to have more specialisation, more standardisation, and more formalisation then smaller organization. Some other studies also confirm this view. However, there are certain studies which do not find any relationship between size of an organization and structure. For example, woodward did not find such a relationship in her studies mentioned earlier. Kimberly has analysed the various studies related to organization size and structure and concluded that there is no definite proof that both are highly related though it can be said that large sized organizations tend to be more formalised. Thus contingency approach of organizational design suggests that the organization structure which integrates the various forces-environment, technology, people, and size—will be more effective. Since these forces differ from organization to organization, an effective structure for one organization may not be equally effective for another if there are differences in contextual variables. Thus managers should not go for universal design but must chalk out a design after careful consideration of the various factors.

Elements of organizational structure

Thus after analysing the classical, the new classical and the modern theories it may be observed that they have suggested some important elements of organizational structure. Some of them form the basis of any organization, following important elements are mentioned.

Division of work: Every organization must analyse total work and allocate them to different individuals. Taylor was the first man to point out that planning should be separated from operation. He mentioned that there should be tow supervisors; operating supervisor and planning supervisor. Later on the classical authors also discussed about vertical division of work.

Thus in any organization there can be two types of division of work (1) Vertical and horizontal. The vertical division of work means chain of command and hierarchy of relationship. The chain of command is essentially for job distinction and job execution. The levels of the job are classified and the individuals are assigned authority on the basis of vertical dimension. Thus even infractional are, there can be individuals with assigned authority to decide policy, other with routine matters authority, while some one else only with the operating authority. They are all vertically related to each other. It relates to delegation or authority.

The horizontal division of work relates to job range and job depth. Job range means the spectrum of task supposed to be performed by individual in performing his job. Thus even one job may have several tasks which can be divided among different individuals, job depth refers to the discretion which the individual may exercise in selecting the means to perform the task and the sequence in which the task can be performed. Thus the horizontal division work refers to assignment of task at the same level among different individuals. Both Taylor and Fayol have given the concept of division of work in organization.

Departmentation: The Division of work leads to the analysis of job into small parts so that each one can be performed by different individuals. There after the jobs are grouped together. The grouping of activities of jobs is commonly known as departmentation.

Departmentation is concerned with horizontal organization on any level of the hierarchy and it is closely related to the classical bureaucratic principle of specialisation. The basic need for departmentation arose due to specialisation of work and for limiting the number of subordinates. It is used for fixing the responsibility, facilitate control and giving autonomy in relation to task performance. Traditionally, purpose, process, person or things and place were recognised bases for departmentation. In more recent terminology 'product is substituted for purpose', functional has replaced 'process' Territorial is used for place'. Besides its customers also form the basis for departmentation.

Function: The grouping of common or homogeneous activities to form an organization unit is known as functional departmentation, that is, the units are resolved around common functions. Functional departmentation is the most widely used basis for organizing activities and is present almost in every large organization at some level. Since functional departmentation can be adopted at various levels of the organization the various functions of the organization are divided in to basic and secondary functions.

Basic functions: The basic or major functions are those which are essential for the organizations and their operations contribute to the organizational efficiency. Davis has called these functions as 'organic functions' because their performance is viral and essential to the basic survival of the organization and values created by them are indispensible. For example, in a manufacturing organization basic functions may be production, marketing, and finance, Similarly, in a finance company, financing activities, of raising and disbursing financial resources may be basic of their importance to the achievement of organizational activities.

Secondary functions: When departments are created on the basis of major functions and a manager effectively or take the advantages of specialisation, he may create departments within the major functional department. Such departments will be created by dividing the major function in to subfunctions. This process may go down further when a secondary function may also be divided into subfunctions. For example, marketing department may be created at the top level. However, in order to perform marketing function properly, particularly in large organization, it may be divided into selling, marketing research, sales promotion, etc. Further sales promotion may be divided into print sales promotion, T. V. sales promotion, etc. Thus the process of functional differentiation will continue through several levels in the organization.

Besides basic and secondary functions, large organizations may also require some functions to be performed which will be helpful for the basic functions. Such functions may be referred to as staff or service functions which provide help to basic (line) functions. Thus a functional departmentation will include both line functions as well as staff functions depending on the organization.

Functional departmentation can continue as long as a sound basis for functional differentiation exists. After that, some other basis of departmentation may be use. For example, in sales department, further departmentation may be on the basis of territorial consideration.

Functional departmentation is most commonly used because it offers certain advantages, which include advantages of specialisation, ensuring performance of activities necessary for the achievement of organizational objectives, elimination of unnecessary activities, easier control over functions, easier way for pinpointing training needs of the managers, and maintaining the relative importance of functions in the organization. However, functional departmentation can not be carried too far in the organization. Moreover, there are many problems associated with functional departmentation such as lack of responsibility for the end results, overspecialisation and consequently lack of general management point to view problems of conflicts and coordination among functions departments.

Product: Product departmentation involves the grouping together of all activities necessary to manufacture a product or product line. As the organization grows in size, it becomes difficult for managers to coordinate the activities of the expanding product lines. One commonly adopted strategy is to establish departments based on products. Product departmentation is preferred for product expansion and diversification when manufacturing and marketing characteristics of each product are of primary concern. It is generally used when the product is relatively complex and a great deal of capital is required for plant and other facilities, such as automobile, electronics. In fact, many large companies are diversifying in different fields and they prefer product departmentation. For example, D.C.M. Limited has more than twenty products and hence products as the basis of departmentation. Within each major product department, major and subsidiary functional departments can be created. The product departmentation can be extended further. For example, if the above organization is manufacturing light commercial vehicles for different uses, this division may be further grouped on that basis like mini bus, delivery van, ambulance, etc.

Product departmentation offers several advantages particularly to an organization having multiple products or operates in a single industry with products for different uses as above. This basis places attention to product lines, reduces problems of coordination for different products, provides opportunities for further diversification and expansion of organization, and provides is different from others. However, it presents problems at the top management level for coordination, multiplicity of efforts because same functional facilities are requires for different products, and problem in maintaining economical central staff services. That is why a mixture of product and functional bases are adopted.

Territory: Territorial or geographical departmentation is specially useful to large-sized organizations having activities which are physically or geographically spread such as banking, insurance, transportation, etc. In such a case, all the activities in a given area of operations are grouped into zones, divisions, branches, etc. The assumption is that if markets are widely disperses, an improved cost-profit situation will result if all activities affecting a product line of service in a specific geographical region are grouped together.

Territorial departmentation is specially suitable to large scale organizations or other organizations whose activities are physically or geographically spread. In such cases, territorial departmentation provides certain efficiency in operation, Local factors such as customers, styles, preferences, etc. always affect organizational functioning. In fact, the same kind of work is always different when location is different. Thus knowledge of local conditions is an important element in effective management.

Moreover, some costs of operations can be saved, for example, serving of customers at different locations. The corresponding facilities are created looking into the needs for local conditions. Further, territorial departmentation may provide training to managers to look after every aspect of organizational operations. Therefore, they can develop the skills of looking the organization as a whole and can progress at the top level of the organization where general management qualities are needed.

Territorial departmentation presents certain problems. There fore, adequate provisions should be made to overcome these problems. The first most important problem is that of communication. However, this problem can be overcome without much difficulty once the system of communication is developed added with modern communication facilities. Another problem which comes in the way is the distance between policy framers and policy executors. Often both of them are at a distance not only in terms of physical distance but also in terms of mental distance because of different local conditions. However, this problem can be overcome by providing suitable training to the managers concerned. Some problems of coordination may also arise between top-level and territorial level managers as some of the functions are to be performed at the head office level. This arrangement requires many managers; level of total processes; maintenance of plant can be done in better way; and manpower can be utilised effectively.

Customer: Customer-based departmentation is basically market-oriented in which departments are created around the markets served or around marketing channels. While both these approaches to departmentation are designed to emphasise marketing an make it more effective, they differ in some respect. Grouping of activities around marketing channels involves making an organization structure reflect the ways an organization reaches an ultimate customer; market-centered grouping supports marketing efforts for different types of customers. Therefore, such a grouping is suitable to those organizations which either serve different customers such as pharmaceutical company supplying to hospitals, government, retail stores, etc., or applying different marketing channels like wholesale, retail, installment and hire purchase, export, etc.

The most important advantage of customer departmentation is that it focuses on customers who are the ultimate suppliers of money to the organization. Therefore, different types of customers can be satisfied easily through specialised staff. In fact the basic idea of this departmentation is to provide service to clearly identified groups of customers. Each group of customers has different purchase behaviour, payment schedule, demand pattern, etc. Therefore, they can be attracted to the organization's business by satisfying them by providing services, payment schedule, demand pattern, etc. Therefore, they can be attracted to the organization's business by satisfying them by providing services most suitable to each of them.

This method may have certain advantages specially when it is followed very rigidily. Coordination between sales and other functions becomes difficult because this method can be followed only in marketing division. Duplication and confusion may arise in product, research and development activities as well as in manufacturing, as the market-oriented mangers demand special attention and service. This may generate more conflicts i the organization. Further, there may be under employment of manpower in some departments specially when demand for that customer group decreases. Therefore, customer oriented departments should be created to the extent they justify their existence. Besides the above major bases of departments, some other bases can be adopted particularly in a major departments, some other bases can be adopted as a base for creating departments like shift systems. Sometimes departments may be created based on serial number such a work group may be called as group number one, two, or so on.

Choice of bases for departmentation

The above discussion shows that each of the bases of departmentation has its suitability, advantages, and disadvantages, Consequently, the selection of bases for departmentation involves a consideration of the relative advantages of each base of the organization. Ideally speaking, a suitable basis of departmentation is one which facilitates the performance of organizational functions efficiently and effectively so that its objectives are achieved. However, since each basis is suitable to a particular type of organization or its part, often a combination of various bases is adopted. Therefore, determination of suitability of departmentation bases is adopted. Therefore, determination of suitability of departmentation bases should be considered in the light of various factors affecting the functioning of an organization. Such factors may be of the following types.

1. *Specialisation*: The basis of departmentation should reflect the specialisation in performing the work. The more an organization structure reflects the division of work in an organization through grouping of activities in departmental form, the more efficiently and effectively it tends to contribute to organizational operation. This is possible because of specialisation of work. Therefore, looking into the organizational framework, that basis should be chosen which results into specialisation.

2. *Coordination*: While specialisation involves that an activity is performed by the most suitable personnel, coordination involves that all the related activities are performed in a way that their performance is synchronised so that each activity contributes to others. In a sense, all activities grouped in various forms have the same objective of achieving organizational goals, though they may skill. Therefore, the best result cane be achieved when all activities are performed in a coordinated way and each activity contributes in the positive way to others. Thus the basis of departmentation should ensure that closely connected operations are put together.

3. *Control*: Control is the process of analysing whether the intended results are being achieved by particular department or not. If not, what can be done to bring the

situation to a desirable level. Control measures and their effectiveness depend on the way in which activities are grouped into departments. Normally more clearly-defined activities and consequently responsibilities of a department are, more are the chances for effective control because the manager can know very easily what is to be controlled. Thus from control point of view, activities whose immediate contributions are similar should be grouped together so that responsibility for achieving results can be clearly specified.

4. *Economy*: A balance should be maintained between the cost of creating a department and its contribution. The existence of a department is desirable only its contributes more than its cost. Creation of departments involves costs on the part of the organization. Costs involves may be of two types. First, when a new department is created, it requires personnel and other matching facilities which involves costs. Second, creation of additional department means creation of additional interactions in the organization requiring additional time of managers which is very important for them. For example, if too many staff departments have been created, they may pose severe time constraints on line managers.

5. *Focus on results*: In an organization, the final results or objectives are achieved through the achievement of subordinate results. Therefore, all those activities which contribute to the achievement of these results should be given proper attention. This will ensure that all necessary activities are performed and there is no duplication of unnecessary activities. Thus activities whose contributions are higher are likely to get more prominence. For example, service activities are grouped separately to support the main activities and also to ensure that they contribute positively to the performance of main activities. However, creation of departments for auxiliary services should not get prominence over main activities.

6. *Local conditions*: While creating departments, adequate consideration should be given to the requirements of local conditions. This is more important to those organization which operate in different geographical areas. As pointed our earlier, the same kind of work is different when the location is different. Therefore, local requirements of the organization should also be taken into account while creating departments.

7. *Human consideration*: Departmentation should also take into consideration the human factor in he organization. Therefore, alongwith technical factors discussed above, departments should be created on the basis of availability of personnel, their aspirations and value systems, informal work groups, and attitudes of people towards various forms of organization structure. Often organization structure is a major source of satisfaction or dissatisfaction to human beings. This also affects the efficiency and effectiveness of the organization. Departmentation scheme providing more human satisfaction is likely to contribute more to the organizational operation. However, departments should not be created merely to suit the needs of few individuals only.

Centralization and decentralization

The terms centralization and decentralization are freely tossed about in both management literature and practice. Most often, both the scholar and the practitioner neglect to define what they mean by the concept. There are three basic types of centralization decentralization. One is the geographical or territorial concentration (centralized) or dispersion (decentralized) of operations. For example, the term centralized can be used to refer to an organization that has all its operations under one roof or in one region. On the other hand, the dispersion of an organization's operations throughout the country or the world is a form of decentralization. The word geographical is often not prefixed, thereby adding to the confusion. A second type is functional centralization and decentralization. A good example is the personnel function of an organization. A separate personnel department that performs personnel functions for the other departments is said to be centralized. However, if the various functional departments, e.g., marketing, production, and finance, handle their own personnel functions, then personnel is considered to be decentralized.

The third type is the only analytical use of the concept. This is where the terms centralization and decentralization refer to the retention or delegation of decision making prerogatives or command. From an organization theory and analysis standpoint, this third type is the most relevant use of centralization and decentralization. They are relative concepts because every organization structure contains both features, and they differ only in degree.

Contrary to common belief, it is not possible to determine whether an organizations is centralized or decentralized by merely looking at the organization chart. The determining factor is how much of the decision making is retained at the top and how much is delegated to the lower levels. This retention or delegation is not reflected on the organization chart.

Determining decentralization: Both management writers and practitioners generally favor decentralization. It represents one of the 'in' concepts and identifies the advocate as a modern-thinking theorist or practitioner. On the other hand, centralization has taken on the connotation of being traditional and even authoritarian. Albers observed that,

> In recent years, decentralization has become the golden calf of management philosophy. It has been lauded by such terms as 'more democratic,' 'a step toward world peace', 'greater freedom of spirit', and 'less authoritarian', The implicit assumption is that centralization reflects the opposite of these worthy qualities.

Although most contemporary managers proselytize the values of decentralization, in reality their use of the concept turns out to be more fiction that fact. A typical case in the executive who gives a speech at the Rotary Club luncheon praising the values of decentralization. More often than not, these individuals are likely to be practicing a high degree of centralization although they may truly think they are running a thoroughly decentralized operation. Obviously, the mere verbalization of decentralization by top management is not sufficient to determine the extent of decentralization.

1. The greater the number of decisions made lower down the management hierarchy.
2. The more important the decisions made lower down the management hierarchy. For example, the greater the sum of capital expenditure that can be approved by the plant manager without consulting anyone else, the greater the degree of decentralization in this field.
3. The more functions affected by decisions made at lower levels. Thus companies which permit only operational decisions to be made at separate branch plants are less decentralized than those which also permit financial decisions at branch plants.
4. The less checking required on the decision. Decentralization is greatest when no check at all must be made; less when superiors have to be informed of the decision after it has been made; still less if superiors have to be consulted before the decision is made. The fewer people to be consulted, and the lower they are on the management hierarchy, the greater the degree of decentralization.

Optimum degree of decentralization: So far, the discussion has probably implied that decentralization is somehow better than centralization. In truth, neither concept is an ideal or intrinsically good or bad. Generally speaking, decentralization is much more compatible with the behavioural aspects of management. This relevancy is due in part to the lower-level participation in decision making that results from decentralization. Increased motivation is an extremely important by-product. Besides the behavioural benefits more effective decisions are possible because of the speed and first-hand knowledge that decentralization provides. Decentralization also affords invaluable experience in decision making for lower-level executives. Finally, it allows more time for top management to concentrate on policy making and creative innovation. On the other side of the ledger, centralization 'produces uniformity of policy and action, lessens risks of error by subordinates who lack either information or skill, utilizes the skills of central and specialized experts, and enables closer control of operation.'

On balance, the answer to the problem of what is the optimum degree of decentralization is that it depends on the situation. Newman, Summer, and Warren suggest seven questions that should be considered in determining the degree of decentralization.

1. Who knows the facts on which the decision will be based, or who can get them together most readily?
2. Who has the capacity to make sound decisions?

3. Most speedy, on-the spot decisions be made to meet local conditions?
4. Must the local activity be carefully coordinated with other activities?
5. How significant is the decision?
6. How busy are executives who might be assigned planning tasks?
7. Will initiative and morale be significantly improved by decentralization?

An analysis and weighing of these seven factors can provide the needed insight into determining the proper degree of centralization-decentralization.

Behavioural implications of decentralization: Although delegation was probably the most behaviorally oriented classical principle, decentralization is an even more concerted attempt to incorporate behavioural ideas into organization structure. Decentralization recognizes and actually capitalizes on the importance of the human element. Most important is that decentralization gives an opportunity for individual responsibility and initiative at the lower levels. Because of the popularity of decentralization, many organizations have been stimulated to incorporate the accompanying behavioural ideas. Yet, as has been pointed out, decentralization may be more fiction that fact, in actual practice. Moreover, as mentioned earlier, there is distinct possibility that decentralization may be occurring. Such a turn of events may wipe out the human advances in organization that have been stimulated by decentralization.

From another viewpoint, there is a convincing argument that decentralization, as practiced, never did have a behavioural impact.

First, we should observe that the principle of decentralized profit-and-loss accounting has never been carried much below the level of product-group departments and cannot, in fact, be applied successfully to fragmented segments of highly interdependent activities. Second, we may question whether the conditions under which middle management has in the past exercised its decision-making prerogatives were actually good conditions from a motivational standpoint.

It is fair to say that, overall, decentralization has supported, and in some cases has stimulated, the behavioural approach to management. At the same time, there is little doubt that a wide discrepancy exists between the theory of decentralization has hand a definite impact on developing a managerial attitude toward acceptance and implementation of behavioural concepts in organization. However, in the future, this may all change because of the movement to recentralize.

Span of control

The grouping of activities to create various departments presents another problem, that is, how may individuals should be place under one superior. This problem is related to the horizontal dimension of an organization structure. In management literature, span of management, span of control, or span of supervision are used to denote the same concept of number of subordinated which should be put under one superior. However, the term span of management appears to be more suitable as compared to its alternatives because a superior is responsible for the total activities of his subordinates which involves not merely controlling or supervising but the total managerial activities.

Span of management refers to the number of subordinates who can be managed effectively by a superior. The number of subordinates who report to superior has two important implications. First, its is influential in determining the complexity of individual managers' jobs. Second, the span of management determines the shape, or configuration of the organization; the fewer the number of people reporting to superior, the larger the number of managers required. Therefore, the number of subordinates reporting to a superior should be fixed which in any case can not go beyond certain limit. However, Soujanen has suggested that span of management is a traditional concept and is not valid because the coordination and control can be achieved through formal and informal group activity. The replacement of old system of individual control by control through management team has changed the whole system of communication and contract in the organization which has affected attention paid to the way executive controls in the command sense. However, Soujanen's contention that modern social science concepts have modified the concept of traditional span of management drew a sharp reaction from Urwick. He brought an article in response and suggested that the contention of Soujanen was wrong and span of control principle held valid.

Determination of span of management

No doubt, management thinkers agree that span of management principle holds true but they do not agree about the number os subordinates that can be put under one superior. The classical approach to the span of management has dealt with generalization embodying specific number of subordinates for effective span. Thee classical writers have suggested between three to eight subordinates as ideal depending on the levels of management with lower the level of management higher the number of subordinates. Graicunas, a French management consultant, has suggested the fixation of number of subordinates based on mathematical calculation. He has analysed superior-subordinate relationships and developed mathematical formulae. Graicunas has identified three types of superior-subordinate relationships: direct single relationships, direct group relationships, and cross relationships.

(i) *Direct single relationships*: Direct single relationships arise from the direct individual contacts of the superior with his subordinates. Thus if there are three subordinates A, B, C under one superior X, there will be three direct single relationships.

(ii) *Direct group relationships*: Direct group relationships arise between the superior and his subordinates in all possible combinations. Thus, the superior may consult his subordinates with one or more providing assistance. With three subordinates, there will be nine such relationships like A with B, A with C, and so on with the superior associated with all groups.

(iii) *Gross relationships*: Gross relationships arise because of mutual interaction of subordinates working under the common superior, such as A and B, A and C, B and A, and so on. The relationship is quite different between A and B than B and A from management point of view because the type of interaction will be different in both the cases. There are six such relationships with three subordinates.

According to Graicunas, most ideal span for a manager is six subordinates involving 222 relationships. No doubt, Graicuna has given a mathematical treatment of the problem of managing subordinates increases with the increase in the number of subordinates, his contribution suffers with a basic limitation. All the relationships are not equally important from management point of view and, therefore, these can not increase the complexity of managing. Moreover, Graicuna has not considered many other possible relationships particularly in cross relationships. Therefore, span based on mere number of relationships can not be fixed.

The recognition that potential managerial effectiveness is limited as the number of subordinates increases has led others to propose definite limits on the span of management. For example, Davis distinguishes between two categories of span of control, an executive span and operative span. Executive span includes the middle and top management positions in an organization. The span for these managers should vary from three to nine, depending on the nature of managers' jobs and responsibilities and the rate of growth of the organizations. The operative span applies to the lowest level of management and it can be defective with as many as 30 subordinates. Similarly, Urwick has proposed span for top management as four built it may be between eight to twelve for supervisory management. Thus span of management has been suggested differently by various writers. Further, differences also exist for different levels of management. Therefore, it is desirable to identify those factors which affect the span of management.

Factors affecting span of management

The basic idea behind limiting the span of management is to enable a manager to manage his subordinates effectively. As such, the important determinant for specifying the span of management is the manager's ability to reduce the frequency and time impact of superior-subordinate relationships. This ability, in turn, is affected by several factors. Therefore, such factors are quite important in determining the suitable span of management. Following are such factors:

1. *Capacity of superior*: Each manager has different ability and capacity in respect of such factors as leadership, communication, decision-making, control, etc. affecting

management of subordinates. Managers having more capacity in respect of these factors can manage more number of subordinates in similar situation. Moreover, the attitudes and personality factors of the manager also determine his span of management. For example, an empire builder may like to have wider span as compared to submissive manager.

2. *Capacity of subordinates*: Capacity of subordinates also affects the degree of span of management. Efficient and trained subordinates may discharge their functions more efficiently without much help their superior. They may just need broad guidelines and rest of the things can be performed by them. In such cases, they require lesser time from their superior who will be in a position to manager larger number of subordinates. Similarly, if there is no frequent changes in subordinates, span can be wider.

3. *Nature of work*: Nature of work affects degree of span of management because different types of work require different pattern of management and hence time from superior. If subordinate are performing similar functions, they require less attention of their superior and span can wider. For example, a study discloses that mean span of management in the case of supervisors subversion similar work was 16 as against only 6.7 for those supervising different work. Similarly rate of change in the work also affects the span of management with work with lower degree of change facilitating higher span and work with higher degree of change restricting the span of management. This is so because work with frequent changes requires detailed instructions from the superior every time when there is change in the work. Type of technology used also affects the span of management. For example, Woodward's study suggests that in the case of mass production and assembly-line technology, the span is highest. Similarly, in unit and batch production, span is higher than process production.

4. *Degree of decentralisation*: Degree of centralisation or centralisation affects span of management by affecting the degree of involvement of the superior in decision-making process. Thus higher is the degree of decentralisation, higher is the degree of span. If a manager clearly delegates his authority and d defines, higher is the degree of span. If a manager clearly delegates his authority and defines it fully, he requires less time to devote to manage his subordinates because most of the actions will be taken by the subordinates because most of the actions will be taken by the subordinates or their own. In the case of centralisation of authority or ambiguity in delegation of authority, the subordinates would require considerable consultation, clarification, and instructions from their superior. This will require more time on the part of the superior an his span sill be narrow.

5. *Degree of planning*: Higher is the degree of plans, particularly standing plans clearly providing rules, procedures, methods, etc. in doing the work, higher would be the degree of span of management. In such cases, the subordinates can take actions of

their own. On the other hand, if they have to draw their own plans they may not know what exactly they have to do and they may require more time for guidelines and consultation. In a situation, where the production foremen were performing repetitive work with well-formulated standing plans, span averaged between 60 and 70.

6. *Communication techniques*: The pattern of communication, its means, and media affect the time requirement in managing subordinates and consequently span of management. If communication is mostly face-to-face, it requires more time on the part of both superior and subordinates. On the other hand, communication tools like electronic devices will save lot of time and span can be increased.

7. *Use of staff assistance*: Use of staff assistance in reducing the work-load of managers enables them to manage more number of subordinates. Many of the managerial functions can be discharged by these staff personnel on behalf of the managers. They can collect information, process communication, and issue orders and instructions on behalf of their superior. This process saves time of mangers and the degree of span can be increased.

8. *Supervision from others*: It is not very uncommon that a subordinate receives supervision from several other personnel besides his direct superior. In such a case, the work load of direct superior is reduced and he can supervise more number of subordinates. The trend is changing towards getting supervision from many persons. For example, Udell has found that it is not uncommon that men in the organizations receive 50 percent or more of their supervisions from someone else that their own immediate superior. He has found that where people were getting supervision from others also besides from their own superior, the average span was 17.6 as compared to 6.7 for those not getting supervision from others.

The analysis of various factors affecting span of management suggests that there cannot be any fixed number of subordinates under one superior. Rather, the span should be decided taking the various factors into account. Therefore, the span of management may vary in the same organization for different levels of management and functions and also in different organizations for similar functions and levels of management. Koontz has analysed the role of various in determining the span of management and has calculated the optimum span based on these factors.

While such an exercise gives an indication about how span of management should be fixed, various research studies have suggested the actual of management followed under various situations. On the basis of review of such studies, House and Miner conclude that (1) under most circumstances, the optimal span is likely to be in the range of 5 and 10; (2) the larger spans, say 8 to 10 are most appropriate at the highest policy making levels of the organization where greater resources for diversified problem-saving appear to be needed; (3) the breadth of effective spans of first-line supervisors is contingent on the technology of the organization; and (4) in prescribing the span of control for specific situations, consideration are given to a host of local factors such as desirability of high group cohesiveness, the environment, task inter-dependencies, the need of the members' satisfaction and the leadership skills available to the organization.

Wide or narrow span

Often there is a controversy whether an organization should adopt the policy of narrow span or wide span of management. While most of the classical writers have suggested a narrow span of management, modern approach suggests a wider trends work in favor of wider span of management. A narrow span throughout an organization causes tall or vertical structure, and a wide span causes a flat or horizontal structure.

Looking into the cost of employment of personnel and their availability, it is preferable to go for wider span of management. The following factors have also made it possible to adopt wider span of management in modern-day organization:

(i) trends towards decentralisation;

(ii) improved communication technology;

(iii) increasing size of organization; and

(iv) the new pattern of leadership with more emphasis on democratic styles.

However, despite the desirability of wider span of management, it is limited by real and important restrictions. An organization can not extend its span of management beyond certain level. Therefore, what is more important in this context is to maintain a precise balance between wise and narrow span of management. One must balance all the costs of adopting one course or the other—not only the financial cost but also costs in morale, personnel development, and attainment of organizational objectives. This requires an understanding of various implications of tall and flat organization structure.

Flat and tall structure

In organizational analysis, the terms flat and tall are use to describe the total pattern of spans of control an levels of management. Whereas the classical principle of span is concerned with the number of subordinates one superior can is concerned with the number of subordinates one superior can effectively mange, the concept of flat and tall is more concerned with the vertical structural arrangements for the entire organization. The nature and scope are analogous to the relationship between delegation and decentralization. In other words, span of control is to flat-tall structures as delegation is to decentralization.

The most noteworthy departure from the tall structural concept of organization is attributed to the pioneering work of James C. Worthy, a former vice president of

Sears, Roebuck and Company. About twenty-five years ago he was involved with a comprehensive organizational study of Sears. The results obtained from surveys of several hundred company units contradicted the classical assumptions about span of control. He found that stores that were organized into flat structures has better sales, profit, morale, and management competence than stores that were formed into tall structures. These results gave empirical evidence to challenge the classical tall structures. Worthy summarized his reasoning as follows: "...the emphasis is constantly on shortening the span, without giving much more than lip service to the fact that circumstances often differ and that under certain conditions there may be positive advantages in lengthening the span."

Advantages an disadvantages: Tall structures assume a role in assessing the value of flat structures similar to that of centralization in assessing the relative merits of decentralization. Tall structure are often negatively viewed in modern organizational analysis. More accurately,, there are advantages and disadvantages to both flat and tall structures. Furthermore, flat and tall are only relative concepts; there are no ideal absolutes.

From a behavioural viewpoint, self-control is much more effective than control imposed from above. This behavioural advantage of flat organizations hinges on the assumption that there are capable people who can produce under conditions of relative independence. In other words, the analysis of flat and tall structures depends a great deal on what hypotheses are made about the basic nature of people. For discussion purposes, McGregor's Theories X and Y assumptions may be used to assess the merits of flat versus tall structures.

Behavioural implications flat versus tall: One behavioural implication that is often overlooked in analyzing flat versus tall structures is the opportunity that tall structures offer for more personal contact between superior and subordinate. This contact is generally assumed to be negative and conflicting, but it need not be. On a tall structure, the superior may create a positive rapport with his subordinate that may not be possible in a flat structure.

Another consideration besides personal contact is the levels of communication in the two structures. In the flat structure there are fewer levels, which means that both downward and upward communication is simplified. There should be less distortion and inaccurate. The red tape and endless communication channels associated with bureaucratic tall structures are not present in a flat structure. On the other hand, the increased equality that exists between subordinates in a flat structure may lead to communication problems. If no status or authority differentials are structurally created, a heavy burden is place upon horizontal communication. As the horizontal communication system is notably deficient in most organizations. The problem may be compounded in flat organizations in flat organizations where more dependence is placed on this type of communication, but it is not structurally facilitated. Also coordination may be seriously impaired by a flat structure for the same reason. Overall, the flat structure, at least from a behavioural standpoint, is generally preferably to the tall. It can take advantage of the positive attribute of decentralization and personal satisfaction and growth. Although managers who have side spans will have to give a great deal of attention to selecting and training subordinates, a flat structure has the advantage of providing a wealth of experience in decision making. Perhaps Worthy best summarizes the behavioural advantages of flat structures in these words: "Flatter, less complex structures, with a maximum of administrative decentralization, tend to create a potential for improved attitudes, more effective supervision, and greater individual responsibility and initiative among employees."

Together with these advantages, however, it must be remembered that flat structures only encourage decentralization and individual responsibility and initiative. The supervisor of a small open does not always keep close control and never decentralize, not does the supervisor of a large span always create an atmosphere of self-control and decentralization. The degree of centralization or its rivers depends on the overall management and organization philosophy and policies and on individual leadership style and personality. All a flat or tall arrangement does is structurally to promote, not determine, centralization or aspects of managing.

Delegation of authority is one of the important factors in the precess of organizing. It is essential to the existence of a formal organization. The organizational units created through the process of departmentation require the authority to the managers changed with their respective management. Assignment of activities to various managers creates responsibilities and in order to carry these responsibilities, managers need appropriate authority. In fact, the authority should match responsibility.

To delegate means to grant or confer. Here delegation means conferring authority from one manager or organizational unit to another in order to accomplish particular assignments. A manager simply does not delegate authority, he delegates authority to get certain work accomplished. By means of delegation the manager extends his area of operations for without delegation his actions and confined to what the himself can perform. Delegation of authority has following features:

1. Delegation is authorisation to a manager to act in a certain manner. The degree of delegation prescribes the limits within which a manager has to decide the things. Since formal authority originates at the tip level, it is distributed throughout the organization through delegation and delegation.
2. Delegation has dual characteristics. As a result of delegation, the subordinate received authority from his original authority. They comments in this phenomenon like this. 'It is something like imparing knowledge. You share with others who then possess the knowledge, but you still retain the knowledge too.'

3. Authority once delegated can be enhanced, reduced, or withdrawn depending on the situation and requirement. For example change in organization structure, policy, procedure, methods, etc. may require change in the degree of delegation of authority.
4. Delegation of authority is always to the position created through the process of organizing. The individual occupying a position may exercise the authority so long as he holds the position. Therefore, the authority is recovered fully from the individual when he moves from the particular position.
5. A manager delegates authority out of the authority vested in him. He can not delegate which he himself does not posses. Moreover, he doesn't delegate his full authority because if he delegates all his authority, he can not work.
6. Delegation of authority may be specific or general. Delegation of authority is specific when courses of action for particular objectives are specified. It is general when these are not specified, though objectives may be specified.

Steps in delegation

The distribution of authority throughout an organization does not occur automatically. Rather, it is deliberate design or plan by which a manager makes his authority effective and influential. This required delegation of authority through particular steps. The entire process of delegation of authority can be completed through the following four steps:

(1) Determination of result expected, (2) Assignment of duties, (3) Authorisation for actions, and (4) Creation of obligation. Let us now explain briefly these steps;

1. *Determination of results expected*: Authority should be delegated to a position according to the results expected from that position. Since authority is intended to furnish managers with a tool for so managing as to gain contribution to the organizational objectives, it is essential that authority delegated to a manager is adequate to ensure the ability to accomplish results expected. It implies that results expected from each position have been identified properly. To the extent, there is clarity in these, delegation will be effective. Therefore, the first requirement is the determination of contributions of each position which is largely a step undertaken at the stage of creating various positions.

2. *Assignment of duties*: The second step is the assignment of duties to the subordinate. Duties can be described in two ways. First, these can be described in terms of an activity or set of activities, for example, selling activity to salesman. According to this view, delegation involves assignment of these activities, by manger to subordinate. Second, duties can be described in terms of results that are expected form the performance of activities, for example, how much sale is to be achieved by salesmen. Assignment of duties in terms of results expected works better because a subordinate is likely to get psychological satisfaction from his work, and he will have

advance notice of the criteria on which his performance is to be judged. A man's duties will be clear to him only when he knows what activities he must undertaken and what goals he must fulfill.

3. *Authorisation for action*: The third aspect involves granting of permission to take actions like making commitments, use of resources, and other actions necessary to get the assigned work done. This problem is essentially one of determining he scope of authority to be delegated to each particular subordinate. In the delegation process, the manager confers upon a subordinate the right to act in specified way or to decide with in limited boundaries. The subordinates. The subordinate exercises the authority in conformity with his understanding of the intentions of the superior who delegates it to him and within the framework of such controls as that superior deems it wise to establish. The process of delegation stakes out the boundaries of permissible action, separating them from actions which are not permissible. The central problem, therefore, is to determine what scope of authority the superior wishes his subordinates to exercise. A ground rule in this context is that the scope of authority allocated to individual by the superior is inseparably linked with the activities allocated to them.

4. *Creation of obligation*: The last aspect of delegation is to treat obligation on the part of subordinate for the satisfactory performance of his assignment. As discussed earlier, a subordinate is responsible for the total activities assigned to him and not only for he activities actually being performed by him. The sense of obligation required arises from the maintenance of responsibility by the superior and an accompanying insistence that the work performed must meet his expectations.

Principles of delegation

Delegation of authority is a conscious effort on the part of the manager. Therefore, in delegating authority, he should observe certain principles so as to make delegation effective. Unless these principles are observed, delegation may be ineffective, consequently organization may ail and the managerial process may be seriously impeded. Following are such principles;

1. *Delegation by results expected*: As discussed earlier, delegation should be based on results expected from a position in the organization. Since authority is intended to achieve certain outcomes in the organization, it should be adequate to achieve those outcomes. A manager is expected to perform better if he knows what he has to contribute and he has commensurate authority for that. Delegation by results expected to perform better if he knows what he has to contribute and he has commensurate authority for that. Delegation by results expected implies that planning exercise has been taken and goals for each position have been set, communicated and properly understood by those who are responsible for achieving these goals. Often managers fail to delegate adequately because either they have very vague idea about the contributions of their subordinates or they just do not bother to determine whether the subordinated have authority to do the things.

2. *Functional definition*: Closely related with principle of delegated based on results expected is principles of functional definition. In an organization, the activities are classified and grouped to create departments or units. Each department contributes to organizational objectives but at the same time has its own objectives. Thus there is a need for coordination of objectives and activities of the department in such a way that they contribute maximum to the organization. This gives rise to the principle of functional definition. The more a department has clear definitions of results expected, activities to be undertaken, authority delegated, and authority and informational relationships with other departments, the more adequately the department can contribute towards accomplishing organizational objectives.

3. *Clarity of lines of authority*: Each position in the organization is linked with others through authority relationships; some directly through line authority, others indirectly. More clearly these lines of authority are defined, more effective is the delegation of authority. In this respect, classical authors have given two principles which guide the delegation or authority. These principles are scalar chain and unity of command. Scalar chain principle refers to the chain of direct authority relationships from superior to subordinate throughout the organization. Clearer the line of authority form the tip manager to every subordinate position in the organization, the more effective will be responsible decision making and organizational the communication. The other principle, that is unity of command suggests that a subordinate should be responsible to a single superior and he should receive instructions from the same superior and he should receive instructions from the same superior only. The more completing an individual has a reporting relationship to a single superior, the less is the problem of conflict in instructions and greater the feeling of personal responsibility for results.

4. *Level of authority*: Authority level principle suggests that maintenance of intended delegation requires that decisions within the authority competence of individuals be made by them and not be referred upward in the organization structure. Thus managers should make whatever decisions they can in the light of their delegated authority and only matters that authority limitations keep them from deciding should be referred upward. This is possible if authority delegation is clear and managers at each level are sure what authority they have.

A problem comes when two or more managers can decide the things jointly without referring the matter upward but singly none of them can decide. Such a matter may be related with inter-departmental functioning. A single manager can not make decision because of splintered authority. Splitered authority exists wherever a problem can not be solved or a decision made without pooling the authority delegations of two or more managers. For example, production manager of plant A can reduce his costs by some procedural changes inn plant B. However, he can not do this unless he pools his authority with manager of plant B. Alternatively, he can refer the matter upward and positive thing can happen by the action of common superior.

In such a case, it is preferable to consolidate and pool splintered authority rather than referring the matter upward for decisions. However, recurring decisions on the same matter may indicated the need for reorganization and delegation of authority.

5. *Absoluteness of responsibility*: Responsibility is an obligation to get the assigned work done. Since responsibility for the activities assigned to his subordinates. Similarly, responsibility of subordinates to their superiors for performance is absolute; once they have accepted an assignment and the authority to carry it out, superiors can not escape responsibility for the organization activities of their subordinates.

6. *Parity of authority and responsibility*: A common saying and in management is that 'authority and responsibility should always be equal'. It implies that since authority is the discretionary right to carry out assignment and responsibility is the obligation to accomplish them, authority should correspond to the responsibility. Thus responsibility for actions can not be greater than implied authority delegated, nor should be less. This parity is not mathematical but, rather, coexistensive, because both relate to the same assignment.

Both under-delegation and over-delegation are equally bad. In an organization, authority is the cement of the organization structure. With the increasing size, specialisation, and need for employee development, adequate delegation of authority becomes a prerequisite for organizational success. Proper delegation of authority increases operational efficiency, satisfaction of need for autonomy, feeling of involvement, and saving time of superiors. Inadequate delegation, on the other hand, creates lack of commitment, lack of commitment, lack of initiative, frustration among employees, and over-burden of superior managers. Similarly over-delegation also affects organizational operation adversely. In this case, a manager may have authority for those actions for which he can not be held responsible. Thus a tendency may develop to avoid responsibility. Moreover, authority without responsibility may develop unhealthy trend in the organization for concerning more and more authority jeopardizing the organizational objectives.

Measures for effective delegation

Effective delegation denotes distribution of authority at various points of the organization so that managers can take actions according to their responsibility. Responsibility for adequate delegation of authority lies mostly with superiors particularly with top management. However, at the same time, role of organizational prescriptions and subordinate managers is also important. In order to make delegation effective, actions should be taken in all these directions. Following are some measures which will help in making delegation more effective.

1. *Making the potential delegator feel secure*: Typically the non-delegator is a hard worker, fully competent, but he may feel insecure in his job. This is partially the reason why he surrounds himself with less competent people or in any event those who lack the courage to challenge him. He wants to continue as the unchallenged

superior and to be looked upon as a necessary man in the organization team. Therefore, there is a need for creating a feeling for security for him. A number of things can be done for this. First, it should be made very clear that his job and position is secure so long he continues to contribute to organization. Second, his contributions for the organization are not being questioned and attempts are to make him even more effective manager. Third, some apparent status like office and other facilities can be grated to him. Granting such privileges reflects in part a manager's appraise through outward manifestation of his subordinate management members.

2. *Creating awareness for need of delegation*: Many managers are not fully aware about the need for adequate delegation of authority. They do not realise that they should do only what their subordinates can not do. In this way, they can multiply themselves and their efforts. This happens specially in the case of those managers who come from operative level and continue to make decisions which their subordinates cân do. Through proper education and training, such managers can be convinced about the need for better delegation.

3. *Determining decisions and tasks to be delegated*: Delegation is adversely affected because there is no clarity about what is to be delegated. A simple and direct means for solving this problem is to list for the delegator all types of decision and tasks that must be performed and then rate each one in terms of (i) their relative importance to the total organization and (ii) the time required to perform. this information will serve to determine what types of decisions and takes should be delegated. Usually those decisions and tasks that are relatively less important and more time-consuming should be delegated.

4. *Establishing conducive organizational climate*: An organizational climate free from fear and frustration goes a long way in determining the success of organizational processes including delegation of authority. Organizational climate is essentially psychological and social in character. In conducive organizational climate. Manager feel confidence that delegation of authority will be rewarded and penalised. Further delegation of authority should have the support of top-label management. It should be reflected in adequate delegation from top level and also in such things as a reasonable and satisfactory compensation, an impartial means for a manager's work, and continuous management development.

5. *Choosing the delegant wisely*: Among unfortunate things that can happen with poor subordinates is that work dos not get done. When the results do not appear, the delegator is accountable to his superior in turn. This requires that the delegator must make a careful selection of the person to whom the work is delegated. He must be sue that the man is able to carry the degree of responsibility and effort contemplated in the assignment. Apart from selection, the delegants have to be properly trained and oriented to certain work because many times spurious consented may not have authority to select their own subordinates. Further, the superior should not delegate beyond the capacity of his subordinates.

6. *Tieing delegation with planning*: A pitfall in delegation is that sometimes it is undertaken without consideration of what is to be achieved by delegation. To delegate without knowing and Keeping in mind objectives leads to chaos. Therefore, authority should never be delegated to the managers before the objectives are clear. Authority is utilised to achieve objective and the extensiveness of the authority should be in keeping the type of activities performed in attaining the objectives. It is better to delegate authority for achieving specific results. Specific results and objectives for each activity can be defined when there is proper planning in the organization.

7. *Delegating authority for whole job*: It is better to give the delegant a chance to participate in a complete undertaking. Broad rather narrow projects serve best imagination and stimulation of ideas. Such assignments serve as an effective means of testing a man's ability to manage and of building his confidence. Frequent delegation on the same subject matter may covey a feeling that the delegator does not want to do the job and wants to get rid of unpleasant job through delegation. However, through the delegation for whole job, this problem can be overcome.

8. *Developing appropriate control techniques*: Since a delegator remains responsible even for the tasks he has delegated to his subordinate, he must ensure that his subordinates get the work done. Therefore, proper control and monitoring techniques should be developed to ascertain that delegated authority is being used properly. This does not, however, mean that control techniques interface unnecessarily with the day to day sanctioning of the subordinates. These should be broad based and should focus attention major deviations from the plans.

Organizational structure

Based on the analyses of classical theories neo classical theories and modern theories of organization the organizational structure can be classified under the following design; (i) Bureaucratic structure, (ii) functional structure, (iii) Divisional structure, (iv) Project structure, (v) Matrix organization, (iv) Free form organization.

(1) Bureaucratic structure

The term bureaucracy has been used widely with invidious connotations directed at government and business. However, the term bureaucracy in this manner, that is, as a synonym for inefficiency is not technically accurate but it should be looked as a type of organization designed to accomplish large-scale administrative tasks by systematically coordinating the work of many individuals. Max weber has given the concept of bureaucratic organization in a systematic manner. He has observed three types of power in organizations; traditional, charismatic, and rational legal or bureaucratic. He has emphasised that bureaucratic type of power is the ideal one.

Features of bureaucratic structure

Weber has given a number of features of bureaucratic structure. Accordingly, following features suggest the characteristics of bureaucratic structure.

1. *Administrative class*: Bureaucratic organizations generally have administrative class responsible for maintaining coordinative activities of the members. Main features of this class are as follows: (i) people are paid ad whole time employees. (ii) They receive salary and other and perquisites normally based on their positions. (iii) Their tenure in the organization is determined by the rules and regulations of the organization. (iv) They do not have nay proprietary interest in the organization. (v) They are selected for the purpose of employment based on their competence.

2. *Hierarchy*: The basic feature of bureauractic structure is that there is a system of ranking various positions in descending scale from top to bottom of the organization. In bureaucratic structure, offices also follow the principle of hierarchy, that is each lower office is subject to control and supervisions by a higher office. Thus no office is left uncontrolled in the organization. This is the fundamental concept of hierarchy in bureaucratic organization. This hierarchy serves as lines of communication and delegation of authority. It implies that communication coming down or going up must pass through each position. Similarly, a subordinate will get authority from his immediate superior. However, this hierarchy is not unitary but sub-pyramids of officials within the large organization corresponding to functional divisions exist. Thus there are offices with same amount of authority but with different kinds of functions operating gin different areas of competence. For example, in Government organizations, we can observe separate office looking after particular functions. This happens in business organizations too.

3. *Division of work*: Work of the organization is divided on the basis of specialisation to take the advantages of division of labour. Each office in the bureaucratic organization has specific sphere of competence. This involves (i) a sphere of obligations to perform function which have been marked off as part of an systematic division of labour; (ii) the provision of the incumbent with necessary means of compulsion are clearly defined and their use is subject to definite conditions. Thus decision of labour tires of ensure that each office has a clearly-defined area of competence within the organization and each official knows the areas in which he operates and the areas in which he must abstain from action so that he does not overstep the boundary between his role and those of others. Further, division of labour also tries to ensure that no work is left uncovered.

4. *Official rules*: A basic and most emphasised feature of bureaucratic structure is that administrative process is continuous and governed by official rules. Bureaucratic structure is the antithesis of adhoc, temporary, and unstable relations. A rational approach to organization calls for a system of maintaining rules to ensure twin requirements of uniformity and coordination of efforts by individual members in the organization. These rules are more or less stable and more or less exhaustive. When there is not rule on any aspect of organizational operation, the matter is referred upward for decision which subsequently becomes precedent for future decision on the

similar matter. Rules provide the benefits of stability, continuity, and predictability and each official knows precisely the outcome of his behaviour in a particular matter.

5. *Impersonal relationships*: A notable feature of bureaucracy is that relationships among individuals are governed through the system of official authority and rules. Official positions are free from personal involvement, emotions, and sentiment. Thus decisions are governed by rational factors rather than personal factors. This impersonality concept is used; in dealing with organizational relations as well as relations between the organization and outsider.

Burns and Stalker have given the concept of mechanistic structure which is largely based on the concept of bureaucratic structure. Their mechanistic structure is characterised by division of labour, specialisation, precise definition of rights and obligations, hierarchical structure of control and communication, emphasis on superior-subordinate relationships, instructions from superiors as the basis of operation, emphasis on obedience and loyalty to the organization and greater emphasis on internal knowledge, skills, and experience.

Problems in bureaucratic structure

Bureaucratic structure has been considered once superior than adhoc or temporary structure. It has been termed as rational and ideal leading to efficiency. The efficiency in bureaucratic organization comes through rationality and predictability of behaviour because every one knows the consequence of his action before actually the action is undertaken. However, bureaucracy has been criticised because of its inefficiency and it has been termed as a symbol of inefficiency. There are many dysfunctional aspects of bureaucracy which is referred to as bureaupathology. Looking into the needs of modern organization, bureaupathology has many shortcomings and is, therefore, not suitable. The major problems of bureaucracy are because of the following factors: invalidity of bureaucratic assumptions, goal displacement, unintended consequences, and inhuman.

Invalidity of bureaucratic assumptions

In fact, the sources of bureaupathology lie in the invalidity of various assumptions of ideal bureaucracy. Many authors have questioned the validity of bureaucracy. In most of the case, either the conditions are not found in practice, or even if found, may not result into efficiency. Specially he following aspects of bureaucracy work against efficiency of the organization, though they are supposed to contribute to efficiency.

1. Rules are normally provided for guidelines but often they become source of inefficiency because of too much emphasis on rules, their misuse, and people's apathy from rules.

2. Rigid organizational hierarchy works against efficiency. It emphasises necessary superior-subordinate relationships which are detrimental to cogenial organizational climate.

3. In dealing with people, total impersonal approach can not be adopted because people have feelings, emotions, and sentiments which affect decision-making. Thus people can not work totally according to rules and prescriptions.

A pioneering criticism of bureaucracy comes from organizational psychologist, Warren Bennis. He sees the model as overly mechanical and no longer useful. the flaws and dysfunctions of the bureaucratic organization are extensive, but the main are as follow:

1. It is inhumane and denies man's needs,
2. It is incompatible with the development of a mature personality.
3. It promotes conformity.
4. It does not consider the informal organization and interpersonal difficulties.
5. The hierarchy interfere with communication.
6. Innovation and new knowledge are stifled.
7. It is ineffective in a turbulent environment.

These criticisms are representative of the lack of human aspect of bureaucracy. The thrust of these criticism is that bureaucratic structure makes inadequate assumptions about the real nature beings and does not address itself to the interaction of people within the organization.

Closed-system perspective

Bureaucratic organization has closed-system perspective. Though a social organization can not be totally closed system but it may lean towards closed system in its working. A closed system is self-contained and self maintaining. It is generally rigid and static. It ignores external conditions and makes no allowances for adopting to changes in the environment. In other words, it is viewed as operating within a vacuum. Specific characteristics of closed-system social organization include predictability, rationality, optimisation, internal efficiency, and certainty. Since behaviour is assumed to be functional and all outcomes predictable, those activities that take place in the environment—that is changes in social, political and economic and other factors—can be ignored.

Bureaucratic structure can work well when environment is highly static and predictable. However, the nature of environment for large organizations of today is highly dynamic and heterogeneous. In dynamic environment, more interaction between organization and environment is required. There is high need for information monitoring and processing. Thus an open-system perspective is more suitable for the management of modern-day organization while bureaucratic structure has closed-system perspective.

Adaptive structure

The term adaptive is used here to describe the models which are opposite to bureaucratic organization structure. Other closely similar terms are organic structure, open-system model, fluid or flexible model, or natural model. All these models convey the similar meaning. This type of structure maintains a high degree of openness to inputs from the internal and external environments, and develops mechanisms by which it remains flexible and amenable to change, innovation, and development. Burns and Stalkar have identified following features of adaptive structure.

1. Adaptive structure is characterised by the realistic nature of the individual task, which is seen as set by the total situation of the organization.
2. There is continuous adjustment and redefinition of individual task through interaction with others.
3. Responsibility is not strictly restricted to a limited field of right, obligations, and methods. Problems may not be posted upwards, downwards, or sideways as being someone else responsibility.
4. There is a network structure of control, authority, and communication as against hierarchical structure.
5. There is a lateral rather than a vertical direction of communication throughout the organization; communication between people of different ranks resembling consultation rather than command. Communication consists of information and advice rather than instructions and decisions.
6. Commitment to the organization's tasks and to the technological ethos of material progress and expansion is more highly valued than loyalty and obedience. Similarly important and prestige are attached to affiliations and expertise valid on the industrial and commercial milieu central to the organization.

Thus it can be seen that mechanistic or bureaucratic and organic or adaptive structure differ considerably not only in terms of structural network of relationships but also in terms of associated organizational processes. We not turn our attention to the basic designs of organization structure and various modifications in the form of overlays.

Functional organization structure is, perhaps, the most widely used in the medium and large organizations with limited number of products. The term functional comes form the idea that there are the functions or activities the organization must perform if it is to carry on its business. It seems natural that an organization begins its operations by emphasising the kind of work it must do to meet its objectives. As it grows and division of labour leads to specialisation, the organization has more to do; it adds new specialities and further divides its presently employed specialities.

Functional structure is created by grouping toe activities on the basis of functions required for the achievement of organizational objectives. For this purpose, all the functions required are classified into basic, secondary, and supporting functions according to their nature and importance. The basic or major functions are those functions. When departments are created on the basis of basic functions and a manager feels that his span of management is too wide to manage effectively, which invariably happens in large organizations, several departments are created on the basis of dividing a basic function into subfunctions. For departments may be finance, accounting, personnel, industrial relations, legal, etc. These departments may be created and placed according to their role in the organization. For example, if the organization emphasises product development and innovation, research and development department may be give high status.

Authority relationships in functional structure may be in the form of line, staff, and functional. In fact, the concept of functional authority is very appropriate for functional structure. Thus functional structure is characterised by the following:

1. Specialisation by functions,
2. Emphasis on sub-goals,
3. Pyramidal growth of the organization,
4. Line and staff division,
5. Functional authority relationships among various departments,
6. Limited span of management and tall structure,

Functional structure has certain potential advantages and disadvantages. Whether or not these advantages are realised depends on the specific organization's situation. The establishment of a functional organization becomes necessary as a small organization grows and business activities become more and more complex. In such a situation, there is a need for more formalised and systematic approach to major activities and for increased delegation of authority of decision making throughout the organization. However, top management will continue to control decisions that involve strategic and coordinative variables. The functional structure works better if the organization has one major product or similar product lines. In such case, the organization may take following benefits.

1. Functional structure can result into high degree of specialisation because a unit or department is concerned only one aspect of total activities. Thus the organization can employ greater variety of skills.
2. Functional structure brings order and clarity in the organization by prescribing what one is expected to do. Every one understands his job clearly which adds to efficiency.

3. It promotes professional achievement as a person is restricted to his own area of specialisation. Thus it provides satisfaction to specialists.
4. There is economy in the use of organizational resources because various units of the organization use the centralised resources of a kind. Thus there is no duplication of activities and processes which save resources.
5. There is high degree of control and coordination of functions because all work of one kind is under one manager. Also there is a clear chain of command for communication and authoritative decision. However, from total organization's point of view, this poses problems in control and coordination.

Problems of functional structure

The relative advantages of functional structure are like two-edged swords; they can cut both ways. In some circumstances, they can lead to disadvantages. For example, specialisation may lead to petrochialism and goal displacement, or control and coordination may lead to overload for a manager. There for, if there is too much emphasis on any aspect, there may be dysfunctional behavior of that aspect. The functional structure is not suitable to an organization which takes up diversification, as the new activity being performed by the organization. Thus diversification can not be managed properly within the context of functional structure, of atleast at some level, there may be violation of functional structure. In such a situation, functional structure presents following problems.

1. Responsibility for ultimate performance can not be fixed in functional structure because no one is responsible for product cost and profit. Each department focuses on its contribution to the product, but not the entire product. Only top man is pulling everything together. Not the operations at the tip, where the emphasis should be on longer-range problems but it makes judging the performance of each department difficult.
2. Functional structure essentially generates slow decision-making process because the problem requiring a decision had to go to various departments as all of them have something to say on the matter. As against this, complex and markedly different activities require decision making because time factor is of prime importance.
3. Functional structure lacks responsiveness necessary to cope up with new and rapidly changing work requirements. For example, if the organization decides to add some new business, there is question mark as how to add this because it may mean a new functional structure as the new business can not be easily absorbed by old functional structure.
4. Functional structure offers usually line and staff conflict and interdepartmental conflict. The heightened degree of such a conflict becomes detrimental to organizational efficiency.

The second basic structural form employed by organizations is the divisional structure. While growth through expansion of same line of business forces a small organization to organize on functional basis, growth through geographic and product diversification necessitates the adoption of divisional structure. In India, many companies have diversified into unrelated business and have found functional structure quite unsuitable for them.

Divisional structure, also called profit decentralisation by newman and others, is built around business units. In this form, the organization is divided into several fairly autonomous units. Each unit is relatively self-contained in that it has the resources to operate independently of other divisions. For example, each division has its own manufacturing, engineering, marketing, etc. Each unit is headed by a manager who is responsible for the organization's investment in facilities, capital, and people as well as for unit's development and performance. Divisional structure is similar to dividing an organization into several smaller organizations but it is not quite the same, since each smaller organization is not completely independent. Each unit is not a separate legal entity; it is still part of the organization. each unit is directly accountable to the organization.

In designing divisional structure, there are several issues which should be adequately taken care of. These are: determination of basis of divisionalisation, number of divisions, provisions of corporate staff activities, and relationship between corporate and divisional management.

Suitability of divisional structure

Divisional structure is suitable to organizations having several products with each product having distinct features, for organizations having coverage of wide geographical area, or having distinct market segments. Dividing the organization into several autonomous divisions allows it many of the advantages of functional structure.

Problems in Divisional structure

There are certain disadvantages and problems of divisional structure. Some of these problems are inherent in the system while others emerge because of wrong approach of managements. Following are the major shortcomings of divisional structure.

1. Divisional structure is quite costly because all the facilities have to be arranged for each division. Therefore, unless a division justifies its cost, it should not be opened but its activities should be carried out by another division.

2. Since there is lack of emphasis of functional specialisation, many professionals do not feel satisfied with this structure.

3. Often there is a lack of managerial personnel when a new division is opened because managers working within a division can not work with same efficiency in

other division as they must have acquired the technical competence of that division.

4. Control system is a major problem of divisionalisation. Though each unit is measured in terms of its contributions to the organization, this system does not work properly specially if information monitoring system is not suitable.

Many of these problems can be overcome through sharp focus on tasks and responsibilities of corporate and divisional management, measurement of performance of divisions, long-term policy for performance and incentives, creating more autonomy and decentralisation of authority, and the explicit strategies for both the organization as a whole and its various divisions.

Project organisation structure

The major reform in the traditional functional structure has come from a group of closely related structures having titles such as project management, programme management, systems organization, product management, brand management, and matrix structure. All these have in common that they provide a horizontal grouping together of a number of functions which might otherwise be labelled functional departments and exercising staff and functional authority. Out of these, project organization structure and matrix organization structure have become quite popular. The basic idea behind these structures is that since environment changes very rapidly, three organization must take up various activities on project basis, that is, adding the required ones and deleting the unnecessary ones. Thus the organization can be organic-adaptive one. The project work can be managed in two forms of organization: pure project organization and matrix organization. The pure project organization is suitable for taking small number of larger projects with long duration so that a separate division can be created for each project. Matrix organization, on the other hand, is suitable for taking large number of smaller projects and the activities of various projects can be accomplished through temporary department.

Project organization appears very like to divisional structure except that in the latter various divisions are created on permanent basis while in the former, they are created only for the life time of a project. When a particular project is completed, the concerned division may disappear. However, since a project may continue for quite long time, project may become a sort of permanent. For example, Middleton observes that "a project organization can also be the beginning of an organization effort that eventually becomes a programme or branch organization cycle. The project may become a long term of permanent effort that eventually becomes a programme or branch organization. The latter, in turn, may become separated from the parent organization and be established as a full-fledged division, functionally organized."

The establishment of project organization calls for appointment of a project manager who is responsible for the completion of the project. He coordinates the activities of the project. He prescribes what is to be done, when it is to be don, and bow much resources are required. The functional personnel are drawn from various functional departments and functional managers decide who in their department will perform the task and how it will be done. Thus project manager is a unifying and focal point for the project activities.

A project manager really does not have vertical authority on the personnel drawn from various functional departments, unlike a divisional manager who has line authority over the people working in various functional departments assigned to his division. In the absence of any vertical authority, the project manager mist convince the functional people so that they help him to finish the undertaking within the time. In reality, project manager faces an authority gap. He has responsibility for completing the project but does not have direct authority over the people associated with his project.

Suitability of project organization

For activities which are undertaken on project basis, project organization is the most suitable. Such an activity has following features:

1. It is one-time task and is definable in terms of a single, specific goal.
2. It is infrequent, unique, and unfamiliar to the present organization. Unfamiliarity usually leads to a disagreement as to how the activity should be managed.
3. It is complex and calls for a high degree of inter-dependence along the tasks.
4. There is a high degree of stake in the successful completion of the project. The time factor is critical because if the project is not completed within the stipulated time, the organization may lose heavily because of fine provision due to delay.

When project organization structure is adopted for this type of activity following advantages emerge.

1. Project organization allows maximum use of specialised knowledge which is available to all projects on equally basis. Knowledge and skills can be transferred from one project to another project.
2. It enables the organization to adapt to environmental demands particularly when environmental factors are fast changing.
3. It provides more flexibility for the utilisation of resources in the organization by allocating them to the projects where these are needed.

Problems in project organization

In fact, many of the flexibilities of project organization may turn into problems if proper arrangement is not made for overcoming these problems. A project manager has to face unusual problems resulting from the project management. Following problems are usually experienced in project organization.

1. Project organization creates feelings of insecurity and uncertainty among people in the organization. It has do not have permanent tenure with any project. Thus there is less loyalty of people with the organization.
3. There is lack of clarity among members about their role in the organization. For example, project relationship are not based on the principles of clarity of authority and responsibility and fixed amount of authority. Thus only those persons can work between who have high level of tolerance for ambiguity.
4. Often project manager faces numerous problems because he has to carry responsibility without authority. Therefore, he has to rely on his personal qualities rather than on his official authority. Therefore, if organizational claims are not very congenial, there is high chance of his failure.

These problems are real and a challenge lies before the project manager. It he believes in traditional system of organization, he may not be able to work. He has to change the total philosophy of managing. For example, Cleaned and King stress that a project manager has to take a new approach to his job. Such approach may be: (i) he must become reoriented away from the functional approach to the management of human and non-human resources; (ii) he must understand that purposeful conflict may very will be a necessary way of life as the manages his project across many vertical organizational lines; and (iii) he must recognise that project management is a dynamic activity where major changes are almost the order of the day.

When a project structure is superimposed on a functional structure, the result is a matrix. Sometimes the matrix organization is considered to be a form of project organization plus a functional organization and the terms are used interchangeable. However, a more accurate portrayal would show that the matrix organization is a project organization plus a functional organization rather than a variation of a project organization. The project overlay provides a horizontal, lateral dimension to the traditional vertical orientation of the functional organization. Fig. 15 represents a very simplified matrix organization. Here, the functional department heads have line authority over the specialists in their departments (vertical structure). The functional specialists are then assigned to given projects (horizontal structure).

Matrix organizations seem to flout the traditional organization principle. The hierarchy principle and unity of command are flagrantly violated. Furthermore, the matrix concept does not coincide with thee usual line-staff arrangements. Obviously, a great deal of conflict is generated in matrix organization. An organizational specialist with IBM has observed that, besides fostering conflict, the matrix structure discourages informal groups and the nurturing of supervisor-subordinate relations. After ten years' experience with the transition form traditional hierarchical to matrix organizations, he concluded that the matrix structure 'has seemingly reduced participant motivation for all but the most aggressive personalities, and has reduced corporate loyalty and identification with the organization'. These disadvantages are countered by many positive aspects of matrix organization. The matrix organization attempts to incorporate the best of both worlds. In an electric manner, it includes the positive aspects of both the functional and project organizations. Cleland and king summarize these advantages are follows:

1. The project is emphasized by designating one individual as the focal point for all matters pertaining to it.
2. Utilization of manpower can be flexible because a reservoir of specialists is maintained in functional organization.
3. Specialized knowledge is available to all programs on an equal basis; knowledge and experience can be transferred form one project to another.
4. Project people have a functional home when they are not longer needed on a given project.
5. Responsiveness to project needs and customer desires is generally faster because lines of communication are established and decision points are centralized.
6. Management consistency between projects can be maintained through the deliberate conflict operating in the project-functional.
7. A better balance between time, cost, and performance can be obtained through the built-in checks and balances (the deliberate conflict) and the continuous negotiations carried on between the project and the functional organizations.

Theorists who advocate a matrix structure maintain that these advantages overcome the inherent disadvantages. Many modern organization which are facing tremendous structural and technical complexity have no choice but to move to such an arrangement. The critical need for coordination and functional interrelationships can be met by adding a horizontal dimension to the formal structure.

In many modern organizations a lateral interface has developed. It occurs when people, departments, or systems must meet to support one another. Interface, more precisely, is 'the contact point between relatively autonomous organizations which are nevertheless interdependent and interacting as they seek to cooperate to achieve some larger system objective.' Such and interface can result in either conflict or cooperation. The matrix organization depends on effective leadership to overcome the obstacles and attain the positive attributes of coordinations and communication. In this regard, Scott and Michelle offer the following conclusion: 'the scalar indeterminacy which exists between project managers and department managers gives rise to a number of transactions that can be only described as political.' Cleland and King maintain that only significant conflicts should be presented to a common superior for resolution. In other words, they recommend that management by exception become the rule in a matrix organization. The right of appeal should not be exercised unless the following two criteria are met:

1. The issue is clearly drawn, with alternatives and costs described.
2. It is a salient project-functional issue.

This type of systematic approach helps to overcome some of the difficulties of matrix organization. This form of organization will undoubtedly become more widely used in the future to meet the demands of increased complexity. It should always be measured against the same high standards that are applied to the classical structures.

Free-form organizations

Closely related to the project and matrix models are the free-form, sometimes called the naturalistic or organic, structures of modern organization. The free-form model is based on the premise that the purpose of an organization is to facilitate the management of change. To accomplish this objective, the structural arrangements are highly adaptable and flexible. There are no prescribed or rigid roles and the internal structure is not allowed to solidify. Under the free-form concept, there is no one way of organizing. Organizations that operate under he free-form concept tailor-make the structure to fit their particular needs at a particular time. Usually, the traditional, departmentalized functional structure is replaced by self-contained profit centers. These organizational units are results-oriented and their members are managed as a team. Individual action within a team attempts to incorporate the behavioral approach to management. Participation, self-control, individual initiative, independent judgement, open communication, and sensitivity are some of the human factors that are encouraged and facilitated by free-form organization.

In a sense, the free-form organization is merely an extension of the 'Great Organizer' afraid Sloan's model of decentralization. An executive group at the tip of the organization maintains centralized control over highly decentralized profit centers. Keeping the profit centers autonomous facilitates the management of change because whole units can be dropped or added with little description to rest of the organization.

Besides the decentralized pattern, there are two major characteristics common to all free-form organizations. First, they make extensive use of computerized information systems, especially to evaluate the performance of various organizational units. Second they are populated by young, dynamic managers who are willing to accept calculated risks. These executives usually have had previous experience in one of the firms which pioneered the free-form concept. The firms include Litton Industries, Xerox Corporation, and Textron, Inc.

Companies that have come to depend on a free-form structure are those which must be highly adaptive to products or services that are on the frontiers of public consumption (for example, pollution control devices). The free-form structure provides the opportunity for technological and operational leverage. Technologically, it can take advantage of external change and the transfer of new knowledge. Operationally, it can easily spread, reduce, or prune to meet economic, technological, or social contingencies, even in the short run. Many types of organizations, including conglomerates and highly technical firms, have found the free-form structure to fit their needs.

Team and traditional management

Team approaches to management have emerged over the last decade as a leding intervention strategy. Their popularity may rival that of job enrichment over the last generation and of human relations training for supervisors two generations back. Just as a variety of constructs, measures, and models were developed to guide research on leader behaviour and job characteristics, students of team-oriented management systems are currently developing approaches that may help guide research on teamwork. Notable contributions in this area have come from Cummings, Hackma, Manz and Sims, and Sundsrtom, Demeuse, and Futrell. Yet much of the work on team-oriented management systems remains conceptual. Empirical contrasts between groups labeled as self-managing teams and other work groups are rare at best, and most of those focus on productivity as an end result. By what mechanism(s) does autonomous team operation change the experience of employees such that these employees might work more productively? Literature reviews such as that of Pearce and Ravlin cite no empirical contrasts between more autonomous and more traditional work groups that would provide evidence for this question. Thus the present study compares members' perceptions of the dynamics of work groups expected to operate as self-managing teams with those expected to operate as traditional work groups in a naturally occurring quasi-experiment.

Perhaps the most widely cited definition of self-managing work teams is that of Hackman. He identified three discrete categories of work teams manager-led, self-managing, and self-designing. Manager-led teams are those responsible only for the execution of assigned work. Self-managing teams are those for which management retains responsibility for the design of the group as a performing unit while team members assume responsibility for monitoring and managing their own performance processes. In self-designing teams, members also take on design responsibilities for decisions concerning task structure, membership changes, and norms for making decisions.

The isolation of areas of authority in Hackman's definition over simplifies the variation between groups with respect to the exercise of participation, influence, and authority. Parties to such decisions will not always agree on the implications of a given decision for task execution, performance processes, and team structures and therefore will often not see that decision as clearly falling into a single responsibility category. Research on Vroom's normative model of decision making indicates that a variety of situational factors and managerial style preferences affect the nature and degree of subordinate group member involvement in workplace decisions.

The relative influence of the affected parties can be expected to vary from one decision to the next. Ultimately work team members and their managers must share control of such decisions, to a greater or lesser extent. Work groups and their managers will settle into some pattern of activity from which one could generalize their relative decision influence. We will regard a team that is generally expected by managers and members alike to exert considerable influence over just what work the group is to do and how the members are to do it as a self-managing team. We will refer to traditional work groups as those in which the members are generally expected to exert little influence in these matters.

If self-managing team are expected to make group decisions on matters typically decided by external leaders, they must establish patterns of interaction among members that would not occur if external leaders made those decisions. Thus we should expect contrasting group dynamics between self-managing teams and traditional work groups. However, none of the self-regulating work group studies reviewed by Pearce and Ravlin tested for differences between work groups expected to be self-managing and those expected to operate as traditional work groups.

Our study of differences between self-managing teams and traditional work groups draws on the work of Seers, which suggested the analysis of social exchange dynamics between an individual and the peer group in the definition of members' team roles. The importance of peer groups in role making has been well documented. In recent years, how ever, most role-making research and most research on work teams has neglected peer group social exchange dynamics even as the latter set of authors all suggest the need for new approaches for understanding team effectiveness.

We should expect peer role making to contrast between self-managing and traditional work teams. The roles of team members are defined and modified over time through the reinforcement of reciprocal actions. Any member of role set can send expectations for the behavior of an individual in a focal role and can respond to subsequent behaviors. An implicit process of negotiation occurs as various role senders interact with a focal role occupant. Some of the sent role expectations may be inherently contradictory, some may be too vague, and some may call for a behavior that a focal member is unwilling or unable to display. When a focal member does exhibit behavior consistent with role sender expectations, those expectations and behaviors are reinforced. Further, each focal member is actually a member of a role set in relation to other individual members. A complete mapping of all these interpersonal interactions and reinforcements clearly exceeds human cognitive capacities. Yet a cognitive map summarizing the general pattern of expectations, behaviors, and reinforcements must emerge such that members can identify behavior that is part of their role and distinguish it from behavior that is not part of their role.

The ideology of team-oriented management systems promotes the development of within-group structures that are more egalitarian and less hierarchical than traditional work groups. This ideology also promotes the taking of roles that are more flexible and less specialized. Pressure for egalitarian structure and role flexibility might temper the forces differentiating peer roles that have been studied in employee groups. The less differentiated the roles, the less important are role messages coming from any one individual, with greater importance becoming attached to convergent expectations. Consistent role messages from many group members signal a focal role occupant that an expected behavior is important to the role being negotiated, and should thus be incorporated into a received role. Divergent messages from undifferentiated peers may simply generate role conflict and role ambiguity. Under a team system, a member's received role should correspond closely to perceptions of what other, in general, on the team expect.

Peer role making must coexist with supervisory role making. Graen analyzes the potential for compatibility or conflict between a leader's preferred role for a subordinate and the role preferred for that subordinate by peer group members. Graen emphasized supervisors as individual role senders because of the position power inherent in this role. Yet one of the hallmarks of emerging team approaches to management is the de-emphasis of formal supervisory roles. Thus spans of control are widened and a number of supervisory jobs are eliminated. To the extent that work groups are expected to be self-managing, members are encouraged to substitute group decision making and consensus formation for the direction of a supervisor. Therefore members of self-managed work teams should experience more peer-directed role-making interaction than their counterparts in more traditional, hierarchically oriented management systems.

Exchange quality in team role making

The team-member exchange construct was designed to address an employee's exchange relationship to the peer group as a team. Team-member exchange quality assesses the reciprocity between a member and his or her team with respect to the member's contribution of ideas feedback, and assistance to other members and, in turn, the member's receipt of information, help, and recognition from other team members. Comparison and contrast of the team-member exchange quality construct to other constructs applied in our literature might be the most effective way to define it. Team-member exchange quality was conceived to be somewhat analogous to the leader-member exchange quality construct developed by Graen and Cashman. Both constructs are based on the logic that relationships rather than jobholder positions are the building blocks of organizational structure. Both constructs focus on the reciprocity between parties to an exchange relationship rather than on attributes or behavioral styles of either party to the relationship. In both cases, the reciprocity must be analyzed in terms of the resources each party may bring to bear on the exchange process. The leader-member exchange construct is designed to joint address employee role making and supervisory leadership, whereas the team-member exchange construct was conceptualized to jointly address employee role making and work team dynamics. Team-member exchange differs from leader-member exchange in that it is not dyadic. Team-member exchange reinvokes a key assumption from Jacobs' work: Individuals can and do aggregate their perceptions of role episode exchanges across members of the work group. Such aggregation may in fact be necessary to establish the identity of a group as a meaningful team in the eyes of its members as well as to give meaning to the members roles within that group. Members expect to receive internally consistent role messages from other team members and must respond in an internally consistent fashion to those role messages to establish identifiable roles within a team. Reciprocal behaviors exchanged between a member and the other who constitute a team thus reinforce the identity of both the member's role and a group as a team.

Team-member exchange should also then be compared to team identification. Team identification is a special case of the more general concept of identification with a psychological group. Identification focuses on the extent to which an individual incorporates his or her role in relation to the group in question within the self-concept. Team identification hinges on labeling the state of existence of the individual member—does the member clearly perceive his or her peers as a meaningful group and the self as an integral part of that group. In contrast, team-member exchange presumes the meaningfulness of the peer group and the member's role within that group but does not presume the member's cognition of that meaningfulness. It reflects the ongoing process of reciprocation between the member and the group rather than an individual's choice of a psychological label. A member high on identification would label her or himself as a team member but may behave in a fashion that is only loosely coupled to that group. The member high on team-member exchange would interact with other group members in a relatively tightly coupled manner, but may or may not cite group membership in order to present oneself to a stranger. Greater team identification is a likely consequence of greater team-member exchange.

To borrow the sports metaphor, team-member exchange quality should therefore reflect the extent to which individuals have established their roles as "team players," whether or not they would invoke that description. Individuals experiencing a high level of team-member exchange quality contribute more cooperative and collaborative efforts and receive more social rewards in the bargain, whereas members low on team-member exchange direct fewer efforts toward the group and receive lesser social rewards. To date, empirical studies have shown team-member exchange direct fewer efforts toward the group and receive lesser social rewards. To date, empirical studies have shown team-member exchange quality to be related to member job satisfaction and performance as well as to the identification, commitment, and turnover rate of team members.

A key extension of the present study is to consider the average level of team-member exchange across a group as a meaningful variable at the aggregate level. Groups in which most members experience high quality team-member exchange relationships should be effective teams as well as provide satisfying experiences to members. Of course, analysis of data aggregated to the group level cannot be interpreted to mean the same thing as the analysis of individual-level data. For team-member exchange, individual-level analysis involves the individual employee's perception of his or her reciprocity with other team members. When these data are aggregated to the group level, we are dealing with the average reciprocity across the group, which may reflect the extent of teamwork in that group. By way of contrast assessment of cohesiveness at the individual level of analysis should reflect the employee's perception of the attractiveness of the group. At the group level, aggregated cohesiveness should reflect the relative capacity of the group to induce member conformity.

If a group's average score on team-member exchange reflects the level of member teamwork, members of self-managed teams should report a higher level of team-member exchange quality than traditional group members, and team effectiveness ought to be positively related to team-member exchange at the group level of analysis. Therefore we state three hypotheses:

1. Members of self-managing teams will report higher levels of team-member exchange quality than more traditional work groups.
2. Team-member exchange will reflect difference between self-managed work teams and traditional work groups beyond those attributable to other internal dynamics such as cohesiveness and coworker satisfaction.
3. The average level of team-member exchange within a self-managed work team will correspond to group effectiveness.

Method

The present study was begun about five years after the opening of a small branch plant within a product division of a major industrial manufacturer. Employee teams established within functionally differentiated departments were given a high degree of autonomy. The original plan, known as "Team Concept," called for teams to decide how they would carry out their tasks, whether individuals had qualified (through proficiency in all tasks performed within the team) for "pay for knowledge"-level moves, and how to handle matters of member discipline. However, much of that autonomy eroded over the years since the plant opened due to reactions to disciplinary problems and union-management power struggles. Complaints from hourly employees to the effect that the team concept had become a farce were common.

Eventually, plant managers and union leaders reached agreement that the team approach needed revitalization. Given the deterioration of team autonomy, a decision emerged to concentrate efforts to revive team autonomy with the manufacturing departments while delaying further effort to nurture team autonomy in support areas such as quality control and production control. Support teams were to present their case if a majority of members voted a preference to have a team leader. The two quality control teams argued that their work directly involved the manufacturing process and self-selected themselves into the revitalization. In the remaining support teams, coordinators lost formal recognition of their role. Thus these teams came under the direct responsibility of a first-line supervisor and became more traditional in their operation.

The revitalization strategy attempted to reinforce the locus of authority within teams by strengthening the role of peer-group leaders within the teams. Manz and Sims, self-managed teams generally have a member who is elected as an internal leader within the team and the new local bargaining agreement defined the role of such an internal team leader. These team leaders would personally perform the assembly line set-up functions of the team that previously had been done by a technically qualified member of the team on a volunteer basis.

Leaders would be expected to act as facilitators for the team's internal accomplishment of traditional supervisory functions. Functions thus falling within the team's scope of responsibility included training for individual team members on all jobs done by the team, scheduling the task assignments of members within the team, setting team goals, establishing housekeeping and safety plans, conducting team meetings, and maintaining a high level of participation by all team members. Team leaders were to serve as liaison to a first-line supervisor on all facets of team responsibility. Thus team leaders were positioned such that they were accountable for the extent to which the teams internally met their responsibilities, even though they retained their union status as hourly workers and lacked the formal authority of a supervisor. Therefore the person that team members elected as team leader had to be a member who was respected both technically and personally. In contrast, the previous role of the peer-group leader, called a coordinator, focused mainly on group maintenance. Once the leaders had been selected by the teams, leadership exchange training sessions were conducted by one of the authors for the new team leaders and for the supervisors with whom they worked.

Design

Management's attempt to revitalize the team approach presented a natural opportunity for a two group quasi-experimental design. In the terminology of Cook and Campbell, this design represents a combination of the reversed-treatment nonequivalent control group design with the nonequivalent variables design.

The manufacturing teams that received revitalization efforts might be expected to show gains in team-member exchange as well as other group dynamics measures, while the support teams, which no longer had to observe the pretense of team concept, should show declines in such team-oriented responses. Yet this expected pattern of change in opposite directions should not be expected for outcome variables that are not oriented toward team or group dynamics, such as task autonomy or satisfaction with the work itself. The combination of these two quasi-experimental design features should between the team and the traditional areas that were not in evidence before the revitalization program as a result of that program. Because management did allow support teams to petition their assignment in the revitalization effort, the possible effects of self-selection on the data must be considered.

Procedure

Questionnaire data had been collected from 156 of the 178 hourly employees before the revitalization was planned. Across the plant, 65% of the employees were male, 63% were under age 41, 73% were White, and 56% had some education beyond high school. None of the demographic variables differed between the team and traditional areas. The follow-up questionnaire was administered to 152 employees 3 months after the separation between team and traditional areas and 12 months after the initial data collection. The matching of the respondents' questionnaires from the pre-and postsurveys relied on the permission of the respondents to identify their surveys with a code number. One hundred and twenty-three employees agreed to the identification procedure. Of these 123 employees, 13 had transferred teams between the team and traditional groups, and were therefore excluded from further analysis. Of the remaining 110 employees, 7 were excluded due to missing data. Among the 103 included respondents were 8 whose faced satisfaction scale averages were computed despite missing data on 1 or 2 of the scale items. Thus 58 employees from seven manufacturing teams participating in the revitalization attempt represent the "team" contrast group used in this study and 45 employees from five support teams who began reporting directly to a first-line supervisor represent the "traditional" contrast group. No significant differences were found between the 103 employees used for this study and those dropped from the sample.

Measures

Group dynamics: Three of these four measures were taken from the work of Seers. Employee perceptions of the cohesiveness of their team were measured with a 4-item scale with an internal consistency estimate of α =.08 at the pretest and α =.75 at the posttest. A sample item reads "Our team seems to have a strong sense of togetherness." The reciprocal exchange quality of an employee's relation to the team was measured with a 10-item scale with internal consistency of α =.83 at both the pretest and posttest. Half of these items asked about the member's contributions to the team while the other half asked about what the member received from the team. Perceptions of the effectiveness of team meetings were assessed with a 4-item scale with α = .83 at pretest and α = .84 at posttest. A sample item reads "our team meetings resolve tension and conflict." The fourth group dynamics measure was an 18-item satisfaction with coworkers scale taken from Graen, Dansereau, and Minami. Its internal consistency was α = .88 at pretest and α = .91 at posttest.

Decision locus. This measure included three items. Each asked respondents to select a description of how a particular kind of decision generally was made. The five descriptions were

1. Supervisor makes the decision *alone.*
2. Supervisor makes the decision *based on team input.*
3. Team leader makes the decision *alone.*
4. Team leader makes the decision*based on team discussion.*
5. Team members make the decision by *group consensus.*

The three kinds of decisions identified addressed work methods, individual task assignments, and qualification for pay-level moves. Internal consistency across the three items was estimated at $\alpha = .61$ at the pretest and $\alpha =.67$ at the posttest.

Nonequivalent dependent variables. These referent variables were included in order to help establish the context for interpretation of differences measured by the group contrast variables. Autonomy was measured by the single item from Section 1 of the Job Diagnostic Survey. Intrinsic satisfaction with the work itself was assessed with a 10-item scale taken from Graen, Dansereau, and Minami. Its internal consistency was $\alpha = .78$ at both the pretest and the posttest. Overall satisfaction was assessed with Hoppock's 4-item general job satisfaction measure. Internal consistency for this measure was $\alpha = .83$ at the pretest and $\alpha = .84$ at the posttest. Supervisory satisfaction measured with a 15-item measure taken from Graen, Dansereau, and Minami. Its internal consistency was $\alpha = .89$ at both the pretest and posttest.

Company records. Records of production efficiency and employee absenteeism were kept only by department and not for individual employees, owing to the de-emphasis on individuals under Team Concept. These records were available for five departments, all of which were manufacturing departments. One department included two teams, but the other four departments each housed a single team.

Results

Because our contrast groups are nonequivalent and not randomly constituted, we must consider ways in which their baseline differences might confound the differences attributable to the distinction between team and traditional management systems. The two nonequivalent groups could have held different opinions on Team Concept as a managerial system, and they could have had important baseline differences with respect to the dependent variables used in this study. Therefore, post hoc *t* tests were conducted between the two groups on all of the dependent variables as well as a single item agreement scale asking whether the "basic idea of team concept is a good idea." The only significant difference existing before the revitalization program was in supervisory satisfaction. Employees assigned to the team area.

A repeated measures multivariate analysis of variance was conducted to assess the overall differences between the team and the traditional groups over time. The main effect for group fell short of significance. However, the main effect for the overall change over time was significant, $F(9,93) = 3.39, p<.01$, as was the interaction test showing the differential change over time between groups, $F(9,93) = 4.37, p<.001$. Thus although our nonequivalent groups were generally comparable with respect to the variables we studied, their reactions to the revitalization differed significantly.

To interpret effects, we examined the accompanying univariate test results. The univariate test results for the overall change across time show significant declines for team-member exchange and task autonomy. For the interaction tests of the differential change between groups, there was no interaction for autonomy or work satisfaction and the meeting effectiveness scale showed only a marginal effect. All of the other measures showed interaction. Inspection of the means indicates that the team area did not differ from the traditional area on any of the group contrast measures before the intervention but did differ on four out of five measures afterwards, including team-member exchange. Thus our first hypothesis was supported. Among the nonequivalent referent measures, the team and traditional areas differed only with respect to supervisory satisfaction before the intervention and only with respect to general satisfaction afterwards.

To examine whether the interaction effect for team-member exchange could be parsimoniously explained in terms of other group dynamics, RoyBargman stepdown *F* tests were conducted. The test for team-member exchange was significant, $F(1,98) = 3.97$, $p<.05$, even after variance associated with cohesiveness, coworker satisfaction, and meeting effectiveness was extracted, thus supporting our second hypothesis.

Although the improvements in the questionnaire data for the team area were generally modest, overall internal production efficiency for the plant increased by 15.4% and the plant's absenteeism rate declined by 16.1%. Additional analysis of the department in absenteeism, efficiency, and the mean levels of the questionnaire measure. Only those questionnaire measures having relatively little within-department variation, were aggregated for these department-level analysis.

The actual changes varied markedly and systematically across departments. Because there were only five departments involved, further analysis used only the ranks of these changes with respect to each variable. Spearman rank order correlations were then computed between these changes in efficiency and short term controllable absenteeism and changes on the questionnaire measures. Increased efficiency was most notable for teams reporting greater team-member exchange, thus supporting our third hypothesis. A similar effect for cohesiveness was marginally significant. Decreased absenteeism was most notable for teams reporting higher overall satisfaction with the job. To test whether differences in team size might explain any of these relationships, the correlations of efficiency and absenteeism with team size were computed but were found insignificant.

Although previous studies have indicated that self-managed work teams may pay dividends for both enhanced productivity and employee job satisfaction, the unique contribution of this study is the contrast of group dynamics between self-managed work teams and more traditional work teams. Prior to the revitalization attempt, teams from both areas shared a common managerial system as well as the same history and company environment. Certainly the contrast groups differed in many ways, especially with respect to the nature of their work. Yet none of those preexisting differences between the contrast groups caused pretest differences on any of the measures reported in this study except for supervisory satisfaction.

The nonequivalent groups changed in opposite directions, so the reversed treatment feature of the design of this study lessens the possibility of a selection-maturation threat to internal validity. Yet the reversed treatment design alone could not rule out additional threats to internal validity such as the possibility of a group-specific maturation effect, local history, and self-selection into the contrasted groups. Here the inclusion of nonequivalent dependent variables in this study facilitates our contrast of the nonequivalent dependent variables in this study facilitates our contrast of the nonequivalent team and traditional groups. Any extraneous factor that could have generally biased employee responses in the different groups toward positive or negative change would have to have been oddly selective toward specific questionnaire measures.

The fact that differences emerged at the posttest on four of the five group contrast variables but on only one of the referent variables helps to establish that the thrust of the changes centered on the way in which team members worked together. Because task autonomy and intrinsic work satisfaction were not sensitive to the changes, we surmise that the autonomy of work groups involves a different set of forces than those brought into play by task autonomy. Operating with a team approach should not be thought of as a group-level analogue of job enrichment.

Our interpretation of the contrast of team and traditional groups is also limited by our selection of variables. For example, the inclusion of measures of internal and external leadership might have allowed for additional insights on the differences between self-managed and traditional work teams. It is possible that the underlying processes of leadership are substantially the same between salaried, supervisory leaders who have formal managerial authority and emergent leaders who retain peer group status as hourly members of the union work force. If that should prove to be the case, then the term "self-managed work teams" would be misleading, and we should be identifying teams as internally led versus externally led.

We did not incorporate a focus on either external or internal leaders for three reasons. The role of team coordinators was quite unstable as we began our research.

Second, there were frequent reassignments of supervisors as well as rotations of the coordinator role within teams. Third, the commonly assessed dimensions of leader behavior were viewed as inappropriate for supervisors under the Team Concept approach.

We did assess supervisory satisfaction, and it is intriguing to note that this was the only variable to show less difference between team and traditional areas after the intervention than before. The interaction for supervisory satisfaction reflects changes operating exactly opposite to the changes underlying all of the other interactions. The differences on all the other variables are consistent with an increase in autonomy for the team area while the traditional area lost team autonomy. A loss of team autonomy may be expected to lead to closer supervision, which is usually associated with decreased satisfaction. Supervisors in the traditional area did have to take on a more directive role in coordinating the activities of employees, but comments from employees suggested that one supervisor who was reassigned to the traditional area during the study was simply a more popular individual than the one replaced, so the increase in satisfaction may be due more to the persons filling supervisory roles than to the nature of that role.

Another aspect of the study that affects our interpretations is the nature of the revitalization program. Trainers were providing attention to the employees in the team area but had much less interaction with those in the traditional area. The colloquial notion of a Hawthorne effect might suggest that more positive responses from employees could be attributed to an increase in attention. As Katz and Kahn point out, the productivity increase observed in the Hawthorne studies was attributable more to group dynamics than to the attention received by employees. Although attention might bed considered as an explanation for the productivity increase observed for the manufacturing area, it is tangential to out research questions because it cannot explain the concentration of significant changes on the group contrast variables, nor does it explain why team changes in production efficiency were related to team-member exchange and cohesiveness.

The revitalization efforts were designed more to reinforce than to extend the existing team system, so we might expect greater change from the reversion to more traditional management in the support area. Yet tests of within-group changes for the support area over time showed a significant decrease only for team-member exchange. Cook and Campbell note that declining or negative responses in group receiving a "less desirable" treatment, such as the withdrawal of formally designated team coordinators for the traditional group, could be attributable to "inadvertent resentful demoralization". The plausibility of such an interpretation, however, is diminished by the absence of significant declines on any of the affective measures.

Thus the most plausible explanation of the results is also the most straightforward. Emphasis on team autonomy in the team area seems to have increased group involvement in decision making and cohesiveness whereas groups placed under the direction of a first line supervisor experienced decline in member reciprocation. In the traditional area, coordination of member efforts became management's responsibility rather than the team's responsibility. Supervisors would find it easier to coordinate activity by directive, rather than by the kind of mutual adjustment expected among peets. Thus traditional teams would have less need and less opportunity for internal coordination and therefore for the reciprocity indexed by team-member exchange.

Our interpretation of team-member exchanges as an indicator of the kind of internal coordination that may most clearly differentiate the dynamics within self-managed work teams from those within more traditional work teams was also supported by the finding from the stepdown *F* test that team-member exchange explained differences between the two groups be you any attributable to the other group dynamics variables. Also, team member exchange emerged from the group level analysis as the variable most closely associated with gains in group production efficiency. These results stand in contrast to those of Gladstein, where no significant relationships were found between objective performance measures and any variable reflecting group dynamics.

Whereas the mean level of team-member exchange was static for the team area as a whole, there was a clear increase in one department, small increase in two others, and decreases in the remaining two. Although we can only speculate as to the underlying causes of differing departmental reactions, such, speculations may prove valuable for hypothesis generation for future studies. Possibilities suggested from our informal observations and conversations in the plant include effects due to workflow technology and the personal attributes of the members of different teams. The two largest increases for team-member exchange were for the two departments with the greatest workflow interdependence, and the largest decrease was for the department with the least workflow interdependence. To the extent that the average level of team-member exchange in a group reflects coordination activity, these results fit Thompson's observation of the concordance of interdependence and coordination. Workflow inter-dependence may be a key determinant of a work group's average level of team-member exchange quality.

Organisation Development Impacts

The espoused goal of organization development or OD is generally recognized as the installation of lasting abilities to manage ongoing change. It is central tenet of OD that real change happens by cultivating the ability and desire of a workface to perform as needed. Such voluntary change in behaviour is distinct from employer-mandated compliance because it is employee controlled and may have associated positive effects on any related work or nonwork activity. In contrast to OD effects, rule-based mandatory compliance programs are likely to induce beneficial change only in specifically targeted and employer-controlled behaviors. However, evaluating voluntary OD-induced change in behavior as distinct from employer-mandatory behaviour and demonstrating the independent effects of rule-based compliance and OD activity have been problematic for OD researches.

This study contrasted Od-induced and voluntary changes in behaviour with later employer-mandated compliance. The behaviors studied were employee time use patterns related to employee absence. Absence research has noted the emergence of legitimacy-based substitution effects in which employees choose to replace forms of time use prohibited under the rukes with nonwork time uses that replace forms of time use prohibited under the rules with non-work times uses that have not been forbidden. With absence control based on policy and forcement, such legitimacy effects are pivotal in accommodating employee non-cooperation with absence control rules. Systems based on employee cooperation differs from this in that substantial gains can be achieved as employees voluntarily seek way of avoiding absence and committing themselves to work. New ways of acting can emerge in relation to values and beliefs rather than in conformance to positional authority, rewards, or punishments.

Research and evaluation of OD has clustered in to several groups. One group investigates the possibility that a positive-finding that a positive-findings bras colors valuative research on OD interventions. Another group compares types of interventions and associated evaluation strategies. Other recent work by Bullock and colleagues explores ways of using meta-analytic techniques to combine results across case studies.

The quality of OD intervention studies has been criticized on several bases. Observed changes following an intervention could be due to various rival hypotheses including maturation, history, self-selection, and related interaction effects. OD evaluation have also been criticized for focusing on short-term changes, subjectively measured dependent variables, weak instrumentation, and lack of independent investigation. Evaluators of OD research have called for more quantitative data, more sophisticated research designs, and appropriate statistical procedures. They also have consistently called for more longitudinal designs and more frequent measurements to assess permanence of OD change effects. Assessing results and their effectiveness almost contemporaneously does not show whether deferent posttest measurements would support different explanations of OD effects. Besides longitudinal measures and more frequent measurement, Morrison also argued for more complete measurement schemata that allow assessing multiple outcomers related to the dependent variable.

The event time line for this intervention

This article a 2-years study of OD and related effects on a major bus system in a Great Lakes state. The bus system executives direction wished to insitutionalize a system that would provide continuous OD and orgnisation renewal activities to his perpetually crisis-ridden organization. He invited proposals from a consulting firm that previously had completed two planning systems projects for the bus system, including many participation mechanisms. A new contract was approved, despite strong public criticism from riders and city politicians and required consultants to perform nearly 600 days of work within 1 year.

Contract approval was conditional. The executive director wanted to focus on runnel, but the city budget office demanded that the consulting firm address the high level of short-term nonlegitimate absences experienced by the buss system. Furthermore, the contract might not be renewed or extended beyond the first year. After much negotiation, an adaptive stray for achieving both the renewal and absence control objectives was collaboratively designed by the consultants, the executive committee, and the director. This corroborates the assertion of Mirvis that challenging clients have the capacity to encourage adaptive approaches to OD.

Employee time use behaviors were monitored daily, but the events that triggered time use shifts in this study can be viewed in terms of four successive time span. A descriptions of events within the four time spans follows:

The base year

During the year before this intervention began, system managers had been exposed to management development training in management-by-objectives and performance problem-solving techniques. All other employees were excluded. Due to the intervention of city authorities, no subsequent activity occurred to install improved performance managements methods. Without the follow-up, this work became simply one ore of a series of managerial training efforts, so that direct and substantial effects on the behaviour of other employees were not expected. Conversely, if any training effects had already occurred, it seemed reasonable to expect them to be consistent with subsequent OD efforts, which would reduce the apparent effect of subsequent intervention basis for evaluating subsequent intervention effects. A database was generated from archival data to include time use data for all employees during that baseline year. This times span has been referred to as the base year.

The OD phase

An intervention making broad use of OD techniques was initiated to collaboratively collect data, to deigns the organization, to design solution options, to build and work in teams, to integrate those teams through a parallel organization, and to invent a new way to improve attendance at the bus system. These activities, refereed to as the OD phase, consumed the first 6 months of the project and involved almost employees. Due to funding constraints, OD activities were abruptly restricted at the end of the first 6 months. Although this sudden restriction of OD contravenes the accepted ideal model of long-term and continues OD effort, it probably typifies the vast majority of attempts to install and apply OD technology. Because the measurement of targeted behaviors continued far beyond the end of the OD effort. The time span of this intensive OD phase was the first 6 months after the base year. OD activities are described below.

A parallel organization

The major strategy recommended was to create a parallel organization to aid upward communication, cooperation across functions, development of staff, and development of executives as leaders of large system change. The seven unions that represented workers in the system we're invited to get directly involved but declined, although they were included in interview activities and did not attempt to block the project. In addition to weekly meting on project and renewal to black the project. In addition to weekly meetings on projects and renewal issues by an executive committee at the top of the organization, a cross-functional, diagonal-slice team called the Issue Analysis Team (I/A Team) was created as the main working entity in the new organization. This term was trained by consultants groups processes. It was to become strongly instrumental in guiding initial OD efforts and in later project design activities.

Data collection, interviews, and nominal groups

The first 6 months of OD were devoted to extensive data collection about absenteeism and related issues. Field interviews were conducted by the I/A Team and consultants with executives, managers, supervisors, employees, and union leaders. These interviews with the I/A Term and external consultants were voluntary and might be either small-group or one-on-one interviews, but virtually every influential party in the organization was invited to participate. Some interviews when conducted by I/A Team members without the external consultants, but when the presence of a disinterested third party seemed important, the consultants were there. In most case, the selection of other interview participants was left to the discretion of the initial contact person invited, but the external consultant, the I/A Team, and other participants did suggest other parties to include when that was likely to be helpful. In addition, dozens of formal nominal group session involved employees in all occupational groups, shifts, and work locations, reaching nearly all bus system workforce.

Members of the parallel organization paired with consultants and designed problem statements around which to focus group problem solving, conducted round-ribbon sweeps of absence-related issues, discussed issues, ranked is sues, and led plenary session. Each session lasted 3 to 6 hours while participants offered ideas about effects of absenteeism, absenteeism solutions, and incentives for improved attendance. Information from employees was summarized in to "white paper" executive summaries and reviewed by the executive committee in their weekly sessions.

White papers

A central focusing mechanism for OD effort during the first 6 months was the collaborate preparation of white papers by I/A Team members and consultants. These papers were an important channel for integration from outside source with feedback from the nominal groups seasonal and interviews. They also served as visible intermediate outcome of intervention activities. Each paper sent to the executive team for review, comment, and decision clarified some aspect of the bus system situation within a context of theory and accepted human resource practice. Papers were responsive to interview data, nominal group process data, and specific technical issues identified by consultants, executives, and L/A Team members.

Technical papers also were prepared on previous absence control efforts, orientation practices, payroll system coding practices, labour relations practices, legal and arbitrator review of absence policies, and actual research in historical profiles of absence within the bus system. Studies of incentive programs and potential uses of information technology also were written.

Widespread Personal Involvement

During the first 6 months, the exposure of the OD/absence control program was high, making it the subject of much discussion, interest, and speculation. Many employees were actively involved in problem solving and collectively brainstorming solutions to the absence control problem. In the course of contributing to this activity, the internalized some of its goals and recognized ways in which they could personally and immediately reduce absence. Personal involvement and the high visibility of this. OD phase ended for most employees at the start of the supervisory pressure (SUP phase), when the intervention activity shifted from extensive data collection and integration to a collaborative but technically oriented design team mode.

The SUP Phase

In the second 6 months, an information system was designed and built to identify, to recommend, and to support managerial actions for absence control. This became the new central thrust of the project. Unfortunately, there was no funding to maintain the investment in OD activity, so that at the start of the SUP phase OD abruptly ended as far as most employees were concerned. As the OD effort became detached from the workforce the stimulus for self-control was gone. Supervisors acted to fill the void.

Supervisory Pressure Tactics

Instead of continued involvement in planning and initiating change, all but 30 employees found they were back in their perproject situations controlled by well-informed and cynical supervisors with a heightened concern about absence. Supervisors began to pressure workers individually and in meeting and briefing not to engage in short-term nonexcused absence. These and hoc pressure tactics varied from situation to situation but included repeated warnings and verbal reprimands, withholding praise and new opportunities, restricting privileges, nonverbal or verbal censure, and when the supervisor believed such punishment would not be successfully grieved and reversed.

Absence Control System Design

The scope of activity narrowed in these second 6 months, and intensity continued as absence program design options were explored in an extensive collaboration between the I/A Team, executives, and consultants. Using an action research mode, data were collected, options were identified, solutions were tested in field setting, and feedback was used to enhance program content and processes. About 20 to 20 members of the organization, primarily the I/A Team and executive management were intensely involved in efforts that were largely invisible to the other 2,000 employees of the bus system. Although OD activity continued for the see few employees, it lacked the visibility of the prior 6 months activities. The unions chose not to become involved in designing the absence control system, perhaps rightly perceiving it to be a political land mine for which they might larger be blamed. On the other hand, they also took no action to block progress and accepted it as a new managerial practice when the no-fault enforcement model with associated information system support was introduced. Some resistance began later, after information system report became an irrefutable basis for disciplinary action after system installation.

Largely due to the history of hard-core unionism and the emphasis mandated by city authority, the philosophical thrust adopted for absence control by the project evolved as two-part plan. Both the director that a positive and productive work culture should mere from the project, but higher city authorities had blocked the intimal momentum toward a long-term OD effort. Instead, positive and supportive work values were to be propagated by working with troubled employees one-on-one in individually responsive procedures to recognize and resolve absence problems. At the same time, problem-solving efforts at the individual level would be supported with clearly defined and implemented corrective discipline for nonresponsive employees.

Design teams stressed that all process and systems had to kept extremely simple and functional due to low levels of literacy among bus system employee and supervisors. The paperwork needed to calculate policy triggers and to document actions for labour relations purpose was seen as a problem. The workforce involved seven different highly adversarial unions with a history of successfully defeating discipline based policies. Further more, largely defensible and successful discipline in a unionized context requires insistent and well-documented adherence to policy. The situation was to support the program with an absence control information system.

Hundreds of hours were invested in needs analysis, requirements definition, system analysis and design, database design, time use codes design, report and screen design, conversion from the old manual system, testing technical training, data entry training, and implementation steps. Coordination with payroll was important because payroll provided unobtrusive collection of time us data for the absence system. Database codes organization's time use control policies. A precise taxonomy of 44 time use behaves that employees tended to exhibit was identified, along with their relationship to short-term nonlegitimate absence (SNA), short and long-term excused absence (SEA and LEA), time worked (TW), and time scheduled off (TS).

The policy status of legitimate absence was anchored in the labour contract language. The contract allowed employees 7 days of paid "causal leave", which covered both sick leave and personal leave and could be taken at employee discretion with short notice to the organization. (Casual leave encompassed most SEA and was later contractual raised to 10 days a year on year on about Day 822 in return for health care cost concessions in the year the system was installed). Under the Organization's no-fault policies, SNAs were absence of up to 5 days taken after the employee had used up the 10-day allotment of casual leave. Under organizational policies, absence in excess of 5 days automatically became LEAs.

Absence control program design issues extended from choosing a philosophical basis for absence control to the creation of problem-solving steps and research-based policy triggers were identified, requiring supervisory action at specified levels of absence hours or occurrence and assigning responsibility for performance of each problem-solving step. Incentives and recognition programs were designed, as well as explanatory training programs for employees. More comprehensive training program were designed for supervisors, managers, personal specialists, executives, and union leaders who would operate the system. OD results took form through design teams as workable programs was conceptualized and installed for a month of operational testing just before B began.

System operation

At the end of the initial contract year, the project consulting contract was not renewed, so that it lasted only 1 year and encompasses only the OD phase and the SUP phase of this study. This possibility had been anticipated when the parallel organization was included in the original project design and formalized. Because program monies were not extended, OD consultants left the organization 1 year just as the implementation year began (referred to in Figures 1,2, and 3 as "System Operation") As originally planned, members of the parallel organization tried to continue OD and design team efforts on their own. However, they often lacked the influence and impact generated by external consultants who were important symbols of management commitment to change. Also, much of the positive and constructive cultural momentum generated in the workforce during the OD phase had dissipated during the SUP phase in the absence of visible OD. Many workers had increased both short-term and long-term excused absence and were pressing for more time scheduled off. Concerned supervisors had begun informally discouraging and refusing to authorize or rearrange scheduled time off to compel increases in time worked. During the last months of the SUP phase, the absences control system was "turned on" and operated in test mode to train both superiors and workers in its operation.

During testing, the absence control system operated in parallel with the old manual system. Employees and supervisors were shown how it would operate and how it would affect them. They were given an opportunity to experience the effect if their actions triggered absence control began on Day 731, on the day following the developing year. Both supervisors and the workforce began to rely on it almost immediately was able to consistently track and report on employee time use and to prescribe mandatory absence control actions. To ensure consistency in application of the rules. All workers were granted a fully renewed bank of 7 casual leave days as the system started up. This was contractual increased to 10 days on Day 822. Supervisors continued to informally restrict the use of time schooled off but otherwise exercised little discretion in time use control. From this point on across the first year of system operation, all participants basically responded mechanistically to the system.

Hypotheses

The 6 months of intensive involvement and highly visible OD effort were expected to induce a combined positive Hawthorn effect and participation effect among employees involved. Voluntary, employee-controlled decreases were expected during OD in all forms of nonwork, including short-term excused absence (casual leave), time scheduled off, and short-term nonexcused absence. Long-term excused absence was already very low and OD was not expected to change it.

> *Hypothesis 1:* Short-term excused absence an time scheduled off will both decrease significantly during the OD phase as will short-term nonexcused absence, where time worked will increase significantly, proportionately, and in inverse association with these voluntary reductions in nonwork time use.

No new effects were originally predicted during the SUP phase because this phase had not brought the consultants into contact with much of the workforce nor involved any formal policy changes. Ad hoc actions taken by the supervisors during these 6 months were not part of the formal design, and the shift from intensive OD activity to other aspects of the project was not recognized at that time as a causal. In retrospect, we offer the following two propositions for future research, and we have examined them below in the light of our findings.

> *Proposition 1*: When OD activity is truncated, any voluntary and constructive action it has stimulated is likely to erode, especially if the workforce is also subjected to competing pressures.

> *Proposition 2*: When ad hoc supervisory pressure is applied to reduce behaviour that conflicts with organizational goals (such as short-term nonexcused absence) significant unintended increase will simultaneously occur in any alternative nonproductive behaviour that has not been prohibited (non work tine uses).

Short-term nonexcused absence was also expected to drop significantly during system operation, although the no-fault policy and supporting information system determined the nature and timing of virtually all supervisory absence was expected to shift directly in to time worked. The automated system was constructed to operas impersonally and consistently and was compelled to act and continue to act on all policy violations. Therefore, the policy and technology effect during system operation were expected to be more powerful and more predictable than the effects of OD involvement in data collection and project design. This led to Hypothesis.

> *Hypothesis 2*: During system operation, short-term nonexcused absence will be significantly reduced and the time use recovered will shift directly in to time worked.

Once again, no legitimacy effects were posited (time use shift form nonexcused absences in to legitimate forms of nonwork) because the bus system believed that it had excellent control over processes managing long term excused absence (longer than 5 days). Nor when the project started would then have seriously considered time scheduled off as a potential problem area. Consistent with the mandate from city authorities, consultants though subsequent events showed that this position was ill advised, no operation began. We offer the following proposition for future researched and have examined it in light of our findings.

> *Proposition 3:* When management pressure is mechanistically applied to reduce an undesired employee behaviour (as with discipline-based absence control under MIS [management information systems] regulation), substitution effects will occur in favor of any other counterproductive behaviors that are not yet forbidden by policy.

Methodology

The methodology adapted for this study includes elements drawn from conventional cross-sectional techniques in the social science, from conventional time series analysis, and from the process control charting methods of production management. An alternative explanation and example of the method is presented in that examines other theoretical and pragmatic aspects of this intervention by using a different time segment of the database.

Exclusive use of time series of group mean movie values conveyed a number of methodological advantages. For examples, conventional cross-sectional methods compare means for distributions of individual values at two or more points in time. They are typically troubled by nonnormal distributions in the individual data that make normality-based inferences suspect. Group mean values, however, are mathematically inclined toward a normal distribution, so that the problems of non-normality inherent in conventional cross-sectional methods could be circumvented in the present model, which relies exclusively on time series of group mean values. All daily cross sections of individual values were simply averaged to create the respective daily group mean values during preparation of the database and before any further analysis began. In the conventional cross-sectional paradigm, conclusions may be highly suspect because discontinuity between points can hide important alternative explanations of events. For the present model, however, the results have been arrayed continuously and graphically, with confidence limits plotted 2 standard deviations about the mean to permit convenient hypothesis testing across any selected interval within the time frame of the study. The standard deviations are based on the continuous time series of daily changes immediately preceding those group means over time. This dynamic representation of confidence limits about a time-serial plot of the mean for each variable is a direct derivative of process control charts in production management, with upper and lower control limits selected represent the 0.95 confidence limits. Because the entire course of change in each variable surrounding any selected time points evident at a glance, discontinuities and spurious comparison of cyclical to through were easily avoided.

The sample

The sample includes all cases of employee data available and adequately represented within the OD phase and the SUP phase of the project. The data for both the baseline year and the development year were retrieved from available archival records, yielding a sample of 320 cases out of about 2.300. On -line data for those cases during the first year following the OD effort were added. As last entry, attrition, and missing values caused this sample size to change over the 3 year of monitoring, the number of cases underlying the mean on any day varied between 227 and 315 case. Eightyeight percent of the sample were African American and 12% were (mostly) white (85% for the entire population). About 90% were nonsupervisory personnel, and the median age was 37 years (both also true of the entire workforce), roughly 55% were bus drivers with the remainder distributed evenly among mechanics and skilled trades clerical, and supervisory work. Demographical, the sample was quite comparable to the workforce as a whole.

The research database

Working independently from the external changes agents, two of the authors developed a database of all absence time use and related time use behaviors. Those behaviors included forms of time worked, time absent, and time scheduled off. To exploit this database, a systemic time-serial methodology supporting graphical analysis was devised. In contrast to the selective focus and cross-sectional model of conventional was desired level of detail.

To encompass the effect of the project on absence and its related time uses the focal system of behaviors for the research had to include all forms of employee time use, accounting for 8 hours of every day, 365 days per year. Every employee time use event was recorded on a time card in off 44 raw subcategories. Data form those subcategories were later reclassified in to one of the following policy-based supercategories. Time worked was all time worked, on or off the job, including such events as jury, training, and time spent in witness duty on behalf of the bus company. Time scheduled off was all scheduled time off, including weekends and statutory holidays, and disciplinary time use, but under the organization's policies, it was unpaid time off with permission. It was not subject to discipline for failure to report to woke, so from a policy standpoint, it belonged in this category. Short-term nonexcused absence was any unexcused absence of 5 days or less. Short-term excused absence was an absence less than or equal to 5 days designated at the employee's discretion as either casual leave (including sick leave) or a single vacation day. (An employee could use 1 vacation day to cover absence). Short-term excused absence was capped initially at 7 days and absence included all absences of more than 5 days, automatically excused as legitimate under the policy. The possibility that employees might voluntarily choose to forefeet pay and absent themselves for over 5 days was almost unthinkable at the start of the project.

Daily hours of time use for each employee in every category were monitored by the payroll system, from the start of the baseline year every day across the course of the study, including the 3-year span affected by OD. All forms of time use were measured in the same units as hours of elapsed time. As 8 hours in every day for every day for every employee had to be accounted for, the sum of time use per day across all categories for every member of the workforce was fixed at 8 hours. Therefore, the mean annual employee time use across all categories also was fixed, at 2,912 hours per employee in a 364-day year. Because the daily and annual total were fixed for the system of time use variables, a rise or fall in any variable had to offset by a fall or rise none or more others.

The segment of the database used in the present study includes a year of preprogram baseline data (a single annual base value represented as a horizontal baseline 6 months of highly visible OD activity, and 6 months of ad hoc supervisory control during design research and development. Then a year of reliance on the absence control policies and information system followed. To present study spans only the first 3 years of our full 6-year database.

Data were aggregated daily to generate an annual moving total in each category of time use for every worker. The moving totals were then averaged daily across all employees in the sample to calculate daily values for the average annual time use in every category. This captures changes in the mean annual employee time use pattern from the beginning of the od intervention until its initial effects had fully dissipated 2 years later. Eight hours of time use had to be fully accounted for within one or more of the time use categories, each day every employee. The systemic annual limit on mean total time use allowed both a time-serial verification of measurement integrity and direct daily tracking of substitution effects induced by the OD effort.

The underlying procedures described above to smooth out day-of-the week phenomena and other (weekly, monthly, quarterly, and annual) cyclical events reflect methods used in conventional time series analysis. They serve to smooth out spurious effects so that the underlying functional forms of observed change were expected to vary with surrounding events over time but were of secondary interest compared to the underlying paths and sizes of time use shifts through which the changes occurred.

Those time use shifts can be effectively discovered and unequivocally verified using the systemic time-serial procedures below.

Graphical procedures for systemic time serial analysis

Three types of graphical summaries present the result for analysis. First is a graph showing the basic integrity of the system of measures. Second is a set of simple time-serial plots showing the contemporaneous changes in the means for all variables across the course of the study. Third is a set of graphical tools for testing hypothesis about the significance of changes observed in the means of each variable across time.

The fourth element in the analysis, the use of systemic time-serial correlation, is necessary to interpret results. Used in combination, changes in means, their concurrent time serial correlations, and the time-serial confidence bands about the means show the size, direction, path, and significance of time use shifts induced throughout the study.

In all aspects of the analysis, an annual basis was used for time use aggregation and, wherever possible, for evaluating changes. Although the study spans 3 years of the database, only 2 years can be tracked graphically because it takes a year for enough daily values to accumulate so the first annual value can be calculated. The first data point (Day 364) for each variable in the OD phase actually represents its mean total time use during the previous 364-day year. The weekly regression test of measurement integrity required at least seven data points for meaningful calculation: the graphical analyses actually begins on Day 367, in the middle point of that first week.

The test of measurement integrity presented at the top of was designed as follows. A multiple regression model was contracted to test internal consistency between the system of variables and their systemic limit weekly over the 2 years of the analysis. Because all five variables share the same systemic relationship, any of them could have been selected a the dependent variables, and several were tried out with almost identical results. However, short-term nonlegitimate absence has been recognized by prior absence research as an unstable variable that tends to confound absence measurement. In a regression system of several variables, the dependent variable is the only one for which instability cannot be hidden by compensating systemic adjustments across the other variables. SNA was therefore selected as the most variables most likely to undermine internal consistency of the system if measures was given the greatest opportunity to do so, and did not, then the system must be sound. Making use of the 2,912-hour systemic limit, the four other variables were regressed against it weekly over the course of the study intervals as follows:

The other three graphs display the time series of daily means for the five time use variables, revealing some powerful substitution effects. Those mean values are the central substance of all the other graphs and of the time-serial correlations. Together with the test of measurement integrity, they are the evidence that analysis must fully explain. Furthermore, to take full advantage of the systemic measurement model, change in the means must not only be explained but can and should be verified for internal consistency in much the same way that an accounting balance sheet cannonade must be checked. That process is outline in the discussion.

All daily values were moving values calculated arose the preceding 364 days, except when the 6-months duration of the OD phase and the basis for the standard deviations to 6 months. Graphical tests for the significance of changes in each variables to 6 any two points in time can be done at a glance as described below.

Pick any two points Time 1 (earlier) and Time 2 (later) along the plot of **the** means for a specific variable. (See the notations on the point A that is vertic**ally** aligned with (directly above or below) the mean at Time 2 and is either on the **lower** 0.9 confidence limit line (for a increasing variable). Imagine a horizontal line 9 a dotted line from A to B in our examples) passing from point A at the 0.95 confidence limit and reaching back past Time 1 and Time 2 beyond the 0.95 confidence level, such as time worked during the OD phase, this imaginary horizontal line would pass above the mean at time 1. Point B would then occur at or above the plot of the means. In the same way, if a decrease in time use level from Time 1 to Time 2 exceeded the 0.95 confidence level (as it did for time scheduled off during the OD phase) then the imaginary line from point A to point B would the plot of the means at Time I so, that point B would fall below the meant at Time 1. A grid of horizontal and vertical lines is plotted in the background of each graph in figure 3 to allow the plots to be used flexibly at the discretion of the leader.

The standard deviations and correlations used in examining change across the OD phase were based on a 6-months calculation period, because that used all days of dare available. To allow direct comparisons between the OD phase and the SUP phases and to isolate effects occurring within the SUP phase, 6-month statistics also were calculate separately for the two 6-month segments of the development year. Correlations spanning more than one phase (such as those across the entire development year) confound the effects of two sets of stimulus events and are not helpful for identifying the paths of change.

Because a positive correlation means two variables are going up and down together, and a zero correlation means they are unrelated any positive or zero correlation over time shows that a given path is inactive within that period. Negative correlations mean one variable is rising, wherever and shows that the path was active over the period.

Because the time use variables are related systemically, the sum of compensatory changes over any interval must be zero. When the path between any two variables is active and one rises while the other falls, the path and direction of a time use substitution is established. When only one path is active between a variable and any other, the path of changes is uniquely established. When more than one path is active the amount of change in each associated variable shows the size and directions of change associated with each path. In special circumstances when two sets of variables may otherwise be confounded, the logic of the situation can also exclude a particulate path are resolve the ambiguity. if a process of changes is still unclear across an interval, one may also choose a shorter time interval, thereby effectively magnifying can be examined as a distinct event. Taken in combination then, the active paths and the size and direction of changes that occurred, the path through which the time use shifted, and the significance of program effects over any selected interval.

OD PHASE

Activities in the OD phase produced many effects. There was a dramatic reduction in time scheduled off compared to levels during the base year (the year before). Dunning this interval, employees also voluntarily reduced their use of short-term excused absence, which fell sporadically, but significantly. This voluntary compliance with underlying project goals made time worked rise by 80 hours per employee per year across that 6 month period. Time serial correlations across the OD phase confirm that those shifts occurred as predicted, directly from each category of nonwork into TW. Anecdotal feedback from the change agent indicates that workers stopped pressing for time scheduled off, and supervisors reexamined and set aside their past practices of using excessive discipline for absence and of favoritism for allocating scheduled time off. The above change were all consistent with a combined Hawthrone and OD effect a predicted.

Another change also emerge within the OD period. As the time-serial correlation show, one hyproduct of the OD effort was to shift some time uses out of the legitimate forms of nonwork (time scheduled off and short-term excused absence) and in to short-term nonexcused absence. Even though it was the time use that the employer wanted most strongly to reduce, short-term nonexcused absence rose by 8 hours per year. Because disciplinary enforcement of the absence control rules was minimal during the OD interval, this path was not yet well restricted.

When examined in context, the implications of this change become clear. Under the time use control policies, no time use would have been assigned to short-term nonlegitimate absence during this OD phase but was significantly reducing it, which rues out the possibility that all employees experienced a rise in short-term excused absence during this OD phase but was significant reducing it, which rules out the possibility that all employees experienced a rise in short-term accused absence and then in short-term nonexcused absence. Could not have come from a relative minority of employees who did not cooperate with the underlying absence-reduction goal of the OD effort and who had used up their personal allotment of casual leave. Further more, that minority of workers contributed so much additional SNA that they drove the average SNA level for the entire workforce up an amount that was nearly significant at the .05 level. So the change within that minority sub group alone must have been highly significant.

SUP phase

Time worked continued to rise during the SUP phase, but at a much lower than during OD. Although the daily increase in time worked were lower than during the OD period itself. Time scheduled off varied during the SUP phase primarily in association with fluctuations in time worked. The long-term net annual effect on time off was negligible because supervisors noted the increase in time scheduled off and began informally restricting its use.

The greatest change induced during the SUP phase was a significant drop in short-term nonexcused absence. No formal policy, or information system, nor any supervisory training in their use had yet been installed. Nevertheless, annual short-term nonlegitimate absence levels fell by 53 hours during that 6 month interval. The time use shifted not one in to time worked as predicted but also into short-term excused absence, both of which rose significantly across the SUP phase. It is noteworthy,that the forms of nonwork (long-term excused absence and short-term excused absence) that rose in compensatory reaction to supervisor-induced reduction of short-term nonlegitimate absence were both subject to worker discretion. Short-term excused absence had shown significant improvement during the OD phase, whereas long-term excused absence was very low and inactive. During the SUP phase however, long-term excused absence rose, and short-term excused absence reversed its trend and began to rise significantly; both of t here show legitimacy effects as workers began to find allowable ways to avoid work, meantime, time scheduled off also started to rise but was brought down again by supervisory pressure.

Supervisory control and pressure tactics characterized time use control for most workers during the SUP phase of development, and participative OD efforts were restricted to a small fraction of the workforce. Because these two stimulus events both occurred over the same time period their significant but unintended effects are logically inferred from the analysis that follows.

Participating in OD activities induced the earlier voluntary reductions in time scheduled off and in short-term excused absence. Furthermore, the supervisory tactics were restricted by the organization's own policies and could not directly act against the excused or "legitimate" forms of nonwork. So it is reasonable to infer that removing the OD activities induced the increases in short-term excused absence and time scheduled off. Increases in short-term nonexcused absence also occurred during the OD phase and were attributed to the permissive conditions and accepting environment that fostered creative problem solving during OD. The ad hoc supervisory action during the SUP phase occurred in replacement of (and to fill the void left by) the withdrawn OD activities. However, it was also a reaction to the minority increase in short-term nonexcused absence, and it was much more repressive than conditions during the OD phase. Except for closing the path for exploitative minority misuse, there is no logical reason to assume that removing OD would induce a drop in short-term nonexcused absence. So we may infer that the shift toward authoritarian control and pressure triggered the dramatic decrease of short-term nonexcused absence observed during the SUP phase.

Development Year overall

Overall changes during development are less revealing of the change dynamics than events during the OD phase and SUP phase separately, and their time serial correlations cannot be used to identify specific paths of time use shifts. As expects, time worked increases and most forms of nonwork decreased (long-term excused absence was the exception). By the end of the development year, a 99-hour (12 day) increase in annual time worked had been achieved. Sixty percent of that (59 hours) came from unpredicted improvements in the scheduling of time off that had not been previously recognized as a problem.

Unfortunately, much of the initial reduction is short-term excused absence under OD had eroded, and short-term excused absence had actually risen to 60 hours a year, 4 hours above its policy limit of 7 days. (Employees could also use 1 day of vacation to cover an absence and some chose to do so). Long-term excused absence had become active and had risen significantly. In general, the improvement in time worked occurred primarily during the OD effort, and the reduction is short-term non excused absences did not begin until after the OD phase ended, when supervisors began to apply pressure. The enforced reduction in short-term nonexcused absence did not only cause simple shifts into time worked. Instead, employees tested the system, found that excused absence offered loopholes in the policies, and began to use the loopholes.

System operation

This phase included the installation and operational start-up of mechanistic control using the absence control information system. As predicted, system operation caused a continuing and significant decrease in short-term nonexcused absence. Time scheduled off also decreased significantly as the absence control information system raised supervisory awareness of it. But none of the time use recovered from either of those appears to have shifted in to work. The paths were inactive (positive correlations) between time worked also dropped significantly. The effects induced by the OD intervention continued to erode, as short-term excused absence rose all the way to the 10-day limit set by policy and a little beyond.

Each path of time use shifts identified above was verified as an active path with in the respective phase by the negative correlation between the two time use variables involved across that interval. Table reports the active and inactive path within each phase in two seaport clusters and comments on their respective implications.

The correctness of these results as system is verified the sum of the mean time use levels across all variables to be a constant for all cross sections, confirming each time use change against the systemic sum of all others as expected. This is consistent with the R^2 results fort the test of measurement integrity. The OD effects on voluntary time use behaviors were highly significant, corroborating the recent meta-analytic finding by Robertson, Roberts, and Porras that OD tends to have positive effects on various work-setting variables and on individual behaviour. We note that prior to the project employees averaged only 1,775 hours (about 10.5 months) of time worker per year, so there was definitely room for improvement. However, the OD results obtained were also less durable than the consultants had hopped, and only the voluntary (and excused) behaviors (short-term excused absence and time scheduled off) were improved and caused shifts into time worked. The least desirable form of absence, short-term nonexcused absence, actually rose instead, showing a strong minority resistance effect to Od. When these results are examined in light of the logic of events across the OD phase, it is clear that a substantial minority of employees were not reached by the OD effects and that these employees exploited the OD phase and were responsible for the rise in short-term nonlegitimate absence.

Two conclusions may be drawn from examining the OD phase. OD was powerfully effective in introducing voluntary changes raising the amount of work done among workers who were included to comply with the organizations goal. Nevertheless, the OD interventions, workers who are inclined to maximize self-interest at the expanses of the organization may find conditions conductive and begin to do so.

Proposition 1 is demonstrated by events immediately following the OD phase. When OD activity was restricted, it triggered a rise in short-term excused absence and time scheduled off, a significant reversal from the low levels of nonwork achieved for these time uses during the OD activity. The noticeably lower rate of increase in time worked during the SUP phase suggests that if short-term nonexcused absence had not been dropping rapidly and forcing time an organization, effects it has induced may be expected to erode very quickly.

Proposition 2 stipulated that when *ad hoc* supervisory pressure is applied to reduce short-tern nonexcused absence, significant reductions would occur in association with significant increases in any excused nonwork time uses and any gains achieved in time worked. In the SUP phase, short-term nonexcused absence was forced down and some additional gains in time worked did occur, but in the course of events, short-term absence and long-term excused absence both began to rise. We directly targeting but caused significant unplanned and undesired consequences elsewhere.

Hypothesis 2 was also partially supported. Under pressure from the mechanistic application of absence control policies with information system support, short-term nonlegitimate absence was dramatically reduced as predicted. But the time nonlegitimate from this reduction did not go into time worked. Instead, strong shifts occurred of time use into other excused forms if nonwork (short-term and long-term excused absence both rose). Mechanistic and authoritarian control effectively changed its direct target variable. However, the end result was not what the organization wanted because punished. These findings prompted and amply support proposition 3.

Proposition 3 states that, during system operation, the shift of short-term nonexcused absence into excused forms of absence instead of work were a classic legitimacy-based substitution effect. This legitimacy effect co-occurred with mechanistic application of absence control policies under informations system control.

Combining proposition 2 and proposition 3, the evidence show's that, when authoritarian discipline-based methods were used to reduce absence and practical alternatives were available, strong legitimacy-based substitution effects tended to occur instead of compliance to system goals. Because this effect emerged in association with both and hoc supervisory action and mechanistically controlled absence control, legitimacy effects appear to be a likely response to external discipline and authority themselves, not merely to the form of its application.

The results of this study show that OD interventions can be a major lever to change organizations but that their long-term effectiveness is pivotal dependent on continued OD activity. Despite the eroded effects of the OD phase, and assuming the average wage rate was only the $4.25 minimum wage, net savings from just these 2 years of the intervention can be shown to exceed $1,122,000. There also were large indirect cost savings from reducing the "hassle costs" associated with high absenteeism, and to the best of our knowledge, the system is still running.

The data show that OD can product powerful behavioral changes, as large as policy and technology effects, and that voluntary and participative effects induced by OD can erode quickly under pressure from other enforcement based managerial policies. However, OD didn't induce reductions in the least desirable from of non work and, in fact, let it increase some what. This suggests a need to extend OD efforts so that the momentum gathered among workers who are already active can spread to those reluctant to get involved. Possible storages might include combining OD with other tactics, perhaps confidential surveys or interviews, tailored to reach workers who need to resolve private reasons for nonparticipation.

Beyond more extensive use of OD, intervention stray would benefit from a better fit between the patterns started by OD and other employment processes. OD effects can legitimize and trigger change. More formal structures may be appropriate to guide, to support, and to maintain it; especially under pressure from adversarial unionism and politically based funding.

A similar 6-years examined absenteeism effects of an interrupted flexible scheduling program. On multiple cross sections of employee data. Absenteeism dropped sharply during the treatment year and returned to baseline levels when management ended the program. Our analysis illustrates a number of interdependent effects during and after the OD phase. It supports the interpretation that management can lose valuable behavioral gains by stopping visible OD involvement and participation in OD-diagnostic activities and studies. Our results argue for continuous OD and contains involvement of employees and teams in improvement process similar to the Japanese Kaizen philosophy integral to total quality management and manufacturing improvement projects. They also indicate that real benefits can be achieved from ongoing real-time data-based feed-back in to OD interventions. It is very probable that had the results of this evaluation been available to city decision makers before OD activities were restricted at the end of the OD phase, contained OD activity would have funded.

Management Training and Development

Management training and development in India is of recent origin. While training programmes in management development are gaining ground, research in training and evaluation processes and practices are few and far between. Studies of training in action are patchy and are done mostly by researchers, who are not directly involved in implementing the findings.

Hence, a longitudinal study on evaluation of management training and development was undertaken. The research team tried to critically evaluate the process of management training and development with a view to highlight the problems of learning in the training institution and then its subsequent transfer to the job. Since any evaluation study seeks to use the data generated for improving future training programmes, this study in evaluation adopted the action research approach.

The study aimed at

1. Measuring the impact of management training and development programmes.
2. Evolving criteria which guide the evaluation of any training activity.
3. Suggesting a model/strategy for evaluation processes which meet the set criteria.
4. Studying the variables/factors—individual, psychological and organisational—that could influence the learning derived through the programme.
5. Preparing the required tools/techniques essential for measuring the impact of training.

Evaluating training has always been a difficult process. By adopting the action research approach, one of the objectives of the researchers was to evolve evaluation criteria which will gradually enhance the effectiveness of the training activity in terms of increased learning and its transfer to the job. The objective of any action research is not only to identify problems but also, based on the data generated through research, develop and implement changes cooperatively with the research client. In other words, the results generated by research are used to influence the situation which is being researched.

Since within the given time frame, it was not possible to cover all the training institutions and organisations about aspects related to training like how training programmes are decided upon planned and carried out, a small sample was selected and a survey study was conducted to gain knowledge on the training and development policies and practices adopted by different organisations and training institutions in the country. It is but natural that in any research, an indepth study may have to be sometimes sacrificed for the sake of broader coverage and coverage of larger samples may have to be sacrificed for the sake of exactitude. Moreover, in any action research situation, indepth analysis can be attempted only in the case of smaller samples because results obtained from the research are directly applicable to the situation which is being researched for purposes of improving it. Doing this kind of a study would be impossible with large samples. Also in action research, the researcher has to be intensely involved in the total process which is difficult if the sample of the research is large.

One feature of this study has been not to rely on a single tool technique of measuring the training effectiveness. It deviated from the normal practices of evaluating programmes on the basis of impressions/reactions of the trainees. The researchers made use of expert opinion, interviews, observations and questionnaires as tools of evaluation. A lot of effort went into preparing questionnaires which were to be used at different stages of the training programme. Given the various approaches used for studying the different stages of training, it was essential that the method of statistical analysis differ depending on its suitability and the type of data sought.

This chapter summarises the findings of this study and besides offering a broad framework for evaluation, also offers suggestions for the training institutions and the organisations for evaluating their training programmes. This is followed by suggestions for future research that emerged as a result of this study.

Evaluation and qualification

At the beginning of this research study, a major issue raised was the problem of qualification in evaluation and the nature of management tasks which was itself a hindrance in measuring the effect of training. Now, at the end of this phase of the research study in the researchers conclude that:

(1) Mere qualification of the training impact is not sufficient by itself but should be a complement to the qualitative assessment of training programmes.

(2) Quantification could be used for comparative purposes also rather than only for drawing conclusions. It aids in the comparison of similar courses and participants of the same course.

(3) Though quantification is not an impossible task in terms of evaluating training, it has its own limitations such as:

   (i) Availability of time to do an elaborate process.

   (ii) Availability of personnel and resources like a computer, a statistician and a programmer.

   (iii) Availability of expertise in interpret the data correctly and purposefully.

(4) Quantification of the transfer of training has its own difficulties because of the nature and variability of management tasks. It can at the most help conclude that there has been transfer of training but to be able to state definitely 'how much transfer' or 'how much improvement' is a difficult task.

Keeping in mind limitations of both the quantitative and qualitative approaches, the researchers used either or both the approaches wherever appropriate. For example, reaction evaluation was more qualitative in nature, but it was not fully relied upon and was supplemented with evaluation findings using the quantitative approach. Learning and linking with biological and organisational variables was done using mathematical and statistical methods. Yet, the Job Improvement Plan again was analysed qualitatively. The researchers in conclusion, feel that for evaluation studies, a blend of qualitative and quantitative approaches best meets all the requirements.

Questionnaire as a tool of evaluation

Apart from evaluation tools such as informal discussion, observation and interview, the questionnaire was the most important tool used by the researchers. Listed below are some of the advantages and drawbacks of using the questionnaire that the researchers found.

(1) The data obtained by using observation and discussions was biased by the personal judgment of the researchers and trainers. For example, the trainers once observed that a participant was not at all active and hardly took any interest in the training activities and felt that this was one trainee who could not have learnt much. But the learning scores gave a completely different picture altogether. Thus, by using a questionnaire they were able to assess the trainee more accurately.

(2) The exercise of questionnaire formulation by the trainers itself resulted in the improvement of training inputs. The test questionnaire in particular, contributed greatly to the improvement in training inputs. The preparation of these questionnaires resulted in trainers questioning the relevance of their own inputs and thus the complete course content underwent changes.

(3) The response and learning both improved by using and constantly modifying the questionnaire from course to course. Modifications were made based on the responses received in each course. For example, the first attempt at framing the pre-training questionnaire resulted in a very generic one with open-ended

questions. The response to it were also rather vague. Gradually, the questionnaire was made more specific which resulted in the trainee and the organisation examining their own needs vis-a-vis training, and thus became a motivational and developmental tool. In another instance, an organisation which received the survey questionnaire became conscious of the fact that they did not have any of the systems that the questionnaire presumed a training department would have. They neither identified any training needs not had a budget nor did any follow-up. Finally, with the questionnaire as a guide to all the requisites of a training department, this organisation has started systematising their own department.

(4) The test questionnaire by the very act of administering increased the motivation of trainees to learn as they got introduced to some of the topics which were to be covered in the course. They anticipated some of the topics and there were instances where they forced the faculty members to cover these topics more clearly so that they could understand them better.

(5) By receiving the follow-up questionnaire, the trainees felt they owned it to their trainers to apply some of the aspects learnt at the programme. Thus, transfer of training increased.

(6) An indirect pay-off of the questionnaire method was increased interaction between training institution and the organisation. The follow-up questionnaire, for example, was a catalyst in the process of interaction. Bosses wrote to the trainers informing them their opinion of the programme. The trainers replied in explanation and thus set the scene for a fruitful interaction.

Some of the drawbacks noticed are:

(i) Sometimes social desirability tends to colour the response. The researchers tried to overcome this problem by constantly reviewing and modifying the questionnaire and also verifying the responses through other methods such as interviews, indepth case studies and observations.

(ii) Another aspect was that some of the finer details leading to a particular phenomenon were not picked up by the questionnaire. Of course, a remedy to this is again interviews and discussions.

(7) Getting sufficient responses to the questionnaire is always a problem. Through persuasion, personal contacts and reminders the researchers were able to greatly increase the response rate.

Thus, the researchers conclude that like a blend of quantitative and qualitative approaches, a combination of all tools is the most suitable method of evaluating training programmes.

Procedure of selecting/nominating trainees

Any organisation normally has certain objectives and criteria in view while selecting trainees for a particular course. Some of the criteria which guide the selection of executives to be trained are:

(1) The content of the programme as given in the brochure by the training institution matching the job needs of the executive.

(2) Training as preparation before promoting the executive to a higher post.

(3) Overcoming the weaknesses of the executives which were identified through his performance appraisal.

(4) Informal discussion between trainee, his boss and training department about training needs.

Organisations mostly tried to match the training programme with the job requirements of the trainee and that of the organisation. Another criteria for selection used by organisations and reported by the trainees was the past experience of the earlier participants with regard to a particular training institution and programme. However, the bosses of these trainees did not perceive this to be an important consideration in the selection. The study revealed that the private sector was more aware of the advantages of using some of the above criteria as compared to public-sector-The most favoured criteria was to train managers in preparation for promotion. Training before promotion was also given as a reason by the participants and bosses in some of the programmes and inn the Production Management Programme it was though to be an important aspect that had to be considered while selecting an executive for training. But in most cases, the selection was made through the combined initiative of the executive and his organisation.

The private sector emphasised training for overcoming weaknesses which were identified through the performance appraisal reports of the executive. Informal observation of the executive by the training departmental and his boss and discussions with the executive about his training needs also sometimes led to the manager being sent for training. The public sector did not follow any predetermined criteria while selecting their executives for training.

A noticeable feature in the entire need identification process is that very little attention was paid by the management to conversion training for changed systems, procedures and technologies. One major objective of any training activity is to avoid executive obsolescence and ensure that he is constantly trained for new developments in the organisations. Most of the organisations responded negatively to this aspect. A substantial number of both private and public sector organisations did not follow any set criteria of selecting executives for conversion training. This shows that most of the organisations in the country have not yet systematised their training practices and consequently are not able to optimize the advantages of training.

The final decision about the selection of managers for training was normally taken by the top management as a team. In most cases, the trainee himself did not take much initiative. The order of priority in taking the decision was top management, line managers and personnel/training department. However, in the public sector, top management had a major say and the immediate boss and the trainee hardly played any role in the final decision about the selection while in the private sector the boss had as major a role as the top management in the selection. The trainee again had only a minor role in his own selection for training.

Absence of the executive's involvement in his selection for the training programme leads to minimising his commitment and motivation to learn. Therefore, it is suggested that the executive himself and his boss, who is crucial in identifying the strengths and the weaknesses of his subordinate, be involved in the process of nominating. The role of the training department/personnel department, besides organising the training set-up, should be more in the nature of keeping an inventory of the executive's strengths and weaknesses. The department should then help choose the right type of training programme for its executives.

As in the case of selecting trainees, while selecting the training programme, most organisations relied on the contents of the programme as given in the training brochure issued by the training institution. In the public sector, considerable importance was also given to the opinion of the executives who had earlier attended the same or similar training programme in a particular training institution.

Need for global congruence

A factor which enhances the learning process and its transfer is the congruency of training objectives between the trainee, his boss and the training institution. A variable which brings about this congruency is a pre-training discussion between the trainee and his boss about their objectives from training and the training objectives as stated by the training institution. In the initial stage of this study it was found that there was hardly any discussion between the trainee and his boss. However, there was an increase in the number of trainees and their bosses reporting discussion, when the training institution specifically requested both the parties to have a joint discussion before the executive came for training. But in spite of this, there were a substantial number who still did not discuss training objectives in relation to their individual and organisational needs.

Another striking feature was that though the bosses reported they had discussed the training objectives in relation to their own, the trainees themselves did not feel it was so. It is quite possible that in the trainees' opinion a thorough discussion was what was intended by the trainers while the bosses felt even an informal chat before training would suffice. This apparent lack of goal congruence amongst parties involved in training, i.e. the supporting organisation, the training institution and the trainee himself does not necessarily affect training negatively but achievement of goal congruence has been found to be a definite facilitator in increasing the impact of training and its subsequent transfer to the job. Goal congruence as a facilitator in increasing the effect of training could be achieved through the process of pre-training evaluation. Discussions about the objectives and expectations from training between the nominee and his boss on the eve of the training programme helps them to see more meaning in the aims and objectives of the programme as set by the training institution. The effect of sending a pretraining questionnaire in itself helps in bringing in awareness of training objectives in the context of the trainees' individual and organisational needs. For the trainers, the process of setting objectives is a continuous one because after every programme they revise the objectives according to the training needs of the participants. They receive this information from the sponsoring organisations either through interaction, personal discussion and use of questionnaires or mainly from the feedback obtained from the participant. There are institutions who tend to ignore this and carry on with the same training model for years.

It was found that very few private and public sector organisations had set pattern of training discussing objectives with their nominees. Till such time the organisations realise the benefits of such a procedure and begin to take corrective steps to regularise this action, it is desirable for the trainee and his boss to themselves take the initiative of discussing the objectives and results to be derived from the training programme. This would be helpful for, when there is clarity of objectives the trainee will gain more insight into the total training process and be able to derive maximum benefit, personally and professionally from the training programme.

Biographic, psychological and organisational variables: learning and its transfer

As assumption the researchers started with was that learning and its subsequent transfer to the job was linked not only to the training but also to the capacity of the trainees to learn. The capacity to learn is sometimes related to the biographical personality and organisational variables of the trainees. In this context the researchers tied to establish a relationship between learning, follow-up and variables like age, previous training experiences, sector and industry the trainees come from, their educational qualification and others. The objective was not to investigate which category of trainees learnt more or less; but which category the training programme was catering to. In case it was found that training was catering to a particular profile then the selection of trainees had to be modified such that all participants derived maximum advantage of training. An example of where this kind of study was found useful can be cited. The Personnel Management programme was initially meant for both Personnel Managers as well as line managers. However, the trainers found that one set of managers always complained that the programme did not cater to their needs. Either the programme was too basic or too advanced. Since it was not possible to alter the inputs and cater to both the groups it was decided to split the two groups and run two separate training programmes, one for Personnel Managers and another for line managers.

Similarly, when it was found only one segment of the participants were able to appreciate the inputs, the inputs in the next programme were modified so as to satisfy all groups. In the sixth programme on Personnel Management covered in this sample, it was seen that learning for all types of participants was almost the same. The researchers feel their intervention has greatly influenced this result.

A personality variable which greatly affects learning is the adaptability of the managers to changing situations. It has been hypothesised that those who are flexible in their attitudes are more susceptible to change, learn more than the those who are rigid and do not change easily. The researchers tried to test this hypothesis by using Rigidity/Flexibility scale to measure the extent of rigidity and correlate it with learning. The results suggested that there was a definite link between the two in some inputs/modules. This poses a challenge for the trainers to see how persons who are less susceptible to change can be made to derive more than they normally do from training. Efforts were made in some of the programmes by giving such executives personal attention. There was also a suggestion that such persons be put through unstructured sensitivity type of training. However, the solution to this aspect needs further investigation and thinking.

The biographical and organisational variables could also be studied in relation to the transfer of learning to the job with a view to find out if any particular category of managers are able to transfer more. If it is so, then the trainers should stress to those who were unable to transfer, the method of tackling organisational constraints if any, or look for factors in their own inputs which were inadequate. The data can also help the organisation in identifying the factors which help or hinder the transfer of learning. Such analysis has utility in terms of identification of training needs. For example, it was found in the Personnel Management programme that persons coming from manufacturing industries got better cooperation from their colleagues, subordinates and superiors are compared to the service industry managers and in the Government sector very often trainees for low cooperation from their subordinates and colleagues while in the private sector, the executives always received high or moderate cooperation. This, the trainers tool as an indication that there was a need to increase the emphasis on human relations to trainees of the service industry and the government sector to overcome this lack of cooperation.

Similar analysis could be done with other variables like age, educational qualification and professional qualification. The objective of the trainer here again will be ensure that every category of trainees is able to get some learning from the course which could be transferred to the job. For example, if certain systems streamlining is taught in the training programme and the participants find it cannot be applied to the job because of the constraints imposed by rules and regulations or the environment, then it is for the trainers to adjust inputs in such a manner that they impart knowledge that can be transferred to the job even within the constraints imposed on them.

Behavioural dimensions and training impact

Trainers do not always know if their inputs have effectively achieved the intended objectives. If the programme director/trainers are evaluating the effectiveness of their inputs purely in terms of the set objectives, they may have a difficult time deciding how well they have accomplished their teaching tasks. However, if trainers are able to develop criteria of evaluating training by translating their set objectives in terms behavioural dimensions, they have more definite standards by which to judge the equality of their teaching efforts.

Therefore, measures of training in terms of observable behaviour while on the job offers a vehicle by which teaching results can be evaluated more precisely. The training institution and the trainers have better direction in planning their training activities. It gives a clearer picture of the instructional intent thus providing a sound basis for selecting appropriate training aids and methods. It also helps select test items that will adequately reflect the trainee's ability to demonstrate the acquisition of desired knowledge and skills. It thus provides both short term and long term objectives to be achieved from the training programme in terms of behavioural dimensions.

The researchers tried to study behavioural dimensions at both the training stage and the stage of its transfer to the job. First at the training stage, the behavioural aspects covered in the inputs were included in the test questionnaire and in the second stage, questions on behavioural dimensions were included in the follow-up study. For example, the test questionnaire included items on the attitude of the manager towards employees, his belief in a democratic/autocratic/participative style of management, etc. The follow-up questionnaire included items on personal dimensions such as his leadership style, development of team spirit, ability to elicit cooperation from his colleagues and subordinates, openmindedness and self-confidence. It may be mentioned that susceptibility to change as measured through the Rigidity/Flexibility scale is also a behavioural dimension affecting training.

Job improvement plan

Preparation of the Job Improvement Plan at the end of the training programme has been perceived to be one of the most important indicators of not only learning but its transfer. When the trainee prepares his action plan on the basis of the training he has undergone, he visualises the modification/changes required in the existing systems, the constraints which he will have to face during the implementation of the change and the time required for the successful completion of the task. It also helps in improving the perception of the trainees and the organisations about the training programme.

The JIP also forms the basis of the follow-up. It indicates the specific problems, if any, faced by the trainee which prevented him from being able to translate his knowledge to action. By following the action steps enunciated by the trainee his organisation is also able to link training with the job. Areas where no action steps have been indicated would be pointers to the fact that the training has been insufficient/inadequate. In the Personnel Management programme, it was found in the initial programmes that in the areas like Absenteeism and Overtime no action steps were given. Later, after this point was taken into cognisance and suitable steps to rectify it were incorporated in the subsequent programmes, there were some steps given in the JIP by the trainees.

The analysis of the JIP gave some idea to the trainers about how relevant their programme was to the organisations to which the trainees belonged. It was found that few organisations had a gievance handling mechanism or a method of dealing with absenteeism. The programme director as a result of this information had two alternatives, either scrapping these input or making only as passing reference to these or making attempts to rectify this situation. The researchers were able to five to the trainers information of this kind which otherwise would have rendered the programme only partially affective or incurred tremendous expenditure in writing to all sponsoring organisations to find out about their practices with relation to the topics covered in the programme.

Follow-up

Transfer of training to the job is an important indicator of training effectiveness. Normally evaluation of training is confined to the reaction evaluation of training is confined to the reaction evaluation of the participants. At times the training faculty discuss among themselves the best method of improving subsequent training activity but it is again based on the feedback obtained from the trainees. The results of the study suggested that immediately after being through the training programme the trainee's reaction to the programme was different from what they reported about the same programme after a gap of six months to year. This is of course natural since the relevance of the programme tends to increase with the passage of time and when the executive is back on the job, he is able to see the utility of training in his day-to day work much more easily. Thus, the follow-up study can given an insight into the relevance and applicability of the training offered.

The study revealed that only few organisations and training institutions had a system of follow-up after six months to a year of the training programme. The few who did a follow-up either asked the trainee to prepare a specific plan of action or just tried to asses the overall performance of the executive subsequent to training.

Input learning and its transfer

The researchers linked the inputs covered in the course with the transfer of these specific inputs/modules to the job. The idea of such an analysis was to see which inputs and modules had greater applicability to the job. In case the applicability was low, the trainers were advised to modify these inputs. It was found in one of the programmes on personnel Management, transfer in the area of Manpower Planning,

Appraisal and Merit Rating and Manpower Information Systems was low. With the shift in emphasis in the subsequent programme, there was substantial improvement in the transfer of inputs in these areas.

Reasons for inability to transfer was also one aspect the researchers concentrated on. This was important since it would point out the reasons due to which the executive did not find the inputs useful to them in their jobs. For example, in the inputs on Organisation Structure almost all the trainees reported that it being a corporate function, they had very little scope to bring in any changes. In spite of this, the trainers decided to continue with this input because they felt that it would come into the purview of the executives' future job functions. But in other instances they modified the inputs according to the profile of the trainees. If training was indicated as a reason then alterations/deletions had to be made in the training programme. If the reasons pertained to organisational factors then the trainers would have to take a different course of action. In this study the read on most often quoted as being responsible for the inability to transfer was organisational constraints. The second one was the function not being related to the job characteristics of the trainee.

Transfer of training to the job

Irrespective of the degree of learning, those trainees who expressed the view that the inputs were relevant to their jobs were the ones who were able to transfer maximum training to the job. This indicated that the opinion of the participants at the end of course had much to contribute in terms of their motivation to implement what was learnt through training. Thus it would seem that a favourable impression about the course promotes transfer training to the job.

To enhance the transfer of training to the job, the trainers can find out the factors which help or hinder this transfer. After identification of these factors he should be able to inform the trainees ways and means of capitalising on those which help and either overcome the hindering factors or work within its confines. The researchers were able to classify into four categories the factors when favourable, helped the transfer and when unfavorable to apply his knowledge for the betterment of the existing method of functioning in the organisation. They are:

(i) Personal development of the trainee like increased personal goals and levels of aspiration, interaction with other managers of different organisations, contact with trainers.

(2) Perception of management training like whether managers are born or can be developed with the aid of proper training.

(3) Organisational climate which when favourable will help the transfer of learning. Organisational climate encompass aspects like autonomy of the participants to carry out his own projects, freedom to set performance goals and make changes in his own department. Factors which contribute to organisational philosophy like

whether the organisation favours innovation as a planned programme for change or is anxious to make use of new ideas are also aspects of organisational climate.

(4) Development of managerial skills like decision-making skills, ability to delegate and act as a leader, development of generalist outlook among others.

Of these four aspects which lead to transfer of learning, two of them are, in general, hindering factors. They are the organisational climate and perception of management training. Unfavourable organisational climate automatically hinders the transfer of learning and a wrong perception of management training hinders learning and hence the transfer. The significance of training as perceived by the manager and his organisation is important in helping the trainee to implement what has been acquired through training. If the trainee himself or those directly concerned with his job performance are conceived that training is only meant for increasing conceptual knowledge and has no practical value, then the organisation will definitely not benefit from training.

While comparing two programmes covered in the simple it was found that in spite of increased learning in the second course as compared to the first, reported transfer was less. There was comparatively a reduction in the personal and managerial skill development in the second programme. On further examination, it was found that a greater number of trainees of the second programme reported an unfavourable organisational climate and fewer of them and their bosses had a positive perception about management training. Of course, training could also have contributed to the inability to transfer. But this suggestion is refuted by the learning scores obtained by participants of the second programme.

In cases where the lack to transfer is primarily doe to the climate of organisation, then merely making efforts towards modifying training programmes would be absolutely of no help in promoting transfer. To promote the transfer of training to the job, training institutions can

(1) During the training itself stress on the development of personal traits like self-confidence, openmindedness, a result oriented attitude and risk taking ability.

(2) During the final phase of training, encourage the trainee to prepare a concrete action plan for the changes that can be brought into his job.

(3) Make the training inputs as relevant as possible to the profile of the participants.

(4) Incorporate in the training programme, some information on how to elicit maximum support and cooperation from various groups of employees in the organisation such as the departmental heads, colleagues, subordinates and trade unions.

(5) Emphasise the importance of a positive attitude towards training for individual and organisational development.

The organisation can help in the process of transfer by:

(1) Nominating the trainees best suited for a particular type of programme as per his training needs and requirements.

(2) Ensuring suitable placement of the trainee after his return from the training programme.

(3) Having systematic procedures of follow-up so that the trainee and the organisation both are aware of the returns from training.

(4) Actively involving the different levels of management to facilitate the implementation process.

(5) Offering a supportive climate the individual on his return from training so as to encourage change and innovation.

(6) Inculcating a training culture in the organisation through the creation of a 'critical mass' i.e. training more than just one executive thus exposing the maximum number of individuals to a training philosophy. In other words, creating a positive attitude to training for individual and organisational development.

While most of the analysis of learning and its transfer was done at a macro level, study of a few trainees and one or two organisations yield details which may be missed out otherwise. This practice was adopted by the researchers in the follow-up study. A case study of one organisation was done and a few individuals studied right from the re-training stage to the follow-up.

The case study of ABC Electric Company and the case studies of individual trainees gave some additional information about the factors which help and hinder the transfer of learning, Some of the factors were:

(1) Those who had a discussion with the boss before coming to the course were able to use their training more effectively while back on the job.

(2) Those who found inputs to be directly relevant to them their jobs were the ones who were able to apply maximum.

(3) The learning was not directly related to the transfer. In other words, those who transferred maximum knowledge to the job were not necessarily ones who had learnt maximum through the training programme.

(4) Resistance from the trade unions to change and accept new systems arising out of training.

(5) Reluctance on the part of the management to change primarily due to lack of information and communication.

(6) Rigid rules and conservative nature of the organisation.

(7) Lack of self-confidence and risk taking abilities of the trainee which could be a result of inadequacies in the training programme itself.

(8) Resistance to changes a group phenomenon in the organisation, i.e. individually one might accept a particular change put collectively as a group there might be resistance to accept any change in the existing rules and procedures.

Another method of assessing the extent of transfer was the preparation of a Job Improvement Plan by each individual trainee. By preparing the action plan, the trainees paved the way of implementing the changes he had planned. The organisation was able to see the effectiveness of the training after the trainee had discussed the action plan with his loss.

Placement

An important factor for the transfer of training, even in spite of the preparation of an action plan is the placement of the executive. Placement of the executive after training has to be in line with the training he has acquired. Most organisations who responded to the survey questionnaire that was sent to them did not ensure that placement corroborated with training. This, the researchers tool as another indicator of the fact that organisations sponsoring their managers for training were not always serious about making use of the training.

External training versus in-company training

An organisation has to make a choice of whether to organise an in-company training programme or send their executives for external training programmes. Normally, financial consideration play a major role in this decision. In other words, if a number of people are to be trained then the organisations normally try to organise in-company training programmes. However, it needs to be clarified that both in-company and external training programmes serve different objectives and cannot be substitutes for each other. In external training programmes, the advantage is that executives come in contact with managers of various other organisations and get a broad idea of what is happening in other organisations. In the case of in-company training, the focus is normally on the organisational problems. Therefore, if the objective is to gain an understanding of the functioning of other organisations and ways of improving one's own performance, then external programmes are ideally suited. But if the goal is to seek solutions to specific problems of the organisation or to prepare the organisation for some new change, then in-company training programmes are best because a large number of executives can be trained in one lot. External programmes are also useful to train executives in key positions to act as change agents after training. Another area where external training could be useful in when attitudinal changes have to be effected in executives who do not subscribe to certain tenets practised in the organisational work environment.

In-company training programmes have some problems in bringing about attitudinal changes because of the hierarchical and organisational constraints. In the external training programme, the group pressure can help in changing attitudes. Of course, long duration programmes can achieve this much better than short term programmes.

Almost all organisations had a set programme of training their executives. In the public sector organisations, a distinction was made between executives of different levels. Higher level executives were sent for external training programmes and junior level executives were trained through in-company programmes. However, while deciding on external training programmes, the organisations said they preferred certain training institutions because of the following reasons:

(1) Relevance of the course content to organisational needs.

(2) Information about the qualification and expertise of the faculty available in the institution.

Organisations have, in general, expressed their dissatisfaction with the external training programmes. The prime reason for this dissatisfaction being the insufficient knowledge on the part of the faculty about the practical problems and needs of the sponsoring organisations.

Training budget

Most organisations do not prepare a training budget on the basis of training needs. Neither do they prepare it in advance and finally resort to ad hoc methods of deciding on the amount they would like to spend on training their executives. From the results of the survey study, it was found that the private sector was much more systematic in allocating the budget according to its training requirements. In these organisations, the budget was first prepared at the departmental level and then incorporated into the central budget, whereas the public sector was comparatively more ad hoc in their approach to the training budget.

It is advisable to link the budget to the training requirements of the organisation. The training department should first conduct an exercise on identification of training needs in close collaboration with the line managers. Having identified the training needs, the priorities could be indicated in the training budget. Preparation of the budget thus would be at the departmental or unit level with incorporation into the central budget later. It is also desirable that within the overall budgetary constraints, certain amount of flexibility be built in so that in case of sudden urgent requirements, the budget can accommodate some more executives who need to be trained.

Review of training activity

Any training function needs a periodical review to assess its utility. Besides an evaluation of the training programmes, a general review of the overall training function is essential. A substantial number of training institutions and organisations engaged in training tend to ignore this important aspect. Training institutions in particular should evolve their own criteria of periodically reviewing their training activity and not find out later that their programmes are out dated and not geared to the needs of the organisations. Review of any training activity would be the shared responsibility of the sponsoring organisations and the training institutions to which they sponsor their executives.

The organisation should itself have its own mechanism of reviewing and evaluating the training activities. Such reviews could be done periodically at least once in three years. The organisation should also evolve its own criteria of evaluation which would begin at the pre-training stage and finish with the follow-up. A basic element of evaluation could be the Job Improvement Plan and preparation of a supportive climate which would help the transfer of learning and at the same time ensure that factors which hinder the transfer are minimised. For deriving maximum benefit from training, the organisation must periodically review systems like that of appraisal, communication and counselling so that all these do not prove to be a hindrance in the psrolless of implementing changes but instead be facilitators so that cache efficiency of the organisation is enhanced.

Interaction between training institutions and organisations

An interesting finding was the mutual rapprochement of the organisations on one hand and the training institutions on the other. There seemed to be a general feeling about training standards being unsatisfactory in spite of the rapid proliferation of the number of training institutions in the country. The private sector was more unhappy over the standards maintained by the training institutions as compared to the public sector. Probably, the reason being that the private sector itself was more organised in its approach to training and alive to the advantages that could result from it.

One of the major drawbacks in training institutions as perceived by the organisations was the inability of the training institutions to keep abreast with practical problems and the growing needs of the sponsoring organisations. They felt training not fully geared to their real life problems had very limited value to them.

The training institutions in turn felt that a factor contributing to the dissatisfaction with the prevailing standards of training was due to the organisations themselves adopting a lax attitude towards training and not being very serious in their efforts to maximise the benefits of training. They felt there was lack of communication and coordination between the Training Manager, the Personnel Manager, the executive to be trained, his boss and the top team.

The organisations felt that it was the responsibility of training institutions to concentrate on appropriate selection of participants and to provide training as closely related to their needs as possible, keeping the kind the environment constraints under which organisations have to operate. On the contrary the training institutions felt that they had very little flexibility in their choice of trainees because of the constraints imposed by the organisations which forced them to accept managers for training though they may not be suitable.

Yet in spite of these complaints about each other, neither the training institutions nor the organisations measured the effectiveness of training by any other means except the reaction evaluation. Organisations relied on the reported reaction of the executive who was nominated for the training. Similarly, the training institutions relied on the impression of their participants to the programme. It is interesting that in spite of the common method of evaluation the factors which were considered responsible for training being ineffective as pinpointed by the two parties were so divergent.

Evidently, to bridge this perception gap a certain amount of liaison between training institutions and sponsoring organisations is required. However, at present very few organisations and training institutions have a regular procedure of interacting between themselves. The study indicated that though almost all the organisations considered interaction to be a desirable and meaningful activity, yet they were apprehensive about whether they would be able to draw any benefits from it. The result is that either interaction is totally lacking or is confined only to individuals of both these acquainted with each other. To straighten out these misunderstandings, it is suggested that a meaningful procedure of interaction be initiated by either of the two parties and be maintained periodically to understand the changing systems, procedures and requirements of the two involved parties. It is when the training institution is clear about its role and expectations in terms of meeting changing systems and requirements of the sponsoring organisation that they will be able to satisfy these requirements. Similarly, when organisations come to realise the constraints under which the training institutions function, they will be less critical and try and make the best use of the efforts that the training institutions make under the circumstances.

The interaction process could be carried out through personal discussions, use of questionnaires, visits to industries and feedback obtained from preceding training programmes. In addition, exchange of faculty and organisational personnel on deputation for professional growth and development would be a welcome feature. Frequent interaction on set lines would also help the two parties in involving a procedure for selection/nomination of participants and in arriving at training objectives which are mutually satisfying.

A factor which prevented the exchange of professionals between the industry and training institutions was the anomalies in emoluments and status of the two. Many professional managers who are more than willing to work in the training institutions for a long duration feel constrained to do so because the training institutions cannot pay them the same amount the industry offers. With the result either the industry has to pay the difference or the managers have to manage within what the training institutions can offer. Obviously, the former is not acceptable to most industries and the latter is not acceptable to the manager himself. Unless some compromise is reached at a national level about this problem, long-term interaction will remain only a theoretical possibility.

Another aspect to this lack of interaction is that in many instances, the industries feel and academician cannot serve a useful purpose in their organisations because of his theoretical approach to problem-solving. Thus, they are reluctant to have them on a long-term basis. This problem to some extent can be taken care of initially by giving the newcomer some specific projects connected with improvement of the organisational systems and structures. He will then gradually gain some idea about the actual functioning of the organisation, its problems and dynamics. Then later on he could be entrusted with specific assignments.

Organisations have indicated certain preference for the training institutions to which they sponsor their executives. These preferences are based on the expertise of the institution in a particular field of management, their ability to relate to the specific problems of the sponsoring organisations and their competence in conducting programmes dealing with particular sectors/industries like the banks, financial institutions, small scale units. The availability of faculty members having academic and industrial exposure is also a strong point which determines the training institution to which determines the training institution to which executives are sent. In order to be able to meet the demands of sponsoring organisations, training institutions would be well advised to take the following steps:

(1) Regularise continuing development of the faculty to maintain high standards and an expert group of trainers.

(2) Systematic evaluation of their training programmes.

(3) Periodical review in order to take stock of existing standards and the need for bringing in improvements.

(4) Above all, undertake problem solving research projects related to the needs of different organisations. It should be a continuous in-built process of teaching and research and these two activities should be combined with a periodic exchange or deliberations with the experience of the trainers/faculty members so that the experiences drawn from consultancy work would help the teaching and research activity or the institution and the experiences drawn from teaching/research could be stored for future use in other consultancy assignments.

(5) Maintain close professional ties with other training institutions.

Some organisations and the researchers feel that there is a need for the constitution of a body at the national level which would try to evolve, maintain and help standardise the quality of the training institutions and the courses offered by them and provide information as and when organisations ask for it. It could also help streamline the areas and fields of training activity which could be covered by different training institutions so that the varied training activities are not all concentrated only in handful of institutions but are properly spread out. The training institutions themselves could have a committee which will regularly look into the quality of its own training programmes and at the same time initiate the process of interaction with its sponsors. Perhaps, the institutional committee could work hand in hand with the national body to ensure that it is continuing to maintain its standards at par with the national level.

Evaluation strategy

The usual question asked in Management Education is how accurately can the effect of a management training and development process be measured. This whole research, as indicated in the preceding chapters is an exploratory attempt to study the effects of a training and development process and how an evaluation strategy could be used to increase its effectiveness. The evaluation model was evolved on the basis of the action research approach adopted by the researchers. It is of course, not a definitive model of evaluation, but can give guidelines to others desirous of evaluating their management training and developmental activities. In this section of the chapter the strategy of evaluation that could be adopted and the advantages of using certain steps of evaluation are summarised and discussed based on the findings of the researchers.

Identification of training needs

(1) The first step in any developmental process is to identify the exact requirements of training keeping in view the individual and organisational needs. The best method of doing this is through a systematic appraisal of the employees 'strengths and weaknesses'

(2) The linking of appraisal with the training needs could be done at the feedback and review stages of the appraisal

(3) The boss and the trainee themselves should play a major role in discussion and identification of training needs.

(4) The training department in an organisation should play a supportive role in suggesting ways of identifying training needs rather than deciding by themselves who should be given training. The training department could also help by being fully aware of the kinds of training available through in-company training and through external programmes which will meet the requirements of the individual and/or the organisation. The final decision of course, will have to be taken after discussion with the trainee and his boss.

Determination of training objectives and design

Setting objectives for a specific training programme is a complicated task. Normally the training institutions give very broad objectives which can encompass almost all directly and indirectly related subjects connected to the main theme of the programme. The problem lies in translating these broad objectives into behavioural dimensions so as to arrive at specific inputs which will be covered in the training. Here the programme director would greatly benefit by having a detailed discussion with other trainers on how best to achieve the stated objectives of the programme. This could be done by asking each of the involved faculty members to prepare a brief document on the following aspects:

(1) The opportunity that is provided to the participant to learn from their input.

(2) Whether they expect this to result in enduring learning.

(3) If so, they expect this learning to influence the way in which the participant subsequently works, and if so how?

(4) If they expect a change in work behaviour, do they also expect demonstrable benefit to their organisations? If so, how?

(5) What do they see as being the objectives of the course as a whole, and how does their part contribute to the achievement of this?

(6) Suggest a simple test/exercise that could be given at the beginning and end of the course to indicate whether they have been successful in bringing about the intended learning.

Choice of training methods

The choice of training methods again will be related to the objectives to be achieved. Research indicates that if the sole objective a programme is information giving, then the lecture method could be adopted and appropriate reading material be given. If the objective is to increase the decision making skills, then exercises and cases are the appropriate tools. Similarly, if attitudinal change is the objective, then role playing and group activities are best. Therefore, the concerned trainers may like to discuss the methodology in relation to the objectives set by them and then decide on the total design.

Congruence of training objectives between the trainee, his organisation and the training institution

(1) For a positive impact of training, it is important that there be congruence of objectives between the parties involved in training. To achieve this the training institution can evolve questionnaires for the trainee and his boss asking them about their expectations from the training in view of the stated objectives of training. This questionnaire would be fruitful if it was filled after the trainee and his boss had a discussion about their expectations.

(2) From the data obtained from this questionnaire, the trainers can make sure that training inputs are by and large, in line with the requirements of the trainee and

his organisation. This process would also help the training institutions in the selection of the trainees for the programme to avoid situations of the kind where the expectations of the sponsoring organisation are totally divorced from the objectives of the training programme.

(3) Any specific requirement of the trainee/organisation that is highlighted in the questionnaire can be better tackled by the trainers when they are aware of it well in advance. Help then could be given in the form of individual discussions, tutorials or through project work.

Preparation for training

It would be of advantage to the organisation and the trainee particularly the one going for a comparatively longer duration training, if he was released from his every day work a few days earlier, thus giving him time to get acquainted with the general functioning of their total organisational departments. In these few days the trainee would also have the time to think and find out about the problems and requirements of the organisation through training. This will enable him to link the subsequent training inputs with his own problems. It would also be helpful if the trainee made himself familiar with the programme objectives, the design and other information provided by the trainers/the training institution.

Measurement of susceptibility to change

The research findings indicated that there is some relation between the trainee's ability to learn and his susceptibility to change. More rigid the personality, the less is the susceptibility to accept new ideas and consequently less is the learning. One method of overcoming this problem would be to first determine if the person is rigid or flexible by nature in the context of his role as an executive. This can be done by administering a questionnaire which will measure the susceptibility to change. In this study the Rigidity/Flexibility scale was administered on the first day of the programme. It may be advisable to get this questionnaire filled much before the executive comes for the course so that the trainers know his Rigidity/Flexibility score in advance.

It is found that an executive is comparatively more rigid then the trainers should try to concentrate on the behavioural aspects in training including tutorials and counselling techniques. If considered desirable, such trainees could be put through a sensitivity kind of training before the regular training programme itself. This may help the rigid executives to overcome their rigidity.

Pre-training test questionnaires

(1) To bring in more clarity about inputs, each trainer could prepare a brief statement about how his inputs are linked to the overall objectives of the programme and the specifics of these inputs.

(2) The trainers may like to know the extent to which his inputs have made an impact on the trainees. It could be measured through a test questionnaire in which the inputs of the trainer are in question form. This questionnaire could be administered to the trainees before and after training thereby giving the learning derived through the programme. Apart from measuring the impact of learning, the questionnaire will also introduce the inputs to the trainee and this by itself can help the trainees to be motivated to learn more.

(3) The responses to the test questionnaire administered before training also gives a feedback to the faculty members about the topics that the participants are not familiar with and the aspects that most of them know. By acquiring this information the trainer can modify his inputs in such a manner that maximum benefit is derived by the participants. The researchers have already discussed how in many cases this exercise of preparing a test questionnaire brought focus into inputs and thus how the action research approach justified its role in the evaluation process.

Evaluation during and immediately after the training process

(1) It has already been discussed that measurement of learning could be done by the administering of the rest questionnaire before and after the programme. Different index of learning can be calculated and can range from the simple difference, i.e. the change score to statistical and mathematical transformations. An index that was neither too simple nor very complex was used by the researchers. It has, of course, some limitations which were overlooked because of obvious advantages.

(2) The learning score then can be related to various organisational and biographical variables like age, educational qualification, experience of the trainee and the kind and nature of the sponsoring organisation. This will give data about the category of persons who are benefiting maximum through training. From this type of information, the selecting of the participants and/or the programme can be streamlined. Some times training institutions could reschedule their programmes depending on the profile of participants who have been nominated. In-company programmes too could be re-looked at on the basis of the information obtained about the biographic factors of their executives.

(3) It is desirable from the point of view of organisational efficiency that the trainees have a commitment to transfer training to the job. It will be present only when they leave the training institution with the right frame of mind. Reaction evaluation would give the trainers an opportunity to apprise themselves of the attitude of the trainees and perhaps, the reasons if any, for a negative frame of mind. The proforma or any other tool of assessing the reaction, if well prepared will also give the trainees an opportunity to think and rationalise their impressions about the programme. Though some times reaction evaluation may not be sufficient to draw conclusions about the programmes, used as an adjunct to

any other method of evaluation, it can give some revealing insights into any particular finding.

Job improvement plan

Preparation of plan for the changes the executives intend introducing is a very effective method of reinforcing training with specific reference to the job and pointing out the relevance of inputs to the work situation. This Job Improvement Plan should be related to related to the subject covered in the training programme.

An analysis of data generated through the JIP could also give indications about the subjects in which maximum number of trainees envisaged some kind of change. It could also indicate these subjects where very few managers attempt any changes. Then by finding out the reasons for this, the trainers could alter the contents of that subject to make it relevant or emphasise/stress more on it if the reason indicated is that many trainees were unable to suggest any changes because it was inadequately covered. Another point in favour of JIP is that is provides information which could be the starting point of a follow-up done six months to one year after the programme.

Follow-up training

The trainer, apart from imparting knowledge has to ensure that this knowledge will be of use to the trainee in his job. While at the training institution neither the trainee nor the trainer can have an accurate picture of how the training is going to improve the trainee's job performance and thus enhance organisational efficiency. Follow-up of the trainee after a gap of time would give a true picture of efficacy of the training programme. Follow-up could be done either through questionnaires or through formal/informal interviews and discussions. It could involve the boss of the trainee, his colleagues, his subordinates or only the trainee.

But the aspect which is of import is that follow-up should be closely related to the expectations of the trainee/organisation, the actual training and the JIP, if any. Help/hinder factors would form an important part of the follow-up since future training must keep in view the factors which are likely to work against the trainee in the transfer of his training to the job.

If some hindering factors pertain to training then of course, the trainer must bear it in mind for subsequent programmes. But if they relate to the organisational culture and climate then the training institution could try and make overtures to win over the top management so that they may in future play the role of facilities in the transfer of training. One method of doing this may be by involving them in the training activity right from the smart so that they then have a vested interest in training and the trained executive.

One method of increasing the commitment of the organisation and of involving them in the complete training activity right from the start is by asking the boss of the trainee at the pre-training stage about the organisational requirements that need to be met through training the executive. After the complete of the programme asking the chief executive/top management whether the training contributed to organisational effectiveness would again draw into the fold of training the boss and top management. This will be so because in nine cases out of ten, the chief executive or the top management will have to refer back to the boss of the trainee about the changed job performance of the trainee. Once again at the follow-up stage asking the boss to consider whether the training programme brought about any demonstrable benefits would go a long way in promoting the idea that training must be made use of to promote organisational effectiveness.

This in short is the broad framework which can be used by trainers/evaluators for evaluating management training and development programmes.

It can be stated that in evaluation of management training and development process, different methodologies have to be adopted each of which will serve different purposes. Each methodology will give its own clues which will be useful to the trainers and the sponsoring organisation. However, it may not be possible to simultareously follow all the methodologies for every course. Therefore, it would be better to adopt a particular methodology in one course, apply its finding in the subsequent and see the improvement in the further courses. Of course, the methodology could also undergo changes to make the evaluation more useful. For example, in the Course in General Management for Senior Executives, the researchers apart from normal evaluation methods as suggested in the model did an indepth analysis of one course based on two types of tools. Similarly, one can do an analysis input-wise, teaching methodology-wise and go on making modification in keeping with the action as a static process but as a dynamic one. Therefore, there will always be scope for improvement and modifications in the methodologies from time to time to keep pace with the changing requirements and situations.

Suggestions for future research

This research was aimed at studying various aspects of management training and development and its evaluation from the point of view of the training institution and the organisation. The major focus was on the identification of training needs, the training process itself acquisition of knowledge in the training institution. In addition, a study of the transfer of learning from the training stage to the job situation was also undertaken. This was with a view to throw light into the actual process of transfer of training in the organisation and to discover areas which are related to this transfer which the researchers intend probing in future. In addition, in course of this study some interesting issues emerged which could be further researched into. Some of the areas where research would be extremely useful are enunciated below:

(1) Though the researchers studied the impact of the variable Rigidity/Flexibility on learning, much more needs to be done before some understanding is reached about the interaction of this variable with various aspects of the learning and how

it facilitates or hinders the transfer of training to the job. This variable according to the research analysis was found to contribute maximum to learning. The exact nature of this relationship would prove very advantageous to trainers.

(2) More often then not discrepancy was observed between the trainees and their bosses response regarding the transfer of training. The most interesting feature was that generally the bosses reported greater degree of transfer than the trainees themselves. Reasons for such discrepancy need to be further investigated.

(3) The findings of the study on follow-up suggested that the transfer of training to the job was immediate for functional courses like Personnel Management rather than the General Management programmes. The point worth investigating is if the transfer of training in the General Management programmes is delayed, what is effect of this time gap on the learning and the application of it to job.

(4) The study led the researchers to tentatively conclude that the nature of the industry which the trainee represents and its climate had much to do with the transfer of training. It may be worthwhile studying whether the organisational climate in the private sector/public sector/government departments were all that different thus leading the trainees of these sectors to report such varying degrees of transfer. In which case, the trainers will have to structure their programmes in such a way that the final outcome of the training for all trainees is the same.

(5) Acquisition of managerial skills was found to be more in the manufacturing industries than service industries. Therefore, investigation is needed to find out whether this is due to job factors, organisational climate or the training inputs itself.

(6) With some insights into the process of transfer of training already achieved from the pilot study, there is need to evolve criteria of evaluation related to behavioural dimensions to appropriately measure the training and its transfer.

(7) The trainers must know the various sources of learning for the trainees. For example, of it is found that a manager is influenced by his boss, then since the boss also bears a responsibility towards teaching his subordinates, apart from learning himself, he should be trained to be an effective teacher on the job situation.

(8) Little is known about the ways in which the ineffective manager becomes effective and effective managers become ineffective. Research on the part of the training institution on some of the parameters of effectiveness could help in making training programme more useful.

(9) The trainers need to know what are the managerial skills that can be taught to improve the manager's contribution to the organisation and what the optimum use of theory and practice in the training activity is how it is to be achieved.

Research related to the learning process could embrace matters such as use of projects, the creation of case studies derived from the real life situations and study of the environment in which managers work.

(10) A charge is often levelled by the managers that the concepts taught in the training institutions are borrowed from advanced western countries, specially USA and UK, and are not suited to the Indian situation. Research is needed in the area of transfer of managerial technology from advanced to developing countries. The studies may include the appropriateness of western managerial techniques to the Indian institution keeping in view the Indian culture, beliefs and value system.

(11) There are gaps between what manager says he does and what he thinks ought to do. There are also differences in the needs of the organisation and the needs of the manager. Similarly, there are gaps between the training needs as perceived by the organisation and the individual himself. The conflict between the personal needs of the executive and organisational needs poses a problem in identifying the actual training needs of the managers.

(12) A trainer needs to distinguish between what can be done in the class-room at work, what can be done in the class-room away from work and what cannot be done in the class-room at all. By understanding this, the trainer will be able to design programmes better, keeping in view the various aspects that can be covered in a particular type of programme. The trainee should also be aware of what the organisation wants for the manager and what the managers want for themselves so that any training design covers all sorts of training in the management development package.

Recent developments in training

The training methods and techniques have been developed in various forms, frequently being modified and tailored to suit particular situations and needs. The profession is, of course, constantly evolving, and training specialists seek to take advantage of any new technologies, methods or approaches which may promise to add to their effectiveness. Often what is offered as innovative is readily recognizable as something from the past simply dressed up in a new guise and described in a new jargon. Training staff should therefore be on their guard against offers of 'new' developments which may only treat them to 'the mixture as before', possible laced with a new flavour.

In a number of areas, training can be justly said to be breaking new ground. While the foundations for such developments may have been laid some years ago, it is only Now, in the mid-1980s, that we can see real progress being made. In a rapidly changing world, one can only take a snapshot of what is happening at the time of writing and this could well be out of date in a matter of months. Specialists developing new ideas may sensibly resist telling the world about their activities until there is adequate evidence that their worth can be demonstrated.

Computer-based training

It was briefly mentioned in the last chapter that the use of computer-based training (CBT) adds a valuable dimension in speeding up decision-making and so compressing the training time-scale. In recent years, micro-technology has contributed to reductions in the cost of computer hardware, opening up opportunities for promoting its use in the training area. Only a few years ago the cost of the computer equipment itself was beyond the means of the training department; most of today's cost is in the program of software.

Facilities for accessing programs may be provided by large computers, which are operated on a time-sharing basis, or by micro-computer. Time-sharing requires a link-up of the terminal a remote computer by telephone line. Difficulties may arise from unsuitable siting of the computer, unfavourable priorities, response delays of equipment breakdown. Sometimes it is possible to limit some of these problem by arranging the use of a computer exclusively for training purposes through a computer bureau. The micro-computer, however, has a distinct advantage over other systems: it offers a comprehensive facility on one's own premises. Computer, terminals and display units can all be accommodated in a limited amount of office space and the complete system is under the user's control. All that is required is a modest electrical power source and suitable programs or software. The training department thus has immediate access to a valuable facility which provides both versatility and portability.

Computer technology in business is now a fact of life, being increasingly used in the larger organizations where the implementation and running costs are more readily justified and absorbed. Smaller businessmen, however, are included to show reluctance to take advantage of new technological developments, not only from the point of view of economics but also because they are apprehensive about being caught up in activities which they do not fully understand. Indeed as entrepreneurs who have been used to holding the business reins and taking all the decisions themselves, they feel that there is a risk that technology could take over completely. It is an important responsibility of members of the training profession to reassure them on this point. The managers need to be shown by non-technical people who do not have a vested commercial interest in the equipment itself that the computer is not something which will take over their thought processes or their jobs, but will only do what they command it to do. In this respect, its obedience may outshine that of some of their employees.

What can training specialists achieve by using computers in their own work? The MSC has urged employers who introduce new technology into their organizations to ensure that they make full use of the computer's teaching and training potential. As with all training media, there must be a pay-off in terms of improved performance at economic cost, so it is logical to assess their applications against this criterion. For some years computers were seen as sophisticated calculators rather than as aids to decision-making. It is true that their facility for producing phenomenally rapid and accurate results where complex mathematics is concerned is of considerable importance. The removal of the drudgery in repetitive arithmetical tasks is certainly welcomed. More recently, however, many other training applications have developed which enable computer technology to make more significant contributions to organizational effectiveness, with the added benefit of economies of scale. The more important of these applications are listed below:

Management of training

The activities of planning, organizing, monitoring, assessing, recording etc. are assumed to involve manual systems. All are extremely time-consuming and some can be quite complicated. Professional training managers who see the trainer or instructor role as the most important part of their jobs are only too pleased to be able to delegate as many of the organizing activities as possible to their supporting staff. The computer can be an extremely useful tool in controlling and speeding up these activities, thus reducing the administrative burden.

There are several ways in which computer programs can be helpful in the management of training. In a large organization the planning of the department's activities and the management of all its resources, such as instructors, training rooms, equipment, training materials, stationery, can involve the control of a large number of variables. This is not always handled as efficiently as it should be and frequently becomes a fire-fighting exercise. Resources are allocated arbitrarily as the need arises and without regard for the effects such action creates elsewhere. A properly designed computer program can take the guesswork out of such decisions, planning the disposition of resources and providing an instant appraisal of their availability.

A trainee's progress through the system can also be more efficiently traced by the computer than by the more common manual means. Details of his educational and occupational background may be stored in the database ready to be retrieved at any time they may be required. This record can also include reports on his training progress, whether as part of a continuing programme or resulting from single modules of training such as technical updating. His future training needs can be fed into the system and the program designed to provide information on the most suitable means of satisfying them. Clearly, a program which provides such detailed data on all the employees trained or under training can also become the source of valuable statistics about the whole training activity in a given period.

Learning aid

The facilities are now being exploited to the full and enable much more sophisticated programs to be designed. To date programmed learning has in effect simulated the page of a book, with a provision for student responses and for revision where the answers given are incorrect. The statements made and questions asked are standard and inflexible. The latest development of a so-called Socratic method in which a more natural dialogue can take place between man and machine. This has led some people to credit the computer with human 'intelligence'. In fact it simply requires a more complex program, which of course demands the employment of more highly skilled programmers.

There have been some interesting new developments in the use of computers in simulations, too. Greg Kearsley, in his informative book *Computer-Based Training,* describes a novel method of training technicians in troubleshooting and repairing electronic circuitry. Circuit diagrams are displayed on the screen and a light pen is used by the trainee to measure to measure voltages at different points in the circuit. When faults are diagnosed, 'repairs' are effected by means of the light pen, this time employed as a 'soldering iron'.

Information source for trainees

There is nothing new in using a computer as a source of information. It is capable of storing a considerable quantity of data. With the increasing preoccupation of trainers with the concept of trainee-based learning, however, it is not surprising that this facility is being used more and more. Learners carrying out training tasks are able to access the information they need through suitable programs in the training room and elsewhere. The computer database provided by MARIS for the Open Tech programme can provide them with detailed information about open learning materials available.

Design of training programmes

Just as scientists and engineers can make use of computer-aided design when developing new concepts and products, so trainers can enlist the help of computers when designing their training programmers. The system lends itself to a high degree of experimentation with various ideas and approaches, with the advantage of instant modification where found necessary.

The discipline required in producing a computer program for particular training application encourages precision in terminology and presentation which may not be present when designing a training programme manually. There is a temptation when writing course materials in the traditional way to be unnecessarily unwieldy in the choice and use of language, making the process more complicated than it need be. The result could well be that the trainees become bored and consequently demotivated. Furthermore, the use of graphical and pictorial representation may not normally be fully exploited, because of the inordinate amount of time necessary to produce something acceptable. A computerized design system, if it does not entirely eliminate such problems, goes a long way towards reducing them. An enormous amount of potential training data can also be stored for retrieval as and when required. Searching for specific information in the database takes a fraction of the time needed to work through books and filing cabiners. The degree of complexity of a computer program suitable for course design raises an important question. The trainer's own training and experience will have concentrated essentially on putting information obtained from practitioners into a suitable learning form. In no way can he be knowledgeable about every aspect of the business likely to be encountered in training. It is probably asking too much that he should be trained in the intricacies of computer programming, which is considered to be a profession in its own right. This suggests that course design has to be a team effort. Detailed information on the topics to be explored has to be obtained from the practitioners, a computer specialist converts that information into a suitable program and the trainer ensures that appropriate training principles are observed and that the outcome meets the agreed objectives.

Testing

A common use of computer programs in training is for test purposes. This application is mentioned here not because it is in any sense a new development, but rather because it is sufficiently important to merit inclusion. For this reason, it is constantly under review and sub,ect to change. As stated earlier, a computer program can provide the basis for assessing a trainees' progress; that is, it can be employed to measure his performance against certain criteria. Those criteria can be incorporated into the program and the computer can carry out the laborious task of comparing performance of a number of trainees against them. The program can also be designed in such a way that it provides a means of selection for training, thus avoiding expensive mistakes in allowing trainees to embark on training programmes to which they are not suited.

By entering appropriate data into the database, tests or exercises may be devised. The correct answers are identified in the program and the accuracy of the trainee's responses communicated either to the trainee himself or to the trainer, as desired. Again, the use of pictorial representation has increased the sophistication of such tests, which do not have to be restricted to the written word. Pictures or diagrams may be used to rest a trainees' capacity to identify certain objects, e.g. an electronic component or sub-assembly which has been shown elsewhere simply by means of symbols.

The flexibility of testing by computer is demonstrated by one of the more advanced forms of interactive testing, known as adaptive testing. Although the program may contain a large number of items designed to test a trainee's comprehension of certain principles, it is not necessary for him to work through all of them or even to satisfy them sequentially in order to demonstrate his understanding. His responses to a limited number of questions will show whether or not he has grasped the appropriate concepts to satisfy given training objectives. The process of testing can thus be speeded up considerably and can proves less frustrating for the trainee.

When evaluating a training programme, for example by the use questionnaires, the collation and interpretation of information from a number of trainees can be an onerous task. Clearly the computer can not only lighten the load by reducing the sheer volume of work, but can also be programmed to interpret the results more meaningfully by drawing attention to the interrelationships between certain responses.

Embedded training

One of the obvious applications of the computer is providing a program which teaches the learner how to use the equipment. Over ten years ago the writer adopted this device on a computerized sales forecasting course. The sales trainees were given instruction through the computer terminal on how to program the computer in the BASIC language. This had the dual advantage of concurrently teaching them about the system and giving them practice in using it. Nowadays it is common practice for suppliers of computer equipment, word processors etc. to include embedded training in the contract of supply.

Do we need computer-based training?

From the above it may be felt that computer-based training (CBT) has a good deal to offer the training manager. Only the salesman is likely to want to convince him that it will provide all the answers to his training problems. It is dangerous, however, to assume that since it is based on new and ever-advancing technology it has to be good. It is equally wrong to avoid trying to evaluate it because it requires radical re-thinking which is somewhat daunting. Some training specialists will be inclined to evade the question by pleading that the cost of implementing CBT would be prohibitive. An honest and detailed appraisal of the alternative means of satisfying an organization's precise training needs is the only way of providing the evidence to support or contest this view. In some businesses, the introduction of CBT has saved money; in others it has cost more than was expected. How does one calculate the cost? If the system is more expensive in hard cash terms but leads to much greater efficiency and effectiveness, is this not an argument for considering it seriously?

It is not at all easy to compare the two alternatives. So much depends on how well the training operation is being carried out without the assistance of the computer. Simply computerizing a sub-standard performance at a higher level of skill, and failure may have more far-reaching effects. For example, in a process industry, the whole costly operation may be brought to a standstill and people and plant put at risk by a single person failing to note and take action on changing conditions in his particular sector. Repetitive manual skills may thus have to be replaced by skills requiring a more intelligent approach to work of a non-recurring nature. An analysis of all possible causes of employee error has to be made in order to provide training which will adequately fit employees for these new tasks. The approach to operator training outlined above goes a long way towards easing the transition from a repetitive manual job to a monitoring or controlling one. If the employee really understands his job, he will more readily see the reasons for change and be more likely to go along with it.

Apprentice training changes

The traditional method of training craftsmen by indentured apprenticeship is rapidly disappearing. The concept of an indenture, a contract 'that binds apprentice to master' and which originally had to be paid for by the unfortunate parents, is an anachronism the removal of which is long overdue. Many 'masters' clung to the idea that the apprentice needed to serve at least five years, i.e. until he reached the age of discretion at 21, before he could be considered suitably skilled to carry out a craftsman's or production worker's job without supervision. Learning by experience in this way was a very long drawn-out affair and depended for its success on the level of instructional skill of the craftsman alongside whom the apprentice worked and on the latter's determination to complete the apprenticeship and 'take up' his indentures. The advances in training philosophy and methods in the years since the war, stimulated partly by the recommendations of the Industrial Training Boards and the Engineering Council, have gradually made the apprenticeship concept redundant. It is now in process of being replaced by 'training agreements'.

The indenture agreement was a remarkably 'open' document. It specified the length of the apprenticeship precisely, but frequently said little, if anything, about what training the apprentice could expect. In spite of this vagueness, the skilled worker who could wave his indentures in front of an employer was more likely to get a job than one who could not.

It was proof that he had completed a programme of training as, for example, a miller or turner, but it seldom identified the skills learned or the standards attained. By contrast, the training agreement is more likely to indicate that induction training, basic skills training, specified skills modules and a part-time course of further education have to be completed to acceptable standards before the agreement may be said to have been discharged. The number and type of skills modules are usually agreed by management and union before the programme is commenced and a statement is made to the effect that the duration will depend upon how long the trainee takes to satisfy the requirements of the various modules.

The implications of these changes for the trainee are self-evident. He knows from the start of a training programme exactly what is going to be required of him, which may allay any fears that he may be used as cheap labour. The training itself will have to be more relevant, because the requirements of each module will have to be satisfied and suitably certificated before he can move on to the next one. This should help to ensure that he is given instruction on skills which are essential, with less attention to those which are simply 'nice to knew'. There are also advantages in his not having to sit out a four-or five-year apprenticeship when he may be quite capable of acquiring the necessary skills in three years. The employer is bound to benefit also. Apart from producing a skilled worker earlier, the standard of training itself is predictably higher, with consequent effects on the quality of output. If the trainee has enjoyed the acquisition of new skills to a high standard within a reasonable period of time and there have been fewer frustrations along the line, it is reasonable to expect him to be better motivated.

Instructional systems development

Training systems fail to meet their objectives for a variety of reasons. The materials may be deficient in important features or may provide too much information of the wrong kind. When training does not meet its objectives of teaching the skills required by employees to carry out their tasks effectively, there is cause for concern. There are also problems of consistency, for example when training manpower resources are supplemented by the part-time use of non-training specialists with appropriate 'technical' knowledge. They may not be familiar with training techniques or the production of training materials, with the result that they develop their own, sometimes in conflict with the training department's philosophy.

A technique known as Instructional Systems Development (ISD) may be helpful in dealing with such problems and others by providing a co-ordinated approach to the training system as a whole. It tabulates what steps have to be taken in each stage of the training process. It does not, however, detail how these steps should be carried out. Nonetheless, most training managers appreciate having checklists to guide them in their activities and ISD fulfils that need in so far as it provides them with prompts in working through the training system and developing training materials.

The various stages in the ISD approach used by the American services will already be familiar to training staff:

- *analysis* - training needs are derived in relation to the requirements of each task or job. Appropriate performance criteria are established.
- *design* - objectives are defined, structure and sequencing determined, tests devised
- *development* - learning media and methods are selected and training materials developed
- *implementation* - the instructional plan is put into effect
- *control* - the programmes are evaluated and the system modified as necessary.

Some of the activities in the above stages are interrelated. For instance, evaluation is something which is taking place all the time and is not simply confined to the control stage. In the event of the training failing to meet the established objectives, it may be necessary to return to the analysis stage and re-start the process.

As will be clear from the earlier section on computer-based systems, there is considerable scope for the use of computers in conjunction with ISD. While it applies to all stages of the process, the areas where it has created greatest interest have been in the design and evaluation of training materials and in testing.

7

Management of Organisational Climate and Organisational Change

The direct teaching approach to the training of apprentices, operators and other individual learners is still used extensively. Whilst an authoritarian style of one-way communication may still survive in some of the smaller establishments where there is no professional training function, it is now widely recognized that successful instruction depends upon an active rather than a passive learner. Directive instruction tends to create dependency, and this is in conflict with the aim to bring a learner up to experienced worker standard at the earliest possible time. This objective requires the use of a systematic method, backed up by a comprehensive two-way information flow, adequate reinforcement of learning and a practical demonstration of that learning under skilled supervision. The work of the Industrial Training Research Unit on instructor performance supports the view that having a systematic approach to instruction does not of itself produce an effective instructor. The learning. Whilst one style may be beneficial another may be a hindrance to meeting the desired objectives.

The research was carried out with a sample of 43 instructors and every statement and action recorded whilst they were supervising their trainees. From this data it was possible to identify different styles of instruction. For example, the instructor who was an automation simply operating the system could be distinguished from the one who was flexible and took into account the specific needs of his trainee whilst still working within an overall master plan. The period of each instruction included basic training and specific operational training.

Information on the past performance and success rate of each instructor was obtained from an independent record source, and a comparison was then made with the identified styles. The results gave a strong indication that there preferred styles of instruction which have a better chance than others of achieving success. These preferred styles were in general centered on the two-way rather than the one-way process of communication. Whilst they conformed to an overall plan which ensured that nothing important was ignored or overlooked, they were characterized by instructor behaviour which showed an awareness that no two trainees and no two tasks were alike but all demanded individual attention and consideration. Each trainee required the right amount of basic information to enable him to learn by doing in a challenging and supportive climate. All the effects of adopting a good instructional style would appear to be positive. They include a better understanding of the job requirements coupled with the ability to carry them out satisfactorily, the generation of enthusiasm for the job and what may be seen as desirable attitudes towards the organization and other employees at all levels.

It is not the purpose of this chapter to give a blow by blow account of every conceivable move in the instruction process but it is felt that the following factors are worthy of mention:

1. The question should be asked initially as to whether one-to-one formal instruction is the best way of imparting the required knowledge or skill. There may be a more suitable method, depending on the objective.
2. The job must be analysed in detail and the learner's present knowledge ascertained. The gap constitutes the learner's training need.
3. An instruction plan must be made, and appropriate targets identified. The most important questions to be asked at this stage are: 'What must the learner be able to do when I have finished the instruction?' and, 'What standards should be able to achieve?' Bearing in mind that there is a limit to the quantity of information a learner can absorb and retain at any time, the instruction should be planned in easily assimilable sections or units, separated by clearly defined breaks. Important points which may make the job easier or affect the quality of the finished work or which may prevent injury to the person or damage to equipment, etc. should be defined so that they may be defined so that they may be impressed on the learner as key parts of the instruction. Where visual aids are deemed to be necessary to reinforce learning they must be appropriate to the information one wishes to impart. They should never be used just for effect, nor to excess.
4. The instructor who organizes himself in such a way as to reduce problems to a minimum clearly stands a better chance of success than one who takes no precautions at all and is content to play everything by ear. There is always the danger of familiarity breeding contempt and important issues consequently being overlooked. It is axiomatic that conditions should be created in which the learner is relaxed and receptive. This requires that the environment is reasonably comfortable and that disruptions to the training process are avoided. Interruptions either visual or verbal not only disturb the learner but can equally give rise to the instructor losing his train of thought. For the same reasons, care should be taken to ensure that everything needed for the instruction, e.g. tools, equipment, diagrams, manuals, are to hand before the process is started.

Accepting that no two learners are alike in personal characteristics or learning capacity, the right relationship has to be established with them, taking into account their particular psychological needs. An extrovert instructor whose manner is overbearing can be very intimidating to a nervous trainee and can thus restrict the learning process. In order to obtain commitment from the trainee, an interest in learning has to be created. This is not always easy particularly where the task is mundane, but that is no excuse for not trying to find some way of making the job satisfying.

5. When carrying out the instruction it is advisable to give the trainee a preview of the task to be performed. This helps him to re-organize his thoughts around the new task before he has to cope with the detail. He needs to know the purpose, the approximate time and the scope of the instruction. An indication of how the job which he is required to perform fits into the general scheme of things is usually in creating interest.

It is important for the instructor to get things right first time, because he is depending on his message getting across so that he does not make problems for the future. This necessitates instructing clearly, patiently, naturally and comprehensively at a reasonable pace, using skillfully whatever tools or aids are required to reinforce learning. Needless to say, any distracting mannerisms have to be controlled.

6. Generally the sooner the trainee can get involved in the instruction process the better, provided the activity is safe and does not risk unnecessary cost. For example, if he is learning how to use a micrometer gauge, his progress will be improved if he is able to handle the instrument at an early stage.

Some instructors, having shown the trainee the job, go away and leave him to practise on his own. This is the very time they should be present, since a trainee left to his own devices will try to take undesirable short cuts and when in trouble may be afraid to call for help. It is important that his early attempts are closely monitored and that his understanding of the activity is thoroughly checked. He should be quite clear at the outset what is required of him and should know what to do if he experiences any difficulty.

7. Operator jobs in a production plant usually demand high speed working to acceptable standards of quality in order to meet output targets. There is a tendency for some instructors to allow trainees to take their time and not concern themselves with speed until they have mastered the skill. This is undesirable in that it introduces two ways of working into the training programme. A crisis in the form of a learning plateau may arise when the transfer has to be made from a low to a high speed mode. The trainee should be encouraged to accept the idea of working at speed from the start, and ergonomic factors and work methods should be established for each process. In other words, the ultimate workplace conditions, including the recommended physical movements and methods involved in the process, should be closely simulated in the training situation. Clearly it is unrealistic for a trainee to be expected to carry out a production process initially at anything like experienced worker performance levels. What can be done,

however, is to introduce the trainee to small units of the process at a time, requiring the achievement of a target speed for each unit before proceeding to the next. When all units in the process have been satisfactorily completed at target speed, it is then necessary to bring them together and to achieve that speed for the total cycle. Extending the number of cycles, or the run, whilst maintaining and improving on the target speed, is known as stamina training and this is the stage at which a trainee may become disheartened if sufficient help and encouragement are not forthcoming. Adequate explanation has to be given for every stage of the training process, and the need to achieve a target speed should not be interpreted by the trainee as slave-driving. It is important that speed is maintained whilst the trainee is actually working but that ample relaxation time is also built into the programme. As the trainee gains confidence and competence, so the relaxation time can be progressively reduced.

8. The record of progress should be freely available to the trainee throughout the instructional process. It is helpful for him to know just how much additional effort is needed to achieve target performance. Frequently it can be quite small and knowing this can remove a good deal of anxiety.

   When teaching skills to, among others, craft and technician apprentices, it is strongly recommended, and indeed is a condition of ITB approval for such training, that the trainee keeps a log book. It records the major elements in the training programme and should be signed by the instructor at the end of each stage of off-the-end instruction and by the supervisor during on-the-job training. This record can make a useful contribution to the reinforcement of learning. It also helps to some extent to assess the trainee's progress and provides him with a handy reference book for the future.

9. Finally, the trainee's progress is monitored at suitable intervals until it is confirmed that target performance is being maintained. There is a joint responsibility at this stage between the supervisor and the instructor. Until the supervisor is happy with the trainee's contribution the instructor should not consider his job complete. The trainee will have built up a working relationship with the instructor during this training and will expect his help and advice to be available until sufficient confidence has been gained to carry out the job required with competence.

Where the initial training is undertaken in an off-the-job area, as recommended for example by the Industrial Training Boards the time that the transfer from training room to workplace is made will vary considerably with the degree of complexity of the job and the rate of progress of the trainee. One important consideration, particularly when re-training adults, who may be over-anxious, is that the move should not be made too soon simply in the interests of getting the work out. Trying to solve one problem in this way may merely result in creating others, such as low morale with consequent low performance, high scrap rate, increased accidents, absenteeism and possibly even higher labour turnover. The work and morale of the longer serving skilled workers can also be affected by their pre-occupation with the problems of the newcomers, with adverse effects on their own productivity.

The lecture is a time-honoured means of communicating with a group. Usually defined as an informative discourse delivered to an audience, it clearly implies a one-way talk to a number of people given by someone who is knowledgeable about his subject. It normally covers a specific, discrete topic rather than a range of subjects, and for it to be successful it demands a high level of skill from the lecturer.

Often a lecture is used when it is necessary to convey messages to a large audience, since other methods of a more participative nature would prove too cumbersome to operate. This creates problems, because the prospect of significant learning taking place with a large group is greatly diminished by the lack of interaction, not only between the lecturer and member of the audience but also between the members themselves. Unless the lecturer is expert at arousing individual attention and creating audience involvement, there is a severe risk of members becoming inattentive and distracted. Some lecturers use humour to create interest, and, if they are naturally humorous people who choose the time and the subject carefully, this can be very successful. The speaker who is not a natural humorist, however, can be a disaster if his jokes are irrelevant and misfire. The danger of relying on humour is that the audience may remember the quips but not the subject matter, and one must always remember the objectives of the exercise and ask oneself whether or not these are being achieved.

It is frequently assumed that someone who is master of his profession is worthy of the attention of his audience. This is very far from the case. The nation's greatest authority on a particular subject can also be the nation's biggest bore in the lecture room. If the object of the lecture is learning, then it is essential that the speaker is not only knowledgeable in his subject but is also skilled in creating a learning climate in which he can get his message across. This requires an understanding of the needs of the audience. Sometimes they are not volunteers and therefore have no vested interest in the topic, finding it unstimulating. They may have their minds full of other problems. Somehow one has to be able to break into their thoughts and re-direct them. Creating the right conditions for learning to be effective requires attention to whole lot of factors. The most important of these are summarized below.

1. The environment, including whatever services have to be provided, must be suitable. As with any other type of training the trainees must be comfortable and reasonably relaxed. Anything short of this will create a distraction and inhibit learning.
2. The needs of the audience in terms of subject matter must be ascertained in advance. There are real problems here, since they may not be a homogeneous

group, that is, their level of knowledge of the subject may vary considerably. Setting the level of the lecture to ensure that the more informed are not bored is likely to leave those with limited knowledge of the topic well behind. Starting from a much lower datum point in order to cater for the less informed may well frustrate those who have heard it all before. This problem is typical of many which managers and specialists have to decide upon, and calls for the exercise of skilled judgement. The lecturer who succeeds in getting it right is hailed as an interesting and absorbing speaker; the one who fails to do so attracts less favourable epithets. One obvious solution to this difficulty is to split the audience into groups, practicable, if only for the reason that one usually does not know who will be coming until they are there. The writer would suggest that a reasonable approach might to be try to set the talk at such a level that the less knowledgeable are stretched but are not entirely out of their depth. This may be tedious for the better informed members in the early stages, but they should be asked to bear with the speaker until he has filled in some of the more fundamental information for the benefit of the newcomers to the subject. Reassurance can be given that the talk will move on to more advanced aspects as soon as is practicable. This avoids the trap of allowing the more knowledgeable to feel that the whole lecture is going to be at a low level. It cannot be over-emphasized that there are dividends to be reaped from letting the audience know right from the start exactly what they can expect.

3. The subject must be thoroughly researched and the lecture carefully planned to meet the perceived need, care being taken to structure it logically insteps separated by natural breaks. Both speaker and audience need time to collect their thoughts between stages. Although there are no hard and fast rules about the duration of such stages, in general it is unlikely that the audience's span of attention will exceed about 20 minutes. It is often advantageous to use the intervals to invite questions or to circulate written information. The vital factor is that no activity is so long that the speaker loses the audience's attention. How the break are used is of less importance.

4. Visual aids and handouts should be used with discretion. It should never be assumed that the use of training aids is essential for a lecture to be successful. Many a lecture has been ruined by visual aids which have been badly produced or equipment which has been inexpertly operated. These devices should be used to reinforce, not to do the lecturer's job for him. Handouts are a valuable means of consolidating and supplementing information provided in a lecture, but they must be well designed and reproduced and must be used at the right time to be effective. Giving them out at the commencement of or during a talk is inviting the audience to absorb itself in reading them and to ignore the speaker. Whenever handouts are distributed, whether during breaks in the programme or at the end, time must be allowed for them to be read without interruption. The audience

should also be told at the beginning how visual aids and handouts will be used, whether or not they need to take notes, the approximate duration of the talk and when questions will be taken.

5. The skills expected of a lecturer differ very little from those required of any public speaker. Creating and maintaining the interest of the audience demands that the speaker considers the following points among others.

   He should adopt a natural, relaxed style. Some people believe that when addressing a group one is expected to behave as a totally different person. Since few are good actor, they fail dismally. Individuality is an essential feature of effective speaking. The lecturer should not try to emulate someone else, but project his own personality. He should therefore behave quite naturally and, as in one-to-one instruction, should avoid mannerisms which are in any way distracting. He should not appear slovenly or take up a stance which impedes his delivery. Needless to say he should also be wary of saying or doing anything which may cause offence to any member of the audience. The way he uses his voice can make or mar a lecture. Its level should be right for the distance it has to travel and the natural acoustics of the room. Variation in tone and pace also helps to maintain interest and so he should try to refrain from speaking in a monotone.

   The lecturer should use straightforward language which may be interpreted by everyone in the audience without too much difficulty. Jargon should be used with care and only when it is known that the audience will understand it. Sentences should be short and to the point and padding should be avoided.

   Every member of the group should be made to feel that the lecture is a dialogue between the speaker and himself even though words may not in fact be exchanged. This requires eye-to-eye contact with as many people as possible, and a determined effort not to direct one's comments to the ceiling, walls or floor or to one's notes. It also means that the speaker has to be able to read the non-verbal signals of the audience and respond to them as if they were spoken. However, a temptation that he should avoid is to address all his statements to one person who gives him a warm feeling by hanging on his every word and nodding sagely!

   The way in which lecture notes are used requires careful consideration. Detailed notes which are read out verbatim often create a dependency which results in a stilted performance. If the speaker expects his audience to respond to him, they deserve more than a mere reading of the lesson. They will expect him to have done his homework and to have planned and rehearsed his talk so as not to have to depend on comprehensive notes. Subject headings on small cards should usually be sufficient to provide the necessary triggers except where the lecture treats a highly technical or involved subject, in which case more detailed information may be necessary.

When expounding a controversial argument, other points of view should not be ignored. Dogmatism may lose an otherwise receptive audience. That is not to say that a speaker cannot be positive or even forceful but he should be wary of sweeping aside views which do not coincide with his own.

The lecturer should be honest with his audience. If he finds that a member of the group knows more about the subject than he does, he should not try to cover up but should make use of the available expertise. This can be done by involving the member and encouraging him to share his knowledge with everyone. Furthermore, if asked a question to which he does not know the answer, it is far better that the speaker should admit it and should promise to find the answer for the questioner at some later time. Most people will accept that the man who knows all the answers has not yet been born, and they will respect a lecturer who is prepared to admit that there are gaps in his knowledge. Trying to bluff one's way through such a situation does nothing for one's reputation.

Control over nervousness is important. Even the most accomplished speakers will say that they are apprehensive when they first goon. Once having got under way and having establish a rapport with their audiences, however, they can relax and even enjoy the experience. A common mistake made by the inexperienced lecturer is to allow himself to be carried along at a fast pace by nervous energy at the start, not giving himself time to think about what has to be said. If he takes his time right at the beginning the audience is able to get used to his delivery. At the same time he has the necessary breathing space in which to marshal his thoughts. The pacing of each of the talk helps in this regard. A lecture should not be a long continuous tirade but a well balanced talk suitably broken up with pauses between statements. A pause of several seconds seems much shorter to an audience than to the speaker and he should rehearse his lecture with the aid of a tape recorder, experimenting with pauses of different duration. The effect if likely to be a reduction in the speed of delivery with marked improvement in the quality of performance.

6. The lecture should always end on a positive note. People like to go away feeling that they have been stimulated and have been given food for thought. The end should never be an anti-climax. Sometimes, a brief review of the main points of the talk is in order and useful in putting everything in perspective. Often a call to future action is required and needs to be put over with conviction. Where such action is being intimated, members of the audience must know precisely what is expected of them.

7. It is usually helpful for the audience to be thanked for their attention and participation and where appropriate an offer of future help may be made.

In spite of criticisms by the advocates of participative learning, the lecture still has its place in certain training situations. Indeed it may be the only practicable way to handle a large audience. Since by its nature it tends to be relatively passive and unstimulating, however, it needs to have a built-in participative element in order to stand a reasonable prospect of satisfying its objectives. It is not only necessary that feed-back is obtained from the audience but also that it is acted upon and not ignored. The skilful use of audience involvement can turn an unstimulating recitation or mere entertainment into a dynamic learning experience for everyone, including the lecturer.

Participative methods

The following training methods rely to a major extent for their success as learning media on the active involvement of the trainees. The degree of this participation varies from one method to another but the overall philosophy implies that learning by doing or by getting personally involved, even if only in discussion, is the most successful route to acquiring knowledge and skill, or towards changing attitudes. The cross-fertilization of beliefs, attitudes, knowledge, experience, etc. between people who have matured in widely differing environments is seen to be invaluable for the broadening of their outlook on life in general and on their work in particular. Furthermore, by inviting total participation of the trainees, a climate is created in which they feel that they are being treated as responsible adults and that their views and their knowledge and experience are valued. The trust and confidence thus engendered go long way towards obtaining optimum contributions from members of the group, and the most effective learning from the activity.

Conference

No apologies are given for including the conference in the list of training methods. Although few conference delegates will consciously think that they are attending a training session, if they do not learn something from it, what is it purpose? They expect to go away wiser than they were before they came, but they may have little idea in advance in what way they will benefit.

The conference is usually a highly structured device for conveying a message or messages on a large scale, often to an audience of several hundred people. It attracts delegates with common interests, usually from a wide cross-section of society, who seek the opportunity to hear and comment on the views of recognized authorities in the areas covered. The literal translation of the word conference implies consultation. In other words, delegates should not only hear an authoritative discourse from the speakers but should reasonably expect to be able to obtain answers to questions concerning the topic or topics covered. It is in this respect that conferences often fail to meet their objectives, either for the reason that the objectives were not properly formulated or communicated to delegates in the first place or because the chairman conducts the discussion badly.

The chairman is a key figure in the conference. He wields considerable power and is expected to have complete control both of the speakers themselves and of the audience. He should know in advance what he can expect from his speakers and should plan adequate question time after each talk. Having to curtail question time due to bad planning can result in a number of dissatisfied delegates, and can turn an otherwise good conference for most into a disappointment for many. One of the weaknesses in the system is that it provides an excellent opportunity for the *prima donnas* to take floor and play to the gallery. They tend not to have anything constructive to say but nevertheless take up an inordinate amount of time, to the detriment of those who may have valuable contributions to make to the debate. Handling this situation demands skill on the part of the chairman and a firmness which cannot be wrongly interpreted as dictatorial. There will, of course, be a good deal of reticence on the part of many delegates to stand up in front of such a large audience to make their points or to put questions. The benefit of the aggregated views and experience of the assembly can thus be lost in the conference situation.

Another major task of the conference chairman is to sum up at the end. Relevance and brevity are the keynotes here. The audience have listened to speakers for a number of hours and are now ready to go home. Prolonging the conference for very long whilst adding nothing to what has already been said does nothing to help send them away with warm feelings about the meeting. What is said depends on the style of the chairman but the temptation to indulge in the expression of personal viewpoints at this stage is to be avoided. Summing up should involve briefly summarizing the major points arising from the conference, and thanking the speakers and others involved for their contributions. It is often appropriate to re-state the objectives of the conference, expressing the hope that they have been achieved. Sometimes valuable feedback is obtained by audience reaction to this.

Many see the conference more as an opportunity for meeting people, particularly the speakers, than for learning much about the subjects discussed. Training specialist are not alone in this. There is certainly a pay-off for them in making contact, at coffee or lunch time, with recognized authorities in fields of direct interest to them and indeed with fellow specialists. The more aware they are of what is going on in their profession the better in terms of keeping up-to-date and coping with change.

Seminar

The more common seminar is a conference on a smaller scale but incorporating a greater degree of participation from the members. The word is derived from the Latin for 'seed-plot' and thus suggest that it is a well prepared situation for sowing, nurturing and developing ideas.

The seminar is usually centered around a single theme which is examined in some depth. The speakers are acknowledged specialists who make brief presentations outlining the topic or topic to be discussed and lead the members towards certain tasks which they want them to explore. The size of the seminar should be such that it can be readily divided up into small syndicate groups. The syndicate size is determined by its effectiveness as a discussion group. Too small a group limits the expertise and views that can be drawn on and so produces frustration and a sense of inadequacy. Too large a group tends to result in domination by a few and the inhibition of members who feel overshadowed by those who are more forthcoming. This suggests, say, a minimum number of four and a maximum of five or six. Syndicates of over six, unless very carefully selected, can suffer from the same problem as the large conference in which valuable contributions are forfeited.

The number of syndicates used depends upon the reporting-back procedure. It is assumed that after each input from a speaker the seminar breaks into separate syndicate groups to examine the task. They are given a time limit to reach their conclusions by democratic processes and they each appoint a spokesman, who is not necessarily chairman of the group, to report back to the full group session. Clearly, if a large number of spokesmen have to report back on the same topic, the full group session becomes a lengthy process with a good deal of repetition. The writer would place a limit of four on the number of groups in these circumstances. Of course, if a number of tasks is allocated concurrently, the limit of four groups can be applied to each different task.

The amount of time devoted to the various activities in a seminar needs to be arrived at very carefully and can be quite critical. It is not an uncommon reaction from members that they feel that they obtain greater benefit from the syndicate discussions than from the full group sessions to which they report back. This is not surprising, since they have explored the problems in some depth in the small groups, where they are more closely involved as individuals, and then find the full group sessions as so much repetition of the same themes. This suggests that more time should be allocated to the syndicate discussions 'where the real work gets done' than to the full group meetings.

Handouts summarizing the man points made by the speakers are useful at the end of seminar sessions to provide reference material for members. To encourage them to make use of the information in the future, handouts should be brief and to the point.

Winding up a seminar may differ very little from closing a conference. The trainer may have to summarize, if appropriate, but again he must be on his guard against spending too much time reiterating points which have been gone over many times already in syndicate and full group sessions. Taking the point that any training activity should end on a positive note, it makes sense to devote time in the winding up session to discussing and taking decisions on future plans arising out of the activity.

The discussion is a common training vehicle which is useful for the presentation of ideas and plans, particularly when issues have to be clarified or expanded and the views of groups of people have to be ascertained. The discussion leader required skill in planning, careful preparation, encouraging the involvement of individuals controlling the debate, summarizing the results of the meeting and ensuring that suitable action is taken.

The objectives of the meeting need to be clearly established and the necessary information gathered in advance. Part of the planning process is to decide who should be present, since a good deal of expensive time can be wasted by people being required to attend all the time when they only have a tenuous, or limited, interest in the topics being discussed. It is suggested that there should be a skeleton membership for the full period of the meeting, and co-opted members should be called as and when required.

Having established the membership of the discussion meeting it is vitally important that a detailed agenda is sent out some time before the event. Lack of precise information about the subjects to be discussed can give rise to members misinterpreting them and arriving at the meeting having briefed themselves for the wrong topics. Needless to say, this results not only in the inefficient use of time but can also be highly de-motivating. When all members know in advance the precise purpose of the meeting and the rules which apply, they start on common ground. If they know the meeting is purposeful, they will be motivated to contribute towards a successful outcome, thus improving the prospects of a practical solution to the problem.

For the discussion leader to be successful, he must be able to handle the debate in such a way that useful contributions are optimized and inappropriate offerings limited. This calls for sensitivity not only in being able to identify practical and workable suggestions but also in being able tactfully to reject the less acceptable ones without offending the contributors. Members should not be allowed to digress from the matter in hand and should be encouraged to be brief. There is a tendency for some groups to go on debating an issue long after everyone has agreed on a course of action. Another time-waster is the practice of some members to carry on private discussions during thy debate and this should again be curbed diplomatically.

Following the discussion, the leader needs to record the outcome of the meeting and ensure that everyone is clear about what future action has to be taken and who has to take it. This last requirement often means that the leader takes on the role of progress chaser between meetings, but this is necessary because failure to follow up the items auctioned in one meeting will lead to time being wasted in the next.

A symposium is a form of discussion meeting. Commonly used by professional bodies, it usually consists of a collection of papers given by a number of speakers. The contributions normally deal with discrete topics within a common theme and are straight lectures, not allowing any immediate feedback in case it may prejudice the talks of future speakers. It is not unusual, however, for a panel discussion to take place at the very end under the leadership of a trainer or chairman, who determines the way in which questions may be put to the speakers.

Team training

In the mid-1950s, when the writer moved from a local government environment to an industrial one, his naively held beliefs as to how manufacturing firms operated were rudely shattered. The books he had consulted led him to the view that management was a team effort and everyone employed was working towards clearly identified corporate objectives. In reality, not only were these objectives completely unknown to a large proportion of the employees, including some managers, but it was quite normal for departmental chiefs to shut themselves away in separate boxes 'doing their own thing' and having little contact with the world outside their departments.

Although over many years this outmoded approach to management persisted in some companies, there has in general been a growing awareness that the contributions of individuals to corporate goals have to be not only optimized but co-ordinated if these orgnizations are to be successful, or indeed survive. People have become alive to the fact that, whatever advantages there may be in giving managers and their subordinates freedom in working out how they should do what they perceive to be their individually jobs, activities which do not promote the organization's objectives, directly or indirectly, are a luxury which is simply not justified. Insularity breeds such luxuries, and it is manifestly unjust that the efficient employees in organizational terms should have to bear the burden of the inefficiencies of others.

It is, of course, widely known among training managers and specialists that problem-solving in groups is generally more productive of solutions than problem-solving by individuals. It should follow, therefore, that there are benefits to be reaped by work groups operating in teams and capitalizing on their combined resources as they work together to meet organizational goals. This policy should prove to be in the interests of the business as a whole, and it would appear to have other desirable by-products. For example, by removing the traditional communication barriers between individuals or departments, it should widen their horizons and enable then to see more of the total action. The effect on morale could be considerable. Much industrial unrest and conflict arises from people being ignorant of management's intentions. Opening up the communications networks and encouraging greater involvement in company operations must surely be to everyone's advantage in the long run.

If management and other work groups are encouraged to work together in teams, it is logical to train them as teams. One of the criticisms of training individuals in isolation is that when they return from a training programme fired with enthusiasm to put into practice what they have learned, they often encounter indifference, or worse, they are flatly denied the opportunity or facilities to implement any changes. The training then is largely abortive, unless the individual is soon promoted and is able to exercise more personal freedom in the way he operates. Training in a team context enables problems to be directly work-orientated and decisions to be taken jointly by those people who have a vested interest. This helps to ensure greater commitment to making decisions work. It also gives individuals confidence that the day-to-day decisions that they are taking in the workplace are not in conflict with the philosophy of other members of their team. The quality of decisions can be improved since more information can be produced and more options explored. Mistakes made by individual team members will more readily come to light and be eliminated, and where decisions require a variety of actions from members, these may be more fairly allocated.

It should not be thought that team work or team training is in fact a panacea for all ills in problem-solving. There can sometimes be difficulties. These may centre around the composition of the team. A team made up of people with largely similar characteristics may be less effective than one with differing philosophies, experience, skills, etc., since the homogeneous group will tend to have a narrower view of problems. A mixed group may give rise to more serious in group pressures and will call for greater expertise from the trainer in handling them. For example, in a team which comprises employees at different organizational levels, there may be a danger of individuals trying to pull rank in order to have things their own way.

As with seminar groups, the desirable size for a team may be between four and six, and one of the dangers of having a greater number is that the team may tend to sub-divide into smaller groups and so disrupt the problem-solving process. Team achievement could also be adversely affected where individuals were permitted to leave the group before the allotted project time expired in order to attend to pressing problems in the workplace.

Team development tends to go through certain identifiable stages before in can be considered productive. Initially there will be a certain amount of confusion in which each member tries to orientate himself and establish his position with respect to the others. In seeking to apply themselves to the task the team members will continue in a stage of uncertainty, whilst searching for support from anyone who is prepared to offer it. Lack of confidence in their ability to carry out the task often leads them to attack it or the trainer and in extreme cases may even give rise to a total withdrawal. This uncertainty is also characterized by conflict within the group, though this should not necessarily be seen as destructive. Frequently conflict is a positive agent which enables people to resolve differences of viewpoint effectively. As the team gradually becomes accustomed to working together on a common task, the individual members begin to appreciate the support they are getting from each other and the first signs of a cohesive group emerge. Trust is built up between them and they come to value each other's knowledge and experience, thus giving each greater confidence. The final stage, which is commonly termed 'maturity', arrives when the team has established its structure and *modus operandi* and its members are working effectively together.

Needless to say, the trainer will usually be able to identify these stages in a team's development by observing the behaviour of its members, and he should resist the temptation to interrupt the process unless specifically asked for help and guidance.

This may not happen, particularly with management groups, since assuming adequate briefing and basic information are given in the first place, the aggregated experience and knowledge present in the group is usually sufficient for it to reach a rational solution to the problem. Frequently the difficulty is not lack of knowledge or expertise but lack of the ability to use it. The team concept of training helps people to test their experience and ideas against those of other members of the group and so check their acceptability. This process thus enables them to decide which aspects of their knowledge are usable and which may have to be rejected or at least shelved until customs or practices change.

Patrick Suessmuth has made some interesting observations on the monitoring of sound levels in groups in order to identify the stages reached in their deliberations:

- the start-up stage in which the sound level quickly peaks and then flattens out
- the thought-collecting stage during which there is comparative silence, which the trainer is advised to respect. Intervention by him at this point would be disruptive and would restrict progress
- the main working stage, in which the sound builds up to a high level and fluctuates for a fairly long period, when the information is being gathered from individual members and consolidated
- the finishing stage where there is a sharp drop in noise level and any subsequent rise is likely to be mere chatting. When this stage is reached the trainer should check that the task has been completed.

When introducing team training into an organization, the trainer has a mammoth selling job to do. The first hurdle will be to get the active support of the top management. However, once obtained, it will provide a springboard from which to integrate the methods gradually throughout the organization. If the management are seen to go along with the idea to the extent of involving themselves in the process, there are better prospects of support at lower levels. This is only one of the prerequisites for success, however, and the ultimate activity has to be worthy of the effort that has gone into selling it. The following suggestions may be helpful in getting the required co-operation:

1. Make it clear to everyone concerned that the problems to be worked on will be real organizational problems and not generalized hypothetical examples. The training, although carried out off-the-job will be part of the member's everyday work.
2. The composition of the teams should be such that they have the basic expertise to carry out the project and the authority to implement their finding rather than having to take them through lengthy procedures of obtaining higher agreement.

3. The activity should not be open-ended. To underline the real life nature of the project, target times should be established and adhered to where possible.
4. The importance of each member's contribution should be stressed and absences from the activity, except in dire circumstances, discouraged.
5. The effectiveness of the team should be monitored and the results communicated to members and examined. It is important that group effectiveness, and thus corporate effectiveness in the organization, is optimized at the earliest possible time. Competition which may be counter-productive is therefore undesirable.
6. The team should be treated as a group rather as individuals. Where any rewards or sanctions are necessary or desirable, these should be on a team basis.
7. The activity should be organized within the rules of any other business activity, e.g. objectives should be clearly defined, budgets of time and cost prepared, suitable resources made available, means of dealing with the results understood.

Some training managers have tried to introduce team training into their organizations relying on one specific method or technique. Those with an organizational or systems orientation have chosen, for example, management by objectives on the assumption that if everyone is shown how to set targets they will work together for the common good. Others who are more behaviourally biased have put their money on, say, sensitivity training, expecting that the enhanced insight and awareness in individual members will improve the effectiveness of the team. Neither of these approaches of itself is likely to provide the desired result. The likelihood is that a judicious combination of both approaches will improve the prospects of making some progress towards team and ultimately organizational effectiveness. One pilot study using this combination of techniques has been described by Iain Mangham. A consultant was invited into an organization in which a particular department employing eight people had been re-organized in the interests of better consultation and employees involvement. The success of this operation had encouraged the management to introduce training aimed at greater and more far-reaching participative management. Team training was therefore seen as a first stage.

The process was introduced by means of a simple questionnaire, the results of which were shared by common consent. It explored the views of each team member on how his team handled its objectives, conflict, etc., and surprisingly brought about widely differing responses. These were examined and explanations sought for the variations. Initially the actual team's problems were disguised, references being made to difficulties experienced by other groups. The scepticism about team work and the feeling that conflict should be avoided were eventually overcome, however, and members gradually became more open and honest with each other, trust being developed to the working group.

The next stage in the study consisted of a practical team exercise in which members were not able to communicate verbally with each other. It provided a bridge to finding solutions to group problems through the use of delegation and shared responsibility and led to discussions on job enrichment and job enlargement as means of optimizing group performance. This was followed by another simple exercise providing members with the opportunity to bring their work related problems out into the open and discuss them. The results of this session and the actions agreed were committed to paper and circulated to members for their confirmation and commitment. Subsequent training followed established management by objectives practice, concentrating on defining the role and objectives of the group in the previous discussions into the future work programme. The final session was one of consolidation and making sure that the results were in no way conflicting.

Although only anecdotal feedback was used to measure the usefulness of the programme, members were in no doubt that it met its objectives by obtaining commitment to the continuous review and improvement of departmental performance through team work. Other observations included a noticeable increase in morale and a wider recognition of the value, both from the individual and the organizational point of view, of members working closely together.

The benefits of team training are unlikely to be felt in the short term. In the long term they will be forthcoming so long as team work is not seen as the magic wand which on its own will convert an ineffective department into a successful one. New problems arise if a highly effective team is created within an organization in which other departments are relatively ineffective. This can only lead to frustration and counter-productive rivalry which will militate against the achievement of the desired objectives. To be most profitable, therefore, team, working needs to be compatible with some form of organization development.

Organization development is often wrongly described as a technique handling change. In reality it is a strategy which depends for its operation on the use of a number of techniques, most of which have been developed individually over many years and are familiar to training managers. The justification for OD, seen by many as being surrounded in mystique, is that orgnizations are in a constant state of flux but, because of the preoccupation with production and profits, their management, systems, procedures, techniques, etc. do not change in sympathy with the needs of the business. Companies can multiply their sales volume, change their product mix dramatically and even transfer their activities to a totally different business sector, without any significant change in organization structure, in administration or in the training of their employees to satisfy the changed requirements. Growth of the business can cause confusion, reduce morale and create friction and conflict, introduce more routine, formality and managerial remoteness, increase controls, perpetuate existing systems and practices to the point of making them unmanageable, and so on. This clearly gives rise to gross inefficiencies and a deficiency in the resources, skills and attitudes required to meet the new challenges.

The pioneers of OD were behavioural scientists and naturally their approach centered around the human aspects of running an organization and keeping pace with change. This may explain why it has tended to mystify some training specialists. In the last ten years or so, however, the skills of the OD consultants have tended to become less specialized, technical and organizational factors having assumed at least equal importance with purely behavioural factors. Employees working in groups are developed in such a way that they are helped, through greater involvement and understanding, to satisfy both their own and the organization's needs within the constraints and influences of the changing internal and external environment. For the training specialist involved with OD the accent is on development rather than simply training. He is committed to creating a learning climate enabling employees to develop themselves in the work situation, optimizing the application of their life experience, rather than simply using the knowledge or skills acquired through conventional training. The latter is sometimes criticized for its lack of relevance when it is carried on outside the work situation. Employee development in the OD context, however, is at the heart of the organization's activities and in the more enlightened business will attract as much attention from the management as technical or other organizational factors. Ideally, work is a continuous learning experience, a way of life which broadens the employee's horizons, is directly related to organizational goals and is dynamically geared to change.

This approach is reflected in the IPM's 'A boost for continuous development' campaign launched in 1984. The most important statement to emerge to date is its *Code for Continuous Department; People and Practice.* It is hoped that the campaign will stimulate greater interest in the idea that employees have to be developed throughout their working lives if they are to keep pace with the constantly changing needs of the business.

Case study

The case study method has had a substantial following in training in the years since the war, its greatest exponent being the Harvard Business School. The object of the case study is to present trainees with a realistic business situation, giving a considerable quantity of background information from which they are expected to analyse, and compute the outcome of, a series of events, or provide solutions to specific problems. Sometimes the information is purely fictitious and is concocted in order to make points in a fairly convincing way. More often, and more appropriately, the case study is a summary of a documented real-life situation in which a named organization has found itself. The actual outcome is usually known to the trainer and he is thus able to compare or contrast the trainees' findings with it. Since the true outcome may not be the most expedient, however, it is more profitable for the trainees to explore the various options that might be available rather than seek the 'right' answer. When dealing with management decisions, for example, it is quite unrealistic to assume that there is only one acceptable answer to a complex problem and it would be undesirable for the trainer to suggest to trainees that decision-making can be so tidy. Nevertheless, there are many trainers who offer trainees neat packaged solutions have been proved the most successful in practice.

Case studies are normally examined in small syndicate groups, and the points already made about these groups apply equally here. It is not unusual for each group to be given a different question to study in depth, so that more ground can be covered in the full group session and duplication is minimized. Many case studies dealing with the practical problems of specific organizations are available from a variety of sources, but the use of these does of course restrict trainees to studying situations which are not always easily related to their own problems and indeed may never be repeated elsewhere. There are therefore advantages in using case studies derived from the experiences of the group's own organization, where there is first-hand information about its successes and failures.

One variation on the case study is the 'action maze'. This is a programmed case study in which the initial issue of information is restricted to that necessary for the trainees to arrive at their first decision. In a similar way to the multi-choice questionnaire, a number of alternatives are given from which the group has to select the one which in their estimation is most appropriate, having studied all the data. When they have made their choice they obtain further printed information from the trainer, enabling them to check their solutions against the 'preferred' answers and to examine the effects of their decisions. The information also leads them into the next set of decisions, which are produced in the same manner. The number of decision sequences will depend upon how many specific issues the trainer wishes the group to explore.

'Incident process' is a further example of the case study approach, its main objective being to sharpen up the trainees' questioning skills. In this method the trainer does not give the groups sufficient data on which to make valid decisions. After due consideration of the available facts, they then have to request such information as they deem necessary to make a judgement. This type of exercise encourages trainees to scrutinize data carefully, to formulate the right questions to elicit further information and to interpret such information before taking decisions. It is therefore a very suitable vehicle for developing the skills required for dealing with industrial relations and disciplinary problems.

Practice in the use of the Socratic method of question and answer is also useful in handling health and safety and other investigations, in most interviewing situations, and in problem-solving generally. This dialectical method is attributed to the Greek philosopher Socrates, although he himself did not commit his experiences to writing and we have to rely for evidence on the written work of his pupils and others. The story goes that after being told by the Oracle that he was the wisest man in Greece, Socrates modestly refuted this and set out to discover who really was. By skilful questioning of other Athenians, giving nothing away himself, he ascertained that they claimed a level of wisdom which they did not in fact possess. Both he and they knew nothing, but whilst they were unaware of the limitations of their knowledge, he was fully conscious of his. He thus had one piece of information which they did not have and he therefore had to concede that he was the wisest man in Greece! W L Reese records in his *Dictionary of Philosophy and Religion* that Socrates' vocation in life was comparable with 'a gadfly, causing the lazy steed of Athens to bestir herself', or 'a midwife helping others to give birth to their ideas'. The method is now widely practised by trainers and teachers and is characterized by their use of patient questioning to bring the trainee or student to a point where he can recognize a true conclusion without actually being told that the conclusion is in fact true.

One of the criticisms levelled at case studies by trainees is that they are bombarded with volumes of information which bewilder them and can introduce considerable stress. In other types of training they often complain that they do not have sufficient data on which to base any useful decisions. In the case study it is helpful to inform them that they may have more information than they need, and as in real life, one of their first tasks should be to reject those facts which are inappropriate or irrelevant.

Since the case study is based on actual events it should provide an ideal vehicle for training in decision-making. Whether it does so or not depends very much on how it is handled by the trainer, how flexible he is and how sensitive he is to the real needs of the group. However realistic the data being used, the training environment, being off-the-job, introduces an artificial element. There is the risk, therefore, that participants will treat the whole experience with detachment and will not enter into the spirit of an activity which can and should have a practically based outcome. The trainer's briefing for the exercise should reflect the reality of the situation and its importance to the organization. He should refrain from introducing hypothetical factors or arbitrary viewpoints into the syndicate discussions but should only dispense true facts about what actually happened in the case. In the final full group session, where the trainer is seeking alternative solutions to the problem, hypothetical outcomes are valid and should be explored. If examples can be provided as to how such solutions were arrived at in similar cases, so much the better.

Role play

Role playing requires the acting out of parts in situations as close to those arising in the real job as possible. It essentially consists of an interview or a series of interviews, each participant having been given a brief specifically relating to his role and the particular set of circumstances to be enacted. The way he carries out his brief depends upon how he sees his role and how he believes the particular situation should be handled. He develops a strategy as to how to approach the task and tries to anticipate the reactions of the other party or parties. Some role playing develops into a negotiating situation and thus provides the opportunity for exploring the skills required in this activity.

Whatever the purpose of role playing exercises, it is important that they reflect the true working environment of the participants. In other words, not only should the everyday conditions be reproduced as far as possible but the roles should be acted out within the limits of existing managerial and supervisory authority and the constraints of organizational systems, procedures and policies. Acting for the sake of acting is purposeless. The over-confident love to demonstrate how clever they are, the more reticent suffer dreadful traumas. And herein lies one of the problems of role playing. It can be stressful for many who are afraid of making fools of themselves in public. Because it involves some practical demonstration of their abilities it makes them feel rightly or wrongly that they have much to lose in prestige and reputation. Their self-esteem is under threat. It is for this reason among others that it is advisable not to carry out role playing exercises in isolation or at the beginning of a training programme. Participants need to get to know each other and get used to working together before they are required to carry out this type of activity. Once the barriers are down and they are relaxed and no longer care what they say to each other, they will be willing and able to embark on role playing, and indeed will be eager to do so. Because of the satisfaction derived from such practical learning activities, it is common for participants to rank these among their most pleasurable and profitable training experiences. It is helpful for role playing to be carried out in small syndicate groups rather than in full group sessions. The pressures are very much less and for this reason learning is less likely to be inhibited. If it is considered advisable that some role playing is undertaken in a larger group, and indeed some participants request this, the experience gained in the more private environment of the syndicate room will remove most of the psychological difficulties.

Where role playing is embarked on in syndicates, the trainer should respect the group's privacy unless they ask for help and guidance. There is no reason why what goes on in the syndicates should not be discussed in a later full group session, but in the interests of removing the barriers to learning the small group activity should preferably not be directly monitored by the trainer.

A variation on role play is 'reverse role play'. This arises when two participants have reached what appears to be an intractable situation in their discussions and they are asked by the trainer to change roles. This move serves to bring home to each trainee the need for him to understand and respect the other man's point of view. It can be a salutary exercise for dealing with someone who delights in putting another on the spot, although the trainer should be on his guard against giving the impression that the ploy is used for disciplinary purposes or to cause embarrassment. It should be seen as a training tool to improve negotiating skills and it does, of course, emphasize the importance of understanding the feelings of others.

Simulation

Simulation, as the term implies, is a combination of case study and role play. Whilst the case study normally deals with the analysis of a historical set of circumstances, the simulation attempts to reproduce a present-day situation to be played out in a lifelike way.

A good deal of information is given about an imaginary organization and about external factors affecting it. Participants are allocated or volunteer for roles within that organization or as consultants to it. They therefore work as a team on specific business problems. Decision points are built into the programme in a similar way to the action maze, the effects of the trainees' decisions being fed back to them, so influencing their future strategy and the next set of decisions. This continuous check on progress makes a simulation a much more satisfying and stimulating experience than other off-the-job training methods. A weakness of many training programmes is that the participants are required to make business or other decisions in isolation and they seldom know what would be the consequences of those decisions in real life. The simulated exercise helps to remove that frustration.

It is increasingly common for simulations to be computerized and this has distinct advantages. It provides participants with training an practice in the use of computer terminals on problems which are directly work-related and also enables them to obtain almost instant feedback on their decisions. The time scale of business activity can thus be greatly compressed in a practicable training period. Unfortunately, this does introduce a degree of unreality into the process and could conceivably give rise to impatience back at work if the results of decisions were not instantly forthcoming.

Where a simulation involves a number of teams in competition with one another, it becomes a 'business game'. A good example of this is where the teams represent different companies competing in a common market or markets. Although some such 'manual' games exist, they demand a good deal from the trainer who has to compute and feedback results to the teams. This often means that time is wasted in waiting. Furthermore, the model is likely to be unrealistic because it would be impossible to build in sufficient variables to simulate a real-life situation. To some degree this problem is overcome by the use of a computer programme. It nevertheless requires a good deal of skill and business know-how to produce a programme which cannot be criticized for failing to reproduce the complex interactions of a real business.

As in other situations, participants should be encouraged to identify with their roles by behaving naturally rather than by trying to put on an act. This applies particularly to simulation where every effort is made to reflect reality. There is little pay-off in training terms for play acting. It merely becomes a diversion from the main purpose of the exercise.

Brainstorming is a practical exercise to stimulate creativity in a group, and is a very useful training technique. The fact that the term brainstorm retains for some people connotations of violent mental disturbance may present the training specialist with an initial difficulty of persuading them that this is a technique which can be used for the organization's benefit, and that it does not involve any psychological stress which they would wish to avoid.

Brainstorming is based on the fact that it is possible to generate more ideas collectively than the sum of the ideas which would be produced individually. This arises from the interaction which enables one member to trigger off new ideas in another. Chain reactions are sometimes set up which ultimately turn an apparently ludicrous idea into a practical one.

The process of brainstorming demands discipline in order to overcome the temptation in most people to pass judgement on ideas as soon as they are revealed. The subject of the session having been decided, the members are required to commit to paper as many ideas as possible for dealing with the problem, without attempting to evaluate them. They should let the ideas flow freely and write them down even if they at first seem impractical. After a suitable period of time, each member reads out his list and the other members are asked not to criticize, however wild they feel a suggestion may be. A combined list is produced and the group is then encouraged to evaluate each item. The cross-fertilization that takes place at this stage leads to the development of new ideas which may or may not be directly related to the original ones.

How the process develops from this point depends on the purpose of the exercise. It is usual for the aggregated list, which is now devoid of impractical suggestions, to be rated and arranged in order of acceptability. When the technique is used for value analysis, the cost of implementing each idea is estimated and this may influence the order in which items are placed.

A variation on this technique involves the use of large boards, at least four feet square, which are supported vertically on either a wall or a movable stand and on which papers may be fixed by means of mapping pins. A generous quantity of pieces of paper, of different colours and approximately 8 x 4 inches, is supplied to the participants. Each idea is committed to one piece of paper and at the end of a specified period of time the papers from all the team members are pinned to the board. The team discusses the contributions, eliminates duplication, re-words ambiguous or inaccurate statements and removes irrelevant or unacceptable ideas. At this point cross-fertilization between members may generate further contributions which are added and agreed.

The next step in the process is to group the ideas in order to be able to produce a suitable structure with headings. A member of the team leads a discussion which results in the papers being re-arranged on the board in new groups, and headings are provided for each group on paper of a different colour. A logical sequence for the various subjects is then established and the total project reviewed.

This technique is extremely useful for generating ideas. Some examples are for incorporation in a report, for establishing guidelines for courses of action, for designing training programmes and for writing books or manuals. The writer used it to effect in his own department when trying to arrive at unambiguous titles for new training programmes. It has the advantage of optimizing the creative abilities of any number of people with a vested interest in, and contributions to make to, a given topic. Further assistance, in order to treat the topic as comprehensively as possible, may be obtained by circulating the ream's product to interested parties for comment.

It has been suggested that brainstorming, if it is to be effective, requires discipline. There are, of course, barriers to thinking in a creative way. Some may unwittingly impose restrictions on ideas by looking at things, as it were, through a narrow tunnel. They way fail to challenge the obvious or may assume that there can only be one answer to a problem. Some are inhibited by the prospect of being ridiculed if they disclose what is in their minds. Others are too eager to assess the value of an idea or pass judgement upon it. When these constraints are overcome, training in the brainstorming technique can be extremely rewarding, not only to the individuals themselves but to the organization which s constantly seeking new ideas and approaches.

Fishbowl

A useful exercise for enabling teams to study group processes is the fishbowl. It is usually carried out with two teams. Team A is assigned a topic which it is required to discuss for, say, 30 minutes. The task is unstructured and the team can elect a chairman or leader if it so wishes or alternatively can cover the topic in a free discussion. Team B is seated around Team A and observes the process. Its members are not free to interrupt the discussion, but when it is finished they are given about 15 minutes in which to criticize and comment on Team A's performance in process terms only. Team A does not have the right to reply or even to comment on any criticisms at this stage.

The roles of the two teams are then reversed, Team B being given the topic to discuss and Team A taking up positions around Team B as observers. After Team A has given its judgement, the two teams come together in a full group session and notes are exchanged on the processes which were observed in the two parts of the exercise. The areas covered may be, for example, the team's interpretation of the task, how its resources were shared, the decision-making process used and the inter-personal relationships developed in the group.

The discussion topic used in fishbowl is sometimes centred around how the team sees its own development in earlier exercises. For reasons of reducing stress in what could be a traumatic experience for some, the exercise would not be at the beginning of a training programme, but rather in the middle or towards the end. The team would therefore have had the opportunity to build up group cohesion over a number of previous exercises.

Group exercises

Until the 1960s group training methods tended to follow a fairly consistent pattern of formal inputs by experts, followed by discussion either in full group or in syndicate sessions. The discussion groups addressed themselves in a structured way to questions posed by the speakers and rigid time limits were set on reporting back for 'judgement' of the results by the specialist, who was seen to be the authority on the topic examined. Even the reporting-back had a formality about it, geared more towards complying with a set of rule and conventions than towards optimizing learning.

As the training profession developed in status, and the work of behavioural scientists attracted more attention, approaches to training began to emerge which caused something of a revolution in methodology. How to optimize learning became the key factor and different means of achieving this end were explored. Management training exercises appeared on the scene, pioneered in the United States by Professor Bernard Bass of the University of Rochester among others and further developed in Europe by the European Research Group on Management. These exercises involved responding to a number of simulated management situations and the results from a large number of managers and students in both America and Europe were fed into a computer and analysed. The data collected provided useful information on the varying responses of different people to the same management situation. It highlighted cultural differences of an international nature and also differences between industries, types of company and levels within an organization. Clearly different people saw things in a different light depending on their knowledge, experience and the environment in which they lived and worked. The value of this in training terms was immense. Rather than rely on an expert to provide a model answer, ie. reflecting his own personal experience or that of a limited group, it was possible to examine the knowledge, beliefs, attitudes and views of a widely differing group of managers and so weigh the different options that were available to solve a business problem. This enabled a group to make full use of its own resources, provided enlightenment for those who approached their problems with tunnel vision and generally improved morale and self-confidence.

The group exercise as it has since developed for training purposes is a written syndicate task which provides clear instructions on the objective, the procedure to be adopted and the approximate timing. The objective can vary considerably. It may involve, for example, learning a technique, skill, procedure, system or policy. The exercise provides an ideal vehicle for developing team work, for problem-solving, decision-making and examining and interpreting data. The procedure usually involves studying the information provided and/or answering the questions posed firstly as individuals and then by syndicate discussion arriving at group responses. Where there is wide disagreement within the group, members are advised to try to persuade the others by reasoned argument rather than to settle readily for a majority answer. They are told that the value of the exercise in not so much in the answer as in the thorough exploration of the issues underlying the question. Preoccupation with seeking the 'right' answer when such does not exist is discouraged.

The trainer role is a relatively passive one. He should not assume that he is welcome in syndicate discussions unless the members say so, and it is advisable to establish this at the commencement of a course. He is a resource on which the groups can draw but he is not an authority in any autocratic sense. He supplies the vehicle for their discussions but they are responsible for their own learning. They are free to manage that learning in whatever manner they agree will be most effective. They are not obliged to appoint a chairman or even a spokesman unless they feel that this will further their objectives. When they report back to the full group they can present their case as a number of individuals and not through a spokesman if they so wish. This freedom and flexibility of working can be a little unnerving for groups experiencing it for the first time. They have been used to being dependent upon a trainer giving the orders, telling them what to do and what not to do, controlling the timing and so on. What they often do not realize is that whatever the trainer does, there is no guarantee that he will achieve learning in the group. In the end they themselves will determine the degree of learning, and indeed, if learning takes place at all.

Flexibility in timing is important. Since what is discussed in syndicate groups should be what is important to its members and to their development, they will be selective about the areas in which they concentrate. This inevitably results in more or less time being spent by different groups on a given exercise than that allotted in the programme. It is counter-productive in both learning and morale terms if a valuable and fruitful discussion is cut short simply because the programme says so. The participants know that one of the reasons why they are provided with off-the-job training is that they may have the opportunity to stand back from the pressures of their jobs and examine problems in depth and without interruption. Trying to reproduce the real work time constraints therefore, conflicts with the requirements of this type of training.

The full group sessions provide the opportunity for the groups to compare their findings in a wider debate. They agree in advance on the way in which this will be done and they are discouraged from looking to the trainer for chairmanship of for arbitration. They are free to request an input from him if they feel it would be helpful. If he thinks that anything vital may have been overlooked, he may tactfully suggest that there might be some benefit in their examining that aspect. Any intervention that he makes should be advisory and supportive rather than authoritarian. At the end of the session he will usually provide handouts which either reflect his own views and/or those of the organization, or give a summary of research which may have been done in the area of the subject which has been discussed.

Group exercises take a variety of forms. In fact, there is probably no limit to the number of variations possible. The choice clearly has to be made on the basis of what is appropriate for the objective to be achieved and some vehicles are more suitable than others for a particular need. The important point to be remembered is that the means chosen must stimulate groups to explore the topic in depth, using all the resources at their disposal. This demands a very clear definition of the objective of the exercise and what is required of the groups. They must be able to relate their knowledge and experience to the problems and although they need to be stretched they should not feel that the goal is unattainable.

One exercise which is widely used in education and is of considerable value in the training field is the multi-choice questionnaire. As the name implies, this consists of a number of questions or statements accompanied by three or more alternative answers from which the participants select the most appropriate tin their considered judgement.

The writing of such questionnaires requires some skill and a knowledge of, among other things, the misconceptions which people have about the particular subjects treated. If it is necessary to provide an easy option because any or all of the other statements may have validity, it is probable the question and/or answers have not been properly formulated. The system is most effective if each statement or answer is so worded that it produces serious discussion and is not simply rejected arbitrarily. One of the problems encountered with this type of exercise is that participants treat it as an examination paper or test, and if everyone comes up with the same answer without discussion the group is content to move on to the next question. They may, of course, arrive at the same answer for widely differing reasons and failing to examine these may defeat the whole purpose of the exercise, which is to explore issues and to challenge beliefs, attitudes, experience etc. It is important for the trainer to brief the groups carefully on how they can get optimum benefit from the exercise and to discourage them from treating it is a purely mechanistic way. The multi-choice questionnaire is a very suitable device for introducing a group to the subject to be studied and establishing common group on which the remainder of the course can be built. It assists participants to warm to the subject and to start to build up the right relationships to achieve cohesive working groups.

An example of one of the questions in an exercise using the multi-choice questionnaire technique is:

Why is employment legislation considered necessary?

(a) to fall into line with EEC countries

(b) to strengthen the hands of the trade unions

(c) to create climate of sound and fair practice in industrial relations

(d) to give the government greater control over the industrial relations scene.

(e) to protect employees.

Each of the responses deserves some discussion even where untrue of not entirely valid, but only one, that is (c), is sufficiently comprehensive to answer the question satisfactorily.

A variation on the multi-choice questionnaire approach is the exercise which invites participants to consider certain statements and to respond by stating whether they believe them true or false. This clearly reduces their options and it is imperative that the participants are required to substantiate their answers in the ensuing full group discussion. It is unprofitable from everyone's point of view if their responses are arrived at by pure guesswork or the toss of a coin.

Another exercise which can be extremely productive in homing a group in on the major subject to be covered in a course and in bringing out their views and attitudes about it is the open question. In its simplest form this type of exercise may merely consist of inviting consideration of the question, "What do you understand by?' followed by a further question,' What are the implications for you as?' Such questions encourage the groups, even when comprised of total strangers, to open up in the privacy of their syndicate rooms and often to expose the problems that really worry them. They seldom have such an opportunity to be frank and honest about their difficulties at work, and the syndicate discussion, if security is assured, provides that opportunity. Enabling them to 'let off steam' at the outset in this way helps to highlight the factors that inhibit their decision-making. Having released their pent-up' emotions, it is then possible for them to concentrate on the real issues. The groups are usually asked to produce the results of their discussion on flip-chart displays, which facilitate their being challenged by the other groups in the later full group sessions.

The use of this type of exercise illustrates how important it is for the trainer to create the right climate for learning to take place. It is very rare for groups not to be inhibited in some way in the training room by constraints which frustrate their efforts at work. The trick is to get these problems out into the open as soon as possible, not only in an effort to find ways of solving them but also to remove the frustration which may prevent learning from being accomplished.

Mini case studies are useful in focusing the attention of groups on specific problems requiring the exercise of judgement based on experience. Often solutions will be produced intuitively rather than by a sound appraisal of all the facts and implications, and this gives the trainer the opportunity to highlight the pitfalls of operating in such a way. Unlike the case studies dealt with, which provide vast quantities of information, mini case studies describe a situation in one or two paragraphs and certain assumptions usually have to be made. Due to the shortage of hard facts, solutions will also tend to be qualified in some way, and will therefore be varied, enabling a number of approaches to be examined and compared.

Although it is quite common for a number of unconnected mini case studies to be used in a training programme, there are clearly advantages in linking them where this is possible. It adds to the realism, for example, if the situations are chosen from one department or from the same company, division or plant. In fact, designing a whole course around a single organization or identifiable part of an organization has its merits, because participants come to identify themselves with the business and are more easily persuaded to enter into the spirit of 'running it'. The use of group exercises when training mature, and particularly experienced, groups has advantages over other methods. The major problem of resistance to training due to arrogance on the one hand or lack of confidence on the other is largely overcome. When trainees can be shown that they are being treated as adults, will not be preached at by someone who thinks he knows it all, will not be embarrassed by exposure of their possible lack of knowledge and will take their fair share of responsibility for the conduct of the training programme, they will respond in such a way as to make the whole exercise more worth-while. Furthermore, learning by discovery and testing their ideas against those of other participants is likely to be much more lasting. The increased self-assurance developed in the process enables them to use their knowledge and experience to more profitable effect in the workplace.

Newcomers to these methods may be spectacle and critical of them on the basis that the trainer is opting out of his responsibilities and is simply leaving the group to their own devices. This is very far from the case. If anything, this type of training is more demanding of the trainer than the direct teaching kind. Frequently the latter may result in trainees going away feeling that they have not learned much from the experience, but, since the trainer has done what appears to have been required of him, they blame themselves for not having been more attention. When they have a joint responsibility they are determined to make the most of the opportunity and any conditions that might arise which place constraints on their learning will be vehemently attacked. The trainer thus has the task of creating conditions which not only provide the most suitable vehicle for learning but which are also acceptable to the trainees. The utmost care has to be taken in writing the exercises. They have to meet the training objectives and be seen by the participants as meeting their own goals. They must encourage the deepest penetration of the topics discussed within the limits of the aggregated knowledge and experience in the group. In the full group sessions the trainer must be prepared to supplement the efforts of the groups with appropriate additional information and guidance once they have exhausted their own resources. Handouts also need to be well written and readable, encouraging participants to use them as reference sources in their future work.

Workshops

The terms workshop has come into popular use in recent years and is often loosely used to describe any form of participative off-the-job training. It is, however, more appropriate to confine its use to describing a method of designing training activities around identified work problems in order to find solutions to them in the training room. The objective is to obtain contributions from all individuals who are affected, and thus to optimize the resources available to solve the problem and agree future action. The workshop differs from other group methods described only in so far as it is set up to tackle specific operational problems and is therefore an extension of the work situation.

Sensitivity training

Sensitivity training, T-group, study groups, group dynamics and group relations training are some of the terms used to describe laboratory-type training which sets out to promote more effective interpersonal relationship in an organization. The goals are:

- to increase awareness of one's own behaviour and how it is received and interpreted by others
- to develop sensitivity to the behaviour exhibited by others and be able to diagnose the causes of that behaviour
- to improve one's skills in handling problems at work by understanding and managing the behavioural factors and constraints.

The technique relies for its effectiveness on creating a climate in which participants are willing to be Frank, open and honest with each other and are prepared to explore in small groups facts about themselves, their backgrounds and their inner feelings without inhibition. Because the focus is on personal behaviour and discussion of one's private thoughts, sensitivity training has given rise to considerable controversy among training and non-training staff alike. Unfavourable criticisms have naturally been levelled at it by those who are prejudiced against any from of behavioural training, but other critics have bee genuinely concerned about the adverse psychological effects T-group training has been known to have on some participants. This fear needs to be put in perspective. There have been instances in the writer's experience, for example, when trainees have suffered some kind of mental disturbance even when he course has been one in which every conceivable effort was made to create a relaxed atmosphere and reduce threats and pressures to a minimum. In other words, any kind of training situation could prove harmful to a trainee who already has psychological problems. This fact leads one to sound a warning that where employees have a previous history of any such difficulties, this should be taken into account before they are considered for participation in group training activities.

Because of the dangers that may be inherent in the study of emotional factors as distinct from job knowledge and expertise, it is imperative that T-group trainers have a high level of skill in the use of this technique. This is certainly not a job for amateur experimenters, but one which demands special training in advanced skills.

It is generally believed that sensitivity training is unstructured and not in any way under the control of the trainer. It is true that there is normally no specific agenda or agreed procedure, and the trainer does not control the group's activities directly. Nevertheless he is usually there all the time and acts as an observer and facilitator, indirectly guiding the group's deliberations and helping them towards an understanding of themselves, their colleagues and the group processes.

The interactive element is a key feature of T-groups. Whilst in many other types of groups training, the accent is on the study of organizational problems *per se,* in T-groups another dimension is added, that of the observation of participants' behaviour and the analysis of their feelings. Those feelings will have a profound effect on how an employee approaches his job, in fact how he develops his relationships with other people generally, and understanding them is essential if objectives are to be achieved. The participants are therefore encouraged to study the behaviour and question the feelings of other members whilst submitting freely to scrutiny of themselves by those members. They discuss how the behaviour of one affects that of another, and how their conception of the way others see them differs from reality. A certain amount of experimentation takes place. Individuals try out different behaviour patterns on their team mates to see the effects that they produce. This eventually leads to insights as to how they need to behave in order to achieve the desired results in others. The interesting thing is that the trainer is seen as one of the group and is therefore equally open to examination by the course members. He may come under fire from anxious participants because they misunderstand his role and accuse him of trying to 'measure with blunt instruments'. The climate of openness and trust created encourages them to say what they really thin about each other. They know that the exercise is a temporary one and that they are not under any threat of long-term repercussions since everyone is a party to the same contract. They therefore enjoy a certain freedom, although this does not remove the anxieties that arise from revelations about themselves. These anxieties are to some extent cushioned by the help and encouragement they get from colleagues, and frequently T-group become highly cohesive. This may of course have adverse effects if they return to the real world of the workplace and discover that similar support is not forthcoming. Perhaps this is a good reason for sensitivity training to be carried out in actual work groups and not with employees from different sectors of the organization. The trainer should however be prepared for the possibility of having to cope with greater conflict between work colleagues than with a group who do not already know each other.

We have stressed the behavioural bias of sensitivity training. One training approach which combines the benefits of this technique with the specific business needs of an organization is Grid Organization Development. This incorporates the well known Managerial Grid concept which relates a manager's concern for production or output with his concern for his subordinates. Various managerial styles may be identified by assessing these two factors. For example a 9:1 manager is motivated almost solely by the task, with minimum regard for the people who have to produce the output, whilst a 5:5 manager tries to give equal weight to the needs of both. There is therefore an implication that the 'ideal' manager has a 9:9 rating, being highly skilled in optimizing employee satisfaction and commitment with organizational performance. Reddin expanded the grid three-dimensionally to include a measure of effectiveness, which was a function of the organization in which the manager worked. The style used, in his view, was not important so long as it was compatible with the organization. Although it is not the purpose of this book to join the debate as to the importance of leadership style, the writer feels from his experience in both manufacturing industry and the public sector that one of the key factors is employee preference. If the work-group favours an authoritarian style, and there are many that still do, that would appear to be the most promising style to achieve results with that particular group. A good deal of behavioural research seems to ignore the individuality of groups.

GOD is an attractive training approach since it incorporates sensitivity training into a structure geared to the corporate strategy of the organization. It therefore goes to the heart of OD by developing team work to the point where its contribution to meeting the organization's short and long term goals is material, and it becomes an essential ingredient of management.

One example in the mid-1960s of the introduction of GOD into an organization has been described by George Clark in 'Managerial Grid training: an application in ICI Pharmaceuticals Division'. In addition to a description of the scheme, its operation and its results, there are usefull guidelines, based on ICI's experience, for anyone interested in using this method.

Transactional analysis

Among the many techniques for studying interpersonal relationships which have emerged since the last war, TA has probably attracted more interest than most. Developed by Eric Berne and others, it overcomes many of the difficulties that managers have in interpreting the language of psychologists when dealing with interpersonal problems. TA provides a simple language which is less likely to be misconstructed by those who wish to use the technique since it is based on concepts within everyone's experience.

Training within industry (TWI)

TWI was phased out in May 1984, but it is included here for historical interest. Originally introduced in America by the War Manpower Board, TWI was a training method devised during the second world war to develop the skills of supervision when it was vital to optimize the performance of work forces in industry in the shortest possible time. It was a good example of the common skills approach to the training of supervision. This makes the reasonable assumption that all supervisors, irrespective of function in an organization, require certain core skills such as leadership, communication and the capacity to instruct subordinates in the requirements of their jobs.

In the UK the TWI service was provided by the Manpower Services Commission which was able to offer both public and implant courses run by their own staff, or instructors' courses enabling an organization to mount its own programmes internally.

Supervisors often had their first taste of supervisory training through TWI courses. Whilst many professional trainers will say the programmes did not go far enough, they could nevertheless be a reasonable first step for employers who wanted to introduce basic supervisory training at a minimal cost. Experienced supervisors were often resistant to training, believing that having been promoted into such a responsible job they were expected to have the skills already TWI could be a fairly painless way of easing them into a situation where they began to realize that they could learn more about the skills of supervision or perhaps re-orientate their thinking concerning them. It could therefore be something on which to build more sophisticated training.

The courses used a discussion leading style which helped to move the group towards certain conclusions. Supervisors were encouraged to exchange their experiences with their fellow trainees to lend weight to those arguments and in this way they began to realize that their knowledge of and approach to dealing with their day-to-day problems did not differ markedly. Where a practical skill was involved, such as instructing a learner, each supervisor was given individual tuition and practice in carrying out the required task using a planned and proven method.

One of the problems encountered in off-the-job training of this kind is that the trainees may find it difficult to relate the tasks presented to them to the jobs that they are responsible for in the workplace. It is desirable, though not always practicable, with a group from a variety of functions, to provide examples which are exactly equivalent to those encountered at work. There are however advantages in suing examples common to everyone's experience and demonstrating a method or system which can be used in any set of circumstances. Training is a systematic approach to learning and helps people to orientate their knowledge around common sets of principles.

This approach was therefore adopted by TWI with a certain degree of success over a period of about 40 years. Supervisors trained under the scheme were not recommended to carry checklists around with them to refer to every time they had to undertake a task. They were persuaded to conform to a tried pattern, however, by memorizing these prompts in the interests of consistency and removing the risks of omitting something vital from their instruction.

Television, film and slide presentations

The reader may be forgiven for making the assumption that these training methods should be listed with those in which communication is largely one-way. They were included in this section because it was considered important to highlight the fact that they should *not* be used is isolation. As visual aids to learning they should only be used as accessories to the main training activity, and should never be relied upon to substitute for it. They can be extremely valuable in providing an additional visual dimension to a programme to underline the message in an agreeable way.

It is not sufficient for a trainer to show a TV programme, a film or a series of 35mm slides and then sit back and assume that learning has taken place. It is highly desirable that the aids used should be associated with a task, and if the trainees know in advance what that task is they are more likely to see them as something which requires their undivided attention and not as an entertainment. Having said that, there is no reason at all why the programme should not be pleasurable. Indeed, if one enjoys an experience one is generally more receptive to learning from it. But however entertaining the visual aids may be, it is often necessary to point out that there are appropriate lessons to be drawn from them and the trainees should be looking for and making due note of them. Small syndicate discussions of the relevant issues following the showing stand a better chance of success than trying to generate a discussion in a full group session, since there fewer opportunities for individuals to 'hide' in the smaller group.

Where aids of this kind are used to supplement training programmes and to reinforce learning it is essential that they are operated skilfully. The slightest hiccup, however small, can prove a major distraction, such that the following discussion centres more on what went wrong with the operation of the equipment than on the subject matter of the programme.

The value of demonstrating a process or activity by means of models should not be underestimated. People in general relate more readily to visual stimuli than to the spoken or written word and showing them a component or a piece of equipment brings the subject to life for them. This is particularly true where practical skills are concerned but again it is important that models are used carefully and are properly integrated into the programme.

Field trips

The point has been in the preceding section that visual stimuli in training can often make a greater impact than verbal or written information. For this reason the value of factory, office or other visits to provide visual reinforcement of information given by other means should not be overlooked.

Unfortunately this method is often avoided either because it is seen to be too much of a disruption to the unit concerned or that it is of doubtful value in learning terms. It is too easy for field visits to be equated with external visits in the eyes of the host unit and so they are not treated as part of a training programme. Most visits tend to be arranged purely for interest and the visitors are nearly always people from walks of life which are remote from that of the host.

The purpose of including field trips in this chapter, therefore, is twofold. First, training specialists may like to be reminded of the value of such visits in terms of reinforcing information and providing atmosphere for trainees who would otherwise not get to know what another environment looks like. The second reason is that in arranging such a visit, every effort should be made to organize it *as a training activity.* This means that objectives have to be set. Trainees are not told that they are going to visit a certain department or establishment because it will be interesting much more specific purpose, the outcome of which is seen by them as an integral part of their training. They should be clear about what they are expected to get out of it and should also understand that there will be some sort of follow-up which will check their learning. Those managers, supervisors or other employees who will have contact with the trainees during the visit should also be carefully briefed so that they know what the objectives are and what their role in the activity will be.

The size of the visiting group must be chosen with care since too large a group will result in less effective transfer of information. There are no hard and fast rules about this because it has to be related to the size of the particular section, department or establishment, the space available, the noise level, the people who will be imparting information, and so forth. As rule of thumb, the recommendations made in earlier sections about syndicate groups may be helpful, although the final answer must be dictated by local conditions. The important thing is that, as with any other type of training, each trainee must enjoy conditions conducive to learning. He should not be adversely affected by the size of the group.

Junior management committee

Many people would argue that there is no better way to learn than by experience. The problem is that this is too often a way of opting out of the responsibility of providing a trainee with the tools and guidance to enable him to learn the job in the most efficient and effective way and so bring him up to experienced worker standard in the shortest time possible.

There are, however, certain types of training in which learning by experience, and often being thrown in at the deep end, so to speak, can achieve satisfactory results, providing there are adequate safeguards. One of these is the junior board, or management committee. The essence of this training method is that young managers or potential managers are appointed to a junior management committee which is set up as near as possible to mirror the structure of the top management committee in the organization. Roles are assigned and procedures agreed. Projects or topics are allocated to the committee on which decisions and recommendations are required.

Trainees have access to their own bosses, the management development adviser, the training, or any other, manager for guidance and they are able to obtain such information as they may need in order to deal adequately with the specific problem. Some decisions may be implemented after agreement with the interested parties but most tasks will have been allocated by the top management and will therefore require their approval before implementation.

Clearly the value of such training depends upon the degree of responsibility that the top management is prepared to delegate to the junior committee. Sometimes it falls into disrepute when the projects allocated are trivial and of no real value to the organization, but in the main a management will not agree to such an activity being set up unless it is prepared to give backing to it. Because of the real-life nature of the problems tackled, this method of gaining experience can be very profitable, giving trainees valuable practice in running meetings, problem-solving and decision-making.

Job rotation

Most organizations suffer to some extent from the problem that people employed in certain functions become somewhat isolated and are not always aware of what is going on in other areas. In fact, they may not even know what is supposed to go on in other functions, which is even worse.

One training method which seeks to deal with this problem is job rotation. This provides an employee with the opportunity to work for specified periods in a variety of different jobs, gaining experience in a wide range of activities. This is on-the-job training and to be effective must be carefully planned and executed. It is not sufficient simply to hand the trainee over to another department and assume that he will receive adequate training and experience. Someone, preferably his boss, needs to have overall responsibility for the programme and, in consultation with the training department, should agree a detailed plan of experience in advance. The supervisor or manager in each department should be prepared to coach the trainee in the requirements of the job and should ensure that he is given appropriate assignments, under supervision, and not simply odd jobs to do. It is desirable that the assignments increase in complexity. This not only stretches the trainee and motivation. Job rotation is not always readily accepted by managers and supervisors. This arises from the fact that it is embarrassing to them to lose an experienced worker to another department and at the same time to have to allocate time to the training of a newcomer. The only way to deal with this is to make it part of company procedure and part of everyone's job description. However sympathetic one may be towards the managers who have to put in that much additional effort to operate the system, they must be shown that it is in the long-term interests of everyone in the organization, including themselves.

In-tray exercise

One way in which training can reflect the realities of the job is by means of the in-tray exercise. This provides the trainees with a typical day's post, both internal and external, which has to be processed to the out-tray. They are required to study all the documents, decide priorities, allocate time and carry out, or if this is impracticable simply indicate, whatever action is deemed necessary.

To add to the realism of the in-tray exercise, other features of normal working, such as interruptions from telephone calls or from unexpected visitors, are often built into the programme. This places time constraints on the activity and can therefore give rise to additional stress. Trainers need to be aware of the symptoms so that action may be taken if it proves necessary.

Frequently the day's 'post' is the same for all participants and at the end of the exercise the ways in which different trainees dealt with the same task are compared or contrasted. There is merit, however, in making the exercise more interactive by allocating roles to the participants and arranging for the action required by the documents to involve more than one trainee.

Transcendental meditation (TM)

Transcendental meditation is a technique which seems to have an increasingly following worldwide. There is justification in regarding it as a training technique since it is claimed that it influences the way in which an employee approaches his whole life and therefore his job.

The essence of TM is that it helps people to reach a state of complete relaxation without any deliberate control on their part. It merely requires 'about 20 minutes twice a day...' when 'the mind is allowed to settle down into a state of complete rest.' There is nothing sinister about TM. No religious or moral commitments are expected and it does not involve any mental or physical effort, or any kind of skill which might make it more suitable for some people than others. Whilst it appears to be a perfectly simple device and does not demand too much from the employee, personal tuition is recommended by the exponents of TM in the first instance and periodic monitoring thereafter in order to obtain maximum benefit from the technique.

One researcher claimed that in a limited survey of 42 managers there was evidence of increased job satisfaction, improved performance in the job, reduced employee turnover and better interpersonal relationship. The conclusion was that it achieved these benefits essentially by the reduction of stress and it should therefore enable the full potential of employees to be exploited.

Coaching

One of the major features of training is the transfer of information from those with knowledge and expertise to those who need to acquire it. It is a tragedy that a good deal of that knowledge and expertise throughout an organization does not get passed on, but is often jealously guarded by those who feel that their positions will be threatened if they disclose it to others.

It is part of the job of anyone who has responsibility for the work of subordinates to ensure that their employees are suitably equipped to carry out their work adequately. Apart from the obvious need for job knowledge, there is a requirement for help and guidance to enable subordinates to find solutions to problems which face them in the execution of their work. They must have a mentor who is preferably one step up in the hierarchy, who is able to advise on the ramifications and difficulties of the job and who is knowledgeable about the interfaces of that job with others in the organization.

The main advantage of coaching as a training method is that it is an on-the-job activity and therefore can be totally relevant. It involves boss and subordinate in a regular dialogue about the department's work and so can reasonably be expected to have a favourable effect on both work performance and morale. It would appear to have everything going for it and yet there is frequently a reluctance to get involved in it. The excuse given for avoidance is usually lack of time, but one suspects that the reasons are more likely to be lack of confidence in the ability to carry it out and a fear that getting too involved will mean more problems to solve. Since it is in the interests of bosses to ensure that their subordinates are effective and can work with the minimum of supervision in meeting the needs of the organization, training specialists should see to it that managers and supervisors are trained in the appropriate skills and encouraged to use them. Coaching is a perpetual activity and provides managers with an ideal opportunity for self-development. It enables them continuously to apprise their subordinates instead of relying on one or two interviews in the course of a year. The progress of the work in their departments can therefore be more easily monitored without subordinates feeling that they are being closely supervised. If handled skilfully it enables a climate of trust and confidence to be built up.

Using coaching as a training medium is also fully justified on the basis that no other training programme can effectively deal with all the day-to-day problems of work. A constantly changing activity brings forth problems on a virtually continuous scale and these cannot be stored up to be dealt with on some future training programme. The machinery for handling such problems therefore has to be available at short notice and the objective is to match the needs of the job and the organization with those of the individual. Tasks are allocated and explained, problems clarified and solved. Expertise and information are passed on and reassurance and encouragement given where necessary Guidance is provided on such matters as cost effectiveness and the management of one's time. Coaching also goes hand-in-hand with delegation, since a boss needs to satisfy himself that a delegated task has been properly carried out.

The training of employees in the skills of coaching has to concern itself with a number of factors. Clearly, since it involves interactive skills, there has to be a substantial behavoural element. The boss has to know what motivates his subordinates and what influences their attitudes to, and performance in, the job. He therefore has to pay attention to his leadership style which must be appropriate to the subordinate he is coaching. He has also to create a learning climate and to encourage his employee to be honest, straightforward, information-seeking and questioning. He needs to be a good listener, must show understanding and be seen to be fair in all his dealings with his subordinates. This clearly demands a much closer boss/subordinate relationship than frequently exists.

Other methods

The following methods do not readily fall into the previous categories and have therefore been listed separately. In general, whilst there is overall supervision in each case, the method relies upon self-activation and self-discipline in order to achieve learning.

Programmed learning

The term programmed learning or programmed instruction is used to describe a number of techniques involving prepared training programmes which are entirely trainee-centred. This means that the trainee directly controls his own learning, the time that he embarks on the training process and the pace at which he progresses through it. He can also decide where the course takes place since the material and/or equipment required is easily transportable. In view of the self-contained nature of the programme, the full-time involvement of a trainer is not necessary.

This system has a number of advantages:

- assuming computer terminals are not involved, it can take place anywhere where the conditions are conducive to private uninterrupted study. This makes training schedules more flexible.
- the time of the staff is not taken up. It is only necessary for the trainee to have arm's-length access to a trainer in the event of anything going seriously wrong. Nevertheless there is good management control because all the ground has to be covered.
- the trainee is able to check his progress continuously and correct errors as they arise. He has to be totally involved and he obtains immediate feedback. The degree of reward in reaching the right answers is greater in this type of training than in many others.
- he can work at his own pace. He does not have to keep up with the rest of the group.
- the programme can be illustrated to aid understanding.
- provided the programme is professionally produced, he should normally have no problems of interpretation. Personal difficulties that may otherwise occur in the relationship between trainee and instructor do not arise.

- it can be better sequenced than any other training programme because it demands greater care from the programmer in analysing and presenting the material.
- there is a built-in revision mechanism which aids learning.
- it is possible to stop the programme and start it again at any time without loss of continuity. That is, the trainee knows precisely where he left off and can review the last part of the exercise if he so wishes before proceeding.
- with the book system there is a permanent record of everything that happens in the learning process.
- where video equipment is used, it familiarizes the trainee with the operation of such equipment.

The disadvantages are:

- It is an impersonal system. The trainee is normally isolated and would therefore have no dialogue with anyone else. This would make clarification of points not properly understood more difficult than usual.
- it requires discipline and motivation to work at a reasonable tempo. If the subject is not particularly absorbing, progress may be slow.
- it assumes that the trainee has acceptable reading and comprehension skills. Educational limitations could prove a drawback
- the programme may be written on a 'one-track' basis and not allow for the exploration of number of options. It therefore tends to be more suitable for the teaching of concrete facts than for the discussion of ideas and management problems or for behavioural subjects. For this reason it may not stand on its own but have to be used alongside other methods.
- programmes are costly to produce.
- learning objectives have to be precisely defined.

Programmed learning can be achieved in three ways, by means of a book, a teaching machine or a computer. The much greater versatility of the computer has meant that teaching machines have been largely superseded, although a few are still in use. In each case the learner is taken through a prepared text or programme in small easily assimilable steps. He is permitted to move on to the next step only when he has satisfactorily answered the questions relating to the current one. In the book programme the model answers appear on the back of the page being studied or on the following page and are therefore not visible until the page is turned after the trainee has written in his responses. If the trainee's answers are correct he is instructed to pass on to the next section. If not, he is referred back in the text to revise the material he has not grasped. Each step in the process, usually on one page if possible, is termed a frame.

Prescribed reading

A problem with training programmes is that they have to take place at a particular time which is not always convenient or most appropriate for some participants. These activities are often seen as disrupting the work programme rather than contributing to organizational effectiveness. It is not unusual, too, for the time limits imposed to restrict learning for those who are not as quick on the uptake as their peers.

In coping with such problems, we should not underestimate the value of self-development. It is probably true to say that most people are eager to learn more, but are not too keen to disclose to others that they need to do so. One of the major constraints to their learning about their jobs by reading is the lack of knowledge as to which book, paper or journal would be suitable to provide the knowledge they require. They may not even recognize appropriate information when they see it. It may only be necessary for the boss to identify the sources to enable them to embark on a useful training activity which they can carry out at work, on the commuter train or in their own homes.

Prescribed reading may be used at any level in an organization, although it is more common with managerial and technical staff than with others, partly because reading is a skill which normally has to be used more by them in their day-to-day business activities. Whoever the learner may be, it is essential that certain safeguards are built into the exercise. First, the boss should take particular care to see that the material recommended is not only suitable in content terms but also in terms of the reading abilities of the learner. Bearing in mind that reading about one's job for work reasons requires a certain amount of self-discipline, it is unlikely to have the desired outcome if the reader is put off by the style or the degree of complexity. Second, there must be some follow-up during which the boss can review the learning which has taken place. This would take the form of a coaching session and it should not be made to appear like an examination, should be a free discussion during which the views and feeling of the employee on the subject and the prospects of implementing what has been learnt, may be explored. In this way there is greater likelihood of prescribed reading becoming of lasting benefit to organization and individual alike. There is a danger that it may be conducted on a *ad hoc* basis without any reference being made to it in the employee's training record. If it is carried out in the way suggested, however, it important that it be recorded as a practical and recognized part of his training.

One of the attractions of prescribed reading is that training cost can be kept to a minimum. At a time when there are severe budget restrictions on training, to the extent that some activities are eliminated altogether, this is a significant factor. There are skills, of course, which all managers are *expected* to have, yet no training help has been provided for them. Sometimes they themselves are reluctant to admit their shortcomings, although they will do so if pressed and will welcome any assistance that may be offered, particularly if it can be given in private. Areas such as interviewing, presentation and counselling are examples of what may be termed 'core skills'. With this problem in mind, the writer produces a series of self-help guides for managers. These are small booklets, of two or three dozen pages, which give advice and guidance on how such skills may be improved in the manager's own time and at his own pace.

Distance learning

It is common, particularly with apprentices and junior trainees, for job training to be supplemented by further education at local establishment such as technical colleges. this sometimes requires day or halfday release from work each week, with or without pay, and it is naturally desirable that practical and academic work are suitably integrated. It is not always possible for employees to attend an external establishment for organizational reasons, because of country transport problems or because a suitable course is not available locally. One possible alternative is the correspondence course. Such courses are offered by independent college or schools which undertake to prepare the student for examinations and usually give a money-back guarantee if he fails after having completed the course to their satisfaction Payment is made in full in advance or by installments over the period of the course. All the work of a correspondence course is normally conducted by post and so suffers from a time lag between the student sending in work and receiving it back marked by the tutor. The dialogue which goes on between student and tutor is protracted, since there will be a considerable delay between either party asking a question and obtaining he answer. This can be vary frustrating if the answer turns out to be unsatisfactory and the process has to be re-activated. Nevertheless, some correspondence schools have carried out sterling work in providing facilities for obtaining qualifications and acquiring knowledge which may not have been possible by any other means. It needs to be said, however, that success in correspondence curses depends for the most part on the tenacity of the student. He has to discipline himself to allocate a suitable amount of his own time to study on a regular basis and must set himself targets which he must be determined to meet. It is all too easy to put off until tomorrow what should be done today and it is in this way that many students starting correspondence course fail to complete them. In an attempt to reduce this risk, some employers will only reimburse the cost of such courses when the students are successful in their examinations.

A highly developed form of correspondence course, introduced in 1969, is the Open University (OU) course. The term 'open' implies that the facilities are available to all UK residents over the age of 21 who are interested in furthering their education and knowledge in their own time. the topics studied may be work-related or simply connected with outside interests. No academic entrance qualifications are required and the curriculum is not restricted to the University's Bachelor of Arts or post-graduate degrees. In addition to the usual postal dialogue by means of written exercises, etc, the OU provides radio and television programmes which are fully integrated into the programme. It has a national network of study centres, based in local education establishments, at which evening tutorials, discussions, etc can be arranged and other opportunities for students to meet their course tutors and colleges are provided at one-week summer schools. The problem encountered in correspondence courses of having to discipline oneself to pace the programme realistically is partly overcome by the need in the OU courses to listen to or watch certain scheduled broadcasts on radio or television.

The programme is in operation and a Steering Group is responsible to the Manpower Services Commission for the scheme's strategic direction. The Group also has consultative and review functions and the Commission provides pump-priming finance to give the necessary stimulus in the stimulus in the scheme's early stages. This financial aid enables projects such as the development of open-learning materials to be carried out by educational establishments, employers or training organizations. It is expected that most of the cost of an employee's participation in the programme will be borne by his employer.

The Open Tech programme sets out to meet part of the third objective in the MSC's *New Training Initiative* which is to widen training and re-training opportunities for adults. Specifically, it is directed towards technician, supervisory and management levels of skill. The methods of achieving its aims are more flexible than in any other form of training. It is 'open' to everyone, irrespective of formal educational qualifications. Limitations as to time, location or the nature of the learning media used are reduced to a minimum. Thus a trainee who is unable to attend a regular course at a technical college is able to satisfy the study requirements by some other means. Learning can take place at home, in a library, at work or in an educational or training establishment. The learning media may include books, tapes, radio/TV, programmes, programmed-learning packages or computers. Tutorial assistance can be provided by letter, telephone, face-to-face discussion where practicable, or computer or interactive video systems. Existing facilities, in whatever mix is considered appropriate in a particular case, are used and it is not intended to set up a separate establishment on the OU or any other model. Clearly the scheme demands for its success the closest co-operation between 'further education and training institutions, examining bodies, sector training bodies and their industries, employers and trade unions'. The writer would suggest that it also requires an ability and a willingness on the part of the trainee to adjust to any form of training which is appropriate and necessary in order to meet his requirements.

The collection of materials suitable for use in open learning schemes is the responsibility of the materials and Resources Information Service (MARIS), managed for the MSC by the National Extension College. It codes the data obtained from the suppliers of learning materials and feeds it into a computer system. The student requiring information completes a form, a search is made in the database and he is provided with a computer print-out of the details requested.

The above and other trainee-centred methods, in which the trainee does not normally come into face-to-face contact with the trainer or teacher, are often referred to as 'distance-learning' methods.

Induction training

The major task of an employer when appointing a new employee, whether from outside the organization or by transfer from another section or division, is to integrate him into the business so that he begins to make a contribution at the earliest possible time. This does not merely mean training him in the specific skills of the job but also involves preparing him generally for his new responsibilities in the concern.

It was once believed that it was only necessary to show a newcomer the job that he was engaged to do and then set him to work. He occupied himself with his work within his own cocoon and did not concern himself with what went on outside it. In more recent years it has been acknowledged that employees should be better prepared to take their place as members of the community forming the organisation. This means providing them with considerably more information about the business and their place in it. Most of the larger employers therefore regard properly organized induction training as essential for all new entrants and some go so far as to arrange talks by the top management on the first day or soon after. Induction training thus consists of two main facets, introduction to the organization and its activities and initial training for the specific job. The former is logically the responsibility of the personnel and training function, with assistance if necessary from certain functional specialists and trade union officials. The latter is a line responsibility, and managers and supervisors should be discouraged from trying to shift the burden on to the training department. The boss is better equipped than anyone to identify the requirements of the job and should therefore see to it that the training meets those needs. When trying to find the best means of satisfying the needs he can enlist the help of the training department.

The main ingredients of an acceptable induction programme are:

A pre-engagement procedures

(i) at interview

- outline purpose and main requirements of job
- provide adequate information on terms and conditions of service, etc
- discuss accommodation arrangements
- answer candidate's questions
- check availability of candidate

(ii) on acceptance

- provide contract of employment

- inform new entrant's manager
- send joining instructions
- send employee handbook, safety policy statement, accommodation addresses or contact, etc.

B On engagement

(i) The organization

- Acquaint employee with:
- organization's history, structure, activities, and provide written information for reference
- corporate objectives, policies procedures
- documentation, obtaining necessary information for national insurance, income tax and personnel records
- terms and conditions of service
- rules and regulations
- grievance and disciplinary procedures
- industrial relations
- general services
- career prospects and training opportunities
- accommodation arrangements

Arrange a guided tour of the establishment, introducing employee to the people he is most likely to have contact with in the course of his work. If there are too many for him to remember all at once he should meet a few at a time over a period of several weeks.

(ii) The job

- introduce employee to his departmental colleagues
- acquaint him with his workplace and the equipment, etc available for his use
- inform him of the departmental systems and procedures
- issue tools, stationery, protective clothing where applicable
- check any personal problems
- provide initial job training

C Follow-up

- check and reinforce understanding of rules, etc as appropriate

- invite questions of clarification
- monitor job performance and coach as required
- review reasons for previous employee(s) leaving and take stops to see that it does not happen again!

It will be seen that induction training does not cease on the day a new employee joins the organization. It is important to think of it as a continuing activity since it is unrealistic to try to acquaint him with all he needs to know within a few hours. It is bewildering to say the least to join a new organization and there is a limit to how much information one can take in on the first day. Furthermore, conditions, systems, procedures, etc are constantly changing and one's knowledge of them therefore requires continual updating.

Special problems of adult re-training

The rapid advance of technology over the last half century has created many problems for employers. For example, difficulties are experienced in deciding what the composition of the workforce should be in order to ensure that it is geared to the organization's changing needs. It is widely accepted that people will need to be trained for two or three jobs in their lifetime, and so employers are now frequently faced with the prospect of re-training adult workers in new skills. Unhappily this brings about a good deal of uneasiness and trauma and is not always successful, often because employers do not understand the nature of the problem from the older worker's point of view. Some valuable research has been undertaken in this field by the Industrial Training Research Unit (ITRU) based in Cambridge, who are able to provide training managers with helpful guidance and advice when confronted with such problems.

There is a popular school of thought that claims you can't teach old dogs new tricks. This saying no doubt came into being because people did not take the trouble to find out why adults sometimes find it difficult to change their pattern of life and therefore tend to resist any change. Those who are concerned about the human aspects of work have identified reasons why adults can experience these difficulties and can provide evidence to show that something can in fact be done about it in a substantial proportion of cases.

Some of the reasons why there is reluctance on the part of older workers to be re-trained may be summarized as follows:

1. Having reached maturity after many years' experience, they consider it a retrograde step to start training all over again.
2. They fear the unknown, believing they will not be able to cope. There is a very real fear of failure which would bring their whole world toppling around them. They may well believe in the old adage mentioned above and it becomes a self-fulfilling prophecy.

3. They are proud of past achievements on which they have established their reputations. What opportunity will there be to build on past experience in the new role?
4. They fear the system which requires them to fill in forms, to answer questions, to be subjected to tests, to be equipped with physical attributes which they my no longer have.
5. They are anxious about the prospect of future competition with younger workers, having hitherto felt that they could hold their own with them.
6. They feel they will not be understood by the trainer and will thus be at a disadvantage when trying to acquire the new skills.
7. Accuracy is more important than speed to them and they think they may be forced to reverse their priorities.
8. They fear that the additional stress involved will make them ill and even shorten their lives. Will they have the stamina needed for the new work?
9. In extreme cases they may even suspicious of the employer's motives, believing that the management is trying to find a way of proving them incapable of carrying out the required work so that they can be paid off.

These reservations and anxieties are understandable among loyal workers who over a period of time have settled themselves into a routine over which they feel they are the masters. The longer this period is the greater effect any change is likely to have on their morale. Their security and self-confidence are under threat, and it is important that training specialists recognize the need to exercise understand again handling the problem. Some of the remedies suggested by ITRU are:

1. Where the change involves moving from one department or establishment to another, induction training should be carefully designed to take into account the special difficulties that an adult worker may have in adjusting to the new situation.
2. There are distinct advantages in selecting a trainer who is sensitive to the needs of adult trainees. The trainer/trainee relationship can be critical.
3. Course design should allow adequate time to cope with new concepts, anticipate possible physical problems including fatigue and make special plans to deal with educational shortcomings.
4. Where training in the use of a new machine is involved, it is helpful to introduce the adult trainee to an associated activity in the first instance, enabling him to see the machine in action without having any responsibility for it.
5. Where practicable, enabling the trainee to talk to another employee with a similar

background who has been trained successfully on the same job will give him some encouragement.

6. To reduce the fear of failure, final tests or examination may be abandoned in favour of monitoring progress on a continuous basis. It sometimes helps for the trainer to take the blame then things go wrong, at the same time indicating that he is confident of the trainee's success. Early success in adult re-training is of course highly desirable in terms of boosting confidence.
7. The method of achieving a satisfactory work pace should be carefully thought out. It will differ with the task, e.g. case of learning and whether accuracy or speed is the more important. Pressure can be applied earlier when the task is relatively sample or when accuracy is not vital.
8. Arranging for trainees to work in pairs may reduce inhibitions in some instances. Indeed there are advantages in carrying on the training in groups with common interests. The shared experience reduces tension and aids learning.
9. Building on the trainee's previous experience is highly desirable because it helps him in relating the new learning to the old. This means, however, that before designing the programme the trainee's previous knowledge must be carefully checked.
10. Uncertainty is a de-motivator and should therefore be reduced to a minimum. The trainee must know in advance what is going to be dealt with in the programme and what will be required of him. He should also be taught in such a way that he fully understands the job rather than merely learning it parrot-fashion.

Educational shortcomings among trainees at any level can create problems for the training department. When they arise with adults they can prove a considerable embarrassment often requiring unique measures to deal with them. A training consultant from head office was invited into an engineering company in the mid-1970s ostensibly to sort out an operator training problem. On investigation he found that the shortcomings were with the supervisors rather than the operators and his report recommended a programme of supervisory training. The report was accepted by the management and he interviewed the supervisors in the process of producing a training needs analysis. He was alarmed to find that there were serious gaps in their numerical ability, in particular in regard to their being able to work with decimals and percentages. Before he was able to embark on the supervisory training programme he had to coach them in elementary mathematics. So that none of them would lose face, however, each was instructed in private without the knowledge of the others!

These are some of the actions that training specialists can take in order to overcome the problems inherent in the re-training of adult workers. Recognizing that these problems exist is more than half the battle. Managing them may not be as difficult as it appears and there are rich rewards to be reaped. Once the early difficulties are mastered, older trainees apply themselves diligently to the job and statistics show that they tend to stay longer in employ meant than younger ones. There is, however, another hurdle to be overcome and that is the transfer from training to the new working environment. Sometimes this phase is difficult because supervisors expect almost immediate integration into the skilled activity. When this does not occur, suggests ITRU, it is more likely to be due to social and psychological reasons than because of poor learning. Help in effecting the transference to everyone's satisfaction may be provided by the trainer who can give moral support to the trainee and who can become a short-term link between him and the supervisor.

The foregoing list represents a cross-section of the more common training methods 'which have been available to the training specialist for some years. The descriptions are of necessity brief, but further reading is suggested in the bibliography. The next chapter explores some of the more recent developments in training approaches.

There is a tendency for certain methods to be used with specific groups, at apprentices, graduates, managers salesmen, regardless of the aims of the exercise or the task. This arises from custom and practice rather than from any attempt to be objective. In general, the training of such groups has not been separately treated in this chapter since by so doing the impression would be given that there was one particular method or group of methods more appropriate than another in each case. It is strongly felt, however, that trainers should resist the temptation of being strait-jacketed in this way. They should keep an open mind about how different functional groups should be trained and, instead of assuming that a particular method is appropriate for a given group at all times, make the decision on the merits of each situation. this applies equally to cross-functional groups involved in, for example, training in industrial relations topics such as negotiating skills.

The variables likely to influence the choice of training method will include the size of the group; its composition and the backgrounds of its members; managerial or supervisory style in the members department; the training objectives and economic constraints. Whatever method is chosen, it is important that it meets certain criteria. It should:

- satisfy the training and organizational goals and the results should be measurable against them. The objectives should be directly work-orientated where practicable.
- motivate the trainees to learn by involvement. Adequate monitoring and reinforcement mechanisms need to be built into the programme.
- provide for ease of transferability of learning to the work situation.

The training system

By using so broad, generic and, in this context, unfamiliar a word as "system" to designate the partner responsible for identifying and organizing training and resources and for providing the actual training and associated consultation that a work organization and its participants need, we have alerted readers to prepare for complexities. Now, starting the practical study of it, "system" also offers three important pointers: a system has many components; these components are interrelated and cohere; and a system has boundaries, a position in an environment, and connections and transactions with this environment that matter greatly. Clearly these pointers to the nature of a training system raise concerns far beyond the usual ones of sending some staff to a training course somewhere, "leaving" training issues to "the training people to get on with since that is *their* business," expecting a new worker or trainer to "pick up" a particular set of competencies by simply being "put with" an old-timer, and other standard but costly simplifications.

To visualize training resources as a system is a useful first step-so long as it is not also the following figure shows the basic model. The "import," "conversion," and "export" subsystems in it represent the more commonly used "inputs," "throughputs," and "outputs." Trainers are quite familiar with these concepts, and also with "boundaries," "environment," "linkages," and "feedback loops."

The environment to which the system relates can also be identified. Only those parts of it that are importantly connected to the particular "task, territory, technology, and time" concern the system sufficiently to warrant attention and proper linkages. These four "Ts", which the Tavistock Institute uses for delineating primary tasks, can also be used for identifying the parts of the otherwise limitless environment that are, in fact, relevant in a particular case. Other classifications are also available. True, a system and its environment become more complex with every traditional task, territory to be covered, or time frame to be addressed. But if developed step-by-step, even a large system can be quite manageable.

Longer-term issues and policy dimensions gain prominence as the system enlarges. Examples of special importance and urgency in developing countries at macro-levels are such conflicting issues as raising the general quality of training across many programs while simultaneously developing new kinds of training capacities and rapidly increasing their volume. Starting specialized training institutions while keeping existing institutions closely linked to operations is also a problem. As the system expands, so does its relevant environment. At national levels it includes, for example, professional associations and specialized research centres.

In a major review in 1983 of its "existing internal training system," which then included three staff colleges, thirty-eight training centers, and a regular "relationship nexus" within the organization that included a deputy managing director and chief general manager, the State Bank of India developed preparatory papers on all the above issues in "a futuristic time frame." This frame took into account the Bank's expansion rates, especially of rural branches, "emerging" positions and roles, technological changes, and other considerations. The report based on these papers and their discussions stressed

> training as a "planned organizational intervention" and proposed means for making the identification of organization development and training tasks into a "continuous process." The "important areas of concern" identified ranged from the need for better "synchronization of organizational growth with the development of the individual employee... through career development" "modifications of the structure" of the system in the light of these considerations.

While each component of a training system can be conceptualized in system terms and these components built into an overall system diagram that incorporates the same concepts, there are important practical differences between systems of different sizes. It is only when all resource components needed for a actual training effort are assembled and synchronized for particular purpose that the training system for it can be solidified. Successive drafts can be tested against particular pertinent question and the constituent parts and the design refined accordingly. Questions about the macro-system are of a different order since they concern overall capacities and leave no scope for shifting resources away from one program or institution to another. For instance, will the nationwide system, perhaps augmented for a while with regional and international resources, yield training on a sufficient scale, and/ or will that output be sufficiently well-paced and coordinated to meet the requirements of the planned projects, expansions and technical and administrative improvements? Can it sustain this level of effort? Are the estimates sufficiently feasible for coping with the imminent retirement of the "independence generation" of experienced administrators and concomitantly for accommodating turbulent changes in the environment. These are the types of questions that system development is meant to address at higher levels in developing countries. That complex scene characteristically includes pressures to develop training capacities in several major sectors at once; to compete for the very same handful of trainers that private enterprises try to attract with better salaries and conditions, to develop training capacities in widely scattered provinces while simultaneously strengthening nationally acceptable standards of training: to multiply training opportunities even at the cost of purpose and quality: to shift experienced trainers away from training into training administration, and from outlying places- but close to the action-to headquarters positions: and to train the work force for foreseeable changes in service needs while also multiplying and improving the quality of the same work force for current basic community services.

At the levels at which these concerns have to be included, training system development is not only larger in scale than simply using systems thinking for developing a component, or a system at program level, or a temporary system, but its complexities are of an entirely different order. In line with this, a readiness to approach the development of a training system as a working proposition, for practical elaboration, improvement and confirmation over time, is of paramount importance in developing countries. Under such conditions the proper use of systems ;concepts and diagrams is as checklist and general map to ensure that all essential components are accounted for, can readily attract necessary attention, and are also plausibly interrelated for charting the territory that lies ahead. Practical considerations will also limit further elaboration of conceptual components and their interrelations in terms of the available capacities for collecting and analyzing data, and putting these results to use in influencing and managing the necessary relationships. The territory itself, full of concrete, stubbornly intricate, and often divergent, if not directly conflicting issues, remains yet to be entered and explored. This step can in turn, guide the further clarification and development of a training system, and the direction for the next steps.

System goals and approaches to system development

Training system development is anchored in its goals-the intended outputs-and it is the acquires of these outputs who are primarily responsible for seeking them. The patterning of roles and relationship is already familiar: establishing training needs-the work organization; taking decision about training strategies and resources-the resource providers; and developing a training program to meet those needs-the training system. The temptation that full time trainers and training institutions must resist-to put forward goals of their own-is likewise familiar. They must constantly remember that their goals are based on extrapolations of past performances or even, merely, past aspirations. No matter if they are better based than that, direct advocacy of a system's goals circumvents the proper trainer functions of helping organizations improve their own processes of goal-setting and of responding professionally to questions concerning technical feasibility, strategy options, and the resources needed for attaining the stated objectives.

A particularly important professional function is to ensure that enough resources are provided for system maintenance and longer-term development so that current activities, however pressing, do not exhaust current system capacities-a constant peril in developing countries. It important that a line be drawn between providing information to assist in processes of decision making and taking responsibility for decisions of policy priorities and resource allocations which all within the purview of national, provincial, or other, broader bodies.

When it comes to establishing the boundaries of the training system, including some sectors and institutions and excluding others, and settling directions and time frames for capacity development, responsibilities are more evenly shared and the processes involve more negotiation between the partners. Differences arise because the training system has to develop internal cohesion and its own capacities for boundary management, and trainers as a cohort have to assume responsibility and feel committed to the results.

Tasks of the training system

In the classic system diagram the tasks that the system exists to performed, managed, and coordinated, the tasks results in the systems's coherent contribution to achieving the goals that users—organization, province, or region—have set for it. The tasks can be classified in many ways. We have grouped them below under eight essential functions.

1. Building and maintaining support

For its very existence and continuation a training system has to merit and keep the support of the organizations that use its outputs. Without active support form the top policy and decision makers in the organizations, training—even good training—may be confined to areas of minor impact, and resources allocated for it consequently remain small and uncertain. For an initial trail period such limitations may serve both system and organizations well by keeping risks low. These risks include unexpectedly heavy demands on organizations following effective training. But if sidelining continues beyond the initial trail, the system risks dismissal or irrelevance. The more far-reaching the development to which training is to contribute, the more important the system's tasks for ensuring support.

The first strategic objective for building support is to involve all levels and parts of the organizations that are prospective users of the outputs, will be involved in their production, and/or will be affected by them. Even the initial list of these, which can be extrapolated from the training needs and strategies for meeting them, goes far beyond the top group who decide whether or not to go ahead with a development at all and the initial levels of effort and funding for it. After policy makers have given training the green light, others in an organization have to be effectively involved in selecting participants, providing space, organizing opportunities, and perhaps arranging equipment, for practice. At every stage staff groups have the power to facilitate, delay, or even effectively negate essential steps in the implementation process, whatever the decision at the top. Modifying existing norms of training and effecting work and organizational change usually involves yet other people. The training and effecting work and organizational change usually involves yet other people. The training strategy may call for new criteria for the selection and subsequent placement of participants at higher production levels and more collaborative work arrangements Support from leaders in these matters is therefore important. Such changes are usually easier and more pleasantly achieved if knowledge about them has already engendered good will in the organization; a general atmosphere of goodwill generates support all around. For thinking through the complexities, for resolving doubts at the inevitable times of perplexity, for copying with stresses which change efforts invariably encounter, and for sharing and learning from the ongoing experiences, trainers and system leaders often took for intellectual and emotional support from professional colleagues.

The theory of institution building classifies linkages according to the types of support that a system needs: enabling, functional, normative, dispersed, and collegial.

Adequate support building, therefore, goes far beyond the initial green light and funds. Aside from the purposes of linkage, it is also important that all eventual users and supporters know they are included in the vision, even if the initial steps involve only a limited set of actors and are heavily influenced by immediate tactical considerations. This means projecting the pattern of support required far into the future. By its pattern of linkages and manner of developing them a system makes its mission concrete, communicates it to its environment, and also establishers its own distinctive style of working and public image.

Detailing linkages goes hand in hand with using them. In each category specific units and contacts can be identified and used in the course of organizing meetings, distributing documents, announcing programs, etc. Establishing ways to keep this information up to date and serviceable deserves early attention, otherwise these tasks tend to became quickly unmanageable.

Building continued mutuality into all relationships is particularly important for maintaining support; all partners need to gain, and also feel that they are gaining, otherwise support wilts. System supports for enabling and normative purposes are at greater risk of neglect than those involved in the more frequent and often discrete functional and collegial linkages. Maintaining top-level support exemplifies the difficulty. Whereas functional linkages are needed and used frequently, and many transactions are directly associated with payments or other benefits to these supporters, top-level support is an obvious and powerful need only at the time of annual budget appropriation or some emergency. But policymakers are amiss if such highly active occasions are the only, or almost only, contacts they have with the system. It is very important that the system find additional and more mutually satisfying ways to keep in touch. The least step is to provide policymakers with information on a regular basis that shows the training system effectively busy on priority developments. When major system developments are proposed and examined policymakers can be heavily involved in thorough reviews.

The following record, made by the head of banking institute, is an example of a thorough review by top-level policymakers initiated by the training system. "In 1983, on the eve of the establishment of... the second apex-level institution for training and development of the State Bank Group (India), a document was presented to the Top management Group... and a two-day seminar. Organized at the new Staff College with following objectives.

1. To have a review of the Bank's Training System in its retrospect and prospect.
2. To have an in-depth ad meaningful in-house debate on the critical areas of the Bank's Training System.
3. To discuss areas of expectations, concern, and action.
4. To crystallize thinking on the Bank's Training System so that it remains continuously attuned to the needs of the User System.

5. To have a productive exchange of ideas for providing direction to the future course of the Bank's Training System-an enabling mechanism for sustaining growth and promoting organizational excellence.

As result of an in-depth date that was highly participative in nature a number of action points have emerged on which we are working at present.

Building organizational support at working levels is also very important, especially wherever trained people are trying to work more effectively and need their colleagues' collaboration to make improvements. Working support goes beyond fostering an atmosphere of general goodwill at the work place. It is very concrete, and often quite pedestrian and routine. Occasionally it requires a training system to organize specific programs in conjunction with formal training in order to address this need.

In 1983-84 the Bank of Baroda decided to relocate training programs in industrial relations for zonal managers from training centres to the zones themselves, to build more of the programs around issues specific to the zone and to involve zonal executives in the programs given the managers. A member of the core faculty writes:

The decision to do this programme on location was based on the feedback from mangers that their effectiveness in managing IR at the branch level depends on the quality of support from zonal authorities. It was, therefore, decided to conduct this programme right at the zone so that it could address the specific needs of the zone and also involve zonal executives.

We have conducted ten such programmes ..... Very important is that before such a programme is launched, we diagnose IR problems of that zone with the help of personnel and trade unions. The programme is designed in the context of this diagnosis. On the last day of the programme is a four-house interface session where the entire zonal team, including personnel specialists, participate and answer the queries of branch managers. Here, during this session, managers raise a variety of issues and quote instances of inadequate support. Later on such issues are thrashed out and, where policy matters are involved, they are referred to higher authorities.

2. Building training competencies and overall training capacity

Increasingly competent planning and running of training sessions and programs is the most obvious outcome of this task. But the task also covers system-wide aspects of training development. At the system level, overall and for all kind of training, consulting, and administrative functions, it involves, for instance, recruiting and building trainers into a coherent staff and making additional trainers available through networks of resources so that both immediate training needs and also broader needs, e.g., for organization development, can be met. The training system's credibility with its constituents rests largely on its displaying the capacities to manage itself well within its own boundaries. Internal management includes program planning, budgeting, and accounting; facilities and materials management; and the management of personnel careers and system change. Increasing competence in training organization and program implementation, in turn, builds the staff's confidence in their system, which probably raises competencies further.

3. Developing training materials

This task supports competency building and also reflects it. The most useful materials are developed from within the work settings in which training is needed. The production of a steady flow of fresh training materials is characteristic of strong training system. Another part of this task is to arrange ready access from larger system to any additional materials needed, and to commission the development of new materials in the larger system when this is appropriate.

4. Building internal structure and process, and developing policy

Developing its internal working and the requisite underpinnings for firming up arrangements and routinizing activities wherever possible is another task of a training system. This task, too, often tends to be postponed, purportedly to that day when pressures for current activities lesson. One result of postponing is the great waste of time and other resources that occurs as people try to cope somehow, *ad hoc* and again and again, with aspects of system's operation that could be routinized. Other results of the failure to carry out this task are the high sense of uncertainty in many systems as to how or whether "things work" and the low morale such uncertainly engenders. This task, like others requires resources. Five percent of the time of system heads and their management teams may serve as a working estimate for it.

5. Strategic planning

Strategic planning is commonly crowded out, a forgotten function, by pressures from current programs on scarce trainers and weak systems. But without it, systems deteriorate fast: resources are wasted, morale plummets, and training becomes the activity of a few idealist and of many who have failed at other work. Strategic planning starts-but does not end—with using projections of training needs for mapping the system required for meeting these needs. This already goes beyond the mechanical scaling up of numbers in work force plans, and dividing projected recruitment among existing and planned training centers, and even beyond using such estimates for extrapolating trainer recruitment and development needs. Estimates-numerical and others-are needed for all system components and all relevant parts of the environment.

It is useful to go down the list of all components inside a system and its relevant environment and map what would be needed by each in an effort as large as the projected scale. Right then constraints on one or two components might rule out the initial goal, e.g. the rate at which new trainers can, in fact, be found and developed, the capacity of the system as a whole for collaborative work, or the capacity of the service organization to place, absorb, allocate, supervise, and manage recruits. Funding usually receives the most attention but other constraints can be far more stubborn. Subjecting all components to systematic review in relation to projected training needs can identify those which are in fact *strategic*. Plants can then be made to concentrate efforts and other resources particularly on these. Even then *some* component(s) will set limit to realistic goals.

Mapping initial planning for components individually and in subjects is followed by two further steps. One is to fit the pieces together into an integrated system under the projected conditions. This produces a composite map of a situation (B), which can be compared to the current situation (A). Strategic planning is complete only when a path has been worked out by which the system will move from A to B and when the decisions, resources, and other external and internal support required for this movement are, in fact, in hand.

Networking training resources

Another task of the training system is to make the best use of the resources available for training, both inside and outside the immediate system. Crossing its own boundaries in order to secure additional trainers, materials, and other resources which it cannot provide from within, or provide as well or as economically, leads to the identification, development, and management of external networks of training resources.

This task, focused as it is outside the system, is least familiar. It runs counter to strong personal and traditional inclinations to reserve resources for internal use only, as if for oneself or for one's family, and to regard their use by others as a weakness, as giving resources "away." In the perspective, calling on outside resources is a regrettable necessity to be terminated just as soon as internal resources can be built up. The perspective for building strong systems is quite different. The strongest systems make the fullest and most systematic use of outside resources. Having decided on their own areas of strength and built these up, they then value the flexibilities and economies of drawing on special strengths elsewhere. They also value the stimulation and assurances that come from working with competent colleagues in other systems.

The second important part of this task is networking within the system itself. It is characteristic of training systems in developing countries that trainers and other resources are either too centralized to be in effective contact with provinces, regions, and local situations where training is needed, or so dispersed and isolated that individual efforts yield little result and slowly peter out one by one. Clustering and networking address these needs

Since August 1983, the Indonesian Ministry of Health has operated a strategy of building training capacity at provincial level through a series of steps:

1. Select 3, then 3 more provinces,
2. Compose any initial provincial "training team" that includes promising and available "trainers" from related ministries and service and educational agencies, private as well as public, i.e., begin the external network.
3. Make a series of technical inputs to this provincial team and develop action projects for putting the new techniques to use. Selected central staff join as active participants, i.e., develop the internal network.

Six months the core training team of six in one a large province developed a network of fifteen additional trainers. Networking is also supported by special funds for provincial team meetings and for joint field activities and materials development. A periodic news newsletter from the center adds to regular communication between all team and network members across the country. By early 1984 direct contact between provinces and occasional work together on provincial programs had also begun.

Improved information gathering and management, he development of resource pools of trainer sand materials at various levels of the system, and ready access mechanisms are important components of this task.

7. Action spin-off and boundary management

Training efforts that are well meshed with training needs tend to spark onward actions. These may require further supportive activities on the part of the training system and/or surface-related training needs beyond those planned and provided for originally. Such spin-off are a good indicator of effective training and will bring training more organizational support.

> The development of training capacity in the initial Indonesian province sparked eight action projects in the first six months, of which three became major multiphase strategies. One of these called for an additional three weeks of senior consultation time. The other two required consultation time and, additionally, funds for provincial officials to participants in a series of local learning opportunities. Together, these two action projects cost half as much again as the initial years work in the province.

Spin-off action projects and other consequences of effective training present dangers which good boundary management can contain. "Successful" systems, especially in understandably success-hungry developing countries, are at a high risk of being overwhelmed and washed away by the overloads organizations urge on them in the wake of successes. Weak systems have the opposite tendency, likewise destructive: they risk insulation and atrophy for lack of contacts across their boundaries.

To cope with the risks of success, two lines of action have yielded promising results, One is to seek a fresh clarification, together with policy and decision makers of organization(s), of the system's of the system's primary task, to sort fresh demands into priorities and sequences, and to attempt only as much and as many as do not endanger the performance of the primary task. Agreement with work organizations along these lines is very important, otherwise pressures on the training system will continue and the organization(s) feel deprived each time the system rejects an attractive project. The next line of action is to ensure that these clarifications and decisions are translated into mutually acceptable work plans and carefully matched with additional resources.

8. Monitoring and evaluation; appraising and controlling performance

Each task to be preformed by a training system has a purpose, and its performance can be assessed in terms of both outcomes and the processes by which they were attained. Regular monitoring yield the data the system needs to improve its immediate functioning, structure, and, looking forward, further development. This task, important to carry out routinely for all tasks, also addresses the often intricate interrelationships between particular tasks and the performance of the system as a whole.

The dynamic of development training systems

There is no one way to develop a training system-training is too dependent on time and local circumstances and on the needs and resources of the work organization, all of which vary widely. The rigorous formulations commonly found in systems literature, comprising tidy and complete steps in one direction, may hide this main point, and by their apparent clarity and finality, confuse newcomers and discourage them. To the overriding generalizations that there is no one way to begin, and that several starts may have to be explored before one works, three other operational steps may be added.

The first practical step is to work on training systems development alongside contributing, through training, to alleviating some severe pressures that organizations are experiencing, e.g. severe shortage of nurses in the health services, patently inadequate supervision of costly materials or technologies, a major shift in technology. Second, no matter what the specific need, and the contribution training can make to meet it, several systemic tasks will certainly surface and demand attention quite quickly as training starts. Support building, trainer competence, resource networking, materials development, and presently, of course, monitoring performance appraisal and control-all predictably appear early. Only just behind will be the other tasks of renewing systemic structures and processes and of ensuring that the new work is part and parcel of deliberate strategies and plans. This emergence of systemic tasks can be counted on no matter what the starting point, because the tasks are closely connected.

The third practical generalization is that none of the eight tasks is ever finished and "laid to rest." A cyclical pattern seems inherent: one or two tasks move to center stage, are reworked to a new level of performance, then give way to the next in line, each comes full circle again for renewed attention, maybe in a fresh sequence and at different levels of system performance. This spiral pattern is true for each task and also for developing the system as a whole. Nothing seems to be gained by hurrying to the "next task" before the current one has been sufficiently accomplished; only then is attention to the next fruitful.

We hypothesize that the upward spiral of system development can continue until it exhausts the readiness of an environment to accept and support it. The immediate and most powerful environment of training is, of course, the work organization but broader culture supports and hindrances to further development may also set early limits, such as the traditions and tolerances of a country's civil service. Until these limits are reached performance levels for each task of a training system and the constituencies with which it is linked can continue to spiral upwards. System malfunctioning and disintegration may likewise be cyclical, but downwards.

The initial six months of work in 1983 on trainer and training system development in the health services of a large Indonesian province showed such a cyclical pattern. The judgment of when "enough" progress with a task has been made to enable system developers to go on to the next is happily easier to make in practice than to define in abstract terms. When the levels of performance in adjoining tasks repeatedly hinder further progress with the task in focus, attention should be shifted to the others. Even after attention has moved on, the momentum may well continue to carry the earlier task forward as information comes in about how well the work is progressing and hindrances to development are removed. So, for instance, there is no such thing as "total" acceptance and support "from the start"; "enough" is well short of that. Initially, especially when an organization's past experiences with training have not been encouraging, proposals for developing the training system may be merely tolerated, and extra resources for it, if any, come through minimal reallocations. Even small amounts of national or international funds can make a crucial contribution, in this first phase. But as developments get underway and some early training yields practical results and promise beyond expectations, tolerance changes to lively changes to lively interest and on toward more active involvement. Later, additional resources are "found," commitment to the developments is publicized, and an active search by the organization for yet more resources produces notable results. In the Indonesian province this progression took six months. Progress with *any* task contributes to and reinforces progress with all the others.

As the training system continues to shift attention to different tasks in turn, round and round, with conscious, deliberate intent informed by orderly monitoring of progress and problems, the map of tasks and their interconnections becomes familiar and using it habitual. Thus, when all levels of the system are routinely receiving general attention, and the system is so organized that it can keep all under regular surveillance and servicing, specific concerns will move in and out of focus at different levels and at different times. When both overall surveillance and shifts in focal attention between components and between levels become routine, system development has been "learned" and become an integral part of operations. This can be said only for the system itself, but also for the organizations which it serves, and to a lesser degree, to its other constituencies.

Rapid success with training systems development is fertile ground for seeds of destruction also. What in good time would be very attractive onward developments can overstrain the planning and management capacities of a barely begun training system, leading to its collapse if undertaken too easily. Regular reviews of system boundaries and careful boundary management offer the best immediate protection. Behind it, the enlarging of resources, improving system structure, and firming program strategy can then receive attention. Top-level support from work organization is essential for deliberate, orderly responses to demands for program expansion and diversification in line with growing system capacity.

By using the catchall word "system" to designate the partner responsible for training and associated consultation. We now have the setting for making three points. One is that the functions we have listed are composites, enveloping manifold variety and application in many possible situations. Second, to be used well and economically, the components required for any particular development effort need to be fitted together, that is, dovetailed into a single system. Any third, while the system may include one or more component units that specialize in training and consulting the other components carry out more, more continuous and, overall, more important "training" functions. If specialized training components in the system are not to spin off into self-serving irrelevance, they need particularly strong ties to the rest of the system and, through the system as a whole, vigorous roots in purposeful action.

Overall, this system perspective allows the same basic question about training resources to be raised at any level for decision and action. Is training-of all kinds and from all sources-of a sufficient scale and quality, and is it sufficiently well-paced and coordinated, to meet the requirements of planned projects expansions, and technical and administrative improvements. "Temporary systems," as well as permanent units of training, are also included in the system and as specially arranged and staffed programs, serve better in many situations. Institutions elsewhere in the country or abroad can also be used. Meanwhile the less formal, altogether more extensive, unobtrusive programs also continue in the system, such as understudy, induction, apprenticeship, and effective on-the-line supervision. All these varied and widely dispersed avenues are integrated by an effective system into cohesive training for organizational purposes. The system also links training with public and private agencies that deal with work force planning and the provision of resources; with work organizations; and with professional associations and resources centres, e.g., for quality maintenance and economies of scale in developing materials and for strengthening support in the general culture for good training.

The training goals, properly set by work organizations, guide decisions about training strategies, about the resources needed for training and their allocations, and—a very strategic consideration-what components to include in the system, i.e., where to draw boundaries. Issue internal to the system, such as task sequences, or development of the kinds and numbers of trainers and other system resources required for achieving the goals, likewise stem from the same set of estimates and considerations.

Organisationl structure

A rapidly growing interest in and need for accurate and useful information related to organizations, their internal mechanisms, and the executives who manage them. Many outside people, such as suppliers and clients who deal with large complex organizations, have exaggerated, almost caricatured, impressions of executives at work in their complex organizations.

One such caricature pictures executives as top mystics who wear their ulcers like a hair shirt and are quietly attended in their air-conditioned retreats by secretaries who whisper low rituals and occasionally give them some paper fetish to contemplate. The paper fetish is usually some ritualized art from such as the annual report of some corporation. Such a report symbolically represents the expenditures of the energy and life of some whole universe, which will show assets of $29,261,834.08 and liabilities of miraculously and precisely the same amount, $29,261,834.08. These are drawn together by the accounting priesthood, a group of highly trained specialists in selection, emphasis, and understatement. The assets and liabilities, of course, must rhyme like the final couplet of an Elizabethan sonnet. And so it goes, on and on. The foregoing is an amusing characterization of what goes on in our complex organizations: however, there is considerably more to the management of a large, complex organization than we find portrayed in this bit of fun.

Organizational theory

Perhaps a brief look at the evolutionary history of organization theory would help our understanding of organizations is general. The early search for greater efficiency in organizational management produced what has come to be known as the classical theory of administration, sometimes known as scientific management. Out of this tradition came the entity described as the formal organization providing the structural format on which organizations normally pattern themselves. Arising as a sort of reaction to the rigid structure which is characteristic of classical theory was the school of organizational thought known as human relations, which emphasized the informal organization and its emotional, unplanned behaviours. There followed a third tradition that attempted to unite the best of the classical and the human relations approaches known as the structuralist approach.

The classical or scientific approach, founded mainly by Max Weber, recognized no conflict between people and the organization, assuming instead that what was good for management was good for the workers. In other words, the classical theory assumed that harder work and higher productivity would produce higher profits which would lead, theoretically, to higher wages and, still more theoretically, to greater satisfaction among workers. The classical administrators used a combination of time and motion studies and a physical capacity assumption that humans are driven by a fear of hunger and a desire for economic gain which will make them respond maximally to financial reward. Such a rational, economic orientation gave rise to such management techniques as bonus systems. The basic problem with the classical approach is the high concern for structure and unconcern for people.

The human relations approach, was basically a reaction to the classical school. Elton Mayo, John Dewey, and Kurt lewin were the chief contributors to this school of organizational thought. Human relations research discovered, among other things, that the amount of work done by workers is determined at least in part by their "social" capacities.

Human relations research findings began mainly with the findings of a classic set of studies known as the Hawthorne studies, which were conducted at the Hawthorne plant of Western Electric in Chicago from about 1927 to 1932. Prior to the studies, the scientific management predictions of the classicists hypothesized that more physical illumination in the work area and its accompanying improved working conditions would increase production. The study actually rejected this hypothesis but revealed the following specific major findings:

1. The level of production is set by social norms, not by physiological capacities.
2. Noneconomic rewards and sanctions significantly affect the behaviour of the workers and largely limit the effect of economic incentive plans.
3. Workers often do not act or react as individuals but as members of groups.
4. The importance of leadership for setting and enforcing group norms and the difference between informal and formal leadership.

The Hawthorne studies revealed the need for the inclusion of at least some social and humanistic thought in organizational theory and analysis. Researchers began, at this point, to be concerned about such variables as morale, social relations, worker attitudes, and the human relations approach to organizational analysis was born. But just as the classical approach was too concerned only with structure and function, the human relations approach has often been too concerned only with people.

The structuralist approach, in its effort to synthesize the classical and human relations approaches to organizational analysis, began to recognize the organizational dilemma. This dilemma encompasses such things as strains between organizational needs and personal needs, between discipline and autonomy, and between management and workers. The structuralists see the organization as a complex social unit with many smaller social subgroups constantly interacting. The synthesis is not necessarily complete since there are still some pure human relations advocates and even some pure classicists; however, the structuralist movement has brought about a broadening of the general approach to organizational analysis. According to Amitai Etzioni, this broader approach to organizational analysis includes:

1. Both formal and informal elements of the organization and their articulation;
2. The scope of informal groups and the relations between such groups inside and outside the organization:
3. Both lower and higher ranks;
4. Both social and material rewards ad their effects on each other;
5. The interaction between the organization and its environment;
6. Both work and non-work organizations.

Our continued examination of the organization in this chapter will follow the broadened general approach suggested by the structuralists.

Organizations defined

What is an organization? Theoretically at least, an organization is a collective group of individuals capable of accomplishments beyond the capacity of individuals acting alone. Because of this notion our society has become highly organized. Most of us now spend most of our waking hours dealing with some type of organization. We work for organizations, we play in organizations, we pray in organizations, we go to organizations when we are sick and even when we die. Obviously then, we consider schools, clubs, churches, and businesses to be examples of organizations, but it is still not easy to pinpoint an exact definition.

Let us reconsider the notion that potentially an organization can accomplish feats not possible for a single human. The implication in such a statement is that an organization, a group of humans acting in concert and pooling their resources and abilities, is potentially capable of more than any single human member of that group would be. The term potentially capable as it is used here can be defined simply as "may be capable but not necessarily." In other words, if individuals band together in a group and then do not work up to their individual capabilities, the effectiveness of this group or organization will certainly be seriously hampered. Of course, the commitment and character of the individuals involved play a part in how fully they each maximize their capabilities.

We have acknowledged that an organization is certainly a kind of group because of its collective nature. We have also looked at some simple concepts of the comparative effectiveness and capabilities of group sand individuals. But our purpose here is to deal with organizations, so it is imperative that we examine the differences between a group and an organized group. Therein should be a workable definition of an organization.

A group is normally composed of three or more persons having something in common and each person interacting at some time with one or all of the others. The organized group, on the other hand, is based on repetitive interaction among members. As a result, the relationships are more permanent and the group has continuity. An organized group can recess or disperse and when reassembled it will repeat the relationships originally established between its individual members. In contrast, when an unorganized group disperses and is reassembled, the similarity between the original group and the reassembled group is often negligible.

An important organizational factor, then, is the repetition of social situations. An apparent prerequisite for this is a definite roster of members because, at the minimum, the members of an organized group must be identifiable to each other. The single most important factor in such identification is a common reference to an entity or a group name. For instance, as an outsider you distinguish one organized group from another by its official name. The members of the group likewise identify with that official name.

It is becoming apparent that an organization is a group of humans bound together by some formal structure. According to almost every organizational psychologist except the classicists, organization means more than just structure. Consensus seems to point to the inclusion of such factors an managerial controls, leadership, technology, and communi-cation networks. An organization is seen by many researchers to be an intricate set of humans strategies designed to achieve certain objectives or goals. We might say, then, that organizations are human groupings deliberately constructed to achieve specific and general goals. Such units as corporations, armies, schools, hospitals, churches, and prisons would fit this description very well.

According to Amitai Etzioni, organizations are characterized by (1) deliberately planned divisions of labor, power and communication responsibilities; (2) one or more power centres which control, evaluate and, where necessary, restructure; and (3) substitution of personnel through hiring, termination, transfer, and promotion. In other words, an organization is much more in control of its own nature and destiny than is any other social group.

Perhaps the definition of an organization which best answers the needs we have thus far delineated is the definition set down by organizational psychologist Edgar Schein. Schein says that an organization is "the rational coordination of the activities of a number of people for the achievement of some common. Explicit purpose or goal, through a division of labor and function and through a hierarchy of authority and responsibility."

Organizational goals

Because specific purposes and goals seem to be so much a part of any description of an organization, perhaps we should take a closer look at these goals. An organizational goal is a future state which the organization is attempting to achieve. Organizational goals serve a variety of functions. They provide orientation, guidelines, legitimacy, and evaluative standards, to name but a few functions. Organizations not only have specific goals, but these goals often become the entire reason for the existence of the organization. Many organizations develop real goals which differ greatly from the original or stated goals. Real goals, in this case, refer to goals that develop along the way as a result of organizational needs, and that command so much of the means, commitment, and resources of an organization that they are definitely of a higher priority than the stated goals.

In most organizations the goals are set by some designated body such as stockholders, members, a board of trustees or, in smaller organizations, by an individual owner. Key roles in the establishment of goals are played by various organizational departments or divisions, by personalities such as a strong leader, and by outside forces from the environment in which the organization exists. An excellent example of environmentally originated organizational goals is the recent addition, by most major industries, of pollution control as a stated and real organizational goal.

Classification of organizations

The classification of organizations according to such factors as size or purpose will help us to define what an organization actually is. There are, of course, many ways to classify or type organizations. One of the most obvious ways is simply to examine the goals of the organization. For instance, what we might call a mutual benefit association would be exemplified by such organizations as political parties, unions, fraternal clubs, religious sects, and professional associations. Another goal oriented organizational type would be business concerns such as industries, mail order houses, wholesale and retail stores, banks, and insurance companies. Under this system of topologies we could classify social work agencies, hospitals, schools, legal aid societies, and mental health clinics as service organizations. Finally, what we will call commonwealth organizations, public benefit organizations, would be organizations such as the State Department, I.R.S., the military, police and fire, and the research functions of a university or hospital.

Etzioni presents still another interesting way to classify organizations when he describes them as being predominantly coercive, utilitarian, or normative. A coercive organization is one in which coercion is the major means of control over participants as in concentration camps, prisons, and custodial mental hospitals. A utilitarian organization is one in which remuneration is the major means of control as in industries, business unions, and farmer cooperatives. A normative organization is described as one in which compliance with norms or normative power is the major source of control as in religious organizations, political organizations, and voluntary associations. Hospitals, colleges, and universities also fall into this category.

It is possible under this typology to have dual organizations that are combinations of the foregoing types. Some examples are a combat unit which would be normative-coercive, or most unions which would be Utilitarian-normative. Organizations such as early industries, farms, and ships might be classified as utilitarian-coercive.

Regardless of the method or typology used, it is important in the study of an organization to begin with some sort of method of classifying that organization.

Formal and informal organizations

The highly structured organization we have been defining and discussing has as its raison d'etre the attainment of objectives or goals through the preplanned, efficient use of available resources. The ensembles of individuals who perform distinct but interrelated and coordinated functions within such structures are really the formal organizations. The implication of the designation "formal" is that there is also such an entity as an "informal" organization. We will examine the latter in a moment, but first we can benefit from a closer look at the formal organization.

The structure of a formal organization is based upon the classical, scientific management principles mentioned earlier. Briefly, these principles assume that a formal organization has:

1. *Task Specialization.* Because a concentrated effort on a limited number of endeavours increases the quality and quantity of output, organizational and administrative efficiency should be increased by specialization of tasks assigned to the participants. A quick look about us shows that this specialization has reached in all-time high, sometimes to the detriment of the individual who is well trained in one narrow field or task and suddenly finds that such jobs no longer exist.
2. *Unity of Direction.* If the tasks of every person in a unit are specialized, the objective or purpose of the unit would then be specialized. The unity of direction notion states that organizational efficiency increases when each unit has a single activity under the direction of one leader.
3. *Span of Control.* The principle of control points out that efficiency is increased by limiting the scope of control of a leader. In other words, the narrower the management responsibilities, either in diversity of tasks or the number of people to be managed, the greater the efficiency. The application of this control principle accounts for what sometimes appears to the outsider to be a top-heavy organizational structure.
4. *Chain of Command.* Task specialization naturally creates many separate but related tasks. However, such a group or individual tasks being performed does not constitute an organization. The actual organization is created by forming these individual tasks into an interdependent and related pattern. The assumption is made that administrative and organizational efficiency is increased by arranging

the individuals in a hierarchy of authority with the individual on top directing and controlling the individual on the bottom.

Such hierarchical patterns, referred to in the army as the chain of command, are what we often call a table of organization or, more frequently, an organization chart. Such a chart often hangs on the office wall proclaiming to all who pass by just what the formal hierarchical structure is supposed to be; a sort of pecking order. The chart is usually the pyramidal structure suggested by the classicists, which might look like the structure. Another format for a formal organization chart is a circle. This particular circular chart is a chart from a middle-sized university. Job responsibilities (including who reports to whom) are very clear. It is even possible to show shared responsibilities such as data processing and budget direction on the circular chart shown.

One factor that determines the type of structure and how formal and well defined the structure must be is organizational size. Clearly, the larger the size, the more formal the structure must be in order to maintain the necessary control. Theodore Caplow in his book Principles of Organizations does a good job of approximating some divisions in organizational size. These divisions are as follows:

1. *Small organizations.* A small organization ranges from about three to thirty members and is small enough to permit them to become a primary group within themselves. A family is an example.
2. *Medium-size Organizations.* These organizations are too large for the development of all possible pair relationships but still small enough that any member, including a leader, would interact with any other member. The medium-size organization ranges from about thirty to about a thousand. An average industrial firm might be an example.
3. *Large Organizations.* A large organization is too large for many members to know each other well but not too large for one or more leaders to be recognized by all other members. These leaders will be recognized by many more people than they are able to recognize. Such an organization ranges from about one thousand to about fifty thousand. Most universities are large organizations.
4. *Giant Organizations.* The giant organization has too many members which are too widely scattered to permit the direct interaction of any individual with all of the others. The range of the giant organizations is from about fifty thousand to infinity. Political parties and business conglomerates are good examples.

One can readily see that the size of an organization does make a great deal of difference, particularly concerning how that organization will be managed. While a formally structured organization has many of the advantages already discussed, it is also faced with certain dilemmas. These dilemmas are, of course, magnified as organizational size increases. Some of the dilemmas of a formal organization are:

1. *Bureaucratic discipline.* It is highly desirable but not always possible to keep everyone operating from a "company" point to view.
2. *Professional expertise.* It is most difficult to find promotable people from within (or sometimes even from outside) to fill all the vital hierarchical slots.
3. *Coordination and Control.* The large formal organization can very easily become awkward and unwieldy.
4. *Managerial planning and initiative.* The formal organization requires an inordinate amount of ability on the part of its managers to plan carefully and then take the initiative in implementation.
5. *Communication.* Last, but certainly far from least, communication is too often hampered. Without communication and constant open interaction, the organization cannot survive and, as was pointed out in the foregoing breakdown by size, communication is far more difficult in a large formal organization than in a smaller organization.

Because of dilemmas such as these, there arise in every formal organization one or more informal organizational structures. A few paragraphs ago we took the opportunity to describe the components found in most formal organizations to illustrate what a typical formal organization chart might look like. If we plan so carefully and control so well how, then, do we find ourselves involved in the chaotic dilemmas just described?

A part of the chaos that may exist in an organization, as the human relations school has pointed out, is the failure to see any dimensions of the organization other than those implied by the formal organization chart on the executive office wall. The formal organization chart is, of course, an important structural factor simply because organizations are traditionally described by organization charts. An organization chart specifies the authority or reportorial structure of the system. The organization chart communicates some of the most important formal attributes of the system. Cyert and March point out that, "The organization chart still provides a lot of information conveniently-partly because the organization usually has come to consider relationships in terms of the dimensions of the chart."

When we study a diagram of the structure of an organization, we learn something about the operation and about the communication patterns which accompany the operation of that organization. Yet when we place human beings into the slots on that organizational chart, we find ourselves with a second, but equally important, structural pattern, a sort of informal organizational chart.

The formal organization has already been described as a conventional methodical structure, a set of rules, and generally refers to the organizational pattern designed by management; a blueprint of the division of labor and the power of control. The informal organization, on the other hand, is a nonconventional methodological structure and often refers to the social relationships that develop among the staff or workers above and beyond the formal one determined by the organization; for example, they do not work on the same team but are friends. The formal aspect of an organization, then, is the classical hierarchical structure which the organization itself recognizes as its structure, that is, who reports to whom. The informal organizations are the less obvious human relations factors within each formal organization which, although not always recognized, are nonetheless present and must be dealt with for example, "the grapevine" or "rumour mill." More will be said about the grapevine in later chapters. Because of the relative obscurity and the lack of recognizable structure, any kind of informal structure is extremely difficult to deal with; however, it still must be dealt with.

The high degree of rigidity of the formal structure may account for the frequently reported growth of informal, and sometimes unidentified, communication channels in organizations. The growth stems from the fact that the informal structure is often better able to meet the changing, fluctuating, and dynamic needs of the organization, whereas the formal structure has a tendency to be more static. Too often the formal structure no longer describes what is, in fact, going on dynamically in an organization. Even more important, in formal organizations more nearly matched the informal organization structurally, the organizations would probably be highly productive, highly cohesive, and enjoy considerably more communication efficiency than they do. Since the informal and formal often do not match structurally, the recognition and understanding of the informal organizational hierarchy within the formal organization is an absolute necessity for an examination of the whole.

The systems approach

For our purposes in this book we will define a system as an organized, complex whole; an assemblage or combination of parts forming a complex whole. We will define a social system as a bounded collection of interdependent parts devoted to the accomplishment of some goal or goals.

The foregoing definition of a social system is closely tied in with our earlier goal-oriented definition of an organization. But why use a systems approach to studying organizations at all? Fundamental to systems theory is the concept of input, throughput, and output. James D. Thompson points out: "Complex organizations exist ultimately as agencies of their environment, acquiring resources in exchange for outputs and, in the final analysis, obtaining technologies from environments. The concepts basic to systems theory, then, do a good job of describing what is going on in an organization and, therefore, provide a useful look at these organizations.

Systems theory itself certainly bears further examination for our purposes here. As stated earlier a system is made up of a series of inputs, throughputs, and outputs. To clarify these concepts it would be helpful to examine the system in an industrial plant for a moment. In the industrial setting, such factors as raw materials, workers, capital, and so on, are considered inputs. The manufacturing process conducted in that plant is the throughput and the finished marketable product is considered to be the output.

Ideally a system should be self-corrective; that is, the system has a cybernetic control mechanism which will tell it when adjustments need to be made. For instance, in a modern heating system the cybernetic device is the thermostat and in a human system the cybernetic device is the brain. But how is that self-corrective? If your human system, your body, is driving a car down the highway and a child darts out in front of you, what do you do? Your eye sees the child and flashes a message to your cybernetic device, the brain, which says, in effect, "Danger ahead-correct at once." Your brain says swerve to the left or right and you will miss the child and so you do. Now if you have over corrected and are heading for the ditch the same process occurs and you are back on course.

This simplified description of a system and its cybernetic is really not any different from the very complex functions of a large social system such as a formal organization. The principles pointed out in this simple example are that, through feedback from the environment, a system may adapt and adjust in a self-corrective fashion and, not only survive, but ultimately reach its original goal. The simple illustration of the child and the car also points to another principle of systems theory known as the law of equifinality. The law of equifinality simply says that there are many ways to get to an ultimate goal, not just by the single course originally planned.

If we return to our industrial example, we will see that the reading of feedback from the environment by the cybernetic portion of the system ultimately becomes important in the profit and loss statement. Basically in our industrial example the sale of the product or output provides the capital necessary to buy the raw material inputs to make more products (output) and on and on continuously. However, in order for the system to continue, it must be under control at all times by its cybernetic and must constantly be adjusting and self-correcting. For example, it would be as unprofitable to have too much unused raw material lying around as it would be to have the throughput ready to operate and have no raw material on hand. On the other hand, it is not profitable to produce a greater output than the market can handle at any given time. It is necessary, then, for the cybernetic-in this case management-to keep correcting the system to maintain a steady process of input, throughput, output, input, throughput, output, etc. What is really involved here is another concept in systems theory known as the principle of optimization. The principle of optimization means that a system attempts to reach a point at which it is getting the maximum output in return for the minimum input. The business of the cost accountant, for instance, is one of optimization. Obviously, one of the main functions of any modern manager is continually to correct flows in the system until it reaches, or at least nears, that point of optimization.

Organizational multiplicity

The subject of interrelatedness, one organization to another or of subparts within organizations, has already been mentioned in this chapter. Most organizations are related to other organizations in one of the following ways:

1. *As a congruent organization.* Congruence in this sense refers to an organization where the membership of organization A is identical with the membership of organization B, but the two organizations have completely separate goals and purposes.
2. *As linked to another organization.* Here we have a situation more of overlapping membership than of congruency. We find that certain members of organization A belong to organization B, and perhaps even to organization C, but still these organizations do not have the same purposes. As the diagram shows, there are three two-way organizational interfaces and one three-way interface.

   As a component of another larger organization. Our concern here is with a relationship of subsystems, systems and suprasystems which, in a complex structure, seems to go on almost to infinity. An example of such a component structure would be General Motors Corporation in which all the employees of the Pontiac Motor Division are at the same time employees of the corporation. Conversely, however, all employees of the corporation are definitely not employees of Pontiac Motor.

According to Daniel Katz and Robert Kahn, most formal organizations function through five basic sybsystems:

1. Productive subsystems concerned with the work that gets done;
2. Supportive subsystems of procurement, disposal, and institutional relations;
3. Maintenance subsystems for tying people into their functional roles;
4. Adaptive subsystems concerned with organizational change;
5. Managerial system for the direction, adjudication, and control of the many subsystems and activities of the structure.

Also, in most organizations such subsystems are not equally powerful in their influence over one another and over the total system. An interesting phenomenon then, which occurs in some organizations, is a leading system. There is an almost infinite number of reasons why one subsystem might lead the other subsystems and exert the greatest influence over the organization. These reasons may range widely from the fact that the chairman of the board came up through that particular subsystem, to the fact that a subsystem possesses technologies that are particularly vital to the total organization, and even to the fact that a certain subsystem such as the sales department provides the income that keeps the blood flowing in the organizational vein. Of course, at various times and for various situationally appropriate reasons, top management may be influenced first by one subsystem and then another. Such multidirectional influence is unquestionably the most equitable and technologically sound way to manage for, the achieve, optimization.

System openness and the organization

Before we can examine the effects of openness upon the functioning of an organization, we must provide at least a limited conceptual definition of system openness. System openness is the degree to which a system exchanges information with sources outside the system. System openness includes open and closed systems and the various degrees found along a continuum stretching between the two. According to Matthew Miles, "An open system is related to an makes exchanges with its environment, while a closed system is not related to and does not make exchanges with its environment."

Basically, then, a closed system is an isolated, self-contained system or at least a system that has fallen into a self-contained operative pattern. In contrast, an open system constantly exchanges information, ideas, energy, and so on with its environment. According to the second law of thermodynamics, the physical world is directed toward chaos, maximum disorder, and disequilibrium. This thermodynamic law applies specifically to a closed system. In other words, where there is no open exchange with the outside environment, a system will stagnate and wither. This stagnating, withering, perishing process is known in systems theory, just as it is in the thermodynamic sense, as entropy. Biologically speaking, entropy is the principle which states that when we are born we begin to die. Entropy in an organizational context may be defined as the tendency for a system to move to a random and chaotic state in which there is no longer a potential for throughput or work.

We have just seen that an open system is a system that is related to and makes exchanges with its environment and that the opposite is true of a closed system. If information is the lifeblood of any organization, then we might expect a closed system to experience a rapidly increasing state of entropy. Conversely, and open system with a steady flow of information at its disposal should experience what we call a steady state. A steady state can be defined as a state where the composition of the system remains constant, or in a state of equilibrium.

We spoke of general systems theory and the concepts of inputs, throughputs, and output. The systems theory option of input and output in an organization is really the maintenance of a steady state or a state of equilibrium between the input and output of that organization.

Because open systems, unlike closed systems, are constantly exchanging energy, materials, and/or information with their environments, these open systems take in (input), process (throughput), and give off (output) in relation to the environment. Of course, open systems experience some entropic tendency toward disorder, randomness, and a loss of energy that goes on in a closed system. But the open system can restore order, cut down on randomness, and replenish energy by adjusting and taking on inputs of greater energy or a higher order than their own outputs.

Besides this organizational life-giving characteristic of an open exchange with the environment and the consequent steady state, there are other characteristics that distinguish an open system from a closed system:

1. Open systems are examples of the law of equifinality already discussed; that is, there is more than one path that may be followed to obtain identical results.
2. An open system is self-regulating. In other words, such a system is able to adjust to adversity and unexpected barriers and still arrive at its original destination with the mission accomplished. It is flexible enough to roll with the punches and correct itself as it goes along and then return to the steady state.
3. Open systems are able to a maintain a steady state and regulate or self-correct through feedback. Whether the feedback refers to materials, information, or whatever, the principle still remains that a system must have a portion of its output fed back into the inputs which will ultimately affect future outputs. It is the ability of a system to adjust future behaviours and outputs by reference to past behaviours and outputs through a proper reading of the feedback portion of the inputs. One basic fact related to this type of feedback is that normally it is negative feedback. It should be clear that the need for self-regulation or self-correction in the systems can only really be pointed out by negative feedback. When negative feedback vanishes, the very reason for correction or regulation also vanishes.
4. Just as we have shown the communication process within a system to be cyclical and constantly in motion, so can we view an open system as a cycle of events. An open system with its input-throughput-output and its self-regulatory feedback is certainly a dynamic rather than a static concept. A simple linear stimulus-response exchange between two entities does not constitute social structure; however, two entities stimulating and responding to each other in a cyclical fashion form the basic dynamic unit in a system. Such a single cycle of events gives us the simple form of structure. A typical complex organization is a system of events cycles made up of many such single cycles, both in and out of the organization, most of which are interrelated.
5. Because of the foregoing features found in an open system, another feature of such systems is negative entropy, sometimes called negentropy. Since an open system, in addition to the foregoing features, can store the imported energic inputs, it can acquire negative entropy. The acquisition of energy, its storage, and subsequent use at the times when it is most needed is one of the main functions

of management. When we manage our systems best, we manage for negative entropy and an ultimate state of organizational equilibrium.

6. The culmination of all features found in open systems is contained in the ultimate goal of any success-seeking organization, the achievement of a dynamic equilibrium. On the surface there seems to be some confusion as to whether an open system provides the impetus for constant change or provides a steady system which resists change. Many people feel that an open system produces stability and infrequent change because of the stable, mechanical system necessary to keep information flowing in and out of an organization. Others feel conversely that the major impetus for change in an organization comes from outside the organization because of the fresh approaches that exogenous information brings with it.

The notion of a dynamic equilibrium, because it is not a motionless or true equilibrium, is the key to this dilemma. Basically, a dynamic equilibrium, with its flexibility, allows for growth and change without loss of the overall steady state. In other words, growth and change are possible in an open system because its self-adjustive factors prevent any extended state of disequilibrium. Such a system reacts to change or anticipates change through growth which assimilates the change into the existing structure. A new operational level is thus established and the organization adjusts and functions around this new level but with the same old internal balance and equilibrium.

Effective management and organizational health

The mere survival of a formal organization such as a business or industrial firm in today's competitive world is almost in itself a tribute to management. What we are talking about when we say survival, is a sort of organizational health or well-being. The healthy state will no more take care of itself than our bodies will survive in a healthy state without sleep, a balanced diet, and proper overall care. The business of taking care of the overall health of organizations is the main function of management.

Systems, be they biological or social systems, are subjected to a force known as entropy. Recall further that the tendency of a system toward maximum entropy is the movement of a system toward disorder, complete lack of resource transformation, and ultimate death. Entropy increases in a system until eventually the entire system stops; if the system is left unattended, the total entropic state and the accompanying system stoppage happens much sooner than one might anticipate. Just as we eat three balanced meals a day, brush our teeth, get plenty of sleep, and so on, in order to prolong life and hold off biological entropy, so must the manager continually be searching for and applying remedial steps to hold social entropy to a minimum in the organization. Clearly, a biological system can only slow down or temporarily arrest the inevitability of the total entropic state. A social system, on the other hand, may be capable of offsetting entropy indefinitely through proper management. However, the principle remains that when a human organism or a social organization is born it begins to die, and everything possible must be done if we are to hold off his process and maintain a healthy state as long as possible. A great deal more will be said about the managerial maintenance of an organization in a healthy state throughout the remainder of this book.

Organizational health would seem to be a prerequisite to organizational effectiveness no matter how effectiveness is measured. There are, of course, many ways to measure organizational effectiveness; however, any evaluation of organizational effectiveness is ultimately a measure of managerial effectiveness.

There are some evaluative factors which should be included in a framework for predicting the effectiveness of any organization. One such factor is stability. In this case stability refers to the ability of the organization to maintain its own hierarchical structure as well as the maintenance of stable input-output relationships. Implicit in such stability is the ability of an organization to remain flexible and maintain itself as a self-corrective system throughout its many internal changes and pressures as well as the external influences by which it is constantly bombarded.

Another criterion of organizational effectiveness is integration, which in this case refers to the level of interaction and the internal flow of information. In other words, what we are really dealing with here is communication integration; who talks to whom, about what, how often, and so on. Integration, then, is affected by such factors as physical proximity of organizational members, by the degree of formality in the organization, and by organizational size.

Morale is yet another important measure of organizational effectiveness. Morale, in this case, means roughly the ability of the organization to provide satisfaction to its individuals and to maintain a desire within those individuals to continue their organizational participation. High morale is apt to cause individuals to conform to organizational norms with a minimum of pressure or coercion. The importance of the morals and integration factors is pointed out by Katz and Kahn when they assert:

> Three categories of behaviour are required to achieve high levels of organizational effectiveness. People must join and remain in the organization; they must perform dependably the roles assigned to them; and they must engage in occasional innovative and cooperative behaviour beyond the requirements of role but in the service of organizational objectives.

One final effectiveness criterion which is probably the most obvious of all is goal achievement. Goal achievement is the result of the total organizational activity and is, of course, a highly objective, results-oriented measure. Such yardsticks usually take the form of productive output, the profit and loss statement or corporate earnings, all of which are undeniably objective and "cold" to a fault.

The best total measure of organizational effectiveness is all of these yardsticks drawn together as a composite approach is necessary because each of these effectiveness factors seem to be interdependent.

There are many other variations and choices for organizational effectiveness criteria but the foregoing seem to be the basic ones. For instance, we have only been discussing the effectiveness of an organization and its management against a predetermined criteria. Another effective evaluative procedure is to compare one organization with another similar organization.

We can say that a system will prevail if the management of that organizational system:

1. Maintains an openness to its environment and to its own suprasystem and subsystems.
2. Watches for and utilizes the existing feedback in a self-corrective manner.
3. Constantly strives to manage toward negative entropy.
4. Constantly strives to manage toward a point of optimization.

The managerial role in an organization

So the managers, in these various ways, are guardians of organizational health and well-being. But how do managers effect such controls? What is the manager's functional role in the organization? One obvious role is that of a task-oriented motivator and mobilizer of the competencies and human resources under the manager's control. If the task-oriented goals of the organization are to be achieved, they will be achieved through the efforts of individuals who ultimately are directed and mobilized into an efficiently functioning team by some manager.

The strong need for managers to assume a task-oriented role cannot be denied; however, it is becoming more and more important to consider carefully another managerial role. According to Warren Bennis:

> This is the paradigm: bureaucratic values tend to stress the rational, task aspects of the work and to ignore the basic human factors which relate to the task and which, if ignored, tend to reduce task competence. Managers brought up under this system of values are badly cast to play the intricate human roles now required of them. Their ineptitude and anxieties lead to systems of discord and defence which interfere with the problem-solving capacity of the organization.

In other words a managerial role equal in importance to the task role is the role of creating a social climate and work environment in which the task is most likely to be accomplished.

It should already be evident that the total management role and the leadership required to be a good manager are much easier to talk about than to accomplish or possess. How, then, do leaders accomplish what at times seem to be superhuman demands made of them? First, effective leaders do not "handle" people. They persuade, guide, and organize the tasks of people in order to accomplish certain desired results. Leader-managers have a number of critical functions that are dependent upon their ability to communicate. They develop and maintain a system of communication and through it develop an effective work environment. The leader in a modern organization must plan, control, and delegate duties and responsibilities in a way which will develop the talents and abilities of subordinates to a point of optimization.

Applying these management functions in an organization is an even greater challenge because, as Katz and Kahn point out, "organizational leadership, like other cases of influence in complex social settings, is always a combined function of social structural factors and of the particular characteristics of the individuals making up the structure."

The attempt to apply such management functions is really an attempt to influence behaviour. Central to the influence of behaviour in an organization is power, authority, and delegation. Power is the ability, sometimes latent, to influence psychological and behavioural change. Authority is a special kind of power which is vested in certain individuals or organizational positions by an organization. Authority is really a form of official permission to use the resources of the organization. Delegation is thus the conferring of a specified authority by someone in a position of greater authority. These authoritative sources of power, organizational position, and job importance are power sources derived from the organization itself. We may find individual sources of power as well. Individually derived power would include such factors as special expertise, interest and tenure, and any personal characteristics. Power may also come about by the coalition of a group of individuals. Because of its organizational nature, we will be mostly concerned with authoritative type of power.

Management involves the kind of roles which coordinate human and material resources toward the accomplishment of an objective. This sort of coordination is ultimately an effective exercise of authority and other types of power. Management's main generalized role is to convert the disorganized resources of people, machines, time, money, space, and material into an effective and efficient enterprise. Perhaps the managerial role is best summed up by Fremont Kast and James Rosenzweig when they point out that the manager manages "toward objectives, through people, via technique and in an organization."

Managerial style

It is difficult to generalize about the effectiveness of various managerial styles in carrying out the managerial role. A strict, autocratic style of management may be the most effective style in some situations, while a very loose, easy-going style may work better in others. The appropriate style depends upon such things as organizational objectives and the willingness of the followers to be led in a certain way. The willingness of the followers is especially important, since practical experience has proven over and over again that we actually only manage with the consent of the managed. The real disparity between managerial styles probably rests in the degree of participation, which in this sense refers to how involved or uninvolved the followers are in organizational planning and decision making. According to Katz and Kahn, "The essential difference between a democratic and an authoritarian system is not whether executive officers issue orders to or consult with those below them but whether the actual power to legislate on policy is vested in the membership or in the top echelons." In other words, participatory management cannot work as long as it is used as a device for getting others to do what management wants them to do. Real, total participation is based on mutual respect.

A strong factor in managerial effectiveness, whatever the style, is flexibility, Managerial flexibility is nothing more than an understanding of, and belief in, the principle of equifinality discussed earlier as a part of the system approach. The effective manager will realize that there is no one right way to manage and lead all followers. Conversely, subordinates can and will be most effectively managed by a managerial style that is failored as much a possible to their individual personalities and needs as followers. Of course, a complex organization can hardly afford to tailor a different management style for each of its followers; however, failure even to consider individual differences can be disastrous. For example, the author has knowledge of a firm which had a very rigid, authoritarian style of leadership with absolutely no flexibility. The managers were supersalespeople themselves and were so inflexible as not even to allow their subordinates to use different wording in the sales talk or a different method of making out a receipt. Punitive measures such as early morning meetings for failing to meet weekly sales quotas were the rule rather than the exception. In a short time the organization found itself facing an employee vote an whether or not there would be collective bargaining through, of all things, a salesmen's union. Out of slightly more than one hundred salesmen voting, the implementation of collective bargaining lost by only seven votes. After the vote a survey was conducted to determine the nature and levels of employee dissatisfaction. One might easily imagine that the dissatisfaction would most likely lie in the areas of punitive measures or oppressive management, but not so. Almost to a man, the area of real dissatisfaction was the lack of flexibility in the system; the lack of enough elbow room to allow for individual human differences.

There are two general managerial styles cited by Douglas McGregor as Theory X and Theory Y. These two theories are mirror opposites and are really better viewed as extreme ends of a continuum and rarely seen as pure management styles being practiced in any given organization. There is a set of underlying assumptions upon which each of these theories is based.

Theory X assumes that:

1. The average human being has an inherent dislike for work and will avoid it when possible.
2. Because of this human tendency to dislike work, most people must be coerced, controlled, directed, threatened with punishment to get them to put forth adequate effort toward the achievement of organizational objectives.
3. The average human being prefers to be directed, wishes to avoid responsibility, has relatively little ambition, and wants security above all.

Theory Y, on the other hand, assumes that:

1. The expenditure of physical and mental effort in work is as natural as play or rest.
2. External control and the threat of punishment are not the only means for bringing about effort toward organizational objectives.
3. Commitment to objectives is a function of the rewards associated with their achievement.
4. The average human being learns, under proper conditions, not only to accept but to seek responsibility.
5. A relatively high degree of imagination, ingenuity, and creativity is widely distributed in the population.
6. Today the intellectual potentialities of the average human being are only partially utilized.

As stated previously, there are clearly few, if any, examples of a management team practicing either Theory X or Theory Y exclusively. Theory X can offer management a convenient set of excuses for the failure of the organizational subordinates to attain their objectives. Conversely, managing by Theory Y could eventually lay organizational shortcomings directly at the feet of management and imply that management had lost control somewhere along the way.

The real concern should be about the potential disaster that could ensue from practicing either Theory X or Theory Y on people whose attitudes were the opposite. For instance, treat an employee with Theory X attitudes using the Theory Y assumptions and obviously you will get no production and perhaps a lot of dissatisfaction. On the other hand, a Theory Y type employee could be ruined by Theory X treatment. This is especially true when one considers the Timothy Leary notion known as interpersonal reflex. Leary says of his concept, "This is a general probability principle. It holds that: interpersonal reflexes tend (with a probability significantly greater than chance) to initiate or invite reciprocal interpersonal responses from the 'other' person in the interaction that lead to a repetition of the original reflex." Interpersonal reflex says simply that, quite unwittingly, our day-to-day actions are really reflexes so that if I shout you will shout back, if I push you will push back, and if I treat you fairly you will probably reciprocate. If this principle is at all accurate, then think for a moment what continued Theory X treatment could do to a dedicated Theory Y person. They might begin to live up or, more appropriately, live down to the label.

There are innumerable examples of dedicated groups of employees who react most peculiarly to continued autocratic Theory X oriented mismanagement. One work unit of competent, well-meaning people known to the author goes absolutely berserk when their Theory X manager leaves the office for anything more than one day. His departure is followed immediately by a cheering, bell-ringing, officewide, extended coffee break type of celebration. Of course, this bizarre reaction to mismanagement is highly counter-productive. Worse than that, however, is the fact that the manager will never be there to witness this brief rebellion and take advantage of what is really a great opportunity for him to see the fruits of his past errors. If only he could see this scene once and take it to heart he would at least have the opportunity to take preventive action in the future.

Perhaps the best measure of the appropriateness of a management style in a given organizational situation is whether the style promotes the loyalty of the work group. It has been proven over and over again that managers who command the loyalty of a group-that is managers who are liked, accepted, respected-will be most apt to have effective managerial control. Of course, such loyalty from the managed would suggest that an office-wide celebration just because the boss is out of sight and has temporarily lost surveillance over the behaviour of employees would be highly unlikely.

Decentralization and the middle to lower-range manager

Our discussion so far has dealt with organizational management in general and top-level management in particular. The focus of the remainder of this book, however, will be directed toward the more pivotal organizational roles, the middle and lower-range managers. We say pivotal roles because managers at these levels are literally the people in the middle; they must be aware of those above and below them and be able to relate effectively in both directions. Most young managers are pretty well aware of the social and psychological needs of their superiors: however, in these lower-range, "firing line" positions where they often find themselves, Katz and Kahn reinforce the obvious fact that:

> In addition to assessing the area in which his superiors will permit movement, the middle manager must fact toward the people below him. He must depend upon subordinates for the efficient accomplishment of the subsystem task, and modifications in structure must be acceptable to them.

If problems in middle management do in fact present a challenging situation the problems seem to be doubled and tripled in field management. Any description of lower and middle-range members of a management team, especially those operating in the field, sounds as if they are each a congiomerate of Superman and Einstein with the hide of a rhinoceros and the endurance of an Olympic miller. Although this seems to be an exaggeration, a field manager can be described as a personal supervisor, the executor of headquarters' plans, a communication link between the market and the home office, and a supersalesperson. Field managers are also literally on their own at times.

How does field management find itself in such a position? Mainly because the manager in the field is usually separated from the immediate personal supervision of the central office. Today one can easily observe the tendency of general management to decentralize and free itself from day-to-day business matters in order better to think about and organize the future of its firms. There is a vigorous effort to force the responsibility for current problems downward, partly because it is evident that those in the field are nearer both the sources of information and the means of treatment.

The typical model of a decentralized reveals a central management executive committee which formulates organizational goals and policies. Then, under the principle of decentralization, the operational management located in the various decentralized branches is mainly responsible for implementation of the general goals and policies developed by central management. Operational or field management is usually free to make decisions and set goals provided that they fall within the broad general framework set up by central management. Branches that are truly decentralized appear to be separate organizations rather than parts of a larger whole. Perhaps the greatest example of a truly decentralized operation is General Motors Corporation. Thus, the manager of the Oldmobile Divisions of General Motors Corporation is responsible for the inputs, outputs, and profits of Oldmobile. He comes as close to being the owner of that company as anyone can be without actually owning it. As Rocco Carza and John Yanouzas point out:

> With this type of organization, General Motors is benefiting from both centralization through centralized planning, financing, and staff services, and decentralization through the fast, "one-the-spot" decision making that characterizes small organization. Decentralization also helps to develop managers by giving them experience in making decisions.

Recall that earlier we defined authority as a sort of official permission to use the resources of the organization. Such authority takes on special importance in a decentralized situation. Traditionally, however, authority and freedom to manage must be approximately equal. In other words, when managers are assigned certain organizational duties, they should have the accompanying permission to use and commit organizational resources in order to carry out those duties. This is harder than it sounds for some top-level managers. For many the delegation of duties and responsibilities is simple; however, the other side of the coin, the right to be wrong occasionally, is much harder to delegate to others.

If management of field operations is more difficult than a centralized operations, and if full management authority is difficult to grant. Why then do organizations decentralize? According to William G. Scott, businesses have traditionally decentralized for one or more of the following reasons:

> *Cost.* The cost factor is operative when the size of an operation becomes uneconomical. Economists refer to this as diseconomies of scale. Product Line. This factor is operative when management considers that it is more efficient to manufacture and market a product through autonomous or semi-autonomous product divisions. Market Area. At times management considers it advisable to manufacture and market through regional divisions geographically decentralized.

Organizational size seems to be the affective factor running ahead of any other need for decentralization. Costs, of course, include such items as transportation of raw materials, finished products, geographical wage differences, etc. When size forces a move to decentralization, the accompanying autonomy often seems to break down better on a product line basis. Geographically separated marketing areas are naturally a big advantage in the area of product development for individualized ethnic and geographical tastes. In the past few years, the advertising business has taken advantage of regional breakdowns in national media. While it has long been possible to buy certain selected network affiliated market areas in radio and TV, it is now possible to advertise regionally oriented products in certain selected circulation areas of national magazines.

Another determinant, which is a growing factor in the decision to decentralize, is communication. Complexity and increasing organizational size are the underlying factors here again; however, they ultimately result in a loss of information flow and the accompanying communication breakdowns. Although these areas will be explored more fully, let us point out here that the need for better and more manageable communication systems is fast becoming a major reasons for decentralization.

Decentralization is not always welcomed with open arms by those affected by it. Without careful central management and thoughtful planning, decentralization may utilize the intended improved communication, improved marketing, and more efficient cost accounting, and nevertheless produce the completely opposite effect. Whether decentralization is wanted and/or welcome or not, it is still inevitable for many rapidly growing organizations. Accompanying this inevitability is an equally rapidly growing need for management to train itself to handle the previously mentioned difficulties encountered by middle and lower-range managers operating in the field.

8

Salary Management

The wage structure must be linked to what the company is trying to achieve. It is not unusual to find a company with a wage structure in direct conflict with the company's overall objectives. For example, a company may plan to produce a high-quality product while at the same time it may have a direct incentive geared to quantity. These questions must be asked:

1. Apart from profit, what are we in business for?
2. Where are we going during the next two to three years; in the next five to ten years?
3. How do we plan to get there?
4. What influence will these plans have on our wage structure?
5. How can the wage structure aid the company in meeting its objectives?

From this a business plan is built up, in simple terms, expressing the company's short-and long-term objectives and how these will affect specific areas. It may be, for example, that in two years' time a massive capital investment is planned. In terms of human resources this will probably affect the way work is organized, manning arrangements and job demands. Care must be taken, therefore, to ensure that the new wage structure will form a satisfactory spring board to cater for future developments. Consideration must also be given to the spin-off which will affect the whole company.

Management style

It is necessary to identify what the company's management style is. Is it predominantly autocratic, paternalistic, participative or laissez-faire? Incompatibi-lities arise if a wage structure is implemented in isolation of this major consideration. An autocratic management style, for instance, is in conflict with a Scanlon/Rucker plan. Since the pay structure expresses to employees how the company values them, a real attempt must be made to draw up a declared wage policy.

Changing a wage structure

The desire to change a wage structure usually springs from an existing structure which management no longer controls. Common features are that the present structure suffers from wage drift, that it has numerous rates which are inequitable in terms of individual contribution and there has been a gradual build-up of 'special' allowances.

Most companies, when faced with the need to change their wage structure, begin by looking for alternative incentives. In reality this is prejudging the issue. The first step should be an initial investigation to ascertain the pressure points which exist in the present structure. Only by discovering the 'lumps and the bumps' in the present system will the way ahead seem clear. A discussion with the senior wages clerk will be an enlightening experience since that individual, more than anyone else, is fully aware of the inadequacies and inequities of the existing system.

Wage analysis

This should be based on a thorough examination of the gross pay earned department by department for, say, a 'typical' week at two points in the year. All special allowances should be examined and the totals expressed as a percentage of labour cost. Consideration should be given to the effectiveness of the incentive element.

Overtime

The number of hours overtime should be broken down and scrutinised to see what indicators exist. Excessive overtime working usually means an unrealistic basic hourly rate. What, for example, would be the result if overtime working were curbed? If overtime earnings were consolidated in the basic rate on the understanding that productivity was maintained, would the need for overtime working cease? And would this be socially acceptable in your locality?

Work study

One of the main reasons why a company decides to change its wage structure is because work study values have worked loose and wage drift has become a dominant feature. For example, is the pace of working closely related to that shown on the time sheets? Too often top management assumes that because performances are high on paper, all is well. If the company's present work study team cannot cope with the situation, the use of consultants should be considered. An alternative is to employ experienced work study personnel on a short-term contract.

Labour turnover

Annual figures should be produced and broken down by the department. These figures are normally associated with the social aspects of employment but it is not by any means unknown for a definite correlation to be established between them and the method of payment. For example, it is possible that a very low labour turnover linked to a very high rate of absenteeism indicates that earnings may be unusually high for the area but working conditions are intolerable, leading to low morale: the employees cannot afford to leave. In other words, it is just as problematic to grossly overpay people as to underpay.

Age and sex

On a departmental basis, figures should be produced for both men and women grouping them by age, for example 16-18, 19-25, 26-40; 41-50, 51-60, 61-65, 65+. Men and women in particular age groups have different attitudes to work and how their pay packet should be made up. Additionally, they will have fairly specific ideas about what they are prepared to do to earn fix per week. It is doubtful, for example, whether a middle-aged male work force would be enthusiastic about the introduction for the first time of direct incentives.

Attitude survey

Ideally an attitude survey should be made to ascertain what needs have to be satisfied through a wage structure. What are the employees' attitudes towards the current pay structure and what are their deeper expectations? The pay structure to a large extent determines and reinforces attitudes. Two of the areas a survey ought to highlight are the reasons why employees work for a particular company and what motivates them. Every company has a reputation as an employer and if it has achieved, for example, a 'quick buck' image, it will attract a particular type of employee. Thought must therefore be given to the kind of image the company wants to have and how it plans to achieve it.

What motivates people in your geographical area? What kind of incentives are socially acceptable, for instance? The whole of the Midlands is almost incurably on direct incentives and a firm that works otherwise is viewed with suspicion. In a free bargaining situation, a company introduced a new incentive scheme which theoretically should have increased take-home pay - and the impact was nil! An investigation highlighted the fact that the social custom was for young people to lay their unopened pay packet on the kitchen table each pay day and to receive in turn a fixed amount of pocket money. A little unusual in the 1980s, perhaps, but knowledge of this factor would have saved the company much time and trouble.

The survey should be done by an outside specialist in order to gain the confidence of the work force.

Influence of production method

Insufficient consideration is normally given to the link between the technological aspects of production and how people are paid. It is obvious that this is important and yet many operatives in a machine-controlled situation are on direct incentives intended to make them work faster! Similarly, it is not unusual for a company specialising in one-offs to have a direct incentive scheme which entails on-the-spot bargaining between, say, a rate fixer and a shop steward for every unit produced: the result is a hardening industrial relation climate.

These questions should be asked:

1. Are runs short, long, one-offs?

2. How important is quality, quantity, accuracy, consistency?
3. Is the operation operator or machine-controlled? And what happens in practice?
4. What are the capital investment plans for the next 3-5 years? Will these developments influence pay structure?
5. What are the market pressures? Are there seasonal fluctuations?
6. Can buffer stocks be kept or is the product perishable?
7. How much is lost through scrap?

Job evaluation

Job evaluation is an essential exercise if a company is to be truly in control of its wage structure. Certainly it is the only answer to leapfrogging pay claims and escalating special allowance.

Job evaluation can be as difficult or as expensive as a company likes to make it. Ranking is quite satisfactory: the basis of job evaluation is ranking anyway and all other methods are, in simple terms, administrative systems which are an aid to maintaining the original rank order of the benchmarks. Points rating is the most commonly used system, however. Nowadays it is normal for a joint management/union committee to introduce job evaluation though this depends to a large extent on the industrial relations climate. It is important, however, for the committee to be trained before embarking on the exercise.

At the other end of the industrial relations scale, however, is the multi-union situation, or long-established union militancy, or a combination of both. In such a situation, the unions should be consulted regarding their role but they will probably prefer to let management make all the decisions while they reserve the right to object on behalf of their respective members. In any case, such unions are probably accustomed to an autocratic management style and a large dose of participation is just as difficult for the unions to countenance as for line management. Obviously, union participation simplifies the situation but involvement does not guarantee instant success: there will still be appeals. What is important is that job evaluation is regarded as a quite separate situation from negotiating actual rates.

Legislation

Two Acts of Parliament are intended to safeguard, among other things, women's wage rates and how they are established:

Equal Pay Act, 1970
Sex Discrimination Act, 1975

In simple terms the legal framework provides for a right of appeal, depending on the case, to an Industrial Tribunal or to the Central Arbitration Committee, for a decision. To avoid such a situation, the following points should be observed:

1. Job evaluation should have been carried out
2. Each job grade should contain jobs carried out by either sex, e.g., there should not be a grade below 'labourer' grade comprising jobs filled entirely by women
3. The jobs in each grade should be 'the same or broadly similar' to each other.

Costing

The basis of a carefully considered wage structure is sound costing. The company accountant, therefore, has an important role to play. Here are the major areas to be scrutinised for key indicators:

1. Budgeted labour cost for the coming year
2. Trend of total labour cost over the last five years
3. General breakdown of cost of the various wage components which contribute to the total labour cost for, say, the last two years
4. Earnings distribution for each department for 2 typical weeks
5. The unit cost of producing each selling line and the proportion of labour cost attributed
6. Cost of employee benefits. Frequently overlooked, these benefits are nonetheless part of the total labour cost
7. Cost of labour turnover. As a rule of thumb, a routine factory worker who leaves after, say, three months, has probably cost the company approximately 750. This figure includes recruitment costs, interviewing time, initial training and a scale linked to the likely contribution an individual will make as his skill and know-how increases. A new employee does not begin to function as a member of a team until one or two weeks have elapsed
8. Cost of absenteeism. It is a useful pulse to take: if, say, absenteeism is running at a steady 20 per cent, possible causes are overmanning, overpaying or simply low morale. The cost of morale is not a balance sheet item but it is nonetheless an important hidden cost which is not be ignored.

Financing the wage structure

It is inflationary to set out to design and implement a new wage structure without first agreeing with the unions concerned that the increase in the wage bill must be found from within the company's resources. The actual cost of changing a wage structure is about 5 per cent of the wage bill, excluding cost-of-living for example. At first glance this figure will appear to be high: in effect a redistribution of cash and control is taking place with a short-term gain for the operatives involved and a medium-term gain for management. In a stable economy, no matter how sophisticated a company's techniques and know-how, it is possible to find savings to cover this cost. Of prime importance at the beginning of the exercise, is agreement by management and unions on how the savings are to be achieved and shared.

Running concurrently with the initial investigation should be the operation of productivity groups or quality circles bent on finding savings. These groups, under the leadership of their supervisors, should comprise operatives meeting on a sectional or departmental basis during working hours or at the end of a shift (on overtime). Their remit should be a broad one here: they may discuss every aspect of the organisation and planning of the work in their immediate working area.

While the structure of the groups will depend on the size of the section or department, the numbers meeting at any one time should not exceed eight to ten. A simple record of decisions made should be kept by each group for the sake of continuity and an effort made to communicate this within the group. Training will be necessary to help the groups to assess each problem and to make recommendations. Many companies underestimate the wealth of untapped potential which exists at shop floor level. However, companies which have attempted a similar exercise, have discovered that operatives are quite capable of using simple problem solving and costing techniques. Provided the groups understand in essence the services supplied by, say, the company's work study or production engineering specialists, the groups will ask for expert advice if the need arises.

Designing the wage structure

Having established the realities of the existing structure, the next step is to design one which will meet the company's needs. The trend is for a company to have a two-tier wage structure: a basic hourly/job rate tier accounting for 80-85 per cent of the wage bill; an incentive tier (if any) accounting for 15-20 per cent.

Number of grades

The trend is to have four to six grades covering all factory personnel. The more straightforward the production process, the less reason for numerous grades. Without prejudicing the situation in the early stages of the investigation, there should be at least 7.50 per week differential between each grade. To have less will act as a disincentive to internal promotion. In effect this means reducing the number of trades to a point where the differential is a significant demonstration that work in a higher grade really is more important to the company. If the pay steps are too small, management will be faced with numerous requests or regarding jobs every time a fraction of responsibility or a grain of dirt is added to the job.

The decision regarding the break point for each grade is largely arbitrary. It will probably be a negotiating point. On the whole, jobs tend to fall into homogeneous groups but no matter where the break points are made, 'grey area' jobs on either side of the line will give rise to much tooth-sucking. It is from this area that job evaluation appeals usually spring.

As an aid to deciding where the break points might be, it is useful to produce some scatter grams showing how, for example, the results of job evaluation compare in relation to job holders' basic rates as well as gross pay, The next step is to determine the 'line of best fit': in simple terms a line is drawn through the centre of the points already plotted. It is then possible to determine roughly what the pay steps might be. In practical terms this is a quite considerable exercise and it may be that a 30 per cent sample, say, of all jobs might suffice.

Yet another statistical aid is the use of bar graphs. In most companies the bulk of the jobs will be in the middle two grades with roughly the same number in the bottom and top grades.

Deciding the basic rate

Traditionally, manual workers have been in a position where the ratio of basic rate to incentive was 2:1. However, this ratio now tends to be nearer 4:1 largely because companies moving towards single (staff) status are rightly challenging the concept that a manual worker's earnings should fluctuate with the company's production throughout.

The case for greater security of earnings should therefore be considered as a matter of course. If nothing else, a proportion of 2:1 is a prime cause of wage drift. Theoretically, a wage survey should be conducted with other firms but since the make-up of gross pay is so variable from company to company, it is difficult to establish any meaningful form of parity. A company must examine its own costing system in terms of budgeted labour cost and the relationship this bears to unit cost. In other words, management must decide how much of the budgeted labour cost should be attributed to basic rate and how much to incentive, if any. Since this is negotiable, management should also know in advance the influence on unit costs of different break points or alternative basic rates.

One company employing about 1000 people avoided this problem by taking the budgeted labour cost for the coming year and giving to the unions concerned three different 'mixes' of total wage cost. This was broken down into 3, 5 and 7 grades complete with incentive calculated at 80, 90 and 100 BSI. (80 BSI is a good average rate of working.) The unions were told that they could produce another option still coming to the same total if they so desired. The company in question, while unused to this level of participation, had a history of good industrial relations. Obviously some unions will question the budgeted labour cost but this does not detract from the principle proposed.

Dealing with anomalies

Once the job evaluation exercise is completed and new basic rates determined, a scatter gram will pinpoint those jobs which are likely to be over or underpaid in relation to the new rates. Provided the old structure was not completely out of control, the bulk of the jobs will be just about right and roughly the same number over as underpaid. The options open to management are:

For overpaid employees

1. Retrain the individuals concerned in order that they can take on work of a more responsible or skilful nature and therefore justify new level of payment.
2. Make the difference between the old rate and the new a personal allowance which would be eroded each time a new basic rate was agreed. In time the new rate would catch up with the old.
3. As for 2, but the old rate—sometimes called a Red Circle Rate—is retained forever and ever. This is not advised. In time this becomes a thorn in the side of other employees.
4. Buy out anomalies by paying a lump sum comprising the difference multiplied by a negotiated figure. This is a strong negotiating area. What must be considered is the percentage of employees involved and whether or not most of the differences will be swallowed up within twelve to eighteen months anyway.

For underpaid employees

There are no options here: the individual's pay must be brought into line.

Incentive element

The word 'incentive' is synonymous with the word 'effort' in the minds of many. But this is not so. An incentive is some form of financial encouragement recognising a particular contribution made by the work force. It is, in effect, a sum of money additional to the basic rate which a company pays to ensure that its most important production aspects are being optimised. For example, a capital-intensive company might have an incentive linked to machine utilisation; a company making diamond-tipped tools might put particular emphasis on a low scrap value while still maintaining quality. Nonetheless many companies insist that effort is the only factor to recognise despite the fact that automation is very much with us.

Thought must be given to the cost of maintaining any one incentive: how many work study personnel, bonus clerks, tally clerks and inspectors are required to maintain standards? Can it be done in a more simple, effective way? Need there be an incentive? Will people only work on a carrot and stick basis? Will you, the reader, only work on this basis or are you different? What contribution does first-line supervision make to motivating people? Will the system encourage or stifle the growth of tomorrow's supervisors?

The basic decisions to be made about the incentive element are whether or not it is going to be individual, group, department or company based or a combination of these. The other important feature is whether the incentive is to be based on a straight-line formula or on a curve where rather less is earned proportionately the more units produced, sometimes with a cut-off point to limit production and thereby restrict bonus. Yet another approach is to have a cut-off point beyond which any bonus earned is placed in a common pool. This is turn is used to help finance basic rates when these are renegotiated.

Direct incentives

Definition. A method of payment whereby a bonus is paid in direct relation to effort.

Advantages

1. Appropriate where a high level of physical effort is necessary and it is difficult to supervise workers effectively.
2. Can generate substantial motivation as payment occurs shortly after achievement.
3. Flexibility in allocating added reward for added effort.
4. Introduction can mean a reduction in labour.
5. Can be useful in the short term to increase the pace of working as an interim step to moving on to a more sophisticated system.

Disadvantages

1. Management is not in control of production.
2. Tendency to ignore avoidance of waste.
3. Supervisors in time may earn less than their subordinates, skilled less than semi-skilled.
4. People learn how to achieve earnings without undue effort, for example by qualifying for special allowances, avoiding promotion to non-lucrative jobs, embarking on slow-downs during 'testing' of new rates.
5. Can ruin industrial relations.
6. Mobility of labour becomes virtually impossible.
7. Supervisors become good progress chasers but rarely good managers.

Measured daywork

Definition. Measured day work is a stabilised direct incentive system where the incentive element is consolidated in the basic rate, thereby achieving a high, non-fluctuating weekly wage or salary.

It is based on sound training, sophisticated work measurement techniques and sound management. It is still payment by results except that the underlying philosophies are one of trust—that an individual will work at an agreed pace provided work is available for him or her. The most common types are:

High day rate, which is suitable in an assembly-line. Each new employee is fully trained before strain work on the factory floor. He or she will be expected to produce work of a specified standard and to maintain a fixed working pace of, say, 90 BSI. The aim is to achieve a controlled work flow: those individuals who have a naturally high pace of working would normally be transferred to indirect work. Those who have naturally slow pace are subject to warnings and then either transferred to indirect work or dismissed, following reasonable warning.

Advantages

1. Simplified pay structure usually based on job evaluation.
2. Considerable operating flexibility.
3. Trust and responsibility given proper emphasis.
4. Management is in control of production and uses work study standards as a condition of employment as well as for management information.

Disadvantages

1. Not always possible to elicit acceptable levels of performance without the 'pull' of a direct incentive.
2. Sophisticated control techniques, such as daily computer data, are necessary.
3. High calibre of supervision is essential.
4. Disputes can be tougher than in direct incentive plants as employees can slow down without impairing earnings.

Philips premium pay plan is stable where individuals can control the pace of work. The same principles as those for high day rate apply except, perhaps, the problem of disputes since PPP is based on individual effort.

The pay structure is a simple one, usually based on job evaluation, but unlike high day rate, it is graded in steps according to the pace of working. Each individual contracts through his supervisor to work for a period of three months at a particular pace. If this pace is not maintained and the faults not that of management, a warning is given. If the pace of working does not meet the agreed standard during the following three months, he or she is either retrained or moved back to a lower pay band. If he or she is unable to maintain an acceptable pace, he or she is liable to dismissal.

Companies employing up to fifty staff normally have an informal salary policy and rightly so. However, when total staff exceed this number, anomalies begin to appear in the system and some form of framework is necessary. This is particularly so when rapid expansion is taking place.

Although there must be a coordinator, the responsibility of salary management is that of line management. What is needed therefore is a salary policy laying down administrative parameters within which discretion may be exercised and providing salary ranges based on simple job evaluation. Involvement of line managers at this point is essential in order that they recognise the need for regularising salary management and make a positive contribution towards drawing up a salary policy.

Communication

As important as the preparation of a salary policy, is the need to communicate it to everyone concerned: indeed there is no reason why every staff member should not have a copy of the actual policy statement.

By far the best way of passing on information is for each departmental manager to call a briefing meeting with all his or her staff to explain what the policy covers and, more important, how it will affect each individual. Care should be taken that each employee's questions are answered sympathetically and honestly. Employees should also be fully aware of the company's intentions regarding possible salary anomalies.

Job descriptions

In every company there are formal and informal arrangements about who reports whom and how work is done. It is important, therefore, to establish and seek agreement on an organization or accountability chart. Job titles can be very misleading and some renaming may be necessary. This in turn involves the writing of job descriptions.

A job description is a basic statement covering such features as:

1. Job title
2. Department
3. To whom responsible
4. Date
5. Tasks/areas of responsibility
6. Job titles of subordinates
7. Training and/or experience required for the job.

Specimen job description

The completed description must be agreed by both the job holder and his supervisor. (Where disagreements arise, the grievance procedure should be operated.)

A specimen job description follows.

Position : Secretary to Chief Mechanical Engineer

Department : Project Engineering

Date :

Overall Aim: To provide a complete secretarial service to Chief Mechanical Engineer by organizing the routine aspects of his work.

Daily tasks

1. On receipt of mail, sort into order of priority, attach previous correspondence, if any, and type routine letters for signature.
2. Take dictation from Chief Mechanical Engineer and deal also with urgent correspondence dictated by senior mechanical engineers.
3. Against a tight timetable, type complicated statistical tables connected with department's project work.
4. Deal with department's travel arrangements and prepare travel itineraries.
5. Maintain simple time records concerning progress of experimental projects. Ensure that progress charts are kept up to date.
6. Act as an assistant to Chief Mechanical Engineer by dealing with the more routine aspects of his work.
7. Act as a 'shield' by dealing with callers personally and on the telephone.

Weekly tasks

1. Prepare for accountant short summary of personal expenses incurred by department during previous week, and allocate to individual projects.

Monthly tasks

1. Collect brief reports prepared by senior engineers on their respective projects and type draft of progress report for the Project Engineering Director.

Six-monthly tasks

1. Transfer old files to basement and make out new files for next six months.

Annually

1. Type statement of account showing income over expenditure on previous year's projects:

Minimum age:	Twenty-one years
Educational qualifications:	Five 'O' levels (including English Language) and secretarial college training
Experience:	Three years' practical office experience including one year in a similar firm
Induction:	Three months
Other information:	The Chief Mechanical Engineer is frequently off site and the job holder is expected to deal with all routine problems arising during such absences.

9
Training and Development

Human resource management is an approach to the management of people, based on four fundamental principles. First, human resources are the most important assets an organization has and their effective management is the key to its success. Second, this success is most likely to be achieved it the personnel policies and procedures of the enterprise are closely linked with, and make a major contribution to, the achievement of corporate objectives and strategic plans. Third, the corporate culture and the values, organizational climate and managerial behaviour that emanate from that culture will exert a major influence on the achievement of excellence. This culture must therefore be managed, which means that organizational values may need to be changed or reinforced, and that continuous effort, starting from the top, will be required to get them accepted and acted upon. Finally, HRM is concerned with integration: getting all the members of the organization involved and working together with a sense of common purpose.

The human resources of an organization can be considered the most significant input an organization utilizes. It is through human resources that all other resources are acquired and used. Decisions about human resources tend to directly affect the quality and use of all other resources.

Human resources differ in another significant manner from other resources. They have intrinsic value. As such, they are treated differently. Four basic assumptions regarding human beings are generally held in our culture.

1. *Individual differences*—While people have much in common, each person is unique in physical appearance, experiences, personality aspiration level, attitudes, etc. Consequently, it's somewhat difficult to lump people together and generalize accurately about their behaviour.

2. *A whole person*—A person is a system. He has ideas, a body, feelings, past experiences, and attitudes which mutually interact. When a person is employed in an organization all of his characteristics are brought into the organization, not just his hands or brain.

3. *Causal behaviour*—All human behaviour is causal. People do things for reasons, and there may be many reasons for a given act. The reasons may not be recognized by

the person nor may they be readily apparent to a researcher, yet they are there. To observe and explain—human behaviour is important to the practitioner of human resource management

4. *Human dignity*—People are of a higher order than other factor of production and need to be treated with respect and dignity. The foundation for this moral philosophy lies in the Judeo-Christian ethic of western culture. Human life, happiness, and the integrity of the individual are key values generally adhered to in our society.

In view of these assumptions regarding human beings, people are not "used" as are other resources in an organization. When we use the term "manage" or "utilize" human resources, we do not mean that they are used as are machines, buildings, tools, cash, or materials. Human beings have a will, free choice, and intrinsic value, machines, tools and buildings do not.

The goal of the human resource management system is to create organizations that are both effective and efficient. Roethlisberger and Dickson, over thirty years ago, stated that:

> ... management has two major functions: (1) the function of securing the common economic purpose of the total enterprise, and (2) the function of maintaining the equilibrium of the social organization so that individuals through contributing their service to this common purpose obtain personal satisfactions...

Therefore, the emphasis of human resource management must necessarily be on establishing systems that accomplish organizational goals (effectiveness) with efficient use of resources. In the past, organizations took this to mean production at the least possible economic cost. Consequently, efforts to increase efficiency often were directed toward reducing per unit labour costs. The adverse personal consequences of such action were ignored unless they resulted in some financial cost to the firm. Today, we realize that this approach ignores some very real and important personal as well as social costs that may be associated with personnel practices in organizations. This book addresses the efficiency of human resource management practices from the point of view of both economic and noneconomic costs and benefits which accrue to those in the larger system: the individuals, the organizations, and society as it pursues its goals.

Simplified human resource system of an organization

Human resources flow through an organization as do other resources. We depicted an organization as a flow of resources through the input-transformation-output process. This section will focus specifically on the human resource flow through the organization.

However, at this point, let us discuss here. The human resources of the organization provide the skills, abilities, talents, ideas, and aspiration levels an organization needs to get its work done. These human resources come from the environment. Some of the sources in this environment include families, educational institutions, and other organizations.

The transformation process in using human resources involves several phases. First, the work of the organization is determined as it relates to the product or service to be produced. This work is the total productive effort of the organization needed to bring about a desired good or service. Then job, are designed based on this work analysis. Next, manpower plans are formulated for acquiring human resources to fill these jobs. People are trained and developed to better perform their jobs. They are also placed, promoted, transferred and discharged as job requirements change. The organization develops a behavioural climate to bring out the highest levels of motivation in its human resources. A communication process is established to facilitate the coordination of human and other resources. Finally, a reward and penalty system is established to encourage good performance and discourage poor performance. Due process is applied throughout to attempt to insure the rights of the people employed.

While the primary outputs of any organization is the production of a product and/or service, we are interested in focusing on the outputs that relate directly to the human resources of the organization. These ouputs mainly include wages, salaries, satisfaction, dissatisfaction, alienation, anomie, security, personal growth, and esteem and status.

Note that all these outputs are generated in an organization. Some of the outputs should not be generated but, never-the-less, often occur. For, example, everyone is paid a wage or salary as a result of their productive effort. However, not everyone is satisfied in their employment relationships. For some, the dissatisfaction received from the job is so extreme that they are in a state of *anomie*, a state of normlessness. They feel there is no meaning to their life. Some are alienated. They rebel against the organization and perhaps society as a whole.

Most people receive security in their employment relationships. Often they also receive status and esteem through their jobs. If they can experience personal growth and development in their jobs, they may also achieve self-actualization. They become all that they can become and reach their full potential. Not many individuals fully achieve this through their jobs. Sentiments are developed among people working in the organization. Sentiments are feelings of liking or disliking among people in the organization.

The users of these outputs are the families of the people employed; educational institutions and other organizations, the economy, and other countries which receive the output produced. Wages and salaries buy goods and services from other organizations, which provide a level of security for the employee's family. Educational services are purchased from educational institutions. For multinational organizations, wages and salaries, security, and so on, are provided for people in other countries.

The attitudes of the users of output, as well as the output itself, are evaluated by the organization in its acquisition and use of it human resources. Organizations should continually monitor wage and salary structures to be sure they are competitive. This will help the organization determine if it is attracting quality human resource inputs. Levels of satisfaction, anomie, and need achievement of human resources should be measured frequently to determine if jobs should be redesigned or if changes should be made in reward and penalty systems, due process, communication, motivation training and development, placement, promotion, transfer, or discharge policies and procedures.

Note in this human resource system a dynamic interaction with the environment is occurring. Human resources are obtained from supply sources in the environment, and the outputs of the system are used by people and institutions in the environment. This aspect of the system is developed more fully in the next section.

The human resource model

This model of the human resource system depicts the relationship the organization has with its environment and the internal processes of the organization involved in its acquisition and utilization of human resources. Emphasis is placed on the interaction of the organization with its environment and the organization's changing use of its human resources over time, as it attempts to institutionalize environmental demands made on it.

In discussing the organization's interaction with its environment, we will use the *macro-intermediate-micro environment* continuum. The *macro environment* is "the broad system in which all the organizations of a given culture exist." The *intermediate environment* is the environment that links a given organization with its macro environment. Some authors also refer to this as a "boundary spanning" environment in that the boundaries between an organization and its environment are "spanned" or "crossed" through the intermediate environment.

The *micro environment* is the organization itself. This environment consists of the structure and internal processes and procedures of a given organization. In our analysis, we will especially focus on the decision-making process in organizations as they use human resources through time.

Since it serves as the basic outline for the remainder of the book, it is important that the student have a clear understanding of this model at this time, Therefore, the rest of this chapter explains the relationships which exist in this model.

The organization's macro environment

The organization's macro environment is the source for the organization's human resource inputs and also receives the outputs generated by the organization. The macro environment influences organizational change. It may exert forces on the organization requiring the organization to change. An example of this would be the legislation passed by government governing employment conditions. The macro environment may also prevent or hold back organizational change. The social values of honesty and integrity usually prevent organizations from adopting programs which may be unethical. Thus, the macro environment sets the broad parameters within which the organization operates.

For purposes of analysis, we focus on six major components of the macro environment:

1. Culture
2. Social institutions
3. Legal environment
4. Product/Service demand
5. Technology
6. Human resource skill mix

These are the most relevant aspect of the macro environment which directly affect human resource utilizations.

Culture

Culture is the underlying glue which holds people together and gives them their identity. It is the values, norms, roles, history, tradition, art and language of a people. It tends to change slowly and provides a sustaining *raison d'etre* for what the people do in a society. In our model, we focus primarily on Western culture changes as they impact on the organization.

Social institutions

Social institutions arise from the culture. They manifest cultural values and norms. While sociologists differ as to a list of basic institutions, they can be classified into four major categories: religious, family, economic, and political. We focus on how institutions are changing as culture changes and how changing institutions affect organizations.

Legal environment

The legal environment consists of the laws of a society, including federal, state, and local laws and statutes. In Western culture it also consists of common law, or court-made law based on precedent. The legal environment also includes the values we hold regarding fair and impartial treatment under the law.

Product/service demand

Customer/client needs and wants as they are manifested in demands for goods and services are the reasons which organizations exist. This includes governmental organizations as well as business organizations. These needs and wants direct organizational activity. They determine the product/service mix and the human resource mix needed to produce this product/service mix.

Technology

Technology is the state of the art employed in producing and delivering goods and services. It includes the level of sophistication of equipment and machinery and its use in the production of goods and services. It also includes the level of scientific advancement in society that leads to the development of new equipment and processes through research and development. Technology has a significant impact in determining the human resource skill mix and its utilization in an organization.

Human resources

People in an organization come from the macro environment. They have varying skills and aspiration levels. They have varying educational levels. They vary in the level of their career goals as well as the importance they place on these goals compared to other goals in their life. They also vary in their mobility, both geographical and occupational.

The intermediate environment

The macro environment interacts with a given organization through an intermediate environment. This environment is a linking environment which spans the boundary between an organization and its macro environment. The intermediate environment manifests the macro environment to a given organization. Thus, it filters, blocks, as well as amplifies aspects in the macro environment.

We will consider eight major groups in the intermediate environment:

1. Special governmental groups
2. Public interest groups
3. Civil rights groups
4. Professional and trade associations
5. Consultants
6. Employment agencies
7. Training organizations

These are groups with which an organization deals in its acquisition and use of human resources. These groups manifest the macro environment to an organization.

Special government groups

Governmental agencies enforce and interpret the law to an organization. These agencies include federal regulatory commissions such as the Federal Trade

Commission, Equal Employment Opportunity Commission, or Securities and Exchange Commission; federal assistance organizations such as the Federal Mediation and Conciliation Service, state regulatory commissions, such as the Environmental Control Board or the Public Utilities Commissions; and city and county regulatory bodies, such as a zoning board, or planning department.

Organizations, be they private or governmental, increasingly interact with governmental bodies. The legal environment changes rapidly and organizations must continually monitor and, to some extent, influence new legislation which affects them. They must also understand and use the court system as needed to obtain important dispute settlements regarding legal interpretations.

Public interests groups

During the past fifteen years, there has been a tremendous increase in the operations and political power of public interest groups. The better known groups which have exerted their influence include John Gardner's Common Cause, Ralph Nader's Center for Corporate Responsibility, and the well-known American Civil Liberties Union. These groups attempt to influence the legal environment and also to directly affect the policies of organizations. For example, in the early 70s at General Motors' annual stockholder meetings, Nader's Center for Corporate Responsibility raised issues dealing with the operations of General Motors in South Africa and the absence of minorities on the GM Board of Directors. Even though they technically lost the stockholder votes at these meetings, much publicity was generated, which resulted in GM adding a Black to the board of directors and in GM changing some policies in their South African operations.

The strength of these public interest groups are a new force with which organizations must deal. The ease with which these groups can focus public scrutiny on a given organization by effectively using television and press coverage for dramatic effect suggests that organizations must continually monitor, understand, and deal with these groups in the future.

Professional and trade associations

Professional and trade organizations bring the organization into contact with organizations of similar industrial and occupational interests. These groups interpret industrial trade, and professional developments to the organization. At the same time, an organization influences the activities of professional and trade associations through its membership. New developments in training and use of human resources often emerge through these organizations.

Unions

Unions have significant impact on organizational use of human resources. Not only is the management of blue-collar operative (non-management) employees influenced by unions, but so is the utilization of professional, technical, and other white-collar occupational groups. The growth of unions in white-collar occupations and in governmental employment has been phenomenal during the past decade.

Unions provide both constraints and opportunities to management. They provide stability to many employee-employer operations and often serve to minimize and control conflict. Craft unions, through the hiring hall, often perform several personnel functions, such as recruiting and hiring, which would normally have to be performed by the employer. On the other hand, unions, especially those in strong bargaining positions, can gain significant concessions from an organization at the expense of organizational productivity or profitability. Management must maximize and capitalize on the opportunities presented by unions and must minimize the adverse consequences that might arise in the union/management relationship.

Outside consultants

These individuals are used by earnestness in dealing with the legal environment and for specialized study and advice on organizational markets, human resource use, and internal operational procedures. They provide skills to the organization on a temporary basis when needed to solve specific organizational problems. Thus, they bring much knowledge of the macro environment to the organization.

Civil rights groups

Civil rights groups have had a organizations impact on organizational human resource utilization of minority groups and women. These groups have not only directly influenced federal and state equal employment opportunity legislation, but have also taken action directly against specific organizations to bring about an end to discrimination in employment.

Public and private employment agencies

Employment agencies often represent the labour market for new employees to an organization. Human resources are filtered through and then directed to particular organizations by these agencies. They often close the gap between the job seeker and the vacant job.

High schools, vocational-technical schools, junior and community colleges, universities and professional schools, and apprenticeship programs provide the organization with its skilled manpower. The essential, basic training which organizations require of its human resources are not furnished by the employing organization but by these intermediate groups. In view of changing technology with its demand for changing and higher occupational skill levels, training and educational institutions will have an even more important role to play.

Human resource planning and utilization in the organization

Organizations make decisions regarding the acquisition and utilization of human resources. The decisions are very directly influenced by the organization's macro environment as it is manifested to the organization through the eight major groups in the intermediate environment. The decisions are also influenced by the mission and objectives of the organization.

We can view the types of decisions made by organizations as being either *strategic* or *administrative*. Strategic decisions are those made to acquire and deploy an organization's resources to achieve objectives in the future. These are crucial decisions because they tend to direct the overall effort of an organization. Most of these tend to be planning decisions and are generally made in a preoperating period. They usually deal with such areas as determining market strategy, developing operational definitions of organizational objectives, and resource acquisition. These decisions also tend to be *preventive* in nature in that they tend to anticipate and minimize the severity of problems before they happen.

The second type of decisions made by organizations are *administrative decisions*. These decisions are the routine, day-to-day decisions that are made in using an organization's assets. Often these decisions are *curative* in nature. That is, they tend to be concerned with solving secific problems after they arise. These are the "fire-fighting" decisions so many managers complain about. These decisions tend to be organizing, directing, and controlling decisions.

In studying we see that organizations make these decisions through time. Strategic decisions are made in the preoperating period for a given organizational program. During the operating period, administrative decisions predominate. Postoperating decisions are also administrative decisions and tend to emphasize the controlling function. Feedback from these decisions influence other decisions to be made in the preoperating and operating periods.

Human resource utilization and decision making

With regard to the organization's human resource decisions, strategic decisions in the preoperating period tend to be job design and evaluation decisions, manpower planning decisions, and recruiting and selection decisions. Once decisions are made as to market strategy and organizational objectives, resource acquisition decision are made. Jobs are designed to fulfil organizational objectives. Immediate and long term manpower needs are determined, including the skill/educational/ability mix needed. The recruiting and selection process begins.

During the operation period, administrative decisions are made to allocate and utilize resources. Human resources are trained and developed for specific job requirements. People are placed, promoted, and transferred in the organization as needed. Motivation, communication, and organizational development programs are designed and implemented.

During the post-operating period, decisions are made which evaluate the use of human resources. It is at this stage that individual performance appraisal is conducted. This performance, appraisal process is usually tied to some reward and penalty system which includes salary adjustment, discipline procedures, and promotion and transfer decisions. In addition, decisions regarding training needs are developed to improve an individual's performance. Throughout these processes, due process to protect the rights of an individual applies.

The separation of organizational decisions regarding human resources into the three operating periods is somewhat artificial. Rarely can a given decision on human resource utilization be classified solely into one of these three categories. For example, decisions on placing, promoting, and transferring individuals are both operating decisions and post-operating decisions.

Yet, from an analytical view, it is useful to classify human resource decisions into one of these three categories to better understand the key decisions made with regard to these resources over time. It also helps to determine whether a given human resource decision is essentially a strategic or an administrative decision. Both types of decisions are important of course, but strategic decisions tend to influence the quality of administrative decisions.

For example, decisions regarding the design of jobs in the organization will have a major influence on decisions made to motivate employees. It is extremely difficult to motivate employees who have been placed in highly repetitive, rationalized, dead-end assembly line jobs. In fact, the whole thrust of job enrichment as a motivational tool requires the redesign of jobs to make them more challenging and hence more "motivating." Likewise, if poor recruiting and selection decisions are made which result in the acquisition of a poorly trained workforce that lacks needed skills, any training and development program the organization adopts will need to be quite comprehensive, time consuming, and expensive to provide the remedial training plus additional training needed.

Thus, it's important to focus on the key human resource decisions, which are often strategic decisions, and improve these first before attempts are made to deal with administrative decisions. Too often managers spend their time making day-to-day administrative decisions— "putting out fires" at the expense of making strategic, preventative decisions which would have kept those fires from starting in the first place.

Organizational output

As the result of the decisions made in the human resource planning and utilization process in the organization, outputs are produced. These outputs include goods and services, wages, salaries and dividends, security and fringe benefits, employee and consumer satisfaction/dissatisfaction, personal growth and development, productivity and efficiency/inefficiency, social costs (e.g. pollution and congestion), taxes (corporate, personal, sales, property), employee status, esteem, and self-actualization, and employee sentiments. Some of these outputs are used by customers and clients in the macro and intermediate environments of the organization. They are also evaluated by these customers or clients, and the results of this evaluation process are fed into the major components of the macro environment, components of the intermediate environment, and into the organization itself. Feedback is also provided directly to the organization from the clients and customers of the organization. This feedback directly affects strategic and operating decisions that organizations make in acquiring and utilizing its human resources.

Some of these outputs are used directly by employees and their families. They are weighed and considered by these people and resultant evaluations are fed back into the organization's operating processes. Much of the feedback from employees is received indirectly by the organization. For example, dissatisfied employees may reduce productivity, increase waste, have more absences and tardiness, file more grievances, or even engage in sabotage. This is their way of manifesting their dissatisfaction to the organization without verbally communicating it directly to managers.

Thus, it is crucial for both public and private organizations to monitor and evaluate information it receives both directly and indirectly from its clients, customers, employees, and intermediate environment. Not only must this information be monitored and evaluated, but it must become a major input to future decisions. A comprehensive study showing poor employee attitudes and low morale is of little benefit if the results of the study do not somehow affect managerial human resource decisions. Labour market research studies showing noncompetitive wages for employees in the organization are worthless unless decisions are made to change the wage and salary structure to attract and hold competent employees.

It is essential for governmental and other public organizations to realize the importance of this feedback. Users of governmental services are rightfully called clients. This includes users of social welfare programs as well as students in state universities, high school and elementary students in public school systems, prisoners in rehabilitation facilities, and farmers who use the agricultural extension service, The attitudes and evaluations of these groups, as well as the attitudes and opinions of employees, need to be better monitored, evaluated, and the resultant information inputed to the decision process. This feedback evaluation is especially important for governmental groups since they often exist as monopolies and are not under the constraints of competition which private organizations usually face.

Integration of formal and informal systems

The nature of an organization cannot be properly understood without an appreciation of how its two major subsystems, or components, operate. Every organization has both a formal and an informal structure. When the formal and informal structures work together harmoniously, the overall organization has the capacity to operate effectively. When the formal and informal organization clash, ineffectiveness (and sometimes chaos is the result. Our discussion of formal versus informal groups referred to the same type of phenomenon under consideration here. The formal organization is the organization as it exists on paper. It is the official, sanctioned way of doing things. The formal organization tells you who reports to whom and how various problems should be handled. A modern definition states, "The formal structure is composed of job descriptions, organization charts, procedures, and other written documents which describe and define how individuals should work with each other."

The informal organization refers to a pattern of relationships that develops to both satisfy people's social needs and get work accomplished. Accordingly, "The nonformal structure is the pattern of relationships that emerges among people that are not specified in written documents. It is their behaviour." A successful integration of the formal and informal structures is illustrated by an incident that took place in a medium-sized company.

A company that manufactured snow shovels found itself suddenly faced with an unprecedented backlog of orders during the winter of 1976-1977. Reliance on the formal structure alone would have made it very difficult to meet such demand. A company policy states, "We shall not incur additional manufacturing costs due to shipping charges levied by suppliers. Suppliers are therefore not authorized to charge us shipping costs for any method of special delivery."

Literal application of this rule would have made it impossible to receive a rush shipment of plastic needed for shovel blades. The head of manufacturing therefore sought an ethical and constructive way around this policy. His decision was to rent a truck for purposes of picking up 1000 pounds of plastic at their usual supplier. The truck rental fee was then allocated to "business travel." By this informal bending of the formal structure, an emergency situation was solved without violating a company rule. This judicious use of the informal organization was possible because the manufacturing head had not used up his business travel budget for the quarter.

A systems viewpoint

A modern perspective for understanding the nature of organizational effectiveness is that of systems theory. As diagrammed an organization is seen as part of a larger system (society itself). An effective organization makes wise use of natural resources (inputs) by processing them (process) into something useful for society (outputs). As these outputs are placed in the environment, the effective organization changes in response to new demands from the environment. Often this means using different inputs.

A business analogy will help explain these relationships further. An automobile dealership uses the *inputs* of (1) new and used automobiles and (2) people in the form of office, shop, and sales personnel in order to provide a service to the public. The cars taken into the dealership are processed to the extent that they are prepared for sale and displayed on a lot or in a showroom. Offering financing and insurance programs to the public is part of the process that takes place in the dealership. The *output* is private transportation for the public. As tastes and requirements change (for example, a demand for more energy-efficient autos), the dealership receives *feedback.* Such feedback helps inform the dealer and the manufacturer what types of inputs (new cars) the dealer should be offering next. As long as the dealership responds to the tastes of the public in an efficient manner (without going bankrupt), it will be able to meet its objective of delivering cars to the public (organizational effectiveness).

The organization as an open system. In recent years, the systems perspective of organizations has become dominant. Fremont E. Kast and James E. Rosenzweig have contributed heavily to this view of organizational life. Their concept of the organization as an open system is particularly helpful in trying to comprehend the complexities of an effective or efficient organization. No organization exists in isolation. Its effectiveness and survival are contingent upon how it relates to the world outside.

Overall effectiveness: A composite measure taking into account a wide variety of factors such as those mentioned in the rest of this list. Overall effectiveness can be measured by combining performance records or obtaining the judgment of people who are familiar with the organization (such as fans or customers).

Goal attainment: Another general measure is how well the organization accomplishes what it set out to accomplish. Assuming that the organization's goals are not destructive or harmful to others, there is much to be said for this criterion.

Profit making: A favourable "bottom line" is often considered to be the single most important measure of effectiveness for a business. Unless a firm makes a profit, it cannot afford to accomplish other objectives such as making charitable contributions or providing job training to culturally disadvantaged people. Yet an overemphasis on profit can result in such practices as firing people indiscriminately or overworking employees.

Staying within budget: This measure is a nonprofit organization's equivalent of making a profit. Unless an organization stays within budget, it risks losing much of its public support. Managers of nonprofit organizations must be as budget conscious as those employed by businesses. Nonprofit organizations that overspend risk "going out of business."

Production of goods and services: An organization that provides what it is designed to provide is justifying its own existence. If a single club affiliated with a church turns out large numbers of events (such as picnics and dances) where singles can meet, that club is effective in at least one important respect.

Efficient use of resources: A modern viewpoint stresses that the ratio of cost to benefit should be favourable. The production of pacemakers (devices to trigger the heart back to normal functioning when it stops beating) represents both an efficient and an effective act. The amount of materials, money, and human resources consumed is small in relation to the output—a life-saving device. In contrast, mining five tons of ore to obtain two pieces of jewellery is a very inefficient act.

Achieving new goals: A successful (effective) organization emphasizes the attainment of new and important goals. An important new goal for a neighbourhood youth center, for example, might be to establish a drug treatment center for young people.

Social responsibility: In recent years this has become an important criterion of organizational effectiveness. Corporate social responsibility has been defined as the serious attempt to solve social problems caused wholly or in part by the corporation. A case in point would be a distillery that chooses to attack the social problem of alcoholism. If it were not for distilleries, people would not have a legal means of consuming alcoholic beverages.

Practicing good ecology: From the viewpoint of ecology, in order to be considered effective an organization must satisfy a number of groups in its environment. Goals set by the organization and those set by strategic constituencies must both be satisfied, Specifically, when certain key groups in society are satisfied, we can say that the organization is doing its job. In one study of 97 small businesses, the researchers identified seven different groups (constituencies) who have a vested interest in the welfare of the company. To the extent that these parties at interest are satisfied, the organization can be classified as effective.

The seven groups are customers, creditors, suppliers, employees, owners, the community, and the government. Many of the expectations these groups have of a small business are similar, for example, all groups want the company to stay in operation. Other concerns are more meaningful to one group than another. The government is strongly interested in a given company obeying safety regulations, whereas a creditor would be more concerned about prompt payment of bills.

Adaptability to change: An adaptable organization has good problem-solving ability combined with the capacity to react with flexibility toward changing environmental demands. Organizations with the ability to adapt to necessary changes have been labelled *organic*. In order to be adaptive or organic, the firm would have to take in and communicate information reliably and validly. An active market-research department could help an organization in this regard. Sears & Roebuck can be considered an adaptive organization because it is generally able to shift with the changing tastes of North Americans. From time to time, however, even Sears has suffered a sales slump because it misjudged the retain preferences of customers.

Stability: An organization that is able to maintain its basic character and size over time is considered to be stable. One such company is Prudential Insurance because it continues to be a dominant influence in the life insurance business and is not subject to wide fluctuations in employment. A company like Lockheed is much less stable, and therefore less effective from that criterion.

Quality: Goods and services of high quality contribute or organizational effectiveness. One of the many reasons for the phenomenal success of IBM is the high quality of both its goods and services (such as programming support for computers).

Growth: This measure is represented by an increase in such factors as total work force, plant capacity, assets, sales, profits, market share, and number of innovations. To many observers, the absence of growth is the equivalent of organizational ineffectiveness.

Favourable departure of clientele: Hospitals, schools, and prisons must all stand up against this criterion. Ideally, a long-range measurement should be taken several years after a client leaves to determine if the organization was successful. If 95 per cent of "cured" clients return to a drug rehabilitation center within six months, we might conclude that the center is not effective.

Readiness to perform: Can the organization successfully perform some specified task if asked to do so? An effective fire-fighting unit, or national guard unit, should stand up against this criterion.

Voluntarism: The extent to which people want to continue as members of the organization is meaningful. When most of the members want to leave at the earliest opportunity, it can be concluded that the organization is ineffective. Among the exceptions are hospitals and prisons, where most of the employees want to remain, but the patients and prisoners, respectively, want an early exit.

Survival: When an organization survives over time, it can be concluded that it in some way is meeting the demands of some section of society. A 100-year college is undoubtedly performing a legitimate service. A home-building company that has been in business in the same community for 40 years has undoubtedly earned a favourable reputation.

Organizational mental health: An organization, similar to a person, tends to be effective when it possesses what amounts to good mental health. Two characteristics of a mentally healthy organization are a sense of identity and integration of the subparts.

An organization has a sense of identity when it is aware of what it is and what it is trying to accomplish. When people in the organization see it as it is seen by others, a sense of identity is fostered. The Mavo Clinic and the Montreal Canadians represent organizations with a strong sense of identity. Integration is achieved when the subparts of the organization are not in severe conflict or working at cross purposes. When employees believe that they can prosper in an organization only by lying and stealing, the opposite of integration has occurred. When the various departments of a company realize that only through teamwork will they all succeed, integration occurs.

Managerial task skills: Few people would argue that an organization can remain or become effective without capable management. Task skills refer to those skills related to work accomplishment rather than to relationships with other employees.

Managerial interpersonal skills: Effective organizations also require that managers deal skilfully with people. Interpersonal skills include the extent to which managers give support, facilitate constructive interaction, and generate enthusiasm for meeting goals and achieving superior performance.

Planning and goal setting: In order to be effective an organization usually has to establish goals and figure out the path to attain those goals. A substantial proportion of published information about the practice of management extolls the virtues of planning and goal setting.

Goal agreement: An organization increases its chances for effectiveness when the vast, majority of members perceive the same goals for the organization. This situation would only take place when top management clearly articulates the goals, or when the goal is obvious. A strike team attempting to free a group of hostages would probably manifest goal agreement.

Control: According to this criterion, effectiveness is enhanced when management has good control over matters of influencing the behaviour of employees. It is also important that the control be distributed among many managers.

Proper management of conflict: An organization may require some conflict to be effective, but too much conflict detracts from effectiveness. When people conform to the same code of conduct, conflict is usually held in check.

Participation in decision making: Many managers and researchers believe that organization effectiveness is enhanced when employees participate in making the decisions which directly affect them.

Absenteeism: Other factors, such as low morale, may contribute to high absenteeism. Nevertheless, the extent of avoidable absenteeism serves as a rough index of organizational effectiveness.

Accident frequency and severity: Accident control is important for both humanitarian and economic reasons. An effective organization does not waste human life nor does it incur needless fines by the federal government, and pay excessive insurance premiums because of poor safely practices.

Job satisfaction: Another indirect measure of effectiveness is job satisfaction. The larger the number of employees who experience satisfaction on the job, the more effective the organization.

Motivation: Effective organization are characterized by large numbers of members who are ready and willing to expend effort toward reaching organization goals.

Morale: High morale contributes to organizational effectiveness although it is difficult to precisely define the concept. A recent definition suggests that morale is a "predisposition in organization members to put forth extra effort in achieving organizational goals and objectives. It includes feelings of commitment and is a group phenomenon involving extra effort, goal communality, and feelings of belonging."

Training and development of members: An effective organization provides for the upgrading of employees through training and development. In the process, the organization benefits.

Value of human resources: An effective organization often has much material wealth. It also tends to have human resources of high value. Similar to a number of measures mentioned above, value of human resources is a composite criterion. The value is expressed in accounting terms, as exemplified by the relatively new discipline of human resource accounting.

Another global measure of organizational effectiveness is the extent to which the organization provides for a high quality of work life. QWL has received so much attention lately that it requires separate mention here.

QWL and organizational effectiveness

The concept of QWL means different things to different people, yet a generally acceptable definition is "the degree to which members of a work organization are able to satisfy important personal needs through their experience in the organization." Many of the internal measures of organizational effectiveness, such as job satisfaction, morale, and participation in decision making, contribute to a high QWL. Hundreds of formal programs have been launched in organizations to help elevate the quality of work life of employees—and in the process, elevate productivity. Sometimes QWL programs have been undertaken because of major problems of organizational ineffectiveness. For example, QWL programs in Scandinavia as well as in the United States have been undertaken as a response to extreme organizational problems involving employee alcoholism, absenteeism, tardiness, turnover, and grievances filed by the union.

Fundamental features of QWL programs: Many different programs are aimed at improving the quality of working life. At different places in this text, human relations techniques have been described which are sometimes included under the category of QWL programs. A recent government report lists fourteen fundamental features of these programs. No one program attempts to accomplish all of them, but worker participation in decision making and some degree of responsibility for and autonomy over the immediate work process are typical. It would require an entire book to describe all the published results about QWL programs undertaken during the last decade. Here we will describe two well-publicized programs, one successful, the other unsuccessful.

Wasteful organizational practices

A general reason that many organizations fail to attain a state of effectiveness is that they engage in many wasteful practices. Several of these practices have been the subject of satire. Although as satire they are exaggerated, a discussion of organizational efficiency warrants some mention of these practices. In the next chapter, mention will be made of the Peter Principle—a famous wasteful practice.

Parkinson's Most Famous Law: Almost anyone who has worked in a complex organization has heard about C. Northcote Parkinson's statement that "Work expands so as to fill the time available for its completion." Parkinson also formulated several other satirical observations, called *laws,* about the waste and inefficiency taking place in so many organizations.

The Organizational Multiplier: Herbert G. Hicks, and C. Ray Gullett use the term *organizational multiplier* to denote a wasteful practice in which an organization feeds on itself more than serving its real purpose. Unlike Parkinson, they are not speaking tongue in cheek. Essentially, the practice refers to a condition in which many people in the organization wind up taking care of each other rather than clients or customers. Many fund-raising organizations, for example, spend about 90 per cent of contributions on administrative costs. When an organization begins to hire additional staff people just to serve other staff people, the multiplier is at work.

An organizational multiplier can work in this fashion: a company grows from 200 to 300 people on the basis of a substantial new contract. No longer can the office manager handle all the personnel problems. So a full-fledged personnel department is formed. The new personnel department of five people soon recognizes that it needs more office space. Since conditions are cramped already, a temporary building is purchased to house the personnel department. The addition of one more building to the company complex now requires that one more worker be added to the maintenance staff. The addition of the new temporary building has also created so much paperwork for the facilities planning department that another clerk is added. In larger organizations, the multiplier effect is even more devastating.

The Administrative Waltz: Two organizational satirists, G. Singer and Meredith Wallace, have formulated the idea of the administrative waltz, whch they difine as "A queer sort of trance dance where the dominant partner is always an administrator. He or she performs all the leading steps and you have no option but to follow." Basically, the waltz refers to the overintrusion of administrators into organizations, thus leading to inefficiency and ineffectiveness.

The doctrine of functional autonomy: states that an administrative unit will tend to develop until it becomes completely independent. Singer and Wallace cite the example of an audio-visual unit in a school system, which is originally set up to improve communications.

Occupational health and safety related practices

A human resource management programme has to include systems which take care of the health and safety at work of employees. The occupational health and safety programme should be based on the following principles:

1. Industrial disease and accidents result from a multiplicity of factors, but these have to be traced to their root causes, which are usually faults in the management system arising from poor leadership from the top, inadequate supervision, insufficient attention to the design of health and safety into the system, an unsystematic approach to the identification, analysis and elimination of hazards, and poor education and training facilities.
2. The most important function of health and safety programmes is to identify potential hazards, provide effective safety facilities and equipment, and take prompt remedial action. This is only possible if there are:
   - comprehensive and effective systems for reporting all accidents causing damage or injury;
   - adequate accident records and statistics;
   - systematic procedures for carrying out safety checks, inspections and investigations;
   - methods of ensuring that safety equipment is maintained and used;
   - proper means available for persuading managers, supervisors and the work force to pay more attention to health and safety matters.
3. The health and safety policies of the organization should be determined by top management, who must be continuously involved in monitoring health and safety performance and in ensuring that corrective action is taken when necessary.
4. Management and supervisors must be made fully accountable for health and safety performance in the working areas they control.
5. All employees should be given through training in safe methods of work and should receive continuing education and guidance on eliminating health and safety hazards and on the prevention of accidents.

To put these principles to work it is necessary to:

- Issue a health and safety statement.
- Introduce an occupational health programme.
- Introduce an accident prevention system.

The health and safety policy statement

The policy statement should be a declaration of the intention of the employer to safeguard the health and safety of his employees. It should emphasize four fundamental points: first, that the safety of employees and the public is of paramount importance; second, that safety will take precedence over expediency; third, that every effort will be made to involve all managers, supervisors and employees in the development and implementation of health and safety procedures; and fourth, that health and safety legislation will be complied with in the spirit as well as the letter of the law.

Occupational health programmes

Occupational health programmes are concerned with the identification and control of health hazards arising from toxic substances, radiation, noise, fatigue and the stresses imposed upon body and mind at work.

Basic approach

In each of these areas the same basic approach is necessary. The first stage is to identify the substances, conditions or processes which are actually or potentially dangerous. The second stage is to evaluate how the hazard arises by studying the nature of the substance of condition and the circumstances in which the danger occurs. This means establishing the point at which a substance or an environmental condition is in danger of becoming harmful, in terms of the intensity and duration of the exposure. It also means that the effect of working methods and processes on the human body and mind has to be examined.

Industrial hygiene research into these matters should be carried out by specialist medical advisers working closely with process engineers and chemists. In particularly hazardous environments, research and advice may be required from members of the growing profession of occupational hygienists.

The final stage is to develop methods of minimizing the risk by exercising control over the use of dangerous substances or over the environment in which the hazard occurs. Control of occupational health and hygiene problems can be achieved by:

- Eliminating the hazard at the source by means of design and process engineering which may, for example, ensure that harmful concentrations of toxic substances are not allowed to contaminate the worker.
- Isolating hazardous operations or substances so that workers do not come into contact with them.
- Changing the process, methods of work or substances used to promote better protection or to remove the risk.
- Providing protective equipment, but only if changes to the design, process or specification cannot completely remove the hazard.
- Training workers to avoid risk by eliminating dangerous or risky practices or by using the protective equipment provided.

- Maintaining plant and equipment to minimize the possibility of harmful emissions.
- Good housekeeping to keep premises and machinery clean and free from toxic substances.
- Regular inspections to ensure that potential health risks are identified in good time.
- Pre-employment medical examinations and regular checks on those exposed to risk.

Accident prevention

The first step to take in preventing accidents is to identify the actual or potential causes. You can then take number of preventive actions as described later.

Identifying the causes of accidents

The process of identifying causes is mainly one of conducting inspections, checks and investigations. Some consideration should be given, however, to the general factors that induce accidents, as these will indicate the approach that should be used at the design and inspection stages.

Fundamentally it is the system of work to which human beings are exposed that is the cause of accidents. Carelessness, fatigue, lack of knowledge, inexperience, inadequate training or poor supervision may, in different degrees, be the immediate causes, but all these factors are related to the basic system of work.

The causes of accidents can therefore be divided into two main areas:

1. Those related to the system of work, which are the basic reasons for most accidents.
2. Those related to personal factors, which in many cases arise from the system of work, but which might not have happened if there had been no human failure at or near the point of time when the accident occurred.

System of work factors

The main factors in the system of work which induce accidents are:

- Unsafety designed machinery, plant and proceses.
- Congested layouts.
- Unguarded or inadequately guarded machinery.
- Defective plant, materials or working conditions; rough, sharp, or obstructive objects; slippery or greasy conditions; decayed, corroded, frayed or cracked containers, wires, conveyor belts or piping; badly maintained machinery.
- Poor housekeeping-congestion, blocked gangways or exits; inadequate

disposal arrangements for swarf or other waste products; lack of storage facilities; unclean working conditions.

- Inadequate lighting, glare.
- Inadequate ventilation or systems for removing toxic fumes from the working environment.
- Lack of protective clothing or devices.

It should be noted that although these factors are all connected with the system of work they all result from a human failure at some time.

Personal factors

The personal factors causing accidents are:

- Using equipment unsafely—deliberately or through fatigue.
- Unsafe loading and placing of materials or parts on machines or transport systems.
- Operating without sufficient clearance.
- Operating at an unsafe speed.
- Making safety devices inoperative to reduce interference and speed up work.
- Distractions from other people, noise or events taking place in the workshop.
- Failure to use protective clothing or devices.
- Any of these factors may result from personal failures such as carelessness, recklessness, laziness, impatience, lack of consideration; or inadequate knowledge, training, skill or supervision.

In this chapter an overview of the basic components that make up an efficient human resource system in an organisation was provided. In the forthcoming chapters some the these concepts would be explored in greater detail.

Human resource development

This organisation concept of this term development will be explained in more detail in the next chapter, but it is essential that we briefly explore it here, particularly in relation to the various kinds of human resource activities that have emerged. There is still no agreement on the terms used in grappling with the whole concept of human resources, and there are many reasons for this. For one, there is no single undergraduate degree in the field, as yet. Therefore, people in the field of human resources come from a variety of disciplines and each brings along his own terminology and concepts. Even at the graduate level there is insufficient distinction among the fields, although programs in HRD are now emerging. At the time of this writing, it is possible to see the clarification of three major areas of human resources, as shown below.

Human resource development (HRD)

This area is the major focus of the book, but it is sufficient to say here only that HRD is concerned with providing learning experiences for people.

Human resource utilization (HRU)

These are obviously the traditional functions of the Personnel Department. They are still needed, and they are very important. Without attention to these activities, few organizations could continue to function, particularly if they are labour intensive rather than capital intensive. In all organizations, HRU is an important activity.

Areas of controversy

At present, and for some time into the future, we can expect to find controversy in organizations capable of producing guerrilla warfare. It is much like the in-company conflicts which were part of the technological boom of the 1960's. Each unit of the company felt that what it was inventing, producing, or marketing was the prime activity of the company. Managers were devoting inordinate amounts of time to reconciling conflicts among various units. This is what is happening in human resources. There are boundary problems as organizations struggle for appropriate placement of some activities.

Workforce planning: Where does this belong? Traditionally, this has been the function of the HRU people. They are the ones who should be in contact with the upper levels of management to know the long-range planning and the human resources needed to staff the future operations of the organization. Yet, the HRE people also want part of this action, for the kinds of people to be recruited and selected will have a direct impact on identifying the appropriate environmental factors. The HRD people, if they think it through should stay out of this conflict. Once plans have been agreed upon, the HRD people have a contribution to make in providing the learning experiences to produce the desired Workforce, identified through the appropriate planning techniques.

Counselling: An outgrowth of concern over the quality of work life, as well as the quality of life outside of work, has led to the growth of what is called career planning or career development. When applied to those who are around the age of 40, it is called mid-career planning or mid-career change. It arises from a variety of sources, including dissatisfaction with the nature and routine of work (environment) or with the present job or future possibilities (utilization). Meanwhile, the HRD people are moving into this field and contributing to the confusion.

Industrial relations: This used to be a well-defined area concerned with union negotiations. Slowly, it broadened into areas concerned with both environment and utilization. With increased talk of worker sabbaticals, it now overlaps with development. But it is none of these, which is why it has purposely not been included. At this time, it is not possible to say whether it can be subsumed under any of the three areas, or whether it is a fourth area. In looking at organizations, it becomes apparent that the relationship and placement of the Industrial Relations (IR) function is more dependent upon history and personalities (both labour and management) than any other concerns.

"Who is in charge here?" This is the major controversy. A new designation of Human Resource Management or Human Resource Administration is emerging on the scene. Some universities already offer degrees in the field, though the behaviours and competency for such a position are far from clear. For many years, we can expect the management position in human resources to be filled on a basis that has little relationship to prior preparation. There are some organizations that have purposely chosen *not* to fill the position with anybody coming from HRD, HRE, or HRU! Rather, they choose a general manager or plant manager and rotate that person through the HRM position. A common title is Vice President for Human Resources.

Obtaining human resources

When you have decided how many and, broadly, what sort of people you want, you set about getting them by knowing:

- What you are looking for?
- Where to find them?
- How to attract them?
- How to choose them?
- How to clinch the deal?
- What to do with them when they start?

What you are looking for?

Most of the people you recruit will probably be replacements and of course you know what you are looking for. But do you? One of the main reasons why people leave is because they should not have been selected in the first place. Mistakes are made because the duties and responsibilities of the job have not been properly analysed, neither has an adequate specification been prepared of what the job holder needs to know and be able to do.

For new jobs, the requirement to analyse the duties and to prepare job specifications based on this analysis is even more pressing. It is likely that only a superficial understanding of what the job is existed when the human resource plans were being prepared.

To know what you are looking for, you need to do three things:

1. Analyse the job, and then.
2. Prepare a job description.
3. Prepare a personnel specification.

Job analysis

Job analysis establishes what the tasks and duties of the job are? The information required covers:

The job title

- An organization chart showing at least the job title of the job holder's immediate superior and the job titles of the staff directly responsible to him.
- A definition of the overall purpose of the job.
- A list of the main tasks or duties that the job holder carries out.
- The initial dimensions of the job—sales turnover, size of budget, number of staff controlled, output or throughput, etc.
- Any special equipment or tools used.
- Information on any special requirements to deal with people—inside or outside the organization.
- Special circumstances, such as travelling away from home, the likelihood of being transferred to another branch or location, unsocial hours, unpleasant or dangerous working conditions.

This information can be obtained by talking to the boss or the existing job holder, if feasible. Questionnaires are sometimes used, but most people are not very good at completing them and you still have to talk it over. It is, however, advisable to warn the person you are seeing in advance of what you will want to know, so that organization charts or any other data can be made available in time for the meeting.

Job descriptions

Job descriptions provide four pieces of information:

1. *The job title:* this should be as precise as possible about what the job is, without being over-elaborate. Try not to allow a proliferation of inflated titles such as director, manager or executive. They may impress other people, but they do not cut much ice within the organization and only serve to devalue jobs where the title means something.
2. *Basic organization:* the person to whom the job holder is responsible and the people responsible to him.
3. *Overall responsibility:* a succinct (one or two sentences) statement of what the job exists to do. It should be possible from this statement to distinguish it from other jobs in the organization and to lead naturally into a description of the main duties or principal accountabilities. For example, the statement of overall purpose for a divisional production director might read:

The divisional production director is responsible for ensuring that the production commitments of the division are achieved in the quantities and qualities required and in accordance with predetermined programmes and cost budgets.

4. *Main activities*: the list of main activities, duties, principal accountabilities or responsibilities is the most important part of the job description. Each activity should represent a key element of the job for which the job holder can be held accountable and which requires specific knowledge or skills. Your aim should be to restrict the number of headings to six or seven so that the crucial aspects of the job can be highlighted. There may, however, be a number of related tasks that can be specified under each activity heading.

   For example, the headings in a retail shop manager's job description might read: selling; display; merchandising; stock control; staff management and training. Under the 'selling' heading, there might be three related tasks which would be described as follows:

   1. Greets customers and passes them to the appropriate sales assistant.
   2. Ensures that customers are handled correctly by the sales assistant.
   3. Sells direct to customers when necessary.

Activity descriptions indicate *what* is to be done. They should not attempt to spell out *how* it is done, although the outline in the job description may be expanded into a task analysis for training purposes, which goes into more detail so that the skills and knowledge required to do each task can be identified.

The three golden rules for writing activity definitions are:

1. The definition should be succinct but informative.
2. Each definition should be expressed in one sentence starting with an active functional verb, e.g.;
   - prepares regional sales forecasts;
   - checks quotations prepared by the sales department;
   - answers customer queries on deliveries.
3. The definitions should be set down in separate, numbered paragraphs to ease identification of the key areas and to assist in cross-referencing.

Other uses for the job description

The job description is a basic tool of human resource management. It is essential not only because it provides vital data for recruitment purposes, but also because it provides key information for use in:

- Organization design and development.
- Human resource planning.
- Training.
- Management development.
- Performance reviews.
- Salary administration (job evaluation).

Overall responsibility

Achieves contribution targets for product by developing and implementing plans, monitoring performance and initiating corrective action.

Main activities

1. Develops a long-range and competitive strategy for the product.
2. Prepares annual marketing plans and sales forecast.
3. Works with advertising agencies to develop and implement promotional and advertising campaigns.
4. Stimulates interest and support for the product among the sales force and distributors.
5. Gathers continuous intelligence on the product's performance, customer and dealer attitudes and new problems and opportunities.
6. Initiates and test product improvements to meet changing market needs.

Personnel specification

The personnel specification tells you six things:

1. The knowledge, skills and personal attributes needed to do the job. These may be classified either as essential or desirable.
2. The qualifications, experience and training which are likely to provide the knowledge and skills required. These may also be classified as essential or desirable.
3. Age limits, if any.
4. Prospects of promotion.
5. Features of the job-location, unsocial hours, travelling, working conditions, likelihoods of transfer.
6. Terms and conditions of employment—basic pay, bonuses, pensions, other fringe benefits, working hours, holidays, periods of notice etc.

The specification is used, together with the job description, first, as a basis for drafting advertisements or briefing recruitment consultants, second, to provide the criteria against which candidates can be assessed and third, as a source of the information which needs to be conveyed to candidates in interviews and offers of employment.

A personnel specification of product manager might read as follows:

1. *Knowledge:*
   - *essential*—techniques of marketing planning, sales forecasting, product analysis, pricing, target marketing and marketing control;
   - *desirable*—techniques of marketing research, new product development and media planning.
2. *Skills:*
   - *essential*—numerate in the sense of being at ease in handling figures and basic statistical analysis, good on paper (report writing), high level of analytical ability;
   - *desirable*—managing and motivating people, persuasive (selling) skills.
3. *Qualifications:*
   - *essential*-graduate or equivalent;
   - *desirable*—first or second degree in business studies with emphasis on marketing, Member of Institute of Marketing.
4. *Training:*
   - *essential* (if no business or marketing qualification)—specialized short courses in marketing techniques, or evidence that he/she is familiar through reading or on-the-job training with basic concepts of marketing;
   - *desirable*—extended full-or-part-time courses in marketing.
5. *Experience:*
   - *essential*—two year's experience after graduation as an assistant product or brand manager in a marketing department or an advertising agency;
   - *desirable*—experience in a FMCG (fast moving consumer goods) business, and/or experience in new product development and launches.
6. *Personal attributes:*
   - *essential*—extrovert, an achiever, articulate, capable of working under pressure.
7. *Age limits:* 23-28

8. *Promotion prospects*: effective product managers can normally expect promotion to product group manager within two years.

9. *Job features*: Based in New Delhi, all India travelling, occasional late-night, even weekend working (i.e., can be pressurized).

10. *Terms and conditions*:

    - *starting salary circa* Rs. X,000 up to Rs.Y, 000 in special circumstances;
    - *salary range* Rs. X, 000—Rs. Z,000;
    - *holiday*—five weeks;
    - *pension scheme*—non-contributory, contracted in;
    - *working week*—basic, 35 hours (9.30-5.30 Monday to Friday with one hour allowed for lunch);
    - *period of notice*—one month;
    - *expenses*—normal, including mileage allowance for using own car on business (NB no company car, allocation starts at product group manager level);
    - *lunch coupons*—x per day;
    - *Leave travel assistance*—after one year's service.

Search for human resources

Internal candidates

You may believe that you already have the ideal candidate within your organization, possibly someone who has been groomed for promotion, but it would be wise to check your assumptions. Compare his or her qualifications with the specification. If they match, that is fine. If they do not fit exactly, think again. You may continue to feel that this is your best bet and, after all, promotion from within is a good thing, isn't it? If, however, a fresh look at the individual means that you have second thoughts, check to see if there is anyone else within the organization. You might want to stick to your first choice, but you will be more certain that you are right.

If no obvious choice springs to mind you should still consider an internal 'trial', if you believe that there are any suitable people around who would be interested because the job will offer promotion, upgrading, wider experience, or just a change. You may know someone, or you can ask around, or look at the records. If your personnel records are computerized you might be able to obtain a printout of people who have the basic qualifications for the job. This implies that the records store the sort of information you need for this purpose. If they don't, then the deficiency should be remedied.

It the trawl brings nothing worthwhile into the net, you can consider an internal advertisement. Many companies do this as a matter of policy in the interest of equal opportunity. This may be highly desirable, but it could be argued that if internal advertisements are mandatory and a manager is absolutely certain about who he wants, then advertising would be an empty gesture and might cause more frustration and disappointment than if an appointment had been made without going through this rigmarole. Alternatively, it could be felt that as there is no one suitable in the company, there would be no point in going through the futile and time-wasting process of advertising inside. The answer to this objection may be that no one can be absolutely certain in any sizeable organization that there are no suitable internal candidates and, in any case, everyone ought to be given the chance. This view has much merit, but there will be circumstances where an internal advertisement is a pointless exercise.

External sources

Even if you have internal candidates or advertise in the company, you may still feel that you have to extend your choice outside. The alternative sources are:

1. *Former employee's*: approach them on a 'Will you come back again?' basis.
2. *Advertisements* : discussed in the next section.
3. *Government employment agencies*: Employment exchanges for manual and junior clerical staff.
4. *Private employment bureaus*/Placement Agencies which deal with general secretarial, clerical or junior professional vacancies, or may specialize in such occupations or areas of business as computer personnel, accountants, graphic designers or publishing. They charge a fairly substantial fee, from 6 to 7 per cent to as high as 17.5 per cent, but save time and trouble and often have direct access to the most appropriate candidates.
5. *Selection or recruitment consultants*, who produce a short-list of candidates for you from advertisement (which may or may not mention the name of your firm) or from their lists of suitable candidates on file. They charge a fee which may be of the order of 15 to 20 per cent of the successful applicant's salary, and they also bill you for the costs of advertising and testing and for travelling and incidental expenses.

The advantage of a good firm is it has expertise in analyzing requirements and writing advertisements and in interviewing. It should also know about salary levels. You save time, although you have to pay for it, and you can, if you wish, remain anonymous so as not to upset your own employees. This sounds an undesirable motive, but there are occasions when employers want to explore the market for a new job without revealing all the details, including salary, to their existing staff.

You should consider the following points when choosing and using a selection consultant:

- whenever you can, use consultants with whom you are familiar and who have given you good service in previous assignments—they know you and your business;
- if you are starting from scratch, obtain recommendations from other users;
- establish which firms have specialist experience in your industry or for a particular occupation;
- check the advertisements of possible consultancies to give you a direct impression of their professionalism and the type and level of firms and jobs they deal with;
- make sure that you meet the consultant who is actually going to conduct the assignment. Check his experience. Assess his competence. If you don't like him, go elsewhere;
- once you have selected the selector, discuss with him the basis upon which he will carry out the assignment, including preparing specifications, advertising, reporting on candidates and the basis upon which the short-list will be drawn up. The consultant may simply hand over details of the short-listed candidates and leaves you to carry out the final selection, but if you wish, he can sit in on the interviews to provide you with further device—at a cost;
- clarify the basis upon which fees and expenses will be charged and get a prior quotation for the full cost or, if that is difficult, set a maximum figure. Make sure you know what the bill for advertising is going to be, otherwise you could get a nasty shock;
- use the consultant's expertise in drawing up the job description, defining the personnel specification and setting the remuneration levels, but don't allow him to persuade you to escalate the salary to an amount which would cause you embarrassment within your firm when it is compared with what equivalent staff are paid. If you agree that the salary should be quoted as *circa* Rs.X,000, make sure that both you and the consultant know what you mean. How far, if at all, will you go above that figure to attract an especially good candidate? What activity, if any, should you give the consultant to indicate that a higher salary is payable? It is best not to allow him—or yourself—to commit yourself to any fixed figure in advance; leave it to negotiation in the final states. Neither should the consultant be drawn into detailed discussion in the early stages about terms and conditions of employment;
- obtain a written confirmation of your brief, together with copies of the agreed personnel specification and draft advertisement for you to approve;

- finally, trust your consultant. Within reasonable limits, give him any sensitive information about your firm he needs to know, but clear with him in advance what he can tell the candidate.

6. *Executive search consultants* (head hunters) approach candidates direct having obtained their names by 'research' or through contacts. The blue-blooded ones with plush offices in Mayfair only deal with top jobs, but there are specialist agencies who cover more junior or professional vacancies. Head hunters are most useful when there is only a limited number of potential candidates, few of whom are likely to be seeking alternative employment. They can make direct approaches to people you or they know who are right for the job and they can also handle with discretion senior people who may not wish to come out into the open. Search fees can be as high as 50 per cent of the first year's salary, and results are not always guaranteed.

   There are a number of reputable and well established search consultancies, but sharks and charlatans also exist. The advice on choosing and using a consultant given above is equally applicable to head hunters.

7. *Schools:* schools can be approached direct through career teachers. It is often worth cultivating local schools—arranging visits, providing holiday jobs or sponsoring events. You will create goodwill and possibly spot promising school leavers.

8. *Universities:* the big firms recruit large numbers of newly qualified graduates through the 'milk round'—visiting universities to interview candidates.

How to attract them?

Basic considerations

Companies which recruit from universities on a large scale produce glossy brochures and even video tapes. They work through the career advisory services and employ specialists who are good at relating to students. If you only want one or two graduates in the UK, you can advertise in the fortnightly 'Current Vacancies' list issued by the Central Services Unit in Manchester, or you can announce your vacancies on Prestel.

1. *Pay*: the first thing to do is to ensure that the remuneration package is attractive. This means paying the market rate unless the job or the company's reputation are good enough to persuade people to settle for less — and this is a rare event. You can find out what market rates are by studying advertisements for comparable jobs. Some people say that these rates are unreliable and, indeed, they, may not reflect what is eventually paid. But you will be competing in the job vacancy pages against other firms, so you must take into account what they offer.

   There is no point in offering less than the average, except in the ultra-special circumstances referred to above. How far you go above the average depends on how badly you want to attract the best available candidates and the extent to which you need to compensate for any drawbacks in the job. When deciding on salary levels and other parts of the remuneration package you must also, of course, have regard to your internal scales so as not to upset relativities, unless there is a good reason for paying a premium to attract a top-rate external candidate.

Check the salary you are offering against any information on salary levels you can obtain from published salary surveys. Advice can also be obtained from the selection consultant, if you are using one.

2. *The job*: you are more likely to get someone good if the job, as described in the advertisement or at the interview, looks, sounds and *is* good from the points of view of interest, challenge and opportunity.

Advertising

You can use a specialist recruitment advertising agency, but if you are doing it yourself the following is a checklist of the points to which you need to pay attention:

1. *Set objectives:*
   - to attract response from suitable candidates;
   - to deter unsuitable candidates;
   - to create a favourable impression of you as an employer;
   - to enhance the reputation of your firm.
2. *Achieving objectives:* to obtain a good response from an advertisement you need to:
   - catch the *attention* of the people to whom it is addressed;
   - hold their *interest* so that your proposition is read thoroughly;
   - arouse *desire* for the opportunity offered;
   - stimulate *action* in the shape of response.
3. *Information content*: a potential employee will want the advertisement to provide him with answers to these questions about the job:
   - is the work interesting?
   - is it relevant to my qualifications and experience?
   - is the pay right?
   - will it advance my career?
   - is it secure?
4. *Creating the advertisement*:
   - catch attention with a bold headline which in a few words will make a potential applicant read on. Illustrations can help;
   - stimulate interest by describing the job in the first paragraph in a way which will make it personally rewarding;

- create desire by mentioning opportunities for advancement early in the copy;
- don't use up too much space describing the company. This is not primarily a public relations exercise. But do tell them where the job is located, and capitalize on a good location;
- Summarize the qualifications and experience. Aim reasonably high. If you understate your requirements you will undersell the job. But be specific; vague references to desirable characteristics such as initiative, judgment or ambition do not add much;
- State age limits, but don't be too restrictive;
- Describe the remuneration package—salary, company car, pension scheme, relocation expenses etc. Concentrate on the key attractive elements. Quoting the salary as *circa* RSX, 000 gives you and the candidate room to manoeuvre; stating that the salary is 'up to' creates expectations which you might not want, to fulfil;
- Stimulate action by telling them how to apply. You can ask them to write a letter of application or, and this often works well, ask them to write or telephone for an application form. If you are raiding a place for a particular category of staff employed locally, you can invite them to attend an informal interview in an hotel;
- Use clear, simple, easy-to-read typography with plenty of white space so that it stands out on the page. Establish a 'house style' if you are advertising frequently;
- Use display advertisements for important jobs. But semi-display, even classified ads can work well for more junior positions;
- use sufficient space in a display advertisement to ensure that it is not swamped by the other ads on the page. But space is expensive and excessively large advertisements are not necessarily cost-effective.

5. *Media selection*: choose media which have been successful in the past or are right for the particular vacancy. If you scan the pages of the 'quality' papers and the more popular press you will soon get a picture of which jobs to advertise where. Some papers have specialist sections, such as the *the Times of India* has got a section called ASCENT. Others go direct to the right audience—the *Economic Times* is appropriate for senior financial posts. The *Hindustan Times* is a good general medium for managerial, professional and technical vacancies. Top jobs may be advertised in *The Times of India,* the *Economic Times.* Your local or evening paper is best for clerical and manual jobs. Journals are useful for specialist posts - *Campaign*, for example, is good for agency and marketing jobs. But circulation may be low and it might be advisable to use the journal as a backup to a general medium. Up-to-date information on each medium is listed in the NRS (National Readership Survey).

6. *Budgeting*: as a rule of thumb, you may have to spend the equivalent of two to three weeks' wages for semi-skilled or skilled workers; over three weeks pay for secretarial and clerical posts; and six to eight weeks' salary for managerial, professional and technical posts. The amount you spend will clearly depend on the extent to which you are in the buyer's or seller's market for the type of person you are looking for. Response analysis of previous advertisements will give you an idea of how much each reply and recruit will cost, but do not rely on data more than 12 months old.

7. *Response analysis*: to assist in budgeting and in analyzing the performance of an advertisement, it is essential to analyse the response you get. Records should be kept for each insertion of the total cost, the number of replies, the number called for interview and the number of joiners. This data can be used to produce these ratios:
   - cost per reply (the basic ratio);
   - cost per interview (an index of quality);
   - cost per recruit;
   - replies per joiner.

8. *Using a recruitment advertising agency*: an agency will be able to provide expert services on copywriting, advertising design and media selection. They are most useful if you are planning a major campaign or are expecting problems in attracting good candidates. Agencies rely for their income mainly on the commission they receive on the space they place with the media. Some agencies work on a fee basis, rebating their commission from the total fee.

How to choose them?

The process of choosing people consists of the following four stages, one of which, testing, is optional:

1. Sifting.
2. Interviewing.
3. Testing.
4. Obtaining references.

Sifting applications

Interviewing is a time-consuming process. Given the choice, you are not likely to want to see more than a dozen people for one vacancy, and if you could reduce this to half-a-dozen, so much the better. Assuming you have had a decent response to your advertisement, you have to sift the applications.

There are six questions you should answer when reading a letter, CV or application form:

1. Does the applicant meet the minimum criteria in the specifications for qualifications, experience and age range?
2. To what extent does the applicant's educational and work history indicate achievement and progression?
3. Are there any features in the applicant's career such as job hopping or mysterious gaps which arouse suspicion?
4. On the face of it, are the reasons given for leaving jobs convincing?
5. If the applicant is unemployed, how long has this lasted and what happened to the last job?
6. Is the letter of application or CV business-like, clear and readable? The more important the job, the greater the weight that should be given to this information. An incoherent, verbose or badly written letter suggests the possession of undesirable characteristics such as an untidy mind, an inability to communicate, or a couldn't-care-less attitude. Don't reject someone who meets the specifications in every respect, just because the letter is somewhat confused, but other things being equal, a badly set out application may tip the balance against the candidate.

If you have received a lot of applications, you will need to classify them. Three categories are enough in the first sift; possibles, doubtful and outright rejects. Don't waste any time with the latter, there are always some job-hoppers who are obviously unsuitable; clear them out of the way.

Unless you are in a desperate hurry, allow a week to go by and then carry out a second sift of the possibles and doubtfuls. This time, classify them into probables, possibles and rejects. Ideally you should have six to twelve probables and as many possibles for one vacancy. Put the rest out of their misery straightaway. As a rule of thumb, try and cover your probables by as many possibles.

When you have sifted twice, invite the probables for the interview. Allow 30 minutes for a clerical or manual vacancy, and 60 minutes for a managerial post—possibly more at a really senior level. Try not to invite too many people on one day; a dozen clerical or manual workers or six managers is enough. If you try and do more you will be unable to—do the tail-end candidates justice, and you could miss a good one. When scheduling interviews, bring in the best candidates first, allow some time between interviews (5-10 minutes) to collect your thoughts and write down your first impressions, and leave some empty slots in the day to allow you to rearrange dates or times.

At this stage you should send the applicant an application form if you have not already done so. The form should elicit all the information you need as a basis for the interview and making the final choice. This covers:

- Personal details—age, sex, marital status, children, if any.
- Education.
- Qualifications and training.
- Job history—for each job, name of company, job title of person to whom the applicant was responsible, starting and leaving dates, final salary or rate of pay and reason for leaving.
- Names of referees.

Interviewing

The best sort of interview is on a one-to-one or, at most, two-to-one basis. The final choice should be made by one person only—whoever is going to be the boss. He can be assisted by a personnel specialist who may carry out a preliminary sifting interview, only passing on suitable candidates for a final interview. If there is a fairly small list of people to be interviewed, the personnel specialist may sit with the line manager. Both approaches have their advantages and disadvantages.

Separate interviews could mean that more ground is covered and different facets of the candidate's qualification and experience are exposed. The personnel specialist may concentrate on educational and job history and on explaining attitudes and motivation. The line manager may deal with the more technical aspects of the job and make his personal assessment of whether or not the candidate will fit into the department. However, separate interviews can be time wasting and inevitably overlap.

The advantage of joint interviews is that both interviewers are exposed to the same information and either of them can follow leads created in advance, and while one interviewer asks the questions the other can sit back and observe reactions. There is a lot to be said for this approach if there is no need to sift at the interview stage. Alternatively, a colleague of the manager can sit in at the preliminary personnel interview or alongside the manager.

As a general rule, using more than two interviewers at a time is counter-productive. The candidate becomes confused, it is difficult to get a natural flow of questions and, because each interviewer feels he has to have his say, leads are not followed up and the candidate is not given enough scope to express himself. Interviewing boards may be desirable, even necessary, in the civil service and local government for political reasons, but they are not an effective way of choosing people.

For the more routine or junior jobs, one interview or a pair of interviews in quick succession is usually enough. At more senior levels, a second interview is desirable to give all concerned another chance to get to know each other thoroughly; selecting someone for a job is a momentous decision and should not be undertaken too lightly.

Purpose

An interview is a conversation with a purpose. The purpose is to obtain information about the candidate so that you can assess his qualifications and personal qualities against the specification and thus make a prediction about his capacity to do the job. This purpose is achieved through a conversation, because by adopting a fairly informal, conversational approach, you are more likely to get the information you want.

Basic approach

The conversational approach is fundamental, but there are three other Cs to which you need to pay attention.

1. *Contact:* establish rapport as quickly as you can. You want the candidate to talk and thus to reveal all you need to know. People can talk themselves out of as well as into a job. A friendly opening is required, but this does not mean that you should not be prepared to toughen up later if you want really to pin down the candidate about what he knows or can do.

2. *Content:* make sure that you cover all the ground by systematically reviewing every relevant aspect of the candidate's education, training and career. Get the facts, but also try to get to know something about his motivation, his attitude to work, his ability to communicate and the way he gets on with people—bosses, colleagues and subordinates.

3. *Control:* your conversation should be controlled to get the information you need within the time available. Control yourself as well as the candidate. Don't talk too much, and keep him to the point.

Interview plan

The best way to get what you want is to determine in advance how you are going to tackle the interview. Read the application form again before you see the candidate. Decide on the questions you need to ask to clarify job history, to explore his depth of understanding of what he does and knows, and to test his ability to cope with the demands of the job for which he is being interviewed.

Also decide how you are going to plan the interview. A typical and logical method is the biographical interview, starting with education and qualifications and then, if applicable, covering each job in turn concentrating on the most recent jobs. Time should be allowed for general questions about personal circumstances and interests and to tell the candidate about the company and the job. He should be given the opportunity to ask questions; the quality of his questions could be revealing.

It is usually advisable to leave the detailed description of the job until after you have interviewed the candidate; there is no point in spending a lot of time telling an unsuitable individual all about a job you are not going to offer him.

Interviewing techniques

The following list summarizes the things you should and should not do to conduct a successful interview:

Do's:

- Ensure you know what you are looking for - read the specification.
- Decide in advance on any technical questions you want to ask to test the candidate's knowledge.
- Prepare, by reading the application form again and deciding how you want to plan the interview - the order in which you want to cover the ground and the particular questions you want to ask.
- Follow your plan and ensure you go over every point.
- Get the candidate to talk freely - offer open invitations for him to respond, such as: "Tell me how you got on at school', What do you find most rewarding about your current job? You don't want 'yes' or 'no' responses; they tell you next to nothing.
- Ask questions which will give you some idea about the candidate's motivation and ambitions, such as: 'What made you study that particular subject?', 'What made you decide to do...?', 'Why did you make that move?', 'How do you think you have progressed so far in your career?'
- Give the candidate the opportunity to reveal his strengths: 'What was your proudest moment at school?', 'What would you say have been your major achievements in your present job?'
- Try to identify any weaknesses or failures. This is not easy; the candidate will do his best to disguise, avoid or gloss over them. All you can do is to press hard to find out the real reasons why he has hopped from job to job, or why he left his last job after only a few months. If, for example, his explanation for leaving his last job is 'I couldn't get on with my boss', probe. Ask him to tell you, with examples, what actually went wrong. Whose fault was it? Ask him open-ended questions such as: 'What sort of problems have you had to deal with?'
- Ensure that any gaps in the candidate's record are filled up. A 12-month space between jobs might have been spent back-packing around Asia, but could have been spent in goal.
- Look for patterns: continuous regression from success to success, or a series of short spells in jobs. Anyone can be unlucky enough to be made redundant or even fired on one occasion. If it happens more than once, you need to watch out. He may have gone on being unfortunate, but it could occur again if he joins your firm.

- Look for evidence of the skills you are seeking. For example, positions of responsibility at school or university, if you want a future manager; making things, if you want a craftsman.

- Seek any evidence you can obtain on motivation. Success at school, university, professional training or in his career is the best guide. You can also find out quite a lot about the degree to which a person is motivated by asking about interests outside education or work.

The sort and range of interests will tell you something about the candidate, but the depth at which he pursues them will tell you a lot more. If, for instance, he says he reads, find out what he reads, how much he reads and if he can talk intelligently about his current reading.

One indicator of motivation is when someone triumphs over disadvantages such as a relatively poor home. One the other hand, a lack of motivation might be indicated if someone has not made the most of his natural advantages.

Don'ts:

- Avoid jumping to conclusions on limited evidence. First impressions can be misleading. Interviewers often seize on one desirable characteristic, such as a lively manner, and allow this reaction to obscure manifold weaknesses. There are plenty of con-artists about in interview rooms as well as on the streets. The candidate, if he wants the job, is out to make a good impression. He will present himself as well as he can and put a bold front over any failings. Your task is to penetrate behind the facade. Avoid indulging in what is known as the 'halo effect', which means letting one superficially attractive characteristic overshadow other less desirable ones. "The halo is only nine inches away from the noose", as Sir Peter Parker said.

- Don't ask leading questions—those that clearly indicate the answer you want. If you ask someone 'Do you think you are good at-so-and-so?' he is almost certain to answer yes, which does not get you very far. You need factual evidence which emerges from questions about achievements and experience and is not simply a matter of following your lead with an assertion of what he believes you would like to hear.

- Try your best not to dominate the interview - the candidate must be able to talk freely. Limit your contribution to well prepared, succinct and open questions and continue by means of encouraging grunts.

- Don't allow the interview to drift—keep control and keep with in your time limit.

Assessing candidates

You should assess candidates against the headings included in the specifications:

- Knowledge.
- Skills.
- Qualification.
- Training.
- Experience.
- Personal attributes.

A simple form can be drawn up with these headings, and for each one you can grade the candidate as follows:

A = exceeds specification

B = meets specification

C = does not meet specification

Anyone with a C in one or more critical areas is eliminated unless there is an overwhelming case for making an exception because of a particularly strong showing in another important area. For example, someone may not have the required qualifications but wins hands down on experience.

The job should not necessarily go to the candidate with the highest number of As or the best test scores. He could be over-qualified, and this could lead to frustration and ineffectiveness. However, this objection could be waived if there is plenty of scope for expanding responsibilities or for promotion.

Some interviewers attempt to weigh each heading by allocating point scores, but this gives a spurious impression of accuracy. Once you have established through the interview and any tests you may administer that a candidate has the required basic qualifications and experience, you are exercising judgment.

Your final choice between two equally well-qualified candidates may be governed by their personal attributes. You have to believe that the candidate will fit into the organization and that you and your colleagues will be able to work with him. This is where subjectivity creeps in. Perhaps it should not but in the real world we want people working in our organization with whom we think we will get along. You must eliminate prejudice when assessing candidates, and this includes, as the law requires, prejudices against race or sex. But if you genuinely feel, other things being equal, that one candidate will fit better than the others, then he gets the job, although your final decision may be delayed until you have checked references.

Testing

It is generally acknowledged that the interview alone can be an inefficient method of selecting people. Interviewers are sometimes prejudiced or they can fail to get the evidence they need, either because their basic techniques are inadequate or because, through poor technique again, they allow candidates to pull the wool over their eyes.

At an interview, the only evidence you have on what a candidate knows or can do, or what sort of person he is, derives from the information the candidate gives you plus your own observations. Can your really say that you have all you need to know about someone who may work with you for years after a 60-minute conversation?

Although tests cannot replace an interview, they can, if properly prepared and administered, provide additional unbiased evidence. The main types of tests that can be used are:

1. *Intelligence tests:* these are the familiar tests which attempt to measure intelligence, especially reasoning power. The most common type produces an intelligence quotient (IQ), which is the ratio of the mental age achieved by the individual and the norm for the population as a whole, which is taken as 100.

   Extensive research has shown that intelligence is distributed across the whole population in accordance with the normal bell shaped curve of distribution. Some intelligence tests do not measure IQ as such, but attempt to grade people into different divisions of the normal curve of distribution of intelligence for the population as a whole or a particular population, such as that of university graduates.

2. *Attainment tests*: these measure abilities or skills that have already been acquired by training or experience. A typing test is the most typical example. It is easy to find out how many words a minute a typist can type and compare that with the standard required for the job.

3. *Aptitude tests*: aptitude tests are designed to predict the potential an individual has to perform a job or specific tasks within a job. They cover such areas as clerical aptitude, numerical aptitude, mechanical aptitude and dexterity. They may come in the form of well-validated single tests, or as a battery of tests developed by test agencies such as, in the UK, Saville and Holdsworth Ltd.

4. *Personality tests*: personality tests attempt to assess the type of personality possessed by the applicant in terms of traits. Personality tests should be treated with caution. They can provide some insight into an individual but they need to be validated by a thorough comparison of test results with subsequent behaviour.

To be useful, tests must satisfy two requirements. First, they must be valid in the sense that they measure what they are supposed to measure and provide an indication of future behaviour. Second, they must be reliable in that they consistently produce the same results in similar circumstances.

Tests are useless unless they are validated by comparing the results achieved in the test with actual behaviour. This should be done scientifically so that norms can be established for evaluating test results. Thus, if it is shown that a job requires above average intelligence, only those whose test results lie in the upper quartile would be considered eligible. The same applies to aptitude and attainment tests. If there is inadequate correlation between test results and subsequent performance, the test becomes suspect. Before introducting a test, it is often worthwhile to administer it to existing staff whose performance has been measured so that the test results and actual achievements can be compared and realistic norms defined.

Tests can be useful for less senior jobs, where norms for intelligence, attainments or aptitudes can easily be determined. They are more difficult to apply at higher levels. Some people say that personality tests can provide valuable insights. This may be so, if they are the right tests, but their results should always be regarded as complementary to the other evidence you obtain from the application form and by the interview. Tests cannot supplant this information.

References

It is up to you to form your own opinion about the merits of a candidate. You cannot rely upon the possibly subjective views of someone else. What you can and should do, however, is to check with the present employer, and maybe the previous one as well, that the facts as given by the candidate are correct—job, length of service, rate of pay or salary and reasons for leaving, if applicable. You can also ask the key question, 'Would you re-employ?', but you will not always get a true answer. Any question asking directly or indirectly for an opinion about the ability of an individual to do a job with your company will as likely as not get a bland reply. People do not always like to commit themselves or damage someone's future prospects and, although references are privileged if they are factually correct and unmalicious, employers are worried about the possibility of an action for libel or slander. Because it is generally felt that it is difficult to make actions for slander stick, you are more likely to get a truthful reply if you get your reference over the telephone.

How to clinch the deal

The first thing to do is to sort out the pay. This presents no problem if there is a fixed rate for the job, but where there is some flexibility, you may have to negotiate around the *'circa'* figure quoted in your advertisement or the initial interview. If you do not offer at least the market rate as established by your research when preparing the job specification, you are not likely to get anyone worth having. You may decide to go above this level if the candidate is really good—but be aware of the danger of upsetting internal relativities and causing alarm, despondency and even anger among existing employees.

Your offer letter should deal with the main points that have to be covered in a contract of employment, namely:

- Job title.
- Starting date.
- Rates of pay and allowances and methods and intervals of payment.

- Hours of work.
- Holiday arrangements.
- Sick pay (if any).
- Pension arrangements.
- Length of notice.

Starting arrangements

It is important to ensure that new employees get off to a good start. You will have spent quite a lot of money on obtaining them; why waste it by creating a bad impression?

Starters should be given all the information they need about the company, the facilities available to them and methods of payment. They should be shown round their department and some time should be spent in explaining how their job fits into the organization.

They may be no more than a cog in a large machine but they will be much better motivated if they appreciate the important part their cog plays.

Induction training should be arranged to ensure that the new employee knows exactly what is expected of him and can quickly master what he has to do.

New employees should be followed up before too long to ensure that they are settling down and have received adequate training. A formal review should take place after a few months when, if the employee is not performing adequately, steps can be taken in good time to warn him that there are problems. Guidance can then be given on what he needs to do to overcome them. This formal review will also provide a check on the effectiveness of the selection procedure.

Defining human resource development

To begin with, let us avoid the use of the word "training." HRD is not synonymous with training, yet it has its origins in that term. When the American Society of Training Directors was formed in 1942, the term "Training Director" was in common usage and was adequate for that period. As time passed and the field began to grow in broader directions, the name of the organization was changed to reflect this, and it became the American Society for Training and Development.

The movement, during the early 1970's, toward human resource development reflects more than a cosmetic change. It reveals significant conceptual changes. In the U.S., in the 1960's, the term was associated with the efforts of the Department of Labor concerning the disadvantaged. Even then, however, there were those who could see broader implications. Fortunately, the Department of Labor ceased using the term and there are probably few who remember that part of its history.

HRD is not new. It is our understanding of the term that is new—or rather, *was* new, since today, increasing numbers of people and organizations are using the HRD term. What we now need is a very clear definition of the term, before we can explore how management relates to HRD.

The term "human resources development" means those learning experiences which are organized, for a specified time, and designed to bring about the possibility of behavioural change.

The term, "learning experience" refers to purposeful or international learning, not incidental learning. Although many of us learn constantly from the incidental learning experiences that flood our lives, HRD is concerned with the learning experiences which meet identified criteria. Below, the components of our definition of HRD are examined separately.

Organized

The learning experience must have some form of organization. This does not mean that it is only formal. On the job learning is certainly organized, or else it is likely to fail. However, it is a non-formal learning experience. Formal usually means taking place in a classroom learning situation, along with other learners. Using a teaching machine, with only one learner at a time, is organized, but is commonly classified as non-formal. The distinction between formal and non-formal is still being explored and it is important to our discussion to emphasize that organized learning includes both.

There has been an increased interest in self-directed learning, and some of the best work in this field has been done by Allen Tough and Malcolm Knowles predict, we will see more non-formal learning situations. These will still be organized and will need the support of the regular HRD function.

For a definite time period

The necessity for a time period helps to clarify both purposeful learning and the organized aspect of the learning. The learner and the organization must set aside specific periods of time for the learning experience, learning never stops, but there is the need for terminal points at which the learner and the organization can assess what learning has taken place and its relationship to performance.

It is important for the learner and the organization to know when a learning experience starts and when it is completed. Think of your own experience. You are scheduled to attend a "management retreat". This is usually held away from the office. Before you go, you need to know how long you will be gone and make the necessary arrangements. A manager's time is important and this prior preparation is essential. Tasks or meetings must be covered, since others in the organization may be relying on your presence. They will need to know how long you will be absent.

As a manager, you also want to know where your people are. This does not mean a constant tracking operation, unless that is your style of management. Still, an organization cannot be run without some mechanism for the manager to know where people are. The manager doesn't have to know where the people are every minute, but he should not have to hit the panic button dependent upon the definite time period allocated for the learning experience.

The possibility of behavioural change

When somebody offers you a learning program that guarantees behavioural change, become extremely cautious. You can find programs that guarantee learning takes place, but that is very different.

Later in this book we will discuss evaluation: what can you expect from HRD and how you will know if programs have met objectives. Learning is sometimes defined not only as the acquisition of new behavioural patterns but also as the utilization of this new behaviour. Knowing and doing are not always the same. Helping people learn is not always easy, but in most cases, it is possible. Helping people change their behaviour is much more difficult.

The emphasis on the word "possible" is an important caution. There are times when HRD people promise too much, and managers expect too much in the way of behavioural change. All your HRD programs may have given all the statistics about eye accidents, indicated the types of safety goggles available in the plant, described how and when to wear them, and even provided each person with his own pair of goggles. The manager responds by saying, "But I am only going to be here about half an hour, and I am only going to observe—I won't be going near the machines. In essence, the manager is conveying the message to the worker that safety goggles really aren't necessary all the time, and each person can choose when to wear or not wear them. Managerial behaviour on-site can wipe out a good deal, if not all, of the learned behaviour in the HRD program.

Another example comes from a sales force of clothing manufacturer that had asked to have a program on "Using Behavioural Science in Selling" designed. Working with the internal HRD people, such a program was drawn up. During the design process, it was identified that consulting selling that management said was wanted. A program was designed, and then conducted. Several managers were involved in developing the program and all gave their approval and support—or appeared to do so. About three months after the program, the internal HRD people followed up, and despite all the apparent support from the managers about the salesman is a consultant, the message some of the managers were still giving their salespeople was, "Don't consult—sell!" These managers were effectively contradicting the learning, and the cost of the program for their subordinates was a total loss to the company.

You, as a manager, must go beyond lip service. You must support such programs by your own actions.

HRD and the organization

HRD is generally found in larger organizations, and there are some identifiable reasons for this, though any organization—no matter what the size-actually provides some kind of HRD. For a particular organization, the HRD program may be insignificant in terms of the 'organization' overall budget. One may not even be able to find HRD in the table of organization, company phone book, or other observable documents.

Even in a small organization, however, somebody is providing learning experiences for new employees. It may be a very brief on-the-job experience, the coaching of one employee by another, or a supervisor telling an employee to read the manual that came with some newly arrived equipment.

No matter what the size of your organization, if you look around you will probably discover more HRD in operation than you realized existed. Some HRD activities are conducted without a specific managerial decision, or even without the knowledge of management. Even these clandestine HRD operations can contribute to the success of your organization.

Larger organizations tend to have much more going on in the way of HRD. There are usually individuals and units identified as having this responsibility. This practice has served to broaden the gap in human resources between more effective and more competitive, but they are the organizations least likely to allocate sparse resources to HRD. Instead, the small organization relies on recruitment of those who have received the benefits of HRD in large organizations. Or, the small organization tends to bridge the gap by other means which usually force them to hover near the survival level and to rely on less well-prepared members of the workforce.

Managers make decisions about HRD

All managers are constantly making decisions about human resources, and most managers are making decisions in the realm of HRD. When a manager chooses *not* to make a decision about HRD, this constitutes a decision *against* HRD! In the absence of some positive decisions by managers, little will be happening in HRD in that organization.

Managers are paid to make decisions, and some of these are made explicitly while others are implicit. Richard III, we are told, thought he was only making an observation when he cried out, "Will nobody rid me of this priest?" It was taken as a decision by his subordinates and the deed was done: the priest was assassinated.

In more recent times, it has been suggested that part of the tragedy of Watergate was this kind of implicit decision-making. It may not have been any direct decision by the then President Nixon, or even some of those around him, though some have been found guilty in the courts for issuing illegal orders. Of more significance is the climate of the organization which leaders produce through their implied decisions, or lack thereof. HRD is an area with which many managers are not sufficiently familiar, and that is one of the reasons for this book's existence. Few of us wish to tread through unfamiliar corporate mazes. Rather, many managers will focus their attention and decision-making on familiar as. From the outside, it may seem that the manager has delegated this function to some other level of the organization as a sound managerial practice. More frequently, a manager will avoid decision-making areas HRD so as to avoid the necessity for processing ignorance or only slight familiarity with this area of organizational operations.

Should we have HRD programs?

The literature in the HRD field tells us that programs are designed and provided based upon specific and identified needs. There are those who contend that HRD programs should only be provided by organizations when there are problems to be solved for which HRD is an appropriate response, Generally speaking, this is true, but it is much too sterile and unrealistic to work as a hard-and-fast rule.

Decisions about HRD programs are reflections of the philosophy and practices of managers. HRD is a response, and it will reflect the kinds of questions managers ask as they move toward decision-making. If managers do not ask questions, those responsible or HRD will try to function in terms of the kinds of questions they *think* the managers would ask. The pitfalls in this vacuum are obvious.

There is an initial decision about HRD which managers must make. Should there be any HRD programs at all? This will definitely relate to the philosophy of management concerning the workforce, as tempered by the availability of physical and financial resources.

Managers of small organizations, with extremely limited resources, try to meet their needs for skilled workers by having high entry level requirements. Such managers look for workers, at all levels, who can be employed and functioning at a high level immediately, with no need for any HRD activity.

This is a short-sighted approach and usually results in labour costs being even more expensive. We know that the more learning experiences an individual has, the more he wants. The small employer cannot provide these, and it should be no surprise that the employee therefore chooses to move to another organization.

Even if turnover does not become a factor, it looms on the horizon. In times of a tight labour market, such as we had in the first half of the 1970's, small organizations benefit from the lay-offs by large organizations of highly skilled workers, including middle managers. When the labour market loosens up and jobs become more plentiful, it is the small organization that loses out in the competition for the available workforce.

Assuming that a worker finds a small organization which meets his financial and emotional needs, does this mean that HRD will not be a factor? Highly unlikely. As changes take place, there is usually the need for some kind of learning experience. The employee may feel the need strongly enough to identify and pay for the learning experience out of his own resources. More likely, he will endeavour to find employment with an organization which can meet those needs. The small organization, then, is once again faced with finding a replacement from the external workforce. It is a constant process which plagues managers of small organizations, and one with which they have received too little assistance.

It should not be assumed that managers in large organizations have no human resource problems. Obviously they do, but the tendency in large organizations is to hire specialists to assist the manager. Historically, that is what happened to the area labelled as the personnel function. As organizations became larger and management more specialized, the tendency was to move all human resource decision-making into one unit, called the Personnel Division or some similar designation. In hindsight, we can see that the result was to withdraw from managers some of the decision-making and any real concern for the HRU functions.

The same history is being repeated with HRD, but with one difference. HRD is still new enough, as an organizational unit, to avoid the isolation which causes non-HRD managers to say "Do it for me, not with me." A well balanced HRD unit is beneficial to any organization, if it is the result of sound and continuing management decisions. The unit should not merely function on the strength of the personality and drive of the manager of the HRD function.

Who should attend HRD activities?

The obvious answer to this question is *those who need the learning experience*. But this is not always the case. Ruth Salinger, of the U.S. Civil Service Commission, found that managers were unclear as to the contribution to HRD to increased productivity. Given this lack of clarity, it is no wonder that managers leave too much decision-making to the HRD staff. Selecting the correct person to take part in the learning experience is more than a matter of determining who needs it. The decision must also reflect the plans of management for the employee, the type of work being done, and the unit in which it will be performed.

An example of this comes from a multinational company which provided extensive learning experiences for those of its employees who would be working overseas. It was obvious to this company that a good employee could be ruined by being sent to a foreign assignment with inadequate preparation. As it was a large organization, and many people were being sent on overseas assignments, the company had developed a specialized HRD unit with the capability for providing these necessary in-house programs.

Suddenly, the unit was advised that it was going to be shut down! This was traumatic for the HRD people, as well as for the employees in the pipeline. Actually, the decision was not sudden. For over half a year, top management had been discussing the need for a change in policy. This organization, like many in the international field, was moving toward staffing its overseas managerial positions with people from the particular country, rather than continuing to send personnel from the U.S. Feeling the need for some secrecy until the decision was final, nothing had been communicated to the HRD unit, which was still geared up for a large effort.

In this instance, with the need for secrecy, there was a possible explanation. Yet, it appears that top management was too security conscious. During the period of their decision-making, they continued to approve increasing expenditures for an operation that they were planning to terminate. They preserved their secret, but gave a message to the organization: *Who would be next*? Which other part of the organization is under discussion with the thought of closing it down or curtailing its operations?

It is not easy to reach a decision on how to handle such a situation as the one described above, but who promised that management would be easy?

On a day-to-day basis, management decisions on who should attend HRD activities will be shared at various levels of the organization. Managers may rely on the HRD people to suggest who should participate, but the final decision must still rest with the managers of the employees who will be attending.

Selecting and approving attendance of specific employees is only part of the involvement of management. The way in which the management decision is conveyed will also communicate a great deal about who should HRD program as some form of reward, the manager should not try to obfuscate by calling it something else. Most people in the organization are wise enough to recognize this situation, and if a manager does not acknowledge the action, doubts will be created about the selection of other participants. When managers select people for HRD programs, the reasons should be stated in such a manner that there is no doubt about the intention.

Unfortunately, there are other areas of ambiguity. These arise most frequently when managers are not fully informed of the basis or need for the learning experience. Then, the management decision may be made on the basis of who can be spared; in other words, who could the unit do without for the time the program will take? The HRD program thus becomes something to avoid. Clearly, this is a waste of the organization's resources, but it does happen.

The selection of those who should attend is an important decision, and one in which each manager should make sure he is involved.

How much should we spend?

It would be helpful if managers could be given some kind of rationale about the limits of expenditures for HRD. At present, all we can do is pose some questions:

- What per cent of the payroll should be spent on HRD?

- How many hours, per employee average, should be made available for HRD?
- What portion of the profit should be allocated for HRD?
- What kinds of problems can HRD solve?

It is almost impossible to give managers any clear answers to these questions, and these are by no means all the questions that could be asked. Many of these questions involve the philosophical base from which management is proceeding.

One study, conducted by The Conference Board, indicated that one in eight employees had participated in HRD experiences in the previous year. This was a study conducted among 600 companies representing 7500 of the largest employers in the U.S. For that year, these companies reported spending about $2 billion. Generally, we do not have sufficient data in the U.S. to enable managers to make any comparisons among organizations, but the total expenditure for *all* employees is probably much higher.

In Great Britain, as in some other countries where the government is much more involved in the HRD picture, it is possible to begin gathering the necessary data. Applying this to the U.S. becomes almost impossible, as we must make allowances for the cultural, philosophical, and economic factors which are so difficult to quantify.

In Japan, the emphasis is on developing internal HRD facilities, rather than relying on the school system. Each major organization has its own company schools which teach theory and skills, usually related only to the company and its products and equipment. The regular school system could not possibly meet the needs of the major Japanese companies, and is not expected to. Compare this with the U.S., where our thrust has been to attempt to bridge the gap between school and work.

Managers are responsible for allocating and utilizing the financial resources of the organization. Yet, at this time, there are insufficient criteria available to help managers make these decisions as related to HRD. This contributes to the kind of fighting and grandiose promises which are, regrettably, a hallmark of some HRD programs.

Should supervisors be instructors?

This question is often asked, and is a misleading one. Instruction is already a crucial element of a supervisor's job. However, not all supervisors agree with this, and it is important for managers to clarify this part of the supervisor's responsibility. As with any similar management decision, if the supervisor is to be an instructor, management must be sure that there are the appropriate rewards and recognition for this behaviour.

There are some obvious examples of how supervisors function as instructor. There is the case where the supervisor must work with each new employee until the employee has reached a suitable level of performance. There is no question but that the supervisor does not feel comfortable serving as an instructor, then it is unlikely that he will give valuable time to being an instructor, even when his services are needed desperately. The HRD unit can help the supervisor acquire the necessary skills to instruct, but without firm management support, it is doubtful the skills will be utilized.

In some situations, the supervisor may not do the actual instruction, but instead, he will rely on a carefully selected subordinate. In one major auto company, they have assigned a "utility-man" for this function. The supervisor, with the approval and support of management, can take an employee off production and use him to instruct new employees or experienced employees who need some additional instruction, the utility-man may either fill in on the production line or do other work as assigned by the supervisor. Such an arrangement cannot succeed unless management has approved it, and, as in this case, reinforced it through the process of union negotiation.

If the supervisor is to be used as an instructor, management must make adequate provisions. Usually, supervisors are rewarded for production, service, or whatever the output of the unit. Management must build in the necessary reward and support for supervisory behaviour based on instruction, as well as giving orders. Managers have to find ways to communicate to supervisors that instructing is not non-productive time, but is necessary if production and quality are to be maintained.

Increased productivity

Particularly in a manufacturing organization, productivity is the crucial element which can spell the difference between profit and loss, survival and collapse. Productivity should not be confused with production. It is possible to increase production by overtime, by hiring additional workers, or by procuring additional equipment. Productivity means bringing about the desired increase in production, not by adding to the workforce or the equipment, but through the greater efficiency of both.

For some managers, this distinction may be difficult to determine. In service situations, where measurement of output is difficult the concept of productivity has less meaning. For other managers, the concept may have been forgotten or may have received less attention in light of other priorities. It is agreed, however, that without a constant increase in worker productivity, a company will have difficulty competing in our industrial world.

To clarify this distinction, let us take an example. If an employee is producing eight widgets in an eight hour period, that is production. If the goal is to increase production, the work day can be lengthened to ten hours and the worker will be expected to produce ten widgets. Productivity would dictate that a manager try to find ways to have the usually accomplished by some kind of speed-up, and the techniques that were used made industrial horror stories. Production might have been increased, and there might have even been some temporary gains in productivity, but the manager usually paid for these gains in other ways—through lowered employee morale and trust, an increase in rejects, breakdowns in equipment and machinery, and provoking the employees to form stronger unions.

When production was tied to machine operation, a manager could obtain equipment that would work faster, thereby forcing the employee to work faster. The famous Charlie Chaplin film, *Modern Times*, depicted how ludicrous and counterproductive this could be.

This does not mean that a manager cannot increase productivity, but it does tell us that other means should be sought.

Organizations that are competing on the international market are very familiar with the productivity concept. Managers in such companies are constantly comparing the productivity of their own workers with that of the workers in the countries with which they are competing. Within the U.S., the term is much more a part of the vocabulary of economists than of managers.

One factor contributing to either a loss of productivity, or to only negligible gains, is the assumption that a worker, once skilled, remains at a skill level. When workers do repetitive functions, they tend to lose some of their skills. Doing the same tasks over and over will not necessarily increase skill level and related productivity, but rather will result in "stale" performance, which lowers productivity.

At first reading, this may seem to be contradictory. After all, the more one does a task, the better one should become at it. Let us take a non-organization-oriented task in which most of us are involved: driving a car. After many years of driving, do you tend to repeat many of your actions without much concern or thought? As long as you do not have accidents, you just keep on driving even if your techniques are not what they were in earlier years. The confrontation comes when you try to back-park, in just the three steps that you used when you were more expert at back-parking. Now, when faced with this need for back-parking, you may exhibit avoidance behaviour by going around the block to find another space which does not require this manoeuvre. Faced with the need to perform, the manoeuvre may take much longer and involve a good deal of curb scraping and bumper contact. Likewise, an employee may have lost some of his skills that were previously at a high level. The employee is now accomplishing the same task, but with diminished efficiency and a resultant higher cost to the organization. This is an area where a manager can use HRD very effectively.

The benefits of HRD for management are not limited to the area of productivity. Some jobs are difficult to measure. For example, in a managerial job, the element of productivity is not as significant. HRD will not help the manager measure his job, or any job. However, if used carefully, HRD programs can contribute to improving some observable elements of job performance. One example is in the area of communications. If it is identified that some members of the organization can benefit from a learning experience in written communications, the HRD people can organize and deliver such a program. At the end, it should be possible to identify how written communications have improved, though there is no productivity measure available for quantifying this change in behaviour.

Internal mobility of the workforce

We have a society in which external movement in the workforce is an accepted way of life. Some people are employed right out of school and remain with the same employer for their entire work life. In our economic society, this is the exception rather than the rule. In some other parts of the world, it is just the opposite: one worker can spend an entire work life with the same employer. Given frequent changes in employment in the U.S., we research and gather statistics and other data relative to these external workforce changes.

Much less has been researched and is known about internal mobility; that is, movement within the same organization. There are many reasons for an organization to want to reduce turnover and keep the same people working for the organization for long periods of time, and this is another area where HRD and HRU must work together through activities such as career planning.

One reason for people leaving an organization where they are functioning well is the lack of opportunity for internal movement. This is sometimes confused with a lack of opportunity for promotion, but not all internal movement is promotion. At higher levels of the organization, there is usually some kind of replacement schedule which is designed to bring about the orderly replacement of executives and managers. It is generally recognized that without some plan, the organization will find itself woefully short of needed leadership because of retirements, deaths, resignations, and other forms of attrition in the workforce. Once we leave the upper levels of the organization, it is often much more difficult to ascertain any plans for orderly movement of people through the organization.

There are organizations that do have good internal mobility plans, but they are too few in number. As a manager, you should look at your organization and find out if such a plan exists. If it does, how is it working, and how do the various human resource activities relate to the plan? If your organization does not have such a plan, it is important to determine what you are losing in its absence.

When the economy is expanding, there is a great deal of room for growth and internal mobility. When conditions are not so rosy, are you likely to lose significant people from your organization because they do not see any place to go? Why should they stay with your organization when there is no expansion, and therefore, perhaps, no movement for them? Part of your workforce will not want to move, and that is fine. People who are supervisors or managers tend to seek movement, which may be one reason they achieved that kind of job in the first place. Have you identified your best people? Do you want to keep them? Then what plans do you and other managers in your organization have for keeping these people: More pay is the usual response, and it is a good one. But it is not sufficient. A "good" employee is one who wants more pay, and the chance to make even more through accepting more responsibility. The good employee will likely also be seeking more opportunity and challenge. As a manager, you can meet these needs, for yourself and others, through carefully prepared HRD programs which have been coordinated with the HRU and HRE functions. You must be cautious not to allow the HRD program to raise expectations that your organization is not prepared to meet.

The question of HRD and internal mobility is a management decision. It pervades the entire organization, revolving around a very important managerial decision: Do you take a good employee who is producing well in the present job, and risk moving that employee to a new job where he may not perform as well? It is a risk decision, which is what managers are paid for. The risk can be minimized through a sound HRD program that will enable the employee to learn what is to be done on the future job before being placed there.

In large organizations, there is, of course, more room for internal mobility. But just moving employees around is not sufficient. There should be carefully evolved career plans for each employee at almost every level of the organization. The articulation between HRD and HRU is essential, with the complete support of management through significant management decisions.

Employee satisfaction

One of the elusive elements in the work situation is the search for job satisfaction. Numerous studies have focused on this area in attempts to understand what is meant by job satisfaction. It became of great concern during the early part of the 1970's, when, for one segment of the work population, it was referred to as "blue collar blues." This was dramatic, and gained much publicity in popular as well as professional journals. It also brought complaints from other parts of the workforce for increased attention to "white collar washouts".

Much of the research has shown that there is no direct relationship between job satisfaction and performance. Despite this, organizations spend significant sums of money, on a variety of activities, to promote job satisfaction. There are even organizations that use HRD programs to try to achieve job satisfaction! They design the HRD program to increase the happiness factor. Employees are sent to programs, not because they have specific learning objectives, but because it makes them feel good. Some managers use the off-the-ranch programs as an unrecorded the organization. For others, it provides a chance to get away at company expense.

When HRD is used in this fashion, it may have some effect on job satisfaction.

Going to one of the outside HRD programs can be considered a perk of the job to which one is entitled by virtue of reaching that position. Perks are fine, and are an essential part of the job, but when HRD is used by management to achieve job satisfaction, there can be disappointments for all concerned.

This should not be confused with the real need for certain kinds of programs to be conducted in plush facilities, with many amenities. This is a function of climate-setting, as part of the HRD experience. It is doubtful if this can be expected to really provide any job satisfaction, though, once the learner returns to the job.

There *are* aspects of HRD which can make a direct contribution to job satisfaction. One has been discussed earlier, showing how HRD can contribute to effective internal mobility. That can produce organization satisfaction, which is hard to distinguish from job satisfaction.

HRD experiences can also be provided to help the employee learn more about how his particular job contributes to organizational goals, product efficiency, and benefits to society. A manager should not expect HRD to take the place of job satisfaction, but HRD can certainly contribute to *increasing* satisfaction with the job.

Organizational goals

One aim of management is to have a high level of congruence between individual and organizational goals. HRD can be one management tool for producing this congruency, but it must be used very carefully. For example, in organizations that have unions, there is the possibility of violating federal laws if the organization and against the union. Such programs need not be eliminated, but should be designed to meet the goals of the organizations and the legal restrictions that might be involved.

HRD can be extremely useful to managers in reaching organizational goals. For most organizations, given technology and materials, there are constant changes in the way the work gets done. Old positions become obsolete and new positions open up. During the early 1970's, with the public clamour for environmental concerns, some organizations responded by creating new positions related to ecology. Unfortunately, too often they went outside the organization to fill such positions. With adequate HRD programs, these new positions could have been filled internally, by employees who had the interest but lacked the qualifications. The goal for meeting ecology needs had not been articulated with the goal for providing opportunities for those currently employed.

More dramatic is the experience of many organizations in endeavouring to comply with equal opportunity laws and regulations. Too many managers view this program as conflicting or competing with other organizational goals. Frequently, the problem is that the managerial decision regarding equal opportunity has not been related to other management decisions regarding HRD.

Let us follow through on a management decision to offer opportunities to minority group members in the organization—whether this was done to comply with the law or because of the value system of the manager. Playing "catch-up," HRD experiences were provided for some of these minority group members who lacked some of the necessary basic skills of communication and computation. The manager made a positive decision that one of the goals of the organizational was to provide compensatory learning for those who had been deprived at an earlier state of their lives.

Unfortunately, this HRD program was not coordinated with total organizational goals. The manager identified a group of employees who had benefited from the program and who were clamouring for the chance to use their new learning in higher level jobs. But the jobs weren't there.

What were the goals of the organization? Was the goal to provide compensatory learning situations, to encourage internal mobility in the organization, or to comply with equal opportunity laws? The activity was conducted, but the goals were not clear.

Quality of work life

A rapidly emerging concern is how to improve the quality of work life. In the present thinking, most of the activity in this area rests in HRU and HRE.

The quality of work life is concerned with the environment in which the employees have to work. This includes not only the physical environment, but also the psychological environment. It is involved with management providing opportunities for employees to have more control over how the work gets done, as long as standards are met.

One of the major evidences of this, at this time, is in the various kinds of flexitime work arrangements which have emerged. An employee, under this arrangement, can have more options. Picture a dreary morning, and the employee is turning over in bed, thinking, "Oh, if I could only sink back into the comfort of the covers and sleep for about another hour—then I would be ready to face the world." Under traditional arrangements, the employee has some limited options. One is to go back to sleep, wake up at some later time, and then call in sick. Another alternative is to struggle out of bed, go through the normal morning motions, and finally get to work.

Under flexitime, the employee could have another option, that of coming in two hours late, and then working two hours later that day. Sound simple? Of course it isn't, but it could be. HRD may be used to prepare back-ups all around so that flexitime does not affect production. Quality of work life is an increasing concern, and the above is only one example. It is still a bit early to clearly identify the range of managerial decisions which will have to be made, particularly those in the area of

HRD. It is included here as an indication of one of the areas where a manager should be exploring new work patterns and keeping in mind that the whole HRD program should be relating to the quality of work life at some point, somehow.

Human resources to match other resources

HRD can benefit the organization, if it is coordinated with how managers make use of other resources. Many examples can be given where the mismatch of human and other resources has proven costly to organizations. One of the most obvious is the experience of "out the back door and in the front door."

In a large organization, where resources are not being matched, employees can be fired or laid off because of changes in production, product lines, or shortage of materials. At the same time, another part of this large organization can be expanding and hiring new workers. This sounds ridiculous, and no competent manager would stand for such a costly arrangement. Yet, during the lay-offs of the 1973-1975 expression, this is exactly what was happening in quite a few companies.

In such a situation, it may not be possible to just take the workers who are due to be laid off and reassign them to other jobs. They probably lack the necessary skills. But this is where the manager can make a decision. It may be more costly, in direct expenditures, to provide HRD experiences for these workers, as contrasted with the cost of recruiting and selecting others. When measured only against direct costs, the "out the back doors in the front door" may look good. But what does this communicate to the workforce? How does this practice relate to the organizational image which managers are constantly striving to enhance?

On the positive side, this is an experience of one organization during the dark economic days of the early 1970's. Corning Glass recognized that they would have to lay off workers and that this could be traumatic for both the employees and the organization. They used their HRD activities to provide a two day workshop on company time. It was geared to helping the employees who were going to be laid off to make the necessary psychological and economic adjustments. The company reported that the workshop contributed to reducing tension in the whole organization. Corning did not promise any jobs, but conducting the workshop on company time and using company resources indicated that management has a concern for their employees. The limitation of resources that require the lay-offs was compensated for by providing increased resources to the HRD unit. This is a good example of how a management decision could be coupled with a management decision to provide appropriate HRD.

Training and development

Organizations of all forms, purposes, and sizes are faced today with the continuing problem of efficiently and effectively integrating employees into working environments, Implicit within this process is the notion that workers and managers must possess the skills and knowledge necessary in order to perform their functions in a satisfactory manner. The central role of employee training and development is to ensure that the human resources of an organization have, and will continue to have, the requisite abilities to perform the work that they have been given to do. Both individual and organizational benefits accrue as a result of systematically planning the training and development needs of the organization's work force. Although today (particularly in high technology and rapidly changing organizations and industries) keeping employee skills and knowledge commensurate with organizational demands is a monumental task, we are learning a good deal about translating work center needs into training and development activities. Additionally, over the past several decades we have managed to understand a considerable amount regarding how people learn and how this learning can be applied in a work setting.

Personnel departments and the training and development specialists within these departments have been given the responsibilities of determining the educational needs of an organization, designating the specific individuals or sets of individuals who would best benefit from educational experience, and designing and in many instances conducting the training. In other instances, personnel training and development specialists will serve as educational brokers for an organization and simply link employees with educational opportunities in the community outside an organization. Whatever the case, it seems clear that training and development of all members of the work force are quickly becoming very important responsibilities within the personnel field. In this chapter we explore not only conceptually what the meanings of training and development are to an organization, but additionally, what types of activities take place under the heading of employee education, the methods for evaluating the effectiveness of employee training and development, and how employee education relates to the overall performance of an organization.

Training will be viewed as a short-term educational process utilizing a planned, systematic, and organized procedure by which nonmanagerial personnel acquire the technical knowledge and skills necessary for increased effectiveness in achieving organizational goals. Development, on the other hand, in reference to staffing and personnel matters, will be viewed as a long-term educational process utilizing a planned and systematic procedure by which managerial personnel acquire conceptual and theoretical knowledge for enhancing general administrative abilities. Under these definitions, training and development differ in four ways: "what" is learned, "who" is learning, "why" such learning takes place, and "when" the learning occurs. Training courses are typically designed for a short-term, stated, set purpose, such as the operation of machinery, while development involves a broader education for long-run general purposes. Training is normally directed at nonmanagerial employees and relates to the technical aspects of doing a particular function, while development activities attempt to enhance a manager's or supervisor's abilities to understand and effectively implement theoretical and conceptual issues and aspects of jobs. It should be mentioned, however, that as clear distinctions between managerial and nonmanagerial employees become less frequent in work settings (this is particularly the case with staff personnel and technical workers), developmental activities will be directed at an ever-increasing percentage of the work force.

This portrayal is usually credited to Robert L. Katz who first presented these ideas in 1955. Nonmanagerial instructional needs are largely technical and not conceptual in nature. Managerial educational needs are generally conceptually and human relations oriented and are not technical in nature. In reality, however, the training and development concepts overlap because there are no clear-cut distinctions or lines of demarcation between and/or among technical, human relations, and conceptual skills.

Goals of training and development

There are many reasons why companies install employee training and management development programs. In general, the reasons for beginning an employee training program are similar to the purposes of initiating management development. These purposes concern (1) productivity, (2) quality, (3) human resource planning, (4) morale, (5) indirect compen-sation, (6) health and safety, (7) obsolescence prevention, and (8) personal growth. We will discuss each purpose briefly. Obsolescence prevention will be covered in greater detail because of its increasing importance.

Productivity

Training and development activities should apply not only to new employees but also to experienced people as well. Instruction can help employees increase their levels of performance in their present job assignments. Increased human performance often directly leads to increased operational productivity and increased company profits. Increased performance and productivity, because of training and development programs, are most evident with new employees who are not yet fully aware of the most efficient and effective ways of performing their jobs.

Quality

Properly designed and implemented training and development programs may also contribute to higher-quality output from the work force. Workers, who are better informed regarding the duties and responsibilities of their jobs and who have the requisite job knowledge and skills, are less likely to make costly errors in their work. Managers who are kept updated on the latest developments in administration are more likely to utilize managerial tactics that take maximum advantage of the multiple skills of the work force. As a result, quality increases naive be evidenced in the company's products or services and within the less tangible employment atmosphere of the organization.

Human resource planning

Proper employee training and development can help a company to fulfill its future personnel needs and requirements. Organizations that have a good internal educational program will have less drastic manpower changes and adjustments to make in the event of sudden personnel alterations. When the need arises, organizational vacancies can more easily be staffed from internal sources if a company initiates and maintains adequate instructional programs for both its nonsupervisory and managerial employees.

Morale

The general organizational climate and atmosphere are usually improved when proper educational programs exist within a company. There are many reasons for this. An endless chain of positive reactions can result from well-planned company instructional programs. For example, productivity and product quality may rise, financial incentives may then be increased, internal promotions become possible, less supervisory pressure is needed, and basepay rate increases result. These isolated events become a synergistic chain of mutually reinforcing activities. Increased morale may be due to many factors, but without a doubt one of the most important of these is the current state of an organization's educational endeavors.

Indirect compensation

Many workers, especially managers, consider educational opportunities part of the total employee-employer remuneration package. They expect the company to pay the bill for programs leading to increased general knowledge and skill expertise. Accordingly, many organizations offer special training and development programs as recruitment techniques to attract highly qualified potential employees. The effectiveness of such incentives in the future may come under serious question as the Internal Revenue Service moves in the direction of tightening Its regulations that consider such benefits as direct income and hence taxable at a fair market value. However, until this type of regulation occurs, indirect compensation in the form of educational benefits will continue to be a major incentive for an individual joining and remaining with a particular organization.

Health and safety

An employee's mental health and physical safety are often directly related to an organization's training and development efforts. Proper training can help prevent industrial accidents and a safer work environment can lead to more stable employee mental attitudes. Managerial mental states can also be improved if supervisors know that they can better themselves through company designed development programs.

Obsolescence prevention

Continuous employee training and development efforts are needed in order to keep workers abreast of the current improvements in their respective fields of work. Old skills and antiquated ideas may bankrupt an organization in the long run. Training and development programs foster employee initiative and creativity and thus help to prevent employee obsolescence. Just as proper planning and investment can reduce machinery obsolescence, the problem of antiquated employees can be at least partially alleviated through a continuous program of educational assessment.

Employee obsolescence may be defined as the discrepancy that exists between an employee's expertise and the demands of his or her job. Many employees lack the training and experience necessary for them to fulfill their work roles efficiently and effectively. Supervisors may be compatibly matched to their positions at one point in time, but jobs change and human personalities evolve at different rates so that people sometimes outgrow jobs and sometimes job outgrow people. Common causes of employee obsolescence include the lack of continuous training, insufficient human intellectual capacity, time constraints, environmental pressures, and cultural and societal alterations. However, the primary cause of employee obsolescence is technological change. Technological change may involve technique, tool, or process alterations. New statistical decision tools and the expanded use of the computer are two technological changes that are affecting production, marketing, finance, personnel, research, and other organizational capacities and capabilities. The accelerating pace of scientific and technological innovation is a continuing threat to an employee's knowledge, expertise, and employability. Every major technological advance threatens the relevance of human knowledge and experience. Managerial obsolescence is often analyzed by the concept of a "half life." The "halflife" idea describes the situation that exists when half of the relevant knowledge in a particular area or expertise has eroded away or become obsolete because of newer scientific innovations and discoveries. While historically such professions as law, medicine, and engineering have been most. Dramatically associated with the halflife concept, today we are beginning to recognize the appropriateness of managerial/supervisorial half-life. Changes in labour legislation, the necessity to store and process vast amounts of historical business data, and the ever-changing composition of the work force individually and collectively provide clear examples of areas worthy of continual managerial updating and education.

Individual adaptability also affects employee obsolescence. Motivation, temperament, and age are basic factors involved in individual obsolescence. Self-actualization, self-development, and self-determination are also crucial variables influencing a person's ability and willingness to adapt. New career paths are always available to the worker who is constantly ready to learn new skills in order to advance him or herself. Promotional inducements have always served to enhance individual coping efforts. Employee audits, job vacancies, new positions, and announced upcoming educational and training opportunities are other organizational inducements.

Employee obsolescence can be controlled through continuing and sophisticated attention to the forecasting of human resource needs, monitoring technological changes in terms of employment impact, and alerting individuals to opportunities as well as to the hazards of technical change. The challenges presented by technological change can only be met through personal supportive relationships, structured organizational training or development, and other programs that bring the full resources of an enterprise to bear on the problems of employee obsolescence.

The relationship of education in general to the more narrow concepts of development, training, and learning. Education is the broadest instructional concept and learning is the most specific of these instructional processes, with development and training falling between these two extremes. Instruction within organizations is moving from the idea of training to development and eventually on to education. This movement progresses from specific job skills to wider organizational concepts and even, at best, includes general personal enlightenment. Although most organizations have not reached the stage where educating employees is done purely for worker self-actualization, there has been at least the beginning of a movement toward this end. Immediately after World War 11, managers began to think of the immense training task that had been accomplished during the war. From this experience arose a new sense of the importance of employees and their potential if they are properly trained and/or educated. For the first time, the idea developed that education and training should be thought of as investments in human resources, or even as capital investment. The next step was to measure the rate of return on this investment. This measurement task, however, was and still is quite complex. Such measurement attempts are called human asset accounting. Human asset accounting shows the value of an organization's human resources on the actual company balance sheet. The education (training and development) of personnel should today be considered as a long-term capital investment of an organization. Historically the investment made in training and development programs was considered as a short-term financial expense, much the same as plant maintenance and advertising. The expectation was that an investment in an educational training program would result in an immediate return on the company's investment. A more contemporary perspective recognizes the fact that employees are human assets of an organization, and similar to other assets, they need a reinvestment in them from time to time in order to keep them properly maintained and performing in a productive manner. Employees, much the same as plant and equipment, may lose their productive capabilities over time and may become obsolete. To guard against this employee obsolescence problem, management in general and the personnel function in particular must continually evaluate the training and development needs of an organization and design and implement educational programs accordingly.

A considerable portion of conventional wisdom with regard to management in general and the quality of work life and job redesign in particular has stressed the notion that employees may be drastically underutilized by most organizations. The general theme here is that workers, if given the proper development and work environment, are capable of considerably greater performance than what they are non normally called on to do. Employees possess untapped intellectual and skill reservoirs that if properly developed can serve as a vast human resource for an organization. Training and development activities may be precisely the key to unlocking this untapped potential.

Throughout the American economy and society, a changed attitude toward education is taking place. Instead of educating an elite group, learning and instruction are meant for the entire populace. Instead of thinking about going to school for a fixed number of years and feeling that this is a terminal education, the idea of continuing education is a reality. Instead of trying to cram everything a person needs to know for the rest of his or her life into a limited number of years while he or she is young, the notion of returning to school from time to time throughout one's life is now evident. Many large U.S. corporations such as IBM encourage employees to take educational leaves of absence and to return to school for additional technical and administrative training. Many other organizations promote ongoing education activities through tuition subsidies and in-house training programs.

Lifelong process

Within any work organization, employee education must be a continuing process. Assembly line workers must be trained and retrained as new automated equipment is introduced. Technicians must attend seminars and conferences to keep abreast of the latest technical developments in their fields. Managers must attend workshops and extension courses to learn the latest planning and organizing techniques. The idea of lifelong education is frightening to many people, but it is now an economic and social fact of life. Those who do not accept this concept usually find it difficult to adjust to and cope with our fast-moving, constantly changing, achievement-oriented American style of life. The modern human resource manager must accept the concept of lifelong learning, and a good portion of his or her time and effort involves establishing procedures and methods for dealing with and implementing this idea within the organization.

As an indication of the importance placed on continuing education over the past several decades, the federal government has established a number of vocationally related educational programs. Additionally, public funds have supported the development of vocational training schools and collegiate level training in law, medicine, education, and business. As early as 1917, under the guidelines of the Smith-Hughes Act, federal support became available for high school courses in agriculture, the trades, and home economics. Later, in 1946, as a result of the passage of the George-Barden Act, this program was provided additional support through the allocation of even more resources.

During World War II a number of specialized training programs sought to provide workers with the skills necessary to ensure the production of war goods. Such federally supported projects as the Training Within Industry program attempted to overcome the problems associated with shortages of certain skills. Following the Korean War the National Defense Education Act of 1958 provided federal support for educating skilled workers in essential defense industries.

Symbolic of public regarding education are the stated intentions of the Manpower Development and Training Act (MDTA) of 1962 and the Vocational Education Act of 1963. The former made it the obligation of the Secretary of Labor to search for and identify skill and capability needs in our economy as well as to initiate and financially support the special educational programs thus prescribed. The latter act initiated the updating of vocational education throughout the nation to attune such programs to present and prospective demands for specialized competence. MDTA programs have been modified and amended by other federal program, such as the War on Poverty, Neighborhood Youth Corps, Job Cops, and especially by the Job Opportunities in the Business Section program (JOBS) of 1967. Many of the original provisions contained within MDTA are now provided for by the Comprehensive Employment and Training Act (CETA) of 1973, which has superseded MDTA.

Although any consensus about the future is not totally clear, some observers believe that public policy can be expected to support a much wider range or educational programs and to provide more financial support in the years ahead. Reasons for this include the growing economic significance of educational attainment and the raid pace of technological change. The shape of things to come and suggestions as to the future of public policy may be seen in the proposed Human Investment Act. This measure, first introduced in Congress in 1965, proposed to grant a tax adjustment for training costs, other than for managerial and professional training, thus encouraging apprenticeship, job training, and MDTA programs. Joseph Yaney, in his Current Issues contribution to this chapter, discusses a number of the social indicators of the 1980s that lead to the conclusion that the education of the American work force will continue to receive increasing attention during the coming decades.

The beginning of education, development, and training is rooted within the learning process. Today there is an emphasis on then learning process itself. Models of human learning are being studied in order to determine why some individuals seem to learn at a faster rate than others. The environmental conditions of the learner and the resources or learning are also being evaluated. Some environmental conditions seem to foster learning, while others hinder it. Human and physical variables are being analyzed in an effort to arrive at a set of general learning principles.

Learning theories concentrate on "how" an individual learns instead of "what" he or she learns. From such studies, learning cycle models similar to life cycle models have resulted. Human learning, like human growth, seems to advance rapidly at some points, to level off at others, and to decline eventually in still other periods. The reasons and conditions for such phenomena are the focal point of learning analysis.

Such research is important because knowing how a person learns can assist individuals, groups, and organizations in specific skill training and general educational development.

Learning concepts and theories are relatively new concerns for organizations, but these concepts are based on firmly rooted and well-grounded educational and psychological principles. We cannot deal with all of the details and developments of teaching-learning theory here, but some of the most significant aspects of current learning theory are listed to serve as a behavioral foundation for the study of current personnel administration practices related to the training and development function.

1. All human beings can learn. Individuals of all ages and of various intellectual capacities have the ability to learn new behaviors.
2. An individual must be motivated to learn. This motivation may exist in a variety of forms, such as self-actualization, promotional possibilities, or financial incentives. However, the best learning motivation is self-motivation.
3. Learning is active, not passive. Effective education requires action and involvement from all participants.
4. Learners may acquire knowledge more rapidly with guidance. Feedback is necessary because trial and error are too time consuming and inefficient.
5. Appropriate materials should be provided. Educators should possess a reasonable repertoire of training tools and materials, such as cases, problems, discussion questions, and readings.
6. Time must be provided to practice the learning. Part of the learning process requires a great deal of time for student internalization, assimilation, testing, acceptance, and confidence.
7. Learning methods should be varied. Variety should be introduced to offset fatigue and boredom.
8. The learner should secure satisfaction from the learning. Education must fulfill human needs, desires, and expectations,
9. Learners need reinforcement of correct behavior. Positive and immediate rewards reinforce and cement desired behaviors.
10. Standards of performance should be set for the learner. Goals or bench marks should be established so that individuals can judge their educational achievements and progress.
11. Different levels of learning exist. Learning may involve awareness, changed attitudes, or changed behavior. Some learning involves mental processes, while other instructional activities concentrate on physical maneuvers. Different time and method requirements are needed to bring about different levels of learning.

12. Learning is an adjustment on the part of an individual. Actual learning represents a change in a person, and all changes require adjustments.
13. Individual differences play a large part in the effectiveness of the learning process. What can be learned easily by some individuals may be very difficult for others because of differences in basic abilities or cultural backgrounds.
14. Learning is a cumulative process. An individual's reaction in any lesson is conditioned and modified by what has been learned in earlier lessons and experiences.
15. Ego involvement is widely regarded as a major factor in learning. Each participant learns most when he or she sees the training opportunity as related to the attainment of personal goals.
16. The rate of learning decreases when complex skills are involved. Simple skills can be learned easier and quicker than complex activities.
17. Learning is closely related to attention and concentration. The learning process is more effective if distractions are avoided.
18. Learning involves both the immediate acquisition and the long-term retention of knowledge. Retention is encouraged by initial understanding, emphasizing, and repeating.
19. There are upward spurts of understanding followed by plateaus in the curve of learning. New knowledge is always gathered in a sporadic fashion.
20. Accuracy generally deserves more emphasis than speed during the learning process. Speed can be improved, but accuracy is more difficult to control.
21. The law of effect states that a particular response becomes more certain the more often it occurs. In other words, repetition tends fix the response or adjustment.
22. Sleep affects learning. Sleeping immediately following a learning experience often improves retention.
23. Learning should be reality based. Education should be highly related to the learner's life experiences.
24. Learning should be goal oriented. Specific purposes and rewards affiliated with the learning effort generally enhance educational attainment endeavors.

From such educational principles and research findings, many management training and development guidelines and adages have emerged. A number of these guidelines and the specific training and development programs they have fostered will be discussed in a latter section of this chapter and in Professor Yaney's Current Issues contribution.

Supervisory responsibility

After policy and planning matters have been decided, the training and development responsibility burden shifts largely to all managers/supervisors. Once the educational program has been established, usually the implementation or application of the program depends on the effort of managers who are either training or developing, their subordinates. No instructional program can succeed without the supportive backing of an organization's managers. They are the ones who serve as the direct training link to the employees. Putting an educational plan, or any other program for that matter, into effect depends ultimately on the cooperative efforts of an organizations supervisors and managers. Operative managers and supervisors must be able to envision the potential return on their time and energy investments if educational program support is to be effective throughout an organization.

Employee responsibility

Some training and development responsibilities also rest with the employees or trainees themselves. It often has been said that ultimately all learning and all education is self-instruction. Without the proper worker attitude or frame of reference, even well-planned and effectively implemented training and development efforts may still fail. Employee motivation, trust, loyalty, and other factors indirectly influence worker receptiveness to training. Virtually all employees have the capacity or ability to be trained, but not all of them possess the willingness to be so developed. Thus, some of the educational responsibility for training and development must be envisioned as vested within the employees themselves. This responsibility when assumed is usually expressed in the forms of feedback and Proposed training and development program revisions. The four basic organizational educational program Constituents with their ultimate respective training and development responsibilities. The starting point for the development and conducting of an employee educational effort begins with the systematic assessment of the training and/or developmental needs of the unit under concern. In some instances the object of the educational training program may be the entire organization. Employee orientation programs and the indoctrination of the work force with regard to health insurance and related benefits are examples of the areas of employee education that have bearing on all the employees of an organization. On the other hand, specific units of the organization may have unique interests that are local to a particular work setting or problem area. For example, certain training in the area of employee health and safety may only affect workers in the production facility of the plant. Finally, employee educational needs may be limited to a particular individual member of the work force. Generally, this type of training is discussed under the heading of performance appraisal, counseling, or coaching and is normally conducted by the direct supervisor of the individual in question. Regardless of the scope of the training/development effort, each need must be systematically assessed.

Determining organizational needs

Assessing organizational needs with regard to training and development normally begins with a company's overall goals and objectives. Once the corporate officers have established the overall direction of the business, and it has been determined that company_ in adequacies or shortcomings exist, then it is possible to construct training and development programs. Again, company needs and the subsequent educational programs that are developed normally relate to problems that concern the entire organization. For example, if management recognizes that effective leadership both at the supervisory and mid-management levels in the organization is an essential ingredient but in short supply internally, the organization may decide to invest in a management development program to address this problem. The solution may involve both classroom instruction and on the job problem solving. In this instance, the design of a management development program began with two sets of organizational data: (1) it was clear that effective management would be critical in the years ahead, and (2) it was assessed that the current leadership was inadequate for facing the problems of the future.

Determining unit needs

In determining specific unit needs, the nature of the task(s) under consideration becomes important. In such instances it may be clear that in order to redesign an existing production setting new machinery and methods will be required. Concurrently with the redesign of the production facility, existing employees must be given the skills and techniques necessary in order to run the machines and to facilitate the production process. In this instance the beginning point of determining the training needs of the work force is not with the goals of the organization, but rather with the requirements of the new production system. Additionally, the determination of the requisite skills inventory for the work force is important. With these data the design of the training program may be accomplished.

Determining employee needs

The most difficult but possibly the most important type of training and development assessment relates to the individual employee. As mentioned earlier, a major portion of this determination rests with the supervisor. A manager must realistically assess the attributes and weaknesses of his or her employees on a daily basis. Employee work related development is largely the immediate supervisor's responsibility. To aid in this assessment, the supervisor is normally provided with some type of routine performance appraisal information as well as his or her own intuitive judgment of worker performance. From these data the supervisor or manager should provide feedback, direction, and counseling to subordinates. Without this process taking place, a major portion of the developmental needs of individual employees will go unaddressed.

Training methods

Earlier it was stated that training is a short-term educational process utilizing a planned, systematic, and organized procedure by which non-managerial personnel acquire the technical knowledge and skills necessary for increased effectiveness in accomplishing organizational goals. This section deals with the methods used to bring about training and the next major chapter section deals with development methods. There are a number of commonly used training methods including (1) on the job, (2) vestibule, (3) demonstration and example, (4) simulation, (5) apprenticeship, (6) classroom methods, and (7) other training, methods. The particular training methods used depends on considerations of time, cost, effort, availability, instructor, preferences, the number of persons to be trained, the depth of knowledge required, the background of the trainees, and many other factors.

On the Job

Most training is of the "on the job" variety. Some estimates are that at least 90 percent of all job knowledge is acquired through on the job training. It is hard io' 'pinpoint exactly what procedures and techniques constitute on the job training, Some of these procedures are informal and haphazard while others are formal and systematic. Simple observation and practice, which are informal techniques, are two of the greatest sources of on-the-job training knowledge. A person may learn his or her, job simply by watching others doing it and then eventually copying these observed behaviors. Other aspects of on the job training may be much more formal. A senior employee may be assigned to a new employee to help "break him or her in" on the proper way to run a certain machine.

The primary responsibility for on the job training rests with ail employee's immediate supervisor. Unfortunately, on the job training is too often envisioned as a burden instead of a necessity. The on the job training function is a role that all supervisors should be taught to perform competently and sympathetically. It is the job of the personnel department to see to it that supervisors are adequately trained so that they can in turn be responsible for the on the job training of their subordinates,

On-the-job training is most appropriate for teaching knowledge and skills that can be learned within a few days or a few weeks. Only a few trainees should be going through on-the-job training at the same time for the same job. The most common types of jobs in which on-the-job training is used are unskilled or semiskilled in nature, such as clerical jobs or sales work. The main advantage of on-the-job training is that the trainee learns on the actual equipment and in the real environment of his or her job. The main drawback of this training method is that it is often highly disorganized and not Properly supervised.

Vestibule

As a training method, the vestibule technique is comprised of a school or workshop, usually organized in an industrial. Plant to introduce new workers into the work setting by means of a few weeks of practice for a specific job, at a separate and generally isolated area of the plant. Vestibule training is often done in a classroom setting for the purpose of teaching semiskilled production and clerical routines. This method is most appropriate when many new employees are being trained for the same kind of work at the same time. Although an attempt is made to duplicate the actual material, equipment, and conditions that will later be found in the real work situation, during the vestibule training period, emphasis is placed on learning instead of production. This training often deals, at, least somewhat, with theory as well as practice. The type of skills being learned usually take from a few days to a few months to acquire. Examples of the types of jobs that are often learned through a vestibule school training method include typists, testers, clerks, bank tellers, machine operators, and inspectors.

Demonstration and example

Demonstration learning involves describing and displaying a, skill through the use of experiments or examples. Often the easiest and most direct way for managers to teach employees how to do something is for the supervisors to actually perform the activities themselves, and to go through a step-by-step explanation of "why" and "how" they are doing the job. Demonstrations are a very effective training method for lower level and repetitive jobs for a number of reasons. One reason is ' because of all the senses, sight is one of the best for learning. Most demonstrations, however, are usually combined with other learning aids including lectures, pictures, text materials, and discussions. Demonstration seems especially appropriate as a training technique, but it may also be used for managerial development purposes.

Simulation

A simulated learning situation is an imitation of reality. In reference to training, a simulation is any kind of equipment or technique that duplicates as nearly as possible the actual conditions encountered on a job. The vestibule training method described earlier is a popular form of simulation. The numerous varieties of the now popular business gaming technique are also in essence business simulations. The idea of simulation involves a physical as well as a mental replication of actual conditions. Life-size models of objects are commonly included. Simulation is usually a very expensive training technique, but it is useful or even necessary Where actual on-the-job practice could result in a serious injury, a costly error, or the destruction of valuable company materials or resources.. Typically, training interest and employee motivation are both high in simulation exercises because the trainee actions taken closely duplicate real world conditions.

Apprenticeship

The apprenticeship training method is a way of developing skilled workers that historically evolved as a descendant of the craft guild system of the Middle Ages. An apprentice is any learner or beginner who is usually bound by a legal agreement to serve in a certain position or capacity for a fixed period of time in order to learn a trade or business. Such training historically was on the job in nature and lasted usually for seven years. In 1937 Congress passed the Fitzgerald Act and new apprenticeship standards were formalized. All apprentices must now be at least 16 years of age. Work experience must now be supplemented with at least 144 hours of trade related classroom instruction per year. Apprentices are now paid on a program that features a progressively increasing schedule of wages. Proper supervision and periodic evaluation are also required within any modern apprenticeship system.

Apprenticeable trades today are those requiring at least 4000 hours (two years) of training experience. Over 300 skilled occupations today have apprenticeship training programs. Although the time period of apprenticeship varies from two to seven years, most programs take four or five years to complete. Apprenticeship programs in various trades are normally administered by committees constituted of both organized labour and management members. These committees establish the criteria by which applicants are admitted into a program, regulate the content of the various programs and review general program guidelines with regard to compliance with established government standards.

The apprenticeship systems in this country do not conform to standard format. Within general guidelines and due to the fact that federal regulations with regard to apprenticeship programs are minimal, employers may operate apprenticeship programs according to specific organizational needs. Thus, journeymen of different caliber are commonly found within the apprenticeable trades. The apprenticeship system permits a continuous supply of highly skilled employees to be continuously introduced into the overall industrial system. Today trainees receive decent wages while learning and later acquire a specialized skill that often commands a wage rate greater than that earned by beginning professional employees. Although the apprenticeship training periods are extended in length, the eventual financial rewards are great enough to attract an abundance of beginners into nearly all of the apprenticeable trades. Many large domestic corporations, such as the Chryslter Corporation and the Ford Motor Company, operate extensive apprenticeship programs in a number of vocational areas. As skilled workers become in greater demand, a projection which has been made for the next several decades, more and more large corporations will find it increasingly necessary to develop their own apprenticeship programs.

Classroom methods

A considerable amount of organizational training that takes place today uses conventional classroom methods of instruction. In many instances, these classroom methods are used in actual classroom locations. However, an alternative setting might be the shop floor or an actual work area. Although there is considerable controversy regarding the effectiveness of traditional classroom methods of instruction, the current lack of more effective pedagogical techniques leads to the use and reuse of conventional teaching methodologies. Certain aspects of all jobs are more easily learned in the classroom than on the job. This is especially true if philosophy, concepts, attitudes, theories,' and problem solving abilities must be learned. Technical, professional, and managerial personnel are examples of positions where trainees are expected to acquire a considerable depth of knowledge during a training period. The classroom methods that the authors will discuss in detail are lecture and programmed or computer assisted instruction,

Lecture

A lecture is a discourse delivered aloud for instructional purposes. Lectures are formal, organized talks on specific subjects. Lecturing permits a topic to be presented in a systematic, organized, and rigorous fashion. The main advantage of the lecture method, however, is that it can be used for very large groups and thus the cost per trainee is low. Nevertheless, the lecture method is increasingly criticized today as an instructional technique for a number of reasons. Trainees or learners are passive instead of active; only one-way communication is involved; little feedback from the audience takes place; lecturing violates the concept of learning by doing; presentations must be geared to a common level of knowledge; lecturing tends to stress the accumulation and memorization of facts and figures; and lectures do not stress the application of knowledge. Because of these disadvantages, it is usually recommended that the lecture technique be combined with other instructional methods so as to at least partially alleviate the aforementioned shortcomings.

Programmed and computer-assisted instruction

Programmed instruction involves a sequence of steps set up, often through the control panels of an electronic computer, as guides in the performance of a desired operation or group of operations. Programmed instruction incorporates prearranged, proposed, or desired plans or courses of proceedings related and pertaining to the learning or acquisition of some specific skill or general knowledge. Programmed instruction can be carried out through a book, manual, computer, or teaching machine.

Programmed instruction involves breaking information down into meaningful subunits and then arranging these segments in a proper way to form a logical and sequential learning program or package. Programmed and Computer-assisted instruction will continue to experience increased popularity as training needs expand and computer technology becomes less expensive. Large, medium, and small-sized businesses will all be using programmed and Computer-assisted instruction more and more. The major advantages of programmed instruction are as follows: students learn at their own pace; the material to be learned is broken down into small units; immediate feedback is available; active learner participation takes place; individual differences can be taken into account; and training can be done at odd times and in odd places. The main disadvantages of programmed learning are the impersonality of the instructional setting, the fact that advanced study cannot occur until preliminary information is learned, only factual subject matters can be programmed, philosophical and attitudinal concepts along with motor skills cannot be taught through this methodology, and the cost of creating any such program and purchasing the necessary hardware and materials may be considerable.

Other training methods

It is virtually impossible to identify and explain comprehensively all the various training techniques and methods used in employee education. Various types and combinations of classes, seminars, lectures, short courses, and the like are provided for rank-and-file and supervisory personnel. In some instances these course are offered exclusive of college credit and in other instances such credit is provided. In either case, the instruction may be provided at a college or university facility, a resort, a company itself, or some other location. These training efforts may take place during the regular workday or may be scheduled in the evening or on weekends. The variety of training methods is almost unlimited in scope and format. However, the intention is clearly to provide employees meaningful training experiences that will meet the needs of the organization and be productive and acceptable experiences to the participants.

ENCYCLOPAEDIA

OF

MODERN MANAGEMENT TECHNIQUES

ENCYCLOPAEDIA OF MODERN MANAGEMENT TECHNIQUES

Volume 3

Edited by
A. K. Chaudhary

ANMOL PUBLICATIONS PVT. LTD.
NEW DELHI-110 002 (INDIA)

ANMOL PUBLICATIONS PVT. LTD.
4374/4B, Ansari Road, Daryaganj
New Delhi-110 002

Encyclopaedia of Modern Management Techniques

First Edition 1999
ISBN 81-261-0321-3 (Set)

PRINTED IN INDIA

Published by J. L. Kumar for Anmol Publications Pvt. Ltd., New Delhi-110 002 and Printed at Mehra Offset Press, Delhi.

Contents

10

Investment Appraisal and Risk Analysis

Any investment involves the outlay of resources at one point in time in anticipation of receiving a larger return at some time in the future. This return must repay the original outlay, as well as providing a minimum annual rate of return on that outlay. If an individual invests Rs.100 in a building society, he will expect to receive that Rs.100 back at some future time, along with compound interest thereon. This is a typical investment situation. The aim will usually be to secure the maximum net cash flow from the investment and this will be achieved only from investments having the highest rate of interest of those available.

Characteristically, a capital investment decision involves largely irreversible commitment of resources that is generally subject to a significant degree of risk. Such decisions have far-reaching effects on a company's profitability and flexibility over the long-term, thus requiring that they be part of a carefully developed strategy that is based on reliable forecasting procedures.

Typical examples of capital budgeting topics are:

(a) expansion projects;

(b) replacement projects;

(c) selection among alternatives; and

(d) buy or lease decisions.

Projects for analysis and appraisal do not just appear—a continuing stream of good investment opportunities results from hard thinking, careful planning, and often from large outlays on R & D. Replacement decisions are ordinarily the simplest to make, as the firm will have a very good idea of the cost savings to be obtained by replacing an old asset, along with the consequences of non-replacement. (A central problem is that of accurately predicting the revenues and costs associated with particular projects for many years into the future). Over-investment in capital assets will result in have fixed costs, whereas under-investment may mean:

(a) a company's equipment is not sufficiently modern to enable it to produce competitively; or

(b) it has inadequate capacity to maintain its share of a growing market.

Good capital budgeting decisions, based on sound investment appraisal procedures, should improve the timing of capital acquisitions as well as the quality of capital acquisitions.

Investment is one of the main sources of economic growth, since it is required not only to increase the total capital stock of equipment and buildings, but also to employ labour in increasingly productive jobs as old plant is replaced by new. The application of reliable means of appraising investment proposals brings out more systematically and reliably the advantages on investing in new plant and machinery where it will increase efficiency, and thus help to secure faster growth.

Various criticisms have been put forward in relation to the methods of appraisal that many companies employ. Among the most important are:

1. Although most companies only make investment decisions after careful consideration of the likely costs and benefits as they see them, these decisions are often reached in ways that are unlikely to produce the pattern or level of investment that is most favourable to economies growth—or even most profitable to the company.
2. Many companies apply criteria for a assessing investment projects that have little relevance to the measurement of the expected rate of return on capital invested (ROI).
3. Even though a calculation of the ROI of each project may be made, the methods used vary widely and are sometimes so arbitrary as to give almost meaningless results. (For instance, a failure to assess returns *after* tax is a frequent weakness of many widely used methods, since alternative opportunities can only be effectively compared and appraised on an after-tax basis.)

This faulty use of means of investment appraisal may result in over-cautious investment decisions in which too high a rate of return is demanded before the equipment is installed. This causes delay in economic growth. Alternatively, faulty methods may mean that investment decisions are made that result in the selection of projects that yield an unduly low ROI. This causes a waste of scarce capital resources, which is also unfavourable to economic growth.

From an information flow point of view, the use of inadequate means of investment appraisal results in a damaging restriction in the flow of information to top management, since these methods are incapable of fully exploiting relevant data. Because a company's future is inextricably linked to its investments, poor methods that give poor information that leads to poor decisions are likely to result in many mistakes.

Realistic investment appraisal requires the financial evaluation of many factors, such as the choice of size, type, location, and timing of investments, giving due consideration to the effects of taxation and alternate forms of financing (or *funding*) the outlays. This shows that project decisions are difficult on account of their complexity and their strategic significance.

The individuality of projects, coupled with technological developments, often means that past experience is of limited value, and the existence of competitors will usually mean that cash flows must be accurately estimated so as to secure adequate but not excessive profit margins.

To aid financial evaluation, investment projects should be broken down into stages, and the time and resources required for the completion of each stage assessed. The sum of the requirements of each stage is the total required investment. Complications arise because of the large number of possible factor combinations, but management science techniques can lead to the best solution. Computer simulation is invaluable on account of the many different possible outcomes that should be considered for any individual project.

No matter which technique is adopted for investment appraisal, the same steps will need to be followed. These steps are:

(a) determine the profitability of each proposal;

(b) rank the proposals in accordance with their profitability;

(c) determine the *cut-off rate;*

(d) determine which projects are acceptable and which unacceptable in relation to the cut off rate; and

(e) select the most profitable proposals in accordance with the constraints of the company's capital budget.

Cash flows

In considering investment decisions, it does not matter whether outlays are termed 'capital' or 'revenue', nor whether inflows are termed 'profit', 'depreciation', 'tax allowance,' or whatever. All outlays and income must be taken into account.

Cash flow in this context is not the same as the cash flow through a bank account, nor is it identical to accounting profit, since changes in the latter can occur without any change taking place in the cash flow.

For purposes of investment appraisal, the cash flow is the incremental cash receipts *less* the incremental expenditures solely attributable to the investment in question.

The future costs and revenues associated with each investment alternative are:

1. *Capital costs*: These cover (a) the long-term capital outlays necessary to finance a project, and (b) working capital. Typically additional working capital will be required to cover a higher inventory, or a larger number of debtors, and to be worthwhile the project must earn a return on this capital as well as on the long-term capital.
2. *Operating costs.*
3. *Revenue.*
4. *Depreciation:* In the case of the discounting methods of appraisal, the recovery of capital is automatically allowed for from the net cash flow, so depreciation need not be included as an accounting provision. This has the important advantage that the discounting profitability assessment is not affected by the pattern of accounting depreciation chosen.
5. *Residual value.* As with working capital, the residual assets of the project may have a value. This residual value should be included with the net cash flow.

An investment decision implies the choice of an objective, a technique of appraisal, and a length of service—the project's life. The objective and technique must be related to a definite period of time. In a static world, that period would quite naturally be taken as being equal to the physical life of the asset that is the purpose of the investment, which would be known with a good deal of certainty on the basis of past experience. However, in a dynamic world, the life of the projects may be determined by:

(a) technological obsolescence; or

(b) physical deterioration; or

(c) a decline in demand for the output of the project—such as a change in taste away from the product manufactured.

No matter how good a company's maintenance policy, its technological forecasting ability, or its demand foresting ability, uncertainty will always be present because of the difficulty of predicting the length of project's life.

The actual assessment of a project's profitability is a team exercise in which the expertise of the economist, the market researcher, the engineer, and the controller must all be brought together. The outcome of their collaboration will be a forecast of the cash flow over a period of years. If this period is incorrectly estimated, the whole analysis will be wrong—or at least grossly inaccurate.

As a rule, in investment appraisal, one of two assumptions is adopted: either the cash flow is assumed to be known with certainty, or the best estimate is used. The assumption of certainty is generally unacceptable, so allowance must be made for the risk inherent in the proposed adoption of the 'best' estimate. To the expected outcome.

Probabilities can be attached to sales, costs, and other elements of the investment proposal to allow for risk.

The application of risk analysis enables management to answer the following questions: (1) What is the profitability resulting from given estimates of costs and revenues from the project, if they are achieved? and (2) What is the likelihood of such estimates being achieved?

This then enables top management to concentrate on those factors that are critical to the financial success of the project, such as selling price, sales volume, capital cost, and so forth.

Time value of money

To permit realistic appraisal, the value of a cash payment or receipt must be related to the time when the transfer takes place. In particular, it must be recognized that Re.1 received today is worth more than Re. 1 receivable at some future date, because Re. 1 received today could be earning interest in the intervening period. This is the concept of the *time value of money.*

To illustrate this, if Rs.100 was invested today at 5 per cent per annum compound interest, it would accumulate to Rs 105 at the end of one year (i.e. Rs. 100 X Rs. 1.05), to Rs. 110.25 at the end of two years (i.e. Rs. 100 X Rs. 1.05 X Rs. 1.05, or Rs. 105 X Rs. 1.05), and so on. In other words, Rs. 110.25 receivable in two year's time is only worth Rs. 100 today is 5 per cent per annum can be earned in the meantime (i.e. 110.25/ (1.05 X 1.05) = 100).

The process of concerting future sums into their present equivalents is known as *discounting,* which is simply the opposite of *compounding.* Compounding is used to determine the *future value of present* cash flows. Whereas discounting is used to determine the *present value of future* cash flows another example will clarify this future. An investor who can normally obtain 8 per cent on his investments is considering whether or not to invest in a project that gives rise to 388 at the end of each of the next three years.

If the investment's capita cost is less than the present value of its returns, say Rs. 800 then it should be accepted, since the present value of the return of this outlay is a larger amount. The gain is the *net present value* of the investment. The interest rate does not always relate to an outlay of cash, as the concept of interest applies equally to the use of internal funds. The reason why interest must be considered on *all* funds in use, regardless of their source, is that the selection of one alternative necessarily commits funds that could otherwise be invested in some other alternative. The measure of interest in such cases is the return foregone by rejecting the alternative use.

Financial evaluation

The stages of financial evaluation are essentially;

(a) the development of a financial standard against which to judge individual proposals; and

(b) the use of a technique to rate and rank each project in terms of its profitability, acceptability, and desirability.

Traditional methods of evaluation

(a) *The payback period* is the most widely used technique, and can be defined as the number of years required to recover the cost of the investment. This is easy to calculate, but is often calculated before tax, and always after accounting depreciation. By definition, the payback period ignores income beyond this period, and it can thus be seen to be more a measure of liquidity than of profitability. In addition, it fails to take account of the time value of money and these limitations make it seriously defective in the aim of reflecting the relative financial attractiveness of projects.

Projects with long payback periods are characteristically those involved in long-range planning, and which determine a firm's future. However, they may not yield their highest returns for a number of years and the result is that the payback method is biased against the very investments that are most important to long-term success.

(b) *Average rate of return* is defined as the profit from the project (after allowing for accounting depreciation but before tax) as a percentage of the required investment. (This investment base is sometimes the initial investment, and sometimes the average investment over the project's life.)

This method is superior to the payback period, but is fundamentally unsound. While it does take account of the earnings over the entire economic life of a project, it fails to take account of the time value of money. This weakness is made worse by the failure to specify adequately the relative attractiveness of alternative proposals. It is biased against short-term projects in the same way that payback is biased against longer term ones.

These traditional methods of investment appraisal are misleading to a dangerous extent. A means of measuring *cash* against *cash* that allows for the importance of time is needed. This is provided by the discounting methods of appraisal, of which there are basically two, both of which meet the objections to the payback period and average rate of return methods.

Discounting methods of evaluation

Both discounting methods relate the estimates of the annual cash outlays on the investment to the annual net of tax cash receipt generated by the investment. As a general rule, the net of tax cash flow will be composed of revenue less taxes, *plus* depreciation. Since discounting techniques automatically allow for the recoupment of the capital outlay in computing time-adjusted rates of return, it follows that depreciation provisions implicitly form part of the cash inflow.

(a) *Time-adjusted rate of return* (also known as 'internal rate of return', and 'discounted cash flow') method consists of finding that rate of discount that reduces the cash flows (both inflows and outflows) attributable to an investment project to zero—this being, in principle, the true rate of return. (In other words, this 'true' rate is that which exactly equalizes the net cash proceeds over a project's life with the initial investment outlay.)

If the time-adjusted rate of return exceeds the financial standard (i.e. cost of capital), then the project is *prima facie* acceptable.

Instead of being computed on the basis of the average or initial investment, the time-adjusted rate of return is based on the funds in use from period to period.

The actual calculation of the rate is a hit- and-miss exercise because the rate is unknown at the outset, but tables of present values are available to aid the analyst. These tables show the present value of future sums at various rates of discount and are prepared for both single sums and recurring annual payments.

(b) *The net present value* (or 'excess present value') method discounts the net cash flows from the investment by the *cost of capital,* and deducts the initial investment to give the yield from the fund invested. If this yield is positive, then the project is *prima facie* worthwhile, but if it is negative the project is unable to pay for itself, and is thus unacceptable. An index can be developed for comparative purposes by relating the yield to the investment to give the yield per Re. 1 invested. This is the *excess present value index,* and facilities the ranking of competing proposals in order of acceptability. (It is not important in their evaluation in terms of profitability that competing proposals require widely different outlays and the index reduces alternatives to a common base.)

Comparison of discounting methods

In ordinary circumstances, the two discounting approaches will result in identical investment decisions. However, there are differences between them that can result in conflicting answers in terms of ranking projects according to their profitability.

In formal accept/reject decisions, both methods lead to the same division, since all projects having a yield in excess of the cost of capital will also have a positive net present value.

EXAMPLE Projects A and B both require an outlay 1000 now to obtain a return of 1150 at the end of year I in the case of A, and 1405 at the end of year 3 in the case of B. The cost of capital is 8 per cent.

Time- adjusted rate of return	A = 15%
	B = 12%
Net present value:	A = (1150 X 0.926) - 1000 = £65
	B = (1405 X 0. 794) - 1000 = £115

Both projects have rates of return in excess of 8 per net *and* positive net present value; but on the basis of the rate of return method, project A is superior, while on the basis of the net present value method, project B is superior.

Confusion arises because the projects have different lengths of life, and if only one of the projects is to be undertaken, the time-adjusted rate of return can be seen to be unable to discriminate satisfactorily between them. As with any rate of return, there is no indication of either the *amount* capital involved or the *duration* of the investment. The choice must be made either on the basis of net present values, or on the return on the incremental investment between projects.

The two methods make different implicit assumptions about the reinvesting of funds received from projects—particularly during the 'gaps' between the end of one and the end of another.

Considering the example further, if it is explicitly assumed that the funds received from project.

All three formulations clearly show project B to be superior, illustrating the importance of project characteristics when only one can be undertaken.

It follows that the comparison of alternatives by either method must be made over a common time period, with explicit assumptions being made about what happens to funds between their receipt and the common terminal date.

Aspects of application

Alternative proposals

The selection of a particular proposal should follow a careful appraisal of both alternative uses for funds, and alternative means of performing a particular project. For instance, a company may wish to double the capacity of its production line, and determine three means of accomplishing this, namely;

(a) introduce double-shift working;

(b) instal a second production line; or

(c) scrap the existing production line and build a new line with double the initial capacity.

The choice of a particular alternative will depend on how it accords with the firm's established investment objectives, and the choice of projects will depend on both corporate objectives and the availability of funds. But the fact remains that if the most advantageous alternative has been overlooked, no amount of technical evaluation and appraisal can overcome this basic omission.

Capital rationing

In terms of financing investment projects, three essential questions must be asked:

1. How much money is needed for capital expenditure in the forthcoming planning period?
2. How much money is available for investment?
3. How are funds to be assigned when the acceptable proposals require more money than is available?

The first and third questions are resolved by reference to the discounted return on the various proposals, since it will be known which are acceptable, and in which order of preference.

The second question is answered by a reference to the capital budget. The level of this budget will tend to depend on the quality of the investment proposals submitted to top management. In addition, it will also tend to depend on:

(a) top management's philosophy towards capital spending (e.g., is it growth-minded or cautious?);

(b) the outlook for future investment opportunities that may be unavailable if extensive current commitments are undertaken;

(c) the funds provided by current operations; and

(d) the feasibility of acquiring additional capital through borrowing or share issues.

It is not always necessary, of course, to limit the spending on projects to internally generated funds. Theoretically, projects should be undertaken to the point where the return is just equal to the cost of financing these projects.

If safety and the maintaining of, say, family control are considered to be more important than additional profits, there may be a marked unwillingness to engage in external financing, and hence a limit will be placed on the amounts available for investment.

Even though the firm may wish to raise external finance for its investment programme, there are many reasons why it may be unable to do this. Examples include:

1. The firm's past record and its present capital structure may make it impossible—or extremely costly—to raise additional debt capital.
2. The firm's record may make it impossible to raise new equity capital because of low yields—or even no yield.
3. Covenants in existing loan agreements may restrict future borrowing.

Furthermore, in the typical company, one would expect capital rationing to be largely self-imposed.

Post-audit

Each major project should be followed up to ensure that it conforms to the conditions on which it was accepted, as well as being subject to cost control procedures.

Venture management and risk analysis

Venture management is an approach to new product development and marketing that is based on the systems approach to corporate planning. Essentially, it requires that management view new product programmes as 'ventures. In other words, from conception to commercialization each new product is treated as one project, and handled by a small team which is responsible for the creation, evaluation, and marketing aspects of new product development and testing.

Venturing is an attempt to make innovation more predictable and less random than it otherwise might be by the managing of new product development as a continuing commitment, rather than as a sporadic or periodic crash programme.

To be most effective, venture management requires that projects be subjected to a rigorous, multi-stage evaluation procedure. At each stage in this procedure the project is subjected to a go/no go decision to determine its eligibility to proceed to the next stage. The criteria on which these decisions are made should be clearly defined corporate objectives. The stages may be:

(a) concept testing;

(b) qualitative screening;

(c) economic analysis;

(d) product testing;

(e) test marketing; and

(f) phased launch/national launch.

Each particular new product venture will be unique, and will require its own specific combination and sequence of evaluation steps. It is the role of venture management to provide a framework within the results of these various tests may be interpreted.

The usefulness of the venture analysis approach is in the viewing of project activities in relation to all other interrelated activities, rather than in total isolation. It enables management to compare alternative courses of action in a systematic way, with such results as:

1. The impact of possible current decisions on the freedom of the firm in the future may be revealed.
2. A clarification of the significance of current assumptions about the future, or the corporate objectives, may occur.

3. A clearly defined and acceptable set of assumptions can be formulated.
4. An internal consistency in the product plan may be achieved.
5. Sensitivity analyses may be applied to each stage of the plan to illustrate the impact of changed assumptions and changes in policy on the end result.

By adopting a systems perspective that allows for interrelationships, it is obvious that present decisions will affect future outcomes. But by making explicit all possible alternatives or strategies—present and future—venture analysis reduces the level of uncertainty, and thus reduces the likelihood of error in making the wrong decision.

Each strategy is a route to an objective, and the problem becomes that of choosing among alternative strategies to ensure that the best one is followed in terms of goal-attainment.

For projects to be effectively evaluated, venture analysis requires that some finite time horizon be specified. Such a planning horizon permits the building-in of the time-related effects of competing strategies, and the life of the project itself is best described in terms of the product life-cycle.

Given the length of the project, and the annual costs and revenues over that life, it is possible to evaluate the project in accordance with the discounted cash flow (DCF) procedure. Decision rules should be devised to facilitate simple evaluation at each stage, in relation to the expected financial outcome. The form of these decision rules may be:

1. *For launch* decision, the likelihood (i.e., possibility) of obtaining at least the ROI that can be obtained from other ventures must be greater than, say, 0.8 (i.e., 80 per cent certain).
2. For a *scrap* decision, the probability of obtaining this ROI must be less than, say, 0.4.
3. If the probability of obtaining this ROI is between 0.4 and 0.8 the decision must be taken to test the product further.

At all stages, due consideration must be given to risk and uncertainty. These matters are now dealt with.

Risk and uncertainty

Risk is used to describe the type of situation in which there are a number of possible *states of nature,* hence outcomes, but in which the decision-maker can reasonably assess the probability of occurrence of each. Thus, risk can be expressed in quantitative terms.

Under conditions of uncertainty, in contrast, it is recognized that several outcomes are possible, but the decision-maker is unable to attach probabilities to the various states of nature. This inability is usually due to a lack of data on which to base a probability estimate. For instance, in launching a new product, the marketing manager may have an idea of what the sales in year 1 are likely to be, but he must accept that the actual level will be one of many possible levels. However, the marketing manager may be unable to specify the probability of each level being achieved, making it an uncertainty situation.

In the case of established products, there is a wealth of historical experience on which to base probability estimates, so this is a risk situation.

There is also, of course, the situation of *complete certainty.* This relates to decisions over which the decision-maker has complete control, and are thus likely to be confined to the production sphere. This is so because the existence of external agents in marketing and distribution means that knowledge is incomplete, and the creative aspect of R & D means that outcomes are unknown in advance.

In relation to decision-making under conditions of risk and uncertainty, the purpose expressing an opinion about the likelihood of an event occurring is to facilitate the development of decision-making procedures that are explicit and consistent with the decision-maker's beliefs.

By convention, probabilities follow certain rules, such as:

1. The probability assigned to each possible future event must be a positive number between zero and unity, where zero represents an impossible event and unity represents a certain one.
2. If a set of events is mutually exclusive and exhaustive, then the total of the probabilities of the events must add to one.

Although analytical methods can be applied to the evaluation of risk and uncertainty, management may prefer to take other courses of action to reduce risk and uncertainty. Perhaps the best method to increase the information available to the decision-maker prior to his making a decision. For instance, marketing research can supply further information prior to new product launches *via* product testing or marketing.

Alternatively, the scale of operations may be increased, or product diversification pursued. Product A having a seasonal demand pattern that is the opposite of the pattern of product B, but in combination. Whereas either product in isolation would result in a loss during part of its demand cycle.

Allowing for risk

In investment decision-making, risk generally derives from five sources:

(a) risk from undertaking insufficient numbers of similar investments;

(b) risk from misinterpretation of data.

(c) risk from bias in the data and in their assessment;

(d) risk from a changing external economic environment, invalidating much of the usefulness of past experience; and

(e) risk from errors of analysis.

The prerequisite to allowing for risks such as these is the establishment of a risk policy. The amount of risk a firm is willing to accept to obtain a given financial return is a general question of values that cannot be rationally determined. A firm may, for instance, opt for a policy of conservatism and require a very high return for risk, or alternatively for a policy of taking greater risks. The major problem is, perhaps, that in pursuing a conservative policy as regards investment, the firm places itself in a risky situation because of its unwillingness to accept risky investments.

Once a policy has been determined, it must be translated into specific rate of return requirements for different types of projects. The categories of project may be;

(a) cost saving investments;

(b) replacement investments;

(c) market expansion investments;

(d) investments required by regulations; and

(e) welfare amenity investments.

Each category will involve different types of risk, and the aim of classifying the various investment proposals by type is to ensure that they all receive equal consideration once due allowance has been made for the differential risks involved.

For practical business decisions, agreement on the exact method of incorporating risk into the analysis is less important than agreement that varying the *discount rate* used in evaluating a project is not a good way of accomplishing the objective of taking risk into consideration. (The discount rate is that rate used to reduce future income streams to their present value, and is the converse of an interest rate.

The application of simple risk analysis is best illustrated by means of an example. Let it be assumed that RST Limited has two new products. A and B, but only sufficient resources to launch one of these. The relevant states of nature relate to competitive activity: no matter which product is launched, it may be assumed that the competition will:

(a) do nothing; or

(b) introduce a comparable product; or

(c) introduce a superior product.

On the basis of past experience and current knowledge, the management of RST

Limited attach probabilities of 0.25, 0.5, and 0.25 respectively to these states of nature. In the light of these alternative condition, the profit of each strategy can be shown in law pay-off matrix.

Allowing for uncertainty

Uncertainty arises from a lack of previous experience and knowledge. In a new venture, it is possible for uncertainty to be attached to the following factors:

a. date of completion;

b. level of capital outlay required;

c. level of sales prices;

d. level of revenue;

e. level of sales volume

f. level of operating costs; and

g. taxation rules;

Inevitably, decision-making under conditions of uncertainty is more complicated than is the case under risk conditions. In fact, there is no single best criterion that should be used in selecting a strategy. Of the various available techniques, company policy or the decision-maker's attitude will determine that which is selected. Four possible criteria are given below:

Maximum-criterion of pessimism

The assumption underlying this technique is that the worst outcome will always come about, and the decision-maker should therefore select the largest pay-off under this assumption.

Maximum—criterion of optimism

This is the opposite of 'maximin', and is based on the assumption that the best pay-off will result from the selected strategy.

Major sources of financing

After deciding on the nature and the amount of his firm's needs for funds, the financial administrator must locate an appropriate source from which to obtain them. We will follow the common practice of classifying sources of business funds according to the period for which they are initially made available: Short-term, repayable within 1 year; intermediate term, repayable within 1 to 5 or sometimes 1 to 10 years; and long term, available for 10 years or longer.

In this chapter we will discuss major sources of short-term funds and management of the current liabilities that result when a business firm employs such funds.

The principal sources of short-term funds are *trade* and *bank credit*. Certain *non-bank lenders* also extend short-term credit to businesses; for some firms with excellent credit reputations, a third source, the *commercial paper markets*, may also be available.

Trade credit

In American business practice, buyers are not generally required to pay cash on delivery for the goods and services they order. Instead, the sellers" invoice," or bill, the buyers on delivery, according to the terms of the particular "trade," or line of business. That is sellers extend credit to buyers, and this extension of credit provides a temporary source of funds to the buyer in the form of accounts or notes payable. Because suppliers are generally more liberal in extending credit than banks are, trade credit has become the most important source of short-term business funds in terms of the dollar volume of credit supplied.

Forms of Trade Credit

There are three avenues of trade credit extension: (1) the open account, which is by far the most common; (2) the promissory note; (3) the trade acceptance.

Open-account credit is ordinarily extended only after the seller conducts a fairly extensible investigation of the buyer's credit standing and reputation. The open account derives its name from the fact that the buyer does not sign a formal debt instrument evidencing the amount he owes the seller, as would be the case if he applied for and obtained bank credit. The only evidence the seller has that credit has been extended is the buyer's purchase order, a copy of the invoice showing that merchandise was shipped, and an entry in his accounts receivable ledger. It is indicative of the extent to which a "credit economy" has developed in this country that, when most trade credit is arranged, this is all that is done and all that is required to be done to establish legal evidence of indebtedness.

In some situations, however, a promissory note may be used in the transaction. A promissory note is a written promise by one person to another to pay on demand or at a fixed or determinable future time a certain sum of money to order of bearer. The promissory note is generally and interest-bearing instrument. Buyers are required to sign such notes most often in cases where their open accounts have become delinquent and the seller wishes to obtain a formal acknowledgment of the debt, a definite maturity date, and, at times, a return in the form of interest on the funds thus committed. Promissory notes appear on the seller's balance sheet as "notes receivable," of course.

In some lines of business, trade acceptances are used in place of the open account. A trade acceptance is generated when a seller, after receiving a purchase order from a customer, draws a time draft on that customer in the amount of the order. A time draft is an unconditional order to pay a certain sum of money at a fixed or determinable future time. The seller then sends the draft through his own bank, together with an order bill of lading from the carrier by which the goods are shipped, for presentation to and acceptance by the customer. An order bill of lading must be presented to the carrier to secure the release of the goods shipped at their destination. The seller's bank forwards the draft and bill of lading to its correspondent bank in the city in which the customer is located; and this bank presents the draft to him for acceptance. The customer accepts the draft simply by signing, dating, and writing the word "accepted" across the face of the draft.

After accepting the draft, the customer receives the order bill of lading from the bank and is able to secure his shipment of goods from the issuing carrier. The accepted draft, now a trade acceptance, is then returned to the seller's bank and thence to the seller, he may either hold it to maturity or ask his bank to discount it for him, since as a trade acceptance it is a full-fledged negotiable instrument. In either event, it will be presented to the buyer for payment on its due date.

When selling an open account is so simple, why should sellers go to all the trouble required to generate trade acceptances? In actual fact, and primarily for competitive reasons, few do; they are attracted by several advantages that trade acceptances possess as compared with open accounts. First, the act of acceptance by the buyers is a clear acknowledgment by him of his debt to the seller. Second, since it is fully negotiable, the seller may use the trade acceptance as collateral for a loan, or he can sell it at any time before maturity if a need for cash should arise. Finally, when it does fall due, few acceptors will chance the damage to their credit reputations that would result from failure to pay. It is one thing—and not necessarily always such a bad thing—to fail to pay an open account payable when it is due; it is quite another and more serious thing to ignore the presentation of a maturing trade acceptance.

Terms of trade credit

Promissory notes and trade acceptances are both used rather sparingly in commercial transactions; therefore, the more relevant terms of trade credit are those pertaining to open accounts. Three aspects of this form of credit warrant discussion: (1) the seize of the cash discount, if any, from the net invoice price which is given for making cash payment within a specified period; (2) the period within which payment must be made if the cash discount is to be allowed; and (3) the maximum period that can elapse before payment of the net invoice price is required if the cash discount is not taken.

It is important to distinguish a cash discount—from both a *quantity discount* and a *functional discount.* A quantity discount—generally expressed as a percentage reduction from a list price—is given for purchasing certain minimum amounts of a particular item. Functional discounts are differential discounts given different types of customers—a wholesaler, for example, may be given a larger discount than a retailer.

Terms of trade credit, which vary from industry to industry, are specified on each invoice and may be categorized according to both the net period within which payment is expected and the terms of the cash discount allowed. In general, cash discounts are rarely set as high as 10 per cent and average closer to 2 or 3 per cent; the discount periods are usually fairly short, in most cases 10 or 20 days.

CBD And COD

"Cash before delivery" (CBD) and Cash on delivery (COD) " are two common forms of payment. Under CBD, a buyer must pay for the goods before the supplier will ship them. When a supplier imposes these terms, he either knows nothing at all about the buyer's creditworthiness or, more frequently, he knows "too much" about the customer's unreliability in managing his business affairs. In the latter circumstance, to eliminate the risk of non-payment completely, he may even wait for the customer's check to clear the bank before shipping the order. Under COD, the supplier will ship the goods ordered, but the buyer must pay for them before taking possession. The only risk involved with COD is that the customer may refuse the shipment and the seller will have to pay shipping costs both ways. Transactions completed under either CBD or COD terms are considered cash transactions since suppliers are required to extend no credit at all.

Net-terms, no cash discount

When net terms are quoted, the supplier specifies the period permitted for payment in full. For example, "net 30" means that the amount of the net invoice must be paid in full within 30 days. If the seller bills of a monthly basis, he may stipulate such terms as "net 15 EOM," meaning that all goods shipped before the end of the month must be paid for in full by the fifteenth of the following month. Sometimes, "bill-to-bill" terms are specified; that is, the bill for a previous delivery is collected at the time a new delivery is made.

Cash discount terms

In addition to extending credit on net terms, suppliers may offer a cash discount for payment more prompt than the net terms require. The terms "2/10, net 30," for example, indicate that the buyer is offered a 2 per cent discount for payment within 10 days of the date of the invoice. If this discount is not taken, the full amount is due within 30 days. When the buyer is far removed from the seller, or the method of shipping the goods is slow, terms may be "2/10, net 30 AOG". That arrangement affords the buyer the opportunity of inspecting the goods before paying for them. More important, it provides all buyers with an equal opportunity to earn the cash discount, regardless of their distance from the point of shipment or the transit time required for the goods to reach them.

Rational for trade credit terms

The variations in trade credit terms described above have a rational. First, the period of time for which credit is granted is related to the nature of the commodity sold. High-style items or perishable merchandise are generally sold on fairly short credit terms because the supplier may not be willing to bear the risk of obsolescence or spoilage. Second, the estimated degree of credit risk is generally reflected in the terms of sale. Retail shops in the apparel trades are characterized by a rather high rate of failure, for example. This may explain the rather large cash discounts usually allowed such retailers—the size of the discount reflecting supplier's desires to be paid as quickly as possible. Third, the nature and extent of competition among suppliers is expressed in credit terms as well as in prices and service. When a product is new, or if a supplier is soliciting business from a new account, granting more liberal credit terms than are customary may be one way of generating additional sales.

Fourth, a supplier short of working capital may offer rather large cash discounts to his customers to induce them to settle their accounts quickly. In this way, the supplier reduces his collection period and thus reduces his total working capital requirements. A thinly capitalized supplier may find that the cost of offering large cash discounts is less than the cost of borrowing or raising additional equity capital to meet his working capital needs.

Finally, the financial strength of the supplier relative to that of his customers is also a determinant of credit terms. Although it might appear that a financially strong supplier could dictate stringent terms, by doing so he may succeed only in losing some customers and possible even putting others out of business. In reality, in many lines of business, smaller companies are "carried" by their suppliers.

Trade credit as a source of funds

Since buyers generally do not pay for goods until some time after they are delivered, trade credit is a short-term source of business funds. If a firm "automatically" pays all its bills a certain number of days after the invoice date, trade credit becomes a built-in source of financing that varies with the production cycle. As the firm increases its rate of production, and thus its rate of purchases, accounts payable increase commensurately, thereby providing some of the funds needed to finance the increase in production. Similarly, as production decreases, purchases, and thus account payable, decrease.

Although changes in the size of a firm's account payable may not be directly proportional to changes in the level of its production because of possible inventory adjustments, there will ordinarily be a strong degree of correspondence between the two. If a firm adheres strictly to the practice of always paying its bills a certain number of days after invoice date, trade credit cannot be considered a discretionary source of financing. Instead, it becomes determinate insofar as it is dependent on the purchasing plan of the firm which, as we discussed earlier, is dictated largely by its production cycle. Although prompt payment of such obligations is generally to be commended, certain advantages may be gained from using trade credit as a discretionary source of short-term financing. To demonstrate the desirability of such a policy, we need only examine the true cost of using trade credit.

Cost of trade credit

For purposes of measuring the true cost, or the effective annual rate of interest associated with use of trade credit as a discretionary source of short-term business funds, it is necessary to consider the effects of its use both when (1) a firm fails to take its cash discounts but nevertheless pays within the net period, and (2) a firm fails to take its discounts and allows its payable to become overdue. These two situations are the only ones that involve an actual cost to the debtor. If no cash discount is offered, then there is no cost for the use of credit during the "net" period, however long it may be. By the same token, if a discount is available and the buyer takes it, there is also no cost for the use of credit during the discount period. However, if a cash discount is offered and is not taken, there is an explicit opportunity cost for the use of third credit.

For example, the Roadman Company purchases its raw materials on terms of 2/10, net 30. It thus has the option of using the funds for 20 days after the discount period if it "passes" the discount but pays on the final day of the net period. Roadman, however, must pay 2 per cent for the privilege of using the supplier's fund for that extra 20 days.

Passed discounts can transform trade credit from a normally castles sources of funds into a very expensive form of short-term financing. Therefore, if banking financing is available, even though relatively high interest rates, say, 12 or 13 per cent, Roadman's financial administrator would be well advised to borrow from his firm's bank in sufficient time it take advantage of any cash discounts offered by its suppliers

Sometimes, firms that are short of cash and lack reserve borrowing power may be forced to not only pass up cash discounts but also postpone payment beyond the net period. This practice is referred to as "stretching" accounts payable or "riding" trade creditors. There are two types of costs incurred by a firm that stretches its accounts payable (1) the explicit cost of discounts foregone, as outlined above, and (2) the implicit cost of permitting its trade credit rating to deteriorate. If a firm rides its creditors excessively, so that its trade payable become noticeably delinquenst, its credit rating among all suppliers in the trade will surely suffer. They will view the firm as increasingly risky to sell to and may quickly begin to impose rather strict terms of sale, up to and including COD or CBD.

Proper use of trade credit

As compared with other kinds of short-term business credit—bank loans, for example-trade credit is almost automatic. And because it may be much more readily acquired, business firms must exercise continuing care to avoid falling into the habit of using trade credit to excess.

Because suppliers regard the extension of trade credit as a part of their overall sales promotion programs, they often extend trade credit to many marginally creditworthy firms—small, new firms and old, declining firms—that do not qualify for and consequently cannot obtain credit from other sources of short-term funds. It is also quite easy to get into debt through the use of trade credit. A firm needs only to order additional goods from its suppliers; and if it is occasionally late in making payment, the sales promotion aspect of trade credit extension may prompt suppliers to "look the other way," so that the firm's credit reputation may suffer no immediate harm.

Finally, trade credit is exceedingly useful and valuable precisely because business firms can usually obtain it when, as, and to the extent that it is needed. When inventory should be increased to anticipate the seasonal expansion of sales, for example trade credit will automatically finance a part of the increase. Then, as the seasonal sales convert inventory into receivables and receivables convert into cash through collections, the firm may use the funds to reduce trade payable. For this reason, trade credit is often termed a "spontaneous" source of funds.

Thus, a firm's financial officer while assuring that his company benefits from the availability of trade credit in every legitimate way, should always maintain the business liquidity required to pay all his firm's bills as they come due. Beyond this, even considering the extremely high cost of passing discounts, he should certainly plan to pay all of his firm's trade bills within the discount period. Doing so will have favourable results, not only on the firm's credit reputation in the trade but, more important, on its current and long-run profitability as well. In a negative but equally significant sense, doing so will automatically avoid the possible financial over-extension of the firm that could result from its succumbing to the temptation to use trade credit excessively "because it is there."

Bank credit

Here we will be concerned only with the acquisition by businesses of short-term bank credit. And we will discuss two specific categories : unsecured loans and secured loans.

Short-term, unsecured loans made by banks to business firms are generally regarded as self-liquidating in that the uses to which the borrower puts the funds are ordinarily expected to generate cash flows adequate to repay the loan within a year. At one time, banks chose to confine their business lending almost exclusively to this short-term, self-liquidating type of loan. While they now engage in a much wider variety of business lending (also by choice), the short-term, self-liquidating loan still meets the specific needs to most business borrowers and thus remains a very important source of business financing.

Forms of unsecured bank loans

A business firm may borrow from its bank on an unsecured, short-term basis either (1) under a seasonal line of credit, (2) under a revolving credit arrangement, or (3) on a transaction basis.

Seasonal line of credit

A line of credit is simply a formal or informal agreement between a commercial bank and a borrowing customer regarding the maximum amount of credit the bank is willing to extend to that customer over a given number of months. Such lines of credit are commonly requested by seasonal business borrowers. By preparing and analyzing a cash budget reflecting his firm's operations over some period, the financial administrator estimates the patterns of his seasonal financing needs and arranges a line of credit with the firm's bank, the upper limit of which equals the firm's forecasted peak requirements, as shown in its cash budget. Then, as seasonal buildups of inventories, accounts receivable, or both create needs for funds, the firm simply signs promissory notes for the amounts required at the times they are required, and the bank credits the firm's account in the proper amounts. Subsequently, the post-seasonal shrinkage in working capital needs permits the firm to repay the advances with funds generated from the sale of inventories and the collection of accounts receivable.

Seasonal lines of credit usually run for a year at a time but can be renewed periodically. Since the loans extended under such lines are made for the purpose of augmenting permanent working capital temporarily, the lending banks ordinarily require their seasonal line-of-credit borrowers to be completely out of debt to the bank at some time during the year. This annual "cleanup" period of a month or two is proof to the bank that funds advanced are being used only for seasonal expansion. From the point of view of the firm's financial administrator, it also serves as an excellent internal control device that helps keep the firm's working capital position in line. Failure of a seasonal business borrower to achieve an annual cleanup of bank debt, moreover, suggests that the firm is using bank funds as permanent working capital. While banks are not averse to helping businesses finance their needs for permanent working capital, they generally prefer to do so with term loans rather than short-term, seasonal loans.

Revolving credit agreements

A revolving credit agreement is a variant of the line of credit. It has become increasingly popular in recent years because of the flexibility it provides to the borrower in using the borrowed funds. As under the seasonal line, the firm and its bank agree on an upper limit of credit. Within this maximum amount, however, the credit may "revolve" more or less continuously. That is, the firm may borrow, repay, and then subsequently reborrow funds as the need arises. This can be done also under a seasonal line, of course, for the one-year period of its life. But revolving lines typically run for more than a year. Many have, in fact, an indefinite length of life—they may extend on and on, so long as the lending bank and the borrowing business are both happy with the arrangement as originally negotiated.

Revolving lines often differ from seasonal lines in yet another way. They are frequently negotiated as formal commitments to lend by the bank, and a commitment fee is charged on any portion of the line that is unused. For example, if a firm has a formal revolving credit agreement with its bank for Rs. 2 million and average annual borrowings for a given year total only Re. 1 million, a commitment fee is payable on the Re. 1 million portion of the line that is used. That is in addition to the interest charged on the Re. 1 million portion of the line that is used. If the commitment fee is ½ of 1 per cent, the cost to the borrower of having the bank keep the unused 1 million available would be Rs. 5,000 for the year. Needless to say, such an arrangement may increase the cost of borrowing significantly under certain circumstances.

Since revolving credit agreements frequently extend beyond one year, many of them involve the extension of intermediate-term rather than short-term credit.

Transaction basis

When a firm borrows only occasionally, for specific purposes that may differ from time to time, it will generally negotiate each loan with the bank as a separate transaction. For example, consider a building contractor requiring funds from his bank to complete a construction job. When the job is completed, the contractor will be paid; and he, in turn, can repay the bank. In such cases, the bank will evaluate each borrowing request as a separate transaction, with its own cash-flow-for-repayment characteristics.

Cost of bank credit

Interest rates on bank loans to business are determined through negotiation between borrower and lender. In unsecured lending, the rate charged tends to vary directly with the credit quality, or the creditworthiness, of the borrower. The largest, soundest companies possessing the very highest credit quality are able to borrow, unsecured, at the prime rate, the lowest rate charged on business loans at any given point in time. The prime rate is the one at which the nation's largest banks lend to their biggest and best short-term business borrowing customers. It is the connecting link between a commercial bank's customer loan rates and short-term, open-market money rates. The prime rate measures, in effect, the opportunity cost to banks of lending rather than investing in short-term, open-market instruments. Since the latter are virtually riskless, it follows that prime-rate borrowers must possess credit qualities of the very highest order to qualify for the lowest bank loan rate.

As relatively few business borrowers qualify for the prime rate, financial administrators must constantly work to raise their firm's credit quality to the highest possible level and maintain it at that point in order to minimize the costs of acquiring funds. An examination of the concept of credit quality from the lender's point of view may indicate how this can be accomplished.

Concept of credit quality

The credit quality of a prospective business borrower is revealed to the lending banker through inquiries made of the company's trade creditors; through reports requested of credit-rating agencies; through analysis of the company's financial statements; and by "trade comparison" — comparisons of the prospective borrower's financial situation with that of other similarly sized firms in the same general line of business activity. With respect to short-term business borrowers, good credit quality includes the following components, indicated by statement analysis and verified by trade comparisons:

1. good reputation in the trade, both for prompt payment of trade payables and for fair dealing;
2. satisfactory current financial position, as revealed by ratio analysis of statement and by trade comparisons of ratios, net working capital position, and common-sized balance sheets;
3. satisfactory equity-debt relationship, as indicated by net worth to debt ratio computation and comparisons;
4. satisfactory record for effective use of working capital, revealed through adequate sales to receivables, cost of sales to inventory, and sales to inventory relationships throughout the past several years;
5. satisfactory cash flows, as demonstrated by a sources and uses of funds statement and a pro-forma cash budget; and
6. satisfactory earning record, as measured by profits to sales and net profits to net worth performances that are comparable with the trade.

In addition to meeting all size criteria of good credit quality for short-term borrowers, prospective term-loan borrowers, must show either (1) satisfactory prospective profits to service the term loan over its anticipated life; or (2) a reasonable expectation of outside financing to "pay the loan out" on schedule.

Non-prime rate borrowers

Borrowers of less-than-prime-rate credit quality pay some rate higher than the prime rate that is related to both their actual credit quality and certain other considerations that the bank will take into account in setting the rate. These other considerations are generally referred to as the "commensurate advantages" attaching to a loan opportunity, as viewed by the bank. They include, first, commensurate balances maintained with the bank by the borrower; and any other commensurate advantages involved in the future relationship between the bank and the business borrower.

Commensurate balances: In setting the interest rate to be charged on a business loan, a commercial bank not only looks at the prospective borrower's credit quality but also at the nature of his deposit relationship with the bank. If the borrower maintains balances that are judged to be "commensurate" with his credit requirements, a lower rate may be placed on the loan than would otherwise be justified. That is, in evaluating any business-loan opportunity, the problem faced by the commercial bank lending officer is that of comparing, and if possible, equating the expected returns available to the bank from making the loan with the risk that the loan will not be repaid at maturity or otherwise handled by the borrowers as agreed. The returns available to banks for lending include the direct interest return on the loan, of course, and may also include the indirect benefits realized from the maintenance of satisfactory commensurate balances as well as other commensurate advantages thought to accrue to the bank as the result of making the loan.

When are a borrower's balances commen-surate with his credit requirements? No single answer to that question can be given, and there are many variations. But for most banks, deposit accounts of about 20 per cent of the outstanding bank loan are considered reasonable. In fact, many banks explicitly or implicitly request a borrowing customer to carry average balances equal to at least 20 per cent of the stated line of credit or contemplated maximum borrowings from the bank. Some banks set the figure at 15 per cent of the expected high borrowing figure or line of credit and a few, at 10 per cent. Other banks request balances equal to 10 per cent of the line when the company is not borrowing and balances equal to 20 per cent when the line is in use. Still other banks—those most desirous of according their customers liberal treatment—consider commensurate balances to be average deposit balances for a 12-month period equal to at least 20 per cent of average loans during the year. This is usually different from balances equal to 20 per cent of maximum loans.

If the minimum level of balances judged to be commensurate is higher than the level a firm would normally keep for operational liquidity purposes, the effect may be to reduce the effective amount of its credit line and to raise its effective cost of credit. To take a simple example, suppose the Willite Company's cash budget indicates that its seasonal borrowing requirements will reach a high of Rs. 475,000 during a year in which current bank credit terms are 6 per cent interest and a commensurate balance equalling 15 per cent of borrowings. The firm's normal needs for operational liquidity total Rs. 50,000.

Other commensurate advantages: Although other commensurate advantages are not susceptible to quantitative measurement in the same sense as interest rates and balances, they are quite real in the banker's mind. While numerous specific instances of such advantages of extending business credits could be cited, for our present purposes a few suggestive examples should suffice. Banks look favourable on loan situation that also generate, or at least have the potential to generate, other advantages to the bank—securing a desirable new customer, obtaining a needed new business or industry for the bank's community, or accommodating businesses whose executives or principals are likely to make, or may be induced to make, substantial use of the bank's trust-department services.

Secured loans

Lenders measure their risk exposure by evaluating the credit quality of prospective borrowers. A business that enjoys a high credit rating among its creditors—by definition, one to whom credit can be granted with little risk—may readily be extended credit on what is called an unsecured basis. Actually, however, it is the firm's high credit quality that stands as security for the loan's repayment. In contrast, a business borrower of lower credit quality may be required to provide some more tangible security than credit quality alone—for example, collateral of various kinds—to compensate a lender for its lack of credit quality high enough to justify unsecured lending.

The collateral most often requested by commercial banks in short-term, secured business lending situations consists of accounts receivable and inventories. The lender's interest in such collateral is defined and protected by law. Under the law when a lender requires a pledge of assets or collateral from a borrower, he obtains a security interest in the collateral. The security interest is created by a security agreement, signed by the borrower and lender and contains a description of the assets pledged as collateral.

Most often, the security agreement also contains the borrower's pledge that he genuinely owns the assets offered as collateral and that these are free from any prior claim. In order to perfect a security interest in the collateral, the lender must file a copy of the security agreement with an appropriate public office in the state in which the collateral is located. Then the leader legally has a prior claim on the assets pledged as collateral and can sell them if need be to liquidate the loan.

The perfected security agreement protects the lender's right to 100 per cent of the liquidating value of the assets pledged, should the borrower default on the loan. If assets are liquidated for less than the total amount of principal and interest due, the lender receives whatever the assets yield and becomes a general creditor with respect to the balance of his claim. Consequently, most lenders will require some "margin of safety" between the estimated market value of assets pledged as security for a loan and the amount of the loan. That is, they will not lend the full amount of the estimated market value of the assets but only some percentage of it. How high the percentage is depends on the borrowing firm's general creditworthiness, the nature of the assets pledged, and the practices followed by the financial institution making the loan.

Bank and non bank secured lending practices

Business may apply to several types of financial institutions beside commercial banks for secured short-term loans. Commercial finance companies lend on the security of inventories, accounts receivable, and sometimes other assets as well. Factors specialize in accounts receivable financing. While in some cases factors lend on the security of accounts receivable, the classic factoring function involves the outright purchase of receivables and includes responsibility for their ultimate collection. Sales finance companies finance the inventories of dealers in automobiles, appliances, and other consumer durable goods. They also buy from the dealers the instalment notes generated when individuals purchase those goods, thus financing the dealer's "receivables" as well.

Accounts Receivable as Security. Business borrowers often pledge their accounts receivable as security for short-term bank loans. And in recent years, commercial finance companies have begun to make similar loans.

Bank lending on accounts receivable is usually done on a non-notification basis, that is, the buyer is not informed that his account has been assigned to the bank by the selling firm. Since approval of the customer's credit is often not required by the bank, it usually lends on "unapproved" accounts receivable only with recourse—that is, the borrowing firm must assume responsibility for bad debt losses by repurchasing such accounts or substituting other, sound accounts receivable for those that failed to pay as agreed.

The borrower is required to sign a collateral note and an assignment-of-accounts—receivable agreement. Under the agreement, the borrowing business firm will investigate the "quality" of its customers before extending credit to them. Then, after each credit sale, it will send a copy of the invoice to the bank, which in turn will remit the previously agreed—on percentage of the invoice's amount. The borrowing firm will also pay over to the bank the agreed—on portion of all payments on receivables from customers, retaining only the "unadvanced" portion of collected receivables. Because customers, of the borrowing firm are not usually informed that their accounts have been assigned, checks collected by the borrowing firm are usually processed without further endorsement by the bank.

The interest cost of borrowing from commercial banks against accounts receivable may range from two to four percentage points above the prime rate. In addition, many banks levy service charges of an additional 1 or 2 per cent of the loan as an administrative fee. Interest and other costs on receivables—secured loans from commercial finance companies are substantially higher, however.

Factoring. In contrast to the assignment of accounts receivable as collateral security for a loan from a bank, factoring involves the outright sale of receivable to a factoring firm or a facstoring department of a commercial bank or other financial institution. Factoring receivables is not a common practice in most lines of business, although in some—textiles, for example—it has been a standard financial operating procedure for many years.

Factors may purchase accounts receivable with recourse, that is, the seller must make good any customer delinquency in payment. But factors ordinarily purchase them without recourse and assume all risks of account uncollectability. For that reason, factors also assume responsibility for approving credit extensions in the first place and for collecting the receivables as well. In contrast with a non-notification assignment of receivables to a bank, the credit customers of a firm that factors its receivables are notified by a stamp on each invoice that the sale has been assigned and that its amount is payable to a factoring or financial institution.

The cost of factoring is usually stated as a flat percentage of the factored receivables *plus* a substantial interest charge on all advances against uncollected receivables. Usually, about 90 per cent of the value of factored receivables is immediately available. The remaining 10 per cent is paid only after the factored accounts themselves become due and payable.s

Inventories as Security. Business firms often uncurl difficulties in obtaining short-term credit secured by inventories because such collateral is less attractive to banks than accounts receivable. Inventories have a longer cash-conversion cycle, for one thing, since they must first be sold, converted into accounts receivable, and the receivables collected. For another, they are frequently heterogeneous both in nature and quality. Finally, establishing and maintaining a lien against inventories, even through the use of a perfected security agreement as provided by the laws, is physically difficult and frequently may be expensive.

Thus, business borrowers who must resort to pledging inventories as security for short-term bank loans are usually charged higher interest rates than borrowers pledging accounts receivables. And sometimes banks may be unwilling to lend on the security of inventories alone, preferring a combination of inventories and accounts receivable as collateral and regarding the receivables as the more significant portion of the security.

When borrowing against inventories, a firm should be prepared to have its bank continually monitor the quantity and quality of its collateral, if the firm maintains physical possession of the assets pledged. Where the inventory is relatively small in quantity and highly uniform in quality, or where each item in it is readily identifiable by serial number, this may not be too inconvenient for either party. But if, as is frequently the case, maintaining adequate controls over the collateral is difficult or expensive, an alternative is to physically segregate the pledged inventory in a warehouse operated by an independent third party, and then to use the security of the warehouse receipts issued to represent the segregated inventory in the credit.

The warehouse utilized to store the segregated inventory may be either a terminal (public) warehouse or a field warehouse. Field ware-housing is preferable to terminal warehousing for goods that are either bulky and expensive to move or to which the borrower needs frequent access—for example, raw materials to put into process or finished goods that have been sold. The borrower can gain this access only with the bank's permission, of course, since the bank holds the warehouse receipts representing the goods. The loan agreement between the borrower and the bank will specify the terms on which access is permitted.

Effective management of any aspect of business life requires a flow of relevant control information which reports the progress of the function being managed. More than this, a manager must possess professional and technical knowledge which will enable him to translate the flow of control data into meaningful instruction and advice. Appropriate actions for achieving the firm's objectives will then have a better chance of being recognised and put into operation. These comments apply to a purchasing executive, just as forcibly as to any other company employee. The flow of control data is not produced for the board's information only. Meaningful cost flow information will, for example, enable a business to be managed more economically and effectively; the various professional and technical skills found in corporate managements can be stimulated to seek reasons for loss tendencies or over costly operations. Thus non-accounting executives, and here we are concerned specifically with the whole supplies function, need to acquaint themselves with the content, nature and significance of accounting data and accounting statements.

Financial accounts, cost statements and balance sheets are valuable parts of the stock of control data available to most managers. These statements generally report what has already happened and they do this in varying degrees of detail. Also, by using the forecasts of business activity, accounting statements can show the likely consequences of proposed future operations. For most managers, their experience of appraising the outcomes of planned future business activities comes with the annual budget exercise—the next year's forecast position. Here, directing and operating managements may be faced with, for example, cost and profitability statements, cash flow forecasts and balance sheets. Each of these documents will contain information, the evaluation of which could be vital for the successful continuance of corporate activity.

Therefore it becomes essential that accounting reports of business activities should be presented in a form that encourages their understanding and use. To this end the user needs to be aware of the limitations of accounting statements generally and the principal conventions customarily used in their preparation. Now the two most important reports prepared by company accountants are the balance sheet and the profit and loss account, and it is to these two statements that we shall direct our attention now. From these studies readers will achieve a better understanding of the content and relevance of accounting reports and will be enabled to make:

1. A more realistic appraisal of the cost effectiveness of their own internal operations.
2. Soundly based judgments of the financial strengths and weaknesses of all companies— suppliers, customers and competitors alike.

Balance sheet and profit and loss accounts

Balance sheet are normally prepared once a year. Such is the statutory requirement for limited companies, but progressive firms produce balance sheets more frequently—once a quarter or once every six months. A balance sheet is an important summary of corporate wealth: it shows the assets and liabilities of a firm on a particular day. It is a stewardship statement in which the directors account for the money and credit made available to the firm, by listing the various assets in the firm's possession at the balance sheet date.

Profit and loss accounts are also prepared once a year: they show the financial results of the firm's trading during the year. As with balance sheets, the reader will find that many firms prepare profit and loss accounts more frequently that once a year. Effective monitoring of the firm's progress requires a continuous appraisal of its profitability. So we find that quarterly profit and loss accounts have become a normal practice for most companies.

Profit and loss accounts summarises the expenditures incurred in the course of corporate trading. The accounts will show the day-to-day running expenses of production, warehousing, selling and administrative departments for the period to which the account relates. When the total expenditures are compared with the total income, the resultant profit or loss is then revealed. At the end of the trading period a new balance sheet will be prepared so as to show the firm's new asset/liability state, and any profit or loss—must be incorporated into that balance sheet. This must be so because a profit signifies a creation of wealth for the firm and is one measure of its economic strength and viability. As the balance sheet purports to show corporate wealth and economic strength, then the new wealth which comes from profitable operations must be embodied therein.

In a more detailed study of balance sheets and profit and loss accounts we have to examine their contents and objectives. A balance sheet has certain well defined characteristics in that it brings items of a similar nature together into meaningful data groups. One of its main objectives is to show the sources and amounts of the various funds and credit which were necessary to enable the firm to acquire the corporate assets.

The depreciation charge

In most balance sheets the description 'Long-term assets' will be replaced by term 'Fixed assets': these items represent the capital expenditure of the business. Now capital expenditures relate to assets which, at the time of acquisition, are intended for long-term use by the firm. Long-term use implies periods longer than one year—the normal trading period for reporting corporate progress. Clearly if these assets are to be in use during several trading periods, it would be manifestly wrong to charge the whole of the expenditure on the asset against one year's income from sales. Long-term assets are expected to contribute to the production of goods for sale, and the making of profit, during several years' operations.

Consequently the whole cost of a capital asset, i.e. the whole acquisition cost *minus* any expected receipts from selling the asset when its usefulness to the firm ends, is shared amongst the various profit and loss accounts prepared during the asset's economic life. This yearly allocation of the fixed asset cost is called depreciation. It is charged in each profit and loss account together with all the other operating expenditures of that period. Another name for the profit and loss account is the revenue account: the expenditures, recorded therein are classified as revenue expenditures a description which denotes resource values which are totally consumed in earning an income. Here is the essential distinction between revenue expenditure and capital expenditure. The latter identifies those resource assets which will have a long life and will not be entirely used up in one operating period.

But even capital assets are eventually retired when their economic usefulness is terminated. In so far as a capital asset has no resale value on retirement, its initial outlay cost—the capital expenditure—has been consumed in the firm's business activities. Thus the depreciation charge, which acts as each year's proportionate 'consumption' of the fixed asset, identifies:

1 A cost of use of the fixed assets.

2 An allocation of some past capital expenditures.

3 A gradual conversation of capital expenditure into revenue expenditure.

Furthermore, so far as the balance sheet is concerned, depreciation operates as a revision of the book valuation of the related capital asset. Fixed assets are not held for resale: they are intended for use in the firm's continued operations.

Materiality and consistency

Profit and loss—or revenue—accounts are prepared on the basis of an input of resources leading to an output of goods and services for sale. The input is expressed in monetary values and thereby gives an aggregate of the day-to-day running costs of operating and managing a business unit. A comprehensive list of running cost would include items such as materials, wages, salaries, rent, rates, insurance, etc.: the cost of use of the available fixed assets would also feature in or list. All of these expenditures must have a factual or realistic foundation for the monetary values given. Thus the depreciation charge will depend upon the related asset's initial outlay cost together with a sensible appraisal of its expected economic life in the firm's business.

But realism demands also that we interpret out definition of capital expenditure in a way that will ensure that revenue accounts are not burdened with depreciation charges of insignificant amounts, for a multitude of low-cost, but long-lasting, assets.

The point is that balance sheets and profit and loss accounts are used as comparative statements of corporate wealth and profitability, both for different periods in the life of a single firm and for comparisons between different firms. Now a desk, a chair or a reading lamp are each assets with potentially long lives.

Clearly, the initial outlay cost of items such as those given above would make only a small impact upon the balance sheet worth of a firm. Moreover the related depreciation charges would not make much difference to the accounting profit reported in the revenue account. They would not be cost or outlay expenditures of significant or material size such as would affect a comparative analysis of final accounts. In these cases it is normal for such costs to be treated as revenue expenditure in the year of asset acquisition. The whole amount will be charged immediately to the year's profit and loss account. In this way the accounting convention of materiality brings realism to the accounting treatment of business expenditure. Materiality is the doctrine of significance and realism. It demands that profit and loss accounts present realistic valuation of resources consumed in earning income: expenditure must be related to, and matched with, income. Thus a series of accounts can be compared one with another, and an analyst may draw conclusions from such comparisons.

Consistency is a further example of the application of accounting conventions in achieving a more realistic comparability of data in final accounts. For example, there are several methods of assessing the depreciation charge for a variety of capital assets. Similarly there are different routines for valuing stocks of raw materials. Each of these alternative methods of capital asset and stock valuations will have an impact upon the accounting profit reported in the profit and loss account. However the convention of consistency demands that whichever method is used, it should be applied uniformly in each year. By these means relevant expenditures and values, recorded in the accounts of different years, can be expected to reflect similar conditions of profitability and wealth. Should it be necessary to vary the methods of valuing stocks or of calculating annual depreciation charges, then the fact of so doing must be clearly stated when the accounts are prepared and published.

In the majority of instances balance sheet values of fixed assets are based upon their initial acquisition costs. Now those historic costs do not reveal the current capital costs of being in business, even where asset replacements are continually being made. Neither does the historic cost concept present a realistic investment sum against which current profits can be compared. Here it must be emphasized that when business profits are determined, they are calculated by matching input/output values-expenditures and incomes, which derive from present-day prices. Clearly a responsible, objective quantification of the investment sum which is necessary to set up a business requires the use of replacement cost in our up-dating of that invested sum.

The act of revising out-dated historic values being attributed to corporate assets is a recognition of the increasing worth of a business' wealth. The funds employed are seen to be represented by higher valued physical assets: the net worth of the proprietors' interest in the firm has grown.

1. Total fixed assets are given a higher book value.
2. The firm's total assets—the employment of funds—have been increased in value.
3. The funds-employed totals will be increased by a similar amount.
4. The worth of the proprietor's investment has been increased to identify the ownership of the growing corporate wealth.

Revaluation of Fixed Assets

Balance sheet extract prior to revaluation

Balance sheet as at ...

Proprietors investment	Fixed assets	Rs.
Ordinary shares, etc.	Buildings at cost	20,000

Balance sheet after revaluation

Balance sheet as at ...

Proprietors investment Rs.	Fixed assets	Rs.
Ordinary shares, etc.	Buildings at	
Revaluation reserve 10,000	revaluation	30,000

The consequences of fixed assets revaluation go beyond the data found in balance sheets. Thus profit and loss accounts, relating to periods subsequent to the revaluations of corporate fixed assets, will have to bear increased depreciation charges. It should be noted, however, that the calculations may not be so straight forward as is given above. At the time of revaluation, one would expect that the remaining economic life of a revalued asset would be appraised. If a longer life appears likely, the depreciation charges would not be varied to such a great extent as the example suggests.

We have to recognise however that the post-evaluation accounting profits will be adversely affected to some extent. The cost of resources consumed is being more realistically stated. Clearly the greatest adverse impacts upon reported profits will be experienced by those firms operating in highly capitalised industries.

Capital invested and capital employed

The proprietors: The final accounts of any business are of interest to a varied public. Each group of interested observers will have its own objectives and requirements. The shareholders of a company will regard their total investment—their capital employed—as the book value of

Subscribed shares + Reserves

But the ordinary shareholders are the residual proprietors of the firm and in order to evaluate the profitability of their investment we have to be more specific. The definition of the equity shareholder's capital employed will be the book value of

Subscribed ordinary shares + Reserves

or

Total shareholder's interest — Nominal value of issued preference shares

As above mentioned the amount involved is 67,000, but if the balance sheet had revealed any fictitious or intangible assets, then these book values would have been deducted from the 67,000. In this connection fictitious assets would include such items as

> expenses of share issues and other capital formation expenses which had not yet been charged to a profit and loss account,

and intangible assets would refer to

> goodwill, which is normally recorded in balance sheets at totally unjustifiable values.

Turning to the profitability rating of the equity shareholders' invested capital, we have to determine the sum of post-tax profits available for the Ordinary shareholders. When this is expressed as a percentage of the equity shareholders' invested capital, it will provide a rate of return figure which can be used in comparative analyses of company accounts. Thus if the pre-tax profits of the Component Manufacturing Company were 15,000, the amount available for the proprietors would be

Pre-tax profits	15,000
Taxation (say 50%)	7,500
Post-tax profits	7,500
Preference share dividend	500
Profits available for Ordinary shareholder Rs. 7,000	

Financial analysts: Financial analysts, long-term investors and lenders of money to the industrial and commercial sector of the economy are more interested in the profitability of the total long-term funds available to a company. In this context, the appropriate definition of the capital employed by a company embraces the book values of its

Fixed assets + Working capital

Which can be alternatively expressed as

Fixed assets + Current assets — Current liabilities

Now working capital measures the book value of the net short-term assets that a business uses to finance its operations—the working of its fixed assets: it is a vital part of the capital employed continuously in the firm's operations. Current assets are described as short-term assets and current liabilities as short-term credit. Thus the Component Company has 100,000 worth of current assets and 63,000 worth of current liabilities giving a value of 37,000 to the working capital at the date of that balance sheet. If we add this sum to the book value of the fixed assets, 45,000, we arrive at the capital employed total of 82,000.

In an appraisal of the overall profitability of the company's operations we shall express the profits before tax and debenture interest as a percentage of the above capital employed sum. Such a percentage rating enables us to compare the firm's profitability progress over a number of years. It also enables comparisons with similarly calculated ratings for other companies.

Company management. On the other hand when management sets out to appraise the profitability of corporate operations, it has to identify the performance of divisions and subsidiary units. Thus when the test of return on capital employed is applied to such units, it will always be necessary to specify those long - and short-term assets which must be counted in the units' respective capital employed sum. In this way a divisional or subsidiary unit's capital employed total will describe the physical assets which they have available for generating their own incomes and profits.

But the appraisal of divisional profitability demands more than an identification of assets *available*. It requires a recognition that subsidiary units need to *control* their asset mix, if they are to be called to account for the effectiveness of their use. Now the existence of debtors and bank balances are frequently determined by Head Office policies towards credit and cash management. These assets therefore cannot be said to be within the control of the management of most divisions and subsidiary units.

Consequently we shall find that concepts of capital employed, used for monitoring the performance of internal divisions and units, will include

1. Their fixed assets *plus* stocks
2. Their fixed assets *plus* stock *plus* a notional sum representing and average monthly cash requirement for the division or unit.

When applied to the data given item (1) above would amount to 112,500. The value attaching to definition (2) would be 112,500 *plus* the notional amount of the monthly cash needs for the unit's operations.

The difficult point arises when we attempt to locate that profit attributable to a segment of the corporate whole. Where goods are transferred from one division or factory to another, the system of pricing inter-unit transfers is bound to affect the outcome. The problem is not insuperable—we can use estimated market prices for input/output calculations and thus derive a workable return on capital rating. It is, however, a complex problem: a study of its implications goes beyond the objectives of this book. Our main object at this stage is to examine how the concept of capital employed can be applied to a study of the effectiveness of separate units of a business, where financing policies are not the prime consideration.

Constituents of return on capital employed

Return on capital employed, the overall average measure of corporate profitability, indicates the rate at which profit is generated by economic use of the amalgam of assets owned by the firm.

The right-hand side of the equation will lead a financial analyst into a detailed study of how and why a firm has achieved its present return on capital rating. The right-hand side of the equation explains how the 23.5 per cent return has been achieved. In particular the figure 2 tells us that 2 worth of sales was generated by each 1 worth of capital employed. Furthermore the 11.77 per cent return on sales shows that each 1 worth of sales earned a profit of 11.77p. These two principal constituents can lead us to a more detailed analysis of the overall 23.5 per cent return on capital employed.

Variations in capital employed

But such performance ratings as those calculated above are reflections of the asset values recorded in company balance sheets. Both net profit and capital employed totals will be affected by management's policies towards:

1. Asset valuation and revaluation.
2. Choice of method of depreciation of those assets.
3. Valuing stock of raw material and work-in-progress.

Moreover, a company which has re-equipped its operating units by replacing older or less efficient assets will, in a period of rising prices, record higher values for the assets employed in the business. Unless net profit also increases markedly from the use of more efficient assets, a lower ROC percentage will result from the increased capital employed sum.

On the other hand, a firm that has continued to work with aged plant and machinery which has not been revalued or modernised, will present a lower capital employed sum. In the cases the ROC percentage could be unrealistically high. So it becomes essential to watch each company's capital spending from year to year, and to verify the rates of depreciation being charge in each years' accounts. To some extent we can test the age mixture of a firm's fixed assets by using the following formula :

$$\frac{\text{Balance sheet value of plant}}{\text{Aggregate depreciation of plant}}$$

And so long as the resultant ratio is greater than unity, then we may infer that the related fixed assets are not being run down. But some firms depreciate their fixed assets at a faster rate than would be required by the firm's own estimates of the expected economic lives of those assets. In such instances the ratio could eventually fall below unity, yet it would not mean that aged and relatively inefficient assets were being used. Here we would have to examine the annual depreciation rates being applied to the various types of fixed asset. In very general terms we would be prepared to accept charges falling within the following ranges :

Buildings between 3 and 6 per cent

Plant between 7 and 14 per cent

Vehicles between 15 and 25 per cent

provided there was evidence of their consistent application from year to year.

Effectiveness of capital employed

The physical content of a firm's capital employed should be examined critically each year in order to identify those assets (a) whose productivity was declining, or (b) were becoming too costly to maintain in operation. Here an appraisal of the viability of each of the firm's assets, and the amount of its working capital may reveal areas of potential reduction in the funds invested in the firm's activities. So the quantum of capital employed might be seen to be capable of reduction in a realistic fashion. In such circumstances the funds released, by selling unused assets or by reducing working capital needs, might be used to acquire more efficient capital assets. Alternatively loans may be repaid or bank overdrafts reduced.

A reduction of 24 per cent in the book value of the firm's capital employed has raised profitability by 32 per cent. Similarly if the sum of capital employed was halved—with the same levels of profits and sales—the return percentage would be doubled. Here we must recognise that the total value of the employed capital and the productivity of its constituent assets are vital in the appraisal of corporate profitability. Equation shows that an increase in sales of capital employed from 2 to 2.65 has brought about a marked improvement in the firm's overall profitability rating.

Return on sales

We will now assume that 20,000 of funds released through reduction of the corporate investment in fixed assets and working capital has been re-invested in more efficient plant and equipment. In consequence of these efficiency studies and the related changes in the asset content of the capital employed, the firm's net profit is expected to rise from 19,300 to 22,600. Similar impacts upon a company's ROC will be achieved by reorganising the flow of work-in-progress through the shop floors. Sound production control methods can improve the output rate from a given mixture of operating assets. Again, as we have seen, the control and reduction of costs through a careful monitoring of the various categories of business expenditure can have a notable impact upon the overall return on capital employed.

Solvency

It would be a grave mistake to restrict one's view of a company to an examination of its profitability performance only. The power to remain in business will be determined, in the last resort, by a firm's ability to settle its debts. Thus corporate solvency, the possession of sufficient liquid assets to meet the demands of creditors as those demands become due, must be our next and most important topic to study.

Trade suppliers and short-term creditors: The suppliers of short-term credit facilities and those who supply raw materials and components on credit are primarily concerned with the immediate security of sums due to them. Their principal concern therefore centres upon the firm's fund of short-term assets, from which their claims will be paid. Thus a surplus of current assets over current liabilities will be a strong feature supporting a sound solvency state for most companies. This surplus has been defined as the company's working capital

However the absolute sum of working capital is not the best of guides for appraisal of a solvency state. Short-term creditors should examine the relationship between the total sum of current assets and the total sum of current liabilities. It is a matter of judgment whether this ratio represents an adequate cover for the current liabilities or not. A firm engaged in business with a strong seasonal emphasis could find itself manufacturing for stock during a large part of the year. In this event current ratios of 3:1 or 4:1 might be necessary, at least during the off- season trading period. On the other hand, a retail business, selling mainly or wholly for cash, would most likely be considered as financially sound with a ratio of unity.

But the current ratio has its limitations also. The asset 'cover' for current liabilities is comprised of stocks, debtors, bank and cash balances - these being the principal components of the quantum of current assets. Debtors, bank and cash balances describe the totals of monies due to, and in possession of, the company. Stocks denote merely the possibility of future income through the conversion of stocks into saleable commodities. Therefore a more precise test of a current solvency state will exclude the book value of stocks from the calculations : this more realistic test will be concerned with the most liquid of the current assets.

Basics of Budgeting Process

Financial planning may be described as a forward-looking appraisal of the financial aspects of an established business program, leading to decisions regarding the most effective course of action to be taken over a future period. It encompasses both the business plan and its translation into terms of the funds needed to carry out the plan. It touches on the acquisition of these funds, control of their expenditure, and the appraisal of the results of the expenditures.

Implicit in that description of financial planning are the two principal components of the job of the financial administrator as he measures his firm's needs for business funds: (1) long-term planning, which involves establishing the objectives of the business and forecasting the conditions that will affect those objectives, and (2) short-term planning and budgeting, which include planning cash flows in the short run, controlling them, and appraising the results of the operations of the business.

We will be primarily concerned with the short-term planning and budgeting component. Although it is difficult to separate the various elements of financial planning and to examine them in isolation from one another, it is helpfull to concentrate on the development and use of budgets in financial planning as the key element in measuring needs for business funds. Financial planning should of course, precede and control the formulation of a budget, since a good budget is the result of good planning. In the final analysis, however, the budget is the expression in financial terms of the plan of operations designed to achieve the objectives adopted by the business firm. Budgeting therefore will receive the major emphasis in this chapter. We will take a look, first, at budgets in general and, then, specifically at the cash budget as one of the most important tools of financial administration.

Nature of budgets in the planning process

All economic units—whether they are individuals, households, civic clubs, businesses, or govern-ments—engage in financial planning and, to a large extent base their economic activities on budgets, those budgets may be voluminous, formal documents, such as those produced by the federal government and the several states, or they may simply be the mental notes of a housewife as she attempts to stretch her husband's paycheck to cover a new party dress for the annual lodge dance. Regardless of what they look like—or whether they even exist in written form—budgets are essentially tools of successful financial administration and an integral part of the process of financial planning.

There is much more to the budget and the budgeting process than simply the production of a document or an organized approach to forecasting cash flows, however. After the business goals and objectiveness have been clearly defined and the long-range forecast of the economic environment has been made, there remain four steps that are necessary to define the budgeting process fully. They are, in their order of performance:

1. preparing the approved budget to be used as an operating plan for the relevant period

2. comparing actual results with the budget at regular intervals
3. analysing the variances of actual from budgeted performance
4. deciding on what, if any, corrective action needs to be taken to eliminate the cause of the variance.

These four steps are the essence of financial planning and control for profit-seeking firms and non-profit organizations alike. Differences in form, degrees of formality and procedures may exists, but the nature and purpose of the budgeting process remain constant.

Preparing the budget

As suggested earlier, all businesses, as well as all governmental bodies and other miscellaneous classes of organizations, operate on the basis of a budget. The budget may be only a seat of the pants forecast, it may be an elaborate system of planning and control, or it may be something in between those two extremes. But if it is something less than a formal budgeting system, the business runs a real risk of making costly mistakes that an adequate budgeting system could help it avoid. It should also be emphasized that each business must develop a system, that will meet its individual needs. No one given system, is suitable for all firms because no two firms operate exactly the same way or have executives who have achieved the same levels of competence or sophistication with regard to planning and control methods. However, all soundly conceived budget systems share certain features which will be described here. While the following discussion deals mainly with the profit-seeking manufact-uring firms, the principles presented are equally applicable to service firms, governmental bodies, and non-profit organizations.

Type of budgets

Budgets may be classified according to their flexibility as planning and control devices. The two main types are the fixed budget and the flexible budget. A fixed budget is one that is established for a definite period in advance and is not subject change for alteration during the budget period. This type of budget is most characteristic of governmental bodies. But it is also used by business firms that can forecast the demand for their products—and, hence, the costs of operating their facilities to meet such demand—over the budget period with a high degree of accuracy. A fixed budget program should be the ultimate goal of every well-run business that manufactures on a stock basis, because it enforces the need for accurate forecasting and planning as well as the need for overall coordination of the entire business operation in an effort to achieve budget objectives.

The flexible budget, in contrast, is especially suited for those firms in which operating costs are variable at different levels of production and for those businesses that encounter difficulties in accurately forecasting their products demands. For example, a company that manufactures highly styled items or produces on a customer-order basis may experience wide fluctuations in sales and consequently will experience significant variations in its operating costs. Similarly, hospitals, whose patient load is unpredictable in large measure, nay operate at full capacity during one period and be left with empty beds in the next. The flexible budget makes allowance for such variations from the initial estimates by providing for constant revisions in the estimates of related income, expenses, and cash flow. Thus, a firm having those characteristics can still achieves good control over its expenditures and plan its operations satisfactorily on a short-term basis by establishing a flexible budget system.

In practice most business firms use a combination budget system comprised of both fixed budgets and flexible budgets. The combinations are, of course, unlimited. For example, fixed budgets are commonly applied to such areas as advertising, research and development, data processing, and capital expenditure, while the actual production of goods or the provision of services is controlled under a flexible budget arrangement. Also, a firm that manufactures both stock items and custom-made items on special order may find the combination budget most appropriate. In this case, the production and sale of the stock items will be controlled under a fixed budget, and the flexible budget will control the production and sale of items produced to customer order.

Budgeting period

There are almost as many budgeting "period" as there are individual managers who establish requirements for budgets. Thus the answer to the questions of how long a budgeting period must be is simply "long enough to provide for effective planning". This makes the specific answer one of individual choice suited to the individual needs of the firm.

The typical business budget covers a period of one year, with a monthly breakdown within that period. In some instances, budgets are made continuous by extending the budgets by 1 month as each month of actual operations comes to a close. For example near the end of January 1976, the budget for January 1977 is prepared and appended to the budget for the 11-month interim. In this way, a 12-months budget is always available. The major advantage of this method is that it avoids the annual budgeting session that usually brings a halt to all other activities within the business, while executives dig out data needed for sales forecasts, productivity estimates, machinery downtime, and so forth. In other words, the monthly "update" permits management to make budgeting and its associated datagathering processes a routine part of normal operations. Also firms that borrow money are usually required to produce projections of operations as part of their loan applications; having a continuous 12 month forecast is a decided advantage. Finally, under a yearly budgeting cycle, in which only one budget is prepared each year, the formal budgeting period averages only 6 months. Thus for the last 6 months of the period, the planning horizon becomes very short; the firm runs the danger of failing to take into account important events that lie beyond the period covered by the budget. The firm under continuous budgeting, however always has a 12 month advance notice of "known" inventory build-ups, loan repayment, dividend dates, and so forth.

Some budgets are by their nature made on a long term basis. Capital improvement budgets are one example. Such budgets include additions to and renovations of plant, equipment, machinery, and other fixed facilities. Individual construction projects may take several years to complete before operations can begin; therefore, the budget period must be extended to cover the entire building phase, at least, in order to insure that the funds for the periodic construction payments are available at the proper times.

The important point to remember is, as with all other aspects of budgeting, that the budget period must be matched with the needs of the individual firm. Manufacturers of women's fashions may budgets from season to season; automobile begins on next year's model; ship-builders work with budgets covering two to three years when involved in the construction of larger vessels. And each of those budgets will probably undergo at least one revision and probably many more before the budgeting period comes to a close.

Budgeting procedure

Although budgeting procedures vary greatly among business firms, the typical procedure, which is also generally applicable to the non-profit enterprise, calls for the separate departments and sub-divisions of the business to prepare individual departmental budgets. The financial admini-strator, who is usually assigned the responsibility of coordinating the budget process, will supply the department heads with certain information on which they will base their estimates. This information will include a statement of the firm's overall objectives, general operating policies applicable to the various departments, and relevant statistical and accounting data covering past results. The department budgets are then brought together to form the preliminary budget, which is subsequently reviewed by the firm's top management.

During the preparation of the preliminary budget, discussions generally take place between the financial manager and the department heads. Such discussions often lead to revisions within and across departmental lines because of the interdependencies among departments which always exist in business organizations. For example, a decision but the marketing division of a large manufacturing firm to, say conduct extensive market research by mailing questionnaires to certain consumer groups will have a direct bearing on the mail room staffing and the work load of the data processing department, which will be called upon to aid in analysing the returns. Unless such plans have been previously coordinated, they might represent a major surprise to departments that must support them. Chances are also that the budgeting process will turn up the need for coordination of plans among departments in several instances, especially in very large organizations.

The form and content of the preliminary budget, again, should be designed to meet the needs of the individual firm's. Some business require detailed budgets, some do not need as much detail, and others require the detail but do not really need it or *vice versa*. The maximum detail required for a manufacturing company budget will probably include the following sections.

1. sales budgets
2. cost of sales budgets
3. inventory increase or decrease budgets
4. production budgets
5. direct materials budget
6. direct labour budgets
7. machine-hour budgets
8. labour budgets for maintenance cleaning internal transportation and so forth
9. utilities budgets
10. indirect supplies budgets
11. other indirect labour and expense budgets
12. selling expense budgets
13. advertising expense budgets
14. administrative expense budgets
15. other operating income and expense budgets
16. non-operating income and expense budgets

All of these budgets—or combinations of them if less detail is required—are useful in the preparation of the three financial or master, budgets common to almost all budget systems:

1. profit and loss budgets
2. capital expenditures budgets
3. cash budgets

These three budgets are generally approved by top management and presented to the board of directors for its approval.

Budgetary control

The finished master budgets can be thought of as the first step of budgetary control. Once the master budgets have been approved and the budget period starts, it becomes necessary for management to begin at once to exert strong efforts to reach the projected goals and to review these efforts as time goes by.

If properly prepared, budgets are forecasts for reasonably attainable results. These results are projected are the responsibilities of the managers who prepared the departmental budgets; consequently, these same managers can be called upon to give an accounting of the activities over which they have jurisdiction, if actual performance is different from their forecasts. Once the budget variance is discovered, the last two steps of budgetary control can then be taken in order: (2) Analysing the causes of the variance, and (3) taking the appropriate course of action to correct the situation.

When the actual results of operations are reasonably close to expectations, there exists a strong presumption that all is well. But there should also exist that extra effort to attempt to improve performance so that a favourable variance will be achieved in the next period. On the other hand, an unfavourable variance always justifies a search for cause followed by a fixing of responsibility.

Cash budgets

The cash budgets, as its name implies, summarizes the estimated cash inflows and the estimated cash disbursements of a business over the budget period. It also shows the resultant cash position, generally on a monthly basis, as the budget period develops. It is the formal presentation of the expected circular flow of cash through the business. The cash budget is an extremely important tool of financial administration because its principal purpose is to predict if, when, and by how much the firm's cash resources will likely either be in excess of estimated requirements or become insufficient to cover the checks it must write during the budget period. Once those predictions have been made, the financial administrator can begin to plan how best to utilize his firm's existing and anticipated cash resources to finances its separations and growth and maintain a satisfactory cash position.

Cash receipts and net income

It is important to keep in mind the earlier discussion about the flow of cash and the point that was made concerning the difference between the net income figure as shown on the income statement and the net change in the firm's bank balance. Many items of cash expenditure are not included as expenses in the income statement; conversely, some items of expense appearing on the income statement do not require a cash outlay in the same period.

Except under rather unusual circumstances, therefore, there will be a difference between the estimated profit for the budget period and the additional accumulation of cash in the firm's bank account. And this deference may be of crucial importance in financial planning; neglecting to take this into account could led the financial officer to wholly mistaken conclusions and the firm into financial difficulties.

Selected transactions and their effects on the income statement and cashs budget

Transaction	*Income Statement*	*Cash Budget*
Cash sales	Yes	Yes
Collections on accounts receivable in previous periods	No	Yes
Credit sales to be collected in subsequent periods	Yes	No
Payment of wages earned in previous period	No	Yes
Cash payment for materials to be used in manufacturing following year's model	No	Yes
Advance payment from customer on order to be filled during subsequent periods	No	Yes
Instalment payment on purchase of fixed assets	No	Yes
Depreciation and amortization expenses	Yes	No
Quarterly tax payment on previous year's income	No	Yes
Purchase of short-term investments	No	Yes
Cash dividend payment to stockholders	No	Yes
Sale of company's stock or issuance of bonds	No	Yes
Bad-debt expense	Yes	No
Repayment of loan principal to bank	No	Yes
Payment of current interest charges to bank	Yes	Yes
Cash sale of fixed assets at less than book value	Yes	Yes
Advance payment of fire insurance Premium for subsequent periods	No	Yes

The transactions selected for inclusions in the Table should be sufficient to show why firm's anticipated results from operations as presented in the income statement can be quite different from the results as shown by the cash budget from the same period.

Selecting budget period and method

The business firm with an established budget system will experience little difficulty in preparing a cash budget, since most of the information required for its preparation is contained in the departmental operating and cost budgets. The financial administrator, in approaching the task of preparing the cash budget, however, must first decide on what time period it will cover and what method he will use. The general considerations involved in selecting a budget period were discussed earlier in this chapter, but it should be pointed out that the cash budget period is largely dependent upon the stability of the firm's sales and production. If the volume of sales and the product prices are stable and production can be scheduled at a more or less constant rate throughout the year, the period can be set quite long, even beyond the usual one-year limit. If, however, dollar sales are subject to erratic movement or production is dependent upon the availability of orders which cannot movement or production is dependent upon the availability of order which cannot be accurately forecast, the period of the cash budget must be shortened.

Normally, the cash budget is prepared separately for each month of the budget period. If the firm's cash position is "tight" or the margin of profit is narrow, such as in the grocery business, it is usually necessary to prepare separate forecasts on a weekly or even a daily basis. It is also advisable to prepare a continuous budget and keep the planning horizon far enough removed from the present to avoid as many "surprises" as possible.

The most commonly used methods of preparing the cash budget are: (1) cash receipts and disbursements, (2) adjusted net income, and (3) pro forma balance sheet. In all three methods, the information with which the final budget is constructed is basically the same. But since they utilise different forecasting techniques the information each provides to the financial administrator is quite different.

The most widely used method is the cash receipts and disbursements method, and it is by far the most flexible of the three. It is consequently, most suitable for companies faced with considerable uncertainty regarding their cash flows, because of volatile sales and earnings records, and for companies that are experiencing tight cash positions. This method permits more frequent interim forecasts, such as for daily or weekly periods, and thus enables the financial administrator to maintain a more effective control over cash flows. Basically, the cash receipts and disbursements method records initially each source of cash receipts and each classification of cash disbursements so that the actual performance during the budget period can be compared with the budget in great detail. That facilitates the timing of cash payments with the firm's cash receipts on a continous basis, thereby reducing idle cash balances to a minimum and avoiding the embarrassment of running short of cash.

The other two methods are similar to one another. The adjusted net income method required that a proforma income statement be prepared for each desired interim period. The net income figures for each period are then adjusted to a cash basis by detailing the transactions that affect the income statement and the cash balance in different ways or that affect one without affecting the other. This approach to cash budgeting as used by Morgan Creek Distillery, Inc. It shows that the firm is expecting to earn increasing profits but will suffer a net cash drain over the quarter.

These effects result from a combination of the seasonal swing that takes place in the distillery industry at year end *plus* the normal cash drains associated with the servicing of debt and the payment of taxes. The firm also purchased $ 12,000 of fixed assets, which added to the loss of cash. Those factors combined to produce an expected loss of slightly over $ 6,000 in cash and will likely cause the cash balance to fall below the minimum the firm has established.

The proforma balance sheet method requires the preparation of as many proforma balance sheets as there are interim periods in the cash budget. Each item of the balance sheet except cash is projected for each period, and the cash balance is "forced," or "plugged," in accordance with the accounting equation asset — liabilities — capital accounts — by subtracting total estimated assets from total estimated liabilities and capital. A minus cash balance or a cash balance falling below the minimum desirable balance would, of course, indicate a need for borrowing funds or otherwise adjusting the circular flow to make up for the anticipated shortage of funds.

These latter two methods have certain disadvantages that tend to limit their use to those firms having stable earnings and sales and those having cash surpluses. First, neither method produces an item by item forecast of cash receipts and disbursements; consequently, it is difficult for the financial manager to plan the timing of the firm's payments closely with its anticipated receipts. Second, the lack of detail also makes it difficult to locate and appropriate individual account for adjusting the timing of cash flows during the budget period. Third, significant budget variance will present the financial manager with the problem of having to reconstruct the entire set of proforma statements in order to revise his cash forecast. This lack of flexibility may cause serious delays in the firm's ability to take appropriate corrective actions, and such delays can often prove costly. For example, a lending institution may wish to see the revised forecasts of cash flows before it would be willing to grant the firm's request for a loan. A one-or two-day delay in producing the proforma statements could cause the firm to lose discounts on purchases, thereby costing it money and perhaps lowering its credit rating.

Because of those disadvantages and because uncertainty characterizes the operations of all businesses, the cash receipts and disbursements method is probably the best method for most business firms to use in constructing cash budgets. The rest of this chapter is therefore devoted to a rather detailed description of the method and the way in which available information may be translated into the cash budget format.

Preparing the cash budget

As mentioned earlier, the first step in preparing the cash budget is the preparation of the departmental operating and cost budgets. To the information that these budgets contain are added the details of probable borrowing and the repayment of outstanding loans, cash flows associated with equity financing and other such transactions that are independent of the firm's operational circular flow of cash. If goes without saying that a failure to assemble careful and accurate estimates of transactions of any sort will likely render the cash budget practically useless. If, for example, the production manager carelessly overlooks an entire step of the firm's manufacturing process in compiling his budget, the cash budget will, obviously, predict a greater cash surplus than will actually exist during the budget period. Borrowing may become necessary, which will increase the unexpected cash outflow by the amount of the interest payment. Most important, however, the financial administrator will have received unpleasent 'surprise', and that is usefulness of the cash budget is highly dependent upon the accuracy of the estimate and the care with which all budgets are prepared.

When forecasts are known to be merely "best guesses," as, for example, in periods characterized by unsettled conditions in supply markets or when a firm introduces an entirely new product to the market the financial manager should be prepared for the worst, even though he may hope for the best. In such instances, more than one cash budget should be prepared so that management knows in advance the likely outcome of the worst combination of future events. Appropriate action can therefore be planned well ahead of an event everyone hopes will not occur. For example, if the cash budget prepared under a pessimistic set of assumptions reveals that the firm's future cash deficit will exceed its borrowing capacity, management will certainly want to protect the firm against insolvency under such circumstances. This may involve arranging for additional financing or adopting a more conservative operating plan for the period. Thus although accuracy in forecasting is always desirable, it is nevertheless possible to develop good plans under conditions of uncertainty. This point should be kept firmly in mind as we review the details of the cash budget preparation in the following sections.

Sales and collections

The sales budget constitutes the foundation upon which the entire budget program of the firm is developed. Only if the sales budget is correctly stated in terms of unit and dollar volume that can be realized during the budget period can the departmental budgets be constructed accurately and reliably. An accurate sales budget is the product of a careful forecast of sales, usually prepared by several different methods to ensure that all factors affecting the firm's sales have been considered. The usual method include an economic, or economic, or statistical, forecast based on past record; a unit sales forecast prepared by the estimating the selling prices of the firm's own sales personnel; and a dollar sales forecast prepared by the firm's own sales personnel; and a dollar sales forecast prepared by estimating the selling prices of the firm's products and relating them to the unit sales forecasts.

The product, or unit, forecasts should be compared with the productive capacity of the firm's manufacturing facilities to see whether the predicted unit sales are within the ability of the firm to produce. If the plant has been oversold, the sales forecasts will have to be adjusted downward or additional plant capacity will have to be acquired either through sub-contracting or constructing or purchasing new facilities. Finally, all of the forecasts are brought together to determine whether they produce a concensus. If the various methods of forecasting produce a wide range of sales predictions, they will have to be reconciled. Once that has been done, the financial administrator can begin the process of constructing the cash flow from the collections of the predicted sales.

First, it is necessary to separate cash sales from credit sale and then to analyze the credit sales for the purpose of determining the time lag between sales and collections. Particular note should be made of the effect of seasonal variations and of the effect of general business conditions on collections and on the length of the collection period. Unless a firm's list of customers changes dramatically from year to year, historical data will usually provide the basis for making estimates about what proportion of the sales of a given month will be collected in that month and each month thereafter and the magnitude of change the firm might expect in its collections, given the forecast of business conditions over the budget period.

Second, other factors affecting the firm's collections must be taken into account. For example, returns and allowance must be estimated, especially if cash refunds must be made. The amount of cash discounts that customers are likely to take should be judged. The effects of any planned changes in either the credit policy or the collection policy must also be taken into account. Finally, the firm's bad-debts experience must be brought into the picture, along with any expected deviations from past history resulting from either changing business conditions or possible changes in operating policies.

One of the many ways in which cash receipts from sales may be budgeted. That form of work sheet provides some of the details of how the forecast was constructed so that actual performance reported in the same detail can be compared with budgeted figures. Variances noted between actual and budgeted cash receipts from sales can be traced back through such details and the source of the variance can be discovered. That type of detail make it easier for the financial manager to fix responsibility for variances and facilitates quick and decisive action to remedy their causes. It also helps to improve forecasting techniques by providing a record that can be reviewed during subsequent budget periods. Such work sheets should be prepared for each section of the cash budget. They are retained on file and used for reviews and for the preparation of subsequent budgets.

In addition to that detail, it is advisable to put into writing the methods of forecasting used for each item listed in the varios work sheets, along with any assumptions that had to be made in order to arrive at the budget figures. This adds immeasurably to the information available for periodic revisions as conditions change. For example, the financial administrator in forecasting the collection of accounts receivable for the first quarter of 1975.

Note: It was assumed that the level of unemployment in the market area would continue to climb during the first quarter, adding significantly to the usual seasonal sales decline. Bad debt losses are expected to remain at a constant 1.25 per cent of credit sales, however.

Other cash receipts

Most businesses receive cash during the course of their operations from sources other than the sale of their products or services. Usually, these receipts are of a relatively small magnitude when compared to receipts from sales; however, if such sources exist, it is necessary to include them in the cash budget.

Examples of other cash inflows include rental income from property owned by the firm, interest and dividends from either permanent or temporary investments, liquidation of such investments, and royalties from licensing arrangements with other firms for manufacturing a product under its patents. Such receipts generally pose only minor problems in forecasting; because they are of small magnitude, inaccuracies in forecasting those flows will have a small impact on the overall cash budget. This does not mean, however, that such forecasts can be carelessly made, for even small errors can sometimes lead to major problems.

Cash disbursements for raw materials of goods for resale

The amounts paid and the timing of payments for raw materials during a given period are closely related to the volume of sales a firm is able to achieve. As with the relationship between sales and collections, however, this relationship is not necessarily precise. It may be upset by a decision to increase or decrease the size of any or all the firm inventories of raw materials, work in progress, or finished goods. Obviously, as increase in inventories would require purchases in excess of those required to support estimated sales; a decision to decrease inventories would lower the volume of purchases needed. Also, a decision to produce highly seasonal goods at a constant rate throughout the year would affect the timing of payments. Therefore, while the volume of sales will set the basic purchase requirements, the production schedule and the inventory policies will influence the timing and the ultimate quantity of goods purchased.

In constructing this particluar forecast for the cash budget, the financial administrator will assemble the information contained in the firm's direct materials budget, the detailed list of the current accounts payable, and the list of suppliers and their credit terms. He will have to distinguish between cash purchases and purchases on account; estimate the likely price changes over the budget period; and try to anticipate external influences, such as the possibilities of strikes, materials shortages, and the like, that would tend to alter the timing of purchases. He will also have to estimate probable return and allowances on goods purchased and plan on taking cash discounts when offered to lower both the cost of production and the cash outflow.

Cash payments for direct labour

The direct labour budget provides the hours worked by employees in the various job classifications. The conversion to money is relatively simple once the respective hourly rates of pay have been estimated for the budget period. To the estimate of direct wages must be added social security taxes, paid holidays, periodic payments into the retirement fund, payments for overtime worked, vocations or payments made in lieu of vacations, and such bonuses as may be prescribed by company policy. Changs in these "extras" over the budget period should also be considered, as should planned organizational changes that may tend to alter the number of employees in the various job classifications.

Cash disbursements for other operating expenses

The remaining cash disbursement for operating expenses is usually listed in the cash budget under the heading of manufacturing, selling, and administrative expenses. The bases upon which their related cash disbursements are estimated are the specific budgets. Those expense categories can also be classified as fixed expenses, variable expenses, and semi-variable expenses for purposes of forecasting the timing and magnitude of each.

Fixed expenses, by definition, are those that are expected to remain constant regardless of the level of production. Such expenses include property taxes: insurance; executive compensation; and most dues, and service constricts. Althogh the level of these expenses independent of the level of production, they cannot be expected to remain constant for ever. Property tax rates and insurance rates do change, especially when new fixed assets are acquired, and executive compensation can be expected to rise from year to year. It can be concluded, therefore, that the same degree of care must be given to estimating payments to cover fixed costs as that required for all other classes of expense.

Variable expenses are those that are expected to vary directly with the level of production or sales. Examples of variable expenses are packaging and shipping costs; salesmen's commissions; and certain pre-printed production, sales, and administrative forms. One of the major problems that is likely to be encountered in constructing forecasts for this class of expenses is the effect relative prices have on then as the level of production or sales change. If, for example, a 10 per cent increase in dollar sales increases salesmen commissions by 15 per cent one year, and both the rate of commission and the selling price of the firm's product are scheduled to be changed during the budget period, the financial administrator must reconcile the effects of these changes on the relationship between the two items before he can accurately forecast that expense. Similarly a change in the price of packaging materials will alter the relationship between shipping costs and unit sales.

Forecasting problems associated with semi-variable expenses arise from two sources. First, the relationship between these expenses and the scale of operation can be either direct or indirect and may change at a changing rate. That is because semi-variable expenses are in part fixed and in part variable. Second, change in relative prices have similar effects on these types of expenses as they do on the purely variable expenses. A forecast of lower sales for the budget period may create a need to increase spending for advertising in order to keep sales from declining even further. In other words, the advertising budget contains a fixed portion that can be looked on as that expenditure necessary to maintain the firm's share of the market. If the market itself expands there may be only a slight need to expand the advertising budget to cover the new portion of the market since sales will probably increase any way. If, however, the firm wants to increase its market share, advertising expenses must increase whether the trend in sales in upward or downward for the budget period in order to obtain maximum sales. Added to this forecasting problems the possibility of change in the rate structures of the firm's advertising media or an internal decision to change the mix of advertising toward either a more expensive package or a less expensive one.

Other cash disbursements

Included in the category of other cash disbursements are items that usually create only minor forecasting problems. Such items are bond interest payable; repayment of loans and retirement of long-term debt; cash expenditures for fixed assets; cash dividends; and acquisitions and maintenance of non-operating assets, such as real estate not employed in the ordinary operation of the business. Of course, outlays for such obligations and acquisition must be as carefully estimated as those directly related to the firm's manufacturing processes, selling efforts, and administration.

Managing working capital

Working capital is normally taken to mean the excess of current assets over current liabilities, this amount being the net current assets. If the balance sheet for ABC PLC is examined the working capital for that company is seen to be 3065539 minus 2505132, which amounts to 560407.

The working capital indicates the liquidity of the company, and there are two commonly used rations to express the degree of liquidity. One is the current ratio which is simply the current assets divided by the current liabilities.

Some accountants consider that it is more useful to ignore inventories when looking at liquidity, since they could take considerably longer to turn into cash than debtors or creditors. They feel that it is more pertinent to compare the quick assets with the current liabilities.

There is no generally ideal current ration since companies differ so greatly from each other. 1.2 may be appropriate for a light engineering company like ABC PLC with a short production cycle. The same ratio, however, may be too low for a company with a longer cycle and a proportionately bigger stock investment. On the other hand, a supermarket with no work in progress and no debtors would very likely have a current ratio of less than 1; that is, an excess of current liabilities over current assets. One should try neither to maximise nor minimise the liquidity rations; one should try to optimise them in relation to the objective, which in the case of a commercial company is probably the maximisation of profit on capital employed. The lower the liquidity rations are, the more vulnerable the company is to pressure from creditors which it is unable to meet. The higher the liquidity rations, the more the capital which is not being fully exploited in terms of the return earned on it. Therefore, one should seek to have as little working capital as is consistent with not being unduly vulnerable to pressure from creditors. This deal level of liquidity would not only vary from company to company but would vary through time in one company as conditions changed.

Like liquidity, stock holding has to be balanced; it should be neither maximised nor minimised but optimised in terms of profit. Too much stock means that there is money tied up in it which is costing more than it is contributing. Too little stock means that the cost of lost sales due to being out of stock exceeds the savings made in not holding the additional stock.

However, there are other factors to be considered in deciding the optimum stock level: for example, whether there are additional costs in holding increased stock rather than just the interest on the capital. If the stock level were to be reduced by a given amount, would the company be able to vacate a warehouse with consequent savings in rates, rent, insurance, heating etc? How many store men could be dismissed or redeployed?

Stock appreciation should also be brought into account. If the company uses volatile commodities, it might save a great deal of money in holding more than its immediate requirements of a material whose market price is expected to rise during the period covered by the holding: this saving may far outweigh the extra stocking costs and throw in as a bonus freedom from the danger of being caught out of stock.

The stock ratio is not ideal in a number of respects. Firstly, the turnover is at selling prices, while the stock is at cost. Secondly, the turnover covers a period, while the stock is at a point of time which may not be typical of the period. Thirdly, the cost of the stock is not factual but is a function of the company's costing system which includes arbitrary assumptions and subjective judgements.

Apart from inventories, a major development of working capital is in the credit taken by customers. This does not of course apply to those retailers and others who do not conduct a credit trade. Alternatively, there may be a strong seasonal bias within the year's total second six months, then the ratio is 1907 x 26 weeks, which is just under 12 weeks. However, this is a problem for the external readers of the balance sheet, since managers with access to the management accounts could take the seasonal bias into consideration in calculating the ratio.

These are the opposite side of the coin to the debtors. They are a source of funds to the company, and the more capital the company can borrow from this source, the less it requires from others, or alternatively the more it can deploy in various assets and build up the activity (and possibly the return) on the same net capital.

The creditors, being money owing in respect of purchases, will be compared with the purchases in the recent period and expressed in weeks. The purchases are not a figure which is required to be shown separately in the published accounts, but once again it will be available to managers. They should use it in the same way as the debtors' ratio by allowing for the seasonal bias.

Readers of the published accounts can make the assumptions that purchases are roughly the same proportion of sales in the recent year as they were in the previous year. Then they can compare the movement of creditors with that of debtors, ABC's debtors increased from 1621 063 to 1 906 981 by 17 1/2 percent. The creditors rose from 545 552 to 938 009 which is over 73 per cent and a considerable relative improvement. Indeed, in absolute terms the increase in creditors exceeds the increase in debtors, so that the net cost of credit to the company may have fallen despite the increase in turnover.

However, the average length of credit taken by the company from its suppliers is still not known. Suppose for the sake of argument that the 938 000 represents two months credit, that is, average monthly purchases have been running at half that level. Then, an increase of one month to three month will, other things being equal, raise borrowing from this source by about 469 000 and at the same time reduce the bank overdraft by the same amount. The total current liabilities will remain the same but the company will have substituted additional borrowing from suppliers for part of what it previously borrowed from the bank. The effect on profit of the change, assuming overdraft interest as, say, 15 per cent pa, is a gain of about 70 000 pa. This is not a once and for all gain but will continue at that rate for as long as the additional credit is taken. This assumes that (a) purchase continue at the current level, (b) interest rates continue at 15 per cent pa and (c) relations with suppliers remain unaltered. If there are changes in either (a) or (b) the effects can be easily ascertained, but assumption (c) requires careful consideration. If we take more credit from a supplier, will that supplier react and if so how will his reaction affect us?

There are a number of things the supplier can do, from writing a letter (which costs the customer nothing) to withholding supplies (which may cost the customer a great deal). Between these extremes, he may reduce quality, increase prices, cut down deliveries and so on. However, there is doubt about the validity of these intermediate reactions.

He may reduce the quality of the product or the frequency of delivery or after-sales service, but this may not be acceptable to the customer who may then withdraw his custom. Before taking any of these steps, the supplier would have to be prepared for this eventuality, the effect of which would be the same as if he himself withheld supplies.

Similarly, if the supplier increases his prices, the higher prices may or may not be acceptable to the customer. If they are, why did the supplier not increase them previously? If they are not, he once again risks losing the business. Therefore, the question facing the supplier is whether or not he can risk losing the business.

From the customer's point of view, he must decide whether he can tolerate loss of supplies from this source because, even though it may not be in the supplier's best interest to stop supplies, he may act irrationally and the customer must be prepared for this. The summary of this discussion is that the customer's ability to take longer credit from a particular supplier depends on the balance of power between them.

Since this varies with different suppliers it follows that an individual credit policy with at least the major suppliers is necessary if optimum credit is to be taken. If a banker credit policy is adopted to cover all suppliers, this assumes that they are all equally powerful, which is most unlikely to be the case. The consequence of this would be to take from some less credit than one could take with impunity; and to take from others more than is wise.

These arguments apply with equal force to debtor control, and since sales exceed purchases tight debtor control is even more important. It is often suggested that if a company takes longer credit from its suppliers, its own customers will in turn extend their credit and the move will be self defeating. This is woolly thinking.

Customers cannot know how a company behaves to its suppliers, save in the exceptional case where customer and supplier are the same and a two-way trade is conducted. In the normal case, the customer will take whatever credit he thinks he can get away with-with impunity. This consideration is based on the same assessment of relative power as already discussed concerning creditors.

However, many companies recognise the importance of intelligent debtor control and designate is as a specific management function, while attention is paid to prompt invoicing and follow-up procedures. It is the treatment of credit obtainable from suppliers that is relatively neglected.

So far we have not considered the effect on one's credit policy if one is offered a discount for prompt payment. For example, a supplier may offer a discount of 2 1/2 per cent on invoice for payment within 30 days.

If one pays two months from date of invoice and forgoes the discount, one has in fact borrowed for one extra month (since the first 30 days would be taken in any event) at a cost 2½ per cent which is equivalent to a straight annual cost of 12 x 2 1/ 2 per cent=30 per cent. The discounted annual rate would be even higher than this. Therefore, it is only worthwhile losing the discount if one can take at least 3 months' credit. However, if bank facilities are scarce it will pay to borrow at more than 15 per cent from suppliers if the benefit derived from the utilisation of the extra credit exceeds the cost.

So far in this chapter the various factors concerning liquidity have been discussed. We have seen that sub optimal utilisation of working capital is expensive. At least, if costs the interest on the unnecessary money used, but it also prevents that money from being properly employed in the company and could inhibit the company's growth through lack of cash.

Liquidity is the life-blood of the company and lack of cash is the only thing which could force the company out of business. Cash flows into the company by direct cash sales and the collection of debts from customers, and also, though less regularly, from the sale of assets. Cash flows out in direct purchases and payments to creditors, in payment of wages and other costs, and in the purchase of capital equipment. It also flows out in payment of taxes and interest on borrowed money and dividends to shareholders. These flows have to be predicted and controlled. This is done by forecasting and budgeting. Cash has always to be available to meet committed expenditure. If not, the company can be forced into liquidation by its creditors even though it has an overall excess of assets over liabilities. The company can also obtain additional transfusions of cash from time to time by means of additional bank facilities, which are likely to be relatively short-term, by raising fresh loans which are likely to be long-term and by rights issues of further ordinary shares which are permanent funds.

11
Accounting Management

One of the major tasks of the sales manager is to manage a pool of prospective or current accounts, or both. All sales management activities should be focused on the generation and maintenance of profitable accounts. That is the very core of our concern. While our prime orientation is not selling, it would be hard to discuss sales management and account management without at least a brief discussion of selling. The objective is not to make everyone a supersales person, but rather to introduce enough material about selling so that the general process is understood and can be managed by those active in it. While our prime interest will be on commercial and industrial selling-one company selling to another-many of the subjects discussed can be applied to consumer selling. The family, in fact, can be looked upon as an organizational buying unit with several participants, each with different needs. Consider, for example, the purchase of an automobile in a one-car family, consisting of a husband, a wife, a 16 year-old son, and an 8-year-old daughter, or a vacation decision for the same family. Each person will have differing needs and a different power position from which to present those needs.

Organizational interaction

Because we are primarily involved with commercial or industrial selling it should be clear that an account must be defined in terms of both the organization and the individuals within the organization.

Selling to an organization is much more complex than selling to an individual. There are two reasons for this: (1) an organization is made up of different individuals with different needs, and (2) these individuals interact with each other in complex ways. While it is impossible to consider organizational buying and selling indepth here, some of the more important points will be considered.

Consider first the different explicit needs of various participants in a purchase decision. When a firm buys a large piece of equipment, the manufacturing managers may desire an efficient machine which will require little repair and which is technically advanced; the treasurers department will be interested in financing terms; while the purchasing department's primary interest may be both total cost of the manufacturing system and out right cost of the machine. The selling company must take account of these various needs and of the importance and power of the persons possessing the needs. That, however, is only the first part. Not only does everyone in the firm have explicit needs based on his position and professional interests, but everyone also has personal needs. Buying decisions, because they involve authority and responsibility, represents a primary focus for the satisfaction of personal needs in the organizational setting. The young treasurer, for example, might be trying to consolidate his newly won power by showing how well he can do the job. The manufacturing people, on the other hand, might be smarting over a recent loss to the engineering people and be anxious for revenge.

The as tute firm, sales manager, and salesperson, of course, work veryhard togather information such as that mentioned above. It is a good deal of what both selling and account management are about.

As the size of the buying and selling companies has increased, and as the importance of major sales-those involving large sums of money-has grown, the selling process has become more complex. More people are involved in the purchase decision, and more needs have to be satisfied. The industrial salesperson, who previously sold capital equipment to engineers and supplies to the purchasing agent, must now sell systems to a buying committee including manufacturing, engineering, financial, and purchasing personnel. The apparel salesperson who sold items to Macy's Herald Square store and its two small branches in 1950 now sells programs to Macy's New York, with almost 2 dozen stores.

The selling process

The process consists of five steps: opening the relationship qualifying the prospect, presenting the message, closing the sale, and servicing the account—with accorted feedback loops.

Opening

The opening has two purposes: (1) to determine the right person in the organization to approach initially and (2) to generate enough interest so that it is possible to obtain the information necessary for qualification. The end result of the good opening should be an appointment with an appropriate and enthusiastic person. Given the complexity of many organizational buying situations, it is crucial to identify the key buying influences and their desires, the important interactions among buying influences,and the allocation of power among the influences. Typically, the salesperson should try to enter the situation with the most powerful buying influence and their desires, the important interactions among buying influences, and the allocation of power among the influences. Typically, the salesperson on his side. It is even better, of course, if all of the people involved are in favour of the seller's position. If the buying decision is a contested one, the salespersons who ally themselves with the weaker buying influences will, of course, be at a great disadvantage. Sometimes, the opening must be made through a particular participant in the decision. Often, the purchasing agent plays this role, In such situations, tradition and policy dictate that the salesperson contact the purchasing department before being allowed to contact other company personnel. In these situations, the purchasing agent can veto a salesperson's proposal but cannot ensure acceptance.

Qualifying

Qualifying is the process in which a salesperson determines whether or not prospect is worth the effort of a sales presentation. The key questions are:

1. Does this company have a need for my product or service?
2. Can I make the people responsible for buying so aware of that need that I can make a sale?
3. Will the sale be profitable to my company?

The qualifications is a very complex process because the answers to these three general questions are really dependent upon the answers to a much longer set of specific questions including:

1. Will be allowed access to enough information to assess the need?
2. Is the risk of changing current suppliers so high that the company will not make the change?
3. Does the current supplier have a special relationship, such as family or close personal friendship, which cannot be broken?
4. Can I identify and satisfy the personal and organizational needs of each major buying influence?
5. Will the sales time be such that the process is not justified by the size of the sale?

The qualification is a difficult activity because it requires the salesperson to be disciplined and objective about the chance to make a profitable sale. Although scholars of selling and sales management tend to gloss over the qualifying process, sales people and sales managers constantly discuss it. The executives of one sales training firm, who are all ex-salespersons, have developed a cassette sales training program which devotes' a whole cassette to this single subject. Two leading salesmanship books, on the other hand, cover the subject only briefly. If the prospect does not quality, then the salesperson can spend the time better somewhere else.

Presenting

The presentation is the core of the selling process and requires astute management on the part of the salesperson, It is the "pitch," the actual attempt at persuasion. There are a great many issues concerned with the presentation, including:

1. Location

2. Attendees
   (a) Who should represent the selling company?
   (b) Of the selling company's participants, who should play which role?
   (c) Who should the selling company want to represent the buying company?
   (d) Should it be a group presentation or a series of one-to-one presentations?
3. Content and order of presentation
   (a) Should material, both positive and negative to the selling company's position, be presented?
   (b) How long and detailed should it be?
   (c) Should it be informal or formal?

Closing

The presentation sooner or later culminates in an attempt to close the sale. Closing the obtaining the final agreement to purchase. This is the Achilles' heel of many would-be-successful salespeople. "Poor old Charlie, he's got a great personality, people like him, and he makes a great presentation but he just can't ask for the order - he can't close." The close is almost always performed with a question such as "When do you want it delivered?" or "Do you want the red one or the green one?

It is not only important to close the sale, but it is important to close it quickly. The salesperson who can close the sale quickly can then be off to make another call. The profit per sale goes down as the amount of time necessary to close goes up. In addition, the risk of losing the sale increases. Until it is closed, it is not a sale, nor is it safe from competitors or from a decision not to buy a product in that generic category.

Servicing

After the actual sale comes the service aspect. Often the salespeople will be responsible for managing installations, training, maintenance support, etc. In addition, they frequently sell supplies, take repeat orders as well as additional and/or larger orders, and perform services. These service functions are important for two reasons. First, they lead to additional sales. Second, they generate sales. In some capital equipment lines, for example, service contracts, supplies, and replacement parts account for greater dollar sales revenue than the initial order. Often, such business also carries very high margins.

Team and multilevel selling

Two lively issues in selling are multilevel selling and team selling Multilevel selling is the process by which several authority levels are called upon. The salesperson selling to a retailer, for example, may attempt to contact the buyer and merchandise manager, so that when the buyer taskes the salesperson's proposal to the mechandise manager for approval, the merchandise manager is presold, or at least receptive. Multilevel selling is, in a sense, a product of system selling, because the chief buying influence in the firms resides at a higher level in the organization than traditional buyers, and because that person is responsible for the total system instead of individual components. Consider, for example, the firm that has a manufacturing system for which one buyer purchases raw material and another machinery. If a selling firm wants to sell a system involving both, it is almost required to move up the purchasing organization to one person in charge of both raw materials and machinery. The sheer dollar size of some commitments or major changes in supplier relationships also forces the buying authority in some organizations to move upward in the organization.

Multilevel selling not only involves selling to different people in the buying firm, but it also often involves people at different levels in the selling firm. This generally occurs when the size of the sale justifies the cost, and the complexity of the buying process necessnates the approach. In a multilevel team sales approach, each level of the selling organization calls upon his counterpart in the buying organization. One reason for this is etiquette-it is more appropriate for the national sales manager to call on the general merchandise manager than for him to climb beyond his own level or to deal with someone beneath his own level. Another reason is that it demonstrates appropriate interest on the part of the management of the selling firm. Still a third reason is that an exchange of power is involved. The two top managers can make arrangements that their subordinates cannot.

Team selling does not necessarily have to involve different levels in the organization, It can involve members of different functional areas in the selling organization. If members of different functional areas in the buying organization have different needs and viewpoints, it is reasonable that those needs can best be met and those viewpoints best understood by the functional equivalents in the selling organization. For example, if the treasurer of the buying firm is concerned about financial arrangements, then the treasurer of the selling firm is probably better suited to deal with him than the salesperson whose primary job is to deal with manufacturing and purchasing personnel.

Three things should be clear about team selling. First it is not always appropriate, since sometimes the sale is simple, repetitive, or small. Team selling is most appropriate for the selling of heavy capital equipment or long-term supply relationships, in the form of either formal contracts of informal commitments. These involve enough dollars and enough different functions in the buying organization to justify the high expenditure of time involved in team selling. Second, team selling is complex and difficult to managed. It is possible for the sales team to spend more time getting coordinated than selling. Or, even worse, it can spend too little time getting coordinated and end up presenting contradictory impressions to the buying influences. Third, team selling is, in a sense, an extension of the marketing concept which stresses the importance of having all parts of the firm directed toward satisfying the customer needs. Although team selling is usually thought of as involving relatively high-level personnel and of being used primarily to "open" an account instead of to provide continuing maintenance selling, it can also be used with lower-level personnel and for maintenance selling. A soft drink bottler may, for example, primarily use a route delivery salesperson for selling, but may supplement his efforts with an in-store display and merchandising expert. In other situations, inside sales liaison personnel, expediters, or even shipping personnel may joint the sales team in keeping the account satisfied.

Selling in nonselling situations

In many industries selling has not been performed in a formal sense. Usually this is because of tradition or "professional ethics." Nonetheless, for example, lawyers and accountants both, who are prohibited from selling by "professional ethics," sell. It may be a very "soft," informal selling process, but it is selling.

The typical approach in such industries is to develop informal contact either through personal social relationships or by referral. The opening and the qualification are handled informally. After that, a more formal presentation may be made, or the presentation may also be informal. Finally, the close is executed. Throughout the process, the lack of explicit selling does not diminish the amount of strong persuasion brought to bear. Recently, "selling" has become more accepted in these situations. This is actually an explicit realization of a situation which has existed for many years. Whether it is called selling or not, it is selling.

The sales manager's role

In some situations, sales managers sell. In all situations, they are responsible for generating profitable sales. Thus, they must constantly focus on the salesperson-customer interaction. All of sales management are devoted to making profitable sales through astute formulation of the sales program and effective management of the sales force.

Personal selling allows the company to segment the market at its lowest level of desegregation, the individual customer, and to respond to the unique needs of that market segment. The sales manager must ensure that the appropriate prospects are approached and that their needs, both personal and organizational, and the needs of existing customers are met by the sales effort. Account management is the process of turning prospects into accounts and of servicing existing accounts in such a manner that they remain long-term, loyal accounts, continually buying more from the selling company. Selling is a part of account management. But account management is much more than selling. Some of the aspects beyond selling are the responsibility of the salesperson in his normal servicing of the account. Others are beyond the typical scope of the saleperson.

Account management is especially important in business selling-one firm selling to another-because, in almost all instances, the selling process is a continuing one. A supplier will sell the same type of merchandise to a buyer over and over again. Since the market for most products is quite finite, each seller must constantly face the same buyers. This is less true for the consumer market where there are many more buying units and where the "rebuy" process is infrequent for many products," such as houses, televisions, etc. Many of the subjects to be discussed here, however, are applicable to consumer selling.

The relationship between sales and account management

The truly astute firm is not interested in only making sales; it wants tobuild account relationships. Account relationships are a major asset of the successful firm. Although account relationships are not a tangible asset which accountants record on a financial statement, they are valuable to the company because they represent the ability to sell mechandise and services in the future relatively easily. If the company does a decent, not necessarily outstanding, job of servicing the customer, the customer is likely to continue to purchase from the seller unless a product or service with a demonstrably clear advantage is offered. In high risk situations and in major sales, the customers are especially hesitant to change suppliers. Thus, the established firm must protect its customer base, and the new growing firm, in addition to attracting new customers, must maintain its position with established customers.

The account relationships, of course, must result in sales sooner or later. The tradeoff between immediate sales and long-term account relationships leads to a phenomenon called the *Pyrrhic sale*. Term is borrowed from military strategy in which a Pyrrhic sale. The term is borrowed from military strategy in which a Pyrrhic victory is one so costly to the protagonist that although he wins the battle, he "loses" the war.

There can be a definite tradeoff between "forcing" a customer to buy something and developing a long-term relationship with that customer. Because the customer is in the position of repeatedly being able to purchase the product, the salesperson must show discipline. He must be willing to forego a sale that is not in the best long-term interest of the account and therefore of his relationship with the account. In forcing a marginal sale, the salesperson often destroys credibility and the opportunity for future sales. The salesperson who can control the desire for the sale in favor of a desire to help the account builds a relationship. For example, the apparel salesperson who is willing to tell a customer that some items in her line do not sell well at retail, in spite of their apparent appeal, is helping the customer and herself over the long run. Or, picture the response to the pump salesperson who says, "Yes, we offer the best pumps for your needs a, b, and c, but unfortunately our pumps are not as good in application d as those offered by competitors x and y." The Pyrrhic sale, on the other hand, is one in which the salesperson gets the sale and loses the account.

The salesperson's role

Account relationship depend upon more than the salesperson's prudence in pushing for orders. The salesperson can perform functions for the customer which make the salesperson a valuable adjunct to the customer's organization.

One of the most important roles of a salesperson is that of ombudsman. In that role the salesperson is the customer's representative to the selling company, and the job is to ensure, that the firm is meeting the needs of the buiyer. For example, the salesperson is responsible for arranging for the return, repair, or replacement of damaged mechandise and for expenditing shipments which are either late or needed quickly. Often, the salesperson is the customer's representative to the credit and billing departments. Obviously, the more effective the salesperson is in dealing with his or her own company the more effective he or she can be in helping customers.

Many salespeople make it a specific duty to get to know order entry, credit, expenditing, and shipping personnel. They attempt to involve these people in the customer's concerns and to alert them to the customer's needs.

The salespeople's roles go beyond the function of ombudsmen. Consumer goods salepeople can be responsible for providing advice or services, or both. It is typical for the better apparel and furniture salespeople to help buyers choose those items which will sell best in their stores. In addition, they will provide advertising and display counseling. Their purpose becomes selling through the store, not to the store, and they do those things which enhance the store's ability to successfully sell their products. Another assistance provided in many situations is careful choice of outlets. Salepeople who place their line in stores of all types often find their best potential customers unhappy because of the poor image the products gain from poor stores.

Some consumer goods salespeople also perform more physically oriented services, usually including display setup and inventory control. Cole National salepeople, for example, are expected to service the Cole key-making machine, inventory keys, and other Cole products, and to maintain displays.

Some companies build their marketing strategy, around strong sales force services. L'eggs stockings and hosiery strategy, for example, depends upon heavy sale force service.

Industrial salespeople are also responsible for both advisory and service functions. many provide applications engineering support, helping customers design their products around the selling company's product. Some salespeople supervise applications engineers. This is typical in the minicomputer industry. Capital goods salespeople provide advice on the use of their product and sometimes provide actual supervision during start-up. Some capital goods salespeople provide maintenance services and others arrange for it. Industrial salespeople are often responsible for maintaining inventory control. Parts suppliers often must check supply room stock and write orders for approval of customers. Again, the importance of the services varies with the situation and the company's marketing strategy.

It is typical for salespeople, both industrial and consumer, to provide training to customers. Industrial salespeople often train machine operators while consumer goods salespeople train retail clerks in how to sell their merchandise. Salespeople who call on distributors often provide management advice and assistance.

Beyond the salesperson

The salesperson should not be the only important aspect of the firm's account management procedures and policies. Many marketers develop special programs to help their customers. Some wholesalers, for example, provide such things as site-selection advice and store-layout help to their retailers. Many firms that sell through distributors provide sales training programs to those distributors. Other firms attempt to help their dealers manage inventories. Special packaging may help some accounts. A producer of materials such as nuts and bols may be willing to package his wares in containers capable of fitting specially designed machinery which uses the products.

Delivery and credit are two other important account management techniques. Fast delivery or emergency backup of spare-parts inventories can cut down the dealer and/or user inventory carrying costs. Special credit arrangements can help customers with their businesses. One important credit arrangement is "dating". Datings are credit extensions provided to highly seasonal industries, such as toys to encourage dealers to accept early delivery.

Some of these programs may be companywide, while others may be directed toward special categories of distributors or even towards particular accounts. It is important to bear in mind that all customers who compete with each other must be treated equally under the Robinson-Patman Act.

It is also important to realize that most of these programs cost money. Sales managers must make careful tradeoffs between their costs and the benefits to their customers. The analytical, creative, and flexible sales manager can probably find a large number of approaches which in fact meet these criteria.

The nonselling parts of the firm have an important role to play in account management. The rude receptionist and the truculent delivery person have probably lost as many accounts as the insensitive salesperson.

Personal versus organisational needs

The people who make purchase decisions are indeed people and as such they have personal needs. An important part of the salesperson's task is to fill those needs. An important part of the salesperson's task is to fill those needs. Different industries have different traditions, but almost all salespeople use personal interest, lunches, and industry "gossip" as appeals to specific customers. In some industries, entertainment is also important. After a point, of course, such expenditures can get beyond the bounds of propriety and eventually become illegal. Bribing a buyer is called commercial bribery and is illegal. There is often a delicate line between treating buyers well and bribing them. Lately the trend has generally been away from lavish entertainment and personal attentions. For most buyers, their greatest personal needs are to do a good job for the organization. Thus, the salespersons often do the best job of serving buyers's personal needs by serving those of their organizations.

Account management is the very essence of the concern of sales managers. All sales management policies should focus on account management. The ultimate success or failure of the sales force is judged primarily upon its ability to manage account relationships.

Consumer goods promotion

Sales promotion activities for consumer goods are usually classified as consumer, trade, or sales force promotions. Some promotions, especially those aimed at salespeople and the trade, are usually designed to "sell in" merchandise so as to increase distribution. Others, especially those aimed at consumers and occasionally some aimed at the trade, are designed to "sell out" merchandise, that is, to create consumer level sales. Often companies will coordinate sell in and sell out programs. For example, a company might run a "Hawaiian Holiday" promotion which includes trips to Hawaii for its salespeople who achieve certain sales goals and similar trips for winners of a consumer sweepstakes or contest. Moreover, an off-invoice merchandise allowance might be offered to wholesalers or retailers to get them to purchase large quantities of the product, and display allowances and special point-of-purchase materials might be provided for the retailers to encourage consumer purchases and participation.

Consumer promotions

Although, in a sense, all sales promotion devices are aimed at ultimately increasing consumer sales, nevertheless, certain devices are designed more specifically than others to attract the consumer to a particular product. The choice of a consumer sales promotion device varies with the nature of the product, its market, and the competitive situation it faces. Three devices- samples, price-off coupons, and refund offers- are most frequently used to generate trials for new or existing products, while price-off deals, premiums, and contests or sweepstakes are most frequently employed to generate repeat purchases and therefore increase the use of a product.

Free samples might be mailed, delivered door to door, placed in bins in retail stores, or attached to or inserted in another package. While sampling is one of the most effective devices for getting consumers to try a product, it usually requires a long lead time to develop programs and is very expensive.

Coupons are certificates which, when presented for redemption at a retail store, entitle the bearer to a stated savings on the purchase of a specific product. Coupons may be issued by either manufacturers or retailers. If the coupon is issued by a manufacturer, the retailer, after taking the coupon in part payment for a purchase, sends it to the manufacturer for reimbursement plus handling fee. If the coupon is issued by a retailer, it s often issued for a kind of product rather than for a specific brand. Coupons can be quickly activated, and their cost is very low. While samples usually produce a higher degree of trial, coupons generally create more triers per dollar spent.[1] The negative side of coupons includes long lapses in redemption time, susceptibility to counterfeit coupon rings, and misredemption. Furthermore, they are, in a sense, little more than price reductions, and price-cutting in any form tends to be rejected by some marketers.

Money-refund offers are propositions in which a sum of money is returned by mail to participants who mail in proof of purchase, such as a box top. Money-refund offers when used alone generate few redemptions and are thought to have little pulling power. Their chief attributed is their low cost to manufacturers.

Price-off deals offer consumers a certain amount of money off the regular price of a product and state the amount on the product's label. These devices are often called cents-off deals or price packs. Price-off deals are the most controversial of all consumer sale promotions. They are strong trial-gaining devices, encourage quantity purchasing by the trade, earn special display locations in stores, and are highly contollable by the manufacturer. On the other hand, frequent price-off promotions tend to cheapen a product's image, are self-defeating in as much as they offer price reductions to regular customers, create only shortlived sales increases, and create additional handling problems for retailers. Furthermore, price-off deals are frequently the object of deceptive practices in that retailers merely raise the supposed "regular" price of the product. Federal Trade Commission regulations now require that the sale price of a product must indeed be different from the established price. However, policing the large number of price-off deals is a difficult task, and additional problems arise with new products that do not have established prices. Usually, price-off deals cannot be offered until 60 or 90 days after a product's introduction.

Premiums are items of merchandise offered free or at a low cost as a bonus to purchasers of a particular product. The most effective premiums are those which offer an obvious, easily understood, and immediately available bonus. Reusable containers, for example, have proved to be extremely strong premiums as have so-called in-pack, on-pack, and near-pack premiums. As their names suggest, these are gifts placed within, attached to, or located near the product being sold. Because visibility tends to increase the impact of the premiums, plastic packages known as "blister packs" and "shrink wraps" are frequently used for on-pack premiums. Because near-pack premiums require a retailer to allot special space for them and his salespeople to handle the premiums, they are recommended only for products whose volume and profit are of significant importance to the retailer.

Free-in-the-mail premiums are gifts sent by return mail to consumers who send in a request for them and include a proof of purchase. Self-liquidating premiums are items offered at well below their normal retail price but at a price high enough to cover the wholesale cost of the merchandise to the manufacturer who runs the promotion. Other costs, such as displays, application blank pads, promotion design, etc., are typically borne by the manufacturer running the promotion as part of its sales promotion budget. In some promotions, the manufacturer and the consumer share the cost of the item. Self-liquidating premiums are by far the most frequently used, even though a redemption rate of 2 percent is usually the maximum that can be expected.

Contests and sweepstakes are also major consumer-oriented promotion devices. These differ in that in a contest the participants compete for a prize or prizes on the basis of their skill in fulfilling a certain requirement, usually analytical or creative. In a sweepstakes, participants merely submit their names to have them included in a drawing of prize winners. Sweepstakes cannot legally require purchase or other significant expenditure of time or effort because to do so puts them in the category of a lottery which is, in general, a form of illegal gambling. The contest avoids this problem because the winner is not chosen by chance but on the basis of demonstrated skill. Many contests require purchase of the product.

Industry experts tend to believe that contests stimulate purchases, since that is usually a requirement of entry, and because entering the contest usually involves significant thought and effort. A contestant, for example, must spend time thinking of an answer "in 25 words or less." Contests, however, typically receive less than 10 percent of the response of sweepstakes.

In the past, legal problems with contests and sweepstakes arose when promoters overstated the value of the prizes, misstated the rules and requirements or presented them in opaque language, or overstated the opportunities for winning.

Another common consumer promotion device is the demonstration, that is, actually showing products in use. As with any promotion that uses direct labor, the cost of demonstrations is quite high. However, for some products, they are one of the most efficient means of promotion. Other very frequently used devices are point-of-purchase (POP), often called point-of-sale (POS), displays. These include outside signs, window displays, all kinds of counter pieces, display racks, self-service cartons, shelf strips, and overhead banners. Similar to these are catalogs, various consumer literature, and price lists.

Trade promotions

Trade promotions are devices designed to obtain special short-term merchandising support from retailers or wholesalers. While some people consider trade deals to be little less than bribery, others feel they are highly acceptable and productive merchandising incentives. Trade promotions generally fall into three categories, according to their objectives.

The first category consists of deals or merchandising devices designed to encourage a wholesaler or retailer to carry a particular product. One such deal is the buying allowance, a short-term offer of a stated reduction in price for a certain quantity of a product purchased. Sometimes buying allowances are escalated-a manufacturer might offer 25 cents off each case if a retailer purchases one size of a brand, 50 cents per case if he buys two sizes, and so on. This is more controversial than the simple buying allowance, however, because many feel that it constitutes unusual and unwarranted pressure from a supplier. Another merchandise deal is the count and recount, an offer of a certain amount of money for each unit of merchandise moved out of a wholesaler's or retailer's warehouse in a specified period of time. It involves a salesperson's taking inventory at the beginning and again at the end of a sale. Yet another merchandise deal is the buy-backallowance, an event which immediately follows another trade deal and offers a certain reduction in price for new purchases based on the quantity of purchases made on the first deal. This device is not used very often. The fourth merchandise deal is the free-goods deal, an offer of a certain amount of a product to wholesalers or retailers at no cost to them, but dependent on the purchase of a stated amount of the same or another product. This differs from the previous three deals only in that goods, rather than money, are given.

The second category of trade promotions consists of deals used to induce retailers to promote a product through advertising and display. The first of these is the merchandise allowance, a short-term, contractual agreement through which a manufacturer compensates wholesalers or retailers for "features"—for example, advertising or in-store displays of the products. Proof of performance is an essential factor in merchanidise allowances. If it is an advertising allowance, for instance, this proof usually takes the form of a "tear sheet" of the advertisement showing the manufacture's product or a radio or television affidavit of broadcasting with the invoice. On display features, reailers furnish written certification or pictures showing compliance with the terms of the agreement. The second device in this category is cooperative advertising, a long-term contract in which a manufacturer pay an allowance based on the quantity of merchandise a retailer orders, and the retailer runs advertisements for both his store and the manufacturer's product with the allowance. In practice, retailers are not paid until the ads are run and they submit proof of performance. This is one of the most widely used of all trade promotions. The final device in this category is dealer-listing promotions. These are advertisements placed by a manufacturer, carrying a message on a particular product, and announcing the names and sometimes the addresses of retailers who stock the product. Retailers receive no payment of money or goods in this promotion. In fact, sometimes they contribute funds to help pay for the listings.

Cooperative advertising and merchandising allowance programs are difficult to control and police. It is a legal necessity as well as good business to ensure that retailers are paid only for services performed. Sometimes, manufacturers who are zealous in their control find themselves in adversary relationships with customers.

Several service companies whose primary business is poli8cing cooperative advertising and merchandising allowances have developed. They take care of the meticulous detail of these programs and deal with the channels of distribution on disputes over reimbursement, thus protecting the manufacturer's relationship with his accounts while ensuring compliance with the program's rules.

The final category of trade promotions is aimed at stimulating retailers and their sales clerks to "push" a certain manufacturer's product rather than that of a competitor. The first of these is PM or push money. It consists of money given to sales clerk in addition to the normal compensation as a reward for selling a particular product. Push money is widely critized by consumer-advocate groups and by many retailers because it encourages sales clerks to emphasize only one line of merchandise rather than showing the variety of merchandise the retailer offers and helping customers select the merchandise that is right for them. A second device is the sales contest. This cannot be alottery, but has to be based solely on the amount of goods sold by each participant. In an effort to allow all participants to have an equal chance in winning, the goal of many contests is a percentage increase over quota rather than the highest total amount sold. The last device in this category is the dealer loader, a premium presented to retailers for the purchase of certain quantities of merchandise. Dealer loaders are of two kinds-buying loaders, or gifts given in return for an order, and display loaders, a premium which is a part of a special display piece. The purpose of dealer loaders is to gain new distribution or to sell an unusually large quantity of goods. Some manufacturers avoid dealer loaders because of the aura of price-cutting. The premium-oriented programs are typically used in industries in which a large amount of sales moves through small owner-operated retailers.

Promotion to salespeople

Promotional devices aimed at motivating a manufacturer's salespeople consist of rewards that supplement their sales compensation plans. While direct sales personnel are the main recipients of sales incentives, many plans include nonselling personnel. There are four basic types of promotional devices aimed at salespeople-sales incentive plans, sales contests, sweepstakes, and recognition programs. In addition, most companies provide a wide range of so-called sales aids for their salespeople.

Sales incentive plans bestow on all participants who achieve certain sales performance goals rewards over and above their regular compensation. The three most common rewards are cash, merchandise, and trips.

In sales contests, prizes are set up for the salespeople who achieve the best performance as spelled out by the contest's rules. Since top performers generally win these contest, average or below average salespeople often acknowledge early that they will not win and therefore do not put forth any extra effort.

Sweepstakes are occasionally used as supplementary activities in a sales-incentive program. They are not considered powerful motivators because rewards are granted not on the basis of an accomplished goal but merely by chance. Recognition programs usually, take the form of titles, trophies, lapel pins, plaques, certificates, etc. They are generally bestowed at sales meetings and again acknowledged in company newsletters, so that the salesperson's accomplishments are known to his fellow salespeople and to company management.

Sales aids include a very wide range of devices and activities designed not to motivate salespeople but to assist them in the actual selling situation. They include such presentation devices as flip charts, price lists, specification data sheets, product bulletins, movies, and things to be left with the customer such as catalogs, advertising specialities which are relatively inexpensive items imprinted with the name of the selling firm, and business gifts which are more expensive items given to special customers and executives. Some companies consider direct mail which supplements or sometimes even replaces a salesperson's visit as a part of their sales promotion activities.

Industrial goods promotion

Sales promotion is generally somewhat different in industrially oriented companies. Those companies, however, which self to many industrial or commercial customers sometimes use consumer-type promotions. Pen companies which sell pens to office managers are typical of this type of operation. Most industrial companies who sell through distributors or wholesalers use promotions similar to those used for the trade in the consumer-goods area. Industrial companies also use promotions oriented toward salespeople.

Sales aids tend to be more sophisticated and complex in the industrial field. Technically oriented companies often offer design guides, or user brochures, which provide a great deal of information. Some offer special calculation aids or small pieces of equipment particularly suited to the industry. Business gifts are perhaps more prevalent in the industrial are where buyer-seller relationship seem more permanent and closer because of intimate design and production scheduling activities.

Management accounting

Introduction

Over the last thirty years management accounting has developed as a practical aid to business managers and as a subject for academic teaching and research. Currently, the management accounting textbooks written by academics describe a coherent set of concepts and techniques which are available to management accountants in practice. Unfortunately, in a number of respects, the practical nature of the subject differs quite considerably from these textbook concepts and techniques. It could be said that there is a gap between the 'theory and 'practice' of management accounting—a gap which is quite wide, particularly when 'theory' includes the various mathematical and statistical techniques available for financial decision making — for example, linear programming and statistical decision theory. However, contemporary developments in management accounting research have provided a basis for understanding the usefulness of textbook concepts and techniques.

A survey of recently published management accounting textbooks indicates a considerable measure of agreement amongst textbook writers at to the nature of management accounting. The contents of those textbooks will be regarded, for purposes of this book, as indicative of the conventional wisdom of management accounting. In general, textbook writers give the impression that the conventional wisdom can provide the 'right answers', while practices which are inconsistent with it are in some sense wrong. Some of the examples and exercises in textbooks illustrate this latter point. For instance, the usual exercise which invites criticism of an absorption costing report 'prepared by the accountant' implies that the practicing accountant is wrong, while the academic textbook writer can provide the 'correct answer'.

Over the past ten to fifteen years researchers have relaxed a number of the assumptions which are implied in management accounting's conventional wisdom. In particular, such researchers have explored the effects of uncertainty, information costs, and the motivations of managers/decision makers on the design and selection of appropriate management accounting techniques. As well as giving the reader an awareness of thinking in management accounting research, this review will place the apparent gap between the theory and practice of management accounting into perspective and provide a basis for evaluating the usefulness of the concepts and techniques contained in most current textbooks.

In particular, the underlying assumptions which were generally accepted by the researchers who developed the basic concepts and techniques will be identified. Emphasis will be given to the user decision approach which is common to most current management accounting textbooks. Such textbooks generally rely on simple economic models which embody the assumptions of profit maximisation and costless information. Much of the research which underlies management accounting's conventional wisdom was undertaken in the 1950s and early 1960s, particularly in the United States; but there were some notable contributions from the United Kingdom as early as the 1930s. No special attempt will be made to identify the geographical origins of particular theoretical developments. Here, however, it will be appropriate to identify, as far as possible, the practice of companies in the United Kingdom and to compare them with practices in the United States. It will be argued that the gap between the conventional wisdom and the practice of management accounting is partly due to the nature of the assumptions used in the research which underlies the conventional wisdom. As indicated above, much of this research was completed by the 1960s. Subsequent research particularly in the early 1970s attempted to remove some of the assumptions implied in the earlier work; for instance, the assumptions concerning certainty about the future. Researchers attempted to extends models for cost estimation, cost-volume profit analysis and cost variance investigation to explicitly recognize uncertainty. Other areas were researched, but these three are described in this book as illustrations of the general trend. Such research led to models which were mathematically very complex and which have not been widely used in practice. It will be argued later in the book that the major problems with these complex models are that they fail to recognize the implementation problems and, more importantly, ignore the cost of information.

A decision maker faced with a complex situation may be quite rational to select a rule-of-thumb, if the costs of providing a more sophisticated solution outweigh the benefit to be derived therefrom.

Some interesting results of studies using agency theory suggest that many of the observed practices of management accounting could be optional, despite their lack of conformity with conventional wisdom. Thus, agency theory may offer a means of closing the gap between the theory and practice of management accounting. But more research is needed. At the present time, agency theory provides few conclusions which can be generalised and empirically tested—most of the results of agency theory are situation specific, i.e., they describe the optimal techniques for a very small range of situations. This book retains the economic perspective of management accounting's conventional wisdom. Developments in behavioral accounting are not explicitly reviewed, although some references are made to them. A review of contemporary developments in behavioral accounting is left to others writers. It is hoped that the theme set up in this book will provide an insight into current economic-based management accounting research and thereby enable the reader to take a more critical view of material contained in management accounting textbooks.

The rise of management accounting

In its simples terms, the conventional view is that management accounting comprises that branch of accounting which seeks to meet the needs of managers—or in general, the needs of users ? to the business. Thus, it could be said that management accounting was first practiced when businessmen began to receive financial information about their business. However, general use of the term management accounting is comparatively new.

Before the Second World War the primary focus of internal accounting was the determination of costs, with particular emphasis on product costing and the control of direct labour, direct materials and overheads. Most of the innovators were cost accounting practitioners. The major concerns of cost accounting included the double-entry recording systems for cost control and the identification of unit cost—i.e. the cost for each product or departmental unit. Attempts were made to identify what could be considered the 'full' cost producing each unit of output. These concerns led to various methods of cost identification and allocation, and to an emphasis on absorption costing. After the Second World War there was an increasing awareness of the view that cost information in particular, and accounting information, in general, should be appropriate to the needs of users—especially managers. In the academic field, a study by Simon *et al.* in 1954 had a profound effect on the perceived role of accounting information for managers. The study identified three uses of accounting information which managers considered important: score-card, attention-directing and problem-solving—all concerned with aspects of the management of organisation performance. This management process can be divided into two elements, planning and control. Management accounting information could be widely used in both managerial planning and managerial control.

A useful distinction between the era of cost accounting and the era of management accounting was made by Horngren:

> In an exaggerated sense, the cost accountants main mission might have been depicted as the pursuit of absolute truth, where truth was defined in terms of getting as accurate or precise costs as possible... [While in management accounting] the theme of 'different costs for different purposes' was stressed—a preoccupation with finding conditional truth.

This change in the perceived nature of the internal accounting function was explicitly recognised by the professional accounting organisations. The Institute of Cost and Works Accountants changed the name of its journal from Cost Accounting to Management Accounting in 1965 and its own name to the Institute of Cost and Management Accountants had changed its name to the national Association of Accountants in 1958.

The management accounting literature expanded rapidly in the 1960s as researchers first developed, and then refined, new techniques for providing accounting information to management. However, these techniques were developed on an ad hoc basis, there was no explicit statement of the underlying theory of management accounting which was used to guide this research. Nevertheless, it is possible to identify some of the assumptions which were implicit in the research and this will be attempted below.

At this stage it would be useful to provide a definition of management accounting, which could be used to structure the present discussion. Unfortunately, this is not an easy task as there is no generally agreed definition. Various definitions are available; but some are too general to provide a suitable structure, while others simply emphasize a particular research approach.

At this stage it would be useful to provide a definition of management accounting, which could be used to structure the present discussion. Unfortunately, this is not an easy task as there is no generally agreed definition. Various definitions are available; but some are too general to provide a suitable structure, while others simply emphasise a particular research approach. The professional management accounting bodies in the UK and US define management accounting in very general terms. Cox, echoing the official view of the Institute of Cost and Management Accountants, argued that management accounting should not be restricted to internal reporting—see also National Association of Accountants. The professional view appears to be that management accountants should be concerned with all aspects of accounting, except the external audit. This wide ranging view of management accounting includes the preparation of financial statements and the general financial management of the organisation within the management accounting function. While such a definition of management accounting might be appropriate from a professional perspective it does not provide a means of structuring a study of management accounting.

Traditionally, the subject matter of accounting has been divided into sections, such as financial accounting and management accounting, for purposes of teaching, research and professional examinations. Undoubtedly, the sections overlap in practice, and the boundaries of each section can be described as arbitrary.

However, the present discussion would be totally unmanageable in the absence of such boundaries. Rather than attempting to provide a priori justifications for the boundaries used in this book, the field of management accounting textbooks. This will provide an indication of the core or conventional wisdom of management accounting as it is understood by academic textbook writers and presumably also by teachers of management accounting.

Scope of management accounting

A sample of 24 management accounting textbooks published in recent years was used to identify the perceived scope of management accounting. No special selection techniques were used, just the books readily to hand. It has to be acknowledged that the sample. Nevertheless, the fact that the textbook market is capable of sustaining at least this number of books suggests that the bias is likely to be shared by a substantial number of accounting teachers. The material included in these textbooks indicates the aspects of management accounting currently being conveyed to most accounting students—many of whom will become the next generation of management accounting practitioners.

As it appears that the terms cost accounting and management accounting now tend to be used synonymously in textbook titles, books with the words 'cost' or 'cost accounting' in the tittle were included in the sample. In a few cases, books with cost accounting titles included additional discussion of cost accounting systems, but in general there was a remarkable consensus in the material covered. Several books included separate chapters dealing with quantitative aspects of management accounting and a few had chapters on behavioral aspects. Some books, notably Amey and Egginton and Doupuch,, Birnberg and Demski attempted to integrate such material into appropriate sections of the text. Some textbook writers included in management accounting such financial management topics as capital investment appraisal and working capital management. However, to avoid expanding the material in this book unnecessarily such topics will not be discussed in detail, although some references will be made to them in order to illustrate certain parallel developments in the field of financial management.

Major topics in the field of management accounting

1.Planning	Relevant costs for decisions Cost-volume-profit analysis Product mix decisions Other decisions:e.g. economic order quantities
2.Cost classifications	Fixed and variable costs Cost estimation techniques Forecasting costs Learning curves
3. Control	Responsibility accounting Budgeting and standard costing Variance analysis
4. Costing	Job order and process costing Variable and absorption costing Cost allocation (including service department costs)
5. Divisionalised organisations	Performance evaluation Transfer pricing

An examination of the earlier editions of several management accounting textbooks suggests that the core material has not changed substantially during the past decade. Although quantitative and behavioral aspects have received more prominence recently, the only major change in the material has been a decline in the space devoted to descriptions of cost accounting systems, particularly in textbooks with a cost accounting title. It is possible that teachers of management accounting at universities and elsewhere, especially in the UK, do not rely entirely on textbooks in designing their courses. But a survey of seventeen universities and nine polytechnicians in the UK suggested that a list of topics taken from Horngren provided an adequate basis for indicating the material covered in management accounting courses, Perks and Morell. Furthermore, textbooks such as Horngren appear prominently in the reading lists for the examinations of professional accounting bodies. Thus, it seems reasonable to assume that such textbooks provide a satisfactory indication of the core material of management accounting.

Much of the material in the above table can be identified with research undertaken in the 1950s and 1960s. Each of the major topics is briefly discussed below and related to management accounting research up to approximately 1970. As will be seen this research provided the basis for the concepts and techniques which comprise management accounting's conventional wisdom. It will be assumed that the reader is reasonably familiar with this material, and so individual topics will not be described in detail. Rather, the origins of the material and its assumptions will be explored.

Planning

As indicated above, the impetus for the development of management accounting came with the acceptance of the view that accounting information should be appropriate for the needs of users. In particular, it was recognised that a single concept of cost could not be appropriate for all purposes. The phrase 'different cost for different purposes' became fundamental to the analysis of short-term planning, and indeed for management accounting in general. This phrase is generally associated with the somewhat earlier work of a US economist. J. Maurice Clark, who, in 1923, took a close look at cost accounting and argued that there can be no unique concept of cost. Similar ideas were developed in the UK, in particular at the London School of Economics, by economists and by accountants trained in economics. These economists argued that relevant costs can only be identified in the context of the particular decision being considered.

In much of the management accounting literature of the 1960s. and also in many current textbooks the notion of different costs for different purposes is developed within a framework which relies on the assumption that decision makers are profit maximisers. For this purpose, the profit maximising objective is expressed in terms of marginal economic analysis, which gives rise to an incremental cash flow approach to decision making. The economic framework also assumes that the decision maker has available, at no cost, all the information needed to arrive at a deterministic solution to his/her choice problem. Most of the quantitative techniques developed in the 1960s are set within such a decision framework—as will be seen in the following discussion.

It is worth pointing out that the marginalist economic theories were never intended to serve as normative theories of how managers ought to behave. They were only meant to generate testable hypotheses about the economic activities of firms in aggregate. It was accountants who gave the theories their normative status. A major attraction of the economic framework was that it permitted a rigorous mathematical analysis of management accounting problems. This provided a considerable measure of academic respectability for the study of management accounting. But it has also meant that on occasions mathematical elegance has taken precedence over practical usefulness. Many of the mathematical models developed by academics are not used in practice—this issue is explored latter.

An early use of mathematical analysis in management accounting was in the study of break-even points. Simple break-even charts are described in many current management accounting textbooks along with discussions of the more general 'Cost-

Volume-profit' (C-V-P) analysis. Some writers have attempted to extends the analysis to the non-linear functions favoured by economists, but linear functions are generally retained for accounting applications.

Two major extensions of C-V-P analysis have been widely discussed in the management accounting literature: (1) uncertainty concerning the models parameters, and (2) production limitations due to scarce resources. Jaedicke and Robichek wrote a seminal paper which explored the effects on C-V-P analysis of allowing uncertainty concerning certain parameters, such as sales volume. This represented a first step away from the conventional deterministic economic framework. Such treatments of uncertainty were not a common feature of management accounting research in the 1960s, nor are they extensively discussed in current management accounting textbooks. Jaedicke was also an important contributor to the second major extension of C-V-P analysis, i.e., for a multiproduct firm with numerous production constraints. He demonstrated that an optimal product mix can be determined by linear programming. By the end of the decade the simple linear break even model had been extended to cover multiple products and multiple constraints. According to Kaplan:

> This progression...highlighted the key feature of the product mix decision—maximizing contribution margin per unit of scarce resource consumed—and demonstrated that departures from the simple linear assumptions can be handled relatively easily within the mathematical programming framework.

Some discussion of linear programming is now included in most management accounting textbooks.

These developments took place as result of, and sometimes alongside, advances in the field of operational research (OR). However, the boundary between management accounting and OR was unclear. It has been suggested that the role of management accounting should be to provide: (1) information for the model builder, (2) data for the model, and (3) monitoring of decision outcomes. The development of linear programming decision models described above could be regarded as operational research, while the provision of information for the development or application of a linear programming model could be regarded as the province of management accounting. Advances in the field of OR were important for management accounting research in the 1960s, and a number of OR models were applied in accounting contexts. Such models were frequently at the center of the user-decision approach. Typically, the models applied in management accounting assumed that the decision maker wishes to maximise contribution and has available the necessary information to arrive at a deterministic solution, i.e., they adopted the economic framework, described earlier.

Cost classifications

The classification of costs as direct or indirect, fixed or variable, period or product, and so on was useful for cost accounting, but became particularly important with the development of management accounting. The recognition that different cost concepts are needed for different purposes gave a new emphasis to cost classifications.

Current management accounting textbooks give particular attention to the classification of costs as fixed or variable. This reflects the short-run decision making orientation of much current management accounting thought. Long-run incremental cost concepts are sometimes included in discussions of relevant costs for decisions, but generally, the decisions situations involve fixed capacity. In such cases, the distinction between fixed and variable costs is particularly important. This is clearly seen in the product mix decisions and C-V-P analysis described earlier.

Statistical regression techniques are frequently portrayed as the preferred methods for classifying costs into their fixed and variable elements. However, there are few empirical studies describing the actual use of regression analysis for cost classification. Scatter graphs appear to have been the only technique widely used in practice in the 1960s, National Association of Accountants, but it was argued by certain writers that regression techniques are superior; Gynther, McClenon and Raun.

In a few textbooks the use of regression analysis for predicting costs and revenues is briefly discussed and occasionally alternative forecasting techniques are mentioned, e.g., time series analysis and exponential smoothing. But in general the decision maker is assumed to have available all the information he/she requires. For instance, if total costs are a function of the units sold it would be assumed that production and sales forecasts are available. This information may be provided by specialists in other fields, such as production engineering and statistics, which are considered to be outside the scope of management accounting. The choice of alternative information sources is not explicitly considered. This consistent with an economic framework which does not address problems of information acquisition.

The raison d'etra of cost classification and estimation is the provision of information for the decision maker. The techniques described above derive from the notion of different costs for different purposes, and have a short-run decision orientation. Considerable attention is given to the separation of fixed and variable elements of total costs. The usefulness of this classification, however, is not restricted planning, it also has relevance in the control process discussed below.

Control

Management accounting, as found in current textbooks, places the notion of responsibility accounting at the very center of the management control system. The techniques practiced in the name of responsibility accounting are many and varied. In an attempt to pin down the nature of responsibility accounting Ferry's definition will be used.

The essence of responsibility accounting is the accumulation of cost and revenues according to areas of responsibility in order that deviations from standard costs and budgets can be identified with the person or group responsible.

Although standard costing and budgetary control had been developed in the early decades of the twentieth century it was in the lat 1950s and early 1960s that responsibility accounting developed rapidly, in the vaguard of advances in management accounting. Its development and popularity was a major step in the movement from cost control to managerial control which typified the emergence of management accounting. The conventional wisdom relating to responsibility accounting is that accounting reports should distinguish elements of performance which are controllable by the recipient of the report from those elements which are uncontrollable.

Responsibility accounting conforms to the classical principles of management which emphasise lines of authority and responsibility. These principles had a substantial impact on organisational design in the 1950s, and it was argued that the responsibility accounting system should be founded upon the company's organisation structure. Initially the motivational role of responsibility accounting was not well understood. But when behavioural theories entered the management accounting could have motivational consequences. Despite this recognition of behavioral research many of the techniques offered in the name of responsibility accounting do not reflect advances in that field.

The use of standard costs and/or budgets to quantify plans for responsibility centres and the measurement of performance in terms of variances therefrom is the primary method of managerial control described in current management accounting textbooks. Budgetary control and standard costing, however, pre-date quite considerably the notion of responsibility accounting. It is the emphasis given to them and the calculation of variance for each responsibility centre which characterises the modern use of these techniques for responsibility accounting.

With the recognition of a need for information for managerial control, traditional methods of calculating variances were criticized for failing to provide relevant information to mangers and alternatives were proposed. These alternatives were derived from the economic framework that was used in analysing decision making situations.

At the simplest level the development of marginal cost and contribution approaches to decision making led to an emphasis in the literature on marginal standard costing, in contrast to the full costing approach common in the earlier forms of standard costing. Today, current textbook writers appear to have a strong preference for the contribution approach The tangible effects of this preference can be seen in computations of sales and overheads variances. It is argued that sales variances. It is argued that sales variances should be measured in terms of contribution margins and that overhead variances should reflect the distinction between fixed and variable costs.

At a more fundamental level attempts have been made to integrate the new management accounting approaches to planning explicitly into the accounting control system. Samuels was probably the first to relate a linear programming formulation of the typical product-mix decision problem to the calculation of variances. He suggested that dual prices on scarce resources computed in terms of opportunity losses. These opportunity loss variances were an attempt to assess the difference between the actual outcome and the best achievable plan. Although the proposed system had detects, it has become recognised as the first attempt at integrating control systems and formal decision models.

In a seminal article, Dopuch *et al.* argued that an extension of variance analysis to the evaluation of the outcomes of formal decision models will require changes in both the types of variances calculated and the methods introduced the notion of opportunity loss variances. Demski provided an illustration of such variances using ex post analysis. He suggested that an opportunity loss variance could becomputed by comparing actual performance against an ex post optimum, i.e., the best performance which should have been possible given the actual environmental conditions. Some of the assumptions of his analysis have been questioned, but the idea of opportunity loss variances seems to have been widely accepted, although not extensively integrated into current textbooks.

The paper by Dopuch *et al.* led to another major development in the literature—variance investigation models. Standard cost systems generate a vast number of variances each period. If the standard cost system is to be effective the variances which are most significant should be investigated to determine their sources and to correct the process if possible. But how should variances be selected for investigation? Essentially this is a decision problem which is no different from those discussed earlier. Statistical control procedures were adapted and operational research type models were developed. Although these later operational research type models were developed. Although these later models were further discussed in the 1970s, only the simplest models are described in current textbooks and these are in general deterministic profit maximising models.

Although considerable behavioural research has been undertaken in the area of budgeting and standard costing, it has had a very limited impact on the the techniques which are offered in current management accounting textbooks. A number of behavioral researchers explored the relationship between behavioral science and management accounting in the 1960s. Most management accounting textbooks now include at least a chapter on 'behavioural implications', but only in so far as they affect the setting of standards, the agreement of budgets and the use of variance reports. In addition, there are a number of specialist behavioral accounting textbooks.

Nevertheless, the effects of behavioral research on the techniques which can be regarded as basic to management accounting's conventional wisdom have been minimal. This is surprising in view of the fact that the economic framework which underlies these techniques is inconsistent with much modern behavioral research, and that economists have developed behavioral theories of the firm, e.g., Cyert and March and alternative models of decision making, e.g., Simon.

Costing

The amount of material on costing topics in management accounting textbooks has been declining in recent years. Current textbooks in general discuss briefly the nature of job-order and process costing systems, the distinction between variable and absorption costing, and cost allocations. As this material is not central to the study of management accounting it is not reviewed in depth, but some comments are appropriate.

Job-order and process costing are used as illustrations of cost-accumulation systems and to provide an introduction to cost allocations. However, the basic principles for these systems belong to the era of cost accounting, when manufacturing processes were typically rather different from those of today. But there have been some subsequent studies.

The distinction between marginal costing and absorption costing was mentioned above, where it was indicated the most management accounting textbooks writers appear to favour the marginal costing approach. The comparison with absorption costing is included in textbooks for two reasons. First, it demonstrates the advantages of marginal costing and the distortions introduced by absorption costing. Second, as absorption costing is widely used to value inventories for the published financial statements, it provides the means of reconciling the financial and management accounts.

Although the origins of cost allocations belong to the era of cost accounting, a considerable literature built up in the 1960s using mathematical methods for cost allocations. Some writers argue that all such allocations are arbitrary. Indeed, some contributors to the literature begin their papers by agreeing with Thomas. They then point out that as cost allocations are observed in practice preferred methods should be identified, e.g., Moriarity. Linear programming and matrix algebra became a feature of this literature in the 1960s and are mentioned in most current textbooks.

Whilst some of this literature is inconsistent with the user-decision approach of management accounting there are connections with the economic framework described earlier. The mathematical programming methods for allocating joint cost, for instance, follow suggestions in the economic literature that in certain circumstances such allocations can provide relevant costs for decision making. An important prerequisite for many of the allocation methods developed in recent years is that they do not distort the decisions which would be made without such allocations.

Divisionalised organisations

It is customary for management accounting textbooks to include at least one chapter dealing with the special problems of divisionalised organisations. However, no new principles are involved. Divisional performance measurement is an application of the notion of responsibility accounting discussed earlier and transfer pricing can be considered a special form of cost allocation.

Return on investment as a measure of divisional performance gained much popularity after the Second World War, but various problems were identified and some refinements were suggested. Solomons proposed the use of residual income, i.e., profit less a notional interest charge computed by reference to divisional capital employed. This proposal appears to have received the support of many textbook writers, especially in the United States, although some remain unconvinced and some are against the proposal.

As an alternative to using return on investment or residual income some writers have suggested accessing divisional performance against budgets. Such proposals put this topic firmly back into the earlier discussion of responsibility accounting and budgetary control. Amey proposed that the divisional budgets should be derived from the solution to the group's linear programming problem. This is a further extension of the idea advanced by Samuels and is related to the use of linear programming for setting transfer prices.

Much of the early analysis of the transfer pricing problem is owned to economists, although some accounts were also interested in the area. An important consideration in the development of transfer prices was that divisional decision makers should be motivated to select courses of action which maximise the profits of the organisational as a whole. Transfer prices based on the dual values derived from a linear programming problem of the group as a whole were offered as a means of ensuring congruence between divisional and group objectives. This approach requires the centralisation of planning, and could defeat the benefits of divisionalisation. From this perspective transfer prices can be viewed as a means of contriving divisional decisions to maximise group profits. Thus transfer pricing can be fitted into the decision-making framework discussed earlier in this chapter.

Some implied assumptions of management accounting

It is hoped that the reader has recognised in the preceding discussion the essential elements of management accounting, as it is currently taught at many universities and colleges in the United Kingdom. North America and many other parts of the world. The particular topics included in this discussion could be criticised for various reasons—for instance, some may argue that the boundaries of management accounting were drawn too narrowly, while others may argue that the focus on particular techniques was inappropriate. All that has been attempted is review of the major topics which are sufficiently accepted to be included in current textbooks. No particular definition of management accounting was adopted. The material discussed above was oriented towards the manufacturing function, as this is the primary focus of most textbooks. This has meant that the distribution and marketing functions have not been explicitly mentioned. However, similar general principles might be applied to these functions, although research in these areas is limited.

The term 'conditional truth' was used to depict the general theme of management accounting, and to distinguish it from the 'absolute truth' theme of cost accounting. The notion of 'conditional truth' is appropriate because management accounting, as described above, implies that different costs are needed for different purposes, or in other words, accounting information depends on the information needs of users. Thus, in developing management accounting concepts and techniques researchers had to identify the information needs of managers. In general, this meant constructing decision models to indicate how decisions are, or should be, made. Once the decision model is postulated the conditional truth approach implies that the appropriate information can be determined by deductive reasoning, i.e., truth can be attained.

It was indicated earlier than an economic framework played a central role in structuring the decision models used by the researchers who were instrumental in the development of management accounting's conventional wisdom. It is not suggested that economics was the only influence. Other subject areas, such as management science, organisation theory and latterly, behavioural science were undoubtedly present, but economics and especially the marginalist principles of neoclassical economics, probably had the dominant influences. This economic approach entails the following assumptions. The decision maker has available, at no cost and without uncertainty, all the information he/she requires to completely structure the decision problem and to arrive at a deterministic profit maximising solution using the principles of marginal analysis.

In management accounting decision models profit maximisation is expressed in terms of profits accruing to the owners of the business. This implies a further assumption that the decision maker either is the owner or shares the owners' goals for the business. Where the decisions makers are not the owners, management accounting relies on the techniques of responsibility accounting to achieve goal congruence. In the early days of management accounting, the way in which such techniques achieved goal congruence was unclear. More recently, research in the field of organisational behaviour has provided some insights. Nevertheless, it is still assumed that the decision maker is a profit maximisers. This is not to suggest that profit maximisation is necessarily an appropriate description of decision making in practice. Rather, it is simply an assumption of the decision models which underlie the conventional wisdom of management accounting.

A further implied assumption of management accounting decision models is that individual decision makers can be isolated from other decision makers within the organisation. This can be seen in that decision makers are identified as individuals, and group decision making is not considered. Group decisions are ignored because they are a trivial extension of individual decisions within the economic framework. All decision makers are assumed to be profit maximisers and complete and perfect information assumptions provide a common information set. As a result, every decision maker within this framework will arrive at the same decisions, and so any one of them can be analysed independently.

The complete and perfect information assumptions permit unlimited mathematical sophistication in quantitative techniques. Decision makers are assumed to have the knowledge to use any mathematical techniques and costless information processing places no limits on the complexity of the information system. Once such a decision is analysed the appropriate accounting information can be determined.

The costs of providing such information in the real world and the uncertainty involved in all practical decision making are only discussed in the most general terms in current management accounting textbooks. It is generally implied that information costs and uncertainty are outside the realm of management accounting techniques and must be handled by management intuition Demeski and Feltham, in a brief review of the conditional truth theme, identified three fundamental defects of management accounting which provide a useful summary of the above discussion:

First, truth—even if desirable—cannot be obtained without incurring a cost. Measurement consumes resources... Second, users operate in an uncertain world and explicit recognition of uncertainty casts doubt on the concept of a true cost, which implicitly presumes a certain world....Third, the concept of a true cost is likely to be both illusory and irrelevant in a multiperson world.

As a response to these defects Demski and Feltham proposed an information economics approach. Although this approach abandons some elements of the economic framework described above, it keeps the study of management accounting firmly within the field of economics. This book reviews contemporary developments in management accounting research from an economic perspective. other perspectives. e.g., organisational and political, may provide alternative explanations of the practice of management accounting—but they are outside the scope of this book.

Before addressing such issues through a description of current management accounting research, it will be useful to briefly examine management accounting in practice.

Accounting practice

Today, it is generally supposed that this research has had only a limited impact on practice. The purpose of this chapter is to review some published empirical evidence. Unfortunately, the available evidence is very limited; there is no coherent body of literature which describes management accounting in practice and there are no publications comparable to the 'survey of published accounts' and 'accounting trends and techniques', which are available in financial accounting. Nevertheless, some descriptions have been published and these are discussed below. In general, however, the assumption of a gap between management accounting in practice and the content of current textbooks appears to be based on anecdotal evidence and impressions gained through informal contacts between academics and practitioners. For instance, the conditional truth approach, with its 'different costs for different purposes' philosophy, is widely accepted. But evidence indicating whether or not such an approach is applied in practice is rather scarce at the present time.

A preliminary examination of the management accounting practices of a small sample of 14 companies led researchers at the University of Aston to conclude that 'three appears to be a substantial gap between theory and practice'.

In the day operation of management accounting systems, Coastes *et al.* observed little formal analysis of cost behavior, even though such analysis was considered to be important by some managers. Most of the sample companies operated absorption based costing systems and there was little use of marginal cost analysis, although some managers claimed to know what their marginal costs were. The predominance of absorption based costing in the UK has been supported by other studies. For instance, Finnie and Sizer found that all the companies in their sample of 22 engineering companies used absorption costing systems.

The conventional wisdom of management accounting textbooks suggests that absorption costing systems cannot provide relevant costs for all purposes. As an illustration, consider pricing decisions in describing relevant costs for pricing, most accounting textbooks use a marginal cost approach. In another study, Scapens *et al.* observed that accounting information routinely provided for pricing decisions is normally based on absorption costing. Such information may not represent the relevant costs for such decisions as no explicit recognition is made of opportunity costs. Only five of the 99 companies which were included in the Scapens *et al.* study make any use of the marginal cost approach in providing information to price setters) may, in practice, modify the accounting information they receive, such that their actions are in fact based upon the concepts implied in the conventional wisdom described. At the present time, it is difficult to evaluate the strength of this argument because of a lack of empirical evidence.

Coasts *et al.* observed a general lack of 'sophisticated' mathematical techniques in management accounting. They found no evidence of linear programming and other mathematical techniques for budget setting, transfer pricing or decision making. In another study, Gregory and Piper found little evidence of sophisticated techniques for stock control. Although many management accounting textbooks describe mathematical models for determining economic order quantities and stock levels, Gregory and Piper found only simple techniques being used in practice. That study and the others cited above support the general view that UK companies tend not to use the various quantitative techniques advanced in the academic literature.

A number of similar studies have been published in North America, describing the use of various quantitative techniques in US industry. Although many of these studies were primarily concerned with the implementation of operational research and management science techniques, their results are of interest in the context of this chapter because the application of quantitative techniques is an important element of management accounting's conventional wisdom. Generally, these studies indicate the whilst some US companies do make use of quantitative techniques in areas such a long range planning and operation management there are a large number of companies which do not make any extensive use of such techniques. Furthermore, it is the simpler techniques which tend to be preferred in most instances —see Green *et al.* for a list of such studies.

The application of quantitative techniques in US industry has increased only gradually over the years, even though one might expect techniques which offer a competitive techniques in areas such as long range planning and operations management there are a large number of companies which do not make any extensive use of such techniques. Furthermore, it is the simpler techniques which tend to be preferred in most instances—see Green *et al.* for a list of such studies.

The application of quantitative techniques in US industry has increased only gradually over the years, even though one might expect techniques which offer a competitive advantage to be readily accepted in practice. In addition to the high cost of using many quantitative techniques various barriers to their use have been identified. These barriers include the absence and/or unreliability of the required data, the inability of some users to understand complex techniques and the lack of time to apply them.

Ackoff has argued that the operational research function in US industry has been pushed down the organisation in recent years because the techniques are of little value to senior corporate executives, although they may be useful for routine planning at lower managerial levels. Such a change would be difficult to discern through questionnaire surveys of the type used in the studies described above, however. Generally, these studies only investigated whether or not certain quantitative techniques are used in the organisation, and not the point in the organisation at which they are used.

In the UK, Argenti asked 'whatever happened to management techniques?. He pointed out that in the mid-1960s modern management techniques, including operational research, were regarded with great enthusiasm. A decade later, those techniques were apparently quite neglected by British industry. One response to Argenti's question was that some of the new techniques would be implemented after they had been fully tested. To Argenti it appeared that the 1970s were the era of simple techniques and that the more complex alternatives were unlikely to be implemented.

This brief discussion suggests that some simple quantitative techniques are used by companies in both the US and UK, but there is rather limited use of the more complex techniques. However, one study appears to have reached a different conclusion. Kiani- Aslani attempted to demonstrate that US management accountants in his sample of US companies—taken from the Fortune 300—used the quantitative methods currently taught in management accounting courses. However, included in his figure of 96 per cent were people who used the techniques were used primarily for operations management, rather than in accounting applications. Thus, Kiani-Aslani's findings are not incompatible with the conclusions of the studies described earlier in this chapter.

More recently, Kaplan argued that quantitative models are being increasingly used in the US. The evidence he cited, basically Kiani-Aslani and a casual examination of articles in the National Association of Accountants' journal, Management Accounting, do little more that suggest that practitioners have heard of the techniques. Such evidence could be quite damaging for the conventional wisdom, if it indicates that textbook methods are not widely used, despite practitioners being aware of them. Even if such a pessimistic interpretation is not accepted, the most that can be claimed from Kaplan's evidence is that practitioners use some of the simple quantitative models which are available in the field of management accounting.

The evidence of the various studies discussed in this chapter does little to contradict the supposition with which the chapter began— namely, that management accounting's conventional wisdom is not entirely compatible with current practice. One commonly expressed reason for the gap between theory and practice is that it takes times for new ideas to become fully developed, accepted and implemented. However, many of the textbook concepts and techniques have been advocated for at least a decade. Thus, it would seem reasonable to expect the textbook methods to be widely adopted if they offer real benefits.

It could be argued that the time lag between theory and practice should actually be quite short if the economic theory which underlies much of management accounting's conventional wisdom is appropriate. In a competitive economy, firms which do not adopt the best available techniques will be placed at a competitive disadvantage, relative to firms which do adopt such techniques. The forces of competition should ensure that new techniques of management accounting will be implemented quite quickly it they assist decision makers to maximise their profits: that is, if the marginal benefits exceed the marginal costs of implementing the techniques. Thus, reasons other than a simple time lag are needed to explain the gap between the theory and practice of management accounting.

In view of the above economic arguments, the lack of acceptance of management accounting's conventional wisdom might be explained by one or both of the following: (1) the failure of the conventional wisdom to meet the needs of decision makers (for instance, because it is not relevant to the decision maker's needs or it is too costly to implement), or (2) the competitive economy assumptions which underlie management accounting's conventional wisdom are not appropriate to the circumstances of management accounting in practice. Accordingly, it would seem reasonable to look for explanations of the gap between theory and practice by questioning the basis of the theory, as well as exploring the nature of practice. In the following conventional wisdom will be explored and the results of recent research will be used to put existing practice into context.

These extensions, however, do not provide models and techniques which are particularly attractive to practitioners. Although the researchers looked to the complexity of decision making in the real world and sought to produce 'realistic' models, the techniques they produced frequently require too much information for their implementation in practice. In many cases, these researchers ignored the costs of providing such information. It will be argued that the use of simple techniques in practice may in fact be an optimal response to the decision making situation and not an irrational rejection of 'academic' techniques—the benefits of using complex techniques may not outweigh the information costs which would be injured.

Principles of accounting

Accounting may be defined as the art and science of recording business transactions in a methodical manner so as to show (a) the true state of the affairs of a business at a particular point of time, and (b) the surplus or deficiency which has accrued during a specified period.

Developments in the application of accounting techniques to assist all grades of management have, however, expanded this original view of the accounting is to assist management in achieving efficiency by the presentation of suitable financial information. Such information will be designed primarily to assist management in making its future plans and controlling the execution of those plans.

It is therefore essential that every manager, whatever may be his function or status, should understand clearly the principles of accounting and have a good working knowledge of its mechanics. A manager must appreciate the extent and limitations of the information which he may demand of the accountant, and he should have a broad knowledge of the cost of producing it. While a good accountant must rest with management. In the end of the value of accounting information depends on the action which it calls forth from the managers of a business.

The first principle: The distinction between capital and revenue

The income receivable and the expenditure incurred by a business must be allocated either (a) to capital account, or (b) to revenue account. Capital may be defined as the wealth which is used to produce income, and it must for this purpose be maintained intact. The items which make up the capital of a business should be recorded in accounts clearly identified as such, so as to show whether capital has been lost or increased.

The remaining accounts record revenue items, comprising income and expenditure; they show in figures the day-to-day transactions of the business, and the difference between income and expenditure represents either profits or losses. Profits can be added to capital or withdrawn from the business, and losses represent deductions from capital.

In a complex business the distinction between the two kinds of transactions is in some cases rather fine and may involve differences of opinion. In such cases it is essential that the treatment be consistent from year to year so as to show a true picture of the trends of income, expenditure, profit or loses. There are certain principles which must be followed, and these principles are discussed in the following sections.

Capital

The capital of a business consists of the assets less the liabilities. The value of an asset will appear on the left-hand side of an account. So as to complete the double entry the theory of which is discussed in the succeeding section the capital is treated as a liability of the business to the proprietors and is therefore also shown on the right-hand side of an account.

If a man sets up in business as, for example, a boot and shoe repairer he requires a certain initial sum of money or money's worth to provide plant, tools, furniture, stocks of leather and ready cash. This initial sum represents his original capital, and he does not consider he has made a profit until he can withdraw cash from the business for his personal use and still show that the original total of capital remains intact. That is to say, there is no profit until income exceeds expenditure.

Income, in this example, consists of the charges made of customers for the work done; expenditure means the wages, cost of material and other expenses incurred in doing work. "Other expenses" include overheads such as rent, right, fuel, power, stationery and repairs to equipment and also include the loss of value which occurs in the machinery and furniture due to wear and tear and old age.

Original capital may be, and frequently is, increased either by: (a) the introduction of fresh funds on a permanent basis, or (b) the allocation of profits to a fund which it is not intended to distribute but which is retained inthe business for the purpopse of earning additional income and maintaining profits.

It should be noted that the loan in the above example is deducted from total funds in order to leave a sum representing the proprietor's capital. B's loan is regarded as a debt due from A, but if B's loan was meant to remain with the business of many years it could be reckoned as part of the capital employeed in the business. Suppose that B's loan had been repaid and, with a view to increasing his income. A retained the business $100 out of the first year's profits and then took into partnership C, who did not bring in cash but a motor van of an agreed value of $500, the capital position would be as follows:

A original capital	$750
Add Retailed out of profit	100
A total capital	850
C capital brought in	500
Capital of the firm	$1,350

Thus, the capital employeed in a business is the capital owned by the properietors, plus loans invested in the business on a permanent basis.

Other uses of the term "capital"

The expression "capital" is used in commercial spheres to mean money or money's worth invested in a business whether by the proprietors or by outside persons, in other words—the capital employeed in a business. Thus investments in industrial undertakings in the form of loans and debentures or provided by banks and finance corporations are regarded as capital, although no rights of ownership of the assests of the undertaking may be conferred.

The authorised or nominal capital and the issued capital of a limited company must be distinguished from its real capital. The amount of capital which can be raised by a company is authorised and limited by its articles and memorandum of association, but no all such authorised capital is necessarily issued. A company's authorised capital may be, say, 1,000,000 shares of ? 1 each, but in fact only half of these may be issued, in which case its issued capital is ?500,000 in shares of ?

Again, the capital issued may be only partly called. If, in the above example, only 50p a share had been called up by the directors the capital called up will be ?250,000, and this amount may, in turn, be further reducedby any amounts which have not been paid by the shareholders under such calls. On 1,000 shares the call of 50 p may remain unpaid.

Owing to the fact that it is the practice of most undertakings to retain part of the profits to meet contingencies or for development, the true value of shareholders' interest in a company is rarely indicated by the authorised or issued shares. The balance of value will be represented by reserve accounts.

The expression "capital employed" is, unfortunately, interpreted in a variety of ways by different writers. In some textbooks the word is synonymous with the total of the assets employed in the business. In this book "capital employed" means the total issued capital, both shares and loans, plus reserves. This is equivalent to the total of the assets less the liabilities to external parties: those liabilities including, for instance, money owing to suppliers, but excluding money on long-term loan to the business, such as debenture capital. It should be borne in mind, in this connection, that accounts recording shares, debentures, reserves and the balance of the profit and loss account merely show the classes of funds towhich the real capital of the concern, i.e. the sum of assets less liabilities, has been allocated. The following illustration of a simplified Balance Sheet illustrates this point:

Balance Sheet

Share capital	£150,000	Fixed assets	£200,000
Reserves	25,000		
Proprietor's capital	175,000		
Debentures	50,000	Current assest	50,000
Capital employed	225,000		
Current liabilities	25,000		
	£250,000		£250,000

The capital employed might be expressed as the "net assets" or total assets less current liabilities, as follows:

Total assets	£250,000
Less Current liabilities	25,000
Net assets or capital employed	£225,000

Note: A Balance Sheet is a statement compiled from the accounts and is not in itself part of the double-entry accounting system. It is, therefore, quite immaterial which side is used for assets and which for liabilities, although assets are usually shown on the right on the U.K., where a double-sided balance sheet is adopted.

Capital in the sense of the difference between assets and liabilities is sometimes called "net worth". The figure of capital employed which can be calculated from the values shown in a Balance Sheet is rarely the same as the realisable value of the net assets if they were sold in the open market. The accounts basically record original cost, not saleable values; although original cost is usually adjusted for inflation, especially in large companies. The capital employed in a limited company is not the same as the total to be arrived at by multiplying the number of shares and debentures by the respective prices at which they are quoted on a stock exchange. The Stock Exchange prices are influenced by, among others, the following factors: (a) supply and demand for the securities; (b) changing money values; (c) the expectation or hope of a certain rate of return on money invested; and (d) prospects of capital profits. Stock

Exchange prices of shares and debentures are not controlled by the company concerned, but merely represent the market price at which the securities change hands.

The fixed and current elements of capital

(i) Foxed and current assets: Funds for use in a business come from three sources:

I Capital obtained when the business was first set up, or subsequently brought into the business, from

(a) shares, i.e. proprietors' capital; and/or

(b) loan capital, such as debentures.

II Credit for goods and services supplied.

III Funds generated from operations, e.g. the excess of receipts over outgoings.

These funds are used to acquire assets which, for convenience, are generally classified as either "fixed" or "current". Fixed assets are those which are acquired to assist the process of earning income over a long term and are not held, as for instance stocks are, for the purpose of earning profit by resale. In this context "long term" normally means at least a year. In a manufacturing business the fixed assets would normally include the land and buildings, the plant and machinery, furniture and fixtures, and vehicles.

Current assets comprise cash and assets destined to be converted into cash in the short term, e.g. under a year. Raw material stores, work in progress, finished stocks for sale, debtors. being largely sums due to the business from creditg sales, bills of exchange receivable and temporary investments, are all current assets.

Because of the immense variety of business transactions which an accounting system must reflect in financial terms, there are exceptions to most of the general accounting rules, and sometimes conventional classifications of assets overlap. For example, it may be difficult to decide whether an investment by a business in a marketable security falls under the "fixed" or "current" classification. If such an investment represented a temporary repository of surplus funds it will be a current asset. In other cases investments are frequently placed in the balance sheet under a separate heading between fixed assets and current assets. Likewise if debtors, such as hire purchase debts, are due for payment to the business beyond a year, they will normally be placed above current assets under the heading of "Long-Term Receivables". The cost of patents and trade marks is also normally shown separately, although some companies treat these items as fixed assets.

The following is a fairly typical presentation of the assets as shown in the balance sheet of a manufacturing company:

Fixed assets

Land and buildings:

- freehold
- long leaseholds (over 50 years)
- short leaseholds

Plant and machinery

Furniture and fixtures

Instruments and test equipment

Vehicles

Patents and trade marks

Investments

Quoted

Unquoted

Long-term receivables

Current assets

- Cash in hand and at bank
- Bills of exchange receivable
- Temporary investments
- Debtors
- Stocks and work in progress

It should be noted that after the initial capital has been obtained for an enterprise the financing of day-to-day requirements should be met as far as possible out of its own resources and not out of further permanent capital. The development of a business may justify the directors obtaining further permanent capital for investment in fixed assets. Thus, fixed assets are often referred to as "capital assets".

(ii) *Fixed and current liabilities*: The net capital employed in a business is calculated by deducting liabilities from assets. The accounts recording liabilities may, therefore, be called "called accounts" for accounting purposes, and in a double-sided account they are shown on the right-hand side. As with assets, liabilities may be grouped as follows: (a) fixed liabilities—those likely to remain for a considerable time; and (b) current liabilities—those which are variable or likely to be soon discharged.

Fixed liabilities include long-term loans obtained by a business, such as debentures in a limited company. Current liabilities include trade creditors, bank or other short-term loans, taxation dues, dividends recommended for payment and bills of exchange payable.

(iii) The necessity for distinguishing between fixed and current capital. It is an essential precept of good accounting that (a) the fixed and (b) the current or variable elements of capital, whether assets or liabilities, should be clearly distinguished both in the accounting system and in any statements which are compiled from that system. This principle applies in particular to the Balance Sheet.

The importance of the classification is that it indicates to the reader of the statement:

(a) The extent to which the funds are invested in fixed assets, which cannot normally be realised except to the determent of the earning power of the business, and probably at a loss; and

(b) The extent to which the funds are invested in current assets which represent idle capital, but are convertible into cash to pay creditors or for further investment in the business operations.

While the maintenance of total capital is the guiding factor in the determination of profit or loss, fixed assets represent the source from which income is obtained, and they must be maintained in a condition to yield the desired income.

From the point of view of an investor in a business the ultimate security of the capital he has invested is represented by the value of the fixed assets less the fixed liabilities. If the investor's money is in the form of loan capital, such as debentures, his ultimate security consists of the gross total of the fixed assets subject only to such charges as may by law rank before by his own. In many cases loan capital is secured on specific assets by way of mortgage.

While attention is directed to fixed capital from the point of view of its intrinsic value and its capacity to yield income, the comparison of current assets and current liabilities will demonstrate the working capital of a business.

Lack of adequate working capital for day-to-day needs may bring an immediate halt to business activity. Working capital is generally calculated as the excess of current assets over current liabilities, and apart from its value as a guide to management, this figure is one of the first considerations by persons contemplating investment in a concern, granting substantial credit or lending it money.

The excess of current assets over current liabilities is not, however, by any means the sole criterion of the availability of funds for current needs. A large proportion of so-called working capital may be tied up in stocks, which may not be easily realisable and which may be subject to fluctuations in market prices. Furthermore, with a manufacturing business the value of work in progress, represented by partly finished goods or work performed, is often problematical.

In such cases an additional calculation is required for the purpose of arriving at liquid capital, that is the amount of cash which can be raised if necessary at short notice. Liquid capital normally consists of cash in hand, cash at bank on current account, good bills of exchange receivable, good debtors' balances and temporary investments valued certainly not higher than current market value. From these liquid assets there must be deducted money which may be demanded at short notice, such as short-term loans, creditors' balances and bills of exchange payable.

Revenue

Revenue may be defined as the surplus of income over expenditure after capital has been maintained. The second main division of an accounting system records revenue, that is it contains the accounts of income and expenditure. For accounting purposes a rather strict meaning is given to the terms "income" and "expenditure". Current income includes moneys due from customers for goods supplied or services rendered. Expenditure is the cost of doing the work, and includes not only payments due for labour, material and other current expenses of the business but also provision for maintaining capital intact.

The expressions "income" and "expenditure" must be distinguished from "receipts" and "payments". The latter refer to cash received and cash paid during a specified period, and include items which may refer to another accounting period, or receipts and payments on capital account, e.g. the sale or purchase of fixed assets. The principle of separating accounting items into their fixed and variable elements is applicable to both income and expenditure.

Fixed income usually covers interest and dividends from investments, fees from royalties and licenses, while variable income includes sales and other income directly resulting from the operations for which the business has its being.

So that management can measure efficiency and control costs it is essential for the accounts and for accounting statements to record the fixed and variable expenditure under separate headings. Frequently a third division, known as sem-variable costs, is found expedient. Examples of items falling within these groups are as follows:

Fixed costs: staff salaries; administration expenses; rent and establishment charges; interest and other financial charges; and depreciation.

Semi-variable cost: indirect hourly labour, which varies more or loss with output but not in direct proportion to it, for example, wages of maintenance man, indirect materials such as nuts and bolts, grease and oil; and other expenses of a semi variable nature such as factory electricity.

Variable costs: direct productive labour; direct materials; and direct expenses, the costs of which all vary closely with turnover or output.

The control of costs, and therefore the correct accounting for costs, is a matter of major importance in any scheme of accounts which is to be used to assist management, and this aspect of the general subject will received extended consideration later in the book.

The nature of profit

It was stated at the beginning of this chapter that one of the basic objects of accounting was to show "the surplus or deficiency which has accrued during a specified period". This is, of course, another way of referring to "profit", but the latter term can take on a variety of meanings depending on the context in which it is used. It is, therefore, desirable to consider the nature of the "profit" which appears at the end of the Profit and Loss Account and is often the result of a protracted analysis of the business transactions, and the application of number of accounting rules and conventions. These rules and conventions rest in part on low and in part on the accumulated experience of businessmen and accountants over the centuries. The reader will become acquainted with the more important conventions as he studies successive chapters of this book. One of the major rules is that transactions on revenue account must be distinguished from transactions on capital account.

The transactions on revenue account, which must include provision for maintaining the capital intact, will indicate how the profit has arisen, i.e. by deducting expenditure from income. In its most elemental orm profit is the amount by which capital has increased over a period, and loss would be the loss of the capital over the period. Thus the final prifit made by a business in, say, a year could be calculated from the Balance Sheets at the beginning and end of the year, because from those Balance Sheets can be calculated the capital of the business at the beginning and at the end of the period. Profit is therefore basically an increase in worth.

It should be noted at this point that an accounting system does not, unless adjustments are made, show the assets of the business in terms of the current purchasing power of the money in which they are expressed. This applies in particular to the fixed assets, which are normally stated at cost less provision for depreciation calculated on the basis of cost. The following discussion of the nature of profit in the accounting sense must be read with this qualification in mind. Many businesses have revalued their fixed assets to conform more closely to current values, but the resulting "book profit" or "holding gain" is separated from the profit from trading by being placed in a Reserve Account which is not available for distribution to the shareholders, e.g. by way of dividend.

Consider the following Balance Sheets of Retailers Ltd. at he beginning and at the end of last year.

Retailers limited

Balance Sheet as at the beginning of the year

Capital:	
Issued shares ?	100,000
Revenue reserves	50,000
Current liabilities	

Trade and other creditors	40,000
Total	£190,000

This Balance Sheet indicates that the capital employed in the business at the beginning of the year was:

Fixed assets	100,000
Current assets	90,000
Total assets	190,000
Less Current liabilities	40,000
Capital employed	150,000

Or the same total derived from the accounts which record how the funds were obtained:

Obtained by subscription from the shareholders :	100,000
Obtained from prifits retained in the business :	50,000
Capital Employed :	150,000

The capital employed at the end of the year thus becomes:

Fixed assets :	90,000
Current assets:	115,000
Total assets :	205,000
Less Current liabilities :	45,000
Capital employed :	160,000

The apparent profit made by the company during the year is therefore:

Capital employed at the end of the year :	160,000
Less Capital employed at the beginning of the year :	150,000
Apparent profit :	10,000

If however, the owners had withdrawn any funds from the business during the year the amount so withdawn would have to be added to the 10,000 apparent profit in order to arrive at the true profit. Let it be assumed that during the year the shareholders had been paid a dividend of, say, 5000 in cash. The net profit would then have been

Apparent profit, as above :	10,000
Add Funds withdrawn :	5,000
Net profit for the year :	15,000

Conversely, if further capital had been introduced into the business during the year (which has clearly not in fact occurred in this example) the amount of that additional capital would need deducting from the figure of apparent profit calculated as shown above.

Profit is therefore basically a question of putting a value on the assets and liabilities of a business, but it should be borne in mind that the value of the assets in accordance with accounting rules and conventions is not necessarily the same as the current saleable value of those assets. The business is looked upon as a going concern, and certainly the fixed assets are not held for resale but to earn income. In view of the prudent convention that profit must not be anticipated, stocks will normally be valued at the lower of cost or net realisable value; if an inflation accounting system is in use, stocks may be valued at replacement cost, but in this case the holding gain due to inflation will not be regarded as a distributable profit. Investments outside the business will normally be shown at cost, but may be written down to market value if it is considered that a permanent falls in that value has occurred.

The priniciple of the double entry

All methodical accounting is based on the principle of double entry, of which the first recorded use was among the Genoese in the fifteenth century. This simple theory is based on the assumption that there are two aspects to every transaction: onthe surrender of a benefit and the other the gain of a corresponding benefit. When the boot and shoe repairer, referred to earlier, buys leather from a supplier he will at some stage surrender cash and receive a stock of leather in return. When he repairs a shoe he will surrender the use of his time, that of his employees, his tools and his premises, and in return he will gain cash or debt representing the price of his work.

The every transaction must be recorded twice in an accounting system, in one case recording the gain of an asset and in the other the loss or liability.

Such a method of accounting enables a full record to be kept of every asset and liability and every gain or loss of assets or liabilities. It has the additional advantage of providing an automatic check on the arithmetical accuracy of the accounting, for the total assets must be made to agree with the total liabilities. Capital will be treated as a liability of the business to the owner or owners for the purpose of this automatic check.

The mechanics of double entry

Entering capital transactions

People unversed in the mechanics of accounting often find difficulty in understanding on which side of an account a particular entry should appear. Income is occasionally confused with liabilities and expenditure with assets. It must be admitted that some of the difficulty is due to the confused state of certain systems of accounts, where, for example, capital accounts are not clearly segregated from those recording revenue transactions. The two kinds of transactions, though closely connected, must be considered separately if the double-entry system is to be understood. This was one of the reasons for proceeding a description of the mechanics of double-entry accounting with observations on the distinction between capital and revenue.

Dealing first with accounts recording capital, it is necessary to keep in mind that (a) assets appear on the left-hand side of a double-sided account, and (b) liabilities (what is owed by the business) appear on the right-hand side.

Entering revenue transactions

It has been stated that revenue transactions comprise (a) income and (b) expenditure. Income is shown on the right-hand side of a double-sided account and expenditure on the left-hand side. Thus, if the boot repairer had during the first year made sales of work to the value of 500 and had incurred expenses of 100, and if depreciation of tools was charged at 150, his revenue accounts would appear as follows:

Sales account
(income)

Cash account : 500

Business expense account
(expenditure)

Cash account : 100

Depreciation of tools
(expenditure)

Tools account : 150

So far as these accounts are concerned, however,the totals on the right-hand side do not agree with the total on the left-hand side. This is because capital and revenue accounts have to be considered together. transactions on revenue account merely record gains or losses of capital.

The sales of 500 recorded in the revenue account would be accompanied by the receipt of assets such as cash or debtors' balances recorded in the Capital Accounts. The payment of expenses entered in the revenue accounts involves the loss of an asset or the creation of a liability; in this case either the loss of cash or the incurring of a liability in the form of creditors' balances. The writing off of depreciation involves the loss of part of the value of an asset; in this case a reduction inthe value of tools.

The complete accounts

With the above considerations in mind the complete set of accounts as they might exist at the end of a year may now be shown. It will be noted that part of the original cash balance has been spent in the acquisition of tools.

The trial balance

In order to test whether the accounts are in balance at this point a trial balance is drawn upon the following form. It is necessary to emphasise that the trial balance is nothing more than the book-keeper's device for checking the arithmetical accuracy of the entries and conveys no other information of any significance, although in some cases it may form a useful summary for preparing the final accounts.

TRIAL BALANCE

Capital Accounts:		
Owner's capital		£750
B. loan		£250
Cash	£1,100	
Tools	150	
Revenue Accounts:		
Sales 500		
Business expenses	100	
Depreciation of tools	150	
	£1,500	£1,500

The two sides of the trial balance being in agreement testify to the fact that the double entry has been carried out in each case. A trial balance will not disclose the following types of error.

1. Errors of omission—items completely omitted from the books of account.
2. Errors of commission—errors in posting to wrong accounts.
3. Errors of principles—errors due to lack of knowledge of accounting principles, i.e. treating revenue items as capital, and vice versa.

A diagram of entries

At this stage the following diagram is introduced with the object of helping readers to visualise the correct side of a double-sided account towhich entries must be posted:

	Left	*Right*
CAPITAL	Assets	Liabilities
REVENUE	Expenditure	Income

The recording of profit or loss

The difference between income and expenditure, following the strict meaning of these terms, indicates profit or loss. Profit, so long as it is not withdrawn from the business, is an addition to capital, and loss is always a loss of capital.

The next stage in accounting for the boot repairer's business is accordingly to find his profit or loss as a result of the year's work. This operation is carried out by transferring the balances on the revenue accounts to a single account in order to find the net total of these items. In a complicated business, as will be explained later, the operation is carried out by stages, involving in some cases a Manufacturing Account, a Training Account, a Profit and Loss Account and an Appropriation Account, the last showing how the profit or loss is appropriated to the owner's and to reserve accounts. In the present simple example it is sufficient to use a Statement of profit account.

The accounts in the revenue section of the ledger are now closed. The accounts in the capital section of the ledger still have balances which are carried forwards into the next accounting period. The financial position of the boot repairers business can be ascertained at this point by extracting the balances of the accounts in the capital section, including the balance of profit, on to a statement usually termed a Balance Sheet, which can be prepared in the following form.

Balance Sheet as at............

Owner's capital	£750	Cash	£1,100
Add Profit	250	Tools	150
	1,000		
B loan	250		
Total	£1,250		£1,250

The organisation of accounts

The elements of the ledger

The preceeding sections set out to provide a general picture of principles on the basis of which an accounting system operates. One of the essential purposes of accounts is to show the extent to which capital has been maintained and to show the gain or loss on revenue account for a period. But the proprietor of a business will not be satisfied merely to learn that he has made a certain figure of profit over a period or has incurred a certain loss, nor is it sufficient for him to be informed that his capital stands at a stated total of money. If the affairs of the business are to be guided and controlled, the accounting system must be so organized that it will reveal the sources of movements in capital and of revenue items.

For such a purpose the accounting system - in a small business contained in one ledger - must be carefully planned so as to show the significant information required. The planning of the accounting system must also ensure that unwanted details and unnecessary clerical labour are avoided. The ledger must therefore be planned in accordance with certain broad classifications or heading available for extension or further analysis only if essential. There is an unfortunate tendency for ledger accounts to multiply until the significant information becomes lost in a mass of detail.

Asset accounts - "What is owned"

The properties, equipment, stocks, debts, cash, etc., owned by the business are called the assets. These assets may be subdivided into (a) fixed assets and (b) current assets.

Fixed Assets

Fixed assets are those held for the purpose of earning income and not for sale in the course of trading, In an industrial concern separate accounts under this heading will be established for:

(a) land and buildings, distinguished between freehold and leasehold property;

(b) plant and machinery;

(c) other fixed assets, such as investments, which are not intended to be disbursed in the course of business;

(d) deferred charges, such as heavy advertising expenditure incurred for the purpose of creating a market in a new product or other initial expenditure for development purposes, the benefit of which will be obtained in future years.

It should be borne in mind that although many assets are described as fixed, they are all, except freehold land, subject to depreciation or other loss of value, and the monetary total of fixed assets continually requires replenishent out of income. The method of accounting for such depreciation in value of fixed assets considered later.

Current assets

Current assets are those which may be expanded or consumed in immediate day-to-day operations of the business. A very necessary characteristic of current assets is that they shall be freely available for conversion into cash. Cash balances and those current assets which may be converted into cash almost immediately the necessity arises are known as "liquid assets".

Thus under the heading of current assets the following accounts may be regarded as the minimum:

Cash in hand.	Temporary investments.	Debtors.
Cash at bank.	Stocks.	

The assets section of the capital division of the ledger may be shown diagrammatically thus:

Liabilities accounts - "What is owed"

Those from whom the business borrows or purchase on account are known as creditors have a claim on the business until they are paid, and those claims are termed liabilities.

Liabilities may also be divided into those which may be regarded as fixed or static, and those which are current.

Fixed liabilities

The owners' capital is for accounting purposes regarded as a liability of the business, i.e. the amount owed by the business to the proprietors, although it is composed of the difference between the assets and the other liabilities, subject to the addition of profit and subtraction of loss represented by the balance in the profit and loss account. In the case of a sole proprietor there will be an account recording his fixed capital, i.e., the amount he will endeavour to maintain intact. In a partnership there will be separate accounts for eachof the partners. In a company there will be accounts for each of the various classes of shares.

In addition to owners' capital, fixed capital will include long-term loans to the business such as, in the case of a company, debentures.

Where amounts are allocated out of surpluses with a view of increasing the permanent capital of the business, such allocations are credited to a "capital reserve" account, which henceforth forms part of the foxed capital of the concern and is not available for distribution to the owners except in the event of the business coming to an end. Profit made on the sale of a fixed asset is also normally credited to capital reserve. Trading profits may be, and frequently are, credited to revenue reserves, which if necessary are available for distribution to the proprietors.

Thus the minimum accounts required to record fixed liabilities are:
(i) owners' capital.
(ii) long-term loans,
(iii) capital reserves.

Current liabilities

Current liabilities are those which may need to be settled in cash at short notice, or in the normal operation of the business. They include trade creditors, short-term loans, such as loans from a bank, and bills of exchange payable.

Contingent liabilities

It is considered appropriate at this point to refer to contingent liabilities, although they are not normally entered in an account forming part of the double-entry system.

Contingent liabilities are those which may become real liabilities and payable on the happening of a specified event. They include guarantees entered into by the business. Guarantees do not, of course, represent real debts until and unless the party guaranteed defaults. A contingent liability arises if, for example, a person or firm becomes a party to a bill of exchange. The contingent liability becomes a real liability if the principal debtor, the drawer or the acceptors of the bill, fails to pay.

Contingent liabilities have to be noted on the Balance Sheet of limited companies in accordance with the provisions of the companies Act, and the practice should be followed by other organisations.

Income

In a trading organisation income may be considered under two headings: (a) sales, and (b) other income. The income which arises from selling the products or services of the business forms the great bulk of "income", while "other income" comprises investment income, other interest and commissions, and exceptional receipts such as damages received in a legal action. Clearly the expression "sales" must be modified in the case of non-trading concerns so as to cover the main source of income to earn which the business exists: thus the main source of income for an insurance company is premium income, and for a transport company fares and freight charges.

Expenditure

Expenditure and "costs"

The expenditure accounts are, perhaps, those which necessitate the most careful planning, for they are those from which stem detailed costing and many other methods of control. It is necessary at this point to emphasise that cost accounts, whether they set out to show unit costs, process costs or departmental costs, represent further analysis and breakdowns of the expenditure accounts which appear in the so-called Nominal or General Ledger. The illogical divorce between "cost accounts" and "financial accounts" has given rise to the modern technique of integrating cost and financial accounts. The use of term "integration" in this context merely implies a reunion of the two systems, which should never have been separated. An accounting system must be dealt with as one entity, not as several independent units.

Because of the temptation for indefinite and, in some cases, pointless analysis of expenditure in the ledger, it is essential for such accounts to conform to a concise plan. Business expenditure falls within three well-defined categories: personnel charges, material charges and other expenses.

Personnel charges

The expression "personnel charges" here means wages, salaries, national insurance, pensions and any expense directly incurred by the employment of people in the business. For a variety of reasons it is necessary to maintain at least three separate accounts recording personnel charges, and these accounts can be shown thus:

For reasons shown later, in all but the smallest concerns the above heading will probably require to be expanded as follows:

Pay: (i) Hourly wages; (ii) weekly salaries; (iii) monthly salaries.

National Insurance: Subdivided as above.

Other personnel charges: (i) Pension contributions; (ii) pensions payable; (iii) other payments, such as welfare expenses, redundancy and severance payments and compensation.

Other expenses

So far the accounts required under the heading of expenditure present little difficulty.

The heading of "other expenses" must, however, be considered with the greatest care because of the miscellaneous nature of expense which it comprises. One answer to the problem of classification is to record separately the largest identifiable groups of expense not being material or relating directly to personnel. The following broad headings may suffice and can be expanded as the need arises:

Financial charges
Administrative Charges,
Selling and distributive charges,
Exceptional charges, and
Sundries.

Under financial charges, separate accounts are normally extracted for cash discount, audit, taxation and legal fees, depreciation and interest payable.

Under administrative charges, separate accounts may be necessary for stationery and postage, employees and general expenses, vehicle charges insurances, rent and rates. Under selling and distribution charges, the accounts include advertising, warehousing, carriage outwards and commission. Commission payable to employed salesmen as part of their remuneration might preferably be included under the personnel heading, but in any event a separate account will be desirable.

Exceptional charges include compensation, damages, fines, losses on exchange, losses on sale of fixed assets and investments.

The economy of ledger accounts

It is emphasised at this point that the growth of a business does not cocessarily entail an increase in the number of main ledger accounts. It is more likely that the small business for which a detailed costing system is not justified would require many more accounts representing analyses of expenditure than a large concern. In a large business the necessary detailed information would be provided by subsidiary systems of accounts or computerised date controlled by and agreeing in total with a limited number of main ledger accounts such as are indicated in the preceding section.

The main or control ledger is thus the chief accountant's personal instrument for watching the progress of the concern and reporting on the results to top management. He should be aware by a rapid scrutiny of the accounts of any trend or change in the financial position which requires immediate investigation; and by the use of a control ledger containing the minimum of accounts he would not be misled by masses of detailed information from which such accounts were made up.

The immediate source from which entries are made in such a control ledger are subsidiary analyses grouping items into, say, monthly totals for posting to the control accounts.

Detailed information is obtainable from subsidiary ledger systems, each self-balancing in itself and each controlled by an account in the main or control ledger. Subsidiary ledger systems of this nature include a debtors' ledger with an account for each debtor, and analogous to the sales ledger, except that a debtors' ledger contains all debtors, not merely those resulting from sales. Similarly, a creditors ledger includes all creditors' accounts and broadly corresponds to the "bought ledger", except that a creditors' ledger is not limited to suppliers' accounts. Further subsidiary ledger systems can, as necessary, be created to show various types of fixed assets, stocks, material purchases and any analysis of other expenses which may be required.

In a substantial business the "ledger" will consist of computerised tabulations, or a computer file; the availability of mini-computers now provides this facility to very small businesses.

Preparation of financial statements

If the accounts in the ledger are organised in the manner shown in the preceding paragraphs the preparation of financial statements for management is simplified. A trial balance can be extracted from the ledger under the main headings required on the financial statements: sub-totals are made for each heading, and the sub-totals extracted on'to a summary financial statement.

Before such a statement is prepared it will be necessary to ensure that outstanding and accrued income have been taken into account. This is dealt with in the next chapter onthe subject of the preparation of the final accounts.

The example which follows is a simplified one, and in practice the number of accounts may be greater than can conveniently be contained in one trial balance. If this is the case schedules of accounts could be prepared and summarised under convenient headings on the trial balance, before being extracted on the financial statement.

TRIAL BALANCE FOR QUARTER ENDED
31st MARCH 19-4

CAPITAL LEDGER	
CAPITAL:	
Ordinary Shares	5,000
Preference Shares	5,000
CAPITAL RESERVES:	
Share Premium	1,250
REVENUE RESERVES:	
General Reserve	1,150
Profit and Loss Account b/f	4,000
This period	2,490
Capital Employed	**18,890**

CURRENT LIABILITIES:		
Trade Creditors		1,950
Accrued Expenses		200
Total Current Liabilities		**2,150**
FIXED ASSETS:		
Land and buildings	3,000	
Plant	1,530	
Fixtures	500	
Goodwill	1,500	
Total Fixed Assets	**6,530**	
CURRENT ASSETS:		
Cash in hand	260	
Bank balances	4,250	
Stocks	4,500	
Debtors	5,500	
Total Current Assets	**14,510**	
Less Current Liabilities	2,150	
Net Current Assets	12,360	
Total Net Assets	**18,890**	

REVENUE LEDGER

INCOME:	
Sales	30,350
Service	4,400
Discounts received	250
Total Income	**35,000**
EXPENDITURE:	
Personnel Charges:	
Pay	3,300
National Insurance	220
Total	**3,520**
Materials:	
Raw materials	20,300
Bought-out-parts	8,050
Total	**28,350**
Other Expenses:	
Financial Charges:	
Depreciation	550
Interest	200

Total	**750**	
Administrative Charges:		
Insurance	200	
Rent and rates	640	
Other	250	
Total	**1,090**	
Selling and Distributive:		
Advertising	100	
Commissions	200	
Total	**300**	
TOTAL EXPENDITURE AND INCOME	34,010	35,000
Stocks to begin and end	**3,000**	**4,500**
	37,010	39,500
Net Profit for Quarter	**2,490**	
	39,500	39,500

SUMMARY FINANCIAL STATEMENT
FOR QUARTER ENDED 31st MARCH 19-4

Capital Employed		£18,890
Employment of Capital:		
Fixed Assets		6,530
Current Assets	£14,510	
Less Current Liabilities	2,150	
Net Current Assets		12,360
		18,890
Income		35,000
Increase in Stocks		1,500
		£36,500
Expenditure:		
Personnel Charges		3,520
Materials		28,350
Financial Charges		750
Administrative Charges		1,090
Sailing and Distributive Expenses		300
		34,010
		2,490
Net Profit for Quarter		£36,500

It will be seen from an examination of the example that the profit for the current accounting period is included. To obtain this figure it will be necessary to total the revenue section first, obtain the profit or loss, and then enter in the capital section. It will be noted that only the totals in bold type are taken on to the summary financial statement.

The source of entries

With the preceding broad picture of the principles of an accounting system in mind, consideration may now be given to the more detailed mechanics of the technique.

In a simple accountancy system, every entry made in an account forming part of the double-entry system of listings originate from a subsidiary book or, as it is otherwise known, a book of original entry. In a more developed system the book will be replaced by a listing made from originating documents, e.g. invoices. Examples of such books are:

Day Books
Journals
Bill Books
Cash Books

The purpose of such books of listings is to collect in chronological order, and if necessary classify transactions, so that totals are available for entry into the appropriate accounts. Thus in accounting for a retails shop the sales account in the ledger cannot be over burdenedc with every single sale, some perhaps for trifling amounts. A sales Day Book or Journal is therefore maintained for the purpose of recording transactions on credit, analysing them by types of sales and providing daily, weekly or possibly monthly totals, for entry in the sales account. Following the principle of double-entry, it should be noted that each subsidiary book constitute the source of entries in at least two accounts. Thus the Sales Day Book or Sales Journal not only provides totals for the credit of the sales account but also the individual debits to the debtors' account. Each entry in the subsidiary books is in turn normally supported by a document to evodence the transaction, such as, for example, an invoice in the case of a sale.

The cash book

The purpose of the Cash Book and the originating documents

The Cash Book of a small business often performs the function of a cash account and a subsidiary book combined.

In many small business the receipt of money over the counter for small sales is not supported by any documentary evidence. It is, however, certainly desirable that some form of slip or receipt be issued, if only for the purpose of providing a check on the accuracy of cash receipts. Money received in the form of Cheques, postal orders, etc., should be paid into the firm's banking account, the counterfoil of the bank paying-in book forming the necessary evidence. Payments of cash should in all cases be supported by a voucher. In the case of cash purchases the voucher will be the receipted bill if obtainable: if not, in common with other petty cash payments, they must be evidenced by a petty cash voucher signed by the recipient and approved by an authorised superior. Cheque payments sent through the post should in the first instance be evidenced by a remittance advice, of which a copy will be retained. The cheques Act 1957, Section 3, provides that: "An unendorsed cheque which appears to have been paid by the banker on whom it is drawn is evidence of the receipt by the payee of the sum payable by the cheque." As a result of this Act the practice of giving receipts for cheque payments, except where a formal discharge is required, has been largely discontinued.

The Cash Book should be written up, at least daily, from the supporting documents, and the procedure can be summarised thus:

Receipts

Cheque and Postal Remittance - from a remittance list.

Cash Sales - total of copies of counterslips or total rolls of cash registers.

Other Receipts - from suitable evidence.

Payments

Cheque Payments - from counterfoils of cheque book.

Cash Payments - from payees' receipted bills or petty cash vouchers.

The three forms of cash books

Three forms of cash books may be found in use and these are:

Separate Cash and Bank Accounts
The Double Column Cash Book
The Bank Cash Book and Petty Cash Book

(i) *Separate Cash and bank accounts.* In the most simple form receipts and payments of money as recorded in one book, and a separate book is maintained for payments by cheque or receipts direct into the bank account.

(ii) *The double-column Cash Book.* In this case the entries are made in a similar manner as before, but with the use of tabular columns both accounts are recorded on the same page side by side. This method has the advantage of keeping all receipts and payments, whether by cash or cheque, in chronological order, and also showing the cash and bank balances adjacent to each other.

(iii) *The Bank Cash Book and Petty Cash Book.* The most methodical system of recording cash transactions depends on the rule that all payments shall be made by cheque and that all receipts shall be banked not later than the morning following the day of receipt. If this rule is enforced the Cash Book will contain an account of transactions with the bank only and will correspond with the bank pass book.

It will be necessary to maintain an independent record of individual cash receipts, since the bank account will show only totals of daily taking paid into the bank. Furthermore, the Cash Book being a medium for posting into the other accounts, an analysis will be required of the receipt by account headings. For this reason separate cash-received and cash-paid books are usually found convenient, and even the entries in such books may require further analysis for statistical purposes.

Small items such as postages and small local purchases are paid out of a cash balance kept for the purpose. The initial imprest is recorded by drawing a cheque payable to "petty cash" for the amount sanctioned. This cheque is exchanged at the bank for the requisite coin and notes and the proceeds entered in the petty cash book and cross posted to a "petty cash" account in the ledger.

The Puchase Journal (Payables)

The objects of the Purchase Journal

So long as a business pays on delivery for everything it buys the purchases account or accounts could be written up from the entries in the Cash Paid Book or the cash paid side of a single Cash Book. Where purchases are obtained on credit it is necessary to operate a separate book of prime entry recording such transactions. This subsidiary book is variously called a Purchase Journal or Purchase Day Book.

The purpose of the Purchase Journal is to provide a medium from which entries can be made: (a) to the creditors' accounts recording the indebtedness of the business to its suppliers; and (b) to the purchases or material account, recording the cost of the material which has been obtained but not paid for immediately.

The basis of entries

The entries in the Purchase Journal are made from the suppliers' invoices. Before an entry is made in the Purchase Journal the accuracy of the charge shown on the suppliers' invoice must be verified. In the case of goods supplied the normal routine is for a goods inwards note to be made out by the goods inwards department after that department has checked that the goods supplied are in acceptable condition and that they correspond with the description shown on the delivery note. The goods inwards note is checked against the order, usually by the buying department, and the invoice, when it is eventually received, is checked against both documents before it is passed for payment.

An order will be preceded by an indent on the buying department made out by the departmental manager authorised to initiate ordering of goods. For stock items, where stocklimits are set up, the stores may submit indents when the stocks have fallen to the ordering level. In the case of invoices for services supplied there will, of course, be no goods inwards note and the invoice will have to be approved by a responsible official who is in a position to certify that the services have been properly carried out.

Where a high standard and precise workmanship are called for from a supplier it may be necessary for the goods to be examined by the inspection department before the charges made for them are accepted. In such a case the indent and orders should be marked to this effect so as to warn the staff concerned that a satisfactory inspection report must be received before the invoice can be passed for payment.

The procedure outlined above must be strictly followed in order to ensure that no unauthorised or incorrect charge is paid for or entered in the accounts. It should be noted, however, that in order to expedite the payment of invoices known and trusted suppliers are often paid on the basis of their invoices immediately the latter have been checked against the goods inwards note. This method has the advantage of maintaining suppliers' goodwill and gaining cash discount as a result of the prompt payment. It may also obviate considerable accounting entries, since no account need be maintained for a supplier whose charges are paid for soon after receipt of his invoice.

Any system of paying on the basis of invoices as compared with the recorded balance on a suppliers' account in the ledger requires, however, close supervision and a well trained staff. In any event, the system of recording and paying suppliers should be subject to investigations from time to time by an internal audit section.

The subsequent entries in the accounts

From the point of view of the ledger keeper the entry in the Purchase Journal is tantamount to acceptance of the charge, and the remaining procedure is automatic. At convenient intervals, say monthly, the entries in the Purchase Journal against each supplier will be credited to that suppliers' account in the ledger. The double entry will be completed at the end of, say, a month, by debiting the total of the entries to a purchases or material account.

The use of the Purchase Journal thus economises in book-keeping, since it avoids the necessity for entering every transactions in the expenditure accounts.

Where it is desirable to record suppliers' charges under different headings, the Purchase Journal will have to be analysed, preferably containing a separate column for each material or other account which is to be posted in the ledger. A Purchase Journal can be used to record every liability incurred. Whether for material, capital items services, or expenditure of any nature obtained on credit. There is otherwise considerable risk that a liability may be created which is not entered in the accounts until payment is made.

Such a use of the Journal necessitates the provision of analysis columns each representing an account or sometimes a group of accounts in the ledger.

The sales journal (Receivables)

The Sales Journal or Day Book is intended to record individual sales on credit. The originating document for entries in the Sales Journal is a copy of the invoice sent to the customer.

A sales invoice is made out, normally by the sales department, (a) on notification from the works that the article required has been completed and has been passed to the warehouse for dispatch, or (b) for stock items on the basis of the sales department's prior knowledge of stocks held. In each case an order will have been previously passed to the works or stores specifying the goods required and the customers' requirements as to packing and delivery. A copy of the delivery note attached to the goods is passed to the sales department for checking against the customer's order and as a basis for preparing the sales invoice.

In a majority of businesses, large or small, it is necessary to analyse sales by types. The Sales Journal requires to be similarly analysed so that totals, say monthly, of each kind of sale, may be posted to the credit of the various sales accounts. The corresponding double entries are made to the individual customer's accounts in the ledger. A brief example of a Sales Journal with analysis column follows:

The Journal proper

At least one further subsidiary book, sometimes called simply "the Journal", is essential for the operation of any efficient accounting system. The purpose of the Journal is to record those entries which cannot be made in the main books of original entry, such as the following:

Opening entries

(i) To record initial assets, liabilities and capital taken over by a new business.

(ii) In an amalgamation, to incorporate the assets and liabilities of the undertakings absorbed.

Transfer between one account and another

Where, for example, an entry has been made in the wrong account; an item has been charged to expenditure or revenue account instead of to capital, the writing-off of bad debts, i.e. transfer from the customer's account to a "Bad Debts" account; transfer of profit to reserve or owners' accounts, etc.

Closing entries

(i) When a business is dissolved.

(ii) To adjust accounts at the year end or other balancing period, e.g. the transfer of balances from the revenue accounts to the Trading and Profit and Loss Accounts, and various other end-of-period adjustments.

Other entries

(i) Where an analysed Purchase Day Book is not kept it will be necessary to record liabilities, such as capital items obtained on credit, in the Journal.

(ii) Other entries, such as infrequent bill transactions, where it is considered unnecessary to maintain a special Day Book got the purpose.

Entries in the Journal should be strictly limited. The Journal should not be overburdened with many entries of a related nature; where this occurs such entries should be accomodated in a separate book of original entry.

Journal entries are made in the following manner:

JOURNAL

Jan.1	Office Equipment account	Dr.	£110	
	To Suppliers Ltd.			£110
	Purchase of calculating machine			
Jan.10	Bad Debts account	Dr.	50	
	To Johnson & Co.			50
	Writing off Johnson & Co.'s A/c			
	Jan.10 Smythe & Co. Ltd.	Dr.	25	
	To Smith & Co.			25
	Correction of error amount posted to Smith & Co. instead of Smythe & Co.			
Jan.10	Depreciation account	Dr.	200	
	To Depreciation Suspense account-Plant			200
	(Being depreciation @ 10% p.a. on 2,000)			

It is not always appreciated that the accuracy of the accounts and hence of accounting statements depends on the information contained in the source documents from which the figures originate. The modern computerised accounting system is tending to eliminate much of the old system of handwritten day books and journals, and even ledgers in double-entry form, but the computer is just as capable as the old system of producing nonsense if the input is incorrect.

There is no difference in principle between a computerised system of accounting and a manual system or one making extensive use of accounting machinery. In a manual system the figure on source documents, such as invoices and material requisitions, etc., are listed, analysed and totalled in books or on analysis sheets called day books or journals. These sheets or journals form the basis from which postings are made to the appropriate ledger accounts, and their purpose is to summarise transactions so that only monthly, or sometimes daily totals need be entered into the accounts. When an accounting system is computerised the essential change which takes place is that the computer itself performs the operations of totalling and analysis and may eliminate the ledger accounts as such. The documents originating the information will continue to be required, although where real time processing a carried out, the computer will receive the information at the same time as the original document, e.g. when an invoice is prepared.

Accounting information and decision-making

Consider the following statements:

1. If accounting information is not considered relevant by a decision-maker to a decision under consideration, a change in the accounting information will not affect his decision.
2. The conception of accounting information held by a decision-maker - his opinion on how well the accountant and accounting system measures significant attributed and characteristics of factors affecting and affected by a decision - will affect the weight given to accounting information in the decision process when other information is available.
3. The availability of other information will be an important determinant of the weight assigned by a decision-maker to accounting information in the decision process.

Each of these statements has many characteristics of a truism. Many more like them, each concerned with the relationship between accounting systems, accounting information, decision-makers, and decision-making could be easily constructed. Though behavioral relationships on which such statements rest are potentially important to the development of accounting theory and the design of information-decision systems, the study of those relationships is in the earliest stages.

Relatively little is known about the way in which information is used in decision-making, and without such knowledge it is difficult to predict the diverse effects which different accounting systems or information will have on decisions. A model developed below explicity identifies and relates some factors which may determine when decisions are affected by accounting systems and information. The hypo these on which this model is based are intended to stimulate and direct part of the study of accounting and decision-making. While the model is not tested here, some implications of the hypothesized relationships for both accounting theory and accounting systems are discussed.

Rationales for research on decision-making and behaviour by accountants

The problem that demand new research in behavioral aspects of accounting are familiar toalmost all who have studied economics and accounting. The relationship between available information and decisions is basic to economic theories of decision-making,. Knowledge about costs, prices, and competitors is assumed in almost all traditional theory, and much effort has been directed towards developing models of decision-making for use when information about one or more of these factors is unknown. As these models have been explored and modified, and as new procedures for analysis of alternative courses of action have been developed, new attention has been given to the role of data as determinants of decisions.

Accounting systems of firms are important sources of information for business decision-making. The information which systems provide for decision-making can be grouped in three classes: financial statements, quantitative reports on selected aspects of operations, and special analyses. Information from each class can be grouped with information from another or with information from sources outside the accounting system in the set of information used by a decision-maker.

Almost all accounting information is affected by the body of rules and procedures called generally accepted accounting principels. Efforts to develop and improve generally accepted accounting principles have been underway since the 1930's, and since 1960 these efforts have found vigorous support from the accounting profession. Thus far, these efforts have not been notably successful for there are few if any bases on which all accountants can agree to select among alternative general principles.

It is possible that much of the effort directed toward resolution of controversy about generally accepted accounting principles has been premature or misdirected. Accounting is a service activity carried out to provide information for decisions within and about business firms, Analyses of alternatives sets of generally accepted accounting principles have often been based on the assumption that the relationship between an accounting report or information contained therein and each decision is direct. But this assumption has not been tested, and alternative hypotheses abound. When these have been tested and efforts to develop generally accepted accounting principles can be based upon knowledge of the manner in which accounting affects decisions about business activity, new and important criteria for selecting among alternative methods and alternative systems will be available.

Defining accounting systems and information

One complication in the task of relating accounting information to decision-making is the fact that "accounting systems" are diverse and "accounting information" describes many different sets of data and information. For purposes of this paper, an "accounting system" will refer to the methods by which financial data about a firm or its activity are collected, processed, stored and/or distributed to members of the firm or other interested parties. It is possible to consider that any data or information which are obtained from or created in the accounting system of a firm are accounting information, whether contained in a financial statement, a special report, or verbal statement. However, for our immediate purposes, that interpretation is too broad to be useful. Hereafter. "accounting information" will refer to written information of the type that might be contained in a complete or partial financial report-balance sheet, income statement or funds flow statement-though in many cases this limitation is not critical to the discussion.

The relevance of accounting information for decision-making

By definition, decision affect future events, for future actions are determined as a decision is made. In the case of management decision, decisions may affect only a single event or they may affect all events subsequent to the decision. But no event which has been completed can be altered by a decision. Furthermore, accounting information, in the sense that we are using that terms here, focuses on past events. Accounting cannot change events or their effects unless it is through the decision process where future events and their effects are determined. Decision-making and accounting information focus on different time periods except to the extent that the decision process employs accounting information. An important question then is, when is accounting information relevant for decision-making?

Selection of a particular decision rule by a decision-maker is affected by many factors, among them his analytical capabilities and objectives. The rule associates inputs with decisions, and selection of a decision rule establishes the degree to which objectives will be met by the expected effects of a particular set of decision. The decision-maker explores the relationship between decisions and objectives prior to the selection of a rule by analysis and through evaluation of the effects of past events similar to those contemplated in the future.

If accounting information affects decisions, it does so through a decision rule which relates decisions to inputs, which include accounting information. The decision-maker uses or selects a decision rule which relates inputs to decisions in a manner consistent with his experience, perceptions, and his objectives. Suppose we let x_1 represent consistent accounting information, one element of a set of all decisions inputs available at the time a set of decisions is to be made. The decision rule weights each decision inputs, which determines each decision in the set Z, and the weight assigned to x_1 will determine what effect, if any, accounting information has on decisions affecting future events. All other decision inputs, x_2 through x_m, are also weighted by the decision rule, and each affects the resulting set of decisions. These inputs may provide nonfinancial information essential to decisions, and in some cases their weights will overwhelm any possible effects of accounting information.

In selecting a decision rule, the decision-maker must consider all inputs available and their relevance to the set of decisions to be made. It is the decision-maker who decides whether any input is relevant or not. The perceived relevance of the decision inputs to the decisions at hand determine whether the decision rule selected will apply a weight different from zero to accounting information. If a weight different from zero is applied, accounting information may affect decisions; if not decisions will not be affected by accounting information. Therefore, we hypothesize; if accounting information is perceived as irrelevant for the set of decisions to be made, accounting information will not affect decisions; if accounting information is perceived as relevant to the set of decisions to be mode, it may affect decisions.

The role of the decision-maker's conception of accouting

Accounting is a systematic process of providing information about wealth and the effects of economic events. The methods, rules, and procedures that comprise accounting are here assued to be familiar to the reader. However, there are reasons to believe that accounting is different things to different participants in economic events, and if so, the conceptions of accounting held by individuals or organizations may influence the impact of accounting information on behavior.

Away from reality, accounting can be regarded as a perfect measure. A perfect measure can be defined as a measure where there is a zero probability that the true measurement of an attribute differs from the reported measurement. We can assume that identifiable objects and legal rights have value and that these values are enhanced or developed as economic events occur, and we can assume that these values and effects are measurable. To many persons, accounting practice, carried out by trained observers applying consistent and objective methods of measurement and attested to by independent agents, holds the image of a perfect measure applied by professionals. There is an aura of authenticity that surrounds accounting data, and to the untrained user of information, accounting may appear to be a perfect source. We must recognize however, that few, if any, of the persons who have processed or reviewed the data and the procedures that have converted it to information would consider it perfect.

More realistically, accounting can be considered as a process by which the value or effects of events is reported as accurately possible but without pretense of being a perfect measure. Here, this conception of accounting will be referred to as an "imperfect measure." Such a measure is defined when the probability that the true value differs from the reported value is greater than zero. This conception is probably closest to that held by most practicing accountants. Errors and inaccuracy in the process of measuring, counting, and reporting are inevitable, and most persons who are familiar with accounting measures and procedures are familiar with these problems. This notion may cause accounting to have a different impact on behavior than the "perfect measure" notion. It allows for a "margin of disbelief" that may in some cases affect the kind of action taken as accounting information is used in decision processes.

A third conception of accounting is fundamentally different from the "perfect measure" or "imperfect measure" notions advanced above. Accounting information may be a goal for actors in economic events., When a businessman seeks profit, he does so for many important to the businessman or manager than the "true" or "perfectly measured" profit. Modern business organization has given this conception of accounting wide significance, and the implications of this notion for accounting warrant close examination. Accounting become a goal when rewards or satisfactions accrue to a decision-maker as a result of accounting information, and the relationship of the true measure to the reported measure is unimportant. For example, if a manager hopes to advance and feels he will be promoted if he can effect cost reductions, and if accounting information will provide the basis for determining whether costs have been reduced, then it is the accounting information, which shows reduced costs that becomes the goal. Likewise, where management is rewarded by stockholders with salary and prerequisites on the basis of reported earnings or growth, the reports which result in these rewards may become more important—the goal of management decision-maker - than the long-run earnings or healthy growth which the stockholders really intend to reward.

While not exclusive, this brief recognition of diverse conceptions of accounting seems essential to understanding the effects of accounting information on behavior and decision-making. Below it will be assumed that any individual in a decision situation conceives accounting information either as a goal or at a point on a continuum on which accounting varies from a perfect measure to an imperfect one. This assumption is necessary to state a second set of hypothese relating accounting information and decisions: the conception of accounting held by a decision-=maker will affect his selection of a decision rule to be used in reaching a set of decisions. This hypothesis can be further specified by stating it in two parts:

1. If accounting information is both a decision input and an objective (goal) sought by a decision-maker, accounting information will affect decisions.
2. The more a decision-maker conceives accounting as being a perfect source of information, the more likely the decision-maker will select decision rules that weight accounting heavily, and the more likely accounting information will affect decisions.

Classifying decision-maker's

Because accounting information can be conceived as a goal, and because accounting information is deteremined in part by an accounting system, a classification of decision-makers provides insight into a final effect which accounting information may have on the set of decisions selected by the decision-makers. Three classes are suggested, first, decision-makers within the firm who make decisions both about operations and about the accounting system used to prepare reports; second, decision-makers within the firm who can make operating decisions but who cannot affect the methods used to prepared reports; and third, those outside of the firm who make decisions about the firm which may affect its environment and operations but who have no direct control over the operation of the firm or any activities in which it is engaged. The reasons for separating the first two classes of decision-makers, both of which are internal to the firm, will later become more obvious.

The first class of decision-makers is comprised of top management. Financial reports are the reports of this group and they are responsible for their preparation and presentation. If a choice must be made between accounting methods, this group is responsible for making that decision. This means that the set of possible decisions available to this class of decision-makers includes modification of the accounting system.

The second class of decision-makers is distinguished from the first only in one important way. Their position in the organization precludes their determining the information included in accounting reports by modifying the accounting system. However, they make decisions about the activities of the firm and we can assume that accounting information enters into their decision processes. They can of course, influence the content of accounting information by their decisions about activities, in which case accounting information may be affecting decisions.

The distinction between top management, who may affect accounting information, and internal decision-makers who cannot, is most critical where accounting information is conceived as a goal. The decision function for such managers may contain important options between operating decisions and decisions to change the methods by which accounting information is prepared. In any event, decisions are affected, but predicting directions of the effects is much more complicated than it is for decision-makers who do not have authority to modify accounting methods or procedures.

Requirements for independent audits and certification of consistency in methods between accounting periods reduces the significance of the two levels of management, though few would argue that this requirement is such that the effects of top management's discretion in accounting can be interested outsiders. Investors, legally the owners of the firm but in fact usually somewhat removed from it, are ostensibly the group for which accounting information in published form is prepared. Creditors, in some cases merely another class of investors, usually seek the some information. A third major set of outsiders consist of government agencies who seek bases for taxation, regulation, and economic analysis. Each of these sets of outsiders makers decisions that may affect the firm and its operations, and to the extent that accounting information is utilized as part of their decision processes, it will affect these decisions. However, the goals of the decision-makers external to the firm presumably may differ from the objectives of the firm or objectives which concern decision-makers within the firm. This possibility makes analysis of effects of accounting information on decisions of this class of decision-makers very difficult. Nevertheless, the classification of decision-makers yields an important hypothesis: if a decision-maker can affect the accounting system as well as the activities of the firm, and if he conceives accounting information as a goal, accounting information will affect decisions about either or both the accounting system and operations.

Non-accounting information

The final hypothesis to be introduced in this model concerns the role played by information which is not a product of the accounting system in determining the impact of accounting information on decisions. Above, accounting information was defined as information of the type that might be contained in a conventional financial report. In many respects, the effects of non-accounting information on decisions can be analyzed in the same framework as accounting information. However, the importance of non-accounting information here is that it may determine the effects of accounting information on decisions.

If non-accounting information becomes a goal or is perceived as having special relevance for decisions undergoing evaluation, the impact of accounting information will be reduced. If non-accounting information is not relevant to decisions, the effect of relevant accounting information will be enahanced. Therefore, we hypothesize: the impact of accounting information on decisions is affected by the perceived relevance of other information also available to the decision-maker.

A model for analyzing the effects of accounting information on decisions

Rather than restate all hypotheses or describe the model in detail, a summary of hypotheses which lead to the principal outcomes predicted by the model will be used to reveal the interrelationships within it.

I. Accounting information will either affect decisions or affect decisions about the accounting system if:

(a) accounting information is relevant to decisions;

(b) the decision-maker conceives accounting as a goal;

(c) the decision-maker is a member of the firm who can control the selection and operation of the accounting system.

II. Accounting information will affect decisions if:

(a) accounting information is relevant to decisions;

(b_1) the decision-maker conceives accounting as a goal;

and (c_1) the decision-maker is a member of the firm who cannot control the selection and operation of the acccunting system;

or (c_2) the decision-maker is external to the firm;

or (b_2) the decision-maker conceives accounting as a perfect measure;

and (c) non-accounting information is not relevant to the decision.

III. Accounting information may affect decisions if:

(a) accounting information is relevant to decisions;

(b_1) the decision-maker conceives accounting as a perfect measure;

and (c) non-accounting information is relevant to the decision;

(b_2) the decision-maker conceives accounting as an imperfect measures;

but (c) non-accounting information is not relevant to the decision.

IV. Accounting information will not affect decisions if;

(a_1) accounting information is not relevant to decisions;

or (a_2) accounting information is relevant to the decision;

but (b) the decision-maker conceives accounting information as an imperfect measures;

and (c) non-accounting information is relevant to the decision.

Some other exploration of the model

This format demands that we state precisely what will happen at each branch of the model. Yet there appear to be some situations in which it would be more satisfactory to think in terms of effects along a continuum.

The model predicts that accounting information perceived as perfect may have some effect on decisions. However, when the decision-maker perceives accounting information as being something less than perfect (for example, recognizes that errors or biases may have been introduced into the measurements reported), the impact of other information becomes less certain. The degree of conceived imperfection and the amount and quality of other information are important variables in such cases. Likewise, even in cases where accounting information is perfect, and other information is relevant, the decision might be affected,but not altered, by accounting information. Similar questions can be raised at other points and simply reinforce conclusions about the need for testing the hypotheses on which this model is based.

While these uncertain conclusions beg for clarification and discriminating research, they are perhaps the least interesting. In cases where decisions may be little affected by accounting information, the choice of a particular accounting system, or particular accounting methods used in that system, may be of little importance. It is at the other extreme, where the model predicts that accounting information will effect decisions that the choice of accounting systems and methods becomes critical.

Interaction within the model

Further complications in interpreting or using the model stem from possible interaction between the method of accounting used and/or the accounting system developed and the perceived relevance of accounting for decision-making purposes. If the decision-maker feels that a particular method or system of accounting is inappropriate as a basis for measurements relating to a particular problem, he will be led to a position where the effective accounting information will be reduced. Unless we know something about the particular class of decision-makers and their perceptions of accounting methods, it is difficult to predict whether any examination of the conception of accounting held by the decision-maker will be of importance. Likewise, if the method chosen, or the process of selecting a method, affect the conception of accounting held by the decision-maker, then this will affect the relationship between a particular method and decisions.

A digression: the meaning of relevance

The proposal made here to recognize relevance as a primary determinant of the effect of accounting on decision-making is not new. The degree of relevance has frequently been suggested as a basis for choosing between alternative accounting methods and form of accounting information. This has been particularly true in the literature relating to accounting within the firm, where it is frequently asserted that those methods that result in revelation of cost-volume-profit relationships are most appropriate. Likewise, in the recent Statement of Basic Accounting Theory, formulated by a committee of the Americal Accounting Association, relevances proposed as a primary standard for selecting among alternative forms of accounting information.

However, the meaning of relevance appropriate for its use as a criterion in the development of accounting methodology and theory is not clear. While users are frequently the point of reference in analysis employing "relevance," the determination of "relevant information" is left to the accountant, who uses some standard, generally accepted model for decision-making as the criterion in determining what should be reported. In the formulation which has been presented above, relevance is determined by the user of the information, and the effect of this choice creates several problems which require careful consideration before this criterion is employed.

If the user determines relevance, we should expect that, in some cases, what the user feels is relevant would not be relevant in those standard, accepted models with which we are familiar, such as those drawn from economics. Suppose the accountant knows the objectives of the firm and those objectives correspond to those in an accepted model of decision-making, but the decision-maker feels the relevant information is different from the called for by the model. The accountant may be placed in a position of second guessing the user, in order to provide the data that will allow him to make a correct decision, because the users idea of what information is relevant is wrong from the standpoint of the decision models. This is a position in which I believe most accountants would feel somewhat uncomfortable.

We must also be concerned with the possibility that the conception of accounting held by the decision-maker affect the perception of relevance to a significant degree. The more a decision-maker conceives of accounting as being perfect, the more relevant accounting information is likely to be for decision-making purposes, and the more importance can be attached to the part that accounting system and methods will play in the decision-making process. In so far as this writer is aware, this relationship has seldom been considered and never carefully explored.

If the hypotheses developed in this paper are valid, then it is clear that relevance alone cannot serve as a primary standard for the development of accounting theory and methods. If accounting is to serve users of accounting information then something besides whether or not the data is relevant must be known. These hypotheses would lead us to believe that critical variables are the conception of accounting held by a decision-maker and the perceived relevance of other kinds of information to the problems under examination at the time the user chooses to employ or not to employ accounting information.

Some examples of the use of relavance and the conception of accounting as bases for accounting systems development

Suppose that research fails to lead to rejection of the hypotheses presented above, and consider a case in which we are concerned with designing an appropriate accounting system to facilitate effective decision-making. Imagine that the organization in question is a business firm. Among the products of an accounting system are financial statements issued at regular intervals. These intervals may vary in length from very short periods to relatively longer periods; that is, financial statements may be prepared for internal use as frequently as daily or weekly, or they may be issued less often, perhaps annually to employees of the firm. It is possible to hypothesize that the more frequently financial reports are issued and attention is drawn to the financial condition of the firm, the more relevant accounting information will appear to people within the firm who are making decisions about prices, promotion policies, and production quantities. Yet, for many decisions of this type, we might argue that other information would be more important and relevant. Therefore, we might be led to a situation in which we wish to reduce the perceived relevance of accounting information by reducing the frequency of reports, so that decisions-makers within the firm would rely more heavily on other information which would allow their decisions to be more appropriate for the conditions, under which the firms was operating.

Consider pricing decisions. In general, economists and other analysts would agree that the financial condition of the firm is not necessarily an appropriate basis for choosing a price strategy and selecting terms of sale their perceived relevance, and the conception of accounting held by decision-makers is such that we might expect accounting information to have some effect, then favorable or adverse profit information and/or other financial information might affect decisions with respect to price. It is possible, then, that by developing an accounting system in which the frequency of reporting reduces the perceived relevance of accounting information we could improve pricing decisions in the firm.

In other cases, we might come to an opposite conclusion. In decision making related to the acquisition and management of working capital, the availability of frequent information on the status of assets and liabilities of the firm may be very important, and we might choose to issue reports to persons concerned with these matters very frequently in hopes of increasing the efficiency of such decisions.

The point of these examples is that changes in the accounting system, may affect perceived relevance of accounting information and may determine the effect of accounting information on decisions, and furthermore, that the interactions between relevance and conceptions of accounting which we have considered above may be important also. In designing an accounting system, relying on cliches like "....the more information, the better...." may lead to surprising results.

Consider another example, in which we are concerned with a choice between alternative accounting methods for reporting on a particular class of assets or liabilities. For sake of illustration, let us consider a choice between two alternative inventory valuation methods—LIFO and FIFO. Assuming that the reader is familiar with the characteristics of these methods, we can quickly conclude that in cases where prices are changing frequently that LIFO will reveal through the income statement the effect of these changes on the profitability of the firm more rapidly than FIFO. To the extent that this is important for the types of decisions being made, this model might provide us with the basis for preferring one method of accounting for inventories over another.

Let us assume that the prices of raw materials for the production process or the price of goods to be resold is rising. From the standpoint of decision-makers within the firm, this is important information and information which we would expect to be important for decision-making purposes within the firm. To the extent that the decision-maker felt accounting information was relevant to his decisions, a conception of accounting as perfect information would make the choice of LIFO more important than if the decision-maker's conception of accounting information was that it was an imperfect measure. If accounting information is not perceived as relevant, or if the decision-maker feels accounting measures are imperfect and other information is also relevant for decision-making, the choice of inventory valuation methods is unlikely to affect decisions.

Here also we can consider the possible usefulness of this model for evaluation the selection of a method for reporting to external users. Assume that external users feel accounting information is relevant for their decisions. The more perfect their conceptions of accounting, the more likely that the choice between methods of accounting will affect their decisions. If the current performance of the firm is important to external users because they wish to use it as a basis for decisions, then LIFO may be more appropriate than FIFO for inventory valuation purposes.

In either of these last two cases, if accounting information were perceived as being irrelevant and/or if accounting information were conceived as being so imperfect a measure that it is not weighted heavily by the decision rule, then a decision on an inventory valuation method might not be very important. Such would be the case in any choice between accounting systems or methods. The implication of this is, quite clear: until we know more about the conditions that affect perceived relevance of accounting information for decision-making and until we know more about the conceptions of accounting held by users we do not have adequate bases on which to reduce diversity in accounting or to increase it selectively.

Implications for further research

It is clear that a great deal more research about behavioral relationship between accounting and decision-making is required. The hypotheses which comprise the model presented here demand that we learn more about the factors that influence a decision-maker's perception of the relevance of accounting information. We need to know more about the conceptions of accounting held by individuals, both within business enterprises and external to them, indite would be useful also to know more about the magnitudes of difference required before perceptions of relevance and conceptions would be affected.

One way of finding data about these variables would be togo into the field and do field research about the perceived relevance of accounting for various decision problems. Some attempts have been made in this direction, and while the results are still inconclusive,they provide a basis for the design of further studies. It is also necessary that something be learned about the conceptions of accounting held by users. Is it true that the majority of users feel accounting is a valid and good source of information? Or do most experienced users of accounting information conceive of accounting as being imperfect in the sense that the term is used here, and hence, the types of decisions made about accounting systems and accounting methods are relatively unimportant?

Another approach to this type of problem is experimental approach, where in a laboratory or a simulated environment, we place people in alternative conditions in hopes of comparing their behavior under the conditions we have created. This, in my opinion, provides a most promising avenue for testing some of the hypothese we have created in this study.

Consider, for example, an experiencement to determine if the relevance of accounting information is a determinant of the effect of that information on decision-making. We could, for example, take a sample groups and partition it to obtain a control section and an experimental section. The experimental section could be instructed as to the types of situations in which, given generally accepted models of decision-making, accounting information is relevant,. Having provided this background, this group could then take part in a simulated exercise-a business game-in which accounting information and other information are controlled. The control group would received no instructions about the role of accounting. The decisions of the groups could be compared, and if there were differences, there might be reasons to believe that when accounting information is perceived as being relevant, it will have an effect and that relevance, then, is something that can be affected through educational experiences.

In like manner, it should be possible to explore in the laboratory the effect of conception of accounting. After determining through tests or interviews the conception of accounting held by subjects, we could partition the group in such a way that those having one conception of accounting are used for a control group, while those having another conception of accounting serve as an experimental group.

Experiments of the types proposed above would have to be replicated many times before we could employ the findings with confidence. Nevertheless, the "obvious" character of the hypotheses developed here gives hope that they may provide keys to new criteria for use in the design of accounting systems and reports.

12

Project Management

The planning of the work is done by experienced people, preferably the leaders who will be in charge of the efforts. Scheduling is done by people experienced in scheduling techniques. The mechanics and arithmetic may be done by less experienced personnel manually or by computer, programs designed for this use. With the advent-of simple scheduling programs for the personal computer, even the smaller jobs can be efficiently entered and processed by the computer. From the beginning the project manager has certain tasks that have to be started even while planning of the entire job is underway. In order to keep control of this work, he relies upon the early work schedule. This schedule is merely a listing of all of these initial activities together with the assignment of responsibility to a specific individual and an assigned date for completion. Following is the sequence in which the various scheduling activities should be done:

1. *Task Identification*: The discrete activities of the proper size for control are chosen. They are selected based upon the system defined by the work breakdown structure. These activities may be entered on an individual input sheet or directly into the computer data bank.

2. *Sequencing*: The work packages and the activities within each package are sequenced following the provisions of the project plan.

3. *Logic Diagram*: A logic diagram of the work packages/major activities is made. Activity restraints are entered in the computer or on input sheets.

4. *Staffing Analysis*: Estimates are made for the normal jobhours required for each of the activities based upon (1) the scope of the activity. (2) historical data input and (3) best judgement for the job. These may be entered in the data bank or on the activity input sheets.

5. *Activity Durations*: Based upon, the activity, its staffing level, and best judgement, the normal activity duration is determined. This is entered in the computer or on the input sheet.

6. *The Critical Path*: Using all of the data entered into the computer, a run is made to determine the critical path or the chain of activities which have zero float. This

sequential linked group of activities determine the earliest completion date based on the logic diagram, the staffing level and the activity durations set. All activities on this chain are critical activities in that any delay in completing any one will delay the project completion.

7. *Resource Profile*: This program or manual determination and the subsequent graphical representation shows each discipline staff level throughout the project. There will probably be conflicting demands for people on the initial runs.
8. *Resource Levelling*: By adjusting non-critical activities, periods of high staffing demand for the individual disciplined may be reduced.
9. *Scheduled Plan*: Once the system has been optimized with respect to calendar time, activity duration and staffing level, the results can be approved, and it becomes the schedule for the project.
10. *Bar Charts*: The schedule is usually communicated to management and to others having a general need to know this information by means of bar charts. These are less cumbersome and more easily understood than the detailed scheduling information developed during the prior step.

Work schedule

A project that gets off to a good start has a better than average chance of being a successful project. On most projects work has to start immediately on some of the activities. These probably are or will become obvious to the project manager. The value of planning is lost if the project ends up in trouble because too much attention is put on formal planning during the first weeks to the exclusion of starting work in some critical areas. The early work schedule, EWS, defines those tasks which require action prior to the issue of formal schedules. It provides an easily developed monitoring document at the very early stages of the project. The early work schedule gives the project manager freedom of mind to know that all of these various activities, once identified, are being taken care of He can then dedicate more of his efforts toward the immediate task of planning the project.

An early work schedule is a simple technique for relieving the project manager's concerns for those activities that need to start rapidly. As he recognizes non-postponable activities, the project manager adds them to a list of those tasks included on the EWS: He assigns the responsibility forgetting the work done and sets target dates for starting and completing each activity. He always specifies the expected deliverable. The EWS may also be put into a bar chart format if the project manager prefers. The project EWS is really a tool for the project manager; however, the technique may be used by any of the discipline leaders or the project engineers for early work assignments in their own areas.

On a small project with a short schedule, the early work schedule assumes a great deal of importance as it may be used to control the project for a relatively greater proportion of the total time. On small projects with tight schedules, the importance of the EWS is even greater. The project manager monitors the early work schedule. If he uses a personal computer for the listing, he can easily generate an exception alarm triggered when a target date is not met. The PC will also let him make hard copies of the schedule for distribution to help improve early communication with the project staff.

The network logic

Sequencing of major segments of work is developed during the planning phase by careful consideration of the objectives, the unique problems and the particular project strategy. The scheduling phase calls for detailed sequencing of the work activities and is dependent upon an extension of the strategic thinking used earlier.

Diagramming techniques: By their nature, some activities will precede others. These activities must be completed before the following activity can be started. In other cases the earlier activity must have been started and have progressed to a certain point before a subsequent, dependent activity may start. The start of some activities depends upon the start of another. Some activities have an end-to-end relationship. These interdependencies may be graphically shown by means of logic or arrow diagram. These diagram chart all of the activities on project depicting how each precedes, follows, or is restrained by others. There are many variations in these charting techniques.

The first use of network diagramming was by dupont in the mid-1950's. Later developments resulted in the critical path method (CPM) which is very closely related to the work- done by duPont earlier and in the program evaluation and review technique (PERT) used first in the U.S. Navy Polaris program. The precedence diagram is similar to a CPM diagram, and represents a subsequent development, probably initiated by the U.S. Navy Bureau of Yards and Docks. Today, variations of these techniques form the basis for the computerized project control programs. The activity interrelationships may now be portrayed very realistically on many of these programs.

Because of the number of activities on extremely large jobs. It may be expedient to develop subnets or fragnets. These are just more detailed diagrams of separate segments of the project. On any project care should be taken to avoid over-controlling by having an excessive number of activities. Maintenance of the computerized program in these instances will require more time than it is worth.

Strategic thinking

Altogether distinct from the obvious emphasis on the mechanics of these various computerized control programs, a most important value lies in the information that can be generated to evaluate alternative sequencing early in the project.

These network programs allow the strategy to be checked in detail. Inoperable execution sequences may be eliminated or modified. Alternatives may be suggested by the results of the trial runs. Use of standard networks may save home office control hours as the logic does not have to be reinvented for each job. Every project offers the possibility of saving a lot of schedule time and a lot of money by innovative thinking in sequencing the project activities. Where there can be a beneficial change in the logic or sequencing of these activities the project manager should be eager to take advantage of the possible improvements. Standard networks may help; but each project is different. The planning, strategy, and scheduling must be individually thought out.

Factors which drive the schedule

In developing a schedule, stepping back from all of the is occasionally important to the project manager in determining whether that schedule is going to what is actually required by the project. The example used for this topic relates to a typical plant construction project, but the methodology is certainly applicable elsewhere where schedules are being developed. The example is taken from work done by the Construction Industry Institute. The premise is that the schedules driven by different factors during the various phases of the project. When you are just starting out a project, the conceptual design the process engineering, and basic engineering concentrate completely on the systems to be included in the plant. All of the drawings, sketches and other data are produced by system. This is true also for the chemical, mechanical, and process control engineers.

When the basic engineering information has been completed and the project moves into the detailed design, then the driving factor shifts and becomes the area. The plot plan is divided into areas, and the design of foundations, structures, piping, electrical, and instrument control wiring proceeds around different areas of the site. When it comes time to requisition equipment and material the driving force changes from area to what has been called the procurement train. Like items are grouped regardless of their system or their area, so that they can be readily handled by the requisitioning bidding, ordering, manufacturing, expediting, inspection, and delivery activities involved in management of materials.

The driving force during the initial construction efforts reverts to the area. Working from the detailed drawing promotes this approach. As construction nears completion, the work has to be completed based on systems as the driving force. This is the way the project must be finished as the job is testing out commissioned, and later started up by system. The graphic immediately following illustrates the process described in the paragraphs above. Unless the scheduler understands the driving forces in play during the different phases of the project and, particularly where the driving force changes, the wrong activities may be scheduled and much time wasted prior to starting the following phase. This is very noticeable in the interface between construction, testing, and startup. There has to be a concerted effort made to integrate the initial work done by area and completion by system in order to optimize efforts.

Staffing analysis

Staffing must be approached from the viewpoint of the numbers of people required as well as the capabilities and experience of the individuals themselves. It is particularly important that the project manager be satisfied that his key managers and the discipline leaders are competent and capable of the work they are scheduled to direct.

Initially, the positions shown on the project organization chart are filled. Timing of the assignments is approximated by the project manager and communicated to each of the functional managers involved. The individuals assigned to the project in a matrix organization are usually selected by their functional managers. The project manager may or may not have a voice in the selection process. Unfortunately for the project manager, one of the prime qualifications in making assignments turns out to be the availability of the individual rather than the ability, related experience, or track record on other projects.

The project manager should have an intense interest in the senior staffing on his project as this one factor will have a definite influence on the success of the endeavour.

Staffing levels

The project activities have been identified, classified, and defined in the work breakdown structure dictionary. It is necessary to evaluate these activities to determine the number of people required to do the work and how these will be organized for the effort.

The project discipline leader must analyze the activities to determine jobhours necessary to accomplish the work. Simultaneously, the leader must consider the optimum length of calendar time required to complete the activity. Total jobhours and duration will give an indication as to staffing levels. For monitoring and control purposes, the estimates must conform to the WBS descriptions. Activity estimates are reviewed by the appropriate project discipline leader and are approved by the project manager. A functional or departmental review is a requirement in many organizations.

The discipline leader relies on his experience to estimate jobhour requirements for each activity. During the estimating process, he necessarily will have to think through in more detail exactly how the work covered by the activity will be done. Relying on past statistics may be somewhat dangerous. Return cost figures will probably include hours spent in recycling, redoing and correcting together with job changes and other inefficiencies. Statistical figures may include not only necessary jobhours for the work, but also hours which were added to cover all of these other items. The project manager should encourage the discipline leader to estimate the work based on the best judgment of what it really should take to do the work. Any allowances or provisions for changed conditions should be expressed separately and clearly as such. Unfortunately there sometimes appears to be a reward for those who are able to include a lot of "generosity" in jobhour estimates. Invariably, hours included in these high estimates are spent on the job except when workloads are high. Project managers should never bypass checking the validity of the discipline jobhour estimates.

The staffing analysis should provide input for the discipline job-hours required for each activity. This input should be made to the computer or manually recorded for later use in resource levelling and optimizing the critical path schedule.

At this time the staffing levels are reviewed in conjunction with the discipline workload for other projects to confirm availability of the number of people required. Staffing plans are formulated and any conflicts are resolved by consultation with all of the project managers involved.

Establishing the proper duration of each activity is critical to the development of a realistic project schedule. There has always been some controversy about what criteria to use in determining activity duration. The duration of an activity may be defined as being that period of time from when the work is started until the work included in that scope has been completed to the point where a subsequent and completely dependent activity may start. Activities may involve follow-up work or cleaning up details which would not exclude the start of other work. This time would not be included in the planned activity duration. All activities should be as described in the work breakdown structure dictionary.

The duration of an activity should be established in concert with the estimate of the work effort required. The duration will be determined by each discipline's project job leader. The initial duration should be a realistic view of the optimal duration for work efficiency. The selected durations should be based on times which can be met under normal conditions. After the durations have been established for all activities, they are used in conjunction with the logic diagram to establish the total project duration. The initial run to determine the critical path will indicate those activities that must be improved to reduce total project length. If very optimistic activity times are used through the exercise, a distorted picture will result. The project length will be too short and improvements will be difficult to achieve. On the other hand, assigning very pessimistic durations encumbered with provisions for possible adversities during execution will create an overly long project schedule. The modification to reduce the project length will be tedious because of the number of activities involved. The effect of known conditions should be reflected in the estimating of the duration of activities. The environment which favours or which handicaps work will have an effect. Rain, snow, or adverse weather may affect progress. These factors are known or have an historical basis for affecting duration and, should be taken into account. Involvement of the functional management through the discipline job leader has been stressed. There are two reasons for this:

- The best experience and historical background available in this organization is brought to bear

- Commitment of the project discipline personnel to the schedule is enhanced by Involving them in the process.

The project manager should be involved if there are problems in establishing a realistic duration for a critical activity in order to be assured that there are no overly pessimistic nor optimistic projections which could influence the end date. Usually the project manager will assure himself that there have been intermediate spot checks run on the setting of activity durations. The project manager's principal involvement, will come later during the intensive analysis of the path activities.

The critical path

The critical path method (CPM) uses, as a basis, the logic diagram prepared earlier. The logic diagram charts a series of activities or events using blocks or nodes interconnected by lines or arrows. Either the blocks or The lines may represent activities depending upon the system selected. Events are the start or completion or some other identifiable point during the activity. In some systems, the nodes represent the events, and the connecting arrows represent the activities or work required to reach the events.

For our purposes we will assume that the blocks represent the activities. The precedence method of CPM is typical of this system of diagramming. The lines connecting the blocks show interdependence and have no time value in the precedence diagram.

Calendar time for the schedule may be expressed as days, weeks or months. Any unit of scheduling time may be used in CPM, but the same unit of time should be used throughout. The level of control desired sets the unit of time to be used. For very large, lengthy projects, job weeks; may be used. Jobdays are used on other projects that call for closer monitoring. On a normal engineering/construction project, use of jobhours as the unit of time is common. Because durations are expressed for a large number of individual activities, the accuracy of the figures is usually good as the errors tend to be compensating when developed by experienced individuals.

The critical path method, using either manual calculations or a computer program, establishes the earliest date that each activity may, start and the earliest that it can finish. The earliest completion date of each activity is calculated by progressively taking the earliest completion date of the preceding constraining activities and adding the duration of the activity in question. By following this procedure repeatedly the duration of the entire project is determined.

The process is then reversed. Taking the completion date of the last activity to finish the activity durations are successively subtracted from the latest completion date of the activity which follows it. The latest completion and start dates are thus determined for each activity. These chains of calculations are referred to as a "forward pass" and a "backward pass" respectively.

The early start and the late start dates for each activity are compared, If these are identical, then the activity lies on the critical path. If they differ, then the time between early start and late start is known as free time or float. Project completion will riot be delayed as long as the activity starts on or before the late start date.

Analysis of the results demands project manager's attention. The initial project schedule invariably needs to be shortened to fall within the date established by the project objectives. This can be done only by improving those activities the critical path. The duration of these activities must be cut, possibly by assigning more people. If this is not possible, the logic of the diagram has to be rethought. The critical path method concentrates project thinking on that small percentage of the activities where the payout will be found.

The critical path method is not a panacea for project managers. It can tell us what work we should concentrate on at a given time during the project and where resources can be used most effectively. It is not a substitute for know-how or experience and it certainly is not a substitute for individual thinking. It is a tool for organizing thought, and, when used with a computer, it is a method of making many calculations rapidly. It is a good communication tool and particularly valuable in playing "what-if- games in evaluating the effect of changing conditions during execution of the work.

Resource levelling

Resource levelling is the process of scheduling work on noncritical activities within their float so that resource requirements on peak days will be reduced. This technique may also be used to protect the resource requirements for critical path activities in order to increase the probability of on time completion of these activities.

The adjusted computer run or manual solution which comes up with an acceptable project duration generally assumes unlimited availability of resources and that the people from the proper disciplines and with the proper skills to do the work will be forthcoming as needed. Most modem programs now provide for a method to identify resource limitations and to restrict assignment of "nonavailable" personnel.

When the consolidated requirements are produced, the critical path activities are considered first as they present the more serious problem. If a critical path activity requires people who are not available, an adjustment to the duration may be the most ready solution. The effect of the corresponding lengthening of the schedule must be against the possibility of somehow increasing staff for that activity by bringing temporary or contract people onto the staff for short periods. Each resource problem on critical path activities is considered separately and an acceptable solution to each resource problem is reached.

Next, the requirements for the whole project are looked at using the early starts for each activity. The numbers of people required for the activities scheduled for each day for each discipline are plotted to give a skyline or the resource demand. There will be peaks and valleys which may be attenuated by delaying noncritical activities within their own float times.

Scheduling of people over the duration of the activity is normally averaged. An activity which required 480 jobhours over the period of 20 eight-hour days would have an average of 3 people assigned. Reflecting the realization that activities don't start off at full speed finish abruptly, many computer programs have additional flexibility to use other than straight line distribution for assigning people to the activity by using a bell curve or an "S" curve as selected by the scheduler.

There may be cases in which an absolutely rigid limitation is placed on resources and no acceptable alternative is open. Computer programs can place this limit as a restraint. The duration of the activities so affected is extended and the overall schedule is correspondingly lengthened.

Resource leveling may be used both as a scheduling tool and as a planning tool for personnel assignment. Crews may be formed to do a specific series of like noncritical activities consecutively rather than two or more crews doing them in parallel.

Planning for project assignments can be done by the functional managers using the same tools. Multiproject requirements from each discipline can be leveled within the constraints presented by the float and after consultation with the respective project managers. Effective functional management in a matrix organization depends upon the ability of the functional manager to use his people effectively, to minimize total staff requirements, and to eliminate the non-productive time of his personnel between assignments.

The scheduled plan

The scheduled plan is the final result of six planning steps:

1. Establishing the objectives, anticipating problems and developing strategy for doing the project.
2. Developing the work breakdown structure to be used on the project. Using the WBS, identify individual project work packages and those activities which make up each work package.
3. Planning the project, preferably on a participative basis, then sequencing all activities on a network diagram.
4. Assigning durations to the activities on the network diagram. Using this information to determine the critical path. Fine tuning by an iterative process to, determine the best schedule.
5. Assigning resource requirements to each of the activities. Making sure that critical

activities have adequate resources. Reconcile resource requirements by changing the timing of non critical activities. Incorporate this fine tuning into the program.

6. Fixing the schedule in accordance with optimized sequencing, critical path determination, and resource requirements.

Contents of the scheduled plan

1. All work packages and activities required by the project are completely described, scoped, and costed. An early start date and the duration for doing the work are both given.
2. All critical work packages and critical activities are identified.
3. The resource utilization requirements for the project are established both in terms of personnel and cost.

This information will be used to communicate expectations to all of the project participants in sufficient detail so that the work can be efficiently and effectively done. In addition, the scheduled plan will provide a basis for continuous monitoring of the status of the on-going project work so that variances can be identified and corrected in a timely manner. Once approved, the schedule is fixed. It is not to be extended arbitrarily. It can only be changed if there are substantial changes of scope or approved changes to the contract which incorporate additional work, and which require corresponding schedule extensions. Internal chancres to portions of the schedule may be adopted as a part of the corrective action to get work which has fallen behind back on the original schedule.

The bulk of computer output from the scheduling process will not be well understood by many of the people who will be working on or associated with the project. Ibis will become less of a consideration as the project staffs become increasingly exposed to working with the computer. Many of the computerized scheduling programs can produce easily-understood bar charts from the data base.

Since the early 1960s, project management planning and scheduling systems based on network analysis have been devised and have been computerized to cope with the vast amount of data associated with increasingly large projects. Typically, the systems are referred to as 'critical path methods' or 'network analysis techniques' and are often extended to cover resource and cost analysis, manufacture control, etc.

The application of these techniques in the past has often proved difficult and expensive. The centralized control department had to be enlarged for input data preparation and sometimes extended so as to have additional staff in operational units to verify the progress made. Even so, where the work-producer's needs were not met by the system, he could thwart the reporting requirements.

From a management viewpoint, despite an excessive flow of paper-work, it was difficult to get a clear picture of the situation in time to take effective action. The planners tended to portray an over-elaborate situation, usually because managers asked for a simple system which would track everything in detail! Whatever the reason, the output was far more complicated than could be assimilated by many of its users. It was often selected by computer specialists in the absence of clear instructions from management as to what was wanted. It seemed that systems worked against managers, nor for them.

The difficulties encountered in obtaining status reports were slightly compared with those found in analysing the cause of shortfalls and deciding corrective action. Trying to determine the reasons for mal-performance was time-consuming and often a distraction. Even worse, it could trigger an out-of-phase corrective action which reinforced the disturbing force. When that happened, the disturbance was recycled or amplified instead of being gradually dissipated.

The situation has improved somewhat in recent years. As computers have become smaller, successful applications have become more common, certainly up to a limited system size. Yet as more people have gained hands-on experience of working with computers, so the machines' limitations have been more generally appreciated, and the need for human organizing ability and management intervention has become more apparent.

Some of the limitations still encountered in computer applications seem to arise from overlooking the general project environment and the individual human beings within the environment. Management control systems which assume a project to be mechanistic are not appropriate tools for project managers.

More complex control theories do exist but not in any readily usable form. An alternative approach, that of cybernetics, considers an organisation such as a project as a living system, too complex to understand or control directly, having problems and solutions not anticipated in the project execution plan or administrative procedures. The whole system works only if the project framework allows its scope for fulfilment of legitimate non-project, such as functional, objectives.

Impact of the environment

Most of the project planning models currently available consider the project as having been developed in a vacuum. Such an approach may be necessary for analytical purposes but is a gross over-simplication. This can be seen by comparing two projects identical in general terms of scope and size but taking place at different times and locations. The end-products would be vastly different, not only as achievements measurable against their predetermined economic and technical criteria, but also in matters such as equipment choices and long-term reliability, which might have a more profound effect on overall project profitability. These differences are created by the project environment.

The most general use of the term 'environment' is in the context of ecology, conservation and safety. Ecology is the study of the relation of living organisms to their environment, and environmental conservation deals with both qualitative and quantitative control of effluents and emissions and with the efficient use of natural resources. Safety includes ecological considerations regarding the public and employees and hazards to property.

Technologists are often severely criticized on ecological and safety grounds. These are extremely complex matters to diagnose and on which to form substantial opinions. In the context of this study, the term 'environment' is used in a wider sense, equally emotive, presenting ample opportunity to criticize technologists and their project managers. The environment includes all relevant aspects of public affairs, economics and the social scene and relates to people. A project, by definition, sets out to make some changes to the environment, usually over a short time period. Hence it ill behoves project management to ignore the environment; it is necessary to develop an understanding of it. But from understanding can develop respect and appreciation, and mutual understanding can lead to constructive working relationships.

In general sense, the environment consists of people inside as well as outside the project: individuals and groups with their own opinions and motivations, and, in this context, the impact of the environment on a project is even more profound.

The five elements contained in project environment are:

- the client
- the project
- the internal department
- the external contractors and suppliers
- the sub-contractors

All five elements are largely, but not entirely, contained in the immediate environment, signifying the local community and the national government and its agencies. The outer solid-line circle represents the international economic and political environment within which the project exists.

Surrounding this is a dotted line, labelled 'people', which is a reminder that people are everywhere within the project and in its environment.

While such a clear cut model is necessary to indicate authority and responsibility, it is inefficient as a method of communication and information.

All people involved in a project need to know what is happening and why, to be able to interpret requirements better and to adapt more readily to changes, and to be alert for undesirable or unacceptable trends. Problems arise if information so obtained is misused in pursuit of control objectives.

The environmental problems for project management may be considered as:

- ignoring the environment or assuming that it cannot be predicted or influenced,
- adopting an over-simplified model,
- attempting to impose a rigid detailed control, without allowing sufficient flexibility for coping with externally imposed changes.

Positive approach to environmental problems

The environment is complex and changing, and it is impossible to define it precisely or to predict its impact in control terms. It will neither go away if ignored nor be passive. It is no respecter of authority or feelings and it is definitely not computer-friendly. Yet an interactive relationship is possible between the project manager and the environment. He can anticipate environmental problems and so minimize their effect and can even lobby people to adopt a positive attitude to his project. It is necessary to develop an awareness of and sensitivity to the cultural, political and environmental situation, and then to use imagination, judgment and persistence in selecting and following up specific issues.

First, the manager has to appreciate what aspects of the environment are relevant to the project. This is not easy, because the significance of different factors varies considerably from project to project. There will be no clearly established written guidelines to compare with a standard checklist, and research and investigation will be called for. It is necessary to develop social awareness, rather than consider only the technology, and this emphasizes the need to stand back occasionally from technical matters, to view the forest as well as the trees. However engrossing the immediate tasks, they can often be tackled better by maintaining a balanced perspective.

Second, the manager has to be alert to changes and trends. The situation is never static. Apart from the environment/project interrelationship, which itself induces change, the expectations of both the public in general and those more directly involved in the project can have a profound effect on their behaviour. Trends and expectations may not have been anticipated fully or correctly at the project inception. It is not sufficient merely to understand the environment. More positive results can be obtained by attempting to influence and change it. This will be considered under the headings of communications and participation.

The immediate and local environment can be influenced to some extent by employee relations. Effective communications can avoid misunderstandings in such vital matters as worker participation, or involvement in planning, and working conditions. In these, trends and expectations, sometimes based on precedents arrived at by default or lack of adequate information, can lead to very exacting legislation.

Project control model

Despite attention to the environmental considera-tions outlined above, some problems will still arise as the project develops, because of external disturbances. Being random and unpredictable, these are difficult to build into deterministic techniques such as CPM, which assumes a rigid numerical information/decision theory.

The scientific approach is to observe a system and its behaviour, to attempt to explain the behaviour in the simplest possible cause-and-effect terms, to experiment in order to test the rules so deduced by comparing actual outcomes from specified causes with those predicted by the rules, and to repeat the process until consistently good correlation is obtained between expected results and actual observations.

How can this method be applied to project management? Time does not usually allow for prolonged observation or experimentation, and the project cannot be isolated from its environment. Nevertheless, some, if not all, of the above steps are often gone through, sometimes intuitively or informally. Let us consider a typical project situation.

The situation is perceived and conceptualized a simplified model. The management role is to direct the system towards the management objective, and to this end some control action may be initiated. However, by the time this action takes effect, the situation may have changed for other reasons. The perceived results will then not correspond to those intended. After some delay for verifying the control action and seeing what effect this has. This still ignores the environment and the system itself. The results will in all probability continue to be unacceptable, because the behavioural model is too simple. In these circumstances, a new model must be devised to enable control to be exercised.

In theory, it would be necessary to design an elaborate mathematical model of the entire project and its environment. In practice, this is not possible. Some small elements of the system may be modelled in simple terms, but the approach becomes unwieldy and misleading when applied to larger components and the overall project. It then becomes necessary to consider different control techniques.

Management control techniques

The techniques that apply to control and communications are grouped together as cybernetics. A basic concept of cybernetics is that there exists a natural law in the way control must operate, whether the system controlled is animate or inanimate, physical or biological, social or economic. Management cybernetics is the application of cybernetic concepts to the control of large, complex and probabilistic systems which occur in government and industry.

The cybernetic school views control as a matter of guidance and modulation, rather than forceful direction. It is most successful if applied by self-regulating, self-adapting sub-units, which, if properly motivated and guided, prove more successful than sub-ordinated systems. The central control must then be considered as, and is effective only in terms of:

- giving general guidance and initial direction,
- ensuring a timely flow of decisions and information,
- setting performance standards and providing guidance in achieving these,
- setting reporting/alarm parameters,
- coordinating interface activities,
- initiating minor stabilizing control action when adverse trends warrant,
- taking direct action only in abnormal situations.

Cybernetic concepts have become more easily applicable to projects with the development of localized mini-and micro-computers. Chemical process, aerospace and aircraft control systems have been devised on the basis of 'distributed intelligence', and further, possibly smaller scale, applications will develop at an increasing rate.

A typical modern system for a large complex may comprise a modular system with a number of local micro-processors each controlling a part of the overall process. Management information on significant control parameters and out of limit alarm conditions is available to the central operator in such a way as to help him make correct decisions by means of coordinated and easily-read displays and by using records of alarm conditions and their trends. Thus he can take early corrective action. The local controller is assumed to be sufficiently intelligent to maintain a predetermined plan, but the supervisor can intervene whenever he considers this to be advisable. A hierarchy of control is also possible, with the supervisor's manager having a similar facility. The following comments are directed towards the application of such a system to project management.

The significance of 'self-regulating and self-adapting' is worth considering further. In a truly cybernetic system, adjustments can be made in order to further the sub-unit's objectives, even if the prevailing conditions were never anticipated when the system was designed. A classical example of this is the human body's control of blood temperature over a wide and possibly artificial range of external conditions.

In project-management terms, this concept and that of 'distributed intelligence' suggest that if the sub-unit's objectives can be aligned to some extent with project requirements, and if the sub-units are allowed to exercise some self-control, then centralized 'control' should become more effective.

It is not necessary for senior management to investigate in detail the reasons for isolated deviations in performance. Care must be taken in any such analysis to avoid distracting first-line supervision from today's and tomorrow's tasks in order to produce an historical account of yesterday's problems, which at best sheds little light on the real issues and at worst reinforces a cyclic or resonant disturbance. However, trends and spread within the sub-group should be highlighted, and first-line supervisors should be encouraged to take any necessary and available corrective action without senior management involvement.

Having outlined in general terms a cybernetic approach to project management control, many details need developing for each particular application, and these cannot be generalized. However, problems in application for managers, programme designers and planners can be reduced if the implications of the cybernetic concept of self-regulating, self-adapting sub-units are fully thought through and accepted. It has to be accepted that it is not possible to plan and control a project centrally, with infinite detail, without allowing for some element of design change, rectification of inadequate fabrication, or poor workmanship.

Project teams

Staff, both permanent and temporary, are part of the project environment. The selection and motivation of project teams entail many factors outside the scope of this report. However, there must be some alignment between the objectives of the individuals and sub-units and those of the project as a whole. Permanent staff should be given the opportunity to broaden their experience, and the core technology of a company and the general project management responsibility should be retained in house.

The transient nature of projects and the corresponding fluctuations in workload require many organisations to augment their permanent staff with temporary assistance. This is a mixed blessing, since there are advantages and disadvantages associated with either, and it is important to decide the appropriate ratio of temporary to permanent staff in any given circumstance.

Permanent staff may be expected to be better acquainted with company philosophy and procedures than temporary staff, but a careful check has to be made that philosophy and procedures are available, that they do relate to the project and that assigned staff understand them sufficiently to apply them correctly. They should also share the long-term company objectives.

Temporary staff are recruited to a project team to provide additional short-term expertise or capacity. Their cost per unit of time will be higher than for permanent staff, but the project schedule and economics may warrant their use. Consultants or other professionally qualified experts can use their experience of other projects and, provided that the project requirements are adequately defined, can make a valuable contribution. Less qualified than consultants, 'agency' staff are engaged to cope with peak demand, for which the company does not wish to engage permanent staff, and, although not necessarily professionally qualified or motivated to the same extent, they do have experience of similar work for different clients on various projects. Motivating agency staff to meet schedule dates can be difficult when the market for their services is slack, since they are paid on a time basis, yet a method must be found on each occasion. The nomination of a project team does not result in a team being created. This takes time, depending on the maturity and experience of the members, the size of the team and the leadership exercised. Developing the project requirements and objectives as a team effort will go a long way to establishing the mutual understanding and trust essential for good teamwork. Subsequently, face-to-face communications will keep it working smoothly.

However well devised and implemented the project-management system, it will founder if insufficient attention is paid to human factors. Too often, the manager is prepared to blame 'the system' for his own failings in human management. Three areas associated with personnel are of particular importance to project management: selection and training of project teams, team building and dealing with conflict.

Selection and training of project teams

Once a project team has been forged and has worked successfully on a project, it would be ideal if the members could be reassigned as a team to the next project. In practice, a number of difficulties arise that prevent this happening: individual release dates may not match the new project requirements; the new project organisation, scope and location may not make a block reassignment possible; and the long timescale may not fit in with individual career prospects.

Often, the project is staffed on the basis of individual suitability and availability, without due regard for team experience or compatibility. The effect of this can be mitigated by training, both prior to and after assignment to the project.

Training prior to or between projects can be provided by companies that have a continuing project workload. It can then serve the purpose of reinforcing the company philosophy and standards, which provides the common ground rules and a solid basis for teamwork.

Team building

Teams can be formed from, and built around, a number of individuals, trained in their separate methodologies and well versed in corporate policy. But they can be developed into a team only by working together towards a common objective. By this means, mutual understanding and appreciation and the overall achievement can exceed the sum of the individual contributions. To some extent, the team-building process begins before project approval during the economic and scoping studies. But the full team will not be established until the project is formally approved and organisational and contractual patterns are set.

At this point, the natural tendency is to proceed as fast as possible with the many tasks needing urgent attention. This can be shortsighted, and may be a case of 'more haste, less speed', since the most important and synergistic task is to establish the project team. It may be that the Western business concept of an informal approach towards solving problems has tended to discount the need to be aware of and understand the cultural differences and values standards which have a profound effect on interpersonal relationships. If so, time and effort should be allocated away from the immediate work situation to set the foundations on which the project members can build as a team during the project cycle.

Dealing with conflict

Conflict, hostility and adverse relationships between groups of people are a chronic problem in most modern organisations. Too often, this emotional effort and involvement goes largely in rewarded because it is destructive rather than constructive. By the same token, conflict releases energy at every level of human affairs—energy that can produce positive and constructive results for organisation renewal. Two realities should be recognized: first, that conflict is an absolutely inevitable and predictable social phenomenon, one that will increase in all organisations as they become larger and more complex; second, that conflict should not be repressed, but channelled into useful endeavours.

The goal of organisational leadership, therefore, is not to eliminate conflict but to use it—to turn the released energy to appropriate problem solving. Conflict is almost always caused by differing points of view. It is inevitable because we have not learned in exactly the same way, because we see and value things differently, because we vary in our beliefs as to what things are or should be, and, most importantly, because our objectives vary in the job situation. The problem is to make the conflict creative for eventual learning. Most of the workable approaches discovered by behavioural scientists have centred on changing the psychological climate and use of conflict.

Emotion is often a cause of conflict between groups as well as individuals. Conflicts between groups can arise by the opposing demands of political aspirations, regulatory agencies, environmental groups, engineering departments, and so on. Very valid and logical reasons and facts are often given. With authoritarian groups or egocentric individuals, the conflict may end in deadlock.

The role of the project manager in dealing with conflict is to identify the people or groups involved, to determine their interests, traits, influence and demands, and to relate these to the project. Conflict can be minimized, or turned to creative use, by understanding and, if possible, anticipating the actions and demands of individuals and groups. Anticipation leads to the development of alternatives as 'insurance policies', a process that also keeps the group on target with its present task and provides an early warning of a deteriorating situation.

There is a natural conflict between 'establishment' groups and innovative groups such as project teams. Such conflict is harmful if not channelled or otherwise kept in perspective. It is essential that key people in the organisation—those with leverage or power—are alert for the signs of this developing. In particular, the project manager must 'build bridges' to overcome conflict and prevent a lack of communication.

The gaps and how to close them

The environment

The environment has a definite impact on a project and may require specialized local knowledge. A great deal of time is required for developing relationships and exploring attitudes and positions. Considerable judgment and persistence are needed in developing plans, obtaining agreement and ensuring commitment to their implementation.

An early key activity in any project is the preparation of an implementation plan. This defines the project objectives, priorities and philosophies and provides a basic reference and briefing document for all who ultimately will be involved in the project. Part of the plan must comprehend environmental considerations and should cover the following:

- a decision as to which aspects local knowledge is necessary and specialized advice may be helpful,
- the preparation of a broadbrush project implementation plan, making some basic assumptions on environmental considerations,
- making an allowance for sufficient time for discussions to test initial assumptions and to reconcile conflicting views and objective of participating organisations and individuals,
- the possibility of revising the original concepts if necessary and developing it into a more detailed implementation plan,
- a record of the plan and the agreement to it by the participants.

Project control

Project control cannot be considered as a simple feedback loop. From a strictly theoretical viewpoint, feedforward and adaptive control both require elaborate mathematical models, but this is impractical in management. The developing manager will make the effort and find the time for a systematic analysis and the recording of problematic project situations as perceived, the actions that were contemplated and taken and the observed results. In effect, he will compile his own databank of case studies in project development, from which future models can be drawn for appropriate control modes, and not leave it to his later recollection of the formal records.

Management control techniques must recognize the potential conflict in the project environment and be adaptive to particular circumstances. The following guidelines are suggested:

(1) There must be some common element in the objectives and aspirations of individuals and sub-units that can be related to the project objectives, including

the time schedule. This may be a financial incentive, professionalism job satisfaction or some other motive. The elements must be identified and reinforced both contractually and in terms of organisation and behaviour.

(2) The work content must be clearly established, explained and detailed in time for all concerned to understand and assimilate the information before the work is due to start. Subsequent changes must be minimized or introduced carefully, since their effect can be to disrupt completely the orderly routine that most human beings find conducive to long-term effectiveness.

(3) The scheduling and reporting system must be accepted as worthwhile and having something to offer to all parties. Otherwise it will fall into disrepute and be ignored or even sabotaged. This aspect needs development and follow-up by management, but can be eased if the previous two have been dealt with resolutely.

(4) When a computerized system is being applied, care must be taken in the selection of both the software and hardware, in terms of capacity and of adaptability to the concepts and scheduling parameters outlined earlier. Emphasis must be placed on the reporting needs at various levels with exceptions, trends and variances highlighted. Great attention should be paid to output reports and their relevance. People are more prepared to provide information when they see a prompt and beneficial reaction to it.

Senior management must be committed to support the project by steps such as:

- promoting a systems view of the situation, stressing the overall goals of the organisation and pointing out the respective roles of the 'establishment' and the project group.
- encouraging teach-ins between groups to improve the passage of information and to bring their respective members together for discussions on shared problems and mutual planning needs.
- arranging for the interchange of personnel,
- arranging a negotiation meeting at which direct bargaining can take place if the situation has been allowed to get out of hand. During this, each group lists the things it would like the other to change, and the lists are clarified by straight questions and answers. The groups then discuss separately their position, come together to discuss their demands and finally agree changes on a *quid pro quo* basis.

Objectives

Once you have gone through the goal-setting process and have a clear idea of where the project is going, you are ready to move ahead. You are ready to add more detail to your project because clearly you cannot operate simply with a goal. Noah, for example needed more detail than just the command "Build an ark." So does your project team. You must add the GO to GO-CARTS and establish objectives

Objectives are guiding principles that direct the efforts of team members in their contribution to the project's goal. Generally speaking, you need an objective for each functional group associated with the project or, in some cases, for each person involved in the project. Team members need to know how each person will contribute to the project. Objectives are similar to goals, but they are focused on each group in the project. They break down the project goal and commit each group to a specific task that helps to accomplish the ultimate project goal. They tell each group or person what to do, when to do it, and how to measure progress. In essence, the project objectives are sub-parts of the overall project goal. Accomplishment of each particular objective leads to the overall project goal.

If, for example, your project is to instal a new computer system, you would assign Group 1 the objective of preparing the site for the computer, Group 2 the responsibility of getting the computer ordered and delivered to the installation site, Group 3 the responsibility of wiring the computer, and Group 4 the responsibility of debugging the computer to make it operate as designed. Once these objectives are reached, your project team has completed the goals of installing a new computer system on the user's premises. In essence, objective resemble goals. But objectives focus on the details and tell you more about what specific people need to accomplish. They set a target for each of the various groups involved in a project. Just as with the goal of the project, you must use a back-and-forth process to establish clear, well-defined objectives. You can apply the SMART criteria to each objective. An objective must be specific, measurable, agreed upon, realistic, and time-framed. Otherwise, objectives cannot guide the behaviour of project participants effectively.

Once you have clear statement of project objectives, you need to identify the key project team members, resources, and inputs necessary to accomplish the overall project goal. By identifying each objective with a specific group and having a dialogue about its formulation, you establish ownership. Ownership leads people to take responsibility and feel committed to accomplishing the objective.

Everyone has a responsibility and must own up to that fact. Each person should understand how fulfilling that responsibility ties into the overall project goal. Many manufacturing organizations have begun to recognize this process. They are redesigning their production flow so that each person feels less like a small cog in the machinery and more like an essential contributor to the production process. People who help formulate their objectives tend to be more committed to accomplishing them. As Ray Abuzayyad, president of Rolm Corporation and Vice-President of IBM, says, "You can't do it all yourself. You must have a team." And objectives define the role of each team member's contribution to the overall project goal.

Just as you did for the project goal, put the project objectives in writing and literally hang them on the wall. That way they constantly remind each individual and each project group of what it is trying to accomplish. Signetics made a company wide commitment to zero defects, and everyone signed a pledge to achieve zero defects. Each of these signed statements was displayed on the lobby walls of the corporate offices. Signetics eventually *guaranteed* perfection in its shipments to all its customers.

And what about Noah and his ark? What are some of the objectives that Noah established to achieve his primary goal? Noah took the overall goal of building an ark and began to specify the responsibilities of the different functional groups that had to contribute to its completion.

Problems in setting objectives

As with goal setting, many people are not very good at setting project objectives. Objectives should be designed so that their accomplishment leads to achievement of the project goal. But as you know, there are times when it just does not work out that way. Why does this occur?

Focusing too narrowly

Objectives alone are not enough. You must look at what tends to happen as your project personnel begin to work on their objectives. The objectives become their focus day in and day out, and it is easy for them to lose sight of the end result or project goal. It is also very easy for a group to lose sight of the objectives of the other groups working on the project. Project personnel readily go off on a tangent or accomplish their objectives in a way that makes it more difficult for the other team members to accomplish their objectives.

Project personnel get lost in the detail of their objectives and lose sight of the big picture—the project goal. In other words, they fail to recognize the forest through all the trees. Manufacturing builds a product that can't be marketed on a cost-effective basis. Marketing promises customized products when operations are based on a mass-production system. The key to avoiding too narrow a focus is to keep the project goal out in the open. As a project manager, you must constantly remind team members of the project goal to combat the tendency to focus too narrowly.

Reward systems

Reward systems in most organizations tend to push team members apart. Instead of fostering cooperation to achieve the project goal, they create competitiveness between groups as each works on its own objectives. Typically, reward systems focus on the accomplishment of the objectives for each functional group and not on the accomplishment of the project goal. A good example of this breakdown occurred at a naval air station that had four squadrons responsible for the maintenance of planes. The stated goal was to have 95 per cent of all planes ready to go at any time. Actual readiness was running around 85 per cent. The new commanding officer decided he would reassert this goal of 95 per cent and backed it up with a reward system. Each month, he would give the particular squadron with the highest percentage of planes a reward, such as a 24-hour pass or public recognition of a job well done. What happened?

The members of one squadron decided that the secret was to have a well-stocked parts inventory. Then if a plane came in with a broken radar part, they could simply take that part out and put in replacement and the plane would be ready to go again. They also realized that if they could increase their parts inventory while decreasing the parts inventory for the other squadrons, they would be well on the way to winning this competition. The obvious solution? Steal parts! This may sound ridiculous, but it is a true story.

One of the squadrons began to engage in midnight requisitions to steal parts from the other squadrons. The other squadrons figured out what was going on and decided to retaliate. Soon four squadrons were stealing from one another. Every squadron put guards on duty 24 hours a day, seven days a week to protect its inventories. Meanwhile, the percentage of planes ready to go was going downhill fast.

The problem was the reward system. People knew the overall project goal but felt that their own squadron's objectives were more important, especially since these objectives were what was being rewarded. A simple change in the reward system solved the problem. In a given month, any squadron that achieved the goal of 95 per cent readiness would get the reward. Now, every squadron could get the reward. What happened? First of all, the stealing stopped. The squadrons started sharing parts to help one another out. The readiness percentage quickly rose to 90 per cent and began pushing toward 95 per cent—all because the reward system was changed to support the accomplishment of the objectives *and* the project goal.

Responsibility but not enough authority

The concept of rewards related to objectives can also help you understand why project managers often have responsibility but lack authority. Think about the typical set up of a project. Suppose the new company computer will affect four departments—data processing, accounting, production and sales. Within each department, people report to the department manager. Several of these people also report to the project manager in charge of the new computer system change over. Thus they have two bosses—their department manager and the project manager. The project accounts for half their responsibilities, departmental matters the other half. But who evaluates these people at the end of the year? The project manager? No. The department manager. So if there is any conflict in what the two managers tell the employee to do, what will the employee do? Ignore or put off the project manager.

But we must go one step further and ask how we can get the data processing, accounting, production, and sales managers to cooperate with the project manager? In many cases, department managers have no real accountability for a project. But in companies where the project manager approach works best, department managers are held partly responsible for the success of the project. The division manager evaluates department managers not only in terms of department activities but also in terms of how well the project is succeeding. The department managers have a reason to cooperate and work with the project manager. Each individual department manager has a stake in the project and knows that rewards and evaluations depend on project success. The department managers focus not only on the project objectives involving their department but also on the overall success of the project. The department managers tend to cooperate and coordinate with one another and with the project manager.

Now, your organization may not have this kind of formalized project accountability for department managers. But if it does not, don't just throw up your hands. Instead, use the informal organisation. Go outside the hierarchy to develop a relationship with each of the department managers and draw them into the project. Get them on your side and make them understand how you are going to help them. In other words, depend on a relationship with the department managers.

For example, Judy Randal is a marketing analyst for a large oil company. To complete her projects, she has to get information from sales people in the field, but she has no authority over them. To go through the organizational channels up several levels, across, and then down several levels to ask a sales rep to provide information would take months. And the sales reps have no stake in Judy's project. So Judy works on her relationship with the sales people. In fact, she goes out and rides the territory with the sales reps, talks with them, and gets to know them. Then, when she calls up to ask for information, it is not just the marketing analyst calling, it is their friend Judy. So even though the system may not support you by coordinating the objectives of different departments, you can ensure that those objectives tie into the project goal by working through the information organization.

Planning

Project planning is an important part of the "deciding" aspect of the project team's job-thinking about the project's future in relationship to its present in such a way that organizational resources can be allocated in a manner which best suits the project's purposes. More explicitly, project planning is the process of thinking through and making explicit the project's objectives, goals, and strategies necessary to bring the project through its life cycle to a successful termination when the project's product or service takes its rightful place in the execution of project owner strategies. This chapter will offer an overview of the project planning function.

Project planning is a rational determination of how to initiate, sustain, and terminate a project. Two authors define the basic concepts of project planning as developing the plan in the required level of detail with accompanying milestones and the use of available tools for preparing and monitoring the plan. Project planning and control are interrelated. Project planning has played a key role in the outcome of successful nuclear power plant projects in an industry where many projects have had grave difficulties. For example, at the Erie Nuclear Power Plant Project, an overall plan was prepared at the project beginning. This plan provided the basis for controlling and coordinating the activities of the participating parties. At Florida Power and Light's St. Lucie Unit 2 plant, adequate project planning contributed to project success by calling for the appointment of a project management organization in the early stages of the project, and early total project schedule, and the planning, scheduling, and implementation of an effective start-up programme.

Planning realities

The planning ethos of the 1970s, rooted in the extrapolation of history, has been discredited by the "bends" in the trends exemplified by the oil crises and the political and social upheavals of the late 1980s and early 1990s, and it is giving way to a new approach to strategic planning. This new approach is based on a *visionary* view of the future gained by a growing awareness of the possibility of long-term strategic alliance building, the sharing of risk in exploiting new technologies and processes leading to earlier commercialization, and continuous improvement of product and process development and implementation in maintaining a complete edge.

Planning is the most challenging activity of a leader or manager. Planning starts with the development of a *vision—the ability to see something that is invisible to others.* People in general find that it is more comfortable to do than to plan. All too often people equate activity with progress—and taking time to think through a plan of action for the future is not considered active management or leadership. Planning involves thinking through the possibilities and the probabilities of the future—and then developing a strategy for how the organizational resources will be positioned to take advantage of future competitive conditions.

Planning is a responsibility of the project leader. Finding ways to get the full-hearted cooperation of team members will facilitate the planning process and improve the chances of the development of a plan of action to which members of the project team are committed.

Planning for the use of resources precedes the monitoring, evaluation, and control of resources. Insufficient front-end planning, unrealistic project plans, and failing to estimate the degree of complexities and the objectives of the project will lead to reduced accomplishment of project objectives. When planning is done by an active, participating project team, the interactions and communications among the team members help to develop the team, give the team members greater ease in dealing with each other, and are a guide for the future use of organizational resources.

A conceptual model of planning

Project planning must be preceded by comprehensive organizational strategic planning, since projects are integral elements of organizational strategies. A conceptual model depicting the strategic context of organizational planning which includes both strategic planning and strategic implementation discussed in this section.

The vision

Planning starts with a *vision*. A manager who has intelligent foresight, unusual competence in discernment or perception, is said to have vision. a vision is a mental image produced by the imagination. Jonathon Swift described vision as "...the art of seeing things invisible to others." A vision and planning are intertwined. For example, Orin E. Smith, president and CEO of Engelhard Corporation, describes the strategic direction of the company in terms of a *vision which is to be a world-class competitor.*

The strategy to accomplish EQ in Engelhard Corporation is to re-examine every step of how products are delivered to customers, fostering complete breakthroughs in the redesign of manufacturing and business processes and the development of more complete and focused long-term strategies for the company's businesses. The main thrust of the company's growth plan is catalysts, particularly environmental catalysts. Further strategies include a rigorous vigilance about costs and through EQ and attempt to overtake competitors and qualify as the supplier of choice. A people-oriented strategy includes unlocking the power of the individual to make a difference.

How important is it to have a vision? One study that benchmarked extraordinary business teams provides compelling evidence on the importance of direction for the teams. Team members stated that the most important factor for high performance was a *clear and elevating vision.* Team members felt the vision was worthwhile.

An effective vision has several key elements: The phrase describing the vision is short and concise and can be easily memorized. The phrase reflects a repeatable basic theme or shared value growing out of a discussion and testing of the vision. And the phrase is meaningful and important to every member of the organization. When the vision statement is believed and frequently talked about by people it takes on a life of its own and becomes important to everyone.

Organizational mission

The apex of the model in the organization's mission—the culminating strategic point of all organizational activity and the most general strategic choice that must be made by the organization's managers. The organization's mission answers the basic question. What business are we in? One project-oriented firm defined its mission thus: "We are in the business of designing, developing, and installing energy management systems and services for the domestic, non-residential market." Boeing company, which uses project management widely, in its 1991 annual report describes the mission of the company as "...to be the number one aerospace company in the world, and among the premier industrial firms, as measured by quality, profitability, and growth."

Organizational objectives

The ongoing end purposes that must be achieved in the long term are organizational objectives, stated in quantitative or qualitative terms. Objectives are organizational performance criteria to be achieved and measured in the utilization of organizational resources. A computer company defines one of its objectives as leading the state of the art of technology in its product lines.

Another company defines one of its objectives in these terms: "To achieve a compounded earnings growth rate of 15 per cent and a 20 per cent return on capital by being the leader in providing scientists and educators worldwide with laboratory products and service systems created through technology, integrity, and a commitment to excellence."

At Wal-Mart, the largest and highest-profit retailer in the world, there is a relentless focus on satisfying customer needs. The company's objectives in this regard are simple to define but difficult to execute: Provide customers with quality goods,, and make the goods available when and where customers want them. Supporting these objectives is a reputation for absolute trustworthiness.

Organizational goals

An *organizational goal* is a milestone, such as a performance goal of 15 per cent return on investment by a specific date. Goals are the basic component for measuring progress in attaining objectives in an organization. Completion of a project's cost, schedule, and technical performance objectives means that an organizational goal has been completed, such as the construction of a production facility. One company's goal was stated thus: "We intend by the end of 1987 to complete the construction of a new manufacturing facility which will complete the transition begun in 1983 from a predominantly R&D services company to an industrial manufacturer."

Organizational strategies

An *organizational strategy* is the design of the means, through the use of resources, to accomplish end purposes. Strategies are also action plans for setting the direction for the coordinated use of resources through the employment of programs, projects, policies, procedures, and organizational design and establishment of performance standards. The equilateral triangles in the strategy tier depict project which have cost, schedule, and technical performance parameters.

Organizational structure

An *organizational structure* is the alignment of the human resources and functions of the organization. Organizational structures are undergoing significant change. Work is being reorganized; the decline of the traditional authoritarian hierarchies is a key change that is gaining favour. Teams, many of which are voluntary relationships, are arising as a basic organizational means to get things done. Continued down sizing of organizations, the reduction in the need for conventional managerial jobs, and the growing quantity of ambitious people with career expectations competing for a diminishing number of positions are other forces of change in the management of contemporary organizations. More than ever, people will have to take more responsibility for their known careers, including a commitment to a lifetime of learning. The old career paths no longer exist; organizations are streamlining their operations as never before. Employees will be rewarded for knowledge and adaptability; specialization will play a less important role, and generalism will grow in importance. The most employable people will be those who can move easily from one specialization to another and who are able to integrate diverse disciplines and perspectives. Teamwork will continue to replace the traditional hierarchy as the dominant form of organizational design. People at all levels in organizations are sharing more power than ever before.

The ability to develop organizational values will be critical to successful leadership. The new workplace will be ferociously Darwinian, both for organizations and for the individuals. "Softer" management issues will become all-important. Although people will have greater empowerment and shared responsibility, the stress on individuals will be greater, and people will have a greater chance of burnout.

Globalization is causing some of the significant changes in organizational structures. ABB, the global electrical equipment giant, is bigger than Westinghouse Electric Corporation and can compare to General Electric Company. ABB is truly an international enterprise without a national identity.

A *master matrix* gives everyone two bosses: a country manager and a business sector manager. The country managers run traditional, national companies with local boards of directors. About 100 such managers exist. Global business managers are organized into eight segments: transportation, process automation and engineering, environmental devices, financial services, electrical equipment, and three electric power businesses—generation, transmission and distribution. The two bosses in the ABB matrix are not always equal. One advantage of this matrix system is that it makes it easier for business managers to use technology from other countries. Company executives say the value of the matrix system extends beyond the swapping of technology and products. For example, if one factory is performing poorly, solutions can be determined and then discussed and worked out across borders.

Organizational roles

Organizational roles are the individual and collective parts played by the members of the organization. Organizational roles bring life to the structure of the enterprise. The material presented earlier on linear responsibility charts bears mentioning again regarding roles.

Manager and follower style

The manager and follower style is the manner in which knowledge, skills, and attitudes are expressed by the people who support the organized effort. Part of the reason for the comeback of Goodyear Tire & Rubber Company has been the new management style brought forth by Stanley Gault, CEO of Goodyear and former CEO of Rubbermaid Company. Factory workers are required to take courses ir business education. A closed-circuit television has been installed in many plants to keep workers informed of competitive developments such as earnings and stock prices. Output per worker-hour climbed 51 per cent between 1985 and 1991. People at corporate headquarters at Goodyear say that Gault's presence "permeates" the headquarters—he is perceived as seldom giving orders, but everyone knows what he wants done. Gault runs the company on the basis of trust. The company's quarterly results are reported at meetings held in the headquarters auditorium, to which about 800 people are invited, and questions are taken from the floor. Every meeting is videotaped, and the tapes are distributed to the company's 88 plants around the world. Gault also is present to chair bimonthly meetings at which employees demonstrate improvements they have made and receive awards. Gault has also steeped up product development through the use of project teams, introducing twelve new tires this year.

At Siemens Company in Germany, the management style is tailored to Germany's consensus-style corporate culture. At Siemens a new generation of executives is moving into power; for these executives a rigid hierarchy is out and an entrepreneurial drive is in. The company has been broken up into smaller units that are headed up by entrepreneurial managers.

At Siemens it has been a tough job to get the civil-service mentality culture to change. Thousands of middle-level managers refuse to take personal initiative and undermine others who do so. These managers were so used to taking and executing orders that they found it difficult to take initiatives on their own.

Systems

Systems include the hardware and software systems that support the organizational activities, such as accounting information, marketing, production, design, and so forth.

Technology embodied in organizational systems changes the way that organizational resources are utilized. For example, at Kao Corporation, Japan's biggest soap and cosmetics company and the sixth largest in the world, an information system developed through project management processes links everything: sales and shipping, production and purchasing, accounting, research and development, marketing, hundreds of shopkeepers' cash registers, and thousands of salesperson's hand-held computers. The information is so complete that year-end financial statements can be turned out by noon of the first day of the new year. Kao people can know if a new product will be successful within two weeks of launch through the melding of point-of-sale information from 216 retailers with a test marketing operation called the Echo System, which used focus groups and consumers' calls and letters to gauge customer response faster than market surveys can. The use of personal computers has changed the way organizations work. Desktop computing power has empowered employees, provided them with increased information, and employees are able to do more things than was ever possible before computers became available. The hierarchy of the organization tends to flatten, process management becomes easier, and many of the things that managers and supervisors used to do (such as providing information needed for employees to do their work) become available to employees. Fewer managers and supervisors are needed. E-Mail is giving employees improved communication capabilities to facilitate the transmission of the intelligence needed to do a job, in particular when the doing of that job requires ongoing and extensive interface with other organizational units and other project teams. Enhanced information capability, utilized through the computer, leads to improved concurrency in both the doing of the work and the management and supervision of the work. Continued improvement in information and computer technology will continue to alter both *how* and *where* people work. People can be part of a project team or other organizational unit without physically being there. Remote information exchanges and telecommunications are enhancing the ability of a person with a computer and a modem to be part of any organization wherever located. As computers, information, and telecommunication technologies are improved, there should be less need for employees to travel to customers, suppliers, and other organizational units.

An added benefit of such technologies will be an expanded work force to include disabled employees and those who have difficulty getting to and from work each day. The advent of state-of-the-art technologies provides and additional bonding needed to hold the project teams and other self-managed teams and business processes together. A feature report, "The New Computer Revolution" in the June 14, 1993 issue of *Fortune* magazine, "holds lessons for every manager." According to *Fortune*, the future course of this revolution will transform the way all businesses work. Project managers—and aspiring project managers—should read this article.

Organizational resources

Organizational resources are the human and non-human resources which are available to the organization to fulfil its mission, objectives, and goals.

Project planning model

Project planning begins within the framework of strategic planning in the organization. For example, the strategic planning phase at a steel corporation led to the approval of a comprehensive facility feasibility study for the location and configuration of the steel plant. As a result of this feasibility study, which evaluated seven alternative sites, the plant location was fixed at Cleveland, Ohio. During the planning for this facility, several options were considered, ranging from turn-key contract to construction management consultant to the owner acting as its own general contractor with sub-contractors and/or in-house personnel. These options were considered in detail before final project planning was carried out with approval estimates and milestone schedules.

The project planning process

Projects often extend for many years into the future. Thus, a project plan for such projects becomes both operational (short-term) and strategic (long-term). It follows that the project planning process requires both operational and strategic thinking. Creativity, innovation, and the ability to "think prospectively" form the basis for the project planning process. The real value of such a process is a framework of things to consider for a project's life cycle. A project planner's philosophy encompasses characteristics such as

- The need to search out objective data that provide the basis for project planning decision-making;
- The value of questioning assumptions, databases, and emerging project strategies to test their validity and relevance;
- An on-going obsession with where the project should go and how it is going to get there;
- A demonstrated ability to view project opportunities in the largest possible context and to constantly seek an understanding of how everything fits together during the project's life cycle
- A faith that, given ample opportunity, a *bisociation* will occur: the fitting together of separate events or forces on the project.

Individuals making key project planning decisions today will have a long-term strategic impact on the organization. Generally, the strategic roles of key individuals involved in project planning are as follows:

- *The board of directors* reviews and approves (or redirects for further study) key project plans and maintains surveillance over the implementation of the plans.
- *Senior management* directs the design, development, and implementation of a strategic planning system and a project planning philosophy and process for the corporation.
- *Functional managers* are responsible for the integration of state-of-the-art functional technology into the project plans.
- The project manager is responsible for integrating and coordinating the project planning activity.
- *The work package manager* is responsible for providing input to the project plans.
- *Professionals* participate as required in contributing to the project planning processes.

Thus project planning is the "business" of many individuals in the organization. By involving these individuals in the roles as described, key people are afforded the opportunity to participate in project planning. Of course, such participation will require relevant knowledge, skill, and insight into both the theory and practice of project planning. By maximizing the participation of key individuals in project planning, the overall value of the project plan should be improved. One large project driven organization recognized the value of project planning like this:

During the early 1960s, after hundreds of projects had been completed, it became apparent that many projects successfully achieved their basic project objectives, while some failed to achieve budget, schedule and performance objectives originally established.

> The history of many of these projects was carefully reviewed to identify conditions and events common to successful projects, *vis-a-vis* those conditions and events that occurred frequently on less successful projects. A common identifiable element on most successful projects was the quality and depth of early planning by the project management group. Execution of the plan, bolstered by strong project management control over identifiable phases of the project, was another major reason why the project was successful.

Project planning may be considered a form of information development and communications. As the project team develops the project plan, the project team should learn more about the project goals, strategies, and team member roles. The project objectives then can be decided in terms of cost, schedule, and technical performance. Satisfaction of project goals is accomplished through the completion of the project work packages. The project strategy is a plan of action with accompanying policies, procedures, and resources allocation schemes, providing general direction of how the organizational effort will be used to accomplish project goals and project objectives.

Project planning considerations

All too often when people think of project planning, they perceive the use of only techniques and concepts such as PERT, CPM, or networking. These techniques will not be discussed in any detail in this book. These techniques are important to use in the development of a project schedule; however, project planning includes a much wider scope of activity. Such concerns as objective and goal setting, cost estimating, and budgeting, technology strategies scheduling, resource usage estimating, and specification of deliverables are key concerns. Project planning also involves a delineation of the organizational design to support the project as well as the information system and the control system which are used to model, evaluate, and reallocate resources as required during the execution of the project plan.

Project planning deals with the determination of what activities and what resources have to be utilized to ensure that the project is adequately executed. Authority, responsibility, and accountability have to be planned so that members of the project team know what their specific roles are and how they relate to other members of the project team who are involved in executing work package activity. When is activity due? and What is the time duration of each activity? are key questions. What human and non-human resources are needed to execute each activity on the project? What are the estimated costs, and how are the budget and financial plans to be established to support the cost considerations of the budget?

One of the changes under way in contemporary organizations is more people involved in and carrying out the management functions.

Participative planning has been used effectively by AT&T. Participation is obtained through the use of workshops that include the entire project team and even customers in joint planning sessions. A planning process facilitator helps to guide the activities and to keep the project planning moving forward. The purpose of the workshops is to have the participants agree on high-level project plans, schedules, and project monitoring and evaluation strategies. Held at the beginning of a project, the workshops achieve the benefits of early planning, including overcoming planning problems and getting the team members involved early in the planning, which leads to more commitment and dedication to their role on the project. In addition, team members are given an early exposure to their individual and collective roles in the project and an opportunity to identify any interpersonal anxieties that might hinder team development and operation at a later date. These start-up workshops have been successful in producing planning deliverables, developing planning skills, and building team interaction and cohesiveness.

The project manager is responsible for initiating action to bring about the development of a plan. In discharging the project leadership role, the project leader has the final responsibility for ensuring that "the right things are done" about the project plan. The complexities of doing the details of the project—doing things right—rests with the specialists who are members of the project plan. Planning becomes a method for coordinating and synchronizing the forthcoming project activities. Project planning should be undertaken after the project has been positioned in the overall strategy for the enterprise; then the detailed planning can be carried out.

Since planning involves thinking through the probabilities and possibilities of the project's future, a detailed cookbook recipe for planning cannot be provided. However, certain key work packages and planning tools have to be addressed in the development of the project plan of action. These planning work packages are described in the next section.

Work breakdown structure

The most basic consideration in project planning is the *work breakdown structure (WBS)*. The WBS divides the overall project into work elements that represent singular work units, assigned either with the organization or to an outside agency such as a vendor.

The WBS process is carried out in the following manner: Each project must be sub-divided into tasks that can be assigned and accomplished by some organizational unit or individual. These tasks are then performed by specialized functional organizational components. The *map* of the project represents the collection of these units and shows the project manager many organizational and sub-system interfaces to manage. The underlying philosophy of the work breakdown structure is to break down the project into *work packages* that are assignable and for which accountability can be expected. Each work package is a performance-control element; it is negotiated and assigned to a specific organizational manager, usually called a *work package manager*. The work package manager is responsible for a specific objective, detailed task descriptions, specifications, scheduled task milestones, and a time-phased budget in dollars and work force. Each work package manager is held responsible by both the project and the functional managers for the completion of the work package in terms of objectives, schedules, and costs.

In the context of a project, the WBS and the resulting work packages provide a model of the products that completely define the project. Such a model enables project engineers, project managers, functional managers, and general managers to think of the totality of all products and services comprising the project as well as its component sub-systems. The model is the focus around which the project is managed. More particularly, the development of WBS provides the means for

1. Summarizing all products and services comprising the project, including support and other tasks;
2. Displaying the interrelationships of the work packages to each other, to the total project, and to other engineering activities in the organization;
3. Establishing the authority-responsibility matrix organization;
4. Estimating project cost;
5. Performing risk analysis;
6. Scheduling work packages;
7. Developing information for managing the project;
8. Providing a basis for controlling the application of resources on the project
9. Providing reference points for getting people committed to support the project

Work packages are the goals to be accomplished on the project. There are certain criteria that should be applied to the project goals:

- Are the goals clear?
- Are they specific?
- Are they time-based?

- Are they measurable?
- Can they be communicated easily to the project team?
- Can they be clearly assigned to the work package managers/professionals?

The WBS provides a natural framework or skeleton for identifying the work elements of the project: hardware, software, documentation, and miscellaneous work to be accomplished to bring the project to completion. The WBS provides an identifier and a management thread to manage myriad aspects of the project. In some projects unique work packages are found. For example, in some global projects a cultural planning work package is included in the work breakdown structure. From this work package successful cultural training and orientation can be carried out.

Project schedules

A key output of project planning is the project master schedule, along with supporting schedules, which is a graphic time representation of all necessary project-related activities. The project schedule establishes the time parameters of the project and helps the managers to effectively coordinate and facilitate the efforts of the entire project team during the life of the project. A schedule becomes an effective part of the project control system. For a project schedule to effective, it must be

- Understandable by the project team
- Capable of identifying and highlighting critical work packages and tasks
- Updated, modified as necessary, and flexible in its application
- Substantially detailed to provide a basis for committing, monitoring, and evaluating the use of project resources.
- Based upon credible time estimates that conform to available resources
- Compatible with other organizational plans that share common resources

Several steps are required to develop the project master schedule. These steps should be undertaken in the proper sequence.

1. Define the project objectives, goals, and overall strategies.
2. Develop the project work breakdown schedule with associated work packages.
3. Sequence the project work packages and tasks.
4. Estimate the time and cost elements.
5. Review the master schedule with project time constraints.
6. Reconcile the schedule with organizational resource constraints.
7. Review the schedule for its consistency with project costs with technical performances objectives.
8. Senior managers approve the schedule.

Project control

Control of the work can also be expressed as those measures that are necessary to make sure that the expected happens. We can never control the project time, but we can control what is done to achieve the schedule. We don't actually control costs, but we do contain the costs to complete the work within the budget.

To effectively control the work, there are several things that must be done:

Establish baselines: Baselines must be established representing expected or acceptable performance. These baselines come from the budget and the schedule, integrated by means of the work breakdown structure.

Monitor status: Performance must be measured regularly or monitored against these baselines. Current status is noted both for budget performance and for schedule performance.

Forecasts: Projections must be made predicting future performance. These projections, when taken with the actual costs to date, result in ongoing predictions of the final job costs and the completion date.

Variances: Current and predicted performance variances must be identified and quantified. The sooner a potential variance can be spotted, the easier the resolution will be.

Analysis: The potential effects of variances on final cost and schedule must be analyzed. Priorities can be established based on this analysis. Reasons for-variances are also investigated to head off other variances stemming from the same or similar sources.

Alternatives: Alternative courses of corrective action must be conceived, evaluated, and compared. The best is selected to remedy the variance.

Implementation: The chosen course of corrective action is implemented by modifying/supplementing the work plan.

Assessment of remedy: The work associated with the corrective action is carefully monitored to assure its success. The results of the corrective action are evaluated for effectiveness in recovering the planned project position.

Project control with respect to schedule, cost, and quality is so important to project success that it must be supported by the entire project staff Project control maybe achieved by fostering a consciousness of cost, schedule, and quality through the project, visibly emphasizing their importance at every opportunity. In this respect-project control is intimately tied in with performance management.

Cost/schedule integration

The basis for cost/schedule integration is the work breakdown structure, Budgeting and scheduling is done following the coding for the work packages and activities as designated by project WBS. Both the budget and the schedule are optimized to come up with the approved project schedule and the -approved project- budget. In graphical format, these become the primary performance baselines for the project.

In past years the individual components of the schedule and the budget were not tied in to each other: In preparing schedule and the budget, the two groups went off in different directions. One came up with a schedule for the project, and the other with a budget for the project. Basically there was no way to tie them, together. This made control of the project extremely difficult. Erroneous interpretation of the status was readily possible. For each of the activities, the resources expressed in jobhours, material quantities, dollars or percentage of forecast totals are spread over the period of time called for by the schedule. A computer program calculates the rate of expenditure as selected from standard profiles in the data bank. The total of the planned resource utilization for each period for all of the activities is calculated over-the life of the project. A curve is then constructed with the cumulative planned use of resources plotted as the ordinate and time as the abscissa. If the use of resources is plotted in dollars, then the resultant curve is known as the budgeted cost of work scheduled (BCWS).

A second curve may be plotted using the above chart as a background and the information gathered during project monitoring for the period. This curve shows the cost of the work done to date. It is called the actual cost of work Performed (ACWP) This curve may, be extended with a dotted line to show projected future expenditures to the end of the job. Progress is measured in terms of actual physical accomplishments. For engineering activities, these are specifications, drawings, purchase requisitions, and the like actually issued or with partial credit taken by means of a preset standard percentage progress allowance. Expenditure of job-hours is not considered a valid measurement of progress except for some elements of management and supervision where no specific measurement is possible. These items are evaluated on the basis of calendar time or as a percent based on the progress for the rest of the project. For equipment and material deliveries and for construction work, actual quantities are used.

Physical progress is plotted against time. If the actual physical progress is converted to dollars at the budgeted amount for doing the corresponding work, a third curve is generated the budgeted cost of work performed (BCWP). This may also be referred to as the earned value. Here, again, the predicted future performance maybe plotted as a dotted line.

Analyzing schedule variances

After monitoring has been completed and the status reports prepared for each reporting period, the actual earned value achieved is compared with the planned earned value. The differences are analyzed to ascertain what the affects have been on the project to date and predict what will be the possible effects in the future.

The work packages that are on the critical path and which are behind schedule are given the highest priority the schedule analysis. Every effort should be made to devise plans for corrective action to return work on these packages to acceptable performance. The project may be on schedule based on the earned value compared with the plan. Nevertheless, if non-critical activities have been completed ahead of schedule and critical path work packages are behind schedule, the project may well be in serious trouble. Once the critical path work packages have been studied, variances in actual earned values are compared to planned earned value and the results analyzed by looking at the schedule variance and the schedule performance index.

Schedule variance is defined as the planned earned value or the budgeted cost of the work scheduled (BCWS) less the actual earned value or the budgeted cost of work performed (BCWP). The result of this calculation will be in dollars.

Schedule Variance (SV) = BCWS — BCWP

The schedule variance in, time units can be obtained from the same curve, by drawing a horizontal line from the actual earned value or the budgeted cost of work performed (BCWP) to the intersection with the planned earned value of the budgeted cost of the work scheduled (BCWS). The length of this line will represent, to scale, the time that the work is ahead or behind schedule.

If we compare where we are at any point in time with where we are supposed to be, we have a measure of our schedule performance. The schedule performance Index (SPI) is defined as the earned value or budgeted cost of work performed (BCWP) divided by the budgeted cost of work scheduled (BCWS). If the value of the SPI is greater than 1.0., then the job is ahead of schedule. If it is less than 1.0, the job is behind schedule. The values for each period may be plotted to see the schedule trends more easily.

On a large project, the schedule performance may be viewed at different levels in the work breakdown structure. The analysis should be directed in successively greater levels of detail to pinpoint precisely where We trouble spots on the project are with respect to the plan. Once the real offenders, those that jeopardize the schedule, have been identified, they are analysed to determine where the problems lie or what is holding back progress.

We don't spend time analyzing schedule variances which will not seriously affect the overall schedule.

Analysing cost variance

The costs are analyzed at the end of each reporting period based on the results of the monitoring information and the cost reports generated. The actual costs are compared to planned cost. If there is a cost variance as a schedule variance, the objectives of the project must be reviewed for guidance as to the possibility of tradeoffs. If cost is the primary objectives, then the schedule may have to slip. If on time job completion governs, then the cost variance may have to be sacrificed to reach that goal. The project costs may apparently be below the plan, but, if the job is also behind schedule, the cost picture may be deceptive. This points out the real value of cost/schedule integration. The cost variance is the apparent budget overrun to date or the difference between what it was supposed to cost for the work done to date versus what it actually did cost. The cost variance (CV) is equal to the budgeted cost of work performed (BCWP) less the actual costs of the work performed (ACWP). A positive number represents a budget overrun.

Cost variance (CV) = ACWP — BCWP

Comparing the budgeted costs for the work done to date with the actual costs, we have a measure of our cost performance on the project. The cost performance Index (CPI) is the budgeted cost of work performed (BCWP) divided by the actual cost of work performed (ACWP).

- for CPI values of 1.0, the project is on budget
- for CPI values > 1.0, the project is under budget
- for CPI values < 1.0, the project is over budget

A running plot of the CPI can be very helpful in spotting cost performance trends. This process of analysis enables the cost engineers and the project manager to spot specific areas within the project which are giving trouble. The elements of the work breakdown structure for which there are budgets and schedules can be studied individually. Any element showing major cost variance should be reviewed to make sure that the allocated charges have been correctly applied. Mischarging should be looked upon as a prime suspect for variance. Here, correcting the mischarge may correct the variance. If the charges are correct, then a review should be made for each element with an overrun sufficient to cause the project cost to overrun. The money to cover these additional costs will have to be provided from somewhere else within the budget. If the work on the elements which are overruning is well advanced, it will be necessary to devise different ways of doing some following activities in a more cost effective manner.

Cost forecasts/projections

We have techniques to identify and analyze variances in project cost and schedule on an ongoing basis. Where we are and how we got there are both important, but they always need to be supplemented by asking, "where are we going?"

The project manager needs to know the current forecast date for project completion and the current projected final cost. The most accurate and straightforward method of determining these two answer is simply to take the work still to be done and reassess the time requirements to complete it. If the project is currently on schedule and going there should be little reason for concern. If the project is behind schedule, those activities without float or with little float would be considered in an attempt to come up with a revised plan to recoup schedule time. If the project is currently ahead of schedule, the remaining work should be reviewed with the objective of moving the completion date forward or in reducing peak resource requirements by extending durations of selected activities. The project objectives would determine which option is selected.

The forecast for the final cost of the project is made by taking costs to date and adding the present estimate to complete all of the unfinished work. If the project is running on budget and performance has been good, final costs will probably be in line with the budget. If the project is running over budget, then a detailed analysis of the remaining costs should be made. The remaining items with the greatest cost sensitivity should receive the greatest attention in this review. If the project is under budget and the projection shows that the project will probably underrun. :he project manager should investigate the desirability of accelerating the completion date, if possible, by spending some of the surplus funds. Ibis option must be carefully studied and any move in that direction in accordance with the project objectives and approved by the proper authorities.

If a project is over forty percent complete, over budget, and behind schedule, there can be little optimism in continuing without a major effort to change the execution plan. At this point the project manager and his staff may tend to justify overruns by reference to the "peculiar difficulties" presented by "this project". If very stringent and possibly unorthodox measures are not taken with a great deal of urgency, the project will not be successful. At the very least, this is the time to redouble efforts to improve productivity and reduce spending wherever possible without further eroding the chances of completing the project successfully.

A project that is consistently running behind schedule but does not concurrently evidence serious budget overruns will probably eventually overrun the budget. A number of the project costs are closely related to time rather than measurable work output. These activities include project management and project control time charges, supervision from most of the disciplines, and accounting and time keeping charges.

The project manager must develop his forecasts and projections realistically. He must present them to his management and to the client honestly, maintaining belief in the predictions that he makes. A project manager's credibility is on the line whenever he changes his completion projection or his final cost forecast. If this becomes a monthly ritual, he will end up with no credibility at all.

Trending

For certain of the job's major sensitive activities, the prudent project manager and cost engineers will not want to wait for return cost information, but will want to do some on-line comparisons with the plan. Many of these techniques will fall under what is called trending. Trending uses a relatively small sample of work for extrapolating future performance

Trending may be used for overall performance of the entire project or for the performance within special areas, systems or disciplines. It shows its greatest payoff for activities with a fairly long duration, a substantial amount of similar or like output, and which are sensitive elements of the estimate. Both cost performance and schedule performance may be trended.

An ideal example of trending would be an analysis of the design quantities specified for one of the initial concrete equipment foundations. Jobhours which were actually used in the design may be compared to those included in the budget for the same work. The design quantities of form work, reinforcing bar, and volume of concrete can be compared with the quantities approved in the control budget. If any of these accounts are significantly higher or lower than the estimate, the possibility of a trend exists. The cost engineer should alert the project manager and discus the problem with the civil/structural job leader.

The effect of changed design quantities will have an effect on both the procurement and the construction efforts. Advance knowledge will allow for adjustment of the work plan. Job forecasts and predictions will be necessary- for the remaining foundations on the job; and, of course, alternative-corrective actions should be examined, a selection made, and then introduced to alleviate the adverse trends. This work should be carefully followed to determine effectiveness of the improvement measures. Trending no matter how it is done, is not a science. It is a procedure for bringing the possibilities of overrun/underrun to management's attention while there is still time for corrective action. It is not a method for obtaining exact numbers. The process should always be kept in perspective. It makes absolutely no sense to trend every activity on the project. Only those few activities with sufficient significance to materially affect the project outcome should be selected for tracking,

Kerridge lists four of the methods of trending being used-on projects:

- Future work will be performed at the budgeted rate.
- Future work will be performed at the actual rate to date.
- Future work will be performed at the budgeted rate to a specific point and afterward at the actual rate to date.
- Performance deviation for individual activities is determined. Future performance for the area, system, or discipline is based on a weighted deviation of included activities.

As with other scheduling and estimating techniques, the project manager should not abandon his common sense in the use of trending techniques. If the forecasts and projections determined by trending methods do not seem reasonable, they should be questioned. Trending Is useful only when properly applied.

Need for timely information

The selection and proper use of an adequate management information system is sometimes difficult for the project manager. Within the limitations afforded him by the available systems, he must assure himself that he has the information at the time that he must make decisions.

Only a few years ago, one of the Project manager's biggest headaches was the length of time it took to get good solid information on the status of his project. This has changed, and there is no longer any excuse for delay in getting current project information.

All but the smallest projects today can support computerized information systems. The best of these are comprehensive data base systems operated in an on-line mode. Even smaller projects can have access to networked personal computers with management information programs to assist the project staff in running the job.

Definite responsibility is assigned for inputting each type of data promptly into the data base. The data are then immediately available to all who have a need for it. Access to input and change data is restricted to those who have the responsibility for it. There are types and levels of information that have restricted access, particularly, in the case of salary and profitability information. No restriction should be placed or,. obtaining the information needed for the work efforts.

On small projects, the need for timely information is critical. The status of the project can literally change completely from one day to the next.

People have two reactions when they don't get information when it is needed. Both are detrimental to the project manager in his effort to run an efficient project. Some people abdicate responsibility if they do not have all of the information needed to work. This causes schedules to slip. Others tend to "invent" the information they need, taking into account their prejudices, perceptions, and bits and pieces of half-truths available to them.

Computer programs have the capability, in effect, of producing information in advance. This is a tremendous advantage for the project manager. If he has a thorny decision to make, he may input "what if" data into the program and come up with nearly instantaeous results. Various alternatives may be compared very rapidly in this manner.

Graphics should be used whenever possible to summarize large quantities of raw, data into a readily understandable form. The computer has made it possible to do this rapidly and at a very low cost once the information has been input into the data base.

Communications technology is changing almost from day to day. Many companies now use electronic mail or "E-Mail" for the project correspondence and reports. It is much easier to get information to the project staff using this system.

Morale is improved because people feel more involved and there is less likelihood that someone will be forgotten W in a distribution list.

Need for the right information

The information collected during the project for control purposes serves as the basis for many of the most important project decisions. The information must be right, not only in the sense of being correct, but also that it is the proper information and that it used properly. The degree of accuracy required is dependent upon what the information will be used for and the urgency for the data. For project control purposes, knowing today that an item cost about a half- million dollars rather than a quarter-million is more important than finding out six weeks from now that it will cost exactly $496,985.13.

During the planning stages of the project, the need for control information should be considered from the standpoint of payout Large, complex computer programs are available, and it may be tempting to follow the easy way and use one of these even for a small project. The capability and complexity of the control program should always be appropriate for the project. This must be determined very early on, and the decision documented in the performance assurance plan. No more information should be collected than is necessary to make the decisions required for the work and to manage the project effectively.

On any project, there will be honest mistakes made in gathering, inputting and interpreting data. The project manager will realize this, and when an important decision is made, he will take pains to confirm the validity of the data used.

The project manager will also insist on honesty on the part of each one on the project staff. He will never tolerate instances of deliberate falsifying or furnishing intentionally misleading information. The project manager will see that procedures for data checking and verification are in place, and will occasionally do some spot checking himself. The information used for control and management information purposes must come from people who are in the best position to know. It must not be filtered or distorted so that it appears more favourable that it is. Numbers must have a basis in fact. Entering data for control purposes into the computer has to be looked upon the same way as making a critical engineering calculation.

The data collected for control are used for feedback on performance, The project: manager's credibility will suffer if the performance statistics are not accurate or are not properly used for that purpose.

Everyone tends to rely on information that is printed on a computer report. It is supposed to be accurate. Many times the figures are right, either because of faulty input or due to a glitch in the software. Those who rely on computer reports should never abandon use of their common sense. If a particular number does not look right, you should follow your instincts and investigate rather than merely accept it.

Information should be received in the form that it car, best be used for the purpose intended. Not so long ago the computer gave us the numbers configured so that it was easy for the computer or convenient for the programmer. Modern technology has left that concept far behind. There is no longer any excuse for not taking advantage of the computer's ability to collect, manipulate, screen, sort, and present information in the most usable format: and then to transmit it electronically via networks or to generate hard copies.

Identifying problem areas

A problem may be thought of as a situation that will create a disruption to project execution, produce an Interruption to the project plan, or jeopardize the success of the project by causing one or more of the objectives to be missed. The most successful project managers seem to live about two months in the future. They thrive on anticipating problems by living out what will be happening on the job a few weeks from now. A more natural course would be to avoid thinking about problems because they involve increased risk. Most people avoid getting entangled with problems because thinking about problems will transport you mentally into the future and the unknown. Dealing with problems is uncomfortable because we are vulnerable and we are concerned about being found wrong.

It is an almost unanimous belief that those problems which are anticipated and for which solutions are determined in advance seldom seem to be the ones that cause difficulties on a job. Some of the project's unique problems will have been identified in the project plan, but identifying problems should be continuous throughout the project. Undoubtedly some of the most frustrating problems will occur toward the end of the job. The project manager will encourage his project staff to continue to undercover problems. Problems have a nasty habit of repeating themselves. Project managers study the patterns of prior jobs to find out where the problems have been. The past is an excellent source of forecasting future problems. The project manager will talk to a wide range of people to get input from various points of view and backgrounds.

Establishing that a problem of the potential for a problem exists is sometimes not easy, but before a problem can be resolved it has to be recognized. Once a problem has been recognized, the project manager must determine if it is serious enough to warrant concern. He should analyze the potential effects on the project.

If the problem is deemed to be sufficiently serious, the next step involves defining the problem. A performance deficiency may be behind a problem. In collecting information about the problem, good communication skills will be required so that the problem is not be aggravated before a solution can be implemented. Quite often, the symptoms of the problem axe initially thought to be the problem itself. Only at the time the problem is being defined are the symptoms unmasked to reveal the true difficulty. While the problem is being defined, try to isolate the root cause of the problem. It is necessary to determine who has responsibility for dealing with the problem, in matrix organization the problem may be a project problem, but the responsibility for resolution may, by definition of responsibility, belong to someone else. If this is the case, the project manager's responsibility is to bring the problem to the proper authority and see that there is a timely response. If he gets no action, he must escalate the issues to higher levels of management. Even though he may not be responsible for the actual resolution, he is answerable to assure that the problem is settled.

Investigation of alternatives

Once an identified problem has been defined and acknowledged to detrimental or potentially detrimental to the project, a solution to the problem must be found, it is always desirable to be able to identify alternative solutions: occasionally there will be instances where finding even one plausible solution will be taxing.

The facts should be examined to determine the cause of the problem. There is always a possibility that removing the cause(s) will eliminate the problem. Most often, even if this is done, additional remedial work may be required. The goals for problem resolution should be clearly expressed. What end result is sought in solving the-problem? In the case of many problems, the end result sought is a return to the original project schedule and budget within a specified time period. There may be premature attempts to resolve a problem, even before it has been defined. The project manager should insist that a sincere effort be made to definite the problem and to develop alternative options before attempting to make a decision as to the proper solution.

Sometimes clues to a possible solution will be given by the indicated path from the present situation to the desired situation. If this approach gives only one possible solution, the search should continue. Alternatives may be developed by using a brainstorming technique which involves group generation of a large number of ideas. The results will depend very much upon the composition of the brainstorming group. The prime prerequisite of the participant should be a creative and innovative nature. Related technical experience may be very helpful, but it may also be a hindrance if it limits the thought process of the group. Every proposed idea should be accepted and investigated including the most far-fetched. One of the benefits of the free-wheeling sessions is the fallout of derivative ideas based upon previous suggestions or combinations of suggestions. If there are a number of alternatives produced, the chances of the optimum solution being among them is correspondingly greater. Once the alternatives have been proposed, they must be evaluated. Each alternative should be ranked with regard to its contribution to resolving each of the results desired of the final solution. The alternative that has the highest ranking should then be "fine tuned."

Finally, the Selected course of action is tested, walked through, or simulated in order to prove its feasibility. There will always be some element of risk present in dealing with a problem area, and the project manager must keep this risk commensurate with the benefits to the project.

Corrective action

The purpose of a continuous monitoring program is to provide opportunity for timely correction of real or anticipated adverse effects on the project scheduled or budget. As soon as there is a definite indication of such an effect, the supervisor should work with the individual assigned the responsibility to develop a program for getting back on track. At times this can be done between, the supervisor and the individual, but sometimes it will be necessary to broaden the focus and bring in other people to help resolve the problem.

Some problems occur repeatedly. Some of the different types of performance problems and ideas for resolution are given below:

Information not available: A very handy excuse for not performing is that the necessary data had not been received. The first question the supervisor must ask is: "What have you done to expedite getting it?" The employee must not be let off the hook unless he has really tried to get the information. He should already have advised the supervisor of the problem before the date has been missed. If he has tried and been unsuccessful, the expediting effort must be escalated. Overtime may be a solution for recuperation after the data has been received.

Optimistic target date: Often the amount of time required to do a specific job is underestimated. A new fix must be made, and its effect on the following project activities analysed. There will be an effect on both schedule and cost stemming from a low estimate. Care should be taken that this does not create a cascading effect on subsequent work. For activities on the critical path, a delay in completion should be considered a serious matter in order to minimize the damage to downstream activities.

Adverse quantity trends: Early material takeoffs may bring up evidence of an uderestimated quantity estimate. The project budget may be sensitive to errors in quantity estimates. An overall evaluation is called for to determine the effect of the actual design on the budget. Redesign is one alternative that must be considered. An offsetting estimate is sometime possible, but this is not usually an option. Far more frequently, a general trend of underestimating may be discovered. At this time all of the available brain power must be brought to bear to reduce the potential budget variance.

Mistakes, errors, and omissions: Even with many of the calculations computerized; and an aggressive checking procedure, errors are possible. If an individual has been directed to proceed with work-based upon assumed data, there will be complications in completing the scheduled work on Lime and within budget if the data turns out to be erroneous. Where critical path activities are involved, serious consequences may arise. The supervisor should make sure that the performance of the innocent employee is not jeopardized because of something for which he is not responsible. They must work together to get the activity back on track with as little disruption to the project as possible.

The substance of project management is composed of many aspects and many types of work tasks and responsibilities. The core and common denominator, of all projects is the activities. These activities are interrelated. Thus, the network of activities is the basis for project management. All human decisions are based, on having and comparing information or, in other words, data. These data are interrelated. Thus relational databases are suitable as the primary background for project management and other management. Values are the real issue for motivation and activities. The values of goods and services are best generated or identified on the market. Thus, the cost or value of the goods and services is the key to project management and other management. Nothing is certain, the world is stochastic. All facts and figures must be seen in terms of their probability of occurrence. The best manager manages risk best. All activities, information, values, and judgments are based on human attitudes, motivation and judgment. Without people working together, nothing can be moved or done. Engaging and organizing people is the most fundamental work of project managers and other managers. Projects should transform an unsatisfying existing or future state to a better state, within a certain time, using a limited effort. The crucial points are the final state to be achieved and the way (intermediate states) to this target. Thus, the project objectives are what project management basically has to be concerned with. Changes are taking place less and less in independent fields. They are realized within a competitive world market, social groups asking questions, and many existing organizations, facilities, and parts of nature. Therefore, project management must not primarily build on the objectives of' its own people and organization, but on the conditions of' a complex environment.

A project is an undertaking that is limited in scope and time. Management is the direction of an organization, including the functions of planning, motivating, and controlling the systems and operations of the organization.

Project management means directing an organization that is responsible for an undertaking that is limited in scope and time. Systemic project management is directing a project organization based on thinking in terms of systems.

Systemic project management

The following reasons led to developing systemic project management:

- The conclusion of the author's situation analysis, at the start of his work in project management in the 70s, was, that the feasibility study is the key to successful project management. It a project is not sound itself, management control cannot help. The most important criterion of the feasibility test was whether the system established by the project cycle continued to be successful during the subsequent operations.

- Many professional fields were created in the past and dozens or hundreds of specialists may be working on a project. There is a need for managing specialists to coordinate the work of all these specialists. But also, the clients want the project manager to cover the overall responsibility.
- Time and again, the method of controlling only some aspects has failed. Time schedules were not acceptable due to an uneconomic use of the resources. The real reason for delays and cost overruns were technical and human problems. Thus, the project manager should have controlled the economic, technical, and human fields, foremost.
- No method was available for the overall planning, and control of complex projects. Often details and major parameters are mixed in the planning and control of project managers. Not even the specific project objective is clear and well understood.
- For advanced research and development work, the structure of the respective professional field should be known. Such work is undertaken to create in-depth knowledge and experience concerning a specific subject for a long time, i.e., for many applications. Theorems showing the rules of the professional field and allowing tests in practice should be developed.
- Every project is different, and every project is the same. Project management should be able to use good theory and good practice in those fields that are known, and to detect the aspects that are new. New aspects may be mastered by learning or by engaging new staff or consultants.

The concise conclusion from the whole analysis was that a basic structure and logic was necessary for both managing projects in a responsible way and expanding project management knowledge.

Basic structure and logic

The end product of a project cycle is a new state of one or several systems that is more satisfying than the initial, pre-project situation. Projects create new potential for the clients and the society, or solve one of their major problems.

A system is composed of a number of subsystems and components that have defined relations to each other and to the environment of the system. Systems are produced and changed by other systems. For example, a products generated by a company. Or a company is established by one or several founders. For project management, we can differentiate:

- The systems to be created or changed or liquidated

- The systems producing the-new state
- The goal systems of the parties involved in the project.

Most systems encountered are dynamic (i.e., changing in time) and open (i.e., related to their environment). The systems keep changing both during their design and construction and (in a different sense) during operation and maintenance. The environment may change or may be changed by the project as well. However it is not assumed to be controlled by project management.

Organizations and technical and natural systems are the most frequent types of systems. The types of management can be derived from the system and work types as follows: Managing organizations (corporate management, company management) Managing the creation or change or liquidation of systems (project management) Managing goods and services (product management).

If the management is systemic, it is based on thinking in terms of systems. This is the common denominator of all three types of management. Organizations, projects, and products are interrelated. Thus, the possibility of interacting presents very substantial demands.

A facility can be broken down into physical entities:

- Operational units (buildings, bridges, road or railway sections, tunnels, sectors of buildings, sections of tunnels, etc.)
- Subsystems (bearing structure, sewerage system, maintenance system, electrical supply, signaling, etc.)
- Components (elements) (reinforced concrete slabs, engines, pipes, repair workers, etc.).

These three levels are typical for constructed facilities. However, the respective units can be integrated to higher-level systems (e.g., the road section is a component of a road system) or they can be differentiated to more detailed systems (the engine is a system itself with subsystems and components).

This structure serves for defining the basic numbering of subsystems and components in the planning, design, construction, and start of operation phases of the project. At a certain time, the actual state as well as past and intended future states of each part of the system can be defined. This structure can be used as well for operation and maintenance management. One of its big advantages is that it can be seen in reality and shown on drawings. Therefore it is an excellent basis for reliable and efficient communication and data administration.

The components, subsystems, and systems have attributes or properties that can be used for engineering and management purposes. For example, a structural component has a certain stiffness, an anchor needs a certain time to be set, a human-machine group needs a certain amount of space, a road section costs a certain amount of money.

The joints between the components, subsystems, and operational units are again locational physical relationships and therefore generally observable. Examples of joints or interfaces are a change of responsibility at the interface between a road section and a tunnel section, a force transfer between two structural components, and a cost information exchange between two positions in the project organization.

The subsystems and the entire constructed facility have boundaries which cut relationships, i.e., are at joints.

The behaviour of the entire system, the subsystems, and the components should allow the fullfillment of the objectives of the constructed facility. The attributes should contribute to achieving these objectives. For example, the quality of a component should be according to standards and its price should be within budget, Project management is concerned with the goals to be set and the functions to be defined.

For data administration, the structure of the physical system can be used as a primary key, the attribute structures can correspond to secondary keys, and views can represent the structure of objectives.

Management model for complex systems

A system is defined by it's components and their topology and attribute data, databases can be used for defining systems and for providing management data.

Complex systems are easier to design and control if the multisystems multidiscipline, and multiphase structure

Several systems allow one to distinguish different purposes and geographical ranges

Several levels display larger and smaller coordination ranges in the organization

Several disciplines refer to a number of professionals involved who are responsible for a type of subsystem or component

Several phases indicate the development to completion stages of the system parts from initiation to completion

The system structure make integration as well as differentiation much easier. They are defined in the project structure lists, graphs, and drawings.

The more complex a system is the more important a well-designed data model and a well-organized data administration become. Both poorly structured heaps of data and sophisticated data accumulation normally do not stand the test.

Theorems of systemic project management

In this section, an attempt is made to define the concept of systemic project management by using theorems. The theorems should allow one to communicate, discuss, test and improve all parts of this concept. For further explanation, examples can be added. Roman numerals are used to identify the theorems. Additions to the theorems are described in brackets.

1. The primary basis of systemic management is the scope and structure of the systems managed.
2. Physical systems serve for producing goods arid set-vices (products) by performing work. (These products themselves are systems which can be subjects for project management, i.e., when they are being created or changed.)
3. The driving force behind the actions of systems is their objectives. (Usually, these objectives are set by persons and organizations or by nature.)
4. Systems are created and operate in a certain environment interacting with them. (All systems should be seen in their context-the physical, economic, and sociopsychological framework conditions which depend on time.).
5. All artificial systems are produced, operated, and maintained by organizations. Organizations may be taking care of natural systems as well.
6. The organizations are systems as well. (The human beings who are parts of organizations can be considered as systems too.)
7. Systems keep changing in time due to their properties and interactions with their environment.
8. The purpose of any activity is to change the state of one or several systems or to maintain a state, by intention. (All activities are related to the systems managed.)
9. The most important function of the management is to direct all activities toward common goals.
10. The decision of how to change a system depends on the attributes and values of the system before and after the action.
11. Systems can be represented by data. (These data are descriptions figures. photographs, etc. which, however, always are simplifications of the system represented.)
12. The primary data structure of a model is defined by its Subsystems and components (which possess attributes) and time. (Many other data structures can be defined using views on attributes of the system and its parts and environment.)

Creation, management, and liquidation of systems

The design and fabrication of new and adapted systems as well as the liquidation of existing systems is done by other productive systems. Such new, or adapted systems may be constructed facilities, products, companies and other organizations, proposals, laws, and so on. The earth is more and more populated by people and their man-made systems. Therefore, the issue of system liquidation and materials recycling is becoming more and, more relevant. Systems that are operated should produce an assortment of goods within a certain time period. The creation and liquidation of systems are value-adding, actions in a multilevel and multidimensional environment of organizations, products, infrastructure, and parts of nature. The systems are interrelated.

The systems, subsystems, and components are usually not designed or fabricated or liquidated by the project management. Its central mission is to assure the planning motivation, and control functions of the design and fabrication or liquidation project. However, the project management should understand the important aspects of these physical systems and may possibly intervene when controlling the project objectives. The design engineers develop, display, and communicate the information about the physical systems schematically and verbally, by drawing components and subsystems and by writing reports. They create an abstract system which defines the real system that shall be fabricated.

The structure of the whole system allows a project to be realized through intermediate targets. The project management concentrates its attention on a certain, subsystem for a limited time in order to drive that subsystem to a certain level of study, investigation, design, realization, or operation. Indistinct or complicated technical systems are often an indication of an inappropriate design, which results in problems of meeting quantity quality, time, cost, and satisfaction targets installation, and operation.

- The conceptual studies mid project definition
- The design
- The fabrication or implementation
- The start of operation and project closedown

The design and design coordination of a constructed facility are governed by the following aspects:

- The desired production output of the facility is defined.
- The geometrical structure and shape of the facility are designed.
- The type and properties of the component with their space and media usage are determined.
- The flows of materials, energy, and information are calculated.
- The feasibility and optimality of the design are checked with reference to the objectives.

The three fundamental elements for the creation, adaptation and liquidation of systems are

- The systems that are going to be created
- The organizations (productive systems) that create or adapt or liquidate them
- The work that is required

Operation and Maintenance

The desired output and the selected methods and conditions for producing it are the basis for the operation and maintenance concept of a system. "The operation and maintenance concept itself includes, for example, in tile case of a constructed facility, the technology, processes, and organization for production and maintenance. This basis is designed, and selected by the industrial engineers. The corresponding activities do not take place in one phase or one stage of the project the general production concept is determined in the conceptual phase; the details of the operation and Maintenance of a component may be defined in the design phase and may even be adapted in the start-up-operation phase. The project management should carefully build up this basis for the creation of systems by the project organization and keep it under control. Otherwise, the operation concept cannot be a reliable starting point for the design and construction of the facility, but is a starting point for change orders propagating throughout the project.

Environment of Systems

Most of the systems are, in practice, open systems. They are affected by or have an effect on the environment of the constructed facility. This is in contrast to physical systems tested in a laboratory where external factors are kept constant. Because the scope of a construction project is often a subject for physical, economic and organizational design, the systems boundary can be an important issue in engineering. The three main types of framework conditions for systems are:

- Physical conditions (technical standards, surrounding facilities and nature, connections to public infrastructure, etc.)
- Economic conditions (market prices, financial limit and conditions etc.)
- Sociopsychological conditions (rules of society, attitudes of stakeholders objectives and experience of persons in the project.)

The first class of framework conditions can be enforced by a second class binds the members of a company or an organization, and a third class represents informal conditions.

The systems created or adapted or liquidated are often interacting with other systems. The project management must identify the interfaces to these systems and allocate the responsibilities for taking them into account in the project organization.

It is essential to be aware of the organizations and persons that may have an impact on the project's success. Tasks are fulfilled by persons belonging, to an environment external to the projects. Each organization and person in this environment as well as each person working on the project, has an identity and a personal interest. The project management should observe potential influences at all times and, if necessary, take steps to maintain the motivation for achieving the project objectives.

Organizations

The project organization is the group engaged in planning and realizing the project. This organization should be tailored to the requirements of the specific project and phase. Organizing means defining the work tasks with the responsibilities allocating them to positions, designing the procedures in the organization, and selecting adequate performers for the positions.

The relationship between project and permanent organizations has been a substantial concern for project managers since the beginning. Good organizational solutions allow a smooth integration of the project work into the company organization, as well as a high responsibility and independence of the project management and project organization.

Specialized labour generally leads to increased quality and productivity of a complex production. The division of work is normal for the creation, adaptation and liquidation of systems and for their operation and maintenance. The definition, coordination, and allocation of work packages and functions to appropriate organization groups and positions are therefore necessary.

Information flows assist the transfer of intermediate products and support the coordination of the work, the allotment of work tasks, and the control and updating of the project objectives.

The project organization (creates a new or adapted system or liquidates an existing system, with its own and purchased resources)

The user organization (operates and maintains an existing system and) is usually considered a part of it)

The physical system that is created or adapted or liquidated can be used as a basis for planning, developing, controlling, and finally reducing the project organization.

A responsible person or group can be assigned to each component, to each subsystem and to the entire constructed facility.

The organization chart, together with the corresponding job description the responsibility matrix, and the definition of important information flows, is tile typical abstract model for developing, displaying, and communicating the information about organizational systems. Responsible persons (components), groups (subsystems) and organizations (systems) are working on certain subsystems and components of the system that is the subject of a project. This fact relates the project organization to the physical system. The project management tries to allocate each work package to the company or group or person offering or assuring the most favourable conditions:

Applying again the idea of realizing a project through intermediate objectives, the project management tends to maintain a constant organization pattern and responsibility through a stage leading to the next set of results. This means that essential reorganization is normally undertaken just before or just after the beginning of a new development stage of a project. An evaluation of the preceding phase of the project, a plan for the next phase, a badge of organizational work, and an improvement or initiation of contracts can be combined at that time by preparing and realizing an initiation meeting.

The response of organizations to work tasks that are given to or found by these organizations can be shown by using the feedback model. In this model, processing activities and information, material, and energy flows are assumed to start according to defined criteria.

The management of the resources (crews, equipments, materials, arid third-party goods or services) is not logical for one project alone. The resources should be managed for a whole organization unit or company (multiproject management).

Value of Systems

Physical systems are seldom an end in themselves. They are designed and built for producing a set of goods and values. This set motivates the owner to allocate the financial resources to the project. However, creating, adapting, and liquidating a system may have effects on other objective systems. New jobs and opportunities for making money new financial commitments, and new qualities of life may be made available and new environmental problems may be created.

Culture is normally related to creating, producing, and building precious works. It is developed and promoted by intention; it is keeping up a set of customary knowledge beliefs, and behaviours. Culture is

- Intentional, therefore it is most important to define the objectives for the project.
- To be realized, therefore the culture of the results shall be evaluated
- Built thereby activities and patterns of behaviour lead to result
- Evaluate nothing happens without motivation which is directly related to the objectives of those who are involved in the project.

Objective functions demonstrate the effect of design and implementation variations on the preference parameters of the client. In the field of cost planning, the client wants answers to three questions: "What is it?," "What is it Worth?," and "What does it cost?". Special attention is directed to the question "What, is it worth?" Answering it determining the subjective preferences of the client. Without knowing the answers, a general optimum cannot he reached.

The physical system is again used as a starting point. Price tags and performance data are attached to file components and subsystems. The structure of the cost estimate and the cost control elements should coincide With the structure of the physical system. Subsystems can be used as cost centers of the cost accounting for the operated systems.

The general and top-level objective is the perform adapted during its operation and maintenance time. For an economic evaluation planned income statements of the organizations involved and the operated system can be used.

The investment costs show up in the expense accounts as interest and depreciation. An alteration in the quality required may change the expenses for operation and maintenance, the depreciation rate, and the revenue. Planned balance sheets and financial plans demonstrate the usage and origin of the financial resources as well as the liquidity as a function of time.

In a capital-intensive system such as a hydroelectric power station, the investment costs incurred during the project cycle have a very significant impact on the facility's economy. On the other hand, investment costs have a relatively small impact off the total income statement of a shopping center. The operation manager should therefore turn his or her attention more to sales effects and material handling solutions.

Technical uncertainties, changes in market and procurement conditions, inadequate working methods unrealistic time and cost estimates, not observing the wishes of stakeholders and the influence of low-cost, poorly qualified consultants can all reduce the probability of achieving intermediate and final targets of a project, In order to achieve the project objectives, the project management must, during the project cycle, successively reduce the probability of outcomes situated outside an acceptable range of variance. This can be achieved by making a risk-analysis and by finding risk-reducing solutions like design reviews, repetition of work items, prefabricated components, and insurance.

Displaying and Communicating Information

An ideal information system would provide, during the whole project cycle, well-presented, understandable, correct, and technically consistent actual data in several degrees of detail for the systems, subsystems, and components and their attributes, at a reasonable cost. New information technology allows one to store, process, display, and transfer data more and more easily and economically. However, (temporary) project information systems are not easy to establish.

The first condition is that each member of the project organization be equipped with a computer processing, display, and memory installation and data transfer unit. In addition, a hard-copy printer and the traditional noncomputer communication equipment should be available.

The second condition is that the data that the user is referring to be available at his or her working place. For example, it should be possible to use standard specifications, contract patterns, cost figures from other projects, standards, and regulations, if possible, in a multitask processing and display mode.

The third condition is related to the decentralized way of working. If the information system should function for a complex, multidisciplinary project structure, the users need to have a common understanding of definitions regarding the data transferred. Clear data structures are necessary for an efficient and reliable data administration as well.

Standard data structures and common terms down to the most detailed level are necessary for

- Developing, implementing, and applying software efficiently
- Being able to interpret correctly incoming information from another company working on the project
- Avoiding the danger of errors propagating over the whole information system

The hierarchical physical system structure can be used as the primary key for work and cost data, for example. Both specifications and cost data for a project usually are related to project-independent databases as well. Often, this information must be adapted and completed according to the size, location, and other project-related attributes and framework conditions before becoming actual project information.

Management strategy

The planning process of an entirely new airport plant—such as that under construction at the new airport of Munich, with about 100 separate facilities and the same number of different planning teams, nearly all of which are related to each other—can no longer be controlled and managed by the traditional boss-subordinate management structure. For successful management, it would be necessary to have an adequate and powerful project-management structure that can coordinate the various project members, control the projects progress, and rapidly react to problems in order to reach the project's main objectives. This structure should realize the possibility of flexible and effective access to the project members skills and resources. Project responsibility should be delegated in an appropriate manner to minimize bureaucratic procedures.

General management structure

The main layout of the New Munich Airport, the schematic diagram of the organization structures and the detail of the main work-breakdown schedule, it is obvious that large-scale construction projects can be treated as a network of simultaneously performed Sub-projects. The management of a network of projects is organized by a steering committee for projects.

In the case of the New Munich Airport, there was, therefore established a Project Coordinator position between the top management and the planning project team members, composed of architects and expert planners for various technical systems.

Principles to allow Management by Projects to become second nature to every team member. It as decided that Project management tasks should be delegated to the team members as necessary, to increase responsibility and flexibility of the team members. The problem in implementing the decision was not the smaller project-team members but rather larger department team members. It was not easy to make them aware of the need to play their new role in a project with as little bureaucratic behavior as possible. In detail, the project teams had to ful-fill the following, additional project-management functions:

- Scheduling and controlling their project contribution within the boundaries set by the project coordinator
- Analyze and prepare necessary decisions for the project coordinator
- Coordinate their project contribution with all related and affected project members

All the team contributors are supported by the project coordinator. Besides such standard project-management functions as scheduling and controlling, the project coordinator has to

- Analyze the quality of project members output
- Maintain and control project communication between the project members
- Analyze and prepare all necessary top-management decisions
- Integrate and maintain communication flow with team members in the post-project phase
- Analyze and control external and internal project influences caused by dynamic changes of the project environment

It is essential that the project coordinator does not plan and design. Nevertheless the coordinator can establish task force teams to do intensive, task-oriented planning when project problems make it necessary.

The main progress information is gathered by the project coordinator in monthly progress reports from all team members and condensed to quarterly progress reports to the top management.

Contract management

Undoubtedly the flat organization structure is possible only when all project members are able and willing to replace the conventional management structures by teamwork, responsive project contributions, and flexibility. This also means that a lot of the usual staff support functions are cut back and responsibilities have more and more to be delegated.

On the other hand, all protect team members are bound together by their contracts to the client's authority. These contracts therefore have to regulate the boundaries in which their new responsibilities and their duties are fixed. It is obvious that the degree of flexibility is limited by the contractual boundaries. This is especially true for all activities that are necessary for the project member's work and have to be done by others. It is therefore necessary to enlarge the contractual agreements with additional coordination tasks for each team member to ensure adequate project progress. This means, of course, additional costs for the client at about 1 percent of the project amount.

Successful interaction of the team members is possible only when result-dependent project members are working simultaneously in adequate design steps and scales to ensure providing the required quality of results. For technical project planning, this is especially important because many of the required results are largely dependent on the finally chosen system. Providing these results is therefore always a part of the company's contract. That means these contracts have to be signed in an early project phase.

Concerning the schematic diagram of the organization structure for the project's design process, it is obvious that the complete design project can be structured in several sub-projects, depending on the functional programs of each object.

Besides the architect's so-called general planning team, including several technical planning sub-teams, which are contractually awarded by the architect, there are several mostly technically oriented planning contributors, who have to involve projectwide System planning in nearly each of the objects, for example, projectwide information systems.

The responsibility for successful intraction between the project members involved in the complete object-design task is delegated to the project members, and the general object planner is the object coordinator for all objects concerning coordination and management tasks.

Management tools

Scheduling. The project coordinator's main management tool is the general work breakdown schedule in the form of a bar-chart diagram. With this general, work, schedule, the project coordinator has to set up the overall time schedule for each object by a detailed time schedule.

At this scheduling level, the project coordinator arranges all design phases the preparation phase of all contracts and all milestone dates for top-management decisions defining the functional program of the object. As a matter of fact, it has to be guaranteed that all project members really can interact with each other.

- The functional and technical program is agreed to by the client
- All necessary planning works are under contract
- The investigation sum is agreed to by the client

Using the above-mentioned schedules the project members have to set up more detailed schedules in order to make visible important milestones for the internal planning project such as the client's decisions and key events dependent on the interaction of project members. The responsibility of working out all necessary milestones for the ongoing planning process is by the project members. There should be the support of a projectwide, personal computer-based datalink system.

Progress Control. It is not necessary to explain the general use of continuous and intensive progress control. Normally this is done by monthly reports. In case of long-term, complex projects, it is useful to prepare a structured list which is used by all project members in the same way. From this, the project coordinator gets the desired information about progress and is able to prepare the next steps as necessary.

As the usable information thereby depends on the contents of the progress report list, the project coordinator may have to make great efforts to get complete reports. Complete reporting should therefore be required in the project members contacts.

Because of the multiproject character of the New Munich Airport, with many different project members, it is nevertheless usually necessary to interpret the contents of the reports in an individual way. We therefore did not integrate progress control into a PC-supported system.

Expert tools

Management of Decisions. All necessary client decisions for keeping the project running such as

- Contract awards for designing works
- Definition of functional programs for each object
- Definition of investigation programs
- Contract awards with later users to define the commercial structure of the building

are combined by the project coordinator within monthly decision lists so that top management is able to make the necessary decisions. The use of PC support is possible and offers the ability to issue monthly decision lists.

Communication in Top Management. By means of weekly or monthly project meetings between top management and the concerned project members, communication can successfully be organized to get a steady flow of information among, the project members. Most of the necessary project decisions are prepared and released here.

Professional data management

Data management with PC-supported systems is an important tool in project management of large-scaled, complex design projects. For nearly all of the mentioned task, in scheduling and preparing management decisions, it is useful to work with data-processing systems.

But due to the fact that there is no efficient, overall management software system that is flexible and powerful enough to enable reliable data management for all cases we decided to use only standard software such as database systems and spreadsheet programs, and adapted these to the desired function with self-written routines.

The use of network scheduling became too complex and ineffective as the project developed. We therefore created a flexible schedule-data pool from which all team members could gain the necessary, scheduling dates. Even when this pool soon expanded to several thousands of activities, it never became a problem to handle and use this instrument.

Experienced project managers know that it is impossible to manage large-scale, highly complex design projects, such as the planning of an entirely new airport-plant, without any failure. Sometimes near-fatal problems come from external and internal sources caused by:

- Dynamic external project environments such as laws, rules and general project acceptance by affected groups
- Business-oriented interests, financing, and marketing aspects
- Resource availability of project teams
- New technical developments

While these can partly be handled by the evolutionary planning approach, mistakes still happen.

Nevertheless, by establishing the described flat organization structure for the Management of the network of projects, it is possible to

- Move responsibility more and more to the directly affected project members to improve flexibility and quality
- Improve project culture by more intensive communication in the network-oriented structure
- Reflect more effectively about the process of planning in the "third level" establishing a project-steering committee.

But is was also not possible to integrate all project teams completely into the organisation structure to the desired degree.

Due to the fact that the new model works only when all project teams are accepting their new level of project responsibility and project-management culture, it still will take great efforts to generally define a suitable environment for establishing the Management by Projects culture. These efforts have to be done also in defining new planning contracts, so that the higher degree of project coordination is also remunerated, for each project team in an adequate way.

As one of the main objectives of management by projects, the traditional top-down relationships have to be replaced. And, as this organization structure is a very practical attempt to establish more project culture by delegating responsibility to all project members it will become eventually the main organization model, accepted by the new type of flexible and quality-conscious project managers. The experiences of the management organization described here suggest that the structure still offers a lot of opportunities for improving project-management success.

Project process

The terms of contract must be precise and definite, and three must be no room for ambiguity or misconstructions therein. Subject to adequate prior scrutiny of terms-general or special-standard forms of contracts must be adopted wherever possible by the project authorities in consultation with legal and financial departments. For instance, many organisations stipulate that no contract involving an uncertain or infinite liability, or any condition of unusual character, should be entered into without a sanction from the competent financial authority. Similarly, the term contract document means and includes, all documents deemed to form an integral part of the contract like tender documents inviting offers, contractors bid proposals, classification letters, material literature, minutes of discussions, letter of intent issued by the project authority, acceptance by the bidder, contract agreement, specifications agreed, variations and special conditions.

Technical specifications, in most cases, to the contractors include the following:

Usually the project manager provides detailed schedules to the contracts which specify Intent of specifications, Scope and terminal points; Technical and engineering data for specific contracts; Standards Material specifications; Design criteria; Technical design specifications; Anticipated deviations in specifications; Shop tests; Site tests; Test certificates; Special inspection requirements; Drawings; Construction details; List of mandatory spares; Liquidated damages for shortfall in equipment performance; Supplies of similar equipments designed and erected; Technical literature and pamphlets; Quality assurance plan; Commercial terms and conditions, including deviations; PERT Network and conditions including deviations; Operating instructions. Stagewise inspection results; Alternate proposals, if any; performance guarantee test; and special maintenance requirements, if any.

Usually bids are typed with sufficient copies and submitted in scaled envelopes. Part I is bid guarantee, Part II is technical and commercial, and Part III is schedule of prices. The bidder has to satisfy himself that full information has been furnished as required in the specifications, as lack of information will be at the risk of rejection of bid. The bids received will be scrutinised by tile project team according to the bid evaluation criteria to ascertain the most suitable evaluation of the bid for the total project. The scope of the contract usually is on the basis of a single bidder responsibility comprehensively covering the specifications of the total project. In the single bid system for evaluation, strict adherence to the specification is a must, which does not provide credit to supervisory officers. In a single bid system, prequalification is a must to eliminate spurious parties. In case of the two bid system, all bids need to be technically evaluated and brought on a common basis of technical capability through discussions with vendors. The two bid system takes more time as discussions with all vendors for technical evaluation consume lot of time. In the single bid system, it is possible to get a lower price than in a two bid system, provided the effect of negotiation does not come into the picture.

Qualifying requirements of bidders

Relevant qualifying clauses indicating qualifying requirements are provided, under the bid specification. The project authority reserves the right for any additional information, and to reject the proposal of an incomplete bid. The bidder has to furnish, along with his bid, PERT chart and other programmes of manufacture, supply, erection quality assurance of subcontracts and other relevant details. The bidder also has to indicate details of the plant, machinery, tools, tackles, instruments, etc., which he proposes to hire and deploy at the project site.

The bidder shall include the quality assurance programmes, and quality management procedures to be followed during various stages of manufacture, installation and commissioning. These include procurement of materials, selection of subcontractors, source inspection, system of manufacturing, fabrication, assembly controls, inspection test procedures at different stages, control of calibration of testing instruments, quality audits, and document control. All deviations/exceptions to the specifications; and or conditions of contract are to be evaluated with respect to the specified value/conditions and categoric recommendations must be made as to their acceptability as follows! (a) Acceptable with no commercial implication-, (b) Acceptable but to be cost-compensated to bring all offers on par; and (c) Not acceptable at present, but to be resolved during contract award tie-up and to be cost-compensated for evaluation

Negotiation

Following consultations or invitations to tender and their progression, a negotiation stage shall be entered into in order to select-suppliers on the basis of the assessment of the supplier and quality requirements. At this stage, it is advisable to ensure that the supplier is in a position to comply with all the terms of the agreement, and that common ground can be negotiated by both parties-in particular for the terms which have not been the subject of previous negotiations, or those of which the parameters defined within the framework of the previous negotiations have been modified. In order to obtain and ensure the quality of purchase/procurements, it is advisable not to overlook elements which could give rise to disputes, and not-to remain in a state of uncertainty, lack of understanding or discord. Negotiations on quality, price, delivery, service and all contractual obligations should take place in an atmosphere of openness.

Spare parts management

The mandatory spares shall be despatched latest along with the last shipment intended for the first machine to be commissioned. Contractors are asked to quote separately for the recommended spares required for long term availability on firm price on a per unit basis. These rates are not considered for bid evaluation purposes. In case, some vital spares are identifiable, the contractor is asked to quote for specific quantities. A complete list of such mandatory spares, and quantity required, is incorporated in technical specifications. Such spares are evaluated with the main bid. All relevant items and conditions of the contract apply to purchase of spares also, except payment and delivery items, which can be agreed to mutually at the time of award. The bidder must also provide the list of subcontractors, and the date of discontinuance of spares supply.

Payment schedule and currency changes

In case of plant or machinery, 90 per cent of the contract price of each consignment despatched to the consignee is paid on production of initial inspection note, and the remaining 10 per cent on final inspection at site. All advance payments are made against bank guarantee, or any other guarantee, acceptable to the project authorities. In the case of a steel craft, the practice in India is that 15 per cent is paid when the keel is laid, 15 per cent when the vessel is framed, 15 per cent when the hull is completed and 20 per cent when vessel is launched. Twenty-Five per cent is paid when vessel is completed and accepted in the final inspection, and the remaining 10 per cent on expiry of the 6 months guarantee period, In the case of central air-conditioning plant, the practice is 80 per cent of the contract price for equipment supplied on initial inspection and delivery at site; 10 per cent on completion of installation, commissioning, and trial run of the plant for 15 days, 5 per cent on successful completion of the major tests with certification against a bank guarantee for 5 per cent of the total contract value, and the balance against final inspection.

The contractors quoting for imported projected machinery in rupee on forward delivery basis should have their prices on a rate of exchange according to T T selling rate as quoted by any authorised exchange banker approved by the Reserve Bank of India, and its ruling on the date of tender. No variation in price is normally allowed if the variation in the rate of exchange remains within the limit of plus/minus one per cent. The exchange variation clause has to be stipulated in the resultant contracts, for supply from East European countries and the USSR should not provide for payment in any currency other than non-convertible Indian Rupees according to the Trade Agreement with these countries. Some suppliers insist on the gold parity which is as follows: The prices specified in the contract are based on current par value of Indian rupee, containing gram of fine gold. In the event of any change in the par value of Indian rupee, the amounts due will be adjusted in proportion to the change in the par value. Some organisations use indices and sophisticated formulae which is announced in the tender documents.

Contracts on, a firm price, as well as on variable price, are considered on the merits of each case. Where firms quote with price variation, the formula of variation including the base, price of raw material etc. should be clearly spelt out. For instance, in the event of JPC steel price, variations are made effective in the price of steel on finished weight from die date-of variation, and can be applicable. Similar is the cases with non-ferrous metals, based on increases by the canalised agencies, similar adjustments are to be made on the statutory levies of sales tax, customs, excise, sctroi, transport, shipping, insurance premium, etc.

Delivery schedules/changes

Delivery is the essence of the project contract, and hence stipulation of the definite date for supply of machinery for contact can hardly be overemphasised. The delivery period to be stipulated should be, worked out such that it is both realise conformity with the offer by the contractor. The time and date of delivery stipulated in the contract are deemed to be the essence, of contract. Tern's like ex-stock, immediate, urgent, etc., must be avoided.

In FOR state of despatch the date on which the dates are placed on rail after inspection and acceptance is the date of delivery. In CIF contracts, the date on policy, packing list, vouchers which the shipping documents-bill of lading, insurance etc., are effectively tendered to the buyer is the date of delivery.

The time to complete the project should be reckoned from the date of issue of the letter of intent to the contractor. The contractor must submit a detailed PERT network for the time frame specified, consisting of key phases of the contract such as design, procurement, manufacturing at works, inspection,, despatch, erection, testing, etc., along. The above PERT network must be reviewed, and periodic review reports must be submitted by the contractor. The manufacturing programme should be reviewed and updated continuously. For supply contracts, the project authority may reserve the right to vary the quantity by plus/minus 20 per cent.

Refixation of delivery period, can be done by the contractor on approval of project authority in the following cases: (a) when the indent or specially states that prior consultation with him is necessary before granting extensions in delivery period. (b) when higher prices have been paid for earlier delivery', (c) where special provisions of recovery of pre-estimated damages have, been included. (d) where the, items are liable to violent market fluctuations; and (e) where there is downward trend in market prices. In order to safeguard the 'right to liquidated damages, the project can extend delivery period, if there is no downward trend in price. It is desirable to, prepare a detailed schedule of deviation pertaining to delivery and price. The contractor should also inform the Purchase Authority-in writing at least 60 days in advance regarding the expity/cancellation/change/renewal of any insurance.

Liquidated damage

When a Contractor is placed on a higher tenderer grade in consideration of the machinery being offered, a price preference clause may be included binding the machinery being offered, a price preference clause between the lowest acceptable offer and the offer accepted as price preference. The clause on disk purchase enables the project authority to repurchase the items, which the contractor fails to deliver within the time allowed and the project authority is entitled to recover from the contractor the loss suffered. If the contractor fails to perform the contract within the time stipulated in the special conditions, the contractor is liable pay to the purchaser liquidated damages, not penalty as specified in the special conditions of the specifications. Unless otherwise stated in special conditions, the contractor shall pay to the purchaser as liquidated damages, not as penalty, ½% of the contract value per week of delay or part there of subject to a maximum of 5 per cent of the total contract value including price variation, Liquidated damages shall be leviable for delays beyond the time stipulated at the rates specified in the special conditions. For a shortfall in equipment performances, there is no limit to the liquidated damages.

Force majeure

The following shall constitute *force majeure*: Acts of God, acts of Government, and ether causes such as strikes, lock-outs or other concerted action of workmen, war, sabotage, riots, civil commotion, police action, revolution, flood, fire, earthquake and epidemic. If the contractor delays in the due execution of the contractual obligations due to delays caused by force majeure as defined above, the agreed time of completion of the work covered by this contract of the obligations of the contractor shall be extended by he period of force majeure, provided that on the contractor immediately reports to the; Purchaser, in writing, the cause of delay with requisite documentary evidence. The decision of the project authority on whether there is a *force majeure* condition or not and whether extension of time shall be granted or not should be final. Force majeure conditions prevailing at the works of the subsuppliers/ subcontractors should not be recognised by the Purchaser on any account, and it should be up to the contractor to make the necessary alternative arrangements to execute the contract within the agreed time schedule, the contractor or the purchaser should not be liable for delays 'in performing his obligations resulting from any force majeure cause as referred to and/or defined above. The, date of completion should, subject to conditions hereinafter provided, be extended by the reasonable time even though such cause may occur after the contractor's performance of his obligations has been delayed because of other causes.

Patent rights and royalties

Royalties and fees for patents covering materials, articles, apparatus, devices, design, equipment or processes used in the works should deemed to have been included in the contract price. The contractor should satisfy all demands that may be made at any time for such royalties or fees and he alone should be liable for any damages or claims for patent infringements and should keep the purchaser, indemnified in that regard. The contractor should, at his own cost and expenses, defend all suits or proceedings that may be instituted for alleged infringement-of any patents involved in the works and, in case of an award of damages, the contractor should pay such damages. India has been raising its voice on TRIPS-trade related intellectual property rights-in this context.

In the case of the purchaser, the same should be defended at the cost and expenses of the contractor who should satisfy/comply any decree order or award, made against the purchaser. The contractor should indemnify and keep indemnified the purchaser, his successors or assignees any and all claims, suits, damages, losses, actions, demands, costs, charges, royalties and expense; arising from, or for, such actions, demands, infringement.

Transportation

The contractor should after proper painting, pack and crate all equipment for and shipment, in a manner suitable to a tropical region, through accredited forwarding and shipping agencies of the Government of India. The contractor should furnish to the Secretary. Shipping Co-ordination Committe full details of the cargo in the prescribed form in triplicate, six weeks in advance of the expected date of shipment. The bill of landing should be drawn as to indicate the project authority on behalf of the buyer as the consignee. The project authorities should not be responsible for any demurrage/wharfage, etc. Documents such as bill of lading invoices, packing list, soundness certificate, certificate of origin, test certificate, invoice of ocean freight; transit insurance, declaration need to be prescribed in the contact, the equipments, both imported and indigenous, should be handled and transported, including interacting, storage at any intermediate point from the shop of the manufactures work, subsuppliers subcontracters to the project site, through accredited reliable/dependable transport carriers. The contractor should assume total responsibility for ocean/inland transport and the freigt charges, port landing, forwading etc., and these must be included in the scehedule of prices. The problems of ovedimensional consignments must be looked into.

Insurance

The contractor should arrange, secure and maintain marine, inland transit, storage and erection insurance, as may be necessary to protect the interest of the project authority against all possible risks. Irrespective of such acceptances, the responsibility to maintain insurance at all times during the period of contract should be that of the contractor alone. Any less or damage to the equipment during handling, transport, storage and erection, till such time the plant is taken over by the purchaser, should be to the account of the contractor. The contractor should be responsible for preffering all claims as applicable, and make good, at his replacement of the portion of the works damaged or lost.

Warranty of taking over and CPG

The contractor should guarantee that the defects in design, material and with the contract specifications, and be free from defects in design, material and workmanship. The warranty period be 24 calendar months from the date of receipt of last consignment at sight in case of supply contract alone; and in case of supply-cum-erection, the same should be limited tot he placement of any defective parts in the equipment of his own manufacture, or those of his subcontractors, arising from faculty design, materials and/ workmanship. The warranty period should be 24 calender months from the date of receipt of last consignment at sight in case of supply-cum-erection, the same should be limited to the placement of any defective parts in the equipment of his own manufacture, or those of his subcontracters, arising from faulty design, materials and/or workmanship. The plant shall be operated as per the opening instructions, and all records, long books and other information about the operation should be maintained. Replaced defective parts should be taken back by the contractor. No repairs or replacement should be carried out by the project authority while the plant is under commissioning, except in the event of serious emergency.

Detailed tests, methods for carrying out tests, value of loss/damages LD for non compliance, test study, etc., are done within two months of completion of trial run The repaired or new parts should be furnished and erected free of cost at site b contractor. If any repair is carried out on his behalf at the site, the contractor should bear the cost of such repair.

The cost of any special or general overhaul rendered necessary during the guarantee period due to defects in the plant, or defective work carried out by the contractor should be borne by the contractor. The acceptance of the equipment by the project manager should in no way relieve the contractor of his obligations under this clause. Upon successful completion of all tests to be performed at the rate, the project authority should issue to the contractor a taking over certificate, as a proof of the final acceptance of the equipment.

Contractor's machinery

The contractor should provide at his own expense all the construction equipment, erection tools, machine tools, power tools, tackles, hoists, cranes, derricks, cables, slings, skids, scaffolding, work benches, tools for rigging, cribbing and blocking, welding machine, preheating and stress relieving equipment, X-ray and all associated protective equipment, commissioning gadgets and instruments, appliances, materials and supplies, required for unloading, transporting, storing, erection, testing and commissioning that may be required to accomplish the work under the contract. Adequacy of such tools should be subject to final progressive determination of the purchaser. Thee contractor should submit a list of all such materials to the purchaser before the commencement of erection work at site. These tools and tackles should not be removed ' from the site without the written permission of the purchaser. The contractor and his workmen should adhere to the disciplinary procedure of the project authority.

The contractor should also provide, at his cost all necessary expendable devices like anchors, grinding and abrasive wheel, rawl plugs, hacksaw blades, random stones, oil stones, wire brushes, necessary scaffolding, ladders, wooden planks, timbers, sleepers, and consumables materials like electrodes, oxygen, acetylene, argon, lubricating oils, greases, cleaning fluids, cylinder oil, graphite powder and flakes, fasteners, gaskets, temporary supports, stainless steel skims of various thickness as required, cotton waste, cheese cloth and all other miscellaneous supplies of every kind required for carrying out the work under the contract. Facilities like access to project site, water, electricity, office accommodation, housing to labour, storage space, communication, security etc., required for normal operations of the contract should be provided by the project authorities.

Disputes/Arbitration

Except as otherwise specially provided in the contract, all-disputes concerning questions of fact arising under the contract should be decided by the project manager, subject to written appeal by the contractor to the project manager, whose decision should be final for the parties hereto. Any disputes or differences, including those considered as such by only one of the parties arising out of/or in connection with the contract, should be, to the extent possible, settled amicably between the parties. If amicable settlement cannot be reached, then all the disputed issues should be settled by arbitration. In case of a dispute or difference of any kind whatsoever between the project authority and the contractor, arising out of the contract, or the performance of the contract, whether during the progress of the contract or after its completion, or whether before or after termination, abandonment or breach of the contract, it should in the first place, be referred to, and settled by the project manager, who, within a period of 30 days after being requested by-the contractor to do so, should give his decision. Except as hereinafter provided, such decision in respect of every matter so referred should be final and binding upon the parties until the completion of the contract, and should forthwith be given effect to by the contractor, who should proceed with contract with all diligence, whether he or the purchaser required arbitration as hereinafter provided. If, after the project manager has given his decision, no claim to arbitration is communicated by either party within 30 days, the said decision, shall become final and binding on the parties.

The arbitration and reconciliation proceedings should be conducted by three arbitrators, one each to be nominated by the contractor and the project manager, and the third to be named by the President of the Institution of Engineers, India. If either of the parties: fails to appoint its arbitrator within 60 days after receipt of notice from the other party invoking the arbitration clause, the President of the Institution of Engineers, India, should have the power at the request of either of the parties, to appoint the arbitrator. A certified copy of the said President making such an appointment should be furnished to both parties. The arbitration should be furnished to both the parties. The arbitration should be conducted in accordance with the provisions of the Indian Arbitration Act 1940, or any statutory modification thereof.

13
Internet Management

Most countries have a government body to run the telephones. In the United States a number of private companies are given licences by the Federal Communi-cations Commission (FCC) which oversees the arrangements. Such licensees are known as common carriers in the USA. The effect of the monopoly given to the licensees is that only the licensee can erect systems to carry signals such as telephone conversations or computer data. The licensees are usually called PTTs and this reflects the arrangements more common in the rest of the world rather than those in the USA. In economically advanced countries the PTTs have established a comprehensive network of telephone connections specially designed to carry speech. This network is called the Public Switched Telephone Network (PSTN). Even if the PTTs did not have a monopoly it would make sense to try to use this existing network for long-distance computer data communications, as all the cables are readily available.

The major problem with the PSTN is that it was designed before anyone even thought of computers. The telephone system is ideally suited to carry speech where a human being can concentrate on decoding the received sounds and try to understand them. There are a number of factors contributing to the PSTN being a poor medium for the type of signals.

Firstly, the equipment has a frequency range of 3003400 Hz, which is not very wide for high-speed data traffic. Secondly, the frequency range is not continuous; some frequencies may be used to operate equipment at exchanges, which explains how phone freaks in the USA can make calls by whistling into the telephone handset and causing the exchange to set up the call. If a data signal produces the wrong frequency the call may be disconnected, This problem is taken up in the section on modulation. Finally, to protect the exchange equipment from damage, no DC (direct current) is allowed through the local exchange. By looking at the type of wave produced by speech against a data signal, in figure, it can be seen that the speech signal never has the same voltage continuously, whereas the data signal consists almost entirely of a continuous voltage at one of two levels. The continuous voltage is the DC part which would be removed by the exchange. Removing the DC part would seriously distort a digital data signal.

The PTTs provide four solutions to these problems

1. Special equipment to convert digital data signals into audio signals which can easily be transmitted through the PSTN.

2. Private four-wire connections to the local exchange, then a fixed circuit to the remote site. This cuts out some parts of the PSTN that cause problems, but not all of them.

3. Direct links of high bandwidth most of the way between sites.

4. More recently, some PTTs now offer digital services directly to the customer, in multiples of 64K bps.

Each of these solutions represents increasing cost, but results in a higher information rate.

Solution 1—This involves the use of a MODEM (MOdulator DEModulator) on the ordinary telephone line, which converts the binary signals into audio signals and back again. Only one two-wire circuit is used, but the available bandwidth is divided to provide two channels, one in each direction. One medium — two channels.

Solution 2—When the bandwidth in solution I is insufficient, an extra two wires are added, and all the wires permanently connected. This means that some of the lost frequencies can be used.

Solution 3— Because of the way the telephone exchanges are connected together, solution 2 does not normally require special connections between exchanges. However when a high bandwidth connection is needed, say 50K bps, then some extra inter-exchange connections have to be made. If special connections are made right through, then modulation techniques may not be required.

A normal telephone handset is connected to the local exchange by two wires, which is sufficient for an electrical circuit. The subscriber can dial any other subscriber on the PSTN by passing through the local exchange. At the exchange, connections are established through a hierarchy of other exchanges. The exchanges are connected together by wideband channels which are subdivided into smaller channels; each small channel is sufficient for one call. When a call is connected the caller is allocated a series of small channels between the exchanges through to the subscriber that is being called. The subscriber can dial-up any other subscriber only by passing through the local exchange which sets up the connection.

The first solution above allows a subscriber to dial-up anywhere and then transfer data by using equipment that will pass data signals through the exchange. This equipment, a slow MODEM, does not have a very high data rate: 300 bps full duplex or 600/1200 bps half duplex. To improve the data rate the local exchange has to be bypassed, but this means the dialling facility is lost. Normally British Telecom provide a four-wire connection bypassing the exchange with a small channel permanently allocated through to the destination. This through connection is called a private circuit as it can only be used by the two subscribers, one at each end. Different MODEMs can be used on private circuits to provide a faster data rate on the better bandwidth. The noise levels on a private circuit are normally lower than on a dialled connection.

The third solution is used to provide a faster data rate. For this, direct connections bypassing several exchanges are made so that the required bandwidth and noise level can be obtained. All of these three methods use some of the existing telephone system. British Telecom have a special data transfer network which is designed for computer data, but uses as many of the existing methods as possible. This data network, known as PSS (Packet Switching Service).

The introduction of digital telephone exchanges will enable the provision of digital circuits direct to ordinary subscribers in the near future. The major piece of equipment needed to transfer data through the PSTN is the MODEM. Modulation is a technique that can enable information signals to be passed through a medium not really suited to them. The original, and still the major, use of modulation is in radio transmission. By using that analogy it is possible to see how modulation can be used to pass digital data signals, through a medium designed to carry voice signals. The human voice does not travel very far on its own, and if more than one person were to try broadcasting at the same time it would be very difficult to separate out the messages. The frequency range of an original signal is called the *base band;* for the human voice a base band of 300 to 3300 Hz is used on the telephone though a wider range is possible. When two people talk at once close together, they confuse listeners because they are both using the same frequency range, the base band. To transmit speech over long distances very much higher frequencies have to be used, and care must be taken to ensure that different frequencies are used for each different transmission. The original base band frequencies have to be increased and no two transmissions should use the same frequency range. The only problems now are how to increase the frequency of the base band signal without losing any information in the signal, and then how to recover the original signal so that the transmission can be heard in the base band. The problems are solved by modulation.

Modulation, very simply, involves superimposing the information signal on to a simple carrier signal in such a way that one, or more, components of the carrier are modified to carry the information.

The technique known as 'differential phase modulation'; there are four possible phase changes (0°, 90°, 180°, 270°) so each possibility represents two bits of data. A continuous frequency simple wave is used so that only the phase component changes; figure shows the phase changes. To be able to detect the phase changes a complete wave, or cycle, is used. In any one cycle there are four possible changes that could occur, so each cycle represents two bits of information. For instance, if we use a frequency of 1200 Hz we can have an information rate of 2400 bits per second. If a stream of zeros is transmitted, no phase change occurs during that time so the receiver and sender (modulator and demodulator) can become out of bit synchronisation. To overcome this an alternative differential, phase modulation encoding scheme is used on newer MODEMs. Notice that every code now has a phase change from the previous cycle, enabling the bit synchronisation to be maintained.

Quadrature amplitude modulation

This modulation technique combines changes in phase with different signal amplitudes. The data is encoded into a specific phase change and signal amplitude. For instance, if there are four possible phase changes and each one can be paired with one of two different signal amplitudes, then there are now eight different combinations giving three bits of information in each baud. This idea is being used on the faster MODEMs above 2000 bps to increase the information rate without increasing the signal frequency. The amplitude of a signal is more likely to be changed by noise than the frequency or phase, so it is not very suitable for use as a modulation parameter for data communication on its own.

The MODEM

This section describes three MODEMs to illustrate the practical arrangements made to use the PSTN for binary data using the modulation techniques previously described. The frequencies mentioned are standard CCITT recommendations; they are not the same as those used on some MODEMs in the US.

A Timesharing Terminal MODEM

A timesharing terminal is restricted by the typing and reading speed of a human being, and as such it has a relatively low data rate. The terminal also needs a full duplex connection. The MODEM used to provide the timesharing terminal with a connection to a remote computer divides the bandwidth on the PSTN into two parts to provide two channels. Normally this MODEM is connected to an ordinary telephone line, allowing the user to dial any computer he wishes, but of course this means passing through the local exchange using a two-wire circuit. The timesharing MODEM uses frequency shift keying to implement the two channels; the frequencies are

Channel 1	binary 0	1180 Hz
	binary 1	980 Hz
Channel 2	binary 0	1850 Hz
	binary 1	1650 Hz

Modulation techniques

This discussion is only related to techniques currently used in MODEMs on the PSTN.

Frequency shift keying (FSK)

The digital data is recoded as frequencies. The binary signal, such as V24 voltage levels, can only have two values, so only two frequencies are needed. This technique is used on slower MODEMs. In FSK the two values of voltage are converted into one of two different frequencies; this is done by a modulator. The electrical circuit *modulates* the input voltage to produce the output. The receiver performs the opposite process, it takes in the frequency signal and *demodulates* it to produce the original voltage signal. Using this technique on the telephone lines is fairly easy; the frequencies can be in the range 3003300 Hz so they are easily passed through the PSTN just as if they were speech signals. The major problem lies in the choice of frequencies, for which there are a number of constraints.

- The chosen frequencies have to be fairly far apart on the frequency range. That is, the cycle time for one should be measurably different from the other.
- In order to detect the actual frequency, half a wave, or cycle, must be transmitted. This means the input digital wave cannot change faster than twice the lowest frequency output from the modulator. Thus the lowest frequency used must be greater than the baud rate of the data signal.
- Certain frequency ranges on the telephone circuit are reserved for use by the switching equipment.
- The higher frequencies on a telephone circuit are attenuated.

Phase modulation

A newer technique that is used to provide a higher information rate whilst using the same frequencies involves coding the data into the phase of a wave. Remember that phase is measured between two waves; it can also be measured between the same signal wave at different points in time. If a wave has phase p_1, at time t_1, we can measure the phase at time t_2 relative to the phase at time t_1. It is very difficult to measure small changes in phase, so MODEMs mainly use large changes.

If channel 1 is used by one MODEM to transmit on a connection it must be used by the other MODEM for receiving, and vice versa. The timesharing MODEM can be used at either end of a connection, terminal or computer. A mechanism is needed to decide which channel should be used for transmitting and which channel for receiving at each end. By international agreement the following mechanism is used. When a MODEM is switched on, but before being connected for a data transfer, it is set to transmit on channel 1 and receive on channel 2. One of the MODEMs in a connection pair must change if data transfer is to proceed: by agreement this is the MODEM associated with the called computer or terminal. The normal situation is for the computer MODEM to be called by the user. Where a MODEM may be used to receive a call, such as at a computer site, the MODEM is arranged so that the incoming call switches the called MODEM over.

This type of MODEM arrangement is the most commonly used; it has been arranged so that a device known as an acoustic coupler can be used to replace the caller's MODEM. An acoustic coupler does not need installation directly into the telephone system. An acoustic coupler uses the same frequencies as the ordinary MODEM, but instead of placing them directly on to the telephone line it whistles into the mouthpiece of a telephone handset and takes the received signals from the earpiece. The acoustic coupler is a very cheap and convenient way of connecting a terminal to any telephone. Unfortunately, using the handset allows other noises from the room to interfere, so it is not as reliable as an installed MODEM.

Higher-speed asynchronous MODEM

Sometimes a faster rate of data transfer is required, say for printing messages, though the input may still be slow. The bandwidth available on the PSTN is not sufficient, given the noise, to allow a full duplex connection faster than 300 bps. However, research is continuing on modulation techniques to achieve faster data rates. A second type of MODEM is used to provide a higher speed in one direction, but a much lower speed in the other direction. Up to 600 bps can be guaranteed on the PSTN in the UK, passing through the exchange in one direction, whilst the return channel has only 75 bps. The return channel is called a 'supervisory channel' and is not expected to carry much data.

Up to 1200 bps may be obtained using a dial-up connection if the noise is very low, but a 'private circuit' will provide a guaranteed 1200 bps. If a connection of 600/ 1200 bps is needed in both directions, then two MODEMs are needed at each end. If the PSTN is used via a dial-up line only a half duplex connection is possible, because the circuit can only manage 600/1200 bps in one direction at a time. If a private four-wire circuit is used then a full duplex connection is possible. Because the direction of the main data transfer is fixed, one type of MODEM is used for sending on the fast channel (600/1200 bps) and receiving the supervisory channel (75 bps), whilst a different model performs the reverse operation at the other end. The 600/1200 MODEM uses frequency shift keying as the modulation technique, with the following frequencies.

Up to 600 bps	binary 1	1300 Hz
	binary 0	1700 Hz
Up to 1200 bp	binary 1	1300 Hz
	binary 0	2100 Hz

The receiving MODEM can always tell if the sender is using 600 or 1200 bps as the idle frequency is different for the two data rates. Note that the frequency range 13002 100 Hz fills the middle of the available frequencies on the PSTN. This means that the supervisory channel is relegated to using the low frequencies, and therefore has a low data rate. The frequencies for the supervisory channel are

binary 1 390 Hz
binary 0 450 Hz

The dial-up MODEM using 1200/75 bps is becoming popular for use with teletex services.

Fast synchronous MODEM

A popular speed for synchronous transfer is 2400 bps. This is provided by a group of MODEMs that use differential phase encoding to obtain the higher data rate within the frequency range of the PSTN. The connection pattern is the same as for the 600/1200 bps MODEM; a simplex connection is available on the two-wire circuit via the exchange with a sending and receiving MODEM. If a sending and receiving MODEM are provided at each end, a half duplex connection can be made by sharing the two-wire circuit. A full duplex connection can be obtained by using a private four-wire circuit. A 2400 bps MODEM is available for use over the PSTN using a dial-up line, but may be limited to 1200 bps by noise. The 2400 bps main data connection can be augmented by a 75 bps supervisory channel in the reverse direction, as in the 600/1200 MODEM. The differential phase encoding uses four possible phase changes on a 1200 Hz signal to obtain the 2400 bps data rate. MODEM speeds of 4800 bps and 9600 bps are also available, but only using private circuits.

Very high-speed MODEMs

For use in inter-computer communications, an arrangement is available for data rates between 40.8K bps and 50K bps over 48 kHz wide band circuits. Some of the larger exchanges in the PSTN are connected by very wide band circuits. These can be utilised for data transfer, although a private high-speed circuit may have bypassed several exchanges on the way to the large exchange. For the high-speed circuit four MODEMS are used, one pair to reach the large exchange, and another pair at the other end. Between the end pairs of MODEMs the data is passed in the base band frequency of the data signals on a special private circuit.

The main uses of MODEMs are listed below.

1. To connect a teletype or slow VDU (110/300 bps) to any computer in full duplex, by dialling through the PSTN.
2. To connect a faster terminal (600/1200 bps); but to get a full duplex connection a permanent private circuit is needed, so only one computer can be used.
3. To provide a synchronous connection using higher data rates (1200/2400, 4800, 9600 bps); but again a private circuit is needed for full duplex and full speed operation.
4. A very high data rate can be achieved, but at a higher cost, using base band signalling for part of the distance on a special circuit.

In terms of cost the acoustic coupler represents the cheapest modulation equipment. The cost then rises through the four types of MODEM described above. The higher the data rate, the higher the cost; however, the relationship is not linear. A 1200 bps service does not cost four times as much as a 300 bps service: it is more likely to cost only about twice as much to install, especially if a private wire is needed, but the rental may only be half as much again. Thus the problem of obtaining the optimum cost/service is not easy.

Digital Data Network

So far in this chapter we have been concerned with using an analogue PSTN that was designed to carry speech signals. The PTTs are currently investing very large sums of money in converting the existing analogue telephone equipment to use digital technology. This digital telephone service is known as ISDN; there is an international standard for this service which includes the interface for connecting private equipment. In the UK, British Telecom are installing equipment to provide the ISDN service in a number of new exchanges and gradually replacing old exchanges and equipment.

The new digital systems convert the analogue speech signal into digital signals using a technique called 'pulse code modulation'. The encoded speech signals are carried through the network as digital signals and converted back to their analogue form for the receiver. Using digital signals for transferring analogue information has a number of advantages.

a. The effects of noise are considerably reduced.

b. Digital multiplexing techniques can be used to make more efficient use of the trunk network.

c. The subscriber circuits can be switched by digital processors using information embedded in the encoded signal.

d. The very cheap VLSI technology developed for computers can be used, thus allowing considerable intelligence to be built into the telephone network.

A further advantage for users of computer communications is that the PSTN can be used directly, and therefore more efficiently. The digital information from the computer is passed directly into the digital network where it is transferred in its original form.

The basic ISDN connection consists of two 64K bps channels, primarily for speech, and an 8K bps channel for control. It is expected that the control channel will be available for data use; this will have a major impact on home computing and personal information services. If required, either or both of the 64K bps channels can be used for data as well.

Standards

The PTTs from all over the world work through a body called the CCITT. The CCITT is a part of the United Nations. It is concerned with enabling the individual PTTs from all over the world to cooperate and provide an international service. The CCITT is one of the most authoritative standards organisations in communications, so any standard adopted by the CCITT is very important.

All of the MODEMs discussed in this chapter conform to international standards for their operation, so it is possible for a terminal user in the UK to use a timesharing computer in Germany by dialling the computer. The German computer uses a German MODEM, while the UK user has a UK MODEM, but because they conform to the same standards they will be able to operate together. The CCITT have had a tremendous impact on computer communications by standardising various interfaces between computing equipment. The most important interface is that between the MODEM and the user's equipment. For instance, for asynchronous terminals the interface standard is called V24. The V24 standard defines all of the control and data signals used to enable the MODEM and the user's equipment to operate together and pass data, including the signal levels.

The result of the standards and their widespread adoption by equipment manufacturers means that any terminal having a V24 interface can be plugged into any MODEM, anywhere. Furthermore computer manu-facturers now use the V24 standard for connecting local terminals as well. This compatibility between equipment is very important in allowing various different types of equipment, from different manufacturers, to be interchangeable. Because the manufacturers in the United States dominate the computer industry the standards adopted by the United States often become the international standards of the CCITT. One of the US standards called RS232C is in fact the same as the V24 recommendation and preceded it. RS232C was the name given to the standard in the US before it became an international recommendation. Many US manufacturers still refer to it as RS232C rather than V24.

The CCITT have defined a standard interface for connecting communications equipment to a digital switched network: this standard is known as X.21. A second interface standard, known as X.21(bis), allows the same mechanisms but over the analogue PSTN, because there are still so few digital services available. The packet switched network access interface, X.25, is defined to used X.21 as its lowest level. However, X.21 (bis), or even V24, may be used where a digital network is not yet available.

Computer network technology

The communications techniques covered so far have been concerned with centralised systems. Terminal networks are all built around a central computer; similarly remote job entry stations are usually connected to a single computer. In the remaining chapters some of the problems and techniques of a network of inter-communicating devices are discussed. The devices at present connected to networks are usually general-purpose computers, with their own terminal networks. One reason for networking multiaccess computers, rather than terminals or smaller devices, is that these computer systems already existed when networking was proposed. A second reason is that the protocols used in computer networks are very complex so that only a large computer system would have sufficient spare computing power to implement them. However, terminals can be directly attached to a network, by using a dedicated computer. In the near future computer networks will become as widespread as the telephone network, and large scale integration will enable cheap processors to handle the protocols. The result will be the networking of every sort of computing device. The current trends indicate that powerful, single user, workstations will replace terminals for network use. The workstations will be directly connected to a local area network and use the resources of larger computers via the network.

This chapter is primarily concerned with the technology used to connect the computers and devices that make up a computer network. For the purposes of description the range of technology has been divided into three areas

1. wide area networks
2. Radio and satellite broadcast networks
3. Local networks

The network technology includes the techniques used to interconnect the computing devices and physically transfer information from one computing device to another.

Wide area networks

The term 'wide area network' is applied to a network that covers a large physical area, say a whole country or large area under one administration. Such an area may be worldwide where a multinational organisation owns the network. The basic communication media used are dedicated circuits, usually of about 50 kHz bandwidth. Where digital circuits are available the bandwidth would be 64K bps. The recent introduction of fibre optics in longdistance trunks has make link bandwidth of 2-3M bps available. Wide area networks will be using these links over the next few years. Examples of such networks are PSS, ARPANET, Tymnet, Telenet, etc.; details of some of these networks are given at the end of this section. For reasons explained in chapter 3, the physical circuits are usually provided by a PTT, although in the case of PSS the whole network is also run by the PTT.

Although 50 kHz bandwidth seems to be a lot compared with the 3 kHz nominal bandwidth of the voice telephone line, it is not very much when highspeed or large-volume transfers of information are required. Even at these high speeds the channel capacity is a resource that needs to be used efficiently.

It is now necessary to see how information can be transferred from one computer to any other on the network. The problem falls into two parts. The first is that of transferring information via a medium, such as a wire. The second part is concerned with addressing and routing. If there were only two computers on a network, then they could be connected by two channels, one for each direction, and whatever one computer transmitted the other would be bound to receive. When more computers are added, the bidirectional connection solution can be extended by having each computer connected to every other computer by a full duplex connection. To send a message to a particular computer the appropriate connection is selected; thus the routing of a message is carried out by the sender. Using a dedicated connection between every computer on the network is very expensive. If there are n computers on the network then $n(n-1)/2$ lines are needed, and have to be paid for! As a single computer would not normally be communicating with every other computer on the network at the same time, most of the lines would be unused in a fully connected network. Therefore to increase the utilisation of the connection circuits, their number is reduced, and switching is introduced within the network. There are three forms of switching that can be used in communications: circuit switching, message switching, and packet switching.

Circuit switching

Circuit switching is used on the PSTN to connect telephone subscribers. To use it for a computer network each computer would have a private circuit to a local exchange, and the exchanges would be connected to form a network.

Whenever two computers wish to exchange information, a physical path is established between them via the exchanges. The path is then disconnected when the connection is closed. The circuit has been ‚switched' by the exchanges. This method of connection is not used on established computer networks. The major disadvantages of circuit switching are

1. The cost of the equipment is very high, whereas the resulting circuit is not necessarily of high enough quality for computer communications.
2. The resulting circuit can only be used by the two computers on the call, thus the equipment is dedicated to the circuit. In particular the connection from the computer to the exchange is dedicated. To enable a single computer to communicate with more than one other computer at the same time, extra equipment is needed for each simultaneous call. If there are no connections all the equipment is idle but being paid for.
3. The time taken to set up the physical path can be very long in computer terms.

As high-speed connection using good-quality circuits is important for efficient computer networks, circuit switching is discounted in favour of the other methods. Circuit switching is used for some networks connecting computers-for instance, the Nordic Data Network.

Circuit switching has two advantages

1. Charges are made only for the time that a call is connected. If infrequent and short connections are all that is required, then circuit switching may be advantageous to the customer. It is expected that many slower devices, such as terminals, will be connected to national computer networks via the PSTN to gain this advantage.
2. Where a single device is used for long periods, such as a facsimile machine, circuit switching is economically advantageous. This is particularly true where digital facilities, such as X.21, are available.

The above discussion is based on the existing PSTN services offered by the PTTs. When the ISDN service is widely available, then it will be an attractive mechanism for some computer networks. Each host will be able to set up calls, use the 64K bps bandwidth, and quickly close the call, as required. The circuits will still carry packets for the end-to-end data transfer; but circuit switching will be the main link-switching mechanism. In the UK it is intended to bring all the PTT communications together into Integrated Digital Access (IDA). This will combine ISDN, X.25 networking and special digital services into a common access interface.

Message switching

To overcome problems in setting up and taking down physical circuits via exchanges, computer networks use permanent circuits and switch the data, A partially connected network is used in which each computer has a permanent circuit to a number of its neighbours, but not to all computers on the network. An example will illustrate the basic operation of *information switching* where the unit of information is a message. If the computer at A wishes to send a message to B, the message must pass through either D or C. The points on the network are called *nodes. A will* address the message to B by placing the address of B in the message header. The message and address are then sent on the circuit to D. At D the node inspects the address; if the address is 'D' the message is given to the computer; if the address is not D the message is forwarded on a circuit that the node believes will enable the message to be delivered, In this case D will forward the message to B. Thus the node at D has switched the message on to the appropriate output circuit. In this example two major characteristics of a computer network can be seen.

Addressing

The message is addressed to a remote destination and sent on the next stage of its route.

Store and Forward

Each message is received into the node storage so that it can be processed as a whole unit. Usually an error check is carried out and the whole message has to be received before this can be completed. The message is then inspected for routing information so that the node can decide which output circuit to use to forward the message.

The nodes have been introduced in the network to carry out the functions of routing and store and forward, so the host computer is separated from the network operation as much as possible. The 'hosts' are the user computers which wish to use the network. Often a number of hosts will be attached to a single node.

The node computers are usually minicomputers chosen for their ability to respond in real time to the communications devices. Each node receives incoming messages and stores them. When a complete message has been received the destination address is inspected so that the message can be placed on the output queue of a circuit to forward the message. If the message is for a host attached to the node, the output circuit will be the one connected to the host. If the message is for a distant host the node must forward the message to another node on the route to the distant host. While the message is in the node store, waiting to be processed or waiting for output, it is, of course, being delayed. The link into any one node may be used to carry messages from several different computers, as may the connection between the node and host. The physical equipment involved is used more efficiently than in circuit switching as a result of this multiplexing. Message multiplexing is the most important advantage of message and packet switching computer networks.

To distinguish between message and packet switching it is necessary to understand what a message is. This has already been introduced in earlier chapters, but a more detailed discussion is given here. The easiest way of defining a message is to say that it is a unit of information which is exchanged by users of a network. This means the characteristics of a message are only dependent on the user or the application. A message could be a few bits or a file, or even a whole database. In a message-switching network the whole message is passed from one node to another as a complete entity. Compared with circuit switching, a message-switching network has the following characteristics.

1. Any computer can communicate with any other computer without having a direct physical connection.
2. Any computer can communicate with several others using the same equipment by multiplexing messages.
3. There is no delay arising from circuit set up, but messages are delayed when they pass through a node *enroute.*

The messages can be transferred between nodes, and nodes and hosts, using an *ARQ* protocol. Characteristic 3 implies that there is no delay arising from the use of a network other than the store and forward operation of the nodes. This is true in some networks using pure datagram techniques. However, in most networks the internode protocol used within the network introduces some delays. Any network using a virtual circuit protocol, at any level, will introduce a delay when the message or packet is given to the network. In many networks the local node negotiates for resources within the network before actually forwarding a message. This is true of an X.25 network when the call is first set up, and is true of every message on the ARPA network.

A user of a message-switching network will pass the network a message, together with a destination address, and the user will receive messages as single units.

Advantages and disadvantages

The advantages of message switching, over circuit switching are

- The sender may dispatch the message when convenient, even if the receiver is not ready, as the network will store the message for delivery, However, if network resources run out, an undelivered message may be deleted and thus lost; this depends on the network protocols.
- Computers can exchange information at different speeds, as the network will buffer the message.
- Broadcasting of a message may be possible.
- Equipment is used more efficiently.
- Messages may be handled by priority.

Each message is treated as a single unit. However, there are also some disadvantages.

- A very long message will hold up other, perhaps more urgent, messages as it monopolises a circuit for the duration of its transmission.
- As a message may be very large, the node computer may not have enough memory to store it before forwarding it; in this case the message is lost. Further, this message will never be delivered as the network does not have the required resources.
- A very large message may monopolise the storage of a node, because it cannot be delivered, so that other messages cannot be received by this node.

Packet switching

The disadvantages of message switching relate to the possible occurrence of *large* messages, where the exact value of 'large' will depend on the network. If a network could be certain of only handling small messages, the disadvantages would disappear. The transfer of messages is a user requirement, so a network that meets user needs must be able to handle very large messages as well as small messages. The solution to these two conflicting requirements is to break the user's message into small *packets* for transfer through the network and have the packets reassembled into the message by the receiver. Note that the message header is included as the data in the first packet and that each packet has its own header. This refinement produces packet switching, which is the most widely used switching technique for computer networks.

The physical organisation of a packet-switching network is the same as for message switching. The network is a partially connected mesh of nodes. For practical reasons most wide area networks use special node computers to perform the switching, with the user computers being attached to the nodes. The term 'host' is now widely used to mean a user computer system attached to a network. The nodes are part of the network, so the hosts use a well-defined interface for accessing the node to enable data transfer across the network. By using a node separated from the host, all of the packet-switching functions, such as storage and routing, are removed from the host. However, the host still needs considerable software to handle the protocols used to access the node and to transfer data to other computers on the network.

The advantages that packet switching has over message switching are

- The small maximum packet size makes storage allocation and management easier in the switching nodes, sufficiently so for minicomputers to be used.
- The multiplexing of packets enables several messages to be interleaved on one circuit, reducing the delay seen by the user.
- The total transmission time through the network is reduced. Figure shows a message passing from A to B which would normally require 6k + d seconds to reach B, where 3k is the transmission time of the whole message on one link and d is the node delay. If the message is broken into three packets, each taking k seconds to transmit, the whole message arrives at B in 4k + d seconds. The difference increases with the number of links traversed and the size of the message.

It would appear that packet switching solves all the problems of wide area network organisation: it uses fixed highspeed lines and minicomputers for nodes; it is also more efficient and responsive than message switching. However, although packet switching is a better technique with which to implement a computer network, users still want to transfer messages. Packet switching introduces another layer of complexity and translation between the user and the physical network transporting the bits. Fortunately, the cost of processing is falling so the extra cost is outweighed by the practical advantages. A second cost, not so easily overcome, is that each packet will have its own overheads as well as those used by each message; this will reduce the efficiency of the physical circuits. The conclusion drawn from consideration of these three switching techniques is that packet switching, especially used in a partially connected mesh of nodes with wideband circuits, is currently the best technique for wide area computer networks. Packet switching is also used in other network technologies, rather than message switching, for the same reasons. Wide area networks have been in existence since the early 1970s. The best known example is the ARPA network in the United States. This network was established by a government research agency to link together computer centres that had contracts for government research so that research workers could share the available computing resources. The network itself also forms part of a research project to evaluate the feasibility of a large computer network, and to investigate techniques that could be used in such a network. The ARPA network has been very successful in showing that the concept of resource sharing by use of a network is feasible. One of the most noticeable advantages that the network has introduced is a mail facility. This allows each user with access to a computer on the network to exchange mail with all the other network users. The mail facility is probably one of the main sources of traffic on the ARPA network and has certainly improved the amount of communication between researchers at different sites.

The basic techniques used within the ARPA network have been influenced by the defence aspects of the research, particularly the need for a fast response and resilience to the failure of any part. The network consists of a mesh of partially connected nodes called Interface Message Processors (IMPs). Each IMP can have up to eight hosts connected to it and may be connected to up to eight other IMPs. Each IMP accepts messages from the hosts of up to 8K bits in length. The IMP breaks the message into IK bit packets which are then forwarded through the network of IMPs to the IMP attached to the destination host. This destination IMP reassembles the message before delivering it to the destination host. If a host wishes to send a message of more than 8K bits it must break the message up itself, into 8K packets, and the destination host must reassemble the message from the 8K packets. Thus the translation between messages and packets takes place at two levels. Within the network of IMPs, packets (1K) are sent individually along whichever route is best at the time, so that packets in a single message may use different routes and may arrive at the destination IMP out of sequence. The destination IMP has to reassemble the message from the packets as they arrive. However, messages passed from the host to the IMP are delivered in the same sequence to the destination host. The technology developed for the ARPANET is now used in a number of commercial wide area networks all over the world.

The British Telecom network PSS (Packet Switching Stream) is an example of a network provided by a PTT as a public service. The design requirements for such a network are different from those of the ARPA network so they have resulted in a network with different characteristics. The network topology consists of a number of *exchanges* which are also partially connected. Each exchange is connected to a number of host computers in its area. The exchanges contain the node computers, the number of node computers in each exchange depending on the number of hosts attached to the exchange. The hosts use an access protocol called X.25 to enable them to make virtual calls to other hosts. A host will give the local exchange the destination address of the host with which it wishes to communicate. The network will route the call to the destination exchange which will then complete the call to the destination host. The call is represented by information kept at all the exchanges on the route. The information is then used to forward the packets transferred on the call. Once the call has been established the hosts may exchange their own information. This is very similar to circuit switching on the PSTN although it is provided using packet-switching techniques. The PSS network techniques are different from those on the ARPA network, where each message is addressed and transferred separately. The hosts can use a single link to the PSS exchange to carry a number of virtual calls to other hosts, thus the link is used to multiplex the calls.

Radio and satellite broadcast networks

These networks differ from wide area networks in the way in which the channel is used for communication between users. Broadcast networks use a channel to which all the users are connected, so all the users receive any transmission made on the channel. At present the two types of channel in use are local radio, covering up to a few hundred kilometres, and satellite channels which are used to span very large distances.

Networks using radio and satellite channels have special problems because noise in the channel can cause errors. There is also the problem of allocating the channel for transmission. The first operational broadcast computer network was built at the University of Hawaii using local radio transmission; many of the techniques and much of the terminology derive from this first network.

Every node receives all packets transmitted on the broadcast channel. When the received packet is complete, the node checks the packet for errors and then checks the destination address. If the address of the receiver matches the packet destination address, it is accepted; otherwise it is discarded. The problems particular to a broadcast network occur in the allocation of the channel to a node for transmitting a packet. Different solutions are used for radio and satellite links. Each node is only able to communicate with each other node via the common channel, so some scheme is needed to coordinate transmission. The schemes that have been proposed and used are discussed here in increasing complexity and are compared for channel efficiency.

The simplest transmission technique is called *pure aloha;* when a node has a packet to transmit it does so immediately. Having transmitted the packet, the node waits for an acknowledgement. This is therefore a positive acknowledgement protocol. If an acknowled-gement is not received within a time out period, the packet is assumed lost. Transmission collisions, which occur when two nodes transmit at the same time and thus interfere with each other's transmission, are detected by the time out mechanism. When a collision is detected, each node waits a period of time of random length before retransmitting the packet to of traffic increases, the rate of collision will increase and more re-transmissions will be needed. As the older packets are re-transmitted, more stations will have newer packets to transmit, causing more collisions, etc. Analysis has shown that a pure aloha scheme can only use a maximum of about 18% of the channel bandwidth. A node may transmit at any time, thus the maximum length of time the channel is wasted as a result of a collision is 2t, where t is the transmission time for one packet. The 2t period is the worst case, where one node begins transmitting just before the previous transmission is complete.

An improvement on pure aloha is *slotted aloha* in which the transmission channel time is divided into time slots of *t.* Each node is then only allowed to begin transmitting a packet at the start of a time slot. The nodes are kept in synchronisation by a time signal on the channel. Now if a collision occurs only one slot *is* wasted, so the maximum efficiency rises to about 34% of the channel capacity. When a collision is detected, a transmitter must wait for a random number of time slots before retransmitting. When the traffic is light the wait can be quite short, but as the traffic load increases the waiting period should be increased.

From the aloha schemes it can be seen that it is collisions that cause problems, so a collision avoidance mechanism should improve efficiency. In packet radio networks a scheme known as Carrier Sense Multiple Access (CSMA) is used. When a node is transmitting all other nodes can receive the transmission, so they can avoid a collision by not transmitting themselves until the channel is free. A transmission is detected by the presence of the carrier signal in the medium. When a node has a packet to transmit it looks for the carrier; if there is no carrier the packet is transmitted. If the carrier is detected the node waits for a random length delay and tries again.

Even in a radio broadcast the signal from a transmitter takes a finite amount of time to reach all the receivers in the network. When two nodes find the channel free, they may both begin transmission because neither has heard the other one. This case is most likely to happen when two stations are waiting for the channel to become free. The length of time it takes to propagate the signal to all receivers is the time band in which collisions may occur, but it is less than the total packet transmission time. As with the aloha technique, the CSMA technique can be improved by dividing the channel time into slots and only allowing the transmission of packets to begin at the start of a time slot. The slot length is set to the propagation delay, not the packet transmission time.

The CSMA technique has been further refined by modifying the action of the node when the channel is busy. When the node samples the channel again and finds it free, it transmits its packet with a probability p, or waits for a further delay of random length, with a probability (1-p). This is called persistent CSMA or p-persistent transmission. If p is high then the delay before transmission occurs is lower, but the possibility of collision increases if two stations are waiting for another station to finish. In persistent CSMA a trade off is made between channel efficiency and delay with the value of p. Channel efficiencies of about 80% may be achieved using these techniques. Packet radio networks have a small delay between the start of a transmission and the detection of the transmission by all stations on the network. On a satellite broadcast network there is a very long delay between transmission and receiving, of the order of a quarter of a second. A satellite network operates by each transmitter sending its signal to the satellite. The satellite then broadcasts the signal to all of the Earth stations, which may be spread over a very large area. One satellite system currently used for packet switching connects nodes in England, Norway and North America using a satellite in stationary orbit over the North Atlantic. A different channel allocation technique is used on satellite broadcast networks because of the long propagation delay.

This satellite channel allocation technique involves making reservations for the future use of slots in the channel. The channel is divided into frames consisting of a number of reservation slots and a number of packet slots. Each reservation slot represents a packet slot in the second part of the frame. All ground stations are synchronised to the frame timing by the satellite transmission. During the first part of the frame the ground stations reserve slots for the packets they have ready by transmitting a marker during the reservation slot time. When the reservation slot is heard on the satellite down channel, the ground station inspects the slot to see if it contains its own marker. If so it can transmit a packet in the corresponding packet slot in the second part of the frame. This scheme uses some of the channel capacity to avoid the collisions which could reduce the network to a pure aloha scheme.

Obviously more than one ground station may attempt to reserve a particular packet slot by transmitting during the reservation slot time. There are a number of algorithms to overcome this, including allocating some slots to busy stations. Thus if a station successfully obtained a packet slot in the last frame, the same slot is allocated to that station in the next frame without competition. If an allocated slot is not used then the slot is open for competition in the following frame. Usually there are some slots that all stations can compete for in every frame. Another mechanism involves using a central allocation station to which each station sends its requirements and the central station allocates the slots. This has two disadvantages: firstly, the central station becomes a weakness in the network reliability, and secondly, the delay between requesting an allocation and receiving the allocation may be of the order of 1 or 2 seconds before the packet can be transmitted. A chapter in the book by Kuo is dedicated to broadcast satellite protocols.

Local area networks

A local, or private, network is a communication system connecting computers in a small geographical area, say less than a few kilometres between the furthest points. The network is wholly owned and run by one administration. There are currently two basic types of technology used on such a network: these are cable, or bus, technology and ring technology.

Whereas wide area networks and satellite networks use nodes to separate the internal network switching from the user hosts, local networks are meant to be as cheap as possible and so the separate node computer is omitted. In both local network technologies all the computers are directly attached to the transmission medium by a special interface, and all the interfaces receive all the packets. The difference between a ring and a bus system is the way in which the channel is allocated. Local networks are designed for use in local computing by allowing the interconnection of very small computers, such as microprocessors, personal workstations and peripheral devices. If the local network is to be useful, the cost of the computer interfaces into the network channel has to be low compared with the cost of the computer or peripheral, and microprocessors are very cheap in computer terms. A widely forecast use of local networks is connecting word processors within a set of offices for the exchange of information and electronic mail. The cost constraints, the limited processing power of the small computers and the protocols used on a local network are different from those used in wide area networks. A local network usually has a very high bandwidth channel of between I and 10 MHz and a very low error rate say one bit in several million might be corrupted. These characteristics permit the use of simple protocols. The lowest level protocol for using the transmission medium is built into the computer interface.

Cable or bus networks

These networks usually use a length of coaxial cable, or an existing cable such as that used for closed circuit television (CCTV). The medium is used in a broadcast fashion, exactly as described in the previous section on broadcast networks. The channel allocation techniques vary slightly on the theme of the CSMA techniques, or on a centralised slot allocation. The most popular broadcast local network is the Ethernet system developed by Xerox. The Ethernet principles can be used on any broadcast medium: radio, telephone lines, coaxial cable and optical fibres have all been used successfully. The Ethernet uses a base band signal, rather than a modulated signal, to simplify the broadcast transmitter and receiver, with a modified CSMA channel access technique. To obtain the maximum efficiency from the broadcast medium an Ethernet transmitter can listen to its own broadcast to detect a collision and abort the transmission. This extra complexity is known as CSMACD (CD = collision detection) or listen-while-talk. As with the other CSMA techniques a station does not begin transmitting until the broadcast medium is free. Two stations waiting for another station to finish a transmission will begin transmitting together, and thus interfere with each other. The collision is detected by the stations and they both abort the transmission immediately. To enforce the protocol a station that aborts a transfer then jams the ether. After a collision each station waits for a random time before trying again.

The CSMA-CD technique enables the Ethernet system to obtain up to 95% of the broadcast channel bandwidth. The improvement in performance over ordinary CSMA is due to the stopping of transmission as soon as a collision is detected. Note that no slots are used so a network-wide timing signal is not required. The transceiver handles all of the CSMACD access, including the retries and delay calculation which is varied with the traffic load. Thus only complete, and checked, packets are passed up to the station interface and only one request is made for a packet to be sent. The checksum generation and checking are carried out within the hardware: bad packets are discarded. A time out mechanism is used to retransmit packets that may have been lost as a result of errors.

Ring networks

The ring technique originated in the USA. The idea was then developed in parallel at Cambridge University in the UK and at two research centres in the USA. The version developed at Cambridge is known as the Cambridge ring in the UK. The computer interface is divided into two parts: the repeater and the interface proper. A ring uses a twisted pair of wires as the transmission medium. However, to improve reliability, the repeater is powered from the ring and electrically isolated from the computer interface, so four wires are used to connect the repeaters. The four wires are used as two pairs for signalling and carry sufficient power for the repeaters. In this way the computer can be switched off and removed from the ring without switching off the repeater. With the ring the medium is terminated at each station, whereas in the cable network it is not. Each station is represented by a repeater, several of which are then connected together into a ring. The repeater is a simple device containing a shift register and some logic to detect certain conditions in the information being passed around the ring. The repeater normally passes any information received on to the next repeater, so transmission only occurs in one direction. When a station transmits data, the repeater transmits the information from the station instead of the information received from the previous repeater.

Slotted ring

There are slight differences in the channel allocation mechanism used in the Cambridge ring and in those rings developed in the USA. In the Cambridge ring a fixed-size mini-packet is used which constantly circulates in the ring, and a special station called a monitor is used to ~generate and maintain the mini-packet and provide the power for the repeaters. In the American versions a variable-size packet is used which may be lost and regenerated as required by each repeater. The current format of the Cambridge mini-packet. Note that only 16 bits of information are carried in a ring mini-packet whereas the broadcast network packet may contain several hundred bytes. The assembly of information into a block has to be done by the computer. The monitor station also provides a buffer if the ring is not physically long enough to hold a complete mini-packet. The monitor performs a check on the mini-packet each time it passes to ensure that it is intact, and to replace it if not. The monitor is an obvious weakness in the Cambridge ring design so far as reliability is concerned; however, experience so far has shown that monitor failures are rare. The advantage of the monitor is that the repeaters can be very simple as well as cheap, which is the purpose of a local network.

To use the ring to send a packet of information, the station will wait until an empty mini-packet is detected by the repeater. When the full/empty bit in the mini-packet passes the repeater it is set to one. If the packet was already full no change has been made to the bit; if the packet was empty (full/empty bit = 0) the mini-packet is now reserved by this station, The repeater will use this mini-packet if the full/empty bit was received as 0. The addresses of the source and destination stations are placed in the address fields followed by the next 16 bits of the information that the station wishes to send; these are placed in the data field from the station buffer. The reserved mini-packet then travels round to all the other stations on the ring. Each station has a source select register in which an address is placed. If the source address in a mini-packet matches the contents of the source select register, and the destination address matches the station address, the data field is copied into the station receive buffer and the accept status is set at the end of the packet. If the packet is refused, or the destination station is busy, the destination repeater will set the appropriate value in the status bits at the end of the mini-packet. No other change is made by the receiving repeater, and all other repeaters will pass on the mini-packet unchanged. Special values which can be used in the source select register are: all ones, which means accept any source station address, and all zeros, which means do not accept the data from any mini-packets.

When the mini-packet returns to the sending station the full/empty bit is reset to 0 and the status bits are checked to see if the information was accepted. As an error check, the station also reads back the 16 data bits and checks them against the data in its buffer. Having reset the full/empty bit, the station must now wait for another empty mini-packet before it can send the next 16 bits of information. In this way the now empty packet becomes available to successive stations around the ring and the packet slot is allocated in a round robin fashion.

The variable nature of packet traffic in a local network makes it difficult to design a system that will provide a very fast response, especially when there is little traffic, and yet not become overloaded or unfair when the traffic becomes heavy. The broadcast techniques provide a low delay, especially in low-volume traffic, as the transmitter can usually send a packet as soon as one is available. However, as the volume of traffic increases, the broadcast system suffers from collisions and longer delays which can eventually lead to an unstable situation. In the slotted ring the channel is allocated by means of a round robin mechanism so collisions never occur, and during a burst of traffic each station is able to continue transmitting with only a larger delay. During periods of low traffic volume the ring does introduce a delay while a station waits for the empty packet to come round.

Proponents of both systems argue that because of the very high bandwidth available on the channel, and the low processing power of the computers attached to the local network, the volume of traffic is nearly always low in a broadcast network and the delay is negligible in a ring.

Token Ring

The token ring attempts to provide the advantages of broadcast access in low-volume traffic periods, with the inherent sharing of the slotted ring during high-volume traffic periods. The physical topology of the ring is the same, but instead of a circulating mini-packet there is a circulating token. Any host requiring access to the ring waits for the token to arrive; it then changes the token to indicate that a packet is following. The modified token is then followed immediately by the data packet, which can be of any size up to some system maximum. All hosts detect the modified token and examine the packet to see if it is addressed to them; if it is the packet is copied off the ring. The receiving host still sends the packet on though, so the data packet goes all the way round the ring to the sender. The sender takes the packet off the ring. Normally the sender receives the front of the data packet before it has finished transmitting the rest of the packet, owing to the short length of the ring. When the receiver detects the end of the data packet it marks its status by changing the last few bits, as in the Cambridge ring mini-packet; thus the sender knows if the packet was accepted or not. Immediately the sender has finished the packet it puts a token on the ring so another host may have a go.

The token ring is a simple idea, but it is more complex than the Cambridge ring and the interfaces are more expensive. The initialise sequence which is required to start the ring is quite complex as the token has to be put on the ring to start data transfer; of course there can only be one token. The mechanisms for detecting duplicate tokens and lost tokens, without the use of a monitor station, add to the cost of the computer interfaces. IBM carried out extensive tests and simulations of all the local area network technologies, and decided that the token ring was the best available. The company now intends to use the token ring as the basis of its local area network products.

The protocols used in a computer network are the mechanisms by which the hosts exchange information over physical distances. In the OSI model, the network layer is the primary layer for host-to-host communication. The network layer makes use of services from the link and physical layers; it also provides an end-to-end service to the transport layer. The network layer can utilise a number of physical networks to provide its services. The two services provided by the network layer are the connectionless services, and the connection-orientated service. X.25 protocol is important as it is being used on all public packet-switched networks operated by the PTTs. The X.25 protocol defines the necessary operation of layers one, two and three.

The X.25 protocol

Within any layer, a connection orientated protocol has two common tasks: error control and flow control. Error control is concerned with detecting, and correcting, errors that may have occurred in the information being transferred. Flow control is concerned with managing the resources of bandwidth and storage so that no single user can monopolise these resources, and the two endpoints are kept in step with each other. This is usually achieved by keeping the sending and receiving rates of information transfer approximately in step. The X.25 protocol covers the three lower layers of the protocol hierarchy. X.25 is defined as an access protocol, which means that it is used between a host and a node (in most X.25 networks the nodes are called 'exchanges') for the host to access the network so that communication between remote hosts is possible. The X.25 protocol has been adopted by the CCITT as a standard, which means that nearly all future networks will use it. The latest version of X.25 will be adopted by ISO as an international standard.

As well as describing the particulars of X.25, the principles of error and flow control will be shown and the mechanisms used to implement them in each layer explained. The description of level 2 is very detailed, as this is the first consequential level to be met in the bottom-up approach. The discussion of level 2 examines a number of problems which occur at many other protocol layers. For instance, the mechanisms used at level 3 for flow control and protocol synchronisation are very similar to those of level 2, so less detail is given in the level 3 explanation and references are made to the level 2 mechanisms. In the X.25 parlance a host is called a DTE (Data Terminating Equipment) and a node is called a DCE (Data Communications Equipment). X.25 provides a standard mechanism for a DTE to access and use a DCE to transport data across a network to a remote DTE via its remote DCE. The protocol used between the DCEs within the network does not have to be X.25, but would probably be very close to it. X.25 is a virtual call (connection-orientated) protocol.

X.25 level 1--the pPhysical circuit

This level provides the physical communication by specifying the electrical signals, voltages, plug shape and pin assignment that the DTE needs to connect physically to the DCE. This would be the normal arrangement, as the supplier of the network (usually the PTT) will provide the MODEM link to the node (DCE) from the user's premises. The actual specification of level I is contained in the CCITT X.21 recommendation. For practical purposes the user will order a computer interface to this standard which plugs straight into the computer at one end and into the MODEM at the other. The user will normally also be able to buy the software necessary to handle the interface.

As the level 1 hardware is bought as a ready-made unit, no further discussion of it is necessary. The important information needed about level 1 is the type of interface it presents to level 2, and the functions it must perform. The level 1 will provide transport for a bit stream from the DTE to a (remote) DCE. The level 2 will present the level 1 with the bits which are then delivered to a level 2 at the DCE. The hardware of level 1 will also indicate if the physical circuit is working correctly, that is whether the MODEMs are switched on and able to exchange synchronised data. So the interface has two parts

1. the sending and receiving of a serial bit stream
2. the control signals indicating the status of the physical circuit.

X.25 level 2 -- link level

The purpose of level 2 is to control the physical link between the two ends of the level 1 circuit to provide a reliable transfer of information for level 3 between the DTE and DCE. X.25 level 2 uses a link control protocol based on the ISO HDLC (Higher Data Link Control) protocol. The advantages of using an existing protocol are greater than those to be gained from designing a new one. For instance, a new protocol would have to be adopted by a large number of people wishing to communicate; adoption of the protocol would then require a lot of effort. Other link protocols have been designed: IBM use one called SDLC (Synchronous Data Link Control) on their SNA network, which is not dissimilar to HDLC; DEC have their own as well.

Information is passed from level 2 to level 1 in blocks called 'frames'. The use of frames enables easier management of storage and error control. Each frame consists of some protocol information added by level 2, and possibly an information packet from level 3. 1 will use the convention of calling level 2 blocks frames and level 3 blocks *packets. The* functions performed by level 2 are

1. To establish the link connection to a level 2 at a remote site.
2. To transfer packets for level 3 securely, and in sequence.
3. To disconnect the link without loss of level 3 information.

To carry out these functions, the X. 25 level 2 uses three types of frame format. The uses of each format are shown in the next section, but first the fields in the frames are detailed

Flag field

This is a unique 8 bit pattern (01111110) which marks the beginning and end of each frame. The use of the flag as a delimiter presents a problem: to ensure that the end of the frame is correctly interpreted by the receiver, the flag pattern must not appear anywhere within the data in the frame. This means that the frame must be transparent to the hardware looking for a flag to mark the beginning or ending of a frame. The problem of transparency occurs in all link level protocols as they all use special bit patterns for synchronisation and for marking various parts of the frame. In X. 25 level 2 the flag is used as the level 1 synchronisation character (see chapter 2 on synchronous character frames). To ensure that the flag pattern does not occur within the frame, X.25 uses a technique called 'bit stuffing'. The bit stuffing technique involves the sender in inspecting the frame contents prior to transfer to level 1. Whenever a sequence of five Is occurs a 0 is inserted.

Notice that the 0 is inserted regardless of the value of the sixth bit. Bit stuffing in this way is easily implemented by hardware and only increases the length of the frame by 1 bit for every sequence of five Is. As the receiving hardware scans the incoming frame, a 0 following a sequence of five Is is removed. If the sequence of five Is is followed by a further 1, then the flag may have been found. The seventh bit is then inspected: if it is a 0 the flag has been found (01111110), whereas if the seventh bit is another 1 (01111111) then the frame is in error. Thus a sequence of seven Is is used to abort the frame.

There are other ways of providing transparency, such as using escape characters, or bit counts, but none is quite so efficient and flexible as bit stuffing.

Address field

This is really redundant in a point-to-point link. The intention in the HDLC protocol was to use this as an address for multipoint lines, but the present X. 25 recommendation does not include multipoint lines. However, X.25 uses the field as an additional check in the protocol, as well as having the field ready should multipoint lines be considered in the future. The addresses used in this field allow commands and responses to be separated. The level 2 link can be thought of as two separate channels.

Channel A for transferring data from the network (DCE) to the host (DTE) and

Channel B for transferring data from the host (DTE) to the network (DCE).

Any frames relating to information flow from the DCE to the DTE carry the address A (11000000) including any frames from the DTE to the DCE relating to information transfer from the network to the host; similarly for channel B (10000000). To help separate the channels, frames are divided into two classes: *commands* and *responses,* Commands always flow in the direction of information on a channel; responses flow in the opposite direction. Responses are obviously the receiver's replies to various commands.

Command field

This 8 bit pattern determines the type of the frame, as well as being used for sequence numbering and acknowledgement. The command field has a different meaning for the three types of frame (information, supervisory, unnumbered). A 0 in bit 1 indicates that this is an information frame. An information frame is the only type that carries a level 3 packet in the information field. Bits 2, 3 and 4 contain the sequence number of this frame, bits 6, 7 and 8 contain the acknowledgement number. The sequence number and acknowledgement number are used in the ARQ techniques explained in chapter 6 for error correction and flow control. Level 2 uses a stop-go flow control. Bit

5 is the poll/final (P/F) bit. This is set in a command frame as a poll bit and the receiver will set the final bit in any response frame that is a reply to a command frame with the poll bit set. The use of the poll/final bit enables the sender of a command to recognise the corresponding response frame. Bits 1 and 2 set to 10 indicate a supervisory frame. Bits 3 and 4 indicate which type of supervisory frame, Supervisory frames are not given sequence numbers as they do not contain any level 3 information, but they may be used to acknowledge information frames and so bits 6, 7 and 8 contain an acknowledgement number. Bit 5 is the poll/final bit which is the same as before.

The command field format for the *unnumbered frame,* so called because it contains neither sequence number nor acknowledgement number. Bits 1 and 2 set to 11 indicate an unnumbered frame and bit 5 is the poll/final bit. The remainder of the bits are used to indicate the type of unnumbered frame.

Information field

This field only occurs in information frames; it is the position in the frame where the whole level 3 packet is placed. The other level 2 fields provide an envelope for the level 3 packet during the level 2 transfer.

Frame check sequence

The FCS field is found by counting 16 bits back from the terminating flag. This is a 16 bit field to contain the CRC remainder used in error checking. The remainder is calculated using the CCITT recommended generating polynomial of $X^{16} + X^{12} + X^5 + 1$.

It is interesting to note that all the fields of the X.25 level 2 header and the CRC are multiples of 8 bits. This makes transmission easier, because the 8 bit byte is the lowest common multiple of most modern computer word sizes, as well as being the character frame size for synchronous transfer. However the information field and the CRC may be increased by bit stuffing for level 1 transmission.

Operation of X.25 level 2

This section describes the semantics of level 2, with the various commands and responses being explained in context. The level 2 at the DTE (host) end of the connection performs the protocol functions with the level 2 at the DCE, using the HDLC protocol over the level 1 physical connection.

Establishing the link connection

An earlier specification of the X.25 protocol included a lever 2 initialisation procedure called LAP (Link Access Protocol) This procedure has been superseded by a simpler *balanced* procedure called LAPB. The LAPB method of initialisation sets up both channels simultaneously.

Data transfer

Level 2 should provide a sequenced, error-free transport of lever 3 packers from the

DTE to the DCE and vice versa. As only 3 bits are allowed for the sequence number and acknowledgement number in the C field, the maximum window size is 7. In X. 25 the link level window size is fixed when the subscriber first applies to use the network. The operation of the data transfer allows the use of limited buffers at the sender (no more than 7) and no requirement for extra buffers to handle out-of-sequence frames at the receiver. The cost of the small buffer requirement is extra channel capacity taken up with retransmission. The use of X.25 to connect hosts to networks would normally involve a fairly high-speed circuit between the DTE and DCE The limiting factor in performance is more likely to be the network and level 3, so a superefficient level 2 is not necessary; thus simpler techniques, such as Go-Back-N, can be used.

The transfer of sequenced frames of information is straightforward but what makes the operation complex (and this applies to every protocol) is the handling of exceptions and errors. There are two basic errors that can occur during data transfer.

1. The frame check sequence indicates an error in the packet.
2. The packet appears to contain no transmission errors but the contents of the A and C fields are not those expected.

In case 1 above the frame is thrown away and no further action is taken by the receiver. Obviously when a frame is discarded the next frame received is not the one expected. In case 2 there are a number of inconsistencies that can be classed as errors. The most common would be a sequence error where a previous packet had been lost or discarded. To ensure that the frame sequence is maintained at the receiver, any frame that does not contain a sequence number matching that of the next expected frame variable, V(R), is an error. If the sequence number of the error frame is within the window, the receiver returns an REJ response to indicate, in the N(R) field, the frame from which the sender should retransmit. If the frame sequence number is not within the window then the sequence numbers of the two ends have become unsynchronised. The only way to recover from a synchronisation problem is to reset the sender and receiver to a known state. The CMDR (command reject) frame initiates a reset which is completed by going through the link establishment exchange. After a reset, the two end-stations will be in a known, initial state. The reset procedure is used to recover from all errors other than the loss of an information frame. A reset may be caused by the receipt of a command or response that is not expected; for instance, a UA if the data transfer is in progress, or the setting of the P/F bit in a response when no command has been sent with that bit set.

The RNR (receiver not ready) frame tells the data sender that the receiver will ignore any further information frames (flow control stop). Once the receiver has returned an RNR response to an information frame, no more information frames are accepted, but the *N(R)* field in the header of any further information frames is inspected so that information frames in the opposite direction are properly acknowledged. The RNR response only stops information on one channel; the other channel is unaffected. When the receiver has more buffer space, an RR (receiver ready) frame is sent to inform the information sender on that channel that more information frames may be transmitted (flow control go), starting at *N(R)*. Note that both RNR and RR have acknowledgement numbers, *N(R)*. The RR frame has another use: if the receiving station does not have any information frames to be sent on the opposite channel, the acknowledgements cannot be piggybacked, and the RR frame is then used to acknowledge the information frames.

A receiver, especially a DCE (node), may not have enough buffers to take a full window for every level 2 link to which it is connected. Instead a statistical allocation could be used which assumes that not all links will be fully active at the same time and that the data is forwarded within a given time. When the network becomes busy this allocation means that a receiver may run out of buffers and need to use some technique to stop the flow of data from one or more links. Every frame, whether it is data or control, needs some buffer space for its receipt. If all the buffers are used up by one link then none of the other links will be able to continue transferring information. Also, if every buffer is allocated, there may be no more buffers to receive a control frame acknowledging a data frame and releasing buffer space! To avoid these problems, complex buffer allocation methods may be used. Normally, enough free buffers are always kept to receive at least one frame on each link so that control information can be exchanged even if data cannot. An information frame would be received, the control information used (for example *N(R)*), and then the frame discarded so that the buffer may be used again.

The loss of information frames as a result of buffer starvation means that information is lost not only because of errors in transmission, but also because of the internal operation of the nodes of a network, especially when the network becomes heavily loaded.

Link disconnection

The LAPB procedure for closing a link requires an exchange of a DISC command and a UA response. The poll/final bit is used to obtain synchronisation between the DCE and DTE.

X.25 level 3—the network level

The function of level 2 is to carry a level 3 packet across a link. The function of the network level is to carry a piece of information from one host (DTE) to another via intermediate network nodes. The transfer of the level 3 information will involve a number of level 2 links. The X. 25 specification only covers the link between the DTE and DCE, but we will assume a similar protocol is used between each node of the network as well. Each level 3 packet contains a certain amount of level 3 protocol information in a header, and possibly some user data (from the transport level). The major differences between levels 2 and 3 are the use of addresses and logical channel numbers. Most hosts will be connected to the network by one level 2 link. This link then has to be used to enable the host to communicate with several other hosts by multiplexing logical channels on to the one physical link. Level 3 is used to achieve this multiple connection via a single link. Using level 3 a host establishes a logical channel to another host by making a connection request using the full address of the remote host. When the connection is established it becomes a logical channel with a unique number, the logical channel number. The logical channel number is unique only for each link. Using the logical channel concept, packets for several calls may pass across the same level 2 link as they are all identified by the unique channel number. At the DCE the channel number is used to decide which route the packet will take. The logical channel is in fact a virtual circuit.

The network level has the same basic functions to perform as the link level.

1. Connection establishment.
2. Data transfer.
3. Connection disconnection.

The difference for the network level is that these functions are now carried out (apparently) between two hosts.

Packet format

The X.25 level 3 headers are used to contain a variety of information, so they are not of uniform size like the level 2 frame headers. The level 3 headers are different for every type of packet, which makes the format quite complex. The general format identifier (GFI) field indicates which format of level 3 header follows. The logical channel group number and logical channel number provide a 12 bit channel-numbering field. Splitting the field may allow subdivisions to be used for, say, different services. Call request and incoming call packets contain the address of the remote host (DTE). The addresses may contain fields indicating a particular process on a host as well as identifying a host. The address fields are of variable length, preceded by a byte count.

Connection establishment

To begin a call, a host uses the full address of the remote host in a call request packet sent from the DTE to the DCE. The DCE will respond with either a call accepted packet if the request was successful, or a clear indication packet if the call was refused.

At the remote host the DCE will send an incoming call packet to the host to indicate that a remote call has been requested. The DTE receiving an incoming call packet will inspect the header to decide if the call is to be established or not. If the call is accepted a call accept packet is sent to the DCE; if the call is rejected a clear request is sent to the DCE. The channel number chosen for a new outgoing call by the DTE is the lowest available number. The channel number for an incoming call is chosen by the DCE as the highest available number. If the DTE and DCE agree on the channel numbers, and the DCE will accept the call, all subsequent packets on that call will only use that channel number, not the full address. A call has been established to a remote DTE when a host receives a call accepted packet having the same channel number as the call request packet. The call is established at the remote DTE when the call accepted packet is sent to the remote DCE.

Information transfer

Level 3 transfers data to the network in a sequenced stream using Go-Back-N ARQ. The techniques of sequence numbers, piggybacked acknowledgements, RNR, RR and REJ responses are the same as for level 2, but they control the data flow across the network and into the remote host for each, independent logical channel. The use of windows and sequence numbers was for error control in level 2 as the level 1 link was prone to errors. At level 3 the level 2 link is assumed to be error free so. the emphasis is different. The windows and sequence numbers are now used primarily for end-to-end flow control. The receipt of acknowledgements allows more information into the network, while the window limits the number of data packets in flight at any one time. Complete suspension of the data flow can be achieved by using a level 3 RNR, but the flow can be partially adjusted by the rate of acknowledgement.

Interrupt

An extra mechanism is used at level 3 to handle what is known as *out-of-band* transmission. Normal user data on an X.25 virtual call is kept in strict sequence; this is called *in band* transmission. However, a user application often requires a special signal which is not subject to the normal flow control. Such a signal is the abort character which a terminal user would type to stop a runaway program. X.25 level 3 uses an interrupt packet to carry this out-of-band signal. The interrupt is not subject to the normal information flow control, the idea being that the interrupt could overtake information packets already in the network. The interrupt packet contains a field to indicate the cause of the interrupt; it is up to the application to decide what to do both with the interrupt and any subsequent data. When the DTE sends an interrupt packet the DCE responds with an interrupt confirmation. The interrupt sequence is shown in figure 9.10. X.25 permits only one interrupt to be outstanding on a logical call at any one time.

Resets and restarts

In level 2 the reset was introduced as a mechanism for recovering from a protocol error where the two ends in the link became unsynchronised. The same thing can happen between the DTE and DCE at level 3, except that there are two areas where problems may occur.

The first problem is due to the information frames and sequence numbers becoming out of synchronisation on a single call. This may be detected by receiving a sequence number outside the window or an acknowledgement for a packet that was not sent. An error may also have been detected by a higher-level protocol, perhaps because of a network failure. In these cases only the one logical channel is affected so a *reset* is used. This sets the level 3 sequence numbers to 0 at the DTE and DCE. The reset will also be propagated to the remote DTE-DCE pair. The reset can be initiated from either the DTE or DCE and requires the usual request-confirmation exchange. A reset may cause the loss of any information packets within the network so a higher-level protocol will need to recover any lost data.

More drastic action is needed if the DTE and DCE become unsynchronised over global level 3 operation. An example is the choice of a channel number for a call request. If the DCE does not agree with the DTE over the chosen channel number (it should be the lowest free number) it means one of them thinks it has more logical calls opened than the other! The freeing of logical channel numbers correctly is the reason for the clear-request and clear-confirmation pair. When the whole level 3 needs resynchronisation a restart is initiated. This affects all the logical channels on the DTE-DCE link. A reset on the level 2 link is propagated as a restart at level 3.

Call disconnection

A DTE wishing to terminate a call issues a clear request packet, to which the DCE will respond with a clear confirmation packet when the call has been cleared in the DCE. This may involve waiting for the forwarding of any information packets still held there. When the clear confirmation is received the channel number is freed for further use. At the remote end the DCE wit send a clear indication packet indicating that the remote host has closed, and no more information packets will follow. The remote DTE will respond with a clear confirmation packet when all outstanding information packets have been acknowledged.

Data flow

The level 3 transport mechanism requires the data from the higher-level protocols to be broken into packets for transfer across the DTE-DCE interface. The X.25 recommendation specifies possible data lengths of 128 256, 512 and 1024 bytes, where 128 is the preferred maximum. It is probable that the PTT networks will guarantee 128 byte data packets. This means a user message must be broken into 128 byte sequences, the last one being perhaps less than 128 bytes. To enable the receiver to reassemble a message from multiple packets, level 3 uses a *more data bit* (M) in the information packet header to indicate that the current packet is not the last one of a message.

Just as the level 2 and level 3 need to include control information in the frames and packets as well as information from the next higher level, it is likely that a higher-level protocol would like to send control and data over level 3. The higher-level protocol may decide to add the control bits to the front of messages it passes to level 3. However, level 3 provides a mechanism that allows a higher-level protocol to multiplex data and control information on to the level 3 packet stream, thus maintaining the sequence of data and control across the network. This mechanism is the Q *bit.* The Q bit is set when the packet contains control information, and is clear when the packet contains data. Thus the higher-level protocol can quickly separate control and data information when receiving level 3 packets.

X.25 implementation

An advantage claimed for X.25 is that it only describes the host-to-node (DTE-to-DCE) interface. The network itself (internode) can use any convenient protocols, even completely different protocols, and the user would be unaware of them. In fact the proposed PTT networks are all planning to use X.25, or variations, within the networks for node-to-node transfer. The problem considered here is the implications of two methods of implementing an X.25 interface in a DCE that produce quite different results for the user. The discussion will show that even standards have complex problems of *meaning* (or semantics).

The two methods of implementation involve the mechanism for generating responses to various DTE packets at level 3. From the above description it can be seen that a command response sequence is used throughout level 3. The X.25 specification indicates quite clearly what responses are required, but leaves it up to the implementer to decide when, and under what criteria, the responses are made.

Consider the implementation that produces the DCE response as soon as the DTE's packet has been processed at the (local) DCE. This means the DCE's answer is sent to the DTE at the same time as the original request is forwarded across the network and well in advance of its arrival at the remote DTE. Such an implementation would give a very quick response to the user host. For instance, as data is passed to the DCE it is acknowledged immediately, even before it has crossed the network. The DCE-DTE flow control would ensure the DCE was not flooded with data, but large amounts could be in transit within the network before the call has been established at the remote end. This implementation would give the host the appearance of high throughput, as the DCE-DTE flow control would be the only restraint. If the DTE receives a level 3 acknowledgement for a data packet, does this mean that the remote DTE has received it, or only that the local DCE has? To be consistent in this implementation it would have to be the latter, so the DCE has taken on the responsibility for delivery of that data. A higher-level protocol would be needed, with its own flow control, to handle the host-to-host transfer.

This implementation has the effect, mentioned above, of apparently providing a fast throughput. A host may be able to open a call (to the local DCE), send data, and close the call, before the remote DTE has received any data. The network, however, will contain a large amount of unacknowledged packets as the DTE-DCE flow control will accept packets as fast as the DCE can forward them into the network. This makes end-to-end flow control in the network difficult and can quickly lead to congestion.

In the second implementation we only allow the DCE to respond to the DTE when the response from the remote DTE has been received by the local DCE. Data sent from the DTE is not acknowledged until the remote DTE has accepted the packet. This gives the host an impression of a long delay. In fact the delay is the round trip to the remote host, plus processing. This end-to-end use of the level 3 protocol reduces the amount of processing required from higher-level protocols. The sending DTE will only be able to have a window of packets outstanding which will represent the maximum number of data buffers which the whole network will need for the call. This makes the resource management within the network easier and is less likely to produce congestion. The cost is the lower performance seen by the user. Each packet takes longer to be acknowledged, thus reducing the throughput. There is also the problem of gaps which occurs when a window full of packets is sent rapidly, which is followed by a delay until the first acknowledgement comes back. This *bursty* mode of operation gives the network an uneven response and is difficult for both the host and DCE to manage.

In the Internet community, the TCP/IP protocol suite is used extensively for computer networking. TCP/IP is very popular because of the simplicity and openness of the protocols. There is a difference between "capital I" Internet and small i" internet. The former is a global network formed by loosely organized and autonomous interconnected networks. It uses Internet Standards such as TCP/IP. Previously, it was called the National Science Foundation (NSF) backbone net. The TCP/IP protocol suite is also known as Internet. The scope of Internet Standards covers TCP/IP protocol suite and protocols, procedures, and conventions used in the Internet context. On the other hand, internet (lower-class) refers to a collection of networks not connected to the Internet, but using Internet Standards. TCP is a stream-oriented protocol and does not bother about record boundaries. It deals with bytes instead of records, as in some other protocols such as SNA. Also in TCP/IP, all computers are generically referred to as *hosts*. Notice that *host* in TCP/IP is a very generic term, which can mean a workstation, a personal computer, or even a mainframe. In the mainframe world, a mainframe is generally referred to as a host, unlike in the Internet arena. Devices which connect networks and forward Internet Protocol (IP) packets are known as *gateways*, which has here a broader meaning and scope than the gateways referred to in the LAN arena. TCP/IP gateways are similar to routers in the LAN arena. Currently, gateways may also be known as IP *routers*. The first layer is the *network interface* (NI) layer. Internet does not have any standards defined for this layer. This layer can have Ethernet, X.25, or token rings. The NI layer corresponds to the physical and link layers of the OSI seven-layer architecture as shown in Figure. Access the ports is achieved in the physical layer. In the link layer, one of MAC layer protocols is used.

The layer above the NI is the IP layer. This is a connectionless layer. Above this layer can be connection-oriented TCP or the connectionless *User Datagram Protocol*

(UDP). On top of these layers are applications such as the *File Transfer Protocol* (FTP), *Simple Transfer Protocol* (SMTP), *TELNET,* and *Simple Net Management Protocol* (SNMP). A *message* or *stream of d* transferred from the application layer to the TCP/UDP layer. When transferred to the lower IP layer along with the TCP/UDP header, this message is called a *packet.* This packet, in turn, is wrapped proper IP headers and becomes an IP *datagram,* which is passe the NI. In the NI layer, the IP datagram is again packaged with the appropriate NI headers; this is known as a *frame.* This frame is transmitted over the network. Internet uses SNMP for network management. In the first version SNMP, security was a weak link. To overcome some of the weaknesses of SNMP, it has been modified. The earlier SNMP is known now as SNMPv1 or SNMP version 1; the new modified protocol known as SNMPv2 or SNMP version 2.

The main objective of this chapter is to introduce to readers the important lower-level protocols used in Internet network management, assuming SNMPs as the higher-layer application protocols. To understand SNMP, important concepts of the lower-layer protocols ",are required. Because this book deals with network management, only an overview of the lower-layer TCP/IP protocol suite is provided.

Internet addressing

In IP, transmission of data and headers is done as shown in Figure. Octet I is transmitted first, then octet 2, and so on. An IP address has two parts: network number and host number. The IP layer recognizes the IP address only. IP address classes are Class A, Class B, Class C, Class D, and Class E. The main distinction among Class A, Class B, and Class C is in the division between network number and host number, also referred to as the *rest field.* In Class D, the first four bits are 1110, and the remaining 28 bits are known as the *multicast address.* When IP packets have to be sent to a group of stations, this is known as multicasting. *Broadcasting* is an extension of multicasting, in which all the stations in a subnet receive the IP packet. In Class E, the first four bits are 1111. Class E addresses are reserved for future uses.

The main advantage of these classes is flexibility for arranging the networks. For example, a large number of workstations may need to be connected to form a network. In such a case, the Class A addressing scheme is convenient. If a relatively small number of workstations are to be connected to form a LAN, Class C may be appropriate. The 32 bits of IP address are divided into four eight-bit fields. The IP addresses in *Dotted Decimal Notation* are formed by decimal numbers obtained from each of the eight-bit fields, and they are separated by periods. As an example, 183.127.2.35, a class B address, is shown in Figure. The network numbers are assigned by the Network Information Center (NIC). At the time this manuscript was written, work on IP version 6 was ongoing. In IP version 6, an IP address will be 16 octets (128 bits). This will solve the present problem of a shortage of IP addresses.

A process in the application layer chooses the transport it requires. It decides whether it wants to use a connection-oriented service such as TCP or a connectionless service such as UDR The next layer (TCP/UDP) wraps its own header to the data it received from the process in the application layer. The action of wrapping a header on the data received from an upper layer is known as *encapsulation.* The internet layer, in turn, adds its own header and sends the data to the local NI. The local NI maps the IP address to the local network address. If a packet is to be transmitted from one host in a network to a host in another network, then the local gateway address must be found and the packet must be transmitted to the right gateway. The gateway maps the IP address to the local network address and routes the packet to the destination host or another gateway in the path of the destination host. A packet may be delivered to a destination host by more than one path. To avoid such a situation, the gateways have algorithms to calculate the right path.

Internet protocol(IP)

he IP is a connectionless best-effort packet delivery service. In this protocol, there is no end-to-end guaranteed delivery, acknowledgment, flow control, retransmission, or error recovery. This protocol tries its best to deliver packets to the destination. The frames are discarded as a last resort. If connection-oriented support is required, then it must be provided by the upper layers. The IP layer deals with four-octet IP addresses.

The IP datagram is as shown in Figure, consisting of the IP header and the data portion. The first field in the IP header is the *version* of IP, which version is provided to furnish details of the IP software. Like any technology, changes do occur to account for advances. The present version is 4. The version field alerts the system to these changes and facilitates compatibility. The IP header length is in multiples of 32 bits. The *length* field extends from the version field to the beginning of the data portion. Total length is inclusive of the IP header and data, and is measured in octets. Because the length field is 16 bits, it can accommodate up to 65,535 octets. However, there is also a restriction that hosts must be able to accept IP datagrams larger than 576 octets.

Though IP imposes an upper limit of 65,535, protocols used in the lower levels impose their own restrictions. For example, Ethernet has its minimum of 64 octets and maximum of 1518 octet frame length limitations. So the length of datagrams sent in networks will be guided by limitations other than the ones imposed by the IP layer. The *type of service* (TOS) field is one octet long. The first three bits indicate *precedence,* for which different levels are defined. High-precedence traffic is regarded as more important than low-precedence traffic.

Bits 6 and 7 of the TOS field are reserved for future use, and they are set to zero. However, RFC 1349 redefines the TOS field. Here the TOS field is taken as four bits; the last bit is labeled Must Be Zero (MBZ), and this bit is unused. TOS values mentioned in Table are the values which will be tried. If the network cannot provide the TOS requested, then values used will be those of the network.

When a datagram is larger than the size that can be handled by a network, then a gateway converts the datagram into smaller-size fragments which are multiples of eight. As an example, the IP datagram shown in Figure can be converted to smaller datagrams as shown. This action of forming smaller datagrams out of a large one is known as *fragmentation,* also sometimes known as segmentation. However, these fragments are reassembled only in the destination host and not in the intermediate gateways.

The *identification* field is 16 bits in length. It has three bits of the *flag* field and 13 bits of *fragment offset.* In the flag field, the fist bit (bit 0) is set to 0. Bit I has two options. If it is set to 0, then it indicates that the datagram may be fragmented. If it is set to 1, then the datagram cannot be fragmented. Bit 2 of flag again has two options. When fragmentation is done, this bit in the last fragment is set to 0. However, in other fragments, this bit is 1, indicating that there are more fragments of the datagram. The other IP field, *fragment offset,* furnishes the offset of the datagram, which is in units of eight octets. The first fragment has a fragment offset of 0. The next IP header field, known as the *time to live* (TTL) field, is eight bits long and has time in seconds. TTL specifies how long a datagram remains in a system. Because a gateway is able to process a packet in less than a second, the TTL count is reduced by one. In such a case, the TTL counter becomes a maximum allowable count of hops for a packet to reach the destination host. When the TTL becomes zero, then a datagram destroys itself. This process is also known as *self-destruction* and prevents a datagram from making unnecessary cycles in the network.

The *protocol* field has the protocol number of the upper layer. For example, ICMP has a protocol number of 1, and the protocol number for TCP is 6. Assigned numbers of higher-layer protocols are furnished in Reference. The *header checksum* field provides the checksum of the IP header field only, and does not include the checksum of the data portion. It is obtained by adding the ones complement of different fields and then taking the ones complement of the sum. The source and destination IP addresses are the addresses of the sender and receiver. The destination IP address does not refer to the addresses of intermediate gateways.

One bit of flag indicates whether the option field is copied into fragments on fragmentation. If it is zero, then the option field is not copied and if it is set to one, then the option field is copied into all the fragments. The option field is quite useful for adding a variety of features, but options cannot be used unless they are accepted by the general Internet community. The *padding* field is used to ensure that the IP header aligns on a 32-bit boundary.

Internet control message protocol(ICMP)

ICMP is used for communicating error or control messages from one host to another host or from routers (gateways) to the host. ICMP is required in every IP layer. The ICMP message occupies the data portion of the IP. It has a header of its own and data. For an ICMP message, the protocol field in the IP header is set to 1.

The ICMP field always has an ICMP type field, which distinguishes different ICMP messages. There is also a code field, which gives more details about messages, and the checksum field, which furnishes the checksum for the ICMP message portion only.

The IP header and first 64 bits of the original datagram refer to the header and the data of the layer above ICMP. The layer above can be either TCP or UDP. The first 64 bits of data are used for matching processes which may use the ICMP message. The ICMP message is quite useful for discovering hosts and routers. The Packet InterNet Groper (PING) is used for checking the connectivity of a host with a remote host and getting the details of a host. It is also quite useful for network management. PING is an echo request and echo reply, and is useful for gathering data on hosts and routers. The ICMP message for an echo request and echo reply is shown in Figure. When an echo request is to be sent, the ICMP type is 8. The destination address is the address of the router or host IP which must send an echo of the message back to the sender. For the echo reply, which has same message sent in the echo request, the ICMP type is 0.

Identifier and sequence numbers are used for identifying and matching a message and its replies. If code is 0, then both identifier and sequence number may be 0. As we have seen earlier, echo request and echo reply can be used to gather data and statistics on the network and hosts and routers. They are also useful for debugging purposes.

Transmission control protocol (TCP)

TCP is a connection-oriented, reliable, packet-switching protocol used for communication between processes in host computers. These host computers are distinct and are part of a communication network. The data transfer is full-duplex, which means that the sender sends data in one direction and can simultaneously receive data from the opposite direction. One of the strengths of the TCP protocol is its flexibility. It does not specifically mandate any protocol for the layer above it or the layer below. Usually, in Internet, the lower-layer protocol is IP. TCP is a stream-oriented protocol, and the combination of TCP layer data and headers is known as a *segment*.

An important concept in TCP is that of a connection. TCP provides for a set of addresses or *ports* within each host. Many processes can be associated with a port. The IP address and port number identify a *socket*. A pair of sockets identify a *connection*. Before communication can take place, a connection must be established between processes. This connection is referred to as a *virtual circuit*, which is analogous to a telephone connection being formed before the start of a conversation.

In a network, segments of data may be damaged or corrupted, lost, duplicated, or delivered out of order. To account for this, there is provision for acknowledgment and retransmission. When data is sent by a sender, the sequence number of the first octet of data in the segment is also sent. At the same time, the sender starts a timer. The receiving end sends an acknowledgment number. This acknowledgment refers to the sequence number of the next expected data octet to be sent by the sender. However, if the acknowledgment is not received before the timer runs out, then the sender retransmits the segment. There is also provision for a checksum of the data to identify whether the data has been corrupted. We have seen earlier that IP does not provide a checksum of the data; it provides for a checksum of the IP header only. So TCP takes account of this fact to provide a reliable communication mechanism.

Flow control is achieved by means of a variable window that can be sent along with an acknowledgment by a receiver. If the receiver does not have much buffer space left, then it sends a smaller window. Conversely, where the receiver is willing to accept and process data at a faster rate, it adjusts the window to a larger number than the existing one. The destination IP address identifies the destination host, and the source IP address identifies the source host address. In this figure, SA1 is the source host IP address, and DA1 is the destination host IP address. The applications Al, A2, and A3 are the source ports. It is assumed that they want to communicate with destination ports B1, B2, and B3, respectively. The process in Host 1, where applications are combined, is analogous to multiplexing, and the process in Host 2, where they are directed to the respective ports, is similar to demultiplexing seen in the data transmissions across a transmission medium.

A TCP segment has a TCP header part and a data part. The TCP header has the following fields:

Source port number: A 16-bit field, containing a source port number.

Destination port number: Also a 16-bit field, with a destination port number where a data segment must be sent.

Sequence number: The sequence number of a data octet of a segment that is being sent from a sender. In the case of synchronization or when the SYN bit is set, it is the *initial sequence number* (ISN). The first octet of data starts from ISN + 1. Here note that the ISN need not always start with 0, or the first octet sequence number need not always start with 1. The sequence number is a 32-bit field.

Acknowledgment number: A 32-bit field, always sent once a connection has been established. This is the number of the first data octet which a receiver expects to receive next. For example, if a receiver has received data up to 100 octets, the receiver puts the acknowledgment number as 101. The receiver next expects a segment in which the data octet starts with 101.

Data offset: A four-bit field. A TCP header is a multiple of 32 bits. This field contains the length of the TCP header measured in terms of 32 bits. In a segment, data offset indicates where the data starts.

Reserved: Intended for future use and set to 0. It is six bits in length. It is a good idea to provide for a reserved field in any protocol. When technology changes or new technologies are incorporated, these reserved bits can be used.

The first six fields in the following list are all one-bit fields.

URG: Urgent pointer significant field. TCP has provided for sending out-of-band urgent data. When this bit is set, the receiver is expected to process this segment first, interrupting all other activities. When the URG bit is set, the urgent pointer field has relevance..

ACK. Acknowledgment significant field. When this field is set, an acknowledgment number is sent.

PSH: Push function field. When this field is set, the sender is expected to send whatever data is available in the buffer instead of waiting for the send buffer to be filled up.

RST. Used for resetting a connection. When this bit is set, depending on the states of sender and receiver, actions are taken. For example, reset is sent when a segment for another connection is received.

SYN: For synchronizing sequence numbers. This is used in the beginning to establish a connection by means of a three-way handshake.

FIN: Used for closing a connection.

Window: A 16-bit field. Because the data in IP segments are in terms of octets, window states the number of octets which a receiver is willing to receive, starting from one.

Checksum: A 16-bit field. The checksum is calculated and includes a TCP pseudo header and TCP segment. The TCP pseudo header has source and destination addresses, eight bits set to 0, the protocol, and TCP length. The pseudo header is used for computing the checksum and is not transmitted while transmitting data. That is the reason for naming it a pseudo header. Here, TCP length is the sum of the TCP header and TCP data. This TCP length does not, however, include 12 octets of the TCP pseudo header. For checksum, header and text octets must be even. To make these even, sometimes the last octet is padded with 0. To form the checksum, the ones complement of the TCP header is taken, then the ones complement of the result is taken.

Urgent pointer: Provides positive offset from the sequence number in a segment. This points to data offset following urgent data. As mentioned earlier, this field is taken into consideration only if the URG bit is set. This is a 16-bit field.

Options: A variable-length field, with length in multiples of eight bits. Here, too, there are two options:

- Case 1: Has one octet of option.
- Case 2: Has one octet of option, one octet of option length, and variable-length options data. Here, as in the IP, length includes two octets due to the option and option length.

User datagram protocol (UDP)

SNMP, Internet Name Server, and Trivial File Transfer use the UDP protocol. This is a connectionless datagram service. UDP, in turn, depends upon the connectionless IP layer. As a result, there is no guarantee that data will be delivered; there may be duplicate frames sent, or data may be received in an order different from the order in which they were sent. Also, there is no acknowledgment that data has been delivered. However, if an application wishes to provide services that are available in a connection oriented service, it is the responsibility of the application to incorporate them in upper-layer software. In UDP, an application that wants to transmit data to another application uses a scheme similar to TCP The data of the application are initially enveloped with a UDP header. Then, at the IP layer, the IP header is appended. In the NI layer, the network header is appended to the IP frame. This frame is transmitted over the Internet to the other end. On the receiving end, the NI layer removes the network layer header, and the IP layer strips off the IP header. The UDP layer, in turn, removes the UDP header and routes data to the appropriate application. If there is a mismatch or the proper frame is not received, the ICMP message can be sent to the original application with causes for the error.

The UDP datagram is as shown in Figure. It has 16 bits each of source port and destination numbers. The length field contains the number of octets of the UDP frame and includes the length of the UDP frame headers. The next field in the UDP header is the checksum field, which is an optional field. If it is not used, then this field has zeros; however, if the checksum field is used, it contains the ones complement of the checksum derived from a pseudo header.

The UDP pseudo header is similar to the TCP pseudo header. The UDP pseudo header has four octets each of source IP address and destination IP address, zero padding, protocol, and UDP length. One octet of zero padding is done to make the UDP frame a multiple of two. One octet protocol field is 17 for IP, and the two-byte UDP length field is the length of the UDP datagram in octets. However ' the UDP length field does not include the length of the pseudo header. Thus, an application that wants to send data needs to know the IP addresses of source and destination beforehand in the UDP layer itself.

The use of checksum is mostly guided by the application. Note here that IP uses only the header checksum; it does not use the checksum over the IP data portion. Hence, if some validation of whether the UDP frame is the correct one is required, then the checksum in UDP is required. In some cases, we may not want to have the overhead of computing the checksum since the loss of some UDP frames may not matter much. One such case is that of monitoring the performance of a resource, where the loss of a UDP datagram may not mean much. Also, in some cases, a network may be very reliable, without the risk of losing frames. In other cases, the application may be critical and the loss of a frame may lead to problems. In such cases, it is better to use checksum. Also, when a network is unreliable, it is appropriate to use the cheeksum to make sure that the data delivered is correct.

Address resolution protocol (ARP)

We have seen that Internet knows only the IP address. Let us investigate how an IP packet is sent to the other end. An IP packet has a destination IP address. Then the local host looks at the ARP table and checks where the destination is. An ARP table is a sort of lookup table which has a mapping between an IP address and its corresponding physical address. Then the NI layer inserts the actual physical address of the destination host. The Ethernet or token-ring frame has this destination physical address. On the destination side, this Ethernet frame is stripped of its physical address and routed to the right IP layer. When this happens, the destination is in the same network. However, it is possible that the destination could be another network, in which case, instead of the physical address of the destination host, the physical address of the IP router is appended in the Ethernet frame. In the IP router, a check is again made with a routing table to see where the destination IP address is. If there are many hops or steps required before a destination can be reached, then the physical addresses of the IP routers are successively inserted. In the last IP router, the destination host physical address is retrieved from the destination IP address to route the IP packet to the correct destination.

The next issue is how to build an ARP table. This is done by broadcasting an ARP request packet, which has a source IP address, source physical address, and destination IP address. When this packet is broadcast, each host examines the IP address and looks whether it matches its own IP address. If it matches, the host puts its IP address and physical address in the source. The earlier source IP and physical addresses are transferred to the destination IP address and the destination physical address, and the response is sent back.

In the original host that sent the ARP request packet, the ARP table now has the mapping of the destination IP address and physical address. It is possible that no host has a matching IP address when an ARP request packet is sent. In such a case, the IP address is not, known.

The manner in which the IP packet handles cases in which mapping between the IP address and physical address is not known is, implementation dependent. In some cases, when the mapping is not there, the IP packet is queued and an ARP request packet is sent. When the destination physical address becomes known, the ARP request packet is received. The IP packet is dequeued and sent to the destination. If the address is not known, the IP layer discards the packets. In some cases, these IP packets may not be queued. If the IP packets are not delivered, the upper layers are alerted by *timeouts*.

Reverse address resolution protocol(RARP)

RARP is the reverse process of ARP, in which mapping is from a physical address to the IP address. A station may have its physical address; it sends a RARP to a server giving its IP address, and the server maps the IP address and sends back the physical address.

Subnet addressing

A network that uses a single access protocol under the control of a single administrative domain is known as a *subnetwork*. As a corollary to this definition, a subnetwork can be a collection of smaller networks. The IP address consists of a network number part and a host number part. The network number part is used for routing from network to network. This provides the first level of routing. The technique of partitioning a network address to cover multiple networks is known as *subnet addressing*. Here, a host number is further divided into a subnet number part and a host number part, which enables one more level of partitioning of networks, and also helps in forming further routing levels.

In subnet addressing, to recover the network number part, a 32-bit subnet mask, which has all 1s in the network number and subnet number part, is used. The subnet mask has zeros in the rest of the mask. So when data is to be sent from station A, it goes to the appropriate router. The router uses the subnet number part to send it to the proper subnet or network; then the host number is used to deliver the data to the right destination host. If all the networks are not using subnet addressing, routers use proxy ARP. According to this, for an ARP on a station address, the router answers by giving its hardware address for the address of a station. This is analogous to saying: I know station B's address; you can send frames meant for it to me. So when station A has to send the frame, it sends it to the correct router. The router, in turn, interprets the address and sends it to the right station.

Network monitors, also known as network analyzers or probes, are quite useful for network management. They basically collect and analyze the packets going through them. These data may be statistics, such as packet sizes, number of collisions, and number of packets per second. In relation to management stations, these network monitors are remote; hence, they are known as *remote network monitors* (RMON). These network monitors, by using the RMON MIB, can be extended to collect data for network management and to communicate with management stations. Note that the RMON MIB extends MIB-II RFC 1271 defined MIB objects primarily for the Ethernet protocol. RFC 1513 is an extension of RFC 1271 and defines the MIB objects required for monitoring networks running on token-ring protocols. RFC 1757 makes RFC 1271 obsolete. RFC 1757 is basically the same as RFC 1271, except it corrects and clarifies some of the terms, such as channel and captureBuffer, used in RFC 1271. Management data collected by a network monitor is sent to management stations. This can be on an exception basis, that is, when changes happen. The location of the network monitors is implementation-dependent. One network monitor can be placed per segment, per subnetwork, or per token-ring network.

As an example, in which there is one network monitor for each subnetwork. FDDI rings have management stations M1 and M2. Remote network monitors are placed in RMON agents Al, A2, A3, and A4, which provide functions such as protocol support for communication with management stations and error recovery for the remote network monitors. RMON agents act as intermediaries between remote network monitors and management stations. For transfer of data to management stations, these RMON agents can use SNMPvl or SNMPv2 protocols. However, if RMON agents are to be implemented, SNMPv2 is preferable because SNMPvl agents must ultimately migrate to SNMPv2 agents. We have made the assumption that RMON agents communicate with only one management station. It is not necessary to have this restriction; an RMON agent carrying a remote network monitor may send data to one or more management stations. Also, these RMON agents can be placed in hosts, routers, and bridges, and there are no set rules prescribed in RFC 1757 or RFC 1513 on the placement of remote network monitors.

This particular approach of having a network monitor exclusively for the purpose of network management has its own advantages. The network monitor can continuously collect data and selectively send it to the management stations. Also, when thresholds are crossed, events may be formed and alarms can be sent to the management stations. This action can help reduce network traffic, because the data collected is logged in agents with network monitors instead of transmitting every piece of data to the management stations. When the management stations need further details, they can access and collect the information required from the agents with remote network monitors.

RFC 1757 covers some of the scenarios where remote networking monitoring may be used. These include:

Offline operation: Primarily relates to cases in which the network monitor operates as a stand-alone monitoring device. These cases can arise due to communication failure between the remote network monitor and a management station, or due to selective collection of data by a management station. Because a remote network monitor can operate independently of the management station, it can continue to perform its operation of continuously collecting and storing data. The management station, in turn, can retrieve these data stored whenever required.

Communication with management stations on an exception basis: Because the remote network monitor can function independently of management stations, it can collect data on the network and log data for analysis at a later time. When problems are observed in the network due to crossing thresholds or failures, notifications can be sent to management stations. Management stations can retrieve the logged data for problem analysis and diagnostics.

Relevant data collection: A monitor can also concentrate on the hosts in its portion of the network that have maximum traffic or errors and can log the data required for management stations. This will help in zeroing in on a portion of the network, as well as with the collection of data on the critical hosts in a network.

Multiple management stations: Management stations may be organized on the basis of actions performed. Under these circumstances, it may be necessary to concurrently deal with more than one management station to which a network monitor is reporting. Also, a breakdown by function, such as accounting, will help reduce the workload in management stations and makes it easy to focus on each of the functions. This can help to centralize the data required for certain network management functions such as configuration management. In many cases, configuration management activities need to be centralized in one management station. Similarly, under certain circumstances, it may be necessary to have centralized fault management, including monitoring, in another management station. So, a scenario where a remote network monitor may have to communicate with more than one management station becomes quite common, especially in large networks with thousands of workstations.

RMON for Ethernet (RFC 1757)

Objects defined in the remote network monitoring MIB are primarily for the Ethernet protocol. They can be expanded to cover token-ring and FDDI protocols. RMON objects are defined using the guidelines furnished in SMI (RFC 1155). However, in addition to the ASN.1 data types mentioned in SMI, RMON defines the following two data types:

OwnerString (DisplayString): Contains information such as IP address, management station name, network manager's name, location, and phone number. This data type is used for identifying the owner of a resource, and helps in resolving conflicts when more than one management station is the owner of a resource. For example, if an instance of a resource is to be deleted by a management station, then there is the possibility that one management station may delete the instance created by another management station. But, by identifying the owner, a rule may be made that only the management station that created an object instance can delete that object instance. Thus, the data type OwnerString is useful when resources are shared by more than one management station.

EntryStatus (INTEGER): Useful when a resource is shared by more than one owner. Suppose that an object instance is created by one owner. At the same time or later, another management station creates an object instance with conflicting values to the one that has been already created. In such a case, there can be major problems regarding the validity of values. The major question is which are the correct values? Under such circumstances, EntryStatus is quite useful because it helps to determine whether an object instance exists.

EntryStatus has these values: valid = 1, createRequest = 2, underCreation = 3, and invalid = 4. As we have seen previously, creating an object instance is equivalent to creating a row entry in a MIB table. So, when an object instance is created, we have the value createRequest. Creating an instance may lead to supplementary actions such as creation of more objects by an agent. During this operation, the value is set to underCreation. When this operation is completed, the value is set to valid, abort, or invalid, depending on the results of the object creation operation. Another management station that wants to create the same entry will get a result of error. Thus, it is prudent for a management station to check whether an object instance has already been created by checking EntryStatus.

After examining the new data types OwnerString and OwnerStatus, we can conclude that their primary objective is for facilitating resource sharing. This is due to the fact that network monitors can send monitored data to more than one management station, which is one of the salient points of RMON. These objects are transmitted across the wires using the BER, which was discussed in earlier chapters. Under the subtree {mib-2 16}, new groups for RMON are defined. Nine main groups are defined in RFC 1757. The tokenRing group, {rmon 10}, has been added in RFC 1513 specifically for monitoring networks working with the token-ring protocol.

Ethernet statistics group

Objects in the statistics group are used to collect statistics on each of the monitored devices. The statistics group has one table, etherStatsTable, which is formed as shown in Figure 9.5. etherStatsTable will have a row for each Ethernet interface. Thus, there are etherStatsEntryl to etherStatsEntryN in the etherStatsTable, and each etherStatsEntry has columns from etherStatsIndex and etherStatsDataSource up to etherStatsStatus. This procedure is followed in forming some of the tables in RMON and is similar to the ones used in MIB-II.

Data types for the statistics group are mainly counters, and they are created with a value of zero. In the statistics group, objects are:

etherStatsIndex (INTEGER): Provides the row position in the etherStatsTable.

etherStatsDataSource (OBJECT IDENTIFIER): Relates to the Ethernet interface from which a remote network monitor is receiving the data.

etherStatsDropEuents (Counter): Provides the number of times packets were dropped in network monitors for limitations of resources, such as lack of storage space.

etherStatsOctets (Counter): Provides the total number of octets received on the network monitor from an Ethernet interface. This includes the total number of data octets and FCS octets. However, these octets do not include the framing bits.

etherStatsPkts (Counter): Includes the total number of packets received, including those packets which had errors.

etherStatsBroadcastPkts (Counter): Furnishes the total number of good broadcast packets received in an Ethernet interface.

etherStatsMulticastPkts (Counter): While in etherStats-BroadcastPkts, the concern is good broadcast packets; in etherStatsMulticastPkts, a count of good multicast packets is kept.

etherStatsCRCAlignErrors (Counter): Provides the number of packets which were between length 64 and 1518 octets or had FCS errors. While counting the length, the FCS octets are included but the framing bits are excluded.

etherStatsUndersizePkts (Counter): Relates to the total number of good packets which had lengths less than 64 octets.

etherStatsOversizePkts (Counter): Refers to the well-formed packets which had lengths greater than 1518 octets.

etherStatsFragments (Counter): Provides data on packets which had bad lengths or FCS errors, and were of lengths less than 64 octets.

etherStatsJabbers (Counter): etherStatsFragments provides details on the bad packets which are of lengths less than 64 octets. We need to have data on bad packets which are over the Ethernet length limit of 1518 octets. etherStatsJabbers provides this data.

etherStatsCollisions (Counter): Provides the number of collisions in a subnetwork.

etherStatsPkts64Octets through *etherStatsPkts1024to-1518Octets:* Provide granularity for counters by breaking them into different counters for lengths of packets ranging from 64 to 1518 octets. Note that these packets also include the error packets.

etherStatsOwner (OwnerString): Identifies the owner that created this row in the etherStatsTable. As we have seen earlier, OwnerString furnishes many details.

etherStatsStatus (EntryStatus): Provides the status of the etherStats entry.

Objects in the statistics group are basically very useful for performance management, but some of them, such as etherStatsDropEvents, etherStatsCRCAlignErrors, and etherStatsUndersizePkts, will be useful for fault management, too. If corrective action is to be taken before a failure occurs, then it may be useful to have thresholds set for objects such as etherStatsDropEvents, etherStatsCRCAlignErrors, and etherStatsCollisions.

History group

In the history group, samples at fixed time intervals are collected and stored. This data can be used for analysis in fault and performance management. As is apparent from the figure, there are two tables: historyControlTable and etherHistoryTable. historyControlTable provides information on how data are to be collected.

Corresponding to a row in the historyControlTable there are one or more rows of data in etherHistoryTable. etherHistoryTable has the actual data which is useful for analysis purposes. This pattern is followed by some tables in RMON MIB. RFC 1757 recommends that while collecting data, it is better to start data collection at the beginning of the next hour of the day. If data is collected for different stations in a network uniformly at the same time, data will be useful and meaningful for comparison purposes. Objects of the historyControlTable are:

historyControlIndex (INTEGER): A unique identifier of an entry in the historyControlTable. Each entry defines a set of entries in the etherHistoryTable on an Ethernet interface.

historyControlDataSource (OBJECT IDENTIFIER): Relates to the Ethernet interface on which a remote network monitor is collecting data.

historyControlBuckersRequested (INTEGER) : Porovides the requested number of sampling intervals.

historyControlBucketsGranted (INTEGER): In a network monitor there may be limitations on resources, so naturally, a network monitor cannot always provide the numbers of sampling intervals as requested in historyControlBucketsRequested. As a result, history-ControlBucketsGranted furnishes the feasible number of sampling intervals, and, as is obvious, the historyControl BucketsGranted value is kept as close to the value requested by historyControlBucketsRequested.

historyControlInterval (INTEGER): Refers to the sampling interval in seconds for each bucket. The value can be set from 1 to 3600 seconds.

historyControlOwner (OwnerString): Identifies the owner which created this row in the historyControlTable. Because management stations will be using the data collected, history Control Owner refers to a management station.

historyControlStatus (EntryStatus): Provides the status of historyControlEntry.

etherHistoryTable has the data which have been collected over an Ethernet interface. Parameters for data collection are guided by historyControlEntry. The columns in etherHistoryTable starting from etherHistoryDropEvents up to etherHistoryCollisions are similar to those in the etherStatsTable, and mean almost the same thing, therefore, we will discuss those objects which are unique to the etherHistoryTable. These objects are:

etherHistoryIndex (INTEGER): Has the same value as historyControlIndex. This entry links the historyControl-Table and etherHistoryTable.

etherHistorySampleIndex (INTEGER): Each etherHistory-Index has one or more entries for etherHistorySample Index. This entry starts from 1, and each sample has a unique value increasing by 1.

etherHistoryIntervalStart (YYrnencks): Refers to the sysUpTime when data collection was started.

etherHistory Utilization (INTEGER): Provides the best estimate of the mean physical layer network utilization in percentage over the time interval during which data collection was done etherHistoryUtilization refers to the utilization over one Ethernet interface.

Alarm group

Implementation of the alarm group is optional. If it is implemented, then the event group must also be implemented because they are interrelated. In the alarm group periodic samples are collected and then compared with the threshold values. If the value of a monitored variable crosses the threshold, then an event is generated. Objects in this group are useful for performance management. Events generated are useful for fault management. The alarm group uses an alarmTable which has entries stating how samples are to be taken and how the alarms are to be generated. The objects in the alarmTable are:

alarmIndex (INTEGER): A unique identifier which identifies a row in the alarmTable. alarmIndex refers to a sample for an object at a particular interval of time.

alarmInterval (INTEGER): States the time interval during which samples are taken from an object being observed.

alarmVariable (OBJECT IDENTIFIER): Refers to the identifier of the object being sampled. The object being sampled should have a data type of INTEGER, Counter, Gauge, or TimeTicks.

alarmSampleType (INTEGER): States how sample values are interpreted. It has two values: absoluteValue = 1 and deltaValue= 2. If the sample value is the absoluteValue, then it is compared against the threshold value for generating alarms. However, if it is a deltaValue, then the previous sample value is subtracted from the current value and this difference is compared with the threshold values.

alarmValue (INTEGER): Provides the last valid sample value. A sample value is complete and available only at the end of a sampling period.

alarmStartupAlarm (INTEGER): Has three values: rising-Alarm 1, fallingAlarm = 2, and risingOrFalling-Alarm = 3. This states what type of alarm will be generated. When a sample value is greater than or equal to alarmRisingThreshold, and, alarmStartupAlarm is equal to risingAlarm or risingOrFalling Alarm, then a single rising alarm will be generated. Similarly, when a sample value is less than or equal to alarm. FallingThreshold and the alarmStartupAlarm is equal to fallingAlarm or risingOrFallingAlarm, then a falling alarm will be generated. These conditions can result in events being generated and sent to network monitors or management stations.

alarmRisingThreshold (INTEGER): Represents a threshold value for a monitored object. A rising event can be generated when the sample value of a monitored object is greater than or equal to alarmRisingThreshold. The previous value should not have crossed the alarmRisingThreshold value. A rising event can also be generated if the first value of this entry is greater than or equal to the alarmRisingThreshold value and the associated alarmStartupAlarm is equal to risingAlarm or risingOrFallingAlarm.

alarmFallingThreshold (INTEGER): Similar to the alarmRisingThreshold, but it represents a threshold value in the opposite direction. When a sampled value is less than or equal to this alarmFallingThreshold and when the value of the previous sampling interval was greater than the alarmFallingThreshold, a falling event is generated. A falling event is also generated if the value of the first entry is less than or equal to this threshold value and the associated alarmStartupAlarm is equal to fallingAlarm or risingOrFallingAlarm.

alarmRisingEventIndex (INTEGER): Used to identify the event generated when a rising threshold is crossed. The value in this entry corresponds to the eventlndex in an eventTable. If there is n corresponding entry in eventIndex, then there is no relationship this alarm entry with the event entry in eventTable. If this value zero, then there is no valid entry in eventTable.

alarmFallingEuentIndex (INTEGER): While alarmRising-EventIndex is used when crossing rising thresholds, alarmFallingEventlndex is used when a falling thresholds is crossed.

alarmOwner (OwnerString): Refers to one or more management stations which configured this entry in alarmTable.

alarmStatus (EntryStatus): Refers to the status of the entry in alarmTable.

Host group

The host group contains statistics on each of the hosts discovered in the network. These are derived by noting good packets received on the network. Each host is identified by the MAC address.

hostControl Table: The entries in this table determine how the statistics on hosts are to be maintained. Based on the parameters' of this table, data is collected and entered in hostTable and hostTimeTable.

hostTable: Has entries on each host based on the MAC addresses. These MAC addresses are used to index into hostTable.

hostimeTable: The rows in this table are arranged in order of hostTimeCreationOrder. The hostTimeCreationOrder column of the table starts from 1, and this is used for indexing into hostTimeTable. There is a subtle difference between hostTable and hostTimeTable. In hostTable, we index into the table using MAC addresses, while in hostTimeTable, we index into the table using hostTimeCreationOrder. The format of the data collected is the same for both tables. By indexing in the order in which the entries are created in hostTimeTable, it is easier to download these tables by means of management stations using SNMP. Also, it is easy to break the packets into manageable SNMP PDUs. The other advantage is that to get details of new hosts added after a download of data from hostTimeTable, entries must be downloaded after a particular value of *N* instead of downloading hostTimeTable all over again.

The entries in hostTable and hostTimeTable are useful for configuration, performance, and fault management. Knowing the addresses of hosts in a network by frequently downloading the entries in hostTimeTable helps in keeping track of the active hosts in the network. When entries are deleted from hostTimeTable, the configuration of the network on the hosts can be accordingly modified. The different objects of the host group are:

hostControlIndex (INTEGER): Each discovered host in a network has an entry in hostControlTable. hostControlIndex is a unique identifier for a row and a host.

hostControlDataSource (OBJECT IDENTIFIER): Identifies t source for data. This source can be any interface on a host and h a corresponding entry in ifIndex.

hostControlTableSize (INTEGER): Corresponds to the number of entries in hostTable for a host. As the entries in hostTable and hostTimeTable have one-to-one correspondence, this number also refers to the number of entries in hostTimeTable.

hostControlLastDeleteTime (TimeTicks): Relates to the time when an entry was last deleted from hostTable. A zero value indicates that no deletions were made in hostTable.

hostControlOwner and *hostControlStatus* have the same significance as described earlier in other RMON MIB groups. In both hostTable and hostTimeTable, only the objects which need explanation will be examined, and we will avoid discussing those objects which are similar in meaning to the ones already explained. Some of the objects which need explanation are:

hostAddress (OCTET STRING): Refers to the MAC address of the host.

hostCreationOrder (INTEGER): A number from I to *N* and having a corresponding row in hostControlEntry. The numbers in hostCreationOrder are increased by one as a new entry is created.

hostIndex (INTEGER): The value in this column is the same as the value in hostControlIndex.

hostInPkts (Counter): Provides the number of good packets received through this host address, furnished by hostAddress, after adding this host to hostTable.

hostOutPkts (Counter): Identifies the total number of packets transmitted by the host, including the error packets.

hostInOctets (Counter): Contains the total number of octets received by this host after it was added to hostTable. hostInOctets does not include error octets and framing bits.

hostOutOctets (Counter): Furnishes the total number of octets transmitted by this host. It includes error octets, but does not include framing bits in the count of octets.

hostOutErrors (Counter): Relates to the number of error packets transmitted by a host after being added to the host table. This object is very useful for performance and fault management. hostOutErrors along with hostOutOctets can furnish solid information on how a host is behaving.

hostOutBroadcastPkts (Counter): A counter for the number of good broadcast packets transmitted by this host after this entry was added to hostTable.

hostOutMulticastPkts (Counter): Counter contains only the packets transmitted to multicast addresses after being added to the host table. Because the distinction has been made between multicast and broadcast, this counter naturally does not include the number of packets broadcast by this host.

The entries in hostTimeTable are:

hostTimeAddress (OCTET STRING): Pertains to the MAC address of the host.

hostTime Creation Order (INTEGER): The index used for hostTimeTable. The entries are arranged sequentially from one to N. This entry has the same value as hostControlTableSize of hostControlTable.

hostTimeIndex (INTEGER): Has the same value as hostControlIndex of hostControlTable.

In hostTimeTable, other entries, from *hostInPkts* up to and including *hostOutMulticastPkts,* have the same significance as described in hostTable.

HostTopN group

The HostTopN group can be used to report the statistics on a group of hosts over a period of time. These statistics on selected hosts over a sampling interval is known as a *report* and is sent to one or more management stations. These statistics are derived from the host group. The interval for collecting data and start and stop times from the host group is determined by management stations. Once the data is collected in hostTopNTable, then it is available for management stations. The implementation of the HostTopN group is optional. However, if this group is implemented, then the Host group must also be implemented. Data collected from the HostTopN group are useful for performance and fault management. The objects in the HostTopN group are:

hostToPNControlIndex (INTEGER): A unique entry which identifies a top *N* report for one interface.

hostTopNHostIndex (INTEGER): The value of this entry and the value of hostIndex in hostTable are the same.

hostTopNRateBase (INTEGER): Identifies an object in hostTable on which data is collected. The values of the objects in hostTopNRateBase are: hostTopNInPkts = 1, hostTopNOutPkts = 2, hostTopNInOctets = 3, hostTopN-OutOctets = 4, hostTopNOut Errors = 5, hostTopNOut-BroadcastPkts = 6, and hostTopNOutMulticastPkts = 7. The significance of these variables is as explained in the host group.

hostTopTimeRemaining (INTEGER): Provides the time remaining in the sampling interval to complete the data collection for hostTopNTable. Only when the value becomes zero will hostTopNEntry be available. If the value is nonzero, then host top N entries cannot be retrieved.

hostTopNDuration (INTEGER): Provides information on the sampling interval in seconds for the previous report, or, if the data is being collected, then this furnishes elapsed time since data collection started. The value of hostTopNDuration is set along with the value of hostTopNTimeRemaining.

hostTopNRequestedSize (INTEGER): Identifies the maximum number of hosts requested for hostTopNTable. Here, the default value is 10.

hostTopNGrantedSize (INTEGER): Furnishes the number of hosts on which data can be collected in hostTopNTable. Because there can be limitations on resources, sometimes this value cannot be equal to the value of hostTopNRequestedSize. This value should be set as close to hostTopNRequestedSize as possible.

hostTopNStartTime (TimeTicks): Provides sysUpTime at which hostTopNReport was started.

hostTopNOwner and *hostTopNStatus* have the same meaning as described previously for corresponding entries in other RMON groups. HostTopN group also has hostTopNTable, which includes the following objects:

hostTopNReport (INTEGER): Identifies a report. Its value is the same as the value of hostToPNControlIndex.

hostTopNIndex (INTEGER): Identifies a row in the hostTopNTable. hostTopNIndex starts from 1 and increases by a value of 1.

hostToPNAddress (OCTET STRING): Refers to the MAC address of a host.

hostTopNRate (INTEGER): Provides the amount of change in the selected object, which is selected by hostTopNRateBase.

Matrix group

In the Matrix group the statistics on conversations between two sets of MAC addresses are maintained in two tables: matrixSDTable and matrixDSTable. Entries in these tables are controlled by the objects in matrixControlTable. In all these tables, when there are shortages of resources, the least recently used entries are deleted. Implementation of the matrix group is optional. matrixSDTable is primarily indexed on the basis of source and destination addresses. However, in matrixDSTable, the statistics on a conversation are indexed on the basis of destination and source addresses. So the major difference between these two tables is in the manner in which the tables are accessed for processing. These tables are useful for configuration, performance, and fault management. In configuration management, granularity may be depicted to the conversation levels, in which case, it is easy to collect data on active conversations from the matrix group. The explanations of objects in the matrix group are:

matrixControlIndex (INTEGER): Uniquely identifies an entry in matrixControlTable. For each matrixControlIndex entry, statistics are stored in matrixSDTable and matrixDSTable.

matrixControlDataSource (OBJECT IDENTIFIER): Represents the identifier of the source device on which conversation statistics are collected.

Other objects, from *matrixControlTableSize* through *matrixControl Status,* have the same meaning as corresponding objects in other *groups.*

matrixSDSourceAddress (OCTET STRING): Refers to the source MAC address for the conversation on which statistics are being collected. Note that the MAC address identifies a host.

matrixSDDestAddress (OCTET STRING): Refers to the destination MAC address.

matrixSDIndex (INTEGER): Has the same value as matrixControlIndex in matrixControlEntry. This entry helps to associate matrixControlEntry with a row in matrixSDTable.

matrixSDPkts (Counter): Provides the total number of packets transmitted from a source to the destination. It also includes error packets.

matrixSDOctets (Counter): Refers to the total number of good octets transmitted from a source to the destination address. It does not include framing bits but does include error octets.

matrixSDErrors (Counter): Includes error packets trans-mitted from a source to the destination address. By subtracting matrixSDErrors from matrixSDPkts, statistics on the number of,: good packets can be recovered.

The objects of matrixDSTable have similar meaning to those in matrixSDTable.

Filter group

The filter group helps in matching the conditions for capturing data or generating events. The concept of channels is used here. Input data is subjected to a set of filter rules stated in different variables in the filter group. Filter rules are applied to packet data and packet status. From the filter operation, a channel is obtained. The channel data can be stored with the aid of captureBufferTable. Note that *channel is* a technical concept and not a physical component. If the channel is enabled, then *events* are generated. An event can also enable the channel on or off. From a channel, we can generate SNMP trap messages and log the events.

The filter group has two tables: filterTable and channelTable. The objects provided are:

filterIndex (INTEGER): A unique index which identifies an entry in filterTable.

filterChannelIndex (INTEGER): Identifies a channel and matches the channelIndex in channelTable.

filterPktData Offset (INTEGER): Points to the starting point in data after which a filter will be applied. The offset is measured after framing bits in a physical layer frame.

filterPktData (OCTET STRING): Provides the data for filtering. It is used along with filterPktDataMask and filterPktDataNotMask.

filterPktDataMask (OCTET STRING): Bits with Is are relevant. filterPktDataMask is extended with Is if it is shorter than filterPktData.

filterktDataNotMask (OCTET STRING): The inverse of the filterPktDataMask. If the filterPktDataNotMask is shorter than the filterPktData, then this mask is extended with 0s.

filterPktStatus (INTEGER): Matched with the input packet, and the input bits relevant here are those corresponding to Is in the filterPktStatusMask.

filterPktStatusMask (INTEGER): Applied to the filterPktStatus, and only those bits which have Is are relevant. Here, as with filterPktDataMask, if filterPktStatus is shorter than the filterPktStatusMask, then filterPktStatus is extended by adding Is.

filterPktStatusNotMask (INTEGER): Operates inversely to filterPktStatusMask.

filterOwner and *filterStatus* have the same meanings as described for corresponding objects in other groups.

The objects in the channelTable are:

channelIndex (INTEGER): Identifies a unique entry in the channel table.

channelIfIndex (INTEGER): Uniquely identifies an interface on the RMON device (just like IfIndex).

channelAcceptType (INTEGER): Controls the actions of the filters associated with the channel. It has values of acceptMatched = 1 and acceptFailed = 2. In accept-Matched, packets will be accepted if there is a match of packet data and packet status. In acceptFailed, for a packet to be accepted, the packet data match or packet status match must fail.

channelDataControl (INTEGER): Controls the flow of data, status, and events through the channel. It has two values: on = 1 an~ off = 2. If the value is on, then data, status, and events can flow through the channel. If the status is off, then data, status, and events do not pass through the channel.

channel TurnOnEventIndex (INTEGER): Controls the generation of events. If an event is generated, then this value has a corresponding value in the eventIndex entry in eventTable.

channelTurnOffEventIndex (INTEGER): Will turn channel-DataControl to off from on, after an event is generated. It also has an entry in the eventIndex entry in eventTable.

channelEventIndex (INTEGER): Will identify the event to be generated when there is a packet match and channelDataControl is on.

channelEventStatus (INTEGER): Used for controlling the flow of events. It has three values: eventReady = 1, eventFired = 2, and eventAlwaysReady = 3. When this object is set to eventReady, an event will be generated and the object will change to the eventFired state. The eventAlwaysReady state will disable flow control, and events will be generated freely.

channelMatches (Counter): States the number of times there has been a packet match, including those cases where channelDataControl is off.

channelDescription (DisplayString): Describes the channel.

channelOwner and *channelStatus* have the same significance as described for corresponding objects in other groups.

Packet capture group

On the basis of filters, packets are captured and stored in, captureBufferTable of the packet capture group tables. A channel is associated with captureBufferTable. bufferControlTable determines how filtered data are stored in captureBufferTable. One row of captureBuffer-Table is used to store data on packets from a channel. The implementation of the packet capture group is optional. If the Filter group is implemented, then this group must be implemented. The objects in the packet capture group are:

bufferControlIndex (INTEGER): A unique index that identifies a entry in bufferControlTable.

bufferControlChannelIndex (INTEGER): Identifies the channel Its value is the same as the value in channelIndex.

bufferControlFullStatus (INTEGER): Shows the status of the buffer which is used to store data received from filters. It has two values: spaceAvailable = 1 and full = 2.

bufferControlFullAction (INTEGER): Will indicate the action to be taken when the buffer becomes full. It has two values: lockWhenFull = 1 and wrapWhenFull = 2.

bufferControlCaptureSliceSize (INTEGER): Furnishes the maximum number of octets of each packet which will be stored in the capture buffer. If it is set to zero, then as many octets as possible will be saved in the capture buffer.

bufferControlDownloadSliceSize (INTEGER): States the maximum number of octets that will be retrieved from a management station by an SNMP GetRequest or GetNextRequest PDUs. The default value is 100 octets.

bufferControlDownloadOffset (INTEGER): States the offset after which data in the buffer will be retrieved by a management station with an SNMP GetRequest or GetNextRequest PDU. The default offset value is 0.

bufferControlMaxOctetsRequested (INTEGER): Furnishes the maximum number of octets which a management station desires a capture buffer to save. A default value of -1 indicates that the request by the management station to the monitoring device is to save as many octets as possible.

bufferControlMaxOctetsGranted (INTEGER): We have noted earlier that a monitoring device may have resource limitations. Under those circumstances, it is not possible to furnish the buffer space requested by a management station. bufferControlMaxOctetsGranted supplies the actual number of octets that can be saved, and if the default value is 1, then the capture buffer" will save as many octets as possible.

bufferControlCapturedPackets (INTEGER): Furnishes the nu ber of packets actually stored at present in a capture buffer.

bufferControlTurnOnTime (INTEGER): Provides sysUpTime when the capture buffer started functioning.

bufferControlOwner and *bufferControlStatus* have the same significance described for corresponding objects in other groups.

The captureBufferTable has the following entries:

captureBufferControlIndex (INTEGER) Provides the index of an entry in captureBufferTable.

captureBufferIndex (INTEGER): Increases in value by 1 from 1, and uniquely identifies an entry in captureBufferTable.

captureBufferPakcetID (INTEGER): An index, in ascending order, describing the order of the packets received on an interface. These packets may be stored in one or more capture buffers, hence aiding in identifying the packets.

captureBufferPacketData (OCTET STRING): Contains the captured data of a packet.

capture BufferPacketLength (INTEGER): Furnishes the length of the captured packet and includes the FCS octets.

captureBufferPacketnme (INTEGER): Furnishes the relative time in milliseconds when a packet was captured since the capture buffer was turned on.

captureBufferPacketStatus (INTEGER): Provides the error status of a packet. The values defined are: packet length greater than 1518 octets = 0, packet length less than 64 octets = 1, packet had CRC or alignment error = 2, first packet in the capture buffer after an error was discovered = 3 and packet's order in buffer is only approximate = 4. The fourth bit definition is an addition in RFC 1757.

Event group

The event group helps in the generation and notification of events. These events might have been generated due to conditions elsewhere in the MIB. It may be determined that when a certain threshold is reached an event is generated. Parameters of events are described in eventTable. When an event is generated, it may be necessary to log the event. Events are logged in logTable. Here an SNMP trap may be generated and used to notify a managing station. The objects are:

eventIndex (INTEGER): Identifies an entry in eventTable.

eventDescription (DisplayString): Provides the description of the event.

eventType (INTEGER): Describes the type of event. The values are: none = 1, log = 2, snmp-trap = 3, and log-and-trap = 4. If an event is logged, then a value of 3 is used and there is a corresponding entry in logTable. If an SNMP trap is sent to one or more management stations, then the value is 3. When the SNMP trap is logged the value is 4.

euentCommunity (OCTET STRING): Names the SNMP community to which the SNMP trap must be sent.

eventLastTimeSent (TimeTicks): Furnishes sysUpTime when an event was last generated. If it is set to 0, then no event was generated.

eventOwner and *eventStatus* have the same signi-ficance as described for corresponding entries in other groups.

logEventIndex (INTEGER): Has the value of eventIndex for which a log was generated.

logIndex (INTEGER): Identifies an entry in the log table.

logTime(TimeTicks): Furnishes sysUpTime when an event that has been logged in logTable was created.

logDescription (DisplayString): Presents the description of the event.

RMON for Token Ring (RFC 1513)

RFC 1513 extends the RMON MIB for the tokenring protocol by adding a new group for tokenRing under RMON.

We discuss RFC 1513 separately, because it neatly describes extensions for the tokenring protocol. Because RFC 1271 is specifically tailored for collecting data on Ethernet protocols, new groups are exclusively added to statistics and history groups for the tokenring protocol. Error counters in a hostEntry for token ring will be incremented for isolating errors such as LineErrors, BurstErrors, ACErrors, InternalErrors, and AbortErrors. In token ring, matrix group error counters are not incremented. For bit mask interpretations for the filter group, refer to RFC 1513. The following new object groups have been added to the token-ring protocol:

Token-ring station
Token-ring station order
Token-ring station configuration
Source routing statistics

New data types in RFC 1513 are:

MacAddress (OCTET STRING (SIZE (6)): Defines the MAC address used in IEEE Standard 802. 1. When MacAddress is used, the source routing bit is stripped off.

TimeInterval (INTEGER): Refers to a period of time, and is measured in intervals of 0.01 seconds.

Token-ring MAC-layer statistics group

The token-ring MAC-layer statistics group consists of one table: tokenRingMLStatsTable. This table has statistics on the MAC layer for one token-ring interface, so the objects defined have significance to the MAC layer. We will discuss only those objects which are unique to this group and will not repeat the explanations of those objects which are similar to the ones we discussed with RFC 1757. As we have seen with RFC 1757, these statistics are useful for performance and fault management. In the following discussion, ML stands for MAC layer. The objects in the group are:

tokenRingMLStatsMacPkts (Counter): Refers to the total number of octets in good MAC packets received. It does not include the packets which had errors. A good frame refers to a token-ring frame defined by IEEE 802.5 standards.

tokenRingMLStatsRingPurgeEvents (Counter): Specifies the number of times the ring purge state has been reached from a normal state. In token ring, data is received when a station is in a *normal repeat mode.* In this mode, a station will receive a frame and transmit it. A ring purge MAC frame must be sent before an active monitor originates a new token. When a ring purge frame is received, timers in stations are reset, and stations enter the normal repeat mode.

tokenRingMLStatsRingPurgePkts (Counter): Refers to the total number of ring purge MAC packets.

tokenRingMLStatsBeaconEvents (Counter): Refers to the number of times a beacon state has been entered. To understand this counter, the concept of *beacoming* must be understood. In token ring, a ring can become nonoperational due to faults in stations, which are known as *hard errors.* A hard error in a station is usually detected by its immediate downstream neighbor. On receiving this frame, the downstream neighbor sends a *beacon frame,* which contains the address of its upstream neighbor and the information on the type of error. By knowing the address of the upstream neighbor, the ring station that has a failure can be pinpointed.

tokenRingMLStatsBeaconTime (TimeInterval): Furnishes the duration of the beaconing state.

tokenRingMLStatsBeaconPkts (Counter): Provides the total number of MAC beacon packets.

tokenRingMLStatsClaimTokenEvents (Counter): Separates the entry to the claim token state into three states: from the normal ring state, from the ring purge state, and from the beacon state. In this counter, only the first two cases are taken, and the total number of times a token enters the claim token state is furnished. Note that the claim token process is done to elect a new active monitor.

tokenRingMLStatsClaimTokenPkts (Counter): Refers to the total number of claim token MAC packets.

tokenRingMLStatsNAUNChanges (Counter): Has the total number of *nearest active upstream neighbor* (NAUN) changes. Note that when an active monitor broadcasts an active monitor present MAC frame, the first ring station that receives this frame saves the source address of the active monitor present frame as the NAUN address. These NAUN addresses are useful for isolating errors in a segment.

tokenRingMLStatsLineErrors (Counter): Provides the total number of line errors.

tokenRingMLStatsInternalErrors (Counter): Refers to the total number of adapter internal errors.

tokenRingMLStatsBurstErrors (Counter): Provides the total number of burst errors.

tokenRingMLStatsACErrors (Counter): Refers to the total number of address copied errors.

tokenRingMLStatsAbortErrors (Counter): A counter of the total number of abort delimiters in error-reporting packets.

tokenRingMLStatsLostFrameErrors (Counter): Refers to the total number of lost frames.

tokenRingMLStatsCongestionErrors (Counter): Provides the total number of receive congestion errors.

tokenRingMLStatsFrameCopiedErrors (Counter): For counting frame copied errors.

tokenRingMLStatsFrequencyErrors (Counter): Provides the total number of frequency errors.

tokenRingMLStatsTokenErrors (Counter): For counting the total number of token errors.

tokenRingMLStatsSoftErrorReports (Counter): Refers to the total number of *soft error* frames. Soft errors mean errors which temporarily make the rings nonoperational, although it is possible to recover from them. These soft errors can pose major problems if there are too many of them.

tokenRingMLStatsRingPollEvents (Counter): Relates to the total number of ring polls initiated by an active monitor.

The other group in the token ring statistics group is the token ring promiscuous statistics group. According to *Webster's New Collegiate Dictionary,* one meaning of *promiscuous is* "composed of all sorts of persons or things." In the MAC layer statistics group' data was collected on just the MAC layer. It is necessary to know data about the physical and link layers too. Hence, there is the tokenring promiscuous statistics group. Data on this group is also useful for performance and fault management. The objects in this group are similar to the data collected in etherStatsTable, thus, we will not discuss each of the objects in the group. Because there is no Ethernet restriction that the packets must be between 64 and 1518 octets, the range of packet length in token ring is greater.

Token-ring history group

Similar to the statistics group, the token-ring history group extends the history group described for RFC 1271. Here, too, history on a token-ring interface is collected and data are saved in tokenRingMLHistoryTable for the MAC layer and in tokenRingPHistoryTable for the non-MAC layer data. Data collected in these tables is useful for performance and fault management. The implementation of the token-ring history group is optional, but it requires the implementation of history groups mentioned in RFC 1757. The meanings of objects are similar to the corresponding ones in RFC 1757 and the token-ring statistics group, so we will not provide individual explanations.

Token-ring ring station group

The token-ring ring station group contains the statistics and status of each station attached to a token-ring network. When there are resource limitations on the network monitor, the resources which have been inactive for the longest time must be freed. The implementation of this group is also optional. The data collected for, this station are useful for configuration, performance, and fault management. RingStationControlEntry has parameters for collecting data on stations in the ring which have been discovered. ringStationEntry has the actual data on the stations. For this group, we will discus those objects that have new meanings.

ringStationControlActiveStations (INTEGER): Furnishes the number of active ringStationEntry in the ringStation-Table.

ringStationControlRingState (INTEGER): Presents the current status of the ring. The values are: normalOperation = 1, ringPurgeState = 2, claimToken-State = 3, beacon-FrameStreamingState = 4, beaconBit-StreamingState = 5, beaconRingSignalLossState = 6, and beaconSetRecoveryModeState = 7. These status values can be useful for depicting status in appropriate colors, while showing the configuration and status of the token-ring network.

ringStationControlOrderChanges (Counter): Contains the number of add and delete events in ringStationOrderTable.

ringStationControlBeaconSender, ringStationControl-BeaconNAUN, and ringStationControlActiveMonitor refer to the address of the sender of the beacon frame, the address of the NAUN in the beacon frame, and the address of the active monitor, respectively.

ringStationTable furnishes statistics on a particular station in the ring. Here, ringStationStationStatus, which can have values of active = 1, inactive = 2, and forcedRemoval = 3, respectively, is very useful for depicting the status of a station in a ring in configuration management. These states of a station may be represented by different colors. In addition, ringStationLastEnterTime and ringStationLastExitTime indicate when a station entered and exited a ring and are also useful for configuration management. The value unknown, indicated by a value of 0 in these variables, can be shown by a specific color when depicting these stations in a ring.

Tokenring ring station order group

The token-ring ring station order group has ringStationOrderTable, in which stations are identified from the station on which the network monitor is placed. The order of a station relative to the station with the network monitor is furnished by ringStationOrder-OrderIndex, and the address of the station is furnished by ringStationOrderMacAddress.

Token-ring ring station config group

The token-ring ring station config group manages token-ring nodes. Another popular term to describe managing token-ring nodes is the *configuration of nodes.* The following describes the nonobvious objects in ringStationConfigControlTable:

ringStationConfigControlRemove (INTEGER): Has two values: stable = I and removing = 2. When RMON agents set the value of this variable to removing, it results in the remove station MAC frame. After this frame is processed, the RMON agent sets this variable to stable.

ringStationConfigControlUpdateStats (INTEGER): Also has two values: stable = I and updating = 2. The behavior of this object is similar to the behavior of ringStationConfigControlRemove. When this object is set to updating, then the configuration information associated with this entry is updated. After this update is over, the RMON agent will set this object to stable.

ringStationConfigTable provides the configuration, entries after a query by the ringStationConfig-ControlUpdateStats',, variable. These data are also useful for configuration management. Some of the associated variables needing explanations are:

ringStationConfigLocation (OCTET STRING(SIZEW): Refers to the actual physical location of the station.

ringStationConfigMicrocode (OCTET STRING(SIZE(10)): Indicates the microcode level of the station.

ringStationConfigGroupAddress (OCTET STRING (SIZE (4)): Pertains to the low-order four octets of the group address recognized by the station.

Token-ring source routing group

The implementation of the token-ring source routing group is optional. Data in this group are collected in source routing bridges and are valid in source routing environments. In transparent bridging or mixed source and transparent bridge environments, the data are not accurate. sourceRoutingStatsTable provides a list of entries with statistics on source routing for tokenring interfaces. Some of the variables in this group are:

sourceRoutingStatsRingNumber (INTEGER): In an internetwork, there may be many rings, which are assigned numbers by management stations. It is this ring number that is entered here.

sourceRoutingStatsInFrames (Counter): Provides the total number of frames sent to a token-ring station from another ring.

sourceRoutingStatsOutFrames (Counter): Refers to the number of frames sent out from a ring.

sourceRoutingStatsThroughFrames (Counter): Provides the total number of frames which went through a ring. Here, frames are received by a ring and they are transmitted to the next ring.

sourceRoutingStatsAllRoutesBroadcastFrames (Counter): Refers to the total number of good all routes broadcast frames that were received.

sourceRoutingStatsSingleRouteBroadcastFrames (Counter): Has the count of good frames received which had single route broad, cast.

sourceRoutingStatsInOctets, sourceRoutingStatsOut-Octets, sourceRoutingStats Through Octets, sourceRouting-StatsAllRoutesBroadcastOctets, and *sourceRoutingSingle-RoutesBroadcastOctets* have counts of octets instead of frames, which we saw earlier. The counts refer to good octets only.

14

Network Management

Business is dynamic. Consequently there is matching growth and decay of the networks that support the business. New requirements may lead to different types of equipment being connected to the network, or different networking technologies, with different behavioural characteristics may be introduced to meet changing workloads. As old equipment becomes obsolete and harder to maintain, it will be phased out to be replaced by newer technology. A network makes such evolution possible. Network management assists the evolutionary process and ensures that it is controllable. Management concerns the *planning, organizing, monitoring, accounting* and *control* of resources and activities. Business enterprises establish policies and provide human structures to carry out the planning and organizational activities to effect a particular management policy. Although computers will probably be used to plan and organize, this use of information technology is usually regarded as lying outside the scope of network management. Rather, network management is more concerned with the day-to-day, operational aspects of maintaining a viable network environment; that is it is concerned with the accounting, monitoring and control functions of management. A particular aspect of management policy in many systems concerns the availability and effective use of resources. The policy may also influence the security of information and its processing in the distributed processing environment. Where the policy demands availability, it is the task of network administrators to achieve this, for example by providing duplicate resources. Where the policy also demands economy, they will find cost effective ways of providing backup. Where security is important they will ensure that the network is operated in such a manner as not to compromise user and management data.

Whereas these tasks can in principle be carried out by people, the responsiveness demanded for monitoring and the complexity of management information is such that many of the tasks are handled by the distributed information processing system itself. The network management team interacts with the processing environment to effect management policies and to provide feedback to policy makers on network behaviour. In short, network management can be implemented as an interactive, distributed processing application where the application task is that of managing the distributed processing environment.

Not all parts of a large network need the same degree of management control, not all will be subject to precisely the same policies. The network environment is therefore composed of many domains of management. We define a *domain* as:

> A set of managed objects that are grouped together, for the purpose of management organization, to support a particular aspect of management.

At the outermost level, domains are determined by the boundaries of different organizations. Within organizations there can be a hierarchy of subdomains, each responsible for a given subset of resources and activities. Domains may also be established on the grounds of delegated responsibility, security, operational reporting, resource naming, etc.

Modelling concepts in network management

A model for network management must cover three main aspects:

- The sphere of management responsibility.
- The delegation of management responsibility.
- The objects of management concern.

The principles of management authority and responsibility require that managers exercise control within their own management domain but that they cannot exercise control outside them. Yet, to provide effective management, managers will need information about activities in other domains which may influence their own domains. They will seek to access that information and even request the delegated authority to effect controlling actions on behalf of particular distributed applications. Management responsibility may be delegated within the management domain. A management entity lying within a domain and carrying out particular management activities is termed an *agent.* These requirements lead to the following dialogue types:

- Manager to manager: to obtain information or authority for control.
- Manager to manager: to request control be exercised on a manager's behalf.
- Manager to management agent: to invoke a management operation.
- Management agent to manager: to report the occurrence of a situation.

A collaborative project in the United Kingdom to develop an advanced network system architecture has adopted a four-level hierarchy of management in which administrators respond to the directives of policy makers and effect management activities. At the base of this hierarchy are the primitive management operations. Control is exercised down the hierarchy and management information flows in the reverse direction. This simple model can be further elaborated to allow for information filtering and for feedback at intermediate levels in the hierarchy.

When a domain is distributed, the interaction between managers and agents becomes explicit. At the operations level there are no peer information flows but at higher levels there can be both peer communication and manager-to-agent communication.

At each level, control is exercised over managed objects and data values are obtained from them. Objects may be passive having values assigned to them or data read from them. Some objects may be active, i.e. changed by agencies external to management activity. Such objects may 'spontaneously' report changes in the values of their attributes to their managers.

Functional areas of management

It is generally accepted that network management covers five areas:

- Fault handling.
- Performance monitoring.
- Accounting.
- Security management.
- Configuration management.

Analysis of these areas identifies the management requirements, specific management functions and the types of managed objects involved. The following examples briefly illustrate this functional decomposition.

Fault handling is concerned with responding to situations when a system no longer meets its specification. For example, comparing a count of the successful number of transactions with a count of failed transactions will show if the error rate for a system has risen to unacceptable levels. A fault-reporting algorithm may contain a threshold to identify the level at which a fault report will be generated.

Performance monitoring records the actual behaviour of systems. For example, operations could monitor the values of the same two counters identified above to see what grade of service was being provided and if the system was meeting its management objectives. Alternatively, the rate at which transactions occur could be monitored to determine throughput.

Accounting management establishes the use that is made of the networked resources, essentially for the purpose of making a charge. Again, counters will be read that total the 'cost' of using a resource. Accounting management can also be used to exercise control over the use of resources by sanctioning only a given amount of resource to be used before warning that an accounting threshold has been reached. A further use of accounting management concerns the maintenance and communi-cation of account records.

Because management operations influence system and network wide behaviour, it is essential that they be properly controlled. Like many other distributed applications, network management will have to demonstrate that authority exists before certain operations can be performed. The need for access control and the authentication of management actions are not of themselves aspects of network management. Rather, *security management* is the set of activities that maintain the security of the environment by controlling the way access permissions are communicated and exercised. Security management also includes activities that monitor the success with which security policies are enforced by, for example, maintaining security audit trails.

Configuration management is needed because the network and the activities within it change. As the network evolves new resources are added and old ones are discarded. The detection and rectification of faults also affects the availability of networking components. Configuration management monitors and controls the following:

- The state of resources and activities.
- The relationships between resources.
- The introduction and removal of resources,

Status is characterized both by administrative and operational attributes. Administratively a resource can be *available, unavailable* or *under test.* Operationally it may be *active* or *inactive.* Relationships characterize resource alternatives and the interconnectivity of resources. In the networking environment, configuration management controls and reports upon the path or route taken to communicate between resources. These aspects of configuration management and the need to create or delete references to both types and instances of managed objects may involve passing considerable amounts of information between systems, for example to update control tables or specify revised management algorithms.

These examples show that individual managed objects do not necessarily belong uniquely to a particular management functional area. Managed objects and their attributes, as typified by counters, gauges, reports, etc., are found in all aspects of management, and although some policy objectives may be satisfied by simple operations of the type described, many will require these simple operations to be compounded into more complex management procedures, For example, a report on the presence of a fault may lead to a check on performance. If this fell below the norm, it could lead to a change of configuration. The faulty component could be placed 'out of service' and made the subject of diagnostic tests to track down the nature of the fault in more detail.

Management standards

Users investing in distributed information technology want an open market for equipment in order to avoid being tied into a single vendor situation. They therefore welcome standardization which also brings the benefit of defined functionality and provides a yardstick against which to judge claims of conformance. These benefits of standardization apply equally to management standards though, because of the diversity of management requirement, the standards are both harder to define and to apply. Standards apply to interfaces and functions, not to the way systems are implemented. Having identified management functions, what are the interfaces? Network management is a distributed processing activity which requires a symbiosis between people and their computing systems. We identify three interfaces of concern to network management:

1. User-system.
2. System-system.
3. Application program-system.

The first two require some form of command and response language. Although the semantic requirements of such languages are similar, the syntax of the first interface is oriented towards human expression. The second interface can be optimized for efficient communication between computer systems. The third interface also concerns language but this time it is the binding between conventional programming languages and the objects of concern to management. These allow systems programmers to write programs to carry out monitoring and controlling operations. All three interfaces provide mechanisms to express the activities which a system is required to perform but, whereas the first and third are handled locally, the second interface involves the communication of the management information between systems. Thus, system-system interfaces require us to consider two aspects of standardization: (1) the end system activity and (2) the open communications between systems. The latter are expressed through open systems interconnection standards.

This distinction between the standards needed to specify the management objects and their associated operations, on the one hand, and the communication standards, on the other, is being developed in a standard document which gives an *overview* of the set of OSI management services. This standard is essentially concerned with the services to manage the OSI environment, that is the communications environment. However, research suggests that the principles it embodies are applicable to the wider aspects of management which are the subject of this chapter. An analysis of the requirements of the open communications environment shows that the OSI basic reference model has to be augmented to handle management. This extension to the reference model is specified in the OSI management framework.

The OSI management framework

The purpose of this standard is twofold:

1. It augments the protocol architecture of the OSI basic reference model by

describing the principles of communication in the OSI environment when applied to communication management activities.

2. It is prescriptive of some of the management standards that will be needed.

The basic reference model encapsulates the concept of protocol exchange between peer entities at seven layers. The service provided by each layer adds value to the communication service provided by lower layers and so provides an enhanced service to a higher layer. The highest layer specifies the application specific protocol. Network management is a distributed processing application so it is not surprising that the system-system communications discussed above should be conveyed by application layer protocol exchanges. This aspect of OSI management is defined as *systems management.* However, some management information is of necessity communicated also in lower layer protocols. This may occur during failure conditions, during system boot-strap or re-configuration. To handle these management communications, the OSI management framework defines the concept of *layer management.* It specifies the circumstances when layer management is appropriate and the constraints upon its use. For example, a network layer operating the X.25 protocol can provide accounting information relevant to a particular instance of communication as a normal part of the layer protocol. Alternatively, in a local area network that offers a broadcast facility, it is appropriate to use data link layer protocols to identify which of the attached systems is acting as manager to control the operation of the network at that level. Systems management is however specified as the norm. Whereas normal protocol exchanges ultimately serve inter-application communications, layer management exchanges are only between the systems connected at that level of protocol. However, the information being transmitted may be destined for a further system or may be transmitted as a result of a request from a distant system. Consider the example of system A requesting system B to place a remote modem into the loop-back test mode. The communication between A and B is a systems management exchange, that between B and the modem occurs through layer management protocol. How the information is handled within system B is an implementation matter. However, the OSI management framework provides an important modelling concept, the *management information base* to cover this type of communication. The management information base is a conceptual repository of information which is accessible for management purposes.

Management information services

OSI management standards encompass the following:

- Those parts of layer protocol standards that help to maintain layer activity on behalf of all users of the layer service.
- Specifications of managed objects that are the subject of systems and layer management communications.

- A naming structure to identify managed objects.
- Abstract definitions of management information together with the specification of operations on the information.
- Procedures that may be invoked to carry out management activities.
- Operations to perform management tasks for a specific management functional area
- The definition of a common application layer service for communicating management operations between open systems.
- A protocol specification for that communication service.
- Mappings between the definition of managed objects and their operations onto their representation in protocol exchanges.

Of these standards, those for the common management information service and protocol are the most advanced. These standards set out the rules for open communication between a manager and a management activity operating as a management agent. The standards are independent of specific management procedures and are applicable to all management functional areas. They distinguish between communications that notify managers of event reports in the agent system and operations that the manager requests of the agent. The general form of the latter is:

< operation type > < managed object identifier > < access right token > < value >

where the operation type is currently defined as one of the following:

- *Get* the value of the identified object.
- *Set* the value of the identified object.
- Perform a given *action* on the identified object.
- *Create* a managed object of a specified type.
- *Delete* the identified object.

Other operations, now being appended to the above list, are those to *cancel* a get operation and to *add* and *remove* members from a set of managed objects. The *cancel get* operation has been introduced to deal specifically with the prospect that a large amount of data may be returned to a manager who has requested a *get* operation of an agent. When network traffic is particularly heavy or the manager does not wish to be overburdened, this operation allows the original *get* to be terminated. The operation may be cancelled at any time. The protocol will ensure that the manager will know, unambiguously, whether the *get* finished normally or prematurely. Because a *get* operation leaves the agent system unchanged, there is no uncertainty concerning the state of the agent system after an early cancellation. There are also proposals to be able to cancel *set* and *action* operations, but these are meeting with resistance because they would leave the state of the agent undefined. Although the common management information protocol is seen as the principal mechanism for the transfer of management information, there is no reason in principle why file transfer protocols should not be invoked for the transfer of very large volumes of information.

All operations and notifications may require the agent system to respond to the communication to acknowledge that the operation has been performed or the notification has been dealt with. However, these standards are not concerned with the consequences of the semantics of the end system operation; these are defined by the specific management information services for each functional area and by the definitions of managed objects.

Some of the standards relating to the fault and configuration management functional areas are well advanced and draft proposals for international standards have recently been registered. One of the difficulties of standardization in this highly integrated area of OSI management standards is establishing an effective structure for the standards documents and meaningful crossreferences between standards. It would be im-practical to publish the whole of OSI management as a single standard since management is a potentially open-ended activity and new aspects of the standards could be added continually. Even if a reasonable subset were to be identified, publishing all those together represents a major editorial task which would delay stable parts of the standard while the less developed parts were refined.

Two sets of documents help to maintain the coherence of this set of standards. One, the management information services overview, has already been mentioned. The other set recognizes that many objects and operations are common to several different management functions. A group of documents defines the structure of management information, the common information types, their attributes and the operations upon them, The documents provide a prescriptive method for specifying new managed object types. For each type the following information is needed:

- The individual *items* of information that can be invoked by management.
- The *permitted* operations on those items.
- The *inherent* properties of the object.
- The *implicit* relations with other information elements.
- The *specific* properties for each instance of an object type.

The documents define such objects and attributes as: status, counter, gauge, threshold, event and log. One aspect of OSI management not included in this figure is the way conformance to management standards is defined. This area still needs further exploration since not only must implementations of the standard conform to the rules of the protocol exchanges but they must also conform to the definitions of the semantics of operations that take place in the end systems where management operations are performed. This presents an interesting problem since tests for conformance cannot expect common implementations of particular management operations. Therefore, indirect methods are needed to test for conformance to a distributed management algorithm and demonstrate that the desired operations have been performed correctly. The difficulties of testing for conformance are further compounded by the nature of the management operations themselves. For example, when testing for conformance to standards related to fault reporting, it is necessary to cause a system to simulate faults to carry out the specified procedure. However, responses may be generated spuriously when the system under test is itself faulty. Also, how may one test for performance without compromising the performance one is seeking to test? Even more significantly, how does one test security management functions without compromising system security? Finally, will it be possible to check re-configuration procedures in such a way that recovery is still possible even if the implementation of the standard under test fails to conform to requirements?

Further developments in open management

Those developing OSI management standards are well aware of the above issues and that they are only scratching the surface of the possible set of management activities that may need to be expressed as standards. So far, most operations and most objects are very simple as are their mappings onto management protocol. Also, they represent only those objects of concern to the open communications environment. It is the author's contention that, in the long run, all aspects of management have to be handled in a coherent manner whether they relate to communications objects, processing resources and activities or to data storage. It will not be possible for managers to monitor and control their distributed processing environments effectively if these areas of their responsibility are handled separately.

Research into distributed systems is now sufficiently mature as to show the appropriate architectures for distributed systems. This is now being complemented by the development of standards for open distributed processing (ODP). More recent work has extended these architectural approaches to encompass management by implementing distributed systems management activities in a wide area networked test bed. As a result, there is growing confidence that the current approach to OSI management is capable of handling all aspects of management. This requires that the current standards are developed with an eye to their eventual extension. Failure to do so runs the risk of constraining the development of open distributed management standards or, worse, of developing mutually incompatible sets of standards requiring different implementation approaches. The consequences for manufacturers would be increased development cost and this would be reflected to users in the costs of products.

What then must be done to extend OSI management? Firstly, the set of objects of concern to all of management and the operations upon them must be defined. Secondly, an extended set of management procedures is needed, though these are still likely to fall within the five functional areas of management that have been established. Then the objects, their operations and the procedures have to be mapped onto the services needed to communicate the management requirement between systems. This will call for extensions to the set of common management information services and protocol. One type of extension will allow for typical control structures to be communicated, for example to express conditional constructs or to request that a set of operations be repeated. Since these constructs can be nested, the syntax of information transfer will take on some of the aspects of a block structured language. A second type of extension will concern the conditions under which groups of activities will be performed. It will define relative priorities for remote operations and whether a group of operations shall be processed as an atomic action or whether a more relaxed processing regime is permitted. Many of these extensions will add to the functionality of the local operating system enabling its functionality to be extended over the distributed processing environment. This will assist in realizing the concept of a distributed operating system when interworking between existing systems with conventional operating systems.

One further benefit which is implicit in this approach to the development of open distributed management is that it handles the open endedness of management requirements and the need to allow managers to manage their systems according to their own policies; that is there is HU requirement to specify a standard way in which management is performed. Drawing upon the analogy of a programming language we see that, by adopting a language structured approach to management communications with a well-defined syntax and semantics we can generate any management procedure *in a standard way* and have it communicated and interpreted *according to a standard* so that it is understood, without having to standardize the procedure itself. With such a language, procedures for remote operation can be specified for immediate action or transferred as named procedures to be invoked by a subsequent *action* primitive.

Current practice

Although progress towards management standards has been slow and there are, as yet, only proposed functional standards for OSI management, manufacturers have recognized the need for some management tools to handle their proprietary networking products. These provide facilities for gathering performance related data, carrying out tests and performing re-configuration of network resources. The products are largely related to managing the communications infrastructure though some local area networking products for personal computer and workstation systems do permit their users to manipulate remote processing and storage resources.

Space does not permit a full analysis of existing products. However, the current ranges of products tend not to integrate their management functions into a single package. Rather, management is performed by a loosely coordinated group of software packages. Nor is communications management coordinated with distributed processing or distributed data management. Many of the current products are concerned solely with the local area communications network on which they reside. They are frequently installed within an IBM personal computer and observe network traffic as it passes; that is on a CSMA/CD network the interface would be instructed to operate in a 'promiscuous' mode, listening to all packets on the network cable. A similar operation is possible on token ring networks and though the packet is not processed by the management computer, it is able to monitor all traffic. Such management devices are well able to produce network traffic statistics, report packet collisions and detect ring failures. They are essentially monitoring devices. Some control can be exercised where such systems are used as filtering bridges between network segments. Also, where networks provide mechanisms for terminal multiplexing, some manufacturers offer proprietary products that restrict the services that may be accessed from a given terminal or by a given user at a terminal.

In some manufacturer's offerings the different aspects of management may have to be performed from different network management devices. For example, some of the products that support the interconnection of local area networks through fibre optic cable only allow the cable environment to be managed from a special management terminal. Management of the attached local networks must be done from other terminals while management of attachments must be done from yet another control system.

These are implementation matters, for even if there is a coherent set of management standards, manu-facturers will not be obliged to place all their management functionality into one box. However, offering a coherent set of standards increases the likelihood of their doing so and, having a compatible set of management standards, allows the users to purchase networking products knowing them to be accessible, for management purposes, in a common way.

Network management has become a critical issue, especially in heterogeneous and multivendor computer networks. Also, for the success of client-server computing, effective and proper implementation of network management is essential. Client-servers with a large number of workstations need network management to manage and control the networks and the components of networks with their associated hardware and software. Like other areas of the computer industry, network management has been undergoing rapid technological advances to meet ever increasing challenges.

It is worth mentioning that, these days, the *computer* has expanded to include desktop computers popularly known as personal computers, workstations, laptops, palm-held computers, and other computing devices, which have the intelligence to do computation and also to communicate with each other. With computer technology growing at an incredibly fast pace, it may not be proper to place limitations on what a "computer" can be. Computers can connect to one another to form a *local area network* (LAN). In LANs, there are two important computer networking scenarios. The most popular scenario is known as *client-server* computing. In client-server computing, a client requests a service from a server and the server provides the service to the client. As an example, compiling a computer program in a client can be done by the compiler located in a server. On the other hand, in *peer-to-peer* computer networking, there are no fixed roles such as that of client or server, and any computer in the network can be a client or server. For our discussion purposes, we include both computer networking scenarios under LANs.

The evolution from hostcentric computer networks to heterogeneous LAN networks has been gradual. This transformation to LAN computing and networking is further complicated by existing applications and protocols from different standards bodies and vendors. However, the limitations of technology, protocols, and topology impose restrictions on the number of computers that can be connected to form LANs. Therefore, clusters of networks have become the trend. Once these islands of networks come into existence, the issue of connecting and managing networks becomes important.

To get a better appreciation of the problems involved in the present-day network management of LANs, let us look at some of the possible LAN environments. Some networks can be connected by *bridges* with similar LAN protocols. Here, networks A and B use similar protocols, and they are connected by bridges. Sometimes, network A and network B are known as *segments*. Here one network is using a token ring and the other network is using Ethernet. *Routers* are used to connect these networks to the backbone network. There are also cases where dissimilar networks have to be interconnected. In this case, as shown in Figure 1.3, *gateways* are used for connecting the networks. Here one network may be using TCP/IP, and another one may be using Open Systems Interconnection (OSI) or System Network Architecture (SNA). Also, these LANs may span buildings and cities to form a *metropolitan area network* (MAN). An extension of the MAN can be found in the *wide area network* (WAN), which covers a larger area than a MAN does.

After having discussed some of the LAN scenarios, let us take some simple examples of problems involved in managing different components of a network. Suppose we have to apply a software fix to all the computers in a network. How do we do it? We cannot take a diskette and apply the fix to all the computers, especially if there are thousands of them. Or what about isolating a fault in one computer? How can we say with certainty that a problem has occurred in X computer? And we need to be sure what caused the problem, and how it can be rectified.

These sets of problems assume serious proportions if computers are from different vendors. These computers may be using different software and hardware architectures. There are various ways of reporting the problems and different ways to rectify them. In some cases, these architectures may be such that the computers attached to different LANs may not communicate with each other. In some cases, it may be necessary to connect these networks to a centralized computer. How do we connect these LANs from different vendors and then manage them from a single, central point?

All of these factors make the network management of computer networks and their components, which may be widely dispersed with multivendor origins and multiprotocol operation, a highly challenging task. How we meet it is the topic of this book.

Network management uses distinctions described by *open systems interconnection* (OSI) seven-layer architecture, it is imperative that we look into it right up front. The International Standards Organization (ISO) brought out the OSI architecture of seven layers for computer networking. The main idea behind partitioning computer networking functions into separate, independent subfunctions is to standardize each layer of activity more easily and expeditiously. Each layer is expected to carry out a set of functions and provide services to the layer above it.

As defined in OSI, a *system* includes computer hardware and peripherals, software, and applications, including those used for communications. *Open system* has different interpretations and connotations. We prefer the following definition: A system is said to be *open* if it supports a widely accepted and well-published set of standards. Openness is not concerned with the system technology, implementation, or how the systems are connected to one another.

The seven layers are as follows:

1. The *physical layer* deals with physical interfaces and details of the physical medium used to connect two open systems. It is concerned with mechanical, electrical, optical, functional, and procedural characteristics of the links used in data transfer.
2. The *data link layer is* responsible for reliable data transfer between two linked open systems. This may require flow control, error control and recovery, and synchronization.
3. The *network layer* provides a path for data transfer between end systems. In this layer, routing of data through a network of intermediate systems may be required. As a consequence, this layer is responsible for making connections when required, maintaining them, and terminating the connections when they are no longer needed.

4. The *transport layer* is concerned with data transfer from one end to another end. For this purpose, end-to-end error recovery and flow control may be required. Note that the network layer is concerned with data transfer from one system to another, whereas, in the transport layer, we are talking about end-to-end data transfer.
5. The *session layer* is responsible for sessions between applications. This layer also provides services for establishing, maintaining, and terminating these sessions.
6. The *presentation layer* is primarily responsible for resolving differences in the way data is represented between two applications on either end. As an example, ASCII to EBCDIC translation, or vice versa, may be done in this layer. This layer also may provide services such as encryption and data compression.
7. The *application layer* provides services and functions required by user applications. In other words, this layer provides applications and services which are not provided by lower layers to support communication between the systems. In this layer, we may include *commitment, concurrency, and recovery (CCR).* Applications such as electronic mail and network management belong to this layer. Network management applications, which use network management, also form part of this layer.

Network management, systems management, and *enterprise management* have been variously defined. This can lead to a lot of confusion and we will therefore clearly define what these terms will mean in this book. We define *management* as monitoring and controlling the resources in computers, the resources used in the connection and communication of computers, and the applications used in the computers. There are, broadly, two models for *network management,* based on how the management activities are accomplished. This, in turn, is dependent on the computing environment. A LAN is a typical *distributed-computing environment.* Management of LAN environments can be done by peer-to-peer network management. Sometimes, this is also known as *distributed-network management.* Here managers, which undertake the network management activities, act more as peers, and there is no one central manager.

The other model is *hierarchical,* or *centralized, network manageinent. In* this model, the network management is controlled from a single point, known as a *manager.* This manager may manage network resources from a centralized computing environment. This may cover the cases where one supermanager or one centralized controlling manager may manage devices via some intermediate managers. This supermanager is also known as the *manager of manager* (MOM). All these cases are grouped under *hostcentric network management.* Some-times, this can also be termed *enterprise management.*

Many definitions are in vogue for network management. We use the one provided by IEEE Standard 802.6-1990. "Network management provides mechanisms for the monitoring, control, and coordination of all managed objects within the Physical Layer and Data Link Layer of a node." The same document also defines systems management as follows: "Systems management provides mechanisms for the monitoring, control, and coordination of all managed objects within open systems. Systems management is effected through application layer protocol." Here we have to note that *skinny stacks* or trivial upper layers can also be used. From the definitions provided by the IEEE, it is apparent that network management is a subset of the activities in systems management.

In the preceding definitions, we have to be clear on the terms *monitoring, control,* and *coordination.* This is central to the concept of systems management. Let us examine the term *monitoring* first. Resources used in computer networks have to be continuously watched, and any untoward behavior leading to the deterioration of functioning of a resource, resources, or network has to be rectified. This is more a proactive action than a reactive one.

The resources have to be controlled. This means that we should be able to control how the resources behave so that they function properly. When resources have to be monitored and controlled, there is a necessary factor: coordination. If there is no coordination, the situation is a free-for-all, and chaos ensues. Not only do the activities of the managed resources have to be coordinated, but so do the facilities that monitor and control them.

Unfortunately, *systems management is* a very generic term. Readers can confuse it with management of systems used in other disciplines. This confusion is compounded by the use of different terms in the computer industry.

While treating the topics of OSI and SNA, especially in the peer-to-peer arena, *systems management* is the popularly used term; thus, it is better to use this term when dealing with these protocols. In Internet, *network management* is the prevalent term; hence, this term will be used when discussing this topic. While discussing IEEE-related management of resources and layer management, we will also use the term *network management.* In other places, where it is not specifically required to make distinctions between network management and systems management, the term *network management* has been used, as well.

Goals

Higher network availability: This involves improving the operational efficiency, which means reducing system and network downtime and improving response times. Problems in a network should be responded to as quickly as possible. In many cases, it should be possible to rectify the problems unattended. But the access and transfer of management information will require processing power and involve network traffic. Therefore, performance must be considered in the design and installation of network management.

Reduce network operational cost: Ultimately, cost reduction is one of the primary motives behind network management. Because the technology changes rapidly, management of heterogeneous systems and multiple protocols is desirable.

Reduce network bottlenecks: In some cases, network administration can be performed from a central site. Under these circumstances, it may be preferable to centrally monitor and control the activity of a network. In other cases, this activity may be distributed.

Increase flexibility of operation and integration: Networking technologies are changing at a fast rate to cater to changing requirements and needs. As new applications are used, protocols used in networking are also changing. It should be possible to absorb new technologies with the least cost. As an example, in LANs, data communication is common, but there may also be a need to integrate graphics, voice, and video capabilities as the application base expands. In addition, computer networks could be used to manage copiers and faxes.

It should be possible to add new technology and equipment without much difficulty. Also, there should not be major problems in migrating from one release of network management software to another version. Network management applications should not be overly platform-dependent for their function.

Higher efficiency: In some cases, some of the goals of network management overlap. If we reduce the network operational cost and improve the network availability, overall efficiency will increase. Here, factors such as utilization, operational cost, migration cost, and flexibility must also be considered.

Ease of use: End-user interfaces are critical for the success of any product. The use of network management applications should not involve a major learning curve. User interfaces based on object-oriented principles and technology are helpful for network management applications.

Security: Some network management functions may need security features. If some critical accounting data has to be secure, then there should be provisions for providing selective security. Here we are making the distinction between computer system and network and network management-related security. Our focus will be on the security of network management functions.

Network management systems architecture

We can organize network management systems as shown in Figure 1.6. This division is based on different functions performed at different levels. To avoid confusion with OSI layers, we have used the term *level* instead of *layer,* It may be noted that this division of functions is made to explain the concepts of overall network management systems. At the lowest level, we have the *operating system and hardware.* The operating system may be DOS, Windows NT, OS/2 Warp, Windows 95, or a combination of these. Network operating systems, such as Novell NetWare or OS/2 LAN server, are also part of this level. The figure shows resources in a separate box, because the intention is to highlight network management of varicus resources. These resources may be on the same workstation as the operating system or they may be separate components, such as a bridge or a router. Over the operating system and hardware, we need *protocol support*. Protocol support provides distinct services; hence, it must be treated as a separate level. Protocol support includes the following:

- Layers below the application layer in OSI, UDP/IP in Internet, or layers which have similar functionality.
- Management protocols such as SNMP, CMIP, or CMOL.
- Conversion of different protocols and multiprotocols which may also be needed for supporting heterogeneous and multivendor protocols.

The level above protocol support is the *network management framework*, which provides the base for various network management applications. In the computer industry, it is becoming a trend to enable and open up this level such that different vendors and alliance partners can write network management applications. The network management framework provides for the following:

- Manager and agent functions.
- Database support such as relational databases and object-oriented databases for storing data for many network management functions and applications support. We prefer to include database support in the network management framework, because network management applications sometimes need close access to the database for topology, status, inventory of resources, logs, and other data.
- View ana user interface support, which are important for the success of software applications. The base for these functions is provided in this layer.
- Network management functions, such as configuration management and fault management.

The *network management applications* area is a growing market and has the potential to produce very innovative applications. Some examples include the following:

- The business management applications area is still largely untapped. With the growing client-server market, this area has challenges and potential, especially regarding the dispersal of computing equipment and environment.
- Easy-to-use view applications can ease the tasks of system administrators. The use of multimedia and artificial intelligence has wide possibilities in this area.
- Fault identification and fault diagnostic applications such as automation

applications will be in greater demand to cater to the highly decentralized nature of networks.

Performance-tuning applications are very important. Even though processor power is increasing at a rapid pace and constraints such as memory are becoming cheaper, demands on them are also increasing at a fast pace. Demands on processing power will increase as graphics, image, video, and audio applications become more prevalent.

The major emphasis is on the resources being managed, protocol support, and the network management framework. It is beyond the scope of this book to either discuss in much detail the operating system and hardware or examine in depth the network management applications area. Management of computer networks involves monitoring and controlling the different hardware, microcode, and software components of networks. Some hardware components that need to be managed are:

- *Physical media and connections:* These include physical and data link layer--related equipment. Many LAN products are coming out for these layers. The protocols used vary from IEEE 802--related products, including FDDI, frame relay, B-Integrated Services Digital Networks (BISDN), asynchronous transfer mode (ATM), Synchronous Optical Network (SONET), and other emerging protocols. Also included are products such as adapters of different protocols, concentrators, and switches.

- *Computer components:* These include storage devices, processors, printers, and others. Though Ethernet, token-ring, and token-bus adapters are considered part of the computer components, they have not been included here. We prefer to lump them under the aforementioned physical media and connections category.

- *Connectivity and interconnection components:* This refers to hardware components such as repeaters, bridges, routers, gateways, hubs, and modems.

- *Telecommunication hardware:* These are modems, multiplexers, and switches, such as, for example, an ATM switch.

Typical software to be managed includes:

- *Operating system software:* This is the bare-bones system software provided on any computer. Some examples are DOS, Windows 95, and OS/2 Warp.
- *Application software and software tools:* The application software makes computers more popular and productive. With increasing integration of video, voice, text, and imaging, applications need to be managed. As the base of multimedia applications grows, multimedia applications need to be managed, too.

- *System software in client-server computing:* Some examples are NetWare servers and OS/2 LAN servers.

- *Interconnection software:* This includes software used in repeaters, bridges, routers, gateways, and hubs. In many applications, extra functionality is provided by adding software functions on the underlying hardware. These software applications are becoming complex, and are as important as the hardware.
- *Application software in client-server computing:* This includes the database server, file server, and print server.
- *Data communication and telecommunication software:* Management of software related to data communication and telecommunication protocols such as FDDI, ATM, and frame relay is necessary. We have specifically included this in the software section, because these protocols rely heavily on software.
- *Backbone telecommunication software:* This is increasingly used to connect different LANs. Though it is included in our earlier categories, we have added backbone telecommunication software here as well to account for the emerging backbone communication protocols.

The above mentioned wide variety of hardware and software to be managed is complicated by various protocols and differences among them. In addition, many proprietary protocols are popular and have a wide application base. Therefore, multiprotocol and multivendor products make connectivity and management daunting tasks. Broadly, the scope of network management is to manage both hardware and/or software products, which may be heterogeneous, multivendor, multiprotocol, and geographically dispersed, as well as managing the people who oversee these products.

Having introduced the topic of network management, we will examine different concepts and standards, including architectures, in the rest of the book. In some cases, to provide a better understanding and appreciation of the important concepts and methodologies involved in network management, lower-layer concepts are also briefly discussed.

Standards

As discussed earlier, there is a paradigm shift in the computing scenario. LANs and WANs are becoming increasingly popular. Also, with the introduction of fiber optics, telephone tariffs are coming down. At the same time, more applications, such as voice, video, text, graphics, and images, are being added to the computing environment. Simultaneously, these applications require bandwidth beyond what we have observed in the traditional transmission of voice or data. This changing scenario is slowly bringing about the integration of data communication and telecommunications, which adds complexity to network management. The management of equipment must include switches and different components used in the telephone industry. In addition, computing and data transmission environments are becoming increasingly heterogeneous. The different types of equipment use a variety of protocols, from standards to the proprietary ones. This adds another dimension to the management of heterogeneous, as well as multiprotocol, environments.

As one guides through the maze of protocols, standards are being advanced by vendors belonging to the telephone industry, computer industry, and government agencies. There are basically two types of standards. *De facto industry standards* become established when a target segment of the user population accepts them or when a majority of vendors uses them. In some cases, such industry standards are the result of prominent players in an industry forming cooperative bodies and introducing products that conform to the guidelines developed by these bodies.

Formal standards are mostly brought out by international, regional, or national standards bodies. In many cases, there is close cooperation among these standards bodies. Governments and their agencies, by and large, prefer formal standards. The ISO is one such body, which, as the name suggests, is an important international standards organization primarily comprising governmental agencies. At the national level, most countries have their own standards organizations. Standardization is becoming important in facilitating the compatibility of hardware and software from different vendors. From this angle, concepts of *portability, connectivity,* and *interoperability* should be emphasized.

Let us examine what each term means. For portability, an application in one computer platform must be able to work with identical functions in another platform, or no modifications should be required to make an application work in different platforms. For portability purposes, application interfaces and functions provided to interact with lower-layer software should be similar. By connectivity, we mean that a system from one vendor attaches to a similar system from a different vendor, and these systems must be able to work together. For example, two computers manufactured by different vendors must work together when connected as LANs.

Interoperability, which is closely related to connectivity, goes a step further. For interoperability, the protocols, formatting of data, and application environments must be similar, such that applications developed on two different platforms must work together. An application developed by one vendor must work with a similar application from another vendor. Let us look at an example. Electronic mail and electronic data exchange applications are quite common. For interoperability, two electronic mail systems must work together regardless of which vendors developed these systems,

Having examined some terms relevant to standardization, let us return to the topic of standards bodies. In the United States and elsewhere, computer networks connected to the Internet follow their own set of standards and have well-established procedures for bringing out standards. In addition, the Institute of Electrical and Electronics Engineers (IEEE) in the United States formulates standards for LANs and in other areas where there is a need for them. Usually, the IEEE concentrates on the standardization of lower layers such as the physical and data link layers. Most standards bodies work closely with one another and adopt each other's standards, where they are available, to avoid duplication of efforts and standards.

As software applications become more sophisticated and are developed by many vendors, there is a trend toward open systems. For open systems, conformance testing to find out whether applications really conform to the standards is becoming a norm. Many variations of standards are available; therefore, it is possible to have a set of implementations with different sets of standards at different layers. To facilitate smooth operation, some standard sets, known as *profiles,* have been developed by standards bodies. This reduces incompatibility and ensures that applications using the same profiles have interoperability.

Standards provide sufficient flexibility in implementation, which may create its own set of interoperability problems. To overcome this, many leading vendors are developing a set of profiles for network management. This effort is being pioneered by the Network Management Forum (NMF), which provides guidelines on how OSI standards must be implemented. In addition to the NMF, there are also vendor consortiums such as the Open Software Foundation (OSF), Unix International, and X/ Open. Many applications are being brought out based on the work done by these groups. These consortiums also active in the network management area.

A common pitfall of standards is that they take a long time to produce. Once a problem is identified, some standards bodies take years before they bring out widely accepted standards. This presents problems in some cases. People in the industry with problems needing immediate solutions cannot wait for many years for standards to resolve these problems. Still, standards are generally useful and good for everyone in the industry.

Another common complaint is that the OSI standards are too complex, and it is difficult to implement them. This may be one reason for the slow implementation of standards. Because standards bodies work on the basis of consensus, there are influences in different directions, leading to frequent changes. As a consequence, it is becoming a practice to wait for standards to stabilize and become international before implementing them.

Network management standard functional model

Different network management standards are prevalent. Some are closely related to one another and, in some cases, they extend earlier protocols, taking migration aspects into consideration. Extensibility is an important part of every standard. General standards must be applicable to specialized cases and applications. In network management standards, we are interested in the following key areas:

Management functional area: This covers how network management functions are organized, how they interact with each other, and how they behave with the external components. The management functional area should also clearly delineate the scope of each network management function.

Informational area: This deals with how resources are represented from the standpoint of management actions. This has to be done in a consistent manner to facilitate smooth and easy definition of new resources. Representation of resources should also cover the scope of the management operations that can be performed on these resources. We stress the scope, because it is very important to precisely define the boundaries of these resources from the management point of view and the interactions possible with external components. There should not be any room for ambiguity, because this leads to confusion during implementation and problems of interoperability.

Communications area: This primarily covers management protocols. As we will notice, in network management, we use entirely different management protocols for communicating management information. The communications area should also include the communication stacks or profiles which are used to support the management protocols.

Conformance area: This is a key area for interoperability. A set of guidelines should be clearly stated for checking whether an implementation has adhered to the standards outlined. During implementation, taking too much liberty may result in incompatible implementations. This can be checked only if there are precise and clear guidelines on how implementations are to be done.

Network interconnection

Networks must be interconnected to allow a user on one network to access services or information located on another network. To satisfy immediate needs it may be possible to connect the two networks together directly or in some ad hoc fashion, but in the more general case it will be necessary to interconnect a variety of networks to achieve communication between many different endpoints, and indeed to transport information between two networks that are situated a long distance apart. A wide variety of networks already exists: proprietary networks such as SNA, heterogeneous WANs based on X.25, token passing and contention based LANs. Standardization should reduce this diversity, but even the standards offer choices and there is a transitional phase as standards are specified, refined and adopted. Networks are often chosen for their suitability for their main body of users, rather than for ease of connection. Also, new types of network are likely to be introduced implying a continuing need for interconnection strategies.

LANs have size limitations, so that interconnection with other networks is essential for wider geographical coverage. All networks must be maintained and managed; separate networks offer a well defined boundary for management control, decisions about the installation and security of a particular network being the responsibility of a single organization. Small networks offer better reliability and performance than large networks; by interconnecting a number of small networks in which the majority of communication takes place within individual networks these advantages can be preserved while wider interworking is made possible.

The nearer the architectures of the networks concerned, the easier it is to connect them. Linking a datagram network to a virtual circuit network presents obvious problems, as does connecting a highspeed local area network with simple access mechanisms to a slower more complicated wide area packet switched system. The following list shows some of the characteristics, which may differ between network architectures and which will therefore have to be considered:

- Addressing and routing
- Multiplexing
- Maximum packet size
- Directionality
- Packet sequencing or resequencing
- Error control
- Connection-oriented and connectionless working
- Flow control
- Expedited flow
- Classes of service

Terminology

A network interconnection system usually connects two networks, but some connect more than two.

1. A *repeater is* often used to connect segments of a LAN and is an extension at the physical level, layer I of the OSI model.
2. A *bridge* connects LAN's at the medium access control layer; bridges may connect similar or dissimilar LANs.
3. A *gateway is* the term normally used when interconnecting two unlike networks, e.g. connecting a LAN to a WAN; the connection is made at layer 3.
4. A *protocol converter is* needed where protocols differ between interconnected networks. This could conceivably be at any level, but the term has been used to describe interconnection at a higher level, e.g. to convert between two message handling systems.

Bridges, gateways and protocol converters generally consist of both hardware and software. A gateway would, for example, have to be capable of implementing protocols on both or all of its interconnected networks up to layer 3, and would also have to make routing, accounting and other decisions associated with information crossing between the networks. Because the actual implementation of such a system may well be at the boundary of two different organizations, or the boundary between a public and a private network provider, in practice a gateway often consists of two processing systems separated by a communications link. In this case the gateway functions are split and each system is called a *half gateway* The interconnection problem is then reduced to agreeing a protocol along the communications link connecting the two half gateways.

A strategy for the interconnection of LANs on a single site is to connect each of the LANs to a *backbone network*. Over a wider area LAN interconnection can be achieved though a metropolitan area network.

Internetworking in the OSI framework

In the OSI model, the decisions and actions involved in forwarding information between open systems are called *relaying*. The highest layer at which relaying can be done is the network layer. Thus the network service ensures that the transport and higher layers need not be concerned with routing and relaying. Indeed, in OSI terms open systems may communicate over a network consisting of a variety of interconnected subnetworks, each of which may, for example, be a LAN, a public WAN or a private data network. There should be no problems in interconnecting subnetworks that provide the full OSI network service. An individual subnetwork will need to use its own lower level services and must be modified to converge with standard relaying functions in order to comply with other subnetworks.

How should the gateway look to the rest of the subnetwork

Should a gateway look like a host or a packet switching exchange to the rest of the subnetwork? If the two subnetworks are very similar, the switching exchange solution may seem easier as the gateway can perform similar functions such as flow control and routing. However, there are problems of addressing. Each exchange will have to know about the address space of the other subnetwork in order to perform routing. If the interconnected subnetworks have totally different strategies for routing and flow control, the problem becomes very complex and a common access interface is needed. If the gateway looks like a host, the operation of the exchanges of the subnetwork is not affected. This technique is suited to the transmission of datagrams, where there is no requirement for packet sequencing or guaranteed delivery. A datagram typically will be wrapped up in the protocol of a specific subnetwork for its passage through the subnetwork, and then unwrapped at the destination host or ongoing gateway.

Approaches to network interconnection

Because requirements have predated the availability of standards, there have been and continue to be a number of ad hoc solutions to network interconnection. However, there are three main areas where standards work has been most evident. The first is the CCITT X.75 recommendation which is intended for the interconnection of connection-oriented public packet switched networks. The second are *Internet* protocols which have been used for some time on the DARPA Internet and offer a connectionless service, and form the basis of an ISO standard. Thirdly, for the interconnection of local area networks, the IEEE project 802 has been looking at LAN bridges for the various IEEE medium access control options. We shall be looking at each of these three areas in more detail, but first discuss more general approaches.

Connection-oriented versus connectionless working

The arguments as to whether interconnection should be based on a connection-oriented or connectionless approach are very similar to those between the two techniques in a single subnetwork. With a connection-oriented approach it will be necessary to enhance connectionlesss subnetworks by providing virtual circuit facilities, and this may be very difficult. However, the advantages of shorter headers, packets being kept in sequence and quick recovery from errors are maintained. Where reliability and predictable response time are of prime importance the connection-oriented approach is preferred With the connectionless approach it is much easier to provide connectionless facilities on a connection-oriented subnetwork, and packets can be routed individually thus offering robustness in the event of gateway failure. However, any error correction or flow control must take place end to end at a higher layer. The connectionless approach may also be suitable for services such as packetized speech which do not require every packet to be delivered reliably.

A general approach to protocol conversion

The following general technique for protocol conversion between different subnetwork architectures which is based on the OSI model was put forward by Green. We can consider conversion as a *mapping* between the protocols of one subnetwork architecture to those of another subnetwork architecture. The first step is to concentrate on the differences between the architectures. In particular, we must find an appropriate conversion level in the hierarchy of each network. In general it will be necessary to map the top of the Nth layer of architecture X onto the top of the Mth layer of architecture Y. The level of interconnection is often dictated by existing system structure, for example specialist hardware may be available to implement the protocols up to a certain level in one subnetwork. The technique can be applied to both host-based and exchange-based gateways, and to a number of conversion methods such as protocol substitution or enveloping one protocol inside another.

Having decided to connect subnetwork X at level N to subnetwork Y at level M, the next step is to examine the services provided by the N-layer and M-layer protocols and look for differences. The protocols of layers M and N must also be taken into account. Since each protocol may have a variety of transient or steady states it is also necessary to examine differences over a certain length of time. Having done this comparison we are left with a well-defined protocol *mismatch,* which must be corrected. This may be very simple. It may prove impossible. Green calls this a *hard mismatch.* On the other hand, it may be possible to perhaps impose some degradation of performance such as extra delay. The gateway must then overcome the mismatch; in the case of a hard mismatch this may be achievable only by inserting an extra complementary layer to enhance the existing architecture.

Service versus protocol data unit mapping

In a more recent paper, Bochmann and Mondain-Monval distinguish two approaches to the mapping between subnetworks—a vertical approach and a horizontal approach. When mapping service primitives there are three main options:

1. Reduce the service available to a minimum level provided by both networks.
2. Enhance the services in one network to correspond to the more powerful services of the other.
3. Provide a common set of extra services on top of existing ones which can be used to enhance both networks to an agreed common level.

The advantages of the service approach are that it is conceptually simple and can use existing protocol implementations which provide the existing services of the interconnected subnetworks. In the protocol conversion approach, the protocol data units (PDUs) from one subnetwork are converted to PDUs of the other subnetwork, thus conforming to the appropriate protocol in each network. This approach is more complex and more difficult to implement than the service mapping approach, but is easier to optimize.

Addressing

The problems of addressing are similar to those within a single subnetwork. The options are

1. *Unique global addresses* This would be the simplest scheme to implement but very hard to manage, and it is already too late to include all subnetworks. The IEEE 802 standard LANs support global addressing with I bit in the 48-bit address field being used to indicate whether addresses are administered universally or locally.
2. *Address mapping* Addresses from outside a sub-network are mapped onto unused addresses within the subnetwork. By performing the mapping only while a call is in progress, a small range of addresses is needed, though care has to be taken not to reuse addresses too soon. This technique was used, for example, in the Universe project, an experiment in highspeed LAN/WAN interconnection
3. *Hierarchical schemes* The address contains a field specifying the subnetwork agreed globally and a field for the address within that subnetwork allocated by the

managing body for each subnetwork. It is probably the simplest and most satisfactory solution when different organizations are involved. Variations of this method are used in X.75 and for the Internet protocols as discussed later.

Routing

Gateways and bridges must keep routing tables which may be fixed or may change. Connectionless schemes offer more flexibility than connection-oriented ones, allowing each datagram to be routed independently and quickly adapting to fluctuations in subnetwork availability. Another desirable feature *is source routing* in which the user specifies the route to be taken. For example for security purposes the user may wish to avoid traversing a subnetwork operated by a rival organization or a user may wish to ensure that a single satellite subnetwork is used rather than a concatenation of several interconnected terrestrial subnetworks.

Packet size and fragmentation

All packet networks have a maximum packet size. When a packet enters a subnetwork whose maximum packet size is less than the length of the packet, it must be fragmented by the gateway. Each fragment must be appropriately addressed and labelled. Fragmentation is relatively easy, but at some point the fragments must be reassembled. If the packet is destined for a host on a subnetwork of small maximum packet size, that host can be expected to cope with reassembly. If the packet is simply passing through such a subnetwork there are two options:

1. Reassemble the packet at the outgoing gateway. Packets travelling through a succession of subnetworks may be subjected to this procedure several times. The gateways must provide buffer space and avoid reassembly lockup.
2. Reassemble only when the packet reaches the destination host. In this case the host must be aware of the fragmentation procedure, but it will save effort and memory in the intermediate gateways.

It may be necessary to indicate within fragments whether the receiving host is capable of reassembly; if not then reassembly must be done by the gateways.

Connection-oriented approaches

In this model the transport layer asks the network layer to open a connection to a specific destination, and that connection will consist of a sequence of virtual circuits created across each subnetwork between source and destination. Each gateway must provide resources, remember all the paths which are currently active, and provide appropriate conversion of packet formats. The result is a transport layer end-to-end connection. Obviously all packets on a single call must pass through the same sequence of gateways.

CCITT recommendation X.75

The CCITT recommendation X.75 is principally aimed at international data communications between public switched data networks. It is based on the virtual circuit model and defines the interface between signal termi-nating equipments (STEs) in two packet switched networks. The STEs must be implemented in the exchanges of each network. X.75 is very similar to X.25 on which it is based. In X.75, the call request packet must contain the full CCITT X. 121 address. The X.75 call request packet has a field for utilities specific to network interconnection such as transit network identification and throughput class. The user facilities of the X.25 call which is being carried are conveyed transparently in the X.75 call request packet. Additional diagnostic codes are defined in the clear request packets which will be conveyed across each of the virtual circuits in turn to the source or destination host.

Connectionless approaches

The ISO *Internetwork protocol (IP)* standard (ISO 8473) is based on an earlier US Department of Defense (DOD) standard. It offers a connectionless service, with the ability to send and receive datagrams, and the protocol is effectively a common datagram format. Since the standards are based on the DARPA Internet protocol we now describe this.

The DARPA Internet protocols

One of the best examples of practical network interconnection is the Defense Advanced Research Projects Agency (DARPA) Internet. The Internet consists of over 150 subnetworks of several types including packet radio networks, LANs, commercial networks, satellite networks and the ARPANET. It is in everyday use as a vehicle of communication between researchers in the United States and Europe.

The Internet protocol (IP) is implemented by all the hosts attached to the Internet and is based on the connectionless approach. Reliability and sequenced delivery are provided if necessary by the transmission control protocol (TCP), a higher level protocol imple-mented in the hosts and offering end-to-end flow control.

The gateways of the Internet have several functions including store and forward for the datagrams, providing interfaces to the appropriate networks, routing, monitoring and control facilities. The Internet address uses a common format, and is therefore easily interpreted by each gateway. IP datagrams are enclosed within the local subnetwork header for transmission across each subnetwork, The local header is stripped off when a datagram arrives at the gateway. A datagram may be destined for the gateway itself, for a host on the connected network or for a host on another network. In the last case the gateway chooses the most appropriate neighbouring gateway for the datagram's onward route, wraps it in the subnetwork's local header and sends it to that gateway. Datagrams are fragmented by the gateway if necessary and reassembled at the destination host. Gateways communicate with each other by a special protocol which allows them to send out echo and probe packets to determine the status of their neighbours. The information obtained is then sent to other gateways as routing updates so that a gateway's view of the status of the network is obtained by dynamic learning. To avoid datagrams circulating endlessly within the Internet each datagram has a *time to lire* field which is decremented on its passage through a gateway. Monitoring systems poll the gateways to collect information on traffic carried.

Bridges

A bridge connecting two identical highspeed LANs is much simpler than a gateway. The interface on each side is identical and some buffering is needed in case the receiving network is busy, but the main objective is to forward information as quickly as possible. Bridges normally make 'best efforts' to forward packets but may discard them if congestion occurs. The IEEE 802 standardization procedure has resulted in three MAC options: CSMA/CD (802.3), token bus (802.4) and token ring (802.5). Interconnection of the three MAC types is not trivial. Tanenbaum gives a detailed picture of some of the problems which we summarize here. Each standard has a different frame format requiring translation in the bridge. They have different data rates making congestion more likely when forwarding, for example, from 802.3 (10 Mbit/s) to 802.5 (4 Mbit/s). They all have different maximum frame lengths. This is very serious as no MAC can cope with fragmented frames, so frames that are too long to be transported have to be discarded. The result of these mismatches makes bridge architecture complicated and in general a degradation of facilities occurs when interconnecting unlike LANs. The IEEE 802 committee have also produced two options for the routing strategies for bridges. The first, produced as an extension to IEEE 802.1 and applicable to all IEEE 802 networks, is the *transparent bridge,* which can simply be plugged in and will learn from its environment. Initially all frames are flooded onto all possible connected networks. As each frame arrives its source address indicates where a particular host is situated, so that the bridge learns which way to forward future frames to that address. To prevent looping, the bridges form a *spanning tree,* a tree structure that has one bridge as a root and in which there is exactly one route between any two bridges. The second bridge type, developed for IEEE 802.5 token rings, is the *source routing bridge,* which requires users to specify the route to be followed. A user can discover a route by sending a discovery frame which proliferates through the network using all possible paths to the destination; each frame gradually collects bridge addresses as it goes. The destination responds to each frame and the source chooses an appropriate route from these responses, for example the route with the minimum number of hops. Thus shorter paths may be found for source routing than for users in an unfortunate position relative to the root of the spanning tree in transparent bridging. However, the proliferation *of* discovery frames can exert a serious extra load on the network. A comparison of the two techniques is made by Soha and Perlman.

FDDI/LAN interconnection

As an example of practical interconnection problems, we consider the use of FDDI as a backbone to link together several lower-speed LANs. This raises a number of issues for bridge design. The issues can be resolved reasonably easily if all the LANs are of the same type, but more complexity is introduced if it is required to have more than one bridge to a single LAN, to interconnect LANs of different types or to allow access to systems directly connected to the FDDI backbone network.

FDDI bridges will adopt one of the LAN bridge routing techniques. We will briefly discuss some other interconnection issues: frame size, frame check computation and MAC address interpretation. It should be noted that there are further issues such as response bit setting for token rings. The maximum size of a frame on a CSMA/CD network is 1518 bytes, on a token ring it can be more than 2048 bytes and on FDDI the frame size could reach 4500 bytes. This can pose problems for frames that are too large to be forwarded onto a network of small maximum size. The easiest solution to this problem is for bridges to discard such frames. Extensions to the LLC layer which allowed fragmentation and reassembly might be possible, but seem less practical.

The second problem is what to do about frame check sequences—should these be passed on unchanged or should they be recomputed by the bridges? Different frame check algorithms are used for each LAN type so recomputation is essential when connecting LANs of different types. For bridging networks of the same type, it would seem sensible to leave the check field unchanged, but as the checksum is often provided by the LAN interface hardware recomputation may be easier. Any doubt about the validity of a checksum at this level may be removed by providing higher layer reliability when it is needed, e.g. at the transport layer.

The third problem, which is considered to be the most serious, is the interpretation of the MAC address. CSMA/CD networks transmit MAC addresses starting with the least significant bit of each byte; token rings start with the most significant bit of each byte. This is not a problem for the bridge as the appropriate bit order can be provided for each LAN, but it Is a problem when the MAC address is used as data by a higher layer. A late decision by the IEEE 802.1 committee is that the least significant bit should be sent first; this implies that all token ring interfaces should be changed, a daunting task. A similar problem could apply if CSMA/CD stations wish to communicate directly with FDDI stations because FDDI is based on token ring conventions.

Commercial Ethernet to FDDI bridges are available, most of which employ *encapsulation,* that is the whole of each Ethernet frame is carried unchanged within an FDDI frame across the FDDI network, and the receiving bridge simply extracts the Ethernet frame for transmission onto the destination Ethernet. This technique, although simple, is not easily extended to enable other networks to be attached or to allow communication directly with FDDI stations.

Network dependent performance

For the lower levels of a local area network, the performance may be measured in terms of the utilization of the capacity of the network. For an individual node, performance is measured in terms of its mean data rate or the mean delays in transmission. Measurements of actual network installations show that most computer networks are rarely used to their full capacity, with typical usage figures of less than 10 per cent. Under these conditions most networks will appear to give the full capacity of the network to an individual node for the duration of the communication. Performance evaluations are, however, undertaken at a much higher network utilization when it is likely that a number of simultaneous transmission attempts will occur. This is valid, as studies have shown that most data communi-cation is of a 'bursty' nature with periods of high data transfer followed by idle periods. If the bursts of a number of transmissions occur at the same time, the presented load may be higher than the maximum network capacity so delays are introduced. It is the performance evaluation *of* the different networks during these periods of high utilization that gives the most interesting results.

Slotted and register insertion rings

For these networks, as more devices attempt simultaneous transmission, the mean delay between packets transmitted from a station increases. This is because the number of free packets is restricted. For a *slotted* ring each device may not reuse a slot after a transmission, so this slot is made available to the next device. This means that the available network capacity is evenly shared between the competing devices. Also, the worst case delay, before a station can transmit again, is defined as the time for a minipacket to be inserted by all other stations, i.e. one slot delay per station. For a *register insertion ring* the delay increases as more registers are inserted into the network.

Multiple access bus with CSMA/CD

For a contention network, as the number of devices attempting to transmit increases, so does the probability of collisions. The utilization of the network therefore depends on the ability of the system to prevent and detect collisions. The effect of collisions and subsequent retries depends on the size of the data packets sent, because for smaller packets the proportion of time spent in resolving collisions to that spent transmitting data is higher. These effects mean that under high loads the system performance is probabilistic and hence that the delay in transmitting a packet is indeterminate. This can be a problem in certain applications, particularly where real time data transmission is required.

Token passing systems

With token passing systems there is the overhead of the transmission of the token, but, as the load is increased, the probability of the token being passed to a device that does not require to transmit is reduced. The throughput of the system will not be wasted in collisions, so high utilization can be achieved. The delay for the transmission of a packet depends on the action of the other devices; it also depends on the token holding time. If the packets have a maximum size then the maximum delay can be calculated.

Performance comparisons

Executing fair performance comparisons is difficult due to the differences between systems and the variance in the parameters for a single system. Performance comparisons have therefore concentrated on specific pairs or groups of LAN systems.

The simple comparison presented here, which follows the technique discussed in Stuck, shows the effect of token passing on the data rate achievable from one station. For the *token ring,* the point-to-point data rate between two stations, ppDR, can be calculated as follows. It is assumed that only one station requires to transmit data in fixed size frames, whose data portion is of length Framesize.

As an example for a 10-station ring operating at 1 Mbit/s, with frames of 1000 bits, a propagation time of 50μs and a delay of 20μs through each station, the following could be achieved:

For one active station: ppDR = 800 kbit/s
For each station when all 10 stations are active: ppDR = 97.5 kbit/s

Token passing has a much greater effect on a lightly used bus network than on a ring network, and also shows how efficient the technique can be in a heavily loaded network. Note that we have assumed that the token holding time only allows one frame to be sent per station; a longer token holding time would give slightly higher data rates but data would be subject to longer delays.

CSMA/CD compared with earlier contention systems

The ALOHA and slotted ALOHA protocols were introduced and an analysis given of the throughput against offered load. Throughput S against offered load G for ALOHA, slotted ALOHA, nonpersistent CSMA and nonpersistent CSMA/CD, all assuming a Poisson arrival distribution.

The curves for ALOHA and slotted ALOHA use equations (2.4) and (2.5) respectively. The two CSMA protocols are plotted according to the following formulae derived in Hammond and O'Reilly. For nonpersistent CSMA

Here a is the normalized propagation delay, i.e. the ratio of the propagation delay to the time taken to transmit a packet. Note that this is non-slotted CSMA. Slotted CSMA offers a slightly better performance.

Comparing token passing with CSMA/CD

A performance comparison between CSMA/CD, token ring and token bus systems is presented in Stuck. Stuck derived performance equations for the three systems; the calculations were for the total network data rate, not that achievable between individual stations. If the load sharing is fair then each station will achieve an equal portion of the network data rate. The analysis of the different systems yielded the following conclusions:

1. For the parameters used, the smaller the mean packet length, the higher the maximum mean throughput rate for token passing compared with that for CSMA/CD. This reflects the fact that, for a given amount of data, smaller packets suffer more collisions under CSMA/CD.
2. Thc token ring is the least sensitive to applied load.
3. CSMA/CD offers the shortest delay under light load, whereas it is the worst under heavy load.
4. When a single station is transmitting, the token passing bus is the least efficient due to the high overhead of the token passing.

Cambridge ring performance

A detailed performance study of a slotted ring, the Cambridge ring, was Made by Blair. The Cambridge ring transmission access rules restrict the maximum slot utilization for one transmitter to be one slot in every $(n + 2)$ slots, where n is the number of slots in the ring. This is because the station must wait for a minipacket to return around the ring and pass the slot on empty, to enable sharing. It then has to examine the response bits at the end of the minipacket, to determine the next minipacket for transmission; while this happens the next slot is allowed to pass. A ring built to the CR 82 standard has 40-bit packets and a 10 Mbit/s data rate.

The actual figure may be lower as the gap can be between 2 and 41 bits depending on ring length. As the access scheme prevents the reuse of a packet, this point-to-point data rate can be obtained between two pairs of communicating nodes. The advantage of the scheme is that if all nodes wish to transmit simultaneously then each node can use one out of every m slots $(m > n + 2)$, where m is the number of stations.

As stations are added to the ring, the delay increases and the bandwidth decreases, until there is sufficient delay to incorporate another slot into the ring which restores some of the lost bandwidth.

Comparing CSMA/CD with slotted and token rings

The performance comparison between CSMA/CD and slotted rings is quite difficult due to the variation of the performance of rings when their parameters are changed. The significant parameters are:

- *Slotted ring.* Slot size, overhead bits per slot, ring length, number of slots.
- *CSMA/CD.* Slot size, network length, number of stations.

The delay/throughput performance of CSMA, slotted and token rings operating under similar conditions at 10 Mbit/s. CSMA/CD shows the best performance at low loads, but for loads greater than 0.4 the delay increases rapidly, showing the degradation due to collisions. The token ring has much more stable delay characteristics. The slotted ring performs worse than the token ring, largely because of the minipacket overheads and the delay caused by the destination release of slots. Blair and Shepherd comment that, although the delays for the Cambridge ring are greater than for Ethernet, the Cambridge ring does have the advantage of a lower variance of delay and the hardware construction of the network interface is simpler and therefore of lower cost and higher reliability.

Network reliability and fault detection

The usability of an LAN is strongly affected by the reliability of its components, the ease with which any faults can be detected and located and the measures taken to repair the faults.

Network reliability

The reliability of an individual device connected to a network is usually considered to be less important than the reliability of the total network. If an individual device connection fails, this only affects the processes running on the device and other processes wishing to access the device. If the network fails then all communication processes are affected. Therefore networks are designed so that failures are unlikely to affect the network as a whole.

All systems are susceptible to the failure of the interconnecting cable. In a star topology, any failure will only cause the loss of the device connected by the faulty cable. In a ring or a bus a shorted cable will cause the failure of the network section. An open circuit cable will cause the complete failure of a ring system but will divide a bus into two sections which may continue to operate.

Reliability in bus networks

In a bus system, the control is decentralized and the connection is usually made to the cable using passive taps. This reduces the possibility of a single failure causing the system to become inoperative. Failures such as shorting the bus, permanently transmitting data and incorrect access behaviour can cause a complete or partial interruption to other devices on the bus.

Reliability in ring networks

In a ring system, the transmitted data is repeated at each device, requiring an active component to be included in the ring. A single failure can thus cause the system to become inoperative. In most systems the operation of the repeater is very simple, consisting of regeneration and re-transmission of the incoming signal, the value of the signal only being changed when data is transmitted. Such repeaters must always be active; they must be provided with a power supply even when the connected device is turned off or if the device is disconnected. This is arranged by distributing the power to the repeaters round the ring, often using the same cores in the cable as used by the signals.

Fault detection and location

The location of faults, particularly intermittent ones, can also be improved by the connection of devices that are dedicated to the monitoring of the network performance and error detection. The Cambridge distributed system incorporated an error logger which produced a hard copy of the source and type of errors detected. The printout produced enabled failing devices to be identified and, due to the error reporting of the Cambridge ring hardware, ring breaks or repeater failures to be detected. In all ring systems individual stations can detect errors in the structure of the incoming signal stream.

On CSMA/CD networks two methods of fault detection are possible. Firstly, periodic enquiries can be made to determine which stations are active. This can be combined with a knowledge of the network configuration to locate faults in sections of the system. Secondly, special monitor stations can be provided which act in promiscuous mode Abnormal behaviour of individual stations can then be detected.

Improving reliability

A possible protection against failure is to provide an alternative communication path. For a bus system the communication path is duplicated to provide an alternative path for use when the main path fails. For ring systems, extra links between repeaters can be added. Then it becomes possible either to form an alternative route for the ring using the extra data paths or to bypass nodes completely. Further discussion of providing alternative communication paths to overcome failures is provided by Zafiropulo.

Wire centres for ring networks

Location and circumvention of faults can be difficult in a ring network which snakes in and out of many offices. One solution employed, for example, in some IEEE 802.5 ring installations is to wire stations in a star arrangement, bringing the wires together at *wire centres* where the ring is completed. It is then a simple matter to remove one of the stations from the ring using bypass relays. For example, station B can be excluded by completing the bypass relay from X to Y. One disadvantage of this method is that, in normal operation, the length of the ring is increased.

LAN management

Most LANs are operated by a single organization and employ a distributed access protocol, so management techniques for LANs must address slightly different problems from those for WANs. Fault management can be carried out as discussed above. The performance of a LAN can be assessed using a promiscuous station to determine, for example, network utilization and to give an early indication of possible overload conditions. This technique can also be used for accounting management.

Protocols above the MAC layer

The discussions above and in the preceding chapter have been concerned with the operation of the lower levels of a LAN system. To consider the operation of a full system, the higher levels have to be included. These higher levels consist of protocol suites or families. Different protocol types have developed to meet system requirements and provide various levels of service to the user processes. In general, the higher the level of service and the more features provided, such as guaranteed delivery, the greater the complexity of the protocol and hence the overhead of operation. Three classes of protocols can be defined: connectionless, transaction and connection-oriented protocols. In general, transaction protocols are considered as special options of connectionless protocols. Each of the different protocol types may support three modes of addressing that control the number of stations to which a message is sent:

1 Individual addressing. Sent to one station only.

2 Multicast addressing. Sent to a group of stations.

3 Broadcast addressing. Sent to all stations on a network.

Addressing types 2 and 3 are more suited to connectionless protocols. In principle, once the details of the network are hidden, i.e. once we get above the transport layer, any accepted protocol can be used. Protocol suites have been developed for each major LAN type. In addition, the IEEE 802.2 LLC offers a standard to complete the data link layer for both connectionless and connection-oriented protocols.

IEEE 802.2 logical link control

Logical link control provides that port' on of the data link layer which is common to every IEEE 802 access technique. The specification details the service interfaces with the adjacent levels and the protocol with peer LLC entities across the network. Two classes of procedure may be supported. Class I is just the connectionless service. Class II provides both connectionless and connection-oriented services. The fundamental unit of information that is passed between two LLC endpoints is the LLC protocol data unit (PDU).

The control field is used by the LLC to indicate which type of data transfer is being carried out—datagram or connection-oriented. In addition, this field contains further control parameters associated with the data being transferred, such as sequence numbers used for flow control. Finally, the information field is made available to the higher level software. This field contains an integral number of octets and can be zero. The maximum size of the information field depends on the MAC layer that the LLC is using for the data transfer. The protocol suffers from only having 8 bits for the service point address and has to incorporate facilities for the control of duplicate addressing within a connected system. If more bits were used the chance of duplicate addressing would be considerably reduced and is generally avoided by other protocol suites.

Cambridge ring protocols

The protocols for the Cambridge ring have been developed to provide connectionless, transaction and connection-oriented communications. Connectionless communication is provided by the basic block protocol (BBP). All the other protocols rely on the BBP to provide a packet or frame communication similar to that supported by the MAC levels in the IEEE 802 systems.

Basic block protocol

Because the Cambridge ring delivers only 16 bits of data in every minipacket, some method had to be devised to send longer packets of information between two stations on the network. A sequence of such minipackets sent between two stations is called a basic block. The first minipacket of the block contains a header that indicates that this is a basic block. The next minipacket is optional and contains the count of octets in the basic block, enabling both stations to know when the block has been completely transmitted and received. The route minipacket includes a 12-bit field called a *port* which is used to address a specific application process in the destination system.

Single shot protocol

The Cambridge ring protocols provide a transaction protocol called the *single shot protocol* (SSP) for simple request/reply transactions. The request contains the port to which the reply should be returned; the station addresses will be found in the ring minipacket and the destination port in the BBP header of the basic block in which the request is sent. Although all this information is in different places, the request includes the full identification of both the destination and the address for the reply.

Byte stream protocols

In order to provide a reliable stream of bytes in both directions between two processes and to ensure that no data is lost, corrupted or duplicated, the *byte stream protocol* was devised. The BSP protocol fragments the user process' byte stream into BSP packets which are sent using the basic block interface. Acknowledgements are used by the BSP protocol to ensure data integrity. However, as the ring error rate is low no negative acknowledgement is used for packets in error; instead a time-out is implemented at the transmitter to recover from unacknowledged packets and retransmit them. During periods when there is no data to send or no available receive buffer, the transmitter or the receiver can stop the traffic and resume responsibility for restarting it. To enable a broken connection to be distinguished from a stopped connection an idle handshake is used in which the two parties infrequently exchange their last messages. This is particularly useful when operating through interconnected rings as it will prevent the path from timing-out and being cleared by the interconnecting systems. The transport service byte stream protocol (TSBSP) is a superset of the BSP including primitives for the provision of a full transport level service in line with interim UK standards.

DARPA internet protocols

Many computer systems attached to LANs implement the Internet protocol (IP) and the transmission control protocol (TCP) at the higher levels. These protocols are collectively known as TCP/IP. This suite of protocols has much wider significance than its use for LANs, as it is the basis for an Internet-a system of interconnected networks of many types. In particular, most of the major research organizations and universities in the United States are connected by an Internet called the Defense Advanced Research Projects Agency (DARPA) Internet, and since 1983 all hosts connected to the DARPA Internet have been required to use TCP/IP. A full description of TCP/IP principles, protocols and architectures can be found in the book by Comer.

The IP is a connectionless network layer protocol; the Internet control message protocol (ICMP) is used for network control messages. Above the IP, connection-oriented working is provided by the transport level TCP; for applications requiring only datagram reliability the connectionless user datagram protocol (UDP) is provided. Above the TCP and UDP, application protocols such as fiie transfer protocol (FTP) and remote log-in use the TCP or UDP as appropriate.

Internet addressing

In order to provide a user perspective of an Internet in which all hosts appear to be accessible, a standard form for network addressing is necessary. For every host on the DARPA Internet, a network connection is assigned a unique 32-bit *Internet address.* A host that exists on more than one network will have an address for each network on which it resides since the address defines a host's connection to a particular network and not an address for a specific host computer. The three highorder bits are used to indicate which form of addressing is applicable. The three main address formats are assigned different sized fields for network address (netid) and host address (hostid), appropriate to networks of large, intermediate and small sizes, respectively. To ensure that hosts of different architectures understand the Internet address, the Internet specifies that bytes should be sent in the big-endian format. The 32-bit address is usually written in a form described as the *dotted notation.* Thus an Internet address may be written as four decimal integers separated by dots where each integer gives the value of one octet.

Address resolution protocol (ARP)

The knowledge of a host's Internet address Is not sufficient to allow communication with it; the physical hardware address is also required. In order that applications can be written which require only a knowledge of the Internet address, a mapping must occur at a lower level. This mapping is commonly known as *address resolution.* One mechanism for address resolution would be for hosts to keep tables consisting of pairs of Internet and physical addressees. Alternatively, the physical address could be mapped using some algorithm to the Internet address. Both methods are unattractive, particularly for Ethernet, which has a large physical address space of 48-bits assigned by the interface or chip manufacturer. The Internet solution is both simple and elegant—a low level protocol provides dynamic binding of addresses. When a host wishes to find the physical address of another host on the Internet, it broadcasts a packet which contains the Internet address of the required host, requesting it to respond with its physical address. All hosts on the network receive the request, but only the host with the specified address should respond. The physical address in the response can then be used for direct communication with the specified host. To reduce the overhead of broadcast packets caused by the protocol, a table of ARP replies is held in a cache on each system for future reference. Also, the initiator of the ARP request sends its own physical address and Internet address in every ARP request, enabling recipients to update the binding information in their local ARP caches. The ARP message is treated as data in the Ethernet frame; details can be found in RFC 826.

The Internet protocol (IP)

The fundamental data delivery service of the TCP/IP suite is the IP which provides a connectionless datagram delivery service, i.e. an unreliable but best attempt packet delivery service. The IP datagram is *encapsulated* in the MAC data frame. The IP datagram contains both header and data parts. Ideally the IP datagram should fit into one MAC frame, making the transmission fairly efficient. Ethernet allows a data unit of 1500 octets but some networks have much smaller data units available. To maintain efficiency on networks such as Ethernet and yet allow networks with a smaller frame size to carry IP datagrams, a strategy of splitting datagrams into fragments is used. These fragments, which are identified by bits in the header, must be reassembled at the destination. The major items of interest concerning the header will be briefly presented. However, the detail of this packet header is not discussed here and the reader is referred to RFC 791 and RFC 894 for details of transmission of the IP across an Ethernet. The *version* field is used to check that all packet handlers are operating with the same version of software for IP data handling. The *length* field specifies the size of the header counted in 32-bit words. The *total length* is the length of the whole datagram including the header and data and is counted in octets. The *type of service* field has several parts. The *precedence* part is generally unused but would allow control messages to be given a higher priority over standard data messages, for example, to implement congestion control. Quality of service can be specified using the D, T *and* R bits: D requests low delay, T requests high throughput and R requests high reliability. The type of service field may be consulted at gateways and applied to the selection of a particular route from several alternatives.

The *ident, flags and fragment offset* fields control fragmentation and reassembly. The ident field together with the source address allows the destination to associate the packet fragment with the correct datagram.

The *time to live* field specifies the time that the datagram should be allowed to remain in the Internet and hence ensures that datagrams do not travel around the Internet forever if routing difficulties occur. The field is decremented by one unit at each gateway on the assumption that each traverse between networks takes one unit of time; when it reaches zero, the datagram is discarded. The *proto* field is used by higher level protocols to specify the protocol in use. The *header checksum is* used to ascertain the integrity of the header field data, the *options* field is largely used for testing and the remaining fields should be self-explanatory.

The internet control message protocol (ICMP)

The ICMP protocol is used by gateways and hosts to send messages concerning error detection and network control. The ICMP messages are transmitted in the data part of an IP datagram and allow messages between the Internet software in two machines. An Internet host might, for example, send an echo request message; if a reply is received the destination is alive and hence reachable. Details of ICMP message types can be found in RFC 792.

The user datagram protocol (UDP)

The Internet user datagram protocol (UDP) provides a datagram service to allow user application programs to send messages to other programs with a minimum of protocol mechanism. The protocol does not guarantee delivery or provide protection. The UDP is achieved by an abstraction for subaddressing called a port. The data is thought of as originating from or being directed to a host at a specific port number. The UDP protocol is normally implemented with a user interface which provides the following:

1. The ability to create new receive ports.
2. Receive operations on the receive ports which return the data octets and an indication of source port and source address.
3. An operation that allows a datagram to be sent, specifying the data, source address and port and destination address and port.

UDP port numbers may be permanently assigned or bound to an application when it is initiated. The UDP protocol is described fully in RFC 768.

The transmission control protocol (TCP)

The TCP makes few assumptions about the underlying network over which it runs. It provides a reliable stream transport mechanism for data and consequently its implementation is rather more complex than the previously discussed Internet protocols. The TCP is responsible for delivering error free data to the destination in the same order as it left the source. The TCP provides a virtual connection which will remain established while the stream is operating. TCP connections are established using a three-way handshake which enables both parties of the communication to be ready for transfer and allows them to agree on the initial sequence numbers. Control packets offer facilities for setting up calls, sending and detecting acknowledge-ments, flow control, multiplexing and security. Data transferred across the network is buffered to provide efficient transfer of data in reasonable sized datagrams, but this may be overridden by a push mechanism, forcing data to be transferred immediately.

The data byte stream is divided by the TCP into entities called *segments,* and each segment is transmitted in an IP datagram. A sliding window protocol at the byte level is used which allows multiple segments to be sent before an acknowledgement arrives, hence providing an efficient data transmission and flow control mechanism. All bytes in the stream are numbered sequentially and three pointers to the byte sequence numbers are maintained:

1. The sequence number reached for bytes sent and not yet acknowledged.
2. The highest sequenced numbered byte which may be sent before more acknowledgements are received.
3. The current byte count for transmission.

The size of the window may be changed dynamically since the acknowledgement contains information on the number of additional bytes that the receiver is willing to accept. The TCP uses a go-back-N scheme and employs timeouts to ensure re-transmission if acknowledgements are lost. The length of the time-out can be adapted to reflect the round-trip delay encountered on a particular virtual circuit. Details of mechanisms for window management may be found in RFC 813. The header contains a number of fields including the source *and destination ports* which are used as in the UDP for directing a stream to the correct application program. The *sequence number* identifies the position in the transmitted byte stream of this data segment. The *acknowledgement number* is used to indicate the sequence number of the highest byte received in the return data stream. Further detail on the fields in the header may be found in RFC 793.

Xerox network systems protocols

The Xerox network systems protocols were principally developed for operation over Ethernets and the interconnection of Ethernet systems over public packet networks. All the protocols are built on the lowest level protocol, the Internetwork datagram protocol (IDP).

Internetwork datagram protocol

Both addressing fields fully specify the location of the source and destination of the datagram. The packet type field, identifies the function of the packet and its association, if any, with a higher level protocol. The checksum provides for additional error detection for the complete datagram, in addition to that provided by the MAC layer.

Packet exchange protocol

The XNS packet exchange protocol (PEP) is the transaction protocol of the XNS protocol suite. PEP is implemented above the IDP and uses type 4 packets. When a packet has been sent the sender will expect a reply. Timeouts are used to retry the exchanges. The ID field is unique for each exchange and is used to identify request and reply pairs.

Sequenced packet protocol

The sequenced packet protocol (SPP) is a connection-oriented protocol which guarantees the integrity and sequence of the packet flow and undertakes re-transmission in the event of errors. The protocol offers three services:

1 Message service, in which a message may comprise a number of packets.

2 Sequenced packet service, in which message boundaries are not distinguished.

3 Reliable packet mode, in which packets are presented in order of arrival without duplicates.

The data is carried by type 5 IDP packets. Connection identifiers (IDs) are unique and identify the call; the call establishment involves the process of agreeing IDs between the parties. The caller has the responsibility for terminating a call, which is achieved by sending an 'end' packet.

Software interfaces for LAN protocols

The above discussion has concentrated on the requirements of network protocols and the facilities provided by implementations. For any protocol implementation to be useful, a software interface has to be provided for the applications programmer. This interface should ideally be uniform between different protocol families and implementations so the programmer can produce portable programs. Uniform interfaces are required for both connectionless and connection-orientated protocols.

As an example, the Berkeley UNIX interprocess communications environment offers an endpoint of communication, called a socket, for different protocol families. Three separate domains are supported: the UNIX domain for processes on the same system, the Internet domain for processes communicating between machines using the DARPA Internet protocols and the NS domain for processes communicating between machines using the XNS protocols.

LAN development direction

The development of local area networks has reached a state where stable commercial products are established in the market place. This does not mean that development and research have stopped but the direction has been changing from new concepts to new applications. The increase in interworking between computers enabled by local area networks is creating an increasing need for interworking between systems on different networks via gateways and bridges. As network interfaces and protocols are standardized, interworking will be simplified, enabling a wide variety of networks and systems to coexist commercially. As a wider choice becomes available the cost/performance of a network will become the overriding factor in choosing a network for an application. Terminals will be interconnected via low-cost networks offering local services and shared resources. These networks will be interconnected by gateways to higher performance networks connecting mini and mainframe systems offering large-scale applications. Again these networks will be interconnected on a metropolitan, regional or national level.

Two areas of development that will have a great influence on local area networks are optical networks, offering higher performance systems, and large-scale integration, which will enable the cost of a network to be reduced due to the scale of manufacturing production.

A LAN can be considered to consist of four elements. The three hardware elements are a transmission medium, a mechanism for controlling transmission over the medium and an interface to the network for the host computer. The fourth basic element is the set of software required in the host computer to implement the protocols which control the communication from one host computer to another. The software functions at different levels to provide a number of protocol layers ranging from packetization to the application level. This combination of layered hardware and software is a noticeable feature of local computer networks. Inexpen-sive hardware, such as a twisted pair or coaxial cable, is used to interconnect systems. The characteristics of LANs are high bandwidth, low error rate and small delay. These characteristics enable LANs to interconnect processors to provide distributed multiprocessor systems which enable the sharing of resources such as secondary storage and other peripherals. The LANs described in this chapter are principally used for data transmission. Other forms of information, such as voice and video, are time critical and will not tolerate the variable delays of LANs.

Network topologies

There are a number of possible topologies for a computer network, the choice of which is usually determined by the purpose for which the network is installed and the physical location of the devices to be interconnected. The number of devices that are to be connected can dictate the choice of topology. If the number is very small, less than say 10 devices, then a point-to-point connection or polling system is possible, but as the number of devices to be interconnected increases then alternatives have to be considered. The basic alternatives, are: the star, where all devices are connected to a central point; the bus, where all devices are connected by a common link between them; the ring, where all devices are successively linked together and the ends of the connection are brought together again to complete a ring; and the unconstrained network, where links can exist between any one device and any number of other devices. There are variations of these basic topologies such as branching buses, trees, etc., but in general these can be considered to be extensions of the basic topologies in which the connected devices are components of another bus, star or ring.

Comparison of the basic topologies

The disadvantage of a star compared with a bus or a ring is that each device requires a connection to a central point which can become a bottleneck and, with a large number of connected devices, that the interconnection costs are comparatively high. The advantage of the star configuration is that the devices can use a simple point-to-point protocol rather than a common access protocol. The interconnection cost disadvantage can be reduced by providing device concentrators located adjacent to a number of devices. This saves the cost of individual connections, distributes some of the control and also allows the possibility of continued operation of parts of the network in the event of the failure of the central point.

The advantage of the bus and the ring is that a simpler interconnection strategy can be used that of single interconnection from one device to the next. A simple topology allows network configurations to be changed as the number of stations varies. With a bus, stations are simply connected to the bus cable. With a ring, the network is temporarily broken and a new station inserted between two existing stations. Most LANs are based on either a bus or a ring topology with common access protocols. The unconstrained topology is uncommon due to the necessity to handle the routing of data between devices and the problem of locating a path between devices. The passage of information through a node will affect its performance and will generally require a processor system of similar performance to the host system.

The physical connection between devices

The physical connection between devices on a LAN is characterized by

- The nature of the medium, e.g. fibre optic, coaxial cable, current loop, etc.
- The method of transmission, e.g. broadband, baseband.
- The signal levels and the modulation schemes used.
- The methods of signal coding.
- The types of connectors used and their pin allocations.
- The logic levels of the signals.
- The use of point-to-point or broadcast techniques.
- The synchronization method used.

Most LAN systems use synchronous schemes. The requirements of the link are specified in terms of data and error rates; this usually results in a compromise between performance and cost. Other important considerations in the selection of a physical medium are its integrity and reliability. These factors will seriously affect the performance of the network and its ease of use. Some successful broadband LANs have also been implemented which carry information on channels of different frequencies. Often, one channel on a broadband network is shared using an access technique similar to those discussed below.

Medium access control techniques

The physical connection ensures that one device can communicate with another. In most LAN topologies part of the transmission system is shared, so some form of control is required to arbitrate between contending devices. This is called the *medium access control* (MAC). In this section, a broad outline is given of the variety of techniques available. In later sections, examples of these techniques are covered in more detail. The techniques to be discussed are token passing and contention for both rings and buses, and slotted and register insertion rings.

Common access control schemes: token passing

A token is a unique control message that conveys the right of access to the medium. The token is passed between devices; the device that received the token most recently is said to hold the token and can access the communication medium. Token passing can be used with both broadcast (token bus) and sequentially connected (token ring) networks.

A number of potential problems exist in token passing systems. The systems must be able to detect and recover from lost or duplicated tokens. These problems have different solutions for ring and bus networks. In a token ring a unique marker is used to delimit the end of a transmission. When this marker is detected by the next device on the ring it looks for a pattern that represents the token and, if found, inserts its message into the ring. If this device does not wish to transmit, it passes the frame marker and token on to the next device. A token bus transmits a unique message for the token and monitors the bus for activity that indicates that the token was successfully received. If this is not so then a token recovery procedure has to be started.

Common access control: contention

Contention control is a distributed control scheme where each device attempts to gain control of the transmission medium. Each device competes against the other devices, so, to ensure fairness, each device must follow a precise set of rules for accessing the medium. LAN contention schemes are derived from the ALOHA and slotted ALOHA approach to multiple access to broadcast networks.

Contention control for network systems

Contention access control methods allow any device to attempt transmission and then take steps to resolve and limit the collisions that will occur. In a LAN, the prevention of collisions is attempted by sensing the activity on the bus before transmission is attempted. Any activity on the bus can be detected by looking for the presence of the carrier on which the data is encoded. This is known as *carrier sense.* The detection of a carrier can be used to prevent a device from corrupting the transmission in progress.

An algorithm is needed to specify what a station should do if the medium is found to be busy. Three approaches or persistence algorithms are possible:

1 *Non-persistent.* The station backs off a random amount of time and then senses the medium again.

2 *1-persistent.* The station continues to sense the medium until it is idle and then transmits.

3 *p-persistent.* The station continues to sense the medium until it is idle and then transmits with some probability p. Otherwise it backs off a fixed amount of time and then transmits with probability *p* or continues to back off with probability (1-p).

The non-persistent algorithm is effective in avoiding collisions; two stations wishing to transmit when the medium is busy are likely to back off for a different amount of time. The drawback is that there is likely to be wasted idle time following each transmission. In contrast, the 1-persistent algorithm attempts to reduce idle time by allowing a single waiting station to transmit immediately after another transmission. Unfortunately, if more than one station is waiting, a collision is guaranteed. The p-persistent algorithm is a compromise that attempts to minimize both collisions and idle time.

If two devices find that the bus is free then both may start to transmit at the same time and their messages will collide. This is detected by each station monitoring its signal on the bus. This is known as *collision detection.* To ensure that the collision is detected by all devices on the network, the devices must continue to transmit for a period after the detection of a collision. After the collision both devices will then wish to transmit. To prevent an immediate collision a random back off delay is used. The system just described is called carrier sense multiple access with collision detection (CSMA/CD).

Other access control techniques for ring systems

A ring can be configured to contain a number *of* circulating data minipackets; this allows two methods of access. In the first method, if a device is able to determine if a packet is empty it can fill this with data. This is called a slotted ring. Alternatively, a device can detect the end of a packet and insert its own packet between two existing packets; this is known as *register insertion.*

Allocated control for buses

In a bus system the access to the bus can be controlled by allocating time slots to connected devices. The simplest form is to divide the time equally between each device using time division multiple access (TDMA). This has the disadvantage that if a device does not wish to communicate then its allocated time is unused and resources are lost. Polling schemes can be used in which one device is allocated the role of bus master to handle requests. When a device wishes to transmit, it waits to be polled by the bus master and either transmits its message or declines the offer.

Both of the above schemes have high overheads when the network traffic is low. This has led to the development of combined contention and allocation schemes. In a combined scheme contention control is used when the load is light and the probability of collisions is low, resulting in low overheads. As the network utilization increases the chances of collisions increases and the throughput decreases. When this occurs an allocation scheme is utilized to ensure the maximum use of the network without contention. For example, see Kleinrock and Yemeni.

Local area network standardization

Local area networks have developed rapidly over a short period of time, presenting the prospective user with a wide choice of systems. To help the prospective users and suppliers, national and international standards bodies have produced standards specifically for LANs, concentrating on the lower levels of the OSI model. The standards developed for wide area networks will also be applicable to the higher levels of LANs. The IEEE is the organization principally involved with the standardization of the lower levels of LAN systems. The standardization was started by the IEEE Computer Society in 1980 by the formation of the IEEE Standards Project 802 whose role is to standardize the means of connecting digital equipment within a local area.

The project has noted that one single standard will not suffice and has accepted three main access methods. The first is the CSMA/CD bus (802.3) and the other two are token passing rings (802.5) and token passing buses (802.4). All three are designed to provide for the transmission of data over the network and are generally not suitable for the transmission of time critical information such as speech and video.

Standardization in metropolitan area networks is closely following that of LANs and will be important for LAN users wishing to interwork between LANs interconnected via gateways to the larger MANs.

The IEEE 802 standardization

The IEEE 802 committee has developed an overall structure into which a family of substandards. These standards have also been adopted by the International Standards Organization (ISO) with the series numbers 8802 (i.e. IEEE 802.2 is the same as ISO 8802/2). The individual IEEE standard numbers are:

802.1 Relationship between the 802 standards and the OSI model

802.2 Logical link control

802.3 Carrier sense multiple access with collision detection

802.4 Token passing bus access method

802.5 Token passing ring access method

802.6 Metropolitan area networks

In addition the following Technical Advisory Groups (TAG) have been initiated which may subsequently produce standards:

802.7 Broadband TAG

802.8 Fibre optic TAG

802.9 TAG concerned with the integration of LANs and digital telephony

IEEE 802.1 standard and the OSI model

The IEEE standard 802.1 describes the interrelationship between the members of the IEEE 802 standard family and their relationship to the ISO OSI reference model for LANs. Each of the access methods includes both physical layer components and a medium access control technique. The 802.2 logical link control (LLC) standard describes a network-independent protocol set used for passing data over any of the standardized systems 802.3-5; The combination of the MAC and LLC layers can be considered to form layer 2 of the OSI model.

The ethernet

The majority of installed LANs are based on Ethernet, which is a passive bus network that utilizes CSMA/CD. The system was developed, in 1976 by Metcalfe and Boggs. The original system operated with a data rate of 3 Mbit/s connecting up to 256 stations with a maximum network length of 1km. The system has evolved into a commercially available system operating at 10 Mbit/s, connecting a maximum of 1024 stations over a branching bus with a maximum network length of 2.5 km. Three of its major manufacturers, Xerox, Intel and DEC, have produced the industry standard definition which has been accepted by the IEEE. The advantages of the Ethernet system are its commercial standard and the fact that commercial interfaces are available for most common computer buses. Two of the disadvantages of the full specification system are the cost per connection and the cabling costs. A number of manufacturers now provide lower cost connection and cabling systems called Cheapernet or thin Ethernet. This has a reduced specification for the number of devices and cabling lengths, but is very suitable for small-scale networks.

IEEE 802.3 CSMA/CD bus

The IEEE standard 802.3 describes a LAN system using a multiple access, broadcast, baseband transmission medium with CSMA/CD.

Physical layer

The 802.3 standard specifies the physical layer of the system which has the following characteristics:

- *Transmission.* Baseband signalling over shielded coaxial cable.
- Topology. Branching non-rooted tree.
- *Network length.* Maximum cable segment length is 500 in, which may be interconnected via repeaters to a maximum system length of 2500 in.
- Data rate. 10 Mbit/s.
- Maximum number of stations. 1024

Frame format

When the frame is transmitted a minimum size limit of 46 data octets is imposed. Shorter, blocks of information presented for transmission are padded to the limit using the PAD field. This is to ensure that a frame will have been sensed by all stations on a maximum sized network before the transmission is completed. The time taken by any transmission must be longer than the *slot time,* that is the maximum propagation time from one end of the network to the other and back. This enables the deference and collision detection procedures to operate correctly.

The *preamble is* a 7-octet field with a bit pattern that results in a transmitted signal of half the transmission frequency; this has a polarity transition at the centre of each symbol time which simplifies synchronization. The SFD is the start of frame delimiter and signifies the start of the frame. The *destination* and *source address* fields are either 2 or 6 octets in length. The address length is constant for a network implementation. The *length* field contains the number of octets in the data field. The *LLCData* field contains the *LLC* information and information from higher layers. The FCS (frame check sequence) field contains a 32-bit cyclic redundancy check (CRC) computed on both address fields, length, LLCData and PAD fields.

Transmission without contention

Transmission is initiated by the MAC on reception of data from the LLC. The MAC constructs a frame, to the above format, with the data provided by the LLC. The MAC monitors the medium for the presence of a carrier, indicating that a transmission in progress, and defers to passing traffic. When the medium is clear transmission is started.

Reception without contention

All stations listen to the network; a reception is begun by the detection of the preamble which is used for clock synchronization. The bit stream up to the end of the start delimiter is discarded and then the frame is reconstructed. The destination address of the incoming frame is checked to see if it should be received by the station, if not it is discarded. If the address matches and the reception was completed without error, this is signalled by the MAC to the LLC and the address and data fields are passed to the higher layer.

Access contention

If more than one station attempts to use the medium at the same time they will interfere with each other, causing a collision between the signals of the two stations. A station can experience a collision during the initial part of its transmission transmitted signal has had time to propagate to all stations on the medium. Once the window has passed, the station has the medium and collisions will be prevented by other stations deferring to it. When a collision is detected the MAC enforces the collision by transmitting a bit sequence called a *jam*. The duration of the jam is sufficient to ensure that all stations will detect the collision. After the jam has been sent transmission is stopped. Transmission is rescheduled to occur after a random period of time, called the back off. If on re-transmission a further collision is detected, the jam and back off sequence is repeated with an increase in the back off. This is continued until a maximum number of retries have been exceeded, in which case a transmission error is signalled to the LLC layer.

Network management and initialization

The CSMA/CD MAC scheme has no separate network management functions to provide detection, control and recovery from abnormal network conditions. This is because these functions are essential for the operation of the CSMA/CD control and are incorporated within it. In addition, as the network is a passive medium with fully distributed control, no medium or common network control initialization is required.

IEEE 802.4 token passing bus

The IEEE standard 802.4 describes a LAN based on a broadcast bus medium with a token passing access control scheme. The physical layer specifications cover a number of coaxial cabled systems with hardware derived from cable television (CATV) systems. The number of stations connected and the total length of the network depend on the physical layer scheme used.

Physical layer

Three different physical layer options are described in the standard. These are:

- An omnidirectional bus using phase continuous frequency shift keying at I Mbit/s.
- An omnidirectional bus using phase continuous frequency shift keying at 5 or 10 Mbit/s.
- A directional bus with active head end repeater using multilevel duobinary amplitude modulation/phase shift keying at 1, 5 or 10 Mbit/s.

Each physical layer option provides a generic interface to the medium access control and to the station management. The MAC interface provides four primitives to control the operation of the physical layer. These are transmission initiation, reception notification, transmission mode control and end of reception indication. The station management interface provides primitives for the configuration and control of the physical layer.

Medium access control

The medium access control scheme used is a token-based system where the token passes sequentially around a logical ring formed between stations on the network. The MAC provides the standard functions of data buffering, station address recognition, frame encapsulation, FCS generation and valid token recognition. The MAC also provides facilities for the maintenance of the logical ring. These are lost token recovery, token holding time-outs, distributed initialization, node failure error recovery and logical ring member addition. The passage of the token between stations on the logical ring has little relationship to the physical connectivity of the stations. The logical ring consists of stations A→B→E→G→C→A; the token is passed between these stations sequentially. Stations D and H are connected to the physical layer and can therefore receive messages but cannot initiate transmission. However, they can transmit a response when a station which is a member of the logical ring issues a *request_with_response*.

MAC operation

The operations performed by the MAC layer involve the management of ordered access to the medium, providing a means for the addition and subtraction of stations and fault handling. The operation of the MAC is based on the following observations about a station's operation:

1. When a station transmits to the medium its signal can be received by all stations; no station can predictably alter the transmission but a transmission can be corrupted.
2. The transmitting station can assume that all active stations received some transmission but cannot assume that its message was received correctly by any station.
3. When a station successfully receives a frame it can assume that all other stations were aware of the transmission.
4. It is not necessary for all stations to be involved in the transmitted sequence, i.e. be members of the logical ring.
5. Each station must be able to handle multiple or lost tokens; there is no common monitor to perform this function.

MAC management functions

The normal operation of the network, when the logical ring has been established and is not changing, simply involves the passage of the token between a station and its logical successor after it has completed its transmissions. A station holding the token may temporarily delegate its right to transmit to any station, including those not in the logical ring, by sending a *request_with_response* data frame. When a station receives a *request_with_response* it can respond with a *response* data frame; after this the right to transmit returns to the original station. After a station passes the token it listens to ensure that its successor sends a valid frame indicating that the token was accepted successfully. If no valid frame is heard the sender attempts to determine the reason why the token was not transferred.

If the sender hears noise or an invalid frame it must attempt to recover the token. If it was just to repeat the token, it could create two tokens in the network. If the station hears a noise burst it continues to listen for four more *slot times*. If nothing more is heard it assumes that its own token was corrupted and as in the case of no activity, repeats the token. The second token is monitored as before; if there is still no activity the sender assumes that its successor has failed. It then attempts to find out its own place in the logical ring by transmitting a Who_follows frame with its previous successor's address. All stations check the address and the station whose predecessor was the successor of the current station responds with a *Setsuccessor* frame. If there is still no response the token holder has to find another station on the logical ring by sending a *Solicit successor* frame containing its own address. Any station wishing to be part of the logical ring responds using a *response windoiv.* A response window is a controlled interval of time after the transmission of a MAC control frame during which the sender waits for a reply to be started. If the attempts to solicit a successor fail, either all stations have left the logical ring or an error condition exists and the logical ring needs to be re-established.

Stations are added to the logical ring by active stations sending a *solicit_successor* frame. This specifies a range of addresses between the sender and its successor. Stations in this range respond during the response window.

It is possible that more than one station will wish to respond. If contention occurs the sending station starts an arbitration procedure by sending a *resolve_contention* frame. A station that responds chooses a delay of 03 slot times before transmitting. If during the delay another transmission is heard the station removes itself from the contention resolution. If nothing is heard it replies, this initiates further *resolve contention* requests. Finally only one station will successfully respond, resolve the contention and become the successor.

The initialization of the logical ring is a special instance of adding stations. This action is started when the bus has been idle for too long. When this occurs, a station transmits a *claim_token* frame and contention is resolved in a similar manner as before.

The station that wins the contention holds the token; it can solicit a successor and build the logical ring.

IEEE 802.5 token ring

The IEEE standard 802.5 describes a ring LAN using a token passing access control scheme for the connection of up to 250 stations with multiple levels of message priority. Information is transmitted sequentially from one station to the next, each active station acting as a repeater for the information. The destination station copies the information from the ring. The information is removed from the ring by the source station. Error detection and recovery facilities and control of the number of bits in the ring are provided by one of the stations acting as a network monitor. This is protected by backup capability in all other ring stations.

Physical layer

The IEEE token ring uses shielded twin twisted pair cable with data transmission at either I or 4 Mbit/s. The frequency is fixed for a particular implementation of the system. Each station is connected into the ring via a trunk coupling unit (TCU) that enables an active station to be inserted into the ring or by-passed from the ring when inactive or failed. Symbols are transmitted to the medium using differential Manchester-type coding which is characterized by having two signal elements per symbol. Two non-data symbols are used within the frame delimiter octets.

The active monitor

The physical layer requires that all stations have the capability to become the network monitor. Only one station acts as the active monitor and signals its presence by regularly broadcasting active monitor present (AMP) MAC frames. The first station to receive the AMP frame resets a timer and sends a standby monitor present (SMP) frame. If the timer expires, indicating the failure of the active monitor, the standby monitor starts the procedure of becoming the active monitor. The SMP frame is passed between all other stations; these stations use a similar procedure to backup the first standby monitor. The active monitor checks the ring for correct transmission and will attempt to restore correct operation when an error is detected. It also checks for AMP frames that are not its own, indicating that two active monitors are in operation. If this occurs it returns to the standby state. The active monitor station provides a variable-length delay buffer, the *latency buffer,* that maintains the minimum length of the ring, specified in bit times. This must be greater than the number of bits in the token sequence, 24 bits. The active monitor also acts as the master oscillator for the network, providing the clock to which all other stations synchronize. Although this provides the frequency to which all segments of the ring should be synchronized, it is possible for segments of the ring to be operating at slightly different frequencies and thereby change the total ring latency. These errors can be up to +- 3 bits, so to maintain a constant ring latency of $\geq$ 24 bits, a variable length buffer, of up to 6 bits, is added to the buffer.

Format of transmitted information

Two formats of information are transmitted around the ring, tokens and frames. The token represents the right for a station to transmit. The frame format is used for the transmission of medium access control (MAC) and logical link control (LLC) messages between stations. To meet the requirements of the LLC each station should be capable of receiving frames up to and including 133 octets. The *end delimiter* contains an intermediate frame bit, I, and an error detected bit, E. The I bit is set to a I to signify that another frame from the same transmitter will follow, and is set to 0 for the last or only frame transmitted. The E bit is set to 0 by the source transmitter. Each station in the ring checks tokens and frames for errors as they are repeated. If an error is detected the E bit is set to I in the frame in error: otherwise the E bit is repeated as received. The *access control field* contains bits for the identification and control of tokens, for message priority and monitor control. The token bit is set to 0 in a token and I in a frame. The priority bits specify the priority of a token allowing a station to determine if it can use the token. There are eight levels of priority with level 0 being the lowest. A station that has a protocol data unit (PDU) awaiting transmission with equal or higher priority than the token's priority may change the token to a start-of-frame sequence and commence transmission of the PDU.

The *monitor* bit is set by the transmitter to 0 in all frames and tokens. When a monitor bit of 0 is detected by the active monitor it is converted to a I to mark its first passage around the ring. If the active monitor detects an access control field with the monitor bit set to I and a priority greater than 0 then the frame or token is aborted; this is because a frame or token should have been removed by its transmitting station. The exception is a priority 0 token which will circulate around the ring when the network is idle.

The frame status field is used to enable the trans-mitting station to receive information about the passage of a frame around the ring. Two bits, the address recognized, A, and frame copied, C, are sent as 0 by the transmitting station. If a station recognizes the destination address of the frame as its own it sets the A bit to 1. If the station also copies the frame into its buffer, it sets the C bit to 1. From the possible combinations of these bits the originating station can determine:

1 If the destination station is inactive on this ring.

2 If the station exists but did not copy the frame.

3 That the frame was copied by the destination station.

Medium access control

The access to the ring, or medium, is controlled by the token. MAC rules specify the usage of the token, the control of the priority of messages and management of the network in the case of errors or failures.

Frame transmission

For transmission, the MAC formats the frame by adding the address and control fields and then waits for the reception of a token with a priority equal to or less than that of the awaiting frame.

When a usable token is received it is converted into a start-of-frame sequence and the frame transmission is started. The frame check sequence is calculated and appended to the information field. Frame transmission will continue until either there are no more queued PDUs with the same or higher priority than the current service priority or the *token holding time* (THT) would be exceeded by transmitting the PDU. The THT ensures that one station does not hog the network and allows fair network usage. When a station has a PDU of higher priority than the current service priority it requests a priority token.

Token transmission

A transmitting station checks that it receives its own frames by looking at the source address of the incoming frames and also checks the response bits to determine if each frame was successfully received. When it has completed its transmissions, it sends a token and continues to receive until all frames that it transmitted have been cleared from the ring. It then repeats the incoming signal. When a token is inserted in the ring it may be necessary to increase its priority either because the received reservation value or the priority value of a frame still queued is higher than the priority of the received token. The station transmits a token of raised priority with the reservation bits set to zero. A station that raises the priority level has the responsibility for subsequently resetting it.

The Cambridge ring

Although there have not been as many implementations of slotted rings as of other LAN types, the most recent approaches to multiservice networks are based on multiple access to a slotted network structure. For this reason it is valuable to discuss the Cambridge ring as an example of a slotted ring LAN. The Cambridge ring was developed, from 1975, by Wilkes, Wheeler and Hopper at the University of Cambridge Computer Laboratory. It has been a popular choice in the UK academic community where it has formed the basis for research into such areas as distributed systems and network interconnection. Up to 254 stations can be connected to a single ring, the total ring length being limited only by the total ring delay. Devices are connected to the ring by *repeaters* which pass on the circulating bit stream. Various technologies can be used in the ring transmission system to cater for differing interrepeater distances. Information is written into a circulating slots in the form of a *minipacket*. The slot structure is established by a special station: the monitor.

Physical layer

The basic transmission scheme uses a twin twisted pair cable providing reliable communication at

10 Mbit/s. The system uses a modulation scheme that enables a 10 Mbit/s data and clock to be transmitted while keeping the bandwidth used to 10 MHz. The scheme uses the two pairs, changing the state of both pairs to indicate a 1, and alternately changing pairs to indicate a 0. This scheme will suffer from any differential delays between the two pairs; this is a significant factor in limiting the interrepeater distance over copper cables to 200 metres. For greater distances fibre optic links can be used to extend the network over a wide physical area.

Ring access scheme

The latest Cambridge rings use a 40 bit minipacket separated by a gap of at least 4 bits. The type bits are used to distinguish between different sequences of minipackets. The data is transmitted at approximately 10 Mbit/s; the frequency is adjusted to ensure that the ring delay is equal to a whole number of bit times. In small rings, where the ring length is less than 44 bits, the ring is padded by a delay in the monitor so that a whole minipacket and a 4-bit interpacket gap exist. An empty minipacket is filled by the transmitting station which sets the full bit and fills in the address and data fields as required. When the minipacket is received by the destination it copies the address and data fields into its internal buffer and sets the response bits to indicate that it *accepted* the data. If the destination station's register is full it sets the response bits to busy. Each station has a source select register which can be set to any station, a specific address or no station. This register is used to control reception so that minipackets from other stations do not interfere with a sequence of minipackets from one station. If the source of the minipacket is from a station the destination has not selected, the station does not copy the data, but sets the response bits to *unselected.* If the destination is inactive or not present on the ring the response bits return *unchanged,* to indicate that the minipacket was ignored by all stations on the ring. The transmitting station waits for the minipacket to return, sets the full bit to empty and stores the response bits for the controlling software. The restriction of waiting for the minipacket to return limits the maximum data rate achievable in a ring with more than one minipacket. The system also prevents a station from reusing the same minipacket, forcing it to send it empty to the next station on the ring. This prevents one station from hogging the ring, resulting in load sharing among the ring stations.

ENCYCLOPAEDIA
OF
MODERN MANAGEMENT TECHNIQUES

ENCYCLOPAEDIA
OF
MODERN MANAGEMENT
TECHNIQUES

Volume 4

Edited by

A. K. Chaudhary

ANMOL PUBLICATIONS PVT. LTD.

NEW DELHI-110 002 (INDIA)

ANMOL PUBLICATIONS PVT. LTD.
4374/4B, Ansari Road, Daryaganj
New Delhi-110 002

Encyclopaedia of Modern Management Techniques

First Edition 1999

ISBN 81-261-0321-3 (Set)

PRINTED IN INDIA

Published by J. L. Kumar for Anmol Publications Pvt. Ltd., New Delhi-110 002 and Printed at Mehra Offset Press, Delhi.

Contents

15

Operations Research

In the sixties and early seventies, operational research become involved in tactical analysis, building financial models "with barehands" using primitive tools and dabbling with new packages. As the significance of financial modelling emerged the popularity of the systems grew, operational research lost its dominances the main modelling distributor. The bridgehead for the continuing contribution of operational research to corporate planning was weakened for the three reasons summarised below.

1. O.R. suffered from the debate and uncertainty as to whether financial modelling etc. was really corporate planning
2. the body of pure O.R. practitioners, worshipping the god of optimisation, frowned upon the mathematical trivialities of such activities as financial modelling
3. there was a tremendous surge of development in both modelling tolls and education for other management disciplines this removed a large part of the O.R. skill in model building.

In 1973, from a survey of practitioners in model building for corporate planning, and Wooler report that 30% were operational research. From 1973 to 1982 their activity incorporate modelling increased by 6% whilst accountants have increased their activity in corporate modelling by 50% and it is apparent today that operational researchers now have limited unique tools to general corporate planning problem and that they have not maintained a proportionate involvement within the surge of modelling activity.

To counter this loss, there has been a determined effort to attack more complex, less popular modelling problems and re-establish specialist skills such as manpower planning, although this remains minor activity attributed with limited involvement in the strategic decisions of most organisations. In practice corporate planning has provided a useful training ground for operational researchers to move upwards into more general business management, exposing the staff to fundamental higher levels of the business activity such as the assessment of a new venture rather than the details of production scheduling within that activity. Because of this lack of long term commitment to corporate planning and the reduced involvement, there has not been enough lateral thinking by operational researchers on different forms of modelling and at different levels of decision making.

Corporate modelling is dominated in practice by financial modelling, accounting for 90% of the activity. Hence the term corporate model is commonly used to describe a financial model which demonstrates the financial consequences overtime of decisions with critical assumptions and within a close range of alternatives. The natural structure of financial reports lend themselves to a mechanical model format that allows the report to be generated repeatedly over time with different prime data.

There are two reasons why financial modelling can become a complex problem that merits the intervention of a specialist; (a) the size of the model/multiple components and (b) the sophistication of forecasts and relationships of elements in the model. In the case of multiple "strategic business units" within an existing or planned investment, there is a need to handle and control the large quantity of data: to provide individual unit reports: and to design the mechanics of consolidated appraisal. The investment involved five strategic business units-crop farming, feedmilling, broiler meat production, egg production and central services. There were approximately five hundred individual data components. The units were structured to provide mutual benefits and joint economies. For example crops were produced on the farm to provide feed for the laying hens-assessing the sensitivity of the results to market changes in the demand for eggs had to link back to the effect on the farm activity etc. as well as the planned flocks sizes and laying cycles. In general there existed a complex lateral interaction of performance between units reflected in the model. Further the vertical impact of changes, for example in a capital cost, filtered through the capital schedule, the depreciation in the profit/loss accounts, the subsequent cash flow, draw down of loan requirement-compounded for interest charges etc.

The quality of the information out of any financial model is dependent on the ability of the model to represent reality. Whilst approximate estimates of revenues and cost can provide reasonable assessment, it may be necessary to include more accurate estimates incorporating sophisticated mathematical techniques. Costs may be projected relationships for simple results. The system has been derived by multivariate statistical analysis relations fuel consumption to the pattern of production activity and whether conditions.

The paper by Shim and McGlade provides a general "state of the art" summary of financial modelling, including both areas of the application how models are used, and a description of tools available-what computer packages are relevant. Modelling packages have developed over the last twelve years in two directions. Firstly, in the range of design, from the large data based main frame packages such as FCS to the micro spread-sheet packages such a VISICALC; secondly, in the quality of design in terms of facilities and use interface. From a survey of financial modelling in The Times 1000 companies, Grinyer has compiled a detailed statistical analysis of user experience in the construction and use of financial models. In contains a particularly useful investigation of experience with modelling packages-important for new practitioners. Bryant's edited collection of case histories gives a practical and detailed insight into financial modelling illustration a wide variety of applications.

Finance is one resource to be considered in any tactical deployment to achieve a particular strategy. A second resource is that of manpower. Whilst manpower planning has not received the same level of attention as financial planning, there have been significant developments over the last ten years in bringing manpower modelling methods into the practical tool kit of corporate planners. Manpower is a considerably more complex issue than money. Its behaviour is subject to a multiply of factors and there are no simple measure of the effectiveness of its application. Developments have gone two ways: firstly more detailed stochastic models that attempt to reflect these additional factors and, secondly, simple modelling packages providing a limited but useful planning tool. Purkiss has summarised the state of the art with respect to the theory of manpower modelling systems. Edwards has described the packages commonly available. These models essentially compromise a system of systems within classes and user defined ruled for flows between classes. The use is limited by the treatment of aggregate behaviour and in most circumstances the same models can be constructed using financial planning packages, although there is undoubted benefit at the user interface from the prespecified manpower format. A common theme of successful applications is that good presentation of results and ease of use are more important to users than theoretical sophistication. Verhoeven discusses these tools as an aid to corporate planning and to the problems of designing alternative policies for promotions, recruitment, etc. through a case study. The application is a typical example of the successful use of models-namely where the profile of the organisation is consistent, there is an inherent rigid class/job description structure and where the stocks of similar personnel within classes are high enough to accept aggregate representation—in this case the Royal Dutch Airforce. The principle applies to planning of all resources. One of the most powerful decision support mechanism for examining the application of resources is simulation. Craig describes the use of system dynamics; a simple simulation mechanism for corporate planning that incorporates non-financial that this case material stocks and cash, using the package GENISM. A more sophisticated model by Newton involves a discrete to play the resources at a new dock for grain export. The resources included grain storage capacity, weigh bridges, conveyer tracking, ship berth etc. -with interacting behaviour. The simulation enables the planners to predict the performance of the dock design with different schedules of grain carried and grain shipped out.

Simulation has two important contributions to planning:

1. demonstrating feasibility—predicting complex interactive behaviour and the ability of the resource to achieve the objectives
2. demonstrating risk—conveying the variability of performance and results.

However, in general, discrete event simulation requires specialist and complex modelling skill, a feature that reduces its applicability and acceptability in routine corporate planning practice. Although system dynamics may be a less powerful tool in predicting behaviour, it undoubtedly has had a larger exposure and application.

Tactical analysis accounts for 99% of the effort in model building within corporate planning and the consequent involvement of operational research. There remains however a significant deficiency of modelling tools for strategic decision making. There is a very important need for decision support system directed specifically at the top level policy making issues.

A group currently active in the manufacture, distribution and export of animal feeds is now deciding whether to diversify, expanding its UK operation base by entering the pet food business. Question—"What decision support system will help to make that decision?" The contribution of modelling practice described within tactical analysis has limited value. A financial model projecting a potential acquisition would be questionable-its past data would relate to the existing management and provide little insight of future performance within the group. It is not easy to attempt to quantify the economies of synergy, operating the business within the group-market access, central management, material purchasing etc. The present financial prospectus for the business might provide a lower bound for the group's expectations but not much more. Further, the less tangible benefits of new distribution exposure for the existing business and the long term opportunities based on the impending decision would be even more difficult to model and quantity. Frequently the error in constructing a detailed financial model with vast quantities of cost/revenue components with solid foundation provide a complex number crunching exercise with limited credibility. The traditional operational research philosophy of linking decisions to outcomes by a mechanical nuts and bolts building operation is not feasible.

At this stage it could be argued that entrepreneurial strategic decision making is an art, and inherent skill within the individual, gut feeling with no room for objective analysis. In the example the chairman of the group might feel that it is chairman of the group might feel that it is right to make successful small business owners who would accept this simple description of their strategic decision making.

A second theory of entrepreneurial behaviour that would rule out the value of strategic modelling is that of the lottery; that decision made on this haphazard approach are in fact a pure toos-of-the-coin gamble; and that some decisions are successful on a random basis. There is no doubt that the unknown outcome of decisions must contribute to the support of this theory and that there is a place for luck in the history of business success. How ever there is also a problem in tying this theory to examples of counting success and in general continuing survival of business organisations.

In practice, in this example the group director identify and debate issues and aspects of the decision that have strategic significance-indication potential success or failure from the outcome.

1. the group has considerable feed technology skills and experience related to pet feed manufacturing.
2. the group already manufacture and sell some of the base component suitable for pet feed
3. the existing distribution systems could be used to distribute pet food, including export business
4. the pet food market is a growth market particularly in new overseas economies
5. the group has surplus cash resources
6. some of the existing animal feed markets overseas are effectively in decline to traditional UK supplier-exhibiting a similar profile to that of a conventional durable product life cycle.
7. there is minimal size of operation in the new product area necessary to sustain the diversification as a success full business unit.
8. the cost of entering the main stream dog and cat food markets of the UK in terms of products promotion and pricing is very high.

The decision making process by the director involves a subconscious strategic modelling exercise with these and other factors as input and the likely results of the decision as output.

Although this is clearly a complex problem to approach, there have been some attempts to formalise this modelling a provide practical tools for corporate planners within limited circumstances.

Qualitative issues

The PIMS study was initiated in 1971 by the American Marketing Science Institute and the Harvard Business School with the intention to examine the profit impact of market strategies through statistical analysis. The PIMS original data base compromised financial and other information on 620 individual businesses supplied by 57 major North American corporations initially for the three year period 1970-72. Since then the survey has been launched in the UK and continues as important collection of business information. Buzzel, Gale and Sutton reported that PIMS project reveals a link between return on investment (ROI) and market share- "the bigger the better". They based this conclusion on the positive correlated observed between ROI and market share from the study data. The findings were supported by the three feasible explanation: economies of scale, market power, and quality of management. Further, the results suggested a predictable change in profit from an aggressive market building strategy.

The idea was enhanced by the Boston Consulting Group and their theory of the experience curve effect. They observed that " each time the accumulated experience of manufacturing a particular product doubles, the total unit cost in real terms.... can be made to decline by a production volume results in a reduction of unit production cost.

Whilst there is considerable debate about the validity of these conclusions and concern for the statistical rigour of the interpretations they represent a new dimension in corporate modelling. This is the concept that the strategic decisions, as input, can be translated into the systematic process. The PIMS finding for example, implied that the direct consequences of a 5% increase in market share etc. could be predicted.

Corporate planning and operational research— the future

In the boarder sense of modelling as a decision support system for corporate planning, there have been attempts to demonstrate the current development of resources and the likely results of strategy decisions through graphic systems. One common theme in corporate modelling is the need to present the decision makers with a critical summary of the large amount of potential data and analysis from a multi-business group. Several matrix representation techniques have been designed the most famous of these systems is the growth-share matrix of the Bostan Consulting Group Strategic business units are plotted on the matrix with two dimensions, business growth rare and market share. The projected movement from one quadrant to the next indicate the weakness in the group structure; the required strategy and the anticipated outcome of that strategy. Whilst again there remains argument about the validity of the inherent analysis the contribution to corporate modelling is very important. Firstly it provides a new line of thought on information representation for strategic decision making a secondary it shows an attempt to advance the one factor model into a two factor model for predicting the decision outcome.

This represent an attempt to model the input of five different factor and the strategic decision from those factors on the implied outcome profit etc. As a decision support system the procedure demonstrates the critical information about the present portfolio of business and the likely outcome from decisions on diversification through acquisition; sellout; market share building; etc.

These matrix system have two futures:

(a) they can only handle the modelling of two factors at any one type.

(b) they are designed for simple accounting factors

Robinson, Hichens and Wade have extended the growth share matrix to include a border range of qualitative factor in assessing the strategic disposition of the organization's business units and those of its competitors with the Directional Policy Matrix. They have expanded market growth to "business sector prospects" a general measure of the health of the industry and market share to company's competitiveness within that industry. The measures are determined by accumulating the simple subjective scores to a series of prescribed questions for each factor. The questions are concerned with qualitative strategic issues rather than quantitative financial analysis. The resulting two-score answer can then be plotted on a two dimensional matrix divided into nine strategic areas and the positions interpreted to assist the planning process.

The tool was further extended by Hussey to include a third factor, environmental risk—a measure of the stability of the external circumstances that directly affect the industry.

Newton showed that the same system, with a rearrangement of priorities and weighting of individual factors could be used to approach potential acquisitions.

The Directional Policy Matrix and its derivatives require three basic assumptions:

(a) that all qualities issues can be assessed in quantitative terms

(b) that all the issues can be clustered into three fundamental dimensions

(c) that the relative significance of different issues within the same dimension can be reflected by a weighted summation process.

McNamee provides a detailed description and comparison of these and other matrix display techniques-how the choice of matrix display to be used by strategic planners is dependent on the objectives of the exercise and the data available. The common theme behind matrix methods is a decision support system that interprets the current disposition of resources in a concise display in an attempt to point to obvious strategic decisions, and their likely affect on achieving the organisation's objectives.

Harris devised the sphere of corporate planning problems into four sectors defined by two dimensions, (a) the degree of change from the existing practice. The paper suggests that (b) operational research can make significant contributions in the three sectors. In the spectrum of decisions within the corporate planning process, problems with these profiles typically fall within the areas of tactical analysis whilst strategic decisions involve high change and at present low understanding.

The contribution of corporate modelling for resource allocation within tactical analysis will continue to provide a powerful tool for planners. The development in corporate modelling popularity should prompt future interest in more modelling mechanisms driven by larger and more varied data bases, and hence a future role for "bread and butter" operational research. Little has been done to link sophisticated forecasting techniques to modelling procedures. There are serious problems in " Controlling" model use, ensuring the data is correct, protecting the logic mechanism and the user!

To encourage the interest and ensure the operational research contribution, the inconvenience of having a specialist between the model and the decision makers needs to be overcome. It is imperative therefore that operational researches have a good education in business principles. Accounting should have the same level of significance in the skills of operational researchers as the more established disciplines such as statistics. Operational research should be examining the process of information presentation to the decision maker, a feature that has been helped by the fact that decision support as well as decision optimisation has been recognised as part of the "approved" subject material. Modelling for strategic decision making the quadrant provides the greatest challenge to operational researchers. Taking our examples a stage further; the animal feed group has now found a potential acquisition, a small family business currently supplying about 30% of a segment within the pet food market. The company has an existing distribution network supplying about 100 wholesalers throughout the UK and is a small profit.

Some issues are not unique to corporate planning. The problems of handling multiple qualitative factors is common to the general development of multi-criteria decision analysis. Such mechanism as Saaty's eigenvector technique for combining multiple qualitative factor is one possible tack to consider. Extending the current matrix methods into more complex strategic maps that allow the presentation of a more complex resource image for portfolio and competitor analysis provides a challenge to operational researchers to stretch their information technology skills and imagination. It has already been suggested that the development in expert systems could close that gap in the loop between resources allocation and its strategic implications." The possibility is clear that within a decade a supercomputer may share or usurp functions of a corporate chief executive functions that up is now have been thought unsharable. Now is the item to begin planning for such as development.

In general if operational research is to regain a significant role in corporate planning and the evolution of its theory, it must think beyond existing of its theory. It must also be prepared to take risk and fall on its nose from time to tome to demonstrate its willingness to consider. Whilst the potential contribution to these "wicked problems" remains unsure there is a very big hole and a demand that is ready to welcome that contribution.

At the turn of the century, a number of Britons believed that every significant invention had already been recorded, and so they instituted a drive to close the Royal Patent Office. Their failure to envisage the countless new inventions developed since that time vividly demonstrates man's inability to foresee the future.

Perhaps this inability to look ahead results from the desire to keep things as they are—to maintain the status quo. The majority has never accepted change as an essential of life. When Richard Arkwright invented the spinning frame in 1769, hostile workmen attempted to destroy any replicas that appeared. Similarly, upon the introduction of steam power, many newspaper publishers urged mother to case bearing children because steam power would rob them of job possibilities. Nevertheless, advances in technology were adopted in the face of widespread resistance, with scores of new economic opportunities opening for the people. In the United States, acceptance of new ideas and adjustment to the changes wrought by innovation have occurred more readily than in most other countries around the world. But this ability to accept and adjust will be tested more rigorously in the future than ever before. The transition which overcame American society in the 1960s was merely a foretaste of tomorrow.

The change is evident everywhere. Since the end of World War II, for example, the population has increased dramatically; in November, 1967, the number of people inhabiting the United States passed the 200 million mark. Whereas it took 35 years for the population to grow from 100 to 150 million, the next 50 million was tacked on in less than half that time, namely, 17 years.

We also experienced tremendous economic growth during the 1960s. The Gross National Product (expressed in 958 dollars) increased from approximately $300 billion in 1950 to nearly $488 billion in 1960 and up to almost $750 billion in 1970. This new wealth generated dramatic increases in personal income, in consumer spending, and in the value of resources allocated for education and public welfare.

The increase in the size of institutions in this country during the same period is of great significance to the function of management. The 20 largest corporations in the United States had combined sales of over $139 billion in 1970—a volume larger than the entire Gross National Product in 1940. Similarly, public organizations greatly expanded their operations. By 1967, one out of every six nonagricultural employees had a job at some level of the government. In 1967, federal, state, and local governments were by far the largest customers in the United States, buying $176.3 billion worth of goods and services, or twenty-two per cent of every dollar spent. The size of giant private and public organizations often defies comprehension, and the growth continues.

Although we are living in an age of intense social change and unrest, many of the problems in our society are not unique to this age. In the midnineteenth century, every major city of the United States had slums so horrible that, in comparison, our contemporary slum areas appear benign. By 1900, New York's traffic problems with the brewery drays, horse trolleys, hackney coaches, and steam locomotives had reached a crisis. Many large cities had areas where anarchy or gang rule went unchallenged. And the history of American cities is replete with accounts of epidemics caused by polluted drinking water, streets made impassable by snow or must, strikes and riots, and operating inefficiencies and corruption in city government.

In the eighteenth century, when the plight of the poor in Ireland became intolerable, Jonathan Swift suggested, in "A Modest Proposal," that if the rich would fatten and eat the children of the poor both food and population problems would be solved. With the resources and know-how available today, Jonathan Swift would be able to suggest more reasonable solutions. For the first time, we are acknowledging the existence of such problems, and we are aware of the urgent need to solve them. The situation presents us with a tremendous challenge and opportunity. Imagine the excitement in redesigning urban centers to rid them of pollution and slums, in creating new economic opportunities to reduce poverty and increase the standard of living, in designing new transportation systems to accommodate the increasing number of travelers, and in developing the knowledge and the means to explore unknown areas of the universe.

The immediate task of our society is to marshall resources to solve these problems—to create public and private institutions which can achieve social and economic goals in the most effective and efficient manager possible. We must structure organizations of the nature to accommodate and adjust to change, to work as a unit toward common goals, and to evaluate the performance of each of the various segments toward accomplishing the master plan.

Unfortunately, the typical functional organization cannot meet current of future requirements efficiently. If traditional organizations had possessed sufficient flexibility the buggymakers of the past would have become today's automobile manufacturers, and the railroads would have used the airplane in their transportation system.

Management by system is more adaptable to change than the typical functional organization. For this reason, we have chosen management by system as a framework for the study of Operations Management. We define Operations Management as the design and operation of systems, including the application of those tools and techniques which are useful in achieving efficient and effective systems performance. Operations Management, as described in this text, has application to all forms of public and private organizations, those engaged in manufacturing, distribution, and service.

General systems theory

What is systems theory? What is system? We might modify the phrase "happiness is different things to different people" and say "systems mean different things to different people." For example, some relate systems to science which they describe as a systematic body of knowledge; an array of essential principles or facts arranged in a rational dependence or connection; a complex of ideas, principles, laws, forming a coherent whole. Scientists endeavor to develop, organize, and classify material into interconnected disciplines. Two well-known works, Darwin's The Origin of Species and Keynes' General Theory of Employment, Interest, and Money, represent attempts to integrate a large amount of related material. Darwin in his theory of evolution, integrated all life into a "system of nature" and indicated how the myriad of subsystems were interrelated. Keynes, in his work, connected the many complicated natural and man-made forces that influence an economy. Both men had a major impact on man's thinking because they were able to conceptualize interrelationships among complex phenomena and integrate them into a systematic whole. The term systems, when used in this context, connotes plan, method, order, and arrangement.

Similarly, general systems theory has been described as the development of a systematic, theoretical framework for describing general relationships of the empirical world. Existing similarities in the theoretical construction of various disciplines become apparent upon examination. Models can be developed that are applicable to many systems, whether physical, biological, behavioral, or social. An ultimate but distant goal of general systems theory is to develop a framework (or systems of systems of systems) that will all disciplines together in a meaningful relationship.

The need for a general systems theory

One of the most important indications of the need for a general system theory pertains to the problem of communication among the various disciplines. Although there is similarity in the general approach (scientific method), the results are not often communicated across discipline boundaries. Hence, the conceptualizing and hypothesizing done in one area seldom are used in other areas even though such work might contribute to a significant breakthrough. Specialists seldom communicate with one another between disciplines. Of course, the conflict of ideas and difficulties of communication are even greater between the various fields of study-the scientific, the social sciences, and the humanistic.

On the positive side, there has been some tendency toward interdisciplinary study in recent years. Areas such as social psychology, biochemistry astro-physics, social anthropology, economic psychology, and economic sociology have been developed in order to emphasize the interrelationship of previously isolated disciplines. More recently, areas of study and research that call on numerous subfields have been advanced. For example, cybernetics, the science of communication and control, draws on electrical engineering, neurophysiology, physics, biology, and several other fields. Operations research is often pointed to as a multidisciplinary approach to problem solving. Organization theory embraces economics, sociology, engineering psychology, physiology, and anthropology. Problem solving and decision making are also becoming focal points for analysis and research, drawing on numerous fields. Unfortunately, the "new" cross-disciplines sometimes create a jargon that tends to compound the communication problem.

With such examples of interdisciplinary approaches, it is easy to under stand the surge of interest in large-scale, systematic bodies of knowledge. However, this trend calls for the development of an overall framework within which the various subparts or disciplines can be integrated but in which they still retain the type of discipline that distinguishes them. The approach of providing a overall framework (general systems theory) extracts phenomena common to many different disciplines and develops general models which include such phenomena.

Within the context of general system theory, we stated that a system an assemblage or combination of things or parts forming a complex unitary whole. In this usage it covers an extremely broad spectrum of concepts-for example, in the world around us, there are mountain system river systems, and the solar system. The human body is a complex organism made up of a skeletal system, a circulatory system, and a nervous system. We come into daily contact with transportation systems, communication systems, and economic systems.

An obvious hierarchy of systems can be created: systems, systems of systems, and systems of systems of systems. For example, the universe is a system of heavenly bodies, which includes many subsystems of stars called galaxies. Within one such galaxy (the Milky Way) is the solar system, one of many planetary systems. Similarly, an organism is a system of mutually dependent parts, each of which might include many subsystems. The human body is, for example, comprised of organs which are themselves subsystems of the organism as a whole.

Now we can use this same framework or philosophy in the task of managing resources. If organizational units are designed and operated as a system, each segment or subsystem can be viewed as a self-contained unit and its relationship or contribution to the next level in the hierarchical structure can be programmed and measured. This means that precise identification of units and of their input and output is an essential part of management by system. Before elaborating in greater detail, however, we should offer a working definition of systems, a definition which can be used as a basis for the study, design, and operation of man-made systems.

We will define a system as an array of components designed to accomplish a particular objective according to plan. This definition contains three significant parts. First, the system must have a purpose or objective to perform. Secondly, components are designed (and sometimes constructed) in a meaningful arrangement. Finally, inputs of information, energy, and materials are allocated according to an operating plan. This definition may be clearer when it is considered in conjunction with, a model of a basis system. Planned resource inputs of information, energy, and materials are transformed by men and/or machines to produce outputs of products, ideas, or service. This output, if the system is effective, achieves the purpose or goal of the system.

Systems may be classified in various ways—for example, natural systems, such as the solar system, as compared to man-made systems, such as a transportation system. Those relationships between objects and sequence of events observed in their natural setting which have meaning for us constitute natural systems. Such systems behave according to the laws of nature and their input-output relationships are predictable in a scientific sense. In contrast, man-made systems are those designed and operated by man. They utilise inputs from natural systems, but retain little of the scientific predictability found in nature, largely because man is somewhat unpredictable.

We may also distinguish between flexible and rigid systems. In a flexible system, the structure or design of the system is adjusting continually to maintain a balance or equilibrium between the system and its changing environment. In contrast, a rigid system is not a self-maintaining unit and a structure does not adjust, at least not in the short run. Most life form as well as economic, political, and social systems are examples of flexible systems. A highway is an example of a rigid system—once constructed little could be done in the short run to adjust to a change in traffic.

Systems and organisations

In arranging and managing the resources of an organisation as a system the achievement of goals and optimization of the input-output relationships of the total system receive primary attention. The preparation and management of a system require a sequence of decisions, each distinct but close related to the others:

1. systems determination,
2. design and creation,
3. operation and control
4. review and evaluation

First, a decision is made to create a system. An entrepreneur decides to open a corner grocery store, a large aerospace organisation decides to establish a missile division, or the government decides to create an agency to resolve the problems of the cities. After the decision is made to have a system, it must be planned—facilities are provided as required, components arranged, and people hired. This the design stage. The grocer must had a location, build or rent a building add facilities in some logical layout to expedite customer service and train clerical help.

After a system has been designed and created, it is ready to function. The grocery store manager, for example will buy and sell foods and notions of various kind to provide a service to the customer and, hopefully, make a profit.

Basic to operation by system is the premise that given certain inputs, the system will produce certain outputs or operate within established limits. However, the relationship between structure and operation may not be predictable. A predetermined equilibrium, particularly in flexible systems, can seldom be forecast by equation, and will change, within limits, as the components of the system are rearranged, or as the inputs are allocated. In most instances, therefore, there must be control of operations, or a means of keeping the system on course in spite of unpredictable variables. Control includes a sensor for measuring output or related characteristics, a means of comparing that measurement with a standard, and an activating unit to adjust inputs to correct any indicated deficiencies. The control should regulate the variables so that the system will tend to stabilise near an established equilibrium. This objective is possible only if a meaningful standard can be determined and if such operating values can be measured. First, control measures operating information and feeds it back to be compared with an established standard. When corrective action is indicated, control releases instructional information to activate a change in input.

The fourth decision level pertains to how well the system has operated. Has it been effective and/or efficient? A system is effective if it accomplishes its objectives, while efficiency is the relationship or resource input to output. A system can be effective while wasting resources (inefficient) and conversely, may transform inputs efficiently without achieving the objectives as outlined (for example, more shoes per man-hour of input, but all for the left foot, or a product few people wish to buy. The answer is to determine a balance between effectiveness and efficiency whenever the two are in position. Obtaining such a balance becomes the optimal course of act and we say the system is optimized. A nonoptimal condition exists to extent that this quality of the product and the cost of production. We try to achieve the quality (effectiveness) and still keep costs (efficiency) acceptable to the competitive environment.

Periodically review and evaluation occur during the life cycle of a system and they may lead to design changes in the present system or recommendations for change which may be incorporated into future system Review and evaluation are often conducted in conjunction with the operations of a system. The feedback of operating information furnishes evidence of how the system is doing, that is whether or not design changes required. Such analysis may bring changes in design, whereas control actual causes changes in operating input.

Input of information energy, and materials are basic to all system Information is needed during the design and creation stage to determine he the stated objective can be accomplished (determination of transformation process); energy (effort spent designing and creating the system) exerted people or the power to operate machines; and materials are transform into the equipment and machines that will be part of the system. In operation and control, all inputs are either inputs of information (for example customer data, quantities, price, discounts, and delivery dates), inputs energy (energy exerted by the workers or the energy used to operate in chines) or input of materials.

Planning or decision making takes place at all four stages. The kind and extent at each stage, however will vary with the nature or king system. For example, an automated oil refinery (rigid system) must carefully preplanned. Most operating decisions are programmed into the system. A department store (flexible system) establishes more general objectives and plans, and uses decision making at the operating level to adjust the system to various environmental influences which are bound to occur.

The case for a systems approach

During the past two or three decades, several concepts and theories has been proposed as a framework for the management or organizations.

Information theory

Information theory or the mathematical theory of communications can used to study various management situations. By making certain base assumptions (ignoring semantics or meaning) a simplified set of mathematical relationship has been developed which is used primarily in the technical aspect of information transmission. Information theory has been applied as a methodology for determining the rate at which information can be transmitted under certain specified circumstances. Some of the factors affecting transmission include the nature of the signal source, whether the signal is discrete or continuous; the nature of the channel and, in particular, its capacity for transmitting information the nature of the noise, if any which disturbs the transmission; and they fidelity criterion by which the adequacy of the transmission is judged.

Although a wide range of applications is claimed for information theory most are in the technical aspects of transmission. Some of the subdisciplines are filtering theory, detection theory, and the analysis of signals statistics. Information theory is cited of automate, the theory of automatic control systems, the analysis of language, theory is cited as operative (applicable) and unified (integrative) are thermodynamics, statistical mechanics, photography language, models, gambling, cryptology, pattern recognition, and computer technology.

Information flow is one of several integral systems in a business or public organization, while systems management is the overall framework within which communication or information flow fits. Communication systems, or systems of information flow, are the vehicle through which the key management can be integrated administered.

Decision making theory

Many theorists have focused their attention on the decision-making processes within an organization. One group concentrates on the human problem solving processes and decisions mechanisms as the primary forces in organizational behavior. According to this their, organizational particulars should not be viewed as mere mechanical instrumentalities, but should be perceived as individuals with wants motive, instrumentalities, levels, and drives and with limited rationality and capacity for problem solving. In other words, this theory regards people not as components but as very complex subsystems contributing to the system. The question is often raised whether the objectives of the system or those of the people participating in the system should be optimized.

Others view the field decision making as synonymous with "managing" in this sense, decision making has three principal stages: intelligence searching the environment for conditions calling for decisions; design inventing, developing, and analyzing possible courses of action: and choice selecting a particular course of action form the available alternative.

Another group of theorists regard the quantitative aspects of decision making as the key to the selection, design, and operation of system. This theorists have concentrated on developing and refining mathematical model and techniques.

Systems analysis

The systems approach may be used as the general model for designing operating organizations, but Systems Analysis is a technique for planning and solving problems, As such it becomes an orderly method used to review and appraise alternative ways of using scarce resources to accomplish particular objective. Considering the integrative nature of a problem (that the cause and effect relationship among the elements), the constant changing environment in which planning must be formulated and the limited resources and time available planning must be formulated, and determining the best alternative, and decision plan developed which satisfies specified objectives.

System analysis is problem-oriented and follows a logical process deductive inductive reasoning. Question considered include:

1. How many distinguishable elements are there to this seeming problem?
2. What cause-and-effect relationship exist among these elements?
3. What function need to be performed in each case?
4. What trade-offs may be required resources, once they are defined?

The reasoning process always goes from deductive to inductive a sit progresses form general objectives to plans and then back in a cyclical, closed loop fashion to redefining objectives and making more detailed plans. The process, goes through several stages of development starting with general objectives and proceeding to plans, then back to refining objectives and detailing plans further then back again, and so forth.

The four main stages are—translation, analysis, trade-offs, and synthesis. Translation represent the statement the problem, including all of the constraint placed on the solution. Organizational policies prescribing general patterns of action, and time or constraints placed on the design and/or operation of the system are examples of constraints. A this stage, selection criteria, such as cost/effectiveness, timing and risk, are outlined and used to evaluate the appropriateness of various trade-offs. The practical reiteration of the cycle until refinements have sharpened the final plan or solution illustrates the feedback features of the model.

At some point, a practical solution or plan may not be feasible. If this occurs, the decision makes review the objectives, along with constraints and selection criteria. A slight modification or adjustments may free the decision makers to increase the alternative solutions, or to develop feasible solutions from among the current alternatives.

Material, energy and information flow are essential elements of any give system or subsystem, although each may be developed as a flow process itself. The design of a system may highlight any one of these elements, it must consider all three. For example, material flow could be tract through a process flow chart. A space and layout study could be tract through a process flow chart. A space and layout study could determine optimal arrangements of facilities and equipment in consideration of flow of raw materials through the system. In layout analysis the human element in the man-machine system is an extremely significant fact Decision makers can develop organizational charts as a matrix to apply specific systems, rather than arranging them in the traditional, function hierarchical manner. The organization structure around the flow of material and information between decision points, would cut across tradition functionally specialised department boundaries. This structure focuses attention on subsystem and total-system objectives and goals.

Systems analysis has been used effectively for planning advance system and technologies. When used with skill and common sense, it has been valuable technique for identifying advanced requirements of complex systems, assessing the impact of environmental changes on de development plans, identifying potential problems in the conceptual stage of program and providing accurate documentation of the decisions made and the supporting reasons for recommended courses of action.

The systems approach

The systems approach is the broad framework to which such concepts information flow and decision theory, and techniques like system analysis relate. These various forms of analysis should not be considered separately, but as segments of something larger when each can contribution enormously to the others for the integrated whole is much greater than the sum of the parts. Each produces an analog of an enterprise system of subsystem and these analogs simulate the behavior of the system can captured.

The system approach is not new: it is a concept borrowed from the natural sciences. Now it is being used as a philosophy for operating organization inputs are identified relative to started objectives. For students of management this philosophy is equally valuable for organizing classifying and simplifying knowledge which can be applied to organization of one kind.

To summarized and also to establish a more formal relationship among the various usages of the term systems in this chapter, we would like suggest that three are three different ways to consider systems: (1) system concepts or philosophy (2) systems management, and (3) systems analysis. All three are included under three most general classification, the System Approach. These relationship showing that systems can be used as a concept or philosophy, as a means of organizing and managing resources and/or as a planning or problem solving technique. In every instance it is the system approach.

At the turn of the century, Frederick Taylor published his concept of Scientific Management, emphasizing the need to organize industrial production more effectively. Several techniques such as methods study, time and motion study, planning and progress charting, and pay incentives were developed in conjunction with scientific management.

Taylor's work had a great influence on production and on the way it was taught in colleges. For many years, the typical book in this field was organized around his philosophy and also included something about every function needed to operate an industrial concern, for example, finance, forecasting, engineering design, and personal management. Since that time, a gradual change has taken place to exclude those general management concepts which warranted a more sophisticated techniques which have been developed (largely mathematical) and to concentrate on certain basic ideas and techniques that apply to all organizations.

This broader application meant that the name, production, was somewhat inappropriate because production means manufacturing to most people. Therefore, a change in name is taking place-from production to operations management. Another problem relates to the difficulty of presenting a group of techniques without an adequate relationship to some general model. Under industrial management, the manufacturing firm was this model, with broader application, there was a need to change the name in order to counter the arguments that manufacturing continued to be the center core of this field of study. The systems approach solves this dilemma because it is a general model to which the operations of any organisation to be related.

We defined Operations Management as the design and operation of systems, but this definitions is too broad. We shall confine our discussion to those principles which relate to analytical consideration of resources.

The choice of subject matter for a text is always difficult decision. We have included those areas which apply to all system, such as design, the scheduling of resource inputs and transformation activities, management of various types of inventory and more generally, control of operations. A question may arise, however, about such activity as purchasing—isn't it common to all organizations? Although this may be true, much of the significant information about purchasing is institutional, and it becomes difficult to make and effective presentation of the subject matter without lengthy review of the nature and character of the items or service to be purchased and of the environment of the organization.

A system can be defined as an array of components designed to accomplish a particular objective according to plan. In other words, components and arranged to transform inputs into output in order to accomplish a stated objective(s) or mission(s). The allocation of inputs of information, energy, and materials into the system occur according to an operational plan.

There are different kinds of systems. Classification can be made relative to the structure or design, for example, natural or man-made, flexible or rigid, and man or machine. On the other hand, a distinction may be made in regard to the kind of output, that is, product or service.

Every system contains components—that segment of a system which performs, or provides the facility for performing, some part of the defined transformation process. A component cannot satisfy the total transformation requirement as defined, even though in another instance it may be regarded as a system. Therefore, the distinction is often a matter of definition, a matter of establishing boundaries for convenience of operations or analysis. Components serve systems, which in turn serve other systems, which serve other systems, and so on.

When the resources of an organization are arranged and managed as a system, we refer to this approach as management by systems. There are four stages to this process: (1) determination. (2) design and creation, (3) operation and control, and (4) review and evaluation. If the relationship between structure and operations were always predictable, we would not need to have control, but this seldom is the case. Control includes four (1) a characteristic or condition to measure, (2) a sense of measuring unit, (3) comparison with a standard, and (4) an activating unit for reallocating inputs.

Whereas management by system relates to the total organization, concepts like information theory and decision theory abstract something less than the total design and operation of organisations. However, the systems theory and are used, along with every other theory, concept of operating organizations. One useful technique, for example, is system analysis, a methodology for planning or problem solving in an orderly or logical manner.

Operational process

In 1919 Frederick Taylor's classic work entitled Principles of Scientific Management was published. From that date on, the management of production processes was never to the same again. The major focus of Taylor's book was in the area of work standards and wage incentives. He showed that outcome of both systematically conceived work standards and wage incentives could materially improve productivity. These work standards were set either by the careful observation of workers or by predetermined standards. Then wage incentive plans were tied to these standards in such a say that the higher-than-average worker would receive better-than average pay.

What Taylor's succeeded in doing was to link the engineering process of the plan with human nature. With a well-designed plant an d a reasonable set of standards, the worker was motivated to achieve a high level of productivity. The payoff to him was higher wages, while the payoff to the firm was larger profits. Everyone could prosper under this new system.

This approach became known a scientific management theory, since it was based on the science of engineering and the "Science" of human nature which drew from psychology, ethics and even psychology. Although by today's standards one might questing how much science was in scientific management, one is easily convinced that Taylor's approach was quite scientific when compared with management practices which preceded him.

From a methodological point of view, of major importance was the way in which Taylor supported his hypothesis. Has was not based, as were so many others, on armchair theorizing. His hypothesis was based on actual studies undertaken at Bethlehem Steel yards. He therefore employed one of the central ideas of the scientific method as we know it today: first the objective investigation of a phenomenon, the formulation of a hypothesis, then its repeated proof by experimentation, and finally its establishment as a theory.

This successful application of the scientific approach was eventually followed by studies directed toward other operational problems. Soon a scientific body of knowledge started to emerge with application to equipment investment replacement analysis, process, design, plant layout plant location, inventory scheduling and quality control. Since many of these applications required the processing of large quantities of data, it was not until the computer arrived that the full potential of this growing body of knowledge became apparent. This realization sparked an intensified level of interest from theoreticians and practitioners alike. Today the interest continues at this pace.

Not only is Taylor's scientific management approach credited with being the father production management school. After his study came the Hawthorne studies are Western Electric and then countless others which have subsequently contributed to a framework within which organizational group and individual production oriented behavioral problem can be analyzed.

Both the scientific management and the behavioural science school have something to offer those who manage operational systems. System skills are not enough by themselves. It takes skills with both system and human beings to effectively by themselves. It take skills with both systems and human being to effectively manage an operation, and frequently skills with human beings are the dominating requirement. The student, therefore, must acquire both. He must become aware of what each has to offer, understand how they interact, and learn their advantage and shortcomings. These then become his tools of the trade.

Although the traditional focus of this field has been on the factory, the management scientist has discovered that its potential is certainly not limited to this environment. The framework can also be applied to any process whose purpose is the transformation of inputs to outputs, included would be applications directed toward a bank airline, hospital, government public, utility, pollution control agency automative repair shop, supermarket library, public education police department and on and on.

Among these seemingly divers fields, there exist several problems which are quite similar in form a although quite unlike in content. For example, if we define inventory as any stock of goods which has potential economic value, then inventory can be applied to problems found in many fields. In a bank, cash stored for customer demand can be considered as an inventory, and seats on an airplane, seats and classrooms in a school beds in a hospital and switching and transmission facilities of a telephone company can all be considered inventories which are stored for future use. Our vast of inventory theory should therefore be capable of giving some insight into the appropriate level at which these resources must be maintained.

You should now understand why the discipline originally called production management became known as operations management. The change in name merely reflected the increase in its range of applicability.

In defining operations management one should therefore be as general as possible. We might say that it is the management of any operational system which transforms inputs into outputs.

The purpose of a system is to transform an into a output. Generally there is some degree of repetitiveness to this procedure. That is once the process is designed and constructed, it will be used over again for the same purpose.

There are two major flows in such as system. These include material and information flows. In a hospital for example the input would consist of the patient. He would then represent the material flow from one work center in the process to the next. Accompanying this material flow would be substantial volume of medical records and billing information. These constitute one part of the information flow. Other information flows include data which are necessary to manage and control the system.

Process design, operation and control

A process can be classified as being either continuous, intermittent, or project. In a continuous process the facilities are devoted exclusively to the transformation of one type of product or service. Flow is serial and usually accomplished by conveyor. Equipment is special-purpose and has little flexibility for use elsewhere. Also prevalent is high level of labor specialization. Typical of a continuous-flow process are automotive assembly lines and chemical and petroleum processing.

Intermittent processes contain a variety of equipment which is shared among several jobs. No job sufficient volume to warrant the exclusive use of one or several pieces of equipment. At the extreme no two jobs would be scheduled through the same sequence of equipment and in the same order. The equipment in these processes is usually general-purpose. The classic example of an intermittent process is a job shop. The project process is employed whenever a sequence of operations is performed once and not repeated. Examples of this include the construction of a new building; a research and development effort designed to develop a new drug; and the design manufacture, and deployment of a communications satellite network.

The decision as to which process orientation is best usually hinges on economic analysis. Whenever the volume anticipated to be high and the process is expected to belong-lived continuous processes are generally chosen. On the other hand, if the volume is expected to be low and the file of the process uncertain or short, the balance shifts to an intermittent-process orientation.

After this major choice is made, other process design decisions must follow. These include selection of equipment detailed design of the process, and major make or buy decisions. Focus then shifts to the work that will be included at each work station. At this point human factors must be considered should the orientation be toward job specialization, in which each person continuously performs a few routine steps, or toward job enlargement where the worker performs more steps, has a more interesting task, and has more control over his environment?

If a project orientation is employed the full set the jobs that comprise the project must be carefully sequenced. Of concern are those jobs which if delayed could delay the entire project. These critical jobs must be identified and carefully monitored. Of some should occur, perhaps additional resources could be channeled in their direction.

The way in which the process facilities are laid out can certainly influence the effectiveness and efficiency of the process. A fresh look at the layout should be undertaken not only when new facilities are opened, but also whenever the process is altered, when is a significant change in volume, or when the mix of jobs processed through the facility changes. Facility location problems can be quite complex. For example either the location of a thermion nuclear power plant an additional to a municipal airport or the location of a steel mill would certainly be expected to create problems. In addition to the usual factors, such as taxes, construction costs, labour pool, and costs, and transportation costs, environmental problems represent a new dimension with which management must continue.

Scheduling, operating and controlling the process

One the process has been designed, it must be scheduled operate and controlled. So that intelligent schedule can be drawn, a forecast is necessary. Sometimes the forecasting process is quite informal and relies heavily on judgment and experience.

This is especially true for new products or in a dramatically changing marketplace. In other circumstances where the product or service has been offered for several years and history demand date are available, statistical forecasting techniques may be employed. It is not uncommon, however to find even these statistical forecasts tempered with good judgment.

After the forecast has been made, an aggregate plan is usually devised. This is a plan, for the next 12 months or so, which sets overall work force and production levels. Planning, however, at this stage does not entail much detail, It is a broad plan which sets the constraints within which the detailed production schedule must fit. For example the manufacturer of a full line of TV sets would first forecast the aggregate demand for all TV sets. Then he would determine overall work force and production level strategies to meet this demand. Detail such as the quantity of each of these models to build, when to build them what category of labor is required, and how much of each category, represents decisions which are made at a later time when the actual production phase is closer at hand.

With thousands, hundreds of thousands, or even millions of items in stock some routine inventory planning and control system must be employed. The system must be capable of determining when forecasted orders can be met from stock, when they cannot, at what levels it is appropriate to institute replenishment orders, and how much should be ordered.

For the month in which processing is scheduled to take place, a full detailed schedule is compiled. In manufacturing for example, this would include the identification of all required parts, subassemblies assemblies, and final assembly. The schedule would show when each of these is to start and when it is expected to be completed. This information is usually provided upon the job's release to the processing system.

Once the job is dispatched to the processing system, it becomes essential to monitor its progress to ensure that its completion will meet the due date. To accomplish this, elaborate computer-based data collection and processing systems are frequently employed. The job's progress is monitored by remote data input terminals located at convenient points throughout the process. In this way the most up-to-date information is assured in the control of the schedule.

Finally, the quality of the product or service must be periodically sampled to ensure that the actual output complies with process objectives. The sampling activity can take place not only at the end of the process, but also at several stages in the process. In this way, whenever, a section of the process is discovered to be out of control, the appropriate corrective action can be taken before a substantial quantity of useless out put is accumulated.

Almost every stage in the design, operation, and control of a system requires the collection, processing and presentation of data. These data serve as and essential ingredient in the decision-making process. Without them decisions can be reached only by hunch, guess, and intuition.

When these data are part of a well-designed and integrated information system whose purpose it is to meet management's information needs, we have a management information system. These system should focus on the routine and occasionally on the not-so-routing decisions that fall under management responsibility, for in these lies the most promising payoff. Above all it should be so designed that it collects, process, and presents data which are relevant, to these decisions. Then the decision maker can combine this source of information with the best or good solutions to the problem.

An example of this can be seen in a job shop situation where mathematical models are used to solve production-scheduling problems. Remote input devices are often used to collect and forward data on the current status of jobs and machines in the shop at the close of each day. Then the central computer, with the help of a mathematical model, proceeds to compute a schedules. The output then serves as the foreman's schedule for the next day.

Before any management information system can be designed, it is absolutely essential that a careful study be made of the decision environment for each particular problem included as part of the information system. Good preliminary design assures that only necessary data will be collected and only useful information will be supplied to the decision maker. Accordingly, the approach that this book will be to analyze decision problems associated with the design, operation, and control, of operational systems. Then the focus will shift to the development of a management information system.

The structure of decisions

Regardless of whether the design, operation, or control problem, and regardless of whether the problem occurs in a factory hospital, school, or bank there seen to be common characteristics that extend across all decision situations. We can postulate that any such situation displays the following five characteristics:

1. Alternative strategies for employing one's resources
2. Environmental states which are out of the control of the decision maker
3. Outcomes that result from a combination of strategy and an environmental state
4. A decision criterion which is used as the basis for comparing outcomes
5. Predictions of the likelihood that each environmental state all occur

Strategies If there were only one way in which to accomplish a task no problem would exist. However it is very infrequent that such is the cases. In the usual situation the decision maker as to make a choice from among several strategies. For example, in the physical layout of facilities, countless, different arrangements can be imagined. The decision maker must determine which of these arrangements will be most effective.

Often the alternatives are not quite so obvious, and then decision maker must creatively general a set. An example of this can be found in new-product development decisions. It is not obvious which products should be included in such a set.

Environmental states and outcomes The outcome of each strategy usually depends upon the prevailing environment state. IF choose, as today's strategy, to carry an umbrella, then the outcomes of this strategy will depend on whether or not it rains. If it rains, I am protected and pleased with my action. However if it does not rain, the umbrella proves to be a nuisance. In this example the environmental states are those factors which affect the outcome of a particular strategy and over which the decision maker has little or no control. Other common environmental factors include the life of a project competitors strategy, market share, and economic conditions.

Frequently some knowledge exist about the likelihood of each environmental state. One might, for example, subjectively feel that the likelihood of a 10 years project life is 10 percent, of an 8-years life, 80 percent, and of a 6-years life, 10 percent. This knowledge may be based on either a subjective evaluation or historical observation.

Criterion The strategy which is finally selected is the one associated with the most attractive outcome. The degree of attractiveness of course, depends upon the criterion by which the decision maker is comparing outcomes. It is much easier if the comparison is based on a single dimension, such as cost, profit, or sales. Whenever there are multiple objectives and the weighing of each one is unclear, it becomes quite difficult to draw comparisons.

In the management of an operational system, the criterion chosen is usually the minimization of cost. This can be defended on the grounds that the generation of sales revenue is usually out of the control of operational decision makers. Therefore the focus of operations managements is on the only variable over which control can be exercised cost.

One way of categorising decision problems is by the state not knowledge about the environment. One of three situations can prevail; decision making under certainly under risk, under uncertainty. In decision making under certainty it is assumed that only one environmental state will exist. That is the state of the environment is known with certainty. For example if you somehow "got the work" and knew that it was going to rain today, our problem would be considered a decision problem under certainty. As you will shortly see, decision making under certainly is not always a trivial exercise.

In decision making under risk, the probability distribution of the possible environmental states is known. For example a decision maker might have the will be 5 years an 80 percent chance that it will be 6 years, and a 10 percent chance that it will be 7 years.

Finally in decision making under uncertainty, it is assumed that nothing is known about possible states of the environment. It is rare however that the decision maker is this ignorant of the future.

Now we will take a closer look at the three categories.

Decision making under certainty Decision making under certainty occurs when there is only possible environmental state. Here the decision maker must choose from four alternatives. The outcomes represent the total cost for each strategy. If the objective is to minimize total cost,, strategy 3 in chosen.

In this example only four strategies had to be searched to find the optimal on. Frequently the problem is much more complex: there can be a very great number of relevant strategies which should be examined.

Consider an inventory problem in which the quantity ordered at any one time can be from 1 to 1,000 pounds. With each strategy there is a cost consequence. To search each of the these strategies for the best one is prohibitive. A better way does exist. We will shortly see how mathematical models can substantially improve our ability to make effective decisions under conditions such as this.

Consider another decision problem under certainty. This time the problem is to schedule 10 jobs through a chemical process. The setup time for each job depends upon its predecessor. When like products are sequenced in succession the setup time is small compared with a sequence of dissimilar jobs. The setup times for a particular set of 10 jobs are shown in Table 1-2. We can see, for example, that if job 3 is followed by job 5 the setup time is 7 minutes.

One feasible sequence for processing these job is 1- 2- 3- 4- 5- 6- 7- 8- 9; its cost is 76. Another feasible sequence is 1- 2- 3- 5- 4- 6- 7- 8- 9- 10 and its cost in 70. In fact, there are 101 or somewhat over 3 million possible strategies for scheduling these 10 jobs, and each one may have a different total setup cost. As you can see, even though the state of the environment setup time is known with certainty, the magnitude of the problem is still overwhelming.

Still another example of decision making under certainty can be found in production scheduling. Here the problem is to absorb fluctuations in forecast demand by some combination of hiring or layoff, subcontracting, overtime, and inventories. Even if the state of the environment—demand—is assumed to be known with certainty, there remain countless strategies which combine different levels of hiring, firing, overtime, and inventories. The decision maker's objective is to uncover that strategy which minimizes production costs.

Suppose in the last example, that demand was not known with certainty. Instead we had a good feel for the likelihood of various levels of demand. The problem would then be classified as decision making under risk. This would, in fact, manage to complicate the issue. Now we turn to a closer examination of these problems.

Decision making under risk In decision making under risk each strategy, S, is associated with several outcomes, Of one for each state of the environment E_1. The probability that any state, will occur is P_1 and 15 must bold that all these probabilities sum to 1.

Consider an inventory problem where four ordering strategies are under review. One of three environment states is likely to occur: demand for the product can below medium, or high. The likelihood that any of these state will exist has been estimated by management to be 1,6,3. The outcomes represent the consequence of a particular strategy occurring together with an environment state. Since it is possible for stockouts to occur, the proper adjustments have been made to the costs associated with each outcome. The expected cost of a strategy is simply the average cost that would be incurred if the process were repeated over and again and if the likelihood of environmental outcomes was accurate.

Suppose, however that the decision maker carefully analyzed the consequences of choosing strategy 4, he had second thoughts. If on occasion his costs should run as high as 20 (and we would expect this 30 percent of the time) he felt his boss would strongly disapprove. He therefore preferred to choose strategy 3. In this case the decision maker has an objective which is more complex than the simple minimization of expected costs. Therefore to maximize the decision maker's utility more than these costs must be considered. Frequently the objective is multidimensional, and this makes the analysis of outcomes quite complex.

This framework which we have develop for decision making under risk is probably appropriate for problems of the short-range to intermediate-range variety—problems where the actual a occurrence of the environmental state is but a few months to a year away. As this time horizon becomes quite long, however it become difficult to assess to the likelihood of these environmental states.

Decision making under uncertainty If nothing is known about the likelihood with which future states of the environment will occur, the problem is classified as a decision problem under uncertainty. Under this condition, expected values for each strategy cannot be computed. Instead other approaches exist which are often used to select a strategy. Since it is rare that decisions are made in total ignorance of the future state of affairs, and since this concept of little help for the kinds of problem which we will be analyzing, the reader is referred elsewhere of a complete development of these ideas.

The role of management science in solving structured problems

The framework which we have just developed is often useful when structuring problems which decision makers face in the management of operating systems. What we need, however beyond this ability to structure the problem is a way to solve it. Management science serves just this purpose.

Formu-lating the mathe-matical model

Recall that even in the simple case of decision problems under certainty it was shown that there could be so many strategies from which to choose that some help was needed. By formulating the decision matrix as a mathematical model we can frequently reduce the problem to a manageable size.

In this mathematical model, the outcome is called the dependent variable while the strategy and state of the environment are independent variables. We generalize these relationship in the following way:

$0 = f(S,E)$

The interpretation is that the outcome is a function of (depends upon) the strategy-selected and the state of the environment. Suppose we make this a little more explicit by considering an actual mathematical model of an inventory problem. It is not important at this state for you to understanding how the model was generated. Later in the book you will have this opportunity.

The total cost corresponds to the outcome, while the order quantity-the only variable which is totally under the control of the decision maker-corresponds to the strategy. The demand represents the state of the environment, and in this analysis we assume that demand is known with certainty. The fixed order cost, per-piece purchase cost, and inventory carrying cost are called parameters. They are different for each firm, depend on its economic and managerial structure, and must be carefully estimated. These parameters are necessary to make the relationship complete between the outcomes, strategies and environmental states.

Solving the model

Consider a situation where the following values were determined for each of the parameters:

C = \$1

A = \$20 per order

I = 20 percent per unit

In addition, demand is estimated to be 1,000 units. Now the outcome for any strategy can be calculated. Take for example the strategy where Q = 100.

The outcome of a strategy which entails ordering 100 units at a time in 1,210 per year. What about the outcomes of other strategies? We could compute the outcomes of many strategies and choose that one which has the lowest total cost. This approach, which is called total enumeration, would be very time consuming and in this very unnecessary.

Mathematical programming Besides the calculus, there are other management science techniques which can be employed to resolve a variety of decision problems. Another such technique—one which will be used several times throughout the text—is mathematical programming. It is useful whenever several factors constrain the choice of strategies, in the inventory problem which we have just considered the objective was simply to minimize total cost. There were no constraints which limited out choice of strategies. Had there been constraints, they might have limited either the space in which inventory could be placed, the funds which could be spent on inventory, or the maximum number of orders that could be placed by the purchasing department. This being the case, it would have become a problem in constrained minimization and mathematical programming techniques could be used tc find a solution.

Simulation In some problem the outcome associated with a certain strategy might be quite difficult to determine. Management science can also help us here. In a later chapter for example a case is printed where the decision maker is faced with a choice from among three alternatives. These include the purchase of a high-speed overhead crane, another medium-speed can to operate alongside the present one, and retention of the status quo. The problem is to determine the outcome for each strategy.

Since the case is developed as decision problem under risk, the determination of the outcome for each of these strategies is complex. To help us, another management science technique known as simulation, is employed. By simulation the behavior of each alternative over several weeks we can determine measure of the performance for each strategy. These outcomes can then be compared and the best strategy chosen.

Heuristic Often rules of thumb called heuristics, are used to solve complex problems. The solutions so obtained, however are most likely not the best ones, but generally they are good enough. The heuristic technique is used whenever time and money do not allow for a better solution to the problem or whenever the problem is so hopelessly complex that better solutions are nearly impossible.

Perhaps the most commonly used heuristic is the First come, firs served rule applied to many queueing situations. At a bank, for example, the customers at a teller's window are processed according to this rule. In a later chapter we will learn that although this rule results in a quick solution to the problem it does not generally provide the best answer. From a practical point of view however, heuristics are often good enough.

A characteristic of modeling as that only a limited number of factors form the real-world problem can be considered. As a result a model of reality is create and not reality itself. If fact it is very seldom, if ever that humans can think in terms of reality.

In most everyday situations we also model reality. For example, our view on civil disorders, campus unrest, war on poverty pollution, politics, and supersonic aircraft are all based on models. No person has a neck long enough to stick out and supersonic aircraft are all based on models. No person has a neck long enough to stick out and thereby consider all the relevant facts, draw out all the necessary interrelationship, and finally reach a conclusion. This is beyond our capability as human beings. No not even the President can think in terms of reality on these major issues. What we actually do is to observe the situation of interest and identify what we consider to the key factors. These serve as the basis for our model. We then make use of the model whenever we need to analyze or process new information or to discuss the issue with others. One must always be sensitive to the fact, however that his analysis and opinions are based on a model and not on reality. It is quite possible that some of the key factors in the environment were overlooked when the model was created. The model itself might display no internal inconsistency, but when used in the real world it may be well off the mark, All model users must therefore maintain a healthy respect for this source of research error.

In operations management the same model-building process is employed First the situation is studied. Then the strategies outcomes, states of nature, and parameters are identified. Next a model is constructed, the relevant data collected, and the model solved. Finally that crucial step from model solution to real-world implementation must be taken. Here the decision maker quite often must take an active role. Based on his knowledge of the model and its assumptions, he may feel that it would be inappropriate on this occasion to blindly follow the model's output. Perhaps time one of those imponderables that was impossible to incorporate in the model is dominating the decision environment. His intervention is a necessary aspect of the decision process. It is unrealistic to expect that all of our models will be comprehensive enough to be left on their own.

16

Effective Communication

Managers are likely to spend most of their time engaged directly in some form of communication process. Even when they are working alone—for example, studying or preparing reports—they are relying on other people's attempts to communicate with them or they are preparing to communicate with others. Accuracy in decision-making depends, in particular, on effective communication. If the communication process is faulty then everything else can be affected.

Experiments, research and sheer personal observation show that most people are far too optimistic about the accuracy of the communication process. This applies not just to communication processes within employing organisations but to life in general. Even when errors are identified, this may be too late, or the inherent faults in the process that will lead to further errors may not be recognised. The barriers to effective communication are far greater than most people realise. The effective communication of factual information can be difficult enough, but often attitudes and feelings need to be communicated and that can be far more complicated. The number and nature of the barriers are such that there is a strong case for communication skills training being given as part of the standard school curriculum. This is not yet the case and in this chapter the attempt is made to give managers practical guidance on how to identify the communication processes in their organisations with a view first of all to evaluating their effectiveness. This evaluation can then provide the basis for the development of the manager's own practical skills of communication.

In Rosemary Stewart's study of how managers spend their time, it was established that on average the 160 managers in her sample spent two-thirds of their time working with other people. The rest of their time was mainly engaged in preparing information reports. It seems reasonable to assume that most managers spend the bulk of their working day in some type of communication activity. Even the 33 managers in the sample in 'backroom'-type jobs spent about half of their time working with other people. This may be through attendance at meetings, the giving and receiving of instructions, discussions with colleagues and contact with customers or suppliers. Such contact may be face to face or over the telephone or a combination of both. Much of the remainder of the time is likely to be concerned with the assimilation or preparation of written information. If managers are to make the correct substantive decisions in their jobs, it follows that they need to be able to handle the communication process effectively.

It is found that managers differ markedly in their ability to communicate effectively. It follows that the need to develop skills of effective communication may be a critical priority for many managers. Regrettably this need is often not perceived and managers may neglect the importance of, and the opportunity for, development in this critical area. Communication skills tend to be taken for granted and lack of skill far more easily recognised in others than in oneself. The process of communication is often far more complex than people realise and this is a further reason why skills development in this area tends to be neglected. It is only when people realise the subtleties concerning effective communication that they may become communication conscious and start to develop their own skills. The complexities are such that even the person who is good at communication is likely to become even better if he systematically evaluates and considers his own effectiveness in this area.

The causes of ineffective communication

Having stressed the importance of the communication process, it is appropriate to develop further the hypothesis is that communication in organisations is a great deal worse than most people realise. This will be done by explaining the nature of communication processes, and the potential for breakdown. Case examples are given to illustrate some of the major points.

Listening problems

It is appropriate to explain one major misconception about communication at this stage. This point is not only important in its own right but develops the argument that the approach of many managers to communication may not be sufficiently sophisticated. Communication is usually seen as the need to brief other people. The reality is that most of a manager's time needs to be concerned with the receiving rather than the imparting of information and views. The reason for this is simple—in any conversation between two people there is a need to alternate between talking and listening. There is not much point in anyone talking if the intended recipient is not prepared to listen. If the two people involved in a discussion take equal turns talking and listening, they will obviously spend half of their time in the listening role. As much of the communication in organisations involves face-to-face discussion between more than two people, it follows as a mathematical fact that most managers will need to spend more time listening than talking. There will, of course, be exceptions to this, but the very existence of exceptions reduces the time available for others to do the talking. Admittedly managers may often need to take the lead in explaining things to their subordinates, but a statistically unequal share of talk in this direction may easily be counter-balanced by the time they have to spend in discussions and meetings involving a number of people when they talk only for a minority of the time. The basic point of this argument is that managers may fail to see that they will normally need to spend more time listening than talking. Effective listening does not come naturally to all managers, particularly if they do not recognise the importance of it. The mistake of assuming that 'good communication' is synonymous with the imparting of information and views is often made by people who set out to improve the quality of communication in organisations. House magazines, letters from the chairman, briefing meetings and training in public speaking are based mainly on the assumption that the problem is in disseminating information. The reality may be that it is more important to unblock the obstructions to information and views flowing in to the decision-makers. The problem may be though that, until such time as communication is effective, managers may not realise that the obstructions are there. In any case if everyone concentrates on imparting information and views, just who will be left to receive all these messages?

One case which illustrates this point concerns a nursing officer who attended a review meeting three months after he had attended a middle management training course. When asked what had happened as a result of his training, he explained that the area on which he had been able to concentrate was the development of his communication skills. He had worked on his listening skills and had put a chair by the side of his desk, on which people were invited to sit when they came into his office. He explained that he was amazed at the extra amount of information that he obtained this way compared with his previous pattern of letting people stand up or sit on a chair the other side of the table. He then realised the limited nature of the information he had been obtaining before and on which basis he had been taking decisions. Before, being unaware of the information that was available, he had not tried to get it. It was only after he had discovered his 'blind spot' that he realised that it existed.

Lack of feedback

The problem of effective communication is unfortunately greater than just the recognition of its scale and importance and the comprehension that one needs to receive information as well as disseminate it. It is all too easy for people to assume that they have effectively communicated and be blissfully unaware that their attempts at communication have been partially successful or, in some cases, totally unsuccessful. We have often used a simple exercise to demonstrate the undue optimism concerning the effectiveness of communication with groups of managers on training courses. This particular exercise involves asking one of the group to tell the rest, without any questions by them, how to draw a diagram consisting of six rectangles.

The manager is asked to sit facing the wall and convert a diagram into words so that the group can reproduce the diagram from his oral instruction. This exercise is described in detail in Leavity's Managerial Psychology. In practice one would not try to explain how to reproduce a diagram by oral instruction, but there are advantages in using this artificial example. It is easy to check the accuracy with which it is reproduced and it is no more complicated than some of the instructions that people do try to explain orally.

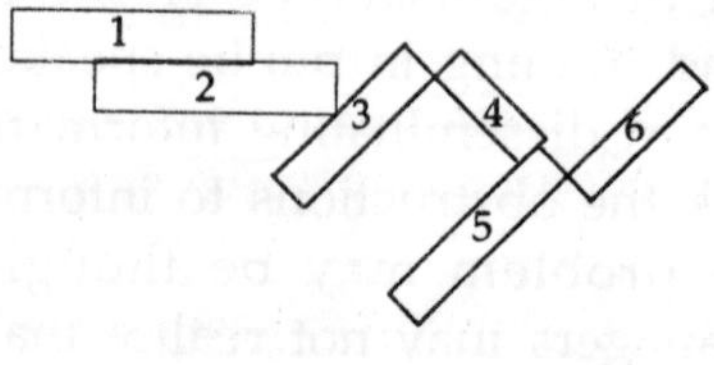

Communication Exercise

All the rectangles are of equal size and the angles either of 45° or 90°. The rectangles touch one another either at the corner or the midpoint. Invariably there is considerable error in the attempts of the groups to convert the oral instructions back into the original diagram. Sometimes the results are devastating. On one occasion a zero score was achieved by a group of 16 managers because their instructor had unwittingly described the rectangles as triangles. But invariably the instructor significantly under-estimates the amount of error made by the group.

After the results of the attempt to explain the diagram using one-way communication have been recorded, the same manager is asked to repeat the exercise but the second time facing the group and with unlimited opportunity for questioning. A similar type of diagram is converted into words and back into a diagram again by the rest of the group. There is a standard pattern to this second stage of the experiment. It takes longer, the accuracy is usually much higher, it is rare for there to be no error, and again the instructor over-estimates the level of accuracy. The assumption is usually made that, if people have queries, they will raise them. The reality is though that, even in the relatively placid context of a training course, people may have inhibitions about asking questions. They may feel embarrassed about their inability to draw the diagram, be confused by the instruction, have wrongly thought that their reconstruction was correct, have failed to catch the eye of the instructor at the right time, or lost interest. The instructor may fail to appreciate that there can be this variety of reasons for people not raising queries and make the common error of assuming that silence means that everyone has accurately reproduced the diagram.

Bogus feedback

One of the crucial points that emerges from the rectangles exercise is that people responsible for initiating communication need to consider both what the evidence is for them assuming that communication has been effective and the consequences of communication being defective. You can be very aware of situations when you are on the receiving end of an instruction that you do not understand. It can be very tempting, for the sorts of reason outlined above, to create the impression by silence that you have understood something when you in fact know that you have not. The problem is that the initiator may be left with quite a false impression of his effectiveness. If a message is particularly important it is up to him to search for more positive corroboration than mere silence that communication has been effective. He will need to consider other forms of feedback and to distinguish between accurate and bogus feedback.

Silence is not the only way in which people give false impressions about having understood explanations. There are occasions when people actually say they have understood when they have not. A common situation when this arises is when you ask the way and are so baffled by the instructions on how to get to a particular place that you may meekly say that you have understood when you have not. This type of breakdown can happen within organisations and for a variety of reasons. These reasons may be the same as those given for people remaining silent when they have the opportunity to ask necessary questions during the rectangles exercise. Another reason can be the fear of admitting ignorance, to authority figures in particular.

In discussing this issue with nursing groups we have been deluged with examples of when this has happened. One example concerned the student nurse who was asked to give a patient an airing. She apparently wasn't quite sure what to do but guessed that the appropriate interpretation was to move the patient's bed on to the verandah and remove the bedclothes. She had in fact been expected to get an airing so that the patient could sit on it and receive a blanket bath. Another student nurse was given the same instruction but with slightly different phraseology—she was told to go and get an airing. Allegedly she returned three-quarters of an hour later saying how much she had enjoyed her walk! Pride of place of the many examples we have been given goes to the case of the student nurse who was expected to give a patient a warm drink of potassium citrate. As is so often the case, an abbreviation was used and the girl was asked to give the patient a 'hot pot cit'. Unfortunately her interpretation of this instruction led to the patient being sat upon a bedpan of boiling water! In these cases the students' guesswork fortunately just led to comic results. That will of course not always be the case and such errors in the communication process may be picked up too late or not at all. The errors in the previous examples may be seen as stupidity or feebleness on the part of the student nurses, but such an interpretation is to miss the point. The fault really lies with the person who gave the instruction not ensuring that he had made himself properly understood. Either he needed to make a positive check that the instruction was understood or have a working relationship with the student nurse such that queries would be raised if necessary. The objective with communication needs to be to see that it is effective rather than being able to lay the blame at someone else's door if things go wrong.

Nursing examples have been given to illustrate the need to get accurate feedback. This is not to suggest that nursing is more prone to this type of problem than other occupations; it is simply that examples come easily to mind from my experience with nursing groups. The culpability of the authority figure can be even worse, than we have so far suggested. Some people may contrive to go through the motions of obtaining feedback when in fact what they want is simply the pretence and alibi that people have had a fair opportunity to raise queries. Rhetorical questions may be used such as 'is that clear?' which do not really invite responses. There was amazement when a person sought to take up a Company's Managing Director's written offer, issued in a standard letter to all new employees, to have an appointment with him concerning a grievance. The technique can be observed with lecturers, or after-dinner speakers, who leave the opportunity for questions until an impossibly late stage in the proceedings. And also recollect it being used in the services, when orderly officers had to go through the routine of asking if there were complaints about the food. Some mastered the technique of asking if there were any queries in such a way that servicemen would deserve a medal if they actually did make a complaint. This of course enabled the orderly officer to maintain the fiction that people had been given an opportunity to complain about the food if they were dissatisfied. The authority figure can of course use his rank to put the blame firmly on subordinates if things do go wrong.

Resistance to criticism

There may be occasions when feedback is sought but resisted if it turns out to be unfavourable. One vividly remembers an occasion when one explained to a subordinate personnel officer that one would always welcome suggestions if she thought there were ways in which the running of the department could be improved. She took at the word and one day somewhat hesitantly started to explain how a change we were planning was, in her view, ill-judged. Our immediate response was one of irritation, but fortunately one was just able to hide this and found to our chagrin that she was right and one was wrong. One was relatively new in the job and realised in retrospect that in the moments when one was seeking to control irritation the future working relationship was being determined. One was able to show, at least with this person, that one would not bite her head off if she expressed views that were contrary to mine. After this incident the personnel officer concerned came when she thought that there was a likelihood of committing other errors. This meant the occasional swallowing of pride when she picked up points that one had missed. There is a strong temptation in situations like this to block off criticism for fear of losing respect amongst subordinates. The conclusion we came to that one was likely to lose much more respect if one simply hid from criticism. The route we chose did at least enable me to get advice before decisions were finalised. There is a much greater danger of losing respect if one cannot accept critical but helpful advice, especially if that is then compounded by decisions that are incorrect.

The importance of these points is sadly illustrated by the problems that the advisers to the late President Lyndon Johnson had in explaining to him that the war in Vietnam was not progressing as favourably as he imagined. President Johnson was not renowned for his sensitive handling of people, particularly those who voiced criticism. Consequently he was more psychologically available to those who reported favourably on the progress of the war, and who suggested that a military solution was possible, than to those who suggested the reverse. It was apparently not until the spectacular Tet offensive by the Viet Cong in 1968 that President Johnson realised that all was not as well as he had imagined. The organisational point to be made is, of course, that there is an understandable temptation to encourage processes which bring good news and a reluctance, if only subconscious, which can still be just as critical, to discourage processes which bring bad news.

It is important to recognise that any manager is going to prefer to hear good news than bad news and the temptation for colleagues and subordinates is to tell people what they want to hear. In the long term this can of course be disastrous, and managers and political leaders alike need consciously to recognise the distortion that can occur in channels of communication and beware of succumbing to it. This can be checked if the danger is consciously recognised and if the ancient Greek tradition of slaying the messenger who brings news of defeat in battle is avoided. It may also be necessary to take independent checks to evaluate the information that is received. It was comprehension of this point which led some Generals, at the time of the First World War, to say that 'if you want to know what's going on you have to go to the trenches.' Having said this, it is necessary also to make the point that there are few people, if any, who can cope with the whole truth all the time. Total exposure could be destructive to the individual concerned. What is needed is a realisation that the information fed to one in organizations needs careful evaluation and that other information may be needed but not passed on. Managers may need to seek out the bad news to the extent that it is necessary and to the extent that they can cope with it. An adage concerning delegation is that 'managers get the subordinates they deserved'. The same adage can be used with regard to communication, i.e. managers get the communication they deserved.

Selective perception and bias

In considering barriers to communication, it is also necessary to deal specifically with the problems caused by selective perception and bias. The sheer volume of data that is available means that one has to have some basis for deciding what to look for and what to react to. However, careful judgment is needed in making these decisions.

A totally open mind can simply mean that a person is swamped with data but a closed mind can mean that a person doesn't respond to what is under his nose. Particular dangers are seeing only what you want to see, making the 'facts' fit what has already been decided, and suppressing unpleasant facts. Norman Dixon, a former Army psychiatrist, explains a number of Western military disasters in terms of such selective perception on the part of the military leaders concerned, in his book *On the Psychology of Military Incompetence*. Three of the many examples the documents concern the Japanese attack on Pearl Harbor, the fall of Singapore and the failure of the Arnhem offensive in Holland. The pattern according to Dixon is clear and recurrent—the warning signs were there but, because they did not fit into the established thinking, they were ignored until too late.

The extent to which people can be misled or even coerced into believing things which are untrue can be alarming. In one experiment conducted with American students it was found that a quarter could be coerced into stating that straight lines were of identical length when one was 25 per cent shorter than the other. This effect was achieved by priming the seven students in the experimental group to say that the lines were identical in length. One must be careful not to overgeneralise about the amount of social coercion possible from the results of a series of experiments in America with a particular group and at a particular time. However, if social pressure can have this effect on such obvious matters of fact, what is the scope for social pressure on matters that are more subjective or where people's self-interest is involved?

As well as having to cope with one's own subjectivity, it must also be recognised that much of the data which is available within organisations is subjective or actually misleading. Most people working in organisations are likely to be concerned with the pursuit of truth, but people in organisations, as in life generally, are under a variety of pressures to highlight some things and not others. There are also pressures to view events in a particular way. This means that a manager, as well as being aware of the pressures on him to see things in a particular way, and to report selectively, needs to evaluate carefully the information that is being fed to him. One of the themes of the TV comedy series *Yes Minister* is that information is fed to the Cabinet Minister by his Permanent Secretary in such a way that the Minister thinks that he is taking the decisions himself. One strategem is that the options are put so that the Minister is bound to choose the one preferred by his Permanent Secretary. It is also necessary to be careful to evaluate the information that this fed down the line. For example, one have found that if one examines carefully the policy decisions that are actually taken by their own Local Education Authority, they bear little relationship to many of the interpretations that work their way down the structure to individual College departments. Selective reporting and misunderstanding are not phenomena confined to upward reporting. Corroboration of the existence and nature of these problems is given by a former civil servant, John Carswell, in a *Sunday Times* article. He explained that, when he was working on the administration of retirement pensions, an experienced superior said to him that there were three National Insurance Schemes, not one: 'The scheme we put in the instructions, the scheme the Permanent Secretary talks to the Minister about, and the scheme they administer in the local offices.'

The skills of effective communication

Much of the skill in effective communication lies in recognising the problem areas one have just identified. Effective communication is achieved as much as anything by avoiding these traps. Positive approaches are, however, also necessary. One positive approach is that of coaxing information out of people.

Coaxing information

It may be necessary for managers to work hard at this, particularly if people feel inhibited about discussing a particular issue. The lament 'why didn't someone tell me' can be as much a condemnation of a manager's lack of skill in developing effective channels of communication as a condemnation of others for keeping him in the dark. It can be very hard for those in authority roles to realise the difficulty that others may have in communicating with them. The authority figure may feel totally relaxed and uninhibited and not appreciate that perhaps the very factors which create his security create difficulties for others. The proprietor of a business may feel totally self-confident and secure and be amazed to find out, if he ever does, that people who are very dependent on him are reluctant to tell him anything unpleasant. The same problem can be encountered by parents with their children. They may forget what it was like to be a child and be blissfully unaware of many of the thoughts and anxieties that their own children have and see any suggestion to the contrary as quite preposterous.

Listening effectively

Adopting a listening role can be far harder than taking the lead by talking. The problem with this can be that, the more the authority figure talks, the less the other person may be inclined to talk. There can be a critical moment when people in the subordinate role might just start saying what they really feel, if only the authority figure stays quiet long enough. Once the 'subordinate' has started talking, things may come out with a rush and to the amazement of the authority figure. One have often found that such a critical moment can occur when one leading classroom discussions. One useful technique in any such situation can be to count silently to five before breaking the silence after a particularly important question has been asked. Time after time one have found that such a delay has resulted in someone making a contribution that one had not thought possible. Once a person has started to talk it can be relatively easy to get him to continue and for any others to join in. The problem is likely to be how to get them started. The authority figure needs to be aware of letting his ignorance, impatience or even his own nervousness prevent such a process starting. Care has to be taken with the timing of invitations for people to open up—it is not only the time and the place that can be important but also the stage in a discussion. It may be necessary to build up rapport gently before the invitation is given. Thought also needs to be given to the way in which questions are put. They can be 'leading' in nature, giving the impression that all that is required is confirmation of the questioner's obvious views such as 'don't you think this is a good idea?' Alternatively they can be probing and phrased in such a way as to encourage the respondents to state their own views.

The choice of time and place

The choice of time and place to invite people to talk can be critical. Just as one knows oneself that there are times when one is prepared to open up, and times when one is not, so this can obviously be the case with other people. One of the skills of communication is picking up the cues as to whether a person is or is not prepared to talk about a sensitive matter. Even if the place cannot always be chosen, sometimes the geography of a room can be arranged to encourage, or for that matter to discourage, a person from talking. The more status symbols surrounding the authority figure, the less likely a subordinate is to feel free to talk. One remember one personnel officer who was over six feet tall always made a point of seeing that he had an able but peppery works superintendent who was short were both seated if anything of consequence was to be discussed. The personnel officer had learned from experience that the superintendent was self-conscious about his lack of height and so he did his best not to emphasise it.

Choice of language

Language difficulties can obviously hamper communication between people who have different national languages. Regional dialects can also, and predictably, complicate matters. However, there can be many other and more subtle language problems even between people who are from the same country, region and class. Technical language may be used in discussion which is beyond the comprehension of some of the participants. In any organisation there are likely to be abbreviations, words with special connotations, and 'in-terms' whose meaning is taken for granted by those inside the organisation. A colleague of mine recently gave an example of two nurses trying to communicate about sterilisation policies in their respective parts of the Health Service. One was a midwife and the other a community nurse. It took a quarter of an hour before they realised that one was talking about sterilisation as a means of birth control and the other about sterilisation as a means of protecting babies from infection! Problems of language invariably get exposed in the rectangles drawing exercise previously explained. The diagram may be explained by the use of geometric language, points of the compass, the hands of a clock or the use of symbols such as 'L shaped' and 'an inverted V'. The language chosen by the instructor is likely to be more convenient to some people than others and a person's ability to understand the instructor will in part depend on whether the instructor chooses a language convenient to him or not.

The recurring problem with language in communication is that the person who is trying to explain something may understandably use the language that is most convenient to himself without perhaps realising that there is a choice of language. The person receiving the explanation may also, understandably, be reluctant to admit that he cannot understand the language that is used. The skill is in recognising that, even when ordinary English is used, there may be problems of comprehension. The initiator of any communication needs to get positive confirmation that the 'language' he is using is one that can be understood.

In identifying the appropriate 'language' for communication, attention needs to be given to the possibility of ambiguity. The more important the consequences of error, the more attention needs to be devoted to avoiding ambiguity. If stress is needed on this point, it can be provided by the ambiguous use of words which contributed to the world's worst air disaster at Tenerife in the Canary Islands in 1977. The pilot of a KLM Jumbo Jet, who was ironically also the head of their Flight Training Department, was preparing to take off at Tenerife. He explained that he was ready to the air traffic controllers and in response was told "Okay. Stand by for take-off I will call you". In the pause after the world "Okay" there was radio interference because of a radio query by the Captain of a Pan-Am Jumbo about the intentions of the KLM Captain. It seems likely that this caused the KLM Captain to assume that the word 'Okay' was the complete message. In any event the KLM Captain then took off and collided with the Pan-Am Jumbo killing a total of 573 people. The investigators commissioned by the American Airline Pilots Association concluded that this was the most likely explanation of events. They also commented on the ambiguous use of the term 'take-off'. Their comments on the use of the term 'Okay' were as follows:

> The word (or letters) 'O.K.' can be ambiguous also: to the controller it was either a word of acknowledgement or a delaying term to allow a moment to think. It can also mean a host of other things, such as a state of well being, a check off of a task accomplished, or a statement of approval. It could have had the latter meaning for the KLM crew.

Cultural differences can obviously present barriers to effective communication as well. Some of the cultural barriers—such as language—are obvious but there may be more hidden obstacles. A recent example given to me which illustrates this point concerned the communication between the male Asian workers and the female canteen workers in a London factory. There was a certain amount of friction when food was being served, part of which was paid by the canteen workers to be because of the surly response by the Asians when they received their food. In particular it was commented that the Asians never smiled. Their response to this was initially one of bewilderment as, in their culture, it was seen as being altogether too familiar for a man to smile at a woman he did't know. Far from trying to create offence they had been trying to avoid it by their impassive expressions. When this incident was recounted to the receptionist at the College where I work, she said that she could now understand why she received so few smiles from Asian callers compared with the broad smiles of other people.

Body language

The expressions, gestures and other body language that people may use, without necessarily realising it, can be important cues as to what they really think. Communication is not just imparting information: if often involves, or needs to involve, understanding people's attitudes and feelings which are not always clearly expressed in words. In some cases people may even feel obliged to say the opposite of what they really think. It is not uncommon, for example, for a person to say 'how interesting' but in a tone of voice which indicates that they are in fact bored. An adage which makes the point that people sometimes accidentally misrepresent themselves is 'listen to what I mean not what I say'. As words can be an inadequate, or even a misleading, guide as to what people really think, it can be important to look for other cues as to people's thoughts. A catalogue could be prepared of what particular physical cues could mean—fidgeting, that a person has other things on his mind; a glazed expression, that a person doesn't understand, and so on. Given that such a list could be very long and only a guide anyway, the point that needs stressing is simply to watch for physical cues as to a person's real thoughts, especially when it is likely that a person is not able to be, or does not want to be, frank about a particular topic. It can be very tempting to rely just on the words that a person uses, particularly if they give the answer that one wants to hear. To rely on words alone can be quite insufficient.

Written communication

The emphasis in the chapter so far has been on oral and visual communication. But much communication is written, and some consideration of the special features of written communication is necessary. The main point that needs stressing is that written communication is one-way and the recipient, or recipients, have, for the time being at least, to rely on the writer's accuracy of expression. The rectangles experiment, described earlier in the chapter, indicated some of the problems with one-way communication. The type of language chosen may not be convenient to the reader, and errors, ambiguities and complicated explanations cannot be questioned until later, if at all. This means that the writer needs to give considerable thought as to how best to express himself. An explanation that seems clear to him may be far from clear to a reader. A person once explained to a friend that he was sorry that he had written him a long letter. This was because he had not had time to write a short one. The point is that it may require considerable effort and concentration to write in a clear and simple manner. It also involves the writer being prepared to state what he really means instead of concealing his real thoughts, or lack of real thoughts, behind a smokescreen of words. Unfortunately people can easily be taken in by verbose or complex explanations, believing that their failure to understand is because of their own limitations rather than those of the writer. It may often be a more appropriate and accurate assumption that, if a person hasn't explained something clearly, the fault is with their thinking rather than with the reader's comprehension.

Sometimes matters have to be expressed in a precise technical way and the use of a particular language is unavoidable. This can be the case with legal documents where the only way of achieving the necessary clarity is to use precise legal expressions. However, even when technical language is used, there are differences between good and bad expression. Whether technical language is used or not, there would seem to be no virtue in explaining matters in a more complicated way than is necessary. All too often, however, sophisticated terms can be dragged in unnecessarily because of a desire to impress or because of clumsy expression or lack of clarity in the actual thinking. The use of many sociological terms in particular can be for these reasons. One of the ironies concerning many Government forms is that those who have to complete them may need a graduate level ability to do so. Persons with that level of ability, though, would not often be applying for many of the services in question. Much of the underclaiming of social security benefit in the U.S. may be because of the difficulty people have in understanding the benefit application forms.

Television as a source of information and its evaluation

The need to evaluate carefully the accuracy and quality of information is not confined to data that is generated within an organisation. All organisations collect much of their information from external sources which are also subject to distortion. Television is an increasingly important source of information for managers and it is appropriate to comment about the problems of distortion which are now becoming apparent in this area. One have become particularly aware of this in teaching industrial relations, and refer to some of the problems of reporting in this area in order to make the general point about the need to evaluate television carefully as an information source.

Industrial relations is an area that has been seized upon by the media generally, and television in particular, for extensive coverage. People's views and knowledge about the subject can be as much influenced by media sources as anything else. This presents difficulties, as increasingly evidence is emerging to suggest that the profile of industrial relations presented by television in particular is not very representative. The obstacles to balanced reporting are considerable and to a large extent stem from the conflict between the obligation of television producers to present fair programmes and the pressures on them to catch the attention of audiences and attain high viewing figures. This can lead to sensationalized reporting, emphasis on the unusual rather than the usual, and 'camera bias' because of the visual impact of anything dramatic. Other problems can include confusion between the symptoms and causes of industrial disputes, the juxtaposition of industrial relations reports with other news items, the limited understanding and work experience of television journalists, and the subconscious judgments and values of those responsible for making programmes. The problem is exacerbated by the simplistic reaction of many television producers and journalists who believe that, because there is no conscious bias, nothing is wrong.

One find that my first task in teaching industrial relations has now become to make people aware of the need to evaluate carefully the information presented on the media rather than simply to accept the pattern of events which is presented. The problems of effective reporting of news and current affairs have led John Birt and Peter Jay to comment on the 'bias against understanding' inherent in television reporting. This observation was based on their own experience as producers for Independent Television and led to them trying in their own productions to strive for balanced reporting, explanation and analysis of the information they presented. The

Glasgow University Media Study Group in their monitoring of news bulletins has been particularly critical of news reporting. In their analysis of news bulletins in January 1975 they found that the five industrial disputes in vehicle building, accounting for 21 per cent of the days lost through strikes in the month, received 125 out of a total of 130 news reports of strikes in the UK. They also established that in 22 news reports of the Glasgow dustcart drivers' unofficial strike in the same year, the unofficial strikers were not represented in any of the 21 interviews shown on the national news during the 13 weeks of the dispute. One may or may not have had sympathy for the unofficial strikers, but viewers were not likely to be able to make that judgment for themselves if one side of the case was not presented.

The criticisms of television coverage of news and current affairs reporting received some endorsement in the Annan report on the future of broadcasting published in 1977. Comment was made about the variability of current affairs presentation and for the need for improvement in news Television News bulletins. This included the observation that 'Both BBC Television News and ITN, but particularly the former, could be improved. News is presented in too stereotyped a fashion; there is too little variety, too little punch and there are too few attempts to give brief explanatory comments. Whilst the Annan report did not endorse all the criticisms made of television reporting, they did point out a large number of other weaknesses in some areas. These included the lack of understanding of industrial life by some producers, the preference by others for presenting current affairs in the style of a boxing promoter, the dangers of social insularity of television producers, and camera bias. These problems are not so pronounced with radio because of the absence of visual images which can have a dominating effect on television programmes. In fairness it should be said that the problems of providing balanced and sensitive TV coverage are immense. The awareness of this and of British achievements in this area has led the TV critic Milton Shulman to describe British TV as 'the least worst in the world'. Readers can judge for themselves the extent to which the media have taken note of the criticisms made in the Annan report in particular. The topic has been stressed because of the increasing importance of television as a medium for communication, particularly in view of the increasing availability of video-cassettes. The point that needs stressing above all others is that one needs actively to evaluate the information with which one is presented when the easiest course of action may be passively to accept it.

Dyadic or interpersonal communication involves face-to-face exchanges between two individuals. Our model of communication and interpersonal relationships and our discussion of non-verbal communication, serial communication, communication networks, leadership and management, com-munication barriers, and methods of improving organizational communication all centre to some degree upon the one-to-one, face-to-face communication situation. In this chapter we shall consider a special form of interpersonal communication: the interview. Since organizational decisions concerning policy, procedures, and personnel often are made on the basis of information gained through interviews, effective interviewing techniques are crucial to organizational success. We shall therefore consider the nature of interviews, kinds of questions often employed during interviews, and specific types of interviews commonly used in organizations.

The nature of interviews

Bingham, Moore, and Gustad suggest that "interviewing is a conversation directed to a definite purpose other than satisfaction in the conversation itself." Similarly, Kahn and Cannell argue that an interview is "a specialized pattern of verbal interaction initiated for specific purpose, and focused on some specific content area, with a subsequent elimination of extraneous material." Goyer, Reading, and Rickey term interviewing "a form of oral communication involving two parties, at least one of whom has a preconceived and serious purpose and both of whom speak and listen from time to time."

These definitions in turn suggest several differences between interviews and other forms of dyadic communication. First, while virtually all interpersonal communication has some underlying purpose, the interview has a purpose which is more clearly defined and more directly sought. Second, interviews typically involve careful preparation by the interviewer. Although we often *"lan"* conversations we anticipate having with others, thinking. Now, if she says so-and-so, I'll say this, rarely is that planning as thorough as the planning preceding an interview. Third, the communication roles of the participants are predetermined to an extent not usually found in other types of interpersonal communication. Both participants realize that the interviewer will ask questions and the interviewee will respond, and both of them usually adhere to those role prescriptions. Finally, while the dominance dimension of an interpersonal relationship usually is determined by situational factors such as organizational role or status, dominance in the interview is determined solely by the communication roles of the participants. Since the interviewer directs the conversation through her or his use of questions, the interviewer always is the dominant individual. While, the company president usually dominates a shop foreman, a foreman interviewer would dominate the president interviewee during the interview itself. Interviews therefore differ from other interpersonal interactions in that they have a specific purpose, are carefully planned, have predetermined communication roles, and generate situation-specific dominance.

Gordon lists several additional benefits of the interview. First, it allows the information seeker greater opportunity to elicit complete and accurate information from the interviewee. The interviewer is able to assess immediately the respondent's answers and to seek further information or elaboration if necessary—things one cannot do when administering a questionnaire. Second, the interviewer can clarify the questions. If someone filling out a questionnaire misinterprets a question, the person collecting the information may wind up with erroneous information and incorrect conclusions; in the interview, however, the interviewer can determine immediately whether the interviewee has understood the question or seen the implications the question carries. Should such comprehension not be present, the interviewer can remedy the situation immediately.

Third, most forms of interviews allow greater flexibility of questioning than does a questionnaire or other information-gathering methods. Interview forms occur along a continuum ranging from extremely structured to extremely unstructured. Although flexibility is minimal in the structured situation, the interviewer still is able to restate or rephrase questions. In unstructured interviews, flexibility is maximized; the interviewer can let the flow of conversation dictate what questions she or he will ask. Fourth, the interview situation allows careful control by the interviewer. Questionnaires may be complete anywhere and letters may be read and answered in any situation. In the interview, however, the interviewer is able to choose and, to some degree, control the interview environment. If the interviewer chooses to speak with a respondent in the respondent's home, the interviewer's control of the situation will be minimal. If the respondent visit the interviewer, the latter's control is maximized. The interviewer can control interruptions, arrange the furniture, dictate the time of the interview, and so on. Finally, the interviewer may obtain more information about the interviewee in face-to-face encounters. By observing the respondent's non-verbal behaviours, the interviewer can evaluate his attitudes toward the questions, his answers, and even the interviewer himself—judgments not always possible with written responses. Thus the interview seems the most desirable means of gathering information; it maximizes immediacy and enhances the interviewer's abilities to obtain complete responses, to guide respondents' interpretations, to adapt to the situation, to control the situation, and to judge respondents' underlying feelings.

Types of Interview Questions

While one probably could generate an infinite list of types and sub-types of questions, we shall begin by distinguishing only two; unrestricted and restricted. Unrestricted questions allow the respondent to discuss almost anything she or he pleases; restricted questions specify the limits of the desired answer. But the differences between the two go far beyond this, and we shall therefore consider each question type in turn.

Unrestricted Questions

Often termed open or open-ended questions, this type includes such inquiries as What's new? and Tell me about yourself. Questions of this sort provide definite advantages to the interviewer. One may learn how much the interviewee knows, the things she deems important or trivial, her beliefs and values, and how well she is able to express herself. Questions such as these convey a sense of warmth to the interviewee, implicitly telling her that she is interesting and that anything she has to say will be important and relevant. However, unrestricted questions present potential problems. They may require a great deal of time, for often the interviewer. They require a great deal of skill on the part of the interviewee spends several minutes relating information of no use to the interviewer, who must know when and how to interrupt the respondent, to encourage her and to provide her with further questions. Finally, they produce unstructured, spontaneous answers which often are difficult to analyse. Nevertheless, for certain situations unrestricted questions are remarkably effective tools for gathering information.

Restricted Questions

The restricted or *closed* question limits the respondent's answers by demanding specific information. The interviewer might ask, How long did you work at your last job? or Where did you go to school? Thus the topic of conversation is specified, and the interviewee must respond within these narrowly defined limits. Such questions are advantageous in that they allow the interviewer to control the conversation more closely, to ask more questions in more areas, to make maximum use of the time available, and to interpret easily the interviewee's answers. On the other hand, these questions lack some of the advantages provided by unrestricted questions. The interviewer gains only the information requested and learns little else about the respondent; the interview is rather impersonal, conveying little sense of warmth; the interviewee has no opportunity to volunteer potentially valuable information. The advantages and shortcomings of restricted questions are thus the reverse of the benefits and drawbacks of unrestricted questions.

Which type of question should be employed? Generally the answer is based largely on the situation. If the interview must obtain maximum amounts of information in minimum periods of time, and if the interview is to be conducted by persons not particularly skilled in interviewing techniques, the restricted form seems most desirable. If, on the other hand, the interview involves personal matters (as in counselling or disciplinary interviews), seeks general kinds of information about the interviewee, is under no pressures of time, and will be conducted by a skilled interviewer, then the unrestricted form is preferable. Clearly the situations described here are extremes; most situations fall somewhere between the two, considering some personal matters, being conducted by adequately skilled interviewers, and so on. But the unrestricted- restricted dichotomy also represent as extremes; questions can be phrased that are somewhat restricted or somewhat unrestricted. Whether extremely restricted, extremely unrestricted, or some moderated forms of questions are chosen, the choice should reflect the situational factors we have considered.

Question Bias

A second distinction among question types can be made on the basis of bias. Most of us probably are familiar with the story of the politician who publicly asked his opponent, "Have you stopped beating your wife?" Often questions such as these occur in interpersonal situations as well. You do want to join the union, don't you?

and How do you feel about those stupid shop rules? are questions that carry as many leading implications as Have you stopped beating your wife? While questions like these may not produce serious problems in everyday conversation, they have definite impact in interviews. To conduct interviews effectively we must be aware of the nature and influence of biased questions.

As with restricted and unrestricted questions, unbiased and biased inquiries range along a continuum from very unbiased to highly biased. The examples used in the preceding section typify unbiased questions. Inquiries such as How do you feel about your job? say virtually nothing about the interviewer's own feelings; the question is stated neutrally. Somewhat more leading is the question. You like to work with machines, don't you? And, at the very biased end of the scale, Do you support our strike, or are you dirty pinko commie scab? Because these three questions vary in their revelations of the interviewer's feelings, they exert different degrees of pressure upon the interviewee to respond appropriately.

In deciding whether to use biased, moderately biased, or unbiased questions, we first must take into account our purpose in the interview. If we are seeking the interviewee's true feelings or attitudes, we probably would avoid biased questions If, however, we are trying to persuade the interviewee, biased questions can be extremely useful. Research in attitude change suggests that if we can get an interviewee to state a certain opinion, he is likely to adopt that opinion as his own. Thus, if the interviewee initially has no intention of supporting our strike but, because of social pressure, responded yes to our "dirty pinko commie scab" question, he would be much more likely to support the strike when it actually occurs. Biased questions also are useful if we are trying to test the respondent. We can determine how independent he is, how well he responds under stress, or how prone he is to provide socially approved responses. For example, if we asked, Are you a sexist? or Are you prejudiced against women in business? he probably would answer no even if he did harbour such prejudices. If, however, we asked, Women really are too emotional to be good administrators, aren't they? we might elicit a true attitude which otherwise might have been suppressed. In any of these situations the biased question, properly applied, would be more useful than an unbiased inquiry.

Question Sequences

Our final consideration here is the order in which questions are to be posed during an interview. While a virtually infinite number of sequences could be identified, we shall consider five types distinguishable by their use of restricted and unrestricted questions.

The first type of sequence, the *pyramid*, begins with unrestricted questions and builds upon them with questions of increasing restrictedness. We might begin by asking a general question about the interviewee's attitude toward work and then become increasingly specific by focusing on particular aspects of the interviewee's position, moving perhaps from conditions in general to her to his supervisors and to one particular supervisor. Rather than focus immediately upon a specific topic which may be personal or difficult for the interviewee to discuss, then, this technique begins with unrestricted questions which are relatively easy to answer and gradually narrows down to more sensitive areas. If the respondent does not touch upon certain areas of interest, the pyramid may be useful in gaining that specific information.

A second sequence, the *inverted pyramid,* is the reverse of the first. The interviewer begins with specific, restricted questions and gradually moves to more general, unrestricted inquiries. This technique is particularly useful when the respondent is reluctant to talk, for often one can be motivated by a restricted question in an area that interests one and, once one begins talking, can be directed toward more general considerations.

The third and fourth sequence types involve combinations of the first two. The *diamond* sequence begins with restricted questions, moves to unrestricted inquiries, and then narrows again to a specific topic through a series of increasingly specific questions. If, for example, we were counselling an employee, we might begin with a situation analogous to his. Through restricted questions, his feelings and thoughts about that situation could be elicited and converted into general principles as the questions become increasingly open. Then, to apply those principles to the interviewee's own situation, a series of questions increasing in restrictedness would again focus the conversation. An alternative to this procedure is the *hourglass* sequence, in which unrestricted questions become increasingly restricted and are then followed by questions which again become increasingly open. Suppose we are interviewing a supervisor who has been sharply criticized by her subordinates for her heavy-handed tactics. We might begin the interview with a discussion of human motivation in general, gradually narrow the topic to her specific situation, and then become general again defining principles of appropriate managerial behaviour. This type of sequence often is useful in changing both the specific behaviours and general attitudes of the interviewee. A fifth type of sequence is the *tunnel.* Interviews of this sort employ questions all of the same degree of restrictedness. If we are interested only in the spontaneous reactions of the interviewee, this sequence may be useful; if, however, we want in-depth information, attitudinal or behavioural change, or a sharing of deep emotions, one of the other formats would be more appropriate. Where these five sequence types are based upon the use of restricted or unrestricted questions, another type of sequence has been developed that takes into account the types of information the interviewer seeks. Constructed by George Gallup, the *quintamensional* sequence presents five ordered question types, each signed to elicit particular responses:

1. Awareness—What does the respondent know about the situation?
2. General Attitudes—What points of view is he aware of concerning that situation?

3. Specific Attitude—What point of view does he himself hold?
4. Reasons—Why does he hold that view?
5. Intensity—How strong is his attitude?

In informational interviews this sequence type seems quite useful in providing a comprehensive view of the respondent's knowledge about and feelings toward a certain situation.

Selection of a question sequence, then, is based largely upon our purpose in the interview and the interviewee's attitude toward us. A reluctant respondent may require use of an inverted pyramid sequence for all or part of the interview period; a disagreeable interviewee may be persuaded through use of a diamond sequence. If information is sought from a willing respondent, the tunnel or quintamensional sequences may be best. As interviewers we must assess the situation as quickly as possible and adjust our questioning accordingly.

Types of interviews

Interviews differ according to their purposes and settings, and each interview type presents unique problems and opportunities. We shall now consider in some detail several of the more common types of interviews: employment, informational, counselling, appraisal, disciplinary, persuasive, and axis interviews. We shall review the purposes of each type of interview and the procedures by which achievement of those purposes might be facilitated.

The Employment Interview

Employment interviews are among the most important types of interviews an organization conducts. These interviews, which according to Taylor occur at a rate of more than ten million per year, determine whether the organization hires the best individual available or whether they hire someone detrimental to the organization. For the interviewee, such interviews determine whether or not one is employed. Obviously, a bad employment interview can be disastrous both to the organization, who may hire the wrong person, and to the interviewee, who may end up unemployed. We shall therefore consider this interview type from the viewpoints of both the interviewer and the interviewee.

Purposes

Although the goal of the employment interview appears obvious—to fill or obtain a job—there are in fact some rather subtle purposes which ought not to be neglected. First, the employment interview seeks information which cannot be presented in an applicant's resume or in a brochure describing the organization. The interviewer must make judgments about the applicant's personality, character and attitude—things difficult to ascertain from written documents. The applicant similarly must judge the climate of the organization, its attitudes towards its employees and the general public, the working situation, and so on, to determine whether working there would be a pleasant experience. Again, brochures or organizational propaganda typically do not allow such judgments.

A second purpose of the employment interview is to create and maintain goodwill for the organization. Often the applicant's sole contact with a company is in an employment interview. If that experience is unpleasant, the interviewee's attitude toward the company probably will be unfavourable, as will the attitudes of other people with whom the interviewee has contact. Therefore, even though an applicant is clearly unsuited for the available position, the interviewer must make the experience as pleasant as possible for the interviewee; failure to do so could seriously undermine the company's public relations efforts.

A third purpose is the reverse of the first: to provide information. Too often applicants and interviewers take an attitude which might be characterized as: We/I want him/them to want us/me. This is dangerous attitude. A candidate who successfully sells herself to a company will be unhappy if that company discovers that she is not qualified or fit for the position. Similarly, a company which receives an applicant in order to hire him will have an unhappy employee when the truth emerges. Thus the third purpose of the employment interview should be to provide honest, comprehensive information. The interviewer must allow the interviewee to decide whether he wants to join the company as it is ; the interviewee must allow the interviewer to decide whether to hire her as she is. Deception or omission by either party usually leads to an unsatisfactory employer-employee relationship.

Procedures: Taken chronologically, the steps of the employment interview include planning, beginning, questioning, and closing.

Planning: The first step in planning an employment interview is to determine the criteria by which applicant will be judged. Shouksmith (1968) emphasizes the importance of determining the "critical requirement" for a job and suggests that four to six factors or abilities be listed to assess interviewees. In hiring a receptionist, for example, we might determine that the factors most necessary for success are friendliness, politeness, attractiveness, and intelligence; we then would look for someone possessing those traits. The interviewer must know what kind of person she or he is seeking, and developing a list of critical requirements seems to be a useful method for specifying desired traits.

A second step on the planning stage involves selecting the types and sequence of questions to be used. This step is somewhat controversial; some writers argue that each interview should be tailored spontaneously to the individual applicant. Research suggests, however, that many advantages lie with careful preparation. Wagner (1949) and Mayfield (1964) both found that highly structured interviews allow the interviewer to make more reliable judgments among all the interviews she or he conducts; hence the interviewer is more likely to select the best candidate. Although some flexibility is necessary within each individual interview, the interviewer therefore should plan the general outline which the interview will follow.

Before each interview the interviewer should review the information at hand concerning the applicant. The interviewer should read any application forms, resumes, and letters of recommendation to determine what information about the applicant she or he possesses and what additional data is needed. By so doing the interviewer will be better able to tailor the questions to the applicant and to avoid asking questions which solicit information already in hand.

Beginning: The applicant should be greeted warmly by name, and the interviewer should introduce himself so that the applicant knows what form of address she should use. When beginning the interview, the interviewer may engage the respondent in friendly conversation to "break the ice" or he may begin immediately to question her. Although idle chatter occasionally is effective in relaxing the interviewee and creating a good atmosphere, it often backfires. Tension and suspense may grow, valuable time may be wasted, and the interviewee may become suspicious of the interviewer's motives for engaging in small talk. Thus it generally is advisable to begin immediately with questioning. If the applicant seems particularly nervous, an open-ended question may allow her time to relax. If nervousness is not apparent, direct, restricted questions may be appropriate.

Questioning: The nature and use of question types has been detailed above, but further cautions are needed concerning the interviewer's behaviours. The fundamental principle underlying these action is this: the interviewee is trying to please the interviewer and will say and what she thinks the interviewer likes. This principle becomes crucial when we consider the interviewer's responses to the interviewee's answers. If he responds favourably to some behaviour, that behaviour probably will increase; if he responds negatively, the behaviour will disappear. As interviewers we must be aware of our own behaviours because of their potency in the interview situation; we should use those behaviours to encourage desired responses but not to condition the applicant's verbal behaviours.

Other principles concerning questioning during an employment interview include:

1. Give the applicant adequate time to answer questions; do not pressure her unduly.
2. Avoid questions answerable by yes or no—they provide too little information.
3. Avoid trick questions unless they are absolutely necessary.
4. Avoid questions which might violate legislation concerning fair employment practices, such as What is your religion?
5. Allow the interviewee to ask questions.

Closing. When ending the interview, either we will be able to make the decision concerning whether the applicant is hired or we will not. If we have the power to hire on the spot, and we have reached a decision concerning the candidate, that decision should be carried out: we should either offer the position or terminate consideration. Too often interviewers are reluctant to do the latter and instead use the old line, We'll call you. By keeping the candidate in suspense and perhaps giving her false hope, this procedure can only disappoint her and perhaps engender hostility toward our organization. If we do not have the power to make a decision on the spot, we should explain the situation as truthfully as possible, in such situations we should have prepared a standard explanation of the follow-up procedure to give the candidate, and we should close as neutrally as possible to avoid giving false impressions. Whatever the ultimate decision concerning a candidate, the letter sent her should be personalized and as pleasant as possible. We still want to maintain her goodwill toward the organization, and some day a position may open *for which she is the best candidate available.*

Participating as an Interviewee

Further consideration of the interviewee's role in employment interviews may be helpful. Just as the first step for the interviewer in planning an interview is to arrive at some criteria by which candidate are to be judged, so must we as interviewee make some decisions concerning what we require from an employer. We must decide what our values in life are, what sorts of material and social rewards we require, what kinds of personal and professional goals we have, and what sorts of organizations we prefer to work in. These decisions will aid us not only in selecting positions for which to apply but in performing better in the interview itself: most employers prefer that we have thought carefully about such matters, and they will ask us questions designed to determine the kinds of decisions we have reached.

First impression at the actual interview are crucial. Research summarized by Wright demonstrates that interviewers form impressions of the applicant very early in the interview and that those impressions typically determine the ultimate decisions. It is important, then that we be punctual, polite, pleasant, and appropriate in appearance. While we might argue that people ought not to be judged by appearance, the evidence we presented in our discussion of non-verbal communication demonstrates that judgments are made on precisely that basis. For practical reasons, then, appearance should conform to the expectations of the interviewer. This is not to say that you should sell out by sacrificing your values to conform to those of the organization; if you do not like the organization's requirements, you should apply somewhere else. If you do decide you want to become part of that organization, you should expect to conform to some of their expectations.

Research by Goetzinger provides a list of behaviours rated offensive by professional interviewers. The list is rather lengthy: it includes dishonesty, lack of interest , belligerence or impoliteness, evasiveness, overconcern with salary, lack of concentration, lack of initiative, indecisiveness, arrogance, feelings of persecution, cynicism, intolerance or prejudice, lateness, limp handshake, unclarity of expression, lack of career planning, lack of acquaintance with the company, lack of maturity, poor moral standards, improper appearance, and overselling of self. While some of these may strike us as trivial, they nonetheless seem important to interviewers—and consequently are worth our notice. In addition to avoiding the behaviours, we can enhance our performances an interviewee by asking intelligent questions. Often interviewers judge the interest, knowledge, and intelligence of a candidate by the questions she or he asks. We therefore would do well to have in mind several reasonable, carefully thought out questions which would both provide useful information to us and demonstrate our competence to the interviewer.

If at the close of the interview no decision has been made concerning our hiring, we should follow up the interview with a personal letter expressing appreciation to the interviewer and sending any additional information which we think might be helpful. Again, this demonstrates our interest in the position while providing the interviewer to respond.

Before leaving our consideration of the employment interview, we want to emphasize the most important element of that situation: honesty. If an interviewer becomes too concerned with selling the organization, or if an interviewee becomes too concerned with selling himself, deception, international or accidental, may occur with the result that the company, the employee, or both may ultimately be unhappy. Regardless of the role you are to play in an employment interview, you should be as open as possible, for only through an honest, complete exchange of information will the best decision be made.

The Informational Interview

As its name implies, the purpose of this interview type is to gain information from a respondent. Given such a broad definition, its follows that this sort of interview is among the most commonly used forms. Included within its boundaries, or example, are asking a supervisor to explain an operation, conducting a market survey or opinion poll, and questioning a prominent person to develop a news story. This interview type ranges from the most informational requests for information to lengthy, prescheduled sessions of intensive questioning. We shall consider only the formal instances of informational interviewing, those interviews which require careful preparation.

Procedures

Planning: When preparing for an informational interview, the first step is to decide what sort of information is to be sought. This involves two questions: what do we want to know? and how are we going to use the information? The answer to the first question dictates the subject-matter to be covered by the interview; the answer to the second determines the types of questions to be asked. We start, then, with a careful analysis of the topic or problem about which questions will be asked. From that analysis should grow a list of topics and sub-topics which need to be covered during the interview and a subsequent list of questions covering those topics. The wording of questions should be appropriate to the ultimate use of the obtained information. Development of a news story, for example, necessitates procurement of detailed information; open-ended questions thus would be the most useful type. If answers are to be reported verbatim or coded into a set of standardized scores, questions requiring only a brief answer would be preferable.

Another decision to be made during the planning stage concerns who is to be interviewed. Occasionally circumstances will dictate that decision; if only one person possesses the information needed, that person must be interviewed. However, if we are interested in consumer buying preferences, public voting behaviours, or other rather general categories of behaviour, we have to decide which of rather thousands of potential respondents we are going to survey. Gordon (1969) suggests four guidelines by which we might choose our interviewees:

1. Who has the information we need?
2. Who among these people is accessible—that is, which of them has the time, proximity, and so on that allow us to talk to her or him?
3. Who among the accessible informants is willing to give us the relevant information?
4. Who among the willing, accessible informants is most able to provide the information?

A variety of factors may affect the last-named consideration. The informant may have forgotten the information, repressed it because of its traumatic nature, distorted it because of bias or prejudice, or reached improper conclusions which affect the report. Each of these potential problems should be taken into account; where possible, the chosen respondents should have a minimum of these characteristics.

Having considered the four processes of elimination Gordon suggests, we still may be faced with a large number of potential interviewees. If we are analyzing voting behaviour, for example, relatively few voters would be eliminated by those four criteria. In such situations we would resort to one of the many sampling techniques available. We shall briefly describe a few of these techniques.

The most common method of selecting a few representative individual from a large population of potential respondents is through random sampling. In effect, we put the names of the entire population in a hat and then pull out the desired number of informants. This "drawing from a hat" technique can be accomplished in a variety of ways but with each method the principle remains the same: everyone in the population has an equal chance of being chosen, and the selections are made purely on the basis of chance.

Other sampling techniques are systematic, stratified, and quota sampling. When sampling systematically, we develop a system by which the sampling will be chosen. We might decide to select every twenty-fifth name in a telephone book, using the resultant group as our sample. Stratified sampling is somewhat more complicated. We divide the population into groups relevant to our interests and then randomly select respondents from those groups. If we are conducting a survey of buying habits, we might want to learn whether sex or age affects buying behaviour. Thus we would divide out population into males and females and young and old—and from the four groups select randomly representatives to be interviewed. The quota method involves selecting a sample which matches as closely as possible the characteristics of the entire population. If we still are interested in the effects of sex and age, and we discover that our population consists of 40 per cent old women, 20 per cent old men, we would select a sample of these same proportions. Although each of these sampling methods involves somewhat different processes, the end is the same: to reduce to a manageable number the group of respondents who are to be interviewed.

Beginning: In opening the interview we must accomplish two things: telling the interviewee the purpose of the interview and establishing rapport. Gordon (1969) suggests that the opining statement contain any of the following facts that are relevant to the situation: introduction of yourself, mention of the person or organization you represent, clear and concise explanation of the interview's purpose, explanation of why the respondent was chosen, mention of the method, if any, by which answers will be recorded and mention of the incentive or reward the respondent will receive for participating. An opening containing all these elements might therefore sound like this: Good morning. I'am Timothy Hill from the Gobbler Meat Packing Company. I'am conducting a survey of the meat-buying habits of people in your community. We believe that the answers you and your neighbours give us will allow us to better meet your grocery needs thus help lower meat prices in this area. Because your answers are important, I'd like to tape record them as we go. Would you be willing to help us by responding to a few questions?

Questioning. Assuming our respondent is willing to be interviewed, our next concern becomes the types of questions we are going to ask. According to Kahn and Cannell (1964), five principles should be kept in view when phrasing questions:

1. *Use language appropriate to the respondent.* We should neither talk down to them nor be too complex; we should not try to imitate them by using their slang or accents. Rather, we should use simple, easily understood language, defining any terms which the respondent seems not to understand.

2. *Be sure the questions are clearly related to the purpose of the interview.* If no relevance is apparent, the respondent is likely to become suspicious or irritated and

stop providing useful information. Therefore, if the relevance of a question is not evident, explain why you are asking it.

3. *Be certain the informant has the information you want.* Even though we have been careful to select only those people we believe to be informed in the areas relevant to our interview, our questions occasionally may stray into areas about which the informant knows relatively little. When this occurs, a variety of responses may follow: the respondent may pretend to know the information so that he will not appear ignorant; she may become annoyed that we have had the bad taste to ask about things with which she has no concern; or she may frankly admit that she does not know and the interview staggers on.

4. *Avoid questions that are overly complex.* Too often questions become mini-speeches that only allow the questioner to state his own opinions and ideas. Following a recent Super Bowl game, an interviewer posed a question to winning quarterback that went something like this: "What did you think of their defense? It looked to me like they were in a rotating zone coverage with occasional man-to-man. But they blitzed every third and long situation. I would have gone to some screen passes or draw plays, but you threw to your tight end. Why?" The quarterback thus had a choice of questions to which he could respond, plus the opportunity to argue with the strategy posed by the interviewer. Not renowned for his quick thinking, and perhaps confused by this array of alternatives, the quarterback answered, "Huh?" To avoid such uninformative answers, the interviewer should ask only one question at a time and state it as simply and straightforwardly as possible.

5. *Avoid questions which ask the respondent to violate a social norm.* For example, the norm that we ought to be modest may cause an interviewee to provide an inadequate response to a question asking him to evaluate himself or his behaviour; norms governing the types of topics discussed in society may hinder one's willingness to discuss questions related to sex income, death, or other personal areas of one's life. If such questions are not vital to the interview, avoid them. If they are necessary, wait until late in the interview to ask them and phrase them as delicately as possible.

Closing: When the questioning has ended, we should offer a brief, planned statement that indicates if and when the results of the interview will be available. In addition, we should provide the interview with an opportunity to ask any questions she may have concerning the interview or its purpose, and we should express our appreciation for her cooperation. Leaving the interviewee with a positive feeling is important; we may wish to obtain further information from her again, and her willingness at that time will be affected by what has happened in this situation. And if we are representing an organization, the feeling she has for that organization will be influenced by our interview. It is in our interests to do everything possible to leave on good terms.

The informational interview should create opportunity and willingness.

Respondents give only the information they have an opportunity to give. If our questions do not provide them the opportunity, the information is lost. In addition, respondents give only the information they are willing to give. In our questions, approach, attitude, or appearance negatively affect the respondent, the willingness may disappear and the desired information may remain undiscovered. Through careful selection of topics, questions, and respondents, coupled with skilful questioning, both opportunity and willingness can be maximized.

The counselling interview

In his article "What Corporation Presidents Think About at Night," John McCaffrey (1953) note that "while a drill press never sulks and a drop hammer never gets jealous of other drop hammers, the same cannot be said for people." His point is that people, by their nature, often encounter emotional problems. These vary widely in intensity, involving minor disputes between workers or major crises at home, but the potential always is present. Whenever these problems become severe enough that a worker's normal functioning is seriously impaired, some treatment may be necessary. In organizations the treatment of emotional problems usually takes the form of the counselling interview.

The primary function of this interview type is to provide the individual with some insight into the problem and to help her or him discover a means of dealing with it. Toward this end, Davis notes, counselling provides advice, reassurance a release of emotional tensions, clarification of thinking, and reorientation. Not all of these may occur during the actual interview; clarification and reorientation, for example, may take place at some later time when the individual reflects on the interview. Nevertheless, these are the essential purposes of this interview type.

Procedures

Planning: In preparing for the counselling interview, we first must learn as much as possible about the interview. Occasionally this may be impossible; clients may arrive without warning, expecting help. In such situations information may have to be obtained directly from the individual. When there is preparation time, we should consult whatever records are available concerning the client in an effort to gain greater insight into her or his feelings and problems.

Beginning: It is crucial that some rapport be established at the outset between interviewer and client. Often this task a considerable amount of time, but it is time well spent, if the situation is at all threatening, or if the client perceives the interviewer to be untrustworthy, the interview is doomed. Our responsibility is to establish a warm atmosphere, one in which the client feels free to discuss whatever he wishes with the knowledge that what he says will be kept confidential and will be accepted by us. We must demonstrate that we are genuinely interested in what he has to say; we must be sensitive to his non-verbal cues to determine the type and strength of his feelings. And above all, we must demonstrate that we truly care about the client's welfare.

Counselling: During the interview our responses to the client may range from extremely directive to extremely non-directive. Directive interviewing involves hearing the client's problem. Deciding with him what he should do, and then telling and motivating him to carry out that action. In extremely directive interviews, the client is ordered to carry out the interviewee's advice, those orders often being accompanied by threats or ultimatums. In more mild forms, suggestions are made but without the exertion of pressure to follow them. In all forms of directive interviewing, however, some direction is given for the client's future behaviours.

While the directive form of counselling serves primarily to provide advice, it also may reassure, give emotion release , and to some degree clarify thinking. However, as Davis notes, it will not achieve reorientation. The directive approach can be dangerous and hence must be used with extreme caution. Nevertheless, if the client needs to be shocked back to his normal state, or if threats can cause him to resume work and forget his problem, this method can be extremely effective.

At the other end of the continuum lies the non-directive or, as Rogers terms it, the client-centerd approach. This approach involves skilful listening to the client, encouraging her to reveal her emotional problems, to analyze them, and to develop for herself some course of action. At its most extreme, the non-directive approach offers no advice or reassurance, although it typically produces emotional release, clarifies thinking, and achieves reorientation. The counsellor provides little or no information or advice but simply encourages the interviewee to continue talking.

Several strategies are used by non-directive counsellors. Silence accompanied by an attentive look may exert pressure on the client to continue talking. So, too, does the non-committal Um-hmm, which shows interest and understanding but provides no input. The reflective or mirror statement, which paraphrases the last comment made by the interviewee, also encourages one to continue. But the most important and most difficult strategy is to pose questions which provide the client with some insight into her or his problem. Usually it takes training and a great deal of experience to become proficient at this sort of probing questioning. The interviewer must have insight into the client's problem, and through her questioning she must lead the client to that same insight and to a solution for the problem—two very difficult tasks. When handled properly, this type of interview has been found extremely effective in handling employee problems.

Despite its advantages, the non-directive approach is not without restrictions. It is an expensive method in terms of the time it requires and the expensive of training competent counsellors. It places considerable responsibility upon the client, assuming him to be motivated to achieve a solution to his problem, to have the insight to ultimately understand his problem and find a solution, and to have the emotional capacity to deal with the problem. Still, the benefits of the non-directive method seem to greatly outweigh any drawbacks it may have.

Closing: The manner in which the counselling interview is closed is as important a determinant of its success as are each of the preceding stages. If the interviewee feels as though she is being rushed out the door, that the interviewer has given her all the time she is worth or that the interviewer's appearances of caring about the client has been an act, any progress made up to that point may be lost. Moreover, if problems again arise, the client may be reluctant to return for further counselling. Thus the interview should close when both client and interviewer feel psychologically comfortable in closing—it should be neither rushed nor drawn out by discussion of irrelevant topics. Although we all tend to seek a neatly tied package at the interview's close, that often is impossible; reorientation often does not occur until some later time. It may therefore be unrealistic and artificial to try to pull together all that has occurred; rather, we should encourage the client to continue grappling with the problem in light of our conservation and to return whenever she or he feels the need. On this positive note the interview should end.

The counselling interview is by no means a cure—all for employee problems. Counselling in many cases is a rather inadequate measure because it returns the client to the environment which may have caused her or his problems in the first place. In such cases lasting change may be attainable only through some changes in the environment, not through any advice we can offer. Often it is appropriate to discuss such cases with management and to suggest changes we feel might be helpful. In any case, the counselling interview must be handled with care. The client usually is emotionally distraught and often has turned to the counsellor as a last resort. A bungled interview consequently could mean disaster. Counselling interviews should not be conducted by amateurs: only after thorough training should one engage in this type of interview.

The Appraisal interview

In some ways the appraisal interview is the antithesis of the counselling form. While in counselling interviews evaluation of the client usually is avoided, the entire function of the appraisal interview is to evaluate the individual's job performance. Davis points out that management profits from appraisal interviews because they give management the opportunity to allocate resources within the organization, reward employees, provide employees with feedback, and maintain fair intergroup relations. Labour also desires this type of communication; research by Howard and Berkowitz and Stolz and Tannenbaum demonstrates that while people prefer positive feedback, and while negative feedback creates anxiety, workers still prefer negative feedback to no feedback at all. These findings also illustrate the paradox attendant on the appraisal interview: the employee desires feedback concerning performance but is anxious about that feedback and likely to behave defensively when it is given. In the appraisal interview, then, the interviewer must provide feedback concerning the interview's performance while making the situation as non-threatening as possible.

Given the difficulty involved in conducting an appraisal interview, it is hardly starting to discover that such interviews often are mishandled in modern organizations. Lahiff reports that appraisal interviewers often tend to dwell upon the individual's negative characteristics—a highly destructive approach. Kay, Meyer, and French found that the more weaknesses the manager mentioned during the interview, the poorer the worker's performance became and the lower he rated the company's appraisal system. In part this tendency to focus on negative characteristics seems to stem from a general lack of daily feedback. Rather than pass problems along as they occur, managers often store them up over a period of time and then unload the entire list during the appraisal. A day-to-day system of feedback would serve to minimize this sort of occurrence and thus avoid some of the tensions of the appraisal situation.

A second misuse of the appraisal interview, Davis reports, is the manager's tendency to "sell" the employee on his need for improvement. This tendency ignores the fundamental differences between appraisal and sales interviews. In the latter, the buyer has the security of knowing that he ultimately will make the final decision, so he feels free to express his true feelings and has the power to say no. The individual being appraised has none of these benefits; the interviewer possesses the power, controls the situation, and has the ability to make final decisions. While the interviewee may go through the motions of "buying" the interviewer's suggestions the sales approach to appraisal is based upon inaccurate assumptions about the situation and typically is doomed to failure.

Procedures

Planning: Having seen the types of strategies to be avoided, we turn now to techniques for effective appraisal interviewing. When planning the interview, it often is useful to develop an outline of topic which the interview is to cover. According to Kindall and Gatza, a five-step structure should be employed:

1. agreement concerning job content and the relative importance of the duties the employee performs
2. establishment of performance targets
3. discussion of the target programme
4. establishment of checkpoints for progress evaluation
5. discussion of the employee's efforts to meet target previously established.

While this approach, *management by objectives,* applies to an ongoing evaluation process that may involve a series of interviews the basic structure may serve a framework for a single appraisal.

Beginning: Because the appraisal interview usually produces tension in the interviewee, it seems best to avoid initial small talk. As Kindall and Gatza indicate, one useful beginning is to reach agreement concerning the duties expected of the worker and how performance on those duties is to be measured. These matters should not be dictated by the manager to the interviewee; rather they should be arrived at cooperatively with input from both participants.

When agreement on these matters has been achieved, the interview should progress to the interviewee's performance record, considering specifically how well her work measures up to the established guidelines. Here the interviewee is presented with whatever information the manager has concerning her performance and is given the opportunity to respond with whatever comments, explanations, defenses, or questions she may have. If the threat present in the situation seems to hinder the employee's responses, the interviewer should ask for them. The function of this portion of the interview is not only to provide the interviewee with information concerning management's judgments of her performance but to allow the employee to react to that information, to assess its fairness and accuracy, and to explain any factors which may underlie the performance figures.

Since the ultimate goal of the appraisal interview is to improve future performance, most of the interviewer's attention should be devoted to finding methods for improvement. While we might be tempted simply to dictate those methods, the best results are obtained by asking the interviewee two questions: What do you think you can do to improve? And what can we do to help? These questions serve several important functions. First, they demonstrate that management respects the worker's intellect and recognizes his ability to make decisions for himself. Second, they provide the worker with an opportunity to determine his own future behaviours and to help establish guidelines by which his performances will be judged. Coch and French found that when employees are allowed to participate in policy-making they show high satisfaction with and commitment to the decisions made. Finally, these questions demonstrate that management is genuinely interested in the employee's progress and in helping him attain it. The employee is given a chance to air whatever grievances he may have, to present any suggestions which may have occurred to him, and generally to engage in some upward communication.

Perhaps the most difficult aspect of the appraisal interview lies not in considering job-related performance but in dealing with the interviewee's interpersonal relationships. Occasionally a worker may not get along well with her co-workers or may not respond well to her boss. Complaints may have been lodged against her by others, or she may have been observed violating company policies. Whatever the situation, these matters are even more threatening than job performance issues, for they focus on the person herself, not just her work. Such matters should be handled directly, objectively, and with whatever evidence is available to support the complaint and minimized the rationalization that "somebody's out to get me" or "that's just somebody' opinion." These matters should be considered only as they affect job performance; other matters of a personal nature belong in a counselling interview. As with matters concerning performance, the interview's input should be sought; best results are obtained if she is able to devise and implement a solution of her own.

Closing: Like other interview forms, the appraisal interview should be closed on a positive note with an emphasis on future performance. The interviewer should express optimism about the employee's future performance, indicate a willingness to meet again with the employee whenever he wishes, provide him with copies of any written performance evaluations available, and give him the opportunity to suggest changes in any factual matters he believes incorrect. Most important, no matter how bad the appraisal has been, the interview should end positively. The interviewer should show that she or he values the employee as a person, feels positively toward him, and is willing to aid in promoting future improvements.

The key to successful appraisal interviewing seems to be the ability to avoid producing defensive reactions on the part of the employee while at the same time providing an accurate assessment of performance. By allowing a maximum of participation by the interviewee, by demonstrating the organization's interest in the employee's achievement, and by showing her or his own concern for the employee's well-being, the interviewer can minimize threat and maximize motivation to improve. By treating appraisal as a daily responsibility and by providing feedback frequently rather than annually, the organization can satisfy the workers' desire for feedback, aid them in improving their performance, and prevent the actual interview from being a traumatic experience.

The Disciplinary Interview

Closely related to the appraisal interview is the interview in which disciplinary action is taken. Occasions arise in which management must attempt to correct a behaviour or an attitude of a worker; common instances involve habitual tardiness, time wasting, improper work procedures, or violation of organization policies. The disciplinary interview is designed first to determine the facts underlying the case and then to produce whatever reforms are needed.

Procedures

Beginning: The interviewer should immediately inform the employee of the situation. Although the employee probably has some idea about why she has been summoned for a conference, doubts may still remain that should be removed as quickly and objectively as possible. The interviewee then should be given an opportunity to explain the situation as she views it, for she may be able to provide information that completely changes the interviewer's perceptions of the problem. Implicit in this is a willingness on the part of the interviewer to listen and to be flexible. Often this is not easily achieved. A disciplinary interview usually is surrounded by a climate of anger and frustration, with either or both of the participants feeling hostile or upset. This climate in turn creates the danger that the interview will become a confrontation in which the interviewer becomes the prosecutor and the employee the defendant or in which the interviewer delivers a sermon demanding that the employee mend her ways or get out. To overcome these tendencies, both participants should resolve to listen and maintain and open mind.

Questioning: As in the counselling interview, our approach can range from extremely non-directive to extremely directive. If threats and ultimatums seem the only viable methods, we must use them and be willing to carry them out. If a gentle application of probing questions can be used to lead the interviewee to self-reform, the non-directive approach is preferable. It allows participation by the employee, makes his opinion seem valued by the company, and increases his commitment to reform measures ultimately agreed upon. But only through a suspension of anger and application of careful listening can this method be effective.

Perhaps the extreme form of disciplinary interview is the one in which the employee is to be fired. If such is the case, this should be clearly stated early in the interview. Typically the action will come as no surprise to the interviewee; he will have been warned before, perhaps in similar disciplinary interviews. As interviews we probably would feel some compulsion to dwell upon any positive characteristics of the employee we can conjure up in an effort to make him feel better. Such efforts usually are wasted; all he wants is to get the information he needs and get out. We therefore should be prepared to explain the organization's termination procedures with regard to such matters as insurance plans and retirement benefits. The employee may ask whether the company will references for him to aid in securing a new job. We should provide an honest answer, telling what we think can be said on his behalf. Situations such as these are unpleasant for both parties and should not be unnecessarily prolonged.

Closing. If the employee has not been fired, clear indication should be given at the end of the interview concerning her situation. If some action is to be taken, such as suspension, demotion, or a pay cut, she should be told about it. Moreover, if the employee has courses of action available to her, such as implementing an appeal's procedure, that too should be described. Most important, it should be made clear to the employee what changes are expected in her behaviour and, perhaps, what consequences will follow should those changes not be made. The ultimate goal of the disciplinary interview is not to discipline but to produce behavioural improvements. Those improvements occur only when the worker knows exactly what she is expected to do.

Although disciplinary interviews usually occur in emotionally changed situations, emotions must be kept out of the interview as much as possible. If you are upset or angry, wait until some later time before speaking with the employee. When the interview takes place, suspend judgment and be willing to listen carefully to what she has to say—it may change your entire perception of the situation. Take a flexible approach to each interview; while organizational rules may seem clear, specific situations may dictate different sorts of enforcement. Finally, deal with the employee only on the job level—do not attack her as a person. Becoming personal in your criticism can only engender hostility and will do little to change a worker's behaviour.

The Persuasive Interview

The persuasive interview is in many ways the most difficult to conduct successfully. This form most often occurs on sales situations that involve used car salesmen, encyclopaedia vendors, retail store clerks, real estate agent, and the like. But persuasive interviewing is by no means limited to the sales context; any one-to-one situation in which one member wants to produce a change in the other involves persuasion. The purpose of the persuasive interview, then, is to change the interviewee's attitudes, values, or behaviours.

Many excellent works, such as that by Cronkhite, explore the process of persuasion, and we shall not attempt to duplicate their efforts. Rather, we shall simply review some of the persuasive influences which operate in interviews.

Procedures

Planning: The first step in the preparation of a persuasive interview is an analysis of the individual to be persuaded. Typically this analysis must be done quickly and on the basis of relatively superficial characteristics. Research suggests, however, that even these characteristic can provide clues about the individual's persuasibility. Investigations of the relationship between sex and persuasibility have found that women are more interested in humanitarian issues than are men, are more susceptible to social pressure, and are more easily persuaded. Educational attainment, often indicated by patterns of dress, also seems related to persuasibility. Well-educated individuals have relatively more stable attitudes, but they too can be persuaded through provision of new information. Studies of age and persuasibility have shown that willingness to take risks decreases with age and that this decrease produces inflexibility in buying habits, living style, and social and political attitudes. Older people tend to have more fixed religious beliefs and typically are less inclined and less able to evaluate complex persuasive appeals. Finally, studieds of persuasibility and socio-economic status have shown people of higher status to be more conservative and resistant to persuasive appeals. Through a quick evaluation of the individual's characteristic, then we can make some judgments about the types of appeals which might persuade her or him.

Beginning: The initial stage of the persuasive interview is the moment at which persuader and persuadee first meet. Burstein says this moment, for the interviewer, is the "point when his appearance, demeanour, and what he says will determine if he will have an opportunity to make an adequate presentation." Thus our concern here shall be the verbal strategies employed in the encounter. Hatfield suggests two approaches which salespersons might adopt. The first, used when the customer seems not to be interested in a specific item, he terms the *service* approach, which is typified by the May I help you? opening. This approach, however, may convey disinterest on the part of the salesperson and tends to elicit a No, I'm just looking response, which stifles further interaction. To minimize these dangers, Hatfield suggests that somewhat unorthodox service openings be employed—such as, Is anyone helping you? or Are you finding what you need? On the other hand, the salesperson may employ the *merchandise* approach, in which some mention is made of the merchandise being examined by the customer. We might begin by observing that, Pontiacs of that year are pretty hard to find, but this one's in great shape. Want to take it for a ride?- thus demonstrating interest on our part, providing information about the product, and giving impetus to further conversation. If the customer is interested in a specific item, the merchandise approach seems best; if she or he seems to be merely wandering around, a "service" opening may be more effective.

Persuading: While each interview is unique and requires custom-designed strategies, some general strategy patterns applicable to all persuasive situations can be identified. One frequently successful approach involves the establishment of common ground between you and the persuadee, that, finding the beliefs and attitudes you have in common and using these as points from which other disagreements and conflicts might be resolved. Stewart and Cash describe three common-ground strategies: *Yes—but*, where the persuader begins the interview in areas of agreement and gradually moves to areas of conflict; *yes-yes*, where a series of agreements or yes answers is used to build a habitual response which in turn produces more favourable reactions when controversial issues are reached; and *implicative*, where the interviewer uses several agreements to imply a conclusion which, if stated explicitly, might be rejected by the persuadee. This last method requires considerable skill, however, for the persuadee may miss the implication and see no point to the questioning. It should therefore be used only after we have become skilled in interviewing—or when we are desperate because nothing else has worked.

Another persuasive strategy takes into account the order in which arguments in support of your position are presented. Should your stronger arguments be presented first, saved for last, or sandwiched between lesser arguments? Researchers have termed these patterns the anticlimax, climax, and pyramidal orders, respectively. Many studies have investigated the effectiveness of each order. Lund, Jersild, and Hovland found support for the anticlimax order. Sponberg Gilkinson et al. and Gulley and Berlo supported the climax sequence. No one has found an advantage in placing the strongest arguments in the middle of the message. While evidence seems equally divided between the climax and anticlimax orders, then, the only certainty is that strong arguments should not be placed in the middle of the message.

Some miscellaneous strategies also seem useful in the persuasive situation. Should we present only our side of the issue, or should we present both sides, refuting the arguments the other side holds? Studies summarized by Bettinghaus suggest that two-sided presentations are more effective with well-educated persuadees, people who initially disagree with your position, and people who are likely to receive later messages opposing your views. On the other hand, one-sided appeals are more effective when the receiver already agrees with you and is not likely to be exposed to later opposing messages. Should we employ appeals to fear in an effort to persuade people by "scaring hell out of them?" If the interviewee thinks you trustworthy, and if the topic is important to her or him, fear appeals usually are effective. To what extent should we use evidence or supporting materials to document our arguments? If the receiver thinks us untrustworthy, is well-educated or intelligent, or already is familiar with the evidence, we should present it. Should humour be used to enhance out appeals? Studies to date of the effect of humour have shown no appreciable gain in persuasive effect produced by its inclusion. However, a recent investigation discovered that a humorous source was rated more trustworthy than a serious one, suggesting that inclusion of humour might be helpful if the receiver perceives you to relatively untrustworthy. Final determination of the role of humour awaits further research.

A last category of persuasive strategies demands inclusion not because we advocate their use but because you ought to be protected from individuals who use them. *Propaganda* devices involve deception and emotionalism rather than sound, rational argument. As miller puts it, "They make us believe and do something we would not believe or do if we thought about it calmly, dispassionately."

Communication concepts

The total field of communication research and opinion embraces work in electronic, psychology, languages, and in a dozen other subjects. This chapter is concerned with one aspect from the field of communication systems—the transmission of ideas and information from one person to another.

Human communication is used to exchange information and opinion, demonstrate and improve status, and to express emotions. In industrial settings three important communication functions occur, gathering information for decision-making, passing decisions on, and attempting to change attitudes.

Some general concepts

Perhaps the commonest of the media used is language. In itself language brings benefits in that it can help clarify thought. A young child replied to her father who had scolded her for 'speaking out of turn'—'But Daddy, how can I watch what I'm saying until I've seen what I've said?

This difficulty in visualizing words, objects, phrases, etc., diminishes as an individual's vocabulary increases. Miller describes experiments which demonstrate that colours become more distinguishable as they are given names. Similarly, Arabs have only one word, tilage, for the English equivalents of snow, ice, and frost, while Eskimoes have five words for snow alone, each one describing a slightly different kind of snow, recognizable to Eskimoes but not to English-speakers. The transmission of concepts is also more difficult to explain when a language has a limited vocabulary. While in New Guinea one was amused to read the pidgin English translation beneath the message 'high voltage,. It read roughly as follows: 'sipos man e holdim disfela, disfela bagarap man, em e dai finis'.

Gestures also can create communication problems. To primitive people a handshake may mean 'I carry no weapons, my hand is open, and not clenched to strike you'. Between friends or politicians, however, the handshake can mean vastly different things. The meaning attached to this gesture will depend on the frame of reference of the person concerned. Not only can the significance of gestures vary with the degree of civilization but also with the type of culture—Arabs speak in a loud voice when sincere; to them a soft voice indicates weakness and deviousness.

In this brief introduction to the concept of 'noise' in the communication process it may be dangerous to draw the conclusion from the examples above that gestures are more capable of being misunderstood than words. The nineteenth- century politician Disraeli said: "Words are just vessels for me to pour meaning into.' Similarly, the expression 'I think they got the message' often implies that the speaker has not been direct in expressing his feelings but instead has purposely pursued a roundabout method to put over his point.

Practising industrialists have no doubt of the importance of communication in organizations. Fayol placed 'unity of direction' in his seven management principles while Barnard, in his popular book *The Functions of the Executive,* saw 'maintenance of organization communication' top of his list of three basic executive functions. Perhaps Bavelas and Barrett expressed this most eloquently when they wrote: 'It is not a secondary or derived aspect of organization—rather it is the essence of organizational activity and is the basic process out of which all other functions derive'.

Growth of public interest

Historically, the need for effective communication in management has been noted since the turn of the century, but few specific works on industrial communication occurred before the forties. One of the first comprehensive books on the subject, published in 1949, had a bibliography of 103 titles with only two references dated before 1940.

The subsequent growth of interest in organization communication can be attributed to:

(1) the marked increase in the size of companies and their international growth since World War I;

(2) the continued specialization of occupations and the resultant demands for co-ordination;

(3) the growth of trade union power and its requirements for information about all matters affecting its member's work or terms of employment with the result that explanations are being seen as a right and authoritarian instructions are being rejected;

(4) the growth of national communication networks, forcing co-ordination in and between firms;

(5) the pressures for increasing occupational mobility which cause the recruit to be heavily dependent on the organization's communi-cation system if he is to 'learn the ropes' as soon as possible;

(6) the 'information revolution'—through the discoveries and use of automatic information storage and retrieval, the automation of information search and analysis, instant physical transmission of information, semi-automatic planning, and decision-making etc.;

(7) the belief that all of these trends seem likely to continue.

The problems outlined

This growth of interest in communication has not been due solely to man's inherent curiosity, but also because ineffective communication has been seen as major industrial problem.

One poll of 650 British works managers put the following problems in their 'top five'.

(a) insufficient cost information to indicate the best areas for improvement in productivity;

(b) frustration at all managerial levels due to lack of clearly defined spheres of delegated responsibilities;

(c) poor communication—upwards and downwards.

Many industrialists define the manager as a person who gets his work done through others, a job which requires clear instructions passed down, and the ability to obtain the details of the results created. These same men would agree that this ideal state seldom occurs. Some refer to the lack of common awareness of goals, others see the head of an organization nestling on a pyramid of communication barriers, many of which are intended to insulate one level from another, while sociologist Dalton refers to a 'fog of uncertainty' which characterizes executive work.

Nor do these problems seem restricted to industry alone. The following comments from a study of American nurses resemble those of many industrial writers:

> A prime factor in any organizational scheme is ease and accuracy of communication both vertically and horizontally. Nursing service, traditionally rigidly disciplined and authoritarian, appears in the observed situation to provide little opportunity or communication except for strictly specified types of information in strictly specified channels and in strictly specified fashion. Not only are such channels cumbersome but they are often insufficient. Nurses apparently find it difficult to secure full information about drugs or medications that may be prescribed. Information placed on the charts is often reduced to a minimum set of hieroglyphics, often illegible, standardized for routine custodial care. The development of personalized nursing plans individual patients would seem to demand that nurses have adequate and pertinent information from appropriate sources. In the situation observed, there appeared to be little communication between units, except via a 'grape-vine' route. It was felt that certain aspects of such communication problems may be related to morale level and job satisfaction.

In the broadest sense, every difficulty encountered within an organization contains some ingredient of distorted, insufficient, or poorly timed information exchange. Communication problems can be the cause and effect of operational or administrative failures, e.g. mistrust can lead to bad communication which in turn intensifies the mistrust.

Having established a frame of reference about the problem, we can proceed to examine research carried out in attempts to measure the extent of these communication gaps.

In a study of two factories, 25 per cent and 66 per cent respectively of the labour force did not understand the calculation of their bonus awards. The workers in the less well-informed factory were consistently more hostile to the incentive scheme and *produced less.* Another shop-floor communication study found that among the work people studied:

35 per cent worried over a lack of clarity about scope and responsibilities;

29 per cent worried over the ambiguity of the expectations of other departments;

38 per cent worried over the lack of adequate information for their job and future prospects.

The research suggests that this feeling of a lack of downward communication might lead to withholding of upward communication.

Nor are white-collar workers immune; in an assurance office 20 per cent of the employees requiring a precise understanding of the operating instructions displayed varying degrees of misunderstanding of the instructional memorandum.

Even among managers the same gaps occur. Maier studied fifty-eight superior-subordinate pairs to assess their degree of agreement over the details of the subordinate's tasks. The results showed that in many ways the communication gaps among managers were often considerably wider than with the more routine positions they controlled. Only on the topic of job duties did the pairs show more agreement than disagreement. More typically, on the important area of the subordinates' work problems, the pattern was reversed. These results occurred despite the fact that all four companies involved had written job descriptions and that two of the companies had performance appraisal programmes. These results indicate that communication failures are not limited to periods of major organizational change but can be an everyday occurrence. Furthermore, these failures seem to occur at all levels of the organization and in a variety of contexts.

Distance

One major cause of these breakdowns is the underestimation of the effects of technical limitations on communication. Research in the forties by Allport and Postman considering distance in terms of the number of links involved in a communication act, proved the commonly held belief that rumours tend to become more inaccurate as the number of links increases—each link liable to produce some distortion. Soon after, Zipf went on to show that physical distance can also reduce the quantity of communication between two locations. He found that the number of long-distance telephone calls between pairs of cities was directly proportional to their populations but inversely proportional to the distance between them. Although cost is a likely factor, it seems reasonable to assume that the extra time involved in connecting distant callers is another factor reducing communication quantity over longer distances. The work of Zipf was confirmed and extended by Cavanaugh in the fifties. Replacing the concept of quantity of communication by rate of interaction, Cavanaugh extended Zipf's hypothesis to cover human transportation.

All of these factors, demonstrated in such a wide variety of contexts, would seem to be relevant in planning the layout of a factory or business premises and in establishing a chain of command—especially in an overseas operation. As Peter Drucker puts it: 'Every additional administrative level makes the attainment of common direction and mutual understanding more difficult. Every additional level distorts objectives and misdirects attention. Every link in the chain sets up additional stresses, and creates one more source of inertia, friction and slack.'

Although many managers would agree with this statement, few companies have gone to the lengths of IBM when they reduced the number of levels in all of their units in the forties. Their grievance procedure, for example, was speeded up by recognizing only three divisions-man, manager, management. The occasional dispute not settled at the man-manager level went straight to the man-board level for settlement. Other see the effects of the problem as being concentrated at the top of an organisation. The top executives have the greatest amount of decision-making power and hence a greater need for information. There may be a tendency for the message flow to them to get increasingly heavy, while they have proportionally less time available to digest the information. In these circumstances they may soon come to depend on briefed-down communication usually interpreted by their assistants. Because of their very position, many chief executives may be totally insulated from what is actually going on. Though most directors like to think of a pyramid of communication centres beneath them, labyrinth of communication barriers might be a more apt description.

Speed

An interesting case in the diffusion of information was the work of the sociologist Dodd, who had leaflets randomly introduced into isolated communities by air-drops. In a series of studies the researcher 'planted' information of various kinds and then traced the speed and range of transmission with a corps of on-the-spot interviewers.

His studies considered the effects of the size of the community; the *potency* of messages; the *time* factor; the *space* factor and the *stimulation* factor. This last factor is of considerable relevance to politicians and managers alike. In Britain, for example, samples of the population taken over a 2-year period showed little increased understanding of the term 'productivity agreements' despite its frequent occurrence on the news media as one of the keys to Britain's economic recovery.

Other studies have shown the effects on industrial relations when communication is delayed. In one factory it was found that management-union agreements were taking an average of 2.8 days to reach the shop floor via union channels but 12.7 days via formal management lines. Many of the first-line supervisors resented this type of information coming to them from their workers rather than their superiors. Typically, workers complained about delays in adjusting pay and working conditions following national agreements. The unions quickly let them know, but the foremen had to wait for their managerial channels to advise them before authorizing increased rates, improved conditions, etc. What little research has been done seems to indicate that speed and accuracy in communication are complementary—as that competent general the Duke of Wellington demanded of his commanders: "Do the business of the day in the day."

Communication frequency

While frequent communication may not *cause* better leadership behavior, good leadership behaviour and frequent communication seem to be associated. A person who is communicating with another is receiving recognition, and his sense of well-being may be enhanced.

As one of the managers in a discussion on the context said: "Those two are just a couple of empire builders—they know all calls are supposed to come through here so that we can keep tabs on everything. But no, they keep giving out their office number. I wish they'd give out their home numbers. There's no empire building at night-Oh, no-we get all the calls then of course!'

One of the two supervisors mentioned above said, after putting the telephone down, 'People are always phoning up about this or that. They see this office as the centre of operations.'

A subordinate's well-being may not be enhanced, however, if he feels that the wall around his boss's office is a mile high. Presumably this is one problem which open-plan areas try to reduce by removing the physical barriers of walls. It is interesting to note here that a common complaint made against open-plan factories is that *too much* communication occurs. In this study only one firm had complete open planning, and their frequency of communication was the lowest of all the firms studied-not the highest as might have been predicted.

Other writers think it is a common mistake to imagine that all organizational ailments can be cured by large doses of official communication. Many well-publicized 'çommunication improvement' and 'management information' programmes are ineffective because they overload the formal system. It would seem that effective organizational functioning depends not upon a maximum but on an optimum of information exchange. The communication studies mentioned already amply illustrate that once a hierarchy of virtually any kind comes into existence, information exchange is no longer 'free' but restricted, shaped, and controlled. The moment a task is delegated the administrator is to some extent insulated from some important aspects of that task. The point is that he not only is insulated but *should be*. Professor Jaques, who did some highly praised work with the Glacier Metal Company, emphasizes that certain barriers to communication frequency are actually necessary if an organization is to get its business done. He refers to 'adaptive segregation' as the automatic process by which barriers are set up, more or less by mutual consent, by sections or levels of a company to keep channels clear for crucial information.

Despite these barriers it was reported of one top executive: "In the sheer volume of all activities demanded of him, verbal interaction is the number one form of contact, consuming upward of 80 per cent of all the executives' time... only 12 times in 35 days of observation was this chief executive able to work undisturbed alone in his office during intervals of *23 minutes or longer*.

This seems to be general in industry as identical findings have been reported in America, Sweden, and Britain. From a similar study, in which managers kept a detailed log of their activities over a period of several weeks, Tom Burns, Professor of Sociology at Edinburgh University, writes:

> ....more important is the picture—the moving picture-such studies give of the management system seen as a communication network. The production of this information itself yields comparative data of considerable interest. For the seven manufacturing concerns, to take one instance, the proportion of all management time spent in spoken communication ran as follows:
>
> 80-71-68-56-55-44-42 per cent

> The order is significant. The firms are arranged from left to right also in terms of their... environmental change. Moreover, the direction of communication changes: in the first firm slightly more than half the communication was lateral, i.e. with colleagues and this proportion dropped until, in the seventh firm, virtually all communication was vertical.

Media

In Western society large numbers of people spend a considerable part of their waking hours in organizations of one sort or another. It is not surprising, therefore, to discover that their main communication media tend to be the same inside or outside the organization, namely speech, writing, gesture, and appearance. Communication may be described as unsuccessful when the received message does not match the transmitted message. As many of the failures have been discovered in the 'coding' and 'decoding' processes, the media involved have come under careful scrutiny.

One might imagine that language—a system of symbols formalized through education, dictionaries, etc., could be expected to transmit messages accurately without any extra organizational help. Many people would not subscribe to this belief and suggest that benefits would be gained by clarifying company terminology through the media of 'terminology dictionaries. Others, however, warn against undue reliance on the written word in the form of bulletins, booklets, magazines, etc., in that they can be looked upon a substitute for face-to-face communication and not as they should be—an aid.

Another difficulty is that more than one media may be used at the same time. Depending on their interpretation, they can reinforce or contradict each other. Consider an applicant at a job interview. If he is telling of his keenness to obtain the opposition but at the same time looks bored, yawns frequently and sports a two-day stubble, then the interviewer may find it difficult to reconcile the conflicting symbols. The whole area of communication through gesture or appearance is fraught with possible errors. Such imprecise meanings exist that perceptual factors can play a large part in the assessment of meaning. These weaknesses can be compounded since gestures and the use of more than one media are often used to create uncertainty deliberately.

Actions themselves are often looked upon as a method of communication. The managing director who informs all and sundry that foremen are his key managers may have difficulty in having his beliefs accepted by the foremen themselves. If they do their paper work at a space temporarily cleared on an oily work-bench while he has a large office, or if they have to walk through a muddy car park in the rain while he is driven past in a chauffeured Rolls-Royce, the credibility gap may be difficult to span.

The following quote from a manager demonstrates this: Well, the director told me that my project was at the top of his list of priorities. After another few weeks of frustration and no action I went back to remind him. "Yes," he said, "your project is still at the top of my list—but the list isn't necessarily in order."

Organizational research into the media of communication has tended to concentrate on the merits and drawbacks of written and spoken messages. Baker and his colleagues of Princeton University found low reader interest in the employee's handbook of the company they studied, and Professor Maier, in the study mentioned earlier, found that written job descriptions did not affect the degree of agreement over job details between superior-subordinate managers, and that firms without this system were rated as highly as firms with it. In general, interest in company magazines increases as the style becomes more informal. Where the company literature is stiff, precise, and full of company jargon, employees prefer to obtain their information from personal contacts.

Many managers recognize these factors although it may be argued that few apply them. In one survey of 100 company presidents, 98 thought the spoken word at least as important as the written word and 40 felt that it was more important. On the other hand, Higgin and Jessop, in a study of the British building industry, pointed out some of the difficulties which resulted from the use of informal spoken communication. They found that many vital pieces of information were committed to memory or the backs of cigarette packets, and that sometimes detail became blurred. These snippets of research, taken in isolation, may seem to contradict each other. Company presidents favour speech as opposed to writing, while the building industry apparently suffers from the use of the same media. Common sense indicates that there is, in fact, no conflict. It is quite obvious that top-grade executives ensure that *important* information is committed to paper but still use speech more often than memos, etc.

Apparently conflicting research results are not always so easy to reconcile, and a general criticism which can be levelled at earlier work of research is that the approach to communication problems has been too narrow.

Often studies have involved only two or three factors in assumed isolation, and the conclusions reached have been used to provide 'simple' solutions with 'universal' applications. These 'formulae' for effective communication have stimulated the current interest in lucid writing techniques, courses in public speaking, visual aids, etc., each advertised as *the* answer to communication breakdowns.

With this in mind, some of the major drawbacks to written instructions can be given:

(1) Policies are often secret and may fall into the wrong hands.

(2) They cannot be all-embracing, and, as times change, the policies can become outdated and even counter-productive.

(3) Over a period of time a mass of 'red tape' may emerge.

(4) One circulated instruction does not take into account the reading ability of the individual readers.

(5) Feedback is more difficult and delayed.

By contrast the major benefits of written communication are:

(1) Authoritativeness.

(2) Accuracy-through being checkable.

(3) Permanence.

(4) Coverage-communications can be reproduced exactly and quickly.

(5) Retention rate is high.

Before decisions are made as to which method of communication should be used in certain circumstances, the comprehensibility of the terminology to be used should be gauged. One such study involved 478 managers from various levels and departments of Scottish industry. Among these executives only 9.6 per cent of the specialist words and phrases commonly used in industry were satisfactorily understood. A further 14.4 per cent were partly understood, 34.9 per cent were wrongly understood, and 41.1 per cent were not known. In terms of levels, senior management knew more financial and quality control terms than other levels; middle management were marginally more knowledgeable in the field of work measurement. Supervisory management showed the worst all-round knowledge, being inferior to that of non-managerial specialists in various fields.

Complicating this picture even more are the results of a study by occupational psychologist Gregson in which he found that departmental loyalties affected the use of communication media. A large transport office contained both a service and a technical section, and had a comprehensive information board devised, installed, and maintained by the service section. Its use by the employees was not related to its visibility alone but also to the degree to which staff felt allegiance to the board, and this in turn varied according to the section for which they worked. A man in the service section working far away from the information board would use it more than a technical section man working close to it. The former seeing the board as a useful tool devised by his section—the other seeing the board as another example of the service section trying to 'muscle into' their work. Having examined some of the basic benefits and drawbacks of the main communication methods and the extent of the problem, we can proceed to look at ways of 'getting message across'—improving the transmission and reception of communication. Although the pages which follow are generally thought to concern one person trying to improve his communication with a group of people, e.g. in a public speech, the comments are equally applicable when communicating to one person only.

Audience identification

Perhaps the first step in organizing one's communication is to 'identify one's audience—the receivers. To take an extreme example there would seem little point in attempting to entertain a 5-year-old child by discussing quantum mechanics. Research by the BBC has confirmed that an intelligent, interested audience will grasp more of the topic being communicated than a less intelligent, bored one. Many industrial writers also realize the importance of knowing the intelligence, interests, attitudes, and technical jargon of an intended audience. Few, however, have gone as far as suggesting sample interviewing' as a means of gaining this knowledge. Nevertheless, it seems self-evident that the amount of effort applied in 'type-casting' an audience should depend, to some degree, on the importance of the intended message. Even with the least important message, however, it would seem rewarding to consider the target audience. Even the least important communication has to be received to avoid a complete waste of effort.

Pitch of communication

Once an audience has been identified, a further factor in successful communication is to pitch the communication in order to maximize its acceptability to the receiver. The credibility of the source of information has been shown to be important. Hovland and Weiss demonstrated early in the fifties how a one-sided presentation, supposedly from a communist source, was rejected by more of a sample audience than the same one-sided presentation supposedly from a non-communist source. An over-emphasis of fear-raising actors in propaganda likewise increases chances of the message being rejected, e.g. an excessive emphasis on the effects of lung cancer can cause heavy smokers to disbelieve that smoking and lung cancer are related.

Considerable work has been done in establishing means of measuring the levels of difficulty in understanding communication. From the early work of Carrol in 1938, who demonstrated that intelligence, age, and education were the principal factors involved in assessing vocabulary range, practical ways of gauging the ease of understanding of individual communications have been suggested, e.g. readability scales. If a person attempting to communicate has not determined what he wants to say, there is little possibility that anyone else will be able to understand his message without some difficulty. The clearest communicators are those who develop a sensitivity to both the viewpoint and the level of comprehension of their audience. Words must be pitched at the correct level and with the right amount of detail to avoid misunderstandings.

There is evidence that little use is made of the readability scales mentioned above. British Government booklets on prices and income policies, using these scales, were 'very difficult' and 'dull'. This may be a cause of the comparatively low levels of understanding Hilde Behrend and her colleagues at the Edinburgh Business School found with such terms as 'productivity bargain'.

For the much-pressed manager with little time to spare, a simple test of his 'readability' is the degree to which his communication is listened to or read. Many a company bulletin goes quickly to the waste-paper bin—the occasional retrieval may show why it was not read and what the manager should avoid in his communication unless he wants his memos to finish in a bin instead of a file. The manager should assess the degree of interest he can arouse in his audience and the extent to which he gets his message across.

From the foregoing it will be apparent that the communicating manager cannot rely upon the simple belief that factual communication will be instantly accepted by the receiver. The concept of matching the communication with the intended audience has had considerable 'lip service' paid to it in industry, but many company magazine failures have been credited to such mismatches. Colby and Tiffin describe one in which they measured the reading ability of industrial supervisors and related this to their age and educational level, while others have delineated the interests of various target audiences. This type of research is providing a base from which communicators, obtaining average details on age, education, interests, etc., from personnel records, can make more scientific attempts to structure their communication acts especially when communicating to large groups of employees. In general, however, company magazines and bulletins leave much to be desired. In an analysis of 69 articles selected at random from 13 representative employee papers, over half (37) were on a readability level of difficult to 'very difficult'—levels which are above the capacity of 67-95 per cent of the adult population. In a similar study a survey of 25 management and 25 union publications for employees showed that, on average, they were pitched at a level of understanding for employees with high school or college education. In terms of human interest, the majority of both company magazines and union newspapers were only 'mildly interesting' or even 'dull'. The authors conclude that both management and union editors alike need to work strenuously towards language simplification. Recent studies indicate that this advice has yet to be taken in Britain.

Identifying the communicator

Finally, it is worth re-emphasizing that the communication act is a two-way process. Not only does a speaker attempt to identify his audience, but the audience tries to identify the speaker through his communication. As the Elizabethan poet and dramatist Ben Jonson wrote; 'language must shews a man; Speak that I may see thee.' Little research has been undertaken in industry into this factor although considerable 'armchair psychology' may be called into play, when a lunch-time chat is commenced with 'I wonder what the boss really meant when he said....." After taking a short look in the next two chapters at the method used to measure the factors affecting managerial communication and the backgrounds of managers involved in the study, we can take the basic ideas of this chapter into the every-day life of the manager. The findings of a study can only be as good as the methods used and might only succeed with management team of similar background.

Interpersonal communication

Industrial psychologist Argyris, in writing about personality, sees seven basic needs in man. Two of these needs, especially relevant to industrial communication are:

(a) to develop from being in a subordinate position in the family and society to aspiring to occupy an equal and/or superior position relative to one's fellow men;

(b) to develop from a state of dependence upon others to relative independence.

In laboratory and industrial research these needs have been interpreted as aspirations towards two main goals—higher status and greater power. The difficulties in separating these ambitions may be due to the fact that they often go hand in hand—especially in industry. However, for the purpose of this book it may be useful to define the terms as used in the text. Status is looked upon as a system of ranking people by some quality, real or perceived, while power is the ability, real or perceived, to affect the lives of others.

Status

Thibaut and Kelley have both clearly demonstrated the adverse effects on group cohesiveness of high achievement desires. In Kellly's study, students took part in laboratory group tasks with artificial status differentials imposed, while in Thibaut's research, boys played games under similar status differentials. Strong individual achievement hopes were found to reduce group cohesiveness in both experiments. Also noticed was the fact that those individuals who wished to move upward in these artificial hierarchies tended to communicate in that direction. These studies and many others all confirm the following conclusions.

Upward communication is likely to contain much information which is irrelevant to the job in hand, and in terms of total volume is likely to be greater from 'lows' to 'highs' than the reverse. Members of low-status groups refrain from expressing pent-up aggressions towards high-status individuals. Similarly, information critical of persons in higher level positions is restricted. Low-status subjects, given no opportunity to move upward, communicate more freely than low-status subjects who have this opportunity. High-status members who are vulnerable to demotion also restrict communication, e.g. regarding 'confusion on the job' and 'negative attitudes about their own job'. In general the intention of the experimental subjects seems to be to retain or improve status, the lowering of status being thought of as highly undesirable. The selective screening of information described above is seen by these researchers as a 'psychological substitute' for actual movement upward on the part of aspiring low-status members.

In industrial pyramids these effects can be translated as a lack of open relationships. Managers become reluctant to upset or contradict their superiors by giving them unpleasant facts—there can be a tendency to keep one's head down, a reluctance to experiment, to take risks, and even to make effective decisions. In many firms more or less specific forms of behaviour become prescribed for the contacts between persons at different levels on the ladder of status. The superior may call his subordinate by his first name, but the junior shows deference in responding by addressing the superior more formally. Even after working hours the boss's wife may use the subordinate's wife's Christian name while she may not reply with a first name unless invited to. The degree of formalization of behaviour patterns varies between organizations. Senior managers might be surprised if their juniors stood to attention when they entered the room, although in the Army this is the norm. Nevertheless, the 'captains' of industry are accustomed to a considerable amount of preferential treatment—the chauffeured car, the parking spot nearest the entrance foyer, the sharpened pencils, and the percolating coffee—to name but a few examples.

As already mentioned, the effects of status divisions on communication have even been shown in the artificial atmosphere of the laboratory. Similarly, Roethlisberger and Dickson showed that each job in their experiment group at Western Electric's Chicago Plant carried its own social status or significance. The group in the Bank Wiring Observation Room could be differentiated into five graduations ranging from the highest to the lowest. Whyte found similar divisions where workers at a salad station in a restaurant were accorded higher status by fellow employees than those engaged in the preparation of vegetables or fish.

From the foregoing it would seem that status differentials can occur at any level of industry. It can also be argued that the status of the job itself—its potential in arousing feelings of pride, worth, and recognition—is an important element in moulding attitudes and in gratifying psychological needs. The existing system of status stratification is itself a fundamental source of the ambition to climb the managerial ladder.

Professor Burns of Edinburgh University suggests that the dislike and rejection of subordination, especially in organic or developing working organizations, created some of the discrepancies in job descriptions he found in his detailed today. He suggests with Stalker that reductions of status differentials will improve industrial communications by breaking down some of these barriers. Status differentials can apply also to whole departments. The British Institute of Works Managers comments on a large poll of their members: 'The relationship between production, design and sales evoked considerable comment; it was suggested that production is not held in the same esteem as the others and sales are allowed too much authority.

While the status of age is a factor over which an organization has little control, it still can cause problems. Sociologist Dalton, who has worked 'undercover' in a number of plants to collect information for his popular book *Men Who Manage*, found the older line officers disliking what they regarded as instructions from the younger staff officers. These factory specialists were typically younger, better educated, and 'smoother' than the production staff. The line managers often wore overalls during their working day, whereas the staff men invariably wore suites. The younger men were regarded as 'green boys still wet behind the ears', and any sabotaging of their ideas was hailed as a great success. Conversely, the staff men regarded the operational staff as 'old fashioned stick in the mud's who would not discuss anything rationally.

Similar problems have been reported in an early Swedish study. The use of formal systems of address decor and situation of offices, and the place and company kept at lunch times, were felt to be the major causes of friction. These systems of status are just as visible in Britain.

In larger firms the elaborations of status can become quite opulent. Wen Hollywood was making *North by Northwest* they borrowed an executive's suite as it was more sumptuous than anything their props, men could design or afford, even having a large number of original paintings valued over $ 10,000 each. Firms at this level of luxury sometimes become a little self-conscious over their executive perks. Company jets may cease to carry the organization's emblem because of the possible adverse effects in the minds of shareholders and union leaders waiting at the airport for their economy flights.

Opinion is divided on the effects of status. Communication can benefit through the informal associations existing in most organizations—associations often grouped by department, status level, etc. Alternatively, Professor Scott of Salford University takes an uncommitted view and looks at status differentials both as an incentive and as a divisive factor in organizations. But even he was surprised when he overheard a canteen waitress commenting on a director's frequent company car changes: 'If he wants to swop his car that often, he's entitled to do it. Who wants to see the head of our business going around in a scruffy old car?

Professor Scott concludes that people relatively deprived of status are not always adversely affected by the system. Others go further and suggest that among managers with jobs primarily defined in terms of performance, differences in responsibilities and status may be psychologically and motivationally unimportant.

The foregoing pages indicate that the theories on the effects of status differentials are numerous and often contradictory. Some of this confusion may be due to the general use of the word status or to the confused manner in which individual people ascribe status. In industry top management has a lot of say in establishing status levels through their power to assign various grades of the visible symbols of status.

Power

The effects of desire for advancement on individual communication when status is the main variable are even more clearly seen when power differentials are substituted for prestige or status differentials. Psychologist Cohen made this substitution in a replication of Kelly's laboratory study. Group members were dependent upon those above them for advancement. Significantly fewer messages critical of those in higher power positions were passed upward by low-power members, who believed they had a chance of promotion, than by low-power members who did not. Zander and his colleagues uncovered similar findings in their study of professional relationships among mental health teams. They found that low-power persons who wished either to advance or improve on their present level communicated less freely with their superiors, and were more likely to tell superiors about their successes than were low-power persons with no ambition to move upward.

Whereas studies in the fifties' stressed centrality as the important dependent variable for morale in their network experiments, later work demonstrated that power was the primary determinant of morale, followed closely by centrality, self-actualization, and activity in the net.

In industry similar divisions of opinions occur. Supervisors at the same level often have varying degrees of influence in their unit, and this variation in power and influence can have considerable effects on the communication process. The superiors, by virtue of their position, can use direct, unsubtle methods, while their subordinates cannot. While one group of writers advocated that more power should be given to supervisors, others are in favour of reducing superiors' control over subordinates. But lack of power can also bring problems; when superiors have little power, then subordinates may react against them—morale can be lowered and performance adversely affected.

That prolific writer on organizational behaviour, Likert, believes that high-producing managers achieve better communication and greater influence than the lower producers. Many examples in management journals suggest that uninfluential managers are often bypassed by subordinates seeking action from higher, more powerful, superiors. The logic of these moves may not be missed by the bypassed manager, and the aggravation and annoyance often caused may reduce what communication effectiveness is left. Many managers recognize that this is a problem of loss of face and go to great lengths to avoid this 'bypassing' action, whether it be upward or downward.

Open-door policies, suggestion schemes, etc., can themselves be interpreted as bypassing methods commonly used by top management, believing that these are good for human relations. These policies often generate suspicion among the bypassed middle management. How far can a subordinate go in pointing out his boss's mistakes—the man often in charge of his progress and salary in the organization? Many managers speculate that they might lose not only their jobs but also their pension rights if they question their superior's judgment too closely. As Arch Patton of the blue chip consulting firm McKinsey says: 'It puts an unrealistically large premium on man's honesty....'

Industrial psychologist Read took this further when he attempted to uncover a significant negative relationship between communication accuracy and the degree of power or influence the subordinate felt his superior to have. The reasoning behind this hypothesis was that the subordinate would again restrict adverse information to the more powerful superior who could have a greater influence on his future salary or promotional chances.

Theories

From the foregoing research two basic theories have emerged. The 'status approximation' theory claims that when 'lows' seek upward movement in a hierarchy of status or power, but cannot achieve it, then their excessive communication to the higher status group members can be looked upon as a 'psychological substitute' for the upward mobility they have failed to achieve. The second theory regards other upward communication as being 'instrumentally oriented' towards promotion. i.e. aspiring lows attempt to maximize good relations with highs in order to achieve the upward movement they desire. Typically they will try to cover up their mistakes and take every opportunity to agree with and praise their superiors. Because of the importance of these theories to managerial communication, more examples of research are worthy of consideration.

Hurwitz *et al.* suggest that upward communication in any social organization is primarily of a kind which serves to reduce tensions and achieve the purposes of the communicator. In their study of social workers they report that 'lows' think of 'highs' as vitally important for the satisfaction of their needs, and so 'lows' attempt to maximize good relations and minimize feelings unease in their interactions with 'highs. In conferences, the 'lows' communicated less frequently than the 'highs', and when they did communicate they directed their talk mainly to 'highs'.

These authors and others have shown that persons in low-status positions also engage in 'facile distortions' in their perceptions of their relationships with superiors, and generally behave in an 'ego-defensive' manner. In lay terms people some way down the social ladder 'fool' themselves that their relationships with their superiors are much more important than they really are. The following quote from one of the managers in the study illustrates this point: 'What I really need to get some of my ideas going, is to report directly to the board, they could see things more clearly.'

There is, however, work by Perlmutter and Hymovitch which has received little attention although it raises some fundamental points about the 'instrumental theory. These academics demonstrated that upward communication may be used specifically to achieve the aims of the communicator but need not always be deferential or approval seeking, the *context* of the communication being of great importance. In a college setting it was found that students communicated *more* critical comments to a group of high-power faculty members than to those with less power. The authors suggest that in this academic atmosphere critical evaluation rather than agreement or acquiescence was the more highly regarded. It may also be the case that comments to do with the work in hand are more often directed to high-power individuals in the hope that suggested changes are adopted—the assumption being that low-power individuals are 'powerless' to implement changes even if they agree with them.

To sum up, many writers suggest that powerful superiors are not likely to receive information about their errors or mistakes. Other writers believe that work-oriented executives might be *expected* to communicate especially about their adverse and difficult problems to individuals who can advise or assist them. As one manager in the study put it: 'An influential boss is the only one worth having—it's no use taking your problems to a fellow who hasn't the authority or resources to solve them.'

Table shows that in this study superiors with greater power received *more* accurate information about their subordinates' problems than their less influential colleagues. The background of the managers may be an important factor in this finding. Like the students and academics of Perlmutter and Hymovitch's study, the managers involved were well educated and many had received technical or science degrees.

Desire for promotion

The striving for status and power of experimental subjects, when translated into organizational terms, usually becomes a desire for promotion. Western society in general admires advancement and rewards it by conferring both status and power on the successful individual. Philosopher Veblen further suggests that the social stratification resulting from this reward system is itself a fundamental source of advancement hopes. No doubt many people have wondered why so many characters from history have risked their secure and luxurious positions to plot and connive continually for even greater power, with failure meaning a certain and horrible death. If one subscribes to Veblen's theory then the extreme divisions of power and status existing then could have been a major reason.

While some research has demonstrated that higher satisfaction can result from higher achievement, others have found that various forms of advancement striving and certain nervous illnesses were quite strongly related. These findings need not conflict if the nervous illnesses found were associated with individuals who had not achieved their expectations. The gap between aspiration and achievement may be a more relevant factor here that the actual achievement itself. The writings of Kahn, Director of Research Programmes into Organizational Behaviour, may provide some insight into these results. He sees the high-advancement-drive individual forced to risk some of his security in search of promotion. It may therefore be a function of the gap between advancement desire and advancement success which gives rise to the problem of management known colloquially in America as "ulcer gulch". We can therefore expect that the manager seeking promotion may be subjected to some internal stress and prepared to adjust his behaviour and communication in order to satisfy these desires.

In our culture the value placed on achievement and success, particularly in industrial society, is well documented. Professor Argyris of Yale makes a similar point to Veblen when he refers to 'climbing the organizational ladder as an adaptive mechanism in reaction to the impact of large scale organizations on individuals'. The Professor also points out that the relationship between advancement aspirations and problems of upward communication in industrial hierarchies has yet to be systematically examined.

Whyte, in his caricature of the American business executive, notes that the 'organizational ladder' constitutes a powerful reward system. For this type of manager, his need for promotion may cause his behaviour to become instrumentally oriented, i.e. he may attempt to meet the expectations of his superiors both in his on- and off-the-job behaviour. He may strive to meet their standards and even exceed them in fulfilling his role in the organization, to maximize his chances of being considered for continued approval and hence promotion, and minimize his chances of being overlooked or even demoted. As one manager I met put it: 'I call it my OJA policy-always be "one jump ahead" of the boss.'

Likewise it can be argued that in communicating work-related matters to his superior, the high-promotion-drive subordinate may structure his communication to his superiors in a way which minimizes 'positive' and minimizes 'negative' information about himself. He may be more likely to withhold or restrict communication of the problems with which he is struggling than more positive matters such as the problems he has successfully solved. Many studies agree that the most silent single characteristic of executives in industry is the striving or advancement through promotion or the gaining of more status or power. Adopting concepts of positive and negative motivations, most morale surveys confirm that promotional opportunities are one of the few factors which operate on both dimensions of this motivational framework.

Jaques, who worked for many years with the Glacier Metal Company, describes many examples in which promotional desire can have an adverse effect on communication effectiveness, especially in what he terms the inverted-T group, with the superior soon to leave and several of his subordinates competing for the position. Similarly, Read demonstrated that subordinates with strong promotional desires tend to 'screen' information to their superior, probably in an attempt to present their superior with a favourably biased picture of themselves.

Sociologists Warner and Abegglen, in their study of American business leaders, have shown that the mobility experiences of executives who have had lengthy climb up the occupational ladder affect their relationships with those above them in the industrial pyramid. These writers point out that the executive who works up 'from the bottom' is relatively isolated socially, has learned to enlist and utilize those who are able to help him in his upward advancement, and has learned to insulate and detach himself from those who are not able to further his career. Similarly, Read's study demonstrated the adverse effect of high work-life mobility on accuracy of upward communication. Inter-generational mobility was, however, not related. The author writes.

The status-seeking tendencies of members who have experienced the long climb up the organizational ladder are related to inaccurate communication. One may only speculate on the lack of significant results for the inter-generational aspect of mobility. It may well be that the psychological remoteness of one's familial relationship for those well long in their career lives would make it less strong as a motivating force than either one's conscious need or desires to advance or one's career experiences.

It would seem to be proven from the work of these researchers that strong promotional desire adversely affects upward communication. What these researches do not tell us is to what degree this desire is inherent in the individual manager or is created by the organization in which he works.

The electronic managers who filled in my questionnaires were no exception to this general rule. Those subordinates who valued promotion highly tended to restrict communication to their superiors. The superiors of subordinates with *high* promotional desires were *less* informed as regards their subordinates' problems than superiors whose subordinates had lower promotional desires. It is interesting to note also at this point that these managers with strong promotional desires *had not* achieved faster rates of promotion than those with lower promotional desires.

These reactions are quite understandable really—for who is most in control of the ambitious subordinate's chances of promotion?—his superior. In nearly every firm there are continuous rivalries for the attention of the top men. Backbiting, lack of co-operation, and empire building are typical phenomena within larger business organizations.

In a similar study by Read an even stronger relationship between inaccuracy in communication and promotional desire was recorded. Read's study involved managers drawn exclusively from the second and third levels of supervision. The present study involves managers from the first four levels of supervision with some 42 per cent of the managers at the first level of supervision—a level which Read did not investigate. As promotional drive was found to be proportionately weaker at lower levels of the hierarchies, a sample drawn only from the second and third levels might well have produced identical findings.

Read suggests that: 'It is unlikely that upward mobility drive would vary markedly from level to level, or that communication upward would be more free at one level than another.

This statement must be questioned however. Among the electronics managers, higher level managers are *more* promotion-minded than their juniors, while communication accuracy generally improves as one moves up through supervisory levels. It would, however, be dangerous for readers to make Read's error of extending results beyond the framework of the research—the location and personal characteristic of the electronic managers involved in this study should be borne in mind when considering the results.

Trust

'The essence of teamwork is mutual confidence, which, in turn is founded upon the exchange of trustworthy information'. This is one of the few principles of management which has been universally accepted. On the other hand, conflict is a prime cause in increasing other areas of tension, creating difficulties in communicating and decreasing trust. Furthermore, the reception of information is often affected by the background of the receiver. For example, distortion may occur when the 'transmitter' is disliked or mistrusted. If these feelings are mutual then double distortions are possible in interpersonal communication. An ex-colleague of mine noted in one of the electronics firms involved in my study that suspicions were created when the managing director conducted his communication on an individual basis and resisted pressure to have group meetings. These suspicions were further compounded by the preference the managing director was thought to have in lunching with a select band from among the departmental heads. The 'outsiders' among the departmental heads suspected that many decisions affecting themselves were made by this clique over lunch without their consultation.

These factors are often recognized by managers themselves. In one large poll of managers, output was said to be restricted when lack of trust between directors often caused decisions to be reversed within hours. Similarly, American psychologist Mellinger found in a large governmental agency that colleagues who felt more trust in each other communicated more frequently and this in turn led to more consensus of opinion and to more accurate perceptions about each other's views. In the absence of mutual trust he found that communication tended to exaggerate existing differences and to diminish any consensus of opinion to such an extent that about a quarter of the subject pairs would have had greater consensus and less distortion of each other's view if they had communicate less, not more.

A study by Ziller among 96 aircrews comprising about 1000 men, found that crews feeling greater 'group confidence' were more flexible and had more open communication systems. None of these factors were related to group productivity, however. Also a detailed study of middle-level managers by the Foundation for Research on Human Behaviour, and by Read confirm these findings, i.e., that high trust between their superior-subordinate pairs tended to produce more accurate communication between the pair of managers in question.

With such a considerable amount of reinforcing research the study of communication among the electronics managers would have been incomplete without investigating the degree of trust between the communicating managers. The results of Figure confirm the widely held belief that really effective or accurate communication will usually not occur unless an atmosphere of trust and confidence occurs.

In terms of the diagram, subordinates who rated their boss highly in the trust section of the questionnaire produced proportionately more accurate communication score than those subordinates who gave their superior a low rating.

Many management books suggest that the more superior-subordinate pairs trust each other the more they will communicate. Among the electronics managers only the *subordinate's estimate* of the trust and communication frequency between the superiors and themselves was measured. Statistical tests indicated that frequent communication occurred when the existing trust was high or low, and similar tests showed that the frequency with which the managers communicated had no effect on their communication accuracy.

Although the speed with which these managers communicate with each other was not measured, the speed with which they completed and returned their questionnaires was. It may be that the subordinate with little trust in his superior was a little slower in returning his questionnaire because of a reluctance to pass on his low opinion of his boss to an almost complete stranger.

Some managers, of course, actively encourage rivalry and ill feeling among all levels of their juniors, attempting to keep all such staff the more firmly allied to themselves and dependent on their favours. One mining supervisor used a similar logic with his night-shift men. His problem was to keep the men working without his continual supervision, coupled with his belief that they were all basically lazy. He would first fill all the jobs in the warm areas of the mine with men who did not get on well together; before sending them off he would do his best to start them arguing expecting that each man would do his share of the work so that the others could not cause him of slacking. He then allocated all the jobs in the cold mine areas to groups of friends. some of these areas were so cold, he maintained, that if the men stopped working for more than a few minutes they would grow cold so quickly they would have to get back to work to keep warm.

Morale

In the involved area of morale and job satisfaction and its relationship to communication, the little research which has been done has produced a variety of results. Some researchers have found morale related to the *perceived* knowledge of group objectives whereas others have found morale not related to the *actual* knowledge of group objectives. These statements are, of course, not necessarily contradictory. At an interpersonal level, however, the findings are more related. Work by many industrial consultants has demonstrated that the morale of subordinates is related to the 'communicativeness' of their superiors.

Frames of reference

In the section on trust it was pointed out that the reception of material can be affected by the background of the receiver. This leads us to consider the effects of frames of reference on interpersonal communication.

Quite apart from the fact that interpersonal communication in organizations, may be affected by the withholding or distortion of information, there is the further fact that the information transmitted is often partial or incomplete, leaving room for bias and elaboration. When one person communicates to another, it is generally assumed that the receiver will understand the message as intended by the transmitter. Some of the errors which can occur in the use of words, gestures, etc., have already been examined, but even when the factual part of a communication is successful, the implications arrived at can be affected by the receiver's own needs, motives, and past experiences. Bullock, among others, would argue the importance of the organization in establishing an individual's frames of reference. In a modern hospital he comments:

> The nurse group is a key segment within this system, which includes such other groups as doctors, administrators, interns, technicians, patients and visitors. The varied demands, expectations and requirements which these groups impose upon the nurse, mark out a role she is expected to play, functions she is expected to accept, behaviour codes to which she is expected to conform and a status position of inferiority or superiority relative to the other personnel groups.

If the expectations of other groups become unrealistic, problems can occur. For example, how often does the stereotyped picture of a foreman's role have little real bearing on the actual shop-floor problems foremen experience?

Perhaps the simplest way of defining a frame of reference is to look upon it as a background of opinions, used to make everyday decisions and based largely on personal experience. Where two people have a similar frame of reference they are often said to be on the 'same wavelength', and usually the communication between such individuals will be both easier and more rewarding than if their frames of reference were vastly different. As a manager in the study expressed it: 'We think along the same lines—we're on the same wavelength—that's my biggest advantage with the boss.

In relation to the questionnaire used one might expect that the way a superior sees his own problems will influence his estimation of his subordinate's problems. The superiors tended to see the subordinates as having the same major and minor problems as themselves despite the fact that the subordinates might have seen their own problems quite differently. Even though most of the managerial pairs demonstrated some degree of agreement, the superior's view of his subordinate's problem tended to be closer to that of his own problems than to those of his subordinate.

Ideally one might hope that the superior could put his own problems behind and look objectively at his subordinate's individual problems. A possible explanation for this general failure may be that superiors do not listen attentively to what their subordinates have to say. A review of bookson communication demonstrates, in a number of ways, the two-way nature of the communication process, so that receiving can be just as important as transmitting. The frequently held stereotype of the business executive has the manager as a dynamic, often aggressive, giver of instructions rather than a listener. The limiting effect that frames of reference have on accurate communication indicates that there may be some truth in this belief, but it also shows the detrimental effect on the two-way communication process.

Cognitive distance

Osgood et al. did much of the pioneering work in establishing ways of measuring the degree of similarity between the frames of reference of two individuals. When facts conflict with a frame of reference, there is an increased tendency for these facts to be rejected, or even a situation in which one has 'two ideas missing each other in psychological space' when the cognitive distance is sufficiently wide.

Sociologist Lerner, in a study involving some 300 Turks, found that his subjects could be classified by the similarity of their frames of reference into modern, transitional, and traditional types. This type-casting was found to be a better predictor of the subject's opinions than any one single measure such as status, country-town dweller, etc. Other research has shown that these groupings can often be affected by culture. A study in the twenties found that children in the USSR had a preference for technical and manual professions as opposed to children in the United States who considered the professions of banker, business man, and minister of religion as being of greater importance.

Although many writers have suggested other factors as being important, e.g., difference in age., social background, educational level, career background, religious beliefs, etc. little research has been carried out in industry to gauge the importance of these factors, and if they do exit, to plan for them. Educational and social snobbery has been a source of argument in Britain for generations. Many people suggest that these status differences, when large, may adversely affect communication accuracy. Statistical tests demonstrate that in the electronic firms studied this was not the case. Social background and educational differences produced results which were inconclusive, while age differences—a measure of the 'generation gap'—on this evidence had absolutely no effect on communication accuracy.

The area of main interest concerning industrial frames of reference has been with superiors who previously held their subordinate's position. Two conflicting beliefs arise—the first that the superior with experience of his subordinate's job can continue his active interest in that area and, coupled with his existing knowledge, be more in touch. Conversely he can keep less in touch because he feels a need to concentrate more on the new positions under his control. These approaches may also have different effects on the subordinate, e.g. the subordinate may look down on the manager with less specialized knowledge than himself *or* dislike the experienced boss whom he sees as 'always muscling in on the only job he knows'.

Norman Maier has twice carried out research in this area. In one study of forty managerial pairs he found no significant difference in communication scores between the two categories, but in the other study of thirty-five pairs he found communication was better when the superior had not previously held his subordinate's job. Neither of the two beliefs mentioned above are founded on conceptual research. Perhaps Professor Maier was coming closer to an explanation of his results when he concluded yet another study.

> It is worth noting that lack of information from their subordinates did not prevent superiors from having ideas about their subordinates' obstacles. Not one superior was reluctant to talk about this area. Superiors obviously perceived their subordinates problems on the basis of either their own past experiences or what they knew about the organization in general; therefore they has little chance of agreeing with their subordinates.

It may be that the frame of reference of the superiors who have had intimate experience of their subordinate's work is more rigid than that of an inexperienced manager. These managers may hang on to old responsibilities as they go higher up the managerial ladder—having little time for their junior's problems but still carrying their slide rule into the board room. Perhaps the extra effort involved in trying to understand the subordinate's work and problems—the need for the inexperienced manager to put himself in the subordinate's place—to role play—is one of the factor involved in this surprising result. A manager in the study seemed to have grasped this point: 'I have to use group decisions and the like. I don't have enough up-to-date information about all the sections I control—I' be blinkered to think that I do.'

This belief seemed uncommon among the managers in my study. More typically the manager of, say, an engineering section, would appreciate less about the problems of his senior engineers than he would about the problems of the 'peripheral' personnel under his control.

More academic work on the distance between frames of reference was carried out when Triandis and Weaver first applied the cognitive distance measurement of Osgood in industrial settings. Their general findings were that individual groups of people—engineers, senior managers, etc.,. tended to have similar cognitive profiles, and that between any two subjects cognitive similarity was related to their degree of liking for one another and to their estimation of how well they communicated together.

The concept of the distance between frames of reference affecting the accuracy of upward communication was taken further by incorporating cognitive distance measure into the questionnaire. Essentially the cognitive distance measure attempted to gauge the degree of separation between the managerial pair with regard to their frames of reference towards a variety of professions.

Management literature suggests that background differences between the managerial pairs will produce greater gaps between their frames of reference and that this in turn will lower trust and decrease communication accuracy. Statistical tests, however, produce a complicated picture. Some background differences increased the cognitive distance but not the separation between the frames of reference. Similarly, greater cognitive distance decreased trust while the separation between the frames of reference of the managerial pair did not affect the amount of trust existing between the managers. Finally, the cognitive distance did not affect the accuracy of communication while the separation between the frames of reference did. Unfortunately these highly important factors are more easy to theorize over than to measure.

Empathy

Argyris writes of the ability to bridge these cognitive gaps as one of the three basic human skills.

Success in imparting information is affected by a willingness to listen—a give-and-take arrangement which is the only true basis of participation. Only through listening can a communicator predict and anticipate the internal psychological state of others. Perhaps who have this ability should be able, more easily, to take on the 'roles' of others, and so predict their actions more accurately. However, there are considerable difficulties in locating and measuring this talent, and, as a consequence, difficulties in devising training for its development.

Professor Mead of the University of Chicago was one of the first writers to stress the importance of role taking ability in communication. He saw many roles in society and that society often expected different roles from the same person. For successful interaction with people, Mead suggested that man must be able to adopt parts of the other's role to be able to predict responses and so continue the activity successfully whatever that activity may be—football or marriage, communicating or crime prevention.

Rose tested Mead's theories in a family setting by having forty-six pairs of relatives predict the replies of each other to a number of set questions, i.e., the closer the role to be predicted was to the role of the predictor, the more successful should be the prediction. Most of Mead's theories were borne out in that, for relations were more successful than in-laws, and subjects of the same sex were more successful than subjects of the opposite sex.

Similar findings have been reported on industry. Organizational theorists Dearbon and Simon demonstrated the effect of departmental identifications when a group of executives from various departments of a large firm were asked to read a case study and identify the most pressing problems presented. The executives tended to suggest the problem most related to their own work; thus salesmen mentioned increased sales as the best solution while personnel executives indicated human relations as the key problem.

These problems may be caused by managers in general, not recognizing communication barriers, and failing to utilize channels most productively-specifically the failure of the superior to listen to what the subordinate has to say before he offers information, comment, or advice. Advice or information may be given without full understanding of the issue or problem being presented. Moreover, there may be a tendency not to listen to the emotional content of what the subordinate is saying, resulting in a failure to understand his feelings on the subject under discussion. When response indicating no recognition of emotional or 'feeling' content is given, and the issue is of real concern to the subordinate, the junior may tend to feel that he has not been fully understood. Without this understanding, further communication in mutually acceptable and useful terms is likely to be restricted: in handling human relations, logic alone will not avail.

Rodgers and Roethlisberger agree with this reasoning, but strike a note of caution on initiating mass 'listening ability training. They believe that many people tend to *avoid* attempting to understand others because:

(a) With understanding may come change in the listener's own philosophies.

(b) Listening attentively to others can heighten emotions—these may be difficult to overcome, especially where the frame of reference of the speaker is vastly different from the listener's.

Where careful listening is *most* important it may be *least* likely to occur.

Even more critical of role-playing training is a study by Zalkind and Costello. They studied a group of senior medical students who deteriorated in perpetual accuracy after such training. Similarly, Whisler and Harper discovered that their own profession-psychologists—was less able to predict ability from interviews than other professional groups untrained in these techniques.

The relevance of communicating ability to individual managers has been demonstrated in a number of studies. In one electric power company manager rated 'immediately promotable' by higher level managers were compared with others whose promotional potential was rated lower or negligible. The comparison was in terms of the way the subordinates of these men described their behaviour in confidential questionnaires. Promotable managers and supervisors were described by their subordinates as being more receptive to discussion of the job and personal problems and more ready to communicative with subordinates in group meetings in which negative feedback could be obtained. The authors conclude.

> The manager's willingness to be accessible to subordinates and to attend to what is said plays a part not only as direct link in the communication process but also as an example to others. Effective managers are typically regarded by their subordinates as being informed, open in communication, accessible, and receptive. They have personal skills in communication and give a great deal of time and attention to the communication processes among their associates. These are skills and attitudes that can be learned.

Lawshe and Bolda confirmed this belief when they concluded that role-playing training increased the sensitivity of supervisors to human relations problems.

Judging by the amount of conflicting evidence, sensitivity-training and role-playing techniques have yet to prove themselves conclusively.

Individual performance

Mann and Dent found supervisors who created an atmosphere of free and easy discussion were more likely to be regarded as promotable by their superiors than those who did not relate this atmosphere. Exkerman *et al.* investigated a brokerage firm with a number of regional offices located in major cities. It was found that official daily information about future programmes and anticipated market changes reached some sales office with a higher speed and reliability than others. Personal sales volume and earnings were higher in those offices where salesmen reported that information flowed freely and speedily. Many of these studies have used the subjects' perception of one of the main variables combined with an objective measure of the other related variable, in this case performance. The Swede Karlsson, however, in a pioneering study involving over 400 married, separated, and divorced couples demonstrated objectively that good marital communication was significantly related to material satisfaction and inversely related to divorce-suppression rates. The subject of interpersonal communication in industry is not a topic isolated by a 9 till 5 barrier from the rest of a manager's existence. There is every reason to believe that the manager who motivates his associates during working hours motivates his family when he returns home.

Improving organisational communication

Various approaches have been made to improve organizational communication which, although often quite different, are widely applied in industry. Few, however, have been subjected to rigorous examination, for their adoption or rejection seems often dependent on the subjective judgments of the top management involved. The results of a study indicate that although all the firms communicated with a certain degree of effectiveness, the communication differences between the firms were quite marked.

By comparing the firms, the degree to which organizational factors were responsible for good or bad communication could be calculated. The practical implications of this analysis are discussed in detail below.

Defining company policy

It is generally assumed that a person will be a more effective member of an organization if he has a knowledge of the purpose of the organization and its operations. Such knowledge should help person to understand his job better and also to appraise his own performance and the performance of others more readily. In the hospital study mentioned the lack of explanations or information regarding personnel policies, promotions, and salary increases were occasionally mentioned as irritating and conducive to snooping and suspicion. One study of the flow of information in an electronic manufacturing firm tested employees' knowledge of company policies. Differences in test scores were uncovered in different parts of the company such that job performance was better on an individual and group basis where the knowledge of the policies was better.

It may be that managing directors have a general reluctance to establish clear policies in case this action reduces their flexibility in the future.

Recruitment

In looking through the personal characteristics of the electronic firms' managers it was noticeable that the only selection procedure that they had in common was that of 'like choosing like'. Thus the social background and type of schooling of the top management tended to be reflected in the junior management. One manager explained his reasoning behind this: 'I don't suppose we do this consciously, but when you talk to an applicant you soon know if you would get on together. If he talks rugby while everyone else talks football, it is clear indication to me that we would have communication problems later on.'

Some managements believe that the sons of professionals, being used to the hustle and bustle of executive life, make the best managers. Others believe that the more gifted sons of the lower classes are better in that they have had to make their way up the managerial ladder solely on their own ability. It is no coincidence that the followers of the first philosophy tend to be sons of professionals while followers of the latter tend to be from the lower classes. These factors should come as no surprise to people interested in human logic, for, after all, the manager who has achieved some degree of success in his career may feel quite justified in selecting subordinates in what he feels is his own image. If this manager has the 'key to success' why should not candidates of similar background have the same gift?

What constitutes the correct management image can, of course, become quite bizarre. One American executive confided to Vance Packard that a good executive should have good ears. Packard thought the manager meant that an executive should be good listener until he noticed the uncommonly large size of the man's ears. There is little doubt that most managers would not use ear size as a means of selection, but there are many managers who would go along with the ex-regular Army officer I met: 'I think most of the other managers here agree with me—if the candidate doesn't have a short head of hair we can reject him without bothering with the interview. It's been my experience in the Army that the "long hairs" were always in the charge room.'

What sort of charges were they on, I asked: 'Oh, usually for having long hair', he replied. It is misleading to think that such preferences are uncommon in industry. One Harvard course in advanced management was attended by over one hundred businessmen; only 40 per cent of them had moustaches and none had beards. These pressures to conform usually start during recruitment interviews. McKinsey Management Consultants Inc. were rumoured to have instructed their consultants to wear suspenders and not self-supporting socks, while a British Consulting firm insists that bearded recruits shave before joining their ranks. These managerial preferences may only be regarded as slightly illogical or mildly inefficient, but they are rather ominous, as indicated by many studies in America which, for example, have shown that religious, racial and political allegiances are of prime importance in the selection procedure.

Returning to the background differences among the electronics managers, the results described that these differences had no effect on the accuracy of communication between managers, while the evidence concerning cognitive distance and frames of references was inconclusive. The only factor uncovered in the study which can be used to aid the selection of good communicators are those of education level or managerial style. An even more direct approach may be to select "high performers' for middle or upper managerial levels, especially where communicating ability is essential.

The suggestion to recruit educational 'whizz kids' or the 'high flyers' of industry may be a daunting prospect for many managers. Some firms are reputed to slow down the progress of their own 'bright young men', fearing the jealousy and anxiety that can be caused among the other managers, but few top managers will admit to being apprehensive about their own job security. It should be remembered, however, that among the electronics managers the well educated and fast movers had accurate communication as their common factor. In neither group were these managers more promotionally minded than less endowed colleagues.

Defining responsibilities

The now retired managing director of Glacier Metal, Wilfred Brown, writes in his best seller *Exploration in Management*.

> When a subordinate is newly appointed to a job, he should, if he has been adequately trained, know a good deal about the general policies on which the operation of the company is based, but he will not know the detailed policies of his new manager. He needs, at this stage, a rapid and decisive introduction to and familiarity with those detailed terms of reference which constitute much of the prescribed content of his new job.

It is essential to give an explicit statement of the situation at the beginning if unnecessary problems are to be avoided. Newly appointed managers often tend to refrain, if possible, from asking many questions because they feel that, if they do, they will give the impression that they are not able to fill the position or because they want to make an immediate demonstration of their competence by doing the job without guidance.

Practitioners of 'management by objectives' would seem to agree in that they see the essence of management success as the achievement of *results* in an area of *responsibility*.

The following is a typical example of the problems which can arise when responsibilities are not clearly defined.

General foreman Jones considers foreman Smith responsible for certain maintenance functions in the department of which Smith is production foreman. These responsibilities include:

(a) Reporting effective equipment promptly to maintenance.

(b) Investigating all breakdowns and reporting improper maintenance which leads to breakdown.

(c) Making the decision to release equipment for repair when requested by a mechanic.

(d) When a breakdown occurs, finding out the cause, how long it will take to repair the machine, and assign operators elsewhere if it is estimated to be over 15 minutes.

(e) Investigating every charge of operator negligence leading to machine down-time and to take corrective action to prevent a recurrence.

Foreman Smith reports that he has no responsibility for maintenance. He does none of the above things. He feels no sense of short-coming since he does not believe that these are his responsibilities. Smith explains this shortcoming as follows: 'After all, the mechanics don't report to me, they have their own boss.

If, as is often the case, general foreman Jones never actually gets around to discussing the specific aspects to the job but is guided in his appraisal of Smith by check-list of personality traits, the unfortunate subordinate may never learn what his job actually consists of.

It would seen that this failure is quite common in British industry as a poll of works managers place 'frustration at all management levels, due to lack of clearly defined spheres of delegated responsibilities, fourth in a list of factors limiting productivity. This is also confirmed by Management Consultants Blake and Mouton who suggest that many managers have the attitude to their new subordinates of 'throwing him into the thick of things'. One manager in the present study used almost the same words: 'I was just flung into the deep end. Mind you it is the quickest way to learn—sink or swim.

It is also important to ensure that any clarification of responsibility is directed to the person able to affect the outcome, for as another manager complained:

> We have full responsibility to draw up the route cards for each lorry so the drivers don't check them at the start of their shift. If there's been a mistake, they'll come back at the end of the day, still half loaded, without a care in the world, and hand us back our mistakes. It is too late for us to do anything then.

More objective work was carried out by Michigan University's Dent and Mann when they studied the accounting section of an electric power company. In this study individual and group performance was found to be related to the individual's knowledge of his responsibilities. Similarly, industrial psychologists Rodgers and Harrison with fourteen superior-subordinate pairs in a laboratory study, and with fifty-nine similar pairs at overhaul shops in a naval air station respectively, found that subordinates who more accurately predicted what their superiors expected of them tended to be given high ranking on job performance.

On the other hand, a similar study of fifty-one foreman-manager pairs found no such correlation, while yet another team of researchers from Michigan University found no improvements in agreement on the subordinate's 'job through the use of written job descriptions. They conclude: 'Job descriptions may be adequate for long term relatively permanent matters, but they are less than adequate for dealing with situations which are constantly changing.'

Many of these apparently conflicting findings may stem from the grouping of all types of communication together. Work in 1964 by Kahn and his associates has made the first step in separating work oriented communication from welfare oriented communication. In their study they found 38 per cent of their subjects received inadequate information on advancement training prospects. The more recent studies by Herzberg, Paul, Lawler and Porter, and Friedlander and Walton, are beginning to put these findings in a conceptual context by a similar separation of motivation into positive and negative, making essential reading for any manager interested in motivating his work force.

Delegation of authority

Communication accuracy was found to be greater at higher levels of the firm studied. Although this may have been due in part to the ability of the managers who have reached these higher levels, there were indications that another factor may have been the greater authority and responsibilities found at these levels. This may bring the subordinate nearer to the point of decision-making and increase his sense of participation in the decision-making process. Even at lower levels, where subordinates believed the power or influence of their superior to be high, communication accuracy was improved. As companies grow it becomes more difficult for top managers to keep tabs on all phases of their operations: many executives in even moderately sized firms would have difficulty if asked to list all phases or products of their firm's activities—an ideal time for them to consider if they can adequately supervise all the functions under their control.

Where subordinates thought their immediate superior had comparatively little power to assist them in their work problems, they tended to bypass him to reach his superior. That this results in 'loss of face' is mirrored in the lower trust scores resulting. One manager in the study complained: 'My boss bypasses me quite often. I've talked to him about it but he says that is the way he works. It can give rise to feelings of insecurity and loss of face. Whenever I have done it—and I *do* try to avoid it—it has been because of a weak link in the chain and that is the link I bypass.'

One can, however, look upon bypassing as a type of feedback and self-corrective adjustment. Weiss and Jacobson noted in their study of the governmental agency mentioned earlier that if the supervisor of a work group failed to fulfil the needed liaison role for his group, some other member would often take over this necessary communication function.

To counteract this tendency and to bring the subordinate nearer the decision-making point, power commensurate with responsibilities could be delegated to lower levels of the organization. Good communication is as important at the bottom of an organization as at the top. By way of example an executive with Sears Roebuck may find he has as many as forty managers reporting to him—not so that he can supervise them properly but precisely because it avoids the necessity for very close supervision and allows the subordinates to take responsibility and speed up decision-making.

It is interesting to note that the firm which believes most strongly in this doctrine—and practises a form of management by objectives—has the highest average power and trust scores of all the firms involved in the study. At the other end of the scale, the firm with lowest trust and power ratings had a managing director who opened all mail before having it distributed to the respective heads of departments allowing them to scrutinize the mail of their juniors before it eventually arrived on the desks of the addresses.

Performance targets

Once the details of an individual's responsibilities and duties have been defined it would seem a logical step to find some way of assessing the person's degree of success in carrying out his duties—in other words assessing his performance.

Many people believe that 'management for results' has often failed through the targets being imprecise, e.g. produce at minimum cost instead of a precise target-reduce production costs by 5 per cent within 6 months. Precise standards, objective in the eyes of both superiors and subordinates, can reduce the amount of subjective criticism often occurring between superior-subordinate managers. At the same time at least some progress towards achieving objectives should be prompt. Some time ago when in a longish period of introductory training with my firm one felt irrationally guilty and considerably frustrated by not contributing to the consultants' 'batting average' the activity or fee-earning ratio.

Even when clearer performance goals have been established, however, co-ordination between related functions may be necessary. British researchers Thurley and Hamblin illustrate a case in point. In examining the inspection section of a manufacturing firm they found that the aims of the supervisors on the three shifts involved were different:

Shift A raised production rates by cutting down on rejecting units.

Shift B concentrated on quality by rejecting even border line cases.

Shift C was permissive and allowed individual foreman to follow their own inclinations.

The authors conclude that the overall result was one of erratic quality which could be stabilized by the establishing of overall objectives common to each shift.

Furthermore the introduction of clear but slack targets, with little incentive to improve on them, can produce additional problems as one manager grumbled: 'Those bright boys upstairs with their targets and deadlines! They sent a circular to all the customers saying orders for delivery the next day should be in by 1.30 p.m. Now hardly anyone sends them in before that and we're going round like trying to cope with the last minute rush.

Feedback

As has been continually emphasized in this book, communication is a two-way process: after passing a message a transmitter looks for some reaction in the receiver—some feedback. It is from this feedback that the transmitter decides how to frame or pitch his next communication act. Only through feedback can an individual build up a picture of the receiver's attitudes and from this picture predict future responses.

The effect of feedback on task performance has been ably demonstrated by Leavitt and Mueller. In their laboratory study four groups of students were required to assemble a design of rectangles from a verbal description given by the researchers. The four groups were differentiated by the degree of feedback they were allowed with the instructor. Summarizing their results, the following essentials were discovered:

(1) Increased feedback increased accuracy.

(2) Increased feedback increased the time involved initially, but eventually similar times to zero feedback trials were obtained.

(3) Zero feedback gives rise to hostility in the receiver.

(4) Zero feedback creates doubt in the receiver.

Similar results were recorded by Zajonc in a laboratory study of twenty groups with seven subjects in each. The experiment involved the reaction time in depressing a key after receiving a set stimulus. A red light would flash if failure occurred. Performance was found to be best when feedback was at a maximum—in this case information could be fed back to the subject on his own performance, his group's performance, and the performance of the other group members. The subjects with slow reaction times improved their performance most quickly under conditions of maximum feedback.

Not only does factual feedback have measurable effects but also perceptual feedback has been shown to change attitudes.

Spector devised an experiment whereby the same poorly delivered lecture was given to different groups of subjects. After 15 minutes the groups were asked to write down suggestions to help improve the lecturer's technique. One group was then told that their suggestions had been accepted, one that their suggestions had been seen but rejected, and another that the suggestions had not been read or accepted. The lecturer then carried on exactly as before—in the same poor style—to all groups. Before-after attitudinal questionnaires found that the group 'allowed' to feedback advice felt that the lecture had improved in style more than either of the other two groups.

Most writers on industry would argue that, in general, an open feedback system would result in a clearer picture of responsibilities, difficulties, and strong and weak points of *both* superior and subordinate. Prompt feedback on performance may be more important in changing behaviour than intensive discussions which only occur infrequently. Furthermore, a human need is satisfied when personnel are informed of their progress and the effectiveness of this satisfaction is governed by the clearness of the performance targets and the accuracy with which they can be measured. Many personnel managers would agree with this and point out that performance feedback based on subjective judgments is often more a mirror of the appraiser than the appraisee as the following Army example shows: 'This officer is keenly analytical and his highly developed mentality could best be used in the research and development field. He lacks common sense.

The supporters of feedback through performance appraisal reject the approach typified by the following manager involved in my study: If subordinates are good men, they will make an objective judgment of their own progress—they don't need me to tell them. We all work in the basis here that no news is good news.'

How much honest feedback could a boss expect to this sort of opening remark: 'I want you to tell me candidly what's wrong with our section—even if it means losing your job!' On a somewhat grander scale one wonders how much honest criticism absolute dictators like Hitler received from their advisors, or kings, like Henry VIII receive from their wives.

A general lack of feedback seems quite common in Britain. A lack of cost information was placed third in a list of problems restricting productivity during the poll of works managers mentioned earlier, and in only two of the seven electronics firms was time set aside at least annually for superior-subordinate pairs to discuss in some detail the problems involved in the subordinate's job.

Without any degree of feedback on his performance, the subordinate will find it difficult to control or correct his behaviour. When performance is thought to be an important factor in promotions and salary increases, this 'non-feedback' may lead to feelings of insecurity and distrust of the immediate superior. As might be expected therefore, the firm with the most formalized system-performance appraisal with the subordinate present—had the highest trust scores of all the firms. Furthermore, only in this firm did all the subordinates believe that their superior was the person most in touch with their problems—an indication that they felt the feedback system to be working both ways.

However, even with this system there is some reluctance on behalf of the superiors to praise their subordinates. As one manager expressed it: 'I really do not like doing his...he has got the same experience, as good if not better qualifications, same background and age more or less—why should I play a little god.'

The problem may be one of managerial style. When the superior believes that the aims of the organization and the subordinate can meet, he can more easily take the step of allowing the *subordinate* to take a major part in deciding what should constitute good performance and what bad. If the superior agrees with his subordinate's ideas, then the junior manager will feel more committed to seeing that the outcome of his proposals are successful—that his targets are met. This method of performance appraisal can reduce a lot of the 'threat' felt during appraisal interviews, as one of the electronics managers discovered:

> I had one of my 'difficult' men come with me on someone else's appraisal to show him the boss's view. Then I go him to fill in his own appraisal form and compare it with mine. It worked very well—I'm sure it helped him realize his own weaknesses without my having to point them out. It is a great value to communication—with a frank talk—may be clear the air. I quite enjoy it.

As this sort of participation should make the subordinate feel closer to the decision-making point, any inadequacies in the authority and responsibilities of the superior may be highlighted in the eyes of the subordinate. Thus one type of organizational change may precipitate another. One of the advantages of feedback at all levels is that weak points may be brought into clearer perspective and corrective action taken.

Performance appraisals

One of the earliest recorded applications of formal appraisals was in the Wei Dynasty where the imperial rater of the emperor appraised the performance of the members of the official family. American industry started taking up formal appraisals before World War I, but the system is still little used in Britain.

In the early days benefits claimed for the system were:

(a) The identification of and concentration upon the most important areas.

(b) Subsequent appraisals identified weak areas and allowed corrections to be attempted.

(c) A record of the conclusions reached was permanently on paper.

(d) Face-to-face communications, increased speed, and interaction.

(e) The motivation of managers through relating reward to performance.

More recently others have highlighted some drawbacks of appraisal systems in common use. These organizational theorists suggest that the power relationship of the dialogue is of paramount importance, such that both superior and subordinate should play their roles with equal openness and frankness, establishing clear targets of performance to which both superior and subordinate are committed. Unfortunately for advocates of annual appraisals, many outstanding men are notably deficient in tact. In a few cases performance reviews stimulate sadistic desires to strip subordinates bare for other than altruistic reasons. Similar beliefs have led to the recommendation or *separation* of performance and reward, i.e. to look upon appraisal as a tool for career development with the superior committed to follow up failings exposed in the process, by giving time or training to correct the weakness.

Not only can subordinates experience difficult in being critical of their more influential superiors but also superiors can be reluctant to criticize as the following quote from a manager to whom I talked indicates: 'Some of my subordinates may complain about some people all the year round but when it comes to appraisal time they tend to say. "Oh, they're a lot better recently". They are very reluctant to criticize or act the headmaster.'

Professor Maier suggests that the lack of agreement he found between superior-subordinate pairs over job details questions the validity of appraisal and the willingness of the subordinate to accept this system. Perhaps, significantly, none of the companies he studied used 'participative appraisals.

Meyer *et al.*, *Kay et al.*, and French *et al.* confirm this belief. in an extended study of ninety-two superior-subordinate pairs at a general electric plant the authors found:

(a) Criticism has a negative effect on target achievement.

(b) Praise had no effect.

(c) Performance improved as targets became clearer, more specific, and realistic.

(d) Performance improved with more frequent feedback.

(e) Mutual target setting improved performance.

(f) Performance interviews should be separate from salary and promotion decisions.

Morale and acceptance of performance appraisals also improved in the same manner. In general these authors suggest that the interview should attempt to decrease the sense of threat to the subordinate's self-esteem and so reduce his defensive behviour.

It is perhaps the uncertainty about the way in which performance is assessed which causes most problems in appraisal interviews. Goal-oriented assessments, produce more agreement, satisfaction, feelings of adequacy, less hostility, and more feelings of responsibility than trait-oriented assessments for both subordinate *and superior* personnel. Perhaps the greatest reward from establishing objective as opposed to subjective appraisals is that interpersonal relations can be improved and greater commitment of the subordinate to his section's objectives is possible.

A study of 567 American companies found a growth in the practice of performance appraisal. Fifty per cent of the firms had, however, eventually dropped the system at executive level because they felt it was too time consuming. Furthermore, it is interesting to note in the light of the foregoing research on participation that over half of the firm using performance appraisal did not involve the subordinate at all, while only eight firms involved three levels of management—subordinate, superior, and his superior—in participative discussion. These figures and tendencies seem even more valid in British industry.

Suggestion schemes and 'open-door' policies

Formal upward communication is often the minimum required by the system in operation. The resulting amount and nature of informal communication can be a direct reflection of the unfulfilled needs, desires, or aims of the people involved. By using informal communication, the subordinate can:

(1) initiate the communication;
(2) control the process;
(3) seek the best channel.

All formal feedback methods can be tested by these three parameters. Meetings usually fail on all three counts, while suggestion schemes are somewhat better in that the first factor is met. Personal contact is often the best method but only when the superior in sensitive to the view of others. Similar faults in suggestion schemes, opinion polls, etc., have been documented by other writers, and certainly 'failure' rates have been as high as 90 per cent, whereas the Socony Mobile Company computed an 800 per cent cash return on their suggestion scheme, other firms have put forward the following disadvantages.

(a) Many companies pay on all suggestions to avoid disappointment.

(b) Many suggestions would have come without the scheme.

(c) There is no evidence that morale is improved.

(d) Turning down suggestions can lower morale.

(e) The result of these schemes is a bypassing of supervisory levels and can create suspicion both among managers and union officials.

(f) Staff personnel excluded from the scheme may pass their suggestions up through eligible workers instead of their superior.

This latter point is illustrated by the following quote from one of the managers I interviewed: 'There is no encouragement from top management for suggestions so I pass my ideas on to other interested people—like you—work study people, etc. They get them implemented because they can get to the right ears and then they get the credit, not me.'

Many supervisors see the 'open-door' policy as an attempt to bypass their levels of supervision presumably because top management believe that communication blocks are occurring among the bypassed managers—an attitude not likely to improve their morale. Another possible problem with an 'open-door' policy is that the manager's office, even with its door open or in open plan, is still his territory. That popular zoologist Desmond Morris, author of *The Naked Ape*, would suggest that for the subordinate to leave his own territory and come to the boss's 'lair' is often itself a sign of submission and perhaps not the best start to establishing 'free open communication'—so often the stated aim of these types of policies. As another manager from the study explained it: 'I try to have an open-door policy. It takes a lot of time but it's the only way of keeping trouble down. Mind you, some fellows I have never seen in this office but I'll be in the yard and they will talk to me there—on their own ground as it were'.

It would seem that for all the schemes mentioned in this chapter, the ultimate success or failure may depend upon the degree of trust and confidence existing between the participants. Any scheme adopted could be judged to a considerable degree upon the 'net growth' of trust and confidence that it generates.

Management by objectives

Of the many books on organization techniques for the improvement of communication and performance, the philosophy which at present seems to be based most closely on the studies already reviewed is that of management by objectives. This theory is itself an example of 'pay-off in organizational studies being developed from the group dynamics research initiated by the late Kurt Lewin of the Massachusetts Institute of Technology.

Briefly, the theory of management by objectives involves the setting of specific performance targets to be achieved in a given time. The targets may be set for the entire organization or for any part of it. The setting of the objectives ideally involves a superior and subordinate jointly, and at the end of the time period, both examine the subordinate's performance in terms of the extent to which the objectives have been achieved. If possible, the objectives should be qualified.

The benefits expected from the introduction of the system are, of course, greater all round efficiency. More specifically:

(a) The operation of the system will identify, and concentrate attention upon, the most important elements of the manager's job.

(b) The subsequent appraisal of performance will identify and enable the correction of factors which have impeded the attainment of the objectives.

(c) The motivation of managers will be increased by their participation in target setting.

A crucial question for the success of management by objectives is whether it will be seen to be a system of imposed control or a system of control exerted by the individual himself, and this in turn requires that both superior and subordinate have some appreciation of the basic pitfalls involved .

Training

Contrary to many industrialists' beliefs, superiors who had *not* previously held their subordinate's job achieved higher communication accuracy scores than those managers who had their subordinate's job. As was pointed out, the answer may have a to do with the extra effort the 'inexperienced' superior has to put into his communication with subordinates who control phases of work with which he is unfamiliar; conversely, the 'experienced' manager may be somewhat more lax. As promotions seem to go more often to 'experienced' men than their 'inexperienced' colleagues, this may be creating major communication problems in industry—problems which training specialists are trying to overcome by the use of job rotation, role laying, and case-study techniques in management development programmes.

Concerning job rotation, it was of interest to note that when subordinates has been with their superior for some time their promotion desire and need for a substitute for promotion were both increased with the possibilities of the resulting adverse effects. Statistical tests also showed that a long relationship was not indicative of low performance or a lack of past promotion—many of the managers having risen together. One manager described his way around this problem: 'I try to move junior staff around to relieve their boredom. When they are in their early twenties, stuck to one section with others in their late twenties and have boss at over 40, it discourages the more ambitious ones. They cannot see ways of getting ahead.'

Returning to the training methods of role playing, job rotation, etc., simultaneous with the expected growth in the ability to see the other man's point of view should come a skill in redefining apparently conflicting aims in terms of common goals. This should also result in improvements in communication accuracy and career achievement. Perhaps of relevance here is the point that the introduction of new techniques and especially ones of a 'psychological' character, require top-management approval for their successful implementation. As one manager in the study complained: 'We go on courses infrequently and when we do we often find that top management knows nothing about the techniques we've been learning and then they won't apply them. I think top management should take the courses before we do.

As training courses are expensive in terms of both time and money, it seems worth describing in some detail a training programme which back-fired in a most costly manner.

> A medium-sized contracting firm called in management consultants to increase the general efficiency of the company. The consultants recommended that training be instituted for all supervisors and that a similar course be given to management. The consultant was called in to run the training programme, which emphasized lectures on good business practices and sound human relations, combined with group-participation discussions and training in becoming more effective in groups. This format stimulated frank exchanges of opinions and feelings and move active participation by the trainees.
>
> The sessions were at first formal but soon loosened up and provided an opportunity for the supervisors to express certain grievances about the company which they had until then only discussed with close friends or held back altogether. Company practices were unfavourably compared with ideal ones as outlined in the lectures. Most of the grievances concerned the behaviour of senior management. Almost all the groups who went through the training unanimously decided that senior management should make certain fundamental changes in their attitudes and behaviour, and that if they did not do so then, with the impetus of an outside consultant, they would never change.
>
> The various grievances were compiled into a report which the consultant submitted to the managing director. It was then decided that the same course should now be run for higher levels of management and that the grievance report should be used as material in the course. It developed in the discussions that senior and junior management both felt that neither the consultant nor the supervisors really understood the practical difficulties they encountered in management. Many of the grievances levelled at them were accepted by senior management but felt to be the fault of junior management. Junior management agreed with the grievances, accepted some blame themselves, but laid most of it on senior management. They frequently attacked senior management for having had bad relations with staff men in the past.
>
> The managing director was left with the conclusion that no blame attached to himself. Following the rather unsuccessful management course, he announced a

number of decisions which had been based on recommendations made by the consultant in line with foreman grievances. These involved adjustments of pay, institution of a better system of communication with supervisors, shorter work week, greater opportunities for promotion from within the company by advertising the jobs internally, and so on. The reaction of the supervisors was 'We'll wait and see'. Shortly after this, the consultant terminated his relationship with the company, having completed his job.

Supervisors suspected that senior management has not really changed their attitudes and this suspicion was borne out by the slowness with which the resolved changes were instituted. Only after a period of months were some of the changes made and some of these were made grudgingly

About one or two months after the training course, foremen started to leave the company. During the year after the course, 20 per cent of the 97 supervisors left and another 25 per cent began to look for jobs elsewhere. In previous years, no more than one or two men had left per year.

An investigation of who left and why revealed three factors; among the foremen who left there was (1) high proportion of intelligent men; (2) a high proportion of men with relatively few years of service, although even among men with over 10 years of service 39 per cent were dissatisfied; and (3) very high percentage of men who had regular contact with senior management. Apparently this last factor was most important, in that it revealed directly to the foremen how little a change of attitude had actually occurred among senior management.

In summary, what started out to be a management-improvement effort not only led in the course of one year to a severe conflict between first-line supervisors and senior management and resulted in no change in management attitudes, but also produced a high rate of turnover among some of the very men whom the company needed to keep. What the organization and the consultant had failed to foreseen was the complex relationships among the several sub-systems of the organization—the forema group, junior management, senior management, and the managing director. Had the training course been adequately thought out in terms of its potential effects on these various sub-systems, the disastrous effects might have been avoided.

Status symbols

Status differentiation in industry is commonly achieved by the use of symbols. Although this topic has received considerable attention in the news media, it has usually been of a comic nature. With the amount of time and money spent in establishing equity in the system, it is perhaps surprising that almost no research work has been done on measuring its effects. One firm's grading system was introduced thus: 'Considerable thought has been given to the most equitable manner in laying down guidelines for the seniority and status of the company's staff.'

This firm had, in fact, the most elaborate system of status of all the electronics firms in my study, having some *sixteen* grades for the *sixty* employees occupying staff positions.

It seems reasonable to presume that a 'perks system' forms part of a reward system for better performance, especially at higher tax levels when salary increases are supposed to lose much of their meaning. It is doubtful that salary levels are the most important status symbols available, particularly at the top of major companies. Robert McNamara, for example, left the presidency of the Ford Company to become US Secretary of Defense. His annual salary shrank from around $400,000 to $20,000, but his reputation expanded from US business circles to the world's informed public.

It seems reasonable to assume that companies with elaborate status differentiation believe, like one director said that: 'If people in business were more clearly identified by the luxury of their offices, those in lower grades would try harder to do a better job and reach higher positions.'

Among the electronic managers, however, this was not the case. The firms with an elaborate system of status symbols had managers of no better past achievement than firms with less elaborate systems. Judging by the comments of the managers in the two firms at opposite ends of the status differential scale, considerable rationalization of each firm's philosophy had occurred after the managers had settled down into the existing schemes. In both of these firms most of the managers interviewed had become content with their respective systems even though the 'logic' behind them was often in direct conflict. A manager from the 'status free' factory commented:

> The British canteen system is disgusting and humiliating—more or less saying to someone 'You're not good enough to eat with us', and the toilet system is even worse. Imagine the directors saying openly to middle management 'Your hygiene is such that you can't with us.' They'd never dare say it but they imply it by having their toilets locked.

While a manager from the firm with the most elaborate system stated that:

> We feel that toilets and works canteens come into the same category, a place where any employee can go and shout his mouth off and not worry about being overhead. By the same token the top executives can discuss confidential matters in *their* own toilet without us overhearing and *vice-versa.*

Presumably this manager had not read about an amazing 1965 American survey in which a quarter of the eighty-seven firms involved eavesdropped by 'bugging' works toilets.

The elaboration of the 'visible' status system tended to have only adverse effects among the firms studied. The desire for promotion was greater as the elaborations increased. In general it seems that the more apparent the status division the more promotion minded are the subordinates. By way of example one firm with higher than average promotion drive scores ensures that following each 'grade' change the manager has his 'new desk' or 'external telephone' installed within a *maximum* of 3 days, proclaiming in a most visible way the change in status. One of their three staff dining rooms caters for two levels of middle management. Not only are the tables graded by the presence or absence of table cloths but also at the coffee section china cups are provided for the higher grade while paper cups are provided for the others. One manager told me of an occasion when a new waitress was working in this section. Seemingly she issued the china cups on a first-come first-served basis and then started to use up the paper cups. There was no problem until the china cups ran out, but after this great embarrassment was caused by a number of the higher grade managers refusing to use the paper cups-insisting on their 'rights'. Because of this and other similar problems, this company is in the process of solving 'this problem by constructing yet another dining room to separate the two grades.

Other visible differentials had the similar effect of increasing the desire for promotion, viz, supervisory level, superior's power, social background differences, and age differences.

Although the status symbol syndrome could not be shown to affect the communication accuracy score directly, it has been already pointed out that strong promotional desires of this sort cause subordinates to restrict adverse information about themselves in attempting to create a 'rosy picture' to their superiors. Firms with an intricate 'honours' system thus tend to create managers with stronger promotional desires. If those managers experience little promotion, then a mismatch of need and achievement may occur. To avoid considerable dissatisfaction an alternative outlet may be sought.

One substitute for upward movement can be upward communication. Whereas managers with little mismatch of need and achievement kept their communications to reasonable levels, managers with a greater need for a psychological substitute tended to communicate more frequently with their superiors.

This finding is somewhat different from the simple instrumental theory which suggests that communicating frequency will be higher towards managers with considerable power—this in fact was not the case. An alternative explanation is possible from other studies although the use of the word 'psychological' may be misleading. The managers dissatisfied with their rate of achieving promotion may consciously 'over-communicate' with their superiors to draw attention to themselves and to ensure that they are not forgotten, especially when promotions are imminent.

It is worth noting that although the 'perks system' did increase this need for a substitute for promotion, few of the other status differences had any effect. It may be again that the important factor is one of visibility of the status difference, and that the perception of visibility may vary according to the type of organization involved. Although this electronics study did not extend to the shop floor, workers in this age of higher education have severely limited promotional opportunities. A *Fortune* magazine study of 900 top executives found that less than 8 per cent had risen from the shop floor. When the study, asked only at managers under 50 years of age this parentage dropped to 5 per cent. If the workers have similar desires for advancement as do the managers, then, like the managers, these desires may be increased by elaborate symbols *devised primarily for managerial and not worker motivation*. Their need for a substitute may be increased by these systems—as they are for the managers—and one form their substitute might take could be stronger demands for wage increases and industrial recognition, e.g. in the form of trade unions. Professor Norman Hunt of the Edinburgh Business School quotes a survey of several hundred American companies which tried to assess the value of profit sharing as a means of promoting industrial peace. Of those companies practising profit sharing at all levels 9.9 per cent had experienced recent strikes, while 23.4 per cent of those companies not practising profit sharing at any level had had strikes. However, of the companies having profit sharing for managers only—an extra status differential—30.6 per cent had had recent strikes.

It would seem easier for firms setting up new plants to start operations with a 'classes' factory. It is, however, noticeable that the older plants have more elaborate 'perks systems' than younger factories. This suggests that the pressures to add to existing status systems become progressively harder to resist. The pseudo-scientific observations of Parkinson's law of the rising pyramid and the Peter principle that in a hierarchy every employee tends to rise to his level of incompetence

Organization performance

Bavelas and Barrett believe:

> It is entirely possible to view an organization on an elaborate system for gathering, evaluating, recombining and disseminating information. It is not surprising, in these terms that the effectiveness of an organization with respect to the achievement of its goals should be so closely rested to its effectiveness in handling information.

Drucker, on the other hand, sees related innovation as one of the prime objectives of any organization, and it can be argued that in electronics—a rapidly developing industry with a high rate of obsolescence-innovation may be the *prime* objective.

These two views did not conflict with the findings of this study. Of the seven firms involved in this study, four have received the Queen's Award to industry for innovation. It may be significant that the same four firms had the highest average communication accuracy scores of the study.

Group communication

Small group studies have emphasized the importance of effective inter-member communication for both high morale and task achievement. Bavelas discusses this facet of group study:

> Although the problem of effective communication is an old one, recent trends are bringing it to a new sense of urgency. More and more it is becoming clear that any fundamental advance in in social self-understanding must rest upon adequate

intercommunication. In areas where effective and highly integrated social effort is required, the problem is particularly crucial.

Considerable research on communication in small groups occurred in the 1950s. Studies of 'communication nets' and their effects on group functioning, combined with studies on the passage of information within hierarchically structured groups, have represented two major lines of interest. Laboratory investigations of experimentally created hierarchies have provided some crucial insights into the existence and nature of communication patterns.

Even now, however, only a beginning has been made in attempts to isolate factors associated with free versus restrained inter-and intra-level information exchange, and generalizations have been limited by the necessary artificialities of the laboratory settings.

Network experiments

In most of the investigations, groups of strangers have been placed around specially designed tables which screen them from their neighbours. By allowing only written messages to be used according to certain plans or networks, tasks could be given and completed in a manner allowing a complete record of the interactions to be made.

Early experimental work found that the relative accuracy in task solving was wheel, all-channel, chain, and circle shown in figure. Leadership was found to be associated with centrality, e.g. position *Y* in the wheel net, while low morale and satisfaction were found to be associated with peripherality—position *X* in the wheel and chain nets.

Classical studies by Heise and Miller proved that 'noise' on the channels increased errors and lowered efficiency, while Macy produced similar results in experiments with two groups—one with 'solid' colour marbles and the test group with 'streaked' marbles. Until the test group developed its own technical language, its performance was below that of the reference group.

Much of the foregoing research was superseded by the more extensive experiments of psychologists Cohen and Carzo. These researchers demonstrated that the group in all the networks tested above continued to learn over longer periods than the earlier studies had investigated. Efficiency tended to a common level, but the morale associated with the various network positions reminded the same.

Liaison people

At the same time as this research was being conducted into experimentally created groups, other academics were looking at communication flow in on-going groups. For example, Festinger *et al.* and Back *et al.* demonstrated the importance of opinion leaders in a study of rumour transmission on a housing estate. The individuals tended to use their friends to receive and pass on the rumours in the fashion of liaison people.

One of the landmarks in the application of social science concepts and methods to the problems of community-wide communication was a study by Katz and Lazarsfeld of the University of Michigan. The study concerned political attitudes and voting behaviour in a small American city, but the conclusions have considerble relevance in business organizations. In their effort to discover how the residents obtained information, and what sources of information were effective in influencing political behaviour, they came to the conclusion that the mass media, although important, had their effects largely through the activation of complex informal inter-personal communication processes.

To explain the development of attitudes, opinions, and behavioural patterns, they came to the view that the community was partially structured into *primary groups*, formed of people who interacted on a person-to-person basis. For many kinds of information intake and outflow these primary groups relied upon one or more *opinion leaders*: these opinion leaders were very active communicators who were responsive to the mass media and had connections with other opinion leaders and with persons who were influential in the community. There was accordingly a 'two-step flow of communication', first from the source to the opinion leaders, and through them by person-to-person transmission to the less active members of the community. The transmission of information and the meanings and implications derived were very much influenced by the beliefs of the primary groups and by the pressure for these individual members to come to the same conclusions as the rest of their groups.

The grape-vine

It is clear that the picture of communication flow in the large communities described above is similar in many respects to communication flow in industrial organizations. Official and controlled communication channels—via mass media, memorandum etc.—convey information to only a small part of the target audience. The content transmitted is often incomplete, so that there is latitude for misinterpretation as well as for selective attention and unintended elaborations of meaning. Many industrialists have noted that the structure of rumour transmission seems to be similar its industrial counterpart—the grape-vine. It has also been suggested that the liaison people in the flow pattern occupy these positions through above average interest in their work and in all factors which might affect it.

Although socio-metric methods have been used to identify these people, proposals to incorporate the liaison people into the formal communication systems have received little attention in management books or journals. Perhaps as a result many industrialists tend to underestimate the extent of the grape-vine among their employees. They may expect some company gossip between wives at cocktail parties, but would they be as surprised as I was when I discovered that one rumour about a highly confidential expansion at one of the electronic plants had originated among the local boy scouts.

Communication linkages

One approach to the description and assessment of information flow in organizations is represented by a study of communication linkages among professional staff members of a government agency. This agency included a number of military and civilian scientists responsible for the administration of a large programme of science development. The study intended to examine the patterning of communication between persons. Reports were obtained from each member about the frequency of his personal contacts with each other member of the agency. Pairs independently reporting their mutual frequency were taken as the basic data and these pairings were analysed to see whether and how there might exist sets, or groups, of members who communicate a great deal with each other and rather little with people not part of their set. A communication structure of the organization could be drawn up for comparison with the 'formal structure. Some results were:

(1) There were, in fact, rather clearly defined sets of members who communicated largely with one another, and these sets were typically rather small, groups of 5-8 being most common.

(2) Each set had at least one *liaison person* who communicated much more than his colleagues and who also had an exceptionally high rate of communication with liaison persons from other sets.

(3) These liaison persons were sometimes, but not always, those designated as supervisors or managers.

(4) There were some people, *isolates* who did not belong to any primary group and who were largely excluded from information sources.

(5) The primary groups tended to match the formal organization plan, but the match was imperfect and some primary groups cut across organizational lines to include people under different supervisors.

It was clear from interviews with these people that some of them were aware of the informal communication system and they relied upon it very much as a means for obtaining, transmitting, and evaluating information needed in connection with their work. Some intentionally used it whenever they thought the official communication system would be too unreliable or too slow.

In another study Davis illustrated one of the ways in which communication flow may be studied. He traced the transmission of specific items of information throughout the organization of a manufacturing firm with attention to their point of origin, their chains and networks of transmission, the speed of communication in different chains and networks, and points of blockage of communication. Among other things in this particular firm, he found:

(1) At every level of the organization except the very top there were some groups of

members who were generally isolated from the flow of information and who got information very late or not at all.

(2) The formal mechanisms for communication were slower and more often resulted in incomplete transmission.

(3) Communication via personal, informal, face-to-face verbal exchanges occurred more frequently and faster than communication via more formal mechanisms.

(4) In this organization there was a severe blockage between the fourth and fifth levels such that only a fraction of information items passed this barrier.

(5) More than half of the information items traced reached their destinations by crossing over organizational line rather than flowing through the intended formal lines.

(6) A unit of information was much more likely to flow *downward* than *upward* from any point of origin that allowed two-directional flow.

Davis concludes from this study that the grape-vine is much more important in organizational communication that some have believed, and that much of the necessary and important communication moves in this way. He observed also that people in staff positions generally received more information and received it earlier than did their colleagues of similar rank in the line positions.

Great quantities of relevant and important information are excluded from formal communication systems: indeed, it is doubtful whether any organization could function when common inaction occurred solely through formal system—overload and failure could result. Fortunately, social organizations are adaptive and readily create means for supplementing formal management information flow systems—commonly called the grape-vine. When described in the language of the social scientist, the grape-vine appears to be a necessary and almost wholly beneficial thing, consisting of complex network of contacts between liaison persons, adapting to the changing needs of its users. The special information generation and flow functions are those of assuring accurate translation of formal communication into the meanings relevant for different kinds of members in different parts of the organization. We notice the grape-vine when it generates false or unrealistic information. We may overlook the same grape-vine when it is doing its normal and necessary work of converting information into more useful forms and into needed derivative forms. We may not realize how much we rely upon it when rapid communication is vital and when advance notice is needed about impending formal communication.

Group pressures

Although most people consider themselves individualists, behaviour is often patterned by the model provided by others. It is, for example, most noticeable how groups of managers at the same level tend to smoke the same brand of cigarettes.

When one manager moves up a level his 'favourite' brand may change quite unconsciously. With this in mind some of the basic research into group pressures is highly relevant to the more important areas of executive meetings, department disagreements, etc.

American psychologists Kelley and Woodruff have shown how an individual' beliefs can be modified if he feels that his 'group' holds different beliefs. Two groups of young teachers listened to a recorded speech loudly applauded by a fictitious audience. The speech rejected most of the modern teaching methods in favour of tried and tested old-fashioned ones—a philosophy at odds with that of the young teachers. The group who were told that the applauding 'audience' were student teachers adjusted their beliefs more than the twin group who were told the audience consisted of a variety of young graduates. In general we find that the more a person feels that his beliefs go against those of his 'group', the more he changes his opinions in the direction of those of his group. What holds members of such groups together is their social cohesion or, more accurately, their ability to transmit relevant messages more accurately to each other than to anyone else.

Even in the clinical atmosphere of psychological laboratories, similar patterns emerge. In one such study, groups of strangers were given tasks to perform; although all the groups were randomly selected, certain ones were informed that they had been specially brought together because of some similarities in their backgrounds, and these groups were termed the more cohesive groups. The research found the more cohesive the group the more communication was directed to obtain agreement. In other studies some subjects in the group were given different information from the main group and hence had the initial tendency to suggest a different solution. The more homogeneous or cohesive the group the more communication was directed at the deviant to obtain a change in his solution towards that of group agreement.

From this and other research Festinger has drawn up some theories to cover group pressures in communication:

(1) Pressure toward agreement is caused by:

(a) social reality—when actual information is low, group pressures can be strong, the 'loner' having fewer concrete facts with which to disagree or argue:

(b) group locomotion—the need to progress, as a group, towards a common goal. This factor is often apparent with political parties on approaching and election when old enmities are temporarily forgotten.

(2) The resulting quantity of communication to create agreement:

(a) increases the greater the discrepancy is thought to be;

(b) increases the greater the perceived importance of the discrepancy;

(c) increases the greater the group cohesiveness;

(d) increases toward the deviants;

(e) increases when a reduction in the difference of opinion is expected;

(f) decreases towards persons thought to be outside the group or not wanted in the group.

(3) The amount of change in opinions:

(a) increases with the pressure for agreement—the more the pressure the more the change;

(b) increases with group cohesiveness;

(c) decreases when the recipient knows of other groups holding his present beliefs, giving him an anchor in an agreement or even a 'new home' if the pressure becomes unbearable.

(4) The tendency to reject members:

(a) increases with the perceived discrepancy;

(b) increases with group cohesiveness;

(c) increases with the relevance of the issue.

In the examination of the information systems of an organization many social scientists attempt first to identify social groupings. From the research reviewed it appears realistic for some purposes to view a business organization as a collection of small social groups of overlapping membership rather than to view it as a set of individuals linked by lines of authority and responsibility. The analysis of information generation and flow throughout the organization can be aided by considering groups as the main units of which the organization is comprised and by consideration of individual behaviour as an expression in part of group processes.

The manager of today needs to choose his methods and strategies in formal communication with some consideration for the existing and desired group structure of his organization and with some consideration for existing group differences. A simple instruction to cut operating costs by x per cent may be accepted at its face value by the firm's accounting section. The engineering section, however, may interpret it as another example of the head office 'pen-pushers' trying to tell them how to run a production line. If the instruction was re-worded along the lines of an explanation of the reasons causing the need to cut costs, the engineering managers might be more encouraged to work out ways of achieving the required economies.

The progressive manager should therefore use group processes to aid effective communication by encouraging the formation of appropriate new groups, by accepting as legitimate the added agreement rising from group interaction, and by utilizing group processes in his own immediate work setting with subordinates, colleagues, and superiors.

Improving oral communication

Since managers spend as much as 50 per cent of their working day listening, they should be accomplished in this skill. Yet, too often we hear such comments as "Bob just doesn't" or "Barbara is hard to work with because she never takes the time to listen" or somebody wasn't listening." In fact, of the four primary communication skills needed for effective management—reading, writing, speaking, and listening—listening is used the most frequently and yet receives the least attention from educators.

A number of essential managerial skills involve listening. First, much of the data necessary for decision making comes through listening to employees, yet poor listeners miss important information. Second, listening makes a person more dependable: people who listen well follow directions better, make fewer errors, say foolish things less often, and generally become the kind of person others will ask for advice or direction. Third, good listeners are more respected and liked by those they work with. Managers who listen compliment those they listen to, in effect telling them they are worthy people. This trait can lead to harmonious labour relations since employees generally trust and support managers who "listen them out."

Fourth, better listening enables a manager to be better informed overall and more sophisticated. Sophistication comes not from talking but, rather, by learning about the world around one. Fifth, good listening spares a person many embarrassments. In many situations, people may miss a name because of poor listening, or they may need to have critical information repeated because of "daydreaming". Worse yet, a direct question may be unanswered because of inapt listening. Such embarrassing situations can quickly label a manager as unconcerned or even apathetic.

Ultimately, the major reason for developing effective listening is to promote understanding between people. People who need to be heard not only for their own emotional well-being but to be understood create gaps by not listening. Mutual understanding is required in any work group.

Listening is not just hearing, and the effective manager differentiates between the two. Hearing is mechanical, an automatic sort of thing often difficult to avoid. A horn blaring, heavy construction equipment groaning, children shouting in a playground—all these sounds, plus others, may be heard even though they are not listened to actively. Hearing usually requires little special physical or mental effort.

By contrast, listening results from a concentrated effort; it requires both physical and mental effort. Listening requires a special effort because physical and psychological factors work against the process. In this chapter we review those physical and psychological barriers to listening and then analyze techniques to reduce these barriers.

Physical barriers to listening

One of the greatest physical barriers to listening arises from our own limitations. The trouble is that people speak approximately 25 per cent as fast as they think. Thus, while most Americans speak at a rate of about 125 words per minute, they are able to think at least four times that fast. As a result, instead of listening carefully, some people tend to think about other things and devote only a fraction of their capacity to taking in what is said. They become impatient with the slow rate of the spoken word and begin to concentrate on topics other than the words being spoken and daydream to remain stimulated. This problem may be referred to as the 25 to 75 problem: a person requires only 25 per cent of his mental time for listening while he spends the remaining 75 per cent on unrelated ideas. No wonder some find it hard to get their attention back to the main topic.

A second type of physical barrier arises from internal distractions that cannot be ignored. Our autonomic nervous system involuntarily pays attention to certain events such as a headache, sore feet, or an empty stomach. It is difficult to divide attention between these internal involuntary distractions and concentrated listening.

A third physical barrier to listening is any overpowering noise that may compete with the main topic of interest. It is hard to listen to a subordinate who speaks softly in a noisy foundry or to a phone conversation mixed with static on the phone line. In these situations, separating the speaker's voice from all the surrounding noise can be exhausting.

These physical barriers are not the only ones to effective listening. Psychological barriers can be equally burdensome.

Psychological barriers to listening

A major psychological barrier to listening is lack of motivation. Many find maintaining the continuous motivation required for listening a challenge. The need for motivation stands out when one recalls the speed of the thought process compared with that of speech. During the 75 per cent of time when the mind is not being stimulated with words, motivation for listening is a challenge. Managers who should be listening may be day-dreaming, making private plans, or even focusing on an emotional problem. During that 75 per cent void many things can take place that overpower the 25 per cent listening.

Researchers have long known that motivation or incentive is a prevalent problem in the listening process. Research completed almost 30 years ago demonstrated that people score better on listening achievement tests when they know in advance that they are going to be tested than when they think they are just supposed to listen. More recent research has also indicated that scores on listening tests rise as the incentive to listen increases. Since listening is hard work, we can expect greater effort when the goal is known, and listeners can observe a positive outcome of the effort. This is why the listening goal discussed later is so important.

Another psychological barrier may be termed "detouring." The listener may become distracted by mannerism, phrase, or concept and detour toward the distraction. This distraction then stimulates thought on another sub-topic more interesting than the central point of the message; consequently, thoughts detour to the more interesting topics.

The "debate" represents a third type of barrier. A listener may suddenly find herself disagreeing with the speaker and begin to plan her rebuttal. As she plans the rebuttal, she blocks out the listener and misses his message. For instance, a manager listening to complaints from another department might prepare a rebuttal as the other person explains the incident. As a result, the manager creates a defensive climate and misses the most important information.

Time, an important factor in every manager's day, can also be a barrier to listening for busy managers. "I just don't have time to listen to this" is a common reaction for managers at one time or another. The saying, "time passes quickly when you're having fun," is really true; being involved in an interesting conversation can use more time than a person realizes. However, time is relative and seems to drag on and on when people have to listen to something in which they have no interest. When listening appears to take too much time, managers tend to stop listening.

Hasty conclusion is one way some terminate listening. This time pressure may lead to the tendency to judge, evaluate, approve, or disapprove a person's statement too hastily. To achieve real communication, resist me temptation to form hasty conclusions.

Perhaps the greatest psychological barrier is lack of willingness. A manager may not want to listen. Before listening is even required, he may have lost any desire to listen. A lack of willingness to listen is an attitude that supersedes all other barriers—both physical and psychological.

Since we have already discussed motivation as a barrier to listening, we must differentiate willingness from motivation. These concepts are closely related, but for the purposes of this discussion, assume that a lack of willingness develops before listening even begins. This is why it supersedes all other barriers. If a person consciously or unconsciously decides not to listen, listening skills are obviously of no advantage.

Why would a manager lack the willingness to listen? Several reasons explain this unfortunate condition. First, most people would rather talk than listen, and even when they ask a question, they often break into the first sentence of the response with another question or an argument. Second, the listener may quickly stereotype the speaker as one who talks a lot but has little to say; consequently, the listener believes that the person has little of value to say. Third, a listener may lack willingness because he may not want to receive negative information. For the speaker who bears "bad tidings,"what incentive is there to listen? Defensive behaviour relates closely to this. Some managers consider the slightest attack on one of their opinions as an attack on them personally; consequently, they will rise, sometimes almost obsessively, to the defense. This defense often involves verbal attacks that preclude the possibility for listening.

This is only a summary of the many barriers to listening. Nevertheless, research indicates that we can improve listening skills. When managers strategically analyze the critical components of communication and apply the techniques suggested in the following section, their listening skills and effectiveness as managers will improve.

General techniques for improved listening skills

Let us first look at the different types of listening to be able to adapt techniques to the appropriate situation and three levels of listening intensity for both types.

For the purposes of this discussion, active listening occurs in situations in which a manager has little or no opportunity to interact verbally with the speaker. People in a large audience use active listening as do those listening to a recorded message or reviewing an audio-visual replay. People use interactive listening when they have the opportunity to interact verbally with the speaker by asking questions or summarizing. Interactive listening occurs with a manager involved in a conversation with one other individual or in a meeting with many people.

The level of intensity at the side reflects the relevance, the importance, or the significance of the information involved. Listening has basically three levels of intensity. Casual or marginal listening is used when the specific or technical information being discussed is not critical. Because no goal for specific information is established, a manager need not be as alert as in other situations. Casual listening occurs in social conversations or when listening to the radio.

The next level of intensity, factual listening, is necessary when specific information needs to be obtained. Probably the most common type of listening in business meetings and conferences, factual listening is the level that most people probably thinks of when they consider the topic of listening. At this level, the listener should ask questions and receive feedback to ensure effective communication.

A manager uses the empathetic level of listening when he wants to understand another person from that person's own internal frame of reference rather than from his own frame of reference. The empathetic listener tries to get inside the other's thoughts and feelings. The listener expresses empathy when he verbally and non-verbally communicates such messages as "I follow you," "I'm with you,"or "I understand."

The empathetic level of listening is not easy to achieve because we naturally tend to advise, tell, agree, or disagree based on our own point of view. It is well worth the effort to become an empathetic listener, however. A speaker who sees that a manager is really trying to understand her meaning will trust the manager and be more willing to talk and explore problems. Empathetic listening can be such a powerful form of listening that, even when it is only partially attained, the mere attempt can be enough to open up communication.

When listening, the first thing a manager should do is to determine the level of listening she needs to achieve. She can accomplish this by establishing a "listening goal," a specific statement of the purpose for listening. In the give-and-take of most communications, the need to adjust one's listening goal arises as the interchange develops. Conversations frequently start with talk about the weather or other topics unrelated to the purpose of the conversation. For example, what may have stated out as a casual conversation with the general listening goal of getting suggestions for the next office social gathering may develop into a serious discussion on possible strategies for improving office performance. Knowing the listening goal permits one to adjust the strategy to the level of listening.

The act of writing out the listening goal is valuable: it forces the listener to analyze the purpose of the listening thoroughly. Also, when the goal is explicitly analyzed, it is easier to maintain the necessary motivation to reach the goal than when analysis is incomplete. As we saw earlier, motivation is often a major problem, so any technique that improves the motivational level is important.

Once she has established the level of listening, the manager must prepare herself physically and psychologically to listen. She should complete the following steps during the preparation state.

1. Pick the best possible place. While it is not always possible to change the place, the manager should not overlook better facilities when available.
2. Pick the best possible time. As with place, it is not always possible to change the time. However, the astute manager must be careful not to eliminate more favourable opportunities.
3. Think about personal biases that may be present.
4. Think about the physical and psychological barriers to listening.
5. Review the listening objectives.

A brief review of these five items shows why they are important in reducing the barriers to effective listening discussed earlier. First, selecting the best time and place helps one avoid the internal and external distractions. In addition, since time influences the psychological barriers of motivation, emotion, and willingness, the choice of time may significantly alter the outcome of the conversation.

However, is it polite to tell another that one cannot listen right at the moment? In a survey involving more than 200 different managers, the managers indicated that they would not be offended if someone asked them to wait for fear that important information might be missed. Of course, if time cannot be changed, it is important that the parties be aware of the barriers present and make a special effort to concentrate on the listening process.

A manager's biases may also have a drastic effect on the outcome of the communication. A manager unaware of personal bias may become selective and hear only what he wants to hear. The person may deal only with preconceived notions and even debate with the speaker on points of disagreement. For example, a manager who believes that women are unreliable may disregard any information indicating that a particular woman is reliable. The first step needed to control this psychological barrier of bias is awareness followed by recognition of the burden it places on the speaker-listener relationship.

Detouring, the psychological barrier that causes a listener to become distracted by a mannerism, phrase, or concept, is closely related to bias. A listener's negative bias toward a mannerism can totally distract from the content of the message. For instance, a speaker may place her hands over her mouth while speaking, or continually play with a cigarette, or look away from the listener. Such mannerisms can distract, and one needs to recognize them as just that—distractions. Mannerisms should not get in the way of messages.

Emotional words or phrases can also trigger listener bias. Such phrases as "typical accountant." "it really isn't my job," "we tried that before, and it didn't work," or "all engineers think alike" can lead to emotional responses. The danger in such phrases is that they cause a listener to hear different parts of a message. When a listener is caught by an emotional phrase, the internal emotional response may overpower the content of the message. Once again, the listener should be aware of the possible emotional responses and not let them distract from the message.

Again, it is important to review and be aware of the listening objective. Without the objective in mind, a manager may use casual listening when factual listening is required, or factual listening when empathetic listening would be more effective. The person who can state in one sentence the specific goal and the type of listening involved is well aware of the listening objective.

The manager who is physically and psychologically prepared to listen could use some specific techniques to improve listening. Let us look at some of them that are appropriate for active and interactive listening. The first techniques reviewed are the only possibilities available for active listening.

Techniques for active listening

One uses active listening in situations where interaction with the speaker is difficult or impossible. For example, a person who is sitting in a large audience or listening to a recording cannot interact. Since asking questions is generally not possible in these situations, a listener usually needs to have a clear and complete understanding of the message the first time around. An active listener should implement the following techniques.

Identify the main and supporting points

A message usually has one or two main points with supporting information in the form of examples, specific figures, or descriptions. One good clue to the main points is the non-verbal techniques that the speaker uses when giving them; she might raise her voice, speak faster, repeat key words, or use gestures. Later discussion will detail non-verbal aspects that can be invaluable when identifying the main and supporting points. In the following example, note the emphasis on main and supporting points in a speech:

The electronic division was pleased with the successful introduction of four new products in the last year. All four of these products sold at a better rate than projected. We were especially pleased with the temperature sensor that sold 14 per cent above projections. This small sensor, which has many applications and is easy to instal, should do as well or better next year.

Besides introducing four new products we expanded the Western Division's sales force by adding 16 high-quality salespeople. These salespeople were recruited from all over the United States, and we're confident of their ability to help us expand in the west. They all have a thorough understanding of the product and the changing nature of our industry.

No immediate changes are seen in the home implement division. It will be necessary to wait and see what happens with the entire housing industry. We're stable here since garage openers, intercom systems, and burglar protection devices are all holding their own. We developed a new burglar protection system that can be programmed by means of a digital device. This has been an interesting project to watch as it developed.

The main points in this example are the four new products, expansion of the Western Division's sales force, and a stable home implement market; the remainder of the message is supporting information. Separation of main and supporting points helps the listener to retain the critical information.

Outline the message

Often, a speaker has some type of organization pattern that a listener may use to outline the message. For instance, a speaker may organize the message by pros and cons, advantages and disadvantages, likes and dislikes, similarities and differences, chronological events, or functional duties. Just as it is easier to remember the outline of a chapter rather than every word in it, it is easier to recall the outline of a spoken message rather than all the specifics.

Summarize the message

Another listening device is the summary, which can take the form of a mental picture of the main points. The summary need not contain elaborate sentences and details; in fact, simple words or sentence fragments may suffice. Summarization does not have to wait until the end of the message as it may be more efficient at major division points. The president's speech given earlier could be summarized in three phrases: (1) four new products in electronics, (2) 16 new salespeople in the western region, and (3) a stable home implement market.

The three techniques listed so far— differentiating between the main and supporting points, outlining, and summarizing—operate together for accurate listening. The effective use of a fourth technique assists in the development of the others.

Visualize the message

Another tactic for active listening, to put the message into a picture, will help keep the listener's mind on the message. In fact, the beauty of this tactic is that it allows one to use some of that 75 per cent of the mental capacity not required to keep up with the message. Consequently, a person can commit more effort to listening, thus reducing the possibility of missing a major part of the message. Finally, the retention of the message improves because a picture can now be associated with it.

In the annual meeting seen earlier, a manager might imagine the 16 new sales personnel in the western region as 16 little people running from different points of a U.S. wall map to California. Absurd as the device might be, these 16 little people running across a wall map will help the manager remember the main point of the message.

Relate the message to personal experiences (Personalize)

Effective listeners are those who search a message for information that has special meaning for them. A topic is naturally more interesting and easier to concentrate on if it personally relates to the listener. In fact, those who relate the message to personal experiences ensure that the key elements of listening, willingness, and motivation are present.

The managers listening to the president in the previous example may also personalize the message by asking questions of themselves: "How will these four products affect my job?" "Will continued expansion of the electronic group affect me?" "Will those 16 new salespeople increase my work load for the western region?" "How will the stable market in the home implement group affect our division?" In answering these questions, the managers find how the message personally relates to them. Then, their incentive to listen to the message will increase as well.

Take notes

All these techniques are strengthened when the listener takes notes. College students generally do not have to be convinced of the importance of notes, but they often lose this good habit once they have left the classroom. A listener can easily make short notations to help visualize and personalize a message. Not only do notes provide a written record of the communication, but they can provide valuable feedback that tells the listener just how well she is listening. If the notes are not well organized with main and supporting points, the listener probably has not mentally organized the message. If a quick review indicates that no notes have been taken for some time, the listener may find that his or her attention has been wandering.

Notes benefit a listener, too, because they keep her physically involved. We have seen that for naturally physically active humans, listening is a predominately mental activity. Since they are not physically active, many people get restless or impatient when listening for long periods of time. Rather than being satisfied by lighting a cigarette or playing with fingernails, this urge for physical activity might be channelled into note taking, which keeps a person involved with the business at hand.

Of course, note taking can be a problem for those people who overdo it. Not every word needs recording, and long sentences are not necessary. In fact, the possibility exists of concentrating on the notes to the extent that major components of the message are missed. Instead, jot down key words and phrases in outline form using abbreviations when possible.

Mnemonics may be used when jotting down abbreviated notes. One mnemonic device is the acronym, a combination of letters, each of which is the first letter of a group of words essential to the message. For instance, suppose that a person is presenting his main objection to taking additional training in computer programming. The objection may stem from the cost, the individual's ability, and the time involved. The mnemonic CAT can be used to record these main ideas whenever the speaker refers to them. In this way, the listener records the main thoughts without becoming burdened by note taking. Later, the listener can rewrite the notes in more detail if an accurate record is needed. This rewriting has the added advantage of acting as a review of the major themes in the message.

A final thought on notes. The listener who takes notes indicates a sincere interest in both the message and the speaker. Notes require involvement, so the speaker will have a greater degree of confidence that listeners are paying attention to the message. The fact that it is important to demonstrate effective listening is discussed in more detail later.

Each of these techniques—identifying the main points, outlining. Summarizing, visualizing, personalizing, and note taking - is useful in either active or interactive listening. However, the techniques are especially critical in situations where the ability to ask questions and observe non-verbal message is limited. The ideal is to ask questions of the speaker for clarity without using them to replace the five techniques just discussed.

Questioning for improved interactive listening

In a variety of situations, the skilful use of questions adds immensely to a manager's ability to communicate. In fact, this book recommends several areas when questioning techniques are appropriate: listening, interviewing, conflict resolution, and coaching. Questions are important because they promote the two-way process of communication. Without the use of questions, feedback and mutual understanding are severely curbed.

Ask questions when the meaning of a message is either unclear or incomplete. When key words, phrases, or concepts are vague or when inconsistencies or contradictions appear, questions help to develop clarity. Listeners are not the only ones to benefit from questions, however; questions may also help a speaker to clarify his thoughts. In fact, a speaker might not be aware of an omission or distortion in a message until asked a question. When questioned, the speaker may be forced to reanalyze his own communication to the listener's benefit.

A manager must strategically determine the most appropriate questions for different situations to ensure mutual understanding. Three classifications of questions are appropriate to this discussion: open-closed; primary-secondary; neutral-directed.

The phrasing of an open-ended question gives the respondent an open choice of possible answers. At the other end of the spectrum is the closed question, which permits a narrow range of possible answers. An example illustrates this point. A frustrated employee has just described to his manager a major problem with a new project. In his agitation, the employee jumped from one point to another while describing the problem. Naturally, this disorderly description has made it difficult to listen, so the manager now needs to ask questions for both clarity and completeness of information. The following questions posed by the manager show the difference between open and closed questions.

What do you think are the major causes of the problem? (open)

Tell me more about it? (open)

Did you check the steam gauge? (closed)

Where do you think we should go from here? (open)

Would it be a good idea to wait until tomorrow? (closed)

While open questions may generate additional information, they also allow possible digression. Closed questions are more direct and help one to focus on the problem. Nevertheless, the lack of openness may cause valuable information to be omitted since the answer is so narrow. Managers must use strategic analysis to determine the best choice of questioning style in each case. Two other options open to managers are primary and secondary questions. A primary question is the first question that seeks clarification or more complete information on a topic. A manager may choose to follow up with a secondary question that probes to obtain still more specific information after the primary question has been answered. A secondary question is not merely an additional question; it seeks to get at a deeper level of information than the first or primary level. The following dialogue shows the strategic use of primary and secondary questioning.

Manager: Do you think you'll be able to have the analysis done by Wednesday? (primary)

Employee: That shouldn't be any problem if everything goes right for a change.

Manager: What would you be afraid of going wrong? (secondary)

Employee: The accounting information is hard to get sometimes.

Manager: What specific part is hard to get? (secondary)

Notice that each secondary question seeks further information on the preceding answer. Managers use the secondary question when they feel that they have not obtained sufficient information through the primary ones.

The third classification involves neutral versus directed questions. While a neutral question seeks information without attempting to lead the speaker to answer in a certain way, the directed question seeks to lead the speaker to a response the inquirer desires. A directed question, often referred to as a leading question, tries to pull the answer in a predetermined direction. Directed questions open with such phrases as "Doesn't it seem logical that...," or "Wouldn't you agree that ...," or "Wouldn't you say..." Directed questions may be used to obtain confirmation or clarification on one specific point, whereas the neutral questions will obtain a more general response.

The use of an appropriate question adds clarity to communication because of the active two-way process that develops. Listening is clearly not a passive activity; rather, it requires the active involvement of the manager through the use of questions and other means.

Listening to non-verbal messages

People listen with their eyes as well as their ears. The renowned communication researcher Mehrabian found that only 7 per cent of a message's effect is carried by words; listeners receive the other 93 per cent through non-verbal means. After conducting extensive research, Bird-whistell suggested that spoken words account for no more than 30 to 55 per cent of all social interaction. Thus, any non-verbal sources of information available to listeners are worth reviewing. Non-verbal communication can be divided into facial expressions, postures, gestures, and spatial messages.

Facial expressions

Facial expression is probably the most universal form of human communication. A smile or frown is known around the world. The wide array of facial expressions used by such communication "experts" as Charlie Chaplin, Buster Keaton, and Jack Benny shows how diverse and dynamic this form of communication can be. Just as Charlie Chaplin developed different masks for the silent movies. adults know the right expression for most communication circumstances. It is relatively easy to turn on and off such facial expressions as anger, disapproval, happiness, and fatigue. For this reason, the face is the most flexible source of non-verbal communication as well as the best at misrepresentation. A manager needs to be aware of the vast amount of information he can read from the face; however, he must be wary of the possibility that it can mask feelings or intent.

Usually, the eyes provide the first facial signal that a person notices. The expressions "shifty-eyed" or "evil-eyed" as descriptions of overall personality probably developed because of this powerful non-verbal cue. Eye contact is a carefully regulated human behaviour. People do not gaze too long without diverting their eyes because they have learned, probably non-verbally, that it is considered hostile, invest, or coercive to give an uninterrupted stare.

The amount of eye contact varies with the relationship between speakers. For example, a person will maintain more eye contact with a subject who is pleasing. People look more at others they like and seek to minimize eye contact with those they do not like. One's eye behaviour has also been linked to the level of anxiety present, a high rate of blinking indicating a high degree of anxiety. Furthermore, the pupils dilate in response to strong emotion of any sort, whether pleasurable or not."

An interesting eye-response test was run recently when a group of supervisors was shown pictures of men and women. Some of the faces on the pictures were retouched to make the pupils large, while other photos of the same persons had small pupils. Those looking at large-eyed pictures usually described the persons with such words as "warm," "loving," or "sincere." Those looking at the same faces, but with small pupils most often described them as "hard" "insincere," or "insensitive."

Managers can use these facts about eyes to improve their listening skills. Observations on eye contact and pupil size can help a manager to determine if an employee is possibly hostile, interested in a particular subject, nervous, or pleased. These cues let a manager listen beyond the spoken word.

The facial muscles around the mouth, forehead, and cheeks are also important because they are so responsive. They make it possible to express pleasure, displeasure, contempt, or doubt. Thus, pulling down the corners of the mouth while furrowing the forehead can signal doubt. Anger may be displayed with an open square mouth or by lips pressed tightly together, accompanied by brows drawn together.

Posture

Most people are probably less accustomed to masking their posture than their facial expressions; thus, posture can serve as a reliable source of information for the manager. The way a person walks, stands, or sits can reveal a wealth of valuable information. Thus, a person can face one person, stand over another, or slump in front of or "give the shoulder" to another. It is possible to lean forward or recline backward, to lean to the right or the left, to sit erect, or to slouch. A person can open up in a sprawling, relaxed pose or be defensive with closed arms and legs locked in tight.

What does all this mean? No specific, irrevocable rules exist, but some general principles apply. First, a person is drawn toward something he or she likes. When a person leans toward a manager in conversation, it is often safe to assume that the person likes the manager. At the same time, since leaning forward may also indicate an aggressive attitude, the context should be considered.

Second, people position themselves in alignment with others. Frequently, the degree of mutual involvement corresponds to the degree that two people mutually align their heads, shoulders, and hips. People in conversation will often make subtle postural adjustments to one another to create their own preferred degree of alignment.

Third, crossed arms and legs generally characterize one who feels wary, distant, angry, or in some way uncomfortable. This posture may suggest that the body is closed off and protected. Of course, an isolated arm or leg cross alone is not enough evidence to judge closedness, because people have other reasons for crossing or uncrossing limbs such as a room's temperature or the need to rest a leg. It is the total posture of the body within a context that helps the manager to determine the openness or closedness of an individual.

Thus, while one can read no concrete messages from posture, the observant and astute manager is better able to listen to the total message if he analyzes the posture of those involved in the communication.

Gestures

Gestures are another way a sender can complement the verbal communication and enable a receiver to understand the message better. When we see a person cupping her hands, pounding on her desk, waving her arms through the air, or pointing a finger while speaking on the phone, we are able to read the message she is sending. An interesting test of the importance of hands to speech requires a person to carry on a conversation while sitting on her hands. An exaggerated use of shoulder and head movement will result as a compensation for the loss of manual gestures.

You should remember that gestures frequently have different meanings in different cultures. The gestures discussed in this chapter are ones that the average American might easily recognize. At the same time, in another culture, the same gestures might have no meaning or one entirely different from that in the American culture. When involved in cross-cultural exchanges, managers are advised to learn some of the gestural vocabulary of the other cultural group.

Gestures can be used to emphasize or demonstrate a point, to regulate a conversation, to present a caring attitude, or to indicate a defensive or offensive orientation. In fact, many use gestures to emphasize key words in a message even as they use punctuation or underscoring in written statements. For example, "until the people upstairs The manager watching for these gestures finds it is easier to listen for the important points.

Some gestures look like what they demonstrate, such as the size or shape of an object. Such gestures are an attempt to draw a picture of an object, but others are more abstract. For instance, the upraised palms and shrugged shoulders gesture of "Who knows?" is abstract, but still easy to understand.

Speakers also use gestures to regulate the flow of the communication. When a person waves his hand upward or inward or cups his hand over the ear, it may be an indication to speak louder. A person can hold another speaker off by holding the other's arm or hand while making a point. Someone may also point to the listener, keep his hands out in space between himself and the listener, or poke a finger into the listener's shoulder. When people want to interrupt with their own point, they put their hand out as if to hold the person down. When people are not ready to answer, they may step back, screw their eyes closed, and scratch their heads in the hope of getting more time. An effective manager can determine the flow of the conversation by observing gestures and strategically adjusting the communication.

People also use gestures to show a caring attitude. Stroking or patting shoulders, arms, hands, heads, or cheeks, and slapping backs are examples of behaviours generally intended to convey good feeling and regard. These gestures relate so closely with caring that people in stress can often be seen giving such attention to themselves.

The final type of gesture to be discussed indicates either a defensive or an offensive attitude. Movements such as hand rubbing, hand clutching, face rubbing, lip pulling, or cuticle picking often reflect a perceived threat. Other defensive gestures that characterize protection include placing a hand to the throat, neck, head, or mouth. Offensive gestures may be clenched fists, a rapid forward movement of the arm, or a pushing motion.

Of course, it is important to listen to the verbal message as well as the gestures of the speaker. However, just as some people speak in a monotone, it is possible that some will use no gestures to complement the verbal message. Thus, managers should observe all the different components of non-verbal communications.

Spatial messages

Edward Hall coined the word " proxemics" for the study of ways in which space, distance, and territory are components of human communication. Skill in reading proxemics can be valuable for managers listening to others in an organization. Through proxemics, one can determine how friendly, worried, or isolated another feels.

Hall identifies three types of space: feature fixed, semi-fixed feature, and informal. Feature-fixed space is the non-moving and clearly defined space found in buildings and rooms. the permanent arrangement of buildings and, in turn, rooms considerably influences the communication environment. First, it reduce the degree to which people may vary their space to correspond to their attitude. For instance person may feel close to another and desire to move physically closer, however, if the chairs and tables are fixed, such a move would not be possible.

Semi-fixed space includes the movable objects such as tables and chairs and their arrangement. A flexible arrangement of furniture allows managers to observe how people arrange their environment and to listen for the messages being conveyed by the arrangement. For instance, when people are at ease with one another, they may move their chairs away from the table so it does not separate them. Research has found that people at right angles to each other produced six times as many conversations as face-to-face situations across a 36-inch span of table and twice as many as the side-by-side arrangement. Thus, two people seated at right angles to one another may be more predisposed to communication that others.

Informal space, perhaps most significant when considering managerial listening, encompasses the distances maintained in encounters with others. Informal space is divided into four distinct distances: intimate, personal, social, and public.

While these zones vary from one culture or group to another, this discussion will be in terms of the American culture. The first zone, intimate, involves fewer than 18 inches of space between two people. Those who feel close, safe, and secure with one another share this zone. A pat on the back or a hand on the shoulder occurs in this space in the business setting, the intimate zone is usually intentionally penetrated only for fleeting periods of time unless artificially enforced by close seating as in a conference setting or a theatre.

The second zone is personal space, which ranges from arm's length to 3 to 4 feet from the body. While friends who feel ease with each other will share this space, strangers would probably feel some discomfort in this zone. The social zone extends from about 4 to 8 feet from the body and is the area in which most conduct ordinary business and social activity. In supervisor-subordinate relationships, anything closer than the social zone requires a special situation.

The public zone extends 8 to 10 feet from the body and is the area over which individuals exert little personal control. A person who moves to this zone may be signalling a lack of interest in the speaker or an unwillingness to become personal or social. Since distractions are a distinct possibility in this zone, listening is especially difficult for two people. It is better for two people to communicate in the social zone unless one of the participants is uneasy.

Paralanguage

The technical term for the vocal melody and the punctuation a person uses to change, emphasis, or reverse the meaning of words is paralinguistics or paralanguage. Paralanguage includes stress, pitch, rate, loudness, timber, inflection, rhyme, and enunciation—all the vocal nuances that accompany the verbal dimension of speech. Moreover, vocalizations that do not qualify as words, for example, laughing, crying, sighing, yawning, coughing, whispering, and the like, are also parts of paralanguage. Even silences, pauses, and hesitations can fall into this category.

Paralanguage can add richness, but also confusion when one listens to a message. A short sentence such as "I'll do it" may mean any on the following:

I' ll be really happy to do it.

I'll do it, but it's the last time.

You always make me do what you want.

All right you win.

Don't worry, I'll take care of it.

You're so dumb I'd better take care of it myself.

Which "meaning" is implied can usually be determined by the tone or inflection of the voice or by the stress placed on each separate word.

Robert J. McCloskey provided an interesting example of the relationship of paralanguage and listening. A former member of the State Department, he was known to have three distinct ways of saying, "I would not speculate. "Newsweek reported that "spoken without accent, it means the Department doesn't know for sure; emphasis on the 'I' means I wouldn't, but you may - and with some assurance, accent on 'speculate' indicates that the questioner's premise is probably wrong."

Effective managerial listening goes far beyond words then. Listening also involves the observation of facial expressions, posture, gestures, spatial arrangement, and paralanguage. One who does not attend to all these factors may miss important information.

For instance, a manager may ask two subordinate if they have been able to work out a satisfactory system to share the services of a secretary. The subordinates say everything is fine, even as they both look at the floor, tense their muscles and lean away from each other. Manager listening beyond the words would see a clear need to pursue this matter further.

Demonstrating a listening climate

In addition to actually listening carefully, managers must also seem to be listening and establish a climate that demonstrates receptivity. Without this climate, the communication environment in an office can become like that in many homes:

Parent: Why don't you ever tell us what you are doing?

Child: I do, but you don't listen. You're always so busy.

Parent: We're never too busy to listen to you, but just don't seem to want to tell us anything.

Are the parents too busy to listen, or do they just act too busy? The same is true with many managers. Is it possible that they act too busy to listen? A manager may unintentionally establish a non-listening climate by subtle behaviour that says to the subordinate, "Why talk if nobody is listening?"

While a manager is responsible for a tremendous amount of information and spends as much as 50 per cent of her working day listening, she cannot listen if nobody is talking. Managers need to demonstrate a listening climate to motivate people to "open up." Consequently, managers should strive to eliminate listening habits that discourage communication. A listener demonstrating these behaviours is not exhibiting a positive communication climate; consequently, the speaker may not feel he is being listened to. This list can serve as a personal checklist for managers to see if they demonstrate any of the irritating behaviours.

A research study asked employees to indicate which of these poor listening habits they found to be the most common. In the results, two items seemed to stand out.

When I'm talking, he finishes sentences for me.

When I come in, he doesn't put down what he is doing and turn his attention completely to me.

This finding is especially revealing. Clearly, the listener needs to give undivided attention to the speaker who does not want to be rushed to complete the message. This fact relates to the "25-to 75" speaking-thinking differential discussed earlier. The listener's mind moves so much more rapidly than the spoken word that the listeners impatience may show as she attempts to complete the speaker's sentence. Even though the listener is paying attention, this impatience to complete the speaker's communication may develop a negative listening climate. The same is true when the listener works on something else while attempting to listen. The speaker may soon get the feeling that the message being delivered is not very important.

It is particularly important to demonstrate a positive climate when involved in empathetic listening. An empathetic listener tries to understand the speaker's inner feelings. Most people have a very difficult time expressing their, so an encouraging, supportive, receptive environment needs to be established . Feelings of elation, sadness. or fear are more easily and willingly expressed when received in a congruent manner by a receiver whose behaviour demonstrates "I'm with you."

Unfortunately, incongrument listener behaviour is too often the norm. For instance, an employee enters a manager's office and says she has a major problem to discuss. Meanwhile, her manager is shuffling papers around of his desk while saying, 'Go ahead. I'll be listening while I get these forms finished up." What kind of an impression will the employee receive? The employee obviously thinks that her problem is important, but the manager acts as if his forms are as important, if not more so. As a result, he has established a negative listening climate with no demonstrated empathy. The manager should give full physical and psychological attention to the speaker by maintaining eye contact, leaning slightly toward the speaker, changing facial expression in relationship to the message, and taking notes. All are ways that demonstrate a positive listening climate.

17
Manpower Planning

One of the hallmarks of modern management is the ability to plan. The skills management has developed to plan for new markets, new capital investment, and new development programs are now being applied to the personnel field. This new approach is called manpower planning.

Narrowly, defined, manpower planning means forecasting: the prediction of the number of people whom the organization will have to hire, train or promote in a given period. Broadly defined, manpower planning represents a systems approach to personnel in which the emphasis is one the interrelationships among various personnel policies and programs. This contrasts with more traditional "piecemeal" concern with selection, training, promotion, and the rest as separate compartmentalized functions.

We shall look first at the narrower and more quantitative view of manpower planning-forecasting-and then we shall turn to the more qualitative, systems implications in this new approach to personnel.

Manpower forecasting

The first step in any planning effort is to get some picture of what has been occurring in a flow of people into and through and out of the organization. Obviously the past isn't going to repeat itself precisely, but some picture of the dynamic interrelationships among these personnel flows will help the organization predict its needs at least in the short run.

Given past experience with managers leaving the organization, on the average, quit, retire, are discharged or become ill in management and managers promoting, the model predicates how many new managers must be hired at each level to maintain a stable system. The model can be used to predict the consequences of other contingencies. If more management training an more promotion from within is practiced, the model shows how much additional recruitment must take place at lower levels and how much recruitment can be reduced at higher levels. Similarly, if turnover can or should be reduced, the implications for reduced hiring are spelled out.

Manpower inventories and computers. The application of new technology to record keeping enables management to make more effective use of employee records in this regard. In addition to personal biographical information, such as age, previous education and training, work experience, and perhaps some psychological factors, such records contain a job history of the employee within the company. When such records are computerized, it becomes possible to answer quickly questions like the following:

How many employees in that jobs will be retiring in each future year? How many employees with appropriate backgrounds will be available for promotion to engineering management type of jobs next year? Who in our present work force is qualified today to be considered for an opening as a commercial underwrite?

Thus, skills and manpower inventories help to answer a range of questions extending from the broader planning type issue to immediate placement problems. The first requires a knowledge of the over-all profile of the current work ; the second needs specific, detailed information on individuals.

The profiles give management an "early warning system" for both bulges and shortages of people at certain points. Since there is usually a relatively long lead time required to get people through the system to reasonably responsible technical or managerial positions, appropriate selection actions must be taken years before the need will develop.

Good forecasting, combined with the use of flow models like the one we have been describing, can alert management to upcoming manpower shortages or surpluses. One the basis of such warnings, management can take measurement to handle problems before they become so serious as to inflict major damage to the organization. Below are two examples of the kind of problem that might be avoided were management given early warning:

The Delevan Company expanded rapidly during and after World War II, and few managers were hired during the 1950's and early 1960's. Thus, its managers are drawn from a relatively compact age group, and most of them are in their 50's and late 40's. There is little between them and the next group of managers, now in their late 20's and early 30's. Further, since the older managers "ran the show" by themselves for all these years, they have not developed the habit of delegating authority. As a consequence, to meet the needs of the 1980's and 1990's, and also to provide middle management in the interim, the company must (1) provide rapid development experience for the younger managers; (2) "pirate" qualified managers in their late 30's from other companies to till middle management slots; or (3) use a combination of these.

Sometimes even more drastic measures must be taken

As of 1977 there were a number of government laboratories which were in very much the same situation as the Delevan Company. A high percentage of their scientists were hired during and immediately after World War II. Since this was a relatively young group at the time, there have been few retirements or deaths. On the other hand, total employment has remained stable, so there have been few new recruits and most members of the work force are in their fifties or early sixties. Over the years a number of old-timers have declined in creative ability; some have narrow skills for which there is little need today. The newer skills are concentrated among the few young men recently hired. Now along come budget cuts and civil service requirements that heavy emphasis be given to seniority in layoffs. Given the age distribution of these scientists, even a slight layoff means that men with 10 or 15 years service are eliminated. Top management of the lab worries that if the cuts get deeper there will be no one left under age 55. With limited funds available, these laboratories do not have the options available to the Delevan Company to hire younger men. Instead, if government civil service regulations permit, they must encourage men in their late 50's to seek early retirement.

Past trends often do not continue and new factors emerge which substantially modify the manpower flows. Then the more static Hairs model we have been utilizing is inadequate.

Changes in demand. Changes in the type of technology employed, in the range of products and services offered, and in over-all company policies will have an impact on future manpower requirements.

An insurance company begins making more widespread use of computers at the same time as it introduces job enlargement. Both have the same impact: a decreased requirement for unskilled clerical personnel. This, in turn, is bound to have an effect on hiring rates, promotions, and the costs of recruitment and training. But the precise impact is difficult to determine without the use of some sort of follow model.

Of course, such calculations are not easy to make. Equipment salesmen and technology enthusiasts often exaggerate the labour-saving results of new installations. Frightening predictions that computers would substantially reduce the need for white-collar employees proved unfounded. In part, of course, such predictions depend also upon sales forecasts.

As the Claridge Company shifts to a more technically sophisticated product line, it must anticipate that he proportion of college-trained salesmen will have to increase. However, the anticipated doubling of sales in these product areas in the next two years will not mean a doubling of manpower. The marketing manager for technical products will have to be consulted as to the relationship between sales volume and sales personnel.

Change in supply. Both a changing labour market and company policies can have a major impact on the supply side of the manpower equation. Perhaps college graduates are harder to hire or the government is placing pressure to hire more minority group members. Over the longer run, it may be realistic to prophesy greater utilization of women, minority group members, and even part-time employees. It will also be useful to observe how the skills profile of the work force is changing over time. For example, if newer employees are better educated than older employees, the company can make use of more internal promotion to fill higher level positions. However, such a change may also be accompanied by higher turnover, since such employees are likely to have more attractive alternatives than do less well-educated employees.

Limitation of forecasting

Forecasting is still far from an exact science. While advance planning is useful in seeking to anticipate personnel changes which are just beginning to show themselves management needs to remember that such forecasts depend upon the continuation of trends, which may easily change. A decline in the economy can change drastically both the need for manpower and even the number of voluntary resignations. The result can be that a predicted shortage in certain jobs becomes a difficult surplus.

Given this discussing of manpower forecasting, let us now look at manpower planning in its broader sense. The manpower system consists of four elements: (1) job structures; (2) career paths; (3) policies to improve employment stability; and (4) policies covering work force reduction by means of attrition, layoffs, and discharge.

Job analysis and job descriptions

The job description is a source of basic information for all of manpower planning. In fact such descriptions are also essential for selection, training, work load, incentives, and salary administration, as will be discussed in forthcoming chapters. All these personnel areas require that the relevant duties, tasks, and employee requirements be made explicit for each organizational position.

Clearly, job descriptions are useful, even though individual deviations from them may be allowed. A new employee will want to know what is expected of him, and when the supervisor detects coordination problems between employees, he will need to know what each should properly be expected to do. Where such mutual role expectations are compatible, there is less likelihood of work flow friction.

Men's furnishings salesman: I get so angry, I could burst. Those stock boys are supposed to place the new merchandise in the display cases; instead they just leave the boxes all over the counter for us to arrange. They say it's our job, but I know it's theirs.

What duties are required in a particular position? The actual job title may be misleading. Some have been inflated to provide ego satisfactions, e.g., the plumber who calls himself a sanitary engineer. Others have just become less accurate because of technological or organization changes, e.g., engineers who have become technical sales specialists. Further, various individuals perform the same job differently. Smith is an accountant who enjoys spending time with lien managers, helping them analyze their cost variances; Jones prefers to stay with his own department doing analytical work. Thus, there can be a number of ambiguities surrounding what is a job, but before dealing with the problems of definition let us look at us look at the process of acquiring and analyzing the relevant information.

Job analysis

Large companies have specially trained job analysts; in smaller organizations the supervisor develops the analysis, ideally in collaboration with the employees involved. The analysis itself consists of two parts: a statement of the work to be performed, and the skills and knowledge which must be possessed by anyone filling the job.

Job or occupational titles in themselves often give a misleading impression of the actual content of a job. A 'milk deliveryman," in addition to being able to drive a truck, must also handle customer accounts and sell the company's products. An engineer may have to spend most of his time *selling* department heads on the importance of using standard parts. Many so-called "clerk" jobs embrace a range of duties that are unrelated to the simple tabulating or recording activities one might associate with the job title.

Particularly at managerial and staff levels, the personalities of the key people with whom the new person will be dealing become an important element in any realistic job specification.

Care needs to be exercised that excessively broad and ambiguous requirements are not established like "intelligent worker" or "hard working" or "good personality." These encourage discriminatory or foolish hiring practices.

Job descriptions

Obviously there are a number of ways to group and organize duties and tasks, and these will vary somewhat, depending on whether we are talking about manual, clerical, professional, or administrative jobs. For purposes of simplification we shall simply list the major categories of analysis that might be included.

Functional categories And	Examples
Procedures, equipment, and subject matter with which job holder should be familiar; typical problems and requests he will receive	Develop new-product quality tests
Scope of responsibility; magnitude of discretion; "time span of control"	Responsible for approving claims up to $500, these decisions reviewed semiannually by Comptroller's Office
Standards of performance and work load	Undertake machining from blueprints to tolerances of .001 inch

Relationships; job interfaces	Calls set-up man to adjust equipment when tolerances can't be maintained
Supervision; reporting relation-work load	Reports to Purchasing Manager but also receives direction from comptroller and Manager of Engineering for special assignments
Qualification, probationary and training period	After 90 days becomes permanent employee
Working conditions, hazards	Operators must stand through most of the work day and be able to lift up to 50 pounds of machine sock; work in hot, humid areas under cranes
Promotion and career opportunities	Secretaries can quality for chief clerk and office manager positions.

If properly handled such descriptions could provide relevant inputs to computer controlled employee information systems that provide a variety of useful manpower data on, for example, the changing character of company jobs, similarities in tasks being performed in various departments that might suggest new promotional ladders or organization changes, and many others.

Ideally the description should distinguish between *prescribed and discretionary* content of each job. Thus, every salesman may be required to submit a field report weekly covering his customer visitations. More experienced and capable salesmen will be expected to use their discretion in providing management with information about changing conditions in the marketplace, its sources and possible remedies in terms of the company's product line.

As noted, management must decide how broad to make jobs; whether , for example, there should be a different category of job for each type of secretary employed or a single job, "Secretary." This can have a critical effect on promotion and transfer.

In much the same vein a decision has to be made as to how specialized or broad the job should be from the point of view of both selection and promotion. Narrow jobs are easier to fill, but they do not build as much qualification for future assignments, and they discourage the employee from reacting to emergencies or changed conditions.

The Carlton Company found that it could not get employees to do even minor maintenance on their machinery, because the job description made no mention of any responsibilities other than production.

Management may be induced to keep the job narrow in order to reduce the evaluated wage rate that will be assigned. However, some supervisors will endeavor to collude with employees to upgrade the job in order to obtain a higher rating, thereby satisfying current employees and making it easier to hire new employees.

Of course, in dynamic organizations, where tasks are constantly changing. It may be useful to keep job descriptions more general, more flexible, and less detailed, particularly when they are developed by central staff groups to cover broad areas of the business.

An organization may wish to compare is job descriptions, or position guides, as they are sometimes called, with those developed for other organizations. The most comprehensive and widely cited reference in the field is the U.S. Department of Labour's Dictionary of Occupational Titles, which contains 22, 000 separate titles. More specialized management and professional job descriptions form representative companies are published by the National Industrial Conference Board.

Job specifications

Experience and judgment should enable the personnel specialist to help management translate job requirements into human requirements: the educational, experience, and personality requirements for anyone filling the job. This doesn't have to be a one-way street; knowing who will be available may exert an influence over how the job will be structured.

The danger here is the temptation to ask for too much background in the way of education and experience, particularly formal degrees and certifications. These requirements can unduly increase salary costs and employee expectations. Similarly there may actually be advantages in bringing in new people who do not have a specific background in the field.

We had always thought that a manager in consumer appliances had to have been in the business for at least four or five years. Now we find that if we take a bright employee from some totally different function of the business, he starts asking some very basic questions about how we do things, and doesn't take much for granted. Often those "dumb" questions about how we do things, and doesn't take much for granted. Often those "dumb" questions of the apprentice are just the kind of perspective our tradition-bound department needs.

It is difficult to specify personality requirements because of the measurement problem. Clearly some distinctions can be made in jobs that require building and maintaining close working relationships with many different people from positions that involve only routine contacts with a small number of nearby colleagues.

Changing jobs to meet people's needs. Our discussion has assumed that job descriptions remain fixed and that people adapt in order to meet these requirements.

While reasonable uniformity may be desirable in some situations, in others management needs to be flexible, as the following example illustrates.

We very much wanted to keep Miss Callaner. She had a number of attractive outside offers and wanted more responsibility, but we thought she just didn't have the math and statistics background to take over the Market Research manager's office. Then we finally decided to upgrade the department's statistician's job to where he became "Assistant to the Manager." Since she would have less to do with survey design and evaluation, we were able to add more liaison duties with our field sales departments to Miss Callaner's new position. In the process we think it's probably a better mix of duties of a Market Research manager than was the old job.

While this type of analysis is often used to reduce the skill requirements to make positions more suitable for minority group members, the same approach encourages managers to think creatively about the whole range of job-person relationships. Particularly within management there can be a number of alternative "clusterings" of duties to assist in the matching of people and jobs.

Designing career paths

Every organization is faced with such questions as: Should employees be promoted within relatively specialized carrier lines or be given broad exposure to a variety of jobs? How much promotional opportunity is desirable? Under what circumstances should openings be filled with an already trained outsider or by training an insider?

The answers depend upon an understanding of the dynamics of promotion systems, including organizational needs and employee expectations.

Employee expectations

Within a given organization, its members come to anticipate a certain pattern of job progression based on what they have observed of the internal mobility of other employees. Below are some examples of quite different types different types of career ladders:

In police departments it is expected that everyone starts at the bottom, as a rookie, and moves up-even though there has been some recent discussion of bringing in college men at higher ranking status as "police agents."

The military traditionally has a two-career ladder system: an enlisted man starts as private and advances as high as warrant officer; an officer starts as second lieutenant or ensign and may end his career as a general or admiral. But there have been increasing opportunities in recent years for some enlisted men to become officers.

The hospital has an even more rigid caste system: nurses aides rarely become nurses; nurses may aspire to be head nurses or even superintendents of nurses, but never doctors, etc.

The university for its academic staff has a well-known ladder: instructor, assistant professor, associate professor, and full professor.

Typical companies have at least four distinct ladders:

— manual workers are hired into unskilled or labour pool jobs and promote on the basis of seniority up to higher paying and/or easier machine-tending positions, or perhaps inspection.

— skilled tradesmen often start as apprentices, or "helpers," and move up to craftsman classifications.

— clerical employees move to more desirable locations and higher paying while-collar jobs.

— managers often start as trainees or as assistant supervisors and can, of course, move to top management. Often there are separate ladders for sales, production, or engineering which converge for the last few steps in upper management. There may also be separate "professional ladders" in fields like accounting, law, and personnel.

Characteristics of career paths: length and breadth

Very obviously the rookie patrolman can move up a much longer career ladder than a hospital medical records librarian, who, in most hospitals, will occupy a "dead-end" job-i.e., one that provides no promotional steps. Most industrial relations experts favour the formal structuring of jobs to provide reasonably long, orderly career ladders, because of the motivation and training they provide.

Where the career ladder leads up to jobs that are much different or much more responsible than those required at the port of entry, special care needs to be taken to be sure that hiring standards reflect this. Thus, petroleum refineries traditionally promote personnel form the labor gang up through many steps to the stillman post, a crew chief responsible for millions of dollars of technical equipment. There can be morale problems associated with new employees being overqualified for their port-of-entry job, marking time until they can be promoted to positions that call for more of their abilities.

On the other hand, in industries like advertising and in many research and teaching posts, while salaries and status go up with movement along the career ladder, there is little difference in the type of work performed at the higher, as compared to the lower, levels. In fact, in many engineering companies, an employee may shift from being a manager of one project to a staff technical person on the next project.

Some companies rely so heavily on the promotion-from-within policy that they cannot afford to keep people who do not qualify or are not desirous of moving ahead. Many universities similarly follow the practice of "up or out," which simply means that instructors and assistant professors must either earn a promotion or seek employment elsewhere.

Breadth of job or career paths vary substantially. In more craft-and professionally-oriented work, the paths tend to be "narrow" and the experience obtained is all in similar function. Many modern managements, on the other hand, pride themselves in providing very diverse exposures to rising executives. Managers shift laterally as they move upward, gaining experience in a variety of functions such as marketing, manufacturing, and finance. Other companies find that while this circuitous routing makes a well-rounded top executive, it tends to diminish the in-depth knowledge and competence of executives in the various functional fields. They, therefore, keep the lines narrow until close to the very top of the pyramid.

Broader career paths increase the likelihood that there will be few or no "dead-end" jobs, because a wide variety of promotional opportunities are made available. A more broadly and less parochially rained work force with wider perspective can be the result. Against these advantages must be weighted the costs of constantly retraining men for new jobs requiring different knowledge and skills.

Technology shapes career ladders

The breadth and length of career ladders can be related to the technology of the industry; it is no simply a management judgement. The manner in which employees move from one job to another is largely determined by he industrial structure. The automobile, steel, and aerospace industries offer examples of quite different patterns.

Dead-end paths

Many times employees are concerned that the promotion ladder on which they find themselves doesn't lead "upward" very far. "In this organization, if you get started in Packaging, you know you've had it."

The organization needs to guard against a situation in which pockets of promotable personnel build up in some areas where promotions are "sluggish"-and a dearth of promotable personnel builds up in other areas where promotional opening are more numerous. It is desirable to have "many roads to the top" so that no group is favoured. Where technology is changing rapidly, this may be difficult to accomplish, and only a major retraining and development program can project promotional opportunities.

"When the computer industry shifted from vacuum tubes to solid state components, a large number of traditionally trained electrical engineers who had been qualified to move to high-level positions found themselves "disqualified" because of their lack of knowledge about solid state physics, just as several years before that, the mechanical engineers had been displaced by the electricals!

A seemingly innocent change in management policy within a given department sometimes wipes out the promotional opportunities of a while group of workers. Whyte describes such a case:

> In view of the rapid scientific and technical development of the company decided that only college graduates should be appointed as foremen. The new ruling hit the HI-Test plant particularly hard, for some of these men had been singled out as especially able and promising...They were at the top now with no place to go.. It was common to hear them say, "We're just bumping our heads against the ceiling here."

When management finds that there are dead-end jobs in the organization where promotions are unlikely, it should try to tie them to other jobs or else fill them with employees who have neither the capability nor the desire to move ahead. Without promotional opportunities, organization effectiveness may suffer.

Manpower hoarding: Departments sometimes try to hoard more employees than they need, particularly employees with scarce talents; for example, engineers were hoarded during the shortages of the 1960's. Understandably, employees grow restless when they realize that the opportunity to advance is being blocked by the piling up of surplus manpower. Excess manpower can mean absence of job challenge; if there are too many people for too little work they get into one another's way.

Interdepartmental competition may also be a factor in restricting promotional opportunities. For example, a department that was carrying on a full-scale training program for tool-makers refused to honor requests from employees who finished the course to accept a promotion to another department, claiming that the other department was "too cheap" to do its own training. On the other hand, there are situations in which everyone recognizes that certain departments will train workers for other departments. The important thing is to insure that the organization's control systems, such as cost accounting, reflect this contribution. Also if some supervisors are reluctant to let their trained workers move on to higher-rated jobs in other departments, serious inequities are bound to develop.

A means of minimizing some of these differences among departments is to require that job opening be announced throughout the organization and candidates be evaluated by some screening body that is not partial to those coming from a given area. This practice, sometimes called "open bidding," serves to tie together a number of individual promotional ladders.

Clarity of career paths

Some career ladders are sharply defined: the head teller is always selected from senior tellers working in her bank, who, in turn have moved up from trainee to teller. Others are less so: In company X the most common route to the presidency has always been through sales, but the most recent top executive had a financial background and currently there are rumors that the Board will bring in someone form outside the company.

There is one obvious disadvantage of clarity in career paths. Some companies are able to transfer ineffective employees to less critical jobs or to positions which don't block others from obtaining promotions, without this appearing to be a demotion. Particularly in large organizations, it is possible to create reasonable ambiguities as to whether a man is going up, sideways, or down. Often salary levels are not known precisely, and even when they are, there is usually enough flexibility in most salary evaluation plans to allow for more generous payment to longer service employees who are no longer eligible for promotion.

Whatever their "shape" or clarity, career paths must be integrated with other aspects of personnel administration. They must be related to the salary structure so that each promotion provides a significant salary increase. Also the various lines must be compared with one another to be sure that there are equitable interrelationships. An assistant department head, which is two rungs up one career line, should have similar pay and responsibilities to other assistant department heads who are similarly situated.

Internal promotion Vs. External recruitment

The above discussion of career paths assumes that the organization is intending to fill most of its job vacancies through internal promotion and employees will gain their qualifications through on-the-job training, perhaps supplemented by additional format training. An alternative policy would be to recruit a candidate for higher level openings from outside organization, someone already filling a comparable job in another firm or with the appropriate formal education. What criteria are available for choosing between training and selection as alternative means of filling job openings?

Thus, the filling of any single job has many ramifications. The proposal here would cut off promotional opportunities for some personnel and increase them for others. In addition, training costs would go up, a least in the short run, and conceivably the company would have to pay higher salaries to recruit college personnel. All of these factors would have to be weighed before a final decision was reached.

The case for promotion form within

Providing better qualified employees. No organization can rely on outside recruitment to fill all its requirements. True, certain jobs are similar from one organization another, but most jobs require specialized knowledge that can be obtained only within a particular firm. Even jobs that do not seem to be unique require familiarity with the people, procedures, policies, and special characteristics of the organization in which they are performed. As we have already observed, career lines allow for on-the-job training insofar as jobs are arranged in such a way that experience gained performing the lower job prepares one for the next rung up.

Internal recruitment is also a means of selection. The most selection procedures, such as interviewing and testing, provide, a far from perfect picture of a new applicant's potential worth. Seeing a man in action, however, over a period of years, enables management to make a realistic assessment of his skills.

Promotion also provides a process of "selective socialization." Over time, those whose personalities and skills enable them to fit into the organization's human relations tend to stay on; those whose personalities conflict tend to leave-either voluntarily or involuntarily. This is called-self-selection.

Providing motivation: People will work harder if they know this will lead to promotion. But employees have little motivation if the better jobs are reserved for outsiders.

Providing job satisfaction: Americans want to keep moving ahead. Being given additional responsibilities is not enough; people want the tangible recognition that a higher-ranking title provides. In addition, most workers look forward to unbroken, continuous service. They like to feel that they can get ahead in their own company without having turn elsewhere.

Cost: It probably is more expensive to recruit an outsider who has already demonstrated high performance and must be lured away form his present employer.

The case for recruitment form outside

Just as many organizations seek outsiders to sit on their boards of directors in order to introduce new perspectives, so they reserve certain lesser positions for newcomers. This infusion of "new blood" keeps the system from growing stagnant, repetitious, and overly conformist. This is probably of less importance in hourly-paid jobs than in staff and managerial jobs, however. Recruitment from outside the firm can reduce the expense of training new employees, which can be very high, particularly for skilled craftsmen and technical personnel.

Different company philosophies: The recruitment vs. promotion decision is partially one of economics: where do you invest your money? Recent research suggests that companies tend to adopt unbalanced strategies: Some invest a great deal in expensive selection testing techniques, while others are more likely to have extensive on-the-job training and stress promotion from within. Rarely do companies have what would seem highly desirable: a balanced program.

Unless expanding very rapidly, most companies are more likely to hire highly trained professionals from outside than to promote their managers from within. However, if, as many observers suggest, management itself is becoming more professionalized, we would anticipate increased job hopping among impatient executives. Anxious to find challenge and increased responsibilities, they may seek out alternative sources of employment to climb a career ladder in contrast to moving up within a single organization.

Administering career paths

This has been a conceptual discussion; now let us move to some of the difficult day-to-day problems of administering these "lines" and "ladders."

Number of promotional steps

The number of promotions possible is not inherent in the technology; management makes the choice. For example, take a clerical department with 20 employees doing various telephoning, typing, filing, and copying tasks. By deemphasizing the differences in job duties, the company could place all jobs in the same salary grade. Contrariwise, by meticulously evaluating differences among the jobs, conceivably each employee could receive a slightly different salary. In the latter case there could be a 2—step promotional ladder.

What is the optimum number? Too few promotional steps may injure morale by eliminating the sense of personal progress and accomplishment. Too many promotional steps may mean that an excessive amount of time and effort must be spent in selecting candidates gaining acceptance for the choices, and shifting employees. The result may be chaos. In approaching this question of frequency of promotions, we must be careful to distinguish between promotion to a better job and periodic wage or salary *merit increases.*

There is a good bit of ambiguity particularly on professional jobs, about when an employee has actually moved to a more important job, for job definitions are often quite elastic. An engineer, for example, may be required to work on a more difficult assignment for several months before the change is officially recognized by what we would call a promotion-that is, a job title with more prestige and increased income. When a man is officially promoted to a more responsible position may be simply a matter of supervisory judgment.

Varying attitudes toward promotion: People differ in what promotion means to them. Many managers tend to project their own feelings about promotion onto their employees, forgetting that not every employee wants to be promoted-at least not in the terms in which management typically conceives of promotion. Employees differ greatly in their "level of aspiration."

Management sometimes makes the mistake of using a highly unpopular job as the required stepping-stone to higher positions. As a result, serious shortage may develop in these higher positions because few candidates are willing to spend time on the undesirable rung of the promotional ladder.

Similarly, when an employee enters into an apprenticeship program he is often required to accept a reduction in pay for a number of years before he wins a craftsman's rating. Management officials assume that employees should be willing to make short-run sacrifices in return for long-run benefits, but they forget that their own time perspective may be quite different form that of their employees.

What management regards as a substantial promotion may not seem like a promotion at all to the employee himself. The nurse or salesman may not want to be an administrator. The additional responsibilities or travel requirements of some jobs may more than outweigh the status associated with the new salary and title. In another situation, technical personnel may be reluctant to give up their specialities to become administrators. In order to motivate and reward these professionals, many companies establish "dual ladders" dual ladders" which allow them to move up through a series of steps without assuming managerial positions. Although this does alleviate some of the inequalities, it is doubtful that, given the present organization of industry, the same status and perquisites, can be given to a "Principal Research Scientist" as to a "Divisional President." The promotional ladders are not really parallel.

Finally, there is always a group of employees what are quite content to stand still, who prefer the known to the unknown. Unwilling to risk what they have in hand, they want to stick close to the people they know and the responsibilities they are familiar with. To these people, improvement means regular wage increases, more security, and perhaps and easier job. Yet in some industries, technology has made it difficult to satisfy this last desire; the majority of jobs are fast-paced and demanding.

Management must provide career ladders that will encourage promising employees to take the risks involved in moving upward. It must not discourage valuable employees from seeking advancement by making service in an unpopular job a prerequisite to promotion. It must provide for employees who do outstanding work but are unwilling to take on new and additional responsibilities. And it must provide alternatives for those who are reluctant to assume supervisory responsibilities.

Selecting who is to be promoted

Having settled on a general promotion program management must face the still more difficult task of deciding who to promote, since there are usually more candidates than openings. The choice usually revolves around evaluations of relative merit, ability, and length of service.

If promotion is to be an incentive, the best-performing employees ought to be advanced. However, since differences in merit may not be readily measurable, the man who was not promoted may feel that favoritism was involved. As a further source of discontent, on many jobs performance reflects the coordinated activities of many people or chance factors-this making individual merit difficult to measure.

But there is also the question of ability-that is, potential performance on other jobs. Jones may be doing fine on his present job but lack the ability to do the work on a higher-ranked job. Smith, on the other hand, may be doing poorly at present because of inadequate supervision or the unchallenging nature of the work. Put him on more difficult work and he may blossom.

Long-term factors are also relevant. The individual best fitted for an immediate promotion may not have the greatest long-term potential. That is, the most deserving candidate at the moment may seem to be a senior employee who has the ability to move only one more step up the promotional ladder, but it may be better to promote a younger man who may eventually advance into higher management.

In addition, ability is as difficult to measure as merit. The specific traits, attitudes, personalities, and skills that make up ability are frequently ambiguous. For this reason companies often rely on objective measurements-years of education, for example.

To complicate matters further, some people may be given special opportunities to acquire valuable skills whereas others are not. Certain jobs give employees an opportunity to move about freely, bringing them into contact with high-level personnel whose opinion are crucial in promotion decision. They "learn their way around the organization" and are on the spot when a promotional opportunity turns up.

What we are saying is that some effort should be made to reward both merit and ability, even though neither is easy to measure. Organizations that have failed to reward excellence in service, or that have relied too heavily on personal relationships or length of service, suffer in terms of both efficiency and morale.

Seniority

The extent to which promotions should be based on seniority is almost always an area of dispute between unions and management.

Arguments for seniority: The use of such criteria as performance evaluation, selection tests, and supervisory opinions leads many employees to feel that promotions are not made fairly. And charges of favoritism and discrimination may lead to declines in morale and productivity. Unions object that as long as managers have the power to select the most suitable candidate for promotion, is a simple matter for them to discourage ambitious employees from speaking out against company policy.

To avoid this difficult, it is often suggested that promotions be based on some objective criterion, and that the only objective criterion is length of service. When management known that it is going to promote the employee with the longest service, chances are that the company will give him the training he needs to move into the new job. Management will also tend to perfect its initial selection procedures, for once an individual gets into the organization his future will be relatively assured.

In certain societies, the older men invariably occupy the highest positions; although we do not follow this practice rigidly, we still feel that it is appropriate for the senior people within an organization to occupy higher positions than their juniors. True, we make a good many exceptions: the long-time employee who is clearly incompetent, and the young man who is a genius. However, ours is at least partially an "age-graded society" where age, position, and prestige are correlated.

Arguments against. Excessive emphasis on seniority, however, may violate employee attitudes about the "right" way of getting ahead: Indeed, the promotion of incompetents solely on the basis of length of service clearly violates another strongly entrenched cultural attitude that rewards should be somehow commensurate with accomplishment.

The top-skilled members of galls-and steel-making crews are typically men who have worked their way up through a lengthy, informal apprenticeship system, in the old days they worked long hours, often without pay, under the far-from-tolerant tutelage of a craftsman who would put up with his younger assistants only in return for numerous services. It was a long, hard, grueling road to the top, and those who have made it frequently resent the rather automatic manner in which men can now work themselves into similar positions primarily by accumulating seniority.

Contribution to ability: Up to some point, it seems likely that the longer an employee works a one job, the more qualified he becomes for promotion to the next-higher job. Research among production workers suggests that the employee with the longest service often is better prepared for promotion than management is initially willing to admit. For many jobs, particularly hose at the lower levels, differences in ability from one employee to another may be less important then noting the most senior employee to another may be less important than management tends to think. Consequently, the gain in morale derived from promoting the most senior employee may more than offset any slight loss of efficiency.

But the correspondence between seniority and ability undoubtedly diminished as length of service increases, and beyond a certain level, continued service brings very little gain. Indeed, after a point, increased length of service on a given job actually *reduces* an employee's ability to change jobs, producing in him what is often referred to as "a rained incapacity to learn"; that is, he becomes so imbued with the problems and procedures of his present job that he is unable to adjust to new circumstances and situations. The expert becomes simply too expert in what he is doing.

Reward for loyalty: In a sense, to grant promotions on the basis of seniority is to reward employees for loyalty. In an organization that wants to keep to its employees and avoid costly turnover, a type of guaranteed promotion plan may be an effective personnel policy. Traditional Japanese industry believed this.

No one would deny that loyal service deserves reward. But the question is how many loyal employees become discouraged about their future with the organization when hey realize that they can be promoted only as fast as length of service permits? Also, the emphasis on longevity induces a "ritualistic devotion to duty" in which perfection in the small things, the job routines, and the avoidance of mistakes take precedence over imaginative and energetic pursuit of more challenging goals. Further, those characteristics that were most associated with job success at lower skill levels may not be as useful in higher level jobs. Balancing this, however, is the reduction in destructive interpersonal competition that can occur when there is too much uncertainty about who will be promoted.

Striking a balance

Every organization must decide on the relative weights it will give to merit, ability, and seniority in making promotion decisions. Even when company policy or the union contract sets up merit and ability as the prime determinants, many an organization succumbs in time to the presumably more objective criterion so seniority. Supervisors in general believe that relations with their subordinates will be easier if they promote the most senior employee. Almost all companies give some weight to seniority in practice, although firms that are unionized give it greater weight than those that are not.

Administering the promotion program

Dealing with the individual

Handling employees who are unlikely to be promoted. A boss must be able to predict what members of his group will be the most likely candidates for promotion when openings occur. And he must try to keep those who are unlikely to be promoted from taking it for granted that they will soon be moving up the ladder. For example, a long service employee may assume he is promotable even if he is not. If his boss allows that misapprehension to continue, the employee will be sadly disappointed when someone else gets the job. And if his buddies encourage him to think that he is wronged, he is likely to create a serious problem.

Problems of this sort can be avoided if the boss makes a point of discussing with the hopeful candidate the exact nature of the new responsibilities long before the opening actually occurs. Then, if the employee is clearly not qualified for the promotion, he may be brought around to accept his unsuitability. The supervisor may be able to suggest a way in which the employee can supplement his background or improve his performance of that he will eventually become eligible for a promotional opportunity. If he shows himself unwilling to make the extra effort required, the job of winning his assent to being "passes over" becomes much easier.

Dealing with the employee who doesn't want to be promoted. In our culture, anyone who odes not want to advance is regarded as somehow queer or lazy. Many individuals take on higher-level jobs even when they are not suited for additional responsibility; but the cost is high to themselves and to the organization. In fact, people who really should not be promoted may come to feel that a failure to show interest in advancement is a black mark against their record. Actually, a clear recognition of each employee's psychological and intellectual limits is valuable both to the organization ad to the individual. The employee who has reached the limit of his ambitions or abilities still has a vital role to plan. The armed services have discovered the value of long service "old-line" master sergeants who stay with a particular unit, providing stability and continuity, while its commissioned officers come and go. So, too, employees who have been in one department for a long time may help to break in newcomers, particularly new supervisors.

But nonmobile people must not be permitted to monopolize the training jobs in which more suitable candidates can be prepared for higher positions.

Helping the successful candidate. Serious problems are experienced by the man who does move up into a new position, particularly if it involves supervision. Unless he has been with the group for a long time, and unless the group has resistance. His new subordinates will be uncertain at first about what his new leadership will mean to their future.

The employee who is promoted to a nonsupervisory position has his problems, too, for he may be facing new responsibilities for which he is not wholly prepared. Nothing is "automatic" in a strange job, and the new man is under great strain. In worrying about what he should do and how to avoid mistakes; he many become so tense that he performs clumsily or forgetfully. If his supervisor is aware of these strains, he can provide the understanding that will help the new man over the hump of the first days on the job.

Craft consciousness

Where promotion ladders are short and narrow, employees are more likely to perceive the job as being a part of their personal property or territorial preserve. Any threat to an element of the job situation becomes a threat to the employee.

This is one of the primary sources of resistance to technological change; the employee is reluctant to see his work modified for fear of his job status. His income, his security derived from knowing everything there is know about the job-any or all may be threatened.

Craft-consciousness-the feeling that no one should work outside his narrowly defined job duties-has traditionally been strong in the construction and maintenance trades. A carpenter will refuse to do any work by carpentry, and he will refuse to let other employees do carpentry work-even if this means that other employees must stand idle or be laid off.

Other groups that lack the traditional craft status of the building trades try to erect barriers around their particular skills. The primary motivation seems to be job security, for workers feel that if they can prevent other men from doing their work, they will be able to make their own jobs more secure. Unions in general encourage craft-consciousness, because they look upon it as a means of restricting management's power to make transfers. And every time management gives in to a union demand to make craft boundaries more sacred, a past practice is established, which is in a sense frozen into the union contract.

In one company, machinists were prohibited from picking up any material that had fallen on the floor. This was the janitors' work! Even valuable parts were sometimes swept away by the cleanup crews because the machinists refused to pick them up.

Management itself, by carrying specialization and division of labour to extremes, may be responsible for proliferating an unwieldy number of narrowly defined jobs. Where jobs are defined narrowly, each with a limited number of highly specific duties, the problem of shifting employees is accentuated. Employees, taking their cue form management, then proceed to erect artificial barriers that inhibit flexible transfers designed to expedite the flow of work and to even out work-load inequalities.

"I am the only girl in the office who can run this mimeograph machine. It's not easy, let me tell you; it's old and has got lots of tricks to it and it takes years to learn. I don't want other girls using it; this way I know they really need me around here. When we occasionally run out of work on the machine, I don't think its fair for me to have to do other odd jobs. After all, this is what I am getting paid for."

Reducing craft-consciousness. How can management deal with excessive craft-consciousness? First, by accepting as natural the work group's efforts to protect its members. Very little is accomplished by accusing employees of "feather bedding", for employees are anxious to strengthen their "property right" in their jobs.

A second way of meeting this problem is to develop job description that define jobs in terms of the work that needs to be done rather than in terms of abstract craft skills. In short, determine job duties by the requirements of the work process, not by traditional concepts of what a craftman is.

In inducting new employees, the supervisor should try to instill in them the broadest possible definition of their jobs. A good recruitment and training policy helps, for employees with diversified skills and good training are more easily transferred.

Transfers

Not all movement is upward. Particularly where career ladders have substantial "breadth", employees many shift sideways. To be sure, the transfer that is a lateral move may involve greater salary and responsibility, but there may also be times in which the individual accepts an assignment at a comparable level in order to broaden his experience or in order to get around a "blockage" in his career ladder. Transfers are also used by management to cope with incompatibilities between the job and the person holding the job. When an employees has trouble doing his work or develops personal friction with his boss or fellow employees, the answer may be to transfer him to another job. Remedial transfers, however, are often used as a means of glossing over serious problems. Where the manager is arbitrary, where newly hired people receive inadequate training or where is arbitrary, where newly hired people receive inadequate training, or where employees discriminate against members of minority groups, it is far better to resolve the problem directly, rather than postpone it through a transfer. After all, the replacement for the man who is transferred may face the same problems again.

Nevertheless, when technological change is introduced or customer demands change, then the manpower needs of some departments may decline while the needs of other departments expand. To safeguard the jobs of long-service employees and to avoid losing the skills of trained personnel, most companies try to transfer employees to other jobs. Moreover, a company that follows a liberal transfer policy and provides retraining for employees who are transferred to new job has less difficulty in introducing changes.

Good evidence of intelligent manpower planning is stability of employment. Erratic "ups" and "downs" in employment levels, expedient hiring, substantial overtime during periods and layoffs and short workweeks in others, are prima facie evidence of poor planning. Well-managed companies seek to avoid hiring surges and plan for cutbacks far enough in advances so that *attrition* will bring employment levels down to efficient levels.

Many companies take great pride in their policy of resisting layoffs and providing stable employment. They claim it pays off in a more secure work force, more loyal to the organization, and less fearful of management changes costing jobs. Obviously a utility or a company fortunate enough or skilled enough to create a stable market for its goods or services finds such a commitment easier to make and keep than a company facing cyclical markets.

There are many incentives to encourage management to provide stable employment.

Many state unemployment insurance plans, as well as company-sponsored supplementary benefit plans, are designed to penalize the employer with a record of unstable employment. In addition, the process of laying off and rehiring is expensive to administer, and valuable employees may eventually be lost to other employers. Change in employment levels involve expensive shifts of workers within and between departments. Just the fear of layoff may encourage employees to consider "stretching out the work" as they mark time, waiting to see "who will be the next to go." Disagreements over seniority criteria result in costly, time -consuming grievances, as do intergroup arguments over short workweeks.

All these possibilities provide a stimulus for the firm to seek means of regularizing employment by using techniques such as the following.

1. Trying to develop a more flexible work force through careful selection and

training, supplemented by contractual provisions that permit relatively free transfers between departments-though craft consciousness makes this more difficult.

2. Using temporary employees or overtime in peak volume periods.
3. Taking on additional products or service lines whose variable demand will complement the demand for existing products-for example, if peak demand occurs in the summer, seeking products that are used primarily during the winter.
4. Exploring the possibility of warehousing goods during periods of slack demand, and offering new incentives for customers to stockpile during normally slow periods or order longer in advance.
5. Contracting out work that would require the employment of new people who might not be needed when the job is completed-for example, maintenance or construction work.

Merely listing alternatives, of course, is an oversimplification of the problem. Temporary personnel agencies typically have higher hourly rates than employees can be hired for directly. Overtime, when continuous, can lead to employee expectations concerning future earnings levels that may be unrealistic and cause resentment when the overtime is reduced. Also excessive overtime reduces efficiency. Inside employees can also resent "losing" work to outside contractors. Among the problems encountered in transfers are the resentment associated with being wrenched out on one's normal work and routines and familiar social group. Also the employee may complain, and often legitimately, that the temporary work is more difficult and is beneath his accustomed status. At the very least the supervisor has to be sure that his earnings are maintained and that if the temporary work is distasteful, such transfers are shared equally.

Whatever its policies or intentions, most organizations at some time do have to face up to the painful decisions surrounding a reduction in the size of the work force.

Reduced employment

Management must provide orderly pathways downward as well as upward and seek to minimize the personal and organizational disruption with cutbacks in employment. If the cutback is a small one, the least painful method is *attrition,* allowing normal turnover, retirement, and cessation of hiring to bring employment levels down.

Reduced Hours or Layoffs

When instabilities in work load persist and attrition is not adequate, then the next choice is usually between shorter work weeks for everyone or laying off the least senior employees, keeping the remainder full employed. Sharing work which is what reduced working hours implies-means in effect that unemployment is distributed equally. Depending on circumstances, this may or may not be an advantage to the firm. Sometimes the exact procedure is specified in the union management agreement, thus making desecration impossible.

What criteria does management use in deciding which procedure to favour? The nature of the industry itself is a critical factor in this decision. A department store could not arbitrarily reduce the hours it is open to the public without seriously damaging its business. Other firms have more flexibility in resorting to a reduced schedule when business warrants.

Naturally enough, longer-service employees are likely to press for the laying off short-service personnel, in an effort to secure higher income for themselves. The availability and the magnitude of *unemployment insurance* benefits may also influence the choice between laying off employees and reducing work hours. At some point it becomes more desirable, from the employees point of review, to accept these insurance benefits and avoid the travel expenses taxes, and effort associated with reporting to work for relatively brief periods.

Seniority vs. Merit in Layoffs

When business is poor and costs are relatively high, management becomes more sensitive to productivity issues. It is regrettable that such slack periods alert management to problems that have probably existed for some periods of time. Layoffs are usually more painful to employees in such a periods when other companies may also be experiencing cutbacks because alternate jobs are scarce.

The first temptation is to dismiss marginal performers, say the bottom 10 per cent in terms of existing appraisals. In fact, this is done in many organizations. However, where there is a union or where very long service employees are involved, there are a number of impediments to this policy.

Most employees and their supervisors will assert:

"Look, James was here almost 20 years before they discovered his work was unsatisfactory. Sure, we know he wasn't the best by any means, but don't you think the company could have noticed this and have done something about it a lot earlier? Now he's got family responsibilities and debts, and a man in his late 40's can't just step into another job that easy if these layoffs should last for long"

Of course, almost every industrial union makes sure that its contract with management includes a clause requiring that employees be laid off in reverse order of their hiring: last hired, first to be dropped.

Ambiguities in counting years of service. But even with the acceptance of this principle of length of service governing such manpower decisions, the question remains as to how seniority is "counted." Here are some alternatives:

1. Company-wide seniority: the length of time an employee has worked of the company.

2. Department seniority: the length of time an employee has worked in a particular department of the company.
3. Job seniority: the length of time an employee has held a specific job in a particular department of the company.

The method used obvious has a significant effect on the choice of which employee is laid when, for example, there is a surplus of clerical in the Accounts Receivable Department.

The "youngest" employee under formula 1 might be a recently hired stenographer in the Engineering Department to take the job of the laid-off stenographer. The employee with least service under formula 2 might be a secretary who has been with the company for several years, but who recently transferred into the department when an opening occurred.

Under formula 3, the company would be required to lay off the youngest employee doing the specific clerical job in the Accounts Receivable Department where the surplus existed.

Bumping. Let us introduce another complication: *bumping.* The application of seniority may mean that a whole series of moves is generated when a single employee is laid off.

Let us look again at our earlier example. Under formula 2, the following would be a more typical sequence of events: The Account Receivable Department has too many stenographers. The stenographer with the least service in that position would lose her jobs. However, she would have the privilege held by an employee with less department service than her own. Thus, the girl first displayed might "bump" a tabulating clerk with less service. In turn, the tabulating clerk may bump a file clerk with even less seniority than hers. And the process repeats itself as long as displaced employees can find other workers with less seniority than themselves occupying jobs that they are able to perform. Larger companies find that cutbacks in manpower may generate thousands of job shifts, which in turn create massive record-keeping and personnel problems. Shifts of this sort are bound to provoke countless grievances and complaints about alleged inequities in the demotions.

Selecting from among Alternative Seniority Systems.

Which seniority system is best form the point of view of the firm? Though there is no simple answer, the following criteria may help management in arriving at a solution.

Reducing frequency of movement. One criterion to apply in evaluating a seniority system is whether it reduces the frequency of job-shifting. Shifts create grievances, and they also give rise to training and efficiency problems. Although management may require that an employee be able to perform the job for which he exercises hi "bumping" privileges, it is hard to measure performance. Under the pressure of events, employee job shifts inevitably result in workers being displaced from jobs which they do efficiently and being placed on jobs for which their performance is marginal. "Bumping" works best when the movement takes place down a promotional ladder and where everyone in the department has worked place down a promotional ladder and where everyone in the department has worked his way up from the bottom jobs. In summary, to satisfy this criterion, management often favors a relatively "narrow" seniority unit, such as job or departmental.

Retaining valuable employees. The use "narrow" seniority units may be costly to the company, however. Assume that the need for machinists has declined temporarily. Under a system of job seniority, the company would be required to lay off machinists with long training and experience. Then, if these machinists accepted jobs elsewhere, expensive recruiting and training would be required to acquire new machinists when business picked up. Obviously, management would like to shift these employees to other jobs, and allow less valuable employees to be laid off. Many times some form of department seniority is a good compromise solution to a problem of this sort.

Encourging requisite mobility. "Narrow" seniority units discourage employees from accepting transfers, for they lose their seniority when they transfer from one unit to another. Thus," wider" seniority units make it easier for the company to provide a flexible work force.

Swift return to normal production. After the need for layoffs has passed, management seeks to return to normal production as quickly as possible. Naturally, key employees must be the first to be recalled. The seniority system usually specifies that those who were laid off last will be called back first. Presumably the more senior workers will have held the more important positions. This correlation is not always a perfect one, however, and management may seek to recall junior employees whose skills are essential to the resumption of production.

Employees desires. Management also wants to be fair. But what is fair is not easy to determine.

In theory, employees and unions favor "wider" or more inclusive seniority units than does management. They argue that it is unfair to lay off employees with 15 years of seniority in one department, when there are employees with only one year of service in another department. Unions have sometimes sought corporation wide seniority agreements to enable an employee whose job is terminated in one company location to shift to another; on occasion, they have even demanded that moving expenses be provided.

In actual practice, employees very often favor narrow units much as management does, only for quite different reasons. Because the employee tends to consider his job as a piece of "property", even though management has a very different interpretation, he seeks out the help of his fellow workers who share the same or nearby jobs to help him protect his valued possession. The importance of seniority and the careful calculations of self-interest that go into employee decisions impinging on this area are revealed by the following case:

Either management or the union may seek modification in existing seniority regulations when changes in technology or in the company's business threaten widespread loss of their jobs.

The Furst Corporation is eliminating is consumer product lines. Under the terms of the existing union-management agreement, even employees with 30 years of service expecting to retire in six months or a year will have to be laid off since the seniority clauses forbid interdepartment "bumping". Recently hired young men in adjacent departments will retain their jobs while these senior employees are separated.

These are very delicate problems of equity and contract. The union finds it difficult to decide what to ask the company, because inevitably some of its members will be injured and others will benefit.

Termination or Layoff

Management has a responsibility to inform the employee when a layoff is assumed to be permanent. Many union-management agreements and company policies specify that an employees' right to be recalled, with a priority determined by his length of service, will not continue beyond one or two years. Thus, if the layoff persists for this length of time, the employee also loses his claim to other employment benefits associated with accrued service. If he is rehired, he will come back as a new employee. Many companies pay a *severance or termination* allowance when an employees loses his hob through no fault of his own.

An alternative to dismissal for older employees is early retirement, an option which is being used with increasing frequency particularly by relatively profitable companies. Realistically they compare the cost of maintaining the employee through to normal retirement at full salary with the additional cost of a more generous early pension.

A systems approach to manpower planning

During recent years the terms *human resource management systems* and *manpower planning* have come to the fore. Their usage reflects a growing concern for personnel systems as distinct from compartmentalized personnel policies. An other way of saying this is that there is growing awareness by managers and personal specialists that the organization is an *organic* entity. All of its parts are so interdependent that a change cannot be introduced in one place in one place without affecting the total.

One of the unfortunate legacies of the scientific management tradition was the encouragement given to managers to compartmentalize their problems. Just as the job of the managers was divided up by the fathers of scientific management into separate components, there is still a tendency to classify personnel problems into watertight categories.

We have a shortage of people qualified to be sales managers: This is a recruitment problem. Too many engineers are requesting a transfer out of the power division: This a transfer problem policy.

We are losing many of our best craftsmen that have been hired in the last several years: This is a turnover problem.

In fact, every one of the above designations may be incorrect. What appears to be a changed recruitment requirement may, in fact, be a training problem. Excessive transfers may reflect inadequate pay or promotion procedures, and turnover can be symptomatic of the same or other defects in internal personnel policies.

In the effort to identify the underlying manpower system that shapes the flows of personnel through the organization, personnel research analysts examine critical comparisons. For example, comparisons like the following may be useful in examining the background and career patterns of those who quite, those who are asked to leave, and those who are promoted.

Do engineers who quit during their first three years of employment graduate near the top or middle or bottom of their class?

Do we lose more young managers who begin their careers with us in our trainee program or more who go directly to a first non-training assignment?

How do the internal company careers of staff people who go "up" rapidly differ from those who promote more slowly?

Traditional management thinking often involved a search for simple cause and effect relationships. Poor performance must mean poor selection procedures. Absence of qualified candidates for a middle-level position must mean poor promotional policies. In practice, it is rare to find such simple causality operating. More often they result from a complex interaction among a number of company processes, including, supervision, remuneration, career paths, performance appraisal, and others. The managerial challenge is to identify the interrelationships among these various organizational processes. Such analyses do not automatically tell the organization what it has been doing right and wrong, but simply what has been happening. However, such new understanding can play a highly useful role in decisions concerning promotion, management development, and selection policy.

Another example of the significance of interrelationships is provided by the manpower implications of various job-security provisions, such as guaranteed annual wages or sub plans. On the surface these appear very costly since they penalize management heavily for layoffs and job insecurities. But these costs have to be balanced against potential benefits to be derived from a work force that feels more secure and, therefore, may be more willing to accept new technology and job changes.

Manpower planning requires management to assess the total impact of existing company procedures on the utilization of manpower. It is not unusual to find organizations failing to recognize that the impact of a given personnel policy depends upon its interaction with other company policies; there is no such things as separate compartments for remuneration, selection, promotion, etc. Decisions made by individual department managers ramify throughout the total organizations.

Companies may have a non-discrimination policy in employment, but unless it is backed up both by suitable training of supervisors and effective monitoring, such policies may be ineffectual. Similarly a great deal of effort may be devoted to selecting high potential graduates of technical schools, but if placement and promotion policies do not reward their abilities, it is likely that the effort placed on selection will be vitiated.

A manager may be reluctant to promote anyone to a middle-level position in his department who does not have a unique and narrowly defined experience; yet this job is a critical stepping stone to broader, general management positions in the company. His immediate needs for fully qualified personnel may have to be modified in the light of the larger organizations' needs.

We cite examples like these to emphasize the need for synthesis and integration in viewing management decisions and policies. Too often their values or "correctness" are assessed independently one from the other.

Long-run vs. Short -run Cost and Benefits

A manpower planning approach to personnel problems should also counter the tendency of all managers to neglect long-run consideration. An investment in training may not pay off for may years and not until the employee has moved up to other jobs. His present manager can be disinclined to "invest" in the future when his incentives motivate him to look only at the present. The organization requires some process by which these longer run considerations can be factored into today's decisions. As in all planning, that is the contribution of manpower planning-to make sure that choices are made today which will assist the organization in moving to the objectives it has set for tomorrow.

A Definition of Manpower Planning

Manpower planning then is an integrated view of the personnel systems of the organization, which allows individual managers to make improved day-to-day decisions that will be consistent with the total organization longer run needs. Its successful operation requires:

1. An understanding of the existing interdependencies among personnel systems and personnel flows.
2. The establishment of guidelines and policies based on this understanding within which managers will make their personnel decisions.

3. Some mechanism to detect when these policies either need changing or are being violated.

If this is done successfully, the organization will be in a better position to decide such questions as :

1. Where should begin hiring people?
2. Where should we reduce hiring and allow attrition to decrease the size of the group?
3. Where should promotion rates be accelerated, slowed down; similarly where is more training required, less?

This chapter outlines approaches that organizations use to effectively match jobs with people. The focus is on the planning process concerned with the acquisition and effective utilization of human resources in the organization. We are especially concerned with the job-person relationship, i.e., with manpower plans that match jobs with people as well as match people with jobs. As we discussed in the previous chapter, the traditional approach of matching people with jobs differs in a subtle manner from the approach of matching jobs with people. With the former, the emphasis is on engineering people to fit available jobs, and the manpower plan emphasize finding the right person with the right qualifications for the job. On the other hand, when one is concerned with matching jobs with people, the emphasis in the manpower plan subtly change to one of engineering jobs to fit available human resources.

This latter approach does not ignore the need to find human resources with the right qualifications to fit the job. Rather it also allow for the desirability, and sometimes necessity, of redesigning jobs to fit the available human resources of a change technological society.

The nature of manpower planning

Manpower planning is the process of making decisions regarding the acquisition and utilization of human resources. In particular, the manpower plan focuses on an analysis of the organization's objectives and the plan for acquiring resources to meet these objectives. The organization's objectives and the resources acquisition process are analyzed in terms of the role that human resources plan in achieving organizational goals.

Planning

Planning is often considered "formal decision making" in the sense that it involves " deciding in advance what to do, how to do it and who is to do it." It involves a determination of objectives to be accomplished at some future date, an assessment of whether existing organizational policies, programs, and procedures are sufficient to accomplish the objectives, a review of alternative approaches to accomplishing objectives, and the organization of resources to implement the alternative chosen.

Strategic planning is the process of allocating resources into new areas whether they be in new product markets, geographical areas, or into new production processes in an effort to more effectively accomplish the goals of the organization. Strategic decisions in organizations are made on a continuous basis, sometimes systematically using sophisticated planning techniques, and sometimes without much involvement in formal processes. The emphasis of this chapter is on the need for a systematic approach to manpower planning and a general model of a manpower plan.

A narrower definition of planning focuses simply on the "how to do" and "when to do" portion of the objectives. Here, laying out a course of action to be followed is considered planning. It is assumed objectives have been identified in a previous step and that making task assignments to accomplish the plan will occur in a later step.

For our purposes, we will use the broader definition of planning since we are concerned with insuring that a given plan is objective oriented that it does indeed focus on the accomplishment of a given goal or end result and that some time sequencing in carrying out the plan is specified. However, we will not be as concerned with making specific task assignments to carry out the plan.

Manpower planning is the sum total of the plans formulated for the recruiting, screening, compensation, training, job structure, promotion, and work rules of an organizations' human resources. It "is a process designed to translate the corporate or institutional plans and objectives into future quantitative and qualitative manpower requirements, together with plans to fulfill those requirements over both the shorter and longer terms, through manpower utilization, human resource development, employment and recruiting, and manpower information systems,"

The emphasis in this definition is on structuring plans to carry out what are considered to be the traditional personnel management functions of hiring, training, compensation, and promotion.

Macro-micro distinction

Manpower planning is done on a national level primarily by the central government aided by the states. This type of planning has a different focus from the manpower planning done by an individual organization. National manpower planning, or *macro* manpower planning, involves the specification of national manpower objectives and programs for their accomplishment. It usually involves federal agencies, such as the Department of Labour, particularly, the Employment and Training Administration, and certain agencies within the Department of Health, Education and Welfare. However, other national organizations, such as the Brookings Institution, are also involved in macro manpower planning activities.

Manpower plans at the national level change as the priorities of a particular Congress and/or administration change. For example, under Presidents Kennedy and Johnson a great deal of effort and funds were spent to develop manpower plans to deal with specific manpower problems. Programs were established for remedial education and skill training, mobility benefits, equal employment opportunity, and labor market information system. Most of these programs in this period were directed at improving the employment relationship of minorities and disadvantaged groups in keeping with the philosophy of the New Frontier of the Kennedy administration and the Great Society Program of the Johnson administration.

However, during the Nixon administration manpower priorities changed. Increased emphasis was given to improving the employment situation of veterans and in improving the already existing federal offices, such as the federal-state Bureause of Employment, to help all levels of manpower. The emphasis on programs for the disadvantaged and minorities was reduced.

The Nixon administration also decentralized the national manpower planning effort by establishing regional offices throughout the nation and, through the revenue sharing program, by asking each state to handle the manpower planning function for the state. Even though the decentralization process has achieved only limited success, the responsibility for national manpower planning has shifted from a centralized federal government in Washington to decentralized regional manpower offices and individual state governments.

Micro manpower planning involves the planning an organization does for the acquisition and utilization of its manpower. As seen in our definition of manpower planning, this is the focus we use in our book. However, this does not mean that macro manpower planning, whether it be done solely by the federal government or jointly by the federal government and the states, has an insignificant impact on micro manpower planning. For example, when federal programs were established to improve the employment opportunities for the so called "hard-core" unemployed, individual organizations were asked to commit extra resources and to develop manpower plans that included programs for recruiting, training, and employing these individuals.

Often federal programs will stimulate an organization to do manpower planning that did little if any manpower planning in the past. For example, government federal law and programs dealings with equal employment opportunity and affirmative action caused many organizations to review their present manpower planning process. The thrust of affirmative action planning involves the development of an organizational plan to recruit, train, and employ more members of minorities and women than are presently employed by the organization. As organizations review the number of employees presently employed in various positions and develop plans to replace these employees to ensure that minorities are being recruited, they usually end up doing a comprehensive review of their total manpower planning system.

For example, an organization may decide to set up a skills bank or skills inventory of all minority and women employees currently employed to insure that they will be considered for future promotion when positions become vacant. As they begin setting up such a skills bank for minorities, they soon realize that this would be a good idea for all employees, whether white or black, male or female. Thus, they are on the way to developing a complete manpower or human resource information system for all employees, which is a critical aspect of manpower planning.

Therefore, the macro manpower planning done on the national level affects the micro manpower planning done by an individual organization. However, there are other aspects of the macro environment, besides national manpower planning, which also affect, in a major way, the micro manpower planning function.

The macro environment of manpower planning

Some major components of an organizations' macro environment. These are the cultural values and norms, social institutions, legal environment, product/service demand, technology, and human resource mix. Each of these components has an impact on the manpower planning system of an organization.

Product/service demand mix

Forecasted demand for an organizations' product/service serve as the primary basis for an organization's manpower plan. As demand for an organizations' product or service increases substantially, people are added to the organization, usually at all occupational levels. As demand decreases, people are usually at all occupational levels. As demand decreases, people are usually laid off or discharged at all levels,. even though individuals at lower occupational levels are usually released first.

Since most organizations have an objective of growth, and since national economic policy is one of growth, the predominant influence of product/service demand forecasts is one of providing additional manpower for the organization as it grows. Therefore, one function of the manpower plan is to ensure that the desired number of people with appropriate skills and abilities are available for appropriate jobs and occupations in the organizations as the demand for the organization's product/service increases.

However, the manpower plan also make provision for organizational manpower decisions for periods or retrenchment, such as during an economic recession. Some organizations, for example, lay off unskilled workers first during a recession rather than skilled, professional, or managerial employees. The rational here is that the unskilled employee is the easiest to replace during an economic growth period. Other organizations tend to lay off employees regardless of skill during a downturn in activity. Aerospace and defense contractors, for example, typically lay off high skilled supervisors, engineers, and technicians along with unskilled and semi-skilled employees during a business downturn.

Still other organizations will reduce the work hour of all employees rather than lay off anyone during a recession. For example, many organizations in Japan will go to a reduced work-week and a cut in wages and salary for all employees, including managers, rather than to lay people off during a business downturn. This reflects the paternalistic managerial philosophy of many Japanese organizations.

Governmental agencies typically reduce budgets for the next fiscal year and rely on normal attrition to reduce the workforce rather than laying off people during periods of economic downturn. As people retire or quit they are replaced until economic conditions improve.

Whatever the particular policy of an organization during periods of economic recession, it needs to be clearly spelled out and implemented in making manpower decisions. Going through the process of formulating a manpower plan that thoroughly considers the effects of economic recession as well as economic growth often provides many unnoticed opportunities for an organization.

For example, some organizations actually add people in certain highly skilled occupational positions during a recession, for it is during this time that an organization can bring on board skilled people who aren't available during normal business activity except at a very high salary premium. Some companies hired skilled engineers rather than laying them off during the 1973-74 recession because they had a wide supply to choose from and did not have to pay a premium. Assuming these engineering skills would be needed when to pay economic picked up, these companies made a wise choice since they obtained skilled manpower at lower salaries than during normal periods. Some colleges and universities also followed this policy during the 1973-74 recession to attract top faculty who would otherwise not be available at the salary these colleges could offer.

Thus, one major function of the manpower plan is to provide an orderly system to add employees to the organization during periods of economic growth and to specify procedures to be followed during periods of economic recession or organizational retrenchment. A good manpower plan allows organizations to smooth out the hiring process so that variations in hiring are not widely divergent from year to year, depending upon market conditions. Organizations without a good manpower plan often find that they hire large numbers of employees one year only to lay them all of the following year.

The key to an effective manpower plan that recognizes the effect of economic conditions is adequate forecasting of these conditions as well as the organization's product/service mix as economic conditions change. An organization should not be at the mercy of economic conditions, but should forecast and develop well-conceived manpower plans is advance of changing conditions.

Changing technology

Technological changes have a profound impact on an organizations' manpower plan. As technology changes, the skills required in particular occupations change. New occupations are created, and old ones cease to exist. The trend over the last fifty years has been to upgrade the skills required in most jobs in our economy. Many of the unskilled jobs, particularly those involving heavy labor, have been eliminated. Labor demand in some skilled occupations has also been eliminated or significantly reduced. We are all familiar with the plight of the blacksmith.

The composition of many skilled jobs change as technology changes. Often the skill components are broken down into separate jobs, which can be performed by semi-skilled workers. For example, the introduction of a highly automated assembly line into the typical manufacturing operations of a company in the 1950s often broke up skilled jobs into several separate jobs requiring lesser skills. These jobs would be routinely performed by workers during the course of a normal day's work on the assembly lines and many became boring because of their repetitiveness.

Another aspect of a technological change is that, while it often eliminates unskilled jobs involving physical labour, it may create semi-skilled jobs requiring repetitive mental and manual labor. The modern auto assembly line has many examples of these.

Changing technology also requires organizations to plan for changes in locating sources of manpower to insure that supplies of needed manpower will be recruited. For example, the introduction of electronic data processing into an organization often requires the organization to recruit skilled computer technicians from technical schools in which they may not have recruited previously.

A technological change often means the organization's own training program must be revised to insure that people with skills needed in the future will be available. Thus, plans have to be made that: (1) forecast future technological change and the skill needs they will create, (2) determine classroom and on-the-job training programs to fill the needs, and (3) prepare instructors, instructional material, and facilities for the training. For many significant technological changes, such as the introduction of electronic data processing, an organization may choose to do little of its own internal training but rely on formal schooling. Any internal training becomes an orientation to show how the organization use the EDP system.

Human resource skill/educational mix

The changing skill/educational mix of the human resource supply and changing technology are closely related. As technology changes to require different skills and abilities, people attempt to change their ability/skill mix to gain skills required in jobs. This matching of the skill requirements of jobs with the skills of people in the work force has been the underlying thrust of government manpower policy. Training and development programs sponsored by the government were established to ensure that people, particularly the disadvantaged and minorities, would be able to secure the needed skills to compete effectively in the labor market.

The tremendous growth in secondary and two year post-secondary vocational and technical schools since 1962 was a result of federal manpower planning, which indicated a need for formal classroom training to provide the skilled work force needed in today's highly technological society. Many regions of the country now have area vocational schools, and many students who might have not gone to college, now receive two years of post-secondary technical training in such fields as electronics, computer technology, aviation technology, automotive mechanics, and the applied medical fields.

When the human resource educational/skill mix differs significantly from the skills required by employers, manpower shortages develop. Employers have jobs open but cannot find people with the skills demand ed. Many people want jobs but are hired because they do not have needed skills. This mismatch between job skill requirements and the skills of the labor force can have a serious negative impact on the economy of a society. For example, in the late 1960s, we had a national unemployment rate under 4.0 percent for 1968 and 1969 a very low rate for the U.S. Employers had many job openings but were not able to find qualified employees. Yet in certain sections of the country, unemployment was very high. People wanted jobs but did not have the necessary skills. In several of our northern inner cities, the unemployment rate approached 50 percent, yet employers in these same cities could not find qualified employees to fill their job openings.

This human resource dislocation had an effect on inflation, since employers tended to bid the wage rate up for what few workers were available, and was also a contributing factor to the inner-city riots during this period since so many were without jobs in such a prosperous period of American history. The federal government reacted to this situation with several programs to hire the "hard-core unemployed" or hard-to-employ persons. The essence of these programs was to provide this advantaged group with remedial education and training, through joint federal-private business action, in the skills necessary for many entry level jobs in industry.

Even though some group have not acquired needed skills to effectively compete for jobs in a highly technological labor market, the vast majority of the U.S. labour force has acquired such skills. In fact the average formal educational level now exceeds a high school education.

The types of skills brought to the labour market by the labor force today are much more sophisticated than they were in the early 1960s. For example, various new engineering, computer, and medical technician jobs require much higher skills than previously required in these fields. Even the automotive mechanic of the 70s must be more highly skilled than his counterpart in the 60s because of the more sophisticated design of automobile engines and related auto systems, and because of the tremendous variety in automotive models within a given manufacturer's line.

Any manpower plan must assess the human resource educational/skill level of the labor market from which it draws, predict future changes in this mix, assess the effect of manpower programs, and then plan recruiting, training, and job design system that take maximum advantage of the forecasted educational/skill mix. An effective manpower plan requires a careful and accurate assessment of the present and forecasted skills of an organizations' potential employees.

Cultural values, norms, and social institutions

Many employers today are asking themselves what happened to the old - fashioned belief in hard work. This concern is but a symptom of a more general concern many people have regarding the nature of fundamental values which have supposedly been held by the work force in the Indian society. Many people believe these values are changing. Others believe that present values are merely being redefined and arranged in a different priority.

Perhaps societal values toward work are not changing, but norms certainly are. Values are basic beliefs which give stability to society and are slow to change. Norms are guides to behaviour. They manifest or represent values. Values tend to be hard to define, norms are more specific. For example, at one time the value of hard work was manifested through the norm of heavy physical labor. Today, hard work often means mental pressure and long hours, but not necessarily physical labour.

The conventional wisdom is that today's employees, particularly younger employees, seem to want jobs that are challenging, personally rewarding, and have opportunities for personal and professional growth. Work is not a necessary evil or something to be avoided, but rather an integral part of life, to be enjoyed to the greatest extent possible.

In addition, many people, particularly youth desire to balance the goals associated with career development with other "life-space" goals such as family life, recreation, church affairs, and civic responsibilities. Long hours of a "work-aholic" may not be personally acceptable if they interfere with goals in other areas of one's life.

These changing norms regarding work mean that organizations should examine job enrichment techniques to determine their applicability. It also means that employers should consider these changes in developing manpower plans. Today's employees expect employing organizations and other social institutions to be more responsive to the demands made upon them by the organizations' various membership groups.

Changing legal environment and manpower planning

The greatest changes in the legal environment have occurred because of legislation and executive orders instituted by the federal government. In particular, the most significant changes have been in equal employment opportunity and affirmative action, occupational safety and health, government involvement in managing the economy to minimize inflation and unemployment and maximize economic growth, and more comprehensive coverage of wage and hour legislation.

At the state level, laws have been passed by many states to legalize collective bargaining in public employment. This means that unions and collective bargaining procedures are becoming increasingly more common in state, city, and county units.

These changes in the legal environment are an extension of a trend begun in the 1930s to give employees more rights, and hence more power, in dealing with employers. From the Federal Wage and Hour law and the Wagner Act, which legalized unions in the private sector in the thirties, to Title VII of the 1964 Civil Rights Act, and the 1970 Occupational Safety and Health Act, employer action toward employees has become increasingly more constrained. No longer can an employer hire only white males, pay them what he wishes, and work them in an unsafe environment. He must now abide by equal employment regulations, pay at least the minimum wage and time and one-half for overtime, and meet the minimum safety requirements in his operations as specified by the Occupational Safety and Health Act.

Why has such legislation been passed to regulate employer treatment of employees? The primary reason is because the operation of the labour market did not regulate such behavior. The economic power of todays' large employers in the labor market would far exceed the power of the individual worker in the absence of protective legislation. If the marked did effectively regulate these practices, how could we have ever had women and children working twelve to fourteen hours per day seven days a week for a subsistence wage under sweat-shop conditions? These conditions were all too common at the turn of the century in our factories.

The role of government is to pass laws to achieve the public good. When the public good outweights private property rights, government will pass laws to constrain these rights. Witness zoning laws, laws against prostitution and drugs, anti-monopoly laws as well as federal and state regulation of various industries such as airlines, railroads, transmission lines, utilities, and communications. In each case, it is believed that the public good would not be served in the absence of such regulations.

The same argument holds with legislation which affects the employer-employee relationship. The effect of the changing legal environment has been to improve wages, working conditions, and terms and conditions of employment for the average employee, thus leading to the accomplishment of the public good. Employer manpower plans have changed over time to be in conformity with the legislation and will continue to change as additional legislation is passed.

Designing a human resource information system-manpower planning in the firm

Our discussion thus far has been concerned with the macro aspects of manpower planning. Macro manpower planning sets the environment for micro manpower planning in the organization. The objective of the internal manpower planning process for an organization is to insure that adequate manpower with the desired skills and abilities are available when and where they are needed.

The manpower planning process is a major component of an organization's *human resource information system*. The concept of the human resource information system developed as a result of the work by Likert, Brummet, Pyle, Flamholtz, and others at the University of Michigan in the late 1960s. A major portion of a human resource information system is the system of human resource accounting. *Human Resource Accounting* is an attempt to assign a Rs. value to an organization's human resources. Such components as the amounts an organization has invested in its human resources through training and development, hiring and replacement costs, employee salaries, and turnover costs are usually used to computer the worth of an organization's human resources.

Human resource accounting systems today have evolved to the point of "identifying, measuring, and communicating information about human resources in order to facilitate effective management within an organization. Management requires information regarding resource acquisition, development, maintenance, and utilization.

Thus, today's human resource accounting system is in actuality a part of the total human resource information system. Not only are the human resources assigned a value for accounting purposes, but other information concerning human resource is gathered, coded, analyzed, stored, and disseminated to managers. This information includes the following components:

1. Demographic information: age, sex, race, educational levels, marital status.
2. Skills and abilities
3. Aspiration levels
4. Performance appraisals
5. Company sponsored training programs or other training and education completed since employed.
6. Past work assignments and job title before and since being hired
7. Special notations

Most organizations gather some or even all of these informational components, but few have developed a total information system that updates this information and makes it available to appropriate managers in a comprehensive fashion. Simply relying on the traditional personnel records system for gathering, analyzing, storing, and distributing information on an organizations' human resources will not produce the quality and quantity of human resource information needed for a comprehensive manpower plan.

Constructing manpower plan

The first step in constructing a manpower plan is to determine the organization's growth and market objectives. These objectives serve as the foundation for estimating the forecasted demand for human resources in the organization. These objectives may be expressed in terms of sales, market share, return on investment, development of new products and services, and development of new markets. These objectives ought to be expressed in terms of some time frame of *planning horizon*- the length of time over which the objectives and the plan for accomplishing them will occur.

The planning horizon for many organizations seldom exceeds fifteen year and is often expressed in terms of short-range, intermediate-range, and long-range periods. As a rule of thumb, short-ranges is a horizon of one year or less, intermediate-range of two to six years, and long-range of seven to fifteen years. Often the long-range objectives are quite general, and the intermediate and short-range objectives much more specific. This specificity is especially true of short-range or *operational* objectives.

Procedures for specifying objectives and the means for their accomplishment generally fall under the heading of *Management by Objectives* in the management literature. The determination of sound, long-range, intermediate-range, short-range organizational and associated departmental objectives is essential for an effective manpower plan, and the management by objectives technique is very effective for developing and specifying objectives.

Once the organization's objectives are specified, communicated and understood by all affected, then the personnel or manpower planning unit should specify their objectives with regard to human resource utilization in the organization. In developing these objectives, specific policies need to be formulated which address the following questions:

1. Shall we attempt to fill positions from within or by hiring individuals from the labor market? More specifically:
   a. What we do hope to accomplish from promotion from within and why?
   b. What jobs shall we fill by promotion?
   c. Does our organization have the needed skills and, if not, can our people be trained and developed for these jobs?
   d. What types of skills exist in our relevant labor market, and can we effectively recruit and attract people from this market?
   e. What effect will bringing in people from the outside have on our presently employed people?
2. Can we meet our commitments to affirmative action and equal employment opportunity?

3. How do our training and development objectives interface with our manpower planning objectives?
4. What union constraints do we face in manpower planning, and what policies should we develop to effectively handle these constraints?
5. What is our policy toward providing everyone in the organization with a meaningful, challenging job? Will we continue to have some boring, routine jobs or should we be eliminating them?

The third step in the process is to estimate the skills and number of people required for the organization by occupational category for the planning horizon. Occupational skills change over time. Therefore, it is important at this stage that an organization have a complete, current listing of all occupational categories in the organization with explanatory job description which specify the duties, skills, and qualifications required for each job. It should also attempt to forecast future changes in the duties, skills, and qualifications for these positions based on changes in technological requirements and the aspiration levels of individuals in the organization and the external labour market.

Fourth, the planner should estimate the manpower shortage or surplus for each occupational and job category and should determine what it plans to do about any estimated surplus or shortage in view of the human resource utilization objectives.

Note that this procedure ties in consideration of human resources objectives in filling jobs from within via internal promotions and organizational growth objectives.

If a surplus is predicted for an occupational category, the human resources planner needs to determine if these individuals will be discharged, temporarily laid off, transferred without any training, provided with training and then transferred, or provided with a cash bonus for quitting. These decisions will probably by determined by the organizations' overall human resource objectives for training and development.

If a shortage is predicted, then the organization must resort to the external labor market if it expects to fill the resulting job vacancies. This decision may cause the organization to review its human resource objectives with regard to hiring in the external market vis-a-vis other objectives.

The final step is to establish specific recruiting, selection, placement, training, compensation, and promotion objectives, plans, and policies to meet the estimated vacancies. The procedures and other information regarding each of these specific areas is discussed in later chapters.

Manpower planning and its development

Manpower planning and development are mutually supportive. While manpower planners want development and training activities to help upgrade the manpower inventory, the development and training function is striving to improve the efficiency of individual and corporate performance, and to prepare individuals for further roles and for the future. The more you can meet your future needs by growing your own, the better the flows through the organization, and there are positive motivational side effects.

It is this role of development which should ensure its integration into the business, for it contributes strongly to the task of supplying people with required skills and abilities. If developing the inventory is the surest and least expensive route to providing the supply, then planning specific individual development to match need has to be seen as a key management responsibility.

It follows that inventory is our primary source of supply for many manpower categories. But the inventory is not likely to stay static in quality and value for long. There will always be a tendency for the less saleable or usable parts on any inventory to age and deteriorate. With our human resource inventory, there is also progressive ageing, but it is slow process, and much effort is generally devoted to improving its quality and utilization, supported by planned development and training. Inputting additional and relevant skills will, as one example, enhance quality, but the primary means of improving the value of existing stock will be by planned deployments and assignments which expand practical experience.

The human resources of any company represent its most critical resources, particularly its managers and future managers. They alone have the capacity to inhibit or enhance business development. The continuity of the enterprise and its continued growth and prosperity are assured only through them. As we emphasized at the beginning, our human resources provide our only real competitive advantage. Planned development ensures that we encourage our people to achieve and use their full potential; that they are prepared for the responsibilities they may have in the future, and are able to achieve optimum efficiency in the present; and that the best of them develop that edge which improves the company's competitive advantage.

The whole development process progressively focuses on the development of individuals. As the process is demanding and time consuming, the return on investment need to be clear. Managers should ensure that, through their efforts, they add value to their subordinates and that they lead them well.

The development process

People grow in number of ways. Their Level of knowledge develops through a variety of learning situations, ranging from reading or watching, and various forms of education and training, to work experience doing a permanent job or part-or full-time assignments or projects. In addition to the acquisition of knowledge, some of these activities build self-confidence and competence, and encourage the development of personality, visible through improved social skills. The ability to make good decisions based on inadequate information while under pressure may be one of the abilities which a young manager develops from an operational assignment. Only by doing can be get a real appreciation of the demands and complexity of higher level work.

People develop far more from doing, from exposure and response to changing opportunities, than by any other means, although the use of training to supplement experience and prepare for further assignments is also important. A planned sequence of jobs, selected to fit developing abilities and personal preferences, and preferably under development-conscious managers, will produce the fastest growth towards ultimate potential.

The process of personal development should designed to maximize the pace of relevant learning and personal growth by planning appropriate deployments, identifying the stage at which learning opportunities will be exhausted, and acknowledging the need to initiate fresh assignments to maintain intellectual stimulate.

The designing and planning of development must be emphasized, for it rarely happens casually. Development assignments have been likened to moving plants from the greenhouse to the garden. The ground needs to be prepared and the seedlings must be brought to readiness; then they will need some protection, particularly in the early stages, and need to be watched initially in case they become battered by the environment. It is the development opportunity, far more than anything else, which enables people to grow.

The elements of development

There are numerous actions or elements in an individual development plan, including:

- Planned work experience, which should be challenging and followed by reassignment when learning opportunities in a job are exhausted, and project work and secondments, either internal or external, full-or part-time.
- Training, to provide the knowledge and skills required in current and possible future jobs, and to bring technical knowledge up to date.
- Further education towards professional qualifications, or to develop language skills, etc. Also, other self-learning and professional reading.
- Coaching, mentoring and counselling.

Most of this list is straightforward, but it is worth commenting that multifunctional project teams provide particularly good developmental experience of other functions and of the working of the business.

Mentors

To facilitate optimum growth, the use of a high level tutor to oversee the progress of each high potential individual, to talk with him periodically and influence the direction of his development, can be invaluable and should be encouraged. The mentor can stimulate and guide the developing individual, and also irritate the company to ensure timely action is taken to prepare the next deployment or relevant training of his charge. With more time to devote to development issues than a direct line boss, and more clout than an adviser from human resources, the mentor can more effectively ensure that the right things are done. In this respect, they provide invaluable support.

In addition to mentors, some direct line managers are exceptionally effective as developers and motivators of their subordinates. These managers need to be identified and utilized as a critically important resource. They deserve to be allocated the best candidates for they are likely to guide the growth of these people through any difficulties and to produce the best development subordinates.

Development jobs

One of the best ways of developing experience is by assignment to carefully jobs. Many companies believe that some jobs are especially valuable for this purpose, and designate them as development jobs. These are reserved exclusively for the higher ability young managers as definitive steps in their personal growth. Such posts include, for example, the general managership of smaller businesses where an individual can get to grips with a full business for the first time and take responsibility for profits.

In practice, we find that development requirements are so diverse that only a small proportion of needs are adequately met by the designated development slots. Only when the total range of jobs is covered in developmental assignments can needs be met fully.

A simple exchange of positions for a set period can be valuable. It allows a manager who is progressing slowly to be returned to his old post after a two year stint elsewhere, while the faster moving manager is assigned to his next career challenge. Alternatively, the manager whose position is borrowed may undertake a project assignment for his own further development.

Although it is advisable not to shuffle managers too frequently, it is equally as important to make sure that no-one stagnates. Development planning should create real pressure for change whenever this appears to be happening.

Individual development plans

A management development system needs to cover every individual with any real potential for personal development. An individual development plan (IDP) should exist, however simple in format, for all of these people, from graduate intake level up to, and including, board members. Based on all available objective information about each individual plus future organization and management requirement data, the IDP should record how we expect the individual to develop over the next several years, including alternative options where appropriate, and detail development plans, training requirements and anticipated appointments.

These are working documents, continually added to and annotated as plans or moves are auctioned, and monitored to ensure plans are implemented. They sit with the line manager as a reminder of his commitment to planned actions, but management development staff should monitor progress. The quality of the evaluation is critically important to the future, both for the individuals and for the company, because it allows any limitations in the process to be identified and corrected.

Ready to move

Within the development process, it is vital to identify those individuals who are ready for fresh assignments and further stretching so that action to move them on to their next assignments can be taken early. Their further growth is essential and must be followed through, however valuable they may be in their present roles. To slow or block the growth of an individual is likely to lead to him leaving the company.

Periodic reviews of the abilities and readiness to move of all career staff are essential, and every vacancy provides a development opportunity. Ideal next assignments should be determined, together with provisional timing, so that moves can be planned ahead to ensure continuity. Where no local opportunity exists able individual who is becoming ready for a move, wider opportunities should be each individual should be evident on his IDP and is part of the overall management inventory.

Individual development plan content

An IDP is a brief summary of key information related to the individual's forward career plan. The form of an IDP can vary enormously, from blank sheets to complex forms. However, it is likely to contain;

Identification:	Name
	Job title, company, location, grade.
	Date of birth/age.
Summary of career/	Qualifications/major training courses
experience:	attended. Dates/companies/positions/major achievements.
Strengths:	Summary of major strengths relevant to future job possibilities.
Limitations:	Notes on any factors which may restrict the scope or direction of his future development, or which need to be overcome by experience or training.
Personal preferences:	Mobility.
	Job type.
	Extent of ambition.

Development action plans:

Job:	Ready for move, when?
	Next job/options/timing.
	Specific appointment planned.
Other factors:	Training plans to meet agreed needs.
	Actions to overcome critical limitations.
	Experience needs to be met.

Preparing an IDP is the easy part. It is implementation which causes the headaches. As with any other plan, it represents the best effort at the time the plan is made, but the business situation and environment change endlessly, as do the pace of individual development, personal preferences and mobility, and the availability of opportunities, so reviews must take place regularly.

Any plan needs to be kept close at hand so that progress can be monitored. Concern only arises when the plans agreed in an managers should audit the progress of development plans within their own area, with some overview by the next managerial level. There should be should business justification for changes, and evidence that the plan has been rethought and individual actions reschedules. If this is not happening, it may be legitimate to ask why expensive management time is being wasted developing plans it is not intending to implement.

Career paths

For many lower level jobs, training and preparation are targeted on one job or a limited range of options, with little expectation that the great majority of incumbents will show any potential for further advancement. A small number will progress into supervisory posts, largely in the area, and a few may show some ability to progress in other ways.

It is in the area of professional and managerial staff that career paths with organized flows are relevant. Career paths are designed to encourage systematic development of numbers of similar individuals, such as the graduate or professional staff intake, to ensure that each has the opportunity to participate in the full range of training and to gain experience in a planned range of relevant activities, and then to progress logically along the most suitable career development route.

These routes can be relatively simple for most people, for the bulk of the further manager intake will enter through a chosen function, and concentrate initially on developing their knowledge and skills within that chosen area. Most will seek a variety of experience to cover all aspects of that function before concentrating on more specific operating roles within it, or a specialist aspect.

The bulk of career progression probably takes place within single functions, with only a relatively small proportion of people deliberately or casually moving between career streams. The company is likely to want a small core of high ability people to gain multi-functional experience as a foundation to general management or to top functional posts, but it would see little advantage from more widespread interchange. Similarly, for employees generally, their market values represent the sum of their knowledge and experience, and their ability to apply it, so any move to a fresh function not subsidized by management would involve a drop in value and this is rarely acceptable.

If early development is within one function, it is logical to define stages and to encourage some systematic progression through them. Normal rates of flow should evolve so that requirements could be forecast, and the core training relevant to each stage should be clear. However, the rate of individual progress should vary with performance, and appraisals will show how quickly an individual gets on top of the demands at each level, and assessments of potential show ability to cope with higher and wider ranging assignments.

Where career development expands to include more than one career path, the pattern may develop with crisscrossing between the line and functional roles within one function, or between primary functions and assignments in other major functions, or by progressive appointments alternating between general and functional management.

There must be purpose behind individual can progressions of this type. The longer term intention might involve developing a high ability individual towards a much more senior post, with a series of hurdles to be overcome in the process. Such a career path has a distinctly higher than normal level of risk, although it may have a similarly high level of potential reward. The responsibility for the risk element should be accepted by the company in that it is the company that is taking the critical decisions to appoint the individual and it will have assessed the form and extent of the risk in advance and judged that it can be overcome. If there is a failure, and there will be some, it must be handled sympathetically as a learning experience, so that career damage is minimized for the individual, who continues to be a valuable corporate resource. Indeed, the reason for failure may be an unexpected change in the business environment which an inexperienced man could not be expected to handle.

Future organizations appear to require greater degrees of specialization, combined with a wider appreciation of where each function's contribution fits into the overall business, plus an understanding of the overall business operation. This will develop in part by the increasing use of project teams, which provide extensive cross-functional experience, and also through management training modules designed to set individual specialist areas in the context of the broader business.

Self-Development

Most employees are acutely interested and active in progressing their own development. The days are long gone when an individual accepted that his development and career would be taken care of by the company and the he would do the jobs to which he was assigned and go where he was sent. Today, individuals not only expect to be involved in the direction of their career development, but are likely to express strong views on their preferences and take initiatives to achieve their career objectives. Ideally, development becomes a partnership, with the company pursuing its needs in open discussion with its staff.

Self-awareness

Self-development is logically proceeded by self-awarenes. Some organizations now run short seminars or development centres for groups of bright younger managers, which are designed to increase self-knowledge or self-awareness and to help clarify the soundness and achievability of personal career objectives and development plans.

These sessions draw out information on a range of aspects. They provide insights into personality and how other people see the individual. For example, a degree of introversion and poor relationship building might be highlighted, which may not have been understood previously and can restrict career development. The process should also explore how individuals learn and their style of learning, and may explore and challenge the personal philosophies of the participants.

Career development options

It is unlikely that the forward view will take the form of a clear single career line. Invariable there will be options but, to some extent, the options which are taken will be heavily influenced by the timing of opportunities becoming available. The chance to take to promotion is difficult to turn down if the preferred alternative is less immediate and less certain.

The task facing each individual is to identify a range if options which seem achievable from the starting point, and then to add some desirable but less realistic possibilities, with notes of the actions which would be required to make them achievable. For example, the individual trained as an accountant is likely to identify a range of straightforward options associated with progression from his initial functional training, but if he wants to progress to general management, there will be range of additional criteria to meet.

Each individual needs to assess the options available from where he is now, weighed against his preferences, ambitions, mobility and what he seeks from life, and then determine the strength of preference for a particular track.

Career development is a partnership owned, jointly by the manager and his manager, but in which neither has total freedom of action and each has different objectives. The boss knows that he must plan to meet the manpower needs of his organization, based on business objectives and environment. In parallel, he will want to deploy his manpower inventory as efficiently as possible while optimizing development opportunities for all individuals, some of whom may have career objectives not available within the company.

Managers who develop subordinates well

In every organization there are some managers who seem to have a golden touch with the development of their subordinates. People in their areas are encouraged and guided to develop rapidly and, subsequently, feature strongly in the lists of promoted individuals. In contrast, there are other manager who appear to place a dead hand on the careers of their subordinates. Inevitably, there is competition amongst the better younger managers to join one of the forcing houses, and great to avoid getting trapped in a dead end.

Observations of the development environment enable an individual to decide whether the company will be supportive in helping him to develop his career along the line he had in mind. However, while this support is invaluable, the main drive and effort must come from himself.

Preferences, ambitions and mobility

Career development is strongly related to abilities but individual preferences, ambitions and mobility have a substantial influence and are liable to change. Knowledge of these influences is an essential ingredient in assembling and agreeing realistic development plans which set out the intended or most likely career paths for individuals.

There is a joint responsibility on the part of manager and subordinate to ensure that the company has sufficient awareness of each employee's view of his future, which should be on the agenda at most counselling sessions.

During the early years of career development, there are generally several avenues open for the next move and many individuals have clear preferences which influence the vacancies they choose to go after. One key consideration will be around the degree of specialization preferred. Those who aspire to top management may seek to broaden their experience through a number of diverse assignments to develop a generalist C.V., while other may find their career satisfaction comes from growing in a specialist function.

Selection of preferred activities may be influence by ultimate career ambition, but other factors are present. Preferred life-style is increasingly influencing willingness to work in some of the more demanding workaholic organizations which attract some individuals who are willing to make such a commitment, but repel others. In this way, the culture of an organization, as perceived from outside, has a significant impact on employment image and its ability to attract able candidates from outside.

We have to learn to live with the view and career preferences of our people, but if we believe that the capabilities an individual fall short of his ambitions, the disagreement may be serious. Participation in a self-awareness seminar with strong feedback from a group of peers my lead an individual to reassess his objectives and achieve greater realism.

When the opportunity arises an attractive appointment involving a significant geographic move, at least one third of the immediate acceptances seem to get reversed after the partner or family become involved. In most of those cases, the partner may have given a casual agreement to the concept of mobility, but react differently when faced with a reality. For the planning of potential overseas postings, the discussion has to be blunt and specific from an early stage to ensure commitment.

Career progression in some large organizations has been linked traditionally to mobility. Development required that an individual did not spend too long in one place, and was rarely promoted without a transfer. The banks and the church were good examples; large multinationals provide another. This policy is changing, and large organizations appear to be seeking new and acceptable rules. Acceptability is recognized because individual attitudes to mobility are far less permissive than a couple of decades back. Company attitudes have been influenced also by the high costs of transfers and the difficulties arising from enormous regional variations in house prices. Associated flow patterns need monitoring.

Career mobility is still expected from high ability, intensely ambitious individuals, who are clearly heading for high positions where some variation in experience and working environments is seen as essential. These committed individuals are likely to accept the opportunities to advance which are offered, and the employer is likely to have strong views on the experience it requires in its top people. The cost factor is irrelevant where the number of people is small and their future vital to the organization.

Mobility seems particularly relevant in large multinationals where those individuals who aspire to senior positions will find themselves managing and doing business across cultural boundaries. It is essential for these people to gain first-hand experience in more than one situation. In these companies, the evolving pattern requires the high performing stream to undertake foreign assignments from an early state, in the knowledge that there are career bars for those who lack international experience.

People following functional careers in categories where organizations employ relatively small numbers also need to be mobile to progress. These may be only limited opportunity for internal career advancement, so individuals are faced with developing their careers by changing employment or accepting slower advancement as they wait for convenient opportunities to arise. Career planning is likely to assume and encourage mobility within the function and across the corporation, so knowledge of the real extent of individual mobility is important.

Development of high potential

The most important resource in the care of any board of directors is the select cadre of high potential younger mangers, which will provide the primary source of candidates for senior management and board positions in ten to 20 years' time. The career development of this elite group is increasing under the hand of the CEO personally.

There is a great deal of difference between our view of the potential of a newly recruited graduate and our view of further potential in an established senior manager. Although significant potential can exist at all levels and age should not be a bar, younger managers do learn and develop fastest.

Mid-20s Up through the mid-20s, there is not likely to be any substantial track record to demonstrate evidence of potential, Judgements made will be based on intellectual strength, personality and perhaps the degree of maturity evident. The first years of post-academic achievements are visible, indicating the ability to adapt to a fresh situation and make things happen. The embrionic track record is likely to look good and early career plans have begun to test and stretch capability. This has been described as the exploratory stage of a career. At this age, the apparent fliers tend to be those who appear more mature, are always quite certain of what they are going to do, aware working hard to get there.

Age 28-32 This period seems to provide the critical decision taking stage in which most employers assess potential. It is at this point that track records seem to be showing clear indications about which individuals learn fast, cope with new situations, and show a grasp of broader business essentials. All of the available information is assembled to determine what is really indicated about future potential as distinct from past performance. The quality of career plans to test and stretch abilities now shows through, for those considered to have above average potential should have been place in appointments and assignments which tested capabilities beyond their present levels.

At this stage, many companies supplement their data by making use of assessment centres which provide more detailed information on the extent and form of potential, and talk out detailed IDPs which take into account apparent potential, individual preferences, and future opportunities.

The 30s These years provide a period of great testing and stretching as individuals climb their chosen paths at varying speeds. Some will continue to show an astonishing ability to grasp the complexities of new situations quickly and make real contributions while, for others, the pace is simply slower, or a ceiling is reached.

The 40s In the 40s, the high potential stream has thinned out considerably, and now contains only the small number of highly placed individuals who are thought to retain the potential for significant further advance. The testing and evaluation of this group to determine their suitability for the highest offices will be ongoing.

There are many individuals who will be assessed as having potential for further advancement well beyond their 40s and no cut-off point is implied here. In fact, most managers have some further potential at all stages of their careers, but high potential implies the ability to achieve significant further advance in a short period of time, and that does become progressively more rare.

Organizations which actively manage the process of development gain a significant competitive advantage. Research in the US has shown a correlation between success in top management and the breadth of experience, showing that slightly less successful top managers in the same enterprise had rather less breadth experience.

Test and stretch

One problem in managing development effectively is that the timing of readiness for advancement is most difficult to predict. The individuals' proven abilities and their needs must be comprehensively understood, and assignments found for them in which they are challenged to the limit and must strive hard to cope. That can be a critical time if any unexpected development occurs, but the next level of management should be on the alert to provide support if necessary. In the process these individuals grow rapidly, but all too quickly they complete or get on top of the task and, once again, begin to show readiness for the next. It is, of course, essential that the next challenge be provided, even if this means giving priority to young high potential managers when more proven ability is available.

Inevitably, not every challenge is tackled smoothly. There can be errors of assignment, or the business may conspire to produce an unplanned set of environmental changes. If failure occurs, there must be commitment to support any individual placed in a test and stretch position. If blame must be allocated for a failure, it falls largely on those who approved the appointment. The main objective in such a situation must be to recover the confidence and upward movement of the candidate by placing him or her quickly in a fresh assignment with a high probability of success, and not recording a black mark. As one CEO noted: 'When they stumble, they should be counselled in a way that shows them how to succeed rather than be shoved off the list of hot prospects.'

People management skills

One group of skills more than any other is gaining importance as a critical characteristic of future senior managers. The role of a manager involves getting things done through other people. He is responsible for some of these people whereas others will be his equals or superiors, or his customers and suppliers. His effectiveness as a manager and his ultimate performance will depend on personal relationships and his ability to get things done. As each manger exist within an enterprise, the task is to manage through the system and structure; to get things done through people within the organization, systems and cultures in which they all exist.

In observing subordinate managers of high potential, the way in which they mange their staff (and other personal relationships) should be watched closely to see whether staff follow their leadership. They should be seen to encourage open communication, be sensitive to others and handle people firmly yet compassionately, handle older subordinates well and gain their respect, and develop their subordinates. If these things are going well, it provides another positive element in the growing track record.

Monitor progress

Feedback of progress on development assignments should be recorded on IDPs so that a comprehensive track record accumulates. If career limiting factors are identified, they must be recorded and action planned to overcome them if possible. They do not disappear if they are ignored and are liable to occur more severely and cause career difficulties if not tackled. Some may limit career prospects, but identification should restrict damage and ensure that evident potential is directed to a career not threatened by the limitation.

The optimum career path for a high potential candidate should be outlined for a five-to 10-year period, with ideal postings noted and selected to provide the mix of experience sought. If one of those positions is filled by a long-term incumbent, and it is considered essential to provide experience in that specific slot, then priority may need to be given to the longer term development of the high potential candidate and a fresh assignment found for the blocking individual. If this seems ruthless, one might also consider the positive aspects of a fresh assignment for a manager who has been stuck, possibly for too long, in a previous position.

Ultimately, further progress becomes more competitive as the numbers of jobs at each level decreases. Even when people reach board level it remains essential to seek indicators of further potential, and continuing growth towards the highest position should be encouraged and tested. The human resource area is an excellent example of where this should occur; senior specialists have the expertise and the time to influence behaviour and systems, and to make things happen. Much of what is in this book makes complete sense to line mangers but also presents then with problems of implementation. It is for the business planning and human resource specialists to quietly guide and assist their collegues in achieving the desired end results.

Increasing specialization is one of the major themes to emerge from predicted future organizations. Hence, specialists are likely to become a more significant element in the organization structures and manpower plans which develop through the 1990s. Specialists will find strong roles in the project management culture, where roles and objectives will be clear and require minimal supervision.

Career development for specialists will change from rather than become more limited. They will be able to move up within their own specialism, but movement specialism will be difficult or impossible. They will have great awareness of other specialism through working in task forces, but few will become true generalists. Generalists are likely to evolve from task force leaders, although leadership will be informal as specialists work together in task forces on equal terms. Compensation potential will be as great for specialists as for generalists. Large consulting and law practices provide parallels already.

Although it is not the intention to deal with the principles and practices of organisation development in this book, it would seem important to emphasise certain relationships between OD and manpower development, which indicate the need for manpower development to be conducted with full awareness of its organisation implications. It can be claimed that the most effective manpower development can only be achieved if the two functions work in close collaboration, and if at the same time general management are fully aware of the overlapping interests, and the interactions, of the two.

It is recognised by those who actually watch organisations at work-as distinct from writing or reading books on organisation-that, whatever the formal nature of an organisation, as reflected in the organisaton charts, the job descriptions and accountability statements, the way it works is dependent on the capabilities, relationship and agreements amongst the people within the organisation. Sometimes these interpersonal relationships are in conflict with the written organisation definitions cannot think of everything.

It is also recognised that the people within the organisation must have freedom to adapt and change, according to their strengths and weaknesses, preferences and dislikes, if that organisation is to keep going in the constantly changing human and economic world in which the company operates. Rigidity beyond a certain point is not desirable if managers and executives are expected to respond rapidly to changes in their workloads and problems. Our interest at this moment is to see the way in which organisaton and changes in organisation, formal or informal, effect the manpower development work which is being carried out within that organisation.

A common impact of manpower development on organisation arises from the deliberate provision of places for trainees. The apprentice requiring real shop floor experience, the graduate who needs to gain wide experience with minimum delay, the supervisors designate who require exposure to apposite aspects of company work, the thin stream of high flyers who must build up expertise faster than anyone else; all of these people may only get what they require in the way or work experience by a special provision. If they all have to wait in the queue all of the time, the training and development may be impossible to achieve. Some will be possible through normal internal posting and transfer mechanisms, but not all. Indeed, it may be seen as undesirable to maximise the movement of trainees through the normal internal cogency opportunities, for this might block many opportunities for those who were members of development schemes but who nevertheless merited a transfer or a promotion.

So some posts or workplaces may have to be created or isolated for development purposes; and this has an effect on organisation structures and the distribution of responsibility. The first effect is the likely increase in the numbers of people in the particular work area, although this need not always be the case when introducing trainees of high calibre. The second effect may then be to create increased supervision, because there are now more employees and the additional ones have an exceptional need for being taught. This is common within apprenticeship schemes. The older and the more sophisticated the learner, the less inclined management are to create new workplaces, and the less inclined are the people already in that work area to accept a stranger in their midst, a stranger who is there to advance his own career at, they may believe, their expense in time and effort.

If the trainees thus posted are good and hard working, and, above all, interested in what they are given to do, they might be quickly assimilated. They may even become indispensable; and this can lead to problems of manpower growth if a strict watch is not kept on the nature of the work undertaken by both trainees and regular employees. A popular trainee group may even create a subtle expansion pressure in the company, should line and manpower managers both prefer to take into their growing establishments such people, beyond their real needs, but too good to let go elsewhere.

Jumping to the other end of the scale we find, for example, the creation of understudy posts at high levels in the hierarchy, in order to provide an insight into more rarified aspects of management for one person, or for a procession of people. Understudy posts can be most successful, it is generally found, if the bulk of the work to be done by the understudy is real and responsible work. Otherwise he is unable to penetrate into the problems and the minds of people around him. If the understudy is given real work to do, where does it come from? From the boss's workload, or from people around him in the organisation? Will the incumbent then inflate the importance of his work until the work becomes recognised as being necessary to the area in which he is working, and so critical that it can never be handed back to those who lent it to him in the first place? Such things do happen. The company may now find itself not only with an extra permanent post, but also with a new division of responsibilities between a group of managers or supervisors in that part of the organisation.

Although these problems may rarely be serious in well established companies in the West, their importance is much greater in companies starting up with inexperienced local labour, or undergoing rapid localisation and growth, in the developing countries. In these cases it would be often unrealistic initially to create hierarchies, structure and job responsibilities based on the Western patterns, although the temptation to do so is extremely great. The existing levels of knowledge and experiences are relatively low, and therefore the capital potential and ready adaptation of people into new work somewhat unreliable. The capability of anyone to teach his colleagues or his juniors much may be also low and therefore organisation and relationships must be developed in some way that will enhance to a maximum the learning opportunities. These should include heuristic principles if this learning and the accompanying interest growth is to be made the most of. Deterministic planning, and manpower development to suit, is most effective where there is high confidence, with evidence to support that confidence; and such planning demands reasonably well worked out structures through which those chosen can worked their way.

Thus organisation development and manpower development must, in these grass roots circumstances, go hand in hand. The work for any individual must not greatly exceed his initial capability, yet it must provide room for 'stretching' and the development on new interest. This may mean that there have to be six in a work unit where otherwise four would be sufficient. But if there are six, with the need for even more supervision than otherwise, attention needs to be paid to the number of supervisors needed, and the levels and sorts of responsibility they are to carry. Clearly their training and development responsibility could be greater than in other older and more experienced companies. With the increase in numbers of supervisory roles at the lower edge of the company, there is an increased pressure on promotion vacancies a little higher up. Does this mean an automatic increase in the number of posts at that higher level? Maybe this is in any case desirable because of the problems for the inexperienced in handling the management workload. Thus one can see a total inflation, vitally necessary perhaps, throughout the company. This increases the fragmentation and decreases the spontaneous communication in the company, both of which are counter-productive and it adds, of course, to the normal manpower control problems of wastage and replacement.

In companies like this, in which a great deal of teaching, learning and personal development is taking place, it is usual to expect to find not only the growth of personal ambition, but also the assumption of a great deal of personal expectation. Socioeconomic studies show how expectation provides incentive to action for some, and a mere demand for satisfaction for others. When the growth rate in the standard of living in any country slows up then dissatisfaction will be felt and expressed, even though there may be no actual decline in the absolute standard of living. Similarly in companies; if the rate of advancement of employees slows up noticeably as the company reaches the end of a growth and promotion phase of localisation there will be a sense of disappointment universally felt amongst the employees.

This disappointment will occur at a time when there is every reason to maintain the stimuli of training and other educational processes, for heuristic and work-day purposes; and this may produce in turn a sourness amongst the employees who associated training and education with pretty rapid promotion and salary advancement, which is now on the wane. This now gives organisation development a new objective. Previously it had been concerned with the structures of a company in which the growth rate will be much smaller, where ambition may have turned to cynicism, but even so where the continued development of management, executive, and all other individual capability is vital.

We must add two further causes of problem to the above. Localisation, in developing countries in particular, can run into age-structure problems from the outset. It is not unusual to find there that much of the educational development in the country is recent. Hence the cadre of people in the company who are regard as being of high technical potential, all fall within a relatively narrow age band, and are probably relatively young. Moreover, those who are the youngest in this group may be the best educated of them all, as a result of the development of educational policies over a period of as little as ten or 15 years.

It would not be surprising to find therefore that there are middle managers in their early thirties, well qualified and trained, who realistically regard their chances of promotion in the foreseeable future as very slight; they know that the ages of those above them are mainly in the middle and late thirties bracket. There must be a very long time to wait before stepping into anyone's shoes unless special measures are taken. Not only has the organisational growth slowed right down, but in addition the natural manpower upward flow rate will in itself be very slow.

This type of problem is met anywhere in the world, and it has become recognised as one which normally needs attention if the resulting stagnation is to be avoided. For the stagnation can produce not merely frustration for the ambitious, but a staleness and loss or creativity and flexibility even in those who are content to accept their lot. At this point organisation development may well become almost indistinguishable from manpower development, for the main question to be dealt with is how to produce structures which provide career satisfaction and progressive work whilst at the same time meet the functional need of the company.

There is a limit to the number of artificial organisation changes that can be effectively made with this short of objective in mind. Some changes may be accompanied by a loss of self respect but this depends on the sensitivity of the person then moved or promoted; and there is a loss in working efficiency in areas where one or more of the appointments inactually unnecessary. But fortunately where are other factors at work which can relieve the pressures inside the company. These we shall consider briefly.

Companies which approach their manpower development in a conscientious way may become over-possessive about the people who work in the company, and may regard the loss of people to the outside world as a sort of failure. But however one regards losses, they inevitably happen, and are part of the manpower equations of the company. Losses in personnel, occurring at the right levels of employment, can actually be an advantage to the company. It would relieve the pressure on management to invent organisational ways of sustaining the motivation of junior and middle executive levels if there were sufficient losses in the middle and senior groups. There can be no question of the company's being unconcerned as to how many, and which, people leave; but there is a definite advantage to be considered as arising from losses uncertain instances.

Fortunately the economic situation which gives rise to the sudden and accelerated growth of a company, may create a demand for skilled and experienced people in the outside labour market. If this is the case then the losses, to other companies, to the government, to education, can be as an advantage to the company in overall terms, and might be encouraged through frank disclosure of the limitations to career and personal development in the company, as it is presently manned.

If, however, the company itself envisages a future growth in its own activities then it may able to use the future growth as a proper means of absorbing that excess fraction of its manpower which, apart from being an extra expense, is impeding its efficiency at present.

The right organisation

We have considered above how the provision of jobs for training and development purpose affects the size, the structure and some of the job responsibilities of a company, and how in the extreme a company's structures may be dominated by factors arising from the need to devote so much effort to the employment and development of people of whom a large proportion have an outstanding learning need. We should look now at the question of what sort of organisation is required to best accommodate people who have learned what they have been set to learn, and are no longer considered as predominantly learners, but as doers, as executives or managers.

This may not seem to be an important question to those who believe that an organisation is created by drawing a chart showing the various hierarchical levels, defining the responsibilities of and relationship between all jobs, and then posting people, suitably chosen, into all the positions in the hierarchy. At any time when the operations of the operations of the company change, that organisation can be changed in all appropriate details, and those affected can be rebriefed and retrained if necessary. This is the classic drawing board approach that is compatible with the deterministic principle of manpower development, but it is not so compatible with the use of the heuristic principle.

We have seen that it is likely that the use of the three principles of development follows the following pattern. For the most junior and elementary trainee and development purposes, heuristic principles may be often used. For middle and junior levels there will less use of heuristic principles and more dependence on a probabilistic approach coupled with a short term deterministic final decision for each ultimate appointment. At the top levels the deterministic approach will predominate. We have seen, however, that wherever heuristics can be used then the interest, energy and capability levels of those involved are likely to be higher than otherwise.

We have been using the word heuristic to apply to learning method. The principle can be extended, and this was referred to earlier, to include the ultimate selection by the person concerned (the learner) of what he is to do. We have seen that some companies attempt to introduce this element of choice into the career development of employees. What is possible, in addition to the normal use of heuristics for individual learning, is its extension into organisation development. One is getting close to this in the exploratory discovery and learning by the individual, when that discovery and learning is about relationship with other people and other functions in his work area. If the other people at the same time are able to examine these same relationships, then, given senior management agreement, there may be an organisational change or development, albeit a small one.

If this is extend further across the organisaton then we would produce organisational development based on the heuristic learning and adaptations of people across the whole network of the organisation. This is familiar concept enough to the OD specialist, who would be interested also in ensuring that the small changes, adaptations and development added up to something that was of advantage to the whole organisaton. There are ways of dealing with this, based on providing information that will enable each person to see and understand the whole situation of which he is a part.

What is of significance to organisational development is that the more the company pursues the heuristic principle for its training more the company pursues the heuristic principle for its training and development, the more likely it is that those who benefit by this may spontaneously employ it in a search for improvements in organisation. The new forms of organisation will reflect, and use, individual capabilities, with a commensurate release of energy and dedication, instead of persuading or forcing people to adapt into roles created by third party decisions.

The more use of heuristics, therefore, for training and development, the more readily and effectively will that same company, in the face of economic or other environmental changes, reorganise and adapt to deal with its new operational requirements.

Around 1800, 90 percent of the *American population worked in agriculture.* More recently it was manufacturing that dominated the economy. But just thirty-five year ago, more than one-quarter of the male labour force was also still self-employed-not only as farmers, but as shopkeepers, repairmen, lawyers. Today less than 10 per cent are self-employed, most work in organizations, and 64 out of every 100 employees are engaged in service activities, not manufacturing: education insurance, social welfare, and a myriad of professional and technical functions. Automated factories, in which products are untouched by human hands, were commonly forecast for the 1990s; but as this time approaches without the forecast being realized, human hands still, proliferate. There is continued demand for office and factory workers, and especially for more professionals-chemists, systems engineers, account managers, and technical personnel. Manpower continues to be a critical resource. Committed, satisfied employees work much more effectively than do those who bored, dissatisfied, or actively antagonistic.

Thus, since most employees work in organizations, at jobs where typically there is no easy measure of personal output, effective methods of personnel management are indispensable. In what is increasingly called our post-industrial society, employees are more sensitive to the quality of work and supervision, and management often has a heavy investment in their technical training.

Although most managers recognize the importance of the human dimension, they differ greatly in how they translate that recognition into action. A great deal of what is thought and practiced today-conceptions about people and the role of personnel-has been inherited from previous generations of managers. To understand the personnel field today, we need to know something about its antecedents.

The autocratic manager

Early managers felt little need for personnel administration. Workers were considered little more than machines; actually, they were considered less worthy of attention, because machines were more expensive to replace. Authority-power over other people-was the key managerial element, unencumbered by concern about employee motivation or satisfaction. At their crudest, these managers forced people to work by threatening to fire them if they didn't. They assumed, of course, people worked only to earn money, and that people will work only if driven to it by fear of losing their jobs.

Autocratic managers assumed that since on one likes work, people will try to work as little as possible. To prevent them from doing so, there must be close supervision. Management must tell every worker exactly what to do and how to do it, giving the worker the narrowest possible discretion. Rules were often promulgated just "to show who's boss." Individuals were kept busy "to keep them out of trouble."

This thinking was inherent in some of the less sophisticated versions of scientific management: people are hired to work rather than to think, and the smallest possible amount of human ability should be used on the job. This has been called the *commodity or contractual theory of labor,* in that it holds that labor can be bought and sold just like material supplies-and can be treated in the same way.

Autocratic managers felt sure that employees were expendable and interchangeable. This approach paid off fairly well in the early days of the industrial revolution, when workers and their families were so close to starvation that their material needs for food, clothing, and shelter were paramount. Nevertheless, this managerial attitude sowed the seeds of its own destruction by producing a frustrated and aggressive work force that eventually sought protection and revenge through unionization. Autocratic managers were also doomed by technological changes that required better trained and more adaptive employees who were motivated more by opportunity than by fear.

The paternalistic manager

In many organizations, the stern, punishing manager was later replaced by a more being authority figure who believed that organizations were just like families. The boss was the good father, and employees were dependent children who had to be taught obedience. The "good" children received special "parental" rewards, such as company housing, gifts at Christmas, a retirement fund, special allowances to cover illness or other family emergencies; the 'bad' children were punished, often simply by discharge.

The impetus for this paternalistic approach came not only from a legitimate sense of employers' responsibility for the welfare of their workers, but also from stirrings of unionism after World War 1. Under the banner of the "new industrial relations," management became interested in a wide variety of projects, from cafeterias and recreation programs for employees to cooking classes for their wives. Some of these programs were designed to change the employees' personal lives as well as their on-the-job performance. The sociology department program of the Ford Motor Company of an earlier day went further than most programs. Headed by a Protestant minister, this department was manned by thirty investigators.

> In what amounted to a brief reign of benevolent paternalism, these gentlemen and their house-to-house canvassers imposed... a set of rules which blended good sense with Ford whims and Puritan virtues.
>
> A worst... its agents became, to some extent, collectors of tales and suspicions... Hearsay as well as fact found its way into a card catalogue where a record was kept of every worker's deviations... Frittering away one's evenings "unwisely." taking in male boarders, sending funds to the "old country"—these things came to be regarded as earmarks of "unwholesome living" The use of liquor was forbidden.... as was material discord that resulted in a separation or divorce action.

Although Ford's program was short-lived, similar patterns of paternalism were developed in other companies. There is little evidence that any of them were particularly successful in eliciting employees' gratitude, in motivating workers to do a better job, or even in staving off the development of unions. In face, some of the companies with the best-known histories of paternalism later became scenes of bitter labor-management strife.

Paternalism resulted in resentment, rather than gratitude; employees were forced to play the role of dependent children who had little or no control over what they received. Further, benefits that are given can be taken away. Troublemakers were summarily dismissed and those unwilling to cater to the boss were deprived of many benefits awarded to favorites. Even where benefits were distributed equitably, their value tended to wear thin over time, as employees took them for granted and felt appreciative only when they were increased.

Although paternalism has become less popular in industrialized countries like the united States, where workers want their benefits guaranteed by contract and the strength of their unions, it still holds sway in more agrarian cultures. For example, the uncertainties of life in Latin America often induce employees to welcome the protection of a powerful *patron*. They give their loyalty and support to their boss in exchange for his personal protection against arbitrary discharge, arrest, or other forms of hardship in the plant and the community. Paternalism flourishes in societies where individuals feel impotent in the face of powerful external forces.

Japan probably provides the best example of paternalism still flourishing in a modern, highly industrialized society. The Japanese company often provides life-time employment guarantees with benefits keyed to worker loyalty. Employees are likely to give up vacation time with enthusiasm and even request additional work assignments when the organization appears to need such contributions. In turn, long-service employees receive a wide range of extra payments and special privileges. For many, the company is almost as meaningful as the family, with neither employees nor management embarrassed by this close, paternalistic relationship.

The bureaucratic manager

In the decades of th twentieth century, businessmen came under the influence of engineers who sought to substitute rational, "Scientific" management for the highly personal, idiosyncratic cycle of the owner-manger.

1) Improving worker performance

Early industrial engineers maintained a rather simplistic, almost mechanical view of employees. They reasoned that employees were analogous to machines, whose output depends on the amount of power input and the frictional drag. Engineers like Frederick Taylor saw employee initiative being stifled by traditional wage systems; they believed that the way to motivate workers was to pay them according to the amount they produced, rather than on the basis of hours worked. Thus began am impressive elaboration of so-called incentive or piecework systems. Complications arising from their administration made work for the Personnel record keepers, and the disputes they engendered created work for a newer generation of Personnel grievance specialists, but that's getting ahead of our story. This simple-minded view of employee motivation may be illustrated by the earlier phases or the now famous Western Electric Studies, or the Hawthorne Research, as it is sometimes called. In some of these experiments, employees were provided with additional food during rest periods at work, almost as if these calories would stoke up the internal furnaces and cause employees to produce more effectively. Thus money and calories were used to increase the energy workers would expand.

Most of the effort to improve employee performance in this period was devoted to reducing the frictional or "drag" elements of the job and work environment. Taylor and others were concerned with designing tools, work methods, and materials that would be more accommodating to the typical employee's physique and perceptual apparatus. This concern with methods was one precursor of Personnel's concern today with training.

2) Better selection

While engineers were endeavoring to make work easier for typical or average employees, psychologists were helping management discover the not so typical employee. After all, management reasoned, if the average employee can produce 100 units an hour, an employee with better than average mental and physical abilities should produce 130 units because the work will be easier for him. As a result of government experience classifying recruits during World War 1. psychologists were brought into industry to help pick out the most able workers. They developed testing techniques for assessing individuals differences, and Personnel began concentrating on selection methods.

The efforts of engineers and psychologists were linked together. Jobs were carefully described, and workers picked whose specific abilities matched these descriptions. It was expected that the selection and matching process would conserve energy by providing well-squared pegs for well-squared holes, with additional energy to be produced by incentive plans.

3) Keeping records and codifying rules

Some of the earliest efforts at substituting rational procedures for intuition and family traditions simply involved better record keeping, for which purpose many personnel departments were first established. Personnel records indicated such information as when the employees was hired, educational background, succession of jobs, disciplinary penalties received, and provided a record of time and production for pavrolls. These were relatively routine clerical tasks that relieved other members of the organization for more productive work. These Personnel functions are still important in view of the growing emphasis on pension and insurance programs, seniority benefits, and a wide variety of in-company social welfare.

From documenting the operations of the business, managers turned to explicit recording of company policies and procedures. Elements that we may how take for granted- such as equal pay for equal work, additional pay for promotion to a more difficult assignment, nondiscriminatory hiring-could be embodied in company policy statements that would minimize *ah hoc* or discriminatory decision-making. For example, without written policies, a manager who needs Brown's skills may give him a raise when he threatens to quit; at the same time, the manager may give Jones additional work without a raise because he knows that Jones needs to work within walking distance of his home.

The defensive manager

The influence of Personnel expanded during the 1930s and 1940s. With their title changed to 'industrial relations,' many personnel departments began to take charge of hiring, firing, wage determination, handling union grievances, and determining who should be transferred or promoted. The personnel department suddenly gained so much power partly because of management's widespread recognition of the importance of the human element, but chiefly because of the threat of unionism. Unions were on the offensive throughout this period. They charged management with setting substandard wages, with encouraging foremen to act as petty tyrants, and with denying employees their human dignity. Faced with such charges, many companies felt the best way to keep unions out was to eliminate the grievance that made workers turn to them. Because management believed that inept supervisors were largely responsible for what observers conceded were still haphazard personnel policies, many companies gave the personnel department broad powers establish and to police uniform payment, promotion, and seniority procedures.

Although unions were organized in many companies despite Personnel's efforts, they increased the department's status. Personnel now has the responsibility for negotiating the labor contract and handling grievances. Moreover, because unions constantly seek inconsistencies in management policies and try to establish precedents in one department that can be used elsewhere, the personnel department was given greater power throughout the organization.

In some ways, this period of defensive management is being repeated today with the increased pressure of government, particularly through fair employment legislation, and vigorous agitation from organized women, blacks, Chicanos, and other groups who feel subject to discriminatory practices. They demand that management prove it will not discriminate in selecting and promoting minority group members and even that it will take affirmative action to make up for past misconduct. This also returns personnel record keeping to center stage, but with more sophisticated records and statistics. Extensive records are necessary to demonstrate nondiscrimination in recruitment, selection, job assignment, advancement, and layoff. Do male employees, for example, receive promotion more rapidly than do comparably skills and motivated women?

Government also contributed to the personnel field by earlier legislation. Since the early 1900s. a growing stream of protective labor laws, both state and federal, have provided social security and regulated wages, hours, and safety and hygienic conditions in the work environment. In addition to proving management's case or finding ways to bolster its response to these governmental pressures, Personnel was also called upon to provide training-for example, to teach supervisors to identify unsafe work practices or to handle grievances stemming from union demands for equitable workloads, pay scales, and disciplinary policies.

The professional manager

In time, the emphasis on specialization that Taylor and others helped introduce at the worker level began to permeate management itself. After all, management is a highly complex task, and few people can be expected to master all its facets. Organization charts blossomed, with finance, production, marketing, engineering, public relations, and-of-course-personnel and industrial relations specialities. Each of these specializations had its own department staffs with university-trained professionals. Not unlike the "functional foreman" Taylor once prescribed, each specialization developed its own set of principles, techniques, and procedures by which it sought to influence the decisions of line management.

With the stimulus of research findings from graduate schools of administration, industrial sociologists, and social psychologists, specialists in industrial relations challenged the simple tenets of scientific management. Worker performance came to mean something more than getting the right person on a well-designed job and paying that person an equitable wage. Emphasis shifted from individual workers to the impact of the group in shaping attitudes, determining productivity, and restricting change. The interaction of personality differences and supervisory styles was explored.

Training programs were designed to communicate more effective methods of supervision that embodied what was known about the impact of leadership methods on employee aspirations. Each company's specialists compared its programs with what professional colleagues in other companies and the universities were doing and saying. And similar developments were occurring in financial management and marketing management.

Some costs of professionalism

Line managers became increasingly restive with this proliferation of programs and specialities. What started as a trickle of additional instructions in the defensive management stage became a torrent of new bosses in the era of professional management. Managers had to gain approval for their actions not only from their line superiors but also from all these technically sophisticated staff specialists such as personnel, finance, and administration. Labor relations specialists argued that such contracting out could cause costly strikes by employees fearful of losing their jobs. Furthermore, there was little integration among techniques within a field. For example, personnel methods, like wage and salary administration, were developed to a fine art, but these techniques were not related to manpower planning. The professional manger took pride in the technical virtuosity with which he approach his job and his ability to base his decisions on research and acceptable formulas rather than intuition and experience. Mangers, however, grew suspicious that specialists were more interested in the growth of their own fields than in the effectiveness of the total business. Line managers employee happiness than productivity, and Personnel was viewed increasingly as a very separate function, far removed from the main business of the organization: producing goods and service efficiency.

The systems manager

Today managers are increasingly taking what might be called a systems view of the personnel function. among the elements that comprise such a managerial style are the following:

1. *Policy integration*: Policies and procedures cannot be evaluated on their individual merit, but only in terms of how well they fit together and work toward and efficient and effective organization.
2. *Adaptation to unique organizational needs*: organizations can be highly distinctive and heterogeneous. (A hospital is not like a factory; the personnel administration requirements of the maintenance staff, for example, are very different from those of the medical staff.)
3. *Recognition of amorphous boundaries*: Organizations are not insulated from the outside community. Race relations in the community, for example, are a part of the system with which the personnel manger must be concerned.
4. *Reconciliation of long-run-and short-run goals.* Organizations need to maintain a balance between satisfying short pressures and providing for long-run organizational needs

Policy integration

The personnel manager should be more than just a technician concentrating on personnel procedures. Not only must the manager e able to see the interdependencies among personnel programs and policies, but he or she must aid top management in perceiving these interpendencies. For example, changes in technology may require the substitution of electronic engineers for mechanical engineers. This will change recruitment patterns, probably create problems in salary differentials between these groups, change promotion patterns, and perhaps affect union relations. Because no single element in a system can be changed without its affecting all the other elements, the wise manager seeks to deal with these interdependencies simultaneously.

This example suggests that personnel policies must be integrated with other company policies. If an organization becomes more oriented to research and development, there will be an obvious impact on the personnel policies that affect the recruitment and retention of highly trained technical personnel.

Adaption to unique organizational needs

Organizations are not all alike. Most industrial relations research and policy analysis assumes a typical factory organization that consists primarily or blue-collar workers, with only a small managerial group. Ann increasing proportion of business, however, is white-collar, heavily clerical, or technical. There are more insurance salesmen than blue-collar steelworkers, and even manufacturing companies may have only a very small proportion of manual workers. White-collar employees may be even more demanding of promotional opportunities, fringe benefits, and salary improvements than their blue-collar counterparts, in part because of their greater educational investments.

In our advanced industrialized society the service sector is growing much more rapidly than the manufacturing industry. In fact, employment in service has grown 116 per cent in the last twenty years, while manufacturing employment has expanded by only 13 per cent. Thus, schools laboratories, government agencies, insurance companies, and hospitals now present a more realistic range of personnel settings than the assembly line and machine shop.

Professional organizations: An increasing number of organizations-law firms, medical clinics, consulting firms- are built around highly trained professionals who are only partly dependent on the company. These professional groups are heavily represented in the nonprofit organizations: hospitals, universities, "think tanks." In such organizations, management is often perceived not as the "boss" but as a service group, and it is very difficult to exercise managerial control. When many specialities are represented, each group grows jealous of the others; prerogatives, and the organization becomes more like a squabbling extended family than the rational bureaucracy Taylor and Max Weber admired. Many people who work in professional organizations do not consider themselves as employees subject to the usual managerial supervision. The physician, for example, uses the hospital for his patients but is reluctant to be managed by the hospital administrators; and many professors consider their universities in the same light.

Government personnel. Today one out of six employees works for federal, state, or local government: teachers, social workers, engineers, accountants. Personnel policies are more likely to be determined by political forces, legislation, or union contract by mangers. Agencies like the civil Service Commission also plays a key role in establishing hiring and tenure standards. On the other side government organizations are having to adapt to unionization, something traditional manufacturing business learned to do a long time ago.

Recognition of amorphous boundaries

Weber and Taylor believed that employees left their personal business at the entrance to their places of work. Family concerns and problems, however, do affect an individual on the job, just as community and political tensions affect the organization as a whole. Increasingly, management is recognizing this interdependence by encouraging employee participation in community social and political activities. more important, Personnel is often assigned the responsibility of relating the organization to community groups. This relationship will be explored in the following chapter.

Reconciliation of long-run and short-run goals

Mangers should recognize that each day they must live with, and successfully cope with, pressures and demands that cannot be postponed. Thus they are tempted to settle union grievances at once, rather than respond to them in terms of the organization's long-run needs. For example, to keep a valuable employee from quitting, mangers may create salary inequities that will trouble the organization for a long period. Personnel is often in the role of trading off today's requirements for tomorrow's responsibilities. It is no easy assignment!

Human resource accounting. "Human resource accounting" is a proposed method of long-run decision making. Many managers are interested in developing the leadership potential in employees whose present skills offer then little chance to exercise more responsibility. On the other hand, many managers are content to exploit their personnel for short-run results, without considering the other skills the employees might develop. Balance sheets do not account for the credit value of the company's human resources, although well-trained workers and motivated mangers may be one of the most significant assets of the firm.

In the past, personnel professionals tended to view techniques and programs a self-contained management goals. A system orientation, however, encourages the development of programs that respond to ever-changing organizational requirements. Alert management perceives the dynamic quality of the work force itself.

Retailed Personnel Director: "Sometimes when I think of the old days, I wonder why we never realized how easy our job was. Just fifty years ago, in fact, a majority of our employees has been born in Europe. They came to work here, almost when they got off the boat. And ho glad they were to be here, and thankful for what they got. The company was their first home, not their second. They worked with friends who may have come from the same town in the old country and them the boss was a god, and they never doubted their responsibilities to him and the company. There was no conflict in their loyalties to work and to their families. How could you be a good family man without being a good worker? Work, God, family, and friends were all wrapped up together.

Employees no longer respond willingly and automatically to instructions or orders. This eroding respect for authority is also demonstrated by increased employee absenteeism and casual neglect of established rules and procedures. Thus, maintaining discipline become more problematic as employees are more willing, even anxious to challenge status and privilege. Although dissatisfactions are frequently channeled through the union grievance process, employees are being bolder about self-expression. Paradoxically, as employees become more reluctant to identify with the organization, they area still increasing the demands they make upon it. Requests for day-care centers, for more paid leisure, for dental and psychiatric care, and other new benefits that are costly and complex to administer are some of these increased demands. And let's not forget the generation gap.

18

Marketing Research Techniques

The purpose of this chapter is to introduce the techniques of qualitative research and their applications in marketing. The value of using such techniques has become increasingly evident over the past several years, as more and more researchers have used qualitative research methods in their effort to generate information on which to base marketing decisions. Intuitively, one can with little difficulty define qualitative research, particularly if it is contrasted with quantitative research. By quantitative research we mean research which provides information to which numbers can be applied. For example, we can determine how many people there are between the ages of 35 and 50 inclusively. We can count each one of these individuals and arrive at a number. Of course, we usually find it impossible to count each individual; therefore, typically we take a sample of people, determine how many people ages 35 to 50 are contained in the sample, then generalize to the entire population. We can similarly measure how many people drink brand X cola or use brand Y deodorant soap. We have objective information (numbers) on which to base decisions.

Qualitative research, on the other hand, involves finding out what people think and how they feel-or at any rate., what they say they think and how they say they feel. This kind of information is subjective since it involves feelings and impressions, rather than numbers.

Sampson defined qualitative research by describing its characteristics, purposes, and techniques:

> Qualitative research is usually exploratory or diagnostic in nature. It involves small numbers of people who are not usually sampled on a probabilistic basis... In qualitative research no attempt is made to draw hard and fast conclusions. It is impressionistic rather than definitive.

Two key arguments can be made which support the belief that in many situations qualitative research provides a reasonable approach in carrying out some part of the marketing research tasks. First, marketing research can be considered to be an applied behavioral science (which is indebted to the behavioral sciences for many of the concepts and techniques which they have adopted). While marketing research has borrowed heavily from the concepts, theories, and techniques of the behavioral sciences, it has also inherited a major limitation of those fields-the lack of accurate measurement systems. Hays indicates the general awareness of the problem as follows:

> In some of the older scientific fields we take for granted such procedures, which give precise, succinct, and numerical specifications of the scientists observations. How to devise similar measurement procedures is still a major problem for psychology and her sister behavioral sciences. The modern psychologist knows that he is only at the frontier of the true application of scientific method to the study of behaviour.

There are many social and behavioural scientists who share this kind of concern about the development of better and more accurate measurement systems in their fields. Past history suggests that any improvements will be quickly incorporated into applied fields such as marketing research. However, it is also true that the search for more advanced measuring instruments may be slowed by the resistance of many practitioners who oppose quantification on philosophical grounds. As an example, Nicosia and Rosenberg have expressed concern for attempts to quantify what may best be left qualitative:

> We are also aware that the blind research for quantifiable regularities in society can lead to ignorance of those aspects of man-the most important ones-that are intrinsically nonquantitative.

Because of the various measurement problems, applied quantitative research has certain practical limitations. First, quantitative researchers have had many successes, but quantitative research techniques have not yet achieved a level of reliability in predicting consumer behavior that is fully satisfactory to marketing management. This can, of course, be in part explained by the cost and time limitations which are inherent in applied research, but the lack of a firm theoretical basis for measurement must also be considered a contributing factor. Other researchers see problems with possible overemphasis on quantitative research and analysis. Demby pointed out that "Blind belief in computer programs has led to some mindless research and senseless analysis..." Einhorn expressed concern that the proliferation of computers and packaged programs is having at least one adverse effect on the quality of research because of a "...temptation to substitute immediate empirical analysis for more analytical thought."

Many other criticisms of quantitative marketing research could be pointed out. However, it is not our intention to indict quantitative research but to show that there is no clearly correct choice to be made between purely quantitative and purely qualitative research. The payoff in business research is improved information for decision making. To the extent that either quantitative or qualitative research achieves this objective, each merits consideration.

The key argument supporting the use of qualitative research is that the research process and the decision-making process retain major subjective elements. The initial steps in the research process, that is, defining the problem and the informational needs, formulating the hypotheses, and defining variables, are essentially subjective in nature. In addition, much of the research design stage, such as determining the type of research, sampling procedure, and designing the measurement instrument, are also qualitative. Quantitative precision is meaningless if the wrong hypothesis is tested, the wrong variables are measured, or if the wrong instrument is chosen for a given problem. Even when these failings are avoided, he research results are subject to the judgmental interpretation of the researcher and of the ultimate decision maker. Clearly, the theoretical precision and objectivity of quantitative research can be substantially diluted by this array of subjective or qualitative factors. Thus the qualitative approach will still have merit in various subjective areas of marketing research even if the problems of accurate measurement can be overcome.

A final point should be made here concerning questions about the validity of the nonquantitative procedures which are now available and the determination of the situations where their use would be most appropriate. Many questions can be raised about specific qualitative techniques, even when used in clinical situations. Dohrenwend has found that "....there is no evidence that open questions possess the advantage of being more productive of depth." Yoell stated that "The TAT Test has been found to measure only the condition or situation immediately preceding a given activity and not the general characteristics of the individual, not the personality." Qualitative techniques are subject to further question when transferred from the clinic to the marketplace. From the discussion thus far, we see that qualitative research has both advantages and limitations. Marketing researchers are thus faced with a need to exercise judgment when determining which type of research technique to use in solving a specific problem.

Focus group interviews

The focus group interview, or group interview, is a technique which grew out of the group therapy method used by psychiatrists. The concept is based on the assumption that individuals who share a problem will be more willing to talk about it amid the security of others sharing the problem. It offers a means of obtaining in-depth information on a specific topic through a discussion group atmosphere which allows an insight into the behavior and thinking of the individual group members. Rather than using a structured question-and-answer methodology, the procedure is to encourage a group to discuss feelings, attitudes, and perceptions about the topic being discussed. One researcher has described the technique as "A chance to 'experience' a 'flesh and blood' consumer...to go into her life and relive with her all of the satisfactions, dissatisfactions, rewards, and frustrations she experiences when she takes the product into her home." In spite of being one of the most frequently used techniques in marketing research today, there are no prescribed guidelines for focus group interviews, no book of rules, no formulas, and no strategies.

Persons interviewed are known to have been involved in a particular situation; ...The hypothetically significant elements, patterns, processes, and total structure of the situation have been provisionally analyzed by the social scientist..On the basis of this analysis he takes the third step of developing an interview guide, setting forth the major areas of inquiry and the hypothesis which provide criteria of relevance for the data to be obtained in the interview. Fourth and finally, the interview is focused on the subjective experiences of persons exposed to the pre-analyzed situation in an effort to ascertain their definitions of the situation.

The groups are generally conducted with women, especially homemakers, but can be conducted with any homogeneous group of consumers. For example, Dr. Alfred Goldman has conducted focus group sessions for National Analysts with computer engineers, personnel managers, heads of manufacturing companies, paper-making chemists, retailers, models, doctors, lawyers, and persons whose net worth exceeds a half million dollars.

Focus group interviews typically last one and a half to two hours, which gives the moderator sufficient time to develop a good rapport with respondents and thus get very candid answers. Often the moderator is able to get below the conscious level, and the respondents reveal their personalities, emotions, and true feelings. This techniques thus allows the researcher to handle sensitive areas more effectively via the group method than with individual interviews.

The technique is particularly suited for new product prototype testing, studying package changes, advertising strategy changes, and advertising copy formulation. It is a very flexible technique, and the interview session can be used to show various products, demonstrations, ads, and commercials or even to conduct taste tests or product usage tests as part of the group interview.

The ideal group is 8 to 12 people. Fewer than 8 is likely to burden each individual, while more than 12 tends to reduce each member's participation. With respect to group member selection, Merton state:

> It appears that the more socially and intellectually homogeneous the interview group, the more productive its reports...Interviewees of widely differing social status often make comments or refer to experiences which are alien or meaningless of the rest...Some continue to be interested in what is being said, but others become restless and ultimately withdraw their attention.

The number of group sessions conducted depends on the topic being considered, the number of segments to be studied, and expenses and time considerations. Covering every possible segment is almost impossible, so the research must concentrate on the few segments most useful to the specific purposes of the study. For example, if the study requires interviews with broad spectrums of age groups from teenagers to retired people, and heavy users and light users are separated, a large number of group interviews will have to be conducted. The objective, of course, is to try to have as few groups as possible, while at the same time realizing the necessity to replicate the focus group interviews for each segment being studied. If there are two with any one age group and they go in totally different directions, a third session should be conducted. It is essential to get as much commonality in a group as possible so that the numerous interacting demographic variables do not confuse the issues; to be most productive, all the participants must be on the same wave length. For example, Young and Rubicam, which conducts approximately 600 focus group interviews per year, almost never puts married full-time homemakers with children at home in the same group as unmarried, working women because their life-styles and overall goals and needs are completely different. They also break teen-age and child groups carefully and rarely interview men and women together.

A number of researchers think age is the most important break after sex, being a better means of separating the group than occupation or income. Great extremes on any of these are bad, however. This is usually not a problem since researchers are typically looking at the middle class only, tending to avoid the extreme of income categories.

Some researchers argue that groups can easily be racially integrated while others feel that separate groups should be conducted with each race. Even those that argue for integration, however, say that one token black may be worse than no blacks at all: it is usually better to have two to three blacks out of ten.

There is much disagreement about the importance of good recruiting to obtain the group members. A minority of researchers feel that because the interview is so subjective and the sample so small and unrepresentative, it does not really matter how you obtain the individuals. A majority of the researchers, however, feel strongly that proper recruiting is essential to the success of the focus group interview. First, it is necessary for the members to have had experience with the product being studied. It is impossible to elicit valuable comments from individuals with no background upon which to draw. Second, people who have participated in group interviews previously (some research firms use a six month limit, some one year, and a very few have no restrictions) should not be allowed to participate. They know what to expect and are too ready to respond, and "show off" for the other participants.

Many researchers believe that an individual should not be allowed to participate in a group containing a friend, neighbor, or relative; they will tend to talk to each other and not to the group as a whole. For that same reason, church groups or organizations should not be asked to send people because he people hat arrive in these groups have already established relationships, with some being leaders and some being followers.

The physical environment is very important to the success of the focus group interview. The atmosphere should be as relaxed as possible to encourage informal, "of the cuff" discussion. An impressive large table in a big corporate conference room may inhibit many participants and should be avoided. The environment should encourage the individuals to give their opinions and feelings, not their judgments; it is imperative to avoid giving the group members the impression that they are experts and you want their intellectual opinions, and the setup of the room is important in this regard.

Most researchers feel it is important for the client or manager to observer the focus group session. This can be done by having him or her actually participate as a group member, or much more commonly, by watching from behind a two-way mirror. It is usually much better to observe from a detached position where there is no danger of disrupting the normal functioning of the group and where the observer can take noted. A short break may be desirable during the session so that the observer can specify to the moderator other things which he or she would like probed in more detail.

The one thing on which everyone agrees with respect to focus group interviews is that the moderator's role is of prime importance to success. Rapport, level of verbal ability, relevance, and direction of the discussion are important responsibilities of the moderator. There have been several good articles written telling the moderator how to carry out these responsibilities effectively. The moderator's skill in achieving interaction among a group of participants who have never met each other before and probably never will meet each other again determines the kinds and the importance of emerging data. Therefore, the moderator, often a trained psychologist must be thoroughly knowledgeable about the category under study and must know when to probe the group members and when to remain quiet. This special talent can be developed only by specific training and by learning from a great deal of trial and error.

A few of the key qualifications are:

1. *Kind but firm.* He must simultaneously display a kindly permissive attitude toward the participants, encouraging them to feel at ease in the group interview environment, while insisting that the discussion remain germane to the problem at hand.
2. *Permissiveness.* While an atmosphere of permissiveness is desirable, the moderator must be at all times alert to indications that the group atmosphere of cordiality is disintegrating. Before permissiveness leads to chaos, the moderator must re-establish the group purpose and maintain its orientation of the subject.
3. *Involvement.* Since a principal reason for the group interview is to expose feelings and to obtain reactions indicative of deeper feelings, the moderator must encourage and stimulate intensive personal involvement.
4. *Incomplete understanding.* A most useful skill of the group moderator is his ability to convey lack of complete understanding of the information being presented.

Although he may understand what the participant is trying to express, by carefully inserting noncommittal remarks, phrased in questioning tones, the respondent is encouraged to delve more deeply into the sources of his opinion.

5. *Encouragement*. Although the dynamics of the group situation facilitate the participation of all members in the interaction, there may be individuals who resist contributing. The skillful moderator should be aware of unresponsive members and try to break down their reserve and encourage their involvement.
6. *Flexibility*. The moderator should be equipped prior to the session with a topic outline of the subject matter to be covered. By committing the topics to memory before the interview, the moderator may use the outline only as a reminder of content areas omitted or covered incompletely.
7. *Sensitivity*. The moderator must be able to identify, as the group interview progresses, the informational level on which it is being conducted, and determine if it is appropriate for the subject under discussion. Sensitive areas will frequently produce superficial rather than depth responses. Depth is achieved when there is a substantial amount of emotional responses, as opposed to intellectual information.

Advantages and uses

When used properly, the focus group interview technique offers a number of advantages over other techniques. John Hess has described some of the potential advantages of the technique as follows:

Synergism—combined group effort produces a wider range of information, insight and ideas.

Snowballing—random comments may set off a chain reaction of responses that further feed new ideas.

Stimulation—the group experience itself is exciting, stimulating.

Security—the individual may find comfort in the group and more readily express his ideas.

Spontaneity—since individuals aren't required to answer each question, the answers given become more meaningful.

In addition, the company whose products are being discussed may benefit by:

Serendipity—key items or concepts unthought of may be discovered.

Specialization—the use of highly trained interviewers can be condensed through group interviewing.

Scientific scrutiny—sessions may be analyzed in detail after the interviews are completed.

Speed—the use of groups speeds up the interview process and the data accumulation.

Structure—group structuring is not so obvious and leading arrangements can be used that are unavailable in individual interviewing.

Major benefits accrue from focus group interviews. These interviews provide the researcher with an opportunity to learn directly from consumers, in their own terms, their reasons for buying a product, their expectations of its performance, and the rewards which they hope to reap from using it." No one has done the original thinking for the woman. No one has locked her into little boxes by 'prethinking' her reactions and responses. She isn't forced into categorizing her spontaneous and uninhibited reactions so she gives them to you as they happen."

Eugene L. Reilly points out an additional advantage of focus group interviewing. He states that "Our own work in traditional focus group inquiry had caused us to respect the ability of consumers (especially in the easily stages of ideation), to assess (through reaction) new product ideas, new concepts, new strategies, etc."

Marketing researchers use the focus group technique in many different ways. The greatest uses appear to be:

1. To generate hypotheses that can be further tested quantitatively.
2. To generate information helpful in structuring consumer questionnaires.
3. To provide overall background information on a product category.
4. To get impressions on new product concepts for which there is little information available.
5. To stimulate new ideas about older products.
6. To generate ideas for new creative concepts.
7. To interpret previously obtained quantitative results.

To generate hypotheses. A researcher has indicated that when you purchase focus group interviews, you are not buying consumer research. "You are really buying the head of the person who will do the research-the key question is can the person organize information and help you define problems?" Which focus groups you are really looking for definitions of problems rather than for solutions. You have a loosely defined problem area and you want the researcher (moderator) to give you a hand with it. The group sessions give him the guidance to help define the particular problems involved. The researcher and client draw up a discussion guide together, and when the focus groups are done, what you have is a good operational definition of what the problems are and how they can be stated in the form of hypotheses which can be analyzed via quantitative research.

Because of the qualitative nature of the technique, focus groups are most successful when they allow the researcher to design a better subsequent research study using experimental design or other quantitative techniques. In many major consumer research-oriented companies, any time a major quantitative study is to be conducted, focus groups will be used first to help define the issues and generate appropriate hypotheses for testing.

With sample sizes typically smaller than 100, data which are only directional in nature, and numbers which are not projectable, it is important to recognize that the conclusions generated from focus groups are only hypotheses and that quantitative research must be used to confirm the results before they can be used for decision making.

Several examples can be cited to indicate how focus groups have been used to generate hypotheses. A major gasoline producer, concerned about the future growth of sales of gasoline through service stations, wanted to find out what consumers felt about the gasoline station of the future. It wanted to identify possible opportunities for sales of alternative products and services through its retail network, and used 12 focus group sessions in five cities throughout the country to select some possibilities which would be worth investigating in some detail, eventually testing the best ideas with test markets and other quantitative techniques.

Another example of he successful use of focus groups for hypothesis generation concerns research on consumer reactions to bank automated tellers. A series of focus group sessions were conducted with potential users, the results indicating that people found the automatic tellers very impersonal and were afraid of losing their money to the machine. The results of the group meetings indicated that the machines should be personalized, the required secret codes should be easy to remember, and an incentive should be given to the consumer to try out the machine. The hypotheses developed were further tested and confirmed, and a program was created which gave he machine a name and personality all its own. Consumers were allowed to create heir own secret code, and free McDonald's hamburgers were given as incentives for using the tellers. The machines now experience the highest usage rate of any automatic tellers in the country, with 30 percent of the bank's customers using them, twice the national average.

A third example concerns the use of focus groups to study why women were rejecting vegetables protein products. The quantitative studies found that women said they did not like the taste, but other research showed women could not taste he difference between these products and equivalent meat products. The focus sessions found that a possible important reason was that the women did not want to deprive their families of meat.

To structure questionnaires. Focus groups are used to help researchers learn and understand he consumer language associated with specific product categories or brands. The language consumers use often may not be at all similar to company technical phrases or buzzwords. One researcher offered semimoist dog food, porous-tipped pens, and demand deposits as representative of corporation words not very relevant to consumers. A major use of focus groups is often to find out the key phrases or words used by consumers in talking about the particular product or service.

As an example, a soft drink company, before doing a major study on brand positioning, needed to define the needs people are seeking to satisfy with soft drinks. They know it is not just thirst or a craving for sweets. Such things as social facilitation and escape are also important needs, and 20 focus groups sessions were conducted throughout the country to identify a complete, all encompassing set of needs which were then incorporated into a questionnaire which was used in a quantitative study.

Focus groups are also used to determine new areas to investigate in a quantitative study. For example, a soft drink company used focus groups to examine consumer reaction of several different package changes, including a new wide month bottle. The participants indicated that they were concerned with the loss of carbonation in the new package, something that the researchers had not been sensitive to previously. Without the focus groups, the quantitative research would not have investigated this important aspect of the package change.

It is sometimes hard for the researcher to know how to structure a particular question, and focus groups can be helpful in this regard. For example, in studying frequency of use of a laundry product, should the question be put in terms of number of times per month, or in terms of proportions of wash loads?

To provide overall background information. Focus groups are often used by advertising agencies before making a new business presentation to a potential client. The creative and account personnel are thus able to hear first hand what consumers feel about the product category, the potential client's product, their likes, dislikes, and level of satisfaction with existing products. They are able to hear directly from consumers how they buy and how they use the product, together with their reasons for buying and using it.

In a similar manner, companies considering a merger, acquisition or product line extension into an unknown category may conduct focus group interviews with consumers and/or distributors to determine the attractiveness of the expansion and factors they should consider in their evaluation. In short, what is the product to consumers, how do consumers talk about the category, and how do they judge and evaluate the product.

The wealth of information generated is of great value in introducing someone to a new product category, and as a result, advertising agencies often will conduct focus group interviews when new account teams are assigned to an account.

To get impressions on new product concepts. One of the most common uses of the focus group technique is the examination of new product concepts to check out ideas at an early stage. As one researcher put it, "So many times the people who work on a project and intellectualize about it almost day and night get so caught up in their reasoning that they no longer can `see' it clearly. As a result, they can miss the most obvious red flags."

The following examples show how focus groups can be used to help new product personnel understand how their product fits with consumer needs. First, Texize Chemicals, producers of a wide line of houschold products including Fantastik, used a series of focus groups for a new product called Glass Plus. Quantitative research had shown that housewives were using Fantastik to clean glass, a use for which the product was not recommended. The company conducted some focus groups to guide their product development effort and found that there appeared to be a need for a product between Fantastik, a heavy duty cleaner, and glass cleaners like Windex. Such a product would be one which could clean glass and also be used as a household cleaner. As a result of the initial concept, they were able to develop Glass Plus, which after a great deal more consumer research, both qualitative and quantitative, was successfully introduced, advertised as an all-purpose light duty spray cleaner. Texize, which has been very aggressive in the new products area, uses focus groups to make preliminary examinations of as many as four to five new product concepts each month, conducting over a hundred group sessions each year.

The focus group technique can also be used effectively by industrial products companies to examine the impressions of dealers toward a new product concept. Owens-Corning Fiberglas is one company which has conducted research of this type. The company's Transportation Marketing Division conducted a series of focus group interviews with mass merchandise, oil company, and private label tire dealers. The research objective was to see what key benefits and merchandising aids would best help dealers sell glass radials. Previous research had shown that consumers would buy fiber glass radials provided they cost less than steel ones. Owens-Corning marketing personnel watched from behind a one-way mirror as a researcher got groups of 3 to 15 dealers talking about the tire business in general and fiber glass radials in particular. The marketers were very surprised by what they saw as they were convinced that product acceptance would be smooth sailing. But dealers talked about the problems they had when glass bias-belted tires were introduced eight years previously. Even though the bias-belted tires had become big sellers, the dealers wee worried that they would have similar initial problems with the glass radials. As a result, the marketing team was able to rework sales themes and promotional copy, with a much higher probability of a successful introduction of the new product.

To stimulate new ideas about older products. Focus groups can also be used to get consumer impressions of existing products. Such things as consumer satisfaction with what is available now, usage habits, which of several forms or package types are best, possible line extensions, and potential product improvements can all be studied with the focus group technique.

To cite and example, a Texize product, Grease relief, whose original concept came out of focus groups, was studied using groups to examine some of the above questions. The quantitative research the company had conducted had not indicated any packaging problems, but some focus group participants were found to have a strong underlying distaste for the package. The focus group interviews indicated that the housewives did not like to handle it (pick it up off the shelf). Analysis indicated that the phallic shape of the package was responsible. The company then conducted a series of focus group sessions in Atlanta, a strong Crease relief market, to determine what type of package might be attractive to the consumers. By the end of each session, respondents had made it clear that a dish detergent-type bottle would be best. In spite of this, participants were sent home with a spray package Texize had developed. Another group session with the individuals was planned for one week later. During these follow-up sessions the participants said the new spray package was a super package and thoughts of a dish detergent package were generally down rated. Because members of the group are sometimes so far removed from reality in these sessions, the results are not necessarily indicative of how the product will do in the store, so the company decided to do further testing. The final result was the successful introduction of a spray package to attract new users and a large economy sized dish detergent-type package without a spray for heavy users. This example shows how qualitative research can be used most effectively, that is, in conjunction with quantitative research, with each type making important contributions. The qualitative focus groups, were able to identify a problem area which quantitative research was unable to uncover. The groups also identified a possible solution, which was then verified and adjusted via a quantitative follow-up study.

To generate ideas for new creative concepts. In addition to helping orient new account teams and gathering information useful for new business presentations, a great number of focus group interviews are conducted by advertising agencies to obtain ideas for new creative strategies for their clients. Myril Axeworld of Young and Rubicam states that:

Group sessions are, for instance, a most valuable way of letting a copywriter know, hopefully before he has become too emotionally committed to an idea, whether his copy is indeed saying what it is intended to say: whether the consumer is "reading" it in the way he wants her to read it: whether it has meaning to her that is relevant to the way she uses the product and to her needs in the category.

Most large scale quantitative studies are concerned with the majority, the numbers, and not the single interesting idea that might emerge. For example, during one series of group interviews designed to select a slogan for a new service system the moderator threw open the discussion for the participants' own ideas. One was particularly succinct and clear, even in perfect rhyme. The phrase was tested further, and now is one General Electric trucks all over the country. While this type of experience is admittedly rare, the group sessions often will provide the creative personnel with a wealth of ideas to pursue in their creative process.

Another use of focus groups in advertising is to pretest advertising. The Marketing Workshop in Atlanta, and undoubtedly other research firms as well, conduct short focus group sessions as part of their normal process of testing advertising. They hold a 20-to 30-minute focus group interview after they have administered a quantitative questionnaire to evaluate the effectiveness of the commercials. The purpose of the short group sessions is to provide further insights into why the individuals feel the way they do about ads and to get ore detailed information on how respondents interpret the ads.

To interpret previously obtained quantitative results. Although not one of the more frequent uses for focus groups, it is one which offers much promise for producing valuable information. This can be demonstrated, using as an example a product of a major soft drink company. The product, a 10 percent fruit juice carbonated soft drink, had an acceptable taste, a price which was a little high, and was oriented toward that segment of the soft drink market which was concerned with nutrition.

In the test market, the soft drink started strong, held up for a while, and then dropped off rapidly. Some 30 percent of the market had tried one of the three flavors in a very short time period. He quantitative research which had been conducted had no predicted he falloff in sales and slow death of he product, and he company waned to know why this had happened.

The panel data they had been gathering showed that repeat purchase was slow, but because of the six to eight week lag for the panel data, it did not tell them "why" the product did not experience a high degree of repeat purchase. They did some focus group interviews and found that the product had a taste that sated very easily, but was a taste hat people described as a kind of thing hat you would "have at a wedding." When asked it that was good or bad, people responded, "It's OK for weddings." In other words, people liked it but thought of it has being only for special occasions. When asked why they were not buying it, they responded, "Because we've already had it." It seemed that one dose every eight weeks or so was enough. If people wanted to get nutrition in what they drank, it turned out they would buy straight juice or vitamins. If they wanted a soft drink, they did not care about the nutrition at all, and they certainly were not willing to pay extra for it.

Limitations of qualitative research

Limitations and ensuing criticisms are inherent in the very nature of qualitative research. The fact that it is often described as nonquantitative, nonobjective and judgmental indicate where its limitations lie. Qualitative research techniques aim at measuring subjective opinions and attitudes, and in order to do so, the methodology involved is also subjective. Questions regarding reliability, that is, would the same results be observed if the research was repeated; and validity, does the technique actually measure what the researcher thinks is being measured, are often raised with respect to qualitative research.

The lack of established norms for use of projective techniques, depth interviews, and focus groups, and the fact that analysis and results are not quantified or readily understood, result in a lack of confidence by many researchers and marketers. Rather than producing numbers and statistics, qualitative research provides hypotheses about behavior, an elusive subject at best.

The interviewer/moderator's role also creates limitations. Because he or she is responsible for gathering relevant data as well as analyzing and interpreting it, the interviewer must be highly trained. The interviewer's role is central in qualitative research, but this may in fact induce a personal bias which is not easily discerned and can only be diminished by using experienced personnel or by checking results with other professional opinions. Such expertise is not only expensive but difficult to locate and acquire.

The samples used in qualitative research are often small and judgmental; this in itself may be viewed as a limitation. Precise inferences cannot be made from such a sample to a larger more diverse population. Since the techniques themselves were designed originally for clinical use, there is also some question about using them effectively in the marketplace.

Each of these limitations has generated criticism of qualitative research, and they are in some sense justified. However, criticism of qualitative research must be evaluated in view of the purpose of this type of research. Qualitative research does not answer quantitative questions relating to population behavior. Instead, it is a systematic exploration that generates well-defined hypotheses, or questions, for further study. Qualitative and quantitative research are most effectively used in conjunction with each other. In view of this role, the limitations described here appear to be at least as acceptable as those inherent in any research methodology.

Trends in qualitative research

Marketing research, like any process, is continually changing to reflect trends in methodological as well as those in the marketplace. Although qualitative research has suffered at the hands of its critics, the need for qualitative data has long been recognized. More and more marketers are recognizing qualitative research as one means of quickly and effectively analyzing today's ever-changing market and of gaining insights into buyer behavior.

There is a trend toward merging qualitative research with other techniques and approaches. The research cycle has progressed from early qualitative research using small samples, through a quantitative orientation using large samples, to the current situation where qualitative and quantitative are used together with both large and small samples. Qualitative intelligence and quantitative data together can improve research results.

In addition, techniques are being developed so that qualitative data can be quantified and subjected to a more systematic analysis. The recent work of Robertson and Joselyn in improving projective techniques through quantitative methods shows that qualitative research can be made more objective and still provide insights into consumer attitudes and opinions.

While less use is being made of depth interviewing and projective techniques focus groups have become recognized as an effective and efficient way to assess consumer views about a product, service, or institution. Focus groups provide consumer feedback that is necessary to the "marketing approach," and as such they are used as part of many research studied. For example, in the development of advertising campaigns, at least one advertising agency always begins the process by conducting focus group interviews. The use of qualitative approaches, particularly in the form of focus groups, is on the upsurge. When coupled with appropriate quantitative procedures, qualitative techniques can be increasingly useful items in the marketer's kit of research tools. Various quantitative procedures and approaches are presented in the following chapter.

Qualitative approaches to primary data collection are designed to probe the thoughts of a selected group of people for impression, ideas, or language concerning a given product, service, or institution. No hard and fast conclusion should ever be drawn from qualitative data, but important insights can be gained. The basic purpose of qualitative research is to generate hypotheses in the exploratory phase of a research effort. These hypotheses can then be tested through more rigorous quantitative study.

Three qualitative approaches are used in varying degrees in marketing research. These are focus group interviews, depth interviews, and projective techniques with focus groups being used much more frequently. With the focus group technique a series of groups with 8 to 12 consumers are interviewed by a moderator. The moderator encourages a free flowing discussion of some specified topic. The group discussions are then reviewed for important ideas and concepts which may be translated into relevant, testable hypotheses. With depth interviews the interviewer conducts a series of one-to-one discussions with a sample of respondents. The discussion centers on the general topic of interest but is not structured with specific questions. The interview is free flowing and the quality of data as well as the analysis depends on the skill of the researcher. Projective techniques are used to encourage the respondent to reveal his attitudes and opinions in an indirect fashion. He is presented with a stimulus (words or pictures) and asked to describe how some other person would react to this situation. The assumption is that he will "project" his own personal thoughts into his description of how others would react. Due to their subjective nature and typically small sample sizes the output of qualitative techniques should never be projected to larger populations. This is the job of quantitative research.

Qualitative marketing research

The development of marketing research over the past seven decades was reviewed, and Lazer's five sequential stages in this evolutionary process were discussed. A whole new armoury of attitude scales and projective techniques was borrowed from the behavioural sciences; a demand arose for depth and insight into consumers and their patterns of consumption.

In the middle and late 1950s, there was, as Joyce noted, a 'wholesale introduction' of behavioural research techniques. This mushrooming activity was encouraged by an over-enthusiastic and at times rather naive adoption of methodologies. Motivation research, in particular, attracted many disciples who, fascinated by its flamboyant claims, failed to discern the preposterous nature of some of its concepts and findings. The early excitement generated by the indiscriminate importation of behavioural methodologies has largely dissipated, and a more stable and realistic use is now made of these techniques in marketing research. This more mature approach has strengthened the theory and practice of marketing research, enabling it to develop creatively and make a significant contribution to marketing strategy.

This has led to a growing interest in improved methods of measuring the behaviour and attitudes of peoples as consumers of a wide range of goods and services. It became apparent that, when investigating people's feelings about some aspects of buying behaviour, a more subtle approach was needed then direct questioning. For many reasons, such as personal prestige or the pressures of social conformity, respondents may feel reluctant to express their true feelings when confronted with direct questions.

> In consumer research, it is rarely much use asking people why they bought a particular product or prefer one brand to another. They may not know. Even if they do, they are not always willing to say. Motives can be socially embarrassing. Moreover, people on the whole like to appear reasonable, both to themselves and to others, and direct questions are apt to elicit plausible but misleading answers.

This greater awareness by marketing researchers of the importance of more subtle forms of investigation has encouraged experiments in the use of some of the techniques applied in psychology and sociology. Interest has centered particularly on the influence of attitudes on consumers' buying habits, and attempts have been made to measure more accurately the motivations, attitudes, and preferences of consumers.

The nature of attitudes and their effects on people's behaviour are fully discussed elsewhere, and it has been noted that the variety and complexity of human behaviour, motivated by so many causes, may of which are not easy to identify, admittedly make the study of consumers difficult. In the process of satisfying their many needs, inherent and also acquired through learning and experience, people develop attitudes which influence their choice of products and brands. Cooper has said 'we prefer to do things for their practical benefits and justify ourselves as rational and worthy, yet underlying this are deeper meanings...of which we may or may not be conscious'. The symbolic power of specific brands, for example, is often influential in buying decisions.

The particular experiences of individual consumers may include the satisfaction—or otherwise—which a brand of product gave them. These experiences will have contributed towards the attitudes which they hold, and it is likely that they will have discussed products with other consumers. In this way, attitudes tend to be acquired or modified. Personal influence is subtle, and studies have shown it to be very important in the purchase of foods, toiletries, clothing, and several other products. The diffusion of new products and the formation of favourable attitudes depend greatly on word-of-mouth recommendation. Opinion leadership has attracted considerable attention among marketing researchers; it is a subject which advertisers should not overlook. If products fail to live up to consumers' expectations, not only will repeat sales to those consumers be lost, but also the chances of selling to their friends and acquaintances will have been reduced.

A special committee of the Market Research Society observed that qualitative research has 'long since extended from its original function of uncovering consumers' motivations to that of providing the constant conceptual link between consumer and decision maker in marketing and advertising development'. It was also noted that qualitative research is not 'scientific' in the way that some quantitative research based on statistical sampling theory and formal methods of interviewing may claim to be. As in some areas of enquiry covered by the behavioural sciences, where observational data lack precise measurement and replication, qualitative research, in general, may be perceived as lacking 'theoretical bonafides derived from any existing philosophy of science'. But it has to be admitted that the indubitable usefulness of qualitative research justifies its existence. Data may be rather inappropriately described as 'hard' or 'soft'; this does not necessarily endorse numeric data as being superior to non-numeric data: they are essentially complementary. As Colin Mclver observed: 'when it is affordable, a combination of qualitative and quantitative research is usually more information than either by itself'. Of course, all data have to be interpreted and '...it is what the individual brings to the data that is important'. Data of any type should result in *insight*; numeric data do not automatically result in that.

This view was also articulated by Crespi in an interesting study of voting turnout in America. To many people, attitudinal data are more interesting than meaningful. Inherently soft, and incapable of providing a reliable theoretical base for understanding how and why people act as they do, attitude research has always attracted vocal critics. However, Crespi's research indicated that attitude measurement and theory, properly understood and undertaken, can provide a basis for predicting voting behaviour.

The upper 'layers of response' are overt, communicable, deal with matters of which the respondent is aware, and can, though subject to the usual problems of bias, be elicited by structured interviews, e.g., brand awareness.

Further down the marked arrow, structured interviewing becomes increasingly difficult, and subject matter more likely to deal with 'private' feelings, irrationalities, 'illogical' behaviour, or repressed attitudes. Cooper and Branthwaite observe that an essential feature of qualitative research is the level of trust developed between interviewer and respondents.

The essence of qualitative research is that it is diagnostic; it seeks to discover what may account for certain kinds of behaviour; for example, brand loyalty. It seeks deeper understanding of factors, sometimes covert, which influence buying decisions. It is impressionistic rather than conclusive; it probes rather than counts. It observes and reflects on the complexity of human activities in satisfying many needs. Intrinsically, it is subjective. For its findings it cannot produce statistical evidence based on probability sampling. But for all its limitations, qualitative research is able to provide unique insights to inspire and guide the development of marketing strategy and tactics.

Sometimes, as the MRS study group notes, marketers seek information that is too subtle and sophisticated to be derived from the structured, standardized techniques of quantitative research. They then seek for methods of enquiry that are unstructured, flexible, and oblique, such as non-directive group discussions, non-directive individual interviews, and projective techniques. Moser observed that the chief recommendation for informal methods of enquiry is that they can 'dig deeper' and get a richer understanding than the formal interview.

Qualitative research has been a term rather freely used to describe several specific kinds of marketing research; for example, exploratory research, unstructured research, motivation research, depth interviewing, attitude and opinion research, etc.

Some of the techniques originally used in qualitative research were generally termed 'motivation research', but this classification is misleading, because since those early days the techniques have been applied to a variety of studies apart from buying motivation. Also, they do not represent the entire repertory of techniques available for researching motivation.

Sampson has warned that because qualitative research appears to be familiar to almost everybody, but really understood by relatively few, there is a danger that it could be presumed to lack subtlety and to require little skill. To the expert, however, the facts are just the reverse: it is a field of research calling for sophisticated and sensitive skills.

Qualitative research has grown significantly in Europe; in the UK it is estimated to represent 20 per cent of all market research, and is the main research technique in marketing activities such as new product development (NPD), concept research and advertising pre-testing. Its growth has been accelerated, in particular, by the pressing need to understand more fully the dynamic opportunities offered by the enlarged European market.

In the US and also in the UK, several different kinds and functions of qualitative research have been classified: (i) *exploratory research*—to generate language, and hypotheses for subsequent quantitative validation; (ii) *pre-testing research*—to check, sort and prioritize potential advertisement, pack, product concepts; (iii) *exploratory research*; and (iv) *everyday life research.*

The distinctive contributions of qualitative research are, therefore, both varies and valuable in marketing decision making. Modern information technologies have resulted in a veritable 'data deluge' on both sides of the Atlantic; qualitative research in partnership with qualitative data, the warp and the weft, form the fabric of a creative research design.

Techniques of qualitative research

The basic techniques of this type of research are 'varied and eclectic'; they include depth interviews—either as individual unstructured interviews or as group discussions, focus groups, synectic groups, extended creativity groups (ECGs), sensitivity groups, brainstorming, Delphi role-playing, various kinds of projective techniques, etc. This imposing battery of qualitative research approaches has, attracted some critical views: Gerald de Groot, for example, is distinctly unhappy about some of the assumptions and practices of qualitative research which, though fascinating, tend to drift away from its main purpose, viz., part of general market research which results in reliable, valid, and usable information.

Depth interviews

Basically, depth interviews are non-directive interviews in which the respondent is encouraged to talk about the subject rather than to answer yes or no to specific questions. Sometimes these interviews take place in groups, as people tend to be less inhibited in a group. The 'funnel' technique may be used-discussion at first on the broadest possible level; gradually narrowed down through progressively more restricted channels. The investigator has a list of points which the interview should cover and he guides conversation (without directly influencing by formal questioning), so that all the principal points are covered adequately.

It is open to some doubt how typical and representative of the total population some discussion groups actually are. Sample should be large enough to permit proper study of sub-groups, as has been noted earlier during discussion of more formal methods of marketing research.

There is little general agreement on what constitutes a depth interview: in 1950 a committee of the American Marketing Association concluded that considerable confusion existed among practitioners, some of whom regarded depth interviewing as any kind of research that goes deeper than conventional fixed-answer questionnaires, while others stressed the 'interviewing' aspects of depth interviewing. By skilful use of 'probes' and other interviewing devices, the informant could be encouraged to respond in depth to the interviewer.

The AMA committee felt that market researchers should abandon the use of the term 'depth interviewing', and replace it with terminology of greater significance and agreement.

Depth interviewing is concerned with the study of one individual, whereas group depth interviewing studies the interaction of group membership on individual behaviour. It is this interaction-this free exchange of ideas, beliefs, and emotions-which helps to form the general opinion of people sharing common interests and responsibilities.

It has been reported that group interviewing is the most prevalent form of qualitative research in both the US and UK, but there has been a resurgence of interest in individual depth or 'one-on-one' interviews.

'A purchasing decision is frequently a social act in that the items are considered in the context of what others think of the product, and what others will think of *them* for having purchased it'. In the atmosphere of a group, individuals react to one another and the way in which they influence personal attitudes can be studied. Sharp criticism of individual beliefs is frequently extremely frank. Goldman cites the case of physicians, who are often difficult to interview alone and yet seem 'considerable more garrulous, frank, and at times argumentative when a group with other physicians'.

The discussion leader, who should have psycho-logical training, acts as a 'moderator' rather than as a formal interviewer. The group is encouraged to discuss freely the subject matter while the moderator aims to keep the flow of conversation within the boundaries of the 'interviewing guide', which sets out the main areas of the subject to be covered. At the same time, the moderator should be sensitive to the value of remarks, which though not apparently directly relevant to the subject, may reveal interesting subconscious motivations.

This technique is widely used, but it is relatively expensive, as it entails interviews lasting from one to three hours and needs expert direction.

Group discussion depend for their success largely on the moderator who must establish the right 'atmosphere' by adjusting his behaviour to suit the type of group involved, so that maximum cooperation is attracted. His methods will vary according to the needs of the group: obviously, highly educated professional groups will react differently from, say, a group a working-class housewives.

Discussions are often recorded on tape, with the full knowledge of the audience, for later analysis. The use of portable tape recorders for individual depth interviews has attracted differing opinions. Sampson, however, feels that the advantages outweigh the disadvantages. 'A friendly relaxed approach and manner, and the clear guarantee of anonymity by the interviewer can very quickly allay any suspicion and anxiety about the tape recorder on the part of the respondent'.

The analysis and interpretation of qualitative research, such as depth interviews, are demanding tasks: they require expert and objective attention. 'Content analysis'—defined by Berelson as 'a research technique for the objective, systematic and quantitative description of the manifest content of communication'—may be used. Critics of qualitative research have suggested that some of the 'findings' of this method of enquiry are too greatly influenced by the individual analyst's training and background, with resultant subjectivity tending to bias analyses.

The group depth interview is particularly useful in the early stages of developing methods of enquiry into a particular problem, and in suggesting areas which questionnaires in a formal survey should cover. Between seven and nine people may be involved over a period of about 90 minutes; individual interviews, on the other hand, may take around 30-60 minutes.

Ciba-Geigy's agricultural division in the US uses several techniques in evaluating new products. Following initial research work, Ciba-Geigy organizes what it terms a 'focus group' which is made up of actual growers who are likely to be users of the products from the company's agricultural division. For example, a group of avocado growers would be asked how they went about their work, problems encountered, such as insect pests, and the kinds of products which they use to meet their needs. From this focused discussion, Ciba-Geigy gathers valuable information for developing market concepts for the proposed new product. These developed concepts are likely to be subject to further focus groups and also survey interviews.

It is significant that Ciba-Geigy uses either an independent research organization or its own research service in order to preserve the objectivity of the research findings. Members of focus groups are screened by telephone to check on their eligibility. Groups are organized to cover topics of interest to farmers, doctors, teachers, housewives, or, in fact, any homogeneous group.

A special form of qualitative research known as ECGs (*extended creativity groups*) combines with depth interviews has been developed in consumer market research. Cooper and Lenton reported a study of groups of medical general practitioners (usually about eight in each group representing high and low prescribes of drugs) over an extended period of time, of three to four hours or longer. A variety of releasing and projective techniques were used. It was made clear to the GPs that the moderators (usually tow per session) were not skilled in pharmacological/clinical matters, but wanted to know 'what really goes on'; they were, of course, skilled in handling these interviewing techniques. Extended creativity groups were also used to explore the values, motives, and attitudes underlying voting behaviour and intention, and reported by Lunn *et al.* at an ESOMAR Congress in 1983. Initially, in 1982, this research focused entirely on the Social Democrat Party (SDP), but it has since been extended to all the major political parties. The primary objective was to probe deeply into the appeal of the SDP; research was conducted, therefore, in two constituencies where voters could have the opportunity of voting either for SDP or its electoral partner, the Liberals. All respondents were aged between 30 and 50 years, and from C1, C2 socio-economic grades.

Findings—'which should be treated as hypotheses and not as firmly established truths'—indicated a segmentation of SDP voters at two levels: at the first level, there was a distinction between 'mainstream', 'liberal', and 'protest' voters. 'Mainstream' voters showed a strong positive commitment; 'liberal' voters appeared as radical thinkers, but without the commitment to join SDP; 'protest' voters were very different, and they wee motivated to support the SDP chiefly to frighten the real party of their choice. 'This could be, in part, a manifestation of the tactical voting'. At the second level, 'mainstream' voters were differentiated as 'idealists' and 'depressives'; the first type were concerned about the decline of social values in Britain; the second type were more self-centred and were inclined to be jingoistic in their comments and feelings about life today.

The declining birth rate in the UK during the late 1970s and early 1980s has, among other matters, posed problems for army recruitment. The traditional sources of many army recruits, the 'working classes' have also been affected by new sets of attitudes and job expectations. 'Marilyn' (Manning and Recruitment in the Lean Years of the Nineties) projected that the army needed a new communications strategy, and its advertising agency together with a marketing group were given the task of formulating one. The army was persuaded to fund some qualitative research in order to discover what young boys rally thought about life in general, jobs prospects, aspirations, etc. The discussion was wide ranging and did *not* directly focus on the army.

From these group interviews, the researchers were able to recommend a new approach to army recruitment advertising: three new TV commercials were aimed at changing the attitudes of this important age-group (under 20 years), and a tracking study made after the first two commercials was said to endorse the key findings of the researchers. Ethnic minorities account for about 5 per cent of the UK population; certain food products have an almost exclusively ethnic market, apart from exotic fruits and vegetables, such as panir and khoya in the Indian Pakistan communities, and bean curd in the Chinese community. But ethnic communities also buy some of the branded products marketed generally and marketers need to be aware of the cultural issues involved in advertising, etc.

> Any sensible advertiser should consider, if a black person is to appear in his advertising, how black people will react to it. It can be extremely difficult, and downright foolhardy, for a white person to speculate on this from behind a disk. Partly because black people appear so rarely in advertising, blacks often show extreme sensitivity to how they are depicted. They are likely to infer messages, intentions, prejudices and so on which, in fact, had never occurred to the advertiser or the agency.

Group discussions and depth interviews are used successfully in ethnic minorities research in the UK. It has, for example, ensured that labelling of ethnic foods provides adequate information to reassure prospective purchasers that the conform to their dietary laws.

Qualitative research has a special role in developing countries, particularly where there are no reliable sources of data available, and where cultural practices may significantly affect patterns of consumption.

Projective techniques

Projective techniques use indirect methods of investigation, borrowed from clinical psychology, in order to obtain data that cannot be secured through more overt methods, e.g., direct questioning. They are also concerned with testing the hypotheses which have been constructed as a probable explanation of the causes underlying people's behaviour as consumers. These techniques are useful in giving respondents opportunities to express their attitudes without personal embarrassment or incrimination.

Oppenheim has listed the following benefits from using projective techniques:

1. They can help to penetrate the barrier of awareness-people are frequently unaware of their own motives and attitudes.
2. The barriers of inadmissibility may be broken-people feel they must have 'rational' motivations for all purchases.
3. The barrier of inadmissibility may be broken- people are loath to admit to some kinds of 'non-ideal' behaviour.
4. The barrier of self-incrimination is penetrated-this is related to (3) and concerns kinds of beliefs, feelings, and behaviour that might lower other people's opinions of the person involved.
5. They can breach the barrier of politeness-where convention and actual politeness inhibit the expression of real feelings.

Projective techniques, according to Ernest Dichter one of the progenitors of motivation research in the US, provide verbal or visual stimuli which, through their indirection and concealed intent, encourage respondents to reveal their unconscious feelings and attitudes without being aware that they are doing so.

These techniques include the following:

1. Third person test.
2. Word association test.
3. Sentence completion test.
4. Thematic apperception test.
5. Story completion test.
6. Rorschach ink blot test.
7. Psychodrama.
8. Cartoons (blank balloons).

Third person test a notable early example involving what is termed 'the third person' method, was the Mason Haire instant coffee in general and the Nescafe product in particular.

When housewives were asked the direct question whether they liked instant coffee or not, most of those who rejected it gave as the reason the taste of this type of coffee. However, there was a suspicion that this was not the real reason and that there were hidden motives. Two shopping lists were prepared, identical except that one had Nescafe instant coffee and the other Maxwell House (drip-grind) coffee. Details of these shopping lists are given below:

*Shopping list*1	*Shopping list*2
11/2 lb hamburger	11/2 lb hamburger
2 loaves of Wonderbread	2 loaves of Wonderbread
Bunch of carrots	Bunch of carrots
I can Rumford's baking powder	I can Rumford's baking power
I lb Nescafe instant coffee	I lb Maxwell House coffee (drip-grind)
2 cans Del Monte peaches	2 cans Del Monte peaches
5 lb potatoes	5 lb potatoes

A group of 100 respondents was asked to project themselves into the buying situation and characterize the woman who bought the groceries. The two lists were distributed (only one list to each person), each respondent being unaware of the existence of an alternative list. The findings revealed that the buyer of instant coffee was seen as lazier, less well organized, more spendthrift, and not as good a wife as the housewife using the conventional type of coffee.

Haire's research has been subject to considerable scrutiny over the years. Arndt undertook a similar survey among Norwegian housewives in 1971 with some slight modifications to product brands: the baking powder was changed to 'Freia', and Nescafe was replaced Friele coffee. Because pilot research revealed criticism of the

Haire shopping list for alleged lack of promotion in the quantities specified for the various items, some modifications were also made to quantities, e.g., carrots were increased from one to two bunches. The results indicated that 'instant coffee' housewife may have become associated with 'modernity and more intense involvement in the world around'.

In 1978, more fundamental evaluation of Mason Haire's research was made by James C. Anderson, senior research psychologist of the marketing research division of Du Pont. He stated that most of the numerous studies had been content with replication and the question of the validity of Haire's research techniques was not adequately considered. What had not been evaluated before were the interactions of other products on the shopping lists with the two test products. Because this factor had been overlooked both by Mason Haire and by those who replicated his research, it was 'not possible to draw valid marketing conclusions about the perceived user characteristics [and] use of the technique for this purpose should be discouraged'. This professional opinion reflects on the fragility of the research design underlying some projective techniques. In addition, changed attitudes towards the consumption of certain kinds of food have, as Sheth pointed out some time age, rendered Mason Haire's original findings out of date. Note only have social taboos against instant coffee almost entirely disappeared, but starchy foods like potatoes are loss favoured.

Another famous Mason Haire investigation con-cerned a brewery company which made two kinds of beer: 'Regular', and 'Light' which was the more expensive. A survey had indicated that more than three times as many people drank 'Light' beer as those drinking the cheaper 'Regular' brew. In fact, for some years the company had been brewing and selling nine times as much 'Light' as 'Regular' beer. It was apparent that direct questioning had aroused defensive responses and had resulted in distorted replies in order to preserve the ego or self-esteem of those questioned.

Alfred D. Goldman records an interesting group study of women shoppers, some of who were strongly determined not to shop in one of the supermarkets in their nieghbourhood, although they were unable to give clear reasons for this decision. They agreed that everything inside the store looked all right, and, in fact, the store at which they shopped was not as tidy ad the other. Spontaneous remarks during a series of group discussions referred to a peculiar odour. There was general agreement that there was a 'bloody' or 'meaty' smell about the store, and that this had given rise to the vague impression of untidiness which they had associated with it. This information enabled the management to trace the cause of the offensive smell, and an improved drainage and air-extraction system was installed in the supermarket's meat processing room.

Word association test—This is probably the best known and oldest projective technique. The informant is given a single word and asked to say immediately what other words come into his mind. A series of words is fired at the respondent so that he is more likely to blurt out a meaningful response. For example, a spontaneous response to 'hot' is likely to be 'cold'; to 'library', 'books'.

Neutral words are mixed in a list of test words in order to overcome mental defensive tactics. Lists are carefully devised to reveal attitudes towards the subject under research.

Responses can be classified by the frequency with which a particular work is used as a response, the interval to time before response is made (hesitation), and by the total failure of some respondents to complete a sequence (blocking).

Hesitation occurs when a respondent takes more than three seconds to respond, and this indicates comparative emotional involvement in the particular word. Sometimes the stimulus word evokes such strong feelings that the respondent 'blocks'—he is unable to give any response.

Obviously, a stimulus word which has both a high hesitation rate and also a high 'blockage' rate, would not be suitable for an advertising message, as use of these words would result either in distortion or complete non-reception by the audience concerned.

There are many variants to this test ranging from one-word response to 'controlled' response, when selection is made, for example, from a given list of products to which respondents are asked to give brand names.

Household products like disinfectants or soap and foods, such as 'prepared meals', could be researched by this method. Successive word association involves the respondent in supplying a chain of associations with the stimulus word. These links can be centred round samples of actual products, illustrations, or complete advertisements.

Word association tests are useful in selecting brand names, and for obtaining consumers' assessments of the relative qualities of a range of competitive goods. Tests could be staged before and after advertising and other promotions to measure the effectiveness of these on a selected panel of consumers.

Sentence completion tests Word association and sentence completion tests are similar, and their value lies substantially in the spontaneity of the answers which they attract. People frequently reveal attitudes which they might otherwise be reluctant, or unable, to disclose consciously. Their responses can be tape-recorded and analysed for attitudinal meaning. In the case of sentence completion tests, respondents are asked to complete a short sentence and an analysis is made of the response. If the area of enquiry is sensitive, the series of sentences opens with a few innocuous sentences gradually 'funnelling' down to more difficult ones.

The responses can be classified into approval (strong, general, qualified), neutral, disapproval (graded), thus revealing attitudes. Like word association tests, the respondent is subjected to some pressure in order to give spontaneous replies. It is possible for some individuals to 'rationalize' their replies, but, in general, the method is one of the most useful and reliable of the many projective techniques in use.

James M. Vicary records that this test was useful where people would not openly express their anxieties and annoyance about increase airport noise near their homes. The depth and type of their hidden fears were revealed by a combination of sentence completion and word association tests.

Thematic apperception test (TAT) The respondent is shown a series of pictures and asked to describe the situations shown, and what led up to those situations, and to give his idea of the outcome.

The most common form of TAT is the cartoon showing, perhaps, the simple outline of a woman at a cosmetic counter. The first cartoon might illustrate her standing near a display of cosmetics marked with a low price; the second cartoon shown her near a display of cosmetics clearly marked with a high price. Respondents are shown one of the cartoons (in random order) and asked to describe the person in the cartoon and also the quality of cosmetic involved.

Story completion test—This is a logical development of the sentence completion test. Respondents are given the opening sentence (or sentences) describing a situation and are invited to continue the narrative. The way in which individuals develop a situation and complete the story will, it is considered, project their own psychological reactions. A marketing example could be concerned with studying women shoppers' attitudes towards trading stamps.

Rorschach ink blot test—This consists of a series of 10 standardized ink blot shapes, named after the Swiss psychiatrist who developed them for the study of psychopathology. These ink blots are shown to informants, who are invited to say what they see in them. It is claimed that what they see guides manufacturers in developing brands of their products to appeal to specific personality types.

Psychodrama—This psychological, techniques has had little application in motivation research, partly because of the difficulty of valid interpretation. People are asked to act a particular buying situation so that their responses can be studied. For example, the event could be typical behaviour when buying a pair of shoes.

Cartoons (bank balloons)—This type of test frequently involves a cartoon or sketch showing two people talking in a particular setting. The comments of one person are shown in a 'speech balloon'; the other person's 'balloon' is empty and the informant is asked to give the reply which he thinks fits the situation. Responses are limited to a few words.

Situations depicted can cover conversations between husband and wife, shop assistant and customer, teacher and pupil, etc. This third party' test is similar to sentence completion and is particularly useful as it allows people to be less inhibited in giving reactions to a situation than they might be if asked to describe their own reactions.

Associated with this type of test is the Roseznweig's picture frustration test, originally developed for personality testing and later used for attitude studies. Cartoon characters are featured in frustrating circumstances in order to arouse the frustration-aggression aspects of the viewer's personality. The reactions of informations can be compared with those established in a set of 24 typical cartoon situations.

Cartoon tests have a variety of uses in testing marketing problems such as store service, packaging, trade-marks, etc.

Can consumer marketing research develop new products? How far consumer marketing research can actually produce viable new product ideas is open to debate. One view is that it is an utter waste of time asking consumers, who often lack knowledge or imagination, about what new products they might like to see marketed.

The difficulty of understanding people's needs and their actual market behaviour is illustrated by *Fortune* of how Campbell's found that about 25 per cent of customers were concerned about salt in their diet. The company responded by introducing a line of salt-free soups which could be seasoned according to taste: they were a flop. What people say they want and what they will actually buy often fail to coincide. This task, it is argued, is best left to the 'experts'-technical and marketing staff already involved in that kind of business. The other view is that consumers are able to make valuable contributions to the development of new product concepts and they should certainly be consulted.

If the second thesis is accepted, the debate is them focused on the most effective method of researching consumers and gathering information useful in new product development.

Principal methods of researching consumer products

Some qualitative research techniques which could be used in developing ideas for new products include gap analysis, depth interviews, action studies, brainstorming, and synectic.

Gap analysis is concerned with identifying potential opportunities of new products from analysis of the positions (as perceived by consumers) or existing products and brands. A simple perceptual model of the market, as viewed by the consumer, is constructed and research is then aimed at discovering 'unoccupied territory'.

A representative sample of consumers would be interviewed and a series of attitudinal measurements relevant to particular products would be collected. By means of multi-variate analysis techniques, the resultant data would be analysed and indications may be given of new product opportunities.

Depth interviews, may be used to discover people's covert feelings about, for example, day-to-day tasks such as housekeeping, cooking, laundry, etc. New product ideas may be sparked off during these interviews.

Action studies-case histories-in which very detailed studies of specific consumers' behaviour are made may provide useful guides to marketers. A panel of housewives may be asked to keep a detailed record ('diary') of their cooking habits-products bought, methods of usage, etc. These records may be used to assist recall in subsequent depth interviews. From these studies it may be possible to detect, for example, irritation with existing versions of products, and suggestions may be given about improved or wholly new product concepts.

Brainstorming as a method of group idea-generation which was developed by an advertising executive, Alex Osborn, in the late 1930s. In Osborn's words the essence of brainstorming is 'to practise a conference technique by which a group attempts to find a solution for a specific problem by amassing all the ideas spontaneously contributed by its members'.

During the idea-generation stage, no judgement or evaluation is to be made; the process is intended to encourage *ideas*. Later, these will be subject to rigorous analysis; many are likely to be rejected, but some may well contain the elements of new product concepts.

Synectics 'is the study of processes leading to invention, with the end aim of solving practical problems, especially by a synectics group, a miscellaneous group of people of imagination and ability, but varied interests'.

This technique is attributable to W.J.J. Gordon who, in 1961, summarized the results of over a decade of research into creativity. He suggested that individual creativity was associated with certain psychological states. If these could be induced, the incidence of creative break-throughs might be increased. He collaborated with George Prince who developed this technique.

The synectics process aims to encourage people to view problems in a new light; to be willing to perceive how strange elements may be fitted into the framework of what is familiar or known. At the same time, people are stimulated to acquire a new way of looking at familiar objects or methods of operation; to break free from the limited perspectives imposed by familiarity.

As distinct from brainstorming, which Gordon felt was inclined to produce solutions before all aspects of a problem had been adequately developed, synectics was intended to give only a very broad indication of the problem so that creative thought would range freely.

One example of the application of this process involved designing a vapour-proof method of closing vapour-proof suits worn by workers who handled high-powered toxic fuels. Conventional devices such as zip, buttons, and snaps, were inadequate. Osborn would have described the problem in just this form to a brainstorming group.

Gordon, on the other hand, would have kept the specific problem a secret and instead sparked off a discussion of the general notion 'closure'. This might lead to images of different closure mechanisms such as birds' nests, mouths, or thread. As the group exhausted the initial perspectives. Gordon would gradually interject facts that further defined the problem. The group then had new fields to discuss. Only when Gordon sensed that the group was close to a good solution would he describe the exact nature of the problem. Then the group would start to refine he solution. These sessions would last a minimum of three hours, and often longer, for Gordon believed that 'fatigue played an important role in unlocking ideas'.

modified approach to qualitative research

While acknowledging the general value of qualitative techniques, Peter Sampson states that 'traditional techniques used in a conventional way provide very little value in obtaining new product ideas *direct* from consumers'. He has introduced variations 'with the hope that these may effect an increase in useful data'.

Sampson's researches involved a 'traditional group' whose group discussions were concerned with the use of existing children's products generally and products especially given to their children. They were asked to suggest new products. Sampson found them 'singularly lacking in imagination', and very little of value came from the group discussions.

A second group were of both men and women from teenagers upwards and ranging over B, C1, and C2 social classes. They were recruited on their ability to give 'divergent' answers to a certain problem: 'How many uses can you think of for a housebrick?' Only those able to give a minimum of six unusual answers to this question wee selected to take part in the group discussions which had three stages.

In the first stage, group members were asked to imagine they were children in considering children's food and drinks. The next stage involved subdividing the group and presenting each sub-group with the task of inventing a viable new product specifically for children; the types of product to be considered were specified as: a drink, a breakfast food, a spread, a dessert, a savoury, and a biscuit. The nine group members were divided into three groups of three to invent the first product, and re-shuffled to consider the remaining products. Hence, each person contributed to two sub-groups which focused on two products. The third stage consisted of evaluation by the panel of each proposed new product. The panel was arbitrarily divided into 'parents' and 'children'.

This modified synectics approach to generating new product ideas resulted in much more imaginative results; six potentially good product concepts resulted.

NOP Market Research, as reported by Sampson, has experimented with brainstorming and synectic groups and believes that consumers may be able to create viable new products, although they are more likely to express new product ideas which can be developed further. To expect 'ready-made' products from such sessions would be unrealistic. The selection of groups and their 'guidance' during discussions are clearly important factors to success.

Marketing research clearly plays, or should play, a central role in the identification and profitable exploitation of new product ideas. This means that firms should constantly monitor the markets in which they operate (or plan to operate), so that trends and market gaps related to resources are identified. Creative flair is not to be frustrated, of course, but the basic analytical approach should be applied to the productive ideas of 'brainstorming' and other creative sessions.

Of course, marketing research itself cannot guarantee successful innovation. Data need interpretation and business decisions have still to be taken. Risk is always present-otherwise managers would largely be superfluous.

Attitude research

The measurement of behavioural factors as attitudes and motivation has been attempted by researchers using a variety of techniques.

None is fully satisfactory, the ones that are the most reliable and valid from a technical viewpoint generally being the most difficult, and expensive, to apply. The selection of the 'best' technique in a particular situation is still a highly controversial question. In practice, researchers endeavour to measure attitudes by means of attitude scales and related techniques such as semantic differential scales. In addition, disguised methods involving projective techniques may also be used for studying motivation.

Two important factors are fundamental to all research activities including the measurement of attitudes, viz., *validity* and *reliability*. The former refers to the extent to which an attitude scale is free from both random and systematic error and measures what it is supposed to measure or what it is believed to be capable of measuring. The latter concerns the consistency of a method of measurement, i.e., that repeated measure-ments under the same conditions will give the same results.

The validity of a test rests on suitable external criteria being available-which is often not the case. Validity can be determined by any or all of these approaches:

1. *Content validity* established by the personal judgements of experts in the particular field.

2. *Predictive validity* involving matching test results against some external criterion; there appear to be few cases of this type of validation.
3. *Construct validity* by testing over 'known' groups or types of respondents who could reasonably be expected to hold certain attitudes which differ towards some defined object.

Reliability can be tested by the following methods:

1. *By repeating a given test* and comparing the two measurements (*test-re-test*). This is done by calculating the correlation between the results of the replicated and original tests.
2. *By comparing measurements* on two comparable forms of the same test (*equivalent forms*).
3. By the traditional methods of *comparing measurements* on one half of the test with those noted on the other half, the result being expressed as a coefficient of correlation (*split-half*).

A certain type of attitude scale may possess the quality of reliability, but it may not be valid to use for a particular research project. Generally, it is easier to check the former than the latter attribute.

types of scales

Before considering specific scaling techniques it will be helpful to review briefly the principal types of scales which are in use. These can be classified as: nominal, ordinal, interval, and ratio.

Nominal

Nominal scales are the least sophisticated; they involve nothing more than simple classification by certain attributes which are then quantified. These may refer to population characteristics based on age or sex, or ownership of a specific consumer durable such as an automatic washing machine.

Ordinal

Ordinal scales, also called ranking scales, rank the objects which are being studied according to certain characteristics. Ranking is a technique which has been widely used for many years in psychology and sociology. While the rank order of a group of items according to some characteristic is indicated, no measure of the differences between the ranks s given. The 'distance' between two ranks may be substantial and yet another pair of ranks may have only a very slight difference between them. For example, the distance between ranking two and ranking three. Ranking is very widely used in grading people, products, and events. It is important to define clearly the attribute which is being ranked; this could refer to competitive products in terms of taste or freshness, or in evaluating shoppers' reactions to various types of grocery outlets (independent shop, 'symbol' shop, large company supermarket, etc.). The method of 'paired comparisons' is sometimes used with ordinal scales. The objects to be ranked are considered tow at a time, and all possible combinations of pairs are considered. This results in a steeply rising number of combinations as the number of objects increases, and because of this the method has rather limited usefulness.

Interval

Interval scales (also known as 'cardinal') use equal of measurement. This makes it possible to state not only the order of scale scores but also the distances between individual scores. The zero point is fixed arbitrarily and measurements are taken from it, as in a temperature scale. This limits the arithmetical calculations, since no value on the scale is a multiple of another. While the differences between pairs of scale positions, e.g., two and three and seven and eight, are identical, it is not correct to say that score eight has four times the strength of score two. This can be checked readily against temperature readings of 80⁰F and 20⁰F, taking the formula for converting Fahrenheit to Centigrade: $T_c = 5/9)T_f - 32)$

Therefore, 80^0F = 26.6^0C and 20^0F = —6.6^0C

If three competitive products were being assessed for buying preferences, the first might attain the highest score of, say, 8, the second score might be 4, and the lowest score 2. It cannot be said, however, that the first product is twice as much liked as the second one, because is an interval scale the zero point, as noted already, is fixed arbitrarily. But it is acceptable to report that the first product is clearly more favoured than the other two, and that the degree of buying preference between the first and second product is twice that existing between the second and third products.

Interval scales permit the use of statistical measures such as the arithmetic mean, standard deviation, correlation coefficient, and tests of significance.

Ratio

Ratio scales have fixed origin or zero points, which allow all arithmetical operations to be used. This means that, among other calculations, multiplication of scale points for comparison purposes is allowable. Ratio scales are found in the physical sciences, e.g., for measuring length or weight. Many marketing measurements, e.g., sales, market share, number of customers, etc., possess the properties of a ratio scale because in each instance a natural or absolute zero exists.

Principal scaling methods

Rating scales are those which measure by means of ordinal, interval, or ratio scales; they may be verbal, diagrammatic, or numerical. It is important to have a knowledge of the principal scaling methods and these are now considered in some detail.

Thurstone's equal-appearing intervals

This classic example of an interval scale entails elaborate preparation and involved sophisticated mathematical procedures. Because of these complications, the method tends to be little used in commercial practice.

In the late 1920s, Thurstone and Chave published a series of scales relating specifically to measuring attitudes towards such matters as capital punishment, evolution, free trade, patriotism, war, censorship, etc. Thurstone scales can be adapted to measure attitudes towards any type of object, using the following procedure:

1. A large number of statements (favourable and unfavourable) relating to the survey subject is collected by the researcher.
2. These statements are independently assessed by a large number of judges, who classify them in 11 groups, from 'most favourable'. The median values of each group are calculated.
3. Between 20 and 25 statements are finally selected, after discarding those which do not attract general support, as indicated by the interquartile range which measures the scatter of judgements.
4. These selected statements are presented, in random order, to respondents, who are asked to confirm all those statements with which they agree.
5. Respondents' total scores are calculated simply by taking the mean or median of the median values of all the statements which have been confirmed.

Critics of this methods feel that the attitudes of those who judge the original collection of statements may bias the selection of those used in the test. Research into this problem does not appear to be conclusive, though Ballachey and colleagues comment that 'the attitude of the judge will bias his judgements of items. However, in most cases this effect will be small. Only judges with extreme attitudes will show substantial distortion'.

It would seem that caution should be exercised in selection judges who are most likely to be similar in their attitudes to the people eventually to be surveyed. Some researchers have speculated on whether Negro judges would be likely to produce the same scale measurements as white judges on a subject such as colour prejudice. Obviously, it would be unwise deliberately to include judges with extreme views about the matter under survey.

Empirical evidence had indicated that reliable scale values for statements can be obtained from a relatively small number of judges. In some of Thurstone's early experiments as many as 300 judges were used; later researchers have obtained reliable scale values with fewer than 50. Clearly, this affects the time and work involved in the preparation of Thurstone scales.

Rensis Likert published 'A technique for the measurement of attitudes' in 1932, in which he described a new method of attitude scaling known as Likert scales-a type of verbal rating scale. The following procedure is used:

1. A large number of statements relating to the particular object being surveyed is collected by the researcher.
2. These statements are then administered to a group of people representative of those whose attitudes are being studied, and they are asked to respond to each statement by indicating whether they:

   (a) strongly agree

   (b) agree

   (c) are uncertain

   (d) disagree

   (e) strongly disagree
3. These five categories are then scored, usually using 5, 4, 3, 2, 1, respectively, for favourable statements, and the reverse order for unfavourable statements.
4. Individual scores are achieved by totalling the item scores of each statement. This total can be compared with the maximum possible score. For example, a set of 12 statements carries a maximum possible score of 60(5x12), and a minimum score of 12 (1x12). If an individual's total score amounts to 50, it would indicate a decidedly positive attitude to the survey problem.
5. Item analysis is now done to select the most discriminating items by computing for each item the correlation between item scores and the total of all item scores. Those with the highest correlations are retained for inclusion in the survey questionnaire. The number of items in a scale is arbitrary and is sometimes quite small.

Likert does not produce an interval scale, and it would not be correct to reach any conclusions about the meaning of the distances between scale positions. Respondents are merely ranked along a continuum relating to the study of a particular attitude. Scores achieved by individual respondents are only relative to other respondents' total scores. Moreover, it cannot be assumed that the mid-point on a Likert scale is necessarily the precise middle between the two extreme scores.

Likert scales are popular because they have been shown to have good reliability, are simpler to construct than Thurstone scales (with which they correlate favourably), and give rather more freedom in expressing their views than restricting them to simple 'agree/disagree' endorsements as used in Thurstone scaling.

Example If Likert scaling is applied to advertising, the collected statements, ranging from positive to negative, could be scored as shown in Table 1. Statements which could be used are as followed (and other statements could be devised):

'Advertising increases the prices we have to pay for products.'

+ 'Advertising is an important source of information for consumers.'

+ 'Advertising makes an important contribution to modern living standards.'

- 'Advertising is socially undesirable and a wasteful use of resources.'

Worcester has observed that not only are Likert scales the most frequently used method of scaling, but they also tend to be most misused because of the relative ease with which they can be devised. While a Thurstone scale demands care in construction, a Likert scale can be constructed fairly easily. All the overworked research executive has to do is to 'think up a few contentious statements, add a Likert agree-disagree scale, and, hey presto, he has a ready-made questionnaire'.

Likert scales are easy for respondents to understand, but this strength is also a research weakness, for wording does not guarantee that perceptual differences will not arise. Is a scale position such as 'very dissatisfied' the precise negative of 'very satisfied'?

Guttman's scales

Shortly before the Second World War, Louis Guttman and his associates developed a method of cumulative scaling which attempted to define more accurately the neutral area of an attitude scale.

The method is rather complicated, but basically it is as follows:

1. Respondents are asked a series of attitude questions on the same subject and relating to the same dimension of that subject.
2. Intensity of feeling is registered by asking after each question: 'How strongly do you feel about this?'

   Answers are classified by such intensities as: strongly agree, agree, undecided, disagree, strongly disagree. 'Favourable' statements are scored 4 to 0.
3. Each individual respondent's content score s computed, e.g., the maximum will be the number of statements times the highest intensity score. (If there are 7 statements and is the highest score, 7 x 4 = 28; the range of possible scores will lie between 0 and 28.)
4. Scores of individual respondents are entered on a 'scalogram' board, which is a device designed to simplify the process against content scores, and the resulting curves are termed 'intensity curves'. The shape of these curves 9s of considerable value in indicating the distribution of attitudes in a given population. A flat-bottomed, U-shaped curve indicates a wide area of neutral attitudes, whereas a sharply angled curve downward and then rising steeply indicates that attitudes are held by two strongly contrasted groups.

Critics of Guttman scales have commented on the method of selecting the initial set of attitude statements, and it does seem that this selection of suitable statements was a matter of intuition and experience. The fact that Guttman's method of scaling tackles the problem of the neutral region of attitude measurement makes it worth serious consideration by marketing researchers. As has already been seen, the other scaling techniques fail to deal with this region satisfactorily.

Apart from classifying responses from 'strongly agree' to 'strongly disagree', intensity of feeling can be conveyed graphically by a scale with divisions printed in various type sizes:

YES	YES	yes	no	NO	NO
SLOW	SLOW	slow	fast	FAST	FAST

A Guttman scale is similar to a Likert scale n that respondents express their agreement or otherwise with a series of statements about a specific subject. However, the distinctive difference between these types of scale arises because the Guttman technique is a cumulative scale, which means that statements are selected so that the responses to succeeding statements can be reasonable inferred from the response given to an earlier one. For example, a set of statements concerning company sales might be drafted as follows:

1. Group sales next quarter year will be considerably higher than this quarter.
2. Group sales next quarter will be higher than this quarter.
3. Group sales will show an improvement next quarter.
4. Group sales in the next quarter will be about the same or better than this quarter.

These statements are termed 'scalable', because if a respondent agrees with statement I it can be assumed that he will also agree with the succeeding ones. It is evident that this respondent has a more optimistic view of future business than another respondent whose agreement is confined to statement 4.

The survey concerned with evaluating people's awareness and attitudes to aircraft noise in the vicinity of Heathrow Airport used a Guttman scale and this technique was also applied to investigate attitudes towards ball-point pens. However, in this particular study, the researcher concluded that the complexity of the Guttman technique rendered it not particularly suitable for relatively simple problems in attitude research.

Semantic differntial

This popular, diagrammatic scaling procedure was developed by Osgood *et al.* of the Institute of Communications Research of the University of Illinois, to measure the connotative meaning of concepts. It rests on the assumption that the meaning of an object for an individual includes both the more obvious denotative meaning, which can readily be given, and also the connotative meanings which are frequently more subtle and difficult to describe. The semantic differential has been shown to be an easy method of quantifying the intensity and also the content of attitudes certain concepts.

The procedure is flexible, reasonably reliable, and much simpler to use than either Thurstone or Guttman scales. Basically, it usually consists of a number of seven-point rating scales that are bipolar with each extreme defined by an adjective or adjectival phrase. It is important that the bipolar terms used define accurately the difference between two extreme feelings. The words should be carefully chosen so that respondents are not confused.

Jean Morton-Williams has commented that some researchers prefer five-point rather than seven-point semantic scales, because the former are easier for interviewers to explain and for informants to understand. From an inspection of answer patterns on seven-point scales, there appears to be a tendency for many respondents to restrict their answers to the extreme position and one other on each side of the mid-point.

Respondents are asked to rate each of a number of objects or concepts along a continuum. They should respond spontaneously as researchers seek first impressions, not studies answers.

As with Likert scales, the mid-point of a semantic differential may not coincide with the precise neutral region between two opposing attitudes. Further, it cannot be assumed that the seven points on the continuum are equally spaced.

Osgood developed 20 rating scales which have wide application:

active/passive	unsuccessful/successful
cruel/kind	important/unimportant
curved/straight	angular/rounded
masculine/feminine	calm/excitable
untimely/timely	false/true
savoury/tasteless	usual/unusual
hard/soft	colourless/colourful
new/old	slow/fast
good/bad	beautiful/ugly
weak/strong	wise/foolish

Scales have also been used successfully for marketing research investigations into consumer attitudes covering corporate image, product image, brand image, advertising image, etc. In these areas it is often difficult for consumers to articulate their feelings, and the semantic differential offers them a convenient and easily understood method of expressing themselves.

The mechanics of operating semantic differential scales are simple:

Fair .X. . . . . . . Unfair

Active . .X. . . . . . Passive

Usual . . .X. . . . . Unusual

Modern . . . .X. . . Old fashioned

Respondents are asked to describe some particular concept along a seven-point scale by placing check mark (X) in the position which reflects their feelings. The seven positions could be shown as:

Extremely fair	Both	Slightly unfair
Very fair	fair and	Very unfair
Slightly fair	unfair	Extremely unfair

Weights are assigned to continuum positions, e.g., 3, 2, 1, -1, -2 (this assumes equal intervals). Total ratings of individual respondents on the same scale can be combined and group mean scores computed which will give profiles for subjects along certain dimensions. Interesting comparisons can be made over time of attitudinal changes towards a company, its products, servicing arrangements and other important areas of activity.

Descriptive phrases instead of bipolar adjectives can be particularly effective in measuring the acceptability of certain features of a product or service. The 'image' which products acquire can be analysed, and the contribution made by individual features can be quantified. Competing brands can be subjected to the same test, and their profiles compared.

Types of consumer can also be scaled and profiles established for different brands of products. This gives rather more qualitative information about consumers than the usual demographic breakdown. For example, housewives could be classified along a scale:

Careful shopper	Free and easy shopper	
'Working' housewife	'Non-working'	housewife
Likes to entertain friends	Likes a quiet life	

Cars could be profiled along some of the following dimensions:

Expense account car	Family man's car
Holds the road well	Domes not hold the road well
Looks a successful man's car	Looks like anyone's car
Quiet running car	Noisy running car
Sturdy looking	Doesn't look well built

Supermarkets have been surveyed using semantic differential scales designed to give profiles of them as seen by consumers: the following bipolar scales were considered to be most relevant in one study:

good bad/
friendly/unfriendly
modern/old fashioned
pleasing/annoying
convenient/inconvenient
clean/dirty
neat/disorderly

large/small
fair/unfair
reliable/unreliable
active/passive
low prices/high prices
roomy/crowded

The position of the positive end of the bipolar scale should be randomized when constructing semantic differentials, in order to minimize biasing responses due to regular positioning.

Semantic scaling was used in comparative studies of product images among Japanese businessmen during 1970 and 1977. Factors researched covered price and value, service and engineering, advertising and reputation, design and style, and consumers' profile.

The versatility of this measuring device is tempered to some degree by two factors identified by an American researcher:

1. There may be subjective interpretation of the adjectives attached to each end of semantic scales. e.g., a 'fast' car may be one capable of 70 m.p.h. to one respondent, and 150 m.p.h. to another.
2. A 'halo effect' may lead to evaluation along one dimension biasing others.

Semantic differential scales are popular in marketing research because of their simplicity and adaptability. They are used by experienced researchers such as the BBC Audience Research, and they are particularly useful in giving fuller information about aspects of consumer behaviour which are not satisfactorily obtained from direct questioning techniques.

There are sometimes used to simplify multi-choice questions. The graphic presentation is readily understood, and is particularly valuable in some overseas markets where difficulties may be experienced in understanding qualitative phrases. The 'thermometer' can be scaled with numerical values and simple adjectives.

Kelly's personal construct theory

It is felt by some leading marketing scholars that the study of attitudes limits the overall appreciation of consumers' needs, and that a more comprehensive approach is needed. A better appreciation is needed of 'how an individual's view of the world interacts with messages, their sources, the message setting, the product and its purchase setting, and consumption, so as to lead to improved understanding of the total process'.

Kelly visualized all as scientists: '...each in [a] personal way assumed more of the structure of a scientist, ever seeking to predict and control...events in which he [or she] is involved'.

Man is active and involved n determining his actions-not a mere pawn in the business game as Vance Packard and other popular writers have suggested. Attempts to understand what is happening and to predict the course of future events use certain criteria in evaluation. The criteria used will be personal to him or her, and these Kelly termed 'constructs'. Within the limitations of these constructs, an individual endeavours to bring some order into the perceptual world. Kelly held that since an individual's behaviour is governed by attempts to predict the future, a detailed study of these constructs will give insight into his or her whole personality and behaviour.

In the course of living, the individual develops a series of constructs to help in dealing with situations which arise. The terms of these constructs may limit, of course, the appreciation of particular situations, but they form, in general, an economical method of dealing with problems and allow the future to be considered within the limits of personal experience and knowledge.

As the individual gains experience of life, some personal constructs may be discarded or modified and new ones developed which will enable a satisfactory relationship with the world about us to be continued. It is conceded that people react differently to events and some, according to Kelly, may exhibit certain inadequacies stemming from deficiencies in their system of personal constructs, of which they may not consciously be aware.

Kelly's personal construct theory is basically concerned with classifying personality along a series of constructs which are bipolar, single dimensional scales. For example, weight is a true construct referring to the bipolar scale light/heavy. But light is not a construct, because it refers only to one extreme of a bipolar scale.

Kelly developed an ingenious technique known as repertory grid analysis which enabled personality to be classified on a scientific basis along set of constructs. The grid is composed on evaluations made by a respondent of a list of people presented to him in sets of three. He is asked to state in what way any of them differs from the other two. In the case of three men, Smith, Jones, and Robinson, the respondent may use the construct of height, with the bipolar scale of tall/short. Other names, in groups of three, are then taken systematically from the list and are considered along the same construct. Different constructs will then be developed by the respondent and similarly assessed until a repertory grid has been constructed of certain criteria or constructs used by the respondent n attempting to classify the persons listed. Correlation analysis of the entries on the grid indicates the way in which the respondent's constructs are related to each other.

Thomas commented that:

Some relation must exist between polar positioning of an object n a construct system and attitudes towards it as conventionally measured. Kelly indicates clearly that the concept of bipolar constructs does not oppose scaling concepts, and that several bases exist for deriving attitude scales from construct systems.

Table 2 Repertory gird analysis

	Tall/Short	Good/Bad	Fat/Thin	Etc.
Smith	0	1	1	
Jones	1	0	0	
Robinson	0	1	0	

A product construed as durable, pretty and cheap will be evaluated extremely favourably, and that evaluation would increase in unfavourability as the product as the product was moved, one construct at a time, to, the contrast poles. In a system of this nature, the superordinate construct indicates the direction of evaluation, and the degree of polarization is given by the positioning of an object at the poles of subordinate constructs.

The value of Kelly's construct theory to marketing analysis has been given relatively little attention. Thomas has suggested that in the field of marketing communication, particularly advertising, knowledge of how an individual views the world and interacts with persuasive messages is of prime importance.

That Kellian psychology can make a valuable contribution to advertising studies is also acknowledged by Francis Harmar-Brown, who points out:

> Advertisements are today quite an important part of the mass of data that a person has to organise and control in order to predict future events. It would be extremely interesting to know what constructs in this area, different sub-groups of people have in common; and in what way these sub-groups are related to existing media groups, for example. Repertory grid analyses on a group of respondents using as data a series of different advertisements n a related product field, would, I think, yield fascinating results. But as far as I know, this has not yet been done. Instead, the advertising business has ignored, almost completely, Kelly's theories of human behaviour and has rushed to apply repertory grid techniques in areas for which they are totally unsuitable, simply because the techniques are objective, scientific, and statistically respectable.

This carefully qualified approval of Kellian psychological techniques deserves further consideration. Harmar-Brown stresses that Kelly's techniques were designed:

> not to classify the data available to a person but to reveal a person's inadequacies, or successes, in attempting the task for himself. As a marketing tool, all that repertory grid analyses tells us is that the mind of the average housewife is totally inadequate to the task of categorising a product market-not a very surprising result.

The application of Kellian methods is seen as having severe limitations as a tool of marketing analysis: 'I have been concerned with only four cases in which repertory grid analysis has been used to categories a market. In very case the results were extremely limited, obvious to the point of banality; or downright incomprehensible'.

The valueless nature of some of the responses derived from repertory grid interviews is also noted by Sampson, who categorizes two virtually useless responses:

1. Those which are too descriptive or irrelevant. ('Those two come in bottles; that one comes n a cardboard packet'.)
2. Those which are too evaluative.

Repertory grids have been used in developing new product concepts, and frequently to obtain attribute for semantic scales.

Qualitative research is essentially diagnostic; it seeks deeper understanding of factors, sometimes covert, which influence buying behaviour. Intrinsically it is subjective but for all its limitations it is able to provide unique insights which direct questioning is unable to obtain. Qualitative research uses depth interviews (group and individual) and projective techniques; there are several variations of both of these approaches. The former cover Synectics, brainstorming, indirect or non-directive interviewing, focus groups, etc. The latter include tests such as: third person, word association, sentence completion, thematic apperception. Rorschach ink blots, story completion, and psychodrama.

Attitude research uses various sealing techniques such as Thurstone's equal-appearing intervals, Likert summated ratings, Guttman's scales (scalogram analysis) and semantic ratings, Guttman's scales (scalogram analysis) and semantic differentials (Osgood, *et al.*) Because some of these scales are versa tile and relatively easy to use, care is need to ensure that the resultant information is valid and reliable.

Kelly's personal construct theory provides a creative approach to understanding better how an individual deals with the many events in his perceptual world. Repertory gird analysis is a technique used to evaluate an individual's constructs, and has been useful in developing bipolar scales.

Market research is an essential tool in the marketing planning process and plays a vital part in the business decision-making process. Its application is effective in all industrial, commercial and consumer markets. More importantly, the results that can be achieved from the market research process are the real objective of the business plan. They are also the most significant element of the marketing mix to influence business decisions.

Therefore, for marketing actions to be taken after the research is completed, it is vital to ensure that, as part of the outcome of the market research, the user is presented with recognizable decision options. The user should also have the confidence in the market research, the market research company and the company's personnel, to make the decisions with certainty and with the backing of the correct detailed analysis of the market.

This confidence must come in the very initial stages of recognizing the need to use market research. It will also come from the initial choice of the market research company, the interaction with its executives and the definition of the marketing problem to be tackled. Therefore, the choice of the market research company becomes the first major decision to be taken before the research can commence.

The first set of key points to consider is as follows:

- Satisfy yourself that the company is competent to understand your market and any technical details, if necessary. Look for details of work carried out in similar fields and that it has been carried out regularly, not as a 'one-off project'.
- Establish that your marketing problem and your company are important to the research executive and the key decision-makers in the organization.
- Ensure that you are aware of who will manage the project and who will carry out the work.
- Try to establish that long-term continuity of personnel can be achieved with the executive involved.
- Question whether sub-contractors such as additional interviewers or special computer services are to be employed. If so, identify their role and the level of briefing they will obtain. Check for confidentiality and conflict of interests with the sub-contractor, as well as the project co-ordinator.
- If quick action is vital, check that the correct forms of communication are available, eg telex, fax, etc.
- The research company's membership of professional associations, such as the market Research Society and the Industrial Market Research Association, and the Institute of Marketing, also provides added assurances through the relevant Codes of Conduct.

A major factor affecting the choice of company to use for the project is the confidence that the user will have in the results of the research. This really comes back to the simple question of the validity of the data in the proposed exercise and whether it will remain valid in the long term.

Taking each type of research technique involved, ask the following questions:

- Is the initial database a reliable source? Will it be published frequently and generally without amendments (unless the amendments are fully recorded)? Is any historical data available?
- Is too much reliance to be placed on estimates from manufacturers in the industry, as opposed to systematic analysis of statistics?
- Is the factual data to be separated from estimated data and the work analysed for variability of the estimated data?

- Are all sources of data to be recorded for future work?
- Will the research give a picture of the whole market, and be properly analysed into accurate market sectors?

Have enough groups been chosen to cover all the demographic profiles such as age, sex, and regional differences?

- Is it important to explore competitive products or services at this stage?
- Is it possible to attend more than one interview session early in the research, to check cross-interpretations of responses.
- Is the market population profile known? Can the sample for the research be related to the population?
- Are the rating scale points in the questionnaire between 'agree' and 'disagree' statements set to measure differentials?
- Does the sample of informants to be interviewed include the non buyer or the non-user of our products or services?
- Does the sample of informants to be interviewed include the user and not the buyer of our products or services?
- Has room been left in the questionnaire to explore alternative uses of the products or services?
- Is there a series of questions to explore future product developments?
- Is it possible to attend at least one briefing and research survey location, to check progress and that the objectives are being achieved by the field research team.

Before looking at some particular examples of how research became actionable for their users, we shall consider the actual briefing of the market research company. It is at this stage, if the correct preparation work is carried out, that the company can ensure that the most actionable results will be produced.

Obviously, most research is commissioned because a marketing problem has been identified. Research can be used for new product development, and market testing, but much of it is used to understand how to approach a market. Good marketers wanting to use their research effectively for decision making will ensure that the research brief and the market research project include all elements of the marketing problem, and are not merely kept within the narrow confines of the 'expected result' of the project. It is therefore important to have good liaison between client and research company to discuss the proposed marketing methods. This will ensure that the results will achieve much more than just being a set of sterile data sheets: they will indicate which of the sales and marketing methods are the most and the least acceptable in the marketing situation being researched.

It is important to include in the brief:

- the effects of competitors' products or services.
- the behaviour of non-buyers or non-users.
- the traditional, current and future uses of the product or service.
- the benefits of the product or service to all consumers in the commercial chain.
- sufficient scope within the context of the research to examine issues beyond the particular marketing activity, giving opportunities in the questionnaire to explore future marketing planning.

It is particularly vital to consider this last aspect in the briefing. It not only provides the basis for any future marketing activities, but forms the basic elements in a strategic market research activity. As has been stressed throughout this book, market research is not a 'one-off' exercise, set down as a set of tabular results. It is an activity at the heart of marketing planning and decision making and it is only through a series of planned, co-ordinated and linked research activities that a company has the basis from which to achieve actionable results leading to success in the marketplace. The key point here is always to include questions designed to elicit information necessary for moving on to next stage of the marketing activity. This will help a company to look beyond the current task and into the future role of its products or services. An ongoing programme of market research is therefore necessary, to ensure that all the answers to today's problems are obtained; some may think that this merely gives full employment to the research company for an indefinite period of time, but in reality it is a recommendation based on a wish to achieve today what will lead towards tomorrow's successes.

Marketing people are looking towards 'tomorrow's markets' and an integrated market research programme provides the stepping stones by which to travel there. For market research to become actionable in terms of total business planning, it must be planned fully and carefully for today and tomorrow.

Once the research has been completed, it is vital that the data are available in a form which will assist the decision-making process. The following points are therefore worthy of consideration.

- Ask for an interim report before agreeing the final report on the research, checking that all the cross-analyses are available.
- Discuss this interim report with the research company, establishing the results of the research and what decision-making data are available. The final report should then highlight all the actions that are possible from the findings.
- Ensure that at least one copy of all data is available, even if it does not appear in the report. It may be required for future work.

- A presentation to he project management team should cover:
  the marketing problem tackled by the research
  the method of research (in outline only)
  the main analytical data produced
  how the results of the research can influence marketing and sales decisions and, in time, the overall business.

Let us now look at a number of case studies which will assist in showing how:

1. market research was used to achieve significant marketing success.
2. market research was used to strengthen a company's advantage over competitors.
3. market research did not provide the results expected by the company, causing management to analyse the situation further and take new decisions.
4. results were used to re-orientate the company's marketing and sales planning.

The first company is involved in supplying artificial flavourings to major food producers. It has as its main competitor a company marketing 'natural flavourings'. In reality, both products were derived from natural raw materials, with the lead company only reprocessing the product to allow ease of use and greater consistency for its customers' processes. As a result it had the major part of the market. However, the competitor tried to emphasize its products 'natural state', despite the fact that productivity gains obtained from the processed product were advantageous to the user and no apparent difference could be detected in the final end product so far as the producer was concerned.

The lead company's American counterpart was experiencing major marketing problems with a similar situation in its home market. Again, there was an alternative 'natural product' produced by a company who successfully used this 'natural' profiles. As a result of exchange rate changes, the prospect of this American product being available at a competitive price in the UK, marketed according to this natural profile, became a possibility.

The UK lead company, recognizing the impending competition from the US product and the possible resurgence of its domestic competition, questioned how this would affect their market. It therefore briefed a market research consultancy to analyse the situation and recommend what activities should be undertaken to protect its markets. It became clear that no one knew what the real effect of the flavouring was on the product, beyond the nor, all technical use. The research consultancy suggested a programme of market research to examine any differences in the three flavourings within the product, in the opinions of the user and the consumer but not the manufacturer.

Conventional consumer quantitative research through hall testing was carried out with all three variants. The expected outcome of the research was that no difference would be perceived by the consumer and that 'naturalness' would not be an issue. In fact, the research, although confirming this latter issue, did not give an even result between the variants, but suggested that the end product with the lead company's flavouring gave an added quality to the product.

The lead company was now in a very strong position to action these results in an aggressive marketing campaign, designed to show its customers that their consumers could differentiate between flavourings and that its product was preferred. The outcome of the research gave a leading edge to the UK company and this was subsequently marketed very efficiently to its benefit.

It is also worth commenting that had the market research findings been negative to the UK company, it would nevertheless have been ready to establish a technical research and development programme to overcome any product deficiencies. Clearly, the market research was the linchpin of the company's decision-making process and the results led to successful marketing activity.

In this situation, the company had recognized a marketing problem, had explored the extent of the problem through market research and, when the results were obtained, used them to influence its market significantly.

The second case study involves the company Devro Ltd, in this instance the company's extensive technical research and development facilities had been working on a project to improve the company's product performance with its customers, as a result of feedback from the marketing department. This feedback indicated that the manufacturing rates of sausage production were increasing rapidly as a result of improved machine technology, and the company's casing products would have to cope with this increased demand. A battery of scientific tests had shown that a new product had a significantly improved operating strength, with no detrimental effect on the eating properties of the sausage product. The question therefore became one of how to use this to the best marketing advantage.

The company had previously used market research to communicate to customers that its casing products gave significantly better eating characteristics with sausages than other competitive casing products. We saw in the previous chapters the type of rating statements that were used to determine preferences for the products. The company decided to use the same technique again to establish the profile of the consumer of this new product.

A series of consumer tasting sessions was carried out using hall tests throughout the UK with sausages in different casing products. Once again, use was made of the same consumer criteria confirmed in previous market research to establish differences particularly in taste, bite, and chewiness for each casing product. Both competitors' and the company's own existing and proposed new products were tested in the research. As was expected from the results of the scientific data, the consumer tests showed no significant difference in eating characteristics between the existing and new Devro Ltd products. The lead over the competitive products was maintained.

Clearly, Devro Ltd was now in a position to use this market research to its competitive advantage. A series of presentations was made to major and potential new customers, highlighting the improved operational qualities of the product, designed to increase user's productivity, without being detrimental to the consumers' perception of the final product. This activity allowed Devro Ltd to strengthen its position in its existing markets, while establishing its credibility with users of other casing products. Once again, market research was able to help Devro Ltd make the initial decision to launch the new improved product and use the results of the research competitively.

The third case study involves a packaging company whose main product base was he manufacturer of high quality printed cartons and boxes. The company had recently invested in the most modern production plant, capable of producing superior quality products at lower costs and with a reduced turn-around compared to their competitors. Once the plant was in operation, it was realized that the necessary production volumes were not being achieved from the sales orders to make the plant viable. So the company decided to carry out market research with its existing and potential customers, to establish its market profile before deciding how to develop a strategy to obtain an increase in market share.

In-depth interviews were carried out with the major purchasers in the market to establish their attitudes towards the leading suppliers of packaging in terms of price, delivery, quality and general company image. Each individual supplier was rated in these terms against the other suppliers. The original packaging company had believed that the results would show the company to be amongst the leaders in quality and delivery performance, but average in terms of price.

The market research results, however, were not as expected. In fact, the results suggested that the company was bottom of the league on all factors except quality. In addition, it showed that the company had an overall image of being a 'slow reacting company', only to be used for special work not required quickly and where price was not important.

These results obviously surprised the company and did not provide the answer to how to increase the volume throughout and the commercial viability of the production plant. As the results were being considered by management, ce ain more positive features became apparent.

First, they realized that the quality image was favourable and that it was a major reason why the company had the image of being a specialist work supplier. Secondly, the comments on poor delivery had been those associated with the company before its investment programme, and the buyers interviewed were not necessarily aware of the new plant and production facilities. Lastly, the perception of specialist work did not link with pricing, which was considered unimportant in this area.

Clearly the company's initial marketing strategy of being a high volume, low cost and quality producer was at variance with the market's image. It was also apparent from the results that a more significant market niche was available. Since its image was specialist, and once the message of increased volume with rapid delivery could be passed into the market, it would be possible for the company to increase its market share. More importantly, as this type of work was not price sensitive, higher profits could be made without direct comparison to competitive suppliers.

Here we have seen that the expected results of the market research were not obtained and the company's initial marketing approach appeared to be failing. As a result of the market research, intuitive analysis of the outcome showed that a definite marketing approach was possible which could provide greater success than had initially been targeted in the marketing plan. The market research gave the company much more actionable results than had been thought possible in the initial marketing planning.

Our last case concerns a distributor of industrial consumable products, whose pricing policy had limited its operation to a sector of user companies who were not sensitive to price. Although acceptable profit levels were achieved in this market sector, little growth was possible. The company was also aware that this sector did not represent the largest share of the market and that growth could also be gained if it moved into other sectors. Clearly, the company had to establish the potential of the remaining market and decide what marketing strategy was appropriate to gain entry.

The initial phase of market research involved conventional desk research to confirm the number of UK establishments who were users of the company's products. In this case, use was made of local government rating statistics, which give a satisfactory breakdown of outlets by type, eg industrial commercial, and retail and of the establishments which were potential users of the company's products.

The second age of the research involved a survey of users to establish annual expenditure on the products across each outlet type. This was carried out over an acceptable representative sample of users and the results cross referenced against government published statistics on population.

Subsequently, the company was able to match both sets of data and confirm the market size in total, and by sector. They found that they operated in 5 per cent of the total market sector, yet they had a 10 per cent marked share overall. In addition, the major user market represented 5 per cent of the market and the company was not represented in that sector in any way. The results also showed that the company was a major supplier to the market as a whole and no other supplier had more than 5-7 per cent of the market. Clearly, the company would achieve its growth targets by entry into the major user market. The key question was how this was to be achieved. It was decided to commission a market research consultancy to carry out in-depth interviews with their main competitors in the major user market, to establish their attitudes to the market and their marketing approach towards the buyers of the consumable products concerned. This project was commissioned in conjunction with a major UK manufacturer, who was concerned by the high level of imported products used in this sector. At this company always operated through distributors, it wished to find a way of improving its own product presentation to the market.

The results of the research suggested that price was perceived as the dominant issue by the suppliers. They also believed that the customer was generally unconcerned with the products' origins, provided quality was maintained. Although lower margins were achieved by the nature of the order volume, acceptable profits could also be maintained. The company was now in a position to work with the major supplier and establish a marketing strategy for both of them to achieve market penetration. Firstly, the manufacturer, by increasing volume through-put, was able to reduce unit costs, which could be used to allow extra discounts to the supplier company. This discount was used in an aggressive pricing policy by the supplier company to achieve market share in the major user sector. Secondly, as the products involved were already supplied to the company's existing market sector, a lower buying cost was obtained and hence higher profit margins were achieved in this mature market sector by the company.

19
Organisational Analysis

Organisations are often defined as collections of individuals seeking common goals. We then attempt to ascertain the common goal being sought and look at the elements in the environments in the environment needed for goal attainment. This is useful in underdeveloped nations characterized by small, comparatively simple units. But in complex societies where organisations are huge and highly specialized, this approach breaks down. For instance, can you state the goal for General Motors that is shared by all of its members?

A key feature of organisations is their ability to act as a collectivity. Recognizing this we define an organisation as any collection of individuals that can enter into a legally binding contract. The legal capacity to make contracts is used because it requires: (1) that the entity be recognized by others; and (2) that it can act as a collectivity.

This definition helps resolve a sticky problem in organisation theory. Complex systems are typically broken down into major components. These components are treated as if they were organisations. If the unit can act as a collectivity we think this treatment is appropriate. State universities typically have this legal capacity even though they are only part of the state government. Likewise, wholly owned subsidiaries have contractual capacity and are frequently treated as organisations.

Organisations can be classified as complex or simple. We may call an organisation complex when it contains more than one unit with contractual capacity. If none of its components possesses this legal capacity, separate from the whole, the organisation may be called simple.

If a unit is part of an organisation but does not possess legal contractual capacity it may be called a subsystem, department, or group. For instance, a state university has an auditing department that reports directly to a board of trustees. It's not an organisation but a subsystem of the university. Units that are recognized externally as collections of individuals but which lack legal contractual capacity are referred to as aggregations or special interest groups. Some units are formed by one or more individuals and/or organisations to accomplish a specific, limited, and short-range objective. Thompson calls these complex configurations. They may have some ability to act as a collectivity. But that ability is frequently limited by sponsoring organisations. Examples of complex configurations include joint ventures or cooperative projects among government agencies. In the construction industry such cooperative ventures are the rule, not the exception. They are also common in oil exploration and basic research.

Our definition of an organisation would apparently lead to straightforward rule for separating it from its environment. What is inside an organisation is that legally controlled by the system. However, this simple rule quickly leads to problems. Individuals, for instance, are typically members of many organisations. Let's use our legalistic approach after developing the notion of domain. Then we will modify the simple rule to include the complexity of defining the boundaries of an organisation.

The domain of an organisation is the set of claims it makes over societal resources. To explain the notion it is necessary to briefly outline the elements organisations often attempt to control and how they may support their claims. What can an organisation attempt to lay claim upon? The literature concerning organisational characteristics suggests the following: goals, outputs, property, technology, structure and members. Earlier we introduced the notion of means-ends chains. We argued it was possible for an organisation to take the overall social function of the system and devise a mission statement. From the mission statement more specific goals could be developed and from this point a strategy for goal attainment could be derived. The strategy would indicate the mix of property, technology, structure, and members needed to create and/or distribute specific outputs. We suggested that organisations that limit their social contribution and develop clear-cut means-ends chain have a better chance for survival. Our arguments centered on the benefits from economies of scale and the synergy received from using related resources. Now we are going to expand the arguments without relying upon the mission of the system as the driving force behind the strategy of an organisation.

It is comparatively easy for an organisation to claim control over goals, outputs, properly, technology, structure, and individuals. Although it's quite another matter for an organisation to actually control any control any of the elements. For an organisation to use any one of the elements, it must exercise some degree of control over it. For instance, members must be willing to work toward organisation effectiveness and goals, follow the structure, and produce the desired outcomes. To gain some degree of control an organisation must back up its claims. It can secure some control with an exchange of resources. For instance, a business hires labor. Organisations can also back up their claims with ideology or a combination of ideology and resources. Let's say the Cub Scouts of America ask parents to volunteer to help all boys in a pack to learn important skills and values. Ideology is preferred since it costs less than tangible resources. The closer the claim to the mission of the organisation, the larger the ideological component can become. In no case does the organisation obtain complete control. The more control desired, the larger the cost in terms of resources and ideology. The concept of domain highlights several important notions about organisations. One, organisations often claim more territory than they are willing to back up with resources and ideology. Two, outsiders may give an organisation more "control" than it wants." For instance, many critics of business argue that pollution control, decaying cities, and the development of equality in employment should be organisational goals. Parents may assume that public schools know to educate children. Thus, the domain is at the same time larger and smaller than desired by the organisation. Three, a claim over a particular element only continues as long as it is backed up with resources and/or ideology. Once a claim is made it must be continually supported, since the value of resource exchanges and ideology decay over time. We should note this aiso holds for goals. For instance, government may claim jurisdiction over police protection. If ineffective, however, vigilante groups may contest this aspect of the government's domain and claim it as part of their domain. Claims over goals establish expectations on the part of subgroups in society. Even organisations given exclusive jurisdiction over goals must provide some valuable output or face competition. Let's take a closer look at competing claims over key organisational elements.

The boundary of an irganisation. The outer limit of an organisation's domain is often called its boundary. At the boundary, control over internal elements is often contested. It may be difficult to clearly separate one organisation from another or delineate control from mere influence. Starbuck has recognized this by likening the organisation to a cloud. At times one cloud is clearly visible and distinct, even though its shape continually changes as it moves across the sky. Two clouds may partially overlap and even merge. It may be impossible to say a particular water droplet belongs to one cloud or another. With organisations, the problem is even more difficult. You are dealing with a large number of elements and potentially different areas of control.

Let's return to our decision rule and modify it. Originally, we stated that an element is inside an organisation if it's legally controlled by the system. Let's refine that. An element is inside the system to the extent that it is legally controlled by an organisation and to the extent that these claims are accepted by other individuals and institutions in society. Obviously, this is not a precise definition. But it appears to be a workable approach to drawing boundaries.

Defining the specific environement of an organisation

Let's restate the basic theme. To maintain control over internal elements an organisation must continually replenish its resources and maintain its ideological legitimacy. The specific environment is the set of external organisations, individuals, and institutions that a given organisation interacts with. An organisation does not exert legal control over these entities, though it may enter into legal contracts with them. These external units are contracted to enhance the probability of growth and survival as a result of an organisation's domain choice.

The primary units in the specific environment of an organisation are its input suppliers and output distributors. Without their support it would be unable to function. Organisations need assured sources of labor, money, raw materials, and equipment. They need distributors and customers to keep the system operating. This is done either directly via exchange of resources for products and services or indirectly via exchange with a supplier for service to a particular client group.

The organisation also interfaces with competitors. We most frequently think of competitors as those offering similar products and services. But organisations face competitors in other areas as well. There is competition for inputs and outputs.

Less well recognized are a number of institutions that develop as a result of organisations attempting to claim jurisdiction over a particular element. As organisations lay claim to labor, unions and professional organisations are likely to develop to offset organisational control. Slowly, large complex organisations are beginning to realize that their claims for control help span special interest groups. Who protects a "free good", such as air, if organisations claim they can use it as they see fit? First came the development of special interest groups. Now the U.S. government claims jurisdiction and limits the manner in which air can be used. Who ensures individual consumers will receive fair treatment from huge corporations? Currently, there are several interest groups pressuring the government to establish a new agency to work toward this end.

Thus, the government is a potential member of every organisation's specific environment. As the allocator of power it can establish organisations or eliminate them. However, the U.S. government is not a single organisation. It is a complex configuration composed of a number of organisations. They compete with one another in a manner not dissimilar to businesses. However, the focal point of the competition often rests with goals and values, not products and services.

So far we have identified suppliers, distributors, customers, special interest groups, and the government as members of an organisation's specific environment. Each of these has been related to the attempts of an organisation to gain control over its internal elements. There is another group of institutions in the specific environment that most organisations tend to dismiss. These are organisations operating in areas not directly related to their mission or domain. Many of these organisations have a different social function. They become a part of an organisation's specific environment because each is part of the larger society. For example, business organisations support charities and universities. Universities, in turn, lend technical assistance to business and government agencies. Churches may provide public schools with meeting rooms. The list is almost endless.

Immediate payoff in not automatically expected in many contacts between institution with different social functions. Many of these contacts appear to be made to improve the image and legitimize the organisation. A few, however, may have direct payoff. For instance, large corporations are most likely to give money to a prestigious private university where their top executives hope their children might attend and from which they hope to obtain new employees. Such "gifts" are often publicized as evidence of the corporation's social responsibility. Universities often lend assistance to local governments as part of their "service obligation to the community." The fact that such help enhances the probability of greater state funding by local legislators is rarely mentioned.

For a large corporation the number of external individuals, organisations, and institutions composing its specific environment can run into the thousands. Even simple organisations may have a specific environment with hundreds of units. But only a comparatively few units in the specific environment receive very much attention by top management. Those external units that do receive attention from the organisation appear to have an impact on its internal operations and decision-making structure.

The enacted portion of the specific environment. Weick argues that organisations only respond to those external forces that are enacted. That is, the system responds to those elements that demand its attention. Not all the institutions just described demand attention. And most managers in complex organisations face only a few portions of the specific environment. The literature on organisational environments splits on this key issue. Is the entire set of units comprising the specific environment important, or just those recognized by the system? While there is no clear-cut answer the following seems reasonable.

Some portions of the specific environment are more important than others. Different portions of the specific environment are relevant to different managers. The system cannot respond to environmental pressures that remain undetected. Thus, we expect alterations in the domain of the organisation to be partially explained by managerial perceptions. That is, the organisation responds directly to the enacted part of the specific environment.

Conditions in the specific environment of the system probably have a direct impact on organisational outcomes whether they are perceived by managers or not. For instance, even if an organisation does not see consumer resistance to a product, sales may suffer. Thus, the objective aspects of the specific environment are important when predicting organisational success.

Managerial perceptions of the specific environment do not automatically correspond to more objective descriptions. However, it appears more likely that managerial perceptions and objective descriptions of the major units in the specific environment will become increasingly similar as you higher into the managerial ranks.

The definition of an organisation as a legal entity should be carefully noted. Assume you are attempting to describe the specific environment of a simple organisation, Sasquash Division, of a complex organisation, Diversified Creatures. The perceptions of the important units in the specific environment of the head of sasquash Division are likely to be very similar to objective measures for the division. It's unlikely, however, that the division head of Sasquash knows very much about the specific environment of Diversified Creatures.

There may be a large overlap between the "enacted" environment and the actual environment when top-level decision makers are asked to describe important outside forces. Lower-echelon managers, however, probably have more difficulty in accurately assessing external pressures. They have a difficult time seeing the "big picture." But regardless of whose perceptions are used, we need to answer a critical question: Which are the most important units in the specific environment?

Important units in the specific environment. We have asserted that supplier, distributors, competitors, and government agencies are particularly important. They have a direct bearing on the short-run survival of the organisation. Let's go a little farther.

If you accept the notion that exchange is the basis for interaction among organisations, it is quite obvious that most individuals or special interest groups have comparatively little to offer organisations. In the case of individuals an organisation can readily substitute one person for another. Special interest groups have difficulty mounting the sustained effort needed to alter existing conditions. Their claims over internal elements may be heavily weighted toward ideology. At the first sign of progress, members of special interests are likely to switch their affiliation to other groups. Unlike organisations, success may spell the death of a special interest group. For example, in the mid 1970s, a loose coalition of housewives boycotted meat to protest dramatically rising costs of beef. The boycott was successful in cutting demand and stemming price increases for a short time. With this success, however, the interest group dissolved. It did not reform when meat prices again jumped some six months later.

In contrast to individual and special interest groups, the organisation relies upon a mix of resources and ideologies. As a legal entity in can make and enforce contracts. Via specialization it can control resources needed by other organisations. It need not be concerned about complete consensus on every issue. Resources can be substituted for ideology to maintain control over individuals. Success does not threaten survival but adds resources for growth and development. Thus, organisations are the most important units in the specific environment of other organisations.

To a large extent, then, the important units in the specific environment of an organisation consist of organisations it must relay upon for growth and development. Suppliers or raw materials, financial institutions, unions, government agencies, and competitors are important for most organisations. Occasionally, individuals and special interest groups are important enough to become a part of the enacted environment.

Most, however, have used a strategy of operating through government agencies, which then become the relevant units of the enacted environment.

Assessing the specific environment of organisation

Three variables appear to be particularly important in analyzing the impact of the specific environment on organisations. These are: (1) the degree of inter-dependence; (2) the extent of uncertainty; and (3) the opportunities for growth and development. Here, we look at each of these.

Interde-pendence, power and reliance

When an organisation establishes its domain it automatically becomes more reliant upon some organisations than others. Via exchange, organisations attempt to grow, develop, and, in Thompson's words, manage their domains. The degree of interdependence of one organisation upon another not only defines the outer boundaries of the specific environment, it also charts the relative importance of various organisations.

We have chosen the term interdependence to highlight the reciprocal nature of exchanges among organisations. If A and B are interdependent, both have some degree of clout over the other. The pattern of dependence in the specific environment appears to have two dimensions. First, to what extent is the focal organisation more dependent upon others than they are upon it? That is, what is the relative power of the organisation? Two, how interdependent are the members of the specific environment upon one an other? Even a powerful system may be forced to adapt if all the weaker units demand it. Perhaps a variation of an Aesop fable will illustrate interdependence.

The lion and the fox agreed to cooperate in the hunt. The fox would chase the game and the lion would come in for an easy kill. Together they killed in one day what each could do alone in a week. When dividing the spoils the fox wisely asked the lion for a fair share. The lion gave the fox more than the fox could have killed along, but still a very small share. The analogy to organisations is clear. The benefits from exchange need not be equivalent. If both parties benefit from the exchange, it is likely the relationship will be voluntarily maintained.

The relative power of an organisation. We said the relative power of an organisation vis-a vis its specific environment is the first aspect of interdependence. But what is the overall pattern of reciprocation? Is the organisation the fox or the lion? The greater the reliance of the organisation upon others, the more responsive the organisation must be to environmental alterations. Why? The organisation receives comparatively less return for its efforts. Thus, it has comparatively little margin for error. Slight changes can eliminate the benefits from exchanges. The organisation has comparatively fewer internal resources to initiate new exchange relationships Note, however, it's still better off with the exchanges than without them.

The pattern of dependence is rarely the same for goals, output, property, technology, structure, and members. Some of these internal elements must be obtained from a single source. As economic theory clearly shows, the monopolist has a more favorable exchange condition. For instance, if a union controls the labor supply, it can bargain for higher wages, fringe benefits, and worker prerogatives than would be found in a free labor market. It tilts the exchange in favor of the union.

However, unfavourable exchange situations can be eased or altered. To continue our example of the union, assume the organisation has developed a favorable exchange relationship with distributors. To some extent higher wages can be passed on to these units which in turn are likely to pass them on to individual consumers. This directly eliminates the unfavourable exchange relationship. An indirect way to reduce dependence might be through the use of other external forces. Assume a business corporation faces the same union as before, but may be unable to pass on extra costs. In previous negotiations the corporation has already bargained away the right to promote employees on the basis of performance. Seniority determines progression. The business might ask the Equal Employment Opportunity Commission to rule that seniority was inherently discriminatory. Seniority reflects previous patterns of discrimination against females and minorities. Given such a ruling, the business has some additional leverage over the union. The seniority system is now bargaining issue.

Domain protection and interdependence. We think organisations will seek areas where favorable exchange relationships are more likely and tend to expand their domain into areas they can dominate. They may even help develop new organisations that will offset the power of an important unit in the specific environment. Thompson argues that such efforts stem from the organisation's desire to protect its "technical core." This means that the organisation will attempt to protect the major processes it uses to produce its products and services. Following Thompson's general notion we expect that an organisation will be particularly vehement in protecting its fixed investment. Protection of an organisation's fixed investment is needed to ensure long-term survival.

To produce the outputs needed, an organisation must often invest in capital equipment, long-term employment contracts, and the like. For instance, producing automobiles requires a huge long-run commitment of resources in machinery and equipment. Only minor shifts from the existing technology are possible in the short run. Major alterations would threaten the existence of the system. This rigidity results primarily from specialization. Specialization is both the organisation's major strength and weakness. It's basis for exchanges with members in the specific environment. But the rigidity inherent in specialization means an organisation must protect its long-term investments. Conversely, if control over less critical elements is challenged, its survival may not be directly threatened. It can move out of one area and seek favorable exchange relationships in others.

These arguments again reveal the critical importance of suppliers, distributors, and government agencies. Suppliers and distributors are needed to protect internal operations. Government agencies can preempt the jurisdiction of an organisation over elements needed to maintain its central technology. A complementary argument is that competitors are a critical feature of the specific environment. They also compete for suppliers and distributors and seek to protect their investments. It's no wonder, then, that organisations attempt to dilute the impact of these important members of the specific environment. This is done by securing several sources of supply, developing numerous distributors, pitting one governmental agency against another wherever possible, and in some cases, trying to expand their domain.

Interdependence within the specific environment. Let's return to the story of the lion and the fox to illustrate another aspect of interdependence. The arrangement between the fox and the lion was so successful that the fox convinced the lion to expand and make the same arrangement with twelve foxes. The kill rate was amazing. The arrangement was so efficient that game started to disappear. After a particularly poor day's hunt the foxes demanded and got a larger share of the spoils.

Collective action is not always needed to alter the policies or internal operations of a more powerful and autonomous organisation. If each demanded a large share separately, the lion might still have trouble. While busy with one fox, another could take more. In much the same fashion, when an organisation faces an interdependent set of organisations in the specific environment, it must often succumb to the desires of less powerful and less autonomous units. Thus, organisations seek a specific environment where the members are not interdependent. It is expected that interdependence among members of the specific environment has much the same impact on an organisation as the degree of reliance upon one external unit. The greater the interdependence, the greater the probability that the organisation will: (a) seek to alter its domain; (b) become more responsive to pressures from members in the specific environment; (c) derive less from exchanges with other organisations; and (d) spend more effort on monitoring external conditions.

The Impact of Interdependence on Organisations. We have already covered some kinds of organisational response to interdependence. Here, as in the Measurement Module, we will distinguish between objective and perceptual measures of interdependence. Let's look at a few studies that have been done about the effect of this on organisational operations and outcome.

In a well-known and often criticized study, Aiken and Hage studied interdependence among health and welfare agencies, as measured by the number of joint programs. Interdependence was positively associated with the degree of professional activity by members, the degree of specialization, the number of new innovative programs, as well as the amount of coordinative activities such as committee meetings.

In another sample of health-related organisations, Paulson found much the same as Aiken and Hage. But his data raise an interesting question of casualty. Most researchers assume that environmental conditions lead to alterations in the internal structure and operations of organisations. Paulson's data, however, suggested that this pattern of causation might be quite the opposite. Namely, a more sophisticated structure leads to greater interdependence. This shouldn't be too surprising if we assume that organisations seek a favorable domain and establish mechanisms to accomplish control. It may very well be that the structure needed to interface with other organisation is established before detailed arrangements, like joint programs, are perfected. There maybe a process of mutual adjustment over time. That is, environmental interdependence is altered by and alters organisational structure. We will continue to treat the major causation chain as moving from environmental conditions to organisational structure and operations. This is the most popular view. But you should be aware of the conflicting evidence. At any rate, interdependence has some influence on an organisation and its members, when measured "objectively."

Studies relying upon executive perceptions of interdependence also show it is an important factor for organisations. Even though top managers may not accurately perceive the degree of interdependence, they act on their perceptions. When top managers see more interdependence they tend to centralize decision making. Specialized units may be formed to meet dependence on powerful units in the specific environment. Greater reliance on outsiders has also been associated with an ideological shift toward the dominant values of more powerful external systems. Freeman shows that reliance upon other units is associated with greater leadership activity on the part of unit heads, particularly in regard to developing more external contacts.

Thus, results for both objective and perceptual measures seem to be consistent. Interdependence is related to organisational structure and operations as well as short-term effectiveness. However, most of the empirical investigations are with small nonprofit organisations and center on "cooperation" as desirable among organisations. To include larger scale organisations and profit-seeking systems we must move to indirect measures of specific environment interdependence. Here the data are somewhat less clear. But the support the general notion that interdependence increases he complexity of an organisations' structure, reduces the perceived autonomy of managers, and is positively related to short-term profitability. The overall impact on long-term survival and growth still awaits empirical investigation. In sum, interdependence is an important variable in assessing the specific environment of an organisation. Yet it is not only important factor. Uncertainty in the specific environment has also been related to internal operations and effectiveness. So let's look at this variable.

Uncertainty in the specific environment

While there are many different views of environmental uncertainty, it is easiest to see in therm of interrelated dimensions: disparity and volatility. We will discuss each of these factors and their association with effectiveness and internal operations.

Disparity. The first aspect of uncertainty in the specific environment of an organisation is called disparity. We have shown that an organisation deals with several other organisations. These outside organisations constitute the core of the specific environment. As the number of types of these external organisations increases, disparity increases. These organisations may be different in many ways. An analysis of key organisational characteristics and of interdependence suggests that differences in goals, outputs, technology, stiucture, size, and employees are important.

Disparity increases the risk for an organisation. It does this in several different ways. The more varied the members, the greater the conflict potential. As the membership of the specific environment becomes more varied, the probability of instability also increases. Organisations face similar pressures from the general environment. When membership becomes more varied, however, the chances of unified pressures from the general environment decline rapidly. The ability of an organisation to influence the specific environment also appears to decline as disparity of the environment increases. Furthermore, greater disparity also reduces the ability of decision makers to accurately predict the actions of outside units. Estimates for one outside organisation do not apply to others.

We should note that such disparity is a two-way street. While it increase risk, it also increases the autonomy executives see in their jobs. At the same time the organisation has less influence over oversiders, outsiders also have less control over the organisation.

There are comparatively few empirical studies showing the association of disparity and organisational processes or outcomes. Yet systems analysts have given disparity a key role in their analyses of organisations. Ashby among others, argues that greater disparity in external factors should be matched with greater variability internal to the organisation. Organisations that follow this "law of requisite variety" are expected to have higher survival potential. At least one empirical analysis suggests that organisations that follow this "law" are more likely to reach their output goals.

Volatility. Many organisations find it particularly difficulty to cope with changes in trends. In panel A, we find little volatility even though there is considerable change. Here there is little uncertainty. The trend is relatively constant. In panel B there is fluctuation and directional instability; but we can still predict the cycle of change. Here, the organisations faces some uncertainty. This is due to the lack of directional stability. Yet a trend is still present. In panel C the velocity, acceleration, and directional stability all appear random. Here the organisation faces considerable uncertainty. There appears to be no trend. In our terms the specific environment would be volatile.

Volatility is the enemy of all organisations. It can upset established patterns of control and interdependence. It reduces the value of the organisation's resources and signals a potential shift in the value of its ideology. Existing patterns of specialization and current outputs may no longer be appropriate.

Organisational and managerial responses to uncertainty. Organisations appear to anticipate the value of future outcomes from current inputs, and discount for risk. Many develop specialized units to cope with uncertainty, which can be linked to specific external units. Environmental uncertainty appears to paralyze some decision makers. When it appears that an organisation no longer controls its fate, decision makers often attempt to build slack to buffer dysfunctional changes.

When first formed, the Equal Employment Opportunity Commission frequently changed guidelines for minority hiring procedures. Many firms responded with centralized affirmative action units. You can imagine what happened. The EEOC issued new regulations for minority hiring that were to be implemented immediately. Regulations were filled with bureaucratic jargon the few could understand, and the EEOC kept reinterpreting the standards. The solution: put someone in charge of the minority relations program. That person can figure out what the EEOC really wants. The head of the new Minority Relations Office obviously needed a staff to cope with the ever changing demands of the EEOC. The Minority Relations Office also needed the support of the top brass for this important effort. Thus, the unit was placed near the top of the organisational hierarchy.

But was this typical response successful? It might be for the derived goal of hiring minority workers. But it might not be in regard to other goals. Several studies have found that firms that resisted the temptation to develop specialized units in the face of greater volatility had higher performance ratings on outputs, which could be directly linked with the mission of the system. In slightly different terms, firms that desire greater overall success must, we think, resist the temptation of overstructuring in the face of environmental volatility. They should not develop specialized bureaus, departments, and agencies with a later increase in the number of rules, policies, and procedures. Instead, the organisation should rely more upon the informal organisation.

Part of the reason for this suggestion is that managers operate in the face of perceptual as well as objective uncertainty. These presumptions influence how they operate. Specifically, fewer good decisions are made by individuals as uncertainty increase. Managers move to a form of decision making where they consult more with each other they abandon rigid decision rules and circumvent the formal relationships dictated by the bureaucracy. Under high risk, then, the individual who has the relevant information becomes important and a key in the decision-making process. Organisations become more flexible and less bureaucratic as manager increase their later contacts. Note that the creation of a specialized unit runs counter to managers' attempts to cope with uncertainty. It forms managers to interact when they don't want to.

The amount of perceived uncertainty may also alter the success of a particular leadership style and particular leader behaviors. Nebecker shows that how a leader perceives environmental uncertainty will alter his other views of opportunities for influence. This, in turn, may alter the impact of leadership style. For example, Hunt and Osborn suggest that since uncertainty cuts the discretion or clout of a leader, managers may withdraw from leadership roles. Several other studies show the same disturbing negative effects of perceived environmental uncertainty on individual behavior and group conditions. As a group the studies combining perceptual and objective uncertainty suggest the following: (1) some volatility seen by managers is not directly traceable to the specific environment; it appears to stem from a combination of personality factors, job experience, and internal organisational conditions; (2) perceived uncertainty appears to foster more informal relations among managers; but such relations may be virtually eliminated if the organisation becomes more bureaucratic; (3) the tendency of the organisation to bureaucratize in response to uncertainty appears to lower effectiveness; and (4) uncertainty appears to have a small negative impact on effectiveness of the organisation but a larger and more profound negative impact on decision makers. In summary, environmental uncertainly appears quite harmful for bureaucracies that rely heavily on centralized decision making and rigidly adhere to rules.

Interdependence and uncertainty. We argued earlier that interdependence has a favorable association with organisational performance. We also noted that uncertainly was generally unfavourable. A logical question is what happens when the specific environment is both highly interdependent and uncertain? The combination of high interdependence and high uncertainty is particularly damaging to the organisation. Put a different way, interdependence can be a double-edged sword. Greater dependence is favorable only when the specific environment has low uncertainty. Some analyses suggest that volatility is the chief culprit. The organisation facing a volatile and highly interdependent specific environment can lose control. It can become a tool of outside interests and be unable to change operations to produce viable outputs. How can a organisation cope with the high interdependence, high variability setting?

When two organisations attempt to control the same resources, there appear to be several techniques that can be used to resolve the conflict. The dispute may be resolved by custom, dominant values, or law. The legal technique is the most expensive and restrictive. We argue it is more likely to be used as the disparity of the specific environment increases. Organisations may also exchange resources, trade existing resources for contested ones, or develop a new ideology that minimizes the conflict. As organisations in the specific setting become more diverse, it is more difficult for any organisation to develop an appropriate medium for exchange or forge a new ideology.

Contesting organisations may agree to disagree, with each claiming a different area of control. For instance, a medical association may share partial control over physicians with hospitals. The association will claim control over how physicians should practice medicine by instructing them in the latest techniques. The hospital will attempt to control physicians by deciding which types of illness it will treat. Since the association and hospitals share similar domains, conflict is not typically extensive.

But now add a quite divergent group to the specific environment of the hospital. Assume it is owned by a religious order. Now the hospital must systematically consider how spiritual concerns will or will not constrain physicians. Again, greater disparity increases the difficulty in resolving conflict with this technique.

Another technique is merger. Here one organisation merely incorporates another. Again as disparity increases it becomes more difficult to use this technique. The benefits of merger are less the more diverse the merging organisations.

Two other possibilities are virtually eliminated by high interdependence. Remember, high interdependence means the organisation must find some way of resolving domain conflict. One, they cannot withdraw without losing power. Two, they can't eliminate the other organisation without suffering the consequences. Thus, where there is considerable disparity among organisations in a specific environment, resolving domain disputes among highly interrelated organisations becomes move difficult and costly. Yet the organisation can still have some control over its fate.

Development in the specific environment

Almost unrecognized in the current literature is the resource base of organisations comprising the specific environment. The composition of the specific environment changes slowly over time. An organisation is typically committed to an ideology and a whole series of long-term investments. Thus, an organisation is stuck with many units in the specific environment. It may be associated with a series of powerful organisations that are growing and contain large reserves of resources. Conversely, an organisation may be interacting wit a series of weak, declining organisations. Does it make a difference? Some data and several theoretical discussions suggest it makes a substantial difference on the outreach activity of the organisation, its internal operations and its annual effectiveness. First, let's briefly look at some different aspects of development. Then we can review the evidence suggesting the importance of development in predicting organisational success.

Development in the specific environment appears to have two dimensions. First, what is the pattern of growth in the specific environment of the organisation? Are the members growing in terms of power, size, technical sophistication, and the like? Or are they on the decline? When an organisation interacts with growing systems there are greater opportunities for domain expansion. Favorable exchange relationships are also more plentiful. Members of the specific environment are less concerned with getting the best exchange than in assuring needed inputs for continued growth. With growth, outsiders are more willing to defer "payment" and accept future assurances. That is, they "bank" some of their excess in other organisations and "invest" resources in new exchange relationships with long-term payoffs. Quite the opposite seems true fro systems experiencing a decline. They cut "investment" in other organisations. They become very concerned with immediate returns. They may attempt to "borrow" from members of the specific environment, placing a strain on existing exchange relationships. For instance, outsiders with excess labor are less likely to let an organisation perform specialized services. They will attempt to use their excess labor even though outsiders could do a better and more efficient job. At the very time outsiders may need cooperative relationships to conserve resources and more efficiently use existing capacity, such efforts are not undertaken. Why? Co-operation among organisations primarily involves long-term payoffs after a period of expensive "investment."

The second aspect of development is somewhat more complex since it involves the notion of the interorganisational set. An interorganisational set is a collection of organisations interrelated either directly via exchange relationship or via the production and distribution of a given product or service. The notion of industry is very similar to that of the interorganisational set. It is an example of a set based on the production and distribution of a given product or service. Those familiar with market channels will not that a channel of distribution is another type of interorganisational set.

What is the relative power of the members of the organisational set(s) that an organisation is a part of? If the set is large and powerful, members of the set are likely to face a more favorable environment. Large organisations facing less competition are more likely to have excess resources they can divert toward their long-term growth and survival. They are likely to be more specialized and maintain a cadre of technical experts. Since organisations rely upon other organisations, some of these excess resources can be diverted to outsiders. For instance, major soda-extract companies have helped local bottlers fight restrictions on disposable containers. They work with bottlers on technical matters and, most of all, supplement local advertising. They will help perform market studies, lobby for the industry, and the like. Similarly, some critics of the auto industry have argued that the major manufacturers are more interested in the dealers that in consumers.

Organisational and managerial responses to development. The power of the set does not without a price. Even argues that it comes at the expense of autonomy. Each organisation must anticipate the impact of its decisions on a whole series of external units. For instance, how do you price a product in an oligopolistic industry? You must consider the pricing strategy of competitors and the impact of the pricing strategy on the channel of distribution. The organisational set and its members are less likely to innovate and anticipate broader social changes as the control and power of the set increase. As Selznick noted, the major units of the set appear to exchange and modify their goals and ideology over time until there is a high degree of domain consensus. Critics of federal regulatory agencies have noted a similar process. Major corporations and government agencies have become an inter-organisational set with a common set of goals and compatible ideologies. Development may have its greatest direct impact on the performance of an organisation and its managers. Just as powerful organisations may tip the balance of exchange in their favor, so can powerful organisational sets. They are in a position to lobby for favorable governmental action including protectionist legislation, direct subsidies, and price controls. By controlling the output of an important good or service they may increase its prices to the society much as the Organisation of Petroleum Exporting Countries has done with crude oil. For governmental units, development also has some very subtle overtones. Via cooperative action, government agencies can legitimize each other so that more funds flow into a given problem area. For instance, state universities operating together can help promote the importance of a college degree regardless of which institution grants the diploma. But one university does not publicly criticize another much as one physician does not testy against a colleague. It's bad for the set. Thus, both resources and performance distortion can occur when the set is growing. However, as a member of the set both the organisation and its managers benefit.

To the extent that resources flow into an organisation as a result of membership in a strong interorganisational set, managers have more resources to work with. Mistakes can be covered with abundant resources. Managers can take credit for growth. They can attract more qualified personnel, reward even marginal performers, and more easily maintain both high satisfaction and performance. However, when the efficiency crunch comes, as it did in education and aerospace, the opposite occurs. Organisations are not given credit for their outputs. Managers can't get the resources they need to maintain high performance and satisfaction. The brightest and the best move on to other areas; the set has problems attracting new blood. And successful administrators are deemed inadequate.

This second aspect of development is the least researched and most controversial. It can be supported by a number of theoretical articles. But we are not aware of any empirical studies relating the power of the interoganizational set to the internal operations or effectiveness of organisations. Thus you should view this aspect of development caution.

What is efficiency in an organisation

Organizations exist to serve a variety of purposes, and the effective organization is one that get things done in such a way as to meet all of its objectives. In manufacturing industry the purpose is to produce sufficient goods of an appropriate specification, quality and price. It is common practice to talk about the 'efficiency' of production. This normally means the relationship between the cost of the inputs and the value of the outputs—a ratio. But is an organization is to serve its purposes, whatever they may be, it needs to know more about what it is aiming to achieve, say than, hopefully, that it would like to be 99.9% efficient.

Once it is decided what it wants to make, and that it has got an appropriate product, an organization needs to meet certain operational objectives. These may be simply stated as:

- achieve output targets
- make products of appropriate quality
- be efficient, making full use of all of its resources, and
- operate in such a way as to ensure survival.

Writers on the subject of management studies have drawn attention to the fact that in organizations there may be multiple goals. They stress the need to stand back and look at the organization as a whole, as well as individual parts of it, and to take a longer term view as well as short term one. Even at the crude level of the above objectives, we can see that there are bound to be these multiple goals, and we have only to look below the surface of each of these to begin to reveal may 'sub goals'.

For example, to achieve output targets we have to have the appropriate tools, machinery and materials, and sufficient numbers of the right kind of employee, properly trained, and who will regularly be available to do the work. They will also need to be well motivated to produce the required output of good quality goods!

If we then considered *how* all of this might be achieved we would begin to generate a long list of further sub goals, and the functions and tasks which need to be performed in order to meet this objective.

To 'be efficient' implies making full use of all of the resources. This should mean not only proper utilization of equipment and materials but also proper utilization of people. In the conventional concept of the term 'efficient', the proper use of people us often seen as 'keeping them at it'. We are often preoccupied with how *hard* people are working, perhaps paying too little attention to *what* they are given to do. As was suggested in the previous chapter, many employees are potentially capable of contributing more in the way of knowledge, talents, experience, skill and goodwill than their present work situation permits. It is just as wasteful to under-utilize the range and depth of peoples' capabilities as it is to have them standing idle, and the consequences for them and for the organization may be even worse.

If we consider the need of an organization to ensure its own survival the simple of 'efficiency' is really put into perspective. It is obvious that it is no use continuing to make products, however efficiently, which people are no longer willing to buy, nor is it sensible to rely on a material, the source of which is drying up. Similarly, it may not be appropriate to continue operating on the assumption that sufficient numbers of people will be available to do the work in the way that it has always been expected it would be done.

Even if survival is not obviously threatened, the really effective organization tries to keep in touch with the reality of its situation. It has the capacity to adapt and maintain itself as changes occur in the environment or in any of the variables with which it has to cope—products, technology, customer expectations, employee expectations and capabilities, and so on.

The nature of an organisation

We have noted that the nature of the environment in which most activities exist is changing very rapidly. It is equally self-evident that an organization which exists in what has been called a 'turbulent' environment needs to be structured and managed differently to one which enjoys a relatively stable and predictable existence. But how? Different in what way?

Burns and Stalker are two social scientists who carried out studies in twenty firms in England and Scotland, with the support of the Scottish Council and the Department of Scientific and Industrial Research. The results of their studies, and their conclusions, were published in 1961 in their book 'The Management of Innovation'. All twenty studies were concerned with the question of what happens when new and unfamiliar tasks confront industrial concerns which are organized for relatively stable conditions. Most of the firms were in the electronics industry, and at the time of the study were subject to many new activities and continuous technical innovation.

There are two contrasting forms of organization and management system. One which they called mechanistic; this they saw as being appropriate to stable conditions. The other they called organic, that is one which is appropriate to changing conditions, i.e. those which give rise constantly to fresh problems, and unforeseen requirements for action. They identify and discuss a large number of features which characterize each form and these may be briefly stated as follows:

a) *Mechanistic Systems*. These are characterized by the breaking down of the tasks of the organization. Each task and functional role is precisely defined. There is a strict hierarchy, each level being responsible for the tasks carried out in the level immediately below, and answerable to the level immediately above. Communication and control tends to be vertical, an accordance with the hierarchy, the ultimate divisions being made at the top, where all wisdom is assumed to reside. There is an insistence on loyalty to the concern and obedience to superiors.

One can recognize here the bureaucratic, scientific management approach, with a highly structured organization, where many employees have limited tasks which are precisely defined. The situation in which this would be at its most appropriate would be a very *static*, i.e. an unchanging one. It ought to be possible to predict technology, products, processes, methods, product market, labour market, etc., and to make firm plans for an unvarying, uninterrupted flow of work. It is also based on an assumption that people prefer simple, undemanding jobs, or that they lack the competence to do more difficult ones.

b) *Organic system*. In this system jobs are not precisely defined, but can changes as conditions change. Individuals contribute any special knowledge or experience which they have to the common tasks of the concern, and responsibilities get distributed on this basis rather than on 'position'. Communication tends to be lateral, but even when people are of different rank it resembles consultation rather than command. Commitment to the concern's tasks is more highly valued than loyally or obedience.

The approach here would therefore be a flexible and adaptable one, with jobs which are more comprehensive, and which allow a high level of employee discretion. The situation in which this would be at its most appropriate would be a varying, unpredictable, unstable one. Collaborative working would replace the rigid divisions of functional demarcation. There would be an assumption that people need to do meaningful work which makes good use of their skills and abilities.

The two forms are seen to be at the ends of a spectrum of possibilities, so that in appropriate circumstances intermediate degrees of the mechanistic - organic ways of organizing work could be used, or both simultaneously in different parts of the organization. If follows that there is no single set of principles for good organization, but there is a need to be sensitive to the conditions which exist, and the changes which are occurring, and to adapt to appropriate management systems.

In other words, the organization, its structure and practices, has an impact on how people behave. If it is restrictive and bureaucratic it will get a limited response.

Many other students of organization have concluded that for an organization to be effective the needs, expectations and objectives of employees have to be integrated with the needs, expectations and objectives of the organization.

We have noted above that motivation is to do with getting commitment, and that the style of the relationships between the members of an organization is important for effectiveness. These relationships are closely concerned with organization structure—that is whether it is highly structured and rigid or adaptive and flexible. Finally, of course, all of these have implications for the design of the individual jobs which employees have to do. Developments in work structuring, job enrichment and the improvement of satisfaction at work have for the most part been directed at the individual job, and there is no doubt that much useful work has and can be done at this level. But individual jobs do not exist in isolation, and even if we start with them we will quickly be faced with the implications for the organization structure, the style of management—employee relationships, and the methods used to motivate employees.

An effective organization, seeking to make changes which will make jobs more meaningful and satisfying, whilst it maintains or improves its effectiveness, should seek to have a co-ordinated policy. This is essential if the desired results are to be achieved, and if they are to be more than occasional experiments, which only result in superficial changes in the details of the work task.

Any grouping or collection of people who are trying to work together to achieve a given objective, be it a number of soldiers trying to win a battle or a number of building operatives and craftsmen trying to build a house, work more effectively and quickly and have more chance of achieving their objective, if they are organized correctly. Without organisations, modern day life quickly degenerate into near chaos. We depend on organisations to bring our food to the local supermarket, to supply petrol to the pumps at the local garage, to educate our children and to look after us when we are sick. We are part of an organisation in our working lives, while at home the family, that oldest organisation of all, has stood the lest of time and change and still survives, loved and cherished by most of us.

Organisations and organizing are so much part and parcel of our lives that we accept the concept of organizing without a second thought. Organizing means whatever resources are available-people, time, money, equipment, services etc.—to achieve objectives. For some people this may not mean much more than organizing their time throughout the day. Manager, however, control substantial resources, and they have to learn how to organize employees and organisations.

For managers the organizing function is made more difficult by the fact that much of their time is spent organizing people, and people change, daily, hourly, even by the minute. Managers are therefore constantly making adjustments to their organisations to cater for such things as the sickness of a key employee, an unexpected resignation, or the shortage of some key component because of a strike in a supplier's factory.

Some of the advantages of organisations were considered during our discussion of types of organisations. We noted, for example, that a partnership could draw on a wider range of expertise and greater financial resources than a one man business, Organisations are also social units; help and advice are provided to the members of the group, worries are shared, and the chances of success are improved when people from different backgrounds, ages and skills work in unison towards an agreed objective.

It is this basic need for human contact, to relate to other people and to have a greater chance of achieving success in any activity, that gives rise to the desire to organize and be organized. We may all be 'loners' occasionally, but we only reach our full potential as part of an organisation, however small. Management is about maximizing potential and management is therefore about organizing.

Principles of organisation

There will always be a limit to the number of manager can effectively control. Some management experts feel that six eight people is the maximum; others have suggested a smaller number. The appropriate span of control will depend on a variety of factors. First, are the subordinates qualified to make decisions without having to constantly refer upwards to the manager? Have they the skills and experience required to take the right course of action and see it through? Second, is the manager concerned prepared to delegate authority to his subordinates? Is this desirable for the manager's own career progression, or is it possible he might delegate himself out of a job? Third, a manager can supervise more people if the organisation has a well-defined planning function and agreed set of objectives, than if the objectives are vague or not widely understood. Similarly, where an organisation has well developed, tried and tested communication systems that feed information quickly, to and from senior management, each manager is able to control a larger number of people. Indeed this may be the primary benefit of the modern communications and information systems discussed.

Finally, some organisations, particularly those in the public sector, depend a great deal on personal contact to operate effectively. These types of organisations will inevitably have small spans of control and involve many levels of subordinates and co-ordinates, the hallmark of a bureaucratic type of organisation.

Unity of objectives

Whatever the organisation structure finally decided upon, all parts of the organisation should work towards common objectives. In these days of international competition and scarce resources no manager can afford the luxury of parts of the organisation 'doing their own thing'. This is particularly true of labour-intensive organisations in the public sector and the service industries in the private sector, where the human resource plays such a key role.

People are more likely to pursue the organisation's objectives rather than their personal interests if these objectives are clearly defined and widely understood. Unfortunately, experience shows that in public sector organisations 'politics' often leads to objectives being blurred or constantly changed, with consequential loss of efficiency.

Delegation

As noted during our discussion of the span of delegation implies that a senior manager gives discretion to a subordinate. Successful delegation requires that attention should be given to the following factors. First, adequate authority must be given to the subordinate to carry out the task. If a junior manager is given the job of running the mailroom, it should be made clear that he has authority over the mailroom staff and can specify the timing of the collection and delivery of the mail.

In situations like this, specifying the limits of authority is often easy. It is much more difficult where a senior manager has only a vague idea of what he wants and gives only broad and general instructions to a subordinate. In this situation there is much more likely to be a dispute later on as to whether the junior manager has exceeded his authority. Consider the situation in which a senior manager asks a subordinate to prepare a report on the feasibility of a proposed new product. The manager feels that a satisfactory report could be prepared as the basis of internal discussions with the production manager, personnel director etc. But the subordinate feels it necessary to obtain information about competitors products and therefore asks the market research department to undertake a survey. Two obvious sources of conflict arise. First, the market research staff may refuse to do what the junior manager requests. Second, if they do accept his authority and undertake the work, the senior manager may complain because of the costs involved. Second, and following from the previous point, tasks delegated must be properly assigned, i.e. the subordinate must understand what is involved, accept the delegated discretion and know that his position and authority are not duplicated elsewhere in the organisation.

Finally, responsibility for the discretion delegated cannot be greater than the authority delegated, e.g. if a manager gives a subordinate the authority to sell certain items, that subordinate cannot be held responsible for high rates of breakage and customer complaints due to a bad design or faulty manufacturing.

Most successful managers are happy to delegate. They see it as being helpful to themselves and their organisations for a variety of reasons:

1 By delegating one can see which subordinates are likely to be 'high flyers', suitable for promotion, and which have reached the limit of their competence.

2 Delegation can provide a useful training tool, in that it enables managers to develop their potential. This may mean that junior managers are given discretion even though they do not perform as well as their seniors in the early stages. As they learn from experience and gain confidence their performance is likely to improve, and senior managers are often pleasantly surprised at how successful subordinates can be, given time and encouragement in undertaking tasks previously thought to be the preserve of the senior manager or 'the boss'.

3 All managers and individuals do some things better than others. If a subordinate is particularly skilled in some tasks it makes sense for a senior manager who may see these tasks as a 'bit of a chore', to let the junior manager do it. The tasks are likely to be performed more effectively and the senior manager will be able to spend more time on tasks for which he is better fitted.

4 Where an organisation is spread out geographically, e.g. with a headquarters and a number of area offices, it may be wise to delegate certain functions to junior managers in the area offices who are in closer touch with customers and the general public.

Whatever degree discretion a senior manager eventually decides to give to his subordinates the general principle is clear cut. Senior managers should concentrate their timed and effort on the major issues facing their organisations. Most senior managers are overworked, with more calls on their time than the working day allows for. Delegation of tasks to subordinates wherever possible makes good business and managerial sense. The tasks will often be done more cheaply, employee job satisfaction will be increased, and senior managers will be more effective.

The 'scalar' principle

In any organisation some individual must take ultimate authority and responsibility for the actions of that organisation. The more clear-cut is the line of authority between this individual and all the subordinate positions within the organisation, the more effective will be the decision-making process and the greater the organisation's efficiency. This unbroken line of responsibility between all individuals in an organisation is known as the 'scalar' principle. Unless the chain of command is clear-cut people will not 'know where they stand', i.e. to whom they are responsible and to whom they refer matters beyond their own authority. Unity of command

Where an individual has responsibility to one clearly defined superior, the less likely it is that he will receive conflicting instructions. He is also likely to obtain more job satisfaction and a greater sense of purpose and responsibility in carrying out instructions, than if he is responsible to two or more superiors. The bigger the organisation, the more specialists it employs, the more difficult it is observe this 'unity of command' principle, with consequent adverse effects on morale and efficiency. For example a personnel officer may be asked by the production manager to provide additional workers; to meet this instruction may conflict with recruitment and induction procedures laid down by the personnel manager.

Types of organisation structure

The formal organisation

There are two types of organisation structure, which exist side by side.

This is the organisation structure designed by senior management to achieve the objectives of the organisation. It is the network of communication, responsibilities and groupings of individuals, that is seen by senior management as being the most effective. This network is often depicted in an organisation chart.

Formal organisation structures are constantly modified by managers in response to a variety to a variety of pressures. Nevertheless it takes times time for a new structure to become fully operational, for all the relevant parts of the formal organisation to be re-organized, and for all the relationships to be modified.

The informal organisation

Within very organisation, alongside the formal organisation structure there exists the informal structure. This is based on relationships between individuals and groups and as such is much more dynamic and less easily definable than the more rigid formal structure. The 'old boy network', the 'office grapevine'; a temporary liaison between two sections to gain a working advantage over a third, e.g. sales and marketing versus production, are all examples of informal relationships.

In many ways, these informal organisations, because they reflect the present, real world situation, rather than what managers think the situation is, more powerful than the formal organisational links. If the two structures seriously diverge, it may become necessary to formalize at least some of the informal relationships; otherwise communication channels may break down and managers' freedom of action become curtailed. However, it is usually undesirable to try to suppress all informal relationships, since they can sometimes help to lubricate the formal machinery and make the organisation a more interesting place in which to work.

Levels within an organisation

Each organisation has its own individual number of levels, determined by an amalgamation of all the issues discussed in this chapter. But most organisations contain certain levels within the hierarchical structure, with clearly defined functions. At the top there are a few senior managers making policy decisions. At the bottom there are a much larger number of employees carrying out the detailed work of the organisation at the 'sharp end' so to speak. In the middle are the co-ordinators, planners and section heads controlling their particular functions, referring issues to senior management and receiving instructions back. The organisational hierarchies of typical public and private sector organisations are depicted.

It will be seen that the hierarchy at the public sector organisation is more complex because of the political element involved. Ratepayers and politicians take a much keener interest in the running of a local authority and are much likely to change their views—with consequent effects on the organisation—than the shareholders of a private company. The bureaucratic organisation and management structure tends to operate so as to deaden and soften the impact of political change in order to aid the organisation's survival and facilitate its management.

Private sector organisations reflect the impact of external changes more quickly and more fully, mainly because the implications of a change are less extreme. Although a loss of sales is a serious matter, it would usually lead to fewer changes in policy than would a change from Conservative to Labour control of a large county council, especially if the political views of the council were not tempered by the advice of permanent officers.

Centralisation versus de-centralisation

Many large organisations have to decide whether all major decisions, responsibility and authority, should be concentrated at head office or whether there should be wider 'power sharing' with, for example, some decisions being made in area offices, There is obviously a connection with delegation, but we are concerned here with the structure of an organisation as a whole, whereas delegation refers to the style of individual managers.

1 Communication systems of all types are made easier by having people and departments alongside one another.

2 Services such as mail, photocopying, plan printing, filing, reception, telephone, canteen, car parking and other support services can be provided on an overall,

rather than departmental, basis. This will produce savings in staff and enable costs to be more closely controlled.

3 The corporate image of an organisation is improved when the organisation is situated in one location. We are all familiar with the Town Hall or County Hall as symbolizing the centre of administration in a town. The large new civic centres and old Victorian 'gothic-style' town halls add a touch of grandeur and dignity to the operation of local services in a way several smaller buildings scattered throughout an area would not.

4 Various aspects of security can be improved in a centralized location, although against this has to be offset the dangers inherent in having all one's eggs in one basket', e.g. all the organisation's could be destroyed in one fire or robbery.

5 It easier to manage the operation and people when everything is under one roof.

De-centralization has the advantage that it decision making 'where the action is.' The sales office on site at a housing estate, the social services area office, the local clinic and the local police station are all examples of de-centralization. These out-stations provide a local link with the people they serve and ease of access for consumers. They enable a local approach to problem solving to be combined with help and advice from a headquarters organisation.

De-centralization only works if the people in the various locations are giver adequate authority to make decisions, and responsibility proportional to the decision-making power of each individual is agreed and exercised at all levels of the organisation.

De-centralization works best when the headquarters provides advice or some specialist support to research activity and this is coupled with good communication systems, widely understood objectives, and control systems which are followed by all concerned.

On-line computer systems now allow constant contact between a network of area or branch office and the main information files at headquarters, and thus help to overcome one of the main problems associated with de-centralization. Previously if you went into your bank, building society or the gas showroom, and wanted detailed information about your finances or accounts, a long wait frequently ensued. Now the answer is immediately available on a visual display screen with print out.

There is no right answer to the question: 'should one centralize or decentralize?' Each case must be treated on its merits and the light of local circumstances. However, it would appear that more and more larger organisations in both the public and the private sectors are taking heed of the maxim 'small is beautiful' associated with the late E F Schumacher and are running their operation with local offices, linked by modern communication systems to a small headquarters organisation that provides policy guidance and advice and specialist help when required. In this way modern advances in electronic communications enable organisations to satisfy the increasing demand by consumers for the personal touch in their dealings with businesses and the public sector.

Departmentation

Having decided, or even before making the decision, on centralization or decentralization every senior manager has to decide how to group the various activities and individuals within his organisation. This organizing function is known as departmentation, and the main forms of departmentation are outlined below.

Where an organisation has a very important customer who requires a particular type of product or standard of service, it makes sense to have a group which can concentrate on the needs of this customer, Advertising agencies have 'account executives' whose job it is to look after the interests of a particularly valuable client and co-ordinate their agencies' approach to the client. Many food manufacturers have 'key account executives' who negotiate terms with the chief buyers of the large grocery multiples.

The use of the various media now requires specialist skills if they are to be fully utilized to the advantage of an organisation. The high cost of advertising time or space makes it worth an organisation's while to develop a co-ordinated approach to the media concerned in order to obtain the preferential rates available to bulk buyers.

Organizing under one head or section the computer operations of an organisation, or a particular type of production process that requires specialist skills, makes for organisational as well as managerial efficiency. Maintenance is made easier and the relevant trade and management 'know how' can be concentrated in one area.

The establishment of a group to provide specialist recruitment advice, or to oversee the development of an engine would be examples of this form of departmentation. This should result in the more efficient use of specialized resources and a more co-ordinated approach to outside individuals and pressures.

Organizing the total resources of an organisation by specialist functions—sales, production, accounts-is common practice in most organisations and dose not really require further comment here. Suffice it to say that the more numerous and more specialized the various departments are, the more difficult is the task of senior management to co-ordinate and manage.

Most readers will be familiar with this type of departmentation. It is particularly common in dividing up an organisation's sales or marketing forces into say the Scottish region, Wales, Northern England, the Midlands and the Home Counties. Regional and local tastes and differences can be catered for in this way, and it also aids overall managerial control in very large organisations that have national or international markets.

Organizing according to time scales, e.g. day and night shifts, makes sense where round the clock production, service, or monitoring systems are in operation, and where, over long time periods, the human response is limited in its operational capability.

Whatever span control is chosen, whatever the of departments or groupings eventually decided upon, management has the choice of certain tried and tested organisational relationships within the organisational structure they finally decide upon.

Line relationships

This refers to the direct working relationships between the vertical levels of an relationship where authority flows from the departmental head to the deputy, to section head and eventually to the person who actually dose the job of work. The communication channels are clear, authority is agreed, and instructions and information flow down and up between the individuals concerned.

Staff relationships

Most textbooks refer to a 'staff' relationship as an advisory function in either a specialist or assistant type of position. This is true insofar as the personnel manager or a management services officer may be regarded as 'advisors' to line managers. But in many large organisations the different between the 'line' and 'staff' function is often less clear cut. In such organisations one often finds staff specialists who also have line responsibility over their own staff. For example the personnel manager or director would have a 'staff' relationship or advisory role to the managing director on personnel policy, but line responsibility over staff in the training, employment, recruitment and safety sections of his own personnel section.

The best guide to the reader in attempting to assess whether a position is 'line' or 'staff' is to remember that the ultimate test is based on the personal relationships, especially in terms of authority, between the individuals concerned and not by purely departmental or sectional activities.

In systems of 'corporate planning' or the 'management team' concept in local government, the two roles are often combined, e.g. the director of education will be acting as a 'line' manager when he comes to speak on educational matters to the other members of the management team, but will act in a 'staff' capacity or advisory role when, as a member of the corporate management team of authority, he criticizes some service aspect of the corporate plan or budget.

Functional relationships

This relationship occurs where a line manager delegates to an individual or section the authority to carry out particular processes, policies, operations etc. The function can be delegated to either other 'line' managers or 'staff' advisors and specialists. This form of delegation is especially common in situations which require a grouping of people and activities to do a particular job, e.g. the move to a new office building, the installation of a new computer or the setting up of a new grievances procedure. Once the job is completed the functional authority often ends and the staff concerned return to their normal work.

Committee relationships

We have already made reference to committees as a system of managing. Suffice it to say here that committees play a large part in organisational structures in both the public and private sectors. Indeed it is often said that they are part of the British way of life; if in doubt then set up a committee. Viewed as part of the organizing function, committees can either be formal, i.e. have written remit and authority to carry out a specific function, or informal or ad hoc, i.e. set up for some temporary purpose to act as a pressure release valve or as a 'sounding board' for management.

(a) Vertical

(b) Horizontal

(c) Circular or concentric

(d) Flow

Working parties

In recent years the increasing need for participation and specialist advice has led to the setting up, particularly in the public sector, of a variant of the committee system, i.e. the working party.

The aim of a working party is to co-ordinate the specialist knowledge of various interested parties to solve a particular problem. This means that the relationships in a working party differ slightly from those in a committee. In principle in a working party the members contribute from their own specialist viewpoint and not as equal participants able to criticize everyone and everything as in a committee.

Matrix relationships

This type of organisational relationship was pioneered by the Americans in their space programme in the 1960s. It combines many of the relationships we have discussed and involves staff having a dual responsibility. First, they have a responsibility to their immediate superior. Second, they have a relationships to the specialist working group and the project team of which they are members. The aim of this structure is to obtain the benefits of multi-discipline project teams at middle management level and below, whilst allowing line managers at senior level control of their specific responsibilities, even though these may be spread over several projects.

Organizing the resources under their control is one of the most difficult functions managers have to undertake and whatever the solution ultimately chosen, most managers will experience one, or combination, of the following problems.

1 The plans paid down by senior management are translated into imprecise, unachievable objectives that have not gained the commitment of the employees concerned.

2 Working relationships within the organisation are ill-defined, vague and exist only on an informal or very personal basis.

3 The degree of delegation is inadequate and inadequate authority is given to those to whom responsibility is delegated.

4 Communication systems are inadequate with the result that management does not really know what is going on or is unaware of the true feelings of the workforce.

5 A breakdown occurs in the chain of command, such as the mixing up of line and staff relationships, the granting of functional authority without responsibility, bad supervision.

6 A period of rapid change leads to constant re-organisations so that the whole structure is in a state of flux, and no one has time to adapt to and fully implement organisational changes.

Experienced managers will recognize the above symptoms and take steps to rectify the situation. In many cases the above issues are the results of 'people problems' and can only be solved by re-training and management development, or at the worst, removal of the individual concerned.

The production function

Here we examine the main work areas covered by the production function: product design and development plant location, layout and equipment; production planning and control.

Some of issues that we discuss apply to all sectors of the economy. But in general the production function is seen as being particularly important in manufacturing. Consequently, our discussion focuses on that sector. The decline of British manufacturing receives constant attention in the media and it is appropriate being a brief examination of this topic.

The decline in manu-facturing

The decline in the importance of manufacturing can be measured in various ways. If we examine employment we find that the number of employees in employment in manufacturing feel by 13 per cent between 1966-75 and by a further 11 per cent between 1975 and 1980 (an even faster rate of decline). By 1980 manufacturing accounted for only 30 percent of to total employees in employment as compared as compared to 40 per cent in services (or well over 50 per cent if the distributive trades are included), increasing productivity has meant that output rose between 1966 and 1975. But a 5 per cent fail in output occurred between 1975 and 1980.

It is quite usual for countries to reach a point in their development at which manufacturing begins to decline in relative importance. But this decline has been greater in the U.K. than in other countries. The U.K.'s share of the value of exports of manufactured goods feel from 26 per cent in 1976, and whilst the subsequent upturn is encouraging, we have of course recovered only a small part of the ground previously lost. Experience has varied from one branch of manufacturing to another. If we look at broad industry groups we find that in the decade 1970 to 1980 the U.K. chemicals and electrical engineering industries increased output albeit to a modest extent. On the other hand, substantial declines occurred in mechanical engineering, vehicles and textiles.

Particularly disturbing is the loss of sales in markets in which Britain was previously very prominent. A virtual monopoly of textile equipment has disappeared; even textile manufactures frequently choose Swiss or German rather than British Machinery, We import the majority of our cars, and B L Ltd., the only remaining major British-owned manufacturer, has seen its share oft he British market dip form 60 to 17 per cent. Imports now account for a large share of the market for domestic appliances-96 per cent of dishwashers, 45 per cent of washing machines, 30 per cent of spindriers-and for nearly 90 per cent of office equipment etc. I.C.L., out sole surviving large computer manufacturer, has been forced to close several factories and substantially reduce its about force, despite the rapid expansion of the world market.

What has gone wrong? Why has the U.K. manufacturing sector done less well than its competitors when the world economy has expanded, and been more vulnerable in times of recession? Diagnoses of the British disease have emphasized the following areas:

1. The level of investment in new plant and equipment has been lower in the U.K. than in most other industrialized countries. Some commentators have argued that the banks have taken too short-term a view of their involvement in industry. Other commentators have suggested that industrial dividends to shareholders rather than plough back profits. An alternative explanation of the low level of investment is its low yield. There is no point in installing machinery if it cannot be fully utilized, either because of union pressure or an inadequate demand for the final product.

2. Many parts of British industry have been characterized by restrictive working practices and overmanning. We have already mentioned that union pressure sometimes prevents the efficient utilization of new plant and equipment. The organization and attitudes of British unions have also resulted in a work force that is less flexible than those of Germany, Japan U.S.A. etc. Demarcation disputes (which union's members have the right to do what more common in this country. The unions also tend to insist that more rigid conditions should be applied to training (including the length of apprenticeships) and re-training. Finally Strikes can disrupts industry and hence cause a loss of efficiency. In fact, overall the U.K.'s

strike record is not very different from the average for all industrialized countries. But a relatively high proportion of strikes in the U.K. are unofficial (without union backing). Since unofficial strikes are difficult to anticipate they tend to be especially disruptive.

3. It is sometimes said that there is no such a thing as poor unions or a poor work-force only poor management. Although this is an oversimplification, it contains an element of truth. Good managers will foster a co-operative attitude on the part of unions and workers. Even if workers and their representatives are determined to be militant, good managers will minimize the number of issues that can be exploited.

Manages are of course concerned with many issues other than those involving the unions, and it appears that in some sectors of manufacturing British managers have proved less skilful than their counterparts in other countries. British firms have a good record in producing new ideas and even in pioneering new products, but frequently fail to translate these into commercial successes.

Sir Freddie Laker built a thriving airline, but was tempted to expand at a time when competition was becoming much more intense. The expansion, which was mainly financed by borrowed money, came to an abrupt end in 1982. The company was unable to meet its financial commitments and a receiver was appointed.

Isolated examples such as these may not in themselves be of much significance. But they are evidence of a more widespread failure on the part of British firms to meet customers requirements. A recent report by the National Economic Development Office identified a number of reasons for loss of sales to overseas competitors including inferior design poor product quality, and a failure to meet promised delivery dates. We have stressed the point that managers can learn to improve their performance. But performance is also affected by native ability and there is no doubt that in the U.K. career opportunities, including prospective salaries, have been less attractive in production, engineering and manufacturing in general than in the City and the professions. In Germany and Japan the best graduates want to go into production, since that is where the money and status are and this undoubtedly help to explain the success of German and Japanese manufacturing companies. In the U.K. on the other hand, the best minds tend to become lawyers accountants or academics. Incidentally these attitudes also to be found among politicians. Conservative government are generally felt to be favorably disposed towards industry. But the members of Mrs. Thatcher's cabinet with full-time experience of business, usually obtained this experience not in manufacturing but in the City in farming or as lawyers.

These then are four fundamental deep-seated reason for the relatively poor performance of British manufacturing industry. In some years these factors may be overshadowed by others, including government policy, For example, the tough economic policy of Mrs. Thatcher governments with high interest rates and a strong pound, contributed to the rapid rundown of industry and the record number of bankruptcies in the early 1980s. But a decline also occurred under the preceding Labour productivity. But a decline also occurred under the preceding Labour government, suggesting that government influence is limited and that we have to look more widely for a solution to our problems.

As suggested above his may require an increase in investment in manufacturing, better training, a change in working practices, more attention to marketing, and so forth. It would be helpful if governments could adopt policies which led to a steady increase in demand, and they could assist the interests of British exporters by persuading other governments to reduce barriers, and in particular non-tariff barriers, to trade.

The production process

Each production process may be regarded as unique. Whether we are talking about the potter moulding clay on his wheel into the shape of a jug, the refining of crude oil into a variety of finished products, or the robot assembly line that produces Maestro cars, each and every process has its own problems, its advantages, its unique style and atmosphere. Among the variables are the machines, the materials the consumables and last, but by no means least, the people involved in the process: shopfloor workers, foremen and supervisors, line managers in charge of departments designers and planners, right up the organizational hierarchy to the production director.

Four main types of production can be distinguished.

1. Mass production is the manufacture of articles in large numbers with few variables as to types or range e.g. modern car assembly plant.

2. Process production also take place on a large scale. But whereas in mass production a large of individual items is produced, the output of process production is usually large volumes of liquids or powders. Moreover process production normally requires large amounts of specially designed plant, operated by a relatively small work-force. The modern, purpose built chemical plants and oil refineries are examples of process production units.

3. Batch production is common in the engineering industry. A number of similar items are produced in batches within a certain time scale. This method is often wasteful in time and resources as it requires stock of materials and semi-finished parts to be stored close to the production unit, and involves the items being transported several times over. It is therefore usually confined to situation where the demand for the item is insufficient to allow mass production methods to operate efficiently.

4. Jobbing involves the production of different products in unit quantities and covers such items as engineering components designed to meet the specifications of individual customers, individual pieces of glassware etc.

The production process may be regarded as the ultimate management test since it requires people, information, machines, materials, buildings, transportation and storage system to be brought together in a given sequence against a required timescale.

A change in one of these variables has an impact on all the others. For example an interruption in the supply of materials due to industrial action may case the whole production process to slow down or stop. This may affect employees take home pay as bonus earnings are reduced. Machines will not be operating at capacity, which will affect their maintenance schedules. The level of finished stocks will be reduced, while stocks of other consumables used in production and not affected by the industrial action will increase, unless management reduces quantities ordered. The amount of finished product available for sale will be reduced, and the sales and marketing people will become involved in explanations to customers as delivery dates are altered. Finally the process come full circle as the production planners alter their schedules and issue new instructions to all the sections involved. Moreover these revised schedules will have to be changed again when the industrial action ends and the supply of materials returns to normal.

A similar set of interaction would result form a change in any of the variables in the process, and production managers are constantly carrying out fine tuning exercises as the resources under their control vary. Patience as well as technical skills is required by managers in this area.

Whatever the type of unit he controls a production manager is concerned with a number of decision areas. These are discussed in detail below, but first it is useful to examine the distinction between long-and short-term decisions. Long-term decisions are generally made by senior management at Board level on the advice provided by specialist mangers, and the production director in particular. They are major decisions determine the shape, size and future activities of the organization as a whole as well as of the production division in or department. Issues decided at this level include:

1. The type of product to be manufactured and its major design features.
2. The type of production process to be used.
3. The detailed design of all the elements in the production process, including that layout of the unit itself.
4. The location of the production unit.

Short-term decisions cover many of the areas of fine tuning mentioned in the previous section, and stem from the flow of information to the production division. The areas involved are:

1. Stock levels
2. Production capacity

3. Maintenance
4. Quality control
5. Financial control
6. Utilization of labour

We now examine the major decision areas relating to production beginning with product design and development.

Design costs

New products often require new machine tools and materials and these retooling and re-equipment costs must always be in the forefront of management's mind when the final design is being decided. Design changes to existing products can also involve expensive modifications to the production process. New or modified design arise from a variety of reasons. A brand new product may be introduced to fill a gap in the market; this may involve an extension of the forefront of science and technology, as with the first television set and the set and the first computer.

In such situations it is often difficult to estimate correctly the overall design, development and production costs, as changes will undoubtedly have to be made to the original design as tests and experience dictate. Being first in the field is find if you get the sums right first time. But experienced managers know that this is rarely the case in practice. Over-runs on budgets are common high technology projects form atomic power stations to multi-role combat aircraft, from Concorde to the Advanced Passenger Train. In other industries, design changes arise from the need to follow the dictates of fashion. The length of hemlines and the width of trouser legs change from year to year. Changes in popularity of particular colours occur in clothes, and also in wallpaper, furnishings etc.

Productions can also become outdated for reasons other than fashion. If one manufacturer introduces a product with superior performance characteristics, competitive products may have to be modified if they are to survive.

New products are sometimes introduced to utilize spare capacity and to keep people in employment. While these are worthy motives it is important to ensure that there is the adequate demand for the new products.

The originator comes up with a good idea and turns this into a rough design or specification. This often involves discussion with the sales and marketing divisions to obtain as much information as possible about likely consumer reactions, the nature of competitive products, if any etc.

Designers, technicians and other specialist staff work on a detailed specification for the product, incorporating such factors as technical requirement, performance statistics and styling. An estimate will also be made at this stage of cost, selling price and output. If in the light of this information the proposal appears to be feasible, the work will continue; if not the idea and the design are dropped.

At this stage a working model is often constructed. Use may also be made of computer design simulation. This allows a comparison between alternatives to be made at a fraction of the cost that would required to construct several working models. Computers can also be to simulate the effects on the different parts of organization: production, purchasing sales etc.

The information collated above is translated into detailed requirements for the production division. Often, a design and development team is set up composed of people with a variety of specialist skills, utilizing a matrix type of organization. The aim of this group is to ensure that the final design can be easily produced; once the production unit is tooled up any changes in design will involve disproportionately heavy production costs.

A 'pilot' or 'test' run is arranged to try out, on a trial basis, the production system and ancillary management functions, and to enable the employees to gain practical experience under actual production conditions. Tools, machines, drawings, work specifications, cost estimates and training requirements are all tested out. At this stage it is not unusual to find easier, more economic means of producing parts of the product. Although computer simulations can be very useful, there is no substitute for practice in a real work situation, and close monitoring and attention by management at this stage will help to maximize efficiency when full production begins.

As part of the quest for greater efficiency in the production process, a technique known as value analysis was oriented in the U.S.A, by L D Miles of the General Electric Company in the late 1940s. The aim of this technique is to ascertain, by mean of a tests and questions, the true value of very part or product used in the production process, and thus to assist management in making resource decisions.

Value analysis questions the whole purpose and function of a part or product, and thus has a broader scope than cost reduction systems which, while aiming to minimize costs, take for granted the functional elements of the part or product.

Value analysis works best when a small multi-disciplinary team can look at all the aspects involved, each member bringing his particular skill and experience to bear on the problem or item in question. The project team would proceed as follows:

1. A product or par (preferably of major importance) is selected.

2. Financial costs are estimated.

3. The number of components used is listed.

4. All possible uses for the product or part are considered and the number likely to be sold is estimated.

5. The major objectives of the part or product is agreed and all the means of achieving this objective are examined. For example is a lubricant additive going to be used solely in the gearbox of a car or can it be used in motor mowers, boat and motorcycle engines? What changes would be required to meet these major aims?
6. The major objective being agreed, detailed financial costs are estimated for each of the options and a final choice is made on the most suitable mix of components in terms of cost, function, design etc.
7. The final involves deciding what other functions or uses for the final product have to be incorporated into this choice of components so that all possible uses are catered for. This may mean that further though and design work is involved before the new product or part is accepted in the market place.

All managers have to set standards. These target are strongly influenced by the sector of the market the organization is aiming at and the price charged, e.g. a Rolls Royce car has a high has a high price and caters for the top end of the car buyer's market, and must therefore maintain the highest quality.

The quality standard achieved depends, of course, on the capabilities of the organization. High quality requires good control standards, and monitoring throughout the production process. Feedback from the sales force and marketing department on customer reaction also helps to maintain high quality standards.

Reliability is linked, but not directly proportional, to the standard of quality. Reliability depends on may factors such as the number of moving parts, usage, the materials and servicing arrangements, Reliability will be enchanced by the following factors.

1. The use of well-proved and tested designs. The closer one approaches the frontiers of knowledge or the current design limits the more likely it is that reliability will suffer.
2. Simplicity of design. The more complex a product, the more faults are likely occur, and the more difficult they may be to correct. Consider the scope for faults in the modern car with it electronic windows, turbocharger, electronic ignition, special lighting systems, heated seats, warning display systems, etc., and difficulties that can face the owner who wishes to service his own car. Even garage mechanics are now having to specialize as no one person can encompass, the necessary knowledge. We now have auto-electricians, fuel specialists, car tuners, in-car entertainment shops etc.
3. The use of reliable components in all parts of the product with high tolerance factors should minimize maintenance and breakdowns. Each component must be tested not only in its own right, but also in conjunction with the other components to be incorporated in the unit or product.

4. The incorporation of fail safe systems or products having set lifespans will assist the user in planning maintenance schedules and avoiding unwarranted stoppages and breakdowns.

5. Production in accordance with the designer's specifications is the greatest guarantee of reliability. Slipshod workmanship, incorrect tolerances, a wrong materials mix will all affect reliability, sometimes with very serious cost implications. For example in 1979 and 1980 the Lancia car company was faced with a massive corrosion problem in some of their models, due in the main to a faulty batch of steel produced several years earlier. In other instance the problem is discovered after an even longer period of time, e.g. corrosion in nuclear power station cooling pipes. In both cases the result was a dissatisfied customer, the spending of vast sums of money to put the problem right, and bad publicity and considerable loss of prestige for the manufacture of the end product.

There are many advantages in locating a new production line in close proximity to existing lines, in adjoining factories or even within the same factory. But in some instances there may not be sufficient space to permit this. In addition, even if there is sufficient space, the manufacturer may decide to locate elsewhere for a variety of reasons. Manufacturers are usually faced with a wide range of alternative locations, and in choosing between these alternatives the following factors will be taken into account.

1. *Proximity to other units within the organization*

In this respect government intervention has often been to the determent of British organizations overall efficiency, by preventing them from locating at their preferred site. In the car industry, for instance particular governments often for purely political reasons, have forced vehicle manufacturers to locate in areas they would not themselves have chosen, putting for example engine assembly plants in Wales, and axle and gearbox plants in Scotland, while the major assembly units remained in the Midlands. The additional transport costs involved, and the co-ordination problems that arise when groups of managers are hundreds of miles apart, have put British manufacturers most of whose activities are concentrated in one huge site.

2. *Labour availability*

With the present high levels of unemployment this factor is no longer so important. Nevertheless firm must ensure that there is sufficient labour to meet their needs. This is especially important when the unit is heavily dependent on one type of labour e.g. skilled engineers or women with the dexterity required for complex assembly operations. Manufacturers often look for workers with the requisite skills and experience. But sometimes they prefer to train 'green' labour since new recruits are less likely to bring with them unwanted habits, including restrictive working practices.

3. Housing availability

This particular applies to temporary housing for their workers. The New Towns are often able to offer a company instant housing for its employees, often in modern surroundings. This gives them a considerable advantage over local authorities which have long waiting lists for council houses from existing inhabitants, and which are, therefore, reluctant to provide housing for newcomers.

4. Amenities

People are now demanding better surroundings and amenities including leisure centres are recreational facilities of all kinds. Public most provision being in the New Towns and in the suburbs of established towns rather than in old, overcrowded inner city areas. (Having encouraged a movement of firms and population away from city centres during the last twenty years, governments are now trying to reverse the trend in order to prevent further decay of the economic and social fabric of these areas).

5. Transport

Another advantage that New Towns are fond of publicizing is the fact that housing is available close to factories and offices, so that workers can avoid long, uncomfortable and expensive journeys to work which are frequently the price of suburban life. Factories built in New Towns or rural areas can also offer better car-parking facilities, a factor of increasing importance with the rise in the level of car ownership. The organization also has to take into account the ease and cost of transporting raw materials, components and finished products. The development of the materials, components and finished products. The development of the motorway system has widened the choice of locations and many industrial development have been established close to motorway intersection points. Similarly the development of airports and container-ports has influenced the location of industrial units.

6. The availability of materials.

The development of the motorway system, discussed above, has made it easier to transport materials over long distances. But there are still advantages to be gained from locating near to the source of materials, especially when these are heavy or bulky. Brick-making factories are located close to clay deposits, coal-fired power stations close to coal mines.

7. Access to markets

Although modern transport systems have made it easier to transport finished goods over long distances, there are advantages in being close to markets. The concentration of population in the South East helps to explain the development of light industry in that region in the post-war period. For manufacturers of industrial goods, and especially of components, nearness to industry is desirable since quick-delivery can be an important competitive weapon.

8. Space

The lack adequate space at the site is the reason why manufacturers choose to expand in new locations. The space requirement can sometimes by very big indeed; when the Nissan car company examined possible sites for a British plant they only considered sites of several hundred acres. In other instances the manufacturer may have special site requirements, e.g. flat land or land which will take the foundations required for high buildings.

9. Climate

Climate conditions were once an important influence on the location of industry, e.g. the cotton industry needed the damp climate of Lancashire. Climate has become of less direct importance as methods of controlling humidity and temperature within factories have been perfected. This has enabled firm to choose locations with a pleasant climate. Note the massive growth of industry in the sun belt and West Coast of America, to the detriment of the traditional East Coast States. Another aspect of climate is the existence of large quantities of water. Some industries use water on a large scalę, either in the production process, or in the treatment and disposal of effluent.

10. Safety

Hardly a day goes by without the press commenting on the dangers from some chemical plant or nuclear power station. The 'Fixborough disaster' of a few years ago awakened the general public to the danger of chemical plants being built close to housing. The danger still exists in many areas, but the trend is to separate tow so that they accidents can be contained without the general public being affected.

11. Finance

This is obviously a vital issue, and most the factors considered above are brought together in a cost benefit analysis of alternative sites. But account must also be taken of the substantial government assistance available in the Assisted Areas.

12. Politics

Jim Callaghan gained notoriety or gratitude, depending on your viewpoint when he persuaded Ford to build their new European engine plant in Wales near his constituency. The arrival of a large multinational in an area means jobs, increased prosperity (or less misery) and this means votes.

In designing the layout of an office building or production unit, a manager has to make decisions concerning;

1. The positioning of departments within the overall site.
2. The detailed design of each department so that the appropriate sections are adjacent to one another.

3. Individual workplace or machine design

Incorrect decisions in many of these areas can give rise subsequently to a variety of increased costs, including the need to rent additional space, inadequate communications, double-handing and other transportation costs.

System of plant layout may be based on:

1. Process or function: example include the catalytic crackers used in the refining of crude oil into Kerosene, petrol, wax, etc., (a process unit), and the designing of one plant, the press shop to make car bodies and another, the spray shop, to paint them, (functional units).
2. A fixed position; this type of layout is used in the construction of large products, e.g., shipbuilding, oil rig construction.
3. The product; in this, the most common type, the layout is determined by the requirements of the manufacture of the product be it beer, whisky, biscuits or bread. This layout often requires long production runs of nearly identical products, usually with a high degree of automation to minimize human fatigue and error.

The detailed preparation of a design for a factory layout involves making use of the information that is available at the time and trying to estimate likely future changes. The marketing department should estimate the likely future demand for product, and the final design should ensure that there is sufficient room for expansion to cater for future needs.

Having completed this investigation the following procedure could be used as brief guide of layout planning.

1. Using a plan of the building and site, ensure the relevant services are available in the right places.
2. Examine the operational sequences, so that operations and sections are located in a correct relationship to one another.
3. Ensure that the major or "key operations are correctly situated, since this is a major determinant of the overall efficiency of the production process.
4. Position the remaining operations and ancillary services, e.g. stores dispatch, canteens, washrooms and all transportation and communication routes.
5. Plan the individual work areas in detail and ensure that all ancillary equipment is correctly located.
6. Test out the plan, either utilizing a model or by carrying out pre-production runs.
7. Fully familiarize employees and management with the layout and make any final adjustments as working experience dictates.

All layout plans may be regarded as a compromise between conflicting process: time, space costs of storage, ease of access. While every unit or plant is unique, and while what is a good layout for one plant may be a bad layout for another, there are certain criteria by which any layout may be judged:

1. It must do the job it was designed to do, efficiently and effectively paying due regard to the human factor, in the production process.
2. Flexibility is vital, Changes in product design will inevitably take place over a period of time and the production process must be capable of adapting to them.
3. The whole process should be well-co ordinated to make maximum use of all the resources involved, eliminate unnecessary storage and minimize waiting time between operations.
4. Visibility and accessibility are important for machine maintenance, safety, and management control and supervision; if you cannot see what is going on, you cannot manage and control it.
5. Handling, particular human handling, should be minimized as it wastes time and money (wages and equipment costs).
6. Health and safety requirements must be and the overall working atmosphere should be a pleasant one. People will only give of their best and take pride in what they produce if management create the right environment.
7. The plant must be secure, well fenced and guarded, with a minimum number of supervised entrances and exits. In some production processes e.g. drugs, chemicals, security is obviously vital and special precautions have to be taken.

In Britain is a shortage of engineers qualified in the production management area. Planning is often carried out by well meaning amateurs or left to architects, who are more concerned with matter of style, than practical work realities. The situation is changing and some of our modern factories are every bit as efficient at those of our overseas rivals. But there are still many manufacturing units housed in old buildings with inefficient layouts. Not surprisingly, their production costs do not compare well with those of the robot-dominated, computer-controlled production system of our rivals in Japan, German and America.

Any purchase of industrial equipment will, of course, make sure that the equipment does the job for which it is required. He will also be concerned with the cost of the equipment, and with the return on his expenditure. (Most equipment is bought for replacement purpose, and if the cost is too high it may be possible to continue using the existing equipment). In considering these issue the purchaser will take account of a range of factors, including the price of purchasing and operating the machines, its reliability, ease of maintenance, its safety standards and the delivery period. A view should also be taken of possible design changes which might outdate the present equipment and thus affect its economic life. This is always an area of potential conflict between the need of the accountant, in terms of finance, and the requirements of the production manager concerned with the job in hand. When sales are booming and capacity is stretched the production manger is more likely to triumph, conversely in times of recession and low profits the hand of the accountant is strengthened. Discounts reflect the benefits of bulk purchasing to suppliers, e.g. longs production runs and easier production planning). These benefits are maximized when all orders are placed with a single supplier.

Centralization aids consistency in purchasing policy and makes standardization in placing orders that good of differing qualities or standards will be purchased.

Expertise and specialization in different areas of purchasing are facilitated, Buyers can for example give all their time and attention to one or two products. In a de-centralized system the buyer is concerned with a wider range of products, with a danger of becoming jack of all trades and master of none. Information, management control and computerized invoicing systems work more smoothly when purchasing is centralized. The changes of losses or mistakes in ordering are minimized.

Finally, a centralized system often has the advantages of being located with a central stores. This makes inspection and quality control easier; stock control is simplified and management of the total operations can be more easily co-ordinated.

The smalls is beautiful, supporters would argue that a centralized system is unwieldy and impersonal, and that there are advantage in having smaller de-centralized units, or individuals working in each operational department or section of an organization.

1. Smaller units can be more flexible. They can purchase according to current requirements rather than to the dictates of some standardization procedure. For example if stock of some materials were about to run out and halt production, it might be better to purchase from a local supplier than to risk a delay in delivery by purchasing from an authorized supplier located further away.
2. Close liaison can be maintained with suppliers, particularly local suppliers, and a more personal as opposed to departmental, relationship built up with salesman.
3. De-centralization puts purchasing responsibility where the action is i.e., alongside line management.

The balance of advantage between these two approaches depends upon the size of the organization, its type and range of products etc. However one of the present authors has had considerable experience of both types of systems and in his opinion the benefits of centralization in particular the opportunity for bulk purchasing, specialization and better management control, far out weight any disadvantages. Moreover it seems likely that these benefits will become even greater in the future; further economics of scale in production arising from technological change will enable bigger discounts to be obtained for bulk purchases.

The responsibilities of the purchasing department

1. The purchasing department's primary responsibility is to form and maintain good relationships with suitable suppliers. This means taking a positive approach: going to exhibitions, reading the trade press, obtaining suppliers names from other purchasers and so forth. There is much more to purchasing than sitting in an office and waiting for salesmen to call. A part of this responsibility, it is necessary to ensure that the vendor organization has a sound financial base (i.e. it is not going to go bankrupt in the middle of delivering a vital order) and that quality standards are maintained.

2. Suitable suppliers having been identified, the purchasing officer must use his negotiating skills and knowledge of the market to obtain the most competitive price possible. However, he must of course, take account of other factors, including quality and speed of delivery. There is often a 'trade-off' among these various factors and a purchasing officer's expertise is put to the test in trade-off situations. He has to decide whether for example, is it worth paying 5 percent more to supplier who offers earlier delivery; or whether he should risk buying from a new company which is selling at a price below that of the existing supplies, whose products have always been of a satisfactory standard.

   When a purchaser accounts for a high proportion of a supplier's output, he must beware of extracting so good a bargain that the supplier's financial viability is threatened. A bankrupt supplier is of no benefit to a purchasing department.

3. It is the responsibility of the purchasing department ensure that the right goods are delivered in the right place at the right time. This involves developing a good relationship with involve developing a good relationship with one's supplier and being aware of their problems. Marks and Spencer's purchasing staff are particularly good at doing this, being helped by the fact that many of their suppliers are former Marks and Spencer managers, who are aware of the company's systems and requirements.

4. If things do go wrong, it is the duty of the purchasing department to notified all concerned, production, sales, research etc., and to try to obtain alternatives supplies. This is where the purchasing function has a particularly close link with the manufacturing function.

5. The purchasing department has two main financial functions to perform. First it has a responsibility to verify invoices and ensure that stock levels are properly costed. Second it can help her department estimate costs and prices by advising them of the likely prices of bought in goods and materials. In providing this advice it may need to predict prices several months ahead.

6. The purchasing department will receive a considerable amount of information from salesmen exhibitions the trade press, T.V., radio catalogues suppliers etc. Much of

this information will help it to discharge the responsibilities listed above. But it should also pass information on to other interested parties within the organization. So for instance it would be helpful for the design department to know that a company has introduced a new component that cold be incorporated in machines currently being designed.

Purchasing departments that try to play things, close to their chest soon one the confidence of their colleagues, and the whole success of the purchasing function can be jeopardized by suspicion and mistrust. Just as the purchasing departments must beware of usurping the purchasing department's authority. If a co-ordinated purchasing policy is to be maintained, personnel in other department must resist the temptations to go behind its back in dealing with suppliers. While it is acceptable for line mangers to discuss their requirements with salesmen, they should not allow themselves to be persuaded to sign orders when the responsibility for doing so has been given to be persuaded to sign orders when the responsibility for doing has been given to the purchasing department.

The purchasing function has developed considerably in recent years. Managers are now aware of the immense saving that can be made in the purchase of materials,components and services, and also of the costs that can arise when supplies are disrupted. With the advent of a professional qualification and training schemes, purchasing staff are now professionals in very sense of the word, and can command appropriate salaries and status in organizations, large and small, in the public and private sectors.

Stores control involves the management of all the items in a store, from the moment they arrive up to the time they leave. One of the major task is checking the quality of the items that come in to the stores. Prior to this acceptance stage it is possible to return faulty goods to a manufacturer for ratification, or to query problems with the carrier.

Staff in the Goods Inward section acknowledge receipt of goods and carry out the documentation required to incorporate the goods in the stock control system. The good are unpacked and checked for quality items are noted and returned, as are packing systems that are re-chargeable to a supplier or carrier. The necessary documentation is then forwarded to the accounts section to ensure that the financial arrangements are progressed. The stores staff also notify other interested departments, e.g. production of the item's arrival.

Stores management in large organizations has been revolutionized by the use of computerized systems. These process all the necessary documentation, maintain checks on stock levels, and notify management to re-order as required. They can even control the location of the stock and of the equipment for extracting and issuing it. The stores counter and shelves has given way to floor to ceiling pallets, stacked to great heights in special artificial environments, handled with modern equipment using the latest micro-chip technology. With such systems man handling is a thing of the past; modern conveyer systems, computer floor tracking systems and a variety of other devices extract and deliver the items to the workplace almost without the touch of a human hand. But however sophisticated the stores system may be, managers are required to make the same decisions as in the past. The major decisions relate to the following areas.

The locations of stock we be influenced by the physical design of the stores, by the need for adequate storage space and for good circulation space, and by the desire to use modern handling equipment and documentation systems. Stock are located partly in stores, and partly in user departments throughout the organization in offices, at particular stages in the production process etc. It is therefore important to have adequate coding and classification.

There is often a tendency to carry too large a stock of certain items just in case. In many instance 80-90% of turnover is derived from products accounting for 15-20% of stocks, therefore turnover and stocks should be fairly closely related. Once the desired level of has been determined systems can be established to trigger ordering procedures once the minimum stock level has been reached.

Nowadays there are often a variety of sources of instant supply for standardized items. For example, garages used to have to maintain stores for all items on the cars they sold an serviced. Nowadays they call on the services of specialized factors small organizations that operate in car electric's, clutch parts, etc. It is cheaper to use these outside suppliers than maintain vast stores of their own.

Standardization of parts between different manufactures, and such system as the British Standards Institute seal of approval on the quality of goods, have helped considerably in this respect.

Handling procedures should be reviewed periodically so as to minimize dual handling e.g. putting an item on to a storage shelf and then getting it out again shortly afterwards for issue. Dual handling involves additional paperwork as well as physical effort. If the stores system is properly managed as part of an overall materials procurement system, there is no reason why some items should not be delivered direct to the workplace, (providing the control procedures are adequate). A periodic review of procedures also ensures that opportunities for introducing new and improved handling methods are not neglected.

The 'people' of stores operations are often high, even in the most mechanized stores operation. Unfortunately, some managers see the stores as a backwater a dumping ground for the old, sick, disabled and troublemakers in their organization. But the approach to stores management is gradually changing as modern accounting systems cause senior managers to re-assess the cost of their stores operations. Well qualified, well trained and enthusiastic staff can be a tremendous help to any organization in achieving efficiency with the sores department and in ensuring that the manufacturing or service section operates smoothly and without interruptions.

Management services refers to a variety of techniques (the main ones being organization and method and work study) that assist management in improving the efficiency of their organizations.

The term 'management services' is based on the title chosen by the professional body which represents staff working in this area. The wide range of activities undertaken by management services personnel was also noted in the Bains Report,' Local Authority Management Structures' which preceded the 1974 local government re-organization.

The term "Management Services" comprises all those services which help management to plan, control and improve the activities of the organization in a general sense. The term is wider than the orthodox interpretation which is generally limited to efficiency and productivity services.

Although management services personnel have extended their range of activities, they still use, in the main, techniques based upon two areas of specialization, O. and M. (organization and methods) and work study. A few years ago these techniques tended to be operated separately. O. and M. was concerned with efficiency in the office, whereas work study was concerned with problems not he shop floor and payment schemes for manual or blue collar workers. But even before the new Institute was formed this demarcation was breaking down and staff were becoming more interchangeable between these two work areas. However, for case of presentation we discuss each of these two, and other techniques, separately.

The formal use of O. and M.can be traced back to 1919 when a small team was set in the Treasury following the Bradbury Report on The organization and staffing of government offices. O. and M. has often been better developed in public than in private sector organizations. This is perhaps no surprise when one considers that much of the public sector operates on bureaucratic lines, in an office type of environment. Nevertheless it shown that innovations in management techniques are no confined to the private sector, contrary to the impression sometimes given by critics of the public sector.

In fact, O. and M. Cover most of the management functions found in either the public or the private sector. It is mainly concerned with:

1. Defining the true problem that exists and the facts required.
2. Examining work methods, i.e. information systems, administrative systems office equipment etc.
3. Analysing how employees spend their and scrutinizing staffing levels.

4. Examining the introduction of the latest types of office equipment, i.e. communications equipment repographics mail etc.
5. Undertaking research into specific areas.
6. Advising on organizational structural and re-organizations including responsibility levels, gradings and salaries common d structures, departmentation etc.
7. Ensuring that the organization has effective communication systems.
8. Advising on office and factory layouts.
9. Introducing computerized systems (and operating the computer in certain organizations).
10. Examining work planning and programming systems

From the above list it will be evident that O. and M. staff are involved throughout the organization, form junior clerical levels up to Board or policy committee level. They use a variety of methods and techniques, statistical, analytical, observational and behavioral as appropriate. But whatever the area of investigation and whatever the methods used, the following steps would normally be involved.

Selecting the material facts: When a situation is first examined, more than one problem area can usually be seen. It is necessary to try to differentiate between those areas that merit more detailed investigation and those which are irrelevant to the main issues. This preliminary survey familiarizes the O. and M. Staff with the main work areas to be investigated, and enables their terms of reference for the assignment to be finalized.

Recording the facts: The terms of reference being agreed, the relevant facts recorded. This often involves direct observation of people in a work situation. Staff may be interviewed as to their duties and responsibilities, questionnaires may be completed and statistical returns analysed.

Examining the information obtained: The information obtained at the previous stage is critically examined in order to obtain answers to the questions: What is done? Where is it done? When is it done? Why is it done? How is it done? Who does it?

Developing ideas for improvement: Ideas for improving the situation are discussed with management and the employees concerned. This discussion helps to reveal any potential snags or problems and to identify the costs involved in the changes, e.g. for retraining. In other words it helps to ensure that the new systems are practical and capable of implementation.

Implementing recommendations: The ideas for improvement modified as required in the light of the discussions, are incorporated in a report. If the report is accepted by the management responsible the O. and M. staff then have to assist with the introduction of their new ideas. This is often a salutary experience which involves overcoming people's built-in resistance to change. This implies that O. and M. staff must have analytical skills and must also be able to 'sell' their ideas and develop good personal relationship with all type of people.

Maintaining new systems: As circumstances and individuals change, the newly introduced systems may have to modified. To ensure that this happens. O.and M. staff undertake a monitoring role.

Work study was pioneered by Frederick Taylor in his attempts to improve efficiency in a factory, unit, and has been developed ever since. The basic technique is work measurement, designed (a) to provide management with information to aid the planning and control of work and (b) to offer an individual a financial incentive for an above average work performance.

Work is measured using either a stop watch or more sophisticated systems incorporating micro-chip technology. The procedures usually adopted are:

1. The job or operation is broken down into easily identifiable sections or elements.
2. The time taken to complete each element of the work is measured.

Because some people work faster than others, and because some employees may try to mislead the work study officer as to the normal pace of work required (e.g. by working more slowly than usual to make the job appear to require longer time and hence a greater allowance), the work study officer applies a ranting estimate to his study. The aim of this rating is to assist with a true estimate of the time necessary to complete the task in a normal work situation with an average employee working at an average pace.

Because of the personal judgment involved in this rating exercise, the factor is often the cause of subsequent disputes. Studies are taken of a variety of employees doing that same job in a variety of work situations to ensure that all types of work situations and conditions are covered.

3. The results are analysed and a time or target issued for the completion of a particular job or operation. This time will include allowances for rest and relaxation, harsh working conditions etc. The work study officer also advises on the best way to do the job, drawing on his observations of perhaps several working methods. On the basis of this information management can plan its work schedules, allocate manpower and equipment train employees to do an operation in the most effective way, and offer them a financial incentive to increase their productivity.

The trade unions, particular in the public sector in the 1960s and 1970s, welcomed work study as a measure of increasing their members take-home pay. It also suited many public sector organizations to encourage work study as a means of retaining skilled craftsmen and other manual workers who were, at that time, on lower wage levels than comparable employees in the private sector. It was not until the early

1970s that efficiency aspects, and the advantages of work study as a management aid, came to be fully appreciated.

It is beneficial for the staff who work in these areas to undertake the training required for membership of the Institute of Management Services. But to be rally successful in these areas of work, personal qualities of a particu'ar type are also required. Since people are the focus of both O. and M. and work study the main qualities required are impartiality, an enquiring mind, patience and the ability to persevere in periods of adversity, a realistic approach to problem solving, and an understanding of and liking for people.

This is a problem-solving technique which uses analytical and statistical techniques to try to measure the factors of change in a given situation, and to compare alternative courses of action. O.R. is now applied to a wide range of issues, e.g., the best route for school buses, optimum stock levels, refuse collection systems and location of warehouse. The Local Government Operational Research Unit operates a central service to local government and has developed considerable expertise in the use of O.R. techniques in the public sector. For example it will advise local authorities on the feasibility of introducing a waste paper collection system.

This technique which is used for planning and co-ordinating large projects such as the construction of a new office building, beings by charting each of the activities concerned. Some can be completed concurrently others are dependent on another activities being completed firs. Each activity has to have a start, a duration and an end. The aim of network analysis is to show all these activities visually and to identify the series of key activities which determine the total duration of the project. This series is known as the critical path.

Because of the time involved in drawing up the network and keeping it up to date, management services staff are often involved in its operation. They have the necessary knowledge of the organization, know the key personnel involved, and have the skills and the time required for this project co-ordination role.

In the private sector the computer system is normally controlled by the manager in charge of the management services function, as shown in Figure 1. This means that there is no problem in co-ordinating the work of management services staff who may be involved in a computer application to a work procedure and require the assistance of systems analysts (who design the system) and programmers (who write the operating procedures for the computers). In this type of combined management services unit the management services staff may well do the systems work and even the programming work themselves. Even if they do not, the control of a multi-disciplinary project team is easier where the management services manager also controls the computer and allied staff.

In the public sector e.g. local government the computer section is often within the finance directorate, whereas the management services section is often is either in the director of administration's department or is directly responsible to the chief executive. This split of responsibility can create problems when it has to be decided who should do the systems analysis work for a particular application, or when putting a management services application on to the computer would conflict with the finance departments priorities. The situation is often resolved by joint working arrangements between the two departments.

In addition to individual management services units in local government, there exists a large central unit, LAMSAC. This operates as a central consultancy unit carrying out research, and developing computerised systems in area of interest common to all local authorities. It also undertakes specific assignments for individual authorities.

LAMSAC operates on private sector in combining management services and computer skills and it may be a forerunner of smaller combined units in individuals local authorities. But one of the authorities. But one of the authors, who spent some years in charge of management services units in local government, feels that progress along these lines will be very slow, if only because finance departments will be reluctant to surrender the powers inherent in the control of the computer and its information systems.

Provided that there is sufficient work to occupy staff on a full-time basis, there are several advantages in having an internal management services unit:

1. As staff of the organization they are more likely to have mangers best interests at heart when carrying out their work.
2. They have to live with their mistakes and will therefore be more careful in framing their reports and implementing their recommendations.
3. Internal staff get to know their won organization's working and develop good relationships with other employees and managers. This helps to overcome mistrust and many of the worries brought about by change.
4. Maintenance of incentive schemes and of re-organization processes is easier when management services staff are on site all the time. They are well placed to pick up problems at an early stage.

Outside consultants have a number of advantages:

1. The organization pays for them only when they are needed; the continuing costs of an internal unit are avoided.
2. Managers can hire consultants with expertise in a particular area rather than having to rely on what is available form within their own unit.
3. Outside consultants are independent, and divorced from office politics. They also

have experience of other organizations that they can bring to bear on a particular problem.

On the other hand outside consultants fees for a given job are usually well above the corresponding costs of an internal unit. Moreover they have to spend some time-at the client expense-getting to know the organization and its management. Furthermore, however effectively they undertake the initial assignment, maintenance problems are likely to arise. The organizations is then faced with either recalling the consultants (at a fee of course) or trying to correct problems with which internal staff may not be fully familiar.

Incentive schemes and productivity agreements are often a major outcome of the work of management services personnel. Before introducing any scheme of this nature management must (a) be clear about what it hoped the scheme will achieve, (b) weigh up the costs of the scheme and (c) try to identify any disruptions that may result.

Incentive schemes and productivity agreements frequently have the following objectives:

Increased output and earnings

Better management control and planning

Increased labour mobility between jobs

Better work methods

Better quality

Reduced absenteeism and staff turnover

Reduced overtime working.

Experience has shown that, whatever the type of scheme or the expected benefits, the scheme will only operate successfully if, when designing it management and the management services staff pays close attention to the following issues:

1. The scheme must be simple to understand and have a minimum of documentation.
2. Employees must accept the work target as being realistic.
3. There must be a clear relationship between increased performance and increased pay.
4. The calculation period and the pay period should be as short as possible and coincide with the normal wage or salary period.

ENCYCLOPAEDIA
OF
MODERN MANAGEMENT TECHNIQUES

ENCYCLOPAEDIA
OF
MODERN MANAGEMENT TECHNIQUES

Volume 5

Edited by
A. K. Chaudhary

ANMOL PUBLICATIONS PVT. LTD.
NEW DELHI-110 002 (INDIA)

ANMOL PUBLICATIONS PVT. LTD.
4374/4B, Ansari Road, Daryaganj
New Delhi-110 002

Encyclopaedia of Modern Management Techniques

First Edition 1999
ISBN 81-261-0321-3 (Set)

PRINTED IN INDIA

Published by J. L. Kumar for Anmol Publications Pvt. Ltd., New Delhi-110 002 and Printed at Mehra Offset Press, Delhi.

Contents

20

Corporate Planning and Management Strategy

It is commonly understood that the business policy is the mater related to top management which is responsible for overall management of the determination of objectives and goals, overall planning, overall control, integration of organisational activity with the external environment. It is true that planning policy and strategy is therefore mainly concerned with the functions of the top management. But the knowledge of corporate planning refers to and focuses on general management of any specific area. It is concerned with the total organisational system in which each manager functions.

Various terms like, Corporate planning, Long range planning, Business planning, Comprehensive planning, Strategic planning, Total planning, Formal planning etc., are used to mean a complete way of running a firm comprising the following steps:

(i) evaluation of firm and its environment

(ii) setting goals

(iii) the listing of assumptions

(iv) gap analysis

(v) strategic ideas in various management areas (such as marketing, personnel, research,) etc., and

(vi) the building of a planning system.

Some treat them as synonymous whereas some have reservation over using the word Long Range Planning as they feel,

(a) Corporate plan is to be appropriate only in a stable environment. For unstable environment, organisation needs a creative strategy which Corporate plan does not signify.

(b) Corporate plan under-emphasizes the comprehensive nature of corporate planning process which is concerned with all aspects, and not only with the Long-range time horizon.

Some of the brief definitions are quoted below, in order to give a broad favour of the meaning.

Planning is seen variously as:

- the design of desired future and of effective ways of bringing it about.
- a process of preparing for the commitment of resources in the most economic fashion and, by preparing, or allowing this commitment to be made faster and less descriptively.
- a formal, systematic, managerial process, organised by responsibility, time and information, to ensure that operational planning project planning and strategic planning are carried out regularly to enable top management to direct and control the future of the enterprise.
- an analytical process which encompasses an assessment of the future, the determination of desired objectives.
- the context of that future, the development of alternative courses of action to achieve such a objectives, and the selection of a course (or courses) of action from these alternatives.
- the formal process of developing objectives for the corporation and its component parts, evolving alternative strategies to achieve these objectives, and doing this against a background of a systematic appraisal of internal strengths and weaknesses and external environmental changes.

Definitions and discussions on corporate planning presented by various authors on close scrutiny depict that they are in agreement with the following aspects:

(i) Planning is a conscious and deliberate intervention for change and corporate planning is concerned with such an effort for sustained growth of an organisation.

(ii) The basic difference in the planning activity carried out of various levels in an organisation is due to the varying quantum of the three parameters viz,:

  (a) the time-span affected by the decisions

  (b) the degree to which company resources can be committed, and

  (c) the risk involved.

(iii) Planning is not a single-shot, once and for-all-affair. It is a continuous activity involving a recyclic process in which the various sections of the plan are progressively modified, reassessed, and refined until a composite plan is achieved, which is compatible in all respects with the objectives and goals that it seeks to achieve, and means available for achieving them.

(iv) There is a gradual change in planning process form traditional planning to the strategic planning. Strategic planning process, typically implies a reappraisal of business in relation to its environment and is primarily concerned with:

(a) development of integrated plans for total organisation, as against plans for a particular department or division only,

(b) long term strategic considerations as opposed to short term operational ones, and

(c) establishment of formal procedure for strategic planning which exists along with short term budgeting.

(v) The planning activity at different echelon of management in organisation hierarchy, in general management parlance, are known as strategic, tactical and operational planning.

It basically includes norm seeking function, goal setting function and administrative function of planning in a three-level structure and a multi-phased process. While the content and procedure for each of these need different methodologies, they are inter-related activities which when put together constitute the total planning function of any organisation. Hence corporate planning is a combination of all the three categories of planning activities. Strategic planning as a top management function is concerned with decisions about the future role and posture of the organisation in relation to the environment of the company. It needs a good deal of informed yet qualitative judgement. The specification of objectives both implicitly and explicitly, is an integral part of strategy formulation.

Corporate planning is the process of translating the aims, objectives and goals set out in the strategic plan into a set of actual implementable plans. The strategic plan sets the boundaries within which corporate planning takes place. The corporate plan forms the frame-work within which operational planning covering various sections of the company can be carried out.

Operational plans, on the basis of tentative constraints on the availability of resources for each functional areas of the company imposed by the corporate management, are prepared, discussed and revised, until a composite operational plan is produced to achieve the following objectives:

(i) an optimal allocation of the corporate resources between the competing operational requirements.

(ii) an optimal allocation of the corporate resources within the individual functional areas of the company.

As planning is the organisation for progress it amounts to deciding in advance what to do, how, when, why and by whom. In other words planning can be defined as rationally perceiving the environment and designing acts whereby either the environment or internal organisation will be altered for the purpose of desired change. Often, objectives/contents of the desired change may also form integral part of planning process.

Thus, planning can be expressed as:

P = f (IV, EV)

IV = internal variables

EV = external variables

Internal variables can be altered by the corporation, but a corporation has practically negligible or marginal influence on external variables, which are to be carefully forecasted or predicted. Hence, planning essentially is concerned with adjusting internal variables in the light of forecasted external variables so as to fix and achieve objectives effectively.

This can be achieved in two ways. One, in which goal is fixed and sought to be achieved by selecting from amongst the available alternatives, by design of end-means hierarchy, described as goal view of planning. In the other, based on the vision of future-state, the performance goals are decided and pursued. Achievement is measured against the set goal. Further, a fresh goal is established based on the state of future vision, achievement in recent past, and organisational capability. This interactive process is termed as process view. These two approaches are also termed by various authors as mechanistic model and human approach model, or means end model/decision model and learning model, closed system view and open system view, normative approach and explorative approach, board approach and institution approach.

Integrated Approach

For successful adoption of planning practices in Indian situation, a combination of both the approaches in a planning methodology is essential. The goal view is appropriate for the operational plans, for middle management level downwards in an organisational hierarchy, and the process view should be considered important at the top management level.

In the early stage of growth cycle of a business, process view is essential. Corporation's top management, which is directly concerned with strategic planning, continuously monitor the progress of the corporation in the light of changing external environment and change the corporation's goals) to adjust to the demands of external environment. This is essentially a learning process or the process view of planning. Once the goals are set, the operating level management should seek to achieve them through goal view of planning process. The reasons for deviations, tensions etc. both inside the company and in the external environment must be examined carefully and be regarded as lessons for:

(a) development of knowledge

(b) creating driving force,

(c) handling obstacles, and

(d) development of resources

Comparison between the goal view and the process view in planning philosophy

The Goal View	The Process View
The decision-maker formulates goals and the alternative plans, which are evaluated in terms of their estimated goals fulfillment.	
Man (and management) as rational decision-makers.	
Suitable in clearly delineated and well-known planning environments, or when the strength of the organisation is so superior that there is no need to take account of environment in any planning.	
Mature stages in the company's growth cycle.	
Tensions and misfits are not desirable and are eliminated by means of planning.	

In the next goal setting process, these informations act as feed forward process in strengthening new vision and feed-back process, thus resulting in an integrated approach to planning combining process and goal views, each feeding into another.

Business Growth Characteristics

Growth planning progresses in stages in which vision and the immediate action taken stand in a dialectic relation to one another i.e. the vision and subsequent actions result again in new vision and further subsequent actions, thus resulting in a cyclic progress.

The art of handling growth is based to a great extent on the art of creating tension and exploiting different types of tensions in the company and its environments.

The special conditions necessary for growth process must be embodied in the organisation structure itself. Creating this special condition would necessitate a type of leadership that aims at maintaining or changing the growth culture rather than steering only individual steps in growth process. Norman has termed this type of leadership as Statesmanship and the management which is responsible for this process as Meta-management. Meta-management system is concerned with the idea-system and with the structure of the company, which are adopted to the changing need of the situation. These tasks need a highly developed capacity to identify and interpret internal political process, and ability to exercise visionary control. Perhaps due to this reason, among the four growth sub-processes viz.,

(a) development of knowledge,

(b) development of resources,

(c) development of driving force, and

(d) handling of obstacles in the power system

Corporate Planning Methodology

The methodology for developing corporate plan differs from organisation to organisation depending upon its external environment, managerial capabilities, organisation in planning and control function, and management information systems etc. However, there is enough similarity in their broad approach.

The methodology for corporate plan can be grouped in four stages:

(i) General frame work of planning activities

(ii) Organisation for corporate plan activities

(iii) Procedure for formulating plans and strategies

(iv) Procedure for monitoring and control.

General Frame Work of Planning Activities

By and large the generalised planning system coverage and broad linkage with various plans of the organisation are similar, though their schematic representation differ. To get concept of frame-work of corporate plan, only selected few are presented here.

Organisation for Corporate Plan

The organisation for corporate plan is generally represented as a three cycle process. Cycle one involves establishing corporate objectives at organisation headquarters.

Cycle two establishes consonant business goals at division levels and cycle three establishes specific strategies and Programmes at the functional levels for allocation of resources. The top management deals with six basic corporate plan processes.

These are:

(i) establishing corporate goals,

(ii) developing the goal setting process,

(iii) environmental scanning,

(iv) understanding the subordinate managers' focus

(v) developing the corporate planners role, and

(vi) developing the linkage between planning and budget.

Procedure for Formulating Plans and Strategies

Henry summarises the strategic planning system a ten steps process as follows:

(i) Determine organisational purpose and managerial philosophy

(ii) Identify internal strengths and weaknesses

(iii) Monitor changes in the external environment

(iv) Forecast future conditions and establish planning premises

(v) Determine threats and opportunities

(vi) Formulate specific goals

(vii) Identify and evaluate alternative policies and strategies

(viii) Select best strategic plan

(ix) Prepare action plans, and

(x) Prepare financial plans.

These planning activities are scheduled over a period of twelve months in most firms, and their results include a strategic plan for the next three to seven years and an operational plan for next one to two years.

To cope with various problems of corporate planning process, a good number of modified approaches have emerged during the last two and half decades. Forecasting techniques not being accurate and computer facility not within the reach of many small and medium size industries, Lineman and Kennell prescribed a ten step shirt sleeve approach as follows:

(i) Identify and make explicit the company's mission basic objectives and policies,

(ii) Determine how far into the future management wish to plan,

(iii) Develop a good understanding of the company's points of leverage and vulnerability,

(iv) Determine factors that management think will definitely occur within the planning time horizon,

(v) Make a list of key variables that will have make or break consequence for the company,

(vi) Determine plausible ranges for variables,

(vii) Build scenarios by:

(a) (a) selecting a value for each key variable

(b) estimating the resulting interaction between variables and assumptions, and

(c) developing a narration describing the future under this set of condition.

(viii) Develop strategies for each scenario,

(ix) Check the effectiveness of each strategy in each scenario,

(x) Select or develop an optimum response strategy.

This methodology provides a better approach to (a) facilitate communication, (b) improve multi-party participation and comprehension, (c) encourage more rigorous thinking in a structured way, (d) develop strategies with better cognizance of potential risks. However, it give too much emphasis on past leverage and vulnerability of the company and does not consider multiperiod fluctuating behaviour of key variables. In case of a larger corporation with multiproducers in complex environment, checking of effectiveness of each strategy in each scenario will be almost impossible in the manner suggested by Linneman and Kennell.

In 1978, Paul Donovan and Taylor discussed two most basic problems inherent in planning viz,:

(a) Producing reasonably accurate forecasts

(b) Misusing the strategic plan itself as an operating document.

To minimise these problems 10 steps in procedure of adopting planning to reality suggested by them are as follows:

(i) Emphasize the process of planning not the financial aspects of the plan,

(ii) Differentiate between risk to the Balance Sheet and risk to the Profit and Loss statement,

(iii) Measure the total market and competitive market shares as accurately as possible.

(iv) Gear the plan to events,

(v) Plan to spend money step by step,

(vi) Build a second plan based on time,

(vii) Decide in advance the criteria for abandoning a project,

(viii) Set up monitoring system,

(ix) Make a new five year plan every year,

(x) Avoid excessive publicity about long term financial goals.

Procedure for monitoring and control of corporate planning function

Key to success of any planning activity is the control function. Adequate and effective control demands a sound monitoring system. As insight into the monitoring and control system has been presented by Hammond while listing the ten following steps of planning models:

(i) Decision must be mad as to where a model may be useful,

(ii) A decision must be made whether to sue a model-

Technically—is it possible?

Economically—is it worth while?

and will the organisation accept and use it?

(iii) Specifications must be fixed—i.e. define the exact purpose of the models, its primary inputs and outputs, the main aspects of its structure and how it could be used?

(iv) A decision must be made as to who shall be the modeller if the company concludes that model will be beneficial.

(v) Actual modelling and data gathering must be forwarded together,

(vi) The model must be debugged i.e. checking thoroughly to see that the model does what it is supposed to do at two levels:

(a) Does the computer program correctly implement the intended concept?

(b) Judging from the output itself, does the concept require modification?

(vii) The users must be educated and the model must gain acceptance,

(viii) The process of user validation must be established,

(ix) The model must be put into actual use. Successful use require an understanding of the model's capabilities and limitations so that its putout can be creatively and intelligently used in the planning process.

(x) The model must be up-dated and modified.

There are various models suggested by different authors such as

(i) Risk analysis Model

(ii) What if Model

(iii) Analytical Port-folio Model

(iv) Optimization Model

(v) Deterministic Model.

None can be said to be uniformly applicable. These models cannot be an integral part of Corporate Planning System in India. The manager should develop a sound satisfactory economic forecast in the background of which he will have to set a planning policy for his own organisation.

Strategic analysis

The approaches to investment appraisal took an individual-project perspective. It was assumed that projects exist either with easily specified cash flows or with easily specified underlying factors which give rise to those cash flows. Some uncertainty was admitted in relation to those factors, and ways of studying the impact of such uncertainties were shown, but then it was assumed that the uncertainties themselves were reasonably structured such that rough probabilities of outcomes could be assigned. This is in general accordance with the state of corporate-finance literature.

While this may be a reasonable stance for finance academics to adopt, even though the problems in analysing cash flows and given probabilities have been shown to be far from trivial, the practising manager has to recognize the limited scope of the 'investment problem' addressed by the current theory of finance. He needs to realize that considerable analysis needs to be conducted in order to form sound judgements of cash flows and underlying uncertainties for large projects, and that too ready a move into discounted cash flow calculations may give the impression of sophisticated analysis which disguises the inadequacy of the underlying assumptions. It may indeed be far more important to get the underlying analysis right than to spend time and effort on refining financial calculations, although the dangers of using incorrect discount rates need to be remembered.

It also seems important to recognize that projects are not all the same. There are differences both in the scale of projects and in their economic profile. It may be appropriate to end up with a net present value calculation for all types of investment, but obtaining the correct decision may depend far more on recognizing the differences, in nature and importance, of the underlying factors which will affect the projected cash flows.

The current financial-management approach to the investment decision not only lacks insight into how the underlying factors should be analysed, but also fails to recognize the different stages of developing projects. Back in 1975, King identified six stages in the development of a major project:

1. triggering the search for an appropriate project
2. screening investment proposals, because it is impossible to conduct an extensive analysis on all possible projects and alternative version of projects
3. definition of the project alternatives
4. evaluation of the alternatives
5. transmission of project information
6. making the decision

He then pointed out that the financial-investment literature concentrated exclusively on stage 4, and with a few exceptions this is still the situation today. Some will want to argue that King is simplifying reality is assuming a single decision-taking point at the end of the project and a neat sequential series of steps, but his message about the limited scope of finance theory is just as important now as it was in 1975.

While few finance theorists have addressed stages other than stage 4, other disciplines have been active in researching what may be appropriate in other stages. In particular, writers in the fields of corporate strategy and industrial economics have made considerable progress in areas which contribute to the types of analysis needed in stages 1-3, and others with a more behavioural perspective to their research have advanced understanding of the organizational and human processes by which these stages are acted out in companies. There have not yet, however, been any far-reaching attempts to tie together the insights of the different disciplines and perspectives. Some limited progress has been made relatively recently in linking up the analysis of corporate strategy and some of the behavioural insights of strategy formulation and implementation, but not much has yet been done to tie that in with financial management.

In case the reader should think that this small book is about to offer the solution to this problem, let it be stated immediately that a complete integration of all these different disciplinary approaches to the investment decision will probably take a considerable time and much research effort by a range of researchers. Moreover, the volume of literature in these other areas is such that only an outline can be presented here. What will be attempted in the remainder of this book is to provide, for accountants and financial-management students, an appreciation of developments in these other fields, together with discussion of some issues which relate to the problem of trying to integrate these different disciplinary views. Consequently, it is recognized that what is offered can only be a highly personal and limited selection of developments in disciplines other than financial management, with a few isolated ideas on linkages between them. It is hoped, nevertheless, that this will encourage students of accounting and finance to be bold in pursuing connections between their own subject and others involved in the study of management.

In this chapter we shall look at corporate resource allocation from the point of view of corporate strategy and industrial economics, summarizing their major contributions in this area over recent years. The discussion will be confined to rational-deductive strategic and economic analysis.

Strategic portfolio analysis

During the 1960s most of the Western world enjoyed steady economic growth and it became increasingly evident that companies' main accounting apparatus provided an inadequate basis for thinking ahead. It was recognized that there was a need for longer-term planning. This generally resulted in processes by which companies tried.

- to identify long-run broad objectives
- to identify gaps between objectives and likely achievement under current policies
- to formulate strategy to achieve objectives
- to select investments to achieve the strategic goals
- to draw up long-term plans
- to ensure that the shorter-term budgets and plans were consistent with where the company wanted to go in the longer run.

While the process did not necessarily proceed without negotiation and iteration between stages, the planning literature emphasized the general logic of the need to integrate short-term budgets with long-term planning.

With the economic recession of 1970-1, corporate managers came to realize that the form of long-term planning that they were conducting, based often on relatively straightforward projections of past growth, did not ensure corporate success. In fact, many corporate planning departments were significantly reduced in size or even abandoned around this time. Those companies that persevered with longer-term planning realized that a mechanism was needed to manage changing emphases in their multiple business interests. It was recognized more clearly than before that most large companies actually held a portfolio of business, and that long-term growth, or indeed survival, might depend more on managing that portfolio rather than assuming continued growth on all fronts. In 1970 the Boston Consulting Group published its product-portfolio matrix, which had and still has, though now through derivatives of that early model, a major influence on strategic thinking in many companies.

The origins of the BGC matrix lie before the 1970-71 recession. That consulting group came to realize earlier than others how important market share was to corporate profitability. This was due not only to economies of scale but also to what came to be known as the experience curve. The experience curve itself was developed from the concept of the learning curve, which had been used for many years in industries where it was observed that labour time fell as the workforce accumulated experience in producing more of a particular type of unit. The BGC accumulated evidence that costs of all factor inputs could be reduced with an accumulation of experience if companies were conscious of the possibility and managed to make savings in labour, develop standardize products, improve equipment and processes, and so on.

The BGC then coupled the importance of market share with the rate of growth in the market to produce a growth-share matrix upon which all a corporate group's main product groups would be plotted. Each product group would be represented as a circle on the portfolio grid, where the size of each circle relative to those for other product groups indicated the proportion of group profits earned by that product group. The growth axis was said to approximate the product life-cycle, with the rate of growth slowing down as the product market entered a more mature state.

The BGC divided its matrix into four quadrants and gave each quadrant a name to signify how the products in it should be treated. BGC also argued that a company with a balanced portfolio of products would use cash flows generated from the cash cows to invest in selected problem children, which would be built up to become the stars of the future. The current stars are generators of profits which may need investment to sustain their position. A star may or may not be able to generate its own cash to provide for its own investment. It was also pointed out that nothing in this picture is static. Stars will eventually become cash cows as they reach maturity. Cash cows will be deprived of any further major investment. Dogs are those cows which have, further deteriorated such that they provide no cash throw-off, due to the effect of a small market share in a very mature market. Companies were advised to get out of dogs as soon as possible.

The BGC matrix, with its implications of a rigid policy for each product quadrant, has been much criticized. For the moment it suffices to say that the BGC-matrix approach was a critical step in emphasizing the need for a balanced portfolio of products within a corporate group in order to sustain longer-run success, and the dynamic nature of managing large corporations. The BGC approach provided the basis for further developments. Various derivatives of the BGC matrix have been developed both by other consultancy firms and by large companies such as Shell, but a description of just one of these will suffice.

The fundamental logic of that matrix is essentially the same as that developed by BGC: namely, that corporate groups can be divided up into sub-categories such that appropriate expansion, hold or contraction policies can be identified for each sub-category. The matrix merely uses a 3 x 3 system of classification, rather than BGC's 2 x 2, to split out the three different policy categories more clearly.

At this time the idea of simply dividing up the group into product groups was also broadened. The relevant units of the matrix came to be called strategic business units. An SBU was taken to be any subsidiary business interest of the group which could be said to be largely separable and could be treated as having a commercial life of its own. An SBU might, therefore, be a product group, a geographical region, a customer group or whatever form of classification seemed appropriate. It was critical, however, that existing organizational units, i.e. corporate divisions, should not automatically be considered the appropriate SBU units. Corporate divisions can incorporate more than one or, indeed, less than one separate economic entity. Divisions may have been formed for administrative or historical reasons, which do not necessarily produce organizational units which are identical with SBUs. This is an absolutely fundamental point. If SBUs with largely separate commercial lives cannot be identified, or are misidentified, the first basic requirement of this type of analysis is not analysis is not met and there is little point continuing with the technique. The point will be taken up again later within an evaluation of these matrix methods.

The McKinsey-GE matrix also recognizes that in many business investment decisions cannot be made simply upon information about market growth and the current share held. Consequently, it redefined the axes as follows. 'Market growth' was replaced by Industry attractiveness - a term that in practice was used loosely, to refer to the attractiveness of being in that area of activity in which the SBU operated. Also 'Market share' was replaced by Competitive strengths, i.e. competitive strengths within the SBU's area of activity. For good measure, McKinsey also decided to exchange the axes.

With these redefined axes. McKinsy concluded that investments should be made in attractive industries where a group was in a strong competitive position and not in less attractive industries, especially where the group's competitive position was weak. It was recognized also that selective investments might be made in unattractive industries if the SBU was the dominant operator in that industry, and similarly where attractiveness was high and the SBU's position weak.

It is at once apparent that the McKinsey-GE matrix has much less definite measurements for its axes. Indeed, I have found that students and businessmen who are using this technique for the first time tend to get confused between the two axes. It is very easy when analysing industry attractiveness to argue that the industry is attractive because the company holds a patent or some other competitive advantage. That is obviously confusing the two axes. A useful piece of advice to avoid this is to tell users that they should be trying to decide how attractive the industry is for some SBU *that is strong in that industry*. Moreover, attractiveness must be defined in terms of looking ahead at the likely state of the industry over the usual sort of investment time horizon for that industry.

In comparison with the BGC matrix, the McKinsey-GE matrix seems at first to be less explicit about building some 'problem children' into 'stars' and identifying 'cash cows' and 'dogs', but the implications are present. The McKinsey-GE model does, however, seem inconsistent with the BGC matrix in two respects, and these seem to have been largely overlooked in the literature.

The first point of inconsistency concerns the investment policy indicated in the top left-hand corner of the grid. BGC does not say 'invest and grow' here, but implies that investment should be made in so far as it is needed to maintain a favorable position; BGC seems to be ambivalent here about the need to invest to increase market share. In contrast, McKinsey says categorically, invest where the market is attractive and where company is strong. Also, BGC is far more explicit about the need to build certain 'problem children' into 'stars', and appears to advocate investment principally in the top right quadrant, in order to increase market in those SBUs where investment can be a vehicle for doing that. The BGC position seems more defensible than McKinsey's.

If the McKinsey-GE matrix is to be similarly interpreted as a guide to the movement of the group's interested through time, one must assume that a substantial amount of investment must take place in the bottom left-hand corner of the grid in order to build future 'stars'. Of course, this conclusion depends of how one interprets the 'Competitive strengths' axis. I prefer to evaluate *current* competitive strength and plot that on the grid. This then forces a consideration of whether investment can than improve the SBU's competitive stance or not. If it can, this implies the possibility of moving the SBU up the vertical axis. If, however, the vertical axis is defined as *attainable* competitive strength, then one expect most investment to take place in the top left corner. This stresses, once more, the need to be extremely careful with the basic definitions used in this apparently simple form of analysis, and to ensure that one's policy deductions are consistent with one's definitions and assumptions. To repeat, however, the interpretation of competitive strength as *current* strength is preferable, because it focuses the dynamic management of the group portfolio on the grid itself, rather than leaving it as an inference of the underlying analysis.

The preference for defining competitive strength as current strength also arises out of the recognition that, if attainable status is used, there will be no clear separation on the matrix of established stars from potential stars, and this seems critical for distinguishing between two types of investment: major investment for the future and sufficient investment to maintain a market position.

The second area of inconsistency between the two types of matrix concerns another aspect of the way they relate to the product life-cycle. The BGC literature shows that the growth rate varies from 0 to 20 percent and above. There is no indication that the BGC matrix includes the negative growth element of the product life-cycles. In contrast, McKinsey claims that its matrix covers the complete life-cycle. The McKinsey position seems more defensible this time, with the negative growth being confined to the dog's quarters.

The McKinsey matrix seems to have more general scope for devising investment and general financial-management policy. But where industries are dominated by the market-share/experience-curve effects, the logic underlying the BGC model can be a useful aid to thinking about the policy of SBUs *in those particular industries*. It is doubtful that the BGC matrix is very useful for *total* portfolio management in many multi-business groups, because, even if the group is involved in SBUs whose business is dominated by the experience-curve effect, it is likely that some its SBUs will not be and hence that they cannot be reliably analysed within just the BGC context.

However, one must not use the McKinsey grid in a deterministic way and infer that most investment must take place in 'stars'. One must distinguish between where the *bulk* of corporate investment must be placed and the location of SBUs on the matrix. The grids states nothing about the degree to which investment is necessary to retain star position or sufficient to build competitive advantage. On the contrary, with intelligent and informed use, it can be a powerful tool for aiding judgment on investment and related financial-management matters. Many companies and consultants have used the approach, and those using it will generally be inteliigent people who are not going to make naive errors through too literal an interpretation of a simple box diagram. It would seem, therefore, that there is considerable benefit to be obtained from the use of portfolio matrices, even if this view is not now so widely held in corporate-strategy literature. The reader is therefore asked to absorb the various arguments for and against portfolio matrices throughout this chapter, but to reserve judgement on the issue until later.

The McKinsey approach to this problem was to avoid oversimplified numerical indices. In McKinsey, General Electric's Vice President in charge of corporate strategy listed two sets of criteria used in his company for determining the location of each SBU on each axis. These were as follows.

Industry attractiveness	*Competitive strength*
Size	Size
Market growth, pricing	Growth
Market diversity	Share

Competitive structure	Position
Industry profitability	Profitability
Technical role	Margins
Social	Technology position
Environmental	Strengths/weaknesses
Legal	Image
Human	Pollution
	People

Allen, the Vice President, stated that classifications as high, medium or low were then made with respect to each axis on the basis of collective judgment by corporate management. Clearly management had to decide

1. what would count as high, medium or low with respect to each criterion, and
2. what weight of importance to attach to each criterion to arrive at an overall assessment for each axis.

industry attractiveness and competitive strengths

The emphasis was on judgement and discussion rather than precise measurement, but Allen said, 'It is surprising how little disagreement there is in positioning of our business on this matrix each year. 'He also stressed that, as the environment changed, the emphasis was shifted to different factors, and that the approach was used to reallocate major investment resource amongst competing needs.

One cannot, of course, say from this description how rigorously each SBU was evaluated, or how well devised the strategies to move SBUs around the matrix were. More recent work by porter has shown, however, that, from a knowledge of industrial economics, it is possible to develop a rigorous basis for solving both of these problems. In comparison with Porter's work, the lists of factors given by General Electric back in the 1970s now seem little more than a tentative beginning at an appropriate form of analysis.

In his 1980 study, Porter argues that the first thing for a firm to understand is the structure of the industry or market in which it operates. It is that structure which determines longer-run profitability. Moreover, industrial structure is not something which can be resolved merely by general debate over a general checklist of factors. There are five main factors which determine the structure of any industry. Three of these are based upon the input-output relationships affecting the production of goods or services in the industry: factors affecting inputs, their conversion into outputs, and saleability. The other two factors are the degree to which it is easy to enter the industry or market, and the degree to which there are substitutes for the products. These five factors can in turn be broken down into a number of subsidiary aspects to produce a specific number of questions to be answered in identifying the likely longer-run attractiveness of the industry. This makes much better sense than the General Electric list, because it places projected profitability as the major element of industrial attractiveness, rather than simply listing it as one of several factors, and provides a sound theoretical basis for determining it.

Following the implications of the McKinsey matrix, Porter states that there is usually little that the firm can do in the short run to affect industry structure and hence attractiveness. It should focus upon understanding that structure in order to develop a competitive strategy. Porter points out, nevertheless, that industry structures do change over time, perhaps due to technological or other developments, and that the firm itself may, through its competitive strategy, change the structure-either inadvertently or not. In particular, a market leader's actions may significantly affect the industry structure. One must therefore develop strategies taking into account the way in which they, and rival responses to them, may change the industry structure and its related profitability. Hence, a dynamic consideration of portfolio analysis, as applied to major investment decisions with their relatively long time horizons, does not just mean moving SBUs up or down the portfolio grid by transferring resources between them. It means identifying, too, how actions on the competitive-strengths axis may feed into the industry-attractiveness axis, which may then create further movement of the SBUs and challenge the relevance of the competitive strategy first devised. There must be an iterative movement between effects of each of the two axis, and a set of matrices, each reflecting a stage of this process.

Despite the comprehensiveness and relative complexity of Porter's analysis, he concludes that, once one has arrived at an assessment of one's competitive strengths by considering how strong an SBU is in terms of the factors which are most important for the relevant industry, there are only three generic strategies open to any SBU to become more competitive. It must

1. aim to be the lowest-cost producer with, usually, a standard 'no-frills' but serviceable, or
2. differentiate its broad product range in some way so that it is not competing directly with lower-cost products, or
3. adopt a strategy of focusing upon a particular niche or segment of the market.

In fact Porter really offers just two possible competitive strategies which can be applied over either a broad range of products in an industry or just in a special niche.

Porter also feels that firms should not get 'stuck in the middle' between differentiation and striving for cost leadership. He does not recognize that it is possible to alternate between the two according to the stage of industry development, and Gilbert and Strebel illustrate how some companies do outpace others in the industry on both cost and quality. Moreover, there seems to be no reason why economic competition should take such a dichotomous form, with a clear separation between the low-cost producers and the differentiators. Phillips, Chang and Buzzell also showed that it was quite possible for there to be several different degrees of differentiation. The main requirement is for each degree of differentiation to be clearly demarcated from others in the eyes of buyers and for each firm to be the lowest-cost producer within each category. One only has to consider the markets for restaurant meals, motor cars and clothes to realize that there are more than two successful cost-quality mixes available in a number of industries. Moreover, Miller and Friesen have tested Porter's position on this point and concluded that differentiators do also employ cost-leadership strategies and that cost leaders do employ differentiation policies. They emphasize, however, that their results relate to the consumer-durable industries, where marketing, branding and economies of scale go hand in hand. In capital-goods industries where knowledgeable buyers are more informed about the technical attributes of different products, Porter's argument about the need to avoid getting 'stuck in the middle' may be more sustainable. This might explain the Gilbert and Strebel finding on IBM and the personal computer market. Perhaps that was just a case where, in the early stages of the life-cycle, corporate managers acted more like private consumers than industrial purchasers of large-scale equipment.

One may also attack Porter's cost-differentiation dichotomy in terms of the logical use of language. He seems to be saying that the product must be seen to be either cheaper or different if people are to buy it. But being different can be due to a whole range of factors. Hill sets great store on identifying relevant order-winning criteria from a set including price, product quality, product reliability, and other factors. He also distinguishes clearly between criteria which qualify a firm's products to be considered and those which actually win the order. From this viewpoint, cost simply becomes one of many ways in which the product may be seen to be different from others. The simple two-way split between cost and differentiation disappears. That does not, however, detract from the value of separating out the notion of cost leadership from differentiation *conceptually* in order to work out the implications for measurement and control.

All this does not, however, detract at all from Porter's basic argument about the underlying analysis needed to identify industry attractiveness, competitive strengths and competitive strategies. Moreover, he shows clearly how strategies can be grouped in terms of broad emphasis into a few types according to whether the industry is in the emergent, mature or declining phase of its life-cycle.

Porter also shows how identifying the precise requirements of a strategy for each SBU require a little more thought that just a broad consideration of that SBU's position in relation to its industry structure. In his 1985 study he de develops the notion of a value chain from earlier similar notions of complete business systems discussed and used by both McKinsey and IBM. A value chain is simply an analysis of the totality of activities associated with adding value to some basic commodity on order to provide end consumption. An SBU should then look at all elements of the chain that it is involved in order to see exactly how it already adds value and might add value in future. This entails examining the SBU's competitive position on each of the dimensions that are shown by the industry structure analysis to be critical to longer-run profitability.

Porter also points out the importance of defining the SBU in terms of the complete network of a value chain within a corporate group irrespective of what that includes in terms of operations in different divisions. This reinforces the statement made earlier about the need to define SBUs very carefully.

Finally, attention needs to be drawn to the possible transient nature of competitive advantage. Even a dominant firm will face rivals seeking to find a window of opportunity to chip away at the dominant position. Competitive strategies therefore need regular review and modification within the realistic rate of change defined by the nature of the industry.

Porter has undoubtedly had a considerable impact upon corporate strategic thinking, and in this brief discussion it has been possible to present only the barest outlines of his ideas developed in two sizable books. Some reference to his views will, however, be inevitable in an attempt to provide an evaluation of the portfolio-matrix approach and concepts associated with it.

portfolio-grid approach

In the first, reports of empirical data are reviewed to see to what extent statistical data on corporate performance support the broad policy guidelines suggested by the BGC and McKinsey-GE matrices. In the second part, some key literature which has challenged the conceptual foundations of these matrices will be examined.

Empirical findings from the PIMS studies

'PIMS' stands for 'Profit Impact of Market Strategy'. It is a large-scale data collection and analysis exercise begun back in the early 1960s by the General Electric Company. Its broad aims were to analyse large American companies in order to discover differences in return on investment, to establish par values for ROI for different industries and their segments, and to attempt to explain variations in ROI across companies and their subsidiary business units by reference to strategic factors. For example, market attractiveness was to be captured by factors such as long-run and short-run growth rates and the stage of the product life-cycle, whereas competitive strength was to be assessed by market share relative product quality and breadth of product line, relative costs, and so on. The PIMS exercise was subsequently taken over by Harvard University and by the mid-1980s a data base had been established including about 250 companies which have provided information on about 3,000 SBUs. More extensive reviews of the results of tests on this data base can be found in McNamee, Abell and Hammond, and Buzzell and Gale. The present discussion will highlight just one or two main conclusions which are of relevance to the main lines of argument in this book.

A major conclusion from cross-sectional studies based on PIMS is that ROI increases significantly as market share increases. ROI as a percentage is in the low teens for market share below 30 per cent and up to the mid to high thirties for market shares above 80 per cent. The PIMS study explains this as due to economies of scale, experience effects and bargaining power. This appears to provide strong support for one of the main planks of the BGC model. It is important, however, to consider this question carefully. The study merely shows a positive relationship between market share and ROI and this is not necessarily a causal connection. A later study by Jacobsen and Aaker examines this proposition and runs regressions including ROI from earlier periods as lagged independent variables as surrogates for other factors which could be giving rise to the positive association between market share and ROI. They conclude that the effect of market share upon ROI is much less than earlier studies showed and that, broadly, a 1 per cent increase in market share led to a 0.1 per cent increase in ROI rather than the 0.5 per cent earlier supposed. Consequently, they state that much of the association between ROI and market share reported earlier was spurious.

Buzzell and Gale contest the Jacobson and Aaker view by arguing that they, in effect, have related the change in ROI to the level of market share. Moreover, Buzzell and Gale argue that, as larger-share businesses, do not continuously increase their ROI differential over small-share businesses, one would expect a zero correlation between the *change* in ROI and market share, which is broadly what Jacobson and Aaker found. Hence, the latter under-estimate the effect of market share on the level of ROI. Buzzell and Gale then regress ROI on both market share and relative quality of product and find a 4.7 per cent ROI differential per ten points of market share. They stress, however, that this is just an overall industry average and that, as market share accounts for only about 14 percent of the dispersion of ROI among businesses, other factors need to be considered. One of these factors is investment intensity.

The next major conclusion of relevance to this discussion is the PIMS finding that investment intensity, measured by investment divided by sales, is negatively correlated with ROI. For an investment-intensity ratio of below 35 per cent, it seems that one gets an ROI above 30 per cent, whereas, when investment intensity is above 70 per cent. ROI falls to about 10 per cent. A not-surprising result is that low market share coupled with high capital intensity spells disaster. The important question, however, is why high capital intensity is associated with lower ROI even when market share is high. A range of possible reasons has been put forward, stressing that it is important to get the right degree of capital intensity for the business and that many business may simply be misled by current profitability and push investment too far. This may have some truth, but seems unsatisfactory as a complete explanation. Part of the reason for getting such a result could well be the cross-sectional nature of the analysis. An SBU with high capital intensity could well be at an early stage of its product life-cycle, when one would expect it to be building up its investment relative to sales and also experiencing low profitability as it fights to establish itself in the market. At a more mature stage, the increase in sales volume should have resulted in a decline in investment intensity, while profit and ROI will increase if the investment is successful. This explanation would be quite consistent with a cross-sectional picture in which capital intensity is inversely related to ROI even when market share is high. It is virtually an obvious consequence of the accounting formulation used with investment as both the numerator of investment intensity and denominator of ROI, while profit in the numerator of ROI is possibly a fairly stable proportion of sales in the denominator of investment intensity. It would therefore be incredibly native to conclude from the PIMS data that it is erroneous for companies to increase capital intensity—when their day to come. This view is enforced when one remembers that investment lead times—that is, the period between basic investment in assets and the time when the product shows up as profitable in the company accounts—can be quite long. As we have already seen, it can take several years for a product to come on stream, let alone break even in reported accounts; seven or more years is possible in some industries.

The PIMS data still give some cause for puzzlement over the question of investment intensity, however, because Buzzell and Gale show that five-year averages of ROI are highly positively related to increases in the long-term value of the business, both being closely and positively associated with initial competitive position. One might infer from this that investment intensity is therefore also negatively correlated with increases in the value of the business over a five-year period. This would be more worrying. One explanation might be that five years is still not a long enough lead time. On the other hand, the explanation might lie in the study by Wagner, who stresses that researchers have usually focused upon PIMS data for an average four-year period. In contrast, he selected those companies that had data in the PIMS system for at least seven and up to thirteen years; this gave him data on 460 US companies. Then, studying changes over time, he set out to test the main conclusions derived from cross-sectional studies. His results are of considerable interest.

He found first that ROI was remarkably stable over time at the *company level,* but that it showed considerable variation over time for *individual business.* Moreover, the rich businesses do not get richer and the poor do not get poorer. In fact, the reverse is true. Those with high ROI tend to experience falls in ROI and those with low ROI tend to have increases, taken across the whole population. Ideally one needs to subdivide the original low-ROI business into those at the beginning of their life-cycle and those at the end, because one would expect ROI to increase in the former but to fall in the latter. Indeed, Wagner found that the position in the life-cycle explained over half the variation in ROI.

Wagner's findings on investment intensity also bring some economic sense to the question raised above. He states that businesses with the highest investment intensity have the greatest chance of improving ROI when one takes the longer run into account. He says that his data showed that those businesses with low investment intensity did indeed start off with high ROI, as the earlier cross-sectional studies discovered, but that this often led managers to over-invest. In contrast, the managers of the longer-run winners did not over-invest, but were in the upswing of the business cycle facing markets with rapid growth. While his explanations do not seem clearly to separate older arguments about managers under-or over-investing from the impact of the business-cycle stage itself, it does seem clear that investment at the right time, i.e. early in the product life-cycle, does lead to increased ROI if management is able to establish its product in the market place and control costs. Indeed, it would be contrary to basic economic laws if this were not so. Nevertheless, given the earlier findings on investment intensity, this matter did need clarification.

It is interesting that Wagner's findings also seem to support Porter. Wagner concludes that managers should strive to increase market share, lower relative costs and/or achieve high product quality, and that any investment activity must be directed at atleast one of these aims if it is to prove successful. He also states that his analysis showed that it is not easy to increase market share through time. The few businesses that do manage to achieve this profit handsomely, but most do not achieve it once the market is established.

So, what can be concluded from the PIMS data base about the relationships implied in the portfolio matrices? First, that there may be a lot more to the relationship between growth and market share established by BGC than has been accepted of late. High market growth, if taken to be an indicator of an early stage in a life-cycle, coupled with high market share should lead to high ROI if the appropriate investment is undertaken. The key words are, however, 'appropriate investment'. One needs a Porter-style analysis to discover exactly what type of investment and competitive strategy is needed to achieve or maintain market share or competitive position; one cannot just assume that any type of investment in capacity in areas of high market share will lead to future success. Nevertheless, given managerial competence in performing and acting upon that analysis, one would expect to find largest positive NPV projects in the regions of the BGC or McKinsey matrix that relate to high growth and high market share. Normally this would be in the region of the matrix indicating early phases of a life-cycle, where competitive advantage can be built up by investment. From Wagner's results we would conclude, however, that building competitive position or market share is really successfully achieved by relatively few businesses. A rigorous porter-style analysis seems to be a more important ingredient in the decision inputs. Buzzell and Gale conclude from the PIMS data that product and service quality is the most significant factor for the longer-run success of a business. The interpretation of quality is variable, however, by product and service and context. It is the economic analysis which Porter demands that determines what quality, product and service mean in each case. It is that form of analysis which indicates what Hill's order-winning criteria are in specific situations.

Conceptual pitfalls of portfolio analysis

While the limited time-series of PIMS to date seems to indicate some broad credibility for the implications of portfolio grids, other criticisms of the approach challenge its underlying assumptions on a conceptual basis. There are a number of different arguments, which will now be summarized.

Some argue that high returns are possible in declining industries and that this is inconsistent with the harvest/divest strategies indicated in the BGC and McKinsy-GE matrices. Indeed, Buzzelled and Gale also point this out. First, it needs to be made clear that high returns now must be distinguished from high returns in the *long run.* In a declining market one might well expect a business that had earlier established a dominant share position in the short run and increase prices and profits, because rivals are unlikely to come into the market or compete strongly for market share. Also, it might be able to increase revenues as rivals drop out of the market. This does not mean, however, that one should invest in that declining industry beyond the level justified by short-run returns. Declining markets are therefore not likely to be receivers of major investment even if *current* returns are high.

In response to this argument it may be observed that even the BGC itself, in a series of articles about strategic investment in the *Financial Times,* November 1981, points out that there can still be profitable niches in declining markets and that 'dogs' may be able to bite back by identifying new possibilities in their industries. That fact is taken into account in a proper definition of an SBU. A significant new niche is tantamount to a new SBU and should be recognized as such and brought into the matrix in its proper place. Labelling a particular SBU as a 'dog' should be seen as a challenge to the people involved with it to search out and propose new SBUs and not just a signal to give up and die. With appropriate management attitudes, the element of the group labelled 'dog' can be encouraged to seek self-renewal, i.e. as an *organizational entity,* not as a particular product line. This would seem to be an obvious recognition that nothing lasts ahead to the need for renewal. In essence, what the portfolio matrix says is, let's have the various business elements at their different stages of growth explicitly on view in the matrix and not lost from view within organizational units. The matrix does not pretend to show organizational units *within which* there may be mixture of growing, mature and declining sub-elements.

It is also quite possible for a 'dog' to find a way of extending its life in a previously unanticipated way. All that says is that this particular product line is not following a smooth transition from youth to middle age and then old age, but that it has managed to find some rejuvenation late in life. In that case it should no longer be defined as a 'dog'. It is a nonsense to say that an SBU is a 'dog' but that it should not be treated as a 'dog' because it is not really a 'dog' at all. Rejuvenation does not invalidate portfolio analysis if the axes are properly formulated and researched. The linking of the life-cycle to the portfolio matrices is a general relationship that is expected to hold. Perhaps it is better to say that it is a *prima facie* relationship which can be used for prescriptive advice to hold back investment *unless* the 'dog' management can establish an exceptional case. The model can handle exceptions. On the other hand, much of this confusion may come from loosely identifying SBUs as industries, rather than products or products groups. While there is some justification for arguing that industries never mature, there is also every justification for arguing that products often do have life-cycles short enough to make sense of this type of analysis.

Another argument sometimes put forward is that the model assumes a capital-rationing situation. Obviously, if there is not such a situation, the company should invest in every positive-NPY product available to it, subject to having the capacity to manage investment on that scale. But the portfolio-matrix approach does not offend that principle. It just says that some parts of the business will throw off cash surpluses, that it may well not be worth investing further in those businesses, and that, in that case, the funds can be used to further investment elsewhere. If the corporate group wishes to raise further funds from external sources or use some of the funds for dividends or to repurchase shares, there is nothing in portfolio-grid analysis to stop it. The portfolio approach does not need to assume that investment has to equal that achievable with internally generated funds, although, of course, most UK and US companies do rely extensively on retained earnings to supply funds for investment.

Others have argued that the axes misleading because they focus on absolute profitability rather than that earnable on marginal investment. Once more, however, that can be handled by a proper definition of the axes; obviously it is future profitability of incremental investment that should go into assessment of SBU attractiveness. If companies do not recognize that they are applying the model incorrectly; it is not the model which is at fault.

Similarly, others have argued that the matrices make little allowance for risk and in their early application this was true, but, if one undertakes a Porter-type analysis to give a solid foundation to industry attractiveness and competitive strengths and the derivation of the appropriate strategies, that will take into account a risk assessment. In fact, by focusing upon the specific factors within the value chain, managers will gain a much better appreciation of the specific risks and uncertainties associated with their strategies than some less well defined, hit-or-miss sensitivity analysis. Derkinderen and Crum raise a rather different point about risk. They stress the need for an organization to build financial resilience, i.e. focus on the necessary financial structure and other factors needed to help it live through adverse times. This may not be covered in the initial simple descriptions of the portfolio grids, but one would expect the underlying risk analysis to include such matters. Derkinderen and Crum do well to remind us of this, but it does not really invalidate the portfolio-grid approach. This argument applies equally to Wensley. He argues that portfolio matrices fail to indicate the considerable risks faced in diversification. On the face of it this is true, but that simply means that there should be a thorough assessment of competitive strengths to underpin the matrix.

A wide range of comments have also been made about the simplistic nature of the grids as specifiers of where investment should be placed. While such criticism was perfectly correct in relation to the early portfolio-grid literature, it should now be clear that, when properly supported by rigorous analyses of industry structure and the value chain, portfolio analysis survives as a valid concept. Porter seems to agree with this view, but says that the extra value obtained from putting the results of the sorts of analyses that he recommends into the matrix form is marginal compared to the value derived from the underlying analysis itself.

All the arguments considered so far against the use of portfolio-grid analysis of the McKinsey-GE type are, in my view, better seen as warnings about simplistic use of the technique rather than as indicating fundamental flaws in it. Intelligent application of the technique can take these warnings into account and still derive considerable benefit from it. We have still, however, to consider one much more fundamental attack upon the use of a McKinsey-GE type analysis.

A range of critics have emphasized that the validity of the portfolio-matrix approach depends fundamentally on the existence of SBUs which have little or no interdependence in a corporate group's portfolio. Porter, in particular, argues that a horizontal strategy affecting a number of different SBUs must be a necessity for a diversified firm, since there is no economic reason for SBUs with distinct lives of their own to be combined into a corporate group. In fact, such separable SBUs with no possibilities of synergy with other SBUs are, he says, likely to be prime candidates for divestment when a good opportunity arises.

While Porter is obviously right to argue that there is no economic reason for *completely* separable SBUs to be combined, it does not follow that they would function any becoming completely independent. There is no economic reason why they should be divested unless it can be shown that they would have synergistic benefits from being combined with SBUs of a different type from those possessed by the groups with non-related SBUs came to be formed in the first place. They may have been formed in the interests of diversification or for political reasons, for example. Alternatively, the corporate management might simply have wanted to acquire them. There is no reason why a professor of history, say, should not also manage a family business if he has the time and energy. Yet the two activities have no obvious relationship. Indeed, the professor's rationale may be that he wishes to be involved in two completely different activities. Similarly, shareholders who rank the capacities of their company management very highly may support expansion on the basis that they can generate larger profits even without synergistic advantages. Hence, corporate groups can continue to exist with separable SBUs and will not inevitably be broken up. At least, therefore, *for such groups*, the portfolio matrices and their separable SBUs are potentially relevant concepts.

A more important question, however, is whether portfolio matrices can be sensibly applied only to such conglomerates. At face value the answer might seem to be 'yes'. Naylor, for example, notes that even General Electric itself ran into difficulties with its portfolio-grid analysis because of the existence of interdependencies. In fact, by 1988 General Electric had reorganized into fewer key business in order to overcome this problem, and in so doing had become more like a conglomerate.

There are basically only two types of interdependencies between SBUs. In Porter's terminology they are tangible and intangible interdependencies. Tangible links are where SBUs have buyers, distribution channels, technology or competitors in common. Naylor also gives an example of a tangible link between SBUs when he cites the interdependence of the multiple car lines at General Motors, where a change in the demand for one line may well be reflected in another. Intangible connections between SBUs are defined as the transference of management know-how. There may be no direct collaboration between upon. For example, beer and cigarettes may both be purchased as recreational products.

Porter first identifies the problem that will be encountered if one proceeds with portfolio planning without explicit management of these interdependencies. SBUs will value these interdependencies differently and this will lead to inconsistencies in the behaviour of linked SBUs. Next, he says, SBUs may well form alliances outside the corporate group to obtain the same benefits as could be obtained by internal linkages while retaining more control over their situation. It is difficult to see why external links should inevitably give rise to greater control over one's actions. Of course, you may prefer to choose outside alliances rather than restrict yourself to the family, but in times of hardship the family may be more dependable. At such times it may be easier to achieve flexibility in a contractual relationship with another SBU in the same corporate group, but there is something in what Porter says. There will be a tendency for joint customers to be ignored and for know-how transfer to be lost.

Porter then develops the argument that the presence of interrelationships between SBUs implies that strategies must be broader than simply build, hold or divest. But must they? Is it not simply the case that the underlying analysis becomes more complex because, before knowing whether it is beneficial to build or hold or divest, it is necessary to know the effects beyond the immediate SBU in question? Surely, no other fundamental policies are possible.

If the interdependencies do not involve all SBUs in a corporate group, it might be possible to form largely separable business clusters and form the portfolio-grid analysis in terms of those rather than smaller SBUs. There is a suggestion of this in both Porter and Chakravarthy, who talks in terms of business families. This may indeed be one possible solution, but it has the disadvantage that the need for analysis of the industry structure and competitive strengths of each of the smaller SBUs may be ignored. After all, when one recognizes the different types of interrelationships which can exist, the linkages may be between SBUs in quite different industries.

So severe does Naylore believe this question of interdependency to be that he devotes the whole of his 1986 study to an attempt to develop an alternative to the portfolio matrix. This alternative, which he calls the strategy matrix, essentially requires top-level corporate management to formulate six to eight key strategies which go across the various subsidiary businesses. Each strategy will be given its own management team, which will be expected to work out all the effects over the whole company, including estimates of resource requirements for each subsidiary business. Naylor says it is important that these corporate-wide strategies should be worked out before the individual businesses commence their planning. While one can see that a certain number of strategies might be conceived at corporate level before reference to the individual businesses, in general it is very difficult to see how this can be done at corporate headquarters unless the central authority has a careful analysis of the attractiveness and competitive strengths of the major SBUs. The main point of the Porter analysis was to establish that form of information was fundamental to any strategic analysis. At the very least, therefore, there must be some preliminary analysis at SBU level, even if that ignores the interdependencies, and this must then be transmitted to corporate level before the central teams can carry out their cross-SBU analyses of the key corporate-level strategies. In other words, some iterative process between SBUs and corporate headquarters will probably be necessary and this may prove to be the key to solving this problem. It seems clear, however, that corporate groups may have many interdependencies between SBUs. When that occurs, the ability to plan resource allocation by looking at independent SBUs becomes impossible. Some overall 'optimization' process and global strategy become necessary. Whereas the wide range of earlier criticisms of the portfolio-grid approach could be countered, this form of criticism, which strikes at the heart of the construction of the matrices and their SBUs seems devastating.

Meanwhile, it can be noted that both academics and businessmen largely working outside the field of corporate finance have contributed significantly to the areas that King said needed addressing. Much of the work evaluated takes us a long way towards identifying mechanisms for triggering the need for investment, screening the proposals and defining them.

Corporate policies

The means by which desired objectives and goals are persued vary in generality from the most particularly, a course of action, through practices plans, procedures and programmes to the most general policies. A carefully selected policy sharpens the meaning of the strategy and guides specific decisions in a direction that supports the strategy. Policies can be regarded as guidelines which make the plan and the strategy work. Policies are rules of guidance which can incorporate all the relevant information available at the time of decision and hence they can provide maximum adaptability and flexibility. Policies, therefore, permit use of all the relevant information that is available at the time of decision. For this reasons they provide more flexibility than a particular course of action. Hence planing is concerned with course of action in the present and policies where course of action will be required in the future. Business policy thus refers to guidelines for decisions about the future of an on going enterprise. In a small single product firm there is very little need for policies in a formal sense. A few decisions which are taken do not involve complex variables and complex issues. The chief executive and his managers have clear understanding of the decision criteria. In a large organisation, however there are many complex issues to be considered in each functional area in the context of multiple decision variables e.g. in a large organisation in the marketing functional area. It is essential to have a rule for guidance for selecting distribution channel or to determine purchase quantity at a particular time in a given situation rather than specify, who will retail or a fixed quantity is always to be purchased. The policies are interrelated as guidelines for decisions at different levels in various segments of a business unit influence each other. Establishment of formal policies is, therefore, inescapable to provide for consistency in decisions and practicability of actions. Even after establishing policies it is necessary to forecast over the planning period the value of the variables that may be relevant to the use of policies.

Policies help in evaluating alternatives in selecting better alternative and in the implementation of the selected alternatives. But it will depend upon the understanding of the system being planned for. Thus business policy refers to decisions, which top managers take after evaluating various factors related to market, environment and the organisation itself. These are vital and strategic for the decisions which the middle and operating managers have to take for operational purpose. These decisions will guide the size of business, product-market position, attitude towards employees, process and technology and functions and responsibilities of different level of managers. Finally it guides the testing of the business. However there are two types of policies:

i. Policies concerned with operations, and

ii. Those concerned with changes in the system

These policies help management in resolving recurring problems at operation level and even a higher level. They did the process of management in: (i) Implementing a plan (ii) delegating duties and authority to subordinate (iii) making coordination easier (iv) developing consistency of action taken by different members of the firm and finally (v) clarifying role of each individual and department in achieving the corporate objective. Policies must be flexible. Policies are a living precepts which guide the organisation in a continuing and consistent pattern of behaviour :

In every organisation the management process is concerned with problems related to:

a. Marketing and Sales

b. Production & Purchase

c. Personnel and industrial Relations

d. Finance

Major Policy Issues In Business Enterprises

Sales

A. Products and Services

1. Diversification vs. Specialisation.
2. Product differentiation
3. Frequency of design change

B. Customers

1. Types of consumers
2. Location of consumers
3. Channels of distribution
4. Size of customers

C. Prices

1. Relation to competing products
2. Relation to costs
3. Prices of individual items
4. Quantity and trade discounts
5. Price Changes

Production & Purchasing

A. Extent of Vertical integration

B. Production Processes

1. Choice of technology
2. Division of labour and automation
3. size and dispersion of plants
4. Involvement in process research

C. Capacity and Facility Balance

1. Peak Vs. normal load
2. Backward taper of capacity
3. Provision for growth

D Maintenance and Replacement

E. Make or Buy Supplies and Services

F. Selection of Vendors

1. Number of vendors
2. Type of vendors

D. Sales Promotion
1. Sales appeal
2. Advertising
3. Personal Solicitation

G. Timing Production and Purchasing
1. Stock Vs. to-order
2. Size of inventory and orders
3. Stabilizing production
4. Anticipating price changes

Personnel

A. Selection
1. New employees
2. Promotion
3. Discharge

B. Training
1. Place in management
2. Specific purpose
3. Types of training
4. Short term creditors

C. Compensation
1. Amount of pay
2. Methods of payment

D. Arrangement for Work
1. Hours of work
2. Vacations
3. Working conditions

E. Employee Services
1. Social and Recreational
2. Protection from risks

F. Industrial Relations
1. Character of relation
2. Support of union
3. Scope of bargaining
4. Use of outside agencies

Finance

A. Use of Capital
1. Fixed asset investment
2. Uses of circulating capital
3. Mergers and acquisitions

B. Sources of Capital
1. Owners
2. Long term creditors
3. Financial structure

C. Protection of Capital
1. Reduction of hazards
2. Insurance
3. Hedging
4. Calculation of Profits

D. Distribution of Earnings
1. Plowing back earnings
2. Stable dividend rate
3. Adequacy of surplus

No single outline can include all policy questions. Any specific company will have problems peculiar to itself or its industry. Also there are many minor policies consideration which would have clustered up the broad picture we have been seeking. The approach to central management planning suggested by the outline of policies is useful because:

(i) almost every enterprise will face probably 90 per cent of the issues in some form, and

(ii) the sequence provides a logical flow of though about a company as a whole.

We need some structure for our thinking about general management problems, and this one has proven to be highly practical in many companies.

A danger in any pattern for analysis into parts and sub-parts is that in identifying each part we loss sight of their interrelationships Real decision problems do not stay in compartments that are helpful to ordinarily thinking. Seeing these mutual relationships, and developing a sense of relative importance, are vital to integrated understanding of the job of central management.

Sales Policy

One of the critical functional area, marketing and sales has received increasingly greater attention in the competitive business world since the early modern era. The old concept of marketing has been replaced by a new concept. The old concept focused on the firm's existing products or services and considered marketing to consist of selling and promotion to maximise sales at a profit. The new concept, in contrast, focuses on the firm's existing and potential customers and seeks to earn profit through customers satisfaction with an integrated marketing programme. Implementation of strategy hinges to a great deal on marketing policy providing guidelines for managerial decision-making and action to carry out the marketing functions in accordance with the chosen strategy.

Marketing decision variables

Before policies are formulated, it may be useful for management to identify and categorize. The decision variables may be classified in different ways. According to Laser and Kelly, marketing decision variables may be divided into three categories:

(i) Goods and service mix: It is concerned with all the ingredients which comprise the bundle of utilities that consumers purchase, including such items as the product per se, the package, price, branding, labelling warranties, and services accompanying the product:

(ii) Distribution mix: It consists of two major components, viz. a channels of distribution including all the middlemen and facilitating agencies involved in getting the goods and title to goods to consumers, and b. physical distribution concerned with transporting, warehousing, storing and handling goods :

(iii) Communication mix: This is concerned with all the persuasive and informational ingredients that are employed in communicating with the market place including personal selling, advertising, sales promotion, merchandising, and special aids.

More or less on the same lines, McCarthy has suggested 'Four Ps' as decision variables: Product, Physical Distribution, Promotion and Price. Another classification proposed by Ferfey is one in which two sets of variables combining the three sets given by Lazer and Kelly are: (1) Product, Packing, Brand, Price and Service - referred to as the offering, and (2) Methods and tools, such as distribution channels, personal selling, advertising sales promotion, and publicity.

Sales Policy Issues

In the marketing policy decisions each firm is naturally expected to use the set of decision variables best suited to its own strategy. But there are certain basic issues which are of common concern to most firms, and it is useful to consider the implications of those issues while formulating policies. The more important issues in marketing with respect to which guidelines need to be provided are:

1. Product related matters.
2. Customers to be served and channel of distribution.
3. Pricing of products/services
4. Sales promotion, and
5. Marketing mix

Product Policy

Product Line and Product Mix

A product line refers to a group of products that are closely related either because they satisfy a class of need, are used together, sold to the same customer groups, are marketed through the same type of outlets, or fall within given policy price ranges, e.g. Willman Razor & Willman Twin Blade. Product mix, on the other hand, refers to the related and unrelated composite products offered for sale by a firm. To illustrate, Godrej 290 litre refrigerators is a product item and Godrej refrigerators, typewriters, detergents and toilet soap, constitute its product mix. The depth of the product mix refers to the average number of items (varieties and grades) offered for sale by a firm within each product line. The width of the product mix refers to the number of different product.

The product mix of a firm may include items which in course of time are likely to suffer a decline in sales and may therefore be required to be replaced by either other items or newly designed ones. The concept of life cycle becomes useful in this context. Many branded products (durable and consumer goods) are known to have a typical pattern of development in terms of sales volume, which is known as the product life cycle.

It may be difficult to predict the length of the cycle and that of its stages governed by the rate of consumer acceptance of the product, the rate of technical change, and the ease of competitive entry. But consideration of the product life cycle brings home to management that products may have a limited life and that the earnings were likely to follow a predictable course through the life cycle. More than that, it may enable management to make necessary changes in its marketing problems during different stages of the product life cycle and thus emphasize one or more of the marketing elements, like price, advertising etc.

Diversification vs. Specialisation

A basic question relating to product policy in marketing is how many products a firm will include in its product mix and the number of varieties or grades that it will offer for sale in a product line. There are four points that need to be considered to decide the issue: (1) Offering a large variety of products. (2) Concentrating on a few terms (3) Offering a complete line, and (4) Customising products. Let us look into the implications of these options.

Offering a large variety. If the differential costs of additional items are low it may be desirable to offer a large variety of products in the same line with some differentiation of quality, price packaging, etc. Such a policy gives widest choice to the customers and may be welcome to salesman in view of the potential appeal of different varieties to particular customer groups leading to increased sale. But a wide diversity of products has cost implications. The sales volume for each item must justify the incremental costs of production and distribution. Besides, while a new item may be paying in the short run, it may not do so after some time. Thus, the policy could be to decide on a limit to the number of items, an existing item being dropped whenever a new item is proposed to be added unless, there is a strong reason to continue with all the items and adding a new one.

Concentrating on a few items. The policy of restricting the number of varieties and grades and concentrating on a few items has the obvious benefit of specialisation and deriving competitive advantage in pricing, unique services, etc. It may enable the company also to gain by way of concentrated attention to customer needs and satisfaction. But with such a policy the volume of sales cannot be enlarged beyond a certain limit, and thus it may not be suitable for a company that seeks to be the market leader.

Offering a complete product line. There are certain product markets in which customers may prefer to buy a complete line of grades and size from a single source of supply e.g. plumbing materials and sanitary fittings, electrical fittings (insulted cables, sockets, plugs, holders, etc.) hosiery goods, hospital equipments, office furniture and so on. Dealers and retailers often find it convenient to stock the whole line of such products to cater to their customer needs. It is also found economical to advertise the products by a single brand name if these are produced by the same manufacturer. Offering a complete line of product for sale may thus be a desirable policy for certain categories of goods.

Customising products. The customising policy refers to the practice of having a standard product and odd in a few options to the customers by way of sizes, colours, accessories, etc. made available only on additional payment. This policy is usually adopted in the case of automobiles, radio and television sets, typewriters, and similar goods. While it has the advantage of giving some choice to the customers, and enables the company to derive the benefits of specifications, the customising policy also poses problems of production scheduling and inventory in so far as customer demands for different sizes, colours, grades etc. may be difficult to predict in a dynamic situation.

The diversification relates to offering a number of products. The number of products are the product mix that a company offers for sale may be aimed at achieving three possible objectives: (1) Improving profitability (2) Securing stability in the face of sales variability, and (3) raising the growth rate of sales. Depending on the objective, the optimum product mix would be one which help in the achievement of objective. However, it may be difficult to determine the optimal product mix with a number of objectives to be served. It is generally easier to recognise the symptoms of sub-optimality than to state positively the characteristics of an optimal mix. A given product mix may be regarded as sub-optimal if any of the following conditions happens to prevail:

(a) Excell productive capacity on a chronic or seasonally recurring basis.

(b) Disproportionately high percentage of total profits from a few products;

(c) Insufficient product with different product lines to exploit sales force contacts efficiently, and

(d) Steadily declining sales or profits.

What type of products optimality of product mix needs a continuous review of the existing mix so as to add new products and eliminate old items Whenever necessary, it may be useful to classify the various items in the mix on the basis of the potential sales growth, profitability and market share. From the product-mix classification may be derived several benefits, indicating (a) whether the rate of product pruning is sufficient and items to be pruned are duly examined, (c) whether and to what extent sales growth, market share of profitability should be stressed for each product, and (d) how should resources be allocated to the products in the mix. Peter Drucker has suggested a six-fold classification of product mix based on the potential sales growth as follows.

(i) Tomorrow's breadwinners - new products or today's breadwinners modified;

(ii) Today's breadwinners - the innovations of yesterday;

(iii) Products capable of becoming net contributors if some-thing drastic is done p;

(iv) Yesterday's breadwinners - typical products with high volume, but badly fragmented into 'specials', small orders, and the like;

(v) The 'also runs' - typically the high hopes of yesterday that, while they did not work out well, nevertheless did not become outright failures;

(vi) The failures.

The static and dynamic aspects of he problems of product-mix optimisation have been defined by Kotler. The static product—mix optimisation problem is defined by him as follows: 'Given product possibilities, Choosen of them (when m n) such that profit is maximised subject to a given level of risk and other constraints'. The problem, he suggests, can be solved by mathematical programming, "the most important condition being the absence of strong demand and cost interactions among the various products being considered". The dynamic problem, according to Kotler," is the problem of timing deletions and additions in response to changing opportunities and resources so that the product-mix remains optimal through time" In this respect, a logical approach is stated to be the simulation f possible sequences and timing of planned product deletions and additions over some future time period.

Differertiation of Products

Product modification may be called for in a competitive market to differentiate and add to the distinctiveness of a product in relation to other similar products. How can a company make its products distinctive? In what respects should products be modified and differentiated? How often should a company introduce changes in product design? These are related issues in respect of which policies are required to be formulated.

In general differentiation f products may be possible in terms of quality, features, or style. The quality of a product may be said to have different connotations depending on the nature of the product, type of customers, and the nature of appeal suited to its sale. Thus quality may refer to durability (as in the ease of speciality goods like photographic camera, electrical gadgets, etc.) or purity (as in the case of pharmaceutical products), or appearance (as in the ease of pressure cookers, air-conditioners, etc.) and so on. Thus, if it is decided to emphasise quality of a product or quality improvement is required for a product to make it distinctive, the policy should be to stress the relevant characteristics suited to the particular product.

Special features of a product may enable its distinctiveness to be established in relation to competing products. Thus the differentiation of a product may be possible in terms of convenience of use, safety, efficiency, or versatility. Makers of pressure cookers often emphasise the safety devices built into the cooker. Electrical irons have been designed with devices to adjust the heat for different types of fabrics (cotton, woolen, silk etc.) Scooters are sought to be made more efficient in terms of fuel consumption, Computers are now being designed as bilingual or trilingual word processors so as to add to the versatility of such equipments in the Indian context. For the convenience of customers, commercial bank offices in residential areas have rescheduled working hours and days operating on Sunday and the morning extended evening hours. These are all instances of special features aimed at product or service differentiation. The main disadvantage of feature distinction is that it is highly imitable.

Style, which refers to the esthetic appeal of a product in contrast to its functional appeal, may be another basis of product differentiation. Salability of automobiles, TV sets, ready-made garments, footwear (shoes), furniture and similar products are known to be enhanced with new models or styles. Sometimes, package re-styling may also make for distinctiveness as in the case of processed fast food and household goods. The appeal of colourful pictures on the containers of confectionery products is well known. The advantage of style distinction is that each firm may achieve a unique market identity on that basis and thus carve out a stable market share. On the other hand, it may be difficult to predict whether and which category of customers would like a new style. Introducing a new style also involves discontinuation of the old style. Introducing a new style also involves discontinuation of the old style and disposal of unsold stock.

Whether it is quality, style, or special features, decisions with respect to the policy of product differentiation should obviously rest on the following factors:-

a. Characteristics of the product which are important from the customer's point of view:

b. Customers' ability and inclination to appreciate the distinctiveness of the product as compared with similar products;

c. Cost of providing the distinctive quality, style or features; and

d. Customers' ability to pay for it.

Product Positioning

Product positioning refers to offering of differential products in a manner such that consumers perceive them to be distinct from competing products. It involves two sets of exercises: (a) assessment of the brand's current position; and (b) determination of the most desirable positioning.

Analysis of the brand's current positioning as by consumers may reveal that the brand is well positioned relative to its competitors and the consumers ideal, or that repositioning is necessary or that introduction of a new product is called for. Among the techniques which may be used for such analysis, the more practicable are Multidimensional Scaling and Clustering, and Conjoint Analysis. Multidimensional scaling and clustering techniques graphically portray consumer evaluation of the objects (brands). This involves preparing geometric representation (maps) on the basis of consumer perceptions and preferences so that brands which are similar psychologically are plotted near each other in the geometric space. Conjoint analysis is concerned with measuring the joint effect of two or more independent variables (i.e. components of differentiating strategy) on the ordering or brand, intention to by, preferences or some other measure). Consumers are required to consider trade-offs among various options and judge the relative attractiveness of different combinations of offerings. From conjoint analysis one can derive a utility function for each factor studied, e.g. specific brand features or price levels. This helps to determine (i) the best possible combination of brand features in term of the highest utilities, (ii) the relative importance of each factor, and (iii) the utility gain and loss associated with changes in any offerings, with a computer simulation, management may then obtain brand-switching matrices revealing the likely outcome of any new product introduction or modification in product offering e.g. change in features. The impact on the market share or profitability of any competitive action or retaliation in response to the firm's own strategies can also be assessed with simulation exercise.

Market Segmentation

A key strategic decision related to the need for product differentiation is the selection of market segments at the corporate product category or brand level. This is because the target market of products is often a small part of the total market. Indeed even for product which are universally consumed, it is quite often found that 80 per cent of the sales are derived from 20 per cent of the market. The questions relevant to marketing strategy are : What parts of the market is a firm in business to serve? What parts it choose not to serve? An automobile manufacturer may decide to serve the requirements of bulk transport operators, not the small operators. A garments making firm may specialise in children's garments rather than ladies outfits. Transistors may be manufactured for defence equipments rather than for industrial customers such as computer manufacturers.

Market a segmentation thus refers to the division of customers into meaningful buyer group's i.e. division of the market into sub-markets. Segmentation can be done on the basis of such variables as socio-economic characteristics of buyer groups (age, se, education, occupation, family size, income level, etc.) or geographic basis (location) or industrial categories, or buyer behaviour (motive, personality, brand loyalty, usage rate, etc.) The foremost benefit of market segmentation is that the firm is alert to the needs of different buyer groups and, hence is in a better position to spot and compare marketing opportunities. Another benefit is that marketing efforts can be directed and marketing budgets allocated on the basis of the knowledge of responses differences to marketing tools among market segments. Adjustments can also be made in the products and marketing appeals on the bass of segmentwise analysis of customer response.

Once market segments are identified it remains for management to decide on the strategic sales policy in that context. Three different approaches are possible. Undifferentiated Marketing, Differentiated Marketing and Concentrated Marketing.

Undifferentiated Marketing: A single product firm may not recognise the differences in demand for the product of different consumer groups. It may thus design the product so as to cater to the common needs and adopt a marketing programme with sales appeal for the maximum number of consumers. Hence, a firm adopting the undifferentiated marketing policy typically develops its product and marketing programme aimed at the broadest segment of the market The common argument in favour of this policy is cost economy which goes with standardised marketing and mass production. But this approach may lead to hyper-competition in the larger segments and low level of consumer satisfaction in the smaller segments. For a long time, American automobile manufacturers produced only large passenger cars. While smaller segments of the car market were served by foreign firms. Over time it was found that largest segments were less profitable because they attracted disproportionately heavy competition.

An alternative approach which may be pursued is that of differentiated marketing. The firm may decide to serve all segments of the product market but with a separate product design and/or marketing programme for each segment. With differentiated products and marketing programmes the firm should normally expect to realise higher sales and attain deeper positioning of the product sin the various segments, and thus strengthen consumers' brand preference in all the segments. To cite a common example, several varieties of toilet sops differentiated by price, quality, etc. happen to be associated with the names of particular firms (like Godrej, Hindustan Lever, Tatas, etc.) However, differentiated marketing also increases the costs of production, administration, inventory holding, and sales promotion. Hence, there is not a priority ground to suggest that this policy may lead to an optimal market positioning.

A third alternative is the concentrated marketing strategy. The firm may decide to serve one or a few market segments so as to gain a substantial market share in those sub-markets rather than spreading the marketing efforts thinly over many segments. Take, for instance, the case of Reliance Textiles which decided in the seventies to cater to be market segment with demand for high quality, high priced fabrics. Many publishers are known to specialise in either college-level or school-level text books. Some publishers serve the market for paperbacks, pocketbooks, etc. Concentrated marketing policy implies tapping up of the future growth to one or a few segments of the market, which obviously it risky. Depending on the mature of demand curves, different segments may also yield different rates of return. On the other hand, producers serving all segments of the market with differentiated or undifferentiated marketing policy can avoid the risks of specialised marketing efforts. However, concentrated marketing is preferable if a firm's resources are limited.

Choice of Strategy: The choice of appropriate marketing strategy in the context of segmented buyer groups should be determined keeping in view the following considerations:

(i) *Resource position*: With limited resources it may not be possible for a firm to serve the entire market consisting of many sub-markets. Concentrated marketing may be most suitable under the circumstances.

(ii) *Product homogeneity*: Marketing of basic consumer goods, e.g. common salt, fuel oil, steel, of which the characteristics in any category are not appreciably different are best taken care of by undifferentiated marketing strategy.

(iii) *Stages in the product life style*: At the introduction stage undifferentiated marketing is more appropriate since varied product designs cannot be offered without evaluating consumer response, and development of primary demand is the main objective at the stage. Differentiated marketing may be preferable at the saturation stage since it is necessary then to search for new and untapped needs.

(iv) *Market homogeneity or heterogeneity*: If the market for any product is such that customers have more or less identical needs, preferences, and price elasticity of demand, segmentation does not serve any useful purpose. Thus undifferentiated marketing is best suited for products with homogenous markets. Conversely, in the case of products with heterogeneous market, the appropriate strategy should be that of differentiated or concentrated marketing.

(v) *Competitor's strategy*: The choice of marketing strategy should take into account the strategy of competitors. If competitors pursue Differentiated marketing policy a firm cannot afford to pursue any other strategy. However, if competitors are committed to undifferentiated marketing, it may be of advantage of the firm decides to follow differentiated marketing policy.

We have discussed above the significance of product positioning as a marketing strategy, and then considered the strategic alternatives for segmented markets. It should be clear that market segmentation and product positioning are not alternative approaches to marketing but are really complementary to each other. Robertson and Wind have suggested four alternative strategies, taking into the two extreme positions in each dimension, viz. (1) positioning of account both the dimensions (segmentation and differentiation) and positioning of a commodity (without any brand preference of consumers), and (II) Market segmentation versus market aggregation. The following matrix is self-explanatory.

	Segmentation	*Aggregation*
Speciality	Cell 1	Cell 2
	Speciality products to specific segments	Speciality Products to the mass market
Commodity	Cell 3	Cell 4

Commodity product to specific segments	Commodity products to the mass market

Consumer needs are ideally met in Cell 1 assuming market heterogeneity. Speciality products are offered to specific segments of the market. This strategy may be expected to maximise sales by meeting consumer needs more successfully in the segments served. Also it usually allows the highest price to be charged. Even with the likelihood of higher costs on product designing, an increased costs due to limited production runs, and higher marketing cost. Cell 1 strategy may be profitable as a result of premium pricing. The strategy suggested by Cell 4 is just opposite to that of Cell 1. A commodity with no brand preference of consumers is offered to the mass market. Premium price cannot be charged, rather if may involve sale at the lowest price. Unless the firm has considerable experience curve advantage or substantial economies of scale, competitive costs may not compensate for the low competitive pricing, and the product is likely to be in demand only on the basis of price competitive. The Cell 2 strategy implies speciality products being offered to mass markets. This may be the only alternative for a firm if its ability to identify and reach unique segments is limited. However, if the consumer needs are heterogeneous, the firm may offer multiple brands to the mass market without clear-cut segmentation which is in any case not feasible, the users of one brand being much like the users of any other brand. If segmentation was possible, the Cell 1 strategy would have been preferable. Cell 3 strategy is generally pursued by service industries like hotels and airlines. Services are offered to unique market segments at different prices and with unique brand to the mass market without clear-cut segmentation which is in any case not feasible, the users of one brand being much like the users of any other brand. If segmentation was possible, the Cell 1 strategy would have been preferable. Cell 3 strategy is generally pursued by service industries like hotels and airlines. Services are offered to unique market segments at different prices and with unique brand names. This strategy really involves discriminatory pricing for different consumer groups with respect to virtually undifferentiated products or service. The differentiation if at all in the products or service is symbolic and is in line with the price-sensitivity levels.

Product Design Policy

With the policy of product differentiation, which involves improvements in quality, style or the features of a products, and changing the product design, the management must also consider how often changes in design should be made. The necessity of design change may arise from technological developments. No company can afford to ignore advancements to technology in such products as colour televisions, computers, internal combustion engines (auto engines), electronic goods, etc. Change of design is a must in those cases, irrespective of the frequency of change that may be required. Pressure of competition is another factor which may compel a company to go in for design change. New brands of competing products often impel companies to follow suit. Take, for instance, the case of TV sets (with remote control device and new cabinet designs), kitchenware (cooking range with multiple uses), electrostatic copiers (with new features) bedsheets, pillow covers and table mats with artistic designs (Biochona), or detergents 'New power packed" Surf), and so on.

While taking into account the compelling reasons for design change, the frequency of change should be governed by : (a) cost implications, (b) inventory problems, (c) provision of after sales service, and (d) the potential benefits likely to secure.

The cost of changing the design of a product may include the following elements:

Technical and marketing research costs

Costs of engineering, testing and tooling up

Manufacturing costs including cost of training men for new skills and additional overhead facilities to be created, and sales promotion costs.

Introduction of a new design or brand involves two problems relating to inventory management. It requires gradual reduction of the output of the old product and building up stocks of the new product for which demand may be difficult to predict. Secondly, anticipation of a new brand or model may cause wide fluctuations in the inventory of distributors and irregular orders for the manufacturer. This may finally lead to the necessity of accepting the return of the unsold stocks of the old product or disposal of the same at concessional price.

Aftersales service including the provision of repair parts for new products require special consideration in the case of new models of automobiles, TV sets, computers office equipments, air-conditioners, and the like. Coupled with the uncertainty of demand for the re-designed product, provision of spare parts of repair services may also be a matter of conjecture. But in the absence or inadequacy of such provision, the usefulness and resale value of the products may be seriously in doubt.

Depending on the nature of the product in respect of which design change in unavoidable, several alternative policies are conceivable for deriving maximum benefits. Thus, the policy may be to change the design annually as a regular practice stressing on changes which may or may or may not imply significant improvements. This policy is found suitable in the case of automobile manufacturers in developed countries. The advantages of such a policy are : (a) it helps the recovery of promotional costs due to the accentuation of changes; (B) it hastens obsolescence of the old model and raises replacement demand (c) The changes are consolidated into an annual package and thus production adjustment can be timed and planned accordingly.

An alternative policy may be that of product leadership which implies design changes being made whenever warranted by technological changes so as to be first in the market with improvements. IBM's policy of developing new generations of electronic computers on the basis of R & D efforts is a typical example of this policy. Clearly, product leadership cannot be the basis of design changes except for companies holding a dominant position in the product market.

A third alternative policy that may be considered is what is called 'leapfrogging'. It implies changing designs only when significant improvements can be made even if it is done with a time lag. In other words, the policy of leapfrogging in one that rests on bringing about major changes once a while, allowing competitors to have their way meanwhile. This may be a suitable policy for products in which technological change is slow.

Yet another alternative policy that may be suitable for certain types of products is that of minimum commitment to change known as 'straddle'. In this policy, the design change is attempted with he standard parts remaining the same, and the stress is on a change of form or appearance. With such a policy additional manufacturing costs and service requirements can be minimised. Watch manufacturing firms in Switzerland are known to follow this policy with success. What is attempted is to make the outer look of watches more appealing (the shape of the casing, dial, minute and second hands, etc.) with the inner parts and components unchanged.

Channel of Distribution Policies

The basic premise of the new marketing concept is customer satisfaction. The most important benefit that flows from this approach to marketing is that merchandising is more effective. To satisfy customer needs, it is necessary that management must identify the customer group that is intended to be served. Thus, one policy issue to be resolved is which category or categories of ultimate consumers the company would like to satisfy. The second policy issue relates to the channels of distribution which would be best suited the reach the existing and potential consumers. A third question of policy is how many customers should the company deal with.

Consumers to be served

A consumer is a buyer who uses the product either for personal satisfaction or for processing it (as a manufacture does). A customer on the other hand, is one who buys a product either for own use or for resale (as a wholesaler or retailer does). It is the satisfaction of ultimate consumers that determines the saleability of any product or service. Hence, every company needs to decide on the category of consumers whose want satisfaction will be the focus in marketing the product along with the convenience, service, as well as aesthetic and symbolic values that buyers seek.

The clientele of firms offering goods and services is identifiable in terms of the nature of the products. One broad classification of goods, based on who the buyers are, is provided by the distinction between (1) consumer goods, and (ii) industrial goods. The former include goods destined for use by ultimate consumers or households and in such form that they can be classified into convenience goods, shopping goods, and speciality goods. Convenience gods are those which the consumers buy frequently for immediate consumption (e.g. soap, confectionery, processed food, newspapers) and for which minimum time and effort is spent in buying. Shopping goods are those which the consumers select on the basis of suitability, quality, price, and style, before making the purchase, as in the case of dress materials, ready-made garments, shoes, furniture, household appliances, used care, etc. Speciality goods have unique characteristics or brand identification for which consumers are inclined to make special purchasing efforts. e.g. specific brands of camera, hi-fi-audio equipments, sports goods, and fancy articles like ladies toiletry.

Industrial goods are the second type of products which are destined to be sold primarily for use in producing other goods or rendering services. These include such items as equipments and accessories, components, replacement parts, raw materials and fabricating materials. But the distinction between consumer and industrial goods does not hold good for certain types of products which may have both consumption and industrial uses. Take, for instance, such goods as paper, diamond, typewriters, fruits, milk and so on. However, the broad classification of products as above is helpful in identifying the consumer groups to be kept in view for policy making.

Identification and Location of Consumers

Even if the type of goods and services are classified on the basis of who the buyers could be, it must be recognised that there are different types of consumers with different needs and preferred values. Users of bicycles in rural areas need sturdy frames and wheels suited to villages roads. Restaurants located near office complexes have to serve midday meals while those in the university campus must provide for snacks, tea and soft drinks for students. The publishers of children's books have to decide on the age-groups of children who will be offered the publications. The clientele of hotels may comprise foreign tourists, or executives, or visitors from other cities. Each of these categories of clients would expect certain facilities and services to be provided by the management. For which category should hotel services be provided and the what price? A product for markets abroad must conform to specific quality standards which may not be essential for domestic marketing. Thus, identification and location of consumer groups to be served become important considerations in determining what is to be offered in terms of consumer satisfaction and at what price. A company cannot be expected to shift from one market to another at short intervals. It takes time and effort to build up the reputation of a company in relation to consumers. Hence, stable policies regarding consumers to be served a very useful.

Channels of Distribution

Whether a firm will sell its product or service directly to the consumers or make use of intermediaries (middlemen) for the purpose constitutes a major policy issue. For certain service organisations direct sale to consumers is invariably called for, like for instance, civil airways, bank's, consultancy firms, passenger and freight transport services. But for most manufacturers of goods, selection of the channel of distribution involves a choice of great significance. For one thing, one channel decisions depend the firm's pricing decisions, advertising decisions and sales force decisions. The firm's pricing decisions depends upon whether it chooses wholesalers or retailers for distribution of its products. The firm's advertising decisions depend upon the degree of co-operation. Secondly, the significance of channel decisions lies in that they involve long-term commitments to and dependence on other firms (dealers, wholesalers and retailers).

Types of Channels

The taps by which products are distributed from the manufacturer to the consumers constitute the channel of distribution. Marketing channel is also referred to as those set of marketing intermediaries linking the producer with the consumers. There may be two or more levels (links) in the channel. Thus, the direct sale of goods by the producer to the ultimate users may be called a two level channel. If there is one selling intermediary (a broker, sales agent or retailer) between the producer and the consumer, it would be a three level channel. A four level channel is typically one with two intermediaries (wholesaler and retailer) between the product and the consumer, and so on.

Factors governing Channel Decision

Selection of an appropriate channel of distribution requires consideration of a number of situational constraints and the channel objectives. Thus, a firm must take into account the characteristics of the customers to be served and the product, the pros and cons of different types of intermediaries, the competitive situation, the environmental conditions, and the organisational characteristics before taking a decision regarding the channel of distribution.

The number of customers to be served, their purchasing pattern, geographical dispersion, and their susceptibilities to different selling methods, are important to be considered in the process of channel decision. Thus, for instance, to serve a large number of customers, particularly if they are dispersed over a wide territory, the producers generally find it more convenient and economical to use to a number of intermediaries in the chain of distribution. Such a policy is also suitable where customers are likely to make purchases in small quantities at frequent intervals, a sin the case of drug and medicines, dress materials, periodicals and journals, etc. On the other hand, buyers of speciality goods, for instance, may be better served through showroom displays.

The characteristics of the product also need to be kept in view in connection with channel decision. Bulky products of low unit value required channels involving minimum number of handling in movement as well as shorter distance in transportation so as to minimise loss can undertake those functions depends on the relative efficiency and effectiveness. In general, if consumer purchases are secured through small retailers scattered over a wide territory, it is found to be more economical to avail of the wholesaler's services. However, product prices are bound to be higher with the addition of margins to cover the cost of services provided by the wholesalers. Besides, sales promotion may not be very effective as wholesalers often handle products of two or more manufacturers.

Direct distribution through retailers may be advantageous in certain ways. The producer has direct contact with the final 'point of sale' and hence may readily obtain consumer feedback regarding their preferences. There is greater control over sales through direct contact with the retailers. Retail prices may be adjusted more easily. Display of good and steps to popularise the products can be conveniently arranged. But selling directly to retailer implies a heavier burden of costs. Selling in small lots and servicing a large number of retailers by way of credit, transportation, and other facilities, along with maintaining account, collection and dues, and follow up, may substantially raise the selling costs and reduce the profit margin.

Brokers or agents are often employed as intermediaries for sale of goods in bulk such as building materials (bricks, stones, sand, etc.) or real estate (property, land and buildings), and also producer goods. Brokers are in close contact with the market and undertake no other function except that of sale. Small producers find it to be a convenient means to sell since it is not possible for them to maintain their own sales force with limited output.

Distribution of goods by the producer through branch offices, showrooms and sales counters requires an organisational setup for the purpose. This facilitates coordination of sales and productions. There is better selling efforts and more direct customer feedback. A company having a wide variety in the product line may find it economical to adopt this method of distribution. Manufacturers of textiles, electrical goods (fans, refrigerators, etc.) and office equipments having nation-wide markets follow the practice of direct sale to customers through retail stores. Specifically products (like computer, office machines, etc.) which require technical knowledge and training on the part of the salesman to explain the method of operation, and where it is in the interest of the producer to ensure that the product is kept in proper repair, direct sale is often of great advantage.

Competitive situation is yet another variable which has a bearing on the channel decision. Using the same channel as the competitors do is an important consideration. It provides a basis for competing on the same footing. Sometimes it may be desirable not to imitate and to void the methods of distribution currently used by competitors.

Distribution through exclusive dealers may be useful in the case of automobiles, drugs and pharmaceuticals as well as speciality goods with a brand image. Even competing firm may have its own dealer.

Environmental factors do have no less significance in the channel decision. In an economic environment characterised by recession or stagnation of business activities, producers must use the least expensive channels so as to minimise selling costs and keep down the price of goods. Moreover, legal regulatory lows may not permit the use of intermediary channels except within certain limits.

Thus, under the Monopolies and Restrictive Trade Practices Act manufacturers cannot engage in re-sale price maintenance, i.e. cannot insist that their goods must not be sold by retailers below the price dictated by them, as it purports to restricting the competition between the actual distributors of the goods and often raises the price that the consumers have to pay. The MRTP Act, as amended in 1984, also provides that any agreement falling within one or more of certain categories shall be deemed to be agreement relating to restrictive trade practice and shall be subject to registration.

The characteristics of the company, like its size, financial strength, product-mix, overall marketing policies, and its past channel experience, among other things, also influence the channel decision. A large company generally has wider market and it is able to secure the co-operation of intermediaries more easily than smaller companies. A company's financial position may compel it to avail the services of intermediaries like storage, transport and customer financing. One which is financially strong may be able to undertake the marketing functions on its own. With a wider product mix it is possible for a company to directly deal with customers. If the product- line includes several varieties, marketing is possible through exclusive or selective dealers. At the same time, marketing policies bearing on delivery and service to consumers, transportation and location of outlets, advertising, and pricing may imply certain channels to be more suitable than other. The past experience with channels in use likewise provides some basis in determining the suitability or otherwise of particular channels.

Pricing Policy

Products in respect of which quality standards can be precisely measured or readily determined, or for products which are normally graded with standard specifications, a producer does not have much scope for pricing his products differently from the established market price. Thus, for highly standardised products like chemicals, mineral ore, metals etc. the going market prices are so fixed on the basis of standard classifications that no producer can avoid competitive reactions if any attempt is made to deviate from the established prices. But for most consumer goods and producer goods, quality may be differentiated in various ways. There is no yardstick to easily measure quality and no commonly accepted standard of quality for products except that in some cases it is prescribed undo law by way of minimum requirements.

The factors that should be taken into account while formulating pricing policy of products are:

1. Prices of competing products;
2. Costs of production and distribution;
3. Implications of discriminatory prices for different customer groups;
4. Prices of different items in the product-line;
5. Scope of changing prices.

Prices of Competing Products

What should be the basic approach to pricing a product in relation to the prices of similar products offered by competitors? One may consider three policy options (a) to set a higher price that of competing products, (b) to set a comparable price (c) to set a lower price.

The policy of charging a higher price is generally based on differences in quality or services rendered, i.e. on some distinctive feature of the product or services offered along with the product. Product and service differences serve to desensitise the buyer to price differentials. For instance, the consumers may be willing to pay a higher price for the superior quality of materials used in the product, or better design, or finish, or workmanship, or convenience of sue. Services offered along with the sales of a product may includes free delivery, credit facility, technical advice, etc. The limiting consideration here is the cost of product differentiation or that of providing special services. Profitability may be enhanced by higher prices only if the additional cost is worthwhile, which depends on how long the product and service distinctiveness can be maintained (that is, on competitors' reaction), whether the differences in quality and services are appealing enough to the customers, and to what extent they are willing to pay for the same.

Fixing a higher price than that of competing products may also be prompted by a firm's market-skimming objective, that is, to take advantage of some buyers' willingness to pay a much higher price than others because they value if more. The skimming price policy is a form of price discrimination over time, for it implies setting a higher price initially and then gradually reducing it so as to attract other consumers with a price-elastic demand. This policy works well if any of the following conditions are satisfied: (a) The product is perceived to be of super quality because of the higher prices; (b) The demand is sufficiently high and is inelastic, (c) Higher unit costs of production and distribution due to the smaller volume of output and sale do not offset the benefit of high unit price charged (d) The policy does not lead to entry of new competitors.

The alternative policy of charging a comparable price while emphasising the distinctiveness of quality and service may be useful for increasing the volume of sale of certain products. But the purpose will be served depending on how significant the quality and service differentiation is to the consumers, as well as on the competitors' reaction. Besides, the volume of sale must be adequately high to justify the increased costs involved in making the product distinctive.

The third alternative is that of fixing a lower price. Often such a policy is prompted by the market penetration objective, which involves setting a relatively low price to build up sales volume and increase market share. The conditions favouring such a policy are likely to be the following (i) the product demand is highly price elastic, (ii) unit costs decline with larger volume of production and sale, (iii) potential competition is discouraged by low prices.

The most important factor to be considered with respect to the policy of setting either a relatively higher or lower price is the competitors reaction. One or two large producers in an industry may be looked upon by others as 'price leaders.' Thus, if such producers initiate a change in price, it is invariably followed by identical changes being made by other firms. On the other hand, a lower price set by any small firm may not lead to a similar action by competitors because only a small part of the market is affected by the price change. Sometimes, informal price agreements among competitors restrict the scope of price changes (fixing higher or lower prices) by any one firm. But formal price agreements are discouraged by law in most countries as such agreements tend to eliminate competition or a competitor. Under the MRTP Act, price control agreements are deemed to be restrictive trade practice and are subject to registration.

Competition-oriented pricing

The pricing policy of a firm may be competition-oriented in the sense that it sets prices mainly on the basis of prices set by competitors. This policy does not necessarily imply setting of an identical price, although it way be so. With a competition-oriented pricing policy, the firm may keep its prices higher or lower than that of competitors by a certain percentage. Actually this policy implies that the firm's pricing decision is not based on cost or products demand, prices are changed or maintained in line with the competitors' prices.

The most common type of competition-oriented pricing is known as going-rate pricing under which prices are maintained at par with the average level of prices in the industry. This policy is usefully adopted by firms selling a homogeneous product in a highly competitive market. In such a product market, there is a market-determined price established through the collective interaction of a number of knowledgeable buyers and sellers. Setting a higher than going market price is not practicable as it would lead to loss of clientele. A lower price is uncalled for since a firm can sell its entire output at the going-rate. Such a policy is also preferred where it is difficult to determine the costs accurately, or when it is difficult to predict how buyers and competitors would react to price differentials.

For a different reasons, firms tend to set prices in line with the competitors' when the market is dominated by a few large firms as in "An oligopolist can gain little by raising his price when demand is elastic or lowering his price when demand is inelastic". Moreover since there are only a few firms, each firm is aware of the others' prices, and so are the buyers. If industry costs and demand change, prices must be changed. This is done in unison by the firms, or one of the firms assumes the role of price-leader and others follow.

Another type of competition-pricing pricing prevails where firms compete on the basis of bid or tenders-as the use of turnkey projects, installation of plant, supply of bulk materials, defence contracts, or construct on jobs. The bid or tender price is based on the probable bid prices of competitors, and each firm tries to set its price lower so as to get its bid or offer accepted.

Costs of Production and Distribution

The policy of setting price essentially on the basis of the total cost per unit is known as cost-oriented pricing. Indeed the costs of production and distribution happen to be the most commonly recognised basis of pricing. This is primarily due to three reasons:-

(i) Administrative simplicity. Costs can be estimated with a fair degree of certainty. The problem of adjusting prices to changing demand is avoided by linking the price to unit costs. The task is simpler to administer.

(ii) Competitive harmony. Price competition is minimised with cost based pricing, for prices are expected to be uniform if all the firms have similar costs and markup policy.

(iii) Social fairness. Cost-based pricing is fairer to both the buyer and the seller. Rising demand does not lead to higher prices, while the seller also earns a fair rate of return on his investment.

There are two approaches to pricing on the basis of costs (a) Markup and Cost-plus pricing, and (b) Target pricing.

Markup and cost plus pricing: Markup pricing and cost plus pricing refer to price-determination by adding a fixed (predetermined) percentage to the unit cost. Usually, the percentage added is the normal profit. Thus, the price is based on cost plus normal profit expressed as a percent age of cost. Markup pricing is mostly found to prevail install trade, while cost-plus pricing is widely used in the case of unique jobs or contracts where it is difficult to estimate cost in advance.

The implications of markup pricing are dependent on what constitutes normal profit. A rigid markup (fixed percent age) may be consistent with the firm's objective of maximising profit only under special circumstances viz, the average (unit) cost must be fairly constant over the range of likely outputs and the price elasticity of demand must be fairly constant over time. These conditions may be satisfied in the case of retail trading, but cannot be expected to prevail in manufacturing firms. Thus, as elasticity of demand changes (may be seasonally, cyclical, or over the product life cycle), the markup should also change.

Target pricing: A type of cost-oriented pricing policy usually adopted by manufacturing firms and public utility concerns is called target pricing. This approach to pricing involves price determination eatunated standard volume of output and sale.

Pricing below cost: Normally, it is not expected that producer will fix his selling price below the total cost. But under special circumstances, a firm may find it useful to set the price of a product so a to recover at least the marginal cost (i.e. variable direct costs and the variable element of the semi-variable costs). In other words, the marginal (out-of-pocket) costs may be the lower limit and the selling price may be established within the range between the marginal cost and the total cost. Such a pricing policy may be pursued (a) where excess capacity exists and the overhead fixed costs cannot be absorbed by regular sales outlets, (b) where it is possible to increase the level of operation by selling products at a reduced price, generally to a different class of customers, and (c) where the additional sales at reduced prices do not affect the long-run pricing option, i.e. lower prices do no become sticky. Typically these conditions may be found to exist in the case of industries with heavy fixed costs relatively to the variable costs, i.e. airlines, hotels, movie houses, etc. Thus, hotels may find it profitable to offer reduced 'off-season' rates provided the additional revenue derived exceeds out-of-pocket costs. Similarly, airlines can afford to offer concessional fares for group travel. Liquidation of cess inventory to anticipation of a general decline in prices may also necessitate selling the products of below cost. Selling some minor item in the product- line at a price below the total cost may also be found useful as service to regular customers.

Sometimes, retailers sell certain standard items below cost so as to attract customers to the store hoping that sale of other items will thereby increase, Products sold at a loss are called 'loss leaders' and the practice is known as 'loss leader pricing.' The rationale of such a policy is based on the assumption that the loss incurred on the sale of certain items below cost will be more than compensated by the increased sale of other items.

Discriminatory Pricing for Customer Groups

Should a company charge different prices from different customer groups? Or, should the company sell its product at a uniform price to all customers? A common practice with many firms is to maintain a list price and then allow discounts to certain categories of customers. Thus, wholesalers or retailers are granted discounts by manufacturers known as trade discount. A special discount may also be allowed for prompt payment, which is known as cash discount. Discounts allowed for bulk orders or trade discounts linked with the services rendered by wholesaler sand retailers are not intended to be price reductions and are granted without upsetting the price structure.,

Price discrimination refers to a form of demand-oriented pricing in which a particular commodity or service is sold at two or more rates that do not reflect a proportional difference in marginal cost. Where prices are settled through bargaining there is obviously a discriminating price policy for it enables a firm to extract higher prices form some customers than from others. Discrimination pricing may be possible due to deferent intensities of demand or .differences in consumer knowledge. Kotler has specified the following conditions under which price discrimination may work.

a. The market must be segmentable and the segments must show different intensities of demand;

b. There should be no scope for consumers in the segment paying the lower price to turn around and resell the product to consumers in the segment paying the higher price;

c. There should be no possibility of competitors under selling the firm in the segment paying higher price;

d. Any extra cost incurred in segmenting and policing the market should be less than the extra revenue derived from price discrimination;

e. The practice should not lead to customer resentment and loss of customer goodwill.

Discriminatory pricing between different regions is sometimes called for on account of the cost of transportation of the product to distant markets, it may be necessary for the manufacturer to absorb a part,; if not the whole, or the transport cost, and keep the price at a competitive level in that region. But it may not be advisable to sell the product in the distant market at a price lower than that being charged in the local area. Price differentiation in the situation should be accompanied by some king of product differentiation.

Pricing of different items in the product line: Product line pricing

Where a firm deals in different grades, brands, or varieties of products in the same line, careful consideration of several factors is needed so as to determine a set of mutual prices that will maximise the profits of the product line.

i. Cross-elasticity of demand: If two products are inter-related in demand, the price of one may affect the demand for the other depending on the cross-elasticity of demand. If the cross-elasticity is positive, the products are substitutable, if it is negative the products would be complementary to each other Thus for instance, lowering the price of three-band radio sets, may lead to a decrease in the demand for two-band sets because the items are substitutes of each other. Lowering the price of colour television sets may, on the other hand, lead to an increase in the demand for its components.

ii. Cost interactions: The costs of by-products and joint products are closely related to the cost of the main product. The costs of two unrelated products may also be interdependent if the same production facilities are used for both. This is because overhead must be absorbed fully by the two products. The cost interactions between colour TV sets and black and white sets in worth considering if the manufacturer decides to raise the price of colour TV sets, for in that case sales of colour TV may fall, and cause a rise in the cost of black and white sets. Hence, management must take into account the cost interactions between different items in the product-line while setting the price of particular items.

iii. Differences in the degree of competition : Different varieties or grades of a product are often exposed to different degrees of competition. If so, the structure of prices in the product-line should reflect difference in the competitive situation of different items rather than deference in their costs. For, otherwise, the profit opportunities associated with competitive conditions may be overloaded.

iv. Accepted market prices : In the case of certain standard products, customers are accustomed to specific prices established in the market, e.g. hosiery goods, undergarments, etc. The manufacture of such products does not have much discretion in the matter of pricing. Better results may be derived by way of product differentiation while setting the accepted price.

Initiating Price-Changes

Pricing decisions not only involve setting prices for the first time but also requires initiating price changes when necessary. A firm may contemplate changing the existing price of a product for different reasons. For instance, a price reduction may be considered necessary to stimulate demand, to take advantage of lower costs, or to squeeze out weaker competitors. Likewise the firm may consider a price increase to take advantage of excess demand, or to pass on higher costs. Any proposal to change prices upward or downward must, however, be considered by management in the light of the likely reactions of buyers, competitors, distributors, and suppliers, to such a move.

Reaction of buyers

To what extent and how buyers will respond to a price change depends essentially on the price elasticity of demand for the product. Simply stated, price elasticity of demand is the ratio of the percentage change in price of the product. It is expressed as the ratio of relative change in quantity of sale to a relative change in price. Thus, unit elasticity reflects a situation where there is perfect correlation between the rise (or fall) in demand following a decline (or increase) in price. (The elasticity in this case is-1) The outcome is that the sales revenue remains unaffected. Greater than unit price elasticity implies a more than proportionate increase (or decrease) in sales resulting from a reduction (or increase) in price. If the price elasticity is less than unity, increase (or decrease) in sales would be less than proportionate to a fall (or rise) price. Greater than unit elasticity is normally expected to prevail in the case of durable goods like automobiles, refrigerators television sets etc. A reduction in price is normally expected to lead to a more than proportionate increase in sales. Demand for essential goods like wheat, rice, etc., is 'inelastic' in the sense that a cut in wheat price is normally followed by little change in demand. But price elasticity of demand for any product is extremely difficult to measure. Price elasticity of demand for any product is extremely difficult to measure. Price elasticity depends on the magnitude of contemplate price change. A small change in price may produce negligible effect on demand. On the other hand, a significant change in price may produce a substantial change in demand. Price elasticity also varies according to the existing level of prices, i.e. the marginal change in price of a low-priced item and that of a high-priced item may reflect different degrees of elasticity. Demand is generally more elastic in the long run because the short-run effect is characterised by the difficulty of rapid adjustment, the existence of market imperfections, and the presence of habit. In spite of the difficulties it may be possible to estimate the degree of elasticity through market survey or test marketing.

The customers' perception of the price change may also determine their response. They may interpret reduction in price differently, e.g. (a) The item is going to be superseded by a new model; (b) The item has some fault and is not selling; (d) The firm is in financial trouble and may not stay in business to supply future parts; (d) The price will come down further and it is desirable to wait (e) The quality has been reduced. The customers interpretation of a price increase may also differ, e.g. (a) The item is in short supply and may not be available unless it is immediately purchased; (b) The item represents an unusually good value and could not yield a profit at the old price; (c) The seller is exploiting the buyers.

Competitors' Reaction to Price Change

A firm intending to alter (move up or down) the existing price of a product is best advised to consider the likely reaction of competitors before taking a decision, even if it is expected that the customers' response will be favourable. If there is one single large competitor, and a price reduction may be looked upon to mean (a) that the company is trying to steal the market from him, or (b) that the company is not doing well and is trying to improve its sales, or (c) that the company is hoping that the whole industry will reduce its price so as to stimulate demand. The reaction of the competitor will depend on what interpretation is pure to the initiative take in changing the price. In a market situation which is characterised by more than one competitors, it may be necessary to analyse the likely reaction of each individual competitor particularly if the reaction is not expected to be identical due to differences in the market share, size, or policies of the respective competing firms. If the response is likely to be identical for all competitors, then it should be enough to analyse the possible reaction of a typical competitor.

Impact on Distributors

Reduction in the product price by a manufacturer invariably causes the distributors to suffer a nominal loss in the value of inventory. So it may be necessary for the manufacturer to reimburse the distributors for the loss. This practice is known as price protection. This is considered necessary for maintaining the distributors' goodwill otherwise such distributors have a feeling of discriminatory treatment vis a vis those who put off buying till the new prices were offered.

Reaction of Suppliers

Retailers intending to increase or to reduce the prices of certain products must consider the reaction of wholesalers or manufacturers. Buyer's reaction to a price change by the retailer may in the final analysis affect the whole-sellers as well as the manufacturer. For instance, if the customers interpret a fall in price to mean that the product is faulty, or that the quality has been reduced the ultimate effect will be a fall in demand—affecting then manufacturer's interest.

Sales Promotion

With a given marketing expenditure budget, management has to formulate policy as to how the budgeted amount will be allocated for product differentiation, customer services, etc. on the one band, and sales promotion advertising the personal selling efforts on the other. In other words, what needs to be decided is the optimal combination of the elements of marketing so that an appealing 'package' of satisfaction (quality, price, services, etc.) may be offered to the target group of customers through appropriate methods of communication advertising, salesmanship, promotion and publicity. Marketing mix policy refers to the decisions bearing on the competing uses of the budgeted sources for fulfilling consumer needs by way of sales appeals (services higher quality, lower price, packaging, etc.) as well as advertising and personal solicitation all of which involve costs to be incurred.

Policy on Sales Appeal Package

Every physical product on sale carries with it the promise of fulfilling some consumer 'needs' by way of material or psychological satisfaction. For instance, household furniture and fixtures, a car refrigerator, colour TV set a polaroid camera, ladies jwellery, and similar products provide the psychological pride of ownership and sue, some articles like a well-designed garment, high-quality eatables, etc. provide the psychological pride of consumption, 'curio' or a rate 'brand' product may satisfy a buyer's ego of getting it at a 'bargain (price, similarly, convenient packaging, lower price or services that may be offered with the product satisfy certain needs which consumers appreciate. The range of sales appeals may include quality, style packaging, price, services or company reputation.

For certain products, the basic sales appeal which may be used by a producer is through a distinctive quality of the products. Quality of processed food, edible oil, fabrics, furniture, and number of other products, may be made more appealing to consumers provided the distinctiveness can be detected by, or is convincing to, the buyers (quality or synonymous with different attributes of products; for instance, it may mean 'purity' in the case of medicines and drugs; 'safety' in the case of household appliances, durability in the case of fabrics, accuracy in the case of scientific precision instruments etc.). To make any product distinctive in terms of quality needs extra cost and effort. To be an effective sales appeal, the difference in quality compared with competing products may involve additional cost of raw materials, processing cost, designing cost, and so on. To make it condensing manufacturers of the guarantee the products offering free repairs and/or replacement of pats during a specified period. This is likely to add to the cost of marketing by way of after sales service. Hence, management must consider alternative dimensions of sales appeal.

Distinctiveness of style may be used as a sales appeal for such products as ready-made garments, handbags and footwear for ladies, decorative furniture, and even household appliances. The degree of importance attached to style as a sales appeal will naturally depend on the nature of the product.

Stylish appearance may be given to certain products through packaging with a view to providing a shelf-appeal, as in the case of tinned confectionery, shampoo and hair lotion, etc. But the package may also enhance the product service, e.g. study containers used for edible oil, water proof cases of folding umbrella, paints in cans fitted with handle which may be used for holding it at the time of painting. Again, the point to be considered is whether the cost of packaging will pay off a in terms of sales increase.

The price appeal is yet another element in marketing which can be used to derive an advantage over competing products. Lower prices often make a favourable impact on consumers' buying preferences, provided the quality aspect is also kept in view. Besides, a lower price cuts into the profit margin, and the effect can be offset only if the volume of sale increases sufficiently and it is maintainable for a recognisable period of time. The chances are that the competitors' reactions will undo the impact of flower prices sooner or later. Even otherwise, the price elasticity of demand is a basic factor to be taken into account to determine the degree of significance of price appeal in the marketing mix.

Customer services constitute a wide range of possible benefits which may add to the consumer's buying preference for a product. Manufacturers of industrial equipments often extend free advice to the customers on the use and maintenance of the machinery. Sometimes manufacturers undertake to train the operating personnel of the user company to assure efficient handling of the equipment. A policy firm which supplied the engine room equipments of an Indian ship, deployed an expert of their own to accompany the crew in the maiden voyage of the ship. Maintenance and repair services are usually made available to customers ensuring prompt and economical repairs of equipments and machinery in the event of breakdown or other defects. personal services are also provided by many firms selling ordinary convenience goods. These customers may be offered different types of buying facility such a home delivery, gift wrapping, return privileges, credit accounts, telephone ordering, and stock held for future delivery To some extent the cost of any of these services can be passed on to the customers. But the customers' reactions and acceptability of the services cannot be taken for granted.

Finally, reputation of a firm is also an important factor which contributes to the sales appeal. It takes time to build up the reputation. Often the existence of a brand image helps in the marketing effort. But to maintain the reputation, a firm has to be continuously on guard, for good reputation arise primarily from sustained willingness to devote extra effort to assure dependability and use of the latest techniques, as well as to avoid exaggerated claims.

Advertising Policy

Advertising, as a means of communicating the relevant sales appeals to target groups, may be defined as 'any paid form of n-personal presentation and promotion of ideas, goods, or services by an identified sponsor. The basic question relating to the policy on advertising is what type of advertising will be worthwhile at the cost involved. Thus the policy issues in advertising decisions are; (a) the purposes of advertising, and (b) the media to be used.

Depending on the nature of sales appeals to be communicated, advertising may be carried out for such purposes as building up the company name, emphasising a brand, information dissemination about a product or service, announcement of a special sale, etc. The media that can be used for advertising are many and include; newspaper and magazine, radio, television, outdoor displays (hoardings, signboards and bill board, posters), direct mail, novelties (calendars, match boxes, window displays, desk diaries), passenger tickets (as in railway, airways, airway and bus tickets), directories and reference books, programmes for public functions, and circulars, catalogues, etc. A firm can hardly afford to use all the media. It must select those that will accomplish the purposes economically. The selection of appropriate media is rendered easier if the special attributes ot advertising are kept in view. Levy has mentioned the following attributes:

i. Advertising is a public mode of communication. Thus it confers a kind of legitimacy to the product and also suggests a standardised offering.

ii. It is a pervasive medium by means of which the advertiser can respect his message many times. Also it permits the potential buyers to receive and compare the messages of different competitors.

iii. It provides wide scope for dramatizing the message through the artful use of print, colour and sound.

iv. But advertising is a form of impersonal communication. The audience does not feel obligated to pay attention or respond to the advertisement.

v. Under the MRTP Act, excessive advertising expenditure may be construed as anti-competitive and a barrier to the entry of new competitors.

Personal Solicitations

Personal selling (or solicitation) refers to some form of oral presentation in a conversation with one or more perspective buyers for the purpose of making sales. A variety of purposes may be served by using personal solicitation, e.g. creating product awareness, developing product preference, arousing interest, negotiating terms of sale and prices, procuring orders, and providing post-transactional reinforcement by follow-up interactions. The most commonly used form of personal selling is that of employing field sales forces for direct contact with consumers. In retail stores, the salesman or sales girls at the counter is expected to do it. At executive level, personal solicitation is often practiced through a lunch or dinner invitation. Depending on the nature of the product, type of customers, size of the market, and the geographical areas to be covered personal selling may be suitable as a means of communicating the sales appeal. Certain basic factors must be kept in view in that context.

a. Advertising may familiarise the potential customers with the product as well as help a favourable opinion to be formed about the company, and thus facilitate personal selling.

b. Personal selling is a mode of communication which involves and interactive relationship between two or more persons. It is likely to be stressful.

c. There is limited scope for constructive salesmanship that a salesman or sales girl can perform at the sales counter.

d. The art of personal selling permits different kinds of relationships to follow. It may develop into a business relationship or may lead to a deep personal friendship between the parties.

e. Personal selling is more likely to invoke the buyer's response. It has also greater possibility of holding the buyers, attention, than advertising.

Publicity

Communication of the sales appeal is sometimes very well carried out through publicity. What is involve is akin to advertising but the method is different. Commercial publicity refer to he non-personal stimulation of demand for a product, a service or business unit by arranging to have company-or product-oriented stories and features included as a news items in the published media, or arranging presentation of the same on the radio or television. This may be regarded as 'free advertising. But to make the publicity writ up acceptable to the press as a news story or feature article, the sponsoring company may have to enlist the services of professional public relations men skilled in the art. This may involve expenses which need to be taken into account. However, the expense could be worthwhile, for effective publicity yields fruitful results due to its unique attributes. One such attribute is that news stories and features are viewed by readers as more authentic in view of these being media-originated reports. Secondly, the messages put across through news stories reach many more potential consumers who otherwise avoid salesman and advertisements. They are taken off guard, so to speak. Thirdly, publicity, like advertising, has a potential for dramatizing a product or company.

Other promotional tools: Marketing efforts may include several other methods of sales promotion and communication of a sales appeal. Lucik and Zeigler have distinguished between three types of these promo-tools as follows:-

i. Consumer promotion, e.g. samples, coupons, money refund offers, trading stamps, contests, demonstration etc.

ii. Trade promotion, e.g. free goods, traders' allowances, co-operative advertising, dealer sales contests, etc.

iii. Sales-force promotion, e.g. contests, bonus, sales rallies, etc.

Use of these methods often has a vital' role in sales promotion during the introductory and maturity stages of the product life cycle. Another feature of the use of promotools is that their effects are immediately known and benefits can be measured more easily than in the case of advertising. In general, these tools have the quality of drawing immediate attention of buyers and breaking through the buyers' inertia towards particular products. The appeal to buyer lies in conveying the message that something special is being offered with may not be available again. At the same time, repeated or careless use of these tools may be counter-productive, for a the buyers may start having second thoughts about the desirability of buying the product.

Simply stated, marketing mix is the set of controllable variables that a firm can use to influence the buyers' response. The variables in the marketing six consist of the sales appeals (in terms of quality, price, services, style and packing) the one hand and the means of communicating the sales appeals to the potential buyers comprising advertisement, personal selling, publicity, and other promotional tools, on the other. Given a marketing expenditure budget, it may be possible to increase sales by altering the marketing mix. Thus, the management

Have to generate a set of plausible marketing mix alternatives in the first instance. As the next step, they have to estimate the volume of expected sales associated with each marketing mix. For a given marketing budget, the amount should be so allocated among the variables that the marginal profit and marginal expenditure on each variable are equal.

Production and Purchasing Policies

Production is the key of all activities. An organisation can rise, grow and develop only when its production department is effective. Essentially speaking, the decision variables with respect to production of goods (manufacturing) and provision of services (e.g. transportation, retailing etc.) are virtually the same. Manufacturing as well as service organisations alike have no decide on policies bearing on capacity, process and technology, purchasing and so on. Retailers for example, may decide to buy provisions in bulk and sell small packs made at their end, or, the packing, may be done by wholesalers and made available to the retailers. On the other hand, producers may decide to undertake only the assembly of some parts and produce others. Thus, production or processing and purchasing functions may be inter-related in various ways. Historically, the basic problem faced by merchants and traders was wherefrom and how economically goods could be produced. With the growth of manufacturing industries and dissemination of modern technology, the decision to be made is; whether a firm should buy or make all the products it sells, and to what extent making should be combined with buying? Let us first consider the policies relevant to production functions.

The major issues in production policy may be said to include the following:

1. Involvement of the firm in production process
2. Choice of the production processes or choice of technology
3. Estimate and utilisation of the production capacity
4. Maintenance/replacement of the existing production facilities.

Involvement in Production Process - Vertical Integration: The relevant question to be asked in this connection are:

a. Should he firm manufacture the product that it intends to sell or buy it?
b. If it is to be manufactured, should the activity consist of assembling purchased components or making the components as well?

Basically the decisions on the above issues determine the extent of firms vertical integration. To start with, why should firm engage in manufacturing rather than trading activities? The only justification for investment in production can be that the same money cannot be deployed more profitably elsewhere in business. But even with such a decision, it remains to be decided what is to be the extent of commitment to production, i.e. vertical integration. At one extreme, a firm may consider manufacturing all the items used in production including standard parts and components and also undertaking complete assembly. At the other extreme, finished articles may be bought and the firm's name attached before selling.

The range of possible alternatives may be illustrated with reference to certain industries. Book publishing companies by and large do not have printing works of their own although printing done outside is definitely more expensive. There are several reasons for it. Fluctuations in the volume of printing work from time to time does not warrant setting up a printing establishment. Besides, there is flexibility of printing design ensured with freedom to get printing done anywhere. Again few publishers have their own paper mills essentially because it does not pay to economise in the cost of paper since supplies are available at reasonable rates under long-term contract. The range of variations in the commitment to production is typically found in the automobile industry. Large manufacturing companies in the United States and Japan produce nearly all the 15,000 parts that go into a modern passenger car. Even then, specialised components like piston rings, speedometers, tyres, etc., are preferred to be purchased. On the other hand, automobile manufacturers in India prefer to buy a large number of parts from the established producers of those items. The scope of vertical integration has also changed over time. In the past, firms in the fruit canning industry mostly produced their supplies of fruits from other firms owning orchards. Increasingly more fruit canning firms on and manage their own orchards. As a result, the location of these firms has also shifted to the countryside.

Factors governing Integration of Production Activities

A number of considerations govern the decision of firms to integrate manufacturing and processing of components and products.

i. Coordination of activities : Manufacture of raw materials and components for the products to be sold ensures supplies in accordance with their required quality, quantity and timely availability. It also provides for flexibility and adjustment to changes in needs.

ii. Saving in costs : The selling costs of the suppliers of materials and components are saved if the user company producers rather than buys the items.

iii. Safeguard against uncertainty or restricted supply : If a company has to depend on a few suppliers with limited capacity, or there is uncertainty of ready availability of supplies, it is always felt desirable that the company should have a captive source of supply of vital raw materials and ingredients. This may not be practicable in the case of patented items. In that case, the company may have to go in for buying the patents.

iv. Limited flexibility : With integrated production activities, it may be difficult to introduce changes in product design. Once heavy investments are made in developing manufacturing facilities or acquiring sources of supply, introducing new products or changing product design with consequential shifts in the plant facilities are likely to be too costly to bear. A company procuring its materials from outside sources can shift from one source to another to suit its requirements besides adjusting the quantity required as and when necessary.

v. Optimum scale and economy of production : Production to be economical must be so planned as to confirm to the volume required for deriving the economy of scale. If the requirements of any component is too small, it may be uneconomical to set up plant with large capacity and make full use of the same. If the requirement is irregular, the plant may be idle at intervals. On the other hand, a large capacity may be installed and the balance of output in excess of internal requirements sold to other user firms. However, this implies deploying resources for a subsidiary activity and diverting managerial attention from the primary activity.

vi. Financial strength and capability : A company with a strong financial position may be able to expand through vertical integration of activities and thereby make substantial improvements in the manufacture of components or raw materials. On the contrary, companies having limited financial capability may not be able to afford making investments other than in the major business activities.

vii. Limitation of management capabilities : Managerial competence based on specialisation in and familiarity with the primary activity is not always capable to undertaking new activities with equal efficiency. Even if new executives are recruited for the purpose, top management must devote some attention to the new activities and thus fail to devote adequate attention to the existing major activities. On the other hand, inadequate attention to the new activities may lead to sub-optimal performance in those areas.

Technology and Production Process

Along with the policy decision on production activities, policies need to be formulated also on production processes. These different aspects of the choice of production process are:

1. Technology to be used
2. Division of labour
3. Mechanisation of operations, and

4. Size and location of plants

Choice of Technology

The technology to be used is uniquely given in the case of certain industries (Products). For instance, in the manufacture of paper or straw boards, cotton and woolen textiles, edible oil, and such goods, executives have no choice in the matter of processes to be used. But it may not be so with respect to many other products. Production of cement may be undertaken using the dry process or wet process, Steel manufacture is possible with electric furnace, open-heart furnace, or oxygen inverters, Airlines may use aircraft's of different type of service in particular regions. On the choice of technology depends the decisions regarding equipments, personnel, methods of operation, and organisation. In the service organisations, too, the process to be used may require a choice to be made out of different alternatives. For instance, a consultancy firm may choose to use standard methods of inventory control, budgeting and planning for different clients. Or design the control system according to the specific requirements of particular clients.

Division of labour

The volume of production and the extent of standardisation of products determine whether and how far line operations could be sub-divided and entrusted to different operatives. Division of labour has been the characteristic feature of large-scale manufacturing works since the industrial revolution. But it has its disabilities, Routinisation of operations is known to produce monotony, boredom, lack of motivation and low morale due top 'anomie' (aloneness among many). Job enlargement is recognised now as a superior means of securing higher productivity and efficiency. Another alternative is mechanisation and automation of routine operations. Thus, in deciding how much emphasis to given to division of labour, management has to take into account the policies bearing on standardisation of products, mechanisation type of labour to be employed, and style of motivation.

Policy on mechanisation and automation

Technological advances over the last half a century have enlarged the scope of mechanisation and automation in any industries e.g. the use of tractors and harvesters in agriculture, automatic spinning and weaving in textile mills, packing of products, loading an downloading of cargo, automatic signaling in the railways, assembly line operations, etc. Computerisation of banking operations, airlines and railway bookings, maintenance and retrieval of accounting records, are being adopted in India to facilitate more efficient performance of tasks. Automatic electronic appliances are fat replacing electrical equipments. But while management is often inclined to fall in line with mechanised and automated work, they have also to face trade union resistance and government concern for the impact of labour saving devices on the employment situation. The recent policy of the Government of India to allow import of foreign technology in certain industries to improve the competitive ability of Indian enterprises is factor which is likely to influence management decisions relating to the introduction of modern technology in new venture.

Size and location of production units

For large enterprises, the decision with respect to the size of plant needs to be examined with two alternatives in view, viz.

i. Large size with centralised location, and

ii. Dispersal of operating units with small size of plant capacity

Centralised location of a large-size plant has both positive an negative implications. Large size offers advantages of large scale operation (economies of scale.) Technologically it is a must for certain industries. Manufacture of steel, cement, heavy and basic chemicals, fertilisers, etc. requires large-size plants to be set up for the sake of operational viability. Centralised location also facilitates top management control from the corporate headquarters. But there are limiting factors which do not permit large size and centralised location to be necessarily economical. One limiting factor is the cost of transportation of raw materials or finished products which may reduce the economies of large-scale production. The high cost of location in urban and metropolitan centers is another constraint. Organised trade union pressure is often found to pose serious problems of industrial relations management in large plants. The relations between the executives and operatives tend to be more impersonal, the communication system is depersonalised, and administration tends to become bureaucratic. The impact of large manufacturing organisations on the community and the environment may create problems and lead to expensive decisions to be taken in accordance with the social responsibilities of management. Industrial concentration is also regulated by Government. In India this is done through the licensing system.

Considerations in favour of decentralised small size plants may be said to arise from technological, administrative and operational advantages. Thus, for instance, the economies of scale cannot be taken for granted under all circumstances. Many a time it is found that the 'optimum size plant is just large enough to support specialised service divisions such as accounting personnel and maintenance. Production technology may be economical in spite of relatively smaller scale of operation. It is claimed that with the Korf reduction process, mini steel plants of 200,000 tpa can be erected at a cost of not more than Rs 150 crores, whereas it costs Rs 2500 crores to Rs 3000 crores to set up an integrated steel plant with a capacity of one million tpa. Smaller plants have certain distinct advantages if located in suburban areas. There is closer and friendly relations among employees, individual workers can be identified with the products they are making, there is greater scope for face-to-face interaction among the executives and operatives, and managers have first hand knowledge of operations. Employees do not have to face the urban problems of commuting to and from the work place. Not only in the case of manufacturing organisations, decentralisation of operating units has been a rewarding experience in the case of retail trading a well. Centrally located super markets have been given rise to overcrowding and traffic congestion problems. Hence there is an increasing tendency towards opening smaller stores in suburban locations. Above all, decentralised location is in keeping with Government policy, and hence it receives encouraging support form the State and Union Governments.

According to Alfred Weber, industrial location is best determined by the least-cost approach and should depend on whether the industry is market-oriented or material-oriented. An example of market-oriented location is the soft drink industry where not only is the transportation cost of the final product much higher than the cost of moving the raw material (i.e. the concentrate) but it also forms a high proportion of the selling price. Most soft drink producers thus have bottling plants located near the market. Coca Cola and bottling plants all over the world. Market oriented location may also be favoured due to factors other than only the transportation cost. In the case of Ashok Leyland Ltd, for example limitations of space and constraints caused by low volume heavy vehicle manufacture tended to suboptimise utilisation or resources and facilities of Ennore (near Madras)

Hence plants were decided to be set up also at Bhandara in Maharashtra and Alwar in Rajasthan for effectively meeting the long-term growth objectives. It was expected that location of units nearer the markets in the north, west and east would accelerate the decentralisation of service support, inspite confidence in market segments, and serve as a major instrument in achieving greater market penetration in the north and east where the vehicle population has been low.

Location of plants on the basis of material orientation due to the heavy cost of transporting materials is typically found in the case of steel, cement, paper, mineral, and agro-based industrial units. Laxmi Starch Ltd, producing starch for industrial use, started operations in Kerala because tapioca could only be obtained there, although its markets are in Bombay and Ahmedabad. Later on plants were set up in Andhra Pradesh and Gujarat for the same reason. For a project to extract drugs and produce medicines from herbs and medicinal plants, Zandu Pharmaceutical Works promoted the venture at Ankleshwar in Gujarat as herbs and medicinal plants are grown nearby. Besides, the firm was to import a lot of raw materials from Arabian countries which could dock at the many small ports near Ankleshwar. An additional factor was that it was a backward area and the company could get various incentives from Government. In a consumer goods industry requiring bulk handling of materials the manufacturing facility is better located near the sources of raw materials. Thus, vanaspati units located in urban centers (as in the case of DCM and Hindustan Lever-now Lipton's have been at a serious disadvantage on account of transport costs as compared with the rural plants particularly because of uniform prices imposed by Government. Yet another consideration in plant location is the need for balancing the transportation costs of raw materials and finished products. Companies like Tomco and Hindustan Lever producing oil, soaps and toiletries which have national wide markets and access to raw materials in different areas have set up production units in multiple locations in different zones. Tomco for instance, had production units in Ernakulam (Kerala), Bombay, Ghaziabad (U.P.) Calcutta, Madras and Guwahati (Assam). Hindustan Lever uses a linear programming model to determine the output of each of the products at each production Unit.

Estimate & Utilisation of Capacity

One of the determinates of the plant size is the desired production capacity. What should be the plant capacity is a major policy matter which needs to be examined by top management on the basis of policy decision on making various buying, estimated sâles, machine productivity and production plans. There are several aspects of policy issue, such as,

i. Norrnal requirement, and peak demand for the product.

ii. Tapering-backward capacity - (backward vertical integration with lower capacity)

iii. Provision for growth, and

iv. Balanced facilities.

In general, long-term forecasts of product line demand given an indication of what capacity might be needed several years ahead. Upon this trend are superimposed the cyclical fluctuations which tend to be much greater in amplitude for industrial than consumer products. Besides, seasonal and periodical fluctuation in business happen to characterise most industries in the market economies of today. Thus fluctuations may be due to cyclical changes or conditions emerging out of international relations (cold war or actual warfare) government regulations, consumer preference, natural calamities (droughts, floods, etc.) and another factors influencing demand. Also peaks and troughs in the state of business are often random occurrences beyond prediction. The choice of production capacity, therefore, enters round two extreme alternatives.

a. Installing capacity to meet maximum demand at all times with idle capacity as a necessary commitment;

b. Installing smaller capacity and allowing excess demand to go unsatisfied provided it does not have unbearable consequences.

But there are policy options which might smoothen the rough edges of these extremes. Establishing capacity to meet peak demand is possible where the demand is predictable as in the case of water and power supply, transport services, warehousing facilities, etc. Sometimes, for certain types of products, customers may be expected to bear with short supply up to an extent during peak demand. This they do during seasonal festivals like Deepawali, Ganesh Chaturthi, Christmas, or Durga Puja when the find the popular varieties of products sold off more quickly and little choice of variety afterwards. Thus, customers often buy their festive requirements earlier than the peak season apprehending price rise and limited choice.

There are several options to adjust plant capacity during peaks period and during slack business which are of periodic occurrence e.g.

a. Standard level production of durable products during the slack season with a view to building up stocks to meet peak demand;

b. Meeting peak demand by overtime work (three-shift Operation) if possible;

c. Having stand by arrangements to meet peak demand by way of sub-contracting excess work, if possible or maintaining high-cost obsolete equipments to be used when necessary; and

d. Off-season stock clearance sales at a discount.

All these options involve additional expenses. For example, level of production and building up stocks during slack season involve additional storage cost. Over-time work or extra shift operation implies higher costs to be borne on various counts, production with obsolete stand by equipments is naturally more costly, sub-contracting is also likely to involve higher procurement costs, Off-peak sales at discount require an appropriate pricing strategy. In short to exercise any of the options management must carry out a trade-off or cost-benefit analysis.

Backward taper capacity

Where a company decides on vertical integration to ensure the supply of raw materials, parts of other ingredients, fluctuations in the volume of business of the final product may be absorbed more easily with a backward tapering capacity, i.e. installing a small capacity for raw material production and meeting additional requirements by purchase from outside suppliers. However, such a policy can be practicable, provided there are potential suppliers ready to meet the fluctuating requirements, If so, the production facilities created for materials, parts or ingredients can be used to full capacity, and meet the minimum requirements.

Provision for growth

To what extent should executives stretch their commitment to the creation of production facilities now in anticipation of future growth of business? Piece meal addition to plant capacity and service facilities involving structural expansion may be inconvenient as well as expensive. Even though investment outlay may be conveniently spread over time, fixed costs may render frequent addition of facilities to be more expensive, Frequent disruption of normal activities also may be undesirable.

But creation of surplus capacity in anticipation of growth may not be continent either. It involves resource deployment of a sizable amount and locking up of liquid funds, besides use of current resources for the maintenance of ideal facilities. Hence, neither piecemeal expansion nor creation of surplus capacity in advance is desirable. The policy under the circumstances should be to provide for future expansion by way of acquisition of space and setting up bare structures of buildings, so that additional machinery may be installed and personnel employed as and when necessary. No doubt, provision for growth will depend upon the magnitude of growth anticipated and the amount f liquid funds to be initially deployed for the purpose.

Balanced facilities

Production, marketing, and various service operations, including maintenance and repairs, materials handling, warehousing, testing, packagings, etc. require adequate capacity in conformity with the volume of business so that of work is not interrupted by bottlenecks in any operational area. Thus, it is essential that facilities in different units and subunits must have balanced capacities, Changes taking place in the methods of operation and changes in personnel in certain units may disturb the existing balance from time to time. The need for balancing facilities thus involves a continuous process of decision making to maintain the balance.

Maintenance and replacement policy

If the existing plant capacity and service facilities are well maintained, there are distinct advantages, and management can accordingly decide on plant capacity to be initially created. Depending on personal preference of the executives and philosophy of management determining the attitude toward up keep and maintenance, the policy may be one of high level conditioning of work environment, or a discriminating policy with deliberate decisions to provide for proper maintenance of only those facilities which are of critical importance like production, and stores.

Machines and equipments, plant services (power, gas, water, sewers, pumps, fire protection), transportation facilities and building (roofs, walls, floors, fixtures and fittings) need repairs and upkeep by way of greasing, lubricating and overhauling so as to prevent breakdowns. The importance of preventive maintenances is recognised in all work places for several reasons. Breakdowns stop production, make men and machines idle, cause lost production, and put orders behind schedule. The biggest cost of maintenance is the cost of down for repairs. Breakdown repairs may have to be carried out on overtime and such repairs may involve bigger jobs, for a breakdown often cause damage also to interconnected parts. Preventive maintenance may thus be the 'stitch in time that saves nine'. It helps to reduce repairs, particularly those caused by breakdown of machines in use.

The cost of maintenance cannot be kept too low. Preventive maintenance costs may be fairly high but the corresponding payoff may justify the same, one way of holding down maintenance cost it to have trouble spots before failures occur. Operations research techniques like the queuing or waiting line theory may also be useful to balance the need for maintenance staff and the maintenance work involved. Whether the repair of replace machine parts and equipments which have worn out is a decision related to the maintenance of facilities. Obviously, it should depend on the cost involved. There are certain types of equipments of which the trouble-free period of use can be estimated irrespective of the apparent condition. Transport vehicles, engines, aircrafts, and facilities like boilers fall in that category. Technological obsolescence may also require equipments to be replaced, e.g. electronic data processing equipments. In the case of old machinery it may be worthwhile to repair, it rather than put in new parts which will outwear the machine. On the other hand, replacement of worn parts may be less costly in terms of labour time and skill requirements while the cost of new part may affect the saving in labour time.

Purchasing Policy Issues

Having discussed the production policies nearing on vertical integration, production processes, plant size and capacity, and maintenance of facilities, we may now turn to the basic purchasing policy matters. While examining the question of vertical integration we have already explained the relevant factors that may influence decisions to produce raw materials, components and parts for the final product, and the extent of backward vertical integration possible under various circumstances. What about supplies and services? Should a company make or buy its requirements of customers, stationery, transport services, water and power supply, and such other items? Thirdly, what kind of policy decisions should govern the condition-coordination of production, purchasing and sales?

Make of Buy Decisions

Research studies have shown that make-or buy decisions are sometimes made on the basis of insufficient data and faulty evaluation of implications resulting in huge wastage from making what could be more advantageously bought. Whether it is the production of containers and packing materials, or printing of forms, circulars and notices, or securing factory and office supplies, or transportation services, if there is no dependable source of procuring the items, obviously the buying option is ruled out. Dependability of reliability of supply should be naturally considered in terms of quantity, quality and timeliness of availability. Thus, for instance, the inadequacy of public power supply has led to the installation of power generators by many companies in certain States.

In general, a decision to make should follow whenever the expected cost savings provide a higher return on the required capital investment then can be obtained from employing the funds. In an alternative investment bearing the same risk. Thus, few firms, if any, consider making the items of office stationery (pencils, writing paper, and hundred other items) worthwhile, likewise, setting up of a printing press to print office forms, circulars and notices may not be worthwhile for most firms since there may not be enough printing work to ensure economic use of the printing machine. But intuitive decisions may not be possible in all cases, particularly when differential' costs are of major significance.

Identifying and estimating the relevant costs of manufacturing a product or creating a service facility require the following aspects to be noted :

i. Fixed costs seldom remain unaffected, particularly the managerial costs. The planning and supervision of any new operation may divert present managers from other responsibilities or require additional supervisory personnel. These costs are somewhat difficult to measure and are often ignored.

ii. Sunk costs (i.e. costs otherwise incurred on creating facilities) have a value depending on whether the same can be utilised by the firm for other internal purposes, rented, or disposed of;

iii. Imputed interest costs have to be taken into account when large investments are involved, which can be done by discounting the future cash flows;

iv. Projecting the cost of raw materials needs consideration of the type and quantity of materials required, probable market trends, availability of reliable suppliers, freight, order size, discount etc.

v. Risk of long-term investment creates a bias in favour of buying. The risk element may be recognised by adding a premium to the rate of expected return;

vi. While calculating the differential cost of making and buying, the purchase cost should include the net supply price plus freight and incremental handling costs.

Apart from the saving in costs and return on capital investments, there are several non-cost factors that also need to be considered. In favour of making there may be such factors:

a. instability of supply

b. poor quality of supply

c. desire to maintain secrecy of process

d. tax considerations

e. ideal facilities

f. maintenance of labour already employed

On the other hand, in favour of buying there may be considerations, such as:

a. lack of capital

b. possibility of passing on the risk of investment to suppliers.

c. lack of managerial experience

d. fluctuation requirements due to uneven production of end products

e. scope of wider selection, and

f. special services rendered by outside suppliers.

Vendor Selection Policy

All companies regardless of the extent of vertical integration have to make purchases of certain materials and supplies as well as services. This is because of the various constraints—mainly financial and managerial— which make downstream integration impracticable beyond a stage. Wholesalers and retailers must buy the products for sale, most manufacturers have to by the factory stores and supplies, if not raw materials, for the final product, or for components and parts to be produced. Assuming that a number of dependable outside sources of supply exist, it needs to be decided :

a. how many suppliers (vendors) should a company make purchases from—several of them, or one of two or two of them, and

b. by what criteria should the company choose the suppliers to deal with?

Is it more advantageous to make purchases from one or two suppliers? If such a policy is contemplated, one must take into account its implications, particularly with respect to the more essential items to be purchased. Let us consider the advantages of making bulk purchases from one or two vendor firms. One advantage is that of quantity discount and obtaining supplies at favourable prices. A supplier can afford to offer favourable prices to large purchasers obviously because of his saving of selling costs. Obtaining suppliers from one or two vendors also ensures reliability in terms of quality and delivery schedule. It may help secure special terms of credit besides accommodation in the matter of collection of dues during financial stress sat any time.

However, the dangers of concentrating purchases and buying from one or two suppliers cannot be ignored altogether. The obvious risk involved in such a policy is that any disruption n supply caused by (say) labour unrest, or unforeseen calamities like fire, may seriously impair the company's operations, since it may be difficult to shift to other suppliers at short notice except on the basis of stringent terms as to price and credit. Thus, it may be advantageous to place smaller orders to a number of suppliers, although this may be somewhat more expensive. Quantity discounts and terms of credit cannot be as favourable as in the case of large purchaser from one or two suppliers. Another advantage of dealing with number of vendors may be that of bargaining each supplier being on his toes lest orders are shifted to competing suppliers if the quality, price and delivery services are not to be buyers' satisfaction.

The policy on the issue should thus be formulated on the basis of favourable price, terms of credit, and other services expected to be derived from concentration of purchases, and the dangers of over dependence on one or two vendors for essential materials and supplies, as well as the advantages of bargaining on the terms of purchase with a number of vendors.

Criteria for Selecting Vendors

Selection of vendors requires careful consideration of several aspects, e.g. conformity with the quality of products, the price, and service available. Quality of the product to be purchased is often an important factor and reliability of the vendor on this account must be ensured even if this involves payment of higher price. However, if the quality of a product can be verified objectively by independent testing, the vendors' reputation may not be vital to consider.

Another consideration while selecting a vendor should be the price. Most purchases are made on the basis of competitive price quotations subject to the product being of the desired quality. If the difference in prices charged by two or more vendors is not significant, consideration of quality and other services provided by the vendors may be the determining factors in selection. The significance of the price factor in purchase basically depends upon the cost of the purchased material relative to the total cost of production. The services provided by any vendor may be important as compensating factors if the price is relatively higher. The services may include delivery on rush orders, technical aid (in the case of machines and equipment), repair services, guarantees, and adjustment in the size and specification of items, etc.

Sometimes, reciprocity may also be a factor determining the choice of a vendor, the basis being you buy from me and I'll buy from you. The reciprocal arrangement may be beneficial to both the parties, but it should not be at the cost of inferior quality, higher price, or poorer services. Reciprocity may have a balancing effect though, for what is lost in buying may be gained on selling. However, reciprocal arrangement may not be possible if only a small quantity is required to be purchased from any large producer. Reciprocity goes well between equals. Back in the old days, Ford Motor Company purchased Firestone tyres for automobiles while Firestone tyre manufacturers used only Ford cars and trucks.

Timing Production and Purchase

Most consumer goods as well as industrial goods are procured or produced in anticipation of demand. Sales are made out of stocks carried. On the other hand, in some industries, procurement and production take place on the basis of orders booked. Manufacture of heavy machinery, quality furniture, aircrafts, ships and trawlers, indeed all products to be supplied according to customer specifications fall in this category. However, even in these cases, it may be possible to carry standard parts and components in stock, and only the final assembly operations many may be done on the basis of order received. It is true that holding inventories in anticipation of customer demand involves certain risks. e.g. the risk of obsolescence, damage and deterioration it also involves locking up of capital, and incurring storage costs. Procuring inventories in accordance with sales orders may reduce the risks and costs involved. However, procurement of inventories for stock may enable management to take advantage of the economy of large scale operations, quantity discounts, and prompt delivery, as well as to avail of the vendors' services. Contrarily, purchasing small lots corresponding to orders booked may result in slow delivery and higher costs.

Thus, the coordination of purchasing and production with sales is essentially related with the timing of procurement. It is not a question of either buying in anticipation of orders or waiting until orders are in hand. Rather it is a question of the extent to which procurement for stock should be combined with procurement 'to order'. The policy on this issue depend on the following considerations:

a. Minimum inventory of raw materials finished goods that is to be carried. This should be adequate to meet unforeseen contingencies like delay in getting supply from the vendor, or the actual use being more than the anticipated requirement, or any possible delay in production operations. The level of finished goods inventory at which replenishment should be ordered, i.e. and re-ordering required for replacement). In the case of raw materials, orders should be placed for replenishment of stock at that point where the level of inventory is adequate to meet the production requirements during the period which the vendor may take to execute the order.

b. Reorder Quality: The size of the purchase order, for replenishment of stocks, is primarily dependent on the economical production runs which can be estimated in terms of the number of days or weeks or month's requirement. On the other hand, there are cost implications, of buying large lots and small lots, with large order size the number of purchase orders is likely to be fewer and hence clerical expenses (ordering costs) may be lower, freight charges and handling costs are also higher carrying costs (cost of storage space, insurance, damage and deterioration, if not obsolescence). Ordering small quantities will imply a larger number of orders, hence higher ordering costs (clerical expenses), but reduced capital investment and interest, freight charges, and handling costs, as well as lower carrying costs. The concept of 'economic lot size' or 'economic order quantity' may be used to resolve the question or order size. The most economical lot size or reorder quantity should be that which minimises the average cost taking into account the aggregate of carrying costs and ordering costs. With different order sizes, the ordering costs will tend to decline and carrying cost to up as the order size is increased. The aggregate cost would be minimum when the two types of costs (one going up and the other coming down) are equal. Thus, the most economical order size is given by the equation.

c. Fluctuations in sales: Purchases and production in the face of seasonal and cyclical in fluctuation in the volume of sales may lead to over-stocking or under-stocking of inventory at different times. The problem can be overcome by (i) adjusting purchase and production in harmony with sales volume (ii) adjusting parches and production in harmony with sales volume maintaining a level rate of production, purchasing and producing for stock during the slack period and using the same to meet peak demand or (iii) sub-contracting instead of expanding production during periods of peak demand, or (iv) leveling out the impact of periodic fluctuations in demand. The first option, that is adjusting purchase and production in accordance with the sales volume, is found useful in the case of products which are subject to periodic changes in customer tastes and fashions, e.g. ready-made garments, ladies handbags, footwear, etc. In these cases, it may be advisable not to carry inventories in excess of the sales needs. But implies higher costs on account of idle facilities and plant capacity, loss of skilled personnel, and discontinuity of operations. Level production (the second option) involves production in excess of demand during slack periods and building up inventory to be available for sale during peak demand. The policy may help the company to retain skilled personnel and enable full use of the production facilities, plant and equipment throughout the year. But it involves additional financial and storage costs to be incurred during the slack season, along with the risks of obsolescnce and deterioration. In industries subject to rapid technological changes, level production may lead to a competitive disadvantage for the company. Moreover, it may not be easy to predict the extent of fluctuations in demand. The third option of subtracting may not permit procurement of adequate quantities during the busy season and hence lead to loss of customers. The fourth option (leveling out the impact of fluctuating demand) may be acted upon in different ways e.g. adding new products that have complementary seasonal fluctuations, allowing off-season discounts on sale, or by changing the time of introducing new models as was done by automobile manufacturers in the United States.

d. Fluctuation in Prices: Should the reorder quantity be adjusted in anticipation of price changes? One normally expects that order quantity should be currently increased if prices are expected to fall. In other words, stocks should be built up in anticipation of a price rise, and cut down in anticipation of a decline in prices. But there are two problems to be taken care of. One is that of forecasting price changes. The other relates to the availability of supply. With anticipatory rise of prices and brisk business conditions procurement is likely to take longer time in view of higher demand. It may be easier to reduce order quantities in anticipation of fall of prices. Besides speculative buying i.e. building up stocks in anticipation of a price rise is risky, particularly on account of the difficulty of accurately forecasting price trends. The policy of adjusting the size of purchase orders and timing thereof should therefore be governed by two considerations: (a) predictability of price changes, and (b) estimation in advance of the volume of demand of particular items of inventory.

Personnel Policies

The significance of personnel policy in strategy implementation hardly needs any elaboration. Both physical and human resources are crucial to the achievement of strategic goals. The basic objective of personnel policy in an organisation is to ensure consistency of action and equity in its relations with employees. These policies constitute the basic for sound personnel practices. They provide the yardstick by which implementation of strategic plans and Programmes can be appraised. Besides, personnel policies are an integral part of the whole policy structure of an enterprise. Any weakness in personnel policy may thus weaken the effectiveness of other functional policies.

The close inter-relation between the quality of personnel and strategic management requires the top executives to be concerned with the following major policy issues bearing on personnel:

a. Recruitment, promotion and transfer

b. Training and development

c. Compensation and supplementary benefits

d. Industrial relations policy

e. Collective bargaining

Recruitment Policy

The appropriate match between strategic goals to be achieved and the kind of people employed require two different but related aspects of staffing to be examined.

On the one hand, there is the necessity of recruiting and maintaining the required number of work people, and on the other it is necessary to ensure that the quality of people employed in terms of skill and competence are suited to the specific requirements of the strategy. As Dale Yoder observed, "the recruitment policy is concerned with quantity and qualifications (vis. the Q_1 and Q_2) of manpower". Several factors are involved in determining a firm's recruitment policy:

i. The relevant public policy on hiring and employment relationships (e.g. Government regulations for employment of persons from scheduled castes/tribes and backward communities, and handicapped persons)

ii. Provision of employment security of individual employees

iii. Provision for an encouragement to each employee in the continuing development of his talents and skill

iv. Assurance to employees of a fair deal in all employment relationships including promotions and transfers

v. Assurance to each employee of the organisational interest in his personal goals and employment objectives

Sources of Recruitment

Most companies recruit personnel from internal as well as external sources. The internal sources include personnel already employed in the organisation. Recruitment involves upgrading, transfer or promotion of the existing employees to fill the vacancies or positions created. The use of internal source has a positive impact on employee morale and motivation. The management can better evaluate the capabilities of the existing staff than outside candidates. It requires little training to be provided to the employees and eventually lead to the building up of a more committed workforce for the organisation. But internal recruitment also engenders the continuation of inbreeding and prevents induction of 'new blood' in the organisation. Jobs which require innovations, application of complex new techniques, and originality of ideas, are thus not expected to be filled up from internal sources. Recruitment from sources outside the organisation may consist of hiring from (1) new entrants to the employment market-mostly young graduates and those who have been trained in various technical/professional institutions (ii) the unemployed possessing skills and abilities, (iii) retired, experienced persons available for employment, and (iv) others employed in other organisations but seeking a change for better prospects. External recruitment obviously provides wider choice from among personnel to select those with skill, training, education and experience required by the firm. For a firm which needs personnel for implementing growth strategy, the process of recruitment from external sources must be planned well in advance. The problems of external recruitment consist of the relatively higher turnover of new recruits and the demoralising effect of outside requirement on the existing work organisation.

Promotion Policy

The ability and versatility of employees are invariably improved with an appropriate promotion policy. These qualities are of great relevance to the implementation of strategic changes. Horizontal and vertical promotions serve two distinct purposes. Horizontal promotion refers to horizontal transfer to a job at more or less the same level but it regarded as a promotion because it represents the normal path of advancement in the company. Horizontal promotion fosters versatility as it enables executives to cope with different kinds of jobs, and they get accustomed to change, which is often a characteristic feature of corporate strategy. The varied experience of men provide a broader perspective to their assignments. It increases the scope of promotion, for the employee concerned does not have to wait for his immediate superior to retire to get a promotion. But the training cost is likely to be higher. With horizontal promotion, a man has more to learn on his new job and he may take decisions without a complete understanding of the total situation.

Vertical promotion serves a different purpose. It enables people to improve their ability and expertise which cannot be developed through horizontal promotion. Also, vertical promotion provides the desired career paths for individuals. Exceptional performance can thus be retained in the organisation and their capabilities enhanced a at the same time. Vertical promotion as a policy is well suited to companies or departments where the harnessing of unusual human talent is a part of the strategy.

The most widely recognised basis for promotion is a combination of both seniority and merit. Thus, for persons of equal seniority merit is the criterion used for promotion. On the other hand, seniority is adopted as the basis for promotion where employed are of more or less equal competence. However, promotion by seniority is preferred by trade unions as seniority can be objectively determined in all cases. It also keeps up employee morale in the organisation for all are assured of promotion in due course of time. But seniority based promotion does not appeal to the young meritorious employees for there is no appreciation of their worth as such. Hence, the more competent among them develop a sense of frustration and are on the lookout for employment elsewhere. They naturally prefer promotion by merit which rewards efficiency and achievement in work performance. From the organisational point of view, merit-based promotion leads to higher productivity and encourages hard work.

Keeping in view the necessity of combining merit and seniority as the basis of promotion, it is necessary that the promotion policy should ensure: (a) that the abilities of personnel receive primary attention in the recruitment programme, (b) that employees have the opportunity of satisfying their own aspirations within the organisational framework, and (c) that a programme of career-planning with periodic assessment is systematically followed by management.

Transfer Policy

Transfer of an employee refers to his lateral movement from one job, a department, or shift to another where his status, responsibility and salary are the same. Transfer of employees may be necessitated by changes in the organisational structure or operations and also occasioned by other factors, e.g. for better utilisation of employee capabilities, to increase the versatility of employees, to accommodate the personal needs and conveniences of individuals. Since strategic management is associated with changes in the organisation structure and working arrangement, transfers are inevitably the handmaid of strategy implementation.

The transfer policy that is formulated must clarify the types of transfers and the conditions under which these will be made. Whether transfers will be restricted within a segment or unit or department, and the persmissibility of inter-departmental or inter unit transfer also need to be indicated. The basis of transfers—ability and competence or seniority or both-is another aspect of transfer to be decided as a part of the transfer policy.

Training and Development Policy

The distinction between training and development has been very well explained by Steiments as follows:

"Training is a short-term process utilising a systematic and organised procedure by which non-managerial personnel learn technical knowledge and skill for a definite purpose. Development is a long-term educational process utilising a systematic and organised procedure by which managerial personnel learn conceptual and theoretical knowledge for general purposes."

In the context of strategy implementation, the need for training may arise for different reasons, e.g. to enable existing employees and new recruits to undertake operations involving new technology, or adapt the existing methods and techniques to changing needs, or improving the efficiency of work performance by employees, to achieve higher productivity, reduce supervision time, minimise spoilage of materials develop the potential abilities of workmen, etc. The basic purpose of training is to help meet company objectives by providing opportunities for employees at all organisational levels to acquire the requisite knowledge, skills and attitudes. More specifically the primary objectives of training are:

a. To impart to new entrants the knowledge and skill they need for an intelligent performance of their tasks;

b. To assist employees to perform their tasks more efficiently;

c. To prepare employees for promotion to positions which require added skill and knowledge, and

d. To bridge the gap between existing performance and potential performance.

The training policy indicates the commitment of top management to provide for employee training and it includes the guidelines for determining the standard and scope of training. Thus, in the process of formulating the training policy, management recognises where training programmes need to be organised, and can allocate necessary resources for the purpose of the basis of priorities.

Management development, which is different from employee training, is as much, if not more, significant in strategy implementation. Factors which have contributed to the increasing importance of organising management development programmes on a continuing basis include; technological changes and changes in the socio-economic conditions, public policy, concepts of social justice, problems of labour-management relations and human engineering, economics (working environment), besides extension of the frontiers, of knowledge in management science and techniques of decision making.

The policy on management development is generally aimed at improving the managerial effectiveness of individual through a planned and deliberate process. This implies a change in the individual brought about through the learning process. The change may consist of change of knowledge, attitude and/or behaviour leading to performance change and/or change in the end-operational results. Depending on the level of management and the objectives of this programme of management development, there are different techniques which may be used for the purpose. Apart from class-room techniques course and group discussion, the methods used include the syndicate technique, incident process, business game, in basket training and sensitivity (T-group) training.

Compensation and Fringe Benefits Policy

Policies with regard to wage and salary administration and policy on supplementary benefits are vial components of personnel policy because it is mainly on the basis of satisfactory compensation schemes that a company is able to attract and retain capable personnel. In the absence of a sound policy with respect to the compensation structure, wages and salaries are likely to be based on personalised arbitrary decisions and thus fall short of the essential elements of adequacy and equity in compensation plans. A satisfactory policy frame is invariably conductive to high morale and minimum frictions among individuals and groups of employees. For, apart from the adequacy of the level of compensation, in equalities in the pay structure happen to be the most common causes of dissatisfaction and grievances among employees.

The basic issues to be resolved while formulating the compensation policy are those relating to:

1. The level of pay and its adequacy
2. The internal structure of compensation or internal alignment of pay for different jobs so as to ensure that pay rates are equitable
3. Recognition of relative efficiency of performance
4. Incentive pay.

Pay Levels and Adequacy of Compensation

The major considerations that influence the pay levels include (a) the competitive rates in the labour market (particularly in the geographical region, (b) industry levels of pay, (c) financial strength of the company and (d) management policies. Wage and salary survey may be designed to determine the general pay levels in the region and industry thus providing the management with a base for setting the rates. The Labour

Bureau of the Union Ministry of Labour, Government of India conducted occupational wage survey on a sample basis in 1958-59, 1963-65 and 1974-79. The survey covered 81 industries—manufacturing (60), mining & Plantation (3) The survey date provide valuable information, but large companies are known to conduct their own survey to supplement the data otherwise available from the industry or employer's associations. While the going market rates of pay in any region or industry may be used as a basis of fixing the pay levels in an organisation, and many companies, do have a policy of paying competitive rates. It does not necessary follow that every company should adopt this policy. When wages and salaries are decided to be paid in line with other, employers in the industry or local market, the company depends on other factors to attract and retain its employees. The policy of adjusting pay levels to the local market rates is generally considered fair, and provides a good basis for defence in negotiations with unions. However, some companies do pay higher than the going rates to attract and secure the services of more competent personnel. Higher rates may have to be paid also to offset unfavourable plant location or working conditions. A distinct advantage of higher rates is the low turnover of employees. On the other hand, some companies decide to pay lower than the average rates to the extent that adequate supply of manpower is obtained. In between, pay levels are found to be different for different companies, in respect of comparable jobs, due to varying corporate requirements, different levels of technology in use, the degrees of skill differentiation and specifically of jobs in industries.

Often companies are required to attach greater importance to industry rates in view of the degree of unionisation and the bargaining strength of unions. Further, the awards of industrial tribunal and tripartite wage boards become the overriding factors in determining the levels of pay of workmen in the relevant industries.

Internal Alignment of Compensation Rates

The external competitiveness of the pay structure is taken care of through the process of setting the pay levels in comparison with the pay structure of the labour market and industry rates. But an equally important aspect of policy is related to the need for establishing on internally equitable pay structure. The importance of securing occupational wage differentials that reflect the job requirements arises from the fact that psychologically employees are as much, if not more, interested in how their pay compares with that of their fellow-workers, as in the actual amount of pay they receive. The basis of wage differentials n naturally to be the relative worth of jobs in terms of skill, education and experience required, the nature of duties involved, responsibilities to be borne, the working conditions including the hazards of the occupation. Job-evaluation or job-rating techniques are helpful n classifying the job in accordance with their relative worth and grading them for purposes of pay fixation.

Efficiency of Performance

Compensating individual employees for the jobs assigned also need consideration of the relative differences in the efficiency of employees in terms of the quantity and quality of work done on the jobs. For one thing, a person newly assigned to a job could not be as perfect as another doing it for a number of year. Even otherwise, persons different in their abilities to pick up the nature of work more quickly than others; the learning curves are not uniformly stretched for all employees. The system of payment by result of price-rate compensation my be used so that pay is adjusted on the basis of differences in performance. However, output is not easily measurable in the case of administrative, supervisory and managerial jobs. To resolve this problem, most companies have a range of pay or pay-scale for each job. New recruits are generally paid at the minimum of the scale and the incremental pay in the scale takes care of their improved performance over time upto the maximum in the scale. A wider range of scale of pay may be provided if the nature of work and the possible of pay may be provided if the nature of work and the possible variations in individual performances warrant it. In that case superior performance may be rewarded by extra increments in the pay scale over and above the time bound increment. However, if the spread in pay scale is wide management control over the salary bill may to that extent become more difficulty.

Incentive Pay

The extra pay that is provided for extra performance in addition to the regular pay for a job is termed incentive pay. Incentive pay plans are designed to stimulate human effort by rewarding the person, over and above the time-rated remuneration, for improvements in the present or targeted results. Thus, financial incentive schemes are essentially regarded as managerial devices aimed at increasing the productivity of employees. While the financial incentive schemes prevalent in Indian Industries are known to have yielded positive results in terms of higher output. Management cannot ignore the significance of non monetary incentives for motivating employees particularly in the supervisory and managerial cadres. A worthwhile generalisation in the aspect is that" the higher the position of a person in an organisation's hierarchy, the greater is his vulnerability to non-financial incentives. Further budgetary restrictions and temporary improvements place a limit on the potency of money as a motivator while non-financial incentives involve only human ingenuity as investment and also ensure a relatively stable improvement in performance.

The most widely practiced schemes of incentive pay in India happen to be the piece-rate and payment of production bonus usually at a differential rate for the output in excess of the normal out-put for a unit of time. The output norms are generally based on job analysis and time studies. Individual as well as group incentive schemes are adopted depending on the measurability of the output of individuals and the inter-dependence of the work of individuals. The problems that arise in the operation of incentive schemes have been found to be as follows:

a. Complex incentive plans are not easily understood particularly with respect to the relation between reward and effort;

b. Where the rate structure comprises many slabs, the basis of calculation of the premium of bonus change, distinctions, between different types of employees as permanent, temporary, supervisory staff, workmen, etc. also lead to the use of multiple bases of calculation:

c. The rate structure of incentive pay does not reflect adequate progressively even when employees shows high levels of performance;

d. Group incentive schemes are more difficult to operate effectively due to the absence of any direct link between effort and earnings.

A satisfactory plant of incentive pay requires the following critical factors to be given due consideration:

i. The effectiveness of pay incentive depends on the total situation or the organisational climate including mutual confidence between management and employees, union-management relations, quality of supervision and the system of communication;

ii. No incentive plan can succeed until there is full understanding of all its implications among the concerned parties, which can be ensured through participation of employees in the planning of the scheme and also negotiations with the union at appropriate stages;

iii. Change of methods and rates of incentive pay at intervals may appear to be attempts at rate-cutting by management, which must be guarded against. A machinery for grievance settlement may be helpful in removing any impression of 'unfair' action by management.

iv. Once output has risen above that required for guaranteed pay, incentive payment should be in proportion to the rise in output.

v. Management of any incentive pay schemes requires supervisors and managers to be trained all the way down the line so that problems may dealt with at the unit or sub-unit level;

vi. Norms of work and output need to be set with great care so as to avoid the rates being too hard or too loose.

Policy on Supplementary Benefits

As also known as 'fringe benefits' the supplements to an employees' regular earnings constitute a very important element of compensation policy. Included in these benefits are: monetary bonus (e.g. profit bonus, festival bonus, attendance bonus, service bonus, etc.) payment for time not worked (vacation and holiday pay, leave travel expenses, paid sick leave, etc.) social security contributions (gratuity and pension payments, contribution to employees' provident fund account, health and insurance schemes), and voluntary benefits like subsidised housing, medical benefits, subsidised canteen facility, educational and cultural facilities, assistance to co-operative societies, childcare, transportation, recreation, group insurance, legal aid, and the like. The policy on providing supplementary benefits and services to employees is governed by several factors, e.g., cost involved and the company's ability to bear the incidence, needs of employees, bargaining strength of the union, tax consideration, public relations, social responsibility, statutory obligations, and the reaction of employees. But the necessity of providing some of these benefits cannot be altogether ignored.

Industrial Relations Policy

The personnel policies and practices of a firm are in many ways influenced by the state of union-management relations. To what extent the basic philosophy of top management vis-a-viz their human resources is subordinated to the bargaining power of employee union depends upon the company's policy with regard to:

i. the nature of relation with the union,

ii. recognition and support of the union organisation,

iii. the scope of collective bargaining, and

iv. settlement of industrial disputes.

Ideally, harmonious relations between management and employee unions should develop on the basis of mutual co-operation. But company executives are often inclined to adopt a policy of belligerency toward union activities. This approach is born out of a strong dislike and mistrust of the union by the executives, who refuse to recognise the union as a bargaining agent, or when forced to negotiate, do it grudgingly with a horse-trading approach. With a hostile attitude of management toward the union, the relationship is inevitably vitiated by mutual suspicion, and there is increase in the militancy on the part of union leaders.

Short of perfect understanding whether union, it may be desirable for management to adopt a policy of straight business relationship with the union leaders. A stable union organisation and the maturity of outlook on the part of executives as well as union leaders can generate mutual confidence and trust, so that demands pressed by he union, even if resisted by company executives, do not lead to strong emotional reactions but are taken in the normal stride of business like dealings.

In India, union-management relations in many companies are affected by a number of factors not so congenial for a co-operative approach. One such factor is the existence of multiple union and acute inter-union rivalry in most industrial organisations. The influence of political parties to which the trade union owe allegiance is another complicating factor. Because of the multiplicity of trade unions at the plant level, no particular union commands absolute majority of membership. This gives rise to the problem of recognition of any union as the sole bargaining agent. Prior to 1946, there was no provision in law regarding grant of recognition to the trade unions. It was the Bombay Industrial Relations Act, 1946 which provided for the recognition of representative unions. The Act is applied in Gujarat and in a modified form in Madhya Pradesh as well as Rajasthan. The Indian Labour Conference as its fifteenth session in 1958 accepted certain criteria for recognition of trade unions as a part of the Code of Discipline approved at the Session. The criteria for recognition are as follows:

i. Where there is more than one union, any union claiming recognition should have been functioning for at least one year before recognition.

ii. The membership of any union claiming recognition should cover at least 15% of the workers in the establishment concerned. Membership should be counted only for those who had paid their subscriptions for at least three months during the period of six months immediately preceding the count.

iii. A union may claim to the recognised as a representative union for an industry in a local area if it has a membership of at least 25% of the workers of that industry in the area.

iv. When a union has been recognised, there should be no change in the position for a period of two years.

v. Where there are several unions in an industry or establishment, the one with the largest membership should be recognised.

vi. A representative union for an industry in any area should have the right to represent workers in all the establishments in the industry; but if a union of workers in a particular establishment has a membership of 50% or more of workers, it should have the right to a call with matters of purely local interest, e.g., handling of grievances pertaining to its own members. The other workers who are not members of that union might either operate through the representative union for the industry or seek redress directly.

vii. Only those unions which observed the Code of Discipline would be entitled to recognition.

As provided under the Bombay Industrial Relations Act as well as the code of discipline, recognised unions can exercise the following rights:

(a) right of 'check off' (i.e., deduction of union dues from the workers pay by the employers);

(b) to use the Notice Board on the premises of the undertaking for union purposes;

(c) to appoint its nominees on the Works Committee;

(d) to represent an employee in any proceeding under the industrial. Disputes Act;

(e) with regard to prevention and settlement of industrial disputes.

(f) to hold discussions on the premises of the undertaking with the employees concerned, who members of the union, but so as not to interfere with normal working of the undertaking.

(g) to meet and discuss with an employer or any other person appointed by him in that behalf, the grievances of employees employed in the undertaking;

(h) to inspect, if necessary, in an undertaking any place an employee of the undertaking is employed.

The existence of multiple unions in an organisation, besides posing the problem of identifying and recognising the representative union, also makes it difficult for company executives to decide on the subjects of collective bargaining. Well organised, stable unions are naturally most conductive to collective agreements, which really consist of rules on the terms and conditions of employment mutually agreed between the representatives of workers and management. As a vehicle of industrial peace and prevention of industrial strife, collective bargaining has no equal and it may be regarded as the most important and significant aspect of union management relations.

Financial Policies

The finance function, like the production and marketing functions, involves decision-making and action, for which managers must be provided guidelines or policies to ensure consistency and uniformity of approach to problems and issues. Essentially, the financial policy issues relate to the procurement of funds and utilisation of funds. In the context of a chosen strategy, financial policy may be said to related to such questions as: what total volume of finance will be required? It ill be influenced by the kinds of investment opportunities available as well as by conditions affecting the sources from which finance is derived. Similarly, the cost and availability of funds depend in part on the quantity and quality of investment purposes for which they will be used.

Following important policy issues in relation to finance function need special consideration:

1. Sources of finance and capital structure decisions
2. Investment decisions
3. Financing decisions and dividend policy
4. Policy for Raising Fund

Sources of Finance

For successful implementation of the chosen strategy, availability of fund is a major precondition. Broadly speaking, finance may be available from two sources (i) External, and (ii) Internal. The external sources of finance may consist of ownership capital and/or borrowed capital. In the case of companies, ownership capital may be raised by issue of (a) equity shares, and (b) preference shares. Borrowed capital, on the other hand, may be raised by issue of debentures, through public deposits, and as direct loans and credits. Internal funds are generated by way of retention of profits (creation of free reserves), and provision of depreciation on fixed assets.

External Sources: Apart from the public issue of debentures, which varying terms and conditions, providing long-term funds, special financial institutions (IDBI IFIC ICICI, and the state level financial and industrial development corporations) also constitute major sources of long-term capital. Public deposits have increasingly become an important source of short-term finance as a partial substitute for bank borrowing which is costlier and requires collateral securities to be offered. Large companies may also have access to foreign sources of capita. Non- resident investors have recently contributed to the equity issues of many companies in view of the government policy encouraging such investments from abroad. Collaboration with foreign companies involving equity participation of the latter is also permitted by government on a selective basis. The ceiling for foreign equity participation is 40 per cent although exception are considered, on merit. For approved projects, the World Bank and the International Finance Corporation (an affiliate of the World Bank) also extend loans to private industrial firms.

Control of Capital Issues : Under the Capital Issues (Control) Act, 1947, companies making public offer of securities are required to obtain the consent of Controller of Capital issues if such issues, in any consecutive period of 12 months, exceeds Rs 1 crore (until recently, the exemption limit was Rs 50 lakhs). But loans from banks for working capital finance as well as loans from financial institutions are exempt. Public limited companies issuing securities other than debentures exceeding Rs 1 crore are also exempt provided the following conditions are fulfilled, e.g. (a) the debt equity ratio does not exceed 2 : 1, (b) Shares are issued at par (c) Calls, if any, are made on uniform basis and shares are fully paid-up over a maximum period of 5 years, (d) The rate of dividend on preference shares and the rate of interest on debentures do not exceed the maximum limit as notified by the Controller; and (e) The offer of shares to the public is such as is eligible for listing on a recognised stock exchange. Private companies are exempt from control over capital issues except where they make an issue of securities in which an amount exceeding 20 per cent is subscribed by a public limited company or companies, and the amount involved exceeds Rs 1 crore during a period of 12 months.

Shares : Companies may issue equity shares and/or preference shares for raising ownership capital, as provided under Sections 86 and 87 of the Companies Act. Preference shares are shares the holders of which enjoy preferential rights over other classes of shareholders in the matter of dividend and return of capital. Different type of preference shares, with dividend rates fixed at the time of issue, can be used by companies to rase long-term capital. Preference shareholders have a right to vote only on the resolutions of the company which directly affect their interests. Government has recently issued guidelines introducing a new type of preference shares known as convertible cumulative preference shares. Companies may issue these shares to rase finance for (a) setting up new projects, (b) expansion or diversification, and (d) working capital requirements. The entire issue of such shares would be convertible into equity shares between the end of 3 years and 5 years as may be decided by the Company and the Controller of Capital issues. The rate of dividend payable on these shares, till conversion, would be 10 per cent. It would be deemed to be equity issue for calculating the debt-equity ratio.

Holders of equity shares do not enjoy any preferential right to payment of dividend or repayment of capital. They are the residuary claimants to profits available for distribution after preference dividend has been paid. They have a right to vote on every resolution relating to the share capital placed before the company. Besides, the equity shareholders enjoy the priority to have shares offered in case the company makes any further issue of shares (Known as 'Right' issue).

Debentures: The creditorship securities most commonly issued by companies are debentures with varying terms and conditions as to interest rate, redemption, and convertibility into shares. A company having borrowing powers under its Memorandum of Association has also the power to pledge or mortgage any of its property as security debentures issued by a company are generally secured by a charge or mortgage on the assents of the company. For public issue of debentures, companies are required to follow the guidelines prescribed by the Government. Some of the requirements prescribed are as follows:

i. The companies must seek the consent of the Controller of Capital Issues for issue of debentures through public subscription;

ii. The object of the issue can be either to rise long-term funds for the financing of any expansion or diversification project or to augment the long-term resources for working capital requirements;

iii. The amount of debenture issue for working capital requirements is not to exceed 20 per cent of the gross current assets, loans and advances. For project financing, the amount will be considered on the basis of approvals of the scheme of finance by the financial institution/government under the MRTP Act, etc.

iv. The debt-equity ratio, including the proposed debenture issues, must not exceed

2:13. But relaxation of this requirement is considered favourably for capital-intensive projects, such as fertilisers, petro-chemicals, cement, paper shipping, etc.

v. The debentures shall not be redeemable before the expiry of seven years, but may be converted into equity shares earlier.

vi. The debentures shall carry a rate of interest not exceeding 14 per cent per annum, as may be prescribed by the Government.

To regulate the issue of 'rights' debentures to meet working capital requirements, certain guidelines are prescribed, some of which are as follows:

(a) The amount of the debenture issue will not exceed (i) 20 per cent of the gross current assets, loans and advances minus the long-term funds currently available for working capital, or (ii) 20 per cent of the paid-up share capital including preference capital and free reserves, whichever is lower.

(b) The debt-equity ration including the proposed debenture issue should not exceed 1:1.

(c) Where 'rights' convertible debentures are offered to existing non-resident shareholders approval must be obtained from (i) the members of the company under Sec. 81 of the Companies Act, 1956, (ii) the Controller of Capital issues, (iii) the Department of Company Affairs u/s 81 (30 (b), and u/s 108A, if the company is registered under the MRTP Act, and (iv) Reserve Bank of India under FERA.

(d) Upon the non-resident shareholders exercising their option to convert the debentures into shares, the percentage holding of the non-residents should not increase.

Convertible Debentures : As the name implies, convertible debentures are debentures which may be exchanged for fully paid shares, either wholly or in part. Conversion can be in the form of either preference shares or equity shares although, in actual practice, the latter is more common. Convertible debentures present a blend of equity and debt. The debt aspect is borne out by the fixed maturity period, regular payment of interest, and repayment par or premium. The equity aspect stems from their conversion into equity after specified period in partial extinguishment of the amount due on debentures. Where under the terms of issue of convertible debentures the holders are to have option to convert or not to convert the debentures into shares, the company is required to obtain the approval of the Central Government u/s 81 (3) of the Companies Act. Where the terms provide for compulsory conversion, no such approval is needed. Also, it is not necessary to seek permission of the Controller of Capital Issues if the issue of convertible debentures is exclusively place with financial institutions

Conversion into equity of loans granted by financial institutions. Companies, which are granted financial assistance by public financial institutions, as under obligation to provide for conversion of the loans into equity and the appointment of nominee directors of the lending institution on the company's board. The more important guidelines issued by the Government in this behalf are as follows:

i. The convertibility clause where required to be inserted in the agreement relating to loans should be in conformity with the provisions of Sec. 81 (3) of the Companies Act.

ii. The convertibility clause is to be stipulated only in respect of rupee loans sanctioned and/or rupee debentures subscribed.

iii. Stipulation of the convertibility clause in the agreement relating to financial assistance is mandatory in all cases where the agreement financial assistance (including outstandings) from the all India financial institutions exceed Rs 5 crores.

iv. The stipulation need not be made here the combined equity holdings by all the all-Indian financial institutions (including the investment institutions e.g. LIC and UTI exceed 265% to the case of non-MRTP companies, and 40% in the case of MRTP companies/large industrial houses.

v. Convertibility clause need not also be stipulated in respect of loans sanctioned for projects both of MRTP and non-MRTP companies being set up in "no-industry districts and special regions."

Under Sec. 94-A of the Companies Act, it is provided that where any public financial institution has converted its debentures or loans into equity, capital of the company shall thereby stand increased by an equal amount and its memorandum altered accordingly.

While negotiating the terms of loans/debentures issues, the financial institutions, in consultation with the IDBI, are to give a clear indication to the assisted industrial concerns of the terms and conditions they have in view in regard to the convertibility of loans into equity. In giving this indication the financial institutions exercise their discretion and best judgement, keeping in view all relevant factors, e.g. the nature of industry, likely gestation period of the project, debt-equity gearing, the projected profit potential, the prospects of expansion, and so on. The concerned lending institutions also determine, in consultation with the IDBI, the maximum amount of loan which can be converted into equity capital in a specified case, the issue price of the share, the stage or stages at which the option can be exercised, the period during which the option shall remain open and the period of notice if any, be given for the exercise of option, and another relevant matter.

As per Government guidelines, nominee directors are appointed on the boards of all MRTP companies assisted by the financial institutions. In the case, of non-MRTP companies, nominee director are appointed on a selective basis, especially where one or more of the following conditions obtain: (a) the unit is running into problems and is likely to become sick, (b) institutional holding is more than 26 per cent, and (d) the institutional stake by way of loans/investment exceeds Rs 5 crores. The nominee directors are expected t ensure that the tendencies of the assisted companies towards extravagance, lavish expenditure and diversion f funds are curbed. For this purpose, the institutions may require that the company should constitute a small audit sub-committee of the board of directors for periodic assessment of expenditure incurred, in all case where the paid- up capital of the company is Rs 5 crores or more. The nominee director is invariably to be a member of the sub-committee. Generally officials of the levels of General Managers and Dy. General Manager represent the financial institutions on the company boards.

Public Deposits : In recent times, acceptance of public deposits for a fixed period has become an important source of short-term and medium-term finance of companies both in the private and public sectors. Companies are thus able to directly obtain funds from the public without financial intermediaries, and can attract investors by offering higher rates of interest than banking institutions. However, there are limits on the acceptance and renewal of deposits load down by the government. A ceiling of 15% on the aggregate of paid-up share capital and free reserves has been prescribed in respect of deposits against unsecured debentures, deposits from shareholders and deposits guaranteed by directors. The overall ceiling on public deposits Including deposits from other sources) is 25% of the aggregate of the paid-up capital and free reserves. No deposit can be accepted or renewed for repayment earlier than six months. But for meeting its short-term requirements of funds, a company may accept or renew deposits for repayment earlier than six months provided such deposits do not exceed 10% of the aggregator of paid-up share capital and free reserves, and repayable not earlier than three months from the date of deposit or renewal. Deposits cannot be accepted or renewed for a period exceeding 36 months.

Besides the limits prescribed on the amount of deposits, the Government has also described several formalities to be observed. Thus, for instance, a company intending to invite or accept deposits is required to publish an advertisement in newspapers disclosing details of paid-up capital, reserves, deposits, etc. The applications from depositors must include a declaration that the deposit is being made from their own savings and not from borrowed funds.

The nominal rate of interest on public deposits now ranges from 12 to 14 p.c. But the actual cost comes to be more than the nominal cost. This is because of the restricted tax deductability of the interest on public deposits. Whereas the entire interest cost in the case of other types of borrowing is an admissible expense for tax purposes, in the case of public deposits the limit is 85% of the total interest.

Sources of Short-term Finance : Short-term capital is generally used for financing the current assets of a business. The more commonly used sources of short-term finance are : (1) Trade credit (ii) Bill discounting, (iii) Bank loans, (iv) Overdraft and case credits. Trade credit as a source of finance is spontaneous in the sense that it arises in the ordinary course of business. It does not require any formal negotiation as with lenders. In so far as it varies in proportion to the volume of operation, it is also a flexible source of short-term finance. The cost of trade credit is the cash discount period. Thus, for example if the terms of credit happen to be 2/10 not 90' (i.e. a cash discount of 2% is allowed if payment is made within 10 days, and the full amount is payable in 90 day), the cost of trade credit may be around 9%, whereas it would be 15% of the credit terms happen to be (say) '2/10 net 60'.

The use of bills of exchange as instruments of credit has obvious advantages for the borrower as payment on bills is predetermined and time bound which enables cash budgeting to be done with some provisions. The system of bill financing also helps banks in credit planning with greater case. But issuance/trade bills, to be eligible for discounting, must conform to the requirements as prescribed by the Reserve Bank of India for re-discounting purposes. The system is also time-consuming in operation, and involves higher costs on account of stamp duty and detailed accounts to be maintained.

Bank loans constitute another source of short-term finance. It requires negotiating the tenure, amount and terms of loan every time, even at the time of renewal. The availability of loan and the conditions as to purpose, rat of interest and security are subject to the available cash resources of the Bank and the credit policy of the monetary authorities. As the loans are tied with specific purposes and granted for a definite period there is a built-in system of review of loans by the banks concerned at short intervals. The borrower's cash budgeting needs to be geared to the schedule of repayment and servicing the loans. Thus, a degree of self-discipline is invariably brought about. But negotiating a loan initially and renewal takes time. Once a loan is granted, it is not possible for the borrower to get the amount increased, so there is a tendency to borrow more keeping in view the future contingencies. Apart from this possibility of funds being arranged in excess of needs, bank loan also implies an element of inflexibility, for it cannot be adjusted with changes in the level of operation which may be caused by fluctuating product market conditions.

Overdrafts and cash credit facilities offered by banks, are the most commonly used method adopted by business firms to meet their working capital needs. The arrangement involves obtaining short-term credit upon a certain limit which is fixed in advance and is based on the value of collateral securities or hypothecation of inventories. The principal advantage of the overdraft/cash credit system is that it can be tailored and adjusted to the levels of operation, and hence guards against borrowing in excess of needs. The cost of funds is lower as interest is payable only on the actual daily balance outstanding. However the flexibility of using overdraft and cash credit facilities is known to have been stretched beyond legitimate needs. This is because security based borrowing through overdraft/cash credit arrangement permits short-term bank finance to be used for long-term purposes. Limits have therefore been prescribed by the Reserve Bank of India on permissible bank financing of working capital. Norms are also prescribed for inventory holding and accounts receivable with respect to 15 major industries.

Financial Leverage

The decisions relating to the sources of capital to be used for raising capital are closely linked with the question of determining the optimum capital structure (the desired mix of equity capital and debt capital). This is, in turn related to the degree of financial leverage and the consequential risks. Financial leverage refers to the use of fixed interest bearing securities (borrowings) in the total capitalisation so as to magnify the effects of changes in net operating income (earnings before interest and taxes).

On the firm's earnings per share (EPS). The degree of financial leverage is thus measured by the ratio of percentage change in EPS to the percentage change in EBIT (earning before interest and taxes). The element of financial risk in debt capital arises from the commitment of fixed charges which must be met whatever be the level of earnings. Thus, in the event of a fall in earnings, the residual surplus after meeting the fixed charges (cost of debt) would be a declining proportion of the earnings and return to shareholders would also declined accordingly if there are losses, payment of fixed charges may be difficult and lead to a position involving technical insolvency of the company. At the same time, debt capital being relatively cheaper than equity capital it may not be desirable altogether to avoid borrowing or depend exclusively on equity financing. Otherwise the rate of return on equity would be relatively lower than what it would have been with a reasonable amount of debt in the total capital.

Capital Structure Policy

The planning of capital structure actually centres round the decisions with regard to the desirable mix of debt and equity capital. There are several considerations which must be weighed in arriving at the optimum mix of debt and equity capital. One important consideration is the norms of debt-equity ratio which is required to be maintained while raising additional capital. The norms are prescribed in India by the Controller of capital Issues and the Public financial institutions. For public sector enterprises, the desired debt equity ratio is 1:1 while it is 2:1 for private sector firms. But relaxations are made in the case of (a) capital-intensive industries (like fertilizer, aluminum, paper and cement where the ratio is permitted to be around 3:1 and in the shipping industry it may be around 6:1 (b) high cost projects in the priority sector (c) projects in backward areas, and (d) projects sponsored by technician entrepreneurs.

Another factor which needs attention is the operating leverage or the proportion of fixed costs in the operating cost structure. Higher the proportion of fixed cost in the aggregate operating costs greater is the operating leverage and higher the operating risk. The risk involved arises from the impact of variation in sales leading to a disproportionate change in the operating profits. Thus, if the degree of operating leverage is high, it is desirable that the financial leverage should be kept low so that the combined effect of operating and financial risk may be tolerable. On the other hand if the operating leverage is low, the firm may plan for a higher degree of financial leverage and financial risk.

A third important variable to be considered in capital structure planning is the overall cost of capital which is the weighted average cost of debt and equity capital. Since the cost of debt is generally lower than the cost of equity due to the tax advantage derived from borrowed funds, a higher proportion of debt in the total capitalisation implies a reduction in the overall cost of capital. But with increasing financial leverage (debt financing) the financial risk also increases. Hence, the cost of both debt and equity also tend to go up and so does the overall cost of capital. The financing decision on financial leverage should aim at minimising the overall cost of capital and maximising the value of the firm. Indeed, the optimum capital structure is defined, in theory, as that mix of debt and equity of which the cost of capital is at the minimum.

The debt capacity of the firm in terms of the adequacy of cash flows to meet the fixed interest burden is yet another factor that needs consideration in capital structure planning. Analysis of the expected future cash flows may be both informative and useful for determining the extent to which debt financing is advisable. The proportion of debt in the capital structure may be increased if the expected future cash flows are predictably high and stable. Under adverse product market conditions with unstable and unpredictable cash flows, the risk of debt financing is obviously to be considered with de caution. The coverage ratio (the ratio of net cash flows to fixed charge) may therefore be used as a guide in deciding the proper mix of debt and equity.

The need for flexibility in the capital structure is another consideration worth nothing. The amount of borrowed capital can be adapted to changing conditions, but equity capital is not so adaptable. The maturity of different interest-bearing securities may be sequentially arranged and some of these may be renewed or redeemed or converted into equity as and when necessary, e.g. when internally generated funds fall short of the requirements or are inadequate to replace debt capital. Similarly, with changes in the structure of interest rates, earlier debts carrying higher interest charges may be replaced by new debts which are cheaper. The element of flexibility or maneuverability with respect to debt capital can be availed of to derive the benefits of lowering the cost of capital and economising the use of funds. At the same time a firm's debt capacity may not be fully utilized so as to leave some scope for raising additional loans in future. The unused part of debt capacity may thus prove to be a reserve to be utilised when necessary.

An additional guiding consideration is the effect of financing decision on management control over corporate affairs. With increases of equity capital in the capital structure, dilution of management control tends to be against the interest of the existing controlling group. Use of debt capital rather than new issue of equity may thus be preferred to retain control. Issues or rights shares or conversion of free reserves into equity involving the issue of 'bonus' share do not pose any problem from the point of view of control by the existing group. However, increasing debt capital may also lead to restrictions on management being imposed by lending institutions particularly in financial matters. This is besides the increasing financial risk involved.

Finally, deciding on the financial leverage requires the industry standards to be kept in view so that the structure of capital is not out of line in relation to firms in the same risk class and the industry as a whole. This is because creditors and investors assess the capital issues may not be acceptable to investors if the mix of debt and equity is out of line either way.

A number of general factors also govern the planning of capital structure e.g. the nature of business and size of the enterprise, the product-market situation and state of the capital market. Thus, the nature of its business may enable a company to resort to higher debt financing if its transactions are mainly on cash basis as in the case of public utilities. On the other hand, a heavy industrial undertaking with large investment in fixed assets and high operating leverage should ordinarily keep down it debt capital. Similarly, the relative proportions of debt and equity have different implications for small and large firms. Raising long-term loans is generally more difficult for small firms on account of higher interest charges and restrictive terms imposed, although small firms in India also enjoy more favourable treatment as regards repayment schedule, etc. for funds provided by a special financial institutions at the state level. For small companies, equity issues involve relatively higher cost and their is greater danger of loss of control, for shares are not as widely held as in the case of large companies.

The product-market situation is of considerable importance in capital structure planning. If the situation is congenial for stable sales and growth prospects, it is obviously a favourable condition for higher debt financing of projects. The state of the capital market determines the marketability of security. The timing of security issue and the methods of financing should naturally be decided in the light of prevailing investors sentiments in the new issue markets for debt and equity.

Investment and Capital Allocation Policy

While formulating policies relating to the sources of finance and financial leverage, it is also necessary to keep in view the uses of capital for different activities including creation of additional facilities, acquisition of plants and equipments, sales promotion, and the like. Implementation of a strategy involves estimating the funds requirements and deciding on the appropriate mix of debt and equity capital, s well as setting limits on the allocation of capital for specific purposes. The main issues in capital allocation policy consist of (a) regulating investments in fixed assets, and (b) restraints on the holding of current assets.

Except in the case of retrenchment strategy, all other strategies leave a wide scope of managers to make proposals for deployment of capital either for increased production or higher efficiency in production or sales. Thus, for instance, executives concerned with production may propose investments in additional facilities or new equipments, while others may propose investments aiming at cost reduction through vertical integration, or investments in R & D, or management training, and so on. Often, a basic policy on the minimum training, and so on. Often, a basic policy on the minimum rate of return helps in the appraisal of investment proposals, so that proposals for the acquisition of additional fixed assets may be accepted or rejected using the acceptable minimum rate of return on investments as a 'hurdle rate'. For instance, if the policy is that any new investment must earn a minimum of 20% return after tax, proposals involving initial capital outlay which are estimated to yield less than 20% annual return would be automatically rejected. But such a policy cannot be operated indiscriminately. For essential projects, e.g. where equipments need to be replaced on technological grounds, or investments in pollution control devices is required under law may be unavoidable, even if its does not fulfil the minimum yield criterion. In general, the minimum acceptable rate of return is based on the weighted average cost of capital with the addition of a risk premium that they may be desired. But a number of other factors also have a bearing on it e.g. growth objective, funds available, necessity of equity issues, and judgement about future risks, Sometimes, the 'hurdle rate' is fixed higher in view of the optimistic estimation of future rate of return by the executives concerned.

Investment Appraisal and Capital Budgeting : Keeping in view the availability of funds and the possibility of multiple proposals emanating from functional departments and divisional managers, top management have to select the proposals that can be judiciously financed. The process of selection is carried out through the steps in capital budgeting. The basic principle involved in capital budgeting for strategy implementation is that it must be consistent with the general investment policy as well as marketing, production, purchasing and personnel policies.

Broadly speaking the investment proposals originating in different business segments of a firm an at different levels of management, may be divided into the following categories.

a. Proposals to add new product

b. Proposals to increase capacity

c. Proposals intended to reduce costs and increase efficiency of operations

The steps involved in the capital budgeting process are generally as follows:-

i. Project generation

ii. Project evaluation

iii. Project selection, and

iv. Project implementation

As a first step, all major proposals need to be described and analysed with estimates of the outlay and potential benefits of each proposal. It is at the stage that there is a screening of all proposals and setting aside those which are not consistent with the strategies adopted for different functional/operational areas. While the outlay and benefits (revenues) are expressed in money terms, the intangible costs and benefits cannot be ignored. The budgeting process emphasises the money value and time of accrual of the benefits. Hence, the listing of intangible, qualitative factors as well as strategic considerations, e.g. the flexibility of a proposal, strategic advantages of entering a new market etc. area important. The next step involves ranking the proposals on the basis of net yield per annum. Finally, selection takes places keeping in vie the overall funds constraint and the cut-off-point (the minimum acceptable rate of return). However, before the projects below the cut-off point are completely rejected, their intangible benefits and other non-monetary aspects should be fully considered, so also the intangible costs of projects, which are otherwise acceptable on the basis of the 'hurdle' rate of return, need to be appraised. It may be that the non-monetary benefits of some projects in the former category may be more than adequate to compensate for the lower monetary benefits and thus make them acceptable. On the other hand, the intangible costs of certain proposals may be so heavy as to make them unacceptable inspite of a satisfactory money rate of return.

The monetary worth of investment proposals are best appraised by using definite measurement criteria which fully recognise the timing of cash inflows and outflows. These are known as the time adjusted or discounted cash flow methods of investment appraisal.

There are two methods based on the discounted cash flow approach to investment decisions viz the Net Present Value (NPV) method, the Internal Rate of Return (IRR) method. The NPV method involves calculation of the present value of estimated future cash inflows using the cost of capital as the discounting rate and subtracting from the aggregate present value of inflows the present value of cash outflows using the same discounting rate. If the net present value derived from the subscription is positive or equal to zero, the investment project is accepted as economically viable. If the net present value is negative, the proposal is rejected, Using the criterion, the investment proposals may also be ranked in descending order of the net present values. The market value of shares is expected to increase if projects with positive NPV are accepted. Thus, the NPV criterion on investment appraisal is consistent with the objective of maximising the shareholders' wealth. It recognises the time value of money and takes into account all ash flows over the entire life of the project.

The IRR method is based on the concept of a rate of return which equals the aggregate present value of cash inflow with that of the cash outflows associated with any investment project. Obviously, this method does not require any pre-determined discount rate (cost of capital) to be used i the calculation. The value of IRR is determined by trial and error, and the project is accepted if the rate so determined is greater than or equal to the minimum acceptable rate of return or the cost of capital. If the rate is lower than the cost of capital, the hurdle rate, the project is rejected. The internal rate of return, besides recognising the time value of money and the entire series of future cash flows, gives an idea about the profitability of a project without any reference to the firm's cost of capital. It suggests the maximum time adjusted rate of return that may be derived from an investment outlay. It is thus compatible with the maximisation of the value of the firm. However, the IRR method has also certain limitations. It involves complicated problems in computation. The implicit assumption is this method is that the intermediate cash inflows generated by the initial investment are reinvested at the internal rate of return, an assumption that is somewhat unrealistic. The NPV method, on the other hand, implies an assumption that the intermediate cash inflows are reinvested at the firm's cost of capital. Such an assumption is more appropriate. The decision signals given by the IRR may also be inconsistent with those of NPV if the projects differ in their expected lives, or cash outlays, or timing of cash flows. Further, the IRR method may result in negative rats or multiple rates in the case of non-conventional projects, i.e. projects in which cash outflows are interspersed with cash inflow.

Benefit-cost ratio or profitability index is another time adjusted cash flow method of investment appraisal. It is the ratio of the present value of future cash benefits (discounted at the required rate of return) to the initial cash outlay. If the ratio is greater than one, the project has a positive net present value and is therefore considered acceptable projects an also be ranked in order of the numerical value of the index. Clearly, if the profitability index is greater than one, the project's not present value will be positive. However, there may be conflicting decision signals given by NPV and profitability index where too mutuality exclusive projects have significant differences in the magnitude of initial outlay and cash inflows. In such a situation, the NPV provides a better decision criterion as it represents a net increase in the firm's value. On the other hand, if the NPV is identical for two projects which requires different amounts of initial outlay, the profitability index provide the precise decision-signal as it evaluates the relative worth of the two projects.

The general significance of investment appraisal in strategy implementation is no doubt to be realised by top management and should be with respect to the projections of estimates cash flows and the relative significance of costs and revenues and other related factors expressed in money terms.

Leasing as an alternative to buying fixed assets

In more recent years, long-term leasing of fixed assets has been found to be an attractive proposition for different reasons. An alternative to buying, long-term leasing may be preferred when the uncertainty of future outlook and the prospects of rapid expansion and relocation may suggest flexibility of assets commitment. It is also found advantageous in so far as the need for immediate outlay of capital is reduced. Long-term (finance) leasing is also termed 'off balance sheet' lease since neither the asset not the source of funds appear on the firm's balance sheet. Where the assets for leasing needs to be constructed so as to serve special technical requirements, it may be built and equipped accordingly and then sold and leased back. The lease agreement may also provide for the lease' option to buy the asset at a depreciated value on the expiry of the lease period. However, long-term leasing involves a binding obligation to make annual rental payments just as periodical payment of interest and principal in the case of debentures or loans The operating cost of the asset and the tax implications of annual lease rentals must therefore be considered carefully before formulating any policy with regard to leasing rather than buying fixed assets.

Divided Policy

Decisions relating to the amount of earnings to be distributed as dividend to shareholders and correspondingly the amount of earnings to be retained as an internal source of finance for the growth of the firm constitute the third most important policy area in financial management besides the financing decisions and investment decisions. The dividend policy (and its observe the profit retention policy) involves determination of the allocation of earnings between dividend payment and retention for reinvestment. The objective of policy is recognised to be maximising the value of the firm to its shareholders but there is an apparent conflict to be resolved with respect to this aspect of policy-making. While retained earnings facilities long-term growth of the firm, dividends are required to be paid to shareholders so as to demonstrate the firm's current performance, and higher the rate of retention, the lower is the dividend payment.

From the point of view of long-term financing of growth, dividend may be regarded as a residual payment. It represents distribution of earnings that cannot be profitably reinvested by the firm. This approach implies that the question of dividend payment arises only if the firm does not have profitable investment opportunities. If the shareholders forego current dividends and the earnings are used for long-term financing of projects, there is faster rate of growth. Retained profits do not involve any flotation costs. On the other hand, in the absence of internal resources (retained earnings), growth may be restricted or it may require the use of more costly external sources of finance. However, because of imperfections of the capital market and uncertainty of earnings, shareholders strongly prefer current dividends rather than future dividends and capital gains through increase in share value due to growth. Thus, payment of dividend meet the investors expectations and increase the value of shares while in its absence, the share value tends to decline. In short, to maximise the wealth of shareholders, management must ensure retention of profits for long-term financing of investments as well as meet the expectations of shareholders as regards dividend distribution. An optical dividend policy is one that maintains a proper balance between the twin objectives.

Typically, most firms retain apart of the earnings and distribute the remaining amount as dividend. Stability of a dividend payment is considered to be a desirable policy and shareholders appreciate it. It has been found that stable dividends have a positive impact on the market price of shares. The dividend policy may thus imply a policy of paying (a) constant dividend per shares, (b) constant percentage of net earnings, or (c) constant dividend per share with extra dividend when earnings are higher than normal. The policy of maintaining the rate of dividend per share over time also provides for raising it when earnings reach higher levels and are expected to be durable. But this policy may be impracticable if the earnings are subject to wide fluctuations from year to year. To overcome the problem of paying constant dividend per share, it is necessary that the company should build up a reserve for dividend equalisation, siphoning a part of the profits for that purpose in years when the earnings are higher than the average. The most serious limitation of the policy is that it does not permit any recognition of investment opportunities within the firm or opportunities available to the shareholders. Equity shareholders are virtually treated as preference shareholders. Hence the policy appeals to individual and institutional investors who depend or the dividend income for current expenses and are not seriously concerned about increases or decreases in the market value of shares. As a result, there is a steady long-term demand for shares and the market value tends to get stabilised.

The policy of paying a fixed percentage of net earnings as dividend, i.e. maintaining a constant dividend payment ratio, is a more flexible policy in as much as it is linked with the firm's ability to pay portion of earnings to be retained as a source of in internal finance. Thus, once the payout ratio has been decided both the amounts of dividend and retained profits increase or decrease in accordance with the changes in earnings level. In a way this policy is somewhat restrictive in that it does not permit management to exercise any discretion either to skip dividend if profits have been currently earned, or to pay dividend in the absence of current earnings.

A third policy alternative is often preferred by companies with fluctuating earnings, that is, to pay a small amount of dividend per share as a regular feature and paying an extra dividend per share whenever higher earnings justify it. With such a dividend policy, shareholders can depend on a minimum amount of dividend income, and do not count on extra dividends to be an increase in the established rate of dividend. There if flexibility in this policy of supplementing the amount of fixed dividend without any commitment on the part of management to maintain the higher dividend in future.

In actual practice the dividend policy of a firm is governed by a set of considerations which include :

a. the shareholders' preference as to current dividend income against capital gains arising out of increases in the market value of shares. Cash dividend is taxable along with other taxable incomes of shareholders. Thus individual shareholders in high income brackets do not favour distribution of cash dividend, rather capital gains are preferred, for the rate of capital gains tax is lower than the rate of income tax.

b. The reinvestment opportunities and financial needs of the firm taking into account the cash position.

c. Constraints on dividend payment e.g. legal restriction non-availability of liquid funds, scope of raising funds from the capital market, restrictions imposed by lenders in loan agreements, risk of dilution of management control involved in additional equity issues, necessity of additional funds for replacement of assets subject to inflationary rise of price etc.

d. Need for stability of dividend distribution.

e. Pros and cons of cash dividend and stock dividend (bonus shares).

21

Conflict Management

Conflict is a daily reality for everyone. Whether at home or at work, an individual's needs and values inevitably come into conflict with the needs and values of others. Some conflicts are relatively minor, easily handled, and simply overlooked. However, other conflicts ate of greater magnitude and require a strategy for successful resolution. The ability to resolve conflict successfully probably is one of the most important social skills an individual can possess. Yet, there are few formal opportunities in our society to learn conflict-resolution skills. Conflict resolution skills can be teamed; and like other skills, they consist of a number of subskills, each separate and yet interdependent. Conflict-resolution skills need to be integrated at both cognitive and behavioural levels.

We develop our own preferred approaches for dealing with conflict when we are children. Even if our preferred approaches do not resolve conflicts successfully, we continue to use them because we lack awareness of alternatives. Conflict-resolution strategies can be classified into three categories: avoidance, defusion, and confrontation. Some people attempt to avoid certain types of conflict situations or avoid conflict situations altogether. These people tend to repress emotional reactions, look the other way, or withdraw from a situation entirely. For example, one may resign from a job, leave school, or become divorced. The person either cannot face the situation effectively or does not have the skills to resolve the conflict situation effectively. Although avoidance strategies have survival value in those instances in which escape is possible, they usually do not provide the individual with a high level of satisfaction. Avoided conflict situations often result in doubts and fear about meeting similar situations in the future and about such valued traits as courage or persistence.

Defusion essentially is a delaying tactic. Defusion strategies attempt to tone down and cool off the situation, at least temporarily, or to keep the issues so unclear that attempts at confrontation are unlikely. Resolving minor points while avoiding or delaying discussion of major issues, postponing confrontation until a more favourable time, and avoiding clarification of the prominent issues underlying the conflict all are examples of defusion tactics. As with avoidance strategies, defusion tactics often work when delay is possible. However, such tactics typically result in feelings of dissatisfaction, anxiety about the future, concerns about oneself, and decreased self-esteem.

The third major conflict-resolution strategy involves confronting conflicting issues or persons. Confrontation can be subdivided into power and negotiation strategies. Power strategies include the use of physical force; and punishment. Power tactics often are very effective from the point of view of the "winner" or "successful" party in the conflict. Unfortunately, the real conflict may have only just begun. For the "loser," getting even, hostility, anxiety, and actual physical damage frequently are the residual effects of win-lose power tactics.

Negotiation strategies, unlike power confrontations, present opportunities for both sides to win. The objective of negotiation is to resolve the conflict with a compromise solution that is mutually satisfying to all parties involved in the conflict. Of the three Conflict-resolution strategies, negotiation seems to provide the most positive and the least negative residuals.

Negotiation skills

Successful negotiation requires skills that must be learned and practiced. These skills include:

— the ability to diagnose the nature of the conflict;

— effectiveness in initiating confrontation;

— the ability to listen and willingness to hear another's point of view; and

— the ability to make use of problem solving bringing about a consensus processes.

Diagnosis

Diagnosing the nature of a conflict is the star ing point for any attempt at conflict resolution through negotiation. The most important issue that must be decided is whether the conflict is a values-driven conflict, a "real" conflict, or some combination of both. Value conflicts are extraordinarily difficult to negotiate. If, for example, one party to the conflict believes that women should be treated as equals in every phase of public and private life, and another party believes that women should be prohibited from performing certain activities, it would be difficult for both parties to arrive at a mutually agreeable solution.

However, differing values are significant only when conflicting views affect the parties in some real or tangible way. As an example, if one's values regarding women's rights results in a woman being denied employment for which she is qualified and that employment is desired by her, then there is basis for a negotiable conflict. Neither party needs to change his or her personal values in order to reach a mutually acceptable resolution on the tangible issue. Notwithstanding, if each opposing party stands on value-laden principles and maintains a value ' conflict, the likelihood of resolution is minimal. But if the conflicting parties focus on the tangible effects within the conflict, they may be able to negotiate a realistic solution.

The Israeli-Arab conflict provides a good example of this point. In order to resolve a tangible element within the conflict i.e., who gets how much land the ideological differences between Israelis and Arabs need not be resolved. Land usage is the tangible element of the conflict that is amenable to a negotiated settlement.

Critical diagnostic skill is an ability to determine whether a conflict is a real or a value conflict. If the conflict is a conflict in values resulting in non-tangible effects on either party, then it is best tolerated. However, if tangible effect exists, then the tangible elements can be resolved.

Initiation

The second conflict resolution skill is effectiveness in initiating confrontation. Confrontation does not mean attacking or demeaning the opposing party. Attack almost always elicits a defensive reaction that blocks a quick resolution of differences. A more effective way of confronting is for one party to state the tangible effects that the conflict has on him or her. For instance, "I have a problem.

Listening

After confrontation has been initiated, the confronter must be willing and able to listen to the confrontee's point of view. If the confrontee's initial response is not what the confrontor had expected to hear, defensive reactions within the confrontor can follow. Argument-provoking replies should be avoided at all costs. The confrontor should not attempt to "defend" himself or herself, explain a particular position, or make demands and threats. Instead, the confrontor must be able to engage in a skill termed reflective or active listening.

In reflective listening, the controntor listens, reflects back, and clarifies the confrontee's position. When the confrontor has interpreted the conflicting position to the satisfaction of the confrontee, then the confrontor should again present his or her own point of view, being careful to concentrate on tangible outcomes and avoid value-laden statements. Usually, when people listen to one another, defenses are lowered and both parties become more receptive to other points of view. When both parties are skilled in reflective listening, the likelihood of successful negotiation is greatly enhanced.

Managing conflict from the inside out

We cannot trust ourselves in conflict Situations because the stress we experience usually short-circuits rational responses. But the more people learn about how they might react to controversy, the greater the chances to act appropriately. Still, the requirement to examine oneself can make one uncomfortable. When one pushes through the discomfort, however, the payoff is a more self-confident and hassle-free lifestyle. For those of us who are not "naturals" at handling conflict, Robert recommends four pathways to self-awareness:

Pathway 1: Intrapersonal awareness. When you are faced with conflict, there is usually a conversation going on inside you. Pay attention to it. If the person with whom you are in conflict can predict your responses better than you can, you are seriously handicapped in emotionally charged situations. To become more aware of your feelings, practice listening to yourself during emotional moments. Avoid lying to yourself or denying your true emotions when you are involved in a conflict.

Pathway 2: Scanning others for clues about ourselves. Redevelop your radar, which may have atrophied from disuse and self-protection. Look for subtle changes in the voices, facial expressions, or body language of others. Pay special attention to people who are not intimidated by you. Analyze reactions to your clothing, adornment, and grooming. Experiment with different behaviours. Pay attention to the teasing you receive.

Pathway 3: Seeking feedback from others and practicing self-disclosure. Feedback prevents us from judging ourselves by our intentions while others judge us by our behaviours.

Pathway 4: Formal and informal behavioural appraisal. Behavioural science instruments provide self-knowledge by a procedure that is less demanding than those mentioned above. The following two instruments are useful:

The Thomas-Kilmann Conflict Mode Instrument (CMI), which measures relative use of five conflict-handling modes in situations in which one's wishes differ from those of another person.

The Conflict-Management Style Survey (CMSS), which reveals a person's style of response to everyday conflict. Robert's book includes the CMSS and activities to help respondents to share results.

We all know people who seem to spend their lives embroiled in conflict. These people probably are doing exactly what they need to do, given their perceptions of reality. Conflict can help to clarify issues, strengthen relationships, solve problems, and enrich our lives. However, conflict also can be unproductive and destructive. Following these rules can help to avoid unproductive conflict:

1. *Know the difference between your principles and your preferences.* Refuse to "sweat the small stuff."

2. *Test your expectations against reality.* When we expect more than others are prepared to give, we run the risk of unwarranted conflict.

3. *Save and spend trust credits.* In the give-and-take of human relations, accounts of trust and credibility credits are slowly built up. Everyone in an inequitable relationship feels uneasy. When trust accounts are out of balance, the potential for unproductive conflict increases.

4. *Handle criticism as a live bomb.* Our species has not evolved enough to accept criticism gracefully. Therefore, consider these cautions:
   - Examine your intent before you criticize.
   - Study the potential recipient's vulnerability.
   - Consider modelling the desired change instead.
   - Describe behaviour *without* a value judgment.
   - Wait five minutes; the critical urge may pass.
   - Criticize kindly and constructively.
5. *Practice the power of optimism.* Emulate the behavioural of cheerful people. Most people with whom you are in conflict want to stop hurting just as much as you do. When involved in a game of "ain't it awful," work to change the focus.
6. *Be aware of personal growth hazards.* Ironically, pursuit of self-knowledge to improve relationships may put us so far "into ourselves" that we lose sensitivity. Examine what is happening; become aware of the responsibilities of living among others.
7. *Recognize day-to-day conflict traps.* Avoid stressors, such as:
   - crowding in the home or work environment;
   - overstimulation by telephones, odors, etc.;
   - rushing to meet time binds;
   - concerns regarding physical safety;
   - problems with transportation;
   - living beyond one's financial means;
   - overcommitment to projects and people; and
   - failure to look after your own physical health.
8. *Avoid assumptions.* The human mind refuses to stay empty in spite of lack of information. Consider what you do when you are unclear about an interpersonal message.
9. *Sensitively anticipate destructive conflict.* Avoid incipient conflicts by sharing information and negotiating expectations, by defining roles, and by renegotiating roles as necessary.

Regardless of what we do to minimize conflicts, we are faced with disruptions. The following techniques can help in coping with them:

- *Systematic Desensitization.* Perform relaxation techniques, vividly imagine the impending conflict until you become tense, and then resume the relaxation techniques. Repeat until the crisis has passed.

— *"Psyching Down" Through Relaxation.* Condition yourself to relax when crises are imminent.

— *Centering and Self-Monitoring.* When conflict strikes, ask yourself whether You are in touch with your inner emotions, whether you are focused on the here and now rather than what might or already has happened, and whether your body language expresses control of yourself.

— *Putting it in Perspective.* Believing that "this, too, shall pass" can be liberating. Situations rarely turn out as badly as anticipated.

— *Examining Ogres.* The worst ogres are in our minds. Identifying and exploring the worst-case scenario can restore emotional equilibrium.

— *Thought Stopping or Diversion.* By rationally blocking anxiety-producing thoughts, we can restore our emotional equilibrium. Some behaviourists suggest placing a rubber band on one's wrist and snapping it to cause pain when unwanted thoughts appear.

Conflict often involves anger. We can deal positively with our own anger by under standing that its source almost always is a perceived threat. We can effectively confront the anger of others by not allowing it to hook us into conflicts that are none of our business; by recognizing the futility of attempting to dissolve fear or anger in others through logic; by stating what we feel and want as clearly and pleasantly as possible; by being reasonable but sticking to our principles; by training ourselves to renege on statements made in the heat of anger; by ignoring abuse and responding only to reasonable statements; and by avoiding escalation.

Robert recommends fourteen strategies for communications that involve conflict:

1. Avoid being judgmental.
2. Deal with present behavioural rather than past or potential injustices.
3. Pay attention to the nonverbal content of communication.
4. Use "I" messages that describe behaviours, feelings, and effects; e.g., "When I did not receive a call back from you, I feared that the deal was off," not, "You never return calls."
5. Practice strategic openness about feelings.
6. Choose your words carefully.
7. Allow the other party to withhold information about feelings, which paradoxically often makes disclosure safe for the other person.

8. Restate what the other party says.
9. Actively listen to the other party.
10. Use questions of clarification; avoid accusatory questions.
11. Break the interruption habit by using silence and delayed response.
12. Do not fear to tell others that they are correct about something.
13. Avoid interpreting the motives of others.
14. Refrain from giving advice.

Conflict sometimes leads to violence. Learn to recognize the signs of potential attack. Identify avenues of escape. Respect other's positions and refrain from escalating passions, maintain nonthreatening body posture; speak calmly, firmly, and soothingly; do not touch a potentially violet person; suggest a move to a more spacious environment; listen intently to your adversary; refrain from mind reading; use distracting questions to defuse violent energy; and begin with the least aggressive methods.

If all else fails, some high-risk methods may head off violence. Although it may be best and most appropriate to keep humorous insights to oneself, sensitively and well-delivered humor can defuse a conflict. Hard-shock methods may startle the other person and prevent escalation, but they are risky. Dire predictions regarding the conflict may interrupt the situation long enough to restore sanity. Finally, if you have exhausted all yours resources to no avail, leave the scene with as much dignity as you can muster.

How to use power and problem

The use of power per se is neither good nor bad. How to use power depends on several circumstances, including what kind of power is being considered. Robert identifies eight types of power:

1. Natural power, which is derived from attributes, such as beauty, size, strength, intelligence, and wisdom.
2. Acquired power, which is obtained by study, hard work, and so on.
3. Top-dog or parent power, the power of domination.
4. Force or coercive power, whose results are risky and unpredictable.
5. Underdog or "helpless" power, achieved by destructive, manipulative resistance, diversion, and delay.
6. Independence power. Others control us only by controlling what we want.
7. Interdependence power, the power derived from the support of friends.

8. Self-confidence power, which helps us manage conflict in ways that enable us to feel good without having to make others feel bad.

Robert suggests two specific methods to solve problems:

1. *Practice Problem-Centered Self-Talk.* Send yourself the following problem focused messages:
   - Self-Talk Message 1: "This is a situation that needs careful attention. How can I (we) work it out?"
   - Self-Talk Message 2: "There is always something that I (we) can do that will work better than this mess we are in now."
   - Self-Talk Message 3: "They [whomever you are in conflict with] are doing exactly what they need to do. I can control only what I do."
2. Practice the Six-Step Problem-Solving Process:
   - Step 1: Define the problem.
   - Step 2: Clearly state what you think.
   - Step 3: Generate possible solutions.
   - Step 4: "Reality test" each solution.
   - Step 5: Make a "what-if" contingency plan.
   - Step 6: Do it.

Most of us are untrained as peace makers. Nevertheless, as parents, friends, lovers, family members, bosses, and colleagues, we are asked to help others work, out their conflicts. Before becoming involved, determine whether you have the resources to be helpful, whether it is too late to be of help, whether the parties could resolve the conflict better on their own, whether your intervention is desired, and whether it feels right to meddle.

If you do intervene, recognize the limits of your power and your own vulnerability. As referee, confer one-on-one with each side to obtain an accurate picture of the conflict., Often, disputants are not equally powerful, so balance power through ground rules on matters such as "equal air time." Negotiate on neutral turf and allow both parties adequate time to prepare. Determine early whether each party is motivated to resolve the conflict. Then help them to identify points of agreement, so that they can make at least one positive connection. Make sure that an alternate third party is available, if the dispute will be protracted. You may not always be available, and the alternate mediator could keep the peace process on track.

As manager of the communication, try this seven-step process of mediation:

1. Elicit a suggested solution to the problem from one of the disputants.

2. Check the suggested solution with the other party.
3. Elicit and check out proposals until both parties agree on a course of action.
4. Work out details of the plan and obtain implementation commitments.
S. Closely monitor the follow-through and make alternate plans as needed.
6. Do not despair if agreement is not reached; look at alternatives.
7. Persist; don't give up.

The law of averages guarantees an occasional interpersonal defeat. Defeat is a stressful experience. For these occasions, Robert recommends one or more of the following coping strategies:

1. Physical activity—aerobic exercise—to relieve stress.
2. Thought control, e.g., positive denial, healthy distraction, altered perception, acceptance reprograming belief systems, patience, and learning from mistakes.
3. Let go of negative thought patterns and stressful emotions.
4. Social and environmental nurturing by distancing oneself from the problem; seeking relief by enjoying pleasant sights and sounds, diversifying interests, or seeking the support of friends.

Various subgroups of organizations are prone to conflict with one another. The divergent interests and perspectives of unions and management obviously lead to controversy. Departments at the same or different levels of an organization often engage in struggles over resources or rewards. In large, multi-unit organizations, there are inherent differences that lead to strife between headquarters and field units. Mergers and acquisitions sometimes create disharmonious marriages between unequally powerful and previously independent organizations. The age, gender, political, ethnic, and racial cleavages of our society often are expressed in organizations as informal subgroup allegiances that result in friction. If organizations are to be effective, it is imperative that they deal with the omnipresent intergroup conflicts. Robert Blake, Herbert Shepard and Jane Mouton developed a theory to analyze intergroup conflict.

Nine classifications of conflict resolution

Blake, Shepard, and Mouton's theory categorizes intergroup conflict into nine classifications of likely conflict resolution. According to the theory, feuding groups choose from the nine methods to resolve their disagreements, in accordance with their basic assumptions about the conflicts. The theory posits that parties will base their assumptions about a conflict on two factors, their orientation toward the conflict and the importance of the issues involved. The theory encompasses three levels of conflict importance and three possible orientations to the conflict. Taken together, the two factors account for the nine different classifications of possible conflict resolution.

Three levels of importance

The three levels of conflict importance are:

— *High-payoff conflicts,* in which the participants are actively involved;

— *Moderate-stakes conflicts,* in which the participants are moderately involved; and

— *Low-payoff conflicts,* in which participants are only passively involved.

Three orientations

Depending on the level of importance the groups give to the controversy, each of the three orientations can lead to one of three different modes of conflict resolution. The orientations and their associated resolutions follow:

*Orientation I. The clash can not be avoided and agreement is unattainable.*If disputing groups view the conflict as unavoidable and irreconcilable, it is likely that they will assume that the disagreement will be resolved by a decision in favor of one party and against the other.

For example, the hypothetical Riverdale and Jefferson campuses of the University of the State of Lincoln are vying to become the location for an institute to research and develop supercomputer technology. Both divisions of the university want to establish the new activity in order to build reputation, to maintain employment, to attract other grant funds, and to provide promotional opportunities for personnel. Each campus has prepared presentations to the state university's board of regents, touting its own competitive advantages. Community leaders in the two potential ?cales have supported the proposals, offering to donate municipal land for the construction and proposing to build access roads. A favorable outcome for both campuses is mutually excluded, because there will be only one center. This is the classic zero-sum game; if I win, you lose, and vice versa.

Under this orientation, there are three possible resolutions:

1. One side will lose a winner-take-all fight over a high-payoff conflict. In the example, both campuses could invest substantial discretionary resources in proposals and public relations campaigns to lobby for a decision that the university's board of regents will make in favor of only one campus.

2. A third party will adjudicate a moderate-stakes dispute in favor of one party or the other. If the two university administrations will be only moderately affected by the outcome but still cannot agree between themselves, they might seek an early decision by an impartial board of regents study group, thus saving one of the campuses the expense of unnecessary plans and proposals.

3. The parties will allow fate to determine the outcome of a low-payoff conflict. If the university's administrations perceive that they have little to gain or lose, they might make little or no effort to influence the decision. The decision by the

regents would almost-but not quite-be a flip of a coin. The regents probably would study the decision systematically, but from the point of view of the two university administrations, the decision would be left to chance.

Orientation II. The clash can be avoided because the groups can act independently. In this situation conflict is avoidable, but the two parties will be unable to agree on a resolution.

For example, each of two identical refineries of a major petrochemical company acts autonomously in its market. In this case, the engineering departments of tile two refineries disagree about the schedule for modernizing certain equipment. The management of one refinery claims that it would be a better strategy to postpone introducing more efficient equipment until the following fiscal year when interest rates for the needed capital are predicted to decline, even though the delay will diminish near-term profits slightly. The management of the other refinery believes that the greater efficiency will decrease costs sufficiently to offset the higher interest costs. Engineers for both refineries concede that it is impossible to predict how efficiently the new equipment will work until it is actually installed.

One of the problems in organizational conflict is that the term has been defined in many different ways by academics and managers. In addition, the definitions are often value-laden or too broad to be useful. There are also problems in confusing conflict with other terms and failing to state whether conflict is being examined on the micro (individual) or macro (organization) level. These important issues are clarified in this section where we (1) define conflict, (2), show how it differs from competition, and (3) indicate the various perspectives from which we can analyse conflict.

Conflict is behaviour by a person or group that is purposely designed to inhibit the attainment of goals by another person or group. This "purposeful inhibition" may be active or passive For example, in a sequential production line, if one group does not do its job and its output is the input for another department, the other department will be blocked from reaching its goal of, say, producing at standard. Alternatively, the blocking behaviour may be active, as in the case of two fighters trying to knock each other out. The key issue in defining conflict is that of incompatible goals. When one person or group deliberately interferes with the purpose of denying the other goal achievement, conflict exists.

The terms conflict and competition are often mistakenly used, interchangeably. Perhaps the most widely accepted view at present is that competition takes place when individuals or groups have incompatible goals but do not interfere with each other as they both try, to attain their respective goals. Conflict, on the other hand, occurs when individuals or groups have incompatible goals and they interfere with each other as they try to attain their respective goals. These definitions suggest that the key behavioural difference in conflict and competition is analogous to the behavioural differences evident in a race and a fight. In the former, the goals are incompatible, but the runners do not interfere with one another. In the latter, the goals are also incompatible, but interfere is an obvious part of conflict.

Using these two definitions allows us to clearly categorize many of the familiar activities in our society. One of the things that becomes apparent immediately is that certain activities which are typically viewed as homogeneous must be further broken down. For example, certain sports (boxing, tennis, football, hockey, etc.) are characterized by obvious blocking behaviour at the activity level. There is also blocking behaviour at the resource-attainment level.

In the past, the New York Yankees have been accused of "buying the pennant." In making this claim, other team owners are really arguing that they have been blocked at the resource attainment stage so their goal cannot be realized. Sports contests in which any of the three types of blocking behaviour occurs are therefore conflict situations. Other sports, however, show little or no blocking at any level. Swimming, horse racing, gymnastics, bowling, and others are classified as competition since blocking behaviour is not part of the game.

The same kind of analysis holds if we analyse business activities. While the general public usually refers to what businesses do to each other in the marketplace as competition, this is an oversimplification. At one extreme, business firms vigorously block one another's attempts to achieve goals, and this is conflict. For example, in an industry where consumer demand is low and industry production capacity is high, conflict is almost certain to result as each film attempts to reach its goals at the expense of the other firms. Blocking activity in these cases often takes place at the activity level. A different situation exists in industries where government contracts are the rule. Here, competition is more likely. Each firm submits bids and strives to reach its goal of getting the contract. Blocking behaviour is not evident, even though there can be only one winner and the goals of the firms are incompatible.

Perspectives in conflict analysis

We can analyse the effects of conflict from four different perspectives, beginning at the individual level and ending at the organization level. These four perspectives.

Intra-individual conflict: This refers to conflict within an individual about which work activities to perform. There may be internal conflict because (1) the individual does not feel that it is morally "right" to do a certain thing, (2) two different bosses are making contradictory demands, or (3) doing a certain job in a certain way will help the individual at the expense of his or her co-workers. Analysing this type of conflict is difficult because "inner states" of the individual must be assessed.

Inter-individual conflict. This refers to conflict between two individuals and is the subject of much research in psychology. Research on this type of conflict often focuses on personality differences and why individuals feel obliged to block the goal attainment of the other person. Within organizations, it appears that tendencies toward inter-individual conflict are exaggerated by the environment of the job. For example, if a person who places a great deal of emphasis on "doing his own thing" is subordinate to a rigid, conservative boss, it is likely that some sort of inter-individual conflict will develop.

Individual-group conflict In organizations, there are two important situations where individuals find themselves in conflict with groups. The first situation is one in which an individual is violating group norms. The reason for this conflict is that groups have a greater ability to block an individual's goal achievement than the other way around. Only in unusual cases will an individual be able to mobilize the resources to block the group's movement toward its goals. This is clearly seen when groups force individuals producing above the group norm to reduce their output. The group does this by threatening to block the attainment of the individual's psychic goals and physical goals.

The second case of individual-group conflict is one in which subordinates of one boss collectively disagree with a course of action the boss wants to take. A conflict exists here because the subordinates are blocking the goal achievement plans of the boss. Although the boss can exercise formal authority to suppress this type of conflict, this is generally an unwise course, since subordinates often find a way to retaliate.

Inter-group conflict This involves conflict between groups of people, irrespective of the group. Included in this category, therefore, is interdepartmental conflict within organizations and conflict between organizations. Specific examples of intergroup conflict are labour-management conflict, United Nations debates, wars, marketplace conflict by firms attempting to outsell each other, conflict between departments in a firm as each fights for a bigger share of the organization's budget, and so on.

The traditional view of conflict, which was popular until the early 1940s, assumed that conflict was bad 'or organizations. In the view of the traditionalists, organisational conflict was proof that there was something "wrong" with the organization. The Hawthorne studies were probably important in shaping the traditional view because in those studies the dysfunctional consequences of conflict were noted. Another likely factor in the traditional view was the development of labour unions and the often violent conflict between labour and management. During the early twentieth century labour unions were struggling for the legal right to bargain collectively. It was not until the 1930s that this goal was reached. Along the way, many confrontation occurred between labour and management. These were almost always viewed as bad for both the organization and The individual, and it is therefore not surprising that the traditionalists viewed conflict as undesirable. Overall, the traditional view assumed that organizational performance declined steadily as conflict increased.

Because conflict was viewed as bad, considerable attention was given to reducing or eliminating it. Perhaps the most general reaction was to suppress it. This was done in an obvious way by simply demanding that people in conflicting situations change their behaviour for the good of the company. It was also done indirectly by rigidly prescribing the limits of authority of each job so that individuals would be less likely to be in conflict. While these tactics sometimes worked, they were largely ineffective because (1) they did not get at the exact cause of the conflict and (2) suppressing the conflict did not allow any of the positive aspects of conflict to come out.

The traditional view of conflict appears to be losing ground as time passes, yet it still describes the views of many people. Why should this view, be so widespread, given that some conflict has been shown to be beneficial? One researcher answers this question by saying that the important institutions in our society—the home, church, and school—are founded on the traditional view of conflict, and these institutions have a powerful influence on society. Since these institutions are very influential when we are young, we are subtly influenced to have a particular view of conflict. In the home, for example, parents suppress conflict by telling their children to stop fighting. In schools, teachers are assumed to have the correct answers, and exams are a check to see whether students are deviating from these. Most churches stress brotherhood and peace, not conflict. If this argument is correct, the change in the view of conflict from traditional to current will take many years.

The current view

The view which prevails among researchers at present is that organizational conflict is neither good nor bad per se, but is inevitable. Thus, conflict will occur even if organizations have taken great pains to prevent it. This situation is similar to that for the informal organization, where it was noted that the informal organization will emerge and be active irrespective of management's attempts to suppress it. Thus, organizations will experience conflict even if they have carefully defined employee jobs and their managers are reasonable people who treat employees well. There are even project some instances in which conflict is purposely created, such as the management structure.

When the amount of conflict is related to organizational performance, we see that there is an optimum level of conflict which maximizes organizational performance. This optimum level is neither low nor high. The argument is as follows: In an organization where there is too little conflict, little impetus for innovation and creativity exists. Employees are comfortable and not concerned about improving performance. As a result, things which might improve performance get very little attention. At the other extreme, organizational conflict is so disruptive that employees cannot give proper attention to performance goals because interpersonal or intergroup conflict saps employee energy. Here again, performance suffers. At moderate levels of conflict, however, employees are motivated to resolve conflicts, but these conflicts do not disrupt the normal work activities.

There are two important implications of the current view. First, much of the conflict in organizations may be good because it stimulates people to find new ways of doing things. If two employees are in conflict about the best way to do a job, the manager might be advised to encourage the conflict to see which individual is correct. The best technique can then be used in doing the job in the future. As an example, consider two departments that are in conflict. Each department tries to get its own way and engages in whatever blocking behaviour it feels is necessary to prevent the other department from attaining its goals. Top management may see this as dysfunctional; but instead of trying to suppress the conflict management might try to induce the departments to find a solution allows each to get what they want.

Second, management of conflict, not suppression, becomes a key activity. If we assume that conflict can be good or bad, it is important that constructive conflict be encouraged and destructive conflict be resolved. But what criterion should we use to make this decision? Robbins suggests that the most practical and important criterion is group performance. Organizations exist to achieve goals, and high performance by groups in the organization increases the likelihood that organizational goals will be reached. Thus, if the criterion of group performance is used, managers must view conflict in terms of its effect on group performance before they move to resolve it or encourage it.

Sources of conflict

There are numerous sources of conflict within formal organizations. Those discussed below have been analysed extensively by researchers and are instrumental in determining how much conflict there will be.

Perhaps the most fundamental fact of organizational life is that resources are finite. Even the most successful companies have found that they are limited in what they can accomplish. With this realization groups and individuals see that there will be times when they will have to fight for what they want. The most obvious manifestation of this problem comes when the annual budget is set. Each department typically submits a request for its needs during the next fiscal year, and top management adjusts the request based on its knowledge of the total organization. Department heads often see their requests cut back because the resources for the total organization are limited. When cutbacks occur, however, the potential for conflict increases because the heads of various departments begin making value judgments about why management decided to cut back one department but not another. As a general rule, the greater the scarcity of resources, the greater the potential for conflict.

Added to the basic problem of finite resources is the problem of organizational units having to work together. It is bad enough to get less than you wanted for your department because of some other department, but then to have to work with the other department may be more than some managers can take. Suppose you are the head of department A, and in the yearly budget just approved by top management, you received considerably less, money for operations than you thought was minimally necessary to run your department. Suppose also that you see that department B got most of what it asked for. If the work activities of your department are interdependent with those of department B, you might well consider purposely slowing down your department's work in an attempt to convince top management that they made a mistake in their allocation of funds.

This is a particularly salient because is so much inter-dependence of work activities in organizations. On a grander scale, inter-organizational conflict is often caused because the activities of many separate organizations must be coordinated, In May 1979, California motorists found themselves in long lines waiting for gasoline. The oil companies, the oil producers, consumer groups, and the government spent considerable time arguing about who was to blame. The problem was most likely caused by the tight interdependence of work activities needed to get oil from the wellhead to the consumer. Any purposeful disruption by one of the organizations in the system would cause conflict among the other in the system. As a general rule, the more interdependent the work activities the greater the potential for conflict.

Differentiation of activities

We noted above that interdependence of work activities is an important source of conflict in organizations. Backing up one step further, we can see that the mere existence of groups doing different functions creates the potential for conflict. As groups become familiar with how they perform their own jobs, they may turn inward and become uninterested in (1) how their work fits in with other groups or (2) the importance of other groups' work. As a result, when difficult issues between the groups must be dealt with, each group behaves in a way that increases the potential for harmful conflict.

This differentiation in work activities leads to differentiation in goals. Production's goals may be to have long production runs with few changes in product styles, because this allows the production facilities to operate at peak efficiency. Marketing's goal, on the other hand, may be to give customers what the, want when they want it. This means rush orders, special orders, and other demands that directly conflict with production's goals.

Communication problems

Both the interdependence and differentiation of work activities demand that communication between individuals and groups be effective. As we saw, however, this often does not occur. At the broadest level, communication problems develop because not all groups have the same information. Each group therefore takes a position based on its view of the world and the information it has. The obvious solution to this problem is to give all groups equal information. However, this is generally not feasible because individuals with important information may want to use it for their own advantage and not share it.

Communication problems are also caused by technical jargon that is so frequently used in organizations. Over time, each group develops its own language, which may mean nothing to another group. When the two groups must deal with a contentious issue, the "us vs. them" mentality more easily develops because of the meanings each group attaches to words.

Differences in perceptions

We all "see" the world slightly differently because we have all had different experiences. These different views of the world can be a major source of conflict in organizations because value judgments flow from these views. One of the classic differences in perception involves the value of experience vs. the value of education. Older, more experienced managers often are in conflict with younger, inexperienced managers about the way in which work should be done The experienced person usually points out how knowledgeable he or she has become over the years, whereas the inexperienced person argues for "new ways" of doing things. Often this conflict is resolved by the older person exercising his or her authority.

It is hard to make unequivocal statements about how differences in perception will influence conflict. It is also difficult to deduce exactly how a person views the world, unless the person is well-known to the manager. Nevertheless, a realization that differences in perception is crucial to conflict means that it must be included in any discussion of the sources of conflict.

The environment of the organization

Thus far we have been concerned with factors inside organizations that cause conflict. However, changes in the firm's environment can cause major conflict within the organization. In the 1970s, for example, college enrollment in liberal arts declined as students began entering disciplines that were more job-oriented. This shift in demand meant that there were pressures to reallocate resources within universities. These pressures caused real problems as the different faculties were in conflict as to how this reallocation should be done. As another example, consider a conglomerate that finds that the demand for the output of one of its divisions is rapidly declining. The obvious thing to do is to cut back activities in that division and channel corporate resources into more profitable divisions. However, if the division having difficulties is an important one and its head is a powerful person, tremendous conflict may develop as other division heads argue for a redistribution of resources within the company.

Other sources of conflict

Numerous other sources of conflict exist in organizations. They include (1) individual differences ; (2) unclear authority structures; (3) differences in attitudes; (4) task asymmetries; and (5) differences in time horizons.

The three important dimensions of conflict are sources of conflict, the actual conflict behaviour, and the outcomes of the conflict." The sources of conflict were discussed in the preceding section. They do not always lead to perceived goal incompatibility, but when they do, the likelihood for open conflict increases. Before that can happen, however, at least one of the parties must see that there is an opportunity to interfere with the other party. If there is no opportunity to interfere, no conflict can take place. Once the conflict is out in the open, any one of several conflict resolution techniques can be used. How the conflict resolution techniques are used influences whether the conflict will be resolved in a functional or dysfunctional way. The resolution leads either to immediate further conflict or to a change in the sources of conflict or perceived opportunity for interference. For example, if the resolution of an inter-group conflict is that the groups are physically separated, the opportunity for interference is altered. Or if the cause of the conflict centres on interdependent work activities and this problem is resolved by consensus decision making, one source of conflict is changed.

The key point in this model is that actual conflict is not an isolated event. It is caused by certain recognizable factors and its resolution is either functional or dysfunctional. The resolution has implications for further conflict in the future.

Conflict outcomes

Earlier in the chapter we argued that conflict can be good or bad. We now should consider the specific positive and negative outcomes that conflict can cause.

Positive outcomes

The positive outcomes of conflict are as follows:

1. *The energy level of groups or individuals increases with conflict.* This increased energy level can be seen when people talk louder, listen more closely to what is being said, or work harder. Two of the benefits organizations get from increased energy levels are increased output and innovative ideas for doing the work better.
2. *Group cohesion increases.* Research has shown that, when groups are engaged in a conflict, their internal cohesion increases. The other group is seen as the enemy," and group resources are mobilized to meet the threat from the outside. To do this, disagreements within the group must be suppressed and all energies diverted toward the enemy. This process can be seen in the Mideast. Arab nations have trouble getting along with one another except when a common threat dominates their relationship. The reason that increased cohesion is considered a positive outcome of conflict is that highly cohesive groups can have high productivity, particularly if they support management's goals.
3. *Problems are made known during conflict.* When conflict develops, management can readily see that something is amiss and can embark on a program to resolve the conflict. If two groups are in disagreement about something but never make it known, they may work at a reduced level of effectiveness without management's being able to determine why. This is particularly likely to happen if the problem

between the groups is caused by some system of work that management has set up. Group members may be reluctant to criticize management about the system, and the conflict will not be made known.

4. *Conflict motivates groups to clarify their objectives, and this increases the group's awareness of its purpose.* Groups are quite often apathetic about their particular function until an external threat emerges. When a threat becomes evident, group members begin thinking seriously about the purpose of their group. This type of analysis can lead to better ways of doing things, making the group more effective. In an organization where two groups are having a conflict, if each group is motivated to think about its objectives the organization as a whole may benefit. On a day-to-day basis, it may also be easier for management to deal with conflicting groups because the conflict has caused a coherence and stability to emerge in the groups. Conflict may also promote a more efficient division of labour.

5. *Conflict encourages groups to protect values they think are important.* Various groups see themselves as the "protector" of certain values. For example, both "pro-choice" and "pro-life" groups vigorously defend certain values concerning family-size management. Right-wing political groups defend one set of values, and left-wing groups defend another. Within a specific organization, marketing people may stress high quality while production people may stress low unit cost. Although these values are somewhat contradictory, the attempt to resolve a conflict like this might result in a solution that will benefit the entire organization.

6. *Individuals or groups are motivated to mobilize information that is relevant to the conflict.* Although this information is biased by the subjective perceptions of the parties involved in the conflict, additional information is usually developed that can be helpful in resolving the problem. If no conflict exists, there may be no motivation to gather additional information or to look for better ways of doing a job.

7. *Conflict can increase an organization's overall effectiveness because it forces groups or individuals to adapt to the changing external environment that the organization faces.* Conflict serves to point out that the environment is constantly changing, and the organization may have to change the way it does certain things if it is going to adapt to this environment. As we shall see in the next chapter, much conflict is politically motivated, as individuals attempt to get a larger share of the organization's resources for themselves. It is not surprising that conflict occurs in this circumstance; we cannot expect people to simply accept a reduction in the resources they have historically received. The outcome of this type of conflict is, however, an organization that is more capable of coping with rapid change in its environment.

Negative outcomes

The negative outcomes of conflict are as follows:

1. *A decline in communication between the conflicting parties.* When individuals or groups are upset with each other, a common development is that they stop speaking. As we have seen, this is very dysfunctional because conflict is often worsened when there is little information passing between the conflicting parties.
2. *Hostility and aggression development* It is a typical human reaction to feel hostility toward someone who is blocking one's attempts to reach a goal. Aggression is also a common behaviour associated with hostility. While this may satisfy the person's urges to attack the person doing the blocking, from the organization's point of view it is undesirable because it channels behaviour into nonproductive areas. For example, if two groups are in conflict about something, they may spend much of the work day devising schemes to block the other group's goal attainment. Obviously a point is reached where the work of each group is not accomplished.
3. *Overconformity to group demands.* We noted above that conflict could cause groups to become more cohesive and this might result in higher productivity. We must also recognize that members of a group faced with an outside threat may overconfirm to the group demands. This involves blind acceptance of the leaders' interpretation of the opposing group and no thinking about solutions by anyone in the group. This prolongs the conflict and makes it more intense. As time passes, the group is unable to view its opposition with any objectivity and perceptions become very distorted.

An examination of the positive and negative outcomes associated with conflict reveals that obviously, both good and bad things can happen. On balance, what can we say about conflict? The most general statement is this: At low levels to conflict there is little incentive for individuals or groups in an organization to perform well. At high levels of conflict, there is too much incentive and people experience anxiety, fear, and reduced performance. But at moderate levels of conflict, the increased incentive to perform causes the positive outcomes of conflict to outweigh the negative outcomes. There is an optimum level of conflict that results in maximum organizational performance. Thus, if a manager observes that organizational performance is not up to standard, it could be that conflict levels are either too high or too low. The material in the following section addresses this very practical issue of what a manager can do to insure that the level of conflict is maintained at a level where organizational performance is maximized.

Conflict management

If we accept the argument that conflict can have either positive or negative effects on organizations, then it follows that managers have considerable flexibility in dealing with conflict. While there are many specific techniques for managing conflict, there are only two broad approaches: (1) stimulate the conflict or (2) resolve it. The specific techniques that can be used in each of these cases are discussed below.

If groups or individuals in an organization are too set in their ways or too willing to accept unquestioningly the views of a powerful individual, management may benefit from stimulating conflict among them. The fact that groups and individuals may come up with inferior decisions because there is too little disagreement has been demonstrated on many occasions. In fact, one of the major reasons for antitrust legislation is that the government assumes consumers will be better off if vigorous competition and conflict exist among firms supplying consumer goods. Without this conflict, the impetus for new product development and technological breakthroughs would be very low.

One laboratory experiment demonstrates this point very clearly. Groups were formed to solve a problem. As in the typical experiment, there were experimental and control groups. The experimental group had a "planted" member whose job it was to challenge the majority view; the control groups had no such member. In all cases, the experimental groups came up with better solutions to the problem than did the control groups. What can management do to stimulate conflict? First, it can openly state that it feels conflict to be desirable on certain occasions. For example, departments managed by individuals who are feared by their subordinates may benefit considerably if conflict with the boss is encouraged when a new department head takes over. Although the goals of the boss may be blocked in the process, if these goals were not reasonable or functional in the first place, the organization will be better off. The same thing is possible on the interdepartmental level. If the sales department succeeds in blocking the production department's goal of smooth department succeed, in blocking the production departments production scheduling and in the process better serves the consumer, the firm will probably be better off than if strictly internal considerations had dictated the decision.

Second, new individuals can be brought into the existing situation. These individuals may know little or nothing about the problems and opportunities facing the organization, but their thoughtful questions and comments may force the long-time members to see new ways of doing things. This is readily seen when "outside" members are asked to join the boards of directors of certain firms. These outsiders may severely question accepted industry practices. In the process, long-time board members may get very upset with challenges to the normal way of doing things, but in the end new approaches often result. Third, the organization can be restructured. When this is done, new reporting relationships develop, and during this development enough uncertainty usually exists that conflict arises. As this conflict is worked out, better ways are sometimes found to do the important tasks of the organization.

Finally, management can implement programs that are specifically designed to induce conflict or competition. The most obvious example of this is sales contests where the winner receives a substantial prize. In many cases these contests are simply competition and not true conflict, but in others dealers are in conflict with one another as they each try to reach the goal. Blocking behaviour such as advertising and price dealing is necessary because the dealers know that there is a limit on the number of cars that can be sold in a given time period.

A variety of conflict-resolution techniques have been used in conflict situations. We will discuss only those that seem to have gained fairly wide acceptance.

Forcing: If two workers are in conflict and the boss says, "You two stop arguing; I will decide which course of action is reasonable," the two workers can no longer disagree about the issue. The manager has "forced" a resolution of the conflict. Obviously, this method leads to quick resolution, but the aftermath of the conflict may be very negative. The one who loses will often try to get revenge for the incident. This behaviour may involve refusal to help out the fellow worker or trying to make the boss look bad.

Smoothing As the term suggests, this conflict-resolution technique involves considerable use of tact by the party doing the smoothing. Smoothing can be an effective strategy in many instances. A manager who is confronted by employees who are in disagreement may find that they are in conflict simply because of a lack of information. Once the manager supplies the relevant information, the conflict may disappear. Suppose that worker A and worker B are having a dispute about work procedures. Worker A argues that B should change the way B does a particular task so that A's work will be easier. Worker B says that the method can't be changed because that is the way B was told to do it by the foreman. If the foreman simply tells A and B why B's job has to be done in a certain way, the conflict is more likely to be easily resolved.

Smoothing is usually an ineffective resolution technique if the employees think that there is an unreasonable rationale for the decision. In the example above, if the foreman resolves the conflict in favour of worker B and A thinks this is only because the foreman likes B, worker A is hardly going to be happy with the decision. On balance, smoothing works most effectively when the parties in conflict are not aware of important information relevant to the conflict. Individuals who have this information and can bring it to the attention of the conflicting parties can often resolve the conflict.

Majority rule Many disputes which drag on for a long time tempt participants to resolve them by a simple vote. For example, in committees discussing a controversial point where there are reasonable arguments on both sides, we often hear the sentiment, "We've heard enough talk on this issue—let's vote!" Although voting and majority rule are important in our democratic society, research has shown that a quick vote on issues usually suppresses thoughtful consideration.

The other problem with majority rule is that one group always wins and another group always loses. The losing side hardly feels that the voting system is fair, hence they will agitate for changes that favour them. In many companies, for example, one department of the business usually has more status than another. People who work in the lower-status department get fed up, over a period of years as they see resources going to the higher-status department when the rational thing to do would be to shift the resource allocation to a more equitable basis.

Compromise Perhaps the most widely used of all techniques, compromise involves giving each of the parties in the conflict some of what they want. This is most easily seen in labour-management conflicts. Labour usually begins bargaining by asking for much more than it actually hopes to get, while management begins by offering less than it actually expects to have to give. Even if an arbitrator is used to settle the dispute, the parties will probably behave this way as they attempt to convince the arbitrator that their position is right.

The main advantage of compromise is that it allows a solution to major conflicts. In many instances it is almost impossible to resolve a conflict unless each party sees that the other is giving up something. The motivation to reciprocate may be the only motivation operating to move the parties toward a solution. The tendency of people to exaggerate their demands in the hope of getting what they really wanted all along is one of the big problems with compromise as a conflict-resolution technique. Consider a conglomerate where the head of each division must submit a proposed budget for next year's operations. These proposals are considered by the board of directors, who adjust the amount as they see fit it would not be surprising to find the division heads asking for more than they need. They reason that, even if their request is cut back, they should still get enough to carry on their division's activities, The division heads therefore find themselves in something of a game with the board of directors, precisely because the board has developed a reputation for cutting back requests. The other major disadvantage of compromise is that neither of the conflicting parties is enthusiastic about the solution. They may both feel they lost because they did not get what they wanted. Their only solace is that the opposing party did not get what it wanted either.

Consensus We discussed consensus as a means of improving group effectiveness. As a conflict-resolution technique, consensus requires the conflicting parties to work together to find the best solution to their problem. While this may sound impractical, there are situations where consensus will be appropriate. When an issue is so important that the conflicting parties can easily see that their conflict must be resolved, consensus decision making is useful. The laboratory parallel of this real world situation is found in the "arctic and desert survival games". In both these cases, the parties can clearly see that their differences must be resolved if they and/or the organization are to survive.

Ground roles should be observed when using consensus as conflict-resolution technique. These are as follows:

1. *Do not vote.* As noted above, voting tends to suppress analysis of the problem and generally results in Poorer decisions. It also creates a win-lose atmosphere.
2. *Do not "horse trade."* One of the tendencies people have when trying to settle a conflict is to say things like, "I'll accept your view on point X if you'll accept mine on point Y." In consensus decision making this is discouraged. Instead, each party is required to decide what the most reasonable position on both X and Y is.
3. *Each person is encouraged to speak.* Some of the most helpful comments are made by individuals who are not aggressive. It is important to create an environment where everyone feels free to contribute to the resolution of the conflict.
4. *Reach a consensus.* It is not necessary to have unanimity. It is important however, that each party to the conflict feels that he or she can live the decision that is reached.

Overall, consensus is a positive conflict-resolution technique because (1) it moves the parties away from the win/lose mentality and (2) it takes advantage of the diverse resources available within the group.

Confrontation The confrontation technique requires the opposing parties to openly state their views to each other. While it may seem that this would happen in the normal course of a conflict episode, the fact is that the conflicting parties may often not state the real problem. Husband-wife arguments, for example, are often characterized by beating around the bush and refusing to state the real problem. While this is often the case because one person doesn't want to hurt the other's feelings, the fact is that the problem cannot be solved until it is known. The same is true in organizational conflict. If two departments are in conflict over an apparently trivial point, we might suspect that sometimes far more fundamental is at stake but the parties are unwilling to admit it.

Once the real reason for the conflict has been brought out, the reasons it came into being and the ways it can be resolved are analysed. The solution is often a fairly simple one, and this is further support for the argument that the reason the conflict wasn't solved sooner was because no one was willing to state the real cause of the conflict.

Integration The integration technique requires the conflicting parties to collaborate in order to resolve the conflict. It requires both parties to have the attitude that, although they may be in conflict, they will strive to develop collaboratively a solution that satisfies the needs of both parties. Thus, the needs of the parties will be integrated by the solution.

That this is a desirable route is often difficult for the conflicting parties to see.

The win-lose mentality is often so strong that the opposing groups assume an integrative solution is impossible. What is needed, therefore, is for the conflicting parties to develop the ability to rise above the usual "we-they" view and assume that integration is feasible. A systematic search for these win-win solutions can then be instituted.

Resource allocations and intergroup conflict

To this point, we have looked at several facets of conflict. We close this chapter with an examination of intergroup conflict because it represents such a crucial and highly visible part of organizational life. All organizations are broken down into formal departments or divisions, and conflict between these groups is very common. How group decisions may be dramatically different from individual decisions how organizational politics can generate tremendous intergroup conflict. Since intergroup conflict can have such a powerful effect on total organizational performance, it is important to analyse what happens during intergroup conflict, and then to consider what management might do to increase the chance that the conflict will be functional.

With the recent economic problems that have been experienced in our society, the issue of intergroup conflict has become even more important. This is because the economic downturn has caused the environment facing both public and private sector organizations to become much harsher. Because organizations have been for forced to cut back, resources available to the various groups in each organization have declined. This almost guarantees conflict between groups, because each of them will fight for a share of the decreased resource pie.

Intergroup conflict can be seen in many organizational activities, but it is particularly evident in the following areas:

1. *Goal setting*—conflicts erupt as various groups in the organization attempt to have their particular goals adopted as the official goals of the organization.
2. *Budgeting*—various groups in the organization fight over the relative share of the budget that each will get.
3. *Organizational effectiveness*—each group attempts to have organizational effectiveness criteria adopted that will make them look the best.

We will examine here only the conflict that develops in the setting of budgets, because this activity has such important implications for the organization as a whole, and because the intergroup conflict follows such a clear pattern.

Resource allocation procedures in organizations

Before an organization can rationally develop a budget, it must have previously made some basic decisions about the goals that it will pursue. Once the budget is adopted, resources are channelled to various parts of the firm in an attempt to reach these goals. When resources are unlimited, there are no problems about where resources should go; since the organization does not need to resolve the merits of each particular group's claims, it simply gives each group everything it wants. Once a group is given resources, it is able to pursue all sorts of new and different activities. Over time, these new activities come to be an accepted part of "normal" operations. So, as long as times are good and resources are abundant, there are few problems. However, when the organization must retrench, these new activities must be curtailed to some degree and it is here that conflict develops. Deciding which group will get fewer resources is a highly political and conflict-generating decision.

Because the conflict over resource allocations can have such a dramatic effect on an organization, it is important that the conflict be properly managed. In most organizations, the process is not managed very well. Instead, when conflicts arise between groups they are usually resolved by the common superior of these two areas imposing a decision. For example, suppose a company has three manufacturing plants. As the annual budget setting deadline approaches, each of the plant managers will make a case to their common boss about the resources they need. The boss will have to resolve these conflicting claims and make a decision about how resources should be distributed among the three manufacturing plants. The boss will usually make some sort of compromise decision, i.e., because the total requests of the three plant managers probably will exceed the amount available, the vice-president will probably cut all the requests by a certain amount.

When the boss makes decisions like this, he or she is actually behaving like an arbitrator and imposing a binding settlement on the conflicting parties. The conflicting parties will probably exaggerate their demands in the hope of the offsetting expected compromise of the manager-arbitrator. So, the plant managers will ask for a larger share of the budget initially, hoping that after the vice-president imposes a compromise they will get what they wanted in the first place. Unfortunately, this leads to budget demands that are extremely high and the organization is continually faced with cutting back on budget demands. This causes all sorts of ill will and increases the conflict between the parties.

Managing intergroup conflict

How can intergroup conflict like this be resolved? As a general principle, what is needed is a budgeting system that motivates conflicting groups to reach a decision on their own, rather than having the manager-arbitrator impose a settlement on them. This, of course, is a rather dramatic departure from the normal way of allocating resources in most organizations. However, it is consistent with a more democratic, participative management system.

One specific technique that might be tried in this context is final-offer arbitration. If this system is used, each of the parties submitting a budget request would be required to indicate what they felt each group or department should receive in the way of resources. The manager-arbitrator would then pick one of the proposed budget packages in its entirely and impose it on all departments. Labour relations research shows that this kind of conflict-resolution technique motivates the conflicting groups to reach an agreement on their own, because they want to avoid the situation where the arbitrator imposes an unacceptable all-or-nothing decision. If the conflicting parties reach an agreement on their own, they will feel more responsibility for the budget allocations and they will have more motivation to stick to its provisions. In one exploratory lab study that analysed the possibility of using final-offer arbitration for budget conflicts, it was found that members of various departments who bargained over budget allocations were closer together at the conclusion of bargaining under the threat of final-offer arbitration than they were under the threat of the typical compromise arbitration that is found in most organizations.

Final-offer arbitration is only one of many techniques that might be used to manage intergroup conflict. The important goal in any of these conflict-management techniques is motivating the conflicting groups to move voluntarily to a resolution that will benefit the total organization. Until groups can be creatively motivated to pursue organizational rather than departmental goals, intergroup conflict will often have negative consequences for individuals, groups, and organizations.

Managerial decision-making

Victor H. Vroom views all managers as decision makers. The managerial task, according to Vroom, focuses on the social process of determining how problems should be solved rather than on finding solutions. Questions concerning what decision-making processes managers should use, what processes managers do use, what considerations affect managerial decisions, and how much decision-making authority should be shared with subordinates, motivated Vroom to seek answers and to formulate a model of managerial decision making.

Vroom believes that the effectiveness of managerial decisions is influenced by three situational factors, *the required quality of outcome, the acceptance* or *commitment required from group members for effective implementation,* and *the time allotted to reach a decision.* Quality refers to the extent to which a decision impacts organizational performance; acceptance refers to the willingness of employees to implement decisions; and time refers to urgency. Vroom noted that managers make decisions *autocratically, consultatively,* and *by group participation.* Any particular style may be effective in one situation and not in another.

Vroom argues that the effectiveness of a managerial decision depends on the manager's ability to adjust his or her decision-making style in accordance with the requirements of the situation. The decision styles and their behavioral characteristics are shown below.

"A" refers to autocratic styles, "C" refers to consultative styles, and "G" refers to group styles. The roman numeral following A, C, or G represents the behavioral variation within the autocratic, consultative, or group style.

Decision rules

Effective managerial decision making, then, is a cognitive process in which situations are assessed and subsequently matched with the appropriate decision-making style. Vroom has formulated seven rules that take into consideration the required quality and acceptance of a decision, for use in decision-making processes. Three of the rules safeguard decision quality, and four of the rules safeguard decision acceptance.

1. *The Rule of Information.* If quality is important, and the decision maker lacks the information or expertise to decide alone, then style AI should not be used. AI in this situation would likely result in a low-quality decision.
2. *The Rule of Goal Congruence.* If quality is important, and group members (subordinates) do not support the outcome to be derived from the decision, then style G should not be used. Style G in this situation will cancel managerial control and potentially result in lack of quality.
3. *The Rule of Unstructured Problems.* If quality is important, the decision maker lacks the information or expertise to decide alone, and the decision maker does not know what information is required, then decision making must involve an interaction with those who have relevant knowledge or expertise. Styles AI, AII, and CI should not be used. Style AI does not allow for gathering information; styles AII and CI are less effective because they do not allow the interaction of those with needed knowledge and expertise.
4. *The Rule of Acceptance.* If acceptance is critical, and the decision maker is not sure if an autocratic decision will be accepted, then styles AI and AII should not be used. AI and AII do not allow for participation; they risk nonacceptance by some group members.
5. *The Rule of Conflict.* If acceptance is critical, and there is probable conflict or disagreement over the decision, then styles AI, AII, and CI should not be used. The decision should permit those in disagreement or conflict to interact and resolve their differences. Styles AI, AII, and CI are one-on-one interactions and risk nonacceptance by some group members.
6. *The Rule of Fairness.* If quality is important, and acceptance is critical and not likely to result from an autocratic decision, then styles AI, AII, CI, and CII should not be used. Style G is the best option because all others risk potential nonacceptance by a few.
7. *The Rule of Acceptance Priority.* If acceptance is critical, and group members can be trusted to pursue organizational goals, then styles AI, AII, CI, and CII should not be used. Style G provides the greatest potential for equal participation in the decision and maximizes the likelihood of full acceptance by all group members without risking quality. All other decision styles risk lack of full acceptance.

Applying these rules to any decision situation results in what Vroom calls a feasible set of decision styles, that is, a group of style alternatives that may be effective in the given situation. For example, the rule of information contends that when decision quality is important and the decision maker lacks information or expertise to make a decision, alternative AI should be eliminated. Once alternative AI has been eliminated, a feasible consisting of AII, CI, CII, and G remains. Vroom suggests that when a feasible set of more than one alternative exists, the alternative that expends the least amount of time should be used.

Decision styles and the need for quality and acceptance

Research in the area of problem solving by Norman R.F. Maier revealed two dimensions that correlate reliably with a decision's effectiveness: quality and acceptance. In Maier's formula, the effectiveness (E) of a decision is a function of the quality (Q) of the decision times the acceptance (A) of the decision, or $E = f(Q \times A)$.

The *quality* of a decision is objective; it depends on the decision maker's utilization of the known facts. Acceptance of the decision is subjective; it refers to how favorably those who must implement the decision react to it--how they feel about it. A high-quality decision that does not have the full support of the persons who are expected to implement it may lack the necessary support to ensure its success. Thus, decisions may be ineffective because they lack quality, acceptance, or both.

A problem arises in decision making because the methods for dealing with facts are different from those for dealing with feelings. The difference is not always apparent because feelings are often hidden behind rationalizations.

Four types of desired outcomes

Problems differ in the degree to which quality and acceptance are vital to success. Normally, and regardless of the nature of the problem, an individual or group will pay more attention either to quality or acceptance. The required degree of quality arid acceptance varies with each decision. Basically, there are four types of desired outcomes.

— High quality-High acceptance

— High quality-Low acceptance

— Low quality-High acceptance

— Low quality-Low acceptance

The proportion of these two factors determines the decision style that is most likely to be effective. The following discussions show how they relate.

High quality-high acceptance: the consultative decision

A high quality-high acceptance decision might involve a manager and a work team in a problem-solving process to reorganize the work distribution and work flow. The quality is in the examination of the existing situation with a logical assessment of areas that could be improved. Although the final decision may be the manager's, all decisions are based on facts presented by the group. Each participant has a psychological investment in the success of the new procedures, thereby enhancing acceptance. In another case, the manager might make the decision after *consulting* with individuals, but without bringing them together as a group.

High quality-low acceptance: the command decision

An example of a high quality-low acceptance--or *command*--decision is the way in which the price is set on a product. In making the decision, management must take into account such facts as production and distribution costs, competition, marketing opportunities, and profit margin. The employees who produce the item are not really concerned with the selling price because they lack the information necessary to analyze it, and the salespeople readily accept the price that is set by the company.

Similarly, solving a mathematical equation is a high-quality, low-acceptance decision--a logical, rational, cognitive process based on fact.

In an organizational setting, when quality is a requirement but acceptance is not, the leader uses the available information and makes the decision without involving the people who will be executing it.

Low quality-high acceptance: the consensus decision

A low quality-high acceptance decision is made when quality is of minor importance but acceptance among the people affected by the decision is very important. For example, two of three employees of equal ability are required to work on Saturday. The manager may be satisfied with any of them, but it may be an important issue for the employees. In an example cited by Maier, three secretaries in such a situation were asked to decide for themselves which of the two of them would work. All had dates for the Saturday: one with her husband, one with her fiance, and one with a man she had just met. Because this date was, to the last woman, critical in the development of the relationship, the other two women decided that they would work so that she could have the day off. The acceptance dimension was met.

In another example, the allocation of a new truck to a repair crew presents a problem of perceived fairness if each member feels that he or she is most deserving. When the leader has the crew members participate in making the decision, there tends to be a redistribution of trucks so that all members stand to gain from the introduction of a new truck. Invariably the worst truck is discarded, but the actual allocation varies greatly from one crew to another. Such situations tend to be tailored to fit the values, attitudes, and personalities of the group members.

In these cases, the persons affected by the decision are brought together and the *consensus* decision evolves from shared information, ideas, and feelings. The decision must be acceptable in some degree to all group members.

Low quality-low acceptance: the convenience decision

A low quality-low acceptance decision is made in a situation in which the choices are equal, the outcome is not really important to anyone, and so on. The manager may make the decision or the group may flip a coin to decide. The leader generally chooses whatever, method is most convenient at the time. No special consideration is given to finding the "best" method.

Individual versus group decision making

The problem of achieving both quality and acceptance is complex because the *quality* of a decision is related to the logic or rational process used in reaching the decision. If it is made by an individual, the quality of the decision depends on the wisdom of the decision maker. *Acceptance* of a decision is related to the emotional factors that influence the decision-making process, such as the affected persons' being allowed to participate in the decision. Because wisdom and participation are not conditions for all decision making, it is necessary to use expertise in some situations, participation in others, and a combination of the two in others.

Decisions requiring acceptance--when quality is not seriously endangered--call for joint participation, and the problem must be stated without offending or blaming. "Tell-and-listen" or "consensus" may be the optimal method in such a case. As the need for both quality and acceptance increases, the "problem-solving" approach becomes more and more feasible.

Decisions requiring a high degree of both quality and acceptance require problem-solving and consultation skills. The consultative approach is an effective way to achieve quality decisions in group situations and, at the same time, to gain acceptance through participation.

Superior-subordinate problem solving applies whenever a manager wishes to influence a subordinate, gain a subordinate's acceptance of a change, set priorities, or have the subordinate accept unpleasant tasks or conditions.

When the need for quality is high and gaining acceptance is not an objective, decisions can be made successfully by individuals alone. Because such decisions need only to be communicated clearly, the "tell-and-sell" or command method is appropriate.

This does not assume that only the two factors of quality and acceptance are to be considered by a leader in selecting a decision style. Other factors, such as time, capability of subordinates, and the level of trust in the group, must be considered as well. For example, regardless of the quality and acceptance factors, time constraints may require the use of the command model. If the level of trust in the group is low, a consensus decision may be difficult or impossible to achieve. If the trust level in the group is high, a consultative decision style may be very effective for achieving acceptable decisions of high quality.

Many of the decision situations facing managers in modern organizations are considerably more complex than those discussed in the previous chapter, This complexity arises from the following factors:

— in many cases, the available options cannot be evaluated simply in terms of a single, well-defined quantitative parameter. It may be that only the preferences of the parties involved can be determined and that these preferences can be expressed only on a nonquantitative ordinal scale;

— the decision situation may involve multiple objectives. Priorities as between individual objectives may vary from time to time and one objective may not always be in the position of first priority. Preferences may therefore vary during the course of the decision process;

— there may be some difficulty in identifying the "opposition" in the decision situation; that is whether it is from purely natural forces, a clearly defined opponent, or a mixture of both;

— the decision situation may be unique and "single-play rather than one that is repeated many times.

If one or more of these conditions exists the quantitative methods of the previous chapter may be difficult or impossible to apply. The purpose of this chapter is to outline methods of studying decision problems under these more complex conditions.

This thread of argument will be reversed in this chapter. Because one of the most generally applicable methods of treating complex decision problems originated from study of conflict situations, this is where the discussion starts. By the end of the chapter, however, the argument will have led back to the treatment of decision situations under conditions of uncertainty.

Managerial decision situations can be related directly to games. In fact, some of the more intellectually challenging games that we play contain many of the elements of everyday decision making found in business and in our personal lives. In such games, however, the rules and the pay-offs are known exactly.

The challenge arises from the very large number of combinations of plays and the need to select a series of plays designed to maximize payoff in the face of another player's opposition. Managerial decisions are seldom so well defined. Nonetheless, some insight can be obtained into the more complicated decisions by studying the conflict implicit in the simpler games. For this reason, this chapter starts with a brief consideration of conflict in the strictly competitive situations found in many games. This is an extension of the treatment of two-person, zero-sum games contained in the latter portion of the previous chapter. The discussion proceeds from there to the more general decision problems found in modern organizations.

Strictly competitive decision situations

In the strictly competitive decision situations discussed in the previous chapter, the gain to one player is exactly equal to the loss to the other. A number of options may be available to each player, but it is assumed that the players must make a choice of strategy simultaneously. Because of the strictly competitive nature of the situation no cooperation or communication between the players can be mutually profitable. Neither player can be assumed at the outset to know what the other's choice of strategy will be.

The "solution" to such conflict situations consists of rules governing the choice of strategies, originally described in complete form by von Neumann and Morgenstern. These have been outlined in the previous chapter. In essence, these rules define strategy choices that bring about an equilibrium in the game. This equilibrium is such that it is not to the advantage of one player to move away from his equilibrium strategy, provided the other player does not. The equilibrium strategies may consist of a pure strategy or a set of mixed strategies for each player. An equilibrium pair is not necessarily unique, although, if other equilibrium pairs exist, they all result in the same value of the game to the players.

The set of strategies providing equilibrium maximizes what may be characterized as the security level for the players engaged in the game situation. The outcome of the game using the equilibrium set may not be the best that either player could desire, but it does represent an outcome that he can be sure of obtaining. Any movement by one player away from his equilibrium strategy cannot cause a deterioration in the other's equilibrium position and may well cause an improvement to the player remaining at the equilibrium. In cases where a pure strategy equilibrium pair does not exist an equivalent equilibrium, providing the same type of security, can be obtained by the use of mixed strategies. In two-person, zero-sum situations, therefore, rational decision makers can be assured of an equilibrium that represents a certain level of security that cannot be broken down by the other player.

In a number of experiments conducted by research organizations and summarized by Lee, players were, in fact, found to search for and move toward equilibrium positions in decision situations involving both pure and mixed strategies. This tends to confirm that the approach to two-person zero-sum games suggested by the theory is likely to be adopted, at least in situations that conform closely to the strictly competitive characteristic of those games.

However, two major questions are outstanding: first, do two-person, zero-sum games ever occur in managerial decision making; and second, how does the mixed-strategy solution apply to a situation in which there is only a single play?

Some authorities hold that the application of two-person, zero-sum theory to real life situations is unrealistic. For example, Nigel Howard states that it is hard to think of real-life situation that is truly a two-person, zero-sum game goes further by stating that a tendency exists to see conflict situations in terms of the zero-sum approach because it is thought to be "... hard-headed, tough minded and realistic." He sees this approach as interesting only insomuch as it is generally invalid and points out that it applies only to such pursuits as parlor games and sports. This being the case, he says, it is unfortunate that these games are used from the earliest age to train people in conflict behavior.

Turning to the second question, is it appropriate to apply the mixed strategy "solution" to a conflict situation with no pure strategy equilibrium, for which there is only a single play? Let us consider such a conflict situation described by Conan Doyle in the adventures of Sherlock Holmes entitled The Final Problem.' Holmes is being pursued by Moriarty and catches a train from London to Dover with a view to escaping to the Continent. The train has one stop. As it leaves the station, Moriarty catches a glimpse of the departing Holmes, who sees Moriarty arrive at the station in pursuit. Holmes reasons that if Moriarty catches up with him he will kill him and deduces that Moriarty will charter a train in pursuit. Holmes now has the choice between getting off at Canterbury or going on to Dover.

The von Neumann-Morgenstern theory tells us that, since no pure strategy equilibrium exists, a mixed strategy policy should be adopted. Holmes should calculate the proportion of times he should get off at Canterbury and the corresponding proportion of times that he should go on to Dover. In a multiple play situation, he should then play each of his available strategies in the correct proportion. However, a problem arises in that Holmes is engaged in a game in which a wrong choice will result in there being no more plays. A manager involved in a major decision may face a similar predicament if the outcome of his first choice of strategy is unfavorable to his company.

Luce and Raiffa suggest that the mixed strategy solution can be implemented by selecting a pure strategy for each play by a simple physical experiment,' such as tossing a coin or throwing a die. That is to say that, provided the experiment is designed to give the same proportions to its outcomes as are desired between pure strategies, the decision as to which strategy to employ in a single play should be made on the basis of the experiment alone. This procedure is intuitively acceptable in a multiplay situation. It is, however, very difficult to accept that it should be used in real-life decision making in a single-play situation. In any case, a manager who is convinced that he should decide between two options in such a situation by tossing a coin would be well advised to do it in the privacy of his locked office. In a single play of a two-person zero-sum game, therefore, unless a pure strategy equilibrium exists, it is probably best to avoid a decision for as long as possible. In practical terms this means seeking delay to gain time for gathering information or reassessing the decision situation and the available options.

The process of gathering information is an endeavor to increase a player's knowledge of the situation. This can be thought of as moving as close as possible to the possession of perfect information within the constraints imposed in terms of time and money available. Perfect information in the simple example discussed above would be knowledge of the other player's selected strategy. If Holmes knew that Moriarty was going on to Dover (for certain), his decision problem would disappear.

An intuitively acceptable procedure in a single-play, strictly competitive decision situation without a pure strategy equilibrium is to endeavor to gain knowledge of the other player's strategy choice before choosing one's own. The difficulty remains, of course, that if both players try to do this, one of them must make the wrong decision. There is no equilibrium that provides a security level to each in a single play of this type of game.

In the case of the two stores advertising simultaneously in the Thursday night's paper, the solution might involve advertising in a different medium once the other store's announcement had been made. This procedure of relating a choice of strategy to the intentions of an opponent comes into prominence later in this chapter in consideration of other decision situations that are found to occur often in the operations of modern organizations.

Personalistic decision theory involves an evaluation of alternatives on the basis of the beliefs and expectations of the decision maker. By projecting the possible consequences of the decision and the possibilities of the alternatives in attaining his or her objectives, the decision maker determines the expected utility of a decision or choice. A decision tree is a graphic representation, similar to a flow chart, of choices that call be used to help to identify alternatives or multiple choices and their possible outcomes. It provides a way to look at and explore possibilities. In form, it is roughly analogous to diagraming a sentence or constructing a mathematical equation. Both quantitative and qualitative choices can be evaluated in this manner.

The possible decisions are represented in a branching mode, i.e., there are points at which one of two or more decisions could be selected. A solid square on the tree represents a decision point, For each possible decision there are potential positive and negative effects, or "consequences." A consequence written on the decision tree is the decision maker's best shot at describing the outcome of a particular decision situation. A "strategy" is the sequence of actions to be taken from an initial decision point through each succeeding decision point, in a linear fashion. Numerical values such as percentage probabilities, estimated costs, possible profits and losses; and so on, can be added to the decision tree, as can other factors such as people and risk.

The decision maker generally identifies preferences between consequences (outcomes) and qualitative probabilities between propositions that reflect the aspects of the situation about which the decision maker is uncertain. Numerical probabilities, called *utilities*, can be assigned to the consequences so that one consequence is preferred to a second one if, and only if, the utility of the first exceeds the utility of the second. In addition, numerical probabilities can be assigned to the propositions about which there is uncertainty, in such a way that one proposition is preferable to a second if, and only if, the numerical probability of the first exceeds the numerical probability of the second. The *expected utility* of a strategy, then, is the sum of the consequence utilities weighted by their respective probabilities of occurrence under that strategy. The consequence utilities and the probabilities can be defined in such a way that one strategy is deemed preferable to another if, and only if, the expected utility of the first is greater than the expected utility of the second.

This method of decision making attempts to establish a balance between the decision maker's preferences and what is known to be factual. Projections and assumptions must be made, and the ultimate analysis is only as good as the decision maker's ability to identify probabilities. However, the decision tree does provide a way to look at several proposed choices or courses of action, to evaluate the possible consequences of each, and to evaluate multiple strategies based on likely probabilities.

As a minor diversion, note that reaction to an opponent's strategy will be seen to be rational only if that strategy is known for sure. If the opponent's strategy choice is wrongly diagnosed reaction to his strategy will be considered to have been irrational. This raises the question of the relationship of rationality to the quality of information in the possession of the decision maker.

For example, it is sensible in hurrying to take a plane to New York to inquire of an airline clerk whether the plane you are about to board is going to New York. If the clerk says yes, it is rational to board the plane on the assumption that you are in possession of information that is as near perfect in the context of the decision to board the plane as it is necessary to obtain. It can be argued, however, that until the plane actually arrives in New York the decision to board the plane can be considered as only subjectively rational. Suppose the clerk was misinformed and the plane was in fact heading for Montreal. It would still be subjectively rational to board the plane on the basis of the clerk's (wrong) information. It would not, however be objectively rationa1, for the simple reason that the plane did not in reality go to New York. If one defines a stable decision as one that would not be affected by additional information, then only an objectively rational decision' would be a stable one for a rational decision maker. In practice, perfect information is rarely available before an event. Nevertheless, possession of the greatest practical amount of relevant information before a decision is the best assurance of closeness to objectively rational decisions and the minimum deviation between desired and actual outcomes.

Problem solvers work under two different conditions. Sometimes things are going along well enough and it does not seem worth the effort to seek improvements. More frequently there are problems to solve and improvements required but there isn't time to do anything about them. Improvements can only be attempted after things get better! This is a not uncommon situation and it is a difficult one. Therefore this chapter considers the implications for management of the shortage of' time and complexity of their job, and then how this knowledge was applied in a particular case to make time for problem solving and improvements. Finally there are observations on the basic skills and organization required for problem solving.

Interesting experimentai work by Mackworth for the Medical Research Council, Cambridge, showed that people with a responsible task, which required them to use information and make decisions had two kinds of difficulties. He called them 'Speed Stress and 'Load Stress'. Speed Stress depends on the rate at which information must be used and decisions made and Load Stress depends on the quantity of information available. The effect of speed stress: the experimental results show that the proportion of wrong decisions increased as the logarithm of the rate at which decisions had to be made. Load Stress depends on the number of items of information considered in a decision. In this case it is found that the proportion of errors increases proportionately to how many items are under consideration. He found that Load Stress depends on the amount of information that may be considered, i.e. although much of the available information may be irrelevant or unnecessary it all adds to Load Stress. Secondly Load Stress is increased by any disorder which means that data has to be arranged or priorities must be decided before action can be taken. Finally Load Stress is increased by the 'Crisis' difficulty that is, when demands for action overlap or appear simultaneously. In brief these theoretical results confirm the statement 'One can only do one thing at a time, and think of one thing at a time.'

Experience suggests that the notions of speed stress and load stress apply to managers, Probably managers fail to make the best decisions because of the rate at which they have to work and the complexity of the task facing them. Very often the first step to improvement is to make things easier for the manager by reducing the load and speed stress on him. A real example may indicate some of the ways of doing so and the result.

Investigation of a tool room 'Some 15 years ago Mr Eric Gray was set the problem of increasing the output of the tool room at the Glacier Metal factory, Kilmarnock. It was rather difficult to see what could be done because of the wide variety of orders coming into the tool room. There were orders for new tools, for replacements, for repairs, for experimental work, and for research equipment. Thus there were 5 sorts of orders, and every one different. It was almost impossible to study such a variety of work.

The manager concerned himself with the costs and technical aspects of tool design and production. Work orders of all five kinds were sent an requisitions to a foreman who consulted with the other foremen to decide whose men should do the work. Then each foreman organized his men to do the appropriate orders.

Three things were done to make work easier for the foreman. First a clerk was added to the tool room. His job was to collect all incoming orders, sort them and send each requisition to the foreman whose section would do that item of work. Now foreman C has 6 fewer lines of communication and 12 of those 14 remaining are devoted to getting the work done. He now only has to deal with about a third of all the orders coming into the tool room. One would expect the new organizational arrangements to reduce the load stress. Anyway it is interesting that the output of the tool room went up from 300 to 420 tools per week. That is for the clerk's wages, a 40% increase in labour cost, a 40% increase in output was achieved. This result was obtained on each of the two shifts.

Some other methods of reducing the load stress were also used, and are frequently useful. When orders were received they were first sorted according to the work place where the order would be done and placed in the corresponding top pigeon hole. When convenient the foreman reviewed the work available in the top holes and from these selected those which the 'due' dates on the requisitions showed should be given first priority. These were placed in the second hole. He transferred requisition the second to the third pigeon hole when he had collected the tools and materials for that job.

The rack reduces the load stress on the foreman because:

(a) He makes a series of simple, separate decisions independently of each other i.e. which work-place should do a particular job; which of all jobs for that particular work-place should be given priority; which of these few jobs can be done next, and which should be done next. Thus the complexity of each decision is reduced and because the decision is made before the workman waits for a job, the speed stress is also reduced.

(b) The load and speed stress is reduced to a very simple decision when a workman is ready for another job. If there is a job available the workman does it; if not the workman must be transferred to a different useful job. In fact the position of cards indicates the state of the workshop and its likely loading a few hours ahead of the present time so adjustments of under-load and bottlenecks can be made before they actually occur.

The device therefore helps to fix priorities, simplifies complex decisions, reduces mental loads and helps control and forward planning. Another device used in this case was a nest of storage boxes which were used to separate and store materials for each order in a similar manner as the rack stored the requisitions. It made it easier to check on the availability of materials for current orders. Thus three ways of reducing the load and speed stress were used. One operated on organizational arrangements, another on the paper work, and the third on the material aspect. We do not know their separate contributions but to ether they increased the tool room Output 40% because they made the foreman's jobs easier.

Implications of this case study This case study has been described in some detail because it highlights many of the procedures and tools of problem solving. Firstly the work arrangements were altered to make the foreman's jobs easier, and thereby he increased output. It illustrates the ergonomics notion that 'the easier way is faster'. Successful innovation almost invariably depends on finding how to do things more easily. Secondly, various devices were used to enable the foreman to see the work situation more clearly. That is, the old pile of work orders was reorganized in a logical manner in the rack so the shop load could be understood easily. Thirdly, responsibilities were reorganized to give people time to solve the problem of increasing output.

The reader may well have some examples where this 'three box trick' or specialists have been introduced and output did not go up. If so analyse the reason. You will usually find that if these devices failed it was because they were not organized so that the load or speed stresses were reduced. For example if the information on the job cards was insufficient to enable the clerk to sort them or for the foreman to understand each job without referring back to the sender, or if dates with priorities were not given, then the three box trick clearly could not save effort until the requisitions were improved

In a similar way if introduction of a clerk complicates the organization structure for any reason, then his work is unlikely to be useful. The test for any such reorganization is, does it make work easier ? Does it actually reduce load and speed stress? These are practical tests and are preferable to blind acceptance of textbook formulae.

The organization for improvement

It has sometimes been asked why was the clerk introduced? Wouldn't it have been possible for the orders to have been sent to the manager and for him to sort them? It could be that would have been more economical, but I am sure it would have required longer than the 6 weeks actually taken for this reorganization. Still, perhaps there was an even better solution possible. However, very frequently it is better to get a partial improvement quickly rather than wait for the appropriate conditions in which to make the best or optimum change. A partial improvement gives people the courage to seek more improvement, so I would suggest it is worthwhile making the partial improvement as quickly as possible. If then this is used as a step to further improvement it may well be that you have the optimum or best path to improvement because of the time saved in implementing each change.

Finally you may wonder who made this improve-ment. Was it the manager who encouraged the changes to be made and seconded the appointment of the clerk and expenditure on the new racks and shelves? Was it the clerk who organized the flow of information and made it easier for the foreman to see how to organize the work? Was it the foremen who in fact controlled their men better? Or was it the workmen who found with the new arrangements that their bosses organized them so that they could do more? Certainly the workmen accomplished more because their time was more fruitfully used. Actually they all contributed to the improvements. The manager by his leadership; the clerk as a specialist helping the others to analyse the problem; the foremen by initially showing what their difficulties were and later by using the new techniques.

In problem solving one usually finds the above three kinds of activities going on:

1. Leadership to provide the environment for problem solving.
2. Specialist analytical help to sort out the problem.
3. Group activity of operational people to give information and implement results.

In small problems one man may play each of these roles in turn; in large problems different people concentrate on each of these roles. The point is to make sure all these roles exist.

Ways of reducing load and speed stress

This chapter has emphasized the need to seek easier ways of achieving organizational objectives, particularly by reducing load and speed stress. Some general ways of doing so are given here, together with the chapters in which these topics are detailed more thoroughly.

1. Organize work so as to reduce the variety of duties which a manager needs to do. Specialization is the technique for doing so, but when specializing duties make sure the communication load is not increased. The check lists in 'Organization and Planning' should be helpful.
2. Make use of step plans. This is the essential 'trick' and enables ordinary people to solve problems which are beyond cleverer people.
3. It is very difficult, in practice, to deal with immediate, medium term, and long term problems simultaneously. Therefore organize duties to keep them separate and allocate these different kinds of decisions to different functions or levels of an organization. In particular, separate long term strategic decision making from short term tactical decision making and day to day operational control. Therefore try to separate, when appropriate, the three stages of pre-planning, planning and control. All work passes through these stages, and as far as possible they should be kept distinct so that each may receive proper attention.

Qualities for problem solvers

The Americans who codified Industrial Engineering, and upon whose techniques this approach to problem solving is based, thought their 'philosophy' was more important than technique. This is because the 'philosophy' underlies all application of technique, the qualities and attributes which the problem solver seeks to acquire and how he uses his knowledge, and it is undoubtedly necessary and significant, but is rarely made as explicit and practical as one would like. Therefore I shall now try to outline a useful philosophy, for the man faced with problems to solve, which is worth cultivating deliberately. It is based on:

Detachment: The Use of Facts and Models. Method: Use of System and Step Plans.

Thoroughness: Progressive, Lateral and 'Crazy' Thinking.

Sensitivity: Appreciating Indicators and Working with People.

These qualities were given by the founder of American medical education Sir William Osler. In his time, 80 years ago, medicine, like turned from a craft into a prolike management today, needed to It is significant that Osler, though well aware of the technical imperfections of his time, thought it important to stress philosophy before technique.

The remainder of this part of the book (Section A) will be devoted to a consideration of these aspects of problem-solving techniques, one chapter being devoted to each topic.

Most research on decision making focuses on how problems are solved. In this chapter, we consider the question of which problems are solved and how alternatives are generated for problem solving. These are fundamental activities underlying effective problem solving and decision making. Clearly, if we spend our time solving the wrong problems, or if we restrict attention to an inferior set of alternative solutions, then no matter how effective our problem-solving procedures may be, the outcome will be poor.

We note the following descriptive and prescriptive aspects of problem finding of interest:

1. *Problem identification*: the process by which a decision maker recognizes that a problem or decision-making opportunity exists.
2. *Problem acceptance*: the decision maker focuses attention on the problem as something worth considering further.
3. *Problem representation*: the problem or decision situation is linked to potential improvements that may be achievable and perhaps some alternatives for problem solving are considered.

From a prescriptive viewpoint, we will be concerned with procedures to improve recognition and acceptance of problem situations. This leads to procedures for clarifying the objectives to be satisfied by problem-solving activity and for improving the management of time and attention so that important problems are dealt with first.

A problem state is perceived. You have a model indicating that improvement is possible. Yet, what is the problem: Is it to come up with an improved living situation with your parents. Is it to change your life-style to conform to your parents' apparent wishes (thereby avoiding any confrontation with them on this issue)? Perhaps you should consider the problem of finding an affordable and convenient apartment. Solving any of these "problems" would involve investments of time and energy. Which problem would you spend time solving and what alternatives should you consider for each problem? This answer would depend on your needs and values and your initial estimates of the costs and benefits of attempting to improve your state through each of the various options. If you solve the wrong problem, you may not remove the underlying problem state.

Note also the importance of problem context in this example. Suppose you rented an apartment and you faced the same kinds of frictions, but this time from a nosy and self-righteous landlord. With this changed problem context, your problem-finding activity might change as well. You would very likely see the problem to be solved as finding another apartment.

Finally, note that we have defined this problem as an individual problem-finding situation. But the context could quite easily be elevated to the level of your family by making them aware of your own problem, bringing them into the problem-finding-problem-solving process and looking in this broader context for the right problem to solve.

In the case of a doctor-patient relationship, the issue is usually diagnostic, determining whether the patient has a problem, and how to treat it. But the patient may be primarily looking for sympathy. The doctor may be only looking for income or professional advancement. What is the real problem here?

The problem-finding activity here is in framing the issues correctly. What are the real objectives of the family reunion? Are there particular family members who have special problems or needs? Do there exist past issues that complicate the decision? One of the greatest challenges for organizations in the private and public sector is improving quality. A typical example of a quality problem is given in the WAD Company Case. Improving quality means finding the right problem(s) to solve.

At a societal level, the LNG siting problem is a good example to how different groups may see problems differently. Environmentalists may see the primary problem as protecting the environment may see the problem primarily as providing adequate energy supplies for a region. If you were a public policy maker with responsibilities for regulating the siting of such a facility, you would have to be very sensitive to these different representations of the same problem.

In all of these examples, additional complexities, such as institutional constraints, naturally arise as we consider more complex levels involving groups, organizations, and social contexts. Nonetheless such issues as problem identification, acceptance, and representation represent common challenges of problem finding and problem definition at every social level. As we shall see, the issue in problem finding is that human decision makers have only limited information-processing capabilities so that we must allocate our attention and energies to only a few of the many problems we might address. We first consider a general framework for problem finding. This framework begins with a simple introspective question. When do I discover I have a problem.

Problems are typically discovered in one of two ways. In *reactive or passive problem finding,* the recognition of problems is triggered by an outside influence such as another person, a reminder letter, or a personal experience that forces you to recognize a problem situation and do something about it. If you are an absent-minded professor, the outside influence could be a bounced check reminding you of the sorry state of your finances. If you are a homeowner, the outside influence could be a theft at a neighbour's house, which alerts you to the fact that your own home may be vulnerable to illegal entry.

Proactive or purposive problem finding involves thinking creatively about the goals you wish to accomplish. This process of imagination and planing may give rise to a recognition that substantial improvements to your current state are achievable. Problems are identified as specific and recognized areas where you believe such improvements may be achieved. Managers engage in such proactive activity all the time, using techniques such as planning and performance monitoring. The purpose of these activities is to look actively for the most important problems to solve to maintain the organization on an acceptable or improving path.

Both reactive and proactive problem finding are responses to differences between the perceived status quo and what an individual believes is possible, desirable, or necessary for his or her well-being. Goals, values, and needs underlying problems finding are determined by the biological, cultural, and social context within which the individual functions. Problem finding is the process triggered when environmental cues indicate that goals, values, and needs are not being satisfied at an adequate level. This leads to problem-solving activity and action. The evolving results of the individual's action become his or her cumulative experience. This experience then conditions the processes determining goals, values, and needs that will trigger future problem-finding and problem-solving activities.

We need to understand how problem states are perceived and attended to by individuals in various contexts. To do so, we first review relevant research on perception, memory, and attention. This research indicates that significant limitations exist in our abilities to perform these information-processing activities. As a result, individuals allocate their scarce attention and information-processing faculties to environmental cues and problems by attending to these sequentially. This leads us to a discussion of goals, values, and needs, all of which are important in determining which problems are perceived and addressed first.

This section is an introduction to perception, memory, and attention. Because each of these areas is a well-developed field in its own right, our treatment will be necessarily selective. Our purpose is to sketch the nature of these processes, to illustrate their linkages, and to understand the limitations they impose on human decision making.

We begin with perception. Following Stephen Pepper, we view the perceptual act as a conscious activity linking an individual through received sense date to the environment. In its simplest form, perception requires a perceived object and an observer. When I say "I see a house," the "house" is the objective reference, and "I" is the observer.

Philosophers have argued for ages whether there is an objective reference independent of the sense data that we perceive. Idealist philosophers have concentrated on sense data as the main focus of concern, whereas realist philosophers attribute objective properties, independent of the observer, to the references of the perceptual act. We follow Pepper and cognitive psychologists in seeking a synthesis between the idealist and realist positions. Instead of focusing on the objective reference, with a passive observer-assimilating sense data, we focus on the observer as an active participant in the perceptual process. This change of focus leads to interesting insights on the nature of perception and its relation to problem finding.

To illustrate, consider the following example. You are thirsty and decide to have a drink of water. You look for and find a suitable glass, fill it, and satisfy your thirst, In this context, the perception of "a suitable glass" as you enter your kitchen is an object of such a shape as to hold water, with anticipated visual and tactile properties. The act of perceiving the glass consists of seeing such an object and, through drinking, fulfilling your expectations of the purpose of the glass. When you find the object you believe to be a glass, you fill it and reinforce the correctness of your perceptions by drinking the water in the glass.

This simple example illustrate the most important characteristics of active perception; it is done as part of some purposeful act and it is consummated by determining that the objective reference of perception fulfills our expectations. These expectations are referred to as schemata. A schema refers to the conceptual model in memory of what we anticipate we shall perceive. If we find what we expected to find, then the schema of this perception is supported. In the example given we would have simple schemata for "glass," "kitchen," "drinking," and so on and more complex schemata integrating these simple schemata into the act of "going to the kitchen to get a drink of water." Note that each of the simple schemata in this example could be further linked to other schemata in our memory. Thus, the schema "glass," "kitchen," "drinking," and so on and more complex schemata integrating these simple schemata into the act of "going to the kitchen to get a drink of water." Note that each of the simple schemata in this example could be further linked to other schemata in our memory. Thus, the schema "glass" might be linked to both a schema of a "typical glass" as well as to particular examples of a glass.

From a philosophical viewpoint, this description of perception underscores Immanuel Kant's famous dictum: "There are no percepts without concepts." That is, to perceive a "glass" requires that we have a notion of what a "glass" is. The act of perception then both assimilates sense data associated with the "glass" we see and reinforces our entire cognitive schema of "glass" and its purposes. In this sense, perception links both subjective sense data and objective references in mutually reinforcing processes, providing an interesting bridge between realist and idealist positions on perception.

From a psychological viewpoint, this same approach has found acceptance and experimental support. In suggests that the faculties of perception, memory, and attention are linked. When we get a drink of water, we have stored in our memory a schema for how this act should proceed and the objects required to accomplish it. Our attention focuses on these objects as a part of satisfying our thirst. When we have done so, all aspects of this process are reinforced.

While perception, memory, and attention are linked, they are also limited resources. Has summarized early research on limitations to our perceptual abilities. To illustrate the nature of this research, consider the following experiment. Suppose that a horizontal line is drawn. Next suppose that a marker is placed on the line toward either the left end or the right end of the line. In a series of trials, almost everyone will unerringly be able to discriminate whether the point placed in each trial is on the left end of the line or the right. Suppose now that additional locations for the point are possible—for example, left, middle, and right, all equally spaced along the line. When the number of possible categories for placement of the point increases, subjects will begin to make mistakes in discriminating which slot the marker occupies in a given trial. In fact, normal subjects can only discriminate roughly 10 locations accurately. Beyond that, their perceptual abilities deteriorate rapidly.

Miller reports other experiments testing the ability of subjects to discriminate unidimensional stimuli, such as musical pitches, concentrations of salt solutions, and loudness of tones. In each of these cases, the number of perfectly discriminable alternatives seems to be in the range of 7 ± 2, leading Miller to dub 7 ± 2 as a magical number reflecting the upper limit to human perceptual discrimination abilities for unidimensional stimuli.

A little thought shows that we can distinguish more than 7 objects from one another, however. For example, many individuals can distinguish the sounds of most of the instruments in an orchestra. All of us can recognize the faces of more than 7 ± 2 people. The key here is that these stimuli are not unidimensional, life loudness, pitch, and position of a point on a line, but multidimensional. For such stimuli, Miller reports results indicating that as the number of independently variable dimensions of the stimuli increases, so do our powers of discrimination. For example, if instead of locating points on a line, we attempt to judge their position in a square, then normal subjects can classify accurately some 20 to 25 positions. Adding the second dimension of vertical position to that of horizontal position thus allows additional discrimination.

What happens when the number of independent dimensions is increased further? Experimental results show that discrimination continues to increase but at a decreasing rate. As a rough estimate, Miller suggest that when the number of independent dimensions is 6 to 7, we can discriminate some 150 alternatives. The question then arises, how many independent dimensions can we actually perceive? This appears to differ across individuals and across stimuli and is further complicated by sequential processing of stimuli—we take in certain dimensions first, then process a second set of dimensions, and so on. In this sequential way, a very large number of independently variable dimensions can be discriminated. Even so, as these examples hint, immediate perceptual discrimination powers of human decision makers are quite limited.

The procedure just suggested of expanding our powers of discrimination by sequentially processing stimulus dimensions introduces memory as a key to discrimination. For we must store and recall successively discriminated dimensions if we are to integrate these into an overall judgment of what we are perceiving. The question of immediate and ultimate limitations to perceptual discrimination is therefore linked to memory limitations. These we now discuss.

Short-and long-term memory. Memory researchers such as Normal and B. Underwood described memory as having at least two levels: short-term and long-term. Short-term memory contains items that relate to the immediate, conscious present. Long-term memory contains items that may have been absent from consciousness for some time; they belong to the past. Items in short-term memory fade if not rehearsed by focusing attention on them. If items are rehearsed, they are more likely to be transferred to long-term memory, where they are integrated into various schemata. Such schemata are also subject to decay over time if not rehearsed through recall.

Memory researchers have studied the span of immediate memory intensively and have found that normal subjects can store about 7 items of information in immediate memory. A simple experiment verifies this. An experimenter reads to subjects strings of unrelated letters, digits, or words with a one-second interval between each successive stimulus. A typical string might be: "A J X R 2 Y 8 Z Z E." The question is, What is the longest string that can be recalled without error? The answer is roughly 7 ± 2.

If we can rely on immediate memory for only 7 ± 2 items, how is it possible that chess masters can look for very brief intervals at a game in progress and then reconstruct the entire chess board without error? The answer seems to be that the "items" stored in immediate memory can be encoded in sophisticated ways, so that each of the 7 or so items in immediate memory can be very large "chunks" of information retrievable from long-term memory. To illustrate this simply, consider the task of remembering the sequence of digits, after only a brief exposure to these digits. If this were attempted in raw form, most people would make errors in recall. However, if this same sequence were encoded in groups of four during exposure to them, then the entire sequence wee encoded in groups of four during exposure to them, then the entire sequence becomes 1492, 1776, 1812, which can be stored immediate memory as three salient dates in American history. Thus, the information content of immediate memory can be enhanced by clever encoding schemes as well as experience that use mnemonic devices to allow us to store significant amounts of information in immediate memory under a single "code name." For example, the name "Pennsylvania" may be stored as one "chunk" in short term memory, with readily accessible facts from long-term memory then retrievable in association with this single word.

The structure of long-term memory has been the subject of considerable research in cognitive psychology. The basic model emerging from this research attempts to answer two questions: How is information stored in long-term memory and how is it recalled? The model suggests the following structure. Memory may be viewed as a network of nodes and links. The nodes might be viewed as "labels" and the links represent associations between various labels. For example, the label "chair" might be linked to the label "table." Further, each label is viewed as being the label for a schema depicting the anticipatory set of various objects, actions, and concepts. For example, the node "chair" might have a schema depicting both the general expectations one has of chairs, as well as links to other nodes with schemata representing specific instantiations of "chair" - for example, a schema representing my favourite easy chair. Also linked to these schemata may be various "episodic schemata" that are the representations of episodes involving general schemata. For example, concerning "chair," there may be schemata representing my anticipations for what my favourite easy chair feels like when I sit in it. There may also be links to schemata representing specific episodes in my experience involving chairs.

We may summarize this discussion of long-term memory by likening long-term memory to an interconnected network of labels, where each label, when focused on, presents a slide or a filmstrip to the mind's eye. These slides and filmstrips are what we have called schemata.

The major limitations to the operation of long-term memory are limitations on our ability to access what is stored there. Such access limitations relate tot he way our "node-link" structure is set up, and the nature of context variables conditioning access. For the present, we wish only to concentrate on the latter issues. What researchers have found is that the context surrounding access to memory may strongly influence whether and what is recalled. This is because we tend to organize information coming into long-term memory so as to integrate it with our current memory structure. Thus, new information will be linked to existing information depending on the context in effect when the information is stored. This organization of the new information and the context surrounding its acquisition then affect the retrieval of the same information at a later point. The most important control process related to retrieval is the process of attention Kahneman defines attention as the allocation of information processing capacity to mental activity. Just as perception and memory are limited in humans, so is our information-processing capacity. Without belabouring the point, one need only compare one's arithmetic abilities with those of a modern computer to conclude that our information-processing capacities are indeed limited. Thus, research on attention is concerned with which activities we attend to and with what intensity. The basic model of attention arising from this research can be stated as follows: We tend to pay attention to those activities that are most pressing within our perceptual field. Activities are attended to in the priority order indicated, until information-processing capacity is exhausted.

Goals, values, and needs

Goals, values, and needs all refer to certain desired results of preferred states. Psychologists and sociologists have argued that our "desires" are many, but our cognitive and physical makeup limits our ability to pursue them. This leads us to structure our "desires" hierarchically so that we attend to the more important ones before we attend to less basic ones. It is this argument of hierarchically structured goals, values, and needs that we shall pursue here. First, however, it will be useful to define and distinguish each of these terms.

A *goal* is a desired end-state resulting from planning activity. The same definition applies to the term *objective*, which may be thought of as more open-ended. An objective can never be fully achieved, whereas goals can. Because goals are generated by proactive planning, they are intentional and purposeful guides to what the decision maker wishes to accomplish.

A *need* represents a basic drive that arises from our biological and cultural background. Tolman and others classified needs into three levels: primary needs; secondary needs; and tertiary needs. Needs are our basic response tendencies and they are conditioned by our cumulative biological, cultural, and social experiences. Milton Rokeach defines a *value* as "an enduring belief that a specific mode of conduct or end-state of existence is personally or socially preferable to an opposite or converse mode of conduct or existence." In other words, values represent personal or social preferences for desired end-states and appropriate means of attaining them. Values can be either personal or social and they can be either instrumental or terminal. Instrumental values include such modes of behaviour as ambition, courage, honesty, and courtesy, whereas terminal values include end-states such as a world at peace, freedom, pleasure, and wisdom.

Let us briefly distinguish now between goals, on the one hand, and values and needs, on the other. Goals are purposefully determined, whereas values and needs need not be. Values and needs may represent desires or drives below the level of our awareness. When they are consciously intended preferences, they become objectives and goals. For example, we may value a comfortable life and purposefully pursue goals to achieve this end.

The distinction between needs and values is more complex. Behaviourist psychologists, such as B.F. Skinner, would see little difference between values and needs since behaviourist psychology deals only with observable response tendencies. The mental states, induced by values, needs, or whatever, leading to these response tendencies are, for the behaviourist, purely conjectural and secondary. Sociologists like Rokeach, however, distinguish between "values" and "needs," seeing needs as basic biological and behavioural drives and values as cultural and social constructs. In this framework, values are viewed as the cognitive representation of individual needs as transformed by social and institutional context.

For example, the need shelter and clothing may be transformed into a value for a comfortable life, the need for security into values of co-operative behaviour and world peace, and the need for dominance into values concerning ambition, courage, honor, or national security. Thus, values may be viewed as transformations of needs into individually and socially acceptable manifestations of these needs. As such, an individual's values reflect needs, but they also tell us something about individually and socially acceptable ways of fulfilling these needs.

Individual: finding suitable living quarters. The basic needs here are shelter and warmth. Beyond these, an individual might also perceive needs related to acceptance and love, both by her family, if she continues to live with her parents, and by friends who might come to visit.

Terminal values in this context would be desirable end-states associated with living quarters, including comfort and status aspects of where we live. Instrumental values would include values associated with how we interact with our family in choosing our living quarters and how we pay the costs of these quarters. These values would co-determine how well our various underlying needs will be satisfied by the process and outcome of our choice of living quarters.

Goals in this context might include the cost of our chosen living quarters, time to work, and space. These would represent specific targets that we might consider reasonable constraints to impose on ultimately acceptable living quarters. They would first arise out of our evaluation of what would fulfill our basic needs and values, and they might be further refined as we proceeded through the process of finding living quarters.

Two-person context: doctor-patient. The patient's needs are to remain healthy. The doctor's needs might be to maintain a secure income and a good professional reputation. A rich set of values surround doctor-patient relationships, however, and these can be in conflict with the basic needs. For example, the doctor may be confronted with tough financial choices in choosing a treatment, since some treatments may make the doctor more susceptible to malpractice suits or some patients may not be able to pay as readily as others. But not selecting the best treatment for a patient, regardless of financial status or possible lawsuits, may conflict with the medical code of ethics and may affect the doctor's professional reputation.

In terms of goals, the patient may have a specific time-frame in mind for getting back on the golf course or to some other normal routine. The doctor may also have a similar temporal goal for treatment effects. Both may have financial goals associated with any treatment.

Organizational level: improving quality. A the organizational level, goals are very much a part of daily life. These pertain to specific targets for cost, time, and quality improvements, as measured by internal measurement systems, by external customer satisfaction surveys, and by the bottom-line results of the business over time. But accomplishing organizational goals requires linking these to action programs, and one of the most important action programs in recent years has been the area of quality improvement. Here goals might be targets for reducing product defects, for reducing delivery time to customers, and for improving other attributes of the organization's products and services.

Whereas identifying goals in organizations is easy, defining needs for an organizational problem context like improving quality is difficult, because needs, as we use the term, apply only to individuals. In fact, one of the greatest problems in launching a quality program at the organizational level is ensuring "buy-in" by organizational participants. In other words, individuals in the organization must want to cooperate in achieving improvements. And they will only want to cooperate if they see their needs and values being satisfied by participating in the quality improvement process. In many organizations, accomplishing this has required very significant changes from traditional hierarchical management styles to a bottom-level, participatory management style, which encourages all employees to look proactively for problems to solve and to find solutions that will benefit the organization. We shall have more to say about organizational and group.

Needs and value hierarchies

These examples illustrate our basic points. Needs are primary; values are derived from these as individually and socially acceptable modes of behaviour and end-states; goals and objectives are more specific states or targets determined through purposeful planning to fulfill needs and values. From the perspective of problem finding, it is important to note that our goals, values, and needs are rarely in a tranquil equilibrium with our environment or with our inner selves. Indeed, the objectives we end up pursuing in problem-solving behaviour are the result of a complex interaction between our instinctive drives, the interest of self vis-a-vis others, and short-versus long-term perspectives in planning. For instance, your desire to learn may conflict with many other objectives, such as earning money, having a good time now, or helping out one's family. Thus, the objectives we ultimately pursue reflect trade-offs between goals, values, and needs that cannot be attained simultaneously. It is important to understand how these trade-offs are resolved in determining an individual's priorities for problem finding.

Maslow's hierarchy. Consider needs. According to Maslow, needs can be ordered hierarchically. Our most basic concern is with physiological needs such as hunger, thirst, sleep, and protection from cold or heat. Once these basic life-support needs are reasonably well satisfied, our concerns will shift to security needs. For instance, if stranded on an island, we would construct some type of shelter, stockpile food, and secure a water supply. These actions are not aimed at the immediate present, but rather safeguard the satisfaction of our physiological needs in the future, especially as many of these are recurring. After security and stability needs are satisfied, social needs become predominant. These include the need for belonging, for friendship, and for love. They concern the human rather than physical environment that surrounds us. When these social needs are adequately satisfied, a fourth level of need manifests itself, self-esteem and the esteem of others. Many people in the economically developed countries of the West are in the fortunate position of having their physiological, security, and social needs satisfied. Yet they may not be fully happy, as their objectives and needs are focused on achievement and recognition thereof. Finally, for those who seemingly have it all—health, money, friends, prestige, power - a last need may manifest itself, the need to self-actualize, to realize one's potential fully in whatever ways one wishes to feel special as a complete person.

Value systems. Just as needs may be prioritized in hierarchies, so also are the values derived from them. For example, Rokeach reports extensive empirical evidence on "value systems" for various cultural and social groups. These value systems are rankings of the various instrumental and terminal values held by different groups. It should come as no surprise that different groups have different values and rankings thereof. For example, comparing low-income groups in the United States, Rokeach reports significant differences. The rich rank "a comfortable life" considerably lower relative to other terminal values than do the poor, perhaps because the rich already possess it. Similarly, the rich rank the instrumental value "clean" much lower relative to other instrumental values than the poor, again because cleanliness is likely taken for granted by the rich. Looking across age groups, educational backgrounds, or cultures presents similar stark differences in value systems. It is clear from these differences in value trade-offs that individuals from these different groups would see problem finding in very different lights. What would be a problem for an individual from one group in not attaining a specific level of some instrumental or terminal value might not even be noticed by someone from another group.

It can be argued, based on Maslow's need hierarchy, that differences in value systems between groups are simply the result of different levels of need fulfillment possible to members of these groups. One individual may be pursuing basic needs of food and shelter while another, having satisfied these needs, is pursuing higher-level needs. But understanding an individual's values goes deeper than this and requires, at the least, an understanding of the social and cultural forces shaping these values. For examples, suppose someone is pursuing a need for "esteem." How will the person operationalize this objective? First, one would identify the reference groups, if any, that are important to this individual as the basis of the esteem he or she seeks. As Douglas and Wildavsky point out, however, the definition of reference groups raises essential cultural issues. In some cultures, there may be no such reference groups; esteem in such cultures is purely self-esteem. In other cultures, such reference groups may be socially defined and in still others there may be a naturally defined reference group. Thus, to understand the operationalization of "esteem," more than just a needs hierarchy is required, although the concept of a structuring of goals, needs, and values into a hierarchy of relative importance is useful in understanding the order in which cues and problems are attended to.

Goals, values, and needs are the conscious and subconscious ends toward which individuals strive. They may be thought of as being organized in a system or hierarchy of objectives, allowing trade-offs between conflicting objectives. From the point of view of problem finding, they hierarchy of objectives presents the basic reference data for triggering the recognition that a problem exists due to perceived unacceptable levels of achievement of one or another of these objectives.

Aspiration levels. One model of the process through which the indicated hierarchy of objectives operates in selective attention is called the *aspiration level* model. According to this model, operational specifications of goals, values, and needs may be viewed as reference points to which the individual aspires. Achieving a comfortable life-style, for example, is specified through an aspiration level of a certain income level, together with levels of other related goal indicators. When these aspiration levels are not met, or are threatened by perceived events, they trigger the recognition of impending problem states. Such problem states are then attended to in order of the value trade-offs incorporated in the individual's hierarchy of goals and objectives. This model, pioneered by March and Simon, goes further in suggesting that aspiration levels are adjusted upward as the objectives in question are easily met, and are adjusted downward when these aspirations levels are difficult to meet. In this manner, one can see how cumulative experience also affects problem-finding activity, tot he extent that such activity is triggered by impending violations of aspiration levels. The aspiration level model has received wide support and application in psychology and consumer behaviour. It is intuitively appealing because it relates to our everyday experience in using reference points, based on our experience, to indicate what we can normally expect from the world. From the point of view of problem finding, the aspiration level view may be viewed as a model of how problem recognition is triggered.

Suppose a potential problem is perceived. What will determine whether a decision maker confronted by this perceived problem will accept the problem as important enough to devote problem-solving energy to it? The preceding discussion suggests the following theory of problem acceptance. Decision makers construct or obtain from their cumulative experience a conceptual representation, against which they judge the existing situation and potential improvements to it. Such a model could be characterized by a set of aspiration levels for a hierarchy of objectives, together with a reasoned basis for believing each aspiration level is desirable and obtainable. These models or views of the world represent reference points or expectations of normally. When these expectations are not fulfilled, a problem state is recognized.

The key to problem acceptance is therefore the models used by the decision maker to represent and define normalcy. At the level of elemental survival needs, such models are the result of biological and social evolution, which determine levels of need satisfaction below which problems are triggered. For goals and values that are more socially and cognitively conditioned, we can identify several types of models of define normalcy. We classify these under the headings of historical models, communicated models, and planning models.

Historical models. These are models based on extrapolations of the past. According to such models, a problem state is recognized when the unfolding present looks very dissimilar from the recent past. For example, suppose that during the period from 1986-1989 a hospital was able to supply blood immediately to over 99 out of 100 patients, whereas in 1990 this figure dropped to 96 out of 100. The hospital's blood bank administrator may see this drop in service level as a problem. In effect, historical models take the past as a reference point to form expectations about acceptable performance in the future and to define problem states when these reference points are violated. Historical models are the most common benchmarks of expectations, both for individuals as well as organizations. We are conditioned by our experience, both in the way we perceive the world and in our conceptions of how the world should operate.

Communicated models. Of course, we learn not only from our own limited experience, but also from that of others. This other experience, passed on through books, the media, and word of mouth, we call communicated models. Such communicated models indicate what others have and have not been able to accomplish, providing inspiration and realism for what we may hope to accomplish. For example, in the marketplace, organizations keep a sharp eye on their competitors has been described by Schumpeter and Nelson and Winter as a determining factor in technological innovation and market structure.

Communicated models come in many forms, from friends and neighbors, from scientific journals, from the media, and so on. What distinguishes these various models is the degree to which decision makers understand and trust them as being relevant to their own situation. Thus, a parent may see in her child's actions great potential harm, perhaps because she has learned from her own experience and from Dr. Freud or Dr. Spock how children should develop. Her child does not share these same models and thus sees no problem in his or her actions. This example also illustrates why problem-finding activity may be quite different from individual to individual, since the models used to define a problem state may be very different.

Planning models. Historical models and communicated models are reactive. Environmental cues are perceived and processed on the basis of a model of how the environment should look under normal conditions. Churchman, Ansoff, Ackoff and Emery, and G. Smith have emphasized the importance of another class of models in defining problem states. These might be called planning models, and they have a proactive or purposeful character. They are carefully thought out conceptions of what is achievable with measurable control indicators and goals to enable the "planner" to understand whether things are going "according to plan." Such models are frequently used in organizations to monitor and coordinate activities and can be as simple as a budget projection. When deviations from the plan are detected, a problem is defined. The essence of planning models is that they embody intentional triggers, defined by the planner, to define problem states.

Summarizing this discussion, we view problem representation and acceptance as the process of setting reference points of acceptability and monitoring environmental cues for deviations from these. The determination of such reference points results from our models of the world based on historically based expectations, information from others, and purposeful planning.

The descriptive aspects of problem finding we have discussed to this point. The major activities involved are labelled the *Scanning Process*, the *Interrupt Process*, and the *Acceptance Process*. Scanning refers to the manner in which data are collected and processed from the environment. Interrupts occur when the decision maker perceives a sufficiently troublesome state to trigger attention and problem identification activity. Acceptance occurs when the decision maker believes sufficient improvement is possible to warrant the costs of problem solving. From a descriptive point of view, one might expect the following shortcomings for each of these problem-finding activities.

Scanning: Scanning is based on our models, expectations, and plans and is constrained by the basic limits on our perception and memory.

Interrupts: Interrupts are based on trigger levels or thresholds. In particular, a hierarchy of interrupts based on objectives determined by our goals, values, and needs determines the sequence in which perceived problems are attended to. The constraints on this process are those implied by limits to our scarce attention (or information-processing) resources.

Acceptance: We accept problems that we perceive and that we believe to be important enough to warrant investing our time and energy further in solving. Problem acceptance is therefore constrained by the accuracy of our evaluation of the importance of perceived problem states.

The pitfalls of problem finding have been summarized pithily by Mitroff and Kilman who suggest the following errors in problem finding:

They I Error: Detecting a problem when there isn't one.

Type II Error: Not detecting a problem when there is one.

Type III Error: Solving the wrong problem.

As should be clear from our discussion, Type III errors may result in particular from limitations to our scarce resource of attention, since another phrasing of Type III error might be, "Solving an unimportant problem when an important one is waiting."

Perhaps one final point should be made on the descriptive side concerning acceptance. A major reason cited for lack of acceptance of perceived problem states is frequently not that we have evaluated them improperly, but that we fear the responsibility of accepting the problem perceived and then not being able to solve it. We have ignored these affective features of acceptance here. In part, these are accounted for by referring to the values and needs that they represent. That is, many of our fears and reasons for responsibility avoidance arise because of conflicting values of accomplishing something personal, but not risking the disapproval of others. To this extent, problem avoidance may be viewed as not compromising the value of the esteem of those whose disapproval we fear. But, as Freud and Pogo have pointed out, frequently those whose disapproval we fear most are none other than ourselves. Thus, the issue of problem avoidance is more complicated than this short description bears out.

Clarifying goals, values, and needs

It would be a pity if we were to solve problems in pursuit of the wrong goals. The first question that naturally arises in prescriptive problem, finding is therefore to clarify what our values and needs are, and what goals and objectives these imply. We shall discuss systematic ways of evaluating value structures. But in the end, these amount to the rather simple dictum of spending some scarce resources of energy and attention to determine whom we are trying to please and in what ways. In somewhat more detail, this amounts to specifying the stakeholders in a given problem context and role-playing their objectives as well as our own. By making a table of the involved parties and what we believe they care about, we clarify two important issues: first, the relevant objectives from their viewpoint and from ours; second, our relationship to these stakeholders from our viewpoint. This table to stakeholders values (including our own) separates and clarifies our personal values and goals in relationship to our social needs of justifying ourselves to others.

One way of visualizing the resulting trade-offs between our social and personal values is through the different roles we play in our lives. A student devotes time to four or five different courses, extracurricular activities at the university, social life with friends, as well as hobbies and interests. Within an organizational setting, a manager assumes many different roles as well. Mintzberg, in his study of managerial work, characterized many different roles for the typical manager, from figure-head and leader to disturbance handler to resource allocator. By recognizing the complexity of our lives through the roles we play, we may be able to understand better the very different objectives that these roles imply and which we embody.

For example, in her role as figurehead, a manager may perceive the importance of attending a particular meeting with a good customer because she perceives that her company's well-being demands her presence for prestige purposes to maintain a high volume of sales in the future. In her role as disturbance handler, the manager may perceive that a particular conflict between two departments should be handled in one way, even though her role as resource allocator might dictate another approach. The point is that the roles we play may be viewed as potentially conflicting value systems, each of which may be justified in certain contexts. By viewing a given context from the vantage point of different roles we believe are justifiable, we help to clarify which values we believe are foremost for the given context.

Ashby has characterized the reasons for our different roles as resulting from our attempt to provide "requisite variety" in our response to a complex world. We cannot deal with all potential problems that emerge in our lives, so we develop responses to important subsets of these problems in a consistent fashion. The roles we play may be viewed as our attempts to provide a livable and consistent response to certain classes of problem contexts. The fact that these responses may not be mutually consistent is just a reflection of our inability, in the fact of a complex world, to design a consistent response to every conceivable problem situation. By analyzing what we would do in our different roles, we nonetheless shed light on both the conflicts between these roles and the underlying needs and values that gave rise to them.

Limitations in our information-processing abilities lead us to attend to problems and potential problems sequentially. To ensure that the right problems are perceived and dealt with two issues arise. First, to avoid spending time on nonproblems, one needs appropriate filters so that unimportant cues from the environment are filtered out and not attended to at all. Next, to avoid not spending time on real problems, one needs alerting systems to recognize when such problems are likely to be present. Both filters and alerting systems are referred to as processes for managing attention.

Let us consider filters first. In this age of information overload, we cannot attend to every cue that might be relevant. In organizations and in our personal lives, the scarce resource today is not information; it is time and attention. By designing proper filters, we can avoid a great deal of irrelevant information. In this regard, we should recognize that the most natural filters are what we read and whom we talk to. These determine in great part the sources of information for our problem-finding activity. By carefully selecting these two filters, we make choices about not only what we will perceive, but what we will not perceive.

In an organization setting, Mintzbery has discussed the importance of filters in making the top manager's various roles manageable. Ackoff provides a similar perspective in arguing that many managers are overloaded with irrelevant information. To avoid irrelevancies, we need to ask what aspects of the environment do I *not* wish to see or her about except in unusual circumstances.

Keen and Scott-Morton describe a successful application of filter design in the form of a computer-based decision support system for the production planning department of a large corporation, similar to the problem. The department's difficulty stemmed from the overwhelming amount of information produced by reports on past sales and inventory records generated by routine computer runs. The reports were three inches thick and so detailed that it was extremely difficult to determine potential problems in the production plans. Therefore, the firm developed an interactive computer model as an important decision aid for the production-planning process. The three key managers could easily check past sales records of selected items by interactive queries, with the results presented in easily digested graphical format. Not only could all the decision makers view the same data profiles, but they could systematically evaluate potential problems and devote their attention to these cases. Models were embedded in the system to determine automatically whether sales and inventory positions for each item were within bounds projected on the basis of past data for the same items. In this way, most items could be controlled automatically and filtered away from the attention processes of managers. The result of this new decision support system was a reduction in managers' time devoted to production planning from 6 days spread over a 20-day period to a half day spread over 2 working days.

The second major tool for managing attention is an alerting system. In an organizational setting, the quality control department has an important role to play in alerting the manufacturing division to when it is making defective units. Samples of produced items are taken periodically and specific characteristics are compared with performance standards. If sufficient numbers of the sample items are unsatisfactory, a problem is signaled.

Clearly, the basic philosophy of alerting systems is no different from the normal triggers we have been referring to in problem finding. Alerting systems simply systematically design these triggers to indicate a problem when there is one. The importance of alerting systems has grown as the computer technology that is frequently used to implement them has improved. For example, credit card companies use them to note a sudden excessive use of a credit card. Typically firms use systems based on a model of expected performance that alerts responsible decision makers when current performance is quite different from what history or the plan would lead one to expect. In so doing, decision makers can set the alerting system so that they will not miss important cues indicating potential problems.

A final important matter for prescriptive problem finding is validating the models, beliefs, and premises that are the basis for representing and evaluating potential problems. The more accurately our models reflect what is achievable and what the status quo is, the more likely we are to accept real problem. For the present, however, let us note that there is frequently a trade-off between postponing judgment on a problem until more information is at hand and acting now. Thaler and Sherfrin have proposed a model of individual choice that reflects this conflict. They postulate that an individual is both a farsighted planner and a myopic doer. In the context of the problem-finding process, the farsighted planner would like to collect more information, whereas the myopic doer prefers to look at the world directly and classify a situation as "a problem" or "not a problem." Frequently, individuals and organizations invoke simplistic rules that enable them to be myopic doers without being fully aware of the consequences of their proposed acting. A hospital may claim that it should always have enough units of blood in stock to satisfy demand. It may have no idea of the implications this policy has for inventory ordering or costs.

Scientific models provide examples of well-validated models. These provide our farsighted planning side with better data on the implications of our otherwise myopic actions. In the blood bank example, data could be assembled on the expected number of shortages as well as inventory storage costs for different ordering policies by the hospital. By formulating and validating a precise model of the inflows and outflows of blood from the blood bank, a more rational choice of stocking policies could be determined. In many cases, of curse, there may be no accurate scientific model to base decisions on. For example, in the liquefied natural gas (LNG) siting problem, it is only possible to specify very crudely the probability of a catastrophic accident because experts degree widely on these figures. In these cases, it is wise to recognize the limits of analysis and human knowledge in the problem-finding process.

By way of summary, we present the various elements of the problem-finding process. These elements are interesting in their own right, but they also condition the problem-solving process, as we now discuss.

First, the goals, values, and needs that trigger problem finding are likely to provide the basic definition of when we will say that a problem, has been solved. From a descriptive viewpoint, therefore, one may expect the problem context that triggered dissatisfaction on one or another dimension of our hierarchy of objectives to influence problem solving strongly. Thus, if the problem perceived in problem finding is based on violating some reference point of normalcy, then one may expect problem-solving activity to be concerned primarily with restoring the condition of the reference point. From a prescriptive viewpoint, we have argued that this conditioning of problem finding by problem, context and objectives makes it imperative that the needs, values, and goals to be satisfied by problem solving be clearly understood. The second key aspect of problem finding influencing problem solving is the representation of the problem in terms of the context, models, and data that were used to determine that it was a problem in the first place. As Newel and Simon and Lindblom have pointed out, problem representations determined during problem finding have a strong influence on problem-solving activities. Thus, generating an appropriate representation of the problem is an important element of the overall problem-solving process.

The third link between problem finding and problem solving concerns the set of alternatives that are generated in problem analysis and solution. How a problem is framed in the problem-finding/structuring phase of decision making can strongly affect the alternatives one considers for problem solution because such alternatives will be generated to restore reference conditions or otherwise remove the problem as recognized. We now consider the alternative generation process in more detail.

Alternatives are usually generated with particular problems, objectives and goals in mind. As rioted already, objectives tend to be open-end whereas goals are more specific. Let us return to an earlier example:, it student is searching for an apartment off campus, then one objective may be to "pay a low rent." This can be translated into a specific such as "pay less than $400 per month." This goal will eliminate merous apartments from consideration, thus reducing the information processing load on the individual.

One easy way of reducing the collection of data is to examine only options that are close to the current solution. Individuals who automatically trade in their old Ford every two years for a new Ford follow this strategy to the extreme. If people limit their search for alternatives to the immediate neighbourhood of their current position, then their present position will be the primary determinant of the set of feasible alternatives generated. Consider the process of job selection by new college graduates. Of the approximately three thousand occupations that exist today, only a small subset is usually examined by any single individual. These tend to be the jobs with which students have personal knowledge, either through others who have worked in this field or their own experience.

New alternatives are often examined only after becoming dissatisfied with the current situation. For example, if one suffers a burglary this may trigger consideration of the alternative "install a burglar alarm." Much empirical evidence suggests that people take protective action only *after* an unfortunate experience rather than before. We usually avoid generating alternatives unless stimulated by a disaster or significant departure from satisfactory performance. We also learn about alternatives from friends and acquaintances. If a friend raves about her new car, we may be influenced by her positive experience. Similarly we may reject other alternatives from consideration because of specific complaints by someone we know.

A classic example of the latter is Whyte's study on the adoption of air conditioners on two blocks in a neighbourhood. One side of the street had no air conditions whereas practically all apartments on the other had the units displayed in their windows. Whyte learned that there had been considerable discussion among those neighbors who had purchased conditioners because their children played together in an adjoining alleyway. Families on the other side of the street did not have such a common play area for their children. The informal conversations and social interaction in one block led over time to widespread adoption of air conditioners, demonstrating a classic pattern in the diffusion of an innovation or alternative.

In case a single choice must be made from many mutually exclusive options, individuals will often examine alternatives sequentially rather than making complete comparisons between them. In a "satisficing" decision rule, this process continues until an acceptable alternative is found. For example, in searching for housing, a particular apartment might be examined. If unsatisfactory, another apartment will be looked at. Once an apartment has been found that is acceptable, the decision process is terminated. The other end of the spectrum would be to consider first all feasible alternatives and then make a final choice. Most decisions lie in between the sequential satisficing rule and an exhaustive evaluation of all alternatives. The links between searching for alternatives and settling on a final choice. At a descriptive level, individuals frequently generate alternatives by engaging in local search and identifying options in isolation of others. Local search is associated with such terms as incrementalism, anchoring, uncomprehensive analysis, business as usual, not changing a winning horse, narrow problem focus, and noncreative decision making. The isolation effect refers to our tendency to simplify problems by breaking them into smaller ones of manageable size. There is no guarantee, however, that the sum of the optimal solutions to the subproblems constitutes the global optimum, or even comes close to it.

Rigidity in problem solving

Closely related to local search is the broader phenomenon of "rigidity in problem solving", a field of research originating with the Gestalt psychologists that shows that learned habits and past history can cause problem finding and problem solving to be so anchored in the past that creativity is stifled. As an example, consider the following puzzle.

Bird and train puzzle: Two trains are 50 miles apart. At exactly 2 p.m. the two trains start toward each other on parallel tracks, each traveling 25 mph. Simultaneously, a bird starts at one train and flies until it meets the other train, turns around and heads back to the first train until it meets it, reverses direction again and continues flying back and forth between the two trains until the trains pass each other. If the bird is flying at 100 mph, how far will it travel in its back and forth journeys until the trains pass each other'?

Another example of rigidity is Bartlett's famous cryptoarithmetic problem, which also stimulated considerable interest in the artificial intelligence literature.

Now what happens in practice when experimental subjects try to solve these two puzzles? In the bird and train puzzle, people who have been exposed to algebra word problems tend to pose quite complicated procedures and mathematical formulations for determining the length of the arc describing the bird's flight path. In reality, this is not necessary. The trains will meet one another one hour after they start since they are 50 miles apart, heading directly toward one another and traveling 25 mph. Thus, the bird will be in the air for one hour and must therefore travel 100 miles, since its speed is 100 mph. What prevents some people from getting this answer quickly (or at all) is that their past experience leads them to represent the problem in too complicated a manner. Similarly, the cryptoarithmetic problem tends to be solved from fight to left, as in ordinary arithmetic. Many subjects solving this problem substitute D = 5, deduce that T must equal 0, but then get no further since no direct clue is provided for L or R as they are working from right to left. Starting from the left, however, makes it clear that E = 9, which thus provides further clues.

In business, such rigidity is sometimes referred to as functional blindness". Marketing managers may only see marketing solutions whereas manufacturing people will favour product improvements. The paradox of creativity is that it requires both great familiarity with a subject matter and the ability to approach it from a fresh angle. For example, workers in a plant making sparkplugs were less able to generate alternative uses for them than workers outside the plant. Nonexperts often envision many more innovative applications. In science, breakthroughs frequently come from the fringes or interfaces of fields. Hence, seeking outside views and challenging one's own assumptions are key to richer alternative generation.

Several other studies exist that illustrate how human decision makers often get locked in by their experience to perceiving and/or solving new problems the way they have solved previous problems. As in the preceding examples, this prior experience is used as a starting point for either problem representation, the problem-solving process, or the alternatives to be considered for a given problem. Thus, although prior experience is critical to our overall cognitive abilities, it can also be a barrier to effective decision making.

Self-imposed constraints

A further characteristic of how people generate alternatives is that they frequently impose constraints on these alternatives that are simply not necessary. The task is to draw four straight lines that pass through all nine dots without lifting one's pen from paper.

Self-imposed constraints often operate as well in those many instances where people fail to do something because they think it will not work or cannot be done, otherwise known as self-discouragement and timidity. An important characteristic of the creative person is that he or she is willing to be ridiculed or declared insane for trying the unusual or "impossible."

Other creativity barriers include social norms and cultural taboos. Going against established norms may well be the key to solving a complex problem. As an example, consider the following puzzle. You are in a barren room. In the middle is a steel pipe sticking out from the concrete floor four inches high. Its diameter is just a bit larger than a ping-pong ball that rests at the bottom of this pipe. In addition, the room has the following supplies: a hammer, thread, safety pin, matches, and a newspaper. Your task is to get the ping-pong ball out of the steel pipe. Try both problems before reading further.

In the nine-dot puzzle, the key to the four-line solution is to go outside the nine dot area. For example, first draw a horizontal line through the top row and continue to the right. Then angle back sharply and go through Dots 6 and 8, and shoot up vertically through the first column. Finally, continue with the diagonal through Dots 1, 5, and 9, which completes the puzzle. The three-line solution centers on the recognition that the points are dots rather than dimensionless algebraic points. Thus vertical lines may be drawn through each of the columns, with slight angles so that the lines touch at some very high and low point. In a related vein, the line to be drawn might be considered to be so thick that just one line covers nine points. The puzzle with the ping-pong ball can be solved by urinating into the steel pipe, which violates a social norm. Such creativity, however, saved at least one bomber crew in World War II. Upon approach to landing, they discovered that the landing gear was stuck because all hydraulic fluid has leaked out. The flight engineer then hit upon the idea of urinating into the hydraulic system, thus temporarily restoring pressure. It worked; they landed safely.

The challenge of breaking out of traditional frames of mind is the hallmark of creativity. Perkins developed an interesting "snowflake" model of creativity, based on laboratory evidence and biographical study. Six traits or characteristics make up the corners of Perkins's snowflake. The first is a strong personal commitment to aesthetic solutions. For example, Albert Einstein was obsessed with simplicity in physics, searching in vain for the unified theory of nature's basic forces. To mathematicians and physicists, a theory or proof has to be elegant, as in Fermat's principle of least time. The second trait concerns good taste in wnat questions to ask. The 1991 Nobel Prize in economics went to Ronald Coase for asking some very basic questions, such as, Why do firms exist? His insightful questions spawned entirely new research fields and journals. Mental agility is the third trait: the ability to think in opposites, also known as Janus thinking. Tolerance for ambiguity, thinking in images or metaphors, and the desire to connect seemingly unrelated ideas all belong to this corner.

These three traits are largely cognitive, although the first one is driven by deeply held values. The remaining two traits address more dispositional characteristics. The fourth corner is about risk taking and not being afraid of failure. Excellence usually requires many attempts. Pablo Picasso is renowned for perhaps 10 or 20 masterpieces. However, these outliers were drawn from a lifelong creative effort amounting to about 20,000 pieces of art, much of it mediocre. This overall output translates into 400 pieces per year for 50 years, or an average of more than one creation per day! The fifth trait concerns objectivity: the courage to seek criticism and outside views. In science, this means openness to new evidence; in the arts, a willingness to listen to and be judged by peers. Lastly, Perkins identifies inner motivation as a key driving force in creative people. Without love or passion for your subject, it is difficult to spend the many hours necessary to create a great book, composition, or scientific work. When Gauss was congratulated on his brilliant proof of a key theorem in mathematics, he replied that there had not been a day in the last 15 years or so that he did not think about that problem. Intense commitment and obsession are common traits in uncommonly creative people.

The snowflake theory has both descriptive and prescriptive elements. It is hard to generate passion for a subject where none exists to begin with, or to be brilliant in science without a certain genetic endowment. However, being open to criticism is a skill most of us can learn to prove. Likewise, seeking simple solutions, tolerating ambiguity, and taking risks are traits we have the power to change. The next section examines the proactive dimensions of creativity in more detail.

Alternative generation: prescriptive aspects

The challenge in improving the process of generating alternatives lies in overcoming the problems associated with bounded rationality, learning and complexity. In order to generate a wider or better set of alternatives, individuals must free themselves from the constraining influences of learned habits, self-discouragement and timidity, and premature problem closure. Essentially, the question boils down to being more vigilant and creative in the generation of options. How is this to be done?

Phases of creativity

Various stages have been distinguished in the process of creativity. The first is preparation and concerns the collection of data and other supporting material. When searching for a job, this might mean utilizing the services of central information sources such as a university placement office or employment agency. When undertaking scientific research, this implies immersing oneself in the literature to study theories and evidence relevant to the problem at hand.

Next the *production phase* involves the actual generation of ideas. This phase is not well understood psychologically and constitutes the essence of creativity. It entails conscious as well subconscious processes and is only partly under rational control. Various techniques exist to enhance idea generation ranging from brainstorming to *synectics*. This latter technique emphasizes the power of metaphorical or analogical thought processes. For example, when Kukule discovered the closed structure of the benzine ring in chemistry, he credited this break-through to a dream in which a snake was biting its own tail. This vision resembled the hexagonal structure of benzine.

The third phase is the *evaluation of ideas*. Recognizing it as a distinct phase highlights that it is often useful to separate the generation of ideas from their evaluation. Brainstorming techniques often emphasize the importance of not evaluating ideas, so that people can freely propose alternatives without having to simultaneously judge them. Importantly, the people who can best generate ideas may not be best in evaluating them, and vice-versa.

The ability to generate different alternatives depends of course on the *complexity of the task*. Apartment selection is normally considerably easier than choosing a job. The preparation phase in either case, however, requires an individual to consider carefully the main objectives and determine how well specific alternatives are likely to meet them. Such coupling of the evaluation phase with the ideation phase may be necessary to narrow down a set of alternatives.

Widening the set of alternatives

As part of the creativity process, there may be considerable learning from others. One person's ideas on a set of alternatives may trigger suggestions from others. The more formal process of *brainstorming*, enables individuals in a group setting to suggest a set of alternatives for consideration by others without being criticized as to their feasibility. At the simplest level, one can begin generating a list of alternatives by envisioning best and worst outcomes and determining alternatives that lead to them. For example, Van Gundy suggests beginning this process by asking two questions: Wouldn't it be nice if? and Wouldn't it be awful if? This type of exercise and other "broadening" procedures are intended to break the bonds that anchor us to our present, limited sets of alternatives.

Sometimes the set of alternatives can be enlarged by combining features of existing alternatives to obtain new ones. For instance, when the National Aeronautical and Space Administration (NASA) had to decide What research activities to engage in, they distinguished between actions, objects, and target features. A long list was created under each heading, and combinations of actions, objects, and features were systematically generated. An exhaustive combination of these yields 48 different research tasks. Some of these are nonsensical, such as "measuring tidal deformation in the interior of the space environment." After eliminating the infeasible combinations, NASA still had more than one thousand meaningful lower-level research tasks left. Also, they had the assurance that few aspects were overlooked.

Metaphors may also be used to highlight unexpected aspects or implications. This technique goes under the name of synectics and uses analogies to join seemingly unconnected elements. The analogies may be personal, biological, or symbolic. For example, an engineer might imagine himself to be a bridge. In so doing, he envisions water splashing against the bottom of the bridge, and thereby may suddenly think of corrosion problems. As for biological analogies, birds have provided inspiration for the design of aircraft, beehives for architectural designs, and so on.

Symbolic analogies may also be useful for more abstract tasks, such as teaching a course. Suppose the instructor views his role in the course as a mother. This analogy directs attention to the importance of birth and caring. The role of metaphor is particularly important in science. For example, in physics Fermat anthro-pomorphized light as seeking the path of least travel time. In doing so, he provided an explanation for the refraction law in optics and proposed various novel hypotheses that subsequently were found to be correct.

We have already alluded to institutional ways of widening the alternative generation process. University placement offices and housing offices often provide comprehensive listing of different jobs and apartments so that students have a centralized data base at their fingertips. In a broader vein, advertising can play a key role in generating information on options.

Unfortunately, people will encounter the problem of information overload in coping with data from these different sources. Here new computer technology may play an important role as a decision aid. For instance, a computer could store a great deal of information related to the characteristics of different apartments so that students can easily retrieve the data in the form they need. Furthermore, the computer might enable individuals to select a subset of alternatives having specific features. It is an open question today how much impact microcomputer technology will have on the alternative generation process. If people are reluctant to consider more than a few options because of memory and other mental limitations, computers may be a useful tool for freeing them from these constraints.

The bird and train problem, the nine-dot problem and the cryptoarithmetic problem all illustrate how rigidity, learned habits, and self-imposed constraints can be significant blocks to creativity. How can we avoid or remove such self-imposed constraints? Several techniques exist to unfreeze people from myopic perspectives. We briefly review some well-known ones here.

Lateral thinking can often be used to expand the range of alternative solutions. Consider, for instance, the problem of how to solve complaints about slow elevators in an office building. Convergent thinkers would accept the diagnosis of "slow elevators" and start to work on ways to speed them up. Divergent thinkers would mentally walk around the problem and note that we are dealing here, in part, with perceptions about time spent waiting. One solution is to change the time perceptions by giving people something to do, from adding bulletin boards to installing mirrors beside the elevators. In the same spirit, restaurants commonly use entertainment to make the waiting time seem less long.

Dialectic reasoning is another important mind-expanding technique. It includes "devil's advocacy" as well as systematic attempts to construct two plausible but opposite interpretations of a case. Our judicial system follows this approach directly by constructing a thesis and antithesis from the same body of evidence, in the hope that a synthesis of these two views will lead to an improved judgment. Royal Dutch/ Shell, the Anglo-Dutch oil giant, uses this approach in its strategic planning process. Every two or three years, the company constructs two to four widely divergent views of the future, ranging from say an economic boom scenario to a world in which environmentalists enact increasingly strict legislation, with a huge price tag. Importantly, the company leaves it up to senior managers to debate the merits of these alternative scenarios. They often spark new ideas for innovations or a better appreciation of the risk--return ratio of the current plans. The creative tension inherent in dialectical thinking can be a valuable impetus to new thoughts or perspectives.

A host of indirect approaches exists as well for improving creativity. Henry devotes entire chapters to such activities as networking, imaging, mental mapping, as well as the honing of intuition and judgment. One company advises newcomers to schedule a lunch with a person from outside their department every week to stay abreast of larger issues. Others train people in the art of remapping, recognizing that changing your world views is a little bit like dying. We can think of a mental map here as a limited set of interwoven assumptions, a domain-specific theory, or an entire life-shaping paradigm. First, there may be shock or anger when discovering that one's view is not as complete or generally accepted as once thought. The stark realization that one's map is in fact not the territory may instill grief or depression, similar to the loss of a friend or relative. Trusted and familiar maps provide security and their loss can be highly upsetting. Finally, acceptance of a new map may slowly set in.

McCaskey describes the personal pain Charles Darwin experienced over several decades in developing his new biological map of natural selection. Few of us will ever personally experience new maps on the order of Newton, Darwin, or Einstein. Yet, our own intellectual and emotional growth requires the destruction of old maps and creation of new maps for the various complexities we encounter throughout life, from developing a career to creating a family and the ultimate acceptance of our own mortality. How well we network, map, imagine, and judge will much affect the problems we encounter in life and the extent to which we shall accept and resolve them.

John Dewey, the famous American pragmatist philosopher, said: "A problem well stated is a problem half solved!" The objective of this chapter has been to pose a framework to help understand why certain problems and decision situations are identified and accepted for problem-solving activity while others may go unnoticed, The framework we have described is based on the fundamental premise, which enjoys support in both biological and social science, that humans are purposeful in their problem-finding and problem-solving activity and that they strive to satisfy a nested hierarchy of needs through this activity. But in so doing they are limited in their information-processing abilities--including their abilities to perceive, remember, and process information. Thus, in Simon's famous phrase, these human decision makers enjoy only bounded rationality.

Organisation training for problem solving

A convenient subdivision of management is according to the phases of Preplanning, Planning and control. Building on Shakespeare's idea 'all the world's a stage and all the men and women merely players', then preplanning is concerned with finding a play, a theatre, backers and identifying the kinds of things that the producer and players will need for their performance. Following this is the producing of the play which may be likened to the planning phase. At the planning stage the objectives and effect to be achieved are worked out in detail, and the timing, and the movements of the actors are developed to secure the right result. A great amount of work has to be done to integrate very many different kinds of skilled work in the rehearsal rooms and theatre workshops. At the final stage the author and producer fade out, the stage director takes over to control the production for its opening night and we hope a long run. If we are to make an artistic or financial success, clearly all three phases of preplanning, planning, and control should be well done.

Clearly the three phases Preplanning, Planning and Control ought to be in sequence., and incomplete work at an earlier stage will increase the effort required at a later stage, and hazard the final effect. Each must be done properly. The cost in money of preplanning is usually less than that of planning, and planning costs are less than those of control and operating because fewer people are required at the earlier compared with the later phases. On the other hand the time span required for preplanning, as it may include research, will probably be more than that for planning, and much more than that for each control action. It is always difficult to get sufficiently thorough preplanning; once a project looks promising it tends to be pushed into production like the cast of a play who after the dreadful rehearsal console themselves with the thought 'it will be all right on the night'. Not all the projects preplanned are worth continuing into the planning phase, nor are all activities planned worth pushing into the production and control phase, and therefore some check mechanism is necessary to select promising projects from all those preplanned, and more rarely to withdraw planned projects which run into unexpected difficulties. This requirement for selection is only common sense. But arising from this is clearly the need to preplan rather more projects than are likely to be planned. Only if rather more than minimal effort is put into preplanning can proper flow of worth while projects be kept up. On the other hand preplanning and planning are overhead expenses and hence bring no return until the control phase is reached. Much more care could profitably be put into determining the balance of effort between 'Preplanning', Planning' and 'Control'.

Frequently, particularly in the one-off type of project like problem solving there is too little planning precisely because it is a one-off job. But in one-off projects there is no second chance to remedy blunders due to poor planning which could be remedied in many-off production. So more attention is needed to planning one-off projects than many-off.

A common reason for skimping on planning is that it appears to be, too costly. The remedy is for more preplanning to reduce the cost of planning and increase the probability that any planned effort will be productive.

In brief this section is a plea for attention to preplanning, planning, and control, and for balanced provision of each. Because of the effects of speed stress, it is usually better to get different people to concentrate on each of the phases preplanning, planning, and control. It is difficult for a particular individual to exercise a daily control, and a medium term planning function and simultaneously think a long way ahead as preplanning requires. No-one can carry these three jobs with different time spans at one instant, although he could do any one of them excellently by concentrating upon one at a time. Therefore in the large organization separate specialization on these three phases is desirable. But it is also desirable to move people from one of these specialized phases to another at intervals. Thus there is no harm and often great benefit in moving from Research (Preplanning' to Development (Planning) to Management (Control) from time to time.

A particular manager, be he in a large organization or a small business, will be sometimes Controlling, sometimes Planning, sometimes Preplanning. He should concentrate on whichever phase occupies film at the moment. But to develop himself lie should preplan, plan and control himself, his activities and his environment. For example if lie Is busy controlling day to day activities lie should set aside some time on planning his future by checking the relation of todays decisions on tomorrows problems; and also be preplanning by reading, studying, noting, and organizing ideas for possible use ill the years to come. He cannot forecast the future but lie can prepare himself for it.

Preplanning for problem solving

The would be problem solver soon faces five kinds of barriers to improvement. These are:

(i) Technological in which shortage of knowledge and, more frequently, lack of experience with techniques leads to material and human losses.

(ii) Personnel Shortage of responsible, trained innovators, the fear of change to which all staff are prone, and the inertia inherent in large organizations, all inhibit change.

(iii) Tools Shortage of equipment, particularly to measure materials' speeds, time and qualities, often makes fact finding difficult.

(iv) Finance There is usually a shortage of money to invest in innovation and to provide for any new or improved capital equipment.

(v) Time Shortage of time restricts the ability to explore alternative or possible avenues to improvement.

The most important shortage is undoubtedly that of time. Given time, training can provide knowledge, and experience can be gained; similarly, people can be recruited and organized; and equipment and tools purchased. Shortage of time also makes it difficult to collect and arrange the facts logically and to weigh them properly, i.e. the psychological load and speed stress on Management is likely to be their greatest barrier to problem solving. Fundamentally preplanning aims to make time for the project.

Although time is the critical factor the first step is not to draw Gantt Charts or make Critical Path Analyses. These tools concentrate on presenting known facts and tend to obscure the need for preplanning to identify, the unexpected and often forgotten difficulties which arise in problem solving. The first requirement is to get an overall picture of what problem solving involves. At the preplanning stage develop only the outline plan, and identify potential human and material shortages so that subsequent planning can make timely provision for the difficult things.

Thereafter preplanning involves developing people and their environment to promote a receptive attitude to change so the programme has a good chance of success. It requires research to develop objectives and identify necessary resources. Preplanning assists the speed and reduces the cost of' innovation by ensuring a thorough job is done using existing resources as far as possible. It seeks to avoid the loss of time and money on ineffective programmes with the frustration and loss of enthusiasm which stems from unsuccessful effort.

The usual way management attempt to solve problems is to choose a useful technique for the purpose, train people in it, do a demonstration project to show the value of the method, and then leave the trainees to practise the technique. Payment by Results, Work Study, TWI, SQQ, CPA, Management Development, OR, Management by Objectives, etc., have all been favoured panaceas in their time, and introduced in this way. Frequently this use of techniques has led to the introduction of specialist empires, and unnecessarily high overheads, because the techniques have become ends in themselves and not a means to an end.

Analysing this process shows 90% of trainees pass examinations in their subject and their demonstration projects are successful but a progress check a year or so later usually shows that only 10% to 40% of trainees will be successful innovators. There are two main reasons for this. Only one-third to two-thirds of successful trainees have the guts to push for innovation in the industrial environment, and only one-third to two-thirds of companies have an organizational environment which will permit anyone, however good, to innovate. Continuing success requires proper technique, adequate innovators, and an appropriate environment. Lack of any one of these three essentials can defeat the training effort.

In the last ten years, major developments of two kinds have occurred. The first is to alter the order of events and to commence by finding the company objective. Then to quantify the objective, and only after this choose the technique and do the training to achieve the quantitative objective. Finally, the company measures the results obtained through training and use of the technique. Notice how training for problem solving is no longer an act of faith, but a process whose efficiency you measure. This is tactical training and is essentially a process with a measurable efficiency.

A second development was necessary because although the magnitude of improvement was great, with this tactical training it took too long to get results. The next step was, therefore, to concentrate on the planning and control of the innovation process. This made greater use of engineering ideas for planning, and of sociology for organizing the work.

A few points may be useful.

1. When we first concentrated on quantitative methods elegant and sophisticated techniques were used which were academically satisfying. These academic niceties had to be stripped away so that organizations could co-operate in innovation, and equivalent simpler techniques were used. Academic jargon or frills must not be allowed to complicate innovation.
2. Previously we concentrated training on a level or a function of management. Now we try to select from different levels and functions the smallest group required to contribute to innovation and train only that group.
3. Previously we tried to train from the, top down, and spread ideas through the chain of command. This leads to sub-optimization as each level accepts smaller objectives and imposes successively greater restrictions on potential gain. Now we try to push training from a middle level upwards and downwards, to achieve integration of objectives, and the sum of the possibilities from each level.

Arising from my work with the United Nations, ILO and Government of India, I am able to compare these three patterns of innovation. Putting in a two-man team and six months training of type (i), produced an annual saving of £16,000. Using type II training, an increase of turnover of £400,000 p.a. from one plant was obtained, but it took four years for management to accept and implement the report! Using type III training, an average increase of, £500,000 p.a. turnover, or similar required result, was obtained for each of 5 six-month periods, together with an average cost reduction of £25,000 p.a. in materials or labour for each period.

Planning of organization training The method study pattern of working, following the steps select, record, analyse, install, maintain, is fundamental to the operation of a task group. For economy, the work must be planned and this requires a forecast of the way in which the project will develop. The forecast will indicate the information required and techniques to be used. With this forecast of what is necessary, then very frequently enquiry will reveal that the things required are already available within the company, and a great deal of time and expense could be saved by making proper use of them. By taking positive steps to uncover existing resources and use them, the cost of innovation can be drastically pruned.

Developing people for problem solving

There are three ways of developing people for problem solving through education, through training, and by practice in solving real problems.

Education is necessary to develop those individuals who will instigate innovation. This education must encourage individual creativity, perceptivity, initiative and receptivity to new ideas. It must be a strategic effort, based on an estimate of future long-term requirements which at best can be only imperfectly forecast. Complementing the strategic educational effort must be training of a tactical kind, designed to achieve new practical company objectives determined by an assessment of product, sales, or financial necessities. A gardening analogy may illustrate the essential difference between strategy and tactics. In winter, the gardener's strategic action is to dig and fertilize the soil, and to sow. In summer lie takes tactical action by weeding, pruning and training, so as to secure only worthwhile growth. The gardener requires that fertilizing be complemented by tactical pruning. In the same way the encouraging and fertilizing effort for strategic individual development must be complemented by tactical training to ensure that work groups integrate their efforts and achieve company goals.

Tactical training must commence by finding the easiest way of making a change and use existing resources and known techniques so far as possible. The trainer must concentrate on trying to eliminate the need for further training, and reducing the input of new knowledge to essentials. On the other hand, strategic education stresses creative thinking, and the creation of new sources of knowledge. It must include material whose relevance is only a matter of faith. Normally, two different kinds of teaching skill are necessary. Tactical training is designed for visible results, strategic education to avoid a management team getting into a rut. Wise spending on developing people for innovation requires that both strategic and tactical aspects be properly done. This demands separate assessment of the tactical and strategic requirements, and proper investment of money and time for teaching of both kinds. The development policy should be explicit. The need for strategic education and tactical training to develop persons for problem solving is a particular, but very important, aspect of the general problem of developing a helpful environment for problem solving. Education and the way techniques are applied have a profound effect on:

1. The Morale of an organization.
2. The Willingness to cooperate in the organization.
3. The Attitude to productivity.
4. The Attitude to quality.
5. The Quality of supervision.

These are intangible qualities of an organization which nevertheless have a very real effect on the time required to introduce new ideas, the speed with which new techniques can be introduced, and the size of change obtained. The strategy of problem solving is concerned with improving these intangible factors; the tactics of problem solving are concerned with using these desirable qualities to achieve practical objectives. At the preplanning stage special attention should be paid to strategic action to improve the intangible factors. Education is one means for doing so. In addition, the way techniques are applied may have a profound effect. For example if an organization chart is required then it might be produced without consultation. Although the chart may be correct, producing it will have no beneficial effect on the intangibles. If on the other hand the need to make an organization chart Is used as an opportunity to discuss their jobs with people and to get to know them better, then the willingness to cooperate is likely to increase. The improvement of intangibles will more than offset the extra effort required to make the chart.

Although this chapter is in the main on the tactical aspects of problem solving, the manager must not neglect the strategic requirement for developing people, their environment and their attitude to change. Equally it is important not to be content solely with strategic action to improve the environment. For example a manager may introduce joint consultation to improve the morale and willingness to cooperate. This is likely to he extremely helpful to problem solving. However cases have arisen where joint consultation has been satisfactorily set up and then has degenerated into a talking shop because the committee are not allowed to solve useful problems. In brief, if tactical action is barred, then successful strategic action eventually fails because there is no complementary outlet of a tactical kind.

The time available before results are required may fix investment in either tactical or strategic effort. The cost of innovation may decide the desirable balance. We have done work on the introduction of personnel management techniques, and find that if, for example, we try to improve the wage bargaining methods by means of job evaluation then, using tactical training only, it may take two years' work and cost, £10,000. On the other hand, strategic education may first be used to ensure the correct objective attitude towage systems and 'job evaluation. It would cost one year of time and £3,000. This education makes it possible for the tactical work of introducing practical job evaluation to be done in a much shorter period of four months, at a cost of about, £2,000. Thus a balance of tactical training preceded by a strategic effort will secure the result in a shorter time (one year four months) at a reduced cost of £5,000. The balanced approach also ensures that the technique is used in a more positive and useful fashion in the future by the managers concerned. In the course of our experiments ' it became clear that managers were generally tending to take too long over innovation because the strategic effort was omitted.

Usually, when innovation is required, there is too little preparatory strategic effort. Also, when the immediate pressure is relaxed, there is too little tactical effort, and concentration is entirely on strategic education. This again produces an imbalance, so that the high overhead costs are apparently not producing any return; and people lose interest in their education when they do not have the stimulus of problem solving and achieving results. At any particular point in time, a company must balance these two types of training. The relative investment in the two types should be between 4 to 1, i.e. we can have from, 80% to 20% of the total training effort in tactical training and the balance in strategic education. So long as there is investment between these limits in each type it is probably not very important to make a precise balance because the two kinds are complementary.

Personnel for tactical effort

Preplanning should make provision for (i) leadership, (ii) group of committee effort and (iii) specialist help. It must:

(i) Decide who of senior management will have time to direct the project, develop its strategy, check that a proper plan is mad and exercise overall control.

(ii) Find which persons must be made available, and perhaps 'conditioned' to serve the programme. Many persons may be needed to provide detailed information at the 'Recording' step and to do most of the 'Install' step of the programme.

(iii) Find who has the technical knowledge and experience to give specialized help in the 'Record' and 'Analyse' steps.

The leader must be of appropriate status to secure sufficient allocation of time to the project by participants and to obtain any money investment required for the project, or for improvements. A common error is to appoint a leader who is not of senior management standing. This is usually reflected in unimportant work taking up the time of participants. The leader need not concern himself with the details of the programme which may be planned by specialist assistants or a junior manager, but he should take part in preplanning and check that a plan is made. He is essential at the final or control stage to ensure that the gains of the programme are not frittered away in new kinds of losses. He *formulates the strategy but avoids detail* so that he can visualize the whole project and direct its external political planning.

Secondly, an advisory group will be necessary to provide information at the early stages of the project and to take positive action to install improvements. Preferably they should assist in *planning objectives* and be taken into full confidence of the leader at an early stage of the project. This makes 'installation' easier. The effort and time required from members of this group will depend on the particular skill that each contributes. All must be selected carefully to avoid 'passengers'. This requires forecasting skill and knowledge of the organization. Frequently the advisory group is too narrowly selected so that a great deal of investigation time is wasted in collecting information which is already available in other functions of the business, such as purchasing, accounts, technical development, sales, etc. The range of skills which can contribute is rarely appreciated at the initial stages.

Finally, some specialist assistance will be required to collect additional facts, make models and analyses of the problems, and record progress. The specialist need not necessarily be an expensive person though he will have to have some training in industrial engineering method. Frequently, a manager may be released from other responsibilities to do this work, which usually has to be full time for the duration of the project.

Basically, the task is company-orientated and the whole object is to make use of existing company skills, personnel and other resources. But the specialist or 'outsider' can be very helpful in at least three ways. Firstly, he can assist the group prepare a plan of work and thus save project time. He should particularly seek within the organization for any additional resources required; for usually participants do not know what is already available within their own companies! He may act as a resource himself, particularly by the giving of information on techniques and their pitfalls. Any previous experience can be very valuable to a company which has knowledge of techniques without the experience of task work.

The specialist acts as a commentator and recorder It is difficult for a working group, subject to the organizational loyalties and schisms which arise from industrial specialization, to be objective. The specialist can assist the group to review and control their work by the preparation of minutes, records or reports. He can be particularly useful if lie ensures that steps of the work are not skipped. This applies particular to the setting up of models, and of quantitative acceptable objectives. Being an 'outsider' permits him to think creatively because he is less tied by traditions which may blind members of an organization.

Thirdly, the specialist can act as a pusher. This needs to be done extremely carefully. The object of Organization Training is to help men within a company make improvements for their company and,, gain experience and confidence by doing so. He should avoid acting as a leader, for if he does, the group would cease to be effective when he withdraws to other jobs. Thus, he has the rather difficult job of helping the group to be thorough and analytical and prevent their jumping to small or incorrect conclusions, to keep to a timetable, and to appreciate the benefit of doing so without dominating their activities.

Sometimes this role is filled by a consultant. Too often the consultant is concerned with his prestige and tends to dominate the situation, for he is trained to believe that in this way he justifies himself and his pay. This concern often prevents him developing the group's expertize and self confidence. A more academic approach which measures success through the achievement of 'students' will be more successful, particularly over a span of six months or more.

Preplanning tactical objectives

At the preplanning stage, objectives should be given careful consideration. We need to develop existing feelings of dissatisfaction into purposive, constructive action. Frank group discussion of existing defects and their causes with suggestions for ways of eliminating the causes of dissatisfaction is useful in generating ideas for feasible and economic action. It is a common error to formulate objectives which are unacceptable or worrying to those who may be expected to install and use improvements. With care it is usually possible to depersonalize the objectives of the programme and frame them, so that all persons concerned will benefit from achieving results, and secure more satisfying work by so doing. Organization training must not be a 'witch hunt', so seek to improve things rather than people.

The problem or situation to be discussed should be presented through a model. People tend to think subjectively about the work situation and their pride in work and desire to dominate make it difficult for them to think purposively or creatively. With a model, it is much easier for participants to be objective and to forego emotions. The models can be charts, or a write-up, or quantitative, or a drawing, or even a physical or working model. It is necessary to concentrate group attention on examining the model rather than the real situation and to try out suggestions for improvement on the model. Only when the ideas are useful in the model situation should any attempt be made to transfer ideas from the model to the real situation. Specialist help is normally necessary to develop and prepare models. At least two kinds of models would be used in any problem. Prepare partici-pants for creative thinking. This is done by encouraging 'wild' thinking on possibilities and preventing committee groups criticizing any possible line of action until a number of possibilities have been identified. There are always many paths to improvement but the easiest way of preventing their identification is to allow someone early in a meeting to say 'we can't do that because'. Usually three-quarters of any early discussion should be developing ideas and only one-quarter of time should be allocated to choosing the useful ones.

Initially objectives will be of a qualitative kind. It is essential at some stage, if possible while preplanning, to put the qualitative objective into quantitative terms. The specialist's help may be useful for this. Project should not continue unless aims are focused in numerical terms for only in this way are objectives likely to be really meaningful.

These aims should also be of sufficient magnitude to be worthwhile a five per cent improvement is too small a target to generate enthusiasm and it is usually easier to get 40 per cent improvement than a smaller one.

At the preplanning stage the leader must:

(a) Beware of getting into details of planning and action too soon. Time on reconnaissance is rarely wasted.

(b) Discuss objectives. Clearly identify the end results expected from technique. Too often a technique is installed for its own sake and a costly empire is built up to serve the technique rather than the business.

(c) Avoid jumping to conclusions. If one method of securing results is available, another could also probably be used. Try to look at a number of possibilities and select the most profitable.

(d) Look for unsystematized areas of work to study. Greatest savings are usually possible in those areas which have never been systematically studied. If a system already exists minor losses are probably easily seen and action is easier but less rewarding.

(e) Organize innovation to simplify rather than complicate responsibilities. Remember every specialist added to an organization increases the difficulties of line management so develop as little but as excellent specialist help as possible.

(f) Check that objectives are written down.

(g) Take strategic action to develop people and the environment for problem solving.

Planning for problem solving

There is no rigid barrier between preplanning and planning, because how much can be preplanned depends on the degree of experience and sophistication of the leader. However preplanning will usually produce a variety of ideas for problem solving and suggest that a particular problem solving project is very desirable and has some chance of success. Thereafter that particular project should be planned with a view to securing a timely result with as little effort and cost as possible. Of course there can be no certainty of success, it would not be problem solving if there were no uncertainty! In general planning is concerned with the tactics of problem solving. Its field should be narrower than that of Preplanning and the study more detailed.

Planning must ensure that:

(i) Objectives are clear, acceptable and in quantitative terms.

(2) Resources of information, tools, etc., required are identified.

(3) Persons who should be concerned with the programme are known.

(4) Provision is made for appropriate resources.

(5) A time plan to ensure quick results is made and checked.

Quantify the problem and objectives

The problem should be specified in numerical terms. A supervisory group trying to reduce rejects in the machine shop used the following figures:

Rejects of Type A Castings 30%
Type B Castings 7%
Type C Castings 10%

Of course the group concentrated their attention on Type A rejects. After 1¼ hours discussion one member asked for the production figures for each type of casting, when the data below was given:

Type	*Cost each*	*Number machined*	*Rejects*	*Cost of Rejects*
A	5	20		6 30
B	10	400	28	280
C	20	90	9	180

It was only then they realized they were concen-trating on a minor problem and neglecting the major problem of type B and C rejects. This sort of thing happens too frequently because we use figures without bothering to understand them. A good rule is to try to avoid ratios, percentages, productivity rates because their simplicity is often illusory. More tangible or directly countable units are preferable.

However, .this was only one of many weekly sessions lead by a works manager for his own staff to study the efficiency of their own workshops. It was an organizational training effort which with some industrial engineering technique produced a 50% increase in turnover within one year in an already efficient company. There must be numerical targets to get this sort of result.

Numerical data will also be necessary to help decide which persons should be trained. For example, if it is desired to improve operating skills to reduce scrap, then clearly figures would help to find which areas have the greatest cost of scrap. But figures may also be useful to find if particular kinds of persons cause more scrap than others. Such information usually helps to reduce the number of people who are to be trained or even show that a change of the grade of labour doing the work may overcome the whole problem, and eliminate the need of training.

Thus data to specify the problem may help to reduce the number of persons concerned. Further, if quantitative targets of performance can be set then the fact that attainment towards the goal is measured will lead to faster improvement and normally to much better performance.

Identify resources

It is extremely helpful to have an overall picture of the work situation in the problem area. One of the first steps is usually to draw Process Charts of the work to be studied or make models of the plant involved. The point to watch is that the complexity of the chart or model does not defeat its purpose.

A chemical plant was used for the study of material losses. It was only after a considerable amount of time was spent in trying to decide the key points of this chart that it was realized a much simpler process diagram was more meaningful to participants because it showed the essential features of the relationship between processes. At this stage, a revised process chart covering the whole plant was prepared which was one-sixth of the size and complexity of the first chart. This was more useful because it eliminated unnecessary detail and con-centrated attention on important parts of the process. Frequently, insufficient time is devoted to simplification of data, charts or models to bring out the salient points.

A chart is helpful for identifying what has to be planned. It is simply a line diagram showing the way activities, things and persons are related to the objective. Numbers are used in the chart to identify people, dotted lines actions and solid lines things produced or used in setting up training. When this chart was constructed it becomes clear that the objective in that problem is not to train persons but to achieve a better performance or cost. Thus information on performance and costs must be provided and it is necessary to find who may be able to do this, and in this way other departments become involved in the project.

A chart enables the resources necessary to be identified well ahead of requirement. A search for required resources normally shows these already exist in the organization so it is unnecessary to employ special people to collect new data. An early appreciation of requirements makes it easier to provide for them.

The first two steps will already have given ideas as to who will be required to help with the programme by giving, and by receiving. A tabulation of this information. 'Schedule of Activities' is useful. The Activities to be undertaken are listed and alongside each are tabulated the Things to be used and the Persons who should be consulted or who may be useful in each activity. Finally we record who should be Responsible for each activity.

It is useful to circulate this list of major activities in order to make certain that the plan is reasonably complete. Preliminary drafts will be necessary to ensure that resources are tapped in an economic manner. At the final stage, the activities are grouped into Sections of work or overall jobs. This is usually necessary because the number of separate activities is inconveniently large for tabulating graphically.

Provide appropriate resources

By this stage we have in the schedule of activities a forecast of the equipment and tools necessary. A convenient way of tabulating the relationship between activities, persons and equipment to show how the work should be done is provided in the

Procedure Analysis Chart. This form of chart has several uses: it may be used to outline the solving programme or record other procedures.

Plan the time scale

The fifth stage of developing a plan is to introduce a time scale. This records the sections of work developed in the Schedule of Activities. The persons concerned with each activity are listed in the separate columns and activities are represented by the numbers in the Schedule of Activities. This time plan gives an overall appreciation of the programme with its preliminary steps and those required for the implementation of results. It is also a convenient device for recording the load or number of people which will be required for the programme at any particular time.

Though devices for planning are simple, they should not be overlooked. The point is that these tools show up any lack of thoroughness in thinking through a plan and enable resources to be developed when the plan is discussed. Each stage of plan assists the next stage. However, it is important to check each stage to ensure that the economic methods are identified and see if improvement in the training process can be achieved. Problems shown up at one planning stage may make it necessary to go back and alter the plan at the earlier stage. Thus reviewing the time scale may make it desirable to add or delete certain resources. Reviewing the resources may make it desirable to modify or amplify objectives. It is important that these planning tools should be used to evaluate the plan critically as well as display what is to be done.

The purpose of a plan is to model what will happen. It should be checked for completeness. A convenient way is to examine it in terms of the factors:

U	Things, Units
R	Activities, Relationships
P	Arrangement Pattern
M	Quantities, Measurements
C	Groups, classes
T	Time
V	Variability and Risk
Q	Quality
T	Profit and Fit

Some tools of planning have been described. Basically, these tools attempt to give a picture of a programme before it is commenced. In so doing, it is possible to save a great deal of time and be more certain of achieving worthwhile results. Because the form of plan is simple, it becomes easier for the people in 'organization training' to make their contribution. Perhaps the most important result of the plan is that any distinction between trainer and trainee or between contributor to and receiver of training tends to be minimized and all see themselves as contributing to worthwhile objectives for the organization. This surely is the crux of organization training. Once a plan is formulated its effectiveness should be periodically checked by measuring performance and adherence to the plan in order to find what additional actions must be taken, which were not forecast. It is important in the plan to ensure that proper provision is made for persons to be responsible for control of the sections of the work and the implementation of the whole plan.

Control must be exercised to ensure that enough time is allowed for all the 5 Steps ill innovation and to 'avoid reaping in spring time. Secondly, control must ensure that the harvest is counted and collected. Thirdly, the overall innovation process must be reviewed to find how future plans can be improved so that we learn from experience. This requires more thorough planning than is common and proper recording and circulation of the plan. Finally the controller must have the courage to look ahead and face future probable but presently unforeseen problems. Too often production and productivity are improved, but because ancillary requirements of increased output are not available after a few months production slips back to its old level. He must not forget to prepare for the innovation's success.

22

Computer Management

Information Technology for Managers

Computers are at the heart of all important new office technology systems. Physical computer equipment, the *hardware,*can memorize, analyse, manipulate and transmit a vast variety of information forms: text, graphics, voices, handwriting and more. Hardware operation is controlled by *software,* detailed *programs* of instructions that define each step that needs to be carried out to perform a task. The versatility of computer-based systems comes from the fact that the hardware can be used to perform a multitude of applications by reprogramming it with new software. Information is stored and processed by computers in an encoded form comprising only the *digits* (bits) 0 and 1. Microelectronics has provided transistors that can act as tiny switches: the *on or off* state of such a switch can be regarded as equivalent to a 0 or 1. Many thousands of transistors can be packed into a *microchip.* This is a thumbnail-sized slice of *silicon,* a constituent of sand, which is a *semiconductor* that enables electronic pulses to flow in only one direction. It can be used either as computer *memory* to store information or, arranged in complex circuits, as the *processor* which executes software instructions. Large volumes of digital computer information can also be stored in *backing storage,* such as *magnetic disks* or *tapes,* similar to music disks and tapes; the direction of magnetization on tiny magnets in the coating of these media is used to indicate a 0 or 1.

Digital techniques are also being used increasingly in telecommunications because they more efficient and reliable than traditional *analogue* methods, which send continuously varying signals that represent, for example, the wave pattern of human voices. The switching exchanges in telecommunications networks are also employing computer systems. The main factor that determines what type of information can be sent on a digital communications link is the *bandwidth,* a measurement of the volume of information, in *bits per second* (bps), that can flow down a channel. *Narrow band* links are suitable for services like telex, computer data or telephone speech. *Broadband* or *wideband* connections are needed either where many different services are to be carried or for providing a service that needs high speed transmission, like colour TV which requires almost 100 million bps.

Data processing and office information systems

The earliest use of computing power was in the from of large *mainframe* computers used for Data Processing (DP) applications which had to be housed in specially maintained environments. Such systems were applied mainly to tasks with a clearly defined set of rules and routines that could operate on large volumes of *data* structured into organized files. Typical DP work consists of managing accounts, processing pay-rolls, and maintaining and updating records, such as in customer, sales or supplier files. In early DP systems, work had to be physically transported to and from the computer, where it was processed as batches. Gradually, however, external links were developed through devices called *terminals,* which could be in direct *online* communication with the mainframe.

In the 1970s, smaller, more robust and cheaper *minicomputers* were introduced which were eventually capable of being operated in ordinary offices. The process of decentralizing computing capabilities was given a dramatic boost in the 1970s when microelectronics made *microcomputers* available that are far smaller, cheaper, more powerful and versatile than even the minicomputer. It became economically and technically feasible to have sophisticated, computer-based systems on the office desk of a manager, secretary, clerk or technical professional.

There is a great deal of overlap between DP and office systems, but it is worth noting some crucial distinguishing characteristics that arise more from the nature of office work than the technology; similar hardware and software elements can be packaged in different ways for different application needs.

(1) DP work is highly structured, routine and predictable. Office work tends to be more unstructured, variable and unpredictable.

(2) The users of DP systems have been relatively highly trained and have often been skilled computing professionals. Office users, from clerks to top managers, have less specialist training, and should require less. Office users therefore need systems that are much easier to understand and use than the type of complex systems that have been accepted by DP users.

(3) DP systems perform a lot of work carried out in offices, such as accounting and order processing, put have been generally regarded as support services, somewhat remote from every-day operations. New office technology is visible in the mainstream of working life. Its success or failure is more clearly seen to have an impact on overall organizational and job performance.

(4) Those in charge of DP, typically DP departments, have generally been technical specialists who inhabited a different arena to the rest of the organization. Those in charge of new office technology must be more integrated into the general running of the organization).

New office technology

Office work that can be assisted by computer based systems can be categorized as follows:

(1) *Document production.* The creation of printed text and graphic material.

(2) *Professional aids.* Tools to help with specific tasks, such as *electronic spreadsheets,* which are simple but effective aids to financial management. and systems honed to assist architects, vehicle designers, doctors, etc.

(3) *Filing/retrieval.* The storage of information that can be subsequently searched to find, analyse and present relevant items.

(4) *Communications aids.* The transmission of information and documents between locations.

The main forces in the office systems industry seeking to fulfil these user needs also fall into four categories.

(1) *Word processors.* Primarily for the production of text documents although some do have basic graphic capabilities.

(2) *Integrated systems.* Provide document production, professional aids, filing/retrieval, and other computing capabilities usually within a communications network.

(3) *Personal computers.* Microcomputers that offer a self -contained, general computing resource suitable for relatively small-scale applications, sometimes without any communications ability.

(4) *Mainframe and minicomputers.* Act as central co-ordinating systems making available computing facilities directly to users via online networks.

A *workstation* is the device from which a user accesses computer-based services. The first type of workstation was a terminal linked to mainframe computers. Initially this was a simple and very slow *teletype.* essentially an advanced form of typewriter that can produce printed material under the control of a computer. The next step was to replace the paper with a screen, in what is known as a *Visual Display Terminal* (VDT), *Visual Display Unit* (VDU) or *video terminal.* A keyboard and screen is now the most common basis for a workstation.

Some workstations rely totally on other systems for their computing power and are called *dumb.* Others, referred to as *intelligent.* have their own in built processor and memory. Many systems can act as *stand alone* devices for some tasks and then be interlinked to share resources and communicate with other workstations. A workstation could be a word processor, a personal computer, a VDT or a device built to provide many services, known as an *integrated* or *multifunction* workstation. Office workstations were originally used mainly for clerical and typing tasks. Systems were also developed for specific professional tasks, such as *Computer Aided Design* (CAD) terminals with high performance graphics capabilities for product designers. *Executive workstations* aimed primarily at management tasks started appearing in the early 1980s. This chapter is mainly concerned with workstations for managers and professionals. There are many techniques and technologies that contribute to new office technology. This chapter, however, concentrates on describing the functions that new office systems can perform in terms of individual services which are aimed at serving one person at a time, in what is called stand alone, or co-operative or corporate services, where users share computing resources.

Individual workstation services

In 1979, Visicorp in the US introduced the Visicalc electronic spreadsheet for the Apple II microcomputer. This system marked a turning point in managers' use of computer-based systems. It gave easy to use evidence that computing can be a practical tool in assisting a manager to perform tasks of importance to him or her. By 1983, over one million spreadsheets were in use in over fifty versions, some more powerful than Visicalc. After sampling the advantages of spreadsheets, many managers started exploring other personal computing services of value to them, such as word processing and personal filing. Word processing software on personal computers has been satisfactory for the requirements on many of its users, but generally has less sophisticated document production capabilities than *dedicated* word processors designed for use by secretaries and clerks. Word processing software for personal computers has, however, improved considerably, while the scope of specialized word processors has been extended to include other services, such as spreadsheets and personal filing.

Word processing and spreadsheets have been important first steps on the road to more advanced computer-based office service. Word processing originally developed as a means of handling text and has now been extended to documents which also have graphs, charts, tables, illustrations, photographs, mathematical and other special symbols. Spreadsheets are a simplified example of software *modelling.* The defines how a system is likely to behave in terms of rules, equations and relationships governing key factors. The user can use the model to find out what would happen if certain variables were altered, so are often referred to as *What if?* systems. Software modelling can become extremely complex, managing far more variables and rules than can be handled in a spreadsheet. Software modelling is an important aid in helping managers to make decisions, but does not necessarily constitute a full decision support system. In addition to document production and spreadsheets, this section describes other facilities of personal interest to a manager, such as the filing and retrieval of information, and enhancements to telephone services.

Document production

There are five stages in the production of a document where computer-based systems can be of benefit

(1) *Input* that creates information in computerized form. The keyboard is the most common input device, usually in association with a display screen. When a key is touched, the relevant character is created in computer storage. A pointer on the screen, typically a square character called a *cursor,* indicates the current position of the information being manipulated.

(2) *Data storage* is where information is memorized electronically so that it can be altered during the drafting of a document or stored for subsequent reference. The most popular storage medium is magnetic disks. *Floppy disks* or *diskettes* are like 45 rpm flexible music records and can hold the equivalent of about 100 to 200 pages of A4 text. *Hard disks,* such as compact *Winchester cartridges,* can contain the equivalent of many thousands of pages of A4 text.

(3) *Editing* software that enables the user to manipulate information.

(4) *Formatting* software to allow the user to define how information is presented.

(5) *Output* that presents information. The two most common forms of output are *hardcopy* printout on paper and displays on a screen. The screen can also be regarded as a *window* onto the text information in data storage. This window may be too small to show all stored information, so it may need to be moved vertically or horizontally to scan all the information.

The key to computer-aided document production is the software for editing and formatting, which is sometimes known collectively as the *editor.* Products on the market provide this software with varying degrees of quality. When evaluating systems, it is important to determine the ease and effectiveness of its human-computer communication and the variety of functions provided which should include the following:

(1) *Editing functions.* The facilities provided by an editor depend on the type of information *objects* being processed, such as:

   (a) Text objects like characters, words, sequences of characters, sentences, footnotes and high level entities.

   (b) Environmental objects, usually associated with text material, such as authors, table of contents, indexes, annexes and appendixes that are concerned with the beginning and ending the document.

   (c) Graphical information, such as circles, lines, multilines, *splines,* freehand drawings, text captions for illustrations, and so on.

   (d) Forms and tables that include areas, such as fields and zones, that need to be manipulated.

There are some basic actions, such as delete copy and move, required for all types of objects although their implementation will differ according to the types of data being manipulated. For text editors, there is a minimum set of functions from which fuller editors can be developed. The types of editing functions needed for graphic systems are illustrated in the above *figure,* which shows a menu from the editor on the kayak Buroviseur workstation that contains actions to create objects or manipulate them.

(2) *Formatting functions.* The formatting process aims to produce a document representing the intentions of the author in terms of meaning and physical appearance. The appearance should not detract from the meaning, for example by having a table split over two pages or confusing the reader with too many different type styles.

Electronic spreadsheets

Spreadsheets consisting of a grid with many rows and columns, produced with paper and pen/pencil, have been used in the past by many accountants and managers using paper and pen/pencil to assist in handling financial information. Electronic spreadsheets provide more efficient, extensive and speedier ways of handling the required data and calculations. The main principles of spreadsheet techniques are:

Table. Basic text editing functions

Text editing function	*Action initiated*
Insert	Allows the insertion of a character, word or other text string at the *active position,* the place currently pointed at by the cursor
Delete	Allows the removal of a character or string of characters
Copy	Causes existing text to be copied from the active position to a target position, with the possibility of repeating the copy at other points
Move	Causes text to be moved from the active position to a target position and deletion of the source text from the initial position
Alter	Leads to the replacement of a character or string of characters with a new value. *Global replacement* alters all occurrences of a particular string by the new value indicated in the command
Find	Searches for a character or string of characters indicated and positions the cursor at the start of the required string

Table. Formatting functions

Element acted on	*Functions that can be performed*
Character	Defines how informations is to be presented, such as: (1) The style *(fount),* weight, size and width.

	(1) The layout of a table vertically or horizontally
	(3) The way information to be presented on a screen is displayed, such as with characters blinking, in *inverse* or highlighted in some other way
Block	Constructs words, sentences and paragraphs in appropriate formats, such as having text lined up to the left or right hand margin or having different levels of indention for blocks that form subsections of other text in a structured document
Page	Organizes blocks in pages, with consideration for the height, width, 'white space' margins surrounding text, and other attributes, such as whether it has a landscape or portrait orientation. It also automatically numbers the pages. Care needs to be taken in the way blocks are split over pages, for example, keeping tables and figures on one page.
Special commands	Carries out special requirements by embedding codes in the source text which are interpreted by the formatter before organizing the blocks into pages. Such commands relate, for example, to footnotes, foreign a special position or updating information that needs to be regularly change.

(1) Each *cell* can have a *label*, a *value* and, optionally, *constraints* such as a maximum or minimum value.

(2) The constraints can link one cell to others, say by a formula using arithmetic operations, percentages, averages, logarithmic, trigonometric, logical and other operations. For example, the value of the value of the cell *profit* could be associated with a constraint that is calculated by subtracting the value of cell *costs* from the value of cell *income*.

(3) The fixed information relating to the cell labels, constraints and inter-relations from a model *template*. When figures are given to particular cells, the model's rules work out the changes to values in all related cells.

An electronic spreadsheet program displays as much of the grid or *table* that can fit in a screen's window. Each cell's *address* is its row and column number in the grid. The total number of columns and rows is fixed, typically from 64 to 2000 or more. The user scrolls the window to view the required cells. Some workstations enable the user to look at more than one part of the grid at the same time, as discussed below in the section on multifunction workstations. The most time consuming and tedious part of using an electronic spread sheet is defining relationships between cells, setting constraints, assigning labels to cells, inserting values, and so on. Such setting up, however, is well worth the effort and is likely to be needed only a few times in many years of use. The task is eased if editing functions are available that assist, for example, copying one or more cells, or moving and swapping cells, columns or rows. Once the spreadsheet model is established, the program automatically performs all the necessary calculations swiftly when the user alters some variables, rules or constraints. In more sophisticated systems, a number of spreadsheets can be interlinked through particular cells; a change in one will trigger the necessary alterations in all others. Electronic spreadsheets are far quicker, more accurate and are able to handle more complex models than traditional paper-based techniques. Spreadsheet programs are used in many different applications, such as sales forecasting, budget planning, currency conversion, and profit-and-loss statements.

Business graphics

Early computer-based systems presented information primarily as text and numbers displayed on green and grey screens or printed, often all in capital letters, on stacks of paper printout. This made many managers shy away from computers because they needed to get on with doing a job rather than spending a lot of time ploughing through difficult to read material.

There are now many *business graphics* software packages that can generate a variety of graphical forms, such as bar charts, line graphs, pie and so on. Such presentations are obviously improved if colour is also available. Business graphics software is often linked to spreadsheet facilities so that results can be translated automatically into suitable graphs. Some systems also have a graphics editor that can be used to modify the figures generated by the software. A suitable printer is needed to produce hardcopy and, preferably, facilities to create slides that can be used directly at a meeting or conference.

Personal information management systems

Some information is private to an individual or a group, and is maintained independently from procedures and rules, maintained independently from corporate procedures, and rules. There are various systems to assist handling such personal information, for example, some microcomputer software helps to create and manage small files of data in the form of the electronic equivalent of a box of reference cards. Systems can also be programmed with *tickler* files which are told by the user to remember certain events and then to given a reminder when the date comes close. *Electronic diaries* can be maintained either as a purely stand alone capability for an individual's private use or in a shared system that allows meetings to be arranged by examining each other's electronic diaries and fixing the appointment automatically.

Images of pictures and pages from a document for personal use can be stored on *video* or *optical disks.* Digital information is stored in a videodisk by shining a laser beam to create holes in the surface; the absence or presence of a hole represents a 0 or 1 bit. Video disks used for entertainment films cannot be recorded over.*Digital Optical Recording* (DOR) techniques, however, enable the user to create new information on a disk via an image scanner. One disk of 30 cm diameter can contain over 500000 pages of typed text or 25000 images of A4 sized pages with photographs and illustrations. Personal information files are stored, maintained and accessed in ways similar to those used for the larger databases described later in this chapter.

Enhanced telephony

Computers can also help to improve telephone services available to an individual, for example, through computerized exchanges and the incorporation of microchips in telephones to offer facilities such as:

(1) *Callback.* Automatic redialling of a number that is engaged until a connection is made.

(2) *Abbreviated dialling.* Initiating frequently used telephone numbers by two or three digits.

(3) *Absent transfer.* Automatically rerouting a call to another specified extension when a person visits another office.

(4) *Hunting.* Routeing an incoming call through a number of possible alternatives until a connection is made. if the originally dialled number is engaged.

In more sophisticated systems, enhanced telephone services can be offered directly from a workstation. For example, a personal information file containing names and phone numbers can be displayed on the screen, and the person being called indicated by reference to a pointer. Computer-based systems can also record voices in digital form. This can be used to record messages for incoming calls, as in an answering machine. The computer can record the incoming message for subsequent replay when the recipient is free to listen. Systems are also being developed that produce synthesized voices from messages typed at a keyboard.

Managers' programming aids

Software is written in special *programming languages* which have rigid, precisely defined structures and grammars with a limited range of commands and vocabulary that can be used with them. Different programming languages are suitable for different types of task. For example, Cobol is appropriate for commercial data processing and Fortran for scientific work. On microcomputers, the most popular language is Basic because it is extremely easy to learn, although it has limitations for complex programs. *Most managers should never have to use a programming language unless they have a special personal interest.* Some professionals may need to learn specialized programming techniques to enable them to develop software tailored to their particular discipline.

There are now many systems available that enable managers to generate software code without having to learn a special programming language. These techniques, known as *end-user, fourth generation or applications languages,* or *program generators,* allow the user to provide information to the system in a natural manner. The system then produces the necessary code with requiring the user to become a programming specialist.

Expert systems

A significant computing development which began to make an impact outside research laboratories in the 1980s is that of the *expert system* which contains the distilled knowledge of one or more specialists in a particular subject or *domain.* Initially, expert systems were applied to narrow scientific fields but are now being extended to broader business applications. They are easier to produce when there are sets of rules to be followed rather than when more qualitative decisions need to be made. Some expert system developments are oriented towards replacing human specialists by computers, but other work aims to apply increased computing knowledge and 'intelligence' in a way which is used co-operatively with human expertise.

Integrated systems

Managers whose main experience of computer-based services has been with personal computers realize that separate software systems are often needed to set up and perform distinct functions, such as word processing, spreadsheets, and communications. One of the most significant trends in new office technology is towards integrating many services into a single system or workstation, as explained later in this chapter.

Co-operative workstation services

People need to share computer-based services to communicate with each other and to gain access to large information libraries or files. The sharing of services can be contained within various levels, such as within a department, a project team that involves individuals from many departments, a building, between organizations, or in a particular discipline or market specialization.

Electronic mail

Post, Telegraphs and Telecommunications were the methods first used to communicate information across long distances. Throughout the world, PTT authorities have been established to provide such services, although it has now become clear that physical postal services are of a different nature to electronic transmission.

Electronic mail, also known as *Computer-Based Message Systems* (CBMS), provides a variety of facilities to assist human communication between locations. There should offer the following basic services:

(1) *Message creation by the originator:* The range of information types used in messages will depend on the workstation available and the capability of the communications network. A secret password should be given as a security check before the system allows a user access to the network.

(2) *Routeing of messages to the recipient(s).* The network control software uses information about where the recipient is located and the transmission channels available to deliver the communication to the appropriate workstation(s) in the most efficient and reliable manner.

(3) *Sorting incoming mail until the recipient is ready to receive it.* After transmission, the message is filed in computer storage accessible to the recipient, known as an *electronic mailbox,* from where it is extracted at the recipient's convenience. This is called a *store and forward* system.

(4) *Delivery of the message.* The recipient can regularly scan an index to what is in the mailbox which indicates who sent it, a headline summary of the content, and the degree of priority or urgency. Specific messages can be selected to be displayed on the screen.

Electronic mail services can be of great benefit in assisting communications within and between organizations by providing facilities such as:

(1) *No time constraints.* The originator can compose and send the message at the time and speed she or he wishes without requiring the recipient to be at the other end of the line at the same moment. This is obviously valuable when communicating across different time zones.

(2) *No interruptions.* The store and forward feature means that the recipient is not interrupted every time there is an incoming message.

(3) *No geographical constraints.* Electronic mail extends the telephone's ability to link people in different locations and can lead to the development of a close community feeling. The *computer conferencing* facility, for example, enables subscribers to share in a continuing dialogue by placing ideas into a common file. A participant joins in at any time, reading the latest comments before making a new contribution.

(4) *Multidestination.* Messages can be sent to many recipients at the same time. Mailing lists can be stored in the system and invoked as necessary for particular categories of communication.

(5) *Voice messages.* If the recipient wishes to add a note before sending it back to the sender and/or someone else, she or he should be able to speak a response that will be digitally recorded and relayed at the appropriate point by the person it is directed at. Speech messages are known as *voice memos* or *voicegrams.*

(6) *Control and monitoring of communications.* The time messages are sent, received in the mailbox and read by the recipient can be recorded. In addition:

(a) The originator can, for example, signal the urgency of the message, causing a light to flash on the recipient's terminal for particularly important ones;

request that he or she is informed when the message is delivered and read: specify alternative recipients if the primary one cannot be reached; and allow recipients to know who else received copies or have some *blind* copies that are not reported to other recipients.

(b) The recipient can, for example, reroute all incoming mail to another workstation if he or she is away for a period, or redirect mail from certain subscribers to other workstations to avoid getting too many unnecessary messages.

(7) *Management of the system.* The system must be administered systematically and effectively. Procedures need to be established to allocate each subscriber an identifying code, password, and appropriate workstation and network facilities. The usage of the system should be monitored to assist in costing and accounting tasks. Distribution lists and other files must be maintained, such as a *directory file* containing names and attributes of subscribers that could help users, for example, to find all subscribers living on the Champs Elysees.

The workstations, computer storage, printers, computers and other elements that comprise a network can be linked together in a number of different ways, such as in the following list, which refers to the four networks in *Figure 2.6*, moving clockwise from the left hand top corner.

(1) *A local site* with workstations serviced by a nearby micro or minicomputer holding mailboxes, directories, and so on.

(2) *Nationwide centralized service* in which minicomputers and mainframes provide co-ordination and control of workstations linked through a network, often run by the public PTT administration or by a private network supplier.

(3) *Distributed round and international Message Transfer Service* (MTS), the newest type of service that can interlink decentralized local networks or allow direct connection by workstations.

(4) *Distributed around a Public Data Network* (PDN) which allows subscribers to various local networks to communicate with each other.

Teleconferencing

Teleconferencing offers an alternative to face to face meetings. The computer conferencing facility provided by computer based message systems described above can be regarded as a form of teleconferencing, but this term is usually used for services that enable people to interact with each other immediately. The two main types of such teleconferencing are:

(1) *Audioconferences* in which people can talk to, but cannot see, each other. Facilities may be provided to exchange documents electronically or the transmit *telewriting* messages using special electronic input *tablets* that transmit movements made by

a pen. Participants must be in rooms with equipment that enables them to talk to and hear others in different locations without the necessity of a handset held to mouth and ear.

(2) *Videoconferences* in which people can see as well as hear each other. The main technical limitation is the need to have high bandwidth transmission links - moving pictures can require a minimum of 1.5 to 2 million bits per second. Instead of *full motion* conferencing, *freeze frame* services can be provided at less cost, operating at only about 50000 bits per second. With freeze frame, a still picture is sent about every thirty seconds. this is clearly not as effective as full motion. Special cameras, studios. TV monitors and other equipment are needed for videoconferencing.

Teleconferencing offers potentially attractive services but its use has grown relatively slowly. This is partly because the costs have been high compared to the benefits. As with other computer-based services, microelectronics is reducing costs, which has made motion videoconferencing a cost effective option in many circumstances. Another brake on teleconferencing growth has been the resistance by managers who have found remote communications awkward, particularly when facing cameras. Increasing experience with live systems is helping to give managers more skill in being able to exploit teleconferencing functions.

The teletex service

The Consultative Committee on International Telephones and Telegraphs (CCITT), which represents tele-communications authorities around the world, has defined standards for *teletex*, a 'supertelex' service for exchanging text messages. Teletex enables messages to be created, edited, transmitted across the network and received. Traditional telex devices had built-in printers with only capital letters, but teletex terminals can have a range of facilities, from being an adapted *electronic typewriter* to specially developed, sophisticated workstations. This gives a vast improvement in quality and speed compared with telex.

Being based on an internationally agreed standard is of great importance for teletex because incompatibilities between computer-based equipment and services is a major barrier to further growth of new office technology. The CCITT teletex standards cover transmission rate, the character repertoire that should be available, the basic range of services to be provided, and the communications *protocols*. Rules and procedures that need to be followed when making connections between terminals, checking that transmission has been error free, and so on, are also given. Teletex systems should also be able to link into the telex network.

Viewdata and teletext

Videotex allows the transmission and presentation of information containing graphics as well as text. Interactive videotex allows the user to send messages and commands to search through 'pages' of data or, say, to order goods displayed in the sales catalogue held in the system's information store. Viewdata can also be used to exchange electronic mail between subscribers. It provides a relatively simple and low cost way of distributing up to date information to many subscribers: for example, from a company to its dealers to between travel agents. Many public viewdata services have been established, such as Prestel in the UK, Teletel in France, Telidon in Canada and Captains in Japan.

Broadcast videotex provides one-way transmission on pages of information to many receivers, such as from a TV transmitter to adapted TV sets, using a spare transmission channel not used for sending moving pictures.

Facsimile document transmission

Telefax or *facsimile* (fax) scans a document, transmits its image and reproduces a copy on the receiving device. Early machines were originally rather slow and generated blurred and indistinct copies. Computer-based digital techniques have improved speed and quality and reduced costs. The CCITT has classified telefax machines into four categories. Groups 3 and 4 are the most interesting for the office of the future. Group 3 systems send the copy of a page in less than a minute, perhaps as quickly as 20 seconds. Group 4 must be equally fast and must also be error free. The other two groups are mainly older machines that transmit an A4 page in up to six minutes or three minutes.

Corporate databases

Filing, storing and retrieving information are common office activities. Filing cabinets with folders and papers have been an integral part of office work. Computerized *databases* provide new means of managing such information to reduce the amount of paper and space needed. Speed up the search to extract relevant information, and enable people at many locations to access the same information source.

One of the problems with any database is getting information into it. Data input via a keyboard can be stored directly in computerized form. Techniques to recognize handwriting and human speech have taken longer to develop. Systems have been available for a long time that can read some printed characters, but it has been harder to get computers to read letters typed unevenly, mixed print and handwriting, drawings and pictures. Storage media that can adequately cope with images, such as optical disks, only started to come on the market in the 1980s.

The most widely used databases have therefore been composed of text and numbers gathered through keyboard entry known as *Database Management Systems* (DBMS). These were developed on data processing systems with highly structured data, such as accounting, orders, delivery, customer, client, inventory, supplier and personnel records, Initially, information was handled in computers as separate *filing systems*, similar to manual systems, with each file containing all its own records and fields, although some information could be common between files, such as a part number in order, delivery and inventory files. Such techniques proved inefficient for large scale information handling although they can be satisfactory for the small-scale personal information needs of many users. Fully scale DBMS software was needed to store and manage data items in a way that avoided unnecessary duplication in data storage but allowed the user flexibility to make an interconnection between items. Three main types of DBMS have been widely used:

(1) *Hierarchical* models structured similarly to an hierarchical organization. A file can be the 'superior' to one or more files beneath it, linked from top to bottom down branches of the hierarchy. This technique is relatively easy to establish and maintain, but can prove to be too rigid and inefficient because it does not allow files or data records to be linked across branches.

(2) *Network* structures that allow data elements to be interlinked in many ways without being confined only to linkages within vertical branches. Like hierarchical files, the structure of the database and the way elements are linked must be defined when the database is set up. As the network approach allows more options for creating links, it is more complex to set up than hierarchical systems but offers the user greater flexibility.

(3) *Relational* databases represent the newest approach, providing great ease of use but requiring extremely complex software controls. The database is regarded as a collection of data items whose structure is not defined when the database is set up, as with network and hierarchical structures. Instead, the relationships are formed dynamically according to the tasks being performed. The difficulty of handling many intricate relations can make this software very slow. Techniques have been developed to give hardware boosts to the speed of relational systems, such as implementing some routines in *firmware,* specially constructed microelectronic circuits, or using microprocessors to aid the search for information on disks.

Information retrieval and query languages

The *query language* or other method available to the user to search through databases, make enquiries and retrieve relevant information is of importance to the effectiveness of the whole system. The following are some of the main query techniques.

(1) *Indexed keyword searches* in which items in the files are associated with explicit search keys. *full text* systems create lists which identify the occurrence of each term and enable the whole text to be searched. *partially indexed* systems, typified by computerized libraries, are based on searching for attributes, such as author, title, and subject selected by a professional indexer.

(2) *Query by Example* (QBE), developed for relational databases, presents the user with a list of attributes; the user fills in the values of those items being looked for.

(3) *Menus* present the user with a number of options from which to select either the required information or another menu taking the user along a trail to the information.

(4) *Natural language* allows the user to express requirements using phrases similar to the way the query would be normally expressed, such as 'Find me all the customers with orders that have been outstanding for more than two weeks'. Such systems usually 'understand' natural languages only within a predetermined context and recognize only a limited vocabulary.

(5) *Question and answer* in which the system finds out what is wanted by asking the user a number of questions.

(6) *Free text* which enables every part of a document to be explored, even if the specification of what is wanted may be incorrect or incomplete.

Image banks

Optical disks, discussed earlier in terms of personal information systems, can be combined into *juke boxes* to provide a source of information, held as images, which may be shared by many users. An image scanner is used to transfer documents to the disks. Information about each page is keyed in from a control workstation by providing details of various attributes that will help an associated database management system to retrieve the relevant image and display it on a workstation screen. It is important to remember that information on such disks is stored as images of whole pages. It therefore cannot be searched in detail, as a text database could.

Office workstations

The most common office workstations have been VDTs for clerical staff, word processors for secretaries and typists, and personal computers for managers. The most important workstation developments for managers have been towards high performance, multifunction workstations which integrate a variety of functions. In addition, there is a growing variety of other executive workstations and terminals.

High performance multifunction workstations

The most advanced workstations are systems that are effectively small computers which can operate as a stand alone device or as part of a network. They were pioneered in the 1970s at Xerox Corporation's Palo Alto Research Center (PARC) in California as a way of integrating different tasks and information types. They first became commercially available in the early 1980s through systems like the Xerox Star and Apple Lisa and Macintosh.Their main attributes include the following facilities:

(1) *Multiwindow displays* that can show different applications being run on the machine at the same time or different parts of the same document or spreadsheet. For example, one window could be used for editing, another for displaying the contents of an electronic mailbox and a third to show an electronic telephone

directory. In addition, windows can come and go displaying, for example, editing menus that can switch automatically from, say, text to graphic tasks. Multiwindows are of great importance to managers whose work is likely to consist of having to keep many tasks active at the same time. It also contributes to good human-computer communication.

(2) *Pointing aids* needed to complement multiwindow systems. They are used, for example, to move windows or other objects on the screen, or to point to a small symbol that represents a function to be performed. The main pointing devices include the following:

   (a) *Mouse,* a small object, with a rolling ball in the base, that can be held in the palm of the hand. the cursor on the screen is moved in the direction followed by the mouse as it is rolled over the desk in front of the screen. The mouse can have one or more control buttons to initiate various tasks.

   (b) *Touch sensitive screen* which registers the point at which the screen is touched. This is suitable for browsing through systems with menus containing large option boxes, but is unsuitable for use as a pointer to small objects with high accuracy.

   (c) *Tablet,* a flat pad sensitized to register the position where it is touched and used particularly in Computer Aided Design tasks where it is necessary to create detailed drawings.

   (d) *Light pen,* an electronic pen-like device used to input graphic images, particularly for Computer Aided Design tasks.

(3) *High resolution displays* that can display crisp images, usually with black characters and images on a white background. Images are formed on the screen as a collection of tiny dots, with each position called a *pixel.* The more pixels, the higher the resolution and the better the quality of image; screens with about 1024 x 768 pixels can reproduce a high quality A4 page.

(4) *Powerful microprocessors* of similar capabilities to those used in micro and minicomputers, typically 16- or 32-bit machines. The basic bit-size of the words used in a processor are a measure of the power and capability of a system, with 4- and 8-bit systems having relatively limited capabilities.

(5) *Large memory and disk storage* containing up to about 512K or more bytes of *Random Access Memory* (RAM) and from 10M to 100M bytes of hard disk store.

(6) *Full page screen* which displays the equivalent of a full page of A4 text, whereas other screens typically have half a page.

Autonomous personal workstations

It was in the mid 1970s that personal computers, like the Apple II, first helped managers lift the grey curtain of jargon and mystique that shrouded computing during the heyday of mainframe data processing. Personal computers could use ordinary domestic colour TV sets and were originally developed for use in the home to entertain and educate. Many managers found that once they got hands-on experience of a personal computer, they began to appreciate what it could do for them at work, particularly when running software, such as electronic spreadsheets, that provide immediate and obvious benefits.

Personal computers have evolved in two main directions since then. On one hand, they have become smaller and more lightweight so that they can be easily carried around. Moving in the other direction, some personal computers have become increasingly sophisticated. A continuous spectrum of personal computing is available to managers, from pocket computers to powerful multifunction workstations. The choice of which system is most appropriate depends on the nature of the tasks involved, the volume of information being handled, and the money available to invest in a system. Many managers may eventually come to have more than one workstation, say one to work with on a plane or train, one at home and one in the office. Each is likely to be capable of being used on its own or connected to a network. The following are the main categories of personal computers, in addition to the multifunction workstations described above.

(1) *Desk-top personal computers* generally have a half page screen, possibly with full colour, keyboard, floppy and hard disks, a minimum of 256K bytes of RAM and options for telecommunications links. The *operating system* software available is of crucial importance.

These are collections of routines that organize the hardware resources and determine which software applications packages can run on the machine. Widely used operating systems, like PC-DOS, MS-DOS, CP/M and Unix, are likely to have a broader range of applications software available to users than an operating system used on fewer machines. Many programming languages are likely to be available, some provided in *Read Only Memory* (ROM), microchip main memory that the user cannot overwrite. They generally weigh between 10 and 20 kgs.

(2) *Transportable or carry-on computers* provide similar capabilities to desk top systems but are lighter, from about 4 to 10 kgs, and come with a case that can be used to carry them around. They may contain a small built-in screen, but can also usually work with a standard display or TV screen. The built-in screen may use a *Cathode Ray Tube* (CRT), which is the basic of TV and VDT displays, or a *Liquid Crystal Display* (LCD), a flat screen also used for calculators and watches.

(3) *Potable or briefcase computers*, generally the size of a book, can be slipped into an ordinary briefcase and are capable of being run off batteries. They usually weigh only a few kilograms, have about two to eight lines of built-in flat screen display, and up to about 32K or 64K or RAM.Cassette tapes or small *microfloppy* disks may

be offered for additional storage. These systems are ideal for note taking, electronic mail and preparing shortish letters and reports.

(4) *Pocket computers,* the size of largish pocket calculators usually with one line display, have a small keyboard, up to about 10K bytes of RAM, and the ability to connect to a small printer.

Connected office terminals

There are many devices in the office which are developments from traditional data processing, such as the intelligent VDT, or from telecommunications-oriented information processing, such as the telephone, teletex and videotex. There are a number of developments to try and combine two or more such terminals into a single workstation, as indicated by the arrows connecting items in *Figure 2.10.* For example, some PTTs are working on terminals that combine teletex and telefax. Videotex and telephone services can be combined in a single unit. The following is a summary of the main types of terminals.

(1) *Intelligent terminal* is typically a VDT including its own microprocessor and main memory.

(2) *Teletypewriter,* usually abbreviated to TTY, is the old fashioned terminal consisting of a keyboard and built-in printer.

(3) *Videotex* terminals are used mainly for viewdata database queries and some electronic mail.

(4) *Telex* is the worldwide text communication system.

(5) *Telephone* network is for voice communications to which computers can add enhanced telephone capabilities.

(6) *Teletex* is text communications as defined by the CCITT.

(7) *Telefax* is document facsimile transmission.

(8) *Smart Card* (SC) is a recent development that puts a microchip on a small plastic card, containing up to 16000 or more characters, which could be used, for example, to assist security checks or to make payments directly.

Networking capabilities

Networks for office work cover either a particular building or set of offices or a broad geographical range. For managers, the establishment of the telecommunications infrastructure is a key strategic and tactical issue. The network effectively lays down the standards that determine the types of workstations that can be linked to it and the services offered.

The ultimate aim is to have *open systems,* where any kind of device can be interlinked with any other. To this end, the *International Standards Organization* (ISO) has denied the *Open Systems Interconnection* (OSI) framework. This is divided into seven levels, starting at the asic physical interconnection and moving up to the interchange of complete software applications. Some detailed standards have been established at the lower levels. The CCITT X.21 standard, for example, covers the lowest level, physical transport, and X.25 encompasses the lower three levels for some networks, including the physical X.21 connection, data transmission, and the routening of messages through a network.

Wide area networks

The telephone and telex networks are traditional examples of *Wide Area Networks* (WANs). The performance of a network is determined by two main factors, the bandwidth of the transmission medium and the method used to route meassages through the system. The copper wire of telephone networks is of low bandwidth, but *coaxial cables,* with a thick conducting core, *optical fibres,* which send signals on beams of light through hair-thin glass fibres, microwave and satellite links provide much higher bandwidths. Two main types of swtiching have been common.

(1) *Circuit switching* is where the circuit connecting the calling device to the network is linked to the receiver circuit by making interconnections through a series of exchanges in the network. This has been the technique used in traditional telephone exchanges.

(2) *Packet switching* is widely used for digital networks. Data is divided into small packets wrapped around with control information, including a header at the front that contains the address to which it is going. Switches in the network send each packet through the most efficient route to the receiver. Checks are made to ensure the packets arrive intact and in the right order. The X.25 standard applies to packet switched networks.

Private automatic branch exchanges

Many organizations have had locally distributed telecommunications networks for many years in the form of intra-company telephone communications controlled by a private exchange, typically a switchboard operated manually. These are being replaced by computer-based Private Automatic Branch eX-changes, known as *PABXs* or *PBXs,* which can offer a variety of office information services, such as enhanced telephony, electronic mail and audioconferencing. One of the long term limitations on a PABX may be that the existing writing does not have sufficient bandwidth to carry high volumes of traffic. An important advantage, however, is that a reasonably powerful network can be established without requiring any major rewiring.

Local area networks

PABXs give a local distribution of telecomunications that provides many additional services in addition to the basic transmission of data. Systems that offer high speed local transmission but with few, if any, addition capabilities are known as *Local Area Networks* (LANs). There are two main LAN families:

(1) *Broadband* can transmit many channels on differing frequencies, so that a mix of information can be carried at the same time.

(2) *Baseband* consists of a single channel that allows the transmission of one stream of data at a time.

Broadband networks can be used for a variety of purposes, such as TV broadcasting, multi-channel audio transmission, environmental control, and for local cable TV networks. They generally cover a greater geographic spread than baseband systems, which are usually restricted to cables of no more than about one to three kilometres in length, although independent LANs can be interconnected. The speed required for a baseband service is typically at least one million bits per second. The following are the main types of baseband LAN techniques:

(1) *Boardcast Carrier Sense Multiple Access* (CSMA) is typified by Ethernet, developed at Xerox's PARC centre, which also pioneered research into multifunction office workstations. In these systems each network *station* can broadcast messages to other stations, which remain constantly on the alert to detect messages addressed to them.

(2) *Ring empty slot systems,* originally developed at Cambridge University in the UK, are where fixed length data slots continually circulate around the link. Stations dump information into vacant slots or detect and pick out data addressed to them.

(3) *Ring* to *bus token systems* are where stations can transmit only when they are in possession of a token, a special code that circulates with other data. A bus layout has stations connected on a linear link, like stops on a bus route.

(4) *Polling* systems have a central controller that distributes to stations the right to access the network on the basis of a controlled polling sequences.

Standards for various aspects of LANs have been established by internationally recognized authorities, such as the American Institute of Electrical and Electronics Engineer (AIEEE) and the European Computer Manufacturers Association (ECMA). Such standardizations are important steps towards enabling organizations to have greater flexibility in choosing devices to link to the network and in joining up networks.

Choosing and mixing networks

Each type of LAN, or the PBX option for local communications, has particular advantages and disadvantages. The choice of the most appropriate technique for any particular circumstances will depend on existing systems, the types of information being communicated, the costs of linking units to the network and of installing the network, overall performance, and so on. For many organizations, a mix of network types may be the solution. For example, it is becoming popular to have baseband systems for local groups, say all offices on one floor of a building, then to link these by a broadband system covering many buildings. It is also possible to have an integrated system consisting of:

(1) One or more local area networks.

(2) Individual computer systems, workstations, databases and input or output devices.

(3) *Gateways* linking up private and public networks.

Financial Accounting System

Highlights

- The Financial Accounting System (FAS) receives accounting information from all of the subsystems.
- FAS produces a general ledger
- Financial statements can be produced from the general ledger
- Budgets are controlled and administered through the Financial Accounting System
- The Financial Accounting System functions as an information traffic cop for the overall system

The pieces of information a manager gives the closest look to are usually the financial statements, primarily the earnings statement or profit and loss statement. Individuals and businesses outside the company use the financial statements in reaching decisions and findings that will have an enormous effect on the company. This chapter discusses the accounting tools used in preparing these statements, and providing financial controls essential to operate a business.

The Financial Accounting System is the heart of the overall distribution system. It functions as a traffic cop to route financial information to the correct file or account. It is very important to plan the accounting system carefully, since it must satisfy an audience of critical observers: an auditor, the managers, the bookkeeper, the company CPA,the IRS, creditors, and owners. Each of these potential users of financial data has expectations that must be met; and frequently, the goals of the use of data between these users conflict. Thus, the financial system must be extremely flexible.

FAS receives the summarization of transactions from each system, recapping them in journal entry form, and posting them to the General Ledger Database File. An audit trail allows an entry to be traced from the general ledger, back through the originating system, to specific transactions such as an invoice or a cash receipt.

Almost all of the financial statements can be prepared from the General Ledger Database. By adding budget and prior-year information, comparative statements can be prepared, making analysis more complete and meaningful.

The company will be required to provide financial information to creditors. To obtain credit, the company must comply with vendor and financial institution demands for information. The quality of the data must be excellent to gain and hold the confidence of these creditors. Most managers prefer to issue financial statements through their CPA, even though he or she may not audit the statements. FAS gives the professional accountant the tools to review the financial records of a client while reducing time spent by the accountant in collecting basic documents, and allows time for more sophisticated analyses. A strong accounting system is one basis for strong management. The proper design of the accounting system is essential, and thorough planning is important.

Entries to FAS

Each of the systems produce transactions that are passed to the accounting system and posted to the general ledger. Refer to the above figure for the flow of data to FAS.

ACRES, the Accounts Receivable System, passes entries recording sales, cash receipts, and other adjustments to the approximate accounts receivable accounts.

ACPAYS, the Accounts Payable System, creates journal entries to record voices and credits for goods and services acquired, and credits to the cash account for cash disbursements when invoices are paid.

INMANS, the Inventory Management System, passes journal entries for the cost of goods sold and other adjustments to the inventory accounts.

Payroll is recorded through PAYSY entries

In addition to these automatic processes, all adjustments to the ledger are entered, via manual input, through manual journal entry. All manual entries produce a paper audit trail record just as automatic entries do. All journal entry report should be saved as part of the audit trail. As a result, the FAS system integrates data from all subsystems in the overall system into a network or fabric. The automation of the Financial Accounting System is an enormous time-saver for the company since many entries are made daily.

The correct accounting period

Accounting period cutoff is extremely important, and a mistake can completely distort the earnings statement of the company. Accounts payable must be closely motored to determine that all expense and costs are recorded for a given month and the none of the following month's transactions are included. If an item is not included in the appropriate month because the invoice has not been received, the ACPAYS system can remain open for a short time into next calendar period to accept these late entries. Such practices are rather common.

One area that has traditionally been problematic is noncash transactions. Appreciation of fixed assets and amortization of prepaid expenses two examples. They may be beyond the experience and ability of the company bookkeeper, but the firm's

CPA can review the need for these entries, and the appropriate amount entered on a quarterly basis. These items lend themselves to accurate projection, and determining each month's entries for a quarter in advance should adequate.

Accounting periods

FAS has 13 accounting periods, one for each month plus a thirteenth period year-end adjustments. The use of this thirteenth period allows the twelfth period be unaffected by usual year-end adjustments. It also allows proceeding to the period of the next year, and periods beyond, while the year-end accounting work being performed.

The 13-period accounting practice is not common, but has some particular advantages. The goal of a closely monitored accounting period program is to mean performance along many dimensions during each period, compare that perform to a variety of benchmarks, and provide data both diagnostic and planning purposes.

At year end, there is always a variety of housekeeping chores that red entries to be made to the general ledger; debts written off as uncollectable, invent adjustments, all types of reversals and compensating en and the like. If these year-end entries were all made in the twelfth period, the ..... twelfth-period performance would be distorted and masked by those "special" entries.

Therefore, an imaginary calendar period is created and used as the dumping ground for all those special entires. In fact, this thirteenth period runs concurrently with the first period. The thirteenth period can remain open as long as necessary. Although the thirteenth period has no definite time limits, it should remain open until all entries have been made and then closed to permit the production of the final financial statements and to update a new year's ledger.

The thirteenth-period concept serves two purposes: it prevents the distortion of the twelfth period by the year-end adjustment and reversal journal entries, and it permits the first period of the new year to accept journal entries while keeping the old year's books open for year-end activity. The thirteenth period is automatically opened with the closing of the twelfth period. It is closed by an option in the EOY program.

All the systems are open for one and only one book period at a time except FAS and ACPAYS. Vendor's invoices for a given month may be received during the following month, requiring the ability to select the month to which an invoice can be charged. An example is a vendor who ships merchandise that is received in a given month but is slow to mail the invoice, resulting in receiving the invoice during the following month. This system allows the recording of the receipt of merchandise in the proper month.

After month end, the usual sequence of events leading to the production of financial statements is:

Recording additional vendor invoices through ACPAYS

Recording noncash entries and adjustments

Requesting financial statements

The additional correcting entries that might be required can be made, and statements requested, a second time. This procedure can be repeated until statement accuracy and completeness is achieved. It is important that no entries be made after final statements are prepared. Formally closing the month assures no change these final monthly statements.

In the discussion here, and in EOM, several types of closing have been described. In summary, they are as follows:

Nominal period closing: at the end of the month, as determined by the calendar date, and accomplished by EOM.

Functional period closing: when the final financial statements are produced after all ACPAYS entries are made. This will normally be sometime after nominal period closing up to the tenth of the following month.

Actual period closing: in reality, true period closing occurs when a period flag is set. This flag is driven by an option in the FAS system. Thus financial statements can be produced and reproduced until the period formally closed by FAS.

The closing of the twelfth period opens four monthly periods in the future period, the thirteenth period. Four months in the new year provide adequate time to close the old year. Often it takes more than a month or two to close a year, and no ...... month can be closed until the one preceding it has been, because asset and liability entries are carried forward.

The closing of period 12 causes the passing of the balance sheet account balances to the first period of the next year. Revenue and expense account balances are not passed to the next year but begin with zero. Period 13 adjustments are passed to period 1 of the next year when period 13 is closed, allowing audit entries to pass to the next year.

One of the most useful exercises in business management is budgeting, not because it is a numerical estimating procedure, but because it forces thorough planning. The successful manager normally spends perhaps one-third of his or her time planning. Planning takes many forms. The Profit Model approach to business is one that implies an MBO approach to management. in MBO, the senior manager is concerned with the global company environment—competition, suppliers, customers, and government. In MBO the lower-level managers are assigned the task of tactical response to the company strategy. For example, how is a 15% return on net worth to be realized? A 3% increase in sales, a 2% improvement in gross margin, and a 1% reduction in selling expense might be a tactical response to such a strategic goal.

Budgeting the reduction of the company's plans to a common denominator, the dollar, for a given period. Budgeting is the test to determine if the plan will achieve the desired results.

Some of the advantages of budget planning are:

The formal process causes thorough study of problems and opportunities.

Goals and objectives are clearly defined.

Others in the company have the opportunity to input their ideas and suggestions.

Capital expenditures are planned and controlled.

Operations are better controlled by comparing actual performance to budget.

The budget should be begin with a written plan covering marketing, people, and capital. Objectives should be set with specific dates by which they are to be accomplished.

A sales goal should be determined and broken down by customer, territories, salespeople, and so on.

Expenses can be budgeted according to the plan and the sales budget.

If the profit result is not equal to the desired level in the plan, the plan may need to be revised, or certain management changes made in the operation, to reduce the impediment to results. Thorough budgeting permits attention to be focused at specific variances, and corrective measures to be targeted at problems rather than broadcast shotgun style.

Budgets and budgeting improve with age. In a company with no previous budgeting experience, the first budgets constructed may be crude at best, but with feedback to performance and through the revision process, succeeding iterations improve in accuracy. Once realistic budgets can be prepared, the budgeting process can be a helpful tool to achieve targeted goals.

FAS allows the budget data to be entered by account and by month. In this manner, budget data always follow actual data, and the financial statements will permit direct comparison of actual to budget. Thus, company performance can be tracked against the same period last year.

Control through FAS

The double-entry accounting method is used in this series of programs. All entries are made in debit-credit pairs which offset or balance each other. The system automatically distributes transactions to the proper accounts, and assures that these accounts balance.

Certain accounts in the general ledger must be reconciled with the appropriate system. Accounts receivable and accounts payable trade general ledger account should be compared to the detail of the appropriate system often, perhaps weekly, certainly no less than once a month. Since all subsystems are integrated, it would be unusual for them to differ. If they are out of balance, it is much easier to locate the difference early. If they do not agree, an error exists, and early detection might prevent presenting an erroneous statement to a customer or paying the wrong amount to a vendor.

The inventory balance in the general ledger should be compared monthly to the Inventory Management System. Because of timing differences in recording receipt of merchandise and vendor invoices, the two systems will seldom be exactly equal, but differences of any size should be explored immediately. This reconciliation may be difficult and require considerable effort. The effort is worth while and should be undertaken, especially in the first year of conversion to the system.

File development

The General Ledger File is the only direct file contact between FAS and the Database The General Ledger Database File is laid out as shown in Table 12.2 Budget fields are loaded via screen. Last-year summary data are calculated as part of EOY and transferred to the new general ledger. The account number and description fields are loaded via file maintenance. The system will not permit an account to be eliminated if it has a status code of "I," indicating that this account is autofed by a subprogram.

The status code can be changed to "0" by using the security-protected Maintenance Menu,but this should be done only after a detailed examination of the systems' documentation to determine which account should be substituted for the deletion candidate, and the appropriate programming changes made.

The data fields are filled period by period as transactions occur. The field for last-year summary data is filled by the EOY program and transferred to the new general ledger diskette as part of EOY. The data elements behave like balance-forward registers; that is, they accumulate to the previous balance the net of new entries, to derive a new balance.

ACRES: The Accounts Receivable System

Highlights

- Accounts Receivable Statements can be produced accurately, and on timely basis, to aid in the collection of outstanding obligations
- Automatic entries can be generated into the Financial Accounting System for cash management
- Past-due positions of customers can be controlled
- Credit history can be collected

- Audit trails can be produced for cash and sales accounting
- Summary data can be provided for cash flow projections
- Salespeople's performance can be reported
- Productivity is increased through clerical efficiency
- Established controls decrease the possibility of embezzlement

The two largest assets owned by a distribution company are the inventory and the accounts receivable. Often, a business must borrow cash to operate because the days of cash outstanding in accounts receivable are excessive. Every effort must be made to reduce the cash investment in receivables and to maintain a no-nonsense attitude toward the establishing of credit and the collection of funds. It this chapter the necessary reports or tools are presented to aid in the monitoring of customers outstanding credit balances and the collection of funds.

The Journal Entry Report is an audit trail report. Each entry of cash applied sales made, credits issued, and adjustments input are reflected. These entries are booked each day to the Financial Accounting System. The Accounts Receivable Statement is a primary tool used to collect funds. The statement must reflect the exact status of the customer's account, and state all terms in an easy-to-understand uncluttered format. The Aged Trial Balance is a cash management and audit trial report which provides the exact status of every entry into the system. This report is used to monitor customers' outstanding obligations, and as a guide to the application of cash.

The Past Due Report is a management information and collections report, and highlights those customers who are late with payments. This report warns the manager that action is required immediately. The Sales by Salesperson is a sales management report which recaps customer sales activity by salesperson with an overall recap for management. This report could be requested weekly to monitor the progress of each salesperson and of each customer. Every opportunity must be exercised to increase sales and improve collections.

System relationships

A full integrated database-driven system requires several files to be available when processing is planned. In the above figure, the relationships of each of the inputs and the outputs are shown.

Daily invoices and credit memos from COPIS are automatically entered into an ACRES Daily Task file and into the Customer Open Invoice Workfile during the EOD procedure. These entries are combined with all other outstanding invoices and credit memos for each customer, and a detail of each account is available for reporting. Payments are direct inputs to ACRES each day and are applied to each customer's account. Invoices increase the customer's liability and payment and credit memos decrease the liability. The customer's outstanding balance, which is maintained on the

Customer Database File, is automatically updated with each entry to the system and is continually compared to the previously established credit limit. This allows automatic credit checking in COPIS and the opportunity for direct inquiry whenever it is desirable. Journal entries that will be fed to the Financial Accounting System in the EOD procedure are recorded on the Customer Open Invoice Workfile when payments are posted, or accounts receivable nonmerchandise adjustments are made. The invoicing and credit memo journal entries are also passed to the Customer Open Invoice Workfile by COPIS in that system. The output reports can be requested when desired. The Journal Entry Report is automatically produced each day as an audit trial of all entries being passed to the Financial Accounting System. Daily balancing is a necessary procedure to ensure that errors are detected as quickly as possible. The aged Trial Balance and the Accounts Receivable Statements should be requested on a fixed date each month. A firm policy of statement mailing dates helps give the customer the impression that the collection of funds is taken seriously by the distributor. The Past Due Report should be requested weekly. A careful review of each delinquent account will pinpoint those customers who are moving to a risk position. Sales by Salesperson could also be requested weekly. This report could be printed in descending sequence by total sales for each customer by salesperson. The salesperson will have a guide to which customers to call on for an order, and management can monitor the progress of each salesperson. This report is not only a history report; more important, it can be used as an action report. After a sales period has ended, it is too late to affect the outcome of that period.

Business considerations

Accounts receivable frequently form a sizable portion of current assets. Retailers have, to a large extent, passed responsibility to others, such as the bank card companies. But companies involved in intermediate distribution have not made this change. They are responsible for administering their own accounts receivable.

The problem/challenge of accounts receivable is both tactical and strategic. The tactical problem is frequently how to collect money from people who may be customers in the future. An information system can affect the tactical problem only indirectly by alerting the manager to potential problems. In terms of strategy, accounts receivable is a critical profit variable and a major component of asset turnover calculations.

The net deterioration in return on net worth is 17% as a direct result of permitting accounts receivable to rise 28%. This emphasizes the importance of controlling even one of the less obvious company assets, such as accounts receivable.

The reports outlined in this section are designed to provide the tools required to monitor sales progress and the collection of funds. The reports also provide an audit trail of sales, cash receipts, and related information.

Journal entry reports

As checks and cash are received, a complete accounting of the funds, including and audit trial, are needed to ensure that control is maintained. The journal entry reports should be produced automatically in each EOD procedure, with clerical checking and balancing being performed by a responsible person. The report shows the application of cash or checks to individual invoices in each customer's account. The customer's check number and the total amount of the check received are displayed in case a question arises about which check was received or for how many dollars. Application of funds are shown as they are applied to each invoice or to unapplied cash. The approved discounts allowed and the adjustments to any line from the Customer Open Invoice Workfile are displayed as an adult trail for balancing purposes. For example, Customer Number 9100-9 refused to pay a service charge (SC) on a late payment. The accounts receivable clerk was authorized to adjust the customer's account for the amount of the service charge forgiven . Customer Number 9495-3, Invoice Number 040616, took 1 cent too much discount. The accounts receivable clerk was authorized to adjust the account for the amount of the service charge for given. The report totals recap the entries to the Financial Accounting System by account number. After clerical balancing is complete, the report should be bound with all other Journal Entry Reports from previous days and held for the auditor.

All invoices processed each day are automatically fed to the Customer Open Invoice Workfile during the EOD procedure. The COPIS Daily Sales Journal—MIS Recap, shows the distribution of all moneys from COPIS into the Financial Accounting System (FAS) by account number and account name. This is part of the formal audit trail and must be balanced each day, bound with other daily sales journals, and held for the auditor. Note the management information that is included in this report: gross margin dollars and percent for invoices and credit memos, service levels and finally, an analysis of the entire accounts receivable aging. All of this information is current as of the closing of each days business and can be a very powerful tool for action—oriented management.

Statements

A distributor's first contact with a customer requesting money is the invoice. The invoice should be simple, complete, and descriptive. The customer should have no trouble understanding the invoice, when the money is due, how much discount can be taken, and item pricing as previously agreed on. These are positive elements of information. Negative elements can also be featured on the invoice. A statement of service charge rates can be shown, together with the company's position on COD (Cash On Delivery of merchandise) order if the customer becomes past due. Finally, the invoice should provide the mailing address for checks. If customers do not pay by invoice, then the statement becomes the next payment request received by the customer.

Again, all the requirements for an invoice are doubly true for the statement. In addition, the statement should show all open debits and credits, including all payments and credit memos submitted since the last statement was issued. all unapplied cash and unapplied credit memos. All service charge records that were unpaid as of the last statement, and the service charges for this statement, should also appear on the statement. If an invoice is in contention, that invoice should be flagged. Blocks for various aging should be used. This aging reminds the customer of the status of the account. Some industry groups may include an aging block for future due invoices.

A modified open item statement will display the cash/checks remitted by the customer since the last statement. This is done to provide the customer with documentation of payments received. A return stub should be provided so that the customer can indicate the amount of payment. This increases the accuracy of clerical processing of cash applications when the remittance is received. Finally, the statement totals should be easily cross-footed by the customer, remembering that accounts probably are not processing the payments. Typical totals are: grand total duc, discount allowed if paid by (date), net due, and the current, and past due position of the account. When statements are requested, several program steps must be performed. Service charges should be calculated for display on the statement. Age tags should be generated for each entry on each customer's account and assigned to that entry. All invoices and credit memos that are paid should be flagged and would remain on the file for days.

The Balance Forward Statement is sometimes used by distributors. A balance forward statement shows one dollar total line for all invoice and credit memos open from previous billing periods and the detail of invoices and credit memos for the current period. this type of statement is almost always used for business-to-individual statements but is not recommended for a business-to-business statement. If the determination is made to use a balance forward statement was business-to-business accounts, a complete open item accounting must be maintained within the microcomputer system and should be displayed on the Aged Trial Balance Report and on the payment application CRT screen. The open item information necessary if a payment problem arises with an invoice and as an audit trail.

Statements and invoices must be submitted to customers on a rigid schedule Invoice should be sent with the merchandise unless the "ship to" and "bill locations are different. Sending the invoice with the merchandise will hopefully the obligation into the customer's accounting system sooner, and will certainly avail postage, envelope, and handling costs. These costs are not insignificant.

Assume postage, envelopes, and handling cost of $2.50 per invoice.
Assume 500 invoices per month

Savings realized by sending invoice with the merchandise are $1250 per month.

Statements should be printed and mailed on the last Friday of the month so that there will be in the customer's office on Monday, or no later than Tuesday. There is available postage bill, so use the same envelope to send promotional materials "Attention Buyer." This will be less effective with some larger companies because the mailroom or accounts payable section may not forward the materials as requested. Larger companies usually pay by invoice and a statement need not be sent if their policy states that they pay by invoice. Use a standard window envelope to mail the statement so that bill-to name and address will show through. Color on the Accounts Receivable Statement form costs more but could be worth the additional cost if the distributor's image demands this extra flair.

The customer has now been presented with a timely and accurate invoice and a timely and accurate statement, both requesting payment. The next logical inducement for early payment is the company's cash discount policy and the willingness to enforce the established policy of not allowing discounts on late payments.

The cash discount policy varies by industry group tradition, and this tradition usually forces the distributor to follow the industry. It is very important that a clearly defined policy be established with the customer and that the policy be enforced.

Cash discounts are given whenever a customer pays a statement totally within a stated period of time after the statement is produced. Typically, the terms are 20% of the merchandise total if paid by the 10th of the next month, with the gross invoice due at the end of that month. The shorthand way to display this method is 2% 10th prox, net EOM. Note that the discount is calculated only on merchandise charges, not on freight, taxes, or other nonmerchandise charges. Also note that a credit memo can have the cash discount charged back. For example, a customer buys one item valued at $100 and takes a 2% cash discount. The customer has actually paid $98 for the item, and if it is returned, the cash discount of $2 should be reversed from the gross of $100.

Another type of cash discount policy that is standard in some distribution industry groups is stated in days after invoice date rather than proximo. This type of cash discount implies that the customer pays by invoice and does not receive a statement. The shorthand way to display this method is 2% 10 days, net 30 days. Two percent of the gross on the invoice may be taken if the customer will pay within 10 days after the invoice is produced.

A copy of the statement should be bound and held for future reference. If the customer calls with a question about the statement, an exact copy is readily available for reference. The statement copy is not normally part of the formal audit trail because no entries were made from this processing run to the accounting system.

Aged trial balance

The Aged Trial Balance Report is a complete and detailed record of the position of each customer's account. The report should show all COPIS invoices and credit memos that were unpaid as of the last statement run or billed since the last statement run. Full and partial payments, unapplied cash, and unapplied credit memos will be shown, as will service charge records that were unpaid as of the last statement run, or were generated on the last statement run. Adjustments should be shown until flagged at the next statement run time. If a contention code is used, it should be displayed until it is removed by changing the status of the invoice or a payment or credit memo is applied against it. If the code is manually removed, aging should be calculated on the original invoice date.

The Aged Trial Balance should be available to print when desired. It is always printed immediately the statement run and at EOM, where it should be bound and held for the audit trail. The customer detail information provided on this report is available on the system simply by requesting a screen display. The application of cash should be performed on-line and normally would not require the clerk to refer to this report prior to applying the cash. Other than as an audit trail, the primary use of this report is for credit and collections decision making, and as a cash planning tool.

Past due reports

A distributors does not need a customer who does not pay his or her bills. Some customers will eventually pay their bills, but require continued correspondence before the payment is rendered. Both types of customers are expensive to do business with, and the distributor must determine how these types of accounts will be handled. Approximately one-half of all new businesses established each year fail. When a business fails, a lot of merchandise suppliers are hurt.

The Past Due Report should be requested at least weekly. A careful review of each customer's status will help spot those customers who are in the early stages of creating a problem for the distributor. Quick, decisive action is required. first, a telephone call should be made to determine if there was a problem with the merchandise received or with the invoice. Any complaint should be resolved immediately and communication reestablished to be sure that the customer is satisfied with the results. If the problem has been resolved, ask when the payment can be expected. If the payment is not received as promised, a decision must be made on the account status. COD is the next recourse. Another phone call should be made to discuss the new account status with the customer. If the distributor has clearly stated its policies on the invoice and on the statement, this step should be routine.

The Past Due Report should also be used to document phone calls to delinquent customers. the report is double-spaced to allow the collection staff to note why the customer has become past due, what agreed upon to resolve the problem, when the payment will be made, or if a request for credit is required. This becomes an excellent credit history, so it should be filed for reference.

Some distributors requires the salespeople to collect past due funds from customers. Sales commissions should be paid on gross profit realized basis so that the salesperson has a vested interest in selling to credit-worthy customers and in collecting the funds due. Other distributors feel that the salesperson should sell and the office collect the funds. this is the good guy, bad guy, and is generally considered preferable.

The Past Due Report is a management information and collections report. The customer's name and phone number are displayed to save look-up time if a phone call is needed. the total balance and the aging are recapped for ease of determining the status of the account, If detail is needed, it can be requested on the CRT secrecy or will be available on the last Aged Trial Balance Report. Finally, the salesperson number is displayed for reference. All customers should be displayed on the report so that the overall total will accurately reflect the total dollars and percentages in each category.

Sales by salesperson

The salesperson needs to know during the month how much he or she has sold and to whom. The salesperson probably has a monthly sales quota established by the company. He or she is on commission, so desires to beat the quota to increase his or her income. Management needs to monitor the progress of sales on a regular base during the month to be sure that the total company can meet or beat the quota. The Sales by Salesperson Report should satisfy both the salespeople and management. This report should be produced by each salesperson, with the accounts for which he or she is responsible sorted by largest gross sales to smallest or no-sales month to date. An example of this report is displayed. For each salesperson, the customer name and number are printed, the type of customer, credit memo information, stock and nonstock sales, noncommission billings, gross sales, contribution dollars and percent, and the past due status of each account. If this report provided to the salespeople each week of the month, they have an opportunity review their accounts to determine where more effort should be applied to meet or beat the quota.

Management is concerned about individual sales and contribution, and the company's performance month to date. On the MIS Recap, Sales by Salesperson, each salesperson's performance is presented on a single line and the overall company performance is shown on the total line. Since the report is produced weekly, management has the opportunity to react to an adverse situation before the month is history. The EOM report can be used to calculate commission for each of the salespeople and as a review of the performance on a period basis.

System inputs

Customer open invoice workfile

At the end of each day, EOD summarizes each invoice and credit memo into a oneline entry that is added to the Customer Open Invoice Workfile. One special customer number could be used for over-the-counter cash sales if a microcomputer-produced individual invoice is not desired. This procedure would be used to relieve the inventory, and account for cash, when an individual audit trail for each sale is not needed. If the over-the-counter cash sales are a large part of the business, an invoice for each sale can be produced. Cash sales will be reflected as accounts receivable, and payments applied from the cash drawer would relieve the account.

Customer payments

As money is received into the company, very careful accounting and application of funds is needed. Checks may come in the mail, or be delivered by customers, salespersons, or a delivery person. Cash may be received from over-the-counter sales or possibly from COD deliveries. As soon as practical each day, cash application must be made to the Accounts Receivable Customer Open Invoice Workfile.

The Customer Open Invoice Workfile contains all open invoices, credit memos, debit and credit adjustments, unapplied cash or unapplied credit memos, and all payments received sine the last statement was processed. As payments are applied, each record is tagged with payment date, discount taken, and remaining balance if any, and is not removed from the file until the next statement run is processed. This allows the history of payments and relievals to be available for reference throughout the month. It allows flexible reporting on the statement, and allows a history file to be built as an audit trail.

Customer payments are applied directly to each individual invoice. The net amount and the discount allowed should be entered. The actual discount allowed should be entered, because program calculations of discount allowed could vary by a penny or a few cents, and the cost to remove this difference from the file would be greater at some future date than simply to allow the difference when first applying the cash. If a partial payment is received, a discount should not be allowed.

For larger Customer Open Invoice Workfiles, other methods of cash application may be considered which could save clerical entry time when applying cash. Application by aged group is an option as well as application by sequence number.

At times, a payment cannot be applied to a specific outstanding invoice. A prepayment may be received for merchandise that would be shipped in the future, or the customer could have paid an invoice a second time by error. The cash should be entered as unapplied cash. A credit memo could have been processed against an invoice that has already been paid. The credit should be entered as an unapplied credit. The unapplied cash and the unapplied credit will reduce the customer's outstanding balance due, but will not relieve any of the outstanding invoices on the file. The unapplied cash and the unapplied credits must be manually applied, as soon as a determination can be made as to where to apply them. A daily review and application of the unapplied entries will keep them to a minimum.

Debit and credit adjustments can be made to the Customer Open Invoice Workfile on a daily basis as needed. these adjustments must be nonmerchandise. All merchandise adjustments must be processed through COPIS. Management may wish to write off a service charge on a specific customer's account, or sales tax may have been entered incorrectly. These are normally minor housekeeping adjustments to the file, but automatic journal entries will be generated to keep the Financial Accounting System in balance and as an audit trail.

Contention code

A customer may dispute an invoice and refuse to submit payment until the problem is resolved. If a solution is not immediately available, a contention code can be entered on the invoice record in dispute in the Customer Open Invoice Workfile. The contention code will be displayed on all listings showing that invoice, including the statement, and should move the contention invoice total to the current receivables position. The invoice in contention should remain in the current aged group until the dispute is resolved. When the contention code is manually removed, the invoice should be calculated on the original invoice date, and moved to the aged group in which it belongs. The system should allow the invoice in contention to be relieved, if a payment is applied, without manually removing the contention code.

Applying COD receipts

COD invoices produced in COPIS will move to accounts receivable during the EOD procedure. COD receipts must be applied against those invoices when the money is received. The cash application procedure is the same as for charge customers.

Over-the-counter sales

Cash from over-the-counter sales should be invoiced on one special customer number. The accounts receivable account should be maintained and payments from the cash drawer applied against that account each day. This procedure will force the daily balancing of the over-the-counter sales cash, and will book the proper entries to the Financial Accounting System. If over-the-counter sales is a "house account" on which separate reporting is desired, a salesperson's number for over-the-counter sales would be coded on the Customer Database File. Special elements of information can be coded on the Customer Database File which will cause the programs to provide specific information, or to perform a special task.

No statement code, when coded on the Customer Database File, would tell the program which produces the statements that this customer pays by invoice and a statement should not be printed. All of the processing, such as aged group calculation and flag, would be performed. the only action that does not occur is the statement print.

A no-service-charge code on the Customer Database File can be made available for those customers on which a service charge should not be calculated. A legal opinion on the selective application of service charge should be obtained before a decision is made to exempt some customers from the firm's service charge policy.

A cash-on-delivery (COD) code on the Customer Database file would tell COPIS that every order processed for this customer must be processed as a COD order. New, unknown customers, and those customers who violate the terms and conditions outlined on the customer invoice and the accounts receivable statement may be examples of COD code usage.

A consolidated customer-accounts receivable statement could be requested by a chain of stores or a buying group. A second customer account number coded on the Customer Database File will allow invoices to be sent to a number of customer buying locations, but one statement would be produced each month that would display all the invoices that were sent to all the buying locations. Obviously, the customer accounts payable group would probably be centrally located, and would pay the outstanding invoices for all the buying locations from this central location. The customer's accounts payable clerk can more easily reconcile a combined statement for payment, and the distributor's accounts receivable clerk can more easily apply the payment to the individual outstanding invoices.

A restricted merchandise code on the Customer Database File would not allow restricted items to be invoiced to a customer who is not authorized to purchase those items. Restricted merchandise items could be private label merchandise, firearms and ammunition, prescription drugs, or any other item that cannot be sold to the general public.

A customer can become inactive, and the distributor may desire to remove his or her name and address from the Customer Database File. A delete or inactive code can be input to the file. The customer number should not be used again for some extended period of time, because history must be maintained in several files. A customer should never be coded as inactive if there is a balance outstanding on the customer Open Invoice Workfile.

File development

In the ACRES system, the primary file of concern is the Customer Open Invoice Workfile. This file is developed as a part of EOD when the COPIS Open Invoice Taskfile is merged into the Workfile.

The Customer Open Invoice Workfile is a small file that contains information about every invoice or credit memo until it is paid, and for a period of time afterward. That period of time could be as short as a month or as long as a year or even two. The determination of the retention period is set by file-size parameters, since in an active business this file could grow quite large over a period of time.

The free field is included since the customer may be using a purchase order number, or other reference number, and this should be recorded to help identify the invoices to which a payment should be applied. the status code indicates the status, both internal and external. The various status codes used are:

0 Invoice due
1 Invoice fully paid but not journalized
2 Invoice fully paid and transaction journalized
3 Invoice partially paid but not journalized
4 Invoice partially paid and transaction journalized
8 Record ready to delete
9 Invoice in contention

These codes facilitate the proper recording of the data when they are summarized by EOD for the General Ledger Database. As in the case with the other status code routines in the system, for the most part, the status codes are maintained automatically by the system.

The Customer Database File is also used in the ACRES system to supply customer name, and to update the customer history and maintain an accurate customer balance.

Screens and procedures

The ACRES Menu is autofed from the Master Menu, and has five options. The first option is to post cash, and it autofeeds Screen 1.

Screen 2 requests input of a customer number, and responds with the customer name for verification. Once approved, the current open invoice lines for that customer are displayed. The line includes the invoice number, a contention code, the discount date, the amount due, the discount amount, the amount paid, the service charge paid, the discount taken, and a field to indicate whether the payment is a partial payment. Since the discount-taken field is supplied by the operator, errors of a penny or two do not create problems. The customer's calculation is accepted, provided that it is reasonably close. Sometimes, customers will refuse to pay service charges, and some companies will not insist that they be paid. By permitting the operator to indicate service charge payment, this policy can be flexible and the system still work.

To aid the operator, a running total of the amount credited during this session, for this customer, is posted and maintained at the bottom of the screen. It may be that the customer has several invoices open and sends a flat amount to cover as much of the debt as possible. After checking with the customer, the operator can apply the cash as directed, and a running total maintained at the bottom is an aid.

Once the end of the customer's list is reached, Screen 3 is autofed to afford the opportunity to input a line number for a change if an error has occurred. Once the total balances, and no more errors are found, Screen 4 is autofed.

Screen 4 requests another posting of cash, or returns control to the ACRES Menu.

Option 2 on the ACRES Menu autofeeds Screen 5 for the printing of statements. The date to appear on the statements is requested, and the statement form is noted to be inserted in the printer. After a carriage return, statements are printed and control is returned to the ACRES Menu.

Option 3, on the ACRES Menu prints reports, and it autofeeds the Report Menu, which is Screen 6. The Report Menu lists three different reports which can be printed, as well as a return to the ACRES Menu. Once the report is printed, the program loops to the beginning of the screen for another report or the optional return to the ACRES Menu.

Option 4 on the ACRES Menu feeds the Inquiry Screen. Screen 7 is the Inquiry Screen. It requests the customer number and responds with that customer's name. The screen then displays, line by line, invoice by invoice, all of that customer's currently open invoices. Essentially, the same data are displayed as when cash is posted.

If another inquiry is desired, the screen is refed. Otherwise, it loops back to the ACRES Menu. The final option on the ACRES Menu is a return to the Master Menu.

System flow and logic

Of particular interest is the logic involved in the creation of statements. First, the aging of receivables must occur. Second, the sequencing, or sorting of the customers, may be recommended to present the statement in a zip-code-sorted arrangement to take advantage of the postal-charge price break.

Aging requires careful consideration of local usury laws, to determine not only the allowable rates, but the necessary disclosure and method of calculation. Legal advice is advised.

The posting of cash also requires some discussion. As payments are made, the amount paid is entered and an appropriate discount made. If the operator deems the payment a partial payment, mark is made. All these option after the status attached to the record. The status code can be changed to contention via the inquire routine. If the customer has objected to the charges, the invoice is placed in contention until resolved. Again, care should be taken to research local statues, to determine legal requirements for invoices in contention.

Microcomputer considerations

The posting of cash is the most interesting procedure in the entire system. It required the maximum amount of screen handing called for in the system. Of note is the suggested format that displays several invoices on the screen and a current balance at the foot of the screen. The procedures is to increment line by line down the record on the screen, enter data, branch to the foot of the screen, display the updated running total, then return to the next field to be filled on the screen. This procedure requires selective address cursor addressing, which may be difficult on some version of BASIC. If the user has difficulty with this enhanced screen version, each record can displayed individually, payment made and checked, and/or passed to the next invoice line. This is not as convenient for the operator as displaying all the customer invoices at once, but it poses fewer screen-handling problems.

ACPAYS: The Accounts Payable System

Highlights

ACPAYS records business transactions involving merchandise purchases and expenses so that:

- Checks can be written automatically at a preselected future date to maximize cash discounts earned
- The general ledger can be posted automatically
- An audit trail is provided to assure appropriate control of funds
- Cash disbursements and requirements analysis are available
- Clerical efficiency is enhanced
- The possibility of embezzlement of funds is reduced through microcomputer control
- Budget versus actual expenses can be monitored
- Historical analysis of business transactions can be analyzed

The continued profitability of a distribution firm may be dependent on the resourcefulness with which funds are controlled. Historically, profit margins have been very this in distribution, and only the most aware and informed managers will have the capability to keep the firm competitive and profitable. The system developed in this chapter provides the tools required to control outgoing cash. This group of tools is usually referred to collectively as an Accounts Payable System. In this system, the daily detail transactions will be key entered into the system and held for future processing. The accounts payable checks, control reports, and the management information reports will be outlined and finally, there will be a discussion of the use of these reports or tools to manage the flow of funds and to increase the profitability of a company.

System relationships

In a fully integrated database-driven management information system, several files will be on line at the same time because they must interact with each other. In the above figure, the relationships of each of the accounts payable activities is graphically represented. When the Accounts Payable System is in operation, the Vendor Database File, the General Ledger Database File, and the Vendor Open Invoice Workfile are used. Detail from the vendors' invoices are the key inputs to the system. The paper or hard-copy outputs are checks and various control and management reports. The electronic outputs are entries to the General Ledger Database File, the ACPAY Daily Taskfile, and to the Vendor Database File.

Business considerations

Controlling the flow of funds is like shooting at a constantly moving target. Merchandise is purchased, services are received, and each vendor who provides the merchandise or services will submit an invoice for payment. Many vendors allow a discount if the invoice is paid by a specified date and a penalty or service charge assessed for all payments received after a second specified date. For example, a vendor's invoice terms may be 2% 10 days, NET 30 days, 1 1/2% service charge on late payments. If the distributor elects to pay the invoice within 10 days after the invoice date, 2% may be deducted from the gross merchandise total. The distributor may pay the net or invoice total in 30 days. After 30 days, he or she will be charged a 1 1/2% service charge per month or 18% annualized.

Prudent payables management is the act of optimizing the use of the vendor's money versus losing his or her goodwill and/or paying a service charge and/or suffering a bad credit rating.

A business cannot remain profitable by accident. There must be a comprehensive plan for the control of accounts payable—both merchandise and expenses. This plan should be continually budgeted, monitored, and adjusted. The National Association of Sporting Goods Wholesalers (NASGW) reported, in a 1980 survey of their members that the average net profit after taxes was 1.95%. The members could obtain a better rate of return from a passbook account in a savings and loan association with no risk.

Once a prudent investment has been made for merchandise or services, controlling the payment of cash for the merchandise or service becomes the responsibility of management. This automated Accounts Payable System does not replace the need for careful reconciliation and approval of every invoice submitted for payment. In fact, no payment transaction should be entered into ACPAYS without an authorized purchase order for merchandise on the major control side, or an "authorized vendor" for the intermediate control items and a known signature approving the payment of each invoice.This system will provide information that will allow management to make decisions in a controlled and informed environment.

Information must be used to be of value. In order to use information, that information must be provided in a logical, timely, and understandable format. The reports presented in this chapter are typical of the reports that should be available as output from an Accounts Payable System. The designer of a microcomputer program may modify some or all of these reports to better fit the needs of a particular distributor but these basic reports are required.

Daily validation report

Approved vendor invoices are entered via keyboard to the ACPAY Daily Taskfile either periodically during the day or batched for input at one time. Since the Daily Validation Report is first used to verify the accuracy of the keyed input, all the invoices that were input should be held for the end-of-day (EOD) output report procedure. Above figure demonstrates the action of key-entering the approved vendors' invoices, system verification of the vendor number, and the storage of the keyed information onto the ACPAY Daily Taskfile.

The end-of-day (EOD) procedure produces the Daily Validation Report, which includes all of the vendor invoices entered that day. The EOD procedure is shown in the following figure. The system will use the Vendor Database File and the ACPAY Daily Taskfile to produce the Daily Validation Report. A simultaneous action that will occur is the updating of the Vendor Open Invoice Workfile with the new entries from today. At the same time, the system will debit appropriate expense or merchandise accounts in the General Ledger Database File and credit the liability accounts.

The Daily Validation Report prints one line for each invoice entered. Important fields of information displayed on the report are payment due date, gross due, and discount. Projections for cash flow and check-writing dates and amounts are determined by the system using these fields of information. If a hand-written check is entered into the system, the date paid and the check number will appear on this report. The totals will reflect the dollars that have been booked into each of the general ledger accounts affected. The handwritten checks will not be displayed on the Cash Flow Projection Report but will appear on the next Cash Disbursements Register that is processed. The report's total routines show the overall report totals and also show the General Ledger Database File account breakdown for merchandise and expense invoices and credit memos entered. Finally, the General Ledger Database File account number and the amount booked to that account by the system are reflected under the report heading distribution of Invoices and Credit Memos. Distribution of handwritten checks is reflected in a separate report control total. These accounting entries are booked to the General Ledger Database File as a debit entry to the liability accounts and as a credit entry to the cash account. Booking these transactions at this time keeps the General Ledger Database File current and the cash balance accurate.

Voids

Voids are the third group of control totals shown on the Daily Validation Report. These are reversals to the general ledger. Occasionally, invoices or credit memos must be removed from the ACPAYS after they have been entered but before being paid. Examples would be invoices posted to the wrong vendor, invoices posted with the wrong account number, wrong accounting data, or other incorrect input data. In these cases, the system must provide for a "void" entry. This entry will remove the vendor's invoice from the Vendor Open Invoice Workfile, and reverse the original' general accounting and history data entries as well as produce a report of voids. When a void has been accepted by the system, the correct vendor invoice entry may be input to the system if applicable. The Void Report is a critical audit trail report, and every void must be reflected on the Daily Validation Report.

Cash flow projection report

In order to control the flow of funds, information must be available on which invoices need to be paid, when the payment is due, how much is to be paid, and what incentives are offered for early payment. The Cash Flow Projection Report is an invaluable cash flow management tool. This report can be current within minutes after the daily invoices have been entered into the system and the Daily Validation Report has been produced.

The information on the Vendor Open Invoice Workfile should be sorted by due date within vendor. This sort allows the report to be totaled by vendor and a simple scanning of vendors can be employed to authorize payment of invoices prior to check writing.

Besides the one line of detail for each invoice or credit memo and a total by vendor, the report displays a breakdown of gross dollars due, discount to be taken, and the net due in increments of 7 days. The overall total routines display the total number of vendors with invoices or credit memos outstanding, the total dollars due for expenses, the total dollars due for merchandise, and the overall total dollars due on all outstanding invoices. These totals must balance to the control liability account in the General Ledger Database File.

Accounts payable checks

Accounts payable checks can be printed on a daily or weekly basis or on the 10th and 25th of the month. The checks can be dated with the due date from the system and mailed on that day in the future, or the date printed on the checks can be any date that is input to the system at check-writing time. The prime consideration is to maximize the discount taken and to maintain cash in the bank as long as possible. Hopefully, cash in the bank will be drawing interest compounded daily, so even a weekend of interest can mean extra earnings.

The remittance statement is positioned over the check. A different form that can be used is the side-by-side check form, which place the remittance statement beside the check. Either form is acceptable. If more invoices and/or credits are displayed than will fit on one remittance statement, void the next check, and use that remittance statement to continue printing. The void check is not sent to the vendor but is handled as a normal void check. A separate remittance statement could be printed on stock paper and included with the check if the overrun was a normal occurrence in a particular firm.

Ideally, accounts payable checks should be triggered automatically by the system based on the due date. Any future date could be key-input to the system when a check run is requested and all invoices and credit memos would be relieved through that date. If cash flow will not allow the distributor to pay strictly by due date, the operator can trigger each invoice to print using a yes/no code as the CRT screen displays each invoice in sequence. The information for the operator could come from the Cash Flow Projection Report.

The original of the check with the remittance statement should be signed and mailed to the vendor on the date due. The envelope should be a standard size with a window so that the vendor's name and address will show through. This simple procedure will save the cost of a custom envelope and the time required to address the envelope.

The copy of the check with the remittance statement should be attached to the original input documents and filed as a physical audit trail in each vendor's accounts payable folder.

Void checks

Another type of voiding is required whenever a check has already been printed. In the case of overpayment, the automated check can be manually voided and rewritten correctly. A handwritten credit memo can be input which will correct the accounting and history data without affecting the Vendor Open Invoice Workfile. If underpayment was the case, the check can be voided as before, but a handwritten invoice can be input to correct all history and accounting files. The voided checks must be saved for the auditors, and if prenumbered checks are used, notes must be made on the Cash Disbursements Register to document the void check numbers.

Cash disbursement register

When the check-writing processing is complete, the CRT should ask the operator to remove the check form from the printer and insert stock paper. Once the starting check number for the checks written has been entered, the cash disbursements register will print. This report will act as an audit trail for all accounts payable checks written and for all disbursements of funds and the General Ledger Database File accounts to which these funds were booked.

Vendor purchases analysis report

This information history report can be requested as needed. It could be of value semiannually or annually when vendor reviews are performed. In negotiating with a vendor for more generous concessions, terms, or credit, knowledge of total yearly payments could be used as leverage. Items purchased from two or more vendors could be purchased from one of the vendors to obtain more generous concessions. Being informed about all vendor relations is a valuable negotiating tool.

System inputs

After the design of all output from the system is complete, the next task is to determine what will be used as input. If the system is automated, it is desirable that as many functions as possible be automated. For example, if the General Ledger Database File account number is coded on the Vendor Database File, the system will always go to this file to determine where ACPAYS entries are to be booked. No General Ledger Database File account number input is required unless split distribution is desired. Split distribution allows multiple entry of general ledger account numbers for any one invoice. The liability is still established but the distribution of dollars could be made to two or more accounts. In effect, the input of multiple account numbers would override the normal account numbers which are coded on the Vendor Database File and direct entries to account numbers specified on input. When the telephone bill is received, it might be company policy to allocate a certain percent of the total bill to office expense. Another percent to selling expense, and the remainder to warehouse expense.

The most obvious input to the Accounts Payable System is a vendor invoice. Vendors' invoices can be delivered in the mail, by hand, or sometimes with a receipt of merchandise or service. Each invoice is an obligation to pay for the merchandise or service that was ordered and delivered. Every invoice should be carefully audited for accuracy and correctness. A valid, signed purchase order should have been issued for all merchandise and services received. Less formal procedures can cost money in overpayments or duplicate payments.

As an audit trail, all invoices should be stamped with the date received. If a question arises about an unpaid invoice and the copy of the remittance statement for paid invoices does not reflect the invoice in question but the actual invoice can be found, the date stamped on the invoice will lead to the window of time when the invoice should have been key-entered into the system. If the invoice is found on the Daily Validation Report for the wrong due date, the wrong vendor, or the wrong invoice number, a correction to the file should be made. If the entire entry is correct, the only reason for not having paid the invoice was that the entry was voided from the Vendor Open Invoice Workfile.

A second input to the accounts payable system is manually prepared entries. Rent normally is not invoiced, but a liability should be established for cash planning. All noninvoiced entries could be input to the system just as if they had been invoiced on a monthly schedule as a regular function of the control group.

Occasionally, a vendor will insist on being given a check immediately, or for some other reason a check must be written prior to the time planned or the availability of the system. There is no real choice but to handwrite an accounts payable check. Even in this rush situation, a purchase order must be written and signed before the check is written.

This request must be handled in a logical way. Select the next accounts payable check number from the stock in the safe, handwrite the check, and complete the remittance statement. Note the date and check number on the purchase order copy and the invoice from the vendor. This invoice should be key-entered into the system with two additional elements of information: the paid date and the check number. By entering the transaction on the daily files, accounting entries will be made and the audit trail will be maintained. The handwritten check will not appear on the Cash Projection Report nor will another check be written for this invoice. The handwritten check will appear on the next Cash Disbursements Resister that is processed. This procedure will help to maintain the established controls.

Occasionally, a check will have been processed, and a determination is made that the check is not valid. The check should be voided and a manually prepared credit entered on the daily input. This will reverse all journal entries and correct the vendor history. The check numbers must be entered as a void on the next Cash Disbursements Register. A note can be written on the Cash Disbursements Register that the check was voided and why it was voided.

Meticulous control of the Accounts Payable System input and output requires very little time, but the benefits can be substantial.

File development

The basic file manipulation in ACPAYS is the building of a Vendor Open Invoice Workfile. This file is built, one record per vendor invoice, from each daily EOD run when the ACPAY Daily Taskfile is merged into the Vendor Open Invoice Workfile. The ACPAYS Daily Taskfile is built as invoice or handwritten check data are entered via keyboard into the system. The Vendor Open Invoice Workfile and the ACPAYS Daily Taskfile are 75 bytes long and contain the same elements.

Status codes

The use of the record status code is important because it enables the system to determine the status of each record in the Vendor Open Invoice Workfile. The code options are:

0 Invoice due

1 Check written but not journalized

2 Check written and transaction journalized

8 Record ready to delete

9 Invoice in contention

As invoices are entered into the ACPAY Daily Taskfile via the keyboard, they are automatically assumed to be "due," that is, to be paid according to the dates in the record.

The status code is passed to the Vendor Open Invoice Workfile from the ACPAY Daily Taskfile. When the check run is made from the Workfile, each record for which a check is written has its status code changed automatically from an "0" to a "1," indicating that the check has been written but not yet entered into the journal or General Ledger Database File. If the data on a handwritten check are entered, it is also given a record status code of "1," since the record has been but not yet journalized by the system.

Upon running the EOD program, each record with a status code of "1" journalized, and the record changed to a "2." The "2" status code will remain months, at which time the EOM program will change the record status code to "8," indicating that the record is to be deleted on the next EOM run. That EOM procedure wipes the record from the file after it creates a paper copy a audit trail.

If the vendor's invoice is in contention, that is, for some reason the invoice not to be paid according to the date schedule on the record, there is a manual procedure to change the record status code to a "9." An invoice might be in contention because the manager disagrees with an aspect of the charge. A listing of invoice contention is printed routinely as part of EOM to remind the manager continue that certain invoices are not paid and need attention.

Vendor database file

The Vendor Database File is also on line when ACPAYS is run so that the very number can be key entered, and the system displays the vendor name. This is a cl on the accuracy of the vendor number key entered. In addition, as payments made, the amount of each payment is added to the activity-to-date file element that accurate historical data can be maintained on each vendor.

23

Supervisory Management

There are differing opinions on management principles and practice. One view is that management science is similar to all other sciences, which rely on explanations and laws applying universally. Another view is that management science varies depending on the culture and environment applying in each instance. Research on this latter topic—comparative management—involves analysis of management in different environments and looks at why enterprises show different results in various countries. Certainly investigations show that *management philosophy* tends to vary in different countries but that organisational structuring and growth rely on logical, recognised practices for success.

Principles of management

All principles of management may be grouped to fit conveniently into seven main aspects of management activity. These are:

- forecasting
- planning
- organizing
- co-ordinating
- commanding
- controlling
- motivating

Forecasting and planning

These activities involve looking ahead and trying to visualise and plan effectively. Certain principles, now described, should be followed from the beginning to cut down the risks of inaccurate forecasting.

Research

Although the value of constant investigation is recognised and attempts are made to carry it out, in practice it becomes too difficult due to lack of time. People who are under pressure work must make decisions based upon less and less information, with the inevitable consequences. However, the sight of everyone working at high pitch pleases rather than bothers some managers. If managers are overworked it is their own fault for not delegating, but there is a limit if top management restricts staff to smaller numbers than are really adequate. Some managers, too, are unable to assess work content accurately, even after research has been conducted and the information is presented to them.

The following minor principles should be intrinsic to any research:

- *cause and effect* a belief that effects can be traced back to particular causes, which is the motivator when pursuing investigations back to sources
- *comprehension* the results must be measurable and presented in an understandable form to be of practical use in forecasting
- *intelligent observation* studying an activity requires a certain of awareness and appropriate background knowledge for intelligent interpretation to be possible
- *recognition and analysis* following from intelligent observation, the recognition of similarities is essential when analysing the information and knowing how to proceed to the next stage of investigation.

Forecasting

Armed with sufficient information, the individual must now find a place where it is possible to think without undue distraction. Having found the most suitable place, there he or she must marshal thoughts logically and try to visualise or predict future happenings. Some people call this process intelligent guesswork, luck or being psychic.

Forecasting is often done with very little information in difficult circumstances, hence the phrase muddling through. The unknown factor must be taken into account to maintenance. Consider the serious punters who attempt to marshal as many facts as possible on the horses in a race. They take everything into consideration, including factors such as the weather and injuries, which make the results unpredictable with any accuracy, in order to lessen the odds as much as possible.

The principles of good forecasting are:

- use all sources of information
- gain the maximum amount of information possible in the time available
- work in surroundings conducive to thought
- take account of the unknown factor.

Planning

The next is to determine the targets or objectives and plan a way to reach these goals.

All industrial activities must be considered in the light of the available resources so that plans will be realistic. The good planner will be thinking along lines of economy, which implies that his or her designs are simple, standardised and make due allowance for changes and each item is weighted depending on its importance to the plan. Scientific control is not possible, unless a plan is based upon a timescale. Planning on this broad front means deciding *what* shall be done, *where, when, how* and *by whom.* It involves not only readjustment of objectives as new information flows in, but also revision of policies, programmes, budgets, systems, organisation and controls.

Top management's task is *strategic* planning of overall policies, objectives, finance and control. This is implemented by managers senior supervisors who are responsible for *tactical* planning, or how the objectives are to be achieved in the time given.

Supervisors then plan - on a short-or medium-term basis - the actual achievement of broad plans using the resources available. This is *process* planning, involving scheduling, progressing, controlling and motivating employees.

The fourth and final phase must logically end with the shop floor or office where employees plan their work in order to complete the jobs allocated to them within the established time limits.

Organising and co-ordinating

Organising means arranging for everything to be at the right place, at the right time, so that work may proceed according to the plan. Co-ordinating means ensuring that all the formal activities of the concern are combined to form a balanced, effective organisation.

The phases that lead to co-ordination are:

- *planning* which includes organisation design or establishing the structure
- *staffing,* which is completed under the aspect of command
- *aligning everyone's efforts,* which is the eventual effect of co-ordination

When employees agree to co-operate and naturally participate willingly, management will be able to co-ordinate successfully. An underlying condition is the ability to lead and motivate people. It is pointless, therefore, for management to complain that employees will not co-operate, when the solution is within its own hands to create the right conditions that encourage and promote co-operation.

Co-ordination is achieved if all the activities are arranged and adjusted in time and situation to ensure smooth economic running and progress towards objectives. Smooth economic operation is an all-embracing term that includes the absence of selfish interests, that balancing of units and adherence to plans.

The problem of balance begins with the co-ordination of main activities or functions by the managing director and continues through to the level of the supervisor who co-ordinates the activities of that section or department with other sections. Balance is made possible by allowing unrestricted input of both information and production assemblies from those who supply the section and unrestricted output to the receiving sections in turn. If the chain of movement is broken, production is off balance and the co-ordinating effect ceases. In this sense, co-ordinating is an intentional active principle.

Commanding

Commanding means giving orders and issuing instructions *and* deciding when and how subordinates should carry out the work. Maintaining command includes making decisions about the relative priority of the jobs that need to be done and ensuring that discipline is kept at a reasonable level that is consistent with good working arrangements. Effective leadership is essential for commanding and motivating.

Although organisation and co-ordination are discussed together because all the principles of organisation are used to achieve co-ordination, in practice command must fall between the two for the following reasons. When the design and planning stage is completed, the next step is to appoint competent staff to the positions drawn up in the organisation plan. Upon completion of staffing, when the individuals are assigned to their jobs and given appropriate duties, authority and responsibilities, they will immediately start to issue instructions. Command becomes operational at this point and its effectiveness will depend upon the ability of managers and supervisors to raise morale by fair and just treatment and to lead in the right direction.

The guiding principles for achieving effective command follow.

Alignment of interest

All effort must be directed towards the general interest. Self-interest must take second place, otherwise command has failed.

Staffing

Appointing managers of the right calibre, consistent with company policy.

Morale

The acid test of command is unmistakably the general feeling of all employees - majority and minority groups - towards management and the company. Much ill-feeling and friction is possible between the two sides, so it takes courage and faith to carry out a long-term programme for morale improvement. A permanent change in management's attitude is essential, otherwise relationships will deteriorate rapidly again.

Adequate payments and appropriate penalties

Adequate payments for services and appropriate penalties for mistakes are two essential principles that should be second nature to the competent manager. Fairness and justice are essential to maintaining a good reputation. Any attempt to show favour to one person results in antagonising the rest. Where it is humane to deviate from the rule, the reason must be made known, whenever possible, if the circumstances are not already common knowledge.

Active participation

People must be allowed to expand their capabilities by using their own initiative, criticising and making suggestions openly with no fear of rebuff. In these conditions they feel more important and develop enthusiasm and drive in response to the progressive atmosphere.

Controlling

Checking performance and taking action to remedy deviations from the plan involves a constant vigil on all stages of the work and the costs incurred.

Effective control demands, *first,* full knowledge of the plans and instructions to proceed, *second,* accurate feedback on operations and results, *third,* a common measure to guage the amount of deviation from the plan and, *fourth,* positive action to correct the deviations.

Scientific control is not a haphazard affair; its operation is very demanding and cannot be switched on and off at random.

The board of directors is supplied with control information by the managing director to check on board policy and programmes, generally from the financial viewpoint. Management accountancy techniques and all the financial control systems connected with them provide the machinery for control throughout the company.

On the production side, information about labour, machines, materials, quality and output provides supervisors and specialist with control figures. Similarly, information about sales in cash and quantity and all the distribution expenses provides management with control statistics. All the information prepared must be worthwhile, providing figures at an economic cost for some positive purpose.

Motivating

Each managerial activity is dependent upon all the others, hence the main difficulty of thinking about a particular one in isolation. Managing is a combined operation that demands a wide, balanced, human outlook, tempered by the use of a multitude of principles.

Probably motivation—the inner force that stirs people from lethargic attitudes into dynamic action—is the most neglected aspect of management. Half-hearted attempts to improve matters, which are most often abandoned, irritate and depress employees; they naturally fail to respond to fresh encouragement and the blame is nearly always laid unfairly on their heads.

Successful motivation of employees requires a complete change in the outlook of most managers who are either unenthusiastic or too cynical or set in their ways to change. Long-term programmes are needed, even though results are sometimes not seen for a few years, to overcome management's faults and misconceptions. The strong tie between motivation and co-ordination is apparent when the principles involved are considered. These include:

- job enrichment programmes
- constant communication to everyone of all relevant information concerning the business
- encouragement of participation and self discipline
- ambitious education and training schemes
- joint consultation
- personnel counselling
- fair schemes of pay, work and welfare

a sincere management.

The skills cycle

Underlying and often permeating the principles described above are certain basic management skills that also apply to supervisors. By appropriate training it is possible to improve these skills through he repetitive process of practice and adjustment.The development of each skill also depends upon the degree of education in certain disciplines or knowledge areas.

Naturally there is a tendency for the disciplines to overlap into more than one skill and in actual operation the dividing line between some of the skills becomes blurred. For the sake of clarity, Fig. indicates these skills in sector form to show the cycle effect, which operates in a clockwise sequence, when logical thought is applied to the work process in any situation. The diagram also indicates some ways of checking on the supervisor's performance as he or she develops. A confusing factor is that, during the course of a working day, the supervisor will have to cope with many situations and people, which means that several of these cycles are in operation at any one time.

The tendency for some supervisors is to think that so long as employees have been told what is required of them that is sufficient to provide the essential motivating factor. 'I told them what to do but they didn't do it' is a very common saying in industry. Two skills are, in fact, necessary: first, action to achieve the plan, which is the communicating skill, followed by the motivating skill, which will decide whether or not the employees will actually do anything, although they may know what is required.

Any person who controls a labour force, whether large or small, must plan ahead as far as can be foreseen. Employees expect to work to a set plan and schedule and be controlled in accordance with the plan and changing circumstances. Absence of planning produces chaos where the work is actually being done. Individuals work from crisis to crisis, frustration develops and productivity is reduced to a minimum. Clearly the supervisor must allocate time for planning insufficient detail to satisfy the requirements of subordinates and production. Time spent on planning is never wasted, provided that the supervisor is reasonably proficient at the task. The extra thought should result in more accurate and detailed plans, with less risk of having overlooked possible difficulties. There is more likelihood, therefore, that the plan will be successful.

Planning supervisory activities

Most supervisory activities lend themselves to planning which leads to more effective supervision. A cross-section of the main aspects is given below.

Production

A large range of separate plans makes up the overall plan for production. Machine capacity, labour utilisation, scheduling workloads, supplies of materials, provisions for tools and equipment, safety devices, batch quantities and all other resources are planned and combined to form the production plan. Within this plan, the supervisor's section generally forms only a part of the whole production, which means that co-ordination with other sections is of primary importance. He or she must allow for this factor and be able to accept work in accordance with the overall production, supply work in sequence to the next section and be prepared to help in emergencies.

Objectives

Objectives must be intelligently planned to fit into a timescale within the capabilities of performance. Establishing unrealistic targets is a waste of time. Progress must be controlled and adjustments made as required. The total collapse of efforts to reach specified objectives is bad for morale; therefore, planning with too much optimism should be avoided.

Control

Effective control does not happen by chance. A plan of the particular activity must be drawn up on a time, cost, quality or quantity basis or some other form of standard by which results can be measured. Variances from the plan are now apparent by reference to the data and control is possible by taking appropriate corrective action. Planning and control must always be complementary.

Organisation

Haphazard growth, rigidity and disregard for organisation principles may be avoided with careful planning. Working towards the ideal organisation and making wise changes when the opportunities occur are made easier by conforming to a plan.

Work study

The introduction of work study can be made easier by planning a careful explanation to employees. The programme may include posters, literature, personal letters, films and introductory talks. Work study can be introduced with a minimum of disruption in this manner.

Planning the actual work to be studied may be based upon those sectors that are:

- causing hold-ups
- expensive to operate
- trouble-spots
- relatively high labour turnover areas
- where an increase in output is contemplated.

Communication

Communication may be improved by having experience in running the particular section and by a plan of methods, routes and check systems. Suitable improvements may be planned to eliminate weak spots. A simple plan would begin with an assessment of each communication between supervisor and subordinates, thus revealing its importance, the time factor, the cost and the confidentiality factor. It should then be possible to select the best means of communication for each kind of message from the methods available. The objective is to ensure that the right person receives the right message at the right time and interprets it in the right way.

The daily routine

Planning the way each day is to be spent is important. Certain daily tasks cannot be neglected and, unless the supervisor plans the day or week, the risk of some vital activity being overlooked is greater. Simple check-lists are useful reminders of daily and periodic tasks that otherwise may easily be forgotten. More elaborate activities that extend over long periods may be charted on the wall by using a time base across the top of a sheet and an activity base down the left-hand side to form a grid. Each square may be either ticked or used to enter details if on a larger scale. Pending jobs may be, similarly, progressed or listed, a pending tray or file being used for the paperwork.

In conjunction with delegation, the supervisor should plan to off-load duties as the opportunities occur and use the freed time for more important tasks that have been rather neglected.

Health and safety

Reducing the accident rate and promoting health depend upon detailed planning by management and the supervisor. Planning for safety is an integral part of reducing accidents to a minimum by making machinery and equipment less hazardous and promoting the right attitudes towards safety. The supervisor's social responsibility cannot be fulfilled unless he or she plans to prevent accidents rather than wait for them to happen and *then* reduce the risk.

Maintenance

Planned maintenance is similar in some ways to planned safety. Time and cost may be cut by planning the maintenance of machines to reduce the risk of breakdown. Replacing those components and assemblies whose life is limited before a breakdown occurs ensures smooth output flow.

Training

Training must be treated seriously as a planned activity to improve productivity by introducing better methods and safer ways of working to reduce fatigue and frustration.

Planned training includes induction training schemes, training employees to use new machines as obsolescent models are superseded, training newcomers at weak points where hold-ups are occurring or are likely to occur and making hazardous operations safer by increasing the skill of the employee.

Motivation

All that was said above regarding management and motivation applies at the supervisory level also. All factors that affect motivation closely interact so the approach must be on a broad front so that employees can develop their capabilities and enthusiasm simultaneously. The plan must be long term and sustained in application. New techniques of leadership and supervision, group activity, organisation, human relations and job satisfaction are essentially long-term projects and need a sustained effort whereas financial incentives are short term and often short-lived as motivators.

Human relations

The supervisor who plans successfully also improves relationships with subordinates. They have more faith in a leader who defines objectives, plans carefully and shows command of the situation. Morale will rise as schemes materialise and employees benefit from effective plans.

The above-mentioned topics are only an indication of the many activities that must be planned by the supervisor. Savings in time and nervous energy and possible by planning any activity. Some guides to better planning are now given, together with the characteristics of a sound plan.

Guides to better planning

- *Planning must not be postponed:* Planning is hare work but, without plans, work becomes much harder.

- *Planning must not be selfish:* The part played by the section within the organisation must be remembered; therefore, co-operative and co-ordinated elements are essential in plans.
- *Always plan within a realistic timescale:* Effective control depends upon measurement of work or a project within a period and, furthermore, employees tend to work within periods related to output, which means they work to time targets.
- *Marshal as much information as possible:* on employees, machines, equipment, materials and other resources. Use up-to-date information and all available resources.
- *Aim to provide as much detail as possible:* There is less chance of overlooking important points and more chance of work proceeding to plan if there is thorough coverage.
- *Ask for opinions and ideas:* Many individuals have something to contribute towards a sound plan; therefore, ask now and avoid adverse criticisms later.
- *Define the problem or objective clearly before planning commences:* Look at the *whole* project and break it down into its constituent parts to ensure full coverage and to provide a workable scheme.
- *A sound, workable and economic plan is the outcome of something more than logical marshalling of information into a set routine:* Certain intangible qualities must be cudgeled into activity within the supervisor's mind. He or she must be imaginative and creative, exercise judgment and perception and yet retain an objective, critical approach to the problem.
- *Have the courage to stand by the plan.*
- *Check and revise the plan as circumstances change.*

The following are ten characteristics of a sound plan:

- economic, within the financial capabilities of the concern
- workable, considering the resources available
- thorough, allowing for most contingencies
- balanced, to blend with other plans
- resilient, to cope with unforeseen changes
- worthwhile, fulfils a desirable purpose
- attractive, creates interest among all who are concerned
- detailed, to establish adequate procedures

- timely, to obtain maximum benefit
- impersonal, avoids personal prejudices.

SWOT analysis

Useful in planning, problem solving, decision making, case studies and projects, SWOT stands for analysing Strengths, Weaknesses, Opportunities and Threats.

Studying situations or organisations under these headings and completing the information in four boxes forces an analysis of the situation from diverse viewpoints. Thus, a more comprehensive base of knowledge about how the company works provides opportunities to build on the company's strengths, minimise its weaknesses, take advantage of opportunities and allow for external environmental difficulties. The technique applies equally at different organisation levels.

APACS

This practical application of SWOT provides a logical framework for study; the letters stand for Adaptive Planning and Control Sequence. The steps are:

- state objectives
- appraise SWOT
- specify activities involved
- evaluate courses of action
- forecast results of alternative actions
- implement the chosen plan
- assess outcome
- modify accordingly

Problem solving

Problems and choices are met in all supervisory and managerial activities and must be dealt with, reputations being built or ruined on individual performance. The supervisors often automatically establish standards for a vast number of control aspects connected with problem solving without fully realising the implications to their subordinates. Human behaviour is a typical example where the supervisors expect a particular code of conduct in many different situations. They are faced with a problem when a standard is violated and if they fail to investigate, find the cause and make a decision, control is lost. Often many managers do not even realise that there is a problem to be solved. Unfortunately problems do not solve themselves effectively, although some managers will openly admit that they believe that if a problem is left for a sufficient length of time it will solve itself. Such managers have not bothered to check on the results of this negative approach, which ultimately brands them as ineffectual.

Standards

Employees also apply their own standards to many aspects connected with their job. One operator, for example, may switch off a machine immediately a fault is suspected, whereas another may wait until a more obvious sign appears. This range of standards among individuals becomes important when it comes to problem solving. One operator, for instance, may report that a machine failed to start when switched on, whereas another may state that when the machine was switched on a smell of burning was noticed. Careful definition of the problem in the latter case immediately narrows down the cause of the fault.

The use of standards - in a broad sense - for gathering information should not be ignored. The approach to obtaining the facts as they appear should be made on a basis of comparison to find a common factor or an isolating component within that factor. A line of machines, for instance, may be powered from the same electricity point; if one machine suddenly ceases to run, the fault may be isolated to a particular section if the basis of comparison is applied by stating whether or not the other machines continue to run. Investigating a problem in this way helps to isolate areas quickly where the cause is likely to be found.

The use of standard practice or standard set-ups is common to many facets of industrial activity. Some examples are the following:

- *the use of raw materials in batches* if faulty work appears it may be isolated to a particular batch that is below standard
- *planned maintenance programmes* when a machine develops a fault it may be possible to trace it to the last maintenance job
- *shift work* a mistake may be isolated to a particular shift or time coinciding with the changeover from one shift to another.

To summarise: problems must be actively solved; the art of recognising and carefully defining problems must be developed the causes of faults may be more effectively located by looking for common factors and isolating the unusual aspects within those factors, thus tracking down the trouble by means of a logical step-by-step approach.

Intuition

This apparently simple, rapid method is essential when coping with common daily problems. The cause is often immediately apparent, thus simple and complex problems may be solved effectively in this manner by the experienced supervisor. The obvious danger lies in not appreciating the *whole* problem because of a lack of experience and knowledge and jumping to conclusions. Automatic problem solving of this nature can also be dangerous when a recurring problem - normally having a standard cause - suddenly occurs through a new cause not foreseen at the time. Nevertheless, fully use of this method is essential considering the time factor.

Using intuition, current experience or *ad hoc* rules of thumb to solve problems is also termed *heuristics*. A heuristic system applies tentative solutions and is subject to alteration as the situation changes. It is therefore useful when problems are vague, which is not unusual.

Analytical thinking

To avoid the dangers of intuitive thinking, logical deduction is often used The approach is to arrive at an indisputable solution by analysing known, factual information. Thus, there must be one, unique answer that is predictable and the assumption is that the problem has only one solution. For example, if 240 working hours were lost in the assembly section last month, 25 per cent of which were due to absenteeism and 10 per cent through sickness, the answer in hours is 60 and 24respectively. However, if the question is how to cut down the high absenteeism rate, there are many answers and imagination is needed, which makes it a *creative problem* requiring creative thinking in its solution.

Creative thinking

If things or ideas that were previously unrelated now *have* to be related to arrive at an answer, the individual must use creative thought. To improve creativity there are various training schemes and techniques that may be applied. A popular method is 'lateral thinking', which was developed by E de Bono.

Group discussion and brainstorming

The use of groups for creative thinking was developed in the Thirties. The techniques generally conform to a number of basic concepts that concentrate on breaking down the inhibiting barriers to creativity. Typical examples are: to suspend judgement on other peoples' ideas; to allow everyone to 'freewheel' so that any ideas - regardless of whether they make sense - are proposed; to produce as many ideas as possible; and to cross-fertilise all the ideas to see if something new emerges. This is called *brainstorming* and is based on the thinking associated with value analysis.

The main barriers to creative thinking are a tendency to think that there is only one answer, to restrict thinking within a narrow self-imposed framework, to give answers that sound reasonable, to allow the obvious statements to go unchallenged and to worry too much about looking a fool. A good group leader will overcome these barriers.

The technique is easily adapted to most problems and, apart from creative thinking, is useful for developing interpersonal relationships.

Lateral thinking

This system is designed to help the mind escape from vertical thinking and move into lateral thinking. By using various techniques associated with challenging preconceptions and rejecting yes/no thinking it is very easy to convert people into a new way of thinking creatively. The system has achieved world-wide success but it is essential to read E de Bono's book, *Lateral Thinking*, first.

Synectics

This series of techniques in imaginative problem solving is complex and really should be practised with the aid of authorised practitioners. The body of knowledge is considerable as the techniques have been developed over a long period. They include overcoming 'right-brain' thinking and involving sophisticated group behaviour.

Morphological analysis

This form of creativity is based upon the use of a series of dimensions that are examined in relation to each other and to the possible elements within each dimension.

The analysis is complicated and demands a considerable amount of preparation. A typical example is to use two dimensions, such as products and markets. Elements for each dimension are listed and combinations are established to trigger off ideas.

Logical approach

A logical approach to problem solving may be established in the following way:

- *set standards* establish standards for as many activities as possible - in other words, set your sights
- *measure activities* measure actual results against established standards to highlight deviations
- *assess deviations* a deviation may be favourable or adverse:
  (a) *favourable* this is a situation nevertheless, the cause should be traced and identified for revising standards and increasing effectiveness
  (b) *adverse* this is a problem that is detrimental to the plan so the cause must be located and decisions made.
- *carefully define the problem* a complete, detailed description of the problem is essential
- *investigate* judge the time factor as the supervisor generally has to work to a definite termscale, then search for information and learn to distinguish between facts, inferences and value judgements
- *analyse and establish the cause* draw up a detailed analysis from the information available, look for indications leading to the source and establish the cause, thus solving the problem - successful elimination of the cause or avoiding a recurrence depends upon making a correct decision.

When assessing information, the source and the number of mouths that have passed it on are of prime importance. The reliability of the source and the distortion factor - as information passes from one person to the next - cannot be ignored. The well-known games of Chinese whispers, making up a sentence and passing it round in a group of, say, ten people, often produces bewildering results, bearing no relationship to the original sentence. This can happen, to some extent, in the workplace. The only sure way to be certain that something is a fact is to see it for yourself; unfortunately there is seldom time and it is impracticable in many instances.

A further confusing point is the inability of some people to distinguish between facts, inferences and value judgements. Each one has its usefulness, but the danger lies in mistaking one for another. Here is a typical example of the three: two people decide to walk from A to B along a street that is often very congested with traffic. The lamp-posts are a standard distance apart and, as the two people walk at a set pace, one takes the time between two lamp-posts and calculates their speed as, for example, two and a half mph. This is a *fact*. From the calculated speed a further reckoning indicates that they should arrive at B give minutes earlier than they intended. This is an *inference* because any number of situations may arise that will affect their estimated time of arrival and therefore it is a conclusion or deduction from a given fact. One then says to the other, 'It is quicker to walk along this road these days because the traffic is so congested'. This is a *value judgement* because it is an *opinion* based upon a series of events over a period that have not been accurately measure or analysed.

Decision making

Making decisions involves the consideration of a number of conflicting factors such as the objective, degree of ruthlessness necessary, humane treatment of people, cost and effectiveness. he supervisor's reputation is directly affected by the ability to weigh these standards sensibly. The choice is tempered also by two conflicting groups, his or here superiors and subordinates.

One method of making decisions is to use a logical approach by placing each standard in priority sequence. The natural priority is to establish and reach the objective. Having stated this, the next priority may be the cost. Assessment is mainly intelligent guesswork based upon considering the courses of action and weighing their probable effect on individuals, general effectiveness and the inevitable undesirable results.

Establishing priorities is a personal matter in which good sense is essential. Which decision is made must depend to some extent on morale and the prevailing industrial atmosphere. Ruthless decisions that cause a deterioration in relationships indicate the inadequacy of the supervisor to appreciate hidden costs and the intangible effects of causing frustration. To complete the cycle of events, new standards must be set to check the effectiveness of the decision, so that variances may be seen and any new problems brought to light for further action.

A logical approach to decision making may therefore be summarised as follows:

- aim to reach the objective
- consider various courses of action
- weigh the factors involved, for example, individuals, cost, undesirable after-effects, morale, etc.
- choose a course of action
- set standards to check after-effects
- follow up and revise if necessary.

Type of decision

Clearly the *type* of decision is an important feature. Low-grade decisions not directly affecting employees, such as cleaning programmes and garden maintenance are acceptable, as are high-grade decisions where specialised knowledge and heavy expenditure are areas for which consultation is pointless. However, high-grade decisions that directly affect employees, such as pay, overtime rates, working methods and automation, obviously need consultation and acceptance, as do low-grade decisions such as holiday arrangements and rest periods.

Discretionary limits

The number of authority levels in the organisation determines the degree of decision making allowed. Typical discretionary limits are easily identified as they will usually be based upon job titles and levels. First, strategic levels include top management to handle policy making and senior management to take structuring decisions. Second, tactical levels include middle managers to make interpretive decisions and supervisors to make situational decisions.

Social aspects

Companies are now expected to make decisions based upon social considerations, but often social issue are vague and only become involved when all aspects are included. Difficulties often arise over interpreting legislation, monopolies and their effects, satisfying all cultural factors and conflicts between what needs to be done for the company's survival and what should be done to provide the best conditions for the workers.

Arguably there could be decisions that would conflict with *shallow* social factors but that are fundamentally sound and would benefit society as a whole. However, excessive appropriations of revenue at the expense of society is obviously suspect and may even warrant state intervention to reduce misuse of such economic power.

Ethical considerations

The supervisor may often be confronted with difficult decisions, conflicting loyalties and cultural conflict when ethics are involved. Ethics are essentially subjective, personal feelings about human behaviour. Everyone behaves within a certain code of morale conduct. Situations arise continually where decisions are tempered by ethical considerations, especially when legality, bribery, theft, loyalty and confidentiality are involved. Such dilemmas cause frustration, stress and often upset relationships within the hierarchy.

Resolving ethical issues depends upon many circumstances, such as acceptable practices in certain countries and companies, the flexibility of individual moral codes, rigid interpretation or adjusting to each case and acting within the best interests of the company, employees, managers or society.

Legal aspects

Bearing in mind the wide range and complexity of legislation, whenever there is doubt, consult a specialist.

There are many general laws affecting supervisory management. These include: contract, tort, company formation, debt collecting, business ownership, consumer protection, credit, agency, fair trading compensation and negligence. Considering the enormous mass of detail and ambiguity, consulting an appropriate textbook is helpful but should not be relied upon if the supervisor is directly involved.

Political aspects

As already indicated briefly, a logical decision-making process may not take into account the external environment and cultural features. Unless explanations, participation at the early planning phased and consultation generally are employed, internal political problems may arise. Although sharing the decision-making process minimises the effects of beliefs, prejudices and attitudes that may upset outcomes, there are limits beyond which personal responsibility is weakened.

Locating information

The telephone can be used to provide much information to help with decision making by accessing on-line databases and View data. ODBs are systems that hold computerised information. they are located world-wide and use he international telephone network. Over 3000 ODBs are available at the time of writing and they cover many subjects. Searching is fast and accessing is easy. Host organisations advise on the equipment required to use the ODBs and provide passwords to access the system. Some charge a subscription while others charge on a time basis, the cost being shown on the screen at the end of the session.

Viewdata is another system employing two-way communication. The user needs an acoustic coupler or modem and a microcomputer. Central computers store information that can be accessed through a keyboard. Other systems are available such as Prestel, a public Viewdata system, and Topic, introduced by the Stock Exchange to give up-to-the-second financial information to subscribers.

Management-supervisor relations

The pressures and heavy responsibilities on managers must be recognised. To appreciate the real situation, the present state of management is now examined, followed by proposals on how to make allowances for managers in the circumstances.

Present state of management

In the UK there are some outstanding managers whose success is known world-wide, but the remaining majority are often accused of being poor managers. According to reports, many are not educated and trained in management, lack drive and initiative and cause more problems than they solve.

Indications of incompetence

In the absence of large-scale surveys, indicators are:

- the poor performance of many companies
- state of the economy
- ignoring outstanding research findings and discoveries that are eventually exploited overseas
- poor individual managerial performance compared with counterparts in other countries
- inability to avoid and resolve disputes successfully
- never-ending accounts of personal experiences from employees, trade unions and customers, all exploited by the media.

The causes

Some of the reasons given by experts for this state are:

- raw graduates are selected then given no further training
- having the right education impresses
- poor selection procedures are followed
- being the right type who mixes well with existing management is considered sufficient reason for employment
- assuming that an effective functional specialist will make a good manager
- possessing the 'right' social background is overvalued
- selecting a ruthless person who, by devious means, impresses
- nepotism, including friends, is practised
- the practice of promoting people according to age, length of service or seniority
- possessing a particular characteristic that overimpresses

- fear of people with management qualifications
- being overimpressed by graduates from certain universities
- failure to attract high-calibre individuals because industry is generally considered to be a dirty general occupation
- lack of financial and physical support of the management education and training system.

Note that many reasons just mentioned have a self-perpetuating effect on managerial selection.

Adverse pressures

Some argue there are conditions that are outside the control of managers but others say that effective managers should be able to *instigate* change. For such former conditions that are often quoted are:

- trying to cope with employees whose national culture or attitude is non-co-operative
- fighting militant trade unions whose selfish aim is to justify their own existence to members by ignoring the national and local effects of their actions
- relying on inadequate supervisors
- trying to combat situations created by poor governmental actions and policies.

Making allowances for managers

To avoid severe frustration, the supervisor must make allowances for managers. Unfortunately individuals usually expect high standards of performance from their superiors but allow their subordinates some latitude.

Five main approaches that help reduce disastrous management-supervisor relations are:

- *be sympathetic* demonstrate an understanding of problems faced by superiors and the difficulties they encounter solving them
- *be mature* show tolerance in any circumstances - eventually mutual tolerance may emerge as the superior recognises the advantages of this kind of relationship
- *set an example* by maintaining due dignity - expect a negative reaction in any situation where the superior is feeling insecure, fearful, confused or inadequate, be ready for rudeness, off-handtreatment and sarcasm, but try to avoid showing contempt
- *be diplomatic* use your knowledge and point out, tactfully, other ways of dealing with situations and solving problems, ensuring that the superior things your suggestions are his or her own ideas and so avoid time-wasting arguments

- *expect strange treatment* and calculate ways of counteracting it, for example:
- for the compulsive talker who has difficulty listening, try interposing and ask question on the subject *you* wish to discuss; surprise might be the response but a reply is also possible
- when the manager keeps you waiting as a way to demonstrate status, try saying, 'Excuse me please, I'll come back later when you're not so busy'.
- for the atmosphere creator who causes a reaction before discussion starts, try withdrawing and telephone or send a memo
- for the snob who intensely dislikes anyone beneath his or her status and ignores you, try avoiding confrontations - you are wasting your time.
- for the intellectual snob who will correct your grammar but miss the message, try a memo.

Time management

Making the best use of precious time is common sense, but, unfortunately, it is all too often uncommon. Time management requires careful planning, control and self-discipline. This straightforward task naturally involves allocating time to avoid having to adopt crisis management and poor performance. Two main features are:

- learn management and organisation principles, supervisory roles, communication techniques and work study.
- use the logical approach detailed below.

Initial check

This involves the following steps:

- *record roles and activities* determine the main tasks and measure the time taken for each one during the working day
- *establish priorities* how important is each activity in terms of its vital nature and how long it takes to complete?
- *list omitted tasks* try to determine the tasks that should have been done but were neglected through lack of time
- *analyse* rearrange items from the above three points to form a comprehensive structure.

Assessing essential aspects

To do this:

- examine the job specification and update if necessary
- determine your main objectives

- check priorities
- clarify responsibilities
- roughly assess the level of performance
- develop a personal plan

Applying principles and techniques

Apart from the management principles already discussed in this chapter, there are the following important aspects.

Using diaries

Examine the range of diaries available to record information. There are elaborate personal organizers with refills, including a diary, addresses references, a notebook and subject tabs; electronic organisers with many facilities; and simple diaries, which are often adequate. Avoid overcomplicated systems, choose one to suit your needs and choose large formats so you never run out of space.

Avoiding timewasters

Activities that waste time are usually glaring as they irritate. Some examples of good strategies are to:

- try to avoid needless switching from one activity to another, concentrating on completing one task before moving on to the next
- take action immediately when information - quantity and quality - is not available to avoid similar problems recurring
- attempt to restrict interruptions by diplomatically establishing periods for discussion with subordinates
- determine quite and busy periods and plan particular tasks accordingly, such as creative work and activities that require concentration
- choose appropriate times to contract others, times when they are able to devote sufficient time to you
- do not rely on memory, write everything down immediately, recording in your notes in the appropriate places later if it is difficult to do so at the time.

Communication aspects

- ensure that communications with subordinates and superiors are clear and understood
- conduct all meetings effectively to avoid unnecessary debate; checking beforehand that they are essential and justify the presence of those who do attend
- always listen attentively and write down important points

- choose times to interrupt carefully and so avoid loss of concentration
- liaise with other sections to check that work is not duplicated
- seek out all sources of information and advice.

Management-supervisor relations

Remember to make allowances, as mentioned in the previous section. Attempt to manage or manipulate the superior, aiming to avoid spending unnecessary amount of time with him or her.

The Supervisor and Supervisory Role

Introduction

Competent supervisor are essential in any business. However many supervisors are poorly trained, neglected by management, usually blamed for unproductive employees and resented by trade union representatives.

Unfortunately many managers do not fully understand the supervisor's role, consequently weak support creates poor relations between supervisors, employees and trade unions. Indeed UK managers fall below standards set in other developed countries. This fault increases the burden on supervisors who must adapt to difficult situations, aggravated now by the accelerating challenge of implementing information technology and other technologies in the workplace.

Effects of the computer

More powerful computer networks have given senior management the opportunity to remove whole layers of middle management. Many specialists, such as accountants and stock controllers, have faced redundancy as much of their work can be done more cheaply and accurately by machine. Senior management has therefore been brought closer to workers. With the aid of networks, more individuals can manage and control themselves. The computer-literate people remaining after lay offs emerge with new roles, new career patterns and more mobility.

Clearly this continual restructuring process creates opportunities for well-trained supervisors as more computer-illiterate individuals retire or become redundant and networking improves. Supervisory development programmes should therefore be a part of top management's strategy.

Definitions of the role of supervisor

This involves looking at the role from traditional and modern viewpoints, taking into account current trends. All tend to conflict. There are four common organisational supervisory categories:

- Supervisors
- managers

- supervision
- management.

In later chapters these terms are discussed in detail and related to organisational and operating problems.

The traditional view

From this viewpoint, a supervisor is any person who is given authority and responsibility for planing and controlling the work of a group through close contact.

In the broad sense, this definition means that supervisors may be delegated the authority to deal with the following matters:

- engagement, transfer, reprimand and dismissal of staff under their control
- staff grievances
- staff discipline
- quantity and quality of output
- recommendations to management.

In the narrow sense it can include anyone who directs the work of others by:

- giving instructions on operations
- co-ordinating specialist departments
- recommending courses of action to management.

The modern view

This is based upon acceptance of supervisors as a part of management and as managers, but the *term* supervisor remains. Typical definitions from this viewpoint are:

- the supervisor is the key front-line manager, the person who can make or break top management plan.
- the supervisor is any manager who control non-managerial subordinates and is wholly accountable for their work
- supervisors, managers and any others who are responsible for the work of people, at any level and in any type of organisation, should regard themselves as managers.

Current trends

These are emerging as a result of the increasing impact of information technology and the realisation that individual initiatives are essential if productivity is to be improved. Such trends give rise to the following:

- the development of direct relationship between supervisors and senior managers through computerised systems, which implies that the concept of an organisational hierarchy is now at least partially redundant

- supervisors adopting a collaborative approach, coaching employees who are established in autonomous teams; such coaching - in collaborative management terms—means close control is removed and replaced with a rapport where team members ask for advice and feel free to discuss their weaknesses and strengths.

Distinguishing features of a supervisor

Five main role relationships remain, regardless of these variations in defining the role of supervisor. These distinguish more clearly the differences between a supervisor and a manager in organisational thinking.

Technician level

Usually a three-tier organisational structure may be identified:

1 higher technology

2 technology

3 technician levels.

In the first tier a specialist controls the technological specialists; in the second tier these specialists control a range of technicians; and in the third tier technicians control the operators and clerical staff.

Sector membership

Supervisory sector membership extends to all organisational levels as all managers and supervisors have a group they are responsible for. The distinguishing feature for supervisors is non-membership of the management sector, which is clearly differentiated by differences in salary, working conditions, status and perks. Although the latter feature conflicts with modern definitions, in practice a demarcation line is apparent to everyone.

Restricted policy interpretation

simplified, top management makes policy, middle management broadly interprets policy, while lower management is restricted to narrow interpretations, which ensure that the day-to-day running of sections conforms.

Decision making

Senior managers make strategic decisions that have a broad effect, such as on marketing, products and services, growth finance, organisation structure, public relations and personnel. Middle managers make tactical decisions to implement the strategies through the use of resources, allocation of duties and various means of control.

Works supervisors make operational decisions involving, say, synchronising production, stock control, labour and machine utilisation and adjustments to the production schedule, while office supervisors make similar decisions on administrative aspects.

Workload limitation

Critical variables affecting the load or stress on a supervisory or managerial job determine the appropriate level and grading. Typical features are the degree of similarity to jobs performed by subordinates, complexity of planning and control, proximity of subordinates to each other, complexity of tasks performed and the degree of supervision imposed by maturity and training levels of subordinates. Theoretically as complexity of features increases, the education, training, qualifications and experience should increase, determining the category and suitability of the individual for that category. Unfortunately this may not always occur in practice, mainly because selection procedures are faulty.

Summary of similarities and differences

To clarify the definitions discussed and avoid blurring later, the similarities between supervisors and managers are outline first, followed by the main differences.

Similarities

These are as follows:

- they are responsible for the work of other people
- they use similar principles, practices and techniques and develop an art to achieve results
- some roles coincide, typically leader, liaison work, various communication activities, handling disturbances and negotiator
- they conform to loose definitions of management, such as the art of dealing with people, the art of getting things done through people and to forecast, plan, organise, command, co-ordinate and control.

Differences

These are as follows:

- additional managerial roles are mainly figure head, entrepreneur, resource allocator and giver of technological expertise
- managers are involved in long-term direction and control of employees as well as short-term activities
- managers conform to comprehensive definitions emphasising policy, strategy, entrepreneurial activities, overall direction and control and technological and specialisms expertise
- managers make strategic and tactical decisions at senior and middle management levels respectively, while supervisors make operational decisions.

Range of supervisor jobs

No two supervisory jobs are exactly alike. Two apparently similar supervisory jobs may in be very different, depending on such factors as status, company size, the product, the type of company and its structure, relationships between management, supervision, trade unions and operators, production tempo, growth problems, staffing and the use of specialists. This variation in supervisory jobs depends mainly upon the range of duties, the complexity of each duty and the particular level of supervision. an understanding of the latter aspect is most important.

The many levels of supervision can be grouped in a number of ways, depending on such factors as titles, salary, number of employees controlled, degree of authority and responsibility. Grouping based on the last two factors, for example, can be further divided into four sub-groups: primary group supervision, section supervision, department supervision and works and administration supervision. These are discussed below. In most cases a supervisor will fit into one of these groups. Generally all four levels are seen in medium and large size companies whereas in the small firm only the second and last would operate.

Primary group supervision

Included are chief clerks, leading hands and charge-hands who are responsible for supervising small groups. This cluster forms a primary working group headed by a primary group leader.

Section supervision

This level generally includes about six primary group leaders headed by a section supervisor, junior foreman, assistant foreman or office supervisor.

A section supervisor rarely does any manual work; instead authority and responsibility is generally restricted to allocating duties, ensuring smooth work flow by co-ordinating the activities of the primary group leaders and dealing with the day-to-day running of the section.

Department supervision

A control group of about six sections is headed by a foreman, department supervisor or department superintendent. General responsibility for the department includes planning and controlling the work.

Works and administration supervision

All senior supervisors come under this category. There are many titles used, including general foreman, senior foreman, production foreman, shop supervisor, shop superintendent and office manager. Whatever the title, the job carries substantial authority and responsibility for effectively controlling the six to eight departments that generally make up the shop, works or office.

Supervisors and employees

In general terms, the difference between employees and their supervisors is that employees perform their own work using their technical knowledge manually, whereas supervisors control the work of others using their technical knowledge theoretically combined with supervisory techniques.

In modern terms the supervisor should concentrate more on developing the co-operation and direct involvement of employees who, it is hoped, will behave more responsibly and feel committed as result. emphasis is placed on teamwork, participation, autonomy and flexibility - key factors that allow employees to work within much wider control limits. Indeed, the supervisor must adopt roles associated strongly with co-ordination, advice, adaptability and associated specialisms, to be successful.

Often logical changes are not acceptable to employees through fear of the consequences, such as less autonomy or redundancy. This apprehension may be reduced by discussion in advance, divulging plans, noting responses and suggestions and endeavouring to gain support. Without ample discussion the supervisor risks ridicule. The usual accusations are discourtesy, ignorance, lack of understanding and having no idea of employees' capabilities and experience.

The old saying still hold good: treat adults like children and they will behave like them; treat them like dogs and they may bite; treat them like idiots and they will behave like them.

Basic elements of supervision

The three basic elements, which are the titles of the three parts of this book, each contain many aspects that demand appropriate techniques, some of which are used instinctively by applying sound common sense. Others demand training and practice. applying the right principles at the right time needs something more than knowledge alone as the basic elements must interact closely, although they are outlined independently.

A representative sample of ten supervisory activities is given for each basic element in. These activities or duties are interdependent in practice. For instance no decision should be made on facts and theory alone; the human factor must be given due consideration, along with control features in a given situation. Finding and maintaining the right balance is difficult, time-consuming and often frustrating.

Responsibilities of a supervisor

A supervisor is responsible for subordinates, the activities and the workplace that he or she is given formal authority to control. Within this overall definition, the finer points of responsibility should now emerge that make possible the performance of the job. One way of thinking about these responsibilities is to examine again the list of duties given under each basic element and to summarise them in a list of responsibilities, as follows:

1 *staff*: morale, consultation, discipline, welfare, safety, employment, induction, training, culture.

2 *work*: quantity, quality and timeliness

3 *cost*: maximum economy

4 *machines and equipment*: maintenance, loading, operation

5 *materials*: supplies, waste, suitability

6 *workplace*: layout, tidiness, good housekeeping

7 *co-ordinating with other sections*: organisational culture.

The above responsibilities can only be fulfilled by giving the supervisor the authority to forecast and plan in accordance with company policy, to organise and execute, to co-ordinate and control. The supervisor, in turn, becomes responsible for these activities.

Social responsibilities

The wider field of social responsibilities covers indirect relationship with the shareholders, the customers, the state and the suppliers. Although these social groups appear remote from supervision, their interests must be considered if a supervisor is to realise his or her full responsibility.

The shareholders or proprietors have invested capital in the business and, naturally, they expect it to earn interest in the form of dividend. The customers expect goods to be priced in relation to quality and delivered on time. Unfortunately, the latter point is often considered too lightly, bearing in mind the chaos late delivery can cause, especially with goods for industry. The question of better designs and a wider range of products for the community presents deeper problems of research, cost and profitability.

The state relies upon industry and everyone connected with it to provide sufficient goods to export and to supply the home market. Economic stability is vital to everyone; success depends largely upon the best use of capital and the effectiveness of labour. Finally, the supervisor's responsibility to suppliers or customers means that promises should be kept whenever possible and wrong impressions carefully avoided. For example, the impression that regular supplies of a commodity will be needed is easily created, leading a supplier to plan accordingly, whereas a limited quantity only may be actually required. Any information of use to the supplier should be given freely, especially on the question of specifications which may be unnecessarily fine, such as tolerances, finish and packing.

Quality of a good supervisor

The main problem when discussing personal qualities is the measurement of degree.

For example, when people refer to intelligence as a quality, they use such terms as average, reasonable, high level, low level and average level. Unfortunately there is no standardised method of dealing with these matters and each individual will naturally interpret these terms in a slightly different way.

It should be appreciated that a general foreman may possess no more qualities than a primary group leader, but he or she will possess them in greater degree. Moreover, a comprehensive list of an outstanding general foreman's qualities would correspond with specifications for general management. Nevertheless, the same qualities appear at the lower levels of supervision, but in a less intensive form.

The main differences in supervisory job specifications occur in the technical and administrative aspects, which vary considerably depending upon the industry, company size of different circumstances within the same factory, e.g., special qualities may be desirable in supervising particular groups that contain an unusual feature.

The five essential qualities are:

drive

leadership

intelligence

skills and knowledge

character

They are discussed below, but not in order of importance as each job demand a different proportion of all these requirements.

Drive

The basic need for vitality, energy and enthusiasm is good health. Physical and mental fatigue impair judgement and are demoralising for subordinates who need to be enthused by the supervisor's example and vigour. Making the best use of time and energy requires careful planning. Whenever possible, over-excitement and bursts of stop-gap measures should be avoided to conserve nervous energy. An even spread of effort sustained over long periods is desirable for good performance, which can then be expected from others. This sustained effort or drive demands self-discipline and conscientiousness in the face of outside distractions and the general pace of living.

Leadership

A good leadership must be an outstanding member of the group who gets along easily with people and has above-average competence. Leadership is difficult to define accurately; its intangible qualities cannot be learned, yet they are easily recognisable.

Naturally, ability is not enough. Previous environment, which moulds personality and character, should provide a balanced background for an individual to feel at ease, mix easily with many types of people and sense the ability to supervise well. some people, of course, manage to overcome an unhappy past, while others who were more fortunate fail to make the grade. Good leaders set high standard of performance for themselves, keep to them and expect similar performance from others. They mix easily with people by understanding them and using clear and constructive methods of handling everyday problems. They are not always more skillful or more intelligent than their subordinates, but they appreciate their own technical and human limitations. They recognise their responsibilities and use their authority in a fair and impartial manner. This implies that they are temperamentally suited for the task of solving problems, are sufficiently far sighted to see potential ones before they arise and can take appropriate early action.

An important management task is to create conditions under which leaders can become effective but, at the same time, avoiding the development of a situation where leaders struggle for power among each other. If the well-known rat race is allowed, subordinates suffer and organisation is badly affected. Given the opportunity and the right conditions, the leader can push people beyond their normal capabilities towards a higher level of effectiveness, with greater work satisfaction.

Intelligence

Most supervisory posts require intelligence, similar to the general level of intelligence found among skilled operators. Some people expect supervisors to be more intelligent than their subordinates, which is naturally desirable. A high level of intelligence is essential in some supervisory jobs, where technical and administrative problems are intricate and demanding. On the other hand, many supervisory jobs contain a large proportion of routine work that would soon frustrate the highly intelligent person.

In reality, supervisors need shrewdness, judgement and an acute mind with plenty of common sense. They must be quick-witted, able to distinguish between major and minor problems, apportioning sufficient time to deal with each problem. They must decide whether permanent or temporary arrangements are needed. They must understand clearly the many and varied written and spoken instructions and be able to pass on information clearly to a number of different types of subordinates.

Skills and knowledge

Three main skills are distinguishable: technical, interpersonal and conceptual. They apply to all managerial and supervisory jobs but the ratios between them differ, depending on the organisational level.

As top levels are approached, technical skills tend to reduce, interpersonal skills should remain the same, while conceptual skills increase. Understandably collaborative philosophies demand more emphasis on interpersonal and conceptual skills for supervisors as a crucial appreciation of the total organisation and the involvement of employees are needed to achieve high performance levels.

These two skills are majority supervisory assets, rated above many other qualities such as IQ, knowledge and job skills.

Technical skills

An inherent part of any supervisory job is technical competence. Supervisors need a good knowledge of every operation or process under their control to be able to eliminate common faults, wastage and any dangerous practices. Practical and theoretical knowledge plus varied experience help to command respect and help others.

To train successfully, supervisors should illustrate:

- *why* a job should be done, so that the criteria used are seen to be right for that task
- *how* it should be done, to demonstrate the proper use of all the knowledge available
- to be aware always that the trainee may be able to contribute through his or her own knowledge or ideas and be innovative.

At the same time a questioning approach should be adopted to discover any problems the trainees may have. Supervisors do not necessarily have to be the best operator in the group, but certainly they should not be the worst.

A reasonable elementary education and further education are essential. Technical skills are learned relatively quickly by repetition and are specific to particular activities. They are classified by referring to an established management principle or methodology and are measurable. Implementation and appraisal are learned through practice. A general definition is the capability to apply knowledge, experience, techniques and methods, to perform specific tasks with the aid of appropriate machines and equipment.

Interpersonal skills

Often called human skills or interactive skills, they use motivational and behaviourist techniques to extract higher performance. They stimulate ideas, concentrate on needs and goals and encourage participation.

A general definition is the capability and judgement to work with employees and to utilise fully their talents through leadership and various behavioural theories. Generally they take a long time to develop as learning and experience are needed, along with patience, perseverance and tolerance.

Sound interpersonal relationships are viewed occasionally as difficult to achieve because of cultural and subcultural factors. These vary widely between countries, areas within countries and with company size. Although some variations in managerial behaviour patterns are noticeable between countries, organisational structuring mostly follows logical patterns that dominate managerial behaviour patterns. On a broader basis interpersonal skills are also applied between management and suppliers, customers, the community, and the government.

Conceptual skills

Abstract in nature, these multiple skills are drawn from knowledge and experience over a long period. for further development the opportunity to gain insight into corporate activities and problems is essential. Conceptual skills concentrate on broader issues, corporate and organisational planning and policy and systems. Collectively, a definition is the capability to act in accordance with the objectives of the company as a whole. Unfortunately conflict often exists between the objectives visualised by the group or section and those of the corporate whole.

The development of though processes that improve conceptual skills requires specialised training, perseverance and close examination of experiences. The mental process of attempting to visualise the future includes not only using data available and experiences, but, also, utilising many aids such as check-lists, systems procedures, statistical frameworks and models. Such forecasting does not rely upon trends or data, but more upon intuition to identify important relevant features and mentally classifying events into significant areas that have causal connections.

Making better decisions and coping with difficulties should be in line with the total organisation scene or corporate whole. This relies heavily on posing searching questions using the normal why, when, where and how approaches and conceptualising or visualising outcomes. In practice, typical observations show that there is more reliance on asking searching questions and less on detailed knowledge as senior levels are approached. Also, the more rapid the change the more reliance there is on asking questions and less reliance on experience to seek appropriate solutions. The real difficulty is knowing the right questions to ask.

Character

Nobody possesses all the qualities of character of the ideal supervisor. A compromise is inevitable and the choice will be governed by the particular circumstances.

Some of the important qualities are honesty and trustworthiness, with a strict sense of fairness and justice. A stable personality is essential for an even temper, steadiness and reliability. A direct, open and positive approach is desirable, giving due consideration all parties when dealing with problems and grievances. Cheerfulness and enthusiasm, coupled with a sense of humour, are essential to provide the right type of industrial atmosphere.

In brief, good supervisors must possess something besides technical competence, clearly placing them above their particular group. Someone without higher intellect can still shine by having more drive or inherent qualities of leadership, A person displaying strength of character who 'bubbles over' with activity can make up for other faults. Each particular combination of qualities suits certain groups in particular work situations. Thus, one person stands out in a group and, provided his or her outlook is reasonably aligned with management policy and not objectionable, he or she is a likely choice.

Selection of supervisors

The importance of careful and fir selection of supervisors is often overlooked by management. Promotions from the shop floor and appointments in the lower levels of supervision are viewed very critically by operatives who are often directly affected.

Poor selection may destroy the efforts of previous supervisors who have managed to improve the industrial climate. Overlooked employees may feel frustrated and suspicious of management if the appointed individual is obviously unsuitable. The working harmony of the group or groups may be upset and resentment tends to spread like a disease - in all directions. The disgruntled individuals, who may have a legitimate complaint, mention the 'injustice' to everyone and a sense of frustration may develop throughout the company.

Some observation on selection

Before considering the methods of selection, some circumstances that can affect selection must be mentioned. A common fault among supervisors is to avoid the promotion of individuals because they are considered to be indispensable in their present positions, even though they are eminently suitable for promotion. Sometimes the supervisor cannot be bothered to train a replacement and the easiest remedy is deliberately to penalise a person's chances of promotion, often forcing the person to seek employment elsewhere.

It is not uncommon for superiors who are able to influence promotion, or who actually select the individual, to allow unimportant incidents to dominate their impressions or opinions of subordinates, sometimes holding a trivial misdemeanour against a person for years. In some cases, even the *suspicion* of wrongdoing is sufficient reason to bypass an individual. A true understanding of reality makes due allowance for human errors and it is wiser and fairer to give other people the benefit of the doubt.

Type suited to management

Managers' opinions on the type of supervisor required are diverse and vary with company size. The manager in a small concern may demand a 'yes man' who carries out orders to the letter; while in a large firm the opposite type may be required, typically one who shows initiative, makes decisions and has a powerful personality. Some prefer the outsider with new ideas; others favour internal promotion. No two managers agree entirely on the qualities they seek for particular position and usually compromise is necessary.

Temperament

Naturally there are many different temperaments that suit a supervisory role, but a certain temperament may suit a particular post. Certainly important general attributes are a stable disposition, reliability and thoroughness. Being able to control emotions in variable circumstances helps greatly when dealing with employees who may exhibit instability or immaturity at times.

Appropriate judgement, perception, sensitivity and intuitiveness are features that highlight potential effective supervisors. What are the best ratios of these four features for a particular post have been the subject of much research.

Methods of selection

The methods of selection can be divided into two groups to highlight the importance of using scientific methods.

Unsubstantiated methods

All methods that do not allow for systematic selection and result in the detrimental effects of poor selection upon employees and the company come under this heading. These methods do not necessarily imply spontaneous selection - some are planned well in advance - but selection is based not on true grounds but on such grounds as:

- favouritism, promoting friends and relatives
- length of service or age seniority
- high standard of skill alone
- haphazard recommendations by a supervisor
- chance, through stop-gap arrangements, i.e., someone being in the right place at the right time.

Scientific methods

Any method that attempts to reduce the possibility of error comes under this heading. The aim is to find the best person available for each vacancy. All employees, therefore, initially have an equal opportunity and those with ability have good prospects of promotion that will not depend upon influence and favouritism. The essential requirements for any scheme with these aims are as follows:

- planning ahead by estimating the vacancies that are likely to occur
- preparation of a job specification, listing all the main requirements of the vacancy
- advertising internally and externally with the understanding that promotion from within will always take precedence where suitable internal applicants are available
- careful investigation of *all* employees as promotion prospects

- interviews of all candidates who are likely to be suitable, conducted by skilled, objective interviewers and supplemented by appropriate tests
- final choice or approval by top management or a selected panel.

Scientific choice, although not perfect, has obvious advantages. Many factors that may have been omitted are now included in the job specification, there is less chance of potential supervisors being overlooked, better assessment of individuals is now assured and unbiased selection is more likely.

Frankness and open dealings are needed to make the scheme acceptable. Any queries should be discussed openly. Every applicant should be fully informed of proceedings and the unsuccessful candidates must be told why they failed.

A fair scheme must be seen to be fair by everyone. This is essential to smooth the way for the new supervisor, who may have to face special problems if he or she comes from the group to be supervised. This type of change can be a big wrench and it will help the person to adjust quickly if everyone accepts that the selection is fair.

Training and development of supervisors

In the UK this has been neglected for over a century by governments and companies. Insurmountable problems face supervisors and managers unless training is taken seriously. Even when many difficulties are overcome without training, they never know *why* they succeeded. Indeed, conversely, when they fail, they are unable to analyse accurately why this happened and discover their weaknesses.

Training is learning information and skills for the present job; development involves learning not only for the present job but also for future jobs and possible promotion opportunities. This difference in emphasis points at how important it is continually to update knowledge and skills to maintain effectiveness and provide ample opportunity for mental growth.

Informal training

Most supervisors learn their jobs by actually doing them, making mistakes and avoiding making them again as a result of these experiences. Although this system of trial and error is considered to be an essential part of training, practical experience must be supplemented by formal training to form a sound framework for future action. Working with an effective supervisor is an invaluable experience but, to gain full benefit, a knowledge of the basic elements of supervision helps considerably. Techniques, built up through the experiences of many supervisors and specialists who have spent years studying supervision, need, ideally, to be learned and integrated with informal training.

Formal training

Many of the half a million supervisors in this country have not received *any* formal training, although various of courses have been on offer for a number of years. Any successful training scheme must have suitable training facilities, the right syllabus, appropriate lecturers and back-up staff and strong support from management, who should ensure adequate follow-up and assessment after the course.

Although managers often agree that some form of supervisory training is essential and show enthusiasm when the matter is discussed, few seem prepared to take any practical steps in this direction. Some managers say either that supervisors cannot be spared or that they are too busy to make the arrangements. Others ignore the facilities offered, possibly because they think the subject is unimportant or perhaps they fear that the supervisor, after training, may know more than they do.

The management charter initiative (MCI)

The latest development in formal training for supervisors and managers is the launching of the Management Charger Initiative by the government-funded Training Agency. The aim is to reach agreement on the competences needed by a range of organisations and to classify what the essential knowledge, skills and qualities are. Thus, basic competence standards for education, training and development would be recognised. Competence—as defined by the Training agency—is the ability to perform activities within an occupational area to levels of performance expected in employment/. A two-part model outlines the competence standards reached by effective managers and the underlying personal abilities and skills required to achieve such standards.

Such standards include managing people, operations, finance and information. Personal competence include displaying self-confidence, taking initiative and coping with stress. The model may be used in many ways and should form the basis for programmes offered by management institutions. These topics have been with us for a long time, but relating the model directly to performance is a new development. A clear distinction is made between courses about knowledge and analysis and those related to competent performance.

Development

This clearly depends on a person's ambition and potential and the seriousness of a company's development programme. Long-term investment is essential in any human resources development scheme, so arrangements must be made and time allowed for supervisors to learn on the job. The process is continuous, with appropriate changes being made along the way to job content, challenges being presented and ample opportunity being given for self-development and initiative. Comprehensive development schemes are easily recognised. Indications are follow-ups to training, assessing individual requirements, discussing future roles and organisational objectives, stressing conceptual skills development, organisational change, environmental aspects and long-term planning.

Understanding the supervisor's Role

What is a supervisor?

Supervision may occur at various levels of an organisation, but normally on the management level nearest to the workers. Viewed in this way, *supervisors are management representatives who direct the work of operating employees.* They perform management activities such as planning, organizing, staffing, directing, and controlling. Almost without exception they operate face to face with their people to accomplish the work that needs to be done. They are where the action is, surrounded by both problems and opportunities. If an organization's work is to be done at all, they are the ones directly involved in getting it done. Their world is one of action, not idle talk or theory.

The supervisor's unique organizational location

It is sometimes assumed that supervisors occupy a position like that of other members of management, but actually their position is somewhat different, as illustrated by the following chain of command in an organization. The presidents manage a middle-management family, and department heads have a management family consisting of supervisors. The supervisors, on the other hand, head a nonmanagement family of workers. Therefore, they must work on a daily basis with managers above them and nonmanagers below them in the organization.

The supervisory job is further complicated, because there often is a union representing employees. Consequently, a supervisor must understand the union's way of life, its leaders, and how to talk with them. In addition there are personnel representatives, engineers, inspectors, and others that supervisors must deal with on a weakly or daily basis. Together, all of these individuals and groups make a complex situation that is difficult to supervise. As the saying goes, supervisors must wear many different hats as they talk with these various groups. Each has a different outlook and way of thinking, so supervisors need to vary their approaches to fit such difference.

Supervisors are made, not born

Many years ago we thought that supervisors needed to be "natural-born leaders." Unless people were born with the right set of personal characteristics, there was little chance for them to be successful supervisors. Potential supervisors were supposed to have strength of character, dominance, and other apparently desirable personal traits. The trait approach sounded reasonable in theory, but the problem was that it did not prove effective in practice. Successful supervisors exhibited a wide variety of personal traits, so it was impossible to identify any one or two traits that cause effective supervision.

We finally came to realise that success comes to supervisors not because of certain personal traits, but because of certain behavior that is appropriate in supervisory situations. Behavior is the key to supervision, not traits. This means that supervisors are made, not born. Supervision can be taught and learned, so there are plentiful opportunities for many types of people to become successful supervisors. This understanding resulted in an increase in supervisory training programs and improvements in the quality of supervision as supervisors learned more about their role. In short, training combined with on-the-line experience was found to provide the very best supervisory development.

Investment in human resources

The supervisor's principal responsibility is to assure that the organization's investment in human, technical, and economic resources is properly used. Supervisors, therefore, are the ones who help the organization gain a return on its investments. This responsibility applies whether the organization is profit making or not, because all organizations seek high outputs in relation to inputs. To do otherwise would be to waste society's resources, and in these times of scarce resources, waste is not acceptable.

The supervisor's responsibility for investments in human resources is particularly important. engineers can determine how to use an organization's technical equipment, and economists can determine uses for economic resources. however, supervisors can make the most effective use of human resources, because they are the ones in direct, daily contact with employees.

Human resources also have a special characteristic. When properly nurtured, people can grow and develop to become more effective and more capable. It is primary responsibility of supervisors to help their people grow so that they can become more capable persons. In this manner everyone benefits. Employee growth helps the organization, the employees, the society in which we live, and the supervisor. The organization is helped, because employees are able through growth to perform better work. The employees benefit, because they are more fulfilled as persons and can advance in the organization. Society especially benefits because better people make a better society. Finally, supervisors benefit because their employees are doing better work and are more satisfied with their jobs. As a result, human growth is perhaps the most beneficial of all the conditions that supervisors influence.

Key persons in the organizational system

Supervisors are key persons in the organizational system. They represent management to the workers, and they also represent workers to management. Workers know management primarily through their supervisors. Likewise, higher management knows the workers primarily through supervisors. They are an essential element, because they sit astride the chains of authority and communication, and can block almost anything going upward or downward. They make decisions, control work, communicate, lead, and generally play an active part in accomplishing organizational objectives.

Supervisors also bear major pressures of all types, both upward and downward. Workers communicate their expectations to supervisors and expect these ideas to move upward in the system, so that they can get more of what they want. Customers also bring pressures on supervisors for better products and services. In a downward direction, management has specific goals that it wants accomplished, and it brings substantial pressure to see that work is done as planned. management has cost standards, legal restrictions, and other controls that put pressure on supervisors. They also receive pressure from various staff groups who help apply management standards. The result is that supervisors are placed under considerable stress unless they have learned to plan and organize effectively.

A supportive role

Essentially, supervisors perform a supportive role for their people. They try to supply the psychological, technical, and economic support necessary to get the job done. By providing such support, supervisors make the workers' jobs easier, more satisfying, and more effective better training is needed, supervisors help the employees get it. If more security is needed, supervisors try to provide it. They move right down the list of employees' job needs, trying to support all of them. As such, the supportive role is a substantial reversal of the old-fashioned role in which supervisors told employees what to do and they meekly followed. Instead, supportive behavior helps develop cooperation and teamwork in the organization, and supervisors are seen as useful and desirable members of the team because they help groups reach their work goals. Psychological support for one's group is especially important. Supervisors can provide psychological support because of their face-to-face contact with employees and their control of the immediate work situation. Psychological support is provided through building job satisfaction, improving motivation, providing security for employees, and other similar actions. Such actions require supervisors who are willing to listen to their employees and learn their needs.

Keystone in the organizational arch

Perhaps the concept that best represents the supervisory role as one bearing pressures from both sides is that portraying supervisors as the keystone in the organizational arch. An arch is held together by the keystone that connects both sides and makes it possible for each to perform effectively. The keystone takes the pressure from both sides and uses that pressure to build a stronger arch. The sides can be held together only by the keystone, which strengthens, not weakens, the arch. This keystone position is the important role of supervisors in all organizations.

A related way of viewing the supervisor is as a linking pin connecting workers with the larger organization so that it may operate as a single entity. If it were not for this linking pin, the organisation would be in shambles. Parts would be separated and heading off in their own directions. There would be unity toward common objectives. From these illustrations it is evident that supervisors are crucial links in organizational systems.

Characteristics of the supervisory role

The supervisory role includes a large number of different activities. Supervisors need to have the flexibility and versatility to perform all of these activities, and most of them must be performed well if supervisors are to be effective. We will now discuss various characteristics of the supervisory role, and most of them will be developed further in subsequent chapters.

Leader

Supervisors are first of all leaders. This is their central role. The organization depends upon them to exercise face-to-face leadership in the front lines. Leadership expands and releases the potential that is in people. It creates motivated, willing followers. Top management and staff people can make beautiful plans outlining what should be done, but plans cannot succeed until supervisory leadership at the point of performance releases the powers in people. Thus, leadership is the ultimate act that brings to success all of the potential in an organization and its people.

Leaders need a balanced combination of three types of skills in order to perform effectively. The three are technical, human, and conceptual skills. Technical skill refers to a person's knowledge about various types of equipment and methods. Examples are skills learned by tool-makers, accountants, engineers, and nurses. At the supervisory level technical skill is not as important as it is at the operating level, but supervisors do need some skill of this type in order to be able to communicate with their people and understand their problems. Supervisors who are know-nothings about the technical activities of their departments will have difficulty getting their jobs done.

The leadership role of supervisors particularly requires human skill. It is the ability to interact effectively with people and to build teamwork, and no organization can do without it. Without human skill a team cannot be built, and people cannot be motivated. All supervisors who intend to hold their jobs must be able to work effectively with people.

Finally, supervisors need conceptual skill, because they deal with plans, complex relationships, and other abstractions. They need to be able to relate items A, B, and C in some reasonable pattern in order to understand what is happening in their department. Conceptual skill deals with ideas, human skill with people, and technical skill with things.

Decision maker

Decision making requires the choice of one alternative compared with another, and it is the ever-present stock in trade that supervisors use day after day. Decision making requires a special type of courage. It is easy to study problems once and then to study them again, but it takes courage to decide what to do about them. Decisions require one to take responsibility and to initiate action. These actions invoke risk, because the decision could be wrong, thereby costing the organization money, discouraging employees, or driving away customers.

For supervisors the goal is not to be right all of the time, because that is impossible. A more modest and realistic goal is to be right most of the time, and that is the level of competence that higher management expects of supervisors. An even more important goal is to improve the percentage of right decisions as one gains more supervisory experience. Growth in competence occurs when a supervisor can move from 90 percent right decisions to 92 percent next year and perhaps 93 percent the year after that.

As a matter of fact, the term "right decisions" is somewhat inaccurate to describe what actually happens with supervisory decisions. In real situations, one can differentiate "right" decisions into "good" and "better" decisions.

Planner

Consider the situation of a supervisor by the name of Mabel Morris. Morris is a whiz with people, and she is an expert in the technical side of her office operation. She is a hard worker, arriving before her employees and leaving after they have departed for the day. By many standards Morris is an effective supervisor. Unfortunately, there is one problem, a small item but a significant one in any supervisor's collection of skills. Morris is a poor planner, or perhaps more accurately, she does not plan at all. Her employees try to make up for her deficiencies because they like her, but they cannot do the whole job. The result is that Morris's department is constantly out of schedule with other departments, because it cannot meet its commitments on time. The people in her department are not sure who should do what, or when they should do it. The situation generally is one of confusion, because Morris does not plan.

Planning is essential for total supervisory success. If it is not done well, then other activities are likely to be different because they depend upon accurate planning. Planning is something distinctly different from forecasting. The act of forecasting requires a prediction of the future, but planning organizes knowledge and resources to cause the future. For example, I forecast the weather, and then I plan a hike into the woods based on my forecast of the weather. The future action is based on the plan. Similarly, a supervisor forecasts work requirements for the next week and then plans how the department will get the work done.

A key supervisory planning activity is to set meaningful goals for subordinates. Group members need to feel that they have something worthwhile to do. Without goals, people go off in different directions and begin to lose sight of what the organization s trying to accomplish. The difficulty will continue as long as there is no common understanding of the goals involved.

Organizer

Modern work environments are complex. Organization is the grand strategy to bring order out of chaos when groups work together. Organizing sets the relationships between people, work, and resources. The necessity of organizing—and the havoc of disorganization—are illustrated by disorganizing a short sentence "riirggnagesnotzt-lsuse." In this form it is nonsense. The parts are not in any meaningful relationship, in the same way that a department can be number of people and resources when it is disorganized. If we reorganise the sentence somewhat, it is workable, but difficult: "organizinggestsresults." By the slight change of converting to a capital "O" and adding two spaces, we achieve a useful, organized sentence : "Organizing gets results." It is rather easy to see that organising achieves a degree of order in work situations, but there is another part of organizing not so evident. Effective organising is a useful way to bring security and psychological support to one's employees. It does so by helping employees know where they stand and to whom they should go for assistance. when people feel that the organization is set up to serve their job needs, then they tend to feel psychologically supported.

A key part of the organizing job is delegating work to people. When employees accept a delegation, they then become their supervisor's "delegate: or representative. If they do not accept, then delegation has been merely attempted, so delegation also requires behavioral skills to encourage people to accept the responsibilities that are delegated to them. The great advantage of delegation is that it permits supervisors to extend their influence beyond the limits of their own personal time, energy, and knowledge.

Inadequate delegation is a primary cause of supervisory failure. Some supervisors feel that delegation is giving away something, so they psychologically cannot bring themselves to do it for fear that it will weaken them. Others are such perfectionists that they have no confidence in letting others do work for which they are responsible. However, all supervisors need to realize that delegation is the act that makes supervision possible. If there is no delegation to others, there is no one to be supervised. Sometimes supervisors have to learn the hard way that delegation is a desirable activity. One supervisor had difficulty delegating special reports to his people. He always felt that he could do a better job than they could, so he would not risk delegating a report to them. On one occasion he decided to prove to himself that he could not depend on others to prepare good reports. He assigned a special report to one of his women clerks, but he also worked privately at night on the same report. In this manner he could compare his report with hers to show that he could do better reports than his employees. when her report was received, he had to admit to himself that it was a better report. Having proved his point - but in the opposite of his expectations—he became more free with delegation in the future.

Motivator

An important part of the supervisory job that nearly all supervisors recognize is that of motivator. Motivation is concerned with the human side of supervision rather than the technical side. The basic strategy is to understand peoples' needs and then to relate those needs to the tasks that the organization is trying to accomplish.

The importance of relating human needs to motivational problems is illustrated by a comparison of machine malfunction and operator malfunction. When a machine malfunctions, people recognize that it needs something. Assume that a machine will not grind a piece of metal to a close enough tolerance. Perhaps it needs oil. Or maybe a nut is loose. First the operator tries to find the trouble. Then the supervisor is called. Finally a maintenance mechanic is called, or an engineer, and so on until the cause of the problem is found and the machine is put back into working order. All of the people who tried to find the cause of the machine breakdown did so in an analytical manner based upon their knowledge of the machine's operations and needs. It would have been wasteful to begin haphazardly to tighten nuts and oil gears hoping that the trouble would be corrected. Such action might aggravate the malfunction.

Now suppose that the machine operator malfunctions. Perhaps the operator is not doing an adequate quality of work. The supervisor may feel like taking immediate action without analyzing the situation, but this approach would be no better than haphazard machine repair. Like the machine, the operator is malfunctioning because of particular needs. In the illustration just given, perhaps the operator lack training, or has a conflict with another worker that is upsetting the operator psychologically. When the appropriate problem can be found and corrected, the operator is likely to perform satisfactory work.

Coordinator and controller

It is necessary for supervisors to coordinate and control the complex environment of their departments. Can you imagine, for example, a football play that is not coordinated? People move in the wrong directions or they are in certain places at the wrong times, or both. The result is confusion and a broken play that often causes a loss for the team. The same situation exists with a work environment. The supervisor plays the role of quarterback and is responsible for assuring that all parts of the organisation are working together smoothly. Control and coordination are closely related to planning, because without plans coordination and control are almost impossible. Consider again the members of a football team. They spend may hours planning their different plays, and then additional hours in practice to be sure that they know how to carry out the plans. Without plans the team would be no more effective than the children's teams that develop spontaneously on playgrounds. They are fun, but they cannot compete with well-planned and coordinated teams. The same situation exists in a supervisor's department. If the supervisor is to be effective, it is essential to develop coordination and control based on sound plans.

Communicator

The importance of communication is made evident by imagining a situation in which supervisors are unable to communicate with their people in any way. The result would be a complete loss of the organization's ability to function. Work could do be done, because people would not know what was needed. Similarly, supervisors would not know what to do, because they would have no feedback from the work situation. The organization would be brought to a complete standstill. Organizations do not face this extreme condition, but many organizations do have such poor communication that there is interference with work performance.

Supervisory plans and ideas, no matter how outstanding they are, become useless unless they can be communicated to employees. Everything that a supervisor does eventually must pass through the bottleneck of communication if it is to reach those involved. Leadership, decision making, planning, organizing, motivating, and all the other supervisory activities require communication before they can take effect. Day-after-day, minute-after-minute, supervisors face a necessity to develop sound communication.

Effective supervisory communication needs to be two-way, upward as well as downward in the organization. The supervisor needs to be an effective receiver of messages as well as sender of them. As a matter of fact, studies show that supervisors usually spend even more of their time listening than they do talking. Consider the process of making a decision. The quality of decisions will depend on the quality of information that supervisors have, and this information is secured by improving inputs from all parts of the organization. Unless supervisors learn from their employees the needs that exist at the work place, the supervisors cannot make effective decisions. similarly, unless supervisors learn what higher management wants done, they cannot make effective decisions. The only way that supervisors can prepare themselves for decision making is to improve their inputs through listening to those both above and below them.

Supervisors are doubly responsible for building communication. First, they are responsible for developing their own proficient communication, as has been discussed. Second, they are responsible for encouraging their subordinates to be effective communicators among themselves and upward to the supervisor and others. In the successful department both the employees and the supervisor are effective communicators. They make up a single team and a single understanding unit that must know what is happening in order to get their jobs done.

From this discussion it is evident that supervisory communication has two broad purposes. First, it provides people the information and understanding they need to do their jobs. But just being able to work together is not enough. People also need suitable attitudes and motivation for working as a team; therefore, the second purpose of supervisory communication is to provide the attitudes for motivation, cooperation, teamwork, and job satisfaction. The accomplishment of both communication goals is required before a supervisor can be successful.

Reward administrator

Another important supervisory activity is that of reward administrator. Supervisors acting as representatives of management provide employees with a proper mix of the rewards available in the organization. There are financial rewards as well as psychological-social ones, such as recognition. Even financial rewards often have overtones of psychological and social value. For example, a raise in pay provides more money, but it also may provide an employee with more status or a greater feeling of accomplishment. Thus, it is impossible for supervisors to separate completely the financial value and the psychological value of rewards.

Supervisors always are interested in getting maximum results from their budget, so they sometimes ask, "Which is more important to employees, financial rewards or psychological-social rewards?" This question is meaningless, because both are important. A more realistic question is how to integrate the two types of rewards so that employees have an effective mix of both.

Supervisors actually administer both rewards and punishments. If a supervisor emphasizes rewards, either financial or psychological-social, then the supervisor is practicing positive leadership. If penalties are emphasized, then the supervisor is applying negative leadership. Most supervisors apply some of both, but the approach that tends to dominate sets the climate in a department.

Negative approaches, such as threats and penalties, do accomplish acceptable performance in many situations, but their human costs are so high that they are not a wise alternative. Negative supervisors act domineering and superior with people. To get work done they hold over their personnel such penalties as loss of job, reprimand in the presence of others, and abusive communications. They display authority with the false assumption that it frightens employees into productivity. These people are really bosses more than supervisors. Positive supervisors offer encouragement to employees. They give employees motivation to come to work in the morning, because the work is rewarding and satisfying to them. Some of the most important rewards do not cost any budget anything. One of these is recognition. Studies show that workers seek and appreciate it. It is a regular source of feelings of worth and fulfillment. when it is offered genuinely, based on actual achievements, it can be a powerful motivator. Another reward that should not cost any budget is a genuine interest in employees as persons. Employees want to know that they are considered important by supervisors, that supervisors do care, and that supervisors are interested in their problems. Even the most competent supervisor will at times fall back upon negative approaches, because positive approaches are not always available. However, the historical trend is clearly toward more and more positive approaches to supervision.

Counselor

Another supervisory activity is the counseling of employees. Counseling has the objective of reducing or removing emotional problems that employees have. As people work together, frictions and problems naturally develop, and it is a supervisory responsibility to reduce these difficulties through counseling. No more complex unit exists than a human being; therefore, it is impossible for a person to be in optimum emotional balance all of the time.

Supervisors need to understand that emotional upsets are not necessarily undesirable or "wrong". Nature gave people their emotions, and sometimes it is more disastrous to suppress an emotion such as anger than to go ahead and express it. But emotional upsets can cause workers to do things that are harmful to their own interests as well as those of the organization. For example, one employee may quit an organization because of some trifling conflict that has been exaggerated until it seems large. In such instances, supervisory counseling may be helpful in retaining employees, thereby helping them as well as the organization. The important point is to channel human emotions along constructive lines rather than destructive ones. Emotions cannot be ignored with the hope that they will go away. They require supervisory efforts just like other parts of the supervisor's job.

When supervisors are working with emotional problems, they are not necessarily seeking the 90-95 percent success rate that is often required in other supervisory actions, such as living within the budget. If only 20 or 25 percent of the employees can be helped, then that is 20 or 25 percent more than would have been helped without counseling, so success has been achieved. However, emotional problems are extremely complex, and supervisors should not expect that they can be easily solved. In many instances, therefore, supervisors will send employees to others such as personnel specialists for counseling.

Trainer

Another activity of the supervisory role is training. Often this activity consumes a substantial portion of a supervisor's time. Training is rewarding both to the supervisor and to employees. If supervisors can develop competent, well-trained employees, then their jobs become easier, because employees can do their work without constant supervision. Employees also are helped. Their self-image and feeling of accomplishment are improved. By becoming better trained they also are more likely to take pride in performing high-quality work. Eventually, training should help them gain wage increases and promotions, because of their added qualifications.

Change agent

A significant activity of supervisors is to administer change in their departments. With the fast technological and social progress that is being achieved in the world, change has become a necessary way life in most organizations. As a representative of management at the work place, supervisors are in the center of the many difficulties caused by change. They need to understand change and how it affects people and organizations. Essentially, their objective is to introduce change with a minimum of upset and in such a way that the organization benefits in the long run. As the saying goes, "Reduce the harm and expand the benefit." Group participation is an effective way to build support for change. Participation helps employees become involved so that they better understand the change, and it increases their commitment to the change. It assures them that management is not trying to put something over on them by deciding on a change and then imposing it by what is derisively called the "bulldozer" method of change. One special benefit of participation is that it may improve a proposed change by adding contributions from those who will work under it. Participation helps to amend poor plans, and almost always it broadens the supervisor's understanding about the change.

Employee resistance to change is not necessarily bad. In some instances resistance uncovers difficulties connected with the change that were not originally evident to the supervisor. Another benefit is that resistance may cause the supervisor to examine more carefully the negative side effects that accompany change, in the same way that they accompany powerful antibiotic drugs. In other instances resistance causes supervisors to clarify their reasons for introducing change and to define more precisely the desirable results that they expect from change. Resistance also may identify pockets of low job satisfaction and poor motivation in the organization, so that supervisors can take corrective action. Resistance can pinpoint weaknesses in communication, because they frequently arise from inadequate communication about change. And finally, resistance to change can cause supervisors to give more attention to building effective human relations in their departments, because they see that it is necessary to reduce resistance to change.

Other activities

Our discussion certainly has not covered all of the activities that make up the supervisory job, but it has described some of the primary ones. There are others, such as handling grievances, maintaining discipline, providing suggestions for improvements, and creative thinking. The important point is that supervisors have a multitude of different duties requiring a wide variety of skills. supervision is not an activity of one, two, or three skills, but of many skills often quite different from one another. It requires persons who are versatile and capable of understanding complex relationships. They are like jugglers, having to keep many events going at the same time as they work back and forth from one to the other.

A favourable organizational climate

We can sum up the supervisory role by saying that most of what supervisors do is covered by the idea of building a favorable climate for job performance and for the personal growth and satisfaction of employees. The supervisory role exists to carry out organizational objectives, but also to accomplish objectives in such a way that people are rewarded.

A sound climate is a long-run proposition. Supervisors need to take an assets approach to climate, meaning that they take the long-run view of climate as an organizational asset. Unwise supervision, such as threatening and putting pressure on people, may temporarily increase production, but it may so alter the organizatinal climate that the department is in worse condition eventually. The far more effective way is to build a positive climate favorable to performance and personal growth in the beginning.

Supervisory Decision Making and Employee Participation

Decisions and decision making

A decision is an act of choice. It takes place when one alternative action is selected in preference to all others. On the other hand, decision making is a process, or series of events, leading to a choice and continuing after a choice is made.

Steps in decision making

To illustrate the nature of decisions and decision making, consider the illustration in Figure. Each stage in the process is important if we are to understand supervisory decision making. Therefore. let us briefly examine each phase.

Establishment of the goal: In making decisions, supervisors are concerned with an objective or a set of goals. This is their standard, their point of reference, when they select among alternative solutions to a problem. The goal may be productive efficiency, work-group satisfaction, industrial peace, or some other end considered desirable and supported by higher management.

Definition of the problem: Before a problem can be solved, it must be accurately defined and analyzed. If, for example, supervisors are concerned about a reduction in the output of their units, care must be taken to analyze the problem thoroughly before taking corrective action. What has changed recently that could cause reductions in performance? Has there been a change in the incentive program? Are there rumors circulating about possible layoffs? Is the union contract up for renewal? These are but a few of the possible questions one might ask.

Search for Alternative: Once the problem has been defined, possible solutions must be generated. It is unusual if only one course of action exists.

Let us assume that we know of rumors about possible layoffs. There are several things that might be done. The supervisor might allow the rumors to go unchecked. In this case, no action is the chosen alternative. Or, he or she may "level" with the group and tell them exactly what the situation is. It might also be advisable to have a member of the personnel department talk to the group. In other words, various alternatives are available to the supervisor.

Selection of the Alternative: After a proper evaluation, the supervisor must decide on the appropriate course of action. This is the point of decision. The choice is made with reference to the goal he is attempting to accomplish. The decision problem is to select the alternative that holds the greatest promise of accomplishing the objective.

Implementation: When the decision is made, the selected course of action must be put into practice. If the group leader decides to hold a meeting of employees to assure them that no plans are being made for layoffs, the conference must be scheduled and the time communicated to the work group.

Follow-up: The supervisor should always be concerned with be coming a better decision maker. Therefore, it is important to monitor the results of a decision. This is a learning process whereby the supervisor reflects on the process and cons of the selected course of action with respect to the goal being sought. Regardless of the outcome, lessons are always learned that can be useful in future decision making.

This we see that decision making consists of several stages, only one of which constitutes the actual decision. We must recognize, however, that decision making does not stop with the evaluation or follow-up phase. Decisions have lasting effects on the person responsible for their implementation. Perhaps the most common effects are the anxiety and frustration that follow human choices. When a supervisor chooses one act over others there are always certain aspects of the rejected alternatives that are favorable. Usually, we overcome frustrations by concentrating on the favourable features of rejected alternatives. Although this can be troublesome if taken too far, such reactions are basically functional in a psychological sense because they allow us to continue with some degree of sanity in accomplishing the complex tasks of supervision.

Before looking in greater detail at the problem-solving process, we must examine some different ways of viewing decisions. This is the goal of the following section.

Basic types of decisions

There are numerous ways to look at supervisory decisions. Although we seldom classify them consciously in our minds, some awareness of each can aid in a more successful implementation of the decisions we make.

Means or ends: One of the most effective ways of emphasising the importance of supervisory decisions is to look at the means-ends relationship they are designed to accomplish. This can be explained with the use of the following illustration.

Morgan Parker is a supervisor on the day shift in the Baker Machine Shop. At the present time he is interviewing several applicants referred by the personnel department for a job opening as a machinist's helper. In screening the applicants, Morgan is primarily concerned with hiring the helpful who will be most effective in increasing the performance of the machinist to whom he will be assigned. The performance of the machinist is important to ensure the efficiency of the department. The department's efficiency of the department. The department's efficiency contributes to the overall profitability of the firm.

The logic of the means-ends relationship is important from the perspective of the firm. The selection of the proper helper is the immediate goal. The accomplishment of this goal, however, is the means to a higher level end—the machinist's proficiency. The machinist's proficiency, in turn, is the means to a more efficient department and ultimately to the profitability of the firm. The view of supervisory decision making emphasis the importance of seemingly routine actions on the accomplishment of organizational goals. In other words, the profitability of a firm, such as the Baker Machine Shop, is dependent on correct supervisory decisions.

Routine and nonroutine decisions: Every supervisory job is a complex mixture of routine and nonroutine decisions. This terminology should not imply that one type is more or less important than the other.

Routine decisions are recurring and predictable. Production scheduling must be done at certain times, and everyone knows it. Schedules can be developed and plans made accordingly. This is also true of shift assignments and released time for vacations. Nonroutine decisions are not recurring and cannot be easily predicted. Sometimes, without notice, a production line breaks down, an employee becomes ill and must be replaced, or your boss puts you in charge of implementing a new process that has not been used previously. Unlike making a schedule, it is impossible to predict exactly when this type of situation will occur, and when it does, little experience is available to guide you in deciding what to do. The point is simple—we can program, plan for, and anticipate routine decisions. Nonroutine decisions must be dealt with as they develop.

Some outcomes of decision making

To this point we have examined the basic decision-making process and noted that it is essentially a means of systematic problem solving. Unfortunately, the supervisor who carefully follows the process is not guaranteed that successful decisions will always result. To illustrate, consider the following situation.

Lois Dodson is the supervisor of Steno Pool Number Three in the Engineering Department of a large petrochemical firm. In this capacity she is responsible for supervising ten senior typists and for assisting the group in completing the consistently heavy work load. The typists are all highly skilled employees because of the technical nature of work. They are not unionized, but there have been rumors of organizing efforts by the local representative of the office workers' union. In the past, vacation time has been scheduled on the basis of seniority. If more than one person applies for vacation time around Christmas, for example, the one with the longest service is given priority. Recently, Lois received vacation requests from Janet Davis and Lawrence Beck for the week of December 25. Only one number of the group can leave on vacation at any given time and both of the applicants have equal time with the company.

Lois knows that Janet Davis' husband is graduate student at the local university and Christmas is the only time they can travel to visit their families in a distant city.

Lawrence Beck, on the other hand, plans to be married on December 23 and wants to combine the vacation with a honeymoon. Sound familiar? Lois is confronted with a serious, although typical, supervisory decision. Let's see what can result.

First, Loid could decide to allow Lawrence Beck to go on vacation because of some criterion such as the alphabetical order or the applicant's last names. It is also possible that Janet might understand and yield to the decision. In this case a decision has been made and a satisfactory outcome has resulted.

On the other hand, Lois may decide in favor of Mr. Beck and Ms. Davis may be dissatisfied. The obvious charge could be that there is no policy for deciding on vacation time based on the alphabetical order of last names. Here, a decision has been made and conflict has resulted. Both of these possibilities could also be repeated with Ms. Davis going on vacation and Mr. Beck remaining at work.

There are, of course, other possibilities. Lois may decide that since both employees have the same seniority, there is no equitable way of resolving the issue and allow no one to leave during the Christmas week. Or, it may be possible to ask the two employees to come together, discuss the dilemma, and work out a compromise.

Obviously, in a decision of this nature, there is no absolute rule for action. What the supervisor does is a complex mixture of judgment, concern for justice, consideration of group performance, and numerous other factors. The important point is that a relatively routine issue can often become quite complex. Recognizing the complexity of the problem, the supervisor must look at the alternatives and select the one considered most appropriate. At times, reformulating the choices in the form of a decision tree like this can help in itemizing and examining alternatives.

The primary danger is to make complex decisions while assuming they are as simple as they appear. Through a more through and systematic analysis, the supervisor can at least anticipate possible outcomes and prevent, insofar as possible, the anxiety and frustration inherent in decision making. He or she can also prepare, in advance, methods of resolving conflicts that might result.

Decision making: from theory to reality

To this point we have looked at decision making as a precise series of steps one follows in arriving at a desired goal. In reality, this is often impossible.

The supervisor often finds problem-solving situations more confusing than our discussion indicates. For example, problems develop from the very beginning of the process. Often the supervisor is not sure of the goal to be accomplished. Although upper management may devote considerable time to emphasizing the importance of profits, good labor relations, social responsibility, and so on, these objectives are difficult to reformulate into precise guidelines for action. For example, will terminating an unsatisfactory employee increase the efficiency of the department and the profitability of the firm? On the surface the answer would appear to be yes. However, we must ask whether or not it would simultaneously, result in unfavorable labor relations, reduced morale, and lower profits?

Another important complication is time. We would all probably agree that systematic problem solving is better than unsystematic behavior. It is also more time consuming. Thus, the practical issue becomes: How much effort can I devote to gathering and analyzing data without using an excessive amount of time? After all, the supervisor's days are far too short already?

Quality control is concerned with excessive waste, sales is concerned that a sufficient supply finished products is available, and inventory control is upset over rising inventory costs. As a result, the logical means-ends relationship becomes less precise. Not only is it impossible to clearly "picture" the organizational goal, but the relationship among the various organizational interest groups in one of conflict. The efforts of the supervisor are thus directed toward comprising the various interest groups rather than maximising the interests of the owners. This is one reason why supervisory decision makers are often said to *sacrifice*; that is, they try to achieve an outcome satisfactory to all the groups by minimizing conflict. This greatly complicates the maximization of performance. But, there is more to the problem.

Limited knowledge

Supervisors also fail to maximize decisions because of the vast amounts of information necessary in even simple situations. In the case of Lois Lodson mentioned earlier, we itemized some of the options she might exercise, but were quick to admit that other alternatives were possible.

Decision makers generally have limited knowledge for one or more of the following reasons.

1. The problem is too complex to understand, or imagine, all possible courses of action.
2. The objective of some decisions makes complete knowledge unnecessary.
3. The cost and time necessary for gathering all information is prohibitive.
4. Search patterns limit the amount and quality of information generated.

Let us look briefly at each of these.

Problem complexity: There are very few problem situations where we are sure that we know all available courses of action. Even if we should be so lucky, we surely could not know the possible outcomes for each alternative. Yet, knowledge of both these items is necessary if we are to maximize the results of our decision making.

Objective of decision making: Sometimes the task facing supervisors is not to generate alternatives but to analyze and select from among those presented to them.

For example, a firm may have a centralized hiring policy where the supervisor reports job openings and the personnel department locates possible candidates. In one case personnel may send three applicants and ask the supervisor to make the final selection. Here, the decision maker may choose may choose any of the three or reject all and ask for more applicants. In earlier event, the supervisor's job is to select among presented alternatives, not to generate new ones. Thus, the objective of decision making is an analysis of alternatives.

Information cost and time: The acquisition of information, or generation of alternatives, consumes time and costs money, neither of which is plentiful in today's organizations. As a result, the supervisor may consciously decide to make a choice after a specific number of alternatives have been generated.

Search patterns: Not all supervisors search for alternatives in the same manner. Some, for example, will generate as many alternatives as possible. Others will make a decision on the basis of only one or a few available options. How supervisors search for information is related to a number of factors such as their personalities, past experiences, time commitments, etc.

Decision making is by its nature an individual activity. At times, however, groups are involved in the process. Probably the most common form of group decision making is the committee, but supervisors may involve others without the formality of a committee structure. Because of this, we must examine the pros and cons of group decision making and the related issue of employee participation.

Group decision making

Supervisors in all types of organizations are frequently faced with the question of whether or not to call on others for assistance in making important decisions. Although we joke about committees and say that no self-respecting supervisor would ever admit that committees are useful, the fact is that most organizations make extensive use of such groups. One survey, for example, found that almost all large firms studied acknowledged the use of committees in decision making. Obviously, groups of this nature are objects of concern to supervisors.

Some oros and cons

If most organizations use committees, they must obviously have some advantages over individuals acting alone. The primary advantages usually include the following:

1. Groups expand the capabilities of individuals. This is particularly true when the groups are structured in certain ways.
2. Group decision making facilities a sense of participation on the part of employees.
3. Representative groups reduce conflict when decisions under consideration have interdepartmental or inte-unit implications.

Let us look in greater detail at each of the proposed advantages.

Expansion of individual capabilities. All of us have, no doubt, experienced the mental stimulation that can be received from discussing things with others. Often, we think of numerous points that might not have been considered if someone had not made a certain statement.

Although we can be easily stimulated by group numbers with similar backgrounds and experience, we can also increase our creativity by interacting with others who view problems from a different perspective. For example, several foremen of production units may talk over a problem and examine numerous alternatives that would have never been considered by each foreman acting alone. Similarly, if a foreman is placed in a group with supervisors from other areas such as sales, finance, and personnel, more dimensions of the problem are likely to emerge.

Increase participation: Since we will deal with employee participation in the final section of this chapter, only a few comments will be made at this point. For our purposes, we can simply note that when people participate in problem solving they feel more a part of the solution. At least, they feel important because someone has asked their opinion. As a result, implementation of the proposed action should be easier.

Aiding in interunit cooperation: Let us assume that production and sales are experiencing a typical conflict. The production department wants to schedule production runs over the year so as to avoid layoffs. Sales, however, recognizing that orders tend to cluster around certain months, wants production increased during such periods to ensure adequate inventory levels.

It is doubtful that either group would approve a solution dictated by the other. However, by working on a solution through representatives of both groups, they can develop a recommendation more satisfactory to each.

To this point, groups, sound like good things. Lest we be misled, however, we must also note some possible disadvantages. A few of the more important are:

1. Groups are expensive and consume valuable time.
2. Some people are not secure in groups and may be inhibited by dominant personalities.
3. Groups make decisions that are too risky since no single individual is accountable for the outcome.

Expensive and time consuming: Everyone in a supervisory position has probably experienced the frustration of attempting to obtain group agreement on some issue. The presentation and discussion of diverse opinions obviously takes longer than a single person's sitting down and making a choice. Also, it is usually difficult, if not impossible, to schedule a time when all concerned parties can attend meetings without disrupting normal operations.

When the group is assembled, each member's attention is also diverted from primary job duties. The person's pay, however, continues. As a result, group decision making becomes expensive in a monetary sense.

Inhibiting effects on individuals: While a group setting stimulates some people, it frightens others. This can be a special problem where groups are composed of people from different levels of authority. For example, if supervisors and their bosses are members of the same problem-solving group, some supervisors may refrain from making suggestions for fear of their bosses' reaction.

Even where groups are carefully selected to ensure that only individuals of equal organizational status are represented, dominant personalities often emerge. Such people who become very stimulated by group discussions can sometimes discourage less dominant individuals from participating.

Groups assume more risk. Some writers in the area argue that groups consistently make riskier decisions than individuals. The idea behind the argument is that when a group recommends a course of action, no single person is responsible for the outcome. Thus, the group feels more comfortable with risky actions. Research on the subject raises questions about this line of thought, since some studies have shown that groups tend to reach compromises that result in less risky recommendation.

The point of this discussion is that groups offer advantages and disadvantages in the area of decision king. They are useful in building involvement and participation but can be expensive and time consuming. The practical issue for supervisors is that groups can assist in solving problems; however, the issue of participation raises additional points and supervisors should consider in the area of decision making.

Employee participation

Rensis Likert, former director of the Institute for Social Research at the University of Michigan, has worked extensively with the question of "how successful managers manage." On the basis of more than three hundred studies in all types of organizations, he developed a list of six characteristics possessed by good managers. These are:

1. The successful manager is technically competent in his or her job.
2. The successful manager formulates high-performance and challenging goals.
3. The successful manager supports subordinates by showing confidence and trust in them and by listening to what they have to contribute.
4. The successful manager builds effective work groups by involving subordinates in decisions affecting them.
5. The successful manager plans and organizes work so that the group knows what is going on.
6. The successful manager ensures that employees are well-trained.

Three of these items relate directly to encouraging employee participation. Item four specially notes that successful managers involve employees in the decisions that affect them. The importance of participative management is becoming recognized by national governments as well as individual organizations. For example, in Sweden it is a low that all companies with one hundred or more employees must have worker representatives on their boards of directors. A similar system exists in West Germany.

In this country, companies like Questor Corporation have involved employees in such basic decisions as workflow design with favourable effects on moral and reduced absenteeism. In 1973, the Conference Board completed a survey of 147 organizations in an attempt to determine the extent of employee participation in decision making. Although this survey used certain types of subcategories of organizations, several interesting results were obtained that are relevant for our purposes. First, it noted that more than 60 percent of the responding firms used participative-group methods of problem solving. However, most restricted the participation to middle and upper management levels in the organization. Less than 10 percent involved lower levels of supervision and rank-and-file employees in participative problem solving. Thus, we see an interesting pattern in participative decision making as it exists in reality. It is used, but involvement is limited. Let us examine the topic in greater detail.

Some advantages of participation: Advocates of participative decision making usually base their position on one or more of the following arguments, listed by Tannenbaum and Massarik:

1. Performance can be improved through higher rates of output and increases in the quality of the work . This is assumed to result from the feeling of greater involvement on the part of employees.

2. Because involvement increases, morale improves. The result is often less absenteeism and lower turnover rates.

3. Better company-union relations develop with a corresponding reduction in the number of grievances filed.

4. There is less resistance to change. Since employees feel a part of what is happening and have been included in decision making, there is less reason for them to resist the implementation of plans.

5. Improved decisions often result because more input has been obtained and a more critical analysis has been conducted.

We see from this list that advocates of employee participation see many desirable effects resulting from the involvement of group members. Production is said to increase, morale is thought to improve, better union-management relations development, individuals become less resistant to change, and better decisions result. If only this were true!

In some cases, no one would dispute the favourable effects resulting from participation. However, there is obviously another side to the coin or no one would be autocratic. Every successful manager would encourage and insist on participation. But this is not the case.

Some disadvantages: All supervisors do not encourage participation because there are certain disadvantages. A few of the more important are:

1. Urgent decisions require fast action. Obtaining inputs from even a few people takes time.
2. Threats to supervisory authority can result from participation. When you ask the opinions of others you have an obligation to consider suggestions seriously. Some supervisors may view this type of inputs as a threat to their position, since they assume that asking the opinions of others is a sign of weakness.
3. The supervisor cannot delegate responsibility. Regardless of how much you involve others in decision making, you alone are responsible for the action taken. Since you are responsible for the action taken, there is less incentive to give up control over decisions to be made.
4. Not all employees want to participate. Some choose not to be supervisors. They do not want to be bothered with decision making and may look upon it as not part of their job.

The choice between autocracy and democracy is not an easy one. For this reason, Le Forest Smith, General director of the YMCA in Orange, New Jersey, suggests that the most effective supervisors are those who can accurately view a situation and decide "when to use group thinking and when to go solo."

24

Material Management

The winds of change are blowing in purchasing and supply. Continued upgrading of conformance quality standards, just-in-time approaches to material availability, long-term relationships with fewer suppliers and a win-win approach to negotiations instead of the more traditional adversarial or win-lose approach, are just some of the changes in the way procurement is managed. These changes are helping organizations to survive and succeed in a very competitive world. Purchasing and supply is a necessary function in almost every organization, from the private household to the national government. This book is mainly about larger organizations which have purchasing and supply departments, but purchasing and supply is just as important in small organizations which do not employ full-time people to do the work, and it is hoped that the latter may also find the book useful.

Smaller organizations

Organizational purchasing is the process by which organizations define their needs for goods and services; identify and compare the supplies and suppliers available to them; negotiate with sources of supply or in some other way arrive at agreed terms of trading; make contracts and place orders; and finally receive, accept and pay for the goods and services required. Purchasing is closely associated with other organizational functions, such as inventory management, stores operation, and transport. Production planning and control, in manufacturing organizations, and merchandising, in distributive organizations, have to work closely with buying. Often some or all of these functions are combined with the purchasing function under a single head, the materials manager or supply manager.

Traditionally, purchasing objectives were defined as: to obtain the right quality of goods, in the right quantity, at the right time, from the right supplier, at the right price. These five 'rights' were often thought of in the context of a static environment, so that by a series of successive approximations it would eventually be possible to arrive at the final right answer for each one.

But in highly competitive world markets the environment is not static but dynamic, tending not towards equilibrium but always towards something new. Purchasing objectives continually need to be updated and revised. Arriving at the final right answer for some old product just as it is discontinued does nothing for the competitive position of an organization. Proactive, rather than reactive; dynamic, rather than static, is the way in which the purchasing role is now conceived. Better quality, in more suitable quantities, just in time for requirements, from better suppliers, at prices which continue to improve, are the sort of aims set by the dynamic purchasing function today.

Long before the large organization appeared with its functionally specialized departments, people bought and sold. Buying, that is acquiring goods and services in return for a price, dates back before the invention of written records. So also does selling, the disposal of goods and services in return for a price. It is likely that human communities have always bought and sold and that culturally and materially then have benefited from these transactions.

Archaeological evidence shows that trade occurred between the prehistoric tribes of Britain's stone age. The distinctive products of a flint axe factory at Langdale in the Lake District have been found hundreds of miles away in South Wales. Did Langdale send out travelling salesmen, or did South Wales have tribal buyers searching the land for better buys in stone age weaponry? We do not know. But what is known is that among the earliest things to be written down were stock records and accounts of commercial transactions. In days when literature and history were still being recited from memory, the pioneer developments in written record, whether incised on baked clay in cuneiform or carved or painted in pictographs, dealt with purchases, stocks and sales.

When books were invented, they dealt at first with higher matters than trade. Yet in the Bible itself, the oldest of all best-sellers, we read: 'It is naught, it is naught, saith the buyer; but when he is gone his way then he rejoiceth'. In Chaucer's *Canterbury Tales*, one of the oldest works in the canon of English literature, several of the horseback pilgrims are described as 'purchasours' or (since the ruling classes had previously spoken a kind of French) 'achatours'. No salesmen made the pilgrimage.

Many of Chaucer's pilgrims have occupational titles which with the passage of time have come to sound more like surnames. There was a 'manciple', for instance, described as an expert catering buyer.

The growth of the firm

Most firms start off as very small organizations, growing in size as they become more successful. The small firm consists of the entrepreneur who runs it and who usually started it, plus a number of other people to whom work is assigned which the entrepreneur either does not wish to do himself (such as perhaps packaging and despatch), or cannot do himself because he does not know how (such as, perhaps, preparation of final accounts), or else because there are not enough hours in the day to do everything. In such a small firm, major purchasing decisions are usually made by the head of the organization and minor purchasing decisions together with the detailed purchasing work fall to those in charge of any departments that exist. When a purchasing officer is appointed, his job may at first be seen as to do the legwork and the paperwork associated with purchasing, rather than to take the basic purchasing decisions.

Eventually, if the firm continues to increase in size, proper departments are set up for all major functions, and it is at this stage that management needs to delegate to purchasing the authority and responsibility to identify and evaluate purchasing problems, and to initiate, recommend and implement effective solutions.

A complex process

Organizational purchasing can be a complex process. Many people may take part, at various levels n the management hierarchy and in several functional departments. It can be a lengthy process: major 'one-off' decisions may take years to finalize. Even routine repeat orders that are placed immediately without consultation may be placed in accordance with policies previously laid down after much consultation and experiment over a lengthy period of time.

It is made more complex by its detailed involvement with other decision and control processes such as:

(1) stock control policies and procedures which determine, control and replenish the range of items stocked;

(2) the physical supply cycle which goods pass through as they are despatched, transported, received, stored and either issued or sold;

(3) production planning and control which determines and controls the quantities of parts and materials required to meet production commitments;

(4) merchandizing which decides which goods will be offered for resale and at what price.

It is when some of all of these other processes are combined in one department or under one head that the term *materials management* is used. The term *purchasing and supply* also suggests a joint consideration of purchasing with stock control and stores management, without necessarily implying that all those concerned with carrying out the relevant activities report to a single manager.

Organization structures

The way purchasing and other supply activities are organized into departments, how tasks and activities are allocated to supply personnel, and the extent to which authority is delegated to the department head to decide matters in the supply area on his own responsibility, are all subject to considerable variation in practice.

A typical organization structure for a medium size manufacturing business which has adopted a materials management approach. This represents one particular organization, and others would be different. Some would not have a product design department, for instance, perhaps because they sub-contract design, or perhaps because they make only to customer design.

The responsibilities of purchasing

Some organizations issue an internal charter or purchasing manual which incorporates a formal statement signed by management of what services the purchasing department is expected to provide and what its responsibilities are. Croell suggests the following:

(1) Provide all materials and services that the company elects not to provide internally. In accomplishing this, purchasing must perform the following basic tasks.

   (a) Select and develop as required, vendors capable of meeting company needs.

   (b) Prepare and sign all purchase orders/contracts, so that the needs of the company and all pertinent terms and conditions related to the purchase are clearly understood by the supplier and documented accordingly.

   (c) Monitor supplier performance and related company activities during the course of the contract to assure that performance is accomplished by both parties in accordance with that originally intended.

   (d) Renegotiate or terminate purchase orders/contracts as required when changes occur, or as other conditions develop that warrant such action.

(2) Provide information to and participate in management planning sessions on subjects related to purchased materials services.

(3) Review purchase specifications and assist operating departments in selection of required materials and services for standardization purposes, and to assure their availability from competent suppliers, at reasonable prices.

(4) Protect the company from all unnecessary or unauthorized commitments which may result from inappropriate contacts or discussions with suppliers.

(5) Dispose of all obsolete materials, equipment, or scrap that is not longer required for company operations.

Marketing and purchasing

The buying department and the selling department are the two departments mainly concerned with external relations, with reaching out into the supply markets and the sales markets outside the firm. To what extent does it make sense to say that both are engaged in marketing? This question is partly semantic (what words mean and how they are used) and partly about what departments do an how their work is perceived.

Definitions and discussions of marketing have certainly been dominated by selling considerations in recent years, although not in earlier periods. Consumer product manufacturers in the West which were competing for discretionary spending by consumers took to the marketing concept in a big way. The marketing concept, so called, could be described as the realization that firms need to find out what their customers want and take steps to provide it if they are to prosper; rather than producing the goods they were interested in producing, they needed to provide the goods the consumer was interested in purchasing. The marketing concept was less prevalent in industrial marketing, where many firms remained firmly and indeed proudly product-oriented rather than customer-oriented.

Industrial marketing differs from consumer marketing in several ways. Firstly, it usually sells different products. It deals in heavy equipment, such as tractors and machine tools; light equipment, such as photocopiers and hand power tools; construction, for example, of factories, docks and housing estates. It sells raw materials, such as iron ore and coal; processed materials, such as steel bar, chemicals and plywood; components, such as ball bearings and electric motors and semi-conductors; consumable supplies, such as cleaning materials and cutting oils; and a variety of services, such as those of the forwarding agent, the contract painter, or machine maintenance.

Secondly, it usually sells to different customers. Consumer marketing aims at households and individuals. Industrial marketing aims at organizations, and these have different and often much more complex buying processes. Consequently, when products such as motor cars or typewriters are sold to both consumers and to organizations the marketing approach tends to be very different for the two.

As Webster and Wind point out,

> industrial and institutional marketers have often been urged to base their strategies on careful appraisal of buying behaviour within key accounts and in principal market segments. When they search the available literature on buyer behaviour, however, they find virtually exclusive emphasis on consumers, not industrial buyers. Research findings and theoretical discussions abut consumer behaviour often have little relevance for the industrial marketer.

Yet the total value of interfirm purchases of raw materials, components and semi-finished parts, finished parts, tools and supplies, is considerably greater than the total of sales to retail consumers. Rowe and Alexander quote an estimate to the effect that interfirm sales are worth about 2.5 times as much as sales to individual consumers-3.5 times as much if sales to the government are included. They conclude that:

> resource allocation, in effect the sorting or matching of needs to supplying ability, is what marketing and selling is all about when looked at from the economist's viewpoint, and nowhere is this function more in need of being expertly carried out than in the area of interfirm transactions where industries are becoming interlocked in increasing interdependence.

This remains at least equally true if the words 'purchasing and supply' are substituted for the words 'marketing and selling'. It could indeed be said that the sorting or matching of needs to supplying ability is what purchasing is all about, and that in the area of interfirm transactions this often calls for marketing initiatives on the buying side.

This is sometimes described as 'marketing in reverse'. But one definition of 'to market', in the most popular dictionary in the United Kingdom, is 'to buy or sell in market', and the very word 'market' derives from a Latin word which means 'to buy' (*mercari*). In earlier days the merchant ventures set forth through unknown seas and distant countries in search, not so much of customers although they had to have something to trade, but more of new suppliers of new products-spices, furs, carpets, turkeys, tomatoes, oranges-as well as of new sources of known materials such as gold, diamonds and tin. Sourcing, and buying generally, was the venturesome and creative part of their marketing effort.

In the distributive industries, the selection and pricing of merchandise of sell is fundamental to marketing plans, and buying is therefore an important part of marketing for the retailer. In the manufacturing industries on the other hand, it is the selection and pricing of products to make which corresponds to this, and the procurement of parts and materials to make them tends to be seen as part of the production process rather than part of the marketing process.

Even here, some buying activities call for creative and entrepreneurial skills, for commercial innovation and persuasion. It is widely feared that shortages of materials and certain products will be increasingly common as the twentieth century draws to a close. And Kotler for instance argues that in times of shortage the marketing problem shifts its location from selling to buying. The development of new suppliers is another example of purchasing firms marketing their buying requirements to the supply markets. And in the negotiation of major contracts (for the design and development of equipment at the frontier of the art) to meet customer requirements, the term marketing may well be equally appropriate to the proposals and arguments coming from each side (if indeed it is appropriate at all in this situation).

The increasing concentration of markets has been a noticeable feature of recent years and accounts for part of the difference between industrial marketing and consumer marketing. For example, if three detergent manufacturers sell to tens of millions of households, scientific studies can be made of the market and how it can be segmented, of marketing methods and how best to apply them. But it an industrial manufacturer sells to six major industrial customers plus a number of minor customers, the scope for science is less, and it is more a matter of art. The shotgum communications of mass media advertising are used in the first case; the sharpshooter methods of field salesmen and low budget advertising in specialist trade journals are used in the second case.

In many industries a small number of manufacturers produce most of the output; and in quite a high proportion of cases, a small number of customers take most of the output. Buying and selling are both affected by the situation; after all, every purchase is someone's sale, purchasing and marketing are the two sides of one coin. Purchase cost analysis, negotiated prices based on mutually agreed figures for cost, larger and more expert departments both for buying and for selling, are typical features.

When two or three large firms supply equivalent or interchangeable products to the same market, at prices which each is reluctant to change because of the risk of retaliation by the others, two obvious ways to increase security as well as profits are: firstly by product differentiation, and secondly by cost reduction. Product differentiation makes the products seem less equivalent or interchangeable to the customer. Cost reduction enables a manufacturer to increase profits without starting a price war.

Cost reduction initially concentrated on manufacturing costs, with much success in many firms. But as one managing director said:

> we have over the years by dint of research, engineering development and good management, reduced operating costs to such an extent that now nearly 80% of total cost consists of purchased materials. Obviously it is important that buyers have an eye for more than the cheap price. Purchasing and supply have a major part to play in reducing cost and increasing profit.

Materials management

If the manufacturing, trading, and profit and loss account of any British manufacturing business is examined it is likely that a large proportion of all costs incurred during a period can be attributed to the requisition and storage of materials and components. Also, from an examination of the balance sheet, a large proportion of funds invested in the business's working capital is likely to be found invested in stocks of raw materials and components. These two observations have not gone unnoticed by business owners and managers who have concentrated their resources on devising ways of organising their firms with the objective of controlling the purchasing and storage of materials and components. The effects of poor buying and bad stock control are increased costs and inefficiency. This chapter looks at the ways business can be organised to ensure that the purchasing and storage functions are carried out efficiently and with the minimum of cost. It also takes a brief overview of the whole production function and the relationship between the departments comprising that function.

Materials management is the name given to the modern approach it purchasing and stock management, it integrates both the purchasing and stock management functions, enabling the firm to benefit from a close liaison between the stores personnel and the buyers. The integrated materials function is managed by a *materials manager*, who is responsible for both the stores and purchasing.

The organisation of the materials function

In many business the materials function is structured as part of the production function, the materials manager being responsible to the *production director or production manager.* This is the traditional organisation of purchasing and stock and is based on the premise that the acquisition of materials and stores are both part of the production function. In practice, materials consumed by a business are influenced by both sales forecasts and the production budget, as there is an interdependence between demand and supply. To recognise the relationship between marketing, production and materials management, a number of firms are now organising their materials function as separate from their production function, the materials manager being responsible to the board of directors. Such a structure recognises that the rate of consumption of materials depends ultimately upon demand.

The responsibilities of the materials manager

The responsibilities of the materials manager are likely to include:

(a) the purchasing of raw materials and components;

(b) the running of the stores and maintenance of stock levels;

(c) participating in product and process design on a consulting basis;

(d) keeping up to date with the development and introduction of raw materials;

(e) providing information for use in the preparation of a purchasing budget.

Purchasing

The objectives of the purchasing department

The objectives of the purchasing department should be to ensure that materials are purchased:

(a) at the right price;

(b) from the best supplier;

(c) of the right quality;

(d) in the right quantity;

(e) at the right time.

The right price

A firm's costs will be minimised only when materials are purchased at their optimal price. This will be the lowest price for which materials can be purchased that satisfies all the other objectives of purchasing. Consideration must be given to bulk discounts, other discounts and credit terms.

The best supplier

Features such as reliability, efficiency at dealing with queries and after-sales service vary from supplier to supplier. The supplier offering the best service that complies with the needs of the purchasing firm should be used. The best supplier will only be found by the buyer using his experience and knowledge of the trade.

The right quality

All materials bought for use in production should comply with the product specification. If they are below standard then can have far-reaching effects on production costs and profits of the firm. The use of substandard materials can result in:

(i) spoilt production;

(ii) high wastage of materials;

(iii) inefficient use of labour;

(iv) increased machine time needed by production;

(v) increased wear on machines.

All of these problems will increase costs and reduce production efficiency. The purchase of materials that are of a better standard than needed may result in a higher price being paid for them, although this may be compensated by other costs being saved because of increased efficiency resulting from their use.

In the right quantity

Materials should be purchased in sufficient quantities to minimise the risk of running our of stock, minimise purchasing costs and keep storage costs to a minimum. Purchase quantities can be controlled by employing stock-control techniques that calculate an optimal order quantity.

At the right time

Materials should be purchased so that they will be delivered when they re needed. If they are bought too early then excessive storage costs will be incurred. If they are bought too late then the firm may run out of materials with the result that production is interrupted.

The objectives of purchasing should be related to the objectives of each business, co-ordinated with the other functions and expressed in detail as its *purchasing policy*.

The function of the purchasing department

The primary function of the purchasing department is to carry out management policy relating to the purchase of raw materials, components, stores and equipment. The purchasing department is likely to have only limited authority expenditure. Most business establish an upper limit for expenditure and allow only specific types of purchases to be carried out by the purchasing department. Materials and components are usually included but authorisation for the purchase of expensive capital equipment is not normally given to the purchasing department, and is normally only sanctioned by senior management. The duties of the purchasing department should include the following.

Carrying out the purchasing procedure

Every business should have a purchasing procedure that is followed whenever a purchase of material is made. A typical procedure is as follows:

(i) A purchase requisition is completed by the appropriate department, e.g. stores, ad is authorised by a person holding the recognised responsibility, e.g. chief storekeeper.

(ii) The authorised purchase requisition is then passed to the purchasing department. A buyer then selects a supplier from the list of accredited suppliers or seeks a quotation from a number of accredited suppliers. Prices and terms are then negotiated and an order is then made out and placed with the best supplier. Orders made by telephone should be confirmed in writing.

(iii) Once an order has been placed with a supplier it should be monitored and if necessary chased up to ensure the delivery of materials is made on time.

(iv) When materials are received they should be checked with the delivery note and the order to ensure that they are as ordered and in the correct quantity. In delivered balances should be recorded as still outstanding. On acceptance of the materials the goods should be recorded in the materials inwards records.

Payment

The purchasing department should agree final acceptance of materials received and that they are as ordered. If they are satisfactory then authorisation should be made for payment to the supplier.

Market intelligence

The purchasing department should keep up to date with new development concerning materials and components available, suppliers and markets. Price trends and forecasts should be studied and projected into the future. Economic factors influencing the market should be studied, e.g. takeover or mergers of suppliers. Businesses whose raw materials suffer from wide fluctuations of price often make purchases in the "future" markets of their raw materials. This means they agree to purchase a specific quantity of a commodity at an agreed price at a fixed future date. The objective of this is to beat anticipated price rises in their raw materials. Future buying is highly speculative and requires considerable expertise on the part of the buyer.

Supplier appraisal

Whenever alternative suppliers exist for materials then each supplier should be evaluated by the purchasing department and a list of accredited suppliers produced.

Suppliers listed as accredited are those which meet the standards of the purchasing firms. A business should not place itself in a position where it is wholly dependent on only one supplier—material suppliers should be encouraged to compete for business. The accredited list of suppliers should be compiled on the basis of buyers' knowledge of suppliers and their experience in the market. It should be regularly reviewed to ensure it is up to date, changes being made whenever necessary.

Purchasing research

Purchasing research is an important activity of the purchasing department. The person responsible for purchasing research should research into:

Suppliers

A researcher should find out what alternative suppliers exist for each material or component and the terms of trade offered by each. Particular attention should be taken in finding out when new suppliers enter a market and who they are. Contact should be made with them as soon as possible. Researchers should also find to as soon as possible if and when existing suppliers are planning to withdraw from a market or discontinue a product line.

Prices

Research should be made into prices to ensure that up-to-date information on price is readily available. Price forecasts should be made so that information is available that can be used in the preparation of budgets and so that the firm can exploit expected falls in prices and minimize the effects of anticipated price rises, e.g. by purchasing additional stocks before a price rise.

Materials

Research into the alternative materials that are available will provide information that can be passed on to the production design and planing and control departments. In formation can also be passed on about new materials as soon as it is known.

The organisation of the purchasing function

As with the other functions of a business, the way in which the purchasing function will be organised depends to a large extent on the size and nature of the business. In smaller firms the number of employees engaged in purchasing will be relatively few, in such cases one person will be responsible for performing many duties. In large, complex organisations, large, extensive purchasing departments may exist, each person employed within the department specializing in only a limited range of activities. Alternative ways of organising the purchasing function are:

Centralized purchasing

When a business organizes its purchasing function centrally only one purchasing department is established. This is located centrally and is responsible for making purchases for the whole organisation. Centralization of purchasing enables economies to be made such as large quantity discounts to be taken advantage of and fewer orders being made. But local knowledge of suppliers will not be available. Smaller businesses with only a small purchasing department are likely to have a centralized purchasing function, as it will be uneconomic to have a number of smaller decentralized departments.

Decentralised purchasing

When a business separates the purchasing function into a number of separately organised divisions, each division is autonomous and is responsible for purchases made within its sphere of operations. An example of decentralised purchasing is when a business is divided into geographical regions, each region with its own purchasing department. A business that organizes its purchasing function in this way will benefit by local knowledge being available. An alternative structure would be to divide the purchasing function into autonomous divisions, each of which is responsible for a group of materials. This would enable each division to acquire and use specialist knowledge and enable the unique characteristics of each group to be known.

A combination of centralized and decentralised purchasing

Many larger firms organize their purchasing function in way in which part is decentralised. Which of the three alternative methods of organisation a firm uses depends on the size of the firm, the nature of its business and management policy. The one selected and used should be the one from which the from will benefit most.

The objectives of materials control

A large proportion of the working capital of a manufacturing business is likely to be invested in stock. This makes it crucial for management to control stock if working capital is to be efficiently used. If stock is not readily available when required then production will be disrupted, if excessive stock is held then unnecessary costs will be incurred. The objective of stock control can be summarized as follows:

(a) to keep storage costs to a minimum;

(b) to ensure materials are available when required;

(c) to preserve and protect materials in stock, e.g. prevent deterioration, pilferage, waste, loss etc;

(d) to facilitate the planning of material requirements;

(e) to co-operate with user departments;

(f) to keep accurate records and provide information to management relating to stock and stock levels.

The usual method for achieving these objectives is to establish and control a store or stores.

Types of stores

The types of stores used in practice vary from firm to firm and not two stores are likely to be identical. Stores are usually classified by type as follows:

(a) *Raw material stores* in which material stocks are kept.

(b) *Component stores* holding parts used for assembling finished goods or sold outside the business as spare parts.

(c) *Finished-parts stores* in which finished parts are stored ready for final assembly

(e) *Tool store* in which loose tools used in the factory or by service engineers are stored when not in use.

(f) *Maintenance stores* in which spare parts for use in the repair of machinery, cleaning materials and incidentals are stored before they are needed.

(g) *General stores* in which all stock is stored irrespective of its intended use. Small businesses will normally only have a general store and a finished-goods store.

The type of stores a firm uses will depend on such criteria as the nature of the industry, size of the form, methods of production used, factory layout and management policy.

Siting of the stores

The siting of the stores is an important decision, as badly located stores will increase costs unnecessarily and result in loss of production and a drop in efficiency, e.g. causing delays while materials are transported from the stores to the user location. Stores should be conveniently situated to facilitate the efficient receiving of materials inwards and the efficient issue and transport of stock to the user departments. The basic choice for the siting of the stores within the factory complex is largely dependent on how many store are decided upon. Management must make the familiar centralization or decentralisation decision regarding the stores.

Centralization of stores

When this is decided upon the stores are centralized in one location only, thus creating one centrally situated store serving all user departments from the same place. A centralized store has the advantages of:

(i) reducing the physical quantities of stock requiring to be kept, which will result in lower stock holding costs, lower risks of obsolescence and deterioration, less working capital needed, less space needed and lower insurance costs;

(ii) enabling specialist storage facilities to be utilized efficiently, e.g. refrigeration, air-conditioning, storage tanks etc.,

(iii) requiring less staff;

(iv) facilitating easier stock control and stock taking;

(v) reducing the amount of recording necessary

However, there are also a number of disadvantages must be offset. The most important disadvantages are:

(i) time and expense is wasted while the user department obtains stores from a remotely located store;

(ii) internal transport costs will be high;

(iii) the individual needs of specialist user departments may not be catered for;

(iv) the specialist knowledge of user departments

Decentralised stores

An alternative to locating stores centrally is to have a number of separate stores strategically placed around the factory complex, e.g. in each user department. The advantages and disadvantages of decentralised stores are those of centralized stores in reverse, i.e. the advantages of a centralized store are the disadvantage of a decentralised one.

Main store with substores

An alternative to locating stores centrally or decentrally is to have a compromise between the two. This involves having a main store sited centrally with a series of substores strategically located near or in the user departments. This benefits from the advantages of a centralized store while overcoming the disadvantages. The substores obtain stocks from the main store when required and issue them to the user departments.

The stores layout

The design and layout of stores is important as stock should be economically and efficiently stored, i.e. storage costs should be minimized and stock should be stored where it can easily be locate and removed. Stock should also be stored safely with the minimum risk of accident or damage. A well-designed stores layout should include the following features:

(a) heavy goods are stored on the floor:

(b) goods prone to damage from damp are kept in a dry location;

(c) valuable and dangerous materials are kept under secure conditions;

(d) fragile goods are stored in conditions which minimize their risk of being damaged;

(e) materials most frequently issued are stored where they are easily accessible;

(f) inflammable and explosive materials are protected from their inherent risks;

(g) the weight restrictions of the building are strictly complied with;

(h) the use of mechanical aids is facilitated;

(i) related matrials are stored near each other.

Once the stores layout has been designed it must then be equipped. Full advantage should be taken of new developments in stores equipment. Stores equipment includes shelving, racks, bins and handling equipment and may be either:

(a) portable, whereby changes can easily be made; or

(b) fixed, whereby changes can only be made with difficulty and at considerable expense.

Organisation of the stores

The stores are likely to be the responsibility of one person. The title of that person varies from firm to firm, common examples being chief storekeeper, head storeman or stores supervisor. He is normally responsible to the materials manager and he will be expected:

(a) to supervise personnel employed in the stores;

(b) to provide management with information and adviser on matters relating to the stores;

(c) to co-operate with the production, planning, purchasing, inspection and any other departments which use the service provided by the stores;

(d) to maintain a comprehensive, accurate and up-to-date set of stores records;

(e) to ensure an economic and efficient service is provided to user departments;

(f) to issue stock when it is required in compliance with the rules and procedures of the business;

(g) to ensure that physical stocks agree with the stores records;

(h) to check goods received from suppliers against delivery notes nd records and report to the purchasing department any variances.

The stores should be organised in such a way that the stores supervisor and his staff can carry out these duties effectively, efficiently and economically. Small businesses may only have one storekeeper performing all duties, large businesses tend to have one or more store together with an extensive and complex stock system requiring a number of stores personnel. In such a situation responsibilities are frequently organised into division of:

(a) warehouse, responsible for the actual receipt, storage and issue of physical stock;

(b) stores accounts, responsible for the maintenance of stores records;

(c) stock control, responsible for stock levels and stock taking.

The objectives of stock control

The main objective of stock control are:

(a) To avoid holding excessive quantities of stock, therefore keeping stock holding costs to a minimum. Holding costs include:

(i) interest on capital tied up;

(ii) loss due to deterioration, obsolescence and pilferage of materials;

(iii) warehouse and handling costs;

(iv) insurance;

(v) storekeepers' wages.

(b) To minimize the risk of running out of stock. If a stock-out occurs if frequently causes a production stoppage resulting in productive resources being lost, delay in completing customer order, lost sales and lost customer goodwill.

(c) To minimize the cost of making purchases. Purchasing costs tend to increase as the number of purchaser orders placed with suppliers increases.

An effective stock control system is one that results in these objectives being achieved. A good stock control system requires:

(a) accurate and up-to-date stores records;

(b) regular stock taking;

(c) the establishment of predetermined stock levels.

Stores records

Methods of keeping stores records that assist stock control are:

Two-bin system

This is a well-tried system that consists of two bins for each individual type of stock. One the working bin and the other the reserve bin. The contents of the working bin are issued until it is empty; the storekeeper then commences to issue the contents of the reserve bin which becomes the working bin. when a working bin is emptied the storekeeper advises the purchasing department, which reorders that particular stock them. When the order is delivered it is placed in the empty bin, which then becomes the reserve bin. Stores records are simple and record keeping is kept to a minimum, a bin and for each bin normally being sufficient.

Imprest system

This system of stores records requires a preprinted stock sheet for each individual type of stock noting the stock level. At regular intervals the quantity of each item in stock is recorded and compared with the normal stock level. The difference is noted and the amount in stock is less than the normal stock level then the quantity required is meted in the documents. The stock sheet is then signed, dated and passed to the purchasing department, as a purchase requisition. The imprest system ensures that purchases are based upon current stock levels and requirements. It also keeps stores records to a minimum and where stores are centrally organised acts as a formal purchase requisition procedure.

Reorder level cards

This system of stores records requires a stock card to be kept for each individual type of stock, each card showing a reorder quantity and reorder level. Issues and receipts of stock are posted by the stock clerk who makes out a purchase requisition for the reorder quantity when the reorder level is reached. The purchase requisition is then passed to the chief stock clerk, stores accountant or stores manager for authorization and is then passed to the purchasing department.

Cyclical reordering

This system involves making purchase orders for standard quantities of stock at regular intervals. This method of stores records is simple to operate but can easily result in a stock-out or overstocking. It is only suitable when consumption of a material is constant. The reorder quantity should be based upon forecast consumption during the period between orders and maintaining a buffer stock. A regular review of the standard quantity is necessary and should be amended to meet any expected changes in conditions.

Stock taking

Any system of stock records should be checked at least once a year by comparing physical stocks with the records. The objective of this is to:

(a) ensure the system is reliable and meets the needs of the business;

(b) detect errors and expedite their rectification;

(c) check for pilferage;

(d) provide information on stock quantities and values in management reports, management accounts and financial statements;

(e) identify obsolete and slow-moving stocks.

There are two basic alternative methods of stock taking. They are periodic stock checking and perpetual inventory.

Periodic stock checking

This involves physically checking and counting all stock on the same day at regular intervals, e.g. annually. Results are noted and compared with the stock records.

Periodic stock checking, even in a moderately sized business, is a considerable task and requires a lot of organising and effort. Disruption to production frequently occurs during stock checking, as issues from the stores must be restricted while stock checking takes place. To complete the check in the shortest possible time, personnel who are unfamiliar with the store may have to be switched from their normal duties. This will necessitate close supervision throughout the procedure.

Perpetual inventory

This is method of counting and checking stock continuously throughout at period by a relatively few specialist staff who are familiar with the stores. This method should be systematic to ensure that all stock items are checked, counted and the results compared with the stores records at least once during each period. Differences should be reported and investigated where, necessary, stores records being amended to show the correct position. Continuous stock checking has a number of advantages over periodic stock checking, including that:

(i) it eliminates the disruption of production;

(ii) errors will be detected sooner;

(iii) it discourages pilferage because it is not known in advance when each stock item is to be checked;

(iv) sow-moving and obsolete stock will be identified earlier;

(v) weaknesses in the system are more likely to be exposed sooner.

Slow-moving stock

These should be identified as soon as possible as reorder levels and reorder quantities may have to be reduced and reorder intervals extended, to prevent over-stocking. If slow-moving stock items are allowed to become overstocked:

(i) the risks of obsolescence increase;

(ii) the stock may deteriorate, resulting in unnecessary waste;

(iii) stocks will become excessive, taking up valuable storage space and increasing stock holding costs unnecessarily.

Obsolete stocks

These should be reported as soon as possible and their cause investigated. Good planning and control should avoid the problem of obsolete stock, which is wasteful and costly. Obsolete stock should be disposed of quickly if no alternative use can be found for it. To hold on to it only increases holding costs and takes up storage space by storing useless materials.

Stock levels

To enable a stock control system to effectively achieve its objective a number of predetermined stock levels should be established and maintained for each individual type of stock. These levels are a minimum stock level, maximum stock level, reorder level and an economic order quantity.

Minimum stock level

This is th buffer stock and is the level of stock below which stocks should not normally be allowed to fall. it should take into account:

(i) the reorder level;

(ii) the normal rate of consumption;

(iii) the reorder period.

Maximum stock level

In the level above which stock should not normally be allowed to rise. If stocks do exceed this level excessive holding costs will be incurred. The setting of this level should take into account:

(i) the rate of consumption:

(ii) the time necessary to obtain delivery;

(iii) the reorder quantity;

(iv) the reorder level.

Reorder level

The setting of a reorder level enables control to be exercised over the requisitioning of purchases. It answers the question of when to reorder, the solution being to calculate the stock level that will take into account:

(i) the quantity of stock expected to be consumed in the period under review:

(ii) the lead time;

(iii) the amount of stock expected to be consumed during the lead time;

(iv) the establishment of a buffer stock to allow for contingencies such as an unexpected rise in consumption or exceptional delays in receiving supplies. Should the buffer stock be used, immediate action should be taken to expedite delivery as a stock-out is threatened.

Order quantity

It is a general business fact that the greater the amount of stock carried by a firm, the higher will be its stock holding costs. However, carrying a large stock will only necessitate the occasional stock holding costs, but to avoid a stock-out will necessitate making frequent purchase orders for each individual type of stock. This will result in high costs incurred by the purchasing department. There is clearly a conflict between stock holding costs which increase as more stock is held and purchasing costs which increase as less stock is held. Establishing a predetermined order quantity answers the question; how many should be ordered? The answer to this is the quantity that will reduce the total costs of purchasing and holding stock to a minimum. This is in fact the point at which holding costs equal purchasing costs, and is known as the economic order quantity. The economic order quantity can be established of each individual type of stock by using a mathematical formula or graphically.

Once the economic order quantity has been established for each material, it should be recorded and whenever the reorder level is reached a purchase order should be made out for that quantity. Reasons why the economic order quantity is important include:

(i) it should ensure total stock costs are minimized;

(ii) it enables maximum and minimum stock level parameters to be set, thus contributing towards the establishment of a good stock control system;

(iii) it facilitates automatic order procedure and is suitable for use in computerized stock control systems.

A stock control system will only be effective if forecasts of stock levels, rates of consumption, lead time and costs prove to be accurate.

Organization structure of the whole production function

An organisation chart portrays a typical organisation structure for the production function of a large manufacturing business. It should be studied carefully, the reader noting the relationship between many of the subdivisions discussed and where they appear. The following is important and should be remembered:

(a) The organizational structure of every business is likely to be unique. It should be designed to suit the individual needs of the business and will be influenced by:

   (i) the size of the business;

   (ii) the nature of the industry and products manufactured;

   (iii) management policy;

   (iv) the objectives of the business.

(b) The purpose of organising the production function is usually to produce an efficient, smooth-running and economical department that contributes to achieving the objectives of the organisation where they related to production.

(c) Ideally the production function should be represented at board level by a production director.

(d) The organisation structure should clearly show the responsibility of each department within the function in a way that will avoid confusion, ambiguity and conflict. Particular attention should be paid to this, as conflict and self-interest are most likely to occur where there is an overlap of responsibility between departments, e.g. quality control and purchasing are both responsible in some way for the quality of materials.

(e) Materials management has been included, but may, as an alternative, constitute a completely separate function responsible to senior management and not to the production manager or director.

(f) The production function is only part of the whole business organisation and must co-operate closely with and be co-ordinated with all the other functions.

Inventory decision

Materials management is the planning and control of all inbound product flows into the firm. It includes purchasing, raw material inventory control, stores, inbound transportation, and production scheduling. Until recent years materials management has been overlooked as an area of efficiency improvement and overall financial gain for the firm. Today, it is the target of attention by production, purchasing, logistics and corporate planners and consultants.

Purchasing is directly involved in the trend toward integrated materials management. Buyers initiate the movement of goods into a firm for use by production and other department. The purchase timing, cost, and specific product chosen all impact the performance of this inbound system. Materials management includes all the control flow and physical goods flow activities in a firm up to and often through the production process. However, not two firms practice materials management in exactly the same manner.

The reporting lines and organizational placement of the individual materials management components vary from firm to firm. In some firms purchasing reports to a materials managers; in other firms, equal purchasing and materials management peers report to production. Some firms include transportation and warehousing in the outbound distribution department, and a small but growing number of firms combine materials management with distribution for a fully integrated logistics organization. Materials management is a new area for purchasing and firms. The combination of purchasing decision making with that of production, distribution, marketing, and finance brings the entire firm's resources into focus. Purchasing decisions cannot be made independently of the rest of the firm nor can other department's decisions unilaterally be foisted upon purchasing where they might result in higher costs. This chapter explores many of the emerging materials management elements that are causing an increasing integration of purchasing with other areas in a firm.

The firm's planning cycle

Materials management is a critical part of the planning and operating cycle activities of a firm. The following subactivities in the overall planning process require specific purchasing and materials management input.

- *Long-range plan*—Purchasing and materials management resources, processes, and capacities (actual and desired).
- *Corporate plan*—Sources as well as material availability, quality, and cost (now and future).
- *Operating Plan*—General timing requirements of goods for production market plan.
- *Production*—Provide goods and services when required.
- *Materials Management and Distribution Plans*—Plan for above production needs, anticipate and advise if possible disruptions foreseen, coordinate with firm's own and vendors' distribution activities, and maintain contact with vendors.

Purchasing and materials management provide periodic planning and continuous operating input to the four activities listed. In more and more firms, the task of production scheduling is being shifted to either materials management, distribution, or both. This shifting is made in recognition of the fact that purchasing materials management-distribution timing and quantity economies are greater than those typically accruing to production alone. Kodak, for example, has integrated the function of production scheduling within distribution so that purchasing, inventory, and warehousing costs can be balanced with production and marketing timing and quantity considerations.

Financial impact of materials management role with inventories

Materials management has stewardship responsibilities over inbound inventories. Inventories, in turn, have a major impact upon the overall financial performance of a firm. The double digit cost of capital experience at the beginning of the 1980s and the memory of products shortages and profit problems in the 1970s has led top management to direct attention to these areas. Inventories represent cash that could be used elsewhere by top management. In fact, excessive inventories have been the reason for some firms' failing. In any case, it is imperative for the purchasing and materials manager to understand the overall role of the inventories he/she is responsible for within the firm. More and more firms are integrating inbound inventory investment, placement, and positioning into the entire strategic decision process.

The income statement shows the results of sales and expenses for the year. It presents the total purchases and usually inbound freight costs for the year. Expenses for holding inventories, such as warehousing, handling, etc., are often found in "operating expenses." The top management of many firms attempts to report low inventory dollar values at year end so that reported profits are low for taxation purposes. This practice assists in cash retention in the firm. During the 1970s many firms switched to LIFO inventory valuation in order to achieve this end.

This is also the reason for year-end inventory liquidation efforts, including sales, promotions, and the write-off or write-down of excess, older or damaged goods and obsolete parts. Thus, what might be a good purchase timing decision during the year may run counter to the wishes of top management and the company treasurer near year end.

On the surface, the income statement shows inventories as a major overall profitability component of the firm. In the JJC Corp., every $1 of sales results in a $.40 margin to cover operating expenses and taxes. These figures are of value when comparing year-to-year trends or looking at similar products sold by competitors.

The balance sheet is a statement of corporate position on a given day. It shows the inventory holding of the firm at the end of the year. In this example twelve and one-half percent of all assets are represented by inventories, which are clearly assets that could otherwise be converted to less risky and more liquid receivables or cash.

The income statement and balance sheet together can be used to show other elements of inventory in the organization, including

1) *Return on Sales*—One measure of the firm often sought by analysis is profit in relation to sales. This ratio is net income after taxes divided by total sales.

2) *Return on Equity*—Return on equity is profit divided by common stock and retained earnings. This figure is $60,000/$925,000 or 6.5 per cent for JJC Corp. It is a measure of how well the owners' investment in the firm is performing for them. Obviously, profit, as it is calculated by using purchases and inventories, is a factor in this measure.

3) *Return on Assets*—A measure of how well the assets of a firm are being utilized is indicated by the return on assets. This figure is determined by dividing net profit by total assets.

4) *Working Capital*—Working capital is the residual when all short-term liabilities are subtracted from short-term assets. Within this context, short term is usually about thirty days. In the ICC Corp. example, this is cash plus receivables plus inventories less accounts payables, or $500,00 less $75,000, or $425,000. This is a healthy position.

5) *Acid Test*—The acid test is current assets without inventories less current liabilities. The argument for this measure is that inventories might not be easily liquidated within the short term. in the ICC Corp. this is $200,000 + $50,000 or $175,000. Within this measure, financial personnel and top managers would prefer the firm's resources in cash rather than inventories. Many firms look healthy from a working capital standpoint but cannot pay bills from an acid test position.

6) *Days Inventory on Hand*—Days inventory on hand is a rough measure of how many days of sales can be covered by the inventory on hand.

7) *Inventory Turnover*—Inventory turnover is determined by dividing sales for the period by the average inventory. In the ICC Corp., this is $1,000,000/250,000 or 4.00 times. This figure is an efficiency measure of asset turnover. Again, industry comparisons are necessary.

The measures described here are keenly watched by top management and financial personnel. Generally speaking, a reduced level of inventory or inventory values is sought for favourable result in these measures. Each factor must be weighed by purchasing and materials manager in day-to-day operations and overall planning. Several of these factors are pertinent for analysis as we enter the mid-1980s.

First, it is still apparent that inventories are not the responsibility of one operating person. Inventories are generally fragmented between purchasing, materials management (when these are separate), production, and distribution. Thus, total inventory control is often spread among many departments. This situation can cause unforeseen shortages or an unmanaged increase of inventories. Often, the inventory flow records of these departments do not correspond to each other. Until there is singular control over goods throughout the firm, there will tend to be problems in controlling this fluid asset.

Purchase and selling terms can have a key direct financial impact upon the firm. Goods purchased FOB receiving plant will reduce the overall holding of inventories by the amount of days in transit, versus those purchased FOB vendor's plant and sold FOB selling destination. While this action might have a favourable impact upon the reporting of the inventory position, it might represent a loss of transportation savings opportunities, especially on the inbound side. Clearly, this is a factor ripe for analysis in the 1980s as the importance of transportation increases for purchasing managers.

The make-or-buy decision plays a major role in inventory decision. The "make" alternative usually requires a larger overall investment in goods unless equipment is already on-hand. This cost and its resulting impact on the financial measures of the firm must become part of the make-or-buy equation.

Vendor performance and lead-time experience come into play here as well. Shipments from a great distance or from unreliable sources require a safety stock or lead-time inventory holdings. Such actions impact detrimentally upon inventory measures. This is particularly a problem with imported goods, which often must be paid for at the exporting port.

Consignment purchasing is a favourable alternative when inventory financial impacts are involved. Consignment purchasing makes goods available without having them "on the books" until actually used. Goods are physically available without lead time and payment for the subsequent sale might actually be received prior to payment to the vendor. Of course, the liability for payment for the total lot of goods must also be considered. The financial aspects of inventories as they affect the overall firm are important considerations for top management. Corporate policy dealing with inventories will no doubt play more of a hand in the future. The purchasing and materials manager must understand these concerns as they relate to day-to-day acquisition and supply management tasks.

Materials management objectives

The objectives of materials management embody those for purchasing including lowest final cost, optimum quality, assurance of supply, and lowest possible administrative costs to the firm. Brought down to an operating level, specific materials management objectives exist.

Minimized inventory investment

Inventories represent cash and other liquid assets that were converted into physical product form having less flexibility and greater risk than cash, marketable securities, or credit power (through increases in accounts payables or other short term debt.) Firms continually seek to reduce inventories because they are seen as one of the cheapest forms of financing available to the firm. That is, cash released from reduced inventories is less expensive to obtain than that available by borrowing.

Inventories are also the subject of reduction efforts because they are a critical variable in the firm's return on investment.

Firms A and B have equal sales, but Firm A has a very efficient materials and distribution management system that keeps its inventories very low. Firm B, on the other hand, has a higher inventory level. This phenomenon will tend to produce some distinctive differences between the two firms that are both overtly and covertly noted in financial records. On the surface, however, both sales and the reported cost of goods sold of both firms are the same.

The first difference between the Firm A and B is that the inventory turnover (inventory on hand divided into the cost of goods sold) is higher in A (5 times) than B (1.2 times). Second, Firm A requires less warehouse space for inventory than Firm B. This is disguised in less fixed plant and facilities assets ($1,500 versus $1,575). Third, Firm A can finance its assets out of short-term cash flow while Firm B must often borrow funds in order to cover its inventory purchases and holdings. This situation will be reflected in higher interest expenses. Fourth, Firm A's profit is higher due to lower interest charges and operating expenses of a smaller warehouse and inventory system. Fifth, Firm A will experience less risk in inventory holding because there is always less inventory on hand that can become damaged or obsolete. And sixth, Firm A has a higher return on investment ration (profit divided by assets), 11.25 percent versus Firms B with 7.7 percent. This occurs from the double impact f higher profits in the numerator and lower assets in the denominator. While this e ample was both hypothetical and simplified, the impacts shown are real inside the firm, and they illustrate the reason why minimized inventory investment is one of the major goals of top, middle, and lower management.

Maximum inventory availability

The second major materials management goal is to maximize that availability of inventory for production, consumption, or resale. This goal appears to be at the opposite end of the spectrum from minimum inventory investment, but it is crucial to the task of materials management, which is: provide all goods to the firms that are economically feasible while minimizing the funds required for doing so. This goal demands that material inventory be tightly controlled.

Firms that fall short of maximum inventory availability will often experience production downtime penalties, stockouts, and an overall loss of production and marketing productivity.

Minimized logistics system costs

This objective requires economical systems for storage, handling, information, communications, and management. This factor is found within the cost of purchased goods, work-in-process inventories, and the various costs for logistics activities that are usually reported in the category of operating costs in the income statement.

The strategic role of materials management

Strategy and its importance for the firm were discussed. On a materials management and production level, strategy encompasses some specific factors, including.

1. *Capacity*—this factor includes physical system capacity and timing potential for handling and processing goods. Some firms actively build capacity in anticipation of product or industry growth.
2. *Facilities*—Production assets, handling entities, and purchasing/materials management system plants, equipment, record, and communication systems all comprise this facet of strategy. Some firms have strategically placed themselves in the marketplace by utilizing their own freight brokerage operation rather than calling one when shipments are needed inbound. By keeping close links with the market in this manner, the firm can take advantage of spot opportunities when they arise.
3. *Vertical Integration*—This forms of strategic placement entails ownership or control of entities supplying the production and materials management system and generally includes private trucking operations that can provide cost and/or service advantages. In the extreme form, vertical integration can be noted with chemical and fertilizer companies that also own pipelines and tank facilities, or the ownership of the Bessemer and Lake Erie Railroad by U.S. Steel Corporation.
4. *Production Technologies*—Production technologies include the processes, machinery,

formulas, etc. that the firm to produce a distinctive product either physically or cost-wise. In the materials management realm, this can include the method employed to maintain tight inventories or the system of maintaining a standardized raw product with final production upon demand. One South American processor obtained an edge on competition by developing a long-term storage system for tomato paste. Previously, the firm would have to rush multistage operations from raw tomato to ketchup, soup, etc. A year's market mix would have to be projected at the beginning of the six-week peak tomato season in March. Forecasting errors would result in some stockouts and other products in excess by November and December. The firm developed a sanitary storage medium for all output from a single stage, making the raw tomato into a standard paste. Any specific tomato-based product could then be made from the paste. This production materials management advantage enabled the firm to reduce the need for future production assets while it cut production scheduling problems and increased subsequent marketplace customer service.

5. *Quality*—This strategic advantage is pervasive from sourcing to handling/storage/inspection all the way through production. Quality is an attribute that exists in materials, design, or manufacturing processes. Adherence to high quality output requires a commitment of the entire firm. In many firms, however, quality assurance is left to the operational level where short-term cost targets can eclipse attention to product quality.
6. *People Talent*—People talent is another important strategic advantage that a firm can possess. This advantage ranges from management persons having special talents to production workers particularly adept at detailed assembly, or working with colors or tastes. In materials management, this can include persons who are able to very efficiently schedule production, negotiate, or conduct low-cost value analyses upon components and processes.
7. *Alternative Recognition*—This strategic advantage is more of a state of mind or an open process in a firm. It is the recognition that physical product handling poses trade-off ranges and decisions in plant and equipment, production planning and control, labor and staffing, and organization and management. Rather than strive for "the one way" of organizing and operating a system, this strategic advantage requires a management perception to problems and opportunities, the possible need for changes and adaptations, and the ability to change or accept alternatives when desirable. Again, alternative recognition is a corporate frame of mind that encourages new input rather than becoming entrenched with fixed methods.

The growth of distribution and materials management has brought an increased awareness of alternative recognition to many firms. There are many combinations of transportation-warehousing alternatives available. Many firms may use just one form large lot distribution. That is, there is no "one way" of distributing. Purchasing personnel are now finding alternative methods of transporting goods inbound from different vendors. One method might be appropriate one time and yet another mode, at a different cost, would be best the next time.

The objectives of materials management are supportive of those of purchasing and the firm as a whole. The key in any one firm is to integrate the individual departmental goals into the overall corporate and marketing goals. Further, the firm must continually check for possible conflicts in both the objectives and the operational practices used by each department in carrying their individual goals out.

Materials management has not always received the attention it is today. Though these activities were always a part of purchasing and manufacturing, materials management as a discipline is a relatively new phenomenon that has grown since the 1950s. Following is a brief discussion about past practices and the trends that have caused materials management to become widely recognized. Traditional organizational structures often had purchasing and manufacturing at an arm's length from each other. Purchasing had the goal of minimum material cost, and production was often evaluated on minimum unit cost obtained through long production runs. Even when purchasing was within manufacturing common emphasis was to supply the production line in ways that optimized purchasing's own operating conveniences and unit costs. Production scheduling was generally contained within manufacturing, and inventories acted as a buffer or reserve so that the operating necessities and conveniences of production could be maintained.

By the 1950s, several factors led to changes in the organizational approach. One factor was product proliferation. The growth in marketing, market segmentation, and an emphasis upon competition caused a growth in the number of separate products most firms produced and sold. This growth complicated the purchasing, manufacturing, and production scheduling tasks. These tasks became particularly problematic when the practice of infrequent long production runs of each product caused delays and stockouts in the delivery of specific products to customers. In this situation, marketing became a department in conflict with production scheduling. Product proliferation also led to large increases in inventory held within the firm.

Vertical integration was another factor that often caused firms to tighten the purchasing-manufacturing processes into what we today refer to as materials management. To achieve vertical integration it is necessary to coordinate the activities of interconnected plants. Production runs, transportation, and work-in-process inventories must be coordinated in order to prevent problems and to optimize any economies sought in such arrangements.

Lead time problems are another factor contributing to the evaluation of materials management. The need to maximize inventory availability in face of uncertain vendor delivery and/or in-transit transportation service requires a close link between purchasing and production scheduling. This problem often grows when procuring internationally or from sources distant from plants. Deteriorated rail service in the Northeast states during the 1970s caused problems for many firms when in-transit time on the Penn Central Railroad both lengthened and become erratic on many lines.

The development of the logistics concept greatly shaped materials management. This concept is recognition that trade-off relationships exist between interfacing functions. Further, whenever trade-offs exist, there are opportunities for total cost and service savings for the entire firm. Thus, many firms recognized that a unit cost increase from a shortened production run might have increased purchase order costs, but the firm saved a greater amount inventory and warehousing. This is only one example of such coordination which suboptimizes each of the major functions for the good of both and the firm.

Many management science techniques, including the use of the computer in production scheduling evolved during this period. These techniques presented new opportunities for analysis and cost/service improvements in the materials management area. The advent of materials requirements planning (MRP) is one such tool that has had a great impact.

Product shortages in the mid-1970s forced firms to link marketing, production, and purchasing in a way that more closely coordinated what was marketed in the best possible production schedule with what component products were available. Some firms made major organizational and coordination changes during this time that resulted in more formalized management entities.

Finally, recognition of the high cost of inventories in the late 1970s and early 1980s has led most firms to seek ways of reducing inventories without penalizing major economies in purchasing, production, and marketing. Inventory investment minimization, while maximizing its availability, requires centralized interdepartmental coordination in materials management.

Materials management literature cities many examples of how specific firms adopted the materials management concept. Each company was shaped by specific events, impacts, and the personalities of those involved. All or most examples point to one or more of the factors highlighted in this chapter. Examinations of firms will also reveal that no two firms are exactly alike in organization, function, or reporting lines of materials management. Boeing, for example, has a much more refined system than does a food processing plant that receives its vegetable supply only once yearly. Each firm has specific products, vendor/supply configurations, manufacturing arrangements, time con-straints, personnel talents, and information systems that all come into play with exactly how a materials management system will evolve.

Alternative approaches to materials management

Literature in the 1980s contains much contrasting information on various approaches used in materials management. In particular, the various approaches are often labeled as the U.S., Japanese, U.S. "just in time," and European approaches. Each approach will be presented and contrasted here to provide insights into how firms can structurally and procedurally address purchasing and production objectives. The U.S. has enjoyed extensive production capacity, labour goals, resource availability, and mass markets. Automation and large productive processes were economical because of large markets.

The quest for minimum manufacturing unit costs in many firms has lead them to optimize production lot sizes. Optimum run lot sizes are a function of balanced set-up costs, variable unit costs, and the scheduled needs of various products produced on each production line. Transportation vehicle sizes also come into play here, too, as rail car, truck, and container capacities enter into the inbound and outbound lot size equation. In the U.S., these capacities are quite large as railroad and highway size and weight limitations are larger in comparison to many other nations of the world. Further, transportation economics generally favour larger vehicles and single handlings of many shipments at once resulting in the form of lower unit carrier prices.

Inventory is used to buffer transportation, production, distribution, and sales when flow rates, availability, or demands are at different rates from each other. Purchasing usually has many materials sources available throughout the country, which requires selection monitoring and expediting efforts. The situation is intensified with the great product variety that is created and expected in our economy. Consequently, U.S. firms have emphasized materials delivery systems.

Many industries, and the automobile industry in particular, have recently been highlighted for quality problems. Quality and its control often are elements that are generally defined by top management but left to lower management levels for follow through and administration. In an effort to reduce unit production costs, line managers often opt for less inspection and the use of less than target quality components in order to avoid scrap, waste, return costs, or production inconvenience. Thus, quality is often treated as a trade-off against purchasing and/or production unit cost. Quality frequently suffers because worker task assignment is often defined in very specialized terms either through the nature of line automation, labour skill rules, job descriptions, or both. This phenomenon creates repetitive and often boring jobs. It can prevent the worker from relating to the overall output of the line and the products of the firm as a whole. Here, too, lax attitude of commitment to the firm, its systems, and the quality of its products can become endemic.

Vendor supply lines, transportation systems, production scheduling, and quality control are approached differently in many Japanese firms.

Large Japanese firms will often procure from small vendors that are in close proximity to their plant. This action minimizes lead time problems and often takes place several times a day, and in some instances a vendor's truck and driver are always at the firm's in bound dock. The driver acts as a production inventory monitor, supplier, and legal party in the purchase of goods. This minimizes inbound inventory for the manufacturer to such an extent that it is nearly nonexistent. Vendors are informed weeks and months in advance of production schedules.

Work-in-process and production activities are often "pulled through" the system according to the firm's sales and delivery requirements. The "pulling" approach is often organized around a system of KANBAN tickets that travel with small lots of goods through various production stages and are posted where all workers can see them. Workers may then relate subsequent production needs with what they are currently producing. This approach often permits a smoother, less hectic production rate than when machinery and manufacturing are running at maximum pace. Observers of Japanese factories note that their high productivity is not necessarily attained through faster work activity. The pull-through system helps pace multiple production stages so there is little or no work-in-process inventory. In fact, safety stocks are regarded as a form of organizational waste.

Inventories are further minimized through simplification of production set-up and changeover processes. Product variety is less than that found in the U.S., and this factor reduces the production lot problem somewhat. But, of most importance, is the drive to reduce production changeover efforts to an absolute minimum. This process is analyzed and implemented as an on-going, all-employee effort. This factor, combined with the almost real-time vendor delivery requirement, reduces the need to optimize production unit costs with run sizes that pay off any high changeover costs.

Quality and its control receives more pervasive attention in Japan that it does in the U.A. Quality problems are minimized in many ways. First quality assurance often involves everyone in the firm from top management down to the individual worker. Production line employees are rewarded for detecting quality problems. A poor quality component is viewed as an opportunity to correct an inherent problem. Correction efforts involve workers who are familiar with the goods and processes, engineers, top management, and the vendors. Firms often hold seminars with vendor's workers to stress quality and how it might be improved. Quality is looked at in a global manner in addition to design and defective parts. It is viewed as a whole concept that includes delivery and inventory problems, communications and anything relating to operations as well. Thus, the materials management process is an attribute of quality. Emphasis upon quality is viewed by many observers as sometimes excessive to the point of being uneconomic, but this is a judgment that is best made in light of market success.

Decision making tends to come from the bottom up in Japanese organizations, which rely highly upon consensus decisions. Production, quality, and other problems are approached with the worker's input along with others in the organization who might be involved or can contribute. This is in contrast to some production setting in Western firms where employee input is minimized; instead, problems are approached by middle management information specialists, and/or consultants. The human resource system must also be included in this contrast of production and materials management. The Japanese culture is very much a part of this analysis. Lifetime employment with one firm is the norm. Inherent to this is a concept of employee trust in the organization. This trust extends to the fact that the employee will not be laid off or have his/her job abolished in slow periods, nor will a suggested improvement in a process eliminate one's employment. Instead of individuals being recognized for periodic improvements, whole teams are involved through consensus decision making. Each employee is generally attuned to the success, operations, and directors of the firm of suborganization. The team concept also extends to worker flexibility. It is common for a production worker to be rotated through many jobs and tasks.

ENCYCLOPAEDIA
OF
MODERN MANAGEMENT TECHNIQUES

ENCYCLOPAEDIA OF MODERN MANAGEMENT TECHNIQUES

Volume 6

Edited by
A. K. Chaudhary

ANMOL PUBLICATIONS PVT. LTD.
NEW DELHI-110 002 (INDIA)

ANMOL PUBLICATIONS PVT. LTD.
4374/4B, Ansari Road, Daryaganj
New Delhi-110 002

Encyclopaedia of Modern Management Techniques

First Edition 1999

ISBN 81-261-0321-3 (Set)

PRINTED IN INDIA

Published by J. L. Kumar for Anmol Publications Pvt. Ltd., New Delhi-110 002 and Printed at Mehra Offset Press, Delhi.

Contents

25

Labour Management

The fifteenth Session of the Indian Labour Conference after considering the report of the Study Group, accepted most of its recommendations and appointed a tripartite Sub-committee to lay down criteria for the selection of undertakings for introducing the scheme. The recommendations accepted by the Conference are as follows:

(1) As the employers were willing to introduce schemes of worker participation in selected industrial units on a voluntary basis, it was not considered necessary to undertake any legislation for the purpose for a period of two years. If, however, this experiment did not succeed, Government might take steps to bring in legislation.

(2) A small sub-committee or 4 persons each from the employers' group and the workers' group and Government should be set up within a fortnight for considering the details regarding the scheme of Worker Participation in Management. The sub-committee would also select undertakings in which the scheme was to be introduced in the first instance. The following recommendations set out in the Report were accepted.

(1) The main functions of the Councils may include provision of means of communication, improvement of working and living conditions and assistance in the administration of laws and agreements. It may be desirable to consult the Councils regarding matters like alterations in standing orders, retrenchment, rationalisation, closure reduction in or cessation of operations, introduction of new methods and procedures for engagement and punishment. They may also have the right to receive information about the general economic situation of the concern, the state of the market, production and sales programmes, organisation and general running of the undertaking, circumstances affecting the economic position of the undertaking, methods of manufacture and work and the annual balance sheet and profit and loss statementand connected documents and explainations and such other matters as may be agreed to by employers and employees.

(2) It would be preferable to exclude wages and bonus and individual grievances from the purview of the joint bodies, but otherwise, the list of functions

should be left flexible enough to be settled by joint consultation betweeen the management and the representative trade union.

(3) To reduce the danger of apathy, Councils of Management may been trusted with some administrative responsibility, such as administration of welfare measures, supervision of safety measures, operation of vocational training and apprentiship schemes, preparation of schedules of working hours and breaks and of holidays and payment of rewards for valuable suggestions.

(4) There should be a strong self-confident trade union, closely connected with the machinery of participation and with a reasonably clear separation of functions. It would be advisable to devise some methods for closely associating the trade unions in the selection of workers' representatives.

(5) It is necessary to enlist the willing cooperation of management at the middle and lower levels such as junior managers, supervisors and foremen.

(6) Joint consultation should be in-build and for this purpose, Government should provide an advisory service on personnel management on the lines of the U.K. Ministry of Labour.

(7) While Government should accept leadership for organising a sustained educational campaign for creating the necessary atmosphere, it should not be made a departmental affair but effort should be made to build up a tripartite machinery of direction by utilising employer's organisations, trade unions, non official bodies, etc.

The Sub-committee approved a draft model agreement regarding the establishment of Joint Management Councils, their constitution, functions and responsibilitees. Later on the Sub-committee itself was reconstituted into the 'Committee on Labour Management Cooperation" to advise on all matters connected with the scheme. In 1958 a Seminar of interested parties was convened by the Government of India to consider and approve the draft model agreement. The Seminar also adopted recommendations on the size, composition, training programme and procedure for the working of the Joint Management Councils.

Size of the joint council

(1) The Joint Councils, to be effective and manageable, should consist of equal number of representatives of management and employees, not exceeding twelve in all. In the case of smaller undertakings, however, the membership should not be less than six.

(2) The quorum should be four, two on each side.

(3) Decisions should be taken unanimously.

Representation to different departments etc.

(1) As one of the essential criteria for the formation of Joint Councils is that the undertaking should have a well established and strong trade union functioning, the rule should be:

(a) where there is a representative union registered under a statute, that representative Union should nominate the employees' representatives on the Council;

(b) where there is now law for the registration of Unions as representative Unions, but there is only one union well established, that Union should nominate the employees' representatives on the Council;

(c) where there are more than one well established and effective Union, the Joint Councils should be formed when the Union, the Joint Councils should be formed when the Union among themselves agree as to the manner in which representation should be given to the employees.

(2) There should be no bar to the members of the supervisory and technical staff being nominated as employees' representatives on the Council.

(3) Employees' representatives should be employees themselves; but, if the trade union so feels, it can appoint non-employee members to the extent of not more than 25% of its quota. If the employers have no objection, the number of non-employee members may be raised to two.

(4) The Joint Council should be set up at the unit level. Where there are a number of departments in an undertaking, having separate identity of their own, the Joint Council may set up subsidiary Departmental Joint Committees to deal with the problems at the departmental level and also to secure proper and effective functioning of the Joint Council itself. Where there are a number of units under the same management in the same area having separate Joint Council of there own, a Central Joint Council might also be established for the group of undertainings.

(5) The Ministry of Labour might request the Ministry of Finance to agree to the formation of Joint Councils in the Life Insurance Corporation of India, for this purpose, a zone may be treated as a unit.

(6) The Ministry of Labour might request the Ministry of Communications to include not only the Posts and Telegraphs Workshops, but also other units functioning under the P & T Department.

Office bearers of the joint council

(1) The question of procedure for appointing a Chairman and a Vice-chairman should be left to the Council itself.

(2) In case the Joint Council fails to come to an agreement on the above, the offices of Chairmanship and Vice-Chairmanship should be made rotating. Again, offer one term the Chairman is selected from the employers' side and vice versa.

(3) The term of office of a Chairman and a Vice Chairman shall be one year and that of the Council shall be two years.

(4) There may be two Joint Secretaries, one from the employees' side and the other from the employers' side., both having equal status. They may be elected by the members of the Council from among themselves.

(5) The employers should provide such secretariat and other assistance as may be necessary for the smooth and efficient functioning of the Joint Councils. If the employees' representatives agree, the Labour Welfare Officer of the unit may be associated with the Joint Council for purposes of secretariat work, e.g. circulation of minutes, notes, etc.

Constitution of sub-committees

(1) It is desirable to appoint Sub-Committees.

(2) For welfare activities etc., a standing Sub-Committee may be appointed.

(3) For other specific points, ad hoc Sub-Committees may be formed.

(4) These Sub-Committees shall submit their reports to the Joint Council.

(5) There should be a parity of employer-employee representation on the standing Sub-Committees. On the ad-hoc Sub-Committees, however, parity need not be insisted upon.

(6) The Sub-Committees might also include in their membership, persons other than members of the Joint Council.

(7) The Sub-Committees shall be working under the general supervision and guidance of the Joint Council. Reports made by the Sub-Committees will be considered by the Joint Council which will take the ultimate decision.

(8) The agenda for the Joint Council meetings should be prepared and circulated in good time, so as to give sufficient publicity to it amongst the employees and invite points for discussion from them. The preparation of the agenda should be the primary responsibility of the Chairman who might make such arrangements as may be necessary for this purpose.

Schedule for the meetings of the joint councils: The periodicity of the meetings of the Council is essentially a matter to be decided by agreement by the Council itself. The Council should, however, meet at least once a month.

Minimum qualifications pertaining to education etc.: No qualifications should be laid down for membership of the Council. The parties are expected to nominate persons who have sufficient knowledge and understanding and who are in a position to deliver the goods.

Liaison between the joint councils and the Ministry of Labour and Employment: The Government of India should make a definite arrangement for liaison between the Joint Councils and the Ministry of Labour and Employment by designating a separate cell for the purpose and giving it all facility. Adequate arrangements should also be made to associate State Governments with the working of the Joint Councils in their respective areas.

Guidance from panel of experts: Having regard to the fact that the experiment is initiated at a few places in the initial stage, an All India Panel should be appointed composed of persons (a) who are nominated by organisations of employers and employees, (b) whom the organisations consider suitable for guiding Joint Councils and (c) who are willing to undertake this responsibility. The advice of the experts shall not be binding on the Joint Councils.

Training Programmes in Units Experimenting with Worker Participation in Management: The representatives of both management and workers on the Joint Councils should continuously keep in mind their joint responsibilities and rights. Towards this end, it should be necessary to ensure that they acquire the requisite attitude and background. Education of a general nature, especially in the issues relating to the satisfactory working of an enterprise must be carried on through different agencies. The representatives of management should be persuaded to actively participate in professional management associations. The trade unions may undertake the education of the workers. The workers' education scheme which is to be launched shortly by the Government of India must devote special attention to this aspect of labour management relations. The Joint Councils at the unit level should also consider the possibility of organising the joint education of all the members of the Council.

Dissemination of information to workers: The Joint Council should have the right to receive information of the various subjects outlined under Clause 6 of the Model Agreement. All arrangements should be made for documentation and dissemination of information to member of the Joint Councils as early as practicable. The technical details in this connection should be worked out. On certain specific matters, information should be given every quarter. The right to receive information also includes the right of discussion. The undertaking having a Joint Council shall also establish a library and a reading room.

Informal meetings: All efforts should be made to increase informal contacts between the members of the Joint Council and top officials of both sides, namely, management and the trade union. The Seminar also discussed other related issues. The conclusions thereon were as follows:—

Joint councils and works committees: (1) Since Joint Councils are working at the policy level, they can function separately without encroaching upon the functions of the Works Committees. (2) Where Works Committees are already working in units where Joint Councils are to be set up, the Works Committees shall continue.

Responsibilities of the council: The Joint Council shall exercise supervisory, advisory and administrative functions on matters concerning safety, welfare etc., as have been indicated in the Model Agreement, though the ultimate responsibility shall rest with the management.

The unanimous decision of the Council should be implemented without any delay. If they are not implemented in time, reasons should be given for the delay.

The Seminar was convinced that joint councils will thrive only in an atmosphere of mutual confidence and goodwill. It took note of the trade unions towards each other, but felt that there was a need for continuous educative work both on the side of labour and management.

The progress of the scheme was reviewed at a subsequent Seminar in 1960 and it was accepted that, pilot stage having passed it should be extended to as many units as possible. It was also agreed that suitable machinery at the Central and State levels be set up to organise promotion drive and exercise a watch over the working of the scheme. The Seminar made a re-statement of the objectives of the scheme and the manner in which it should operate and other related matters in the following manner:

1. Effective consultation leads to participation
2. The main objectives of the scheme are:—
   (a) establishment of cordial relations between management and workers and building up understanding and trust between them;
   (b) substantial increase in productivity in the interest of management, workers and building up understanding and trust between them;
   (b) substantial increase in productivity in the interest of management, workers and the nation;
   (c) securing better welfare facilities etc.: for workers; and
   (d) training and education of workers to understand and share the responsibilities of management.
3. Though a written agreement between the management and workers to participate in management on the lins of the model Agreement would be desirable and helpful, it is not absolutely necessary.
4. Though the existence of one strong union would considerably facilitate the introduction of the scheme, it could be set up also where the unions agree to co-

operate with each other or the workers themselves come out with a concrete proposal for participating in the Scheme.

5. The Joint Councils machinery for participation may be considerably modified to fit the actual conditions of the unit and the industry. Where for example, the union is large as in the case of Tatas, the single Joint Council could be very unwieldy. There, the division of functions widely on some rational basis helps. Where there are many units as in the Simpsons Group of industries one Joint Council for each unit proves useful. The set up of sub-committees of the Joint Council for welfare, canteen management, production, suggestions etc. composed of suitable persons considerably facilitate work and prove effective for achieving best results.

6. Management should share the benefits of increased production with their workers in the shape of better welfare amenities, introduction of schemes for incentive bonus etc.

7. Management should consult the Joint Council more and more on matters indicated in the Model Agreement and the unanimous decisions of the Joint Council should generally be accepted and promptly implemented. Should it not be possible to do so, the Council may be informed as soon as possible and the reasons explained.

8. Irrespective of what name the Joint Council for Participation is called by,. it may be considered as a Joint Council sharing in management if it meets the following conditions:

   (a) it is entitled to receive information on the general working of the concern etc. as indicated in Clause 6 and is consulted by management on all or in all the matters referred to in Clause 5 of the Model Agreement ;

   (b) management of canteens and administration of welfare measures and/or in all the other matters refereed to in Clause 7 of the Model Agreement are entrusted to it. A committee could further examine the essential criteria of Joint Councils of Management.

9. The success or failure of the scheme in any unit should be determined by examination of the following:

   (a) Industrial peace.

   (b) Increase in productivity both before and after introduction of the scheme and waste reduction.

   (c) Elimination of outside intervention in disputes i.e. the number of maters settled mutually.

   (d) The amount of general activity undertaken by the joint Council.

(e) Concrete results achieved in the field of welfare.

(f) The amount of administrative matters that have been handed over to the Joint Council.

(g) The number of meeting already held by the Joint Council and the attendance.

10. Participation in management should not be handled by a few persons. The general mass of workers must in some may be participating in its work. For this purpose the interest of workers is to be maintained by publicising and explaining to them the results of the scheme. Inviting suggestions and awarding prizes for accepted suggestions is one of the effective ways of creating a sense of participation and a sense of belonging amongst all the workers. All general information of the type mentioned in the Model Agreement should be supplied by management to the Council. This will facilitate working. In requesting for the supply of any specific information of more detailed nature the Joint Council should as far as possible relate the same to the matters under consideration or discussion so that inconvenience, suspicion or embarrassment is avoided. Information obtained should not be divulged outside.

We suggested earlier that there were some indications that what we called the 'openness' of management to external communication channels and associations was connected both with the state of its labour relationships and with its activity in internal consultation.

To measure 'actual consultation' we had necessarily to adopt a rather more complex assessment system than the simple 'yes/no' record which sufficed to rank plants in the immediately preceding analysis. In this case, we first distinguished nine heads of management decision as follows.

General administration and policy

Production management

Inspection

Maintenance

Employment

Training, welfare and job security

Sales and service

Buying and control

Research and development.

Each of these heads was then broken down again into appropriate subheads; thus the subheads for 'production management' were:

Allocation of work

Manning scales

Choice of equipment

Methods of work

Working hours

And under each of the subheads again, establishments were scored on a six-point scale according both to the extent of the consultation actually reported in each case, and to the formality of the procedure through which it operated. Thus 'no consultation' was scored as zero, while at the other extreme joint decision-making was scored as 5, for management-worker consultation when through formal negotiations, and for 'within-management' consultation when done by a formal committee of managers. The actual level of consultation practised was thus measured from several viewpoints and in a graduated way.

One point which immediately emerged from this analysis was that the general level of actual consultation is distinctly higher 'within management' than between management and workers. This is true even if one considers only the first six broad heads of consultation above-abstracting 'sales and service', 'buying and control', and 'R & D' on the ground that these areas of management decision are much less likely than the others to be of interest to workers-indeed, are ones in which the actual level of management/worker consultation was reported as negligible. It is notable, however, that the level of consultation 'within management' appears inversely related to that obtaining between management and workers-a point of some possible significance, in the light of subsequent aspects of this analysis.

Meanwhile, we can also record that the only areas of decisions where worker/management consultation is more highly scored than for operational production are 'maintenance' and 'training, welfare, etc'.. It is remarkable that the score under 'employment' is rather low-about 13% of the possible maximum, which is perhaps symptomatic of the extent to which traditional employer insistence on 'hire and fire' as a managerial prerogative was still preserved in practice, up to the employment protection act of 1974 at least.

The size effects are important, not only in themselves, but because they would again lead to an expectation of a similar pattern in the relationships between consultation and the plants' incidence of working days lost from disputes. This was not at all the case; management/worker consultation increased quite markedly between firms with a low and those with a high strike incidence. But table shows that consultation 'within management' first jumped sharply between plants with zero strike experiences and others, but then declined as the strike incidence of establishments rose.

For each type of consultation , moreover, the appropriate effect was more or less visible under all heads of decision-making. So that in view especially of that effect's variances from the expected influence of size, there seems little doubts as to the conclusions which follow. The degree of actual consultation between management and workers depends on the militancy of the labour force; but management/worker consultation on the whole seems to take place at the marginal expense of consultation within management. So we have, again, an inverse relationship, in practice, between the two types of *consultation.*

One argument for increased 'employee participation in management' which has been often put forward in the past has been that it would help to improve efficiency; but this would be obviously weakened if the price of such an increase were to be a decline in communication and coordination between the members of management themselves. As regards what some might call the 'morale' effects of management/ worker consultation, however, we also now have a paradox. As we showed previously, the introduction of formal joint consultative machinery apparently reduced the liability of plants to labour unrest. But the extent to which such machinery is actually used, and the effective level of management/worker consultation in general, depend on the demonstrated level of employee militancy. How can this paradox be explained?

One explanation might link the effect of the nominal existence of formal joint consultative machinery with the similar effect of various other 'communication' devices and of fringe benefits, which we also previously traced. To the extent that these things are volunteered by employers, they constitute a recognition of employee status; most of them, indeed, were historically part of the employment conditions which distinguished 'staff' from 'operatives' in industry. Thus, the suggestion is that the concession of such symbols of status to workers, irrespective of whether or not they also have a material content, will reduce the liability of plants to labour unrest. But on the other hand, genuine 'worker participation' makes demands that could imply a reduction of effective contact or communication between the members of management themselves, and is therefore likely to be resisted unless it is imposed on managers from board level, perhaps as a consequence of active employee pressure.

The Work Situation: Incidence of Strikes

From the analysis of the process of industrialization we can isolate several major factors contributing to stability or change in industrial relations at company level. The *structure* and organization of work is a major factor determining both individual and collective relationships. We have argued that the trend towards greater bureaucratization has contributed to the growth of unions. But company organization is strongly influenced also by the *ideology* of senior managers; an ideology contained in the 'charter' and chose of each individual company as well as in the national administration of the country. However, the available *technology* and type of *product* markets set constraints on the choice of organization and the style of management adopted. The technological influence becomes greater as one moves nearer to the point of production.

Employees derive status wither personally or a as a group from the structure of tasks allocated in the workplace which tends, even today, to contribute to their occupational status and way of life *outside* the place of work. For this reason, the rewards attached to a job become more than just an economic indicator of a person's present position and future aspirations; there is usually an expectation that the level and forms of rewards are concomitant with the status of the occupant. Within the place of work there is an equal expectation that he/she will carry the authority required to perform the job. However, the market situation of the employee as well as his/her contribution to the process of production gives him a power that is not necessarily 'legitimate' within the formal structure and purposes of the company management. it is, of course, this power that is crucial to the establishment of the industrial relations system of the firm-given that before 1971 there has been little legal or statutory support for union recognition of 'union security' in the place of work. Before this power can be realized, however, there has to be some form of group identify and cohesion within the workforce sufficient to sustain itself against what is - or has been- the opposition of management.

For this reason we start outside the place of work with the market situation of employees and employers and examine their orientations first to work and then to industrial relations. We shall then suggest how these are mediated by the work situation and finally how their bargaining behaviour and strategy is conceived in the light of these influences. We have summarized the situation diagrammatically and you can see the role played by 'expectations in the labour market'. The behavioural strategy adopted by employees may be directed through the formal procedures of the firm's industrial relations system or may lead to individual or collective 'protest' actions- which for the firm constitutes wastage- and the short-run costs of under-utilized plant and equipment, and possible loss of product markets in the longer run.

It suggests that the firm offers a particular structure of rules such as the make-up of rewards to labour. These rules relate to the technology used to produce the products or services and to the nature of the product market. The sheer size of organization will also affect the rules governing the employees, rights and obligations. Perhaps more important from the sociological view-point is the effect of management ideology on industrial relations in the plant. However, neither this ideology not the most uncontrollable and independent element in the model, that of labour market expectations can realistically be isolated from factors external to the workplace. When aspirations of employees grow more rapidly than the employers believe consistent with their ability to pay, conflict becomes built into the system. For this reason a whole new set of rules have brought into being a division of labour within the company.

If an industrial relations system is to remain viable, it must them be an open system, one which interacts with its environment, however variable and unpredictable, in a manner that keeps the system in being. We must, therefore, as students of industrial relations, as well as of sociology, go beyond the factory-gate for out explanations of group behaviour in work. We must indeed look at the wider institutional framework of society at large for unless we know something of the *sources* of workplace behaviour it is unlikely that we shall be able to design rules or behavioural norms that will both contain actions and satisfy the social needs aspiration of all parties.

Employee orientations

Research suggests that the *work-ethic* is most salient in the thinking of the middle-classes: we find most interest in the intrinsic satisfaction in work and most ego-identification with their work role and status among white-collar workers and skilled tradesmen. Among manual workers, the primary meaning of work is more likely to be solely as means to an ends or *instrumental*. This instrumental view of work appeared to be strong among the small sample of Luton workers surveyed by Goldthorpe, *et al.* Common to many of the 229 employees interviewed in three plants, was the fact that they has moved to Luton in order to earn more money and a proportion has left higher-status jobs in order to gain higher earnings on the shop floor. The lives of these workers focused in their nuclear family and their domestic standard of living: some retained ambitions of a wider future for their children through achievement at school. This instrumental view of work can be contrasted with a 'bureaucratic' orientation and a 'solidaristic' one. The bureaucratice view sees work as service to the organization in return for steadily increasing income and social status and for long-term security- tha is, in return for a career. Work, therefore, represents a central life interest to the worker in that his/her 'position' and 'prospects' contribute to his/her self-identity. Involvement in the organization contains a moral rather than simply calculative commitment. The solidaristic worker sees work 'not simply as a means to an end but also as a group activity'. Economic returns are likely to be sacrificed where 'maximizing' behaviour would offend group norms. We can identify a fourth major congifiguration of attitudes and belief which are consistent enough to have deserved a separate title: these are usually described as 'cosmopolitan' and are contrasted with those of the 'local'. Although originally coined to describe managerial groups it is also appropriate for a wide range of occupations in which the major reference group of the employee is *outside* the firm, that is within a craft or professional *membership* group. I the Goldthorpe study these employees have a much higher intrinsic interest in their work than the semi-skilled operatives, and a wider social life. They differ from the more 'local' bureaucratic and solidaristic employees in their wider view of their market opportunities and from the instrumentally oriented workers in their extended community of interest shared with other craftsmen, a community differentiated by status, rewards, culture and language.

Se we have four categories that emphasize differences in their perceived ability to move outside the internal labour market of their present employer. They also identify differences in their degree of *group consciousness* and *readiness to act collectively* as against an individual movement between jobs.

The solidaristic and cosmopolitan orientations may well be associated with a traditional community feeling. In the first type this is likely to be of the Bethnal Green variety: the tightly knit urban village made up of extended family networks in which work and leisure are closely linked. The ascribed family status is retained in the work situation and the achieved work status is recognized in the community. This may give rise to orientations which Lockwood has described as 'traditional differentials', workers who value the social bonds they enjoy with management as well as with their work mates. In contrast 'traditional radicals' mirror their social isolation from the middle calss in their workplace attitudes. There is considerable evidence of a duality in employee orientations. for example, Daniels has suggested that mutually inconsistent attitudes can be held in respect to satisfactions derived from the job itself and to the rewards and recognition given to it by management. It is possible to pursue a militant *market* strategy whilst placing a high value on intrinsic interest in work and holding one's immediate superior in considerable respect. This was, for example, the norm among many of the cosmopolitan technicians and scientists surveyed by Roberts *et al.* For them it was possible to retain high aspirations in their personal career whilst pursuing a militant collective bargaining stance. However, bureaucratic orientations among supervisory workers appeared to lead to a greater weight being placed on individualism while collective strategy offered a defence against over- dependence on a single employer.

There is a suggestion that employee orientations may be moving in the direction of instrumentalism as bureaucratization increases. However, such tendencies are mediated by other counteracting ones. Large movements of employees have taken place at regular intervals during the process of industrialization. Former groups of itinerant workers such as the Irish peasants who moved into the London and Liverpool docklands in the latter part of the nineteenth century, and the Welsh, and Northern workers who migrated to the motor car cities of the Midlands in the 1950s have tended to settle and form communities around their place of work.

Manager orientations

Chamberlain's classification of management attitudes to collective bargaining divides managers into short-time maximizers in purely economic terms, legalistic sticklers to contract, and the politically 'aware' who are willing to share power with other interest groups. All these ideological alternatives seem possible ways of justifying the reaction of managers to the conflict inherent in activating the various aspects of their role.

The primary role for the most senior executives is laying down the strategic guide-lines for the firm. Their general orientation is *outward*; towards potential competitors, towards suppliers and towards government, i.e., towards the environments through the firm's 'boundary regulation'. They are generally well insulated from the internal consequences of their decisions, especially in the areas of production and industrial relations. This 'outward orientation' has caused many directors to treat labour at one and the same time as members of their team and an encumbrance which drains profits made by the finance department from sales generated by marketing! They have only reluctantly moved towards a pluralistic structure at shop floor lever, mainly in response to government pressure. Since these managers know each other intimately they *are* a team. The unitary ideology is perfectly natural explanation of their role. Unitarism is less apparent at plant level where the coordinative role of the manager becomes important. However, at this level the career orientation of managers cause them to respond to directions from above more readily than to the contingencies of the workplace and the requests of junior managers. The disjuncture between the expectations of their superiors and the actualities of day-to-day operations may cause them to adopt the view of 'labour' held by their seniors and to demand a legalistic adherence to 'contracts'. But the line-manager, and behind him the specialists feeding the line, have to confront the conflicting objectives of technical efficiency and representative democracy. It is the line manger who has to meet the day-top-day production dead-lines *and* consult with all parties concerned. His/her role is the most stressful and is made more so by apparent isolation and lack of understanding or even response from the coordinative managers. To the line manager the short-term deadlines arise out of the policy decisions of superiors who appear to have little knowledge of, or insight into, the consequences of their planning.

Structure, orientation and ideology

It is, however, by no means clear that all firms need or posses 'tall' organizational hierarchies which give rise to these divisions among management. The Aston University work suggests that a number of factors are important, not least of which are the age and ideology of senior management. However, perhaps the best known explanatory scheme is that of Woodward who related organizational structure to technology and the product market. Form an empirical study of 203 manufacturing firms she developed ten levels of 'technical complexity' from small batch or unit production in which the work was hand done and labour intensive to process production of continuous-flow type, employing few people or flow-line production in which assembly work represented the final stage of a complex series of operation.

Woodward's conclusions were , briefly, as follows;

(1) The number of levels of authority in the management hierarchy increased with technical complexity.

(2) The ratios of indirect workers increased with technical advance.

(3) The span of control of the chief executive increased with technical advance.

(4) Percentage labour costs decreased with increasing technical complexity.

However,

(1) The span of control of the first-line supervisor was greatest in half-way technology-large batch production.

(2) Both specialization in roles and formality in communications were greatest in large batch technology.

(3) Specialist administration such as production planning and control, methods of engineering and work study were most separated from the administration of production in large batch technology.

(4) Organization was less flexible in terms of role definition in large-batch technology.

The implications of Woodward's findings for the climate of industrial relations in a company are considerable, for they 'explain' many of the differences between industrial levels of conflict. However, they are somewhat modified by her complementary findings that the form of *technology* generally relates to the type of product *market*. Hence much of the stress in the car industry or in any large batch industry, stems form the cyclical nature of the product market and the interdependence between the assembly state of production and a range of commodity suppliers. In a small-batch technology the bespoke market creates problems for the payment of installments on the price, be this motorways, houses, boats, or radar sets. The more customer-oriented the service provided by the company, the more crucial this becomes.

At the other end of the spectrum, process- production plant has to be set up to produce continuously for five years or more in order to pay off the enormous capital investment.

Planning decisions are, therefore, based on the assumption that markets will be available for a flow of plastic, oil, steel, or other such commodities. This measure of *variability* in the environment is now more widely accepted by theorists as a predictor of organizational form. The historical association of craft occupations with small-batch technology has already been discussed. The same associations has been observed in the *laissez-fair* economy of the United States, and in Tyneside ship yards. In the latter craft groups were extremely solidaristic in both work and out-of-work behaviour, but traditionally antagonisms between these occupational communities were strong. In work, the skill groups were largely autonomous with respect to management, but after each ship's launch all group suffered the same fate-immediate lay-off.

Traditions of solidarity and self help within separate and autonomous groups bedeviled the domestic building industry for many years-as, of course, did the tradition of transitory implement from which it sprang. However, the groups has, and have, real power to hold up production at every dead-line when a cash instalment becomes due from the customer. In the primary producing industries even the manual methods that preceded the present automated plant were extremely capital intensive. The tradition in coal, steel, textiles, etc. was for the large single employer to become identified very closely with a geographical community. Perhaps the outstanding modern example is the association of Pilkingtons with the town of St. Helens. Work and community were and are closely intertwined in such communities and inter-generational employment at the same plant is common. Employees develop solidarstic but generally deferential attitude. In such industries the introduction of increased career opportunities for the operatives of complex automated machinery has changed attitudes, but it has always been possible, through seniority and expertise, to advance from the shop floor in such industries. This, combined with their greater security of employment, gives workers in process plants a much more bureaucratic orientation than other solidaristic workers. Their power to a large extent is self-negating: a process plant once stopped may take months to restart, hence short-time strikes are not usually feasible for production workers. Outright confrontations may be ruinous to both parties and long-run strikes are likely to prove costly to whole interdependent community.

Even today a minority of the workforce are engaged in mass-production technology, and these are confined to a few industrial and are concentrated in the Midlands and South East. As we suggested earlier the combination of job mobility and alienative work seems to have created a largely instrumental orientation among these itinerant employees. In face, out own research seems to suggest that in the Midland's car industry the orientation of employees is much more solidaristic than instrumental . A high value is placed on the twenty years of experience typical of 25 per cent of the employees of at least one major car manufacturer.

The integrative logic in technological processes tends to cause social identity to re-emerge in the most unprepossessing circumstances. However, in order for the group to cohere in the place of work"

(1) the structure of the work situation must allow inter-personal communication;

(2) the work situation must present issues or problems that are held in common by a number of people, and

(3) workers must have or believe themselves capable of obtaining sufficient power to articulate and influence other on the matter in dispute.

The process by which cohesion occurs is different across different technologies, labour markets and organizations. In large-batch industry, in spite of the high concentration of workers in line or machine shops, communication is usually difficult. However, the nature of the workflow gives rise to vital *nodal* points where components come together for assembly. From their connection with these key points, some groups gain considerable disruptive power whose effects can be felt over a wide area. In process production communication is more informal and the stress much less. Conflict can be more easily handled on an inter-personal or inter-group level, and in any case, workers tend to be more dispersed geographically. Confronation can have severely disruptive effects and both parties are usually aware of this. In small batch production, group cohesion around the manufacturer of the product is high.

Sources of conflict may stem from the value put on inter-personal relationships between employer and employee, or different groups of employees. In a research and development laboratory we studies, the major conflicts originated from the disdainful treatment of 'locally' oriented technical staff by 'cosmopolitan' scientists and of the latter by bureaucratically oriented senior administrators. Long-term power in this situation lies with the professional or craft workers whose *replacement* value gives them strategies significance: both ancillary workers and administrators have only a short-term power to disrupt the work process.

Much will depend upon the response of management to the attempts by the group to gain recognition. Again we can look to the structure of the organization as an influence on ideology. Senior executives are much more likely to wish for some form of worker-participation within a unitary framework than to recognize an outside body like a union.

Line managers, particularly in large batch industries, may resort to a form of informal pragmatism in order to meet their dear-lines and to avoid confrontation with union representatives ensuing from attempts to operationalize their own sharply defined supervisory responsibilities. However, Harrison has suggested that managers can be categorized according to their views on organizational structures:

(1) power orientation-the organizational success depends on one 'great man' whom all others trust and attempt to emulate.

(2) role orientation-the effective organization depends on clear goals, prescribed functional responsibilities and well- defined roles.

(3) Task orientation- the organization must relate to the task or product and specialists must combines as equals within integrated teams.

(4) Person orientation-the people who posses the skills and abilities must be place first in all organizational servicing.

These orientations may be juxtaposed with Woodward's categorization of technology. These may be crudely represented as a complementarity in structure and orientation.

The sort of confrontation typical of the engineering industry may, therefore, be seen as the product of a juxtaposition of cosmopolitan and power-orientations in small batch production, or of instrumental and role orientations in large batch. In process control the confrontation of bureaucratic employees and equally bureaucratic, or 'person oriented' employers is nothing like so volatile. However, the very effectiveness of the relationship between 'master' and 'men' resulted in very intense conflicts in the primary sector industries. The nature of both the technology, the product market and the solidaristic feeling of the work-based community also prolonged strikes.

We now turn to a more speculative area-the effects of managerial practice on labour unrest. As an index of labour conflict we take the *incidence* of strikes in each establishment surveyed, rather than the reported *number* of stoppages. We were obliged to use the latter figure as a basis for our initial selection of firms, because it is one that can be derived from press reports- which previous experience has shown to give figures not very different from those yielded by Department of Employment record. But the experience also indicated that from neither source is the number of strikes reported a very accurate comparative measure of strike-proneness: and that the total of officially reported 'working days lost' is, for most purposes; much more reliable. Nearly all the companies interviewed agreed to out using the Department of Employment records to obtain their own figures in this respect even where they kept records of their own. We used the DE records because they are based on common definitions, and are thus comparable between plants. The basis of our calculations was the five full calendar years for which we had analysed these records by the time our interview programme was completed, and for which data were available for all the plants interviewed.

Our establishments' respective strike incidence was correlated statistically with several parameters of our survey, some of which have already been noted, while others will be referred to later. For the moment, we shall consider only the relationship between dispute liability and the managerial characteristics already considered in relation to size of plant.

Again, no very definite relationship emerged at first between a plant's strike liability and its degree of management centralisation. For 'standardisation' and 'formalisation', however, the case is rather different. Under these heads there appears to be slight but definite tendency for the incidence of disputes to increase with the managerial characteristic concerned- especially if one excludes the 'oddball' establishment shown in the extreme position for days lost per employee in both diagrams, which is also among the lowest scorers on both 'standardisation' and 'formalisation'.

Here, however, we are dealing with very general characteristic of management practice. If we turn to those bearing on industrial relations specifically, we find that the tendency for the incidence of disputes to increase with 'formalisation' is perhaps a little more marked when that characteristic applies to labour relations. And it is perhaps still more definite if we consider, again, the relation between the facilities provided to shop stewards by firms and their respective dispute incidences. So we arrive at the position that, so far from declining with the establishment and development of formal collective agreements, conciliation procedures and consultative arrangements, *or* with increasing provision for regular union activities and representation within the enterprise, the incidence of labour unrest appears, if anything, to increase.

Of course, this conclusion, while it *suggests* a causal connection, does not indicate the latter's direction. It is, for instance, quite possible that the formalisation of labour relations within the plant, and the accompanying acceptance of the shop steward system, were responses to labour unrest, not causes of it. There are many cases in industrial history where acceptance of union negotiations or workplace representation has been brought about by strikes; and though we found very few instances of such a direct relationship in the plants we surveyed, it was not impossible that a generally higher degree of labour militancy might produce increased formality in industrial relations, and more elaborate shop steward facilities, as a secondary effect of that militancy's secondary effect of that militancy's immediate objectives .

If this were so, the observed relationships would tell one nothing about the reverse effect that more elaborate and more formal bargaining and representative arrangements at the plant level might have on labour unrest. However, one rather curious phenomenon displayed by our results is the quite close similarity between the shapes of the last three diagrams- a similarity which extends also in some degree to diagram E as well. the suggestion, on other worlds, of these observations is that a firm which has a high degree of standardisation and of formalisation in its managerial processes in general will tend also to have a high level of formalisation in its labour relations and more systematic arrangements for internal union representation. And this was confirmed by our statistical analysis, which showed very strong correlations between the degree of standardisation or formalisation in the plants' labour relations and that recorded in other aspects of their managerial practice.

This seems sin any case a very likely relationship, on commonsense grounds. But it seem *unlikely* that the *general* qualities of a management would derive from those it had developed in dealing with its employees, and much more probable that its behaviour in industrial relations would reflect its broader managerial practice and attitudes. And if that is so, then the causal connection between 'formalisation', etc., in labour relations and the establishment's incidence of strikes presumably runs from the former to the latter. At the least, the proposition that formal arrangements for bargaining and union activity at the enterprise level necessarily arrangements for bargaining and union activity at the enterprise level necessarily encourage industrial peace must be highly suspect.

Industrial Relations and Mobility of Labour

Recruitment policies in firms, if they are to be sensibly planned, must take account of the availability of suitable supplies of labour, both in the local labour markets where their plants operate and, for certain types of skills, in the national and possibly international labour markets. This might seem a simple enough statement-perhaps tending towards the obvious-but exercise in meeting firms and discussing recruitment problems has shown that many firms exist on a day-to-day basis of notifying vacancies and simply hiring casual callers to staff their positions. Increased awareness in firms. however, of the importance of adequately skilled and trained labours has drawn attention to the planning of recruitment and this, in turn, demands a better understanding of the operation of the labour market and the mobility of labour.

Many factors condition supplies of labour to different markets; for example, the type of educational system through which prospective employees pass, and the attractiveness of the working environment offered by employers relative to those offered in other areas or in other firms. Relative wages ar clearly important, although there is not a great deal of evidence for the proposition that higher relative wages are clearly important, although there is not a great deal of evidence for the proposition that higher relative wages will induce transfer of labour from areas of abundant supply to areas where labour is scarce. Some firms are fortunate enough to operate in areas where the interaction of these factors provides plentiful supplies of labour with the right skills and experience, located at the right place and available at the right price. But, as the market' tightens', management has to search further afield for people, and it is in this situation that the importance of the relative mobility of labour becomes apparent.

The recruiter needs to know what kinds of people, with what training and what experience, are physically and mentally able to cope with the job offered. He must know what will attract a man or woman to do a certain type of job, to enter a new firm or even industry, or to uproot his family to move to another part of the country. It helps him also to know the extent to which such movement is prevalent among different occupations in order to ensure that his recruitment strategy is realistic and relevant.

Internal and external mobility

Mobility can take two forms: it can involve a change of job within an existing firm this is normally referred to as. Both types of mobility are important to the recruiter. As far as the first type is concerned, the job structure within the firm an opportunities for promotion clearly affect the extent to which the recruiter has to look outside the firm for additional labour. The extent to which manpower planning has been developed in the firm will greatly determine the extent of internal mobility—whether it is positively encouraged or whether it just happens. More significant to the recruiter, however, is the second type of mobility, namely external mobility. This normally involves a change of occupation, industry or area of work, and possibly a combination of all three. Since this is more important to the recruiter, we shall limit most of our discussion of labour mobility to external mobility for the remainder of this chapter.

The facts about external mobility

Previous studies of job changes show that labour is less static than is often assumed. In the UK, some one-third of the labour force change jobs in the course of a year, frequently involving a change of employer. For example, a study in South-east England found that one third of all job changes involved a change of area or industry, and of occupation; one-half of the job changes involved changes in occupation, whilst three-quarter involved a change in industry.

Thus external mobility can be geographical, occupational or industrial, or these can be interrelated. The Government Social Survey, which investigated labour mobility in Britain between 1953 and 1963 found that almost half the people surveyed had lived at their present address for ten or more years, whilst one-quarter had lived at their present address for twenty years or more. More recently, another government survey of households in Great Britain[3] has brought these mobility figures up to date, and these. The 1971 Household Survey shows, for example, that 35.7% of the population aged 15 or over had moved within the previous five years. and between 1958 and 1963 about 31.6% had done so. There was little significant difference between the findings of the two surveys. A further comparison can be made with earlier housing surveys. A 1960 housing survey estimated the annual rate of movement of households living within England and Wales at 8%, and a 1964 housing survey at between 7% and 8%. These figures ignored multiple moves by some households and revealed no difference between London and the rest of England and Wales. The 1971 survey found the annual rates of movement to be 11% for Greater London and 8% for the rest of England and Wales.

By contrast, inter industry mobility is even greater. For example, as much as three-quarters of those leaving a hob in commerce move to another industry[4]. But no systematic patterns seems to occur in the movements between industries. As far as movement between occupations is concerned, many studies have shown occupational mobility and skillto be inversely related, occupational change becoming less frequent the higher the qualification level of the occupation group.

The simple result of labour movement should be to shift a person from one job to another where productive performance will be higher and satisfaction greater. For the economy as a whole, if knowledge about individual capabilities and job opportunities is good, the net result will be a gain. But, the pay-off for the employer and employee can differ with the circumstances.

The main benefit to the employer is that he can maintain a flexible labour force which can be adapted to the needs of the moment. With skillful manpower planning he can adjust the size of his work force to a change in the demand for his products or to changes in the technology he uses. If the age structure of this staff is no longer likely to provide him with a stable pattern of career development he may alter it by replacing those who leave with people in the right age bands. Less frequently, but as important, he can relocate his factory or offices effects to where critical resources or good communications are more readily available, yet still draw to himself the skills he needs. Against this, the employer must set his costs of recruitment, relocation, induction and training. Rapid turnover can upset the social cohesion of work groups. An inability to retain the younger worker can worsen rather than repair the damage to his age balances.

The employee sees things differently. If he is escaping from a poor position, he is seeking to meet his basic needs: adequate earnings, relief from over stress, good working relations. More positively, movement may mean the furtherance of career aspirations, the possibility of developing new skills or the chance of establishing himself in a location where job opportunities are more plentiful. Against this he must weigh up any loss of job security consequent on his established position in the hierarchy, losses of pension benefits, the need to establish himself with new colleagues, and the problems of housing and schooling. The recruiter will need to help the potential recruit to make a fair judgment of the balance, if he is to retain as well as to recruit him.

Characteristics of the mobile person

We now consider what kind of people change jobs in the population and whether there are any differences between people in respect of occupations and locations which will tend to make them more mobile. We shall draw on two main sources of information for this and we shall look at the main factors involved.

Age

This is probably the most important factor affecting mobility. The pattern for the younger age groups follows that for the middle age groups, as younger people living with their parents will share their experience of house-moving. This is shown in

In contrast to the lower mobility of the very young and the middle age groups, only one-third in the 20-24 age group and as little as one-seventh in the 25-30 age group had not moved. In general, the age pattern of mobility shows high mobility in the age 20-24, after which the number of moves falls off rapidly.

Education level

The higher the level of education, the higher the proportion of people who are likely to move[1]. Amongst those educated in UK, the people with the most moves are those who attended university; about one-third of movers were found to have moved three ties or more Grammar and public school leavers showed a slightly higher degree of mobility than those leaving commercial or technical schools. The least mobile were those who last attended comprehensive or pre-1947 central schools.

Confirming these facts, the Government Social Survey showed that people with academic, technical or commercial qualifications are among those most likely to be willing to move. Over 60% of men with degrees or similar qualifications said they would move compared with 50% of men who are skilled. Men who had no skills or qualifications were the least likely to be willing to move.

Marital status

The government survey also investigated the characteristics of those who would not move compared with those who could be encouraged to move. Two of the most frequently quoted characteristics can be highlighted: first, marital status and, second, type of housing possessed. The willingness of males and females to move, according to marital status. It is clear that, if anything, a slightly higher proportion of married men say they would move if conditions were suitable. Married men say they would move if conditions were suitable. Married women an widows, on the other hand, are less likely to be willing to move than single women.

Housing

The government survey also showed that the least likely to move according to type of housing were local authority tenants, followed closely by those in controlled rent dwellings. Owner occupiers were more willing to move but the highest proportion of possible movers was found among those renting accommodation from private landlords, or living rent free.

Regions

Analysis of national patterns of inter regional mobility show that certain regions are more popular than others. Some difference can be observed between industrial and nonindustrial areas and, in general, nonindustrial areas are more favoured than industrial areas. The area most favoured as a place to move to is Southwest England, as is indicated. The next preferred areas are London, together with the nonindustrial part of the Midlands.

Managers

A special study has been made of the mobility of British managers. They exhibit certain behaviour patterns which are of particular interest to the recruiter of management staff. This study concluded that the mobility of managers, both geographically and between employers, had doubled in the last 30 years; specifically it found that younger managers are more mobile than those of previous generations. One-third of managers had never moved region, whilst 15% had moved region four times or more during their careers; confirming the results of the previously mentioned surveys, those with qualifications were more likely to move around. The study also confirmed that managers attached importance to the same kind of social and economic factors as other professional workers in deciding on whether or not to move. The particular characteristics they are looking for in a new job are complex and cover such features as self-expression, creativity and job interest as well as the more basic considerations of pay and security.

Attitudes to mobility

The reasons for people moving

A large proportion of recruits are those men and women moving from one firm to another. The government survey found that half of all those who moved had a job to go to before leaving their old jobs. Bowey has written a useful summary of the reasons why people leave a job and these illustrate the kinds of motivation which the potential recruit will have when applying for a post. Under the positive factors which attract a person to a company are included higher earnings, career development or a wider range of job opportunities within the firm or in its locality. At the other extreme are the stresses from which a man or woman may be withdrawing. These can be due to interpersonal conflict, early recognition of a bad choice of firm or job overwork, changes in working requirements or a redundant job. The recruiter must identify the prime motivations of the potential recruit in order to ensure that these will not continue to be a barrier to satisfactory employment.

The Government Social Survey investigated the reasons which would encourage workers under retirement age to move away from their areas of residents to other work. Gives a list of these factors, together with the percentage of those asked who responded positively. Prominent in the list are pay, promotion prospects, housing and job security. Very little mention is made of other factors relative to these. Higher pay, improved prospects and so on are clearly positive inducements to people to move, but we also know, from the same survey, the conditions that need to be satisfactory before people will decide to move, whatever the financial inducement they are offered. The single factor of concern to most people is housing, with over 80% of people mentioning this as a condition, and, when prompted, 95% agreeing it to be important. Of importance to fewer people, but still a major concern, is the security of the job, the attractiveness of the surroundings and the availability of good schools. In general, men tended to attach more importance to these conditions in their employment than women. Manual workers were slightly more concerned about security than others; professional and managerial people specified more than others the importance of good schools and amenable surroundings.

Implications for recruitment and selection policy

It is too easy to assume that every vacancy must be filled by a recruit; it is also too often thought that labour turnover cannot be controlled at all. The recruiter's job could more aptly be described as resourcing; he can draw on the skills of people already within the firm as well as without. No recruitment decision should be ad hoc; each should if possible be made with reference to other parts of corporate and manpower policy in the firm.

The recruiter needs to know, too, what is happening to those he recruits— are they leaving a short time after recruitment? Are the vacancies arising in the same jobs time and time again? The proper analysis of labour wastage requires that the rates of loss of people recruited at different times into each type of job are constantly monitored. If the loss rate is high for any particular group, then the cause needs investigation. Although mobility between firms may be characterized by general statements of the kind discussed previously, labour wastage from an individual firm is much more subject to local peculiarities.

Job and man specifications

To link up with available knowledge about potential movement of people to a firm, job specifications need to be expressed in terms relevant to the labour market in general. They should also relate to other jobs in the firm so that a shortlist of internal candidates with relevant experience can be drawn up. Terms like 'manager', 'supervisor' or 'clerical worker', used in many surveys of employment in firms, are simply not informative enough or used consistently. A good job classification needs to be able to identify the work to be done, its complexity, the authority held and the kind and level of knowledge required[6]. It is a basis for the man specification, but separate from it; ideally a classified file of all jobs should be held.

The man specification, in addition to what it normally includes, needs to bring out any characteristic which will limit the sources of recruitment: age, problems of travel to work outside of normal hours, the areas of the country for which the costs of relocation are likely to be unreasonable.

Identifying recruitment sources

Many jobs are normally filled by people living locally. The Employment Services Agency has carried out experiments in parts of the country to identify and bring togethr the kinds of information which the recruiter needs to have in order to access the potential local labour supply: information on school leavers, female participation, housing, principal travel routes, new business developments, redundancies pending and so on. Some agencies have introduced a newsletter; most are worth approaching for advice. Otherwise the recruiter will need to build up his own picture. Further information for certain areas and occupations, on wage rates, labour wastage and other manpower statistics, can be got from the Census and the various surveys organized by the Department of the Environment, CBI, BIM, IPM, Industrial Society, Institute of Manpower Studies and other specialist bodies.

We have shown that managers and professional people move more easily than others from one part of the country, or from one industry, to another. The reports already mentioned give limited but dated information on this. Again, up-to-date information on the potential labour supply outside one's immediate area is most likely to be got through the ESA and the Professional and Executive Recruitment Service.

Once a potential labour market has been chosen, the need is to identify what kind of man or woman is most likely to move. We have described the characteristics of the mobile person. Briefly, we know that in general a worker who is in the 25-30 age group, married and well qualified is more likely to move than one who is not. The recruiter must know in his own situation which factors are likely to be most critical.

Costs as a limiting factor on recruitment

It can easily cost 10000 or more to recruit a senior executive. The recruiter needs to work through a complete checklist if he is to evaluate properly his policy, the cost of prerecruitment, search, evaluation and selection, training and relocation. A list of over 30 items under these heads has been prepared by the Manpower Society[7]. Relocation costs, involving hotel charges, disturbance allowances, premiums, travel subsidies and so on, can be large and limit the range of locations from which labour can be attracted.

Making the job attractive

The factors which, if not satisfied, cause a man to leave one job and those which attract him to another have been described. The recruiter must ensure that the pay and security of the job are clear to the potential recruit. Where relevant, he should explain the prospects for promotion. If he is aiming to move a man from one location to another he should be prepared to provide information about housing, schooling, public transport and possibly even shopping facilities and social amenties. For manual occupations he may need to emphasize the security of the job, and for professional and managerial occupations schooling and social amenities as well. If a person is married, he or she may move more readily if aware that employment opportunities for their wife or husband are plentiful.

Wider implications

Some locations simply do not have and cannot attract people to work in them. In certain occupations there is a general shortage of skilled and qualified people. In these, labour wastage may be high, the working population mobile and retention difficult. The employer needs to be able to recognize whether his problems are unique to himself or more general. He needs benchmarks. Is he getting a fair proportion of school leavers with 'O' and 'A' level qualifications? What is his competitors in certain jobs, age groups, locations or after a certain length of time has elapsed since recruitment? If his recruitment position has deteriorated, has it done so relative to that of his competitors? Government statistics can provide a good indication of what is happening in the economy at large. But, they are too broad-based to give a proper understanding of these problems. Many companies exchange information with colleagues in local firms on an ad hoc basis; others have come together to organize an exchange in a more comprehensive and systematic way[8].

If the problem is low retention relative to others, internal policies need to be reexamined; if it is more general, different statics must be employed. Possibilities include restructuring and deskilling jobs, training unskilled people or retraining existing workers; proposals for more concerted action by government or central agencies can be put forward—for more relevant training in government training centres, by industrial training boards and professional institutions, for resettlement allowances, for the provision of suitable housing and so on.

What is industrial relations?

Industrial Relations as a discipline has been defined in various ways during the past three decades. Dunlop has said that the centre of attention in any industrial relations system is the establishment of procedural and substantive order as well as the containment of conflict. Flanders has put forward the view that industrial relations is oriented to the containment of conflict through the mechanisms of institutionalization and regulation. There have been several subsequent efforts to develop conceptual frameworks in order to enhance the understanding of industrial relations. However, most of the formulations have either reinforced the systems and pluralist approaches or have disagreed with these approaches in order to present alternative approaches. The divergence has been more often than not on an ideological basis on the liberal—pluralist and the radical—Marxist continuum. Hyman, for instance, has taken the position that viewing industrial relation as a rule-making or job-regulating process not only does not give due significance to the human aspects of the drama of industrial relations but also does not give adequate importance to the reality of the dynamics of power and conflicts. And the result, according to Hyman, is the "reification" of the processes of industrial relations.

1. Industrial relations is a rule-making process.
2. Industrial relations is the process of interaction among institutions of job regulation.
3. Industrial relations is a process of struggle for control over work structures and work processes.

Industrial relations, therefore, may be viewed as the dynamics of contradiction between menmployers and employees and the struggle for control over work structures, processes and relations, in which regulation and institutionalization are significant elements.

The management of industrial relations

There have been several attempts to conceptualize the modalities of the management of industrial relations. Fox wrote about the unitarist as well as the pluralist approaches in the management of industrial relations. Within the unitarist perspective, the right to manage is considered the presere of management while the pluralist perspective recognizes several competing power centres. Fox later added a third "radical" perspective in which he challenged the "balance-of-power" advocates, whose basic premise was that the mere recognition of plural centres of power brings about a balance of power. Fox went on to formulate his own typology of management approaches to industrial relations with the traditional mode at one end of the continuum and the continuous challenge mode at the other end with classical conflict, sophisticated modern, standard modern and sophisticated paternalist modes between the two ends of the continuum.

The mid-70s saw the emergence of the "control" theory of industrial relations with the focus on various tyupologies of management control. Braverman in his seminal work stated that the main mechanisms of control of industrial relations by management was through job fragmentation and job specialization. Friedman wrote of two perspectives—one which advocated direct control and another which postulated the responsible autonomy approach. Edwqrds described technological control and bureaucratic control. Burawoy's fascinating account of how consent is organised at the point of production throws up three types of control—despotic control, hegemonic control as well as hegemonic despotism, While Brayverman had spoken of control through job fragmentation and specialization, Gospel identified other mechanisms through which management exercises control over industrial relations—the putting out system, job contracting and the wage earning foremen mechanisms.

Hence, early theorizing on the management of industrial relations has focused on the unitarist/pluralist paradigm, and on the underlying logic, as well as the modalities of the control paradign of the management of industrial relations.

Several studies in the mid - 80's have directed attention to the fact that the management of industrial relations is characterized by adhocism, opportunism and pragmatism. The orientation is to live from crisis to crisis and the tactic has been to play by the ear. Expediency is the underlying logic and fire fighting is the pervasive stance. A certain cynicism is also associated with this approach since the actors within this framework of industrial relations indulge in games manship, one-upmanship as well as in brinkmanship.

The disenchantment which goes with this approach gave bith to a new perspective on the management of industrial relations which drew its inspiration from the strategic choice perspective.

Strategic management perspective

An understing of some of the contributions to strategic management is necessary, in order to be able to get a better appreciation of what strategic industrial relations management signifies. It might even be possible to argue that Dunlop's seminal contribution contains the seeds of what today is referred to as strategic industrial relations management, considering that he not only directed attention to the complex structure of interacting constituents, but also the the contextual complexity in which the interactions take place.

Hierarchies of managers and their representatives, hierarchies workers and their spokesmen, specialized government agencies interact in a given environment which has certain technological characteristics, market constraints as well as certain power structures in the larger society. Industrial relations within such a conceptualization will essentially have to be strategic given the need for sensitivity to the structure of stockholder interactions, as well as to the situation in which these interactions take place.

Strategic management literature is vast but in essence it began with the postulates that environmental changes determine corporate strategic initiatives determine internal structures and processes. Strategic management, as studies have shown, involves strategic decisions like investment, disinvestment, relocation, merger bankruptcy. In the Indian context changes in the structure of ownership, changes in the structure of management, new enterprise development, mergers and acquisitions, diversification, foreign collaboration, new technology introduction, relocation, decentralization of production, sick unit turnarounds, retrenchment and closure in response to internal as well as environmental pressures are some of the more significant strategic management concerns.

Peters and Waterman, based on their research on the elements which go into the search for excellence in the American corporate context, came up with the conclusion that strategic management is a function of seven interrelated dimensions - strategy, structure, systems, skills, staff, style and shared values. In other words, strategic management is not just a response to the environment, not just a strategic choice for the organization's survival or growth, but it covers a whole gamut of mechanisms, processes and human concerns, A key element is of course, the choice of a strategic thrust in relation to a firm's products, markets and technology with the option of continuing with current strengths at one end of the continuum and with the option of continuous innovation at the other end of continuum.

Strategic management, therefore, is not a static but a dynamic process in which the organization continuously defines the environment and responds appropriately. It is a continuous process of redefining its own core in order not only to remain in existence but also to change in order to be able to grow. This involves not only structural changes and systemic innovations but it also involves the skills and shared values of the people in the organization. It is this broadening of the scope of strategic management which opens up possibilities for proposing an approach to industrial relations which can be conceptualized as strategic industrial relations management.

Strategic industrial relations management

Broadly speaking, there are two schools of thought in contemporary thinking related to strategic industrial relations management. One school of thought views industrial relations decisions as second order decisions which are deeply influenced by first order business decisions. For instance industrial relations strategy would be determined by whether one is looking at any of the following situations which a firm may be facing at a given moment: new enterprise development, new product development, new technology introduction, mergers and acquisitions, investment or disinvestment, sick unit turnaround, nationalization or privatisation, retrenchment or closure. Strategic industrial relations initiatives activate industrial relations structures and systems, and in the process not only challenge the existing skill levels but also the prevailing shared values of the organization.

The other school of thought is represented by a model of strategic industrial relations management as represented in the writing of Kochan and Katz. Basically, what the model is trying to do is to conceptualize not only industrial relations management at the strategic, functional and work place levels but also to link the strategic, choice perspective at the firm level with the macroeconomic, microeconomic, political, social, technological, demographic and public policy constituents of the environment. In other words, the term strategic is not just confined to firm level decision processes but an attempt has been made to look at industrial relations processes within a multiple interest perspective, after making the assumption that there is an inherent conflict of interest between employers and employees.

One can draw a parallel between the approach of Kochan and Katz and Hyman's approach to industrial relations, which can also be viewed as emanating from a strategic perspective. Hyman, however, has taken the position that the drama of industrial relations is enacted within a politico-economic totality which is characterized by contradictions. The transformations of the contradiction ridden totality is brought about by the praxis of the labouring classes. In Hyman's "strategic" perspective, the focus is one the direct producer and the politico-economic framework of the praxis of the direct producer.

Hence, it may be suggested that strategic industrial relations management is not just the decision-making processes which are activated as a sequel to certain strategic business decisions, but it is a complex process which involves the totality of societal configurations. Confining the concept as well as the attendent techniques to the firm level, is perhaps, not only not strategic industrial relations management, but only one more instance of old wine in a new bottle in the sense that it is really adhocism and opportunism in a new garb.

Strategic industrial relations management—a humanist perspective

The traditional approach to strategic industrial relations management at the firm level as discussed earlier, begins with top management decisions and then works out implications at the functional and workplace levels. And the underlying logic of top management strategic decisions is oriented to products, markets and technology. In this scheme of things, the direct producer is "commodity" and an "input cost" to be minimized. Such an approach merely serves to sharpen the contradiction which are inherent in employer-employee relations. The modalities of strategic industrial relations management, however, take on totally differently connotations in the employer-employee relations as well as the standpoint of the praxis of the direct producers.

The notion of praxis needs some clarification as this point. The term has been interpreted in different ways by different authors. Kappen sees two distinct patterns from the plethora of interpretations - one neutral, the other value laden. Peraxis in the neutral sense means the totality of sense experience which includes both action and passion, perception and need, man's whole relationship with his environment through seeing, touching, hearing, feeling,loving, willing, acting and suffering. Praxis, in the value laden sense, derives from the historical dialectic phases: the praxis of alienation, the praxis of disalienation and the praxis of humanized social systems. Kappen's perceptive interpretation of praxis can be taken as a basis for conceptualizing the strategic industrial relations management from a humanist perspective. The strategic industrial relations management approach from the humanist perspective can be conceptualized as a function of three interrelated processes - the praxis of alienation of the direct producers, the praxis of disalienation and the praxis of humanized patterns of socio-economic organizations. The direct producers as the subjects of history are, therefore, actively involved in the praxis of alienation and disalienation as history evolves in the directions of the praxis of the liberated man under more humane, more just, more egalitarian patterns of society.

The praxis of alienation has two conceptually distinguishable elements - the macropraxis of alienation and the micropraxis of alienation. The macropraxis of alienation includes the socioeconomic formation in a given context and the concomitant industrial relations processes within which trade unions as well as managements live, move and have their being. An understanding of the socioeconomic formation and the role played by industrial relations structures and processes is vital for enhancing not only the understanding of trade union praxis, but also for enhancing the understanding of the praxis of strategic industrial relations management.

The micropraxis of alienation also has two conceptually distinct dimensions - the manner in which work itself is organized to generate surplus value and the manner in which the direct producers experience alienation from work. The understanding of the micropraxis of alienation, therefore, on the one hand involves the analysis of the structure and processes of work organizations in a given politico-economic context. On the other hand, the analysis of the modalities of the alienation of the direct producers is also important to enhance the understanding of the praxis of trade unions.

The alienation of the working classes impels them to participate in democratic institutions and processes—right to livelihood, eight to associate, right to be recognized, right to represent, right to strike and the right to self-determination.

Participation in trade unionism and recourse to direct, legislative and legal action activates the praxis of disalienation of the working classes. The praxis of strategic industrial relations management, therefore, is determined by the praxis of alienation as well as the praxis of disalienation of the direct producers. And the objective of strategic industrial relations management would be to orient its structures and processes to the praxis of humanized patterns of socio-economic organizations.

Strategic industrial relations management from the humanist perspective entails the following assumptions :

1. It recognizes the inherent contradictions in employer-employee relationships given the praxis of alienation and the praxis of disalienation of the direct producers.
2. It is committed to the praxis of humanized patterns of socio-economic organizations.
3. It not only is pluralist rather than unitarist in its stance towards labour, labour organizations, the agencies of the state as well as the judiciary, but the approach is principled, democratic and unconditionally constructive. Management respect trade union and collective bargaining rights.
4. The approach is not one of adhocism and opportunism but one of a conscious and continuous search for laying down sound principles to govern the relationship between employers and employees. The principles may emanate from management itself or from interactions with labour or through judicial pronouncements or through legislative enactments.
5. The orientation is to work towards consensus, to enhance cooperation with trade unions in a principled framework and also to enhance commitment of the direct producers through information sharing, employee involvement and participative management strategies and the systems and processes of Human Resources Development Interventions.

The strategic industrial relations management perspective and HRD mechanisms and processes

This Unit addresses itself to the following questions:

1. The conceptual basis of changing the praxis of industrial relations management from a reactive mode to a strategic mode.
2. The operational implications of the HRD concept in the context of labour management relations.

The basis of changing the practice of Industrial relations management from a reactive toa strategic mode could revolve around the following concepts and proportions:

1. The concept of alienation is the key to analysis of the condition of wage labour given the reality of contradiction-ridden organizational and societal totalities.
2. The concept of lienation is also the key to a better understanding of the interface between human resources development and industrial relations.
3. Any consideration of change from reactivity to strategic proactivity, in the process of considering the effect of the concept of human resources development on industrial relations should, therefore, be founded on the evolution of strategies oriented to the disalienation of the direct producers.

Conceptual basis

The notion of totality refers to the axiom that any issue, any problem, any practice, any subsystem should be seen in perspective. A blinkered approach could not only distort but could even distract the attention from the core of the problem. The concept of totality has two dimension—a static dimension and a dynamic dimension. For instance, the static dimension of any given society would be the definition of that society at a particular moment of history. The dynamic dimension would be that stages of the evolution of that society upto the moment of the present analysis. The totality of the static dimension of society would include the techno-economic, politico-legal, socio-cultural structures and processes. The dynamic aspect of any society would focus on the mode of production relation of production and relations in production. Hence, an analysis of any aspect of society should be sensitive not only to its present mode but should also be sensitive to how the present mode has evolved. Any discussior of strategic industrial relations management should take into account the mode of production and the relations of production as well as the techno-economic,politico-legal and socio-cultural structures and processes given the dominant mode of production.

The "totality" referred to above is not by any means a harmonious configuration of parts. There are inherent contradictions in the totality given the relations of production of a given mode of production. A sensitivity to the structural contradictions of the totality is essential to any analysis of human resources management. The structural contradictions flow from the struggle between those who own and/or control production and those who sell their labour for wages. The forms of these struggles will vary depending on the mode of production and the relations of production. Labour-management relations and human resources development are conceptualized and operationalized within the framework of a contradiction-ridden totality both at the societal level as well as at the organizational level.

The worker experiences the work organization at alienating. The politico-economic structure of the work organization, the drive towards profit generation, the hierarchy of control, division of labour, the dehumanizing structure of work processes, exploitative management practices and procedures, the manipulation of worker behaviour in organizations and other factors combine to form the basis of the workers experience of alienation.

The alienation of the worker consists in a complex of factors:

1. That work is external to the worker. It does not flow from his own creativity, farmhouse own volition, from his own aspirations. The politico-economic structure of the work environment divests the worker of his power to control the modalities of his working life.
2. Work is forced on the worker because of the urgent need for satisfying his various survival needs. Work itself is not the satisfaction of a need but merely a means.
3. As a worker, he surrenders his freedom to the organization and to impersonal market forces in return for wages. His condition amounts to wage slavery.
4. The alienated worker, therefore, has no control over what work he has to do, what his work is going to produce and also over the structure and processes enveloping his working life. He, on the contrary, through his work, creates power structures and processes which in turn contribute relentlessly to his own oppression and exploitation.

HRD : Implications for strategic industrial relations management

The picture which emerges from the discussion of the conceptual framework earlier is one of alienated labour given a contradiction-ridden totality. It is within this perspective that the implications of the HRD concept for industrial relations will be discussed. In order to facilitate this process, the following questions need to be addressed:

- What are the HRD instruments, processes and outcomes?
- What is the most important dimension of the HRD concept?
- What is the profile of industrial relations in the Indian context?
- What are the likely implications of the HRD concept for industrial relations?

A schematic presentation of what HRD means developed by Rao, T.V. is presented on the next page. The scheme is self-explanatory and demonstrates clearly the shift in focus which has taken place along with the change from the term "Personnel function" to the term "HRD function". While the term personnel function has somehow or the other been associated with perspective, critical-evaluative, punitive connotations, the term HRD function vibrates with images of a positive, dynamic development-oriented approach.

The central theme in the HRD approach is the development of the individual. The emphasis has shifted from "maximization of performance" and "compensation" towards "employee potential awareness creation" and "employee potential realization". The focus is now on enhancing employee involvement in internalizing organizational objectives through vibrant HRD efforts in order to release the springs of dynamism and creativity of individuals. The HRD approach holds the view point that the personnel function has reduced human resources in organizations to mere objects while the HRD approach views the people in organizations as the subjects of the organization's history and destiny. The employees are no longer cogs in the organizational wheel but the active agents shaping not only their own futures but also the future of the organization. The HRD approach therefore postulates a proactive rather than a reactive approach, a visionary stance rather than a firefighting orientation, a developmental strategy rather than a constrictive strategy. The discussion of the conceptual basis for considering the modalities of shifting from a reactive mode to a proactive mode, however, has tried to demonstrate that the contradiction-ridden totality of society forms the framework for there alienated condition of the working classes. Workers experience powerlessness, self-estrangement, cultural estrangement, meaninglessness, and normlessness given the politico-economic profile of the prevalent mode of production as well as the relations of production. Anyone familiar with life in organizations knows that the HRD approach appears to pull in one direction while the reality of industrial relations appear to pull in an opposite direction. Rules, regulations, enforcement, grievances, discipline, transgressions, inquires, sanctions, unions, more unions, disputes, negotiations, litigation, appeals, banners, slogans, go-slows, gheraos, strikes, lockouts, mandays lost, wages loss, production loss, damage, violence, intimidation, terror, despondency, despair, death—such are the stuff industrial relations realities are made of.

The HRD approach makes many assumptions which further appears to increase the distance between the HRD orientation from the realities of industrial relations:

1. The employee is an individual employee isolated, insulated, from other organizational and extra-organizational forces.
2. The individual employee is amenable to "developmental" overtures.
3. The organization can establish a direct relationship and rapport with the individual employee who is generally satisfied with the organization.
4. The organization is the sole custodian of the individual's growth and development.
5. The organization is capable of magnanimity and impartiality in transcending social,cultural, economic inequities, so much a reality in the Indian organizational context in its dealings with employees.
6. The organizational - individual relationship is homogeneous, harmonious, stable, cohesive, vibrant.

It must be recalled here that the conceptual basis evolved earlier, yielded the picture of an alienated labour given a contradiction-ridden totality. A perusal of the history of industrial relations in India, an analysis of the legal foundations of industrial relations and an appraisal of the empirical realities of industrial relations yields a certain profile of industrial relations, which calls into question many of the assumptions made by the HRD approach.

The industrial relations system has given employees the following rights:

1. The right to hire employees.
2. The right to frame the terms of contract with employees.
3. The right to enforce discipline at the workplace.
4. The right to activate the machinery for resolving disputes.
5. The right to form trade union.
6. The right to layoff, to retrench and to dismiss workers.
7. The right to lockout employees as well as to close down operations.

Employees have been given the following rights:

1. The right to form and register a trade union.
2. The right to activate the machinery to resolve disputes.
3. The right to strike to redress grievances.
4. The right to defend themselves in disciplinary proceedings.
5. The right to layoff and retrenchment compensation.
6. The right to withdraw by resignation.

The rights conferred on employers and employees have given rise to a certain kind of employer-employee relationship in the Indian industrial relations scenario :

1 The employer-employee relationship is a contractual relationship.
2. The employer-employee relationship is a struggle for power to gain control over work processes.
3. The employer-employee relationship is a political relationship.
4. The employer-employee relationship is conditioned by legislative enactments, executive authority and judical pronouncements.
5. The employer-employee relationship is disputeridden.

The characterization of industrial relations presented above provides an insight into the basis of the alienated condition of labour. The discussion of the conceptual basis has shown that labour experiences alienation as powerlessness, self-estrangement, cultural estrangement, norlessness and meaninglessness. The vital question therefore is: Given the alienated condition of labour in a contradiction-ridden organizational totality, to what extent are the assumptions of the HRD approach valid? If not valid, is there some way some aspects of the HRD spirit, the HRD philosophy, the HRD approach can be made to spill over, to transform the current modalities of industrial relations?

The most fundamental reason why the assumptions of the HRD concept are subject to debate is that the employer-employee relationship is not just a relationship but a relationship but a relationship which is contractual, combative, political, legalistic, contradictory. Any HRD practitioner will testify to the experiential fact that HRD overtures at the employee level, especially where labour is organized, are usually viewed with distrust and suspicion. This fact explains why the HRD approach more often than not does not inform all levels of the organization, but is confined only to the managerial and supervisory levels.

The HRD concept is certainly a dynamic concept and it seemingly has tremendous potential to bring about a qualitative change in organizations. But the danger lies in isolating the HRD innovations and the HRD interventions from the realities of industrial relations. Hence, when considering the prospect of moving away from a reactive mode to a proactive mode in the context of managing people in organizations, the potential of the HRD concept as a means to the above end, can only be gauged within the perspective of the modalities of idustrial relations in India. A change from reactivity to proactivity cannot be achieved by the HRD concept if the strategy is one of employers trying to reach out directly to individual employees or groups of employees, without taking into consideration the complexities and contradictions of industrial relations.

Hence, in order to move forward from reactivity to proactivity, given the HRD orientations and industrial relations realities, the following ideas, emanating from a strategic industrial relations perspective, are proposed for critical reflection and action:

1. The HRD concept and interventions should be addressed not only to individuals or work groups but also to organized labour. If the goal is to introduce a development-oriented approach tohuman resources in organizations, this should be done at all levels of the organizations and in dialogue with the worker organizations. Although the process may take longer if this approach is adopted, the long-term advantages to the worker and their organizations will be much more tangible. Or else, if the HRD initiative comes from above and does not have the sanction and support of the rank and file and their representative organizations, the initiative itself will contradict the "developmental" dimension of the HRD concept. The HRD initiative should recognize the fact that organized labour is the subject of its own destiny in organizations and is also the subject of the destiny of the organization itself.

2. For too long, industrial relations in this country have been handicapped by a dependency syndrome, mainly because of the debilitating dependence of the entire disputes resolution machinery on the state and its agencies. The executive, the bureaucracy and the judiciary have had a strangehold on employer-employee relations. Legalism as well as extra legal political interventions have been detrimental to the development of bilateralism. Thus industrial relations has never been allowed to grow into a proactive mode. A reactive, or what is popularly known as the firefighting approach, has become the order of the day.

Hence, it is evident that while the HRD approach is avowedly proactive, the reality of industrial relations shows that it is predominantly reactive. The question therefore is whether the proactive orientation of HRD could in some way spill over to the industrial relations functions function, and in the process contribute to the shift of IR from a reactive mode to a proactive mode. The answer to this question perhaps lies in focussing on the central theme of the HRD concept—the theme of "development". The shift from reactivity to proactivity could best be achieved by considering how there can be genuine "development" of industrial relations. One likely direction of this change could be by weaning industrial relations away from the dependency syndrome as well as from legalism. Alternatively bilateralism could be promoted by encouraging a principled mutuality as a means for chalking out the modalities of employer-employee relations. Such a strategy would also require that the following four rights should be given to the actors in the drama of industrial relations :

1. Right to form associations.
2. Right to recognition.
3. Right to represent as bargaining agent.
4. Right to withdraw labour or operations.

The contentious issue of determining the bargaining agents should also be resolved with a certain sense of urgency. An acceptance of the strategy of bilateralism, along the lines delineated above, will in the long run promote genuine development of bilateral relations and hopefully will also contribute to a proactive approach to bilateral relations.

3. A third possible issue flowing from the dialogue between the HRD approach and the IR reality, given the mandate of changing over from a reactive to a proactive mode, revolves around the question of democratization of the ownership and management of organization. Can there be genuine human resources development if a vast majority of the contributors to an organization has no stakes in owning the organisation or sharing power in the organization? Various forms of ownership and models of participative management have been identified, dissected, discussed and experimented within some organizations, but there has been little political will or corporate commitment to the dissemination of these

concepts. Except for certain sporadic demands, trade unions too have not seriously addressed themselves to this issue. Human resources development without democratization of the ownership and power in organizations, will not contribute to the resolution of the contradictions in the organizational totality, but will also ultimately intensify the alienation of labour in organizations. HRD without democratization will be an elitist concept and will ultimately contribute to the development of the privileged groups in organizations, thus increasing the gap between the managerial cadres and the direct producers.

From the substantive angle, strategic industrial relations management should also give due attention, as well as new direction, to three interrelated HRD systems:

- Human Resources Planning and Staffing
- Human Resources Commitment to Performance and Review
- Human Resources Training and Development.

Human Resources Planning and Staffing is a condition for sound performance. Since it is management which has the right to hire, the onus is on management to hire the right people, for the right job, in the right numbers. Improper as well as inefficient methods in this function leads to deleterious consequences for industrial relations. Stuffing should be based purely on the ability and competence of the individual, for the requisite job, within the parameters of affirmative action enjoined by state policy.

5. Strategic industrial relations management should orient its actions to enhance the commitment for efficient and high quality on the job. The focus here should shift from individual performance to workgroup performance. While individual performance needs to be monitored and improved, the unit of performance review should be well defined workgroups, consisting of managers, supervisors and workers. This will reduce disparate and dysfunctional individualism and also facilitate workgroup empowerment and collective pride. Rewards and recognition should be linked to commitment as well as demonstrated competence and performance. Perhaps reward and recognition should also be collectivized in addition to being individualized if a dent is to be made in the work ethos of Indian organizations. Performance review should become progressively open, participative and collective, rather than a closed, unilateral, superior-subordinate activity. Developmental initiatives should not also be divorced from disciplinary concerns.

6. Strategic industrial relations management should also give due importance to training and development activities.

Training should cease to be and "elitist" activity in the sense that only managers and supervisors benefit. The focus should shift to a Total Training Approach where the training unit is the workgroup including managers, supervisors as well as direct producers. The goal should be to empower the entire workgroup rather than increase the comnpetencies of managers only. It is this dichotomy between the managerial cadres as well as the direct producers which further accentuates the alienation of the direct producers. Again, the more privileged in terms of education, training and knowledge should have the responsibility of developing direct producers through on-the-job monitoring systems.

The strategic industrial relations management perspective, therefore, seeks to strike a balance between the individual needs and organizational interests, the inherent contradictions in employer-employee relations and the search for a principled collaboration between management and the direct producers.

26

Total Quality Management

For any project there is a limited supply of resources, such as capital, materials, energy, and labour. Further, competitive environments demand a better quality product or service at the existing price or at a lower price. Survival through acceptable profit levels requires maintaining the current market share or improving it as much as possible. In order to attain the end goal of profit, a business unit typically has multiple objectives. Problems arise when allocating scarce resources to the variety of alternative purposes competing for their use. Matching objectives with resources to attain end results is not an easy task. Only those organization that manage productivity and quality as an ongoing activity will be able to deal with these problems. At the global level, the problems of inflation, international trade competition, and unemployment are directly affected by the level of productivity growth and the quality of goods and services. In this age, every nation concerns itself with a high standard of living and better quality of work life and every organization concerns itself with high profit levels and an increased market share. For consumers who are concerned with the quality or "fitness for use" of the goods and services offered, therefore, productivity and quality management constitute the major driving force for survival.

Productivity was mentioned for the first time in an article by Quesnay in 1776, and since then most authors have defined it in different ways. A careful examination of these definitions reveals that some authors have defined productivity in a vague manner and others, precisely. One major similarity that could be inferred from these various definitions of productivity is that most authors viewed productivity as a "measure" of output, to one input, or total input.

The measure also pertains to how well resources are utilized. Three different forms of productivity have been accepted universally by most researchers and practitioners. For the purpose of this text, the three forms of productivity are presented as follows:

1. Total productivity is "the ratio of total output to all input factors".
2. Total factor productivity is "the ratio of total output to the sum of associated labour and capital (factor) inputs."
3. Partial productivity is the "ratio of total output to one class of input."

Juran defines quality as "fitness for use." The unique aspect of this definition is the inclusion of the concept of the user. Quality is viewed as one that requires every member of the organization to provide the next person in the process with an acceptable product or service. This means that everyone is responsible to perform a task in such a manner that the product can be used immediately and in the most efficient manner possible. Juran further identified four important parameters of fitness for use as:

1. Quality of design
2. Quality of conformance
3. The abilities
4. Field service

Quality is a term that has valuable meaning to both producer and customer. The producer views fitness for use in terms of the ability to process and produce with less rework, less scrap, minimal downtime, and high productivity.

There are two other aspects of quality; the quality of design and the quality of conformance. Quality of design pertains to quality obtained through changes or manipulation in design parameters. The differences in quality are a result of differences in size, materials used, tolerance in manufacturing, reliability, equipment utilized, and temperature. Quality of conformance is a measure of how well the product conforms to the specifications and tolerances required by the design. Such factors s training, the production process, motivation levels, procedures, and quality assurance systems can have an effect on the quality of conformance.

Quality characteristics

These are elements of fitness for use hat typify the variety of uses of a given product. Quality characteristics may be of several types:

1. Time-oriented (serviceability, reliability, maintainability)
2. Sensory (colour, taste, beauty, appearance, and others)
3. Structural (including frequency, weight, length, and viscosity)
4. Commercial (warranty)
5. Behavioral or ethical (fairness, honesty, courtesy, and so on)

Improvements in quality are therefore made by examining the design and conformance phases with their associated characteristics through the application of techniques and methods (changes in design, timing, inspection procedure, process control procedures, and so on). Productivity and quality management will be defined as follows. 'Productivity and quality management is an integrated process involving both management and employees with the ultimate goal of managing the design, development, production, transfer, and use of the various types of products or services in both the work environment and the marketplace. The process requires the total involvement of everyone in the planning, measurement, evaluation, control, and improvement of productivity and quality at the source of production or service center.

The productivity and quality management triangle

The productivity and quality management triangle (PQMT) encompasses an information system that provides input of information relevant to the planning, performance, and measurement processes and implementation of corrective actions and techniques that improve productivity. For an organization initiating comprehensive productivity and quality management, measurement, control, and evaluation is the first stage in the PQMT triangle. Once a set of measures has been developed, plan targets and strategies are formulated. Based on these strategies, short-range objectives are formulated and operational improvement techniques are then used to implement short-and long-range objectives. In order to assess the extent to which the improvements were successfully implemented, measurements, control, and evaluation are performed again. This triangular relationship thus continues as long as the comprehensive productivity and quality program exists in the organization.

Benefits of productivity and quality management

The management of productivity and quality can provide the following benefits to organizations:

1. Productivity and quality management will enable the consumer to pay low price for goods and services because the cost of production is reduced owing to reduced rework and gains in productivity.

2. Productivity and quality management enable the effective utilization of resources. More goods and services are produced for a reasonable amount of expended resources.

3. Productivity and quality management provide the basis for higher real earnings for employees. The reduction in the cost of production of goods and services can allow increases in wages without significantly offsetting gains in total productivity.

4. Productivity and quality management components provide an organization with the strength to deal with internal operating weakness and external competition.

5. Productivity and quality management will enable an organization to be more profitable because quality improvement results in reduced rework, reduction in scrap, better utilization of tools and equipment, and less work in process inventory, which in turn leads to higher productivity. Minimization of the cost of manufacture for goods and services improves the profit margin. The production of good quality products also improves the market share because the satisfied customer will buy more and will recommend the product to another consumer.

6. Productivity and quality management enable the public to realize greater social benefits through increased public revenues from organizations.

Top management role in productivity and quality management

Deming discusses what top management must do to improve both productivity and quality. The fourteen points offered by Deming have been successfully implemented in Japan and most of the industrialized countries in the world. A summary of Deming's fourteen points follows:

1. Create constancy of purpose toward improvement of product and service, with a plan to become competitive and to stay in business. Decide to whom top management is responsible.
2. Adopt the new philosophy. We are in a new economic age. We can no longer live with commonly accepted levels of delays, mistakes, defective materials, and defective workmanship.
3. Cease dependence on mass inspection. Require, instead, statistical evidence that quality is built in to eliminate the need for inspection on a mass basis. Purchasing managers have a new job and must learn it.
4. End the practice of awarding business on the basis of price tag. Instead, depend on meaningful measures of quality, along with price. Eliminate suppliers that cannot qualify with statistical evidence of quality.
5. Find problems. It is management's job to work continually on the system.
6. Institute modern methods of training on the job.
7. Institute modern methods of supervision of production workers. The responsibility of foremen must be changed from sheer numbers to quality. Improvement of quality will automatically improve productivity. Management must prepare to take immediate action on reports from foremen concerning such barriers as inherited defects, machines not maintained, poor, tools, and fuzzy operational definitions.
8. Drive out fear so that everyone may work effectively for the company.
9. Break down barriers between department. People in research, design, sales, and production must work as a team, to foresee problems of production that may be encountered with various materials and specifications.
10. Eliminate numerical goals, posters, and slogans for the work force that ask for new levels of productivity without providing methods.
11. Eliminate work standards that prescribe numerical quotas.
12. Remove barriers that stand between the hourly worker and the right to pride of workmanship.

13. Institute a vigorous program of education and retraining.
14. Create a structure in top management that will push every day on the other thirteen points.

Causes of productivity decline in companies

Mail presented twelve causes for the decline of productivity in organizations:

1. The inability to measure, evaluate, and manage the productivity of white-collar employees can cause a shocking waste of resources.
2. Rewards and benefits given without requiring the equivalent in productivity and accountability causes spiraling inflation.
3. Diffused authority and inefficiency in complex organizations cause delays and time lags.
4. Organizational expansion that lower productivity growth results in soaring costs.
5. There is low motivation among a rising number of affluent workers with new attitudes.
6. Late deliveries may be caused by schedules that have been disrupted by scarcity of materials.
7. Unresolved human conflicts and difficulties in team work result in the firm's ineffectiveness.
8. Increased legislative intrusions or antiquated laws result in constrained management options and prerogatives.
9. Overspecialization in work processes results in monotony and boredom.
10. Rapid technological changes and high costs result in a decline in new opportunities and innovations.
11. Increasing demand or leisure time causes disruption of time commitments.
12. A practitioner is unable to keep pace with the latest information and knowledge.

Although Mali's points focus on productivity, much the same reasons are applicable to the decline of quality within organizations

Quality Costs

Quality costs are those various categories of costs that are associated with identifying, avoiding, producing, maintaining, and repairing products that do not meet specifications. Quality costs are in four categories. Each quality cost category will now be described.

Prevention Costs

Prevention costs are associated with designing, implementing, and maintaining a quality system capable of anticipating and preventing quality problems before they generate avoidable costs. All costs related to efforts in design and manufacturing that are directed toward the prevention of nonconformance are in this category.

Appraisal Costs

Appraisal costs are associated with measuring, evaluating, or auditing products, components, and purchased materials to assure conformance to quality standards and performance specifications.

Internal Failure Costs

Internal failure costs are associated with defective products, components, and materials that fail to meet quality requirements, and this failure is discovered prior to delivery of the product to the customer.

External Failure Costs

External failure costs are generated by defective products shipped to customers. The product generally does not conform to requirements and fails to meet the satisfaction of the customers.

Effective system management for productivity and quality improvement

In order to improve productivity and quality, an effective management system must be in place. Such a management system requires applying common sense and creativity in making the required changes in policies, organizational structure, and procedures that allow a fertile environment for productivity and quality improvement. The following are basic requirements:

1. Management philosophy must be one that is geared toward continuous productivity and quality improvement at the source of production or service. Management of productivity and quality is not a one-time action. It is a continuous process that involves both management and employees, in producing and delivering good products and services.
2. Management and employee commitment to quality and productivity improvement can be translated into a written policy. There must be documentation of such a policy and clear specifications of all the necessary details to assure it.
3. Management philosophy must accept no levels of defect. Low productivity is not acceptable.
4. There must be a system in place for measurement, control and evaluation, planning and analysis, and improvement and monitoring of all activities.
5. There must be a data base for the strong and retrieval of information about the process.

6. There must be a clear definition of process parameters and variables. Input and output elements must be clearly identified.
7. All process parameters must be characterized with complete understanding of repeatability and variability.
8. There must be process ownership by everyone involved in the management process.
9. Productivity and quality improvement based on the implementation of key actions must be documented and rewarded on a timely basis.
10. The management information system must provide a real time feedback mechanism to everyone involved in the productivity and quality improvement efforts.
11. There should be a provision for ongoing management and employee training in productivity and quality improvement techniques.
12. There should mechanisms for the identification and removal of barriers between functional departments to facilitate open communication.
13. Management must provide clear guidance and clear goals and objectives, specify short- and long-term commitments, and set the direction for excellence.
14. The attainment of a good quality product should be through prevention of defects, not through detection of defects.
15. The removal of defects from a process should be done through root cause analysis and the implementation of proper corrective action. Cost inspections should be discouraged. The strategy should be that which utilize sampling inspection when necessary and no inspection when it is not warranted.

Productivity and quality management hierarchy

In order for a productivity and quality management system to provide useful and meaningful results, it is important for the level of emphasis to be clearly specified and understood within the productivity and quality management hierarchy (PQMH). The productivity and quality management hierarchy suggests that productivity and quality management should start at the basic levels. If all the associated inputs and outputs are clearly identified and managed properly at this level, the results have tremendous impact. It becomes less cumbersome to quantify and manage productivity and quality at the other eight different levels. The PQMH also provides a basis to identify the productivity and quality issues from a global perspective. Most importantly, it shows that the productivity and quality management of any nation starts from the basic units. At each level of the PQMH, techniques and methodology are required for the planning and analysis process, performance and measurement process, and improvement and monitoring process. Aggregation technique is usually applied to understand productivity and quality management issues at the higher levels. It is usually helpful if there are consistent and conducive policies affecting productivity and quality at the higher levels of the PQMH. In Japan, for example, there is partnership between the government and industry on issues that affect productivity and quality.

The quality manager (or chief inspector) reports directly to the plant manager and is responsible to determine by sufficient inspection that the company products conform to all pertinent company/customer specifications and drawings. Products deviating from specifications will be withheld from shipment and will be reviewed jointly by the plant manager and the quality manager for disposal and corrective action.

Such a statement clearly identifies that quality is an independent function and that the task is limited to one of inspection and the accumulation of defect data for review. Inasmuch as no mention is made of the accumulation of historical data, it must be assumed that none is required.

At the other end of the spectrum the statement of responsibility, accountability, and authority for the quality manager of a very large corporation can be extensive and detailed; for example:

Under the policy guidance of the vice president and general manager, responsibility, accountability, and authority is vested in the director/manager of quality as follows:

Responsibility

1. Plan, control, direct, develop, and evaluate the operations of the functional departments assigned to his or her area:
   a. Quality assurance, which includes:

      Product assurance

      Quality audit

      Laboratories

   b. Quality control, which includes:

      Internal quality control

      Supplier quality control

   c. Quality program management
2. Ensure that products delivered to customers meet all standards of quality contained in contracts and specifications.
3. Ensure that operations or processes affecting quality standards and performance are tested, audited, and evaluated.

4. Ensure that program areas are supported and assisted in terms of systems, techniques, and trained personnel necessary to enable such programs to meet quality standards and requirements.
5. Examine quality policies, instructions, and procedures to ensure that they are effective, appropriate, and congruent with the accomplishment of division objectives.
6. Establish a work environment that ensures the development and effective utilization of personnel and the proper combining of resources necessary to carry out quality programs and meet objectives.
7. Maintain a continuing liaison with customer personnel and agencies which generates a positive understanding of quality systems and commitment.
8. Communicate division goals; develop and disseminate concise statements of the quality groups tasks and standards of performance, and evaluate results against these standards.

Accountability

1. Products delivered to customers meeting all specified standards of quality contained in contracts and specifications.
2. Achievement of required quality at cost within limits of allocated funds.
3. The performance, morale, and motivation of assigned personnel.
4. The integration of his assigned functional departments with the remainder of the division.
5. Prepare data that identify for management trends in hardware quality, costs related to scrap and production errors, and overall cost of the quality function.

Authority

1. The supervision, administration, and execution of programs, policies and functions assigned, so as to ensure the division's capability of attaining its profit and long-range commitments.
2. Develop and maintain systems, controls, and techniques which provide for the timely detection, solution, and elimination of quality problems and their causes.
3. Approve program personnel certification board requirements.

Whatever the dimensions of the task—is it is clearly defined-both the quality organization and the rest of the production operation understand what the quality department is required to do.

An equally important element in organizing for quality is the recognition that the production of a quality product is the responsibility of every division of the company involved in the production process: engineering, manufacturing, material handling, and purchasing, as well as quality. This responsibility begins at the point of initial design and continues throughout the life of the product. All company divisions must keep the requirement for quality basic in their activities. Only by working as a team can the goal of a product that delivers ultimate customer satisfaction at the lowest cost be achieved.

The basic quality task

An understanding of the basic task to be accomplished is fundamental to developing an organization. Although there are many variations of emphasis, the fundamental tasks of the quality organization can be identified as follows:

1. *The Prevention of defects through analysis of requirements*: 'It is axiomatic that elimination of potential problems before production begins will result in lower cost and a better-quality product. Unaccountably, this is an area all too frequently ignored. The inclusion of manufacturing and quality personnel in the early review of preliminary designs can reap handsome rewards by way of a more realistic tolerancing, dimensioning for easier machining, elimination of difficult assembly processes, better understanding of test requirements, and so on.

Quality reviews at this stage can establish the proper sequencing of inspection requirements, eliminating unnecessary inspections which make no real contribution to product quality. The review will also pinpoint similarities in design to past products which have suffered from failures or defects. Early identification of such problems can lead to corrections or changes that will eliminate the probability of recurrence.

2. *Control of the manufacturing and test operations*: To achieve product quality it is necessary to be certain that every manufacturing action is performed according to predetermined standards and instructions. There is no substitute for the discipline that ensures this control. In theory it makes no difference who exercises such control. The factory workers who are properly motivated can be just as effective in controlling their output as the inspector who normally checks their work. This is equally true for all other functions involved in product manufacture.

In real life, however, the practicalities of meeting cost schedule commitment generally mitigate against production personnel being an effective force for sustained and improved quality. It falls to the quality organization to exercise this control or restraining activity. It is incumbent that they be equipped both mentally and technically to accept the responsibility. Failure to do an effective job has sometimes been due to the reluctance of quality management to accept the fact that the company really meant for them to control the production operation to the degree necessary to produce satisfactory hardware.

3. *Detection of defectives in the hardware*: Detection of hardware and test errors is the traditional role of the inspection force within the quality organization. The effectiveness of this function has a marked effect on overall control of the product

4. *Corrective action to prevent repetition of mistakes:* Repetitive mistakes are costly, interfere with schedules, and are unnecessary. Every company, however small must have a system to recognize repetitive problems and eliminate their cause. It is important to recognize that the elimination of some problems may be so costly as to prohibit any constructive action. A conscious decision to take no action must be carefully weighed against the possible results of such a decision.

5. *Planning for a more effective operation*: One of the more noticeable shortcomings in many quality organizations is the absence of effort directed toward the future needs of the division. All too frequently the planning effort is concentrated on today's problems, with little thought given to future developments. Clearly, a function of quality is to provide expertise to consider possible changes or modifications in order to be more effective and meet future challenges.

Organizational Concepts

At the outset it should be recognized that there are no absolutes with respect to the manner in which the quality function is organized. The basic tasks of quality must be satisfied in some manner, but the organization required is dependent on a variety of factors. It should be developed to fit the job at hand: what is required for complex mechanical hardware is patently different from that required for a supplier of simple parts, a chemical processing concern, or a supplier of services.

The opening paragraph of this chapter identified the need for a commitment by management; a definition of the quality charter— what, precisely, does the management expect from the quality group? The size of the task has a marked influence on the nature of the ultimate organization. The most effective group is one that accomplishes its task with a minimum of organizational requirements.

There is also no common agreement with respect to what the organization for quality is called. Quality Control, Quality Division, Quality Assurance, Product Assurance, and Quality and Reliability Assurance are all titles that appear on company organization charts, and it matters little what the organization is called as long as its charter is properly defined. Quality assurance, for example, has been used to designate a total, complex quality organization; a small audit group in such an organization; a group responsible for all non-inspection quality tasks; and a separate organization independently auditing and reviewing all aspects of quality within a company.

The specific task requirements may also influence the basic approach to organization. A limited responsibility may be best served by a quality assurance group acting in a staff capacity as mentioned above. Some large organizations consider it desirable to monitor the quality function by having a group of operating executives act as a quality committee, or quality council, establishing basic policy and ensuring that such policy is communicated to the operating divisions. The important factor is to recognize the scope of the work and organize for it. It is also necessary to recognize that flexibility and the ability to change must be allowed for in the structure.

In every company there are built-in contraints that can have an effect on how a task it organised, and these constraints must be recognized and taken into consideration. Identified below are a number of such constraints with a short paragraph outlining their effect. These are by no means all that could be developed, nor are they examined in detail. Rather, they are indicators of real-life situations that must be faced in the development of a good quality organization. Organizational theorists sometimes choose to ignore these constraints, but they are real and must be a consideration in any organizing effort.

1. *Company operational and organizational guidelines*: Every company has developed over its history certain guidelines relating to how it organizes and operates. Usually, but not always, these are written down in the form of policy or standard practice manuals. Although these are not necessarily inviolate, the wise manager will find it prudent to stay within these guidelines unless they prevent the proper accomplishment of the quality objective.

2. *Management style*: Over the years, most companies develop a management "style." This style or attitude is reflected in the way the management team operates, both within the organization and in the marketplace, for example; some companies are highly disciplined, outlining in written procedures all possible situations and following the procedures to the letter. At the other end of the spectrum is the laissez-faire approach; nothing very formal, each executive doing his or her own thing and keeping in touch with peers in the organization. In some organizations nothing gets done unless the top executive personally decides. This is not the place to comment on the merits of the various styles but only to point out that the company style must be considered in organizing for quality. It would be unrealistic to propose a highly formalized procedural system in a company where day-to-day problems are attacked by informal meetings of management. This is not to say that quality discipline should be ignored, but it must be organized in a manner that will fit the ongoing style. Traumatic changes can occur when a new chief executive arrives who operates with a completely different organizational style.

3. *Customer influences*: More frequently than not, the quality organization is dictated/affected by requirements of the customer. This may come from specifications, process controls, or even certain administrative actions required in order to do business. This is particularly true for companies having contracts with government agencies, each of which has its own special set of requirements or regulations. One of the quality manager's more difficult tasks is to develop an understanding in all levels of management that these customer requirements are real and must be satisfied. Unfortunately, requirements of different customers are sometimes divergent to the point where multiple systems may be required. The challenge is to meet the intent of

the requirements with the minimum disruption of the normal quality system. Quality costs can become exaggerated if the organization is expanded to over every eventuality. This problem has always been particularly acute for those companies that act as subcontractors to a variety of other manufacturing concerns. Those who have a sound quality system based on well-established controls are usually able to negotiate an agreement substituting their procedures or the customer's requirements.

4. *Company size*: It would seem to go without saying that the size of the company itself has a marked effect on the Quality organization. Although the basic quality task must be accomplished, the function has to fit into the frame-work of the overall organisation. Large organisations have the facilities and finances to maintain systems and records, which, although desirable, may be well beyond the means of a smaller company. Conversely, a pitfall of some quality management teams is the urge to expand and grow simply because the company is large. Size and number of systems are not the measure of superior quality operation-effectiveness is!

5. *Diversity and complexity of product line*: The diversity and complexity of the company product line have a strong influences on the development of the quality organizational structure. An organization that is suitable for the manufacture of a few, large, highly sophisticated, and individually costly articles may not resemble at all that required to produce volume deliveries of small, diverse, highly precise parts from automatic machinery. It is erroneous to conclude that any given quality system or technique, however successful in the past, is necessarily useful when the manufacturing product-line changes radically or becomes completely different. As has been mentioned previously, the quality system must be adapt itself to the environment in which it operates. The quality control system that is unable to change with product-line variations will eventually have to bear either the stigma of unnecessary cost or the failure to produce satisfactory hardware.

It is true that the same type of controls are often a requirement for entirely different products. It does not follow however, that the technique of application must be the same. Indeed, the technique may be so radically different as to require a different organizational pattern. For example, precision castings for a space vehicle may have the same tolerance requirements as those for an engine block on an automotive assembly line. Automatic gaging would be prohibilitively costly in the case of the space vehicle where the few castings involved would probably be checked individually by a highly skilled inspector, either by actual layout on a surface plate, or through the use of an inspection measuring machine. The automotive assembly line would probably have automatic gaging equipment built into the assembly line, which would be monitored by less-skilled checkers or by the production personnel. Both methods achieve the same end but through different techniques and a different organizational alignment.

6. *Stability of the product line*: Product stability can also have an influence on

organizational structure. A product line that is relatively the same from year to year can generate economies, both in the use of personnel and selection of the most useful and economic equipment. Less supervision, more use of production checking data instead of direct inspection, and elimination of formal corrective action teams are ready candidates for system improvement is a stable manufacturing environ-ment.

Improvements such as the above cannot be achieved when the product line changes frequently. a different structure is required to identify problems as they occur and to take the required action to correct them. The manager of the quality function must be alert to recognize when a change in product requires a change in the quality system.

7. *Financial stability*: Quality is a part of the business aspect of every company and its operation is dependent on the overall profitability of the concern. Quality managers cannot ignore, as some would have us believe, the cost of doing business and the financial stability of the entire organization. Quality managers should get their fair share of the money but must recognize that the program has to be developed to fit the funds available. If risk taking is involved, the risks should be clearly identified to the company management.

8. *Availability of personnel*: The organization must always be formulated around the requirements of the task at hand. It would be unrealistic, however, not to recognize that the availability of certain by personnel may affect the formation of the ideal organization. Lack of certain skills in quantity may make it necessary for supervisory personnel to head more than one element where normally a separate grouping would be preferable. This can be true in lower-level technical assignments, where either cost or inability to hire creates a necessity for doubting up of responsibility. This may end up being cost-.effective but usually involves the risk of missing some important element in the inspection cycle.

Quality functions to be considered in organizational planning

The spectrum of functions that have been assigned to the quality organization is very broad. Some of these functions are universally accepted as a part of the quality role, whereas others are considered by many managements as being outside their conception of the quality charter. The following paragraphs identify the tasks that can be considered as part of the quality charter in the broadest sense. It should not be assumed that every organization must involve itself with each of these activities. The basic premise still holds that the organization should fit the job at hand, and cover only those tasks necessary to produce a quality product. Every production environment has need for different controls, and the quality charter should be structured around those needs, not to a list of possible functions. The general management of the company should be made aware of all of the personnel quality tasks in order to support and, indeed, demand the controls required. Further, the paragraphs below are intended only as a brief outline of the principal elements of the function. Specific methodologies for the various tasks are covered in other chapters.

1. *Product design reviews*: Earlier, a basic quality function was identified as being the prevention of defects through analysis of requirements. Inclusion of quality engineers in the design review process at the earliest possible time is the medium for accomplishing this object. Where formal design re-views do not exist, or where products are manufactured from another company's design, the quality engineers should still begin to critique the design as early as possible. This review should emphasize ease of manufacture and inspection, required process controls, similarity to past products which developed defects, and consideration of tolerancing problems in manufacture and assembly. It is not the responsibility of quality personnel to be the design checking function of the engineering department. Although glaring design deficiencies should not be allowed to develop without comment, the quality critique should be limited to matters that affect the manufacture and quality of the product. The danger in design reviews results from quality engineers frequently wishing to instruct the engineering department on how to design the product in its entirety.

2. *Quality planning*: Every quality organi-zation should have a planning function, however small. In very small operations it may be part of the department head's duties, but it must exist for quality to survive. The many aspects of quality planning are diverse and will be covered in detail later in this chapter.

3. *Purchase order review*: The review by the quality group of all purchase orders for production materials is similar to the requirement for design review. History shows that purchased material is usually subject to more problems and uncompensated cost losses that that produced in-house. A considerable portion of these problems are the result of incomplete communication between the supplier and the company. Inasmuch as the department usually involved in stopping the flow of incoming material is the quality organization, it is imperative that they be represented as the order is placed. A review of purchase orders prior to release tends to minimize rejections by ensuring (a) that the proper specifications have been included, (b) that the necessary documentation has been requested, (c) that any additional inspection requirements are clearly stated, and (d) that the supplier selected is a satisfactory source and has been approved by the quality department.

This requirement for review must be organized as a function of volume. The quality group must make certain that the flow of the documentation through the division does not impede the placement of orders. The quality function can be handled by a single individual or a group, depending on the volume to be processed. In large organizations where the purchase order system is computerized, the quality input can be made a part of the system and input fed into the purchase order through a terminal located in the quality area.

4. *Supplier control*: A large part of the dollar cost of many manufactured products is spent in the plants of suppliers: in some companies it is actually a majority of the total cost. Many of these companies, however, spend virtually no money in the control

of this supplier effort. The role of evaluating and checking the performance of these suppliers falls largely to the quality organization. A separate quality function dedicated to ensuring that the suppliers are attempting to meet all the requirements of the contract can result in significant savings. This is reflected principally in the elimination of defectives found in receiving inspection or even after in the production cycle where delay can be more costly than the actual part. This identifiable quality function is one of the most undervalued, and often unused, tools in the quality system.

5. *Receiving inspection*: This group is charged with determining that the parts and materials received from suppliers do, in fact, meet the requirements of the purchase order, including the receipt of proper documentation. The tasks vary from simple inspections to highly sophisticated tests using the most modern computerized techniques. The receiving inspection group also develops historical records of supplier performance for use in the placement of future orders. Some companies include purchase order review as part of the receiving inspection function.

6. *Stores inspection and control*: Parts and materials need to be well controlled once they are manufactured or received from suppliers. It is the responsibility of Quality to determine that the system devised by the company for this control is being followed and that different materials and parts are not mixed together or issued incorrectly. Depending on company size, this task can either be a separate function or an added responsibility of another segment of Quality.

7. *Tool and fixture inspection*: The majority of manufacturing operations employ the use of specially manufactured tools and assembly fixtures. To minimize future rejection of hardware, the quality organization should be required to inspect such tools for adherence to the tool drawings and to inspect the first production lot for adherence to the engineering specifications prior to release of the tools for production.

8. *Product inspection*: Product inspection is the day-to-day chore of sorting the good from the bad. The inspection force is divided generally into three groups.

a. *Fabricated parts*: All the piece-part hardware and the processes that produce them are controlled and inspected. This may be accomplished by sampling during a production run, by lot inspection prior to moving to the next production station, or at the end of the production of the finished article. Depending on the repeatability of the production equipment and the experience of the work force, this inspection can be very intense or simply an occasional check on a proven process.

b. *Subassembly inspection*: As individual parts are assembled into larger components or subassemblies, a further check is required to ensure conformance as well as completeness. Frequently, a part of subassembly inspection involves test routines where operating components have been installed. Here again it should be recognized that the earlier problems are discovered, the lower will be the ultimate cost.

c. *Final assembly*: The last critical inspection takes place during and after the final completion of the hardware. The degree to which this is emphasized has a relationship to the inspections and tests accomplished prior to this point; where subassembly inspections has been minimal, final inspection must be rigorous and all-inclusive. A system built on a heavy inspection and test cycle prior to final assembly may require only a rigorous final test. The variations in philosophy are limitless with respect to the degree of inspection at various stations. The true test is the production of satisfactory hardware with minimum losses due to bad hardware.

9. *Test control*: The role of the quality group with respect to the test function varies widely from industry to industry and from company to company. Each method has its strong adherents and it is sufficient to say that with the right management environment any of them can be successful. Some of the most widely recognized methods for quality monitoring and control are outlined briefly below.

a. *Quality operation of the test department*: In this system the quality division is directly responsible to write test procedures, design the test equipment, and run the actual tests as an independent agency.

b. *Direct control of test by monitoring all phases*: The quality group is responsible to review and approve test procedures written by others,verify that the test setups are in conformance with the approved procedures, monitor the testing as it is being performed, and certify the test results as being acceptable. Their responsibility involves stopping the testing at any point where the results are not in accordance with procedures or specifications.

c. *Monitoring of tests written and performed by other departments*: In this system the quality role is limited to observing the tests as performed by a test organization and certifying that the results match the written procedures.

d. *Minimum role*: The minimum role that quality personnel can perform in the test area is to verify that written procedures exist, that they are being followed, and that a spotcheck of the test results indicates compliance to the requirements.

The gamut of quality participation actually involves combinations of systems outlined above. Again, the objective is to be certain that for the product involved sufficient independent quality control is exercised to ensure satisfactory hardware.

10. *Final acceptance*: Final acceptance of the product prior to delivery is basic quality task. Organizationally, this can take different forms: a part of a test; the last inspection station; or in the case of large complicated items, a final review of product and paperwork in a separate department.

11. *Customer interface*: The customer interface that pertains particularly to the quality organization is the one that has to do with those who make acceptance for the customer. The quality department, having the records and history of the product, as well as the customer's specifications, is charged with the task of interfacing with the customer to assure acceptance of the hardware. One of the pitfalls that some companies make for themselves is the mistake of having salespeople attempt to "sell the customer the finished product, and then try to explain any questionable items. Not only does this not, satisfy the customer, it frequently generates general distruct of the producer's intentions. Quality personnel are best equipped to handle this sensitive interface.

12. *Process control*: The control of the basic processes used in the production of hardware and other products is fundamental to achieving acceptable end result. Heat treatment, chemical processing, batch mixing, surface preparation, and protection are examples of the types of processing that must be rigorously controlled if rejection costs are to be kept within bounds. In the non-hardware industries, such as petroleum, medicines, and foodstuffs, process control is the only real control prior to sampling the final product. The staffing of the process control function is dependent on the number and type of processes involved. Where it fits organizationally within the quality group is determined by its size relationship to other quality operations.

13. *Laboratory operations*: All quality organizations do not end the services of a full-time laboratory, but most need some laboratory work performed on a routine basis. Chemical and physical analysis of materials, process control checks, requirements for x-ray, and so on, are all laboratory operations essential to good quality control. These services may be obtained in a more cost-effective manner by the use of outside laboratory facilities. Where the work is sufficiently extensive to justify an in-house quality laboratory, it is often expanded to include process control, calibration, and basic measurement standards.

14. *Calibration of equipment*: Calibration of equipment presumes the existence of non-production use standards to which the day-to-day working equipment can be compared and adjusted. These working standards must, in turn, be regularly checked against master standards, usually traceable to the U.S. Bureau of Standards. The services of special laboratories for this service are often employed in preference to developing an in-house capability. The use of these special laboratories is a perfectly satisfactory method of maintaining calibration as long as the system employed is under the control of some element of the quality organization. As mentioned previously, where a quality laboratory exists, calibration, or at last the maintenance of standards is often an element of the laboratory organization. Organising for the collaboration function must encompass all equipments used througout the operation—developmental equipmental as well as production. A common mistake is to assume that engineering equipment used for product development does not need the rigorous calibration requirements that production equipment requires. It is impossible to

develop products that will perform according to the specifications if the equipment used in development is not held to the same requirements that the production force will use. Those engaged in government contracting are subjected to very rigorous controls in the area of calibration. Much of the success of many of our national programs can be traced to adherence to these standards.

15. *Certification of operators*: In the somewhat distant past the journey-man machinist, welder, and so on, was exceedingly well trained, having served a long apprenticeship. Today when many critical production operations are, or can be, in the hands of newly trained semiskilled employees, a minimum level of proficiency must be obtained before new employees are allowed to proceed on their own. The practice of ensuring this skill level by a mandatory training and certification program is becoming increasingly common among companies anxious to protect their reputation and their profits. After classroom training, on-the-job experience, and testing the employee is "certified" capable of doing the work assigned. Achieving this certification may take only a few hours or several weeks, depending on the assignment.

The quality organization should be responsible for monitoring this program, issuing the evidence of certification, and systematically checking for violations of the prescribed rules. In some companies the quality organization has been given the responsibility for the testing as well.

16. *Corrective action*: Corrective action is the quality function designed to review discrepancies, determine their cause, and ensure that a solution to the problem is implemented. Corrective action is more than finding a solution corrective action is not complete until the solution has been implemented into the system. The solution may affect various divisions of a company: engineering, manufacturing, quality, purchasing, and so on. Repetition of mistakes represents an unnecessary loss of production dollars that fast, accurate, and complete corrective action can minimize.

Organizing for corrective action can be as simple as assigning the responsibility to an area quality supervisor. In the smaller company this supervisor is the one relatively unbiased person who has access to all the information pertaining to the problem.

Large organization find corrective action to be most effective when it is set up as separate group within the quality structure. This group has its own staff of engineers to analyze problems and seek permanent solutions. Frequently, special projects within a company have quality corrective action engineers assigned directly to the project.

17. *Statistical analysis and data reporting*: Adequate record are paramount in any quality system. The "build history" of a products is often required to prove exactly what actions took place during manufacture or processing. Such records are usually the output of the planning operation.

Equally important is the gathering and analysis of statistical data relating to the production output from the viewpoint of the quality management. The availability of computer storage and printout has increased enormously the ability of quality personnel to produce data. These data can include every aspect of the quality function. Receiving inspection reports, process and manufacturing trend data, repetitive non-conformances, test yields, and so on, must be produced in a form that when reviewed by other than quality personnel is understandable and complete. Data are useful only when their meaning is clear and leads to some constructive action. It is a common fault of programmers to load data into the system that will never be retrieved for use. Only that information required for regular management use should become a part of the permanent data base.

Audits : Audit of the quality function-indeed, of the entire manufacturing process—is a historical element of the quality system. The degree of responsibility given to the quality audit function varies with respect to the size of the company, the historical performance of the product in the marketplace, and the desire of the company management to have independent reviews of the performance of the manufacturing operation. Some companies extend the audit function in areas other than those closely related to manufacturing on the premise that such audits identify problems that might otherwise go unnoticed, and can be wasteful of both time and money. In some companies quality audits are considered an important enough element to warrant an independent unit reporting directly to the quality manager. Usually, they are considered to be a part of the quality engineering function, separated specifically from the "hands-on" elements of quality control.

19. *Administration*: The administrative element of the quality organization is charged with the responsibility for writing and issuing quality procedures; developing hiring and training plans; preparation and control of the quality budget; and frequently has the added responsibility of some elements identified previously, such as data accumulation and certification or operators. In organisations where such elements represent few actual personnel, the administration department offers the leadership capability that can be used to minimize supervisory overhead. Most often the administrative department manager reports directly to the top quality executive.

20. *Facilities acquisition*: The acquisition of the necessary facilities for the quality operation is an increasingly important element of developing quality system. The equipment available has become more diverse and in some cases very sophisticated. Selection of such equipment requires more detailed analysis, both from the standpoint of application as well as cost-effectiveness. Where and how this analysis should be performed is not as important as the concept that the quality organization is a part of the approval cycle. In smaller companies the details of selection and ordering are often done by a separate facilities group with the head of Quality approving the package and suggesting rivisions. Larger organizations, where considerable quantities of equipment/tools are to be ordered, require a group of quality engineers who review

requirements, search for acceptable equipment, evaluate the alternatives for cost-effectiveness, and make the ultimate selection for presentation to the management facility control group. Where such a quality function is required, it is also frequently a part of the administration department.

21. *Advanced quality technology*: In today's rapidly changing engineering and manufacturing environment it is incumbent on the quality department to keep abreast of these techniques and to determine what new quality methods are required. In recent years many larger organizations have funded separate quality research programs to advance the state of the art in measurement techniques, process control, computer applications, and defect detection. Although this has not been as widespread as desirable, it recognizes that quality must be a part of the development process and not be left in "catch-up" posture. It should be an organizational entity, usually a part of quality engineering or the quality laboratory, that must be considered in the development of the system.

22. *Additional responsibilitie:;* Some management have seen fit to strengthen the quality role by assigning tasks not traditionally accepted as a basic quality function, although they do have a bearing on the customer' formulation of a total quality system the following elements should be reviewed to make a determination as to the best organizational assignment.

a. *Reliability*: Reliability studies, projections, and analysis have, for the most part, been a traditional element of the engineering department. Recent history indicates that this role, at least in part, is being assigned as a quality function, particularly with respect to reliability assurance, the degree to which the product meets the predicted reliability.

b. *Safety*: Safety, particularly as relating to the design and manufacture of the product, is also being assigned to the quality organization. The independent and impartial assessment that can be made by Quality is the principal reason for this approach by top management. Safety has become such an important part of the manufacturing scene that an impartial review is mandatory.

c. *Product liability*: Although safety and product liability go hand in hand, it is not mandatory that they be assigned to the same personnel. We must remember that we are considering product liability and safety in terms of design, manufacture and use, not in terms of the legal aspects that prevail once a product liability suit is instigated. Safety, for example, might respond to a problem regarding assembly practices with the plant which would have no affect whatever on the ultimate use by the customer. Product liability, on the other hand, may be concerned with an ultimate fatique failure, one which never could occur during manufacture and test.

d. *Field service reporting*: Reporting of field service usage, including warranty claims, is a certain indicator of the reliability and usability of the product. Failure to analyze these reports and compare them to in-house failure rates can lead to ctastrophic warranty and reshipment costs. The quality department is the keeper of the in-house failure history. Some organizations have simplified their handling and correction of field failures by making them a responsibility of the quality organization.

e. *Configuration management*: In more complex products where changes to the design are to be expected, the configuration management system must be accurate and timely to preclude delivery of incorrect material and to ensure updating of hardware with a minimum cost impact. Before the general use of computers to maintain and update configuration data, it was usually the responsibility of the quality department to manage configuration control by means of a manual system. Although the computer has simplified this task so that the inputs can more readily be matched against the hardware, some companies still look to the quality department to operate and manage the system.

Types of organization

We have defined the basic quality task, discussed some organizational concepts with regard to quality, and outlined the functions that must be considered when developing a quality system. The form of the organization can now be considered. It must be emphasized that all the elements previously identified are not a requirement for every organization. Only the larger and more diversified company would need them all. In developing the organization all functions must be considered, however, and a conscious decision made with respect to each one. To overlook or disregard an obvious need can only lead to catastrophy.

There are certain fundamental organizational patterns that should be considered when putting the quality group together. As mentioned previously, company policy and tradition often have an impact on the structure of any organization. An adequate quality system can be developed irrespective of the basic format employed.

Staff versus line function

An important philosophical concept concerning organizing quality group is the determination of its role as either an operating department in the line organization or as a quality assurance group operating in a staff position reporting to the chief operating executive. A staff group has the ability to move freely outside the normal operating environment, monitoring the results of the system and reporting its findings to management. In such a setting the inspection work is usually performed by personnel reporting to an inspection chief. Other functions relating to the quality system may be assigned to departments within the manufacturing or engineering organizations. A major disadvantage of this type of staff assignment is that the group is often not empowered to do other than report the situation. The group must achieve corrective action by discussion and persuasion, with the chief operating executive as the final arbiter. In the absence of any operational authority there arises a normal reluctance to force many problems to their ultimate solution, the result being that proper corrective action is never pushed to a conclusion. There is the tendency to become more interested in finding fault that in eliminating troublesome company problems. This attitude can develop when the quality assurance group is made to feel like "outsiders" and not part of the team. There are, of course, companies that empower the quality staff to enforce corrective action by literally stopping the work effort if necessary. Such actions can be successful only where the quality staff is exceptionally well qualified and respected.

When the quality function is established as a part of the operational line organization the quality department manager should report to the same management level as those in charge of manufacturing, engineering, and material. As an operating executive the quality manager has the responsibility not only to assure that acceptable hardware is delivered to the customer but also to minimize operational costs through rapid and responsive creative action and preventive quality control. The form of the organization may vary, as we shall see, but the focus should be on implementing the controls necessary to carry out the established quality role.

Small versus large companies

The problem of the smaller company is to achieve the proper result with resources that are limited by comparison to larger organizations. Personnel must be selected who are capable of doing more than one function. Specialists are a luxury that can seldom be justified. Once the quality charter has been identified and agreement reached relative to the scope of activities to be pursued, the work must be organized in as simple a manner as possible. Smaller companies tend to adopt the horizontal from of organization, with all the principal supervisors reporting directly to the department head. This simplifies communication and allows for rapid top-level decision making.

As a case in point, consider a shop whose output is relatively straightforward sheet metal and machine shop detail parts. The quality task has been described as:

1. Inspection, including raw materials
2. Collection of data regarding shop defects and losses
3. Process control of certain chemical operations, such cleaning, painting, and chemical finishing
4. Monitoring customer complaints.

A more effective alignment would be to have a strong supervisor over all of the inspection effort, with all the other functions continuing to report to the quality manager. Such an arrangement would still give the manager instant access to problem areas from both plant and customer, and at the same time minimize the number of upper-level supervisors required. As the organization increases in both size and complexity of function, the need develops to reduce the span of control of the upper-level supervision. The organization tends to change from a horizontal orientation to a more vertical alignment. This allows the department manager to devote time to those matters which he or she considered important to the well-being of the department and the company. It presumes more highly qualified leaders reporting directly to the manager: supervisors who are expert in their particular discipline and capable of making decisions regarding their part of the operation.

No set rules govern the choice of organization but in a quality group it is particularly important that sufficient leadership be available to respond quickly to problems that affect the production process. There is an ever-present danger in very extended horizontal arrangement that problems may get set aside because of the press of other business demanding the attention of the top decision maker. As has been stated previously, the best organization is one that gets the job done effectively, at minimum cost, recognizing that cost sometimes gives way to certain preferences in organizational concepts. What cannot be allowed to suffer is effectiveness.

The large organization has the need for specialists in many of the quality disciplines. The generalist who has broad knowledge and responsibility appears higher and higher in the organization and his or her skills are managerial as contrasted to technical.

In a every large corporation that is involved with the majority of the functions outlined as the quality task, the organizational possibilities are endless. Certain real-life situations tend to establish patterns; for example, grouping of similar activities, such as receiving inspection, source inspection, and control of stores. These are not only related but are often physically located in proximity to one another. The ability to share equipment and space may also dictate an organizational alignment. If the quality laboratories and receiving inspection are close together, a sharing of equipment offer substantial savings. Some companies require that very expensive equipment be shared between divisions, such as quality and engineering. These considerations should be uppermost in the mind of the quality executive when planning an organization.

The second plan reduces the number of people reporting to the quality executive from eight to five; it raises the quality audit to a more important level, reporting to the director; all the projects are consolidated under one project manager; and the inspection and test group now has responsibility for all inspection, including source and receiving. The large company with more personnel available has a better opportunity to match skills with job requirements and to organize around the elements of the job, whereas the smaller company may have to organize more around the available talent.

Multi-divisional or international corporations

Many multidivisional or internationally oriented corporations have a headquarters staff group for quality. A vice-president or director of quality reporting to the chief operating executive is responsible for corporate wide activities in the quality field. These responsibilities generally include:

1. Development of general policies, objectives, and standards
2. Preparation of basic training criteria
3. Consulting and audit service to the divisions
4. Review of capital equipment requirements
5. Preparation of reports to top management
6. Representing the corporation in interchanges with government and industry groups

It must be noted that the responsibility of such a quality executive is frequently not supported by the authority necessary to achieve the objective. Different product mixes, the degree of autonomy of the individual division managers, and even cultural differences in the case of multinational corporations mitigate against much real achievement by a headquarter's staff unless the chief executive is constantly and pointedly supportive. Even with such support the quality headquarter's staff personnel must be persuasive and tactful if they are to obtain the necessary cooperation from the divisions.

The final organization

It must now be clear that there is no "best" way to organize the quality function. The definition of the quality role identified the scope of the job and the elements needed to satisfy that role. The organizational framework to support that role must be tailored for every company, keeping in mind the various influences that have been described. It is particularly important that the organization be oriented toward those elements that have the greatest impact on the ultimate worthiness of the product and the cost to produce it.

Several alternative organizations have been suggested, but they should not constitute a boundary, only a basis for further development. The quality executive should be ever mindful that "large" is not synonymous with excellence and that every organization should be no larger than necessary to accomplish the assigned quality role.

Quality planning

Quality planning can be defined as the sum of those actions taken in preparation for the accomplishment of the assigned quality task. In the early stages of the development of inspection systems it was usually limited to planning where inspection points were to be identified within the production cycle. Planning now involves a myriad of tasks, depending on the size and complexity of the production operation. The development of the organizational structure determines to a considerable degree how much planning is required and who must do it. Wherever there is a requirement for a quality task there must be a plan to accomplish it. Someone in the quality department must develop and identify the steps and actions to be taken. The scope of the quality planning effort is therefore similar to the basic role identified in the quality charter. The number and type of plans required become a function of the complexity of the work effort and the experience of the work force. The requirement for detailed planning usually increases in proportion to complexity of product or system, lack of experience in the work force, and the amount of customer regulation imposed. Conversely, "plans can simplified when the products or system are less complex" where the personnel are highly qualified and the amount of customer regulations are minimal. In the real world, where these factors may vary from department to department, it is necessary to be certain that the plan prepared recognizes the conditions that exist.

Quality planning can be classified as administrative plans, having to do with the operational and business aspects of the system; and product-oriented plans, which relate to the activities in solved in producing the product.

Administrative planning

Administrative planning begins with the preparation of the overall quality program plan for the company. It is a reflection of the basic quality charter agreed to between chief operating executive and the quality manager. In many cases it is one and the same. Other administrative plans are:

1. *Policy and procedures manual:* A quality policy and procedures manual is the resources document for all additional planning, as it contains the guidelines for the entire quality activity. The procedures themselves are often the actual step-by-step plan of operation for certain tasks, particularly ones that are repetitious and unlikely to change suddenly. The manual is the framework on which the rest of the quality plans can be overlaid.

2. *Special program plans:* The customer/company program leadership may require that special quality plans be developed. Such plans usually describe special paperwork and reporting systems, but they may also dictate the manner in which certain inspections or tests are to be accomplished. These controls may be more stringent than normal or they may call for a relaxation of some existing controls. Such plans are usually developed by the quality personnel assigned to the program. They must be carefully controlled in order that the personnel working on the shop floor will not be confused by the exceptions to the normal procedures.

3. *Planning for audits:* The audit group, regardless of size, must develop audit plans and schedules in order to have a consistency of approach and reporting within the company. Audit plans must be sufficiently detailed and clear that changes in the audit personnel will not affect the efficiency of the audit program.

4. *Personnel planning:* Every organization must have well-identified requirements for the number and type of personnel required for the year ahead, with acquisition requirements by the month. The employment department must be given adequate time to hire the proper personnel. When ample numbers of qualified people are not available in the area, a training plan and schedule will also be required. Even in the smaller company where personnel acquisition is handled personally by the quality manager, a plan must be made to indicate when additional personnel are needed.

5. *Equipment acquisition:* Equipment acquisition is similar to personnel acquisition in that it requires a plan that indicates month by month the new equipment required, the justification for its use, estimated lead time, and cost. Irrespective of the approval cycle for such equipment, the quality department is responsible for planning to meet its needs and for justifying the expenditure of the capital dollars.

6. *Other administrative plans:* Depending on the size of the organization and the charter given the quality department, many other plans of an administrative nature maybe required, such as:

   a. Long-range forecasts of personnel, equipment, and space

   b. Accumulation of cost data by work center/ department

   c. Plan for the accumulation, storage, and retrieval of non-conformance and yield data

   d. Plan for the training and certification of employees in certain critical manufacturing and test skills.

Product-oriented planning

All of processing or manufacturing work effort is controlled by some type of written plan or instruction. Such plans may be written by a singular group within the manufacturing organization, or they may be distributed to a number of different elements, such as tool engineering, manufacturing engineering, manufacturing test, or in the case of test design and planning, may come from the engineering organization.

In every case the quality group must be a part of the team developing the plans to ensure that the product will meet the requirements of the contract. Insertion of specific inspection points in the processing and test cycle must be a part of every manufacturing plan. In some instances a special inspection plan must be developed separately from the manufacturing information for quality personnel to assure proper conformance.

In addition to those plans generated for use by production personnel the quality department develops other plans relating to the product:

1. *Supplier plans:* An overall methodology for the approval and control of suppliers to the company is usually contained in the quality procedures manual. In addition, specific instructions/inspections are frequently required. These should be transmitted to the supplier as a part of the purchase order.

2. *Receiving inspection:* The quality department must develop the inspection/test plans for the multitude of parts and equipment that are received by the company from outside sources. These plans must recognize what has taken place at the plant of the supplier and what subsequent inspections will be done during the in-house processing cycle.

3. *Laboratory and calibration:* The amount of laboratory testing and the general rules for the maintenance of standards and calibration of equipment are usually contained in the quality procedures manual. Individual calibration and laboratory testing procedures must be separately planned and maintained in a current file in the work area. In an organization with much diverse equipment, this can be a very heavy planning load. although some calibrations can be done by the use of the equipment manufacturers' manuals, the planners must be certain they meet the requirements of in-plant usage.

4. *Process control:* Plans for the control of special processes used during the production process are an extremely important part of the quality control operation. Heat treatment, metal finishing, batch control, and chemical formulation are examples of processes that must have well-written for each step of the process and an indication of what physical action the quality group must take to unsure a successful result.

5. *Planning for inspection*: The actual inspection of parts, components, and assemblies is the original and traditional function of a quality organization. The plans associated with this effort range form the very simple (such as a dimensional checkoff card) to an extensive step-by-step document outlining in detain the plan for acceptance of the product. There is no substitute for the planning required to assure a satisfactory product. As in all aspects of quality control, it is possible to overemphasize the planning of inspection points and produce more paper than product. The mark of the proficient quality planner is to cover every important element without inserting unnecessary checkpoints that are unproductive in terms product use.

The inspection planner must work closely with those planning the test procedures when tests are required. Frequently, the test and inspection planner may be the same quality engineer.

6. *Planning for test:* Testing of many products has become the major element in the

proof of acceptability and usability. Testing covers an extreme breadth of activity, from simple tension tests of material samples to hours-long runs of equipment undergoing changing environmental conditions. Organizationally, the quality group may not be the leaders in the formulation of test plans and the development of test equipment. The quality organization in all cases must have competent personnel reviewing and approving both plans and equipment, In some cases the level of testing required at receiving inspection may be so sophisticated that a special quality engineering group may be required to write the test plans, set up the equipment, and monitor, if not run, the tests.

Organization of the planning function

The manner in which planning for the quality operation is organized is similar to that of the overall quality organization in that it depends on the scope and size of the assigned quality task. The most effective planning operation is one that gives the quality department all the necessary tools (i.e., direction, documentation, and equipment) at a reasonable administrative cost. In some small companies the planning can be accomplished by consultation between the inspectors and the supervisors, with the ultimate plans being produced on simple inspection forms. As the size of the company grows and the complexity of the products increase, the need for specialized planners becomes a necessity. Where these special planners should report organizationally becomes an administrative decision of the quality manager, as there is no clear pattern historically.

Central versus decentralized planning

Centralized planning implies that all planning is performed by one group. Such an approach is not practical because of differences in both discipline and physical location. It is, however, possible to group large segments of the various planning operations into one or two central operations, usually with substantial savings in efficiency and cost. For example, all inspection and test type planning could be located in one area adjacent to the corresponding manufacturing planning organization. This could include piece-parts inspection, process control, subassembly and assembly inspection, and all associated test operations. In addition to probable cost savings in the number of personnel required, such a central planning group would ensure uniformity of inspection between different products and programs. The preparation of receiving inspection plans could also be a function of such a group. Similarly, all administration planning could be grouped together, either as a part of the quality engineering function, or as the responsibility of a responsibility of a quality administrator reporting directly to the department head. As the responsibilities and size of the quality function increase, it is doubly important that the control of the business aspects of the department be grouped together and monitored closely.

Some quality planning, such as laboratory and calibration work, are most effectively handled in the functional areas involved, where the personnel are particularly those with several large, important, and non-similar programs, prefer to decentralize a large part of the inspection, test, and administrative planning and have it done within the confines of the quality program staff. The peculiar requirements of each program may differ to such a degree that special instructions are required. This may even be reflected in plans for receiving inspection. Program funding restrictions usually prohibit the use of specialists in every discipline, so the program planner has to be more versatile and qualified to plan a variety of inspection requirements. Certainly this approach is proper for cases where the requirements differed extensively from the rest of the plant operation, but the quality department head must be ever watchful to be certain that the need for decentralization is real. The tendency for overall program management to want everything under its control does not necessarily lead to the most efficient quality effort.

Planning for the quality group's participation in extensive test programs frequently requires a special test group with a preponderance of highly qualified engineering personnel. Where the role of the quality organization is to personnel must be located in close proximity to the engineers responsible for the initial planning. In companies where the engineering department is heavily involved in the test program, their quality department counterparts must have the same level of technical expertise as those planning the operation.

Skill requirements for planners

All skilled quality personnel do not make good planners, even through their technical capability may be very high. It requires a special talent and disposition to do a good planning job, day after day. Some employees are temperamental unsuited or the task because of its confining nature, and planners must be selected by temperament as well as technical ability. A checklist of planner prerequisites would include:

1. An understanding of the technical process
2. The ability to recognize what elements are truly important
3. The ability to use simple language and terminology in order to help the inspector to understand the requirements
4. An understanding of the interrelationships that exist on the production line so as not to create unnecessary delays
5. The ability to foresee "what if" situations in order to have a recovery plan available
6. A personality that can accept and work under the pressure of constant changes in plans and requirements.

Organization and planning are the keys to success in quality control. They both begin with the establishment of the quality role by management. The development of the organization to fit the task also establishes the basic parameters of the planning required. Organizational development or improvement should not be used as an excuse for growth. Organization implies an orderly approach to a defined goal, which is achieved by the use of intelligent planning. Excesses in either organization or planning are both costly and ineffective.

Quality control

Quality control is concerned with observing a process, identifying the variable characteristics of its content, and then tracking these variables through scientifically devised statistical methods. The measurement of the variables while they are being accomplished, permits holding the process its specified performance limits. This prevents defects from occurring; or at least finds them at the earliest possible moment.

Quality management

Quality management treats the company as a process and the various management systems within that process as the variables that require measurement and control. However, each of these variables is devised and conducted by a group of individuals, whereas in quality control the variables are accomplished by a chemical or physical process. That is why quality management requires an understanding of the way the whole company operates. It also requires a comprehension of the company goals, which are not spelled out and a process plan or blueprint; a familiarity with other functional management systems, such as marketing, engineering, finance, and purchasing; and a willingness to spend time helping other function measure and control their own operating characteristics.

Quality control is thing and process oriented; quality management is people and system oriented. The purpose of quality management is to make the company run more smoothly and more profitably by preventing problems. It also serves as the key element in solving those difficulties that do escape the prevention system. In many ways quality management serves as a catalyst-bringing together activities with a common purpose and different methods. Quality management must report organizationally in such a way that it is free of control by those whom it is measuring and assisting. In most cases this means that it should be working for the chief executive officer. It should never be part of operations because this is only a small part of its activities.

Quality engineering

Quality engineering is major element contained within the quality management function. It is responsible for activities within other departments and particularly engineering assists the appraisal function in establishing acceptance methods and procedures, conducts failure analysis, and reports results and needs for corrective action.

Purchasing

Quality engineering assists purchasing in vendor selection, Prepares the buyer rating results, and trains supplier personnel in quality concepts and techniques. It determines the need for sources control or inspection and sets up the appraisal plan for products or services in conjunction with purchasing.

Engineering

A major role of quality engineering is to help arrange design reviews, products qualification, life testing, and other objective performance measurements oriented to prevention. It provides engineering with data concerning manufacturing and customer experience with products.

Marketing and sale

Marketing depends on quality engineering to provide product performance data to assist in the selling of the product, conduct quality seminars for the customer, and handle consumer affairs activities. Quality engineers share results with marketing concerning specific causes of complaints and ways or preventing them. They also experience data to assist in developing new specification.

Comptroller

Quality engineering assist the comptroller in identifying the characteristics of the cost of quality within both product and service areas. Another responsibility would be to devise quality control programs to evaluate clerical accuracy.

Manufacturing

In the manufacturing area, quality engineering determines appraisal activities for each product and process, assists in selecting test equipment and devising sample techniques, and conducts quality orientation or manufacturing personnel.

Administration

Quality engineering arrange new employees orientation programs in cooperation with personnel and conducts company-wide quality awareness activities. It also provides measurement guidance for internal programs.

Top management

Top management is furnished quality status information showing areas where problems are occurring and listing specific causes, responsibilities, and actions under way. Quality engineering also provides continuing status chart visible in work areas (both whit and blue collar) and gives smaller, desk-size copies to key management.

Quality department activities

Appraisal Analysis

The inspection a test functions-ranging from suppliers' plants, through receiving, in-process, assembly clerical, engineering, field, and wherever applicable—for the company should be designed specifically by quality engineering. No appraisal activities should conducted by chance; all must be part of the overall concept of treating the company as one large process that continually needs to be measured.

Failure analysis

This is one of the most important jobs in the quality engineering task list. Analysis must be conducted primarily to determine the integrity of the overall quality management system, as well as getting the specific problem surfaced and resolved.

Appraisal

All appraisal function having to do with the acceptances of the company's products or services must be accomplished by the quality department. In turn, quality engineering assume responsibility for training and leadership of the personnel involved. The data generated by appraisal are the quality department's most significant product. It is these data that from the prevention strategy for the company; they also tell, on continuing basis, a clear story of the status of the output.

Consumer affairs

Customer with complaints need someone to talk with who one their side. This function must be carefully oriented to think in customer's terms. All complaints must be handled within two working days and departments that caused the problems must take corrective action immediately.

Quality education

Administering the professional and other employee training necessary to maintain the competence of the quality function itself and the awareness's of other departments is a key function. Actual training will be accomplished by quality management's functional personnel, but quality education must provide the spark and coordination.

Product quality

The handling of product safety problems must be assigned to special teams consisting of quality engineers, lawyers, and appropriate specialists. Quality must chair this team.

Environmental quality

This function is the liaison between the regulatory agencies and the company to make certain that all regulations are known and met. It must conduct continual self-audit within the company manage, the environmental quality functions policies.

Strategy of quality management

Installing a quality management system in a company is a never-ending, long-range effort. There are six phased of evolution. They are listed in sequence, yet all of them occur in parallel since a company is a growing entity with new members coming and old member leaving on a regular basis. Each person must be taken through these phases in some manner; otherwise, he or she will not be in step with the remainder of the company.

Comprehension

There must be a solid understanding of what quality is all about, how the company feels about it, and a recognition that the goal is to "do things right the first time." In the case of management this is the stage when it decides there has to be a better way reaching its goals than continuing with the waste that faces it. All members of the company are included in the orientation.

Commitment

Everyone must in some way signify that they understand the quality concepts, agree with the goals, and will do their best participate. The method of accomplishing this depends on the personality of the individual company. Some companies from a "quality club," some just request show of hands, some sign pledges, some take group photos. No one way is best. However the strategist should recognize that the step cannot be ignored. If the commitment is not registered as a conscious act, it will not be remembered.

Competence

Committed,people who understand what has to be done will want to put their own houses in order. This is where the functional department can begin its won internal quality control programs with the assistance of the quality management function. Also, it is very important that quality function assurance that all its activities are accomplished with the maximum effectiveness. There is a significant responsibility and burden in leading quality improvement program—you must always work harder than anyone else in getting things right the first time. Zero effects has to be the performance standard of the quality department at all times.

Communication

Quality awareness activities expose the desire on the part of employees (of all levels) to have their problems heard. It is best to reach out early and ask to hear the problems rather than wait to be approached. Error-cause identification programs, group meetings, and discussions are very helpful and practical, particularly when set up on continual basis. Professionally designed and marketed programs such as Buck-A-Day provide employees with an interesting program that will improve moral and communications. They will also save the company money. An important part of the communication phase is that you must be ready to continue to work at it for a long time.

Correction

When people contribute ideas and participate, management must be ready to do something. Most of the problems that occur in a company can be corrected only by management. When employees see that management is really taking action, thy will believe that management is serious about the whole business of defect prevention. Corrective action should be organized through natural interfaces and a methodical listing or problems taken to the proper activities for correction. Follow-through should be in a disciplined manner. Employees who list term must be notified immediately that their input has been received and be told of the disposition of the items.

Continuance

As noted, the phases must be conducted on a continuing basis. However, this will not happen unless they are scheduled exactly and someone is responsible for continuing and conducting them. Planned acts range from a visit to a new executive in the manner of "welcome wagon," to the orientation of new employees as they join the company (not after they have been there for a whole), and to the recommitment of the entire population to quality improvement on an annual basis.

Policies

A company management must state clearly its method of operating if it wants its employees to understand and implement it. The six C's apply to running a company, as well as to installing a defect prevention quality program. Managers of all functions and professions traditionally blame their senior management for not supporting them or for not providing the proper leadership. In reality, individual managers must make certain that the polices necessary to their functions exist and that everyone understands them.

In quality management there are three key policies that have to exist to smooth the way for installing the company-wide program.

1. The company management must state its standards concerning the subject of quality. The policy should be couched in words typically used within the company, but the policy should state these things.

It is intent of the X Company and its management that all products and service supplied by this company will conform exactly to the specifications and advertisement our customers have used to purchase from us. The quality department is responsible for assuring that all products or services received by the company met this requirement and for reporting any difference immediately so that corrective action can take place.

Quality means conformance to the requirements. Our standards is zero defects, which means "do it right the first time." Our performance measurement is the cost of quality, which is the expense of doing things wrong. The comptroller reports the cost of quality.

Each department will conduct its own internal, continual quality improvement program (with support from the quality department) to guarantee is ability to meet these standards, and each employee is expected to do everything he or she can to help all of us accomplish this necessary goal. Communication programs will be conducted continually to assure that each of us can hear the other on this subject.

Stage three - control

The major cost in this stage is the cost associated with scrap and rework. The focus here shifts from eliminating non-conforming products to reducing the internal failures. Management realizes that sorting is not a long term solution and that the process producing the non-conforming has to be controlled. Control charts and other techniques for listening to the process are introduced. The investment in control techniques to reduce scrap and rework is an additional 3 units. The benefit is a decrease in the internal failures from 12 to 8, a decreased need for sorting, reducing sorting costs from 3 to 2, and a further decrease in the proportion of defective units escaping to the field from 3 to 2.

Fourth Stage—Prevention and total quality control

The next step is a more detailed and systematic investigation into the process for the non-conforming products; it includes improved process studies designed to remove the causes of the defects and increase the process capability. Greater attention is paid to improving the quality control systems. This investment into doing it right the first time is rewarded by further decreasing all other costs categories. Control costs are decreased because the source causing the problem is eliminated. Sorting costs, internal failure costs, and external failure costs are all further reduced because the non-conformity has less of a chance of occurring.

Studies relating failure costs and profits

Although quality-related cost is a good tool for thinking about the distribution of quality-related cost, there may be better indicators that correlate better profit. A study, by Francis X. Brown and Roger W. Kane at Westinghouse, indicates that failure costs may be better correlated with profit than other measures. This study, which was based on 64 business units, showed that every dollar decrease in failure costs, profits increased an average of $5.45.

One possible explanation for this multiplier effect is that many of the costs of quality failures are not easily identified as failure costs, but that they affect profit anyway. Failure that cause shortages at subsequent operations increase production downtime. Some rework is absorbed in productivity and reported as labour variance. Chronic rework or excessive shrinkage may necessitate scheduling of overtime or purchase of additional production facilities. A completed product that fails in final test may result in increased work-in-process inventory and reduced billings for the month. Product failures in the field can, at least in the long run, contribute to reduced market share or poor price realization. They may also contribute to past-due or uncollectible receivables.

The second dimension of quality is the grade of quality. Products may conform to the specifications, but there are differences in specifications. For example, there is a perceived difference in quality between a Chevrolet and a Cadillac although each may conform to its respective specifications.

The higher selling price for a perceived higher quality can be summarized in a statement by Stanley Marcus, past chairman of Nieman-Marcus: "As long as oranges are two different sized, people will pay more for the largest and juiciest." This can be verified by taking a five-minute survey of food prices in your local grocery store. Compare the prices of the generic foods with those of the brand name products.

This has also been researched and documented on a scientific basis. One of the first studies to try to identify and analyze the factors that impact profit was the Profit Impact of Marketing Strategies (PIMS) research. The PIMS team studied the effect of hundreds of variables with long-term financial performance. The analysis gave strong support to the proposition that market share is a major influence on profitability. It also identified other factors that had significant impact. One was perceived product quality. The score for the perceived product quality was appraised in the following terms: What was the percentage of sales of products or services from each business in each year that were superior to those of the competitor? What was the percentage of equivalent products? Inferior products? These factors included various quality and service delivery traits.

The combined impact of market share and perceived product quality is shown in figure. The best of all possible worlds is to have both hight market share and superior quality. Businesses in this category averaged 28.3% return on investment. Even with a weak market position, however, superior quality producers earned 17.4% .

There have been other studies conducted since the initial PIMS research that are wholly consistent with the analyses of the PIMS team. In Search of Excellence, for example, researched 75 of the most financially successful companies. Of these 75, 5 were in the resource-extraction business. For those companies, efficiency may be an apropriate first principle. Of the remaining 70, 65 were successful by focusing on quality and service.

A similar study conducted by McKinsey and Co. for the American Business Conference focused on the management strategic practices among the 45 top performers. The study showed that management practice in most of these companies was to provide higher value added products. In 43 of the 45 cases, the following was observed: "winners compete by delivering a product that supplies superior value to customers."

One belief has been that lack of motivation on the part of the worker is the cause of most errors. There have been, however, significant data published to refute this belief. Some of the earliest data were published by Dr. Joseph Juran. Dr. Juran uses a non-industrial example, the golfer, to emphasize that motivation is not the issue.

The golfer is obviously in a state of self control. He knows very well what he is supposed to do. He can observe with his senses what his actual performance is. He has tools identical to those used by experts. Why then are there so many golf balls in

b. Process quality control- that portion of compensation and costs associated with implementing the quality plans and procedures

2. Design and development of quality measurement and control equipment
3. Quality planning by functions other than quality control
4. Quality training
5. Other prevention expense

Appraisal

1. Receiving or incoming test and inspection
2. Laboratory acceptance testing
3. Inspection and test
4. Checking labour
5. Setup for inspection and test
6. Inspection and test material
7. Quality audits
8. Outside endorsements or approvals
9. Maintenance and calibration of test and inspection equipment
10. Review of test and inspection data
11. Field testing
12. Internal testing and release
13. Evaluation of field stock and spare parts

Internal Failures

1. Scrap
2. Rework and repair
3. Troubleshooting
4. Reinspect, retest
5. Scrap and rework—fault of vendor
6. Material review activity
7. Downgrading

External Failures

1. Complaints

2. Product of customer service
3. Returned material processing
4. Returned material repair
5. Warranty replacement
6. Engineering error
7. Factory or installation error

Quality cost and profit

A useful aid for explaining the interrelation among the quality costs is the Veen Model shown in Table:

First Stage - No Special Action

In this model, the quality-related costs at the outset total 24 (arbitrary)

Table: The Veen model for Quality-Related Costs

Cost Category	Stage 1	Stage 2	Stage 3	Stage 4
External Failures	20	3	2	1
Internal Failures	1	12	8	4
Sorting	1	3	2	1
Control	1	1	4	2
Prevention	1	1	1	2
Total	24	20	17	10

units due primarily to defects reaching the users and causing high external failure costs. The high external costs are those costs associated with fixing products that have been shipped or the cost of having those products returned.

Second stage - sorting

The second stage occurs when the high external failures attract the attention of management. Inspection stations are established to prevent non-conforming products from being shipped to the customer. Very often this sorting operation is not 100% effective. If the sorting operation is 85% effective in eliminating the non-conforming, the cost of shipping defectives to the field decreases from 20 units to 3 units.

There are two costs in doing this. Inspection costs increase 3 units. Serap costs, rework costs, and the cost associated with non-conforming material also increase. This results in 12 units of cost. The net gain in making this change is a decrease in cost from 24 units to 20 units.

2. The management must clearly state the organizational responsibility and reporting relationship of the quality department. The department itself must issue an operating policy concerning all the activities that take place within it.

The company quality department must always be organizationally independent of those operations it is charged with measuring. For that reason the quality director will report to the chief executive officer.

The quality department will assist other departments in division and conducting the appropriate internal quality control programs, and will conduct company-wide quality awareness functions.

In addition, the department will perform all appraisal activities, report the results, and conduct corrective action systems. Quality engineering, consumer affairs, environmental quality, product safety, reliability, and other appropriate functions shall be included in the department's responsibility.

3. The management policy must stake what it means by requiring other departments to.

Conduct appropriate internal quality control programs in their operation. This means "spelling out of how those departments can identify the necessary actions to develop Comprehension (rewriting the quality logic so that it fits the terms of their professions); Commitment (deciding to do some reviews and inspection inside); Competence (conducting internal audits with the support of quality engineering); Communication (conducting quality awareness and error-cause removal or make certain activities); Correction (setting up an action team); and Continuance (having their own quality improvement team to review status continually).

The astute quality department will supply guideline to other functions—which they will be delighted to receive—concerning some actions to be taken and methods of measuring non-hardware activities. All of these policies, and the procedures necessary to implement them, should be included in the company quality manual.

Quality management and the defect prevention system it creates must be treated as a living system requiring continual nourishment and attention the quality department does not need to be large in terms of numbers of people or budget. It needs only to be large in terms of action and strategy.

Dimensions of quality

We have beliefs about quality as about other things. Some of these beliefs are hidden. Some are complementary. Some are true and we act in accordance with them. Some are not true and we act in accordance with them as well.

One word, two (Independent) dimensions

The fact that quality has at least two independent dimensions was made very clear to me about eight years ago. Figure illustrates the two dimensions of quality. In one direction is the conformance of the product to the requirements. It focuses on a uniform, consistent product meeting specifications. It is concerned about doing things right the first time. The place where the quality of conformance becomes an issue is typically in the factory. The second dimension of quality occurs in the marketplace. In this dimension the issue is the perceived grade of the product. It is concerned with the competitive position of the product relative to other products that are being sold. It is concerned with doing the right things.

Some beliefs about quality have been identified, studied, and in some cases quantified. Three beliefs about quality are the following:

1. The quality of conformance decreases the cost.
2. Perceived quality increases the selling price.
3. Most errors occur because the criteria for self control are not met.

Belief 1: The quality of conformance decreases the cost

The first dimension of quality is the quality of conformance. Improving the quality generally reduces the cost. Products that do not have to be reworked or scrapped can be made more efficiently.

The American Society for Quality Control has standardized the quality cost structure. The categories are listed here:

1. *Prevention*: The cost associated with personnel engaged in designing, implementing, and maintaining the quality system. Maintaining the quality system includes auditing the system.
2. *Appraisal*: The costs associated with the measuring, evaluating, or auditing of products, components, and purchased materials to assure conformance with quality standards and performance requirements.
3. *Internal failures:* The costs associated with defective products, components, and materials that fail to meet quality requirements and result in manufacturing losses.
4. *External failures:* The costs which are generated because of defective products being shipped to customers.

The committee recommends that systems be established to record costs according to the following detailed categories:

Prevention

1. Quality planning and process control planning:
   a. Quality planning—quality control engine-ering type work

the lakes? Under conventional logic, the reason is that the golfer is not well motivated. Such a conclusion would be laughed at by anyone who plays golf or has observed golfers at play, since few people are as intensely motivated as golfers.

In Dr. Juran's analysis of errors, the causes of 80% of the errors was not lack of motivation, but a result of the worker not being in a state of self-control. The three criteria for self-control are:

1. Knowledge of what is supposed to be done, i.e., the budgeted profit, the schedule, the product specification;
2. Knowledge of what is actually happening, i.e., the actual profit, the delivery rate, the extent of the conformance of the product to specifications; and
3. Means of regulating what is happening in the event that the goals are not being met. These means must always include the authority to regulate and the ability to regulate either by (1) varying the process under the person's authority or (2) varying the person's own conduct.

At face value, wilful errors seem unexcusable. Closer examination, however, makes clear that these errors arise from many reasons, good as well as bad.

One major category of willful errors could be considered management initiated. Three forms of the management initiated errors are caused by

1. Conflicting priorities. Management is faced with meeting multiple standards of performance: quality, schedule, cost, safety. Obviously life is easier if all standards are met, but if unforeseen events occur, one of the standards may need to be compromised. One standard may have priority over the others.
2. Conflicting quality specifications. Management action in failing to enforce specifications also creates conflict, since repetitive actions become unofficial specifications. With no explanation, operators are led to believe that the unofficial specifications are acceptable.
3. Management apathy. In some cases managers fail to face up to quality problems encountered by operators; this forces the operators to find their own solutions.

27

Marketing Management

Consumption is the sole end and purpose of all production; and the interest of the producer ought to be attended to, only so far as it may be necessary for promoting that of the consumer. The maxim is so perfectly self-evident that it would be absurd to attempt to prove it. In order to protect the consumer while applying the concept of private enterprise that Smith endowed us with, the government often finds it necessary to formulate rules of the game for the guidance of the producer. In a complex society like ours, agencies are developed to carry out this rule-administering function. The purpose of this chapter is to give an overview of these ideas. There must be mutual understanding between the two, regulators and regulated, for effective adjustments to occur. Otherwise there may be chaos, and both will be less effective in performing their respective tasks. We believe that regulators should understand the marketing system and, moreover, know the means by which regulation enters into the decision processes of the regulated, that is, the professional marketer. The marketer should understand the techniques of marketing, the marketing system in which he is operating, and the nature of the regulatory process if regulation is a central feature of the environment of that marketing system.

To an earlier generation, a book serving both sides might seem heretical. The younger generation feels differently. As an associated brand manager which three years experience for one of the largest advertisers in the country put it:

In the past, business made its decisions through its stockholder constituency. But to make business decisions is no longer a right. It is privilege that must be earned. We will be permitted to make these decisions in the future only if we can prove our right to do it well.

We have used the term "marketing system" without defining it. Our system is highly complex, as it is in any modern society with advanced technology in mass communication and great amounts of new-product innovation. Therefore we will examine it in some detail; the reader who is already familiar with it can skip the following section.

The term "system" is used because it aptly describes the phenomenon we are dealing with a set of elements that interact with one another. The key elements of concerned with adequacy of information to the consumer and the effects of marketing upon the basic character of Americans. These goals give rise to such questions about marketing as: Does it make Americans more materialistic and more cynical?

That these emerging criticisms should develop in the pos-twar technological environment is not surprising. Food is a prime example. Traditionally it came basically from the soil. We had developed a culture which included rules for wise eating. Almost suddenly, edible things can be made by chemistry. But we have neither the culture to guide us in the consumption of foods from these sources nor the time for the thousands of years necessary to build it up by trial and errors. If we are to maintain our standard of living, we must investigate these new products, to do so we need an enormous amount of information, which it is the role of the manufacturer to provide. He uses the most effective means he can—often television. Television is an intrusive kind of medium; it is no wonder, that the public becomes concerned about its effects on children or on basic human values. It allegedly causes people to buy things they do not need, thus littering the earth with the trappings of a materialists civilization it has abetted, if not created. Similarly, appliances add immensely to the standard of living but entail serious problems of service and repair, even to the point where they are replaced rather than repaired when they fail. New toys bring vastly greater opportunities to please the kids, but when combined with another technological change—television—they open up equally vast opportunities for deception.

Because most of the criticism of the marketing system focus upon the consumer segment, they might seem irrelevant to those engaged in industrial marketing.

Further, for many industrial companies, what happens in the ultimate consumer market is a major consideration in the success of their sales. Government regulations applied to consumer markets will also inevitably 'rub off' on the industrial markets, thus stimulating criticism there. Finally, if the consumer marketing end of the system fails to perform adequately, the whole system will probably be called into question.

Before addressing ourselves further to criticisms of the marketing system, however, we should obtain a better understanding of the system and how it works, in some detail. This examination is particularly necessary because some of the well-intentioned criticism springs from the premise that all marketing management-decisions are well-informed, rational choices.

A commonly held view is that modern psychological research techniques enable the seller to attack the vulnerabilities of the consumer and render him helpless. If this premise is not valid, it may be that one of the major areas of improvement in the operation of the American marketing system can come about through better management of the marketing operation of the companies that make up some of the central elements of the marketing system.

Aside from the possibility of improving internal management in terms of its own objectives of better meeting society's needs, we must somehow change the system if it is not performing adequately, as judged by society. To change it requires that the rules influence managerial behaviour in as appropriate way.

Thus, as regulators we must understand the managers decision process. This is complicated by our lack of knowledge, as we will see below in discussing public policy as an environmental influence on decision.

Marketing management: decision, planning and control

In considering how the individual selling unit in the marketing system operates, we will investigate the question: what is marketing, management? Some readers will be students who intend to be in marketing management, others already are marketing managers, and still others may be in related activities that bear on marketing management in either a managerial or a regulative capacity. To meet all their needs our main objective in this book is to develop a structure, a "theory," of managerial marketing around which they can organize their reading and experience in order to arrive at a better understanding of it.

This understanding can serve two objectives. First, it will help them obtain new insights from the experiences they will be acquiring on the job in the future. Inevitably they will develop from experience some such structure to serve this crucial need anyway, so they can profit from new experience and new knowledge. To acquire such a structure from experience alone, however, is a slow and often uncertain process. Formal education can help them to speed this up so they grow in marketing skill much faster. Second, understanding of marketing management will permit a better grasp of the role of marketing in economic development, which many countries are so earnestly seeking. This structure is culture-free and can be applied to any environment. In general, study of marketing management leads to a better evaluation of marketing activity in terms of its performance in meeting the consumer's needs.

Marketing management is the process of decision-making, planning and controlling the marketing aspects of a company in terms of the marketing concept, somewhere within the marketing system. Before proceeding to examine some of the details of this process, comments on two aspects will be helpful background.

The marketing concept is simple in principle but often very difficult, if not impossible, to fully implement. The marketing concept is that a company can more effectively serve its own objectives if it will integrate the various aspects of its marketing activities, explicitly so as to meet the preferences of its customers. To one unfamiliar with company practice the need for implementing the concept and the capacity to do it would seem to be so obvious as not to merit discussion. This is typically not so, however, for many reasons which will be presented in the following chapters.

urbanism, economic regions, and standard metropolitan areas. These are especially helpful in delineating the dynamics of marketing because market potential is in effect a moving target, as economic conditions fluctuate, consumers needs change, and populations move.

Retailer level

The retailer's general function, analogues to the wholesaler's, is to collect products from a number of wholesalers, to sort these products into groupings that meet consumers' needs, and then disperse the products geographically. The difference is that the retailer disperses directly to the consumer. Each retailer in the C level competes with other retailers in his market area. He too bargains for a satisfactory price from his wholesaler and from his consumer, but government rules, can limit this. Much of the bargaining to hidden, however, and occurs slowly through the myriad ways the retailer employs to adjust his margin of profit.

Consumer level

The magnifying glass on level D shows how each retail store serves many consumers. The consumer compares the price, product, and service of different retailers in deciding which brand to buy. This ultimate user of the product is the focus of attention of the manufacturer's marketing manager, whose task is to translate the company's offering into a description—a "package" of ideas—that fits the consumer's way of conceptualizing according to his needs and then to translate these needs back to the production manager so that the factory's output will more closely conform to them. Because the marketing manager is so far removed from the consumer in both a geographic and an emotional sense, he may become preoccupied with the intermediate levels and tend to ignore the consumer. But if he does this for long, he does it to his sorrow. When the consumer finds a better brand and shifts to it, a marketing manager's sales may not reflect it immediately because inventories of his brand will be accumulating at the retailer and wholesaler levels; neither of these anticipate the change in consumer purchases and so fail to adapt to it by reducing their buying. When he does catch on to what is happening. A few bitter experiences of this type teach a marketing manager that unless his product pleases the consumer his efforts at good wholesaler and retailer relations may go for naught.

Industry distribution system levels

The function of the marketing system is to collect, sort, and disperse the product in meeting the needs of the consumer. Both wholesalers and retailers perform these functions. The wholesaler buys from a number of manufacturers; this serves to collect geographically. He sorts the products of these various supplying manufacturers in such a way as to meet the needs of particular retailers; this disperses these assortments geographically. Retailers collect, sort, and disperse in an analogous way but at one level lower in the system and to a much more restricted market geographically.

Diversified needs of an adequate marketing system

Thus far we have considered only one distribution system and only one channel, one route, within that system—manufacturer to wholesaler to retailer to consumer. In actually, there is a large number of other possible channels. A manufacturer also often uses more than one channel for the same product and so has a marketing channel system made up of more than one channel. In North-Eastern Statesand Ladakh, where population is sparse, for example, he will use a wholesaler, while in New Delhi, where population is concentrated, he will sell direct to the retailer.

Evaluating a total marketing system

It is much too premature to attempt to evaluate a marketing system here. But we can set the stage so that the reader will have some points of leverage for thinking about evaluation as he considers the details of how a marketing system works.

One important but perhaps non obvious point is that the level of marketing activity of an economy appears to grow with the standard of living. Perhaps this is because a more complex society increases the need for the manufacturer to communicate directly with the consumer. At the same time, better communication technology encourages this communications, and there are more new products to require it.

The criterion by which we have tended to judge our marketing system industrially has been a growing standard of living. Earlier generations in the United States felt that this criterion would give people the satisfaction they wanted, as is the case now in the less developed countries. When the standard of living is how, a growing standard probably accomplishes this. But when the standard is high, people begin to want their marketing system to satisfy other goals as well.

One of the new goals is sensitivity to the consumer's need for improved products, which becomes especially important in an economy of rapid technological change. Its application in the Russian and Yugoslavian economies was pointed by Khrushchev in a fascinating description of an exchange he had with Tito:

"We don't really have that problem here," said Tito, "and I'll tell you why. When some items becomes fashionable among our young people, we buy the necessary equipment for a factory and start manufacturing the item ourselves. Of course, consumer tastes are always changing, but all you have to do is use your head and make sure your industries keep up with fashions and adapt to changing consumer demands."

This goal became especially important in the United States following World War II, which initiated a period of exceedingly rapid product change that changed the nature of much of the consumer industry. But success in meeting this goal helped to precipitate new problems and a corresponding new set of goals that have to do with what traditionally has been through of as the means of marketing. These are marketing system are two: the companies which produce and market goods and services and the households which purchase these goods and services for its members. There are many kinds of each element.

In the part of the American marketing system that deals with consumer products, these elements are manufacturers, wholesalers, retailers, and ultimate consumers. In the part dealing with industrial products those bought to be used in further manufacturing, the terms are a little different-manufacturers, mill supply houses, and users—but the functions served are roughly the same. The manufacturers provide the product which is the input to the marketing system, and this product directly or indirectly reaches the ultimate user, the consumer. Alcoa mines bauxite and converts it into aluminium, which it sells to a can manufacturer. The can manufacturer converts the aluminium into cans, which it sells to food manufacturers. The food manufacturer packs the can with food which it sells to a wholesaler, who in turn sells it to a retailer, who finally sells it to a consumer. Thus the output of the system is products and services to the consumer. An opposite flow in the form of money payments from the consumer for the product purchased reaches the various elements back through the system.

A marketing system is for an economy as a whole. It is the means by which all of the goods and services flow to the consumer from the various stages of manufacturing and all of the funds flow in the reverse direction from the consumer to each of the preceding stages of distribution and manufacturing.

Such a system is essential to the efficient flow of the product to the ultimate consumer. Other functions of the middleman contribute further to economical distribution. The nature of this system is important because the economic welfare of an economy is strongly determined by its efficiency and sensitivity to the changing needs of consumers. For the manager, it affects his entire marketing operation in the company.

To convey the nature of this complex system, we will examine that part of the marketing system that relates to a single industry—an industry's distribution system. Further, only a part of that system will be considered because we will only the most immediate level of production—the manufacturers producing the consumer goods—and omit the earlier stages on the production process.

The interaction of parts of a distribution system is also complex clarifies this interaction by considering two characteristics of the marketing system: hierarchy, or levels, and geographic space or plane. Hierarchy is shown by the different levels at which the parts work: manufacturer (A), wholesaler (B), retailer (C) and consumer (D). In this schema, we assume that all manufacturers in the industry use the same distribution system. Each manufacturers in the industry use the same distribution system. Each manufacturers sells to wholesalers, each of which, in turn, sells the product to a set of retailers, and, finally, each retailer sells to a set of consumers.

The concept of market plane is essential because it shows the geographic dispersion of each of the respective parts—manufacturer, wholesaler, retailer, and consumer—over the country, but with each set on a different plane. This dispersion, particularly in a country as large as ours, renders the marketing problem infinitely more difficult because of the variety of conditions found in different geographic areas.

Each manufacturer, for example, Hindustan Levers or Godrej Soaps sells a brand. Assume that each manufacturer produces in a single plant. A producer of radios in Delhi, must somehow conceptualize his ultimate market, his potential consumers. Here the real complexity of a marketing system begins to be apparent. We can see that his market or his way of marketing it, he will be in serious difficulty, because they will turn to his competitor's products. Further, these disgruntled consumers have no ready means to tell him why they are dissatisfied; the easiest thing for them is to buy another brand providing a satisfactory competing brand is readily available. He must somehow conceptualize these consumers in order to understand why they are deserting him and to conceive reasonable solutions to the problem (for example, price is too high, the advertising doesn't tell them enough his retailers are out of stock because his salesmen are ineffective). The conceptualizing task is difficult because the consumers are myriad, literally millions in fact, and they are not all alike. They can be remarkably different in various parts of the country; for example, those in the South India like dark, heavy coffee, while those in the North prefer it light. The densities of people—how closely they live together—are also highly varied; contrast the New Delhi area with the Andaman Islands. Further, these people differ not only geographically but also demographically—some areas have relatively younger or older people, more women, more tribals, and so forth. They also differ psychologically, or in how they respond to marketing effort.

Wholesaler level

A wholesaler's role is to collect products from a number of manufacturers, to sort these products into groupings that serve the retailer's needs, and then to disperse them geographically by shipping the groupings of products to the respective retailers. In one part of the country the consumers want only electricity-powered radios, in another, both electricity—and battery-powered, and in a third, only battery. From the wholesaler's view, each wholesaler competes in the process of carrying out these functions with other wholesalers. He must persuade as many effective retailers as possible to handle his product. He bargains with his supplying manufacturer for a satisfactory buying price and with his retailer for a satisfactory selling price. His market area is more restricted geographically than that of the manufacturer because the wholesaler is expected to supply a retailer quickly when the retailers needs the products the manufacturer is typically too far away to provide this fast service.

To conceptualize their markets in order to achieve effective market planning, both wholesalers and manufacturers need detailed information on and explanation for the geographic location of customers. For this the wholesaler uses such concepts as

This process of marketing management takes place "somewhere" within the marketing system. Having seen the marketing system portrayed, you know that "somewhere" can be within any of the many, companies—manufacturing, wholesaling and retaining-that make it up. Marketing management is practised in every one of them. Assume, to simplify, that we are concerned only with the manufacturing level in a direct sense because the manager we are considering occupies a marketing management position there. What is the nature of each of the three elements making up the marketing management process: decision-making, planning, and control?

Marketing Decision-making

Adaptation of controllable to uncontrollable: The manager makes decision about things he can control—the controllable. In very general terms, what does he decide? Roughly, he decides the kind of a product to produce, the kind of a distribution system to use, the price to charge, advertising messages and media, and the salesmen's message to customers on whom they call.

In making these decisions he learns from experience to use an operating principle which simplifies his task and avoids substantial frustration. It might be called the "law" of marketing management, like other rules of behaviour such a Aristotle's Golden Mean and Golden Rule. This "law" of marketing management, like other rules of behaviour such a Aristotle's Golden Mean and the Golden Rule. This "law" of marketing management states: Since some things are controllable and others are not, separate the controllable from the uncontrollable and don't waste your time and energy trying to change the uncontrollable. Rather attempt to understand it so you can adapt the controllable to the uncontrollable in such a way as to satisfy your company's needs as effectively as possible. The application of this law is an art in which analytic tools from science can aid.

As suggested by the discussion of the marketing system, there is a complex of more or less uncontrollable forces operating on the manager. These can be summarized, as competition, demand, non-marketing cost, structure of distribution, public policy and company organization. Underlying these are, of course, the much more fundamental forces of technological, social, political and economic change. While over the long term these factors will shape the nature of the uncontrollable forces, the manager is forced by such aspects as convenience and lack of adequate data to concern himself mainly with the immediate uncontrollable item. The art of marketing management is the effective adaptation of these elements to the uncontrollable in the marketing environment so as to optimize the company's welfare. This optimum welfare can be thought of as the maximum area attainable in the inner pentagon within the constraints of its environment, the outer hexagon.

Controllable features. These relate to (1) product or service variation, (2) selection and management of marketing channels for distributing the product, (3) setting prices, and (4) fixing and allocating the promotional budget to advertising and selling.

Product variation. A company's modification of the nature of its offering is achieved through product and service decisions which are essentially of two types. Some decisions are concerned with change of an existing product to conform more nearly to the demands of the market. These changes may be superficial or fundamental (for example, the use of a new package as opposed to a revolutionary redesign of the product). Other decisions concern dropping or adding an item to the product line. These decisions of product change and change in product line are common, since few companies in the India produce a single product. They are also serious decisions for most firms. A marketing manager must be constantly on the alert to exploit new-product opportunities and to avoid continuing an unprofitable item.

Marketing channels. All companies must choose the set of channels they think will be most effective. The possibilities, as we have seen, are almost unlimited. Selecting the correct channel requires careful analysis, particularly since the decision usually involves a heavy investment of time by managers and salesmen and goes far in the rest of the marketing plan for some time into the future. The spatial aspects of the structure of distribution, for example, the geographical concentration of buyers in each market, will make a great difference in determining the best set of channels for a particular situation.

Prices. Prices must be set. Competitors prices typically establish significant limits to the range of choice, but there is usually some discretion. There are many pricing problems. Not only must a number of products be priced, but if a marketing channel other than direct-to-user is employed, consideration must often be given to the prices set at each level of the marketing channel. Finally, some buyers may receive a different price (or discount as it is usually called), based on such factors as the quantity they purchase.

Promotion. Most companies must use some type of promotional effort. The function of both types of promotion—advertising and personal selling—is to provide potential buyers with information about the products as quality, its availability, and its price. A salesman may well perform functions, such as delivery and repair, but, to simplify he will be here as a conveyor and receiver of information. Thus advertising and personal selling are alternative methods of performing the function of conveying information, but a particular blend of the two may be more effective than either of them alone. In many companies promotion decision require much of the marketing manager's time.

Advertising is concerned with deciding how much advertising to use, what media to use; the frequency with which the advertisements will appear; and the message to be employed (this involves the artwork and copy prepared for printed media and the commercials prepared for radio and television). Personal selling deals with the selection, supervision, and training of salesmen; the allocation of salesmen to territories; and the evaluation of salesmen.

"Promotion" is also often used in the trade literature in a restricted sense of special pricing arrangements to retailers and consumers.

Uncontrollable features. The uncontrollable or environmental elements that the decision-maker must adapt to, as shown in the outer hexagon, are not uncontrollable in an absolute sense. Instead they can best be viewed as controllable, but only a cost. They are (1) demand, (2) competition, (3) non-marketing costs, (4) structure of distribution, (5) public policy, and (6) company organization.

Company demand is the expected sales volume of a brand or service for a given period of time, which given marketing practices and under given environmental conditions, for instance, the sales of company A last year were Rs. 125 crores. Undoubtedly, this sales figure would have been different had the company used different marketing practices or had the environmental conditions surrounding the company been different. The analysis of demand is the study of buyer behaviour, which is the source of sales. In recent years the economist, the general psychologist, the social psychologist, and the sociologist have made contributions to the understanding of buyer behaviour. Demand is the marketing man's special province—on this topic he should be the recognized authority in his company. For this reason he should be a key number of overall planning groups in the company.

Competition is the degree of rivalry among companies in terms of the number and size of the companies in the industry and other market characteristics that limit a marketing manager's freedom to manoeuvre. These market characteristics, make up the *structure of competition* that a company faces, and they determine the kind of rivalry that will appear in a market. The rivalry may be stable, for example, or it may be highly chaotic, as exemplified in a "price war", how competitors are likely to respond is often one of the critical considerations in a marketing manager's decisions in such matters as where to position a brand.

Marketing decisions usually involve some estimate of *non-marketing costs*. The marketing manager, however, is concerned only with those cost outlays that are affected by his decisions. For example, assume the problem is to be decided whether to establish an advertising budget of Rs. 1 million or Rs. 2.5 million. At least two costs are involved: the cost of the advertising, which is a marketing cost, and the cost of producing the quantity of product necessary for the additional sales volume resulting from each of the advertising expenditures, which is a non-marketing cost. Both costs are affected by the marketing manager's decision, but only advertising is controllable from his point of view. The cost of producing the additional units he must take as given, and thus it is an environmental constraint. Just as there are several significant concepts of demand, there are numerous cost concepts, each one having its use, in dealing with cost, the marketing manager usually must rework the conventional cost data found in his company in order to make it useful for his purposes, and therefore he must be familiar with appropriate cost concepts.

Another uncontrollable feature is the industry's *distribution* system. It is made up of all of the marketing channels currently in use by the industry, and a manager must decide which channels are best for his needs. The spatial features of the market, for example, the geographical concentration of buyers, are key dimensions of the structure of distribution. Because the concept of a distribution system was explained earlier it will not be dealt with in the discussion of environmental constraints. Instead it will be covered as a part of the management of marketing channels.

Becoming increasingly influential in marketing decisions is the law, which embodies *public policy*. It is the rules of the game laid down by public bodies to influence the company to market in such way as to better serve the public interest. In some decisions, public policy is the consideration bearing the most weight. Also, the MEPTC is continuing to be concerned with deceptive advertising and is questioning whether advertising adequately informs the consumer. Public policy also exerts an unobtrusive but pervasive influence which must be considered in long-term predictions concerning marketing channels. The efforts of the anti-trust agencies to limit such things as exclusive dealing and the practice of vendors selling only to certain buyers instead of to all buyers, for instance, will probably result in a greater number of available marketing channels.

Unfortunately, the current state of the art of regulating marketing does not permit us to deal effectively with it. True, we do have a fairly adequate formal way of looking at competitive practices called the market structure concept, and we will use it in, on competition. But for the newer area of consumer information and the one which is currently in the greatest state of change, we have almost no structure. For marketing peruse, regulation is much the most important area of public policy. It is very complex because, like all public policy, it involves bringing society's values to bear upon the phenomenon of marketing practices.

Finally, there is *company organization*. The uncontrollable factors that we have been discussing up to now are the more general, global kinds of influences. For the manager, however, nothing is much more important than the fact that he makes his decisions in an organization. It dominates the criteria by which he makes his decisions and influences the information he applies to these criteria in coming to his decisions, until this central nature of organization is recognized, he can engage in marketing management only in a superficial way. It is like talking about modern physics and chemistry with it considering the concept of the atom.

Marketing planning

Decisions are basic. Yet individual decisions are only the ingredients in the central activity of a marketing manager, which is to plan. Individual decisions are put together in a mosaic which provides the systematic, coherent, comprehensive, and unified approach to marketing a brand that is represented by a *marketing plan*. Constructing the annual marketing plan for a brand or group of products is one of the major task of marketing management. There are a variety of plans, but the annual plan is considerably the most important. It is a detailed description of each of the decision areas for the coming 12 months period. To give some grasp of its magnitude of detail however, you might bear in mind that the annual plan for Surf detergent at Hindustan Levers is a bulky document.

Marketing control

A plan is a statement of what the marketing manager intends to do. A central question always facing him once he has executed a plan, however is the retrospective one: How well did it do, in fact? How successful was I?

Control attempts to answer such question by providing a measure of performance, such as market share. *A* standard for that measure of performance is also required. Is 10 per cent a "good" share, or does 20 per cent represent "good" performance? In addition, he must have a feedback system tells him the market results of the plan—sales computed as a share—compared to the standard. Finally, he needs these measure regularly, and so he develops a market monitoring system by which he keeps his performance within acceptable limits. He thus keeps his marketing operation under control. The central point made here are intended only to serve as an introduction. It is, however, the chief means by which a marketing organization maintains sensitivity to the market, which is essential to its own welfare and to its capacity to meet society's needs.

Management and promotion of rock concert is a vital part of the service industry. In a short span of time concerts one marketed to millions of fans in many countries. The work is demanding. Event manager needs to supervise a small army of seventy-eight people who were responsible for a bewildering variety of tasks. These included erecting a specially designed huge stage with special lighting and sound systems, taking care of security, arranging transportation, even obtaining doctors and lawyers on a retainer basis in each city. The event management organization obviously fill a consumer need.

With the development of economy a considerable interest to marketing is the shift to increased spending for consumer services. Services-ranging from such necessities as electric power and medical care to such luxuries as foreign travel, backpacking guides, ski resorts, and tennis schools—now account for *two-fifths of the average consumer's total expenditures*. In addition, the increasing complexity of modern business has created almost unlimited growth opportunities for such business service firms as management consultancy, market research, insurane, event management and security. For most consumer and business service firms, marketing is an emerging activity for two reasons: (1) the growth potential of the service market represents a vast marketing opportunity, and (2) increased competition is forcing traditional service industries to emphasize marketing in order to compete in the marketplace.

Opportunities for marketing careers in service firms have also grown rapidly. Such service organizations as banks and public utilities have now recognized the marketing concept and placed emphasis on marketing research, service development, and promotion in an attempt to better satisfy their market targets. Because some service companies are just beginning to recognize their marketing problems and opportunities, there is a great need for creative, imaginative marketing managers. Challenging opportunities also exist for men and women interested in sales careers. For many major service industries, such as insurance and specialized business services, personal selling is a key element of their marketing strategy. These companies are working hard to select and develop effective sales forces. The future growth of service industries can be seen by examining projections for next decade. The ten industries projected to show the largest increases in number of jobs in this period are :

1. Education
2. Miscellaneous business services
3. Retail Trading
4. Hospitality and Tourism
5. Health services
6. Financial Services
7. Construction
8. Miscellaneous professional services
9. Non-profit organizations
10. Wholesale trade

It is estimated that these ten industries will account most of the additional jobs in our total economy. Nearly all of them can be classified as service-producing, and many are just beginning to realize the contributions marketing can make.

Why emphasize services?

In an earlier we defined marketing as the efficient development and distribution of *goods and services* to chosen consumer segments. In a fundamental sense, marketers approach the development of marketing programs for both products and services in the same manner. Such programs begin with an investigation, analysis, and selection of a particular market target and follow with the development of a marketing mix designed to satisfy the chosen target.

Yet, while there are many similarities, there are also sufficient differences between tangible products and the intangible services to justify the special analysis of the marketing of services. An economy seat on the 10 A.M. Indian Airlines flight from

New Delhi to Bombay is similar to the purchase of a Casio pocket calculator in that both provide consumer benefits.

The overwhelming size of the service market dictates special attention. An area of the economy that represents about 40 per cent of total consumer spending deserves careful analysis and understanding by present and future marketers.

Services are difficult to define. In fact, the failure to agree on a workable definition appears to be one reason for the slow development of marketing in service industries. Personal services, such as haircuts and dry cleaning, are easily recognized as services, but these are only a small portion of the total service industry. The industry now includes such diverse elements as legal and medical services, electricity, insurance, and apartment rentals.

Some firms provide both goods and services. A security firm may market alarms (a good) as well as uniformed guards. A dentist's business may also be divided into goods and service components. A bridge, crown, or filling is a good, while the dentist's professional skills are a service. Some services are an integral part of the marketing of physical goods. Thus, a computer sales representative may emphasize his or her firm's service capabilities to minimize machine down time.

One potential solution is a products spectrum that shows most products to have both goods and services segments. A tyre is a classical good, although services like balancing may be sold along with the product. Hair styling, or the other end of the spectrum, is a pure service. The middle of the continuum consists of products with both goods and services components. The satisfaction that comes from dining in an exclusive restaurant is derived not only from the food and drink but also from the services rendered by the establishment's personnel.

While it is difficult, if not impossible, to describe in one definition all of the services that are available to consumers, a general definition does seem in order. Services can be defined as intangible tasks that satisfy consumer needs when efficiently developed and distributed to chosen consumer segments.

The preceding discussion suggests that services are varied and complex. The key features of services that have major implications for marketing include:

- Services are intangible.
- Services are perishable.
- Services can rarely be standardized.
- Buyers are often involved in the development and distribution of services.

Services are intangible

Services do not have tangible features that will appeal to a consumer's sense of sight, hearing, smell, taste, and touch. Because they are intangible, services are more difficult to demonstrate at a trade fair, to display in retail stores, and to illustrate in magazine advertisements. It is also nearly impossible to sample services or to use many other forms of sales promotion. Consequently, imaginative personal selling is usually essential in the marketing of services. A second consequence of intangibility is that buyers are often unable to judge the quality of a service prior to purchase. Reputation of the service vendor then becomes a key factor in the buyer's decision.

Services are perishable

Since the utility of most services is short-lived, they cannot be produced ahead of time and stored for periods of peak demand. Vacant seats on an airplane, idle dance instructors and unused electrical generating capacity represent economic losses that can never be recovered. Idle facilities during slack periods must be tolerated in order to have sufficient capacity for peak demand periods. Electric and gas utilities, resort hotels, the Bell System, and airplanes, to cite a few examples, all face the problem of perishability.

Services can rarely be standardized

Services are dissimilar since it is usually impossible to standardize offerings among sellers of the same service, or even assure consistency in the services provided by one seller. For instance, no two hair styles from the same beautician are identical. Creative marketing is needed to adapt satisfactorily a non-standardized services to the unique needs of individual customers.

Buyers are often involved in the development and distribution of services

The buyer often plays a major role in the marketing and production of services. After examining the buyer's role in service marketing, one writer commented that "productivity in many service industries is dependent in part on the knowledge, experience, and motivation of the consumer". It is this feature of many services that requires service marketers to be very skill ful in helping buyers identity and satisfy their service needs. Another writer noted, "The adequacy of an insurance policy will depend on the buyer's ability to communicate his specific insurance needs as well as on the salesman's skill in perceiving these needs and adapting an insurance policy to them".

Buyer behaviour

Important elements of buyer behaviour were discussed in an earlier chapter. These are many similarities between buyer behaviour for goods and for services, yet some important differences exist. These differences may be grouped into three categories—attitudes, needs and motives, and purchase behaviour. In most of these the personal element of the services is the key to the consumer's decision of which services to purchase.

Personal element of services

Service marketers are sometimes perceived as more personal, friendlier, and more cooperative than good marketers. These and other distinctive personal elements often differentiate service marketers from goods marketers and thus provide the service marketer with a unique marketing opportunity.

The personal feeling consumers have toward service industries is an important marketing advantage, but there is evidence that some service industries are losing this advantage. In addition, some service industries have surrendered some of the advantages inherent in the personal nature of services. The recent history of the insurance industry illustrates this. Several large insurance companies have introduced mass merchandising techniques with a resulting decline in the role in of the insurance agent. Although buyers have a large choice of conveniently packaged insurance policies at lower prices, they may resent the loss of close personal contact with an agent. As service industries expand, they may be in danger of losing a marketing advantage that they may have over goods marketers.

Attitudes

For almost any product or service a consumer's attitudes will directly influence his or her buying decision. Attitudes seem to be especially pertinent to services marketing since services are intangible. It is likely that this characteristic of services causes buyers to emphasize subjective impressions of a service and its seller when making a service purchase. This is less true when tangible goods are bought. Two attributes appear to represent important distinctions between goods and services. Services are perceived as being more personal than goods, and consumers are sometimes less satisfied with purchase of services.

For many service buyers dissatisfaction with the personal elements of a service, such as an unfriendly flight attendant or impolite bank teller, is likely to lead to an attitude of dissatisfaction with the entire service. For example, one woman reported that her vacation to Mauritius was marred only by her annoyance with an airline's flight attendant. She expressed a preference for one airline over another because the latter's flight attendants "were not as competent". When pressed for a further explanation, it was learned that her annoyance resulted from an attendant's cold, distant attitude. This impression contrasted with the warm, friendly personalities of the personnel on another airline.

The comments of a young man sum up the outlook of many consumers. Although he is not satisfied with a local dry cleaner, this consumer has not bothered to consider others. Previous experience has convinced him that there are really no satisfactory dry cleaners, and, at least, "this is the best of the worst". He has begun increasing his satisfaction by purchasing clothing that does not require dry cleaning. It is likely that consumers feel the same way about many other services and have taken steps to substitute for these services.

Needs and motives

A comparison of needs and buying motives for goods and services suggests that similarities dominate. Essentially the same types of needs are satisfied whether a person buys the materials for a home repair, or hires a service organization to perform the task. Although service needs have increased in importance, these needs usually can be satisfied by new or modified goods as well as by services.

A need that often does stand out is the consumer's desire for personal attention. By appealing to the consumer's desire for personal attention, the barber, the banker, or the insurance agent provides a form of satisfaction that the seller of a good cannot easily match. The desire for personal attention is often the dominant need satisfied by a service.

Purchase behaviour

Research suggests that differences between goods and services are most noticeable in the case of purchase behaviour. Goods-selection decisions are normally concerned more with the question of whether to purchase, while service-selection decisions emphasize proper timing and selection of a source. This situation suggests several distinctions between purchase behaviour for goods and services. In particular, the degree of pre-purchase planning may differ, influences on the buyer may differ, and the buyer may be more personally involved in a service purchase.

Consumers are influenced more by others such as friends, neighbours, and sales-people—when services are bought than when goods are bought. Since services are intangible, it is difficult for the service buyer to judge quality and value. Buyers are usually unable to inspect or try out a service prior to purchase, so they may depend on the experiences and observations of others.

A buyer is less likely to depend upon the opinions of others when adequate information about the alternatives is available. However, the buyer will rely heavily upon the advice of others when uncertainty due to limited information prevails. This is precisely the predicament a service purchaser is in. For example, one study explored the decision-making process used by consumers when selecting a physician: "For new residents to a community, information sources such as friends, neighbours, and co-workers were sought in over 60 per cent of the physician-selection-situations."

Closely related to the consumer's lack of personal knowledge about buying a service is the risk involved. One strategy for reducing the risk in a purchase decision is to rely on the advice of others. When buying a service, the consumer's lack of personal experience magnifies the uncertainty associated with the purchase. To reduce the perceived risk, the service buyer seeks information and advice from others, such as neighbours, friends, and relatives.

The dominant role of personal influence in the selection of services has two principal implications for services marketing. Added emphasis must be placed upon developing a professional relationship between service suppliers and their customers, and promotional efforts must be aimed toward exploiting word-of-mouth promotion.

The status of marketing in dervice industries

Although spending for services has grown substantially, the development of marketing as a major business activity has Some slowly to most service industries. This is largely due to what Theodore Levitt has called "marketing myopia". *His thesis is that* top executives in many industries have failed to recognize the scope of their businesses. Future growth is endangered because they are product-oriented rather than customer-oriented. Specifically mentioned as examples are several service industries, including dry cleaning, motion pictures, railroads and electric utilities.

Indicative of the low status of marketing in many service industries are the findings of a survey of manufacturing and service firms. It was concluded that the marketing function appears to be less structured in service companies than in manufacturing firms." The following major findings were reported:

In comparison to manufacturing firms, service firms appear to be (1) generally less likely to have marketing mix activities carried out in the marketing department, (2) less likely to perform analysis in the offering area, (3) more likely to handle their advertising internally rather than go to outside agencies, (4) less likely to have an overall sales plan, (5) less likely to develop sales training programs, (6) less likely to use marketing research firms and marketing consultants, and (7) less likely to spend as much on marketing when expressed as a per centage of gross sales.

For many service industries the shift to a marketing orientation will require a change from traditional ways of doing business. Fortunately, this change is already taking place in some of the leading service industries. The emphasis for airlines has shifted from the technical aspects of operation to marketing considerations. Long-range, high-capacity jets forced airline managements to think in terms of "the kind of marketing that consumer product industries had development and of the requirements of adapting these profit-oriented techniques to the marketing of a service." Banking and insurance are other service industries that have begun to emphasize marketing coordination.

The marketing environment for service industries

In many ways the economic, societal, legal, and competitive, forces exert the same type of pressures on service firms as they exert on goods producers. However, certain features of the environment for service marketing need to be highlighted.

Economic environment

Since liberalization an economic reforms the Indian economy has undergone extensive social and economic transformation. A significant change has been the shift to increased spending for services. It has already been pointed out that the average consumer now spends roughly 25 per cent of his or her income for services.

A corollary to the growth of consumer expenditures for services is the further expansion of business and government services to keep pace with the increasing complexity of the Indian economy. The sharp increase in spending for services and the development of the service industries as the major employer of labour is one of the most significant economic trends in our post-liberalization economy. Most explanations of this trend are based upon changes associated with a maturing economy and the byproducts of rapid changes associated with a maturing economy. In the first, and most primitive stage, the vast majority of an economy's population is engaged in farming, grazing, hunting, fishing, and forestry. As an economy becomes more advance, emphasis shifts from agriculture-related to manufacturing activity. The final, and the most advanced, stage occurs when the majority of labour is engaged in the so-called tertiary industries.

Also contributing to increased spending for consumer services are technological advances, population shifts, and changing consumer needs. The evolution of science and technology has altered productivity trends, and higher productivity in the manufacturing industries brought about the shift of workers to service industries. Technological advances created a higher standard of living for the average person, who spends a larger portion of his or her increased discretionary income for services. Psychological and sociological factors and also relevant. The desires for personal service, for convenience, and for service differentiation are three emerging consumer needs that must be recognized.

Perhaps even more spectacular that the growth of consumer expenditures for services has been the increased spending for business services. Servicing business has become big business, and companies in this field range from suppliers of temporary help to highly specialized consultant services.

Business services have grown rapidly specialized function more cheaply than the purchasing company can do it itself. Enterprises providing maintenance, cleaning, and protection services to office building and industrial plants are common examples. For instance, the demand for security services has risen as the nation's crime rate has soared. Second, many companies are unable to perform certain services for themselves. Marketing research studies, for example, often require outside specialists.

Societal environment

It is clear that major societal changes have contributed to the increased spending for services.

> Our society is marked by the emergence of secularized services rendered outside the family. A service revolution has, in fact, followed on the heels of the industrial revolution. This service revolution brings with it not only great new markets for the distribution of intangibles, but a new and highly significant dimension in the division of labour—the active participation of the consumer in the production of many services.

Society has a significant impact on the marketing of services. Consumers are offered a wide array of services; some are accepted, others rejected. Tastes also can shift over time. For instance, the increased use of counsellors and consultants influence many aspects of modern personal, family, and work lives. A few years ago some of these services were not even available, let along influential. Societal needs clearly influence the marketing of services.

Various societal trends are relevant. For example, there is evidence that the American consumer's tastes are shifting to a preference for services as status symbols. Travel, culture, health and beauty, and higher education have partially replaced durable goods as status symbols in the minds of many consumers. Other trends include a growing emphasis on security, which has expanded the market for insurance, banking, and investment services; greater stress on health, which has less to a greater demand for dental, medical, and hospital services; and the changing attitude toward credit, which has credit, which has expanded the demand for the services of banks and other lending agencies.

Legal environment

Service businesses are more closely regulated than most other forms of private enterprise. There are few service firms that are not subject to some special form of government regulation in addition to the usual taxes, monopolies legislation, and restrictions on promotion and price discrimination. An airline cannot change its fares without the approval of the Regulatory Board, a local bus company must have the approval of the public bodies before adding or dropping a route, and a doctor must be licensed in most states.

Marketers of services must recognize the impact of government on their competitive strategies. It has been suggested that regulation affects the marketing of services in at least three significant ways:

1. It typically reduces the range of competition; if competition remains, its intensity is typically increased.
2. It reduces a marketer's array of options and introduces certain rigidities into the marketing process.
3. It introduces into the marketing decision process a new and exceedingly relevant variable—the fact that the regulatory agency's decisions are controlling and that it is therefore necessary predict those decisions.

Other authors have reviewed the myriad of government regulation in the service industries. Many service industries are regulated at the national level by special government and regulatory agencies. Other service industries— insurance, banking, and real estate—were always traditionally regulated. In addition, many personal and business services are restricted at state and local levels by special fees or taxes, certification, and licensing. Often included in this category are the legal and medical professions, barbers and beauticians, accountants, engineers, and similar professions.

Government regulation has significant impact on marketing. It is possible that one reason for the lack of marketing innovation by service industries is excessive regulation. Because of their regulated, semi-public status utilities, service enterprises, transportation companies, and communications firms are constantly confronted with the threat of increased regulation or perhaps government ownership. A favourable public image is essential since any significant outburst of public displeasure will almost certainly mean government action.

Competitive environment

The competitive environment for services is a paradox. For many service industries competition comes not from other services but from goods manufacturers or government services. Internal competition is almost non-existent in some service industries. Price competition is severely limited in such services as transportation, communication, and legal and medical services. Moreover, many important service producers like hospitals, educational institutions, and religious and welfare agencies are not even operating for a profit in the business sense. Finally, many service industries are difficult to enter and may require a major financial investment or special education or training, many be restricted by government regulations.

Competition from Goods Direct competition between goods and services is inevitable since competing goods and services often provide the same basic satisfactions. Consumers may satisfy their service requirements by substituting goods. Competition has become greater because manufacturers, recognizing the changing desires of consumers, are building services and added conveniences into their products. Wash-and-wear clothing has replaced some laundry and dry cleaning services; improved appliances have reduced the need for domestic servants; and television competes with motion pictures and other forms of entertainment. Consumers often have choice between goods resulted in higher prices for some services and has led to increased competition from a variety of "do-it-yourself" products.

Competition from Retailers and Manufacturers The entry of retailers and manufacturers into consumer and service markets is also increasing the intensity of competition for the service money. Large retailers are providing services such as optical centres and automobile repair facilities that go far beyond traditional department store offerings. Sears Roebuck in the U.S. has been a leader in the trend to diversify into services with its entry into insurance. These large retailers have apparently decided that the mass merchandising of consumer services is possible and profitable.

Large manufacturers are also entering service markets, and *sources* predict that the "next revolution" in manufacturing will be in the production of services.

Competition from Government An expanded number of services are now provided by all levels of government. Some services can only be provided by government agencies, but others compete with privately produced goods and services. Often, the consumption of government services is mandatory as are contributory provident fund and compulsory education. Government services limit the consumption of private goods and services whether they are mandatory or not.

The marketing mix for services

Satisfying the service needs of buyers requires the development of an effective marketing mix. Service policies, and distribution, promotional, and pricing strategies must be combined in an integrated marketing program.

Service policies

Services may be classified in the same categories as tangible products. A distinction is made between consumer services and industrial services. Even when the same service is sold to both consumer and industrial buyers, a service firm will often have separate marketing organizations for each market segment. Consumer service may also be classified as convenience, shopping, and speciality services. Dry cleaning, shoe repairs, and similar personal services are commonly purchased on a convenient basis. Auto repairs and insurance are services that usually involve considerable shopping to compare price and quality. Speciality services may include professional services, such as financial, legal, and medical assistance.

There are many similarities between the services policies of service firms and the product policies of goods manufacturers. The product life cycle is applicable to services, and service marketers must make major decisions at various stages of the life cycle. Unfortunately, many service organizations have been slow to respond to their customers' needs for new or diversified services because they do not have a marketing orientation. In recent years some service firms have begun to develop new services or to diversify their some service mix, and consumers have responded favourably. The homeowner's insurance policy, packaged vacation tours, and air-travel family plans are examples of expanded service offerings that have caught on with consumers.

New services are often an improved method of delivering an existing service.

Some important differences between service policies and product policies should be noted. First, because services are intangible, packaging and labelling decisions are very limited. Service marketers are rarely about to use the package to promote their services. Second, the lack of a tangible product limits sampling by service marketers as a means of introducing a new service to the market.

Distribution strategy

Channels of distribution for services are usually simpler and more direct that channels of distribution for goods. In part, this is due to the intangibility of services. The marketer of services is often less concerned with storage, transportation, and inventory control, and shorter channels may be employed. Another consideration is the need for continuing, personal relationships between performers and users of many services. Consumers will remain with the same insurance agent, bank, or travel agent if they are reasonably satisfied. Likewise, public accounting firms and lawyers, are retained on a relatively permanent basis by industrial buyers. When marketing intermediaries are used by service firms they are usually agents or brokers. Common examples include insurance agents, securities brokers, travel agents, and entertainment agents. Another distribution strategy that is becoming more prevalent is franchising. Automobile rental, temporary help, motels and hotels, and dry cleaning are examples of services that are distributed through franchises.

Studies have indicated that a dominant patronage motive for many consumer services, such as banks, motels, and car rental agencies, is a convenient location. It is absolutely essential that careful consideration be given to retail site selection. Banks, in particular, have been sensitive to locating branches in suburban shopping centres and malls to meet the needs of customers in these areas. A recent retail banking development has been automated vending machines that enable customers to withdraw funds and make deposits during times when a bank's offices are close.

Promotional strategy

Promotion is an important aspect of the marketing mix for most services. Like goods, the importance of each particular form of promotion will vary.

The *advertising* of services is somewhat more challenging than the advertising of goods since it is more difficult to illustrate intangible services. Several strategies may be used. One is to make the service seem more tangible by personalizing it. This may be done by featuring employees or recognizable entertainment or sports personalities.

A second strategy is to attempt to create a favourable image for the service or the service company. Some of the themes used by service organizations are efficiency, progressiveness, status, and friendliness. For example, the Modi Luft advertisement, emphasizes efficiency and helpfulness. A third advertising strategy is to show the tangible benefits of purchasing an intangible service. An airline shows grandparents greeting a granddaughter as she arrives for a visit; a local bank shows a young couple enjoying a new home purchased through a home loans or a retired couple relaxing because of a savings plan they had established years ago. These and many similar themes help buyers relate to the benefits of the particular service that they may be unable to visualize. The desire of many service buyers for a personal relationship with a service seller increases the importance of *personal selling*. In fact, unless a very simple or highly standardized service is sold, personal selling is usually the backbone of service marketing.

Life insurance marketing provides a good illustration of the sales representative's key role. Because insurance is a confusing, complex subject for the average buyer, the agent must be a professional financial advisor who develops a close personal relationship with the consumers. Life insurance companies and other service firms must develop well-trained, highly motivated sales, forces to provide the high-quality personalized service that customers require.

Sales Promotion Is difficult because services are intangible. Sampling, demonstrations, and physical displays are severely restricted, but service firms often do use premiums and contests. Publicity is also important for many services, especially for entertainment and sports events. Television and radio reports, newspaper articles, and magazine features inform the public of events and stimulate interest. Many closely regulated service industries use publicity releases to create a favourable impression of the organization and its employees. Contributions to charitable causes, employees' service to non-profit organizations, sponsorship of public events, and similar activities are publicized to influence the public's opinion of the service firm. Pricing in service industries pricing practices are not substantially different that those in goods industries. The service marketer must consider the demand for the service, production, marketing and administrative costs, and the influence of competition when developing pricing strategies. However, for many services price competition has been limited. Prices of transportation, communication, and other utilities are closely regulated by federal, state, and local agencies. For many other service firms, such as advertising agencies, there is a traditional pricing structure that is closely followed.

Price negotiation is an important part of many professional service transactions. Consumer services that sometimes may involve price negotiation include auto repairs, foreign travel, and financial, legal, or medical assistance. Specialized business services, such as equipment rental, market research, insurance, and maintenance and protection services, are also priced through direct negotiation.

Pricing has been used by many firms to overcome the problems associated with the perishable nature of services. Lower rates for long-distance calls are in effect during evening hours and on weekends. Airlines offer "night coach" prices for late evening departures. The offering of off-season rates by resort hotels and motels is another example. For instance, several Goa resort hotels feature special "get-away" rates during the rainy months and promote their indoor pools, saunas, exercise rooms, restaurants, and the like at special weekend package rates.

Service—A future perspective'

In some ways the service industries are a new frontier for marketing. Many service firms have remained very production-oriented even in the face of a changing business environment. But even these companies are beginning to realize the value of an effective marketing strategy. Government data and projection clearly suggest that service will be a growth sector of our economy over the next decade. Consumers will spend more for services, and significant employment gains will come in this area. These advances can be achieved only if the service industries improve their productivity record, and this can probably come only through improved marketing.

28

Information System Management

Information, for the modern organisation, is a resource parallel in importance to land, labour, and capital. Here, we examine the concept of information as it applies to organisations and individuals in organisations. We see how data and information are different. We look at the sources and uses of information. Communication, the process of transmitting data and information from one person or location to another is another topic. After identifying some of the internal and external sources of information, we examine how and to whom it is transmitted. We also assess the value of information. Being able to judge this value is important to any organisation. Finally, we look at information processing in perspective.

Information is input to be acted upon, a stimulus that results in some action being taken by managers or others, or the product of some other action. Without it, an organisation is incapable of survival. In this section, we study the meaning of information and how it is different from data. Then we look at the attributes of information that should concern us when using information for managerial decision-making. What is information? There are a seemingly infinite number of definitions for this term, both in a data processing context and in common usage. Information is meaning assigned to data. For the purpose of any system or organisation, information is data that have been processed into a form that is meaningful to the recipient or user and is of real or perceived value in current or prospective decision processes. It must add to what we already know about an event or place; it must tell the recipient something that he or she did not know or could not predict. Information, in other words, adds to knowledge but must be relevant to some event, state, or process. The lack of knowledge but must be relevant to some event, state, or process. The lack of knowledge, that is, the absence of information about a particular entity, is uncertainty.

Information distinguished from data

The term information is often used imprecisely, partly because of confusion over the difference between information and data. Data (the plural of datum) are facts, records of an event that has occurred or is about to take place. Facts are independent, unrelated, and unlimited in number. For example, the items Rs 100 million sales, 10-day strike, and four pizza ovens are all data. By themselves, however, these items of data are meaningless; they must be changed to a usable form and placed in context to have value. All data are facts, but information is not facts, even though it is based on data. Similarly, while all information originates from data, not all data may become information. Relevance is one of the key facts in distinguishing between the two. As we saw earlier, information must be relevant to a particular problem or event. Therefore, all information must be based on factual data, but only data that are relevant to the situation are information. Not all data or facts can be relevant at a given moment. Indeed some data may never be relevant to any event. For a marketing manager planning the sales program for the upcoming year, the figure of Rs 100 million in sales for the company's product X is relevant knowledge, that is, information that effects the decision-making activities. Likewise, the fact that a 10-day strike of the production personnel may occur during the first quarter is relevant information. However, the fact that the Wimpy's Restaurant just purchased four new pizza ovens is not relevant to the manager in developing a sales program.

Data become information when they undergo a transformation involving infusion with purposeful intelligence (Figure 1). That is information is actually data transformed so that they communicate meaning or knowledge based on data that have, through processing, been infused with intelligence, (meaning, purpose, and usefulness).

Another part of the confusion between data and information is due to the fact that what is information for one person may not be for another. In the same sense, one person's information may be data for someone else. This analogy from a manufacturing operation will demonstrate. Company A receives daily shipments of metals and chemicals from its suppliers. These materials are used to produce copper wire. Company B purchases the wire from Company A and used it to manufacture lamps and lights fixtures. The two companies operate two distinct production processes. In the first case, the raw materials include copper and the product is copper wire. In the second case, the raw materials include copper wire and the finished goods are lamps. What is a finished good for company A is actually raw material for company B.

The same relations exists between data and information. The copper wire produced by company A might be considered analogous to information. It has undergone a transformation to give it a specific value to the business. At the same time, copper wire is analogous to data (or raw material) for company B. The wire is transformed to be part of the finished product, lamps, themselves analogous to information. In each case something more—intelligence—has been added to the data of the operation to create information.

The same transformations occur all the time in the modern organisation. A cost accountant, for example, collects data on materials costs, labour costs, the hours of labour needed for a job, overhead rates, and so on, in order to develop standard product or production costs for given items. However, for someone developing contract bids, the standard costs are only one part of the larger cost package needed to develop information on break-even and profit points and levels.

The Attributes of Information

Information adds to relevant knowledge, reduces uncertainty, and supports the decision-making process in an organisation. There are, however, different kinds of information and various ways of describing an entity, object, or situation. For the moment, however, let's focus on the general attributes of information, both for an item of information and for a set of information. The attributes of individual pieces of information are characteristics that are meaningful to the user on an item-by-item basis. That is each individual item of information can be described as to accuracy, form, frequency, breadth, origin, and time horizon.

We have dealt quite extensively with both data and information as they apply to organisations and management. It is now evident that there is a strong relationship between data and information. Data are processed to produce information needed for decision-making and problem solving. Now we need to put the subject of using computers to produce information into proper perspective so that the reader has a better understanding of how computer systems can be effective tools to assist managers. Organisations regularly deal with a lot of data, particularly as the result of transaction processing where important data from routine events such as ordering merchandise, controlling inventory, or giving medical treatment or diagnosis are collected, sorted, classified, summarized, and stored. Furthermore, they are used to produce reports that convey certain facts about an aspect of the business to managers and other users. The term that we assigned to these activities is transaction processing.

But there is another kind of processing, namely, information processing. Information processing is the use of a set of procedures that transform data into information needed in management. In many cases it involves using data that are stored as a result of transaction processing. However, as we have seen, information can also be drawn from sources outside the organisation. Not all data available to a person will be needed or wanted for a specific task. For instance, a hospital administrator probably will not want or need data about the maintenance of surgical wards if the task at hand is formulating a charge policy for outpatient care in the emergency room. However, if the administrator is establishing charge policies for the use of surgery facilities, the maintenance data will be relevant and important. The point is that only selected data are processed to transform them into the needed information. Even though there is a vast resource of data available because of transaction processing, only certain items of data will be needed.

After the data are selected, the necessary processing takes place. In computer-based systems, this is performed with computer programs that carry out the calculations and manipulations to make the transformations. Access is made to different files of data and the data reduced to a manageable and relevant form—the information. Thus, information processing is data reduction, organising a high degree of detail in the data into a form that the user can work with. Processing a set of sales data, such as one containing the date, quantity, and dollar value of each individual sales order, into sales information such as total dollar sales, total item sales and sales by the product type is data reduction. Without it, managers would have a difficult time applying all of the data to the problem at hand; it would be too cumbersome and time-consuming to sift through each sales record to assimilate the needed information. As we have pointed out, computers can significantly assist managers in data reduction like this.

A major problem in information processing is delay. In both manual and computer-based processing operations, data can be processed one at a time as soon as transactions occur, or the transactions can be grouped into batches and processed later. Batching transactions thus causes delays in processing. In some cases delay will be tolerable as, for instance, when payroll data are collected on Friday and processed during the following week. But in other instances, delay is not tolerable and, in fact, immediate processing may be needed. The Strategic Air Command, which provides air protection for the United States around the clock, cannot tolerate delay in information processing when it needs to know if a certain aircraft over the country is friendly. In this case, immediate response by quick information processing is essential. Delay could be devastating.

There are many tools and techniques that can be used to help in computer-based information processing. The way in which they will be used depends on the needs of managers and organisations. But first, we need to develop a perspective on information and information processing in organisations. In the next section, we see that information is an integral part of the processes taking place within systems like organisations. The system model is our framework for examining organisations and their information gathering.

Concept of information systems

The concept of a system is that a business organisation, or more specifically, managers, place a scheme of order on the greatly varying environment in which they operate. In effect, managers try to simplify their surroundings so they can understand them and their implications. For a retail marketing manager, for example, the environment includes people, other business, the existing body of laws and regulations, different governments, competitors, and so on. The environment in this context is the set of all objects that can change or be changed by the system. It its simplest terms, a system is a set of components that interact with one another for some purpose. It is a set of objects that are related to one another and that may be described in terms of their attributes or their component parts.

Types of systems

Systems may be abstract or physical. An abstract system is conceptual, a product of the human mind. That is, it is not a system that can be seen or pointed to as an existing entity. Examples of abstract systems include social systems, theological systems, and cultural systems. None of these entities can be photographed, drawn, or otherwise physically pictured. However, they do exist and can be discussed, studied, and analyzed. A physical system in contrast, is a set of elements—rather than ideas or constructs—that operate in relation to each other to accomplish a common goal or purpose. Examples of physical systems include:

Computer systems : Collections of hardware elements that work interdependently under some means of control to process data and produce outputs reports.

Communication systems : Collections of components that can represent and transmit bits of information from one point to another.

Marketing systems : Collection of people, equipment, and procedures that develop, produce, and distribute commodities, ideas and other entities to a consumer or user.

The fact that a system may be classified as abstract or physical does not imply any judgment of worth value. That is, a physical system is not more meaningful or more necessary than an abstract system. The distinction is for analytical purposes only.

System definition and element

A system is a set of components that interact with one another to accomplish a purpose or goal. Within this basic definitional framework, elements necessary for the very existence of any system may be identified. These system elements include the environment, boundaries, input/output, and components.

System Environment

All systems operate within an environment. The environment surrounds the systems, both affecting and being affected by it. What we call the environment depends on the system's goals, and activities, as well as whether it is a physical or an abstract system. For example, a sociologist studying interpersonal behaviour in a social group would probably consider everyone and everything not in the group as the environment. However, a psychologist studying the personality of one group member would undoubtedly consider the other group members to be part of the environment. Similarly, a computer specialist studying the processing efficiency of the central processing unit would place the user in the environment, since he or she is not part of the CPU. However, if a computer specialist is examining the role of an organisation's computer processing system in terms of reducing operating costs and decreasing errors in handling data and information, the user would definitely be a part of the system. These examples show how different environments can be defined for systems. Further, the environment is a function of the individual who is observing or interacting with the system.

Systems boundaries: The system boundaries distinguish or separate the environment from the system. The system exists, within the boundaries, and anything lying outside them constitutes the environment. The system's boundary line determines what is included within the system and what is not.

The particular characteristic of a boundary vary according to whether a system is physical or abstract. In a physical system, the boundary is a natural line of demarcation determined by the basic system structure and the system's goals and purposes. In abstract systems, on the other hand, boundaries are typically imposed by an observer. The arbitrary boundary line may therefore vary from observer to observer, unless everyone can agree on criteria for its selection. Under any circumstances, the abstract system's boundaries are determined by the observer's level of inquiry, the intent and purpose in drawing the line, and the observer's perceptions of the internal working of the system. In a physical system, like the central processing unit of a computer, the boundaries are fixed to contain the arithmetic/logic unit, the control unit, and the primary storage unit. However, the boundaries for an abstract system like production work group, may or may not include the foreman of the group, depending on the definition of the observer. One observer may feel the foreman is a part of the work group; another, that the foreman is outside the boundaries of the group.

Information as a corporate resource

This section propagates the view that information is a corporate resource and goes on to survey the characteristics one looks for in Computer Based Information Systems, (CBIS). It also seeks to find managerial needs for various functional activities. An information scientist has said that, like the sun, we take Information for granted until it ceases to "shine". Another has said that whereas the power of steam was seen and harnessed. It was a century, and more, till the laws of thermodynamics were postulated. We do not propose to set the Thames on fire with earth shaking "Informatics laws" but review some well known behaviour patterns of Information.

As a corollary to Toffler's identification of the "third wave" we note that some management scientists have seen a shift in management paradigms. Of interest to us is the identification of the most important resource to be managed, "third wave" organisations : it is no surprise to see "information" getting pride of place, unseating the traditionally supreme "cash". Before seeking to draw the profile of Information, it is essential to reiterate difference between Data and Information. Data is an event, an occurrence or an action that also has historical value. Viewed from the environment and its interaction with other items of data, it becomes Information; what needs emphasis is that they are not synonymous.

Some important facets of information are as follows:

- It is highly subjective—the meaning, or interpretation of an item of occurrence depends on the recipient's slant on that event;

- It has to meet the differing needs of the various levels in the management hierarchy;
- It should possess a flexibility in the presentation of Information e.g. a bar chart is more useful than a mass of numbers;

A cynical, but often true statement, is that we do not really know what we want till we see the information presented verbally, in writing or as a display.

Desirable features in information systems (IS) are:

- It must provide information and not data that managers have to subsequently process to extract information; thus sparing the manager the pain of unnecessarily spending time on infructuous activity;
- Every change in status of the data—consequent on decisions and resultant action—must be instantaneously reflected in the data base;
- Must deliver information in formats, at desired times, to the concerned level, in the hierarchy;
- Should automatically take care of programmable decisions;
- There should be one and only one source to change the status of concerned data in the data base;
- Access to a modification of data should be capable of being governed by "need-to-know" policies.

Consequent to research by well known consultants, some canons, rules or tenets arise:

The 80:20 rule : Information scientists have arrived at a very interesting finding. Component units at any level in the hierarchy will have access to 80% of its data of interest within itself and hence it only goes out to other echelons for the other 20%. This has led to the concept of Local Area Networks (LAN) and Wide Area Networks (WAN) in the interconnection of segments of the organisation. It further hypothesises that 40% would be at call of the manager's terminal without having access to other data bases.

The 50% rule: Investigators have seen the volume of "Communicating" in the average organisation. Over 50% of a worker's time—be he a manager or whatever—is spent on handling information irrespective of mode viz speech, data, text etc. Integrating, through use of digitizing, would be highly beneficial.

Harnessing information

This section will not take on the "analysis and system design" aspects that are dealt with elsewhere. Rather we are looking at the philosophy of infusing IT into the organisation. These can be further classified into—policy, method and *modus operandi* as discussed below:

Policy of approach: There is a trichotomy: Centralised, decentralised and distributed as discussed below:

Centralised—It is decided to have one computer serving the needs of the whole organisation; a hang over of the early days when computers were thought to cost a lot of money and managers fought shy of investing money on many computers.

(a) Advantages:

— Good control of all resources used—equipment, space, people etc.; and optimal utilisation;

— One policy, hence, better systems, standards, monitoring etc. will result;

— There is an economy of scale;

— Corporate level information is of high standards;

— Incorporation of new trends, techniques, add-ons etc. are easy;

— Will attract "quality" staff.

(b) Disadvantages:

— End user made distant; it-is-somewhere-in-the-company-and-not-my-system attitudes, result;

— There will be a clash of priorities;

— Turn-around times will be high, resulting in lack of faith;

— System "down" would have cataclysmal aftermath; the famous all-eggs-in-one-basket syndrome;

— The "computer culture" is retarded;

— Almost negligible co-operation from the end users who do not see it as "their" system;

— MIS will be just another management aid remaining the toy of the professional, in the view of managers;

— The manager-in-charge acquires an undue importance, resented by other users.

Decentralised—The concept that anyone that wants it, gets a computer, which arrived with the microcomputer, and reinforced with the PC explosion that has changed CBIS all over the world.

(a) Advantages

The manager sees the computer as his/hers and therefore:

- end user motivation is very high;
- there is an urge to participate in IS building;

- controls are stronger;
- priority contention does not exist;
- extra capacity available;
- responses are to suit management needs;
- meets the 80% rule adequately.

(b) Disadvantages

— There will be duplication and even triplication of effort and so sub-optimal use of the computing power;

— Information as sluggish as in manual systems; as said by a management specialist, "the garbage only gets churned out faster";

— bound to be incompatibility in systems, equipment etc.;

— Information ceases to be a "corporate" entity and the management will lose out on the benefits of the computer as a tool;

— there would be a dilution of specialist personnel;

— overall, would be an expensive policy as expressed by a cynic "it is not only dispersed computing but also dispersed systems and people; increases cost and breeds incompetence".

Distributed—Distributed data processing (DDP) is a progeny of the Microcomputer and the Communications field. It may also be seen as the culmination of many developments:

— systems approach of the late 60s:

— cheap computing, harbinger of which was the Integrated Chip (IC);

— the 80 : 20 rule emergence and awareness of it;

— digital communications:

This last policy is a good mix of all the advantages of the other two and eliminates many disadvantages.

Method—This can also be seen as a trichotomy of methodology of data manipulation: batch; interactive; online.

Batch—All transactions are collected, the master files updated on set dates and outputs to management generated on predetermined schedules. The various advantages and disadvantages can be easily catalogued.

Disadvantages worth highlighting are as follows

— There is a high degree of manual intervention involved, such as keeping a tag on transaction tiles, mounting programs, media etc.; such an environment is fraught with less potential;

— errors/duplicates will need careful trace, to ensure that they do not re-enter the system after rectification;

— all too often, there is a proliferation of unwanted reports;

— it is difficult to keep priorities in proper perspective;

— computer awareness is the first causality since users tend to lose interest by the remoteness resulting from this mode.

Interactive—The first development to put the user in contact with the system, in which transactions are entered through terminals and all "off-line" work is shut down. A high degree of data discipline is necessary and the end user becomes responsible for the data updation. It requires very comprehensive verification through validation programs which will ensure that only "clean" data is accepted. Very clear procedures will have tọ be built in, in order to ensure that only entitled personnel would update and other such "security" measures will have to be incorporated.

On-line—Extending the above, to a global scale, so that users anywhere have access to databases through communication networks linking many computer and terminals. In this, not only are those that input data linked but also many others using data for their decisions. It is the current trend and brings with it, the need for very rigid security measures. A super-set of this mode is "real-time" systems. The term "real" will depend on the environment and the user's need for response; for example the response time for passenger reservation systems could be 5 seconds whereas, that of an Air Force Operations Systems could be much less than a second.

Modus Operandi—The exact way to develop the IS needs can be seen also as a trichotomy; integrate now or total; integrate later; systems perspective. These are briefly covered below:

Total system—The aim is to take every application in the organisation and implement all of them simultaneously. At first sight, this seems very attractive but is full of potential disaster, due to some very sound reasons:

— to complete the work of design, test etc., most medium sized organisations would need very large resource investment of people, space etc.; often these would not find favour since the management would be hard put, firstly to find them and, secondly, to absorb the task force; getting a temporary force would be impractical;

— during the interim, that would vary from three to five and more years, the management would lose the advantages of the computer as an aid to their management; needless to say getting them enthused later would be a mammoth problem;

— no system is static; hence the teams will be on a "chasing their tail" hunt and the systems developed would be sub-optimal;

— at the end of it all, if the teams survive, the MIS would be a very poor one.

Integrate later—Systems are developed haphazardly with the hope that some one, some time, will integrate them. Such artless thinking will end up with "islands" of "CBIS" with very little mutual support. There is many a professional who has ruled the day that he/she adopted this philosophy.

A system perspective approach—It is probably the most pragmatic one which also, by instinct, is the most palatable since it is a "Systems" approach. There is a two stage framework that is involved; noteworthy is the intimate partnership necessary between the management and the DP team:

— a macro level assessment of the functions, their mutual dependence, on further hierarchies, input/output interfaces;

— drawing up priorities, safeguards etc. and installing systems on a building block basis.

Information in the organisation

We have seen the various shades of information and the characteristics that it possesses. It is said to deserve as much, Business scene. So some authors talk about Information Resource Management (IRM) at par with other resource management. We have heard, from Forester for example, about the business enterprise having innumerable information channels coming up to decision-making points. The modern concept of LAN, is only to be an expected development as also the Data linkages now possible by carriers like the PTTs Telecommunication agencies etc. Where the two disciplines of communications and computers developed individually, their reliance on each other and the IC's appearance, has made the two converge to a synergism rarely seen in history.

If information is so all pervasive, it would be only logical that its role in the various classical functions of POSDCORD be examined. Before we do so it is worth looking at some well known terms like MIS and DSS.

Window to MIS

Ushering in the "Systems Approach", the sixties saw MIS as the binding force it encircles the classical functions, management aids etc. and is visualised as omnipresent. Not that MIS is a new concept; only its computerisation and its new role, as a binding force, to every nook and corner of the organisation, is of recent origin. Some information techniques did exist, to provide information that allowed planning and control functions: the computer has added new dimensions—speed, accuracy, ability to handle a large volumes etc. and hence give managers the feasibility to consider many alternatives before a decision.

MIS also suffered from "over selling" by DP persons; this led to a degree of suspicion of the "unknown" distorting its usefulness, the accent being more on the machine and not on what it could do for management. It led to the well known consultants, McKinsey and Company, to comment in terms of achievement: "the computer revolution in the US has been out running all expectations. In terms of economic payoff on new applications it has rapidly lost momentum". Booz Allen and Hamilton, made an even more pertinent (pertinent in our underdeveloped context) comment that "modern generation equipment was being used for first generation System Design". Irrespective of all these disconcerting views, it would appear that in the not too distant future, the manager who cannot use the computer will become, organisationally, a misfit and dysfunctional. Computer literacy should be a *sine qua non*, at all levels.

MIS is made up of three elements— Management, Information and System. We will need to define each of the component parts to really understand MIS.

Management—This is too vast a subject to be undertaken as a precis but, for this chapter, it comprises the process/activities that describe what managers do in the operation of their organisation: plan (setting strategies/goals and selecting the best course from alternatives available); organise (tasks assigned to selected groups along with authority/delegation); control (through standards and assessing deviations). Decisions, in all these, is a fundamental necessity and our MIS has a major role to play.

The role of MIS in these functions are dealt with later in this chapter.

Information—As we have seen earlier, Information and Data are not synonymous; a fact that is highly relevant in our discussions.

Some characteristics have been looked at earlier in this chapter.

Systems—Simply put again, it is a set of elements put together, for a common objective. All systems are part of a larger system.

In areas like manufacturing, some high degree of integration has been achieved by automation; sub-systems have been linked together to achieve "synergism". Unfortunately, this has not happened in business organisations; particularly as it applies to integration through information exchange of sub-systems. For example, marketing, operations and finance are often on diverse paths and at cross purposes. The systems concept of MIS is, therefore, one of the optimising the output of the organisation by connecting the operating sub-systems through the medium of Information exchange.

Objective of MIS—To provide Information for decision-making on planning, initiating, organising and controlling the operations of the sub-systems of the firm and to provide a synergistic organisation in the process.

Of recent origin, it is seen by some writers as the evolution from MIS. We, however, view it as one already encompassed in the term MIS since

— it supports decision-making in both structured and unstructured environments;

— supports decision-making at all levels;

— it, far from being a stand-alone concept, is woven into the fabric of the organisations;

— supports all aspects of decision-making processes;

— is made up of people, procedures, interactive systems etc.; intended to be evolutionary/adaptive and easy to use.

Thus MIS can be viewed as a superset of DSS.

DSS vs MIS—MIS has the following characteristics:

— gives reports and access to data; the latter by retrieval on data bases;

— involves structured Information flow:

— Information flow centered around specific functions like production, marketing, finance etc.;

— Transaction processing giving Information in consistent manner; time focus is retrospect;

MSM—Visualises structured tasks leading to a decision or action. The focus is on better solutions in the current environment. Use of modelling techniques.

DSS—Is generally interactive to the Manager to expedite the decision process and its communication, that could be direct or through storage.

— prepare models relevant to function and/or level in hierarchy;

— stand alone models for specific tasks but integrable to other models;

— efficient query languages interacting with the data base;

— effective mechanisms to extract data, for manipulation, from the data base;

— input flexibility in modification;

— desirable to have batch-interactive mode;

— follow, exactly, the changing patterns;

— be highly "user friendly".

— allow *ad-hoc* enquiries; hence usually around DBMS packages (DBMS is covered elsewhere; but what is relevant is that the Data Base Management System aggregates the organisation's data with benefits of flexibility, uniqueness, expandability etc.);

— support financial/statistical analyses of desired data streams;

— a planning language for "what if ?" queries of managers;

— ability to invoke graphics;

— report generation to any desired format.

Objectives - The above leads to state the objectives of DSS as:

— assist organisational decision-making process;

— improve the effectiveness of such decision making;

— add value to the existing corporate data base.

— personal systems like spreadsheet, own application and the more recent electronic mail;

— access to corporate entities like key company data, linkage to external data, forecast, budget etc.;

— flexible presentations through menus, graphics etc.

One often hears the term Computer Based Information Systems (CBIS) which seems to cover all types of ISs; the comparison of a few is given below:

CBIS Type	Inputs	Processing
MIS	Processed transcation data, some management data management originated programmed models	Report generation,
DSS	Some Processed data management-oriented data; unique models.	Query response; management science/OR Modelling Simulation
TPS	Transaction data	Classifying, sorting, adding deleting, updating.
OAS	Appointments, documents; address lists.	Scheduling, word processing, data storage and retrieval.

a) A Transaction Process System (TPS) is an euphemism for Data Processing (DP). It can be defined a computer based system that captures, classified, stores, maintains, updates and retrieves transaction data for record keeping and for input to other CBIS.

b) An Office Automation System (OAS) is also known as the automated office; defined as a multifunction, integrated CBIS that allows many office activities to be performed in an electronic mode.

c) The relationship of these CBIS links with management hierarchy is often depicted as below; also shown are other management aids:

— Top Mgmt—DSS; part of OAS; MSM & OR;

— Mid Mgmt—MIS; part of OAS; Organisation theory;

— First lines—TPS; part of OAS; accounting;

— Clerical—based on OAS; Office work.

d) The growth is interesting to follow;

— mis 50s, DP; supporting first-line and some middle management need;

— early 60s, MIS; aid to first line and middle level;

— mid 60s; TPS; and MIS extending some support to top management;

— late 60s/early 70s, OAS;

— mid 70s; DSS introduced.

A very legitimate question that arises, in the mind of the manager, that needs an immediate answer, after all these views projected, on Information as a corporate resource.

Fact 1: The information worker is a big chunk in the work force and even small improvements will have great impact;

Fact 2: Putting in order the 80% (of the 80 : 20 rule) information will improve efficiency as well as productivity.

Fact 3: People slow down communications. For example, the delays in our day-to-day work. Let us take the number of person, each a delay center, that are involved if a letter is to be sent from person A to B. A dictates, the secretary prepares a draft, this may go through one or more cycles of correction; the letter, as finalised, may await for a period for the person to sign; remain for further period in the pending/out tray; taken by a messenger to in/out registration; it will await documentation; it is then carried by a messenger, when free, and after delays in the carrier, goes through a registry, the PA and then to B.

The above, along with the more than adequate support to management in the areas dealt with later, make a CBIS an attractive proposition. It is the answer to management's problem and with the integration of the various modes of image, speech, data and text being digitised, will improve the Information sector of management.

It is used to utilise scientific analysis for firstly developing and managing operating systems (e.g. cash flow or personnel) and, secondly, designing Information Systems for decision-making. The basic tenet is that the system is held together by Information exchange. The need for this and for the greater emphasis, is due to two factors that have accelerated management thinking to a system approach;

— the increased complexity of business and

— the increased complexity in management.

— technological advances which presuppose a simultaneous managerial revolution consequent of the great need for Information;

— great emphasis on Research and Development;

— Product changes becoming necessary due to rapid obsolescence and the need to extract optimum ROI on products in shorter time spans;

— the information explosion; as the decision-maker, the manager is a processor of Information; to remain ahead of competition, she/he must be able to take decision based on a plethora of data, organised in the most optimal way.

— Feed back: the output of the IS leads to a decision, leading to some action that corrects the output, which, in turn, leads to another decision;

— Automating/programming decisions by rules;

— Management sciences techniques like Linear Programming (LP), simulation etc.;

— The electronic computer with inherent capacity of handling voluminous data.

The manager of tomorrow will face a number of changes in physical processes and operations; the systems look is the only way to tackle it and that presupposes the availability of good, and flawless, ISs. This will be one that takes note of environmental changes, a highly reliable internal data bank and a model bank.

To arrive at this, perhaps utopian state, we see some essential ingredients;

— a systems approach to managing, to meet challenges, is implicit;

— the systems approach to Management must precede the design and use of MIS;

— it must be realised that the computer is only a component and not the MIS or the central focus of MIS;

— Management must get fully involved in design of MIS; islands of automation" or a string of DP systems.

The general model of managing is described below taking note that the functions of management are not performed sequentially; planning is involved in organising and control; organising is required for planning and control.

— Planning (setting objectives; perception of opportunities, problems, and alternatives surrounding the achievement of the objective; diagnosis of opportunities, analysis of objectives and selection of a course of action; design a program of action to achieve the objective);

— Directing (leadership in the organisational action required to achieve; includes communication and motivation of subordinates)

— Organising (supervision of action plan through an organisation whose task relationships are defined and understood);

— Controlling (observation and measurement of performance against standards for achieving the plan and correction of performance deviation if required; observation of significant trends within and without the Manager's activity so that goals and programs may be modified as necessary).

— Feedback (recycling of Information concerning plans, actions and progress at different stages of the management process to ensure that proper programming to achieve the objective is being met).

Note that the management process is interactive. Note also that a good Management System is a *sine qua non* for a MIS; it is only then that the Manager gets the Information needed in the form, place and time to perform a task. The management system helps to develop plans for achievement of objectives, to organise for implementing plans and to control performance so that plans and actions occur on schedule.

The "material control" and "transportation" processes are representative of the current approach of integrating the various processes through well planned basic information. For example orders and movements from the warehouse can be used to optimize warehouse space; based on each order, that show the cubic content and weight, as also the destination, loading and routing of trucks can be optimised.

Let us add another process to the integrated model we are building; the "purchasing" process, whose schematically at Fig 6. A well designed inventory control process provides for automatic ordering based on many factors-customer Service, EOQ, and lead times. Orders are then screened against inventory record and when the level of a particular item reaches the reorder point, the "inventory" process directs the "purchasing" process to issue a purchase order to the concerned vendor. The vendor fills the order, ships the material to the warehouse and submits his invoice to be entered into the "account" process. This process triggers the "accounts payable" activity and the eventual reconciliation of cash points. Note that from the Materials control process, on receipt of material from trade, receipts enter the Inventory control process.

So far we have considered some basic processes. There are two connections that have been left out:

— one that connects inventory control and accounting functions; necessary since inventory data is a requirement of accounting;

- the second is to show some important outputs of the accounting process; it is to be remembered that accounts is a "score-keeper", so to say, of all processes; it accumulates and outputs reports of the type shown (Inventory statistics, Sales statistics and PL statements) in many ways, as desired by management.

Note that although we have mentioned Product 'X', it should be apparent that these models would cover most applications, covering as they do, the Operational control and some management control activities.

The Marketing process uses the basic source data that has been collected and filed but processed in diverse ways to answer specific queries of management like— effort of promotion on sales, effect of price changes, product mix, diversification etc. One key output is the sales forecast based on historical sales movement (from accounting process) as well as on environmental/projected external events (buying trends, economic factors, Government policy changes etc.).

The Strategic planning process is the core of the business model; all major company decisions are made here, based on reports of the accounting process (these are digested, reviewed and analysed).

We could view the "Business Process" as made up of the "Main stream", a "Support stream" and an "Administrative stream", the component parts of which are covered in the next sub-section. A later Sections we shall examine some characteristics within these streams.

The main stream : Can be said to be made up of:

(a) Sales order processing which, in turn, is built up by

- Customer billing, which, in turn,
- Order filling.
- transportation;

(b) Inventory reporting and control which, in turn, can be seen as -

- stock status reporting,

- statistical replenishment;

(c) Requirements generation, further seen as -

- gross requirements generation,
- net requirements generation;

(d) Production scheduling, consisting of -

- fabrication and assembly scheduling,
- shop loading;

(e) Production control made up of,

- performance vs plan analysis,
- variance reporting;

(f) Purchasing; - numerical control,

(g) Receiving; - configuration management,

(h) Quality control; - industrial engineering,

(i) Maintenance; etc - BOM generation; etc.

The supportive stream : which can be seen to be made up of -

(a) Marketing made up of-
- sales analysis,
- sales forecasting,
- sales administration,
- advertising;

(b) Strategic planning built from-
- econometric models,
- market models,
- simulation,
- decision theory,
- investment analysis,
- facilities planning;

(c) Engineering and Research, consisting of -
- design automation,
- project control,

The administrative stream: that can be seen to be made up of -

(a) Financial, consisting of -
- accounts receivable;

- accounts payable,
- general ledger,
- cost accounting,
- fixed assets accounting,
- budgeting,
- financial Models,
- Key-rated analyses,
- Profit and Loss (P & L) statements;

(b) Personnel, made up of-
- payroll
- payroll reports
- wage and compensation analyses;

(c) Legal,; etc.

Computer have come to the aid of the Design activity. Some of the benefits of CAD are:

— drafting—that makes the life of the draftsman easy;

— the design that enables optimisation of space, density, and modification easy not only in two dimensions but three;

— the ability to effect changes and see the results from any perspective etc.

The use of computers in the Manufacturing field would cover all aspects of the manufacturing activity including the Numerical control of Machines. Flexible Manufacturing Systems (FMS) CIM. etc. are other concepts in the field where the whole process is optimised. Some of the more common terminologies used are : Computer Aided Production Engineering, Computer Aided Storage and Transportation, Computer Aided Production Planning, Computer Integrated Manufacturing etc.

Some of the basic features one would expect are:

Geometry creation

— creation of a complex drawing out of a set of primitives that will include point, lines, arcs, circles and polygons;

— identify any part of this drawing as a unit and repeat in a rectangle or a circle and arranging like bricks in a wall or teeth of a gear;

— identified units to be made to move, rotate, change scale, get mirror image etc.,

— zoom, layering, reference grading etc.,

Any new technology will always have its share of antagonists, who will number as many as the protagonists. It must be remembered that the Industrial revolution was on which automated the manual operations of mankind and it brought in its wake a high degree of opposition led by one Capt Ludd. The computer is viewed as one that is attempting to automate functions that are mundane and repetitive in the Information field and ultimately automate many of the applications requiring "thinking". Managers and Computer people would do well to study the implications of the introduction of computers; particularly in developing countries, where the sceptre of unemployment raises its head.

This is a major concerns of labour; there is fear that because of the introduction of computers there will be retrenchment. Their concern does not stop here but there is fear that future generations will suffer. Management argues that far from displacing labour, there is, firstly opportunity for a new and better class of workers and, secondly, the result of higher productivity is greater employment potential.

Peter Drucker has dubbed the individuals dealing with information "knowledge workers". He says "the substitution of knowledge of manual effort as a productive resource in work is the greatest change in the history of work". He says that in 1900, out of 20 workers, 18 were manual workers but by 1965, in a vastly increased work force, out of 2-workers, 5 and only 5 were involved in manual labour—an indirect effect of introducing the computer.

It is common knowledge that change is to any individual particularly if there is a threat, real or imagined to his position, his job or any such.

At the shop floor level, the threat is more perceptible and it is with great difficulty that organisations have been able to get the labour Unions to agree to computerisation. It is the white collar worker who has shown the greatest resistance. Examples are galore and the student should investigate the happenings in Banks, Insurance companies in the private and public sector. It says much for the Unions that they have readily accepted computerisation where they see that the manual systems are not capable of handling volumes. We quote the example of the Inter Branch Reconciliation of Banks that, almost a decade ago went in for computerisation as long as the computer was not in house.

Researchers have found that the middle range manager has always viewed the computer with suspicion. His fear is based on the fact that many of the programmable decision can now be delegated to the computer and two factors are to be remembered:

— his/her importance reduces: He/she is no longer in a position to do favours; equally, they are in no position to suppress facts that could be compromising;

— there is speculation in journals that the Development of Information Systems, on the computer, the middle management cadre will shrink if not disappear altogether.

Strange as it may seem some top level executives also resent the coming of the computer into their sphere changing the way they perform their functions and changing their ways of functioning and learn complicated, new procedures whose effectiveness they question in the first place. Mixed up with this is a "fear of the unknown" since the computer is a best about which his/her generation had NO knowledge whatsoever.

What kind of modern Luddite action do we visualise?

— at the operational level, there could be subtle ways of introducing errors and generally making systems fail; to be borne in mind as security measures;

— at higher levels, is by ducking from involvement in systems and suppressing vital information parameters.

There is tremendous scope for choosing what to do on computer and what should be left to the human. This is a dilemma of all developing countries where there is fear of unemployment.

One great fear of the person-in-the-street is what one may term "Big brother is watching you" syndrome. Quite rightly citizens are afraid that their data on various files may be misused.

Appreciating this point of view, many countries have introduced laws to afford protection against misuse.

Even in advanced country there is criticism on the amount of money sent on projects at the cost of development of computer based projects for example in Medicine. Citizens are getting more concerned on this aspect.

There is criticism about introducing computers at schools or fond parents buying computers for their children. The feeling is that the child tends to neglect studies, equally, the absence of remembering tables, they take easy way out using the computer even for simple additions. This is one view offset by the contrary view that it leaves the child time to learn more useful things.

The after effects of working on the terminal is still to be fully investigated.

It is said that the greatest rate of obsolescence is in the field of electronics. A thinker has said that were such strides made in the automobile field, we should have a car sold at ridiculous prices (like ten paisa) and it would give mind boggling performance (like a thousand km. per litre of petrol). The field of computers is a sub-set except that apart from the electronics, the juxtaposition of its components (in the form of an architecture); the driving force is software, giving scope for not only obsolescence, but also the for power never before achievable. The very fact of rapid growth makes it difficult to forecast to any degree of accuracy.

Technology: Rapid strides are being made here:

— Integrated circuits are reaching limits set by the laws of physics;

— Memory devices are getting to terrabytes storage potential;

— for recording, for printing and so on, new techniques like Laser and optical devices are giving greater speeds for peripherals;

Architecture: The juxtapositioning of devices and components to achieve throughputs show greater innovation; distributed computing, parallel processing etc. will make the dividing line between the current concepts of PCs to super computers hazy. As Dr. Seshagiri said in an address to the Computer Society of India, in the not too distant future, there will be only two families of computers; Super Computers and Microcomputers.

Reliability: In a lighter vein, it was said that when the early valve based computers worked for an hour there was cheering on the sidelines. Tomorrow, reliability, maintainability and availability would be essential ingredients to give NO down time and 100 per cent "up" time, a combination of the other development would contribute to that status; allied would be the need for communication linkage reliability through not only good channels but also through efficient re-routing, confidentiality etc.

Software: The efficiency of which has always lagged behind technology by decades. The trend will be a synergism of technology, architecture and software to give users the best environment.

Applications: Is what the user wants; menu driven user-friendly systems will proliferate making the user to make full use of computer power;

Internal user: Whose demands will be satisfied by free access.

Society: Obligations to and observance of external factors; there would be greater emphasis on privacy: for example through Governmental pressures, economic constraints with emphasis to : prevention of industrial espionage etc.

Traditionally CBIS has been Technology driven. Tomorrow the emphasis should be not on whether or not the product will work but what kind of work it will is; the criterion should be not the ability to do something but the advisability of doing it; the concentration should not be on how something done but on what is done.

We can visualise the inclusion in the home, in addition to the power, water, gas, the telephone, and devices working on these, an *information* outlet. Also contingent is distributing it around the house and equally, provide control of home devices like temperature control and perhaps security with connections to the Police and Fire Services all through the use of computer power. We already have some systems claiming to be of this category. These are off shoots of Artificial Intelligence (AI) and parallel processing developments. These are termed Knowledge Based Systems (KBS).

The nucleus is a knowledge base which contains data as well as assertions about the data; assertions are in computer processible form which are stored by it and inferences gleaned after duly organising and processing.

One type of KBS is the Expert System that is designed to support a non-expert to arrive at decisions. MYCIN is one such in the medical field to help diagnose certain infectious diseases. Its success rate is said to be very high *vis-a-vis* a general practitioner. The future is very bright and with processing powers increasing manifold, they may even learn by experience.

The second, third and fourth generations of computers were mere technology upgrades, dramatically ushered in. It was the Japanese that postulated "a discontinuity in idea seem inevitable" and, with fanfare, announced plans for the next generation; the West was caught by surprise but were not very far behind in planning for studies.

The Japanese stated that western computer technology is stuck in a mire, trapped by:

— Von Neumann architecture;

— Vast operating systems;

— Dedication to third generation languages;

— Avoiding relational databases or rather slow in developing them

— huge customer investment in existing programs;

— Vested (financial) interests in avoiding as opposed to evolution change.

The aim of the fifth generation is to enable socially valuable functions being handled by the man-in-the-street. Means of representing and possessing knowledge is necessary so that the computer can appear intelligent and provide expertise far beyond the capability of the human brain for certain highly specialised areas. Pictures, speech and human language should be employed between the machine and its users.

On the route to that target is the evolution of KBS and expert system that we have briefly seen.

The Japanese target is to produce, by 2000, a KB machine that cam access upto 100 million data items (each of which will require a thousand bytes of storage) and 20,000 assertions (called rules). Initially, the KB machine will employ a separate inference machine for processing the assertions; the inference machine will be fused with the KB machine. It is said that the inference machine will be able to process 100 million to 1 billion logical inference per second. To a large extent the inference can be processed in parallel. A highly parallel architecture capitalising on the cost of future microprocessors will therefore be used. The control mechanisms and software for this will be complex and highly innovative says James Martin.

Challenges in Developing Organizational Information Systems

Developing an organizational MIS involves considerably more challenge than does the development of personal and workgroup MIS. Some of the reasons for this arise from within the system to be developed and some arise from outside the new system; some, however, arise from the nature of the organizational systems themselves. We will address each group of challenges. To understand this discussion, however, first consider the needs for a new organizational system in a manufacturing organization.

Scott Orthodontics

Scott Orthodontics manufactures exceptionally high-quality orthodontic appliances for orthodontists, oral surgeons, and dentists. Over 90 percent of the orders that Scott receives are for custom, one-of-a-kind items. Depending on the item, if may require from two days to several weeks to process the order. On rare occasions, when the required raw materials are out of stock, it may take six to eight weeks to manufacture an item. Scott's customers, the dental professionals, want to provide prompt and efficient service to their patients. When they order from Scott, they need to know how long it will be before their order will be processed, so that they can schedule their patients' visits. Further, if there are going to be extensive delays in the manufacturing of an item, they need to know this so they can reschedule their patients, order a different product, or order from another source.

When there are delays, the sales force bears the brunt of the customers' complaints. The salespeople need to know the status of an order, what problems exist, if any, and how long it will be until the order is shipped. Unfortunately, Scott's order-tracking system is informal and inadequate. There is no single point of contact for salespeople to call. Consequently, salespeople often are forced to call production supervisors who, if sufficiently charmed or bludgeoned by the salespeople, will track down an order. The current situation is unacceptable to all, and as a consequence, Scott has decided to develop an order-tracking information system.

The Flow of Order Processing

The entities involved in Scott Orthodontics order processing are shown in. Although this diagram uses dataflow diagram symbols, this is not a dataflow diagram. Instead, it shows the flow of an order. An order is received by sales and submitted to Order Processing where the customer's credit is verified and the order is validated for accuracy. The approved order is then sent to Manufacturing where it is produced. Raw materials are received from suppliers to produce an order. Finally, the order is transferred to shipping, where it is sent to the customer.

At a point in time, an order can be in any one of these processes, or it can be in transit between any two of them. When there is a delay with an order, the salespeople need to know not only where an order is in this process, but also how long it will be until the order is received by the customer. Knowing that the order is in Manufacturing is of little value if it will be six weeks until a required raw material is received.

Although there is no order-tacking information system, there are other information systems. There is a revenue generation system that includes sales, Order Processing, and Accounts Receivable. There are information systems in Manufacturing that are used to plan production and purchasing activity and to schedule people and machines. There are information systems in Purchasing and there is a general ledger system in Accounting. All of these systems are effective in accomplishing their function, but none of them provides information about the status and shipping date of a particular order.

Challenges to Development from Within the System

One purpose of an organizational information system is to integrate the activities of different departments into a single business system that produces coordinated, consistent responses to its Environment. To do this, the information system must bring together a diverse group of people, policies, procedures, goals, and expectations. This diversity creates a number of challenges to the development activity; they are listed.

First, as stated in the previous chapter, different departments will maintain different views of shared data. Further, Departments will vary in the ways in which they need to process data. Sales can delete an undesired customer record from the data sooner than Accounts Receivable can. Also, some departments will need to enter data that is only used by a different department. In this case, the quality of the data will suffer.

Allied with the differing views of data is the fact that users will employ the same terms to mean different things. A shipping date to manufacturing may be the date the order is completed. To Shipping, such a date is the date that it is delivered to the carrier. To Sales, it may be the date the shipment is received by the customer. Until the inconsistencies are known and understood, they will confuse the development activity.

Additionally, each department has its own goals and expectations. For example, at Scott Orthodontics, personnel in Order Processing are evaluated on the basis of the number of orders they process; personnel in Manufacturing, on the other hand, are evaluated on the quality of their product. As a result, characteristics of the new system that enable orders to be processed more quickly will be applauded by order Processing: They may, in fact, be resisted by Manufacturing.

Departments will also have different goals and expectations regarding the type of system to be developed. Order Processing may want a system that is, in its basic character, a TPS. Manufacturing, on the other hand, may want a system for production supervision that is primarily an MIS. Shipping may want a system that primarily addresses product delivery, While Sales may want a system that improves product quality (Where the product includes sales support). Another complication is that, very often, there are major differences in the competencies of departments. Manufacturing quality was of great concern to Scott's founder. Consequently, Manufacturing is full of well paid, hard-working, ambitions, capable. On the other hand, Order Processing was an afterthought. Hiring was done with less care, salaries are lower, promotions have been infrequent: as a result, the level of competency is lower. When the system development team convenes meetings among Order processing and Manufacturing personnel, This difference may become a problem. For example, Manufacturing may so overwhelm the discussion that Order Processing's needs may never become apparent.

Yet another complicating factor is that the departments compete with one another for dollars, management time, promotions, salary increases, and other resources. While it is all very good to state that the new system is to be created for the greater glory of all, when the system places one department in an advantage with respect to another, problems will result. Furthermore, it is possible for one group to gain control over the development activity and tern the project into an internal competitive weapon. Markus states.

> Designers have been known to build systems to change the balance of power among departments or other units in the organization. Because this design intention is not viewed as legitimate in most organizations, systems designed to increase one party's power and control over others are frequently masked in the language and appearances of improved efficiency or decision-making performance.

While such manipulation is undoubtedly rare, elements of it, or threats of it, do complicate the development activity.

Finally, systems often change the flow of work and the interactions among personnel both within and across departments. As this occurs, the Organization will change. Such change, however, is normally perceived as threatening and is resisted. The organizational change does not even have to be real; if the system is perceived as changing the organization, it may well be resisted. Impact of such resistance is great because it is seldom openly stated.

Challenges to Development Outside the System

Other factors that complicate development arise from sources outside of the boundaries of the system. These factors are listed. To begin, every information system resides in an environment of other information systems. In the case of Scott Orthodontics, the new order-tracking system will reside amidst existing revenue generation systems, manufacturing systems, purchasing systems, general ledger systems, and others.

The development activity of a new system must take cognizance of existing systems. If the new system will obtain data from or send data to an existing system, then this need will form part of the new system's requirements. In many cases, this is no problem. In others, however, the interface will be awkward. Consider an example from Scott. The goal of the new system is to track customer orders. To do this, the new system could utilize data that is processed by the existing manufacturing scheduling system. That system, however, keeps track of production work orders, which are very different from customer orders. Thus, for the new system to use data from the existing manufacturing systems, some type of data conversion must be done.

Another complicating factor is that the new system may require more data from existing systems than they can provide. At Scott, it may be that the order-tracking information system will be able to obtain 90 Percent of the manufacturing data that it needs from the current manufacturing systems. Obtaining the other 10 percent, however, may require a substantial change to those systems. When this situation arises, the development team has a choice of three undesirable alternatives. They can develop an incomplete system, they can wait for the manufacturing system to be changed in the necessary way, or they can duplicate the functionality that properly belongs in a manufacturing system. All of these alternatives involve an unwanted compromise.

There are other external sources of complication besides existing systems. One is that the new project will compete for both dollars and development personnel with other systems development projects. Sometimes the development team is forced to compromise and cut back on necessary system capabilities because of a lack of money or time. The users whose requirements are unmet will be dissatisfied; their dissatisfaction will then pose another problem to be solved. The organizational prioritization of information system projects is an important issue and will be discussed later in this chapter. Another problem is organizational politics. The new system may alter the organization external to the system as well as the organization internal to it. Or, the new system may give certain departments more power, more competency, more time, or some other resource. This change may be viewed jealously by departments that do not benefit from the new system's capabilities.

Sometimes, too, there is conflict between the user's needs and those of the MIS department. The MIS department may believe that it requires control over processing that the users do not want to give. For example, sometimes users want to make changes to organizational data on their own computers. The MIS department may prohibit this. The reasons may be valid, such as limiting the processing of partitioned, replicated data bases, as discussed in the previous chapter. Their reasons may also be suspect, such as a concern for loss of budget, personnel, or priority with management.

Challenges from the Nature of Large Systems

In addition to challenges that arise from within the new system and from outside the new system, there are other challenges that have to do with the very nature of organizational systems. These factors are listed. First, organizational information systems are often far more complex than personal and workgroup systems. Complexity in this sense means more functionality against more types of data. Whereas workgroup systems provide functions needed by the workgroup, an organizational system provides functions needed by many departments. Furthermore, the data to be processed is often more complicated. As stated, there may be many views of data as well. Second, organizational information systems are larger. There are more concurrent users, there is more data input and stored, and there are more reports and output produced. Although size does not directly impact the design activity, size does impact the amount of activity required for requirements definition and implementation.

Another complicating factor is that organizational systems integrate departments whose underlying activities may be inconsistent or incompatible. For the order-tracking system, It might be that Order processing has been blaming certain delays on Production for years, and that manufacturing has been blaming other delays on Order Processing for years. To substantiate these claims, Order Processing and Manufacturing may have set up independent business reporting systems. The new order-tracking system may bring these incompatibilities to light.

Organizational information systems often require considerably more work and longer periods of time to be developed than do personal or workgroup systems. The increased complexity and size means that more time must be spent in all five stages of development. There are two consequences of this fact. First, to shorten the development time, organizations sometimes increase the size of the development staff. Unfortunately, there are diminishing returns on the addition of people to development projects. In short, the more people there are, the more human interfaces must be maintained, and the more time must be spent on communication and coordination. Larger projects are harder to manage. Second, the problem with long projects is not just the delay that occurs before the system's benefits are realized. Another problem of lengthy projects is that, while development is underway, the business will change and the needs for the new system will also change. For a long project, it often occurs that, by the time the system has been developed, it is out of date. The organization must respond to market needs, new laws, and changes in ownership and management; as it responds to these things, the original requirements may be invalidated.

Finally, because of the increased complexity, size, and time required for organizational information systems development, it is more difficult for the development team and for any one individual to have an overall understanding of the system. In a classic book, Fred Brooks, one of the pioneers in large hardware systems development, discusses the importance for a single individual to have a vision for the conceptual integrity of the entire system. Without such vision, the system is vulnerable to inconsistencies, errors, omissions, and general ugliness. The larger the system becomes, the more difficult it is for anyone to have such vision. Additionally, the longer the project takes, the more likely it is that key personnel will be transferred or change jobs.

Organizational Information Systems Planning

As stated, the development of an organizational information system is far more difficult than the development of a personai of workgroup system. Consider a construction analogy. Building a personal information system is like constructing a single-family house; building a workgroup system is like constructing a small office building; building an organizational system is like constructing a skyscraper. To build a skyscraper, much more planning and organization is required than for building houses or small office buildings. Furthermore, as described in the previous section, the new system will reside amidst existing information systems, and it will compete with other project for resources. In terms of the construction analogy, he new skyscraper will need to be compatible with existing buildings; and it will compete with other skyscrapers that are being constructed or planned.

Business organizations need a family of organizational information systems that enable them to accomplish their business goals and objectives. They need a city of skyscrapers. At any one point in time, a number of different groups will propose the construction of a number of different systems. All of these proposed systems may be equally critical; some may be more critical than others; some may not be critical at all. There may even be other systems not being proposed that are more critical than those being proposed. To deal with this problem, the organization must have some means of planning and prioritizing projects. We will consider a number of planning alternatives in this section. First, however, we will discuss the role of the MIS steering committee.

The MIS Steering Committee

Every organization has some means for setting priorities among information systems development projects. Initially, as organizations first develop information systems, that means is simply a de factor system involving an informal committee. Perhaps the MIS director meets with the CEO and one or two other senior officers before making important or large dollar decisions. Such a de factor system is not generally effective in the long run, except for small organizations. As the organization develops more and more information systems. The planning issues become more involved. And it becomes apparent that a formalized forum for such decisions is needed.

To meet this need, most organizations establish a formal group that sets priorities for information systems development projects. This group, called the MIS steering committee, or some similar name, consists of senior level managers or executives from all of the organization's major departments. The major functions of the MIS steering committee are listed. First, the MIS steering committee has the responsibility for setting priorities among information systems projects. As stated, most often a number of different projects compete for the same dollars and human resources. The MIS steering committee resolves such conflicts. The committee may also take a proactive role in suggesting systems that should be developed or in approving planning projects whose goal is to determine which projects should be developed.

Another function of the MIS steering committee is to approve project plans, schedules, and budgets. Along with this, the committee often has responsibility for reviewing progress at major milestones in large or important projects and in giving "go" or "no-go" decisions for initiation of the next project stage. The MIS steering committee also can have responsibility for approving the acquisition of hardware and/or major programs. Sometimes organizations establish a budgetary limit for the MIS director; if the cost of an acquisition exceeds that limit, then the committee's approval is required. Similarly, the committee can also be involved in the selection and hiring of key MIS department personnel.

Additionally, the MIS steering committee often sets high-level policy and standards. For example, the committee might establish the policy that users can buy only certain types of personal computer hardware or programs. Or, the committee might stipulate that the MIS department is to determine lists of approved hardware and programs from which suers must select. Finally, the MIS steering committee provides advice and assistance to the CEO, the board of directors, and other senior executives on an as-needed basis. An evaluation of the use of MIS steering committees can be found in an article by Drury.

Top-Down vs. Bottom-Up Planning

There are two general categories of information systems planning: top-down and bottom-up. Top-down planning starts with an analysis of the overall business objectives and works down to specific systems. Bottom-up planning starts with the needs of a particular system, develops the needs for that system and other systems on the same level, and works upward toward an integration of systems.

To understand the differences between these two, suppose that Scott Orthodontics sets out, without any further planning, to build the order-tracking system. If they do this, they are following a bottom-up strategy.

Now suppose that, in the development of requirements for the order-tracking system, it becomes clear that many information systems need work. Suppose manufacturing systems are totally inadequate, not only for the needs of order tracking, but also for manufacturing in general. Then suppose that the team learns that the order-processing system needs substantial rework as well. As the order-tracking system development progresses, it may turn out that the order-tracking system development progresses, it may turn out that the order-tracking system development progresses, it may turn out that the order-tracking system cannot be completed without an entire revamping of Scott's information systems.

To revamp so many of their systems, Scott will most likely use a top-down strategy. They will review the general business objectives and translate those objectives into the need for specific Then they will prioritize the development of those systems and set to work.

The advantage of top-down strategies is that systems will be developed with an overall perspective of the needs of the business. Correct and appropriate systems will be developed on a timely basis. The disadvantage is that substantial lead time will be required to perform the top-level studies. This results in substantial delays before the first system is developed. Further, because of the lengthy time required, the business needs may change before the first system is developed. When this occurs, there is a danger that the top-level analysis will never be finished, a situation that is sometimes not so humorously referred to as analysis paralysis. The advantage of bottom-up strategies is that specific systems are developed more quickly. The disadvantages are that the wrong system may be developed, that incomplete and ineffective systems may be developed, or that the system that is developed may have a short lifetime because it fulfills only a short-term need.

In the next three sections we will consider two top-down planning methodologies and one bottom-up planning methodology.

Critical Success Factor Planning

A critical success factor (CSF) is an operational goal that must be attained to achieve success. Individuals, departments, and organizations all have CSFs. For example, a salesperson may believe that it is critical for her to identify at least two new leads per day, or an inventory manager may believe that it is critical to turn the inventory at least six times per year. CSFs are used in information systems planning to identify information needs, to identify types of information systems, and, ultimately, to identify requirements for information systems.

The underlying assumption in CSF-based information systems planning is that systems must exist that provide the information necessary to help management achieve the CSFs. If they do not exist, they must be created. The first step is to interview managers and to define the CSFs. Then the individual CSFs are combined into departmental and organizational CSFs. Finally, the CSFs. Finally, the CSFs are analyzed to determine which information systems need to be added and which of the existing systems need to be changed. Usually all top-level many midlevel managers are interviewed and asked to specify personal and departmental CSFs. For example, the manager of Customer Support at legacy Systems believes it is critical for his to call three dissatisfied customers per day. That is one of his personal CSFs; typically, a manager will have several or many. At the departmental level, this manager may believe it is critical for the Customer Support staff to keep a customer on hold an average of less than 30 seconds and in no case longer than 3 minutes. Senior mangers are also asked to specify organizational CSFs. Examples of their CSFs are that should exceed 20 percent of sales.

Once all of the managers have been interviewed, the CSFs are combined. Herien lies one of the problems of this method. There is no clear-cut, well-delineated algorithm for combining CSFs. Four individuals in Customer Support may specify 10 different CSFs. Using this method, somehow these 10 CSFs must be combined into 2 or 3 CSFs. Similarly, five different organizational officers may specify a large number of organizational CSFs, which also must be combined into a few. One advantage of the CSF method is that, by identifying the most important information needs, it focuses the planning and development of information systems on the highest-priority issues. It is broad in scope and thus unlikely to leave important information needs unaddressed. It is also simple and intuitive to understand.

The disadvantage are that the CSF method is time-consuming to perform, that the process of combining the CSFs is difficult and sometimes ambiguous, and that the result is no better than the ability of people to specify the CSFs. Also, this method focuses primarily on high-level managers. While such mangers may be able to specify good CSFs at their level, they may not know and understand how the company truly functions at lower levels. Thus, the information needs of lower-level personnel may remain unaddressed. This disadvantage is compounded because the CSF method is not concerned with the details that must be specified to develop operational TPS systems. Because of these disadvantages, the CSF methodology is more likely to facilitate the development of MIS and ESS systems.

Enterprise Analysis

Enterprise analysis, or, as it is also known, business systems planning, is a second top-down method for planning information systems. Whereas the CSF method is primarily concerned with generalized objectives, enterprise analysis is concerned with details-with identifying and correlating groups, their processing, and their data use. The CSF method asks each manager to consolidate his or her understanding into a few objectives. Enterprise analysis asks the managers for details about processes and data use; then the myriad details are combined, often with the assistance of computer processing, to identify which information systems are needed and what functions those systems should have. Enterprise analysis was invented by IBM personnel under the name Business systems planning.

Enterprise analysis is concerned with processes, organizations, data classes, and logical application groups. A process is an activity performed in dataflow diagrams. An organization is a group within the overall organization; usually organizations are formal groups and have names like department, office, and group. A data class is a group of data items that are created, changed, deleted, or used by one or more processes. A logical application group is a group of processes and organization that utilize the same data. The first step in enterprise analysis is to select a group of managers who represent all the important activities of the organization. Then this group is interviewed to determine what processes they or their organization performs and what data is involved in those processes. The result of these interviews is recorded in a number of different matrices and other documents.

Shows a portion of an example process/oraganization matrix for an enterprise analysis at Scott Orthodontics. The rows of the matrix list processes and the columns list organizations. An M means the organization has a major involvement with the process while an S means the organization has some involvement. The absence of a letter means there is no involvement in that process.

Shows a process/data class matrix that relates processes (rows) to data groups (columns). A C means the data is created by that process, a U means the data is updated by the process, and an R means the data is read by that process. Processes that utilize the same groups of data are called logical application groups. These are shown by the shaded regions.

A logical application group associates processes and data classes. Using the process/organization matrix, process can be related to organizations. Thus, the result of an enterprise analysis is a set of logical application groups with the data classes, processes, and organization units for each. This set of groups can then be used to plan the development of information systems to support each application group.

Most logical application groups are applications within one of the seven major organizational functions defined. They identify specific systems that need to be developed within these functions. Usually, to a logical application group will involve a mixture of systems types. Often a single logical application group will indicate a need for TPS, MIS, and ESS within that group. Another way of saying this is that a logical application group serves all five of the basic business functions on the why face of the MIS cube.

The major advantage of enterprise analysis is that it provides a comprehensive review of the information requirements across the organization. It documents the use of data for all major processes and organizations. It is particularly useful for large organizations that require a thorough review of their processing and information needs. For example, the Social Security Administration used enterprise analysis in documenting its information requirements when revamping its information systems.

There are three major disadvantages of enterprise analysis. First, as with CSF, only mangers are interviewed. Critical information needs of workers and first-line managers are interviewed. Critical information needs of workers and first-line mangers can be missed. Second, enterprise analysis is a time-consuming and expensive process. The Social Security Administration scheduled 10 years for their systems modernization plan. It began in 1982 and is scheduled for completion in 1992. Finally, enterprise analysis documents what is and not necessarily what ought to be. The results of an enterprise analysis are a set of logical application groups that are required to facilitate the existing processes, data needs, and organizations. Enterprise analysis does not suggest better ways of organizing business activity and dataflow.

Evolutionary Planning

Whereas CSF and enterprise analysis are top-down methods, evolutionary planning works from the bottom, up. With this approach, the need for information systems and their requirements are allowed to evolve as the business evolves. This does not mean that development is unplanned or uncontrolled. Rather, it means that projects are proposed as the need for them becomes apparent. The proposals are periodically reviewed by the MIS steering committee and prioritized against projects underway and projects scheduled to be started. Newly proposed projects may preempt existing projects, or they may supplant projects that were about to be started.

The advantage of evolutionary planning is that projects can be started with a minimum of study time and expense. The intuitive judgment of the MIS steering committee members replaces the lengthy analyses performed using CSF or enterprise analysis. Furthermore, evolutionary planning is adaptive. Priorities for projects change as the business needs change. New system development projects can be started without having to reconsider or repeat portions of an extensive planning process.

The disadvantage of this approach is that it can result in a hodgepodge of systems that have clumsy and ill-fitting interfaces. It can result in a number of separate systems in search of a centralized theme. Furthermore, it places a great burden on the judgment of the members of the MIS steering committee. While these people may be wise and experienced, with the evolutionary planning process, they may not have enough data on which to base good decisions. Also, the MIS steering committee typically is a consensus-oriented, group decision-making body. Such groups can be dominated by one or two powerful individuals. If this occurs, the information needs of certain groups may receive undue attention.

Finally, evolutionary planning can cause systems development to proceed in fits and starts. It may be that, of three systems-say, systems A. B, and C- system C is the most important. If, at one point, the MIS steering committee is only aware of system A, then they will approve the initiation of this project. If, later on, the committee learns about system B, they will probably decide to place system A on lower priority and then start system B. When, finally, the committee becomes aware of the need for system C, it may decide to place system B on a lower priority and start system C. At this point, the management and staff of the MIS department may begin to lose confidence in the directions they are receiving.

Realize that evolutionary planning is not an unplanned or ad hoc approach. There is a plan, but it is a plan based on the needs that have been discovered, without an active attempt to determine what other needs may exist. A truly ad hoc approach would allow projects to be started as they are proposed to the MIS department, as long as the money holds out and with little intervention or prioritizing.

Choosing a Strategic Planning Method

Compares the characteristics, strengths, and weaknesses of the three strategic planning methods described in this section. None is superior to the others in all cases. They each have situations in which they excel. Proponents of the top-down approaches argue that they are superior because the business needs an overall strategic systems implementation plan to avoid incomplete and duplicative systems and costly rework. Proponents of the evolutionary or other bottom-up approach argue that they can build several incorrect systems for the time and cost that must be invested in top-down plans. Even if the systems are ineffective and incomplete, the process of building them will reveal more true requirements than will ever be identified by a strategic study. Sometimes businesses elect to follow a hybrid approach. For example, the MIS steering committee might request a quick top-down overview of needs using either CSF planning or enterprise analysis. Given the results of this review, they would then follow evolutionary planning.

CASE

CASE is an acronym that has two meaning. Sometimes it stands for computer-aided software engineering, and other times it stands for computerised systems engineering. In this text, we will use the acronym CASE to stand for the latter meaning. It will refer to the process of using information systems to build information systems.

CASE technology developed as information systems professionals sought ways to use computer technology to improve their own productivity Some professionals found it ironic that there were so many people in the computer field attempting to increase others' productivity but ignoring the computer's potential for improving their own.

While many of the ideas that form the foundation of CASE have existed for quite some time, it was not until the advent of the microcomputer that CASE technology began to see widespread use. Today there are dozens of case technology began to see widespread use. Today there are dozens of CASE products; almost every major corporation is experimenting with, if not operationally using, CASE products and methodology. CASE, however, is more than a set of computer programs. CASE is an information system that includes all five components. There is CASE hardware, and there are CASE programs: these are sometimes called CASE tools. But, as CASE is used to develop systems, CASE database of system descriptors and other system parameters are also developed. Further, there are CASE procedures, which are sometimes called the CASE methodology. Finally, CASE requires a staff of CASE trained systems development personnel. It is a mistake to think of CASE as a set of programs. Technology without methodology is a waste of money. Organizations that have acquired CASE programs without changing their methodology have found little benefit from the too.

We will now survey the important components of CASE methodology and then discuss the capabilities of CASE tools.

CASE Where It Came from Where Its Going

Most significant applications of technology have come from the synergistic combination of existing elements. This is certainly true of computer-aided software engineering. Micro-computer-based analysis tools and mainframe database and code generators are coming together to address the entire software development life cycle. Artificial intelligence is the most recent technology to contribute to CASE.

The personal computer provided a break-through in software engineering by giving analysts the ability to generate high-resolution graphics, easily revise diagrams, and produce high-quality paper copies for delivery to users. While this constitutes significant automation of previous approaches, the use of local computer power to validate diagrams, enforce conventions, and capture information about processes took software engineering another step forward.

Developments in code generators progressed in parallel with those in micro-assisted design. Generators translate information combined from diagram, painted screens, and well structured descriptive text into code that can be compiled and executed. Early versions of these products did have shortcomings. Some generated only about 80 percent of a program's logic, leaving the additional 20 percent, usually the most difficult part, to be done by programmers, some produced code in a proprietary language or in a COBOL style barely decipherable by programmers. While the ultimate goal is to introduce changes by regenerating the application, maintainable code is good insurance until the technology matures, Finally, in some cases, the generated code required that the code generator be resident as the generated program runs, representing considerable resource overhead.

Recently, products have combined frontend analysis and design tools with back-end code generators and central repositories for information describing the data entities and relationships uncovered in business analysis.

These repositories-a third-party DBMS or proprietary file structure-allow for the generation of more complete programs. The repositories also help enforce data naming standards and design methodologies.

These application base management systems allow more or less seamless movement from graphics-based design to generation. The ease with which information captured by the design tools fulfills the code generator's input requirements depends on how well the vendor has integrated the front-and back-end components of its product....

Most of the progress in CASE has been directed at the process of building new applications. What of the massive investment in existing applications? Several restructuring tools convert existing code, usually COBOL, into structured code and create some documentation to make the structure evident....

Re-engineering of code is certain to require some fuel-based processing. More artificial-intelligence technology will find its way into CASE products in the near future. Knowledge of popular hardware and software environments and other information junior programmers are expected to know will be embedded in future

CASE tools when they are shipped. Business policies, such as accounting and control standards and government regulations, might also be described to and then enforced by CASE tools.

In the near term, we can expect continued improvement in code generation, user interfaces, and consistency checking. It will still be necessary for a human operator to have a clear idea of what a system should do. The analyst will also continue to need the ability to communicate a large volume of information about a system and its environment to the CASE tool. In the long run, the continuing technological synergies tapped by CASE developers will result not only in higher productivity, but also in the redefinition of systems development.

CASE Methodologies

While there is no single step-by step CASE methodology, there is general agreement about the stages and basic activities that need to take place for developing systems using CASE tools. This generally agreed-on process is a variation and extension of the five-stage process you studied. Consider which summarizes this process. It begins with strategic systems planning, using one of the top-down methods. Enterprise analysis is frequently mentioned in CASE literature, though other methods are feasible. The result of the first stage is a set of specific systems to be developed. These systems may be submitted to the MIS steering committee for approval, and one of the goals of CASE tools is to provide documentation for that purpose. The remaining activities are repeated for each system to be developed. The development of two systems.

First, a systems analysis is performed. During this stage, requirements are developed, including dataflow diagrams and data dictionaries. A double arrow labeled Shared Data. This means that, with some CASE tools, requirements developed for one system can be used as input to others. This is useful when an office or department is common to both systems. In this situation, the dataflow diagrams and data dictionary that have been developed for one system can be used as a starting point for the analysis of a second. The next stage is database design. Here, the data dictionary data is used to develop a design of the database. Next, system design is undertaken. In CASE literature, the word system refers to the design of programs, user interfaces, forms, and reports. It does not generally include the design of hardware specifications, procedures, or job descriptions.

The next stage is system construction. This term also refers just to the creation of programs, user interfaces, forms, and reports. Finally, the last stage is system management. During this phase the system is monitored, and changes are made to it in a controlled fashion. Versions of programs and other system components are managed so that configuration of the system is always known and under control.

Two activities underlie the development of the system. Process support refers to activities used to ease the development process and to ensure that it complies with the MIS department's development standards. It includes support for group communication, for creating, editing, and reviewing work, for provision of security and backup and recovery, and for compliance with quality assurance standards. Project management support refers to activities used to accomplish planning, scheduling and allocating resources, and controlling the development project. The process described here is similar to the five-sage process you learned previously, but it emphasizes different aspects of the development effort. With organizational systems, much more time must be placed on the coordination of the new system with the existing systems. Also, since organizational systems are typically more complicated than personal or workgroup systems, this methodology places greater emphasis on design activities; and, since organizational systems are larger, the methodology places more emphasis on systems management.

This process, however, is not incompatible with the five development stages. The definition stage occurs during strategic systems planning; the requirements and evaluation stages occur during systems analysis, the design stage occurs during database and system design, and the implementation stage occurs during system construction and management. Again, this process is an extension and adjustment of the five stage development process.

CASE Tools

The goal of CASE is to use computer technology to facilitate the development of information systems by automating or at least improving human productivity for each of the activities. The general architecture of a CASE product, which is a collection of CASE tools and a database of systems development data. The databse, shared among all of the tools, is often called the CASE encyclopedia. The advantage of sharing the database is that the results from one stage of development are automatically available to tools in a subsequent stage of the process.

Not all CASE products have all of these tools, though most CASE vendors are developing a complete set, or are cross-licensing tools with other vendors to form a complete set. Not all CASE products have the same strengths. One product may have a particularly good systems analysis tools, while another product may have a particularly good database design tools. Consequently, some organizations mix and math tools from different products. They use a tool from one product for one stage and another tool for a different product or for another stage.

Unfortunately, there is a problem with using multiple CASE Products: there is no standard structure for the encyclopedia. The data in an encyclopedia for one product may be incompatible with the data in an encyclopedia for another. Different products have different data standards. For example, one product restricts data element names to 10 characters; another product allows them to be up to 30 characters. Names from the second product cannot be input to the first. Organizations that plan on using several CASE tools must therefore restrict their encyclopedia data to the lowest common denominator. There are CASE tools for each of the activities. Starting with strategic planning, some tools store, organize, and present the results of an enterprise analysis, CSF plan, or some other type of strategic planning analysis. Using these tools helps to organize the strategic plan as well. The matrices are examples of the kinds of output that such strategic planning tools could produce.

There are dozens of CASE tools that facilitate the creation of dataflow diagrams. These tools are graphical and driven by mice. They provide a standard set of symbols that can be placed and moved about the screen, and they allow the input of both text and drawn art. Using them, dataflow diagrams can be developed with far greater ease and productivity than when drawn by hand. In addition, these tools provide automatic validation checking. For example, they ensure that, as a dataflow process is expanded to another level, no input or output is left out nor is any extraneous input or output added.

Analysis tools also provide capabilities for creating the data dictionary. Each dataflow, file, and process can be defined as described. These definitions are then carried forward into the design construction processes.

CASE products generally include a database design tool, although the capabilities very widely. Some such tools are simply graphical systems that aid humans in documenting a manually developed design. At the other end of the spectrum, some tools will construct a database design from data descriptions recorded in the CASE encyclopedia. Generally, there are problems with automatically generated designs, however, and such designs usually serve only as a starting point for human designers.

CASE products also include system design tools to facilitate the design of programs, menus, forms, and reports. By the time the system design tool is used, the data dictionary data and the database design will be stored in the CASE encyclopedia. The system design tools can access this data to make it easy for the human designer. For example, the user need only specify the name of a table when designing a report, and the system design tool can obtain the name of all columns of that table and guide the designer through the process of locating the columns on the form.

CASE products vary widely in their support for system construction. Some provide little, if any, support. Others provide tools thet generate application program code, menus, and form and report descriptions. Many products produce large sections of source code that application programmers then move into the programs they write. This saves considerable time and eliminates the need for much of the programming work that is boring and repetitive.

There are also CASE tools to facilitate systems managements. Many of the tools are used for configuration control over programs and database structures. Changes are made to programs or to databse structures either to correct errors or to adapt the system to changes in system requirements. Either way, it is important to know what changes were made when, for what reason, and by whom. Concerning process support, many CASE tools include word-and other text-processing programs, paint and draw programs, and a limited version of electronic mail. They also include facilities to control concurrent processing by development personnel and to protect the database against accidental, unauthorized, or criminal loses.

Finally, many CASE products include project management tools. These products include programs for developing plans and budgets, for scheduling system development tasks, and for allocating resources. These tools are used to organize and control the project and to report on progress to management and the MIS steering committee.

From this discussion, you can see that CASE is exactly what it sounds like. It is computer-aided systems engineering. CASE is not automated systems development. Instead, it is a methodology and a set of tools for developing systems with high productivity.

Prototyping

In its general sense, the word prototype means a sample, a pattern, an example, or the first thing of its kind. As applied to systems development, a prototype is a simulation, a demonstration, a piece of a system, or the first instance of a system. Usually prototypes are limited to hardware, programs, and data while there is no reason for prototypes not to involve the procedural and people components, they usually do not.

Why Prototype?

Prototypes are used for a number of reasons. For one, prototypes are used to demonstrate a concept or to sell or market an idea. It is often difficult for information systems professionals to indicate the benefits of a new system to management or end users from a description of product specifications. The prototype is constructed to show the benefits. Within an organization, prototypes are used to generate enthusiasm for a concept or to obtain financial or other resources. For example, start-up software companies prototypes to raise money for product development.

Another use of prototypes is to demonstrate the feasibility of an idea or an approach. Such prototypes are sometimes called proof-of-concept prototypes. Here, the essence of the idea is developed sufficiently in the prototype to demonstrate its technical feasibility. Such a demonstration might be required to show that the idea works at all, to show that it works with acceptable performance, or to show that it works within the constraints of a particular hardware configuration.

Another use of prototypes is to better understand requirements. users and professional systems developers come from two different cultures. Often, after an exchange of words, the two parties wonder whether or not they have understood one another. One way to check on the clarity of the communication is for the developers to build a sample of the entity being discussed, say, a report, and show that sample to the users. The users can then agree, or they can better describe what they want in the context of the prototype. Yet another use of prototypes is to determine requirements. It may be that users and developers agree that they do not know what is required. One way to learn more about the need is to build a prototype and then apply it to the problem to be solved. The deficiencies of the prototype will then lead to more questions and further understanding of the requirements. The reasons for building prototypes are summarized.

Components of a Prototype

The most common use of a prototype is to simulate the user interface. Prototypes are used to demonstrate the structure and processing of menus and other user commands. They are also built to represent data-entry forms. Often such prototypes simulate the user's action in processing the form. Users can employ the prototype in a sample situation and see how well it works. Awkwardness in the order of processing or missing features for special cases are identified in just this way.

Similarly, prototype reports are often constructed. Here, the users employ the report to perform whatever function they need to perform with it, and then they evaluate its effectiveness. From such firsthand experience, they can better comment on the appropriateness and usefulness of the form's design.

Another type of prototype is used to evaluate an algorithm, or processing method. Here the essence of the algorithm is programmed and tested, and sample data are submitted to it. Then the performance of the system is measured to determine technical feasibility. Performance is measured in terms of CPU cycles used, main memory required, disk accesses needed, and the like.

The last type of prototype we will consider is a prototype of an interface to another system. The new system may need to obtain data from or send data to another information system or even another computer. The only way to know for certain that the interface is as expected is to build a prototype and see. If data can be exchanged in the manner expected, then likelihood of surprises in the interface is greatly reduced.

Types of Prototypes

There are a number of different types of prototypes. The simplest is a simulation, or slide show. This type is most often used for prototypes of user interfaces. With it, dummies of menus, data-entry forms, or reports are constructed. The user then uses the keyboard as he or she would with the actual system. Behind the scenes, a program reads files of canned screens and data to simulate what would happen with the actual system. The advantage of simulated prototypes is that they are quick to develop. They also can provide a realistic feel of the character of the users interface. Usually, however, this type of prototype is restricted to a canned script or only minor variations from a canned script. This means that users cannot perform realistic tests against such a prototype. When, as a business professional, you use or review a prototype, be certain to ask what type it is. If it is a simulation, or slide-show, prototype, keep in mind that none of the actual work in building the system has been done and that the prototype only indicates the nature of the idea. it does not indicate that the interface being demonstrated can actually be built.

A Second type of prototype was mentioned previously: it is the proof-of-concept prototype. Such prototypes are developed when there is substantial risk that the proposed design will not work. Building the prototype reduce the amount of dollars and other resources that must be placed at risk. Proof-of-concept prototypes typically have a very rough user interface. Little time is spent developing program instructions to accept data or return results. Instead, the programming activity is focused on the particular aspect of the problem whose feasibility is unknown.

Most end users and managers are not qualified to evaluate a proof-of-concept prototype. Instead, the prototype should be evaluated by competent information systems professionals who are disinterested in the results of the evaluation. Those whose idea is being tested are obviously not disinterested, nor are the opponents of the concept. A third prototype is a partial-function prototype. Here a part of part of the actual system is developed and tested. Such prototypes are constructed to demonstrate a key feature of the system. Unlike simulation and proof-of-concept prototypes, the assumption behind a partial-function prototype is that the programs that are written will become part of the operational system. Thus, the programs, even though they only implement a part of a part of the system, are written with the same care and control as the operational system.

The advantage of such a prototype is that it need not be thrown away. The work invested in such a prototype saves work later. The disadvantage of such prototypes is that they are slower to develop and more expensive than either simulations or proof-of-concept prototypes.

The final type is pilot prototype. Here, all of a part of the operational system is developed. All of the features and functions, the user interface, the error processing, and the other aspects of some piece of the system are developed. AS with partial-function prototypes, these prototype programs are assumed to become part of the system. Thus, the prototype is not thrown away. The advantage of such prototypes is that the user can truly test the system for adequacy. The disadvantage is that considerable time and expense are required to develop such a prototype. Types of prototypes are summarized.

Problems with Prototyping

While there are substantial advantages of building a prototype there are also important disadvantages. First, the rapid development of a prototype may set an expectation in the users' minds that the system can be developed faster than it can. A complete system must not only process all of the features and functions, but it must also handle exception cases and errors. It may take more time to develop the program code for the latter items than it takes for the former. Second, The prototype may gloss over important issues. It may not reveal what later turns out to be the most critical and difficult to accomplish requirements. It may make the system appear to be easier to develop than it is and thus generate a false sense of optimism.

Third, Prototypes can lead to a false sense of how much has already been accomplished. Particularly with simulations and slide shows, if the reviewers do not understand that they are seeing a mock-up, they may believe that the technical challenges have already been overcome. They will later be surprised to learn that problems have been encountered in building something they thought already existed.

Prototypes for Personal and Workgroup Systems

Although prototypes are described here for organizational MIS, they can be used for personal and workgroup MIS just as well. Prototypes for personal systems are usually simulations of user interfaces. They are developed quickly, often using form and report generators of personal DBMS products. Such prototypes are developed to understand and document requirements. They must be developed quickly because the cost of the system is too low to support extensive prototype development.

Prototypes for workgroup systems are more like those for organizational systems. All of the types of prototypes described here are used for workgroup systems.

Organizational Systems and the Development Process

The five-state development process you learned also has a role in the development of organizational MIS. We have not focused on that method in this chapter, however, because you are already familiar with it. Do not conclude from its omission here, however, that the five-stage process cannot be used for the development of organizational systems.

The five-stage process can follow any of the methods of strategic planning. The strategic plan indicates which systems need to be developed; once the needed systems are identified, the five-stage process can be used to develop them. As described in the section on CASE, the standard CASE methodology differs only in emphasis and perspective from the five-stage process. CASE focuses on the development of programs and databases; the five-stage process focuses more on the development of all five components. Thus, if you use Case, much of what you learned about how to use the five-stage process to develop procedures and personnel components can be used to augment the CASE methods. Finally, prototypes are easily combined with the five-stage process. A simulation, or slide-show, prototype can be used to help during problem definition and requirements definition stages. Partial-function and pilot prototypes can also be used for requirements analysis. Proof-of-concept prototypes can be used in feasibility assessment during the definition stage or to verify designs during the design stage.

29

Advertising Management

Advertising is complex subject—a valid activity to some people, and a social blight to others. If such diverse viewpoints are possible, even with the same person, it is true that there is much more to this subject than appears on the surface and reason enough to consider not only definitions of advertising but also an examination of the various components that make up advertising. One of the major problems in attempting to define advertising is that the definition will vary depending upon the perspective of the individual. From the point of view of the consumer, advertising is considered either a source of information or a form of entertainment. Thus, a typical homemaker might define advertising as the supermarket ads that appear in the local newspaper every Wednesday. Her husband football fanatic, might define advertising as those funny Pepsi commercials that appear on the television every commercial break. The children in family might define advertising as the kellogy cornflakes commercials that describe all the great giveaways that can be exchanged by three box-tops. Although these definitions focus on the advertisement rather than advertising, they do point out several important considerations.

First, advertising is just one of many types of information employed by consumers that may ultimately shape their wants, attitudes, predispositions, and purchase of particular product. These alternative sources of information include conversations with friends about products and institutions and visits to stores to name but a few. Such information is often judged by the consumer to be more credible and reliable than information received through advertising about the same institutions and products.

Second, the role of advertising is strongly affected by the physical and emotional setting in which it is received. For example, an avid football fan is watching a football game in an intent and serious manner. He probably would not be receptive to advertising messages that create more anxiety. Rather, he responds positively to messages that provide a type of comic relief. This may mean that the advertiser is forced to use a great deal of repetition and to hope for positive cumulative effect. The toy manufacturer has long tried to design advertisements that carry through the cartoon format, so that in many instances the child cannot distinguish between the ad and the program.

A third consideration is the fact that in many instances the advertising message may have a low priority for the individual. If the intensity of a particular need is low or non-existent, then the person is less likely to show much interest in any message related to that need area. A host of factors can influence the level of importance a person may place on a particular good or service. For example, an individual who purchase a new automobile six months ago and is pleased with her choice, will probably pay very little attention to automobile ads. Conversely, a person who has a ten-year-old automobile that doesn't start in cold weather may exhibit a great deal of interest in new car advertisements.

Therefore, if we define advertising from the perspective of the consumer, it might sound like the following

Advertising: One of several incoming messages directed at the consumer, the salience of which is influenced by the emotional, physical, and need state of the individual.

Advertising can also be defined from a societal perspective. Advocates of advertising would argue that advertising provides a valuable service to society and its members. In general, it helps define the meaning and the role of products and institutions for the consumer. It also provides consumers with information that indicated the differences that exist between product brands and the distinguishing characteristics of companies and institutions. This information also tells the consumer what a particular brand should do when used, how to evaluate this performance, and how to compare brands and institutions.

Advocates of advertising would also claim some economic benefits. There is little doubt that advertising does create greater product turnover, which in turn produces greater profitability for the company, which in turn produces more jobs and higher wages, and so forth. Thus, our improved standard of living can be tied directly to advertising. Another economic virtue attributed to advertising is the contention that advertising assists in ridding our society of ineffectual businesses. That is, businesses that are well-run and offer meaningful products tend to be helped through advertising. Businesses that are poorly managed and offer unwanted products tend to be eliminated through the impact of advertising.

Many critics of advertising feel that advertising is a detrimental force in our society. At one extreme, some people believe that advertising represents a waste of economic resources because of its large volume. Because advertising is so pervasive, some people also believe that advertising leads consumers to purchase things that they should not or do not need, thus misallocating economic resources and creating social pressures that lead people to act in ways that they would not if it were not for advertising. These critics feel that a great deal of advertising is misleading and that it takes advantage of the inherent weaknesses found in the consumer. A definition considered appropriate from a societal perspective would be:

Advertising: An institution of society that has the capability of informing the citizen, stimulating economic growth, and providing knowledge useful in decision-making, as well as the tendency both to misallocate scarce economic resources and lead consumers to engage in behaviour that may not be in their own best interests.

The final and perhaps most common, perspective of advertising is that of business. Business managers are most concerned with the benefits they obtain as a result of advertising. Most business managers believe that advertising is an important selling tool. They believe that it facilitates the sale of products or builds the reputation of companies by making consumers aware of the existence of both, in addition to conveying compelling information about the characteristics of products and companies to consumers. They also believe that advertising can help create sales by cultivating consumer readiness to buy.

Business managers also recognize the limitations found in advertising. They realize that some advertising is more effective, that advertising seems to work better with certain types of products. They acknowledge the fact that certain consumers will not buy in spite of extensive advertising and that some will buy without any advertising. Not all institutional reputations are enhanced by advertising. Many other marketing forces may affect product and institutional success. And the effect of specific advertisements may vary widely from consumer to consumer, both at a particular point in time and over a period of time.

Both critic and advocate agree that advertising is just a part of the total marketing effort required for success. They know that they must make a quality product that performs its function well, and that this product must be priced fairly and competitively. They know that the product must be available to the consumer in locations where they expect to find it. Finally, they know that the product must be sold through an aggressive promotional strategy that may include all the elements of promotion, or just one.

When it gets down to the final analysis, advertising is only valuable to businesses if it can create easy consumer identification of the advertised brand or institution. With this benefit comes a serious risk. Although advertising helps consumers identify the brand they wish to buy, it also helps them make a positive identification of those brands or institutions they wish to avoid because of bad reports or bad experiences. Essentially, the continued advertising of a particular brand or institution over several years is an implied warranty to the consumer that the product has met the test and is being used. The measure of success for any products is repeat purchase. The greater the consumer's satisfaction and the more repeat purchases, the bigger the economic base from which continuing advertising expenditures can be generated.

The definition of advertising that is most meaningful to business managers is one that identifies the parameters of advertising as well as its immediate and long-range goals. This is the definition provided by the American Marketing Association several years ago: Advertising is any paid form of non-personal presentation and promotion of ideas, goods, and services by an identified sponsor.

However, this definition doesn't really incorporate all the factors that are important to business managers. A better definition was offered by Wilkes and Wilcox. This definition describes the purpose of advertising, a more meaningful perspective.

Advertising's function is primarily to inform potential buyers of the problem-solving utility of a firm's market offering, with the objective of developing consumer preferences for a particular brand.

Classifying advertising

There are several bases for classifying advertising. Understanding the various ways in which advertising can be classified should be useful to the decision-maker because different types of advertising will be called upon depending upon the company's objectives in its advertising program.

Audiences

A variety of audience types exist to which advertising is directed. Some ads are directed at the ultimate users of the product who are referred to as the *consumer* audience. Others are directed to the companies or middlemen that distribute the product; these are referred to as the *business* audience. Both of these major categories can be further broken down into smaller and smaller sub-categories. For instance, the two most important business audiences are *dealers* and *manufacturers*. Consumer audiences can be reduced to a myriad of smaller groupings, for example, upper class, wine drinkers, Spanish-Americans, golfers, and so on.

Advertiser

National advertising is that sponsored by manufacturers or other producers. *Local* advertising is advertising placed by retailers or wholesalers that have markets usually confined to one locality. A further distinction between a manufacturer's and a retailer's advertising is that a manufacturer's advertising is designed to build a demand for the product, regardless of where it is purchased. In retailer's advertising, the stress is on the store. Retailers do not care what brand you buy, as log as you buy it in their store. Consequently retail advertising tends to emphasize patronage motives such as good location, good service, free delivery, and so forth.

Intention

Another basis for classifying advertising is in terms of the intention of the advertising. The two most general categories are *product* or *institutional*. In product advertising, advertisers are informing or stimulating the market about their products or services. This category can also be further sub-divided into *direct-action* and *indirect-action* advertising. The former advertising is intended to require a quick response to the advertisement. Ads that include a coupon with an expiration data or a sale with a date deadline would fall under this heading. Indirect-action advertising is designed to stimulate demand over a longer period of time. Advertisements are intended to inform customers that the product exists and to indicate its benefits and where it can be purchased.

Product advertising can also be classified as being *primary* or *selective*. In the case of primary advertising the purpose is to promote the demand for generic products or services. Thus, in the case of the American Dairy Association, the emphasis is on the product milk, it really doesn't matter which brand of milk you purchase. Selective advertising is used by a particular firm in order to create a demand for a particular brand. It typically follows primary advertising which more or less sets the stage for selective advertising.

Institutional advertising is designed to create a positive attitude toward the seller. Rather than selling a particular product or service, the objective is establishing a high level of good will. Institutional advertising can be further sub-divided into three areas: public relations, public service, and patronage.

Public relations institutional advertising attempts to create a favourable image of the firm among employees, stockholders, or the general public. To illustrate, for several years Phillips Petroleum has been running ads that highlight their contributions to medical technology and the environment.

Public service institutional advertising is illustrated by ads urging the public to give to the United Way or to use their seat belts. The National Football League continues to highlight the volunteer work of a football player with a United Way-supported organization.

Patronage institutional advertising, is designed to attract customers by emphasizing a patronage-buying motive rather than a product-buying motive. For example, a retailer might inform the public of her new sheltered parking lot or extended store hours. A manufacturer might describe his new warranty policy.

The importance of advertising

Advertising is one of the most pervasive entities in our business society in that it is used by virtually all manufacturers and retailers. The importance of advertising is easy to document—one need only look at the figures. One quantitative indication is the total amount spent on advertising in the several countries all of than are on upswing. The number one medium in terms of total money spent is still newspapers, although television is gaining. The growth in advertising expenditures have been rising faster than the gross national product, national income, or any other measure of business activity. Even the cost of producing a commercial is increasing rapidly.

Most of the growth in advertising has occurred since World War II. After the war, companies in western Europe and the Far East once again started to compete in the world markets, making advertising and other types of promotion essential parts of the new economy. Large corporations like General Motors and Coca-Cola have long been active all over the world, but since late 1960s many small and medium-sized companies have become international. Today, most large advertising agencies of the United States, western Europe, and the Far East have offices in several different countries.

Another dimension of advertising that alludes to its tremendous size is the number of people it employs. Although the exact number of people employed in all phases of advertising is unknown, the American Association of Advertising Agencies estimates that at least 200,000 work in the four primary areas of advertising: agencies, media, advertisers, and suppliers and special services.

Frequently, advertising expenses are expressed as a percentage of company's sales. It is interesting to note that some of the largest advertisers actually devote a very small percentage of sales to advertising. Many drug, cosmetics, and clearing firms, on the other hand, allocate a large percentage of their sales revenue toward advertising. A study conducted by the Conference Board showed that the average advertising as a percentage of sales was less than 2 per cent across the various types of manufacturers, middle agents, and retailers.

The history of advertising

Attempting to identify the progression of advertising through the ages is not an easy task. Although it is interesting to discuss the fact that advertising messages have been discovered on ancient pieces of papyrus or on cave walls, this has little relevance to our understanding or appreciation of advertising. Clearly, ever since individuals have attempted to sell goods or services they have engaged in various types of persuasive communications. Because of the extremely high rate of illiteracy, almost all early advertising was oral. Thus, the major media employed was the barker or town crier. Probably the next most common advertising medium was the sign. Again, because of the high illiteracy rate, most signs included both the name of the company and the product sold as well as a picture representing the product. In many societies, an elaborate system of codes was developed that told the consumer what was inside. Eventually, individual businesses began to customize their signs in order to differentiate themselves from other similar business. Soon, the customized signs were printed on the product itself and served as the basis for the trademark of today.

Perhaps the event that provided the greatest push for advertising as we understand it, was the invention of the newspaper in the early seventeenth century. It was in conjunction with the newspaper that the word advertisement first came into use. It was used as a heading for the commercial announcements section of the newspaper. Most of the ads were for books or for medicines.

Benjamin Franklin is considered the father of American advertising. From 1729, when he began publishing his newspaper. *The Pennsylvania Gazette,* until his death, he was the ultimate promoter. The *Gazette* had the largest circulation and the largest advertising volume of any paper in colonial America. In it one could find ads for ship sailings, quills, books, wine, tea, chocolate, and so forth. Franklin also made several innovations in newspaper advertising. For instance, he was the first to separate ads from one another by placing a border of white space. He also was the first to use a large heading for each ad, as well as the first to use illustrations and drawing within the ads.

Despite this interesting beginning, advertising as we have come to know it really had its beginnings in the mid-1800s.

From the period 1875 to 1905, a great many aspects of modern business setting had their birth. The first was the development of the factory system and mass production. As manufacturers began to make more than could be consumed in their immediate market, advertising developed in importance. In turn, as consumers began to depend upon brands that were manufactured by companies unfamiliar to them, they had to rely more and more on advertising.

Another business institution that had its birth during this period was the departmental store. Americans such as Jordan Marsh of Boston, John Wanamaker, and R. H. Macy, all began their newfangled stores during this time. The concept, as well as the products they carried, were new to the customer. These retailers found it necessary to aggressively advertise though all the media forms available—newspapers, magazines, and handbills.

At about this same time, A. Montgomery Ward of Chicago started the first general mail-order house in this country. Sears, Roebuck and Company soon followed in 1886. This innovation, the mail-order catalogue, was truly unique in that it was advertising with no story content at all. The success of the mail-order business brought a great deal of credibility and respectability to the activity of advertising.

The history of advertising is also entwined with the development and availability of media forms. Although there were probably several hundred newspapers in the late nineteenth century, no single newspaper was able to provide national coverage because of the problems of printing in one location and then delivering it across the country. But there emerged a vehicle that did not depend on the day-to-day events as its lifeblood—the magazine.

Although the publishers of early American magazines did not think of them as a means for carrying advertising, advertisers had different ideas. The first successful magazine in America was *Godey's Lady's Book,* a fashion magazine that appeared in 1830. The growth of the magazine industry was nothing less than phenomenal. Several reasons are posited for this success. First, Congress approved low postage rates, which allowed magazines and newspapers to be distributed economically. Second, some Americans viewed magazines as being the vanguard of culture. Finally, many Americans felt that magazines were truly American and could serve as a basis for establishing our own culture.

A final factor that helped the cause of advertising during the late nineteenth century was the emergence of the advertising agency. Volney Palmer is considered by most advertising historians to be the earliest advertising agent in the United States. He established himself as an agent in Philadelphia in 1841 and established branch offices in Boston and New York. These early agents were simply street salespeople who learned that they could earn more commissions if they represented not one but several newspapers and, later, magazines. Some also contracted annually with certain publications and, in effect, became brokers of advertising apace. George P. Rowell, a former bill collector for the Boston Post, brought ingenuity and stability to the agency business. He was interested in all media, and anticipating the needs of advertisers, he brought space in large quantities and resold it to advertisers in smaller lots at a profit. The publishers were happy to sell him space at reduced rates and let him act as a middleman. He was the first agent to guarantee payment to publishers for their space, instead of asking them to wait until the advertiser paid the agent. In 1888, he founded the first major magazine devoted to advertising in the United States, *Printers' Ink.*

During the first two decades of the twentieth century, advertising continued its phenomenal growth, spurred on by a society that was now on wheels. In 1915, the automobile industry was spending heavily on advertising. Now that millions of people were zooming along the highways, a new form of advertising emerged the billboard.

It was also during this period that trust-busting, expose, and reform programs became popular. It is not surprising that advertising was caught up in this cleanup movement. The Associated Advertising Clubs of America helped launch a campaign to promote truthful and ethical advertising. Several codes for truth in advertising were devised. Probably the most famous was the Printers' Ink Statute published in 1911. It was a model that indicated the types of activities that were considered ethical, unethical, and questionable.

The Roaring 20s were good times for advertising as well. By 1929, advertising was a $ 3.5 billion dollar industry in the U.S. Marketing, including advertising and personal selling, became important and respectable elements of business. A major new advertising medium, radio, was introduced during this period. By 1930, more than 50 per cent of the homes in the United States had radios.

In 1929, advertising plunged into the despair of the depression. Advertising billings dropped $ 2 billion in 1930. With over 14 million people unemployed, products remained on shelves because no one had money to purchase them. The public was looking for scapegoats for their troubles, and advertising became a prime target. The critics struck, at the very concept of advertising—advertising waste helped bring on the depression. Consumer unions were formed to evaluate and restrict all advertising. Laws were passed that were directed at advertising, such as the Wheeler-Lea Amendment of 1938, which granted the FTC the power to curb false advertising. Unfortunately, laws such as this were passed after the damage was done.

A positive outcome of the depression was that it brought research into advertising. With the heavy consumer resistance to advertising and product purchasing, learning more about the behaviour and motivations of the consumer became very important. It was during this time that A.C. Nielsen, George Gallup, and Daniel Starch started their research organizations and developed much of the technology that we are still using today.

The period since the end of World War II represents the modern era of advertising. Actually, during the war, advertising gained back much of its respectability. During this time, it was either patriotic or institutional, and the War Advertising Council was staffed by volunteer experts coming from all phases of professional advertising. This advertising genius quickly turned to the tremendous needs of the consumer following the war. People wanted new homes, automobiles, second cars, vacations, and a plethora of new products that they has not yet imagined. Most importantly, the development of television meant that a vital new vehicle for advertising had emerged.

As we approach the last decade of the twentieth century, advertising is still an extremely healthy business. With the advent of the satellite and computer technology, the potential appears unlimited. Nevertheless, a great many questions still need to be answered. What role will the government play in the future of advertising?

Is there still a place for the small advertiser or the small advertising agency? Will advertising be held more accountable for what they do and do not do? What new technologies lie over the horizon?

The administration of advertising

It is clear that advertising is big business, both in terms of dollars and complexity. During the last two decades, advertising has moved away from its more traditional business patterns and has adopted a more formal managerial approach. Today, most advertising results form careful planning implementation, control, and staffing, in order to make the advertisement' as effective and efficient as possible.

Within the advertising industry, a wide variety of means is available by which advertising is created and placed in media. At one extreme, advertisements are created, approved, and placed in media for dissemination by a single individual. The individual who writes and places a classified advertisement in a newspaper with the hope of selling his automobile is a good example of this kind of advertising activity. At the other extreme, a great deal of specialization is involved. The advertiser will retain the services of a full-service advertising agency to create and place her advertising retaining only the function of final approval of advertising and advertising plans developed by that agent. Within the full-service advertising agency organization, significant specialization is developed to discharge the various functions involved in planning and executive advertising programs for the various advertisers or clients that the agency serves.

At both of these extremes in the preparation and placement of advertising programs, and in between as well, a wide variety of skills and solutions must be applied to advertising problems. The greater the advertising appropriation, the more likely the work will be done by a full-service advertising agency and the many specialists employed by the agency. Whether or not the advertiser uses an advertising agency or does the advertising in-house, or some combination of the two, depends upon a host of factors unique to each organizations. Regardless of the decisions, a number of basic functions must be performed by someone if creative and effective advertisement are to be placed.

An overview of responsi-bilities

Individuals who are in charge of the advertising effort in any business have a variety of ultimate responsibilities—some of which they accomplish themselves and some of which they may delegate to an advertising agency. They must:

- decide what products, institutions, or ideas are to be advertised;
- decide whether to prepare advertising programs themselves or turn the work over to an advertising agency;
- engage and give policy and other direction to the advertising agency if an agency is used;
- develop their own advertising work or approve the advertising programs brought to them by the advertising agency;
- pay the advertising bill; and
- determine the extent to which the advertisements helped reach the stated objectives.

If an advertiser chooses to use an advertising agency, the role of the agency will typically revolve around the creation and production of advertising materials and the placement of these materials in the advertising media. To do this, the agency must be familiar with the advertiser, the products, problems, opportunities, and peculiarities. The advertisements produced by the agency should be consistent with all of these in order to maximize benefits the advertiser can bring to the particular situation.

The advertising media also can play a facilitating role in the advertising process. Media institutions can provide a host of technical expertise, as well as consumer information, scheduling advice, and assistance in the design of advertisements in particular mediums. Media assistance will tend to be more useful with the smaller advertiser who may not be able to afford the services of the advertising agency. In addition, there are a wide variety of suppliers of various production, research, and other services that are critical to the success of the advertising enterprise. Sometimes the advertiser contracts for such services directly; sometimes the advertising agency will contract for them in behalf of the advertiser.

The net result is that most national and regional advertising and some local advertising reflect the collective efforts of several individuals and institutions. Rather than attempt to discuss all of these institutions, the two most prominent ones, the advertising department and the advertising agency are presented.

The company advertising department: An advertising department can be a one-person operation or can employ fifty or more employees as is the case with Pepsi-Cola and Proctor and Gamble.

Regardless of the size, advertising departments have similar responsibilities: the formulation and supervision of an overall advertising program.

Unfortunately, most companies do not give advertising departments top priority. This is reflected by the fact that advertising departments receive only a small part of the total corporate budget. In addition, everyone in the organization tends to second-guess how this money should be spent. Sometimes this interference involves redirection of budget dollar spending.

The organizational structure of an advertising department depends heavily upon the size and complexity of that particular business. In an advertising department with fewer than ten employees, everyone usually reports to one individual who supervises the entire process. In larger companies, two structures tend to emerge. In companies like Black and Decker in which marketing operations are divided by product or division, each division has its own ad manager and staff that work solely for that one division within the corporation. In other large companies, such as Proctor and Gamble, brand mangers are responsible for the success of specific products and they select staff specialists who perform the advertising function. The types of specialists are assigned by the ad manager, who in truth will confer with brand and product mangers as well as distribution managers in order to initiate and develop programs.

Advertising managers tend to be held responsible for everything classified as *advertising* and *sales promotion*, even if it is designed by an advertising agency. The following activities tend to be the responsibility of the advertising manager:

1. Formulating the advertising program.
2. Implementing the program.
3. Controlling the program.
4. Presenting the budget.

5. Maintaining relationship with suppliers.
6. Establishing internal communications.
7. Setting professional standards.
8. Selecting an advertising agency.

The advertising agency: An advertising agency is an independent business organization that specializes in providing one or more advertising-related services to companies. The relationship continues from year to year until one side or the other decides, for whatever reason, to end it. It is amazing that, for the most part, these relationships tend to last for several years.

Although there are over many agencies, they vary tremendously in respect to size, service provided, skills, profitability, and the kinds of clients that are served.

When the term full-service agency is used, it does not necessarily refer to large agencies, for even relatively small agencies may qualify. A full service agency would tend to have five functional areas:

1. Creative—This includes the designing, recommendation, and creation of advertisements.
2. Media—This includes planning and purchasing the media units specified.
3. Financial—Maintain proper records in order to pay all of the individual media whose facilities have been used on behalf of a particular client.
4. Support Services—This may include marketing research, sales promotion, retail advertising, direct-mail, yellow pages, talent, and so on.
5. Account Management—The account manager is responsible for client-agency relationships.

In a typical agency most of the staff would work in the creative area, followed by the account management area. The advertising agency houses a wide variety of disciplines and perhaps an even wider range of educational backgrounds and personality types.

Advertising agencies earn their money through media commissions, production *add-ons,* and fees. The commission system is the best known of these techniques. Based upon a 15 per cent commission allowed by the media proprietor, the advertising medium presents a bill to the agency for the cost of the media service rendered to the agency as a purchaser on behalf of the advertiser. The agency bills the advertiser for this cost. The advertiser pays the agency the gross amount of the bill. The agency, in turn, remits the gross amounts less the 15 per cent commission back to the medium.

Under a fee arrangement, the agency and advertiser agree upon what the agency's compensation will be, without reference to the 15 per cent commission. The advertiser then pays less than the cost of media bills when rendered if they agreed upon fee amounts to less than 15 per cent. And the advertiser pays the agency an additional amount, beyond media bills, for agency service if the agreed fee exceeds the 15 per cent commission. This fee system tends to emerge when agencies have been undercompensated because clients have demanded excessive service, or when clients believe that the agency is overcompensated under the 15 per cent commission.

Agencies can also earn money through production additions. When agencies subcontract for services for their clients, they charge their clients for the service plus a markup of 15 to 20 per cent, with 17.65 per cent being the norm. This markup is the agency's attempt to earn the equivalent of its traditional media commission on non-commissionable purchases of photography, typography, engraving, printing, and so forth.

Media-buying services

Another service option available to advertisers is the media-buying company. This institution is relatively new in the industry, and since it only buys media, it can coexist with client's conventional agency. The basic organization operates as a wholesaler of media: buying large blocs of time or space at a wholesale rate and then selling them to clients at special prices below what conventional agencies can buy. More sophisticated services offer media planning, buying, and post-evaluation services. Some media services are paid a negotiated fee: others split the savings they realize with the advertiser. Agencies are not very receptive of these media specialists.

Boutique agencies

A boutique agency is a speciality shop that deals in a few services. Most concentrate on the creative services—art and copy. Since they do tend to specialize they keep their costs down and can charge lower fees. Owners of boutiques claim that they are restoring the basic purpose of the ad agency—creating ads.

Social and ethical issues in advertising

Very few industries have been more widely criticized than advertising. Even people who have little understanding of the technical or strategic elements of advertising are more than willing to assess its worth. These judgments are often based on nebulous criteria, partial information, hearsay, and emotions. Furthermore, these standards vary among factors such as culture, religion, race, age, and so forth.

Although it is impossible to provide a detailed discussion of all the social and ethical issues related to advertising, a brief discussion is beneficial.

Is advertising deceptive

Despite the importance placed on identifying deception in advertising, there is still great controversy in determining exactly what constitutes deception. Do advertisements have to be literally true if they are not to be deceptive? Do they merely have to give a true impression of the products or service? Unfortunately, even the FTC, the governing agency, had not clarified this issue either to the satisfaction of advertisers or consumers. Strong critics of advertising suggest that the FTC should go much further in defining deception and that all types of *puffery* should be considered deceptive and illegal. Consumer advocate Ralph Nader posits that he would regard as deceptive ads that claimed a brand contained "ingredient X" unless that ingredient was unique or unless the ad carried a statement disclosing the fact that it was not unique. Advertising advocates, such as Theodore Levitt, argue that if the products deliver the benefits the consumers expect, then the advertisements for them are perfectly acceptable, whether true or not.

Regardless of how deception is defined, most advertising practitioners agree that deception causes consumers to turn against a product and is consequently self-defeating. In addition, there is no evidence to show that deceptive advertising results in any more sales than non-deceptive advertising. A final deterrent to deception is the observability of advertising. Advertising is on record, inviting scrutiny that tends to keep dishonest people from using it regularly.

Is some advertising offensive or in bad taste?

If deception is a difficult concept to understand, terms like *offensive or bad taste* are even more difficult. This is such a totally subjective process that what is considered offensive by one segment of people may be considered quite mild by another. Criticisms of taste in advertising are provoked both by the products themselves and the manner of presentation. The National Association of Broadcasters, for example, recommended that certain intimate products, such as vaginal deodorants, should not be advertised on television because commercials promoting them would offend large numbers of people no matter now carefully they were written. The ban was later lifted, however, subject to restrictions such as "sexual themes or connotations are to be avoided." Of course, some people will be offended by any liquor advertisement or any ads having a sexual overtone, no matter how innocuous.

Some products are not offensive *per se*, but the advertising used to promote them may be objectionable. For instance, promoters of certain movies and books tend to over-emphasize the sensational aspects in order to attract customers. Even basic products such as perfume, jeans, and underwear are portrayed in a sexual or vulgar manner having very little to do with the function of the product.

This question of taste will continue to be one of the most controversial areas in advertising. There will always be creative people who insist on gaining attention by shocking people. Because copywriters are normally rather sophisticated, they can easily underestimate the shock value of a particular ad. Although this problem will probably never be totally eliminated, advertisers will continue to abide by the accepted rules of decency and taste of the audience they expect to reach.

Does advertising cause people to buy things they don't really need?

Assuming that advertisers create wants and desires is really much too simple. The creation of wants is a complex process governed by many factors, most of which are beyond the control of the advertiser. Despite criticisms to the contrary, advertising has a limited influence on the consumer. It is true that advertising does have the power to awaken desires, conscious and sub-conscious, but there is not trickery in this effort. As long as advertising is honest and presents relevant information, it will remain a valid partial basis for making purchase decisions.

The dilemma of creative advertising

Marketing people, as everyone else, have a sincere and understandable interest in observing the effects of their own activities. How else are they to know if their activities have real significance?

However, the vast majority of advertising men are denied this privilege. It is a pleasure reserved only for that small minority engaged in the preparation of advertisements which have some criterion of effectiveness built into them, such as mail-order ads.

Nevertheless, the experiences of this privileged minority have made possible the statement of certain principles which can be applied to advertising in general. Unfortunately, most of the advertising in our national media is witness to the fact that these principles are not very widely practised.

On the other hand, advanced consumer research leads to conclusions almost identical to those which have been arrived at by advertising people who have been permitted to see directly the results of their own work. What are some of the conclusions about effective advertising which have emerged from consumer studies and experiments?

Not Gimmicks for advertising's effectiveness

One conclusion is that intellectual gimmicks, cleverness, wittiness, or ingenious and tricky word combinations do not add to, but rather subtract from, the effectiveness of advertising. Even slogans are of doubtful value. In fact many of these so-called attention-getting devices actually operate as distractions.

Efficiency in advertising seems to depend on the use of simple language—simple direct presentation of sales arguments—and the avoidance of tricky attention-getting devices unrelated to the product itself. Here are a few examples.

An advertisement for phonograph records uses an illustration of a woman breaking a phonograph record by stepping on it. Presumably this illustration is intended to catch the consumer's attention and lead to the next revelation: that steel needles also ruin phonograph records. To be sure, the needles do not ruin them as thoroughly or as quickly as a woman stepping on them, but nevertheless they do serious harm. After this devious opening gambit, we are finally permitted to learn the moral of the story—the true sales point: diamond needles preserve records.

The creator of this copy apparently had convinced himself that the consumer would not be interested in the simple fact that phonograph records are ruined by steel needles but can be preserved by using diamond needles. Therefore, the copy writer felt compelled to try to catch the consumer's attention by the "more interesting" picture of a record being brutally broken by a woman's foot.

In another advertisement, traveller's cheques were offered as the right way to carry money. But in the headline the word "right" was spelled "write". The copy writer seems to assume that the reader of the advertisement wants to be entertained, to be impressed by wittiness and by an unusual use of the English language. He assumes that the reader will be pleasantly surprised to see this game of words. This pleasant feeling, he hopes, will generalize to the traveller's cheques and will increase the reader's interest in using them instead of cash when he travels.

These examples are so extremes as to be almost unrealistic. However, in almost any copy of a national magazine we can find milder forms of the same disease: tomato catsup described as "what eggs scramble for," television picture-tube purchasers exhorted not to be "Vidiots," or a telephone instrument described as a "conversation piece." We can also find roses growing out of liquor bottles, dogs dressed policemen, and women apparently walking on clouds. Are the products to be sold so pitifully drab and uninteresting that the consumer must be entertained or shocked before he will attend to them?

An even more innocent appearing example was brought to light several years ago. For many years the Socony Mobil Oil Company used the symbol of "the flying red horse" to identify its service station outlets. The argument in favour of using this symbol rather than the simple word "Mobil" was that the flying red horse gave pleasure to the motorists who viewed it, and suggested lightness, power, and speed, whereas the single word "Mobil" was drab and colourless. Considerable evidence had been accumulated that the horse was an inefficient communication.

As a final assault on this question, the following experiment was designed:

An automobile equipped with movie camera was driven along roads where Mobilgas and other gas stations were located. As the camera moved along, it photographed every gasoline outlet on the way. After the film was developed, the number of Mobil stations and other brands was equalized. To avoid bias, the selection was random.

Various audiences were invited to see the movie thus prepared, and afterwards every member in each audience was requested to tell what brands of station signs were on the road, and approximately how many of each he thought there were. The frequency of the flying red horse sign was underestimated down to about one-half of that of its most efficient competitor. The outcome of this experiment revealed that the station sign of Socony Mobil Oil Company was losing substantial parts of its competitive sales opportunities by clinging to a symbol which has associations which were pleasant but irrelevant to the problem of identifying Mobil stations.

These advertisements and signs communicate in a manner that deviates drastically from communication as it takes place in other phases of our daily life... in the editorials of newspapers and magazines, in teaching, in simple conversation, and in ordinary sales talk. Directness and simplicity have been replaced by carefully contrived detours, which can be very costly indeed.

A simple change in the wording of a headline may increase the efficiency of an advertisement by several hundred per cent. For example, in a split-run test the following two headlines were compared: "New Jobs Are Offered In Television Station" and "Television Courses for $11.60 per week." The first of these headlines returned six times as many orders as the second—six times the value for an identical investment in advertising space. If a change only in a headline can produce differences of this order of magnitude, imagine how these differences might be compounded by changes in the whole copy treatment.

It seems a modest hope that an increase in the knowledge of the principles of advertising will enable an advertiser to double, at least, the value he receives for each advertising dollar invested.

The overlooked familiarity principle

The average "expert" in advertising must apply a substantial part of his ingenuity and inventiveness to tricks and gimmicks which *lower* the efficiency of advertising, rather than *raising* it. If it is true that a simple change in the wording of a headline can produce a six-fold change up or down in the efficiency of the ad, why do we not more often notice advertising campaigns leading to business disaster?

The reason is that at least two mechanisms operate in advertising. One of these, the "Persuasion Principle," has been widely discussed in writings on advertising. The second, which we may call the "Familiarity Principle," has been much neglected.

The familiarity mechanism in advertising is often overlooked in analytical discussion of advertising. However, it is possible for this mechanism to operate effectively even in an advertisement in which persuasion operates at an almost negligible level.

Thus, a consumer confronted with two products, and having no knowledge of the physical characteristics of either of them will almost certainly choose the one whose brand name is more familiar to him. Consequently, a piece of advertising which does nothing else but mention the name of the product will contribute something to the sales of that product, simply by creating an awareness of the brand name that generates this minimum amount of confidence. Advertising can survive, and even give the appearance of some efficiency, by trading on this unavoidable, minimum effect of familiarity. Many advertisers, in fact, can afford to rest their whole case on it. Marketers of chewing gum, soft drinks, and cigarettes often have gained a powerful position through the deliberate use of advertising that concentrates on simply making the brand familiar by merely showing the brand name.

Copy and flexibility

But advertising copy is intended to perform a function *beyond* the mere development of familiarity with the brand name. Copy is intended to shape motives and desires, to build believability, and to provide a reason for selecting a particular brand over all others. It is the most flexible part of the advertising message. In the development of advertising, it is the copy function which demands the greatest skill, creativeness, and intelligence.

Every advertising man wants to create "good" copy. And yet what criteria can the advertising man appiy in deciding that one piece of copy is good and another bad? What are the criteria of efficiency in copy? The great problem is that we cannot relate a *specific* sales increase or decrease to a *specific* advertising act such as a copy treatment, a sound effect, a headline or a sales point. Indeed, it is almost naive to imagine that any relationships can be established between specific advertising actions and sales.

The reasons are manifold. For one thing, even in the most favourable marketing situation which we can contrive, it is difficult to separate the *familiarity* effect from the *persuasive* copy effect of advertising. A piece of advertising with "depressing" copy can fall back upon the familiarity principle as long as a brand name is mentioned. Many advertising successes which are attributed to copy are in reality simply the unavoidable minimum success solidly secured by the Familiarity Principle.

Furthermore, when we attempt to relate specific advertising actions to specific sales effects, we must get rid of the cumulative effect of advertising over a period of years. For an old established product, the cumulative effect of previous advertising will greatly outweigh any specific contemporary advertising action. Therefore, old established products make the observation of causal relations between specific copy and specific sales impossible. Nor do we realize any advantage if we are dealing with an entirely new product. It is never possible to separate advertising's effect from the contributions of ingenuity in product design, packaging, or distribution. Thus, the copy writer must always be denied the advantage of being able to observe the effect of a specific copy action in a specific sales success.

In almost every other field of human endeavour, the development of proficiency and skill depends upon being able to observe the effects of our actions. Let us imagine that builders of pianos were forever forced to build their products in a vacuum where there is no sound and sell them to "clients" without ears. After forty years or so of working under such conditions, we should expect that the piano designers would be turning out very attractive pieces of furniture, but we should have no right to expect that this furniture could product music. If we should happen to mention to the piano builder that his instruments do not sound good and that his activity is inefficient, he would probably not be surprised. Indeed, he would consider us unreasonable if we blamed him for his inefficiencies, so long as she is denied the privilege of hearing the results of his activity.

Today the copy writer creates his message in the vacuum of the modern distribution system without being able to see the effects of that message unfold. Then he sells his creations to a client who has no sensory organs to observe what a specific phrase does to a prospective consumer.

The creative advertising man is deprived of the natural rewards that any sincere individual wants. He wants to see the results of what he does; and yet our entire marketing system forces a blind-fold over his eyes. The primary rewards of seeing the results of his actions are replaced by the secondary rewards of praise from his colleagues, bosses, and clients. And the people who confer these rewards are in no better position to see the results of the man's action than is the copy writer himself.

Let us imagine that the copy writer proposes an entirely efficient piece of copy for his client. This copy consists of simple language and uncluttered, straight-forward sales presentations—without gimmicks, tricks, or intellectual surprises—copy equipped with the most ingenious and most invisible device of letting the product impress the listener or reader. The client reviews the copy and before approving it, happens to think. "This copy writer does not seem to be using his imagination. He talks only about the product itself, and does not add anything of his own." So, the copy writer efforts but it actually rebuked for failing to show "imagination."

It is quite natural, then for the copy writer to resort to the use of tricks, gimmicks, and devices that will entertain, startle, or humour himself, his intellectual friends, and the client. The emphasis is shifted from ends to means—from *what* advertising should say, to *how* it should say it. It is unfortunate, but not surprising, that the creative man now diverts his efforts from making the *product* interesting to making the *advertising* interesting . Ultimately he is no longer selling the product to the consumer, but selling the advertising to his client.

The difficult and even unfair position in which the creative man finds himself may be illustrated by the following analogy. Imagine a room with a large window that looks out on a beautiful countryside. On the wall opposite the window are three mirrors. The first mirror is uneven, spotted, and dirty looking. The second mirror is clean and neat, and in addition is framed by a beautiful ornamental engraving. The third mirror has no frames or ornament, and is nothing but a plain, but perfectly flawless mirror. Now, an observer is taken into the room and his guide points to the first mirror and says, "What do you see?" The observer says, "I see a bad mirror." His guide points to the second mirror and asks again, "What do you see?" The observer says," "I see a beautiful mirror." Finally his guide point to the third mirror and says, "What do you see?" The observer says, "I see a beautiful scene out of an open window."

Obviously, the third mirror has done the most efficient job. It is the function of an efficient mirror to reveal with perfect clarity the object to be mirrored without interference—that is, without making the mirror itself visible.

It is likewise the function of perfect advertising to step behind its own means—its own tricks and gimmicks—and push the products so much into the foreground that the advertising itself, psychologically speaking, can be overlooked. It may be disappointing to the maker of mirrors to discover that his most efficient mirror is one which the prospective customer is unaware. The very perfection of the mirror conceals itself from the observer. The advertising man, unless he takes pleasure in perfection, will also be disappointed to discover that the more perfect he makes his advertising, the less it becomes noticeable as "Advertising."

The advertiser's opportunity

How can advertising rise above this situation in which only its inefficiencies are capable of producing reward for its creator?

We cannot normally expect the copy writer to take the initiative. He is human, and must respond to the rewards and punishments which are offered to him. His client, the advertiser, on the other hand, is in a much better position because he controls the rewards and punishments meted out to the copy writer.

Let the client relieve the copy writer of the burden of having to prove his " imaginative" and "creative" powers by forcing him to resort to tricks and gimmicks. Let him trust the copy writer's professional competence to use correct grammar and an attractive style. Let him then concentrate on *what* the copy writer says, rather than *how* he says it. This would surely have the effect of restoring the sales point to its rightful position of importance in advertising.

The development of a sales point is one of the most challenging problems in advertising. Sometimes the best sales point is intimately related to the main function of the product. For example, the function of antihistamines is to relieve cold symptoms, and this turns out to be their best sales point. On the other hand, the main purpose of face soap is to clean the face. But the cleaning power of face soap is not an interesting sales point for face soap. It is not always easy to decide for a particular product what will be an efficient sale point. For hair tonic, for example, is it better to say that it prevents quenches thirst or that it has a distinctive flavour?

Advanced marketing research justifies its existence in terms of its ability to discover the most efficient sales points for a particular brand. This is the real core of advertising and its most challenging problem area. This is the center where creativeness can makes it most fruitful contribution. Only the advertiser has the opportunity to bring the sales points back into advertising... to make the advertising product-oriented rather than advertising-oriented.

Comfortable illusion about creativeness

Superficial reasoning easily sinks to the level of platitude where the following pseudo-logical argument sounds convincing. First of all, advertising has to get the attention of viewers, readers, and listeners. A given advertising message competes within an inexhaustible number of other advertising messages. Therefore, a given, piece of advertising, to meet this competition, must put something out of the ordinary before the eyes and ears of the potential consumers. Ideally, a given piece of advertising should look or sound different from any other piece of advertising.

This kind of reasoning bypasses the product and, therefore, the advertising function. The ideal statement should be to formulate: "A given piece of advertising should make the product look different from all other products, without violating the truth."

That the easiest and least "creative " mental effort leads to the "Attention-getting advertising" escapes superficial reasoning.

A printed ad under the headline "Your Father in the Cesspool" would get good attention. Not much useful imagination goes into the headline. However it requires a surplus of intelligence, analytical power, and useful imagination to find an interesting headline which leads the reader to read the text in the anticipation of learning about a useful product.

In advertising discussions, the term "create" and its derivatives are partially misused and misunderstood. "Imagination" is confused with "creativeness." Imagination is a fundamental and elementary requirement. Creativeness denotes the *advanced* form of imagination where it is *purposively* used by abiding to rigid rules and by meeting practical conditions.

Children on a playground and many patients in mental hospitals display extraordinary imagination. But the imagination in these instances is usually without the discipline of organization, selection, and constructiveness. It is not, in other words, *creative*. An advertising man who claims that the acceptance of rules and conditions interferes with his creativeness is probably unaware of the fact that he is seeking a licence which the real creative geniuses in arts and sciences would consider embarrassing. Creativeness is the opposite of pure freedom of imagination. To create something means to *build* something along rules of usefulness or purposiveness... to build an intellectual or mechanical organism.

Leonardo da Vinci spent a lifetime seeking the rules within his visual imagination which could produce more powerful creations. To be creative in advertising means to have so much imagination that it does not "fizzle out" as soon as product orientation is imposed. If the advertising man believes that the product itself has no virtues worth the attention of the consumer, be should suggest taking it off the market. If he believes that the product has a right to be on the market, and yet believes that it has no property worth the attention of the public, he is obviously overlooking the most serious and most creative obligation of advertising—*to find an approach which makes a good product look good and thereby interesting*. If, in the advertising man's opinion a product is justified in being on the market, then the advertising man's consider it justifiable that consumers pay money for the product. Where should we position advertising in our company and how should we organize it?

This question is being asked by a growing number of chief executive officers and top marketing men today, and the reason is clear. They are experiencing advertising problems and inefficiencies that no longer respond to conventional treatment: hiring a hot new agency or injecting new faces in the advertising department lends hope for a time, but when the dust has settled the same old problems and the same inefficiencies are often there, framed against a background of rising marketing costs.

A Liggett & Myers marketing executive, speaking to an audience of advertising and marketing executives a few years ago, asked, "Would you believe that the marketing problems which many companies are now experiencing might stem not from people but from the *way that management has the people working?"*

In the light of studies made since then, his insight looks increasingly sound. In particular, we find compelling evidence that the primary problems of advertising are rooted in the basic plan by which companies handle the work of advertising.

"The plan for handling the work" is, of course, one of the simplest definitions of organization. But advertising organization—the plan for handling the work of advertising—is anything but simple today. Advertising work is no longer a sideline speciality handled mainly by the advertising department and the agency. As advertising has grown unimportance it has received a growing work input from sales, product, and brand managers; from marketing heads, from general managers and top management, and from many others in engineering, manufacturing, and finance who often play a part in the approval and budgeting of advertising.

Getting this growing band of persons—including some who have little feeling for advertising—to team together on the delicate job of turning out consistently effective advertisements or commercials is a challenge that relatively few companies meet. Surprisingly, the challenge has evoked relatively little organized thought and effort, despite signs that growing organization problems are cancelling much of the nation's growing investment of advertising dollars and advertising creativity.

Large multi-division companies have the lion's share of knotty advertising organization problems today and the most to gain by applying the principles and practices covered in this chapter. At the same time, other companies, including smaller, non-divisionalized firms, will find that most of the problems discussed here apply equally well to them, and that the problems which are not yet acute will became so as their companies grow, acquire more divisions, decentralize, or possibly merge with a multi-division company. In short, these other companies have much to gain by anticipating and avoiding serious problems around the bend.

The studies on which this chapter is based emphasize that the big opportunities for improving marketing communications are not concentrated in the consumer-product companies in which advertising is obviously such a big factor in corporate success. Instead, the opportunities are widespread. Most large multi-division industrial product companies—especially those that have products and markets that are reasonably kindred —can usually benefit just as much as the company selling toothpaste, toasters, or biscuits. They can do so because they are usually able to implement more of the principles and practices that follow in this chapter and extend them to a much broader range of marketing and corporate communications.

Root of the problem: marketing fragmentation

The chief executive can often trace his most serious advertising problems to a series of vital, and successful, operating decisions which he or his predecessors made in the preceding decade or so: decisions to add products and grow, to acquire, diversify, divisionalize, decentralize, and then continue diversifying.

In this process, he necessarily transferred much of the direct responsibility for line marketing from headquarters to his division heads. As their individual operations grew, they usually were forced to delegate much of it to marketing managers who, in turn, delegated part of it to product or brand managers.

For companies with a swelling list of products and markets, this fragmentation of the overall marketing effort has usually given it increased vitality, flexibility, and effectiveness. Clearly, more managers are needed at lower levels to get the company to grasp the many marketing programs and the increasing complexity of modern marketing.

But what about the advertising sector of marketing? The record indicates that, to date, it has not proved nearly so adaptable to decentralization and fragmentation as have other marketing functions. Where line marketing has matured, it is true that advertising, along with other marketing functions, has received better marketing direction, better decisions on what marketing objectives to pursue, what products to promote to what market, and what to spend on each program. More often than not, this important gain in *direction* has been largely offset by losses in the follow-through stages of advertising *execution*, that is, in the delicate and increasingly complex process of determining how to say it.

The problem plainly hinges on the difficulty of transferring responsibility for the creative execution of advertising from a few individuals to many. Because of this difficulty, relatively few companies have found a way to fragment their advertising activity and still retain for top management a business like control of its quality and effectiveness.

The main symptom: spotty advertising

In the multi-division company the dominant symptom of advertising organization problems is the spotty quality of advertising done for the various divisions and subsidiaries.

This is emphasized today by the fact that some of it is top-notch, usually better than anything done in the past. Most of it, however, has to be labelled run-of-the-kill, a trail of wasted opportunities to the professionals who turn out the top programs. A part of it is usually so mediocre that even the unhappy agency that turned it out will privately agree that it is probably wasteful.

Thus, when the marketing minded chief executive officer and his associates go to the conference room for that periodic review of company-wide advertising, they witness a growing quality-control problem that would set off no end of alarms on the production line. Frequently, it sets off an explosion in the conference room too. Too often, nothing comes of it because the responsibility for advertising effectiveness is so widely diffused that top management, and even top marketing management, has lost control of it.

In companies that are marketing leaders, the chief executive is weary of being told he needs advertising; he knows it. He is wary of those who continually tell him, with a commissionable glint in the eye, that he needs more of it; he knows that better advertising could obviate the need for more. He stands ready, however, to welcome and reward the rare marketing man, advertising manager, agency head, or management consultant who can tell him what he needs to do get strong, professional advertising for *all* his divisions, to support *all* his major marketing opportunities.

Conventional advertising wisdom no longer holds

What, he asks, does it take to upgrade the bottom 80 per cent of that advertising and boost the return on the large investment it represents?

Quick answers and conventional wisdom no longer help him very much. Advertising, he is reminded, is a "people business." A creative-people business. If he wants top-notch advertising right across the board, he must have top-notch creative people in all his agencies and, it is hoped, in his headquarters and division advertising staffs. To the degree that he fails to procure the needed creative personnel, his company-wide advertising display on the conference-room wall will contain large patches of mediocrity.

Why, he asks, do those same advertising people who made such a big splash for another division, or another company, create scarcely a ripple when they take on some of his divisions that most need help in advertising and marketing? Indeed, why do some of them with the best records even decline at times to tackle some of his toughest problems?

If he will follow through on these questions, the chances are that he will head directly into the subject of advertising organization, into the way that management has the advertising personnel, the product and brand managers, and all the others working on the process of planning and creating his advertising programs.

Guidelines for effectiveness

He will find, too, that there are ways in which he can provide a relatively small group of creative persons with the leverage needed to improve that bottom 80 per cent of his division advertising.

The eleven guide rules that follow are those that others have used most effectively to do that.

1. *Put Your Advertising Organization Plan in Writing:* This is the first decision to make. Doing so permits you to get the plan endorsed by the chief executive officer and distributed by him to all those who play a key role in funding, planning, approving, and creating advertising.

Without this step, and without continuing top-level interest and support, the record shows that the best advertising organization plan is soon pulled out of shape, and the work of the best advertising personnel is watered down.

Decide, too, right at the start, that your company advertising plan will go beyond the general objectives, the organization charts, and the all-purpose position guides that so often pass for a plan. To work, your plan must face the sensitive questions of basic responsibility that today are usually swept under the rug with the explanation that it is better to "play it loose" and leave these things to "collaboration". The collaborators are very apt to produce unhappy compromises if you do not make it clear who sets the marketing direction the advertising is to follow, who is responsible or executing the advertising and approving it and who has the last word in the hiring of a new advertising agency.

The remaining guide rules that follow are intended to help you write this plan. They deal with basic factors in the order in which most companies will want to consider them.

2. *Nail Down the Major Advertising Objectives:* These objective must provide a clear written understanding of what you are organizing to do. This most obvious of needs is the most overlooked.

Naturally, these objectives will often be framed at lower levels, but in their final approved form, they should reflect the considered advertising needs of the company as seen by the chief executive officer. Then, they are most apt to provide not only for the needs of the individual operating divisions, but also for company front advertising or marketing programs he considers vital, and for coordination of advertising with other company communications programs.

For example, the president of one integrated, multi-division company with a wide range of kindred products and markets established this relatively ambitious priority of needs:

a. Provide highly effective skills for improving the advertising programs of all divisions.

b. Integrate advertising fully with the marketing of individual products of the divisions.

c. Establish effective cross-division or company-wide advertising programs to support marketing programs in which a group of related products from various divisions are promoted as a group to common markets.

d. Coordinate product advertising of the divisions with other related communication programs whenever this will increase the combined impact and lower the overall cost of these programs.

Why, some ask, is it necessary to formalize objectives such as a and b? Surely, everyone in a multi-division company would agree and work for them. The reason for emphasizing them is painfully clear to anyone who, over the years, has grappled with the realities of providing both of these requirements. One finds these two "obvious" needs to be largely in conflict if he adopts one of the more common methods of positioning and organizing advertising in a multi-division company. For this reason, much of the advertising of multi-division companies is apt to be weak on either marketing integration or on creative technique, or both. For this reason, keeping both of these basic objectives up front and centre, on paper, provides a healthy stimulus to innovate and to adapt the advertising organization in ways that will fill both needs in good measure. It is even more important to do so when other objectives such as c and d are added.

3. *Position and Structure the Advertising Department to Achieve Top-management Objectives.* When should the product advertising activity be centralized in a multi-division company? When should it be decentralized? How can you strike the balance that best fills your specific needs?

Usually, the man who organizes the overall marketing operation has a quick and simple answer: Advertising, an integral part of marketing should be centralized or decentralized to the same degree and in much the same way as marketing. How else, the reasons, can we hold the operating divisions in a multidivision company responsible for overall results and for profit?

This quick answer sounds logical and is usually adopted because it is the simplest way to decide the matter in the decentralized multi-division company. Nevertheless, it should be questioned by the executive who is intent on increasing the effectiveness of his overall advertising investment. By investing some extra thought and effort, a knowledgeable task group can usually come up with a better solution.

If its members have an intimate grasp of the sensitive advertising process and of the marketing operation in an operating division, they will be able to evaluate the relative advantages of centralization and decentralization in terms of the company's specific marketing and advertising needs?

The "scores" for centralization and decentralization, in the two right-hand columns, were agreed on by a task force in the same company at the start of its study of the advertising organization.

In arriving at the scores, the task force was influenced by past experience in their own companies and in other companies it studied. This told them that a centralized advertising department has a clear advantage in providing effective advertising skills, in handling multidivision or corporate advertising, and in coordinating advertising with other communications programs such as public relations. It also told them, however, that it usually had difficulty in integrating advertising programs with individual division marketing programs as effectively as a decentralized advertising organization.

Filling out this chart will seldom point out any sure answers, but it can reveal the major problems and opportunities. In this case, it showed the task force that they were unlikely to fill their basic advertising needs if they followed any of the conventional patterns for centralizing or decentralizing the advertising function. This, in turn, caused them to break trail later on in developing a sound blend of centralization and decentralization, one that in actual experience is now scoring high on all four of the advertising objectives set forth by the chief executive officer. They did this by implementing a number of the basic principles and practices discussed later in this chapter.

Other Alternatives: After determining the degree of centralization or decentralization needed, we must decide where the advertising function can best be positioned in the headquarters or division organization, and how it should be structured. Although there is no end of possible variations of the most common methods, a task force having a good feeling for both advertising and overall marketing and narrow the alternatives quickly and logically by following the same basic discipline described above, that is, by matching the various alternatives against the company's established advertising objectives. In this chapter, we can include only a few of the most helpful insights:

a. Don't be unduly influenced by what other companies do. To date, few have given their advertising organization the study it deserves, so copying even the leaders in your field can put you far behind where you would be if you wisely organized to fill your specific needs.

b. Frequently, you can best fill your needs by combining the advantages of two alternative methods, and taking specific steps to overcome the inherent disadvantages of each. The guide rules that follow will help you do this.

c. When the marketing organization is organized by product or by market, the product advertising activity should usually be structured in the same way to integrate best the advertising and marketing effort. However, when the marketing organization is structured by function, it does not follow that advertising should be organized by advertising sub-function.

d. Organization by advertising sub-function is most feasible in companies marketing basic materials or services which do not require the advertising men to acquire deep knowledge of a wide range of products and complex applications. Frequently, supporting functional units attached to a product-or market-type organization provide the best balance. In general, going to a basic productor market-type advertising organization offers these advantages over a functional organization:

1. It minimizes the functional fences between advertising sub-function and simplifies development of unified programs.

2. It helps develop marketing minded advertising men who talk the language of the product and marketing managers, work with them more effectively, and become better prepared for higher marketing responsibilities within the company.

3. *Make Sure That Advertising Gets Sound Marketing Direction*: It is helpful when everyone concerned with advertising thinks of the direction setting and the execution parts of advertising as the first and second halves of a single process. This is a healthy reminder that a poor job on the direction-setting first half of the process assures poor advertising results regardless of the dollars, zeal, and creativity poured into the creation of the advertising program.

This helps to flag the unfortunate fact that, at all levels in the company, attention is apt to be focused primarily on the more exciting, ever-changing second half, the final execution. Too little thought and effort go into the fact-getting and painful decision-making that must often precede it. Consequently, the advertising, even though bright, creative, and provocative, often runs like a loose pulley on a shaft.

Although many marketing heads are well aware of this, it is safe to say that providing sound, clear-cut marketing direction is seldom done well unless a marketing-minded top management insists on firm practices for doing the job thoroughly.

The written marketing plan—approved and supported by division management and in line with corporate level plans—is far and away the most effective management tool for giving sound direction to advertising and to all other marketing functions as well.

Written marketing plans capable of doing this are still relatively uncommon, as any candid survey of advertising and marketing men will quickly reveal. This is true despite all the emphasis on modern marketing since the early 1950s, and despite broad agreement that a sound written marketing plan is the key to its implementation.

Actually, many of these companies have in the past made an earnest effort to initiate written marketing plans for all major programs, only to have the effort bog down. The trouble, it seems is that they tried to go too far in a single leap. Their people were not ready for the fact-getting and planning disciplines that are required. The plans were bulky but inadequate, division management did not use them as a plan of action, and the whole effort was, in many cases, talked into disrepute.

With this in mind, the following method is suggested for the many companies who desire but still do not have adequate written marketing plans, and whose advertising still suffers for lack of unified direction. Many companies have used this method to develop written marketing plans in a logical transition.

a. *Move first to a plan that provides sound marketing direction for product advertising.* A real marketing plan—like real marketing itself—has two main parts:

1. *An analysis of the problem* that provides a basis of fact for major conclusions and marketing objectives.

2. *A plan of action* that calls for integrated teamwork of all functions involved. It tells who is in charge, who does what and when to achieve the established marketing objectives.

The follow-through plan of action is, of course, the payoff part of modern marketing and of corporate-level planning as well. It is also the point at which marketing planning and corporate-level plans often stumble. The great majority of organizations that meet difficulty or defeat in trying to go all the way in one step may well consider a preliminary step that takes them well past the midway point. This is to prepare what some companies call a *marketing audit* for advertising and sales promotion alone. The first part includes, necessarily, the same analysis of the problem needed for a complete marketing plan. The plan of action, however, is limited *initially* to the plan of action for advertising and sales promotion.

b. *Upgrade the marketing audit into a real marketing plan.* This marketing audit will provide sound marketing direction for advertising. It will also give all the operating people who are exposed to it some feeling of what a full marketing plan could do for them. The first part of the marketing audit—the analysis of the overall marketing problem, basic conclusions, and resulting marketing objectives—is naturally useful for the other marketing functions, and adds some degree of marketing coordination.

However, its inadequacy as a real marketing plan stands out. Missing is the follow-through plan of action for functions other than advertising. Why do all that work for advertising alone? Why not include our plan of action too? At this point, a marketing-minded management can fan this dissatisfaction into positive action that adds the plan of action for all major functions, plus clear-cut management responsibility for carrying out the entire plan.

Why should management use the advertising plan in this way to spearhead full marketing planning? Actual experience offers two reasons:

1. In many companies, the annual advertising plan is usually the best annual written plan in the area of marketing. Advertising men, by necessity, are familiar with planning techniques.
2. The discipline of planning to communicate publicly with customers and prospects creates an ideal climate and a sharp needle for digging up available marketing facts and initiating marketing research to get what is not them available.

For this reason, a team of marketing-minded advertising and line marketing people can usually do the best job of annually updating the first part of a marketing plan, that is, analyzing the overall marketing problem, arriving at conclusions, and setting objectives. What's more, this job, very costly if done separately, gets done at little cost as a natural by product of the advertising process. It provides, each year, a stimulus for division management to add the follow through plan of action for all functions and create a real marketing plan.

5. *Organize to Attract, Encourage, and Protect Creativity.* To do this, we return again to one of the most practical organizing concepts of advertising, the allocation of advertising responsibility into the direction-setting "what" of the product or marketing manager and the functional or creative "how" of the advertising man.

While most top executive and marketing managers readily support the concept of dividing advertising responsibility in this way, few of them ever do what it takes to go from the concept to the actual practice of it. Firming the responsibility at the "What" "How" line, they fear, will introduce human problems and further diffuse advertising responsibility. Even the advertising mean often hesitate to push for it, apparently feeling that the marketing trend of the past decade—in which many of them have lost control of the "how"—has gone too far to arrest, and that, despite the spotty advertising, they are no longer in a position to bell the cat.

For these reasons, the understanding and personal support of the chief executive is usually essential to implement this sound principle of advertising organization. And he, along with his marketing people, has a compelling reason to do so: all signs indicate that those companies that have really taken the step have almost always been able to upgrade the quality of their advertising throughout their various divisions and to boost the return on their advertising investment. In implementing the concept, he can draw on a sound rationale and on specific practices that leading companies have used successfully.

The Rationale: Men who excel in making the hard "what" decisions in marketing and in other functions of a business usually come from a different mold than those who excel in making the "how" or creative decisions in advertising. The record throughout industry indicates that relatively few can make both types of decisions without turning in a mediocre performance in one area or the other.

How about the product or brand managers who are making an important contribution in many consumer-product companies? To an increasing degree, they and their marketing managers work directly with the advertising agency and give the final stamp of approval to both the "what" and the "how" of their advertising. Do they not disprove the above rationale, and perhaps point the way for the successful integration of advertising within the line marketing organization throughout all industry?

Would that they did and could! For then the advertising organization problems of the multi-division company would be far simpler. But we must note that the product manager's direction of advertising "how" is, increasingly, being questioned. And we must also note that the product or brand managers who wear both "what" and the "how" hats successfully are usually in companies that a management consultant is apt to classify as "advertising companies" insofar as advertising is a prime factor in their marketing success. Consequently, advertising is the major part of the job—the part in which they have the most clear-cut responsibility and authority. Indeed, some of those who wear both hats successfully are marketing-minded former advertising men recruited from the company advertising department or the agency—men who have a good feeling for advertising quality themselves and who know how to give adequate rein to a capable creative agency. Their other marketing duties are mainly as a coordinator of functions over which others exercise line responsibility. As product managers, they are primarily advertising men, and they are as much the exception as the product manager in a science oriented company selling complex equipment for space exploration, who is apt to be 95 per cent engineer.

The great bulk of product managers through industry have heavy responsibilities other than advertising, with experience and aptitudes to match. The growing problems of advertising organization in multi-division companies attest to the fact that they cannot successfully wear both the "what" and the "how" hats of advertising.

6. *Use the advertising agency for all the work it can do best—without relinquishing self-sufficiency in providing marketing direction.* An ANA study conducted by Booz, Allen & Hamilton shows that the agency services used by leading United States marketers extend across this entire range:

1. Advertising only

2. Advertising and selected services in areas such as sales promotion and marketing research.
3. Advertising and other selected services plus marketing counsel in areas such as product and marketing planning.
4. Advertising and other selected services, plus important marketing contributions that make the agency a marketing partner and sometimes enable it to exercise marketing leadership.

What are the guidelines to follow in seeking the right level of agency services?

Selecting the right agency. As the ANA study points out, nearly every leading marketer agrees that agencies can create better advertisements than marketers can. The advertising agency, they say, can provide creative skills and specialized services that a company cannot match economically. In truth, many companies could not match the agency contribution at any price, because they cannot maintain the objectivity provided by a strong, creative agency that is not too dependent on the client. Objectivity, the lifeblood of good communications is very hard to maintain within most company hierarchies, and this is the main reason why the advertising agency is such a durable institution. A prime organizing principle in most leading marketing organizations is to preserve and use this objectivity of the outside agency in the creation of advertising and in other areas of marketing in which agency has competence.

In what other areas, beyond advertising, should you expect your agency to contribute?

Prudence dictates that a company remain self-sufficient in those marketing functions, such as marketing planning, that are vital to its survival. But many alert companies with strong agencies do not hesitate to draw on the agency for help even in marketing planning when this will speed the day when the company is more self-sufficient in that area. As they develop new products and diversify, these companies frequently find themselves with a product or market with which they are relatively unfamiliar. Short-term outside help in marketing planning, from an agency or marketing consultant that knows the market, is then needed to get the product off the ground and also to speed the day when the company has adequate in-house marketing leadership.

7. *Reduce the advertising approval line to the minimum—Preferably to an advertising approval point.* Top management does not normally consider the process of approval of advertising to be a part of the advertising, "organization." Yet, organization is "the plan for doing the work"—all the work. The advertising approval process is a critically important part of the work of advertising, one in which needed improvements must be supported by top management.

The approval of print advertisement or commercial is usually a drown-out process involving eight or nine persons, frequently a dozen or more. Moreover, it is usually carried out in a way that saps much of the potential effectiveness of the advertising submitted. This is a needless waste which many alert companies are taking steps to eliminate.

Authority in a single individual. Most advertising and marketing men have apparently accepted long advertising approval lines as inevitable. While applauding the principles behind methods 2 and 3, they feel that those who try to implement them are dreaming. However, actual experience shows they can be implemented and work splendidly—provided top management is interested enough to support the governing principles and the advertising people are firm enough in applying them.

In his excellent series entitled "The Management of the Marketing Function," marketing consultant Clarence Eldredge endorses this general thinking, and adds vital point when he states that "nothing would make a greater contribution to advertising creativity than to scrap the multi-approval process and delegate to a single individual the authority to approve advertising, provided always that the basic advertising and marketing strategy has been formally approved by the marketing director and general manager."

Eldridge reminds us that there is a precondition for effective, streamlined approval methods: firm, clear marketing direction. Long approval lines and continuing revisions of advertising programs usually reflect indecision on basic marketing and advertising strategies that should have been settled long before. Short, effective approval lines, or one-man approval points, are a blessing available to heads-up marketing groups who think through their marketing and advertising strategies, put them on paper, and make them known in advance to those who would otherwise be in along approval line.

8. *Combine the advertising and sales promotion functions whenever they require the same basic skills and source material.* Should advertising and sales promotion be combined or should they be separate functions in your company? The answer depends on what the term "sales promotion" means to you. However, there is a good guide rule that can be used by any company: Combine the two functions whenever the actual preparation of advertising and sales promotion material requires the same basic skills and source material.

In some packaged—goods companies, for example, sales promotion consists mainly of "promotions" such as off-label deals that are little more than price reductions; give-away promotions of contests that offer special inducements to consumers, the trade, or dealer organizations. The skills and information needed to stage such promotions often have little in common with those needed for creating or directing advertising, and so the advertising and sales promotion functions may logically be separated. They may even report upward through different marketing executives and compete furiously for the same budget dollars.

In most companies, however, the term "sales promotion" is a catchall referring to a broad range of sales-support activities other than space and broadcast advertising. In some cases as in consumer durable companies and in those marketing industrial parts and equipment, much of the sales promotion may be directed to the trade, sales force, or dealer organization. When this deals mainly with the same product-market information, and draws on the same communications skills as does the advertising, the sales promotion function may logically be positioned directly alongside the advertising function, supervised by a manager who directs and coordinates both.

In many industrial companies that sell direct, and in many consumer-product companies as well, nearly all advertising and sales promotion communications focus on consumer benefits of their products and services and draw on the identical skills and source information. In these companies, a tight integration of advertising and sales promotion is obviously best, and there is no better way to achieve it then to combine these related efforts at the supervisory level.

There are many companies in which advertising and sales promotion clearly draw on the same skills and source material, but are nevertheless separated, sometimes in apparent competition. In these cases, marketing management will wisely review the original reason for separating the two functions. More often than not, they will find that a former advertising and sales promotion manager, and his agency, became too enamored of the space or broadcast advertising programs and neglected the sales literature and related promotion materials needed to make the advertising pay off. Consequently, sales promotion was broken out solely to get the difficult, time-consuming work of sales promotion done. When this is the case, management has much to gain by combining the two functions again, under a manager who sees the big advantage and economy of coordinating them and who can manage to do so.

9. *Encourage the advertising and sales promotion department to provide related marketing services whenever practicable.* A growing number of companies are combining the advertising and sales promotion function with other specialized marketing services that are closely related. The additional serices usually begin with assistance in marketing research and extend naturally to include teamwork in marketing-planning activities and other areas. In some cases, they include marketing-training programs to help in the operating units achieve more effective marketing teamwork. Frequently, the broadened activity takes on the title of "marketing services" or "marketing communications."

Companies seeking to get this over-and-above contribution from their advertising activity may benefit from these observations drawn from successful marketing services groups of this type:

a. The first requirement is that the advertising department head and his division contact personnel by marketing minded advertising men, with a good feeling for effective advertising and a grasp of modern marketing and the disciplines that make it effective. Men of this type will invariably begin collaborating closely with their product managers on marketing research, marketing planning, and other related activities that have to be done before an effective advertising program can be initiated.

b. This good teamwork accelerates when management takes the step recommended under guide rule 4, above. A firm management requirement for written marketing audits or marketing plans, together with an offer of assistance from advertising and other marketing support groups, speeds the process of getting advertising and sales promotion men working closely with the line marketing people who most need help in fact-finding and marketing planning. This assistance should, of course, be provided as a catalyst rather than as a permanent service, to encourage the line marketing group to become wholly self-sufficient in this area.

c. The fact-getting and planning resulting from this teamwork directly benefits all areas of the operation. It is done, furthermore, at very low cost. In the area of marketing research, for example, little additional administrative costs are incurred, because the personal contacts, the close collaboration, and the research that is often required to define the basic needs are done as a normal part of the advertising and sales promotion job; getting the research work done requires relatively little additional time, because it can usually be done most objectively and economically by outside research personnel.

d. The former advertising department becomes increasingly aware of the realities of the marketing situation, and the marketing organization provides increasingly good direction not only for advertising but also for other marketing functions. Rapport between advertising and marketing men improves, and advertising recommendations, including budget proposals, gain in credibility.

e. The broad challenge offered by a marketing services activity of this kind increases the company's ability to attract and developable, marketing-minded advertising men. It broadens their experience and capabilities, and it also helps to hold those who rise to top positions. There, they are no longer deal-ended in a specialized advertising job, with no place to go except other companies and agencies. Instead, they frequently move into line-marketing activities where their combination of marketing and communications skills prove valuable.

10. *Coordinate advertising and sales promotion with the public relations activity.* The advertising and the public relations departments are organizationally separate in some companies. They are also separated, and relatively out of touch, in many other companies where both logic and experience indicate they should be working together very closely, under a director of public relations and advertising.

One way management can help decide how closely to coordinate the two functions is to ask these two questions.

a. To what degree do the communications objectives of your advertising and your public relations programs overlap? In many companies, a thoughtful effort to determine the communication goals for all major public relations and advertising audiences will reveal that some goals are common to many of them. A primary goal, for example, might be to show all public relations and advertising audiences that the company is competent, reliable, diverse, growing, progressive, and profitable. The secondary communication audiences such as employees and the financial community will, of course, vary widely and call for disseminating distinctly different information. Achieving the primary goal may be very important, and require the same basic communication skills for all audiences. When this is the case, a close organizational tie between advertising and public relations is suggested. To determine how close the tie should be, it is well to ask the second question.

b. *How valuable to your public relations programs is specific news and information on your company's products and markets?* The value of such information may be relatively small in a company marketing, let us say, only salt or a basic industrial material that meets common industry specifications and has no readily apparent product advantages. The same is doubtless true for many packaged-goods products.

Many other products and services have very interesting and distinctive features and advantages. News concerning them can be used effectively throughout all the company's public relations programs to help achieve the primary communication goals. This may be true for products running from heavy capital goods equipment through office machines, small appliances, software, and drugs. In all these the advertising and public relations functions are frequently combined.

Answers to these two questions will often suggest a close coordination of advertising and public relations when, in fact, they are separate and striving hard to remain independent and self-sufficient. In this case, as in the case of separate advertising and sale promotion functions, a study will often show that the company does not need separate, specialized functions but, instead, a director who is interested in both functions and able to manage them.

Corporate advertising. Corporate-level advertising, like public relations, may be focused on any one or a combination of different audiences. In deciding where to position it, we must go back to basic communication objectives. Where these overlap substantially for the corporate advertising and for product advertising, and where both draw on the same basic skills and source material, the corporate advertising can regularly be handled most effectively and economically by the advertising department. In other cases, the corporate advertising may be focused solely on the financial community or some other special audience, and contain little or no product or market information; it may be that it can be handled best by a public relations group that is in close touch with the chief executive and his top financial and legal aides.

Product news publicity. Positioning the product news publicity function very often presents a Hobson's choice. The case for positioning it with the public relations activity is usually strong. Having within the company a single contact for all product and corporate news can be a decided convenience for the news media. It also makes possible a valuable degree of control and coordination within the company. When the company's products are unique, with a strong potential for making news in the general press and broadcast media, positioning the product and corporate news relations group in the public relations department offers clear benefits to the corporate-level news activity.

In the same company, however, we may also find compelling reasons for making the product news activity an integral part of the product advertising and sales promotion group.

One reason for this is that a vital part of the public relations activity is usually done for and under the watchful eye of top management. This work, understandably, has an urgency and priority that frequently cause the trade-magazine level of product releases and signed article activity to get lost in the shuffle. Meanwhile, the product advertising department, with no responsibility for product news relations, is not motivated even to plan for optimum use of it in their programming and budgeting. As a result, they use more costly media for goals they could achieve at much less cost in the news columns.

Where product news coverage can carry an important part of the marketing communications load, it seems wise to position the product news activity with product advertising, making that activity clearly responsible for transmitting to the public relations group the 10 per cent or so of product news that many have potential for coverage in the general news media.

11. *Make advertising organization changes in a transition rather than a revolution.* Most of the changes required in an advertising organization can be foreseen, often years in advance. This is particularly true of changes that are required to adapt to a major restructuring of the corporate organization, and those that are needed to help increase the effectiveness of advertising and marketing.

Communications functions can be severely disrupted by organization upheavals, and management has much to gain by planning ahead so that advertising and marketing personnel can collaborate on a reasonable transition. Important changes in advertising organization can often lead to related changes in the company organization structure. The big advantage is that it can avoid changes that overshoot the mark and cause the quality of advertising to deteriorate, as has so often been the case during the decentralizing and marketing revolutions.

The process of developing a recommendation for the allocation of media dollars entails a series of steps which are logical and simple in concept, but require a great deal of analytical skill, media expertise, and sound judgment to execute successfully.

This chapter will outline the allocation procedure and explore in detail some of the more important elements of a sound media plan. A good deal of pertinent information is now available from syndicated research services such as W.R. Simmons, Brand Rating Index, and others, which was not available a few years back. This information, together with the advanced analytical techniques made possible by the application of electronic data processing equipment, has introduced a degree of precision into the media selection process that was not possible a few years ago. There are still many areas where judgment must be applied, but these judgments can now be based on a more solid foundation of knowledge.

Changes in media research

As background, it may be worthwhile to review briefly the changes that have taken place in media research and explain how they have affected media planning techniques. First, and most importantly, the new research is more relevant to the critical job of matching media to markets.

The key element is that it combines research into the media habits of people with product-usage data. Information on both is taken from the same people, making it possible for the first time to assess the product-purchase rates of a medium's audience in meaningful and specific terms. This is a big step forward.

Second, the new data provide a better identification of audiences in terms of people rather than households. Until a few years ago, most media audience research reported on the coverage of media vehicles by the number and kind of households reached. But obviously households do not read or view media; people do. With the old research, it was not clear whether it was the housewife, the husband, or the teen-age daughter who was being exposed to the magazine or television program once it got into the home. Today, the trend is toward measuring the media habits of individuals, who can then be qualified as prospects according to either personal or household characteristics or individual purchase patterns—a much tougher assignment for the researcher but an essential step forward in defining media values in meaningful marketing terms. Third, we are now getting a better fix on the interaction of various kinds of media. These new services are finding out from the same people the extent of their exposure to the various types of media, television as well as magazines, and radio, and newspapers. While this still does, not tell us which media form is the most effective, it is now possible for planners at least to assess the numerical contributions of various media to a media problem more accurately than ever before.

Finally, much of the new research is available on computer tape, making it possible to utilize the incredible speed and memory capacity of the computer in data analysis. For those agencies that do not have their own computer installations, service bureaus or shared time operations are available.

The computer, however, has contributed much more to media planning than a superior computational capacity. It has enforced a more stringent discipline on the decision-makers. Because the computer is, in fact, a "logic machine." it has forced us to define and evaluate audience objective more carefully, to proceed in a rational step-by-step fashion throughout the analytical process, and to make explicit decisions with regard to the relatives values of media forms and media vehicles which were sometimes evaded in the past.

Importance of new advances

The importance to the advertiser of this improved information and new-found analytical expertise is self-evident. Budget requirements have multiplied, and the role of advertising as a marketing tool has increased over the past two decades. Advertisers have quite understandably come to expect a more careful accounting of dollars allocated for media. They want a well-reasoned rationale and documentation for the specific media proposed and the plan for using them most effectively.

The reason is simple. The media decision is critical to the success of the advertising campaign. It determines, for example, the characteristics of individuals exposed to the advertising, and it controls the place and the circumstances, form, timing, and frequency of advertising exposure.

Beyond exposure, the media decision influences the whole complex of advertising perception and communication. It selects the senses through which communication takes place. It affects their response to the advertising.

Beyond its direct effect on consumers, the media decision may even affect distribution, dealer interest, and the kind of retail selling support the brand receives.

It is obvious that a decision of this magnitude must be approached in a carefully reasoned, highly disciplined way. While the kinds and amounts of information that will be appropriate will vary from problem to problem, and the analytical techniques required may change, it is possible to set down a general procedure that will serve as a guide to the media planner and a check list for the advertiser. Such a procedure is outlined at the end of this chapter.

Areas to be Explored: The remainder of the chapter will examine the most critical problems and decision to be faced in media planning and describe some practical methods for resolving them. Specifically, these areas will be explored:

1. Setting the media objectives
2. Fulfilling creative requirements
3. Defining audience goals
4. Allocating advertising dollars geographically in relation to sales opportunities
5. Scheduling the advertising

6. Establishing reach and frequency goals
7. Test marketing
8. Media plan outline

Setting media objectives

The media objectives are, in effect, a listing of all the things the media planner must take into account in selecting the components of his plan. Carefully expressed, they serve two basic purposes: They are the means of arriving at complete agreement on the part of everyone involved as to what is to be accomplished, and they provide guidelines for the actual purchase of media time and space.

Unfortunately, media objectives are often couched in such vague terms as to be inadequate for either of these purposes. Generalities such as "provide broad national coverage," "deliver maximum reach with adequate frequency," are crutches for the careless or superficial thinker. They obviously provide neither a specific goal for the execution of the plan nor a yardstick by which to measure results.

They must be consistent with the Advertiser's Overall marketing Objectives and Strategy: The successful media plan is not an end in itself but a means to an end. An objective that calls for "the lowest possible cost per thousand" is irrelevant unless the goals against which this cost per thousand are to be measured are spelled out and are consistent with the product's marketing targets.

They must be consistent with the Copy Strategy and the Requirements of the Creative Approach: There is little argument that the most important element in an advertising campaign is the message. Thus the media specifications must take into account the requirements for an effective message. Obviously, a discussion between the media planner and the creative supervisor is highly desirable before the process of media selection begins.

They must give adequate consideration to competitive activities: In making media decisions, we should consider the likelihood that the individuals covered by each medium will be heavily or lightly reached by competitive advertising. On occasion, alternative media choices may be about equally desirable, except that one is being used by competitive brands. If these are brands against which our product will have no special advantage in copy or dollar expenditures, the competitive advertising may largely nullify the response to our own advertising and diminish its profitability. If good alternative media are available, we should seriously consider using them.

On the other hand, if we are in a position to dominate other competing advertisers in a particular medium, or if a consumer comparison of copy will leave our brand with a clear advantage, we may profit from direct media competition.

In some cases, where media serve a sort of shopping-guide function, i.e., the so-called shelter magazines in home decoration, it is desirable for competitors to group together. Or, when the market saturation for a product category is low and promotional funds are limited, the total market may best be expanded by parallel competitive efforts.

Expert media selection requires a knowledge of competitive activity, and the proper use of this information involves imaginative thinking and a good sense of strategy.

They must take realistic account of budget restrictions: All media plans are a compromise between the ideal and the practical. Large space and time units may be creatively desirable, but their high cost may defeat their value because of a critical reduction in exposure levels. Budget will also affect the definition of the audience target, whether the advertiser can afford to reach the total market or would be better advised to direct his limited funds toward a high potential segment. The size and shape of the media plan will depend upon the bolt of cloth from which it must be cut.

Critical specific questions

These are the general requirements. More specifically, the media objectives should contain concisely summarized answers to the following questions:

1. To whom should the advertising be directed? (Demographic description of target groups, and indication of relative value assigned to each. male *versus* female? users *versus* principal purchasing agents?)
2. Where should the advertising messages be delivered? (nationally? Regionally? By client sales territories? Are geographic or major market variations in message weight desirable? If so, what levels, by area?)
3. When should the product be advertised? (Taking into account seasonal requirement, anticipated competitive activity, etc.)
4. What creative requirements must be taken into account? (Does the copy strategy dictate certain media capabilities, such as colour, sound, motion? Is a special frame of reference or editorial environment needed? What units of time or space are needed and affordable?)
5. What are the special requirements or priorities for reach, frequency, or frequency distribution?
6. What other marketing requirements must be met? (Is retail merchandising support required? An unusual degree of budgetary or timing flexibility? Support for consumer promotions? Other?)

As indicated earlier, the answers to each of these questions usually require considerable analysis of market and media data, a though understanding of the overall goals of the advertising campaign, and the application of a very large pinch of judgment based on this knowledge. The critical need throughout is to be as precise and specific as possible in order to provide guidelines that will help maximize the efficiency and effectiveness of the advertising dollars in accomplishing the objectives of the campaign.

Creative requirements

Advertising is communication, and effective communication depends on the presentation of the message. One of the media planner's most important responsibilities, therefore, is to provide the most appropriate vehicle for the advertising copy. All the advantages gained through a careful allocation of dollars in the marketplace can be wiped out if the message does not come across to the potential consumer:

Communication between media and copy

As mentioned earlier, close communication between the media planner and the copy group is highly desirable in the early stages of plan development. A discussion at this time will serve two important ends:

It will help the copy group understand clearly the exposure opportunities and limitations which will result from the use of various media forms or units of time space.

It will provide the media planner with an understanding of the intended creative approach which will guide his thinking in the selection of media.

Impact versus *Exposure:* An understanding of the limitations which the use of large units of space or time imposes is always important. An actual situation comes to mind in which a better assessment of this factor could have made a difference to the success of the product.

A well-known advertiser in the household-products field introduced a new coloured brand (Brand A). The creative group devised an excellent campaign using four-colour, full-page magazine advertisements. The objective of this approach was to dramatize the new colours and give the product a high-quality, "decorator" image. Copy tests revealed an excellent reaction and good playback of copy points. Initial reaction in the marketplace was also good.

The strategy might well have worked except for one factor. A leading competitor came out with a similar product (Brand B) shortly thereafter. Ignoring the "need" to show the product in colour, the second advertiser elected to use 20 second and 30 second television spots. With about the same budget he was able approximately to double the amount of exposure against the primary target group.

The gamble on greater exposure at the sacrifice of a more dramatic creative approach paid off. A decreasing brand share indicated trouble for Brand A. Field research revealed that consumer familiarity with the advertising campaign was low, though it was well liked by those who claimed to have seen it. Most distressing, many who claimed familiarity with it actually attributed Brand A copy to Brand B. Obviously, the more frequent repetition of the Brand B name had enabled it to attain a substantially greater share of mind—a critical factor in the marketplace.

In this case, the Brand a budget was obviously inadequate to provide for both expensive units and competitive frequency. An otherwise excellent campaign had failed for lack of exposure.

The relative importance of creative impact through expensive space or time units *versus* greater exposure through less costly units must be resolved on the basis of judgment, experience, and a full awareness of the media alternatives. Little progress can be made on the media plan until a decision on this point has been reached.

Once this decision has been made and the creative strategy settled, the media planner is in a much better position to select media which will (1) provide the physical characteristics needed to present the message most effectively, and (2) take full advantage of the general media environment.

Media environment. Much has been written and little has been proved about the ability of a medium to enhance the impact of the advertising it carries. A majority of advertising men believes that a medium does act as something more than a simple carrier; that an advertisement seen in the environment of a reader's favourite magazine or a viewer's favourite program will have an edge in terms of both perception and response over one seen in a neutral or unfavourable environment. If the copy approach is congenial with the spirit and the content of the medium, so much the better.

This phenomenon, if real, is the result of two factors: (1) the amount of attention given them media vehicle by the individual exposed, and (2) the psychological rapport between the medium and the reader or viewer. In door-to-door selling a salesman will find that this success depends on both the degree of interest his prospect has in the product and the amount of customer rapport he is able to achieve. The same may be true of a media vehicle, which, like a salesman, has a definite style and personality.

Demographic audience information, based as it is on simple exposure, is only partially useful in analyzing this subtle aspect of media selection. The medium may reach many people, but it will probably be most effective among those viewers or readers who find it congenial enough to absorb their full attention. Syndicated attitudinal studies such as TV Q. magazine Q, and several studies done by individual media, all shed a glimmer of light if not a full beam on the media preferences of different kinds of people.

However, whether the media planner uses research or simply judgment, the important thing is for him to make an explicit decision regarding the value of the medium as a communicator of the advertising to appropriate target groups.

Defining audience goals

The most critical job the media man must face is the establishment of audience objectives. Once an advertisement has been put into finished form, the next step is obviously to see that it gets adequate exposure. Every advertising exposure costs money. Thus, the determination of how many exposures should be bought, and who should receive them, occupies a great deal of the media planner's time.

We know, of course, that not everyone uses the product or service to be advertised, and that many people can never be induced to use it either because it does not fit into their way of life, they cannot afford it, or because it simply does not appeal to them. There is a temptation to generalize about such people—to say that single persons or old or rural people or some other broad groups are not prospects and therefore should be eliminated from consideration.

Establishment of audience goals

What is needed, then, is a method of establishing advertising audience goals which takes into account the elusive nature of the prospect group. If the market data are reliable, such an approach should enable the media planner to improve the efficiency of his media selection by helping to identify and evaluate potential consumers, and to select media which are most efficient in reaching those potential customers who have been selected as targets for the advertising.

It is important at this point to face one of the more frustrating aspects of the media planner's job. That is the knowledge that no matter how precise he is in setting his audience targets, the nature of media is such that he will inevitably reach many individuals who are of little value as customers. Mass media are by definition. They offer something for everybody and thus cut across the demographic segmentations that determine product usage.

There is no perfect case of media and marketing matching. Any medium, no matter how selective, will reach some people other than the ones who are prospects for a manufacturer's product. Any market of heavy users, no matter how concentrated, will include many people beyond the reach of a selective medium.

In any attempt to correlate media and consumption habit some very important simplifications have to be made. To the extent that there is a relationship at all, it is rarely a direct relationship between the two. Instead, it usually arises because of the intrusion of a third element which reflects such things as the consumer's age, education, or income, of more subtle matters of personality and taste.

Recognizing that a perfect market and media match is unattainable, the media planner must nevertheless make every effort to minimize the waste circulation by carefully describing his consumer target in terms that can be related directly to his knowledge of media audiences.

How to Identify Targets: There are two methods of identifying audience targets and evaluating media which are in general use today.

First, a demographic-matching approach. Under this system, market and media audience characteristics are matched in an effort to put messages in front of designated prospects with minimum cost. This is the traditional approach, but it has recently become much more scientific as a result of computer technology.

Second, the so-called product-user (or direct-match) approach. With this method the number of actual users of a given product in a medium's audience is taken into account as well as the approximate volume they consume in a specified period of time. Different media can then be compared on the basis of their efficiency in reaching users or "heavy users" of a product category, or when information is available, of the advertiser's own brand or competitive brands. In some cases, the total volume of product consumed by each medium's audience can be measured.

The principal weakness of this approach is that it cannot be used to analyze the demographic components of the current market—an essential first step in pointing the direction toward market expansion opportunities. Neither is it of value in the selection of media for the introduction of new or drastically altered products.

On the other hand, it is a very useful measure of the efficiency of media when the marketing strategy calls for either (1) increasing the volume of product used by present customers, or (2) increasing brand share within the present market.

The demographic approach has some value in almost any situation. An understanding of the demographic characteristics of users is basic in developing the overall advertising strategy and determining the best copy approach. However, as a media selection tool, demographic matching also has its weakness.

This weakness lies in the implicit assumption that for any demographic group there will be about the same percentage of users in a medium's a audience as in the population as a whole. This is not always true. For example, let us assume that a product is bought by 40 per cent of all housewives aged twenty-five to thirty-four years and living in middle-income families. A given media vehicle may reach 25 per cent of such housewives. The trouble is that there is no real assurance that a *proportionate* share of the 40 per cent of these housewives who are *users* are included in the 25 per cent of similar women covered by the media vehicle.

This variance is the result of the selectivity of media vehicles. A family's product usage will be strongly influenced by its demographic characteristics—its size, income, age of children, etc.—but the *media exposure* of the family's chief purchasing agent is the result of such subtle matters as personality and taste. Thus there can be no assurance that two women who are equally heavy users of, say, bacon are also interested in the same magazine or television show.

Researchers are attempting to improve current methods of relating purchasers and media audiences through a new measurement which involves a blending of demographic and psychological characteristics. This new measure is currently referred to as *psychographics*, or in a slightly different form, *attitudinal segmentation*. It promises to lead a step closer to the goal of matching media to markets, but as yet it is in a very elementary stage of development. Until further progress is made, media planners must utilize as best they can the two current systems described earlier.

This approach requires the type of information currently made available through syndicated research services such as Simmons, Brand Rating Index (or, through the blending of market data from any one source with media data from another). Data must be drawn from a sample of the population which is reasonably representative of the whole and is large enough to be statistically stable when broken down into the required number of sub-segments. The following information is needed:

1. A description of each individual in the sample in demographic terms—his or her age, household income, education family size.
2. A record of each individual's usage of the product or brand to be advertised over a specified period of time.
3. A record of each individual' s media exposure

By relating the product usage history of each individual in the sample to his or her personal or family (demographic) characteristics, it is possible to identify those characteristics which separate users from non-users or heavy users from light users—the characteristics, in other words, which serve as *predictors* of the potential of each person as a customer.

Contribution of the Computer: The important contribution which the computer has made to this process is to enable us to take into account the complex correlations which exist between different characteristics. For example, it is useful to know that women aged eighteen to thirty-four have an above-average probability of purchase, but it is more useful to know that within that large group, those women with two or more children are twice as valuable as the remainder, and of those with two or more children, the segment having a family income of more than $ 8,000 a year is 25 per cent more likely to buy.

The Computer, with its capacity to perform thousands of calculations in a matter of seconds, can identify sub-segments of the market in multi-demographic terms and specify the value of each group in relation to the average of the entire sample. It thus enables the planner to be far more precise in defining and evaluating his audience targets, and as a consequence, to develop a more efficient media plans.

Market in Multi-demographic Terms: In this example, an analysis of the purchase patterns of the respondents (adult women, in this case) disclosed that the most important predictors of usage of product. A were age, income, and family size. By dividing the universe into seven mutually exclusive groups (that together account for the total adult female population) based on these characteristics and relating the usage levels of each group to the average for the entire sample, it was possible to assign each group a relative value, expressed as an index, with the overall average expressed as 100.

This first step provides an important insight into the productivity level of each group. However, it could be misleading unless the total potential of the group is taken into account.

As pointed out earlier, this approach reduces the likelihood of oversimplification. If the planner had generalized that younger, larger, upper-income groups were the "best prospects" and set these people as his audience target, he might have unwittingly overlooked or undervalued the older or less affluent people who together account for almost half of the total. By showing the value of each group in terms of both their productivity and their overall importance in the marketplace, such a generalization is unlikely to be made.

This is not to say that the media plan should necessarily strive to distribute advertising impressions against prospect groups in direct relation to their current usage rate. Other factors such as budget, recent or expected changes in the market situation, competitive considerations, or a change in the advertising approach may dictate an entirely different strategy.

For example, if the budget is too small to develop competitive impact against the whole market, it may be more sensible to attempt to concentrate advertising weight as much as possible against a relatively small, potentially productive segment.

If it is determined that the greatest current opportunity lies in expanding the market as a whole by increasing consumption on the part of light or moderate users, a quite different allocation of advertising weight may be in order.

Positions of Competitive Brands: On the other hand, if the market is mature and approximate "saturation usage" has already been achieve, the advertiser's main marketing task may be to attract customers away from his competition. In this case, an analysis of the relative position of competitive brands within each group can often reveal an opportunity in one or more areas of the marketplace which the shrewd media strategist can turn to his advantage.

In this product category, a packaged food product, three brands have a 70 per cent penetration overall.

Brand A and Brand C are competitive in price and are the leaders in the field. Brand B is a "price brand", relying heavily on trade and consumer promotions.

In advertising, Brand A features quality and taste using media aimed at housewives. Brand B is highly promotional. Brand C has divided its effort between housewives and children, stressing quality but in a much lighter vein.

A study of brand penetration by demographic groups points up some interesting differences as a result of these varying strategies. Brand B, as would be expected, has its highest share in the lower income, older groups. This is a function of price promotion. Advertising can probably not do a great deal about it, nor are these groups productive enough for the product category as a whole to justify a major effort by Brands A and C. Brand C. However, is considerably stronger than Brand A in Groups 1 and 4, both of which have above average product penetration and are worth cultivating. These groups contain large families, and after further study, it is apparent the success of Brand C is because of its appeal to children.

Brand A, which does well among smaller, middle and upper-income families, might well decide to invest some of its dollars in media aimed at young people, children's television shows or comics, for example.

The point is that such a demographic analysis provides a good basis for making a marketing strategy decision because the decision-maker knows the rate at which different people currently buy. Once this marketing strategy is set, it should be reflected in the statement of media objectives where it will serve as a guide in evaluating alternative media plans.

A short discussion of this media evaluation phase may be in order here before we move on to a discussion of the product user approach.

Alternative Media Combinations: A truly meaningful analysis of the delivery of alternative media combinations against various sub-segments of the market involves complex mathematical computations, the volume of which calls for the use of the computer. This assumes that the planner wants to know the reach and frequency against each group—as well as the simple gross-rating point count the plan delivers.

Before any media analyses were undertaken, the following decisions were made:

1. The advertising would be directed to adult females within the groups specified.
2. The objective would be to distribute advertising weight as nearly as possible according to the current sales potential of each demographic group.

These decisions having been made, it was then possible to determine which of several media combinations would meet the objectives most efficiently.

There are, of course, computer models in use which will select the one most efficient plan. These so-called maximization programs are not infallible, however, owing to the many areas requiring personal judgment. Its is frequently desirable to supplement such an analysis with additional evaluations which include other media or revised judgmental decisions.

In this example, three combinations of magazines plus daytime and nighttime television were run off. Five factors were considered in evaluating the plans:

1. Total message weight
2. The distribution of messages by groups
3. The reach and frequency against each group
4. The cost per thousand adult women
5. The cost per thousand units of potential (women weighted by their usage rate)

1. Plan 2 (magazines and prime evening network TV) does a better job than either plan 1 (magazines plus day network TV) or plan 3 (magazines plus day network TV and fringe spot TV) in distributing advertising impressions in relations to sales.
2. While Plan 2 has the best skew, it is the least efficient of the three plans in reaching women. It does place more actual impressions against all those groups with above-average sales-indices, and yet, in spite of this, the lower cost media used in Plan 1 (daytime TV as opposed to prime evening TV; and less magazine space) which has resulted in substantially greater advertising tonnage against all women has given plan 1 an efficiency advantage in coverage of "units of potential." This emphasizes the need, where two or more media forms are involved, for an explicit decision as to the relative worth of each type of impression. Is an exposure in magazines equal to one delivered by television, is it half as valuable, or worth twice as much? In totalling impressions, such differences must be taken into account if one plan is to be equated with another.
3. Plan 3 provides greater reach and frequency than plan 2 in the twenty-six Nielsen A counties in every demographic group. However, it gives slightly less reach and substantially lower frequency in the remainder of the country in Groups 1 though 3. The choice between these two plans would depend on the geographic distribution objectives (discussed in detail in a later section).

While an analysis of this type based on a demographic matching approach does not solve all the problems of the media planner, it does substantially narrow the areas of choice in deciding on the most appropriate media strategy.

This system for evaluating media is more direct than demographic matching. It eliminates entirely the need to determine the demography of the customer. The information required is (1) knowledge that a given respondent in the research sample is a user of the product or brand under consideration; (2) some measure of the quantity of usage; and (3) a report on his or her media exposure over a period of time.

With this information (which is provided by the syndicated research services) it is possible to identify media known to be read or viewed by people who have purchased the product and to compare them on the basis of lowest cost per thousand users.

The product in this example is in the alcoholic-beverage field. Magazines have been ranked in order of the cost per thousand adult male readers, with each magazine's relative position on this basis indicated in parenthesis. It is easy to see that substantial differences exist in the two rankings.

A refinement on this type of analysis is to categorize all individuals in a medium's audience into groups labelled "heavy", "medium," "light," or "non-users," and rank each vehicle on its efficiency in reaching one or more of these categories. If the marketing strategy calls for a high degree of concentration against "best prospects." the heavy user approach would be the best method for the problem.

An even more exact measure of media value is usually possible through a further step in this type of analysis, based on the total volume of product usage.

In most cases an estimate of the volume of usage for each individual in the sample is available. It is thus possible to compute the total volume accounted for by the audience of each vehicle and develop a ranking based on cost per thousand "units of potential" covered.

The mechanics of this are simple. The computer identifies users in each medium's audience, multiplies each user by the number of units of the product purchased or consumed (cans of food, bottles of beverage, number of trips, etc.), totals these, and divides the sum into the cost of the unit of space or time selected.

There are occasionally secondary audience targets of considerable importance to the advertiser.

For example, if retail distribution is the problem or shelf space is being encroached upon by competition, it may be of particular importance to impress the store manager or distributor with the size and nature of the consumer advertising being put behind the product.

Advertisers frequently attempt to do this by describing their campaigns in appropriate trade magazines. However, actual exposure of the retailer to the consumer advertising is even more effective. In addition to convincing him that the advertiser really means business, it enables the retailer to judge for himself the effectiveness of the advertising copy and form some estimate of probable customer response.

Where such firsthand exposure is considered important, the planner will attempt to include in the schedule media which provide exposure to the trade. Newspapers are generally considered to be effective for this purpose (most retailers use them for their own advertising), as are outdoor, general magazines, and prime-time television.

With the growth of chains and discount houses and the concomitant development of central buying committees and automatic inventory control, the need for special pressure at the store-manager level is somewhat reduced. Nevertheless, many advertisers consider a media plan which can be merchandised to the trade a definite plus, while recognizing that this should never take precedence as an objective over effective impact against the consumer.

In addition of evaluating the market demographically, it is essential that one thoroughly understand geographic sales patterns and establish a strategy of area allocation of advertising dollars. Although the development of such a strategy, which involves a knowledge of current sales and recent trends, product distribution, transportation costs, long-range plans for expansion, competitive manoeuvres, etc., is not primarily the responsibility of the media planner, its successful implementation is. He must plan media strategy in such a way as to place advertising dollars where they will be most productive.

This assignment is complicated by the fact that marketing strategy will frequently dictate a pattern of expenditures which is at odds with the audience distribution of the national media under consideration. It is indeed a rare situation where this is not the case. The media planner must utilize techniques which give him maximum capability to take into account the advertiser's unique sales pattern. He must consider these variations both by geographic region and by market size, sometimes on an individual market basis.

Perhaps the least complicated approach to the problem of matching media dollars to sales potential by geographic region is to take a map of the advertiser's total sales area, describe on it the boundaries of each regional marketing division and within each of these areas develop a media expenditure goal which reflects the marketing strategy.

This goal is often expressed in terms of dollars per thousand homes, or people, or housewives—whatever the target audience happens to be.

If the market is basically national in character alternative notional media plans can be analyzed on the basis of their audience delivery in each area. Such an analysis will show the fit of each plan, and demonstrate where major weaknesses occur. These can then be corrected through the addition of local or regional media.

Use of television in sales areas: In this case the advertiser has provided the agency with sales forecasts by market area for each quarter of the year. Estimates of the advertising-sales ratio on a national basis have been developed and the agency media department instructed to try to approximate that same A/S ratio in each area.

The primary medium for all products in this case happened to be nighttime network television. Brands were rotated through a sizeable stable of corporate program buys. The media planner's first step then is to determine the distribution of the net television dollars by market area.

The coverage of all programs Product d will participate in during the quarter has been ascertained, and the network television expenditures have been allocated to each of these sales districts on that basis.

This does not, of course, reflect only the fluctuations in the network television coverage, although these can be considerable. It reflects primarily the fact that the variation in sales potential by market area is quite substantial. Any medium, no matter how even its geographic distribution, would almost certainly result in the same kinds of variation in A/S ratios across the country.

With the national pattern established, it remained to estimate the number of dollars required to bring each underspent division up to a point where the A/S ratio would approximate the national average.

The overspent divisions, such as Des Moines and Toledo, could only be corrected by reducing the total network effort or running cut-ins for other products—an expensive business because of station cut-in charges. In this case, since the overspent markets were relatively small and the amount of overspending nominal, no action was taken.

Money invested and advertising messages. Efforts are often made to translate money investments in each area into advertising messages generated. This is theoretically a far more precise measure of advertising input since it takes into account such factors as local rating levels, readers per copy, and variations in market by market media costs. In cases where media audience surveys are both frequent enough and accurate enough, such a refinement can be made.

It should be kept in mind, however, that in cases where a combination of media forms is involved, a decision to base the comparison on message input carries the obligation to place a value on messages derived from different media forms as well as on different units of time or space. Is a 1-minute television commercial equal to a black-and-white magazine page? Should a 30-second commercial message be given a value of one-half the minute, two-thirds, three-quarters? How about a magazine spread *versus* a colour page?

An analysis based on dollar input assumes that equal dollars generate equal impact. It implicitly accepts the theory that the law of the marketplace, which has governed the pricing of media forms and units of space and time over many years, has taken into account the buyer's combined judgment of the value of the media product. Full colour reproduction, for example, would not be saleable at its premium cost unless in the experience of advertisers the value of colour justified the price.

This is undoubtedly an overly simplified view, since it does not take into account the creative requirements of individual campaigns. Nevertheless, many advertisers feel that after eliminating certain obviously unsuitable media, this approach is as realistic as attempting to assign a relative weight to each different kind of message delivered.

It is also pertinent to keep in mind that the profitability of the brand is based in large part on the dollar expenditure required to market it. A careful marketer, therefore, cannot afford to lose sight of the dollar investment required to support the product in each area. If the finds the advertising costs in one market to be so far out of line as to make the market unprofitable, he will either reassess his media approach or eliminate the market in favour of another, more profitable area.

There are many possible variations on the allocation procedures described above. But regardless of the technique, it is essential that advertising dollar allocations bear a direct relationship to the requirements of each geographic area based on the advertiser's judgment of its current value or future potential.

Of all the problems the media planner must cope with, one of the most complex has to do with scheduling advertising. This problem must be considered on several levels.

The least complicated level is timing the advertising. For example, for those products which have a clear-cut seasonal sales curve, it generally makes sense to time the advertising when most people are in the market. However, even this axiom should be subjected to careful scrutiny.

Coca-Cola decided in the 1930s to attempt through advertising to develop an almost non-existent winter business. It introduced a new sales theme, "Thirst Knows No Season," and plugged it hard off-season with considerable success.

Charts of new-car sales show relatively moderate variations by season. Yet automobile companies spend from one-third to one-half of their total budgets on the two to three months new models are introduced. The theory is that during this period consumer interest is at a peak, and the advertising will work harder to build a predisposition toward the particular line advertised.

These exceptions, and there are many others, prove that in media scheduling no traditional pattern should be accepted without a careful analysis of the possible results of breaking the mold and trying a new approach. While the cases cited represent an advertising and marketing decision as opposed to a strictly media consideration, an alert media man can often, from his own knowledge of media usage, suggest similar opportunities to steal a march on competition. For example, where no important seasonal variations occur, a study of competitive advertising patterns may reveal an opportunity for a low-budget advertiser to dominate the field at a given time of year.

Timing can also mean taking advantage of the availability of the desired audience to the medium. For example, running a food ad in newspapers on the traditional Thursday or Friday grocery shopping days when women are "shopping" the food page. Or reaching teen-agers on weekend radio. Or businessmen in the early morning or evening drive times. A study of the times and days when the target audience is likely to be the most available and most receptive is an important ingredient in media planning.

An additional consideration in scheduling is the need, on occasion, for *flexibility.*

In a highly competitive market there is often a need for quick tactical manoeuvring to take advantage of a competitive weakness or to capitalize on a favourable market development. The likelihood of such a contingency should be assessed by the media planner and provision for the necessary flexibility made in advance.

Such provision can take the form of a contingency fund to be held aside until the need arises. However, unless there is a reasonably strong probability that such action will be needed, it is usually wiser to incorporate the funds in the media plan in such a way that they can be transferred on short notice. Newspapers, spot radio, and spot television are examples of media where minimal contractual commitments are required and funds can be shifted in time or place on short notice.

A much more complex scheduling problem involves the *rate* of advertising—the knotty question of scheduling on a continuous basis *versus* short flights of advertising spaced at intervals throughout the year.

Again there is no rule of thumb to follow. The size of the advertising budget related to that of competition is a key factor, and this in turn must be related to the product itself and its current position in the marketplace.

The gravest risk is to spread the advertising too thin—to fail to break through the "noise level" and attract the attention of the potential consumer. At the other extreme is the possibility of wasting costly impressions after the job has already been accomplished.

In examining this problem, it may be useful to see what happens when an equal number of television spots is spread over a thirteen week period, or concentrated in shorted "flights," say, nine weeks or six weeks.

First, if the program schedule is the same, the total gross rating points in a given quarter will produce the same reach, average frequency, and frequency distribution by viewing quintals whether the TRPs are spread over the entire thirteen weeks or concentrated in a shorter period. A flighting pattern does not increase the proportion of total impressions delivered in the heaviest quintiles during the total advertising period.

Since the total number of exposures does not change as a result of adopting a flighting pattern, the effect of compressing the same total number of exposures into a shorter period is to increase the average number of exposures a week during the advertising period.

While no one as yet has been able to shed much light on "how much is enough," most strategists will agree that the share of advertising is a key factor in arriving at a judgment in any given situation.

If competition spending at a level which is substantially greater than is affordable on a continuous basis by the brand to be advertised, it is usually wise to move in periodically with bursts of sufficient intensity to assure awareness of the advertising.

In the example, given, the determination of which period of time is most appropriate will depend on judgment, which in turn will be based on knowledge of such factors as:

The purchase cycle of the brand

The brand-switching probabilities

The anticipated level of competitive activity

The life cycle of the brand

With so many factors involved, it is safe to say that the With so many factors involved, it is safe to say that the same flighting pattern would not produce the same results for a different product or for the same product in very situation. The dynamics of media require that the dimension of time be carefully considered. There is some laboratory evidence that consumers can be *unsold* by a barrage of advertising extended beyond a given point; there are indications that at a certain point in the life cycle of a product, it is wise to with-draw all advertising to allow the public a "period of gestation," and then to come back with renewed vigour; there is evidence that for some products short bursts of advertising will produce more sales than the same amount of advertising run every week.

The effect of timing, or *periodicity* as it is sometimes called, is one which requires more study. In the meantime, the creative media planner should not close his mind to the possibilities inherent in experimentation with varying scheduling patterns.

A key decision in any media plan involves the proper balance of reach and frequency. It is seldom possible within any specified budget to reach as many people as often as one would like. Since a compromise is usually required, a decision must be reached as to whether a plan should be designed which will maximize coverage of the total defined market without much regard to how many impressions any individual receives, or conversely, whether a frequency goal against a prime segment of the market should be set up, with secondary consideration given to expanding coverage beyond that segment if funds turn out to be available.

Plans A and B both cost approximately the same. Plan A might be classified as a reach plan, while the objective of plan B is to obtain heavier frequency against a smaller audience. Plan A reaches 89 per cent of all women; over two-thirds receive five or fewer impressions, while only 6.4 per cent are contacted more than either times. Plan B, which emphasizes frequency, reaches 69 per cent of all women, but of these more than one-third are exposed eight or more times.

It is apparent from these differences that the choice of alternative media plans must depend heavily on the reach and frequency strategy established at the outset.

This decision would be relatively easy if there were available some empirical data which indicated how many advertising messages are required to ensure maximum consumer response. Obviously, no such certain knowledge exists. Advertising works differently on different people—and may work differently on the same individual from time to time depending upon the message, the media, and the individual's stage in the decision process. Thus, it is impossible to say that X number of impressions is just the right number to put against a single individual, much less an entire "prospect group."

Elements in a decision: Nevertheless, an explicit decision on this critical question must ultimately be made and a number of considerations will be involved in the decision. First among these will be *the budget available relative to the size of the potential market.*

Ideally, a media budget would be fixed only after a careful assessment of the goals of the advertising plan and the estimated cost of meeting those goals. Unfortunately, in the real world, the budget is more often based on an arbitrary percentage of sales or sales quota and is frequently subject to alteration, up or down, as the year progresses. The media planner's options under these circumstances are limited. He is not in the ideal position, as a rule, of saying how much reach and frequency should be delivered; rather, he must assess the objectives of the plan in the light of the dollars available and recommend the most effective practical plan. In doing this, he will of course analyze a number of alternatives to arrive at the one which will come *closest* to the ideal distribution of impressions he would like to achieve. This is often a hard decision and requires a careful assessment of several other factors.

A second key consideration will be *the competitive environment in which the advertising will be working.*

A study of competitive media schedules will provide a reasonably accurate estimate of the volume of advertising being put against sub-segments of the potential market by competing brands. It should also be possible to estimate the monthly reach and frequency achieved by these schedules.

With this information it will then be possible to form a judgment as to where advertising dollars have the best chance of achieving a positive response, or conversely, where competitive advertising may largely nullify response to our own advertising and diminish its profitability

If there is no real alternative but to meet competition head-on, such information will indicate what level of advertising is needed in order at least to rise above the "noise level" of competing coy claims. We can then circumscribe the "reach" goal in order to achieve the frequency level necessary to get into the range of optimum effectiveness.

Another consideration which will affect this decision is *the degree of brand switching or brand loyalty in the product category.*

Information on the intensity of consumer loyalty to the particular brand and other brands in the product class is available from consumer panel studies and from special surveys of brand attitudes and brand switching. Where brand loyalty is naturally high and it appears that a heavy weight of advertising may be required to induce switching, an advertising strategy concentrated against only a fraction of the total market may be very productive, and only such a policy may, in fact, produce the frequency required for effective communication.

Finally, it is necessary to take account of *the stage in the product's life cycle—is it in a growth period, sustaining, or on the decline?*

A new product building its market will probably set as its advertising goal brand awareness among the maximum number of potential users. A strategy of broad exposure, therefore, may seem appropriate in the first year or two of its development.

Once the product becomes well known, the market has stabilized, and inevitably, competition has moved in, a strategy of maintaining competitive weight against the best customer groups may be more productive. Such a strategy change will lead to more emphasis on frequency of impression delivery against the selected market segments.

In the declining phase a gradual retrenchment in spending may further circumscribe the reach objective. Maximum affordable frequency against enclaves of loyal customers will be the objective in an effort to stave off the inroads of new, more dynamic competition.

Selection of media. Once a reach-frequency strategy has been agreed upon, the media planner has the responsibility of selecting those media which, in combination, offer the greatest potential for successful implementation. Media audiences differ in their extent and rate of duplication, and these differences must be taken into account.

A valuable attribute of the computer in media selection is its ability to do just this. One system in use at J. Walter Thompson and perhaps at other agencies provides the opportunity to place differing values on a first impression going against an individual the simulated population as opposed to the second, which in turn can be evaluated differently from the third, etc. If a first contact is given a greater value than any subsequent exposure to the same person, the computer will be forced to search for media vehicles which add the greatest number of new viewers or readers at each stage in the selection process. The result maximizes reach.

The computer, however, is not able to set the strategy. This can be done only by the media decision makers on the basis of a careful evaluation of each specific situation.

In the actual selection of media vehicles, there are certain pitfalls in the analysis of reach and frequency which must be avoided.

a. Coverage versus *selectivity.* If the media strategy calls for "maximum coverage" of a carefully defined target-prospect group, it will be important to implement that strategy as efficiently as possible. A television program or magazine with mass appeal may well provide excellent coverage of the selected market segment but be a very inefficient vehicle because of the additional *waste* circulation which the advertiser must buy.

On the other hand, a selective vehicle which at first glance may appear to have a high cost per thousand in terms of its total audience may be comparatively efficient when measured against potential prospects only.

The three factors to be considered are (1) coverage. (2) selectively, and (3) efficiency against prospects. Efficiency in reaching the selected target is, of course, the result of selectivity related to cost and is the key criterion.

It should be reiterated here, however, that reach cannot be rigidly controlled. The relationship between market goals and media audiences is tenuous at best. Except for those specialized media aimed at such select groups as flower growers, boating enthusiasts, or skiers, or those few publications offering demographic editions, it is not possible to pinpoint a target group exactly. Thus, there are always practical limitations on our ability to achieve reach goals, and alternative media plans must be evaluated on their *relative* capabilities in this area.

b. The high cost of adding reach. A second important consideration is the cost of adding few percentage points of reach to a schedule. As can be seen in the following Table, a daytime network television investment of $32, 000 might provide a reach of 40 per cent of all housewives, for example.

c. The quintile distortion: Every individual tends to spend more time with one medium than another. Television has its devotees, as do magazines. Some people spend an hour or two with the daily newspaper; others race through it in a few minutes. While the demographic characteristics of individuals may have some influence on these predilections, the connection is tenuous at best. Thus a heavy investment in any one medium will create imbalances in the distribution of impressions among market segments or demographic groups.

On the other hand, the addition of a second medium will almost invariably tend to level these imbalances.

The evening network television schedule provided a reach of 47 per cent of all adults in the United States over a four-week period. However, if these viewers are divided into quintiles on the basis of number of hours of television viewed per week, it can be seen that 79 per cent of the heaviest-viewing quintile is exposed to the message as contrasted with 10 per cent of the lightest-viewing quintile. Frequencies are also heavily skewed, ranging from 1.0 to 1.6.

The addition of a second medium, in this case magazines, levelled the reach substantially. The magazine schedule added 400 per cent to the reach of the lightest-viewing television quintile and 10 per cent to the heaviest.

While magazines tend to complement television particularly well, any other medium added to the television schedule would have had the same effect to some degree. It is safe to say that if level coverage of any target audience is desired, a mix of more than one medium will achieve the objective better than a single media form used exclusively. On the other hand, while there undoubtedly is a point beyond which it is economically unsound to pile more impressions against an already overexposed quintile of viewers or readers, it is not always easily determined when the addition of a second media form to balance the skew is desirable. The excitement and impact that can be engendered by a concentrated effort in a single medium may, in fact, be the secret ingredient which makes the total campaign a success. A degree of "overexposure" may be critically important to tip the scales in favour of the product advertised.

30
Productivity and Technology

Managements worldwide are generally never satisfied with productivity levels in their organisations. Although the American worker remains slightly ahead in the productivity race, the gap is closing rapidly as the rest of the industrial world accelerates. The capital-intensive United States, home of industrial engineering and the assembly line, production planning and the computer, has recently witnessed its first productivity decline in output per working hour in three decades. Japan and the leading nations of Western Europe bettered USA in rate of growth as it fell to ninth place among the dozen leading industrial nations in the rate of productivity increase.

Reversing this trend is of significant concern to this large nation. At the national level it is the best way to stop inflation and improve real income. At the company level it is the only way to reduce costs and improve profits. And for the individual managers, improving their own productivity is central to their jobs. For each, it means the way to increased responsibility, satisfaction, and growth.

Getting better results by productivity improvement is the most important task of all managers, whatever their level in the company. Many middle-management and only that group is responsible. This is not so. Without some measurable productivity objective, neither the organization nor the individual manager have a sense of direction. Planning, if done at all, proceeds without any definable goal. Control cannot be exercised because there is no method for measuring performance against plan. The extent there is no method for measuring performance against plan. The extent to which resources are made productive becomes the primary test of the manager's ability as well as productive becomes the primary test of the manager's ability as well as the standard by which we can compare the performance of organizations.

Peter Drucker, the popular management writer, says that making work productive and the worker achieve is the major dimension of the management task. This dimension is also a challenge. It is a challenge because productivity improvement has no mature body of knowledge or group of tested methods, nor does there exist a clearly defined yardstick by which it can be measured. Add to this the accelerating social change and the uncertain knowledge of human motivation and we do indeed face a challenge.

Productivity is somewhat like the weather; many people are talking about it but few are doing anything. If you asked the question: "Who's in charge of productivity?" the typical company would reply, "Nobody!"

Richard C. Gerstenberg, former chairman of General Motors, says he is astonished at how few major companies "even know what productivity is." In a 1975 survey of 6,000 business managers, the American Management Association found serious worry over productivity, but two thirds of the respondents in the survey reported their companies were making no special effort to evaluate executive productivity.

Some industries are particularly lax in efficiency. This appears to be higher than average in service industries which make up about fifty per cent of our gross national product. When you combine this with the "service" or overhead departments of other types of business you have an enormous sector that is not being gauged by any value-added measure. A senior executive in a large insurance company says, "The service industries cannot answer some of the basic questions relating to their operations. We spent three years installing our information system but we can't tell how much it cost since we don't have a cost accounting system to tell us. However, as slow as the insurance industry is, it appears that the banking industry is still behind us."

Government agencies and industries regulated by the government come in for their share of criticism. Twenty years ago the railroads guaranteed delivery of a head of lettuce from California to the East coast in six days. Today it takes eleven days. It is estimated that a rail car is moving under load only seven per cent of the time. Productivity varies by as much as one thousand per cent in some government operations.

During the most recent period for which data are available, productivity in Japan increased at five times the rate of the United States. Japanese government expenditures on productivity improvement are over six times the amount spent by the U.S. government, despite the fact its federal budget is five times larger than Japan's.

The people problem: Who's to blame?

What's the problem? Whatever your personal view, you can probably find support for your conclusion. Each of the causes listed has come in for its share of the blame.

Many executives think that militant labour unions restrict improvements in productivity. No doubt this feeling has some validity. In some companies it appears that an imbalance of power between management and labour has occurred. In some extreme cases unions may have as much to say about day-to-day operations as management. One frustrated official remarked, "Workers believe that since they come to the plant forty hours per week they can't be expected to work too!"

The government is everybody's whipping boy. It is said that efficiency is being stifled by regulations. Additionally, many companies complain that the U.S. government, unlike governments in other countries, does little to encourage private investment in plants and equipment, nor does it take additional measures to support free enterprise. While there may be some truth in these complaints on a company basis, they are hardly justification for individual managers to become lax.

The rise of the service industries has changed the "blue collar blues" to the "white collar blues." It is said that a growing proportion of the work force are "knowledge workers" and since it is difficult to define the output of this type of worker, it is difficult to measure their productivity. Moreover, some manual workers have adopted self-defeatist attitudes because they perceive themselves as second class citizens.

Some managers blame egalitarianism for the "the world owes me a living" attitude of some workers. This accelerating philosophy is causing near-apoplexy in some board rooms. Broadly defined, the movement seeks equality of condition—more equal distribution of income, housing, consumer goods, and social status—as well as equality of rights. The modern egalitarians have placed their hostility queerly at the door of the corporation and have demanded government intervention to assure equality. Opponents of the movement point to the management and financial fiasco in New York city as an example of the likely consequences of a welfare state.

The increasing role of technology

The potential for replacing power muscle by technology such as the wheelbarrow is easily understood and applied by both worker and manager alike in the United States. During the twentieth century it has become the most capital-intensive nation in the world. Its capital resources have combined with innovative engineering to provide it with a technology base that is unsurpassed. It has traditionally depended upon technology to solve everything from defense needs and environmental problems to its increasing standard of living. The remaining two components of increased productivity, labour and management, have played a secondary role.

This emphasis is changing fast. Some feel that perhaps technological interventions have gone about as far as it can go until the human element catches up with technology. The 3M chief executive, Harry Heltzer, reflects this conclusion in his comment: "You can't press the button any harder and make the automated equipment run any faster. In a rising cost spiral you've just got to find ways of pressing it more intelligently." In other words, working harder is not the total answer; we've got to work "smarter" too.

In the American Management Associations survey mentioned earlier in the chapter, greater capital investment ranked thirteenth on a list of factors considered very important in terms of influencing an organization's productivity. In the survey of 6,000 managers, only twenty seven per cent ranked capital investment a very important and only thirty five percent ranked technology as very important. The overwhelming choice for improved productivity was better management.

The leverage of management

Despite the popular belief that the biggest roadblock to productivity is people, the evidence seems to indicate otherwise.

Most people understand and appreciate the principle of muscle or mechanical leverage. Mental leverage is not so widely appreciated or understood. To demonstrate this for yourself, close your eyes and try to multiply five numbers in your head without benefit of paper and pencil. Most people give up after ten or fifteen minutes. Yet with the aid of simple technology such as a pencil and paper we are able to perform the calculation in fifteen seconds. With a hand-held calculator, another generation of technology, the time is reduced to three seconds. Consider yet a higher level of technology.

Unfortunately, the potential for mental leverage with the computer, a special case of technology, goes largely unrealized.

Now consider these questions: (1) Is it likely that the application of good management can provide increased leverage to operational improvements and hence to productivity increases? (2) Can we consider the management of productivity a special case of technology? The answer to both of these questions must be in the affirmative.

The improvements resulting from better management are not so easily identified and quantified, therefore the multiplier effect is often overlooked. However, we do known that failure to apply good management can result in disaster.

The answer: Better management

Management consultant John Patton, who has been studying the subject for thirty years, says, "Declining productivity is not entirely the fault of organized labour....it is not entirely the fault of our patronizing, interfering government....it is not entirely the fault of the shifting attitudes of our younger generation....the real fault lies squarely at the feet of management, for not seizing the initiative to take remedial action."

A number of productivity studies make it clear that there is room for blame across the board. The productivity problem is no more the fault of the production line worker than that of the middle manager or supervisor or even the president of the company. To quote former chairman Gerstenberg of General Motors again, "Better productivity results from better management."

If this is the case, why do so many people overlook the leverage potential of improved management? It is probably because the managers themselves so frequently overlook; look it or they are unaware of the techniques and methods at their disposal.

Productivity—the ratio of some measure output to some measure of input—a difficult measure at best, is usually attributed to the improved efficiency of some specific resource such as capital, money, materials, or technology. For example, one familiar output-input measure is kilometers per litre of petrol. We use this measure not as a gauge of the efficiency of the gasoline but as an indicator of the efficiency of the car's performance. We overlook the accumulated technology and capital that has been managed by the petroleum companies. More recently, the energy shortage has demanded increased efficiency of automobile engines. We have assumed that this increase is solely a function of engineering design whereas it resulted from the volume and quality of other inputs that were planned, organized, and controlled by management. And here management implies process of management and not a group of persons.

There exists a paradox among managers. On the one hand there is a growing consensus that the most important factors in improving productivity depend on management: better planning, more effective job procedures, better communications, more effective human resource policies, improved decision making, and so on. On the other hand there is a reluctance to tackle the job. Managers at all levels need to roll up their serves and get to work.

Top level managers have two tasks. First they must develop and disseminate a strategy that will guide each member of the organization in a unified sense of direction. They must answer the questions: What kind of company do we want to be? What is our purpose and mission? What is our product/market scope and our competitive edge? What are our major objectives and the plans to achieve them?

The second task of top management is to determine the necessary investment to make in productivity. They have done it for technology and they have done it for marketing. It is now time to make a commitment to productivity. Part of this investment should be in management development.

Individual managers and supervisors need to stop thinking in terms of performing activities and think instead in terms of results. They must think in terms of motivating subordinates and managing work. Objectives must be achieved through action plans arrived at in an orderly manner through better problem solving and decision making.

Productivity, job development and appraisal

It is widely agreed that the greatest untapped potential for increasing productivity lies in the motivation and management of people in the work situation. This idea, somewhat slow to catch on, is now being promoted by management and labour alike. At General Motors, the "organization person's organization," many managers believe that recapturing the interest of their workers—or at least getting them to tolerate life on the assembly line—is one of the crucial problems to be solved in the remainder of the century. Most chief executives will freely admit that their most important decisions are about people. Even unions, historically concerned with little more than pay and benefits, are now adopting policies regarding the quality of work life as it relates to motivation and participation.

The modern manager must consider not only what is right for the company but what is right for the individual as well. In the past we have ordinarily considered these two requirements as conflicting. The problem now is to combine them into a single approach that meets the seeds of the company as well as its personnel. It can be done.

In this chapter we will examine those factors which affect productivity and relate them to modern motivational philosophy and practice. Throughout it is argued that a management by results approach is the central theme and the operational vehicle by which we can achieve productivity. Results management motivates the manager and the subordinate to action because each decides the job necessary to get the results demanded by the work. It is a philosophy of management that rests on the concepts of human action, behaviour, and motivation.

Motivation and productivity

Most of the readers of this book have probably been exposed to the basic conceptual aspects of human motivation as it applies to the job situation. The fundamental notion is that when employees are provided an opportunity to utilize their talents and potential, they will perform at a higher level of productivity, made fewer mistakes, and achieve a higher level of personal satisfaction. The mainstream of existing theory is summarised by presenting a thumbnail sketch of the principles developed by three contemporary experts. Abraham Maslow, Douglas McGregor, and Frederick Herzberg.

Maslow, the father of humanist psychology, concluded that human wants from a hierarchy which runs from lower to higher order needs; from basic physical divers to higher order psychological needs. The highest order need he called self-actualization. As one level of the hierarchy is reasonably satisfied, the next level becomes the more potent motivator. His statement that "man lives by bread alone—only when there is no bread" illustrates the point that as the economic wants become increasingly satisfied, it becomes less and less satisfying to obtain more economic rewards. Hence the promise of money or other economic rewards is not a motivator once basic needs are met.

Maslow's theory has two important lessons for the manager. First, within most organizations, sizable numbers of employees move swiftly to the satisfaction of lower order needs but become frustrated because their opportunities for self-actualization are thwarted and full utilization of their talents in blocked. They must either be satisfied with something less than optimum job satisfaction or find outside involvement to fulfill their needs for meaningful accomplishment. The second lesson to be learned from Maslow is that money is not the motivator we thought it was. This may be hard to accept but a moment's reflection may convince you that although a person may work harder because of the promise of money, he or she is not motivated. There is a substantial difference. The problem with money is that the worker must constantly be re-cycled by some form of behaviour reinforcement with either the carrot or the stick. Neither case illustrates motivation. The worker "moves" but isn't motivated. Only self-actualization related to the job will achieve that.

A second highly popular theory of motivation and human behaviour has been advanced by Douglas McGregor: the concept of the Theory X and the Theory Y managerial styles. The classical approach to management is represented by Theory X, which maintains that there is no satisfaction in the work itself, that humans avoid work as much as possible, that positive direction and tight control over workers is necessary, and that workers possess little ambition or enthusiasm for their work. The human relations approach of Theory Y, the antithesis of Theory X, states that workers exercise self-direction and seek responsibility if properly motivated. Theory Y is a participative approach.

It remained for Frederick Herzberg to show how managers can move toward adopting Theory Y assumptions while satisfying the higher order needs of self-actualization for their subordinates. He pointed out that when economic rewards and other lower-level needs are met, they are diminished in importance as positive incentives, but their capacity to create dissatisfaction rapidly increases if they are not satisfied. He said that economic rewards cease to be "incentives" and become "hygiene factors." If not properly taken care of—that is, if there is dissatisfaction with the economic rewards—they become deterrents. On the positive side, Herzberg found that another group of factors, the motivators, tended to produce job satisfaction and productivity. These motivators center around the job itself or the job content and included achievement, growth, participation, and responsibility.

Herzberg's role in motivational theory cannot be denied. He has refocused management's attention from the classical Theory X assumptions and hygiene factors to the far more important motivator factors of achievement, recognition, and the work itself. These factors are the ones that hold promise for increased productivity and job satisfaction. Too often in the past, management's motivational attempts have been limited to the hygiene areas.

It is important to understand the difference between hygiene and motivational factors surrounding the subordinate's job.

What does all this mean in terms of our system for managing productivity? It means that first we must identify those job factors that motivate and hence affect the productivity of subordinates. It means that second we must operationalize these factors. In other words, we combine theory and practice in order to achieve results through managing subordinates.

Factors affecting productivity

Research and observation tell us that there are nine important factors that need to be taken into account if an organization is to effect the changes that are necessary to increase productivity and profitability. These are summarized here:

1. Work that is challenging, creative, and interesting and provides an opportunity for "stretch" performance.
2. Participation in decisions that have a direct effect on the individual's job.
3. Compensation that is tied to performance and to sharing in productivity gains. This requires realistic appraisal.
4. Communication and authority channels that are simplified.
5. Supervision that is competent.
6. Recognition of achievement
7. Self-development opportunity.
8. Opportunity for stewardship, care of and attention to customer and co-worker needs.
9. Organizational style and patterns that are more flexible.

Providing for these job satisfaction and motivational needs is not a simple task. Indeed, it is very complex. No simplistic change or group of changes, such as revised pay schedules or job enrichment, alone will suffice, nor will any misdirected notions of "human relations" or paternalism.

We do know that certain basic techniques, methods, and programs are available to the organization and to the individual manager that, taken together, can go a long way toward creating the proper climate for productivity. We will call these Results Management Methods and they form the basis of our system of managing subordinates. They are:

1. *Job Development*: Matching the content and level of an employee's job responsibility to his or her skills and abilities.
2. *Performance Appraisal*: The process of appraising a subordinate's performance against previously established goals. This provides feedback on performance, a tool for self-development, and a device for recognition for performance.
3. *Subordinate Development*: Providing the environment for continuous learning, self-development, and growth on the job.
4. *Communication*: Improving the communication process using upward communication so that subordinates are informed about matters which affect their jobs.

5. *Leadership Style*: The adoption of leadership and supervisory styles that promote "results thinking" and hence productivity and job satisfaction.
6. *Delegation and Control:* Learning and practicing the art of delegation utilizing self-control by subordinates.
7. *Organizational Style*: Adopting an organizational form that provides for flexibility in authority and communication and overcomes the inflexibility of the classical bureaucracy.

Job development

History goes that job development or job enlargement was discovered at IBM when the company's founder, Thomas J. Watson, Sr., saw a woman operator sitting idly at her machine. When asked why she was not working, the women replied: "I have to sit and wait for the setup man to change the tool setting for a new run." Watson asked: "Couldn't you change the tool setting yourself?" The woman replied: "Of course I could but I am not allowed to." Upon further examination Watson learned that in addition to waiting for setup men, additional idle time was spent waiting for inspectors to inspect the finished products of the same workers. Watson reasoned, correctly, that little time would be required to train the workers to perform both additional tasks of setting up the machine and inspecting the finished product. He instituted these changes and the resulting job development and elimination of excess task specialization resulted in better quality, fewer losses due to scrap, and a steady increase in productivity. Moreover, workers reported greater job satisfaction and more interest in their work. This philosophy has provided IBM since that time.

There is little doubt that millions of employees at all levels of organizations are underutilized and misutilized. This waste of human resources can result in serious consequences for company productivity. In the personnel management area it can account for turnover, tardiness, accident, high rates of grievances, strikes, and even outright sabotage. In the product and service areas these consequences can range form low product quality to disinterest in or ever antagonism to wards customer requirements.

Two actions can go a long way toward improving productivity through better personnel utilization: match the job with the person; and remove the boredom from the job.

Matching the job with the person involves developing or engineering the job so that the job responsibilities, content, and level match the employee's skills and abilities. It is worth nothing the difference between *content* and *level* of the match. If a job calls for a level of responsibility that is lower than the person's ability, it is not a good match even through the job content and employee overlap. A good job-employee match includes a reasonable overlap between skill and job demands and a level of responsibility that provides room for growth and development of the individual.

Removing the boredom from the job is becoming an increasing challenge. Popular expressions like "blue collar blues" and "white collar monotony" are becoming commonplace but these trite phrases mislead people into thinking that job monotony, boredom, and dissatisfaction are confined to the assembly line or the clerical level. This is not the case. In many organizations dissatisfaction occurs at all levels from the floor sweeper to the executive suite.

The manager who wants to improve the job-employees match or to remove some of the boredom from work is faced with two contradictory arguments. On the one hand, traditional "scientific management" and the industrial engineer calls for the programming and standardization of specialized tasks using the techniques of work simplification, methods design, process and activity charts and so on. On the other hand the emerging approach of the behavioural scientists tell us that task specialization is bad and we should engineer the job so that employees want to channel their interests toward their work.

Appraisal

Any manager with "hands on" experience with performance appraisal almost invariably finds the job distasteful. Research has shown that in those companies without a formal control system over the process, fewer than half of the appraisals are ever completed. In my own experience with hundreds of supervisors and middle managers I have found that the appraisal process and communication are the two most frequently mentioned problems. They don't like either role, whether it be the "appraisor" or the "appraisee." The process inhibits more often than it promotes communication.

In general, there are three reasons for supervisory resistance to the appraisal process: Supervisors don't like to criticize a subordinate and have to handle the inevitable argument that follows; they feel that they are not equipped to properly perform the appraisal of a subordinate or to handle the accompanying interview; and they have a general mistrust of the techniques and procedures surrounding the appraisal process.

The subordinates usually dislike the process also. Unless they are one of the few selected for high praise, the employees almost always feel that their performance has been judged unfairly.

The general failure of the appraisal system to operate as expected is unfortunate. Properly used, the performance appraisal can become fine tool for improved motivation, communication, self-development, and hence productivity.

The problems with performance appraisal

Most organizations with appraisal programs have two things in common. They follow the textbook definition and consider the appraisal process as a formal evaluation of the employee actions over a previous time period. Secondly, virtually all have some performance appraisal form. The similarity among companies ends there.

Deficiencies in practice can be summarized under the five broad areas discussed below.

1. Focusing on the *reward/punishment* aspects tends to detract from the real purpose of an appraisal session. When viewed this way, the interview frequently turns into either a whitewash job or a faultfinding session. If the former, the employee may go away with false hopes for promotion or pay increases or a false sense of job security. Faultfinding appraisal frequently regress into personality clashes resulting form statements about behaviour and performance that have not been previously communicated. In any case, both the boss and the subordinate frequently depart with feelings of distress or ill-will.
2. Appraisals based on *personality traits* are bad news. They obscure the real purpose of appraisal which is focus on results. In particulate no case is the subordinate motivated to better productivity.
3. *Emphasis on the system* is an all too frequent complaint. When it is viewed as a mandatory technique or procedure, or something the Personnel Department "demand up", they system becomes the ends and not the means.
4. There is a general *confusion about the objectives* of performance review. Rarely is improved productivity a stated objective of appraisal not it is viewed as a vehicle to focus on results. Instead, its purpose is frequently seen as a catch-all of procedures related to general personnel administration: wage and salary review, placement, development, and advancement. When this approach occurs, both employee and manager become confused and adopt defensive behaviour regarding the process.
5. *Nonproductive behaviour* is a frequent result of appraisal. Although the process implies precision, in reality it is quite imprecise and filled with personal judgment and emotion. There is a tendency to do something *to* the employees, not *with* them. The appraisal becomes, at best, a hygienic aspect of motivation, at worst, an emotional letdown for both superior and subordinate.

The job description problem

Some of the difficulty surrounding the focus on activities can be traced to a great American industrial institution—the job description. Often these are written in terms of activities and general statements of responsibilities rather than in terms of what is expected from the job.

A solution to this difficulty lies in including a statement of expected results in the job description. Aside from all the other advantages we have mentioned, such action would provide a basis for appraisal.

One question tends to rear its head at this point in a book like this: will the reader be stimulated to action as a result of the material that has been presented? This chapter has been designed as an impetus for action to provide incentive to utilize this book's ideas and thereby improve team productivity.

The most obvious and compelling reason for a serious study of how teams work is the need to improve the productivity of teams in all organizations. This reason is so obvious that it is often overlooked, and managers may be inclined to ask, "Why should I do this?" or "What's in it for me?" The answer is simple: "What's good for the organization is good for you." A serious examination of teamwork can lead to valuable discoveries that can make the difference between a moderately productive and a highly productive group of people. Improved quality and increased output will be a direct result of the talents of team members being unleashed. Many organizations in other parts of the world have discovered how to unleash the dormant talent within their work forces.

If improved output alone is not reason enough to begin looking at team productivity, managers might consider team productivity from the point of view of their own career development. The changing direction of management requires that managers of the future be fully versed and qualified in all the functions of managing, including managing team productivity. If the competitive position of an organization is that it has achieved the past is to be maintained, managers and members of organizations must have not only a solid business education but also skills in the following essential areas; team-work, oral communications, listening, learning how to learn, goal setting, motivation leadership, self-esteem, problem solving, creative thinking, personal and career development, and interpersonal negotiation.

Once a manager had realized the significance of learning how to improve team productivity, the next question is how to take charge and move ahead. Organization politics can often work against a manager who is attempting to assume responsibility for making needed changes. However, a manager can take action by discovering the positive ways of being political and entrepreneurial. A manager can either maintain the status quo, remaining cautious and dependent on the organization, or be courageous and autonomous. The results of following one's entrepreneurial instincts honestly and affirmatively can be extremely beneficial for both the individual and the organization.

In the typical bureaucratic organization, politics tend to be destructive, forcing people to say things that they do not really believe, breeding suspicion and concealment, and causing issues to be dealt with in guarded and ineffective ways. If managers believe in the power of teams, they can take on the responsibility and authority for improving their own organizational while encouraging the same type of action in people working around them. It is through a strong commitment to the idea that improved teamwork really can make a difference that a manager can exert a constructive form of organizational politics. In short, to make things change and to improve productivity in an organization, the manager should do the following:

1. Make a commitment to yourself to improve.
2. Be an architect of your own organization.
3. Set goals that are unique and that others have not achieved.
4. Choose the path of highest resistance rather than the one with the least resistance. The payoff will always be higher.
5. Take some risks because it is the right thing to do and needs to be done.
6. Recognize that you are an entity in yourself and that you can initiate change.
7. Know that you are responsible or your own problems. What you have is what you have made?
8. Do not wait for the signal from above. The ball is in your court, and you can throw it any time you wish.

Managers sometimes run into stagnation resulting from old habits and ideas that have become entrenched within an organization, and such stagnation can drag down innovative efforts at improvement. There are ways to circumvent such problems and resistance by taking advantage of the positive feelings and the desire to move ahead that are found in all organizations. People do look forward, and they do want to improve and win; when changes are linked to these human desires, positive responses and results will follow. A second problem commonly encountered when change is undertaken in insufficient time to make the change. Managers are often so caught up in day-to-day ire fighting that they never set aside the time to work on general improvements in areas such as problem solving. Time must be spent working on projects that will lead to improvement, not just on keeping the organization from slipping below its present level. Although this extra time is difficult to find and sometimes painful to spare, it is very productive time.

As managers start to change the way they manage their groups, they often find a clear and pronounced drop in productivity. Every effort at change entails a learning process, and it is during this learning process, this transition period, that productivity temporarily drops. Be assured, however, that the drop will be followed by an increase in productivity that will surpass the previous level. Managers also frequently encounter resistance. The solution is not to try to clash directly with those who resist but to work around them. Find ways to war with those who are receptive and enthusiastic and simply avoid those who are resistant. In time, those who resist may see the light and come around to your position. Finally, managers attempting to initiate change may experience the feeling of a loss of power. Managers have been taught over the years to feel powerful and to strive for power within their organizations. A manager who delegates power or responsibilities to members of the team may feel that he or she is giving up something important. In reality, however, the manager is not giving up power but simply sharing it with other people. The manager will still be held accountable and will in fact be seen as more powerful for having made the team more productive.

Manager can do a number of things to initiate change on their own. First of all, they can develop their own vision of how they see the organization working, commit this vision to writing, and then share it with members of the team. The vision serves as a picture or target that people can easily identify with, and it can stimulate them in a similar direction. The second thing managers can do is start changing their own styles of managing. This can be done by simply introducing new behaviours and actions, one at a time, watching the results of these actions and behaviours, and then making them a part of a permanent leadership approach. Third, managers can seek out support from members of the team who are interested a more team-oriented approach to managing. Fourth, a manager can experiment with specific areas in the way the team works. For instance, problems such as poor team meetings can be addressed directly with the team. Team members will view this as improvement and moving ahead. After one or two successes, the whole process of changing the team will begin to unfold. Finally, managers can observe other successful teams, read about self-directed teams and team productivity, and attend seminars and workshops on the subject. The following steps are suggested as an agenda for action:

1. Start by preparing a vision of how you see your team working two or three years from now. Discuss this with your team members, visualize it with them, and gain their commitment to reaching it.

2. Study and understand your team members. What are they like? What do they need? What do they want? What can they contribute to the team? How can you set up a culture that will tap their unused and unleashed resources? Work with them in this process.

3. Analyze the way your team is working today. Use a survey or whatever method is best suited to your needs to help you diagnose and understand the team problems that you are now experiencing. Share these problems with your team. Get them to help you develop action steps to correct the problems.

4. If needed, enlist the help of outside resources. Most organizations have their own specialists who are qualified to assist as facilitators and team builders. If there are no such specialists or resources within the organization, go outside.

5. Once a team has started to make the change, be sure that you have designed ways to monitor the improvements. Provide ways to reinforce the change in a positive way, and reward the team for the successful adoption of action steps that increase its productivity. The improved results will themselves be rewarding, but it is helpful to offer more tangible rewards as well: special recognition, favours,

opportunities for personal development, financial rewards. If possible, try to design your system so that the more people produce, the greater the financial reward.

The whole issue of managing productive teams boils down to what is in it for you, the team leader. When you get improved performance from your team, you will feel greater satisfaction with yourself, your work will be more fun, your career position will improve, and you will be on the way to greater financial reward.

Management control

In recent years, manufacturing firms worldwide have been directing increasing attention to the need for improving productivity in order to strengthen their competitive position. To monitor and evaluate productivity changes, and to communicate and reinforce this new emphasis on productivity improvements, appropriate measures of productivity are required. Productivity measurement can generate information that may be useful for management control purposes in two ways. First, such measurement may identify dimensions on which productivity improvements are possible, in which case targets may be generated to guide future operations. The productivity measures may be employed to identify products or processes for which the firm has a competitive edge in productivity or similarly evaluate new technologies or investment projects that are likely to increase the firm's profitability. The second role for productivity measures in management control systems arises from their use in evaluating the performance of managers. In conjunction with the usual profit or cost accounting system, a productivity measurement system can be designed by the corporate managements so that it motivates the divisional managers to select actions that are consistent with the overall corporate plans and priorities.

Recent surveys, however, have documented that most large corporations do not use direct measures of productivity. Instead, they continue to use surrogates for productivity, such as labour variance, capacity utilization, or production cost standards. Sumanth's survey of 61 manufacturing companies indicated that partial productivity measures were used in 19.3% of the cases, aggregate productivity measures were used in only 0.3% of the cases, and simple surrogate measures were used in 80.4% of the cases. Furthermore, considerable confusion prevails about the definition and implementation of productivity measures. This is likely due to the fact that the direct productivity measures that have traditionally been used are simplistic, and they generally do not reflect the complex nature of most production processes encountered in practice. In particular, the traditional approaches assume linearity, separability, and other restrictive features for the production technology to simplify the calculations. As a result, improvements in productivity as measured by the traditional approaches are frequently found, in practice, to be inconsistent with improvements in the firm's competitive position and its short-term or long-term profitability. This arithmetic simplicity may have been necessitated in the past by computational concerns. However, with the increasing availability of inexpensive computing facilities, it is imperative that new productivity measure be developed that are appropriate for today's technologies.

A management control system is sometimes described as consisting of a device for measuring what is actually happening, a device for assessing the significance of the measured quantity relative to a standard, and a device for influencing the behaviour of managers, with evaluation of performance based on this measure and standard. Similarly, a productivity measurement system requires first a proper definition and development of a productivity index that reflects the actual productivity considerations in complex technologies. Second, it requires benchmarks for comparison purposes. These benchmarks, or standards, may be based on the information about the organization's performance in the past. Such information need not be restricted to just the performance in the preceding period. The standards could also be based on the performance of other similar organizations. This is particularly appropriate for corporations with a number of similar plants or branches or divisions which are evaluated relative to each other. Such benchmarks could also be developed from extensive engineering simulation models. This approach is appropriate for evaluating the productivity impact of new or potential technologies.

Finally, a productivity measurement system must be integrated with other systems for evaluating managerial performance. Productivity measurement is not very meaningful without an appropriate accounting and reporting system to support it. However, currently in most corporations, much of productivity oriented information remains at the shop floor level and is rarely reported to higher levels of management. If productivity accounting is to be employed for management control purposes it must be defined and developed carefully, and integrated with existing accounting and reporting systems, and further, it must maintain consistency with other corporate objectives such as profit maximization.

Productivity, as defined in this framework, measures the extent to which the actual input consumption exceeds the minimum inputs necessary to produce the actual input levels. The minimum input consumption is determined in a manner consistent with out current knowledge of the available production technology. Thus, a distinction is made between resources controllable by the responsible manager, and resources that are fixed, or beyond his discretionary control. In a manner analogous to responsibility accounting, the productivity variations are analyzed to emphasize which manager controls what parameters of the firm's operations, and to what extent each manager is responsible for the observed productivity variations.

For the price of the output relative to the labour usage rate depicted by the relative price line, it is also apparent that profits will be maximized if, in fact, the activity level is increased. But this implies a reduction in the traditional productivity measure. In this situation, therefore, the criterion of increasing "productivity" leads to a decision that is contradictory to the objective of increasing profits. This remains the fundamental problem with the traditional methods, where productivity improvement does *not* always imply profitability improvement. In fact, many corporations experimenting with productivity measures have found that some divisions making great strides in improving productivity have actually been showing lower profits. This is one of the principal reasons why we have not seen the acceptance of productivity measures as an integral part of a management control system, even though considerable attention has been focused for so long on the problem of productivity management.

The simple situation depicted done involves only output measured in number of units. But this notion can be directly extended to wider range of competitive issues. For instance, a reduction in labour hours may imply a lower quality of service or product, even if the same number of units are still produced. Further, such reduction may also affect the resilience of the organization to respond to change, or the investment in terms of time and effort in new products to improve the competitive position in the future. The use of just the traditional productivity measures may, in this manner, bias decisions against considerations for maximization of profits or competitive benefits.

It is thus important to emphasize the impact of reduction in an input, such as labour, on the level of output measured broadly, possible on multiple dimensions. Reduction in labour without reducing the output is desirable—it is true trimming of excess fat. But on the other hand, a decision to reduce input consumption that will also reduce the output must be evaluated with due regards to overall competitive considerations.

A framework for 'productivity analysis'

The productivity measurement approach described in this section builds on the pioneering work of Farrell in measuring relative technical and allocative inefficiencies, and is based on the theoretical constructs of production economics developed in Shephad. Farrell's early work was cast in a ration form, with an equivalent linear programming formulation, by Charnes, Cooper, and Rhodes. Its formal links with production economics were axiomatized by Banker and Banker, Charnes, and Cooper, to extend the efficiency analysis to the case of nonconstant returns to scale and distinguish between the purely technical and scale effects. Banker introduced the notion of the most productive scale size, and in suggested a framework for productivity measurement and variance analysis. Banker and Maindiratta provide the link between this efficiency and productivity analysis and the neoclassical nonparametric production analysis of Variance.

For concreteness, we describe the productivity measurement method for the case of a firm having two outputs and four inputs. The actual identification of the principal outputs and inputs requires the exercise of managerial judg… the particular circumstances for each firm. The estimation of … indexes is based on the following data:

a. Actual values of inputs consumption, outputs produced, an… prices.

b. Similar values for a set of referent points relative to which product… will be assessed. These referent points will depend on the actual … application of this model, but it could consist of time series data … performance of the firm, cross-sectional data available for the performance of other firms, or technical estimates of various production possibilities in case a new technology is being considered.

c. Additional knowledge about the actual production technology, such as separability, substitutability or linearity of the production function, and the controllable or fixed nature of the input.

Technology management

Technology has a competitive impact in two primary ways. First, it provides a market advantage through differentiation of value added; and second, it provides a cost advantage through improved overall system economies. To use technology effectively, companies must be explicit about its role. This requires answering four elementary questions: (1) What is the basis of competition in our industry? (2) To compete, which technologies must we master? (3) How competitive are we in these areas? (4) What is our technology strategy? In embryonic and growth industries, technology frequently drives the strategy, while in more mature fields, technology must be an enabling resource for manufacturing, marketing, and customer service. The U.S. excels at technology-driven innovation that creates whöle new enterprises. By contrast, Japan excels at incremental advances in existing products and processes.

Product, process, and support design

The technological aspects of projects are related to the design, manufacturing, and support of the product or system for which the project exists. Design activities begin with an analysis of the client's or organization's needs, which are translated, these requirements are transformed into functional and technical specifications. The last link in the chain is detailed product, process, and support design. Product design centers on the structure and shape of the product. Performance, cost, and quality goals must all be defined. Process design deals with the preparation of a series of plans for manufacture, integration, testing and quality control. In the case of an item to be manufactured, this means selecting the processes and equipment to be used during production setting up the part routings, defining the information flows, and assuring that adequate testing procedures are put into place.

...gn is responsible for selecting the hardware and software that will be ...d monitor activities once the system becomes operational. This means ...databases, defining report formats, and specifying communication ...for the exchange of data. A second support function concerns the ...ion of manuals for operators and maintenance personnel. Related issues ...n the design of maintenance facilities and equipment, and the development of ...es for inventory management. Both process design and support design include ... design of training for those who manufacture, test, operate, and maintain the system.

Design efforts are present in many nonengineering projects. Such efforts are required to transform needs into the blueprint of the final product. For example, consider the design of a new insurance policy of a change in the structure of an organization. In the first case, new needs may be detected by the marketing department: for example, a need to provide insurance for pilots of ultralight airplanes. The designer of this new policy should consider the risk involved in flying ultralights and the cost and probability of occurrence associated with each risk. In addition the risk to the pilot due to accidents, damage to the ultralight or to a third party needs to be considered. The designer of this new policy has to decide what options should be available to the customer and how the different options should be combined with each other.

In the second case, new products, changes in the business environment, and new technologies may generate a need to change the structure of an organization. For example, if a new product is very successful in a traditional organization and the business associated with this product becomes a major part of the total organizational business, a special division may be needed to manufacture, market, and support this product. The designer of the new organizational structure should consider questions related to the size of the new division, its mission, and its relationship with the existing parts of the organization.

In some projects, the design effort represents the most important component of the work. An example would be an architect who is designing a new building, or a team of communication experts designing a satellite relay network. Usually, design is the basis for production or implementation, depending on the context. In many situations, the design effort may consume only a small portion of the assigned budget and resources. Nevertheless, decisions made in the conceptual design and advanced development phases are likely to have a significant effect on the total budget, schedule, resource requirements, and overall success of the project.

Management of the design effort, from identifying a specific need to implementation of the end product, is the core of the technological aspect of project management. The fact that design takes place in the early stages of the most projects does not imply that technological management efforts cease once the blueprints are drawn. Changes in design are notoriously common throughout the life cycle of a project and have to be managed carefully.

The project manager has to consider four major factors when dealing with the management of technology: quality, cost, risk, and performance, the latter being measured by the functional attributes of the system. The tools for assessing each of these factors in the initial stages of a project were, Engineering Economic Analysis; Project Screening and Selection; and Multiple-Criteria Methods for Evaluation. We discuss life-cycle costing and show how decisions made early in the project affect the total life-cycle cost. To underscore the importance of good tools, we cite a National Science Foundation study which has shown that over 70% of the life-cycle cost of a product is defined at the conceptual and preliminary design stages. Information and decision support systems play a dynamic role in these stages by focusing management's efforts on the technology and providing feedback to the design team in the form of assessment data.

Our aim here is to indicate how the techniques discussed previously can be used throughout the life cycle of a project to manage its technological aspects. Frequently, the design is subject to change due to newly identified needs, changing business conditions, and evolution of the technology. Therefore, the management of the design is a continuing process that ends only with delivery of the finished product to the customer and perhaps, not even then. Manufacturer warranties and an insistent desire for product improvement in some markets may keep a project alive well after delivery of the products(s).

Importance of time

In the global market, successful companies will be those that learn to make and deliver goods and services faster than do their competitors. These "turbo marketers," as Kotler and Stonich term them, will have a distinct advantage in markets where customers value time compression enough to pay a premium or to increase purchases. Moreover, in certain high-tech areas such as semiconductor manufacturing and telecommunica-tions, where performance is increasing and price is dropping almost daily, survival depends on the rapid introduction of new technologies.

Once a company has examined the demand for its product, it can begin to reduce cycle time. In general, three principles can be applied: (1) reorganize the work, (2) organize and reward to encourage time compression, and (3) pursue cycle time reduction aggressively. Although the implementation effort and cost required to educe cycle time will be substantial, the payoff can be great. To create a sustainable advantage, companies must couple the so-called "soft" aspects of management with programs aimed at achieving measurable time-based results.

In this regard, a recent trend in technology management is to perform all major components of design concurrently. This approach, aptly known as *concurrent engineering,* is based on the concept that the parallel execution of the major design components will shorten project life cycles and this reduce the time to market for new products. In an era of time-based competition where the shelf life of some high-tech items may be as short as 6 months, this can make the difference between mere survival and material profits.

Studies by the consulting firm McKinsey & Co. have shown repeatedly that being a few months late to market is even worse than having a 30% development cost overrun. The figure points up the difference in revenue when a product is on time or late. The model underlying the graph assumes that there are three phases in the product's commercial life: a growth phase, (where sales increase at a fixed rate regardless of entry time), a stagnation phase (where sales level off), and a decline phase (where sales decrease to zero). The figure shows that a delay causes a significant decline in revenue. Suppose that a market has a 6-month growth period followed by a year of stagnation and a decline to zero sales in the succeeding 8 months. Then, being late to market by 3 months would reduce revenues by 36%. Thus a delay of one-eighth of the product lifetime reduces income by over one-third. Such a loss can be especially server since the largest profits are usually realized during the growth phase.

The application of concurrent engineering principles to technology management requires thoughtful planning and oversight. There is a clear need to inform the product engineers, process engineers, and support specialists of current status of the design and to keep them updated on all change requests. Due to the rapid propagation of errors, the risk of cost and schedule overruns. Faltering performance, and team bickering is greatly increased when control is lax. An error in one expect of the design may have repercussions that quickly extend to all functional areas.

In the following sections we explore the issues surrounding concurrent engineering and describe the risk aspect of technological management. We also discuss several approaches for managing design information and introduce the concept of total quality management for projects.

Concurrent engineering and time-based competition

The ability to design and produce high-quality products that satisfy a real need at a competitive price was, for many years, almost a sure guarantee for commercial success. With the explosion of electronic and information technology, a new factor-time has become a critical element in the equation. The ability to reduce the time required to develop new products and bring them to market is considered by many the next industrial battleground, For example, the Boeing 777 transport design took a year and half less than its predecessor the 767, permitting the company to introduce it in time to stave off much of the competition format the European Airbus. Similarly, John Deere's success in trimming development time for new products by 60% has enabled it to maintain its position as world leader in farm equipment in the face of a growing challenge form the Japanese. This was done using the concurrent engineering (CE) approach to support time-based competition.

The basic idea of concurrent engineering is to use project scheduling and resource management techniques in the design process. These techniques, have always been common to the production phase but are now recognized as vital to all life-cycle phases of a project form start to finish. In a CE environment, teams of experts from different disciplines work together to ensure that the design progresses smoothly and that all the participants share the same, most recent information.

The concurrent engineering approach replaces the conventional sequential engineering approach, in which new product development starts by one organizational unit (e.g., marketing), which lays out product specifications based on customer needs. These specifications are used by engineering to come up with a product design, which in turn serves as the basis for manufacturing engineering to develop the production processes and flows. Only when this last step is approved does support design begin.

Sequential engineering takes longer because all the design activities are strictly ordered. Furthermore, cycles are quite common throughout the project's life cycle. This is the case when product specifications prepared by marketing cannot be met by the available technology (unless, perhaps, a risky or costly R&D effort is undertaken). Similarly, manufacturing engineering may not be able to translate product design into process design, due to technological difficulties or the absence of adequate support (e.g., it may not be economically practical to develop test equipment for a product that has not been designed with testing in mind). In each of these examples, primary activities have to be repeated, creating cycles, and thus lengthening the entire design process, making it that much more expensive.

Put succinctly, concurrent engineering depends upon designing, developing, testing, and building prototype parts and subsystems concurrently, not serially, while at the same time designing and developing the equipment to fabricate the new product or system. This does not necessarily mean that all tasks are performed in parallel, but rather, that the team members from the various departments make their contribution in parallel. A prime objective of Concurrent Engineering (CE) is to shorten the time from conception to market (or deployment in the case of government or military systems), so as to be more competitive or responsive to evolving needs.

The basis of CE is teamwork, parallel operations, information sharing, and constant communication among the team members. To be most effective, the group should be multi-disciplinary, comprised of one or more representatives from each functional area of the organization. The watchword is cooperation. After a century of labour-management confrontation and sequestering employees in job categories, hierarchies, and functional departments, many manufacturers are now seeking teamwork, dialogue, and barrier bashing, if only for survival. By performing product, process, and support design in parallel there is a much greater likelihood that misunderstanding and problems of incompatibility will be averted over the project's life cycle. By reducing the length of the design process, over head and management costs are reduced proportionally, while the elimination of design cycles reduces direct costs as well. From a marketing point of view, a shorter design process results in the ability to introduce new models more frequently and to target specific models to specific groups of customers. This strategy leads to higher market share and consequently, higher sales and profits.

The implementation of CE is based on shared databases, good management of design information (this is the subject of configuration management), and computerized design tools such as CAD/CAM (computer-aided design/computer-aided manu-facturing). It is also important to understand that CE is risky and that without proper technological management the results can be calamitous. The two most prominent risks are:

1. *Organizational risks.* The attempt to cross the lines of functional organizations and to introduce changes into the design process is usually met with resistance. Once way to overcome this resistance, often manifested by interia and subtle acts of neglect, is to form, prior to the implementation of CE, project teams made up of people from the various functional areas. In addition an educational effort aimed at teaching the advantages and the logic of CE can create a positive atmosphere for this new approach.
2. *Technological risks.* The simultaneous effort of product, process, and support design should be well coordinated to ensure that the information used by all the designers is current and correct. The risks associated with a failure to manage this design information in the CE environment is much higher than in sequential engineering, where it is possible to freeze product design once process design starts, and to freeze process design once support design starts.

Companies thinking about using concurrent engineering techniques for the first time should consider projects that have the following characteristics:

1. The project is of a developmental (novel applications of known technology) or applications (routine applications of known technology) type.
2. The team has experience with the technology.
3. The team has received in total quality management and has had the opportunity to apply the concepts in its work.
4. The scale of the project falls somewhere in the range of 5 to 35 full-time staff members for a period of 3 to 30 months.
5. The goal is a product or family of products with clearly defined features and functions.
6. Success is not dependent on invention or significant innovation.

One of the goals of concurrent engineering is to reduce the time it takes to develop and market new products. Before we can say that a reduction has been achieved, we must have some idea of what the current standards are and what controls them. This is not as clear cut as it sounds because few projects proceed smoothly without interference from outside forces. Also, most companies modify their goals as work progresses, making it that much more difficult to measure project length.

Every industry and its constituent firms are in continuous flux, but they are all limited in their flexibility to achieve change. A number of inhibiting factors combine to create a rhythm or tempo in a company that is very difficult to break. The table lists some of these factors for manufacturing companies, although each may not be universally applicable at all times. Thoughtful engineering managers develop a feeling for the important factors in their business and how these affect their operations. As far as possible, they quantify them. This provides a baseline against which improvement can be measured. It is clear that many time-sensitive decisions have an impact on the successful operation of a business and that focusing on only one or two factors to the exclusion of the others is rarely optimal. Concurrent engineering is a business activity, not just an engineering activity.

The principles are the same, but their implementations are somewhat different. Two notorious time wasters are senior people doing junior work and everyone repeating the same tasks. These are both addressed by forming a multifunctional project team from the appropriate departments and carefully assigning responsibilities to the members. Not everyone is needed full time on every team, but the organizing plan should indicate where to get resources when needed on a part-time basis. All team members, whether or not active, should be kept in formed of progress so that they do not have to waste time catching up when called into play. Examples of person falling in this category are patent attorneys, illustrators, and technical specialists needed for tricky problems.

The participation of staff from all major functions—marketing, development, manufacturing, finance, and so on—from day 1 makes a direct contribution to the reduction of duplicate effort. The marketing person can immediately comment on the desirability of some feature before the development person has spent time on it. Similarly, the development staff can get immediate feedback from manufacturing on the producibility of a particular design.

Tools. The team organization will lose effectiveness if the members are not provided with appropriate tools; today, this usually means access to personal computers, applications software, and system support for CAD, CAE, CIM, and other computer-aided disciples. Team members must also be trained in the effective use of the tools. Just as the craftsman can do better work than the journeyman, so the trained specialist with a detailed understanding of the capabilities of computer-aided systems can do better work than an untrained person using the same tools.

Team empowerment. The team organization will also lose effectiveness if there are unnecessary delays in decision making. This is another major source of time wasting. The solution is the well-known empowerment approach, which gives the team the authority to make the great majority of the decisions. This is not to say that upper management should not be informed of those decisions on a regular basis, but that the natural tendency to second guess those doing the work should be restricted. The initial program plan should include some major review points when upper management can influence the course of the project. These meetings should not be determined by the calendar but rather by progress. The same principle is true of meetings among team members. Setting them every Tuesday at 8.00 A.M. usually leads people to spend all day Monday preparing for Tuesday and all day Wednesday responding to Tuesday. Have frequent team meetings but schedule them at short notice to deal with issues as they arise. To use the project scheduling terminology, team meetings are activities, not events. Many companies have difficulty implementing the empowerment requirement because it encroaches on established lines of authority. This is one area where concurrent engineering can actually increase risks, not reduce them, unless special attention is paid to it.

If there is an important role for upper management to play during the course of day-to-day activities, it is in assigning access to limited resources. If two or more teams need access to a special piece of equipment, say, for production trials, there has to be a responsive mechanism in place to set priorities. Again, the initial project plan must cover this situation.

Use of design authorities. Another approach to facilitate decision making is to appoint design authorities in various areas. For example, there could be a technology design authority, a product design authority, a process design authority, and an equipment design authority. The authorities must be legitimate experts in their fields. They do not necessarily do the design work and may not, in fact, be full-time members of the team. Their role is to help the project manager make the final decision when two or more conflicting approaches have been documented in equivalent and identified in the plan with their role clearly spelled out, it is possible to facilitate decision making evening complex situations. Nevertheless, the ultimate decision maker is the project manager. The design authorities are consultants who are called on only to evaluate competing solutions and offer their expertise.

Quality. A major time waster is repeating work because of poor quality. This is where the principles of total quality management come into play. Every person on the team must realize that they have "customers", many of whom are fellow team members, while some are outsiders who will use their products. Developing procedures and habits that focus on delivering satisfaction to the customers, both internal and external, goes a long way in reducing the need to correct or redo work. Obviously, careful selection of team members also goes a long way in assuring high-quality results. Here is where the best interests of a CE team can conflict with the best interests of individuals. Unless the company implementing the procedures takes special steps to prevent it, working on a CE team can limit growth opportunities for individuals and even eliminate career paths. The project manager wants to be assured of high-quality work in all areas and will tend to select people who have already demonstrated their ability to deliver. The problem can be especially acute for junior staff members who have demonstrated their skills in one area but are not given a chance to expand into other areas because they are continually asked to work on projects that require their known skills.

Bureaucracy. The final time waster of note is lengthy administrative and bureaucratic proce-dures. Eberhardt Rechtin, a former vice-president of engineering at Hwelett-Packard, once said that an approval takes $2n$ days, where n is the number of levels of approval needed. The obvious solution to this problem is to empower the project team in advance with all the necessary approval authority. Again, this means that the initial project plan must be prepared very carefully. Another approach to shortening the time required for administration is to provide the team leader with the authority to eliminate competitive bidding procedures on certain development items involving known vendors. Other bureaucratic red tape should also be eliminated, although this makes sense even in the absence of concurrent engineering. Many companies assign a full-time administrator/facilitator to CE teams to relieve the project manager of the burden of handling all the details.

External participation. The best users of concurrent engineering also extend the concept of the project team to involve key vendors and customers. The customers can help minimize the time required to define and specify the product, they can facilitate product acceptance procedures, and they can reduce project risk by either ordering early or at least indicating through a letter of intent what their purchases may be. Vendors can be extraordinarily helpful members of the team by providing technical support for the application of their products and materials, and by providing preferential access to scarce resources. In return, they get some indication of likely sales. If a company uses formal vendor certification procedures, they should extend them to "certifying" selected key vendors as participants in concurrent engineering development programs.

Guideposts for success

On the surface, the idea of multifunctional product design and development teams along with self-managing work groups seems unassailable. Nevertheless, a critical issue remains: How do you keep such teams from becoming committees with plenty of talk but little action? Tome Peters, a well-known management consultant, has postulated the following guideposts to help organizations implement the team concept:

1. *Set goals/deadlines/or key subsystem tests.* Committees deliberate. Project teams *do.* Successful project teams are characterized by a clear goal, although the exact path

is left unclear to induce creativity. Also, three to six strict due dates for subsystem technical and market tests/experiments are set and adhered to religiously.

2. *Insist on 100% assignment to the team.* Members must be obsessed by the project. Forget "one-fifth obsession": key function members must be assigned full-time for the project's duration.

3. *Place key functions on board from the outset.* Members from sales, distribution, marketing, finance, purchasing, operations/manufacturing, and design/engineering should be part of the project team from day 1. Legal, personnel, and others should provided full time members for part of the project.

4. *Give members authority to commit their function.* With few exceptions, each member should be able to commit resources from his or her function to project goals and deadlines without second-guessing from higher-ups. Top management must establish and enforce this rule form the start. If commitments from members' primary functional areas (e.g., engineering) are conditional, you've got a committee.

5. *Keep team-member destiny in the hands of the project leader.* For consulting firms such as Booz Allen & Hamilton and McKinsey & Co., life is a series of projects. The team leader might be from San Francisco or Sydney, Australia; either way, his or her evaluation of team members' performance will make or break a career. In general, then, the project boss rather than the functional boss should evaluate team members. Otherwise, the project concept falls flat.

6. *Make careers a string of projects.* A career in a "project-minded company" is viewed as a string of multifunction tasks. How one does not these determines career prospects.

7. *Live together.* Project teams should be sequestered away from headquarters as much as possible. Team camaraderie and commitment depend to a surprising extent on "hanging out" together, isolated from one's normal set of functional colleagues.

8. *Remember the social element.* Spirit is important: "We're in it together," "Mission impossible." High spirits are not accidental. He challenge of the task per se is central. Beyond that, the successful team leader facilitates what psychologist call "bonding". This can take the form of "signing up" ceremonies upon joining the team, frequent (at least monthly) milestone celebrations, and humorous awards for successes and setbacks alike.

9. *Allow outsiders in.* The product development team notion is incomplete unless outsiders participate. Principal vendors, distributors, and "lead" (future test-site) customers should be full-time members. Outside not only contribute directly, but also add authenticity and enhance the sense of distinctiveness and task commitment.

10. *Construct self-contained systems.* At the risk of duplicating equipment and support, the engaged team should have its own workstations, local area network, database, and so on. This is necessary to foster an "its-up-to-us-and-we've-got-the-wherewithal" environ-ment. However, the additional risk created by too much isolation must be balanced with the need for self-sufficiency. Problems may arise when it comes time to integrate the project with the rest of the firm.

11. Permit *the teams to pick their own leader.* A champion blessed by management gets things under way. But successful project teams usually *select* and *alter* their own leaders as circumstances warrant. It is expected that leadership will shift over the course of the project, as one role and then another dominates a particular stage (engineering first, then manufacturing, distribution later).

12. *Honour project leadership skills.* No less than a wholesale reorientation of the firm is called for away from "vertical" (functional specialists dominate) and toward "horizontal" (cross-functional teams are the norm). In this environment, horizontal project leadership becomes the most cherished skill in the firm, rewarded by dollars and promotions. Good team skills, for junior members, are also valued and rewarded.

Few experts or practitioners disagree: To halve product development time and constantly improve quality and service, all companies must destroy the walls between functions and commit to perpetual "horizontal" improvement project. But to become project focused requires more than appointing teams. Teams and task forces have often ended up adding to, rather than subtracting from, bureaucracy. Care must be taken to avoid the project-turned-committee trap.

Industrial experience

The success stories of CE implementation in companies such as Boeing, Hewlett-Packard, Raytheon, and John Deeree have been amply documented and reported at professional conferences such as those sponsored by the Computer-Aided Acquisition and Logistics Support Society, the Society for computer-Aided Engineering, the Institute of Industrial Engineers, and the Society of Manufacturing Engineers. We cite a few examples briefly to gain a better appreciation of the issues.

For Cadillac, a 1990 winner of the Malcolm Baldrige National Quality Award, concurrent engineering has come to mean a new culture and a new way of designing and building its extraordinary complex product-luxury cars. Engineers, designers, and assemblers are now members of vehicle, vehicle-systems, and product (parts) teams that work in close coordination rather than belonging to separate, isolated functional areas as before. Assembly line workers, dealers, repair shop managers, and customers provide insight to engineers involved in all stages of design. To inspire cultural change, Cadillac created a position of champion of simultaneous engineering (a role that combines keeping the process son track, preaching to the believers, and motivating the recalcitrant) and sent 1.400 employees to seminars on that quality management. They also established an "Assembly Line Effectiveness Center" where production workers rub shoulders with engineers,critiquing prototypes for manufacturability.

John Deere's industrial equipment division in Illinois, has had two concurrent engineering efforts. The first, begun in 1984, failed because management retained the traditional manufacturing departments. Designers and process engineers who were assigned to task groups remained loyal to the interests of their disciplines rather than to the overall enterprise. In 1988 the division reorganized. Staff members now report to product teams and answer to team leaders, not to functional department heads. Early in the design stage, teams, create a product definition document that describes the product precisely. sets deadlines, and lays out the manufacturing plan. Products no longer change as departments work on them. The result has been gradual improvements in manufacturing processes. There are now fewer experimental designs, and it is possible to produce prototypes in the production environment. The advantage of this is that in addition to checking for flaws in the prototypes themselves engineers can simultaneously perfect the manufacturing process.

The third example comes from *Federal-Mogul*, a precision parts manufacturer in Southfield, Michigan. The first Federal-Mogul unit to adopt concurrent engineering was its troubled oil-seal business. Other units quickly followed. Success in the oil-seal business, where products are simple but must meet exacting standards, requires rapid turn-around on bids and prototypes and strong customer service. By providing estimates to customers in minutes instead of weeks and producting sample seals in 20 working days instead of 20 weeks, market share has soared. Federal-Mogul accomplished this by adopting a cross-functional product team approach to manufacturing, encouraging consensus building and empowerment, and introducing new information technologies. Key applications include networks allowing all plants to share CAD drawings and machine tools, a scheduling system that notifies appropriate team members automatically when a new order comes in, an engineering data management system, and on on-line database of past orders.

Unresolved issues

From a technical point of view, what makes concurrent engineering possible are the recent advances in hardware and software, database systems, electronic communications, and the various components of computer-integrated manufacturing. At the first International Workshop on Concurrent Engineering Design sponsored by the National Science Foundation four themes emerged from the discussions: models, tools training, and culture. Participants identified measurement issues and trade-offs that will inform future models of new product development. They concluded that tools must focus on expanded CAD/CAM/CAPP capabilities with strong interfaces. Training is needed for multiple job stations, in the impact of design on downstream tasks, and in teamwork and individual responsibility. Corporate culture, and how to change it, must be better understood. Important aspects of culture to be clarified include incentives and performance, myths that inhibit an organization's progress, and the management of change.

One of the primary roles of CE is in identifying the interdependencies and constraints that exist over the life cycle of a product, and ensuring that the design team is aware of them. Nevertheless, care must be taken in the early stages to avoid overwhelming the design team with constraints and in stifling their creativity for the sake of simplicity. A truly creative design that satisfies customer requirements in a superior manner may justify the expense of relaxing some of the development and process guidelines.

Although a basic tenet of CE is that input to the design process should come from all life-cycle stages, there is much ambiguity about how to achieve this. At exactly what point in the CE process should discussion of assembly, sequences, tolerances, and support requirements be introduced? Also, trade-offs abound. For example, consolidation of parts is desirable, yet too much consolidation implies costly and inefficient procurement and inventorying. A balance must be struck between meeting the customer's specifications, designing for manufacturability, and life-cycle cost. This means that cost information should be available to the design teams, not just the accounting department, throughout the project.

Risk management

Risk is a major factor in technological management. Whenever the design process or the design itself deviates from current procedures and established techniques, technological risks are introduced. These risks can be related to the product design, to the process design, or to the design of the support system, and can vary widely in magnitude. For example, in product design a low-level risk might be one associated with the modification of an existing subassembly. A moderate-level risk would concern the design of a new product based on currently used technologies and parts (integration risks); a third, even higher level of risk is related to the use of new materials, such as ceramics, in product that was previously fabricated out of conventional metal alloys.

The development of the first transistor was a high-risk project involving a completely new technology. SONY's work on the first radio transistor was also a high-risk project because this technology was being implemented in a new product—the portable radio. However, development of subsequent models of the transistor radio represented much lower risks, as both the technology and the basic product were known.

The probability of success (or the risk of failure) should be estimated and monitored throughout the life cycle of a project. The selection of projects for implementation, the evaluation of alternative designs for a specific project, the decision to adopt or to reject proposed design changes, and the implementation of such changes measurably affect out-comes. Risk management is therefore part of the project manager's responsibilities. The scope of associated activities includes risk assessment, risk analysis, risk reduction, and risk handling.

Risk can be defined as a function of the probability of an undesirable event and by the severity of the consequences of that event. In general, high risk corresponds to a strongly adverse event that has a high probability of occurrence. while low risk corresponds to a low probability of occurrence and low severity. Moderate levels of risk correspond to combinations of probabilities and consequences that fall between these extremes.

Consider, for example, the risk associated with flying. the possible outcome of an accident is death, but due to high safety standards in the airline industry the probability of accidents is very low, and therefore the overall risk is low. This is evidenced by the cost of traveller insurance policies. when the probability of an undesirable event is higher (e.g., with parachuting or hang gliding), insurance policies that cover the same outcome (death) are much more expensive. This the level of risk depends on both the severity of an adverse outcome and its probability of occurrence.

It is possible to develop a scale for assessing the level of risk based on these two measures. Each risk, however, may affect one or more of the dimensions of project success. Thus a project may face a schedule risk related to the event of delays, a cost risk associated with the event of a schedule risk related to the event of delays, a cost' risk associated with the event of a budget overrun, one or more performance risks accompanying the failure to achieve technical/operational goals,and a program risk related to the success of the project as perceived by the participating parties.

Risks are caused by several factors.

Technology. The rapid pace with which (e.g., information systems and integrated circuits) is expanding may make a new product obsolete the day the first unit rolls off the production line. To avoid this risk, design engineers prefer to use the latest technologies available, which frequently are immature and unproven. This increases the risk of technological failure. Simple lack of experience heightens the chances that the project will be saddled with unforeseen problems. The trade-off between well-proven technologies with lower performance levels and new, unproven technologies requires detailed risk analysis. When NASA decided to build a new space shuttle in 1987 to replace the *Challenger,* which exploded on launch, it opted for a design that was nearly identical to the original. Rather than exploit recent advances in microelectronics, expert systems, and robotics, 20-year-old technology was used to avoid additional risks.

Complexity and integration. The adoption of well-known technologies for a project reduces the risk of component failure but may do little to mitigate the risk of integration failure. Modern, complex systems are based on the integration of parts and subsystems, the compatibility of software modules, and integration of hardware and software. the interfaces between components of a system are a source of integration problems and risks. For example, problems related to RFI (radio-frequency interference) or EMI (electromagnetic interference) should be considered in the design of electrical devises. Parts of the same system may affect each other in an undesired and unexpected fashion. Complex interfaces within a system, between systems, and between systems and humans are sources of risks that need management attention throughout the project.

Changes. Virtually all projects are subject to design changes throughout their life cycle. A reassessment of needs, revitalized competition, and emerging technologies are some of the factors that may call the original design into question. Design changes are risky, as each change may have a different effect on the system or its components. As a result, the risks of integration may go up sharply. A control system that evaluates each proposed change and its possible consequences is required. This system should provide information on approved changes to the design engineers in an effort to reduce the risk of the integration failure. The same system should provide updated design information to manufacturing and quality control so that the product is manufactured and tested according to the most recent configuration.

Supportability. Good design and workmanship are to enough to guarantee a successful project. The ultimate test of success is customer or end-user satisfaction. To achieve this goal, the design should be based on the customer's needs, and the product should conform to the design. At the conclusion of the project,the product or system, delivered should be operational (i.e., all the support required for maintenance and operations should be available). In the case of the rough-terrain cargo handler, for example, this includes trained personnel, transportation, storage and maintenance facilities, spare parts, and manuals. To prepare for worst-case contingencies, the design effort should cover the risks of a system delivered without adequate logistics support.

The multiple sources of risks and the different aspects of a project that are subject to failure or delay make risk management a demanding, time-consuming activity. Because technological risks affect performance as well as cost and schedule, we shall discuss the relationship between technological management and the effect these risks have on overall project success.

To demonstrate the problems faced by management during the various project phases, consider an organization that has decided to initiate a project aimed at automating its production planning and control system. Among the large variety of available options, the organization focuses on two alternatives: (1) purchasing the most suitable system off the shelf and modifying it according to its individual needs, or (2) developing a system that will support all of the specific production planning policies and procedures currently in use. In this example, the first alternative represents a project of relatively low development risk; however, the benefits may be minimal. This is because most off-the-shelf software packages have limited flexibility and can only rarely be made 100% compatible with the existing work environment. The second alternative offers a higher chance of achieving the technological and functional goals but involves a significant software development effort. As such, development and integration risks, and consequently the risk of schedule delays and budget overruns, are higher.

To perform a trade-off analysis between the two alternatives, the techniques presented in earlier chapters can be implemented. This should be done in such a way that all parties feel involved in arriving at the final choice and are satisfied with the decision-making process. Consensus building is the key. Achieving a high level of satisfaction depends on the process used in selecting and implementing the alternative. When management, potential users, and future operators of the new system select alternative and define its specific configuration, the probability that the project will be successful is greatly increased.

In addition to the economic scheduling, and cost aspects that have to be analyzed, risk analysis is part of the selection process. Risk analysis starts with the identification of all possible events that might have a negative impact on the project. in the example above, typical negative events for the first alternative are an inability to modify the software to accommodate a given need, and an inability to integrate the package with existing management information systems and databases. Negative events for the second alternative include unexpected difficulties in integrating the modules of the new software package, and excessive CPU time requirements that slow down information processing and retrieval.

In the next stage of the analysis, the severity of each event is estimated and the level of risk (based on the analysis, the severity of the event and the probability of occurrence) is calculated. The events are then ranked, with those exhibiting the highest risks placed at the top of the list. Next, the source of high-risk events is investigated. Technological risks are usually generated by one or more of the following factors.

- Unproven technology
- System complexity
- Integration requirements
- Physical or chemical properties
- Modeling assumptions
- Interfacing with other systems

- Interfacing with operators, service personnel, and so on
- Operating environment

Major sources of risks require special attention. The risk management plan starts by identifying each of these sources, their magnitude, their relation to the various design stages, and their possible effects on cost, schedule, quality, and performance. the next step is to look for modifications or alternatives that would permit risk reduction. Continuing with the example above, the thoughtful selection of a computer language or operating system may reduce some of the integration risks. If management decides to develop a new software package, contingency plans that cut expenses and development time at the cost of lower performance should be prepared. these plans are used in case the undesired event takes place. By preparing contingency plans in advance time is saved when the anticipated problem surfaces.

Special techniques for the analysis of risk include fault tree analysis, event tree analysis, synergistic contingency evaluation and review technique, and reliability analysis evaluation and review. The specifics are explained in books dealing with risk analysis, such as that of Cooper an Chapman, and in technical articles such as that by Rasmussen. The analysis of risk is based on experience gathered in past projects, expert opinion, and physical or mathematical models. If the project manager does not have the technical expertise to perform the task, he or she should call upon those in the organization who are more qualified. In some cases it may be appropriate to contract an outside consultant to undertake the assessment. By initiating a risk management activity at the outset of the project, unnecessary risks can be avoided while those deemed necessary can be minimized or transformed.

Configuration selection

In large, technologically sophisticated projects, selection of the best design by a direct comparison among the functional efficiencies of the alternatives is difficult and sometimes impossible, due to technological uncertainties, the absence of a single agreed-upon objective, the size of the system, and system's complexity. In such projects it might not be appropriate to make a decision based solely on the cost of development and manufacturing. Once the system is put into place, its operations and maintenance costs may be significant enough, even after discounting over the useful life, to warrant consideration when the original decision is being made.

Cost-effectiveness and benefit-cost analyses are intended to assists in the selection of the most appropriate design alternative for system development or system modification projects. These techniques are supported by a variety of models used to estimate the functional efficiency, the risk, and the life-cycle cost of each technological alternative.

The selection process may be driven by the available budget or by the functional requirements. In the first case, the available budget for the project is viewed as a binding constraint and an effort is made to design a system with the best possible capabilities without exceeding the budget. This is know as the *design-to-cost* approach. In the second case, the design effort is aimed at minimizing the ratio between the cost of the system and its effectiveness. This is know as the *cost-effectiveness* approach. In either case there is need to define and estimate the value of some performance measures for cost and effectiveness. Both approaches are used the process of configuration selection. This process takes place before and during the detailed design phase, when the exact configuration of the system and each of this components is selected.

The techniques discussed earlier in this book for project are used for configuration selection as well. Checklists and scoring models, benefit-cost analysis, cost effectiveness analysis, and multiple-criteria methods all have a role. In the configuration selection process, each alternative design (configuration) is analyzed by a life-cycle cost model and is evaluated with respect to its expected performance. Performance measures are project dependent (they would be different for the development of a new car and for the construction of a new building), but some are common to many systems:

1. *Operational or functional capability.* This is a measure of the system's ability to perform tasks and satisfy the market or customer's needs. For example, the range of an electric passenger vehicle, is payload, and its speed are possible measures of operational or functional capabilities. In the software selection example, the ability to perform all planning and control activities required within acceptable time standards is an operational performance measure.

2. *Timeliness.* This measure relates to the point of time when the system is available to perform its mission (i.e., the successful completion of acceptance tests and the start of regular operations). In the software selection example, an off-the-shelf system can perform better with respect to this measure.

3. *Quality.* The measure of quality relates to the degree that the system's design reflects the market or customer needs, and to the degree that the product or service meets its design specifications. Therefore, the quality of an alternative refers to the system's components, the integration of those components, and the compatibility of the proposed system with the environment in which it will interact. Quality is defined in specific terms for military systems (known as MIL-STD or military standards); for nonmilitary systems such as planes,boats, buildings and computers, a host of national and international standards exist. *The Institute or Electrical and Electronics Engineers* is in the forefront of setting standards for electrical equipment and devices. If adequate standards are not available, desired quality for electrical equipment and devices. If adequate standards are not available, desired quality levels should be specified for both the operational (functional) and technical (design and workmanship) aspects of the system. The

relationship between these aspects through QFD (quality function deployment) is explained later. Returning to the software selection example, in addition to specific needs and requirements, a set of standards and testing procedures has been established for software quality and reliability. *The Software Engineering Institute* based at Carnegie-Mellon University has taken the lead in this effort.

4. *Reliability.* This measure is a function of how well the system performs for a given period of time under specific operating conditions. The two factors used in the calculations are the mean time between failures (MTBF) and the mean time to repair (MTTR) the system.

There is a correlation between reliability and quality, as high quality of design, workmanship, and integration usually leads to a high level of reliability. However, reliability also depends on the type of technology used and the operating environment. In the software selection example, the presence of bugs and the average time required to repair them affect the reliability of the system.

5. *Compatibility.* The measure corresponds to the system's ability to operate in harmony with existing or future systems. For example a new management information system has a higher degree of compatibility if it can use existing databases. Electronic systems are said to be compatible if they can operate without interference from the electro-magnetic radiation put out by other systems in the same vicinity. In the software selection example, the ability to import and export data from other information systems and data bases in the desired format is an important measure of compatibility.
6. *Adaptability.* This measure evaluates a system's ability to operate in conditions other than those initially specified. For example, a communication system designed for ground use would be considered a highly adaptable system if it could be used in high adaptabilities are preferred when future operating conditions are difficult to forecast. In the software selection example a highly adaptable software package is one that can run on different computer types under a variety of operating systems in addition to the computer and operating system specified.
7. *Life span.* This measure has a direct impact on both cost and effectiveness. Due to learning and efforts at continued process improvement, systems with a longer life span tend to improve over time. This eliminates the need for frequent capital investments and hence reduces total life-cycle cost.
8. *Simplicity.* The process of learning a new system while it is being introduced into an organization depends on its simplicity. A system that is easy to maintain and operate is usually accepted faster and creates fewer difficulties for the user. Furthermore, complicated systems may not be maintained and exercised adequately, especially during startup or periods of change, when there is high

turnover in the organization. In the software selection example, a software package that is simple to operate and maintain is one that is developed according to software engineering standards regarding modularity, documentation, and so on.

9. *Safety.* The methods by which a system will be operated and maintained should be considered in the advanced developed phase. Safety precautions should be introduced and evaluated to minimize the risk of accidents. As with quality, designing a safe system from the start can provide significant benefits over the long run.

10. *Commonality.* A high level of commonality with other systems in the organization should be a driving force in the design of a system. Commonality has many facets, such as common parts and subsystems, and maintenance. Many airlines insist that all aircraft they buy within a particular class, regardless of manufacturer, have the same engines. In a similar vein, the U.S. Department of Defense developed the computer language Ada in the late 1970s and now requires that all program commissioned by any of its branches be written in Ada.

11. *Maintainability.* Providing adequate main-tenance from a system is important. There is a question, though, as to how much preventive maintenance should be scheduled. When a system is out of service, it cannot perform its assigned tasks. This loss in operational time must be weighed against the probability of system failure and the need for unscheduled maintenance, which in turn, reduces the system's overall effectiveness. Higher levels of maintainability lead to better labour utilization and lower personnel training costs. Part of maintainability is testability—the ability to detect a system failure and pinpoint its source in a timely manner. Higher levels of maintainability and testability contribute to the effectiveness of a system. In the software selection example, a well documented source code as well as clearly defined interfaces between the modules of the software package help in the detection and correction of bugs.

12. *Friendliness.* This performance measure quantifies the effort and time required to learn how to operate and maintain a system. A freindly system requires less time and skill to learn, an hence reduces both direct and indirect labour costs. In the software selection example, the use of menus, on-line help, and pointing devices such as a mouse can increase the friendliness of the software package.

The measures listed above form a general, nonexhaustive list of indicators that should be taken into account when evaluating a system from a technological point of view. By combining them with specific project objectives related to budget and schedule, they provide a framework for selecting the design configuration and foreshadow the capabilities of the final system.

For a particular project, each of these measures should be subdivided until the desired level of detail is reached. Foe example, compatibility might be broken down by hardware, software, operations and maintenance personnel, training requirements, and logistics support. Software then might be decomposed into database, controls, interface protocols, and applications. Quantifying each element in the resultant hierarchy for each alternative is the first step in the analysis. the selection process itself can be supported by scoring models.

The cost of each alternative must also be evaluated. the notion of life-cycle cost is widely used for this purpose. the life-cycle cost of a system is defined as its total cost from the start of the conceptual design phase until it completes active service.

Along with a benefit-cost analysis, a risk analysis of each alternative design should be conducted. Risk analysis includes the following steps:

- Identification of risk drivers
- Estimation of probabilities of undesired outcomes
- Evaluation of the impact of each undesired outcome (on cost, schedule, quality, and operational and technological capabilities)
- Elimination and reduction of risks
- Preparation of contingency plans

The procedures used for selecting the best design alternative can also be adopted for managing configuration changes. This is discussed presently, but first we offer some guidelines for system definition. The selection process is complete when the specifications of the proposed system are robust enough to at least answer the following questions:

Technological specifications

- *Operational functional:* What tasks should the system perform, and what performance levels are expected?
- *Timeliness*: When should the system be operational?
- *Quality:* Which standards are applicable? Which customer needs are to be supported by the system, and to what extent?
- *Reliability:* What are the expected MTBF and MTTR in the environment in which the system has to operate?
- *Compatibility*: With which other systems must the system contemplated operate in harmony? What interfaces are required?
- *Adaptability*: Under what environmental conditions is the system designed to operate, be maintained and stored? Under what conditions is the system required to operate, be maintained, and stored?

- *Life span*: For how long is the system expected to be in service?
- *Simplicity*: What level of training is required to operate and to maintain the system?
- *Safety*: What safety standards are applicable to the system?
- *Commonality:* What level of commonality is required with each existing or planned system?
- *Maintainability:* What logistics support is required: spare parts, training, technical manuals, test equipment, and so on?
- *Friendliness*: What features should be included in the system to enhance its friendliness?

Life-cycle cost

- What are the estimated costs of design, manufacture, operation, maintenance, and phase out for the system?
- What is the expected timing of each cost component?

Risk assessment

- What are the major risk drivers?
- What are the probabilities of undesired outcomes?
- What is the expected impact of each undesired outcome?
- What are the plans to handle undesired outcomes?

The selected design alternative defines the technological aspects of the project. Based on the specification, estimates of cost and schedule are made and the proposed project is either approved or rejected. Project approval is a management decision that may affect the entire organization. When several projects are being considered, the final choice is based on strategic and tactical considerations including:

General considerations

- Organizational goals
- Current or pending projects
- Existing and future products and markets
- Introduction of new technologies
- Image of the organization
- Organizational growth

Research and development

- The availability of required technology
- Future use of new technologies developed or acquired for the project
- Development risks
- Opportunity to acquire new technologies developed or acquired for the project
- Development risks
- Opportunity to acquire new technologies and new knowledge
- Availability of resources required
- Future use of new resources acquired for the project

Logistics and production

- Project's need for logistics support
- Future use of investment in logistics support
- Project's production resource requirements
- Availability of production resources needed
- Effect on utilization of existing resources
- Need for new facilities
- Future use of facilities required for the project

Marketing

- Potential markets
- Estimate of future sales or business
- Availability of marketing resources
- Effect on existing products markets

Finance

- Project net present value
- Project rate of return
- Project payback period
- Project budgetary risks
- Project cash flow

This partial list, together with nay specific considerations unique to the organization, underlies the selection process. Once again,. actual decision making can be based on multi-criteria techniques or any of the other methods discussed for evaluating and selecting alternatives.

Configuration management

Configuration Management (CM) concentrates on the management of technology by identifying and controlling the functional and physical design characteristics of a system, and its support documentation. The medium of implementation is a set of tools designed to provide accurate information on what is to be built, what is currently being built, and what has been built in the past. The mission of CM is to support concurrent engineering and to assist management in evaluating and controlling proposed technological changes. Through quality assurance activities CM ensures the integrity of the design and engineering documentation, and supports production, operation, and maintenance of the system.

In configuration management, a baseline is established in each phase of the system's life cycle with well-defined procedures for handling proposed deviation. The initial baseline, known as the *functional (or program requirements) baseline*, is prepared in the first phase of the life cycle—the conceptual design phase. This baseline contains technical data regarding functional characteristics, demonstration tests, interface and integration characteristics, and design constraints imposed by operational, environmental, and other considerations. Approval is subject to a preliminary design review (PDR).

The advanced development phase produces the second baseline, the *allocated (or design requirements) baseline*. This document contains performance specifications guiding the development of subsystems and components, including characteristics derived from the system's design. Laboratory or computer simulation may be used to demonstrate achievement of functional characteristics, interface requirements, and design constraints. This baseline is subject to a critical design review (CDR).

The *product (or product configuration) baseline* is last and includes information on the system as built, including results of acceptance tests for a prototype, supporting literature, operation and maintenance manuals, and part lists. Acceptance is subject to a physical configuration audit (PCA). In addition to these three baselines, other baselines and additional design reviews are frequently needed when complicated systems are involved. Examples are a baseline that defines the initial design and a baseline that defines the detailed design of the system. The transition from one baseline to the next is controlled by design reviews.

The configuration management system ensures smooth transition and provides updated information on the configuration of the system and all pending change requests at all times. To function properly, it should perform the tasks discussed in the following subsections.

Configuration identification

Configuration identification sets the foundation of the CM system, It starts with the selection of configuration items (CI), both software and hardware, that have one or more of the following characteristics:

- End-use function
- New or modified design
- Technical risk or technical complexity
- Many interfaces with other items
- High rate of future design changes expected
- Logistic criticality

The selection of configuration items is a critical task of systems engineering. Too few configuration items will not provide adequate management control, and too many may overload the system, sparking a waste of time and money.

Next, a coding system is adopted and configuration identification numbers are assigned. These numbers are designed to assist in providing the following information on each configuration item or a lower-level item:

1. Technical requirements which form the basis for detail design. These are provided by *specification numbers.*
2. Identification of the equipment designed and built to the applicable specification. These are provided by *equipment numbers.*
3. Technical descriptions for the equipment and its lower-level items. These are provided by *drawing and part numbers.*
4. Description of the sequence of manufacturing the equipment and its lower-level items. These are provided by equipment and item *serialization numbers.*
5. Change documents. These are *provided by change identification numbers.*
6. Sources of manufacture at all levels. These are provided by *manufacturer's code identification numbers.*

As an example, consider configuration item 123. For this CI, the following identification numbers are defined:

Specification number	SPEC 123
Equipment number	CI 123
Drawing number	123 A
Serial number	123 SN5

Manufacturer number	00375
Change identification numbers:	
Engineering change request	ECR 123 N 005
Engineering order	EO 123 N 005

To control the allocation of numbers, they should be assigned from a singly point and a standard procedure established to prevent errors in identification.

Configuration change control

Configuration change control involves the development of procedures that govern three steps:

1. *Preparation of a change request.* This step requires that a formal change request be prepared and submitted. The initiation of a change can be internal (the project team) or external (the customer, a subcontractor, or a supplier).

2. *Evaluation of a change request.* A team of experts representing the different organizational functions is responsible for the evaluation of change request. This team, known as a change control board (CCB) or configuration management board, evaluates each proposed change based on its effect on the form, fit and function of the system, logistics (manual, training, support equipment, spare parts, etc.), and project cost and schedule. This review leads to a decision to approve or reject the change request, or to reconsider it after more data are collected.

Changes are classified as either permanent or temporary. A temporary change might be needed for test programs or debugging software. Approval can usually be obtained in a short item compared to a request for a permanent change.

All information regarding each proposed change is accumulated and analyzed by the change control board, which also functions as a central repository for historical records. The CCB decision is based on cost-effectiveness and risk analysis in which the need for the change and its expected benefits are weighed against implementation and project life cycle costs, its impact on project quality and schedule, and te expected risks associated with implementation.

3. *Management of the implementation of approved changes.* Approved changes are integrated in to the design. This is accomplished by preparing and distributing a change approval form or an engineering change order to all parties involved, including engineering, manufacturing, quality control, and quality assurance.

The CCB is responsible for the pivotal task of conducting a comprehensive impact analysis of each change proposed. A well-functioning change control system assures tight control of the technological aspects of a project. In addition, it provides accurate configuration records for the smooth, coordinated implementation of changes and effective logistics support during the life cycle of the system.

Configuration status accounting

This task provides for the updated recording of:

- Current configuration identification, including all baselines and configuration items
- Historical baselines and the registration of approved changes
- Register and status of all pending change requests
- Status of implementation of approved changes.

Configuration status accounting provides the link between baselines of the system. It is the tool that supports the CCB in its analysis of new change requests. The effect of these changes on the current baseline must be evaluated and their relationship to all pending change requests must be determined before a decision can be taken.

Review and audits

This configuration management task provides both the contractor and the customer with assurance that test plans demonstrate the required performance, and that test results prove conformance to requirements. Functional configuration audit includes a review of development test plans the test results, as well as a list of required tests not performed, deviation from the plan, and waivers. In this task, the relationship between quality assurance and configuration management is established. Configuration management provides the baselines and a record of incorporated and outstanding changes. Quality assurance first checks the configuration documentation to gauge requirements; then it verifies that the system conforms to the approved configuration.

Configuration management is a tool designed to help the project team know what they are developing, producing, testing, and delivering so that the appropriate support and maintenance can be given to the product throughout its life cycle. It specifies the procedures and information required for the project to be carried out in the most cost-effective manner.

Technological management of projects

The technological aspect of project management is the link between the engineering, science, and management disciplines. The understanding of these links and the connection between product design, process design, support design, cost schedule, resources, and project success are the main contributions that the project manager makes to the technological aspects of a project.

Technological management starts when a need is identified for a new product, service, or system. The first step is to assess the feasibility of providing that need. Favourable results from a feasibility study and a positive economic evaluation of the proposed project trigger the next step-the definition of specifications and design characteristics that satisfy the needs in the best possible way. As an example, if the development of an electric passenger vehicle is being considered, questions related to the required driving range on a single charge, the payload required, and the maximum speed are translated into design attributes such as vehicle size, battery type, and power consumption. These attributes are then translated into the blueprint of the finished product through a detailed design. In the car example, questions as to the types of materials that should be used and the best manufacturing process are answered by teams of engineers. If a concurrent engineering approach is adopted, issues such as logistics support throughout the life cycle of the product are studied simultaneously.

The organizational aspect should be addressed at the outset of the project during the conceptual design phase. The structure of the CCB is a critical decision. Functional areas such as engineering and quality assurance should be included along with the various representatives of the project. The role that each CCB member plays and the procedures adopted for change request evaluations are central to the technological management process.

A time aspect is present because each phase of the project ends with an updated, more complete, and more detailed configuration baseline. The baselines and the corresponding design reviews—the functional baseline and system design review, the allocated baseline and preliminary design review, the product baseline and critical design review, and any additional baselines and design reviews—are key milestones in the project life cycle. Well-prepared reviews and a supporting configuration management plan provide the necessary foundation. In addition, many products and systems require ongoing technological manage-ment, due to a continuing stream of engineering change requests.

Finally, the cost aspect of technological decisions and the analysis of risk should be integrated within technological management. Each design decision has an impact on the project's life-cycle cost and on its probability of success. The ability to integrate all the different factors affected by technological decisions, and consequently to produce the best design based on all these factors, is the essence of technological management.

Total quality management in projects

The industrial world is in the midst of a quality revolution brought on by the Japanese. The introduction of the just-in-time philosophy supported by kanban for production and inventory control, continuous process improvement on the shop flow, and the general goal of zero part and product defects has allowed Japanese firms to capture the bulk of the consumer electronics market, a large share of the semiconductor market, and a troublesome proportion of the U.S. automobile market. This success, which has come in less than two decades, can be attributed to a knack for squeezing a few more percentage points of performance out of a system or process after logical and economics indicate that diminishing returns have long set in. But such an explanation is too glib. At the heart of Japanese manufacturing is an emphasis on education and training, a cross-functional workforce, teamwork, and a commitment to excellence—some of the basic components of total quality management.

What is total quality management?

TQM is a system that combines quality control techniques and organizational models developed over the last 40 years in both the United States and Japan. It is logical evolution of management by objectives, strategic planning, quality circles, quality assurance, and many other systems. TQM offers a structural approach to creating organization-wide participation in planning and implementing a continuous improvement process that exceeds the expectations of the customer or client. It is built on the assumption that 90% of our problems are process related rather than employee related.

TQM has three major components:

1. *Breakthrough planning, sometimes called Hoshin planning*

- Clarify a vision of where the organization wants to go in the next 5 or 10 years.
- Identify goals and objectives that move the organization toward its vision.
- Identify critical processes that must deliver the goods and services provided to clients in a way that exceeds their expectations.
- Select a few (no more than four) breakthrough items that can help the organization reach its vision quickly.
- Communicate the vision and the methods to reach all employees
- Provide a structure for monitoring progress toward the vision

Vision planning allows the organization to identify and focus on key areas. The ultimate objective is to facilitate full development of the methods and pathways by which vertical levels of the organization then participate in the planning, development, and deployment of the strategic breakthroughs identified.

Breakthrough planning is an evolution of strategic planning that adds value statements, reminding us that "how we got here" is just as important as where we are going. A related concept is *breakthrough thinking,* which has recently been formalized by Nadler and Hibino.

2. *Daily management.* This system shows people what they must do personally and what they must measure and control to keep the organization running smoothly. It helps them define and understand the process they use in producing goods and services to meet customer needs and expectations. Once these processes are understood, individuals and departments can continuously improve them, then standardize the methods to ensure that gains are maintained.

This continuous improvement is achieve by problem-solving teams who engage in identifying customer problems, finding solutions, and then providing ongoing control of the improved process. Use of several basic quality control tests and statistical methods symptoms. Problem solving requires the collective effects of everyone in an organization working in study teams following a multistep procedure. This includes customer surveys identification and selection of issues, establishment of performance measures, data collection, modeling and analysis, action, and feedback. Daily management is te most revolutionary of the three components of TQM. It empowers employees at all levels of the organization and focuses management improvement efforts on process problems.

3. Cross-functional management. This is the integration of team activities across divisions/departments to achieve organizational goals. It is the vehicle for breaking down department/divisional barriers. Through cross-functional management, top-level managers can ensure that all groups in the organization-technicians, engineers, staff, and so on—are working together with commonality of purpose.

Concurrent engineering and configuration management establish the framework in which TQM can be implemented. The impacts can be felt throughout the life cycle of the project. In the detailed design and production phases TQM is geared toward customer needs and preventing future defects. After completion of the production process, TQM is aimed at detecting defects and more important, eliminating their sources. The third aspect of TQM is to achieve control by trend analysis and preventive actions.

The TQM approach is based on the philosophy that quality should be designed into the product and process, and that defects should be avoided at almost all cost. This is because defect detection by itself is expensive and prone to error. Once a defect is created, it might be a nightmare to find and remove it. In electronic assembly, for example, an oft-cited rule of thumb is the cost of finding a defective component goes up by a factor of 10 for each level of assembly: device, board, system, and field installation. Furthermore, even if te defect is found, correction is not only expensive and time consuming but is likely to reduce the quality of the product. A reworked part will often not measure up to the same standards of one manufactured properly the first time.

Breakthrough thinking methodology

1. *Assemble the problem-saving team.*

- Brainstorm major functions that could be improved.
- Use consensus to select one function on which to work.
- Size the work group between 5 and 8.

- Select people who will contribute to the success of implementation.
- Include one "outsider"—someone unconnected to the issue—and a customer.

2. *Develop the function statement.*

- Discuss the uniqueness of this particular issue.
- Expand the function statement.
- Select the largest function that can be addressed with the resources available.
- Review the chosen function and function expansion with decision makers.

3. *Establish measures to gauge improvement.*

- Select ways to measure your improvement progress.
- Use existing data and systems whenever possible.
- Establish goals for improvement.

4. *Brainstorm general solutions.*

- Define regularly occurring conditions or assumptions.
- Brainstorm solutions for the chosen function. Ask the question, "How can we achieve our selected function?"
- Ask, "What would be the solution after that ?" Focus on an ideal future.
- Organize solutions into major alternatives.
- Add limited details to each solution: who, when, where, how, how much.
- Review solutions with decision makers.

5. *Select the ideal solution.*

- Narrow the solutions to those two or three that best address the function.
- Add further details to these solutions, including plans for irregularities.
- Analyze the remaining solutions, Which solution provides the best answer, taking into account the entire system and any irregularities?
- Select the solution to implement.
- Establish a plan of actions to achieve implementation.
- Review solution and plan with decision makers.

6. *Implement the plan of action.*

- Individuals or small teams working within their own areas of responsibility further develop the details of implementation.

- Further analysis or tests may be required as the detailed plan is implemented.
- The team leader acts as the projects manager to coordinate diverse activities.

7. *Monitor progress and repeat process.*

- Manage at your own level of responsibility. Do not micromanage implementation.
- At regular intervals, ask each participant what barriers exist to the success of the implementation. Exercise control at the group rather than at the individual level.

Cost quality

The modeling and analysis of trade-offs is at the very foundation of decision making. In manufacturing, one of the trade-offs most enshrined in our thinking has been the perceived relation between quality and cost. Vaughan points out that when people go to buy a product, they usually want it to be perfect at a minimum price. However, defect-free products are impossible to attain in any production environment at any cost.

The traditional view holds that near approaches to zero-defect operations are too expensive for manufacturers of most products to attempt to reach. When the manufacturer must work to such high quality standards, production costs require that the price charged be outrageously high.

What drives this trade-off according to this traditional view? Vaughan explains that efforts to reduce rework, repairs, warranty costs, and liability losses generate increasing costs associated with the time, materials, engineering, and overhead required to achieving quality 1 unit is just equal to the marginal loss due to poor quality is the point at which the optimum is achieve. Even Juran, the guru who has long been at the forefront of the quality improvement movement, encouraged this kind of thinking. In his optimization model, he shows how failure costs decline until they are overtaken by the increasing costs of appraisal and preventation. At this point, total quality cost begin to rise.

Why, then, have the Japanese been so successful in increasing quality while simultaneously bringing down production costs? As Cole asks: "Have they abolished the laws of economics?" Moreover, continuous improvement makes perfect economic sense as long as the search follows a minimum cost path. In terms of organizational dynamics it has long been observed that quality achievements tend to regress over time. If one is not going forward, one is going backward. Thus to press for continuous improvement at least helps ensure that no ground is lost.

According to Cole, the Japanese achievement has been six fold. First, Japanese managers realized that the traditional calculations dramatically underestimated the costs of poor quality. Typically, such calculations ignored the customers who were lost or who had never bought the product. A declining reputation among customers and the effects of negative work-of-mouth publicity were never considered, partly because they were difficult to quantify. There is very reason to believe that these effects are substantial. Japanese managers recognize these costs. They stress the fragility of their reputations with their customers and the importance of winning the customer's trust. They find it entirely appropriate to spend generously for this purpose. In short, once one recognizes the high costs associated with poor quality, one sees that it is economically rational to invest more in quality improvement.

Captains of quality

The TQM approach was developed over the last 40 years by many researchers and practitioners. Four of the most prominent are W. Edwards Deming, Joseph Juran, Philip Crossby, and Masaaki Imai, their message is basically the same:

- Commit to quality improvement throughout the organization.
- Attack the process. not the employees.
- Strip down the process to find and eliminate problems that diminish quality.
- Identify you customers and satisfy their requirements.
- Instill teamwork an create an atmosphere for innovation and permanent quality improvement.

The leitmotif is worker enablement and empowerment: that is, train the workers and give them responsibility. In the remainder of this section we highlight the main points made by each of these pioneers and mention how they can be applied to project management. Like any discipline, a unique vocabulary has grown around TQM.

Deming approach. Deming, originally a physicist with a Ph.D. From Yale, after many years in industry came to believe. "Improve quality and you automatically improve productivity. You capture the market with lower prices and better quality. You stay in business and you product jobs. It's no simple. In his work he stresses statistical process control, statistical quality control, and a 14 point plan for managers that emphasizes the human element. The philosophy is to threat people as intelligent human beings who want to do a good job. Although statistical control methods are difficult to implement in a project environment due to the one-of-a-kind nature of projects, the 14 points are readily adoptable.

Deming was the American who took his message to Japan in 1950 after being shown the door by most major U.S. corporations. It was a time when U.S. firms dominated international markets: there was virtually no competition from abroad, so as long as the product worked. The concern for quality was minimal. Deming was instrumental in changing this attitude and in turning Japanese industry into an economic world power. This 14 principles for achieving competitiveness through quality are as follows:

1. Create constancy of purpose toward improvement of products and services: emphasize long-term needs rather than short-term objectives. This principle should guide management throughout the life cycle of a project. In early stages of project selection, long-term goals should be emphasized. The acquisition of new knowledge and the ability to master new technologies are leading considerations. Furthermore, the specific configuration selected for a project should support these long-term objectives as well. The required constancy can be achieved only by a learning process that promotes improvement from one project to the next. Whatever learned during project execution is as important as the final results and deliverance. Top management has to facilitate the diffusion of knowledge throughout the organization and the transfer of technology between different projects. This calls for an investment it, resources and the development of procedures to support these activities.

2. Adopt a new philosophy. The philosophy that productivity and cost are the most important performance measures should be modified based on the recognition that improved quality can reduce cost and improve productivity while increasing customer satisfaction. Thus, quality is the most important performance measure. Defects are unacceptable and problem-solving tools should be used at all levels of the organization to eliminate their sources.

3. Cease dependence on mass inspection. Quality should be built into the product design, the process design, and the support design. The responsibility for quality should not be with quality control and quality assurance but rather with all members of the organization regardless of function and level. Advanced presentation analysis should be used to support group problem solving so that improved process capability will be maintained.

4. Reduce the number of vendors; don't select vendors on the basis of cost. The decision on project structure and selecting subcontractors should be based on quality considerations; i.e., employ a limited number of high-quality subcontractors with whom long-term relationships predicated on loyalty and trust can be established. Quality should be the predominant factor in choosing a subcontractor, rather than price tag alone.

5. Search for problems and improve constantly. Successful project management is based on good design and good planning, and a dogged determination to remain on course. Thus, an ongoing effort to identify and solve problems is the key to smooth implementation. The earlier a problem is detected, the easier it is to correct. control systems should be established with this adage in mind. One way of doing this is with trend analysis in areas such as cost, schedule, and quality.

6. Institute on-the-job training to make better use of human resources. Instituting training in technological and managerial fields supports continuous improvement in the process. Training employees in new technologies developed in one project

enhance the likelihood of success for future project It is an investment that will pay for itself many times over. Promulgating the philosophy of built-in quality enables the whole organization to move in the direction of quality improvement. Training in managerial techniques used for planning, scheduling, budgeting, and control is important for the project manager and the project team. Input from the various team members on all problems relevant to their expertise should be continually sought, and the reasons behind all decisions should be made explicit.

7. Improve supervision. The role of supervision is leadership aimed at helping people do a better job. Since recognition an reinforcement are critical to good job performance, supervisors should be trained to support this continued improvement process by proving leadership. example, and training to their teams. Managers should become coaches rather than feudal lords.

8. Drive out fear. Encourage open communication. Open communication lines and the ability to report problems without fearing the consequences are essential to the ongoing improvement process. Employees are the first to know about problems in their specific areas of responsibility. Problems can be resolved early in the project life cycle by encouraging open discussion. Furthermore, employees usually know their part of the project better than anybody else. By encouraging them to initiate change in the product, process, or support design when they see fit, a continuous improvement is likely to take place. management should institute an "open door" policy and a "How can I help you in doing your job?" approach to promote communication and to effectively use its most important resource-people.

9. Break down barriers and promote communication among the different organizations participating in the project. By eliminating communication barriers between functional areas, departments, and subcontractors, concurrent engineering can be implemented. All the participants in the project should be viewed as a team with a common goal. The organizational breakdown structure should clearly define the formal communication channels within the team. However, informal communication between the members of the project should also be encouraged. Each organization participating in a project should learn to view the other organizations as its customers (or suppliers), striving to understand their needs in performing their tasks. By adopting the customer-provider point of view, integration between the various elements of the WBS assigned to different organizations in the OBS greatly increases the likelihood that it will be smooth and error free.

10. Eliminate slogans, posters, and targets for the workforce that ask for a new level of productivity without appropriate methods and solutions. The focus should be on the process as well as the outcome. An effort to improve the process of design and implementation will result in higher levels of achievement. Management

should help employees develop better ways of performing their tasks; i.e., provide leadership in problem identification and problem-solving methodologies.

11. Use work standards (quotas) carefully. Work standards used in a project environment can be dangerous, especially when they depend on environmental factors external to the project. Standards and quotas are important in the planning process, but should be carefully used as a foundation for performance evaluations. When standard time or cost goals are not achieved, the source of the problem should be determined. It is rarely a good idea to apply sanctions solely on the basis of cost or schedule overruns, as the cause may be outside the worker's control.

12. Remove barriers that eliminate the worker's pride of workmanship. The responsibility of supervisors must be changed from sheer numbers to quality. Employees should be annual or merit rating and of management by objectives. By assigning the responsibility of better quality to the employees who perform the work, a link is established between their satisfaction and the improvement process. This link is necessary to promote improvement in quality.

13. Institute an education and training program to teach workers new skills as new technologies are developed or assimilated by the organization. Technologies developed or acquired for one project can serve the whole organization in future projects if proper training regimens are established. In addition to on-the-job training, a training program should be instituted to transfer knowledge between different parts of the organization.

14. Everyone in the organization should team up in the quality improvement process. This process should not be an isolated effort of the quality control or quality assurance departments. Everyone in the organization should be involved in the transformation to quality. Too often, advice and opinions of low-level staff are either not sought or ignored. Too many times, managers act as if they know the answer to every problem.